OCT 2015

KU-546-583

THE ROUGH GUIDE TO

South America
ON A BUDGET

written and researched by

Alasdair Ba~~~~ ~~~~ Kiki De~~~~ ~~~~ Ge~~~~ ~~~~ Villi~~~~
India Dowle~~~~
Stephen Ke~~~~
Shafik Megh~~~~
O'Brien, Ph~~~~

roughguides.com

Contents

Introduction to
South America

From the palm-smothered tropical beaches of the Caribbean to the wild and windswept archipelago of Tierra del Fuego, South America is a dizzying trove of landscapes, legendary cities and ancient ruins that have fuelled the imagination of adventurers for centuries. Trace Darwin's voyage through the Galápagos, the devastating path of the conquistadors in Peru or Che Guevara's route across the snowcapped peaks of the Andes. Discover Eva Perón's Buenos Aires, a truly beautiful, stylish metropolis, or pick up the trail of Bruce Chatwin across the lonely plains and ice-bound fjords of Patagonia. Whether exploring the elegant cities of Colombia, soaking up Aymara culture in Bolivia, or just chilling on a white-sand Brazilian beach, options for budget travellers remain extensive and highly alluring.

Much of the continent's dynamism is a result of the collision of cultures here over the last five hundred years. South America's peoples were devastated by European invasion in the sixteenth and seventeenth centuries, not least by the introduction of diseases that killed thousands. Yet **indigenous culture** never entirely disappeared and is especially strong in Peru, Bolivia and Brazil to this day. Indeed, much of the continent's people are proud of their **mestizo heritage**; indigenous, Spanish and Portuguese cultures dominate, but West African, British, Italian, German, French and Dutch influences have also contributed over the years, supplemented more recently by waves of Japanese, Chinese and Middle Eastern settlers. As the Argentine saying goes, "Peruvians come from the Incas; Argentines come from the boats".

This blending of races and cultures across the continent means that South American nations have a lot in common. **Catholicism** has provided a foundation for spiritual life here for centuries – sometimes blurring with far more ancient indigenous beliefs, especially in the Andes, it has created a legacy of magnificent churches and exuberant fiestas. When it comes to natural wonders the continent is equally blessed, with just about every terrain – from deserts and glaciers, to grasslands, rainforests and wetlands

ABOVE BOY ON A BICYCLE, NEAR MEDELLÍN, COLOMBIA **OPPOSITE** PERITO MORENO GLACIER, ARGENTINA

– and a range of **wildlife** found nowhere else: rheas, llamas, giant anteaters, jaguars and armadillos among them. The mighty Amazon River connects the Atlantic with the Brazilian jungle and the Peruvian Andes, while the lofty mountain chain itself runs from Colombia and Ecuador in the north, through Peru and Bolivia to the south of Chile and Argentina. This shared cultural and natural heritage is reflected in the ease of crossing borders, with multi-nation itineraries relatively simple to put together, whether traversing the River Plate between Argentina and Uruguay or the Atacama between Chile and Peru.

Today, South America is booming: Portuguese-speaking Brazil, the largest, richest and most populated country in South America, is a global power in the making, while Peru, Chile, Colombia and Argentina are important regional players. It's an exciting time to visit; backpackers will still find an extensive range of accommodation on offer, with plenty of options for the tight budget. South America also sports some of the best camping and hammock-slinging spots in the world, as well as many exhilarating **adventure tourism** destinations. Travelling within the continent varies wildly from country to country; sometimes it will require a little patience, initiative and navigating of red tape, but the colourful bus journeys, sunrise ferry crossings and people you'll meet along the way will be impossible to forget.

Where to go

Brazil alone could occupy several months of travel, though many pan-continental itineraries also begin or end with **Rio de Janeiro**, one of South America's most alluring cities: with the world's most exuberant carnival, hip nightlife, trend-setting beaches and that mesmerizing skyline, it's hard to beat. South of Rio lie the wealthier parts of the country, from the

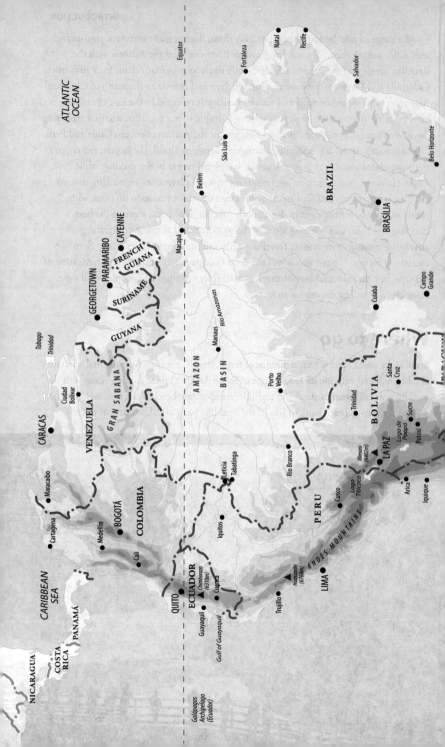

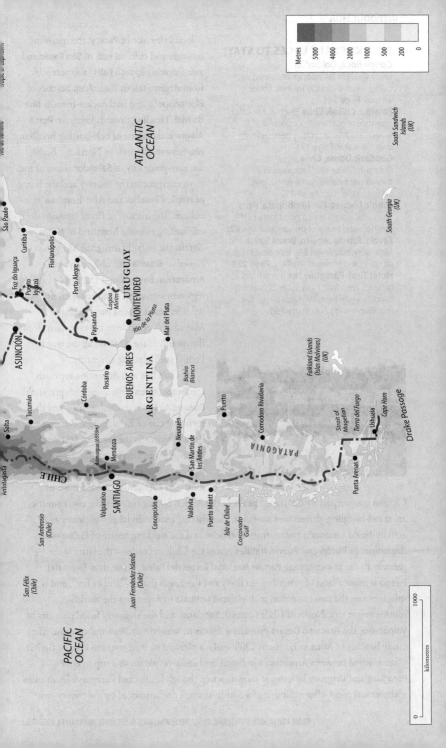

SIX UNUSUAL PLACES TO STAY

Coffee finca, Colombia
Enjoy views of lush slopes crammed with coffee shrubs, and the freshest coffee around. **Page 546**

Palafito, Chiloé, Chile Sleep in a *palafito* guesthouse (pictured), a colourful fisherman's house on stilts perched right over the water. **Page 451**

Geodesic Dome, Chile
Glamp in Chiloé and Patagonia in a two-storey, heated dome with a glass ceiling to the stars. **Page 457**

Jungle Lodges, Río Tambopata, Peru
The rustic lodges give a good taste of the rich flora and fauna of the jungle. **Page 828**

Favela, Rio de Janeiro, Brazil Stay in *The Maze*, a friendly *favela* B&B that doubles as a jazz club and triples as a gallery. **Page 250**

Hotel Tirol, Paraguay Not many hotel grounds are a forest sanctuary containing capuchin monkeys, 190 bird species and four swimming pools. **Page 705**

colonial elegance of **Paraty**, the sprawling business and cultural hub of **São Paulo** and awe-inspiring **Iguaçu Falls** (also accessible from Argentina), to the golden beaches of **Florianópolis** and backpacker-friendly **Ilha do Mel**. Heading towards Uruguay, **Porto Alegre** is the home of belt-busting Brazilian *churrasco* (barbecue). In Northeast Brazil, the easy-going city of **Salvador** is one of the most energetic in the country and the home of tropical beaches and Afro-Brazilian culture. The interior of Brazil contains the enchanting colonial heartland of **Minas Gerais**, the unfairly maligned Modernist capital of **Brasília** and ultimately the **Amazonian Basin**, an unimaginably vast region of rivers and rainforest, rich in wildlife, best accessed from Belém or Manaus. It's possible to travel by boat from the mouth of the Amazon all the way to Peru, a spell-binding adventure.

Trips to **Chile** and **Argentina** are easily combined, often beginning with grand old **Buenos Aires**, Argentina's capital and the ravishing city of Evita, tango, Borges and Boca Juniors. To the west sits **Mendoza**, centre of Argentina's ever-improving wine regions, while across the pampas to the south lies **Patagonia**, divided from its Chilean counterpart by the jagged peaks of the Andes. Slicing between the two countries are mind-boggling glaciers and ice-fields, shimmering mountain lakes, volcanoes and activity-based mountain towns, from **Bariloche** and the trekking centre of **El Chaltén** in Argentina, to **Pucón** and **Puerto Natales** across the Chilean border – the latter is the gateway to the jaw-dropping **Parque Nacional Torres del Paine**. These days **Tierra del Fuego** is more a land of penguins, sea lions and flamingos than a "land of fire", and is also split between the two countries, with isolated **Ushuaia** in Argentina the world's southernmost city. North of Chile's capital, **Santiago**, and the elegantly faded port city of **Valparaíso**, the **Atacama Desert** provides a dramatic, witheringly beautiful contrast. The sandy beaches of **Arica** in northern Chile make a pleasant stop en route to Peru or Bolivia.

Sandwiched between Argentina and Brazil, and easily tacked on to a trip to either, **Paraguay** and **Uruguay** lack major showstoppers, though landlocked Paraguay's Jesuit ruins and national parks offer a glimpse of a South America untrammelled by the twenty-first

PARTY CONTINENT

South America loves a fiesta, by far the most famous being **Carnaval**, the legendary flesh-fest closely associated with South America's greatest city, Rio. Expect hardcore partying with two million people packing the streets every day. Rio's might be the most famous but other cities boast spectacular Carnaval celebrations, with Salvador and Recife in Brazil both renowned, and distinctive versions filling the streets in Bolivia's Oruro, Encarnación in Paraguay and throughout Ecuador.

For something spiritual, head to **Inti Raymi**, a week-long Inca festival in Cusco, Peru, where thousands of revellers honour the sun god in lavish and theatrical celebrations. An equally visual and religious party in Peru is **Fiesta de la Virgen del Carmen**, Paucartambo (pictured). Beautifully costumed dancers blend pre-Columbian and Catholic traditions in this magical Andean celebration. Down in Argentina, the **Feria de Mataderos** lets you mingle with gauchos, snack at *parrillas* and peruse local crafts at one of Buenos Aires' most exhilarating events.

century. While adventure tourists may not flock to Uruguay, its relaxed, cultured capital **Montevideo** (an easy day-trip from Buenos Aires) sports crumbling churches and enlightening museums. **Punta del Este**'s upmarket beach resorts are only a couple of hours from here and are worth checking out, if only briefly, by those on a budget.

Bolivia is perhaps the continent's most intriguing destination, encompassing snaggle-toothed peaks, dense jungles and a dynamic indigenous culture, best absorbed in the capital **La Paz**, around **Lake Titicaca**, heartland of the Aymara and especially on the **Isla del Sol**, said to be the spiritual centre of the Andean world. The silver-mining city of **Potosí** funded the kings of Europe for centuries, while **Sucre** is one of the most captivating colonial cities on the continent.

Backpackers continue to flock to **Peru**, globally renowned for the great Inca ruins at **Cusco**, the **Sacred Valley** and especially **Machu Picchu**, the jaw-dropping mountain hideout on which all images of "lost cities" are now based. Many travellers reach the city on foot via the **Inca Trail**, a truly magical experience. Yet Peru has a lot more to offer, from virgin Amazonian jungle protected in parks such as the **Pacaya Samiria National Reserve** and a long dry coastline where *ceviche* became an art form, to the booming nightlife and innovative culinary scene in **Lima**.

Ecuador has much in common with Peru and is easily combined with a trip to its larger southern neighbour. The highland capital, **Quito**, is crammed with absorbing museums and colonial architecture, while the rest of the country is littered with volcanoes, old Spanish towns and beguiling indigenous markets. Naturalists, however, should head straight for the extraordinary **Galápagos Islands**, home to some of the world's most astonishing wildlife.

At the northern end of the continent, **Colombia** continues to be an up-and-coming travel destination, much safer after years of drug wars and guerrilla insurgencies. Immerse yourself in the salsa-soaked nightlife of **Bogotá**, the coffee-growing landscapes of the **Zona Cafetera** and the romantic colonial towns of **Cartagena** and **Popayán**. The mesmerizing scenery around **Villa de Leyva** is perfect for hiking, while **San Gil** is the base for adventure sports, especially white-water rafting. Far to the north, closer to Nicaragua than South America, the **Isla de Providencia** is part of the remote San Andrés chain, home of palm-fringed Caribbean beaches and a spectacular reef ideal for divers.

Neighbouring **Venezuela** remains a far more challenging country to visit, but the rewards for doing so are considerable; experience untouched national parks, spectacular Caribbean beaches and the Amazon region of Guayana, which contains the **Angel Falls**, the world's tallest waterfall.

The **Guianas**, comprising the former British and Dutch colonies of **Guyana** and **Suriname** and the French overseas *département* of **French Guiana**, are often overlooked. However, their three capital cities, Georgetown, Paramaribo and Cayenne respectively, are home to cool bars and colonial wooden architecture in picturesque decay, while French Guiana has the added appeal of the **Centre Spatial Guyanais**, **Devil's Island** (immortalized in *Papillon*). English-speaking Guyana offers a taste of West Indian culture – with cricket, rum and rotis, it's more Barbados than Brazil.

When to go

With about two-thirds of South America near the equator or the tropic of Capricorn, visitors to most destinations can expect a tropical or subtropical **climate** all year round. Temperatures rarely drop below 20°C, while rainforest regions average maximum temperatures of about 30°C. As you get further south (and don't forget the southern hemisphere reverses the seasons), you'll find colder winters from June to August and milder summers from December to February, with the extreme south of the continent freezing between April and October. It's important to plan around the **rainy season** in each country, particularly when travelling in the Andes.

Domestic tourism, especially in the richer countries of the south, is booming, meaning that hostels, hotels and transportation can become fully booked during the summer (December to March), especially on the coast, so book ahead if possible. Expect hordes of local tourists to hit the road in any country on major religious holidays, especially **Christmas** and **Semana Santa** (Easter).

Incredible Journeys

1 INCA TRAIL, PERU
Page 756

Tackle the four-day hike between Cusco and Machu Picchu, a spell-binding mountain trek into the Inca past.

2 CARRETERA AUSTRAL, CHILE
Page 455

Wend your way along this spectacular Patagonian highway, rounding ice-fields, vast glaciers and jagged fjords.

3 CYCLING THE DEATH ROAD, BOLIVIA
Page 168

A hair-raising adventure on two wheels in the mountains near La Paz.

4 RUTA 40, ARGENTINA
Page 131

Travel this epic 5000km highway along the Andes, from the Bolivian border to the bottom of Patagonia.

5 SERRA VERDE RAILWAY, BRAZIL
Page 349

This enchanting train ride winds around mountains and traverses one of the largest Atlantic Forest reserves in the country.

6 THE CIRCUIT, TORRES DEL PAINE, CHILE
Page 476

This seven- to ten-day hike is the best way to soak up the charms and wildlife of the rugged national park.

Architectural Wonders

1 VALPARAÍSO, CHILE
Page 392

Colourful half-painted houses cascade down the hills alongside distinctive *ascencores* (funiculars) in Chile's quirkiest city.

2 HISTORIC CENTRE, SALVADOR, BRAZIL
Page 277

Locals know it as Pelô and love this UNESCO World Heritage Site for its pastel-coloured buildings in their restored Renaissance glory.

3 CUSCO, PERU
Page 742

This former capital of the Inca empire charms with its colonial and Incan architectural treasures, which often battle it out on the same site.

4 NIEMEYER'S MASTERPIECES, BRAZIL
Pages 255 & 317

Latin America's greatest architect, Oscar Niemeyer, designed the capital, Brasília, while his Museum of Modern Art, in Niterói near Rio, clings to the cliff like a recently landed flying-saucer.

5 CARTAGENA, COLOMBIA
Page 517

The walled Old City is a beauty, its narrow old streets crammed with picturesque corners, while cool, new Afro-Colombian music blows in from Cartagena's neighbourhoods into the night.

6 LA COMPAÑÍA DE JESÚS, QUITO, ECUADOR
Page 575

Opulence? Try seven tonnes of gold to dress up this decadent wonder, which took 163 years to build.

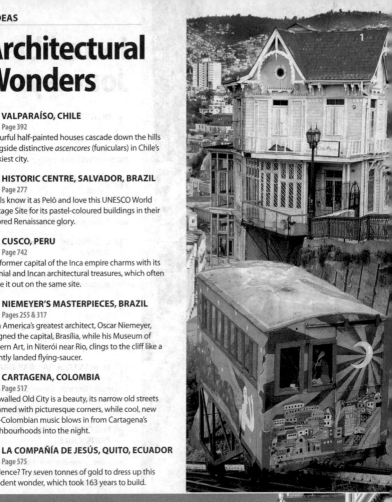

Amazing Wildlife

1 THE PANTANAL, BRAZIL
Page 326

The world's largest wetland is home to thousands of animal species; giant river otters, giant anteaters, jaguars, pumas and capybaras among them.

2 GALÁPAGOS ISLANDS, ECUADOR
Page 633

Witness the giant tortoises, marine iguanas, penguins, sea lions and flightless cormorants that Charles Darwin observed, developing his theories on evolution here.

3 AMAZONIAN BASIN, BOLIVIA, BRAZIL, ECUADOR, PERU AND VENEZUELA
Pages 216, 303, 611, 815 & 879

Explore the Amazon and you'll find everything from poison dart frogs to snapping piranhas.

4 COLCA CANYON, PERU
Page 782

The best place in the Andes to see condors rise up the sides of a mesmerizing canyon wall.

5 BEAGLE CHANNEL, ARGENTINA
Page 148

Take a thrilling boat trip to see the sea lions, penguins, whales and seabirds of Tierra del Fuego.

6 LOS LLANOS, VENEZUELA
Page 896

This tropical grassland supports hordes of capybaras, crocodiles, anaconda, armadillos, scarlet ibis and over sixty species of waterbirds.

Local Flavours

1 PISCO SOURS, CHILE AND PERU
Page 404 & 771

There's a fierce rivalry between Chile and Peru about where the spirit pisco originates, but everyone agrees it's best drunk in a pisco sour. You can visit pisco distilleries in Chile's Elqui Valley and Ica in Peru.

2 ASUNCIÓN, PARAGUAY
Page 790

Eat fresh street food at Mercado 4, one of Latin America's great markets, or make for the neighbourhood of Loma San Jerónimo where local houses have been converted into homespun restaurants, and roof terraces into bars.

3 MENDOZA'S BODEGAS, ARGENTINA
Page 98

Splash out on a degustation – and a glass of wine, naturally – among the vineyards with views of the cordillera.

4 CÓRDOBA, ARGENTINA
Page 72

A wining and dining delight for everyone, the city offers fashionable restaurants in converted mansions, tasty *empanadas* on the go and edgy bars in revamped warehouses.

5 MIRAFLORES AND BARRANCO, LIMA, PERU
Page 738

These swanky neighbourhoods are Lima's sparkling coastal highlights; treat yourself to delicious lime-marinated *ceviche* and ocean views.

6 RIO DE JANEIRO'S NIGHTLIFE
Page 253

Head to the neighbourhood of Lapa on Friday night for its street parties and samba.

Itineraries

You can't expect to fit everything South America has to offer into one trip – or two or three or four, to be fair – and we don't suggest you try. This selection of itineraries will guide you through the different countries and regions, picking out a few of the best places and major attractions along the way. For those taking a big, extended trip around the continent you could join a few together, but remember that the distances you'll be covering can be vast. There is, of course, much to discover off the beaten track, so if you have the time it's worth exploring smaller towns, villages and wilderness areas further afield, finding your own perfect hill town, deserted beach or just a place you love to rest up and chill out.

SOUTHERN BRAZIL

❶ Rio de Janeiro The beaches, the samba, the towering statue of Christ the Redeemer looming over it all – Rio has every base covered to kick off your trip in style. **See p.235**

❷ Costa Verde Backed by forested mountain peaks, the coastline between Rio and São Paulo contains hidden gems like colonial Paraty and spectacular beaches at Ilha Grande. **See p.256**

❸ Minas Gerais This state inland from Rio offers some of Brazil's most stunning historic towns – none more attractive than Ouro Preto. **See p.261**

❹ Brasília Come see the vision of the future, circa 1960, courtesy of Oscar Niemeyer's Modernist architecture. **See p.316**

❺ The Pantanal If you're not going to make it out to the Galápagos during your travels, consider checking out the huge array of wildlife in this vast wetland. **See p.326**

❻ Ilha de Santa Catarina Some of the best beaches in the country can be found on the coast near Florianópolis. **See p.356**

❼ Serra Gaúcha The mountain bases of Canela and Gramado serve two nearby parks with crashing falls and challenging climbs and hikes. **See p.364 & p.365**

ABOVE PARQUE NACIONAL TAYRONA, COLOMBIA

NORTHERN ARGENTINA, PARAGUAY AND URUGUAY

❶ Buenos Aires The most cosmopolitan of all South American cities, worth a few days of anyone's time. **See p.52**

❷ Colonia del Sacramento If you're just going to dip into Uruguay, you can't do better than the historic centre of this charming town. **See p.845**

❸ Eastern beaches, Uruguay Beach getaways to suit every budget, from quiet Cabo Polonio with no roads or electricity to the flashy surf resort of Punta del Este. **See p.851**

❹ Rosario The perfect spot to launch yourself into the Paraná Delta. **See p.78**

❺ Córdoba Wander from the colonial centre to Nuevo Córdoba, a neighbourhood chock-a-block with cool bars and restaurants in converted mansions. **See p.70**

❻ Mendoza Undoubtedly the best stop for wine-lovers, a sophisticated city with great restaurants and hundreds of nearby *bodegas*. **See p.100**

❼ Cerro Aconcagua Whether you take two weeks to scale the summit or just see a section on a day-hike, the tallest mountain in the western hemisphere will sear itself into your memory. **See p.104**

❽ Salta Its central plaza is a lovely place to begin an evening stroll. **See p.89**

❾ Parque Nacional el Rey The lush cloudforests here hold colourful toucans, as well as other exotic fauna and flora. **See p.93**

❿ Iguazú Falls Better to see the crashing waters from the trails and catwalks on the Argentina side. **See p.86**

⓫ The Ruta Jesuítica Visit Paraguay's famous Jesuit ruins; Trinidad and Jesús are a four- to five-hour coach ride from Iguazú Falls. **See p.704**

CHILE AND ARGENTINA: THE LAKE DISTRICTS AND PATAGONIA

❶ Volcán Villarrica Skiing, snowboarding, mountaineering – you can experience the smouldering volcano up close. **See p.436**

❷ Lago Llanquihue A sparkling blue lake with volcanoes, white-water rafting and waterfalls. **See p.440**

❸ Western and southern Chiloé The protected areas have some great coastal hiking through fishing villages, forests and beaches. **See p.446**

❹ San Martín de los Andes A lower-key version of Bariloche and a hub for getting out to the nearby lakes and Parque Lanín. **See p.113**

❺ Parque Nacional Nahuel Huapi Well-marked trails, plentiful campsites and huts, crystal-clear lakes and much more make this the most popular Patagonian park on the Argentine side. **See p.121**

❻ Península Valdés Consider an eastern detour here to see abundant birdlife, a sea-lion colony and – if you time it right – whales on their migration route. **See p.129**

❼ Perito Moreno Glacier The unquestioned highlight of Parque Nacional Los Glaciares, a calving glacier that provides theatrical drama for onlookers. **See p.143**

❽ Parque Nacional Torres del Paine The most famous destination on the Chilean side of Patagonia – and perhaps the best trekking in the entire region. **See p.472**

BOLIVIA

BRAZIL

PARAGUAY

CHILE

URUGUAY

ARGENTINA

ATLANTIC OCEAN

0   400
kilometres

NORTHERN ARGENTINA, PARAGUAY AND URUGUAY

CHILE AND ARGENTINA: THE LAKE DISTRICTS AND PATAGONIA

❺ **San Pedro de Atacama** An oasis town chock-full of natural attractions in the surrounding *altiplano* wilderness. **See p.411**

❻ **Salar de Uyuni** You'll have to go on a tour, but it's worth the trip to see the flat, white salt "lake", perfectly reflective in summer when covered with water. **See p.195**

❼ **Potosí** The colonial architecture and lively cafés make an uneasy contrast with the tragic legacy of the nearby silver mines at Cerro Rico. **See p.191**

NORTHERN CHILE AND SOUTHERN BOLIVIA

❾ **Ushuaia** If you've made it here you're practically at the end of the world – send a postcard, eat some seafood, ski in winter and dream of Antarctica, 1000km away. **See p.145**

NORTHERN CHILE AND SOUTHERN BOLIVIA

❶ **Santiago** Relatively developed Santiago is a gentle introduction to South America, with some interesting museums and neighbourhoods to explore. **See p.380**

❷ **Valparaíso** Ride the *ascensores* (funiculars) around the hilly streets by day, then eat, drink and carouse in the gritty port area at night. **See p.392**

❸ **Pisco Elqui** This charming village, with views over the Elqui valley, is the perfect place to sample a pisco sour. **See p.405**

❹ **Parque Nacional Nevado de Tres Cruces** Drive by arid salt flats, spot vicuñas and guanacos, and stay by a lake populated with colourful flamingos. **See p.407**

8 Santa Cruz One of the rare places in Bolivia known for its excellent restaurant and club scene. **See p.209**

ECUADOR, PERU AND NORTHERN BOLIVIA

1 Guayaquil An alternative introduction to Ecuador than more traditional Quito; the Malecón and nearby beaches make it seem like a different land entirely. **See p.623**

2 Otavalo Few can resist the town's famous Saturday market, the ultimate place to purchase a hammock or woodcarving as a keepsake. **See p.586**

3 Quito Base yourself in the old town, where plaza after plaza provides a vantage point for historic churches and narrow walkways. **See p.573**

4 The Quilotoa Loop Hike for a few days around the peaceful waters of a volcanic crater lake. **See p.593**

5 Nariz del Diablo train ride A five-hour journey starting in Riobamba and slicing its glorious way through the Andes. **See p.601**

6 Cuenca Ecuador's third-largest city and possibly its most beautiful, with cobbled streets and the vibe of an Andean town. **See p.603**

7 Huaraz This lively city, nestled in a valley, affords you an approach to trekking in both the Cordillera Blanca and Cordillera Huayhuash. **See p.789**

8 Lima Love it or hate it, you can nevertheless find plenty to occupy you in the Peruvian capital, and the proximity to the sea makes it a great place to try out *ceviche*. **See p.726**

9 Trails to Machu Picchu Discover less expensive and less crowded alternative Inca Trails deep in the imposing jungle. **See p.765**

10 Cusco As much of a hub as Lima and closer to many of the country's highlights – though its plazas, museums, restaurants and nightlife certainly stand on their own. **See p.742**

11 Lake Titicaca Whether you visit the Uros islands on the Peru side or the sacred Isla del Sol in the Bolivian section, you're certain to be awed by the high-altitude lake. **See p.787 & p.176**

12 La Paz Now this is what an Andean capital city should be: delightfully situated high up in a

ECUADOR, PERU AND NORTHERN BOLIVIA

COLOMBIA

ECUADOR

PERU

BRAZIL

PACIFIC OCEAN

BOLIVIA

CHILE   ARGENTINA   PARAGUAY

0   200
kilometres

canyon, full of interesting and inexpensive places to eat, drink and stay, and with an undeniable energy all its own. **See p.164**

⑯ Sucre The official capital's beautifully maintained colonial architecture accounts for the nickname "White City", but don't overlook this pretty town's excellent bars. **See p.200**

COLOMBIA AND VENEZUELA

❶ Bogotá Colombia's densely packed, cosmopolitan capital divides opinion, but is a worthwhile first or last stop for its colonial architecture and raucous nightlife. **See p.497**

❷ San Agustín A crazy array of monolithic statues, with a lovely mountain landscape serving as a backdrop. **See p.557**

❸ Cali This might be Colombia's most fun and freewheeling city, with plenty of salsa clubs and streetlife to balance out the sober array of churches. **See p.550**

❹ Medellín From Cali you can travel up to Medellín – an attractive, modern city that's had quite a makeover in the past decade – via Colombia's coffee country. **See p.537**

❺ Cartagena The jewel of the Caribbean coast, a gorgeous colonial city and a must on any Colombia trip. **See p.517**

❻ Parque Nacional Tayrona Beautiful beaches, lush flora and pre-Columbian ruins are the highlights of this pristine coastal park, accessed from Santa Marta. **See p.529**

❼ San Gil Colombia's best spot for adventure sports is known for its white-water rafting, but you can also try out paragliding, kayaking, abseiling and more in the mountains north of Bogotá. **See p.512**

❽ Villa de Leyva Under an hour from San Gil, this is a thoroughly unmodern and relaxed colonial town; from Villa de Leyva or San Gil you can loop back to Bucaramanga for buses to the border with Venezuela at Cúcuta, though don't linger here. **See p.508**

❾ Mérida Contemplate adventures to nearby mountains, a trip to wildlife-rich Los Llanos or just chill out in this laidback city. **See p.891**

❿ Ciudad Bolívar Venezuela's most lovely colonial town and the gateway to Angel Falls and the Orinoco Delta. **See p.901**

⓫ Angel Falls Journey by boat and on foot to reach this towering waterfall. **See p.905**

⓬ Orinoco Delta Visit the delta jungle region for a truly mind-blowing experience. **See p.909**

⓭ Parque Nacional Henri Pittier A great mix of beaches, wildlife and walking trails – and it's

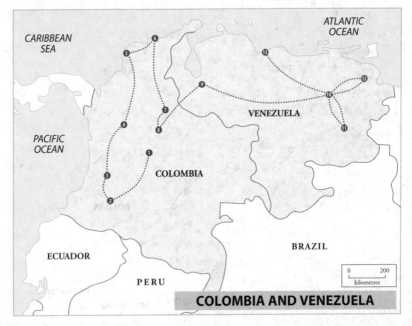

COLOMBIA AND VENEZUELA

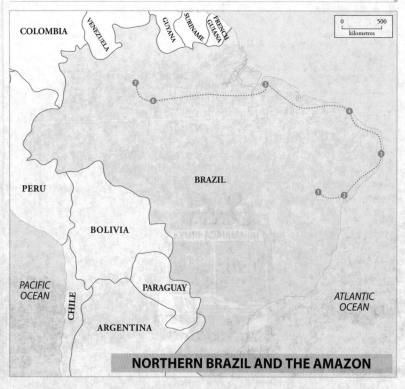

NORTHERN BRAZIL AND THE AMAZON

relatively near Caracas, which makes your exit or travel connections easier. **See p.881**

NORTHERN BRAZIL AND THE AMAZON

❶ **Chapada Diamantina** Some of the best hiking and waterfall hunting in the country is to be found in this canyon-filled national park. **See p.287**

❷ **Salvador** For candomblé, capoeira or Carnaval, Bahia's capital is practically the country's capital. Seek out fine beaches, diving and surf at nearby Morro de São Paulo. **See p.277**

❸ **Olinda** You won't find a prettier array of churches, plazas and houses anywhere in the north of the country. **See p.295**

❹ **Fortaleza** The central market is a sure bet to buy a hammock; take it with you to Jericoara, the best beach in the area. **See p.298**

❺ **Belém** Great restaurants and bars, but the main reason to come is its location at the mouth of the Amazon. **See p.303**

❻ **Manaus** After seeing the astounding Teatro Amazonas, grab some of the fine street food on offer and head to the lively port area. **See p.311**

❼ **Amazon river trip** Float along the Rio Negro to a jungle lodge or even just a clearing where you can string up a hammock – or head along the Amazon all the way to Iquitos in Peru. **See p.315**

BUS IN NORTHERN ARGENTINA

Basics

Getting there

The easiest way to reach the northern parts of South America is by air via the US, usually through a hub such as Houston, Atlanta or Miami. Flights from Europe alternatively may go via another city in the EU or, for the southern part of the region, stopover in São Paulo or Rio. The national South American airlines, such as Aerolíneas Argentinas, Latam (previously LAN and TAM) and TACA, provide a reasonable choice of schedules and routes. Many immigration departments in South America insist that you have an onward or return ticket to enter the country, but the application of such rules is more strict in some countries than in others.

Airfares are seasonal, with the highest around July, August and mid-December to mid-January; you'll get the best prices during the dry winter (May, June and late Sept) and the wet summer (in most of the region Feb–April, excluding Carnaval and Easter). Flying on weekends is often more expensive. You can generally cut costs by going through a specialist flight agent, booking flights well in advance or taking advantage of web-only offers and airline frequent-flyer programmes. Another way to cut costs is to book with a tour operator that can put together a package deal including flights and accommodation, and tours as well.

Flights from the UK and Ireland

Book months, not weeks, in advance for cheaper flights to South America from the UK, unless you manage to get a last-minute deal – not always to be banked on. If you're prepared to not fly direct, you'll also get a cheaper price, but this could mean a long stopover in a US airport while waiting for a connection. Return flights from the UK and Ireland start at around £400–500. British Airways operates direct flights to both Rio de Janeiro and São Paulo in Brazil and Buenos Aires in Argentina (for the latter you'll sometimes have to touch down in Brazil but don't have to change planes) – but fares tend to be more expensive than those of their European and South American rivals. Only London Heathrow has direct flights from the UK. The best value-for-money airline depends on the country you are flying to, but generally a flight with a European airline such as Iberia, TAP or Air France, via their main airport in Madrid, Lisbon or Paris, is cheaper than flying via the US.

Flights from the US and Canada

Most South American airlines serving North America operate flights from New York or Miami. US airlines tend to fly out of their hubs: Delta from Atlanta and Continental from Houston. Flying through Miami affords you greater flexibility in travel planning and cheaper prices, though American Airlines have closed their hub there. There are flights to all major South American cities from at least one of the above. Direct flights from Canada are very limited; it's generally best to transfer at a US hub. From either the US or Canada, return flights are available from around US$450.

Flights from Australia and NZ

The best deals to South America are offered by the major South American airlines Aerolíneas Argentinas and Latam (previously LAN) in conjunction with Qantas and Air New Zealand. Aerolíneas Argentinas flies from Sydney to Buenos Aires, with connections across the continent; Qantas has code-shares with Latam via Auckland to Santiago and beyond. There are also plenty of flights via the US, but most are not scheduled through to South America and therefore tend to take longer and cost more. From Australia and NZ expect to pay at least US$1500 – but you can sometimes pay much more. Often airlines will charge more if you wish to stay in South America for longer than a month.

ESTA CLEARANCE

The US government requires those travellers coming to or through the US (even just transiting) on the **Visa Waiver Program** to apply for clearance via **ESTA** (Electronic System for Travel Authorization). This is not something to ignore – if you arrive at the airport without having done it, the airline won't allow you to check in. To apply for clearance visit ⓦcbp.gov/travel/international-visitors/esta. Make sure you do this at least 72 hours before travelling; you'll need your passport to hand, and the admin fee is US$14. Once a traveller has received clearance, it remains valid for two years for unlimited visits.

A BETTER KIND OF TRAVEL

At **Rough Guides** we are passionately committed to travel. We believe it helps us understand the world we live in and the people we share it with – and of course tourism is vital to many developing economies. But the scale of modern tourism has also damaged some places irreparably, and climate change is accelerated by most forms of transport, especially flying. All Rough Guides' flights are carbon-offset, and every year we donate money to a variety of environmental charities.

From Central America

Crossing overland from Panama into Colombia is not recommended as it entails traversing the Darién, a wild, lawless region occupied by guerrillas. The safest option is to fly – Bogotá and Caracas are the main points of entry – or take a boat from Panama to the Caribbean coast of Colombia. There is a ferry service from Colón in Panama to Cartagena, Colombia.

AIRLINES

Aerolíneas Argentinas Ⓦ aerolineas.com.ar
Air Canada Ⓦ aircanada.com
Air Europa Ⓦ aireuropa.com
Air France Ⓦ airfrance.com
Air New Zealand Ⓦ airnewzealand.com
Alitalia Ⓦ alitalia.com
American Airlines Ⓦ aa.com
Avianca Ⓦ avianca.com
British Airways Ⓦ ba.com
Caribbean Airlines Ⓦ caribbean-airlines.com
Delta Airlines Ⓦ delta.com
Gol Ⓦ voegol.com.br
Iberia Airlines Ⓦ iberia.com
KLM Ⓦ klm.com
LAN Ⓦ lan.com
Qantas Ⓦ qantas.com.au
TACA Ⓦ taca.com
TAM Ⓦ tam.com.br
TAP Air Portugal Ⓦ flytap.com
United Airlines Ⓦ united.com

AGENTS AND OPERATORS

Dragoman UK ☎ 01728 861133, Ⓦ dragoman.com. A range of South American overland trips on a giant 4WD bus, with a choice between accommodation in a hotel or tents.
Exodus UK ☎ 020 8675 5550, Ⓦ exodus.co.uk. Walking and cycling – and everything in between – from Argentina to Venezuela.
Expedia Ⓦ expedia.com. Discount airfares, all-airline search engine and daily deals.
HostelTrail Ⓦ hosteltrail.com. A great source for hostels and budget tour companies in South America.
Hotwire Ⓦ hotwire.com. Last-minute savings of up to forty percent on regular published fares. Travellers must be at least 18 and there are no refunds, transfers or changes allowed. Log-in required to purchase.
Intrepid Australia Ⓦ intrepidtravel.com. Global travel company with almost three decades organizing adventure group travel – also has a "basix" option for those on a budget.
Journey Latin America UK ☎ 020 3432 1550, Ⓦ journeylatinamerica.co.uk. Knowledgeable and helpful staff, good at sorting out stopovers and open-jaw flights. Also does package tours.
Lastminute.com Ⓦ lastminute.com. Package holiday and flight-only deals.
Opodo Ⓦ opodo.com. International flight comparison site where you can also book everything from car rental to hotels.
REI Adventures US ☎ 1 800 622 2236, Ⓦ rei.com/adventures. Climbing, cycling, hiking, cruising, paddling and multi-sport tours to many countries on the continent.
Skyscanner Ⓦ skyscanner.net. International flight comparison site.
STA Travel UK ☎ 0333 321 0099, Ⓦ statravel.co.uk. Low-cost flights and tours for students and under-26s, though other customers welcome.

AIRPASSES AND ROUND-THE-WORLD TICKETS

If you're visiting South America as part of a world trip, a **round-the-world (RTW) ticket** offers the greatest flexibility – and if your starting point is Australia or New Zealand, it may even be cheaper. Many international airlines are now aligned with one of two globe-spanning networks: "Star Alliance" (Ⓦ staralliance.com), which has 27 members including Air Canada, Air New Zealand, Lufthansa, Avianca/TACA and United; or "One World", which combines routes via twelve airlines including American, British Airways, Cathay Pacific, Iberia, LAN and Qantas. Fares depend on the month, point of origin and number of continents or distance travelled, and in general the more expensive options include South America, but they are worth exploring.

If you plan to do a fair amount of travelling within South America consider buying an **airpass** (see p.30) with your main ticket. These passes offer substantial savings, but can be bought only outside South America when buying an international ticket.

Trailfinders UK ☎ 020 7368 1200, ⓦ trailfinders.com. One of the best-informed and most efficient agents for independent travellers. Good for round-the-world tickets.

Travel Cuts Canada ☎ 1 800 667 2887, ⓦ travelcuts.com. Canadian student-travel organization.

Tucan Travel Australia ☎ 029326 6633, ⓦ tucantravel.com. Specializing in adventure and backpacker holidays – and also has a budget option. Based in Australia but offices worldwide.

Wilderness Travel US ☎ 1 800 368 2794, ⓦ wildernesstravel.com. Adventure travel and wildlife tours throughout South America.

Getting around

Most South Americans travel by bus, and there is almost nowhere that you can't reach in this way. The major routes are comfortable and reliable and always cost effective. Moreover, you will see more, and meet more people, if you travel by bus. Remember, though, that distances between towns can be huge, and that in more remote areas such as Patagonia there are few bus and no train services. If you have a little spare cash and limited time, you may want to fly occasionally, or rent a car to explore at leisure. There are frequent flights within and between South American countries; the former are generally much cheaper. Public transport options vary within each country. Most places will have collectivos (which are minibuses that depart when full and take set routes; not to be confused with colectivos, a name for city buses in the south), as well as rickety local buses. There are also mototaxis in some places (similar to those in Thailand and India), which are good for covering short distances within towns.

By bus

This is by far the cheapest way to see the continent. While you can, technically, travel all the way from the tropical north to Tierra del Fuego by bus, there are few direct international services and you usually have to disembark at the border, cross it, then sometimes get on another bus to a large city in the new country. The process is repeated at most border crossings. The best bet for an international service is in capital cities or major hubs near borders; in places with limited transport you may just have to buckle down and take what's on offer.

Terminals are often situated on the outskirts of towns – follow the signs to the *terminal* (in Spanish-speaking countries) or the *rodoviária* (in Brazil). Levels of comfort vary, so a quick visual check in the terminal will give you an idea of which company to go for. With better bus companies on long-distance routes, the **seating options** usually include normal seats, seats that partly recline (*semi-cama*) and seats that recline fully (*cama*) to become beds. They are priced according to the level of comfort, with the most expensive options including on-board meals and drinks. Some of the cheapest companies only have one level of comfort and that can mean anything from wooden seats to standing in an aisle.

By car

South American **roads**, especially outside the major cities, are notorious for their bumpy, potholed and generally poor conditions. Most car rental companies in South America do not allow their vehicles to be driven across borders, making independent exploration of the continent by car difficult.

If you are determined to go it alone and drive around South America, you will find car rental companies at all airports and in most major cities. Hotels can advise you of better-value local places, but often it's better to book in advance online. Costs are high thanks to skyrocketing insurance rates, but the independence of a car may be worth it. An international driving licence is recommended although most of the time you will probably be able to use the one issued by your country of residence (and may not even be asked for the international one). Check your **insurance** carefully for exclusions, as car theft, vandalism and general security are renowned problems in many parts of South America, especially Argentina and Brazil, and you may not be covered for these. Damage to tyres or the underside of the car may also be excluded. Consider the state of the roads you'll drive on before choosing your vehicle type.

Rental charges vary from country to country and depend on the model of car. You will be required to present a credit card and valid driving licence. Most international rental companies won't allow crossing a border with a rental car. Buying can be an option, and with the industry booming in South America – and more cars on the road every day – most countries have competitive secondhand markets. If you want to buy a car, make sure you check the quality of vehicle (standards are lower than in Europe and the US) and your insurance cover. Driving standards are poor, so beware, especially at night. Honk your horn before going round any corner – the locals do this with great gusto, so no one will find you rude. South Americans drive on the right except in Suriname and Guyana. A useful website for driving in South America is Ⓦdrivetheamericas.com.

By air

Several budget airlines have sprung up in recent years, although they are still more expensive than US or European counterparts. That may change when the Viva airlines chain, backed by Ryanair and which already includes VivaColombia and Mexico's VivaAerobus, expands into Costa Rica, Peru and Ecuador. You can normally check-in online, but always find out whether flights need reconfirming. On certain flights in Peru, LAN and TACA charge a fee at the airport for passengers who can't prove Peruvian residency or citizenship; check the small print. Remember that distances are large and may involve a stopover. Budget airlines include Brazil's Gol (Ⓦvoegol.com.br), Chile's Sky (Ⓦwww.skyair line.cl) and Colombia's EasyFly (Ⓦeasyfly.com.co) and VivaColombia (Ⓦvivacolombia.co).

Airpasses

If you plan to do a lot of travelling around South America, consider one of the reasonable **airpasses**. These are a godsend if you want to see as much as possible in a limited time.

All Airpass (Ⓦallairpass.com) is a useful website for checking the different "airpass" offers out there from regional airlines. The passes are only available to travellers with a scheduled international return ticket and they have to be purchased outside South America. After you have used the first sector on your pass the ticket is non-refundable. Prices range from US$500 to US$1300 depending on the number of stops and area covered.

The **Mercosur Airpass** covers travel in Argentina, Brazil, Chile, Paraguay and Uruguay. Prices are calculated on a kilometres-flown basis. There is a maximum of two stopovers and four flight coupons for each country, and the pass is valid for seven to thirty days. The pass is available directly from the participating airlines (including Gol, Aerolíneas Argentinas and Austral). You can rebook to change dates (but not reroute); contact the individual airlines for more details. Both LAN (Ⓦlan.com) and TAM (Ⓦtam.com .br) also offer their own airpasses for routes they fly.

By train

Trains are much less frequent and efficient than South American buses, but if you have a little time to spare they provide a wonderful way to see the countryside and wildlife, as they tend to travel more exotic routes. Typically they are less expensive than buses, but services in popular tourist areas can be pricey. Two of the most famous routes are from Cusco to the start of the Inca Trail (see p.764) in Peru and the Serra Verde Express (see p.349) between Curitiba and Morretes in Brazil. There are several types of train, including the fast and efficient *ferrotren*, stopping at major stations only; the average *tren rápido*; the slower *expreso*, which stops at most stations; and the super-slow and amazingly cheap *mixto*, which stops for everyone – and their livestock too.

By boat

There are several ferry and catamaran services on South America's **lakes**, especially in Chile, Argentina, Peru and Bolivia, providing unforgettable views, including the Southern Lakes Crossing (see p.442) between Argentina and Chile, and trips on Lake Titicaca (see p.787) between Bolivia and Peru.

One of the finest ways to soak up the slow pace of South American life is to travel some of the continent's **rivers** by boat. Unfortunately, the riverboat industry is in decline, especially on the Amazon, with more passengers flying and cargo-only replacing many travel boats. However, several riverboat services survive, recommended for anyone with time and patience, particularly on the narrower, less-frequented rivers. Shop around, as boats vary hugely in quality. Your ticket will include hammock space and basic food, but drinks are extra and will probably be expensive on board – it's best to bring your own supplies. You should also bring a hammock, rope, insect repellent and a sleeping bag, and aim to be on board well before departure to ensure that you don't get put right next to the toilets.

By bicycle

If you're fit and hardy enough to consider cycling in South America, there are a few common-sense rules. Given the terrain, a mountain bike is best, unless you stick to paved roads and well-travelled routes. Taking on some of the Andean roads, though, is an experience hard to rival. In adventure travel centres, especially in Argentina and Chile, bikes can be rented for short periods, but if you're doing serious cycling, bring your own. Bikes and bike parts tend to be of a lower quality in South America than in other parts of the world, so give your bike a thorough check before you go. Carry a basic repair kit and check the bike daily when you arrive. Weather can be a problem, especially in Patagonia, where winds can reach 80km/hr, and be aware that bicycle theft – particularly in larger towns – is common; bring a good bike lock. Finally, remember that South American drivers can be a hazard, so try to avoid major roads and motorways if at all possible.

Hitchhiking

Hitchhiking is still fairly common in rural South America, and it isn't hard to get a lift if you're on the road early. Be aware, though, that many drivers now expect to be paid – it's only in the Southern Cone (Argentina, Chile and Uruguay) that hitchhiking seems to be understood to be free. Prices are usually around that of a bus fare, but if you head to the local truck park or refuelling station (most towns have one), ask around for the going rate. Hitchhiking in South America, like anywhere in the world, is a potentially perilous enterprise – travellers should be aware that they do so at their own risk. Couples and groups are safest; women should never hitchhike alone.

Accommodation

The range of accommodation available in South America – and the variety of price and quality that goes with it – is enormous and, should you be embarking on a multi-country tour, you'll find that the US$10 that buys you a night's rest in Ecuador won't even stretch to breakfast in the Southern Cone or French Guiana.

Most local tourist offices will provide a list of available accommodation, but bear in mind that establishments often pay to be included and that they may include little outside the main tourist hotspots. Generally, tourist boards will not recommend specific accommodation, nor book it.

Usually there is no shortage of places to stay, but use common sense if you plan to be somewhere at the time of a local festival, such as in Rio for Carnaval. Obviously, accommodation fills up quickly at these times, prices skyrocket and it's best to book well in advance. While the types of lodging described below offer an overview of your options in South America, names, classifications and prices vary from country to country. Unless alternatives such as dorms or camping are specified, **prices** quoted for accommodation throughout the guide are for the **cheapest double room in high season**. A good resource for budget accommodation in South America is ⓦ hosteltrail.com.

Hospedajes, residenciales, albergues and pensiones

These categories of accommodation are all used throughout South America and are interchangeable terms, although **pensiones** (known as *pensões* or pousadas in Portuguese) and **residenciales** are officially the most basic forms of accommodation. Generally, the Andean countries are the least expensive, and you should be able to find a decent room in a *residencial* or *pensión* for under US$15 (US$8 for dorms). For this price you should expect a bed, shared bathroom and intermittent hot water. In Brazil, the room cost will usually include breakfast but most other places are room only. In the south of Argentina and Chile, you can expect to spend around US$45 a night – check out the quality of the local *casas familiares* (family houses where you stay with a local family in a room in their house), which can be the best value for money in these areas.

Hostales, hosterías and haciendas

Hostales tend to fill the gap between the totally basic *pensión* and hotels, and come in many shapes, sizes and forms. Usually they include private bathrooms and hot water, clean towels and maybe a television, and cost from US$5 to US$20 per night. In the southern countries, though, *hostales* may be youth hostels.

Hosterías and **haciendas** are often old, sprawling estates converted into hotels, and are perhaps the grandest places to stay on the continent. They can be furnished in period style and offer excellent home-cooked meals, fires, hot water and maybe a swimming pool. Be aware that *hostería* can also refer to a family-style hotel complex out of town, so check which kind of *hostería* you're getting first.

Camping

Camping is most popular in the southern region of Latin America, particularly in the Southern Cone areas of Argentina and Chile. It is wise to stick to official sites, which are usually well equipped, with hot, running water, toilets, firepits and maybe even a self-service laundry. Camping is not really a popular or viable option in the northern countries unless as part of an organized tour, and is practically non-existent in Colombia, French Guiana and Paraguay, though French Guiana does offer *carbets*, shelters where you can hang a hammock.

ACCOMMODATION ALTERNATIVES

Useful websites that provide alternatives to standard hotel and hostel accommodation:

Airbnb ⓦ airbnb.com
CouchSurfing ⓦ couchsurfing.org
Craigslist ⓦ craigslist.org
Roomorama ⓦ roomorama.com
Vacation Rentals by Owner ⓦ vrbo.com

Youth hostels

Youth hostels are not always the most viable option in South America, but in the more expensive southern countries like Argentina and Chile, they are a more attractive choice: competition means that many have great facilities and offer extras, from free internet to party nights. Prices average US$10–15 per night and most are open all year, although some only open in January and February for the South American summer. If you are planning on using hostels extensively, consider getting an official **HI card**, which will quickly pay for itself in discounted rates.

HOSTELLING ORGANIZATIONS

Argentina Hostelling International Argentina/Red Argentina de Alojamiento para Jóvenes (RAAJ) ☎ 011 4511 8723, ⓦ hostels.org.ar.
Argentina, Brazil, Chile, Peru and Uruguay Che Lagarto ⓦ chelagarto.com. Regional chain of hostels.
Brazil Federação Brasileira dos Albergues de Juventude (FBAJ) ☎ 21 2531 1085, ⓦ hostel.org.br.
Chile Asociación Chilena de Albergues Turísticos Juveniles ☎ 02 577 1200, ⓦ hostelling.cl.
Peru Asociación Peruana de Albergues Turísticos Juveniles, Av Casimiro Ulloa 328, Miraflores, Lima ☎ 01 446 5488, ⓦ limahostell.com.pe.
South America Hostelling International ⓦ hihostels.com. Membership cards and worldwide hostel booking.

Health

The potential health risks in South America read like a textbook of tropical diseases and the possibilities could easily deter nervous travellers before they even set out. But if you prepare for your trip carefully and take sensible precautions while travelling, you will probably face nothing worse than a mild case of "Montezuma's revenge" (traveller's diarrhoea) as your system gets used to foreign germs and unhygienic conditions.

It is important to get the best health advice before you travel – prevention is always better than cure. Consult a medical specialist (see p.34) on each of the countries you wish to visit. About ten weeks before you travel, **vaccinations** can be arranged with your doctor or a specialized tropical diseases clinic. Bring your vaccination record when you travel. If you are taking any prescription drugs, your doctor can prescribe enough for the time you are away, and you should also take a list with you and a covering letter in case of emergencies. Good **medical insurance** (see p.38) is essential. It is important to declare any pre-existing conditions, and also to ensure that you have sufficient cover for all the extra activities you may undertake (particularly diving, extreme sports and hiking at high altitudes).

A common affliction is **heat stroke**, for which you should seek immediate treatment. Avoid dehydration by drinking bottled water and staying off alcohol, and stay out of the sun during the heat of the day (midday until around 4pm).

Pharmacies abound in every town but bringing a basic first-aid kit is sensible. Essentials in remote areas include insect repellent, bandages, painkillers, anti-diarrhoeal tablets and antiseptic cream.

Bites and stings

The general advice is to use an **insect repellent** containing at least 35 percent DEET, especially in rural areas or where malaria is endemic, and to wear light clothes that cover as much of your body as possible. It is wise to use a mosquito net or a mosquito coil containing permethrin at night, especially in the cheaper hotels.

Venomous **spiders and snakes** exist throughout the continent and bites from these, while rare, merit seeking medical advice as soon as possible. Most responsible tour companies carry antivenin, but in the absence of this, prompt medical attention is the only answer. A photo or description of the offending species may be useful, but never attempt to catch or kill it as this can provoke further bites, and don't listen to so-called local knowledge involving tourniquets, sucking venom or anything else – go to hospital.

If travelling to remote areas, consider a rabies vaccination – this will not make you immune to infection, but will buy you time to seek medical treatment after exposure. The majority of reported cases are from contact with dogs, and licks and scratches can be as dangerous as being bitten. If this happens, wash the area thoroughly with soap and water and disinfect it with alcohol or iodine solution. Always seek medical advice.

ALTITUDE SICKNESS

If you don't take care, altitude sickness, known locally as *soroche*, can seriously affect your trip. The most common symptoms are **headache**, **nausea** and **dizziness**, but when climbing at high altitude (above 2400m), symptoms can lead to more serious conditions such as **HAPE** (high altitude pulmonary oedema) or **HACE** (high altitude cerebral oedema), when medical attention should be sought immediately.

Soroche can affect anyone regardless of physical fitness. The key is to allow a few days to **acclimatize** when you arrive in a high-altitude region. When hiking, ascend slowly and follow the rule "sleep low and hike high" (sleep at a lower altitude than you ascended to that day), which allows your body time to recover. Drink plenty of water and eat light food, including carbs. Avoid alcohol and caffeine and, most importantly, pace yourself. Don't attempt to climb a mountain like Cotopaxi or Chimborazo after just a few days at 2800m in Quito – you need a couple of days above 2500m, then a couple more above 3500m before climbing over 4000m. If you are hiking as part of a tour and not dealing well with the altitude, alert your guide. Better to turn back than risk your health. In the Andean region locals swear by "*mate de coca*" – coca leaf tea – as a cure.

A much more likely nuisance when visiting wilder areas is the itchy **bites** given by tiny black sand flies or painful bites of ants and ticks. Hairy caterpillars are also capable of giving nasty stings similar to burns.

Mosquito-borne diseases

Malaria is present throughout the continent; check before travelling on current advice on the countries you plan to visit. Malaria prevention is two-fold; in addition to avoiding mosquito bites as detailed above, travellers should be sure to take a prescription anti-malarial drug, typically malarone (usually the best option), chloroquine or doxycycline – consult with a doctor before taking any. These should generally be started several weeks before you travel, and the full course must be completed which means continuing to take them after leaving a malaria zone. Symptoms can occur any time up to a year after travel, so it's important to inform your doctor about your travel history. Initial symptoms of malaria are a raging thirst and an aching upper back. Seek medical attention immediately if you think you may have picked it up.

Yellow fever is a serious disease carried by mosquitoes, which, like malaria, can be avoided by vaccination and taking sensible precautions against insect bites. It is present in most of South America except the far south. You'll need to show a certificate if travelling from one endemic country to another (although you won't always be asked for it, it's best to have one anyway). The following countries are considered the greatest risk areas: Bolivia, Brazil, Colombia, Ecuador, Peru and Venezuela.

Dengue fever is also mosquito-borne and there is no vaccine. The mosquitoes carrying the virus tend to live near stagnant water so it's more of a problem in poor areas. It has become a serious health issue in Brazil, Bolivia, Paraguay and Argentina, but is present in most countries in South America. Symptoms include high fever and aching limbs. Drink fluids, take paracetamol to reduce fever and seek medical attention immediately.

Intestinal problems

Common illnesses such as traveller's **diarrhoea** can be largely avoided by steps such as washing your hands before eating, and drinking bottled water. Unpasteurized dairy products and all un-refrigerated food should be avoided and fruit and vegetables should be washed and peeled. Take care with shellfish, lettuce and ice. If you do fall ill, rest and replace the fluids you have lost by drinking plenty of water and an oral rehydration solution. A home-made option is 1tsp salt and 8tsp of sugar in 1 litre of water. An anti-diarrhoeal tablet can usually alleviate symptoms.

Other than diarrhoea that usually lasts no more than a few days there are a number of more serious problems that you can encounter on your travels. **Cholera**, for example, is an acute infection with watery diarrhoea and vomiting; **dysentery** has similar symptoms but includes bleeding. If your diarrhoea persists for a week and your symptoms include a chill or fever or bleeding, or if you are too ill to drink, seek medical help. Typhoid is also a problem in the poorest, most rural areas and is transferred through food or water. Symptoms include fever, headache and occasionally a bleeding nose or spotty rash. Seek medical advice immediately – the fever can be easily treated with antibiotics but is serious if not caught early.

To avoid problems, always use bottled water, even for cleaning your teeth. Avoid buying food from street vendors unless the food is piping hot, and think carefully about swimming in lakes and rivers. If bottled water isn't available, there are various methods of treating water: boiling for a minimum of five minutes is the most effective method. Filtering alongside chemical sterilization is the next best option. Pregnant women or people with thyroid problems should consult their doctors about chemical sterilization formulae.

MEDICAL RESOURCES FOR TRAVELLERS

UK AND IRELAND

Fit for Travel Ⓦ www.fitfortravel.nhs.uk. NHS website with information about travel-related diseases and how to avoid them.
MASTA (Medical Advisory Service for Travellers Abroad) Ⓦ masta-travel-health.com. Comprehensive website for medical advisory services for travel abroad. See website for the nearest clinic.
Tropical Medical Bureau Republic of Ireland; see website for different branches Ⓦ tmb.ie.

US AND CANADA

Canadian Society for International Health ☎ 613 241 5785, Ⓦ csih.org. Distributes a free pamphlet, "Health Information for Canadian Travellers", containing an extensive list of travel health centres in Canada.
Center for Disease Control ☎ 1 800 232 6348, Ⓦ cdc.gov/travel. US Department of Health and Human Services travel health and disease control department. Offers comprehensive and up-to-date advice on health for travellers. Publishes outbreak warnings, suggested inoculations, precautions and other background information.
International Society for Travel Medicine Ⓦ istm.org. Has a full list of clinics specializing in international travel health.
Travel Health Online Ⓦ www.tripprep.com. Travel Health Online provides an online comprehensive database of necessary vaccinations for most countries, as well as destination and medical service provider information.

AUSTRALIA AND NEW ZEALAND

Travellers' Medical and Vaccination Centres Ⓦ traveldoctor .com.au. Contains a list of all Travellers' Medical and Vaccination Centres throughout Australia, New Zealand and Southeast Asia, plus general information on travel health.

Culture and etiquette

South America is a vast continent and it's difficult to generalize about how to dress or behave; ultimately, you should try to behave unobtrusively and dress modestly if not at the beach.

Cultural hints

People usually shake hands upon introduction and women generally kiss acquaintances on one cheek or two (dependent on the country), although you can defer to a handshake if you prefer. It is common to wish people you meet on the street *"buenos días"* (*"bom dia"* in Brazil) or *"buenas tardes"* (*"boa tarde"* in Brazil). Politeness is a way of life in South America, and pleasantries are always exchanged before getting to any kind of business. Dress with respect in official or religious buildings.

Remember that in most South American countries, locals have a lax attitude to **time**, so expect people to arrive late in social situations and don't get annoyed if they do.

Tipping is generally common in restaurants and cafés but is lower than the norms in Europe and the US. If in doubt, ask a local (and not a waiter!).

Shopping

Shops and markets in South America tend to offer a wide range of beautifully crafted goods and antiques for the visitor. Prices are usually reasonable; you can **bargain** in markets and outside the tourist drags, but only do so if you really think the item is worth less than its asking price. If you decide to buy something, be firm – ask the price and confirm it before offering cash. Be polite to street vendors, no matter how annoyed you get with them. Remember that this is their livelihood and smile, saying *"no, gracias"* or *"não, obrigado"*. Check that you are not purchasing objects plundered from the jungle or made from endangered species.

As a rule of thumb, native crafts are usually of the best quality and cheapest when bought close to the source. Buying such items, rather than mass-produced alternatives, is a good way to help local *artesania* and give something back to the communities you're visiting.

Public holidays and festivals

Travelling through South America entails negotiating a variety of **public holidays** (*feriados* in Spanish and Portuguese) that differ from country to country. Bear in mind as well that, particularly in more remote areas, some towns and villages celebrate saints' days and other local holidays that shut down businesses and make travel difficult. Check with local tourist information offices (where they exist) for more details. South Americans are not known for passing up an excuse to celebrate.

Every country in South America has a take on **Carnival** (known in Spanish and Portuguese as *Carnaval*); the exact time varies, but official celebrations usually take place on the days before Ash Wednesday and Lent. There are national variations, of course: in Ecuador, for instance, the festivities are most visibly represented by the water fights throughout the country. There are a couple of locations where Carnaval has become famous internationally, such as Oruro in Bolivia and Encarnación in Paraguay. The most famous Carnaval of all, however, is in Rio de Janeiro, Brazil, which lasts for weeks before and after the "official" Carnaval time and is an extravagant mix of dance, sweat, drink, laughter and colour.

South America remains largely a devoutly Catholic continent, although Argentina and Uruguay are the most secular nations – expect lots of festivals around Semana Santa (Holy Week in Easter). Show respect and dress modestly when entering a church or religious site.

Work and study

Opportunities for volunteer and non-profit work abound, but be prepared to pay something towards your upkeep. Paid opportunities are few and far between, and some are likely to be illegal.

Teaching English

Qualified English teachers with a CELTA, TEFL or TESOL should be able to find work, but you are strongly advised to arrange a placement before you travel. Qualified schoolteachers from English-speaking countries can also find teaching opportunities, and if you have a Master's degree, you can teach at university. However, turning up and looking for work is likely to leave you frustrated and/or violating local laws – officially you will require a work permit. The British Council (Ⓦbritishcouncil.org) and the TEFL website (Ⓦtefl.com) each has a list of English-teaching vacancies. Most jobs are in the larger cities.

Language study

South America has long been a hugely popular destination for people wishing to brush up on their **Spanish**: Cusco, Peru; Buenos Aires, Argentina; Sucre, Bolivia; and Quito, Ecuador, are the most popular destinations and a huge variety of courses and levels is available. In Brazil, most of the large cities are great

locations for learning **Portuguese**. You can also learn **indigenous languages** such as Quechua in Bolivia or Guaraní in Paraguay. Typically, three types of course are on offer: a classroom-based course, a more active learning course through activities and excursions, or the live-in option with a host family.

LANGUAGE SCHOOLS

Academía Latinoamericana de Español Ⓣ 1 801 268 2468 (US), Ⓦ www.latinoschools.com. Spanish classes in Ecuador, Peru and Bolivia.

Amerispan Ⓣ 1 800 511 0179 (US), Ⓦ amerispan.com. Spanish courses and volunteer opportunities.

Apple Languages Ⓣ 703 835 9762 (US), Ⓣ 01509 211612 (UK), Ⓦ applelanguages.com. High-quality Spanish schools throughout South America.

Bridge Linguatec Ⓦ bridge.edu. Spanish and Portuguese classes in Argentina, Chile and Brazil.

Don Quijote Ⓦ donquijote.org. High-quality, internationally recognized courses offered in Argentina, Bolivia, Chile, Ecuador and Peru.

Escuela Runawasi Ⓣ 04 424 8923 (Bolivia), Ⓦ runawasi.org. Quechua, Aymara and Spanish-language and literature lessons in Cochabamba, Bolivia.

Latin Immersion Ⓦ latinimmersion.com. Spanish immersion courses throughout the continent.

Simón Bolívar Spanish School Ⓣ 07 284 4555 (Ecuador), Ⓦ bolivar2.com. Based in Cuenca, Ecuador, with courses based on a study of the country.

Spanish Study Holidays Ⓣ 01509 211612 (UK), Ⓦ www.spanishstudyholidays.com. Courses from one week to nine months.

Volunteering

Volunteer opportunities are available in social, environmental and conservation work in many South American countries, though you will be expected to pay for the privilege. Working alongside local people on a worthwhile project that captures your interest can be an unforgettable experience.

VOLUNTEER ORGANIZATIONS

While many positions are organized prior to arrival, it's also possible to pick something up on the ground through word of mouth. Noticeboards in the more popular backpacker hostels are always good sources of information.

Earthwatch Institute Offices worldwide, Ⓦ earthwatch.org. Long-established research company offering environmental and social volunteer programmes throughout the continent.

Global Volunteer Network Ⓣ 0800 032 5035 (UK), Ⓦ globalvolunteernetwork.org. Volunteer opportunities in eight different community projects in Peru.

i to i Volunteering Ⓣ 0800 011 1156 (UK), Ⓦ i-to-i.com. Offers everything from conservation work in the Galápagos Islands to archeology work in Lima, Peru.

Projects Abroad ☎ 01903 708 300 (UK), ⓦ projects-abroad .co.uk. Teaching, conservation and community projects throughout South America.
Volunteer South America ☎ 01903 708 300 (UK), ⓦ volunteersouthamerica.net. Lists free and low-cost volunteering opportunities across the continent.

Crime and personal safety

South America is a continent that suffers from high levels of poverty. This tends to go hand in hand with crime levels, which, while much magnified by tales in the foreign news media, shouldn't be ignored. In general, cities are more dangerous than rural areas, although the very deserted mountain plains can harbour bandits. Many of the working-class *barrios* of big cities are "no-go" areas for tourists, as are the marginal areas near them. One of the biggest problems in urban areas is **theft**, and bag snatching, handbag slitting and occasional armed robbery are problems in cities such as Buenos Aires, Lima, Rio, Salvador, Recife, Georgetown, Quito and Cusco. Caracas has also experienced an upsurge in violent crime in the last few years, so extra precaution is recommended there.

Take particular care on the street, in taxis and in restaurants. Any unsolicited approach from a stranger should be treated with the utmost suspicion, no matter how well dressed or trustworthy they may look. There are obvious preventative measures you can take to avoid being mugged: avoid isolated and poorly lit areas, especially at night; never walk along a beach alone at night, or even in a pair if female.

Keep a particular eye out in busy areas and watch out on public transport and at bus stations, where **pickpocketing** is rife. If travelling by bus, keep your valuables in your carry-on luggage rather than stowing them below with your backpack. Make sure that you are given the numbered receipt corresponding to your bag. If you need to hail a taxi, get someone at your hotel to recommend one, or hail a moving one – never get into a "taxi" that just happens to be parked at the kerbside or which has two drivers. Avoid wearing expensive jewellery and watches, dress down, and keep cameras out of sight.

Car-jackings can also be a problem, particularly in certain areas of Brazil. When driving in the city, keep doors locked and windows closed, particularly at night, and be especially vigilant at traffic lights. Kidnapping of tourists in South America is extremely unlikely.

Colombia has been in the grip of a **civil war** for decades and there are still flare-ups between the army and FARC. In general, though, the areas mentioned in this guide are safer than ever.

Drugs

Just say no! In South America **drug trafficking** is a huge, ugly and complicated enterprise, and large-scale dealers love to prey on lost-looking foreigners. Don't let anyone else touch your luggage, be sure to pack it yourself and don't carry anything – no matter how innocuous it may seem – for anyone else. You will find that drugs, particularly marijuana and cocaine, are fairly ubiquitous in the region, but you should be aware that they are illegal and that punishments are severe. The law is in flux in Uruguay (see box, p.836), but marijuana remains illegal for visitors to buy. Tourists are likely to come off much worse than locals at the hands of the South American police, something of which the dealers and pushers are very aware. If you happen to visit a region famed for drug trafficking, stay well away from anything that looks (or smells) like trouble.

The only **legal high** on sale in South America is the leaves of coca (locals will be keen to point out it has nothing to do with chemically produced cocaine), which are particularly popular in Bolivia and Peru. They are usually used to make *mate de coca*, a hugely popular tea in the Andes, and one that's claimed to cure altitude sickness (among other things). Some people chew the leaves as this is meant to produce a mildly intoxicating state, but the taste and texture may well convince you that you can do without the alleged high. If you want to try *mate de coca* or chewing on coca leaves, be aware that there is a possibility that you could test positive for cocaine use in the weeks following your trip. Do not take any leaves out of the country as they may be illegal elsewhere.

Reporting crime

In case you are mugged or robbed, you should make sure that you have a photocopy of your passport and plane tickets in a safe place. Call the local police immediately and tell them what happened. It's likely that they won't do much more than take a statement, but you'll need it for insurance purposes. In some South American countries there is a special "tourist police" force, used to dealing with foreigners and, hopefully, able to speak English.

Women travellers

Though violent attacks against women travellers are not very common, many women find that the barrage of hisses, hoots and comments in parts of South America comes close to spoiling their trip. Latin American men are not renowned for their forward-thinking attitudes towards women's emancipation, and genuinely see nothing wrong with the heady sense of machismo that rules much of the continent. You may find that attitudes are less polarized in country areas.

There are measures you can take to avoid being hassled. Don't go to bars or nightclubs alone – this is an activity only undertaken by prostitutes in the region, and you will be considered fair game. If you are approached and feel uncomfortable, try to avoid antagonizing the guy, but make it clear that you're not interested (in Spanish *"no estoy interesada"* or *"não estou interessada"* in Portuguese). It's sometimes easier to invent a boyfriend or husband than to get into a protracted dispute. Watch how the local women behave and where they go, and never be afraid to ask for help if you feel lost or threatened.

Solo women travellers should also avoid going to remote locations alone, and if you go as part of an organized visit, check the credentials of the tour company. However, if you are attacked, you should not only get medical attention and go to the regular police, but also contact the tourist police and your country's embassy.

Travel essentials

Costs

South America is not as cheap as it used to be, but, if approached in the right way, you can still travel for less here than you would on other continents. French Guiana, Suriname, Argentina, Chile and Brazil are the most expensive countries, with prices often

---

PRICES

At the beginning of each country chapter you'll find a guide to "**rough costs**", including food, accommodation and travel. These costs are quoted in US$ to make comparison easy; within the chapter itself prices are quoted in local currency. Note that prices and exchange rates change all the time – they are particularly volatile in Argentina (see p.51) and Venezuela (see p.861), where parallel black market rates operate – which may affect the accuracy of those figures we have quoted.

---

comparable to North America, Europe and Australia. Bolivia, Peru and Ecuador still remain budget destinations, but the highlights such as the Galápagos Islands, the Amazon jungle and mountain climbing can add a lot of expense to the trip.

Electricity

The standard electrical current in most South American countries is 220V, 50/60Hz. The main exceptions are Colombia, Ecuador and Venezuela, where a 110/120V, 50/60Hz current is used, and Suriname, where 127V is standard. Some major tourist cities also use a 110V, 50Hz current, at odds with the rest of their country, including La Paz and Potosí in Bolivia and Rio de Janeiro and São Paulo in Brazil. For the most part **plug sockets** are flat two-pin (as in the US), but three-pin sockets are sometimes found. Your best bet if visiting several countries is to travel with a universal adaptor and make sure you check appliances' compatibility before plugging them in to South American sockets.

The South American attitude to safety can be lax and you may see plugs that obviously don't fit, forcibly pushed into sockets. Take particular care with electrical showers, common in the poorer countries.

BUDGET TIPS

- Take local transport, which means buses and *colectivos* instead of taxis or tourist shuttles.
- Avoid the most touristy destinations. Get off the beaten track and you'll notice the price difference.
- Eat and drink as the locals do. Eat street food from popular vendors and in restaurants choose local staples over the tourist menu. Buy from stores and markets as opposed to hostels or hotels.
- You can make big savings on bottled water, which many hostels will refill for free or a small fee.
- Be prepared to barter – bargaining can be fun. Don't be afraid to confront taxi drivers or chancers who you suspect are trying to rip you off. However, don't be too ruthless – bargaining over a few cents is not cool.

ROUGH GUIDES TRAVEL INSURANCE

Rough Guides has teamed up with Worldnomads.com to offer great **travel insurance** deals. Policies are available to residents of over 150 countries, with cover for a wide range of **adventure sports**, 24hr emergency assistance, high levels of medical and evacuation cover and a stream of **travel safety information**. Roughguides.com users can take advantage of their policies online 24/7, from anywhere in the world – even if you're already travelling. And since plans often change when you're on the road, you can extend your policy and even claim online. Roughguides.com users who buy travel insurance with Worldnomads.com can also leave a positive footprint and donate to a community development project. For more information go to Ⓦ **roughguides.com/travel-insurance**.

Gay and lesbian travellers

Rural, Catholic South America is not overly welcoming towards homosexuality but there is more acceptance in urban areas. Gay and lesbian travellers would probably be safest following locals' example – public displays of affection between two men or two women could invite trouble on much of the continent.

Things are generally easier in the big cities, though, and there are a couple of major destinations where anything goes. Brazil boasts most of them – Rio de Janeiro, Salvador and São Paulo provide safe and welcoming havens for any sexual orientation, as do Buenos Aires and Santiago. If you are looking for thumping nightlife and a very "out" scene, then these cities are the best on the continent. A useful website for LGBT travel companies is Ⓦ iglta.org/south-america.

Insurance

A typical **travel insurance policy** provides cover for the loss of baggage, tickets and – up to a certain limit – cash, as well as cancellation or curtailment of your journey. Most of them exclude so-called dangerous sports unless an extra premium is paid: this category can include scuba diving, white-water rafting, windsurfing and trekking, though probably not kayaking or jeep safaris. Many policies can be changed to exclude coverage you don't need. If you take medical coverage, ascertain whether benefits will be paid as treatment proceeds or only after your return home, and whether there is a 24-hour medical emergency number. When securing baggage cover, make sure that the per-article limit will cover your most valuable possession. If you need to make a claim, you should keep receipts for medicines and medical treatment and, in the event you have anything stolen, you must obtain an official statement from the police.

Internet

Internet access is now almost ubiquitous in cities and towns across South America (though it is more restricted in the Guianas), and only in rural areas is it difficult to come by. Connection speeds and costs vary from country to country, and in some cases from area to area. Wi-fi is now increasingly common in hostels and hotels, but also in cafés and restaurants (especially in the Southern Cone).

Mail

Post offices in cities and major towns offer a wide range of services; those in villages are much more basic, with shorter opening hours and slow service. It's often quicker and safer to use a courier service – although you'll pay much more. Hotels in capital cities may sell stamps and have a postbox – if you are staying in one, this can be the most convenient way to send a letter home. Expect airmail to take from a week to a month to Western Europe and the US.

Maps

Excellent maps of South America, covering the region at a scale of 1:5,000,000 and individual countries, are produced by Canada's International Travel Maps and Books (Ⓦ itmb.com). In South America the South America Explorers Club (Ⓦ saexplorers.org) is a good point of reference, and often the only source of accurate maps is the military – check at the local tourist offices on where to purchase them. If you'd rather be sure, buy maps at home and bring them with you.

Money

ATMs are widely available in most large cities, but in smaller towns and rural areas don't expect to rely solely on using international debit cards to access funds. Travellers' cheques are much less widely accepted than they once were, and you'll often get a fixed exchange rate: pre-paid **currency cards** are an excellent alternative, though these, too, require access to an ATM. There is still nothing as easy to use as cash, preferably US dollars, and it makes sense always to carry at least a few small-denomination notes for when all else fails.

Credit card fraud is a problem on the continent, particularly in Brazil and Venezuela; be sure to keep an eye on your card and to retain your copy of the transaction slip. In many countries credit cards will only be accepted in the biggest hotels and shops, and banks will sometimes refuse to offer cash advances against them. Payments in plastic may also incur high surcharges when compared to cash payments.

When **exchanging money**, you should use only authorized bureaux de change, such as banks, cambios and tourist facilities, rather than deal with moneychangers on the streets. In remote and rural areas, and for shopping in local markets and stalls, **cash** is a necessity – preferably in small denominations of local currency. Some countries, including Venezuela (see box, p.861) and Argentina, have a flourishing black market with much better exchange rates.

Phones

The ubiquity of mobile phones means **public phone boxes** have all but disappeared in many South American countries. Where phone boxes exist, they usually operate with cards, available from newspaper kiosks. There are, however, plenty of *locutorios*, stores originally dedicated to telephone communications, most of which have now branched out into internet access as well. You can make direct-dial international calls from most South American phones, apart from remote areas, where calls must be made through an operator. International phone calls are, in general, expensive from South America, so you're best off trying to buy international calling cards where they exist or using web services such as Skype – most internet cafés will be set up with webcams and headsets.

Mobile phones

If you want to use your **mobile phone** in South America, you'll need to check with your phone provider whether it will work abroad, and what the call charges are (beware of amassing a fortune in data charges and use wi-fi wherever possible).

You are likely to be charged extra for incoming calls when abroad, as the people calling you will be paying the usual rate. If you're in the country for a while, and assuming your phone is unlocked (most contract phones are locked so that they can only be used on one network – your provider can usually unlock it for

CALLING FROM ABROAD

To phone abroad, you must first dial the international access code of the country you are calling from, then the country code of the country you are calling to, then the area code (usually without the first zero) and then the phone number. In some South American countries there may be different international access codes for different providers. See below for details.

INTERNATIONAL ACCESS CODES WHEN DIALLING FROM:

Argentina ☎00
Australia ☎0011
Bolivia ☎0010 (Entel), ☎0011 (AES), ☎0012 (Teledata), ☎0013 (Boliviatel)
Brazil ☎0014 (Brasil Telecom), ☎0015 (Telefónica), ☎0021 (Embratel), ☎0023 (Intelig), ☎0031 (Telemar)
Canada ☎011
Chile ☎00
Colombia ☎009 (Telecom), ☎007 (ETB/Mundo), ☎005 (Orbitel)
Ecuador ☎00
French Guiana ☎00
Guyana ☎001
Ireland ☎00
New Zealand ☎00
Paraguay ☎002
Peru ☎00
Suriname ☎002
UK ☎00
Uruguay ☎00
US ☎011
Venezuela ☎00

COUNTRY CODES WHEN DIALLING TO:

Argentina ☎54
Australia ☎61
Bolivia ☎591
Brazil ☎55
Canada ☎1
Chile ☎56
Colombia ☎57
Ecuador ☎593
French Guiana ☎594
Guyana ☎592
Ireland ☎353
New Zealand ☎64
Paraguay ☎595
Peru ☎51
Suriname ☎597
UK ☎44
Uruguay ☎598
US ☎1
Venezuela ☎58

TIME ZONES

Most of South America is spread across only two time zones, with the outlying islands spread across five:

GMT–6: Galápagos Islands and Easter Island
GMT–5: Colombia, Ecuador and Peru
GMT–4.5: Venezuela (a new time zone created by former president Chávez in 2007)
GMT–4: Chile, Bolivia, Guyana, Paraguay, western Brazil and the Falklands
GMT–3: Argentina, Uruguay, French Guiana, Suriname and most of Brazil
GMT–2: Fernando de Noronha (Brazil) and South Georgia

a fee), you can buy a **SIM card** from a local telephone company and use it in your phone. These are usually pretty cheap and your calls will be charged at a local rate. If you don't have a mobile phone and are staying a few months in one country, consider buying a local phone, easily done for less than US$50.

Tourist information

The quantity and quality of tourist information varies from country to country, but in general, don't expect too much. While almost every city in Brazil, Argentina and Peru will have at least one well-equipped tourist office, they are much thinner on the ground in countries like Paraguay and the Guianas. We've listed websites wherever pertinent throughout the guide; the following is a general list of useful ones.

SOUTH AMERICA ON THE INTERNET

Ⓦ **buenosairesherald.com** English-language newspaper, updated weekly.
Ⓦ **clarin.com** The largest Spanish-language daily newspaper on the continent, printed in Buenos Aires.
Ⓦ **lab.org.uk** News, information and analysis on Latin America.

Ⓦ **lapress.org** Non-profit news organization based in Lima, producing independent news and analysis.
Ⓦ **latinnews.com** Real-time news feed with major stories from all over South America in English.
Ⓦ **planeta.com** Excellent selection of online ecotravel and ecotourism resources for South America.
Ⓦ **roughguides.com** Travel articles, online community and guides covering the whole of South America.
Ⓦ **saexplorers.org** The website of the South American Explorers Club, a non-profit organization with the latest research, travel and adventure information.
Ⓦ **zonalatina.com/Zlmusic** Regional music links and information, covering everything from Sertaneja to Shakira.

Travellers with disabilities

South America is not the friendliest of destinations for travellers with disabilities and many places are downright inaccessible. The more modern the society, the more likely you are to find services for travellers with disabilities – this means that while Bolivia and Paraguay are pretty impenetrable, much of inhabited Chile and Argentina, as well as several cities in Brazil, is more accessible. Unfortunately, though, you may need to compromise over destination – big hotels in major cities that are very much on the tourist trail are much more likely to have facilities to cater to your needs than idyllic cabañas in the middle of nowhere. You might be limited as regards mobility, too, as local buses will probably prove difficult and you might need to settle for taxi services or internal flights. In any case, check with one of the agencies below before planning anything.

Access Travel UK ☎ 01942 888 844, Ⓦ access-travel.co.uk. Small tour operator that can arrange flights, transfers and accommodation. Personally checks and can guarantee accommodation standards in many countries.
Directions Unlimited US & Canada ☎ 1 800 533 5343, Ⓦ www .empressusa.com. Tour operator specializing in custom tours for people with disabilities.
National Disability Services (NDS) Australia ☎ 02 6283 3200, Ⓦ nds.org.au. Can supply lists of travel agencies and tour operators for people with disabilities.

YOUTH AND STUDENT DISCOUNTS

Various official and quasi-official youth/student ID cards are available and are worth the effort to obtain: they soon pay for themselves in savings. Full-time students are eligible for the **International Student ID Card** (ISIC; Ⓦ isiccard.com), which entitles the bearer (any student no matter their age) to special air, rail and bus fares and discounts at museums, theatres and other attractions. For Americans, there's also a health benefit, providing up to US$300,000 in emergency medical care, plus a 24hr hotline (☎ 1 800 353 1972).

You have to be 26 or younger to qualify for the International Youth Travel Card, which carries the same benefits. Teachers qualify for the International Teacher Card, offering similar discounts. All these cards are available from student travel specialists including STA.

PARQUE NACIONAL LOS GLACIARES, PATAGONIA

Argentina

HIGHLIGHTS

❶ **Buenos Aires** Tango and football rule in this European-style capital. **See p.52**

❷ **Iguazú Falls** The world's largest waterfalls are framed by lush, subtropical jungle. **See p.86**

❸ **Salta** This beautifully preserved colonial city is surrounded by epic mountain scenery. **See p.89**

❹ **Bariloche** An outdoor adventure hub with stunning mountain vistas. **See p.117**

❺ **Perito Moreno Glacier** A frozen landscape that splinters and creaks. **See p.143**

❻ **Ushuaia** The end of the earth and just 1000km from Antarctica. **See p.145**

HIGHLIGHTS ARE MARKED ON THE MAP ON P.43

ROUGH COSTS

Daily budget Basic US$50, occasional treat US$80

Drink Beer (1ltr) US$2.50 (shop) US$5 (bar/restaurant)

Food Asado barbecue US$20

Camping/hostel/budget hotel US$10/15/40

Travel Bus/airfare from Buenos Aires to Córdoba US$50/140

FACT FILE

Population 40 million

Official language Spanish

Currency Argentine peso (AR$)

Capital Buenos Aires

International phone code ☎54

Time zone GMT -3hr

1

Introduction

Even without the titanic wedge of Antarctica that its cartographers include in the national territory, Argentina ranks as the world's eighth-largest country. Stretching from the Tropic of Capricorn to the most southerly reaches of the planet's landmass, it encompasses a staggering diversity of climates and landscapes: from hot and humid jungles in the northeast and bone-dry Andean plateaux in the northwest, through endless grasslands, to the windswept steppe of Patagonia and the end-of-the-world archipelago of Tierra del Fuego.

A country influenced by generations of immigration from Europe and elsewhere, Argentina offers a variety of attractions, not least the great spectacles of tango and football in the seductive European-style capital **Buenos Aires**. Moreover, the extent and diversity of the country's natural scenery are staggering. Due north of the capital stretches **El Litoral**, a subtropical region of riverine landscapes featuring the awe-inspiring **Iguazú** waterfalls. Highlights of the northwest are the spectacular, polychrome **Quebrada de Humahuaca** gorge and the **Valles Calchaquíes**, stunningly beautiful valleys where high-altitude vineyards produce the delightfully flowery *torrontés* wine.

West and immediately south of Buenos Aires are the seemingly endless grassy plains of the **Pampas**. This is where you'll still glimpse traces of traditional **gaucho** culture, most famously celebrated in **San Antonio de Areco**. Here, too, you'll find some of the country's best *estancias*. As you move west, the **Central Sierras** loom on the horizon: within reach of **Córdoba**, the country's vibrant second city, are some of the oldest resorts on the continent. In the lee of the Andes, the vibrant city of **Mendoza** is the country's wine capital, from where the scenic Alta Montaña route climbs steeply to the Chilean border, passing **Cerro Aconcagua**, the highest mountain in the Americas and a dream challenge for mountaineers from around the world.

To the north of Mendoza, San Juan and La Rioja provinces are relatively uncharted territory but their star attractions are **Parque Nacional Talampaya**, with its giant red cliffs, and the nearby **Parque Provincial Ischigualasto**, usually known as Valle de la Luna on account of its intriguing, moon-like landscapes.

Argentina claims the lion's share of the sparsely populated expanses of **Patagonia**, one of the world's biggest deserts, and the frigid isles of **Tierra del Fuego**. An almost unbroken chain of national parks hugs the mountains, making for some of the best trekking anywhere on the planet – certainly include the savage granite peaks of the **Parque Nacional Los Glaciares** in your itinerary. For wildlife enthusiasts the **Peninsula Valdés** is also essential viewing, famous as a breeding ground for southern right whales.

CHRONOLOGY

1516 The first Europeans reach the Río de la Plata and clash with Querandí natives.

1535 Pedro de Mendoza founds Buenos Aires.

1609 The first missions to the Guaraní people are established in the upper Paraná.

1806 The British storm Buenos Aires, only to be expelled within a few months.

1810 The first elected junta is sworn in to replace Spanish leaders.

1816 Independence is officially declared in the city of Tucumán.

1854 The country's first railways are built.

1912 Universal male suffrage is introduced.

1930 Radical Hipólito Yrigoyen is overthrown in a military coup.

1943 A coup led by Juan Domingo Perón results in the ousting of the constitutional government.

1946 Juan Domingo Perón is elected president.

1952 Perón's wife Evita dies at the age of 33.

1955 Perón is overthrown in a military coup and exiled.

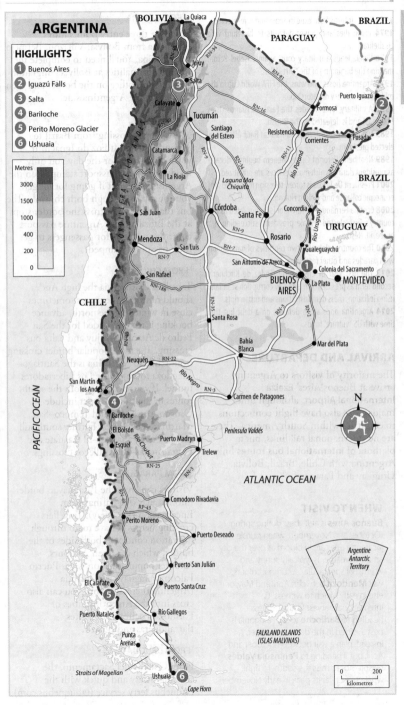

ARGENTINA

HIGHLIGHTS

1. Buenos Aires
2. Iguazú Falls
3. Salta
4. Bariloche
5. Perito Moreno Glacier
6. Ushuaia

Metres

3000	
1500	
1000	
400	
200	
0	

BOLIVIA
La Quiaca
PARAGUAY
BRAZIL

Jujuy
Salta
Cafayate
Tucumán
Santiago del Estero
Catamarca
La Rioja
Laguna Mar Chiquita
San Juan
Córdoba
Santa Fe
Concordia
Mendoza
San Luis
Rosario
San Rafael
San Antonio de Areco
Santa Rosa
Bahía Blanca
Mar del Plata
Neuquén
San Martín de los Andes
Bariloche
El Bolsón
Esquel
Puerto Madryn
Trelew
Comodoro Rivadavia
Perito Moreno
Puerto Deseado
Puerto San Julián
El Calafate
Puerto Santa Cruz
Puerto Natales
Río Gallegos
Punta Arenas
Ushuaia
Cape Horn

Puerto Iguazú
Formosa
Resistencia
Corrientes
Posadas
BRAZIL
Rio Paraná
Rio Uruguay
URUGUAY
Gualeguaychú
Colonia del Sacramento
BUENOS AIRES
La Plata
MONTEVIDEO

CORDILLERA DE LOS ANDES

CHILE

PACIFIC OCEAN

Río Negro
Carmen de Patagones
Península Valdés
Río Chubut

ATLANTIC OCEAN

Argentine Antarctic Territory

FALKLAND ISLANDS (ISLAS MALVINAS)

Straits of Magellan

RN-9, RN-34, RN-40, RN-16, RN-81, RN-12, RN-11, RN-14, RN-9, RN-7, RN-188, RN-35, RN-3, RN-2, RN-22, RN-25, RP-43, RN-40, RN-3

N

0	200
kilometres	

1

1973 Perón returns from exile in Spain and is re-elected.

1974 Perón dies and power defaults to his third wife "Isabelita".

1976 Videla leads a military coup against Isabel Perón, marking the beginning of the "Dirty War".

1978 Argentina hosts, and wins, the FIFA World Cup in the middle of a military dictatorship.

1982 A military force invades the Falkland Islands (Islas Malvinas) and is defeated by the British.

1983 Democracy is restored and Radical Raúl Alfonsín is elected president.

1989 Neoliberal Peronist Carlos Menem begins a decade as president during which most services are privatized.

2001 President De la Rúa is forced to resign in the midst of economic collapse and violent rioting.

2008 Cristina Fernández de Kirchner is inaugurated as the country's first elected female president, succeeding her husband, Néstor.

2010 The country celebrates two centuries of nationhood with parades and other festivities.

2012 The first year of Cristina Fernández de Kirchner's second term as president is marred by corruption scandals, rising inflation, mass demonstrations and urban riots.

2014 Argentina once again defaults on a debt but this time with US "vulture" funds.

ARRIVAL AND DEPARTURE

The majority of visitors to Argentina arrive at Buenos Aires' **Ezeiza International Airport**, although other major cities also have flight connections to countries within South America. There are no international **rail** links, but a plethora of **international bus routes** links Argentina with Chile, Brazil, Bolivia, Uruguay and Paraguay.

WHEN TO VISIT

Buenos Aires is at its best during spring (October and November), when purple jacaranda trees are in bloom all over the city and the weather is typically sunny and warm. For spectacular autumnal colours, visit **Mendoza** between April and May, or else in early March to witness its international harvest festival. Unless heading to **Bariloche** to ski, Patagonia is best avoided in the depths of winter. Instead, plan a visit between October and April, but if heading to **Peninsula Valdés**, be sure not to miss the southern right whale season, at its peak in early November.

FROM BOLIVIA

There are three entry points into Argentina from Bolivia: Villazón, Bermejo and Yacuiba. You'll need to complete the requisite formalities at Bolivia's migration and customs office on the border and then register on the Argentina side.

FROM BRAZIL

Most people crossing from Brazil to Argentina do so at Foz do Iguaçu. If you're just going for the day you only need to get your passport stamped on the Argentine side, but if going for longer you must pass through both controls. The bus that takes you across the border stops at the Brazilian and Argentine passport controls and waits for passengers to get their passports stamped.

FROM CHILE

Travellers crossing via the high Andes should note that the passes sometimes close in winter. In the north, advance booking is recommended for the San Pedro de Atacama–Jujuy and Salta bus crossing. The most popular border crossing from Chile to Argentina is the Santiago–Mendoza route via the Los Libertadores tunnel. If you're coming from the south, routes in the Lake District include Osorno–Bariloche, and Temuco–San Martín de Los Andes. Further south still are the Puerto Natales–El Calafate and Punta Arenas–Río Gallegos crossings.

FROM PARAGUAY

Visitors can cross the Paraguayan border into Posadas (Argentina) from Encarnación (Paraguay). Travellers crossing here will have to go through migration control at both sides of the border, which are open 24 hours. Another popular option is the Puerto Falcón (Paraguay) to Clorinda (Argentina) crossing, but you can also cross into the Argentine cities of Formosa, Pocitos, Corrientes, Barranqueras and Iguazú.

FROM URUGUAY

From Colonia del Sacramento, the crossing is easy and quick with the Buquebus ferry service (@buquebus.com), with a fast service taking an hour and the slower but cheaper service three hours. Otherwise opt for the more scenic route with Cacciola Viajes (ⓦcacciolaviajes .com) from Carmelo to Tigre. If travelling by car, you can cross the border in Fray Bentos further north.

VISAS

Citizens of the EU, US, Canada, South Africa, Australia and New Zealand do not require visas, though Argentina charges reciprocal entry fees for nationals of countries that charge Argentine citizens to enter: the US, Canada and Australia are subject to **one-off arrival fees** that need to be paid in advance by signing up at ⓦreciprocidad.provincianet.com.ar. This fee only applies if you enter Argentina at either of the Buenos Aires airports on an international flight; no fees are payable if you enter via one of the land borders. Tourists are routinely granted ninety-day entry permits – the easiest way to renew your tourist visa is to cross the border into a neighbouring country.

GETTING AROUND

Argentina is a huge country and you are likely to spend a considerable proportion of your budget on travel. Air travel is relatively expensive – and tourists also get charged a much higher rate than local residents – so most people travel by bus (though that is increasingly pricey, too). Car rental is useful in places, but too expensive for most budget travellers, unless they can share the cost. Extra fees are charged for drivers under 25.

BY AIR

Argentina's most important domestic airport by far is Buenos Aires' **Aeroparque Jorge Newbery**. There are connections (with Aerolíneas Argentinas, LAN and LADE) to most provincial capitals and major tourist centres; Andes serves Puerto Madryn and Salta among other destinations. Some cut-price deals booked in advance can work out to be not much more than the bus. One of the best deals is the "Visit Argentina" airpass, sold by

Aerolíneas Argentinas (ⓦaerolineas.com.ar) and valid for domestic flights on Aerolíneas and its subsidiary, Austral, covering more than thirty destinations. This pass must be bought abroad; it is not sold in Argentina.

Many smaller airports are not served by public transport, though some airline companies run shuttle services to connect with flights; otherwise, you're stuck with taxis. When leaving Ushuaia airport, you must pay the airport tax after checking in (US$20).

BY BUS

There are hundreds of private **bus companies**, most of which concentrate on one particular region, although a few, such as TAC, operate pretty much nationwide. Most buses are modern, plush models designed for long-distance travel, and your biggest worry will be what video the driver or conductor has chosen. On longer journeys, snacks and even hot meals are served (included in the ticket price), although these vary considerably in quality. The more luxurious services are usually worth the extra money for long night-rides; some even have waiters. *Coche cama* services have wide, reclining seats, and *semi-cama* services are not far behind in terms of comfort. Most companies also offer *cama suite* or *cama ejecutivo* services, which have completely reclining seats and include an on-board meal.

Buying **tickets** is normally a simple on-the-spot matter, but plan in advance if travelling in peak summer season (mid-Dec to Feb), especially if you're taking a long-distance bus from Buenos Aires or any other major city to a popular holiday destination. In Buenos Aires look for kiosks advertising *venta de pasajes* – these are authorized ticket sellers and will save you having to visit the Retiro terminal before you leave.

BY CAR

You are unlikely to need a car for your whole stay in Argentina, but you'll find one useful if you hope to explore some of the more isolated areas of Patagonia, Tierra del Fuego, the Northwest, and Mendoza and San Juan provinces.

1

To **rent a car**, you need to be over 21 (25 with some agencies); most foreign licences are accepted for tourists. Bring your passport as well as a credit card for the deposit. Before you drive off, check that you've been given insurance, tax and ownership papers. Check too for dents and paintwork damage, and get hold of a 24-hour emergency telephone number. Also, pay close attention to the small print, most notably what you're liable for in the event of an accident: excess normally doesn't cover you for the first AR$5000 or so, and you may not be covered for windscreens, headlights, tyres and more – all vulnerable on unsurfaced roads. Look for unlimited mileage deals, as the per-kilometre charge can otherwise exceed your daily rental cost many times over given the vast distance you're likely to be covering.

BY TRAIN

Argentina's **rail** network, developed with British investment from the late nineteenth century, collapsed in the 1990s with the withdrawal of government subsidies. The few remaining services are generally unsavoury, running on routes that are of limited use for visitors. However, the country's famous **tourist trains**, where the aim is simply to travel for the sheer fun of it, are a major attraction. There are two principal stars: *La Trochita*, the Old Patagonian Express from Esquel; and the *Tren a las Nubes* (see p.93), one of the highest railways in the world, which climbs through the mountains from Salta towards the Chilean border.

ACCOMMODATION

You can often tell by a hotel's name what kind of place to expect: a **posada** for example suggests a slightly rustic feel, but generally comfortable or even luxurious. In a similar vein, **hostería** is often used for smallish, high-end hotels – oriented towards the tourist rather than the businessperson. **Hostal** is sometimes used too – but doesn't refer reliably to anything – there are youth hostels called *hostales* as well as high-rise modern hotels.

Residenciales and **hospedajes** are basically simple hotel-style accommodation. Most are reasonably clean and comfortable and a few stand out as some of Argentina's best budget accommodation. Rooms start at around AR$280, but prices fluctuate.

A very different experience is provided by Argentina's *estancias*, as the country's large ranches are called. **Estancia** accommodation is generally luxurious, and with a lot more character than hotels of a similar price; for around US$500 per person a day you are provided with all meals, invariably including a traditional *asado* or barbecue. At working *estancias* you have the chance to observe or join in ranch activities such as cattle herding and branding, while almost all include activities such as horseriding and swimming. To book *estancia* accommodation, either approach individual establishments or try one of the two specialist agencies in Buenos Aires: Comarcas, Laprida 1380 (☎011 4821 1876, ⓦcomarcas.com.ar), and Estancias Argentinas, Diagonal Roque Sáenz Peña 616, 9th Floor (☎011 4343 2366, ⓦestanciasargentinas.com).

HOSTELS AND CAMPSITES

Youth hostels are known as *albergues juveniles, albergues de la juventud* or simply *hosteles* (you might wish to avoid *albergues transitorios* or motels, which are places that rent rooms by the hour). Accommodation is generally in dormitories (a dorm bed costing AR$80–130, depending on where you are), though most places also have one or two double rooms, which are often excellent value. Facilities vary from next to nothing to internet access, washing machines, cable TV and patios with barbecues.

There are plenty of **campsites** (*campings*) – most towns and villages having their own municipal site – but standards vary wildly. At the major resorts, there are usually privately owned, well-organized sites, with facilities ranging from provisions stores to volleyball courts and TV rooms. In less touristy towns, municipal sites can be rather desolate and not particularly secure: it's a good idea to check with locals before pitching your tent.

FOOD AND DRINK

Traditionally, Argentine food could be summed up in a single word: **beef**. Not just any beef, but succulent, cherry-red, healthy meat raised on some of the greenest, most extensive pastures known to cattle. The **barbecue** or *asado* remains a national institution, but it's not the whole story. An *asado* is prepared on a **parrilla** (grill), and is served everywhere, at restaurants also known as *parrillas*. Usually there's a set menu, but the establishments vary enormously. Traditionally, you start off by eating the offal before moving on to the choicer cuts, but you can choose to head straight for the steaks and fillets. The lightly salted meat is usually served with nothing on it, other than the traditional condiments of *chimichurri* – olive oil with salt, garlic, chilli pepper, vinegar and bayleaf – and *salsa criolla*, similar but with chopped onion, tomato and red pepper added.

Alongside the *parrilla*, pizza and pasta are mainstays of Argentine cuisine, a reflection of the country's Italian heritage. Those staying in Argentina for a while may get frustrated by the lack of choice, particularly in rural areas, although the variety of restaurants in the cities, especially Buenos Aires, reflects a mosaic of communities who have migrated to Argentina: not just Italian and Spanish but Korean, Middle Eastern, German, Welsh, Japanese and Peruvian. **Vegetarians** will find that there are few options on most menus, but staples such as basic salads, *provoleta* (delicious melted cheese) and *tartas* (a kind of quiche) are almost always available, as well as pasta with meat-free sauces. In larger towns vegetarian restaurants are growing in popularity.

There are plenty of *minutas* or **snacks** to choose from. *Choripán*, a large sausage in a soft roll, is a national favourite, as is the ubiquitous *milanesa*, a breaded veal escalope. *Lomitos* are grilled steak sandwiches, the local answer to the hamburger. Excellent local-style fast food is also available in the form of *empanadas*, pasties that come with an array of fillings, from the traditional beef or mozzarella cheese to salami, Roquefort and chard. *Humitas* are made of steamed creamed sweetcorn, served in neat parcels made from the outer husk of corn cobs. *Tamales* are maize-flour balls, stuffed with minced beef and onion, wrapped in maize leaves and simmered. The typical main dish, *locro*, is a warming, substantial Andean stew based on maize, with onions, beans and meat thrown in.

WHERE TO EAT

Argentines love **dining out** and, in Buenos Aires especially, places stay open all day and till very late: in the evening hardly any restaurant starts serving dinner before 8.30pm, and in the hotter months – and all year round in Buenos Aires – very few people turn up before 10pm. By South American standards the quality of restaurants is high. You can keep costs down by taking advantage of restaurants' *menú del día* or *menú ejecutivo* – good-value set meals for as little as AR$70 served primarily, but not exclusively, at lunchtime. In the evening *tenedor libre* restaurants are just the place if your budget's tight. Here, you can eat as much as you like, they're usually self-service (cold and hot buffets plus grills) and the food is fresh and well prepared, if a little dull.

Cheaper hotels and more modest accommodation often skimp on **breakfast**: you'll be lucky to be given

ARGENTINE WINE

Argentina is the world's fifth-largest producer of wine, and more than three-quarters of the stuff flows out of **Mendoza**. Enjoying around three hundred days of sunshine a year and a prime position at the foothills of the Andes, Mendoza's high-altitude vineyards produce premium vintages on a par with Chile's. The idyllic desert climate (cool nights, little rain and low humidity) works especially well for reds: **Malbec** – brought over from Cahors in southwest France – remains Argentina's star grape, producing rich fruity flavours that go down superbly well with the ubiquitous steak. For a dry yet fruity white alternative, give **Torrontés** a whirl. Others that are having an impact include **Bonarda** and **Cabernet Franc**, while many sparkling wines are well priced.

1

more than tea or coffee, and some bread, jam and butter, though *medialunas* (small, sticky croissants) are sometimes also served. The sacred national delicacy *dulce de leche* (a type of caramel spread) is often provided for piling onto toast or bread.

DRINK

Fizzy drinks (*gaseosas*) are popular with people of all ages and are often drunk to accompany a meal. Although few beans are grown in the country, good, if expensive, **coffee** is easy to come by in Argentina. In most towns and cities you can find a decent espresso or *café con leche* (milky coffee) for breakfast. *Mate*, the bitter national drink, prepared in a special gourd and drunk through a metal straw known as a *bombilla*, is a whole world unto itself, with rules of etiquette and ritual involved. It is drunk everywhere – at home, in parks, at the office, and always with friends.

Argentina's **beer** is more thirst-quenching than alcoholic and mostly comes as fairly bland lager. The Quilmes brewery dominates the market with lagers such as Cristal; in Mendoza, the Andes brand crops up all over the place, while Salta's eponymous brand is also good. Most breweries also produce a *cerveza negra*, a kind of stout. Patagonia produces some excellent craft ales, some of them available in bottles. If you want draught beer ask for a *chopp*.

Argentine **wine** is excellent and reasonably priced – try the red Malbec grape variety. The locally distilled *aguardientes* or firewaters are often deliciously grapey. One national alcoholic spirit – an orange-flavour beverage called Hesperidina – is undergoing a comeback, while a number of Italian-style vermouths and digestifs are made in Argentina. **Fernet Branca** is the most popular, a demonic-looking brew the colour of molasses with a rather bitter, medicinal taste, invariably combined with cola, whose colour it matches, and consumed in huge quantities by students and young people.

CULTURE AND ETIQUETTE

Argentines are generally friendly, outgoing and incredibly welcoming to foreigners. In all but the most formal contexts, Argentines greet with one kiss on the cheek (men included), even on first meeting. In general, visitors are unlikely to find any huge culture shock in Argentine etiquette. Service in shops or restaurants is generally very courteous; conversations should be started with "*buen día*", "*buenas tardes*" or "*buenas noches*".

SPORTS AND OUTDOOR ACTIVITIES

Argentina is an exciting destination for outdoors enthusiasts, whether you're keen to tackle radical rock faces or prefer to appreciate the vast open spaces at a more gentle pace, hiking or on horseback. World-class fly-fishing, horseriding, trekking and rock-climbing options abound, as do opportunities for white-water rafting, skiing, ice climbing, and even – for those with sufficient stamina and preparation – expeditions onto the Southern Patagonian Icecap. The Patagonian Andes provide the focus for most of these activities – particularly the area of the central Lake District around Bariloche and El Calafate/El Chaltén, but Mendoza and the far northwest of the country, around Salta and Jujuy, are also worth considering for their rugged mountain terrain. If you're planning on doing any of these, take out appropriate insurance cover before leaving home.

HIKING AND CLIMBING

Argentina offers some truly marvellous **hiking** possibilities, and it is still possible to find areas where you can trek for days without seeing a soul. Most of the best treks are found in the national parks – especially in Patagonia – but you can also find less well-known but equally superb options in the lands bordering the parks. Most people head for the savage granite spires of the Fitz Roy region around El Chaltén, an area whose fame has spread so rapidly over recent years that it now holds a similar status to Chile's renowned Torres del Paine and is packed in high season (late Dec–Feb).

NATIONAL PARK INFORMATION

The **National Park Headquarters** at Santa Fe 690 in Buenos Aires (Mon–Fri 8am–8pm; ☎011 4311 0303, ⓦparquesnacionales.gob.ar) has an information office with introductory leaflets on the nation's parks. A wider range of free leaflets is available at each individual park, but these are of variable quality, and limited funding means that many parks give you only ones with a basic map and a brief park description. Contact the headquarters well in advance if you are interested in voluntary or scientific projects.

The other principal trekking destination is the mountainous area of Nahuel Huapi National Park, which lies to the south of Bariloche, centring on the Cerro Catedral massif and Cerro Tronador.

For **climbers**, the Andes offer incredible variety – from volcanoes to shale summits, from the continent's loftiest giants to some of its fiercest technical walls. You do not have to be a technical expert to reach the summit of some of these and, though you must always take preparations seriously, you can often arrange your climb close to the date through local agencies – though it's best to bring as much high-quality gear with you as you can. The climbing season is fairly short – generally November to March, though December to February is the best time. The best-known, if not the most technical, challenge is South America's highest peak, **Aconcagua** (6962m), accessed from Mendoza. In the far south are the Fitz Roy massif and Cerro Torre, which have few equals in terms of technical difficulty and grandeur of scenery. On all of these climbs, but especially those over 4000m, you must acclimatize thoroughly, and be fully aware of the dangers of altitude sickness (see p.33).

SKIING

The main **skiing** months are July and August (late July is peak season), although in some resorts it is possible to ski from late May to early October. Snow conditions vary wildly from year to year, but you can often find excellent powder. The most prestigious resort for downhill skiing is modern Las Leñas, which offers the most challenging slopes, followed by the Bariloche resorts of Cerro Catedral and Cerro Otto. These are the longest established in the country and are still the classic Patagonian ski centres, with their wonderful panoramas of the Nahuel Huapi region. It is also possible to ski in Ushuaia. Ski gear is widely available to rent. For updates on conditions and resorts, check out the Andesweb website (ⓦandesweb.com).

COMMUNICATIONS

There are Correo Argentino **post offices** throughout the country, and you will also come across *locutorios* offering postal services and phone booths. International post is relatively expensive and not always reliable; use registered post if possible and try to avoid sending items of value.

Making **local phone calls** in Argentina is cheap and easy. In cities and towns, you are never far from a *locutorio*. It's worth asking about phone cards offering cheap minutes if you are planning to make a number of **national calls**. **Mobile calls** are expensive, but mildly cheaper if calling someone with the same phone company. The main ones are Claro, Personal and

ARGENTINA ON THE NET

ⓦ**turismo.gov.ar** The official tourist website for Argentina.

ⓦ**welcomeargentina.com** Information about accommodation and activities, and detailed transport advice.

ⓦ**buenosaires.gob.ar** City government site for Buenos Aires, with up-to-date details on cultural events.

ⓦ**buenosairesherald.com** Buenos Aires' English-language newspaper, with national and international news.

ⓦ**bubblear.com** Satirical website poking fun at Argentina's news.

ⓦ**argentinaindependent.com** Online magazine with articles in English about Argentine culture and travel.

1

Movistar. If you're in Argentina for more than a couple of weeks, you may want to buy a pay-as-you-go SIM card to avoid extortionate roaming fees on your mobile.

Cheap **internet** cafés are everywhere, and in all but the most remote areas the connections are fairly fast. Many cafés and restaurants, as well as most hotels and hostels, have free wi-fi.

CRIME AND SAFETY

Argentina is one of the continent's safest countries and, as long as you take a few basic precautions, you are unlikely to encounter any problems during your stay. Indeed, you'll find many of the more rural parts of the country pretty much risk-free: people leave doors unlocked, windows open and bikes unchained. More care should be taken in large cities and some of the border towns, particularly the northeastern ones, where poverty and easily available arms and drugs make opportunistic crime a more common occurrence. Some potential pitfalls are outlined here, not to induce paranoia but on the principle that to be forewarned is to be forearmed.

By Argentine standards, **Buenos Aires** is currently suffering something of a crime wave, and incidents of violence and armed robbery are on the increase. It's sometimes difficult to know how much local anxiety is due to a genuine increase in crime and how much to middle-class paranoia, a lot of it provoked by sensationalist news channels. In general, serious crime tends to affect locals more than tourists. Nevertheless, you should not take unmarked taxis; it's better to call a radio taxi (hotels and restaurants will do this for you), or flag one down, rather than take a waiting cab, particularly in affluent or tourist areas. Avoid walking around the quieter neighbourhoods after dark, and be especially wary near the main bus and train stations in Once, Retiro and Constitución; avoid carrying valuables around with you. In La Boca, stick to the main touristy areas such as Caminito – the non-touristy part is to be avoided and is considered dangerous. In the rare event of being held up at gunpoint, don't play the hero.

> ### EMERGENCY NUMBERS
> Ambulance ☎ **107**
> Fire ☎ **100**
> Police ☎ **911/101**
> Tourist Police ☎ **011 4346 5748**

Theft from hotels is rare, but, as anywhere else in the world, do not leave valuables lying round the room (most have a safe). Some hostels have lockers; it's worth having a padlock of your own.

Drugs attract far more stigma than in most European countries, and Argentine society at large draws very little in the way of a line between "acceptable" soft drugs and "unacceptable" hard drugs. Although they are commonly found in clubs and bars, you're advised to steer clear of buying or partaking yourself – the penalties are stiff if you get caught.

HEALTH

Health issues are rarely a problem in Argentina, which has a generally good health service and clean drinking water. Vaccines are not really needed, but if you're planning on significant travel in rural areas within Salta, Jujuy or Misiones provinces, **malaria** tablets are recommended. **Yellow fever** vaccinations should be considered before visiting forested areas in the north of Argentina, including Iguazú Falls. All travellers over 1 year of age are advised to ensure they have the **hepatitis A** vaccination at least two weeks before arrival. If you're heading off the beaten track, vaccinations against typhoid and rabies are also recommended.

INFORMATION AND MAPS

Argentina's main **National Tourist Office** is at Santa Fe 883 in Buenos Aires (Mon–Fri 9am–5pm; ☎ 011 4312 2232, ⓦ turismo .gov.ar) and offers maps of the country and general information about getting around. Every province maintains a *Casa de Provincia* in Buenos Aires too, where you can pick up information about what there is to see or do. The standard of information you'll glean from them varies wildly.

The clearest and most accurate **map** of the country is *Rutas de la Argentina*, which you can get free from the national tourist office; it has small but clear inset maps of twenty towns and cities as well as a 1:2,500,000 national map. Another useful resource for route planning is the website ⓦruta0.com. The ACA (Automóvil Club; ⓦwww.aca.org.ar) produces individual maps for each province, which vary enormously in detail and accuracy.

MONEY AND BANKS

The **Argentine peso** is divided into one hundred centavos. In Argentina, it's represented by the dollar sign ($), but to avoid confusion we have used the symbol AR$ throughout this section. Notes come in 2, 5, 10, 20, 50 and 100 peso denominations, and 1 and 2 peso and 5, 10, 25 and 50 centavo coins are also in circulation. Guard your loose change in Buenos Aires as you will need it for the buses. Try to cash large notes in hotels and supermarkets – never in taxis – and look out for counterfeit money. Check your notes for a watermark, and that the number is printed in shiny green.

Argentina has an unpredictable **economy**, with high inflation and currency controls. The situation is fluid, and it's advisable to check the latest situation before you travel. At the time of writing there were two dollar/peso exchange rates – an official rate, used by **ATM**s (*cajeros automáticos*) and banks, and an increasingly divergent black market (confusingly known as the "blue") rate, which you will be offered (illegally) in the street. If you offer to pay cash dollars for services such as hotels and tours they will

often give you a rate just short of the blue rate, that equates to a substantial discount (as much as 50 percent), so you may wish to take a supply of dollars with you.

ATMs are plentiful in Argentina, though you can sometimes be caught out in very remote places, especially in the northwest. **Travellers' cheques** are not a viable option.

At the official rate of exchange, Argentina currently ranks as a fairly expensive destination by Latin American standards, though it's still cheaper than Brazil, Chile and Uruguay, and, if you travel outside the main tourist areas, you can still find some surprisingly good bargains.

OPENING HOURS AND HOLIDAYS

Most **shops and services** are open Monday to Friday from 9am to 7pm, and Saturday till 2pm, although later in large towns, including Buenos Aires. In smaller towns they may close at some point during the afternoon for between one and five hours – sometimes offset by later closing times in the evening, especially in the summer. Supermarkets seldom close

---

PUBLIC HOLIDAYS

January 1 New Year's Day (*Año Nuevo*)
Carnival (varies) Shrove Tuesday and the day before (usually in February)
March 24 Day of Truth and Justice
April 2 Malvinas Remembrance Day
Easter (varies) Easter Friday is a public holiday (Easter Thursday is optional)
May 1 Labour Day (*Día del Trabajo*)
May 25 May Revolution Day
June 20 Flag Day (*Día de la Bandera*)
July 9 Independence Day (*Día de la Independencia*)
August 18 Remembrance of General San Martín's death (*Día del Paso a la Inmortalidad del General José de San Martín*)
October 12 Columbus Day (*Día de la Raza*)
November 20 Day of National Sovereignty (fourth Monday of November; *Día de la soberanía nacional*)
December 8 Day of the Immaculate Virgin Mary
December 25 Christmas (*Navidad*)
Note that for some holidays the exact date may vary slightly from year to year.

STUDENT AND YOUTH DISCOUNTS

An **ISIC card** will entitle students of any age (over 12) to substantial discounts for many museums, travel and cultural events, as well as other services. See ⓦisic.com.ar for details. For travel discounts, contact Al Mundo ☎011 4345 7227, ⓦalmundo.com.ar.

1

during the day and are generally open much later, often until 8 or 10pm, and on Saturday afternoons. Large shopping malls don't close before 10pm and their food and drink sections (*patios de comida*) may stay open as late as midnight. Most of them open on Sundays, too. **Banks** mostly open on weekdays only, from 10am to 5pm, while casas de cambio more or less follow shop hours. In the northeast, bank opening hours may be more like 7am to noon, to avoid the hot, steamy afternoons.

In addition to national **holidays**, some local anniversaries or saints' days are also public holidays when everything in a given city may close down. Festivals of all kinds, both religious and profane, celebrating local patrons such as Santa Catalina or the Virgin Mary, or showing off produce such as handicrafts, olives, goats or wine, are good excuses for much pomp and partying.

Buenos Aires

With a huge variety of high-class restaurants, hotels and boutiques, as well as an eclectic mix of Neoclassical and modern architecture, **BUENOS AIRES** is deservedly known as the "Paris of South America". The influence of immigrants from all over the world, Italian and Spanish above all, can be seen in its street names, restaurants, aesthetics and language. Sip a coffee in the famous *Café Tortoni*, visit a dark and romantic tango hall to watch the nation's famous sultry dance, or simply walk the streets of Recoleta and watch the ladies in fur coats walking tiny dogs on Chanel leads. If you grow weary of the people, noise and buses of the capital you can head out of the city to the waterways of the Paraná Delta, the quiet streets of La Plata or San Antonio de Areco, home of Argentina's gauchos.

WHAT TO SEE AND DO

The city's museums and sights are well distributed between the central areas of Recoleta, Retiro, Palermo and San Telmo, and the *microcentro* lies east of Avenida 9

de Julio between Retiro and San Telmo. The historic *barrio* (neighbourhood) of San Telmo is one of the most interesting for visitors, on account of its atmospheric streets, surviving (if often faded) nineteenth-century architecture, and its Sunday antiques and handicrafts street market. The *microcentro* has the greatest concentration of shops and commerce, but Palermo Viejo should also be on every visitor's itinerary for its leafy streets lined with design and fashion shops, and hip bars and restaurants.

Plaza de Mayo

The **Plaza de Mayo** has witnessed the best and worst moments of Argentina's history – host to founding presidents, devastating military coups, the fanaticism of Evita, the dark days of the "Dirty War", and desperate crowds after the economic crisis. It has been bombed by its own military, filled to the brink with patriots, and left deserted, guarded by the federal police, in times of uncertainty, and even now it is still the spiritual home of the **Madres de la Plaza de Mayo**. These women, whose grown-up children "disappeared" during the Military Dictatorship (1976–83), marched in the plaza every week for over thirty years demanding information about their children's whereabouts. The huge pink building at the river end of the plaza is the **Casa Rosada** (free tours Sat & Sun 10am–6pm; ☎011 4344 3804, ⊛www .casarosada.gov.ar), home to the offices of the president and the executive branch of government. To the south of the building is the underground **Museo del Bicentenario** (Wed–Sun 10am–6pm; free; ☎011 4344), an extravagant but impressive propaganda exercise on the good of Peronism as compared with the evil of all other political movements in Argentine history.

At the opposite end of the plaza is the **Cabildo**, which, though much altered, is one of the few examples of colonial architecture left in this part of the city. During the week there is a small crafts market, as well as a **museum** of historical artifacts (Wed–Fri 10.30am–5pm, Sat & Sun 11.30am–6pm; AR$10; guided tours

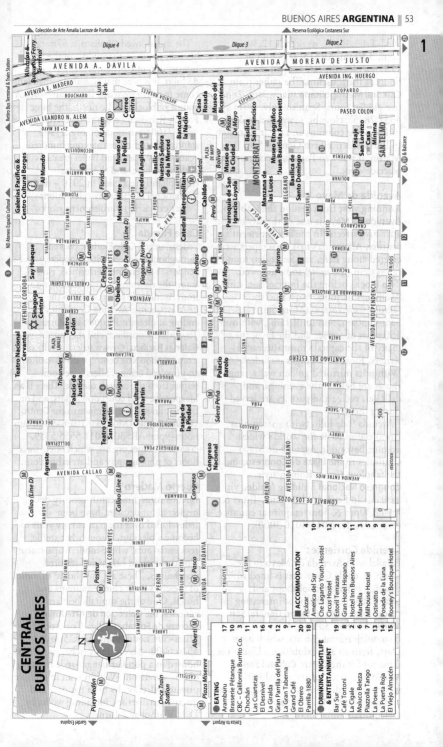

CENTRAL BUENOS AIRES

Colección de Arte Amalia Lacroze de Fortabat

Reserva Ecológica Costanera Sur

Dique 4

Dique 3

Dique 2

AVENIDA A. DAVILA

AVENIDA MOREAU DE JUSTO

AVENIDA ING. HUERGO

AVENIDA E. MADERO

BOUCHARD

Luna Park

Retiro Bus Terminal & Train Station

Milviaductes & Buquebus Ferry Terminal

AVENIDA LEANDRO N. ALEM

25 DE MAYO

L.N.Alem

RECONQUISTA

SAN MARTIN

FLORIDA

TUCUMAN

LAVALLE

VIAMONTE

ESMERALDA

SUIPACHA

Correo Central

Al Mundo

Galerías Pacífico & Centro Cultural Borges

Museo de la Policía

Florida

Museo Mitre

SARMIENTO

Catedral Anglicana

Basílica de Nuestra Señora de la Merced

PTE. PERON

MAIPU

AVENIDA ROSALES

ESPORA

AZOPARDO

PASEO COLON

Casa Rosada

Museo del Bicentenario

Plaza De Mayo

Basílica San Francisco

Banco de la Nación

PLAZA DE MAYO

Museo de la Ciudad

Catedral

Bolívar

MONTSERRAT

Museo Etnográfico 'Juan Bautista Ambrosetti'

DEFENSA

Pasaje San Lorenzo

Casa Minima

SAN TELMO

& Balcarce

Catedral Metropolitana

Cabildo

Perú

Manzana de las Luces

Basílica de Santo Domingo

BELGRANO

BOLIVAR

PERU

CHILE

VENEZUELA

AV. 40 & Balcarce

NO Ateneo Espacio Cultural

Say Hueque

P.R.S. PEÑA

Parroquia de San Ignacio Loyola

Rivadavia

MEXICO

CHACABUCO

ESTADOS UNIDOS

Sinagoga Central

AVENIDA CORDOBA

C. Pellegrini

9 De Julio (Line D)

Obelisco

Diagonal Norte (Line C)

Piedras

Lima

Av. de Mayo

H. YRIGOYEN

MORENO

Belgrano

PIEDRAS

TACUARI

BERNARDO DE IRIGOYEN

9 DE JULIO

CERRITO

AVENIDA

LIBERTAD

MITRE

AVENIDA DE MAYO

ALSINA

Moreno

Teatro Nacional Cervantes

Teatro Colón

PLAZA LAVALLE

Tribunales

Palacio de Justicia

TALCAHUANO

URUGUAY

Centro Cultural San Martín

Teatro General San Martín

PARANA

Palacio Barolo

Sáenz Peña

SANTIAGO DEL ESTERO

SAN JOSE

SALTA

AVENIDA INDEPENDENCIA

DEL CARMEN

DELLEPIANE

Agreste

MONTEVIDEO

RODRIGUEZ PEÑA

Pasaje de la Piedad

PTE. L. SAENZ

PEÑA

VIRREY

CEBALLOS

SOLIS

AVENIDA BELGRANO

500

metres

0

AVENIDA CALLAO

Callao (Line D)

Callao (Line B)

Congreso

Congreso Nacional

RIOBAMBA

AYACUCHO

AVENIDA ENTRE RIOS

MORENO

COMBATE DE LOS POZOS

VIAMONTE

Pasteur

AVENIDA CORRIENTES

JUNIN

Pasco

RIVADAVIA

H. YRIGOYEN

ALSINA

TUCUMAN

LAVALLE

PTE. J. E. URIBURU

BARTOLOME MITRE

AVENIDA

AZCUENAGA

LARREA

Alberto

J. D. PERON

PASTEUR

Plaza Miserere

Once Train Station

Puerredón

PASO

SARMIENTO

CASTELLI

AVENIDA RIVADAVIA

N

Ezeiza to Airport

Gardel Esquina

EATING

Aramburu	17
Brasserie Petanque	10
CBC – California Burrito Co.	3
Chochán	11
Las Cuartetas	5
El Desnivel	16
La Giralda	4
Gran Parrilla del Plata	12
La Gran Taberna	9
Grand Café	1
El Obrero	20
Parrilla 1880	18

● DRINKING, NIGHTLIFE & ENTERTAINMENT

Bar Sur	19
Café Tortoni	8
La Cigale	2
Maluco Beleza	6
Marbella	7
Piazzolla Tango	13
La Poesía	3
Ostinatto	5
La Puerta Roja	14
El Viejo Almacén	15

■ ACCOMMODATION

Alcázar	4
America del Sur	10
Che Lagarto Youth Hostel	7
Circus Hostel	12
Estoril Terrazas	6
Gran Hotel Hispano	2
Hostel Inn Buenos Aires	11
Marbella	3
Milhouse Hostel	9
Posada de la Luna	8
Rooney's Boutique Hotel	1

1

Wed–Fri 3.30pm, weekends 12.30pm, 2pm, 3.30pm; AR$15; ☎011 4334 1782); a pleasant café is open the same hours as the museum. The rather plain **Catedral Metropolitana** (daily 9am–7pm; free guided tours, Spanish only; ☎011 4331 2845), close by, is worth a look for its imposing columns and the **mausoleum** to Independence hero General San Martín; it was also Pope Francis' previous place of work.

Avenida de Mayo

Running west from behind the Cabildo, **Avenida de Mayo** is one of the city's most attractive streets. In the late nineteenth century, Argentina's first skyscrapers were erected along here, and an underground rail system (the *subte*) soon followed. Two blocks before the intersection with Avenida 9 de Julio, you'll find the famous *Café Tortoni* (Mon–Sat 8am–3.30am, Sun until 1am), with over 150 years of service and the favourite of many of the capital's most successful writers, Jorge Luis Borges included. Within its mirrored golden walls, tango shows are held in the evenings, and delicious coffee and pastries are served during the day.

Avenida 9 de Julio (with sixteen busy lanes) claims to be the world's widest avenue: beyond it, Avenida de Mayo continues to the **Plaza de Congreso**, and the fabulous Greco-Roman-style **Congreso Nacional** building (guided visits available in English Mon, Tues, Thurs & Fri 12.30pm & 5pm; enquire at entrance on south side; ☎011 4010 3000).

Avenida Corrientes

Parallel with Avenida de Mayo to the north, Avenida Corrientes is lined with theatres, cinemas, bookshops and pizzerias. One of the most interesting places to stop is the **Teatro General San Martín** (☎0800 333 5254, ⓦcomplejoteatral.gob.ar), which hosts plays, festivals and exhibitions. Under the same roof is the **Centro Cultural San Martín** arts space, featuring exhibition spaces and auditoriums for music, drama and film (☎011 4374 1251, ⓦelculturalsanmartin.org).

The much-loved **Obelisco**, a 67m-tall obelisk, stands in the middle of the busy intersection of Corrientes and Avenida 9 de Julio. It is here that ecstatic football fans come to celebrate when their team wins. A couple of blocks to the north, the huge French Renaissance **Teatro Colón** (☎011 4378 7100, ⓦteatrocolon.org.ar) still stands tall after more than one hundred years. Many opera and ballet greats have performed here, and the theatre triumphantly reopened in 2010 – during the national bicentenary celebrations – after extensive refurbishment works.

Calle Florida

Pedestrianized **Calle Florida**, packed throughout the week with shoppers, street vendors, buskers and performers, runs across the downtown area, heading north from Avenida de Mayo, close to the Plaza de Mayo, across Avenida Corrientes and ending at pleasant Parque San Martín. Towards the northern end the impressive **Galerías Pacífico** (ⓦwww.galeriaspacifico .com.ar) shopping centre, with its vaulted and frescoed ceiling, offers a welcome respite from the crowds outside. There is an inexpensive food court downstairs, and on the first floor is the entrance to the **Centro Cultural Borges** (Mon–Sat 10am–9pm, Sun noon–9pm; AR$30; ☎011 5555 5359, ⓦwww.ccborges.org.ar), which offers three floors of photography and art exhibitions.

Puerto Madero

Buenos Aires' nineteenth-century docks, neglected for decades, have been redeveloped over the past twenty years to become a pleasant, if somewhat sterile, residential area, where modern apartment blocks surround bright-red restored warehouses. These are now home to some of the city's most chic restaurants and hotels. One of the capital's best art galleries, the **Colección de Arte Amalia Lacroze de Fortabat**, Olga Cossettini 141 (Tues–Sun noon–9pm, AR$25; ☎011 4310 6600, ⓦcoleccionfortabat.org.ar), is housed in a peculiar hangar-style building on the waterfront. Within is an impressive private collection by both national and international artists, including works by Dalí, Warhol and Turner.

Also of note is the **Faena Arts Center**, at Aime Paine 1169 (Tues–Sun 11am–7pm; AR$30; ⓦba.faenaarts.com), which frequently rotates contemporary exhibits and installations.

Nearby along the river's edge is the **Reserva Ecológica Costanera Sur** (entrance at Av Tristán Achával Rodríguez 1550; Tues–Sun 8am–6pm; free; ☎011 4893 1588), a large expanse of reclaimed and regenerated land. It makes a delightful afternoon stroll, and they hold full-moon tours once a month. In front of the entrance, a small craft market is held on weekends.

Montserrat

Cobblestoned **Montserrat**, just south of Plaza de Mayo, is one of the oldest neighbourhoods of the city, and the most popular until a yellow fever outbreak in the nineteenth century forced wealthier families to move to Recoleta and Palermo. The *barrio*'s principal street is Calle Defensa, named after the event when residents trying to force back British invaders in the early 1800s poured boiling water and oil from their balconies onto the attacking soldiers.

The neo-Baroque **Basílica San Francisco** (Wed–Sun 11am–5pm; ☎011 4331 0625), at the corner of Alsina and Defensa, has an intricately decorated interior that can just about be made out through the atmospheric gloom. Nearby is the small **Museo de la Ciudad**, Alsina 412 (daily 11am–6pm; free; ☎011 4331 9855), which houses informative and well-presented changing exhibitions about the city. Two blocks west of Defensa is the collection of buildings known as the **Manzana de las Luces** (guided visits daily at 3pm, Sat & Sun also 4.30pm & 6pm, Spanish only; AR$25; info at Perú 272; ☎011 4342 9930, ⓦmanzanadelasluces.gov.ar), which dates back to 1686. Originally housing a Jesuit community, it has been home to numerous official institutions throughout its history, and today it accommodates the **Colegio Nacional**, an elite high school, and Buenos Aires' oldest church, **San Ignacio** (daily 8am–8pm; ☎011 4331 2458), begun in 1675.

San Telmo

San Telmo begins further south along Defensa from Montserrat, on the far side of Avenida Belgrano. With its myriad antique stores and junk shops, as well as a range of busy, late-opening restaurants and bars (especially around the intersection of Chile and Defensa), it's a great place to wander. For fresh food and eclectic antiques head to the **Mercado de San Telmo** (Mon–Sat 7am–2pm & 4.30–9pm, Sun 7am–2pm). The market takes up an entire city block, with an entrance on each side, including one on Defensa near the corner of Estados Unidos.

A few blocks further, **Plaza Dorrego** is a great place to pause for a coffee under the leafy trees, at least on weekdays when it's quieter. On Sundays the area is completely taken over by the **Feria de San Pedro Telmo** (10am–5pm; buses #8, #24, #86, #93 or #152 easily picked up downtown). Vintage watches, posters, clothes and jewellery are all on display at this huge open-air antiques market, enlivened by street performers and live tango acts. Another great place for antique-spotting is the **Pasaje de la Defensa**, Defensa 1179, a converted mansion filled with hidden shops, cafés and workshops.

Calle Defensa continues, across the busy, ugly avenues of San Juan and Juan de Garay, to leafy **Parque Lezama**, home to the **Museo Histórico Nacional**, Defensa 1600 (Wed–Sun 11am–6pm; free; ☎011 4307 1182). This small museum has an interesting permanent exhibition on Argentina's history. The collection at the **Museo de Arte Moderno de Buenos Aires (MAMBA)**, Avenida San Juan 350 (Tues–Fri 11am–7pm, Sat & Sun 11am–8pm; free; ☎011 4342 3001, ⓦmuseos.buenosaires.gob.ar), focuses mainly on Argentine art from the 1920s until the present day, and includes pieces by Xul Solar and Antonio Berni. Next door is sister museum, **Museo de Arte Contemporáneo de Buenos Aires (MACBA)**, San Juan 328 (Mon & Wed–Fri 11am–7pm, Sat & Sun 11am–7.30pm; AR$30; ☎011 5299 2010, ⓦmacba.com.ar), which shows contemporary works.

1

La Boca
Easily accessible from Parque Lezama, the suburb of **La Boca** is known for the Caminito and as home to one of Argentina's leading football clubs, **Boca Juniors**, arch-rivals of the River Plate team on the other side of town.

The **Caminito** is a small area of brightly coloured buildings along the river, created in the 1950s by the neighbourhood's most famous artist, **Benito Quinquela Martín**. These days the Caminito is a serious tourist trap, though it has an interesting open-air **arts and crafts fair** (daily 10.30am–6pm), street performers, and cafés charging tourist prices.

A visit to the Boca Juniors' stadium, **La Bombonera** (Brandsen 805, three blocks west of Av Almirante Brown; ☎011 5777 1200), is definitely worthwhile, even if you can't score tickets to a game. The starting point is the fascinating **Museo de la Pasión Boquense** (daily 10am–6pm; AR$75; ☎011 4362 1100, ⓦmuseoboquense.com), a must for football fans; guided tours of the stadium start from here (daily 11am–5pm hourly; AR$15 extra).

La Boca can be reached by **bus** #29 from Corrientes or Plaza de Mayo, #86 from Plaza de Mayo or #53 from Constitución. Note that La Boca has a bad reputation for **robberies**, so leave your valuables at home and do not stray from the touristy area around Caminito.

Recoleta
Immediately north of the city centre, the wide streets of upper-class Recoleta are most famously home to the **Recoleta Cemetery** at Avenida Quintana and Junín (daily 7am–5pm; free), surrounded by café-lined streets and their designer-clad denizens. The cemetery is the resting place of some of Argentina's leading celebrities, including Evita herself, buried under her maiden name of Duarte. A map is available at the entrance to guide you around the great monuments of dark granite, white marble and bronze.

Next door are the white walls of the **Basílica de Nuestra Señora del Pilar** (Mon–Sat 10.30am–6.10pm, Sun 2.30–6.10pm; free; ☎011 4803 6793,

ⓦbasilicadelpilar.org.ar). The eighteenth-century Jesuit building has been beautifully restored, and is much in demand for fashionable weddings: inside, the magnificent Baroque silver altarpiece, embellished with an Inca sun and other pre-Hispanic details, was made by craftsmen from the north of Argentina. Adjacent, the **Centro Cultural de Recoleta** (Tues–Fri 1.30–8.30pm, Sat & Sun 11.30am–8.30pm; free; ☎011 4803 1040, ⓦcentroculturalrecoleta.org), at Junín 1930, is a fabulous art space with interesting temporary exhibitions.

If by now you're in need of a coffee or a shopping fix, head to **Buenos Aires Design**, a shopping centre focusing on chic design products and homeware, which adjoins the cultural centre. The large terrace upstairs overlooks a park, and is a great place for an afternoon drink.

Visible from the terrace of Buenos Aires Design, the **Museo Nacional de Bellas Artes** (Tues–Fri 12.30–8.30pm, Sat & Sun 9.30am–8.30pm; free; ☎011 4803 0802, ⓦmnba.gob.ar) is at Avenida del Libertador 1473. Within the imposing, columned building is a traditional art gallery, primarily displaying European paintings but also with a small but valuable collection of colonial and modern Argentine work. For more local artworks, go to the **Museo Xul Solar** (Tues–Fri noon–8pm, Sat noon–7pm; AR$20; ☎011 4824 3302, ⓦxulsolar.org.ar), further to the southwest at Laprida 1212, near the corner of Calle Mansilla, which focuses on the bright and colourful Cubist paintings of twentieth-century Argentine artist Alejandro Xul Solar.

Palermo
Expansive, middle-class **Palermo** stretches around Avenida del Libertador as it heads north from Recoleta, taking in the high-rise apartments near the north of Avenida Santa Fe, the chic cafés and hotels of Palermo Viejo, and the leafy streets and late-night bars of Palermo Hollywood. On or near tree-lined Libertador are three unmissable museums. The **Museo de Arte Decorativo**, Libertador 1902 (Tues–Fri 2–7pm, Sat & Sun 12.30–7pm; AR$50, Tues free;

1

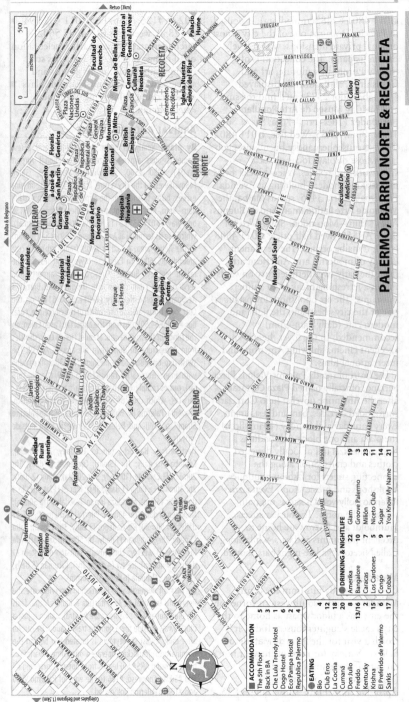

PALERMO, BARRIO NORTE & RECOLETA

Retuo (3km)

Malba & Belgrano

Colegiales and Belgrano (1.5km)

■ ACCOMMODATION	
The 5th Floor	5
Back in BA	3
Che Lulu Trendy Hotel	1
Dogo Hostel	6
Eco Pampa Hostel	2
Republica Palermo	4

● EATING	
Bio	4
Club Eros	12
La Cocina	18
Cumaná	20
Don Julio	8
Freddo	13/16
Kentucky	2
Krishna	15
Los Cardones	6
El Preferido de Palermo	9
Sarkis	17

● DRINKING & NIGHTLIFE			
Amerika	22	Glam	19
Bangalore	10	Groove Palermo	3
Caracas	7	Millón	23
Congo	9	Niceto Club	11
Crobar	17	Sugar	14
		You Know My Name	21

1

☎011 4801 8248, ⓦmnad.org), is housed in Palacio Errázuriz, one of the city's most original private mansions, with a lovely café in its patio. The collection is of mainly European sculpture, art and furnishings, all beautifully displayed.

At Libertador 2373 you'll find the small and inviting **Museo de Arte Popular Hernández** (Tues–Fri 1–7pm; Sat & Sun 10am–8pm; AR$5, Wed free; ☎011 4802 9967, ⓦmuseohernandez.buenosaires.gob .ar), whose displays focus on local silverwork and textiles. A few blocks away, in a striking modern building at Avenida Figueroa Alcorta 3415, stands **Malba**, the **Museo de Arte Latinoamericano de Buenos Aires** (Thurs–Mon noon–8pm, Wed till 9pm; AR$50, Wed half price; ☎011 4808 6500, ⓦmalba.org.ar). The permanent display of modern Latin American art from the early twentieth century onwards makes a refreshing break from stuffier museums. The art bookshop downstairs is one of the city's best, and the light and modern café (daily 9am–9pm) is recommended. In the foyer there is an excellent cinema showing Argentine and international films.

The heart of trendy **Palermo Viejo** is Plaza Serrano, officially named **Plaza Cortázar** after the Argentine novelist Julio Cortázar, surrounded by cafés, bars and restaurants. Every Saturday and Sunday (10am–8pm) the plaza and one block of Honduras is host to markets full of locally designed clothes and crafts. Stroll along the connecting streets for fashion boutiques, bookshops and music shops. Even jazzier **Palermo Hollywood** is across the train tracks to the north. The busiest streets, Humboldt and Fitzroy, are home to excellent restaurants and bars, while along Calle Niceto Vega late-night bars abound.

Mataderos

Over an hour by bus from the centre, **Mataderos**, in the southwestern corner of the city, has a bloody past as home to the city's cattle slaughterhouses. Today, it is worth a visit for the **Feria de Mataderos**, held on Sunday for most of the year but on Saturday evenings in summer (Jan–March Sat 6pm–midnight, April–Dec Sun 11am–sunset; buses #36,

#92 & #126; Mon–Fri; ☎011 4323 9400 ext 2830, weekends 011 4687 5602, ⓦferiademataderos.com.ar). A celebration of all things gaucho, the Feria has stalls selling leatherwork, *mate*, gourds and silver, as well as folk music and displays of horseriding, plus some of the best *empanadas* in the city.

ARRIVAL AND DEPARTURE

By plane Nearly all international flights and a few domestic ones arrive at Ezeiza International Airport (☎011 5480 2500, ⓦwww.aa2000.com.ar), 35km (45min) west of the city centre. Manuel Tienda León runs express buses to and from the airport (every 30min; daily 6am–9pm, less frequent outside these times; AR$130 one-way; ☎011 4315 5115, ⓦwww.tiendaleon.com.ar), which use its terminal at Av E Madero 1299 (at San Martín) in the Retiro area. A taxi or *remis* (radio cab) will cost around AR$250 from Ezeiza to town, a bit less for the return journey. Buenos Aires' domestic airport (also serving some connections with Uruguay and Brazil) is Aeroparque Jorge Newbery (☎011 5480 6111) on the Costanera Norte, around 6km north of the city centre. Local bus #33 (AR$4.50) runs from the airport to Paseo Colón, on the fringe of the *microcentro*. Manuel Tienda León shuttles from Aeroparque to downtown are around AR$30. The swish hop-on ArBus (6am–midnight; AR$30, only payable with an electronic SUBE card; ☎4845 0429, ⓦarbus.com .ar), comes complete with wi-fi and a/c and has six direct services, which drop off passengers at Retiro, Obelisco, Saavedra, Palermo (Av Bullrich & Av Santa Fe, Alto Palermo Shopping Mall) and Belgrano. Pick-up is from outside arrivals.

Destinations Bariloche (up to 10 daily; 2hr 20min); Córdoba (10 daily; 1hr 15min); Corrientes (1 daily; 1hr 20min); El Calafate (10 daily; 3hr 20min); Jujuy (2 daily; 2hr 10min); La Rioja (1 daily; 3hr); Mar del Plata (up to 5 daily; 1hr 15min); Mendoza (up to 7–9 daily; 1hr 50min); Neuquén (4 daily; 1hr 40min); Puerto Iguazú (up to 10–12 daily; 1hr 50min); Rio Gallegos (3 daily; 3hr 15min); Salta (3 daily; 2hr); San Juan (1 daily; 1hr 50min); San Martín de los Andes (3 weekly; 2hr 20min); Santiago del Estero (1 daily; 1hr 40min); Trelew (4 daily; 2hr); Tucumán (5 daily; 1hr 50min); Ushuaia (6 daily; 3hr 40min).

By bus All domestic and international services use the Retiro bus terminal, at Av Antártida & Ramos Mejía. Taxis are plentiful and the Retiro *subte* (metro) station is just a block away, outside the adjoining train station. Be careful after dark; a vast shantytown is located just behind the terminal and pickpockets operate around here. A variety of buses (around AR$4.50) leaves from outside, including #5 and #50, to Congreso, #106 to the edge of Palermo Viejo and #106 to Palermo Hollywood.

Destinations Frequent domestic services to Bariloche (19–25hr); Córdoba (9–11hr); Mendoza (14–16hr); Neuquén (14–19hr); Puerto Iguazú (17–18hr); Puerto Madryn (18–20hr); Rosario (4hr); Salta (20–22hr); Tucumán (16hr). Daily international services to La Paz (48hr); Montevideo (8–9hr); Santiago de Chile (19hr); São Paulo (34hr); Rio de Janeiro (40hr).

By ferry Ferries and catamarans cross the Río de la Plata from Montevideo and Colonia del Sacramento in Uruguay. More convenient are services by Sea Cat (Av Antartida Argentina 821 ☎011 4314 4100, ⓦseacatcolonia.com) and Buquebus (Av Antartida Argentina 821; ☎011 4316 6500, ⓦbuquebus.com), which use the Terminal Dársena Norte (often just known as the Terminal Buquebús) at Viamonte & Costanera Sur, just a few blocks from the *microcentro*. Meanwhile, *Colonia Express* (☎011 4317 4100, ⓦcoloniaexpress.com) operates a third service from a terminal called Dársena Sur located at Pedro de Mendoza 330, close to La Boca.

Destinations Colonia (8 daily; 1–3hr); Montevideo (4 daily; 4hr).

By train The main stations are Retiro, Constitución and Once but are mostly used only for urban and provincial travel. Retiro station (Av Ramos Mejía, just to the east of Plaza San Martín) is the departure point for trains to Tigre and the northern suburbs. There's a twice-weekly scenic train from Retiro to Tucumán (see p.89).

INFORMATION

Tourist information There are a number of *centros de informes* around the city run by the Secretaría de Turismo, including one at Av Alicia Moreau de Justo 200 in Puerto Madero (daily 9am–6pm; ☎011 4313 0187, ⓦturismo .buenosaires.gob.ar). The best is on Florida 100, at Av Diagonal Roque Sáenz Peña (daily 9am–6pm, Sat & Sun until 7pm). You can also pick up information from the well-organized National Tourist Office at Santa Fe 883 (Mon–Fri 9am–5pm; ☎011 4312 2232, ⓦturismo.gov.ar), which has details of the provincial tourist offices within the capital.

GETTING AROUND

By subte The easiest part of the public transport system to get to grips with is the underground railway or *subte*, which serves the central neighbourhoods from 5am until 10.30pm (Mon–Sat) and from 8am to 10pm (Sun & public holidays). There are six lines – Lines A, B, D and E run from the city centre outwards, while lines C and H (the latter still under construction) run between Retiro and Constitución, connecting them all. Tickets cost AR$6 for a single trip and are bought from booths at each station. If you are going to travel a lot, invest in a pre-pay swipe SUBE card for AR$20, which will give cheaper subway as well as bus fares – subway fares cost AR$4.50 with a SUBE card. Buy one from Av de Mayo, 9 de Julio, Independencia or Federico Lacroze subway stations.

By bus Buses (ⓦloscolectivos.com.ar) are one of the most useful (and cheap) ways of getting around the city – and indeed the only way of reaching many of the outlying districts. Invest in a combined street and bus-route booklet, such as the Guía "T", widely available from street kiosks, to work out the routes. One-way tickets (AR$4.50) are bought from a machine on the bus, which gives change for coins (no notes); however, it's better and cheaper to use an electronic SUBE card: fares start at AR$3. Many services run all night.

By remís These are radio cabs or minicabs, plain cars booked through an office (and therefore preferred by some wary locals). Not particularly economical for short journeys, they're cheaper than taxis for getting to the airport; try *Remises Uno* (☎011 4638 8318). It's safest to call a radio taxi at night, although there is an extra fee of AR$8 for the privilege. Ask your hostel for their preferred company or try *Taxi Alo* (☎011 4855 5555).

By taxi The city's black-and-yellow taxis are spectacularly plentiful. The meter starts at AR$14.30 (charges increase at night), and you should calculate on a ride costing around AR$35 per twenty blocks.

By bicycle Buenos Aires not only has an extensive cycle route known as the *bicisenda*, it also lends bikes for free (ⓦecobici.buenosaires.gob.ar). With more than 30 stations dotted around the city, you can borrow a bike for a 4hr period. Visitors can take advantage of the scheme – sign up with a photocopy of your passport and date of entry visa, and Ecobici will do the rest.

ACCOMMODATION

Finding accommodation in Buenos Aires shouldn't be a problem but advance planning is advised, especially for high season. Discounts can sometimes be negotiated, particularly if you are staying for more than a few days. Most backpackers head for San Telmo, where the hostels are concentrated, but you can also increasingly find good-value, pleasant accommodation in leafier Palermo.

HOSTELS

Most hostels have communal kitchens and offer free or cheap internet, breakfast and laundry.

CENTRAL BUENOS AIRES

★ **Estoril Terrazas** Av de Mayo 1385 (1st & 6th Floors), at Uruguay ☎011 4382 9073, ⓦhostelestoril.com.ar; map p.53. Directly opposite the Palacio Barolo, one of Buenos Aires' most stunning buildings, *Estoril* has to be among the top hostels in the world. Extremely comfortable and always impeccably clean, it offers all amenities and has a roof terrace with perfect views of Av de Mayo and Congreso. Ask for the roof-top dorm. Dorms **AR$180**, doubles **AR$350**

Milhouse Hostel Hipólito Yrigoyen 959, at Bernardo de Irigoyen ☎011 4345 9604, ⓦmilhousehostel.com; map

BUENOS AIRES TOURS

Walking tours are offered by the city government (free; in English and Spanish) around a given *barrio*, or with themes such as "Evita" or "Carlos Gardel". Ask at a tourism kiosk for the schedule. **Buenos Aires Bus** (daily 9am–5.30pm, every 20min; ❼buenosairesbus.com) are city hop-on hop-off bus tours stopping at various points of interest, including Boca, the Reserva Ecológica and the Rosedal in Palermo. $120 per day or $160 for two days represents good value compared to taxis – if you're planning to cover a lot of ground.

TOUR OPERATORS

Al Mundo Florida 825 ☎011 4114 7600, ❼almundo.com. A young and dynamic travel agency, offering some of the cheapest flight deals in the city as well as international packages; student discounts available.

ANDA tours ☎011 3221 0833, ❼andatravel.com.ar. Organizes responsible tourist visits with a difference, such as their "La Boca Beyond Caminito" walking tour of Boca, which includes stop-offs at local art collectives and community organizations.

MacDermott's Argentina Borges 2470, Office 1C ☎011 4773 2522, ❼macdermottsargentina.com. Organizes horseriding tours all around Argentina including Andes treks.

Say Hueque Thames 2062 ☎011 5258 8740, ❼sayhueque.com. A professional tour operator covering all of Argentina (and parts of Chile).

---

p.53. A large, lively hostel in a colonial-style building with a huge range of activities on offer. One of the city's most popular, so book well in advance. Breakfast included. *Milhouse* also has another outpost at Av de Mayo 1245. Dorms AR$150, doubles AR$500

PALERMO, RECOLETA AND RETIRO

Back in BA El Salvador 5115, at Uriarte ☎011 4774 2859, ❼backinba.com; map p.57. Small, friendly hostel with a low-key vibe, bar and a good-sized living area, as well as comfy beds and decent linen. Great location close to the heart of Palermo. Dorms AR$130, doubles AR$380

Dogo Hostel Cabrera 4716 ☎011 3968 7800, ❼dogohostel.com; map p.57. Intimate and colourful five-room Palermo hostel run by its owners. Some rooms have terraces and private bathrooms. Its ample terrace and *parrilla* barbecue area make this a great spot to meet other travellers. Dorms AR$115, double AR$460

Eco Pampa Hostel Guatemala 4778, at Borges ☎011 4831 2435, ❼hostelpampa.com; map p.57. Dubbing itself the city's first green hostel – the vibrant lime-hued facade sets the tone – *Eco Pampa* is comfortable as well as eco-friendly, with its leafy terrace and low-energy computers. Dorms AR$150, doubles AR$680

SAN TELMO

America del Sur Chacabuco 718, at Chile ☎011 4300 5525, ❼americahostel.com.ar; map p.53. A blockish new build, now a San Telmo classic; pop art and contemporary furnishing abound, giving it a hotel feel. That extends to the rooms too, as dorms are for a maximum of four. All rooms have private bathrooms, doubles include TV. Dorms AR$150, doubles AR$325

Che Lagarto Youth Hostel Venezuela 857, at Piedras ☎011 5218 6701, ❼chelagarto.com; map p.53. Rooms are standard but the sociable atmosphere, cool bar/restaurant (meals AR$40–75) and lovely tree-shaded back garden make *Che* a top traveller hangout. Dorms AR$100, doubles AR$500

Circus Hostel Chacabuco 1020, at Humberto Primo ☎011 4300 4983, ❼hostelcircus.com; map p.53. Offering a variety of private rooms and four-bed dorms, breakfast is included at this smart hostel. When summer gets too steamy, slip into the outdoor swimming pool. Dorms AR$120, doubles AR$420

Hostel Inn Buenos Aires Humberto Primo 820, at Tacuarí ☎011 4300 7992, ❼hostel-inn.com; map p.53. A restored mansion for a hostel could only be located in the heart of historical San Telmo. A plethora of activities is organized, such as free walking tours, movie nights and pizza parties. There's another hostel at Avenida de Mayo 1111. Dorms AR$115, doubles AR$150

Ostinatto Chile 680, at Perú ☎011 4362 9639, ❼ostinatto.com; map p.53. Falls squarely in the category of "hip" hostel, with cool minimalist design, spacious dorms and friendly staff. Hosts free tango, yoga and Spanish classes as well as film and barbecue nights. If you feel like treating yourself, there are two self-contained apartments, the loft (AR$460) and penthouse (AR$480). Dorms AR$125, doubles AR$420

HOTELS AND B&BS

CENTRAL BUENOS AIRES

Alcázar Av de Mayo 935 ☎011 4345 0926, ❼hotelalcazar.com.ar; map p.53. This old hotel with a lovely central staircase features basic rooms, all with heating, a fan and private bathroom. AR$440

Gran Hotel Hispano Av de Mayo 861, at Tacuarí ☎011 4345 2020, ❼hhispano.com.ar; map p.53. Metres from the famous *Café Tortoni*, this family-run classic retains its original Spanish-style architecture. Most rooms are centred on a beautiful old courtyard, while some have balconies looking onto the street below. **AR$595**

Marbella Av de Mayo 1261 ☎011 4383 8566, ⊛hotelmarbella.com.ar; map p.53. Calm, good-value lodgings (discounts for cash) in a central location. Rooms are modern with cable TV and decent-sized bathrooms, and there is also an economical restaurant. **AR$520**

Posada de la Luna Perú 565, at México ☎011 4343 0911, ⊛posadaluna.com; map p.53. Attractively decorated B&B set in a colonial townhouse on the cusp of San Telmo. Home-made bread and jam is served with breakfast and there's a jacuzzi and sun deck. No hotel sign outside the door means it's still a relatively well-kept secret. This corner can be a bit dodgy so keep your wits about you. **AR$420**

Rooney's Boutique Hotel Sarmiento 1775, at Callao ☎011 5252 5060, ⊛rooneysboutiquehotel.com; map p.53. Run by an Irish expat, the former residence of writer Leopoldo Lugones, this 14-room hotel is a hop from the Obelisk yet is zen enough to retain calm. **AR$980**

PALERMO, RECOLETA AND RETIRO

The 5th Floor Vidt, at Santa Fe ☎011 4827 0366; map p.57. Take the cramped lift to the fifth floor and step into a spacious Art Deco B&B that spans two floors. With terraces and shared spaces galore, this is a friendly option in a more residential part of Palermo, but still a stone's throw from the buzz. English breakfast included. **AR$1020**

Che Lulu Trendy Hotel Pasaje Emilio Zola 5185, at Godoy Cruz, Palermo Viejo ☎011 4772 0289, ⊛chelulu .com; map p.57. On a colourful *pasaje* in Palermo, *Che Lulu* offers a down-to-earth and relaxed experience. Includes dorms as well as private rooms. Dorms **AR$170**, doubles **AR$850**

Republica Palermo Costa Rica 4828, at Borges ☎011 4833 5834, ⊛republicapalermo.com; map p.57. Sleek twelve-room B&B, with designer features and a neat location in the heart of Palermo's Soho area. **AR$170**

EATING

Buenos Aires has a busy, increasingly diverse, restaurant scene. Many restaurants offer a good-value *menú del día* (lunchtime set menu) on weekdays, usually including a drink, an excellent way to sample the best of BA's restaurants for less. It is wise to book ahead at the more popular places.

CENTRAL BUENOS AIRES

CBC – California Burrito Co. Lavalle 441 ☎011 4328 3057; map p.53. Busy central burrito joint, ideally placed for lunch on the go. White-flour tortillas are packed with seemingly endless combinations of fresh ingredients; portions are enormous. Three burritos and drink special from AR$60. Mon–Fri noon–9pm, Sat & Sun noon–7pm.

Las Cuartetas Av Corrientes 838 ☎011 4326 0171, ⊛lascuartetas.com; map p.53. Big, brightly lit theatre and pizzeria, opposite the Gran Rex. Large pizzas from AR$140. Mon–Fri 11am–1.30am, Sat noon–1.30am, Sun 7pm–1.30am.

La Giralda Corrientes 1453 ☎011 4371 3846; map p.53. Brightly lit and austerely decorated Corrientes café, famous for its *chocolate espeso con churros* (thick hot chocolate with fritters, AR$40). A perennial hangout for students and intellectuals, and a good place to observe the *porteño* passion for conversation. Mon–Sat 7am–2am.

La Gran Taberna Combate de los Pozos 95, Montserrat ☎011 4951 7586; map p.53. A popular, bustling and down-to-earth restaurant a block from the Congreso. The vast, reasonably priced menu offers a mixture of Spanish dishes, including a good selection of seafood, *porteño* staples and a sprinkling of more exotic dishes such as *ranas a la provenzal* (frogs' legs with parsley and garlic, AR$250). Many dishes are large enough to share. Mains AR$80–105. Daily noon–4pm & 8pm–2am.

Grand Café Basavilbaso 1340 ☎011 4893 9333; map p.53. Adorable, friendly café serving well-priced modern Argentine dishes. Kick back in an armchair with a daily lunch special such as fried chicken with mash and tartar sauce, a soft drink and dessert (AR$120). Also serves up a delectable croissant (AR$15) and large coffees (AR$30). Mon–Fri 8am–8pm & Sat 10am–4pm.

PALERMO, RECOLETA AND RETIRO

Bio Humboldt 2192 ☎011 4774 3880 ⊛b1orestaurant .com.ar; map p.57. Vegetarian restaurant with lots of wholesome ingredients – wholemeal *empanadas*, quinoa risotto, tofu salad and so on – with a good-value (AR$70) lunch with drink. Organic wine and beer are also served. Daily 10am–midnight.

Club Eros Uriarte 1609, Palermo Viejo ☎011 4832 1313; map p.57. Fun, noisy cantina at a neighbourhood sports and social club, offering Argentine standards at bargain prices. Daily noon–4pm & 8pm–midnight.

★ TREAT YOURSELF

Aramburu Salta 1050, San Telmo ☎011 4305 0439, ⊛arambururesto.com.ar; map p.53. At this intimate and award-winning establishment, chef-owner Gonzalo Aramburu, who trained in Europe and the US before returning to Argentina, shows off his culinary wizardry. Splash out on the divine twelve-course tasting menu with wine pairings – it will set you back around AR$1000 but will be worth every sip and bite. Book in advance. Mon–Sat 8.30–11.30pm.

1

La Cocina Pueyrredón 1508, Recoleta ☎ 011 4825 3171; map p.57. Tiny budget place serving *locro* (a filling corn stew from the northeast of Argentina) and a selection of delicious Catamarca-style *empanadas*. Mon–Sat noon–4pm & 7pm–midnight.

Cumaná Rodriguez Peña 1149, Retiro; map p.57. Popular with students and office workers, this is a good place to try *mate*, served from 4pm to 7.30pm with a basket of crackers. There's also a selection of provincial food, such as *empanadas* and *cazuelas* (casseroles). Daily from noon.

Don Julio Guatemala 4699, Palermo Viejo ☎ 011 4831 9564 ⓦ parrilladonjulio.com.ar; map p.57. Excellent *parrilla* with choice cuts of meat, a superb wine list and smart, efficient service. *Lomo*, fries, salad and wine will set you back AR$320. Daily noon–1am.

Freddo Branches throughout the city, including Alto Palermo Shopping and Armenia 1618, ⓦ freddo.com.ar; map p.57. Buenos Aires' best ice-cream chain. *Dulce de leche* fans will be in heaven, and the passion-fruit mousse flavour (*maracuyá mousse*) is superb. Prices from AR$30. Daily 10am–late.

Kentucky Santa Fe 4602, Palermo Viejo ☎ 011 4773 7869, ⓦ pizzeriaskentucky.com; map p.57. A Buenos Aires institution that's been around since 1942, serving excellent pizzas and *empanadas*. Expect old-school waiters in white shirts and bow ties, and a grungy clientele. The *empanadas* are abundant and worth the higher than normal price. Sun–Thurs 6am–2am, Fri & Sat 24hr.

Krishna Malabia 1833, Palermo Viejo ☎ 011 4833 4618, ⓦ krishnaveggie.com; map p.57. Tiny bohemian spot on Plaza Palermo Viejo run by the International Society for Krishna Consciousness and serving tasty vegetarian Indian food. Go for the mixed *thali* with a ginger lemonade. Mon 8pm–12.30am, Tues 12.30–5pm & 8pm–12.30am, Wed–Sun 12.30–12.30am.

El Preferido de Palermo Borges 2108, at Guatemala, Palermo Viejo ☎ 011 4774 6585, ⓦ elpreferidodepalermo .com; map p.57. Fun, *pulpería*-style diner with bottles and cans packing the shelves and hams hanging from the ceiling. Menu choices include a lentil and bacon stew and *milanesa* (breaded escalope) with potatoes. Mon–Sat noon–4pm & 8pm–midnight.

Sarkis Thames 1101, Villa Crespo ☎ 011 4772 4911; map p.57. Excellent tabbouleh, *keppe crudo* (raw meat with onion – much better than it sounds) and falafel at this popular restaurant serving a fusion of Armenian, Arab and Turkish cuisine. Close to Palermo Viejo, and great value for money (very popular so expect long queues). Daily noon–3pm & 8pm–1am.

SAN TELMO AND AROUND

Brasserie Pétanque Defensa 595, San Telmo ☎ 011 4342 7930, ⓦ brasseriepetanque.com; map p.53. Authentic and chic French-owned brasserie, serving French classics (onion soup, steak tartare, crème brûlée and even snails). Weekday lunch deal AR$120 (main course and drink). Tues–Thurs 12.30pm–4pm, 8pm–midnight, Fri & Sat 12.30pm–4pm & 8pm–12.30am, Sun 12.30pm–4.30pm & 8pm–11.30pm.

Chochán Piedras 627 ☎ 011 4342 7930; map p.53. In an unusual culinary twist for Argentina, this cantina deals specifically in pork, and even the name is backslang for pig in Spanish (*chancho*). From sweetbreads to pulled pork sandwiches loaded with home-made kimchi (AR$90), the menu changes on a daily basis. Mon–Sat 7pm–midnight.

El Desnivel Defensa 855, San Telmo ☎ 011 4300 9081, ⓦ parrillaeldesnivel.com.ar; map p.53. Classic San Telmo *parrilla* with accessible prices, great meat and a friendly, slightly rowdy atmosphere; popular with tourists and locals though quality has taken a hit in recent times. *Lomo* steak AR$130. Mon 8pm–1am, Tues–Sun noon–4pm & 8pm–1am.

Gran Parrilla del Plata Chile 594, San Telmo ☎ 011 4300 8588, ⓦ parrilladelplata.com; map p.53. Excellent-value steakhouse whose *asado de tira* ribs (AR$150) have to be one of the tenderest cuts in town. Mon–Sat noon–4pm & 8pm–1am, Sun noon–1am.

El Obrero Caffarena 64, La Boca ☎ 011 4362 9912; map p.53. With Boca Juniors souvenirs on the walls and tango musicians moving from table to table at weekends, the atmosphere at the hugely popular and moderately priced *El Obrero* is as much a part of the fun as the simple unfussy food (*lomo* steak AR$80, pasta dishes AR$60). Very popular, so prepare to queue at weekends. Take a taxi as the local area can be unsafe. Mon–Sat noon–10pm.

Parrilla 1880 Defensa 1665, San Telmo ☎ 011 4307 2746; map p.53. Extremely good *parrilla* joint, opposite Parque Lezama. Its walls are lined with photos and drawings from the restaurant's famous and mostly bohemian clients, and the friendly owner makes sure everyone is happy. Mains AR$75–110. Mon–Sat noon–4pm & 8pm–1am, Sun noon–4pm.

DRINKING AND NIGHTLIFE

Buenos Aires offers a lively nightlife every day of the week. The only exception is perhaps on Monday, when some venues, especially in the centre, tend to close. Wednesday is known as "After Office", when the city's bars and clubs start to fill from 6pm. Keep in mind that Buenos Aires starts – and finishes – late, so clubs don't fill up until the early hours. Check out *What's Up Buenos Aires* (ⓦ whatsupbuenosaires.com) for articles on the city's cultural and nightlife happenings, or *Wipe* (ⓦ wipe.com .ar; Spanish only) and *Aires de Bares* for bar reviews (ⓦ airesdebares.com; Spanish only). The *Buenos Aires Herald*'s Tues–Sat listings are also invaluable for up-to-date events.

BARS AND PUBS

Bangalore Humboldt 1416, Palermo Hollywood ☎011 4779 2621, ⓦthebangalorebar.com; map p.57. Fine traditional pub in Palermo Hollywood, popular with locals, expats and tourists. Happy hour until 10pm; pints and curries served. Daily noon–2am.

Caracas Guatemala 4802, Palermo Viejo ☎011 4776 8704, ⓦcaracasbar.com.ar; map p.57. Trendy Palermo Viejo venue attracting a cool crowd. Has a lovely roof terrace and serves Venezuelan food. Mon–Sat 6.30pm–4am.

Los Cardones Jorge Luis Borges 2180, Palermo ☎011 4777 1112, ⓦcardones.com.ar; map p.57. One of the best *peñas* in town – a bar where traditional folk musicians play. Wed–Sat from 9pm.

La Cigale 25 de Mayo 597, Centro ☎011 4893 2332; map p.53. One of the Centro's most happening bars, attracting an up-for-it crowd. Regularly hosts live music and DJs. Also hosts a monthly pub quiz in English. Mon–Fri from 6pm & Sat from 8pm.

Congo Honduras 5329, Palermo ☎011 4833 5857; map p.57. Sleek interiors and atmospheric lighting at this popular hang-out. Particularly heaving in summer thanks to a stunning outside area. Wed–Sat 8pm–5am.

Milión Paraná 1048, Recoleta ☎011 4815 9925, ⓦmilion.com.ar; map p.57. Stunning bar that occupies an early twentieth-century townhouse. Packed with gringos and Argentines on the prowl for good times, this is a fun if pricey place to start the night and another venue with a superb garden. Mon–Fri 10am–late, Sat noon–late, Sun 8pm–late.

La Poesía Chile 502, San Telmo ☎011 4300 7340; map p.53. Old-fashioned establishment that feels a bit like a Spanish tapas bar. From the owners of the equally excellent *El Federal* (Carlos Calvo 599), *La Poesía* serves three types of artisan beer (AR$20–40) and does a wide range of *picada* tasting platters (AR$85–145). Daily until midnight.

La Puerta Roja Chacabuco 733, San Telmo ☎011 4362 5649; map p.53. Old men, bohemians and night owls while away the small hours in this traditional wood-panelled bar overlooking Parque Lezama. 24hr.

Sugar Costa Rica 4619, Palermo ☎011 4831 3276, ⓦsugarbuenosaires.com; map p.57. Not the place to come if you're looking for an authentic *porteño* night out. This American-run bar feels more US frat party than BA boozer. But if you fancy a hamburger and a lengthy, well-priced happy hour (7pm–midnight), then *Sugar* is your bar. Daily noon–late.

NIGHTCLUBS

Amerika Gascón 1040, Villa Crespo ☎011 4865 4416, ⓦameri-k.com.ar; map p.57. Opening in 1999, it's still the city's biggest gay club, with three dancefloors playing mainly electro. Fri–Sun from midnight.

Crobar Marcelo Freyre s/n & Paseo de la Infanta, Palermo ☎011 4778 1500, ⓦcrobar.com.ar; map p.57. Glitzy club near the Hipódromo Argentino that plays commercial dance music and regularly welcomes international DJs such as Armin van Buuren. Fri & Sat from 10pm.

Glam Cabrera 3046, Barrio Norte ☎011 4963 2521, ⓦglambsas.com.ar; map p.57. One of the city's hottest gay bar-discos. Several lounge areas and dancefloors play everything from Latino beats to 1980s classics. Thurs & Sat from 1am.

Groove Palermo Av Santa Fe 4389, Palermo ⓦpalermogroove.com; map p.57. Club specializing in live music, often rock and international bands. Also one of the host venues of legendary alternative rock/reggae nights *Fiesta Clandestina*. Open Saturday night for club nights and for live music during the week.

Maluco Beleza Sarmiento 1728, Centro ☎011 4372 1737; map p.53. Long-running Brazilian club, playing a mix of *lambada*, afro-samba and reggae to a lively crowd of Brazilians and Brazilophiles. Wed & Fri–Sun from 10pm.

Niceto Club Niceto Vega 5510, Palermo Hollywood ☎011 4779 9396, ⓦnicetoclub.com; map p.57. One of BA's best clubs, *Niceto* has a roster of live music during the week – local and international artists have played here – mainly reggae and electronic music at weekends, with the outlandish Club 69 dance parties on Thursdays.

You Know My Name M T de Alvear 1540, Recoleta ☎011 4811 4730, ⓦyouknowmyname.com.ar; map p.57. Laidback club formerly known as *El Living*, this space is in a rambling old building with two bars, a coffee stand and a

MILONGAS

Milongas – regular dance clubs, usually starting with lessons (beginners welcome) – are popular with tango dancers young and old. They are a great way to try the moves for yourself and to get a feel for the scene, for a fraction of the price of a dinner show (entrance usually costs around AR$30). Among the city's best *milongas* are **La Viruta** (Armenia 1366, Palermo; ☎011 4774 6357); **Salón Canning** (Scalabrini Ortiz 1331, Palermo; ☎011 4832 6753); **La Catedral** (Sarmiento 4006, Almagro; ☎011 5325 1630); and **Centro Cultural Torquato Tasso** (Defensa 1575, San Telmo; ☎011 4307 6506). **Confitería Ideal** (Suipacha 380–384, San Nicolas; ☎011 5265 8069), a beautiful if crumbling relic of a dancehall, also holds afternoon classes.

1

long, narrow dancefloor that packs out. Plays a fun, danceable mix of funk, disco and rock music. Thurs from 7pm and Fri & Sat from 10pm.

ENTERTAINMENT

CULTURAL CENTRES

Buenos Aires has a number of excellent and popular cultural centres. Entry is free, although special temporary exhibitions occasionally charge a fee.

Centro Cultural Borges Viamonte 525 ☎011 5555 5358, ⓦ www.ccborges.org.ar. Named after Argentina's most famous writer; there's a permanent area dedicated to him, as well as exhibitions, a cinema and workshops. Mon–Sat 10am–9pm, Sun noon–9pm.

Centro Cultural Recoleta Junín 1930 ☎011 4803 1040, ⓦ centroculturalrecoleta.org. Located next to the famous cemetery, this is an excellent centre with a particular focus on visual arts; it's also the occasional home of anarchic theatre troupe Fuerza Bruta/De la Guarda. Tues–Fri 1.30–8.30pm & Sat & Sun 11.30am–8.30pm.

Ciudad Cultural Konex Sarmiento 3131 ☎011 4864 3200, ⓦ ciudadculturalkonex.org. Atmospheric cultural centre in converted warehouse, located in the Almagro part of town. Hosts film and theatre productions as well as live music. Also the home of legendary drumming outfit La Bomba de Tiempo (shows on Mon at 7pm). Daily.

ND Ateneo Espacio Cultural Paraguay 918 ☎011 4328 2888, ⓦ ndteatro.com.ar. Cultural space and theatre with an emphasis on live music. Has shows from 9pm most evenings and there are also regular evening debates.

TANGO SHOWS

Tango shows are expensive, but they are the best way to see a series of top tango dancers in one evening, and most are well worth the splurge. All the following have nightly shows, and most include dinner. Prices range from around AR$250 (without food) to VIP treatment with haute cuisine for over AR$1000.

Bar Sur Estados Unidos 299, at Balcarce, San Telmo ☎011 4362 6086, ⓦ bar-sur.com.ar; map p.53. This cosy little joint puts on fancy shows and encourages audience participation.

Café Tortoni Av de Mayo 825, Centre ☎011 4342 4328, ⓦ cafetortoni.com.ar; map p.53. Buenos Aires' most famous café offers an affordable and rather theatrical tango show downstairs at AR$80–100.

Esquina Carlos Gardel Carlos Gardel 3200, Abasto ☎011 4867 6363, ⓦ esquinacarlosgardel.com.ar. Although very touristy, this smart venue, named after the king of tango, remains a classic. Nearest subway Carlos Gardel. Shows from AR$96 (without food).

Piazzolla Tango Florida 165, Microcentro ☎011 4344 8200, ⓦ piazzollatango.com; map p.53. Housed in a grand old theatre in the centre, the show here is made up of two singers, an orchestra and a set of tango dancers, with prices starting at AR$1100.

El Viejo Almacén Av Independencia 300, at Balcarce, San Telmo ☎011 4307 6689, ⓦ viejoalmacen.com.ar; map p.53. Dinner and show from 8pm or show only from 10pm.

SHOPPING

Buenos Aires offers some of the best shopping in South America. Best buys include leather goods (handbags, belts, shoes), wine, home design and handicrafts (particularly handmade jewellery). Top shopping areas include Avenida Santa Fe, Palermo Viejo and San Telmo. Downtown Calle Florida is a famous shopping street from yesteryear but is a bit of a tourist trap today. Most of the Argentine clothing chains and designers have outlet stores in Villa Crespo, around Gurruchaga and Aguirre.

Malls The city's malls house Argentina's most successful brands, as well as big international names; they open every day of the week until 10pm. Try Alto Palermo (Santa Fé and Coronel Díaz, Palermo, ⓦ www.altopalermo.com.ar), Galerías Pacífico (Florida and Córdoba, Centre, ⓦ www .galeriaspacifico.com.ar) or Paseo Alcorta (Salguero 3172 and Figueroa Alcorta, Palermo Chico, ⓦ www .alcortashopping.com.ar); the last has a large Carrefour hypermarket downstairs. The largest of all is Unicenter (ⓦ unicenter.com.ar), north of the city in the outer suburbs, full of designer shops, a cinema, and with an IMAX close by. You can get there on the #60 bus from the centre, or by taxi.

Markets The city's ferias usually take place on weekends and are an excellent place to pick up inexpensive local handicrafts. The most extensive are: the Feria "Hippy" next to Recoleta cemetery (Sat & Sun); Plaza Dorrego in San Telmo, spanning a dozen blocks along Defensa (Sun); and on Sat or Sun depending on time of year, the Feria de Mataderos (see p.58). For locally made and designed clothes head to Plaza Serrano in Palermo, weekends from 3pm onwards, when the cafés surrounding the plaza are converted into indoor markets filled to the brim with affordable clothes and jewellery.

PALERMO VIEJO

After the economic crash of the early noughties, this low-rise area became a hotbed of creative and design talent, and the streets have since filled to bursting with tiny, beautifully presented boutiques. The area is perfect for browsing, but choice boutiques include: **Condimentos** (Honduras 4874) for attractive local jewellery designs; **28 Sport** (Gurruchaga 1481) for top-quality shoes for men and women; and **Pesqueira** (Gurruchaga 1750), cool print heaven.

DIRECTORY

Banks and exchange Many casas de cambio foreign exchanges have closed down due to the double exchange rates that vary wildly, and many people with dollars change them at *cuevas* or unofficial exchanges as they get more bang for their buck; ask your hotel or hostel for more info. Banks will also change to or from dollars but at the official rate.

Embassies and consulates Australia, Villanueva 1400 (☎011 4779 3500); Bolivia, Av Corrientes 545, 2nd Floor (☎011 4394 1463); Brazil, Cerrito 1350 (☎011 4515 2400); Canada, Tagle 2828 (☎011 4808 1000); Chile, Tagle 2762 (☎011 4808 8601); Ireland, Av del Libertador 1060, 6th Floor (☎011 5787 0801); New Zealand, Carlos Pellegrini 1427, 5th Floor (☎011 4328 0301); UK, Dr Luis Agote 2412 (☎011 4808 2200); United States, Av Colombia 4300 (☎011 5777 4533); Uruguay, Av Las Heras 1907 (☎011 4807 3040).

Hospitals Private hospitals: Hospital Británico (Pedriel 74 ☎011 4309 6400) has some English-speaking doctors and 24hr emergency care; for non-emergency visits there is also a more central location at Marcelo T de Alvear 1573 (☎011 4812 0040). Hospital Alemán (Av Pueyrredón 1640, between Beruti and Juncal ☎011 4827 7000), emergency (entrance on Beruti) and non-emergency care; English spoken. Public hospital: Hospital Juan A Fernández (Cerviño 3356, at Bulnes ☎011 4808 2600).

Laundry Laundries are plentiful and inexpensive (though not usually self-service). Expect to pay around AR$35 for a wash and dry.

Left luggage Retiro bus station and both the domestic and international airports have left luggage services. Your hostel may be prepared to look after your luggage if you have a return booking.

Pharmacies Farmacity (🖥farmacity.com.ar) has numerous branches, many open 24hr (for example, at Santa Fe 3880, and Vidt, Palermo ☎011 5778 3276).

Police In an emergency call ☎911. Tourist Police, Comisaría del Turista, Av Corrientes 436 ☎011 4346 5748 or ☎0800 999 5000 (24hr), English spoken.

Post office Correo Argentino has branches all over town (🖥www.correoargentino.com.ar).

Around Buenos Aires

Argentina's most spectacular scenery lies far from the capital but, thankfully, Buenos Aires province offers several rewarding and easily accessible destinations for a day-trip or a peaceful

overnighter. The lush mini-Venice of **Tigre**, just north of Buenos Aires, is the gateway to the watery recreation of the Paraná Delta. A trip to the provincial capital, **La Plata**, is essential for natural history enthusiasts; the city's Museo de la Plata is home to an extraordinary array of megafauna skeletons. For a slice of gaucho life you can visit **San Antonio de Areco**, where late nineteenth-century houses and cobbled streets combine with gaucho culture to charming effect. Taking the ferry across the Río de la Plata to **Colonia**, in Uruguay (see p.345), also makes a great day out.

TIGRE AND THE DELTA

A short train ride north of the city centre, the river port of **TIGRE** distributes the timber and fruit produced in the delta of the **Paraná River**. Originally a remote system of rivers dotted with inaccessible islands, the Delta is now crowded with weekend homes and riverside restaurants.

WHAT TO SEE AND DO

The river itself is the principal attraction; head for Tigre's **Estación Fluvial** from where inexpensive local wooden ferries leave every twenty minutes or so. Take one of these to "Tres Bocas" (AR$40) where there are two or three good restaurants and cafés with riverfront verandas, or simply enjoy a cruise. The tourist office at the Estación Fluvial can give you a map of the islands and details of the numerous boat companies serving them, among them Río Tur (☎011 4731 0280, 🖥rioturcatamaranes.com.ar), leaving from the Los Mimbreros dock; and Sturla (☎011 4731 1300, 🖥sturlaviajes.com.ar), from the Estación Fluvial. The town of Tigre also has some interesting places to visit. About eight blocks from the Estación Fluvial at Sarmiento 100 is the colourful **Puerto de Frutos** (daily 10am–6pm) where hundreds of baskets made from Delta plants, spices, wooden furniture and handicrafts are on sale. Across the bridge you'll find the ageing but well-thought-out **Museo Naval**, at Paseo Victorica 602 (Mon–Fri 8.30am–6pm, Sat & Sun

1

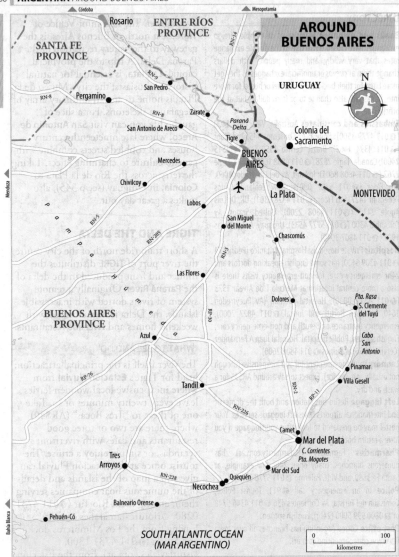

AROUND
BUENOS AIRES

10am–6.30pm; AR$10), and if you keep walking up the river the spectacular **Tigre Club**, now the **Museo de Arte Tigre** (Wed–Fri 9am–6.30pm, Sat & Sun noon–6.30pm, AR$20), will come into view. The carefully restored early twentieth-century building gives an idea of how the other half lived; there is a fine art collection inside and great views from the terrace.

ARRIVAL AND DEPARTURE

By train To get to Tigre you can either take a direct train from Retiro (Mitre line, every 10min; 1hr; AR$2, use a SUBE card) or take the commuter train to Bartolomé Mitre (every 15min); walk across the bridge to Maipú station, and jump on the touristic *T ren de la Costa* (every 20min; AR$40 one-way for tourists), which runs through the leafy suburbs, stopping at scenic stations to the north of the city.

★ TREAT YOURSELF

Delta Eco Spa Río Carapachay Km6, Tigre
☎ 011 5236 0553, ⓦ www.deltaecospa
.com. A beautiful riverside setting with two
swimming pools, this is an idyllic spot to
kick back and unwind, especially during
the week when it's quieter. Book a
massage at the time of reservation for a 10
percent discount. **ARS2800**

ACCOMMODATION

Delta Hostel Coronel Morales 1418, Tigre ☎ 011 5245
9776, ⓦ tigredeltahostel.com.ar. This friendly hostel offers
free massages and organizes a host of activities such as
boat trips and kayaking on the Delta, as well as typical
Argentine *asados*. Dorms **ARS120**, doubles **ARS300**

EATING AND DRINKING

There are numerous cheap and cheerful *parrillas* on the
mainland. A more romantic option, however, is to stop off
by boat at one of the secluded riverside restaurants.
Beixa Flor Arroyo Abra Vieja 148 ☎ 011 5228 1367,
ⓦ beixaflor.com.ar. This quiet and colourful restaurant
serves up delicious home-made food (ranging from river
fish to *bife de chorizo*) out in its peaceful garden or by its
private beach. If you can't bear to tear yourself away, book
yourself into one of their rooms for the night. Three-course
meal around ARS200. Daily noon–3pm & 8–10pm.
El Gato Blanco Rio Capitán 80 ☎ 011 4728 0390,
ⓦ gato-blanco.com. A family favourite, *El Gato Blanco* has
an attractive deck area and flower-filled garden, as well as
a mini playground. Inside is an elegant tea room. Three-
course meal around ARS300. Daily noon–3pm.

SAN ANTONIO DE ARECO

The refined pampas town of **SAN ANTONIO
DE ARECO**, set on the meandering Río
Areco 110km northwest of Buenos Aires, is
the spiritual home of the gaucho or
Argentine cowboy. A robust tourist
industry has grown around the gaucho
tradition: silver and leather handicraft
workers peddle their wares in the town's
shops, historic **estancias** (ranches)
accommodate visitors in the surrounding
countryside and an annual **gaucho festival**
draws massive crowds every November.
While bicycles rule the streets here, you'll
also spot beret-clad *estancia* workers on
horseback, trotting about on the cobblestones.

WHAT TO SEE AND DO

The leafy town centre is laid out in a grid
fashion around the main square, **Plaza Ruiz
de Arellano**, and is full of genteel, slightly
decaying, single-storey nineteenth-century
buildings, many of them painted a
blushing shade of pink. On the south side
of the square is the plain white **Iglesia
Parroquial San Antonio de Padua**, the
town's first chapel, dating from 1728. A
sculpture of San Antonio graces the
exterior. One block north, in a refurbished
former power plant at Alsina 66, is the
Centro Cultural Usina Vieja (Tues–Sun
11am–5pm; AR$5), home to the **Museo
de la Ciudad**, with nineteenth-century
objects and temporary art exhibitions that
depict life in rural Argentina.

Just north of town, across the Río
Areco, lies **Parque Criollo**, home to the
Museo Gauchesco Ricardo Güiraldes
(Mon & Wed–Sun 11am–5pm; guided
visits Sat & Sun 12.30pm & 3.30pm;
AR$12). Just four of the nine rooms can
be visited following a devastating flood in
2009, but the museum, set in a replica
nineteenth-century *estancia*, has a

ESTANCIAS

Reflecting Argentina's changing economic climate, many of the country's **estancias** – vast
cattle and horse estates once lorded over by wealthy European settlers – have been converted
into luxury accommodation. For anyone with latent aristocratic or cowboy aspirations, *estancias*
offer the chance to milk cows, ride horses, go fly-fishing, play polo or simply tuck into a juicy
slab of steak plucked straight off the *asado* while swanning poolside with a glass of Malbec.

Running the gamut from simple family farmhouses to Pampas dude ranches and
ostentatious Italianate mansions, *estancias* are a character-filled throwback to the Argentina of
yesteryear. For a list of *estancias* offering accommodation in and around San Antonio de Areco,
see ⓦ sanantoniodeareco.com or ⓦ sanantoniodeareco.org. For more **information** on
estancias in other parts of Argentina, visit ⓦ estanciasargentinas.com, ⓦ estanciastravel.com,
ⓦ estanciasenargentina.com or ⓦ ranchweb.com.

1

collection of gaucho art and artefacts and pays homage to the life of author Ricardo Güiraldes, whose classic novel, *Don Segundo Sombra* (1926) – set in San Antonio de Areco – served to elevate the *mate*-sucking, horse-breaking, cow-herding gaucho from rebellious outlaw to respected and romantic national icon. Demonstrations of gaucho feats are held every year in the Parque Criollo during November's week-long **Fiesta de la Tradición** celebrations.

ARRIVAL AND INFORMATION

By bus The bus station (☎02326 453 904) is at General Paz & Av Dr Smith, a six-block walk from the town centre along C Segundo Sombra. There are buses to and from Buenos Aires (every 1–2hr; 2hr) and Rosario (6 daily; 4hr).
Tourist information The tourist office, which loans bicycles, is a short walk from the main square towards the river at the corner of Arellano & Zerboni (Mon–Fri 8am–7pm; Sat & Sun till 8pm; ☎02326 453 165, ☜areco.gob.ar).

ACCOMMODATION

While San Antonio de Areco can easily be visited on a day-trip from Buenos Aires, you might well be charmed into staying the night. Book ahead at weekends (the town is a popular destination for *porteños*) and well in advance for the Fiesta de la Tradición in November, or contact the tourist office, which can arrange homestays with families.
Hostal de Areco Zapiola 25 ☎02326 456 118, ☜hostaldeareco.com.ar. Centrally located in a pink colonial building, this B&B has a nice sunny garden and offers decent doubles with private bathrooms. AR$340
Club River Plate ☎02326 453 590. This campsite is 1km west of town along Zerboni. The price is for two people. Camping AR$80
Hostel El Puesto Belgrano 270 ☎02326 15 402 159, ☜hostelelpuesto.com.ar. Located in a former stately home, *El Puesto* is just three blocks from the main square. Friendly staff, an outdoor swimming pool and free access to the all-important barbecue equipment are all part of the attraction. Dorms AR$190, doubles AR$750

EATING AND DRINKING

Many of San Antonio de Areco's restaurants and bars have been given Old World-style makeovers, and their continued patronage by weathered *estancia* workers gives them an air of authenticity.
Almacén de Ramos Generales Zapiola 143 ☎02326 456 376, ☜ramosgeneralesareco.com.ar. Old bottles and gaucho paraphernalia line the walls of this delightful *parrilla;* the rabbit and trout specials and waist-softening desserts ensure a steady stream of regulars. Mains around

AR$100. Daily noon–3pm & 8–11pm.
La Esquina de Merti Arellano 149 ☎02326 456 705. Dolled up like a traditional corner store, this spacious and atmospheric plaza-side restaurant excels in fast and friendly service. *Parrilla* for two AR$180; pasta dishes around AR$70. Daily until 1am.
La Olla de Cobre Matheu 433 ☎02326 453 105, ☜laolladecobre.com.ar. A small chocolate factory and sweet shop selling superb home-made *alfajores*. Sample before buying. Mon & Wed–Sun 10am–1pm & 2.30–7.30pm.

LA PLATA

LA PLATA became the capital of the province of Buenos Aires in 1880, when the city of Buenos Aires was made the Federal Capital. Close enough to make an easy day-trip, it has a relaxed, small city feel. The geometric design, by French architect Pedro Benoît, and grid-numbered streets, were meant to make navigating the city easy but at times do exactly the opposite.

WHAT TO SEE AND DO

The most famous attractions can be found north of the city centre, next to the zoo, and in the middle of the pleasant lush parkland, **Paseo del Bosque**. The **Museo de la Plata** (Tues–Sun 10am–6pm; AR$6) was the first museum built in Latin America and has a wonderful collection of skeletons, stuffed animals and fossils, set in a crumbling building in the midst of the university. Though desperately in need of refurbishment, the museum is well worth visiting to see the vast whale bones and the models of prehistoric animals.

From the Paseo del Bosque (Av Iraola), avenidas 51 and 53 lead down through the historic centre to the **Plaza Moreno**. On its far side stands the colossal, neo-Gothic brick **Catedral**, with an impressive marble interior of thick columns and high vaulted ceilings. Roughly halfway between the two is **Plaza San Martín**, the lively heart of the city. On the western side, the **Centro Cultural Pasaje Dardo Rocha** (daily 9am–10pm; free) occupies the city's former train station, taking up an entire block between avenidas 49 and 50, 6 and 7. Behind the elegant, French- and Italian-influenced facade are housed a

MAR DEL PLATA

Argentina's **beaches** are somewhat overshadowed by neighbouring Uruguay's golden sands, in particular glamorous Punta del Este (see p.851). Still, a seaside outing in summer is a quintessential Argentine experience – and **Mar del Plata**, boasting some 50km of beach 400km south of Buenos Aires, is the country's number one resort. In the summer season (mid-Dec to March), millions of city-dwellers descend on the place, generating vibrant eating, drinking and entertainment scenes (or overcrowding and overpricing, depending on your point of view).

Though Mar del Plata may have lost some of its lustre, glimpses of glamour still abound in the city's restored early twentieth-century mansions – check out French-style Villa Ortiz Basualdo, now the **Museo Municipal de Arte**, at Avenida Colón 1189, the **MAR Museo Municipal de Arte Contemporáneo**, Avenida F.U. Camet and Dardo Rocha, and the **Centro Cultural Victoria Ocampo**, Matheu 1851. The renowned **International Film Festival** is held in Mar del Plata in November, showing new Argentine and international films.

Nearby **Cariló** and **Mar de los Pampas** are both eco-resorts that provide a more laidback seaside experience, set within beautiful pine forests. Rent a house or stay in a luxury hotel and chill out for a few days – but be warned, these are boutique resorts for Argentina's rich and famous, so you won't find much in the way of mid-range or budget accommodation.

There are numerous daily **buses** from Buenos Aires to Mar del Plata (6hr), or (not recommended) you can make the journey less comfortably (from ARS200) by **train**, from Constitución station (3 daily, 6hr), or **fly** across in less than an hour (2–3 daily).

cinema and various exhibition spaces, including the excellent **Museo de Arte Contemporáneo Latinoamericano** (daily 9am–10pm; free).

ARRIVAL AND INFORMATION

By bus Buses for La Plata leave from Retiro bus station every 30min (1hr 10min; ARS28 one-way).
Destinations Mar del Plata (12 daily; 5hr); Puerto Madryn (4 daily; 18hr).
By train The train journey from Constitución station is much slower than travelling by bus. Trains leave approximately every 40min (1hr 30min; ARS2.85 with SUBE, ARS5.80 without one-way, fast train four times a day ARS16).
Tourist information There's a tourist office inside the Pasaje Dardo Rocha cultural centre (daily 10am–8pm; ☎0221 427 1535). Many of the best places to eat and drink are just south of here, around the junction of avenidas 10 & 47.

EATING AND DRINKING

Cervecería Modelo Diagonal 54, 496 ☎0221 421 1321. Old-school classic restaurant and café housed in a century-old building with legs of ham hanging from the ceiling. Serves excellent draught beer; paella and home-made *pan dulce* (*panettone*) are the house specialities. Daily 8am–1am.
Cinco Sabios Brewing Co C 13 between 63 and 64 ☎0221 457 3333. Brewer run by young handcraft-beer enthusiasts making waves in the city. Also tuck into home-made burgers and fries (ARS50). Tues–Sun from 7pm.

Córdoba Province

CÓRDOBA PROVINCE, 700km northwest of Buenos Aires, marks Argentina's geographical bull's-eye. Serene towns dot its undulating **Central Sierras**, the second-highest mountain range in Argentina after the Andes, and the region is one of the country's more affordable travel destinations, except perhaps in high season when many city-dwellers flock to its cool heights. Córdoba province is a relaxed place for exploring the great outdoors – via hikes, horserides or even **skydives** – or just hanging out sipping *mate* with the super-friendly locals.

Most of the action takes place in and around **Córdoba city**, which has the country's highest concentration of bars and clubs outside Buenos Aires. South of Córdoba city in the verdant **Calamuchita Valley**, towns such as **Alta Gracia** and Germanic, beer-brewing **Villa General Belgrano** have historically served as getaways for Argentina's elite. Northwest of the capital in the **Punilla Valley**, laidback towns such as **Capilla del Monte** are growing in popularity among bohemian *porteños* looking for a clean, green break from city life.

1

CÓRDOBA

Argentina's second-largest city, unpretentious **CÓRDOBA** boasts some beautifully restored colonial architecture, plentiful restaurants and a legendary nightlife at its best when the university students are around. It is a good base for exploring the province, though during the city's stiflingly hot summers you'll soon be lured west to the Sierras' cooler elevations.

Plaza San Martín and around

Once the bloody stage for bullfights, executions and military parades, **Plaza**

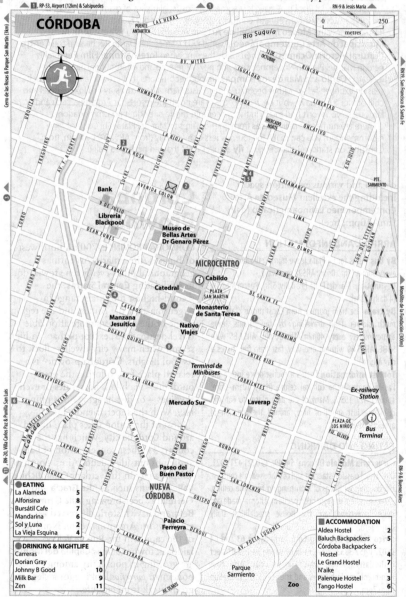

CÓRDOBA

● EATING
La Alameda	5
Alfonsina	8
Bursátil Cafe	7
Mandarina	6
Sol y Luna	2
La Vieja Esquina	4

● DRINKING & NIGHTLIFE
Carreras	3
Dorian Gray	1
Johnny B Good	10
Milk Bar	9
Zen	11

■ ACCOMMODATION
Aldea Hostel	2
Baluch Backpackers	5
Córdoba Backpacker's Hostel	4
Le Grand Hostel	7
N'aike	1
Palenque Hostel	3
Tango Hostel	6

San Martín was converted into a civilized public square, replete with fountains and semi-tropical foliage, in the 1870s. Free tango events are hosted here most Saturday nights at 9pm.

On the square's western side, the two-storey, sixteenth-century **Cabildo** was once the city's colonial headquarters and has now been turned into the **Museo de la Ciudad** (Mon–Fri 9am–12.30pm & 3–5pm, Sat & Sun 9.30am–1pm & 3–7pm; free; ☎0351 433 2758). It also hosts concerts, art exhibitions and, in the summer, tango evenings.

Alongside the Cabildo is the **Catedral**, one of the oldest in the country. Construction began in 1577 but wasn't completed for another two hundred years, rendering the cathedral something of an architectural mongrel, with a mix of Neoclassical and Baroque styles and a Romanesque dome thrown in for good measure. Note the trumpeting angels in indigenous dress gracing the bell towers.

Manzana Jesuítica

The seventeenth-century **Manzana Jesuítica** (Mon–Sat: summer 9am–1pm & 4–7pm; winter 9am–6.30pm, Sun closed; AR$10; ☎0351 433 2075), or Jesuit Block, a short walk southwest of the plaza, is Córdoba's top attraction. A testament to the missionaries who arrived hot on the heels of Córdoba's sixteenth-century colonizers, the **Templo de la Compañía de Jesús**, built in 1640, is Argentina's oldest surviving Jesuit temple. It has a striking Cusqueño altarpiece, and its barrel-shaped vaulted roof is made of

---

★ TREAT YOURSELF

Córdoba is the most affordable place in Argentina to jump out of a plane. Tumbling out of the door at 2500m, you get a bird's-eye view, after 20 seconds of face-flattening freefall, of city sprawl, a patchwork of green fields and the Central Sierras. **Skydive Córdoba** (☎0351 15 687 8471, ⊛skydivecordobaargentina.com) have almost 40 years of skydiving experience and charge from AR$1560 for a tandem jump.

Paraguayan cedar. The block also houses a private chapel, the **Capilla Doméstica**.

Monasterio de Santa Teresa

Southwest of Plaza San Martín at Independencia 146 is the **Iglesia Santa Teresa**, part of a working convent that contains the **Museo de Arte Religioso Juan de Tejeda** (Independencia 122; Mon–Fri 9am–1pm; AR$10; ☎0351 428 1540, ⊛museotejeda.wordpress.com). It has perhaps the finest collection of sacred art in the country, including Jesuit artefacts and religious paintings from Cusco in Peru.

Museo de Bellas Artes Dr Genaro Pérez

The municipal art gallery, the **Museo de Bellas Artes Dr Genaro Pérez**, Avenida General Paz 33 (Tues–Sun 10am–8pm; free; ☎0351 434 tttttttt), is housed in a late nineteenth-century French-style mansion and features nineteenth- and twentieth-century Argentine art. The permanent collection has numerous landscape paintings from the **Escuela Cordobesa**, a movement led by master Genaro Pérez.

Nueva Córdoba

The neighbourhood of **Nueva Córdoba**, just south of the historic centre, is full of late nineteenth-century mansions converted into hip bars and restaurants. Diagonal Avenida Hipólito Yrigoyen cuts through the neighbourhood, which extends from Plaza Vélez Sarsfield to Parque Sarmiento (see p.72). Just over halfway down is the **Paseo del Buen Pastor**, Avenida Hipólito Yrigoyen 325, a former women's prison converted into a culinary and cultural precinct featuring art exhibitions and free concerts. Flanked by fountains and landscaped grassy knolls, it is one of the city's most popular spaces for chilling out in the summer.

Museo Superior de Bellas Artes Palacio Ferreyra

An exemplary art museum, the **Museo Superior de Bellas Artes Palacio Ferreyra**, Avenida Hipólito Yrigoyen 511 (Tues–Sun 10am–8pm; AR$15; ☎0351 434 3636), features four floors of works in an

1

opulent 1916 palace built in the French classical style. The top floor has rolling contemporary art exhibitions, while the basement level is devoted to photography. In between, some three hundred artists are represented, including Pablo Picasso and Argentina's Fernando Fader and Lino Enea Spilimbergo. A little further south is the hilltop **Parque Sarmiento**, one of the city's most popular green spaces.

ARRIVAL AND DEPARTURE

By plane Córdoba's Aeropuerto Internacional Taravella is 11km north of the city centre. It has domestic flights to Buenos Aires, Bariloche, Mendoza and Rosario, as well as international services to cities in Brazil, Chile and Peru. Taxis (around AR$140) and minibuses connect the airport with the city centre.

By bus The long-distance bus station (☎ 0351 433 1692) is several blocks east of the centre at Blvd Perón 380. Public buses run downtown; a taxi costs around AR$25. Local buses for some provincial destinations leave from the Terminal de Minibuses behind the Mercado Sur market on Blvd Arturo Illia.

Destinations Alta Gracia (every 15min; 1hr); Buenos Aires (frequent; 9–11hr); Capilla del Monte (hourly; 2hr 30min); Mendoza (15 daily; 9–10hr); Rosario (hourly; around 6hr); Salta (8 daily; 11–13hr); Villa General Belgrano (every 45min–1hr; 2hr).

INFORMATION AND TOURS

Tourist information The main tourist office is in the Cabildo (daily 8am–8pm; ☎ 0351 434 1200, ⍟ www .cordobaturismo.gov.ar). There are several smaller (and often more helpful) offices dotted around the city, including at the bus station (daily 7am–9pm; ☎ 0351 433 1982), the airport (Mon–Fri 7am–9pm, Sat & Sun 8am–8pm; ☎ 0351 434 8390) and the Paseo del Buen Pastor (daily 8am–8pm; ☎ 0351 434 2727).

Tour operators Servicio de Guías de Turismo de Córdoba (☎ 0351 15 593 1700, ⍟ guiasdecordoba.webnode.com .ar) runs regular walking tours of downtown sights with English-language guides. City Tour (☎ 0351 15537 8687) offers sightseeing tours on a red double-decker bus starting from the Plaza San Martín near the cathedral. For day-trips and tours of the province, try Nativo Viajes, Independencia 174 (☎ 0351 424 5341, ⍟ cordobanativoviajes.com.ar).

ACCOMMODATION

Córdoba has some of the best-value hostels in the country, as well as the odd decent guesthouse, but its lower-cost hotels are generally pretty poor. All the establishments listed offer tour-booking services and include internet/ wi-fi, breakfast and use of kitchen.

★**Aldea Hostel** Santa Rosa 447 ☎ 0351 426 1312, ⍟ aldeahostelcordoba.com. This bright, ambitious hostel has space for one hundred people and is bursting with extras including a café/bar serving lighter meals, a TV lounge, a leafy patio and a roof terrace. Discounts for extended stays. Dorms AR$100, doubles AR$300

Baluch Backpackers San Martín 338 ☎ 0351 422 3977, ⍟ baluchbackpackers.com. This popular hostel has a cosy lounge area, helpful staff and hosts weekly barbecues on its roof terrace. The dorms sleep up to six people, and the private rooms have a/c. Late risers, however, might be put off by the ambient street noise. Dorms AR$90, doubles AR$200

Córdoba Backpacker's Hostel San Martín 414 ☎ 0351 422 0593. A lively bar, tour desk, roof terrace with a small bouldering wall and laundry service are just some of the perks of this bustling, spacious HI hostel. Dorms AR$80, doubles AR$200

Le Grand Hostel Buenos Aires 547 ☎ 0351 422 7115, ⍟ legrandhostel.com. The largest hostel on the scene, located in Nueva Córdoba, an area popular with students. There's a chill-out room with huge flat-screen TV, an excellently equipped kitchen and decent outside area. There are also smart private en-suite rooms with a/c. Dorms AR$95, doubles AR$380

N'aike Fresnal 5048 ☎ 0351 589 0501, ⍟ naike.com.ar. This friendly, well-run guesthouse is located in the quiet Villa Belgrano neighbourhood, a few kilometres northwest of the centre. There are six colourful rooms with a/c, and guests have access to a kitchen, a plunge pool and a jacuzzi. AR$445

Palenque Hostel General Paz 371 ☎ 0351 423 7588, ⍟ palenquehostel.com.ar. Noisy but fun hostel in a converted nineteenth-century townhouse. The dorms and private rooms are reasonable value, and the wood-panelled common areas are good for meeting other backpackers. Dorms AR$80, doubles AR$300

Tango Hostel Fructose Rivera 70 ☎ 0351 425 6023, ⍟ tangohostelcordoba.com. In a convenient location, close to the Paseo de las Artes, this hostel has a sociable atmosphere and a collection of decent, no-frills dorms, plus a few private rooms. Dorms AR$105, doubles AR$270

EATING

Córdoba is a real delight for winers and diners. There are restaurants for refined tastebuds, boisterous drinking holes serving pub grub, and plenty of eat-on-the-run *empanada* joints for lining your stomach before a night out on the town. The pick of the fashionable restaurants is in Nueva Córdoba.

La Alameda Obispo Trejo 170. Savour inexpensive Argentine staples like *empanadas* and *humitas* for a few pesos, while sitting outside on wooden benches, or indoors where customers' poetry and art adorn the walls. Mains around AR$40–70. Mon–Sat noon–2am.

★ **Alfonsina** Duarte Quiros 66 ☎ 0351 427 2847. Antique typewriters, exposed brickwork and a jolly crowd of students are the hallmarks of this restaurant-bar, which offers a taste of Argentina's northwest (mains AR$60–110) and is popular for an evening *mate*. There are other branches at Belgrano 763 and Viamonte, at Lima. Mon–Sat 8am–4am, Sun 8pm–2am.

Bursátil Cafe Ituzaingo, at San Jeronimo ☎ 0351 711 3333. In Córdoba's small financial district, this café takes its name from the Spanish for "stock exchange". Food includes classics like *locro* (stew) and international dishes such as Caesar salad. Mains from AR$60. Mon–Fri 8am–7pm, Sat 9am–4/5pm.

★ **Mandarina** Obispo Trejo 171 ☎ 0351 426 4909. This chilled-out crowd-pleaser is more inventive than the norm, with Chinese, Japanese and southeast Asian dishes, as well as plenty of vegetarian options. Mains from AR$65. Daily 8am–1.30am.

Sol y Luna Av Gral Paz 278 ☎ 0351 425 1189, ⓦ solylunaonline.com.ar. Load your plate with a variety of hot and cold dishes at this lunchtime vegetarian buffet: a good feed costs less than AR$80 (AR$18.50/100g). There's another branch at Montevideo 66, Nueva Córdoba. Mon–Sat noon–3.30pm.

La Vieja Esquina Caseros, at Belgrano ☎ 0351 424 7940. This tiny local joint serves up excellent *empanadas* (around AR$9), *humitas* and *locro*; you can eat at one of the counters, take them away or even have them delivered to your room. Mon–Sat 11.30am–3pm & 7.30pm–midnight.

DRINKING AND NIGHTLIFE

Córdoba is no wallflower when it comes to partying, with Nueva Córdoba the late-night destination of choice. Hipsters gravitate to the revived warehouse district of El Abasto, just north of the centre, for its edgy bars and clubs. Further afield, in the Chateau Carreras neighbourhood, chic discos cater to a young crowd who love *cuarteto* music – a Córdoba speciality.

Carreras Av Cárcano, at del Piamonte, Chateau Carreras ☎ 0351 676 2342. One of the city's biggest and liveliest clubs, *Carreras* focuses on house and electro, though early on in the evening the sounds are a bit more varied. Fri & Sat 11.30pm–5am.

Dorian Gray Blvd Las Heras, at Roque Sáenz Peña ☎ 0351 6205 025. Bizarre decor and an alternative ambience draw an eclectic crowd who throw shapes well into the small hours to mostly electro music. Fri & Sat midnight–5am.

Johnny B Good Av Hipólito Yrigoyen 320, Nueva Córdoba ☎ 0351 424 3960, ⓦ jbgood.com. This busy, rather cheesy restaurant-bar serves up good US-style food, a wide range of *tragos* (alcoholic drinks; from AR$52) and a rock-dominated soundtrack (live music most weekends). There's another branch at Rafael Núñez 4791, Cerro de las Rosas. Mon–Wed 7.30pm–2am, Thurs 7.30pm–3am, Fri 7.30pm–4am, Sat 10am–5am, Sun 6.30pm–2am.

Milk Bar Laprida 139 ☎ 0351 664 3009 ⓦ lovemilk.com.ar. Put on some of your fancier rags, forget about Fernet and coke and order some fine cocktails (around AR$60) at the trendiest bar in town. The big chandeliers in the ceiling and hipster bartenders give it an old-school, although slightly pretentious, touch. Wed–Fri 9.30pm–5am, Sat & Sun 6.30pm–5am.

Zen Av Julio A Roca 730 ☎ 0351 15 513 9595, ⓦ zendisco .com. This renowned gay-friendly club has two throbbing dancefloors and hosts kooky live shows. Fri & Sat midnight–5am.

SHOPPING

Bookshops Librería Blackpool, Deán Funes 395 (☎ 0351 423 7172). Sells English-language novels and travel guides. March & April Mon–Fri 8.30am–7pm; rest of year Mon–Fri 9am–6.30pm, Sat 9am–1pm.

Markets On weekend evenings (5–9.30pm) there is an arts and crafts market at the Paseo de las Artes on the western edge of Nueva Córdoba in the bohemian Güemes neighbourhood, around Belgrano and Archaval Rodriguez streets.

Shopping centres Nuevocentro Shopping, Duarte Quirós 1400 (daily 10am–10pm; ☎ 0351 482 8193, ⓦ nuevocentro.com.ar).

DIRECTORY

Banks Change money at Citibank, Rivadavia 104, or BBVA, 9 de Julio 450. ATMs are everywhere, especially around the Plaza San Martín.

Hospital Hospital Sanatorio Allende, Av Hipólito Yrigoyen 384 (☎ 0351 426 9200, ⓦ sanatorioallende.com).

Laundry Laverap, Chacabuco 313, at Belgrano 76.

Police Colón 1200.

Post office Av General Paz 201.

ALTA GRACIA

The pleasant colonial town of **ALTA GRACIA**, 38km south of Córdoba at the entrance of the Calamuchita Valley, was once a genteel summer refuge for the *porteño* bourgeoisie. Today it continues to bask in the reflected glory of its former residents: Jesuit missionaries, Spanish composer Manuel de Falla and Che Guevara have all left their mark here.

WHAT TO SEE AND DO

Easily walkable on foot, the town centre is dominated by an impressive Jesuit *estancia*, one of the finest examples in Argentina. But it's also a great springboard for walking in the nearby countryside or, for the more adventurous, skydiving.

1

Plaza Manuel Solares and around

Alta Gracia came into its own after
1643 when it was chosen as the site of a
Jesuit *estancia*. When the Jesuits were
expelled in 1767, the *estancia* was left to
the elements, only briefly reinhabited in
1810 by Viceroy Liniers. The *estancia*

buildings have been well preserved and
overlook the town's main square, **Plaza
Manuel Solares**. The **Iglesia Parroquial
Nuestra Señora de la Merced**, dating
from 1762, stands alongside the Jesuits'
original living quarters, which have
been converted into the UNESCO

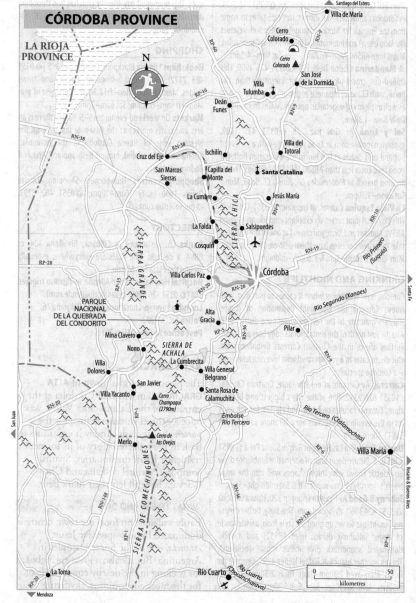

World Heritage-listed **Museo de la Estancia Jesuítica de Alta Gracia – Casa del Virrey Liniers** (summer Tues–Fri 9am–8pm, Sat & Sun 9.30am–8pm; winter Tues–Fri 9am–7pm, Sat & Sun 9.30am–6.30pm; AR$15; free guided English-language tours on request; ☎03547 421303, ⊚museoliniers .org.ar). Here, a dramatic Baroque doorway leads to a cloistered courtyard and a motley collection of furniture and religious paintings.

Ernesto "Che" Guevara house and museum

A twenty-minute walk uphill from the plaza brings you to the leafy residential neighbourhood of **Villa Carlos Pellegrini**, whose crumbling mansions once served as holiday homes and residences for moneyed socialites. The Guevara family moved within these circles after relocating from Rosario to Alta Gracia in the 1930s in the hope that the fresh mountain air would alleviate the asthma plaguing their 4-year-old son, **Ernesto "Che" Guevara**. The family's former home, Villa Beatriz, at Avellaneda 501, has been converted into the **Museo Casa de Ernesto "Che" Guevara** (Tues–Sun 9am–7pm; AR$75; ☎03547 428579), showcasing Che's personal effects as well as photographs charting his progression from carefree kid to revolutionary icon. Among the museum's highlights are video interviews with Che's childhood companions, a handwritten resignation letter to Fidel Castro, and photos from a visit Castro and Hugo Chávez made to the house in 2006.

ARRIVAL AND INFORMATION

By bus Regular buses from Córdoba (every 15min; 1hr) stop at the bus terminal on C P. Butori, at Av Presidente Perón, around eight blocks west of the Tajamar reservoir; minibuses tend to stop nearer the centre on Lucas V Córdoba street. Buses to Villa General Belgrano (every 1hr; 1hr) stop on Ruta 5, at Av L.G San Martín by the main entrance to town.

Tourist information The tourist office is in the clock tower alongside the Tajamar reservoir on Av Padre Viera, at C del Molino (Jan, Feb & July daily 8am–10pm; March–June & Aug–Dec Mon–Fri 7am–8pm, Sat & Sun 8am–8pm; ☎03547 428128, ⊚altagracia.gov.ar).

ACCOMMODATION AND EATING

Alta Gracia Hostel Paraguay 218 ☎03547 428810, ⊚altagraciahostel.com.ar. A cosy little hostel, five blocks away from the main square, with a basic dorm, a couple of private rooms, a kitchen and a patio area at the back. There are bikes for rent. Dorms __AR$120__, doubles __AR$390__

Hispania Urquiza, at Mateo Beres ☎03547 426 772. Popular with locals and tourists, this Spanish seafood restaurant fills up fast at night. The extensive menu includes seafood *paella* (ARS$85), king prawns in sherry sauce (ARS$80), gazpacho (ARS$40) and other Galician-styled dishes. Tues–Sat noon–3pm & 8pm–midnight; Sun lunch only.

VILLA GENERAL BELGRANO

The twee resort town of **VILLA GENERAL BELGRANO**, 50km south of Alta Gracia, founded by the surviving seamen of the *Graf Spee*, which sank off the coast of Uruguay in 1939, unabashedly exploits its Germanic heritage with all kinds of kitsch. The town's main street, **Avenida Julio Roca**, comes over like an alpine theme park, with folksy German beer houses and restaurants resembling Swiss chalets. You'll either love it or hate it.

WHAT TO SEE AND DO

The best (and some might say only) reason to visit Villa General Belgrano is to sink steins of locally brewed beer at the annual **Oktoberfest**. Held during the first two weeks of October in Plaza José Hernández, it is considered the continent's best celebration of this German tradition. The most popular day-trip from Villa General Belgrano is 30km west to the alpine-flavoured village of **La Cumbrecita**, where there are good opportunities for hiking, abseiling and cooling off in the Río Almbach.

ARRIVAL AND DEPARTURE

By bus The bus terminal is on Av Vélez Sarsfield, a 10min walk northwest of the main street, although all buses make drop-offs and pick-ups in the town centre.

Destinations Alta Gracia (8 daily; 1hr) and Córdoba (every 45min–1hr; 2hr). Pájaro Blanco (☎03546 461709; call for the latest timetable) runs a minibus service several times a day to and from La Cumbrecita (7 daily; 1hr); its bus stop is on Av Ojo de Agua, in front of *Hotel Edelweiss*.

1

INFORMATION

Tourist information Av Julio Roca 168 (daily 9am–9pm; ☎ 03546 461215, ⓦ vgb.gov.ar).
Mountain bike rental Cerro Negro Bikes, Av Champaqui 100 (☎ 03546 462785).

ACCOMMODATION

The hotels in town are generally overpriced, but *cabañas* (self-contained cabins) make a good alternative for groups of four or five – ask at the tourist office for suggestions.
Camping Rincón de Mirlos 9km west of the centre, off the RP-5 ☎ 0351 15 5164 254, ⓦ rincondemirlos.com.ar. The best of several campsites around town, *Rincón de Mirlos* has a bucolic riverside setting, clean dorms, isolated camping pitches among the trees, a restaurant-bar, and long stretches of sandy beach. Camping/person **AR$60**, dorms **AR$160**
Posada Nehuen San Martín 17 ☎ 03546 461412, ⓦ posadanehuen.com.ar. This central guesthouse has a selection of comfortable en-suite rooms with TVs, mini-fridges and phones, though the decor throughout is a bit old-fashioned. **AR$590**
★ **Hostel El Rincón** Alexander Fleming 347, 15min walk northwest of the bus station ☎ 03546 461323, ⓦ hostelelrincon.com.ar. This laidback, HI-affiliated hostel offers dorms, en-suite private rooms, and a place to pitch your tent, as well as kitchen access and a small pool. Camping/person **AR$90**, dorms **AR$120**, doubles **AR$370**

EATING AND DRINKING

Café Rissen Av Julio Roca 36 ☎ 03546 464100. Situated on the main strip, this kitsch café is probably the most popular in town. Excellent cakes (from AR$48) and sandwiches are on the menu: the Black Forest (*selva negra*) gateau, in particular, comes highly recommended. Daily 8am–around midnight.
El Ciervo Rojo Av Julio Roca 210 ☎ 03546 461345, ⓦ confiteriaelciervorojo.com. Dating back 50 years, this appealing restaurant serves up an array of German and Central European dishes (mains AR$85–110) including smoked pork racks, goulash, spätzle, sausages and sauerkraut. There's live German music on Saturday nights. Daily 8am–midnight/1am.
Viejo Munich Av San Martín 362 ☎ 03546 463122, ⓦ cervezaartesanal.com. The trout, goulash and venison

mains aren't too bad, but the beer – eight different varieties, all brewed on-site – is the real star of the show. Free brewery tours (end Dec–early Feb: daily noon, rest of the year Mon, Tues, Fri, Sat & Sun noon). Mon, Tues & Thurs 11am–3pm & 7–11.30pm, Fri–Sun 11am–midnight.

CAPILLA DEL MONTE

CAPILLA DEL MONTE attracts more alternative-lifestyle types in summer than you can shake an incense stick at. Situated 102km north of Córdoba city, the idyllic mountain town lies at the base of **Cerro Uritorco**, which, at 1979m, is the Sierra Chica's highest peak and is claimed by many locals to possess an inexplicable magnetic pull.

Set at the confluence of two (often dry) rivers on the northern edge of the Punilla Valley, Capilla del Monte's former glory can be glimpsed in its slowly decaying nineteenth-century mansions.

WHAT TO SEE AND DO

Capilla del Monte makes a good base for outdoor adventure sports, including **horseriding** in the surrounding countryside, **rock climbing** the strange sandstone formations around the hamlet of **Ongamira**, **hiking** to the summit of Cerro Uritorco (4hr or so to the top – register at the base of the mountain and start your return by 3.30pm; AR$130; ⓦ cerrouritorcoam.com .ar), strolling through the multicoloured rock formations of **Los Terrones** (daily 9am–dusk; AR$68; ⓦ losterrones.com) or **paragliding** in the Sierras.

ARRIVAL AND INFORMATION

By bus The bus station is near the centre at Corrientes & Rivadavia. There are regular buses to and from Córdoba (hourly; 2–3hr).
Tourist information Pick up a map and information at the tourist office in the old railway station on Av

---

THE TRUTH IS OUT THERE

Capilla del Monte hosts an international **UFO convention** every November, organized by local "research" group Centro de Informes OVNI, Juan Cabus 397 (☎ 03548 482485, ⓦ ciouritorco.org – OVNI is Spanish for UFO). **Mystical tourism** is gaining in popularity, with local tour operators jumping on the extra-terrestrial bandwagon by offering guided tours to sites of supposed UFO landings as well as night excursions to observe celestial happenings on remote mountaintops. You'll be in good hands with Angeluz (☎ 03548 15 634 532), Diagonal Buenos Aires 161, which does a (fairly) convincing range of otherworldly tours.

Pueyrredón s/n (daily 8am–8pm; ☎03548 481913, Ⓦ capilladelmonte.gov.ar). It can also provide information on the town's New Age healers.

ACCOMMODATION AND EATING

Calabalumba Calabalumba s/n ☎03548 489601. The closest campsite to town is the riverside *Calabalumba*, which has tent pitches and cabins sleeping up to six. Camping/person AR$45, cabins AR$512

★**El Duende Azul** Chubut 75, at Aristóbulo del Valle ☎03548 15 569667, Ⓦ cordobaserrana.com.ar/

elduendeazul.htm. A guesthouse in tune with the town's hippy vibe where you can frolic in the big garden or hang out in the common area overrun by pixie and elf figurines. The simple but pretty rooms are en suite and the lovely owners arrange various detox programmes. AR$300

Maracaibo Buenos Aires 182 ☎03548 482741. This unpretentious restaurant is a good all-rounder, serving fish, pasta and chicken mains, as well as lots of vegetarian options; the vegetable and corn lasagne is filling and tasty. Mains from around AR$40–150. Mon–Wed & Fri–Sun 11am–4pm & 7.45–11.45pm.

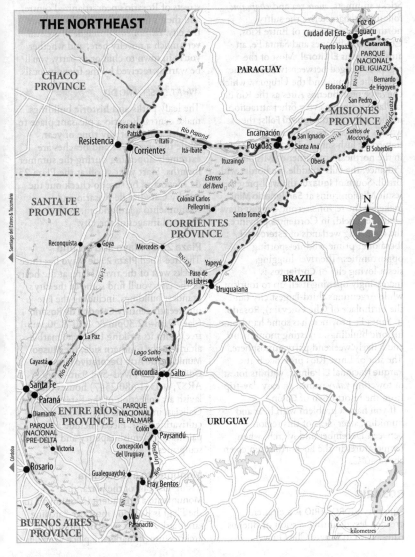

1

Los Tres Gómez 25 de Mayo 452 ☎03548 482647, ⓦhostellos3gomez.com.ar. Hostelling International-affiliated joint with a lurid colour scheme in the communal areas – the dorms and private rooms, by contrast, are plain and a little bare. There's a kitchen, garden and a restaurant-bar. Dorms AR$120, doubles AR$380

The Northeast

Sticky summers, *mate* tea and *chamamé* folk music characterize the sultry northeastern provinces of Entre Ríos, Corrientes, Misiones and Santa Fe, an area known as **El Litoral**. Most of the region is wedged between two awesome rivers, the Paraná and the Uruguay, which converge near Buenos Aires as the Río de la Plata. Eclipsing every other attraction in the region are the **Iguazú Falls**, the world's most spectacular waterfalls, framed by lush subtropical forest. Located in the northeastern corner of Misiones Province, the falls straddle the border with Brazil. South of **Iguazú**, the well-preserved Jesuit Mission ruins at **San Ignacio Miní** make for the region's second-biggest draw.

Further afield, in Corrientes province, the sprawling wetlands of **Esteros del Iberá** offer prime wildlife-spotting opportunities. The river-hugging, siesta-loving city of **Corrientes** is increasingly opening itself up to tourism, while Argentina's third-largest city (and the birthplace of Che Guevara), **Rosario**, in Santa Fe province, has some handsome historic buildings, arresting monuments and a lively weekend party atmosphere. The star of Entre Ríos province is the **Parque Nacional El Palmar**, with its forest of towering *yatay* palms, an easy day-trip from the resort town of **Colón**.

If you have a problem with heat and humidity, steer clear of this region between December and March, when temperatures in the far north often creep above 40°C.

ROSARIO

Super-stylish **ROSARIO** is a cleaner, greener, less daunting version of Buenos Aires. The city where Che Guevara

learned to crawl and Lionel Messi learned to kick a ball is home to a handsome, academic and culturally inclined population of just over one million.

Sprawled on the banks of the **Río Paraná**, Rosario's assets are its riverside beaches, parks, restaurants, bars and museums. For an enjoyable day-trip, the sandy beaches of the subtropical **Alto Delta islands** are just a short boat or kayak ride away. Stylish shops line the streets of Rosario's pedestrianized centre, and there's free public wi-fi throughout the city. *Extranjeros* (foreigners) are still very much a novelty here, and whether you're in town to chill or to party, you'll be warmly received by the friendly locals.

WHAT TO SEE AND DO

The leafy parks and historic buildings make central Rosario a pleasant place to wander around at any time of year, while the riverfront and beaches are extremely appealing during the summer months. Start your stroll at the Plaza 25 de Mayo and be sure to check out the nearby Catedral de Rosario and Monumento a la Bandera, both postcard images of the city.

Plaza 25 de Mayo and around

The tree-lined **Plaza 25 de Mayo** lies three blocks west of the river. Here, at the heart of the city, you'll find some of the city's grandest buildings, including the late nineteenth-century **Catedral de Rosario** (daily 9am–12.30pm & 4.30–8.30pm; free), with its striking Italianate marble altar. On the southern side, the **Museo Municipal de Arte Decorativo Firma y Odilio Estévez** (Wed–Sun 9am–5pm; AR$7; ☎0341 480 2547) houses the lavish art collection of the Estévez family, Galician immigrants who struck it big cultivating *mate*. Pieces include a Goya painting, a Flemish tapestry and Greek sculptures.

Monumento a la Bandera

Rising just east of the plaza, the **Monumento a la Bandera** (Monument to the Flag) is Rosario's most eye-catching landmark. A stark piece of nationalistic architecture, it marks the place where, in

1812, General Belgrano first raised the Argentine flag. Take the **lift** up its 70m-high tower for panoramic city views (Mon 2–6pm, Tues–Sun 9am–7pm; AR$5; ☎0341 480 2238).

Costanera

Rosario's **Costanera** (riverfront) extends for around 20km from north to south, providing plenty of green space to sunbathe or sip *mate*, as well as waterfront restaurants, bars and museums. The central **Parque Nacional de la Bandera** – a narrow strip of parkland – is the main setting for regular markets and festivals. As you stroll north, the park merges with **Parque de España** and the large brick **Centro Cultural Parque de España** (Tues–Sun 3–8pm; free; ☎0341 426 0941, ⊛ccpe.org.ar), which hosts changing modern art exhibitions. Half a kilometre north is the **Museo de Arte Contemporáneo de Rosario** (daily 2–8pm, closed Wed; AR$10; ☎0341 480 4981, ⊛www.macromuseo.org.ar), a kitsch temple to modern Argentine art housed inside a converted grain silo, its facade painted in pastel shades. The building – as well as the views from the top floor – outshines the displays, while the gallery's riverfront café-bar, *Davis*, is a great place to watch boats floating by over a drink or two.

Most of the summer beach action happens 8km north of the centre at the **Balneario La Florida** (Dec–April; daily 9am–8pm; AR$25; ☎0341453 3491; bus #153). Just south of here is the Rambla Catalunya (with a free beach) and Avenida Carrasco, a strip of upmarket restaurants, bars and clubs that is the hub of Rosario's vibrant summer nightlife.

Parque de la Independencia

The **Parque de la Independencia**, 3km southwest of Plaza 25 de Mayo, is one of Argentina's largest urban green spaces. Within its extensive grounds are a football stadium, a racetrack, a theme park, a rose garden and two museums. The **Museo Municipal de Bellas Artes Juan B. Castagnino** (Mon & Wed–Sun 2–8pm; AR$10; ☎0341 480 2542, ⊛www .museocastagnino.org.ar), Avenida

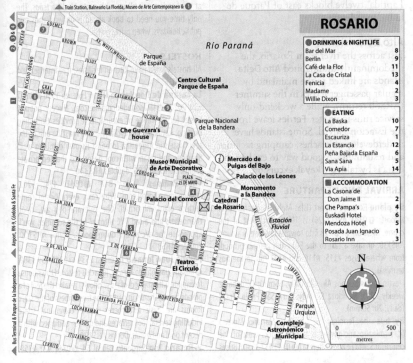

ROSARIO

DRINKING & NIGHTLIFE

Bar del Mar	8
Berlin	9
Café de la Flor	11
La Casa de Cristal	13
Fenicia	4
Madame	2
Willie Dixon	3

EATING

La Baska	10
Comedor	7
Escauriza	1
La Estancia	12
Peña Bajada España	6
Sana Sana	5
Via Apia	14

ACCOMMODATION

La Casona de Don Jaime II	2
Che Pampa's	4
Euskadi Hotel	6
Mendoza Hotel	5
Posada Juan Ignacio	1
Rosario Inn	3

1

Pellegrini 2202, has an important collection of European and Argentine fine art. West of the lake, the **Museo Histórico Provincial Julio Marc** (Tues–Fri 9am–6pm, Sat & Sun 3–8pm; AR$5; ☎0341 472 1457, ⟨w⟩museomarc.gob.ar) is strong on religious artefacts and indigenous ceramics from across Latin America.

Che Guevara's house

Though there's little of the fanfare about it that you might expect given his international icon status, **Ernesto "Che" Guevara** was born in Rosario in 1928. He lived in an apartment on the corner of Entre Ríos and Urquiza until the age of 2, now an office not open to the public, although there's nothing to stop you gawking from the street. One block north and one block east, at the corner of Tucumán and Mitre, a **mural** of Che's intense and haggard-looking face dominates a small neighbourhood square, while there's a bronze **statue** of him on a rather forlorn plaza on 27 de Febrero, at Laprida, twelve blocks east of Parque de la Independencia.

Alto Delta islands

Just across the river from Rosario, the predominantly uninhabited **Alto Delta islands** are linked to the mainland by regular passenger ferries in the summer (AR$60 return), while a weekend-only service runs in winter. **Ferries** leave from the Estación Fluvial. Some islands have underdeveloped beaches, camping facilities and restaurants. A good way to explore the delta is by taking a **kayak excursion**.

ARRIVAL AND DEPARTURE

By plane Rosario's airport (Islas Malvinas International Airport; ☎0341 451 1226) is 10km northwest of the centre. There are no buses into town; a taxi ride is around AR$130, or take a taxi to the Fisherton neighbourhood, from where buses #115, #116 and #133 run to the bus terminal.
Destinations Buenos Aires (5 daily; 55min); Córdoba (2 weekly; 1hr); Mendoza (2 daily; 3hr); São Paulo, Brazil (daily; 2hr 50min).
By bus The Terminal de Omnibus Mariano Moreno (⟨w⟩terminalrosario.gov.ar) is twenty blocks west of the centre, at Santa Fe and Cafferata (☎0341 437 3030). Buses

#141 and #146 go to the centre. Fares must be paid in exact change (AR$5) or using pre-paid passes.
Destinations Buenos Aires (every 30min; 4hr); Córdoba (every 30min; 6hr 30min); Corrientes (7 daily; 10–12hr); Montevideo, Uruguay (1 daily; 9hr); Puerto Iguazú (3 daily; 19hr); Salta (6 daily; 16hr).
By ferry The Estación Fluvial (☎0341 448 3737), in Parque Nacional de la Bandera, has ferries to the Delta islands (Dec–March daily; year-round Sat & Sun).
By train The train station (☎0800 333 3822) is 3km northwest of the centre.
Destinations Buenos Aires (2 weekly; 7hr).

INFORMATION AND TOURS

Tourist information The riverside tourist office is on the corner of Av Belgrano and C Buenos Aires (Mon–Fri 8am–7pm, Sat 9am–7pm, Sun 9am–6pm); ☎0341 480 2230, ⟨w⟩rosario.tur.ar). An information kiosk in the bus terminal has maps and hotel listings.
Bike Rosario ☎0341 15 571 3812, ⟨w⟩bikerosario.com.ar. Cycling tours of the city run by multilingual guides ($120); they also do kayak tours of the Alto Delta islands (AR$185/3hr).

ACCOMMODATION

Rosario has experienced a hostel boom in recent years and at weekends many fill up with party-hard *porteños*. The only time you need to book ahead is on weekends and public holidays, when prices go up.

HOSTELS

All hostels listed have kitchen facilities, free internet and breakfast.
La Casona de Don Jaime II San Lorenzo 1530 ☎0341 530 2020, ⟨w⟩lacasonadedonjaime.com. Hugely popular hostel for the range of excursions it provides (including boating, kayaking and cycling) – this must be one of the few hostels in Argentina to boast its own climbing wall. Spacious and clean with cool decor and themed private rooms. Dorms AR$85, doubles AR$330
Che Pampas Rioja 812 ☎0341 424 5202, ⟨w⟩chepampashostel.com. Why can't every hostel come with a giant mirrorball, Che Guevara pop art, neon chandeliers and a red PVC throne? In the summer, you'll appreciate the a/c in the dorm rooms. Dorms AR$100, doubles AR$300
Posada Juan Ignacio Tucuman 2534 ☎0341 439 1380, ⟨w⟩posadajuanignacio.com.ar. Ignacio's restored townhouse (complete with stained-glass windows) retains the feel of a private home, thanks in part to the friendliness of the staff. Rooms are basic but there's ample communal space including several roof terraces and garden equipped with a decent pool and *asado*. Dorms AR$120
★**Rosario Inn** Sargento Cabral 54 ☎0341 421 0358,

ⓦ www.rosarioinn.com. With a fantastic location near the river, this light-drenched hostel has two patios to hang out in and bikes for rent. Tango and theatre classes offered. Dorms <u>ARS118</u>

HOTELS

Euskadi Hotel 3 de Febrero 1244 ☎0341 421 4549, ⓦ hoteleseuskadi.com.ar. This modern hotel is light and airy; the best of the budget options. Rooms have all the expected facilities (private bathroom, cable TV, a/c and wi-fi). Breakfast included. <u>ARS320</u>

Mendoza Hotel Mendoza 1246 ☎0341 424 6544, ⓦ hotelmendozarosario.com. Functional and comfortable, all rooms in this humble hotel feature private bathrooms, cable TV, a/c and wireless internet. Breakfast included. <u>ARS290</u>

ALTO DELTA ISLANDS

El Pimpollal ☎0341 549 4777, ⓦ elpimpollal.com.ar. Offers transport to and tours of the islands, including birdwatching, horseriding and boat trips. Overnight stay in a dorm can be included at <u>ARS290</u>

EATING

The bulk of Rosario's restaurants are clustered along Avenida Pellegrini, although in summer you'll want to take advantage of the waterfront aspect and pull up an outdoor chair at one of the many popular restaurants along the Costanera, many of which are open until the small hours (during winter most close by around 10pm, later at weekends).

★**La Baska** Tucumán 1118 ☎0341 426 7573. The *empanadas* here are piping hot and come with a huge range of heavenly fillings including prawns, tuna, mushrooms and Roquefort cheese. Great for a cheap bite. Daily 11am–2pm & 6–11pm.

Comedor Balcarce 1 ☎0341 425 6765. Popular with locals, this is the place for generous portions of traditional food (*empanadas, milanesa, parilla*) at very affordable prices. Mon–Sat noon–3pm & 8.15pm–midnight.

Escauriza Paseo Ribereño, at Escauriza ☎0341 454 1777. Highly regarded *parrilla* specializing in fish, on the riverfront near the access to the Victoria road bridge. *Surubi* and *dorado* (river fish) are on the menu as well as more conventional meat, and the prices are very reasonable. Daily lunch & dinner.

La Estancia Av Pellegrini 1510 ☎0341 440 7373. Rosario's most popular restaurant is a (pricier) old-fashioned place with a vast menu. The emphasis is on – you guessed it – beef, and it's fun to watch the impeccably suited waiters rush around with exotic cuts of sizzling cow. Daily 8.30am–1am.

★**Peña Bajada España** Av Italia, at España ☎0341 449 6801. Restaurant with a tranquil wooden terrace overlooking the river and serving cheap barbecued fish feasts. Access is by elevator. Daily lunch & dinner.

Sana Sana Alvear Bis 14 ☎0341 438 2036. Great option for vegetarians/vegans or those wanting a break from meat-heavy Argentine cuisine. Veggie lasagne, risotto and hamburgers alongside an interesting selection of salads and wraps in brightly coloured surroundings. Mon–Sat 9am–midnight.

Vía Apia Av Pellegrini 961 ☎0341 481 3174. It's easy to miss this small Italian restaurant among the vast neon-lit food palaces of Av Pellegrini, but the crisp stone-baked pizzas are arguably the best in the city. Mon–Sat 6–11pm.

DRINKING AND NIGHTLIFE

Rosario's party spirit makes it a great place to go out. In summer, the clubs and bars in the riverfront Estación Fluvial attract a modish crowd. Summer fun also transfers to Rambla Catalunya, a waterfront avenue in the city's north. Nightlife in Rosario doesn't really get going until well after midnight, with some clubs not opening until after 2am.

Bar del Mar Balcarce, at Tucumán. A restaurant-bar with an aquatic theme and colourful mosaics; good for people-watching before painting the town red. Wed–Sun 8.30pm–6am.

Berlin Pje Zabala 1128, between the 300 block of Mitre & Sarmiento ⓦ elberlin.com.ar. Regular events and a steady flow of German beer keep locals coming back to this trendy bar. Thurs–Sun 11pm until late.

Café de la Flor Mendoza 862 ⓦ cafedelaflor.com.ar. Live music, DJs and pizza fuel the boisterous alternative crowd at this cavernous joint. Thurs–Sun; shows start around 8pm.

La Casa de Cristal Av Pellegrini 1159 ☎0341 15 645 8601, ⓦ lacasadecristal.com.ar. This gay-friendly nightclub is super-slick and stylish; the place to go for a break from the backpacker scene. Fri & Sat 10.30pm–5.30am.

Fenicia Av Francia 168 ☎0341 423 2376. The only pub in Rosario with a brewery on site, their Californian draught beer is arguably the best in the city, if not Argentina. With excellent food to soak up all that extra liquid, this place gets very busy, especially at weekends. Tues–Thurs 6pm–2am, Fri & Sat 6pm–3am, Sun 6pm–2am.

Madame Brown 3126. This is *the* club for party animals – a mainstream disco with three dancefloors blaring *cumbia*, reggaeton, electronica and rock. Over-21s only. Fri & Sat 2am until late.

Willie Dixon Suipacha, at Guemes ⓦ williedixonblues club.com. Live music venue hosting quality Argentine acts; *the* place to watch (and partake in) *salsa* and *cumbia*. See website for schedule.

SHOPPING

Bookshop Ameghino, Corrientes 868 (☎0341 447 1147), stocks English-language books.

1

Clothes The pedestrianized Av Córdoba is a busy shopping street flanked with handsome historic buildings, many of which now house chic boutiques. Falabella, at Cordoba & Sarmiento, is a vast department store with good bargains to be found during end-of-season sales.

Markets The Mercado de Pulgas del Bajo flea market is on every weekend afternoon in the Parque Nacional de la Bandera, near Av Belgrano 500. Handmade crafts, used books and antiques are on sale.

DIRECTORY

Banks and exchange Banco de la Nación Argentina, Córdoba 1026; many other options along Santa Fe 1064, San Martín 902 and Córdoba 1770/72. Rosario Transatlantica casa de cambio generally offers decent exchange rates and has branches at Rioja 1198 and Córdoba 1463.

Laundry 5àsec, at Maipú and Santa Fe.

Post office Buenos Aires, at Córdoba on Plaza 25 de Mayo.

PARQUE NACIONAL EL PALMAR

Only after ranching, farming and forestry had pushed the graceful *yatay* palm to the brink of extinction did it find salvation in the **PARQUE NACIONAL EL PALMAR**. The 85-square-kilometre park, on the banks of the Río Uruguay, lies 50km north of Colón at Km199 on the RN14, and is a stark, but beautiful, reminder of how large chunks of Entre Ríos province, Uruguay and southern Brazil once looked. Many of the **palms**, which can grow up to 18m tall, are over three hundred years old. Trails wind through the park, past palm savannah, streams and riverside beaches. Sunset is the perfect time to pull out the camera, when the palms look stunning silhouetted against a technicolour sky. El Palmar's creation in 1966 also did wonders for the habitat of local subtropical **wildlife**, including capybaras, viscachas, monitor

lizards, raccoons and the venomous *yarará* pit viper. Parakeets, egrets, *ñandúes* (large, flightless birds similar to ostriches) and storks are some of the bird species that can be spotted here.

ARRIVAL AND INFORMATION

By bus To get to the park, catch any Concordia-bound bus from Colón (9 daily; 30min) along the RN14 to the entrance (where you pay AR$12 entry). From here it's a 10km walk, drive or hitchhike to the visitor centre and adjacent Los Loros campground.

ACCOMMODATION

Amarello Hotel C Urquiza 865, Colón ☎ 03447 424 063, ⓦ colonentrerios.com.ar/amarello. Plain en-suite rooms in a range of sizes; breakfast included. **AR$120**

Los Loros campground ☎ 03447 423 378. This campsite in the park has showers and a basic store. Camping **AR$8** plus/person **AR$20**

CORRIENTES

Subtropical **CORRIENTES** is one of the northeast's oldest cities (it was founded in 1588) but doesn't offer much in the way of conventional attractions. That said, its compact historic centre, elegantly crumbling buildings and shady riverside area make it an ideal place for a leg stretch between long bus rides. Party people will be at home here during the heat of summer – Corrientes has been dubbed Argentina's "Capital of Carnaval", and each January and February the city explodes in a riot of colourful costumes and thumping drums.

WHAT TO SEE AND DO

Corrientes' historic core fans out in grid fashion from the shady main square, **Plaza 25 de Mayo**. The square is framed

---

CROSSING FROM COLÓN INTO URUGUAY

Colón, on the Río Uruguay 320km north of Buenos Aires, makes an inviting base for visiting the Parque Nacional El Palmar (see above), 50km to the north. Colón is also a prime gateway to Uruguay, and is linked to the city of Paysandú, 16km southeast, by the Puente Internacional General Artigas. It is 8km from Colón to the **Uruguayan border** (immigration office open 24hr) and a further 8km to Paysandú: approximately four buses daily make the journey. Colón's bus terminal is on the corner of Paysandú and 9 de Julio. There are frequent services to Concordia (9 daily; 2hr 15min), passing Parque Nacional El Palmar, and plenty of connections to Buenos Aires (14 daily; 5hr 30min). Colón's helpful tourist office is in the port area on the corner of Avenida Costanera and Gouchón (Mon–Fri 6am–8pm, Sat & Sun 8am–8pm; ☎ 03447 421 233, ⓦ colon.gov.ar).

FEELING HOT, HOT, HOT!

Despite the oppressive heat that strikes in summer, the city manages to muster up heroic levels of energy for the annual, Brazilian-style **Carnaval Correntino** (Ⓦcarnavalescorrentinos.com), which takes place throughout January and February in the open-air Corsódromo at Avenida Centenario 2800. Raucous street parties, which frequently include bucketloads of iced water being thrown over the sweaty hordes, take place each weekend throughout Carnaval season.

If you're in town over the second weekend in December, check out the **Festival del Chamamé** (Ⓦcorrienteschamame.com), a celebration of regional folk dancing and music.

by some of the city's most important nineteenth-century buildings, including the pink Italianate **Casa de Gobierno** and the plain **Iglesia de Nuestra Señora de la Merced** (daily 7am–noon & 4–8pm; free). On the plaza's northeast corner, the **Museo de Artesanías Tradicionales Folclóricas de la Provincia** (Mon–Fri 7am–noon & 4–7pm; free) showcases regional basketwork, leather and ceramics within a whitewashed colonial residence.

One block south of the main square is Corrientes' 2.5km riverside avenue, the **Avenida Costanera General San Martín**, flanked by pretty jacaranda and native *lapacho* trees. It is the favoured haunt of fishermen, *mate-* and *tereré*-sippers, joggers, mosquitoes, daydreamers and courting couples. Locals flock to its promenades on summer evenings after emerging refreshed from siestas. There are a few small riverside **beaches** here, but swimming is not recommended, as the river's currents are notoriously strong.

ARRIVAL AND INFORMATION

By plane Corrientes' airport (☎03783 458 340) is 10km northeast of the city centre. Free shuttle services can take you from the airport to the centre. Aerolíneas Argentinas (☎03783 458 339) flies to Buenos Aires (2 daily; 1hr 30min).
By bus The bus terminal (☎03783 449 435) is 4km southeast of the city centre. Local buses run frequently between the terminal and the centre; a taxi will set you back around AR$15.
Destinations Buenos Aires (6 daily; 12hr); Posadas (9 daily; 5hr; change here for more regular services to Puerto Iguazú); Puerto Iguazú (1 daily; 10hr); Rosario (3 daily; 10hr).
Tourist information The provincial tourist office is at 25 de Mayo 1330 (Mon–Fri 7am–1pm & 3–9pm; ☎03783 427 200, Ⓦturismocorrientes.com.ar); there is a municipal tourist office where the Costanera meets Pellegrini (daily 7am–9pm; ☎03783 474 702).

ESTEROS DEL IBERÁ

A vast area of marshy swampland, the Esteros del Iberá comprises a series of lagoons, rivers, marshes and floating islands, much of which is protected in the **RESERVA NATURAL DEL IBERÁ**. The islands are created by a build-up of soil on top of a mat of intertwined water lilies and other plants; these in turn choke the flow of water, creating what is in effect a vast, slow-flowing river, draining eventually into the Río Paraná. The wetlands make up nearly fifteen percent of Corrientes province – spreading annually in the rainy season and gradually contracting until the rains come again. With the protection of the natural reserve, the area's **wildlife** is thriving, and there's an extraordinary variety: three hundred species of birds, including storks, cormorants, egrets, ducks and around the edges of the lake the *chajá* (horned screamer), a large grey bird with a startling patch of red around the eyes; snakes (including the yellow anaconda) and caimans; and forty species of mammals, including capybara, marsh and pampas deer, otters and howler monkeys. The capybara, the world's largest rodent, makes an unlikely swimmer, but spends most of its time in the water – listen out for the splash as it enters. Take a trip out onto the water, and you can enjoy remarkably close encounters with many of them.

WHAT TO SEE AND DO

Access to the reserve is from the tranquil village of **Colonia Carlos Pellegrini**, on the banks of the Laguna del Iberá. At the approach to the village, immediately before the rickety wooden bridge that is the only way in, former poachers staff the Centro de Interpretación, the reserve's visitor centre, which has useful information as well as a fascinating photo display. A nearby forest trail is a good place to spot (and hear) howler monkeys. The **Laguna del Iberá** itself is covered in water lilies, especially the yellow-and-purple *aguapé*, and its floating islands teem with a rich microcosm of bird and aquatic life.

ARRIVAL AND DEPARTURE

Access to the reserve is from Colonia Carlos Pellegrini. The village has very little to it; a grid of sandy streets around the Plaza San Martín, with very few facilities – bring enough cash to cover your entire stay.

By bus Colonia Carlos Pellegrini is 120km from the village of Mercedes (3hr approx; departures Mon–Sat at noon; AR$50 one-way). Ten buses run daily from Corrientes to Mercedes (3hr). Access to Colonia Carlos is also possible from Posadas, to the northwest, but this is still slower, and frequently impassable in the wet (3 buses weekly with Nordestur, 5–6hr; AR$140 one-way; ☎03722 445 588).

INFORMATION AND TOURS

Tourist information Mercedes has a helpful tourist office (daily 8am–noon & 4–8pm; ☎03773 420 100) and you can also arrange private 4WD transfers from here, through your accommodation in Colonia Carlos. For more information on the reserve, visit ⓦ esterosdelibera.com.

Tours Guided tours are highly recommended – and obligatory for visiting the lagoon and wetlands. Best organized through your accommodation, they are often included in the price. Trips on offer include by boat (you'll be poled through the marshier sections, where a motor is useless), on foot or on horseback. There are also moonlit night-time boat tours (Sat nights only) and walks to see nocturnal species.

ACCOMMODATION

Accommodation is provided by a handful of gorgeous posadas; they are more expensive than hostels but provide food (often as full-board) and organize tours.

Posada El Yacare Curupi y Yaguarete ☎03773 499 415, ⓔ ibertatours@hotmail.com. Posada built using natural materials. Rooms are spacious with all the expected amenities and there's a luscious garden at the front. Doubles AR$600

Posada Ypa Sapukai Yacare at Mburucuya ☎03773 1551 4212, ⓦ ypasapukai.com. This charming lakeside place has a small pool, lookout tower, impeccable rooms and beautiful garden. Excursions can be organized for AR$150 upwards. Cost includes full board. AR$750

SAN IGNACIO

The riverside town of **SAN IGNACIO** is home to one of the major sights of northern Argentina – the dramatic remains of the Jesuit missions at **San Ignacio Miní**. There's little clue of that in the centre, though, where this is just another hot, sleepy town. If you time the buses right you can visit the missions and move on the same day, but there are a couple of other attractions worth visiting should you be staying longer.

WHAT TO SEE AND DO

The main street south will lead you past the **Casa de Horacio Quiroga** (daily 8am–6pm; AR$10; ☎0376 447 0130), a museum to the Uruguayan-born Argentine writer of Gothic short stories, who made his home here in the early twentieth century. The same road continues to **Puerto Nuevo** on the Río Parana, a couple of kilometres away, where a sandy beach offers wonderful views across the river to Paraguay.

San Ignacio Miní

SAN IGNACIO MINÍ (daily 8am–6pm; AR$90; ticket valid for 15 days) was one of many Jesuit missions set up throughout Spanish America to convert the native population to Christianity. Originally established further north in what is now Brazil, the missionaries gradually moved south to avoid attack from Portuguese *bandeirantes* (piratical slave traders), eventually settling here in 1696. The mission became a thriving small town, inhabited by the local Guaraní, but, following the suppression of the Jesuits, was abandoned in the early nineteenth century. Rediscovered around a hundred years ago, the ruins are now among the best preserved of their kind in Latin America, a UNESCO World Heritage Site with some spectacular Baroque architecture.

At the entrance, at the northeastern end of the village, an excellent **Centro de Interpretación Regional** looks at the life of the mission and its Guaraní inhabitants. Rows of simple *viviendas* (stone-built, single-storey living quarters that once housed Guaraní families) lead down to a grassy Plaza de Armas, overlooked by the **church** that dominates the site. The roof and most of the interior have long since crumbled away, but much of the magnificent facade, designed by the Italian architect Brazanelli, still stands, and many fine details can be made out. Twin columns rise either side of the doorway, and the walls are decorated with exuberant bas-relief sculpture executed by Guaraní craftsmen.

ARRIVAL AND INFORMATION

By bus The bus station is located in town on RN12.
Destinations Posadas (hourly; 1hr); Puerto Iguazú (hourly; 4–5hr).
Tourist information There's a small Centro de Informes on Av Sarmiento, at RN12, at the entrance to town. Ask here, or at the ruins' entrance, about the musical and visual shows, held daily at 7pm at San Ignacio Miní.

ACCOMMODATION AND EATING

There's not a great deal of quality when it comes to food, but for budget eats, try one of the pizzerias and snack bars near the ruins. There is a decent supermarket on San Martín, between Av Sarmiento and Belgrano.
La Carpa Azul Rivadavia 1295, ☎0376 4470 0096, ⊚ lacarpaazul.com. Conveniently located just across from the ruins, it may be touristy but the traditional Argentine dishes are good quality and the prices reasonable. Daily for breakfast, lunch and dinner.
Residencial San Ignacio San Martín 823, at Sarmiento ☎03752 470 047. The largest hotel in town is located right in the centre. Comfortable and modern rooms with TV and a/c. Internet on site. Great value and within walking distance of the ruins. **AR$210**
Residencial Yvy Pyta San Martin 1363 ☎03764 470 751, ⊛ residencial-yvypyta.com.ar. Rooms are simple but brightly decorated and there's a lovely outdoor seating area. Conveniently located close to the ruins and there's an on-site tour desk. Doubles **AR$200**
San Ignacio Adventure Hostel Independencia 469, ☎03752 470 955. Don't be put off by the name; the general air of this HI hostel is one of tranquillity. Set in an expansive garden dotted with hammocks, facilities include a decent-sized swimming pool and barbecue. The high-ceilinged rooms are light and airy and it's a short

walk to the ruins. Breakfast included. Dorms **AR$90**, doubles **AR$210**

PUERTO IGUAZÚ

PUERTO IGUAZÚ is an inevitable stop if you're visiting **Iguazú Falls** (see p.86) on a budget – it's a perfectly pleasant town with all the facilities you need, if a little dull. On the western edge of town, the **Hito Tres Fronteras** is an obelisk overlooking the rivers Iguazú and Parana at the point where they meet and form the three-way border between Argentina, Brazil and Paraguay.

ARRIVAL AND DEPARTURE

By plane The airport is 25km southeast of Puerto Iguazú (☎03757 421 996). Buses meet flights and run to the bus terminal (AR$15; ☎03757 423 006).
Destinations Aerolineas Argentinas has several daily flights to Buenos Aires (1hr 45min). For international destinations, TAM (⊛ tam.com.br) flies from the larger airport at Foz do Iguacu on the Brazilian side of the border. Taxi drivers will take you from your hotel to the airport at Foz, allowing time for completing visa formalities, for around AR$200.
By bus Rio Uruguay buses for the National Park depart from the obelisk at Hito Tres Fronteras every 20min (7am–7.15pm; 30min; AR$25 each way); you can also pick them up at intervals all the way along the main street, Av Victoria Aguirre. All other services use the bus terminal on Av Córdoba, at Av Misiones. For destinations in Brazil buses departing from Argentina are cheaper and more comfortable than those departing from across the border in Brazil, although it is often necessary to book well in advance. Crucero del Norte (⊛ www.crucerodelnorte .com.ar) has regular departures to destinations across Argentina as well as to São Paulo and Rio de Janeiro in Brazil, and Asunción in Paraguay.

INFORMATION AND TOURS

National Park office Av Victoria Aguirre 66 (Tues–Sun: winter 8am–5pm; summer 8am–6pm; ☎03757 420 722).
Tourist information Av Victoria Aguirre 311 (Mon–Fri 7am–9pm, Sat & Sun 8am–noon & 4–8pm; ☎03757 420

CROSSING INTO BRAZIL

To make your trip to Iguazú Falls complete you should really visit the **Brazilian side** (see p.353), where the view is more panoramic, and the photography opportunities are excellent. There are direct **buses** from Puerto Iguazú to the falls on the Brazilian side; services are run by Crucero del Norte or Rio Uruguay (AR$80). Get some Brazilian cash before you go, for bus fares and the like, and bear in mind that, from October to March, Brazil is one hour ahead of Argentina.

1

800). ⊕ iguazuturismo.gov.ar is a useful website and there are also a number of private information booths and travel agents at the bus terminal.

Tour operator Iguazú Jungle (☎ 03757 421 696, ⊕ iguazujungle.com) offer boat tours, from AR$120 for a gentle nature ride to AR$400 for white-water fun.

ACCOMMODATION

There are a number of big resort hotels near the falls, but budget travellers stay in Puerto Iguazú, where there are plenty of good hostels and inexpensive guesthouses. In high season, July and around Easter, reservations are recommended.

Lilian Fray Luis Beltrán 183 ☎ 03757 420 968, ⊕ hotellilian@yahoo.com.ar. One of the slickest of the budget options, offering spotless modern rooms with good bathrooms. AR$390

Marcopolo Inn Av Córdoba 158 ☎ 03757 425 559, ⊕ marcopoloinniguazu.com. Popular HI hostel with six-bed dorms and double rooms. There's a pool, free internet and wi-fi, large kitchen and friendly ambience. Dorms AR$120, doubles AR$430

Noelia Residencial Fray Luis Beltrán 119, between Moreno and Belgrano ☎ 03757 420 729, ⊕ hostelnoelia .com. Excellent-value, family-run hotel not far from the bus station, with a/c, private baths and a lovely patio where breakfast is served. AR$285

Porämbá Hostel El Uru 120 ☎ 03757 423 041, ⊕ porambahostel.com. A quiet hostel surrounded by nature. Lovely pool, simple, clean rooms and an excellent breakfast. Dorms AR$90, doubles AR$260

EATING AND DRINKING

With a few exceptions, restaurants in Iguazú serve bland and touristy fare. At the falls there are several cafés, but the food is expensive and uninspiring, so consider packing a picnic.

Las Canitas Av Victoria Aguirre, at El Pindó. This lively local *peña* is a little off the main restaurant strip, but worth the walk for the warm welcome, live music and tasty grilled meats. Non-carnivores can tuck into vegetable kebabs and some interesting salads. Mains AR$40–65. Daily 6pm until late.

Gustos del Litoral Av Misiones 209. This pocket-sized restaurant and bar serves lip-smackingly good dishes from neighbouring Paraguay. Try the *chipá guazú* – a warm, crumbly combination of fresh corn and white cheese; covered here in tangy tomato sauce. Good cocktails too. Mains AR$40–45. Daily 8.30am–midnight.

La Rueda Córdoba 28 ☎ 03757 422 531. Pleasant restaurant, with outdoor seating. Fish is a speciality (mains AR$50–110). Mon–Tues 8pm–midnight, Wed–Sun noon–midnight.

La Vitrina Av Victoria Aguirre, at Curupi. Probably the best in town; a good-looking ranch-style *parrilla* on the main street, with outdoor seating on a veranda. Cover charge of AR$14 per person includes unlimited access to the inviting salad bar. Mains AR$45–95. Daily 11.30am–late.

IGUAZÚ FALLS

Around 275 individual cascades, the highest with a drop of over 80m, make up the stunning **IGUAZÚ FALLS** (*Cataratas de Iguazú*, or simply *Las Cataratas*). Strung out along the rim of a horseshoe-shaped cliff 2.7km long, their thunderous roaring can be heard from many kilometres away, while the mist rises 30m high in a series of dazzling rainbows. In the Guaraní language Iguazú means "great water", but clearly the Guaraní are not given to overstatement, for there's little doubt that these are the most spectacular falls in the world: only the Victoria Falls in Africa can compare in terms of size, but here the shape of the natural fault that created the falls means that you can stand with the water crashing almost all around you.

This section of the Río Iguazú makes up the border between Brazil and Argentina and the subtropical forests that surround the falls are protected on both sides: by the **Parque Nacional Iguazú** in Argentina, and the **Parque Nacional do Iguaçu** (see p.353) over the border. These parks are packed with wildlife, and even on the busy catwalks and paths that skirt the edges of the falls you've a good chance of seeing much of it. Orchids and serpentine creepers adorn the trees, among which flit vast, bright butterflies. You may also see toucans overhead and – if you're lucky – shy capuchin monkeys. Look out too for the swallow-like *vencejo*, a remarkable small bird, endemic to the area, which makes its nest behind the curtains of water.

Parque Nacional Iguazú

Thanks to an extensive system of trails and boardwalks that lead around, above and below the falls, the Argentine side offers better close-up views of Iguazú, while the Brazilian side has sweeping panoramic views. Everything lies within the **Parque Nacional Iguazú** (daily 8am–6pm; AR$215, get your ticket stamped to receive half-price entry the next day; ⊕ iguazuargentina.com), whose entrance is 18km southeast of Puerto Iguazú along RN12. Buses drop passengers off here, and the visitor centre just inside can provide a map of the park and various leaflets. It's also the departure point of the **Tren de la Selva**, a natural-gas-fuelled train for Cataratas Station (daily every 30min 8.30am–4.30pm), which gives access to the walking trails and the Garganta del Diablo walkway.

Several well-signposted trails (most wheelchair-accessible) take you to the park's highlights. The **Paseo Superior**, a short trail that runs along the top of the first few waterfalls, makes a good introduction. For more drama, and a much wetter experience, the **Paseo Inferior** winds down through the forest before taking you to within metres of some of the smaller falls. At the bottom of this trail, a regular free boat service leaves for **Isla San Martín**, a rocky island in the middle of the river. Note that the boat doesn't run when water levels are high after heavy rains. The same jetty is also the departure point for more thrills-oriented boat rides, such as those offered by Iguazú Jungle (see opposite).

At the heart of the falls is the truly unforgettable **Garganta del Diablo** (The Devil's Throat), a powerhouse display of natural forces in which 1800 cubic metres of water per second hurtles over a semicircle of rock into the misty river canyon below. The 1km boardwalk takes you to a small viewing platform within just a few metres of the staggering, sheer drop of water. Often shrouded in mist during winter mornings and early afternoons, the Garganta del Diablo is best visited later in the day, when the views tend to be clearer.

The Northwest

Argentina's northwest is an area of deserts, red earth and whitewashed colonial churches, punctuated with pockets of cloudforest and lush green jungle. The bustling city of Tucumán is an assault on the senses and a must-see for anyone interested in the political history of Argentina, while its diversity gives it a contemporary edge. The pretty and inviting city of **Salta** is known for its well-preserved colonial architecture and makes a great base for visiting the wonderful natural formations of the **Quebrada del Toro** and **Quebrada de Cafayate**, as well as the stylish wine-producing villages of the **Valles Calchaquíes**, such as **Cafayate**. To the north of Salta loom three jungle-clad **cloudforests** – El Rey above all is worth a visit – along with the busy market town of **San Salvador de Jujuy**, with its palm trees and wild Andean feel. As you head further north, the seven-coloured **Quebrada de Humahuaca** ravine can be seen from the small mud-brick towns of **Tilcara** and **Humahuaca**.

SAN MIGUEL DE TUCUMÁN

Argentina's fifth-largest city and the seat of Argentine independence, **TUCUMÁN** (officially **San Miguel de Tucumán**) has a cosmopolitan air and lively cultural scene that attracts young people from across the country. By day, the energy can be overwhelming – it's noisier, dirtier and busier than neighbouring Salta – but the abundance of theatres, galleries, universities, bookshops and bars can't help but draw you in.

WHAT TO SEE AND DO

Walking is the best way to appreciate the city and its attractions, which can easily be explored in a day. The main sights surround **Plaza Independencia**, where Tucumán's rich heritage can be seen in the French and Italian architecture of the **Casa de Gobierno** (daily 8.30am–8.30pm; free; ☎0381 484 4000) and the adjacent **Museo Casa Padilla** (daily 9am–12.30pm & 3.30–7.30pm; free; ☎0381 431 9147), house of former governor José Frías (1792–1874). In the northwest corner of the square stands the Neoclassical **Iglesia San Francisco**, while the south is dominated by the impressive cathedral. It's particularly beautiful at night when the buildings are illuminated and locals relax among the lapacho and orange trees surrounding the marble Statue of Liberty. A couple of blocks south of the plaza is

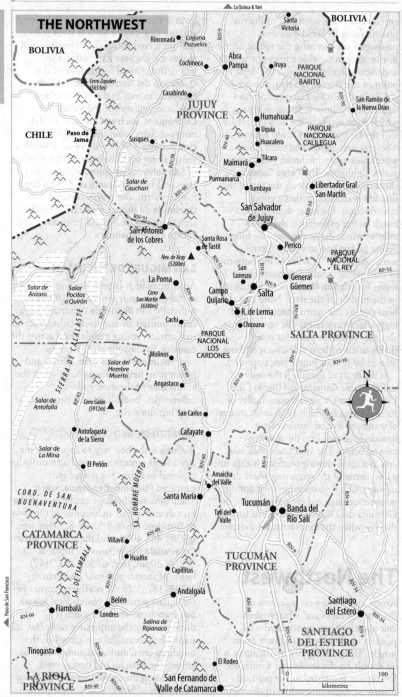

THE NORTHWEST

La Quiaca & Yavi

BOLIVIA

BOLIVIA

Santa
Victoria

Rinconada   Laguna
            Pozuelos

Cochinoca   Abra
                Pampa   Iruya

Cerro Zapaleri   PARQUE
(5653m)   NACIONAL
                            BARITÚ

CHILE   Casabindo   San Ramón de
                                                        la Nueva Oran

                JUJUY PROVINCE   Humahuaca

                                          Uquía   PARQUE
                                          Huacalera   NACIONAL
         Paso de   CALILEGUA
         Jama   Susques   Maimará Tilcara

                                    Purmamarca
                                                        Libertador Gral
Salar de   Tumbaya   San Martín
Cauchari
                                    San Salvador
                                    de Jujuy

Salar de   San Antonio   Perico
Arizaro   de los Cobres Santa Rosa
                               de Tastil
         Salar   San
         Pocitos   Nev. de Acay   Lorenzo   PARQUE
         o Quirón   (5200m)   NACIONAL
                                                              EL REY
                La Poma   General
                      Cerro   Güemes
                      San Martín   Campo
                      (6380m)   Quijano   Salta
                      Cachi   R. de Lerma
                                         Chicoana
                      PARQUE
                      NACIONAL   **SALTA PROVINCE**
Salar de   LOS
Antofalla   CARDONES
         Cerro Galán   Molinos
         (5912m)
                      Angastaco   **N**

                      San Carlos

      Antofagasta   Cafayate
      de la Sierra
                                              Amaicha
Salar de   del Valle
La Mina
      El Peñón   Santa María
                                                        Tucumán Banda del
                                    Tafí del   Río Salí
C O R D. D E S A N   Valle
B U E N A V E N T U R A
                                                    TUCUMÁN
CATAMARCA   Villavil   **PROVINCE**
PROVINCE
                      Hualfin
                                    Capillitas   Santiago
                                                      del Estero
                      Andalgalá
                                                      SANTIAGO
         Fiambalá   Belén   **DEL ESTERO**
                     Londres   **PROVINCE**
                             Salina de
                             Ripanaco
      Tinogasta   El Rodeo
                                                    0   100
LA RIOJA   San Fernando de   kilometres
PROVINCE   Valle de Catamarca

1

the **Casa Histórica de la Independencia**, where congressmen signed the Declaration of Independence from Spain on July 9, 1816. It now serves as the **National Museum** (daily 10am–6pm; free; ☎0381 431 0826, ⓦmuseocasahistorica.org.ar), where you can see the room in which the signing took place, lined with portraits of the signatories. Free English tours are available and there's a good sound-and-light show (daily except Thurs, AR$10, tickets from the tourist office). Once you're up to speed on Tucumán's political history, head to the **Museo Folclórico** (daily 9am–1pm & 4–8pm; free; ☎0381 421 8250) for a lesson in indigenous and gaucho culture, including traditional instruments, pottery and weaving.

ARRIVAL AND INFORMATION

By plane Tucumán's airport (☎0381 426 5072) is 13km east of the city centre. A taxi should cost no more than AR$80.
Destinations Buenos Aires (8 daily, 1hr 45min).

By bus All buses arrive at the mammoth bus terminal on Av Brígido Terán 250 (☎0381 400 2000, ⓦterminaltucuman.com).
Destinations Regular buses to Buenos Aires (16hr); Cafayate (6hr 30min); Córdoba (7hr); Jujuy (5hr); Mendoza (13hr); La Quiaca (11hr); Salta (4hr 30min).

By train Departs twice weekly to Buenos Aires (Wed & Sat; 25hr; AR$45–400 depending on class; ☎0381 430 9220). This is a scenic route with many stops along the way; book well in advance.

Tourist information The tourist office is opposite the Plaza Independencia at 24 de Septiembre 484 (☎0381 4303 644, ⓦtucuamnturismo.gob.ar).

ACCOMMODATION

A La Gurda Maipú 490 ☎0381 497 6275, ⓦlagurdahostel.com.ar. Excellent downtown location in a beautiful colonial house with high ceilings and tiled floors. Homey but fresh, it's got ample communal space including a roof terrace, patio and courtyard. Dorms

AR$99, privates AR$280
Backpackers Tucuman Laprida 456 ☎0381 430 2716, ⓦbackpackerstucuman.com. The only HI-affiliated hostel in town, it's centrally located with amenities beyond standard hostel expectations (including a stereo system and PS2), making it a great place to meet fellow backpackers. Dorms AR$100, doubles AR$280

EATING, DRINKING AND NIGHTLIFE

Plaza de Almas Maipú 791 ⓦplazadealmas.com. A lively "cultural eatery" in central Tucumán; fresh international dishes and traditional food at reasonable prices are served up with live music, independent cinema or theatrical performances. Nearby *El Arbol Galeano* and *Muna Muna* (vegetarian/vegan restaurant) are part of the same cooperative. Mon–Sat 12.30pm–3am, 8pm–2am.

El Portal 24 de Septiembre 351 ☎0381 422 6024. Rustic restaurant with a cosy feel serving expertly cooked Argentine specialities including *empanadas*, *tamales* and *locro*.

La San Juan San Juan 1059 ☎0381 421 7590. The place to go for an evening of Latino fun; this vibrant resto-bar in a colonial building comes alive at night with *salsa*, *bachata*, *merenge* and *chachacha* dancers. Tues–Sun 9pm–3am.

SALTA

SALTA is one of Argentina's most elegant provincial capitals, with leafy plazas, well-preserved colonial architecture and, thanks to the altitude, a pleasantly balmy climate during the summer. In the winter months temperatures drop dramatically, and snow is not uncommon. Throughout the city, and in its hotels, restaurants and museums, there's a strong emphasis on the culture of the Andes, and you'll notice that the food is spicier than in the south of the country. Attractions include the cable-car ride to the top of **Cerro San Bernardo**; a peach-coloured Neoclassical church; and wonderful *peñas* that mix spicy food and live Andean music.

Salta is a great jumping-off point for the

TAFÍ DEL VALLE

Lying 107km north of Tucumán in the Sierra de Aconquija, the hillside town **Tafí del Valle** is the gateway to the **Valles Calchaquíes** and a base from which to explore the surrounding scenery. The area is steeped in history, from ancient Tafi monoliths in the **Valles Calchaquíes Parque de los Menhires** to the eighteenth-century Jesuit ruins of **Capilla la Banda** (☎0386 742 1685). The surrounding mountains, lakes and rivers mean it is also an excellent place for outdoor activities, including horseriding, fishing, trekking, paragliding and windsurfing. Don't miss the National Cheese Festival in February. For information see ⓦtafidelvalle.com. Aconquija is the only bus company from Tucumán (6–9 daily; 2hr 30min; ☎0381 422 7620, ⓦtransporteaconquija.com.ar).

1

high passes of the **Quebrada del Toro** – ideally viewed from the **Tren a las Nubes** – and for the **Valles Calchaquíes**, where you can stay overnight among the vineyards of **Cafayate**. A less-visited option is the cloudforest national park of **El Rey**, to the east. Salta has scores of good backpacker

hostels, but these tend to fill up quickly at weekends and during public holidays, making advance booking essential.

WHAT TO SEE AND DO

The verdant **Plaza 9 de Julio** lies at the heart of Salta, with scenic cafés nestled under its

SALTA MICROCENTRO

● **EATING & DRINKING**
Bartz	1
Boliche de Balderrama	8
La Casona del Molino	4
Fili	2
Ma Cuisine	3
Mercado Central	7
El Patio de las Empanadas	6
El Solar del Convento	5

■ **ACCOMMODATION**
Backpacker's Hostel	6
Bloomers Bed & Brunch	4
Hostel Coloria	2
Hostal Prisamata	1
Munay	5
Las Rejas	3

arches – in the evening the whole place is lit up, and half of Salta seems to descend on the square for an evening stroll.

Plaza 9 de Julio

On the southern side of the leafy plaza, the whitewashed **Cabildo** houses the **Museo Histórico del Norte** (Tues–Fri 9am–7pm, Sat & Sun 9am–2pm & 3–7pm; AR$20, free 9–10am; ⓦmuseonor.gov.ar), which displays an eclectic array of artefacts, from horse-drawn carriages to everyday objects. The balcony here offers a great view over the goings-on in the square. Facing the museum is the ornate Neoclassical **Catedral**, built in 1882, which has some interesting frescoes inside.

Just east of the plaza, Calle Caseros leads to two more interesting churches. The blood-red **Iglesia y Convento San Francisco**, designed by architect Luigi Giorgi, is one of the most impressive religious buildings in the country. Its exuberance makes a fascinating contrast with the whitewashed walls of the **Convento San Bernardo**, a lesson in simplicity and tranquillity of design.

Archeological museum

MAAM, the **Museo de Arqueología de Alta Montaña**, on the west side of Plaza 9 de Julio (Tues–Sun 11am–7.30pm; AR$40; ⓦmaam.gob.ar), is a modern and controversial museum displaying the mummified remains of several high-mountain child sacrifices; many locals argue that the perfectly preserved remains should be laid to rest instead. The beautiful exhibits of Inca clothing and jewellery are well organized and have labels in English.

Cerro San Bernardo

To the east of the *microcentro* a steep path leads you up **Cerro San Bernardo** hill (1458m; 45min), or you can take the easy option and hop on the **teleférico** (cable car; daily 10am–7pm; AR$85 return) from Avenida Hipólito Yrigoyen, between Urquiza and Avenida San Martín, at the eastern end of Parque San Martín. At the top are gardens and a small café with sweeping views over Salta and out to the Lerma valley and Andes mountains beyond.

Calle Balcarce and Museo de Arte Étnico Americano Pajcha

The liveliest part of the city is the area around **Calle Balcarce**, especially the pedestrianized blocks north of Avenida Entre Río, about half a dozen blocks from the centre. Arts and crafts are on sale in the evenings and on weekends, and this is where you'll find the largest number of restaurants, bars, discos and folk-music venues. There is also an outstanding museum of American ethnic art, the **Museo de Arte Étnico Americano Pajcha**, 20 de Febrero 831 (Mon–Sat 10am–1pm & 4–8pm; AR$30; ⓦmuseopajchasalta.com.ar), featuring handicrafts from Argentina and elsewhere in South America, with Mapuche silver jewellery and Andean ceramics the highlights.

ARRIVAL AND INFORMATION

By plane Salta's airport (☎0387 424 7356) is 12km southwest of the city centre. A taxi should cost no more than AR$100.
Destinations Most parts of Argentina, including: Buenos Aires (2–3 daily; 2hr 30min); Córdoba (2–3 daily; 1hr 30min); Tucumán (2–3 daily; 40min).

SALTA TOURS

A wide variety of highly professional **tours**, **expeditions** and other **activities** all around the northwest region can be arranged from Salta city.

TOUR OPERATORS

Clark Expediciones Mariano Moreno 1950 ☎0387 497 1024, ⓦclarkexpediciones.com. Small ecotourism company specializing in birdwatching tours.
MoviTrack Safaris Buenos Aires 28 ☎0387 431 6749, ⓦmovitrack.com.ar. Lively 1–2-day overland safaris and sightseeing tours.

Norte Trekking Av del Libertador 1151, oficina 1 ☎0387 155 093 299, ⓦnortetrekking.com. Sightseeing, trekking and mountaineering adventures.
Salta Rafting Caseros 177 ☎0387 421 3216, ⓦsaltarafting.com. Fun white-water rafting and zipwire excursions on the Río Juramento. Can also arrange horseriding and mountain-biking trips.

1

By bus All buses arrive at the bus terminal (☎ 0387 401 1143) eight blocks east of the main plaza along Parque San Martín. It has luggage storage, cafés, chemists and bakeries but no internet.

Destinations Regular buses to Buenos Aires (20hr), Rosario (16hr), Córdoba (13hr), Tucumán (4hr), La Quiaca (7hr 30min) and Mendoza (19hr).

By train Bus #5 links the bus terminal with the train station, at Ameghino 690, via Plaza 9 de Julio. The only trains that serve Salta are the tourist *Tren a las Nubes*, which departs weekly, and infrequent goods and passenger trains to the Chilean border.

Tourist information The office for Salta city is housed in a converted Neoclassical building at Caseros 711 (daily 8am–9pm; ☎ 0387 437 3341) offers leaflets and a good city map. For information on Salta province there's an office at Buenos Aires 93 (daily 8am–9pm; ☎ 0387 431 0950).

ACCOMMODATION

There are plenty of budget accommodation options within walking distance of the bus terminal and the central plaza.

HOSTELS

Backpacker's Hostel Buenos Aires 930 ☎ 0387 423 5910, ⓦ backpackerssalta.com. One of three HI-affiliated hostels in Salta, this lively spot wins points for its free dinners, large pool, LCD TV and fun events such as five-a-side football. Doubles have TV and private bathroom. Dorms AR$100, doubles AR$240

Hostel Coloria General Güemes 333 ☎ 0387 431 3058, ⓦ coloriahostel.com. Super stylish (rooms are colour themed) and clean, this modern hostel is conveniently located close to the historic centre. There's ample communal space – including a small pool – and a decent Argentine breakfast. Dorms AR$70, doubles AR$200

Hostal Prisamata Bartolomé Mitre 833 ☎ 0387 431 3900, ⓦ hostalprisamata.com. Located close to the nightlife in Balcarce, the large communal spaces and indoor hammocks in this restored colonial house make it perfect for socializing. Choose a room towards the back to avoid noise from the road. AR$95

Las Rejas General Güemes 569 ☎ 0387 421 5971, ⓦ lasrejashostel.com. Family-owned and run, this converted 1900 building offers hostel accommodation with dorms and doubles with breakfast, as well as more luxurious accommodation at the adjoining B&B, where rooms start at AR$475. Dorms AR$100, doubles AR$300

HOTELS

★**Bloomers Bed & Brunch** Vicente López 129 ☎ 0387 422 7449, ⓦ bloomers-salta.com.ar. Five beautifully decorated rooms, with private bathrooms and a spectacular breakfast (there's an in-house pastry chef), which changes daily. AR$690

Munay Av San Martín 656 ☎ 0387 422 4936, ⓦ munayhotel .com.ar. Good-quality budget hotel, with basic but clean rooms with private bathrooms. Breakfast included. AR$360

EATING, DRINKING AND NIGHTLIFE

Salta has a good range of budget eating options, ranging from simple snack bars where you can enjoy delicious *empanadas* to atmospheric cafés and lively folk-music *peñas*, with the latter staying open well into the small hours at weekends and during peak tourist seasons; most charge extra for the entertainment.

Bartz Santiago del Estero 686 ☎ 0387 461 0160, ⓦ bartzsalta.com. Excellent little tapas restaurant serving delicious tasting plates from octopus to carpaccio at reasonable prices. Mon–Sat 7pm–12.30am.

Boliche de Balderrama San Martín 1126 ☎ 0387 421 1542, ⓦ boliche-balderrama.com.ar. Somewhat pricey but popular *peña* with local music, and sometimes dancing while you eat. Mon–Sat lunch & dinner.

★**La Casona del Molino** Luis Burela, at Caseros ☎ 0387 434 2835. It's a 30min walk or a quick taxi ride to this rambling old building, but well worth it for the delicious local food and lively atmosphere. The fairly priced menu includes *empanadas, locro, guashalocro, tamales* and *humitas*. The house wine comes by the litre and is dangerously drinkable. Tues–Sun 9pm–5am.

Fili Av Sarmiento 229 ☎ 0387 422 3355. This ice-cream parlour, housed in a natty Art Deco building, has been attracting locals for some sixty years with its vast selection of flavours, including a delicious *dulce de leche* with almonds, cinnamon or both. Daily 9am–10pm.

Ma Cuisine España 83 ☎ 0387 576 8786. Fresh ingredients, crisp decor and a chalkboard menu of pasta, meat, seafood and vegetarian dishes which changes daily. Mon–Sat 8pm–midnight.

Mercado Central Av San Martín 750. Good for lunch, with a range of inexpensive food stalls offering everything from *panchos* and fries to *locro* and *humitas* throughout the day.

El Patio de las Empanadas Caseros 117. Pleasant place serving northwestern treats, with an outdoor patio. Try the famous *empanadas, humitas* and *tamales*. Mon–Fri 7am–midnight, Sat 7am–1am.

★**El Solar del Convento** Caseros 444 ☎ 0387 421 5124. Stylish decor, attentive service and thoughtfully prepared traditional dishes combine to make this restaurant a standout on Salta's dining scene (without being *too* expensive). The wine list is extensive, and local "champagne" is served on the house. Sometimes closed during low season but otherwise open daily for lunch and dinner.

DIRECTORY

Banks and exchange There are several banks with ATMS at Plaza 9 de Julio, and Av España is lined with banks including HSBC, Banco Francés, Santander and Citibank.

There are further cashpoints and exchange services on España, at Mitre.

Car rental Turismo Marina Semisa, Caseros 489 (☎0387 431 2097, ⓦmarina-semisa.com.ar).

Hospital San Bernado, Doctor Tobias 69

Internet Salta Internet, Florida 55.

Post office Deán Funes 170.

Tourist police Mitre 23.

LA QUEBRADA DEL TORO

There are several ways to experience the dramatic, ever-changing scenery of the **Quebrada del Toro** gorge and its surrounding town; you can rent a car, take an organized tour or hop on the **Tren a las Nubes** – a fabulous if expensive experience (March–Dec only, twice weekly; check ahead, closed at the time of writing AR$830; ⓦtrenalasnubes.com .ar). Leaving early from Salta and the Lerma valley, you start to ascend the multicoloured gorge of the Río El Toro, usually tranquil but sometimes torrential in spring. The rail tracks ascend to a dizzying 4200m above sea level, allowing you to experience this exceptional engineering achievement. There are 21 tunnels and more than 13 viaducts, the highlight of them the 64m-high, 224m-long **Polvorilla Viaduct**, almost at the top of the line. Along the way there are various stops and photo opportunities, usually including the town of **Santa Rosa de Tastil**, the pre-Incan site of **Tastil**, and the small mining town of **San Antonio de los Cobres**, where local artists sell their jewellery, clothing and toys by the train station.

PARQUE NACIONAL EL REY

The spectacular cloudforests of the **PARQUE NACIONAL EL REY** (9am–dusk; free) lie just under 200km from Salta. El Rey features an upland enclave covered in lush green vegetation, with high year-round humidity and precipitation but with very distinct seasons – very wet in summer, dry (or at least not so wet) in winter. The park is frequently covered in a low-lying mist, the signature feature of cloudforests, protecting the plants and animals beneath it. El Rey is particularly good for **birdwatching**: the giant toucan is

the park's symbol, and is easily spotted, while at least 150 other bird species also live here, as well as jaguars and howler monkeys.

There is just one access road to the park (the RP20). The easiest way to discover the park is on an **organized trip** from Salta (see p.91), but if visiting independently you're advised to take a 4WD and check in with the **guardaparques** at the park entrance before you set off. The only option for an overnight stay at the park is to pitch a tent at one of the two official **camping** spots, basic but with toilets and showers. Again, check with the *guardaparques* at the entrance for directions and prices.

VALLES CALCHAQUÍES

To the south of Salta lie the stunning **VALLES CALCHAQUÍES**, the valleys of the Río Calchaquí, fed by snowmelt from the Andes. Here you'll find some of the highest vineyards in the world. You can rent your own car from Salta to explore the area, which allows you to loop round via the amazing **Cuesta del Obispo mountain pass**, visit the wonderful cactus forests of the **Parque Nacional Los Cardones**, stop off in the little towns of **Cachi** and **Cafayate**, and return to Salta via the incredible rock formations of the Quebrada de Cafayate. There are also tours from both Cafayate and Salta, and Cachi and Cafayate are both connected to Salta by bus (though not really to each other).

Cachi

CACHI lies around 160km southwest of Salta, along an incredibly scenic route with mountainous views across lush valleys. Small and still quite undiscovered, but what Cachi lacks in services, it makes up for in scenery and location. The permanently snow-covered **Nevado del Cachi** (6380m), 15km to the west, looms over the town.

WHAT TO SEE AND DO

Truth is, there's not a great deal to detain you in Cachi other than the picturesque nature of the place itself. A small **Plaza Mayor**, shaded by palms and orange trees, marks the centre of town and on the north

1

side you'll find the well-restored **Iglesia San José**. Its bright white exterior gives way to an interior made almost entirely, from pews to confessional, of porous cactus wood. Not far away, the **Museo Arqueológico Pío Pablo Díaz** (Mon–Fri 10am–7pm, Sat & Sun 10am–6pm; AR$10) displays local archeological finds in an attractive building with a wonderful patio. For the more energetic, a hiking track to the west of the village will lead you to **Cachi Adentro** (6km), where you'll have wonderful views of the surrounding landscape and may see the fields of drying paprika which line the route from March to May.

ARRIVAL AND DEPARTURE

By bus Buses drop passengers off at the main square. From there all services are within walking distance. There are frequent services to Salta (4hr 15min) and local destinations.

ACCOMMODATION

There are relatively few budget places to stay in Cachi.
Art Hostel Viracocha Federico Suarez at Ruiz de los Llanos ☎03868 491 713, ⓦrestaurantviracocha.com.ar. Low-key little hostel with decent rooms at reasonable prices. The lack of kitchen might have something to do with the fact they have a (nice) restaurant just down the road. Breakfast included. Dorms **AR$85**, doubles **AR$190**
Llaqta Mawka Ruíz de los Lanos s/n ☎03868 491 016, ⓦhotelllaqtamawka.todowebsalta.com.ar. Welcoming inn that has made a concerted effort to respect local building and decoration customs and techniques and offers interesting tours of the immediate region. **AR$490**
Municipal Camping Av Automóvil Club Argentina (at the end) ☎03868 491 902. Basic clean campsite, with cabins on offer. Pool and shaded areas. Camping **AR$30**

EATING

ACA Sol del Valle Av Automóvil Club Argentina ☎03868 491 904, ⓦaca.tur.ar/hoteles/vinculados/salta/cafayate. The restaurant of the pricey *ACA Hotel* serves local food,

including hearty soups and stews, as well as cakes, sandwiches and pastries at the adjoining café-bar. The setting is wonderful and the staff friendly.

Around Cachi

The 157km drive from Cachi to Cafayate takes you through some of Valles Calchaquíes' most spectacular scenery and some delightful little towns. A short stop in **Molinos** (60km from Cachi) is recommended to view the local crafts, see the picturesque adobe houses and check out a fabulous church, the eighteenth-century **Iglesia de San Pedro Nolasco**. Beyond the town of Angastaco, the red sandstone **Quebrada de las Flechas** gorge is filled with dangerous-looking arrowhead formations. Shortly afterwards the road passes through **El Ventisquero**, the "wind-tunnel", and the natural stone walls of **El Cañón**, over 20m high.

Cafayate

The largest town in the region, and the main tourist base, is **CAFAYATE**. Set amid apparently endless vineyards, it makes a perfect place to hole up for a few days while exploring the surrounding area on horseback or sipping the local wines at nearby *bodegas*. The town is lively, filled with inviting plazas and popular restaurants.

WHAT TO SEE AND DO

The pleasure of your visit lies in getting out into the countryside, though there are also craft stalls and a couple of museums to fill the hours. The sleek, modern **Museo de la Vid y el Vino**, on Güemes Sur at Cesar Fermin Perdiguero (Tues–Sun 10am–7.30pm; AR$30), uses poetry and audiovisuals to bring to life the oenologist's craft and explain why the climate in the area is so good for the grapes. The **Museo Arqueológico** (Mon–Fri 11.30am–9pm, Sat 11.30am–3pm; free; ☎03868 421 054), at the corner of Colón and Calchaquí, is the private collection of late collector Rodolfo Bravo. On display alongside archeological relics are local ceramics, and everyday items from the colonial period.

ARRIVAL AND DEPARTURE

By bus Buses from Salta and nearby villages use the small terminal on Belgrano, east of the plaza, though some will drop you off at your destination as you pass through town; ask the driver. Buses from Tucumán arrive at the terminal on Güemes Norte & Alvarado.

Destinations Salta (6 daily; 4hr); Tucumán (4 daily; 4hr).

INFORMATION AND TOURS

Tourist information A kiosk on the plaza (daily 8am–9pm), dispenses information. Look for the helpful map of the wineries.

Tour operators Ipuna Turismo, San Martín 81 (☎03868 421 808), can arrange horse rides, trekking, 4WD tours, winery tours and mountain-bike adventures. Majo Travel, Vicario Toscano 80 (☎03868 422038, ⍵majoviajes.todowebsalta .com.ar), offers a huge variety of tours and adventures across northern Argentina. Turismo Cordillerano, Camila Quintana de Niño 59 (☎03868 422 137, ⍵turismocordillerano.com.ar), offers trekking and excursions in the valleys.

ACCOMMODATION

There is a range of options for budget accommodation; all are within walking distance of the plaza and can advise on winery visits.

Casa Arbol Calchaquí 84 ☎03868 422 238, ✉casaarbol84@gmail.com. New hostel centrally located in a small colonial house with a real home-from-home vibe. Run by ex-backpackers who have lots of tips on the surrounding area. Dorms A̲R̲$̲8̲5̲, doubles A̲R̲$̲2̲5̲0̲

Rusty K Hostal Rivadavia 281 ☎03868 422 031, ⍵rustykhostal.todowebsalta.com.ar. Central, friendly hostel with a pleasant garden to relax in. Dorms A̲R̲$̲1̲2̲5̲, doubles A̲R̲$̲2̲5̲0̲

Ruta 40 Güermes Sur 178 ☎03868 421 689, ⍵hostel-ruta40.com. The liveliest hostel in town, with clean dorms and small doubles. Dorms A̲R̲$̲9̲0̲, doubles A̲R̲$̲3̲5̲0̲

Los Toneles Camila Quintana de Niño 38 ☎03868 422 301, ⍵lostoneleshostal.com.ar. Friendly budget hotel half a block from the plaza with barrels of character – literally, with giant beer barrels serving as decoration and as tables in the small patios off each room. A yard with benches that resembles an English pub garden completes the picture. A̲R̲$̲2̲5̲0̲

★ Hostal de Valle San Martín 243 ☎03868 421 039. Large, light spacious rooms, set around a luscious patio. Ask for a room upstairs. A̲R̲$̲3̲6̲0̲

EATING AND DRINKING

Restaurants and cafés surround the main plaza, where in summer you can join crowds of locals strolling through the city at dusk with an ice cream.

Las Dos Marias San Martin 27 ☎03868 422 463. A more intimate option than the other touristy restaurants on the

WINERY VISITS

There are some world-class wineries around Cafayate and most offer **tours** in English and Spanish with a tasting afterwards. Ask at the information centre on the small plaza in Cafayate for a winery map of the area. Two of the most popular are **Bodega Etchart**, on RN40 (Mon–Fri 9am–5pm, Sat & Sun 9am–1pm; ☎03868 422 220, ⍵bodegasetchart.com), and **Bodega Nanni**, on Silverio Chavarría 151 (Mon–Sat 10.30am–12.30pm & 2.30–6.30pm, Sun 11am–12.30pm & 2.30–5.30pm; ☎03868 421 527, ⍵bodegananni.com). Both are within walking or cycling distance, and offer free tours.

plaza, serving high-quality Argentine fare at more reasonable prices. Daily lunch & dinner.

El Almacén Camila Quintana de Niño 59, ⍵elalmacenhostelbar.com. This remodelled house has retained many antique fittings, providing an atmospheric setting for enjoying the house *picadas* and very reasonable *torrontés*, made from vines that grow just behind. The building also houses a decent hostel (dorms AR$55). Daily noon–late.

Baco Güemes Norte, at Rivadavia. Simple decor and friendly staff make this corner restaurant popular, as do its pizzas, trout and local wines. Daily lunch & dinner.

Carreta de Don Olegario Güemes Sur 20, at Quintana de Niño on the east side of the plaza. Popular for its reasonably priced local dishes, this well-located restaurant features live traditional music as well as hearty goat and veal stews, veggie-friendly tortillas and pasta dishes, and delicious cheeses. There's a good selection of wines from local *bodegas* too. Daily noon–3pm & 7–11pm.

Miranda Av Güemes, half a block north of the plaza. Gourmet ice creams in exotic flavours; try the famous wine sorbets. Daily noon–8pm.

SAN SALVADOR DE JUJUY

Generally playing second fiddle to its prettier cousin Salta, **SAN SALVADOR DE JUJUY** (known as Jujuy) lies 90km to the north. Although it's the highest provincial capital in the country, at 1260m above sea level, Jujuy is set in a lush pocket of humidity and greenery. It's a busy place, with a frantic, market feel, where crumbling colonial buildings are juxtaposed with neon signs. Most travellers pass through for just one night

1

on their way to **Tilcara** and **Humahuaca**, and, to the north, the spectacular colours of the **Quebrada de Humahuaca**.

WHAT TO SEE AND DO

If you have time to kill in Jujuy, head to the lively **Plaza General Belgrano**, east of the city centre. This large, green open space is generally crowded with young locals, checking out the craftsmen and market sellers who set up stalls here. On the west side of the plaza, the late eighteenth-century **Catedral** (daily 8am–1pm & 5–8pm; free) makes up for a plain facade with a wonderfully decorative interior, above all a spectacular pulpit decorated by local artists over two centuries ago. This has a rival in the intricate pulpit of the nearby **Iglesia San Francisco**, whose tiny human figures, columns and scenes are thought to have been carved in Bolivia.

ARRIVAL AND DEPARTURE

By plane Jujuy's airport (Gobernador Horacio Guzmán International Airport; ☎0388 491 1102) is 32km southeast of the city. A taxi will cost around AR$200.

By bus The ugly bus terminal (☎0388 422 6299) on Iguazú, at Av Dorrego, is just south of the centre across the Río Chico, which serves all local, regional and national destinations, and also offers services to Chile and Bolivia.

Destinations Buenos Aires (3 daily; 22hr); Córdoba (3 daily; 14–15hr); Salta (2 daily; 2hr); Tucumán (regular; 5–6hr).

INFORMATION AND TOURS

Tourist information Secretaría de Turismo y Cultural, Canónigo Gorriti 295 (Mon–Fri 7am–10pm, Sat & Sun 9am–9pm; ☎0388 422 1343, ⓦturismo.jujuy.gov.ar).

Tour operators Noroeste, San Martín 155 (☎0388 423 7565, ⓦnoroesteargentino.com), is a youth travel agency attached to *Club Hostel*.

ACCOMMODATION

★**Hostal Casa de Barro** Otero 294 ☎0388 422 9578, ⓦcasadebarro.com.ar. Wonderful and welcoming, with clean spacious dorms and private rooms, an excellent on-site restaurant and a pleasant common area. Dorms AR$100, doubles AR$250

Club Hostel San Martín 155 ☎0388 423 7565, ⓦclubhosteljujuy.com.ar. Busy, lively hostel with a small pool, within walking distance of the bus terminal and the centre. Dorms AR$100, doubles AR$300

Dublin Hostel y Bar Independencia 946 ☎0388 422 9608. A long-running Jujuy hostel offering a handful of high-ceilinged dorms as well as a couple of doubles. There's a bar (which closes at midnight) with a good selection of beers tacked on the side. Dorms AR$90, doubles AR$240

Munay General Alvear 1230 ☎0388 422 8435, ⓦmunayhotel.com.ar. Just north of the centre, this friendly, budget hotel has clean, rather dark rooms with private bathrooms. AR$370

EATING AND DRINKING

The open-air market, next to the bus station, is a great place to fill up on *empanadas*, grilled meat sandwiches and coffee for just a few pesos.

Cacao Sarmiento 330 ☎0388 423 2037, ⓦcacaorestaurante.blogspot.com.ar. Sophisticated formal dining, good tapas and an extensive list of local wines. Mon–Sat noon–3.30pm & 8pm–2am.

La Candelaria Alvear 1346. West of the city, this *parrilla* is a local institution, and a must for any meat-lover. Tues–Sat noon–3pm & 8.30pm–1am, Sun noon–3pm.

★**Macedonio** Lamadrid 524 ☎0388 424 1606. Wonderful cultural centre and café bar in an 1860s adobe house, with a palm-fringed patio where folk and jazz bands play (Wed–Sat). Inexpensive meals – hearty sandwiches, salads and pasta – are served. Tues–Sat 10am–1.30am.

Madre Tierra Belgrano 619 ☎0388 422 9578. Fresh salads, juices and vegetarian/vegan food. Mon–Sat 7.30am–10pm.

Zorba Belgrano 802 ☎0388 424 3048, ⓦzorbacafebar.com.ar. Large, two-storey restaurant serving Greek food, as well as local favourites. Mon–Sat 8am–2am, Sun 6pm–1am.

DIRECTORY

Banks and exchange Alvear is lined with banks that accept foreign cards, including HSBC at Alvear 970.

Car rental Sudamerics, Belgrano 601 (☎0388 422 9034, ⓦsudamerics.com).

Post office La Madrid, at Independencia.

★ TREAT YOURSELF

Just 19km west of Jujuy are the thermal hot springs of the **Termas de Reyes** and the **Hotel Termas de Reyes** (☎0388 392 2522, ⓦtermasdereyes.com; double AR$1242, day visits also possible). Sinking into a hot mineral spa bath, or relaxing with a mineral mud mask, is just the way to shake off a long bus ride. There are fourteen private thermal baths for three people, with stunning panoramic views, as well as two saunas. Bus #14 runs to Termas from the main bus terminal (4 daily; 20min).

QUEBRADA DE HUMAHUACA

The scintillating, multicoloured **QUEBRADA DE HUMAHUACA** gorge stretches 125km north of Jujuy, past the small village of **Purmamarca** and the town of **Tilcara**, with its pre-Columbian archeological site, all the way to the busy village of **Humahuaca**. From there you can carry on to reach the border crossing with Bolivia at **La Quiaca**, nearly 2000m higher and 150km further on. The region is popular with Argentine holidaymakers, who come to stay in the many swish spas and resorts, to hike and take in the extraordinary mountain scenery.

Purmamarca

As you head north, the first substantial settlement you reach along the RN9 is **PURMAMARCA** at Km61. This small town sits at the foot of the stunning **Cerro de los Siete Colores** (Hill of Seven Colours) and is an ideal base for horseriding and hiking excursions. Purmamarca is home to scores of luxury hotels as well as more budget-friendly options, and, despite the tourist influx, retains plenty of rustic Andean charm, thanks to its traditional adobe buildings and colourfully dressed locals. The village has a fantastic seventeenth-century church, the **Iglesia Santa Rosa de Lima**, at its heart – faithfully maintained and still in use today.

Tilcara

The busy tourist town of **TILCARA** is a favourite with holidaymakers for its fantastic restaurants, attractive hotels and a pre-Incan **pukará** or fortress (daily 10am–6pm; AR$50). Discovered in 1903 and heavily reconstructed in the 1950s, the site enjoys a wonderful, commanding location, covered in giant cacti. To get here, follow the signposted trail from the centre of town over the bridge across the Río Huasamayo. Keep your entrance ticket for admission to the **Museo Arqueológico** (same hours), on the south side of the square in a beautiful colonial house. The well-presented collection includes finds from the site and further afield, including anthropomorphic vases and a humanoid standing stone from another *pukará*.

Humahuaca

HUMAHUACA is a small, attractive place, originally founded in 1591 and popular with backpackers, with a wider spread of budget accommodation than elsewhere. Numerous shops, restaurants and craft stalls stand all around the leafy plaza. On the east side, the tiny **Iglesia de la Candelaria** (daily noon–1pm; free), constructed in 1631 and rebuilt in the nineteenth century, has some interesting artworks. Beside the church, steps lead up to the base of the **Monumento a la Independencia**, a masculine and dramatic sculpture. There are awesome views from here, pocked by human-size cacti.

ARRIVAL AND DEPARTURE

By bus Buses leave every hour from Jujuy and run up the Quebrada to Purmamarca (1hr), Tilcara (1hr 30min–2hr) and Humahuaca (3hr), dropping off locals at farms and houses along the way. Only certain companies go all the way to La Quiaca – look for El Quiaqueño, Panamericano and Balut. Tilcara and Humahuaca have a central bus terminal that offers luggage storage; at other towns you will be dropped off at the main plaza.

INFORMATION AND TOURS

Tourist information The region's best tourist office is in Tilcara, Belgrano 590 (daily 8am–noon & 1–9pm; ☎0388 495 5720). It has lists of accommodation in the region and free maps. Otherwise there is a small tourist office in Humahuaca (daily 7am–9pm), in the white colonial *cabildo* building on the plaza.

Tour operators Tilcara Tours, Necochea 250 in Jujuy (☎0388 422 6113), organizes guided tours into the Quebrada de Humahuaca.

ACCOMMODATION

The best budget accommodation is in Tilcara and Humahuaca, although campsites can be found in nearly every town in the valley.

TILCARA

★**Albahaca Hostel** Padilla, between Ambrosetti and Sarmiento ☎0388 155 855 194, ⓦalbahacahostel.com.ar. The panoramic views of the gorge from the lovely sun terrace (where you can enjoy a breakfast of home-made bread) place this hostel above the rest, while the central location, cheerful furnishings and helpful staff (on hand to arrange tours and activities from dance classes to barbecues) do not disappoint. Dorms **AR$120**, doubles **AR$220**

Malka San Martín (at the top of the hill) ☎0388 495 5197, ⓦmalkahostel.com.ar. It's a strenuous uphill walk

1

to this hostel, which has comfortable cabañas for up to six people – great value if travelling in a group – as well as dorms. HI discounts. Dorms ARS180, cabins ARS500

HUMAHUACA

Hostal Humahuaca Buenos Aires 447 ☎0388 15500 1726, ⏍humahuacahostal.com.ar. Located just off the main plaza, this small hostel has slightly dark but cool dorm rooms set around a bright patio. Dorms ARS85, doubles ARS200

Posada el Sol Barrio Medalla Milagrosa (across the river) ☎0388 742 1466, ⏍elsolhosteldehumahuaca.com. Follow the signs from the bus station to this small rustic house on the outskirts of town. Small, comfortable dorms and doubles in peaceful surroundings. Dorms ARS80, doubles ARS220

EATING AND DRINKING

TILCARA

El Nuevo Progreso Lavalle 351 ☎0388 495 5237. This intimate, candle-lit spot serves delicious Andean cuisine in hearty portions. The llama steaks are good, and there's a decent wine list sourced from local *bodegas*. Live music some evenings. Daily 6–11pm.

Los Puestos Belgrano, at Padilla ☎0388 495 5100. For a meal in exceptionally beautiful surroundings, *Los Puestos* rules supreme: the varied menu features tender grilled llama, mouthwatering *empanadas*, juicy *humitas* and succulent pasta, all at reasonable prices. Daily 11.30am–3pm & 8.30pm–midnight.

HUMAHUACA

El Portillo Tucumán 69. This hotel restaurant serves traditional food including llama meat, quinoa and Andean potatoes in a rustic environment. Daily 7pm–midnight.

Pacha Manka Buenos Aires 457, at Córdoba ☎0388 742 1265. Charming café-restaurant serving home-cooked

food (both international and local) on terracotta plates. Sit outside to enjoy the mountain sunshine. Daily breakfast, lunch & dinner.

Mendoza and San Juan

The vast midwestern provinces of **MENDOZA** and **SAN JUAN** are sparsely populated, sun-fried playgrounds for lovers of mountains and vineyards. The highest peaks outside the Himalayas rise to the west, capped by the formidable **Cerro Aconcagua**, whose icy volcanic summit punctures the sky at nearly 7000m, an irresistible magnet for experienced climbers. Further south down the Andean cordillera is the see-and-be-seen resort of **Las Leñas**, whose powdery slopes deliver some of the best skiing in South America. Come summer, snowmelt rushes down the mountains, swelling rivers and creating ideal **white-water rafting** conditions, especially along the Cañon de Atuel near the small city of **San Rafael**.

At the foothills of the mountains, the same sunshine that pummels the region's inhospitable, parched desertscapes also feeds its celebrated grapevines. Wine enthusiasts will feel right at home in the eminently liveable city of **Mendoza**, the region's urban hub, which offers easy access to Argentina's best *bodegas*.

VISITING WINERIES

Barrel-loads of wineries near Mendoza offer free tours and tastings (some also have restaurants offering gourmet lunches), with the majority in the satellite towns of **Maipú** (15km southeast), **Luján de Cuyo** (7km south) and the eastern suburb of **Guaymallén**, all accessible by public transport from the city centre. Many Mendoza-based tour companies offer half- or full-day winery excursions, but if there are four of you, it can be more fun and cheaper to **rent a taxi** and hit the *bodegas* of your choice independently (call ahead for appointments; most closed Sun). Or if you want to exercise between swills (but maybe spit the wine out?), **rent a bike** in Maipú from Mr Hugo (ARS80/day; ☎0261 497 4067, ⏍mrhugobikes.com), arm yourself with their winery map, and cycle a 40km circuit, stopping at vineyards along the way. To reach Maipú from downtown Mendoza, catch *colectivos* #171, #172 or #173 from Rioja (between Catamarca and Garibaldi) and ask to be let off at Plazoleta Rutini (45min).

If time only allows for one winery, walk around the corner to **Bodega La Rural** (Mon–Sat 9am–1pm & 2.30–5pm; ☎0261 497 2013) at Montecaseros 2625, which has an informative on-site wine museum. For expert advice on which wineries to visit, pick up a free copy of *Wine Republic* magazine from the tourist office or speak to the helpful staff at *Vines of Mendoza* (see p.103).

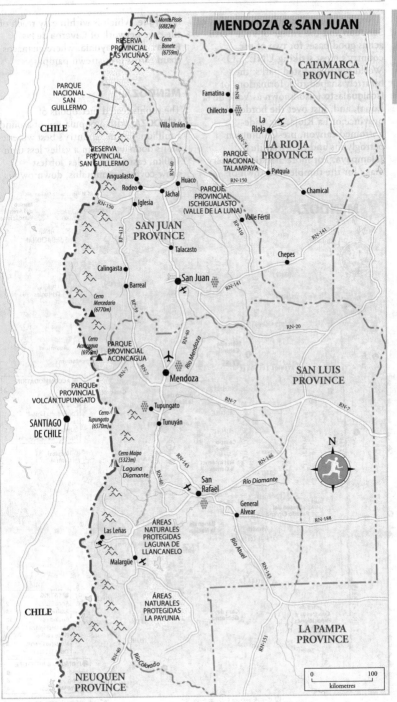

MENDOZA & SAN JUAN

Monte Pissis (6882m)

Cerro Bonete (6759m)

CATAMARCA PROVINCE

RESERVA PROVINCIAL LAS VICUÑAS

Famatina · RN-60

Chilecito · La Rioja ✈

PARQUE NACIONAL SAN GUILLERMO

Villa Unión ·

CHILE

RN-74

RESERVA PROVINCIAL SAN GUILLERMO

RN-40

PARQUE NACIONAL TALAMPAYA

LA RIOJA PROVINCE

Patquía · RN-150

Angualasto
Rodeo · Huaco
Iglesia · Jáchal

RN-150

RN-412

PARQUE PROVINCIAL ISCHIGUALASTO (VALLE DE LA LUNA)

Chamical ·

Valle Fértil

RP-510

RN-141

SAN JUAN PROVINCE

Talacasto ·

Chepes ·

Calingasta ·

San Juan ✈

RN-141

Barreal ·

Cerro Mercedario (6770m)

RP-39

Cerro Aconcagua (6959m)

PARQUE PROVINCIAL ACONCAGUA

RN-40

Río Mendoza

RN-7

SAN LUIS PROVINCE

RN-20

PARQUE PROVINCIAL VOLCÁN TUPUNGATO

RN-7

Mendoza ✈

RN-7

RN-7

SANTIAGO DE CHILE ·

Cerro Tupungato (6570m)

Tupungato

Tunuyán ·

RN-143

RN-146

Cerro Maipo (5323m)
Laguna Diamante

RN-40

Río Diamante

San Rafael ✈

RN-143

General Alvear

RN-188

Las Leñas ·

ÁREAS NATURALES PROTEGIDAS LAGUNA DE LLANCANELO

Río Atuel

Malargüe ✈

RN-143

ÁREAS NATURALES PROTEGIDAS LA PAYUNIA

CHILE

LA PAMPA PROVINCE

RN-151

N

RN-40

Río Colorado

| 0 | 100 |

kilometres

NEUQUEN PROVINCE

1

North of here, the provincial capital of **San Juan** and the village of **Valle Fértil** act as good bases for two of the country's most striking UNESCO World Heritage-listed parks: the bizarrely shaped rock formations of **Ischigualasto** (also known as Valle de la Luna), and, just over the border in the province of La Rioja, the wide-bottomed canyon, pre-Columbian petroglyphs and rich wildlife of **Talampaya**. For more arresting scenery, make for the tumbleweed town of

Malargüe, which is within easy reach of the cave network of **Caverna de las Brujas** and **La Payunia**, where guanacos roam across lava-strewn pampas.

MENDOZA

The sophisticated metropolis of **MENDOZA**, with a population of around a million, has the country's best wineries on its doorstep. Set in a valley less than 100km east of the Andes' loftiest snow-covered mountains, downtown is

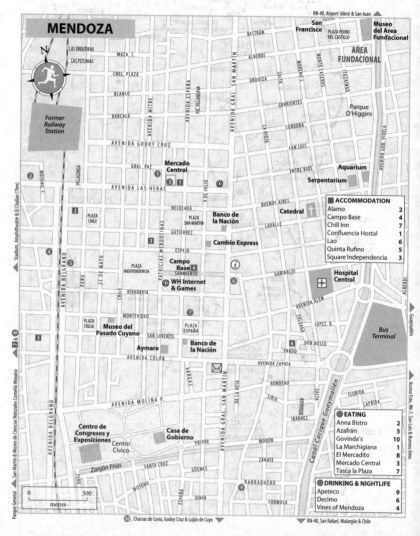

MENDOZA

ACCOMMODATION

Alamo	2
Campo Base	4
Chill Inn	7
Confluencia Hostal	1
Lao	6
Quinta Rufino	5
Square Independencia	3

EATING

Anna Bistro	2
Azafrán	5
Govinda's	10
La Marchigiana	1
El Mercadito	8
Mercado Central	3
Tasca la Plaza	7

DRINKING & NIGHTLIFE

Apeteco	9
Decimo	6
Vines of Mendoza	4

characterized by elegant, fountain-filled plazas and wide, sycamore-lined avenues. An earthquake in 1861 laid waste to Mendoza's former colonial glories, but the modern, low-rise city that rose in its wake is certainly no eyesore. *Mendocinos* know how to enjoy the good life, and, along with taking their siestas seriously (many businesses close between 1pm and 4pm), they enjoy dining at the city's many fine restaurants and alfresco drinking along the spacious pavements.

Mendoza makes an ideal base for exploring some of Argentina's undisputed highlights. Hundreds of *bodegas*, offering wine-tasting tours, lie within easy reach of downtown. **Tour operators** run a range of white-water rafting, horseriding, paragliding and skydiving excursions, and those looming peaks offer skiing in winter and world-class mountain climbing in summer.

WHAT TO SEE AND DO

At the junction of the city's two principal thoroughfares – Avenida Sarmiento and Avenida Mitre – the spacious **Plaza Independencia** is the physical and cultural heart of Mendoza. Fountains and sycamore trees create an ideal space for chilling out or, over summer, taking in one of the regular outdoor concerts. One block east and south of here, **Plaza España** trumps Independencia in the beauty stakes, thanks to the Andalucian tilework gracing its stone benches, tree-lined paths, pretty fountains and monument to Spain's discovery of South America.

Museo del Pasado Cuyano

The **Museo del Pasado Cuyano** (Tues–Fri 10am–2pm; donation), at Montevideo 544, is the city's history museum, housed in a mansion dating from 1873. The collection includes an exhibition on General San Martín along with religious art, weaponry and period furniture.

Parque General San Martín

A four-square-kilometre green space you could easily spend a day exploring, the forested **Parque General San Martín**, 1km west of Plaza Independencia, is one of the most impressive urban parks in the country. Whether you're navigating it by foot, bike, horse or public bus, be sure to grab a map at the **information centre** (daily June–Sept 9am–6pm, rest of year 8am–7pm; ☎0261 420 5052, ext 221) just inside the park's grand gated main entrance.

Within lie some fifty thousand trees, a rose garden, tennis courts, an observatory, swimming pool, lake, zoo, football stadium, amphitheatre and, in the southeastern corner, the **Museo de Ciencias Naturales y Antropológicas Juan Cornelio Moyano** (undergoing refurbishment at the time of writing. Check with the tourist office for latest information). This contains an intriguing collection of pre-Columbian mummies, fossils and stuffed animals. Sweeping city views are to be had from the top of **Cerro de la Gloria** (Glory Hill), crowned by a bronze monument to San Martín's liberating army.

MENDOZA TOURS

Mendoza province is not just about wine, and its mountains and rivers offer plenty of opportunities for trekking and adventure sports, for which you'll need the services of the region's highly professional tour operators.

TOUR OPERATORS

Argentina Rafting Potrerillos ☎0262 448 2037, ⊚argentinarafting.com. Runs white-water rafting trips down the Class III–IV rapids of the Mendoza River.
Aymara Av España 735 Mendoza ☎0261 420 2064, ⊚www.aymara.com.ar. Specializes in guided Aconcagua treks.
Campo Base Peatonal Sarmiento 229, Mendoza

☎0261 425 5511, ⊚campobase.com.ar. Offers adventure excursions that combine trekking, mountain biking and abseiling in one action-packed day.
Mr Hugo Urquiza 2288, Maipu ☎0261 497 4067, ⊚mrhugobikes.com. Organizes bicycle tours to wineries.
El Rincón de los Oscuros Av Los Cóndores, Potrerillos ☎0262 448 3030, ⊚rincondelososcuros .com.ar. Horseriding specialists.

1

ARRIVAL AND INFORMATION

By plane The airport (☎0261 520 6000) is 7km north of downtown. A taxi or *remise* to the city centre costs around AR$80.

Destinations Buenos Aires (9–13 daily; 1hr 50min); Córdoba (2 daily; 1hr 20min); Santiago de Chile (2 daily; 40min).

By bus The bus station (☎0261 431 5000) is just east of the centre on Av Gobernador Videla, at Av Acceso Este (RN7); a taxi to the centre costs AR$25.

Destinations Bariloche (1–3 daily; 18hr); Buenos Aires (every 30min from 5.30pm, also 7am & 2pm; 14–17hr); Córdoba (14–16 daily; 9–12hr); Salta (5 daily; 19hr); San Juan (hourly; 2hr 30min); San Rafael (hourly; 3hr 15min); Santiago de Chile (8 daily; 7hr).

Tourist information The city tourist office is on Garibaldi, at San Martín (daily 9am–9pm; ☎0261 420 1333), and the provincial tourist office is at San Martín 1143 (daily 9am–9pm; ☎0261 413 2100, ⓦturismo .mendoza.gov.ar). Ask staff for a list and map of wineries.

ACCOMMODATION

Mendoza has dozens of outstanding backpacker hostels, the best of which have gardens and swimming pools; all listed here include breakfast, kitchen, internet and tour-booking services. Book well in advance if travelling in early March, as the city packs out for the *Fiesta de la Vendimia* wine festival.

HOSTELS

Alamo Necochea 740 ☎0261 429 5565, ⓦhostelalamo .com. On a quiet residential street, this yellow mansion is a real godsend for those looking for a sociable but well-mannered backpackers' retreat. The massive supermarket opposite will delight self-caterers, as will the hostel's glassed-in dining area looking onto a Zen-like garden. Dorms AR$110, doubles AR$280

Campo Base Mitre 946 ☎0261 429 0707, ⓦhostelcampobase.com.ar. Although the dorms are a bit cramped, this well-located hostel is a hit with party people and Aconcagua climbers (treks are organized through the affiliated tour company). Dorms AR$100

Chill Inn Arístides Villanueva 385 ☎0261 420 1744, ⓦhostelchillinn.com. A modern and clean hostel smack in the middle of the city's main bar and restaurant strip. Dorms are a bit sterile, but the back garden with swimming pool and barbecue area is livelier. Extra points for the two very friendly and helpful owners. Dorms AR$130, doubles AR$420

★**Lao** Rioja 771 ☎0261 438 0454, ⓦlaohostel.com. The most inviting of the city's hostels, this English-run place is often full. Chilled-out but buzzing, it has plenty of common space, travel photography graces its walls, there's a large garden with a pool and hammocks, a roof terrace, wi-fi and very clean dorm rooms. Wine flows when the owner is feeling generous. Dorms AR$140, doubles AR$360

Square Independencia Mitre 1237 ☎0261 423 1806, ⓦsquareindependencia.com.ar. Boisterous party hostel in a gorgeous mansion. The location and common areas are among the best in the city; the bathrooms, sadly, are not. If you're sensitive to noise or alcohol, go elsewhere. Dorms AR$130, doubles AR$500

HOTELS

★**Confluencia Hostal** Av España 1512 ☎0261 429 0430, ⓦhostalconfluencia.com.ar. Perfect for couples who want more privacy and sophistication than your average hostel, this place offers spacious and clean doubles (and quadruples) with wooden floorboards and private bathrooms. There's a TV lounge and large roof terrace with mountain views. Breakfast included. AR$390

Quinta Rufino Rufino Ortega 142 ☎0261 420 4696, ⓦquintarufino.com. A B&B offering large rooms with private bathroom and cable TV in a converted villa. It's a short stroll to the city's bar strip. Breakfast included. AR$290

CAMPSITE

El Suizo Av Champagnat in El Challao, 6km northwest of Mendoza ☎0261 444 1991, ⓦcampingsuizo.com.ar. A shady spot for campers to pitch their tents, with a swimming pool, restaurant and outdoor cinema. Bus #115 runs there from Av Alem, at San Martín. Two people AR$150, additional person AR$50

EATING

Mendoza has some exceptional restaurants, many specializing in local produce, Pacific seafood and regional wine.

Anna Bistro Juan B Justo 161 ☎0261 425 1818, ⓦannabistro.com. Cocktail-sipping diners lounge outside on white leather couches amid fragrant foliage and romantic lighting at this top-notch French-run restaurant. The eclectic menu features standouts like prawn pasta (AR$137). Set lunches are good value (around AR$100). Daily 8am–1am.

★**Govinda's** San Martín 948, bus ride or taxi from centre ☎0261 424 3799, ⓦgovindavegetarian.com. Simply the best vegetarian restaurant in the city; load up your plate with lovingly prepared dishes from the gigantic buffet (AR$105/kg). No alcohol served. Daily 12.30–3.30pm & 7pm–midnight.

La Marchigiana Patricias Mendocinas 1550 ☎0261 423 0751, ⓦmarchigiana.com.ar. This airy, family affair is widely considered to be the city's best Italian restaurant and has very fair prices (mains start at under AR$100). Daily noon–3pm & 8pm–midnight, Fri until 12.30am, Sat until 1am.

El Mercadito Arístides Villanueva, at Viamonte ☎0261 463 8847. Feeling a bit beef and wine heavy? Order a freshly squeezed apple and cucumber juice (AR$27) to go

Azafrán Sarmiento 765 ☎0261 429 4200, ⓦazafranresto.com/home.html. From goat ravioli to trout with squid ink risotto, the dining experience at this lauded restaurant is pure gourmet. The sommelier will guide diners on a rummage in the wine cellar, where more than 450 vintages from 80 different vineyards are stocked. Mains AR$89–138. Daily noon–12.30am.

with your Ceasar salad (AR$65), soak up the sun at a table outside at this friendly restaurant and you will soon feel like a new person. Mon–Sat 12.30pm–midnight.

Mercado Central Las Heras between España and Patricias Mendocinas. This bustling indoor market is full of inexpensive cafés offering local dishes such as *humitas* and *empanadas*, and is a great place to try goodies such as Andean goat's cheeses. Most snacks AR$7. Mon–Sat 9am–1pm & 5–8pm; food court 9am–11pm.

★ **Tasca la Plaza** Montevideo 117 ☎0261 423 1403. Flickering candles set off the wooden floorboards, bright-red walls and funky *Mendocino* art at the city's coolest tapas bar and restaurant where you can indulge in a bottle of red (from AR$75) and bacon-wrapped shrimps (AR$99). Daily 7.30pm–midnight.

DRINKING AND NIGHTLIFE

Mendoza's bar scene is concentrated along trendy Aristides Villanueva, where pavement tables fill with drinkers on summer evenings. The best nightclubs are in outlying neighbourhoods like El Challao to the northwest, Las Heras to the north and Chacras de Coria to the south. Women generally get in free, and while *Mendocinos* like to party late, keep in mind that a city law stipulates that last entry is at 2.30am.

Apeteco San Juan, at Barraquero. A sophisticated crowd packs into this sleek, cavernous club on weekends. Following the midnight live music set, punters lose their cool on the dancefloor to a mixed soundtrack of electronica, rock, reggaeton and salsa. Free entry until 11pm, then AR$70 for men. Wed–Sat 10pm–5.30am.

Decimo Garibaldi 7, 10th floor of Edificio Gómez. Yuppie wine bar and restaurant *par excellence*. Set on the top floor of a downtown apartment block, it offers a winning combination of city and mountain views along with a hundred Argentine wines to wrap your palate around (small bottles from AR$55). Put on your glad rags and live the high life. Mon–Sat 6pm–3am.

Vines of Mendoza Belgrano, at Espejo ☎0261 438 1031, ⓦvinesofmendoza.com. A swanky wine-tasting room with more than forty wines from regional *bodegas*. Let the English-speaking staff talk you through a tasting session (from AR$150) or nurse a glass of *vino tinto* at the sleek bar. Mon–Sat 3–10pm.

DIRECTORY

Banks and exchange Banco de la Nación Argentina accepts foreign cards and has branches across the city, including San Martín, at Gutierrez, and España 1275. Cambio Express, at Espejo 58, and Cambio Santiago, at Av San Martín 119, will exchange foreign cash.

Car rental Alamo Nacional Rent, Pvo de la Reta 928 (☎0261 429 3111); Avis, Pvo de la Reta 914 (☎0261 420 3178); Hertz, Espejo 391 (☎0261 423 0225); Via Rent a Car, San Juan 931 (☎0261 429 0876).

Internet The WH Internet & Games chain has internet cafés at Las Heras 61 and España 1076.

Laundry Lavandería Necochea, 25 de Mayo 1357.

Post office San Martín, at Colón.

Shopping There is a handicraft market on Plaza Independencia every weekend. The upscale Mendoza Plaza shopping mall (ⓦwww.mendozaplazashopping.com), at

Try to make time (and room in the budget) for a trip out of town for a gourmet lunch among the vineyards at a nearby **bodega**: ask at the tourist office or pick up the *Vines of Mendoza* magazine for further listings.

Melipal Ruta 7km 1056, Agrelo, Luján de Cuyo; bus to Luján and then a taxi for AR$100 ☎0261 479 0202, ⓦwww.bodegamelipal.com. Surrounded by a moat and situated in a sleek building looking over the vines and Andes, this restaurant belongs to one of the region's smaller wineries and prepares gourmet Argentine food with an international touch. Try their five-course tasting menu (AR$495) with exciting dishes like citric terrine with *torrentes* gel and zucchini fritters on plum marmalade. Guided

tour and wine included. Mon–Fri 11am–5pm; Sat prior reservation only.

Ruca Malen Ruta Nacional 7km 1059, Luján de Cuyo ($AR100) ☎0261 15 454 0974, ⓦbodegarucamalen .com. The restaurant here looks out on to vineyards and mountains, and lunch is a belly-busting five-course degustation (AR$600), with each delectable plate – from smoked bacon with pine mushroom powder to honey and orange ice cream – perfectly paired with *bodega* wine. Lunch daily.

1

Av Acceso Este 3280 in Guaymallén, to the east of the city centre, has around 200 shops and restaurants, plus a cinema. **Spanish school** Intercultural, at Rep de Siria 241 (☎0261 429 0269, ⓦwww.spanishcourses.com.ar), offers one-week courses.

ALTA MONTAÑA

The cathedral-like peaks of the Parque Provincial Aconcagua lie just three hours west of Mendoza, easily visited on a popular day-trip dubbed the **ALTA MONTAÑA ROUTE**. Leaving behind verdant vineyards and climbing into barren hills, this scenic excursion follows the RN7 (the highway to Santiago de Chile), following the former Trans-Andean railway and the Río Mendoza into the spectacular Uspallata Valley, where *Seven Years in Tibet* was filmed. From the crossroads village of Uspallata (105km west of Mendoza), it's a further 65km to **Los Penitentes**, a winter ski resort with 28 pistes (☎0261 429 9953, ⓦlospenitentes.com), and, in summer, a base for Aconcagua climbers (see below). Some 6km west of Los Penitentes is one of the area's most photographed landmarks, the **Puente del Inca**, a natural stone bridge traversing the Río de las Cuevas at 2700m. Beneath it, thermal waters seep among the ruins of an abandoned 1940s spa resort. The route passes Parque Provincial Aconcagua and

ends at the Chilean border where a statue of **Cristo Redentor** (Christ the Redeemer) commemorates the 1902 peace pact between historic enemies.

PARQUE PROVINCIAL ACONCAGUA

At 6959m, **CERRO ACONCAGUA** – "the roof of the Americas" – lords it over the 710-square-kilometre Parque Provincial Aconcagua. The highest mountain in both the western and the southern hemispheres, Aconcagua's faces are ringed by five glistening glaciers. In 1985, the discovery of an **Inca mummy** at 5300m on Aconcagua's southwest face lent further weight to the theory that the Incas worshipped the mountain and offered it human sacrifices.

Inca worshippers have been replaced by ardent mountain climbers, who ascend in droves throughout summer. Only the most experienced attempt the **climb** without a professional guide. Taking into account acclimatization time, it should take at least thirteen days to reach the summit. There are three possible routes – south, west or east – with the least difficult being the western route, leaving from the Plaza de Mulas (4230m). For **route details** and advice, see ⓦaconcagua .mendoza.gov.ar. Easier **day hikes** are also

---

CLIMBING ACONCAGUA

To trek or climb in the Parque Provincial Aconcagua between mid-November and mid-March, you need to obtain a **permit** (bring your passport) from the Dirección de Recursos Naturales Renovables (mid-March to mid-Nov Mon–Fri 8am–1pm; mid-Nov to mid-March Mon–Fri 8am–6pm, Sat & Sun 9am–1pm; ☎0261 425 8751), at San Martín 1143, 2nd floor, in Mendoza. Foreign trekkers pay between US$90 and US$760 between December and March (depending on the date and length of trek). The rest of the year snow cover makes the climb extremely dangerous; the fee at this time is around US$1150 plus a staggering US$30,000 deposit and climbers must apply for a special permit (for update see website ⓦaconcagua.mendoza.gov.ar).

TOUR OPERATORS

Owing to the mountain's unpredictable weather (storms claim lives every year), climbers are advised to go on organized trips with experienced local guides. The following are Mendoza-based operators that specialize in Aconcagua trips. Fernando Grajales Expeditions and Aconcagua Trek can make the arrangements for mule hire.
Acomara Rivadavia 430 ☎0261 425 1983, ⓦaconcaguaexpeditions.com.

Aconcagua Trek Barcala 484 ☎0261 15 466 5825, ⓦaconcaguatrek.com.
Aymara España 735 ☎0261 424 4773, ⓦaconcaguaaymara.com.
Fernando Grajales Expeditions ☎0261 428 3157, ⓦgrajales.net.
Inka Expediciones Juan B Justo 345 ☎0261 425 0871, ⓦinka.com.ar.

possible in the park as well as multi-day treks to base camps and mountain *refugios*.

ARRIVAL AND DEPARTURE

By bus Buttini operates three buses daily from Mendoza to the base camps at Los Horcones and Punta de Vacas.

ACCOMMODATION

For accommodation at or near the base camps, there are options at Puente del Inca (where many people spend a couple of days acclimatizing), Las Cuevas and Los Penitentes.

Hostel Campo Base Penitentes Los Penitentes ☎0261 425 5511, ⓦ penitentes.com.ar. This lively, 27-bed hostel, with well-equipped kitchen, is a jumping-off point for organized ski trips in the winter and Aconcagua climbs in the summer. Breakfast and dinner included (prices lower in Oct–May). Dorms AR$281

Plaza de Mulas ☎0261 425 1983, ⓦ aconcagua expeditions.com. It is possible to overnight here on day two of the mountain trail. Three meals a day can be arranged for an extra fee (AR$1342). Dorms AR$850

Refugio El Nico Ruta 7 s/n Puente del Inca ☎0261 15 592 0736, ⓦ elnicohostel.com. A simple and small hostel just 1.5km from the Aconcagua park entrance. It has heated dorms and communal bathrooms. Excursions can be arranged in summer and winter. Dorms AR$140, doubles AR$290

EATING AND DRINKING

Make the most of hostel kitchens, and bring plenty of food supplies, as refuelling opportunities are few and far between once inside the park itself. During ski season, the resort hotels of Penitentes offer decent, if unspectacular, food, while snacks and hot drinks can be found at Puente del Inca's outdoor market.

SAN RAFAEL AND AROUND

In the heart of wine country, the laidback city of **SAN RAFAEL**, 230km south of the provincial capital, likes to think of itself as a smaller, friendlier version of Mendoza; its wide, flat streets are filled with cyclists and its leafy plazas are squeaky clean. The city itself offers few distractions, beyond strolling around the main square, **Plaza San Martín**, and visiting the **Museo de Historia Natural** (daily: summer 7am–8pm; winter 8am–7pm; AR$5), on Isla Diamante, 6km south of the centre, where the pre-Columbian displays include ceramics from Ecuador and a mummified child dating from 40 AD.

There are, however, worthwhile sights just beyond the city itself in the San Rafael department, including six hundred square kilometres of vineyards and around eighty **bodegas**. Most of the wineries are small, family-run affairs; the tourist office has a list of those open to the public. For **white-water rafting** enthusiasts, the **Cañon del Atuel**, a short journey to the southwest, is one of the top destinations in the country for riding the rapids.

ARRIVAL AND DEPARTURE

By plane San Rafael Airport is 5km west of downtown, with one daily flight to and from Buenos Aires. There are buses to the centre (AR$5); a taxi costs around AR$55.

By bus The centrally located bus terminal is at C Géneral Paz, at Av Granaderos.

Destinations Buenos Aires (4 daily; 13hr); Las Leñas (June–Sept 1 daily, Dec–Feb 3 weekly on Tues, Thurs & Sat; 2hr 40min); Malargüe (3 daily; 2hr 30min); Mendoza (hourly; 3hr 15min).

INFORMATION AND TOURS

Tourist information The friendly tourist office is on Av Hipólito Yrigoyen, at Balloffet (Mon–Fri 8am–9pm, Sat & Sun 9am–9pm; ☎0260 442 4217, ⓦ sanrafaelturismo .gov.ar).

Tour operator Risco Viajes (Av Hipólito Yrigoyen 284; ☎0260 443 6439, ⓦ riscoviajes.com) is a San Rafael-based tour operator for adventurous types. Offers everything from one-day wine-tasting trips (AR$560) and two-day excursions to climb Cerro El Nevado (AR$3400 including accommodation), to mountain-biking and climbing adventures in the surrounding peaks.

ACCOMMODATION

San Rafael's accommodation options lack the range and quality of Mendoza.

Camping El Parador Isla Río Diamante, 6km south of downtown, ☎0260 443 6756. If you're camping, make for this shady site. Per person AR$30, plus per tent an extra AR$8

Tierrasoles Hostel Alsina 245 ☎0260 443 3449, ⓦ tierrasoles.com.ar. An HI-hostel run by two friends offering modest dorms, a simple breakfast and wi-fi. You have to be a contortionist to use the toilets, though. Dorms AR$100, doubles AR$300

Trotamundos Hostel Barcala 300 ☎0260 443 2795, ⓦ trotamundoshostel.com.ar. A cool hostel in a converted historical building with a large, open-plan kitchen and plenty of activities laid on for guests. Includes breakfast and wi-fi access. Dorms AR$120, doubles AR$360

You! Hipólito Yrigoyen 56 ☎0260 442 2177. This bright hotel on the main drag has spacious, although a bit soulless, rooms arranged around a quiet courtyard. Cable TV, breakfast and parking included. AR$480

EATING AND DRINKING

San Rafael springs to life post-siesta, when locals pack the restaurants, bars, nightclubs and ice-cream parlours along Hipólito Yrigoyen.

Jockey Club Belgrano 330 ☎0260 443 0237. Upscale and with an Old-World feel, this much-loved restaurant serves well-prepared, filling mains including good pasta, beef and chicken dishes. Mains starting from AR$65. Daily 8–11pm.

Pettra Hipólito Yrigoyen 1750 ☎0260 443 9837. The most popular *parrilla* in the city, where you can tuck into a massive steak (AR$125) straight from the outdoor *asado* and quaff local wine. Daily 1–4pm & 8.30pm–1am; Mon dinner only.

La Quinta Hipólito Yrigoyen 1850. The dancefloor at this popular bar is often shaking, thanks to a mixed soundtrack of rock, retro and electronica. On steamy nights, the drinking spills into the garden. Occasional live music. Fri & Sat until late.

Tienda del Sol Hipólito Yrigoyen 1663 ☎0260 442 5022, ⌨tiendadelsol.net. A hip, modern restaurant with outdoor tables, serving imaginative beef, chicken and fish mains (around AR$90), along with a wide range of regional wines. Daily 12.30–2.30pm & 8pm–midnight.

LAS LEÑAS

Some 180km southwest of San Rafael and 445km south of Mendoza, the exclusive ski resort of **LAS LEÑAS** is to winter what Uruguay's Punta del Este is to summer – a chic party playground for *porteño* socialites. Between June and September (snow permitting), they flock here on week-long packages. As well as après-ski glamour, the setting of Las Leñas is exquisite. The resort, which sits at 2240m, has the dramatic Cerro Las Leñas (4351m) towering over its 29 runs and 13 lifts. Pistes range in difficulty from nursery slopes to hair-raising black runs, with night-time and cross-country skiing also possible.

In summer, Las Leñas transforms into an outdoor action hub, offering horseriding, white-water rafting, trekking, climbing, abseiling, 4WD tours, mountain biking, summer skiing and even scuba diving in high-altitude lakes.

ARRIVAL AND INFORMATION

By bus During the ski season there are daily buses from Mendoza (6hr), Malargüe (1hr 30min) and San Rafael (3hr). Chartered direct buses also run from Buenos Aires twice a week (14hr; book through the central tourist office).

Tourist information The resort's office for booking ski packages and accommodation is in Buenos Aires at Bartolomé Mitre 401, 4th floor (Mon–Fri 9am–7pm; ☎011 4819 6000, ⌨laslenas.com).

Lift ticket office Mid-June to late Sept daily 8.30am–5.30pm (☎0260 447 1100 ext 1130, ⌨laslenas.com). Daily lift ticket prices range seasonally from AR$395 to AR$585.

ACCOMMODATION

Las Leñas accommodation needs to be booked through the resort's central Buenos Aires office; there is only one low-priced lodging. If you are in a group, the most affordable places are the self-catering apartments known as "dormy houses": *Laquir*, *Lihuén*, *Milla* and *Payén* cost around AR$1500/night and accommodate up to five people.

Leñas Hostel ☎0260 447 1172 ✉hostel@laslenas.com. This 72-bed modern hostel is Las Leñas' only budget accommodation, so book ahead if you're tight on cash but not keen on commuting to get to the slopes. It has ten shared rooms with all the basic amenities: lockers, shared kitchen and communal bathrooms and showers. Dorms AR$380

EATING AND DRINKING

Innsbruck A log cabin *confitería* in the ski village where you can buy expensive fast food (a steak is AR$170) to enjoy over a beer from a terrace with piste views. Open for breakfast, lunch and dinner, as well as cocktails until the small hours. Winter only.

El Refugio In the central Pirámide building ☎0260 447 1100, ext 1238. Dip into cheese fondue (AR$180) at this pricey French restaurant. Reservations necessary. Daily 10am–1am in peak winter season.

UFO Point The appetizing pizzas served here have earned this restaurant a devoted following, but at around AR$170 (serves two), they're not cheap. The restaurant is open for breakfast, lunch and dinner; at night it turns into a club with electronic music.

MALARGÜE

Set at the arid base of the Andes, 186km southwest of San Rafael, **MALARGÜE** is a small, nondescript town that's a jumping-off point for some of Argentina's most remarkable scenery. In winter its *raison d'être* is as an affordable base for skiing at the resort of Las Leñas (see above), while in summer the surrounding landscape offers ample opportunities for hiking, horseriding, fishing and white-water rafting. Worthwhile day-trips from town are to the underground limestone caves of **Caverna de las Brujas** (73km southwest), the volcanic wonderland of **La Payunia** (208km south), and to **Laguna de Llancanelo** (see below).

WHAT TO SEE AND DO

Malargüe's flat, compact centre is easy to get your head around: the wide main drag is the RN40, known in town as **Avenida San Martín**. Here you'll find the tourist office, shops and the main square, **Plaza General San Martín**. Just south of the tourist office is the landscaped greenery of **Parque del Ayer** ("Park of Yesteryear"), filled with sculptures and native trees. Opposite, you can take a free guided tour at the **Observatorio Pierre Auger** (Mon–Fri 5–6pm; ☎ 0260 447 1562, ⓦ www.auger .org.ar), an astrophysics centre that studies cosmic rays.

ARRIVAL AND DEPARTURE

By bus Malargüe's bus terminal (☎ 0260 447 0690) is on Av Gral Roca, at Esquibel Aldao, five blocks south and three west of Plaza San Martín.

Destinations Las Leñas (1 daily during ski season; 1hr 30min); Mendoza (10 daily; 6hr); San Rafael (10 daily; 2hr 40min).

INFORMATION AND TOURS

Tourist information The tourist office (daily 8am–10pm; ☎ 0260 447 1659, ⓦ malargue.gov.ar) is on the RN40 four blocks north of the plaza.

Tour operators Many local companies run tours to La Payunia, Laguna de Llancanelo (when not dried out) and Caverna de las Brujas, as well as horseriding and other adventure activities. Check out Karen Travel at Av San Martín 54 (☎ 0260 447 2226, ⓦ karentravel.com.ar), where you can also rent 4WDs.

ACCOMMODATION

Malargüe has plenty of affordable places to stay, including a handful of well-run hostels. Prices rise significantly during winter.

Cabañas Newen Mapu Av Roca, at Villa del Milagro ☎ 0260 469 7724. Buy yourself some space with a two-storey cabaña (sleeps 6) complete with cable TV, full kitchen, fireplace and mountain views. Prices go down in the low season. Cabaña <u>AR$900</u>

Camping Polideportivo Capdevila, at Aldao ☎ 0260 447 0691. This municipal campsite is conveniently located in the north part of town, but is open summer only. Camping/person <u>AR$5</u>, plus for the tent <u>AR$30</u>

Hostel La Caverna Cte Rodríguez 445 Este ☎ 0260 447 2569. This hostel has a spacious common area and plenty of dorm beds. The self-catering apartment out back is ideal for groups. There is laundry service and wi-fi. Dorms <u>AR$150</u>, doubles <u>AR$380</u>

Ecohostel Colonia Pehuenche I, Finca N. 65, 5km south of town (free transfer from the Choique Turismo Alternativo office on San Martín, at Rodríguez) ☎ 0260 15 440 2439, ⓦ hostelmalargue.com. There's some serious stargazing and R&R to be had at this rustic HI hostel set on an organic farm. Home-made meals and horseriding excursions offered. Dorms <u>AR$135</u>, doubles <u>AR$390</u>

EATING AND DRINKING

El Bodegón de Maria Rufino Ortega, at General Villegas. Trout and meat get all the attention at this welcoming rustic-style restaurant. Mains from AR$72. Daily 11.30–4pm & 8pm–midnight.

Cuyam-Co 8km west of Malargüe in El Dique. Catch your own meal and have it cooked to perfection at this trout farm. AR$160 for full menu and AR$80 to fish for your dish and then have it cooked. Daily noon–10.30pm.

Río Grande RN40 Norte ☎ 0260 447 1589. The restaurant in this upmarket hotel serves decent steaks (AR$80), pastas (AR$60) and trout ($AR100). Daily for breakfast, lunch & dinner.

AROUND MALARGÜE

Some 65km southeast of Malargüe is the nature reserve of **LAGUNA DE LLANCANELO**, a vast high-altitude lagoon famous for its abundant birdlife. Alongside the flamingos that flock here in their thousands, herons and black-neck swans can be easily spotted. Also look out for the *coipo*, a rodent similar in appearance to the capybara but a little smaller in size. The best way to visit the reserve is with a guided tour (see above); note, however, that it can become dried out, so check with operators on its condition.

The **CAVERNA DE LAS BRUJAS** ("Witches' Cave") is an incredible limestone cave filled with mesmerizing many-coloured rock formations, including **stalactites** and **stalagmites**. The cave, located 73km southwest of Malargüe and 8km along a dirt road off the RN40, is within a provincial park and

1

is staffed by *guardaparques*. Guided visits (AR$150) are restricted to nine people at a time and are the only way to see the various underground chambers. The **temperature** inside the grotto can be 20°C lower than outside, so be sure to wrap up.

Continuing along the RN40, you'll reach the entrance to **LA PAYUNIA** at El Zampal. This expansive, wildlife-rich reserve spans 4500 square kilometres. Flaxen grasslands, black lava flows and eight hundred threatening-looking volcanoes (the highest concentration of volcanic cones in the world) provide a starkly wild backdrop for the guanaco, puma and condor that call it home. The best way to see La Payunia is on an organized **day-trip from Malargüe** (see p.106) that takes in the Caverna de las Brujas along the way.

SAN JUAN

SAN JUAN is a modern, low-rise provincial capital. In 1944, one of South America's most powerful earthquakes (8.5 on the Richter scale) razed the city, killing more than ten thousand people. Essentially a poorer, smaller and less attractive version of its southerly neighbour Mendoza, San Juan is unlikely to capture your imagination. It does, however, make a convenient base for sampling the fruits of nearby wineries as well as for excursions to the sculptural desert landscapes of **Parque Provincial Ischigualasto** and the surreal rock formations of **Parque Nacional Talampaya**. Try to avoid visiting in the summer, when *Sanjuaninos* cope with the midday heat by taking long, sluggish siestas.

WHAT TO SEE AND DO

The leafy Plaza 25 de Mayo, flanked by a couple of inviting cafés, marks the city centre. On its northwestern side, the modern cathedral's 50m-high brick campanile is a nod to St Mark's in Venice. If the mood takes, climb the **bell tower** (daily 9.30am–1pm & 5–9.30pm; AR$20) for great city and countryside vistas. Not far away at Sarmiento 21 Sur, opposite the tourist office, is the whitewashed childhood

home of former Argentine president **Domingo Faustino Sarmiento** (1811–88), now a museum (April–Oct Mon–Fri 9am–7.30pm, Sat & Sun 10.30am–4pm; Nov–March Mon–Fri 9am–8.30pm, Sat & Sun 11am–6pm; AR$20; guided tours every hour). Although damaged in the 1944 earthquake, the house has been lovingly restored and displays belongings and paraphernalia from Sarmiento's eventful life.

For a more artistic day head to **Museo Franklin Rawson**, Av Libertador 862 Oeste (summer daily noon–9pm; winter Tues–Sun noon–8pm; AR$10; ☎0264 420 0598), where fine art and contemporary photography by local and national artists are displayed in an airy glass-walled building.

Finally, if all that has left your mouth dry, drop into the historic **Bodega Graffigna** (Mon–Sat 11am–4pm; free; ☎0264 421 4227), at Colón 1342 Norte, which houses the Museo de Vino Santiago Graffigna, and a wine bar where you can sample provincial vintages.

ARRIVAL AND DEPARTURE

By plane Las Chacritas Airport (☎0264 425 4134) is 12km east of the city centre. A taxi downtown costs around AR$90. Destinations Buenos Aires (3–4 daily; 1hr 50min).

By bus The bus station (Estados Unidos 492 Sur; ☎0264 422 1604) is eight blocks east of Plaza 25 de Mayo. Destinations Buenos Aires (7 daily; 16hr); Córdoba (5 daily; 8hr); Mendoza (hourly; 2hr 30min); San Rafael (2 daily; 5hr 30min); Valle Fértil (3 daily; 4hr). Most long-distance buses, including two daily services to Santiago de Chile, require a change in Mendoza.

INFORMATION AND TOURS

Tourist information The tourist office at Sarmiento 24 Sur has good city and provincial information (daily 8am–8pm; ☎0264 421 0004, ⓦ www.turismo.sanjuan.gov.ar).

Tour operators Companies offering Ischigualasto and Talampaya excursions include CH Travel, at Gral Acha 714 Sur (☎0264 427 4160, ⓦchtraveltur.com.ar); and Yafar Destinos, at Rioja 428 Sur (☎0264 420 4052, ⓦyafardestinos.com.ar).

ACCOMMODATION

Cheap accommodation is of a reasonable standard in San Juan.

Camping Don Bosco 3km east on RN20 ☎0264 425 3663. A conveniently located campsite with hot showers

and a swimming pool. Catch bus #19 from the centre.
Camping/person AR$100, tent AR$50
Jardín Petit 25 de Mayo 345 Este ☎0264 421 1825,
ⓦjardinpetithotel.com. A welcoming hotel with cosy, simple
rooms and an inviting patio and pool. Breakfast included and
discounts can sometimes be arranged. AR$400
El Refugio Ramón and Cajal, at San Luis ☎0264 421
380, ⓦelrefugioaparthotel.com.ar. A peaceful and
relaxing apartment hotel in a quiet neighbourhood
thirteen blocks from the city centre. Rooms are spotless
and arranged around an atrium with pool. Breakfast and
wi-fi included. Doubles AR$500
San Juan Hostel Av Córdoba 317 Este ☎0264 4201
835, ⓦsanjuanhostel.com. Helpful staff, a central
location and a comfortable common area make up for
the depressing dorms and basic bathrooms at this
backpackers' pad. Includes breakfast and internet. Dorms
AR$90, doubles AR$260
Zonda Hostel Caseros 486 Sur ☎0264 420 1009,
ⓦzondahostel.com.ar. Conveniently located four blocks
from the bus station, this 35-bed HI hostel has a TV room,
patio, kitchen, free internet and breakfast. Dorms AR$90,
doubles AR$250

EATING AND DRINKING

Antonio Gómez e Hijos Supermercado, General Acha at
Córdoba. The heaving paellas (AR$75) draw the lunchtime
crowd at this Spanish-centric market stall. Lunch only.
Remolacha Av José Ignacio de la Roza Oeste, at Sarmiento.
Traditional and hugely popular *parrilla* with a vast range of
meaty treats to be enjoyed indoors or alfresco. Vegetarians
won't starve either, thanks to some decent meat-free pasta
dishes, mixed vegetable grills and interesting salads. Mains
from AR$60. Daily noon–4pm & 8pm–3am.
El Rincón de Nápoli Rivadavia 175 Oeste. Noisy and
cheerful fast-service restaurant whipping up pizza, pasta,
burgers and plenty of grilled meat (mains AR$45). Daily
7am–2am.
De Sánchez Rivadavia 55 Oeste. The city's classiest restaurant
serves beautifully prepared salmon (AR$176) and beef
(AR$165) with a fine selection of local wines by the glass and
bottle. After the meal, browse the adjoining book and music
shop. Mon–Fri 12.30–5pm & 9pm–12.30am, Sat dinner only.
★ Soychú Av José Ignacio de la Roza 223 Oeste. Slip into
something elasticated before gorging yourself on one of
the continent's best vegetarian all-you-can-eat buffets
(AR$52). Don't pass up the offer of a freshly squeezed juice.
Mon–Sat lunch & dinner, lunch only Sun.

DIRECTORY

Banks and exchange Several banks on General Acha
accept foreign cards, including Banco Macro at Gral Acha
41, HSBC at Gral Acha Sur 320 and Banco de la Nación
Argentina at Av Rioja Sur 218.

Car rental Avis, Sarmiento 164 Sur (☎0264 420 0571).
Internet Late opening and good connections at Cyber le
Red, Tucumán Norte 910; Cyber 51 at Av Libertador General
San Martín Oeste 51; and Upe at Mendoza Sur 21.
Laundry Laverap, Rivadavia 498 Oeste.
Post office Av José Ignacio de la Roza 259 Este.

AROUND SAN JUAN

The UNESCO World Heritage-listed
parks of **Ischigualasto** (better known as
Valle de la Luna) and **Talampaya** lie in the
provinces of San Juan and La Rioja
respectively. The former is known for its
other-worldly rock formations, the latter its
red sandstone cliffs. Located close together,
both can be visited on day-trips from San
Juan, but the sleepy village of **San Agustín
de Valle Fértil**, 250km northeast, is a much
closer base. Some **tour operators** pack both
parks into one day-long excursion,
stopping off at Talampaya in the morning
when the wind is low and the light best
illuminates the red in the sandstone, before
journeying 93km to visit Ischigualasto in
the mid- to late afternoon.

San Agustín de Valle Fértil
Set in a valley carved out by the Río San
Juan and surrounded by olive groves and
sheep pasture, **SAN AGUSTÍN DE VALLE
FÉRTIL** is a verdant oasis amid desert-like
terrain. Take cash as the only cashpoint
regularly runs dry and cards are rarely
accepted.

ARRIVAL AND INFORMATION

By bus The bus terminal is on Mitre, at Entre Rios; there
are three daily services from San Juan (4hr) and three
weekly from La Rioja (4hr).
Tourist information The super-friendly tourist office
(daily 7am–midnight; ☎02646 420 104,
ⓦischigualastovallefertil.org) is at Plaza San Agustín,
on General Acha, and can advise on tours and transport
to the parks, as well as bicycle and horseriding
excursions to view pre-Hispanic petroglyphs in the
nearby mountains.
Tour operator Turismo Vesa, at Mitre s/n (☎02646 420
143, ⓦturismovesa.com), offers daily trips from Valle
Fértil to Ischigualasto and Talampaya.

ACCOMMODATION

Altos del Valle Rivadavia 114 ☎02646 420 194,
ⓦaltosdelvallesj.com.ar. A cosy and intimate apartment

1

hotel with clean en-suite rooms facing a peaceful garden with a small swimming pool in the corner. Not really a budget option, but good value. Doubles __ARS450__

Camping Municipal Rivadavia, at Ischigualasto ☎ 0264 15 5172 411. Managed by a lovely couple, this campsite has the friendliest ambience in town. Situated by the river with plenty of shade. An extra ARS40 for the first night. Camping/person __ARS40__

Campo Base Valle de la Luna Tucumán s/n between San Luis & Libertador ☎ 02646 420 063, ✆ hostelvalledelaluna .com.ar. This modest but welcoming hostel has a kitchen, TV lounge, free breakfast and tour advice. Dorms __ARS95__

Eco Hostel Mendoza 766 Norte ☎ 02646 420 147. A cooling swimming pool and nightly tango lessons make this basic hostel popular with backpackers. Two blocks from the bus station. Dorms __ARS100__, doubles __ARS200__

★ **Hostería Valle Fértil** Rivadavia 5400 ☎ 02646 420 015, ✆ alkazarhotel.com.ar. The village's most inviting accommodation, thanks to its setting on a breezy hillside overlooking the Dique San Agustín reservoir, though it looks a bit sorry for itself these days. Some of the small, modern rooms have lake views. There's a restaurant and guests can use the swimming pool in the hostería's cabaña complex down the hill. __ARS452__

EATING AND NIGHTLIFE

La Cocina de Zulma Tucumán 1576 ☎ 0264 154 508 026. Tuck into pesto pasta served with steak for a bargain ARS75. Daily 11am–4pm & 7.30pm–midnight.

La Gran Picada Rivadavia s/n, at Tucumán ☎ 02646 420 267. The only cervecería and decent bar in town. Has plenty of beverages to cool you down on a hot day. Daily noon–3pm & 7pm–midnight.

Hostería Valle Fértil The restaurant here is open to non-guests in summer (for dinner only) and serves unpretentious dishes such as omelettes, salads and soups (mains from ARS60). It's the only restaurant in the town to accept cards. Daily 8.30–11pm.

Parque Provincial Ischigualasto

Sculpted by more than two million years of erosion, wind and water, the **PARQUE PROVINCIAL ISCHIGUALASTO**, otherwise known as the Valle de la Luna (Moon Valley), is San Juan's most visited attraction. Set in a desert valley between two mountain ranges some 80km north of Valle Fértil, it is considered one of the most significant **dinosaur graveyards** on the planet. Skeletons dating from the Triassic era around two hundred million years ago have been unearthed here.

Given its size (150 square kilometres), you need a **car** to explore the park properly; rangers accompany visitors in convoy on a bumpy 45km circuit of the park's highlights (2–3hr), imparting explanations of its paleontological history, photogenic moonscapes and precarious sandstone rock formations. The southern section resembles the arid lunar landscapes of Cappadocia in Turkey, with surreally shaped rock formations dubbed El Submarino (the submarine), El Esfinge (the sphinx) and Cancha de Bolas (bowling alley); further north on the circuit lie stark white fields strewn with petrified tree trunks. If you're lucky, you might catch a glimpse of hares, red foxes, armadillos, lizards, guanacos, snakes and condors.

INFORMATION AND TOURS

Park information The park entrance, where there's a helpful guardaparque post, is along a signposted road off the RP510 at Los Baldecitos. Entrance (daily: April–Sept 9am–4pm; Oct–March 8am–5pm) is ARS160/person and includes a 3hr tour following a ranger in your own vehicle. An extra ARS420 buys you a range of special tours, including 2hr guided bicycle excursions, full-moon night tours and 3hr treks to the top of Cerro Morado (1748m), with tremendous views of the park. Make use of the toilet facilities and cafés at the entrance, as there are none within the park.

By bus The easiest way to visit the park is on an organized tour. To get there independently, Empresa Vallecito buses from San Juan to La Rioja run on Mon, Wed & Fri and pass the Los Baldecitos checkpoint, a 5km walk to the park entrance. It is sometimes possible to accompany rangers on a tour of the park, or hire a vehicle at the entrance, but always check this in advance before showing up.

ACCOMMODATION

Campers can pitch their tents for ARS40 next to the park visitors' centre, where there is also a bathroom and small café. Most people spend the night in nearby Valle Fértil (see p.109) and get a transfer to the park with one of the village's tour operators.

Parque Nacional Talampaya

Familiar from regular appearances on posters promoting Argentine tourism, the smooth sandstone cliffs and surreal rock formations of **PARQUE NACIONAL TALAMPAYA** are even more eye-boggling in reality. The centrepiece of the park is a 220-million-year-old **canyon**, with 180m-high rust-red sandstone cliffs rising on either side, rendering everything in between puny and insignificant. At the centre of the canyon, armadillos and grey foxes scurry among groves of cacti and native trees in a lush **botanical garden**. Elsewhere, erosion has carved out towering columns and gravity-defying **rock formations** where condors and eagles have found nesting sites. Other park highlights include a series of pre-Hispanic **petroglyphs** and **pictographs** etched onto gigantic rock faces. Thought to be around a thousand years old, the etchings depict llamas, pumas, hunters, stepped pyramids and phallic symbols.

INFORMATION AND TOURS

Park information The closest urban centre to the park is Villa Unión, an entirely forgettable town in La Rioja province, 55km away along the RP26. Organized tours from San Juan, Valle Fértil or Villa Unión are the best option, as private vehicles are not allowed. If you want to visit the park independently, the *guardería* (daily: May–Oct 8.30am–6pm; Nov–April 8am–6.30pm; AR$80 entrance fee; ☏03825 470 397, ⓦtalampaya.com) is staffed year-round and you can explore on foot (not recommended) or take an excursion with an official guide in their truck (2hr 30min, AR$235/ person; 6hr, AR$435/person).

By bus Buses from Villa Unión to La Rioja and Valle Fértil can drop you off on the main road (check when the last bus goes past or you'll be stuck overnight).

ACCOMMODATION AND EATING

There is a basic, windswept campsite (AR$25/person) next to the *guardería*; it can get brutally cold at night. A small shop here sells snacks and simple meals.

The Lake District

The Argentine **LAKE DISTRICT** in northern Patagonia is an unspoiled region of azure glacial lakes, pristine rivers, snow-clad mountains, extinct volcanoes and verdant alpine forests. Dominated until the late nineteenth century by the indigenous Mapuche people, the Lake District is now Argentina's top year-round vacation destination – the place to go for hiking, camping, fishing, watersports, biking, climbing and skiing.

A series of spectacular national parks runs down the region's serrated Andean spine, providing easy access to the wilderness. The northernmost of Patagonia's national parks is **Parque Nacional Lanín** in Neuquén province, accessible from both the sleepy fishing town of **Junín de los Andes** or its dressier neighbour **San Martín de los Andes**. As you head south, the dazzling 110km route between San Martín de los Andes and the upmarket village of **Villa La Angostura** affords roadside vistas of snowcapped peaks reflected in picture-perfect lakes as well as the first glimpse of the gigantic **Parque Nacional Nahuel Huapi**.

The route continues south to the lakeside party town of **Bariloche**, the region's transport hub and base for hiking in **Nahuel Huapi** in summer, skiing in winter, and gorging on chocolate and locally brewed beer all year round. Further south, in the province of Chubut, the dusty town of **Esquel** is within day-trip distance of the **Parque Nacional Los Alerces**, a dramatic wilderness area of lakes, rivers, glaciers and thousand-year-old alerce trees; it also boasts one of the world's most famous trains, the **Old Patagonian Express**.

PARQUE NACIONAL LANÍN

The imposing snow-clad cone of extinct Volcán Lanín rises 3776m at the centre of its namesake **PARQUE NACIONAL LANÍN** (entrance AR$80). Lanín sits on the Chilean border, spanning 4120 square kilometres of varied Andean terrain. Fishing enthusiasts flock to its glacial lakes and trout-filled rivers, campers enjoy lakeside pitches at free or Mapuche-run campsites, while trekkers take advantage of the park's hiking trails. Forests of monkey-puzzle trees (also known as araucaria or *pehuén*) are the trademark of the northern section of the park. Volcano views are best from **Lago Huechulafquen**, 22km northwest of Junín de los Andes.

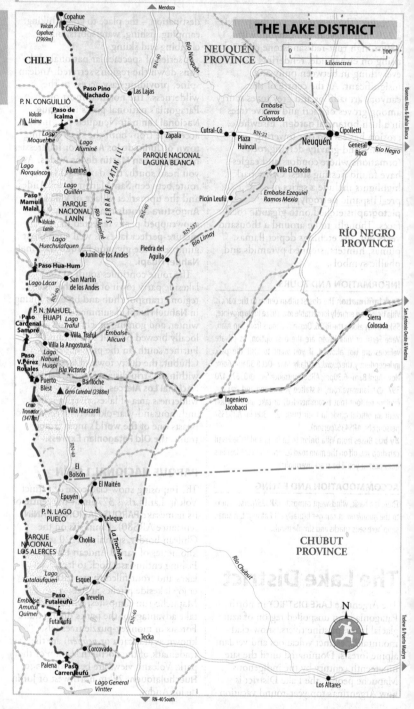

THE LAKE DISTRICT

0 — 100
kilometres

CHILE

NEUQUÉN PROVINCE

RÍO NEGRO PROVINCE

CHUBUT PROVINCE

Mendoza

Copahue
Volcán Copahue (2969m)
Caviahue
Paso Pino Hachado
Las Lajas
Río Neuquén
RN-40
Embalse Cerros Colorados
Cipolletti
P. N. CONGUILLÍO
Volcán Llaima
Paso de Icalma
Lago Moquehue
Zapala
Cutral-Có
Plaza Huincul
RN-22
Neuquén
General Roca
Río Negro
Lago Aluminé
PARQUE NACIONAL LAGUNA BLANCA
Lago Norquinco
Aluminé
SIERRA DE CATAN LIL
Villa El Chocón
Lago Quillén
Paso Mamuil Malal
PARQUE NACIONAL LANÍN
Río Aluminé
RN-40
Embalse Ezequiel Ramos Mexia
Volcán Lanín
Picún Leufú
RN-237
Lago Huechulafquen
Río Limay
Junín de los Andes
Paso Hua-Hum
Piedra del Aguila
Lago Lácar
San Martín de los Andes
RN-40
Sierra Colorada
P. N. NAHUEL HUAPI
Lago Traful
Paso Cardenal Samoré
Embalse Alicurá
Villa Traful
Villa la Angostura
Paso V. Pérez Rosales
Lago Nahuel Huapi
Isla Victoria
Puerto Blest
Bariloche
Cerro Catedral (2388m)
Cerro Tronador (3478m)
Villa Mascardi
Ingeniero Jacobacci
RN-40
El Bolsón
El Maitén
Epuyén
P. N. LAGO PUELO
Leleque
Cholila
La Trochita
CHUBUT PROVINCE
PARQUE NACIONAL LOS ALERCES
Lago Futalaufquen
Río Chubut
Esquel
Paso Futaleufú
Trevelin
RN-40
Embalse Amutul Quimei
Futaleufú
Tecka
Corcovado
Palena
Paso Carrenleufú
Lago General Vintter
Los Altares

Buenos Aires & Bahía Blanca

San Antonio Oeste & Viedma

Trelew & Puerto Madryn

N

RN-40 South

Lanín's southern sector is best explored from **San Martín de los Andes** (see below), set on the eastern shores of the park's **Lago Lácar**, or on the nearby section of the Seven Lakes Route (see box, p.116). Optimal visiting months are from October to mid-May, when there are organized excursions and regular buses.

JUNÍN DE LOS ANDES

It is impossible to avoid trout in pint-sized **JUNÍN DE LOS ANDES**; they not only populate the Río Chimehuín, but decorate every street sign and dominate every menu. Junín is well positioned for tours to the **Parque Nacional Lanín**, in particular the area around **Puerto Canoa**, the main base for treks around the volcano and boat trips on **Lago Huechulafquen**. Castelli (☎02972 491 557) runs buses to Puerto Canoa from Junín twice daily in summer (1hr; AR$57.50), skirting alongside the lake and passing campsites and fishing spots such as the **Boca del Chimehuín** along the way.

For something to do in town, take a stroll around the **Vía Christi** sculpture walkway, which starts at the base of Cerro de la Cruz, a fifteen-minute walk west of Plaza San Martín at the end of Avenida Antártida Argentina. A path winds through a pine-forested hillside dotted with sculptures and mosaics depicting the Stations of the Cross, which fuse Catholic and Mapuche symbolism. If you are thwarted by bad weather, check out the **Paseo Artesanal** instead. Behind the tourism office on the main square various cabins (daily 10am–1pm & 5–9pm) sell Mapuche crafts alongside woollen knits and handmade wooden crockery.

ARRIVAL AND INFORMATION

By plane Chapelco Airport (☎02972 428 388), which Junín shares with San Martín de los Andes, is 19km south of town. A taxi to the centre costs around AR$300; on your return, the hourly bus run by Castelli between Junín and San Martín will drop you off at the airport on request (AR$7).
By bus The bus station is three blocks from the main square at Olavarría and F.S. Martín.
Destinations Neuquén (7 daily; 6hr); San Martín de los Andes (16 daily; 1hr).

Tourist information The tourist office is opposite Plaza San Martín (Padre Milanesio, at Coronel Suárez; open 8am–9pm; ☎02972 491 160, ⓦjunindelosandesturismo .wordpress.com). Fishing licences can be purchased here. Next door is the helpful Parque Nacional Lanín information office where you can register for hikes to Volcán Lanín (Mon–Fri 8am–2pm; ☎02972 492 748, ⓦparquesnacionales.gob.ar/areas-protegidas/region-patagonia/pn-lanin/).

ACCOMMODATION

Hotel prices hit Andean peaks in the summer, when advance bookings are recommended.
Chimehuín Coronel Suárez, at 25 de Mayo ☎02972 491 132, ⓦhosteriachimehuin.com.ar. The rooms in this good-value B&B have windows that look out onto a landscaped garden with porch furniture. Wi-fi and breakfast included. AR$550
La Isla ☎0294 15 4288 881. This pretty campsite is within easy reach of the main plaza, on an island at the eastern end of Gines Ponte. It has hot showers and a shady riverside setting. Camping/person AR$80
Marisa Rosas 360 ☎02972 491 175. A neat and friendly budget option near the bus terminal, this *residencial* is peaceful, despite its central location. AR$400
Tromen Lonquimay 195 ☎02972 491 498, ⓦhosteltromen.com.ar. A characterless but serviceable budget option with a variety of dorm rooms and doubles scattered around a large house. There is a TV room and kitchen. Dorms AR$80, doubles AR$240

EATING AND DRINKING

Junín's culinary offerings are mostly mediocre pizza joints and rotisseries, strung out along the main road. Stock up on fresh produce at the supermarket on 9 de Julio, at Panil.
Panadería La Ideal Gral Lamadrid, at O'Higgins. Seemingly the whole town gathers here each morning for coffee, newspapers and fantastic sweets and sandwiches. Daily 7.30am–1.30pm & 4–9pm.
Ruca Hueney Padre Milanesio, at Coronel Suárez The best restaurant in town serves trout alongside the traditional *parrilla* choices. Less expected are the Middle Eastern dishes such as *hummus*, *tabbouleh* and *baklava*. Closed Wed.

SAN MARTÍN DE LOS ANDES

Pleasant but pricey, **SAN MARTÍN DE LOS ANDES** is a smaller version of neighbouring Bariloche, albeit without the gobsmacking vistas, tacky hotels or packs of party-hard students. Alpine-style chalets, boutique chocolate shops and upscale restaurants line the holiday

1

town's impeccably clean streets. San Martín is set on the shores of **Lago Lácar**, in a peaceful valley wedged between two forested mountains. The lake offers great summer splashing, while hiking and biking trails lead off to lakeside viewpoints.

WHAT TO SEE AND DO

The **Museo de los Primeros Pobladores** (check at the tourist office for opening hours, which change frequently; ☎02972 428 676; free), set in a 1930s wooden house on the main plaza, puts the area in a historical context with changing exhibitions. If you're here in winter (June–Oct) and wondering where all the people are, your answer may lie 19km south on the slopes of

Cerro Chapelco (☎02972 427 845, ⓦcerrochapelco.com), where there are 29 ski runs, excellent options for beginners and a snowboard park and night skiing. San Martín is also the northern starting or finishing point for the **Seven Lakes Route** (see box, p.116).

ARRIVAL AND DEPARTURE

By plane Chapelco Airport (☎02972 428 388) is 25km from town, with minibus connections to the centre (AR$85). If flying out of Chapelco, the hourly bus to Junín (run by Castelli) will drop you off at the airport on request (AR$12).

Destinations Buenos Aires (daily; 2hr).

By bus The bus terminal is on General Villegas between Juez del Valle and Coronel Diaz.

Destinations Bariloche (4 daily; 4hr); Junín de los Andes (16 daily; 1hr); Villa La Angostura (4 daily; 2hr 30min).

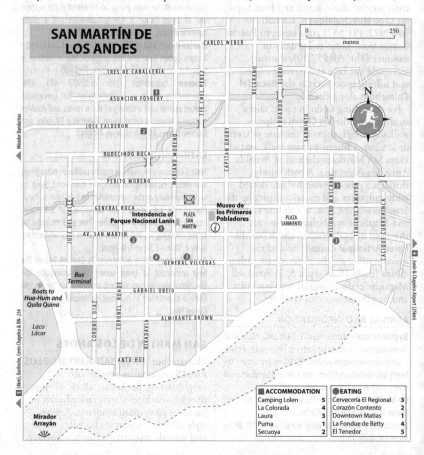

SAN MARTÍN DE LOS ANDES

0 — 250
metres

N

ACCOMMODATION
Camping Lolen	5
La Colorada	4
Laura	3
Puma	1
Secuoya	2

EATING
Cervecería El Regional	3
Corazón Contento	2
Downtown Matias	1
La Fondue de Betty	4
El Tenedor	5

INFORMATION AND TOURS

Tourist information The helpful tourist office is on San Martín, at J.M. de Rosas (daily 8am–9pm; ☎ 02972 427 347, ⓦ sanmartindelosandes.gov.ar). For trekking and camping maps as well as general park information, head to the Intendencia del Parque Nacional Lanín, on Perito Moreno, at Eduardo Elordi (daily 8am–7pm; ☎ 02972 420 664).

Tour operator Pleasure boats run by Naviera Lacar Nonthue (☎ 02972 427 380), based at the lake pier, depart for excursions to Paso Hua-Hum near the Chilean border (daily; AR$600) and to the bay of Quila Quina on Lácar's southern shore (6 daily; AR$240).

ACCOMMODATION

San Martín's prices reflect its popularity with the Argentine elite. Advance reservations are recommended during the height of summer and in the ski season, when prices can double. Backpackers can choose from a handful of good hostels, although prices are somewhat inflated.

Camping Lolen 4km southwest of town. The pick of the town's three campsites is run by the Currühuinca Mapuche community. The site is beautifully positioned on the lake at Playa Catritre. Camping/person **AR$60**

La Colorada Av Koessler 1614 ☎ 02972 411 041, ⓦ lacoloradahostel.com.ar. This hostel, housed in a bright-red cabin, has a fireplace, big back yard and well-equipped kitchen. Some of the dorm rooms have private bathrooms. Breakfast included. **AR$230**

Laura Misionero Mascardi 632 ☎ 02972 426 475. There's plenty of charm and comfort to the simple little rooms in this unassuming wooden house. Breakfast included. **AR$650**

Puma Fosberry 535 ☎ 02972 422 443, ⓦ pumahostel.com .ar. A serviceable enough hostel with kitchen and laundry and plenty of party potential. Breakfast included. **AR$220**

Secuoya Rivadavia 411 ☎ 02972 424 485. The welcoming staff, tranquil vibe, spotless kitchen and wooden floorboards make this superb little hostel feel more like a guesthouse. The doubles are a bit pokey, but the three-bed dorm rooms are a treat. Dorms **AR$170**, doubles **AR$480**

EATING AND DRINKING

Dining out is an expensive pastime in San Martín, but generally worth every peso.

★**Cervecería El Regional** San Martín, at Mascardi ☎ 02972 414 600, ⓦ elregionalpatagonia.com.ar. This brewery is the local favourite for its familial atmosphere, home-made pilsner on tap and massive *tablas* (antipasti platters) of pâtés, smoked trout, boar sausage and other local delicacies. The deer ravioli with wild mushroom sauce (AR$150) is to die for. You won't get warmer service anywhere else in town. Daily noon–4pm & 8pm–midnight.

Corazón Contento San Martín 467 ☎ 02972 412 750. Bustling café and takeaway offering a wide variety of filling sandwiches and burgers, though the quiche

generously stuffed with veggies is most popular with locals (around AR$35 each). Daily 9am–11pm.

Downtown Matías San Martín 598 ⓦ downtownmatias .com. This is where all the nocturnal action is – a cool Irish pub and restaurant that shakes its drunken groove well into the small hours. Daily 8pm to late.

La Fondue de Betty Villegas 586 ☎ 02972 422 522. Warm your hands on a fondue pot at this European-style, intimate restaurant. Cheese, meat and chocolate fondue are served up by the owners, alongside French favourites like beef bourguignon. Cheese fondue for two people from AR$340. Daily 7.30–11pm.

El Tenedor Villegas 776 ☎ 02972 427 597. The cheapest place to fill up on grilled meat. Go nuts with endless refills of *parrilla* (AR$146) and unlimited sides of French fries, salads and *milanesas*, as well as *empanadas*, goulash and other appetizers. For about 20 pesos more you can replace the *parrilla* with a main course of trout or deer. Daily noon–3.30pm & 8–11.30pm.

VILLA LA ANGOSTURA

A hit with well-heeled Argentines, **VILLA LA ANGOSTURA** is a lovely little wooden village spread loosely along the northern shores of Lago Nahuel Huapi. It makes a tranquil alternative to Bariloche and is the obvious place to stay overnight before taking a stroll in the unique woodlands of **Parque Nacional Los Arrayanes**. Most of the village's shops and restaurants are in the commercial area known as **El Cruce**, spread along Avenida Arrayanes, a squeaky-clean main street with twee log-cabin buildings. Heading 3km downhill from here, along Boulevard Nahuel Huapi, you'll find a handful of pretty lakeside teahouses known as **La Villa**, as well as two jetties and the entrance to Parque Nacional Los Arrayanes.

Ten kilometres northeast of town is **Cerro Bayo** (ⓦ cerrobayoweb.com), a lovely small winter ski resort that caters for hikers and mountain bikers in the summer. Villa La Angostura is also the southern start (or end) point for the scenic Seven Lakes Route (see box, p.116), which heads north to San Martín de los Andes.

Parque Nacional de los Arrayanes

A mini-park nestled within the mammoth Parque Nacional Nahuel Huapi (see p.121), the **PARQUE NACIONAL DE LOS**

1

ARRAYANES (daily: 9am–1pm if arriving by land, till 2pm if arriving by bike; 9am–7pm by boat; AR$80) lies on Península Quetrihué, which dips into **Lago Nahuel Huapi** from Villa La Angostura. Its key feature is the **Bosque de los Arrayanes** at the peninsula's tip. The *bosque* (wood) hosts the world's last stand of rare *arrayán* myrtle woodland, where some of the trees are more than 650 years old. The myrtle's corkscrew-like trunks, terracotta-coloured bark and white flowers are a stunning contrast to blue sky or the shimmering lake.

To **get to Bosque de los Arrayanes**, you can either hike, bike or take a boat. To hike, follow the undulating trail (12km one-way) from the park entrance to the end of the peninsula; allow for a five- to six-hour round trip. Cycling is allowed on the trail; bikes can be rented at half-a-dozen places in Villa La Angostura. Leave early to get to the *bosque* before the catamarans full of tourists arrive at about 11.30am.

ARRIVAL AND INFORMATION

By bus The bus station is at Av Siete Lagos 35, just uphill from the main avenue.
Destinations Bariloche (12 daily; 1hr 45min); San Martín de los Andes (4 daily; 2hr 30min).
Tourist information You can pick up a map and organize accommodation at the tourist office (daily

8.30am–10.30pm; ☎0294 449 4124, ⓦvillalaangostura .gov.ar), at Av Arrayanes 9, next to the bus terminal.

GETTING AROUND

By boat Catamarans depart for Bosque de los Arrayanes from the two jetties that are right across from each other in La Villa – Bahía Mansa and Bahía Brava. Futaleufú (☎0294 4494 405) runs three daily boat trips from Mansa (AR$280), and Patagonia Argentina (☎0294 4494 463) two daily trips from Brava (AR$250). It's also possible to visit the *bosque* on a boat trip from Bariloche, usually stopping off at Isla Victoria on the way (AR$420; ⓦturisur.com.ar).

ACCOMMODATION

Built solely to accommodate tourists, Villa La Angostura is luxury central, with the most exclusive hotels hugging the lakeshore. But there are some reasonable budget options.
Hostel La Angostura Barbagelata 157 ☎0294 4494 834, ⓦhostellaangostura.com.ar. It's a short uphill walk west of Plaza San Martín to this enormous green house fronted by wind chimes. The comfortable dorms are en suite and the front room is a huge chill-out space, with pool table, TV lounge and kitchen. Breakfast and wi-fi are included and staff can help with bike rent. Dorms AR$180, doubles AR$520
Camping Unquehué 0.5km west of the bus station on Av Siete Lagos ☎0294 4494 103, ⓦcampingunquehue .com.ar. This very lovely site is the closest campsite to downtown. Camping/person AR$70, plus/tent AR$30
★**Italian Hostel** Los Maquis 215 ☎0294 4494 376, ⓦitalianhostel.com.ar. Two blocks south of the main street, this lovely hostel has spacious dorms as well as doubles and triples set in a large wooden-beamed house

---

SEVEN LAKES ROUTE

The **Ruta de los Siete Lagos** is one of South America's most picturesque drives. It winds for 110km between San Martín de Los Andes and Villa La Angostura along the RN40 traversing the dense alpine forests, snowcapped Andean peaks, brilliant blue lakes, trout-stuffed rivers and plunging waterfalls of two magnificent Patagonian national parks – **Lanín** and **Nahuel Huapi**. In summer the road is lined by purple and yellow wild flowers, and the dramatic snow-covered mountains make the view in winter.

Seven principal photogenic **alpine lakes** are visible or accessible from the roadside. From north to south they are: Machónico, Falkner, Villarino, Escondido, Correntoso, Espejo and Nahuel Huapi. You can spend the night en route at numerous free and serviced lakeside campsites as well as at *refugios* and lodges. *Camping Lago Falkner* (AR$90/person; ☎0294 154 411 607, ☎0294 154 411 772) has lots of facilities, including a restaurant and shop, and is popular with Argentine students and young families, who come to cool off in the lake, camp and party. The first half of the road is paved, while the final stretch, between Lago Villarino and Lago Espejo, is a bumpy dirt track, with vehicles spewing up walls of blinding dust in their wake, though tarmac is gradually being applied. Regular buses run the route, though check you are going on the "7 Lagos" route rather than the "Rinconada" alternative route that some buses take between San Martín and Villa Angostura. La Araucana (ⓦaraucana.com.ar) runs two minibus trips daily (AR$154), picking up and dropping off on request along the way. Despite obvious hazards from rip-roaring cars and buses, the route is also extremely popular with cyclists. Check in with the tourism office before setting out in winter, as parts of the road can be closed due to snow.

1

★ TREAT YOURSELF

Tinto Bistro Nahuel Huapi 34 ☎ 0294 4494 924, ⊛ tintobistro.com/angostura. Serving food fit for royalty (literally – the owner's sister is Queen Máxima of the Netherlands), the bold fusion menu here is well versed in the ways of the world – think Thai, Mediterranean and Peruvian influences. Pasta is teamed with lemon, mushroom and sautéed prawns (AR$192), while their *ceviche* features local trout as well as prawns (AR$165). A wine list of more than 150 vintages seals the deal. Mon–Sat 8.30–11pm.

with plenty of smaller communal nooks to have a chat, backyard hammocks and a herb garden. Extras include wi-fi, breakfast and well-equipped kitchen with a recycling system. Dorms AR$200, doubles AR$550
Verenas Haus Los Taiques 268 ☎ 0294 4494 467, ⊛ verenas-haus.com.ar. The town's most affordable B&B-style option offers six impeccable if dark private rooms (ask for discounts in low season). Board games, wi-fi and a good breakfast are on offer in the living room. AR$950

EATING

Most restaurants in town are of the upmarket variety, although many of the tea houses serve inexpensive sandwiches. That said, it's not impossible to eat full meals on the cheap.
La Caballeriza Av Los Arrayanes 44 ☎ 0294 4494 248. A good-value restaurant that locals will direct you towards for the best beef. Hard-to-find vegetable *parrilla* with pumpkin, courgettes, peppers and more is big enough to share (AR$130). Daily noon–3.30pm & 8–11.30pm.
Gran Nevada Av Los Arrayanes 106 ☎ 0294 4494 512. This bare-bones eatery is always full because of the gigantic portions of dirt-cheap food. Daily noon–3.30pm & 8.30–11.30pm.
La Luna Encantada Belvedere 69 ☎ 0294 4825 999. Skip the usual dinners; the draw here is the wood-fired pizza. The locally smoked trout or salmon makes the perfect topping. Tues–Sun 12.30–3.30pm & 8.30–11.30pm.

BARILOCHE

Set on the southeastern shores of sparkling Lago Nahuel Huapi and framed by magnificent snowcapped Andean peaks, **BARILOCHE** has its breathtaking setting to thank for its status as one of

Argentina's top holiday destinations. Argentines will tell you that it is the country's most European or Swiss-tinged city, but Bariloche itself is a rather ugly hotchpotch of high-rise hotels, garish souvenir stores and faux chalets. That said, the lake and surrounding landscape are stunning – snowy evergreens in winter and covered with purple and yellow wild flowers in summer. The lake is at its best when the sun is reflecting off a placid, cobalt-blue surface, but it can rapidly transform into a tempestuous sea, lashing icy wind through the streets and sending every warm-blooded being indoors to drink hot chocolate or huddle around a pot of cheese fondue.

Aside from lake views, Bariloche's forte is as an **outdoor adventure** hub. The town's proximity to the lakes, mountains, forests and rivers of Parque Nacional Nahuel Huapi makes it one of the top spots in the country for white-water rafting, zip-lines, kayaking, paragliding, mountain biking, trekking and climbing. Come winter, the fun shifts to the nearby pistes of Cerro Catedral (see p.121). To avoid the crowds, come in **spring** or **autumn**.

WHAT TO SEE AND DO

Bariloche's heart is its **Centro Cívico**, a spacious plaza dominated by an equestrian statue of a defeated-looking General Roca. Forming a horseshoe around the square is a set of attractive, mid-twentieth-century public buildings constructed of local timber and green-grey stone, a collaboration between Ernesto de Estrada and famed Argentine architect Alejandro Bustillo, who also built the **cathedral** a few blocks away. On Centro Cívico, the **Museo de la Patagonia** (Tues–Fri 10am–12.30pm & 2–7pm, Sat 10am–5pm; AR$30) traces the area's Mapuche and European history. Bariloche's main drag, **Calle Mitre**, runs east of the plaza.

In the height of summer, you might be tempted to dip a toe beneath the lake's icy surface; the most popular **beach** is rocky Playa Bonita, 8km west of town (buses #10, #20, #21 or #22), or, for a warmer and more secluded dip, head

1

EATING
El Boliche de Alberto	7/9
Butterfly	4
Covita	1
Dias de Zapata	6
La Fonda del Tío	2
Helados Jauja	5
La Marmite	3

ACCOMMODATION
41 Below	7
1004 Penthouse	4
Bariloche Hostel	5
El Gaucho	9
Hostel Inn Bariloche	6
Nogare	8
Patanuk	3
Periko's	10
La Selva Negra	2
Sur	1

DRINKING & NIGHTLIFE
Antares Brewery	10
South Bar	8

BARILOCHE

Lago Nahuel Huapi

13km southeast to Villa Los Coihues on Lago Gutiérrez (buses #41 or #50). Pick up a map and schedule for the useful network of municipal buses at the tourism office.

ARRIVAL AND DEPARTURE

By plane Bariloche Airport (☎029 444 0516) lies 14km east of the centre. Local bus #72 runs into town every couple of hours; a taxi or *remise* will set you back around AR$190. Agencies including Quetrihue (Inacayal 13 1st floor ☎0294 449 4803) operate transfers to Villa La Angostura (AR$350).

Destinations Buenos Aires (8–11 daily; 2hr); Córdoba (2 weekly; 1hr 20min); El Calafate (1 weekly; 1hr 45min); Esquel (weekly; 30min); Mar de Plata (weekly; 1hr 30min); Mendoza (2 weekly 1hr 15min); Puerto Madryn (weekly).

By bus The bus terminal (☎0294 443 2860) is a couple of kilometres east of the centre. Local buses #10, #20 and #21 run into town along C Moreno; a taxi to the Centro Cívico costs around AR$50. Many intercity buses also drop off at the C Moreno stop in the city centre, so check with your driver.

Destinations El Bolsón (13 daily; 2hr); Buenos Aires (10 daily; 21–24hr); El Calafate (1 daily; 28hr); Esquel (6 daily; 4hr 30min); Mendoza (3 daily, 18hr); Puerto Madryn (4 daily; 12hr); Puerto Montt in Chile (5 daily; 6hr); San

Martín de Los Andes (5 daily; 3hr 40min); Villa La Angostura (8 daily; 1hr 30min).

By boat Cruce de Lagos (☎011 5237 1246, ⓦcrucedelagos.com) organizes boat crossings (all year round; 12hr; US$280) from Bariloche to Puerto Varas in Chile (see p.440). The scenic journey cruises lakes Huapi, Frieas and Todos Los Santos, with the overland segments traversed by bus. Optional overnight stops at Puerto Blest and Peulla.

INFORMATION AND TOURS

Club Andino Bariloche 20 de Febrero 30 (daily: summer & winter 9am–9pm; rest of the year 4.30–8.30pm ☎0294 452 7966, ⓦclubandino.org). The must-do stop before you set off hiking in Parque Nacional Nahuel Huapi (see p.121).

Intendencia del Parque Nacional Nahuel Huapi Av San Martín 24 (Mon–Fri 8am–5pm, Sat & Sun 10am–5pm; ☎0294 442 3111, ⓦnahuelhuapi.gov.ar). Pick up official national park pamphlets here.

Tourist information The busy tourist office (daily 8am–9pm; ☎0294 442 9850, ⓦbarilochepatagonia.info) is in the Centro Cívico.

Tour operators Aguas Blancas, Morales 564 (☎0294 443 2799, ⓦaguasblancas.com.ar), runs rafting excursions; Bike Cordillera at Av Bustillo Km18.6 (☎0294

452 4828, ⓦ apurabici.com) rents bicycles; Turaccion (ⓣ 0294 442 7507, ⓦ turaccion.com.ar) offers a range of backpacker-friendly excursions, including a four-day Ruta 40 trip to El Calafate in summer; Pura Vida (ⓣ 0294 441 4053, ⓦ puravidapatagonia.com.ar) offers kayaking trips on the lake; Turisur, at Mitre 219 (ⓣ 0294 442 6109, ⓦ turisur.com.ar), specializes in boat trips.

ACCOMMODATION

Bariloche's accommodation is among the most expensive in Argentina. Bookings are recommended in high season (mid-Dec to Feb, July & Aug), though there is always somewhere with a spare room. Many of the cabins and hotels that lie west of town along Av Bustillo offer great lake views and are a quieter alternative to staying in town. A large number of excellent backpacker hostels have kitchens, internet and tour-booking services.

HOSTELS AND CAMPSITES

★41 Below Juramento 94 ⓣ 0294 443 6433, ⓦ hostel41below.com. A chilled, Kiwi-owned hostel with 24 beds, friendly staff and quality music grooving in its common area. Most dorms and doubles have partial lake views, as the hostel has a completely glass front. Dorms AR$180, doubles AR$560

1004 Penthouse San Martín 127 ⓣ 0294 443 2228, ⓦ penthouse1004.com.ar. Swan around this hostel and take in the panoramic mountain and lake vistas from the tenth floor of an apartment block. Travellers hang out in the mellow living room, or watch the sunset – *vino* in hand – from the balcony. The dorms are not as stylish as the common area. Dorms AR$200, doubles AR$600

Bariloche Hostel Salta 528 ⓣ 0294 442 5460, ⓦ barilochehostel.com.ar. A nine-bedroom mountain-hut styled hostel with great lake views. A good place to come to relax in the small communal/kitchen area or on the wooden sun deck at the back. All rooms are en suite. Dorms AR$180, doubles AR$400

El Gaucho Belgrano 209 ⓣ 0294 452 2464. A friendly German/Argentine couple run this spick-and-span operation four blocks from the main plaza. Hanging carpets liven up the rather bare dorms and nicer doubles. Dorms AR$180, doubles AR$550

Hostel Inn Bariloche Salta 308 ⓣ 0294 455 2782, ⓦ hostelbariloche.com. This HI hostel, smack in the middle of town, offers both breakfast and dinner included in the price. While the atmosphere is a little sterile, one benefit is a number of smaller common areas including a DVD player. Dorms AR$200, doubles AR$540

Patanuk Juan Manuel de Rosas 585 ⓣ 0294 443 4991, ⓦ patanuk.com. Right on the lake with its own private pebble beach, this hostel wins hands down in the

atmosphere category. The six-bed dorms enjoy gorgeous views and the doubles have private bathrooms, though all rooms have seen better days. Breakfast included and bicycles for rent. Dorms AR$180, doubles AR$550

Periko's Morales 555 ⓣ 0294 452 2326, ⓦ perikos.com. Recharge at this rustic cabin with a big backyard swinging with hammocks. The four- and six-bed dorms are en suite and there are four bright doubles. Dorms AR$180, doubles AR$480

La Selva Negra Av Bustillo, 3km west of town ⓣ 0294 444 1013. The closest campsite to town is surrounded by forest. Good facilities include a wi-fi area and bar/café. Price decrease if staying more than one night. Camping/person AR$100

HOTELS

Nogare Elflein 62 ⓣ 0294 442 2438, ⓦ hosterianogarebariloche.com. A welcoming, central budget hotel, with five pleasant blue-and-white rooms with cable TV. Internet is included, as is a hearty breakfast. Discounts in low season. AR$770

Sur Beschtedt 101 ⓣ 0294 442 2677. This two-star hotel may not be the most beautiful, but it does offer clean hotel rooms with all of the amenities including wi-fi. They can also help arrange excursions. AR$550

EATING

El Boliche de Alberto Elflein 347 (ⓣ 0294 443 1433) and Bustillo 8800 (ⓣ 0294 446 2285); ⓦ elbolichedealberto .com. Make a glutton of yourself at this popular local *parrilla* that serves massive portions; be prepared to wait for a table (they don't take reservations). An outrageously large *bife de chorizo* is AR$160. Daily noon–3pm & 8pm–midnight.

Covita Rolando 172 ⓣ 0294 442 1708. This second-floor restaurant does gourmet but affordable takes on dishes

---

★ TREAT YOURSELF

Butterfly Hua Huan 7831, Playa Bonita ⓣ 0294 446 1441, ⓦ butterflypatagonia .com.ar. "An Irish chef, Argentine hostess and German sommelier walked into a restaurant" may sound like the beginning of a joke, but it is the actual story behind this six-table restaurant with a view of the lake. *Butterfly* has caused quite a stir by serving Michelin-worthy meals at a reasonable price. Call ahead to reserve, and let them know of any dislikes and they will craft a meal for you with courses such as *foie gras* or fillet of lamb with cypress mushroom. From AR$490 for seven courses, more with wine pairings (AR$730). Seatings at 7.45pm and 9pm.

1

like aubergine quiche with borscht, pizza with chargrilled vegetables, or Asian curries. Loads of vegetarian and vegan options, with a good-value set lunch (AR$85). Mon–Wed lunch only, Thurs–Sat lunch & dinner.

Días de Zapata Morales 362 ☎0294 442 3128. This colourful Mexican-owned restaurant serves mains like quesadillas and tacos, as delicious as they are generous. Arrive between 7 and 9pm for cheap cocktails. Daily 12.30–4pm & 7.30pm–12.30am.

La Fonda del Tío Mitre 1130 ☎0294 443 5011. Packed to the fluorescent-lit rafters with ravenous locals, this unpretentious, economical diner does outstanding versions of Argentine staples (beef, *milanesas* and pastas). *Milanesa Napolitana* (AR$139). Mon–Sat noon–3.30pm & 8pm–midnight.

★ **Helados Jauja** Moreno 48. In a country known for its ice cream, *Jauja* is recognized as the best. Try a scoop of white chocolate, *dulce de leche* with chocolate chips, or blackcurrant. Daily until late.

La Marmite Mitre 329 ☎0294 442 3685. This old-fashioned joint hung with antlers is a bit of a wallet-sapper; the traditional afternoon tea or cheese fondue will set you back around AR$250 for two. Mon–Sat noon–12.30am, Sun 8pm–12.30am.

DRINKING AND NIGHTLIFE

Exhaustion after a day on the slopes/rapids/trails leaves many travellers tucked in bed by 10pm, but those with more energy can enjoy any number of bars and after-midnight action in lakeside discos such as *Cerebro* (Av Juan Manuel de Rosas 406) and *Roket* (Av Juan Manuel de Rosas 424). Come the winter, most are filled with young Brazilian ski bunnies.

Antares Brewery Elflein 47. Sip the Antares microbrew at a comfortable pub right at the source. Decent pub snacks and a range of artisanal beers (approx AR$50 a pint). Happy hour 6.30–8.30pm. Daily 6.30pm–late.

South Bar Juramento 30. Locals and tourists meet at this no-frills Irish bar to share cheap pints and mixed drinks. Stay out late until the tables are pushed aside and the dancing commences. Daily 8pm–late.

SHOPPING

Books Cultura Librería, Elflein 74, stocks some English-language books and travel guides.

Chocolate C Mitre has numerous chocolate shops selling eye-wateringly expensive gourmet chocolate. The local favourite is Mamuschka, at C Mitre 216, though Abuela Goye, at C Mitre 258, is cosier and has shorter queues.

Markets The bustling Fería Municipal (known colloquially as Mercado de Artesanias) is held daily behind the Centro Cívico on Urquiza between Mitre and Moreno, and sells locally made crafts.

DIRECTORY

Car rental Avis, at San Martín 162 (☎0294 443 1648, ⊛andesrentacar.com.ar); Budget, at Mitre 717 (☎0294 442 2482, ⊛budgetbariloche.com.ar).

Hospital Moreno 601 (☎0294 442 6100).

Police Centro Cívico (☎0294 442 2772).

Post office Moreno 175.

DAY-TRIPS FROM BARILOCHE

Most day-trips from Argentina's outdoor adventure capital involve conquering – or at least ogling – the nearby mountains, rivers and lakes. Outside the winter months, when **skiing at Cerro Catedral** reigns supreme, the most popular excursions are cycling or driving the scenic **Circuito Chico** route (see below), **white-water rafting** on the class III–IV Río Manson some 80km southwest of Bariloche, and hiking in **Parque Nacional Nahuel Huapi** (see opposite). Local tour operators also offer kayaking, kitesurfing, windsurfing, scuba diving, horseriding, canyoning, rock climbing, mountain biking, parapenting (paraskiing), scenic flights, bus tours on the Seven Lakes Route (see box, p.116) and boating trips.

Shopaholics and beer-lovers will find their spiritual home 123km south of Bariloche in the hippy-ish town of **El Bolsón**, where the outstanding **fería artesanal** (Tues, Thurs, Sat & Sun 10am–5pm) sells locally crafted wares and food. Afterwards, sample a pint of the local brew at *Cervecería El Bolsón*, at RN258 Km124 (⊛cervezaselbolson.com), or stay on in the valley for exemplary hiking in the surrounding mountains.

Circuito Chico

The **CIRCUITO CHICO**, a 65km road circuit heading west of Bariloche along the shores of Lago Nahuel Huapi, is a popular day excursion, with a variety of possible stop-offs. It can be explored by bike, rental car, minibus tour (4hr) or by catching a public bus and jumping on and off wherever you fancy. The first point of interest – and a decent half-day excursion on its own – is **Cerro Campanario** at Avenida Bustillo Km18. Take the chairlift (daily 9am–5.30pm, summer until 6.30pm); AR$100) or trail (a 30min steep walk) to the lookout for camera-battery-depleting 360-degree **views**; tours don't usually stop here, so you'll need to come under your own steam. The next point of interest is the luxurious, mountain-framed **Llao Llao Hotel and Spa** at Km25 (☎0294 4448 530, ⊕llaollao.com), an alpine-style creation by architect Alejandro Bustillo. Non-guests can feast on pastries at the hotel's decadent afternoon tea (daily 4–7pm).

Just after the turn-off for the *Llao Llao* is **Puerto Pañuelo**, where boats leave for leisure trips to Puerto Blest, Isla Victoria and the Parque Nacional Los Arrayanes (see p.115). Beyond here the traffic dissipates and the circuit follows an undulating road flanked by thick forest. The scenery is superb, with worthwhile stops at **Villa Tacul**, **Lago Escondido**, **Bahia López** and **Punto Panorámico**, the last of these offering the most recognized postcard shot of the region. For a detour, the pretty Swiss village of **Colonia Suiza** offers an enjoyable opportunity for a lunch or afternoon tea break.

Cycling the circuit allows the flexibility to leave the main road and ride along forested trails to hidden beaches and lakes. As traffic is heavy along the first 20km stretch west of Bariloche, it's best to take a bus (#10, #11, #20 or #22) from downtown to Avenida Bustillo Km18.6, where Bike Cordillera (see p.118) rents **bicycles**. To see the circuit by **public bus**, take #20 along the lakeshore for *Llao Llao* and Puerto Pañuelo or #10 inland for Colonia Suiza. In summer, #11 does the entire circuit.

Cerro Catedral

Named for a summit (2405m) that resembles the spires of a Gothic cathedral, **CERRO CATEDRAL** (☎0294 4409 000, ⊕catedralaltapatagonia.com) is one of South America's top ski resorts from June to October, offering bedazzling lake and cordillera views, more than fifty runs, forty lifts and descents up to 9km long. **Villa Catedral**, a village just 20km south of Bariloche, lies at the base of the mountain and has hotels, restaurants and ski-rental shops. When the snow melts, Cerro Catedral stays open for trekking; a

cable car (AR$205) and chairlift (free) provide access to **Refugio Lynch** (1870m) and spectacular mountain vistas. A tough but worthwhile trail leads along the ridge and past glacial lakes to **Refugio Frey** (4hr); you can overnight there or push on to descend through spellbinding forest back to Villa Catedral (4hr). Mountain biking, abseiling and horseriding are other popular summertime activities on the mountain. Buses marked "Catedral" leave from Moreno 470 in Bariloche.

PARQUE NACIONAL NAHUEL HUAPI

Spanning a whopping 7050 square kilometres, the magnificent **PARQUE NACIONAL NAHUEL HUAPI** (⊕nahuelhuapi.gov.ar) is deservedly one of Argentina's most visited national parks. It incorporates both Bariloche and **Lago Nahuel Huapi**, a sapphire-blue glacial lake flanked by forest-quilted slopes. In the park's wild heart lie forests of cypress and beech trees, crystal-clear rivers, cascading waterfalls, lupin-filled meadows, ancient craggy glaciers and formidable snowcapped summits. Nahuel Huapi's crown is **Cerro Tronador**, an extinct volcano whose three icy peaks (around 3500m) straddle the borders of Argentina and Chile. Wildlife includes Patagonian hares, guanacos and condors, although, in the height of summer, humans rule the roost.

WHAT TO SEE AND DO

Nahuel Huapi has three distinct **zones** – northern, central and southern – and helpful *guardaparques* are stationed at key points to advise on trekking, fishing and camping.

The northern zone

The park's **northern zone**, which lies just south of the town of San Martín de los Andes (see p.113), adjoins Parque Nacional Lanín (see p.111). This zone is defined by sky-blue **Lago Traful**, accessible from a turn-off on the Seven Lakes Route (see p.116). Also here is the **Paso Cardenal Samoré**, a popular overland pass into Chile.

1

TREKKING IN NAHUEL HUAPI

Parque Nacional Nahuel Huapi has an outstanding network of well-marked trails as well as numerous campsites and *refugios* (basic staffed mountain huts, AR$100–250) to overnight in. Trails link many of these *refugios*, allowing hikers to embark on multi-day treks or return to Bariloche every couple of days for a hit of civilization.

The **hiking season** runs from December to March, although snow at high altitudes sometimes cuts off trails. January and February are the warmest and busiest hiking months, although this is also prime time for *tábanos* – intensely annoying biting horseflies that infest the lower altitudes. Spring in the park can be quite windy, while in autumn the leaves of the *ñire* and *lenga* trees turn a brilliant shade of red. Before heading for the hills, trekkers should visit **Club Andino Bariloche** (see p.118), where knowledgeable staff give out trekking maps and can answer questions about the status of trails, campsites and *refugios* as well as transport to trailheads. They also register solo hikers for safety reasons. Club Andino offers regular guided trekking tours to **Pampa Linda** (AR$500), 90km southwest of Bariloche, from where you can hike to Refugio Otto Meiling, which cowers dramatically beneath Cerro Tronador, nestled between the Castaño Overa and Alerce glaciers.

ACCOMMODATION

All of the park's *refugios* are spectacularly sited in the park's southern zone and have bathrooms with cold water and dorms (bring a sleeping bag, supplies and a torch). There are campsites at all major park locations, including *Lago Roca* near Cascada Los Alerces, *Los Rápidos* (☎0294 15441 6120, ⚫losrapidos.com.ar) at Lago Mascardi, and *Los Vuriloches* at Pampa Linda. *Hosterías* within the park are expensive; pleasant *Hostería Pampa Linda*, at the base of Cerro Tronador

(☎0294 4490 517, ⚫hosteriapampalinda.com.ar), costs AR$960 half-board.

EATING AND DRINKING

River water is safe to drink untreated, as is the water from *refugio* taps. Fully equipped kitchens in the *refugios* can be used for a small fee, and hot meals, snacks and an impressive selection of alcohol can be purchased (although prices reflect the fact that everything has been lugged up the mountain by porters).

The central and southern zones

The **central zone**, which incorporates the pretty Bosque de los Arrayanes (see p.116) and Isla Victoria, has **Lago Nahuel Huapi** as its centrepiece. In summer, this zone buzzes with tourists on boating, kayaking, cycling and hiking excursions. The southern zone has the best trails and facilities for hikers, and is focused around **Lago Mascardi**, ideal for swimming and diving in summer.

ESQUEL

Cowboys and urban sophisticates should feel equally at home in **ESQUEL**, the main town in the north of Chubut province. Some 340km south of Bariloche, Esquel means "bog" in the Mapuche language, a name that says nothing of the town's arresting mountainous backdrop. Although Esquel is often relegated to a pit stop en route to Bariloche or Chile, the town makes a perfect base to explore the lush **Parque Nacional Los Alerces** and for riding the historic **Old Patagonian**

Express steam train (see box, p.124) on a touristic loop. Other local draws include the tea-house-filled Welsh settlement of **Trevelin**, 23km south, and, in winter, the ski resort of **La Hoya** (☎02945 453 018, ⚫skilahoya.com), 12km northeast, where there are 22km of runs, plenty of off-piste skiing and a season that often extends into early October.

ARRIVAL AND DEPARTURE

By plane Esquel Airport is 21km east of town; a taxi will set you back around AR$170.
Destinations Bariloche (1 weekly; 30min); Buenos Aires (daily except Wed; 3hr).

By bus The bus terminal (☎02945 451 584) lies eight blocks from the town centre on the corner of A.P. Justo and Av Alvear, the main street.
Destinations Bariloche (6 daily; 4hr 30min); El Bolsón (6 daily; 2hr 30min); El Calafate (daily; 24hr); El Chaltén (3–4 weekly; 18hr); Comodoro Rivadavia (3 daily; 9hr); Futaleufú in Chile (Jan & Feb 2 daily 3 times a week; rest of year 2 daily twice a week; 2hr); Mendoza (daily; 24hr).

By train The train station from which the *La Trochita* steam train departs is on Roggero, at Brun.

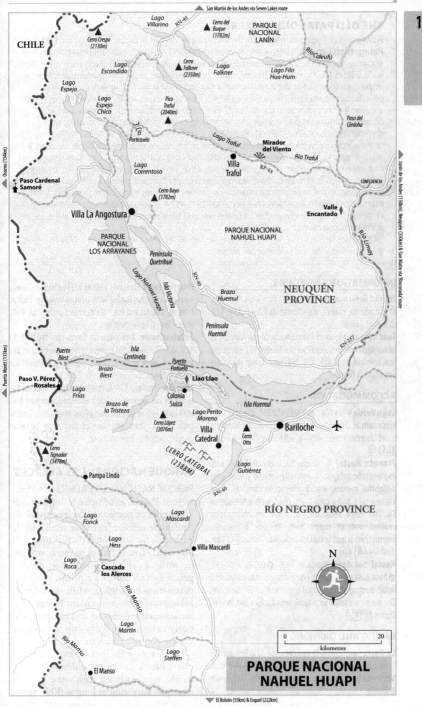

San Martín de los Andes via Seven Lakes route

CHILE

Lago Villarino

Cerro Crespo (2130m)

Cerro del Buque (1782m)

PARQUE NACIONAL LANÍN

Río Caleufú

Lago Espejo

Lago Escondido

Cerro Falkner (2350m)

Lago Falkner

Lago Filo Hua-Hum

Lago Espejo Chico

Pico Traful (2040m)

Paso del Córdoba

El Portezuelo

Lago Trauful

Mirador del Viento

Río Trauful

Lago Correntoso

Villa Trauful

RP-65

Osorno (134km)

Paso Cardenal Samoré

CONFLUENCIA

Cerro Bayo (1782m)

Villa La Angostura

Valle Encantado

Río Limay

PARQUE NACIONAL LOS ARRAYANES

Península Quetrihué

PARQUE NACIONAL NAHUEL HUAPI

NEUQUÉN PROVINCE

Lago Nahuel Huapi

Isla Victoria

RN-40

Brazo Huemul

Península Huemul

RN-237

Puerto Blest

Isla Centinela

Puerto Pañuelo

Puerto Montt (133km)

Brazo Blest

Llao Llao

Paso V. Pérez Rosales

Lago Frías

Colonia Suiza

Isla Huemul

Brazo de la Tristeza

Cerro López (2076m)

Lago Perito Moreno

Bariloche

Cerro Tronador (3478m)

Villa Catedral

Cerro Otto

Pampa Linda

CERRO CATEDRAL (2388M)

Lago Gutiérrez

RÍO NEGRO PROVINCE

Lago Fonck

Lago Mascardi

RN-40

Lago Hess

Lago Roca

Cascada los Alerces

Villa Mascardi

N

Río Manso

Lago Martín

0   20

kilometres

Río Manso

Lago Steffen

PARQUE NACIONAL
NAHUEL HUAPI

El Manso

Junín de los Andes (130km), Neuquén (350km) & San Martín via 'Rinconada' route

El Bolsón (55km) & Esquel (222km)

1

THE OLD PATAGONIAN EXPRESS

Puffing and chugging its way across the arid Andean foothills at around 25km/hr, the **Old Patagonian Express** is both a museum on wheels and a classic South American train journey. Known as "*La Trochita*" ("little narrow gauge" in Spanish), the locomotive's tracks are a mere 75cm wide. Built in 1922 to connect sheep farmers in isolated, windswept communities with faraway markets for their goods, the train was put out of commission in 1993 when the railways were privatized. Immortalized in Paul Theroux's 1979 train-travel narrative, the express is today mostly involved in short, round-trip tourist jaunts. Passengers pile into antique wooden coaches, complete with wood-burning furnaces and dining cars, to puff from Esquel to a Mapuche community plus museum called **Nahuel Pan** and back (44km return; 3hr; AR$300). Peering out of the window, you might spot guanacos, rheas and hares – and you will certainly see cows. If you are really lucky, you may even see "bandits" that hold up the train on occasion – rest assured that it is an organized part of the experience and no one will be relieving you of your jewellery.

The train leaves throughout the year on Saturdays at 10am and then puts on extra trips depending on the season and demand – up to five departures a week in high season. Ask the tourist office for the latest schedule or call ☎02945 451 403. Renovations or strikes sometimes close the line completely, so check that it is running before you come to Esquel if the train ride is the main objective of your journey.

Occasionally, the train makes the 165km journey all the way from Esquel to El Maitén, where there is a museum and railway repair shops.

INFORMATION AND TOURS

Tourist information The tourist office is on Av Alvear, at Sarmiento (daily 7am–10pm; ☎02945 451 927, ⓦ esquel.gov.ar).

Tour operator Tours of Parque Nacional Los Alerces can be booked through Gales al Sur (Av Alvear 1871, inside the bus terminal ☎02945 453 379) and leave every day according to demand.

ACCOMMODATION

Lago Verde Volta 1081 ☎02945 452 251, ⓦ patagonia-verde.com.ar. Small but impeccable rooms set behind a quiet family home with a cute rose-filled garden. **AR$380**

Planeta Hostel Av Alvear 1021 ☎02945 456 846, ⓦ planetahostel.com. A centrally located hostel with delightful owners, wacky artistic touches, an open kitchen area and a cosy living room with a flat-screen TV. The dorm beds are just what the chiropractor ordered and all rooms have en-suite bathrooms. Internet, wi-fi and breakfast included. Dorms **AR$180**, doubles **AR$480**

Hostel Sol Azul Rivadavia 2869 ☎02945 455 193, ⓦ hostelsolazul.com.ar. The cosiest hostel in town boasts a wood-burning stove, heated floors and an all-stone bar. The dorms are small with bunk beds for four and lockers. Dorms **AR$150**

EATING AND DRINKING

La Barra Sarmiento 638 ☎02945 454 321. This *parrilla* serves big juicy slabs of tenderloin accompanied with home-made mayonnaise on lacy tablecloths. Daily lunch & dinner.

Fitzroya Pizza Rivadavia 1048 ☎02945 450 512. Cheesy, inexpensive pizzas loaded with creative toppings such as broccoli, salmon and trout are delivered piping hot. Daily noon–3pm & 8pm–midnight.

Futalaufquem Ameghino, at Sarmiento ☎02945 15 429 357. The delightful owners serve decent dishes like trout and home-made lasagne. Mon, Tues & Thurs–Sun lunch & dinner.

Moe Bar Rivadavia 873. Cocktails and classic rock are the orders of the night at this dark and rowdy drinking hole with half a yellow car protruding from its entrance. Tend to your hunger pangs with one of their tasty pizzas or *picadas*. Daily 8 or 9pm until late.

PARQUE NACIONAL LOS ALERCES

PARQUE NACIONAL LOS ALERCES, 40km west of Esquel, encompasses 2630 square kilometres of gorgeous, glacier-carved Andean landscape (entrance fee AR$65). Although far less visited than Parque Nacional Nahuel Huapi to the north, its network of richly coloured lakes and pristine rivers makes it a prime destination for anglers, while countless hiking trails through verdant forests attract summer walkers and campers. It's easily navigable on a day-trip from Esquel via the popular lake tour.

The *alerce* (or Patagonian cypress) that grows here is one of the oldest living species on the planet, with some examples surviving as long as 3000 years.

In size, they're almost comparable to the grand sequoias of California, growing to 70m tall and 4m wide. Though the *alerce* gives the park its name, the flora is wildly varied: **Valdivian temperate rainforest** thrives in its luxuriant western zone near the Chilean border, which is deluged by around 3000mm of annual rainfall. Elsewhere, incense cedar, bamboo-like *caña colihue*, *arrayán*, *coihue*, *lenga* and southern beech thrive.

WHAT TO SEE AND DO

Most visitors gravitate towards the park's user-friendly and photogenic **northeast sector** where there is a network of four dazzling lakes – **Rivadavia**, **Verde**, **Menéndez** and **Futalaufquen**. The emerald-hued Lago Verde is often the first port of call for day-trekkers and campers. Spilling over from Lago Verde is the **Río Arrayanes**, crossed by a suspension bridge that marks the start of an easy hour-long interpretive loop walk.

Some hikes, including the trek to the summit of **Cerro Alto El Dedal** (1916m), require registration with the park ranger's office (see below) first. The most popular day excursion is the **boat trip** run by Brazo Sur (Rivadavia 891, Esquel; ☏ 02945 456359, ⊛ brazosur .com.ar), which leaves from either Puerto Limonao (3km north of the ranger's office, 9.30am departure, AR$510) or Puerto Chucao (halfway around the Lago Verde/Río Arrayanes loop trail, 11.30am departure, AR$440). The boats cross Lago Menéndez to visit **El Abuelo** (The Grandfather), a 57m-high *alerce* estimated to be more than 2600 years old.

ARRIVAL AND INFORMATION

By car One main dusty, bumpy road (the RP71) runs through Los Alerces and is usually accessible year-round, although it is occasionally blocked by snow in winter. There is no public transport outside of peak season, so a vehicle is recommended; otherwise, hikers need to walk along the road between trails, enduring clouds of body-coating dust from passing cars and trucks.

By bus Peak season is Jan–Feb, when Transportes Esquel (☏ 02945 453 529, ⊛ transportesesquel.com.ar) runs two daily bus services to the park; it takes three bumpy hours to reach Lago Verde.

> **CROSSING INTO CHILE**
> Esquel is well placed for crossing into Chilean Patagonia, with several buses weekly making the two-hour trip to the settlement of **Futaleufú**, (see p.457) where there is excellent white-water rafting. Feryval and Lago Espolón buses leave Esquel (travelling south via Trevelín) around four times a week. At the Chilean border (immigration 8am–8pm), passengers transfer to a minibus for the final 10km to Futaleufú.

Tourist information The ranger's office (daily 8am–9pm; ☏ 02945 471 020) is at Villa Futalaufquen, a village on Lago Futalaufquen, 12km past the park entrance point, with a smattering of shops, public telephones and eating and accommodation options (which close in winter). It can provide information on camping, park accommodation, hiking and fishing, and sells fishing permits.

ACCOMMODATION

A number of cabañas, *hosterías* and campsites lie within the park, including pricey lodges that cater for anglers. There are a dozen free campsites with no facilities at all, some very cheap basic ones with cold-water bathrooms and a handful of slightly more expensive organized campsites with hot water, gas and electricity; enquire at the tourist office in Esquel or at the park ranger's office.

Patagonia

Vast, windswept and studded with glaciers, **PATAGONIA** has an undeniable mystique, a place where pioneers, outlaws, writers and naturalists have long come in search of open space and wild adventure. While few corners have been left unexplored, there's still plenty of scope for adventure, whether you're watching a southern right whale swim metres under your boat or strapping on crampons to hike across the Southern Patagonian Ice Cap.

For those short on time, flights allow you to hop between Patagonia's key attractions, but to appreciate the region's size, it's best to travel overland. After hundreds of kilometres of desolate steppe, nothing bedazzles quite like the sight of serrated Andean peaks rising up on the horizon.

1

ARGENTINA PATAGONIA

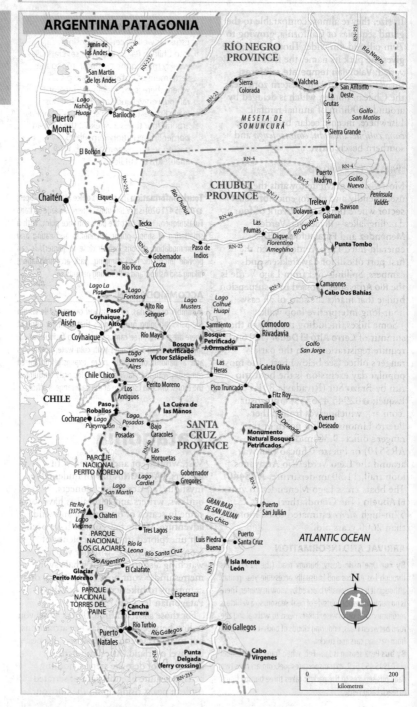

RÍO NEGRO PROVINCE

Junín de los Andes

San Martín de los Andes

RN-40

RN-237

RN-251

Río Negro

Sierra Colorada

Valcheta

San Antonio Oeste

La Grutas

RN-23

Lago Nahuel Huapi

Puerto Montt

Bariloche

MESETA DE SOMUNCURÁ

Golfo San Matías

El Bolsón

Sierra Grande

RN-3

RN-4

Chaitén

Esquel

RN-258

CHUBUT PROVINCE

Río Chubut

RN-40

RN-11

RN-4

Puerto Madryn

Golfo Nuevo

Tecka

Las Plumas

RN-5

Trelew

Rawson

Península Valdés

Paso de Indios

RN-25

Dique Florentino Ameghino

Dolavon

Gaiman

Río Pico

Gobernador Costa

RN-40

Punta Tombo

Lago La Plata

Lago Fontana

Alto Río Senguer

Lago Musters

Lago Colhué Huapi

RN-3

Camarones

Cabo Dos Bahías

Paso Coyhaique Alto

Sarmiento

Comodoro Rivadavia

Puerto Aisén

Río Mayo

Bosque Petrificado J.Ormachea

Golfo San Jorge

Coyhaique

Bosque Petrificado Víctor Szlápelis

Las Heras

Lago Buenos Aires

Caleta Olivia

Chile Chico

Perito Moreno

Pico Truncado

Los Antiguos

La Cueva de las Manos

Fitz Roy

Río Deseado

CHILE

Paso Roballos

Jaramillo

Puerto Deseado

Cochrane

Lago Pueyrredón

Lago Posadas

Bajo Caracoles

SANTA CRUZ PROVINCE

Monumento Natural Bosques Petrificados

Posadas

Las Horquetas

RN-40

PARQUE NACIONAL PERITO MORENO

Lago Cardiel

Gobernador Gregores

RN-3

Lago San Martín

GRAN BAJO DE SAN JULIÁN

Río Chico

Puerto San Julián

ATLANTIC OCEAN

Fitz Roy (3375m)

El Chaltén

Lago Viedma

PARQUE NACIONAL LOS GLACIARES

Río la Leona

Tres Lagos

RN-288

Río Santa Cruz

Luis Piedra Buena

Puerto Santa Cruz

Lago Argentino

Glaciar Perito Moreno

El Calafate

RN-3

Isla Monte León

PARQUE NACIONAL TORRES DEL PAINE

Esperanza

N

Cancha Carrera

Puerto Natales

Río Turbio

Río Gallegos

Río Gallegos

RN-9

Punta Delgada (ferry crossing)

Cabo Vírgenes

RN-255

0   200
kilometres

Two main arteries traverse Patagonia. The RN40 runs parallel to the Andes and links some of Patagonia's major sights: the 10,000-year-old rock art of the **Cueva de las Manos**; the Fitz Roy sector of **Parque Nacional Los Glaciares** around the town of El Chaltén; and the **Perito Moreno** and **Upsala** glaciers in the park's southern sector, both easy day-trips from El Calafate. To the east, the RN3 loosely traces the Atlantic seaboard, passing the town of **Puerto Madryn**, a launching pad for the marine-wildlife-rich shores of **Península Valdés**, before heading south to the Welsh heartland of **Trelew** and **Gaiman**, a short jump to the continent's largest penguin colony, **Punta Tombo**.

December to February are the warmest months to visit Patagonia, but to avoid the crowds, inflated prices and high winds, March and April are better.

PUERTO MADRYN

Sprawling, windblown **PUERTO MADRYN**, an aluminium-producing fishing port, founded in 1865 by 153 intrepid Welsh families, that clings to the featureless coastal pampas of northern Patagonia, is an unlikely visitor destination at first sight. Its attractions lie more in its proximity to one of the world's most significant marine reserves – the **Reserva Faunística Península Valdés** – as well as to South America's biggest penguin colony. Scuba diving, snorkelling with sea lions and whale watching are among the area's draws. Puerto Madryn also makes a convenient base from which to explore the nearby Welsh towns of Trelew and Gaiman.

WHAT TO SEE AND DO

In the southern part of town, at Julio Verne 3784, is the excellent **Ecocentro** (daily 3–7pm; AR$90; ⓦecocentro .org.ar), with interactive exhibitions on Patagonian ecosystems, breeding habits of southern right whales, sea-lion harems and more, as well as a changing art exhibition. Just outside is the skeleton of a whale that was beached nearby in 2001. Take bus #2 from the town centre to its last stop and walk another 1km south along the waterfront.

Around 20km north of town, and reachable via a fairly strenuous bike ride or shared taxi (AR$200 one-way), is **El Doradillo**, a pristine stretch of beach where between June and December you can spot whales swimming right near the shore.

Seventeen kilometres southwest of Puerto Madryn via a good gravel road is **Punta Loma**, with a viewpoint overlooking a sheltered beach that's home to a few hundred sea lions, plus a gulp of cormorants, best seen at low tide. Some agencies organize trips (2–3hr), but you can get here by bike or taxi.

ARRIVAL AND DEPARTURE

By plane Puerto Madryn's airport (Aeropuerto El Tehuelche; ☎0280 445 1909) is around 5km west of town (taxi about AR$100). There are regular flights to Buenos Aires, but nearby Trelew Airport serves more destinations.

By bus The bus terminal is at Avila and Independencia, on the northern edge of the centre. Bus timetables and accommodation details are displayed on the wall, and there are luggage lockers. Bus companies 28 de Julio (☎0280 447 2056) and Mar y Valle (☎0280 447 2056) serve Trelew; Andesmar (☎0280 447 3765) runs to Mendoza, Jujuy and Iguazú, Don Otto (☎0280 445 1675) serves Buenos Aires, Comodoro Rivadavia, Neuquén, Bariloche and Esquel; TAC (☎0280 445 7785) runs to Río Gallegos and Jujuy. Chaltén Travel can arrange bus tickets along the Ruta 40.

Destinations Bariloche (daily at 9.30pm; 14hr); Buenos Aires (10–11 daily; 18hr); Comodoro Rivadavia (5–7 daily; 5–6hr); Esquel (2–3 daily; 7–9hr); Jujuy (5 daily; 36hr); Mendoza (2–3 daily; 24hr); Neuquén (2 daily; 12hr); Puerto Pirámides (1–3 daily; 1hr 15min); Río Gallegos (4–6 daily; 15–20hr); Trelew (every 30min–1hr; 1hr).

INFORMATION

Tourist information The tourist office is on Av Roca 223 (daily 7am–9pm; ☎0280 445 3504, ⓦmadryn.gov.ar/ turismo).

TOUR OPERATORS

Chaltén Travel Roca 115 ☎0280 445 4906, ⓦwww .chaltentravel.com. Tours of Península Valdés and Punta Tombo ($AR560 each). Also arranges onward travel and tours along the Ruta 40.

1

PUERTO MADRYN

● EATING, DRINKING & NIGHTLIFE	
El Almendro	7
Ambigú	3
Café Martínez	2
Cheers Patagonia Bar	6
Lupida Taberna Mejicana	5
Margarita	4
Mr Jones	3
Plácido	1

■ ACCOMMODATION	
ACA Complejo Turístico Punta Cuevas	1
Casa Patagónica	2
Casa de Tounens	3
Chepatagonia Hostel	3
El Gualicho	5
Hi! Patagonia Hostel	4
Hotel Petit	8
La Tosca	6

Trelew (65km)

Estación Marítima Puerto Rawson ☎ 0280 449 8508, ⓦ estacionmaritima.com.ar. Runs dolphin-watching boat trips from Rawson.

Lobo Larsen Roca 885 ☎ 0280 447 0277, ⓦ lobolarsen .com.ar. Hugely popular snorkelling and diving with sea lions trips.

Scuba Duba Brown 893 ☎ 0280 445 2699 ⓦ scubaduba .com.ar. PADI-affiliated, reputable diving operator.

ACCOMMODATION

Most accommodation is close to the centre and within walking distance of the bus terminal (many hostels offer pick-ups if you call ahead). Prices drop outside high season (Jan–March). Rates include breakfast unless stated otherwise and all have free wi-fi.

HOSTELS AND CAMPSITES

ACA Complejo Turístico Punta Cuevas Punta Cuevas ☎ 0280 445 2952, ⓦ acamadryn.com.ar. This well-run complex has camping spots (tents provided), simple rooms and self-contained apartments best for groups. Breakfast costs extra. Camping/person AR$100, doubles AR$360, four-person apartments AR$1350

Casa de Tounens Pasaje 1ero de Marzo 432 ☎ 0280 447 2681, ⓦ lacasadetounens.com. A block from the bus terminal, this friendly French-run place has a little patio, a compact living room, guest kitchen that's a magnet for socializing in the evenings, several spartan private rooms and a swing-a-cat dorm. Dorms AR$170, doubles AR$450

Chepatagonia Hostel A. Storni 16 ☎ 0280 445 5783, ⓦ chepatagoniahostel.com.ar. Right on the waterfront, this compact hostel is run by a friendly local couple. Dorms have good mattresses and individual reading lights, there are bikes for rent (AR$150/day) and the owners throw the odd barbecue. Also has a fully equipped five-person apartment (AR$800). Dorms AR$170, doubles AR$500

El Gualicho Marcos A Zar 480 ☎ 0280 445 4163, ⓦ elgualicho.com.ar. The biggest, slickest hostel in town, *El Gualicho* welcomes a young backpacking clientele to a rock soundtrack. Dorms and doubles are large and spotless, the hammock-hung garden, beanbag-strewn lounge with guest computers and pool table are good and staff will book you in for every conceivable tour, but the sheer size (120 beds) makes it a little impersonal. Dorms AR$150, doubles AR$590

Hi! Patagonia Hostel Av Roca 1040 ☎ 0280 445 0155, ⓦ hipatagonia.com. Small, sociable hostel run by a young Argentine owner, which attracts active travellers who make use of the climbing wall and bike rentals. Top-notch backpacker facilities include a hammock-festooned garden with a bar and a/c in the rooms, and there are occasional communal barbecues. Dorms AR$150, doubles AR$550

★ **La Tosca** Sarmiento 437 ☎ 0280 445 6133, ⓦ latoscahostel.com. Curving around a placid garden, this professionally run hostel caters to all backpacker needs. Besides providing information on the area's attractions, pluses include two guest kitchens, a range of snug rooms with private and semi-private bathrooms, good beds, and ample locker space. Owners also bake cakes for their guests. Dorms <u>AR$80</u>, doubles <u>AR$210</u>

B&BS

Casa Patagónica Av Roca 2210 ☎0280 445 1540, ⓦcasa-patagonica.com.ar. This homey, family-run B&B has four twins and triples which share a bathroom, plus one en suite. Guests have access to a microwave and fridge (though not a full kitchen), and owners are happy to help you plan your stay. <u>AR$470</u>

Hotel Petit Marceló T. de Alvear 845 ☎0280 445 1460, ⓦhotel-petit.com.ar. The rooms at this anonymous motel-style budget hotel are on the small side, but are all en suite with cable TV and some come with kitchen facilities. Avoid during hot weather as they lack fans. <u>AR$450</u>

EATING AND DRINKING

El Almendro Alvear 409, at 9 de Julio ☎0280 447 0525, ⓦelalmendro.ucoz.com. Simple, stylish decor, good service and an imaginative menu of Mediterranean-inspired dishes characterize this local favourite. The steaks are among the best in town, and the home-made pasta is good, but the paella lets the side down. Mains from AR$84. Tues–Sun from 8pm.

Ambigú Roca, at Roque Sáenz Peña. The menu at this bustling café-restaurant features everything from steaks and pastas to stir-fries, but it's particularly popular for its pizzas – the large ones are more than enough for two people. Small/large pizza from AR$95/145. Daily noon–2.30pm & 7.30pm–midnight.

Café Martínez Roca 143. The national chain's Chubut branch is Puerto Madryn's answer to Starbucks, serving sandwiches, wraps, salads, milkshakes and ample breakfasts involving fry-ups or granola. Coffee is not the cheapest (from AR$24) but it's consistently good. Mon–Sat 9am–8pm.

Cheers Patagonia Bar Belgrano 323. Cavernous restaurant/bar/microbrewery with faux-Grecian columns and photos of ye olde Puerto Madryn, with its own beer on tap and steaks, Patagonian-style lamb and fish with creamed spinach gracing the menu. Steer clear of anything too ambitious-sounding. Mains from AR$105. Tues–Sun noon–3pm & 8pm–late.

Lupida Taberna Mejicana Av Gales 191. With a psychedelic cactus mural and strategically placed sombreros, this is the Argentine take on Mexican food (so not spicy), but the portions of burritos and quesadillas are generous and it makes a change. Mains AR$45–68. Daily 8.30pm–midnight.

Margarita Roque Sáenz Peña 15. Visit this cosy, brick-walled pub to enjoy some good (and often live) music and rub shoulders with the locals over their long list of cocktails

and a few local beers (from AR$30). Mon–Sat 7.30pm–3am.

Mr Jones 9 de Julio 116. A bustling pub, popular with locals and young gringos alike, who fill up the wooden benches and spill out onto the streetside tables. The menu is overly ambitious but you can't go wrong with a beer (from around AR$30) and a *picada* (cold meat and cheese platters). Mon–Sat 6pm–1am.

★ **Plácido** Roca 506 ☎0280 445 5991, ⓦplacido.com.ar. Besides great sea views, this upscale but relatively inexpensive restaurant offers some of the most imaginative dishes in town, from salmon ravioli in curry sauce to pumpkin cannelloni in cheese fondue. Mains AR$90–135. Daily noon–3pm & 8pm–midnight.

DIRECTORY

Banks and exchange Banco Galicia, at Mitre 25, changes money and has an ATM, one of dozens in the city.
Car rental Most rental company branches are along Av Roca. Rates start from AR$700/day.
Laundry Servicios de Lavandería Morenas, Sarmiento, at Marcos Zar (Mon–Sat 8.30am–8.30pm).

DAY-TRIPS FROM PUERTO MADRYN

For animal lovers, it's hard to top the **Península Valdés** marine reserve, with its whale-watching boat trips and sightings of other marine fauna, though a trip to South America's biggest penguin colony at **Punta Tombo**, a little further afield, gives it a run for its money. South of Puerto Madryn is the excellent dinosaur museum in nearby **Trelew**. To delve into the region's Welsh heritage stop by tiny **Gaiman**, easily combined with Trelew on a single day-trip.

Península Valdés

PENÍNSULA VALDÉS is brimming with life. More than a million Magellanic penguins make their summer home here, along with numerous colonies of elephant seals and sea lions, while the waters hide dolphins and orca (killer whales). Topping even that is a pod of southern right whales – vast, barnacled leviathans that come here to breed and raise their young, and that can be observed directly from the beach of **Puerto Pirámides**, the peninsula's tiny port surrounded by desert scrubland. If you're lucky, you can sometimes spot

1

VISITING PENÍNSULA VALDÉS

Most people visit Península Valdés on an organized tour (around AR$560, 10–12hr round-trip; bring warm clothes), most of which follow the same itinerary, with minor variations according to the season and weather. The first stop, a short drive out of Puerto Madryn, is to pay the park entrance fee (AR$180) and visit the **information centre**, followed by an impressive look out over the Isla de los Pájaros (Bird Island). Next, across the isthmus on the peninsula proper, you'll stop off in Puerto Pirámides, where hugely worthwhile **sea-lion**- and **whale-watching** boat trips are offered (AR$650). From here, most buses head east to Punta Cantor and Caleta Valdéz to see the **elephant seals** and their pups on the long gravel beach, with a brief stop at El Parador where there's a colony of **Magellanic penguins**. Some tours may instead head north to Punta Norte, to the huge colony of elephant seals and sea lions. **Orcas** are found here year-round, and between February and April they are most likely to stage stealth beach attacks on seal and sea-lion pups. Marine life is present year-round but some viewing stations close from Easter to June; optimal viewing is between September and February, but whales can be seen from June to December. Other than on day tours, the only other way to reach the viewpoints is by car, which can be good value if you are travelling in a group; most of the roads around the peninsula are dirt-and-gravel ones, so cautious driving is imperative.

them from the beach, but you need to go on a boat trip to get close up.

ARRIVAL AND DEPARTURE

By bus There are daily buses from Puerto Madryn to Puerto Pirámides (8.55am, 5pm & 6.55pm, returning 11am, 7pm & 8.45pm; extra departure at 6.30am on Mon, Wed & Fri, returning 8.15am; 1hr 15min; double check the frequently changing timetable at the bus terminal).

ACCOMMODATION AND EATING

If you prefer picturesque villages with a slow pace of life to cities, Puerto Pirámides has far greater appeal than Puerto Madryn. Dining options are either along Av Ballenas or in a cluster by the boat dock.

Hostal Bahía Ballenas Av de las Ballenas s/n ☎ 028015 4567104, ⓦ bahiaballenas.com. The only hostel in the village consists of two 12-bed dorms, divided by gender. Don't expect peace and quiet, but it's a good place to meet travellers and the guest kitchen is a boon for self-caterers. Dorms __AR$150__

La Casa de La Tía Alicia Av de las Ballenas s/n ☎ 0280 449 5046, ⓦ hosteriatiaalicia.com.ar. This eye-catching pink house decked out with knick-knacks hides four compact en-suite rooms. Breakfast is basic, but there's plenty of *buena onda* (good vibes) and the *Guanaco* pub/microbrewery next door is a welcome bonus. __AR$600__

Trelew

An hour south of Puerto Madryn across some wind-blown pampas, **TRELEW** is a busy commercial centre, proud of its Welsh history – "Trelew" in Welsh

means "village of Lewis", in honour of Lewis Jones, the town's founder. It's only worth staying here to cut down on travelling time to Punta Tombo and Gaiman.

It also has, at Fontana & Lewis Jones, the excellent **Museo Paleontológico Egidio Feruglio** (April–Aug Mon–Fri 10am–6pm, Sat & Sun 10am–7pm; Sept–March daily 9am–8pm; AR$70; ⓦ mef.org.ar), which houses Patagonia's most important paleontological finds. You can touch an enormous sauropod femur, wander among the skeletons of giant flightless birds and immense herbivores and predators, and check out the remains of a theropod predator, the *Tyrannotitan chubutensis*, discovered on a farm in Chubut in 1995.

ARRIVAL AND INFORMATION

By plane Almirante M.A. Zar International Airport (ⓦ www.aeropuertotrelew.com), 5km northeast of the town, has flights to Buenos Aires, Bariloche, Esquel, Ushuaia and El Calafate. A taxi to/from the centre costs about AR$70.

By bus The bus station is next to the Plaza Centenario. Destinations Bariloche (1 daily; 13–16hr); Buenos Aires (10–11 daily; 19–21hr); Gaiman (every 30min; 25–35min); Puerto Madryn (every 30min–1hr; 1hr); Río Gallegos (4–5 daily; 15–16hr).

Tourist information The well-stocked tourist office is on San Martín, at Mitre (Mon–Fri 8am–8pm, Sat & Sun 9am–9pm; ☎ 0280 442 6819, ⓦ trelewpatagonia.gov.ar).

ACCOMMODATION AND EATING

Hostel El Ágora Edwin Roberts 33 ☎ 0280 442 6899, ⊛ hostelagora.com.ar. Run by friendly young owners, this is the only hostel in town and a nice one at that, with spacious, tiled rooms and spartan dorms with lockers and a kitchen. The owners sometimes throw a barbecue for guests. Dorms AR$150, doubles AR$400

Miguel Angel Trattoria Fontana 246. All dark wood and exposed brick, this is a stylish spot for thin-and-crispy pizza (the large is big enough for two) and home-made pasta. Small/large pizza from AR$65/150. Tues–Sun 12.30–3.30pm & 8.30pm–midnight.

Touring Club Fontana 240, ⊛ touringpatagonia.com.ar. Antoine de Saint-Exupéry, author of *The Little Prince*, and (reportedly) Butch Cassidy and the Sundance Kid have stayed at this faded Art Deco hotel. Its cavernous dining area with an imposing antique bar is worth lingering in with a drink, though the food's overpriced and mediocre. Daily 7am–2am.

Gaiman

Some 17km west of Trelew, **GAIMAN** is the most visitor-friendly of the region's Welsh settlements, an oasis of greenery thanks to the Río Chubut. Founded in 1874 by Welsh settlers – a third of its population still claims Welsh ancestry – and it's renowned for its immense **Welsh teas**; even the late Princess Diana stopped by for a cuppa in 1995. Served from 2 or 3pm every day in quaint cottages (or their gardens), they consist of tea, home-made cakes (including *torta negra*, a traditional Welsh fruitcake), scones, breads, tiny sandwiches and jams.

ARRIVAL AND INFORMATION

By bus There are regular 28 de Julio buses to and from Trelew (every 30min; 25–35min); they arrive and depart from the central square.

Tourist information The tourist office (Mon–Sat 9am–8pm, Sun 9am–7pm; ☎ 0280 449 1571) is at Belgrano 574, a 5min walk from the main square. You can pick up a map here to do a self-guided tour of Gaiman's historical buildings.

ACCOMMODATION AND EATING

Tea houses charge around AR$150–170/person for tea; some are closed on Monday.

Gwalia Lân Eugenio Tello, at Jones. Just off the main square, this well-loved local restaurant is run by a Welsh-speaking descendant of original settlers and serves the best steaks (AR$130) in town, as well as home-made pasta and fish dishes, washed down with the local Patagonia ale. Tues–Sat 12.30–3pm & 7.30pm–midnight, Sun 12.30–3pm.

Ty Gwyn 9 de Julio 147, ⊛ tygwyn.com.ar. A block from the main square, this spacious *casa de té* has tables set with blue-and-white china and teapots with cosies. *Ty Gwyn* also has clean, compact rooms with wooden floors and partial views of the Río Chubut. AR$700

Ty Nain Yrigoyen 283. The abundant tea (AR$150) is served by a descendant of the first Welsh woman born in Gaiman inside this gorgeous ivy-clad building that dates back to 1890. There's a tiny museum at the back. Tues–Fri 3–7pm, Sat & Sun, from 4pm.

★ **Yr Hen Ffordd** Michael Jones 342 ☎ 029 654 91394, ⊛ yrhenffordd.com.ar. Presided over by young, friendly owners, this appealing B&B with antique touches and tiled floors has just five rooms, all with a/c and TV and bathrooms. Breakfast includes home-made scones. AR$500

Punta Tombo

Around 180km south of Puerto Madryn and 110km south of Trelew, the **Reserva Provincial Punta Tombo** (Sept–late March daily 8am–6pm; AR$100) is the largest penguin nesting site on the continent. Around a million Magellanic penguins come here to breed and raise their chicks, and wander freely across the paths (give them plenty of room). Penguins aside, you'll see a vast array of birds, from rock cormorants and kelp gulls to giant petrels. The reserve can be visited independently by car or on a long day tour (around AR$560) from Puerto Madryn or Trelew; tours often include stops at Rawson's Playa Unión for dolphin-spotting trips (AR$500) and Gaiman.

RUTA 40

Ruta 40 (or **RN40**) runs from the top to the bottom of Argentina, following the line of the Andes all the way to the far south from the border with Bolivia in the north. It covers 5000km and 11 provinces, crosses 18 important rivers on 236 bridges, and connects 13 great lakes and salt flats, 20 national parks and hundreds of communities. The section between **El Calafate/El Chaltén**

1

TRAVELLING RUTA 40

The **best time to travel** Ruta 40 from El Calafate/El Chaltén to Bariloche by public transport is from November to the end of March. Outside of these months, buses are infrequent and much accommodation shuts down. The Cueva de las Manos can only be visited from December to February.

Bus services between El Calafate and Bariloche, via Perito Moreno, are offered by the well-established **Chaltén Travel** (W www.chaltentravel.com), which has offices in El Calafate, El Chaltén, Puerto Madryn and Bariloche, as well as less reliable Taqsa/Marga (W taqsa.com.ar); both run frequent services every other day between November and the end of March. Check the latest timetables before planning a trip.

If you have more time and money, plus a sense of adventure, the best way to see the region is to rent a **car** either in **Bariloche** or **El Calafate** and drive the route at your own speed (though one-way drop-off fees for rental cars can be as high as US$900).

It's a huge territory, and even though large chunks of the route have been paved, the rest is still dirt-and-gravel and fuel stops are few and far between (so fill up at every opportunity). Watch out for wildlife in the road, carry spare tyres, food and water, and stop to help if you see anyone who's broken down, as there's no other roadside assistance. Two places to break for fuel are Bajo Caracoles, 130km south of Perito Moreno, and Gobernador Gregores, around 440km north, essential for petrol and food; Gobernador Gregores has better lodging options.

There is little in the way of budget **accommodation** along the route (especially as the windy, hard plains make camping virtually impossible), but there are a few *estancias*.

If you want to take an **organized tour** on RN40, the appropriately named Ruta 40 agency (T 0294 452 3378, W www.ruta-40.com) is a small, multi-lingual company that shows small groups of travellers the highlights of the route between Bariloche and El Calafate.

and **Bariloche** has long been popular with backpackers, with much of the route paved and buses running its length almost daily in season. It still retains a sense of isolation, however, thanks to the endless pampas scrubland, interrupted only by the occasional tiny settlement or *estancia*. The ancient **cave paintings** near the unappealing crossroads town of Perito Moreno are a worthwhile detour.

PERITO MORENO

Named after the explorer who rerouted the Río Fénix that provides the town with water, **PERITO MORENO** (not to be confused with the Perito Moreno glacier) is a small, unappealing, wind-blasted town roughly halfway between El Chaltén and Bariloche, and a convenient stopover along Ruta 40. Perito Moreno's main point of interest is as a base for excursions to the **Cueva de las Manos**.

ARRIVAL AND DEPARTURE

By bus The bus terminal is a 15min walk north of the centre. Sportman (T 02963 432303) passes through en route between Comodoro Rivadavia and Los Antiguos; buses are frequently late; Taqsa/Marga (T 02963 432675 W taqsa.com.ar) serves all destinations along Ruta 40, as does Chaltén Travel, leaving from Hotel Belgrano, San Martín 1001 (T 02963 432019, W www.chaltentravel.com) on alternate days (Nov–April).

Destinations Bariloche (5–6 weekly; 11hr); El Chaltén (5–6 weekly; 11hr), Comodoro Rivadavia (2 daily 3.20am & 3.30pm; 6hr), Los Antiguos (2 daily 11.30am & midnight; 45min).

INFORMATION AND TOURS

Bank Banco de Santa Cruz on San Martín at Rivadavia has an ATM, but not always functioning; the nearest reliable sources of cash are El Calafate and Bariloche.

Tourist information The helpful tourist office on San Martín at Gendarmería Nacional (mid-Dec to Feb daily 8am–9pm; shorter hours rest of year; T 02963 432732 W peritomoreno.gob.ar) has maps of the town and province.

Tour operators Guanacóndor, Perito Moreno 1087 (T 02963 432303, E jarinauta@yahoo.com.ar), run trips to the Cueva de las Manos, including an excellent hike. If you're heading to El Chaltén, you can combine a half-day tour of the Cueva de las Manos with a bus south from Bajo Caracoles with Chaltén Travel.

ACCOMMODATION AND EATING

There are a couple of small supermarkets along San Martín. Most lodgings double as basic restaurants. If arriving on a late bus, notify your lodgings in advance.

Hotel Americano San Martín 1327 ☎ 02963 432 074, ⓦ hotelamericanoweb.com.ar. The nicest place to stay in town, and one with the friendliest welcome, this budget hotel has compact, clean, warm rooms with small bathrooms and a reasonable restaurant on-site. Book rooms in advance, particularly for Sundays. AR$280

Camping Municipal Mariano Moreno, off San Martín ☎ 02963 432130. Next to the brackish Laguna de los Cisnes in the southern part of town, this campsite has little shelter from the wind, but there are hot showers, an indoor cooking/eating area and rustic four-person cabins. Camping/person AR$20, cabaña AR$300

Salón Iturrioz Rivadavia at San Martín. Food at this atmospheric café is limited to toasted sandwiches and empanadas, but you can check out the beautiful antique tills (one's silver) and the collection of pioneer photos while sipping a coffee, fruit shake or a submarino (frothy hot milk with a melting chocolate bar). Daily 8am–8pm.

LOS ANTIGUOS

West of Perito Moreno, the landscape changes and for much of the 57km journey to the border town of **LOS ANTIGUOS** the RN43 skirts the shore of the impossibly blue **Lago Buenos Aires** (the second-biggest lake in South America, after Lake Titicaca), with the Andes looming beyond.

Small, pretty and more cosmopolitan than Perito Moreno, Los Antiguos is the cherry capital of Argentina and home to a scattering of chacras (independent farms) where you can buy delicious fruits in season. Besides being an attractive stopover along Ruta 40, Los Antiguos is also the gateway to Chile via Chile Chico (see p.461), a mere 12km away.

ARRIVAL AND DEPARTURE

By bus The bus terminal is on Av Tehuelches, a 10min walk to the parallel Av 11 de Julio, the town's main street.

Sportman (☎ 02963 491175) runs to Comodoro Rivadavia via Perito Moreno; La Union (☎ 02963 491078) runs twice-daily shuttles across the border to Chile Chico; Taqsa/Marga (☎ 0297 15419615, ⓦ taqsa.com.ar) serves Bariloche and El Chaltén, as does Chaltén Travel, the latter leaving from Albergue Padilla on alternate days (Nov–April).

Destinations Bariloche (5–6 weekly; 12hr); Chile Chico (2 daily at 12.30pm & 6.30pm; 30min); El Chaltén (5–6 weekly; 12hr); Comodoro Rivadavia via Perito Moreno (2 daily at 2.30am & 2.30pm; 7hr).

INFORMATION AND TOURS

Tourist information The tourist office on 11 de Julio at Lago Buenos Aires (daily 8am–8pm; ☎ 02963 491261) gives out maps of the town and surrounding farms.

Tour operators The Way Travel, Lago Buenos Aires 656 (☎ 0297 5045325), run trips to the Cueva de las Manos on weekends for a minimum of four (AR$580 each). 9am departures from the bus terminal.

ACCOMMODATION AND EATING

Albergue Padilla San Martín 44 ☎ 02963 491140. Family-run guesthouse that attends largely to the needs of Chaltén Travel passengers who get dropped off here in the wee hours. Owners can book onward Ruta 40 tickets. For dorms, bed linen costs extra. Dorms AR$100, doubles AR$450

Camping Municipal RP43 ☎ 02963 491265. On the approach to town, 1.5km away, this lakefront campsite is sheltered from the wind and has hot showers. The windowless cabins sleep up to four but get very hot in summer. Camping/person AR$20, cabaña AR$300

Viva el Viento Av. 11 de Julio 447 ⓦ www.vivaelviento .com. With its eclectic decor and a menu of steaks, pizzas, burgers and milkshakes, this bright Dutch-Argentine-run restaurant is the buzziest place on the strip. Dollars, Euros and Chilean pesos accepted. Steak AR$120. Oct–April daily 9am–9pm.

CUEVA DE LAS MANOS

A couple of hours south of Perito Moreno along Ruta 40 and a wonderfully scenic, steep gravel road that offers marvellous canyon views and plenty of wild animal sightings, the **CUEVA DE LAS MANOS** (daily 9am–7pm; guided tours AR$50) is an astonishing cave displaying 9000-year-old cave paintings depicting guanacos, hunters hurling bolos and, most famously, 829 hand stencils made by ancient local inhabitants using mineral pigments. The cave, a UNESCO World

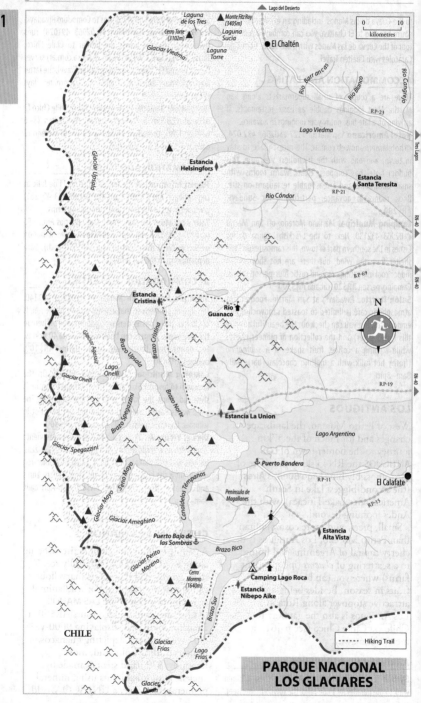

Parque Nacional Los Glaciares

Heritage Site, is easily accessible from Perito Moreno or Los Antiguos via an organized day-trip (AR$580); you can also combine a tour with same-day travel south to El Chaltén with Chaltén Travel.

ACCOMMODATION

Hostería La Cueva de las Manos 7km off the RN40 ☎ 02963 432207, ⓦ cuevadelasmanos.net. The cave is actually located inside this *estancia*'s perimeters and group tours approach it via a fairly tough guided trek that descends into the canyon. There are dorms, private rooms and a restaurant, and staff can organize transport, horse rides, hikes and trips to nearby Charcamata, another rock-art site. Book in advance through the Perito Moreno office, as there's no phone signal or internet at the *estancia*. Closed May–Oct. Dorms AR$320, doubles AR$1400

PARQUE NACIONAL PERITO MORENO

Consisting of over 1150 square kilometres of windy Patagonian steppe and the jagged peaks of the Sierra Colorado, **PARQUE NACIONAL PERITO MORENO** comes complete with herds of guanacos and condors wheeling overhead. Not to be confused with the glacier of the same name (see p.143), the remote national park is located along a rough dirt-and-gravel road that branches off Ruta 40 around halfway between Perito Moreno and El Chaltén; the closest town is Gobernador Gregores. You need a sturdy car to reach the park and you have to bring all your own supplies, including warm gear. Water in the park is drinkable. As the park receives few visitors, you may have it practically to yourself.

There's an information centre at the park entrance where you must register, and where guided hikes can be arranged. Trails include an easy hour's ramble to Pinturas Rupestres (cave paintings), a longer trail leading to Lago Belgrano, a 16km trek to Lago Burgmeister and a tough three-hour ascent of Cerro León (1434m) from *Estancia La Oriental*.

ACCOMMODATION

There are three basic campgrounds with pit toilets and no showers: a wind-battered one at the information centre, a tree-shielded one at Lago Burgmeister and one at El Rincón; no fires permitted. There are two *estancias* which border the park.

La Oriental 1km from Lago Belgrano ☎ 011 4237 4043, ⓦ estanciasdesantacruz.com. This working *estancia* is beautifully situated, and makes a good base for trekking and horseriding. You can bed down in the triples or double in the main house or the triples and a quad in the annexe; room rates include half board. Closed April–Oct. Doubles AR$650

PARQUE NACIONAL LOS GLACIARES

The **PARQUE NACIONAL LOS GLACIARES** hugs the eastern slopes of the Andes, extending for 170km along the border with Chile. A UNESCO World Heritage Site, nearly half of the park's 6000 square kilometres consists of virtually inaccessible continental ice fields. Elsewhere, thirteen glaciers sweep down from craggy mountains into two parallel turquoise lakes – Argentino and Viedma – while dry Patagonian steppe and sub-Antarctic forests of *ñire* (Antarctic beech) and *lenga* (lenga beech) trees provide exceptional trekking country and a home for endangered *huemul* deer, red fox and puma.

The park's northern section can be reached from the village of El Chaltén, where the jagged jaws of the Fitz Roy mountain range dominate a dramatic skyline. Tremendous glaciers, including the show-stopping **Glaciar Perito Moreno** (see p.143), are the stars of the park's southern sector, within easy reach of the town of El Calafate.

EL CHALTÉN

Argentina's self-proclaimed "national trekking capital" **EL CHALTÉN** lies within the boundaries of the Parque Nacional Los Glaciares, 217km northwest of El Calafate. It is set at the confluence of two pristine rivers, overlooked by the granite spires of Monte Fitz Roy (3405m) and Cerro Torre (3102m). El Chaltén means "smoking mountain", a name given to Monte Fitz Roy by the Tehuelche.

El Chaltén is Argentina's youngest town, officially created in 1985 as an

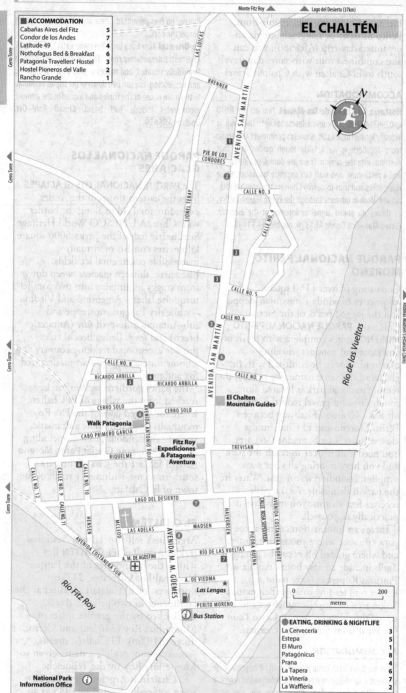

EL CHALTÉN

Monte Fitz Roy ▲   ▲ Lago del Desierto (37km)

ACCOMMODATION
Cabañas Aires del Fitz	5
Condor de los Andes	7
Latitude 49	4
Nothofagus Bed & Breakfast	6
Patagonia Travellers' Hostel	3
Hostel Pioneros del Valle	2
Rancho Grande	1

EATING, DRINKING & NIGHTLIFE
La Cervecería	3
Estepa	5
El Muro	1
Patagónicus	8
Prana	4
La Tapera	6
La Vineria	7
La Wafflería	2

Street labels: LAS LOICAS, BRENNER, AVENIDA SAN MARTIN, PJE DE LOS CONDORES, LIONEL TERAY, CALLE NO. 3, CALLE NO. 4, CALLE NO. 5, CALLE NO. 6, CALLE NO. 7, CALLE NO. 8, RICARDO ARBILLA, CERRO SOLO, AVENIDA ANTONIO ROJO, CABO PRIMERO GARCIA, RIQUELME, CALLE NO. 12, CALLE NO. 9, CALLE NO. 10, CALLE NO. 11, HENSEN, MCLEOD, LAS ADELAS, A. M. DE AGOSTINI, AVENIDA COSTANERA SUR, AVENIDA M. M. GÜEMES, MADSEN, HALVORSEN, RÍO DE LAS VUELTAS, CALLE ROSA SEPÚLVEDA, AVENIDA COSTANERA NORTE, PIEDRA BUENA, A. DE VIEDMA, PERITO MORENO, TREVISAN, LAGO DEL DESIERTO

Río de las Vueltas

Río Fitz Roy

Andrés Madsen's estancia (2km) ►

El Chalten Mountain Guides

Walk Patagonia

Fitz Roy Expediciones & Patagonia Aventura

Las Lengas

Bus Station

National Park Information Office ⓘ

0		200
	metres	

Cerro Torre ◄ (×5)

Lago Viedma & RN-40 to El Calafate ▼

outpost against Chilean encroachment. Since then it has experienced a tourist boom, and during the peak season of December to March, campers, hikers and climbers descend in large numbers, but there are enough trails in the immense park to keep them from getting crowded. From El Chaltén you can also cross over to Chile on foot and by boat (see box below).

Hikes from El Chaltén

Fitz Roy and Torre peaks offer some of the planet's most challenging technical climbing, but there are plenty of paths for beginners. Those short on time can enjoy a number of day-hikes in the national park with trailheads that start right in town.

The most popular trail is the relatively flat hike to **Laguna Torre** (11km; 6hr round-trip), which follows the Río Fitz Roy to a lake resplendent with floating icebergs, overlooked by Cerro Torre. A more strenuous hike is to **Laguna de los Tres** (12.5km; 8hr), which ascends sharply to a glacial lake with in-your-face views of Fitz Roy; this is impassable in the winter.

For the best panoramic views in the area – of both Fitz Roy and Torre as well as Lago Viedma – hike uphill to 1490m-high **Lomo del Pliegue Tumbado**

(12km; 8hr). Short walks include those to the **Chorrillo del Salto** waterfall (4km; 2hr) and uphill to the **Los Condores** viewpoint (1km; 1hr 30min) overlooking the town. A classic multi-day hike is the **Monte Fitz Roy/ Cerro Torre loop** (3 days, 2 nights), which leaves either from El Chaltén or just beyond the park's boundaries at *Hostería El Pilar* (15km north of town; ⍵hosteriaelpilar.com.ar). There are three free **campsites** (with latrines only) along the route.

A tough five-day, anticlockwise loop takes in Laguna Toro, Paso del Viento, amazing views of Glaciar Viedma, and Paso Huemul, before skirting Lago Viedma on the way back to town. Tougher still, and requiring a guide, is the multi-day trek from Río Eléctrico that crosses Glaciar Marconi and involves overnighting at least twice on the Southern Ice Field.

There are good hikes and no crowds in the Lago del Desierto area, and a 25km network of beautifully maintained trails at the private *Reserva Los Huemules* (AR$100; ⍵loshuemules.com), 17km north of El Chaltén (Lago del Desierto transfers pass by it).

The park office produces an excellent **free trekking map**, but for something more detailed, the 1:50,000 *Monte Fitz*

HIKE, BIKE AND SAIL INTO CHILE

From El Chaltén, it's possible to cross to **Villa O'Higgins** (see p.463) in Chile (⍵villaohiggins .com) via an adventurous two-day trip by boat and foot (or bike) in the summer. Start by catching a morning bus from El Chaltén (1hr 30min; AR$260) in time to take the 10am **boat** across Lago del Desierto (late Dec–late Feb: Tues, Fri & Sun; early Dec & March to mid-April fewer departures; AR$260). The lake's northern shore can also be reached by **hiking** (16km; 5hr) along its eastern shore to a free campsite next to the Argentine border post, where you get an exit stamp from the police. From there, a narrow, hilly trail (you'll have to carry your bike part of the way) runs to Laguna Larga (2hr 30min) and beyond to no-man's-land in between. On the Chilean side, the trail turns into a wide dirt-and-gravel road that winds its way down to the Lago O'Higgins and the Chilean border post at Candelario Mancilla (4hr 30min), a handful of houses by the lake. There's a very basic campsite near the dock; the owner also has several rooms to rent (CH$26,000) and can sell you bread. Bring plenty of food, as the ferry from Villa O'Higgins is weather-dependent and you may find yourself lingering here for an extra day or two.

Boats to Villa O'Higgins run on Mondays, Wednesdays, Thursdays and Saturdays in January and February; fewer departures in November, December and March to mid-April. This border crossing is only open from November to March; check ⍵villaohiggins.com for up-to-date boat schedules and prices. Horses can be hired from Lago del Desierto via the website to help with luggage (CH$20,000 per horse, CH$40,000 minimum).

1

Roy & Cerro Torre map published by Zagier and Urruty can be purchased in El Chaltén.

ARRIVAL AND DEPARTURE

By bus The bus terminal is in the southeastern end of town on Güemes, at Perito Moreno. Chaltén Travel (☎ 02962 493092, ⓦ www.chaltentravel.com), Taqsa (☎ 02962 493068, ⓦ taqsa.com.ar) and Cal-tur (☎ 02962 493801, ⓦ caltur.com.ar) all run buses up to three times per day to El Calafate (typically 8am, 1pm & 6pm); Chaltén Travel and Taqsa also run buses up the Ruta 40 every other day (Nov–April). Las Lengas (☎ 02962 493023, ⓦ transportelaslengas.com) run shuttle services to El Calafate Airport, Lago del Desierto, Río Eléctrico and *Hostería El Pilar*. Buy tickets at least a day in advance for all services.

Destinations Bariloche (1–2 daily; around 27hr); El Calafate (3–9 daily; 3hr); El Calafate Airport (1–3 daily; 3hr); Perito Moreno (1–2 daily; 11hr).

INFORMATION AND TOURS

A useful website is ⓦ elchalten.com. Bring plenty of cash: the single ATM at the bus station is unreliable. Dollars, furos and Chilean pesos are widely accepted. There's a basic *puesto sanitario* (health clinic) on Agostini, but for anything major, go to El Calafate.

Parque Nacional Los Glaciares office The excellent park office is at the entrance to town (daily: Dec–Feb 8am–6pm; March–Nov 9am–5pm; ☎ 02962 493004), with free maps, wildlife exhibits, video screenings and advice on leave-no-trace camping. All buses that arrive in El Chaltén stop here for an English- or Spanish-language introduction to the rules of the park. Climbers, multi-day trekkers and those using the Laguna Torre campsite must register here first.

Tourist information There's a helpful tourist office (daily 8am–8pm ☎ 0292 493370) in the bus station.

Tour operators El Chaltén Mountain Guides, San Martín 187 (☎ 02962 493320, ⓦ ecmg.com.ar), run ice-climbing and rock-climbing trips – from half-day introductions to multi-day ventures. Fitz Roy Expediciones, San Martín 56 (☎ 02962 493110, ⓦ fitzroyexpediciones.com.ar), organizes trekking on Glaciar Torre, teaches ice climbing and leads expeditions on the continental ice cap. In the same office, Patagonia Aventura (☎ 02494 436424, ⓦ patagonia-aventura.com) offers boat excursions across the lake to the snout of Glaciar Viedma, and ice-trekking on the glacier itself (AR$1200), which is more interesting than ice trekking on Glaciar Perito Moreno. *Patagonia Hostel* offers transfers to Lago del Desierto (37km) from where you bike back to town with the wind at your back. The Anglo-Argentine-run Walk Patagonia, Antonio Rojo 62 (☎ 02962 493275, ⓦ walkpatagonia.com), can help

you with onward travel planning and booking. Most agencies shut down in the winter.

Walking tour The first European settler to the area, Andreas Madsen, came here from Denmark in 1915 and built the Estancia Cerro Fitz Roy, a 40min walk along the Río de las Vueltas, on the side opposite town. Every day at 3pm, Madsen's great-grandson Fitz Roy leads a walking tour in Spanish, English and German from the bridge (2hr; AR$150; ☎ 02966 15 344540) to the restored *estancia*.

ACCOMMODATION

Reserve a bed in advance if you are coming between December and March. Few places open year-round. Rates include breakfast, unless stated otherwise and all listed accommodation offers (slow) wi-fi. Several basic campsites are scattered throughout the town.

HOSTELS

Condor de los Andes Av Río de las Vueltas, at Halvorsen ☎ 02962 493101, ⓦ condordelosandes.com. A well-run HI hostel that provides all the services that backpackers expect: tour and transport booking, laundry, guest kitchen and lunch boxes for hikers. The four- and six-bed dorms and doubles are all en suite and in the evenings guests congregate in the appealing lounge with stone fireplace. Open mid-Sept to April. Dorms AR$200, doubles AR$660

Hostel Pioneros del Valle San Martín 451 ☎ 02902 492217, ⓦ caltur.com.ar. Located on the main street, the Cal-Tur-affiliated behemoth is fairly impersonal yet professional, and there's a large range of amenities including currency exchange and bus pick-up and drop-off, friendly staff and large, sparsely decorated en-suite, good-value private rooms. Dorms AR$150, doubles AR$500

★**Patagonia Travellers' Hostel** San Martín 493 ☎ 02962 493019, ⓦ patagoniahostel.com.ar. With its slate walls, a beautiful, airy common space with TV and well-equipped guest kitchen, this chalet-like hiker refuge is the most appealing of the town's hostels. Downsides are lockers located outside the simple four-person dorms and school-gym-like communal bathrooms, though private rooms are en suite. Their biking tours from Lago del Desierto are justifiably popular. Mid-Sept to mid-April. Dorms AR$170, doubles AR$750

Rancho Grande San Martín 520 ☎ 02962 493005, ⓦ ranchograndehostel.com. This large Chaltén Travel-affiliated hostel is a backpacker factory, but they're good at what they do. There are snug four-bed dorms, an appealing, two-tiered dining/hangout area, café/bar, small kitchen and staff who help you plan your stay. They also change currency, accept credit cards and sell onward bus tickets. Open year-round. Dorms AR$150, doubles AR$720

GUESTHOUSES

Cabañas Aires del Fitz Ricardo Arbilla 124 ☎ 02962 493134, ⓦ airesdelfitz.com.ar. An effusive hostess runs four split-level cabañas sleeping either two/three or six people; beautiful living spaces include a fully equipped kitchen and satellite TV in the common area, and nice touches such as blackout curtains and drying racks in bathrooms. Open year-round. No breakfast. Cabaña AR$900–1800

Latitude 49 Ricardo Arbilla 145 ☎ 02962 493347, ⓦ latitud49.com.ar. A justifiably popular place with spick-and-span en-suite rooms, plus a couple of self-contained apartments. Closed June & July. Doubles AR$450, apartments AR$600

★ **Nothofagus Bed & Breakfast** Hensen, at Riquelme ☎ 02962 493087, ⓦ nothofagusbb.com.ar. A bright and homely B&B with wooden furnishing and a rustic feel; three rooms are en suites, while the other four share a bathroom; some have views of Fitz Roy. Besides the good breakfast, there's a small library and book exchange. Closed Easter–Oct. AR$700

EATING AND DRINKING

Opening times given are for high season; many places close Easter–October.

La Cervecería San Martín 564. One of the most sociable spots in town, with locals and hikers perching on rough-hewn wooden seats to savour pints of bock or pilsner microbrews or tuck into ample portions of stew, pizza or pasta. Daily 11am–midnight.

★ **Estepa** Cerro Solo, at Antonio Rojo. Featuring snug booths and posters of Jack Daniels, Warhol and Che Guevara, *Estepa* has plenty of culinary creativity. Treat yourself to lamb sweetbreads with lemon butter, smoked trout ravioli (AR$145) and slow-cooked lamb in calafate (berry) sauce with gnocchi (AR$250). Tues–Sun 11.30am–midnight.

El Muro San Martín 948. Steak with peppers and bacon, sweet and sour ribs, salmon *sorrentinos* and slow-cooked lamb with mint are just some of the tempting creations dished up at this hungry hiker haven. There's a climbing wall out back to help you work up an appetite. Mains from AR$130. Daily 7.30pm–midnight.

Patagónicus Güemes, at Madsen. Consistently the best pizza in town (twenty types, including plenty of vegetarian ones), served at big wooden tables. The good range of beers includes their own Chaltén and Patagonicus brews. Small/large pizza from AR$40/80. Mon & Wed–Sun noon–11pm.

Prana San Martín. Indian wall hangings decorate the salmon-pink walls of this snug vegetarian bistro, while delicious smells lure you in to try the likes of brown rice risotto, beetroot gnocchi stuffed with sheep's cheese and lentil stew. Fantastic selection of gourmet teas, too. Mains AR$100–130. Daily noon–11pm.

La Tapera Av Antonio Rojo. Adorable, split-level log cabin with a roaring fire, packed full of hungry punters tucking into pork shoulder cooked with beer, beautifully seared steak, salmon with spring onion and ginger, a smattering of tapas and a couple of cold weather warmers such as lamb and lentil stew. Mains AR$97–192. Daily 12.30–3pm & 7.30–11.30pm.

★ **La Vineria** Av Lago del Desierto 265 ☎ 02962 493301. This busy, buzzy little joint is the place to sample a couple dozen craft beers and wines from all over Argentina, accompanied by sharing platters (AR$330) of cold cuts (smoked venison, trout, black pudding) and local and imported cheeses, as well as gourmet sandwiches (AR$120). Hugely popular, so form an orderly queue. Daily 4pm–midnight.

La Wafflería San Martín. Colourful, snug and run by two friendly guys, *La Wafflería* sates your cravings for waffles. Toppings vary from calafate ice cream with *dulce de leche* to blue cheese, black olives and nuts (AR$49–75), and tipples range from seven types of hot chocolate to El Chaltén's very own Supay brew. Daily 11am–9pm.

EL CALAFATE

If global warming were suddenly to lay waste to the Perito Moreno glacier, **EL CALAFATE** would promptly fizzle out in its wake. Settled by wool traders in the 1920s and named after the edible purple berry that pops up in summer, the town expanded rapidly following the creation of Parque Nacional Los Glaciares in 1937. Perito Moreno glacier remains the main draw for visitors, who flood the town particularly between December and March. The glacier aside, El Calafate makes an excellent base for boat trips, ice trekking, hiking into the remotest corners of this slice of wilderness and visits to local *estancias*.

WHAT TO SEE AND DO

The main drag, Avenida Libertador, is lined with tourism outfits and restaurants, with many lodgings located within a few blocks.

The **Centro de Interpretación Histórica** on Brown, at Bonarelli (Sept–April daily 10am–8pm; May–Aug Mon & Wed–Sun 11am–5pm; AR$80; ⓦ museocalafate.com.ar), does a dramatic job of recounting the area's natural and cultural history in Spanish and English, complete with re-creations

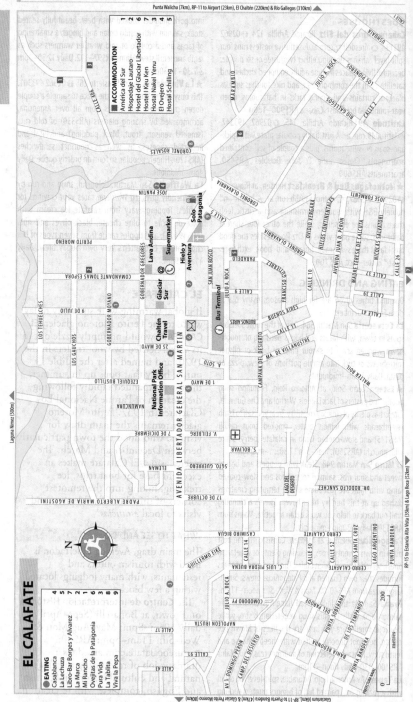

EL CALAFATE

Punta Walichu (7km), RP-11 to Airport (23km), El Chaltén (220km) & Río Gallegos (310km)

■ ACCOMMODATION
América del Sur	1
Hospedaje Lautaro	2
Hostel del Glaciar Libertador	6
Hostel I Keu Ken	7
Hostel Nakel Yenu	3
El Ovejero	4
Hostal Schilling	5

● EATING
Casablanca	4
La Lechuza	5
Libro-Bar Borges y Alvarez	7
La Marca	2
Mi Rancho	1
Ovejitas de la Patagonia	6
Pura Vida	3
La Tablita	8
Viva la Pepa	9

Laguna Nimez (500m)

Glaciarium (6km), RP-11 to Puerto Bandera (47km) & Glaciar Perito Moreno (80km)

RP-15 to Estancia Alta Vista (33km) & Lago Roca (52km)

Lava Andina
Supermarket
Solo Patagonia
Hielo y Aventura
Glaciar Sur
Chaltén Travel
Bus Terminal
National Park Information Office

of Patagonian megafauna and the skeleton of locally found *Austroraptor cabazaii*.

The Glaciarium

The town's main attraction is the Glaciarium (daily: Sept–April 9am–8pm; May–Aug 11am–8pm; AR$180; ⓦglaciarium.com), a superb interactive museum dedicated to glaciers. Displays recount the discovery of the two Patagonian ice fields and the tiny creatures that have adapted to live on the ice. The videos – a 3D documentary on the Parque Nacional Los Glaciares and one on environmental issues – are particularly worthwhile. Free shuttle buses to the Glaciarium depart from the car park on 1 de Mayo, between Avenida Libertador and Avenida Roca (hourly on the hour 9am–noon, then every 30min until 6pm; reduced service May–Aug).

ARRIVAL AND DEPARTURE

By plane El Calafate's airport (ⓦaeropuertoelcalafate .com) is 22km east of town; taxis (AR$200) and minibuses run by Ves Patagonia (AR$90; ☎02902 497355, ⓦvespatagonia.com) connect it with El Calafate.

Destinations Daily flights to Bariloche, Buenos Aires, Trelew, Río Gallegos and Ushuaia.

By bus The bus terminal is at Av Roca, one block up a flight of steps from Av Libertador.

Destinations Bariloche (summer only; 1 daily; 30hr); El Chaltén (high season 3 daily, typically 8am, 1pm & 6.30pm; Chaltén Travel; ☎02902 492212, ⓦwww .chaltentravel.com; Taqsa; ☎02902 491843, ⓦtaqsa .com.ar; and Cal-Tur (☎02902 491842, ⓦcaltur.com.ar); Puerto Natales (Chile; 3–4 weekly; 6hr); up the Ruta 40

(Nov–April every other day; Chaltén Travel and Taqsa). Río Gallegos, change here for daily departures to Ushuaia (4–5 daily; 4hr–4hr 30min; Taqsa and Sportman; ☎02902 492680).

INFORMATION AND TOURS

Parque Nacional Los Glaciares office The national park office on Av Libertador 1302 has maps and can provide up-to-date information (Mon–Fri 8am–6pm, Sat & Sun 9am–6pm; ☎02902 491005, ⓦparquesnacionales.gov.ar).

Tourist information There's a kiosk in the bus terminal (daily: summer 8am–10pm; winter 8am–8pm).

Tour operators Hielo y Aventura, Av Libertador 935 (☎02902 492205, ⓦhieloyaventura.com), offers trekking and ice-trekking trips on Glaciar Perito Moreno (from AR$640) and boat excursions to the glacier. Glaciar Sur, 9 de Julio 57, Local 2 (☎02902 495050, ⓦglaciarsur.com), is the only operator allowed to take small groups of visitors into the pristine, remote southwestern corner of Parque Nacional Los Glaciares (see p.135). Solo Patagonia, Av Libertador 867 (☎02902 491115, ⓦsolopatagonia.com), runs full-day boat trips to Upsala, Spegazzini and Perito Moreno glaciers.

ACCOMMODATION

Reserve in advance for high season. Rates include breakfast, internet/wi-fi access and kitchen use.

HOSTELS AND CAMPSITES

★**América del Sur** Puerto Deseado 151 ☎02902 493525, ⓦamericahostel.com.ar. A well-designed, spacious and friendly place with wonderful views of Lago Argentino and knowledgeable staff who can help you organize a wide range of trips. The four-bed dorms and private rooms are clean, bright and have under-floor heating. It's a 10min uphill walk from the centre. Dorms AR$280, doubles AR$700

Hostel del Glaciar Libertador Av Libertador 587 ☎02902 491792, ⓦglaciar.com. This enormous (and somewhat anonymous) wooden house sleeps more

---

ESTANCIAS IN PATAGONIA

Patagonia's empty steppe is speckled with isolated *estancias* – the legacy of the first pioneers – and many of these open their doors to visitors. As lodgings, most cater to high-end tourists, but many are accessible on day visits if you wish to take part in hiking, horseriding, *asados* and perhaps witness a sheep-shearing demonstration.

Estancia Cristina ☎02902 491133, ⓦestanciacristina.com. Completely devoted to tourism these days, and one of the most popular day-trips from El Calafate, involving a boat ride across the northern arm of Lago Argentino and plenty of scope for hiking and horseriding.

Estancia Nibepo Aike ☎02902 492797, ⓦnibepoaike.com.ar. A working *estancia* by Lago Roca where you can take a peek at the world of cattle ranching, go horseriding, cycle around the property and enjoy an evening barbecue.

than a hundred, has spotless dorms with private bathrooms and lovely private rooms. Walls are thin, and the service is professional but impersonal. Dorms AR$180, doubles AR$740

Hostel I Keu Ken FM Pontoriero 171 ☎ 02902 495175, ⊛ patagoniaikeuken.com.ar. An intimate but lively hilltop hostel with a balcony that enjoys the afternoon sun and lake vistas. Dorms and bathrooms are pretty ordinary, although the two adjacent, fully equipped cabañas are good bets if you're travelling with friends. Dorms AR$190, doubles AR$580 cabañas AR$760

Hostel Nakel Yenu Puerto San Julián 244 ☎ 02902 493711, ⊛ hostelnakelyenu.com. This refurbished, bright yellow hostel, with psychedelic mural, dreamcatchers and guitar for guest use, is one of the cosiest and most chilled-out in town. The kitchen/lounge are in a separate building next door so as not to disturb early sleepers, six- and four-bed dorms have lockers and the owners throw barbecues most weekends. A 10min uphill walk from the centre. Closed June–August. Dorms AR$200, doubles AR$700

El Ovejero José Pantín 64 ☎ 02902 493422. Just a block from the main street, this clean campsite is protected from the wind by a row of trees and sits alongside a babbling brook and a *parilla* restaurant. Price includes hot showers and there are picnic tables and *fogones* (fire pits for cooking; firewood costs extra). Pitches across the stream are cheaper (AR$60) but have a longer trek to the bathroom. Camping AR$60

GUESTHOUSES

Hospedaje Lautaro Espora 237 ☎ 02902 492698, ⊛ hospedajelautaro.com.ar. A super-friendly option where you'll feel just like one of the family, *Hospedaje Lautaro* has a mix of dorms and private rooms, a communal lounge and free tea and coffee, and particularly shines when it comes to hospitality. Dorms AR$180, doubles AR$480

Hostal Schilling Gobernador Paradelo 141 ☎ 02902 491453, ⊛ hostalschilling.com. This professionally run guesthouse offers spacious, comfortable but featureless en-suite rooms and a single dorm. Its vast lounge wall has been decorated by globetrotting guests of all ages, there's a bar on site, and the owner runs the excellent Glaciar Sur trips. Dorms AR$170, doubles AR$440

EATING AND DRINKING

Outside of the high season, most places have reduced opening hours.

Casablanca Av Libertador 1202. Buzzing café-bar that serves good coffee and fifteen types of beer (from around AR$45), plus tasty *lomitos* (Argentine steak sandwich), burgers and other alcohol-soaking delights. Classic film posters and signed hockey and rugby shirts decorate the place. Mon, Tues & Thurs–Sun noon–midnight.

La Lechuza Av Libertador 1301 ⊛ lalechuzapizzas.com.ar. This deservedly popular place serves up thirty or so varieties of what are arguably the best pizzas in town (AR$103–148) from its wood-fired oven, plus pasta dishes, make-your-own salads and huge sandwiches. There are a couple of other branches. Daily noon–midnight.

Libro-Bar Borges y Alvarez Av Libertador 1015. This small, warm café-bar with a cave-like, book-covered lounge attracts bibliophiles and cocktail lovers alike. There's an extensive range of Argentine and South American coffee-table books to flick through while perusing the long list of cocktails (AR$85–99), or sipping an Antares beer or coffee. Mon, Tues & Thurs–Sun 10am–3am.

La Marca Jose Pantín 64. Attached to a campsite and hostel, this is a local favourite for all-you-can-eat *parilla*; AR$178 will get you your fill of lamb, steak, chicken, chorizo, morcilla (black pudding) and *chinchulines* (crispy lamb entrails). Daily noon–11pm.

★ **Mi Rancho** Gobernador Moyano, at 9 de Julio ☎ 02902 490540. All exposed brick and homey touches, this intimate little restaurant offers some wonderfully creative and surprisingly affordable dishes, including king crab ravioli with Vermouth sauce and lamb T-bone with calafate reduction. Round off with a passion-fruit parfait or apple crumble. Mains AR$120–175. Reserve ahead. Daily noon–3pm & 8pm–midnight.

Ovejitas de la Patagonia Av Libertador 1370. The best of the El Calafate's ice cream places, *Ovejitas* specializes in a couple of dozen flavours of extra-creamy gelato delight, ranging from fruity to *dulce de leche*, white chocolate and mascarpone. From AR$30. Daily noon–10pm.

Pura Vida Av Libertador 1876 ☎ 0290 493356. A fantastic little restaurant specializing in refined Argentine home cooking, *Pura Vida* provides a reprieve from steakhouses in the form of "Granny's lentil stew", country chicken pie, lamb *empanadas* and gnocchi in saffron sauce. Save room for dessert. Mains AR$110–160. Mon, Tues & Thurs–Sun 7.30–11.30pm.

★ **La Tablita** Colonel Rosales 28 ☎ 02902 491065, ⊛ la-tablita.com.ar. An El Calafate institution for over 25 years, this large hall heaves with discerning carnivores who come for the spit-roasted Patagonian lamb, slabs of steak and traditional gaucho fare, such as lamb chitterlings and sweetbreads. If there's two of you, go for "Mix Carnes" (AR$400), and unless you're ravenous, half a steak (AR$110) is plenty. Evening reservations recommended. Daily noon–3.30pm & 7pm–midnight.

Viva la Pepa Emilio Amado 833 ⊛ vivalapepacalafate .com. Cheerful, whimsical café decorated with children's paintings and specializing in sweet and savoury crêpes – think lamb with honey and rosemary, chicken with blue cheese and pear and *dulce de leche* with chocolate-covered banana (AR$68–90) – as well as soups, sandwiches, fresh juices and coffee. Mon–Wed & Fri–Sun noon–8pm.

DIRECTORY

Banks There are three banks with ATMs including at the Banco de la Nacion, Av Libertador 1133, and Banco de Santa Cruz, Av Libertador 1285.
Car rental Avis, Av Libertador 1078 (⊕02902 492877, ⓦavis.com); Fiorasi, Av Libertador 1341 (⊕02902 495330, ⓦfiorasirentacar.com). Prices start at around AR$700/day.
Laundry Lava Andina, Espora 88.
Post office Av Libertador 1133.

PERITO MORENO GLACIER

The **PERITO MORENO GLACIER** is one of Argentina's greatest natural wonders. It's not the longest of the country's glaciers – Upsala is twice as long (60km) – and whereas the ice cliffs at its snout tower up to 60m high, the face of Spegazzini can reach heights double that. However, such comparisons prove irrelevant when you make your way along the extensive network of boardwalks facing the towering wall and seemingly endless field of immense white and blue spikes, and hear the muffled cracks as enormous chunks of ice cleave from the face of this immense glacier and drop into the lagoon. Afternoons are the better time to visit, as the majority of tours arrive in the morning.

Perito Moreno is considered to be "stable" in the sense that it is neither advancing nor retreating. It periodically pushes right across the channel, forming a massive dyke of ice that cuts off the Brazo Rico and Brazo Sur from the main body of Lago Argentino. Isolated from their natural outlet, the water in the *brazos* (arms) builds up against the flank of the glacier, flooding the surrounding area, until eventually the pressure forces open a passage into the canal once again. Occurring over the course of several hours, such a rupture is, for those lucky enough to witness it, one of nature's most awesome spectacles.

UPSALA AND OTHER GLACIERS

Although receding fast, **GLACIAR UPSALA** remains the longest glacier in the park and indeed in South America. The same height as Perito Moreno (60m), Upsala is twice as long (roughly 60km), 7km wide and known for calving huge, translucent icebergs that bob around Lago Argentino like surreal art sculptures. Located 45km west of El Calafate, Upsala is accessible by **catamaran excursion** along Lago Argentino's northern arm (boats leave from Puerto Bandera). Full-day tours (AR$1200, plus the park entry fee), usually called "All Glaciers" and taking in the Upsala, Spegazzini and Perito Moreno glaciers, are run by Solo Patagonia (Av Libertador 867; ⊕02902 491115, ⓦsolopatagonia.com). Upsala is occasionally inaccessible when icebergs block the channels.

LAGO ROCA AND AROUND

The southern arm of Lago Argentino, and also known as Brazo Sur, **LAGO ROCA** is fringed by dense forest and hemmed in by mountains. This is the least visited and the most serene corner of the park, but to reach the most spectacular part – an unnamed glacial lagoon full of enormous chunks of ice, fed by two glaciers and with Glaciar Dickson peeping from the border of Chile's Torres del Paine National Park

---

VISITING PERITO MORENO GLACIER

The **entry fee** for the Perito Moreno section of the park (daily 8am–7pm) is AR$150, payable at the park entrance, 30km before the glacier. Most people visit on a guided **day-trip**, which is offered by virtually all the agencies in El Calafate and allows for around four hours at the ice face. They cost around AR$430–450, excluding the entry fee. To visit independently, take one of the **buses** that leave from El Calafate's terminal (2–3 daily; around 1hr 30min).

One-hour **catamaran cruises** (daily Oct–May hourly 10am–4pm; June–Sept noon; AR$220) to see Perito Moreno's southern face leave from Puerto Bajo de las Sombras; regular minibuses shuttle here from the main viewing boardwalks, 6km away. For an even closer view of the glacier, Hielo y Aventura (see p.141) offers **ice-trekking** trips (wearing crampons) across its surface from AR$1200, excluding the park entry fee.

1

CROSSING INTO TIERRA DEL FUEGO

Reaching **Argentine Tierra del Fuego** or, specifically, **Ushuaia**, from the Argentine mainland requires travelling through Chilean territory. The journey, which takes the better part of a day (there are no night buses along this route and the border post in Tierra del Fuego is no longer open at night), involves crossing two borders, thus getting stamped in and out of Chile and Argentina twice, and a thirty-minute ferry ride across the Magellan Strait. If you book a bus ticket from Río Gallegos to Ushuaia, the ferry crossing is included in the ticket price and the bus driver will guide you through the border crossing formalities.

(see p.472) – you have to go via organized tour. Glaciar Sur (see p.141) is currently the only company allowed to bring a group of up to fourteen people three times a week here. The tour involves a boat ride to the southern end of Brazo Sur, an hour's stiff hike to the smaller Lago Frías, a zodiac boat ride across and then a spectacular, mostly flat, hike along a dried riverbed to the lagoon, with waterfalls cascading down the mountains on one side.

RÍO GALLEGOS

The grim and windy oil refining port of **RÍO GALLEGOS** is an inevitable (but mercifully brief) stop for travellers travelling by bus between El Calafate and Ushuaia (if not heading to Punta Arenas in Chile) or between El Calafate, Ushuaia and destinations along the east coast of Argentina.

ARRIVAL AND DEPARTURE

By plane Río Gallegos Airport is 7km west of the city. A taxi to the centre costs around AR$120–150.
Destinations Daily flights with Aerolíneas Argentinas to Buenos Aires and several weekly to Ushuaia; several weekly flights with LADE to El Calafate, Buenos Aires and Ushuaia.
By bus The bus terminal is 3km west of the city at the corner of Av Eva Perón and the RN3. Bus marked "B" or "terminal" connects the bus terminal with downtown; a taxi costs AR$50–60.
Destinations Buenos Aires (several daily, 36–40hr); El Calafate (4–5 daily; 4–5hr); Puerto Madryn (7 daily; 15–19hr); Ushuaia (daily; 12hr). In Chile: Punta Arenas (2 daily; 3hr 30min); Puerto Natales (3 weekly; 4hr).

INFORMATION

Tourist information There's a tourist information booth in the bus terminal (Mon–Fri 7am–8pm, Sat & Sun 7am–2pm & 4–8pm; ☎02966 442159).

ACCOMMODATION

Accommodation caters mostly to business travellers, so budget options are thin on the ground.
Hospedaje Elcira Pje Zuccarino 431 ☎02966 429856. Handy for the bus station, this neat guesthouse is sweetly adorned to look like a stereotypical grandma's house, with a TV lounge and a kitchen for guests. Dorms AR$130, doubles AR$360
Sehuén Rawson 160 ☎02966 425683, ⊚hotelsehuen .com. An efficiently run little hotel with a range of decent rooms; each has a TV, phone and boxy private bathroom, and breakfast is served in a vaulted room. AR$480

EATING

British Club Roca 935 ☎02966 432668, ⊚britishclub .com.ar. A port of call for Bruce Chatwin, this atmospheric place has more than a hint of a gentleman's club about it. The weekday lunch menu (AR$50) is a bargain and the à la carte temps with the likes of Lancashire hotpot and black hake with vegetable risotto. Mains from AR$130. An English high tea is served around 5pm. Daily noon–midnight.
★ **Laguanacazul** Gob Lista, at Sarmiento ☎02966 444144. Chef Mirko Ionfrida doesn't shy from using locally sourced game in his Patagonian cuisine, so expect the likes of guanaco and rhea. At this waterfront restaurant, slow-cooked lamb is a worthy splurge; don't even think about turning up in backpacker gear. Mains from around AR$130. Tues–Sun noon–3pm & 8pm–midnight.

Tierra del Fuego

A rugged and isolated archipelago at the extreme southern tip of the continent, **TIERRA DEL FUEGO** (Land of Fire) marks the finish line for South America. Here the Andes range marches into the chilly southern waters; deciduous forests and Ice Age glaciers lie a stone's throw from a wildlife-rich shoreline, penguins and sea lions huddle on rocky islets, salmon and trout thrash about in the rivers, and sheep and guanacos graze on arid windswept plains.

The archipelago is shared, with historic hostility, by Argentina and Chile, and only about a third of Isla Grande (Tierra del Fuego's main island) belongs to Argentina. This includes **Ushuaia**, however, the region's top destination. As locals will proudly point out, it is the planet's southernmost inhabited city. It's a fantastic base for exploring the lakes and mountains of **Parque Nacional Tierra del Fuego**, wildlife-watching trips on the **Beagle Channel**, and summer cruises to **Antarctica**.

High season is from December to March, when days are longest and warmest. Spring (Oct to mid-Nov) is beautiful and lush, but can be seriously windy. In autumn (late March to April) the countryside lights up in warm shades of red and orange. But Ushuaia's growing status as a winter-sports playground ensures it is now a year-round destination.

USHUAIA

Sandwiched between the Sierra Venciguerra range and the deep blue of the icy Beagle Channel, **USHUAIA** has one of the most dramatic locations of all Argentine cities, its colourful houses tumbling down the hillside, and the bay protected from southwesterly winds and occasional thrashing storms.

The city lies 3500km south of Buenos Aires and just 1000km north of **Antarctica**, a fact you'll have no problem detecting: even in summer you may need to wrap up warm.

WHAT TO SEE AND DO

A former penal colony, Ushuaia is not the best-planned city, but it has a clutch of absorbing museums, and an excellent dining scene. Most of the tourist and commercial action is centred on **San Martín** and **Maipú** streets, while boats leave on wildlife-watching excursions from the Muelle Turístico. The post office issues end-of-the-world stamps, conveniently forgetting about Puerto

Williams (see p.475). There's good **hiking** in Parque Nacional Tierra del Fuego, plus ice climbing or trekking on nearby glaciers, horseriding in nature reserves, scuba diving in the chilly harbour, boating to penguin and sea-lion colonies and skiing and dog sledding in winter. You can also visit the historic *Estancia Harberton*.

Museo del Fin del Mundo

The **Museo del Fin del Mundo**, Maipú, at Rivadavia (Mon 2–7pm, Tues–Fri 10am–7pm, Sat & Sun 2–8pm; AR$90), has exhibits on the region's indigenous peoples – the Yámana, Selk'nam, Alakalúf – and the arrival of the Christian missionaries, including a rare example of the Selk'nam–Spanish dictionary written by the Salesian missionary José María Beauvoir. There's also a section on bird life, with stuffed specimens, while the figurehead of the *Duchess of Albany*, a ship wrecked in 1893, looks on overhead.

Museo Yámana

A small gem of a museum at Rivadavia 56 (daily: summer 10am–8pm, winter noon–7pm; generally closed July & Aug; AR$60), **Museo Yámana** explores the remarkable lifestyle and egalitarian society of the Yámana people who lived along the Tierra del Fuego coast for over seven thousand years and, tragically, were wiped out after the founding of the 1869 Anglican mission, which introduced European diseases. Dioramas re-creating their dwellings and fishing techniques demonstrate how the Yámana lived in harmony with nature despite the inhospitable climate.

Museo Marítimo y Presidio

Housed inside the city's former prison, the excellent **Museo Marítimo y Presidio**, at Yaganes & Gobernador Paz (daily 10am–8pm; AR$150; ⓦmuseomaritimo .com), displays exhibits that range from the maritime exploration of Antarctica and its wildlife to life in the prison and its most notorious inhabitants, arranged inside the cells. Most engaging are the

1

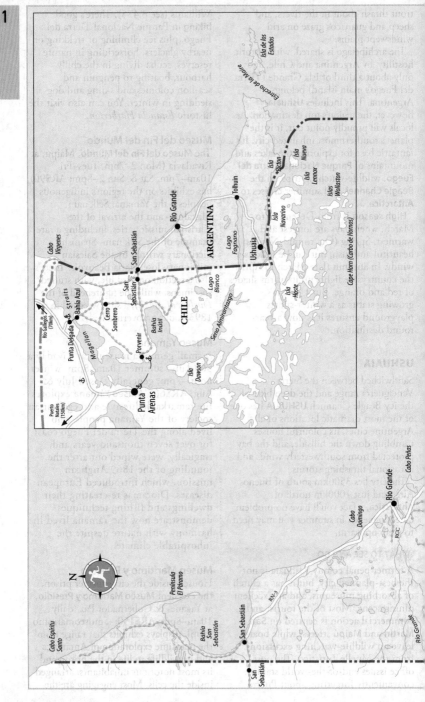

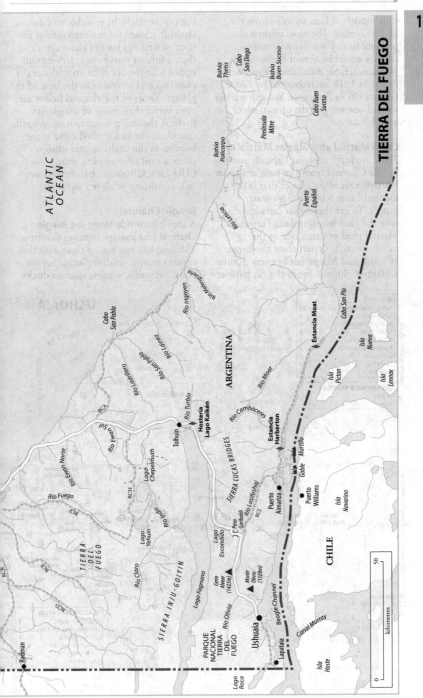

TIERRA DEL FUEGO

ATLANTIC OCEAN

Bahía Thetis

Cabo San Diego

Bahía Buen Suceso

Cabo Buen Suceso

Península Mitre

Bahía Policarpo

Puerto Español

Río Leticia

Cabo San Pablo

Río Irigoyen

Río Malengüena

Cabo San Pío

Estancia Moat

Isla Nueva

Río Moat

Río Cambaceres

Isla Picton

Isla Lennox

ARGENTINA

Río Turbio

Hostería Lago Kaikén

Tolhuin

Río Ladrillero

Río San Pablo

Río Claro

Río Ewan Sur

Río Ewan Norte

Lago Chepelmuth

SIERRA LUCAS BRIDGES

Estancia Harberton

Isla Gable

Río Gable Martillo

Puerto Almanza

Puerto Williams

Río Fuego

RCA

RCH

RC9

Río Olivia

Río Claro

Lago Yehuin

TIERRA DEL FUEGO

Lago Fagnano

Lago Escondido

Paso Garibaldi

Cerro Alvear (1425m)

Monte Olivia (1328m)

Isla Navarino

CHILE

Isla Hoste

SIERRA INJU-GOIYIN

PARQUE NACIONAL TIERRA DEL FUEGO

Río Olivia

Ushuaia

Lapataia

Beagle Channel

Canal Murray

Lago Roca

RCH

RC8

RCD

RL-5

Redman

0   50
kilometres

1

scale models of famous ships from the island's history. The most celebrated prisoner to stay was early twentieth-century anarchist Simón Radowitzsky, whose miserable incarceration and brief escape in 1918 are recounted by Bruce Chatwin in *In Patagonia*. You can wander around one wing of the prison, which has been left bare.

Cerro Martial and Glaciar Martial

There are lofty views of Ushuaia and the Beagle Channel from the base of **Glaciar Martial**, a receding glacier that is the source of much of the city's water supply. To get there, you can either take the 7km winding Luis Fernando Martial road or catch one of the minibuses that depart from the corner of Fadúl and Maipú (daily every 30min 8.30am–6.30pm). From the car park at the top, it might be possible to take the chairlift (closed for maintenance at the time of writing) part of the way; it's then a further one-hour-thirty-minute uphill hike (or 2hr hike up without the chairlift) and scramble to the base of the glacier. Views of the channel below are even better than those of the glacier itself. A charming mountain *refugio* sells snacks, coffee and mulled wine at the bottom of the chairlift, and canopy tours are on offer in peak season (AR$230–320; ⓦcanopyushuaia.com .ar), consisting of eleven zip-lines.

Beagle Channel

A scenic boat ride along the **Beagle Channel** (the passage heading east from Ushuaia) lets you get up close with the region's marine wildlife, including sea lions, penguins, whales, steamer ducks,

USHUAIA

EATING
Almacén de Ramos Generales	10
BarDPizzas	5
Bodegón Fueguino	4
Kalma Resto	8
María Lola Resto	2
Placeres Patagonicos	1
La Rueda	7
Tante Sara	6
El Vagón	9

DRINKING & NIGHTLIFE
Dublin	3
Kuar	11

ACCOMMODATION
Antarctica Hostel	5
Camping Pista del Andino	1
La Casa de Alba	9
La Casa en Ushuaia	4
Los Cormoranes	2
Cruz del Sur	6
Galeazzi-Basily B&B	3
La Posta	8
Yakush	7

cormorants and albatrosses. Excursions, in vessels that range from small fishing boats to large catamarans, generally last three to eight hours (AR$450–800). The more popular trips take in the sea-lion colony at **Isla de los Lobos** and the sea-bird-nesting site at **Isla de los Pájaros**, and then sail past **Faro Les Eclaireurs**, often incorrectly dubbed "the Lighthouse at the End of the World". Some longer trips take in the penguin colony at **Isla Martillo** (Oct–May only) or head west into the national park or east to *Estancia Harberton* and the Reserva Yekapasela penguin colony. A number of agencies (see p.150) offer tours from the Muelle Turístico.

Estancia Harberton

Tierra del Fuego's oldest farmstead, **Estancia Harberton** (mid-Oct to mid-April daily 10am–7pm; AR$150, includes a guided tour and museum; Ⓦestanciaharberton.com), perches on a secluded peninsula in a sheltered bay overlooking the Beagle Channel. Founded in 1886, this working sheep station lies 85km east of Ushuaia along the paved RN3 and then the scenic, bumpy, dirt-and-gravel RC-j route. The land was a government donation to the English missionary Reverend Thomas Bridges in recognition of his work with the local indigenous population and for rescuing shipwreck victims from the channels. His descendants now run the *estancia*, offering guided tours that take in Tierra del Fiego's oldest house and a replica Yaghan dwelling – cooking up meals (around AR$90) at the on-site restaurant, serving tea at the old teahouse, overnight stays in the cottages and free camping on the property (ask permission first).

The excellent **marine wildlife museum** on the property (Ⓦacatushun.org) features murals and skeletons of large whales, dolphins, and more, their remains recovered after sea mammals were left stranded at Bahía San Sebastián. Minibuses for the *estancia* leave Ushuaia from 25 de Mayo and Avenida Maipú at 9am, returning at 3pm. Some day-long Beagle Channel boat excursions stop here (see above).

Cerro Castor

With a ski season that runs from late May to early September, the Sierra Alvear ranges, northeast of town and accessible from the RN3, are home to a growing number of resorts. The pick of the bunch, 26km away, is **Cerro Castor**, the world's most southerly ski resort, with 22km of downhill runs (ski passes from AR$470 per day; Ⓦcerrocastor .com), cafés, lodges and more. Minibuses leave frequently from the waterfront at the corner of Juan Fadul and Avenida Maipú.

ARRIVAL AND DEPARTURE

By plane Ushuaia Airport is 4km southwest of the centre of town; a taxi costs around AR$55–75.

Destinations Daily flights to Buenos Aires, El Calafate and Trelew, and less frequent services to Puerto Madryn and Río Gallegos.

By boat At research time, the larger Fernández Campbell boats from Ushuaia to Puerto Williams, Isla Navarino (see p.475), were no longer running, so if you wish to cross the Beagle Channel to Chile, the only option is to take one of the eight-person daily zodiac boats with Ushuaia Boating (Ⓣ02901 436193) or Piratour (Ⓣ02901 424834, Ⓦpiratour.com.ar). One-way tickets cost US$125. These boats are notoriously weather-dependent; if it's too windy, they can be delayed for hours and sometimes days. Both companies have kiosks at the Muelle Turístico.

By bus There's no central bus terminal; instead buses depart from their company offices. These are the summer season timetables; out of season, services are reduced drastically. Book well ahead in peak season. Buses Pacheco (San Martín 1267; Ⓣ02901 437073, Ⓦbusespacheco.com) runs buses to Punta Arenas (6 weekly; 12hr). Bus Sur (San Martín 245; Ⓣ02901 430727, Ⓦbus-sur.cl) has services (4 weekly) to Punta Arenas (12hr) and Puerto Natales (15hr). Tecni Austral also has services to Punta Arenas and a single one to Río Gallegos (daily 5am; 12hr); book through Tolkar (Roca 157, Ⓣ02901 431408, Ⓦtolkarturismo.com.ar). Taqsa (Godoy 41, Ⓣ02901 435453, Ⓦtaqsa.com.ar) has a single daily bus (5am) to Río Gallegos. Buses for Punta Arenas leave at either 5am or 8am.

INFORMATION AND TOURS

Tourist information The main tourist office is at Av Prefectura Naval Argentina 470 (Mon–Fri 9am–10pm; Sat & Sun 9am–8pm; Ⓣ02901 437666, Ⓦturismoushuaia .com), by the passenger boat terminal.

Parque Nacional Tierra del Fuego office Av San Martín 1395 (Mon–Fri 9am–4pm; Ⓣ02901 421315,

ⓦparquesnacionales.gov.ar). Fishing licences are available from here.

Tour operators Canal Fun, Roca 136 (ⓣ02901 435777, ⓦcanalfun.com) runs 4WD trips to Lago Fangano, including a barbecue, and kayaking trips; Companía de Guías, San Martín 628 (ⓣ02901 437753, ⓦcompaniadeguias.tur.ar), organizes trekking, mountain biking and sea kayaking excursions; Rumbo Sur, San Martín 350 (ⓣ02901 421139, ⓦrumbosur.com.ar), offers a range of tours and day-trips, from kayaking to beaver-spotting. Piratour, at Muelle Turístico (ⓣ02901 424834, ⓦpiratour.net), is the only boat company authorized to offer a walk with the Magellanic penguins on Isla Martillo, which allows you to see the birds close up; Tres Marías Excursiones at Muelle Turístico (ⓣ02901 436416, ⓦtresmariasweb.com) are the only company allowed to land on Isla H, taking eight passengers at a time on hiking/birding excursions. Ushuaia Divers (ⓣ02901 444701, ⓦtierradelfuego.org.ar/divers) operates diving trips in the Beagle Channel.

ACCOMMODATION

In the December to March high season, book accommodation well in advance. All those listed below provide kitchens, free breakfast and internet/wi-fi access.

HOSTELS AND CAMPSITES

Antarctica Hostel Antartida Argentina 270 ⓣ02901 435774, ⓦantarcticahostel.com. This hostel's best feature is the huge, light-drenched lounge with colourful wall hangings, mini-library, guitars for guest use and a bona fide bar serving a range of beers and cocktails. However, the plain upstairs dorms are a bit of a hike from the downstairs bathrooms. Dorms AR$170, doubles AR$500

Camping Pista del Andino 3km uphill at Av Alem 2873 ⓣ02901 414664. This site has bay views and good facilities, including a kitchen and bike rental. They offer free pick-up from town. Camping/person AR$80

Los Cormoranes Kamshen 788 ⓣ02901 423459, ⓦloscormoranes.com. A stiff hike (or short cab ride) uphill from the city, this hostel has plenty *buena onda* (good vibes), lounge for swapping stories from the road and lovely, helpful staff. The facilities are a bit worn, but some rooms have great city views and breakfast includes make-your-own eggs and fresh oranges for squeezing. AR$180

Cruz del Sur Deloqui 242 ⓣ02901 434099, ⓦxdelsur .com.ar. A dorms-only hostel, with rather compact, mixed gender four- and six-bed dorms. There's plenty of beanbag-strewn common spaces for socializing and walls graffitied by happy customers. Dorms AR$200

★**La Posta** Perón Sur 864 ⓣ02901 444650, ⓦlapostahostel.com.ar. A 20min walk south of the centre, this sparkling hostel ticks every box: two kitchens, free

laundry, well-scrubbed dorms, private rooms and self-contained apartments. It has a sense of guest camaraderie without it being a party place, plus staff who will bend over backwards to help you. Dorms AR$210, doubles AR$630, apartments AR$1100

Yakush Piedrabuena 118 ⓣ02901 435807. Spacious and with good guest chill-out areas, this central hostel gets high marks for the helpfulness of its staff. The dorms are roomy enough to spread out in, one of the doubles is en suite and breakfast is good but unexceptional. Dorms AR$200, doubles AR$645

GUESTHOUSES

La Casa de Alba Belakamain 247 ⓣ02901 430473. Congenial Alba (who speaks a little English) presides over a set of cosy, sparsely furnished rooms connected by a creaky staircase. There's a kettle for guest use in the dining area (but no kitchen), and wi-fi comes and goes like a stray cat. A 15min walk southwest of the centre. AR$400

La Casa en Ushuaia Gobernador Paz ⓣ02901 423202, ⓦlacasaenushuaia.com. Run by the helpful, trilingual Silvia, this set of comfortable, cream-coloured doubles benefits from its central location, good breakfast and plenty of city-related information on hand. Solo travellers get an AR$160 discount. The only downside is the ratio of rooms to shared bathroom. AR$710

★**Galeazzi-Basily B&B** Gobernador Valedéz 323 ⓣ02901 423213, ⓦavesdelsur.com.ar. Run by hospitable English- and French-speaking owners, this large family house on a quiet residential street a few blocks uphill from the centre has simple twins, double, kitchen access, and hot drinks and cakes on offer all day. The two self-contained cabañas in the backyard offer more privacy and sleep up to four. Doubles AR$710, cabañas AR$1400

★**TREAT YOURSELF**

Kalma Restó Antartida Argentina 57 ⓣ02901 425786, ⓦkalmaresto.com.ar. Still the culinary king of Ushuaia, chef Jorge comes out to explain the dishes to diners at this intimate restaurant. His menu changes, depending on the season, but you may be treated to crab and roast pumpkin ravioli with saffron sauce, his signature black hake and the "deconstructed" *chocotorta*. The presentation and service are flawless, with dishes often adorned with edible flowers and delicate sauces. Mains from AR$140. Reservations essential. Mon–Fri 12.30–3pm & 7–11.30pm, Sat 7–11.30pm.

EATING

Seafood is king here, especially the local *centolla* (king crab), though *cordero al palo* (spit-roasted lamb), a Fuegian speciality, is also well represented. Many places operate restricted opening hours during the low season (May–Sept).

Almacén de Ramos Generales Av Maipú 749. At this half-museum, half-café/bakery, the antique-dotted surroundings are as much of a draw as the hearty soups, sandwiches, cakes and *picadas* (shared platters; from AR$170). See if you can spot the porcelain chamber pots, the splendid antique bank till and the harlequin doll peeking out of a chest. Daily 9am–midnight.

BarDPizzas San Martín 753 ⓦ bardpizzas.com.ar. Centrally located pizzeria catering to vegetarians and mighty meaty lovers alike with their decent thin-and-crispy offerings. On Wednesdays there's a two-for-one Beagle beer on tap. Pizzas from AR$45. Daily noon–midnight.

★ **Bodegón Fueguino** San Martín 895. Park yourself down on a sheepskin-draped wooden bench in this historic wooden house (built in 1896) and order the likes of lamb with orange and honey sauce or pork leg with mustard and sweet potato croquettes. There's fish and pizza on the menu too, but this place really shines with its meat. Good home-brewed beer too. Mains AR$105–186. Tues–Sat 12.30–3pm & 8pm–midnight.

Maria Lola Resto Deloquí 1048 ☎02901 421185, ⓦ marialolaresto.com.ar. Besides its superb hilltop views of the bay, this slick, professional restaurant really delivers for creative and classic dishes. Feast yourself on pumpkin ravioli with blue cheese, southern sea bass with ginger or Fuegian lamb (mains from AR$150). Mon–Sat 12.30–2.30pm & 8–11.30pm.

Placeres Patagónicos Deloquí at Godoy. This low-key restaurant serves a good selection of local beers, platters of cold cuts and cheeses, pastas, fish, and a good-value *menú* on weekdays. Mains from AR$80. Daily noon–1am.

★ **La Rueda** San Martín, at Rivadavia. This all-you-can-eat *parrilla* is the best place in Ushuaia to get your fill of spit-roasted lamb, chorizo, beef, chicken, *morcilla* (black pudding) and *chinchulines* (crispy lamb chitterlings), with bottomless salads thrown in (AR$230). Also offers à la carte meaty choices. Daily noon–11pm.

Tante Sara San Martín 175 ⓦ tantesara.com. Popular *confitería* and *panadería*, which does a fine line in cakes, sandwiches and salads, as well as decent coffee (AR$24), though skip the mediocre pasta. There's another branch at no. 701. Mon–Thurs & Sun 8am–8.30pm, Fri & Sat 8am–9pm.

El Vagón Av Maipú 771. Decked out like an antique, wood-panelled train carriage, with glimpses of labouring convicts out of the "windows", this café offers an

PARQUE NACIONAL TIERRA DEL FUEGO

1

inexpensive menu of burgers, *milanesas* (meat fillets) and *picadas* (mains from AR$80). Or else you can just sip your *mate* or coffee while making use of the free wi-fi. Mon–Fri 8am–1am, Sat 10am–1am.

DRINKING AND NIGHTLIFE

Dublin 9 de Julio 168. This green-walled, red-roofed pub is a good place for a draught Beagle beer (around AR$55), with a buzzing atmosphere and occasional live music. Daily 8pm–3am.

★ **Kuar** Perito Moreno 2232 ⓦ kuaronline.com. Set in an attractive stone-and-timber building right on the seafront, on the road to Río Grande, this bar-restaurant has stupendous views and a blazing fire, as well as imaginative fish and pasta dishes, locally smoked meat, their own delicious home-brewed pale ale, amber ale and dark porter (each around AR$55), and an extensive wine list. Daily 3pm–4am.

DIRECTORY

Banks and exchange There are numerous ATMs in the city centre, including the HSBC at Maipú and Godoy.
Car rental Avis (☎ 02901 433323, ⓦ avis.com) and Hertz (☎ 02901 432429, ⓦ hertz.com) both have offices at the airport.
Post office Gob. Godoy 118.

PARQUE NACIONAL TIERRA DEL FUEGO

Located 12km west of Ushuaia along RN3, **PARQUE NACIONAL TIERRA DEL FUEGO** (daily 8am–8pm, slightly shorter hours during winter; AR$140; if visiting the following day, let the park staff know, and you won't have to pay twice) stretches from the Beagle Channel in the south to Lago Fagnano in the north and the border with Chile in the west. Encompassing 630 square kilometres of mountains, waterfalls, glaciers, lakes, rivers, valleys, sub-Antarctic forest and peat bog, the park offers a number of good day hikes; the rest of the park is off-limits to the public. Guanacos, Patagonian grey foxes, Fuegian foxes, Southern river otters and some ninety bird species are among the park's fauna; introduced Canadian beavers and European rabbits also run amok, wreaking environmental havoc.

Highlights include the **Costera Trail** (8km; 4hr), which starts at the jetty and follows the shore of Bahía Ensenada through coastal forest of deciduous beech trees, meeting the RN3 near the Lapataia park administration centre. It affords spectacular views of the Beagle Channel, passing grass-covered mounds that were former campsites of the indigenous Yámana and offering birdwatchers prime opportunities for spotting Magellanic woodpeckers, cormorants, gulls and oystercatchers.

For the park's best views, take the steep, picturesque route to the top of 973m-high **Cerro Guanaco Trail** (8km return; 7hr) from the car park at Lago Roca. Another popular route, **Hito XXIV Trail** (7km; 3hr), is a level path that starts from the same trailhead, traces the shores of Lago Roca and ends at a small obelisk that marks the border with Chile.

ARRIVAL AND DEPARTURE

By bus Regular buses (high season every 30–40min 9am–6pm; 20–30min) run from the corner of Maipú and Fadul in Ushuaia to various points in the park. Services are reduced during off-season. It's only worth taking a taxi if there are four of you.
By train El Tren del Fin del Mundo (2–3 departures daily at 9am & 3pm, plus noon if minimum 4 passengers; 50min; AR$380 round trip; ticket office at the Muelle Turístico; ☎ 02901 431600, ⓦ trendelfindelmundo.com .ar), is a scenic ride on the narrow-gauge train that used to transport wood in the days of the penal colony, departing from its main station, 8km west of Ushuaia, and arriving at the park station, 2km from the main gate.

ACCOMMODATION

There are four rudimentary free campsites which tend to get crowded and dirty; a couple are a bit of a hike from the nearest toilets. Take all your trash out of the park.
Camping Lago Roca ☎ 02901 433313. By the shores of the eponymous lake, this is the only serviced campsite (with hot showers, a café and an expensive shop). It also has a *refugio* with dorm beds. Camping/person AR$60, dorms AR$120

Bolivia

HIGHLIGHTS

❶ **Death Road** Cycling the spectacular road between La Paz and Coroico. **See p.168**

❷ **Isla del Sol** The spiritual centre of the Andean world. **See p.180**

❸ **Cerro Rico** An unforgettable glimpse of the miners' life. **See p.190**

❹ **Salar de Uyuni** The world's largest salt flat. **See p.195**

❺ **Samaipata** Laidback town surrounded by lush cloudforest. **See p.212**

❻ **Parque Nacional Madidi** A pristine and diverse Amazonian rainforest. **See p.218**

HIGHLIGHTS ARE MARKED ON THE MAP ON PP.156–157

ROUGH COSTS

Daily budget Basic US$25, with the occasional treat US$45

Drink Small beer US$2.50

Food Fixed three-course lunch menu US$3–4.50

Hostel/budget hotel US$6.50–13.50/US$15–27

Travel Bus: La Paz–Copacabana (155km) US$4

FACT FILE

Population 10.5 million

Language Spanish (also more than thirty indigenous languages)

Currency Boliviano (B$)

Capital Sucre is the official capital; La Paz is the de facto capital

International phone code ☏591

Time zone GMT -4hr

Introduction

Surrounded by Brazil, Paraguay, Argentina, Chile and Peru, Bolivia lies at the heart of South America. Stretching from the majestic icebound peaks and bleak high-altitude deserts of the Andes to the exuberant rainforests and vast savannahs of the Amazon basin, it embraces an astonishing range of landscapes and climates, and encompasses everything outsiders find most exotic and mysterious about the continent.

Three centuries of Spanish colonial rule have left their mark, most obviously in some of the finest colonial architecture on the continent. Yet the European influence is essentially a thin veneer overlying indigenous cultural traditions that stretch back long before the Conquest: while Spanish is the language of business and government, more than thirty indigenous languages are still spoken.

Bolivia is dominated by the mighty **Andes**, which march through the west of the country along two parallel chains. In the north and east, they give way to the tropical rainforests and grasslands of the **Amazon and eastern lowlands**, in the southeast to the dry thornbrush and scrub of the **Chaco**. Yet, despite its extraordinary biodiversity and myriad attractions, Bolivia remains one of South America's least-visited countries.

Most visitors spend a few days in the fascinating city of **La Paz**, which combines a dizzying high-altitude setting with an intermingling of traditional indigenous and modern urban cultures. Close by is the magical **Lake Titicaca**, and the towns of **Coroico** and **Sorata**, good bases for trekking, climbing or mountain biking in the **Cordillera Real**, a range of high Andean peaks that plunge precipitously down into the Amazon basin through the dramatic, deep valleys of the **Yungas**. The best base for visiting the Bolivian Amazon further north is **Rurrenabaque**, the jumping-off point for exploring **Madidi National Park**.

South of La Paz, the southern **Altiplano** – the bleak, high plateau that stretches between the Andes – has historically been home to most of Bolivia's population. In **Potosí** you can experience underground life in the mines of **Cerro Rico**, while to the southwest, Uyuni is the gateway to the astonishing landscape of the **Salar de Uyuni** and the **Reserva de Fauna Andina Eduardo Avaroa**. Also well worth visiting are the towns of **Sucre**, with its fine colonial architecture, **Samaipata**, which has designs on Rurrenabaque's crown as the country's best ecotourism base, and **Santa Cruz**, a brash, lively tropical metropolis – and a good base for exploring the rainforests of the **Parque Nacional Amboró** and the immaculately restored Jesuit missions of **Chiquitos**.

WHEN TO VISIT

Climate varies much more as a result of altitude and topography than it does between different seasons.

Winter (May–Oct) is the **dry season**, and in many ways the best time to visit Bolivia, with sunny, trek-friendly highland days and slightly lower temperatures in the generally hot and humid **lowlands**. While highland temperatures hover in the mid-teens most of the year (albeit with chilly winter nights), the summer **rainy season** (December into March and sometimes April) can see lowland temperatures reach 31°C. Rain affects the condition of roads throughout the country, especially in the Amazon, where river transport takes over from often impassable overland routes. The parched Altiplano and mountainsides nevertheless briefly transform into lush grassland, as wild flowers proliferate and the earth comes to life.

CHRONOLOGY

1000 BC Founding of Tiwanaku on the shores of Lake Titicaca, centre of a colonial empire comprising much of modern Bolivia, southern Peru, northeast Argentina and northern Chile.

c.1000 AD Tiwanaku dramatically collapses, most likely as a result of a prolonged drought.

Eleventh to fifteenth centuries The Aymara take control of the Altiplano, maintaining a more localized culture and religion.

Mid-fifteenth century The Aymara are incorporated into the Inca Empire, albeit with a limited degree of autonomy.

1532 Francisco Pizarro leads his Spanish conquistadors to a swift and unlikely defeat of the Inca army in Cajamarca (Bajo), Peru.

1538 Pizarro sends Spanish troops south to aid the Aymaran Colla as they battle both the remnants of an Inca rebellion and their Aymara rivals the Lupaca. Spanish control of the territory known as Alto Peru is established.

1545 The continent's richest deposit of silver, Cerro Rico, is discovered, giving birth to the mining city of Potosí.

1691 San Javier is founded as the first of the Chiquitos Jesuit missions.

1767 The Spanish Crown expels the Jesuit order from the Americas.

1780–82 The last major indigenous uprising, the Great Rebellion, is led by a combined Inca-Aymara army of Túpact Amaru and pac Katari.

1809 La Paz becomes the first capital in the Americas to declare independence from Spain.

1824 The last Spanish army is destroyed at the battle of Ayacucho in (Bajo) Peru.

1825 The newly liberated Alto Peru rejects a union with either (Bajo) Peru or Argentina, and adopts a declaration of independence. Bolivia is born.

1879 Chile begins the War of the Pacific by occupying the entire Bolivian coastline and invading Peru.

1899 The Federal Revolution consolidates power of the new tin-mining barons and creates a new administrative capital in La Paz.

1904 Bolivia finally cedes its coastline to Chile, in addition to losing the Acre to Brazil.

1932–35 The Chaco War with Paraguay ends in stalemate and huge loss of life.

1952 The National Revolution sees armed civilians defeat the army in La Paz and the ascension to power of the Revolutionary Nationalist Movement (MNR).

1964 A resurgent army led by General René Barrientos seizes power, beginning eighteen years of military dictatorship.

1967 Che Guevara is captured and executed in the hamlet of La Higuera.

1970s General Hugo Banzer heads a brutal military regime, coinciding with an unprecedented period of economic growth.

1980–81 The most brutal and corrupt regime in modern Bolivian history is led by General Luis García Meza.

1985 Bolivia plunges into a recession as the bottom falls out of the tin market, and the economic vacuum is filled by the production and export of cocaine.

Late 1990s US-backed coca eradication policies provoke widespread resistance, led by indigenous activist Evo Morales.

2005 Morales is elected as Bolivia's first indigenous president with an absolute majority and a programme of nationalization and agrarian reform.

2008 Morales suspends US Drug Enforcement programme, accusing agents of espionage. In retaliation, the US adds Bolivia to its drugs blacklist and suspends trade preferences.

2009 New constitution agreed, giving greater rights to indigenous people. Morales is elected for a second term.

2011 Mass demonstrations lead to a suspension of government plans to build a Brazil-funded highway through the TIPNIS reserve.

2013 The Constitutional Court rules Morales can run for a third presidential term.

2014 Research suggests Bolivia's economy grew by 6.5 percent the previous year, among the strongest rates in the region.

ARRIVAL AND DEPARTURE

At present there are only **direct flights** to Bolivia from Miami in the US (including with American Airlines; ⓦaa.com), Madrid in Spain (with Air Europa; ⓦaireuropa .com) and neighbouring South American countries, the most frequent connections being from São Paulo in Brazil, Buenos Aires in Argentina, Santiago in Chile and Lima in Peru. The principal Bolivian international **airports** are El Alto in La Paz (see p.169) and Viru Viru in Santa Cruz (see p.211). Passengers departing Bolivia on international flights must pay a B$175 ($25) **airport tax** in cash (bolivianos or dollars), sometimes included in ticket prices, but if not you'll have to pay it at a separate kiosk after checking in.

FROM ARGENTINA

The principal **border crossing** is from La Quiaca in Argentina to Villazón in the southern Altiplano (see box, p.197), with regular bus and train connections to the desert town of Tupiza. There's also a crossing between Pocitos in Argentina and Yacuiba in the Chaco (see p.216), from where it's possible to travel by bus or train to Santa Cruz.

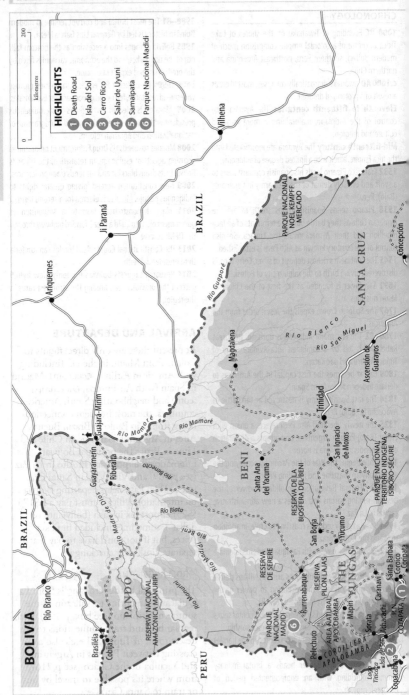

HIGHLIGHTS

1. Death Road
2. Isla del Sol
3. Cerro Rico
4. Salar de Uyuni
5. Samaipata
6. Parque Nacional Madidi

0 ___ 200

kilometres

BOLIVIA

BRAZIL

Rio Branco

Brasiléia

Cobija

PANDO

RESERVA NACIONAL AMAZÓNICA MANURIPI

Rio Manuripi

Rio Madre de Dios

Guayaramerín

Guajará-Mirim

Riberalta

Rio Beni

Rio Biata

Rio Madidi

PERU

PARQUE NACIONAL MADIDI

6

Pelechuco

ÁREA NATURAL APOLOBAMBA

CORDILLERA APOLOBAMBA

Lago Titicaca

Isla del Sol

Copacabana

Rurrenabaque

Mapiri

RESERVA DE SERERE

RESERVA PILON LAJAS

THE YUNGAS

San Borja

Yucumo

San Ignacio de Moxos

PARQUE NACIONAL TERRITORIO INDIGENA ISIBORO-SÉCURE

Santa Ana del Yacuma

RESERVA DE LA BIOSFERA DEL BENI

BENI

Trinidad

Magdalena

Rio Blanco

Rio Mamoré

Rio Mamoré

Rio Benecito

Rio Guaporé

SANTA CRUZ

PARQUE NACIONAL NOEL KEMPFF MERCADO

Concepción

Rio San Miguel

Ascensión de Guarayos

BRAZIL

Vilhena

Ji Paraná

Ariquemes

Sorata

Santa Barbara

Coroico

Coripata

Caranavi

Adhuachi

P.N. COTAPATA

Quiapata

CORDILLERA

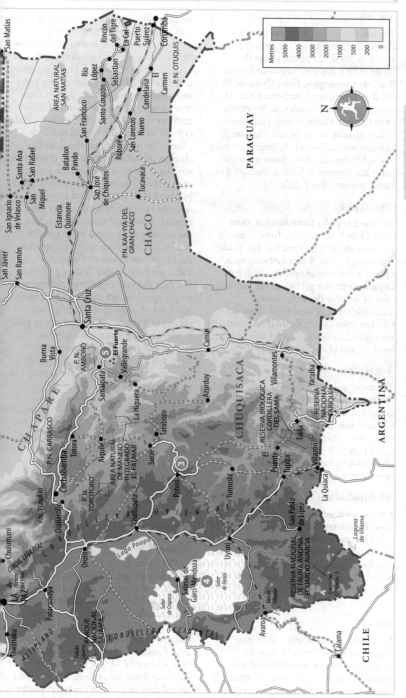

2

FROM BRAZIL

The busiest crossing is the **rail border** at Puetro Quijarro (see p.214), near the Brazilian city of Corumbá, where the Bolivian Pantanal meets its more famous Brazilian counterpart. From Quijarro, it's a full day's train journey to Santa Cruz. There are also a couple of borders in **Amazonia**, from Guajará-Mirim (transit point Porto Velho) by boat across the Rio Mamoré to Guayaramerín, from where there are regular onward flights; and from Brasiléia (transit point Rio Branco) to Cobija, the capital of Pando province (see p.222).

FROM CHILE

The most popular **trans-Andean route** from Chile is the road up from Arica on the coast to Tambo Quemado (see p.188), and on to La Paz. A more adventurous option is the remote border crossing of **Laguna Verde** (see p.196), at the southern edge of Reserva Eduardo Avaroa, accessible via organized tours from the Chilean town of San Pedro de Atacama. A weekly train also runs from Uyuni to the border town of Avaroa (see p.194).

FROM PERU

The most widely used land border of all is the **Yunguyo-Kasani crossing** (see p.179) at the southern tip of Lake Titicaca near Copacabana, easily accessible from Puno in southern Peru. Less busy but just as easy to get to from Puno is the crossing at **Desaguadero** (see p.169), with regular onward transport to La Paz.

FROM PARAGUAY

For the adventurous only, the **trans-Chaco** border between Bolivia and Paraguay (see p.210) is navigable only in the dry season, during which the route – all the way from Asunción to Santa Cruz – is served by an endurance-testing two- to three-day bus journey.

VISAS

Many visitors to Bolivia – including citizens of the **UK**, most European countries, **Canada**, **New Zealand** and **Australia** – don't need a visa. Citizens of **South Africa** do need a visa ($55); these are generally available on entry (for cash only), but it is better to get one in advance if you can. Citizens of the **United States** can apply for a tourist visa in advance or on arrival (US$160/person, paid in cash). They're valid for five years and allow visitors to enter Bolivia three times a year, with a maximum of ninety days per year spent in the country; check ⓦtravel.state.gov for further details.

For other nationalities, the situation changes periodically, so always **check** with your local embassy or consulate a month or two before travelling. On arrival, you'll be issued with a **tourist card** (*tarjeta de turismo*) valid for thirty or ninety days, depending on your nationality – check the number of days and make sure the border officials give you the stamp with the maximum number of days your nationality allows you. If they give you less than the maximum, you can request it on the spot (though there's no guarantee you'll get it) or go to the immigration office in La Paz or the nearest city to your border crossing and receive another stamp. The annual limit is currently restricted to ninety days, and, officially at least, you cannot just cross the border and get another ninety-day card.

GETTING AROUND

Bolivia's topography, size and lack of basic infrastructure mean that getting around can be a challenge, especially in the rainy season. However, buses are inexpensive and numerous, flying within the country is very affordable, and convenient, especially in rainy season, and trains follow some spectacular routes.

BY PLANE

La Paz, Santa Cruz, Sucre and Cochabamba are all connected by **daily flights**, and there are also frequent services to Tarija, Trinidad, Rurrenabaque and a number of remote towns in the Amazon and the eastern lowlands. State-run Boliviana de Aviación (ⓦboa .bo), Amaszonas (ⓦamaszonas.com) and military-run TAM (ⓦwww.tam.bo) are the main domestic carriers. Book at least several days in advance for busier routes.

Flights are often cancelled or delayed, especially in the Amazon, where the weather can cause disruption.

FCA (Empresa Ferroviaria Andina; ⓦwww.fca.com.bo) runs two passenger lines – *Expreso del Sur* and *Wara Wara del Sur* – from Oruro south across the Altiplano via Uyuni and Tupiza to Villazón on the Argentine border. **Ferroviaria Oriental** (ⓦwww.fo.com.bo) runs two lines in the lowlands: one from Santa Cruz east to the Brazilian border at Quijarro (a service known as the "death train" – a reference to its speed, not its safety record); the other from Santa Cruz south to Yacuiba in the Chaco, on the Argentine border.

Bolivia's **buses** are run by a variety of private companies and ply all the main routes in the country. Road conditions continue to improve greatly, but journey times are still unpredictable, and you should be prepared for major delays, especially in the rainy season. In the highlands, always bring warm clothing and a blanket or sleeping bag, as journeys can be bitterly cold.

Other forms of transport include: minibuses (minivans that chug along fixed routes in the bigger cities); *micros* (similar to but bigger than minibuses); *trufis / colectivos* (shared taxis that run along fixed routes); and *mototaxis* (motorbike taxis).

Although Bolivia is landlocked, there are still several regions – particularly the Amazon – where travelling by water is the best way of getting around. There are two main forms of **river transport** in the Bolivian Amazon: dugout canoes, powered by outboard motors, are used to visit protected areas such as the Parque Nacional Madidi; more economic but less comfortable cargo boats ply the Río Mamoré, between Trinidad and Guayaramerín on the Brazilian frontier, and the Río Ichilo, between Trinidad and Puerto Villaroel in the Chapare.

Renting a car (from around US$35/day) is an option, though it's often easier and not much more expensive to hire a taxi to drive you around for a day or longer. Outside the main routes, many roads are unpaved and in very poor condition, so a **four-wheel drive** (4WD) is essential. Petrol stations are scarce and breakdown services even more so. A recommended car rental company with offices at El Alto airport and Santa Cruz (on the second ring road) is Barbol (ⓣ02 2820675, ⓦbarbolsrl.com). You'll need to be over 25, and to leave a major credit card or large cash deposit as security; most rental companies will include insurance cover with the hire price, but it is worth checking.

ACCOMMODATION

While **accommodation** in Bolivia is generally good value, the standard is not particularly high, especially in smaller towns. Room rates vary according to season, rising during the high tourist season (May to September) and on weekends in popular resort towns, and doubling or tripling during major fiestas.

The prices we quote are for the cheapest doubles in high season, often with shared bathrooms – you can usually get one in a clean, simple hotel for around B$100–200. In some towns there are backpacker-conscious places (not always hostels) that offer **dorm beds**. Even in the coldest highland cities, heating is usually non-existent; in the lowlands, heat, rather than cold, is often a problem, though all but the cheapest rooms are equipped with a fan. Most places usually have **hot water**, although it's generally intermittent and often courtesy of individual electric heaters that you'll find attached to the tops of showers; don't touch the apparatus while the water is running.

With few designated **campsites** and an abundance of inexpensive accommodation, few travellers camp in Bolivia unless exploring the country's wilderness areas. Beyond the cities and towns, you can camp almost everywhere,

2

usually for free; make sure you ask for permission from the nearest house first; local villages may ask for a small fee of a few bolivianos. In some **national parks** you'll also find shelters where you can stay for a minimal charge.

2 FOOD AND DRINK

The style of eating and drinking varies considerably between Bolivia's three main geographical regions – the Altiplano, the highland valleys and the tropical lowlands. Each region has *comidas típicas* (traditional dishes). Generally, be wary of street food and take recommendations before trying the real locals' restaurants – food hygiene can be an issue.

Restaurants almost all offer enormously filling good-value set lunches (*almuerzos*) usually costing between B$15 and B$40, while a smaller number offer a set dinner (*cena*) in the evening and also have a range of à la carte main dishes (*platos extras*), rarely costing more than B$30–40. For B$40–70 you should expect a substantial meal in more upmarket restaurants, while about B$70–120 will buy you most dishes even in the best restaurants in La Paz or Santa Cruz.

FOOD

While Altiplano cuisine is dominated by the humble **potato**, often served in hearty soups (llama and mutton are common), the valley regions cook with **corn**, often used as the basis for thick soups known as *laguas*, or boiled on the cob and served with fresh white cheese – a classic combination known as *choclo con queso*. Meat and chicken are often cooked in spicy sauces known as *picantes*: a valley mainstay is *pique a lo macho*, a massive plate of chopped beef and sausage fried with potatoes, onions, tomatoes and chillies. In the tropical lowlands, **plantains** and **yucca** take the place of potatoes; beef is also plentiful – the lowlands are cattle-ranching regions, so beef is of good quality and relatively cheap.

Although Bolivia is obviously not the place to come for seafood, fish features regularly on menus, especially the succulent *trucha* (trout) and *pejerrey* (kingfish) around Lake Titicaca, and the juicy white river fish known as *surubí* and *pacú* in the lowlands. Ordinary restaurants rarely offer much in the way of **vegetarian food**, although you can almost always find eggs and potatoes of some description (usually fried), as well as the ubiquitous potato soup, often cooked without meat. The situation changes a great deal in cities and in popular travellers' haunts, where a cosmopolitan selection of vegetarian dishes, salads and pancakes is widely available, and there's a growing number of wholly vegetarian restaurants.

The most popular snack throughout Bolivia is the **salteña**, a pasty filled with a spicy, juicy stew of meat or chicken with chopped vegetables, olives and hard-boiled egg. It's usually eaten in the mid-morning accompanied by a cold drink and a little chilli sauce if desired.

DRINK

Mineral water is widely available – avoid the tap water – and a variety of delicious fresh juices is sold by market stalls and on the streets from handcarts across the country. **Tea and coffee** are available almost everywhere, as well as *mates*, or herbal teas – *mate de coca* is a good remedy for altitude sickness, but many others are usually available.

Locally produced alcoholic drinks are widely available in Bolivia and drinking is a serious pastime. **Beer** (B$12–25) is available almost everywhere – Paceña, produced in La Paz, is the most popular, followed by Huari, made by the same company but with a slightly saltier taste. Although not widely consumed, Bolivia also produces a growing variety of excellent high-altitude – and highly underrated – **wines** (*vinos*), mostly from the Tarija Valley; the best labels are Campos de Solana, Concepción and Kohlberg. A glass of red wine (*vino tinto*) costs B$15–30. While production is still a fraction of Argentina's and Chile's, Bolivia's wines deserve a higher profile. One problem is that much cultivation is dedicated to muscat grapes, which, rather than being used for fine **wines**, are used to a produce a white grape brandy called *singani*, the beverage most Bolivians turn to when they really want to get drunk. It's usually mixed with Sprite or 7 Up, which creates a fast-acting combination known as *chuflay*. Finally, no visit to the Cochabamba is complete without a taste of *chicha*, a thick, mildly alcoholic yeasty-flavoured beer made of fermented maize and considered sacred by the Incas.

CULTURE AND ETIQUETTE

There isn't really such a thing as an all-encompassing Bolivian culture, as traditions vary widely according to different regions and climates, as well as according to social class and ethnic background. There are around forty official **ethnic groups** in the country,

while a distinction is often made between the "camba" (people from the lowlands) and "colla" (those from the highlands). Tensions between the two regions have heightened as a result of sweeping reform on land distribution and nationalization introduced by President Evo Morales.

Spanish is the official language in Bolivia, and it's a great place to brush up on your language skills as Bolivians speak slowly and clearly compared with their Chilean or Argentine neighbours. **Indigenous languages** including Aymara, Quechua and Gurani are also widely spoken. **Catholicism** is the predominant religion, though many festivals and celebrations involve a mishmash of Catholic and indigenous beliefs with offerings made to both the Virgin Mary and Pachamama (mother earth).

ORGANIZED TOURS

Tours to the salt flats, the jungle and Bolivia's national parks are offered by most operators and agencies across the country. Some agencies are less reputable and responsible than others, and it is always worth shopping around before booking a tour.

TOUR OPERATORS

Amboró Tours C Libertad 417 2nd Floor, Santa Cruz ☎ 03 3390600, ⓦ amborotours.com. Specializes in trips to Amazonian national parks.

America Tours Ground-floor office 9, Edificio Avenida, Av 16 de Julio 1490, La Paz ☎ 02 2374204, ⓦ america-ecotours.com. Efficient and reliable, they're the main booking agent for *Chalalán Ecolodge* in Parque Nacional Madidi, and a good place for booking internal flights.

Andean Epics Ground-floor office 10, Edificio Avenida, Av 16 de Julio 1490, La Paz ☎ 02 2313849, ⓦ andeanepics.com. Excellent option for mountain biking and trekking in the Sorata region. Their April–Dec five-day bike, jeep and canoe trips from Sorata to Rurrenabaque are recommended.

Bolivian Journeys Sagárnaga 363, La Paz ⓦ bolivianjourneys.org. Highly regarded mountaineering specialists, offering professionally equipped expeditions into the Cordillera Real.

Fremen Av 20 de Octubre 2396, 10th floor Edificio María Haydee, La Paz ☎ 02 2421258, ⓦ andes-amazonia.com. Highly respected agency offering a wide range of tailor-made tours throughout Bolivia, including river trips on the Río Mamoré on their own floating hotel.

Kanoo Tours C Illampu 832, Zona Rosario, La Paz

☎ 02 2460003, ⓦ kanootours.com. Englishman Phil is a top source of information for the budget traveller, with quality tours and bookings arranged across the country. Also has a branch in the *Adventure Brew Hostel*.

La Paz On Foot C Indaburo and Jaén, La Paz ☎ 7154 3918, ⓦ lapazonfoot.com. Offers an interesting range of trips in the immediate vicinity of La Paz, not least the "Urban Trek", but also heads further afield with an ethos of responsible, rural community-supporting travel.

Ruta Verde Tours C 21 de Mayo 318, Santa Cruz ☎ 03 3396470, ⓦ rutaverdebolivia.com. More expensive but excellent Dutch/Bolivian-run tour operator offering trips to the salt flats and jungle, with sustainability as a priority.

Topas Travel C Carlos Bravo 299, in Hotel El Consulado, La Paz ☎ 02 2111082, ⓦ topas.bo. A wide-ranging, well-respected operator.

Travel Tracks Sagárnaga 366 ☎ 02 2316934, ⓦ travel-tracks.com. Run by affable Dutch woman Aly Bakker and specializing in climbing, trekking and Uyuni tours.

Zig Zag C Illampu 867 ☎ 02 2457814, ⓦ zigzagbolivia .com. Climbing and trekking specialists, including the Yunga Cruz trail.

2

Generally speaking, Bolivians are friendly and will go out of their way to help you. It's polite and common practice to pepper any requests with "por favor" and "gracias", and greet people with "buenos días" or "buenas tardes" before starting a conversation. There is little concept of personal space in Bolivia and people typically stand very close when speaking to you.

Chewing **coca leaves** is an integral part of daily life for many Bolivians. The controversial leaf is commonly chewed into a round ball, and kept in the side of the cheek, or used to make herbal tea. It is said to combat tiredness and altitude sickness, and to quell hunger, and is also used in ritual ceremonies.

When eating out at a restaurant, or taking part in a guided tour, a ten percent **tip** is appreciated, and increasingly expected. Many museums and historical landmarks charge higher fees to foreigners, which some travellers find frustrating. If you are not sure of what you are being asked to pay, it is best to ask around to establish the going rate before assuming you are being ripped off. Haggling is not common.

SPORTS AND OUTDOOR ACTIVITIES

Dominated by the dramatic high mountain scenery of the Andes, Bolivia is ideal for **trekking**, **mountain biking** and **climbing**; whether you want to stroll for half a day, take a hardcore hike for two weeks over high passes down into remote Amazonian valleys, or climb one of the hundred peaks over 5000m, it's all possible. The best season for outdoor activity is between May and September, while the most pleasant and reliable weather is between June and August.

The easiest way to go trekking or climbing is with a tour operator. There are dozens of these in La Paz and in several other cities (see box, p.161). Prices depend on group sizes.

Many travellers say one of the highlights of South America is a bike ride down the road from La Paz to Coroico in the Yungas, a thrilling 3500m descent along what was once dubbed the **world's most dangerous road**. There are plenty of tour companies – beware unscrupulous operators – and it is easy to organize as a day-trip from La Paz. You don't need any previous experience, but bear in mind that several bikers have been killed on this route in the past, and though the most dangerous stretch was bypassed in 2007, some vehicles still use it. Attempting the trip in the rainy season (Nov–March) is not recommended.

COMMUNICATIONS

Airmail (*por avión*) to Europe and North America tends to take one to two weeks; mail to the rest of the world outside the Americas and Europe takes longer. Letters cost about B$10–15 to Europe, the US, Canada, Australia or New Zealand. For a small extra charge, you can send letters certified (*certificado*), but even then don't send anything you can't afford to lose.

There are **ENTEL** phone centres in all cities and most towns, where you can make local, national and international calls. While there are still a few coin-operated **telephone booths** in the street, most use **prepaid cards**. These are widely available at street stalls, which often have their own phones for public use. Consider buying an inexpensive mobile phone, or bringing one with you, and getting a Bolivian pay-as-you-go chip (SIM card). If you're dialling long-distance within Bolivia, you'll need the respective **area code**, which for La Paz, Oruro and Potosí is ☎02; for Beni, Pando and Santa Cruz ☎03; and for Cochabamba, Chuquisaca and Tarija ☎04. Mobile phone numbers have eight digits wherever you are.

Calling internationally, the cheapest option is via an internet phone or Skype service. **Internet cafés** themselves are ubiquitous in all but the most remote corners of Bolivia, though connections are often slow. Expect to pay about B$3–6/hr. Many hotels and restaurants offer free (though generally far from fast) **wi-fi**.

2

EMERGENCY NUMBERS

Police ☎ 110
Ambulance ☎ 118
Directory assistance ☎ 104

CRIME AND SAFETY

Despite being among the poorest countries in the region, Bolivia has lower levels of theft and violent crime than neighbouring Peru and Brazil, though in recent years levels have risen. The vast majority of crime against tourists is opportunistic theft, and **violence is rare**. One scam is for **fake policemen** to approach you in the street and ask to search you or see your documents (before making off with them), or ask you to go with them in a taxi to the "police station". Be aware that real policemen would never do this, so on no account hand over your documents or valuables and never accompany a stranger in a taxi.

Another trick is for **fake taxi drivers** or even minibus drivers to pick up unsuspecting passengers before either stopping in a deserted part of town where they and/or their associates rob the victims, or, in even worse scenarios, kidnap and seriously assault the victims to force them to reveal their PIN. Always check the ID of any taxi you take and only ever use official ones; better still, whenever possible ask your hotel to order one for you.

Another common means of theft starts with you being spat on or having some substance spilt on you; a "helpful passer-by" will stop you, point out the offending substance and attempt to clean it off you (while their partner in crime quickly relieves you of your valuables). If this happens to you, don't stop, but walk on as quickly as possible before cleaning yourself up.

Political upheaval is a regular feature of everyday life in Bolivia. Keep an eye on the news and ask around before you make travel plans – road blockades are the go-to form of protest for many groups, and can easily disrupt your schedule. Street protests are also common.

HEALTH

Though levels of hygiene and sanitation are generally poor in Bolivia, you can reduce the risk of getting ill. Avoid drinking tap water and watch out for ice in drinks, as well as uncooked or unpeeled fruit and vegetables. Appreciate the risks of buying food from street vendors and always check that food has been properly cooked.

Altitude sickness is a common complaint in La Paz, Potosí and on the salt-flats tour. Mild symptoms include dizziness, headaches and breathlessness. Bolivians swear by coca tea (*mate de coca*), but resting and drinking plenty of non-alcoholic fluids should also help. You can buy small bags of coca leaf around the witches' market area of La Paz for a few bolivianos. Anyone with more severe symptoms should get immediate medical help.

It is advisable to get vaccinated against **yellow fever** before you travel to Bolivia; bring a doctor's certificate with you. Use mosquito repellent with a high DEET content and wear long sleeves and trousers to avoid insect-borne diseases such as malaria and dengue fever.

Bolivia is home to a wide range of venomous **snakes and spiders**. Watch where you step and seek medical advice if you are bitten or stung.

When looking for healthcare, it is always best to opt for **private clinics** (*clínica*) rather than state-run hospitals,

BOLIVIA ON THE NET

ⓦ **www.bolivianexpress.org** Website of a free monthly English-language current affairs magazine.

ⓦ **boliviabella.com** Fascinating website set up by a woman with detailed knowledge of the Santa Cruz region and a passion for everything related to the country.

ⓦ **chiquitania.com** In-depth site about visiting the Jesuit Mission churches and the surrounding region.

ⓦ **lab.org.uk** The UK-based Latin America Bureau provides news, analysis and information on the continent, including Bolivia.

2

which are often overcrowded and poorly equipped.

INFORMATION AND MAPS

Most major cities have a regional **tourist office**, run either by the city municipality or by the departmental prefecture. Tour operators, however, are often a better source of information, and are happy to answer queries, often in English, though obviously their main aim is to sell you one of their tours.

MONEY AND BANKS

The Bolivian currency is the **boliviano**. It's usually written "B$" or "Bs" and is subdivided into 100 centavos. Notes come in denominations of 10, 20, 50, 100 and 200 bolivianos; coins in denominations of 1, 2 and 5 bolivianos, and of 5, 10, 20 and 50 centavos. At the time of writing, the **exchange rate** was roughly B$7 = US$1; B$9 = €1; B$11.50 = £1.

US dollars can be **withdrawn at ATMs**, and changed at banks and some hotels, shops and by street moneychangers, so they're a good way of carrying emergency backup funds. Most day-to-day costs will be charged in B$, though tourist-based activities – especially the more upmarket kind – will often be quoted in US$. The easiest way to access funds in cities and larger towns is by using plastic; Visa and MasterCard are most widely accepted. In rural areas and smaller towns carry plenty of **cash**, as plastic and travellers' cheques are fairly useless.

OPENING HOURS AND HOLIDAYS

Public offices in Bolivia have adopted the *horario continuo*, whereby they (theoretically at least) work Monday to Friday straight through from 8.30am to 4pm without closing for lunch.

Bank opening hours are generally Monday to Friday from 8.30am to noon and 2.30pm to 6pm; some branches are also open on Saturdays from 9am until noon.

Bolivians welcome any excuse for a party, and the country enjoys a huge number of national, regional and local **fiestas**, often involving lengthy preparation and substantial expense.

La Paz

Few cities have a setting as spectacular as **LA PAZ**, founded in 1548 as La Ciudad de Nuestra Señora de la Paz – the City of Our Lady of Peace – and now the political and commercial hub of Bolivia. Home to just under a million people, and sited at over 3500m above sea level, the sprawling city lies in a narrow, bowl-like canyon, its centre cradling a cluster of church spires and office blocks themselves dwarfed by the magnificent icebound peak of **Mount Illimani** (6439m) rising imperiously to the southeast. On either side, the steep slopes of the valley are covered by the ramshackle homes of the city's poorer inhabitants, which cling precariously to even the harshest gradients. From the lip of the canyon, the satellite city of **El Alto** sprawls in all directions across the Altiplano, a dirt-poor yet dynamic locus of urban Aymara culture and protest. The fact that its gridlocked main streets control access to La Paz below has often been exploited by the Aymara, with roadblocks used for political leverage.

WHAT TO SEE AND DO

There are still some fine colonial palaces and churches in the centre, with one of the main squares, **Plaza San Francisco**, bisected by the frantic thoroughfare of Avenida Mariscal Santa Cruz and its continuation, Avenida 16 de Julio, collectively known as **El Prado**. Though most of the surviving colonial buildings are in a poor state of repair, there's at least one street, **Calle Jaén**, where you can get a sense of how La Paz used to look. Many of the city's museums are also here. To the west of the Prado, lung-busting lanes sweep up to the travellers' enclave of **Calle Sagárnaga** and the Aymara bustle of the **market district** beyond. To the south lies the wealthy suburb of **Sopocachi**, where you'll find some of the city's best nightlife and restaurants.

Plaza Murillo

Though it remains the centre of Bolivia's political life, **Plaza Murillo** – the main square of the colonial city centre – has an endearingly provincial feel, busy with people feeding pigeons and eating ice cream in the shade. On the south side stands the **Catedral Metropolitana Nuestra Señora de La Paz** (Mon–Fri 8am–noon & 4–8pm, Sat & Sun 8am–noon; free), with its imposing facade but relatively unadorned interior, and the **Palacio de Gobierno** (Presidential Palace; closed to public), abutted by thin, elegant columns and ceremonial guards in red nineteenth-century uniforms.

Museo Nacional de Arte

On the southwest corner of Plaza Murillo at Calle Socabaya, the Palacio de Los Condes de Arana, one of La Paz's finest surviving colonial palaces, houses the **Museo Nacional de Arte** (Tues–Fri 9am–12.30pm & 3–7pm, Sat 10am–5.30pm, Sun 10am–1.30pm; B$20; ⓦmna.org.bo). The palace itself is a magnificent example of Baroque architecture, with a grand portico opening onto a central patio overlooked by three floors of arched walkways, all elaborately carved from pink granite in a rococo style with stylized shells, flowers and feathers.

Contemporary Bolivian artists are represented, but the museum's permanent collection is based firmly around colonial religious works, featuring several by the great master of Andean colonial painting, Melchor Pérez de Holguín. Look out for temporary exhibitions, which often stray from the colonial theme.

Templo de Santo Domingo

A block northwest from Plaza Murillo, the **Templo de Santo Domingo** (C Ingavi, at Yanacocha; Mon–Fri 9am–noon & 4–7pm, Sat & Sun 9am–noon; free) has a richly detailed eighteenth-century facade carved from soft white stone in Mestizo-Baroque style, exemplifying the combination of Spanish and indigenous symbolism characteristic of Andean colonial architecture.

Museo Nacional de Etnografía y Folklore

The small but rewarding **Museo Nacional de Etnografía y Folklore** (C Ingavi 916, at G. Sanjinez; Mon–Fri 9am–12.30pm & 3–7pm, Sat 9am–4.30pm & Sun 9am–noon; B$20; ⓦmusef.org.bo) is housed in an elegant seventeenth-century mansion, with a variety of costumes and artefacts representing three of Bolivia's most distinctive indigenous cultures: the **Aymara**, formed of thirty ethnic groups in the Cordillera Oriental; the **Uru-Chipayas**, who subsist in the Altiplano around Oruro; and the Quechua-speaking **Tarabuqueños** from the highlands east of Sucre.

Calle Jaén and its museums

Calle Jaén is the best-preserved colonial street in La Paz and home to no fewer

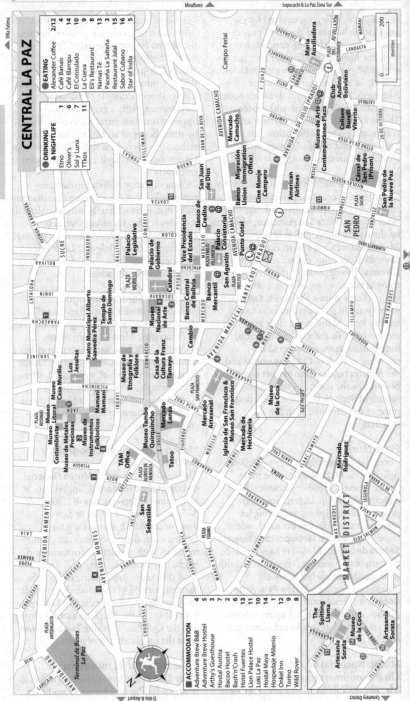

CENTRAL LA PAZ

● EATING

Alexander Coffee	2/12
Café Banaís	4
Café Illampu	14
El Consulado	10
La Cueva	9
Eli's Restaurant	8
Namas Té	13
Paceña La Salteña	3
Restaurant Jalal	15
Sabor Cubano	16
Star of India	5

● DRINKING & NIGHTLIFE

Etno	1
Oliver's	6
Sol y Luna	7
Tkos	11

■ ACCOMMODATION

Adventure Brew B&B	4
Adventure Brew Hostel	5
Arthy's Guesthouse	3
Hostal Austria	7
Bacoo Hostel	2
Bash'n'Crash	6
Hotel Fuentes	13
Lion Palace Hostel	11
Loki La Paz	10
Hostal Maya	14
Hospedaje Milenio	1
Onkel Inn	12
Torino	9
Wild Rover	8

than five museums, four of them accessed on a single B$10 ticket (all Tues–Fri 9.30am–12.30pm & 2.30–7pm, Sat & Sun 9am–1pm), sold at the **Museo Costumbrista Juan de Vargas** at the top of the street (entrance on Av Armentia, Plaza Riosinho). This museum gives a good introduction to the folkloric customs of the Altiplano and history of La Paz, as well as holding an extensive collection of grotesque yet beautiful folkloric masks and a room dedicated to the city's icon, the **chola**. This is the vernacular term for the ubiquitous Aymara women dressed in voluminous skirts and bowler hats who dominate much of the day-to-day business in the city's endless markets. Housed in the same building but accessed from Calle Jaén, the **Museo del Litoral Boliviano** is dedicated to one of Bolivia's national obsessions: the loss of its coastline to Chile during the nineteenth-century War of the Pacific. Next door, the **Museo de Metales Preciosos**, also known as the Museo del Oro, has a small but impressive hoard of Inca and Tiwanaku gold ornaments, and informative displays explaining the techniques used by pre-Columbian goldsmiths. On the other side of the road, inside the sumptuous mansion which was once the home of the venerated independence martyr after whom it's now named, the **Casa Museo de Murillo** houses an eclectic collection, ranging from colonial religious art to artefacts used in Kallawaya herbal medicine.

Set around yet another pretty colonial courtyard a little further down at Calle Jaén 711, the delightful **Museo de Instrumentos Folkloricos** (daily 9am–1pm & 2.30–6.30pm; B$5) features an astonishing variety of handmade musical instruments from all over Bolivia, including the indigenous *charangos*, some of which you can pick up and play.

Plaza San Francisco

With traffic crawling through its centre, the all-concrete **Plaza San Francisco** lacks the charm of the city's other major plazas, and is no longer a major focus for the Aymara. Instead it's an important bus stop and a focus for tour groups, thanks to the looming Iglesia de San Francisco that dominates the whole space. **Protests** and demonstrations still take place here, but are generally small scale and mostly colourful pieces of political theatre. For a bewildering choice of cheap, home-cooked Aymara and Bolivian food, check out **Mercado Lanza** at the plaza's northern end.

Iglesia de San Francisco

On the south side of Plaza San Francisco stands the **Iglesia de San Francisco** (Mon–Sat 4–6pm; free), the most beautiful colonial church in La Paz, established in 1549 and rebuilt between 1743 and 1784. The richly decorated facade is a classic example of the Mestizo-Baroque style, showing clear indigenous influence, with carved anthropomorphic figures reminiscent of pre-Columbian sculpture as well as more common birds and intertwined floral designs. Attached to the church is the **Museo San Francisco** (Mon–Sat 9am–6pm; B$20; ⓦmuseosanfranciscobolivia.com), a museum set in a beautiful renovated Franciscan monastery, with a large collection of seventeenth-century Franciscan art and furniture.

Calle Sagárnaga and Witches' Market

Heading west from Iglesia San Francisco, **Calle Sagárnaga**, La Paz's main tourist street, is crowded with hotels, tour agencies, restaurants, handicraft shops and stalls. It's also the

---

TIWANAKU MUSEUM

One of the most important museums in La Paz, the **Museo Nacional de Arqueología Tiwanaku**, Tiwanaku 93 at Federico Zuazo (inside the bizarre Palacio Tiwanaku, completed for archeologist Arturo Posnansky in 1916), has been closed since 2011. At the time of writing it still wasn't clear when (or if) it would open again. Ask at the tourist information office (see p.169) for the latest.

2

gateway to the main Aymara neighbourhoods of La Paz, one of the most distinctive parts of the city, with steep, winding lanes filled with lively markets. The **Mercado de Hechicería**, or Witches' Market – a cluster of stalls on calles Linares and Jiménez, leading off Santa Cruz – offers a fascinating window onto the world of Aymara mysticism and herbal medicine. The stalls are laden with a cornucopia of ritual and medicinal items, ranging from herbal cures for minor ailments like rheumatism or stomach pain to incense, coloured sweets, protective talismans and dried llama foetuses. The area offers plenty of great photo opportunities, but remember to ask permission or buy a memento.

Museo de la Coca

The small but enlightening **Museo de la Coca** (C Linares 906, a block south of Sagárnaga; daily 10am–7pm; B$13; ⓦcocamuseum.com) is dedicated to the small green leaf that is both the central religious and cultural sacrament of the Andes and the raw material for the manufacture of cocaine. The museum gives a comprehensive overview of the history, chemistry, cultivation and uses of this most controversial of plants.

Market district

A few blocks west of the Witches' Market is the **market district**, a vast open-air bazaar sprawling over some thirty city blocks where La Paz's Aymara conduct their daily business. The market area goes by many names – locals tend to refer to specific streets where certain products are sold – but is generally known as **Mercado Negro** where Max Paredes meets Graneros (shoes and clothing), and **Huyustus** (or just "Uyustus"), further west around the street of the same name (clothing, bedding, toys, shoes and musical instruments). Street after street is lined with stalls piled high with sacks of sweet-smelling coca leaf, mounds of brightly coloured tropical fruit, enormous heaps of potatoes and piles of silver-scaled fish; there are also smuggled stereos and televisions, and endless racks of the latest imitation designer clothes. In the last week of January, the area, as well as most of the rest of the city, is taken over by stalls selling all manner of miniature items during the **Feria de las Alasitas**, which is centred on representations of Ekeko, the diminutive mustachioed household god of abundance.

Museo Tambo Quirquincho

Just northwest of Plaza San Francisco, **Plaza Alonso de Mendoza** is a pleasant

---

CYCLING THE DEATH ROAD

One of the most popular trips in Bolivia, and some travellers' sole reason for crossing the border, is a chance to hurtle down the infamous Death Road. This exhilarating 3500m descent, along the old road from **La Paz to Coroico** in the Yungas, is easy to organize as a day-trip from La Paz. Cyclists have been killed or seriously injured on this rough, narrow track chiselled out of near-vertical mountainsides, and you must choose a tour operator with great care – some are truly unscrupulous. As well as the Death Road, there are many other excellent mountain-biking alternatives if you want to get off the beaten track.

TOUR OPERATORS

Gravity Assisted Mountain Biking Ground-floor office 10, Edificio Avenida, Av 16 de Julio 1490 ☎02 2313849, after-hours number ☎7721 9634, ⓦgravitybolivia.com. The original and still the best downhill mountain-biking operator, offering daily Death Road trips (B$750) with excellent US-made bikes and experienced, enthusiastic English-speaking guides. They also offer a range of single-track options for more experienced bikers – their Chacaltaya–Zongo descent plummets 4300m. Gravity helped set up the

lower-cost Barracuda (C Illampu 750, office 4, inside *Hostal Gloria*; ☎7672 8881, ☎02 2459950, ⓦbarracudabiking.com), Zzip (see p.184) and Urban Rush abseiling (B$150) in central La Paz (ⓦurbanrushbolivia.com).

Vertigo Biking Jimenez 836, between Santa Cruz and Sagárnaga ☎02 2115220, ⓦvertigobiking.com. A recommended agency for cycling the "world's most dangerous road" (from B$480), with top-of-the-range bikes, a good safety record and English-speaking guides.

THE FIGHTING CHOLITAS

One of the main reasons to visit El Alto – other than for its airport – is to watch slightly kitsch, Mexican-style wrestling matches featuring the bowler hat-wearing indigenous women known as **cholitas**. The shows take place on Sundays (4–7pm) and can be booked through hostels or La Paz-based tour operators (all-inclusive trips including transport and tickets are typically B$80).

square named after La Paz's founder, whose imperious statue stands at its centre. On the southern side of the square on Calle Evaristo Valle, the **Museo Tambo Quirquincho** (Tues–Fri 9.30am–12.30pm & 3–7pm, Sat & Sun 9am–1pm; B$8) is a showcase for Bolivian contemporary art. More interesting is the museum's setting: inside one of the largest examples of an eighteenth-century *tambo*, a compound that served during the colonial era both as accommodation and as marketplace for rural Aymaras.

Museo de Textiles Andinos

The **Museo de Textiles Andinos**, Plaza Benito Juarez 488 (Mon–Sat 9.30am–noon & 3–6.30pm, Sun 10am–12.30pm; B$15; ⟡ museodetextiles.org), in the student suburb of Miraflores, northeast of the Prado, is a must-see for textile lovers. Set in a beautifully kept house, the museum has an interesting display of textiles from all over the Bolivian Andes. The museum's gift shop sells products made by Quechuan women.

ARRIVAL AND DEPARTURE

By plane International and domestic flights use the small El Alto airport (flight information on ☎02 2157300, ☎02 2810240), on the rim of the Altiplano, about 11km from La Paz and at over 4000m above sea level. The easiest way into town from here is by taxi; they wait right outside the terminal (30min; B$60–80). Cotranstur run shuttle minivans (*minibus*) down into the city and the length of the Prado to Plaza Isabella La Católica (Mon–Sat every 10–20min 6am–8pm, Sun every 30min; B$3.80).

Destinations Cochabamba (12 daily; 35min; AM/TAM/ BOA/Ecojet); Oruro (1 daily; 30min; AC); Potosí (1 daily; 1hr

5min; AC); Puerto Suárez (3 weekly; 2hr; TAM); Rurrenabaque (7 daily; 30–40mins); Santa Cruz (12 daily; 1hr; AM/Ecojet/BOA); Sucre (3 daily; 1hr; AM/BOA); Tarija (2 daily; 1hr 5min; AM/BOA); Trinidad (4 daily; 1hr 5min; AC); Uyuni (2 daily; 1hr; AM).

By bus Most international and long-distance inter-departmental buses arrive at and depart from the Terminal de Buses La Paz on Plaza Antofagasta, about 1km northwest of Plaza San Francisco. Minibuses and *micros* depart from the Lago Titicaca region, Copacabana, Sorata and Tiwanaku depart from the cemetery district, high up on the west side of the city. Plenty of *micros* and minibuses ply the route to and from the city centre (marked "Cementerio" on the way out), but consider taking a taxi as it's an edgy part of town. Buses from Coroico and Chulumani in the Yungas, and from Rurrenabaque and the Beni, arrive in the Villa Fátima district, in the far northeast of the city. The different companies all have offices around the intersection of Av de las Américas and C Yanacachi. Again, plenty of *micros* and minibuses head to and from the city centre, but a taxi is preferable.

Destinations from Terminal de Buses La Paz Arica, Chile (2 daily; 8hr); Cochabamba (hourly; 7–8hr); Copacabana (2 daily; 3–4hr); Cusco, Peru (2–3 daily; 12–15hr); Lima, Peru (2–3 daily; 27hr); Oruro (every 30min; 3hr 30min); Potosí (2 daily; 8–9hr); Puno, Peru (2–3 daily; 8hr); Santa Cruz (15–20 daily; 16–18hr); Sucre (2 daily; 14–15hr); Tarija (2 daily; 24hr); Uyuni (3 daily; 10hr 30min–11hr 30min).

Destinations from Cemetery District Charazani (1–2 daily; 10hr); Copacabana (every 30min; 3hr 30min); Desaguadero, Peru border (every 30min; 1hr 30min); Sorata (hourly; 4hr 30min); Tiwanaku (every 30min; 1hr 30min).

Destinations from Villa Fátima Chulumani (hourly; 4hr 30min); Cobija (1 weekly; 48hr); Coroico (every 30min; 4hr 30min); Guayaramerín (1 daily; 32hr); Riberalta (1 daily; 30–40hr); Rurrenabaque (1 daily; 20hr).

INFORMATION

Tourist information There's a small office (Mon–Fri 8.30am–noon & 2.30–7pm; ☎02 2371044) on Plaza del Estudiante at the end of the Prado, which has plenty of information on La Paz and the surrounding area. The main tour agencies are the best places to go for information on the rest of the country. There is also a very helpful kiosk in the bus terminal – especially handy at weekends (Mon–Fri 6am–10pm, Sat 8am–4pm, Sun noon–10pm; ☎02 2285858).

GETTING AROUND

Minibus, micro and trufi There are two main forms of public transport in La Paz: rickety city buses, known as *micros*, and privately owned minivans, confusingly known

2

MI TELEFÉRICO – LA PAZ BY CABLE CAR

In 2014 the commute between El Alto and La Paz became a lot more serene with the opening of a Doppelmayr-built cable-car system that includes three colour-coded **Mi Teleférico** routes running down the slopes of the city (with five more lines planned). Though it's not billed as a tourist attraction – the first stage (**Línea Roja**) connects the former train station (Av Maco Capac), the cemetery district (Av Entre Ríos) and El Alto (Zona 16 de Julio, Av Panorámica Norte) – for around B$3 each way this is a scintillating ride across the rim of the Altiplano (take a taxi to the El Alto station and ride down). Each cabin seats ten passengers, leaving every twelve seconds, seventeen hours a day. See ⓦ miteleferico.bo for the latest information.

as "minibuses" (even though they are smaller than *micros*). Minibus destinations are written on signs inside the windscreen and bellowed incessantly by the driver's assistants. Your third option is a *trufi* – basically a car operating as a minibus with a maximum of four passengers and following fixed routes (mostly between Plaza del Estudiante and the wealthy suburbs of the Zona Sur). *Trufis* charge a flat rate of about B$3, *micros* about B$1–2 and minibuses B$1.50 for journeys in the city centre (B$2.40 for trips to the Zona Sur; fares increase to B$2 and B$3 respectively after 9pm). The city is currently developing a more integrated mass transit system dubbed "La Paz Bus", which includes the new cable car (see above) and new "Pumakatari" buses, though for now this is primarily targeted at commuters.

Taxis To reduce your chances of being robbed, assaulted or worse, it's advisable to only ever take a radio taxi: they're marked as such, usually with a telephone number painted on the side. Radio taxis charge a flat rate of B$10–12 to anywhere in the city centre regardless of the number of passengers (agree the price before you get in).

ACCOMMODATION

There's plenty of budget accommodation in La Paz, though things get pricier from June to August. Most places are in the city centre within a few blocks of Plaza San Francisco, within walking distance of most of the city's main attractions.

NEAR THE BUS STATION

Adventure Brew B&B Av Montes 533 ☎02 2461614, ⓦ theadventurebrewbedandbreakfast.com; map p.166. This B&B operation is a sister property to the hostel 50m down the road (see below), but don't confuse them – this place offers more comfortable private en-suite rooms as well as four- and eight-bed dorms, a "SkyBar" on the roof, fast wi-fi and micro-brewed Saya beer on tap. Doubles B$180, dorms B$80

Adventure Brew Hostel Av Montes 503 ☎02 2915896, ⓦ theadventurebrewhostel.com; map p.166. Popular hostel with a range of dorms, excellent free wi-fi, one free beer a day (there's an underground bar with pool table), DVD lounge and a breakfast of coffee and pancakes. Staff are incredibly friendly. Access to the facilities of its associated B&B included; book online in advance. Dorms B$49

Arthy's Guesthouse Av Montes 693 ☎02 2281439, ⓦ arthyshouse.tripod.com; map p.166. The best non-hostel option near the bus terminal, this peaceful, welcoming retreat offers clean, whitewashed, carpeted rooms with bedside lamps, as well as a TV room and communal kitchen. Wi-fi is free, but use of computer terminals is B$3/hr, and breakfast is B$10 extra. B$90

Bacoo Hostel Alto de la Alianza 693 ☎02 2280679, ⓦ bacoohostel.com; map p.166. Bright yellow walls line the approach to this airy, peaceful hostel, which is well situated for the Calle Jaén museums. There's a social room that gives good views of the city, a garden, and an outdoor hot tub (not always operational). Dorms B$60, doubles B$160

Bash'n'Crash C Ingavi 681 ☎02 2280934, ⓦ bashand crashbackpackers.com; map p.166. Less slickly managed than the foreign-owned "party hostels", but part of its appeal is that it is run by a team of welcoming locals. Accommodation consists largely of dorm beds, along with a few private rooms, while the communal areas retain enough charm (if a little too much tobacco smoke). Wi-fi is not the best (there are also two shared computers) and there's no kitchen. Dorms B$39, doubles B$144

PLAZA MURILLO AND EAST OF THE PRADO

★**Hostal Austria** C Yanacocha 531, on the left at the top of the stairs ☎02 2408540, ⓔ hotelaustria@acelerate.com; map p.166. With its lofty ceilings and maze of wood and glass corridors, this place oozes history. The rooms are real period pieces, with undersized doors and an unintentionally shabby chic-cum-1960s minimalist feel. The only downside is the complete lack of private bathrooms and the rather dodgy gas-powered showers. Nevertheless, a must for retro fans and a real bargain. Fast wi-fi, one shared computer and laundry available (B$10/kg). B$70

★**Loki La Paz** C Loayza 420 ☎02 2119024, ⓦ lokihostel .com; map p.166. The raucous La Paz branch of this Peru-based party hostel chain is located in a dandy pink townhouse draped with red velvet – it's probably worth staying here for the gilt-trimmed showpiece bar alone, located in the old ballroom and the focus of the hostel's no-curfew, party-hard

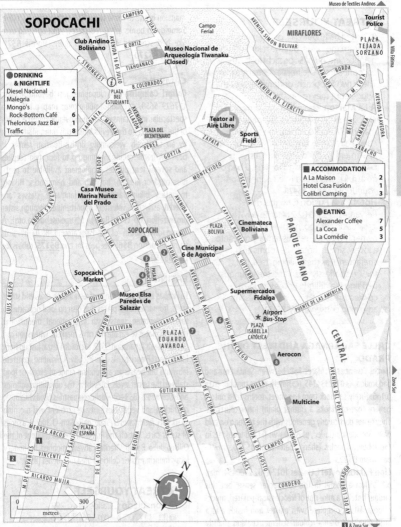

SOPOCACHI

● DRINKING & NIGHTLIFE

Diesel Nacional	2
Malegria	4
Mongo's	
Rock-Bottom Café	6
Thelonious Jazz Bar	1
Traffic	8

■ ACCOMMODATION

A La Maison	2
Hotel Casa Fusión	1
Colibri Camping	3

● EATING

Alexander Coffee	7
La Coca	5
La Comédie	3

2

philosophy. Rooms are clean and comfortable with duvets, there's a small roof terrace and breakfast is served till 1pm. Free wi-fi. Dorms B$45, doubles B$160

Hospedaje Milenio C Yanacocha 860 ☎02 2281263, ⓦ hospedajemilenio.blogspot.com; map p.166. Friendly family-run place on a cobbled street. Several rooms are comically tiny, most are without natural light and some bed frames are covered in stickers, evidence of their past existence in a child's bedroom. Breakfast is B$8–13 extra. Free wi-fi. No en-suite bathrooms. Doubles B$80

Torino C Socabaya 457 ☎02 2406003, ⓦ hoteltorino .com.bo; map p.166. Facing the crumbling north flank of

the cathedral, the site includes a beautiful cloistered courtyard, which, unfortunately, the guest rooms are entirely apart from. Doubles (shared bathroom) B$100, private bathroom B$140

Wild Rover C Comercio 1476 ☎02 2116903, ⓦ wildroverhostels.com; map p.166. One of La Paz's big gringo party hostels, centred on a pleasantly open-air, canary yellow-painted courtyard and an in-house bar that keeps the Guinness flowing till well into the wee hours (there's an Irish theme). They also claim to have "the comfiest beds in South America". Free wi-fi and computer terminals. Dorms B$45, doubles B$170

2

CALLE SAGÁRNAGA AND WEST OF THE PRADO

Hotel Fuentes C Linares 888, between Santa Cruz and Sagárnaga ☎02 2334145, ⊛hotelfuentes.com.bo; map p.166. Nicely set back from the street, rooms lead onto a gallery that overlooks a (rather plain) inner courtyard. They're not particularly generous with the heating on cold days. Breakfast included, plus slow wi-fi (and terminals in the lobby). Doubles (shared bathroom) B$180, private bathroom B$225

Lion Palace Hostel C Linares 1017 ☎02 2900454; map p.166. Not a hostel in the backpacker sense, but this budget hotel is a mini riot of Neoclassical-pillared, mock-colonial kitsch complete with plaster lion heads and a lurid blue and orange colour scheme. Looking slightly tattered in places, but it's comfortable and clean enough, and decent value. Free wi-fi on the ground floor only. Doubles B$90

Hostal Maya C Sagárnaga 339 ☎02 2311970, ⊛hostalmaya.com; map p.166. Tucked within one of the many warren-like mini shopping arcades hereabouts, this place is spick-and-span, though the sickly lighting and garish wallpaper are turn-offs. Prices include a basic breakfast. Doubles (shared bathroom) B$130, private bathroom B$170

Onkel Inn C Colombia 257 ☎02 2490456, ⊛onkelinn .com; map p.166. Blessedly light and airy and not a shot glass in sight, this HI-affiliated hostel in an 1886 mansion is one to come to for R&R rather than partying. Some dorm bunks are three-storey, with one odd den-like bed screened off for B$20 more. Dorms B$70, doubles B$270

CAMPING

Colibri Camping C 4, Jupapina, just beyond Mallasa ☎7629 5658, ⊛colibricamping.com; map p.171. In a spectacular mountainside location overlooking the Valley of the Flowers and the Devil's Molar, this tranquil site is run by an extremely welcoming British-Bolivian family. It boasts A-frame cabins sleeping up to four, two teepees and several tent pitches (equipment available to rent), plus outdoor kitchen, hot tub and hammocks. Hiking, mountain biking and Spanish-language classes are offered, as well as volunteer opportunities through sister organization Up Close Bolivia (⊛upclosebolivia.org). A 30min drive south of La Paz; around B$70 by taxi. Camping/person B$68, teepees for two B$175, cabins for two B$350

EATING

La Paz has an excellent range of restaurants, cafés and street stalls, from traditional places that dish up local delicacies to tourist-orientated spots with international menus. The cheapest places to eat are the city's markets, where you can get full meals for around B$12. Mercado Lanza, just up from Plaza San Francisco, is an initially uninviting concrete labyrinth but boasts an astounding range of excellent food stalls on the upper levels. Elsewhere, the ubiquitous *salteñas* and *tucumanas* (B$3–6) – delicious pastries filled with meat or chicken and vegetables – make excellent mid-morning snacks. Try *Tucumanas El Prado* (daily 8am–1.30pm), a series of street carts, just off the Prado on México (in front of the Coliseo Julio Borelli Viterito), always mobbed by hungry locals munching their delicious fried *tucumanes* (B$6).

CAFÉS

Alexander Coffee Av 16 de Julio 1832, map p.166; C Potosí 1091, map p.166; Av 20 de Octubre 2463, Sopocachi, map p.171; ☎02 2433402, ⊛www.alexander-coffee.com. This serves the city's best coffee in an almost eerily westernized setting (it's often dubbed the "Bolivian Starbucks"), though the C Potosí branch has plenty of atmosphere with a vaulted brick ceiling and free wi-fi. Salads from B$20 – try the quinoa option, with broccoli, courgette, and alfalfa sprouts. Mon–Fri 8am–11pm, Sat & Sun 9am–11pm.

Café Banaís Sagárnaga 161 ☎02 2311214; map p.166. This elegant tourist-hub café has a pleasant central courtyard and tasty breakfasts, with huge bowls of muesli, cereal and fruit (from B$22), and very good-value buffets (B$33). Strong wi-fi. Daily 7am–10pm.

★ **Café Illampu** Linares 940 ☎02 2971543; map p.166. The La Paz branch of Swiss expat Stefan Anders' Sorata institution (see p.166) occupies the first floor of an elegant mansion – morning sun pours through big colonial windows. Visit for breakfast (B$35–47); there's home-made bread, good jams and rustic crockery. A couple of tables are squeezed onto the wardrobe-width balcony. Mon–Sat 7.30am–8pm.

RESTAURANTS

CENTRAL LA PAZ

La Cueva C Tarija 210B ☎02 2147115, ⊛4cornerslapaz.com; map p.166. Part of the "Four Corners" enterprise that has something of a local monopoly, this authentic-feeling Mexican restaurant is all terracotta walls, wooden benches and Day of the Dead theming. Chilli, tacos, burritos and quesadillas start at B$35 with generous sharing plates for B$95 (veggie) or B$105. They have at least forty types of tequila on offer, too. Mon–Sat 11am–11pm, Sun 5–11pm; the bar stays open later.

Eli's Restaurant Av 16 de Julio 1491, at Bueno ☎02 2335566; map p.166. This sweetly kitsch place was founded in 1942 (Che Guevara is rumoured to have worked or at least eaten here in the 1950s). The diner-style decor is a shrine to the silver screen, with a portrait of Humphrey Bogart in pride of place. Get into the spirit of the age with huge, Technicolor ice-cream sundaes (all around B$20). Don't confuse the restaurant with the *Eli's Pizza Express* mini chain. Daily 11am–11pm.

★ **Namas Té** Zoilo Flores 1334, at Almirante Grau ☎02 2481401, ⊛namastebolivia.com; map p.166. Run by Gonz Jove, an artist/sculptor responsible for several of the murals around La Paz, this bohemian enclave offers the best-value vegetarian (much of it vegan) *almuerzos* (B$23) in the city, prepared with healthy doses of quinoa and a flair for traditional adaptations. The fruity desserts are likewise imaginative, and they do delicious takes on the usual sandwiches, burritos, tacos, etc. Mon–Fri 8am–7pm, Sat 8am–4pm.

Paceña La Salteña Loayza 233 ⊛pacenalasaltena.com; map p.166. A La Paz institution with several branches in the city, and probably the best of the *salteña* joints in the city, where a couple of tasty pastries won't set you back much more than B$10 (meat, chicken and veggie options). Mon–Fri 8am–2pm, Sat & Sun 8.15am–3pm.

Restaurant Jalal Sagárnaga 392 ☎7759 8088; map p.166. Don't be put off by the shabby entrance to *Jalal* – walk up the stairs for delicious tapas-like portions of falafel, hummus, *tabouleh, babaganoush* and other Middle Eastern classics for around B$10–12 each. The decor and ambience still need a bit of work (it's like eating in the owner's sitting room), but the food makes a trip worthwhile. Mon–Sat noon–10pm.

Sabor Cubano C Sagárnaga 357 ☎02 2451797, ⊛saborcubanobolivia.com; map p.166. Excellent-value Cuban cuisine including *almuerzos* (B$25) in a cave of a bar-restaurant plastered in photos and graffiti. There's often live music on Thursday and Friday evenings. Mon–Sat noon–midnight.

Star of India C Cochabamba 170 ☎02 2114409; map p.166. A self-proclaimed "British Indian curry house" (albeit one that serves llama tikka masala) with a low-lit interior and tiled floors. They promise their vindaloo is "silly hot". Curries from B$45, naans B$8, *almuerzo* B$35. Mon–Sat 9am–11pm, Sun 4–11pm.

SOPOCACHI

La Coca Rosendo Gutierrez 482 ☎02 2410892; map p.171. Located in the Sopocachi neighbourhood, this pleasantly rustic bistro is a shrine to the wonders of pan-Andean, and specifically coca-inspired, cuisine: pizzas with coca flour, quinoa hamburgers, coca-infused crab, mouth-watering red quinoa soup and even coca ice cream. Mains range B$25–50. Daily 11am–midnight.

La Comédie Pasaje Medinacelli 2234 ☎02 2423561, ⊛lacomedie-lapaz.com; map p.171. With expensive-looking art on the terracotta-coloured walls and wine glasses on tables, this Sopocachi restaurant is a notch up in class from almost everywhere else in the city. Mains are upward of B$50, and the French-influenced cooking is generally exemplary. Mon–Fri noon–3pm & 7–11pm, Sat & Sun 7– 11pm.

DRINKING, NIGHTLIFE AND ENTERTAINMENT

Many travellers spend the majority of their partying time in the hostel bars, not moving on until *Loki, Wild Rover* and – to a lesser extent – *Adventure Brew* kick out in the small hours. The Sopocachi neighbourhood – a 30min walk or 10min cab ride – is a good target, with venues running the gamut from live jazz to raucous travellers' hangouts. Although La Paz's club scene isn't what it was, you can still find a busy dance floor heaving to just about any kind of music. For more traditional

2

entertainment, head to one of the folk music venues known as *peñas*, where – with varying degrees of authenticity – you can witness age-old Andean music and dance.

BARS AND NIGHTCLUBS
SOPOCACHI

Diesel Nacional Av 20 de Octubre 2271, between Rosendo Gutiérrez and Fernando Guachalla ☎ 02 2423477; map p.171. Industrial-chic bar with an extraordinary steam-punk design, complete with aircraft engines (circa 1948) hanging from the ceiling (cocktails from B$25). Mon–Thurs 7pm–midnight, Fri & Sat till 2am.

Malegria Pasaje Medinacelli 2282 ☎ 02 2423700; map p.171. Tribal-themed nightclub with ethnic masks, stone walls and a middling music policy that runs between ska, Mexican and Argentine rock, and the usual generic stuff. The real reason to come here is the live Thursday-night Afro-Bolivian music (aka "Saya"), a veritable orgy of rhythm and colour. Thurs–Sat 10pm–3.30am.

Mongo's Rock-Bottom Café Hermanos Manchego 2444 ☎ 02 2440714; map p.171. Not quite the gringo rendezvous it once was, but its cocktail of televised sports, decent food, serious drinking, live music and raucous dancing still pulls a crowd at weekends. Live Cuban music on Tuesdays; it hosts salsa classes too. Daily 6pm–3.30am.

★**Thelonious Jazz Bar** Av 20 de Octubre 2172; map p.171. Venerable jazz venue with an intimate basement atmosphere, hosting excellent live jazz, Brazilian music and occasional Gypsy swing (Wed–Sat). The cover charge (Wed & Thurs B$20, Fri & Sat B$25; no charge for the jam session on Tues) is tacked onto the end of your drinks bill rather than paid upfront, but is usually worth every centavo. The only downside is how chokingly smoky the place gets later in the evening. Tues–Sat 8pm–4am.

Traffic Av Arce 2549 ☎ 02 2118107; map p.171. Garishly designed bar-restaurant-club, with a chandelier-lit, brick-arched dining area, though it's more famous for its Friday/Saturday-night roster of big-name national – and occasionally international – DJs. The salsa nights (Wed or Thurs) are actually a lot more fun. Mon–Sat noon–2pm & 6pm–4am.

CENTRAL LA PAZ

Etno Jaén 722 ☎ 02 2280343, ⓦ etnocafecultural.blogspot .com; map p.166. Artsy bar/café tucked away in La Paz's most charming street, with dimly lit wooden tables, the city's best *café con leche*, Amazonian whisky and a relaxed vibe. Mojitos from B$20 (it's also the only place in La Paz serving *Ajenjo*, Bolivian absinthe). Mon–Sat 11am–3am.

Oliver's Murillo 999, at Cochabamba ☎ 02 2120764, ⓦ 4cornerslapaz.com; map p.166. The infamous *Oliver's Travels* has been reborn down the road, right above *Sol y Luna*, as an "English tavern". Honest-to-goodness pint glasses of beer (Saya, Paceña etc), superb ginger and tomato curries (B$40), breakfast served till 3pm, live English Premiership and Champions League football, free wi-fi and classic British indie sounds. Daily 8am till late (or "until we get bored").

Sol y Luna Murillo 999, at Cochabamba ☎ 02 2115323, ⓦ solyluna-lapaz.com; map p.166. Dutch-owned institution serving strong coffee and cold beer in a mellow, stone-walled, candlelit atmosphere. There are pool tables, a book exchange, an excellent range of beers (including local microbrews), and live music on Monday and Thursday. Daily 9am–1am.

TTkos C Mexico 1555 ☎ 7011 5660; map p.166. Hot, dark, sweaty and often packed subterranean bolthole with a jumping local crowd losing themselves in some of the best live music, DJs and club nights in La Paz, including live reggae (Tues), electronica (Wed) and world/Afro-beat (Thurs). Cover charge is usually a mere B$10. Mon–Sat 10pm–4am.

CINEMAS AND PEÑAS

Cinemateca Boliviana Oscar Soria 110, at Rosendo Gutiérrez ☎ 02 2444090, ⓦ cinematecaboliviana.org. An excellent arthouse cinema with a café that gives good views north towards Miraflores. Usually showing one or two blockbusters, too. Tickets B$30.

Multicine Av Arce 2631 ☎ 02 2112463, ⓦ www2 .multicine.com.bo. A modern, comfortable multiscreen place in Sopocachi, within walking distance of central La Paz. All manner of fast-food joints here, too. Mon–Thurs B$30; Fri–Sun B$30 before 4pm, B$35 after 4pm (3D movies B$45–50). Daily 10am–1am.

Peña Markatambo Jaén 710 ☎ 02 2280041, ⓦ markatambo.com. This is no longer the most authentic traditional music and dance show in La Paz, with a mostly tourist audience, a mix of American and Bolivian songs and mediocre food, though the setting in an old colonial mansion is atmospheric and it can still be lots of fun if you adjust your expectations accordingly. B$35 cover charge. Shows Thurs–Sat 10pm (doors open at 8pm).

Peña Parnaso Sagárnaga 189 ☎ 02 2316827. A very touristy peña, slap-bang in the middle of gringo alley. The food isn't bad (and they also have some vegetarian options), and reasonably compelling shows take place amid colonial cornicing, columns and a particularly tacky backdrop. Cover charge B$80, though you can sometimes pick up flyers offering a free drink. Shows Mon–Sat 8.30pm.

SHOPPING

With its many markets, La Paz has a wide range of *artesanía* (handicrafts) on sale from all over the country. You'll find dozens of outlets along Sagárnaga and the surrounding streets selling traditional textiles, leather items, silver jewellery and talismans. Most fossils sold on this street are fake, though. Illampu also has lots of outlets selling fake big-name gear.

Artesanía Sorata Sagárnaga 303, at Linares ☎02 2454728; and Sagárnaga 363 ☎02 2393041; ⓦ artesaniasorata.com. One of the best – and most ethical – handicraft shops. Mon–Fri 9am–8pm, Sun 9am–2pm.

The Spitting Llama Linares 947 ☎7977 0312, ⓦ thespittingllama.com. An excellent family-owned, community-tourism-minded bookstore with a formidable selection of used books and travel guides in English, German, Spanish, French and even Quechua and Aymara. Daily 10.30am–7.30pm.

Tatoo E. Valle 235 ☎02 2451265, ⓦ tatoo.ws. The best of a number of shops around Sagárnaga selling clothing and equipment for trekking and climbing. Mon–Fri 10am–7pm, Sat 10.30am–5.30pm.

DIRECTORY

Banks and exchange There are plenty of banks with ATMs in the centre of town, especially on Av Camacho, and a growing number of freestanding ATMs line both the Prado and Calle Sagárnaga. The best places to change cash and travellers' cheques are the cambios on Av Camacho and the Prado.

Car rental Avis, Av Costanera and Pablo Guillén 24 ☎02 2111870; Barbol, Av Héroes 777 (Km7), opposite El Alto airport ☎02 2820675, ⓦ barbolsrl.com; Budget, at the airport but also Capitán Ravelo 2050 (near the *Camino Real Hotel*) ☎02 2417698, and Fernando Guachalla 639 in Sopocachi ☎02 2418768.

Doctor Clinica del Sur, Av Hernando Siles 3539, corner of C 7, Obrajes, Zona Sur, 2881 (☎02 2784001, ⓦ clinicadelsur .com.bo), has a 24hr emergency facility and is used by most embassy staff. Try Clinica Cemes, Av 6 de Agosto 2881 (☎02 2430350), for less serious ailments.

Embassies and consulates Australia, Av Arce, Edificio Montevideo (☎02 2971339, ⓦ dfat.gov.au/missions/countries/bo.html, honorary consulate only; see embassy in Lima ⓦ peru.embassy.gov.au); Canada, Victor Sanjinés 2678, Edificio Barcelona (☎02 2415141, ⓦ canadainternational.gc.ca/peru-perou/index.aspx), full services available at embassy in Lima; Ireland, Pasaje Gandarillas 2667, Sopocachi (☎02 2411873), see embassy in Buenos Aires for full services; UK, Av Arce 2732 (☎02 2433424, ⓦ gov.uk/government/world/Bolivia); US, Av Arce 2780 (☎02 2168000, ⓦ bolivia.usembassy.gov).

Emergencies Ambulance ☎118, police ☎110, tourist police ☎02 2225016.

Immigration For visa extensions go to the Oficina de Migración at Av Camacho 1433 (Mon–Fri 8.30am–12.30pm & 4.30–6.30pm; ☎02 2203028). It should be a same-day service, but don't count on it.

Internet An internet café beckons at every other doorway; most charge about B$2–3/hr and are pretty much interchangeable. Punto Cotel branches throughout the city usually have internet terminals.

Laundry Most hotels have a laundry service, and there are plenty of *lavanderías* around town. Try Lavandería Maya, Sagárnaga 339, inside the same gallery as *Hostal Maya Inn*, or the friendly Finesse, Illampu 853.

Pharmacy There's a 24hr pharmacy on Av 16 de Julio 1473, near the Monje Campero cinema (☎02 2331838). Farmacias Bolivia (ⓦ www.farmaciasbolivia.com.bo) has branches all over the city.

Post office Correo Central, Av Mariscal Santa Cruz 1228, at Oruro (Mon–Fri 8am–8pm, Sat 8am–6pm, Sun 9am–noon); little office in the corner of the *Angelo Colonial* courtyard, Linares 922 (Mon–Fri 9am–noon & 3–7pm; Sat till 1pm, Sun till noon).

Telephone centres One of the cheapest places to make international calls is the small Punto Cotel on the Prado (no. 1270), opposite the main post office (internet section at the back, B$2.50/hr, B$1/20min; Mon–Fri 8.30am–10.30pm, Sat & Sun 8.30am–8pm).

Tourist police Edificio Olimpia, Plaza Tejada Sorzano, opposite the stadium in Miraflores (24hr; ☎02 2225016). Come here to report thefts for insurance claims.

TIWANAKU

The most worthwhile attraction within a few hours of La Paz is the mysterious ruined city of **TIWANAKU** (also spelled Tiahuanaco), set on the Altiplano 71km to the west. It's Bolivia's most impressive archeological ruin, and was declared a World Heritage Site by UNESCO in 2000.

Founded some three millennia ago, Tiwanaku became the capital of a massive empire that lasted almost a thousand years, developing into a sophisticated urban-ceremonial complex that, at its peak, was home to some fifty thousand people. Tiwanaku remains a place of exceptional symbolic meaning for the Aymara of the Altiplano, who come here to make ceremonial offerings to the *achachilas*, the gods of the mountains. The most spectacular of these occasions, the **Aymara New Year**, takes place each year at the June winter solstice, when hundreds of *yatiris* (traditional priests) congregate to watch the sun rise and celebrate with music, dancing, rituals and copious quantities of coca and alcohol.

Though the city of Tiwanaku originally covered several square kilometres, only a fraction of the site has been excavated, and the main ruins (daily 8.30am–5pm, last

2

entry 4pm; B$80) occupy a fairly small area that can easily be visited in half a day. Two **museums** by the entrance house many of the smaller archeological finds, as well as several large stone monoliths. The main ruins cover the area that was once the ceremonial centre of the city, a jumble of tumbled pyramids and ruined palaces and temples made from megalithic stone blocks, many weighing over a hundred tonnes. It requires a leap of the imagination to visualize Tiwanaku as it was at its peak: a thriving city whose great pyramids and opulent palaces were painted in bright colours and inlaid with gold, surrounded by extensive residential areas built largely from mud brick (of which little now remains) and set amid lush green fields, rather than the harsh, arid landscape you see today.

ARRIVAL AND INFORMATION

By minibus Minibuses to Tiwanaku depart from the corner of Aliaga and Eyzaguirre in the cemetery district in La Paz (every 30min; 1hr 30min; B$15); on the way back they leave from the square in Tiwanaku town, just under 1km walk away down Av Ferrocarril, though you can flag them down as they pass the entrance to the ruins.

Tour operators Most tour agencies in La Paz run full- or half-day trips to the site (B$80–140/person).

Guided tours Though foreigners tend to get charged a lot more than locals (you'll be lucky to pay less than B$100 for a 1–2hr tour), it's worth investing in an English-speaking tour guide once you get to Tiwanaku. Official site guides operate out of an office next to the ticket counter (*boletería*), and make a huge difference – there are very few signs or explanations on the site itself and it's easy to miss important objects. The same guides will also lead you around the museums, where all the labelling is in Spanish only.

Lake Titicaca, Cordillera Real and the Yungas

To the northwest of La Paz lies one of South America's most beguiling and romantic destinations, the vast, high-altitude **Lake Titicaca**, with its sacred Inca islands, **Isla del Sol** and **Isla de la Luna**, and lakeside pilgrimage town

of **Copacabana**. East of here is the **Cordillera Real**, the highest and most spectacular section of the Bolivian Andes, easily explored from La Paz, or else from the magical outpost of **Sorata**. Sweeping down from the Cordillera Real, the **Yungas** is a rugged region of forest-covered mountains, rushing rivers and fertile valleys, with the humid languor of **Coroico** at its heart.

LAKE TITICACA

Some 75km northwest of La Paz, **Lake Titicaca**, an immense, sapphire-blue lake, easily the largest high-altitude body of water in the world, sits astride the border with Peru at the northern end of the Altiplano. The area around the lake is the heartland of the Aymara, whose distinct language and culture have survived centuries of domination, first by the Incas, then by the Spanish.

Titicaca has always played a dominant role in Andean religious conceptions. The Incas, who believed the creator god Viracocha rose from its waters to call forth the sun and moon to light up the world, also claimed their own ancestors came from here. The remains of their shrines and temples can still be seen on the Isla del Sol and the Isla de la Luna, whose serene beauty is a highlight of any visit to the lake. Nor did Lake Titicaca lose its religious importance with the advent of Christianity: it's no coincidence that Bolivia's most important Catholic shrine can be found in Copacabana, the lakeside town closest to the Isla del Sol.

COPACABANA

The small town and backpacker hangout of **COPACABANA** overlooks the deep blue waters of Lake Titicaca and is the jumping-off point for visiting Titicaca's sacred islands. The main drag, **Avenida 6 de Agosto**, is pleasant enough, lined with cafés, bars, cambios, tour agents and street entertainers. As home to Bolivia's most revered image, the Virgen de Copacabana, hordes of Catholic pilgrims descend on

2

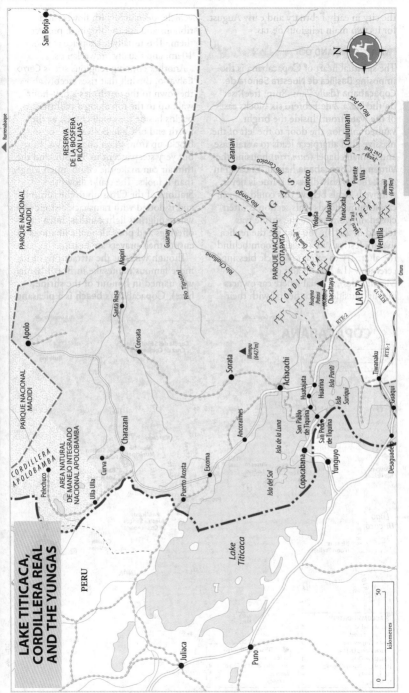

LAKE TITICACA, CORDILLERA REAL AND THE YUNGAS

2

the city in early February and early August for its two main religious fiestas.

The spiritual heart of Copacabana is the imposing **Basílica de Nuestra Señora de Copacabana** (daily 7am–8pm; free), set on the Plaza 2 de Febrero six blocks east of the waterfront. Inside the bright, vaulted interior, the door to the left of the massive gold altarpiece leads to a staircase and a small chapel (*camarín*) housing the **Virgen de Copacabana** herself. Encased in glass, the lavishly dressed statue is never removed: locals believe this could trigger catastrophic floods (this section is often closed, however, since the shrine was robbed in 2013). You can see the replica used in festivals in a special room behind the altar. Try to catch a "vehicle blessing" ceremony (La Benedición de Movilidades), a ritual where car owners line up outside the cathedral with their

vehicles decorated with flowers and ribbons and ask the Virgin to protect them. This usually takes place at about 10am, and usually on weekends.

Another enticing religious site is **Cerro Calvario**, the hill that rises steeply above the town to the north. It's a half-hour walk up to the top along a trail that begins beside the small church at the north end of Calle Bolívar, five or so blocks up from Plaza Sucre; it's a short but very steep ascent to 3973m, and the thin air can make the climb much longer than it looks. The trail follows the Stations of the Cross up to the summit and is dotted with ramshackle stone altars where pilgrims light candles, burn offerings and pour alcoholic libations to ensure their prayers are heard.

Though without the attractions of its more famous namesake in Brazil (which was named in honour of the shrine here), Copacabana's **beach** is a pleasant

COPACABANA

0   200
metres

Cerro Calvario

Kusijata & Yampupata

Capilla del Señor de la Cruz de Colquepata

PLAZA DE TOROS
Bullring

AVAROA
BALLIVIAN
JUNIN

MICHEL PEREZ
AVENIDA GENERAL JAUREGUI
BAPTISTA
AVENIDA 6 DE AGOSTO
BUSCH
AVENIDA 16 DE JULIO
RIGOBERTO PAREDES
AVENIDA COSTANERA

SAN ANTONIO
ZAPANA
BOLIVAR
3 DE MAYO
BENI
ORURO
PANDO
BOLIVAR
PANDO

COCHABAMBA
MICHEL PEREZ
J. PEREZ
LA PAZ

Museo Poncho

Boats to Isla del Sol

Lago Titicaca

Kioscos (Food Stalls)

Buses to La Paz
PLAZA SUCRE
Buses to Kasani

@
i

Mercado
Alcaldía Municipal
Police Station & Post Office
Banco Los Andes

PLAZA 2 DE FEBRERO

Prodem
Bank Bisa

Basílica de Nuestra Señora de Copacabana

JOSE MEJIA
JOSE BALLIVIAN

Capilla de Velas

ENTEL

MANUEL MEJIA

POTOSI

MURILLO

PLAZUELA MANCO KAPAC

AVENIDA FELIX TEJADA

N

Intikala

La Paz

ACCOMMODATION
La Casa del Sol	5
Hostal La Cúpula	2
Hostal Emperador	7
Hostal Flores Del Lago	4
Hostal Las Olas	1
Hostal Las Olas del Titicaca	6
Hostal Sonia	8
Hotel Utama	3

EATING & DRINKING
Café Bistrot	2
El Condor and the Eagle	4
Nemos	3
La Orilla	1

Kasani & Peru

Horca del Inca

place for a lakeside stroll and a bite to eat; there are also plenty of pedal boats to rent.

ARRIVAL AND DEPARTURE

By tourist bus "Tourist buses" run by agencies and hostels in La Paz (but still fairly basic) will usually pick you up from your accommodation; they terminate at central Plaza Sucre in Copacabana. Return buses usually drop you at the main Terminal de Buses La Paz. Companies include: Milton Tours, Illampu 1123 (daily at 8am; ☎ 02 2368003, ⊚ hotelmiltonbolivia.com), which are more reliable than others; and Titicaca Bolivia, Illampu 773 (daily: 8am, pick-ups from 7am & 2pm from Terminal de Buses La Paz; 4hr; ☎02 2462655, ⊚ titicacabolivia.com).

By public bus A little older and rougher, but cheaper: they depart the cemetery district in La Paz (roughly every 30min; 3hr 30min; B$20), from the depots at Manco Kapac or 2 de Febrero (taxi drivers will know where these are). Cooperativa 6 de Junio runs minivans from the same area, but these are very cramped. You must disembark when the bus crosses the Estrecho de Tiquina (the section of the lake that separates La Paz and Copacabana), and pay and cross over separately (B$2) before re-joining the bus. The last departure from Copacabana to La Paz is usually around 6.30pm.

Crossing the Peruvian border Minibuses (minivans) to the border at Kasani (every 30min or so; 15min; B$4) leave from the other side of Plaza Sucre in Copacabana (you can also take shared taxis for B$5; three people minimum). At Kasani, get your exit stamp at passport control (8.30am–7.30pm) and then walk across the border. On the Peruvian side, *micros* and taxis wait to take passengers to the town of Yunguyo (10min), from where regular buses head to Puno and on to Cusco and Arequipa; there are also places to stay in Yunguyo. Alternatively, catch one of the tourist buses (daily 9am, 1.30pm & 6.30pm; 3hr to Puno, 12hr to Cusco); tickets are available from travel agencies in Copacabana.

INFORMATION

Tourist information There's a rudimentary tourist office just off Plaza Sucre on 16 de Julio (daily 8am–noon & 2–6pm; ☎7191 5544), but the tour agencies are often better placed to answer your questions.

Money and exchange The handful of ATMs in town rarely accept international cards (try Banco Los Andes on Plaza 2 de Febrero or Banco Bisa on Av 6 de Agosto), but Prodem (Tues 2.30–6pm, Wed–Fri 8.30am–6pm, Sat & Sun 8.30am–3pm) on Av 6 de Agosto can usually service Visa and MasterCard transactions at a hefty charge of five percent. Cambios all along Av 6 de Agosto change dollars and travellers' cheques.

★ TREAT YOURSELF

These equally charming hillside neighbours have the same owner, but quite different atmospheres.

Hostal La Cúpula Michel Pérez 1–3 ☎02 8622029, ⊚ hotelcupula.com. A delightful hotel built in neo-Moorish style, overlooking the town and lake. It offers light and airy rooms, a nice garden overlooking the bay, plus hammocks, kitchen, laundry and a somewhat inconsistent restaurant. Breakfast is included and reservations are recommended. **B$196**

Hostal Las Olas Michel Pérez (Final) ☎02 8622112, ⊚ hostallasolas.com. Eccentrically constructed and decorated apartments with wonderful views of the lake, kitchenettes and tranquil outdoor spaces. No breakfast, and free but weak wi-fi throughout. **B$310**

ACCOMMODATION

Owing to its role as a pilgrimage centre, Copacabana has an enormous number of places to stay, though they fill up fast and prices double or triple during the main fiestas.

La Casa del Sol Ballivián ☎7158 6731. Owned by Ligia and Samuel (a former mayor of Copacabana, who can impart insights into local life, should you so wish), this peaceful hotel on the edge of town upholds high standards and irrevocable cleanliness at budget prices. **B$60**

Hostal Emperador Murillo 235 ☎02 8622083. A solid budget option – the place is bright and friendly, though the narrow beds have seen far better days. Rarely has hot water. Breakfast is B$10–15 extra. No English spoken. Doubles **B$50**

Hostal Flores Del Lago Jáuregui (Final) ☎02 8622117. Overlooking the ferry dock, this budget hotel option is fine if you just want somewhere to crash while passing through, with cheap, 1970s-style private rooms (some with lake views), the usual patchy but free wi-fi and a pleasant terrace. **B$175**

Hostal Las Olas del Titicaca Av 16 de Julio ☎02 8622205, ⊚ olasdeltiticaca_@hotmail.com. Not to be confused with its posher namesake (see above), this is probably the best of Copacabana's bargain-basement traveller haunts, in a central location and with hot water. Spacious and clean en-suite doubles, but the staff can be tetchy on occasion. Basic breakfast and free but patchy wi-fi. **B$80**

Hostal Sonia Murillo 256 ☎07196 8441, ⊚ hostalsoniacopacabana@gmail.com. A notch up from nearby *Emperador*, this place has warm water (albeit

2

sporadic), very slow wi-fi, en-suite bathrooms and kitchen facilities. The roof-top terrace has lovely views. Breakfast B$15. B$80

Hotel Utama Michel Pérez 60, at San Antonio ☎02 8622013, ⓦutamahotel.com. The modern central courtyard has an odd ambience, glowing yellow from the plastic corrugated roof and decorated with huge international flags. But this is a friendly place, with free tea and fruit, en-suite rooms, and breakfast included. B$250

EATING AND DRINKING

There's no shortage of restaurants in Copacabana, most catering to travellers and pilgrims, and some doubling as bars and evening hangouts, though Copacabana is not a party town. Virtually all offer big plates of the delicious Titicaca trout (*trucha*), including a number of food stalls on the waterfront (B$25; most daily 10am–7pm). At the market you can get a coffee, plus a *pastel* (a bloated, bubbled morsel of fried dough) or *buñuelos* (a sort of doughnut) for around B$3.

Café Bistrot C Zapana, at Av 6 de Agosto ☎715 18310. Backpacker favourite, mostly thanks to the Bolivian owner Fatima (who speaks French, English and Spanish) who is a fount of local information. Her tasty Bolivian-international fusion menu features decent espresso, plenty of veggie dishes, Thai curry and seasonal fresh fruit juices – there's even Marmite and Vegemite for hardcore fans. Chilled-out music and free wi-fi. Mains B$25–40. Daily 7.30am–2pm & 5.30–9pm.

★**El Condor and the Eagle** Av 6 de Agosto, just off Plaza Sucre. A sophisticated café (owned by an Irishman and his Bolivian wife) serving excellent organic coffee, Barry's Irish Tea and hot chocolate (all B$10–20), home-made dishes like baked beans on soda bread, and cakes and muffins. Free wi-fi. Mains B$20–70. Mon & Wed–Sun 7am–1.30pm.

Nemos Av 6 de Agosto. A simple little bar with a good playlist run by a Brit and a Bolivian, with Bolivian micro-brewery beers including Saya and Ted's Cervecería, plus international favourites like Erdinger. Daily 5–11.30pm.

La Orilla Av 6 de Agosto ☎02 8622267. Perennially popular restaurant, usually packed full by 6pm. *Orilla* tends to divide opinion despite the hype, and it really depends on your expectations. It's not bad if you've been on the road for a while, but don't expect international standards of haute cuisine – the food is a bit hit and miss. The pizzas are usually solid choices (B$28–30), and it's a great place to sample the local trout (B$48). Mon–Sat 4–9.30pm.

ISLA DEL SOL

Just off the northern tip of the Copacabana peninsula, about 12km northwest of Copacabana town, **ISLA DEL SOL** (Island of the Sun) is a world

apart from the mainland, a beautifully preserved slice of old Bolivia. Now a quiet backwater, the island was one of the most important religious sites in the Andean world in the sixteenth century, revered as the place where the sun and moon were created and where the Inca dynasty was born. Scattered with **enigmatic ancient ruins** and populated by traditional Aymara communities, Isla del Sol is an enchanting place to spend some time hiking and contemplating the magnificent scenery. Measuring 9.5km long and 6.5km across at its widest point, it's the largest of the forty or so islands in Lake Titicaca, with three main settlements – Yumani, Ch'alla and Ch'allapampa. You can visit the island, along with nearby **Isla de la Luna** (see p.182), on a day- or even half-day trip from Copacabana, but it's really worth spending at least one night on the island to appreciate fully its serene beauty.

WHAT TO SEE AND DO

The best way to see the Isla del Sol is to walk the length of the island from Ch'allapampa in the north to Yumani in the south (or the other way round) – a three- to four-hour hike. You can do this on a day-trip or, much more comfortably, stay the night and depart Yumani the next day.

North island (Parte Norte)

The island's northernmost settlement, **Ch'allapampa**, is a pleasant and peaceful village founded by the Incas as a centre for the nearby ceremonial complexes. At the dock you'll find public toilets (B$2), and a couple of stalls selling sandwiches, water and snacks, while a short walk from the village lie several fascinating **Inca sites**. Note that local guides (free) meet the boats from Copacabana and try to shepherd day-trip visitors around these Inca sites at a healthy pace (worried they will miss the boat back) – you'll learn a lot (if you speak Spanish or someone translates), but this can also be a little restrictive, and you are not obliged to join them. The tiny **Museo del Oro** (daily 9am–5.30pm; B$10 for museum and

Inca ruins; buy your ticket here and keep hold of it, as there are a couple of checkpoints) has pre-Columbian artefacts found both on the island and at sites off the coast. From the village it's a forty-minute walk northwest along an easy-to-follow path to a cluster of Inca sights and ruins, including the **Roca Sagrada** or **Titikala**, the sacred rock where the creator god Viracocha is believed to have created the sun and moon. Nearby is the **Chincana** (daily 9am–5pm; included in ticket for Museo de Oro), an Inca complex of rambling interlinked rooms, plazas and passageways.

From Chincana you can return to Ch'allapampa for the boats or the trail south along the coast (see below), or take the much more scenic **Ruta Sagrada de la Eternidad del Sol (Willka Thaki)**, paved for most of the way to resemble an old Inca road. The trail runs along the central ridge of the island, with spectacular views throughout its 7km length (allow 3hr–4hr 30min). About halfway along there's a checkpoint where you pay a B$15 fee. The path runs just below 4000m, so it can be a strenuous hike if you've just arrived in Bolivia. Just before Yumani you'll pass through another checkpoint to pay the B$5 village entry fee.

South island (Parte Sur)

The coastal trail between Ch'allapampa and Yumani is a slightly easier route, running at a lower altitude than the ridge path, through small farms and villages. The main attractions along the way are the small village of Ch'alla (village admission B$15) with its **Museo Arqueológico** (daily 9am–5.30pm; free) and **Playa Ch'alla**, a picturesque stretch of sand.

Straggling up the slope from a small harbour about an hour and a half south of Ch'alla, **Yumani** (village admission B$5) is the island's largest village and home to most of its accommodation. If you arrive by boat (as opposed to by trail from the north part of the island), the climb up to the best accommodation on the ridge (200m up) is a very steep, breathless hike. Yumani's only sight is the **Escalera del Inca** (222 steps), a stairway

running steeply for 60m up from the dock through a natural amphitheatre covered by some of the island's finest Inca agricultural terracing, irrigated by bubbling stone canals. There's a small but evocative multi-roomed Inca site called **Pilko Kaina** (daily 9am–5.30pm; B$5) a thirty-minute walk from Yumani. Overlooking the lake, one room, whose small window is aligned with Isla de la Luna, floods with light at sunrise.

ARRIVAL AND DEPARTURE

By boat Boats leave from the waterfront in Copacabana at around 8.30am (for a full day; B$40–50), with half-day boats at 1.30pm (B$30–40). For full-day tours you normally have a choice between "Parte Norte" and "Parte Sur" boats. Parte Norte tours go straight to Ch'allapampa (B$25 one-way), before going to Yumani and returning to Copacabana around 3.30pm. Parte Sur tours go to Yumani (B$20 one-way) for a brief stop, then usually on to Isla del Luna at 9.30am for an hour or so, then return to Yumani for the rest of the day before also leaving around 3.30pm (B$35 for just the Yumani-Luna-Copa leg). There are also one-way boats that depart Yumani for Copacabana at 10.30am and 4pm; it is very rare for any boat to leave Yumani after 4pm, so you'll have to hire a private boat if you get stuck (at least B$350/US$50 for two people to Copacabana).

ACCOMMODATION

Yumani is home to the majority of the island's accommodation, most of which offers sporadic (and usually cold) water, and basic conditions. There are also a couple of simple but friendly places to stay in Ch'allapampa.

CH'ALLAPAMPA

Hostal Inca Uta Near the northern landing jetty at Ch'allapampa ☏ 7151 5246. Large yellow building with basic en-suite rooms, friendly owners and limited electricity. __B$60__

Hostal Pachamama Just beyond the museum ☏ 7353 0261. A friendly place, overlooking the beach, with claustrophobic ground-floor rooms but better, more spacious ones upstairs; both have shared bathrooms. There are also basic laundry facilities. Cash only. __B$60__

YUMANI

Hostal Imperio del Sol Near the church on the left-hand side of the steps ☏ 7196 1863, ✉ hotelimperiodelsol @gmail.com. This modern peach-coloured *hostal* has great views and clean, though still pretty basic, rooms with shared or private bathrooms, plus a restaurant, internet café (B$15/hr) and pet alpacas. Usually no hot water.

2

Shared bathroom B$60, private bathroom B$120
Hostal Inti Wayra Near the church, Yumani ☎ 7194
2015. A slightly better budget choice with sizeable, balconied rooms (with shared and private bathrooms) and excellent east-facing lake views. Those of a spiritual bent can avail themselves of the meditation room, and there's also a decent restaurant. B$90

EATING

There are plenty of basic restaurants serving pizza, pasta and freshly caught Titicaca trout upon request.
Las Velas Yumani, high up near the eucalyptus forest ☎ 7123 5616. Run by a former chef at a top Bolivian resort, *The Candle* (it really is lit by candles, no electricity; bring a torch) has a similar menu to the other restaurants in Yumani, but significantly higher standards: try the vegetable pizza or trout in wine sauce. Mains around B$30–50. Mon–Sat noon–2.30pm & 6–10pm.

ISLA DE LA LUNA

About 8km east of the Isla del Sol, the far smaller **Isla de la Luna** (Island of the Moon) was another important pre-Columbian religious site. For much of the twentieth century, the island was used as a prison for political detainees, yet for the Incas it was a place of great spiritual importance. Known as Coati ("Queen Island"), it was associated with the moon, considered the female counterpart of the sun, and a powerful deity in her own right. The main site on the island – and one of the best-preserved Inca complexes in Bolivia – is a temple on the east coast known as **Iñak Uyu** (daily

8am–6pm; B$10), the "Court of Women", probably dedicated to the moon and staffed entirely by women. From the beach a series of broad Inca agricultural terraces leads up to the temple complex, a collection of stone buildings with facades containing eleven massive external niches still covered in mud stucco, all around a broad central plaza.

ARRIVAL AND DEPARTURE

By boat Tour boats from Copacabana to Isla del Sol sometimes call at Isla de la Luna if there's enough demand (see p.181). Otherwise, you can charter a private boat from Copacabana or Yumani (around B$550 or US$80).

ACCOMMODATION AND EATING

Although far fewer (and more basic) than the accommodation options on Isla del Sol, there is a handful of simple, locally run lodges dotted throughout the island; a double room costs around B$60–80. There are also a few shops to buy food, though you should bring some with you too.

THE CORDILLERA REAL

Stretching for about 160km along the northeastern edge of the Altiplano, the **Cordillera Real** is the loftiest and most dramatic section of the Andes in Bolivia, with six peaks over 6000m high and many more over 5000m forming a jagged wall of soaring, icebound peaks separating the Altiplano from the tropical lowlands of the Amazon Basin. Easily accessible from La Paz, the mountains are

---

TREKKING AND CLIMBING IN THE CORDILLERA REAL

The easiest base from which to explore the Cordillera Real is **La Paz**. Many of the best and most popular treks start close to the city, including the three so-called "Inca trails" which cross the Cordillera, connecting the Altiplano with the warm, forested valleys of the Yungas. Two of these ancient paved routes – the **Choro Trail** and the **Takesi Trail** – are relatively easy to follow without a guide; the third, the **Yunga Cruz Trail**, is more difficult – bring at least two days' worth of drinking water. You can do all of these treks, as well as many more challenging routes, with many of the adventure tour agencies based in La Paz (see box, p.161).

The other major starting point for trekking is **Sorata**. From here, numerous trekking routes take you high up among the glacial peaks, while others plunge down into the remote forested valleys of the Yungas. The **Sorata Guides and Porters Association** (see opposite) provides trekking guides, mules and porters.

With so many high peaks, the Cordillera Real is also obviously an excellent place for **mountain climbing**, for both serious and inexperienced climbers. **Huayna Potosí** (6088m), near La Paz, is one of the few peaks over 6000m in South America which can be ascended by climbers without mountaineering experience (albeit with the help of a specialist agency – check carefully that the guide they provide is qualified and experienced, and the equipment adequate).

perfect for climbing and trekking (see box opposite) – indeed, walking here is the only way to really appreciate the overwhelming splendour of the Andean landscape. Populated by isolated **Aymara communities** that cultivate the lower slopes and valleys and raise llamas and alpacas on the high pastures, the cordillera is a largely pristine natural environment. Here, the mighty **Andean condor** is still a common sight, pumas, though rarely seen, still prowl the upper reaches, and the elusive Andean spectacled bear roams the high cloudforest that fringes the mountains' upper eastern slopes.

SORATA

Set at an altitude of 2695m, **SORATA** is an enchanting little town, and the most popular base for trekking and climbing in the Cordillera Real. Hemmed in on all sides by steep slopes, often shrouded in clouds and with a significantly warmer climate than La Paz, it was compared by Spanish explorers to the Garden of Eden. There's not a lot to do in Sorata itself except hang out and relax either side of some hard trekking or climbing, or less strenuous walks in the surrounding countryside.

ARRIVAL AND DEPARTURE

By bus Minibuses from the cemetery district (Manuel Bustillos, at Av Kollasuyo) in La Paz (hourly 4am–6pm; 3hr 30min–4hr) pull up in front of the offices of Trans Unificada Sorata (☎02 2381693) on Plaza Enrique Peñaranda. The only way to reach Copacabana without going via La Paz is to take a La Paz-bound bus and change at Huarina (in the past there have been high-season direct services between Copacabana and Sorata – ask at your accommodation); for Coroico you'll have to go via La Paz.

INFORMATION

Tourist information For information and advice on trekking in the surrounding mountains, try the Sorata Guides and Porters Association (Asociación de Guías de Turismo Sorata), whose office is opposite the *Residencial Sorata*, just off the plaza on Calle Sucre (☎7327 2763). They can arrange guides for all the main trekking routes around Sorata for around B$200/day; they also organize mule hire and have a limited amount of camping equipment available for rent. La Paz-based Andean Epics

offer some fantastic all-action expeditions leaving from Sorata (see p.161).

Money There's no ATM in Sorata, but Prodem, Plaza General Enrique Peñaranda 136 (Tues–Fri 8.30am–12.30pm & 2.30–6pm, Sat 8am–3pm) changes US dollars and gives cash advances for a five-percent commission fee.

ACCOMMODATION

Altai Oasis ☎7151 9856, ⓦwww.altaioasis.com. A series of imaginative cabins, rooms and dorms on the folds of the riverbank, including a psychedelic log cabin (sleeping 3–4), a tree-house-like hideaway, a conical yurt-like construction, as well as more humble abodes. Follow the path past the *Hostal El Mirador*, take the first right down the hill, then the next right-hand turning to drop steeply down towards the hostel. Alternatively, take a taxi for about B$20. Camping/person B$30, dorms B$85, doubles B$315

Hostal Jordán III C Murillo, at Bolívar, 1 block from the plaza ☎7328 8144, ⓦsoratajordan.com. With terraces overlooking the square, this is an excellent place to watch the world go by. Facilities include a kitchen and a comfy DVD room. Continental breakfast available (B$10). B$90

Hostal Panchita Plaza Enrique Peñaranda ☎02 2134242. A welcoming, simple place with a sunny courtyard and clean rooms (though the "hot" shower doesn't quite live up to its name). There's a TV lounge and access to kitchen facilities. B$80

Hostal Las Piedras Villa Elisa C 2, near the football field ☎7191 6341, ✉laspiedras2002@yahoo.de. A 10–15min walk out of town, the German-run *Las Piedras* offers spotless rooms (with or without bathrooms) with great views and styled with an attention to detail rare at budget level. Friendly owner Petra Huber is a mine of local information in German, English and Spanish, while her partner – owner of *Café Illampu* – supplies artisan breads, yoghurt, honey and marmalade for breakfast (for B$35). B$80

Residencial Sorata Plaza Enrique Peñaranda ☎02 2136672. Set in the delightful, rambling nineteenth-century Casa Gunther, this *residencial* makes you feel you've stepped back in time by at least eighty years. There are lovely gardens, attractive simple rooms and a huge, wonderfully decorated drawing room. B$120

EATING AND DRINKING

Restaurant opening times are erratic: most places are open everyday except Tuesday, from around 9/10am to 9/10pm. Some restaurants have shorter opening hours during the rainy season (Nov–March), and a few close completely.

Altai Oasis ☎7151 9856, ⓦwww.altaioasis.com. You can dine to the peal of wind chimes and distant rattle of campground bongos on *Altai*'s idyllic outdoor deck. It's one

2

ZZIP THE FLYING FOX

Ziplines have made it to Bolivia, with this incarnation a 1555m beast in three sections, swooping 200m over the forest canopy at speeds of over 85km/hr. **Zzip the Flying Fox** (daily 9–11am & 1–5pm; around B$260; ☎02 2313849, ⓦziplinebolivia.com), a Kiwi-Bolivian-run outfit, is located in Yolosa, 6km from Coroico, with most organized "Death Road" trips (see p.168) including a stop here as an optional extra.

of Sorata's best places to eat, with Eastern European dishes like goulash and *borsht*, vast T-bone steaks, veggie options and a wide range of breakfast choices. Mains B$35–50. Daily 8am–8pm.

Casa Reggae One block west of *Hostal El Mirador*. A basic outdoor bar, with drinks and sandwiches (from B$12) in the evening and a chilled out, hippyish feel. Daily 6pm–late.

El Ceibo Muñecas 339. This first-floor restaurant is the pick of the local joints, serving standard Bolivian fare at moderate prices (mains B$15–30) in a rustic, low-lit dining room. The filling set *desayunos*, *almuerzos* and *cenas* are all good options. Daily 8am–9pm.

Restaurante Jalisco Plaza Enrique Peñaranda. This simple restaurant boasts a rather varied menu of Mexican and Italian food, as well as more traditional dishes. The enchiladas are surprisingly tasty (B$25). Daily noon–9pm.

THE YUNGAS

East of La Paz, the Cordillera Real drops precipitously into the Amazon lowlands, plunging down through a region of rugged, forest-covered mountains and deep subtropical valleys known as the **Yungas**, abundant with crops of coffee, tropical fruit and coca. Three of the well-built stone roads that linked the agricultural outposts of the Yungas to the main population centres before the Spanish conquest, the so-called "Inca" trails – the **Takesi**, **Choro** and **Yunga Cruz** – are still in good condition, and make excellent three- to four-day hikes from La Paz. The most frequently visited Yungas town is the idyllic resort of **Coroico**, set amid spectacular scenery and tropical vegetation. From Coroico, the road continues north towards Rurrenabaque and the Bolivian Amazon (see p.218).

COROICO

Rightly considered one of the most beautiful spots in the Yungas, the peaceful little town of **COROICO** is perched on a steep mountain slope with panoramic views across the forest-covered Andean foothills to the icy peaks of the Cordillera Real beyond. It enjoys a warm and pleasantly humid climate, and this, combined with the dramatic scenery and good facilities, makes it an excellent place to relax and recuperate – especially if you've spent the day cycling the "Death Road" (see box, p.168). Most cafés and restaurants are closed on Monday mornings and Tuesdays, and the town is often without electricity on Mondays.

WHAT TO SEE AND DO

Most visitors to Coroico spend much of their time relaxing on the peaceful **Plaza Principal**, lounging by a swimming pool and enjoying the fantastic views. However, there are some pleasant walks through the surrounding countryside, with forested mountain slopes covered in a lush patchwork of coffee and coca plantations, and banana and orange groves. If you're feeling adventurous, consider a canyoning trip with community ecotourism agency, El Vagante (☎02 2413065; ask at the office on the corner of the main square).

ARRIVAL AND DEPARTURE

By bus Buses, *micros* and minibuses (minivans) to Coroico (every 30min; 2hr 15min–3hr 30min) depart from La Paz from the Villa Fátima district (last bus back around 6pm); they depart from and return to the bus station on the south side of Coroico (Av Manning). If you're coming to Coroico from anywhere else, you'll have to catch a pick-up truck (B$5) for the 15min ride from the main road at Yolosita – these drop passengers off outside the Mercado Municipal, on Sagárnaga.

INFORMATION

Money and exchange Various shops change US dollars; Banco FIE and Pronam, on the north side of the plaza, offer cash advances on Visa and MasterCard (Sat & Sun am).

Tourist information There is a tourist office staffed by local guides on central Plaza García Lanza (daily 8am–noon & 2.30–7.30pm; ☎7250 5402), which has a

★TREAT YOURSELF

La Senda Verde Animal Refuge & Eco Lodge ☎ 7472 2825, ⊛ sendaverde.com. Situated twenty minutes outside of Coroico (a taxi will be about B$40) and set in a beautiful valley next to a river that you can swim in, this animal sanctuary is the kind of gorgeous hideaway you won't ever want to leave – it's a home for animals rescued by illegal traffickers, including monkeys, toucans and parrots, ocelots and even spectacled bears (reserve daily 10am–5pm; 45min tours B$69, B$89 including bears; no shorts, short skirts or children under 10). There are sprawling, lush grounds to wander around, pretty views and a restaurant that serves home-made pasta and salads. Accommodation is in two- to five-person cabins, which are dotted around the grounds. Prices include breakfast and monkey encounter. Basic huts B$260, treehouse B$300, doubles B$360

selection of flyers and maps, and can give advice in Spanish; guides are available for trips to nearby Afro-Boliviano communities, the Camino del Inca and waterfall hikes. The bus station also has a tourist office, though it's only intermittently open.

ACCOMMODATION

For a small town Coroico has a good range of places to stay. At weekends and on public holidays everywhere gets very full and prices go up, so it's worth booking in advance.

★**Hostal Chawi** In front of the petrol station, just off the road to La Paz ☎ 7355 5644, ⊛ hostalchawi.com. The friendliest and cosiest budget option in town. Rooms are basic but comfy, with dorms or private doubles with hot showers. Dizzying views, lush gardens, wonderful Bolivian hospitality and amazing home-cooked food and home-grown coffee add to the experience. Breakfast included. Dorms B$55, doubles B$150

Hotel Esmeralda Julio Zuazo Cuenca 725, 400m above the plaza ☎ 02 2136017, ⊛ www.hotelesmeralda.com. This large hotel has great views, an attractive garden and pool, a reasonable restaurant, table football, internet access and a book exchange, and breakfast is included. There's a wide range of dorms and rooms; the best rooms have private bathrooms and bamboo balconies with stunning vistas. If their free transfer service isn't there to pick you up from the plaza or bus terminal, they'll refund your taxi fare. Dorms B$75, doubles B$200

Hostal Kory Linares 3501 ☎ 7156 4050. The genuinely spectacular views of the valley are the real draw here

– you can see Death Road winding its hair-raising way. A good-value choice with a huge pool (open to non-guests for B$10) and clean, parquet-floored en-suite rooms. There are also some cheaper options with shared bathrooms, plus a restaurant, communal kitchen and laundry service. B$160

★**Hostal Sol y Luna** Just under 1.5km outside town, uphill on Julio Zuazo Cuenca, beyond the *Hotel Esmeralda* ☎ 7156 1626, ⊛ solyluna-bolivia.com. Tranquil hideaway in beautiful hillside grounds that overlook the valley, with hammocks, fire pits, a yoga room and plunge pools. Cooking facilities are available to guests, but the restaurant does excellent, simple dishes too (daily 8am–10pm). Breakfast costs B$35–40 extra, and a taxi from town is around B$20–25. Camping/person B$40, doubles B$120, cabins B$310

Villa Bonita C Héroes del Chaco, 100m past *Hotel Bella Vista* on the road to Caranavi ☎ 7191 8298, ⊟ Villa_Bonita05@yahoo.com. Amid the laidback, familial environs of their raspberry-coloured home and leafy garden – site, too, of a great café (see p.186) – friendly Bolivian-Swiss couple Ninfa and Gianni Pedetti have three lovely, wooden-shuttered rooms and a four-berth cabin. Cash only. Breakfast at the café included. Dorms B$65, doubles B$160

EATING AND DRINKING

Back-Stube Pasteleria Alemana Linares, off Plaza Principal. German café-bakery serving excellent breakfasts, home-made cakes (B$13), salads, sandwiches and main meals (B$30–50): for a hearty feed, try the *saurbraten* (a thick beef stew served with noodle-style dumplings; B$47). It has a wonderful terrace affording yet more amazing views. Wed–Fri 9.30am–2.30pm & 6.30–10pm, Sat & Sun 9.30am–10pm.

El Cafetal Miranda (near the hospital, 15min walk up from the plaza). Great-value French-run hotel restaurant with panoramic views and delicious food (B$20–50), including trout lasagne, steak in Roquefort sauce, crêpes, soufflés and curries. All that's missing is the French wine, although Tarija supplies a fine substitute. Wed–Mon 8.30am–4pm & 6.30–9.30pm.

Carla's Garden Pub Pasaje Adalid Linares, 50m down the steps beyond *Hostal Kory*. Down a flight of steps that you won't relish climbing back up, *Carla's* is a cute, tucked-away little bar that does good simple food (sandwiches from B$12, pasta from B$32) and a fine range of beers (B$17–20), including the punch-packing "Judas". Wi-fi use is B$5. Tues–Sat 3pm–midnight (sometimes later).

La Casa C Julio Cuenca (two blocks east of the plaza). German/Bolivian-run restaurant where walls are adorned with an eclectic range of trinkets. Specializes in fondues from B$45. The opening hours are one benefit in a town

2

which shuts up shop once the weekending *paceños* have fled. Daily 6–11pm.

Villa Bonita C Héroes del Chaco ☎7191 8298, ✉villa_bonita05@yahoo.com. It's a 10min walk from the plaza, but come for the friendly, boho atmosphere, shady garden, and delicious home-made ice cream (B$4/scoop) and vegetarian dishes. Daily 8.30am–6pm.

The Southern Altiplano

South of La Paz, the **Southern Altiplano** stretches 800km to the Chilean and Argentine borders. Set at an average altitude of around 3700m, this starkly beautiful landscape is the image most frequently associated with Bolivia: a barren and treeless expanse whose arid steppes stretch to the horizon, where snowcapped mountains shimmer under deep-blue skies.

The unavoidable transport nexus of the Altiplano is the tin-mining city of **Oruro**, 230km south of La Paz, a grim monument to industrial decline that nevertheless comes alive once a year during the **Carnaval**. Some 310km further southeast of Oruro is the legendary silver-mining city of **Potosí**, a city of sublime colonial architecture, marooned at 4100m above sea level and filled with monuments to a glorious but tragic past.

The Altiplano grows more desolate still as it stretches south towards the Argentine border. From the forlorn railway town of **Uyuni**, 323km due south of Oruro, you can venture into the dazzling white **Salar de Uyuni**, the world's largest salt lake. Beyond the Salar in the far southwestern corner of the country is the **Reserva de Fauna Andina Eduardo Avaroa**, a nature reserve of lunar landscapes, brightly coloured lakes and a surprising array of wildlife.

Southeast of Uyuni, the Altiplano changes character. The pleasant little mining town of **Tupiza** is surrounded by arid red mountains and cactus-strewn badlands eroded into deep gullies and

rock pinnacles. In the far south of the country lies the provincial capital of **Tarija**, a remote yet welcoming city set in a fertile grape-growing valley that enjoys a much warmer climate than the Altiplano.

PARQUE NACIONAL SAJAMA

Southwest of La Paz, the road to Chile passes through a desert plain from the middle of which rises the perfect snowcapped cone of Volcán Sajama. At 6542m, Sajama is the tallest mountain in Bolivia and the centre of the country's oldest national park, **Parque Nacional Sajama**.

The mountain's slopes support the highest forest in the world while the surrounding desert is home to pumas, rare Andean deer and the rarely seen, flightless, ostrich-like rheas.

Mountain climbers are drawn by the peak's relative ease of ascent – only permitted between April and October, when the ice is sufficiently frozen. The lower slopes contain bubbling geysers and hot springs which make for excellent hiking.

The administrative centre, where you can register to climb the mountain and arrange guides, mules and porters, is **SAJAMA** village.

There is very basic accommodation in the village (the park office can arrange this; around B$50–70/person) and various places serving simple, inexpensive food. Bring warm clothing – it can get chilly.

ARRIVAL AND INFORMATION

By bus There are two ways to reach Sajama by public transport from La Paz. The first is to take any Oruro-bound bus (every 30min; 1hr 30min) as far as the crossroads town of Patacamaya, from where a *micro* (3hr 30min) goes to Sajama every day at about noon–1pm (get there a couple of hours early), returning to Patacamaya at 6am the next day. Alternatively, get on a bus from La Paz (2–3 daily; 3hr 30min–4hr) headed for Arica in Chile and alight at the village of Lagunillas (Lagunas on some maps), 2.5km beyond the turn-off to Sajama, from where you should be able to hire a taxi to Sajama village for B$80–100.

Information For pre-trip information, contact SERNAP, Av Mariscal Santa Cruz, Edificio Litoral no. 150, La Paz (☎02

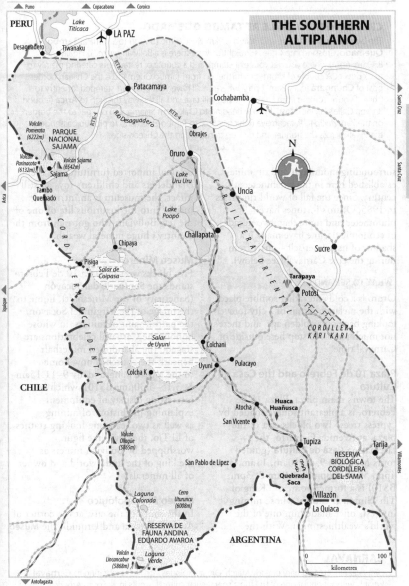

THE SOUTHERN ALTIPLANO

2111360, Ⓦ sernap.gob.bo). On arrival in Sajama village you must register at the park office (daily 8am–noon & 2.30–7pm; ☎ 02 5135526) and pay the B$30 entrance fee. **Organized trips** Andean Summits (☎ 02 242 2106, Ⓦ andeansummits.com) offer trips to the park with accommodation at the rather pricey *Tomarapi Ecolodge* (doubles B$550/US$80).

ORURO

Huddled on the bleak Altiplano some 230km south of La Paz, the grim mining city of **ORURO** was the economic powerhouse of Bolivia for much of the twentieth century, thanks to the enormous mineral wealth in the

2

CROSSING INTO CHILE AT TAMBO QUEMADO

The **border** between Chile and Bolivia is 9km west of the turn-off to Sajama at **Tambo Quemado**. Crossing into Chile is straightforward: there is a Bolivian *migración* (daily 8.30am–6pm) where you get your exit stamp, and a couple of restaurants catering mainly to truck drivers. A couple of kilometres further on from Tambo Quemado is the Chilean border post of **Chungará** (daily 8am–6pm), where you'll have your passport stamped for entry to Chile. If you're coming from La Paz, the bus will take you all the way through to **Arica** (around 8hr) on Chile's Pacific Coast. If you're heading to Chile from Sajama, you can get to the border on the 7am *micro* to Patacamaya (which comes to Tambo Quemado to pick up passengers), then walk across the frontier and pick up transport on the Chilean side.

---

surrounding mountains and tin mines established here in the late nineteenth century. Since the fall of world tin prices in 1985, Oruro's fortunes have plummeted and more than two decades of economic decline have made it a shadow of its former self – apart from during the epic Carnaval (see below).

WHAT TO SEE AND DO

Oruro is a cold and rather sombre place, with the melancholic air of a city forever looking back on a golden age, and there's not much reason to stop here outside of Carnaval time.

Plaza 10 de Febrero and the Casa de Cultura

The town's main plaza, Plaza 10 de Febrero, is a pleasant square shaded by cypress trees. Two blocks east of the plaza, at Avenida Galvarro, the fascinating **Casa de Cultura** (guided tours Mon–Fri 9am, 10am, 11am, 3pm, 4pm, 5pm & 6pm, Sat 9am & 3pm; B$10) is a former home of "King of Tin" Simón I. Patiño, whose mining interests once made him one of the world's wealthiest men. With the

original imported furniture, decadent chandeliers and children's toys all still intact, the museum is an intriguing insight into the luxurious life of one of the few Bolivians who got rich from the country's huge mineral wealth.

Museo Minero

Five blocks west of Plaza 10 de Febrero stands the **Santuario del Socavón** (Sanctuary of the Mineshaft), home to the image of the Virgin del Socavón, the patron saint of miners, in whose honour the Carnaval celebrations are staged. The abandoned mineshaft beneath the church is now home to the **Museo Minero** (daily 9–11.15am & 3.15–5.30pm; B$10), which has an interesting display of equipment explaining the history of mining, as well as two fearsome-looking statues of El Tío, the devil-like figure worshipped by Bolivian miners as the king of the underworld and owner of all minerals.

Museo Antropológico

In the south of the city, at the corner of Avenida España and Urquidi, the **Museo**

CARNAVAL

Every year in late February or early March, Oruro explodes into life, celebrating its **Carnaval** in what is without doubt one of the most spectacular cultural events in all South America. Tens of thousands of visitors flock here to watch a sensational array of costumed dancers parading through the streets, and there's always a good deal of heavy drinking and chaotic water-fighting. At the centre of the festivities are two events: the **Entrada** on the Saturday before Ash Wednesday, with a massive procession of more than fifty different troupes of costumed dancers passing through the streets, and the **Diablada**, or Dance of the Devils, led by two lavishly costumed dancers representing Lucifer and St Michael, followed by hundreds of devil dancers who leap and prance through the streets. If you're coming to Oruro at this time of year, be sure to book accommodation in advance.

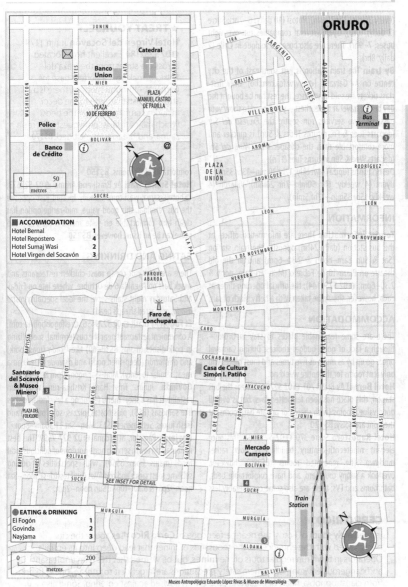

ORURO

ACCOMMODATION

Hotel Bernal	1
Hotel Repostero	4
Hotel Sumaj Wasi	2
Hotel Virgen del Socavón	3

EATING & DRINKING

El Fogón	1
Govinda	2
Nayjama	3

Museo Antropológico Eduardo López Rivas & Museo de Mineralógia ▼

Antropológico Eduardo López Rivas

(Mon–Fri 8am–noon & 2–6pm, Sat & Sun 10am–6pm; B$5) has an extensive archeological and ethnographic collection from the region, with displays featuring arrowheads, stone tools, jewellery and a wonderful collection of traditional masks.

ARRIVAL AND DEPARTURE

By bus All long-distance buses pull in at the Terminal Terrestre, ten blocks northeast of the city centre on Villarroel except those from Tarija, which drop you off on Ejército on the eastern outskirts of the city. A taxi into town costs B$10–15; alternatively, take any *micro* heading south along Av 6 de Agosto.

Destinations Cochabamba (6–7 daily; 5–8hr); La Paz

2

(every 30min; 3hr 30min); Potosí (10 daily; 6–7hr); Sucre (2 daily; 10hr); Uyuni (several companies run overnight buses; 7–9hr). There are also buses to Iquique in Chile (2 daily; 8hr).

By train The train station is just southeast of the city centre on Av Galvarro (ⓦ www.fca.com.bo). Only first-class tickets are sold in advance; the rest can be bought the day before travel at the earliest – you'll need to show your passport. Two services run south: the *Expreso del Sur* (departs Tues & Fri, returns Thurs & Sun) is quicker and more comfortable than the cheaper *Wara Wara del Sur* (departs Wed & Sun, returns Tues & Fri).

Destinations Tupiza (4 weekly; 12hr 30min–13hr 35min); Uyuni (4 weekly; 6hr 50min–7hr 20min); Villazón (4 weekly; 15hr 35min–17hr 5min).

INFORMATION

Tourist information There are information offices at the bus station (daily 24hr), opposite the train station (Sat & Sun 8am–noon & 2.30–6pm) and in the old theatre on Plaza 10 de Febrero (Mon–Fri 8am–noon & 2.30–6pm; ☎ 02 5250144); the official opening times at each, however, should be taken with a hefty pinch of salt.

ACCOMMODATION

There are some reasonable places to stay in Oruro – though a lack of good budget choices. During Carnaval prices go up by as much as five times and most places will only rent rooms for the entire weekend.

Hotel Bernal Av Brasil 701 ☎ 02 5279468. Near the bus station, this place has seen far better days, but is overall good value. Rooms (with shared or private bathrooms) at the front are noisy. **B$120**

Hotel Repostero Sucre 370 ☎ 02 5258001. This once elegant nineteenth-century building is now rather rundown. The renovated rooms (B$200), however, overlook a sunny courtyard, and have comfortable beds, bathrooms and TVs; there are also some considerably less

Hotel Virgen del Socavón Junín 1179 ☎ 02 5282184. Excellent hotel located across the street from the Plaza del Folklore, making it a perfect base for Carnaval. Although modern, there is a strong Christian theme to the decor, including crucifixes above the beds, which may surprise some guests. There's a sauna, and breakfast is included. **B$370**

comfortable older rooms. **B$150**

Hotel Sumaj Wasi Av Brasil and Aroma ☎ 02 527673, ⓦ hotelessamaywasi.com. Handily located just opposite the bus terminal, this good-value, mid-range option has clean and comfortable en-suite rooms with TVs. Road noise can be an issue, however. **B$250**

EATING AND DRINKING

There are plenty of cheap roast-chicken restaurants and snack bars on Avenida 6 de Octubre, where late on Friday and Saturday night stalls serve the local speciality *rostro asado*, or roasted sheep's head.

El Fogón Av Brasil ☎ 02 5279456, ⓦ elfogonbolivia.com. A convenient restaurant near the bus terminal, specializing in pork dishes (mains B$30–60) like *lechón* (roast pork) and *chicharrón* (deep-fried pork) and *charque* (dried llama meat, similar to jerky). Mon–Sat noon–2pm & 6–10pm.

Govinda Junín. This Hare Krishna-run vegetarian restaurant has a short menu featuring a few Indian dishes like samosas (B$5), plus pastas, pizzas, soya burgers and fresh juices. Set lunches B$13. Mon–Sat 11.30am–8pm.

Nayjama Pagador, at Aldana ☎ 02 527 7699. The best restaurant in town, serving huge portions of delicious local food (mains from B$50), with specialities including sublime roast lamb and *criadillas* (bull testicles). Mon–Sat noon–2pm & 6.30–10pm, Sun noon–2pm.

CERRO RICO

Immediately south of Potosí the near-perfect cone of **Cerro Rico** rises above the city, pockmarked with the entrances to the thousands of mines that lead deep into its entrails. Operators in town run regular tours of the **mines**, but be warned that this is an unpleasant and dangerous environment, where safety precautions are largely left to fate; anyone suffering from claustrophobia, heart or breathing problems is advised against entering. Some also question the ethics of making a tourist attraction of a workplace where conditions are so appalling. It is, however, also an extreme and unforgettable experience.

Tours of the mines begin with a visit to the **miners' market** on and around Plaza El Calvario. Here you can buy coca leaves, dynamite, black-tobacco cigarettes, pure cane alcohol and fizzy drinks as gifts for the miners you'll be visiting. Tours cost around B$130 per person. Recommended operators include **Koala Tours** (Ayacucho 5, ☎ 02 6222092, ⓔ koalabolivia @hotmail.com), with trips run by experienced multilingual guides, and **Green-Go Tours** (Junín 15–17; ☎ 02 6231362, ⓔ greengotours@hotmail.com).

POTOSÍ

Set on a desolate, windswept plain amid barren mountains at almost 4100m above sea level, **POTOSÍ** is the highest city in the world, and at once the most fascinating and tragic place in Bolivia. Given its remote and inhospitable location, it's difficult to see at first glance why it was ever built here at all. The answer lies in **Cerro Rico** ("Rich Mountain"), the conical peak that rises imperiously above the city to the south and that was, quite simply, the richest source of silver the world had ever seen (see box opposite).

The **silver rush** of Cerro Rico was triggered in 1545 by a llama herder who was caught out after dark on the mountain's slopes. He started a fire to keep warm, and was amazed to see a trickle of molten silver run out from the blaze. News of this discovery soon reached the Spaniards, the rush was soon under way, and the town's population mushroomed to more than 100,000 over the next twenty years, making it easily the largest metropolis in the Americas.

By the beginning of the seventeenth century, Potosí was home to more than 160,000 people and boasted dozens of magnificent churches, as well as theatres, gambling houses, brothels and dance halls. For the **indigenous workers and African slaves** who produced this wealth, however, the working conditions were appalling. Estimates of the total number who died over three centuries of colonial mining in Potosí run as high as nine million, making the mines of Potosí a central factor in the demographic collapse that swept the Andes under Spanish rule.

WHAT TO SEE AND DO

Potosí is a treasure-trove of colonial art and architecture, with hundreds of well-preserved buildings, including some of the finest churches in Bolivia.

Plaza 10 de Noviembre

The centre of the city is the **Plaza 10 de Noviembre**, a pleasant tree-shaded square with a small replica of the Statue of Liberty, erected in 1926 to commemorate Bolivian independence. On the north side of the square, the site of the original church (which collapsed in 1807) is now occupied by the twin-towered **Catedral**, completed in Neoclassical style in 1836 and recently renovated (entrance at Matos 24; Mon–Fri 8am–noon & 2–6pm, Sat 8am–noon; B$15). To the east of the square lies the **Plaza 6 de Agosto**, at the centre of which is a column commemorating the Battle of Ayacucho in 1824, which secured Bolivian independence early the following year.

Casa Real de la Moneda

West of the Plaza 10 de Noviembre on Calle Ayacucho stands the unmissable **Casa Real de la Moneda**, or Royal Mint (by guided tour only; 1hr 30min–2hr; Mon–Sat 9am–12.30pm, last tour 10.30am, & 2.30–6.30pm, last tour 4.30pm, Sun 9am–noon, last tour 10.30am; B$40, camera B$20, video B$40). One of the most outstanding examples of colonial civil architecture in all South America, it is now home to one of Bolivia's best museums. The collection includes the original minting machinery, some of the country's finest colonial religious art, militaria, archeological artefacts and a display of coins and banknotes.

Built between 1759 and 1773, La Moneda is a formidable construction, built as part of a concerted effort by the Spanish Crown to reform the economic and financial machinery of the empire to increase revenues. The rambling two-storey complex of about **two hundred rooms** is set around five internal courtyards, and housed troops, workers, African slaves and the senior royal officials responsible for overseeing operations. A vital nerve centre of Spanish imperial power in the Andes, it also served as a prison, treasury and near-impregnable stronghold in times of disorder.

La Torre de la Compañia de Jesus

On Calle Ayacucho, west of the Casa Real de la Moneda, stands **La Torre de la Compañia de Jesus** (Mon–Fri 8am–noon & 2–6pm, Sat 9am–noon & 2–6pm, sometimes closes earlier; B$10), a bell

2

2

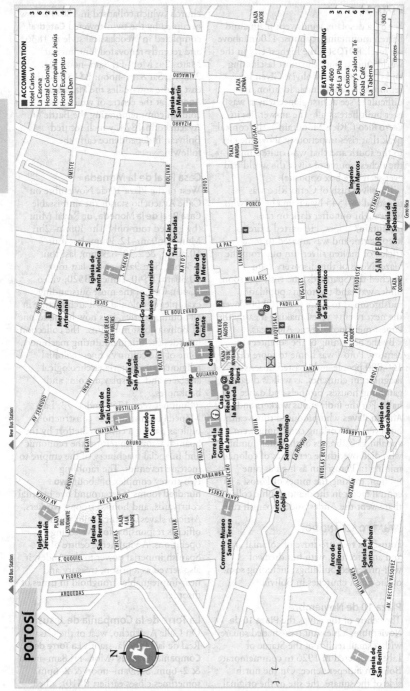

POTOSÍ

New Bus Station
Old Bus Station

■ ACCOMMODATION
Hotel Carlos V	3
La Casona	6
Hostal Colonial	2
Hostal Compañía de Jesús	5
Hostal Eucalyptus	4
Koala Den	1

● EATING & DRINKING
Café 4060	3
Café La Plata	5
La Casona	2
Cherry's Salón de Té	6
Koala Café	4
La Taberna	1

0   300
metres

Iglesia de San Martín

Iglesia de Santa Mónica

Mercado Artesanal

Iglesia de San Lorenzo

Iglesia de San Agustín

Casa de las Tres Portadas

Iglesia de la Merced

Teatro Omiste

Catedral

Green-Go Tours
Museo Universitario

Lavarap

Mercado Central

Casa Real de la Moneda
Koala Tours

Torre de la Compañía de Jesús

Iglesia de Santo Domingo

Iglesia y Convento de San Francisco

Ingenio San Marcos

Iglesia de San Sebastián

Iglesia de San Pedro

Iglesia de Copacabana

Convento-Museo Santa Teresa

Arco de Cobija

Arco de Mejillones

Iglesia de Santa Bárbara

Iglesia de Jerusalén

Iglesia de San Bernardo

Iglesia de San Benito

Cerro Rico

tower which is all that now remains of a Jesuit church founded in 1581. Completed in 1707 and recently restored, the grandiose tower is one of the finest eighteenth-century religious monuments in Bolivia and a sublime example of the Mestizo-Baroque style. You can climb to the top, from where there are excellent views of the city and Cerro Rico.

Convento and Museo Santa Teresa

The **Convento-Museo Santa Teresa** (Calle Ayacucho; Mon–Sat 8.30am–12.30pm & 2.30–6.30pm, Sun 9am–noon & 3–6pm; B$21) is a beautiful colonial church and convent worth visiting both for its fine collection of colonial religious painting and sculpture, and for a somewhat disturbing insight into the bizarre lifestyle of nuns in the colonial era. Visits are by guided tour only, so you need to get here at least an hour before closing.

ARRIVAL AND DEPARTURE

By bus The new bus station is on Av Banderas, near the Centro Recreasional Los Pinos. All services depart from here apart from the Uyuni ones, which still use the old terminal on Av Universitario, on the way out of town towards Oruro. A taxi into the centre from either costs around B$10–30.

Destinations La Paz (up to 10 nightly; 9–11hr); Oruro (10 daily; 6hr); Sucre (hourly; 3hr); Uyuni (6–7 daily; 4hr).

Taxis A quicker and more comfortable way to get to Sucre is to take a collective taxi (2hr 30min). Drivers wait at the old bus station until the vehicle is full.

INFORMATION

Tourist information Oficina de Turismo Municipal (Mon–Fri 8am–noon & 2–6pm, Sat 9am–noon; ☎02 622 7404), through the arch of Torre de la Compañia on C Ayacucho, a block west of Plaza 10 de Noviembre.

ACCOMMODATION

A primary consideration when choosing where to stay in Potosí is warmth – some places have central heating, but otherwise make sure there's adequate bedding.

Hotel Carlos V C Linares 42 ☎02 6231010. This place feels clean and fresh and offers kitchen facilities to guests (breakfast is included in the price), plus there's a living room-like TV area. B$150

La Casona Chuquisaca 460 ☎02 6230523, ⓦ hotelpotosi .com. They're not the friendliest bunch here, but there's an atmospheric feel to the place with its cloisters and dimly lit passageways. You can take your free breakfast in the pleasant courtyard. Dorms B$45, doubles B$110

Hostal Colonial C Hoyos 8 ☎02 6224265, ⓦ hostalcolonialpotosi.com. The dated rooms don't live up to the grand communal spaces, but they're spacious and well heated, and staff are accommodating. Comfortable but overpriced. B$374

Hostal Compañía de Jesús Chuquisaca 445 ☎02 622 3173, ⓦ hostalcompania.galeon.com. The welcome, as frosty as the Potosí nights, is on a par with *La Casona* across the street, but the building, a beautiful colonial conversion, makes up for it. Showers are steaming hot, even if the rooms are a little chilly. B$60

Hostal Eucalyptus Linares 88A ☎7240 1884, ⓔ koalabolivia@hotmail.com. Run by the Koala Tours agency (see p.190), this popular hostel has spick-and-span en-suite rooms, as well as a roof terrace with great views, and rates include a simple breakfast. B$200

Koala Den Junín 56 ☎02 6226467, ⓔ koalabolivia@hotmail .com. A travellers' favourite, this charming, amicable hostel owned, also run by Koala Tours, features decent dorms and inviting private rooms. Heating throughout means you won't feel the chill, and there are great showers, a comfortable communal area, kitchen and large DVD collection. Internet, wi-fi and breakfast are included. Dorms B$50, doubles B$150

EATING AND DRINKING

Potosí's popularity with travellers is reflected in the city's growing variety of places to eat. The Mercado Central – on Bolívar, between Bustillos and Oruro – is your best bet for cheap local food.

Café 4060 Hoyos 1 ☎02 6222623. Named after Potosí's altitude, this popular café/pub has a pretty, stylish interior. Offers the dreaded "international" menu (a bit of everything from steaks to burgers to pizza; B$17–18), beer and good coffee. Mon–Sat 4pm–midnight.

Café La Plata Plaza 10 de Noviembre ☎02 6226085. With its earthy tones, warm lighting and creaky floorboards, this elegant place screams hot chocolate and their spiced version is up to the task; fine coffee (B$8–30) and light meals are available too. Snooty service, however, lets the side down. Mon 1.30–11pm, Tues–Sat 10.30am–11pm.

★**La Casona 1775** Frías 41 ☎02 6222954. This is the liveliest bar in town (beer from B$13), housed in an eighteenth-century mansion with graffiti-covered walls, plus good food (mains B$25–50) and occasional live music. Mon–Sat 6pm–12.30am.

Cherry's Salón de Té Padilla 8 ☎02 6226753. Appealing tearoom with orange walls, faux wrought-iron furnishings and plastic flowers. The economical menu features breakfasts (B$17–23), coffee, cakes, sandwiches and ice-cream sundaes, as well as a few more substantial meals. Daily 8am–9pm.

Koala Café C Ayacucho 5. Those who appreciate shabby, higgledy-piggledy places will warm to *Koala*, spread across two creaky upper floors. At B$40 their *almuerzo* is not the cheapest, but it's generous, offering four courses (there's also a veggie alternative). Daily 7am–9pm.

La Taberna Junín 12 📞 02 6230123. Smart, downstairs restaurant decked out with French posters, wine racks and antique typewriters. The excellent-value four-course lunch (B$45) is one of the best deals in town. Daily 9am–11pm.

DIRECTORY

Banks and exchange The Banco Nacional de Bolivia on Junín changes cash and travellers' cheques, or try Casa Fernandez on Padilla between Bolívar and Matos. Several shops along Bolívar change US dollars. There are numerous ATMs.

Internet There are plenty of internet cafés: try the nameless place near *Cherry's* cafe on Padilla (B$2/hr).

Laundry Lavarap, Quijjaro at Matos (B$10/kg).

Post office Correo Central, a block south of Plaza 10 de Noviembre on Lanza, at Chuquisaca. Mon–Fri 8am–8pm, Sat 8am–6pm, Sun 9am–noon.

UYUNI

Set on the bleak southern Altiplano 212km southwest of Potosí, the chilly railway town of **UYUNI** is useful as a jumping-off point for expeditions into the beautiful and remote landscapes of the far southwest. In its heyday, the city was Bolivia's main gateway to the outside world and a symbol of modernity and industrial progress. Today, its streets are lined with a collection of shabby, tin-roofed houses and semi-abandoned railway yards filled with the decaying skeletons of redundant trains. A small town, it holds everything you might need within a few blocks; the effective centre is the nineteenth-century clocktower at the intersection of avenidas Arce and Potosí. That Uyuni hasn't become a ghost town is thanks to the ever-growing number of travellers who come here to visit the spectacular scenery of the **Salar de Uyuni** and the **Reserva de Fauna Andina Eduardo Avaroa**, which are usually visited together on a three-day tour.

ARRIVAL AND DEPARTURE

By plane There's a small airstrip just north of Uyuni; a taxi costs around B$10. Amazonas and military-run TAM fly to/from La Paz (2–3 daily; 45min).

By bus Buses from Potosí, Oruro and Tupiza pull up in front of the various bus company offices (an area optimistically described as "the terminal"), three blocks north of the train station along Av Arce. Todo Turismo

(📞 02 6933337, 🌐 todoturismo.bo), on Cabrera, has easily the most comfortable services, though considerably more expensive, to La Paz (around 10hr) via Oruro. Several buses make the scenic but rough journey to Tupiza; you may have to changes buses midway at Atocha; quicker and more comfortable jeeps sometimes run for part of the journey.

Destinations La Paz (3–4 daily, usually departing around 8pm; 10–12hr); Oruro (several overnight buses; 7–9hr); Potosí (6–7 daily; 4hr); Tupiza (2–3 daily; 6–9hr).

By train Trains (🌐 www.fca.com.bo) south to Villazón via Tupiza and north to Oruro depart from the train station on Av Ferroviaria, in the centre. The *Expreso del Sur* is quicker and more comfortable than the cheaper *Wara Wara del Sur*. There's also a weekly service to the border post of Avaroa from where there are connections to destinations in Chile.

Destinations Avaroa (Mon 3am; 4hr 30min); Oruro (4 weekly; 6hr 50min–7hr 20min); Tupiza (4 weekly; 5hr 20min–5hr 45min); Villazón (4 weekly; 8hr 25min–9hr 15min).

INFORMATION

Internet Mac Internet on Av Potosí (B$5/hr).

Money There are numerous ATMs. Banco de Crédito on Av Potosí between Arce and Bolívar changes dollars.

Tourist information There is a small tourist office (officially Mon–Fri 8.30am–noon & 2–6pm, though it's often empty) in the clocktower on Potosí, though it's only really worth coming here if you want to complain about a tour agency – tourist police officers share the office. The numerous travel agencies are generally more helpful, though their main aim is to sell you a trip.

ACCOMMODATION

There's a limited range of accommodation and most of it is fairly basic.

Avenida Av Ferroviaria 11 📞 02 6932078. A vast, narrow and rambling place. Though rooms are very basic, most have windows out onto the central area and are bright enough. B$80

Julia Av Ferroviaria, at Arce 314 📞 02 6932134, 🌐 juliahoteluyuni.com. Decent choice if the other budget hotels are booked up. Rooms have TVs and shared or private bathrooms. B$200

Kory Wasy Av Potosí 350 📞 02 6932670, 📧 kory_wasi@hotmail.com. Although the gloomy rooms lack natural light, the welcome is friendly enough and it's one of the better low-cost places in town. Doubles B$200

La Maison Martinet Av Potosí 16 📞 02 2732631, 🌐 lamaisonmartinet.com. The layout is akin to a hotel, but the rooms on offer are actually apartments, each with a mini-kitchen and sitting room. Sleeping three to four people, they work out as good value if you're in a group. The place is decked out with antique apothecary and medicinal artefacts. Apartments B$450

Hostal Marith Potosí 61 @02 6932174, @marithotel
.com. A few blocks from the centre, the bright, clean rooms
are set round a courtyard (though this is rather spoilt by
the plastic sheeting stretched across it). B$50
Piedra Blanca Backpackers Av Arce 27 @7643 7643,
@piedrablancabackpackers.hostel.com. Ramshackle
place set back from the street with some charm, not least
thanks to the row of stained-glass windows down one side
of the U-shaped building. Guests get breakfast and can use
the kitchen. Private rooms are overpriced though. Dorms
B$70, doubles B$250

EATING AND DRINKING

The range of places to eat in Uyuni is pretty limited, though
the food market on Potosí and Avaroa has cheap and
decent local dishes.

Arco Iris Plaza Arce @02 6933177. The best pizzas and
pasta dishes (from B$40) on this tourist strip, and, with its
brick arches, it's a little more atmospheric than most.
Drinks are relatively cheap. Daily 4–10pm.

Extreme Fun Pub Av Potosí 9 @7573 4008. It really
depends on your idea of fun, but you can't deny this place's
dedication to boozing with a wacky twist (how about a
"Llama Sperm" shot?). One room has a floor of salt. Prices
(cocktails B$35–65) are pretty high, though there are
drinks promotions early in the evening (happy hour
7–9pm). Daily mid-afternoon till 1am.

La Loco Av Potosí @02 693 3105. An endearingly weird

railroad-themed bar and restaurant. From the outside, its
long low block looks every centimetre the frontier town
saloon; inside, the bar itself is a riveted railway carriage,
and there's a large circular fireplace for cold nights. Mains
from B$40. Happy hour 7–8pm. Mon–Sat 4pm–2am.

Minuteman Pizza In the *Toñito Hotel*, Av Ferroviaria
@02 6933186, @bolivianexpeditions.com. Oddly located
directly outside the army barracks, this place is renowned
for its buffet breakfast, which is expensive but bountiful
(B$50), from porridge to pancakes with maple syrup. Their
pizzas (from B$45) are equally good. Daily 7.30–10am &
5–9pm.

Pizzeria Doña Isabella Camacho at Colón @7375 9824.
The chef-patron has ambitions to move closer to the train
station, but for now the strange dining room is part of this
place's appeal. Set up like a family sitting room, with just
four tables, the pizza oven sits incongruously in one corner.
The pizzas (from B$45) can be made with quinoa flour
bases, and are better than those at many of the more
touristy places. Quinoa beer is available too. Daily 6–9pm.

SALAR DE UYUNI

One of South America's most
extraordinary attractions, the **Salar de
Uyuni**, covering some 9000 square
kilometres of the Altiplano west of
Uyuni, is by far the largest salt lake in the

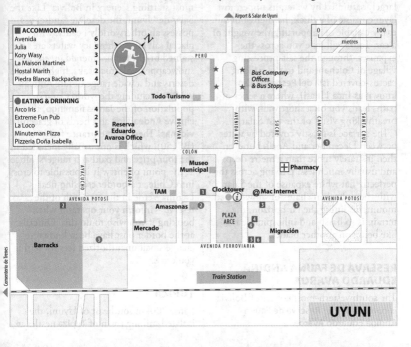

2

VISITING THE SALAR AND THE RESERVE

Pretty much the only way to visit the **Salar de Uyuni** and **Reserva de Fauna Andina Eduardo Avaroa** is on an organized tour, which can be easily arranged from Uyuni. The standard three-day tour price is usually B$800–1100 (US$118–163) including food, accommodation, transport and a Spanish-speaking guide. You'll pay more if booking in La Paz, and often significantly more for an English-speaking guide. An additional B$30 is payable for the visit to Isla del Pescado and B$150 for entering the reserve. The tour is by 4WD around a circuit comprising the Salar de Uyuni and **lagunas Colorada** and **Verde** in the reserve; trips ending in San Pedro de Atacama in Chile (see p.411), starting or ending in Tupiza, and lasting four or more days, are also available. Note that wind-chill temperatures can drop to anything from -25°C to -40°C. You should bring high-factor sunblock and sunglasses to counter the possibility of snow blindness, as well as a good sleeping bag (available to buy or rent in Uyuni), a torch and plenty of warm clothing.

Late departures, inadequate accommodation and vehicle breakdowns are problems that may occur no matter which agency you choose, but it's definitely worth paying a little more to ensure good safety conditions. The cheaper agencies tend to have older cars, bad food and unfriendly, occasionally drunk drivers.

The best method of choosing an agency is to talk to travellers just returned from a tour. You should also visit several companies, ask for written itineraries, check the vehicles and confirm how many other people will be in the jeep with you: six or fewer is preferable; seven or eight can be very uncomfortable. Agencies regularly swap drivers, guides and vehicles, and many travellers find that they booked with one company only to be put on a tour run by another.

Despite all the hassles and potential pitfalls, however, these tours are well worth the trouble, and almost everyone who goes counts them among their best experiences in Bolivia.

world. The blindingly white Salar is not a lake in any conventional sense of the word – though below the surface it is largely saturated by water, its uppermost layer consists of a thick, hard crust of salt, easily capable of supporting the weight of a car. Tours will take you across the expanses, through the salt-processing village of **Colchani** and to the striking cactus-covered **Isla del Pescado** (also known as Inca Huasi), where a series of paths leads you on a short walk with breathtaking vistas of the vast Salar.

The surface is mostly covered by water between December and April, but even then it's rarely more than a metre deep, and usually much less. Driving across the perfectly flat white expanse of the Salar, with the unbroken chains of snowcapped mountains lining the far horizon, the terrain is so harsh and inhospitable it's like being on another planet.

RESERVA DE FAUNA ANDINA EDUARDO AVAROA

The southwestern-most corner of Bolivia is covered by the **Reserva de Fauna Andina Eduardo Avaroa**, a 7147-square-kilometre wildlife reserve, ranging between 4000m and 6000m in altitude and encompassing some of the most startling scenery in Bolivia. Like the Salar de Uyuni, the desolate landscapes possess an otherworldly beauty, with glacial salt lakes whose icy waters are stained bright red or emerald green, snowcapped volcanic peaks, high-altitude deserts and a wide range of rare **Andean wildlife** including the world's largest population of the **James flamingo**, the elusive **Andean fox** and herds of graceful vicuñas. There is an entrance fee (B$150), which is not usually included in the tour price and paid at a rangers' office at the point of entry. It is possible to cross into Chile at a **border crossing** near Laguna Verde in the far south of the reserve – inform your operator when booking if you wish to do this. Officials at the border post have been known to charge small unauthorized fees for letting you cross.

TUPIZA

Some 200km southeast of Uyuni, the isolated mining town of **Tupiza** nestles in a narrow, fertile valley that cuts through the harsh desert landscape with its cactus-strewn badlands, deep canyons and strangely shaped rock formations and pinnacles. In the late nineteenth and early twentieth centuries, Tupiza was the home of one of Bolivia's biggest mining barons, Carlos Aramayo. His mines were rich enough to attract the attention of the infamous North American gunslingers **Butch Cassidy and the Sundance Kid**, who reputedly died in a shoot-out in the town of **San Vicente**, some 100km to the northwest. The town draws visitors largely because of the surrounding landscape, ideal for hiking, horseriding or just touring by jeep, activities that are easily arranged through local operators (see box, p.198), who also offer Butch-and-Sundance-related excursions.

ARRIVAL AND DEPARTURE

By bus The bus terminal is on Av Arraya, three blocks south and two east of the main square, Plaza Independencia. Several buses make the journey to and from Uyuni; you may have to change buses midway at Atocha; quicker and more comfortable jeeps sometimes run for part of the journey.

Destinations Tarija (2–3 daily, departing early eve; 6–7hr, much longer in rainy season); Uyuni (2–3 daily, generally leaving am; 6–9hr); Villazón (4–6 daily; 2–3hr).

By train The train station is three blocks east of the main plaza on Av Serrudo. Trains (ⓦwww.fca.com.bo) head south to Villazón and north to Uyuni and Oruro. The *Expreso del Sur* is quicker and more comfortable than the cheaper *Wara Wara del Sur*. Buy tickets in advance.

Destinations Oruro (4 weekly; 12hr 35min–14hr 5min); Uyuni (4 weekly; 5hr 20min–5hr 45min); Villazón (4 weekly; 2hr 45min–2hr 55min).

INFORMATION

Money and exchange There are ATMs on the main square. Several cambios east of the plaza on C Avaroa will change travellers' cheques, as well as US dollars, Argentine pesos and sometimes Peruvian soles.

Tourist information There is no formal tourist office, but the tour operators (see box, p.198) can tell you all you need to know.

ACCOMMODATION

There is a small range of accommodation in Tupiza, aimed specifically at backpackers on limited budgets. If arriving late, it is best to call ahead.

Mitru Av Chichas 187 ☏02 6943001, ⓦhotelmitru.com. A sunny central courtyard and swimming pool, clean, comfortable rooms and a buffet breakfast make this a popular choice, with prices depending on whether you're in the newer or older parts of the hotel. Run by the same owners are *Anexo Mitru*, C Avaroa (☏02 6943002), and *Refugio del Turista*, Av Santa Cruz 244 (☏02 6943155), which has dorms and doubles, with use of a kitchen and *Mitru's* pool. *Mitru*: doubles **B$230**, *Anexo Mitru*: doubles **B$215**, *Refugio del Turista*: doubles **B$90**

La Torre Av Chichas 220 ☏02 694 2633, ⓦlatorretours-tupiza.com. A friendly, family-run place with a handsome black-and-white tiled floor and a homely social area. Kitchen use is offered (though no eggs, garlic or onions are permitted because of the smell). **B$185**

Hostal Valle Hermoso Av Pedro Arraya ☏02 694 2370, ⓦvallehermosotours.com. Split between two main buildings and a smaller "backpacker" annexe, the Hostelling International-affiliated *Valle Hermoso* has a range of clean and sunny dorms and private rooms, with shared or private bathrooms; most also have TVs. There's a book exchange, laundry service, common rooms with TVs, a DVD library and a roof terrace. Dorms **B$45**, doubles **B$100**

EATING AND DRINKING

There's a limited choice of places to eat and drink in Tupiza. As usual, the cheapest place is the market, on the first floor of the corner of calles Chichas and Florida. Local specialities include *asado de cordero* (roast lamb), usually served at weekends, and *tamales* stuffed with dehydrated llama meat – the best are sold outside the Mercado Negro on Av Chichas.

Il Bambino Florida at Santa Cruz. Eating at this first-floor restaurant feels a little like dining in someone's house, and appropriately the food has a home-made touch. It's a good-value spot for a hearty lunch (around B$15–20). Mon–Sat noon–2pm.

CROSSING INTO ARGENTINA AT VILLAZÓN

The main border crossing between **Bolivia** and **Argentina** is at the dusty ramshackle frontier town of **Villazón**, about 92km south of Tupiza by road or rail. Just walk south from the plaza down to the frontier along Avenida Internacional and get an exit stamp at the Bolivian *migración* office (open 24hr), then walk across the bridge into Argentina, where immigration is open 7am–11pm. From the Argentine border town of **La Quiaca** there are regular buses to the city of **Jujuy**, from where there are connections to the rest of the country.

2

ORGANIZED TOURS FROM TUPIZA

Tupiza's tour agencies all offer broadly similar guided excursions into the desert landscapes around the town. Often referred to as a "triathlon", they combine **4WD excursions**, **trekking**, **horseriding** and sometimes **mountain biking** (in the case of Valle Hermoso Tours). The full-day tours usually cost around B$300–400/person depending on numbers, and half-day tours are often offered for a little over half the price. You can also do longer but not terribly rewarding trips to **San Vicente**, where **Butch Cassidy and the Sundance Kid** are thought to have died. These same agencies organize trips to the Reserva de Fauna Andina Eduardo Avaroa and the Salar de Uyuni (see p.195), usually as a four-day circuit that should cost about B$1300 (US$192), ending at Uyuni (though returning to Tupiza is usually possible). The advantage of doing the trip from Tupiza is that you hit the highlight of the salt flats on the last day.

TOUR OPERATORS
La Torre Tours Hotel La Torre ☎02 6942633, ⓦlatorretours-tupiza.com.
Tupiza Tours Av Chichas 187, inside the Hotel Mitru

☎02 6943003, ⓦtupizatours.com.
Valle Hermoso Tours Av Pedro Arraya, inside the Valle Hermoso hostel ☎02 6942370, ⓦvallehermosotours.com.

El Rinconcito Quilmes Suipacha. The best food (B$15–50) in town, popular with locals for its filling set almuerzos, excellent meat dishes, including delicious Argentine-style steaks, and special lamb roasts at the weekend. There's live music on Sunday afternoons. Mon–Sat noon–2pm & 6–10pm, Sun noon–5pm.
La Torre de Italiana Florida. As well as reasonable pizza and pasta (from B$30), this touristy restaurant has decent Mexican food, Spanish-style tortillas and a good range of coffees, though service takes an age. Daily 8am–10pm.

TARIJA

In the far south of the country, the isolated city of **TARIJA** is a world apart from the rest of Bolivia. Set in a broad, fertile valley at an altitude of 1924m, Tarija is famous for its **wine** production, and the valley's rich soils and mild climate have historically attracted large numbers of Andalucian farmers. The surrounding countryside is beautiful, particularly in the spring (Jan–April), when the vineyards come to fruit and the whole valley blooms.

WHAT TO SEE AND DO

Tarija's tree-lined avenues and temperate climate give the city a laidback ambience. The two main squares, tranquil **Plaza Luis de Fuentes**, named after the city's founder, whose statue stands in the middle, and **Plaza Sucre**, two blocks southeast, are lined with excellent restaurants and cafés – perfect

for a glass of the region's increasingly well-known wine. At nightfall, the streets around the Mercado Central, at the corner of Sucre and Bolívar, transform into a bustling street market, while Plaza Sucre is the centre for much of the town's nightlife.

Museo Paleontológico

A block south of the Plaza Sucre on the corner of Virginio Lema and Trigo, the **Museo Paleontológico** (Mon–Fri 8am–noon & 3–6pm, Sat 9am–noon & 3–6pm; free) offers a fantastic collection of fossils and skeletons from the Tarija Valley. Most of the specimens on display are of mammals from the Pleistocene era, between a million and 250,000 years ago, many of them from species similar to ones that still exist today, such as horses, bears and llamas.

Casa Dorada

On the corner of Ingavi and Trigo is the **Casa Dorada** (Mon–Fri 8.30am–noon & 3–6pm; B$5; ⓦcasadelaculturatarija .com), also known as Casa de la Cultura. Built in the nineteenth century in the Art Nouveau style by a wealthy merchant, the house has been restored and declared a national monument. You can wander through its rooms with photo displays depicting the history of Tarija, or check out one of the many cultural events hosted here, including concerts and dance performances.

WINE IN THE TARIJA VALLEY

There are some worthwhile excursions close to Tarija in the warm and fertile Tarija valley, which is notable as Bolivia's prime **wine-producing region**. A visit to one of the **bodegas** (wineries) to see how the wines are produced and sample a few glasses makes an excellent half-day trip. Generally, you can only visit the closest *bodegas* on an organized trip with a Tarija-based agency (from B$150). However, you can visit the lovely **Casa Vieja** bodega, about 25km from Tarija, independently. *Micros* marked "v" leave from the corner of Campero and Corrado every half-hour or so and will drop you off in the village of Concepción, from where it's a ten-minute walk from the plaza to the *bodega* – ask the driver or anyone in the village for directions. You can taste the wine, wander around the pretty vineyards and eat lunch in the restaurant.

2

ARRIVAL AND DEPARTURE

By train The airport (☎ 04 6642195) is a few kilometres east of the bus station along Av Las Américas. A taxi into the centre costs B$35–50; there are also frequent *micros*; to return to the airport (or the bus station) catch a *micro* heading east along Av Domingo Paz, which runs alongside the market. Departure taxes are B$11 for domestic flights.
Destinations Cochabamba (1–2 daily; 45min); La Paz (1–2 daily; 1hr); Santa Cruz (1–2 daily; 50min).
By bus The bus terminal is ten blocks or so southeast of the city centre on Av Las Américas – roughly 20min on foot. Alternatively, take a taxi (around B$10–15) or one of the frequent *micros* that run along Av Las Américas.
Destinations La Paz (4 daily, generally late pm/early eve; 24hr); Oruro (4 daily, late pm/early eve; 20hr); Santa Cruz (2 daily, late pm/early eve; 24hr); Tupiza (2–3 daily, generally am; 6–7hr, much longer in rainy season); Villamontes (2 daily, late pm/early eve; 10–12hr); Villazón (1–2 daily, generally am; 8hr). There are also buses to the closest border crossing with Argentina, Bermejo (5–6 daily; 4hr).

INFORMATION AND TOURS

Tourist information There are two tourist information offices: the Oficina Departamental de Turismo, Ingavi at Trigo (Mon–Fri 8am–noon & 2.30–6.30pm; ☎ 04 6672633); and the Oficina Municipal de Turismo (Mon–Fri 8am–noon & 2.30–6.30pm, Sat 8am–noon; ☎ 04 6633581) on Bolívar, at Sucre. Alternatively, speak to VTB Tours or Viva Tours.
Tour operators VTB Tours (☎ 04 6643372, ⓦ vtbtourtarija.com), inside *Hostal Carmen* at Ingavi 784; and Viva Tours, Bolívar 251 between Campos and Sucre (☎ 04 6638325, ⓔ vivatour@cosett.com.bo), run one-day tours (around B$150) of the city and the vineyards and *bodegas* of the Tarija Valley.

ACCOMMODATION

Tarija has a good range of accommodation, mostly in the centre of town, with a cluster around the bus terminal.
★**Hostal Carmen** Ingavi 784 ☎ 04 6643372, ⓦ hostalcarmentarija.com. This rightly popular *hostal* has

a range of well-decorated en-suite rooms; all have TVs and phones; there's also an apartment with a kitchenette (B$230). Perks include free wi-fi, filtered water, tea and coffee. **B$190**
Grand Hotel Tarija Sucre 762 ☎ 04 6642893, ⓦ grandhoteltarija.com. Aimed predominantly at business travellers, the rooms here are very comfortable – each has a/c, TV, safe and minibar – though lacking in character. There's also a restaurant-bar, sauna and wi-fi. **B$250**
Hostal Miraflores Sucre 920 ☎ 04 6643355. Converted colonial house with a sunny central courtyard and helpful and efficient staff. Choose between comfortable (and significantly more expensive) rooms with cable TV, private bath and breakfast, or small, spartan and much cheaper rooms without. **B$170**
Hostal Segovia Angel Calabi, right by the bus terminal ☎ 04 6632965, ⓦ hotelsegoviatarija.com. Friendly hostel with clean rooms, with or without bath and all with cable TV, conveniently located right by the bus terminal. **B$170**
Hostal Zeballos Sucre 966 ☎ 04 6642068. Although the exterior could do with a fresh coat of paint, this *hostal* is still a decent option. It has plain, clean rooms with private bathrooms – plus gloomy ones with shared facilities that are best avoided – and a patio overflowing with plants. There's also a laundry service. **B$120**

EATING AND DRINKING

Nowhere is Tarija's strong Argentine influence more evident than in its restaurants. Good-quality grilled beef features strongly, ideally accompanied by a glass of local wine, while *Tarijeños* are also proud of their distinctive cuisine of meat dishes cooked in delicious spicy sauces – try *ranga-ranga*, *saice* or *chancho de pollo*.
Café Mokka Plaza Sucre ☎ 04 6650505. In a good people-watching spot, this busy café has a lengthy menu featuring over twenty types of coffee (from B$10), as well as Argentine-style *submarinos* (hot chocolate), cocktails and beer. Food-wise the breakfast and snacks are good, but the mains are a bit overpriced. Mon–Sat 10am–11pm.
Club Social Tarija Plaza Luis de Fuentes ☎ 04 6632473. Good-value traditional *almuerzos* (around B$25–40) and

2

more expensive à la carte options for dinner in a rather staid atmosphere. Mon–Sat noon–2pm & 6–10pm.

El Fogón del Gringo Madrid 1051, five blocks west of the cathedral ☎ 04 6643399. In culinary terms this is as close as you'll get to Argentina without actually crossing the border. Succulent steaks (B$60–90) come with free access to a well-stocked salad bar, and there's a fine selection of wines. Daily 6–11pm.

Nougat Plaza Luis de Fuentes ☎ 04 6642259. Sophisticated stone-walled café-bar serving tasty salads, sandwiches and wraps (B$20–40), pasta dishes and steaks, cakes and sundaes, plus cocktails and local wines. Mon–Sat 8am–midnight.

Pizza Pazza Macondo Lazcano 317 ☎ 04 6654020. Eccentric, arty pizza parlour serving superior thin-ish crusts (from B$40) with an array of inventive toppings. There's live music at the weekends. Mon–Sat noon–2.30pm & 6pm–late.

★**Taberna Gattopardo** Plaza Luis de Fuentes ☎ 04 6630656. Vintage typewriters, radios and rifles, jazz paintings and discreet booths give this stylish restaurant-bar plenty of character. The vast menu includes sandwiches, pizzas, pasta, grilled meat and chicken, and the odd Mexican dish (mains from B$40), plus good coffee. Daily 8am–10pm.

DIRECTORY

Banks and exchange The Banco Nacional de Bolivia on Sucre changes cash and travellers' cheques and has an ATM. There are also numerous other ATMs.
Internet Consultel, Plaza Sucre.
Laundry La Esmeralda, Madrid between Campos and Colón.
Post office Correo Central on Lema, between Sucre and Trigo.

The central valleys

East of the Altiplano, the Andes march gradually down towards the eastern lowlands in a series of rugged mountain ranges, scarred with long, narrow valleys and blessed with rich alluvial soils. Both in climate and altitude, the **central valleys** are midway between the cold of the Altiplano and the tropical heat of the lowlands.

The administrative and political centre of Bolivia during Spanish rule, and still officially the capital of the republic, **Sucre** is a masterpiece of immaculately preserved colonial architecture, filled with elegant churches and mansions, and some of Bolivia's finest museums. The charms of **Cochabamba**, on the other hand, are more prosaic. Although somewhat lacking in tourist attractions, it's a pleasant and interesting city. It is also the jumping-off point for an adventurous journey south into the **Parque Nacional Torotoro**, Bolivia's smallest national park, boasting labyrinthine limestone caves, deep canyons and waterfalls, dinosaur footprints and ancient ruins.

East of Cochabamba, the main road to Santa Cruz passes through the **Chapare**, a beautiful region of rushing rivers and dense tropical forests, where the last foothills of the Andes plunge down into the Amazon basin. The area is notoriously the source of most of Bolivia's coca crop, so it isn't wise to stray too far off the beaten track.

SUCRE

Set in a broad highland valley on the eastern edge of the Altiplano, **SUCRE**, declared a UNESCO World Heritage Site in 1991, is the most beautiful city in Bolivia, with some of the finest Spanish colonial architecture in South America and a spring-like climate all year round. Neon signs are banned, and municipal regulations require all buildings to be whitewashed once a year, maintaining the characteristic that earned Sucre another of its many grandiose titles: "La Ciudad Blanca de Las Américas" – the White City of the Americas. It is also the administrative and market centre for a mountainous rural hinterland inhabited by the Quechua-speaking indigenous communities, particularly renowned for their beautiful weavings. These can be seen – and bought – in the city itself or on a day-trip to **Tarabuco**, a rural town about 60km southeast of Sucre that hosts a colourful Sunday market.

Founded between 1538 and 1540 and initially named Chuquisaca, Sucre's official title subsequently changed to Villa de la Plata (City of Silver). After independence, it was made the capital of the new **Republic of Bolivia** and renamed **Sucre**, but the city's

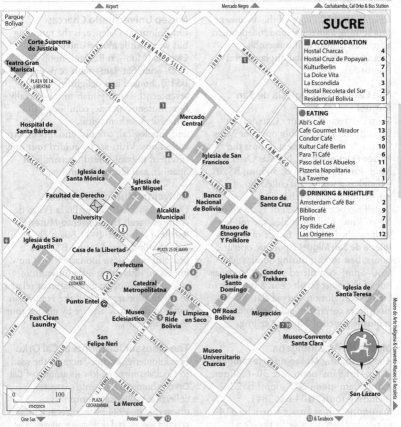

SUCRE

ACCOMMODATION

Hostal Charcas	4
Hostal Cruz de Popayan	6
KulturBerlin	7
La Dolce Vita	1
La Escondida	3
Hostal Recoleta del Sur	2
Residencial Bolivia	5

EATING

Abi's Café	3
Cafe Gourmet Mirador	13
Condor Café	5
Kultur Café Berlin	10
Para Ti Café	6
Paso del Los Abuelos	11
Pizzeria Napolitana	4
La Taverne	1

DRINKING & NIGHTLIFE

Amsterdam Café Bar	2
Bibliocafé	9
Florín	7
Joy Ride Café	8
Las Orígenes	12

economic importance declined. When the seat of both congress and the presidency was moved to La Paz after the civil war between the two cities in 1899, the transfer merely confirmed long-established realities. Sucre remained the seat of the supreme court and was allowed to retain the title of official or constitutional capital, which it still holds today.

WHAT TO SEE AND DO

The extravagance of Sucre's silver-funded past is evident in the city's beautifully preserved architecture. Most visitors enjoy a few hours or days wandering the streets and admiring the grandeur of the city centre; the attractive **Plaza 25 de Mayo** is the best place to start. The **Casa de la Libertad** offers an excellent insight into the significance of the city in Bolivia's history. Within easy walking

distance, you'll find a plethora of lavishly decorated churches, as well as excellent restaurants and some lively bars. When you're ready to explore beyond the centre, consider a visit to the dinosaur footprints at **Cal Orko**.

Casa de la Libertad

On the northwest side of the Plaza 25 de Mayo stands the simple but well-preserved colonial facade of the original seventeenth-century Jesuit University. Now known as the **Casa de la Libertad** (Tues–Sat 9am–noon & 2.30–6.30pm, Sun 9am–noon; B$15 including guided tours in Spanish, English and French; ⩎casadelalibertad.org.bo), this was where the **Bolivian act of independence** was signed on August 6, 1825, and it now houses a small but very interesting museum dedicated to the birth of the

2

republic. Inside, a copy of the document proclaiming a sovereign and independent state is on display in the assembly room (with the original displayed every August 6).

The Catedral and Iglesia de San Miguel

Sucre's sixteenth-century Catedral on Plaza 25 de Mayo is only open for Mass (Thurs & Sun 9am); next door is the **Museo Eclesiastico** (C Nicolás Ortiz 61; Mon–Fri 10am–noon & 3–5pm; B\$20), which has a wonderful collection of important religious relics.

Half a block northwest of Plaza 25 de Mayo along Calle Arenales, the modest whitewashed Baroque facade of the **Iglesia de San Miguel** (sporadic opening hours; best to visit during Sunday Mass, 6.30–8pm), completed in 1621, conceals one of the most lavish church interiors in Sucre, with glorious carved Baroque altarpieces covered in gold leaf and an exquisite panelled Mudéjar ceiling.

Museo de Arte Indígena

The fascinating **Museo de Arte Indígena** (Mon–Fri 9am–noon & 2.30–6.30pm, Sat 9.30am–noon & 2–6pm; B\$22 including tours; ☎04 6453841, ⓦasur.org.bo), at Pasaje Iturricha 314 opposite *Hotel Kolping* in the Zona Recoleta, is dedicated to the distinctive weavings of two local Quechua-speaking indigenous groups, the Jalq'a and the Tarabuqueños, and provides an excellent insight into a distinctly Andean artistic expression.

Museo Universitario Charcas

On Bolívar, at Dalence, is the rambling but worthwhile **Museo Universitario Charcas** (Mon–Fri 8.30am–noon & 2.30–6pm, Sat 9am–noon & 3–6pm; B\$15), housed in a delightful seventeenth-century mansion. It is really four museums in one, combining the university's archeological, anthropological, colonial and modern art collections. Visits are by guided tour only (no need to book ahead), generally in Spanish, and last at least an hour.

Convento-Museo La Recoleta

On the southeast side of Plaza Pedro de Anzures stands the **Convento-Museo La Recoleta** (Mon–Fri 9–11.30am & 2.30–5.30pm, Sat 3–5pm; B\$10), a peaceful Franciscan monastery that now houses an interesting little museum of colonial religious art and materials related to the missionary work of the Franciscan order in Bolivia. Visits are by guided tour in Spanish only.

The dinosaur footprints at Cal Orko

Five kilometres outside Sucre on the road to Cochabamba, the low mountain of **Cal Orko** is home to the world's largest collection of **dinosaur footprints**, discovered in 1994 by workers at a local cement works and limestone quarry. The site is a national monument, and has become a major tourist attraction for its five thousand or so prints from at least 150 different types of dinosaur that cover an area of around 30,000 square metres of near-vertical rock face; it requires

---

SUCRE TOUR OPERATORS

Most agencies in Sucre offer a Sunday tour to the Tarabuco market as well as city tours and trips to the salt flats and mines of Potosí. Some offer more adventurous biking and hiking excursions in the surrounding countryside.

Condor Trekkers Calvo 102, at Bolívar or Loa 457 ☎7289 1740, ⓦcondortrekkers.org. A not-for-profit tour agency, with the focus on trekking (and good food) on one- to three-day trips (ask about the trip to the Maragua crater). They also run a café (see p.204).

Joy Ride Bolivia Next door to the *Joy Ride Café* at Ortíz 2 ☎04 6425544, ⓦjoyridebol.com. Popular

Dutch-run operator offering a wide range of adventurous activities – mountain biking, paragliding, climbing, horseriding – as well as city tours.

Off Road Bolivia Ortíz 30 or at *Café Florin* ☎7033 8123. Quad and motorbike tours into the countryside around Sucre, including the Maragua crater and Yotala. Two-day trips also offered, spending the night at a mountain lodge.

binoculars, a good guide and some imagination to appreciate the footprints, as they're not easy to spot at first sight. The prints are on quite unstable rock, and some are at risk of crumbling away, so visitors are not allowed to get too close. To visit, head to **Parque Cretácico** (Mon–Fri 9am–5pm, Sat 10am–8pm, Sun 10am–5pm; B$30 including a guided tour). Micros A and 3 take you to outside the site; a taxi costs around B$20 one-way. Alternatively, take one of the Sauro Movil buses, which theoretically leave daily around 9.30am, noon and 2.30pm from outside the cathedral (though the service is prone to cancellations).

ARRIVAL AND DEPARTURE

By plane The airport (☎04 6454445) is about 8km northwest of the city; *Micros* I and F run into the centre along Av Siles (30–45min); a taxi costs about B$30. The domestic departure tax is B$11.

Destinations Cochabamba (1–2 daily; 30min); La Paz (1–2 daily; 40min); Santa Cruz (3–4 daily; 30min).

By bus The bus terminal (☎04 6456732) is about 3km northeast of the centre on Av Ostria Gutiérrez. From here it's a short taxi ride (around B$20) into central Sucre, or catch *Micro* A, which runs to the Mercado Central, a block north of Plaza 25 de Mayo.

Destinations Cochabamba (several early eve; 10–12hr); La Paz (4 daily, early eve; 12–14hr); Oruro (2 daily, early eve; 10–12hr); Potosí (hourly; 3hr) Santa Cruz (several daily from late pm onwards; 14–16hr; some travel via Samaipata).

By taxi Collective taxis are the quickest and most comfortable way to get to Potosí (2hr 30min); drivers wait just outside the bus station (by the clock) and depart when full. They will drop you off anywhere in central Potosí.

INFORMATION

Tourist information There is a wealth of information available, including on the first floor of the Casa de Cultura on C Argentina (Mon–Fri 8.30am–noon & 2.30–6pm; ☎04 6427102). The Oficina Universitaria de Turismo (Mon–Fri 8.30am–12.30pm & 2.30–6.30pm; ☎04 6452283) on C Estudiantes, just off the Plaza 25 de Mayo, is run by enthusiastic student guides.

ACCOMMODATION

Sucre has a good range of accommodation, almost all of it conveniently located in the heart of the old city centre.

Hostal Charcas Ravelo 62 ☎04 6453972, ✉hostalcharcas@yahoo.com. A little gloomy-looking, but the friendly welcome really goes a long way to endearing this place to you. B$80

Hostal Cruz de Popayan Loa 881 ☎04 6440889, ⓦhotelsucre.com. This popular place is based in a restored seventeenth-century townhouse. Although the rooms are a bit scruffy, most are en suite and come with TVs and wi-fi. There is also a dorm. Dorms B$45, doubles B$168

KulturBerlin Avaroa 326 ☎04 646 6854, ⓦkulturberlin .com. Also known as *Hostal Berlin*, this attractive German-run hostel has two six-bed dorms and several private rooms set around a courtyard. Facilities include a café-bar (see p.204), Spanish lessons, and cookery classes. Dorms B$55, doubles B$180

★**La Dolce Vita** C Urcullo 342 ☎04 6912014, ⓦdolcevitasucre.com. Central guesthouse, run by a friendly, informative Franco-Swiss family, with good views from a relaxed terrace and big, nicely decorated rooms. B$110

La Escondida C Junín 445 ☎04 6435792, ⓦlaescondidahostal.com. The name means "hideaway" and you'll be glad that it is, as it's located down a little passageway that runs off one of the city's most bustling streets. Rooms are smart and set around a sunny courtyard where you can enjoy the free breakfast. B$180

Hostal Recoleta del Sur Ravelo 205 ☎04 6454789, ✉mairusta34@hotmail.com. This reliable mid-range choice, a 10min walk from the main square, has comfortable, carpeted, en-suite rooms with TVs in a converted colonial house with a glass-roofed patio. B$200

Residencial Bolivia San Alberto 42 ☎04 6454346. This friendly *residencial* has spacious rooms, though there are some duds, so ask to see a few. They are set around a courtyard with plenty of plants and a questionable mauve and peach colour scheme. B$100

EATING

Sucre is home to an excellent variety of restaurants where you can try everything from the spicy local cuisine to authentic French and Italian plus good vegetarian food, at reasonable prices. The markets are great places to find cheap, filling lunches: try the second floor of Mercado Central on C Zabelo and the food hall in Mercado Negro on C Junín; don't miss the huge fresh fruit salads at the former.

Abi's Café Plaza 25 de Mayo 32 ☎04 6467738. Come to this popular café on the plaza for two things dear to travellers far from home – a decent cup of coffee and strong wi-fi. Snacks B$5–15. Mon–Fri 8.30am–10pm, Sat & Sun 8.30am–midnight.

Café Gourmet Mirador Pasaje Iturricha 297, Plaza de la Recoleta ☎04 6452330. A short taxi ride from the centre brings you to this shady, dusty length of garden overlooking the town and strewn with deckchairs. Come for Italian chef Marco Castiglion's home-made pasta (around B$50) as much as the views – the *alfredo* and *ragù bolognese* are both recommended. Daily 9am–8pm.

2

Condor Café Calvo 102 ☎ 7343 3392, ⓦ condortrekkers .org. Non-profit vegetarian restaurant run by travel agency Condor Trekkers (see p.202), with a menu featuring salads, *empanadas*, fresh juices and good organic coffee (B$7–16). Mon–Sat 8.30am–10pm, Sun noon–8pm.

Kultur Café Berlin Avaroa 326. A winning German-South American fusion (mains from B$30), with sauerkraut and sausages, *papa rellena* (mashed potato stuffed with a filling then fried), German beers and cheap *almuerzos*. Daily 8am–midnight; later at weekends.

Para Ti Café Audiencia 68. Sucre's finest chocolatier also has a tiny café and a short menu of delicious chocolate-flavoured milkshakes, coffees and liqueurs (from B$10). There's also home-made cakes and – of course – a vast array of chocolates and sweets to choose from. Daily 9am–7pm.

Paso del Los Abuelos Bustillos 216 ☎ 04 6455173. Smart *salteñeria* where Sucre's wealthiest citizens go for their mid-morning snacks: at B$6–8 each, the *salteñas* are relatively expensive, but worth every cent. Mon–Sat 8am–1pm.

Pizzeria Napolitana Plaza 25 de Mayo 30 ☎ 04 6451934. It's a bit gloomy inside, but Sucre's longest-established Italian restaurant serves tasty pizza and pasta, home-made ice cream, strong coffee and a daily choice of different set lunches (B$35). Mon & Wed–Sun 8.30am–10.30pm.

La Taverne Arce 35 ☎ 04 6455719, ⓦ lataverne.com.bo. Alliance Française-backed restaurant serving classic dishes like *coq au vin* and *boeuf bourguignon* with flair. Quite pricey (mains around B$60–70), so consider coming for their generous four-course *almuerzo* (set lunch) rather than dinner. Mon–Sat 9am–11pm, Sun 7–10.30pm.

DRINKING AND NIGHTLIFE

A large student population and a stream of party-loving backpackers ensure Sucre has a good range of bars and clubs.

Amsterdam Café Bar C Bolívar 426 ☎ 04 6436650. This intimate, two-roomed place is heavy on the timber and red brick – the perfect surroundings for their regular live music. There are frequent drinks promotions (for example, two Heinekens for B$30 8–10pm), while food is of the snack variety, though there's often a daily hot dish. Mon–Thurs 2pm–2am, Fri 2pm–3am, Sat 4pm–3am, Sun 4pm–midnight.

Bibliocafé N. Ortíz 50 ☎ 04 6447574. Bohemian bar-café (beer from B$12) attracting a good mix of locals and travellers from early evening until late with its mellow live music and intimate atmosphere. Snacks and light meals are also available. Tues–Sat 11.30am–2pm, Sun 7pm–2am.

Florín C Bolívar 567 ☎ 04 6451313. A booze-focused venue with drinks promotions (mixology quality dips during the 9.30–10.30pm happy hour) and microbrewery beers (from B$20). There's good food too – try their

generous salads or their decent take on *pad thai*. The decor is pleasant, with antique portrait photographs on the walls. Mon–Thurs 7.30am–2am, Fri & Sat 7.30am–3am, Sun 7.30am–midnight.

Joy Ride Café N. Ortíz 14 ☎ 04 6425544, ⓦ joyridebol .com. Part of a Dutch-run mini empire (there's also a travel agency and a shop), this bar-restaurant serves local and international dishes (B$25–65), as well as cocktails and beer (from B$18). There are film screenings, pool tables, a heated patio, and a book exchange. Mon–Fri 7am–late, Sat & Sun 9am–late.

Las Orígenes Azurduy 473 ☎ 02 645 7091. Venue staging a folkoric show with traditional dances from across Bolivia. Not just for gringos, and worth visiting if you're missing out on Carnaval – B$125 with dinner. Tues–Sun from 8.30pm.

DIRECTORY

Banks and exchange Casa de Cambios Ambar, San Alberto 7, and El Arca, España 134, both change travellers' cheques and cash dollars at reasonable rates. There are also plenty of ATMs, including at Banco de Santa Cruz and Banco Nacional de Bolivia, on San Alberto, at España.

Cinema Cine SAS, Juan Jose Perez 331. Shows subtitled new releases. Tickets around B$20.

Internet There are internet cafés all over the city, most of which charge about B$3–5/hr. Try Punto ENTEL on Bustillo, at Dalence/Olaneta.

Laundry Limpieza en Seco, Audencia 81.

Police If you get into difficulty or need a report for insurance purposes, make for the office on C Bolívar, at Camargo (the continuation of Av Hernando Siles).

Post office Correo Central, Junín, at Ayacucho. Mon–Fri 8am–8pm, Sat 8am–6pm.

TARABUCO

By far the most popular excursion from Sucre is to the small rural town of **TARABUCO**, set amid undulating mountains about 65km southeast of the city. The town itself is an unremarkable collection of red-tiled adobe houses and cobbled streets, but its real claim to fame is the Sunday market. This is the focus for the indigenous communities of the surrounding mountains, the Tarabuqueños, who come to sell the beautiful weavings for which they're famous throughout Bolivia. The market is actually a bit of a tourist trap, but the stalls selling weavings and other handicrafts to tourists are still far outnumbered by those selling basic supplies such as dried foodstuffs, agricultural tools, sandals made from tyres, big bundles of coca and pure alcohol in great steel drums.

ARRIVAL AND DEPARTURE

Buses and trucks to Tarabuco from Sucre (1hr) leave most mornings from Av de las Américas returning in the afternoon; however, it's much more convenient to go in one of the tourist buses (around B$35 return) organized by hotels and tour agencies in Sucre. Every tour operator will offer a trip to Tarabuco, some with guided tours in English (see p.202).

COCHABAMBA

Set at Bolivia's geographical centre, midway between the Altiplano and the eastern lowlands, **COCHABAMBA** is one of the country's most vibrant and youthful cities and the commercial hub of the rich agricultural region of the Cochabamba Valley, the breadbasket of Bolivia. It's a friendly and unpretentious city, also known as the "City of Eternal Spring" for its year-round sunny climate, and is perfect for relaxing in one of the cafés around Calle España.

WHAT TO SEE AND DO

Though Cochabamba isn't the place for colonial architecture, there are at least a couple of historic sights. Shopaholics will love the huge outdoor market of La Cancha, and there are also opportunities for exploring the understated attractions of the surrounding valleys.

Plaza 14 de Septiembre and the Museo Archeológico

The centre of Cochabamba is **Plaza 14 de Septiembre**, a placid and pleasant square with flower-filled ornamental gardens and plenty of benches where *Cochabambinos* sit under the shade of tall palm trees. A block south of the plaza on the corner of calles Aguirre and Jordán stands the extensive **Museo Archeológico** (Mon–Fri 8.30am–5.30pm, Sat 8.30am–2.30pm; B$25), which explains the evolution of pre-Hispanic culture in the Cochabamba region.

Convento de Santa Teresa

The lovely **Convento de Santa Teresa** (entrance on Baptista through the café; Mon–Fri 8.30am–11.30am & 2–5pm; B$20) on Baptista, at Ecuador, is worth visiting. As well as the convent, this beautiful building houses a church built within a church (the original church was destroyed in the 1700s). The nuns still live on the site, though they are now housed in the complex next door.

La Cancha

The commercial heart of this market city is in the south, with its massive rambling street markets. An entire block between calles Tarata and Pulucayo is occupied by the covered street market known as **La Cancha** (Quechua for "walled enclosure"), where *campesinos* and merchants come to buy and sell their produce, in this sprawling labyrinth of stalls.

Palacio Portales

About 1km north of the city centre, with its entrance off Avenida Potosí, the luxurious **Palacio Portales** (visits by guided tour only Tues–Fri: Spanish 3.30pm, 4.30pm, 5.30pm & 6pm, English/French 4pm; Sat: Spanish 9.30am, 10am & 11am, English/French 10.30am & 11.30am; Sun: Spanish 11am, English/French 11.30am; B$15) was built for the Cochabamba-born "King of Tin", Simón Patiño, though he never actually lived here. Built between 1915 and 1922 in a bizarre mix of architectural styles, including French Neoclassical and Mudéjar, the palace's interior is decorated with astonishing opulence. If anything, it's the magnificent **gardens** (Tues–Fri 3–6.30pm, Sat & Sun 9am–noon; free) that really impress, laid out in perfect proportion by Japanese specialists and featuring a rare ginkgo tree.

Cristo de la Concordia

About 1.5km east of the city is the Cristo de la Concordia – a statue of Christ modelled on the one in Rio but just slightly taller. To reach the summit, the risk of muggings means you shouldn't walk: take the five-minute cable-car ride (Tues–Sun 10am–7pm; B$8 return) for excellent views of the city.

2

2

COCHABAMBA

EATING & DRINKING

Café Paris	5
La Cantonata	2
Casa de Campo	1
Casablanca	3
Gopal	4
Sucremanta	6

ACCOMMODATION

Americana Hotel	5
City Hotel	4
Hostal Casa Vieja Colonial	2
Hostal Jardin	1
Hotel La Fontaine	3

Micros to Cliza & Tarata ▼   Jorge Wilsterman Airport ▼   ▼ Buses to Torotoro & Micros to Arani

ARRIVAL AND DEPARTURE

By plane Jorge Wilsterman airport (☏ 04 4222846) is a few kilometres southwest of the city; a taxi into the centre costs B$30–50; alternatively, take Micro B, which goes up Av Ayacucho to Plaza 14 de Septiembre. In addition to domestic flights there are a few services to neighbouring countries.

Destinations La Paz (6–11 daily; 30min); Santa Cruz (8–11 daily; 45min); Sucre (1–2 daily; 30min).
By bus Most long-distance buses use Cochabamba's bus terminal, in the south of the city on Av Ayacucho just south of Av Aroma. The surrounding area can be rough, especially at night, so take care. A taxi to the city centre costs B$10–20.

Services to the Chapare region (including Villa Tunari; 3hr–3hr 30min) depart when full from close to the junction of Av Oquendo and Av 9 de Abril, southeast of the city centre. Destinations La Paz (hourly; 7–8hr); Oruro (6–7 daily; 5–8hr); Santa Cruz (10–12 daily, most leaving in the morning or eve ; 10–12hr); Sucre (several early eve; 10–12hr).

INFORMATION

Tourist information The tourist office (Mon–Fri 8am–noon & 2.30–6.30pm, Sat 8.30am–noon; ☎04 4662277, ☎04 4258030) is on the east side of Plaza Colón.

Tour operators Fremen Tours (Tumulsa 245; ☎04 4259392, ⓦandes-amazonia.com) offer a variety of regional tours including a four-day "Essential Cochabamba" trip that takes in the Torotoro and Carrasco national parks. Bolivia Cultura (Ecuador 0342; ☎04 4527272, ⓦboliviacultura.com) offer Spanish lessons with host family options, and volunteering opportunities, with a minimum of three months for placements (ⓦvolunteerbolivia.org). Andes Extremo (La Paz 138; ☎04 4523392, ⓦandesxtremo .com) offer Torotoro, climbing, trekking, rafting and paragliding trips (the latter cost around US$60).

ACCOMMODATION

Budget accommodation in Cochabamba is underwhelming. The only time you really need to book ahead is in mid-August during the Fiesta de la Virgen de Urkupiña in nearby Quillacollo.

Americana Hotel Arce 788 ☎04 4250552, ⓦamericanahotel.com.bo. A good-value high-rise hotel with attentive staff and comfortable, well-equipped en-suite rooms with TVs and good views. The area isn't the safest, however, so take care at night. B$300

Hostal Casa Vieja Colonial Junín 134 ☎04 4583791, ✉hostal.colonial@hotmail.com. The garden is cool and shady (though a little untidy) and features a religious shrine, with the rooms in a cloister-like arrangement around it. They're fairly spacious, though the bedspreads and decor look washed out. B$130

City Hotel Jordan 341 ☎04 4222993, ⓦcityhotelbolivia .com. Although a little frayed around the edges, this central hotel is a sound choice. Its en-suite rooms feature phones, TVs and faded decor – those at the back are the best. B$240

Hotel La Fontaine Hamiraya 0181 ☎04 4252838, ⓦfontainehotel.com. Small and comfortable business-traveller hotel offering decent rooms equipped with fridges, TVs and private bathrooms, and decorated with colonial religious paintings – but beware the hazardously low ceiling beams. B$180

Hostal Jardin Hamiraya 0248 ☎04 4247844. This *hostal*, a 10min walk from the central plaza, has compact but reasonably comfortable rooms (with private bathrooms) that open out on to a peaceful garden with outdoor seating. B$120

EATING AND DRINKING

The best places to eat if you're on a tight budget are Cochabamba's many markets, and the choice of restaurants in the city is broad. Boulevar Recolta, a modern pedestrianized strip on the right-hand turning from the roundabout before Av Pando, is a popular night-time place for a meal and a drink; there's an abundance of modern restaurants, bars and a few karaoke joints too.

Café Paris España, at Bolívar ☎04 4503561. Sophisticated café with Parisian posters, wrought-iron chairs and a stained-glass-covered bar. There's a concise menu of coffees, sweet and savoury crêpes (B$13–25), ice creams and snacks. Mon–Sat 8am–10pm.

La Cantonata España, at Mayor Rocha ☎04 4259222. Smart Italian restaurant serving decent pizza (from B$40) and pasta (from B$49) at reasonable prices. Daily noon–2.30pm & 6.30–11pm.

Casa de Campo Blvd Recoleta at Pando ☎04 4243937. An attractive, if tourist-orientated, restaurant, *Casa de Campo* offers classy versions of traditional local dishes (mains B$32–77) around a pleasing central courtyard. Mon–Thurs & Sun noon–10pm, Fri & Sat noon–11pm.

Casablanca 25 de Mayo 344 ☎04 4521048. Hollywood-themed bar serving cold beer (B$15–25), fruity cocktails and the usual fare of pizzas, pasta, breakfasts and sandwiches to a tourist-heavy clientele. There's a pile of magazines to peruse, plus occasional jazz gigs. Mon–Thurs 10am–1am, Fri 10am–2am, Sat 11am–2am.

Gopal España 250 ☎04 4234082. This Hare Krishna restaurant serves up inexpensive and tasty vegetarian meals, including a buffet lunch that features twenty different salads, as well as numerous other dishes (B$20–40). Mon–Sat noon–3pm.

Sucremanta Arce 340 ☎04 4222839. A cool place in this hot town, with white walls and a vaulted ceiling, and otherwise sparse but tasteful decoration of old maps, paintings and iron chandeliers. Try the *fritanga* pork stew, the *chorizo* sausages or the *salteñas*. Mains B$17–42. Daily 9am–2pm.

DIRECTORY

Banks and exchange There are exchange offices on the southwest side of Plaza 14 de Septiembre and street moneychangers in the centre of town. There are also plenty of ATMs in the city centre.

Cinema Cine Center north of Plaza Quintanilla (☎04 4533731, ⓦcinecenter.com.bo).

Internet Internet cafés abound and most charge around B$3–5/hr. There are two good places on Arce to the southeast of Plaza 14 de Septiembre.

Outdoor equipment The Spitting Llama (Mon–Fri 9am–1pm & 3–8pm, Sat 9am–1pm; ☎04 4894540,

2

ⓦ thespittingllama.com) on Ecuador, at España, is a useful place which rents bikes and camping equipment, as well as selling novels and guidebooks.

Post office Correo Central, Av Ayacucho, at Av Heroínas (Mon–Fri 8am–9pm, Sat 8am–noon).

PARQUE NACIONAL TOROTORO

Some 139km south of Cochabamba, the **Parque Nacional Torotoro** covers just 165 square kilometres, making it Bolivia's smallest national park. But what it lacks in size it makes up for with its powerful scenery and varied attractions – high valleys and deep canyons, ringed by low mountains whose twisted geological formations are strewn with fossils, dinosaur footprints and labyrinthine limestone cave complexes. The park's cactus and scrubby woodland supports considerable wildlife – including flocks of parakeets and the rare and beautiful red-fronted macaw. The main attractions are the limestone caves of **Umajallanta**, the beautiful, waterfall-filled **Torotoro Canyon**, and hiking expeditions to the pre-Inca ruined fortress of **Llama Chaqui**.

ARRIVAL AND INFORMATION

By bus Buses to Torotoro leave Cochabamba from the corner of avenidas 6 de Agosto and Republica (Wed, Thurs, Sat & Sun 5.45–6am & 6pm; returning Mon, Tues, Fri & Sun 6am; 6–7hr). In the rainy season the journey takes much longer and is sometimes impossible.

Tourist office On arrival you must head to the tourist office (officially daily 8am–noon & 2–5pm), on the village's main street to pay the B$30 park admission fee. The office has basic information about the park and can find you a guide (affiliated with SERNAP) for about B$100/day for groups of up to five people (slightly more for larger groups).

Tours It's also possible to visit Torotoro on a tour – which is significantly easier but obviously more expensive. Try Fremen Tours (see p.207), which offer three-day, all-inclusive packages for about B$2600.

Accommodation There are a couple of simple places to stay in the village, and locals will prepare inexpensive meals.

THE CHAPARE

Northeast of Cochabamba, the main road to Santa Cruz drops down into the **CHAPARE**, a broad, rainforest-covered plain in the Upper Amazon Basin and an

area of natural beauty. However, it's also Bolivia's largest provider of coca grown to make cocaine, so this is not the place for expeditions far off the beaten track. The peaceful towns along the main Cochabamba to Santa Cruz road are perfectly safe to visit, unless you go during one of the sporadic road blockades by protesting *cocaleros*; these are usually announced in advance, so ask around or look through the local newspapers before your trip.

Villa Tunari

The small, laidback town of **Villa Tunari** is a good place to break a journey between Cochabamba and Santa Cruz and also to get a brief introduction to the Amazon lowlands.

ARRIVAL AND INFORMATION

By bus In Cochabamba, regular minibuses and *trufis* (shared taxis) leave from the Av Oquendo, at Av 9 de Abril (3–4hr); alternatively, you can take a bus heading to Santa Cruz and tell the driver you want to get off just after the Espíritu Santo Bridge.

Money Villa Tunari's ATM is sporadically operational, so bring sufficient cash.

ACCOMMODATION AND EATING

Hostal Los Cocos Near the church ☏ 04 4136578. A good choice for accommodation, with decent rooms and hot showers. Doubles B$180

★ **Hotel de Selva El Puente** About 4km east of town ☏ 04 4259392, ⓦ frementours.com.bo. Villa Tunari's best option is *Hotel El Puente*, which has simple cabañas set amid a patch of rainforest. There's a swimming pool, fourteen natural river pools and a restaurant. B$260

The eastern lowlands

Stretching from the last foothills of the Andes east to Brazil and south to Paraguay and Argentina, Bolivia's **eastern lowlands** were until relatively recently among the least-known and least-developed regions in the country; however, the area has undergone astonishingly rapid development, while its economy has grown to become the most important in the country, fuelled by oil and gas, cattle-ranching and massive agricultural development. At the centre of this economic boom is the regional capital of **Santa Cruz**, a young, lively city and the ideal base for exploring the many attractions of the surrounding area. West of the city are the pristine rainforests protected by the **Parque Nacional Amboró**; the beautiful cloudforest that covers the upper regions of the park can be visited from the idyllic resort town of **Samaipata**. From Samaipata, you can also head further southwest to the town of **Vallegrande** and the hamlet of **La Higuera**, where Argentine revolutionary, Ernesto "Che" Guevara, was killed in 1967. East of Santa Cruz, the railway to Brazil passes through the broad forested plains of **Chiquitos**, whose beautiful **Jesuit mission churches** bear witness to one of the most extraordinary episodes in Spanish colonial history, when a handful of priests established a semi-autonomous theocratic state in the midst of the wilderness. Finally, south of Santa Cruz, the vast and inhospitable **Chaco**, an arid wilderness of dense thorn and scrub, stretches south to Argentina and Paraguay.

SANTA CRUZ

Set among the steamy, tropical lowlands just beyond the last Andean foothills, **SANTA CRUZ** has emerged in recent decades as the economic powerhouse of Bolivia. An isolated frontier town until the middle of the twentieth century, the city has grown in the past fifty years to become the biggest in the country, as well as the locus of Bolivia's wealthy right wing. The election of Evo Morales and his plans for constitutional reform met with violent opposition here; in recent years, this tension has calmed down somewhat. The city layout consists of a series of rings – called *anillos* – with the colonial city centre inside the Primer Anillo, and almost everything you need within the first two or three.

WHAT TO SEE AND DO

Santa Cruz has little to match the colonial charm of highland cities like Sucre and Potosí, and few conventional tourist sights beyond a handful of museums. While some travellers find its unapologetic modernity, commercialism and pseudo-Americanism unappealing, others enjoy its blend of dynamism and tropical insouciance. Be careful walking around the city centre at night as there have been several reports of muggings.

Plaza 24 de Septiembre

At the centre of Santa Cruz is **Plaza 24 de Septiembre**, a spacious, lively square with well-tended gardens shaded by tall trees. On the south side of the plaza stands the salmon-pink **Catedral** (daily 7am–7pm; free), or **Basílica Mayor de San Lorenzo**, a hulking brick structure with twin bell towers built between 1845 and 1915 on the site of an original church, which dated back to 1605. The cool, vaulted interior has some fine silverwork around the altar, but the best religious art is tucked away in the adjacent **Museo de Arte Sacro** (Mon–Fri 8.30am–noon & 3–6pm, Sun 10am–noon & 4–8pm; B$10); the entrance is just to the right as you face the altar. To the west of the cathedral on Independencia is **Manzano Uno** (Tues–Sat 10am–12.30pm & 4–9pm, Sun 4–9pm; free; ☏03 3395792, ⓦmanzanauno.org.bo), a small exhibition space showcasing some excellent displays of national and international sculpture, photography and painting.

Museo Etnofolklórico

Four blocks north and a block east of Plaza 24 de Septiembre inside the Parque Arenal (a little park with an artificial lake), the **Museo Etnofolklórico** (Mon–Fri 9am–noon & 3–6pm; free) houses a small but varied collection of artefacts that provides a good introduction to the different indigenous ethnic groups of the eastern lowlands. Exhibits include photographs, traditional dress, including feather headdresses worn by dancers at religious festivals, and wooden animal masks.

Biocentro Güembé and Jardín Zoológico

About a thirty-minute taxi ride from the city centre, at Km7 Camino a Porongo, Zona Los Batos, **Biocentro**

Güembé (daily 8.30am–6pm; B\$150; ⓦbiocentroguembe.com) is a tranquil park retreat with more than enough to keep anyone entertained for a day or two. There are ten swimming pools, as well as opportunities for mountain biking,

kayaking and beach volleyball. There's also a large butterfly house and orchid display.

ARRIVAL AND DEPARTURE

By plane Aeropuerto El Trompillo, south of the centre in the Segundo Anillo, is sometimes used by TAM and some smaller carriers. Aeropuerto Viru-Viru (☎03 3852400) is 17km north of the city centre, B$60–80 by taxi; alternatively, catch a *micro* (every 20min; 30min) to the old bus terminal, seven blocks southwest of the city centre. In addition to domestic flights, there are international connections to Miami, Madrid and several cities in neighbouring countries.

Destinations Cochabamba (8–11 daily; 45min); La Paz (8–13 daily; 1hr–1hr 35min); Sucre (3–4 daily; 30min); Tarija (1–2 daily; 50min). Less frequent services to Cobija; Guayaramerin; Riberalta; Puerto Suarez; Trinidad.

By bus Long-distance buses and all trains arrive and depart from the Terminal Bi-Modal de Transporte, the combined bus and train terminal about 2km east of the city centre. There are always plenty of taxis outside (B$15–20 into town); alternatively, catch any *micro* heading west along Av Brasil and marked "Plaza 24 de Septiembre".

Destinations Cochabamba (hourly; 10–12hr); La Paz (around 20 daily; 16–18hr); Trinidad (around 10–12 daily; 9–10hr). Less frequent services: Asunción, Paraguay (24hr); Buenos Aires, Argentina (34–36hr); Camiri (5–6hr); Oruro (12–14hr); Sucre (14–16hr); Tarija (24hr); Yacuiba (10–14hr); Villamontes (8–12hr).

By train There are several trains (☎03 3488482, ⍟fo .com.bo) east to Quijarro (6 weekly; 13hr–16hr 39min), from where it is 5min taxi ride to the Brazilian border town of Corumbá; these trains travel via San José de Chiquitos (5hr 8min–6hr 10min). There are also weekly trains south through the Chaco (see p.216) to the Argentine border at Yacuiba (16hr 35min) via Villamontes (13hr 45min).

INFORMATION

Tourist information Santa Cruz's tourist office (Mon–Fri 8am–7pm, Sat & Sun 9am–noon & 3–5pm) is in the government building on the north side of Plaza 24 de Septiembre.

ACCOMMODATION

Most budget accommodation is conveniently located in or close to the old city centre.

Alojamiento Santa Bárbara Santa Bárbara 151 ☎03 3321817, ✉alojstabarbara@yahoo.com. No-frills budget option. The rooms, set around a courtyard, are clean but ultra-basic and equipped with threadbare camp beds. Doubles B$60

Amazonas Hotel Junín 214 ☎03 3334583. Rooms here vary widely, so choose carefully: some resemble darkened cells, but others are far nicer, with more space and light, and less of a tropical-damp feel. All have TVs and phones. Doubles B$180

Los Aventureros Av Pedro Rivera Mendez 600 ☎03 343 4793, ⍟losaventureros.net. Welcoming, family-run hostel with a mix of dorms, a/c private rooms and tents (with electricity and bathrooms), as well as a kitchen, bar and

pool. The only downside is that it's out in the third *anillo*. Dorms B$60, tents B$140, doubles B$200

★**Jodanga Hostel** El Fuerte 1380, near Parque Urbano ☎03 3396542, ⍟jodanga.com. Run by an extremely helpful Bolivian-Australian couple, this excellent Hostelling International-affiliated backpacker haven is a 20min walk from the plaza. It has private rooms (with shared or en-suite bathrooms) and six- to ten-bed dorms, plus a swimming pool, jacuzzi, TV/DVD room, communal kitchen, internet/wi-fi and laundry service. Dorms B$80, doubles B$200

Residencial Bolívar Sucre 131 ☎03 3342500, ⍟residencialbolivar.com. Long-standing backpackers' favourite with helpful staff and small but clean dorms and rooms (with fan and private or shared bathroom) around a cool, leafy patio with hammocks and a resident toucan. Prices include a generous buffet breakfast. Dorms B$91, doubles B$210

Residencial Ikandire Sucre 51 ☎03 3393975, ⍟residencialikandire.com. The building hails from Santa Cruz's early days and has real historic charm, with high ceilings, original doors and a well in one courtyard. The grounds are teeming with local plants, trees and faux naïve art depicting Santa Cruz's history. Doubles B$215

Hostal Rio Magdalena Arenales 653 ☎03 3393011, ⍟hostalriomagdalena.com. A solid, mid-range choice with spick and span a/c rooms and a pool. It's a 10min walk from the main plaza. Doubles B$210

EATING

Santa Cruz's relative wealth and cosmopolitanism are reflected in the city's wide variety of restaurants.

El Aljibe Potosí, at Ñuflo de Chávez ☎03 3352277, ⍟elaljibecomidatipica.com. Charming family-run restaurant specializing in traditional *Cruceño* cooking (B$30–50). Keep an eye out for hummingbirds in the lush courtyard garden. Mon 11.30am–3pm, Tues–Sat 11.30am–11pm, Sun 11.30am–4pm.

La Casa del Camba Av Cristóbal de Mendoza 539 ☎03 3427864, ⍟casadecamba.com. The best of the many traditional *Cruceño* restaurants on this stretch of the

---

★**TREAT YOURSELF**

Yorimichi Av Busch 548 ☎03 3347717. A cool, modern space with a Japanese garden built into it, you can splurge here in a way that's rarely possible in Bolivia, with portions of sushi reaching beyond B$200. But it's worth it, and if you tend towards the soups and bento box-style platters, that will keep costs down – many of them include a sushi sampler anyway. Mon–Sat 11.30am–2pm & 7–11.30pm.

2

second *anillo*, and a great place to enjoy moderately priced *parillada* (barbecued meat), *keperi* (spicy, marinated brisket beef), *majao de charque* (rice with dried meat, fried egg and bananas) and *pacumutu* (massive shish kebab). Mains from B$40. There's a small "Express" branch in the Patio de Comidas Los Immigrantes food court at Libertad 153, near the plaza. Daily 11am–midnight.

La Casona Arenales 222 ☎03 3378495, ⊚bistrolacasona .com. Smart bohemian restaurant-bar in a nineteenth-century building. There's live jazz and blues (Thurs–Sat nights), as well as refined German, Italian and local dishes (mains B$64–136) and a lengthy menu of beers (B$18–45), including some pricey imported German options. Mon–Sat 11.30am–late.

Kiwi's Bolívar 208 ☎03 3301410, ⊚kiwiscafeteria.com. The narrow front leads into a big, airy space with a slightly hippy vibe (that's the power of a few carefully placed shisha pipes). Salads (around B$40–50) are good value – try the "Samurai" of chicken, beef or tofu with greens, crispy noodles and sesame seeds, or the hefty burgers. There are tango dances and classes on Saturday evenings. Mon–Sat 2.30–11.30pm.

★**República** Bolívar 175 ☎03 3347050, ⊚republica .com.bo. Contemporary photography and paper sculpture on the walls, well-chosen music, and just-so cooking, with excellent pasta (B$39–69) and salads (B$39–49), plus pizzas, panini and steaks. The exterior courtyard has a bar. Mon 6pm–midnight, Tues–Sun 10am–midnight.

DRINKING, NIGHTLIFE AND ENTERTAINMENT

The Equipetrol area, to the northwest of the city, is the main area for nightlife. After 10pm, the streets are lined with people going out and cars blaring loud music. Head to clubs on Av San Martín for dancing and drink deals, or, for a slightly calmer scene, check out Av Monseñor Rivero, between the first and second *anillos*. Dress up smart for clubs, as doormen will refuse scruffy-looking backpackers.

Café Lorca Sucre 8 ☎03 3340562, ⊚lorcasantacruz.org. Popular café-bar with excellent but expensive food (mains from B$75). A good place for a drink in the evenings, and they hold regular art exhibitions, events and live music. Mon–Thurs 9am–11.45pm, Fri & Sat 9am–3am, Sun 6–11.45pm.

Cinecenter 2nd Anillo, Av El Trompillo between Monseñor Santiesteban & René Moreno ⊚cinecenter .com.bo. Multiscreen complex with fast-food joints and coffee bars, as well as a range of international films (usually subtitled but worth checking individual films).

Duda Florida 228, between España & 21 de Mayo ☎7760 0655, ⊚facebook.com/dudapub. Funky bar decked out with old photos, toys and other knick-knacks. The music is as eclectic as the decor, and the joint is particularly lively on Wed nights. Tues & Wed 9.30pm–2am, Thurs–Sat 9.30pm–3am.

Irish Pub Plaza 24 de Septiembre ☎03 3338118. On the first floor of the Bolívar shopping centre, with tables overlooking the plaza, this bar gets very lively with locals and travellers in the evenings, especially on weekends. Sadly, they don't serve Guinness. Beer B$18–27. Daily 9am–midnight.

DIRECTORY

Banks and exchange You can change US dollars and travellers' cheques at the Casa de Cambio Alemán (Mon–Fri 8.30am–noon & 2.30–6pm, Sat 8.30am–noon) on the east side of Plaza 24 de Septiembre, and there are plenty of banks with ATMs: try Banco Mercantil on Av Moreno, at Figueroa.

Internet There are many internet cafés around the city centre (around B$5/hr), especially in the shopping complex on the east side of the main plaza.

Laundry Lavandería Marc Torres, La Paz 42, offers a same-day service (B$15/kg).

Spanish lessons *Jodanga Hostel* (see p.211) offers good-value language classes (B$60/hr guests, B$80 non-guests), as does *Residencial Bolívar*.

PARQUE NACIONAL AMBORÓ

Forty kilometres west of Santa Cruz, the **Parque Nacional Amboró** covers some 4300 square kilometres of a great forest-covered spur of the Andes jutting out into the eastern plains. Amboró's steep, densely forested slopes support an astonishing biodiversity, including more than 830 types of bird and pretty much the full range of rainforest mammals, including jaguars, giant anteaters, tapirs and several species of monkey, while its enormous range of plant and insect species is still largely unexplored.

The northern gateway to the park is the picturesque and peaceful town of **Buena Vista**, some 100km northwest of Santa Cruz along the main road to Cochabamba. You can arrange a tour into the park from there, or with one of the operators in Santa Cruz (see box opposite) or Samaipata (see opposite). Overnight camping trips start at US$150–175/ person each day, depending on duration and number of people in the group.

SAMAIPATA

Some 120km west of Santa Cruz, the tranquil little town of **SAMAIPATA** is growing in popularity as a tourist destination among Bolivians and foreign travellers. Nestled in an idyllic valley surrounded by rugged, forest-covered mountains, it's the kind of place where many travellers plan to stay a couple of days and end up staying for a week or longer. Just 9km outside town stands one of Bolivia's most intriguing archeological sites – the mysterious, ruined pre-Hispanic ceremonial complex known as El Fuerte (see box, p.214).

WHAT TO SEE AND DO

At the centre of town lies the small **Plaza Principal**, the core of the grid of tranquil streets lined with whitewashed houses under red-tiled roofs. A few blocks north on Bolívar, the small **Museo Arqueológico** (Mon–Fri 8.30am–noon & 2–6pm; Sat 8.30am–4pm; B$5, free with El Fuerte ticket) shows a short film explaining the significance of El Fuerte, and houses a small collection of archeological finds from all over Bolivia, including beautiful Inca-carved ceremonial *chicha*-drinking cups, Inca stone axes and mace heads, and a range of pottery.

Innumerable walking trails run through the surrounding countryside, the beautiful cloudforests of the Parque Nacional Amboró (see opposite) are within easy reach, and most tour companies offer **day-trips** to nearby valleys where you might spot condors, climb mountainous ridges for breathtaking vistas or enjoy an afternoon splashing around in some of the area's spectacular waterfalls.

ARRIVAL AND DEPARTURE

By micro *Micros* leave Av Grigota in Santa Cruz for Samaipata (daily at 4pm; 3hr) and arrive in Samaipata's

Plaza Principal (returning to Santa Cruz: Mon–Fri 4am & Sun noon–4pm). Buses to Sucre (6.30–7.30pm) and Vallegrande (11.30am–12.30pm & 3.30–4.30pm) pass by the highway: catch the bus from outside *Restaurant El Turista* on the main Sucre–Santa Cruz highway. You can also buy bus tickets to Sucre from Amboró Tours on Bolívar. They charge around B$30 commission, but it guarantees you a seat.

By taxi From Santa Cruz, shared taxis (*trufis*) depart when full from the corner of Chávez Ortiz and Solís de Olguín. Returning to Santa Cruz, take one from the main plaza or the petrol station on the main highway (10min from the main plaza). You may have difficulty finding a taxi after 6pm.

INFORMATION AND TOURS

Tour agencies Samaipata's tour agencies make it easy to visit the area's less accessible attractions; they're also the best source of tourist information. One of the most popular excursions is along the Ruta del Che, a two-day, one-night trip that traces the last steps of revolutionary Che Guevara (see p.215). Michael Blendinger Nature Tours (C Bolívar; ☏ 03 9446227, ⓦ discoveringbolivia.com) and Roadrunners (Bolívar; ☏ 03 9446193, ⓔ theroadrunners @hotmail.com) are both reliable and have English-speaking guides. If you speak Spanish, contact the experienced Don Gilberto Aguilera (☏ 03 9446050, ☏ 7261 5523).

ACCOMMODATION

There's a good range of budget accommodation in Samaipata, including a couple of tranquil tucked-away options. Prices go up at weekends and on public holidays, particularly between October and April.

Hostal Andorina C Campero ☏ 03 9446333, ⓦ andorinasamaipata.com. A peaceful place to stay (though beware the mosquitoes), with sunny patios and hammock-strewn balconies, characterful rooms and dorms. A good, generous breakfast is included and there's a library and book exchange. Dorms B$50, doubles B$130

Cabañas Traudi Outside town, 800m south of the plaza ☏ 03 9446094, ⓦ samaipata-traudi.com. A wide range of quirky cabañas sleeping up to eight people, with kitchens

---

TOUR OPERATORS IN THE LOWLANDS

If you plan to head to Amboró National Park, it is cheaper to organize a tour from Samaipata, and you'll get more time in the rainforest for your money. However, the following companies in Santa Cruz are all well established and have good reputations:

Amboró Tours C Libertad 417, 2nd Floor ☏ 03 3390600, ⓦ amborotours.com. Long-established Bolivian firm offering trips to the Jesuit Missions, multi-day trips into Amboró National Park, and cultural tours.
Fremen Tours Beni 79, Edificio Libertador ☏ 03 3338535, ⓦ andes-amazonia.com. Specializes in river tours in Trinidad but can also help with Jesuit Mission

trips and other all-inclusive tours in Bolivia and Peru.
Ruta Verde Tours C 21 de Mayo 318 ☏ 03 3396470, ⓦ rutaverdebolivia.com. Highly recommended Dutch/ Bolivian-run tour operator with excellent local knowledge, who organizes tours to national parks like Amboró and Noel Kempff Mercado, as well as trips further afield.

2

EL FUERTE

Located 10km east of Samaipata, **El Fuerte** (daily 9am–5pm; B$50) is a striking and enigmatic ancient site with a great sandstone rock at its centre, carved with a fantastic variety of abstract and figurative designs and surrounded by the remains of more than fifty **Inca buildings**. The easiest way to reach El Fuerte is by taxi from Samaipata (about B$40–50 one-way, B$80–100 return with 2hr waiting time), or to join a guided tour with one of the tour agencies in town. While it is possible to walk to the ruins in about two to three hours – follow the road out of town toward Santa Cruz for a few kilometres, then turn right up the marked side road that climbs to the site – it's a tiring, very hot walk, so it's advisable to take a taxi to the site and walk back, otherwise you might be too exhausted to appreciate the ruins.

and fireplaces. They are set amid spacious grounds with a large pool, sauna and a talkative pet parrot. B$140

★ **Finca La Víspera** ☏ 03 944 6082, ⍵ lavispera.org. You can camp in this secluded haven with comfortable lodgings, an idyllic location amid orchards and terraced herb, vegetable and flower gardens and a friendly young Dutch-Bolivian couple overseeing the place. Guests can use the kitchen and harvest food from the grounds. Camping/person B$40, doubles B$290

La Posada del Sol Three blocks north of the plaza (look for the sign) ☏ 03 9446366, ⍵ laposadadelsol.net. Fresh rooms set in beautiful grounds with views of the mountains bordering Amboró National Park, and there are even dorm beds. Breakfast is served alfresco, and the restaurant is excellent. Doubles B$150

EATING AND DRINKING

As a resort town with a significant international community Samaipata has a varied range of restaurants and cafés. *La Posada del Sol* also has a fine restaurant.

La Bohème Plaza Principal ☏ 6091 1243, ⍵ facebook.com/labohemebolivia. A warm welcome from owners Kirsty and

Dave, a cool-looking space, and excellent drinks from fresh cocktails to locally brewed beers. Great snacks too (B$16–22). Tues–Thurs 5pm–midnight, Fri & Sat 5pm–3am, Sun 5pm–1am.

Café 1900 Plaza Principal. A simple place overlooking the plaza with strong wi-fi, a laidback atmosphere, decent coffee and tasty meals. Mains B$30–45. Daily 8am–10pm.

Café Jardin At *Finca La Víspera*. The focus here is on fresh and organic vegetarian food, with much produce grown on their gently sloping terrace plots – when you order, staff will come into the garden to snip herbs and pull up veggies. Breakfasts B$14–55, mains B$35–55. Daily 8am–3pm.

La Chakana Plaza Principal ☏ 7260 6331. Small café serving good coffees, juices, breakfasts, snacks, more substantial meals (B$34–75) and a good-value two-course menu of the day (B$28). It has a small book exchange and runs tours. Daily 8am–9pm.

La Cocina Sucre. Snazzy little eatery with a handful of tables and a concise selection of high-quality burgers, sandwiches, quesadillas and the like (B$16–22), as well as tempting brownies. Tues–Thurs 6.30–9.30pm, Fri 7.30–10pm, Sat 12.30–3pm & 7–10pm.

DIRECTORY

Internet *Café 1900* has a decent wi-fi connection, or try the internet café on the corner of Campero and Rubén Terrazas.

Money There's a Banco Union (and a not especially reliable ATM) on Campero, just east of the plaza.

VALLEGRANDE AND LA HIGUERA

West of Samaipata on the old road from Santa Cruz to Cochabamba, a side road leads to the market town of **VALLEGRANDE**. Vallegrande leapt briefly to the world's attention in 1967, when it witnessed the end game of a doomed guerrilla campaign led by Cuban revolutionary hero, **Ernesto "Che" Guevara** (see box opposite). There is a small **museum** (officially Mon–Fri 8.30am–noon & 2–5pm, though not

---

EAST FROM SANTA CRUZ TO THE BRAZILIAN BORDER

From Santa Cruz, the railway line runs some 680km east to the **Brazilian border** across a seemingly endless expanse of forest and tangled scrub, gradually giving way to the vast swamplands of the **Pantanal** as the border draws near.

The last stop on the railway line in Bolivia is **Puerto Quijarro**, a dismal collection of shacks surrounding the station. If you're heading on to Brazil, you're better off pushing on to the border at Arroyo Concepción, 2km away and connected to Puerto Quijarro by *trufis*. The border town on the Brazilian side is Corumbá (see box, p.328).

REVOLUTIONARY CHE

Probably the most famous revolutionary of the twentieth century, Ernesto "Che" Guevara was executed in the hamlet of **La Higuera** about 50km south of Vallegrande on October 9, 1967. Visitors to the area may be surprised to learn that this iconic hero spent his final days hiding out in a remote ravine with only a few bedraggled followers. An Argentine-born doctor, Che became a close ally of Fidel Castro during the Cuban Revolution and then turned his sights to Bolivia, which he hoped would prove to be the kick-off point for a continent-wide revolution.

With a small band of rebel followers, Che tried to drum up support for change, but CIA-backed Bolivian troops were determined to quell any kind of revolution, and he was soon forced into hiding.

When Che was eventually captured, his last words were: "Shoot, coward, you are only going to kill a man". His body was flown to Vallegrande and put on display for the world's press in the town hospital. Today Che's grave and the hamlet of La Higuera attract a steady trickle of pilgrims.

always kept to; B$10) in the municipal **Casa de Cultura** on the central Plaza 26 de Enero, which houses an unexciting collection of local archeological finds and photographs of Che.

La Higuera

La Higuera, the hamlet where Che Guevara met his end, lies about 50km south of Vallegrande. It's a miserable collection of simple adobe houses with tiled roofs and a one-room **Museo Histórico del Che** (opening hours timed with tours so ask around; B$10), with the atmosphere of a shrine, complete with relics including Che's machete, bullets and ammo clips.

ARRIVAL AND INFORMATION

By bus Daily buses run to Vallegrande from Samaipata and Santa Cruz. La Higuera can be reached by taxi or lorry from Vallegrande in 2–3hr, or by getting buses to Pucará from Vallegrande and getting local transport from there.

Tours Both Vallegrande and La Higuera can be visited on a tour; try agencies in Samaipata (see p.213) or Santa Cruz (see p.213).

ACCOMMODATION AND EATING

Hostal Juanita Vallegrande ☏03 9422231. The most comfortable place to stay is this friendly *hostal* with private bathrooms. B$120

El Mirador Vallegrande. German-run restaurant which offers a daily selection of tasty meat and trout dishes. Evenings only; closed Mon.

CHIQUITOS: THE JESUIT MISSIONS

East of Santa Cruz stretches a vast, sparsely populated plain which gradually gives way to swamp as it approaches the border with Brazil. Named **CHIQUITOS** by the Spanish, this region was the scene of one of the most extraordinary episodes in Spanish colonial history. In the eighteenth century, a handful of Jesuit priests established a series of flourishing mission towns, where previously hostile indigenous Chiquitanos converted to Catholicism, adopting European agricultural techniques and building some of the most **magnificent colonial churches** in South America. This theocratic, socialist utopia ended in 1767, when the Spanish Crown expelled the Jesuits from the Americas. Six of the ten Jesuit mission churches have since been restored and are recognized as UNESCO World Heritage Sites. Their incongruous splendour in the midst of the wilderness is one of the most remarkable sights in Bolivia.

The six missions can be visited in a five- to seven-day loop by road and rail from Santa Cruz. A rough road runs northeast to **San Javier** and **Concepción**, then continues to **San Ignacio** (from where the churches of **San Miguel**, **San Rafael** and **Santa Ana** can all be visited by taxi in a day). From San Ignacio, the road heads south to **San José**. Buses connect all these mission towns as far as San José, from where you can get the train back to Santa Cruz or continue east to the Brazilian border. Alternatively, many agencies organize tours to the missions, including shorter two-day trips that take in San Javier and **Concepción** only; tours can be arranged in Santa Cruz (see p.213); ⓦchiquitania.com is a good source of information.

2

THE CHACO

South of the Santa Cruz–Quijarro railway line, the tropical dry forest gradually gives way to **the Chaco**, a vast and arid landscape that stretches beyond the **Paraguayan border**. The Chaco is one of the last great wildernesses of South America and supports plentiful wildlife, including jaguars, peccaries and deer – much of it now protected by the 34,000-square-kilometre **Parque Nacional Kaa-Iya del Gran Chaco**, the largest protected area in all South America. There are no organized tourist facilities in the Chaco, so your view of the region will likely be limited to what you can see from the window of a bus or train, either down the region's western edge to the towns of **Villamontes** and **Yacuiba**, which is on the Argentine border, or along the rough **trans-Chaco road** which makes for the Paraguayan border at **Hito Villazón**.

The Amazon basin

About a third of Bolivia lies within the **Amazon Basin**, a vast, sparsely populated and largely untamed lowland region of swamp, savannah and tropical rainforest, which supports a bewildering diversity of plant and animal life. Roads are poor in the best of conditions, and in the rainy season between November and April they are often completely impassable; even in the dry season sudden downpours can quickly turn roads to quagmires.

Linked by road to Santa Cruz, the capital of the Beni – the northeastern lowlands region – is **Trinidad**, the starting point for slow boat journeys down the

Río Mamoré to the Brazilian border or south into the **Chapare**. From Trinidad, a long and rough road heads west across the Llanos de Moxos, passing through the **Reserva del Biosfera del Beni** before joining the main road into the region from La Paz at Yucumo.

North of Yucumo, the small town of **Rurrenabaque**, on the banks of the Río Beni, is the obvious destination for anyone wanting a taste of the Amazon, given its proximity to the pristine forests of the **Parque Nacional Madidi**, one of Bolivia's most stunning protected areas. From Rurrenabaque a dirt road continues north across a wide savannah-covered plain towards the remote backwater of the **Northern Amazon Frontier**, more than 500km away. As the road draws near to **Riberalta**, the largest city in the region, the savannah gives way to dense Amazonian rainforest. East of Riberalta, the road continues 100km to **Guayaramerín**, on the banks of the Río Mamoré, which is the main border crossing point if you're heading north into Brazil.

TRINIDAD

Close to the Río Mamoré, the city of **TRINIDAD** is the capital of the Beni and a modern commercial city dominated by a vigorous cattle-ranching culture and economy. Hot and humid, with few real attractions, Trinidad doesn't really merit a visit in its own right. It is, however, the jumping-off point for adventurous trips into the surrounding landscape.

WHAT TO SEE AND DO

Though most of its buildings are modern, Trinidad maintains the classic layout of a Spanish colonial town, its streets set out in a neat grid around a central square, the

---

THE FLOODS OF 2014

In the rainy season of 2013/14, the Bolivian Amazon and especially the Beni region was devastated by a series of major **floods**. Unusually heavy rainfall, climate change, deforestation and two dams across the border in Brazil were all variously blamed. More than 68,000 families were displaced, with 59 people reported dead, crops destroyed and up to 50,000 cattle lost – damages are reckoned to top US$110 million (B$770 million). At the time of research things were slowly getting back to normal, but you'll need to check the latest before travelling in this area, and needless to say, visiting during the rainy season (Nov–March) is not a good idea.

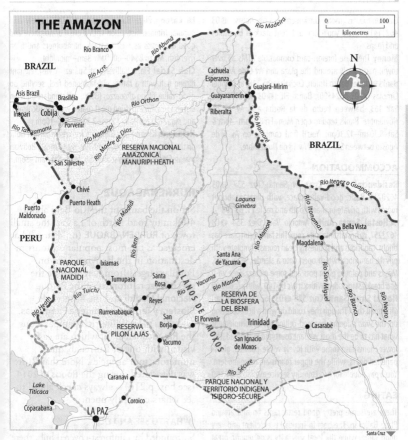

THE AMAZON

BRAZIL

Río Branco

Río Acre

Río Abuná

Río Madeira

Asis Brazil
Brasiléia
Iñapari   Cobija
Río Tahuamanu
Porvenir

Río Orthon

Cachuela
Esperanza
Guajará-Mirim

Guayaramerín

Riberalta

Río Manuripi
Río Madre de Dios

San Silvestre

RESERVA NACIONAL
AMAZONICA
MANURIPI-HEATH

Río Mamoré

BRAZIL

Chivé

Puerto Heath

Puerto
Maldonado

Río Madidi

Río Beni

Laguna
Ginebra

Río Itenez o Guaporé

Río Itonamas

Bella Vista

Magdalena

Río Mamoré

Río San Miguel

Río Blanco

Río Negro

PERU

PARQUE
NACIONAL
MADIDI

Ixiamas

Tumupasa

Río Tuichi

Santa
Rosa

Reyes

Rurrenabaque

RESERVA
PILON LAJAS

San
Borja

Yacumo

Santa Ana
de Yacuma

L L A N O S   D E

Río Yacuma

Río Maniqui

M O X O S

El Porvenir

RESERVA DE
LA BIOSFERA
DEL BENI

Trinidad

Casarabé

San Ignacio
de Moxos

Río Sécure

Río Heath

Caranavi

Lake
Titicaca

Copacabana
LA PAZ

Coroico

PARQUE NACIONAL Y
TERRITORIO INDIGENA
ISIBORO-SÉCURE

0   100
kilometres

N

Santa Cruz

2

Plaza Ballivián, shaded by tall trees hiding three-toed sloths. A popular place to go for the afternoon is the former river port of **Puerto Varador**, about 12km southwest of Plaza Ballivián, where simple restaurants serve up fresh fish (Varador now sits on a landlocked lagoon, not the shoreline of the constantly meandering Río Mamore). Take a *mototaxi* to the Mercado Campesino on Avenida Oscar Paz Hurtado, where *micros* leave regularly for Varador (about 30min).

ARRIVAL AND DEPARTURE

By plane The airport is 2km northwest of town; a *mototaxi* into the centre should cost B$10–12; regular taxis charge at least B$25. Between them, Amaszonas, 18 de Noviembre 267 (☎ 03 4622426), TAM, Bolívar, at Santa Cruz (☎ 03 4622363), and Aerocon, Av 6 de Agosto, at 18 de Noviembre (☎ 03 4624442), cover most destinations.

By bus Buses arrive at, and depart from, the Terminal Terrestre on Av Mendoza between Viador Pinto Saucedo and Beni, eight blocks east from the centre of town (buses from San Borja arrive just behind the terminal on Av Beni).
Destinations Guayaramerín (1–2 daily; 25–28hr); Rurrenabaque (2 daily; 20hr); San Ignacio de Moxos (2 daily; 3–4hr); Santa Cruz (18–22 daily; 9–10hr).

By boat If you are arriving by boat from Guayaramerín (2–3 weekly; 3–7 days) to the north, or Puerto Villarroel (2–3 weekly; 7 days) in the Chapare to the south, you are likely to dock at Puerto Almacén, 9km southwest of Plaza Ballivián on the Río Ibare. *Mototaxis* ply the 15min route into town (B$15).

INFORMATION

Tourist information The main municipal tourist office is at Felix Pinto Saucedo, at Nicolás Suárez (Mon–Fri 8.30am–12.30pm, 2.30–6pm; ☎ 03 4621322). The small, very helpful office on Av 6 de Agosto, next to *Hotel*

2

Campanario, is more convenient (same hours; ☎03 4621141), where you'll find a decent stack of brochures and maps.

Money There are foreign-card compatible ATMs all over town, particularly around the plaza and Av 6 de Agosto. Banks include: Banco Unión, Cochabamba 118, at Manuel Limpias (☎03 4624500); Banco FIE (☎03 4652578), La Paz 163, between Pedro de la Rocha and Av 18 de Noviembre. Banks tend to open Mon–Fri 8.30am–4pm & Sat 8.30am–12.30pm. You'll find cambios on Av 6 de Agosto between Suárez and Av 18 de Noviembre.

ACCOMMODATION

Residencial Santa Cruz Av Santa Cruz 537 ☎03 4620711. Basic, good-value place, with pleasant, bright rooms with private or shared bath and cable TV. **B$100**

★**Hostal Santa Anita** Antonio Vaca Díez 354 ☎03 4622257, ✇hostalsantaanita.com. This family-run place has bright, capacious and spotlessly clean rooms, complete with private hammock, which open onto a slender, leafy patio. Masks and painted plant pots add some pizzazz. Free wi-fi and breakfast included. Without a/c **B$160**, with a/c **B$200**

Hostal Sirari Santa Cruz 526 ☎03 4624472, ✉hsirari @hotmail.com. Though they could do with a little sprucing up, the *Sirari*'s ageing, beamed-ceiling rooms complement what has to be the most verdant courtyard in Trinidad. The lower rooms also come with lovely white-painted, glass-panelled doors, while the upper rooms are more modern. You'll pay double for a/c. Laundry service available. **B$160**

EATING

There are some pretty good restaurants on and around Plaza Ballivián. The beef in Trinidad is excellent and very good value, while the local speciality is *pacumutu*, great chunks of meat marinated and grilled on a skewer.

Bistrot Carambar Av 6 de Agosto 224, between Santa Cruz and Villavicencio ☎6021 3007. A French-run place with fine crêpes (from B$8–12), a scattering of alfresco tables, reggae soundtrack and a buzzy atmosphere. Wed–Sun 5–11pm.

La Casona Plaza Ballivián ☎03 4622437. Lively and popular Trinidad institution with a great atmosphere and good *almuerzos* as well as steak, hamburgers and fried river fish. Mains B$40–60. Daily 8am–midnight.

Club Social Plaza Ballivián, at Suárez. A vast, elegant dining hall with a rather old-fashioned feel, serving up good-value, filling *almuerzos* (B$20) and standard Bolivian dishes like *milanesa* (fried meat coated with breadcrumbs) and *pique macho*. Daily 11am–2.30pm & 6–10pm.

Heladería Kivon Plaza Ballivián. Ice-cream parlour right on the plaza serving cakes, sandwiches and meaty Bolivian mains. Single ice-cream scoop B$5. Mon–Sat 9am–8pm.

RURRENABAQUE

Set on the banks of the Río Beni about 400km by road north of La Paz, the small town of **RURRENABAQUE** (or "Rurre") has emerged as the most popular ecotourism destination in the Bolivian Amazon. Popular targets from here include the spectacular rainforests of the **Parque Nacional Madidi** and the **Reserva de Biosfera y Territorio Indígena Pilón Lajas**, as well as the wildlife-rich pampas along the **Río Yacuma**, all of which are easily visited with one of Rurrenabaque's numerous tour agencies. Note that Rurre was devastated during the **floods of 2014** (see box, p.216) – always check ahead to see what's currently open.

WHAT TO SEE AND DO

Surrounded by rainforest-covered hills, there is little in the way of formal sights in Rurre but it's an enjoyable town to watch the boats go by on the mighty Río Beni or just relax in a hammock. If you've an afternoon to spare, head up to one of the swimming pool miradors, either **Oscar's Swimming Pool**

RAINFOREST TRIPS FROM TRINIDAD

Trinidad makes a great base for birdwatching excursions into the surrounding wilderness, or as the starting point for river cruises or camping expeditions into an area where tourists rarely venture. Recommended tour operators include:

Fremen Tours Av Cipriano Barace 332 ☎03 4622276, ✇andes-amazonia.com. This La Paz-based agency specializes in four-day/three-night cruises on the Mamoré aboard its luxury floating hotel, the *Reina de Enín*. Prices range B$6175–10,290 (US$882–1470 for two people per cruise).

Turismo Moxos Av 6 de Agosto 114 ☎7113 0122,

✉moxosibc@hotmail.com. Various one- to three-day trips (from B$1260/US$180 for 3 days) into the rainforest by motorized canoe along the Río Ibare, a tributary of the Mamoré, with plenty of opportunity for seeing wildlife (including pink dolphins) and visiting indigenous communities. They also offer shorter, two-night blue-throated macaw viewing trips.

(B$40), or the nameless, quieter one (B$20) a minute further up the same road. Both have great views of the town and river, while *Oscar's* is also a popular bar (p.220). Ask a *mototaxi* to take you (B$10).

ARRIVAL AND DEPARTURE

By plane Due to often impassable roads, many people choose to fly to Rurrenabaque – the alternative is a nightmarish bus journey of at least 18 hours. Amazonas fly from La Paz several times daily, with all flights arriving at the airstrip a short distance north of town, and are met by free hotel minibuses for those with reservations, or an airline shuttle bus (B$6) that will take you to the Amazonas office (10min; Comercio and Santa Cruz; ☎ 03 8922472, ⓦ amaszonas.com).

Destinations La Paz (2–6 daily; 30–40min); Trinidad (4 weekly; 30min).

By bus/micro Buses arrive at the Terminal Terrestre, a few blocks away from the centre of town on the corner of calles Ayacucho and 18 de Noviembre; you can get a motorbike taxi into the centre for about B$5. Daily departures to La Paz (3 daily; 20–24hr) and Trinidad (2 daily; 20–30hr), and, when possible, to Guayamerín and Riberalta.

By boat When the road is closed in the rainy season, motorized canoes occasionally carry passengers between Rurrenabaque and Guanay, a small town about 230km northwest of La Paz (6–8hr) and Riberalta (8–10 days). Book in advance with one of the tour agencies.

INFORMATION

Tourist information There is a small office at Vaca Diez, at Avaroa (Mon–Sat 8am–noon & 2.30–6pm).

Internet There are numerous hole-in-the-wall internet cafés along Comercio, though prices are high (B$6–8/hr) and speeds hardly the fastest. Entel on Comercio also has internet for B$6/hr. For decent wi-fi try *Café de la Jungla* (see p.220) on Comercio.

Money Banco FIE (Comercio, at Aniceto Arce) and Banco

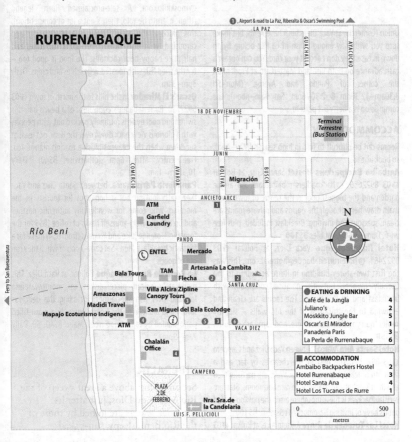

RURRENABAQUE

Río Beni

Ferry to San Buenaventura

● Airport & road to La Paz, Riberalta & Oscar's Swimming Pool ▲

LA PAZ

GUACHALLA

AYACUCHO

BENI

18 DE NOVIEMBRE

Terminal Terrestre (Bus Station)

JUNIN

COMERCIO

AVAROA

BOLIVAR

BUSCH

Migración

ANICETO ARCE

ATM

Garfield Laundry

PANDO

ENTEL

Mercado

Bala Tours

TAM

Artesanía La Cambita

Flecha

SANTA CRUZ

Amazonas

Villa Alcira Zipline Canopy Tours

Madidi Travel

San Miguel del Bala Ecolodge

Mapajo Ecoturismo Indígena

ATM

VACA DIEZ

Chalalán Office

CAMPERO

PLAZA 2 DE FEBRERO

Nra. Sra.de la Candelaria

LUIS F. PELLICIOLI

N

● EATING & DRINKING
Café de la Jungla	4
Juliano's	2
Moskkito Jungle Bar	5
Oscar's El Mirador	1
Panadería Paris	3
La Perla de Rurrenabaque	6

■ ACCOMMODATION
Ambaibo Backpackers Hostel	2
Hotel Rurrenabaque	3
Hotel Santa Ana	4
Hotel Los Tucanes de Rurre	1

0   500
metres

2

Unión (Comercio, at Vaca Díez) both have ATMs, but make sure you withdraw enough cash in La Paz before flying down in case they don't accept your card. You can obtain a cash advance on both Visa and MasterCard at Prodem on the corner of Pando and Avaroa (Mon–Fri 8.30am–12.30pm & 2.30–6pm, Sat 9am–noon); the commission is a hefty 5.3 percent.

ACCOMMODATION

Rooms can be difficult to find in high season (May–Aug), so book ahead.

Ambaibo Backpackers Hostel Santa Cruz, at Bolívar ☎03 8922686, ⓦbackpackersambaibo.com. An ample garden and the biggest pool in the centre of town is the main draw here, though the dorms and private rooms are clean, spacious and inviting. Breakfast included, plus free wi-fi. Dorms B$80, doubles B$100

Hotel Rurrenabaque Vaca Diez, at Bolívar ☎03 8922481, ⓔhotelrurrenabaque@hotmail.com. This was the first two-storey building in Rurre according to the friendly owners, but it's in good condition, with breakfast and wi-fi included. The rooms are clean and – owing to the thickness of the old walls – slightly cooler than you'll find elsewhere, and some are en suite. B$150

Hotel Santa Ana Avaroa, between Vaca Díez and Campero ☎03 8922314. The best of the cheapies by far, and a labyrinth of leafy courtyard rooms. Walls are partially tiled and there's a choice of shared or private bathrooms. Staff are very laidback, as is the atmosphere amid the *palalpa*-roofed patio's bevy of inviting hammocks. Free wi-fi. B$100

Hotel Los Tucanes de Rurre Aniceto Arce, at Bolívar ☎03

8922039, ⓦhotel-tucanes.com. Popular and spacious hostel with hammocks hung around the grounds, a huge roof terrace, pool table, free but slow wi-fi and free breakfast. B$100

EATING AND DRINKING

Café de la Jungla Comercio at Vaca Díez. For breakfast there's no beating this petite Argentine-owned café, with pavement-side seating to enjoy their nut-filled muesli (with coffee and juice B$15–25). The house speciality is hot chocolate with red chilli, and they also do gourmet sandwiches filled with fillings such as teriyaki chicken or lentil burger. Free wi-fi. Mon–Sat 8am–8pm, Sun 8am–2pm.

Juliano's Santa Cruz at Bolívar ☎7392 0088. This is the fanciest Rurre gets and the prices are a little higher than elsewhere. As well as the usual fish, meat and pasta dishes (B$30–40), they also do hummus and falafel, starters of fried cheese and other lesser-seen delicacies. Daily 6–11pm.

Moskkito Jungle Bar Vaca Díez ☎03 8922267, ⓦmoskkito.com. A self-proclaimed Rurre legend (though, truth be told, there's not a lot of competition), this place is the town's main hub of drinking and carousing, with pool tables, tree-trunk furniture, and half-price happy-hour cocktails. The food is good too – try the fried fish with roasted vegetables and chips. Daily 3pm–3am.

Oscar's El Mirador In the hills to the north of town ☎03 8922710. Rurrenabaque's equivalent of a beach bar, this swimming pool eyrie is routinely packed out with people, with a glorious view back down over the Beni, not least at sundown when the heavens blush a roaring orange-red. Free entry after 6pm (otherwise B$40). Daily 10.30am–1am.

Panadería Paris Avaroa, between Santa Cruz and Vaca Díez. Tatty-looking but a honeypot for tourists in the morning, who come for wonderfully authentic pastries and bread rolls. Help-yourself flasks of coffee (B$5 for the "organic"), orange juice and *licuados* (from B$4) make for a fantastic breakfast. Mon–Sat 6am–noon or when they run out of goods.

La Perla de Rurrenabaque Bolívar, at Vaca Díez. This moderately priced place dishes up mouthwatering lowland river fish specialities, including the delicious *surubí a la plancha* in the house sauce, in a plant-filled patio shaded by tall mango trees. Mains B$40–50. Daily 7am–9pm.

RIBERALTA

Set on a bluff above a great sweep of the Río Madre de Dios, just after its silt-laden waters are joined by those of the Río Beni, sleepy, sun-baked

TOUR AGENCIES IN RURRENABAQUE

A growing number of tour agencies offer trips to the rainforest and the pampas lowlands, generally lasting three nights. Most guides speak only Spanish, but agencies can usually arrange an English-speaking interpreter for larger groups. Prices for all-inclusive two-night trips to both the pampas and the jungle start at about B$500 (not including park entrance fees; B$150 for the Santa Rosa reserve on the Pampas Tour, and B$125 for the Madidi National Park) – though expect to pay much more if you want anything more than the most basic accommodation.

TOUR OPERATORS

Bala Tours Av Santa Cruz, at Comercio ☎ 03 8922527, ⓦ balatours.com. Specialize in longer five- to eight-day camping tours into Parque Nacional Madidi, as well as standard *selva* (jungle) and pampas programmes. They're more expensive, but the jungle tours in particular are very highly recommended and they own their own solar-powered camp.

Madidi Travel Comercio between Santa Cruz and Vaca Díez ☎ 03 8922153, ⓦ madidi-travel.com. Environmentally conscious agency offering tailor-made tours. Profits go towards conservation and community work. Accommodation at its private reserve, Serere (3hr by boat from Rurre), is in spartan, yet stylish, two-storey cabañas, located by Lago San Fernando.

Mapajo Ecoturismo Indígena Comercio between Vaca Díez and Santa Cruz ☎ 03 71127800, ⓔ mapajo .ecoturismo.indigena@gmail.com. Indigenous community-run agency specializing in three-,

four- and five-night lodge-based trips (from B$1890/US$270) into the Reserva de la Biosfera y Territorio Indígena Pilón Lajas (3hr by motorized canoe from Rurre); the *Albergue Ecológico Mapajo* is fully operated and owned by the Río Quiquibey communities.

San Miguel del Bala Ecolodge Comercio between Vaca Díez and Santa Cruz ☎ 03 8922394, ⓦ sanmigueldelbala.com. Not the best option for spotting animals but excellent for a cultural experience of a Tacana community, and near enough to Rurre for a day-trip if you're in a rush (30min by motor canoe). Two days, one night B$1120/US$160 person.

Villa Alcira Zip Line Canopy Tours Comercio, between Santa Cruz and Vaca Díez ☎ 03 8923875, ⓦ ziplinecanopy.amawebs.com. A chance to fly through the trees on a series of high-speed zip-lines (1200m total) at the Tacana community of Villa Alcira (15min from Rurre by boat). Trips depart daily at 8am and 2pm (B$250).

RIBERALTA is the second-biggest town in the Amazon lowlands, with a population of about 78,000, largely employed in the processing and export of brazil nuts. At least twelve hours by road from Rurrenabaque when conditions are good in the dry season, there's no great reason to stop unless you're heading for Brazil (see box, p.221), though there's an indolent charm about the place that makes it perhaps the most likeable of the Northern Amazon outposts.

ARRIVAL AND DEPARTURE

By plane The tiny airport is about 1km south of town (B$4–5 on a motorbike taxi, or 20min walk from Plaza Principal). Aerocon, Plaza Principal (☎03 8523899); Ecojet, Av Bernardino Ochoa 966 (☎03 852 4837); and TAM (no office; ☎03 8522646) all operate from here. Maddeningly, most flights are routed via Trinidad.

By bus Buses arrive at, and depart from, the pot-holed terminal at the eastern edge of town, 2km from Plaza Principal on the road to Guayaramerín (B$3–4 on a motorbike taxi).

Destinations Cobija (2 daily; 12–16hr); Guayaramerín

(4–5 daily; 2hr 30min–3hr); La Paz (2 daily; 35–40hr); Rurrenabaque (when possible; 12hr); Trinidad (1 daily; 28hr).

ACCOMMODATION

Hotel Las Palmeras Suárez 855 ☎ 03 8522354. Basic but cosy family home operating as a guesthouse, with en-suite rooms, a short walk from Plaza Principal. B$150

Residencial Los Reyes Sucre 781, between Oruro and Chuquisaca ☎ 03 8522628. Pleasant hotel near the airport, with a garden, hammocks and pretty tiled walkways creating a cool ambience. B$80

EATING AND DRINKING

Cabaña Tom Sucre 669, southeast corner of Plaza Principal. *Tom's Cabin* does decent *almuerzos* as well as the two Beni stalwarts: beef steaks and river fish. Mains from B$25. Daily noon–7pm.

Club Social Progreso Plaza Principal ☎ 03 8523024. Of all Beni's *Clubes Sociales*, this one – over 90 years old – has by far the most ramshackle charm. Under ancient ceiling fans, amid rickety chairs and huge window shutters, dine on cheap *almuerzos* (B$15–20), refreshing fruit juices and fantastic omelettes. Daily 9am–midnight.

2

CROSSING INTO BRAZIL: GUAJARÁ-MIRIM

From the port in Guayaramerín, **regular passenger boats** (daily 6am–6pm; every 30min; additional services 6pm–6am at irregular times; B$10 each way) make the five-minute crossing to Guajará-Mirim in Brazil. The Bolivian *migración* (Mon–Fri 8–11am & 2–6pm, Sat 8am–noon) is to the right of the port as you face the river; you should get an exit stamp here if you're continuing into Brazil, but it's not necessary if you're just making a day-trip across the river. If you need a visa, the **Brazilian consulate** (Mon–Fri 11am–3pm) is on Calle Beni, at 24 de Septiembre, a block east of the plaza in Guayaramerín. Note that to enter Brazil you need to have an international certificate of yellow-fever vaccination. From Guajará-Mirim there are frequent buses to Porto Velho, from where there are connections to other destinations in Brazil.

GUAYARAMERÍN

On the banks of the Río Mamoré some 86km east of Riberalta, **GUAYARAMERÍN** is the main crossing point on Bolivia's northern border, a modern and prosperous frontier town with a distinctly Brazilian flavour and a thriving economy based on duty-free sales. Most people only come here to cross into Brazil (see box above).

ARRIVAL AND DEPARTURE

By plane The airport is four blocks east of the plaza along C 25 de Mayo. Flights are operated to here by Aerocon, 25 de Mayo and Beni (☎03 8555035), and Ecojet at Sucre between Beni and 16 de Julio (☎03 8559176). Most flights are routed via Trinidad.

By bus Buses from Riberalta and beyond arrive at the Terminal de Buses, about 3km from the centre of town along C Beni; a motorbike taxi from here should cost about B$5. Buses to Riberalta leave throughout the day (3hr); in dry season, services attempt the long journeys to Trinidad (around 30hr), Rurrenabaque (around 26hr) and Cobija (around 15hr) – the length of the journeys varies significantly due to road conditions.

INFORMATION

Tourist information There's no tourist office, but Mary Tours, on the north side of the main plaza

(☎03 8553883, ✉mary-tours@hotmail.com), is a good source of information.

Money and exchange Cooperativa Jesús Nazareno (Mon–Fri 8.30am–12.30pm & 2.30–6pm, Sat 9am–12.30pm; ☎03 8553039), Mariscal Santa Cruz at Av 24 de Septiembre, on the northeast corner of the main plaza, has an ATM that should accept foreign cards, and you can also obtain a cash advance on a credit card (five percent) and change dollars and Brazilian reais. Prodem on Plaza Principal can also give cash advances on Visa and MasterCard.

ACCOMMODATION AND EATING

There is a reasonable choice of budget hotels and guesthouses in town, though very few tourists choose to stay much more than a night here. The best places to eat are on and around the plaza; the two *heladerías* are good for ice cream, coffee, juices and snacks.

Hotel Anexo Plaza Plaza Principal (west side) ☎03 8553650. Long established, but they haven't let their standards – either of cleanliness or friendliness – slip. It's a bit overpriced because of the central location. B$140

Hotel Santa Ana 25 de Mayo 611, at 16 de Julio ☎03 8553900. With an inviting courtyard garden and timber-ceilinged rooms, located just east of the plaza, this is another reasonable option. B$140

CHRIST THE REDEEMER, RIO DE JANEIRO

Brazil

HIGHLIGHTS

❶ **Rio de Janeiro** Sunbathing and samba in a stunning urban setting. **See p.235**

❷ **Cidades Históricas** Cobbled colonial streets, architectural gems and great food. **See p.261**

❸ **Salvador** Take in pulsating street life and the Afro-Brazilian martial art capoeira. **See p.277**

❹ **Chapada Diamantina** Hike canyons and jump waterfalls in the Northeastern interior. See p.287

❺ **Iguaçu Falls** Straddling Argentina and Brazil is one of the planet's most impressive natural wonders. **See p.353**

HIGHLIGHTS ARE MARKED ON THE MAP ON PP.226–227

ROUGH COSTS

Daily budget Rio de Janeiro, São Paulo and Brasília: US$65/The North and Northeast: US$45

Drink beer (600ml bottle) US$2

Food *Prato comercial/prato feito* (basic set meal) US$5–9

Hostel/budget hotel US$16–50

Travel Rio–São Paulo (352km) by bus, US$35

FACT FILE

Population 200 million

Language Portuguese

Currency Real (R$)

Capital Brasília (population 2.8 million)

International phone code ☎ 55

Time zone GMT -3/-4hr

Introduction

Brazil has an energy like no other nation on earth. Unified through open-armed hospitality and the combined passions of football, the beach and all that's beautiful, even the glaring gap between rich and poor somehow fails to distract Brazilians from a determination to succeed – and party hard along the way. It's a huge country (larger than the United States excluding Alaska) with all the diverse scenic and cultural variety you'd expect, from Bahian beaches to Amazonian jungles. But Brazil is cosmopolitan too. You could as easily find yourself dancing samba until sunrise as you could eating sashimi amid a crowd of Japanese Brazilians. Rio and São Paulo are two of the world's great metropolises and eleven other cities each have more than a million inhabitants.

Brazilians are one of the most **ethnically diverse** peoples in the world. In the south, German and Italian immigration has left distinctive European features; São Paulo has the world's largest Japanese community outside Japan; while centred principally in Salvador and Rio is the largest black population outside Africa. Amerindian influence pervades the entire country but is especially evident in Amazonia and the northeastern interior. Enormous natural resources and rapid postwar industrialization have made it one of the world's ten largest economies, but **socio-economic contradictions** mean that this hasn't improved the lives of many of its citizens: there is a vast (and growing) middle class, yet all Brazil's cities are strewn with **favelas** and slums.

Nowhere, however, do people know how to enjoy themselves more – most famously in the orgiastic annual four-day celebrations of **Carnaval**, but also reflected in the lively year-round nightlife you'll find almost everywhere. Brazil's vibrant arts, theatre and design scenes are accompanied by the most relaxed and tolerant attitude to **sexuality**, straight and gay, of anywhere in South America. And the country's hedonism also manifests itself in a highly developed **beach culture**, superb music and dancing, and rich regional cuisines.

WHEN TO VISIT

If **Carnaval** is the main thing on your mind, then try to arrive in Rio, Salvador, Recife or Minas Gerais well before the action – dates change each year from February to early March. This is also the main tourist season and warmest part of the year for most of Brazil (Jan–March), with higher accommodation prices and crowded beaches and hostels. The other big draw is **Reveillon** (New Year), when beds in Rio are especially hard to find. As you go further south it gets noticeably **cooler**, so it's best to visit places like Foz do Iguaçu, Florianópolis and São Paulo between November and April. In the Amazon the less rainy and humid months are between May and October, while the Northeast has pretty good weather all year round.

CHRONOLOGY

1500 Off course, en route to India on behalf of Portugal, Pedro Álvares Cabral lands in Bahia.

1502 Amerigo Vespucci enters Guanabara Bay and calls it Rio de Janeiro.

1537 Olinda founded.

1549 King João unifies 15 hereditary captaincies under governor-general Tomé de Sousa, who founds Salvador, the first capital. Portuguese settlers begin to flow in.

1555 French take possession of Rio area and are finally expelled by the Portuguese in 1567.

1574 Jesuits given control of converted Indians.

1630 Dutch West India Company fleet captures Pernambuco.

1654 Brazilians, without Portuguese aid, defeat and expel the Dutch.

1695 *Bandeirantes* discover gold in Minas Gerais.

1757 Slavery of indigenous peoples abolished.

1759 Jesuits expelled from Brazil by prime minister Marquis de Pombal.

1763 Capital shifted from Salvador to Rio.

1789 First rebellion against Portuguese ends in defeat when José Joaquim da Silva Xavier, known as Tiradentes, is executed.

1807 Napoleon I invades Portugal. Portuguese prince regent Dom João evacuates to Brazil.

1808 Dom João declares Rio temporary capital of the empire, opens harbours to commerce and abolishes restrictions on Brazilian trade and manufacturing.

1822 With Dom João (King João IV) back in Portugal, his son, Dom Pedro I, declares Brazil independent and crowns himself emperor.

1825–28 Cisplatine War: Uruguay gains independence from Brazil.

1830 Slave trade abolished, but slavery continues.

1864–70 War of the Triple Alliance: Argentina, Brazil and Uruguay crush Paraguay.

1888 Princess Isabel, acting as regent, signs the "Golden Law" abolishing slavery. The following year Dom Pedro II is overthrown and Brazil becomes a republic.

1930 Great Depression leads to revolution. Getúlio Vargas rises to power.

1937 Vargas declares himself dictator, creates the "New State", the Estado Novo.

1944 Brazil accepts US aid in return for bases, joins Allies in World War II, and sends force to fight in Italy.

1954 Vargas commits suicide after military tells him to resign or be overthrown.

1956 Juscelino Kubitschek elected president with an ambitious economic programme. Construction of Brasília begins.

1958 Brazil wins its first World Cup – it wins again in 1962, 1970 and 1994.

1960 Brasília declared capital of Brazil.

1964 Massive population growth, disparity in wealth, economic inflation and fears of a rising proletariat lead to a military coup.

1968–73 Economy experiences spectacular growth.

1969 General Emilio Garrastazú Médici assumes presidency. Censorship and torture are routine and thousands are driven into exile.

1983–84 Mass campaign in Rio and São Paulo for direct elections.

1985 Tancredo Neves elected first civilian president in 21 years, but dies shortly afterwards. Military rule ends.

1994 Inflation peaks. President Cardoso introduces Real as new currency along with new economic plan.

2002 Liberal former trade union activist Luiz Inácio Lula da Silva elected on promises to curb hunger and create jobs; Brazil wins the World Cup for a fifth time.

2006 Lula re-elected; raises minimum wage by 13 percent and announces new economic plan.

2010 Lula succeeded by Dilma Rousseff, Brazil's first female president, on the promise of continuity assisted by discovery of vast new Atlantic oil reserves.

2013 Major protests and riots erupt all over the country in response to high transportation prices, corruption and funding of upcoming sports events.

2014 Brazil hosts the World Cup – despite a humiliating 7–1 defeat to Germany in the semi-final, the tournament is considered a success.

2014 Dilma Rousseff is narrowly re-elected president.

ARRIVAL AND DEPARTURE

There are direct **flights** to Rio and São Paulo from Europe, North America, Asia, South Africa, and from most major Latin American cities, while easy connections are available from Australia and New Zealand via Argentina or Chile. Brazil also has a well-developed network of domestic flights. **Direct crossings** are possible from most South American countries, with Colombia and Peru accessed **by boat**, and flights available from Chile, Ecuador and Suriname. If you enter Brazil **overland**, remember that crossing points can be very remote.

FROM ARGENTINA

Most people crossing between Argentina and Brazil do so at the frontier at **Foz do Iguaçu** (see p.353). Another handy crossing further south is at the Argentine city of Paso de los Libres, across the border from **Uruguaiana**, 694km west of Porto Alegre. There are daily **flights** from Buenos Aires to Brazil's main southern and central cities.

FROM BOLIVIA

You can reach Bolivia's southeastern border by train from the station a few kilometres out of Puerto Suárez or by hourly bus from Quijarro. From the border there's frequent transport to the *rodoviária* in **Corumbá**, where you'll find regular onward buses to Campo Grande (5–7hr), São Paulo (21hr) and Rio de Janeiro (26hr). In the north, passenger boats make the ten-minute crossing to **Guajará-Mirim** in Brazil, where there are frequent buses to Porto Velho, for connections to other destinations in Brazil. There are daily **flights** from La Paz

3

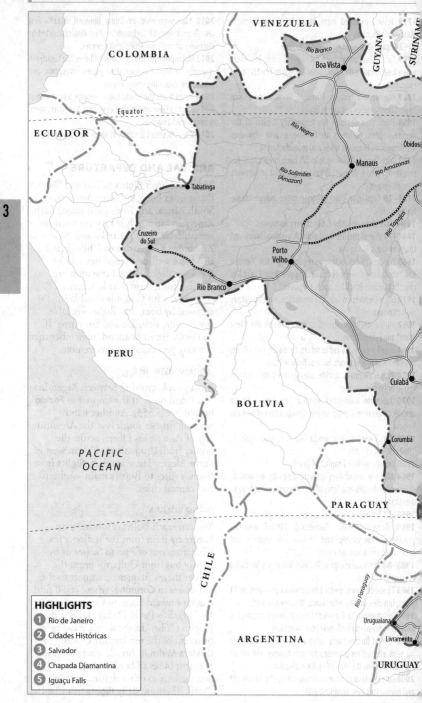

HIGHLIGHTS

1. Rio de Janeiro
2. Cidades Históricas
3. Salvador
4. Chapada Diamantina
5. Iguaçu Falls

3

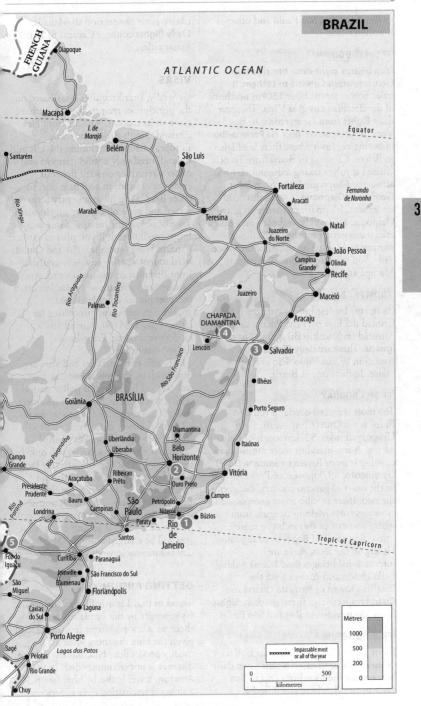

BRAZIL

ATLANTIC OCEAN

FRENCH GUIANA

Oiapoque

Macapá

Equator

Santarém

I. de Marajó

Belém

São Luís

Fortaleza

Fernando de Noronha

Aracati

Teresina

Marabá

Juazeiro do Norte

Natal

Rio Xingu

João Pessoa

Campina Grande

Olinda

Recife

Rio Araguaia

Rio Tocantins

Palmas

Juazeiro

Maceió

CHAPADA DIAMANTINA

Aracaju

Lencóis

④

③ Salvador

Rio São Francisco

Ilhéus

Porto Seguro

BRASÍLIA

Goiânia

Diamantina

Itaúnas

Uberlândia

Uberaba

Belo Horizonte

Campo Grande

Rio Paranaíba

② Ouro Prêto

Vitória

Ribeirão Prêto

Araçatuba

Campos

Presidente Prudente

Bauru

São Paulo

Petrópolis

Rio Paraná

Campinas

Niterói

Londrina

Paraty

Búzios ①

Santos

Rio de Janeiro

Tropic of Capricorn

⑤

Curitiba

Paranaguá

Foz do Iguaçu

Joinville

São Francisco do Sul

São Miguel

Blumenau

Florianópolis

Caxias do Sul

Laguna

Bagé

Porto Alegre

Lagos dos Patos

Pelotas

Rio Grande

Chuy

Metres	
	1000
	500
	200
	0

┄┄┄┄┄ Impassable most or all of the year

0 ┄┄┄┄┄ 500

kilometres

to Rio, Salvador, São Paulo and other Brazilian cities.

FROM THE GUIANAS

It's a bumpy eight-hour bus ride from Georgetown in Guyana to **Lethem**, a quiet border town about 130km northeast of the Brazilian city Boa Vista. There are daily **flights** from Georgetown to Boa Vista, or you can connect via **Paramaribo** in Suriname, from where there are flights to Belém. Crossing to Brazil from French Guiana involves taking a dugout taxi-boat across the Oiapoque River from Saint Georges to **Oiapoque**, a small dirt-road settlement. It's smarter to arrive in gritty Oiapoque by daylight and plan on a quick exit; buses depart for the twelve-hour journey to Macapá on the Amazon, twice daily. You can also **fly** from Cayenne to Macapá and Belém.

FROM PARAGUAY

Paraguay's busiest border crossing is from Ciudad del Este over the Puente de la Amistad (Friendship Bridge) to **Foz do Iguaçu**. There are daily **flights** from Asunción to São Paulo, Rio and other major destinations in Brazil.

FROM URUGUAY

The most travelled overland route to Brazil is via **Chuí** (Chuy on the Uruguayan side), 527km south of Porto Alegre. A less-used but more atmospheric crossing is from Rivera to **Santana Do Livramento**, 497km west of Porto Alegre in the heart of gaucho country. Between the two, there are also more complicated crossings from Melo to Aceguá, from where you can easily reach the more interesting town of **Bagé**, or to **Jaguarão**. Finally, in the west, there are international bridges (and buses) linking Bella Unión and Artigas with the Brazilian towns of **Barra do Quarai** and **Quarai** respectively. There are daily **flights** from Montevideo to Rio and São Paulo.

FROM VENEZUELA

From Santa Elena de Uairén in Bolívar (Venezuela's southeastern state) two daily buses make the four-hour trip to **Boa Vista** in Brazil, where you'll find a twelve-hour connection to Manaus. Daily **flights** connect Caracas to Brazil's major cities.

VISAS

Generally, Brazil requires **visas** based on the principle of reciprocity of treatment given to its citizens. Visitors from New Zealand, South Africa and most European nations, including the UK and Ireland, need only a valid passport and either a return or onward ticket or evidence of funds to purchase one, to enter Brazil. You fill in an entry form on arrival and get a ninety-day tourist visa. Try not to lose the receipt of this entry form; you'll need it if you plan to extend. Citizens from **Australia**, **USA** and **Canada** need **tourist visas** in advance, available from Brazilian consulates abroad; you'll usually need a return or onward ticket, a passport photo, completed visa application form, and processing fee (US citizens pay US$160; Australians US$35-equivalent; Canadians US$65-equivalent).

In Brazil, entry permits and visas are dealt with by the **Polícia Federal**. Every state capital has a federal police station with a visa section: ask for the *delagacia federal*. You can extend your stay for an additional ninety days if you apply at least fifteen days before your initial permit or visa expires, but it will only be extended once; if you want to stay longer, you'll have to leave the country and re-enter. A US$10 charge, payable in Brazilian currency, is made on tourist permit extensions. If you stay past the permit date without having extended it you will be charged around R$8.50 per day before you leave the country.

GETTING AROUND

Travel in Brazil is usually straightforward: it's generally by bus or plane, though there are a few passenger trains, too, and given the long distances involved it's usually good value. Hitchhiking over any distance is not recommended. In the **Amazon**, travel is also by boat (see p.306), a slow yet fascinating river experience.

BY AIR

Brazil relies heavily on air travel. **TAM** (Ⓦtam.com.br), **GOL** (Ⓦvoegol.com.br) and **Azul** (Ⓦvoeazul.com.br) serve most domestic destinations, while **Avianca Brasil** (Ⓦavianca.com.br) also offers competitive fares. If you plan on flying within Brazil at least four times in thirty days, and don't mind sticking to an itinerary, it makes sense to buy an **airpass** with TAM or GOL. These need to be purchased from an agent before you travel (you can't buy them in Brazil); each costs somewhere between US$532 and US$1282 for between four and nine flights. **Departure tax** is included in the price of your international ticket.

BY BUS

Hundreds of bus companies offer services that crisscross Brazil. **Bus travel** prices range from 25 to 75 percent of the cost of air travel, and this is usually the best-value option for journeys of under six hours – although in more remote areas buses tend to be packed and the roads in poor condition. Intercity buses leave from the **rodoviária**, a bus station usually built on city outskirts. **Prices** are standardized even when more than one firm plies the same route, and there are often two levels of bus service: the perfectly comfortable *convencional* and marginally more expensive *executivo*; on the latter you're usually supplied with a blanket, newspaper and snack. **Leitos** are luxury buses that do nocturnal runs between major cities, with fully reclining seats in curtained partitions. All long-distance buses are comfortable enough to sleep in, however, and have on-board toilets. Bring water and a sweater for the often-cool air conditioning.

For most journeys it's best to buy your ticket at least a day in advance, from the *rodoviária* or some travel agents. An exception is the Rio–São Paulo route, with services every fifteen minutes. If you cross a state line, you may be asked for proof of ID (your passport is best).

BY CAR

High accident rates, poor signposting, immense urban congestion and heavily potholed rural roads make driving in Brazil hardly a recommendation. Nonetheless, vehicle **rental** is easy, from about R$130/day for a compact car. International companies operate alongside local alternatives like Interlocadora, Localiza and Unidas – offices (*locadoras*) are at every airport and in most towns. An **international driving licence** is recommended: foreign licences are accepted for visits of up to six months but you may find it tough convincing police of this.

Be wary of driving at night as roads are poorly lit and lightly policed – specifically avoid the **Via Dutra**, linking Rio and São Paulo, due to the huge numbers of trucks at night and the treacherous ascent and descent of the Serra do Mar, and the **Belém–Brasília highway**, whose potholes and uneven asphalt make it difficult enough to drive even in daylight. Outside of big cities, service stations don't always accept international credit cards, so bring cash. If you're stopped by police, they can be intimidating, pointing to trumped-up contraventions when they're probably angling for a bribe. If such an on-the-spot **multa**, or fine, is suggested, it's your choice whether to stand your ground or pay up. Whatever you do, always appear polite. If your passport is confiscated, demand to call your consulate – there should always be a duty officer available.

BY TAXI

Metered **taxis** are easy to flag down and relatively inexpensive, though base fares vary from place to place and rates have risen a lot in recent years. An alternative is the radiotaxi, a metered cab you can call to pick you up.

ACCOMMODATION

Hostels (*albergues*) usually offer the best value, in most cases with dorms (*dormitórios*) and private rooms (*quartos*). There's an extensive network of Hostelling International-affiliated hostels, so it's worth taking out an HI membership (Ⓦhihostels.com). In most bigger cities and resorts you'll find numerous **private hostels** for R$35–45 a night per person. Slightly higher in price are small, family-run hotels called **pensão** (*pensões* in the plural) or *hotel familiar*. *Pensões* are often better in small towns than in large cities. You'll also find **pousadas**, which can be just like a *pensão*, or a small, luxurious or offbeat hotel. In the Amazon and the Pantanal pousadas tend to be purpose-built **fazenda** lodges geared towards upscale ecotourism.

Hotels run the gamut from cheap dives to ultra-luxe. The Brazilian star system (one to five) depends on bureaucratic requirements more than on standards – many perfectly good hotels don't have stars. A **quarto** is a room without a bathroom; an **apartamento** or suite is en suite (with private shower); an **apartamento de luxo** is an *apartamento* with a fridge/mini-bar. A **casal** is a double room, a **solteiro** a single. *Apartamentos* normally come with telephone, air-conditioning (*ar condicionado*), TV and fan (*ventilador*). Room **rates** vary tremendously by region and season. Generally, for R$80–150 a night you can stay in a reasonable hotel or pousada with private bathroom and fan or air-conditioning, though you can expect to pay a lot more in **São Paulo** and especially **Rio de Janeiro**, where rates have sky-rocketed in recent years: the cheapest one-stars charge R$120, while mid-range places are more likely to be R$300–350.

In many cases (especially smaller towns) the price of a double or twin room may be little more than two hostel beds – and the breakfast could be much better. During the off-season hotels in tourist areas offer hefty discounts of around 25 to 35 percent – and even in high season at hotels and pousadas it's worth asking *"tem desconto?"* ("is there a discount?").

Brazilian **campsites** are usually found on the coast near larger beaches. These have basic facilities – running water and toilets, a simple restaurant. Elsewhere camping is prohibited in most national parks, and is usually only undertaken on organized jungle treks or with local guides to ensure safety.

FOOD AND DRINK

Brazil has five main **regional cuisines**: **comida mineira**, from Minas Gerais, is based mainly on pork with imaginative use of vegetables and thick bean sauces; **comida baiana** (see box, p.283), from Bahia, has a rich seafood base and an abundance of West African ingredients; **comida do sertão**, from the interior of the Northeast, relies on rehydrated, dried or salted meat and regional fruits, beans and tubers; **comida amazônica**, based on river fish, manioc sauces and the many fruits and palm products of northern Brazil; and **comida gaúcha** from Rio Grande do Sul, the world's most carnivorous diet, revolves around *churrasco* – charcoal-grilling every meat imaginable. **Feijoada** is the closest Brazil comes to a national dish: a stew of pork, sausage and smoked meat cooked with black beans and garlic, garnished with slices of orange. Eating it is a national ritual at weekends, when restaurants serve *feijoada* all day.

Alongside regional restaurants, there are **standard meals** available everywhere for about R$12–15: **prato comercial** and **prato feito** (literally, pre-made dish) are two very budget-friendly phrases you'll see on (usually lunchtime) menus, consisting of *arroz e feijão* (rice and beans), a choice of steak (*bife*), chicken (*frango*) or fish (*peixe*), and often served with salad, fries and *farinha*, dried manioc (cassava) flour that you sprinkle over everything. *Farofa* is toasted *farinha*, and usually comes with onions and bits of bacon mixed in. The **prato do dia** (plate of the day) or set-menu **prato executivo** are similarly cheap and usually very filling (R$15–25). Also economical are **lanchonetes**, ubiquitous Brazilian snack bars where you eat at the counter. These serve a *salgados* (savoury snacks) like *pão de queijo* (cheese profiteroles), *pastel* (fried pastry with meat or cheese filling) and *coxinha* (shredded chicken in corn dough, battered and fried), or cheap meals like a *bauru* – a basic filling steak meal with egg, fries and salad.

Restaurantes a quilo (or kilo) are the lunch choices of most Brazilian office workers, where you choose from (sometimes vast) buffets and pay by weight (*por quilo*); less lavish ones will cost you anything from R$12–24 for a decent plateful. **Rodizio** restaurants can be fantastic deals – specialized restaurants (such as pizza or sushi), where you pay a set fee and eat as much as you want of the endless supply food waiters bring around. The *churrascaria*, the classic Brazilian **steakhouse**, operates similarly, with a constant supply of charcoal-grilled meat on huge spits brought to your table.

There are more **fruits** than there are English words for them. Some of the fruit is familiar – *manga* (mango), *maracujá* (passion fruit), *limão* (lime) – but most of it has only Brazilian names: *jaboticaba*, *fruta do conde*, *sapoti* and *jaca*. The most exotic fruits are Amazonian: try *bacuri*, *cupuaçu* and *açaí*. The last-named is often served *na tigela* with *guaraná*, crushed ice, sliced bananas and granola.

DRINK

Brazil is famous for **coffee** and you'll find decent espresso in many cafés, but in lots of local places the coffee comes ready loaded with copious amounts of sugar (Brazilians add it to *everything* and you'll draw looks if you don't follow suit; ask for it *sem açucar* to have them offer you a sugar substitute instead). **Tea** (*cha*) is surprisingly good: try **cha mate**, a strong green tea with a caffeine hit, or one of many herbal teas, most notably that made from *guaraná*. Fruit in Brazil is put to excellent use in **sucos**: fruit is popped into a liquidizer with sugar and crushed ice to make deliciously refreshing drinks. Made with milk rather than water, it becomes a **vitamina**.

Beer (*cerveja*) is mainly of the lager/pilsner type, though craft beers made in microbreweries are becoming popular in the South, São Paulo and Minas Gerais. Brazilians generally drink beer ice-cold, mostly from 600ml bottles. Draught beer is *chopp*. The regional beers of Pará and Maranháo, *Cerma* and *Cerpa*, are generally acknowledged as the best; of the nationally available brands, *Skol*, *Brahma*, *Antarctica* and *Bohemia* are all popular, though mild. Despite the undoubted improvement in the quality of Brazilian **wines**, those imported from Chile and Argentina remain more reliable.

As for spirits, stick to what Brazilians drink – **cachaça**, sugar-cane liquor. The best way to drink it is in a **caipirinha** – *cachaça* mixed with fresh lime, sugar and crushed ice – one of Brazil's great gifts to the world. One thing to remember when enjoying Brazil's beverages: most clubs and some bars will give you an **individual card** when you enter upon which your drinks are tabulated. Don't lose it. Even if you have paid, unless you have the receipt at the door, you will have difficulty leaving and may even have to pay again.

CULTURE AND ETIQUETTE

The most widely spoken language in Brazil is **Portuguese**. Educated Brazilians often speak a little English, and there are plenty of Spanish-speakers, but knowing Spanish is of limited help in interpreting spoken Portuguese. You will do yourself a huge favour and likely make several new friends if you learn some Portuguese – even a little effort goes a long way.

On the whole, Brazilians are very friendly, open people (you'll be guided to your stop by passengers on public transport if you ask for help). The pace differs depending on the region. In major cities things operate fairly quickly and on a schedule. Things work in the Northeast too, but in their own special way – you're better off slowing to their pace.

Though attitudes vary regionally, in general Brazilians are remarkably open with their **sexuality**. Brazil's reputation as a sex destination is not completely without merit – prostitution is legal and you'll see love motels (hourly rates) everywhere. Also be aware that while Brazilians are very accepting of gays and lesbians during Carnaval, Latin machismo still applies here and Brazilians can be as bigoted as anybody.

3

3

SPORTS AND OUTDOOR ACTIVITIES

Brazilian football (*futebol*) is globally revered and a privilege to watch, at its best reminding you why it's known as "the beautiful game" – despite being humiliated 7–1 by the Germans on home soil in the 2014 World Cup. Brazil have been **world champions** a record five times, and **Pelé** – born in Minas Gerais – is still regarded as the best player of all time. Indeed, you won't really have experienced Brazil until you've attended a match. Stadiums are spectacular sights, games enthralling and crowds are wildly enthusiastic. **Tickets** are not expensive, ranging from R$20 to R$150 depending on whether you stand on the terraces (*geral*) or opt for stand seats (*arquibancada*) – major championship and international matches sometimes cost more. You can usually pay at the turnstile, though there are long last-minute queues. Regional rivalries are strong; fans are seated separately and given different exit routes to prevent fighting. In Rio, **Flamengo** and **Fluminense** have long had an intense rivalry; in São Paulo there are **São Paulo** and **Corinthians**.

The other major national sport is **volleyball** (*volei*), mostly played on the beach, though the hard-court game is also popular and sand is imported inland for beach volleyball championships elsewhere. In Rio especially, beach **foot-volleyball** (*futevolei*) has gained massive popularity in the last decade.

A full range of **outdoor activities** is available across the country, with regional highlights including hang-gliding in Rio, hiking and waterfall hunting in the coastal forests of the Serra do Mar or Bahia's marvellous Chapada Diamantina, river-based pursuits in the Amazon and Pantanal, and exploration of the lunar-like dune systems of Maranhão's Lençóis Maranhenses.

COMMUNICATIONS

There are **internet cafés** (here called *LAN houses*) everywhere in Brazil – even obscure jungle towns have air-conditioned places with web connections – and **wi-fi** is now standard in hotels and cafés in major cities. Prices vary from R$3 to R$7/hr.

If you have a compatible (and unlocked) **phone** and intend to use it a lot, it can be much cheaper to buy a Brazilian **SIM card** (R$10 or less) to use during your stay. Currently, **TIM Brasil** (Ⓦtim.com.br) is your best bet for a SIM card (look for TIM outlets or visit a branch of the Lojas Americanas chain store). Once the SIM is installed you should opt for a pre-pay plan ("*pré-pago*"); to add credit, just go to TIM shops, newspaper stalls or pharmacies and ask for TIM "*cargas*". Bear in mind that rates will apply only to calls within the same state – calling to and "roaming" within other states is charged at a hefty premium.

Public phones are operated by phonecards (*cartão telefônico*), available at newspaper stands, and are often cheaper for local landline calls than mobile phones. Different phone companies compete within different areas of Brazil, and pay phones display which company code should be used. This doesn't affect **local calls** – just dial the seven- or eight-digit number – but for **long-distance or international calls** (long-distance charged at around R$7/min; calls to the US or Europe cost about US$1.50–2/min), you must first select a phone company (Claro/Embratel, code 021, is reliable; from a TIM phone use 041). Dial this code first, then the area or country code. To call Rio from anywhere else in Brazil, for example, dial 021+21 (phone company code + city code) followed by the eight-digit number. For international calls, add an extra zero before the company code. International calls can also be made from booths in a *posto telefônico* (though these are becoming far less common as Brazilians switch to mobile phones) – you're billed at the end.

Post offices (Ⓦcorreios.com.br) – *correios* – are identified by their bright yellow postbox signs.

BRAZIL ON THE NET

ⓦ **brasil.gov.br** Government site with information on Brazilian culture, environment and current affairs in English.
ⓦ **visitbrasil.com** Official site of the Brazilian Ministério do Turismo.
ⓦ **brazilmax.com** Self-proclaimed *Hip Guide to Brazil* covering travel, arts and politics across the country.
ⓦ **www1.folha.uol.com.br/internacional/en/** São Paulo newspaper with a helpful English-language version.
ⓦ **gringoes.com** Brazilian culture, arts, sports and travel in English.
ⓦ **riotimesonline.com** Focused on news and entertainment in Rio, but with information for travellers across Brazil.

International stamps cost R$1.80 for up to ten grams (letters and postcards). Airmail letters to Europe and North America take around two weeks, and, though generally reliable, it's better not to send valuables.

CRIME AND SAFETY

Brazil's reputation as a rather dangerous place is not entirely undeserved, but it is often overblown, and many visitors arrive with an exaggerated idea of the perils lying in wait. **Street crime** can be a problem, especially in the evenings and late at night (the targeting of tourists is worst in Rio, Salvador and Recife), but the key is to be sensible and not let fear grip you. Criminals are also getting more sophisticated – there has been an increase in the **cloning of ATM cards**, so you should check your online account often.

EMERGENCY NUMBERS

Ambulance ☎ 192
Fire ☎ 193
Police ☎ 190

TOURIST POLICE

Rio ☎ 21 3399 7170
São Paulo ☎ 11 3214 0209
Salvador ☎ 71 3222 7155

PERSONAL SAFETY

Being a gringo attracts unwelcome attention but it also provides a measure of protection. The Brazilian police can be extremely violent to criminals, and law enforcement tends to take the form of periodic crackdowns. Therefore criminals know that injuries to foreign tourists mean a heavy clampdown, which in turn means slim pickings for a while. If you are unlucky enough to be the victim of an **assalto** (a mugging), remember, it's your possessions that are the targets. Don't resist: your money and anything you're carrying will be snatched, your watch yanked off, but within seconds it will all be over. Most *assaltos* happen at night, in backstreets and desolate areas of cities, so stick to busy, well-lit streets, and where possible take taxis; city buses generally run late too, though mind your belongings when it's crowded.

BUSES, BEACHES AND HOTELS

Long-distance **buses** are pretty secure, but it pays to keep an eye on your things. Get a **baggage check** on your luggage from the person loading it and keep an eye on your possessions until they are loaded. Overhead racks are less safe, especially during night journeys.

On city **beaches**, never leave things unattended; any beachside bar will stow things for you. In tourist areas and busy cities avoid walking on the beach at night. Shared **rooms** in pousadas and hostels usually have lockers (bring a padlock) and even many cheap hotels have **safes** (*caixas*).

POLICE AND DRUGS

If you are robbed or held up, it's not necessarily a good idea to go to the **police**. Except with something like a theft from a hotel room, they're unlikely to be able to do much, and reporting something will likely take hours even without the language barrier. You may have to do it for insurance purposes, when you'll need a local police report; this could take a full and very frustrating day. If your passport is stolen

3

in a city where there is a consulate, get in touch with the consulate first and take their lead.

Both **marijuana** (*maconha*) and **cocaine** (*cocaína*) are fairly common, but be warned: if the police find either on you, you will be in serious trouble. The following cannot be overstated: under no circumstances do you want to spend any time in a Brazilian jail.

HEALTH

Public healthcare in Brazil varies tremendously from poor to sometimes quite good, but private medical and dental treatment is generally more reliable; costs are significantly less than in North America (a doctor's visit will cost on average the equivalent of US$50–80). Check directories at the end of each section for hospital information and refer to advice from your country's embassy or consulate. Standard drugs are available in *farmácias* (pharmacies) without prescriptions. Note that **malaria** is endemic in **northern Brazil**, and anyone intending to travel in Amazônia should take precautions very seriously. Getting a **yellow fever vaccination**, which offers protection for ten years, is recommended if you're going to Amazônia, Goiás or Mato Grosso.

INFORMATION AND MAPS

Popular destinations in Brazil have friendly and helpful **tourist offices**, as do most state capitals, many of which distribute free city maps and booklets. Generally the airport information offices have the best English-speakers and are usually open the longest. They also have decent free maps but little else in English. EMBRATUR is the national tourist organization and has a useful website (ⓦvisitbrasil.com).

MONEY AND BANKS

The Brazilian currency is the **real** (pronounced "hey-al") and is made up of one hundred centavos. Its plural is **reais**

(pronounced "hey-ice"), written R$. Notes are for 2, 5, 10, 20, 50 and 100 reais; coins are 1, 5, 10, 25 and 50 centavos, and 1 real. At the time of writing, US$1 = R$2.4, £1 = R$3.9 and €1 = R$3. **ATMs** are available all over Brazil, though not all accept foreign cards and many non-airport ATMs are inactive after 8pm or 10pm for security reasons. Banco do Brasil offer the most reliable machines; Bradesco and HSBC also accept foreign cards.

OPENING HOURS AND HOLIDAYS

Basic opening hours for **shops** and **businesses** are weekdays from 9am until 6pm and Saturday 9am to 1pm. Shopping centres are usually open 10am to 10pm, with larger ones also open Sundays from 3pm to 9pm. Banks generally open weekdays from 10am to 4pm. **Museums** and historic **monuments** generally cost just a few reais and follow regular business hours, though many are closed on Mondays. In addition to the public holidays listed, there are plenty of local and state holidays when you'll also find everything closed.

PUBLIC HOLIDAYS

In addition to those below, between one and three further days are offered by each state; **Carnaval**, which takes place on the five days leading up to Ash Wednesday, is an "optional" rather than official national holiday (though almost every Brazilian takes at least one day off), as is **Corpus Christi** on June 11.
January 1 New Year's Day (Ano Novo)
March/April (varies) Good Friday
April 21 Tiradentes Day (Dia de Tiradentes)
May 1 Labour Day (Dia do Trabalhador)
September 7 Independence Day (Dia da Independência)
October 12 Feast Day of Nossa Senhora Aparecida (Our Lady of Aparecida, patron saint of Brazil)
November 2 Dia dos Finados (Day of the Dead)
November 15 Republic Day (Proclamação da República)
December 25 Christmas Day (Natal)

FESTIVALS AND CELEBRATIONS

Carnaval is by far the most important festival in Brazil, and when it comes, the country comes to a halt as it gets down to some of the most serious partying in the world. The most familiar and most spectacular celebration is in **Rio** (see p.237), one of the world's great sights, televised live to the whole country. **Salvador**'s Carnaval (see p.277) is now almost as commercialized, with big headline performers, and a reputation for being even wilder than Rio's. **Olinda** and its winding colonial hilltop streets next to Recife make for a fun and perhaps less frenzied experience, while **Fortaleza**, and **Diamantina** in Minas Gerais, also host great parties.

Reveillon New Year's Eve. Major cities along the coast compete with fireworks displays. Rio's is nearly always the biggest.

Festa de Iemanjá February 2. Devotees make offerings on beaches along the coast to celebrate the goddess of the sea. Salvador's Praia Vermelha hosts one of the largest.

Lavagem do Bonfim Second Thursday of January. Hundreds of women in traditional Bahian garb clean the steps of Salvador's beloved church with perfumed water (food and music follow).

Bienal de São Paulo Biennial in March (next in 2016) ⓦ bienal.org.br. The largest arts event in Latin America.

Paixão de Cristo (The Passion Play) Ten days leading up to Easter. Latin America's largest passion plays are enacted in Nova Jerusalém, outside Recife.

Bumba-meu-boi June 13–29. The people of São Luís re-enact the folk tale of a farmer who, having killed another farmer's ox, must resurrect it or face his own death. Costumes, dancing, capoeira, heckling and hilarity ensue.

Festa de São João (Festa Junina) June 13–24. Celebrations of St John happen across Brazil, but Salvador, Pernambuco and cities in the Northeast are the most raucous, with *forró*, drinking and eating.

Paraty International Literary Festival (FLIP) Early August ⓦ paraty.com.br/flip. Some of Brazil's and the world's best authors converge on Paraty, with events and talks in Portuguese and English, and performances by top Brazilian musicians.

Rio International Film Festival October ⓦ festivaldorio.com.br. The country's biggest film festival, showcasing 200 mainstream and independent releases.

Círio de Nazaré Second Sunday in October ⓦ ciriodenazare.com.br. An effigy of the Virgin of Nazaré is carried across the water from Vila de Icoaraci to the port of Belém.

Oktoberfest October 10–27 ⓦ oktoberfestblumenau .com.br. German-settled Blumenau has all the beer-swilling, German food and traditional garb you'd expect.

Grand Prix November ⓦ gpbrasil.com. Brazil's Interlagos circuit near São Paulo is one of the most atmospheric Grand Prix venues.

Rio de Janeiro

The citizens of **RIO DE JANEIRO** call it the *cidade marvilhosa* – and there can't be much argument about that. It's a huge city with a stunning setting, extending along 40km of sandy coast and sandwiched between an azure sea and jungle-clad mountains. The city's unusual name has a curious history: Portuguese explorers arriving at the mouth of Guanabara Bay on January 1, 1502 thought they had discovered the mouth of an enormous river which they named the January River or Rio de Janeiro. By the time the first settlement was established and the error was realized, the name had already stuck.

Although riven by inequality, Rio has great style. Its international renown is bolstered by a series of symbols that rank as some of the greatest landmarks in the world: the **Corcovado** mountain supporting the great statue of Christ the Redeemer; the rounded incline of the **Sugarloaf mountain** standing at the entrance to the bay; the beaches of **Copacabana** and **Ipanema**, probably the most famous lengths of sand on the planet. Then there's the **Maracanã stadium**, a huge draw for football fans, which was renovated to host the World Cup final in 2014 and Olympic Games in 2016. It's a setting enhanced by a frenetic nightlife scene and the annual sensuality of **Carnaval**, an explosive celebration which – for many people – sums up Rio and her citizens, the Cariocas.

3

WHAT TO SEE AND DO

Rio's sights are scattered across three main sectors of the city, and improved metrô links make getting around fairly straightforward. **Centro** contains the last vestiges of the metropolis's colonial past, and its major sites are easily walkable in one day. The most obvious place to start is historic **Praça XV de Novembro**, while the other main focal point, Cinelândia, has numerous places of interest nearby. Just south of here are the lively *bairros* of **Lapa**, capital of Brazil's samba scene, and bohemian **Santa Teresa** sprawling across the hills above. It's the **Zona Sul** (south zone), however, where you're likely to spend most of your time – in no small part due to the 16km of sandy **beaches** that line its shores – though visits to the Corcovado and Sugarloaf mountains should not be missed. Although somewhat run-down, parts of the **Zona Norte** (north and west of Centro) are being renovated in advance of the Olympics; fans of the "beautiful game" should make the pilgrimage to the **Maracanã football stadium**, while for the more culturally minded there's the **Museu Nacional**.

Praça XV de Novembro

Taking its name from the day in 1889 when Marechal Deodoro de Fonseca, the first president, proclaimed the Republic of Brazil, "**Praça Quinze**" (10min walk from Metrô Carioca) was once the hub of Rio's social and political life. On the south side of the square is the striking **Paço Imperial** (Tues–Sun noon–6pm; free), which serves as an exhibition space. It was here in 1808 that the Portuguese monarch, Dom João VI, established his court in Brazil, and the building continued to be used for royal receptions and special occasions: on May 13, 1888, Princess Isabel proclaimed the end of slavery here. Just south is bold, Neoclassical **Palácio Tiradentes** (Mon–Sat 10am–5pm, Sun noon–5pm; free), the Rio state parliament, while to the north is the **Arco de Teles**, constructed on the site of the old *pelourinho* (pillory) in around 1755, and leading through to Rua do Mercado and Rua do Ouvidor, a lively street with restaurants, cafés, bookshops, bars and clubs.

On the Rua I de Março side of Praça Quinze, the **Antiga Sé** (Mon–Fri

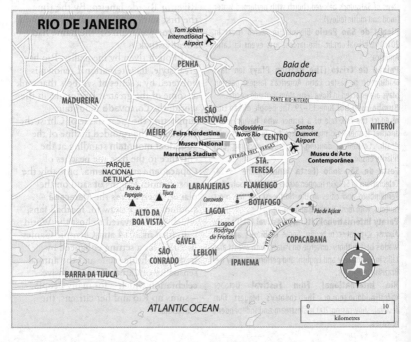

RIO DE JANEIRO

Tom Jobim International Airport

PENHA

Baía de Guanabara

PONTE RIO-NITERÓI

MADUREIRA

SÃO CRISTOVÃO

Rodoviária Novo Rio

MÉIER — Feira Nordestina

Museu National

Maracaná Stadium

AVENIDA PRES. VARGAS

CENTRO

Santos Dumont Airport

NITERÓI

Museu de Arte Contemporânea

STA. TERESA

PARQUE NACIONAL DE TIJUCA

Pico do Papegaio

Pico da Tijuca

Corcovado

LARANJEIRAS

FLAMENGO

BOTAFOGO

Pão de Açúcar

ALTO DA BOA VISTA

LAGOA

Lagoa Rodrigo de Freitas

AVENIDA ATLÂNTICA

COPACABANA

GÁVEA

LEBLON

N

SÃO CONRADO

IPANEMA

BARRA DA TIJUCA

ATLANTIC OCEAN

0   10
kilometres

CARNAVAL

Carnaval is celebrated in all of Brazil's cities, but Rio's is the biggest and most famous of all. From the Friday before Ash Wednesday to the following Thursday, the city shuts up shop and throws itself into the world's most famous manifestation of unbridled hedonism. Rio's carnival ranks as the most important celebration on the Brazilian calendar, easily outstripping either Christmas or Easter. In a poverty-stricken city, it represents a moment of release, when Cariocas unite to express their aspirations in music and song.

THE ACTION

Rio's street celebrations (known as *blocos* and *bandas)* happen all over town from the beaches to the distant suburbs, and you should keep your ears open for the biggest and best parties (🖳 todorio.com has listings). The processions feature loudspeaker-laden floats blasting out frenetic samba, and thousands of hyped-up revellers. **Avenida Rio Branco** (Metrô Carioca) is the most traditional spot, but Santa Teresa, Laranjeiras, and of course all the beach districts have loads going on. Many neighbourhoods also have their own **samba school**, competing in three leagues, each allowing promotion and relegation. It's a year-round occupation, with schools mobilizing thousands of supporters, choosing a theme, writing the music and learning the dances choreographed by the **carnavelesco** – the school's director. By December, rehearsals have begun and the sambas are released to record stores. From September to February a visit to a samba school is a must (see p.254), while you can check out the *Cidade do Samba* (Rua Rivadávia Correa, Gamboa, Centro 🖳 cidadedosambarj.globo.com), a huge complex where carnival floats are constructed and touristic samba spectacles take place (due to reopen in 2015).

The main **procession** of *Grupo Especial* schools – known as the **Desfile** – takes place on the Sunday and Monday nights in the purpose-built **Sambódromo** at Rua Marques de Sapucaí (Metrô Praza Onze/Central do Brasil), a concrete structure 1.7km long that can accommodate ninety thousand spectators. Some schools may have thirty thousand participants; they compete for points awarded by judges according to the presentation of their song, story, dress, dance and rhythm. Each school must parade for between 85 and 95 minutes, with the **bateria**, or percussion section, sustaining the cadence that drives the school's song and dance. The **carros alegóricos** (decorated floats) carry prominent figures, and the **porta-bandeira** ("flag bearer") carries the school's symbol. The bulk of the procession behind is formed by the **alas** – each with hundreds of costumed individuals linked to a part of the school's theme.

The **parade** at the Sambódromo starts at 9pm, with six schools (see p.254) parading on each of the two nights, and it goes on till 4am. The *arquibancada* (high stand) in sector 9 has numbered seats largely reserved for foreign visitors (R$1058 per night), while stand 3's *arquibancada* is the best value for a reasonable view (from R$398). Stands 2, 12 and 13 have slightly lower prices (from R$368) but more restricted views. **Tickets** are available from the organizers (🖳 rio-carnival.net), or from agents such as Rio.com (☎ 1800 260 2700 in the US or Canada, ☎ 020 3129 3573 in the UK, ☎ 02 8015 5419 in Australia, 🖳 rio.com) or Bookers International (☎ 1866 930 6020 in the US or Canada, ☎ 020 3355 7907 in the UK, ☎ 02 9191 2901 in Australia, 🖳 camarotecarnaval.com), or at premium prices from travel agents in Rio, and should be booked well in advance.

Carnival balls (*bailes de Carnaval*) and other live shows are a big feature of festivities before and during the main event. Check out Lapa's *Fundição Progresso* (🖳 fundicaoprogresso.com.br) for appearances by top samba schools in the run-up, and Leblon's *Scala* (🖳 scalario.com.br) for no-holds-barred affairs each night.

7am–3.20pm, Sat 10am–2pm; guided tours every 30min; R$5) served until 1980 as Rio's cathedral. Inside, the high altar is detailed in silver and boasts a beautiful work by the painter Antônio Parreires. Below, in the **crypt**, rest the supposed remains of Pedro Álvares Cabral, Portuguese discoverer of Brazil – though his final resting place is more likely to be Santarém in Portugal.

North to São Bento and the port

Heading north up **Rua 1 de Março** from the *praça*, you'll pass the church of **Santa Cruz dos Militares** (Mon–Fri 1.30– 3.30pm; free), dating from 1628 and rebuilt in granite and marble by the army in 1780; a display of ecclesiastical and military oddments is to be found inside. The grand interior of the **Centro Cultural Banco do Brasil** (Wed–Mon 9am–9pm; free; ⓦculturabancodobrasil.com.br), Rio's most dynamic arts centre, is just north of here and well worth a look around. Just beyond, the enormous **Candelária church** (Igreja de Nossa Senhora de Candelária; Mon–Fri 7.30am–4pm, Sat 8am–noon, Sun 9am–1pm; free) looms into view, luxuriously decorated inside in marble and bronze. A short way from the entrance a simple wooden cross inscribed with eight names (and with flowers usually laid nearby) commemorates police shootings of street children that took place here in 1993, and serves as an ongoing plea for respect of human rights in Rio. Accessed by elevator from Rua Dom Gereardo 40, the hilltop **Igreja e Mosteiro de São Bento** (daily 7am–5pm, Sun Mass at 10am; free) was founded by Benedictine monks in 1633. The facade is pleasingly simple with twin pyramid-shaped spires, while the interior is richly adorned in gold designs and statues of saints, popes and bishops executed by the deft hand of Mestre Valentim. Further north again is Praça Mauá, part of a redevelopment featuring the new **Museu de Arte do Rio** (Tues–Sun 10am–5pm; R\$8; ⓦmuseudeartedorio.org.br), a museum dedicated to the city's own art from colonial times to the present day.

Museu Histórico Nacional

The **Museu Histórico Nacional** (Tues–Fri 10am–5.30pm, Sat & Sun 2–6pm; R\$8; ⓦmuseuhistoriconacional.com.br), housed in the former military arsenal, is located south from Praça XV de Novembro in the shadow of the Kubitschek flyover. The exhibits contain some pieces of great interest, from furniture, firearms and locomotives to displays on indigenous societies and the sugar, gold, coffee and beef trades. Information about slavery – so important to Brazil's history – is scarce, while the monarchy is granted ample space. Audio-guides (R\$8) are available in English, and the varied collection makes it one of Brazil's most important museums.

Carioca

The bustling square **Largo da Carioca** (Metrô Carioca) is dominated from above by the cloistered **Igreja e Convento de Santo Antônio** (Mon–Fri 8am–6pm, Sat 8–11am; free; ⓦconventosantoantonio .org.br), though the square's other historical buildings were, sadly, lost to ugly new high-rises. Built between 1608 and 1620, this is Rio's oldest church, a tranquil refuge decorated in marble and Portuguese tiling. Adjoining it, the striking **Igreja de São Francisco da Penitência** (Tues–Fri 9am–noon & 1–4pm; R\$2) contains extensive gold and silver ornamentation. Lively shopping street Rua Uruguaiana heads north from here towards the Candelária.

Saara and Campo de Santana

West from Metrô Uruguaiana ruas Alfândega and Passos run through Rio's best (and cheapest) market area, known as **Saara**, originally peopled by Jewish and Arab merchants.

A block south of Saara, the **Igreja de São Francisco de Paula** (Mon–Fri 9am–4.50pm; free), the site of the Mass to "swear-in" the Brazilian Constitution in 1831, contains meticulous decoration by Valentim da Fonseca e Silva, known to Cariocas as Mestre Valentim, Brazil's most important eighteenth-century sculptor. One of Rio's most impressive ornate interiors is to be found two blocks west, however, at the **Real Gabinete Português de Leitura** (Mon–Fri 9am–6pm; free; ⓦwww.realgabinete.com.br), dating from 1887 and containing a library with 350,000 leather-bound volumes. At Saara's western end you come upon a surprisingly peaceful park, the **Campo de Santana** (daily 6am–5pm; free), where Emperor Dom Pedro I proclaimed Brazil's independence from Portugal in 1822 – now complete with ponds, strutting peacocks and scuttling agoutis.

Nova Catedral and around

To the southwest of the Largo da Carioca, the unmistakeable form of the

Nova Catedral Metropolitana (daily 7.30am–6pm) rises up like some futuristic tepee, 75m high and with a capacity of 20,000. Built between 1964 and 1976, it's an impressive piece of modern architecture, resembling the blunt-topped Maya pyramids of Mexico. It feels vast inside, its remarkable sense of space enhanced by the absence of supporting columns and four huge stained-glass windows, each measuring 20m by 60m. Over the road is the bizarre Cubist-style **headquarters of Petrobrás**, the state oil company. Immediately behind it is the station for *bondes* (trams) up to Santa Teresa (see below).

Cinelândia: Praça Floriano

At the southern end of Avenida Rio Branco, the dead-straight boulevard that cuts through the centre from north to south, you reach the area known as **Cinelândia** (Metrô Cinelândia), named for long-gone 1930s movie houses. At the centre of impressive square **Praça Floriano** is a bust of **Getúlio Vargas**, still decorated with flowers by an anonymous mourner on the anniversary of the former dictator's birthday, March 19. At the northern end is the **Theatro Municipal** (guided tours Tues–Fri noon, 2pm, 3pm & 4pm, Sat 11am, noon & 1pm; R$10; best reserved in advance on ☏21 2332 9220), modelled on the Paris Opera Garnier – all granite, marble and bronze, with a foyer decorated in Louis XV-style white and gold with green onyx handrails. If you can, come to a performance here (ⓦwww .theatromunicipal.rj.gov.br) featuring Rio's symphony orchestra and guest ballet schools and singers from across the globe.

Across the road is the superb **Museu Nacional das Belas Artes** (Tues–Fri 10am–6pm, Sat & Sun noon–5pm; R$8; ⓦmnba.gov.br), a grandiose construction imitating the Louvre in Paris. The European collection includes Boudin, Taunay and Frans Post, but the painting and sculpture by all the modern Brazilian masters are of much greater interest. Neighbouring **Biblioteca Nacional** (guided tours in Portuguese hourly Mon–Fri 10am–5pm, Sat 10am–2pm, in English Mon–Fri 1pm only; free but photo ID required; ⓦwww.bn.br) is also noteworthy, for the high Art Nouveau ceilings of its reading rooms and its stairway decorated by important artists like Visconti, Amoedo and Bernadelli. Ten minutes' walk southeast, at the edge of the Parque do Flamengo, is the **Museu de Arte Moderna** (Tues–Fri noon–6pm, Sat & Sun 11am–6pm; R$14; ⓦmamrio .com.br), which contains a range of twentieth-century Brazilian art. Start upstairs with the pieces from the 1920s.

Lapa

Immediately southwest of Cinelândia is the *bairro* of **Lapa**, a gracefully decaying neighbourhood and the beating heart of Rio's **samba and nightlife scenes** (see p.253). Its **Passeio Público** park (daily 7.30am–9pm; free) was opened in 1783 and is now a little past its best, but this green oasis still charms – with busts of famous figures from the city's history by Mestre Valentim. Lapa's most recognizable feature is the eighteenth-century aqueduct known as the **Arcos da Lapa**. Built to a Roman design and consisting of 42 wide arches, in its heyday it carried water from the Rio Carioca to the thirsty citizens of the city; now *bondes* (trams) pass across it on their way up to Santa Teresa. Each Friday night thousands of people throng the surrounding streets. Just off Rua Joaquim da Silva, a remarkable ascending tiled mosaic lines the **Escadaria Selarón** stairway into Santa Teresa, a feat of obsession by the murdered Chilean artist Selarón.

Santa Teresa

Just above Lapa to the southwest is **Santa Teresa**, a leafy *bairro* of labyrinthine, cobbled streets and *ladeiras* (steps), clinging to a hillside, the streets lined with atmospheric but slightly dishevelled early nineteenth-century mansions and walled gardens, with stupendous views of the city and bay. Santa Teresa enjoys something of a bohemian reputation and is Rio's main artistic neighbourhood: in July or August around one hundred

CENTRAL RIO

AVENIDA PERIMETRAL

AVENIDA RODRIGUES ALVES

AVENIDA PERIMETRAL

Novo Rio Rodoviária

RUA DA GAMBOA

RUA RIVADAVIA CORREIA

RUA DO PRÓPOSITO

AVENIDA VENEZUELA

RUA PEDRO ERNESTO

Cidade do Samba

SAÚDE

S Família

R LIVRAMENTO SECADURA CABRAL

R LIVRAMENTO SECADURA CABRAL

RUA ORLDS SANTOS

RUA BARÃO DA GAMBOA

GAMBOA

Palácio de Conceição

POMPEU

Cemitério dos Ingleses

R LADEIRA DO BARROSO

Vila Olímpica da Gamboa

R AMÉRICA

R DO RIBEIRO

R VISCONDE DA GÁVEA

RUA SENADOR

RUA CAMERINO

MORRO DA PROVIDÊNCIA

RUA BARÃO DE SÃO FELIX

Palácio Itamaraty

AVENIDA MARECHAL FLORIANO

Train Station

RUA SENADOR POMPEU

PRAÇA DUQUE DE CAXIAS

Pres. Vargas

Central

SAARA

CIDADE NOVA

PRAÇA 11 DE JUNHO

Casa de Deodoro

Campo de Santana

RUA DA CONSTITUÇÃO

AVENIDA PRES. VARGAS

AVENIDA PRES. VARGAS

Casa de Moede

RUA GENERAL CALDWELL

RUA VISC. DO RIO BRANCO

AVENIDA G. FREIRE

RUA BENEDITO HIPÓLITO

De Santana

Solar do Conde dos Arcos

RUA SANTANA

RUA M. DE POMBAL

CANECA

FATIMA

RUA DO SENADO

RUA DE INVALIDOS

Praça Onze

R. MARQUES DE SAPUCAÍ (SAMBÓDROMO)

AVENIDA TRINTA ULM DE MARCO

DE SÁ

RUA FREI

AVENIDA MEM. DE SÁ

VALADARES

CATUMBI

PRAÇA DE CRUZ VERMELHA

AVENIDA MEM. DE SÁ

AVENIDA SALVADOR

AVENIDA H.

RUA SENHOR DE MATOZINHOS

RUA PAULA MATOS

RUA DO RESENDE

RUA DE CATUMBI

RUA REI CANECA

RUA RIACHUELO

RUA MONTE ALEGRE

RUA ANDRE CAVALCANTE

RUA JOAQUIM

LARGO DAS NEVES

LARGO DE CATUMBI

RUA PADRE MIGUELINHO

RUA TERPTU

R. COQUEIROS

Museu do Chácara do Céu

SANTA TERESA

0 ——— 400

metres

Maracanã Stadium & Feira Nordestina

4 & 18 ▼   ▼ 19   Largo do Guimarães ▼

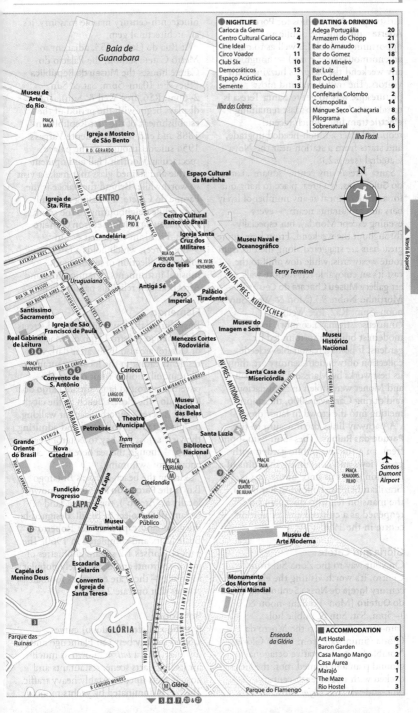

artists open their studios for **Portas Abertas**, offering the public an opportunity to look (as well as to enjoy an enormous street party) – though on any weekend the *bairro* is buzzing with visitors. The traditional and most picturesque way to get to Santa Teresa is to take the *bonde,* Rio's last remaining **electric tram** line, which recently reopened after a much-needed upgrade, and starts from a station near the Nova Catedral (see p.238).

Santa Teresa's tiny centre "square", **Largo do Guimarães**, is a great place to hang out for a drink or meal at any number of lively bars and restaurants nearby – every evening except Monday, but especially throughout the weekend. From here, more great bars are staggered along the bus/tram route westwards, while downhill to the east it's an enjoyable ten-minute walk to art gallery **Museu Chácara do Céu** at Rua Murtinho Nobre 93 (Mon & Wed–Sun noon–5pm; R\$2, free Wed; Ⓦmuseuscastromaya.com.br), in a modernist building surrounded by gardens. It holds a reasonable, eclectic collection of twentieth-century art, though its best works by Matisse, Picasso, Dalí and Monet were stolen in an audacious raid during Carnaval 2006, the culprits melting into the crowd in fancy dress.

A pathway links the museum to the **Parque das Ruínas** (Tues–Sun 8am–6pm; free), an attractive public garden with great views and containing the ruins of a mansion that was once home to a Brazilian heiress. Following her death, the mansion fell into disrepair, but reopened as a cultural and exhibition centre in the 1990s.

Glória and Catete

On your way to the Zona Sul from Centro, it's worth visiting the eighteenth-century **Igreja de Nossa Senhora da Glória do Outeiro** (Mon–Fri 8am–noon & 1–5pm, Sat, Sun & public hols 8am–2pm; free), atop the Morro da Glória (5min walk from Metrô Glória). Notable for its innovative octagonal ground plan and domed roof, the latter decked with seventeenth-century blue-and-white *azulejos* and

nineteenth-century marble masonry, it's an architectural gem.

At Rua do Catete 153, adjacent to Metrô Catete station, the Palácio do Catete houses the **Museu da República** (Tues–Fri 10am–5pm, Sat & Sun 2–6pm; R\$6, free Wed & Sun). The displays begin with the period of the establishment of the first Republic in 1888 and end with Presidente Vargas's 1954 suicide, though it's the palace's spectacular Moorish Hall and opulent marble and stained glass that make a visit so worthwhile. Behind the palace is the Parque do Catete, a pleasing tranquil spot, while neighbouring to the south is the **Museu de Folclore Edison Carneiro** (Tues–Fri 11am–6pm, Sat & Sun 3–6pm; free), which holds a fascinating folkloric collection of leatherwork, musical instruments, ceramics, toys and Afro-Brazilian religious paraphernalia.

Flamengo

Busy during the day, the tree-lined streets of **Flamengo** (Metrô Largo do Machado or Catete) are also lively after dark with residents eating in the local restaurants; it's tranquil enough to sit out on the pavements around large square **Largo do Machado**. The closest **beach** to the city centre is here, a superb place for walking, people-watching, volleyball and admiring the view across the bay to Niterói (see p.255) – though the sea here is not clean enough for swimming.

Skirting the beach as far as Botafogo Bay is the **Parque do Flamengo** (known locally as "Aterro"), the biggest land reclamation project in Brazil, designed by the great landscape architect Roberto Burle Marx and completed in 1960. The park comprises 1.2 square kilometres of prime seafront, and is extremely popular for sports – there are countless football pitches that operate 24hr.

Botafogo

Botafogo (Metrô Botafogo) curves around the bay between Flamengo and the Sugarloaf, a *bairro* known as much for its lively arts scene, restaurants and hostels as its uncomfortably heavy traffic. The bay is dominated by yachts moored near Rio's yacht club, while seven blocks inland the district's top attraction is the **Museu do Índio** (Tues–Fri 9am–5.30pm, Sat & Sun 1–5pm; free; ⓦmuseudoindio .gov.br) at Rua das Palmeiras. Housed in an old colonial building, the museum has broad and imaginative multi-sensory displays, as well as utensils, musical instruments, tribal costumes and ritual devices from many of Brazil's dwindling populations of indigenous peoples, plus an extensive library. A block north of here off Rua São Clemente, the bright colours of *favela* Santa Marta light up the Corcovado mountainside. The first of Rio's *favelas* to be pacified by police in 2008, it's now fine to walk around or to take the cable car up to the summit, for fantastic views. In the *favela*'s upper west area you'll find a life-size bronze sculpture of Michael Jackson, a tribute to the late singer's (then controversial) shooting of the video *They Don't Care About Us* here in 1995, directed by Spike Lee.

To the south of the *bairro*, at the foot of Rua São João Batista, is the **Cemitério São João Batista**, the Zona Sul's largest resting place, with extravagant tombs for the Rio elite – Carmen Miranda and Bossa Nova master Tom Jobim are both near its central area. Botafogo's best bars and restaurants lie westwards around Rua Visconde de Caravelas. The **Cobal de Humaitá**, a partially covered complex of some twenty eateries, lies nearby on Rua Voluntários da Pátria.

Urca and the Sugarloaf

The small, wealthy *bairro* of **Urca** stands on a promontory formed by a land reclamation project and flanked by golden beaches. Facing Flamengo, the **Praia da Urca**, only 100m long, is frequented almost exclusively by the *bairro*'s inhabitants, while in front of the cable-car station (see below) is **Praia Vermelha**, a gorgeous cove sheltered from the Atlantic and popular with swimmers.

The beaches aren't the main draw, however: a cable-car ride up the **Pão de Açúcar** is not to be missed. Rising where Guanabara Bay meets the Atlantic Ocean, **Sugarloaf** is so named because of its similarity in shape to the moulded loaves

in which sugar was commonly sold in the days before granulated took over. The **cable-car** station (daily 8am–8pm; every 20min, last car back down at 8.40pm; R$62; ⓦbondinho.com.br) is located at Praça General. Tibúrcio (bus "Urca" or "Praia Vermelha" from Centro or #511 and #512 from Zona Sul). The 1325m journey is made in two stages, first to the summit of **Morro da Urca** (220m), then onwards to Pão de Açúcar itself (396m). It is possible to hike the first section and take the cable car for the second stage only, but it will not save you any money and you must first buy a ticket for the whole journey from the cable-car station, as tickets are not sold at the halfway stage. Aim to arrive well before sunset on a clear day and you'll find views as glorious as you could imagine right over the city.

Copacabana and Leme

Leme and **Copacabana** are different stretches of the same 4km beach. At the northeastern end of the Praia do Leme, the Morro do Leme rises up to the ruined **Forte do Leme** (Tues–Sun 9.30am–4.30pm, but closed in bad weather; R$4), a thirty-minute cobblestone walk from the army's sports club, great for more wonderful views of the Zona Sul and Guanabara Bay. Leme morphs into Copacabana at Avenida Princesa Isabel. The **Praia de Copacabana** runs a further 3km to the military-owned **Forte de Copacabana** (Tues–Sun 10am–8pm; museum 10am–6pm; R$6; ⓦfortedecopacabana.com), certainly worth a wander around and a drink at its branch of *Confeitaria Colombo*. The area's newest attraction is the **Museu da Imagem e do Som** (ⓦmis.rj.gov.br/nova-sede), due to open in 2015, covering the history of Brazil's film, recording and broadcast media, and the new home for memorabilia from the now-defunct Carmen Miranda Museum, dedicated to Brazil's best-known Hollywood star. Copacabana's **beach** is stunning, right down to its over-the-top mosaic pavements, designed by Roberto Burle Marx to mimic rolling waves. The seafront is backed by a line of high-rise hotels and apartments that have sprung up

3

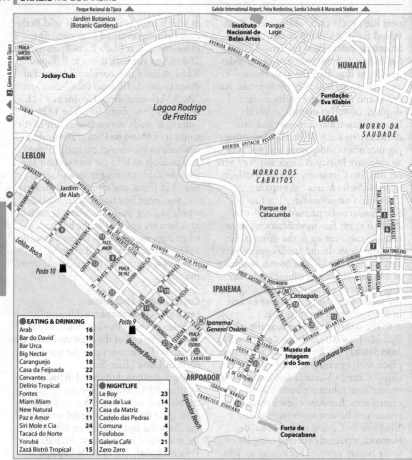

Parque Nacional da Tijuca ▲   Galeão International Airport, Feira Nordestina, Samba Schools & Maracanã Stadium ▲

Jardim Botanico
(Botanic Gardens)

Instituto
Nacional de
Belas Artes

Parque
Lage

HUMAITÁ

PRAÇA
SANTOS
DUMONT

AVENIDA BORGES DE MEDEIROS

Jockey Club

Fundação
Eva Klabin

TURIBA

Lagoa Rodrigo
de Freitas

LAGOA

MORRO DA
SAUDADE

AVENIDA EPITACIO PESSOA

LEBLON

MORRO DOS
CABRITOS

Jardim
de Alah

Parque de
Catacumba

Leblon Beach

Posto 10

IPANEMA

Cantagalo

Posto 9

Ipanema/
General Osório

EATING & DRINKING
Arab	16
Bar do David	19
Bar Urca	10
Big Nectar	20
Caranguejo	18
Casa da Feijoada	22
Cervantes	13
Delírio Tropical	12
Fontes	9
Miam Miam	17
New Natural	17
Paz e Amor	11
Siri Mole e Cia	24
Tacacá do Norte	1
Yorubá	5
Zazá Bistrô Tropical	15

Ipanema Beach

NIGHTLIFE
Le Boy	23
Casa da Lua	14
Casa da Matriz	2
Castelo das Pedras	8
Comuna	4
Fosfobox	6
Galeria Café	21
Zero Zero	3

Museu da
Imagem
e do Som

Copacabana Beach

ARPOADOR

Arpoador Beach

Forte de
Copacabana

since the 1940s, while a steady stream of noisy traffic clogs the two-lane **Avenida Atlântica**. A strong undercurrent at Copacabana means that it is dangerous even for strong swimmers – don't do anything the locals don't do. Another problem is theft: take only the money and clothes that you will need.

Arpoador, Ipanema and Leblon

On the other side of the point from Forte de Copacabana, the lively waters off **Arpoador** are popular with families and the elderly, as the ocean here is calmer than its neighbours – and the "Arpoador rock" often draws crowds to applaud the sunset. From here, as far as the unkempt

and balding greenery of the **Jardim de Alah**, 3km away, you're in **Ipanema**; thereafter lies **Leblon**. The beaches here are stupendous and packed at weekends. Stalls sell fresh coconuts, while for bars and restaurants you'll need to walk a couple of blocks inland. Ipanema's beach is unofficially divided according to the particular interests of beach users; the "rainbow beach" between Rua Farme de Amoedo and Rua Teixeira de Melo is where gay men are concentrated, while posto 9 beyond is firmly for the party crowd; posto 10 is a little more low-key. On Sunday, the seafront road is closed to traffic, and given over to strollers, skateboarders and rollerbladers. At the far

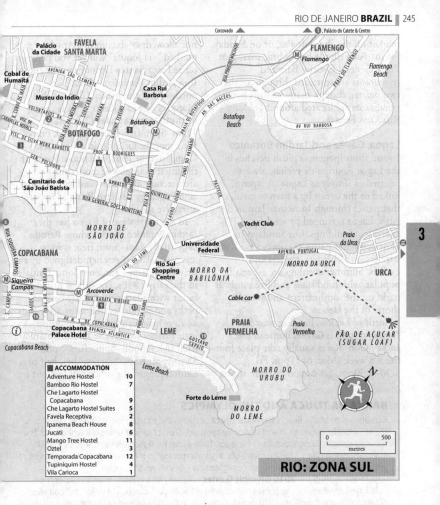

Corcovado ▲   ▲ ① Palácio do Catete & Centro

RIO: ZONA SUL

ACCOMMODATION	
Adventure Hostel	10
Bamboo Rio Hostel	7
Che Lagarto Hostel Copacabana	9
Che Lagarto Hostel Suites	5
Favela Receptiva	2
Ipanema Beach House	8
Jucati	6
Mango Tree Hostel	11
Oztel	3
Temporada Copacabana	12
Tupiniquim Hostel	4
Vila Carioca	1

end of Leblon, the marvellously located Vidigal *favela*, "pacified" by police in 2011 along with neighbouring Rocinha, covers the hillside, and completes the sweep around the bay.

Since the 1960s, Ipanema and Leblon have developed a reputation as a fashion centre, and are now seen as among the most chic *bairros* in all of Brazil. Try to visit on a Friday for the **food and flower**

THE GIRL FROM IPANEMA

It was at a bar called **Veloso** in 1962 that master composer-musicians Tom Jobim and Vinicius de Moraes sat down and penned *Garota de Ipanema* – **The Girl from Ipanema** – which put both bossa nova and Ipanema on the global arts map. The song was inspired by 15-year-old local girl Heloisa Paez Pinto, who would pass each morning on her way to the beach. These days the bar has been renamed *A Garota de Ipanema*, and is located at Rua Vinicius de Moraes 49 – changed from Rua Montenegro in honour of the lyricist – while the song has been kept alive through numerous cover versions by the likes of Frank Sinatra and Shirley Bassey. Heloisa posed as a *Playboy* playmate in 1987 and 2003 – the latter at the age of 58 – and now runs a chain of fashion stores (one next door to the bar, at Rua Vinicius de Moraes 53). No prizes for guessing the name.

market on the Praça de Paz, or on Sunday for the **Feira Hippie** bric-a-brac market at Praça General Osório. Bars and restaurants are scattered throughout the two *bairros*, though many of Rio's best restaurants are located around Leblon's Rua Dias Ferreira.

Lagoa, Gávea and Jardim Botânico

Inland from Ipanema's plush beaches is the Lagoa Rodrigo de Freitas, always referred to simply as **Lagoa**. A lagoon linked to the ocean by a narrow canal that passes through Ipanema's Jardim de Alah, Lagoa is fringed by wealthy apartment buildings. On Sundays, its 8km perimeter pathway comes alive with strollers, rollerbladers, joggers and cyclists. Summer evenings are especially popular, with food stalls and live music at parks on the southeastern and western shores of the lagoon.

North of Leblon, heading west from Lagoa's shores, is **Gávea**, home of the **Jockey Club**. Races usually take place four times a week (Mon 6–11pm, Fri 4.30–9.30pm, Sat & Sun 2–8pm; shorts not allowed; ⓦjcb.com.br). Any bus marked "via Jóquei" will get you here; get off at Praça Santos Dumont at the end of Rua Jardim Botânico. About 3km northwest of the Jockey Club, at Rua Marquês de São Vicente 476, is the **Instituto Moreira Salles** (Tues–Sun 11am–8pm; free; ⓦims.com.br), one of Rio's most beautiful cultural centres. Completed in 1951, the house is one of the finest examples of modernist architecture in Brazil – and the gardens, landscaped by Roberto Burle Marx, are attractive too.

To the northwest of Lagoa lies the **Jardim Botânico** *bairro*, whose **Parque Lage** (daily 8am–5pm; free; ⓦwww .eavparquelage.rj.gov.br), designed by the British landscape gardener John Tyndale in the early 1840s, consists of primary forest with a labyrinthine network of paths and ponds, as well as its artsy *Café do Lage* inside an Italianate mansion. A little further west is the **Jardim Botânico** itself (Mon noon–5pm, Tues–Sun 8am–5pm; R$6; ⓦjbrj.gov.br), half of it natural jungle, the other half laid out in

---

BARRA DA TIJUCA AND THE OLYMPICS

Rio's answer to Miami Beach, **Barra da Tijuca** occupies the coastal plain of the city's west zone (Zona Oeste) between an inland lagoon system and 23km of almost unbroken white sand. The natural setting is stupendous, but unless you have a love for skyscrapers and shopping malls (Barra Shopping offers a full kilometre of consumer therapy), not to mention your own wheels, you're unlikely to find a trip here very enlightening – or easy on the pocket.

Half the events of the **2016 Olympic Games** will take place in Barra, mainly in a purpose-built Olympic village on the shores of picturesque Lagoa de Jacarepaguá (30km by road west of Leblon), a development which includes the vast RioCentro conference centre, famous for hosting the 1992 UN Earth Summit. Unusually, the main Olympic stadiums are located a good distance away: the Maracanã will host the opening and closing ceremonies and much of the football, while the athletics is scheduled for Engenhão stadium in the Zona Norte (accessed by train from Centro and bus from the Olympic village), an arrangement already rehearsed at the 2007 Pan-American Games.

Controversy has nonetheless followed Barra's land speculation boom in advance of the games. Voracious **development** here monopolized city resources for a quarter century from the late 1960s, yet planners failed to account for the area's working-class builders, maids and other service personnel. As with other areas of Rio, *favelas* grew quickly, the most famous of which is just inland from Barra at Cidade de Deus (City of God), immortalized worldwide in the namesake Oscar-nominated film. While long-standing conflict ended with the implementation of a police "pacification" unit in 2009, removal of other irregular housing around Barra remains a matter of extreme contention – not least because many of their residents were forcibly removed from *favelas* in Rio's Zona Sul under the military dictatorship in the 1970s. New hotels, a golf course, bus routes and metrô extensions offer a mixed bag for a region not known for its social inclusion. Journalists and campaigners are eagerly following Olympic developments: check out the excellent sites ⓦriorealblog.com and ⓦrioonwatch.org.

impressive avenues lined with immense imperial palms that date from the garden's inauguration in 1808. A number of sculptures are dotted throughout, notably the Greek mythology-inspired *Ninfa do Eco* and *Caçador Narciso* (1783), the first two metal sculptures cast in Brazil.

Corcovado and Christ the Redeemer

The unmistakeable Art Deco statue of **Cristo Redentor** (Christ the Redeemer), gazing across the bay from the **Corcovado** ("hunchback") hill with arms outstretched in welcome, or as if preparing for a dive into the waters below, is the city's most famous emblem. The immense statue – 30m high and weighing over 1000 metric tonnes – was scheduled for completion in 1922 as part of Brazil's centenary independence celebrations. In fact, it wasn't finished until 1931. In clear weather, it's every bit as awe-inspiring as you'd imagine – the journey up to the statue is breathtaking day or night – though what ought to be one of Rio's highlights can turn into a great disappointment if the Corcovado is hidden by cloud. By day the whole of Rio and Guanabara Bay is laid out

magnificently before you; after dark, the flickering city lights of this vast metropolis create a stunning visual effect far more impressive than any artificial light show, enhanced by your position at Jesus's feet.

Most people reach the statue by the **Corcovado cog train** (daily every 30min 8am–7pm; tickets must be bought in advance, R$50 online, or R$55 at Rio Sul shopping mall in Botafogo or from Riotur at Rua Candelária 6 in Centro or on Av Atlántica in Copacabana opposite Rua Hilário de Gouveia, round trip and Parque Nacional da Tijuca entrance fee included; ⓦcorcovado.com.br). The train leaves from the station at Rua Cosme Velho 513 (bus #180 from Centro or Catete, #570 or #584 from Copacabana, Ipanema or Leblon, or express bus #580 from Largo do Machado metrô station with through metrô–bus tickets available) and proceeds slowly upwards through lush forest as it enters the **Parque Nacional da Tijuca** (see box below). You still need to buy the same ticket in advance if you take a taxi to the top or if you walk from Parque Lage (see opposite), a steep and gruelling two- to three-hour climb on which, although there hasn't been a

---

PARQUE NACIONAL DA TIJUCA

The mountains running southwest from the Corcovado are covered with forest, representing the periphery of the **Parque Nacional da Tijuca** (daily: winter 8am–5pm; summer 8am–6pm; R$32 weekends, holiday periods and December, R$22 other times, but included in Corcovado ticket; ⓦparquedatijuca.com.br). The park offers sixteen walking trails and some excellent views of Rio, and makes an appealing day retreat away from the city. The trails are steep and not for the unfit, but if you have the energy climb 2–3hr for staggering views from coastal Pedra da Gávea (842m; guide essential), or in the far north of the forest, Pico da Tijuca (1021m) above popular picnic spot Bom Retiro. **Public transport** to the park is not especially convenient so it's most easily visited by car, taxi or on a tour. Alternatively, take metrô Linha 1 to Saens Peña and catch bus #301, #302 or #345 towards "Barra da Tijuca", asking to be let off at Alta de Boa Vista right by the park entrance. Also accessible on foot from here is the Museu do Açude (Estrada do Açude 764; Wed–Mon noon–5pm; R$2, Wed free; ⓦmuseuscastromaya.com.br), built by the man responsible for the reforestation of the park, and containing wonderful Chinese bronze sculpture, painted vases and, outside, well-maintained forest trails interwoven with art installations.

Excellent small-group **hiking tours** are run by Rio Hiking (half a day from R$228/person; ☎21 2552 9204, ⓦriohiking.com.br). For a bird's-eye view take a tandem flight with a **hang-gliding** instructor from the Pedra Bonita ramp above São Conrado near Pedra da Gávea; an experienced and reliable operator is Go Up Brasil (R$400; ☎21 3322 3165, ⓦgoup.com.br), with daily flights when weather permits; price includes pick-up and drop-off. If you want to **cycle**, enter the park in the Zona Sul at Rua Pacheco Leão, which runs up the side of the Jardim Botânico to the Entrada dos Macacos and on to the Vista Chinesa, from where there's a marvellous view of Guanabara Bay and the Zona Sul.

robbery for some years, it's still advisable to walk in a group.

Maracanã Stadium

Sports fans will not want to miss the **Maracanã** (Metrô Maracanã; Linha 2) – the world's most famous football stadium, steeped in soccer history, which was refurbished before the 2014 World Cup, with a capacity of 78,800. The real name of this monumental arena is actually **Estadio Mario Filho**; *Maracanã* is a nickname derived from the Brazilian word for a macaw and given to a nearby river. But it's not just football that earns the stadium its place in the record books. In 1991 former Beatle Paul McCartney played to a crowd of 180,000 people here, the highest ever concert attendance. It's certainly worth coming to a game, but if your visit doesn't coincide with a match, you can **tour** the stadium (daily 9am–5pm; R$30; ⓦ maracanaonline .com.br), visiting the dressing room, dug-out, press stand, and of course the hallowed turf itself.

Quinta da Boa Vista

The area covered by the **Quinta da Boa Vista** (daily 9am–5pm; free; Metrô São Cristóvão) was once incorporated in a *sesmaria* (a colonial land grant) held by Jesuits in the seventeenth century, before it became the country seat of the Portuguese royal family in 1808. The park, with its wide expanses of greenery, tree-lined avenues, lakes and games areas, is an excellent place for a stroll, though it can get crowded at weekends. Looking out from a hilltop in the centre of the park is the imposing Neoclassical **Museu Nacional** (Mon noon–5pm, Tues–Sun 10am–5pm; R$6; ⓦ www.museunacional .ufrj.br). Its archeological section deals with the human history of Latin America; in the Brazilian room, exhibits of Tupi-Guarani and Marajó ceramics lead on to the indigenous ethnographical section, uniting pieces collected from the numerous tribes that once populated Brazil and with displays on Brazilian folklore and Afro-Brazilian cults. The surprisingly spacious **Rio Zoo** (Tues–Sun 9am–4.30pm; R$6; ⓦ www.rio.rj.gov.br/ web/riozoo) is located next door.

ARRIVAL AND DEPARTURE

By plane Tom Jobim International Airport, known as Galeão (☎ 21 3398 5050, ⓦ aeroportogaleao.net), is 15km north of the centre and also handles many domestic flights. Santos Dumont Airport (☎ 21 3814 7070, ⓦ aeroportosantosdumont.net), southeast of (and walking distance from) Centro, handles mainly short-haul domestic services, including the São Paulo shuttle. Frequent executive buses (every 20min 5.30am–10.30pm; R$12–13.50) link the airports with the *rodoviária* (bus

---

RIO DE JANEIRO TOURS

You can get around most of Rio's sights independently, but for off-the-beaten-track exploring such as to *favelas* and football matches, or for outdoor activities, experienced guides are on hand to help. All operators listed below speak English. Book tours personally rather than through commission-hungry hostels/hotels.

TOUR OPERATORS

Cruz the Coast ☎ 21 8076 5743, ⓦ cruzthecoastbrazil.com. Operates an excellent guided minibus service north to Bahia with a ten-day suggested itinerary including accommodation and numerous excursions (from R$1700).

Favela Adventures ☎ 21 8221 5572, ⓦ favelatour .org. Offers a variety of tours of Rocinha, including opportunities to party with the locals.

Favela Tour ☎ 21 3322 2727, ⓦ favelatour.com.br. Responsible, community-approved trips to Rocinha by minibus for R$75.

Heli Rio ☎ 21 2437 9064, ⓦ helirio.com.br. Arranges helicopter trips over the city.

Rio Hiking ☎ 21 2552 9204, ⓦ riohiking.com.br. Offers a variety of trips around the city and state, as well as nightlife tours and adventure sports.

Rio's Surf Bus ☎ 21 3546 1860, ⓦ surfbus.com.br. Four daily buses connect Largo do Machado, Botafogo, Copacabana and Ipanema with the top surf spots and gorgeous beaches west of the city such as Barra, Macumba and Prainha – an ideal day-trip for surfers and beach bums alike.

Robert Shaw ☎ 21 2275 8811, ✉ brazsoc@hotmail .com. Football tours and organized trips to football matches – covers all stadiums and clubs.

terminal), city centre and the Zona Sul beaches, passing through Flamengo, Botafogo, Copacabana, Ipanema and Leblon. To take a taxi at Galeão, buy a pre-paid ticket at one of the desks in arrival (around R$80 to/from the Zona Sul); at Santos Dumont city taxis (yellow with a blue stripe) are on hand outside the terminal (around R$35 to Copacabana, more at night).

Destinations São Paulo (approximately every 15min 6am–10.30pm; 1hr); Belo Horizonte (every 30–60min; 1hr 5min); Foz de Iguaçu (3 daily; 2hr 10min); Salvador (13–15 daily; 2hr 05min); Recife (7–10 daily; 2hr 50min).

By bus Buses arrive at the vast Rodoviária Novo Rio (❶21 3213 1800), 3km northwest of the centre at Av Francisco Bicalho. Late at night take a pre-paid taxi (from R$30 to Copacabana/Ipanema), otherwise take an executive bus (R$6–13.50) or the Metrô Integração bus #133 to Largo do Machado metrô station (R$4.55 for bus and metrô combined), or cross the street to Praça Hermes for (slower) city buses including #127 and #128 to Centro and Copacabana. Book intercity services a couple of days in advance at the *rodoviária* or from agencies such as Dantur in the Galeria do Condor mall on the south side of Largo do Machado.

Destinations Belo Horizonte (25 daily, most overnight; 6hr 30min); Foz do Iguaçu (2 daily; 23hr); Salvador (1 daily; 25hr); São Paulo (approximately every 15min; 6hr); São João del Rei and Ouro Preto (2 daily; 7hr); Paraty (13 daily; 4hr 30min); Mangaratiba/Angra dos Reis (for Ilha Grande; 4 daily; 2hr 30min). Buses for Petrópolis (every 40min; 90min) depart from both the *Rodoviária Novo Rio* and the city terminal at Castelo between Metrô Carioca and Praça XV de Novembro.

INFORMATION

Tourist information Riotur (⊛www.rio.rj.gov.br/riotur) has an English-speaking telephone information service, Alô Rio (Mon–Fri 9am–6pm; ❶21 2271 7000), plus 24hr desks at Rodoviária Novo Rio (❶21 2263 4857) and Galeão airport (❶21 3398 4077, ❶21 3367 6213), and information booths with more limited hours around town.

GETTING AROUND

By bus Buses are frequent and many run 24hr; numbers and destinations are clearly marked on the front. Get on at the front and pay the seated conductor; guard your valuables closely. Bus routes/numbers are available at ⊛vadeonibus.com.br.

By ferry Frequent crossings from the terminal at Praça XV de Novembro to Niterói (see p.255) cost R$4.50 and take 20min.

By metrô Mon–Sat 5am–midnight, Sun 7am–11pm. *Linha 1* (orange) links Ipanema, Copacabana, Botafogo and Flamengo with Centro (downtown) and several

stations to the north; *Linha 2* (green) runs from the northern suburbs to Centro and Botafogo. A third line (silver) is under construction linking Ipanema and Leblon to Barra da Tijuca in the west, to be ready for the Olympic Games in 2016. Tickets are R$3.50, with no discount for multiple journeys, but combined metrô and bus tickets (*superfície* or *integração*) are available for certain routes.

By taxi Rio's taxis come in two varieties: yellow with a blue stripe, or white with a red-and-yellow stripe; the latter are pricier, more comfortable radio cabs, which you order by phone. Both have meters and you should insist that they are activated (except from the *rodoviária* or Galeão airport; pick up a ticket at the booth). Radio cabs include Santo Amaro Táxi in Glória (❶21 2252 0054) and Coopertramo in Bonsucesso (❶21 2209 9292).

ACCOMMODATION

Rio is by no means cheap, and during Carnaval and *Reveillon* (when you should book well in advance) you can expect to pay way over the odds. That said, there are numerous youth hostels, catering to a massive crowd of budget travellers. Accommodation is cheapest in Botafogo, Catete and Lapa, with Santa Teresa marginally more, Copacabana more still, and chic Ipanema/Leblon the most expensive. Most options include breakfast. For a more authentic Carioca experience get in touch with *Cama e Café* (daily 9am–4pm; ❶21 2225 4366, ⊛camaecafe.com), who arrange fairly priced rooms with families in Santa Teresa and elsewhere.

LAPA AND SANTA TERESA

★**Casa Áurea** Rua Áurea 80, Santa Teresa ❶21 2242 5830, ⊛casaaurea.com.br; map pp.240–241. Lovely pousada in a charming old house with an attractive courtyard garden and friendly, multilingual staff always on hand for local advice. Dorms R$75, doubles R$180

Casa Mango Mango Rua Joaquim Murtinho 587, Santa Teresa ❶21 2508 6440, ⊛casa-mangomango.com; map pp.240–241. A wide range of bright and airy rooms in a large historic house, complete with pool, lounge with wi-fi and guest kitchen. Attractive, great-value dorms. R$150

Marajó Rua São Joaquim da Silva 99, Lapa ❶21 2224 4134, ⊛hotelmarajorio.com; map pp.240–241. Excellent choice for budget travellers not keen on the hostel scene. Modern facilities, clean, spacious rooms and friendly service in the heart of vibrant Lapa. Rooms at the front can be noisy at night. R$140

Rio Hostel Rua Joaquim Murtinho 351, Santa Teresa ❶21 3852 0827, ⊛riohostel.com; map pp.240–241. A cool backpacker hangout with a small pool and bohemian feel – plus a great bar serving *caipirinhas* until dawn. Stay seven nights and get one free; cheap packages combined with their sister hostel in Ipanema. Dorms R$40, doubles R$130

3

3

CATETE, FLAMENGO AND BOTAFOGO

Art Hostel Rua Silveira Martins 135, Catete ☎ 21 2205 1983, ⓦ arthostelrio.com; map pp.240–241. In a nineteenth-century building near the metrô, this is an artsy place with bags of atmosphere. Ask to see several dorms before choosing one. Café with wi-fi at front, roof terrace and video room. Dorms R$39, doubles R$120

Baron Garden Rua Barão de Guaratiba, Morro da Glória ⓦ barongarden.com; map pp.240–241. A colonial house with grand views, pool and garden, a short walk from Flamengo beach and Metrô Catete, aimed at the 30-plus budget traveller. Dorms R$75, doubles R$160

Oztel Rua Pinheiro Guimarães 91, Botafogo ☎ 21 3042 1853, ⓦ oztel.com.br; map pp.244–245. A modern hostel with cosmopolitan designer chic, but thankfully it has all the facilities and friendly staff to match. Dorms R$46, doubles R$135

★ **Tupiniquim Hostel** Rua Paulo Barreto 79, Botafogo ☎ 21 2244 1286, ⓦ tupiniquimhostel.com.br; map pp.244–245. Billed as an alternative hostel, there's no denying the facilities on offer: fast internet, pool table, bar, terrace, and more. Great value, but fills fast. Dorms R$40, doubles R$160

Vila Carioca Rua Estacio Coimbra 84, Botafogo ☎ 21 2535 3224, ⓦ vilacarioca.com.br; map pp.244–245. Small and friendly hostel near the metrô, with neat, balconied dorm rooms, patio and chill-out area. Has internet access and a/c. Dorms R$35, doubles $130

COPACABANA

Bamboo Rio Hostel Rua Lacerda Coutinho 45 ☎ 21 2236 1117, ⓦ bamboorio.com; map pp.244–245. Three blocks from the beach in a quiet, leafy suburb, *Bamboo Rio* is a hostel with refreshingly colourful, a/c rooms, a good pool (though not exactly a "spa" as advertised) and a pleasant garden with wild monkeys. Great value. Dorms R$45, doubles $170

Che Lagarto Hostel Copacabana Rua Barata Ribeiro 111 ☎ 21 3209 0348, ⓦ chelagarto.com; map pp.244–245. They pack them in here, but if big hostels are your thing and you don't mind the Copacabana price you won't regret staying here. Clean, with numerous facilities

and the organization for which the name is known. Dorms R$71

Che Lagarto Hostel Suites Rua Santa Clara 305 ☎ 21 2257 3133, ⓦ chelagarto.com; map pp.244–245. This branch of the most established chain of hostels in Rio has gone upmarket, with smart, comfortable rooms and decent facilities, 10min walk from the beach. R$240

Jucati Rua Tenente Marones de Gusmão 85 ☎ 21 2547 5422, ⓦ edificiojucati.com.br; map pp.244–245. On an attractive residential square, this is a bargain if you're travelling in a group (always ask for a discount at booking). Apartments have a double and two bunks, TV, kitchenette and wi-fi. R$280 (four people R$360)

Temporada Copacabana Edificio Av Atlantica 3196 ☎ 21 2255 0681, ⓦ temporadacopacabana.com.br; map pp.244–245. It won't win awards, but if you always dreamt of staying by the beach and can't afford the *Copacabana Palace*, this is your place. No breakfast. R$180

IPANEMA AND LEBLON

Adventure Hostel Rua Vinicius de Moraes 174 ☎ 21 3813 2726, ⓦ adventurehostel.com.br; map pp.244–245. Don't let the name put you off: this is a well-maintained HI hostel, and while they don't have many beds, the rooms are spacious. Dorms R$75, doubles R$200

Ipanema Beach House Rua Barão da Torre 485 ☎ 21 3202 2693, ⓦ ipanemahouse.com; map pp.244–245. Actually three blocks from the seafront, but a welcoming, laidback hostel nonetheless, with hippy-chic rooms and great socializing at the outdoor pool and bar. Dorms R$70, doubles R$200

★ **Mango Tree Hostel** Rua Prudencio de Moraes 594 ☎ 21 2287 9255, ⓦ mangotreehostel.com; map pp.244–245. A block from posto 9 on the beach, this is easily Ipanema's best cheap option. Spacious dorms, grand bathrooms and an overgrown garden with hammocks. Dorms R$60, doubles R$170

EATING AND DRINKING

Rio offers a huge variety of cuisines to discerning diners. In general, Cariocas eat well at lunch, so you'll find most restaurants in Centro and other office districts only open

---

STAY IN A FAVELA

Contrary to what the media would have you believe, Rio does have safe *favelas*, and staying in one can be an enjoyable, enlightening experience.

Favela Receptiva Estrada das Canoas 610, São Conrado ☎ 21 99848 6737, ⓦ favelareceptiva.com.br; map pp.244–245. A well-organized network of clean and comfortable host homes within small, friendly community Vila Canoas. Good breakfasts included; cultural tours and dance classes available. R$130

★ **The Maze** Rua Tavares Bastos 414, Casa 66, Catete ☎ 21 2558 5547, ⓦ jazzrio.com; map pp.240–241. An eccentric, Gaudí-esque pousada/hostel with a truly inspirational view across Guanabara Bay. Huge British-Brazilian breakfast on offer, and also hosts a popular monthly jazz night. Dorms R$60, doubles R$150

during the day. At night eating and drinking are always done together, whether in an informal bar with shared *petiscos* (tapas plates) or pricier fine dining. Santa Teresa, Botafogo and Leblon are the city's key districts for innovative options.

CENTRO AND LAPA

Bar Luiz Rua Carioca 39 ☎ 21 2262 6900; map pp.240–241. This hectic, but essentially run-of-the-mill, restaurant and bar, serving German-style food and ice-cold *chopp*, was founded in 1887 and is quite an institution. Still a popular meeting place for intellectuals, the food is good but a little overpriced; try the kassler smoked sausage (R$43.50). Mon 11am–8pm, Tues–Fri 11am–10pm, Sat 11am–6pm, Sun closed.

Bar Ocidental Rua Miguel Couto 124, Centro ☎ 21 2233 4728; map pp.240–241. On a small pedestrianized street that runs alongside Rio Branco all the way up from Sete de Septembro, this is a cheap little bar where you can sit at a table outside and enjoy an early evening *chopp* (R$5) with a plate of fresh sardines (R$1.90 per fish). Daily 7am–10pm.

Beduino Av Presidente Wilson 123 ☎ 21 2524 5142, ⓦ arabebeduino.com.br; map pp.240–241. Popular and inexpensive Arabic restaurant, which, unlike its rivals, offers a decent meze and falafel meal – a great option for vegetarians and carnivores alike. Mon–Fri 7am–midnight, Sat 7am–3pm.

Cosmopolita Travessa do Mosqueira 4 ☎ 21 2224 7820; map pp.240–241. An excellent Portuguese restaurant established in 1926 with a loyal and bohemian clientele. Fish dishes are firm favourites especially those based on saltfish (all R$99), as is the Oswaldo Aranha steak, invented here in the 1930s, with heaps of garlic (R$48). Mon–Sat 11am–3am.

★Mangue Seco Cachaçaria Rua do Lavradio 23 ☎ 21 3852 1947, ⓦ www.manguesecocachacaria.com.br; map pp.240–241. This great bar, offering the twin night-time pleasures of samba and *cachaça*, in the daytime also serves really good meals for a reasonable price. Specialities include *moqueca* (fish stew in coconut milk, R$86), with *pratos executivos* (cheap lunchtime dishes) from R$37, and seating indoors or on the pavement. Mon–Sat 11am–4am.

Pilograma Rua Carioca 53 and eight other addresses in Centro; map pp.240–241. Just up from *Bar Luiz*, this place is hugely popular with office workers who take advantage of the extensive buffet of eighty different dishes for cheap eats. Meals from around R$20. Mon–Sat 11am–4pm.

SANTA TERESA

Bar do Arnaudo Rua Almirante Alexandrino 316; map pp.240–241. An excellent mid-priced place to sample traditional food from Brazil's northeast, such as *carne do*

Confeitaria Colombo Rua Gonçalves Dias 32, Centro ☎ 21 2505 1500, ⓦ confeitariacolombo.com.br; map pp.240–241. Take the lift for a peek at the grand salão upstairs (after 4pm) or indulge in the excellent and huge Franco-Brazilian buffet lunch (Mon–Sat noon–4pm, around R$50). Downstairs relax over coffee or afternoon tea. An unmissable Rio institution. Mon–Fri 9am–8pm, Sat 9am–5pm, closed Sun.

Miam Miam Rua General Góes Monteiro 34, Botafogo ☎ 21 2244 0125, ⓦ miammiam.com.br; map pp.244–245. Splashing out here is more than worthwhile, with creative international fusion dishes (salmon with spinach, mash and pistachio pilaf, for example, at R$51.80). They also do a R$110 tasting menu. Tues–Fri 7pm–midnight, Sat 8pm–1am.

Siri Mole e Cia Francisco Otaviano 50, Copacabana ☎ 21 2267 0894, ⓦ sirimole .com.br; Mlpanema/General Osório; map pp.244–245. Excellent but pricey Bahian restaurant serving beautifully presented and often deliciously spicy dishes such as crab in coconut milk and palm oil (R$168) and prawn bobó (with manioc, nuts and coconut oil; R$110). Daily noon–11pm.

sol (sun-dried meat, served with sweet manioc; R$41.50), and *caldinho de feijão de corda* (bean soup with pork scratchings; R$6). Mon, Sat & Sun noon–6pm, Tues–Fri noon–10pm.

★Bar do Gomez (aka *Armazém São Thiago*) Rua Áurea, 26; map pp.240–241. Santa Teresa's best bar and Portuguese grocery, doing a roaring trade in red wine, *chopp* and *petiscos* (try the succulent *bolinhos de bacalhau*) to a friendly crowd of locals and visitors. On the Paulo Mattos bus and tram route. Mon–Sat noon–1am, Sun noon–10pm.

Bar do Mineiro Rua Paschoal Carlos Magno 99 ☎ 21 2221 9227, ⓦ bardomineiro.net; map pp.240–241. Inexpensive and authentic country-style food in an old bar that could be in any small town in Minas Gerais. Try the *carne seca abóbora* (dried meat in manioc purée; R$62), and there are also good beers and an excellent range of *cachaça*. Tues–Sun 11am–1am.

Sobrenatural Rua Almirante Alexandrino 432; map pp.240–241. Fairly pricey fish restaurant (*moquecas* and Amazonian fish dishes are the highlights; R$78 for two), but nearly always has great live music. Deliberately rustic decor and an inviting place for a leisurely meal. Daily 11am–11.30pm.

FLAMENGO, BOTAFOGO AND URCA

Adega Portugália Largo do Machado 66a, Catete ☎ 21 2558 2821; map pp.240–241. Don't miss out on the delicious house speciality at this popular bar/restaurant: casserole of tender roast goat (R$38.90), washed down with copious quantities of cold *chopp*. Daily 8am–2am.

Armazem do Chopp Rua Marquês de Abrantes 66, Flamengo ☎ 21 2225 1796, ⓦ armazemdochopp.com.br; map pp.240–241. Beer hall serving decent-quality food in large quantities. The terrace overlooks the street, and the *bolinhas de bacalhau* (saltfish croquette balls; R$23 for five) are an excellent accompaniment to an ice-cold glass of *chopp*. On Fridays in particular it tends to stay open late. Daily 11am–2am (or later).

Bar Urca Rua Cândido Gaffrée 205, Urca ☎ 21 2295 8744, ⓦ barurca.com.br; map pp.244–245. Traditional neighbourhood gathering-point, with a bar on the street and a restaurant upstairs, where daily specials include an excellent *feijoada* on Fridays (R$55), and low-priced *pratos executivos* (Mon–Fri till 3pm) include prawn risotto (R$40). Restaurant: Mon–Sat 11.30am–11pm, Sun 11.30am–8pm; bar: Mon–Fri 6.30am–11pm, Sat 8am–11pm, Sun 8am–8pm.

Tacacá do Norte Rua Barão do Flamengo 39, Flamengo ☎ 21 2205 7545; map pp.244–245. A *lanchonete* (cheap diner) with a difference: here you can try delights from the Amazon like the signature dish, *tacacá* (yellow shrimp and cassava hot pepper soup; R$17), and easily the best *açaí* in Rio, served with tapioca and granola (R$15). Mon–Sat 8.30am–11pm, Sun 9am–9pm.

Yorubá Rua Arnaldo Quintela 94, Botafogo ☎ 21 2541 9387; map pp.244–245. Friendly restaurant serving moderately priced Bahian cooking with strong African influences. Service is slow, but the *bobó* and *moquecas* are well worth the wait. Wed–Fri 7pm–midnight, Sat & Sun noon–7pm.

COPACABANA

Arab Av Atlântica 1936 ☎ 21 2235 1884; map pp.244–245. Reasonably priced Lebanese and North African restaurant, where you can enjoy *meze* (Lebanese hors d'oeuvres such as hummus or tabbouleh) at R$13 a portion, with main courses such as lamb couscous for R$44. Mon 5pm–1am, Tues–Sun 9am–1am.

★ **Bar do David** Ladeira Ari Barroso 66, *favela* Babilônia, Leme ☎ 21 7808 2200; map pp.244–245. Officially "pacified" *favelas* are slowly opening up to the business potential of tourism: chef David has received press accolades for excellent shrimp bobó, seafood croquettes, and at weekends his signature seafood *feijoada* – all at knockdown prices (R$12–25). Tues–Fri noon–5pm; Sat & Sun noon–9pm.

Big Nectar Av Nossa Senhora de Copacabana 985, at Xavier Silveira ☎ 21 2522 1354; map pp.244–245. A cut above the average *lanchonete* in Copa, serving pretty

decent steak or chicken combo dishes for R$10–15, and quality juices. Daily 24hr.

Caranguejo Rua Barata Ribeiro 771, at Rua Xavier da Silveira ☎ 21 2235 1249, ⓦ restauranteocaranguejo .com.br; map pp.244–245. Excellent street-corner seafood joint, where you can start with a dozen crab claws for R$29 before you tuck into a succulent prawn stroganoff (R$110). Daily 11am–2am.

Cervantes Av Prado do Júnior 335 (restaurant) and Rua Barata Ribeiro 7 (bar) 5 ☎ 21 335 2275-6147, ⓦ restaurantecervantes.com.br; map pp.244–245. Doing a roaring trade day and night, this restaurant/bar linked at the rear serves speciality thick-wedge meat sandwiches (steak with cheese and pineapple R$23). Tues–Sun noon–4am.

IPANEMA AND LEBLON

Casa da Feijoada Rua Prudente de Morais 10, Ipanema ☎ 21 2247 2776, ⓦ cozinhatipica.com.br; map pp.244–245. *Feijoada*, traditionally served only on Saturdays, is offered here seven days a week (R$78), along with other traditional, moderately priced and extremely filling Brazilian dishes. Daily noon–midnight.

Delírio Tropical Rua Garcia D'Ávila 48, Ipanema ☎ 21 3624 8164, ⓦ delirio.com.br; map pp.244–245. Just a block from the beach and the best value for lunch you'll find anywhere near it, with lots of veggie options such as salads (R$11.20–16.30) and vegetarian burgers (R$7.50), as well as light fish or meat options. Mon–Sat 11am–4pm, Sun in winter 11am–7pm, Sun in summer noon–8pm.

Fontes Galeria Astor, Rua Visconde de Pirajá 605 ☎ 21 2512 5900, ⓦ fontesipanema.com.br; map pp.244–245. Does inexpensive dishes made with only natural ingredients, including several vegetarian options. There's gnocchi made with manioc (R$11.45), and at weekends, a hearty *feijoada* is served – R$12 for the vegetable option, R$24 with meat. Mon–Sat 11am–9.45pm, Sun noon–8pm.

New Natural Rua Barão de Torre 167, Ipanema ☎ 21 2287 0301; map pp.244–245. Really good vegetarian *por quilo* lunch place (R$55/kg) that always has a couple of meat choices too. Expect numerous salads, soya dishes and fresh juices. Daily 7am–11pm.

Paz e Amor Rua Garcia D'Ávila 173, Ipanema ☎ 21 2523 0496, ⓦ restaurantepazeamor.com; map pp.244–245. One end of this Brazilian bar/restaurant serves the best-value *prato feito* set-plate for miles around. R$14.50 will buy you the bargain *carioquina comercial*, a filling heap of rice, beans and meat. Daily 10am–11pm.

Zazá Bistrô Tropical Rua Joana Angelica 40, Ipanema ☎ 21 2247 9101; map pp.244–245. Light-hearted, imaginative fusion cuisine, colourful decor and a terrace with a street-life view make this a popular spot with tourists and locals alike. There's a lunch menu for R$39, and à la carte dishes such as chicken curry in coconut milk for R$49 or flambéed scampi for R$65. Mon & Tues

7.30pm–12.30am, Wed & Thurs noon–12.30am, Fri noon–1.30am, Sat 1pm–1.30am, Sun 1pm–12.30am.

NIGHTLIFE

LIVE MUSIC

Lapa is Rio's nightlife heart and the undisputed capital of samba: every Friday night around Avenida Mem de Sá and Rua do Lavradio one of the world's biggest street parties takes place, with numerous bars offering the real deal. Despite Lapa's obvious appeal, be careful walking around after dark; if in doubt, take a taxi. Other currently popular outdoor (free) parties include samba at Pedra do Sal (off Rua Sacadura Cabral, nr Praça Mauá, Centro; Mon from 8pm), and street jazz at Praça Tiradentes, Centro (Thurs from 10.30pm). During rehearsals for Carnaval (Sept–Jan), don't miss a trip to a Samba School (see box, p.254).

Carioca da Gema Av Mem de Sá 79, Lapa ⓦ barcariocadagema.com.br; map pp.240–241. Samba bar-cum-pizzeria, this is a more upmarket but very fun place, especially lively on Monday and Friday nights. Daily from 6pm.

★**Centro Cultural Carioca** Rua do Teatro 37, Centro ⓦ centroculturalcarioca.com.br; map pp.240–241. For serious music lovers, this bar/dancehall offers a cross section of the best Brazilian music to a grown-up crowd. Thurs from 7pm, Fri & Sat from 10pm, Sun from 9pm.

Circo Voador Rua dos Arcos, Lapa ⓦ www.circovoador .com.br; map pp.240–241. Rap, funk and fusion samba-punk-rock in a large circus tent, with a young crowd who come to dance and discover new bands. Fri, Sat and sometimes other days, usually from 10pm.

Democráticos Rua do Riachuelo 93, Lapa ⓦ clubedosdemocraticos.com.br; map pp.240–241. Never short on atmosphere, this traditional *gafieira* (dance hall) has been going since 1867, with popular live *forró* (Wed) and usually samba other nights. Wed–Sat 10pm–late.

Feira Nordestina Campo de São Cristovão, São Cristovão (near Quinta da Boa Vista) ⓦ feiradesaocristovao.org.br. A 48hr non-stop party in a stadium every weekend might sound far-fetched, but exactly that has been hosted here for decades. *Forró*, funk and reggae for the Zona Norte and Northeastern Brazilian masses, with food and crafts stalls. Popular in the early hours post-clubbing. Tues–Thurs 10am–6pm, Fri 10am–Sun 9pm.

Semente Rua Joaquim Silva 138, Lapa ⓦ barsemente .com.br; map pp.240–241. A small bohemian bar, but also one of Rio's hottest music spots, where some of the biggest current names in samba cut their teeth. Daily from 9.30pm.

NIGHTCLUBS

Rio's vibrant club scene offers a music mix from pop and rock to hip-hop and *funk* Carioca, as well as superb Brazilian electronica, samba and MPB (*Música Popular*

Brasileira). Most places don't get going until midnight; entry fees R$20–60.

★**Casa da Matriz** Rua Henrique Novaes 107, Botafogo ⓦ casadamatriz.com.br; map pp.244–245. Stylish and perennially popular club with different music each night, from rock to reggae and samba to drum 'n' bass.

Castelo das Pedras Estrada de Jacarepaguá 3600, Favela Rio das Pedras, Jacarepaguá ⓦ castelodaspedras.com.br; map pp.244–245. Rio's premier *funk Carioca* venue, with 3000-strong crowds of sweating, gyrating bodies. Fri–Sun from 11pm.

Club Six Rua das Marrecas 38, Lapa ⓦ clubsix.com.br; map pp.240–241. Three dancefloors featuring anything from reggae, trance or hip-hop to old-school Brazilian sounds such as *forró* and *zouk*, depending on the night. Thurs–Sat from 10pm.

Comuna Rua Sorocaba 585, Botafogo ⓦ comuna.cc; map pp.244–245. A split personality of electronica parties, art exhibitions, film screenings and even food makes this warehouse-style space a truly communal entertainment centre. Tues–Sun 6pm–2am.

Espaço Acústica Praça Tiradentes 2, Centro ⓦ espacoacustica.com.br; map pp.240–241. Helping along the resurgence of one of Rio's most historic central squares, this is a hip yet unpretentious place to catch some of the best DJ talent in town. Electro/pop/rock/Brazilian mash-up. Fri & Sat from 10pm.

Fosfobox Rua Siqueira Campos 143, Copacabana ⓦ fosfobox.com.br; map pp.244–245. This small, highly rated and long-standing basement club plays underground techno and alternative music for an animated crowd. Brazil's best DJs often pass through. Thurs–Sun from 11pm.

Zero Zero Av Padre Leonel Franca 240 (in the grounds of Gavéa planetarium), Gávea ⓦ 00site.com.br; map pp.244–245. A trendy club frequented by a wealthy but music-loving crowd. Some of Brazil's top DJs play an eclectic mix. Sunday draws a gay crowd. Tues–Thurs from 10pm, Fri & Sat from 9pm, Sun from 6.30pm.

GAY AND LESBIAN

Rio has one of the world's liveliest gay scenes, though you may be surprised that many venues are "GLS" ("gay, lesbian and sympathizers") with clubbers of all persuasions hanging out – for example, at *Fosfobox* and *Zero Zero* (see above). Gay Pride takes place in Copacabana each September; the wildest weekend on the Gay Rio calendar. For up-to-date information check out ⓦ timeout.com.br/ rio-de-janeiro/en/gay-lesbian.

Le Boy Rua Raul Pompéia 102, Copacabana ⓦ leboy .com.br; map pp.244–245. Based in a former cinema, this huge gay men's club has three dancefloors, drag shows and much more besides. Daily from 11pm.

Casa da Lua Rua Barão da Torre 240, Ipanema ☎ 21 3813 3972; map pp.244–245. A low-key lesbian bar and

3

SAMBA

From September to February the ultimate highlight of Rio's nightlife is a visit to a **samba school**, when the emphasis is as much on raising funds for their extravagant Carnaval parade (see p.237) as it is on perfecting routines. Expect drummers and dancers en masse, and thousands of hyped-up revellers. There are many schools, of which a few are listed here; each has its own weekly programme. Check the websites and keep your ear to the ground.

SAMBA SCHOOLS

Beija-Flor Rua Pracinha Wallace Paes Leme 1652, Nilopolis ☎21 2247 4800, ⓦbeija-flor.com.br. Founded in 1948, their colours are blue and white; champions in 2003, 2004, 2005, 2007, 2008 and 2011.

Mangueira Rua Visconde de Niterói 1072, Mangueira ☎21 2567 3419, ⓦmangueira.com.br. The largest and most famous school; weekend events attract many tour groups – so nights out here, while fun, sometimes lack a traditional feel.

Portela Rua Clara Nunes 81, Oswaldo Cruz ☎21 2489 6440, ⓦgresportela.com.br. Thought of as a highly traditional school, with *feijoadas* (usually first Sat of the month), but haven't won since 1984.

Salgueiro Rua Silva Telles 104, Andaraí ☎21 2238 9226, ⓦsalgueiro.com.br. Most recently champions in 2009. Easily accessed from the Zona Sul and events here are often a great night out.

Unidos da Tijuca Clube dos Portuários, Av Francisco Bicalho 47, São Cristovão ☎21 2263 9679, ⓦunidosdatijuca.com.br. Carnaval champions 2010, 2012 and 2014; popular with a gay and straight crowd.

---

restaurant known for its *batidas* (*cachaça* and fruit juice cocktails). Tues–Sun 11.30am–3.30pm & 5pm–2am.

Cine Ideal Rua Carioca 64, Centro ☎21 2221 1984, ⓦcineideal.com.br; map pp.240–241. This young and often-wild GLS club in a former cinema calls itself "the temple of house music". Open-air terrace and mezzanine, as well as an open bar, and a crowd eager for *beijos* (kisses). Fri & Sat from 11.30pm.

Galeria Café Rua Teixeira de Melo 31, Ipanema ☎21 2523 8250, ⓦgaleriacafe.com.br; map pp.244–245. Spinning an original music mix from old classics like Chico Buarque to self-styled drum 'n' bossa, this small artistic venue also has theatre and art exhibitions, as well as Sunday's long-standing Café Bazar (noon–9pm) featuring fashion shows and music. Otherwise open Wed–Sat from midnight.

DIRECTORY

Banks and exchange Banks are located throughout the city, and especially along Av Rio Branco in Centro. Banco do Brasil is best for foreign cards.

Car rental Most agents are located along Av Princesa Isabel in Copacabana. Avis (☎0800 725 2847); Hertz (☎0800 701 7300); Localiza-National (☎0800 979 2000).

Consulates Argentina, Praia de Botafogo 228 (☎21 2553 1646); Australia, Av Presidente Wilson 231, Centro (☎21 3824 4624); Canada, Av Atlantica 1130, Copacabana (☎21 2543 3004); UK, Praia do Flamengo 284, Flamengo (☎21 2555 9600); US, Av Presidente Wilson 147, Centro (☎21 3823 2000).

Hospitals Private hospitals with good reputations include Hospital Samaritano, Rua Bambina 98, Botafogo (☎21 2537 9722, ⓦhsamaritano.com.br), and Hospital

Copa d'Or, Rua Figueiredo de Magalhães 875, Copacabana (☎21 2545 3600, ⓦcopador.com.br).

Police Emergency number ☎190. The beach areas have police posts at regular intervals. The efficient, English-speaking Tourist Police are at Av Afrânio de Melo Franco (opposite the Teatro Casa Grande), Leblon (☎21 3399 7170).

Post office Central branch on Rua 1 de Março (Mon–Fri 9am–5pm).

Shopping Rio is replete with high-class shopping malls and designer stores. Budget shoppers, however, should head to Saara (see p.238) or the Hippie Fair market held every Sunday at Praça General Osório in Ipanema, with souvenirs, street shows and typical foods. For handicrafts check out Brasil & Cia, at Rua Maria Quitéria 27 in Ipanema (☎21 2267 4603, ⓦbrasilecia.com.br).

Visas Apply at the Polícia Federal's Registro de Estrangeiros at Galeão Airport, 3rd floor, Terminal 1, Sector A (Mon–Fri 10am–4pm; ☎21 3398 3182, ⓦdpf.gov.br).

Rio de Janeiro state

Though many travellers dash through the state in order to reach its glorious capital city, there are enough regional attractions to more than reward visitors. Either side of Rio lie two idyllic sections of coast. To the east beyond Rio's neighbouring city **Niterói** is the **Costa do Sol**, an area of gorgeous white beaches peppered with a string of low-key resort towns and three large **lakes**. The trendy and commercial resort town of **Búzios** is popular with the affluent but less of a draw for budget travellers, while nearby **Arraial do Cabo** offers a slice of beach paradise. To the south of Rio is one of Brazil's most magnificent landscapes, the **Costa Verde**, dotted with charming resort towns and blessed with dreamy stretches of deserted beach. The colonial town of **Paraty** is one of the region's highlights, while **Ilha Grande**'s verdant forests create a stunning unspoilt setting. The mountainous wooded landscape and relatively cool climate of the state's interior make a refreshing change from the coastal heat. Immediately to the north of Rio, high in mist-cloaked mountains, lies the imperial city of **Petrópolis**, with the magnificent **Parque Nacional Serra dos Orgãos** nearby. In the far west lies another breathtaking protected area, the **Parque Nacional Itatiaia**.

NITERÓI

Cariocas have a tendency to sneer at **NITERÓI**, typically commenting that the best thing about the city is the view back across Guanabara Bay to Rio. The vistas are undeniably gorgeous, but there are a few things to see too – without the need to stay overnight.

WHAT TO SEE AND DO

The Oscar Niemeyer-designed **Museu de Arte Contemporânea** (MAC; Tues–Sun 10am–6pm; R$10; ⓦmacniteroi.com.br) is Niterói's biggest draw. Opened in 1996 and located just south of the centre on a promontory, the spaceship-like building offers breathtaking 360-degree views of the bay and a worthy, though hardly exciting, permanent display of Brazilian art from the 1950s to the 1990s, plus temporary exhibitions. But the real work of art is the building: trademark Niemeyer curves which even his most hardened critics find difficult to dismiss.

Beautiful **Praia de Icaraí** lies near the city's centre, but as the water in the bay is none too clean, take a bus to **Camboinhas** or **Itacoatiara**, long stretches of sand every bit as good as Rio's Zona Sul.

ARRIVAL AND INFORMATION

By bus Services from N.S. de Copacabana and Largo do Machado, via the 14km Rio–Niterói bridge, take you into the centre of Niterói; MAC and the Icaraí neighbourhood are a further bus journey (numerous services; look on front of bus) or a 30min walk.

By ferry The best way to get to Niterói is by ferry (see p.249). MAC is just 1.5km from the ferry terminal; you pass the Universidade Federal Fluminense en route.

Tourist office Estrada Leopoldo Fróes 773, São Francisco (ⓣ0800 282 7755, ⓦniteroiturismo.com.br), with a kiosk by the ferry terminal.

EATING

There are plenty of cheap eating places in the backstreets of central Niterói.

Da Carmine Rua Mariz e Barros 305, Icaraí ⓣ21 3617 6109, ⓦdacarmine.com.br. Serves the city's best pizzas by far, and, though most cheap, offers cheap "executive lunches" weekdays until 4pm. Tues–Sun noon–4pm & 6–11.30pm, Mon 6–11.30pm.

★**Mercado de Peixe São Pedro** Av Visconde do Rio Branco 55. This fish market, a 5min walk north from the ferry terminal, has some forty fish restaurants upstairs. Expect to pay around R$25–50 per head. Tues–Fri 6am–4pm, Sat & Sun 6am–noon.

BÚZIOS

The most famous resort on the Costa do Sol, a sandy stretch of coast east of Rio, "discovered" by Brigitte Bardot in 1964 and nicknamed "Brazil's St Tropez", is Armação dos Búzios, or **BÚZIOS** as it's commonly known. A former whaling town, it's now cashing in on the upscale tourist market. Bardot described the sea here as "foaming like blue champagne", and the seafront promenade, the **Orla Bardot**, now bears a statue of her in homage. From December to February the population swells from 20,000 to 150,000, and boats take pleasure-seekers island hopping and scuba diving along the very beautiful coastline. If a crowded 24-hour resort full of high-spending beautiful people and buzzing nightclubs is your thing then you're sure to fall for Búzios; if not, give it a miss – at least in high season.

ARRIVAL AND INFORMATION

By bus Direct buses from Rio (3hr) run eight times a day, arriving at the *rodoviária* on Estrada da Usina Velha.

3

Tourist information The helpful tourist office is on Travessa dos Pescadores, just off Praça Santos Dumont (☎ 22 2633 6200, ⓦ buzios.com.br).

ACCOMMODATION

Búzios Central Hostel Av José Bento Ribeiro Dantas 1475 ☎ 22 2623 2329, ⓦ buzioscentral.com.br. An HI-affiliated hostel with attractive gardens and a plunge pool. Dorms are a little cramped but reasonable, and small doubles the cheapest you'll get in town. Dorms R$60, doubles R$118

El Misti Yellow Rua de Mandrágora 15, off Av José Bento Ribeiro Dantas, 1km southeast of central Armação ☎ 22 2623 3174, ⓦ elmistihostelbuzios.com. It's a bit of a walk to the beach from this hostel, but the company here is congenial and there's even a small pool. Dorms R$29, doubles R$159

EATING, DRINKING AND NIGHTLIFE

Restaurants in Búzios are, predictably, expensive; cheaper options include the grilled fish stalls on the beaches and numerous pizza places in outlying parts of town.

Bananaland Rua Manoel Turíbio de Farias 50 ☎ 22 2623 2666, ⓦ restaurantebananaland.com.br. On a street parallel to Rua das Pedras, this is one of the best *por kilo* restaurants in Búzios (R$67.50/kg), and one of the cheapest for a solid meal. Mon–Fri & Sun 11.30am–10.30pm, Sat 11.30am–11.30pm.

Chez Michou Crêperie Rua das Pedras 90 ☎ 22 2623 2169, ⓦ chezmichou.com.br. Thanks to its open-air bar, cheap drinks and imaginative crêpes (*doce de leite* crêpe R$12, chicken curry crêpe R$15), this has long been Armação's most popular hangout. Open until dawn, when it serves breakfast to the patrons pouring out of the nearby clubs. Daily noon–around 6am.

Pacha Búzios Rua das Pedras 151 ☎ 22 2292 9606, ⓦ pachabuzios.com. The venue of choice for trendy clubbers, Ibiza-based *Pacha* has helped bring Balearic glitz and top-name DJs to Búzios; entry from R$44. Fri & Sat from 10pm.

Privilège Av José Bento Ribeiro Dantas 550 ☎ 22 2623 8585, ⓦ privilegenet.com.br. Despite *Pacha's* rise as venue of choice in the last few years, *Privilège* is still the town's biggest club, and has a great party atmosphere. Half the entry price is redeemable as drinks; entry R$100 for men, R$70 for women. Thurs–Sat from 10pm.

Sawasdee Av José Bento Ribeiro Dantas 422 ⓦ sawasdee .com.br. Excellent spicy Thai food, based around vegetables and seafood – one of the best creations is "Khao Tom", a delicious spicy shellfish risotto (R$65). Daily except Wed 7pm–midnight.

ARRAIAL DO CABO

Tipped by those in the know to have the best beaches east of Rio, the small fishing town of **ARRAIAL DO CABO** has many of the attractions of Búzios, 40km northeast, but without the crowds, nightlife and price tag. The draw here is relaxing on a stunning peninsula between sea, sand dune and lagoon, with beaches like the 23km **Praia Grande** and smaller turquoise gems **Praia do Forno** (for snorkelling), **Prainha da Pontal** and **Praia Brava** (for surfing). All have a rich marine life and excellent diving. Boat trips are available to the beaches of nearby **Ilha do Farol** and the aptly named **Grotto Azul** (Blue Grotto), a cavern famous for its deep blue water.

ARRIVAL AND DEPARTURE

By bus Direct buses leave Rio (daily every 2hr, with a couple extra in the morning and early evening; 3hr 5min). Frequent buses also ply the route from Arraial do Cabo to neighbouring Cabo Frio (14km), where you can pick up buses to Búzios.

ACCOMMODATION

Marina dos Anjos Rua Bernardo Lens 145 ☎ 22 2622 4060, ⓦ marinadosanjos.com.br. Drawing Brazilians from Rio and Minas Gerais for the easy-going beach life, this HI hostel is pleasingly social with great communal areas. Dorms R$65, doubles R$184

ILHA GRANDE

ILHA GRANDE comprises 193 square kilometres of mountainous jungle, historic ruins and beautiful beaches, excellent for some scenic tropical rambling. The entire island, lying about 150km southwest of Rio, is a state park with limits on building development and a ban on motor vehicles.

★ **TREAT YOURSELF**

Hibiscus Beach Hotel Rua 1 No. 22, Quadra C. Praia de João Fernandes ☎ 22 2623 6221, ⓦ hibiscusbeach.com.br. Gorgeous bungalows, each with a small terrace and wonderful sea views, at this welcoming, British-owned pousada with a good-sized pool in a flower-filled garden. The area's best snorkelling beach is just seconds away. R$296

WHAT TO SEE AND DO

Ilha Grande offers lots of beautiful **walks** along well-maintained and fairly well-signposted trails. As you approach the low-lying, whitewashed colonial port of **Vila do Abraão**, you'll see the mountains rise dramatically from the sea, and in the distance there's the curiously shaped summit of **Bico do Papagaio** ("Parrot's Beak"), which ascends to a height of 980m. There's little to see in Abraão itself, but it's a pleasant base from which to explore the island. A thirty-minute walk along the coast west are the ruins of the **Antigo Presídio**, a former prison for political prisoners that was dynamited in the early 1960s. Among the ruins you'll find the *cafofo*, the containment centre where prisoners who had failed in escape attempts were immersed in freezing water. Just fifteen minutes inland from Abraão, overgrown with vegetation, stands the **Antigo Aqueduto**, which used to channel the island's water supply. There's a fine view of the aqueduct from the **Pedra Mirante**, a hill near the centre of the island; close by, a waterfall provides the opportunity to cool off.

For the most part the **beaches** – Aventureiro, Lopes Mendes, Canto, Júlia and Morcegoare, to name a few – are wild, unspoilt and most easily reached by boat, though most have some basic accommodation or campsites. Araçatiba is home to a sizeable village, accessed by boat direct from Angra dos Reis on the mainland.

ARRIVAL AND INFORMATION

By bus Three daily buses from Rio's *rodoviária* connect with boats from the ferry ports at Mangaratiba, Angra dos Reis and Conceição de Jacarei (total journey time 4hr 30min).

By ferry CCR Barcas (ⓦ grupoccr.com.br/barcas) run ferries to Ilha Grande's Vila do Abraão from Mangaratiba (daily 8am, Fri also 10pm, returning daily 5.30pm; 80min; R$4.80) and Angra dos Reis (Mon–Fri 3.30pm, Sat & Sun 1.30pm, returning daily 10am; R$4.80). Private boats also do the crossing to the island, especially from Angra (R$25).

Tourist information There is a tourist office in Angra dos Reis at Av Ayrton Senna (ⓣ 24 3369 7704) and in the ferry

terminal, but not on the island itself. Online try ⓦ ilhagrande .org. Bring plenty of cash: there's no ATM, nowhere to change money and few places accept credit cards. The Elite Dive Center (ⓣ 24 3361 5501, ⓦ elitedivecenter.com.br) is the only PADI-registered dive centre on the island.

ACCOMMODATION

There are some great pousadas all over Ilha Grande, though Abraão has the largest choice (generally mid-priced). Reservations are essential in the high season, but prices may be halved off-season. When you arrive you'll probably be approached by youths intent on taking you to a room in a private house (around R$50/person). Camping at a designated site is a decent alternative (R$50–75/person). Abraão has a number of basic campsites (ask at the jetty) while nearby Praia das Palmas is a more scenic alternative: ⓦ campingparaiso .com and ⓦ campingflorestinha.com.br both have facilities, including a restaurant and kitchen. For the more adventurous, try one of the tiny campsites at stunning and secluded Praia do Aventureiro on the island's southwest coast.

Holandês Rua do Assembléia, Abraão ⓣ 24 3361 5034, ⓦ holandeshostel.com.br. Always popular, this trendy HI hostel is behind the beach next to the Assembléia de Deus. Accommodation in dorms or lovely chalets (which sleep up to 3) in lush gardens. Dorms R$65, chalets R$180

★ **Lagamar** Praia Grande de Araçatiba ⓣ 24 9978 4569, ⓦ pousadalagamar.com.br. Superb-value pousada surrounded by lush jungle in a quiet fishing hamlet at the island's western end. Generous seafood dinners and large breakfast are included. Boat available direct from Angra. R$180

Oásis Praia do Canto, Abraão ⓣ 24 3361 5549, ⓦ oasis .ilhagrande.org. Cosy and friendly, this is one of the nicest pousadas on the island, with unpretentious and simply furnished rooms. It's located at the far end of the beach, a 10min walk from the jetty. R$160

EATING

Café do Mar Praia do Abraão ⓣ 21 3361 9446. A great little bar and beach restaurant serving up the day's catch in various formats, notably with coconut or mango sauce (R$32). For those in need of a wake-up, they do a nice espresso too, but they're best known for their thrice-weekly barbecues (Mon, Wed & Sat 7.30pm). Mon–Thurs, Sat & Sun 10am–midnight.

Rei dos Caldos Rua Santana, Abraão ⓣ 24 3361 5511. A good fish restaurant that specializes, as its name suggests, in soups – in starter size (R$8–9) or meal size (R$6–18) – giant crab (*siri*) being the house speciality. To follow, if you still have room, fish in passion-fruit sauce goes down a treat at R$70 between two. Mon, Tues & Thurs–Sun noon–10pm.

3

PARQUE NACIONAL DO ITATIAIA

On the border with Minas Gerais, 167km west of Rio, the **Parque Nacional do Itatiaia** takes its unusual name from an Indian word meaning "rocks with sharp edges". Holding the distinction of being Brazil's first national park (1937), it's incredibly varied, from dense Atlantic forest in the foothills, through to treeless, grassy summits. The park's loftiest peak, **Agulhas-Negras**, is the second highest in Brazil, at 2789m.

There's no shortage of **walking trails** here, as well as a couple of two-day walks for serious hikers. The better, but more difficult, of the two is the Jeep Trail, which scales the valley and ultimately reaches the peak of Agulhas-Negras. The other is the Tres Picos Trail – easier, but care should still be taken as the path becomes narrow and slippery as it rises. A **guide** is recommended for both trails (available from hotels within the park) and essential for the Jeep Trail, for which you should seek prior permission from the IBAMA office at the park entrance. Itatiaia is also a popular **birdwatching** destination, thanks to its varied terrain and flora: highland species present in the park include the Itatiaia spinetail – a small, brownish, skulking bird that occurs only in this range of mountains.

ARRIVAL AND INFORMATION

By bus Access to the park is via the town of Itatiaia – buses between Rio and São Paulo stop here. Local buses (30min) run from the footbridge in Itatiaia, a short walk from the *rodoviária*, to the park visitors' centre. Staying in the town of Itatiaia is the cheapest way to visit, despite the 30min bus ride. Penedo offers alternative accommodation but is further away, served by local buses roughly hourly (20min).

ACCOMMODATION

Rio das Pedras Rua Resende, Penedo 39 ☎ 24 3351 1019, ⓦ hotelriodaspedras.com.br. A quiet place by a river (the "Rio das Pedras" of its name), where you can stay in a room with a veranda or in a pretty little alpine-style chalet in the grounds. Two day minimum-stay at weekends. R$100

PARATY AND AROUND

PARATY, 236km from Rio along the BR-101, is the Costa Verde's main attraction, and rightly so. Inhabited since 1650, Paraty remains much as it was in its heyday as a staging post for the eighteenth-century trade in Brazilian gold. Today, UNESCO considers the city one of the world's most important examples of Portuguese colonial architecture, with all the narrow cobbled streets and churches you'd imagine, and it has been named a national monument. Besides the town's charmingly relaxed atmosphere, the main draws are its great restaurants and bars, and stunning surrounding scenery, from rainforest and waterfalls to hidden coves, islands and **beaches**. Paraty really comes alive for its annual Literary Festival ("FLIP"; ⓦflip.org .br) in July or August, which in past years has drawn such figures as Tom Stoppard and Brazil's own Chico Buarque; book accommodation well in advance for this.

WHAT TO SEE AND DO

One of Brazil's first planned urban projects, Paraty's centre is a warren of narrow, pedestrianized cobbled streets bordered by houses built around quaint courtyards. The cobbles of the streets are arranged in channels to drain off storm water and allow the sea to enter and wash the streets at high tides.

Churches

Paraty's **churches** traditionally each served a different sector of the population. **Nossa Senhora dos Remédios** (daily 9am–5pm), on the Praça da Matriz, is the town's most imposing building. Originally built on the site in 1668, the current construction dates from 1873 with building having begun 84 years earlier. Along Rua do Comércio is the smallest church, the **Igreja do Rosário** (Mon–Fri 9am–5pm), once used by slaves, while at the southern edge of the town, the Portuguese Baroque **Igreja de Santa Rita** (Mon–Fri 10am–noon & 1–5pm) served freed *mulattos* and dates from 1722. The oldest and most architecturally significant of the town's churches, it now houses the **Museu de Arte Sacra de Paraty**, with religious artefacts from all of the town's churches.

Beaches and islands

From the **Praia do Pontal**, across the Perequé-Açu River from town, and from the port quay, boats leave for the **beaches** of Parati-Mirim, Iririguaçu – known for its waterfalls – Lula and Conceição. In fact, there are 65 islands and about two hundred beaches to choose from – ask around for the current favourites. Hotels and travel agents sell tickets for trips out to the islands, typically for around R$50 per person, leaving Paraty at noon, stopping at three or four islands, giving time for a swim, and returning at 6pm. For a short **hike**, walk the trail to perfect **Praia do Sono**, 12km southwest of town.

Beyond Praia do Sono (21km from Paraty) and reached by a steep winding road is the village of **Trindade** (17 daily buses; 45min). Sandwiched between the ocean and Serra do Mar, it's crammed with backpackers and trippers in peak season, camping on the beaches or staying in one of numerous pousada/ hostels. Famed for its **beaches**, the best are across the rocky outcrops to **Praia Brava** and **Praia do Meio**, some of the most attractive mainland beaches on this stretch of coast, and completely unspoilt.

ARRIVAL AND INFORMATION

By bus The *rodoviária* is about 0.5km from the old town on Rua Jango de Padúa.

Destinations Angra dos Reis for Ilha Grande (roughly hourly; 2hr); Rio (13 daily; 4hr 30min); São Paulo (5 daily; 5hr); Trindade (17 daily; 45min); Ubatuba (6 daily; 2hr).

Tourist information On the corner of Rua Costa and Rua do Comércio opposite the Igreja do Rosário (daily 8am–7pm; ☎24 3371 1222).

ACCOMMODATION

Casa do Rio Hostel Rua Antonio Vidal 120 ☎24 3371 2223, ⓦparatyhostel.com. A well-organized HI hostel with a large communal area, social vibe and a variety of dorms – compare a couple before choosing. Helpful staff and tours on offer. Dorms R$50, doubles R$150

★**Pousada Guaraná** Rua Cinco 13, Portal de Paraty ☎24 3371 6362, ⓦpousadaguarana.com.br. An artistic, spacious and very good-value pousada 10min from the Centro Histórico. Superb breakfast, free use of bicycles, a pool, plant-filled garden, soft music and attention to detail all make this an ideal choice. R$250

Solar dos Gerânios Praça da Matriz ☎24 3371 1550. Beautiful Swiss-Brazilian-owned place filled with rustic furniture and curios. Rooms are spartan but impeccable, most have a balcony and all are en suite. Great value. Reservations advised; request a room overlooking the *praça*. R$150

EATING AND DRINKING

Camoka Praça da Bandeira 3 ☎24 3371 1063. Between the pier and Santa Rita church, genial owner Marcão has found a business niche in inexpensive eats (try the baked *escondidinha* pie, or *torta vegetarian*) and good beer served until late at night. Tues–Sun noon–midnight.

★**Istanbul** Rua Manuel Torres, Shopping Colonial ☎24 9974 9638. Home-cooked Turkish kebabs (R$12) as well as falafel and choice of teas at this friendly and great-value snack bar with tables upstairs, just across from the bus station. Tues–Sat noon–9pm.

Sabor da Terra Av Roberto Silveira 180 ☎24 3371 2384, ⓦparaty.com.br/sabordaterra. Paraty's best *por kilo* restaurant (R$36.80/kg), offering a wide variety of inexpensive hot and cold dishes that include a choice of grilled meats. Daily 10am–10pm.

PETRÓPOLIS

Some 66km to the north of Rio, high in the mountains, stands the imperial city of **PETRÓPOLIS**, so named because in the nineteenth century Emperor Dom Pedro II had a summer palace built here, rapidly making the place a popular retreat for Brazilian aristocracy. En route the scenery is dramatic, climbing among forested slopes that suddenly give way to ravines and gullies, while clouds shroud the surrounding peaks. You can easily tour Petrópolis in a day – its cultural attractions and stunning setting make it well worth the trip.

WHAT TO SEE AND DO

The **Palácio Imperial** on Rua da Imperatriz (Tues–Sun 11am–6pm; R$8; ⓦmuseuimperial.gov.br) is a grandiose colonial structure, set in beautifully maintained gardens. Upon entry, you're given felt overshoes with which to slide around the polished floors of this royal residence, and inside there's everything from Dom Pedro II's crown to the regal commode. The cathedral of **São Pedro de Alcântara** (Tues–Sun 8am–6pm)

3

blends with the surrounding architecture, but is much more recent than its neo-Gothic style suggests – it was finished in 1939. Inside lie the tombs of Dom Pedro himself and several royal personages.

The town's most recognizable building is the **Palácio de Cristal** (Tues–Sun 9am–6pm) on Rua Alfredo Pachá, essentially a greenhouse erected for the local horticultural society in 1879, though competing for the honour is the alpine chalet **Casa Santos Dumont** (Tues–Sun 9.30am–5pm; R$5), which is well worth visiting for the collection of the personal oddments of the famous aviator.

ARRIVAL AND INFORMATION

By bus Buses leave Rio for Petrópolis every 40min (journey time 90min) – sit on the left side of the bus for best views – arriving at the *rodoviária* on Rua Dr Porciúncula, from where it's a further 10km by local bus into town.

Tourist information Praça da Liberdade (daily 8.30am–5.30pm; ☎0800 024 1516). Other branches (same hours) at the *rodoviária* and Palácio de Cristal.

ACCOMMODATION

There are a few reasonable options in town, though most are very classy former colonial mansions.

Albergue Quitandinha Rua Uruguai 570 ☎24 2247 9165, ⓦalberguequitandinha.com.br. Ten rooms and a dorm within wooden cabins, a bus ride from the Centro Historico. **R$140**

Comércio Rua Dr Porciúncula 55 ☎24 2242 3500. One of the cheapest options in town, though by no means a bargain. Rooms without a bathroom are cheapest. **R$100**

Pousada 14 Bis Rua Buenos Aires 192 ☎24 2231 0946, ⓦwww.pousada14bis.com.br. A themed pousada based on the life of aviator Santos Dumont. Rooms are nothing flashy, but decorated in attractive colonial style. **R$180**

EATING

Restaurants are surprisingly lacklustre in Petrópolis, most of the best being some distance from town.

PARQUE NACIONAL SERRA DOS ORGÃOS

The **Parque Nacional Serra dos Orgãos** is breathtakingly beautiful and refreshingly easy to visit from Petrópolis's less attractive neighbour, **Teresópolis**. The park is dominated in its lower reaches by lush Atlantic forest, with bare mountain peaks emerging from the trees to create a stunning effect against the backdrop of a clear blue sky. It is these peaks that give the park its name, the rocks reminding the early Portuguese explorers of the pipes of cathedral organs.

There are a number of **walking trails** in the park, most of them short, easily accessible and suitable for people who like their hiking easy, though all have uphill stretches. Many of the park's most recognizable landmarks are visible on the horizon from Teresópolis. The most famous of all is the **Dedo de Deus** (Finger of God) – a bare, rocky pinnacle that points skyward – while arguably more picturesque is the **Cachoeira Véu da Noiva** waterfall. The longest and most challenging trail is the **Pedra do Sino** (Stone Bell), starting some distance from the park entrance, passing the bell-shaped rock formation (at 2263m the park's highest point) and emerging some 30km further on (close to the town of Petrópolis) – a guide is strongly recommended.

ARRIVAL AND INFORMATION

By bus Buses to Teresópolis run from Rio (hourly) and Petrópolis (7 daily), arriving at the *rodoviária* on Rua 1 de Maio. Teresópolis is located right at the edge of the park, the entrance being just to the south of town (head towards the Dedo de Deus).

Tourist information Praça Olimpica (Mon–Fri 9am–5pm, Sat 10am–3pm; ☎21 2742 5561). The park office at the entrance (daily 8am–5pm) rents out camping equipment and can provide information on local guides. There is a R$25 entrance charge.

ACCOMMODATION AND EATING

If you're not camping or walking to Petrópolis, you'll probably want to base yourself in Teresópolis, where there are a couple of reasonable accommodation options. There are plenty of *por kilo* lunch places.

Recanto do Lord Rua Luiza Pereira Soares 109 ☎21 2742 5586, ⓦteresopolishostel.com.br. It's a steep climb to reach this well-equipped youth hostel (the house numbers go up to 300, and then start again before reaching 109), but you do get great views to compensate. Dorms **R$35**, doubles **R$80**

Várzea Palace Hotel Rua Sebastião Teixeira 41 ☎21 2742 0878. Once the most elegant place in town to stay, only faint traces of its former luxury remain, but it's clean, welcoming and good value, with discounts midweek. **R$130**

Armazem 646 Rua Visconde de Itaboraí 646 ☎ 24 2243 1001, ⓦ armazem646.com.br. Welcoming bar-restaurant with live music most nights and a varied menu of meat and fish that will suit most tastes. Try *camarão com catupiry*. Daily noon–last customer.

Bordeaux Rua Ipiranga 716 ☎ 24 2242 5711, ⓦ bordeauxvinhos.com.br. In the converted stables of a stately home, moderately priced Italian- and French-influenced offerings include smoked local trout to start (R$29.90) with solid meat dishes such as steak *au poivre* (R$44.90) to complement the excellent wine list. Daily noon–midnight.

Casa d'Angelo Rua do Imperador 700 ☎ 24 2242 0888, ⓦ casadangelo.com.br. A *chopperia* (beer bar) and restaurant, slap-bang in the centre of town. Lunchtime *pratos executivos* (till 4pm) go for R$14.90, or you can tuck into a supper-time stroganoff for R$28, and of course wash it down with an ice-cold glass of *chopp*. Daily 8am–midnight.

Rink Marowil Praca da Liberdade 27 ☎ 24 2243 0743. Reasonably priced restaurant right on the square. The food is nothing to write home about but you'll struggle to find better value for money. At night it functions as a bar with food. Daily 8am–11.30am.

Minas Gerais

Explorers flocked to **MINAS GERAIS** following the discovery of gold in 1693, and with the unearthing of diamonds and other gemstones the state has been exploited for these abundant natural resources ever since. For a hundred years the region was by far the wealthiest in Brazil, but as the gold reserves became exhausted so Minas Gerais declined, and by the mid-nineteenth century it was a backwater. Coffee in part served to stem the decline, and alongside extraction of workaday minerals like iron ore it continues to sustain much of the region today. Visitors flock here, too, enjoying a series of startlingly beautiful towns left behind by the boom.

Minas Gerais's **CIDADES HISTÓRICAS** started life as mining camps, as rough and basic as imagination can make them. But the wealth of the surrounding mountains transformed them, and today they are considered to be among the most beautiful cities in the Americas, with cobbled streets and alleyways, glorious churches encrusted in gold – built in the over-the-top local version of Baroque architecture *Barroco Mineiro* – and beautifully preserved colonial buildings. And all of this is set in an area of rugged natural beauty, with a few towns connected by historic trains.

Ouro Preto and **Diamantina** are both UNESCO World Heritage Sites and are the best places for budget travellers to base themselves; **Tiradentes** is pricier though barely less impressive, with attractive and affordable **São João del Rei** worth a brief visit nearby.

BELO HORIZONTE

Founded in 1893 and the first of Brazil's planned cities, **BELO HORIZONTE** is the booming capital of Minas Gerais. The third-largest urban area in Brazil may at first appear daunting and uninspired, but what this cosmopolitan metropolis lacks in aesthetics it makes up for in some eclectic architecture, enticing museums and superb food.

WHAT TO SEE AND DO

For all its size, the centre of Belo Horizonte is fairly easy to explore on foot. Heading south from the *rodoviária*, walk to Praça Raul Soares and then take Rua dos Guajajaras for the bustling **Mercado Central** (Mon–Sat 7am–6pm, Sun 7am–1pm), which has more than four hundred stalls and restaurants selling anything from cheeses to bamboo artefacts and bric-a-brac.

If you are in town on a Sunday morning (8am–2pm), don't miss the **Feira de Arte e Artesanato** (Arts and Crafts Fair) on Avenida Afonso Pena, the largest open-air fair in Latin America, with three thousand stalls.

Praça da Liberdade

At the traditional heart of the city lies park-like **Praça da Liberdade**, with its celebrated **Edifício Niemeyer**, designed by renowned Brazilian architect Oscar Niemeyer, the elegant Neoclassical-style

3

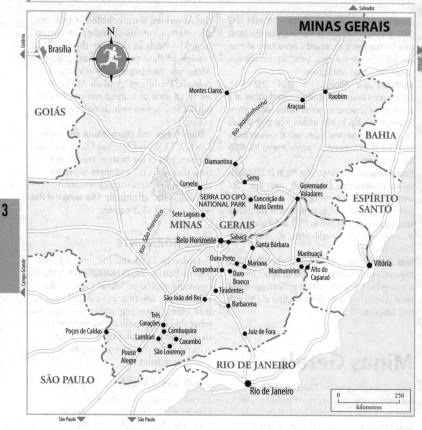

Palácio da Liberdade and a fine ensemble of **museums**. The highly imaginative, entertaining galleries of the **Memorial Minas Gerais Vale** (Tues, Wed, Fri & Sat 10am–5.30pm, Thurs 10am–9.30pm, Sun 10am–3.30pm; free; ⓦmemorialvale.com.br) are more like artistic representations of various aspects of Minas Gerais culture and history than a typical museum, while the artfully designed **Museu das Minas e do Metal** (Tues–Sun noon–6pm, Thurs till 10pm; last entry 1hr before closing; free; ⓦmmgerdau.org.br) successfully makes the otherwise dry subjects of mining and minerals utterly absorbing.

Museu de Artes e Ofícios
On Praça Rui Barbosa, the **Museu de Artes e Ofícios** (Tues, Thurs & Fri noon–7pm, Wed noon–9pm, Sat & Sun 11am–5pm; R$5; ⓦmao.org.br) highlights traditional trades and industries within the wonderfully enigmatic premises of the renovated **train station**. Essentially this is a huge display of old machinery and tools from the nineteenth and twentieth centuries, but there are some truly intriguing exhibits, including a video of the process of traditional sugar refining, huge, antique sugar boiling vats, leather tanning drums and copper alambiques (distilleries).

Museu Mineiro
The tiny but beautifully presented art collections in the **Museu Mineiro**, at Av João Pinheiro 342 (Tues, Wed & Fri 10am–7pm, Thurs noon–9pm, Sat, Sun & hols noon–7pm; free; ☎31 3269 1109),

are enhanced by the elegant Neoclassical building it occupies, completed in 1897 as the state senate. Today its gorgeous rooms house a variety of religious statuary, the work of local painters from the twentieth century (mostly landscapes) and a small collection of six vibrant paintings by Minas Gerais Baroque master **Manuel da Costa Ataíde**.

Pampulha

Set around an artificial lake that is home to cormorants, grebes, ibis, egrets, herons and even large **capybara**, the surburb of **Pampulha**, 10km north of the city centre (1hr by bus #2215A, B or C from Av Paraná between Rua Tamoios and Rua Carijós), boasts some architectural gems, the work of great modern Brazilian designers Oscar Niemeyer and Roberto Burle Marx. The **Museu de Arte de Pampulha** (MAP; Tues–Sun 9am–6pm; free; ☎31 3277 7996), on a peninsula in the lake, is one of the finest, a work of art in itself (though also housing a small collection inside), which was built as a casino in 1942 before becoming a museum in 1957. Also on the lakeshore is the **Igreja de São Francisco de Assis** (Tues–Sat 9am–5pm, Sun 9am–2pm; R$3), among the finest works of Niemeyer, Burle Marx and Cândido Portinari, who created the beautiful *azulejo* tile facade in 1943.

ARRIVAL AND DEPARTURE

By plane Confins Airport (☎31 3689 2700), officially called Aeroporto Internacional Tancredo Neves, is 38km

north of the centre. Airport buses (1hr) run every 15–30min (24hr) to the main *rodoviária* in the centre (R$9.50 or R$7.75 local; ⓦconexaoaeroporto.com.br), while posher *executivo* buses (every 15–30min, 24hr; R$21) drop you in the centre at Av Alvares Cabral 387, near the corner of Rua da Bahia. Taxis to the centre from Confins cost around R$100–120 on the meter, depending on traffic. Some domestic flights use Pampulha Airport (☎31 3490 2001), 9km from downtown; take a regular city bus to the *rodoviária* (4am–11.45pm; R$9.50).

Destinations Brasília (12 daily; 2hr); Rio de Janeiro (12 daily; 1hr); Salvador (5 daily; 3hr); São Paulo (20 daily; 1hr 30min).

By bus The *rodoviária* (☎31 3271 3000) is on Praça Rio Branco, at the northern end of the city centre. Note that some services (primarily to and from the Northeast, Espírito Santo, Belém and Brasília) have been moved to the Estação de Integração José Cândido da Silveira, in the far less convenient suburb of Santa Inês (though it's connected to the metro system), until a new bus station is completed (though there is no date set for the latter). Taxis from here into the centre are around R$30–40; metro tickets are R$1.80.

Destinations Brasília (4 daily; 12–13hr); Diamantina (6 daily; 6hr); Ouro Preto (hourly 6am–11pm; 2hr); Rio de Janeiro (20 daily; 6hr 30min); São João del Rei (7–8 daily; 3hr 30min); São Paulo (hourly; 8hr).

By train The train station (☎31 3273 5976) at Praça da Estação serves just one route, to Vitória on the coast (daily 7.30am, returning at 7am; 13hr; R$58; ☎0800 285 7000). You can buy tickets at the station or online; the Vitória station is "Cariacica" (ⓦtremdepassageiros.vale.com).

GETTING AROUND

By bus The city's bus system (ⓦbhtrans.pbh.gov.br) is colour-coded: blue buses run up and down the main *avenidas* within the city centre (R$2.65); yellow buses have circular routes (R$1.90); green buses are "express", stopping only at selected points (R$2.65–2.80); and red

---

INHOTIM

It comes as a bit of a shock to find the world's largest open-air art museum 60km from Belo Horizonte. But that's exactly what's on offer at **Inhotim Instituto Cultural** (Tues–Fri 9.30am–4.30pm, Sat & Sun until 5.30pm; Wed–Thurs R$20; Fri–Sun and hols R$30; free Tues; students pay half-price; ☎31 3571 9700, ⓦinhotim.org.br), an exhibition of 400 pieces of contemporary art across **twelve pavilions** and set amid an incredible 500,000 acres of botanical reserve (though only 110 acres are accessible via walking trails). Opened in 2006, the collection includes paintings, sculpture, photos, videos and installations by Brazilians and international artists dating from the 1960s to the present. Inhotim's appeal goes beyond art, however, with **gardens** of orchids, palms and rare tropical species landscaped by Burle Marx.

You'll need a full day (or more) at Inhotim. Special **direct buses** (R$23.90 one-way; around 2hr) operated by Saritur leave from the *rodoviária* in Belo Horizonte (Tues–Sun at 8.15am, returning at 4.30pm, Sat & Sun at 5.30pm; ⓦsaritur.com.br). Converted golf carts whisk visitors around the park if walking gets too much (R$20 per ride). Cafés and restaurants on-site.

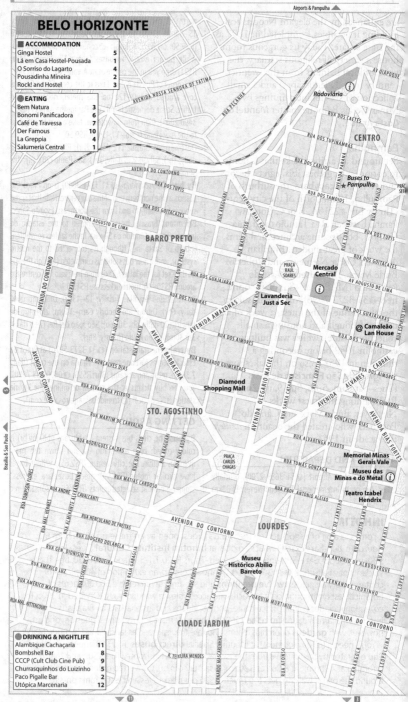

Airports & Pampulha

BELO HORIZONTE

■ ACCOMMODATION

Ginga Hostel	5
Lá em Casa Hostel-Pousada	1
O Sorriso do Lagarto	4
Pousadinha Mineira	2
Rock! and Hostel	3

● EATING

Bem Natura	3
Bonomi Panificadora	6
Café de Travessa	7
Der Famous	10
La Greppia	4
Salumeria Central	1

● DRINKING & NIGHTLIFE

Alambique Cachaçaria	11
Bombshell Bar	8
CCCP (Cult Club Cine Pub)	9
Churrasquinhos do Luizinho	5
Paco Pigalle Bar	2
Utópica Marcenaria	12

Rodoviária

CENTRO

Buses to
Pampulha

PRAÇA
SETI

Mercado
Central

PRAÇA
RAÚL
SOARES

Lavanderia
Just a Sec

Camaleão
Lan House

BARRO PRETO

Diamond
Shopping Mall

STO. AGOSTINHO

PRAÇA
CARLOS
CHAGAS

Memorial Minas
Gerais Vale

Museu das
Minas e do Metal

Teatro Izabel
Hendrix

LOURDES

Museu
Histórico Abílio
Barreto

CIDADE JARDIM

Brasília & Sao Paulo

3

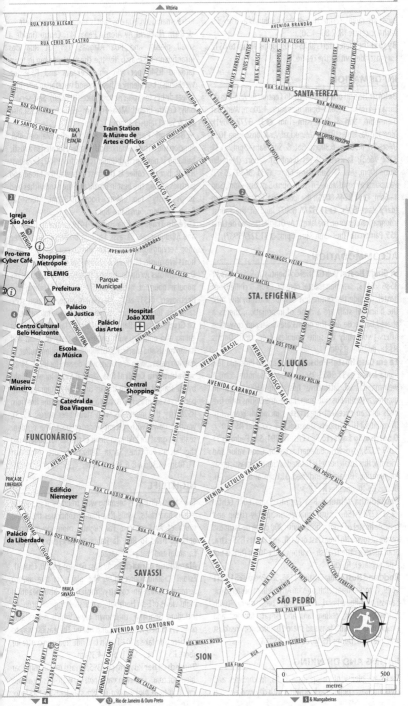

Vitória

RUA POUSO ALEGRE
RUA CERIO DE CASTRO
AVENIDA BRANDÃO
RUA POUSO ALEGRE
RUA MATIAS BARBOSA
AV. C. DOS SANTOS
RUA G. MASCI
RUA BUENOPOLIS
RUA ESMALTINA
RUA SALINAS
RUA ANHANGUERA
RUA PROF. GALEA VELOSO
SANTA TEREZA
RUA MÁRMORE
RUA EURITA
RUA RIO DE JANEIRO
RUA GUAICURUS
AV SANTOS DUMONT
PRAÇA DA ESTAÇÃO
Train Station & Museu de Artes e Ofícios
AVENIDA DO CONTORNO
RUA BUENO BRANDÃO
AV ASSIS CHATEAUBRIAND
AVENIDA FRANCISCO SALES
RUA AQUILES LOBO
RUA CRISTAL
RUA CAPITÃO PROCÓPIO
❶

❶
❷
Igreja São José
AVENIDA
Pro-terra Cyber Café
Shopping Metrópole
TELEMIG
AVENIDA DOS ANDRADAS
AL. ÁLVARO CELSO
RUA DOMINGOS VIEIRA
RUA ALVARES MACIEL
Prefeitura
Parque Municipal
STA. EFIGÊNIA
❸
❷
❹
Palácio da Justiça
Palácio das Artes
Hospital João XXIII
AVENIDA PROF. ALFREDO BALENA
AVENIDA DO CONTORNO
RUA GRÃO PARÁ
RUA MANAUS
Centro Cultural Belo Horizonte
AFONSO PENA
Escola da Música
RUA DA BAHIA
RUA JOÃO PINHEIRO
RUA DOS OTONI
AVENIDA BRASIL
AVENIDA FRANCISCO SALES
S. LUCAS
RUA PADRE ROLIM
Museu Mineiro
RUA SERGIPE
RUA AL. ALAGOAS
RUA PERNAMBUCO
RUA PARAÍBA
RUA RIO GRANDE DO NORTE
Central Shopping
AVENIDA BERNARDO MONTEIRO
AVENIDA CARANDAÍ
RUA CEARÁ
RUA PIAUÍ
RUA MARANHÃO
RUA GRÃO PARÁ
RUA DANTE
Catedral da Boa Viagem
FUNCIONÁRIOS
AVENIDA BRASIL
RUA GONÇALVES DIAS
RUA POUSO ALTO
PRAÇA DE LIBERDADE
Edifício Niemeyer
RUA CLAUDIO MANOEL
AVENIDA GETULIO VARGAS
❻
RUA MONTE ALEGRE
AV. CRISTÓVÃO COLOMBO
RUA PERNAMBUCO
RUA DOS INCONFIDENTES
RUA STA. RITA DURÃO
AVENIDA DO CONTORNO
RUA PROF. ESTEVÃO PINTO
RUA CICERO FERREIRA
Palácio da Liberdade
RUA RIO GRANDE DO NORTE
AVENIDA AFONSO PENA
RUA LUIZ
SAVASSI
RUA TOMÉ DE SOUZA
RUA ALUMÍNIO
SÃO PEDRO
PRAÇA SAVASSI
RUA PALMIRA
RUA SERGIPE
RUA AL. ALAGOAS
❾
❼
N
AVENIDA DO CONTORNO
RUA MINAS NOVAS
ERNARDO FIGUEIREDO
RUA VICOSA
RUA RAUL POMPEI
RUA PADRE PEDRO
RUA LAVRAS
AVENIDA N.S. DO CARMO
RUA GRÃO MOGOL
RUA CALDAS
SION
RUA PIAUÍ
RUA FINO
❿

0	500
	metres

▼ ❹   ▼ ⓬ , Rio de Janeiro & Ouro Preto   ▼ ❺ & Mangabeiras

buses are radial, connecting outlying suburbs and *favelas* with the centre (R$2.80–4.50).

By taxi The meter starts at R$4.10; budget for up to R$12 for most rides within the centre.

INFORMATION

Belotur Helpful offices at Mercado Central, Av Augusto de Lima 744 (Mon 9.40am–6pm, Tues 8am–4.20pm, Wed–Sat 8am–6pm, Sun & hols 8am–1pm ☎ 31 3277 4691); Mercado das Flores, Parque Municipal, Av Alfonso Pena 1055 (Mon–Fri 8.30am–6.30pm, Sat & Sun 8am–3pm; ☎ 31 3277 7666); Tancredo Neves (Confins) airport (Mon–Fri 8am–10pm, Sat & Sun 8am–6pm; ☎ 31 3689 2557); Pampulha airport (Mon–Fri 8am–5pm, Sat 8am–4pm, Sun 1–6pm; ☎ 31 3246 8015); the *rodoviária*, Praça Rio Branco (daily 8am–6pm; ☎ 31 3277 6907), and at the tourist information centre on the lake at Av Otacilio Negrao de Lima 855, Pampulha (Tues–Sun 8am–5pm; ☎ 31 3277 9987).

ACCOMMODATION

★**Ginga Hostel** Rua Gabriel dos Santos 165, Serra ☎ 31 3586 6113, ⊛ gingahostel.com.br. Fun, chilled-out hostel, outside the centre but easy to reach by city bus; the bilingual staff are a mine of information, there's a shared barbecue and the dorms are clean and cosy. Also offers two comfy en-suite doubles. Free wi-fi. Dorms R$38, doubles R$90

Lá em Casa Hostel-Pousada Rua Capitão Procópio 18F, Santa Tereza ☎ 31 3653 9566, ⊛ laemcasahostel.com. A well-maintained, attractive hostel in BH's bohemian quarter, a 10min bus ride from the centre. Dorms have five beds and an excellent breakfast is included. Free wi-fi. Discount for HI members. Dorms R$43, doubles R$120

O Sorriso do Lagarto Rua Cristina 791, São Pedro ☎ 31 3283 9325, ⊛ osorrisodolagarto.com.br. Good value and friendly, this small hostel is located in trendy Savassi, great for nightlife. Breakfast included, kitchen and free wi-fi. Dorms R$40, doubles R$90

Pousadinha Mineira Rua Espírito Santo 604, Centro ☎ 31 3273 8156. Institutional yet incredibly cheap and reliable hostel (it's not a hotel) with 200 dorm beds, in the centre of town. No breakfast or wi-fi, and sheets R$5 extra. Staff speak a little English – curfew after 10pm (this is not a party place). R$25

Rock! and Hostel Rua Cristina 1185, São Pedro ☎ 31 2531 0579, ⊛ rockandhostelbh.com.br. An excellent hostel in the Savassi neighbourhood, with clean, basic dorms (with hardwood floors, ceiling fans and private lockers) and simple doubles with fans and shared bathrooms; breakfast and free wi-fi. Dorms R$40, doubles R$115

EATING AND DRINKING

There are plenty of cheap restaurants, *lanchonetes* and *churrascarias* – popular at lunchtime with city workers – on Rua Pernambuco, Rua dos Caetés and around Praça Sete.

★**Bem Natural** Av Afonso Pena 941, Centro (inside a small plaza), and Rua Alagoas 911, at Rua dos Inconfidentes, Savassi. Not the cheapest *por kilo* in town (around R$40 per kilo on weekdays and R$48 on weekends), but plenty of healthy and vegetarian offerings (meat dishes too) plus natural juices (R$2.80). Self-service only; Centro branch Mon–Fri 9am–6.30pm, Savassi also Sat & Sun 11am–3.30pm.

★**Bonomi Panificadora** Rua Cláudio Manoel 488, Funcionários. This upmarket café/bakery located in a rustic building is not strictly budget (cakes from R$7; breakfast R$30), but the coffee is the best in town, the bread and pastries among the best in Brazil, and the sandwiches and soups tasty too. Mon noon–10.30pm, Tues–Sat 8am–10.30pm, Sun 8am–8pm.

Café de Travessa Rua Paraíba 1419, between Tourinho and Albuquerque, Savassi. Enticing bookstore and coffee shop, serving light meals, cakes and decent espresso – also hosts live music. Mon–Fri 4–10pm, Sat noon–4pm.

Der Famous Av do Contorno 6399, São Pedro. Justifiably popular gourmet hotdog joint – try the "Ludwig Van Beethoven" (R$17.80) – featuring huge, German-style sausages. Tues–Sat 6pm–1.30am, Sun 6pm–midnight.

La Greppia Rua da Bahia 1196, Centro. Classic 24hr spot for eating and drinking, with great-value tasty Brazilian and Italian meals and snacks. R$30 unlimited lunchtime buffet, or evening pasta *rodízio de massas* with dessert for R$22. 24hr.

★**Salumeria Central** Rua Sapucaí 527, Floresta. Right by the train station, this Italian-Brazilian restaurant-cum-bar serves salamis, hams, pasta, cheeses and the like from R$20 (try the meatballs with stout beer sauce; R$25), washed down with decent wine or beer. The outdoor seating's great for taking in views of the station square and the arches of the Santa Tereza viaduct. Mon–Sat 11.30am–3.30pm & 6.30pm–1am.

NIGHTLIFE

The Savassi district is teeming with trendy – if expensive – bars and clubs, while Rua Pium-í continues the trend south of Av Contorno. For slightly more downmarket options, head to Rua da Bahia anywhere between Av Carandaí and Praça da Estação.

Alambique Cachaçaria Av Raja Gabáglia 3200, Chalé 1, Estoril ⊛ alambique.com.br. The place for live *música sertaneja* (Brazilian country music), but also beautiful night views of Belo Horizonte, a massive range of *cachaças*, including Germana, their own brew which is available plain or infused with herbs and honey. The easiest way to get here is to take a 10–15min taxi ride from the centre for about R$30. Tues–Sat 10pm–4.30am.

Bombshell Bar Rua Sergipe 1395, Savassi ⊛ bombshellbar .blogspot.com. Contemporary *boteco* with DJs spinning anything from *funk carioca* to jazz standards or rock/pop:

check the schedule. Tasty eats for sharing, too. Mon & Sun 6pm–midnight, Tues–Fri 6pm–1am, Sat 1pm–1am.

★**CCCP (Cult Club Cine Pub)** Rua Levindo Lopes 358, Savassi ⓦcultclubcinepub.com.br. Hip spot just off the Contorno that used to be a cinema but now serves a variety of craft beers on tap. Also hosts frequent gigs (most rock, folk and especially blues) and film screenings. Sun, Tues & Wed 6pm–2am, Thurs & Fri 6pm–4am, Sat 8pm–4am (also serves lunch Mon–Fri 11.30am–2.30pm).

Churrasquinhos do Luizinho Av Francisco Sá 197, Prado ⓦchurrasquinhosdoluizinho.com.br. Packed on Thursdays with up to 500 people, *Luizinho's* serves the usual drinks and delicious *espetos* (grilled beef on a skewer) – owner Luiz says the secret lies in the sauce, a recipe of his mother's. Free shot of *cachaça* with your *espetinho* on Mon. Mon–Fri 5pm–midnight.

Paco Pigalle Bar Av do Contorno 2314, Floresta (between Av dos Andradas & Av Assis Chateaubriand) ⓦpacopigalle.com.br. Plays a mix of hip-hop, reggae, salsa and disco to a high-spending, trendy crowd. Fri & Sat 10pm–5am (also Thurs for special events).

★**Utópica Marcenaria** Av Raja Gabáglia 4700, Santa Lúcia ⓦutopica.com.br. Popular live music venue, located a few kilometres south of Centro. Samba Thursdays, rock/MPB Friday, funk/soul on Saturday and *forró* on Sunday. Cover R$15–30. Thurs–Sun 9pm–3am (sometimes open Tues & Wed for shows).

DIRECTORY

Banks and exchange Concentrated downtown on Av João Pinheiro, between Rua dos Timbiras and Av Afonso Pena. Bank ATMs throughout the city.

Car rental Numerous options at the airports, plus Hertz, Av Prof. Magalhães Penido 101, Pampulha (☎31 3492 1919); Alpina Serviços Automotivos, Rua dos Timbiras

2229 (☎31 3291 6111); Localiza, Av Bernardo Monteiro 1567 (☎31 3247 7956); Localralpha, Av Santa Rosa 100 (☎31 3491 3833).

Consulates Canada, Edifício Lumière, Hospital de Olhos Dr Ricardo Guimarães, Rua da Paisagem 220, 3/F, Vila da Serra (☎31 3047 1225); UK, Rua Cláudio Manoel 26, Funcionários (☎31 3225 0950).

Hospital Ambulance ☎192. Pronto Socorro do Hospital João XXIII, Av Alfredo Balena 400, Santa Efigênia (☎31 3239 9200).

Laundry Lavandaria Just a Sec, Rua dos Guajajaras 1268, Centro (Mon–Fri 8am–6pm, Sat 8am–1pm).

Police ☎190. For visa extensions go to the Polícia Federal at Rua Nascimento Gurgel 30, Gutierrez (☎31 3330 5200).

Post office Main post office, Av Afonso Pena 1270 (Mon–Fri 8.30am–6pm, Sat 9am–noon); Savassi branch, Rua Pernambuco 1322 (Mon–Fri 9am–6pm, Sat 9am–noon); also a branch at the bus station (Mon–Fri 9am–7pm, Sat 9am–noon).

Taxis Coomotaxi (☎31 3419 2020); Coopertáxi/BH (☎31 3421 2424).

OURO PRETO

The most enchanting of all the colonial towns in Minas Gerais, **OURO PRETO** ("Black Gold") lies 100km southeast of Belo Horizonte, its narrow, cobbled streets straddling impossibly steep hills topped with Baroque churches and lined with an assortment of candy-coloured eighteenth-century homes and mansions. The former capital of Minas Gerais (until 1897) was also the birthplace of renowned sculptor **Aleijadinho** and the focal point of the

---

SERRA DO CIPÓ NATIONAL PARK

In a country of few mountain peaks the upland landscapes of the **Serra do Cipó** stand out as one of the finest places in the country for outdoor activities. This dazzling national park lies 100km northeast of Belo Horizonte, encompassing limestone hills, rugged valleys and grasslands, Atlantic forest and numerous pools and waterfalls. Rare bird species like the Cipó canastero and hyacinth visorbearer attract serious birders, while other fauna includes wolves, jaguars, monkeys and the *sapo de pijama* (pyjama frog).

Six **buses** daily (2hr 30min; R$25) ply the route from Belo Horizonte to the small town of **Serra do Cipó** (formerly Cardeal Mota) at the edge of the park – an attractive place for backpackers with a low-key atmosphere, plus bars and pousadas. From here (and with the right gear) it's quite feasible to hike on your own from the park entrance, but there are also guides and **organized trips** available; for information contact Bela Gerais Turismo (☎31 3718 7394, ⓦserradocipogeraes.com.br) or Cipó Aventuras (☎31 9974 0878, ⓦcipoaventuras.blogspot.com).

Entry to the park is free, and though at weekends the principal trails draw day-trippers in numbers, during the week it's often near-deserted. Check the websites ⓦserradocipo.com and ⓦserradocipo.com.br for details on accommodation.

3

Inconfidência Mineira, a failed attempt in 1789 to end Portuguese rule and form a Brazilian republic. People flock to Ouro Preto from all over Brazil for **Semana Santa**, with its grand processions and Passion plays in open-air theatres, while **Carnaval** also attracts large crowds; book in advance at both these times.

WHAT TO SEE AND DO

The town is best explored on foot, taking in the cobbled passageways between its handful of stunning churches, excellent museums and numerous shopping and eating options – but be prepared for lots of uphill climbing.

Praça Tiradentes

Praça Tiradentes lies at the heart of Ouro Preto, with several sights right on the square. The **Museu da Inconfidência** (Tues–Sun 10am–6pm; R$10, students R$5; ⓦmuseudainconfidencia.gov.br), inside the old Paço Municipal and jail, chronicles the town's fascinating local history, though it is primarily a shrine to the doomed *Inconfidência Mineira* rebellion of 1789. The spiritual heart of the museum is a solemn room containing the tomb of Tiradentes, leader of the rebellion, and the remains of his fellow conspirators, marked with simple, flat tombstones. On the opposite side of the

square, inside the vast **Escola de Minas**, the former governor's palace dating from the 1740s, the **Museu de Ciência e Técnica** (Tues–Sun noon–5pm; R$6) houses a large geological and mineralogical collection, though the main draw is the gallery containing gold, huge amethyst and quartz crystals, silver, diamonds and other precious stones.

Museu do Oratório

Just behind the Igreja de Nossa Senhora do Carmo, off Praça Tiradentes, the intriguing **Museu do Oratório** (daily 9.30am–5.30pm; R$5, students free; ⓦmuseudooratorio .org.br) displays a high-quality collection of eighteenth- and nineteenth-century oratorios (small Catholic altars or shrines) from throughout Brazil. Although there are some glittering examples featuring gold and silver (and even sea shells) on the top floor, including a fine example by Manoel da Costa Ataíde, the most touching shrines are the portable and "bullet" oratorios in the basement, carried by muleteers and other travellers to protect themselves from danger.

Igreja de São Francisco de Assis

The most beautiful church in Ouro Preto, the **Igreja de São Francisco de Assis** (Tues–Sun 8.30am–noon & 1.30–5pm; R$10, including entry to

---

ALEIJADINHO AND CONGONHAS

The most important sculptor in colonial Brazil, **Antônio Francisco Lisboa** (1738–1814), aka Aleijadinho, was born in Ouro Preto to a slave mother and a Portuguese architect father. Self-taught, Aleijadinho was exceptionally prolific, turning out scores of profoundly original works, an achievement made all the more remarkable by the fact that from his mid-30s he suffered from a degenerative disease (presumably leprosy) which led to loss of movement in his legs and hands, eventually forcing him to sculpt using chisels strapped to his wrists while apprentices moved him around on a trolley (the name **Aleijadinho** translates literally as "little cripple"). His extraordinary works reflect his Christian spirituality and abound in many of the *cidades históricas*, particularly Ouro Preto. His most famous works, sculpted towards the end of his life between 1796 and 1805, and credited with introducing greater realism into Baroque art, are the 76 life-size figures at the **Santuário do Bom Jesus de Matosinhos** (Tues–Sun 7am–6pm; free) in the otherwise utterly unremarkable town of **Congonhas**. Thankfully you don't have to stay there to visit them – Congonhas is a convenient stop-off between Ouro Preto (or Belo Horizonte) and São João del Rei: leave your baggage at the Congonhas *rodoviária*. To get to Bom Jesus, catch a local bus (every 30min–1hr; 15min) marked "Basílica", which takes you all the way up the hill to the church; it's impossible to miss. The bus to take you back to the *rodoviária* leaves from the parking bay behind the church. Taxis charge R$15–20.

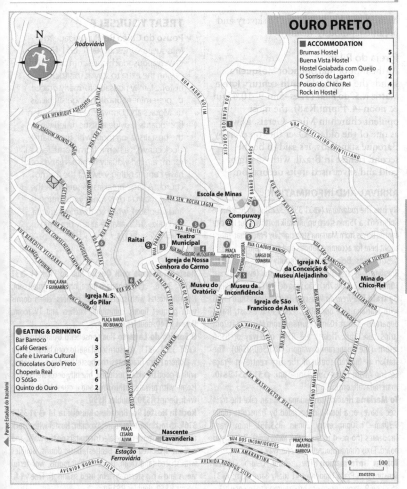

OURO PRETO

ACCOMMODATION	
Brumas Hostel	5
Buena Vista Hostel	1
Hostel Goiabada com Queijo	6
O Sorriso do Lagarto	2
Pouso do Chico Rei	4
Rock in Hostel	3

EATING & DRINKING	
Bar Barroco	4
Café Geraes	3
Cafe e Livraria Cultural	5
Chocolates Ouro Preto	7
Choperia Real	1
O Sótão	6
Quinto do Ouro	2

the Museu Aleijadinho), east of Praça Tiradentes, was begun in 1765, and no other contains more works by Aleijadinho (see box opposite). The exterior was entirely sculpted by the great master himself and the ceilings painted by his partner Manoel da Costa Ataíde. With the **Igreja Matriz de N.S. da Conceição** closed for renovation at the time of writing, precious artworks from the **Museu Aleijadinho** (same hours; ⓦmuseualeijadinho.com.br) are temporarily located inside São Francisco, in the side rooms and sacristy at the back.

Mina do Chico Rei
Close to the Igreja Matriz de N.S. da Conceição, at Rua Dom Silvério 108, is the **Mina do Chico Rei** (daily 8am–5pm; R$10). Founded in 1702, the long-abandoned mine has claustrophobic tunnels to explore, and gives a good sense of the scale of the local mining operations. Constructed on five levels, it contains an astonishing eighty square kilometres of tunnels, vaults and passages. It's also an intriguing place to learn more about Chico Rei ("Little King") himself, a legendary figure said to have been an enslaved African king who bought

himself and his people out of slavery and became fabulously wealthy.

Igreja do Pilar

At the foot of **Rua Brigador Mosqueira** stands the early eighteenth-century **Igreja Matriz N.S. do Pilar** (Tues–Sun 9–10.45am & noon–4.45pm; R$8), the most opulent church in Minas Gerais, as well as one of the oldest. Over the top even by Baroque standards, it's said to be the second richest in Brazil, with 434kg of gold and silver used in its decoration.

ARRIVAL AND INFORMATION

By bus The *rodoviária* (☎31 3559 3225) is on Rua Padre Rolim 661, a 15min steep uphill walk northwest of the city centre. Buses from Mariana stop right by Praça Tiradentes: alight here for accommodations and restaurants.
Destinations Belo Horizonte (hourly 6am–8pm; 2hr); Brasília (daily at 7.30pm; 11hr); Mariana (every 20min; 30min); Rio (2 daily; 7hr); São João del Rei (2 daily; 4–5hr).
By train The *Trem da Vale* tourist train links Ouro Preto with Mariana (see opposite), 12km to the east. Trains depart Fri–Sun at 10am, returning from Mariana at 2pm (trips take 1hr). Tickets are R$40 one-way or R$56 return (the "panoramic wagon" is R$60/R$80). The station is located south of the city centre at Praça Cesário Alvim (Tues–Sun 9am–5pm; ☎31 3551 7310, ⊚tremdavale.org).
To Mariana Heading to Mariana you can take the train (see above) or a local bus operated by Transcotta (daily 5.30am–11.30pm; every 20min; R$3.15), from Praça Tiradentes (no need to go to the *rodoviária*). Pay as you board. Taxis charge around R$50 one-way.
Tourist information The helpful Centro Cultural Turístico is at Praça Tiradentes 41 (daily 8am–7pm; ☎31 3559 3269, ⊚ouropreto.org.br, ⊚ouropreto.mg.gov.br).

ACCOMMODATION

Make sure that you book in advance in high season and at weekends. Expect substantial discounts midweek and off-season.
Brumas Hostel Rua Antonio Pereira 43 ☎31 3551 2944, ⊚brumashostel.com.br. Part of the HI network (reduced prices for members), this place offers basic dorms, kitchen, breakfast and laundry facilities. Dorms R$45, doubles R$180
★**Buena Vista Hostel** Rua Henri Gorceix 198 ☎31 3551 4677, ⊜buenavistahostel@hotmail.com. Close to the bus station, this spotless hostel with a helpful owner has newish dorms, pool table, kitchen, cosy communal areas and small, simple doubles. Dorms R$40 (towels R$3), doubles R$90

Hostel Goiabada com Queijo Rua do Pilar 44 ☎31 3552 3816, ⊜goiabadacomqueijohostel@gmail.com. No-frills hostel with super-helpful owners, clean dorms with parquet floors, communal kitchen and TV room. Dorms R$40, doubles R$120
O Sorriso do Lagarto Rua Conselheiro Quintiliano 271 ☎31 3551 4811, ⊚osorrisodolagarto.com.br. A 10min walk from Praça Tiradentes, this hostel has big clean dorms with a good breakfast included, brightly decorated rooms (some with private bathrooms) and a guest kitchen. Free wi-fi. Dorms R$30, doubles R$90
Rock in Hostel Rua Brigadeiro Musqueira 14 ☎31 3551 3165, ⊚rockinhostelouropreto.com.br. Hostel with a rock music theme (posters and electric guitars on the walls, and a room dedicated to the Beatles), basic dorms, doubles with shared (and clean, modern) bathrooms, wonderful views and a big stereo system, used sparingly. Free wi-fi. Dorms R$50, doubles R$120

EATING AND DRINKING

Good cheap places to eat are scattered throughout Ouro Preto. Night-time action is centred on Rua Direita (aka Rua Conde de Bobadella) where students spill out of the bars, while there are a couple of options along Rua Barão de Carmargos.
★**Bar Barroco** Rua Conde de Bobadela (Rua Direita) 106. Hip student dive bar with wooden benches and graffiti-smothered walls. Live music (mostly MPB and jazz) and tasty *coxhimba* (fried chicken or cheese-filled *pasteles*). Mon–Sat noon–2am.
Café Geraes Rua Conde de Bobadela (Rua Direita) 122. Café with fairly priced sandwiches and soups, delicious cakes and wine, as well as more extensive dinners, all served inside the gorgeous interior of an old townhouse

(mains R$30–50). The hip *Escadabaixo* bar is downstairs. Daily noon–midnight.

★**Cafe e Livraria Cultural** Rua Cláudio Manoel 15. Great artsy space below the tourist information desk in the Cultural Centre, serving quality coffee (R$3.50), quiche (R$16.50) and a superb range of local Ouropretana microbrews (R$8–9) as well as some Belgian imports (R$10–12). Free wi-fi. Daily 9am–7pm.

Chocolates Ouro Preto Praça Tiradentes 111 (also Rua Getúlio Vargas 66). Ouro Preto's most popular chocolatier offers excellent espresso (R$2.90) as well as hot chocolate (R$5.90–6.60), rich, tempting brownies (R$12.50) and even local microbrews from Cervejaria Ouropretana (R$13) in its casual café. Free wi-fi. Daily 9am–7pm.

Choperia Real Rua Barão de Camargos 8. A few psychedelic paintings decorate this popular joint with tables on the cobbled street in front, perfect for a *chopp* on a warm evening. Live bossa nova or MPB most nights from 8pm. Daily noon–2am.

O Sótão Rua São José 201. Fun, colourful paintings decorate this student-friendly place with straw lightshades casting shadows on the walls. Cheap buffet at lunch and excellent rodízio (Tues–Sun from 5pm; R$25), as well as *cachaças* and light bites such as filled pancakes. Live and relaxing samba, MPB and bossa nova sets the mood from 8pm. Tues–Sun noon–2am.

Quinto do Ouro Rua Conde de Bobadela (aka Rua Direita) 76. This attractive *lanchonete* is famed for its excellent *por kilo* buffet of typical mineira food – at around R$42 per kilo it's not especially cheap, but you can have a decent plate (and a taster of everything) for around R$20. Daily 11am–3pm.

DIRECTORY

Banks and exchange All the major banks with ATMs and exchange facilities are located along Rua São José. HSBC is at Rua São José 201.

Hospital Santa Casa de Misericórdia (24hr), Rua José Moringa 620, Bairro Bauxita (☎ 31 3551 1133).

Internet Compuway, Praça Tiradentes 52 (Mon–Fri 8am–9pm, Sat until 6pm); Raitai, Rua Paraná 100 (daily 9am–9pm).

Laundry Ask at your hotel/hostel as there are no laundries downtown. Nacente Lavanderia, at Rua dos Inconfidentes 5 (Mon–Fri 8am–5pm, Sat 8am–noon), picks up and drops off washing.

Post office Rua Conde de Bobadela 180 (Mon–Fri 9am–5pm; ☎ 31 3551 1855); also at Rua Getúlio Vargas 233 (near Rosário church; Mon–Fri 9am–5pm, Sat 9am–noon).

Shopping Ouro Preto is littered with jewellery stores selling the region's precious stones, notably tourmaline, topaz and imperial topaz (the latter is only found here).

Quality is usually very good, and, despite the touristy focus, prices are much cheaper here than in the US or Europe and the trade is well regulated. Try Brasil Gemas at Praça Tiradentes 74 (☎ 031 3551 4448).

MARIANA

A thirty-minute bus ride from Ouro Preto, lovely **MARIANA**, founded in 1696 and named after King Dom João V's wife Maria Ana de Austria, is home to two of Minas's most elegant town squares and a beautifully preserved colonial centre. The town can be visited as a day-trip from Ouro Preto, but it's also a great place to stay should you wish to escape the hordes of tourists elsewhere.

WHAT TO SEE AND DO

Buses drop you at the base of the hill and colonial district along the main commercial drag, Avenida Salvador Furtado. Rua Padre Lopes leads one block south to Praça Cláudio Manoel and the impressive, elaborate **Catedral de N.S. da Assunção** (Tues–Sun 8am–6pm; R$2). The church was designed by Aleijadinho's father in the early eighteenth century and contains many carvings by the man himself. The *tapa o vento* door, painted by Mariana native Ataíde, is considered by many to be the most beautiful in South America. Further riches include 365kg of gold leaf and a beautiful German organ with 1039 flutes and a keyboard made of elephants' teeth. **Organ concerts** are held on Friday at 11.30am and Sunday at 12.15pm (R$25).

Not far away, at Rua Frei Durão 49, the elegant former bishop's palace now houses the **Museu Arquidiocesano de Arte Sacra** (Tues–Fri 8.30am–noon & 1.30–5pm, Sat & Sun 9am–3pm; R$5), which displays religious treasures, paintings by Ataíde and sculptures by Aleijadinho. Two gorgeous Baroque churches stand on **Praça Minas Gerais**: the **Igreja de São Francisco de Assis** (Tues–Sun 9am–noon & 1–4pm; R$2), with yet more Aleijadinho carvings, is the final resting place of Ataíde; the relative restraint of the **Igreja de N.S. do Carmo** (Tues–Sun 9–11.45am & 2–5pm; R$2) makes an interesting contrast.

3

3

Minas da Passagem

Four kilometres from Mariana (on the road to Ouro Preto), **Minas da Passagem** (Mon & Tues 9am–5pm, Wed–Sun 9am–5.30pm, tours last 1hr; R$30; ⓦminasdapassagem.com.br) is one of the oldest and richest deep-shaft gold mines in the region. From 1719 to the mine's closure in 1985, 35 tonnes of gold were extracted from here. Once you've purchased tickets, walk to the mine head via the tiny museum (full of rusting equipment), and line up to board what for many tourists is the main attraction: a rickety open-seat railcar that trundles 315m down a steep slope into the main tunnel (be careful of bumping your head). At the bottom, guides lead you around the dripping, muddy but fairly spacious main tunnel, with smaller galleries branching off in all directions. Take the Ouro Preto–Mariana bus (R$3.15) and ask to get off at the stop opposite the mine; taxis from Ouro Preto charge R$30 one-way, and R$20/hr to wait for you.

ARRIVAL AND INFORMATION

By bus Transcotta buses from Ouro Preto (daily 5.30am–11.30pm; every 20min; R$3.15) stop right in the centre at Praça Tancredo Neves (Av Salvador Furtado). If you're coming from Belo Horizonte or São Paulo, you'll arrive at the *rodoviária* (☎31 3557 1122), on the main road a couple of kilometres from the centre; if you don't wish to walk into the centre, catch one of the buses from Ouro Preto, which pass through the *rodoviária*.

By train The *Trem da Vale* (see p.270) connects Mariana with Ouro Preto. The train station is near the centre at Praça Juscelino Kubitschek (Tues–Sun 8.30am–5.30pm).

Tourist information The tourist information office is at Praça Tancredo Neves, opposite the bus stop (Tues–Sun 8am–noon & 1.30–5pm; ☎31 3557 1158). There's a smaller office at Rua Direita 91, a short walk into the old town, which can also supply maps (Mon–Fri 8am–5pm; ☎31 3558 2314). See also ⓦmariana.org.br.

ACCOMMODATION

Hotel Faísca Rua Antônio Olinto 48 ☎31 3557 1206, ⓦhotelfaisca.com.br. Hotel with 35 smart, spotless rooms in the centre of town; excellent value with breakfast and wi-fi included. **R$78**

Mariana Hostel Rua Mestre Vicente 41 ☎31 3557 1435. Clean, popular hostel 5min walk from the centre, with sparkling rooms and bathrooms, a communal area, breakfast and wi-fi included. Dorms **R$40**, doubles **R$130**

EATING AND DRINKING

Chantilly Confeitaria Rua Frei Durão 32. The best café on Praça Gomes Freire, in a building completed in 1925, offering mouth-watering cakes, coffee, quiche and *empadas*. Daily 8am–9pm.

Rancho Praça Gomes Freire 108. Excellent local cuisine kept warm on a wood-fire stove, as well as a selection of pizzas (from R$28). Lunchtime buffet (R$24), soups (R$6) and *petiscos* (from R$10) at night. Tues–Sun 11am–3pm & 6pm–midnight.

Scotch & Art Bar Praça Minas Gerais 57. Great location for an evening tipple, with a terrace overlooking the churches on the plaza and a menu of tasty bar snacks. Tues–Sun 6.30pm–2am.

SÃO JOÃO DEL REI

SÃO JOÃO DEL REI was one of the first settlements in the region, dating back to a mining camp established in 1704. Though its historic centre boasts several imposing Baroque churches, it is one of the few gold towns to have found a thriving place in the modern world. Given that São João's neighbour Tiradentes is the prettier town, you may wish to stay there and visit here for the day, even though it is the more economical option. On Fridays, weekends and public holidays you can ride between the two towns on the *Maria Fumaça* **steam train**.

WHAT TO SEE AND DO

Not far from the city's wide central artery (which has a rather fetid stream running through the middle), on Hermílo Alves at Andrade Reis, is the **Museu da Força Expedicionária Brasileira** (Brazilian Expeditionary Force Museum; Mon–Fri noon–5pm; R$1), which tells the story of the country's involvement in World War II, with combat gear, radios, photographs, weapons, banknotes and fascinating news clippings from the period.

The **Museu Ferroviário** (Railway Museum), at the station four blocks east at Hermílio Alves 366 (Wed–Sun 9–11am & 1–5pm; R$3, free with a train ticket), has interesting facts on the origins of the *Maria Fumaça* in the 1880s, and also houses the first engine to run on the track here.

On Rua Getúlio Vargas, the stunning 1721 Baroque **Catedral de Nossa Senhora de Pilar** (Mon 8–10.30am & 5–8pm, Tues–Fri 8–10.30am & 1–8pm, Sat & Sun 8–10.30am & 5–8pm; free) has extensive gold gilding over the altar and attractive tiling. Close by, the **Museu Regional**, Rua Marechal Deodoro 12 (Tues–Fri 10.30am–5.30pm, Sat & Sun 1.30–5.30pm; R$1, Sun free), has a rich collection of historical and artistic objects from furniture to paintings, housed in a beautifully restored mansion.

Igreja de São Francisco de Assis and Tancredo Neves

The most impressive and important of the city's churches, the 1774 Baroque **Igreja de São Francisco de Assis** (daily 8am–5.30pm, Sun until 4pm; R$5) looks over the palm-filled Praça Frei Orlando. A deceptively large place with carvings by Aleijadinho and his pupils, the church has a graveyard to the rear where President Tancredo Neves is buried. Just around the corner at Rua Padre José Maria Xavier 7 is the **Memorial Tancredo Neves** (Fri–Sun & hols 9am–5pm; R$2; ⓦmemorialtancredoneves.com.br), containing a collection of personal artefacts and documents relating to the former president's life. One of the nation's most revered politicians, Neves was born here in 1910, and is credited with masterminding Brazil's return to democracy in the 1980s.

ARRIVAL AND INFORMATION

By bus The *rodoviária* (☎ 32 3373 4700) is 2km northeast of town; outside and across Rua Cristovão Colombo, take a local bus (R$2.30) from in front of the *drogaria* and get off at Av Tancredo Neves (10min). Taxis (☎ 32 3371 2028) charge R$15–20.

Destinations Belo Horizonte (8 daily; 3hr 30min); Ouro Preto (2 daily; 4hr); Rio (3 daily; 5hr); São Paulo (8 daily; 7–8hr); Tiradentes (every 30min; 30min).

By train The *Maria Fumaça* leaves São João (Av Hermílo Alves 366; ticket office Wed & Thurs 9–11am & noon–5.45pm, Fri & Sat 9am–1pm & 2–5pm, Sun 9am–2pm; ☎ 32 3371 8485; ⓦ trilhosdeminas.com) for Tiradentes on Fri & Sat at 10am and 3pm, returning at 1pm and 5pm, and on Sun at 10am and 1pm, returning 11am & 2pm (R$40 single, R$56 return; 45min).

Tourist information The tourist office (daily 8am–5pm; ☎ 32 3372 7388) lies across from the Catedral at Praça Frei Orlando 90.

ACCOMMODATION

Brasil Av Tancredo Neves 395 ☎ 32 3371 2804. Facing the river, the biggest hotel in town gives a whole new meaning to faded grandeur, with fifty very simple, clean rooms (some with private bathrooms) that surely haven't changed much since the place opened in 1881. Free wi-fi. **R$90**

Pousada Estação do Trem Rua Maria Tereza 45 ☎ 32 3372 1985, ⓦ pousadaestacaodotrem.com.br. Wooden furnishings, rugs and soft lighting make this historic house a lovely option, good value for the price, right by the train to Tiradentes. Wi-fi and breakfast included. **R$130**

EATING AND DRINKING

Biscoiteria Tradição Mineira Travessa Lopes Bahia 18. Close to the train station, seek out this small store to load up on traditional *mineira* sweets and biscuits. Mon–Sat 9am–5pm.

Del Rei Cafe Av Tiradentes 553. Open until the early hours, this restaurant-cum-chopperia serves reasonable pizza, lunchtime *pratos feitos* and tasty filled crêpes. Some outdoor seating. Daily 9am–late.

Pelourinho Rua Hermílo Alves 276. A decent and cheap self-service place with a great variety of *mineira* food, near the train station; buffet by kilo, so you can stuff yourself for well under R$30. Daily 11am–4pm and 6pm–midnight.

Restaurante Rex Rua Marechal Deodoro 124. Perfectly adequate and cheap *por kilo* restaurant, with a huge selection of traditional items in a spacious, clean dining room. Try and get a table on the balcony. Daily 11am–4pm.

Villeiros Rua Padre José Maria Xavier 132, close to São Francisco church ☎ 32 3372 1034, ⓦ villeiros.com.br. The best *por kilo* restaurant in town, with a good range of typical *mineira* food (budget for R$30–40 with drinks). Daily 11.30am–4pm; buffet served till 3pm.

DIRECTORY

Banks and exchange All banks and ATMs are on Av Tancredo Neves.

Internet World Game Internet, at Rua Ministro Gabriel Passos 281 (daily 9am–10pm).

Post office Av Tiradentes 500 (Mon–Fri 9am–5pm, Sat 9am–noon).

Shopping The Feria do Artesanato, held every Sun on Av Presidente Tancredo Neves, sells local crafts.

TIRADENTES

With its quaint historic houses, cobblestone streets and horse-drawn carriages, **TIRADENTES** could be mistaken for a film set. Surrounded by mountains, the charming town is better appreciated during the week, as Brazilian tourists swarm in at weekends for a romantic break or to shop at the many little boutiques around town. Costs here are the most expensive in Minas, but despite this it's worth staying a night or two to fully appreciate the rich atmosphere, explore the town's cobbled alleyways – and, if you like the outdoors – go walking for an hour or two in the surrounding countryside.

WHAT TO SEE AND DO

Despite being described as a *cidade histórico*, modern Tiradentes is little more than a village, which at least ensures that everything is easily found. The chief landmark, pretty much at the highest point in town, is the **Igreja Matriz de Santo Antônio** (daily 8am–5pm; R$5). Among the largest and most gold-laden of Minas Gerais' Baroque churches, it also features some of Aleijadinho's last works, and the classic view from the church steps is the most photographed in the state. Nearby, at Rua Padre Toledo 190, in the former home of one of the heroes of the *Inconfidência Mineira*, where the conspirators first met in 1788, the **Museu Padre Toledo** (Tues–Sun 9am–5pm; R$10) has period furnishings, art and documents dating back to the eighteenth century, and a preserved slave quarters (now converted into toilets). The slaves themselves built, and worshipped at, the small, dignified and supremely attractive **Igreja da N.S. do Rosário dos Pretos** (Tues–Sun 10.45am–5pm; R$3), down the hill, which also contains three sculptures of black saints.

ARRIVAL AND INFORMATION

By bus The *rodoviária* is in the centre of town off Rua Gabriel Passos. Buses leave regularly for São João del Rei (every 45min–1hr; 30min), from where you can connect to other destinations.

By train The *Maria Fumaça* links Tiradentes with São João del Rei (see p.273). The train station is 1km southeast of the main square on Praça Estação.

Tourist information The Secretária de Turismo is on the main square at Rua Resende Costa 71 (Mon–Thurs & Sun 9am–6pm, Fri & Sat 9am–8pm; ☎ 32 3355 1212).

ACCOMMODATION

Tiradentes caters primarily for the well-to-do, but try visiting midweek when pousadas offer discounts – or stay in São João.

Pousada Arco-Iris Rua Frederico Ozanan 340 ☎ 32 3355 1167, ⓦ pousadarcoiristiradentes.com.br. Basic singles close to the old town for just R$70 per person. The added bonus of a pool makes this one of the best budget choices in Tiradentes. No wi-fi. Doubles R$120

Pousada da Bia Rua Frederico Ozanan 330 ☎ 32 3355 1173, ⓦ pousadadabia.com.br. Set in a beautiful plot of land with a little herb garden and pool, and offering a variety of comfortable, multi-coloured rooms in rustic converted outhouse surroundings. Small charge for wi-fi, but buffet breakfast included. R$150

Hostel Raiz Rua Silvio Vasconcelos 141 ☎ 32 3355 2256. Simple but elegant rooms with tiled floors and shared bathrooms in the centre of town – shared kitchen and free wi-fi. Singles just R$50. Doubles R$120

EATING AND DRINKING

Most popular restaurants and bars are centred on Largo das Forras. Your best bet if in a small group is to share a *comida mineira*, usually large enough for two or three people.

Chico Doceiro Rua Francisco de Morais 74. Lauded local sweetshop, with all the traditional *mineira* treats inside handmade by octogenarian Chico "the candyman" since 1965; try the exquisite *doce de leite* or *doce de banana* (R$6–7). Take away only. Daily 9am–6pm.

Confidências Mineiras Rua Ministro Gabriel Passos 26. Warm, candlelit place serving large (for three) portions of *mineira* delights such as mashed pork and bean Tutú cooked in *cachaça* (R$55), or *petiscos* to accompany your choice of their near-infinite range of *cachaças*. Wed–Fri 6–11pm, Sat noon–11pm, Sun noon–6pm.

Divino Sabor Rua Gabriel Passos 300. Popular lunch-only place in simple surroundings with wooden tables on a patio outside. *Mineira* buffet for R$22 or reasonably priced *por kilo*. Tues–Sun noon–3.30pm.

Panela de Minas Rua Gabriel Passos 23. Right by the square, the town's most popular lunch spot serves typical *mineira* food *por kilo* laid out on a raised hearth, plus decent pizzas on weekends. Tues–Sun 11.30am–4pm.

Virada's do Largo Rua do Moinho 11 ⓦ viradasdolargo .com.br. On a backstreet a 5min walk behind the *rodoviária*, this is considered the best value in town for *comida mineira*. While not cheap, the huge portions (R$40–70) serve up to three, most guests seated around large antique tables. Mon & Wed–Sun noon–10pm.

NIGHTLIFE AND ENTERTAINMENT

See ⓦ tiradentes.net for what's-on listings (in Portuguese).

★**Centro Cultural Yves Alves** Rua Direita 168, ⓦ tiradentes.net. The town's cultural hub features theatrical performances, films, concerts and temporary exhibitions by local artists (free), as well as a tranquil, blossom-filled garden.

DIRECTORY

Banks and exchange All banks with ATMs are located off Rua Gabriel Passos, close to Largo das Forras.
Internet Game Mania Lan House, Rua dos Inconfidentes (daily 9am–10.30pm).
Post office Rua Resende Costa 73 (Mon–Fri 9am–5pm).

DIAMANTINA

Six hours by bus from Belo Horizonte, **DIAMANTINA** is the most isolated of the historic towns yet well worth the trip. Nestled in the heart of the Serra do Espinhaço, it is surrounded by a breathtakingly wild and desolate landscape. Named after the abundant diamond reserves first exploited in 1729, the town is rich in history and was designated a UNESCO World Heritage Site in 1999. It retains a lively, friendly atmosphere and is the hometown of visionary 1950s president **Juscelino Kubitschek** who founded Brasília; a statue is dedicated to him on Rua Macau Meio. Diamantina justifies a couple of days' wandering around in its own right, but you should also try to follow a trail outside of town to take in the scenery and nearby waterfalls and rock pools – details of routes and guides can be found at the tourist office (see p.276).

details of routes and guides can be found at the tourist office (see p.276).

WHAT TO SEE AND DO

Diamantina's narrow streets are set on two exceptionally steep hills. Fortunately, almost everything of interest is tightly packed into the central area close to the main cathedral square, the Praça Conselheiro Mota. The **Museu do Diamante** (Tues–Sat 10am–5pm, Sun 9am–1pm; R$2; ⓦ museudiamante .blogspot.com) is right on the square at Rua Direita 14, bringing the colonial period vividly to life through an extraordinary variety of exhibits. They include real gold, real and fake diamonds, mining paraphernalia and a number of swords, pistols, guns and torture instruments that were used on enslaved Amerindians and Afro-Brazilians.

Mercado dos Tropeiros, and Casa da Glória

The old **Mercado dos Tropeiros** on Praça Barão de Guaicuí, just below the cathedral square, was once the focus of trade for the whole region, and is worth seeing for the building alone – an exceptional tiled wooden structure built in 1835, with a facade of rustic but very elegant shallow arches. The **market** (Fri 6–11pm & Sat 6am–3pm) itself has a very Northeastern feel, with its cheeses, *doces* made from sugar and fruit, blocks of salt and raw sugar, *cachaça* sold by the shot as well as by the bottle, and mules and horses tied up alongside the pick-ups – these days there are also cheap snack stalls and handicrafts for sale, as well as live music on Friday evenings.

More worthwhile for the building than its contents is the eighteenth-century **Casa da Glória**, which is uphill from the tourist office at Rua da Glória 298 (Tues–Sun 1–6pm; R$1); it was inspired by Venetian structures. This former residence of diamond supervisors is now part of the Centre of Geology and contains a collection of maps, gemstones and minerals. The premises span both sides of the street, linked by the Passadiço da Glória (1878), Diamantina's own "Bridge of Sighs".

Casa Chica da Silva

Generally unknown outside of Brazil, Chica da Silva (1732–96) remains something of a legend inside the country, inspiring movies and telenovelas; the **Casa Chica da Silva** at Praça Lobo de Mesquita 266 (Tues–Sat noon–5.30pm, Sun 8.30am–noon; R$2) is dedicated to her story. Chica was born a slave, but grew rich and powerful nonetheless, becoming the mistress of her owner, João Fernandes de Oliveira,

3

the government overseer of diamond mining in the region. She was eventually freed by him, and lived in this house and bore his thirteen children, though they were never married. The house is beautifully maintained to mirror how it would have looked in Da Silva's time, though the entertaining guides that bring the story to life rarely speak English.

Two churches

The **Igreja de N.S. Senhora do Carmo** on Rua do Carmo (open sporadically Tues–Sun, not lunchtimes; R$2), built between 1760 and 1765, is the most interesting of Diamantina's churches, with an exceptionally rich interior including an organ built in 1782 on which Lobo de Mesquita, considered the best composer of religious music of the Americas, performed many of his own works. Just downhill from here, the **Igreja de Nossa Senhora do Rosário dos Pretos** (same opening hours; R$2) was built in 1728 to serve local slaves and features an intricately painted ceiling.

ARRIVAL AND INFORMATION

By bus The *rodoviária* is on a steep hill, about a 10min walk above the centre of town (20min if walking uphill); a taxi costs around R$12–14. Buses for Belo Horizonte leave at midnight, 6am, 10.45am, 3.30pm and 6pm daily (5–6hr). There is no service from Diamantina to Brasília, and usually just one bus a day to São Paulo (13–14hr).

Tourist information at Praça Antônio Eulálio 53 (Mon–Sat 9am–6pm, Sun 9am–2pm; ☎38 3531 9532, ⓦ diamantina.mg.gov.br).

ACCOMMODATION

Diamantina Hostel Rua do Bicame 988 ☎38 3531 5021, ⓦ diamantinahostel.com.br. This HI hostel is spotless and has a great view, yet the rooms are dark and not especially inviting. A 15min (uphill) walk from town and 10min from the *rodoviária*. Laundry and free wi-fi. R$5 discount with HI card. Deposit required. Dorms <u>R$40</u>

Pousada Presidente Rua Oscar Batista 365 ☎38 3531 6369, ⓦ pousadapresidente.com.br. Basic but charming pousada a short walk from the centre, with cosy rooms equipped with fans, free wi-fi and some with private bathrooms (R$120). Good breakfast included. <u>R$70</u>

★**Tijuco** Rua Macau do Meio 211 ☎38 3531 1022, ⓦ hoteltijuco.com.br. This 1951 Oscar Niemeyer creation has fairly spartan but perfectly adequate rooms. It's worth paying for one of the slightly more expensive "panorâmico" rooms (from R$100), which are larger and brighter and have balconies offering wonderful views across Diamantina. <u>R$90</u>

EATING AND DRINKING

There's a decent variety of budget options around the town centre, most serving *comida mineira*. Bars around Rua da Quintanda such as *Café A Baiúca* have tables spilling onto the square – perfect to watch life go by as you sip a *chopp*.

★**Apocalipse** Praça Barão do Guaicuí 78. A popular and classy *por kilo* restaurant across from the market, worth a visit as much for the unintentionally hilarious English translation of the menu (baked *namorado* fish comes out as "boyfriend to the oven") as for the genuinely good food: Italian and *comida mineira*, plus sublime desserts (expect to pay R$20). Daily 11am–3pm, Thurs–Sat also 7–11pm.

Casa Velha Rua Direita 106. Located in the Casa de Juscelino Kubitschek, this popular pizzeria knocks out decent thin-crust pies and classic *comida mineira*, the walls adorned with Kubitschek memorabilia. Mon 11am–2.30pm, Tues–Sun 11am–2.30pm & 6pm–midnight.

Livraria Café Espaço B Beco da Tecla 31. Just off the cathedral square, this is the place for good coffee and cakes late into the evening, in sophisticated bookshop surroundings. Free wi-fi. Mon–Sat 9am–midnight, Sun 11am–2pm.

Recanto do Antônio Beco da Tecla 39 (an alleyway off the Praça Barão do Guaicuí). Chilled-out spot with the appearance of a country tavern, serving beer, wine, sausage and *carne do sol*. Tues–Sun 11am–3pm & 6pm–midnight.

DIRECTORY

Banks and exchange All banks with international ATMs are located around the central squares.

Internet Padaria Central, Rua Joaquim Costa 34 (Mon–Sat 6am–9pm and Sun 6am–1pm), is an internet café/bakery behind the Mercado Central.

Post office Praça Monsenhor Neves 59A.

Bahia

Gateway to the Brazilian Northeast (see p.288) and, after Rio, the state drawing the most foreign visitors, **BAHIA** is a clear highlight of South America. Portuguese Brazil began here in the historic capital of **Salvador**, a legacy reflected today in its colonial architecture, political conservatism, and the significant population of Brazilians with African heritage. The syncretism of the African with the European in Brazilian culture is reflected in all aspects of daily life here – but especially in the city's food, music and religion.

Roughly the size of France, Bahia comprises an extraordinary natural landscape, from 1000km of stunning coastline to the vast semi-arid *sertão* of the interior. Rising up at the state's heart, the wide valleys and table mountains of the **Chapada Diamantina** provide some of the best trekking and climbing possibilities in the country – the perfect antidote to the resorts or laidback hideaways along the coast.

SALVADOR

High above the enormous bay of Todos os Santos (All Saints), **SALVADOR** has an electric feel from the moment you arrive. This is the great cultural and historical centre of Brazil, where Afro-Brazilian heritage is strongest and where capoeira, *candomblé* and *samba de roda* were created. The Centro Histórico is a magical place, a melange of narrow cobbled streets, peeling purple walls, grand Baroque churches, kids kicking footballs, rastas, locals sipping bottled beer on plastic chairs and the almost constant beating of drums, especially as

the sun sets. Salvador was officially founded in 1549 by Portuguese conquistador **Tomé de Sousa**, who chose the city for its inaccessible perch high above the water. It was the scene of a great battle in 1624, when the Dutch destroyed the Portuguese fleet in the bay and stormed and captured the town, only to be forced out again within a year by a joint Spanish and Portuguese force. For the first three hundred years of its existence, Salvador was the most important port and city in the South Atlantic – Rio only replaced it as capital in 1763.

If you tire of the city, go down to the pier and grab a boat for the choppy ride over to **Morro de São Paulo**, an island with beautiful beaches that's just two hours away.

WHAT TO SEE AND DO

Salvador is built around the craggy, 70m-high bluff that dominates the eastern side of the bay and splits the central area into upper and lower sections. The heart of the old city, **Cidade Alta** (upper city, or simply Centro), is strung along its top – this is the administrative and cultural centre of the city where you'll find most of the bars, restaurants, hostels and pousadas. This cliff-top area is linked to the old, shabby commercial district, **Cidade Baixa** (lower city), by precipitous streets, a funicular railway (Mon–Fri 7am–7pm, Sat 7am–1pm; R$0.15) and

3

FESTIVE SALVADOR

Lavagem do Bonfim Second Thurs in Jan. The washing of the church steps by *baianas* (local Bahian women) in traditional dress is followed by food, music and dancing.
Iemanjá Feb 2. A celebration of *candomblé*, a popular Afro-Brazilian religious cult, with a procession and offerings to the sound of Afro-Brazilian music.
Carnaval Week preceding Lent. The largest street party in the world takes place in Salvador. There's an accepting atmosphere but it's worth bearing in mind that all-black *blocos* (street bands and groups) may be black culture groups who won't appreciate being joined by

non-black Brazilians, let alone gringos; be sensitive or ask before leaping in.
Festa de Santo Antônio June 13. The main celebration of the patron saint of matrimony is held at Largo de Santo Antônio.
Dia de São João June 24. The biggest holiday in Bahia outside Carnaval celebrates St John with *forró* (Northeastern Brazilian folk dance), straw hats and traditional food.
Independência da Bahia July 2. Celebrating the expulsion of the Portuguese and the province's independence since the year 1823.

SALVADOR

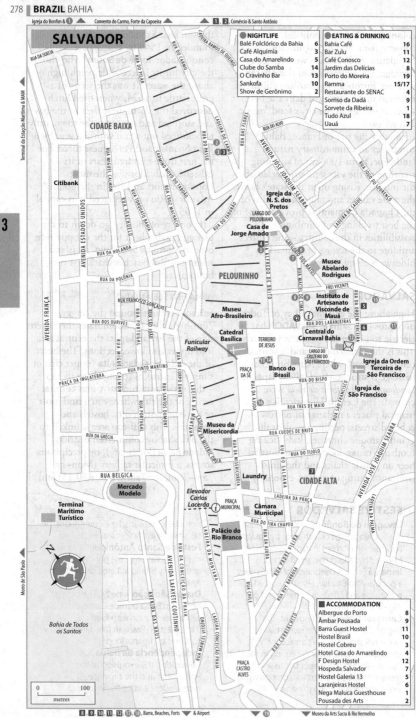

● NIGHTLIFE

Balé Folclórico da Bahia	6
Café Alquimia	3
Casa do Amarelindo	5
Clube do Samba	14
O Cravinho Bar	13
Sankofa	10
Show de Gerônimo	2

● EATING & DRINKING

Bahia Café	16
Bar Zulu	11
Café Conosco	12
Jardim das Delícias	8
Porto do Moreira	19
Ramma	15/17
Restaurante do SENAC	4
Sorriso da Dadá	9
Sorvete da Ribeira	1
Tudo Azul	18
Uauá	7

■ ACCOMMODATION

Albergue do Porto	8
Âmbar Pousada	9
Barra Guest Hostel	11
Hostel Brasil	10
Hostel Cobreu	3
Hotel Casa do Amarelindo	4
F Design Hostel	12
Hospeda Salvador	7
Hostel Galeria 13	5
Laranjeiras Hostel	6
Nega Maluca Guesthouse	2
Pousada des Arts	1

the towering Art Deco lift shaft of the **Carlos Lacerda elevator** (daily 24hr; R$0.15), the city's largest landmark. Stretching south along the coast are beaches, forts, expensive hotels, and **Barra**, where you will find more restaurants and pousadas. From Barra, a broken coastline of coves and beaches, large and small, runs east along the twisting **Avenida Oceânica**, which runs along the shore for 22km through the other main beach areas, **Ondina**, **Rio Vermelho** and Itapuã (near the airport).

Praça Municipal

Praça Municipal, Cidade Alta's main square overlooking the bay, is the place to begin exploring. Dominating the *praça* is the **Palácio do Rio Branco** (Tues–Fri 10am–6pm, Sat & Sun 9am–1pm; free), the old governor's palace, burnt down and rebuilt during the Dutch wars. The fine interior is a blend of Rococo plasterwork, polished wooden floors, painted walls and ceilings. The exhibit inside, the **Memorial dos Governadores**, houses pieces from the colonial era and portraits of former governors. On the east side of the square is the **Memorial da Câmara Municipal** (Mon–Fri 9am–6pm; free), the seventeenth-century city hall, now a small, well-presented museum charting the history of the city.

Just north of the square is the **Museu da Misericórdia** (Mon–Sat 10am–5pm, Sun noon–5pm; R$6), Brazil's first hospice and shelter for the sick and hungry. It's now a large colonial-period art museum with dazzling carved Baroque ceilings, mahogany panels and period furniture throughout. Head up to the mansion's upper rooms for stellar views across the bay.

Praça da Sé

Rua da Misericórdia leads into the **Praça da Sé**, the heart of Cidade Alta. The square lies at the southern end of **Pelourinho** or Pelô, the area of Cidade Alta famed for its gorgeous architecture, shops, music, dining and nightlife, though less than twenty years ago it was decaying and run-down. At the end of the Praça da Sé, facing the adjoining square known as the **Terreiro de Jesus**, the **Catedral Basílica** (Mon–Sat 8.30–11.30am & 1.30–5pm; R$3) was once the chapel of the largest Jesuit seminary outside Rome. To the left of its altar is the tomb of **Mem de Sá**, third governor general of Brazil (1556–70). You're likely to see some capoeira in full swing as you exit the cathedral, as groups often perform on the front steps.

Museu Afro-Brasileiro

Next to the cathedral in what used to be the university medical faculty, the **Museu Afro-Brasileiro** (Mon–Fri 9am–5pm, usually open Sat mornings, but check in advance; R$6; ⓦwww.mafro.ceao.ufba.br) is the city's best museum, offering an enthralling overview of Brazil's (and especially Bahia's) African roots. The ground floor covers popular culture, including carnival, capoeira, religion and music, with special rooms dedicated to the famous **carved wood panels** by Carybé, Bahia's most famous artist, while the basement contains the **Museu Arqueológico e Etnológico**, given over to ceramics, basketware, textiles and artefacts from Afro-Brazilian burial sites, alongside coverage of the Jesuit conversion of Amerindians. Across all floors you'll see striking objects from ancient African civilizations, including jewellery, musical instruments, masks and sculptures of the *orixás* (African gods), widely worshipped today in the Brazilian *candomblé* religion.

São Francisco

On Largo do Cruzeiro de São Francisco, an extension of the **Terreiro de Jesus**, are the superb carved stone facades of two churches dedicated to St Francis: the **Igreja de São Francisco** (Tues–Sat 9am–5.30pm, Sun 10am–3pm; R$5), completed between 1708 and 1723, and the **Igreja da Ordem Terceira de São Francisco** (Mon–Fri 9am–5pm; R$5). The former contains a small cloister decorated with one of the finest single pieces of *azulejo* (decorative glazed tiling) work in Brazil, while the latter, with an especially ostentatious sandstone facade, was completed in 1703 as a

3

display of wealth and power by Portuguese colonizers keen to demonstrate to the world their imperial might in the Americas. Over 100kg of gold was transported here and used to decorate the interior; the opulent walls display imperious paintings as well as *azulejos*.

Largo do Pelourinho

The beautiful, cobbled **Largo do Pelourinho**, down narrow Rua Alfredo de Brito, has changed little since the eighteenth century and remains the heart of the Pelô. Lined with solid colonial mansions, it's topped by the oriental-looking towers of the **Igreja da Nossa Senhora do Rosário dos Pretos** (Mon–Fri 8am–6pm, Sat & Sun 8am–noon; free), built by and for slaves and still with a largely black congregation. Across from here is the **Casa de Jorge Amado** (Mon–Fri 10am–6pm, Sat 10am–4pm; R$3; free on Wed; ⓦjorgeamado.org.br), a museum given over to the life and work of the hugely popular modern novelist, author of 25 works including the critically acclaimed *Captains of the Sands* and *Gabriela, Clove and Cinnamon*; the displays here are devoted both to the author's life and to the contrasting (and controversial) themes of his books, from social realism to sexual mores.

Museu da Arte Sacra

Despite the concentration of riches in Cidade Alta, you'll have to leave the old city proper to find the **Museu da Arte Sacra** on Rua do Sodré 276 (20min walk south of Praça Municipal via Rua Chile and Carlos Gomez; Mon–Fri 11.30am–5.30pm; R$5; ⓦwww.mas.ufba.br), one of the finest museums of Catholic art in Brazil. It's housed in a magnificent former convent with much of its original furniture and fittings still intact, and with a maze of small rooms stuffed with a remarkably rich collection of colonial art, primarily dating from the sixteenth to eighteenth centuries. The collection of Baroque work by **José Teófilo de Jesus** and **José Joaquim da Rocha**, founders of the Bahian school of painting, is especially good.

Mercado Modelo

Cidade Baixa has few sights, but it is well worth the effort to get to the **Mercado Modelo** (Mon–Sat 9am–7pm, Sun 9am–2pm), which is full of Bahian handicrafts, trinkets and beachwear – great for gifts and souvenirs – though be prepared to haggle a little. You'll find it across the street from the bottom of the Lacerda elevator, behind a row of outdoor handicraft stalls.

SALVADOR'S BEACHES

All of these beaches (apart from Aldeia Hippie) can be reached by bus (heading to either "Vilas do Atlântico" or "Praias do Flamengo") from Praça da Sé.

Praia da Onda This beach in Ondina is good for surfing (although watch the rocks) and even fishing.

Praia de Aleuluia The perfect spot to grab some lunch at one of the many bars or restaurants along the beach. Good waves for surfing too.

Praia de Itapoã One of the most scenic beaches, mainly because of its tall, lilting palm trees.

Praia de Jaguanibe Strong winds make this a perfect spot to surf, windsurf and kite-surf.

Praia de Stella Maris Good for long walks

as well as surfing.

Praia do Farol da Barra Windswept palms and thatched huts punctuate this small, rocky beach near the lighthouse.

Praia do Porto da Barra The closest swimming beach to historic Salvador is calm and narrow, and just a short bus ride away.

Aldeia Hippie In Arembepe, about 50km from Salvador, the long beach here was made famous by Mick Jagger and Janis Joplin in the 1960s. Though often crowded, there are still peaceful spots to be found, and many people come to take a dip in the Capivara River. Frequent buses from the *rodoviária*.

Museu Náutico da Bahia

The **Museu Náutico da Bahia** (Tues–Sun 8.30am–7pm, daily in Jan & July; R$10; ⓦmuseunauticodabahia.org.br) sits within the picturesque **Forte de Santo Antônio** on the windy Barra point, where the Atlantic Ocean becomes the bay of Todos os Santos (local buses and the *executivo* service to Barra leave from the Praça da Sé). It houses a collection of seafaring instruments, maps, model boats, art and documents (all labelled in English). Founded in 1534 as a wattle-and-daub construction, this was the first European fort on the Brazilian coast (the current fortifications date from 1696–1702). Most people come for the views from the terrace above the museum; it's a popular place to have a cocktail as the sun sets.

Igreja do Bonfim

The **Igreja do Bonfim** (Mon 8.30am–5.30pm, Tues–Thurs & Sat 6.30am–noon & 2–6pm, Fri & Sun 5.30am–noon & 2.30–6pm; free), located at the top of the peninsula of Itapagipe, is worshipped at by *Candomblistas* (followers of the Afro-Brazilian religion, *candomblé*) and Catholics alike, an intriguing hotchpotch of city dwellers from *favelados* to wealthy matriarchs and rural *mestizos* to naval officers. The church houses the **Museu dos Ex-Votos do Senhor do Bonfim** (Mon 9am–noon, Tues–Fri 8am–noon & 2–5pm, Sat 8am–noon & 1–4pm; R$3), lined with heart-wrenching photos of supplicants, written pleas for divine aid and thanks for wishes fulfilled. Hanging from the ceiling are a hundred body parts made of plastic and wood, offerings from the hopeful and the thankful. The church is a thirty-minute bus ride from the centre (take the buses marked "Bonfim" or "Ribeira" from the bottom of the Lacerda elevator).

ARRIVAL AND DEPARTURE

By plane Aeroporto Deputado Luis Eduardo do Magalhães (ⓣ 71 3204 1010) is around 30km northeast of the Cidade Alta, connected to the centre by an hourly shuttle express bus service (daily 7.30am–8pm; R$6.50), marked "Praça da Sé/Aeroporto", that leaves from directly in front of the terminal and takes you to Praça da Sé bus station via the beach districts. The length of the ride varies according to traffic, but if you're going back the other way make sure you allow two hours just to be safe. A taxi to the centre will cost around R$130 (fixed rate).
Destinations Daily flights to Miami, Buenos Aires, Lima, Madrid and Lisbon. Belo Horizonte (8 daily; 1hr 40min); Brasília (10 daily; 1hr 50min–2hr 10min); Recife (11 daily; 1hr 15min–1hr 30min); Rio (14 daily; 2hr 5min–2hr 35min); São Paulo (30 daily; 2hr 35min).
By bus Salvador's well-organized and large *rodoviária*, Av Antônio C. Magalhães 4362, Pituba (ⓣ 71 3616 8300), is 8km east of the centre. To get to/from the Cidade Alta an *executivo* bus runs between the Iguatemi shopping centre (across the busy road from the *rodoviária*) and Praça da Sé. The bus costs R$6 and makes stately progress via the beach districts of Pituba and Rio Vermelho. Alternatively, take a taxi (about R$25).
Destinations Belo Horizonte (1 daily; 23hr); Lençóis (4–5 daily; 6–7hr); Recife (4 daily; 12–16hr); Rio (4 daily; 28–30hr); São Paulo (4 daily; 33–35hr).
By boat Numerous launch services depart from the

CRIME AND SAFETY

Salvador (especially Centro) has more reported **robberies** and **muggings** of tourists than anywhere else in Bahia (and possibly Brazil). However, trouble is much easier to avoid than the statistics suggest. The vast majority of tourists who get mugged go exploring along pretty, but deserted, narrow streets. However enticing this might seem, never wander off the main drags or down ill-lit side streets in the day or at night, and don't use the **Elevador Lacerda** (see p.279) after early evening. Again, though it seems tempting (because it's so close), never walk up and down the winding roads that connect the Cidade Alta and the Cidade Baixa. Be careful using ordinary **city buses** on Sundays when there are few people around – the *executivo* bus is the safest option – and avoid wandering the backstreets of Barra at night.

If you stick to these rules you should have no problems: the main tourist area around **Pelourinho** is heavily policed and busy until quite late at night, and is therefore relatively safe. Needless to say, leave expensive jewellery, watches and electronics in the hotel while touring the old city, and if you are mugged, do not resist.

Terminal Maritimo Turístico, the blue building at the water's edge behind the Mercado Modelo. Popular destinations include the island of Itaparica, visible directly across the bay from Salvador, and Morro de São Paulo (see p.286) on Tinharé.

INFORMATION AND TOURS

Tourist information Helpful English-speaking staff can be found at the tourist office at the Lacerda elevator on Praça Municipal (daily 8am–6pm; ☎71 3321 3127, ⓦbahia.com.br). There are also information desks at the airport (daily 7.30am–11pm; ☎71 3204 1244), in Cidade Alta at Rua das Laranjeiras 2 (daily 8.30am–9pm; ☎71 3321 2463) and at the *rodoviária* (daily 7.30am–9pm; ☎71 3450 3871). An additional source of information is the tourist hotline, "Disque Bahia Turismo" – call ☎71 3103 3103 (24hr) and you should be able to get an English-speaker.

Tour operators Salvador Bus (Mon–Sat; tickets from R$50; ☎71 3356 6425, ⓦsalvadorbus.com.br) operate double-decker buses for various city-tours with tickets available at hotels and travel agencies; Privé Tur, Rua Manuel Andrade 55, Sala 310, Pituba (☎71 3535 0707, ⓦprivetur.com.br), organizes city tours, beach trips and schooner cruises. Tours Bahia, Cruzeiro de São Francisco 4/6, Pelourinho (☎71 3322 4383, ⓦtoursbahia.com.br), offers a range of good-quality services, covering city tours, airline tickets, transfers and money exchange.

GETTING AROUND

By bus The bus system is efficient, cheap (R$2.80) and easy to use, running till 11pm on weekdays and 10pm on weekends. To reach the centre, any bus with "Sé," "C. Grande" or "Lapa" on the route card will do. Buses with route card "Flamengo" leave from Praça da Sé passing Barra, and stopping off at all the beaches to the north – the last stop is Ipitanga. Air-conditioned "*executivos*" buses run most of the same routes, though less frequently (R$6).
By taxi Taxis are metered and plentiful and are recommended at night, even for short distances within the Cidade Alta. Meters start at R$3.75 and will quickly top R$50 for rides across the city. Radio Taxi Cometas (☎71 3377 6311); Chame Táxi (☎71 3241 2266).

ACCOMMODATION

The best area to head for is Cidade Alta, not least because of the spectacular view across the island-studded bay. The exception is if you want to be near the beach, in which case Barra offers great value for money and a good choice of party-vibe hostels. While pousada prices generally stay within reason, be aware that during Carnaval rates double or even triple. Out of season discounts are nearly always on offer, so make sure you ask for one ("*tem desconta?*").

CIDADE ALTA

Hostel Cobreu Ladeira do Carmo 22 ☎71 3117 1401, ⓦhostelcobreu.com. A steep staircase leads you up to colourful dorms with polished parquet floors. The corridors are decorated with vibrant graffiti by a renowned local artist, as is the little communal chill-out area, which has nice views over town. Dorms R$43, doubles R$85

Hostel Galeria 13 Rua da Ordem Terceira 23 ☎71 3266 5609, ⓦhostelgaleria13.com. Have an afternoon dip in the pool or unwind in the dimly lit Moroccan chill-out room before heading out on the town at this English-owned hostel with comfy wooden bunks. Owner Paul is always more than happy to point you in the right direction. Breakfast served until noon. Dorms R$38, doubles R$140

Hospeda Salvador Rua Sao Francisco 26 ☎71 3266 6923, ⓦhospedasalvador.com.br. Basic inn with clean dorms (sheets and towels included), filling breakfast including as much coffee as you need and the real feeling of a family home, just a 5min stroll downhill from the main Pelô drag. Dorms R$25

Laranjeiras Hostel Rua da Ordem Terceira 13 ☎71 3321 1366, ⓦwww.laranjeirashostel.com.br. Always booked-up HI hostel with long thin dorms that have unbelievably high top bunks. The crêperie in the lobby and the mezzanine chill-out area are great for mingling, while the long windows offer the perfect

---

TREAT YOURSELF

Hotel Casa do Amarelindo Rua das Portas do Carmo 6, Pelourinho ☎71 3266 8550, ⓦcasadoamarelindo.com. Step into a little oasis in the heart of Pelo, with terracotta floors, tropical plants and sculptures of orixas (gods) dotted around the tranquil reception area. It's worth the splurge for the lovely rooms, which have comfy beds and flat-screen TVs, as well as DVD and CD players. There's a small rooftop pool, and a panoramic terrace from which you can soak up the views of the Baía de Todos os Santos. R$470

★**Pousada des Arts** Rua Direita de Santo Antônio 90 ☎71 3012 5964, ⓦpousadadesarts.com.br. Set in a stunning four-storey colonial mansion dating from 1740, this elegant pousada has palatial rooms, some with excellent views of the Santo Antônio Church. *Berimbaus* (percussion instruments) decorate the walls on the ground floor, while upstairs local wooden furniture gives the place a warm, cosy touch. Good discounts in low season. R$280

vantage point for people-watching in the colourful cobbled streets below. Dorms R̲$̲4̲4̲, doubles R̲$̲9̲6̲
★**Nega Maluca Guesthouse** Rua dos Marchantes 15 ☎71 3242 9249, ⓦnegamaluca.com. This Israeli-owned hostel has dorms with deposit boxes for valuables, as well as sockets and lamps above each bed. There's a rooftop terrace with hammocks overlooking the upper part of Salvador, as well as a chill-out area at the back. Free wi-fi and breakfast buffet, free coffee all day and a "free shoulder to cry on in times of need". Dorms R̲$̲3̲0̲, doubles R̲$̲1̲0̲0̲

BARRA AND THE BEACHES
Albergue do Porto Rua Barão de Sergy 197, Barra ☎71 3264 6600, ⓦalberguedoporto.com.br. Comfy hostel with a relaxed vibe, good-sized dorms and hammocks slung in between the rooms. There's also a pool table, PlayStation, big TV and a good selection of films in the living room, as well as a kitchen and a supermarket just next door. Free internet and discount for HI members. Dorms R̲$̲4̲7̲, doubles R̲$̲1̲2̲0̲
Âmbar Pousada Rua Afonso Celso 485, Barra ☎71 3264 6956, ⓦambarpousada.com.br. The breakfast room has an old-fashioned feel but the rooms are clean and some open onto the inner courtyard. Staff are helpful and Barra beach is just a 10min walk away. Dorms R̲$̲5̲6̲, doubles R̲$̲1̲7̲0̲
Barra Guest Hostel Rua Recife 234, Barra ☎71 8774 6667, ⓦbarraguesthostel.com. Set in a colonial house, this comfy hostel has clean dorms with lockers and personal reading lamps. There's also cheap European grub, a free caipirinha every night at 7pm, as well as weekly barbecue nights and surfboard rental. Free wi-fi. Dorms R̲$̲3̲5̲, doubles R̲$̲1̲1̲8̲
Hostel Brasil Rua Recife 4, Barra ☎71 3264 9637, ⓦhostelbrasil.com.br. Fun and welcoming hostel, 10min from the beach. The spacious dorms all have individual lockers and there's a chill-out area with colourful beanbags that are perfect to sink into after a long day's surfing. Laundry and internet facilities available, and they can also help with travel arrangements. Dorms R̲$̲4̲0̲, doubles R̲$̲9̲0̲

★**F Design Hostel** Travessa Prudente de Moraes 65, Rio Vermelho ☎71 3035 9700, ⓦfdesignsalvador.com.br. It's a bus ride from the historic centre, but you get a fabulous, friendly hostel, with designer dorms, cool bar-like lobby, excellent wi-fi, decent breakfast, rooftop pool and bar and excellent a/c doubles. Dorms R̲$̲6̲5̲, doubles R̲$̲1̲6̲0̲

EATING AND DRINKING

Eating out is a pleasure in Salvador. There's a huge range of restaurants and the local cuisine (see box below) is deservedly famous all over Brazil. Street food is fabulous too and readily available, with plenty of vendors selling local delicacies (try the acarajé stalls in Rio Vermelho district, including the celebrated Acarajé da Dinha). While the Cidade Alta has a growing number of stylish, expensive places, it's still relatively easy to eat well for under R$25.

RESTAURANTS
CIDADE ALTA
Bar Zulu Rua dos Laranjeiras 15 ☎71 8784 3172. Come here if you're craving cheap comfort food or veggie options, including curries and fish and chips. It's lively in the evenings and the high wooden chairs are the perfect spot to enjoy a drink overlooking the street. Try their unique fruity zumorangi caipirinha (R$9.50). Daily 11am–2am.
Jardim das Delícias Rua João de Deus 12 ☎71 3321 1449. A hidden tranquil world within the Pelourinho, this courtyard restaurant offers high-quality ingredients that are definitely worth splashing out for. Try the badejo Jardim das Delícias (white fish marinated with herbs and served with plantain). Mains cost R$46–58. Mon & Wed 11.30am–4pm, Tues & Fri–Sun 11.30am–4pm & 6–11pm.
★**Porto do Moreira** Largo do Mocambinho 28 ☎71 3322 4112. Unassuming local spot with creative Bahian dishes and a long history – it was founded in 1938 by Portuguese immigrant José Moreira da Silva and is now managed by his two sons (the restaurant and the plaza featured in Jorge Amado's novel Dona Flor and Her Two Husbands). Dishes R$25–40. Mon–Sat 11.30am–4pm, Sun 11.30am–3pm.

COMIDA BAIANA
The secret of Bahian cooking is twofold: a rich seafood base and the abundance of traditional West African **ingredients** like palm oil, nuts, coconut and ferociously strong peppers. **Vatapá**, a bright yellow porridge of palm oil, coconut, shrimp and garlic, looks vaguely unappetizing but is delicious. Other dishes to look out for are **moqueca**, seafood cooked in the inevitable palm-oil-based sauce; **caruru**, with many of the same ingredients as vatapá but with the vital addition of loads of okra; and **acarajé**, deep-fried bean cake stuffed with vatapá, salad and optional hot pepper. Bahian cuisine also has good **desserts**, which are less stickily sweet than elsewhere: **quindim** is a delicious small cake of coconut flavoured with vanilla, which often comes with a prune in the middle.

Ramma Praça do Cruzeiro de São Francisco 7 (off Terreiro de Jesus), Pelourinho ☏71 3321 0495. Excellent vegetarian restaurant (though be warned, meat dishes are also served), with a fabulous salad bar and desserts. Buffet-style meals cost R$45/kilo, but R$15–20 will get you a good meal. Mon–Sat noon–4pm.

★**Restaurante do SENAC** Largo do Pelourinho ☏71 3321 5502, ⓦwww.ba.senac.br. Municipal restaurant-school in a finely restored colonial mansion (once a legendary *capoeira* school). It looks very expensive from the outside, but it's good value for what you get. You pay a set charge for the lunch *buffet típico* upstairs – about R$48 – and take as much as you want from a choice of around forty dishes (and twelve desserts), all helpfully labelled so you know what you're eating. On street level is a simpler *"buffet à quilo"* option (R$34.90/kilo; Mon–Fri). Mon–Sat 11.30am–3.30pm & 6.30–10pm, Sun 11.30am–3.30pm.

Sorriso da Dadá Rua Frei Vicente 5 ☏71 3321 9642. You certainly won't get much of a *sorriso* (smile) here, but locals still rave about the famous Bahian cuisine on offer, though you get less for your money than a few years ago. Classic dishes for two will set you back around R$75–80. Daily 11.30am–midnight.

Uauá Rua Gregório de Matos 36 ☏71 3321 3089. A smart option with interior decor evocative of the mud huts of northern Brazil. There are plenty of seafood dishes (stewed shrimp and fish in coconut and palm oil R$55 for two) on the menu, alongside meat dishes. Mon–Sat 11am–10pm.

BARRA

Ramma Rua Lord Cochrane 76 ☏71 3264 0044, ⓦrammacozinhanatural.com.br. This classic wholefood café (sister to the old town branch) provides an excellent range of tasty and healthy *comida por kilo* at lunchtimes. Get there well before 1pm to avoid the crowds. Figure on R$15–20. Daily 11.30am–3.30pm.

Tudo Azul Av Sete de Setembro 3717 ☏ 71 9104 8011. This modest Swiss/Brazilian fusion place is great for a relatively cheap meal (R$15–22) and cold beer, with the names of customers scribbled on the walls. Think "Swiss" potatoes, *moqueca* and fresh shrimp. Staff hand out salted popcorn while you wait for a table. Daily noon–11.30pm.

CAFÉS AND ICE CREAM

Bahia Café Praça da Sé 22 , Pelourinho ☏71 3322 1266. Sandwiches, soups and salads (R$10–20) alongside superb coffee (R$3.50) at this chilled-out café in a hotel bang in the centre of town. There's also free wi-fi access and airy windows opening onto the street. Daily 8am–11pm.

Café Conosco Rua da Ordem Terceira do São Francisco 4, Pelourinho. Attractive café set in an early eighteenth-century house; good coffee, quiche and cakes (R$4–5) made by owner Nilza Ribeiro, free wi-fi and a tranquil

escape from the hubbub of the streets. Mon–Fri 10am–7pm, Sat 10am–4pm.

★**Sorvete da Ribeira** Praça General Osório, 87, Ribeira (a short taxi ride from Igreja da Bonfim) ⓦsorveteriadaribeira.com.br. Open since 1931, this ice-cream parlour offers numerous flavours including local fruity ones such as tamarind, tapioca, *umbu* and *jenipapo* (R$3 per scoop). Eat your ice cream while watching the fishermen organize their haul in the evenings. Daily 9am–10pm.

NIGHTLIFE

You'll find Salvador's most distinctive bars and nightlife in Pelourinho, though Barra also attracts the party crowd and other venues are scattered all over the city (Amaralina and Pituba are probably the liveliest areas to head for, and Friday and Saturday nights are best). Other than the weekend, Tuesday is a big night out, a tradition known as Terça da Benção ("blessed Tuesday").

Café Alquimia Ladeira do Carmo 22, Pelourinho. This small, often crowded bar and café, located underneath the *Hostel Cobreu*, serves cold beers and wonderful falafels. It's a popular meeting place where English is spoken, but it can get rowdy. Daily 5pm–late.

Casa do Amarelindo Rua das Portas do Carmo 6, Pelourinho. Smart, intimate hotel bar with a leafy indoor area serving superb *maracujá caipirinhas*. Wind your way up the spiral staircase to the terrace, where there's a small pool and lovely views across the bay. Daily 4–11.30pm.

Clube do Samba Largo do Terreiro de Jesus 5 ☏71 8726 9609, ⓦclubedosamba.com.br. Often hosts live samba acts on Saturdays and Sundays, and various local groups during the week. Cover R$10. Wed–Sun 5–11pm.

O Cravinho Bar Terreiro de Jesus 3, Pelourinho ⓦocravinho.com.br. *The* place to kick the night off with a few drinks before heading to *Fundo do Cravinho* at the back to try some frenetic salsa (cover R$4). The speciality here is *cravinhos*, flavoured *cachaça* shots with essence of clove or ginger (R$3). Daily 11am–late.

★**Sankofa** Ladeira de São Miguel 7, Pelourinho ☏71 3321 7236. The hippest African bar and club in town and a true local hangout. Spread over two storeys, the ground floor has live bands as well as DJs spinning anything from reggae to samba-rock and Afro-pop. A more chilled-out area with a tiny smoking terrace awaits upstairs. Entry R$10. Mon & Wed 7–11pm, Tues 9pm–3.30am, Fri & Sat 9pm–3am.

ENTERTAINMENT

A soulful, foot-tapping weekly event worth heading to is the jazz concert at MAM, Av Contorno (Museum of Modern Art; Sat 6–11pm, entry before 9pm; R$3–6; ☏71 3117 6139, ⓦjamnomam.com.br), near the marina in the Cidade Baixa (take a taxi).

CAPOEIRA

The Brazilian martial art **capoeira** is widely considered to originate from ritual fights in Angola to gain the nuptial rights of young women, though in Brazil it developed into a technique of anticolonial resistance, disguised from slave masters as a dance. Although outlawed for much of the nineteenth century, capoeira is now practised across the country, a graceful, semi-balletic art form somewhere between fighting and dancing. Usually accompanied by the characteristic rhythmic twang of the *berimbau* (single-string percussion instrument), it takes the form of a pair of dancers/fighters leaping and whirling in stylized "combat" – which, with younger *capoeiristas*, occasionally slips into a genuine fight when one fails to evade a blow and tempers fly. There are regular displays on Terreiro de Jesus and near the entrances to the Mercado Modelo in Cidade Baixa, largely for the benefit of tourists and their financial contributions, but still interesting. The best capoeira, though, can be found in the *academias de capoeira*, organized schools with classes you can watch for free. If you want a really cool capoeira experience, leave the Pelourinho and head up to the Forte Santo Antônio, just a short walk up the hill. Inside the renovated white fort are several schools where the setting may make you feel more like a Shaolin monk in training.

CAPOEIRA SCHOOLS

Academia de João Pequeno de Pastinha Largo Santo Antônio, Forte Santo Antônio ☎71 3323 0708, ⓦjoao-pequeno.com. You can watch, or if you want to join in, there are classes (Mon, Wed & Fri, 9am, 7.30pm; 2–3hr).
Associação de Capoeira Mestre Bimba Rua das Laranjeiras 1, Pelourinho ☎71 3322 0639, ⓦcapoeiramestrebimba.com.br. Probably the most famous *academia*, it sometimes has classes open to tourists.
Forte de Santo Antônio Praça Barão do Triunfo, Largo de Santo Antônio ☎71 3117 1488, ⓔfortesanto antonio@gmail.com. Classes open to tourists.

Balé Folclórico da Bahia Rua Gregório de Matos 49, Pelourinho ☎71 33221962, ⓦbalefolcloricodabahia .com.br. Frantic drumming as radiant dancers in colourful dresses spin around tapping their feet and moving their bodies to Afro-Brazilian music at the Teatro Miguel Santana. Performances Mon, Wed, Thurs, Fri 8–9.15pm; buy tickets (R$45) in advance from the box office (open from 2pm).
Show de Gerônimo Ladeira do Carmo, Pelourinho. Don't miss this weekly live performance by Gerônimo (a veteran Salvadorian songwriter) on the steps leading up to the Igreja do Santíssimo Sacramento (best viewed from the Ladeira do Carmo around the *Café Alquimia*), supported by his band Mont'Serrat, renowned for its classy horn section. Tues 7–10pm.

SHOPPING

Instituto de Artesanato Visconde de Mauá Rua Gregório de Matos 27, Pelourinho ⓦmaua.ba.gov.br. This place was founded by the government to promote regional artists. You'll find carving, ceramics and hammocks at fixed prices, among other handicrafts. Mon–Fri 10am–6pm.
Mercado Modelo Praça Visconde de Cayrú 250, ⓦmercadomodelobahia.com.br. Handicraft market in Cidade Baixa. Mon–Sat 9am–7pm, Sun 9am–2pm.
Shopping Barra Av Centenário 2992 ⓦshoppingbarra .com. Large mall that's handy for the Barra beaches. Mon–Sat 9am–10pm, Sun 1–9pm .

DIRECTORY

Banks and exchange There are several places to change money in the Pelourinho area, while Banco do Brasil has several branches, all with Visa ATMs, including one on the Terreiro de Jesus. Citibank has a branch at Av Estados Unidos 558, Cidade Baixa.
Consulates UK, Av Estados Unidos 18B, 8th Floor, Comércio (☎71 3243 7399); US, Av Tancredo Neves 1632, Room 1401, Salvador Trade Center, Torre Sul, Caminho das Árvores (☎71 3113 2090).
Hospitals Hospital Aliança, Av Juracy Magalhães Jr. 2096, Rio Vermelho (☎71 2108 5600); Hospital São Rafael, Av São Rafael 2152, São Marcos (☎71 3281 6111).
Internet Try Baiafrica Internet Café on the Praça da Sé (R$4/hr) or Internet do F@rol, Av Sete de Setembro 42, in Barra (R$4/hr).
Laundries O Casal at Av Sete de Setembro 3564, Barra (☎71 3264 9320); Wash & Dry, Ladeira da Praça 4, Pelourinho (☎71 3321 0821).
Pharmacies Farmácia Sant'ana, Largo Porto da Barra, Barra (☎71 3267 8970); Drogaleve, Praça da Sé 6, Pelourinho (☎71 3322 6921).
Police The tourist police, DELTUR, are at Praça José de Anchieta 14, Cruzeiro de São Francisco, Pelourinho (☎71 3116 6817, ☎71 3116 6512).
Post office Largo do Cruzeiro de São Francisco 20, Pelourinho (Mon–Fri 9am–5pm, Sat 9am–1pm).

3

MORRO DE SÃO PAULO

Covering the tip of the island of **Tinharé**, some 60km south of Salvador by sea, the beach resort of **MORRO DE SÃO PAULO** is quite unlike anything else in Bahia. Safe, friendly, and with no cars and a string of gorgeous beaches lined with palm trees, reggae bars, hip pousadas and great seafood restaurants, it boasts a tropical, laidback beach scene reminiscent of Thailand or the Philippines – the main beaches are backed by jungle-clad mountains and you're as likely to hear Daft Punk as Sergio Mendes in the bars. However, this is no longer a backpacker haven. Brazil's middle class have been coming here for a while now, and though cheap hostels remain, more upmarket pousadas, lounge bars and restaurants are far more prevalent. Between November and March (especially at weekends, which are best avoided), Morro is swamped with visitors, though at other times it can still seem relatively peaceful and undeveloped.

WHAT TO SEE AND DO

There are four main beaches in Morro, known simply as **First**, **Second**, **Third** and **Fourth beaches**, with the first being the closest (and therefore most popular) to the village centre and the fourth being the furthest away and thus quietest.

On arrival, expect to be besieged by tenacious locals offering to be your "guide" – shake them off relatively easily by heading straight to the **Tiroleza do Morro Zipline** (daily 10am–5.30pm; R$35), a 70m-high and 340m-long zip-wire that will whizz you down to the First Beach in no time. To get to the zipline, head along the coastal path up the hill and make your way to the back of the lighthouse (Farol do Morro de São Paulo). Of course, you can just as easily, if less dramatically, walk to the beach in five minutes from the pier.

ARRIVAL AND INFORMATION

Though you can fly to Morro via chartered air taxi from Salvador, most people take the ferry. You must pay the R$15 "Taxa de Preservação Ambiental" to enter the village at the dock. When you leave, you must pass through the Cais do Porto on the pier itself to pay the R$0.81 "Taxa de Embarque" (don't pay this coming in).

By boat Several boats run back and forth between the Terminal Maritimo Turístico in Salvador (see p.281) and the ferry dock in Morro every day (8.30am–2pm, roughly hourly; returning 9am–3pm). Fares start at around R$75–85 for a one-way trip on a fast boat (*lancha*) or larger catamaran (usually a bit cheaper coming back); trips take about 2hr 30min, but be warned, the sea can be rough, even on a fine day. See Bio Tur (⊚ biotur.com.br) or Passeios às Ilhas (⊚ passeiosasilhas.com.br) for more information.

Tourist information Behind the pier lies a small tourist office that hands out useful maps (daily 8am–10pm; ☎ 75 3652 1083, ⊚ morrosp.com.br, ⊚ morrodesaopaulo .com.br).

ACCOMMODATION

Accommodation on the island is generally expensive, particularly at holiday times. Most of the larger places are pousadas with their own restaurant and bar. Nearly all of them are within a stone's throw of the beaches, and those listed have free wi-fi.

Che Lagarto Hostel Rua Da Fonte Grande 11 ☎ 75 3652 1018, ⊚ chelagarto.com. Basic rooms and dorms, all with a/c, and a shared TV room, bar, table tennis and barbecue area – drinks are cheap and the owners lay on free popcorn to munch. Dorms R$36, doubles R$122

Hi Hostel & Pousada do Reggae Travessa da Fonte Grande 7 ☎ 75 3652 1094, ⊚ pousadadoreggae.com.br. Cheap, clean dorms and doubles with free wi-fi, lockers, a/c and shared bathrooms. Linens and towels are provided. Buffet breakfast included. Dorms R$50, doubles R$130

Hostel Rosa dos Ventos Rua Chalon, Terceira Praia (Third Beach) ☎ 75 3652 1316, ⊚ rosadosventoshostel .com.br. Solid, clean budget choice 25m from Third Beach with a communal kitchen (till 11pm) and a sociable bar where you can swap stories with other travellers. There are a/c doubles and larger rooms with two bunks that can function as dorms. Adequate breakfast included. Dorms R$45, doubles R$140

EATING AND DRINKING

There are several good restaurants around the Praça Aureliano Lima and Caminho da Praia in town, with cheaper menus in the smaller, no-frills places towards the Fonte Grande. Most restaurants on the beaches double as bars, and drinks prices are usually standardized – R$10 for 3 beers, R$8 for *caipirinhas* – but look out for happy-hour deals. Second Beach can be smothered in tables on summer weekends, and you'll need to arrive early to snag one; further along, the scene is more laidback.

Chez Max Between Second and Third Beach. Good thin-crust pizza for your *reais*, with Italian chefs, relaxed vibe and good music. Pasta dishes for R$25–27 and pizzas R$24–32. Daily 11am–10pm.

Morena Bela Rua da Fonte Grande. This cheap local favourite knocks out stews, chicken, seafood and especially tasty *moquecas* for just R$15–20 per plate, with seating on plastic chairs and tables in a sleepy street. No sea views, but this is a real bargain. Daily 11am–10pm.

★**Pedra Sobre Pedras** Second Beach. Right at the north end of the beach, where the path comes down the hill, this bar is perched on a wooden deck with magnificent views, cold beers, snacks and decent *caipirinhas*. Open 24hr.

NIGHTLIFE

Clubs, bars, beach and full moon parties – there's always something going on in Morro and you won't need much help in finding it. Second Beach is the place to start (and often end) the evening, with dozens of caipirinha vendors and bars playing beats catering to all musical tastes – dancing goes on until the small hours. To get to the clubs, follow the path through the town centre and head up the hill.

Pulsar Disco Club Caminho do Fortaleza 1 (the path to the Fortaleza do Tapirandú) ⓦ pulsardisco.com.br. Surrounded by thick vegetation, Morro's party central is an Ibiza-style club that really gets going in the summer, with decent guest DJs from all over Brazil. Cover charge R$10–50. Fri & Sat midnight–8am.

Toca do Morcego Rua Caminho do Farol 11 (on the path up to the lighthouse) ⓦ tocadomorro.com. Friday night is legendary at this club a 5min walk from the centre. Soak in the sea view as you sip on unbelievably potent *caipirinhas* and groove to dance tunes until the early morning. Cover R$35–50, but get flyers in advance for reductions. Sunset sessions Tues–Sun 4.30–9pm; club Fri & Sat midnight–6am.

THE CHAPADA DIAMANTINA

One of Brazil's most exciting locations for hiking, climbing and rural sightseeing, the **PARQUE NACIONAL DA CHAPADA DIAMANTINA** offers 38,000 square kilometres of awe-inspiring table mountains, jagged rocky peaks and wide-open canyons interspersed with gigantic waterfalls, rivers, scrubland and forest. Once here, most visitors undertake a three- or six-day organized trek (guide essential; seven days from R$1350), staying in local houses along the way with meals included. The experience is like no other in Brazil: you gain a glimpse of the slow *sertanejo* pace of life and rural northeastern hospitality while taking in stunning scenery. The challenge of a long hike is not for everyone, but guides tailor trips to your ability and fitness. It's advisable to come here in the cooler months between April and October – though conversely the region's waterfalls are at their most spectacular in rainy (and high) season, from December to March.

Though the sizeable and attractive ex-diamond-mining town of **Lençóis** provides the most obvious access to the northern half of the park – and offers consummate facilities – most independent/budget travellers choose to go directly on to the community of **Vale do Capão** within the park boundaries itself. Long a bohemian hangout, in recent years smarter pousadas have opened, adding a new level of alternative-chic with meditation, massage and saunas, and drawing a broader age group.

WHAT TO SEE AND DO

There is almost endless potential for hikes in the national park. Some of the most famous or accessible locations are not too far from Capão or Lençóis and can be visited on day or multi-day excursions. The (guided) hike between the two communities is usually undertaken over three days, though its most famous sight – Brazil's highest waterfall, the **Cachoeira da Fumaça** – can be visited on a circular hike from either location. Here, a stream tumbles 385m over a cliff face, vaporizing into a fine mist before it reaches the bottom. Jagged overhanging rocks provide dizzying viewing points. Hiking to the base of the waterfall is a somewhat more difficult trek than that of reaching the top, however, and in high season the caves that serve as overnight sleeping spots (camping gear provided or pre-arranged by guides) can get overrun with visitors.

Another celebrated sight is the **Morro do Pai Inácio**, a 1120m high mesa peak with fabulous views over the cactus-strewn tablelands, while the **Gruta do Lapão**, a kilometre-long gorge formed from layered sandstone, lies just 5km north of Lençóis.

ARRIVAL AND DEPARTURE

By bus Real Expresso (ⓣ75 3334 1112; ⓦ realexpresso .com.br) buses run between Salvador and Lençóis (4 daily; 6hr), all arriving at the main *rodoviária* in town and continuing on to Palmeiras (45min); *colectivos* shuttle between Palmeiras and Capão for around R$10 (30min); a taxi is R$60–70.

By plane Azul (⊕voeazul.com.br) operates one daily flight (1hr) between Salvador and the tiny airport outside Coronel Octaviano Alves (20km from Lençóis), where taxis will take you into town (R$40) or to destinations inside the Parque Nacional da Chapada Diamantina.

INFORMATION AND TOURS

Guides are most often arranged by pousadas, but you can arrange your own. Standard rates for independent guides are R$150–160/day for a group of five or six people, though it can be tough to find someone that speaks good English. Information is available from the Associação dos Conductores de Visitantes at Rua 10 de Novembro 22 in Lençóis (daily 8am–noon & 2–8pm; ☎75 3334 1425). See also ⊕guiachapadadiamantina .com.br.

Chapada Adventure Daniel Praça Horácio de Matos 114, Lençóis ☎75 3334 1933, ⊕chapadaadventure.com.

Extreme Eco Adventure Av 7 de Setembro 15, Lençóis ☎75 3341 1727, ⊕extremeecoadventure.com.br.

H2O Travel Adventures Rua do Pires, Lençóis ☎75 3334 1229, ⊕h2otraveladventures.com.

ACCOMMODATION

Numerous pousadas are located in Lençóis and more are scattered throughout Vale do Capão. Book as far in advance as possible. Capão also offers a few basic restaurants, including a great pizzeria.

Hostel Chapada Rua Boa Vista 121, Lençóis ☎75 3334 1497, ⊕hostelchapada.com.br. Attractive and brightly painted HI hostel in the middle of town. Basic breakfast served and free wi-fi. Cheaper for HI members. Dorms R$58, doubles R$150

Pousada Pé no Mato Ladeira da Vila 2, Caeté-Açú, Vale do Capão ☎75 3344 1105, ⊕penomato.com.br. Offers simple but adequate rooms with fans, dorms and more comfortable suites and chalets with verandas, TVs and fans. Dorms R$50, doubles R$140, suites and chalets R$175

Pousada Safira Rua Miguel Calmon 124, Lençóis ☎75 3334 1443, ⊕pousadasafira.com. This is one of the friendliest budget options but with just a few small rooms, all with their own bathroom – singles pay R$70. Free wi-fi in public areas and breakfast is included. It's a little hard to find in the backstreets at the heart of town. R$100

★**Pousada Tatu Feliz** Vale do Capão ☎75 3344 1124, ⊕infochapada.com/pousadatatufeliz.htm. Friendly multi-lingual service, free wi-fi and an excellent breakfast make this pousada a really good bet for exploring the park. Dorms (minimum of 3 people required) R$60, doubles R$130

The Northeast

Long regarded as one of Brazil's poorest areas, **THE NORTHEAST** has benefited from the nation's economic boom and is now a region on the rise. Despite having the most dazzling coastline in South America, a buzzing beach scene and an exuberant culture that blends samba, reggae and African influences, the area, divided politically into eight separate states, has not been spoilt by tourism. There are major cities along the coast: some, such as **Recife**, **Olinda**, **São Luís** and **Fortaleza**, have deep colonial histories; others, such as **Natal**, have developed mostly in recent decades. All have their own city beaches plus more idyllic and deserted resorts hidden up and down the coast. The **Ilha de Fernando de Noronha**, hundreds of kilometres offshore, is one of the finest oceanic wildlife reserves in the world, an expensive destination but perfect for ecotourism.

RECIFE

The Northeast's largest metropolitan area, **RECIFE** ("her-see-fey") is a dynamic, sprawling city of over four million with a booming economy and two major ports. The city centre – the three islands of Santo Antônio, Boa Vista and Bairro do Recife – remains a chaotic, shabby place, where scrappy street vendors, markets, polluted drains and heavy traffic contrast with crumbling Art Nouveau buildings and a profusion of colonial churches. It's a compelling mix, once you get used to it, and the regenerated **Bairro do Recife** area in particular is a real gem, more akin to *belle époque* Europe than the rest of Brazil. Most of the money – and the middle class – lives in the beachside district of **Boa Viagem**, a forest of high-rise condos and beach hotels to the south. Just to the north lies **Olinda**, one of the highlights of Brazil (p.295).

WHAT TO SEE AND DO

Modern Recife sprawls over the mainland, but the broad **Avenida Dantas Barreto** forms the spine of the central island of

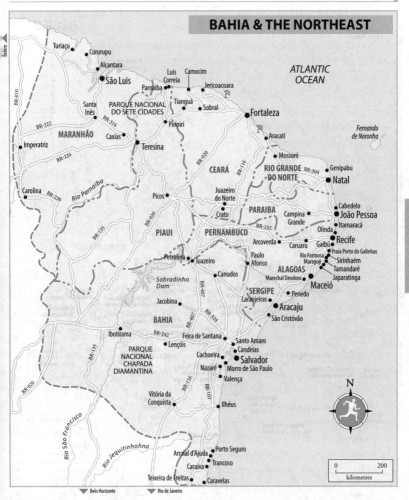

BAHIA & THE NORTHEAST

3

Santo Antônio, lined with street markets almost its entire length, and crisscrossed with a web of crowded, narrow lanes lined with stalls and shops. It ends in the much quieter **Praça da República**, filled with majestic palms and surrounded by Recife's grandest public buildings.

Convento de Santo Antônio and the Capela Dourada

The most enticing attraction in central Recife is the **Capela Dourada** (Golden Chapel), housed inside the Franciscan complex known as the **Convento do**

Santo Antônio on Rua do Imperador (Mon–Fri 8–11.30am & 2–5pm, Sat 8–11.30am; R$5). The convent, established in 1606, was incorporated by the Dutch into their fortress here in the 1630s, and it was largely rebuilt between 1702 and 1777. You enter via the **Museu Franciscano de Arte Sacra**, a small but precious collection of religious carvings and statuary (all with good English labelling), before walking through a quiet cloister to the Golden Chapel itself. Finished in 1724, the Baroque interior is smothered in lavish wall-to-ceiling

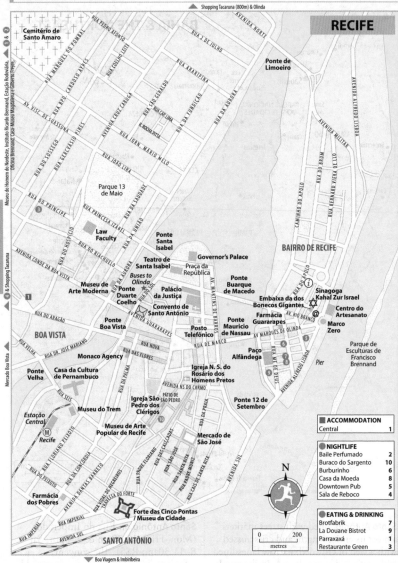

RECIFE

ornamentation, everything covered with gold leaf, while its crowning glory is the series of ceiling panels by **Manuel de Jesus Pinto**, an *alforriado*, or freed slave, whose work graces many of the city's finest religious buildings.

Pátio de São Pedro and around

Just off the Avenida Dantas Barreto, the impressive **Igreja São Pedro dos Clérigos**

(Mon–Fri 8am–noon & 2–4pm; free) stands on the graceful **Pátio de São Pedro**. Inside there's some exquisite woodcarving and a trompe l'oeil ceiling by Manuel de Jesus Pinto. The colonial buildings that line the square have been beautifully preserved, and in the evenings you can soak up the view over a beer at one of the many bars that set up tables outside. Browse the stalls lining the square's adjacent winding streets for crafts, or head west to the T-shaped **Casa da Cultura de Pernambuco**, a former prison turned crafts gallery, located on Rua Floriano Peixoto (Mon–Fri 9am–7pm, Sat 9am–6pm, Sun 9am–2pm; free; ⓦcasadaculturape.com.br).

Forte das Cinco Pontas

The star-shaped **Forte das Cinco Pontas**, at the southern end of Santo Antônio (built in 1630 by the Dutch, and the place they surrendered in 1654), currently houses the **Museu da Cidade** (Mon–Fri 9am–6pm, Sat 1–5pm; free; ☏81 3355 3108). Though the fort is worth visiting for its splendid sea views, the museum offers a window into the city's myriad past lives with temporary exhibits, often with an architectural theme.

Bairro do Recife

The once run-down district of **Bairro do Recife** (aka **Recife Antigo**) now has a thriving nightlife scene and is also a pleasant place during the day to explore, with grand, brightly painted *belle époque* buildings. Check out the **Sinagoga Kahal Zur Israel** or simply the **Centro Cultural Judaico**, Rua do Bom Jesus 197 (Tues–Fri 9am–4.30pm, Sun 2–6pm; R$8; ☏81 3224 2128), the site of the first synagogue built in the whole of the Americas; it dates back to 1639 when Jews started to coming to Dutch-controlled Brazil. When the rather less tolerant Portuguese resumed control of the city in 1654, the Jews were booted out and the synagogue destroyed – today all that remains is the foundation, the excavated Mikvah (ritual bath) and some brick walls. Upstairs there's a re-creation of what it might have looked like in its heyday.

Nearby at Rua do Bom Jesus 183, the **Embaixada dos Bonecos Gigantes** (daily 8am–6pm; R$10; ⓦbonecosgigantesdeolinda.com.br) is a small, quirky museum displaying some of the giant **puppets** used in the Olinda Carnaval, many of them celebrities, from Lampião to a scary-looking Michael Jackson.

At the heart of the Bairro do Recife's regeneration is Praça Barão Rio Branco, known simply as **Marco Zero** for the "Km 0" marker in the centre. On the other side of the plaza lies the **Centro do Artesanato** (see p.295), with views across the river to the totem-like 32m-high Torre de Cristal in the **Parque de Esculturas Francisco Brennand** (boats there daily 7am–5pm; R$5).

Museu do Homem do Nordeste

Though it's a fair distance from the centre, it's worth making the trip to the fascinating **Museu do Homem do Nordeste** in Casa Forte, Av 17 de Agosto 2187 (Tues–Fri 8.30am–5pm, Sat & Sun 1–5pm; R$4; ⓦwww.fundaj.gov.br). Founded by Brazilian anthropologist Gilberto Freyre (see below) in 1979, the museum depicts everyday life and folk culture with more than twelve thousand exhibits ranging from carriages used by seventeenth-century sugar barons to present-day northeastern carnival costumes. To get here, take the "Dois Irmões – Via Barbosa" bus from the post office or from Parque 13 de Maio, at the bottom of Rua do Hospício in Boa Vista, a thirty-minute drive through leafy northern suburbs. The museum is on the left, but hard to spot: ask the driver or conductor where to get off.

Casa Museu Gilberto Freyre

Anyone with even a passing interest in anthropology, or Brazil's cultural identity, shouldn't miss the chance to root around in the sugar-pink nineteenth-century mansion of **Gilberto Freyre**, whose 1933 book, *The Masters and the Slaves*, remains one of the most iconic texts ever written on the country. Located a shortish taxi ride away from the Museo do Homem do Nordeste (or via bus #522 or #930 from Av Agamenon Magalhães), at Rua Dois Irmãos 320, Apipucos (Mon–Fri 9am–5pm, R$10; ☏81 3441 1733), the interior is stuffed with his collection of over forty thousand books and all manner of fascinating ethnic antiques and curios.

Instituto Ricardo Brennand

One of Recife's most incongruous attractions is the **Instituto Ricardo**

3

3

Brennand on Alameda Antônio Brennand in the outlying suburb of Várzea (Tues–Sun 1–5pm; R$20; ☎81 2121 0352, ⓦinstitutoricardobrennand.org.br). This mock-Tudor castle belongs to one of the sons of the city's renowned Brennand family, and is home to a fascinating gallery dedicated to the **Dutch occupation of Brazil** (including the world's largest collection of paintings by Frans Post), as well as Greco-Roman mythological figures, suits of armour and a collection of Swiss-army knives. To get here, catch bus #040 on Avenida Domingos Ferreira (in Boa Viagem) or Avenida Agamenon Magalhâes (bordering Boa Vista) and take it to the end of the line. Continue on foot to the end of the road, and turn right onto Rua Isaac Buril. The institute is at the end of this road on the left. Taxis will charge at least R$110 round-trip from Boa Viagem.

Oficina Brennand

A short walk south of the Instituto, on Propriedade Santos Cosme e Damião, you'll find the studio of the Brennand clan's most famous scion, sculptor Francisco (the cousin of entrepreneur Ricardo). A renovated ceramics factory-cum-Brazilian Parque Güell, **Oficina Brennand** (Mon–Thurs 8am–5pm, Fri 8am–4pm, Sat & Sun 10am–4pm; R$10; ⓦbrennand.com.br) displays thousands of his whimsical sculptures, decorated tiles, paintings and drawings in what is actually a vast open-air sculpture park surrounded by pristine *Mata Atlântica* forest.

Boa Viagem

Regular buses make it easy to get down to the district of **BOA VIAGEM** and the beach, an enormous skyscraper-lined arc of sand that constitutes the longest stretch of urbanized seafront in Brazil (over 7km), protected by the slim *arrecife* (reef) just offshore.

The narrow **beach** is packed at weekends and deserted during the week, with warm natural rock pools to wallow in just offshore when the tide is out. Pavilions punctuate the pavement along the noisy road, selling all sorts of refreshing drinks from coconut water to pre-mixed *batidas* (rum cocktails). There have been a small number of shark attacks over the years, but they usually involve surfers far offshore.

ARRIVAL AND DEPARTURE

By plane Recife's modern Aeroporto Internacional dos Guararapes is only 11km from the city centre, at the southern end of Boa Viagem; TAM and Gol connect it with the rest of the country. You can pay for fixed-rate taxis at the arrivals halls (COOPSETA; ☎81 3462 1584), which will cost R$17–32 to Boa Viagem, R$40 for Santo Antônio (city centre) and R$63 for Olinda, or opt for a pay-by-meter *taxi comum*, which are about the same, assuming it's not rush hour. Alternatively, for Boa Viagem take either the a/c bus #042 from outside the airport (every 20min, 5am–11.55pm; R$2.80), or bus #040 (every 20min, 5am–11.55pm; R$2.25) from nearby Praça Ministro Salgado Filho. For Boa Vista (city centre), take bus #163 (every 20min, 5am–11pm; R$2.25) from the same *praça*. The metrô (R$1.60) also runs from just south of the airport (connected by walkway) to Estação Central terminal (not the beach).

Destinations Fortaleza (11–12 daily; 1hr 15min–1hr 30min); Lisbon (1 daily; 7hr 35min); Miami (1 daily; 8hr 20min); Panama City (1 daily; 7hr 20min); Rio (26–32 daily; 5hr 20min–7hr 50min); Salvador (7–10 daily; 1hr 10min–1hr 20min); São Paulo (11–15 daily; 3hr–3hr 30min).

By bus The *rodoviária* is about 14km west of the centre at BR-232 km 15, Coqueiral (☎81 3452 1103), though this is not really a problem since the metrô whisks you very cheaply (R$1.60) and efficiently into the centre, gliding through various *favelas*. It will deposit you at the old train station, called Estação Central (or simply "Recife"). To get to your hotel from there, you're best off taking a taxi. Taxis from the bus station direct to Boa Viagem or the city centre should run R$45–55 on the meter.

Destinations Belo Horizonte (3 daily; 35hr); Brasília (3 daily; 48hr); Fortaleza (3 daily; 13hr); Natal (10 daily; 4hr 30min); Porto de Galinhas (every 30min; 1hr); Rio (3 daily; 38–40hr); Salvador (3 daily; 12–15hr); São Paulo (3 daily; 48hr).

GETTING AROUND

By bus Most city buses originate and terminate on the central island of Santo Antônio, on Rua Cais de Santa Rita. They range in price from R$2.25 to R$3.50 (R$1.15 on Sun). To get from the city centre to Boa Viagem, take either bus #042, #039, #032 or #071. For up-to-date timetables see ⓦgranderecife.pe.gov.br.

By taxi Taxis use meters that start at R$4; reckon on R$15–20 between Boa Viagem and the city centre, and R$30–35 between Boa Viagem and Olinda.

INFORMATION AND TOURS

Tourist information The most helpful tourist information point is at the airport (daily 8am–6pm; ☎ 81 3462 4960, ⓦ www2.recife.pe.gov.br), where you may find English-speaking staff. There area also branches at the *rodoviária* (daily 7am–7pm; ☎ 81 3182 8298) and Pracinha de Boa Viagem (daily 8am–8pm; ☎ 81 3182 8297). There's the tourist hotline, the Disque Recife Turístico (Mon–Fri 8am–5pm; ☎ 81 3355 8409), on which you should be able to find someone who speaks English.

Tour operators Martur, Rua Dr Nilo Dornelas Câmara 90, Loja 02, Boa Viagem (☎ 81 3312 3666, ⓦ martur.com.br), organize flights, cruises and trips to Fernando de Noronha. There's also an office at the airport (☎ 81 3213 1404).

ACCOMMODATION

By far the cheapest place to stay is Boa Vista in the centre, though most of the city's hotels and hostels are located in Boa Viagem. If you don't mind staying in a soulless high-rise, the beach may compensate for the steep prices. Olinda (see p.295) is also expensive, if offset by the charm of its colonial conversions. As ever, if you want to visit during Carnaval, you'll need to book months in advance.

BOA VISTA

★ **Central** Av Manoel Borba 209 ☎ 81 3222 2353; map p.290. This handsomely decaying old hotel (opened in 1927) still has many of its original features including window shutters, stone steps and cage lift. While the en suites have a/c, the clean, spartan *coletivo* (shared toilet) rooms are probably the best bargain in the city. Ten percent discount if you book two nights or more. Breakfast included. R$75

BOA VIAGEM

Arrecifes Hostel Rua João Cardoso Ayres 560 ☎ 81 3462 5867, ⓦ arrecifeshostel.com.br; map opposite. One of Boa Viagem's newer hostels, this HI-affiliated place is perfectly pitched between the airport and the beach. The tiled rooms are basic but spotless, with a choice of a/c or fan, and there's also a kitchen, paved patio with hammocks, a pool table and wi-fi. Breakfast included. R$10 discount for HI members. Dorms R$52, doubles R$120

Cosmopolitan Hostel Rua Paulo Setúbal 53 ☎ 81 3204 0321, ⓦ cosmopolitanhostel.com; map opposite. Modern budget option, with basic en-suite doubles and spotless dorms, stylish TV lounge (cable TV, DVDs and free wi-fi), shared kitchen and breakfast included. Dorms R$45, doubles R$140

Estação do Mangue Rua Raimundo Gomes Gondim 26 ☎ 81 3049 2626, ⓦ estacaodomangue.com.br; map opposite. Justly popular hostel, a short walk from the beach, with communal TV room and kitchen, simple dorms and free wi-fi. Buffet breakfast included. Dorms R$50, doubles R$180

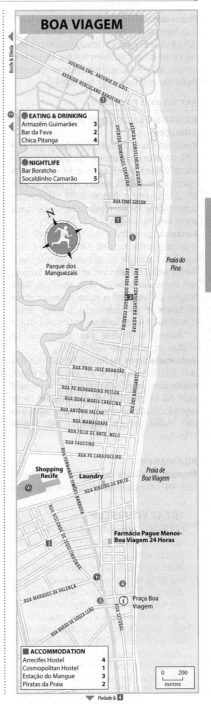

BOA VIAGEM

● EATING & DRINKING

Armazém Guimarães	3
Bar da Fava	2
Chica Pitanga	4

● NIGHTLIFE

| Bar Boratcho | 1 |
| Socaldinho Camarão | 5 |

Parque dos Manguezais

Praia do Pina

RUA TOMÉ GIBSON

RUA PROF. JOSÉ BRANDÃO

RUA PE BERNARDINO PESSOA

RUA DONA MARIA CAROLINA

RUA ANTÔNIO FALCÃO

RUA MAMAGUAPA

RUA FÉLIX DE BNTO. MELO

RUA FAUSTINO

RUA PE CARAPUCEIRO

Shopping Recife

Laundry

Praia de Boa Viagem

RUA RIBEIRO DE BRITO

Farmácia Pague Menos-Boa Viagem 24 Horas

RUA MARQUES DE VALENÇA

Praça Boa Viagem

RUA BARÃO DE SOUZA LEÃO

■ ACCOMMODATION

Arrecifes Hostel	4
Cosmopolitan Hostel	1
Estação do Mangue	3
Piratas da Praia	2

0 200 metres

Recife & Olinda

Piedade & 4

Piratas da Praia Av Cons Aguiar 2034 (3rd floor), at Rua Prf. Osias Ribeiro ☎ 81 3326 1281, ⓦ piratasdapraia.com; map p.293. Neat pastel dorms with primary-coloured portraiture and a choice of fan or a/c. Lockers available, discount for HI members, and wi-fi. Also some rooms and small apartments. Breakfast included. Dorms R$48, doubles R$160

EATING AND DRINKING

BAIRRO DO RECIFE, BOA VISTA AND THE SUBURBS

Brotfabrik Rua da Moeda 87, Recife Antigo ☎ 81 3424 2250, ⓦ brotfabrik.com.br; map p.290. Bakery that almost pulls off the Dutch theme in a spacious old warehouse with espresso (from R$3.10), pastries, rye bread, salgados (R$2.50), sandwiches (R$8.90–10.50) and bite-sized pizzas (*brotinho*; R$8.60); popular, as the constant queue attests. Mon–Fri 7am–8pm.

Parraxaxá Rua Igarassu 40, Casa Forte ☎ 81 3463 7874, ⓦ parraxaxa.com.br; map p.290. A little piece of the desert transplanted to the city, this celebrated *por quilo* place is themed around the talismanic *sertão* bandit, Lampião, with *cantina*-style tables and chairs, and a daily buffet featuring specialities such as *paçoca*, sun-dried beef and all manner of deliciously stodgy puddings (around R$49.90/kilo). A perfect lunch stop after the nearby Museu do Homem do Nordeste (see p.291). Mon–Sat 11.30am–10pm, Sun 7am–10pm.

Restaurante Green Rua Gervásio Pires 577, Boa Vista ☎ 81 3221 3531; map p.290. The food at this friendly neighbourhood *por quilo* joint isn't going to set the world alight but it's cheap (R$22/kilo), healthy and largely vegetarian (usually including decent veggie *feijão*), with some chicken and fish options as well. Mon–Fri 11am–3pm.

BOA VIAGEM

Armazém Guimarães Rua Baltazar Pereira 100 ☎ 81 3325 4011, ⓦ armazemguimaraes.com.br; map p.293.

> ## TREAT YOURSELF
>
> **La Douane Bistrot** Paço de Alfândega 35, Recife Antigo ☎ 81 3224 5799, ⓦ ladouane .com.br; map p.290. Located in the Alfândega shopping mall (see opposite), a beautifully renovated customs house. Waiting staff are immaculately turned out and the food is Mediterranean in flavour with a Brazilian bent – if you're feeling flush, splash out on the *bacalhau gratinado* with garlic purée (R$110); if not, go for the veggie pasta with artichoke and palm heart (R$40). Mon–Fri 10am–10pm, Sat noon–10pm, Sun noon–5.30pm.

This is the place for authentic wood-fired pizza in Recife. What the barn-like interior lacks in romance, the food makes up in quality, with prices in the R$30–40 range. Mon–Thurs 6pm–midnight, Fri & Sat 6pm–1am, Sun 5pm–midnight.

Bar da Fava Rua Padre Oliveira Rolin 37A, Jardim Beira Rio, Pina ☎ 81 3463 8998, ⓦ bardafava.com.br; map p.293. Renowned for its exquisitely prepared *favas* (broad beans) that accompany virtually every meal. Most dishes are priced for two to three diners, though they do an *executivo individual* for R$20, and the grilled cheese starter (R$10) is heavenly. Best take a taxi as it's difficult to locate. Mon & Tues 11am–6pm, Wed–Sat 11am–10pm, Sun 11am–7pm.

Chica Pitanga Rua Petrolina 19 ☎ 81 3465 2224, ⓦ chicapitanga.com.br; map p.293. Long one of the most popular *por quilo* places in Recife, with a bright, stylish interior and tables that you'll likely have to wait patiently to snag. At R$59 per kilo (R$69 at weekends), it isn't cheap but you get what you pay for, with a dazzling buffet heavy on seafood. Mon–Fri 11.30am–3.30pm & 6–10pm, Sat & Sun 11.30am–4.30pm & 6–10pm.

NIGHTLIFE

Recife lives and breathes live music. While Carnaval throbs to *frevo*, *afox* and *maracatu*, they've long been hybridized into the city's most famous musical export, *manguebeat*, a style that continues to exert a huge influence on acts you can either see for free, in the Pátio de São Pedro (see p.290), or on the big stage at Marco Zero or, for a modest fee, in the bars and clubs of Bairro do Recife. Look out, especially, for performances by Orquestra Contemporânea de Olinda, perhaps the most celebrated of the area's *manguebeat* inheritors. For upcoming shows see ⓦ www.acontecenorecife.com.br.

BAIRRO DO RECIFE AND SUBURBS

Baile Perfumado Rua Carlos Gomes 390 ☎ 81 3414 1241, ⓦ baileperfumado.com.br; map p.290. Recife's newest live music venue, with a capacity of 5000 and an already impressive list of rock/pop performances including Céu, Arnoldo Antunes and Alceu Valença, as well as local heroes Otto and Mundo Livre S/A. Tickets are usually in the region of R$50. Located well out in the suburbs (5km west of the centre), so take a taxi. Opens according to show times.

Buraco do Sargento Pátio de São Pedro 33, Santo Antônio ☎ 81 3224 7522; map p.290. Classic old-school bar and café on the plaza since 1955, housed in the headquarters of the Batutas de São José (one of Recife's *blocos de carnaval*). Stand around the granite counter-top or sit on a table outside, sipping Brahma or *cachaça* and snacking on *galinha cozido* (chicken gizzards; R$15). Mon–Sat 9.30am–10pm.

Burburinho Rua Tomazina 106, Barrio do Recife (Recife Antigo) ☎ 81 3224 5854, ⓦ www.barburburinho.com.br;

map p.290. Long *the* venue in Recife to hear local music in a sweaty nightclub setting, this place puts on everything from the new generation of local artists influenced by the '90s *manguebeat* explosion, to homages as diverse as The Cure and Creedence Clearwater Revival. Cover usually R$8–15. Hours vary; currently runs Blues sessions Mon 10pm–1am, Beatles night Wed 8pm–1am and stand-up comedy Thurs 8–10pm.

Casa da Moeda Rua da Moeda 150 Bairro do Recife (Recife Antigo) ☎81 3224 7095, ⓦcasadamoedabar .com.br; map p.290. For a taster of Recife's bohemian side visit the bar run by local photographer and artist Sergio Altenkirch, decorated with his work. Join the alternative crowd to drink *cachaça* and snack, and to enjoy live music (from jazz and blues to rock). Mon–Sat noon–late, Sun 6.30pm–late.

Downtown Pub Rua Vigário Tenório 105, Barrio do Recife (Recife Antigo) ☎81 3424 6317, ⓦdowntownpub.com.br; map p.290. Though the "casa do rock" – given a swanky makeover and definitely more of a club than a pub – lays it on thick with the Anglophone rock and tribute nights, you can sometimes land lucky with decent live reggae. Cover R$20–50. Fri & Sat 11pm–5am.

Sala de Reboco Rua Gregório Júnior 264, Cordeiro 264 ☎81 3228 7052, ⓦsaladereboco.com.br; map p.290. If you're really keen to pick up some authentic *forró pé-de-serra nordestino* (Northeastern Brazilian folk dance) skills, then it's worth your while heading out to the suburbs (bus #040 if you're not taking a taxi; ask the driver where to get off) to one of the country's best *casas de forró*, drawing a loyal crowd as well as some of Brazil's best *forrozeiros*. Thurs–Sat 10pm–late.

BOA VIAGEM

Bar Boratcho Galeria Joana D'arc, Av Herculano Bandeira 513, Pina ☎81 3327 1168; map p.293. With its name practically inviting a good drinking and dancing session, this cool fairy-lit shack is one of the best places in town to hear quality DJs. They also do Mexican food, should you need something to soak up all the tequila. Tues–Thurs 7pm–1am, Fri & Sat 7pm–3am, Sun 7pm–midnight.

Socaldinho Camarão Av Visconde de Jequitinhonha 106 ☎81 3462 9500; map p.293. If you fancy some footie action, head here and join the locals for a beer over a gripping game of Brazilian *futebol* as you munch on some *peixe a móda* (R$40 for three people). Mon–Thurs 11.30am–1.30am, Fri & Sat 11.30am–3am.

SHOPPING

Centro do Artesanato Av Alfredo Lisboa (Marco Zero), Armazém 11, Bairro do Recife (Recife Antigo) ☎81 3181 3451, ⓦwww.artesanatodepernambuco.pe.gov.br. Former warehouse on the waterfront that acts as a showcase for

folk art and the traditional crafts of Pernambuco. Mon–Sat 8am–6pm, Sun 9am–5pm.

Mercado de São José Rua São José, Santo Antônio. Opened in 1875, this is the oldest public market in Brazil. Stock up on some local crafts, or simply peruse the stacks of curious herbal medicines and everyday items as locals go about their daily shopping. Mon–Sat 6am–6pm, Sun 6am–noon.

Shopping Paço Alfândega Rua Alfândega 35, Bairro do Recife (Recife Antigo) ⓦpacoalfandega.com.br. Chic, refurbished former customs building on Recife Island, housing the typical range of Brazilian chain stores and fast-food outlets as well as the swanky *La Douane Bistro* (see opposite). Mon–Sat 10am–10pm, Sun noon–9pm.

DIRECTORY

Banks and exchange Most banks have ATMs. Banco do Brasil has branches at the airport (daily 10am–9pm), at Av Dantas Barreto 541, at Av Rio Branco 240 (4th floor), and on Rua Sete de Setembro in Boa Vista, all charging commission. Shopping centres all have ATMs, banks and money-changing facilities that stay open until 9pm Monday to Saturday. The Bradesco bank on Conde de Boa Vista has an ATM that accepts most Visa cards.

Consulates UK, Av Agamenon Magalhães 4775, 8th floor (☎81 2127 0200); US, Rua Gonçalves Maia 163, Boa Vista (☎81 3416 3050).

Hospital Real Hospital Português de Beneficência, Av Agamenon Magalhães 4760, Boa Vista (☎81 3416 1122).

Internet Caravela's Cyber Café, Rua do Bom Jesus 183, Recife Antigo (daily 8am–6pm; R$3/hr); Espaço Net, Rua Visconde de Jequitinhonha, Boa Viagem (Mon–Sat 7am–7.30pm; R$3/hr).

Laundry Aqua Clean Lavanderia, Av Eng Domingos Ferreira 4023, Boa Viagem (☎81 3466 0858).

Pharmacies Farmácia Pague Menos, Av Cons Aguiar 4635, Boa Viagem, 24hrs (☎81 3301 4209).

Post office The main post office is the Correio building at Av Guararapes 61 in Santo Antônio (Mon–Fri 9am–5pm). There's also a branch in the Bairro do Recife at Av Marquês de Olinda.

OLINDA

Founded in 1535, **OLINDA** is, quite simply, one of Brazil's most impressive examples of colonial architecture: a maze of cobbled streets, hills crowned with brilliant white churches, pastel-coloured houses, Baroque fountains and graceful squares. The city is also renowned for its street **Carnaval**, which attracts visitors from all over the world.

Despite its size, Olinda can effectively be considered a suburb of Recife: a high proportion of its residents commute to the city so **transport links** are good, with buses leaving every few minutes.

WHAT TO SEE AND DO

Olinda's colonial highlights include more churches than you could wish to see in an afternoon, and a curious puppet museum. Much of the appeal lies in wandering through the picturesque streets.

Alto da Sé

A good spot to have a drink and plan your day is the **Alto da Sé**, the highest square in town, not least because of the stunning view of Recife's skyscrapers shimmering in the distance, framed in

the foreground by Olinda's church towers, gardens and palm trees. The main attraction on the Alto da Sé is the **Igreja de São Salvador** (daily 9am–5pm; free), or just Igreja da Sé, reconstructed between 1656 and 1676 after the Dutch had destroyed the original. Inexplicably, the facade was given a bland Mannerist makeover in the 1970s, and the interior is now more of a museum than a living church, its former chapels used to display desultory religious art. At the back of the church is a patio from where you'll have the best views of the surrounding area and Recife.

Convento de São Francisco

If you only have time to visit one of Olinda's churches, head to the impressive

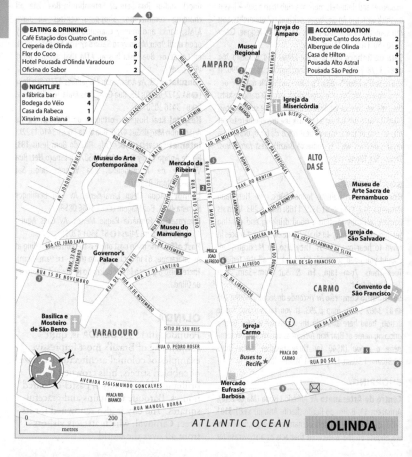

● EATING & DRINKING	
Café Estação dos Quatro Cantos	5
Creperia de Olinda	6
Flor do Coco	3
Hotel Pousada d'Olinda Varadouro	7
Oficina do Sabor	2

● NIGHTLIFE	
a fábrica bar	8
Bodega do Véio	4
Casa da Rabeca	1
Xinxim da Baiana	9

■ ACCOMMODATION	
Albergue Canto dos Artistas	2
Albergue de Olinda	5
Casa de Hilton	4
Pousada Alto Astral	1
Pousada São Pedro	3

ATLANTIC OCEAN

OLINDA

Convento de São Francisco on Rua São Francisco (Mon–Sat 9am–12.30pm & 2–5.30pm; R$3; ☎81 3429 0517), the country's oldest Franciscan convent. Established in 1577, most of what you see today was rebuilt in the eighteenth-century. Particular highlights are the cloister adorned with sixteen tiled *azulejo* panels depicting the lives of Jesus and St Francis of Assisi, and the sacristy's ornate Baroque furniture carved from jacaranda wood. Behind the convent there's a patio with grand panoramas across the ocean.

Museu do Mamulengo

The most enticing museum in Olinda is the **Museu do Mamulengo** at Rua São Bento 344 (Tues–Sun 10am–5pm; R$2), its galleries and passages festooned with flowery wallpaper and an excellent collection of traditional puppets arranged by theme and type (with English labelling). Don't miss the hand-turned mechanical diorama downstairs, and the depictions of bandit Lampião on the upper floor.

ARRIVAL AND INFORMATION

By bus From Recife, take bus #983 or #993 from Rua do Sol to Praça do Carmo, just by Olinda's main post office and a 2min walk up into the old city. From Boa Viagem, take bus #910 (every 30min).

Tourist information Information and maps are available from the Secretaria de Turismo in the Biblioteca Pública at the foot of Rua do São Francisco near Praça do Carmo (daily 8am–6pm; ☎81 3305 1060, ⓦolindaturismo.com.br). For all Carnaval-related information see ⓦcarnaval.olinda.pe.gov.br.

ACCOMMODATION

★**Albergue Canto dos Artistas** Rua Prudente de Moraes 351 ☎81 3493 2169. Popular hostel in an old house in the centre, with bright, tastefully decorated dorms and rooms, buffet breakfast and free wi-fi included. There's a sister property, *Albergue Canto dos Artistas II*, at Rua de São Bento 274. Dorms R$40, doubles R$120

Albergue de Olinda Rua do Sol 233, Carmo ☎81 3429 1592, ⓦalberguedeolinda.com.br. Located on a busy main road by the seafront, this bright HI hostel has a little garden with hammocks and a pool, ideal for mingling with other travellers. Rooms are a bit plain with just the bare necessities, but they're clean enough and the place itself has a friendly vibe. Wi-fi. HI discount available. Breakfast included. Dorms R$45, doubles R$100

Casa de Hilton Rua do Sol 77 ☎81 3494 2379, ⓦcasadehilton.com.br. The Hilton rents out a few vibrantly painted rooms in this bright yellow house at an unbeatable price; the tatty furniture has seen better days but the rooms are adequately comfortable for a few nights, and there's a communal kitchen. Dorms R$45, doubles R$90

★**Pousada Alto Astral** Rua 13 de Maio 305 ☎81 3439 3453, ⓦwww.pousadaaltoastral.com. Decorated with naïve art with a handsome wrought-iron staircase and a breakfast area (lavish spread included in price) that is perfect for socializing. The staff are incredibly friendly, rooms are warm, wildly painted and superb value, plus there's a pool and wi-fi. Ask for any of the rooms at the back, or, if there are four of you, ask for room 8 – spacious and with leafy views over the city. Single rooms available. R$100

★**Pousada São Pedro** Rua 27 de Janeiro 95 ☎81 3439 9546, ⓦpousadapedro.com. A spiral staircase leads up to the more expensive rooms in the main house of this charming pousada, while the cheaper rooms are around the pool area at the back. All have a/c. Breakfast included. R$100

EATING AND DRINKING

If you want to eat for less than R$20 in Olinda, try the *comida por quilo* places along the seafront. For a bit more, you can eat far better in the old town. Best and least expensive of all, though, is to join the crowds drinking and eating street food at the Alto da Sé. The charcoal-fired delights sold here include addictive Bahian *acarajé*.

Café Estação dos Quatro Cantos Rua Prudente de Moraes 440. Laidback café, art gallery, handicrafts store and cultural space, with decent espresso and snacks but also live samba in the evenings. Tues–Sat 2–9pm, Sun 3–9pm.

Creperia de Olinda Praça João Alfredo 168 ☎81 3429 2935. This agreeable crêperie is decorated with

---

★**TREAT YOURSELF**

Oficina do Sabor Rua do Amparo 335, Recife Antigo ☎81 3429 3331, ⓦoficinadosabor.com. After two decades of supplying Recife and Olinda's chattering classes with exquisitely prepared Pernambucan cuisine, the reputation of this place precedes it. And with an interior that's hardly ostentatious, the emphasis is squarely on the food; blowing a day's budget on dishes such as their pumpkin stuffed with shrimp in a passion fruit and coconut sauce (R$110) is all too easy. Tues–Thurs noon–4pm & 6pm–midnight, Fri noon–4pm & 6pm–1am, Sat noon–1am, Sun noon–5pm.

knick-knacks, local art and exposed brickwork, and has an open-air patio. The scrumptious crêpes come in both sweet and savoury (from R$6–35) varieties and they even do a curried version (R$22.50). Daily 11am–11pm.

Flor do Coco Rua do Amparo 199 ☎81 3429 6889. Pousada restaurant boasting excellent regional cuisine, including both local fish dishes and great pastas. Mon–Fri 6–11.30pm, Sat & Sun noon–5pm & 6–11.30pm.

Hotel Pousada d'Olinda Varadouro Rua 15 de Novembro 98 ☎8134391163, ⓦpousadadolindavaradouro .com.br. Tasty, unfussy and cheap *por quilo* food (R$29) at this small restaurant on the ground floor of *Pousada Varadouro*. Locals swarm in on their lunch break so get here early; if you'd rather not sit indoors, head to the back and eat by the pool. Mon–Fri 11.40am–3.15pm.

NIGHTLIFE

a fábrica bar Praça do Fortim do Queijo ☎71 3429 9258, ⓦafabricabar.com. This is Olinda's hippest bar and club, semi-alfresco with a great location close to several hostels on Rua do Sol and a busy schedule that includes live samba (Wed) and pop rock (Sat). Cover R$10 and under. Mon–Fri 5pm–4am, Sat & Sun 4pm–4am.

★ **Bodega do Véio** Rua do Amparo 212 ☎81 3429 0185. A convivial general store-cum-neighbourhood bar of the kind you still find in rural Brazil and Cape Verde, with brooms propped up against the walls and shelves stacked to the ceiling with everything from soap powder to packets of beans and, of course, booze. From mid-afternoon onwards, people are crammed up against the counter and spilling onto the cobbled streets, and there's usually some kind of live music at weekends. Mon–Sat 9am–11pm.

Casa da Rabeca Rua Curupira 340, Cidade Tabajara ☎81 3371 8197, ⓦcasadarabeca.com.br. A legacy of the late Mestre Salustiano and a community focal point for the music that made his name, *forró da rabeca*, alongside *maracatu* and other traditional Pernambucan styles; the place comes into its own during Carnaval. It's a bit out of the way, so best take a taxi. Opening times and cover charge vary (some events are free), though there's usually always something happening. April–Sept Sat 9pm–late.

Xinxim da Baiana Avenida Sigismundo Gonçalves 742 ☎81 3439 8447. Bahían-themed bar where local *forró de rabeca* stars, Quarteto Olinda, made their name. Still a good place for music new and old, as well as other myriad cultural happenings. Tues–Sun 7pm–3am.

DIRECTORY

Banks and exchange There are no ATMs in Olinda's historical centre so you'll need to take out money in Recife before heading up here.

Pharmacies Farmácia Bicentenária, Rua S Miguel 277, Novo Olinda (☎81 3429 2148).

Post office Praça João Pessoa s/n ☎81 3439 2203 (Mon–Fri 9am–5pm).

Shopping Crafts aplenty are available at the Mercado da Ribeira, Rua Bernardo Vieira de Melo (daily 8am–6pm).

FERNANDO DE NORONHA

Recife is one of the main launch points for this beautiful archipelago 545km off the coast of Pernambuco. It boasts pristine beaches and it's absolutely stunning for scuba diving; the water is clear for more than 30m in many places, with turtles, dolphins and a wide range of fish species to observe. Since 1988 much of the archipelago has been protected as a marine national park to maintain its ecological wonders (it's also the breeding territory for many tropical Atlantic birds). The main island, **ILHA DE FERNANDO DE NORONHA**, has plenty of gorgeous beaches. While you can no longer swim with the dolphins, you're likely to see quite a few should you visit, though you'll have to wake up early – they enter the bay every day between 5am and 6am.

It's not cheap to get here (one-way fares rarely dip below R$300; two daily flights from Recife with GOL or Azul), and you're also charged the **TPA** (Taxa de Preservaçao) **tax** at a *daily* rate of R$48.20 for first four days, then increasing by varying amounts for each extra day (which goes towards protecting the archipelago), and a one-off park admission fee (R$150) – but this can be quite an experience. For more information, including restaurants and places to stay, check the government-run website, ⓦwww.noronha.pe.gov.br.

FORTALEZA

The languid state capital of Ceará, **FORTALEZA** is a sprawling city of over 2.5 million inhabitants, an oddly provincial place compared to Northeast rival Recife, despite its size. The city itself contains a smattering of sights, though there's nothing special to see, and it's the bar scene and shopping opportunities that make it an obvious pit stop on the road to the state's celebrated **beaches:**

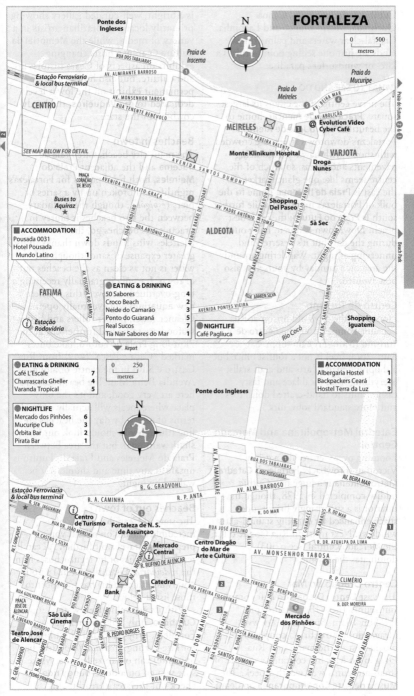

FORTALEZA

0 ___ 500
metres

Ponte dos Ingleses

Praia de Iracema

RUA DOS TABAJARAS

AV. ALMIRANTE BARROSO

Estação Ferroviaria & local bus terminal

AV. MONSENHOR TABOSA

RUA TENENTE BENÉVOLO

CENTRO

Praia do Mucuripe

Praia do Meireles

AV. BEIRA MAR

AV. ABOLIÇÃO

MEIRELES

Evolution Video Cyber Café

RUA PEREIRA VALENTE

VARJOTA

Monte Klinikum Hospital

Droga Nunes

AVENIDA SANTOS DUMONT

PRAÇA CORAÇÃO DE JESUS

AVENIDA HERACLITO GRAÇA

Shopping Del Paseo

5à Sec

AV. PADRE ANTÔNIO

Buses to Aquiraz

RUA JOÃO CORDEIRO

RUA ANTÔNIO SALES

AVENIDA BARÃO DE STUDART

ALDEOTA

AV. DESEMBARGADOR MOREIRA

AV. SENADOR VIRGÍLIO TÁVORA

AV. SENADOR COLOMBO SOUSA

RUA BARBOSA DE FREITAS

RUA ABAKEN SILVA

AVENIDA PONTES VIEIRA

Rio Cocó

AV. ENG. SANTANA JUNIOR

Shopping Iguatemi

FATIMA

AV. VISCONDE RIO BRANCO

Estação Rodoviária

Airport

SEE MAP BELOW FOR DETAIL

Praia do Futuro 2 & 3

Beach Park

3

■ ACCOMMODATION	
Pousada 0031	2
Hotel Pousada Mundo Latino	1

● EATING & DRINKING	
50 Sabores	4
Croco Beach	2
Neide do Camarão	3
Ponto do Guaraná	5
Real Sucos	7
Tia Nair Sabores do Mar	1

● NIGHTLIFE	
Café Pagliuca	6

● EATING & DRINKING	
Café L'Escale	7
Churrascaria Gheller	4
Varanda Tropical	5

● NIGHTLIFE	
Mercado dos Pinhões	6
Mucuripe Club	3
Órbita Bar	2
Pirata Bar	1

0 ___ 250
metres

■ ACCOMMODATION	
Albergaria Hostel	1
Backpackers Ceará	2
Hostel Terra da Luz	3

Ponte dos Ingleses

AV. A. TAMANDARÉ

RUA DOS TABAJARAS

R. DOS POTIGUARAS

AV. BEIRA MAR

R. G. GRADVOHL

R. A. CAMINHA

R. P. ANTA

AV. ALM. BARROSO

R. DO MAR

Estação Ferroviaria & local bus terminal

R. SEN. JAGUARIBE

Centro de Turismo

RUA DR. JOÃO MOREIRA

Fortaleza de N.S. de Assunção

RUA JOSÉ AVELINO

AV. NEREU RAMOS

RUA JOSÉ S.

TV. TUPI

RUA GUAINACES

RUA ARARIUS

R. DO MAR

R. ALVES

R. DR. ATUALPA DA LIMA

AV. MONSENHOR TABOSA

RUA CASTRO E SILVA

RUA SEN. ALENCAR

Mercado Central

Centro Dragão do Mar de Arte e Cultura

AV. A. NEROMICENO

R. RUFINO DE ALENCAR

RUA PEREIRA FILGUEIRAS

RUA TENENTE BENÉVOLO

R. P. CLIMÉRIO

AV. 24 DE MAIO

RUA SÃO PAULO

RIO BRANCO

Catedral

AV. DOM MANUEL

RUA DOM JOAQUIM

RUA COSTA BARROS

R. DEP. MOREIRA

RUA GUILHERME ROCHA

Bank

R. V. SABOIA

AV. 25 DE MARÇO

RUA RODRIGUES

Mercado dos Pinhões

PRAÇA JOSÉ DE ALENCAR

FACUNDO

R. SENA MADUREIRA

R. CORONEL FERAZ

SANTOS DUMONT

RUA BOQUEIRÃO ACIOLI

RUA JOÃO CORDEIRO

RUA AUGUSTO

RUA DELFONSO ALBANO

São Luís Cinema

R. LIBERATO BARROSO

R. PEDRO BORGES

RUA 25 DE MARÇO

RUA FRANKLIN TAVORA

RUA GONÇALVES LEDO

Teatro José de Alencar

R. BARÃO DO RIO

R. MAJOR

R. GENERAL EZERIEL

RUA PINTO

R. GEN. SAMPAIO

R. SEN. POMPEU

R. PEDRO PEREIRA

R. PEDRO PRIMEIRO

Cumbuco, Jericoacoara, Canoa Quebrada, Morro Branco and Lagoinha. Crystal-clear waters and palm-fringed sands are just one selling point – this is a kite- or windsurfer's paradise.

WHAT TO SEE AND DO

The nerve centre of the city is its largest square, **Praça José de Alencar**, home to the beautiful **Teatro José de Alencar**. Fortaleza's downtown streets are crowded with shops, with hawkers colonizing pavements and plazas, so much of the centre seems like one giant market. To the east is **Praia de Iracema**, home to the bulk of Fortaleza's nightlife, while further south is **Praia do Futuro**, the city's best beach. Downtown is fine to hang out in during the day, but it's deserted and unnerving at night. Wandering around the area on a Sunday by yourself is also best avoided.

Centro de Turismo

Housed in the city's old prison at Rua Senador Pompeu 350, the **Centro de Turismo** (Mon–Fri 8am–6pm, Sat 8am–2pm; free) is not a tourist office but a shopping mall of arts and craft stalls, everything from local lace and tasty cashew nuts to hand-crafted dolls, toys and more standard souvenirs.

Catedral Metropolitana and Mercado Central

Looming over Centro like a grimy Victorian throwback, Fortaleza's **Catedral Metropolitana** is a huge neo-Gothic oddity completed in 1978, though its interior is a surprisingly bright, open space enhanced by dazzling stained-glass windows. Next to it, on Rua Conde d'Eu, the **Mercado Central** (see p.303) dominates the skyline.

Centro Dragão do Mar

The vast **Centro Dragão do Mar** complex (museums Tues–Thurs 9am–7pm, Fri–Sun 10am–8pm; free; ⊕www .dragaodomar.org.br), a couple of blocks east of the market on Rua Dragão do Mar 81, contains a couple of small museums well worth a peek. The **Museu de Arte Contemporanea do Ceará**

is a bright, well-curated gallery showing primarily local and Brazilian artists in a variety of media, while the **Memorial da Cultura Cearense** hosts changing exhibits on aspects of Ceará history, art and culture, but also houses a permanent exhibit on the lower levels dedicated to the **Vaqueiros**, the hardy cowboys of the state.

Beaches in town

The main city beaches are **Praia de Iracema** and the adjacent **Praia do Meireles**, both focal points for Fortaleza's nightlife and broken up by a series of piers (*espigões*), though the boundary between the two beaches is blurry in practice. As beaches go, the Praia do Meireles wins hands down thanks to its greater expanse of sand, though the water is not as clean as the beaches out of town. Iracema is gradually receiving a long-overdue makeover (this is where a new **aquarium** will eventually open). Cleaner water, higher rollers and better seafood are to be had further out at the 7km-long **Praia do Futuro**: take buses marked "Caça e Pesca" (#49) from Rua Castro e Silva in the centre or along Avendia Beira Mar. The beach *barracas* here are very good, and it's the only place where locals will actually swim. In terms of safety, by day the beaches are fine (though you should look out for **shark warnings**), but the area between Praia do Meireles and Praia do Futuro is unsafe at any time and should not be walked by night.

Beaches out of town

The state of Ceará has plenty of incredible beaches on offer if you are prepared to travel a bit further. All can be reached on tours or by regular buses from the *rodoviária*. Lisatur (⊕85 3219 5600, ⊕www.lisatur.com.br) has transport to those listed below.

With its emerald-green waters, **Cumbuco**, only 35km north of Fortaleza, is by far Brazil's best beach for kite-surfing. *Pousada 0031* (see box opposite) can organize lessons. Make sure you go on a **dune-buggy ride** to check out the area's breathtaking scenery. Further up is the popular **Canoa Quebrada** (@canoa-quebrada .com), which has dramatic cliffs and fun nightlife that goes on until the early hours. Heading further north you come to Ceará's most famous beach, **Jericoacoara** (@jeri-brazil.org), with fine white sands and high dunes, especially popular with wind- and kite-surfers. The second half of the trip up here is by 4WD, and it can take up to seven hours to make the 312km journey. Finally, in the opposite direction is **Morro Branco**, 80km to the south of Fortaleza and renowned for its beaches backed by maze-like cliffs of multicoloured sand.

ARRIVAL AND DEPARTURE

By plane Fortaleza's Aeroporto Internacional Pinto Martins is just 6km south of the centre. A fixed-rate taxi costs R$45 to Meireles, Iracema and Centro or R$32 to the *rodoviária*. Pay first at the Coopaero desk in the terminal (higher rates apply Mon–Fri 8pm–6am, Sat after 1pm and all day Sun). You can also take a by-the-meter "Taxi Comum" that are nominally a little cheaper, but only if traffic is light. Buses with the route card Aeroporto/ Benfica/Rodoviária (#404; R$2.20) run regularly to Praça José de Alencar in the centre via the *rodoviária* (daily 5.10am–10pm).
Destinations Belém (5 daily; 1hr 50min–3hr 40min); Recife (10 daily; 1hr 15min–1hr 35min); Rio (12–24 daily; 5hr 40min–8hr 15min); Salvador (7–9 daily; 1hr 40min–4hr 20min).
By bus The bus station, Rodoviária Engenheiro João Tomé, Av Borges de Melo 1630 (@85 3230 1111), is about 3km from the centre, and served by the same Aeroporto/ Benfica/Rodoviária bus. A taxi costs around R$25–30 from the *rodoviária* to most places.
Destinations Belém (3 daily; 24–26hr); Jijoca de Jericoacoara (16 daily; 5–6hr); Natal (7 daily; 8hr); Recife (6 daily; 12–13hr); Salvador (2 daily; 22hr); São Luís (3 daily; 18hr 30min).

GETTING AROUND

By bus Fortaleza has plenty of local buses (R$2.20). Useful routes that take you to the main beaches and back to the city centre are marked "Grande Circular I" and "Caça e Pesca/Centro/Beira Mar" or #49. The local bus station in the centre is known as Praça Da Estação, a large square by the old railway station.
By taxi Taxi meters start at R$4 – it's around R$15 between Meireles and the centre. Cooperativa Rádio Táxi de Fortaleza (@85 3254 5744, @radiotaxifortaleza.com .br) runs 24hr.

INFORMATION AND TOURS

Tourist information Fortaleza boasts a multitude of tourist information outlets including kiosks in the airport (daily 6am–11pm; @85 3392 1667), *rodoviária* (daily 8am–6pm; @85 3230 1111) and Centro do Turismo, Rua Senador Pompeu 350 (Mon–Fri 8am–7pm, Sat 8am–3pm, Sun 8am–noon; @85 3101 5508), as well as offices in the Mercado Central (Mon–Fri 8am–5pm, Sat 8am–noon; @85 3105 1475), on Praça do Ferreira (Mon–Fri 9am–5pm, Sat 9am–noon; @85 3105 1444) and on Av Beira Mar near the Anfiteatro Flávio Ponte (Mon–Sat 9am–9pm, Sun 9am–8pm; @85 3105 2670).
Tour operator Lisatur, Av Monsenhor Tabosa 1067, Praia de Iracema (@85 3219 5400, @www.lisatur.com.br), has good day-trips to beaches and other attractions.

ACCOMMODATION

The budget hotels, as ever, tend to be downtown, which hums busily during the day but empties at night – it's best to stay elsewhere. Close by is Praia de Iracema, with a decent enough range of accommodation, while Praia do Meireles further along is home to more upmarket hotels.

CENTRO

Albergaria Hostel Rua Antônio Augusto 111, Praia de Iracema @85 3032 9005, @albergariahostel.com.br. Cheerful hostel close to the beach and nightlife, with a/c, free wi-fi and small clean dorms and doubles with tiled floors. Basic breakfast included, and there's a pool table and cold beers (for sale) at the bar. Dorms R$30, doubles R$100
Backpackers Ceará Av Dom Manoel 89 @85 3091 8997, @backpackersce.com.br. Somewhat camouflaged until you notice the animated wall painting, this place buzzes with travellers, though it can feel a little impenetrable, with its barbed wire, CCTV and coded locks. Rooms are comfortable, but be ready to battle against the worn-out fans. Wi-fi. Dorms R$20, doubles R$50

★ TREAT YOURSELF

Pousada 0031 Av das Dunas 2249, Cumbuco @85 8617 9119, @www.0031 .com. A little tropical paradise at this Dutch-run pousada forty minutes from the centre of Fortaleza. Management couldn't be friendlier, the restaurant is the best in town, the rooms – in individually styled thatched-roof apartments – are spotless, the pool refreshing, and the golden sand dunes and pristine beaches only two minutes' walk away; "huge breakfast" included. R$165

3

Hostel Terra da Luz Rua Rodrigues Junior 278 ☎85 3082 2260, ⓦhostelterradaluz.com. This hostel has a cosy atmosphere and scribbled guests' notes coat the upstairs walls. The dorms are clean and colourful, equipped with both a/c and fan, and there's also a communal kitchen and free internet. Breakfast included. Dorms R$35, doubles R$100

PRAIA DO MEIRELES

Hotel Pousada Mundo Latino Rua Ana Bilhar 507, Meireles ☎85 3242 8778, ⓦmundolatino.com.br. The breakfast room and communal area are not exactly alluring with their PVC-covered sofas, but staff are helpful and the a/c rooms are spacious. Internet facilities available, plus wi-fi. Breakfast included. R$137

EATING AND DRINKING

Downtown, Praça do Ferreira offers a few *por quilo lanchonetes* (self-service cafeterias), and Iracema has a few good restaurants, while the Centro Dragão do Mar is a popular spot, particularly in the evenings, with at least seven pavement cafés overflowing with people. The beaches all have a smattering of good restaurants as well as beach huts offering some of the best deals on seafood.

CENTRO

Café L'Escale Rua Floriano Peixoto 587. Excellent local pit stop right on Praça do Ferreira (in an Art Nouveau building dating from 1914), with the usual selection of *salgados*, drinks and self-service buffet options. Mon–Thurs 8am–9pm, Sat 8am–4pm.

Real Sucos Heráclito Graça 1709 ☎85 3244 3923, ⓦrealsucos.com.br. Veteran chain serving renowned fresh fruit juices (R$5–10), including *açaí, graviola, carambola,* tamarind and papaya – the *cajú* juice is especially good – as well as lots of sandwich options (from R$8). Mon–Thurs 7am–2am, Fri & Sat 7am–5am, Sun 5pm–2am. Also at Shopping Aldeota ☎85 3458 1104, Shopping Benfica ☎85 3281 4029, and Center Um Shopping ☎85 3224 0121 (all 10am–10pm).

Tia Nair Sabores do Mar Rua Ildefonso Albano 68, Praia de Iracema ☎85 3219 1461, ⓦtianair.com.br. Despite the menu's unappetizing photos, this seafront place has good food at reasonable prices. A range of ambitious two- and three-person fish dishes (in the region of R$80) mix it up with shrimp and lobster. Daily 11am–1am.

Varanda Tropical Av Monsenhor Tabosa 714, Praia de Iracema ☎85 3219 5195. Open-fronted restaurant on the main road serving a solid range of meat, fish and seafood options, many of which will fill two bellies; if you're alone try the shrimps in garlic (R$9.90). The buffet is R$27/kilo. Mon–Sat 11am–midnight, Sun 11am–5pm.

PRAIA DO MEIRELES

50 Sabores Av Beira Mar 3958, Mucuripe ☎85 3032 5850, ⓦ50sabores.com.br. This decades-old Fortaleza institution hides its light under a proverbial bush, with almost double the titular 50 flavours of ice cream, all of which change with the seasons, even if it feels like the weather never does. Try the plum, *caipirinha* or *maracujá* (R$12 for two huge scoops). One of six branches spread around town. Daily 9am–11.30pm.

Churrascaria Gheller Av. Monsenhor Tabosa 825 ☎85 3219 3599. No-nonsense steakhouse where the buffet is just R$19.90 on weekdays (with salads, sushi, pasta and vegetables), though the *rodízio* is so-so. Drinks and desserts are extra. Daily 11am–11.30pm.

★**Neide do Camarão** Av da Abolição 4772 Mucuripe ☎85 3248 2680. You buy your shrimp at the door (R$29 *por quilo*), choose how you want it prepared, hand it to the waiter, then eat the crispy shrimp, shell and all, washed down with ice-cold beer. Local, authentic and awesome. Daily 5–11pm.

Ponto do Guaraná Av Beira Mar 3127-A, Meireles ☎85 3086 5650. *Guaraná* addicts should head here – there's plenty of flavours to choose from including lemon, *acerola* and *açai* (drinks R$5–7). Sandwiches are also available (from R$8). Daily 6am–10pm.

PRAIA DO FUTURO

Croco Beach Av Zezé Diogo 3125 ☎85 3521 9600, ⓦcrocobeach.com.br. Probably Futuro's most popular beach restaurant, serving huge sharing platters of seafood and a buffet for R$49.90/kilo, as well as sushi (from R$22) and plenty of meat dishes (most mains for two R$25–75). Also lays on live local bands and MPB Tues & Thurs (R$20 cover) and DJs/live music at weekends (R$5 cover). Mon, Wed & Fri 8am–6pm, Tues 8am–midnight, Thurs 8am–3am, Sat & Sun 8am–9pm.

NIGHTLIFE

Fortaleza is justly famous for its *forró*. There's no better way to see what Cearenses do to have fun than to spend a night in a *dancetaria*. One of the busiest nightlife areas is the streets around the Ponte dos Ingleses. Most *dancetarias* open at 10pm, but they don't really get going until about midnight. Other nightlife is mainly out by the beaches: Praia Meireles appeals to a broad cross section of locals and tourists, whereas Praia Iracema is slightly younger.

Café Pagliuca Rua Barbosa de Freitas 1035 ☎85 3324 1903, ⓦcafepagliuca.com.br. An arty, rustic-bohemian vibe makes this one of the mellowest spots in town for a quiet drink and live jazz, bossa and MPB (Tues–Sat 9.30pm–midnight). Food includes a range of authentic Italian risotto, and *feijoada* on Saturdays (R$34). R$8.80 cover. Tues–Fri 6pm–1am, Sat noon–midnight.

Mercado dos Pinhões Praça Visconde 41 ☎85 3266 9866. Perhaps the best place to get a sense of how locals take their *forró* and *chorinho* seriously, this old 1890s mercado is an arts and craft market by day (Mon–Fri 9am–noon & 2–5pm), but morphs into authentic *forró* dance hall on Friday to Sunday evenings. Thurs–Sun 5pm–midnight.

Mucuripe Club Travessa Maranguape 108, Centro ☎85 3254 3020. Veteran superclub hosting some of the country's biggest DJs, singers and bands in several themed areas including a film-set-like, colonial-style street, a huge "arena" for live shows and a hi-tech clubbing area, with a music policy covering everything from rock, funk and electronica to samba, *axé* and *forró*. No flip-flops or shorts. Cover varies (usually R$30–60). Fri & Sat 10pm–5am.

Órbita Bar Rua Dragão do Mar 207 ☎85 3453 1421, ⓦorbitabar.com.br. A Fortaleza institution, with live Brazilian and international indie/alternative, blues, electronica and even – for those who like their twang – a night (Wed) dedicated to the delights of surf-rock. Check out their radio station, ⓦorbitaradio.com.br. Cover R$20–30. Thurs–Sun 9pm–4am.

Pirata Bar Rua dos Tabajaras 325 ☎85 4011 6161, ⓦpirata.com.br. The most famous place in Fortaleza (and Brazil) to get your fix of *forró*. By cannily cornering the club-less wilds of *segunda-feira*, this unashamed tourist trap has generated more than its fair share of publicity – the *New York Times* famously called it "the craziest place on earth on a Monday night". Cover is a hefty R$40 (ask at hostels for R$30 advance tickets). Mon 8pm–5am.

SHOPPING

Mercado Central Rua Alberto Nepomuceno 199 (ⓦmercadocentraldefortaleza.com.br). Fortaleza's modern Mercado Central and the nearby shops diagonally across from the cathedral are the best places in the city to buy a hammock. This huge complex resembles a parking garage crowded with hundreds of small stores, most selling *artesanato* for which the city is famed. Mon–Fri 7am–6pm, Sat 7am–4pm, Sun 7am–2pm.

DIRECTORY

Banks and exchange HSBC and Bradesco have 24hr ATMs in the city centre on Rua Major Facundo, near the corner with Rua Senador Alencar. HSBC also has branches at Av Monsenhor Tabosa 1200, Praia da Iracema and Av Santos Dumont 3581, Aldeota, typically open Mon–Fri 10am–4pm.

Consulates UK, British Honorary Consulate, Rua Leonardo Mota 501, Meireles (☎85 242 0888); US, Torre Santos Dumont, Av Santos Dumont 2828, Suite 708, Aldeota (☎85 486 1306).

Hospital Monte Klinikum Hospital, Rua República do Libano 747 (☎85 4012 0012, ⓦwww.monteklinikum.com.br).

Internet Evolution Vídeo Cyber Café, Av da Abolição 3230, Meireles (Mon–Sat 8am–6pm; R$4/hr).

Laundry Lavanderia São Luíz at Av da Abolição 2679 (Mon–Fri 8am–noon & 1–6.30pm, Sat 8am–1pm) for drop-off service; the branch of Lav & Lev (ⓦlavlev.com.br) next door at Av da Abolição 2685 has self-service coin-operated machines (powder available).

Pharmacy Farmácia Santa Branca, Av da Universidade 3089, Benfica (☎85 3223 0000).

Police The tourist police are open 24hr and can be found at Av Almirante Barroso 805, Praia da Iracema (☎85 3101 2488).

Post office The central post office is at Rua Senador Alencar 38 (Mon–Fri 8am–5pm & Sat 8am–noon); in Miereles there are branches at Av Beira Mar 3960 (Mon–Fri 8am–6pm & Sat 8am–noon) and Av Monsenhor Tabosa 1561 (Mon–Fri 9am–5pm).

The Amazon

The Amazon is a vast forest – the largest on the planet – and a giant river system, covering over half of Brazil and a large portion of South America. The forest extends into Venezuela, Colombia, Peru and Bolivia, where the river itself begins life among thousands of different headwaters. In Brazil, only the stretch below Manaus, where the waters of the **Rio Solimões** and the **Rio Negro** meet, is actually known as the **Rio Amazonas**. The daily flow of the river is said to be enough to supply a city the size of New York with water for nearly ten years, and its power is such that the muddy Amazon waters stain the Atlantic a silty brown for over 200km out to sea.

BELÉM

Strategically placed on the Amazon River estuary, **BELÉM** was founded by the Portuguese in 1616 as the City of Our Lady of Bethlehem (Belém). Its original role was to protect the river mouth and establish the Portuguese claim to the region, but it rapidly became established as an Indian slaving port and a source of cacao and spices from the Amazon. Belém prospered following the rubber boom at the end of the nineteenth century but suffered a disastrous decline after the crash of 1914 – it kept afloat, just about, on the back of brazil nuts and the lumber industry. Nowadays, it remains the economic centre of northern Brazil, and the chief port for the Amazon. It is also a remarkably attractive place, with a fine colonial centre, offering some of the Amazon's finest cuisine.

WHAT TO SEE AND DO

The old town or **Cidade Velha** is at the southern edge of the centre, where the cathedral and fort sit around the Praça da Sé. Immediately north on the waterfront lies one of the city's highlights, the **Ver-o-Peso market**, the largest open-air

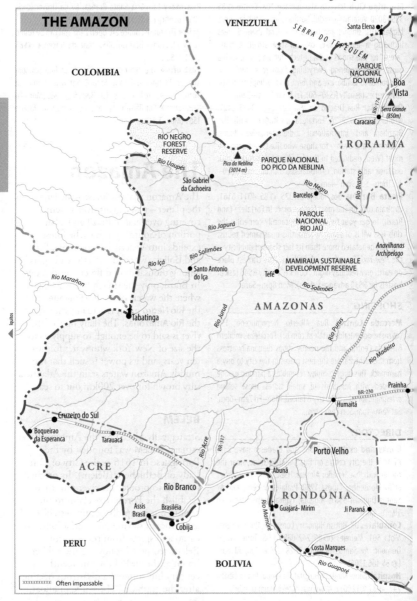

THE AMAZON

VENEZUELA

SERRA DO TEPEQUÉM

Santa Elena

COLOMBIA

PARQUE NACIONAL DO VIRUÁ

Boa Vista

BR-174

Serra Grande (850m)

Caracaraí

RORAIMA

RIO NEGRO FOREST RESERVE

Rio Uaupés

Pico da Neblina (3014 m)

PARQUE NACIONAL DO PICO DA NEBLINA

São Gabriel da Cachoeira

Rio Negro

Barcelos

Rio Branco

Rio Japurá

PARQUE NACIONAL RIO JAÚ

Anavilhanas Archipelago

Rio Solimões

Rio Içá

Santo Antonio do Iça

MAMIRAUÁ SUSTAINABLE DEVELOPMENT RESERVE

Tefé

Rio Marañon

Rio Solimões

AMAZONAS

Rio Juruá

Rio Purus

Tabatinga

Rio Madeira

Prainha

BR-230

Humaitá

Cruzeiro do Sul

Boqueirao da Esperanca

Tarauacá

Rio Acre

BR-317

Porto Velho

ACRE

Rio Branco

RONDÔNIA

Assis Brasil

Brasiléia

Cobija

Guajará- Mirim

Ji Paraná

Rio Mamoré

PERU

Costa Marques

BOLIVIA

Rio Guaporé

Iquitos

xxxxxxxxxx Often impassable

3

market in Latin America – visit in the morning when the market is bustling, its stalls overflowing with spices, potions, crafts, exotic fish and foodstuffs. Carrying on up the waterfront you reach the **Estação das Docas** cultural centre (Mon & Tues 10am–midnight, Wed 10am–1am, Thurs–Sat 10am–3am, Sun 9am–midnight; Av Boulevard Castilho s/n; ☎91 3212 5525, ⊛estacaodasdocas.com .br) where some (rather pricey) *artesanato* stalls compete with restaurants, cafés, a cinema and exhibition and live music spaces in a refurbished warehouse area.

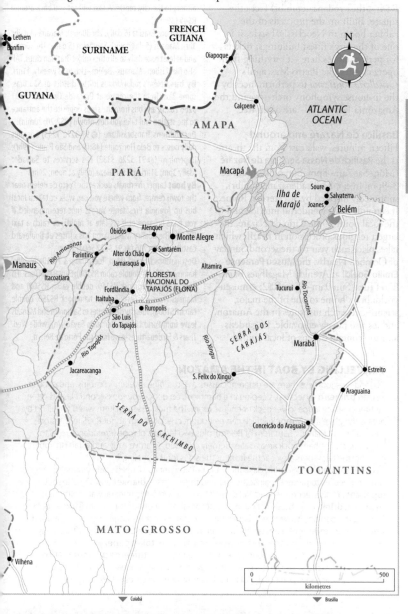

Praça da Republica

Heading inland up Avenida Presidente Vargas, you reach the shady Praça da República, a popular place to stroll. The magnificent **Theatro da Paz** (Tues–Fri 9am–noon & 2–5pm, Sat 10am–noon & Sun 11am–noon; hourly guided tours R$4; ⓦtheatrodapaz.com.br) faces the square. Built on the proceeds of the rubber boom in Neoclassical style, it is one of the city's finest buildings; tickets for performances here – everything from opera classics like Pietro Mascagni's *Cavalleria Rusticana* to performances by the in-house symphony orchestra and the Amazônia Jazz Band – are often free.

Basílica de Nazaré and around

Fifteen minutes' walk east from the theatre is the **Basílica de Nossa Senhora de Nazaré** (Mon–Sat 7am–8pm, Sun 6.30–11am & 3–9pm; free; ⓦbasilicadenazare.com.br), supposedly inspired by St Peter's in Rome. It certainly has a wonderful interior, and is the focal point of the Cirio de Nazaré, the largest religious procession in Brazil, which takes place each year on the second Sunday of October. Nearby, the **Museu Paraense Emílio Goeldi** at Avenida Magalhães Barata 376 (Tues–Sun 9am–5pm; R$2; ⓦmuseu-goeldi.br) is home to one of the major scientific research institutes in the Amazon, and it's also hugely enjoyable. Its gardens and zoo contain dozens of local animal species, including spider monkeys, caimans and macaws.

ARRIVAL AND DEPARTURE

By plane Belém's Val-de-Cans/Júlio Cesar Ribeiro Airport (☎ 91 3210 6000) is about 15km north of town. Regular buses (every 15min; 40min; R$2.20) connect the airport to the city centre. A taxi will set you back around R$45 (30min).

Destinations Brasília (5 daily; 2hr 30min); Macapá (1 daily; 1hr); Manaus (5 daily; 2hr); Santarém (5 daily; 1hr 30min) and at least once daily to all other major Brazilian cities. TAP also flies Lisbon–Manaus–Belém–Lisbon (3 weekly; 11hr).

By bus Belém's *rodoviária* is in the district of São Bras, some 3km from the centre at Praça de Operário (☎ 91 3266 2625); any bus from the stops opposite the entrance to the station will take you downtown (R$2.20; 20min).

Destinations Transbrasiliana (☎ 91 3226 1243) operates daily buses to Belo Horizonte (48hr) and São Paulo (49hr); Itapemirim (☎ 91 3226 3382) has services to Salvador (daily 3pm; 31hr) and Fortaleza (daily at noon; 24hr).

By boat Larger riverboats dock at the Porto de Belém near the town centre, from where you can walk or take a local bus up Avenida Presidente Vargas (not recommended if you have luggage or if it's late at night), or catch a taxi (R$15). The agency Macamazon has offices at Boulevard Castilho França 716 (☎ 91 3222 5604).

Destinations Macapá (Mon, Tues, Thurs & Fri 10am; 24hr; hammock R$130, double cabin R$500); Santarém (Tues–Fri 6pm; 3 days; hammock R$150, double cabin R$500) and Manaus (Tues–Fri 6pm; 5 days; hammock R$250, double cabin R$1000). Tuesday departures to Santarém and Manaus leave from Porto Líder at Bernardo Sayão s/n), while Wed, Thurs & Fri departures leave from the Porto de Belém.

TRAVELLING BY BOAT IN THE AMAZON

On long river journeys there are different classes: avoid *cabine*, sweltering cabins, and choose instead **primeiro** (first class), sleeping in a hammock on deck. *Segundo* (second class) is often hammock space in the lower deck or engine room. The most essential item when travelling by boat is therefore a **hammock**, which can be bought cheaply (from about R$25 in the stores and markets of Manaus, Santarém or Belém), plus two lengths of rope (*armador de rede*) to hang it from. The hammock areas get extremely crowded, so arrive early and establish your position: the best spots are near the front or the sides for the cooling breezes.

Loose **clothing** is fine during daylight hours but at night you'll need some warmer garments and long sleeves to protect against the chill and the insects. A **blanket** and some **insect repellent** are also recommended. Virtually all boats now provide mineral water, although enough to **drink** (large bottles of mineral water are the best option) and extra **food** – cookies, fruit and the odd tin – to keep you happy for the duration of the voyage may also be a good idea. There are toilets on all boats, though even on the best they can get filthy within a few hours of leaving port – it's advisable to take your own roll of **toilet paper** just in case.

The most organized of the wooden riverboats are the larger **three-deck vessels**. All of these wooden vessels tend to let passengers stay aboard a night or two before departure and after arrival, which saves on hotel costs, and is handy for travellers on a low budget.

INFORMATION AND TOURS

Tourist information Paratur is at Praça Waldemar Henrique (Mon–Fri 8am–5pm ☎ 091 3110 8700); there is also a Paratur kiosk at the airport (daily 8am–10pm; ☎ 91 3210 6330).

Tour operators Valeverde Turismo, in the Estação das Docas (☎ 91 3212 3388, ⓦ valeverdeturismo.com.br), organize good-value river tours around Belém, as well as city tours. Amazon Star Turismo, Rua Henrique Gurjão 210 (☎ 91 3212 6244 or 24hr line ☎ 9982 7911, ⓦ amazonstar.com.br), is an excellent French-run agency specializing in ecotours, including visits to Ilha de Marajó and half-day tours (R$140) through the streams of the Rio Guamá. Both offer excursions to Ilha dos Papagaios, an island near Belém where tens of thousands of parrots zoom out of the trees at dawn (R$160).

ACCOMMODATION

Amazônia Hostel Av Gov. José Malcher 592 ☎ 91 3278 4355, ⓦ amazoniahostel.com.br. An immaculately kept Hi-affiliated hostel in a lovely old mansion, with polished hardwood floors and stratospherically high ceilings, though the usual colonial layout means rooms face on to a corridor rather than an outside window. There's a kitchen, internet facilities, lockers, free wi-fi and a/c in all dorms. Breakfast included. Discounts (of around R$10) for HI members. Dorms R$50, doubles R$99

Fortaleza Travessa Frutuoso Guimaraes 276 ☎ 91 3212 1055. This rambling old colonial house, frayed but with character to spare, is often full of French backpackers en route to or from French Guiana. Rooms and dorms are basic but you'll be made to feel at home. There's hammock space too for R$15. Take care at night as the area can be dangerous. Dorms R$20, doubles R$50

Grão Pará Av Presidente Vargas 718 ☎ 91 3221 2121, ⓦ hotelgraopara.com.br. A great-value mid-range hotel on the busy Vargas thoroughfare just a few steps from the Theatro da Paz, offering comfortable a/c rooms on fifteen floors, all with fridge, cable TV and private bath. R$120

★ **Portas da Amazônia** Rua Doutor Malcher 15 ☎ 91 3222 9952, ⓦ portasdaamazoniabelempara.com.br. Right on the picturesque Praça da Sé, this excellent pousada offers welcoming breezy rooms that give off a shaded leafy patio. All have high ceilings and are decorated with lovely antique furniture. There's wi-fi throughout and also an attached pizzeria. R$120

EATING AND DRINKING

Belém boasts plenty of excellent cheap restaurants, which have especially good deals at lunchtime. The stalls of Dona Miloca, in front of the Goeldi museum, and Maria do Carmo, in front of the Colégio Nazaré on Avenida Nazaré, just before the Basílica, serve excellent *tacacá* (shrimp soup with jambú leaves) and *acai*. In the evenings, head to the Estação das Docas where all places stay open till late.

Higashi Rua Ó de Almeida 509 ☎ 91 3230 5552. An informal *por quilo* (R$48) restaurant with a good range of dishes on offer, including shrimp, crab and salmon; the all-you-can-eat buffet on the first floor (daily excluding Sat; R$18) is a bargain. Daily 11am–3pm.

Lá em Casa Estação das Docas ☎ 91 3212 5588, ⓦ laemcasa.com. Founded in the early 1970s by the late Slow Food advocate and pioneer of Amazonian cuisine, Paulo Martins, no other restaurant in Belém commands quite the same combination of die-hard local following and international media coverage, with its excellent all-you-can-eat lunchtime buffet (R$47) between noon and 3pm. Mon–Wed & Sun noon–midnight, Thurs–Sat noon–1.30am.

Point do Açaí Boulevard Castilho França 744 ☎ 91 3212 2168, ⓦ pointdoacai.net. As the name suggests, this place has *açaí* aplenty – this refreshing Amazonian drink of crushed berries is served with most dishes – try the *chapa mista paraense* (serves two; R$82), a platter of local fish, meats and vegetables. Mon 6–10.30pm, Tues–Sun 10.30am–3.30pm & 6–10.30pm.

Sorveteria Cairú Travessa 14 de Março at Gov José Malcher 1570 ☎ 91 3242 2749. With over 65 exotic ice-cream favours on offer (R$5 per scoop), including an exciting selection of regional fruit flavours such as *cupuaçu*, *graviola* (soursop) and *acai*, this ice-cream chain is one of the best in town. There's another branch at the Estação das Docas. Daily 8am–11.45pm.

NIGHTLIFE

Belém has some excellent nightlife, although most of the action takes place outside the centre of town; you'll find many bars along Av Almirante Wandekolk and in the Estação das Docas.

Amazon Beer In the Estação das Docas ☎ 91 3212 5400, ⓦ amazonbeer.com.br. Beer-lovers will be in heaven at this bar with an in-house brewery and a mouth-watering selection of artisan brews on tap (R$5–10). Mon–Thurs 5pm–midnight, Fri 5pm–1.30am, Sat & Sun 11am–1.30am.

★ **Bar Palafita** Rua Siqueira Mendes 264, Cidade Velha ☎ 91 3212 6302. One of Belém's most famous treasures: an atmospheric bar on stilts right on the Amazon River with truly incredible views, especially at sunset. Drinks and grub (mains R$35) are served to the sound of live *carimbó*, *forró* and pop-rock bands on weekends. Tues–Sun noon–midnight.

Casa do Gilson Travessa Padre Eutíquio 3172, Condor ☎ 91 3272 7306. For 25 years now, this place has championed the delicate, folky strains of classic *choro* and MPB in the unlikely environs of Belém, with live performances at weekends. Cover charge R$5–10. Fri 7pm–midnight, Sat & Sun noon–midnight.

DIRECTORY

Banks and exchange Banco da Amazônia, Av Presidente Vargas 800; Bradesco, Av Presidente Vargas

3

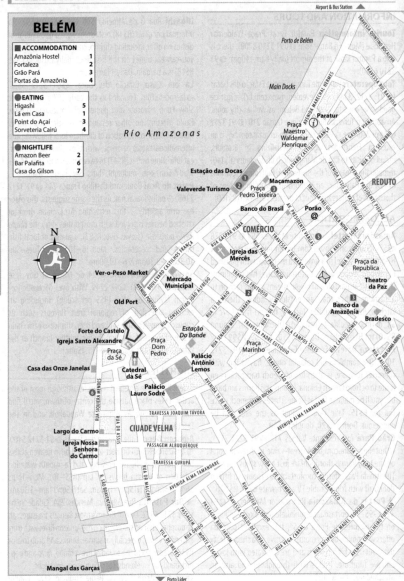

BELÉM

■ ACCOMMODATION
Amazônia Hostel	1
Fortaleza	2
Grão Pará	3
Portas da Amazônia	4

● EATING
Higashi	5
Lá em Casa	1
Point do Açaí	3
Sorveteria Cairú	4

● NIGHTLIFE
Amazon Beer	2
Bar Palafita	6
Casa do Gilson	7

Porto de Belém

Main Docks

Paratur

Praça
Maestro
Waldemar
Henrique

Río Amazonas

Estação das Docas

Valeverde Turismo

Maçamazon

Praça
Pedro Teixeira

Banco do Brasil

Porão
@

COMÉRCIO

REDUTO

Ver-o-Peso Market

Igreja das
Mercês

Praça da
Republica

Mercado
Municipal

Theatro
da Paz

Old Port

Banco da
Amazônia

Bradesco

Forte do Castelo

Igreja Santo Alexandre

Estação
Do Bonde

Praça
Dom
Pedro

Praça
da Sé

Palácio
Antônio
Lemos

Praça
Marinho

Casa das Onze Janelas

Catedral
da Sé

Palácio
Lauro Sodré

Largo do Carmo

Igreja Nossa
Senhora
do Carmo

CIUADE VELHA

PASSAGEM ALBUQUERQUE

Mangal das Garças

▼ Porto Lider

988; Banco do Brasil, 2nd floor, Av Presidente Vargas 248. There are also a number of ATMs in the Estação das Docas.

Hospital Hospital Guadalupe, Rua Arciprestes Manoel Teodoro 734 (☎ 91 4005 9877).

Internet Porão at Rua Senador Manoel Barata 943 (Mon–Fri 8am–4pm; R$2/hr; ☎ 91 3222 1776).

Laundry Lav & Lev Travessa Dr Moraes 576 (Mon–Sat 8am–6pm; wash R$10, dry R$10; ☎ 91 3223 7247).

Post office The central post office (Mon–Fri 8am–5pm) is at Av Presidente Vargas 498.

Shopping Belém is one of the best places in the world to buy hammocks (essential if you go upriver) – look in the street markets between Av Presidente Vargas and Ver-o-Peso, starting in Rua Santo Antônio.

Taxi Cooperdoca Rádio Táxi ☎ 91 3241 3555; Águia Rádio Táxi ☎ 91 3276 4000.

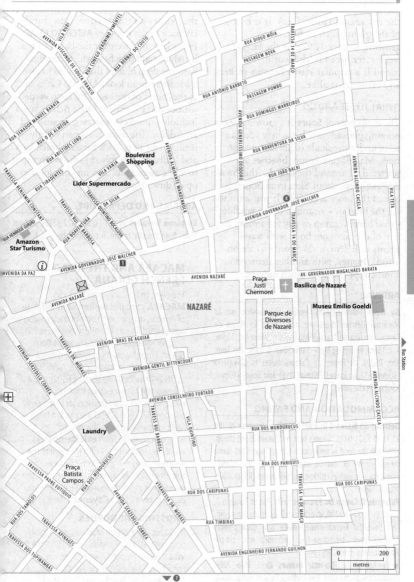

3

Bus Station

Tourist police Travessa Castelo Branco 239 (24hr hotline ☏ 91 8123 1178).

ILHA DO MARAJÓ

The **ILHA DO MARAJÓ** is a vast island in the Amazon delta, opposite Belém, consisting of some forty thousand square kilometres of largely uninhabited mangrove swamps and spectacular freshwater beaches. Created by the accretion of silt and sand over millions of years, it's a wet and marshy area, the western half covered in thick jungle, the east flat savannah, swampy in the wet season (Jan–June), brown and firm in the dry season (June–Dec). It is home of the giant *pirarucu* fish, which, growing to over 180kg, is the largest freshwater breed in the world. The island is a popular resort for sun-seekers and ecotourists alike.

WHAT TO SEE AND DO

The main port of **Soure** is a growing resort offering pleasant beaches where you can relax under the shade of ancient mango trees. Magnificent empty **beaches** are scattered all around the island – the **Praia do Pesqueiro**, about 8km from Soure, is one of the more accessible. If you want to see the interior – or much of the wildlife – you have to camp or pay for a room at one of the *fazendas*: book with travel agents in Belém or take your chance on arrival. **Joanes**, with another tremendous wind-swept beach, is much quieter.

ARRIVAL

By boat From Belém's Terminal Hidroviário on Av Marechal Hermes there are daily boats to Ponto de Camará on Ilha do Marajó (Mon–Sat 6.30am & 2.30pm, Sun 10am, returning Mon–Sat 6.30am & 3pm, Sun 3pm; 3hr; R$22). At Ponto de Camará buses to Salvaterra (30min; R$5), Joanes (20min; R$5) and Soure (40min; R$6) meet the boats.

ACCOMMODATION AND EATING

Delícias da Nalva 4 Rua 1051 between Travessa 20 and 21 ☎ 91 8301 0110. Soure's best restaurant is not cheap, although the food is well worth the splurge. Chef Nalva serves plenty of buffalo meat dishes – the island's speciality – as well as chicken and fish mains (R$50). Daily 10am–10pm.

Pousada O Canto do Francês Sexta Rua at Travessa 8, Soure ☎ 91 3741 1298, ⓦ ocantodofrances.blogspot.com. This beautiful French-owned place is a good choice, offering cool, terracotta-tiled interiors and simple whitewashed rooms. **R$130**

★**Ventania do Rio-mar Joanes** ☎ 91 3646 2067, ⓦ pousadaventania.com. This laidback Belgian-run pousada is set on a windy headland with spectacular views over a freshwater beach. Accommodation is in rustic colourful rooms with mosquito nets; bathrooms have cold water only. **R$130**

SANTARÉM AND ALTER DO CHÃO

The main reason to visit **SANTARÉM**, roughly halfway between Belém and Manaus and the first significant stop on the journey up the Amazon, is to visit the laidback beach resort of **ALTER DO CHÃO**. From July to November the bay is fringed by **white-sand beaches**, which combine with the deep blue of the Tapajós to give it a Mediterranean look. Alter do Chão sits at the shores of the beautiful **Lago Verde**, surrounded by verdant forest rich in fauna including monkeys, macaws, agoutis and armadillos. The town has a particularly mellow vibe to it, with friendly beach bars and laidback atmosphere – the perfect spot to while away a few days on your journey up or down river.

ARRIVAL AND DEPARTURE

By plane Santarém airport (☎ 93 3522 4328) is about 15km from the city centre. A taxi from here to Alter do

---

MACAPÁ AND THE ROAD TO FRENCH GUIANA

Travellers mainly only pass through **MACAPÁ**, capital of the impoverished state of Amapá, on the north side of the Amazon across from Ilha de Marajó, to get to French Guiana. You'll need to fly to Macapá from Belém. From Macapá's *rodoviária* catch a bus to **Oiapoque** (daily 5pm & 7pm; 10hr, up to 24hr in the rainy season; R$92); there are also 4WD services that shuttle passengers (7hr, can take longer in the rainy season; R$150). In Oiapoque catch a boat (every 5min; 10min; €10) across to Saint-Georges. Brazilian **exit stamps** can be obtained from the Polícia Federal at the southern road entrance into Oiapoque; on the other side you have to check in with the *gendarmes* in Saint-Georges. From here you can hop on a bus to **Cayenne** (3hr; €35).

CROSSING THE BORDER

If you are not a citizen of a European Union country, the US or Canada, you will need a **visa** to enter French Guiana. There is a French consulate in Macapá at the *Hotel Pousada Ekinox* (Rua Jovino Dinoá 1693; ☎ 96 3223 0086), though it's better to try to arrange the visa before you leave home. If you're going to travel overland, buy **euros** in Belém or Macapá. You can get them in Oiapoque but the rates are worse, and you can't depend on changing either Brazilian currency or US dollars for euros in the border settlement of Saint-Georges in Guiana.

Chão is R$80. TAM, Azul and Gol have connections to Belém (8 daily; 1hr) and Manaus (5 daily; 1hr).

By boat Boats from Manaus and Belém dock at the Estação das Docas on Av Cuiabá to the west of Santarém.

Destinations Belém (Fri & Sun 10am, Sat 10pm, with an added service every 15 days on Mon at 2pm; 48hr; hammock R$160, cabin for two R$700); Manaus (Mon–Sat noon, also Tues 1pm; 42–50hr; hammock R$150, cabin for two R$600).

By bus The *rodoviária*, 3km from the city centre, is connected to Santarém by local buses (every 20min; 10min). From Praça Tiradentes in the centre you can catch a bus to Alter do Chão (hourly; 45min).

Destinations Cuiabá, Mato Grosso (daily, 6.30am, 2pm, 3.30pm & 9.30pm; 36hr); Campo Grande, Mato Grosso do Sur (daily 6.30am, 2pm, 3.30pm & 9.30pm; 48hr).

ACCOMMODATION AND EATING

★**Albergue da Floresta** Tv Antônio de Sousa Pedroso s/n ☎ 93 9132 7910, ✉ alberguedafloresta@hotmail.com. A laidback, welcoming place offering rustic accommodation that blends in with the jungle's environment: timber walkways lead to a series of cosy rooms, and there's an airy kitchen for guests' use. Bed sheets are an extra R$10. Hammock R$25, dorms R$40, doubles R$160

Farol da Ilha Rua Ladro Sodré s/n ☎ 93 9209 5614. On the riverfront, this open-air restaurant with wooden tables offers great takes on local dishes including *peixe ilha dos macacos* (R$65), stuffed fish with shrimps, banana and *farofa* cooked and served wrapped in a banana leaf. There are also some tasty spaghetti dishes (R$22) made using local ingredients. Thurs–Sun 11am–10pm.

Mae Natureza Praça 7 de Setembro s/n ☎ 93 3527 1264, ⓦ maenaturezaecoturismo.com.br. Travel agency by day and a fun and happening bar at night, *Mae Natureza* hosts live *carimbó* and MPB bands on Friday and Saturday evenings. Tables spill on to the street, with drinking and dancing until closure. Sadly the food is nothing to write home about, although the drinks are positively potent. Daily 6pm–2am.

Pousada do Tapajós Hostel Rua Lauro Sodré 100 ☎ 93 9210 2166, ⓦ hosteltapajos.com.br. A friendly HI-affiliated hostel with clean tiled dorms equipped with personal lockers and private baths. The leafy garden has hammocks and a barbecue area and there's also a kitchen for guests. Call ahead to organize airport pick-up (R$70). Lower rates for HI members. Dorms R$45, doubles R$120

SHOPPING

Artesanato Rua Dom Macedo Costa ⓦ araribah.com.br. This excellent Araríba arts and crafts shop displays beautiful pieces of indigenous art from ninety ethnic tribes. Daily 9am–8.30pm.

MANAUS

MANAUS is the capital of Amazonas, a tropical forest state covering around one-and-a-half-million square kilometres. The city actually lies on the Rio Negro, 6km from the point where that river meets the Solimões to form (as far as Brazilians are concerned) the Rio Amazonas. Arriving in Manaus may at first seem overwhelming given its near-two million inhabitants, noise and confusion, though it'll have you under its spell soon enough.

Towards the end of the nineteenth century, at the height of the rubber boom, architects were summoned from Europe to redesign the city, which rapidly acquired a Western feel – broad, Parisian-style avenues were laid down, interspersed with Italian piazzas centred on splendid fountains. Innovative Manaus was one of the first cities in Brazil to have electricity, trolley buses and sewage systems. However, by 1914 the rubber market was collapsing fast, leaving the city to slumber in past glories for much of the twentieth century. Today, however, Manaus is thriving again: an aggressive commercial and industrial centre for an enormous region.

WHAT TO SEE AND DO

To start with the real flavour of Manaus, head for the riverfront and the **docks**, a constant throng of chaotic activity set against the serenity of the moored ships as they bob gently up and down. During the day there's no problem wandering around the area (although watch your wallet), and it's easy enough to find out which boats are going where just by asking around. At night, however, the port is best avoided: many of the river men carry guns.

The port and the market

Known locally as the Alfândega, the impressive **Customs House** stands overlooking the floating docks. To cope with the river rising over a 14m range, the concrete pier is supported on pontoons that rise and fall to allow even the largest ships to dock all year round. Across the main road from the port is the **Praça Tenreiro Aranha**, where there are

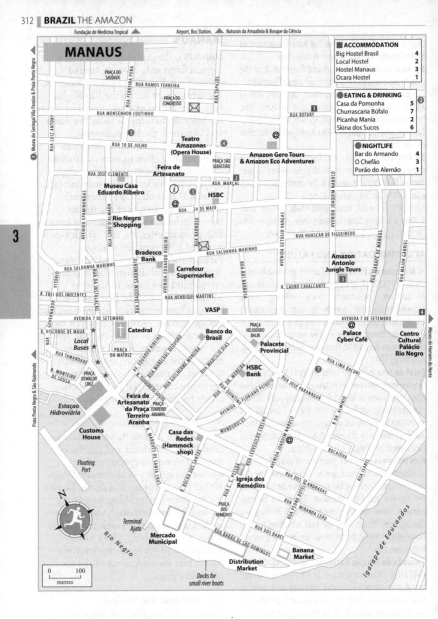

several craft stalls selling indigenous Amazon tribal *artesanato*. Along the riverfront is the covered **Mercado Municipal** (Mon–Sat 6am–6pm, Sun 6am–noon), displaying tropical fruits and vegetables, herbal remedies, and all manner of exotic freshwater fish, along with indigenous crafts.

Teatro Amazonas and around

The sumptuous **Teatro Amazonas** on Avenida Eduardo Ribeiro (20min guided tours only, leaving every 15min; Mon–Sat 9.15am–5pm; R$10; ☎92 3232 1768) remains the architectural embodiment of Manaus's rubber boom: a *belle époque* extravagance built with materials brought from Europe and entirely decorated by European artists. Inaugurated in 1896, its main feature, the fantastic cupola, was created from 36,000 tiles imported from Alsace in France. In front of the theatre, the wavy black-and-white mosaic designs of the **Praça São Sebastião** represent the meeting of the waters. The beautiful little **Igreja de São Sebastião**, on the same *praça*, was built in 1888 and only has one tower, the result of a nineteenth-century tax payable by churches with two towers.

Museu Casa Eduardo Ribeiro

This brightly painted rubber boom mansion at Rua José Clemente 322 (Tues–Sat 9am–5pm, Sun 9am–1pm; free; ☎92 3631 2938) was once home to the governor responsible for Manaus's neo-European spending spree. As such, it's a suitably opulent window on how the city's original other half lived, though pretty much everything that you see, apart from the walls, has been re-created, or, in the case of the antique furniture, brought in from elsewhere.

Museu do Homem do Norte

The wonderful **Museu do Homem do Norte** at the Centro Cultural dos Povos da Amazônia on Praça Francisco Pereira da Silva (Mon–Fri 9am–5pm; free; ☎92 2125 5323; bus #611, #705, #706, #712, #713 or #715 from Praça da Matriz) houses a collection of over 2000 objects that offer an insight into the life and traditions of the Amazon's tribes. There are informative displays on pre-colonial societies, tribal rituals, medicinal herbs and exhibitions on rubber production.

Palacete Provincial

Housed in the former military police headquarters, the Palacete Provincial on Praça Heliodoro Balbi, commonly known as Praça da Polícia (Tues & Wed 9am–5pm, Thurs–Sat 9am–7pm, Sun 4–8pm; free; ☎92 3631 6047), is a cultural and educational centre housing a number of curious museums and exhibition halls; among these are the Museum of Image and Sound, the Numismatic Museum and the

Archeological Exhibition. The pleasant leafy square and the building itself are also worth checking out.

Bosque da Ciência

Occupying an area of approximately 130,000 square metres, the **Bosque da Ciência** (Tues–Fri 9am–noon & 2–5pm, Sat & Sun 9am–4pm; R$5; ☎92 3642 3192, ⊛inpa.gov.br) on Avenida Otávio Cabral, Aleixo, is a plot of forest home to plenty of animals, including monkeys, manatees, otters and snakes. Don't miss the giant leaf of the coccolba plant that's on display in the museum within the grounds – measuring 250cm by 144cm, it's the largest ever found in the Amazon. To get here catch bus #125, #215, #515 or #517 from Praça da Matriz (1hr; R$2.75).

The meeting of the waters

The most popular and most widely touted day-trip from Manaus is to the **meeting of the waters**, some 10km downstream, where the Rio Negro and the Rio Solimões meet to form the Rio Amazonas. For several kilometres beyond the point where they join, the waters of the two rivers continue to flow separately, the muddy yellow of the Solimões contrasting sharply with the black of the Rio Negro, which is much warmer, and more acidic. Most one-day river trips stop here (see p.315).

Parque Ecológico do Janauary

Most tours to the meeting of the waters stop in at the **Parque Ecológico do Janauary**, an ecological park some 7km from Manaus on one of the main local tributaries of the Rio Negro. Usually you'll be transferred to smaller motorized canoes to explore its creeks (*igarapés*), flooded forest lands (*igapós*) and abundant vegetation. One of the highlights of the area is the great quantity of *Victoria Amazonica*, the extraordinary giant floating lily for which Manaus is famous, and which reaches a diameter of two metres.

Praia Ponta Negra

At weekends, the river beach at **Praia Ponta Negra**, about 13km northwest of Manaus, is packed with locals. It's an enjoyable place to go for a swim, with plenty of bars and restaurants nearby serving freshly cooked river fish. The bus to Ponta Negra (#120) leaves from Praça da Matriz (every 30min; 40min).

Museu do Seringal Vila Paraíso

The **Museu do Seringal Vila Paraíso** in Tarumã Mirim (Tues–Sun 8am–4pm; R$5; ☎92 3631 3632) re-creates the living and working conditions of rubber barons and tappers from the beginning of the twentieth century. The rubber baron's mansions displays antique pieces of furniture including a 1911 piano, while within the grounds you will also be able to see a rubber-smoking hut where liquid latex was solidified into rubber bales. To get here catch a boat from the Marina do David in Ponta Negra (hourly; 40min).

ARRIVAL AND INFORMATION

By plane The Aeroporto Internacional Eduardo Gomes (☎92 3652 1212) is at Av Santos Dumont 1350, Tarumã, 17km from the town centre. The airport is served by bus #059, #126 and #306; if travelling from the centre, catch a bus from Praça Matriz. A taxi to/from town is about R$70. Many tour operators offer airport pick-up if you're booked with them; Antônio Gomes of Amazon Antônio Jungle Tours (see opposite) offers airport pick-up for R$60 (up to four people), while Geraldo Mesquita of Amazon Gero Tours (see opposite) can organize a van pick-up for up to ten people (R$120).
Destinations Belém (5 daily; 2hr); Brasília (5 daily; 3hr); Rio de Janeiro (2 daily; 4hr); São Paulo (several daily; 4hr).
By bus The *rodoviária* (☎92 3642 5808) is at Rua Recife 2833, Florês, some 6km north of the centre; buses #201, #202, #203, #222, #214, #223, #227 and #228 connect the station to the city centre (40min; R$2.75).
Destinations Boa Vista (5 daily; 12hr); Porto La Cruz, Venezuela (with a change of bus in Boa Vista; Tues, Thurs & Sat at 7pm; 36hr); Puerto Ordaz, Venezuela (with a change of bus in Boa Vista; Tues, Thurs & Sat at 7pm; 30hr). For Santa Elena in Venezuela, grab a taxi from Boa Vista's *rodoviária* – it's actually cheaper and less time-consuming than the bus as there are plenty of Brazilian drivers keen to fill up with cheap fuel in Venezuela.
By slow boat Slow boats dock at the Estação Hidroviária where you also need to go to buy boat tickets to most destinations.
Destinations (via slow boat) Belém (Wed & Fri 11.30am; 4 days; hammock R$180, double cabin R$800); Porto Velho (Tues & Fri 6pm; 4 days; hammock R$200, double cabin R$600); Santarém (daily except Sun 11am; 30hr; hammock R$100, double cabin R$400); Tabatinga (Wed & Fri 11.30am; 6 days; hammock R$350, double cabin R$1000).

By speedboat Speedboats depart from the Terminal Ajato (☎92 3622 6047, ⓦterminalajato.com.br) on the riverfront by the Estação Hidroviária.
Destinations (via speedboat) Tefé, for the Mamirauá Sustainable Development Reserve (Mon, Wed, Thurs, Fri & Sat 6am; 14hr; R$220); Tabatinga (Wed & Fri 7am; 9hr 30min; R$520).
Tourist information Amazonastur is by the Opera House, Av Eduardo Ribeiro 666 (Mon–Fri 8am–5pm, Sat & Sun 8am–noon; ☎92 3631 1142, ⓦvisitamazonas .am.gov.br). There's an information point at Mercado Municipal (Mon–Sat 8am–5pm, Sun 8am–1pm; ⓦmanauscult.manaus.am.gov.br), and a 24hr information desk at the airport (☎92 3652 1656).

ACCOMMODATION

Big Hostel Brasil Av 7 de Setembro 1653 ☎92 3086 3083, ⓦbighostel.com.br. A lovely hostel with warm and welcoming rooms, some with bare brick walls, to the east of the city centre. Facilities include a kitchen for guests' use as well as a garden area with hammocks. Dorms R$30, doubles R$90
Local Hostel Rua Marçal 72 ☎92 3213 6079, ⓦlocalhostel.com.br. A stone's throw away from the Opera House, this pleasant hostel offers comfortable four- to ten-bed dorm rooms with lockers, privacy curtains, personal reading lamps and electricity sockets. The friendly staff will make you feel right at home. Dorms R$39, doubles R$130
Hostel Manaus Rua Lauro Cavalcante 231 ☎92 3233 4545, ⓦhihostelmanaus.com. Aussie-owned HI-affiliated hostel with firm comfortable dorm beds with lockers in lovely old high-ceilinged colonial rooms (some dorms with a/c) and a sweetly eccentric and eclectic bunch of staff. Cheaper for HI members. Dorms R$29, doubles R$63
Ocara Hostel Travessa Rotary 72 ☎92 3302 3975, ⓦocarahostel.com.br. Tucked away on a side street off Avenica Getùlio Vargas, this hostel offers neat, tiled dorms with slightly spartan decor; there are hammocks and a billiard table in the communal area. Dorms R$33, doubles R$90

EATING AND DRINKING

There is plenty of cheap street food everywhere, especially around the docks, the Mercado Municipal and in busy downtown locations like Praça da Matriz, where a plate of rice and beans with a skewer of freshly grilled meat or fish costs about R$9.
Casa da Pamonha Rua Barroso 375 ☎92 3233 1028. All the atmosphere of a doctor's waiting room yet a godsend for vegetarians who don't eat fish/seafood – though slightly pricey, the lunchtime buffet (R$37.90 *por quilo*) includes regional dishes like *tapioca* with Brazilian nuts and *tucumã* (palm); the bread is home-made and the freshly squeezed juices (R$5–8) are well worth a try. There

are a handful of vegan, sugar-free and gluten-free options too. Mon–Fri 7am–7pm.

★**Churrascaria Búfalo** Av Joaquim Nabuco 628A, Centro ☎ 92 3633 3773, ⓦ churrascariabufalo.com.br. An excellent restaurant with over five locations in and around town, *Búfalo* offers an excellent *por quilo* lunch buffet (R$48), with succulent meat and fish dishes to choose from. Daily 11am–3pm.

★**Picanha Mania** Rua Ramos Ferreira 1684 ☎ 92 3234 8054, ⓦ picanhamania.com.br. This bustling restaurant with speedy service specializes in excellent *picanha* (fillet steak) dishes. There are plenty of other meats on offer too such as beef ribs (R$7.50/100g), pork ribs (R$16) and spring chicken (R$16), with sides of your choice (R$16). Mon–Sat 11am–3pm & 6–11.30pm, Sun 11am–3pm.

Skina dos Sucos Av Eduardo Ribeiro 629 ☎ 92 3233 1970. This no-frills café packed with fruits just south of the Opera House is the perfect spot to grab a freshly squeezed juice on the go – there are plenty of exotic flavours on offer including energizing *guaraná*-based drinks and *açaí* (R$7). Mon–Sat 7am–6.30pm.

NIGHTLIFE

The bulk of the action is outside the centre in Ponta Negra, Vieiralves and Adrianópolis, along with Avenida do Turismo in Tarumã, 18km north of the city centre, which is lined with restaurants and bars (taxi R$70). In the centre, the bars by the Praça do Teatro are frequented by tourists and locals alike – the rest of the centre can be unsafe, so don't head off anywhere on an evening stroll.

★**Bar do Armando** Rua 10 de Julho 593 ☎ 92 3232 1195. As old-school as it gets, this local institution has beer crates stacked high against the back walls and ancient football strips dangling from the ceiling. For forty years now, it's where people have been heading for an ice-cold beer (Skol R$7), accompanied by exquisite *bolinhos de bacalhau* (bacalhau fritters; R$23). Mon & Tues 10am–1am, Wed–Sat 10am–2am, Sun 5–11pm.

O Chefão Rua Ferreira Pena 50, Centro ☎ 92 3234 2202. A cosy Irish-style pub set on two floors dotted with comfy armchairs and curios. Good selection of local and imported beers (R$6), along with comfort food like fish and chips (R$25) and burgers (R$25), plus a courtyard at the back and live rock music on weekends at 11pm. Mon & Thurs–Sat 8pm–3am.

Porão do Alemão Estrada da Ponta Negra 1986 ☎ 92 3239 2976, ⓦ poraodoalemao.com.br. There's no getting away from the fact that Brazilians can't get enough of their hoary Anglophone rock – this place is Manaus's original, a hugely popular shrine to the genre. Live music most nights, with the usual mix of tribute acts and young hopefuls; R$20 cover for the bigger shows. Beers start at R$7. Wed–Sat 9pm–late.

JUNGLE TRIPS FROM MANAUS

The nature and quantity of the **wildlife** you get to see on a standard **jungle tour** depends mainly on how far away from Manaus you go and how long you can devote to the trip. Birds like macaws, jabiru and toucans can generally be spotted, and you might see alligators, snakes and a few species of monkey on a three-day trip. For a reasonable chance of glimpsing wild deer, tapirs, armadillos or wild cats, a more adventurous trip of a week or more is required.

There are scores of agencies offering jungle tours and lodge stays around Manaus, and competition is fierce. Touts roam the streets around the Opera House and pounce on tourists at the airport – just ignore them. Whatever you do, do not hand over money to someone who approaches you; always travel with a reputable tour operator. We have listed some of the most reliable operators below.

Amazon Antonio Jungle Tours Rua lauro Cavalcante 231, Centro ☎ 92 3234 1294, ☎ 92 9961 8314, ⓦ www.antonio-jungletours.com. Run by native tour guide Antonio Gomes, this experienced operator located within *Hostel Manaus* organizes jungle tours with stays at a pleasant ecolodge powered by solar panels 200km from Manaus along the Rio Urubu. Accommodation is in native-style chalets, bungalows and dorms.

Amazon Eco Adventures Rua 10 de Julho 695 ☎ 92 8831 1011, ⓦ amazonecoadventures.com. A one-man outfit run by experienced Pedro Neto whose office is in the same building as Amazon Gero Tours. His tours are slightly pricier than the rest as he only works with small groups – seeing the meeting of the waters from Pedro's very own speedboat instead of from a large boat packed with tourists is well worth it, though.

Amazon Gero Tours Dez de Julho 679, Centro ☎ 92 3232 4755, ☎ 92 9983 6273, ⓦ amazongerotours .com. One of the most reliable and experienced operators, the owner Geraldo (Gero) Mesquita organizes tours mainly to the Mamori and Juma areas. Great rainforest accommodation is available in Gero's own *Ararinha Jungle Lodge*, located on the scenic and peaceful Lago Arara just off the Parana do Mamori.

3

THE THREE-WAY FRONTIER: CROSSING TO PERU AND COLOMBIA

From Manaus to **Iquitos** in Peru (see p.816), the river remains navigable by large ocean-going boats as well as the occasional smaller, more locally oriented riverboats. In spite of the discomforts, such as long delays and frequently broken-down boats, travellers still use this route as it's the cheapest way of travelling between Brazil and Peru.

The point where Brazil meets Peru and Colombia is known as the **three-way frontier**, and it's somewhere you may end up staying for a few days sorting out red tape or waiting for a boat. The best place to stay is in Leticia in Colombia, from where you can also head out on jungle trips.

If you want to break the journey before you reach the three-way border, you can do so at **Tefé**, around halfway. The main reason to call here is to visit the **Mamirauá Sustainable Development Reserve** (ⓦmamiraua.org.br), a beautiful and wild area of rainforest upstream from the town.

Staying at the rustic **Uakari Floating Lodge** (ⓣ97 3343 4160, ⓦpousadauacari.com.br) makes it possible to explore the area from a comfortable base within the reserve.

GETTING THERE

Slow boats from Manaus Tabatinga (Wed & Fri 11.30am; 6 days; hammock R$350, double cabin R$1000).

Speedboats Speedboats depart from Manaus's Terminal Ajato (ⓣ92 3622 6047, ⓦterminalajato .com.br) on the riverfront by the Estação Hidroviária.

Destinations Tefé, for the Mamirauá Sustainable Development Reserve (Mon, Wed, Thurs, Fri & Sat 6am; 14hr; R$220); Tabatinga (Wed & Fri 7am; 9hr 30min; R$520).

By plane Azul (ⓦvoeazul.com.br) has one daily flight to Tabatinga (1hr 40min).

SHOPPING

Casa das Redes Rua dos Andradas 106 ⓣ95 3234 9814. The best place to buy hammocks with a huge variety of all colours and sizes; prices for singles start at R$45, for doubles R$59. Mon–Fri 8am–6pm, Sat 8am–1pm.

Feira de Artesanato Praça Tenreiro Aranha. The best place to buy crafts at reasonable prices is at the Feira de Artesanato by the riverfront (Mon–Sat 8am–6pm).

Feira de Artesanato Av Eduardo Ribeiro. The Sunday-morning street market that appears out of nowhere in the broad Avenida Eduardo Ribeira, behind the Teatro Amazonas, displays crafts, herbal remedies and food. Sun 7am–1pm.

DIRECTORY

Banks and exchange Bradesco, Av Eduardo Ribeiro 475; HSBC, Rua Dr Moreira 226 and Rua 24 de Maio 439; Banco do Brasil, Guilherme Moreira 315.

Consulates Bolivia, Av Ephigênio Salles, Condomínio Greenwood Park, Quadra B, Casa 20 (ⓣ92 3236 9988); Colombia, Rua 24 de Maio 220, Centro Rio Negro (ⓣ92 3234 6777); Peru, Rua Mato Grosso 10, Parque das Laranjeiras (ⓣ92 3228 9312); UK, Rua Poraquê 240, Distrito Industrial (ⓣ 92 3613 1819); Venezuela, Rua Rio Jurai 839 (ⓣ92 3584 3828).

Hospital The Fundação de Medicina Tropical, Av Pedro Teixeira 25 (ⓣ92 2127 3555, ⓦfmt.am.gov.br), also known as the Hospital de Doenças Tropicais, specializes in tropical illnesses.

Internet Palace Cyber Café, Av 7 de Setembro 1428 (daily 8am–11pm; R$2/hr); Top Cyber, Av Getúlio Vargas 5815 (Mon–Sat 8.30am–9.30pm; R$2.75/hr; ⓣ92 9154 5815).

Laundry Lavanderia Brilhante, Rua Lima Bacuri 126 (Mon–Fri 7am–5pm, Sat 7am–noon; ⓣ92 3635 1485).

Police The tourist police is in the same building as the tourist office on Av Eduardo Ribeiro (ⓣ92 3231 1998).

Post office Praça do Congresso 90 and at Rua Barroso 226, corner of Rua Saldanha Marinho (both Mon–Fri 8am–4pm, Sat 8am–noon).

Brasília

Much of central Brazil, including most of the state of Goiás, the north and west of Minas Gerais and the east of Mato Grosso, is dominated by the Planalto Central (central highlands), a largely dry and savannah-like *cerrado*, once covered with low vegetation and now a centre for ranching and plantation agriculture. In this inhospitable landscape almost 1000km northwest of Rio lies **BRASÍLIA**, the largest and most fascinating of the world's "planned cities". Declared capital in 1960 and a UNESCO World Heritage Site in 1995, the futuristic city was the vision of

Juscelino Kubitschek, who realized his election promise to build it if elected president in 1956. Designed by **Oscar Niemeyer**, South America's most able student of Le Corbusier, it is located in its own federal zone – Brasília D.F. (Distrito Federal) – in the centre of Goiás state.

Intended for a population of half a million by 2000, today the city is Brazil's fastest growing, with 2.8 million inhabitants. At first glance the gleaming government buildings and excellent roads give you the impression that this is the modern heart of a new world superpower. Look closer and you'll see cracks in the concrete structures; drive ten minutes in any direction and you'll hit kilometres of low-income housing in the *cidades satélites* (poorer satellite cities). This is a city of diplomats, students, government workers and the people who serve them. Prices are high. Still, there are beautiful sunsets, two or three days' worth of things to see (more if you want to take in the best of Goiás), and an exuberant bar and restaurant scene.

WHAT TO SEE AND DO

Brasília's layout was designed to resemble an airplane (some say a bird, others a bow and arrow). At its centre is a sloped, grassy plain and two central traffic arteries, the **Eixo Monumental** (north/south) and the **Eixo Rodoviário** or **Eixão** (east/west), which neatly divide the centre into sectors: administrative, shopping, banking, commercial and embassy. These are the treeless (and thus shadeless) parts of Brasília where pavements are provided and you can actually walk between many of the sights. North and south of the centre are self-contained **residential areas** – each with its own shops, restaurants and nightlife; each one is spaced a long way from the next. The city is designed for the car, which means you can end up spending a lot of cash on taxis. To take advantage of better and cheaper food in the city's wings, pick an area with several restaurants and bars, take a bus there and walk between *quadras* (blocks).

Esplanada dos Ministérios

Brasília's *raison d'être* is the government complex known as the **Esplanada dos Ministérios**, focused on the iconic 28-storey twin towers of the **Congresso Nacional** (the nose of the plane or the bird's "beak"). The buildings here, designed by Niemeyer, can all be seen in a day for free (though you'll need to plan carefully around their different opening hours) and are regarded as among the world's finest examples of modernist architecture. The white marble, water pools, reflecting glass and flying buttresses on the **Presidential Palace** and **Supreme Court** lend the buildings an elegance made more impressive at night by floodlights. A taxi or bus ride around the Esplanada in the early evening before the commuter traffic (6–8pm), when the buildings glow like Chinese lanterns, is a must.

Praça dos Três Poderes

At the complex's centre is the **Praça dos Três Poderes** (Plaza of the Three Powers), representing the Congress, judiciary and presidency. Two large "bowls" on each side of the Congresso Nacional house the **Senate** (the smaller, inverted one) and the **House of Representatives** (☎61 3303 1581, ⓦcongressonacional.leg.br/visite/agendamento). There are free guided tours (weekdays every 30min 9am–5pm; English-speaking tours need to be booked by phone or online). You need to bring photo ID, and you cannot come wearing sandals, shorts or sleeveless T-shirts.

Behind the Congresso Nacional on the *praça*'s northern side, the **Palácio do Planalto** houses the president's office (tours Sun only 9.30am–2pm; dress code as above), whose stunning interior is dominated by sleek columns and a curved ramp. On weekdays, visitors must content themselves with a changing of the guard outside (daily 8.30am & 5.30pm).

Also on the *praça*, at its edge near the Avenida das Naçoes, is the **Panteão da Pátria Tancredo Neves** (daily 9am–6pm; free), dedicated to ten Brazilian national heroes, with murals and painted glass. Nearby, the **Museu Histórico de Brasília** (Mon–Sat 9am–6pm; free) is a curious oblong marble structure balanced on a plinth, which is currently largely empty.

3

3

Palácio da Justiça and Palácio Itamarati

The **Palácio da Justiça** (interior not open to the public) is beside the Congresso on the northern side of the Esplanada dos Ministérios. The bare facade was covered with fancy – and, to many, elitist – marble tiles during the military dictatorship, but with the return to democracy they were removed, revealing the concrete pillars and waterfalls between them, cascading pleasantly into pools below.

A more worthwhile visit is the **Palácio Itamarati**, the vast foreign ministry building directly opposite (tours Mon–Fri 2pm, 3pm & 4pm, Sat & Sun 10am, 11am, 1pm, 2pm & 3pm, dress

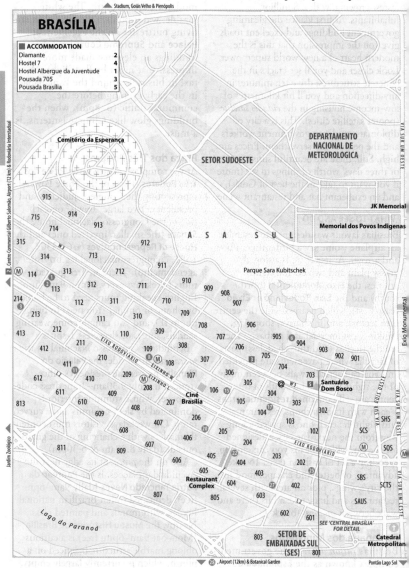

BRASÍLIA

■ **ACCOMMODATION**

Diamante	2
Hostel 7	4
Hostel Albergue da Juventude	1
Pousada 705	3
Pousada Brasília	5

Stadium, Goiás Velho & Pienópolis

Cemitério da Esperança

SETOR SUDOESTE

DEPARTAMENTO NACIONAL DE METEOROLOGICA

Centro Comercial Gilberto Salomão, Airport (12 km) & Rodovia Interestadual

VIA SUR UM OESTE

915

715   914   913

714

913

315   713

314   713

712

114   313   312   711

113

214   213   112   311   310

413   212   211   210   209   208

412   411   410   409

612   611   610   408

813   609   407

811   809   608

807

Lago do Paranoá

A S A   S U L

Parque Sara Kubitschek

912

911

910   909   908   907

906

707   706   905   904   903   902   901

708

709   710   308   307   705   704

109   108   107   306   703

110   207   305   304   303   302

106

206   105   104   103   102

205   204   203   202

405   404   403

406   605   604   603   602   601

606

Restaurant Complex

Ciné Brasília

W3

Santuário Dom Bosco

SEE 'CENTRAL BRASÍLIA' FOR DETAIL

SETOR DE EMBAIXADAS SUL (SES)

803   801

JK Memorial

Memorial dos Povos Indígenas

SCS   SOS

SHS   SBS   SCTS

SAUS

Catedral Metropolitan

Eixo Monumental

VIA SUR DOIS OESTE   VIA SUR UM LESTE

Jardim Zoológico

Airport (12km) & Botanical Garden

Pontão Lago Sol

code as above; free; ☎61 2030 8051). Combining modern and classical styles, it's built around elegant courtyards, gardens, and a surfeit of sculptures, including Bruno Giorgi's stunning marble *Meteor*. Inside, the building's spaciousness, set off by modern art and wall hangings, is breathtaking.

Catedral Metropolitana, Museu Nacional and Teatro Nacional

Between the ministries and the downtown *rodoviária* (within walking distance of both), the striking **Catedral Metropolitana Nossa Senhora Aparecida** (Tues–Fri & Sun 8am–5pm, Mon & Sat 8am–6pm, but no entry during mass, and no shorts allowed) marks the spot

▲ Parque Nacional de Brasília & Chapada Imperial

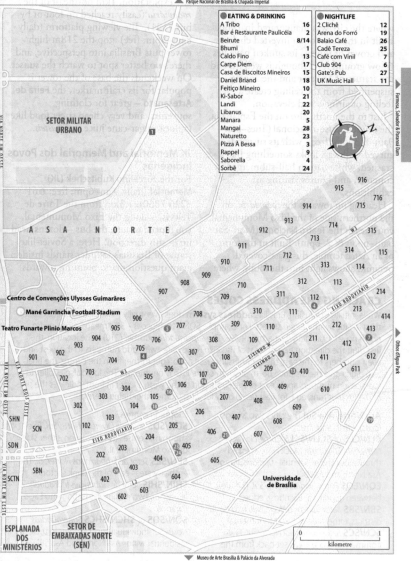

● EATING & DRINKING	
A Tribo	16
Bar é Restaurante Paulicéia	2
Beirute	8/14
Bhumi	1
Caldo Fino	13
Carpe Diem	17
Casa de Biscoitos Mineiros	15
Daniel Briand	18
Feitiço Mineiro	10
Ki-Sabor	21
Landi	22
Libanus	20
Manara	5
Mangai	28
Naturetto	23
Pizza À Bessa	3
Rappel	9
Saborella	4
Sorbê	24

● NIGHTLIFE	
2 Cliché	12
Arena do Forró	19
Balaio Café	26
Cadê Tereza	25
Café com Vinil	7
Club 904	6
Gate's Pub	27
UK Music Hall	11

SETOR MILITAR URBANO

A S A   N O R T E

Centro de Convenções Ulysses Guimarães

Mané Garrincha Football Stadium

Teatro Funarte Plinio Marcos

ASA NORTE

SHN
SCN
SDN
SCTN
SBN

ESPLANADA DOS MINISTÉRIOS

SETOR DE EMBAIXADAS NORTE (SEN)

Universidade de Brasília

0 — 1 kilometre

Formosa, Salvador & Paranoá Dam

Olhos d'Água Park

▼ Museu de Arte Brasília & Palácio da Alvorada

3

ONLINE BRASÍLIA

ⓦ aboutbrasilia.com Facts and information along with city satellite maps.

ⓦ vemviverbrasilia.com.br Decent what's on guide supported by Brasília tourism agency Setur.

ⓦ vejabrasil.abril.com.br/brasilia *Veja* magazine's online selection of the city's best restaurants and bars (in Portuguese).

where the city was inaugurated in 1960. Built in the form of an inverted chalice and crown of thorns, its sunken nave lies below ground level though is well lit, and the statues of St Peter and the angels suspended from the ceiling create a feeling of airiness and elevation.

Just to the north, also on the Esplanada, the domed **Museu Nacional** (Tues–Sun 9am–6.30pm; free), with its suspended curved walkway, looks something like a crashed, white Saturn half-submerged in concrete, and houses visiting art exhibitions.

Heading up towards the *rodoviária*, on the northern side of the Eixo Monumental, you'll reach the **Teatro Nacional** (Mon–Sat 8am–noon & 2–6pm). Built in the form of an Aztec temple, this glass-covered pyramid allows light into the lobby, where there are often art exhibitions, while there are three performance halls inside. Most productions are in Portuguese but the venues are also used for classical and popular music **concerts**.

Torre de Televisão

The landmark TV Tower, the **Torre de Televisão**, makes a good place to start a city exploration, 1km northeast of the *rodoviária* (easily reached on foot or by bus #131). The viewing platform (daily 8am–8pm; free) atop the 218m-high tower puts Brasília into perspective, and there's no better spot to watch the sunset. On weekends the base of the tower is popular for its craft market, the **Feira de Artesanato** – great for clothing, souvenirs, and very cheap street food like tapioca, sugar-cane juice and *pasteis*.

JK Memorial and Memorial dos Povos Indígenas

For the **Juscelino Kubitschek (JK) Memorial** (daily 9am–6pm; free; ☎ 61 3226 7860), 1.5km from the Torre de Televisão along the Eixo Monumental, you'll need to take the bus – dozens head up in this direction. Here, a Soviet-like statue of Brasília's founder stands inside a giant question mark, pointing towards

CRACKING THE ADDRESS CODES

While initially confusing, Brasília's **address system** does eventually make finding places easier than in cities with named streets. For example: SQN 210, Bloco B – 503, means *superquadra* north no. 210, building B, apartment 503. The *superquadra* number (210) is the location, the first digit the direction east or west of the Eixo Rodoviário, with odd numbers to the west and even numbers to the east; the numbers increase as you get further from the centre. The final two digits give the distance north or south of the Eixo Monumental. The logic also applies to roads: even numbers apply east of the Eixão, odd to the west; a letter in front indicates the side of the Eixão it runs, eg L for east (*leste*) or W for west. Some other helpful terms:

Asa Norte/Asa Sul The city's two "wings" (*asas*), north and south.

CLN/CLS or **SCLN/SCLS** *Comércio Local Norte/Sul*. Shopping blocks interspersed throughout the residential *superquadras* of Asa Norte and Asa Sul.

EQN/EQS *Entrequadras Norte/Sul*. The area between *quadras* at Eixinhos's edge.

SBN/SBS *Setor Bancário Norte/Sul*. Two bank districts, either side of Eixo Monumental.

SCN/SCS *Setor Comercial Norte/Sul*. Two commercial office areas set back from the shopping centres.

SDN/SDS *Setor de Diversies Norte/Sul*. Two shopping centres (*conjuntos*) on either side of Eixo Monumental.

SEN/SES *Setor de Embaixadas Norte/Sul*. The embassy areas east of the bank sectors.

SHIN/SHIS *Setor de Habitações Individuais Norte/Sul*. Two peninsulas jutting into Lago Paranoá.

SQN/SQS or **SHCN/SHCS** *Superquadras Norte/Sul*. Individual *superquadras* in the residential wings Asa Norte and Asa Sul.

the heart of government. The museum has many personal mementos and books of Kubitschek, the extraordinary force behind much of Brazil's twentieth-century development, and features a fascinating display on the construction of the city. JK himself lies in state in a black marble sarcophagus, backlit by purple, violet and orange lights.

Across the road is another trademark white Niemeyer building, the **Memorial dos Povos Indígenas** (Tues–Fri 9am–5pm, Sat & Sun 10am–5pm; free; ☎61 3344 1154), which houses a good collection of

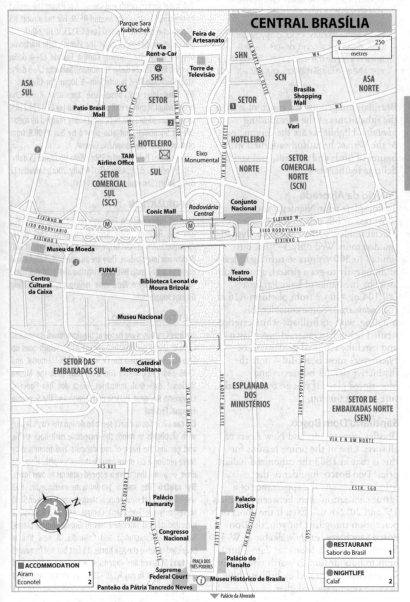

CENTRAL BRASÍLIA

0 — 250 metres

ACCOMMODATION
Airam 1
Econotel 2

RESTAURANT
Sabor do Brasil 1

NIGHTLIFE
Calaf 2

CLAIMING THE RIGHT OF WAY

Brasília has many cars, few traffic lights and an endless number of roundabouts. At most road crossings you'll see a yellow sign on the asphalt near the curb depicting an outstretched hand with the words, "*Dê sinal de vida*", a prompt to claim right of way. If you see approaching cars a fair distance away, do as the locals do and raise your hand with authority. As long as you don't do it at the last second, drivers are well trained to cede the road to you. Trying this elsewhere in Brazil may be your last act.

Brazilian indigenous art, much of it from the inhabitants of the surrounding *planalto*. Highlights are the ceramic pots of the Warao, beautifully adorned with figures of birds and animals, and vivid, delicate featherwork.

Palácio da Alvorada

To complete your Niemeyer tour take a short taxi or bus ride to the president's official residence, the **Palácio da Alvorada** (guided tours Wed only 3–5pm, but limited to 300 visitors so turn up at least an hour early to get a ticket), about 3km away by the banks of Lake Paranoá (#0.104 or #104.2 from platform A16 at the *rodoviária*). Some consider this building, with its brilliant-white exterior nestled behind an emerald-green lawn and carefully sculpted gardens, to be Niemeyer's most beautiful – note the distinctive slender buttresses and blue-tinted glass. If you go by taxi, make sure it waits for you.

Santuário Dom Bosco

Brasília attracts cults and New Agers of all sorts. One of the prime reasons for this is that in 1883 the canonized Italian priest **Don Bosco**, founder of the Salesians, foresaw the appearance of a "great civilization" here between "Parallels 15° and 20° South". Even if the doors of perception thing isn't for you, the **Don Bosco Sanctuary** (easily walkable at W-3 South, Bloco 702; Mon–Sat 7am–7pm), built to honour him, is worth visiting for the atmosphere created by brilliant blue floor-to-ceiling stained glass.

ARRIVAL AND DEPARTURE

By plane Brasília International Airport is about 12km south of the city, served by bus #0.102 and #102.1 from platform A17 of the Rodoviária Central (R$3.80), with the #113 *executivo* service (every 30min 6.30am–7pm; R$8) following the same route and also going onwards to the Esplanada dos Ministérios and the Setor Hoteleiro Norte e Sul (hotel sectors north and south). A taxi from the airport to the hotel sector costs around R$50. For the airport it's slightly cheaper with Unitaxi (☎61 3323 3030; 24hr).

Destinations Belém (4 daily; 1hr 35min); Belo Horizonte (11–14 daily; 1hr 15min); Campo Grande (2–4 daily; 35min); Rio (18–24 daily; 1hr 40min); Salvador (7–9 daily; 1hr); São Paulo (1–5 hourly 5am–9.30pm; 1hr 45min).

By bus Inter-city buses use the new Rodoviária Interstadual at the far end of the Asa Sul (☎61 3234 2185, ⓦrodoviariadebrasilia.net), most easily reached by metrô (Metrô Shopping), but also served by bus #108.8 from platform A1 at the Rodoviária Central.

Destinations Belém (daily; 36hr); Belo Horizonte (5 daily; 14hr); Recife (2 daily; 48hr); Rio (4 daily; 20hr); Salvador (2 daily; 26hr); São Paulo (17 daily; 14hr).

INFORMATION

Tourist information The city's tourist office is in Praça dos Três Poderes (daily 8am–6pm; ☎61 3325 6376, ⓦconhecabrasilia.com.br), with desks at the airport and Rodoviária Interstadual. They are all extremely helpful and give out a free map with information about all the main sights. The *Correio Brasiliense* newspaper has a daily listings supplement.

GETTING AROUND

By bus City buses are based at the downtown Rodoviária Central. Useful services include the #131, which goes up Eixo Monumental past the TV Tower and JK Memorial, and #108 and #104, which run frequently past the Museu Nacional, cathedral, ministries, Praça dos Três Poderes, Congresso Nacional, Palácio do Planalto and the Supremo Tribunal Federal.

By car Lúcio Costa didn't seem to design the city's layout with stoplights in mind; the incredible rush-hour traffic and getting the hang of roundabouts and tunnels may make renting a car more trouble than it's worth. If you do drive, be aware that there are speed cameras all over town.

By metrô The metrô (ⓦwww.metro.df.gov.br; R$3 weekdays, R$2 at weekends; system closes at 7pm on Sun) serves only the Rodoviária Central, Asa Sul, Rodoviária Interstadual and satellite cities of Guaraí, Águas Claras, Samambaia, Taguatinga and Ceilándia. A new line is projected to serve the Asa Norte. It's fast but not frequent.

By taxi Metered and expensive (especially at night and on Sun); expect to pay R$20–25 for quick trips and R$30 wing to wing.

ESCAPING THE CITY

There are parks and gardens on the outskirts of the city that can be reached on foot or by local bus. Wilder natural attractions and tourist towns a little further out require renting a car, hiring a taxi or taking a long-distance bus.

CITY PARKS AND GARDENS

Parque Sarah Kubitschek If you sicken of all the city concrete, visit this park sprawling west of the TV Tower, which has ponds and walking trails for a quick and easy escape. Daily 5am–midnight; free.

Olhos d'Água Park Asa Norte, entrance by Bloco 414 ☎61 3447 8194. Trails and playgrounds at this park within the residential wing. Take one of the buses running along Eixo Rodoviária Norte to Bloco 213 and walk one block to the park. Daily 6am–7pm; free.

Jardim Zoológico de Brasília Av das Nações, South Exit, Via L4 Sul ☎61 3445 7043, ⓦwww.zoo.df.gov.br. The zoo has more than 250 species of birds, reptiles and mammals. Take one of the buses running along Av das Nações. Tues–Sun 9am–5pm; R$2.

Parque Nacional de Brasília EPIA Highway, North Exit ☎61 3233 6897. Trails and two

swimming pools with running mineral water, about 6km northwest of the city centre. Take bus #128.1 or #128.3 from platform A at the Rodoviária Central. Daily 8am–4pm; R$15.

Botanical Garden Setor de Mansões Dom Bosco, Module 12 (entrance by QI-23 of South Lake) ☎61 3366 2141. Gardens with more than 100 species of native herbs, a 9km taxi-ride (R$30) southwest of the city centre. Tues–Sun 9am–5pm; R$2.

Pontão Lago Sul ☎61 3364 0580. The beautiful people come to this lakeside area to eat, drink and be seen. Walk along the lake and check out the JK Bridge, a series of spectacular modernist arcs. There's no bus so take a taxi (20min; R$40); a line of waiting cabs is there for your return. Mon, Tues & Sun 7am–midnight, Wed & Thurs 7am–1am, Fri & Sat 7am–2am.

FURTHER AFIELD

Salto de Itiquira ☎61 3981 1234. A lovely park with a spectacular 168m waterfall 40km from Brasília, near the town of Formosa. There are hourly buses from Brasília to Formosa although buses from there to the park are less frequent. Daily 9am–5pm; R$15

Pirenópolis In the Serra dos Pireneus mountains, a five-hour drive from Brasília (regular buses ply the route). This attractive market town is a popular weekend retreat

with cobbled streets, pousadas, river swimming, and numerous arts, crafts and hippy/alternative-lifestyle stores.

Goiás Velho One of the prettiest colonial towns in Brazil, entirely unhurried and almost completely surrounded by steep hillsides. Two buses per day operate the six-hour route from the *Rodoviária Interstadual*. Stay a night or two in a pousada to take in the cobbled streets and museums of this UNESCO World Heritage Site.

ACCOMMODATION

There's a lack of centrally located hostels. The hotel sectors are aimed at diplomats and expense accounts, though many do offer discounts of up to 50 percent at weekends (be sure to ask). In general, the taller the hotel, the more expensive, so go for the squat, ugly ones. Cheaper pousadas (though often very poor quality or even semi-legal) are located in the wings. The best-value accommodation in town is found through private B&B rentals like ⓦairbnb.com.

HOTELS

Airam SHN Q.5, Bloco A ☎61 2195 4000; map p.321. A good-value mid-range hotel midweek, with fine views from the upper floors, but no weekend discounts. It's seen better days, but it isn't bad value for the price. R$229

Diamantes QS5, Lote 30, Taguatinga ☎61 3356 5011, ⓦhoteldiamantes.com.br; arrowed off map pp.318–319. Way out of town but only 300m from Taguatinga Sul metrô station. Together with its nearby sister hotel the *Dallas*, it isn't luxurious, but it's clean enough, and rooms have a/c, TV, a fridge and free wi-fi, with (unlike central Brasília) shops nearby. R$143

Econotel SHS Q.3, Bloco B ☎61 3204 7337, ⓦhoteleconotel .com.br; map p.321. The cheapest of the city-centre hotels. It's housed in a squat grey building that doesn't look too prepossessing, but it's actually fine inside: the rooms are cool and quite spacious, and all have TV, a/c and a fridge. R$219

HOSTELS AND POUSADAS

Hostel 7 705 Norte, Bloco I, Loja 20 ☎61 3033 7707, ⓦhostel7.com.br; map pp.318–319. Clean and modern,

3

with mixed and girl-only dorms, in a residential area near some handy shops, but the price of a dorm bed here is much the same as that of a single room in a pousada. Dorms R$80
Hostel Albergue da Juventude Setor Recreativo Parque Norte (SRPN), Quadra 2, Lote 2, Camping de Brasília ☎61 3343 0531, ⓦbrasiliahostel.com.br; map pp.318–319. A bit of a trek from town (bus #143), but this HI hostel has Brasília's best-value budget accommodation; book well in advance. Dorms R$68, doubles R$150
Pousada 705 705 Sul, Bloco M, Casa 184 ☎61 3244 6672, ⓦpousada705sul.com.br; map pp.318–319. Marginally better than surrounding "low-budget" options but still very basic. A meagre breakfast is served and a/c costs extra, but the place is clean. R$140
Pousada Brasília 703 Sul, Bloco A, Casa 61 (facing W3) ☎61 3321 9889; map pp.318–319. The best of a little huddle of pousadas in 703 Sul, with rooms that are clean and neat, if rather poky, and not all with windows, although all have attached bathrooms and wi-fi. R$140

EATING AND DRINKING

There are great restaurants in Brasília, though they're pricey. Eating and drinking is often done in tandem, with restaurants open until at least midnight. Asa Sul is especially popular, peppered with places ranging from Mexican and Chinese to Italian or fondue; good areas are around 206/205, 204/203 and 405/404.

RESTAURANTS

A Tribo 105 Norte, Bloco B; map pp.318–319. Excellent organic/vegetarian food including a *por kilo* buffet Tues–Sun lunch only, with a couple of fish/meat options thrown in. Prices are R$40.90 Tues–Sat, R$44.90 Sun. Tues–Sat 11.30am–3pm, Sun noon–4pm.
Bar é Restaurante Paulicéia CLS 113, Bloco A, Loja 20 ☎61 3245 3031; map pp.318–319. A cheap, local dive excellent for *picanha*, salty snacks and for sipping ice-cold beer as smoke from charring meats wafts over the patio. Patrons range from old men to students and office workers. Weekend *feijoada* R$45 for two. Mon–Sat 11am–midnight.
Beirute 109 Sul, Bloco A, lojas 2/4 and 107 Norte, Bloco D, lojas 19/29; map pp.318–319. Two branches of this all-ages institution where you often have to wait for a table; the Asa Sul branch has been open for 44 years. A selection of hot meze goes for R$34, a selection of cold ones for R$27.50. Daily noon–11pm.
Bhumi 113 Sul, Bloco C, Loja 34 ☎61 3345 0046; map pp.318–319. The vegetarian lunchtime self-service is wonderful (R$47.90/kg), although the soups they serve in the evenings are pretty hearty too. Daily noon–3pm (self-service) & 5–10pm (soups).
Feitiço Mineiro CLN 306, Bloco B, Lojas 45/51 ☎61 3272 3032, ⓦfeiticomineiro.com.br; map pp.318–319. Even without the live music at weekends this place would be

worth patronizing for the food: a buffet of *comida mineira*, heavy on pork, beans and vegetables, served the traditional way on a wood-fired stove (lunch R$36.50/kg, supper R$62/kg). Daily noon–1am.
Ki-Sabor SHCN 406, Bloco E, Lojas 20/30/34 ☎61 3036 8525; map pp.318–319. Popular student self-service lunch buffet with patio seating. Salads, *feijoada*, grilled meats and decent desserts (R$28.90/kg). Mon–Sat 8am–4pm.
Libanus CLS 206, Bloco C, Loja 36 ☎61 3244 9795; map pp.318–319. Perennially crowded spot serving up good-value, hearty Lebanese food daily (meze platter for three R$89.90), with a young and buzzing scene at night. Mon–Thurs & Sun 11.30am–1am, Fri & Sat 11.30am–2am.
Manara 706/707 Norte, Loja 60, Bloco E ☎61 3273 2324; map pp.318–319. This is a simple self-service place with good-quality Brazilian and Lebanese food – hummus, *kibe* and the like (*rodizio* R$49.90 weekdays, R$59.90 Sat), Mon–Sat 11.30am–3pm.
Mangai SCES, Trecho 2, Conjunto 41, Asa Sul ☎61 3224 3079, ⓦmangai.com.br; map pp.318–319. A really novel spot with a beautiful view of the Paranoá lake, seating for 800, and hammocks waiting for you after you eat. Oh – and there's food, too (R$58.90/kg). Mon–Thurs noon–3pm & 6–10pm, Fri–Sun noon–10pm.
Naturetto Asa Norte 405 ☎61 3201 6223, ⓦrestaurantenaturetto.com.br; map pp.318–319. You can eat well here, selecting from a large menu of vegetarian options, pastas, pizzas, and meat and fish too (R$46.90/kg). Mon–Fri 8am–10pm, Sat–Sun 8am–4pm.
★Pizza À Bessa CLS 214, Bloco C, Loja 40 ☎61 3345 5252, ⓦpizzaabessa.com.br; map pp.318–319. This excellent pizza *rodizio* serves forty different slices including dessert pizza. It's all-you-can-eat for R$33.80, so you can try each kind if you dare – though that would be some achievement. Daily 8am–midnight.
Sabor do Brasil 302 Sul, Bloco A ☎61 3226 5942; map p.321. A big, varied lunchtime buffet with lots of salads, fish, meat and good vegetarian options (R$40.90/kg Mon–Sat, R$45.90/kg Sun), and in the evenings a R$25.90 *rodizio*. Mon–Fri 11.30am–2.30pm & 5pm–1am, Sat & Sun noon–2.30pm & 5pm–1am.

CAFÉS, SNACKS, ICE CREAM

Caldo Fino SQN b/n 409/410, Bloco B; map pp.318–319. Great soup (R$10) served nightly under an open tent that workers put up and take down each night. Try the pumpkin and gorgonzola or the *verde* (potato, leek and sausage). Mon–Sat 6pm–midnight.
Casa de Biscoitos Mineiros 106 Sul, Bloco A, Loja 7 ☎61 3242 2922; map pp.318–319. Decent bakery with bread, cakes, great biscuits and coffee served outside at the rear. Mon–Fri 8am–8pm, Sat 8am–6pm.
Daniel Briand 104 Norte, Bloco A, Loja 26, Asa Norte; map pp.318–319. Upmarket French-owned patisserie and

★ TREAT YOURSELF

Carpe Diem 104 Sul, Bloco D, Loja 1 ☎ 61 3325 5301, ⓦ carpediem.com.br; map pp.318–319. Deservedly the best-known bar/restaurant in town: great atmosphere, renowned politico hangout and reasonably priced. Famous among locals for the best salad bar (R$29) and lunch buffet (R$52) in the city, and for the Saturday *feijoada* (R$52). Mon–Sat noon–2am, Sun noon–midnight.

coffee-house serving Brasília's best quiche lorraine (R$15.50). Great for coffee, cake, late weekend breakfast or afternoon tea. Tues–Fri 9am–10pm, Sat 8.30am–10pm, Sun 8am–10pm.

Landi 405 Sul ☎ 61 9987 7351; map pp.318–319. Hot dogs are taken to a new level here, with fresh bread and toppings including tomato and *catupiry* cheese, at R$6 a go. Mon–Fri & Sun 5.30–11pm.

Rappel 210 Norte, Bloco B, Loja ☎ 61 3272-2426; map pp.318–319. Very respectable coffee and a good selection of sweets, *salgados* and ice cream. A nice place to start the day. Mon–Sat 11am–6pm.

Saborella 112 Norte, Bloco C, Lojas 38/48 ☎ 61 3340 4894, ⓦ saborella.net; map pp.318–319. A smart yet small modern ice-cream parlour with a choice of exquisite flavours; you'll want to taste several before deciding, sadly, on just two, served as standard. Also has decent coffee. Mon–Sat noon–10pm, Sun noon–9pm.

Sorbê CLN 405, Bloco C, Loja 41, Sudoeste ☎ 61 3447 4158, ⓦ sorbe.com.br; map pp.318–319. Artesanal *sorveteria* that has exotic fruit sorbets and unusual, enticing flavours like tapioca, toasted coconut and cheese. Daily 11am–7pm.

NIGHTLIFE

★ 2 Clichê CLN 107, Bloco C, Loja 57 ☎ 61 3201 5749; map pp.318–319. Around 300 different kinds of *cachaça* line the walls of this *cachaçeria*, which plays good music and gets filled with narghile smoke. Terrific on Saturdays, when drinks are half price. Local media folks love this place and nearby bars. Mon–Wed 5pm–1am, Thurs–Sat 5pm–2am.

Arena do Forró Setor de Clubes Sul, Trecho 3 ☎ 61 9982 0123 ⓦ arenadoforro.com.br; map pp.318–319. *Arena do Forró* is the place for those who love swing from the Brazilian northeast. Every Thursday (and sometimes other nights) as advertised on the website, from 11pm.

Balaio Café CLN 201, Bloco B, Loja 19/31 ☎ 61 3327 0732, ⓦ balaiocafe.com.br; map pp.318–319. Artsy place for a drink, food and live music from samba to jazz. Daily 9am–1am.

Cadê Tereza CLS 201 Bloco B, Loja 1 ☎ 61 3225 0555; map pp.318–319. Get down to some serious dancing at this popular joint for samba, zouk, MPB and much more, alongside the usual choice of food and *cerveja*. Tues–Sat from noon, Sun from 4pm.

Café com Vinil SHCN 413, Bloco E, Lojas 3/5 ☎ 61 3037 1110, ⓦ cafecomvinil.com; map pp.318–319. Exactly what it says on the can: 3000 LPs will keep vinyl junkies happy, while a good few types of coffee, fancy food and fine wine completes the sensory experience. Tues–Thurs & Sun 5pm–1am, Fri & Sat 5pm–2am.

Calaf Edifício Empire Centre, Quadra 2, Bloco S, Sétor Bancário Sul ☎ 61 3325 7408, ⓦ calaf.com.br; map p.321. Busy after work until late, this is *the* place in Brasília on Mondays for samba-rock, or samba on Tuesdays and Saturdays. *Veja* magazine named it the best place in town to flirt. Mon–Sat 11.30am–3am.

Club 904 (Asceb), 904 Sul ☎ 61 3321 6745; map pp.318–319. Open every day bar Sunday, but especially good on Friday when it hosts Play!, one of the top nights on the Brasília club scene, with an eclectic rock, electro and house soundtrack. Mon–Wed 5pm–2am, Thurs–Sat 5pm–5am.

Gate's Pub 403 Sul, Bloco B, Loja 34 ☎ 61 3225 4576, ⓦ gatespub.com.br; map pp.318–319. This dark Londonesque pub has two stages and is bigger inside than it seems, with live rock, pop and blues most nights. Tues–Sun 9pm–4am.

UK Music Hall SCLS 411, Bloco B ☎ 61 3346 5214, ⓦ ukmusichall.com; map pp.318–319. Known locally as the "UK-Brasil Pub", this small-ish music venue spins a Brit-rock-leaning music selection with some reggae, blues and soul thrown in for good measure. Most importantly, it serves a nice pint of (very non-UK) Murphy's stout. Thurs–Sat 8pm–2am.

SHOPPING

Feira de Artesanato The market at the base of the TV Tower sells clothes and crafts, from hammocks to meticulously pin-pricked dried leaves and *capim dourado*, attractive golden-grass jewellery. Stalls and food stands open every day but busiest weekends. Fri–Sun 7am–6pm.

Indigenous Crafts Market Outside the FUNAI building, SBS Q.2 Lote 14 (behind Banco da Amazônia). A couple of impromptu stalls outside the headquarters of the federal agency for indigenous peoples, where some indigenous people sell crafts such as basketware, wood carvings, ceramics and jewellery, so avoiding middlemen. Do give them a fair price for their wares. Mon–Fri 9am–5pm.

DIRECTORY

Banks and exchange Most ATMs take foreign cards; try Banco do Brasil or Bradesco. There's a centrally located *Citibank* near Brasília Shopping. Cambios are located at the airport and at Pátio Brasil shopping mall (unit 2).

3

Car rental Airport branches include: Avis (☎61 3664 9905); Hertz (☎61 3365 5151); Locadora (☎61 3366 2096); Movida (☎61 3364 9681).

Crime You'll feel pretty safe walking the streets by day, but at night the central area is mostly deserted, so take care. Remember, there are few traffic lights outside the centre and crossing main roads requires either entering dodgy tunnels or getting through gaps in traffic, so it's often safer to take a taxi instead of walking late at night. Lastly, beware of pickpockets in the *rodoviária* and on public transport at rush hour.

Embassies and consulates Australia, SES (Setor de Embaixadas Sul) Quadra 801, Conjunto K, Lote 7 ☎61 3223 7772; Canada, SES, Av das Naçies, Quadra 803, Lote 16 ☎61 3321 2171; Ireland, SHIS QL 12, Conjunto 5, Casa 9, Lago Sul ☎61 3248 8800; South Africa, Av das Nações, Quadra 801, Lote 6 ☎61 3312 9500; UK, SES, Quadra 801, Conjunto K, Lote 8 ☎61 3225 2710; US, SES, Av das Nações Quadra 801, Lote 3 ☎61 3312 7000.

Hospital Hospital de Base do Distrito Federal, SMHS 101, Bloco A ☎61 3315 1200.

Laundries There are *lavanderias* in residential *quadras*. Try the ubiquitous 5 à Sec, at CLN 309, Bloco D, Loja 35.

Left Luggage Both the airport and the *rodoviária interstadual* have 24hr baggage storage facilities.

Post office The main post office (Mon–Fri 9am–5pm) is a small, white building in the open grassy space behind the *Hotel Nacional*. There are branch offices at most shopping malls.

The Pantanal

An open, seasonally flooded wetland larger than Spain, extending deep into the states of Mato Grosso and Mato Grosso do Sul, THE PANTANAL has some of the most diverse and abundant wildlife in Brazil. The word Pantanal is derived from the Brazilian word *pantano* (meaning marsh), reflecting its general appearance, but originally it was the site of a giant, prehistoric, inland sea. Today, with an area of 195,000 square kilometres, it represents the world's largest freshwater wetland and is one of the most ecologically important habitats in Brazil. Travelling alone in the Pantanal is difficult, and the easiest way to experience it is by taking an economical **organized tour** or, if your budget stretches far enough, spending a night or two at a **fazenda-lodge** (called pousadas in the north). The *fazenda*-lodges

are generally reached by jeep; those deeper in the interior require access by boat or plane. At least one night in the interior is essential if you want to see animals; three- or four-day excursions will greatly increase your chances of seeing the more elusive species. Most tours enter the Pantanal by road and spend a couple of days exploring in canoes, small motorboats or on horseback from a land base.

There are three main entry points: **Cuiabá** in the north, **Corumbá** in the west and **Campo Grande** in the east. You can visit the Pantanal any time of year, but you're more likely to see the biggest congregation of wildlife from April to October. Renting a car is not recommended unless you hire a local guide who knows the area well to accompany you – you will need a 4WD.

CORUMBÁ

CORUMBÁ was founded as a military outpost in 1778 and rose to prominence due to its strategic location on the Paraguay River. Located in the western Pantanal, today it dedicates itself to the more peaceful pursuits of ranching, mining and ecotourism. Of the three main Pantanal towns, **Corumbá** is best placed for getting into the Pantanal quickly by bus or jeep, and has a fair few guides and agencies to choose from, as well as boats for hire, though is more accessible from Bolivia than from Brazil. The town is not safe at night, so you do need to take care and avoid walking the streets after 10pm.

Museu de História do Pantanal

One of the city's highlights is undoubtedly the **Museu de História do Pantanal** on Rua Manoel Cavassa 275, Porto Geral (Tues–Sat 1–6pm; free; ☎67 3232 0303, ⓦmuhpan.org.br). The museum, designated a national heritage building in 1992, was erected in 1876 when Corumbá was Latin America's third major river port; curiously, most of the materials used for its construction were imported from England. The museum covers over 8000 years of the region's human history in a highly interactive manner, with a variety of archeological and ethnological artefacts complemented by modern resources in a high-tech setting.

ARRIVAL AND INFORMATION

By plane Aeroporto Internacional de Corumbá (☏ 67 3231 3322) is located 3km from the centre on Rua Santos Dumont. From here, all flights go via the regional hub Campo Grande (see p.328). The bus with route card "Popular Nova" runs to and from Rua Antonio João in the centre.

By bus The small *rodoviária* is located at Rua Porto Carreiro 750 (☏ 67 3231 2033), a 10–15min walk south of the city centre.

Destinations Andorinha (🌐 andorinha.com) serve Campo Grande (9 daily; 6–7hr).

Tourist information 🌐 corumba.com.br is a half-decent tourist web portal on the town and surrounding area.

ACCOMMODATION

Laura Vicuna Rua Cuiabá 775 ☏ 67 3231 5874, 🌐 hotellauravicuna.com.br. A peaceful and friendly place, very neat and tidy with clean rooms (all with TV, a/c and wi-fi), and a quirky line in sculpture (look out for the Don Quijote and Sancho Panza), as well as free wi-fi and internet. Breakfast included. **R$130**

★ Pousada do Cachimbo Rua Alan Kardec 4, Bairro Dom Bosco ☏ 67 3231 4833, 🌐 pousadadocachimbo .com.br. On the site of a former cattle farm, this delightful colonial pousada is located 5min from Corumbá on the edge of the Bay of Tamengo. It's ideal for a small taster of what the deeper Pantanal will be like, with birds tweeting as well as the occasional duck strolling around the garden. All rooms have a/c, there's a pool, wi-fi and even a football pitch. **R$100**

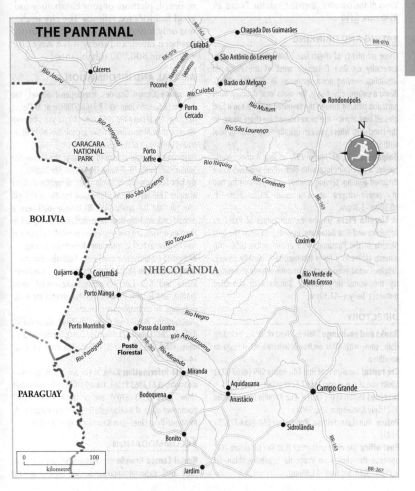

3

ENTERING BOLIVIA FROM CORUMBÁ

Crossing into or out of **Bolivia** from Corumbá is a slightly disjointed procedure. **Leaving Brazil**, you should get an exit stamp from the Polícia Federal at Praça da República 51 in Corumbá (easiest daily before 11am or Mon–Fri 2–5pm), before picking up a **Bolivian visa** (if you need one) from the consulate at Porto Carrero 1650 (☎67 3231 5605). After that, it's a matter of taking the **bus** (from the Praça Independência on Rua Dom Aquino Corréa) for the 10km to the border, checking through Bolivian immigration and receiving your passport entry stamp. **Entering Brazil** from Bolivia (see box, p.214) is essentially the same procedure in reverse, although US citizens should remember to pick up visas in the Brazilian consulate in Santa Cruz before leaving.

Salette Rua Delamare 893 ☎67 3231 6246, ⓦsalettehotel.com.br. Convenient central location and *muito* atmosphere, with original mosaic tile floors, crisp white linens, handsome period sinks and battered antique beds and furniture. Some rooms with decent views of the cathedral. Breakfast included. TV and a/c R$40 extra. **R$90**

EATING AND DRINKING

There are plenty of cheap snack bars throughout town, especially on Rua Delamare west of the Praça da República, serving good set meals for less than R$10. Being a swamp city, fish is the main local delicacy, with *pacu* and *pintado* among the favoured species. You'll find bars all over town – the more relaxed are those down on the riverfront, where you can usually get a game of pool with your drink.

Galpão Rua 13 de Junho 797, at Rua Antônio Maria Coelho. A cavernous local with cart-wheel windows and a thatched awning, serving cowboy-sized portions for two of *comida caseira* at a bargain R$20. Mon–Sat 10.30am–3.30pm.

★**Fiorella Pizza** On the eastern corner of Praça da República and Rua Delamare. In with a shout as the best pizzeria in the Pantanal, with decent prices (R$8–30), alfresco tables in a quiet location, fast, friendly service, delicious wood-fired bases and mouth-watering toppings; try the wonderfully garlicky Buffalo with sun-dried tomatoes. Daily 6–11.30pm.

DIRECTORY

Banks and exchange There is a host of banks, including HSBC, some with ATMs, on Rua Delamare west of Praça da República.

Car rental Localiza is at Rua Edu Rocha 969 (☎67 3231 6000) and at the airport (☎67 3232 6000).

Internet M@bo Cyber Coffee, Rua Antonio Maria Coelho 192 (daily 8am–6pm; R$2.50/hr).

Police Rua Luiz Feitosa Rodrigues 664 (☎67 3231 2493).

Post office The main post office is at Rua Delamare 708, opposite the church on Praça da República (Mon–Fri 8.30am–5pm, Sat 8am–11.30pm).

CAMPO GRANDE

Capital of the state of Mato Grosso do Sul, **CAMPO GRANDE** is the most popular gateway into the Pantanal on account of its excellent transport links with the rest of Brazil, plethora of tour companies and good facilities for visitors. The city itself was only founded in 1877 but its growth has been rapid, and today it is a large city with some 800,000 inhabitants.

ARRIVAL AND INFORMATION

By plane Campo Grande's international airport, the Aeroporto Antonio João (☎67 3368 6000), is at Av Duque de Caxias. Local bus #408 (R$2.70) will take you into town via central Av Afonso Pena, while a/c minibus #015 (R$8) makes the rounds of the downtown hotels.

Destinations Rio de Janeiro (8–15 daily; 3hr 25min–6hr 30min); São Paulo (6–7 daily; 1hr 45min–6hr 20min).

By bus The *rodoviária* is 20min south of town at Av Gury Marques 1215 (☎67 3026 6789). Local bus #87 or #85 will take you into the centre (R$2.70) though you'll need a prepaid card, available from the central information kiosk in the station; without a card, you'll need to get off and pay (and wait for another bus) at the nearby Morenão interchange. Andorinha (ⓦandorinha.com) serve Corumbá, Rio and – along with Viação Motta (ⓦmotta.com.br) – São Paulo. Motta and São Luiz (ⓦviacaosaoluiz.com.br) serve Brasília, and Eucatur (ⓦwww.eucatur.com.br) serve Foz do Iguaçu. All companies serve Cuiabá.

Destinations Brasília (3 daily; 22–23hr); Corumbá (9 daily; 6–7hr); Cuiabá (21 daily; 11–12hr); Foz do Iguaçu (1 daily; 18hr); Rio (2 daily; 21–22hr); São Paulo (8 daily; 14–15hr).

Tourist information Kiosk at the airport (daily 6am–midnight; ☎67 3363 3116), a small office at the *rodoviária* (24hr; ☎67 3313 8705) and a large, very helpful downtown office at Av Noroeste 5140, on the corner with Av Afonso Pena (Tues–Sun 8am–6pm; ☎67 3314 9968).

ACCOMMODATION

Hostel Campo Grande Rua Joaquim Nabuco 185 ☎67 3321 0505, ⓦhostelcampogrande.com. Located directly

PANTANAL TOURS

Organized tours inevitably include at least some water-based transport and a guide who can tell you about what you see. Numerous tour companies are based out of the main access towns Corumbá, Campo Grande and Cuiabá; as ever, you get what you pay for, and the cheaper options don't always enjoy a good press.

CORUMBÁ TOUR OPERATORS

Águas do Pantanal Av Afonso Pena 367, Miranda ☎ 67 3242 1242, ⌨ aguasdopantanal.com.br. This company organizes programmes in the southern Pantanal, as well as fishing trips and visits to traditional local farms where you can stay overnight. They also own a pleasant pousada offering both upscale and economical rooms in Miranda, between Corumbá and Campo Grande.

CAMPO GRANDE TOUR OPERATORS

Brazil Nature Tours Rua Terenos 117 ☎ 67 3042 4659, ⌨ brazilnaturetours.com. Dutch/French-run company offering a wide range of activities and packages from one-week-long 4WD trips exploring the Nhecolândia region to cave diving in Lagoa Misteriosa and the Gruta do Lago Azul.

CUIABÁ TOUR OPERATORS

Ecoverde Tours Pousada Ecoverde, Rua Pedro Celestino 391 ☎ 65 3624 1386 or ☎ 65 9638 1614, ⌨ ecoverdetours.com.br. Well-established company run by respected guide Joel Souza from his inimitable pousada (see p.330). Keen to foster sustainable ecotourism and offering a variety of nature tours, from birdwatching to jaguar treks deeper into the Pantanal. Stay at a *fazenda*-lodge or camp.

opposite the old bus station, with vivid naïf murals on the walls, a small pool and adjoining breakfast area. The clean, comfy, mini-dorm rooms have fans and can accommodate up to four people. There's free internet and wi-fi, and *gratis* airport and *rodoviária* pick-up. English spoken. Dorms R$50
Nacional Rua Dom Aquino 610 ☎ 67 3383 2461, ✉ hotelnacional@ig.com.br. One of the best value of the budget places around the old *rodoviária*, with internet access and a big breakfast featuring tropical fruit and freshly baked breads, cakes and pastries. Rooms come with TV and a choice of fan or a/c. R$80
★ **Pousada Dom Aquino** Rua Dom Aquino 1806, near the Clube Libanes ☎ 67 3382 9373, ⌨ pousadadomaquino .com.br. Comfortable and secure, this charming pousada in the centre has a peaceful ambience, lounge area and a pretty courtyard. Rooms are clean, airy and pleasant, and the decor is inspired by local tribes. R$126

EATING

Comitiva Pantaneira Rua Dom Aquino 2221 ☎ 67 3383 8799. Buzzing, cavernous *por quilo* restaurant (R$35 weekdays, R$40 weekends) that "preserves the culture of our Pantanal", with waiters in cowboy outfits, seriously good meat and fish-based grub sizzling away on an open stove and the odd antique saddle to gee up your appetite. Mon–Fri 11am–2pm, Sat & Sun 11am–3pm.
★ **Fogo Caipira** Rua José Antônio 145 ☎ 67 3324 1641. Award-winning, modern-rustic shrine to gourmet *comida de fazenda*, with prices that won't break the bank. An inviting and intimate patio-cum-garden is perfect for feasting on the likes of fried spaghetti with cubes of *carne do sol* (R$36), and, incredibly for a traditional restaurant in

this part of the world, there are even a couple of vegetarian options, and imaginative ones at that. Tues–Thurs 11am–2pm & 7–11pm, Fri 11am–3pm & 7pm–midnight, Sat 11am–midnight, Sun 11am–4pm.
★ **Sabor En Quilo** Av Afonso Pena 2223 ☎ 67 3321 4726. An exceptionally hospitable, high-quality cross between a Japanese restaurant and a typical *por quilo* lunch joint, with eat-as-much-as-you-like prices held, at the time of writing, at an incredible R$15 for men and R$13 for women on weekdays (slightly more on weekends). The spread features everything from freshly prepared sushi to aubergine tempura and four-cheese cannelloni, and they even throw in dessert; try the excellent peach flan if it's on. Mon–Fri 10.45am–2.30pm, Sat 10.45am–3pm, Sun 11am–3pm.

DIRECTORY

Banks and exchange There are ATMs that accept foreign cards at the airport and an HSBC ATM at Av Afonso Pena 2440.
Car rental Localiza, Av Afonso Pena 318 (☎ 67 3311 0800).
Consulates Paraguay, Rua 26 de Agosto 384 (☎ 67 3384 6610).
Hospital Hospital Santa Casa, Rua Eduardo Santos Pereira 88 (☎ 67 3322 4000).
Internet Cyber Shot, Rua Dom Aquina 1083 (R$2/hr; Mon–Fri 8am–6pm, Sat 8am–3pm).
Pharmacy Drogaria Rui Barbosa, Rua Rui Barbosa 2721 (☎ 67 3314 3710).
Police Emergency number ☎ 190.
Post office Av Calógeras 2309, on the corner with Rua Dom Aquino (Mon–Fri 8.30am–5.30pm, Sat 8am–noon).

3

CUIABÁ

Capital of Mato Grosso and one of the hottest cities in Brazil, **CUIABÁ** is located at the dead centre of the South American continent, broiling home to over half a million people, many of whom speak with one of the country's most distinctive local accents. The city's unusual name is of disputed origin but probably comes from an indigenous term meaning "arrow-fishing", a reference to the local Bororo Indian hunting technique. The installation of Brasília as the nation's capital in 1960 revived Cuiabá's fortunes and its recent growth has been rapid. The city is the main gateway to the northern Pantanal, and is the least frequently used of the three main access points.

ARRIVAL AND INFORMATION

By plane Marechal Rondon International Airport (☎ 65 3614 2500) is located 10km from the centre at Av João Ponce de Arruda, Varzea Grande. Bus #24 (R$2.75) runs between the airport and the small, turnstyle-controlled mini-terminal on the southeastern corner of Praça Ipiranga. Taxis to the centre cost around R$20. At the time of writing, a new tram system that will run from the airport to the centre is being built, due to open at some point in 2015.

By bus The hulking *rodoviária* (☎ 65 3621 3629) lies west of the centre on Av República do Líbano. Bus #204 and #302 (R$2.75) run between the station and Av Getúlio Vargas, just off Praça Alencastro. Taxis to the centre cost around R$15. São Luiz (☎ viacaosaoluiz.com.br) serves Brasília; Andorinha (☎ andorinha.com) and Eucatur (☎ www.eucatur.com.br) serve São Paulo, with the latter also serving Porto Velho and – together with Verde Transportes (☎ viagemverde.com.br) – Cáceres, while Viação Motta (☎ motta.com.br) serve Rio. Most companies serve Campo Grande.

Destinations Brasília (7 daily; 17–22hr); Cáceres, with connections to Santa Cruz, Bolivia (10 daily; 3–4hr); Campo Grande (22 daily; 11–12hr); Porto Velho (9 daily; 23–24hr); Rio (1 daily; 35hr); São Paulo (6 daily; 26–27hr).

Tourist information There's a Sedtur office at Rua Voluntários de Pátria 118 (Mon–Fri 8am–6pm; ☎ 65 3613 9313), and also a kiosk at the airport (daily 8am–6pm; ☎ 65 8419 8310).

ACCOMMODATION

Hostel Pantanal Av Isaac Póvoas 655 ☎ 65 3624 8999, ☎ portaldopantanal.com.br. HI hostel painted in bright colours that organizes trips to the Pantanal. There's wi-fi, a half-decent kitchen and basic laundry facilities. Breakfast included. Dorms R$56, doubles R$96

★ **Pousada Ecoverde** Rua Pedro Celestino 391 ☎ 65 9638 1614, ☎ ecoverdetours.com.br. Very possibly unique in Brazil, at least at this price level: a tastefully rambling, shabby-chic, five-room pousada with hospitality and atmosphere to spare, crammed with bric-a-brac and antiques. Cats and hens roam freely around the communal library and book exchange to an original vinyl soundtrack of Herb Alpert, Frank Sinatra and Chico Buarque, while birds peck from feeders in a large, happily un-manicured garden with fruit trees and

---

PANTANAL WILDLIFE

First-time visitors to the Pantanal will be struck by the sheer quantity of **animals** that populate the region, allowing for some great photo opportunities. Undoubtedly the most visible inhabitants of the region are the **waterbirds**, vast flocks of egrets, cormorants and ibises that flush in the wake of your boat as you cruise the channels – an unforgettable spectacle. The most impressive of the region's waterbirds is the immense **jabiru**, a prehistoric-looking snow-white stork as tall as a man and the symbol of the Pantanal.

Another species that will undoubtedly catch your eye is the **spectacled caiman** (*jacare*), a South American alligator whose regional populations are estimated at more than ten million. The mammal you'll see most of is the **capybara**, a rodent resembling a huge guinea pig that feeds in herds on the lush plant life, but you will need a bit more luck to see the rare **marsh deer** or the endangered **giant armadillo**. Listen out too for the squeaky calls of the **giant otter**, a species that inhabits the more isolated parts of the Pantanal, but which is often overcome by its own curiosity when approached by a boat-load of tourists.

Jaguar and **puma** are present in the area but are active mainly at night; you will need a huge dose of luck to see either, and you shouldn't count on seeing **maned wolf** or **bush dog** either. **Lowland tapir**, looking something like a cross between a horse and a short-nosed elephant, are sometimes seen bathing in streams. You will likely be serenaded each morning by the far-carrying song of the **black howler monkey**, often observed lying prone on thick branches, while the gallery forests are the preserve of the **black spider monkey**, considerably more svelte and active as they swing acrobatically through the trees.

CHAPADA DOS GUIMARÃES AND AROUND

The mountain village of **Chapada dos Guimarães** is located bang on one of the oldest tectonic plates on the planet. It is on this plateau that the true geodesic centre of South America was pinpointed by satellite, much to the chagrin of the Cuiabanos who stick resolutely to their old 1909 mark; the actual spot, the Mirante da Geodésia, is located on the southern continuation of Rua Clariano Curvo from Praça Dom Wunibaldo, 8km away.

Mato Grosso's oldest church, the **Igreja de Nossa Senhora de Santana do Sacramento**, built in 1779, dominates the top end of leafy Praça Dom Wunibaldo. These days, the village has something of a reputation as a centre for the Brazilian "New Age" movement, with crystal shops, health food stores and hippy communities all springing up over the last years.

Over three hundred square kilometres of the stunning countryside around the village of Chapada dos Guimarães is protected as the **Parque Nacional da Chapada dos Guimarães**; at 800m it's the highest land in Mato Grosso.

Park highlights include the impressive and weird rock formations of Cidade da Pedra, the spectacular waterfalls of Cachoeira da Martinha, and a couple of interesting cave systems. The most spectacular sight of all is the Véu de Noiva waterfall, which drops over a sheer rock face for over 60m, pounding into the forested basin below. All visits must be accompanied by a guide – all of the operators based in Cuiabá, including Ecoverde Tours (see p.329), can arrange a guide and/or transport for a day-trip or longer excursions.

ARRIVAL

By bus Nine daily Expreso Rubi buses make the 90min journey from Cuiabá's *rodoviária* to Chapada dos Guimarães.

ACCOMMODATION

Pousada Bom Jardim Praça Dom Wunibaldo 641 ☎65 3301 2668, ☎65 3301 1244. Located right on the central square, this clean and very friendly hotel is good value for money and serves decent breakfasts; some rooms have a/c and are nicer than others. R$120

---

hammocks. Laundry, cooking facilities and internet (all free) are also available, as well as free airport and *rodoviária* transfers. Highly regarded tours (see p.329) to the Pantanal can be organized. R$60

Samara Rua Joaquim Murtinho 270 ☎65 3322 6001. A rather dingy but friendly and clean hotel in the centre that's a good option if other budget places are full. All of the rooms have private bathrooms and you can choose between a/c or fan (the latter obviously cheaper). R$90

EATING

Choppão Praça 8 de Abril ☎65 3623 9101. Traditional and hugely popular open-fronted restaurant-bar countering Cuiabá's ferocious heat with a frigid, turbo-charged fan and delicious pints of ice-fortified, hangover-free *chopp* (draught beer). They serve traditional *escaldo* (egg- and fish-based soup) and have some fascinating historical photos on the walls. Mon–Sat 11am–3pm & 6pm–midnight.

Conde de Azambuja Praça da Mandioca, s/n. This laid-back restaurant-bar is one of three on the square serving up a small, simple menu and bottles of ice-cold beer. On weekend nights, the place gets busy with locals who come to enjoy the live bands. Daily 7pm–late.

Mistura Cuiabana Rua Pedro Celestino 8 ☎65 3624 1127. Set in an airy colonial mansion with handsome old shutters and timber ceiling, this excellent *por quilo*

restaurant (R$23) hums with activity at lunchtime and has a particularly fine selection of vegetarian and salad options. Mon–Fri 11am–3pm.

DIRECTORY

Banks and exchange There are ATMs that accept foreign cards at the airport.

Car rental Localiza, Av Dom Bosco 965 (☎65 3624 7979).

Internet Nameless copy shop inside the same colonial mansion that houses *Mistura Cuiabana* (see above). R$1/15min; Mon–Fri 8am–8pm, Sat 8am–3pm.

Police Av Tenente Coronel Duarte 1044 (☎65 3901 4809; 24hr).

Post office Praça da República (Mon–Fri 9am–6pm, Sat 9am–noon).

São Paulo

South America's largest city, **SÃO PAULO** – or "Sampa", as the locals call it – makes up for a lack of beach and leisure culture with all the urban buzz and modern grandeur that you would expect from a place that's home to a staggering half of Brazil's industrial output. With an exceptionally vibrant cultural scene, the city boasts 150 theatres and performance spaces, more than 250 cinemas, countless nightclubs and no fewer than 90 museums. São Paulo is Brazil's New York, and there are echoes of that city everywhere: in Avenida Paulista, it has South America's Park Avenue; in the Edifício Banespa its Empire State Building.

As a city of immigrants, with a heritage of Italian and Japanese influx – it has the largest Japanese population outside Japan

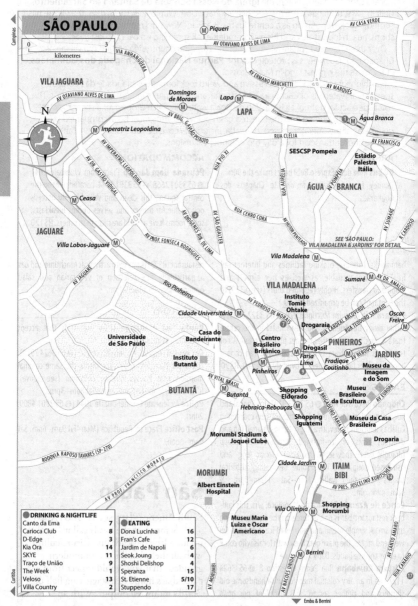

SÃO PAULO

0 — 3 kilometres

● DRINKING & NIGHTLIFE		● EATING	
Canto da Ema	7	Dona Lucinha	16
Carioca Club	8	Fran's Cafe	12
D-Edge	3	Jardim de Napoli	6
Kia Ora	14	Seok Joung	4
SKYE	11	Shoshi Delishop	4
Traço de União	9	Speranza	15
The Week	1	St. Etienne	5/10
Veloso	13	Stuppendo	17
Villa Country	2		

Embu & Berrini

– this is easily the best place to eat in Brazil. São Paulo's denizens, known as Paulistanos, like to live the good life and party hard at night. While many people will always want to contrast workhorse Sampa with the beauty of Rio, the city somehow manages its underdog status well, and its friendly population simply gets on with making money – and spending it. If you're someone who gets a thrill out of buzzing cosmopolitan streets and discovering the hottest bar, club or restaurant, then you'll

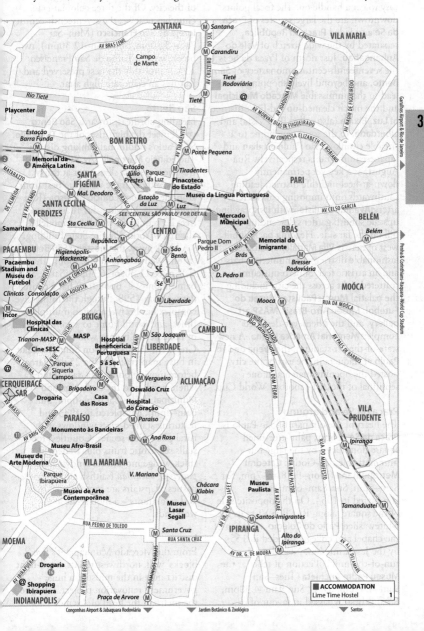

■ ACCOMMODATION
Lime Time Hostel   1

love São Paulo – a city of both pure grit and sophisticated savoir-faire.

WHAT TO SEE AND DO

São Paulo is vast, but the central neighbourhoods and metrô lines are fairly easy to get a handle on. The focal points downtown are the large squares of **Praça da Sé** and faded **Praça da República**, separated by the wide stretch of **Vale do Anhangabaú**. Just north of Praca da Sé is the seventeenth-century monastery of **São Bento**, and beyond lively shopping streets lead to the unmissable **Mercado Municipal** and the much cleaned-up red-light district of **Luz**. **Bixiga** (also called Bela Vista) and **Liberdade**, to the south, are home to a sizeable chunk of São Paulo's Italian and Japanese immigrants respectively. Rua Augusta is a key yet permanently down-at-heel nightlife district, leading southwards onto imposing commercial artery **Avenida Paulista**, with its sprawling upscale suburb gardens descending the hill on the far side. Heading back uphill west of here is **Vila Madalena**, another fashionable district with numerous bars and an artistic feel. Superb museums are scattered right across the city, including the palatial **Museu Paulista**, **Museu do Futebol**, **Museu Afro-Brasil**, **MASP art gallery**, and the Niemeyer-designed complex **Memorial América Latina**. A new state-of-the-art stadium, the **Arena de São Paulo** at Itaquera in the east of the city, hosted the opening match and one semifinal of the 2014 football World Cup.

Praça da Sé and around

The heart of the old part of São Paulo is **Praça da Sé**, a busy, palm-tree-lined square dominated by the large but unremarkable neo-Gothic **Catedral Metropolitana** (Mon–Fri 8am–7pm, Sat 8am–5pm, Sun 8am–6pm; free), completed in 1954. On the opposite side of the square, along Rua Boa Vista, is the whitewashed **Pátio do Colégio**, a replica of the chapel and college founded in 1554 by the Jesuit mission. Next door the run-of-the-mill collection of relics at the **Museu Padre Anchieta** (Tues–Sun 9am–4.45pm, Sat & Sun 9am–4.30pm; R$6) is best bypassed in favour of its

lovely patio café. Around the corner is São Paulo's sole remaining eighteenth-century manor house, the **Solar da Marquesa de Santos** (Rua Roberto Simonsen 136; Tues–Sun 9am–5pm; free), with a few displays telling the story of the city. Of the three colonial-era churches near Sé, the seventeenth-century **Igreja de São Francisco** (Mon–Sat 7am–3.30pm, Sun 7am–12.30pm), two blocks west at Largo de São Francisco 133, is probably the best preserved and features an elaborate high altar.

São Bento

Heading northeast towards **São Bento** you'll meet the high-rises of the **Triângulo**, São Paulo's traditional banking district. The **Edifício Martinelli** (Av São João 35) was the city's first skyscraper at thirty storeys, although the views are best from atop the 36-floor **Edifício Banespa** (Rua João Brícola 24; Mon–Fri 10am–5pm; free; ID required), which was modelled after New York's Empire State Building.

A block away, the **Mosteiro São Bento** (Mon–Wed & Fri 6am–6.30pm, Thurs 6–8am & 11.30am–6.30pm, Sat & Sun 6am–noon & 4–6pm; free) has a church dating from 1598, though the impressive complex has been renovated multiple times, and is still home to a community of Benedictine monks who sing Gregorian chants early on Sundays. Take in busy market street Rua 25 de Março before moving on to Rua da Cantareira, where you'll find the city's **Mercado Municipal** (Mon–Sat 6am–6pm, Sun 6am–4pm), completed in 1933 and featuring stained-glass windows with rural plantation scenes. Countless food stalls sell exotic fruits plus trademark thick-wedge mortadella sandwiches and *pasteis de bacalhau* (saltfish and potato pasties). Upstairs are some terrific bars and restaurants – a mob scene at weekends.

Luz

From the Mercado Municipal it's five blocks' walk northwest to **Luz**, a red-light district now in the midst of a huge government renovation project. Close to the metrô at the head of Avenida Cásper

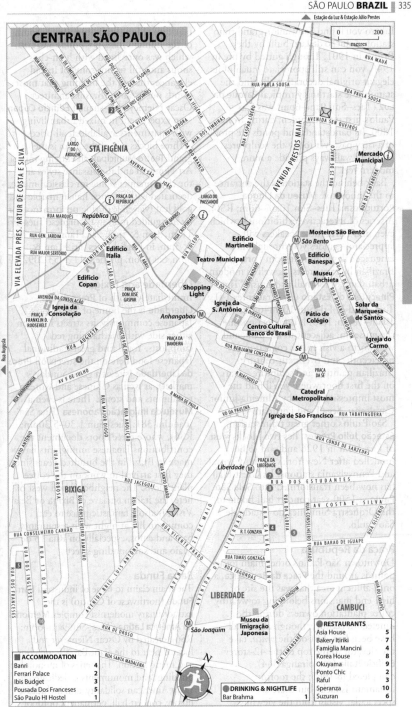

Estação da Luz & Estação Júlio Prestes

CENTRAL SÃO PAULO

0 · · · · 200
metres

ACCOMMODATION

Banri	4
Ferrari Palace	2
Ibis Budget	3
Pousada Dos Franceses	5
São Paulo HI Hostel	1

DRINKING & NIGHTLIFE

Bar Brahma	1

RESTAURANTS

Asia House	5
Bakery Itiriki	7
Famiglia Mancini	4
Korea House	8
Okuyama	9
Ponto Chic	2
Raful	3
Speranza	10
Suzuran	6

Avenida Paulista

Líbero you'll find São Paulo's grand train station, **Estação da Luz**, built by the British in 1901. Though gutted by fire in 1946, you can still appreciate much of its elegant original decoration. Behind the station, the startlingly tropical **Parque da Luz** (Tues–Sun 9am–6pm) was São Paulo's first public garden, dating from 1800. Its bandstands and ponds are proof of a ritzy past, yet today the sculptures lining its walkways provide a more modern feel.

Back behind the station is the entrance to the innovative **Museu da Língua Portuguesa** (Tues–Sun 10am–6pm; R$6). A series of interactive exhibitions – which even non-Portuguese speakers will appreciate – guides you through the language's development from Portugal to Brazilian literary greats, as well as modern urban slang in football and music. The **Pinacoteca do Estado** (Av Tiradentes 141; Tues, Wed & Fri–Sun 10am–6pm, Thurs 10am–10pm; R$6) is directly opposite the museum, adjacent to the park, and well worth a visit for its collection of nineteenth- and twentieth-century Brazilian painting and sculpture – start on the first floor where you'll find the most impressive pieces by Almeida Junior, Cavalcanti, Segall and Portinari.

São Paulo's other great train station, **Estação Júlio Prestes**, lies two blocks west of Luz, built in 1926 and said to be modelled after New York's Grand Central and Pennsylvania stations. Its Great Hall has now been transformed into **Sala São Paulo**, a 1500-seat concert hall home to the Orquestra Sinfônica do Estado de São Paulo.

Praça da República

Downtown São Paulo's other main focal point is around the **Praça da República**, a once-affluent area that was the site of high-end mansions belonging to wealthy coffee plantation owners during the nineteenth century, though almost all have been lost. Just off the *praça*, take the elevator to the top of the 42-storey **Edifício Italia** (Av Ipiranga 344), completed in 1965; the rooftop restaurant is tacky but there are spectacular vistas from the viewing platform (Mon–Fri 3–4pm; free). South of the Edifício Italia is **Avenida São Luis**, which was once lined with high-class shops and still retains some of its old elegance, though the building that most stands out is famed Brasília architect Oscar Niemeyer's S-shaped **Edifício Copan** – an experiment in mixed urban living with apartments available at all prices.

Three blocks east of the *praça* is the grand **Teatro Municipal**, an enticing mix of Art Nouveau and Renaissance styles and the city's premier venue for classical music, decorated with mirrors, Italian marble and gold leaf (viewable during performances or by free guided tour, in Portuguese Tues–Fri 11am, 3pm & 5pm, Sat 11am, noon, 2pm & 3pm, in English Tues–Fri 11am & 5pm, Sat noon; phone ☎11 3053 2092).

Liberdade and Bixiga

Immediately south of **Praça da Sé**, **Liberdade** is the home of São Paulo's Japanese community, its streets lined on either side with overhanging red lampposts. You'll find great traditional Japanese food here on the streets off **Praça da Liberdade** (site of a good Sunday market), as well as Chinese and Korean restaurants and stores. There is even a **Museu da Imigração Japonesa** (Rua São Joaquim 381; Tues–Sun 1.30–5.30pm; R$6), whose three floors document the contributions Japanese immigrants have made in Brazil in the hundred years since they first arrived to work on the coffee plantations. The neighbourhood west of here, the Italian enclave of **Bixiga** or Bela Vista, is also a fantastic place to eat, coming to life at night with restaurants, bars and clubs, especially on Rua 13 de Maio and surrounding streets.

Barra Funda

The main claim to fame of industrial **Barra Funda** (northwest of Centro) is the extraordinary modernist complex **Memorial da América Latina** (Tues–Sun 9am–6pm; R$6), created by Oscar Niemeyer and located next to the giant Barra Funda bus and metrô station. The series of monolithic buildings and monuments is dedicated to Latin American solidarity, and includes a library, concert hall, permanent outdoor exhibition and sculpture of a giant bloodied hand. Linked by one of Niemeyer's trademark curvaceous walkways, to the south side of the highway is the anthropological museum **Museu Darcy Ribeiro**, containing crafts, bright costumes, and an impressive three-dimensional map of the continent beneath a glass floor.

Estádio do Pacaembu and Museu do Futebol

A bus or taxi ride south from metrô Barra Funda along Avenida Pacaembu brings you to **Estádio do Pacaembu** (also reached by bus #917M from Av Paulista or #177C from Vila Madalena, or a 15min walk from metrô Paulista or Clínicas), former home to Corinthians football club, who now play at the Arena de São Paulo in Itaquera. The impressive 40,000-seat stadium was designed by Brasília's other great designer, Lúcio Costa; it stands at one end of a large square, Praça Charles Miller, that is named after the Englishman who introduced football to Brazil. The main reason for coming here, however, is the superb **Museu do Futebol** (Tues–Sun 9am–5pm, match days; R$6; allow 3hr). Piecing together how football became Brazil's greatest national obsession through enthralling multimedia displays, the museum has an appeal far beyond the game itself, from the players, fans and commentators to the controversies of race and dictatorship in twentieth-century Brazil.

Avenida Paulista and Jardins

South of Bixiga, **Avenida Paulista** is central São Paulo's third major focal point, a 3km stretch that in the early 1900s was lined with Art Nouveau mansions owned by coffee barons. Redeveloped in the 1960s, it's now lined with skyscrapers topped by helipads and TV antennas dramatically lit by different colours at night. The **Casa das Rosas** (Av Paulista 35; Tues–Sat 10am–10pm, Sun 10am–6pm; free) gives some sense of what the avenue once looked like, a French-style mansion set in a walled garden that's a huge contrast to the surrounding steel-and-glass hulks, and

now a state-run museum. Also worth a look is the **Museu de Arte de São Paulo** or **MASP** (Av Paulista 1578; Tues–Sun 10am–6pm, Thurs 10am–8pm; R$15, free Tues), standing on four red stilts floating above the ground and allowing a view of the city behind. Upstairs contains a large collection of Western art, while the basement below has a very enjoyable and reasonable buffet. Opposite MASP make sure you take a stroll along the trails of the eminently peaceful Parque Siqueira Campos, pure Atlantic forest landscaped by Roberto Burle Marx.

Separated from Bixiga by Avenida Paulista is **Jardins**, one of São Paulo's most expensive and fashionable neighbourhoods, modelled in 1915 according to the principles of the British Garden City movement, with cool, leafy streets leading down the hill. Actually a compendium of three smaller neighbourhoods – Jardim America, Jardim Europa and Jardim Paulista – it's home to swanky villas, top-end restaurants and bars. Have a walk on and around **Rua Oscar** and **Rua Augusta**, with their expensive shops and boutiques.

Vila Madalena, Pinheiros and Itaim Bibi

West of Jardins, the *bairro* of **Vila Madalena** is also chock-a-block with nightlife and restaurants, though with a younger, more bohemian feel than its neighbour. Southwards, **Pinheiros** is rougher around the edges but also home to some decent nightlife. Cutting through Pinheiros is Rua Teodoro Sampaio, a street lined with music stores, some of which feature free music performances on weekends. Further south, **Itaim Bibi** is a chic neighbourhood with galleries, bars and more good restaurants. **Avenida Brig. Faria Lima** is the main drag here, while the nearby **Museu Brasileiro da Escultura** at Avenida Europa 218 (Tues–Sun 10am–7pm; free) is home to travelling exhibits of Brazilian artists and sculptors.

South of Itaim Bibi is the impressive new financial district, **Berrini**, within whose skyscrapers the largest sums of money in Latin America are now transferred. South

3

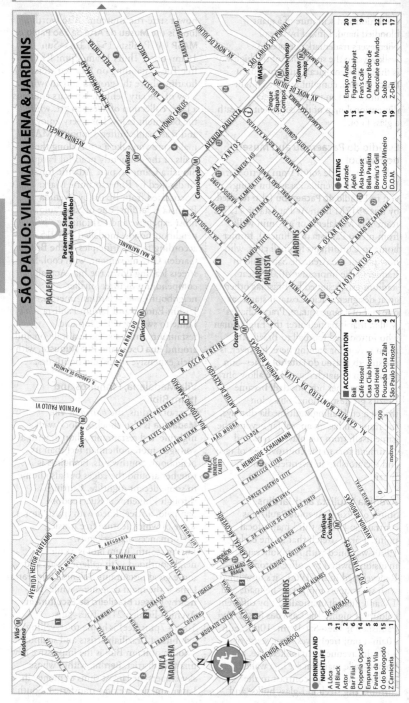

SÃO PAULO: VILA MADALENA & JARDINS

● EATING

Andrade	16
Apfel	13
Asia House	11
Bella Paulista	4
Bovinu's Grill	7
Consulado Mineiro	10
D.O.M.	19
Espaço Árabe	20
Figueira Rubaiyat	18
Fran's Café	9
O Melhor Bolo de Chocolate do Mundo	22
Subito	12
Z-Deli	17

■ ACCOMMODATION

Bali	5
Café Hostel	1
Casa Club Hostel	6
Gold Hotel	3
Pousada Dona Zilah	4
São Paulo HI Hostel	2

● DRINKING AND NIGHTLIFE

A Lôca	3
All Black	21
Astor	2
Bar Filial	16
Chopería Opção	14
Empanadas	5
Favela da Vila	8
O do Borogodó	15
Z Carniceria	1

again, and worth driving over (especially when dramatically lit at night), is the 138m-tall, cable-stayed **Octavio Frias de Oliveira Bridge**, a picture-postcard image with separate roadways passing under a giant concrete "X".

Parque do Ibirapuera

South of Jardins and sandwiched between Itaim Bibi and Vila Mariana, **Moema** is a wealthy district with some really good restaurants, although its main feature is the **Parque do Ibirapuera** (daily 5am–midnight; free; 10min walk from the bus stops on Av Brigadeiro Luís Antônio), opened in 1954 to celebrate the 400th anniversary of the founding of São Paulo. Outside its main north entrance is the **Monumento às Bandeiras**, a 1953 sculpture by Victor Brecheret that celebrates a *bandeirante* expedition. Inside the park, a triad of inspiring Niemeyer-designed buildings houses the **Museu de Arte Contemporânea** (Tues–Sun 10am–6pm; free), with regularly rotated works by twentieth-century European and Brazilian artists; the **Museu de Arte Moderna** (Tues–Sun 10am–6pm; R$6; free Sun), a smaller museum featuring mostly temporary exhibits of Brazilian artists; and the **Auditório Ibirapuera** concert hall. The **Museu Afro-Brasil** in the northern part of the park (Gate 10, just off Av Pedro Álvares Cabral; Tues–Sun 10am–5pm; free) is an interesting collection exploring the African–Brazilian experience through paintings and artefacts, with sections on religion, slavery and oral history, as well as visiting exhibitions and occasional theatre.

Vila Mariana and Ipiranga

East of the park is the **Museu Lasar Segall**, at Rua Berta 111 (daily except Tues 11am–7pm; free), which houses the work of the Latvian-born, naturalized-Brazilian painter, originally a member of the German Expressionist movement. In nearby Ipiranga (avenidas Dom Pedro and Nazareth) is the impressive **Museu Paulista** (also known as Museu do Ipiranga; Tues–Sun 9am–5pm; R$6; short bus ride or walk from metrô Ipiranga), modelled on the French Palace of Versailles. Very good exhibitions on the *bandeirantes*,

coffee and slavery, alongside paintings and furniture that once belonged to the Brazilian royal family, bring the city's history to life. The museum stands in the park where Brazilian independence was declared in 1822; at its southern end stands the Independence Monument.

ARRIVAL AND DEPARTURE

By plane São Paulo has two airports: Guarulhos, about 25km from downtown, serves international destinations and many domestic flights; and Congonhas, right in the city, for the shuttle (Ponte Aérea) to Rio and other relatively local domestic flights. From Congonhas taxis to downtown cost about R$60; from Guarulhos about R$120. An executive bus service (ⓦ www.airportbusservice.com.br) runs between the two airports, and from Guarulhos to Tietê bus station and Praça da República (24hr; infrequent at night), and from Guarulhos to the Paulista/Augusta hotel circuit and other central destinations (every 30min 6am–11pm); all services R$36.50. The cheapest option is local bus #257 or #299 from Guarulhos to Tatuape metrô station (5am–midnight; R$4.55; 1hr 30min). CPTM (metropolitan overground) line 13, due for completion in 2015, will connect Guarulhos airport with Engenheiro Goulart station on line 12.

Destinations Belo Horizonte (3–10 daily; 1hr 30min); Foz do Iguacu (6–9 daily; 1hr 40min); Salvador (3–4 hourly 6am–10pm; 2hr 20min); Recife (23 daily; 3hr 5min); Rio (2–12 hourly 5am–11pm).

By bus Almost all inter-state and international buses arrive at the vast Tietê Rodoviária north of the centre, which lies on the metrô line. Rodoviária Barra Funda serves towns throughout São Paulo State and some inter-state services to the west, while Rodoviária Jabaquara serves Santos and the São Paulo coast (both also on the metrô).

Destinations Belo Horizonte (29 daily, mostly overnight; 8hr); Curitiba (1–2 hourly; 6hr 15min); Foz do Iguaçu (5 daily; 16hr 30mn); Ouro Preto (2 daily; 12hr); Paraty (5 daily; 5hr); Rio (4–8 hourly; 6hr); Salvador (3 daily; 32hr).

INFORMATION AND TOURS

Tourist information São Paulo Turismo (ⓣ 11 2226 0400, ⓦ cidadedesaopaulo.com) maintains information in Praça República (daily 9am–6pm), at Av Paulista 1853 (daily 9am–6pm), in Galería Olido at Av São João 465 (daily 9am–6pm), in the Mercado Municipal (Mon–Sat 8am–5pm & Sun 7am–4pm), and in the arrival areas of Guarulhos airport (terminals 1 & 2; daily 6am–10pm) and Tietê bus station (daily 6am–10pm).

Tour operators São Paulo Free Walking Tour (ⓦ saopaulofreewalkingtour.com) offers free walking tours in English: on Mon, Wed and Sat a 4hr city-centre tour starts at 11.30am by the tourist information booth in Praça República; on Thurs and Sun a 3hr Rua Augusta and

3

Av Paulista tour begins at 3.30pm at the Banco do Brasil by Consolação metrô station – turn up 15min before it starts. City Tour São Paulo (☎ 11 5182 3974, ⓦ circuitosaopaulo .com.br), offer city, shopping, culinary and nightlife tours (not on foot) starting at R$50.

GETTING AROUND

Avoid travelling around 4–7pm when the metrô and road network suffer from serious overcrowding.

By metrô Quiet, comfortable and fast, São Paulo's metrô (ⓦ www.metro.sp.gov.br) is by far the easiest way to move around the city. Although only four lines of the metropolitan train system are actually classed as metrô lines – there are also overground (CPTM) lines, plus an underground line run by an independent firm – it matters little because a R$3 ticket covers all twelve lines with free interchange between all of them. The metrô runs every day from 5am until midnight, although the ticket booths close at 10pm. You can buy a bunch of tickets in one go to avoid having to queue each time, and there are integrated bus and metrô tickets too.

By bus Sampa's notoriously congested roads and 1500 bus routes make navigating the city above ground seem unduly complicated; it's best to use buses from metrô stations, where you can ask advice on which lines go to your destination. Standard fares are R$3. Buses run 4am–midnight.

By taxi Taxis are metered and start at R$4. You can also call the following cab companies: Coopertax (☎ 11 2095 6000, ⓦ coopertax.com.br), Ligue-Taxi (☎ 11 2101 3030, ⓦ liguetaxi.com.br), Rádio-Táxi Vermelho e Branco (☎ 11 3146 4000, ⓦ radiotaxivermelhoebranco.com.br).

ACCOMMODATION

All options serve breakfast unless otherwise indicated.

HOSTELS AND POUSADAS
VILA MADALENA AND JARDIM PAULISTA
Café Hostel Rua Agissê 152, Vila Madalena ☎ 11 2649 7217, ⓦ cafehostel.com.br; map p.338. Small, low-priced hostel, very friendly, if a bit squashed together, with minimal breakfast, but handy for Vila Madalena's nightlife and metrô. Dorms R$35

Casa Club Hostel Rua Mourato Coelho 973, Vila Madalena ☎ 11 3798 0051, ⓦ casaclub.com.br; map p.338. A lively hostel in a corner house in this artsy *bairro*, a 25min walk from the metrô and close to nightlife. Great downstairs bar/kitchen under a mango tree. Dorms a little crowded, but wi-fi included. Dorms R$30

Pousada Dona Zilah Alameda Franca 1621, Jardim Paulista ☎ 11 3062 1444, ⓦ zilah.com; map p.338. The only real pousada in town: it has a great location near Av Paulista, friendly, family touches and superb breakfast buffet, and there's always someone on hand to offer local advice. R$215

São Paulo HI Hostel (Vila Madalena) Rua Girassol 519, Vila Madalena ☎ 11 3031 6779, ⓦ hostelsampa.com. br; map p.338. Smarter and cosier than the downtown option, with consummate facilities and close to great bars. HI discount available. Dorms R$47, doubles R$160

CENTRAL SÃO PAULO AND BIXIGA
Lime Time Hostel Rua Treze de Maio 1552, Bixiga ☎ 11 2935 5463, ⓦ limetimehostels.com; map pp.332–333. Won't win awards for its dorms but more than makes up for it with friendly vibes: great caipirinhas, free use of computers and wi-fi, kitchen (no breakfast), PlayStation, and guided nights out. Near Bixiga and Av Paulista. Dorms R$35, doubles R$100

★Pousada Dos Franceses Rua dos Franceses 100, Bixiga ☎ 11 3288 1592, ⓦ pousadadosfranceses.com.br; map p.335. More smart hostel than pousada, in an ideal spot near Av Paulista and Bixiga. Fresh, blue rooms, small garden, guest kitchen and a mix of accommodation. Dorms R$55, doubles R$140

São Paulo HI Hostel (Downtown) Rua Barão de Campinas 94, Centro ☎ 11 3337 3305, ⓦ hostelsp.com.br; map p.335. The downtown area is grimy but this gigantic hostel is near the metrô, safe, friendly and with numerous facilities, including a roof terrace. HI discount available. Dorms R$50, doubles R$103

HOTELS
VILA MADALENA AND JARDIM PAULISTA
Bali Rua Fradique Coutinho 740, Pinheiros ☎ 11 3812 8270, ⓦ hotelbali.com.br; map p.338. The mirrors behind the beds remind you that this is primarily a "love motel", and it's often fully booked, but if you can get a room, it'll be one of the cheapest in town. Near Vila Madalena. R$90

Gold Hotel Alameda Jaú 2008, Jardins ☎ 11 3085 0805, ⓦ hotelgold.com.br; map p.338. On a noisy corner two blocks from Av Paulista, but has some serious personality, with decor that's Greek diner meets kitsch Taj Mahal. Jolly red rooms with doors with room-service openings. R$110

CENTRAL SÃO PAULO AND LIBERDADE
Banri Rua Galvão Bueno 209, Liberdade ☎ 11 3207 8877; map p.335. There may be cracking plaster in the hallways but this is one hotel where the rooms are better than the public spaces. Good value, almost stylish, and near great Japanese restaurants. R$150

Ferrari Palace Rua Conselheiro Nébias 445 ☎ 11 3337 7689, ⓦ ferraripalacehotel.com.br; map p.335. While not exactly a palace, this hotel, located on a side street full of motorbike repair shops near Praça da República, is clean and comfortable and, not surprisingly, popular with bikers. R$120

Ibis Budget Av São João, 1140, Centro ☎ 11 2878 6400, ⓦ ibis.com; map p.335. A couple of blocks from Praça da República, good value but the last word in characterlessness.

Other Ibis Budget hotels are dotted around São Paulo, but the ordinary Ibis hotels (of which there are more) sometimes offer cheaper deals; all are cheaper if booked online. R$154

EATING

With its profusion of immigrant communities – notably Japanese, Italian, Jewish and Arab – São Paulo hosts by far Brazil's best selection of restaurants, and you may well feel a need to splurge. Take advantage of the excellent Mercado Municipal at lunchtimes (its upstairs food court is good value, too). A range of cheap *por quilo* restaurants is located along Rua Augusta, north of Av Paulista. Also keep in mind that at night all bars serve food, with Vila Madalena known for high-quality options.

BRAZILIAN

Andrade Rua Artur de Azevedo 874, Pinheiros ☎ 11 3085 0589, ⓦ restauranteandrade.com.br; map p.338. Northeastern food is the speciality here, including *carne do sol* (sun-dried beef) served with pumpkin, sweet potato and manioc (R$81 for a full portion that'll serve two people, or R$49 for a half-portion). Live *forró* music. Tues–Thurs noon–3pm & 7pm–1am, Fri & Sat noon–3pm & 7pm–4am, Sun noon–5pm.

Bovinu's Grill Rua Augusta 1513, Consolação 1513 ☎ 11 3253 5440, ⓦ bovinusaugusta.com.br; map p.338. Excellent-value *churrascaría* (branches around town, but this is the best), which has a huge selection of salads, Brazilian stews and other dishes, and, of course, lots of meat. At lunchtime there's an unlimited R$39 buffet. Mon–Fri 11.15am–3.30pm, Sat & Sun noon–4pm.

Consulado Mineiro Praça Benedito Calixto 74, Pinheiros ☎ 11 3064 3882, ⓦ consuladomineiro.com.br; map p.338. Satisfying fare from Minas Gerais at this popular choice in Jardins/Pinheiros. Crowded at weekends. Two can share one (huge) portion for around R$80. Tues–Fri noon–midnight, Sat noon–8pm, Sun noon–11pm.

★**Dona Lucinha** Av Chibarás 399, Moema ☎ 11 5051 2050, ⓦ donalucinha.com.br; map pp.332–333. Excellent unlimited lunch buffet (R$49 Mon–Fri, R$59 Sat & Sun) at the best *mineiro* restaurant in São Paulo. Try the full range of typical meat and vegetable dishes (vegetarians catered for), *cachaças* and desserts. Daily noon–3pm & 7.30–10pm.

Ponto Chic Largo do Paissandú 27, Centro Novo ☎ 11 3222 6528, ⓦ pontochic.com.br; map p.335. Established in 1922, this low-key sandwich bar is where they invented the traditional *baurú* sandwich (roast beef, tomato, pickle and a mix of melted cheeses in a baguette; R$20.80), and it's still the best place in town to try one. Mon–Sat 8am–8pm.

ITALIAN

For really decent Italian food, head to *bairro* Bixiga, where you can take your pick of moderately priced places along Rua 13 de Maio.

Famiglia Mancini Rua Avanhandava 81 (off Rua Augusta) ☎ 11 3256 4320; map p.335. Established by a prominent local Italian–Brazilian family who bought up this run-down street and turned it into a popular eating venue, this is the flagship: an Italian restaurant specializing in pasta. There's a choice of pastas with a big choice of sauces (pesto, carbonara, *arrabiata* and *palermitana*, for example, all go for R$82), as well as lasagne, risotto and some meat dishes. Daily 11.30am–1am.

Jardim de Napoli Rua Dr Martinico Prado 463, Higienópolis ☎ 11 3666 3022, ⓦ jardimdenapoli.com.br; map pp.332–333. A simple cantina where some of São Paulo's best Italian food is served at moderate prices. Justifiably famous for its *polpettone* (giant meatballs; R$55), it also does excellent pasta. Mon noon–3pm & 7–11pm, Tues–Fri noon–3pm & 7pm–midnight, Sat noon–4pm & 7pm–midnight, Sun noon–4pm & 7–11pm.

Speranza Av Sabiá 786, Moema ☎ 11 5051 1229, ⓦ pizzaria.com.br; map pp.332–333. This labyrinthine pizza house with balcony seating has been open since 1958, and successfully replicates genuine Neapolitan pizza (from R$42). Also delivers, and now has a branch at Rua 13 de Maio 1004, in Bixiga. Mon 6pm–12.30am, Tues–Thurs 11.30am–3pm & 6pm–12.30am, Fri 11.30am–3pm & 6pm–1.30am, Sat noon–4pm & 6pm–1.30am, Sun noon–midnight (Bixiga branch daily 6pm–1am; map p.335).

Subito Av Paulista 2073 ☎ 11 3266 3250, ⓦ subitorestaurante.com.br; map p.338. Popular with nearby office workers at lunchtime, this place offers good-value salads, risotto and pasta dishes (lasagne or *quattro formaggi* R$23.90), and also serves a *por kilo* breakfast (R$28.90/kg). Outside of mealtimes and at weekends, it

3

dispenses ice-cream-style sweet frozen yoghurt. Mon–Fri 6–10am & 11.30am–10pm.

JAPANESE AND KOREAN

São Paulo's best East Asian food tends to be Japanese and Korean. Liberdade, the city's Japanese quarter, is full of restaurants and sushi bars. More recently, a number of low-priced Korean restaurants have been opening up in Bom Retiro to cater for the neighbourhood's large Korean community.

Asia House Rua da Glória 86, Liberdade ☎ 11 3106 1159; map p.335; Rua Augusta 1918, Jardins; map p.338; ⓦ asiahouse.com.br. Great-value *por quilo* lunch buffet (R$46.70/kg), with a range of Japanese soups, sushi and noodle dishes. Mon–Sat 11am–3.30pm.

Korea House Rua Galvão Bueno 43, Liberdade ☎ 11 3208 3052; map p.335. One of the first Korean restaurants in São Paulo, where the inexpensive, often spicy, dishes are very different from the Japanese places in the same neighbourhood – try the Korean beef broth (R$52). Mon, Tues, Wed, Fri & Sat 11am–2.30pm & 6–10pm, Sun 11am–10pm.

★ Okuyama Rua da Glória 553 ☎ 11 3341 0780; map p.335. Great-value Japanese food and lots of it: the "festival de sushi" (R$46) – with vast amounts of sushi, sashimi and other dishes too – takes some getting through. Mon–Sat noon–3pm & 6pm–2am, Sun noon–3pm & 6–11pm.

Seok Joung Rua Correia de Melo 135, Bom Retiro ☎ 11 3338 0737, ⓦ seokjoung.wordpress.com; map pp.332–333. The most sophisticated of the numerous Korean restaurants in this *bairro*. Very authentic – and inexpensive – dishes (the speciality being *gogi gui*, or Korean barbecue; R$80) are served to largely Korean diners. Across the road at no. 142 is a slightly simpler Korean restaurant, the *Gogung*. Mon–Sat 11.30am–3pm & 5.30–9.30pm.

Suzuran Rua da Glória 234, Liberdade ☎ 11 3101 1938; map p.335. The unlimited *rodizio* of wonderful sushi, sashimi, tempura and other delicious Japanese specialities served here is a bargain at R$37.90 on weekday lunchtimes (until 3pm) and R$48.90 on evenings and weekends. Mon–Sat 11.30am–10pm, Sun 11.30am–6pm.

ARAB AND JEWISH

Espaço Árabe Rua Oscar Freire 168, Jardins ☎ 11 3081 1824, ⓦ espacoaraberestaurante.com.br; map p.338. This large and welcoming restaurant does great, tasty chargrilled chicken (R$35.90), hummus (R$9.90) and other excellent Middle Eastern food. Branches around town. Mon–Thurs & Sun 11am–11pm, Fri & Sat 11am–midnight.

Raful Rua Abdo Schahin 118, Centro ☎ 11 3229 8406, ⓦ raful.com.br; map p.335. This bright Lebanese diner is a great spot for meze, or just a coffee, and in case you're hungrier than that, it also offers an unlimited Arabic *rodizio* (R$59). Mon–Fri 7am–6pm, Sat 7am–4pm.

Z-Deli Alameda Lorena 1689, Cerqueira César ☎ 11 3064 3058; map p.338. A small Jewish deli-restaurant with an outstanding all-you-can-eat spread of Ashkenazi Jewish specialities (R$49 weekdays, R$60 at weekends, when the selection's bigger). Mon–Fri 12.30–6pm, Sat 12.30–5pm.

VEGETARIAN

Apfel Rua Bela Cintra 1343, Jardim Paulista ☎ 11 3062 3727; ⓦ apfel.com.br; map p.338. An excellent and largely organic vegetarian buffet – a hundred percent veggie, ninety percent organic, they say – features hot and cold dishes, including salads, soups, sweets and savouries, for R$26 on weekdays, R$30 at weekends. Mon–Fri noon–3pm, Sat & Sun noon–4pm.

CAFÉS, BAKERIES, SNACKS

Bakery Itiriki Rua dos Estudantes 24, Liberdade ☎ 11 3277 4939, ⓦ bakeryitiriki.com; map p.335. Brazilian and Japanese pastries and savoury snacks, with upstairs seating. Daily 8am–7pm.

Bella Paulista Rua Haddock Lobo 354 ☎ 11 3214 3347, ⓦ bellapaulista.com; map p.338. Handy for a drink, a meal, a coffee and cake or just an ice cream at any time of the day or night: it's a rare hour of a rare day that it isn't buzzing. Daily 24hr.

Fran's Cafe Praça Benedito Calixto 191, Jardins ☎ 11 3083 5351; map p.338. Rua Cubatão 1111, Vila Mariana ☎ 11 5083 0350, ⓦ franscafe.com.br; map p.332–333. Excellent coffee, and free wi-fi access. Part of a chain with branches around town and nationwide. Daily 24hr.

O Melhor Bolo de Chocolate do Mundo Rua Oscar Freire 125, Jardins ☎ 11 3061 2172, ⓦ omelhorbolode chocolatedomundo.com; map p.338. Its name ("the world's best chocolate cake") gives it away – and after tasting their creations here, modelled on those of a renowned Lisbon bakery, you may well agree. Mon–Fri 11am–7pm, Sat 10am–8pm, Sun noon–8pm.

★ Shoshi Delishop Rua Correia de Melo 206, Bom Retiro ☎ 11 3228 4774, ⓦ delishoprestaurante.com.br; map pp.332–333. In among the Korean eateries is this inexpensive Jewish-Brazilian lunch and snack joint. Super-friendly and ideal if you're visiting museums in Luz. Mon–Sat 8.30am–3.30pm.

St Etienne Alameda Joaquim Eugênio de Lima 1417, Jardins ☎ 11 3885 0691, & Av Diógenes Ribero de Lima 2555, Alto de Pinheiros ☎ 11 3021 1200, ⓦ santaetienne.com.br; map pp.332–333. Busy, unpretentious 24hr cafés/bars with pavement seating, great sandwiches and, if you're really hungry, a variety of unlimited breakfast/lunch/tea buffets. Daily 24hr.

Stuppendo Rua Canário 1321, Moema ☎ 11 5093 2967, ⓦ stuppendo.com.br; map pp.332–333. A great place for top-notch ice cream, with flavours galore rivalling Italy's best. Mon 12.30–7pm, Tues, Wed, Thurs & Sun 12.30–10pm, Fri & Sat 12.30–11pm.

DRINKING AND NIGHTLIFE

São Paulo's nightlife is fantastic – a good enough reason alone for visiting the city. Options are scattered all over town, with things really getting going after midnight: Rua Augusta north of Av Paulista is the unofficial nightlife (though also red-light) centre; Vila Madalena (corners of Morato Coelho and Aspicquelta) is good for more upscale drinking; nearby Pinheiros is a mix of the more artsy and Brazilian down-at-heel; Barra Funda has big dance music clubs; while Bixiga and Itaim Bibi also both offer good bars and live music. The São Paulo edition of the weekly magazine *Veja* contains an excellent entertainment guide, and the daily newspaper *Folha de São Paulo* lists cultural and sporting events and, on Friday, contains an essential entertainment guide, the *Guia da Folha*. Great-value performances by famous Brazilian singers and dance troupes often take place at Auditório Ibarapuera: see ⓦ auditorioibirapuera.com.br.

BARS AND PUBS

All Black Rua Oscar Freire 163, Jardins ☎ 11 3088 7990, ⓦ allblack.com.br; map p.338. São Paulo's best Irish pub for those dying for a Guinness. Mon 6pm–12.30am, Tues 6pm–1.30pm, Wed 6pm–2am, Thurs 6pm–3am, Fri 6pm–3.30am, Sat 7pm–3.30am.

Astor Rua Delfina 163, Vila Madalena ☎ 11 3815 1364, ⓦ barastor.com.br; map p.338. This well-established bar done out in Art Deco style, with an impressive stack of Johnny Walker bottles behind the bar, plus excellent beer and *petiscos* (snacks), is a great place to start a night out in Vila Madalena. Mon–Wed 6pm–2am, Thurs–Sat noon–3am, Sun noon–7pm.

Bar Brahma Av São João 677, Centro ☎ 11 3224 1250, ⓦ barbrahmacentro.com; map p.335. One of the city's oldest bars (opened 1948). Once a haunt for musicians, intellectuals and politicians, today it hosts musical acts most nights. Mon–Sat 11.30am–3am, Sun 11.30am–midnight.

Bar Filial Rua Fidalga 254, Vila Madalena ☎ 11 3813 9226, ⓦ barfilial.com.br; map p.338. Looks like a simple local bar, but is actually quite a sophisticated locale with a chequered floor, bow-tie-wearing waiters and a wide range of *cachaças*. Mon–Thurs 5pm–3.30am, Fri 5pm–4am, Sat noon–4am, Sun noon–3.30am.

Choperia Opção Rua Carlos Comenale 97 ☎ 11 3288 7823, ⓦ choperiaopcao.com.br; map p.338. Just metres from Av Paulista and MASP, this is a really popular after-work place, with an outdoor terrace that's great for watching workhorse Sampa go by. Daily 4pm–late.

Empanadas Rua Wisard 489, Vila Madalena ☎ 11 3032 2116; map p.338. The simple but effective selling-point of this busy bar is that, in addition to beer, it serves *empanadas* (savoury pastries popular throughout South America but usually referred to as *empadas* in Brazil) at R$6.90 each or R$28 for half a dozen. Mon–Thurs 12.30pm–1am, Fri & Sat 12.30pm–3am, Sun 1pm–1am.

Kia Ora Rua Dr Eduardo de Souza Aranha 377, Itaim Bibi ☎ 11 3846 8300, ⓦ kiaora.com.br; map pp.332–333. With its live rock bands, Kiwi-owned *Kia Ora* is a popular pub among expats and *Paulistanos* alike. On some nights there's a long wait to get in, although you can reserve ahead. Be aware that there's a dress code – no shorts or football shirts, for example. Tues 6pm–1.30am, Wed & Thurs 6pm–3am, Fri 7pm–4am, Sat 8pm–4.30am.

★**SKYE** Hotel Unique, Av Brigadeiro Luis Antônio 4700, Jardim Paulista ☎ 11 3055 4702, ⓦ hotelunique.com.br; map pp.332–333. This is the place to start your night, on the roof of the "watermelon hotel" sipping a cocktail along with the beautiful people and a 360-degree view of the skyline. Chic and luxurious. DJs from 9pm. Sun–Thurs 7pm–midnight, Fri & Sat 7pm–12.30am.

Veloso Rua Conceição Veloso 56, Vila Mariana ☎ 11 5572 0254, ⓦ velosobar.com.br; map pp.332–333. Perennially popular bar voted for serving Sampa's best *caipirinhas* and *coxinha* savouries. Inevitably neither comes cheap, but they are worth it. Tues–Fri 5.30pm–12.30am; Sat 12.45pm–12.30am, Sun 4–10.30pm.

Z Carniceria Rua Augusta 934, Jardim Paulista ☎ 11 3231 3705, ⓦ zcarniceria.com.br; map p.338. Meat-cleaver door handles adorn the entrance to this rather macabre, dark cocktail bar on the site of an old butcher and abbatoir, which still preserves many of the original butcher-shop props. The house speciality is a "mad butcher", made with vodka, peach liqueur, passion fruit juice and tabasco. Tues, Wed, Thurs & Sun 7pm–1am, Fri & Sat 7pm–2am.

CLUBS

A Lôca Rua Frei Caneca 916, Bixiga ☎ 11 3159 8889, ⓦ aloca.com.br; map p.338. Crazy-busy place, which gets crammed with people (many of them gay), especially on Thursdays. The music is mostly house and techno, but Sunday is rock night. Wed–Sat midnight–late, Sun 7pm until not quite so late.

Canto da Ema Av Brig. Faria Lima 364, Pinheiros ☎ 11 3813 4708, ⓦ cantodaema.com.br; map pp.332–333. You can hear the *forró* outside despite the airlock entrance. Inside, it's all dancing fun and *cachaça*. Opening hours vary; usually Thurs–Sat 10.30pm–late, sometimes Wed & Sun.

Carioca Club Rua Cardeal Arcoverde 2899, Pinheiros ☎ 11 3813 8598, ⓦ cariocaclub.com.br; map pp.332–333. This great dance hall features live *forró*, funk or samba nightly, with friendly people not averse to showing newcomers the ropes. Some acts start early (7–11pm), and others late (11pm–5am). The website has comprehensive details of what's on.

D-Edge Alameda Olga 170, Barra Funda ☎ 11 3665 9500, ⓦ d-edge.com.br; map pp.332–333. Sampa's premier electronica club, with nightly DJs playing anything from techno to (*baile*) funk, and a mixed crowd ready to dance. Mon–Sat usually from midnight.

Favela da Vila Rua Mourato Coelho 1272, Vila Madalena 419 ☎ 11 3031 8927, ⓦ faveladavila.com.br; map p.338. Live rock, Brazilian pop (MPB) or samba at this hip and friendly spot. Saturday *feijoada* buffet from 1pm at R$39.90 for two people, with live samba. Fri 10pm–late, Sat 1pm–late, Sun 4pm–late.

Ó do Borogodó Rua Horácio Lane 21, Pinheiros ☎ 11 3814 4087; map p.338. This is the real Brazil: a gritty, authentic samba bar where everybody dances with everybody. Mon–Fri 9pm–3am, Sat 1pm–3am, Sun 7pm–midnight.

★Traço de União Rua Claudio Soares, Pinheiros ☎ 11 3816 7693, ⓦ tracodeuniao.com.br; map pp.332–333. One of the city's top samba venues, especially busy on Friday nights, but also known for its Saturday *feijoadas* and always with a good vibe. Fri 10pm–3am, Sat noon–3am.

Villa Country Av Francisco Matarazzo 774, Barra Funda ☎ 11 3868 5858, ⓦ villacountry.com.br; map pp.332–333. *Serteneja* (Brazilian country music) is massive right now thanks to a certain Michel Teló, and this 1800-capacity venue needs to be seen to be believed. Expect crowds of cowboy hats and cowgirl hotpants. Thurs–Sun 11pm–late.

The Week Rua Guaicuras 324, Lapa ☎ 11 3868 9944, ⓦ theweek.com.br; map pp.332–333. São Paolo's biggest and most famous gay and lesbian club attracts top DJs and a fair few VIPs (not necessarily gay). Fri & Sat midnight–9am.

DIRECTORY

Banks and exchange There are cambios at the airports and sprinkled throughout the city, with several banks and money changers along Av Paulista.

Car rental (Centro) Hertz, Rua da Consolação 431 ☎ 11 3258 9384; Localiza, Rua da Consolação 419 ☎ 11 3231 3055; Movida, Rua da Consolação 293 ☎ 11 3151 4450.

Consulates Argentina, Av Paulista 2313, Cerqueira César (☎ 11 3897 9522); Australia, Alameda Santos 700, 9th floor, suite 92, Cerqueira César (☎ 11 2112 6200); Canada, Av das Nações Unidas 12901, 16th floor, Itaim Bibi (☎ 11 5509 4321); Ireland, Alameda Joaquim Eugenio de Lima 447, Jardim Paulista (☎ 11 3147 7788); New Zealand, Alameda Campinas 579, 15th floor, Cerqueira César (☎ 11 3253 6296); South Africa, Av Paulista 1754, 12th floor, Cerqueira César (☎ 11 3265 0449); UK, Rua Ferreira de Araújo 741, 2nd floor, Pinheiros (☎ 11 3094 2700); US, Rua Henri Dunant 500, Campo Belo (☎ 11 5186 7000).

Crime São Paulo has high crime. Keep valuables hidden and be careful at all times, especially in crowded areas like bus stations and markets. At night, much of downtown, including Luz and Praça da República through to São Bento, gets very seedy.

Hospitals The private Hospital Albert Einstein, Av Albert Einstein 627, Morumbi (☎ 11 2151 1233, ⓦ einstein.br), is considered to be the best hospital in Brazil. For dentistry, Banatti, Av Paulista 925, 13th floor, Cerqueira César (☎ 11 3141 1061, ⓦ benattiodontologia.com.br), is central and

English-speaking.

Laundries HGM, Praça Julio Mesquita 13, at Sta. Efigênia, and Rua Castro Alves 437, Aclimação; 5 à Sec, Praça da República 177 E 199 Loja 9, and Brigadeiro Luis Antonio 2013, Loja 4.

Left luggage Guarulhos, Congonhas and Tietê Rodoviária have 24hr lockers.

Police Emergencies ☎ 190. DEATUR, a special police unit for tourists (☎ 11 3257 4475), is located at Rua Consolação 247, and has posts at the two airports.

Post offices The main post office is downtown at Praça Correio, at the corner of Avenida São João (Mon–Fri 9am–6pm, Sat 9am–1pm). Smaller offices (Mon–Fri 9am–5pm), with their distinctive yellow signage, are scattered throughout the city, including several along Avenida Paulista (see ⓦ correios.com.br).

Visas To extend your visa, visit the Polícia Federal, Rua Hugo D'Antola 95, 3rd floor, Lapa de Baixo (Mon–Fri 8am–2pm; ☎ 11 3538 5000; Metrô Lapa).

SANTOS

Half the world's coffee, oranges and sugar pass through **SANTOS**, Latin America's biggest port. Inevitably a big chunk of the city is given over to industrial complexes and shipyards, but the surprise beneath the grit is a charming historical centre that attests to its foundation by the Portuguese in 1535. Lying on the island of **São Vicente**, the city is surrounded by water and has some popular beaches that draw the crowds in from São Paulo at weekends (you may wish to give swimming a miss here, however, as the water is not especially clean).

WHAT TO SEE AND DO

You can see Santos's sights in a few hours, making it great for a day-trip or a stopoff if you're travelling from São Paulo along the coast to Paraty via São Sebastião.

A **tourist tram** (Tues–Sun 11am–5pm; weekdays half-hourly, weekends every 20min; R$5) runs from Praça Mauá by Rua do Comércio for a fifteen-minute trip. The centre is easy to navigate on foot. Walk past the attractive colonial-era houses on Rua do Comércio towards the nineteenth-century train station. Nearby, the grand **Bolsa de Café** (Rua XV de Novembro 95; Tues–Sat 9am–5pm, Sun 10am–5pm; R$7; ⓦ museudocafe.com.br) is Santos's main museum space. It hosts a remarkable permanent exhibition on the history of Brazil's coffee industry, partly responsible for the country's ethnic make-up given its enormous demand first for African slave labour, then for Italian, Japanese and other migrant workers in the late nineteenth and early twentieth centuries.

International football legend Pelé learnt his trade at **Santos Futebol Clube**, a legacy followed in part today by the club's newest young prodigy, Neymar. The stadium makes a worthwhile visit (Rua Princesa Isabel 77; Tues–Sun 9am–7pm except match days; R$6, guided tour R$10).

ARRIVAL AND DEPARTURE

By bus The *rodoviária* is in the Centro on Praça dos Andradas. From São Paulo, Santos buses (every 15min; 1hr 15min) leave from the Jabaquara *rodoviária* and not from Tietê. Santos's *rodoviária* has left luggage and tourist information. Executive buses to São Sebastião depart daily at 7am, 1pm, 5pm and 7.30pm (3hr 40min; R$47; ⓦ litoranea.com.br).

ACCOMMODATION

HI Santos Hostel Rua Barão de Paranapiacaba 22 ⓣ13 2202 4566, ⓦsantoshostel.com.br. Smart, friendly and well organized, it's a 10min taxi ride south of the centre. R$50

THE SÃO PAULO COAST

Between São Paulo and Rio the coastline is fantastic, and while Paraty (see p.258) and Ilha Grande (see p.256) get all the credit, a couple of days along the São Paulo section is a really worthwhile diversion. Founded on sugar and fishing, **São Sebastião** is a pretty colonial town popular with Brazilian and Argentine backpackers and trippers. A calming place after the urban clamour of São Paulo, you can also visit the island of **Ilha Bela** from here, home to fantastic beaches and waterfalls – though it's on the radar of São Paulo's rich list and has no budget accommodation aside from camping. Stunning coves and Atlantic forest mark the route onwards to **Ubatuba**, an energetic yet plain town best known for its 72 beaches on nearby islands and inlets. Though some now resemble hotel resorts, they're still the state's best, and numerous secluded spots remain. A car or plenty of time on buses is needed to explore them, but you'll most probably find plenty of like-minded beach seekers to do it with.

ARRIVAL AND DEPARTURE

By bus 12 buses/day ply the route from São Paulo's Rodoviária Tietê (R$54) to São Sebastião, while there are 4/day from Santos (both 3hr 40min). To get from there to Ubatuba, change at Caraguatatuba. 2 buses daily go from Ubatuba direct to Rio (5hr), or 4 to Paraty (1hr 30min; R$12.50).

ACCOMMODATION

HI Maresias Hostel Rua Sebastião Romão Cesar 406, Maresias ⓣ12 3865 6612, ⓦmaresiashostel.com.br. A great place to relax after the rigours of the big city, and also lively with Paulista and Argentine surfers in season. Dorms R$38; doubles R$90

HI Tribo Hostel Rua Amoreira 71, Ubatuba ⓣ12 3842 0585, ⓦubatubahostel.com. Consummate facilities include free wi-fi, large buffet breakfast, games and book/DVD rental, while the lively party atmosphere is aided by the Praia do Lázaro right on hand. Dorms R$35, doubles R$90

Hotel Roma Praça Major João Fernandes, São Sebastião ⓣ12 3892 4622, ⓦwww.hotelroma.tur.br. A simple but handsome old hotel on São Sebastião's main square, where there's a range of rooms, sleeping one to four people, newer ones with a private bathroom around an attractive garden, and older ones without bathrooms in the main building. R$85

The South

Southern Brazil – the states of **Paraná**, **Santa Catarina** and **Rio Grande do Sul** – is a land of gauchos, barbecues and beaches. It's also generally considered to be the most developed region in the country and shows little of the obvious poverty found elsewhere. As a result the South can be an expensive place to travel, and hotel and restaurant prices are equivalent to those in Rio de Janeiro. Choose wisely, though, and you can still find good-value places to stay and eat out.

The spectacular **Iguaçu Falls** are deservedly the South's most visited attraction, though it's the subtropical southern coast that provides much of the region's allure in the summer (Nov–March). Building is virtually forbidden on the beautiful islands of the

3

3

Bay of Paranaguá in Paraná – the most frequently visited being the gorgeous **Ilha do Mel**. By way of contrast, tourism has encroached along Santa Catarina's coast, but development has been restrained and resorts around **Florianópolis**, particularly in the south of the **Ilha Santa Catarina**, remain small and in tune with the region's natural beauty.

Beyond the pretty German enclaves of Gramado and Canela, the highland areas and the pampas of southern **Rio Grande do Sul** are largely given over to vast cattle ranches and latter-day **gauchos** – who share many cultural similarities with their Uruguayan and Argentine neighbours. The haunting remnants of **Catholic missions** pay homage to the brief but productive Jesuit occupation of the area.

CURITIBA

Founded by the Portuguese in 1693, **CURITIBA** was of little importance until 1853 when it was made capital of the newly created state of Paraná. Since then, the city's population has risen steadily from a few thousand to 1.8 million, its inhabitants largely descendants of Polish, German, Italian, Ukrainian and other immigrants. Home to a pristine old town and some enticing art museums, notably the eye-catching **Museu Oscar Niemeyer**, to visit Curitiba is to experience the best of the Brazilian economic boom: on average, *Curitibanos* enjoy Brazil's highest standard of living, the city boasts facilities that are the envy of other parts of the country, and its eco-friendly design is a model that many urban planners try to emulate.

WHAT TO SEE AND DO

Most of Curitiba's attractions can be visited relatively easily in a day or so on foot, with the **Rua das Flores** – a pedestrianized precinct section of the Rua XV de Novembro – the centre's main late afternoon and early evening meeting point. However, if you have limited time, take the Linha Turismo **bus tour**, which departs from Praça Tiradentes (Tues–Sun; first bus at 9am, last bus 5.30pm; R$29). Stopping at 25 attractions around the city centre and suburbs, it takes two hours thirty minutes to complete the full circuit. Tickets allow passengers five hop-on hop-off stops.

Praça Tiradentes and the historic quarter

A couple of blocks north from Rua das Flores is **Praça Tiradentes**, home to the neo-Gothic **Catedral Basílica de Nossa Senhora da Luz** (daily 6am–7pm; free). From here a pedestrian tunnel leads to Curitiba's **historic quarter**, an area of impeccably preserved eighteenth- and nineteenth-century buildings of Portuguese and central European design. The **Igreja da Ordem**, on Largo da Ordem, dates from 1737 and is the city's oldest surviving building. Plain outside, the church is also simple within, the only decoration being typically Portuguese blue and white tiling and Baroque altar and side chapels. The church contains the **Museu de Arte Sacra** (Tues–Fri 9am–noon & 1–6pm, Sat & Sun 9am–3pm; free), with relics gathered from Curitiba's churches.

A short distance uphill from here, on the same street, is the **Igreja Nossa Senhora do Rosário** (Tues–Fri 1.30–5.30pm, Sat 2–6pm, Sun 8am–noon; free), built by and for Curitiba's slave population in 1737, though it was completely reconstructed in the 1940s. The **Museu Paranaense**, nearby on Rua Kellers 289 (Tues–Fri 9am–6pm, Sat & Sun 10am–4pm; free), contains paintings by twentieth-century Paranaense artists as well as arts and crafts made by the region's first indigenous population.

Modern Curitiba

The futuristic **Museu Oscar Niemeyer** (Tues–Sun 10am–6pm; R$6; ⓦmuseuoscarniemeyer.org.br) lies about 3km to the north of Curitiba's old town, on Rua Marechal Hermes. Designed by the Brazilian architect after whom it was named, the building's most notable feature resembles a giant eye. The galleries inside house primarily modernist art, including works by *paranaenses* Alfredo Andersen, Theodoro de Bona and Miguel Bakun, and many by Niemeyer himself, best known for designing much of Brasília (see p.317).

West of the *rodoferroviária* along

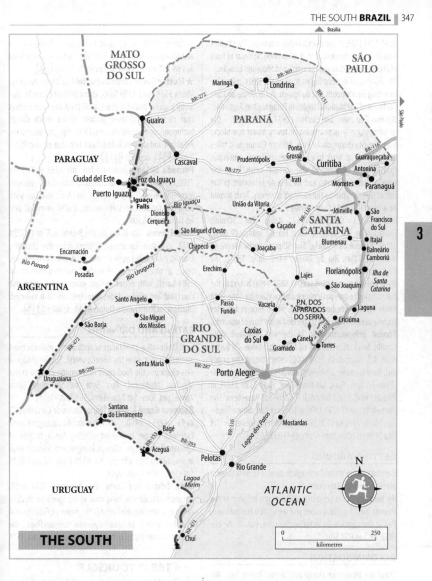

Brasília

MATO
GROSSO
DO SUL

SÃO
PAULO

São Paulo

Maringá • • Londrina

Guaíra •

PARANÁ

Ponta
Grossa

Prudentópolis

Guaraqueçaba

PARAGUAY

Cascavel •

Curitiba

Antonina

Irati •

Morretes

Paranaguá

Ciudad del Este •

Foz do Iguaçu •

**Iguaçu
Falls**

Puerto Iguazú •

Rio Iguaçu

União da Vitoria •

Joinville •

São
Francisco
do Sul

Dionísio
Cerqueira •

São Miguel d'Oeste •

Caçador •

**SANTA
CATARINA**

Itajaí •

Encarnación •

Chapecó •

Joaçaba •

Blumenau •

Balneário
Camboriú

Rio Paraná

Erechim •

Lajes •

Florianópolis •

Ilha de
Santa
Catarina

Posadas •

Rio Uruguay

São Joaquim •

ARGENTINA

Santo Angelo •

Passo
Fundo

Vacaria •

P.N. DOS
APARADOS
DO SERRA

Laguna

São Borja •

São Miguel
dos Missões

**RIO
GRANDE
DO SUL**

Criciúma •

Caxias
do Sul •

Canela •

Uruguaiana •

Santa Maria •

Gramado •

Torres

Porto Alegre

Santana
do Livramento •

Bagé •

Mostardas •

Acegúa •

Pelotas •

Lagoa dos Patos

Rio Grande •

URUGUAY

Lagoa
Mirim

ATLANTIC
OCEAN

N

Chuí •

THE SOUTH

0   250
kilometres

Avenida Sete de Setembro is the city's converted former railway station, now the **Shopping Estação**, an atmospheric mall incorporating the small **Museu Ferroviário** (Tues–Sat 10am–6pm, Sun 11am–7pm; free), which houses relics from Paraná's railway era as well as temporary exhibits.

Finally, it's worth a trip out to Curitiba's most popular attraction, the **Torre Panorâmica** (Tues–Sun 10am–7pm; R$3.50) on Rua Prof. Lycio Grein de

Castro Vellozo, the only telephone tower in Brazil with an observation deck (109m), offering sensational views across the city.

ARRIVAL AND INFORMATION

By plane The ultramodern Aeroporto Internacional Afonso Pena is about 18km from the city centre. Taxis to the centre charge about R$58 on the meter. Regular city buses ("Aeroporto") trundle between the Centro Cívico and the airport every 20–30min (6am–11pm; R$2.70); there is also a faster Linha Aeroporto Executivo bus (R$12; every 15–20min;

41 3381 1326, ⓦaeroportoexecutivo.com.br). The shuttles stop at the *rodoferroviária*, at Rua Visconde de Nacar in front of Rua 24 Horas (name of the stop), and Shopping Estação.

Destinations Frequent flights to all major cities in Brazil – including Florianópolis, Foz do Iguaçu, Porto Alegre and São Paulo – and international flights to Paraguay and Argentina.

By bus The main bus station (☎41 3320 3232) – the *rodoferroviária* – is southeast of town, about ten blocks from the city centre on Av Pres. Affonso Camargo. It takes about 20min to walk to the centre, or there's a minibus from almost in front of the station: catch it at the intersection of Camargo and Av Sete de Setembro, to the left of the entrance to the station's driveway. Taxis should be around R$12–15 to the centre.

Destinations Camboriú (22 daily; 2hr 30min); Florianópolis (23 daily; 4–5hr); Foz do Iguaçu (9 daily; 10hr); Paranaguá (hourly; 1hr 30min); Porto Alegre (8 daily; 12–13hr); Rio de Janeiro (4–5 daily; 13hr); São Paulo (hourly; 6–7hr).

By train The train station (☎041 3888 3488) is next to the bus station. The only passenger train from Curitiba is the Serra Verde Express (see box opposite), which runs to Morretes (service to Paranaguá was suspended at the time of research).

Tourist information Go to the well-organized Visite Curitiba head office on Rua da Glória 362 (Mon–Fri 8am–noon & 2–6pm; ☎41 3352 8000, ⓦturismo.curitiba.pr.gov .br); there are more convenient branches in the *rodoferroviária* (Mon–Fri 8am–6pm, Sat 8am–2pm; ☎41 3320 3121); in Palacete Wolf, Praça Garibaldi 7 (Mon–Sat 9am–6pm, Sun 9am–4pm); ☎41 3321 3206; at the Torre Panorâmica (Tues–Sun 10am–7pm; ☎41 3339 7613); and at the western end of Rua 24 Horas (daily 9am–7pm; ☎41 3225 4336).

GETTING AROUND

Curitiba's centre is small enough to be able to walk to most places within the city centre.

By bus City buses (ⓦurbs.curitiba.pr.gov.br) stop at the strange glass boarding tubes you see dotted around town. Pay at the turnstile on entering the tube, not on the bus (R$2.70; Sun R$1.50).

ACCOMMODATION

There are numerous cheap and secure hotels near the *rodoferroviária*. Places in the city centre are within walking distance of most attractions and are generally excellent value.

Curitiba Hostel Rua Dr Claudino Santos 49, Largo da Ordem ☎41 3232 2005, ⓦcuritibahostel.com.br. Fabulous location right in the heart of the old town, with clean dorms featuring triple bunks, single rooms (R$80), buffet breakfast, hot showers, strong (free) wi-fi, and extra-friendly staff. Dorms R$60, suites R$250

Knock Knock Hostel Rua Isaías Bevilácqua 262 ☎41 3152 6259, ⓦknockhostel.com. Stylish, modern hostel featuring six dorms, a fully equipped kitchen, laundry, barbecue area and terrace, a 10min walk from the centre. Free breakfast and wi-fi. Taxis from bus station R$15. Dorms R$42

★**Motter Home Curitiba Hostel** Rua Desembargador Motta 3574 ☎41 3209 5649, ⓦmotterhome.com.br. This justly popular hostel a short stroll from the centre offers four clean dorms, three private rooms (with shared bathroom), communal kitchen, TV lounge and pool table. Breakfast and wi-fi included. Taxis from bus station R$14. Dorms R$41, doubles R$130

Pousada Betânia Monteiro Tourinho 1335 ☎41 2118 7900, ⓦpousadabetaniacuritiba.com.br. Cosy, tranquil accommodation, 20min from the bus station, with compact, modern en-suite rooms. Buffet breakfast and wi-fi included. R$98

Hostel Roma Rua Barão do Rio Branco 805 ☎41 3224 2117, ⓦhostelroma.com.br. A block from the Shopping Estação, midway between the *rodoferroviária* and the centre, this is an older, standard HI hostel (converted from an old 1909 hotel), with dorms, private rooms and an attractive courtyard and garden. Light breakfast and wi-fi included. Discount for HI members. Dorms R$60, doubles R$134

EATING AND DRINKING

Curitiba boasts a good range of restaurants, with the most interesting located in the historic centre. For the cheapest eats check out the food court in Shopping Estação or the Mercado Municipal, Rua Sete de Setembro (Mon 7am–2pm, Tues–Sat 7am–6pm, Sun 7am–1pm).

Bouquet Garni Alameda Doutor Carlos de Carvalho 271 ☎41 3223 8490, ⓦrestaurantebouquetgarni.com. Excellent veggie restaurant offering lunch buffets of stroganoff chickpeas, spinach lasagne and *feijoada* with onion, turnip and coconut for R$20 Mon–Fri and R$25 Sat–Sun. Daily 11am–3pm.

Mein Schatz Rua Jaime Reis 18 ☎41 3076 0121, ⓦmeinschatz.com.br. Next door to the Igreja do Rosário, offering a variable and affordable menu of German and Brazilian dishes in quasi-Bavarian surroundings; the popular starter plates of red and white sausages are R$16

★**TREAT YOURSELF**

Durski Rua Jaime Reis 254 ☎41 3225 7893, ⓦdurski.com.br. This is Curitiba's only Ukrainian restaurant, located in a renovated house in the heart of the historic centre, looking onto Largo da Ordem. The food (including Polish and Brazilian dishes) is attractively presented and very tasty: try the delicious filet mignon with mash and sautéed mushrooms in Madeira wine. Mains R$60–90. Tues–Thurs 7.45–11pm; Fri & Sat 7.45–11.30pm.

(mains from R$25). Mon–Sat 11.30am–2.30pm, Sun 11.30am–3.30pm.

★**Montesquieu** Rua Des. Westphalen 918 ❶41 3233 7065. Legend with students and staff at the technological university (UTFPR), who come to fill up on the famous X-Pastel burgers (R$7), X-Montanha (burger with meatloaf; R$7.50), and other cheap plates. No tables – just sit around the bar. Mon–Fri 9.30am–9.30pm.

Oriente Árabe Rua Kellers 95 ❶41 3224 2061, Ⓦorientearabe.com.br. Excellent, reasonably priced Arabic food, with mains starting from R$15. If you want to try a bit of everything go for the *rodízio* buffet (Sun around R$58, Thurs–Sat R$53; Tues & Wed R$90 for two people). Belly-dancing shows feature in the evenings. Tues–Sat noon–2.30pm & 6.30–11pm, Sun 11am–3pm.

Schwarzwald Rua Claudino dos Santos 63 ❶41 3223 2585, Ⓦbardoalemaocuritiba.com.br. Also known as the *Bar do Alemão* (German bar), this pub and restaurant has outdoor seating and a spacious, kitsch interior. A popular evening student meeting in the heart of the old town, it serves excellent German food with cold beer (half a litre for R$7.50). A plate of pork knuckle and sausages for two will set you back R$40. Daily 11am–2am.

DIRECTORY

Banks and exchange Main offices of banks are concentrated at the Praça Osório end of Rua das Flores.

Hospital In emergencies use the Nossa Senhora das Graças hospital at Rua Prof Rosa Saporski 229, which has a 24hr hotline ❶41 3240 6555.

Internet Try e-motion (open shopping hours; ❶41 3019 6706) inside Shopping Estação (turn right at the central entrance); R$3/15min or R$7/hr.

Laundry Auto Serviço Gama at Rua Tibagi 576 (Mon–Sat 8am–8pm; wash from R$15; ❶41 3019 1699), near the intersection with Rua Nilo Cairo, is a good central option.

Post office The most convenient central office is at Rua Marechal Deodoro 298 (Mon–Fri 9.30am–6pm; Sat 9.30am–1pm).

PARANAGUÁ

Brazil's second most important port for exports, **PARANAGUÁ**, 92km east of Curitiba, has lost some of its former character, though the colonial-style pastel-coloured buildings along the waterfront retain a certain charm. It was founded in the 1550s on the banks of the Rio Itiberê, making it one of Brazil's oldest cities, but only recently have measures been taken to preserve its colonial buildings. Today it's the main departure point for ferries to Ilha do Mel (see p.350).

WHAT TO SEE AND DO

The appeal of Paranaguá lies in wandering around the cobbled streets and absorbing the faded colonial atmosphere of the town. Almost everything worth seeing is concentrated along **Rua XV de Novembro**, a block inland from the waterfront. At the corner of Avenida Arthur de Abreu is the very pretty **Igreja São Francisco das Chagas** (Mon–Sat 9–11am & 2–6pm, Sun 2–6pm; free), a small and simple church built in 1784 and still containing its Baroque altar and side chapels. Further along is the **Mercado Municipal do Café** (daily 6am–6pm), an early twentieth-century building that used to serve as the city's coffee market. Today the Art Nouveau structure contains handicraft stalls and simple restaurants serving excellent, very cheap seafood.

Just beyond the market is Paranaguá's most imposing building, the fortress-like **Colégio dos Jesuítas**, the old Jesuit school, opened in 1755. Today it is home

3

SERRA VERDE EXPRESS

The **Serra Verde Express** (❶41 3323 4007, Ⓦserraverdeexpress.com.br) is one of the most scenic train rides in Brazil, winding around mountainsides, slipping through tunnels and traversing one of the largest Atlantic Forest reserves in the country; make sure to sit on the left-hand side of the train for the best views (or on the right if you're not good with heights). Though the express used to go as far as Paranaguá, at the time of research trains were only going from **Curitiba** to **Morretes** (daily 8.15am, arriving 11.15am; Sat & Sun also 9.15am, arriving 12.15pm; return trains depart 3pm, arriving in Curitiba at 6pm), a lovely colonial town 16km inland from the Atlantic. A variety of tickets is available, from coach class (*economica*; R$72 one-way, R$50 extra return) to R$290 each way on the special *Litorina* service. For the cheaper tickets book several days in advance, as they are limited and sell out quickly. Morretes bus station lies just outside the centre; from here buses run to Paranaguá (every 30min; 1hr; R$8.50), and back to Curitiba (9 daily; 1hr 30min; R$15–16).

to the **Museu de Arqueologia e Etnologia**, Rua XV de Novembro 575 (Tues–Sun 8am–8pm; free; ⓦwww.proec.ufpr.br), with exhibits on prehistoric archeological finds, indigenous culture and popular art – the poor old Jesuits don't even get a mention. Three blocks inland from here on Largo Monsenhor Celso is the town's oldest church, **Igreja de Nossa Senhora do Rosário**, dating from 1578 (daily 8am–6pm; free).

ARRIVAL AND INFORMATION

By bus Buses arrive at the *rodoviária*, in the southwest of town on the waterfront at Rua João Estevão 403. Buses depart for Curitiba hourly (1hr 30min).

By train The *ferroviária* is three blocks from the waterfront at Av Arthur de Abreu 124, but at the time of research the Serra Verde Express from Curitiba was no longer running to Paranaguá.

By ferry Services depart from the Estação Nautica (Rua General Carneiro 258) to the bay islands, including Ilha do Mel (daily 8.30am, 9.30am, 11am, 1pm, 3pm, 4.30pm & 6pm in summer, with 9.30am & 3.30pm crossings in winter; R$34 return); the boats stop at Nova Brasília (1hr 30min) then Encantadas (2hr). See ⓦabaline.com.br.

Tourist information The Fumtur tourist office (Mon–Sat 8am–6pm, Sun 11am–2pm; ☏41 3420 2940, ⓦfumtur.com.br) is at Av Arthur de Abreu 44, near the train station, which has useful maps of the city and boat, bus and train information. There's also a small kiosk at the bus station (daily 9am–6pm; ☏41 3425 4542).

ACCOMMODATION

There is no real reason to hang around in Paranaguá, but should you need to, you can choose from a cluster of reasonably priced hotels within walking distance of the major transport terminals.

Hotel Palácio Rua Correia de Freitas 66 ☏41 3422 5655, ⓦhotelpalacio.com.br. Centrally located hotel with clean but spartan rooms for up to four people. A good option for families on a budget. Breakfast, parking and wi-fi included. R$120

EATING

Cheap seafood and the local speciality, *barreado* (slow-cooked meat stew baked in clay pots), are the order of the day at most restaurants. There are some excellent inexpensive seafood places in the Mercado Municipal do Café, on Rua General Carneiro at Prof. Cleto, though they are open at lunchtimes only.

Casa do Barreado Rua Antonio da Cruz 78 ☏41 3423 1830, ⓦcasadobarreado.com.br. The best place to try the regional speciality *barreado* (R$25, with dessert included);

the lunchtime buffet of Brazilian dishes is also good. Sat & Sun noon–3pm.

Lar do Má Rua João Estevão 574 ☏41 3425 2156. Next to the Colégio dos Jesuítas, this place offers a reasonably priced Chinese lunch buffet (R$25–30), as well as à la carte seafood in the evenings. Daily 11.30am–2.30pm & 7pm–midnight.

ILHA DO MEL

Famed for its golden beaches and tranquil setting, the idyllic **ILHA DO MEL** ("Island of Honey") in the Bay of Paranaguá is a hit with backpackers and surfers looking to enjoy the simpler things in life – and the island's waves. It's an unusually shaped island, to say the least. Its bulbous northern half, a protected Atlantic Forest ecological reserve (entry is prohibited), is joined to the slender south by a bridge of land where the lively main village of **Nova Brasilia** is located. The island's other major settlement, **Encantadas**, near the southwest corner, has the atmosphere of a sleepy fishing port. It's little more than 12km from north to south, but given the hilly topography of the island most walks hug the coast. Bear in mind that there are no cars, no banks, no public transport and no shops on the island and electricity for only a short period each day – so come prepared.

WHAT TO SEE AND DO

Praia do Farol is the closest beach to Nova Brasilia, curving in a wide arc around the "neck" of the island. It's a 4km walk north along these sands to the Portuguese fort of **Fortaleza Nossa Senhora dos Prazeres** (open daily; free), completed in 1769. Encantadas' nearest sandy beach is **Praia de Fora**. The entire stretch of coastline along the southeast side between Praia de Fora and Praia do Farol is dotted with enchanting coves, rocky promontories and small waterfalls. The rocks are slippery here, so take care, and the three-hour walk along the beach from Praia de Fora as far as the fort should only be attempted at low tide or you risk being stranded. The southern tip of the island, known as **Ponta Encantada**, is where you will find the **Gruta das Encantadas** (Enchanted Cave), focal point for a number of local legends.

ARRIVAL AND INFORMATION

By boat In summer 7 daily ferries (1hr 45min; R$34 return) link Ilha do Mel with Paranaguá. You can also catch a bus from Curitiba (5 daily; 2hr 30min; R$30) to Pontal do Sul, from where boats leave every hour or so from the beach to the island (daily 8am–6pm; 30min; R$29 return; ⓦabaline .com.br); all ferries usually serve Encantadas then Nova Brasília. There are fewer boats to the island in winter.

Tourist information There is a small tourist information booth at the dock in Nova Brasília (summer: daily 7.30am–8pm). See also the useful ⓦilhadomelonline .com.br.

ACCOMMODATION

If you plan to visit in the height of summer, it's best to arrive during the week and as early as possible, as accommodation books up quickly during the weekends. The island is always full to capacity over New Year and Carnaval, when reservations are essential and are accepted only for minimum stays of four or five nights.

★**Ilha do Mel Hostel** Praia do Farol (Farol), Nova Brasília ⓣ41 3426 8065, ⓦilhadomelhostel.com.br. Not really a hostel but a hotel with two compact but stylish rooms near the main beaches. There is a "cyber lounge" with four computers and Sky TV, breakfast is served on the deck; beach chairs and umbrellas available. R$180

Pousadinha Caminho do Farol, Nova Brasília ⓣ41 3426 8026, ⓦpousadinha.com.br. Popular backpacker hangout (180m inland from the dock) with leafy gardens and relaxing hammocks for chilling out. Rooms are simple but good value, and multilingual staff can assist with booking activities. Cabañas R$100, doubles R$90

Pousada Lua Cheia Praia das Encantadas ⓣ41 3426 9010, ⓦluacheiatur.com.br. Ten simple en-suite wood cabins that hold up to four people each, equipped with TV, fridge, fan and a/c. Breakfast included. Cabañas R$130

Pousada Marimar Praia das Encantadas ⓣ41 3426 9052, ⓦpousadamarimar.com.br. Simple, rustic accommodation, with free wi-fi, private bathrooms, shared kitchen and TV room; dorms have fans and private lockers. Buffet breakfast included. Dorms R$60, doubles R$225

FOZ DO IGUAÇU

The city of **FOZ DO IGUAÇU** is the Brazilian gateway to the magnificent **Iguaçu Falls**, one of the world's greatest natural wonders, which lie 20km south. Much larger than its Argentine counterpart **Puerto Iguazú** (see p.85), it makes a livelier, if pricier, base for exploring the falls, with the advantage of decent restaurants and nightlife.

WHAT TO SEE AND DO

Foz do Iguaçu is a modern city with no real sights of its own, but on the road to the falls (Av de Cataratas), the parrots and showy toucans at **Parque das Aves**, Km17.1, just 300m from the falls entrance (daily 8.30am–5pm; R$28; ⓦparquedasaves.com.br), are well worth the expense, with enormous walk-through aviaries in dramatic forested surroundings (all birds have been rescued from traffickers and would not survive alone in the wild). There is also a large walk-through butterfly cage – butterflies are bred throughout the year and released when mature. All the butterflies and eighty percent of the eight hundred bird species are Brazilian, many endemic to the Atlantic Forest.

ARRIVAL AND INFORMATION

By plane Foz do Iguaçu International Airport (ⓣ45 3521 4200) is 12km southeast of town, halfway along the road to the falls (12km north of the falls themselves). It is served by flights from Curitiba, São Paulo, Rio de Janeiro, Brasília, Salvador and Belém. A taxi into town costs around R$45 (R$25 to the falls and R$75–85 to Puerto Iguazú), or take bus #120 (Mon–Sat 5.45am–12.40am, every 20min, Sun 5.30am–12.40am, every 45min; R$2.85), which shuttles between the falls and the local terminal in town on Av Juscelino Kubitschek.

By bus The *rodoviária* (ⓣ45 3522 2590) is 4km north of the centre on Av Costa e Silva; buses #105 and #115 from here, marked "Rodoviária", can take you to the local bus terminal (TTU or Terminal de Transporte Urbano) on Av Juscelino Kubitschek in the city centre (R$2.85); taxis cost around R$20. At the TTU you can pick up bus #120 to the falls ("Aeroporto Parque Nacional"; R$2.85).

Destinations Buenos Aires (1 daily; 19hr); Curitiba (10 daily; 9hr); Florianópolis (9 daily; 16hr); Porto Alegre (6 daily; 14hr); Rio (3 daily; 24hr); São Paulo (5 daily; 14–15hr).

Tourist information There are tourist offices at the airport (daily 8am–10pm; ⓣ45 3521 4276) and at the *rodoviária* (daily 7am–6pm; ⓣ45 3522 1027). In town, there are offices at the Terminal de Transporte Urbano (daily 8am–5pm; ⓣ45 3523 7901), and the Centro Municipal de Turismo, Av das Cataratas 2330, Vila Yolanda (daily 7am–11pm; ⓣ0800 451516, ⓦpmfi.pr.gov.br/ turismo).

ACCOMMODATION

When choosing where to stay, your main decision is whether to pick a central option or to go for somewhere closer to the falls. Being central has the advantage of proximity to good restaurants and bars, while staying close to the falls, where there are a number of excellent hostels and a great campsite, cuts down your travelling time.

CENTRAL

★**Concept Design Hostel** Rua Vereador Moacyr Pereira 337, Vila Yolanda ☎45 3029 3631, ⊛conceptdesignhostel .com. This stylish, budget boutique hostel has spacious doubles with individual colour themes, slick dorms, each bed equipped with reading lights and power sockets, a central pool, bar and communal kitchen. Close to the bus stop for the falls. Dorms R$65, doubles R$180

★**Favela Chic Hostel** Rua Major Raul de Mattos 78 ☎45 3027 5060, ⊛favelachichosteliguassu.com. Hostel run by friendly English owner, Nick, near the bus stop for the falls. It's all nicely done, with bright, comfy hang-out areas, hammocks and two dorms with a/c and shared bathrooms. Includes cooked breakfast, free yoga classes and wi-fi. Dorms R$35, camping R$20

Iguassu Guest House Rua Naipi 1019 ☎45 3029 0242, ⊛iguassuguesthouse.com.br. A short walk from the bus station, this small hostel offers spotless dorms but also excellent private en-suite rooms (R$120–150) with all the amenities – free wi-fi, bar, book exchange, pool table, PC terminals. Dorm R$50

Hostel Paudimar Falls Rua Antônio Raposo 820 ☎45 3028 5503, ⊛paudimarfalls.com.br. Run by the same people as the *Paudimar Campestre* (see below), this gives you the same great service and facilities in a central location, and with free internet. Dorm R$40, doubles R$110

Pousada Evelina Navarrete Rua Irlan Kalichewski 171 ☎45 3574 3817, ⊛pousadaevelina.com.br. Extremely friendly place with a youth hostel atmosphere that mainly attracts foreign backpackers. Rooms are simple but spotless, breakfasts are adequate, there's internet access (wi-fi R$2.50/day or R$2.50/30min on terminals) and multilingual Evelina goes out of her way to be helpful. Well located for buses to the falls. R$106

ROAD TO THE FALLS

Camping Clube do Brasil ☎45 3529 8064, ⊛campingclube.com.br. This excellent campsite is at Km17 on the road to the falls; the site is surrounded by jungle, and facilities include a laundry area and a clean swimming pool. Tents can be rented for R$3–10. Camping/person R$24

★**Hostel Paudimar Campestre** Av das Cataratas Km12.5 ☎45 3529 6061, ⊛paudimar.com.br. This excellent HI establishment has superb facilities, from basic shared dorms sleeping six to eight people and family apartments (with double bed, bunk bed, a/c and private bathroom) to pretty cabins for two. The extensive grounds include a swimming pool and bar. Kitchen facilities are available, and they also serve evening meals. The hostel organizes daily trips to the Argentine side of the falls. Camping R$25, dorm R$43, private cabin R$142

EATING AND DRINKING

While it's no gastronomic paradise, Foz do Iguaçu is a good place to eat cheaply, with a proliferation of buffet-style *por kilo* restaurants. The main drag for restaurants and bars is Av Jorge Schimmelpfeng, south of the city centre – taxis should be around R$10 (on the meter) from most hotels in town.

Búfalo Branco Rua Engenheiro Rebouças 530 ☎45 3523 9744, ⊛bufalobranco.com.br. Top-notch *churrascaría* with the all-you-can-eat *rodízio* system and a vast, excellent salad bar. Normally R$60 per person, but look for lunchtime special offers (R$35). Offers free transfer from your hotel. Daily noon–11pm.

Capitão Bar Rua Jorge Schimmelpfeng 288 ☎45 3572 1512, ⊛capitaobar.com. One of a series of lively bars on this stretch, playing loud music and serving "Torre de Chopp" (beer towers, R$19.90), a cheap lunch buffet (R$17.90) and affordable pizzas. Outdoor tables fill quickly so arrive early in summer if you want to sit outside. Daily 11.30am–2am.

Clube Maringá Rua Dourado 111, Porto Meira ☎45 3527 3472, ⊛restaurantemaringa.com.br. Justly popular for its superb *rodízio de peixe* lunch and stunning views of

---

IGUAÇU FALLS TOURS AND ACTIVITIES

The Iguaçu Falls has become a major adventure travel centre with a bewildering range of activities available. Every fifteen minutes the **Helisul helicopter** (☎45 3529 7474, ⊛helisul .com) takes off just outside the park entrance, offering ten-minute flights over the falls for R$255 per person (minimum three people); sensational views, but controversial thanks to the noise pollution (which scares wildlife).

TOUR OPERATORS

Macuco Safari ☎45 3529 6262, ⊛macucosafari .com.br. At its own dedicated bus stop in the park, Macuco operates a jet-boat ride through white water right up to and into the falls (daily 9am–5.30pm, every 15min; R$170/person). Macuco also operates Cânion Iguaçu (accessed at the Path of the Falls bus

stop), which comprises a canopy trail – a series of ropes and ladders above the forest (R$80) – and a 55m cliff face that you can abseil down (R$70).

Martin Travel Travessa Goiás 200 ☎45 3523 4959, ⊛martintravel.com.br. A reliable local travel agency that specializes in ecotourism and puts together groups to go canoeing, rafting or mountain biking along forest trails.

★ TREAT YOURSELF

Ipê Grill Parque Nacional do Iguaçu ☎ 45 2102 7000, ⓦ belmond.com/hotel-das-cataratas-iguassu-falls. The only hotel restaurant worth a splurge. Located by the pool in the *Belmond Hotel das Cataratas* (overlooking the falls), it offers an extensive but very pricey buffet dinner of typical Brazilian dishes and "gaucho" style barbecue for around R$125. Even if you can't afford to stay here (rooms start at around R$950), you should take a wander around the hotel grounds just to have a look. Daily 6.30–10am & 7.30–11pm.

the Rio Paraná. As well as a vast selection of local freshwater fish – golden dorado, pacu, tilapia – mostly fried and battered but some soups and grilled fish, there's an excellent salad bar and desserts (buffet for R$42 per person). Take the "Porto Meira" bus and ask for directions, or take a taxi (R$20). Tues–Sat 11.30am–10.30pm; Sun till 3pm.

Recanto Gaúcho Av das Cataratas Km15, near the turn-off to the airport ☎ 45 3572 2358, ⓦ recantogaucho .com. A favourite Sunday outing for locals and tourists, but the atmosphere's lively, the meat's excellent and cheap (R$35/person for all you can eat), and the owner, who always dresses in full gaucho regalia, is a real character. Turn up early; food is served until 3pm. It's advisable to phone ahead. Taxis R$18–21. Sun 10.30am–6pm. Closed Dec & Jan.

Trigo & Cia Av Paraná 1750 ☎ 45 3025 3800, ⓦ trigoecia .com.br. Ten minutes by bus from the centre of town, this busy café serves tasty savoury snacks, good coffee and the best cakes in Foz (R$5–7), at all hours. Daily 24hr.

DIRECTORY

Banks and exchange Dollars (cash or travellers' cheques) can be easily changed in travel agents and banks along Av Brasil; the banks have ATMs.

Consulates Argentina, Eduardo Bianchi 26 ☎ 45 3574 2969; Paraguay, Rua Marechal Deodoro 901 ☎ 45 3523 2898.

Hospital Ministro Costa Cavalcanti, Av Gramado 580, ☎ 45 3576 8000, is a good private hospital.

Police Tourist police ☎ 45 3523 3036.

Post office Praça Getúlio Vargas 72, near Rua Barão do Rio Branco (Mon–Fri 9am–5pm).

Taxi Coopertaxi Cataratas ☎ 45 3524 6464.

IGUAÇU FALLS

The **IGUAÇU FALLS** are, unquestionably, one of the world's great natural phenomena. They form the centrepiece of the vast **Parque Nacional do Iguaçu** (**Iguaçu National Park**), which was first designated in 1936 though the falls were discovered as early as 1542 by the Spanish explorer Alvar Nuñez Cabeza de Vaca. To describe their beauty and power is a tall order, but for starters cast out any ideas that Iguaçu is some kind of Niagara Falls transplanted south of the equator – compared with Iguaçu, Niagara is a ripple. About 15km before joining the Rio Paraná, the Rio Iguaçu broadens out, then plunges precipitously over an 80m-high cliff in 275 separate cascades that extend nearly 3km across the river. To properly experience Iguaçu it is essential to visit both sides. The Brazilian side gives the best overall view and allows you to fully appreciate the scale of it;

CROSSING THE BORDER TO PARAGUAY AND ARGENTINA

Buses bound for **Ciudad del Este** in **Paraguay** depart across Av Juscelino Kubitschek from the Terminal de Transporte Urbano (every 30min or so; 7am–8.50pm; around R$4); taxis charge around R$40. You need to disembark at the Brazilian customs for your exit stamps – the bus will not wait but your ticket is valid for the next one. You will then cross the Friendship Bridge to the Paraguayan customs, where you will again be asked to disembark.

For **Puerto Iguazú** in **Argentina**, Crucero del Nord buses depart from Rua Mem de Sá, at Rua Taroba, the street just north of the Terminal de Transporte Urbano (Mon–Fri every 40min 7am–7pm; Sat & Sun every hr, 45min past the hr; R$4); you can also flag them down at stops en route. They terminate at the bus terminal in the centre of Puerto Iguazú where there are regular buses to the Argentine falls. Taxis charge around R$50 to the town, and R$100 to the Argentine falls (R$190 return); you'll have to stop at both the Brazilian and Argentine immigration posts in both directions, but wait times are rarely more than a few minutes. Taxi drivers will wait for you while you clear immigration, but buses may not; keep your ticket and take the next one coming through. It's unlikely that your Brazilian reais will be accepted across either border, so change money as soon as you can.

3

the Argentine side (see p.86) allows you to get up close to the major individual cascades.

The falls are mind-blowing whatever the season, but they are always more spectacular following a heavy rainstorm. Weekends and Easter are best avoided if you don't want to share your experience with thousands of Brazilian and Argentine holidaymakers.

WHAT TO SEE AND DO

At its best in the early morning, a 1.2km cliffside trail runs alongside the falls, offering predictably jaw-dropping photo opportunities. A stairway leads down from the bus stop to the start of the trail. The path ends by coming perilously close to the ferocious "**Garganta do Diabo**" (Devil's Throat), the point where fourteen separate falls combine to form the world's most powerful single cascade in terms of the volume of water flow per second. Depending on the force of the river, you could be in for a real soaking, so if you have a camera with you be sure to carry it in a plastic bag. From here, you can either walk back up the path or take the lift to the top of the cliff and the road leading to the *Belmond Hotel das Cataratas* (see box, p.353). You'll undoubtedly come across coatis on the trails (though raccoon-like, they are not raccoons, whatever the local guides may say) – don't be fooled by their cute and comical appearance; these little creatures are accomplished food thieves with long claws and sharp teeth.

ARRIVAL AND DEPARTURE

It costs foreigners R$49.20 to enter the park (concessions available for MERCOSUR and Brazilian residents), after which a shuttle bus (included) will deliver you to the trails. See ⓦ cataratasdoiguacu.com.br for more information.

By bus Bus #120 ("Aeroporto Parque Nacional"; $2.85) from Foz do Iguaçu terminates at the entrance to the falls (daily 9am–5pm).

By taxi Taxis (using the meter) will cost around R$50 from town.

ILHA DE SÃO FRANCISCO DO SUL

Travelling 135km south from Curitiba into the state of Santa Catarina, the coastline becomes the main attraction, with the beaches of **ILHA DE SÃO FRANCISCO DO SUL** well worth a diversion off the main highway. A low-lying island separated from the mainland by a narrow strait some 40km east of the industrial port city of Joinville and the site of a major Petrobras oil refinery, it might be reasonable to assume that São Francisco should be avoided, but this isn't the case. Both the port and refinery keep a discreet distance from the main town, **São Francisco do Sul**, and the beaches blend perfectly with the slightly dilapidated colonial setting. On the east coast, **Praia de Ubatuba**, 16km from the centre, and the adjoining **Praia de Enseada**, 20km from town, offer enough surf for you to have fun but not enough to be dangerous. A ten-minute walk across the peninsula from the eastern end of Enseada leads to **Praia da Saúdade** (or just Prainha), where the waves are suitable for only the most experienced surfers.

São Francisco do Sul

One of the oldest settlements in the south, the gorgeous *centro histórico* of **SÃO FRANCISCO DO SUL** (aka "São Chico") is separated from the main commercial part of town by a ring of small hills, giving it a relaxed, languid air unusual in this part of Brazil – it's also one of the few places in Santa Catarina where a concentration of colonial and nineteenth-century buildings survives.

WHAT TO SEE AND DO

Dominating the city's skyline is the **Igreja Matriz Nossa Senhora da Graça**, the main church, originally built in 1699 by Indian slaves, but completely reconstructed in 1926. The **Museu Nacional do Mar** on Rua Manoel Lourenço de Andrade in the historic centre (Tues–Fri 9am–6pm, Sat & Sun 10am–6pm; R$5; ⓦ museunacionaldomar.com.br) has a vast maritime collection with an emphasis on southern Brazil and its people. The prettiest beaches, **Paulas** and **Praia dos Ingleses**, are also the nearest to town, just a couple of kilometres to the east. Both are small, and have trees to provide shade. Surprisingly few people take advantage of the calm and shallow waters here, which are ideal for gentle swimming.

ARRIVAL AND INFORMATION

By bus The easiest way to reach São Francisco do Sul is by Verdes Mares (hourly; 1hr 30min; R$8.50–12.50; ⓦ vmares .com.br) bus from Joinville's *rodoviária* (though there are less frequent direct buses from Curitiba); you can get to Joinville from Curitiba (hourly; 2hr) or Florianópolis (hourly; 2hr 30min). Buses from Joinville terminate at the *rodoviária*, inconveniently located outside São Francisco do Sul centre on Rua Dom Fernando Trejo Y Sanabria (just off the main highway); most people get off the bus at the junction of Afonso dos Santos and Barão do Rio Branco in the commercial heart of town – from here it's a fairly straightforward 20min walk to the *centro histórico* (ask if you get lost), or R$4–8 by taxi (ⓣ 47 3444 2047). Similarly, heading back to Joinville you can pick up the bus from the bus stop in town (taxi drivers all know it). Local buses to the beaches (R$2.85) depart from the plaza near the church (Praça da Igreja); bus #5440 to Prainha; and numerous buses to Enseada along the coast road in both directions.
Destinations Curitiba (daily; 3hr); Joinville (hourly; 1hr 30min); São Paulo (daily; 8hr).
Tourist information The helpful local tourist office is on the waterfront at Rua Babitonga 62 (daily 8am–5pm; ⓣ 47 3444 5380, ⓦ saofranciscodosul.tur.br).

ACCOMMODATION

Most of the island's visitors bypass the town and head straight for the beaches to the east, so, even in midsummer, there's rarely any difficulty in finding a central hotel.
Kontiki Rua Babitonga 33, near the market in São Francisco do Sul ⓣ 47 3444 2232, ⓦ hotelkontiki.com.br. Located in the heart of the old town directly in front of the bay, this comfortable hotel has wonderful views and a "colonial-style" (which basically means indulgent) breakfast. R$164
Pousada Farol da Ilha Enseada, just behind the beach on Rua Maceió 1156 ⓣ 47 3449 1802, ⓦ pousadafaroldailha.tur.br. This little family-run place, only 300m from the beach, also has its own pool. The rooms are decorated in a rustic style and it's particularly popular with couples. There is a discount for rooms with a shared bathroom. R$120
Zibamba Rua Fernando Dias 27, São Francisco do Sul ⓣ 47 3444 2020, ⓦ hotelzibamba.com.br. The town's top digs is a gorgeous old property near the waterfront, with relatively plain rooms (free wi-fi), pool and decent seafood restaurant – try and get a room with a balcony. R$200

EATING AND DRINKING

Eating out holds no great excitement, with the *Zibamba*'s restaurant the best of a generally poor bunch serving up a seafood buffet at lunch and typical Brazilian dishes à la carte in the evenings. Enseada does have a lively nightlife, though.
Bar do Banana Av Brasilia at João Pessoa, Prainha ⓣ 47 3444 0785, ⓦ bardobanana.com.br. Popular with 20-somethings (and cruise-ship passengers) looking for reasonably priced drinks, food and fun by the sea. Daily 11am–11pm.
★**Café do Museu** Rua Manoel Lourenço de Andrade 133 ⓣ 47 3444 8071. Opposite the main entrance to Museu Nacional do Mar (and attached to the exit), this small café is by far the most atmospheric place to drink or grab a snack in town. It's a mellow, artsy space with old shed walls, part shop, part snack bar, with coffee, beers and light meals on offer. Tues–Fri 9am–6pm, Sat 10am–midnight, Sun 1–6pm.

BALNEÁRIO CAMBORIÚ

If you are travelling in search of the Santa Catarina party scene, look no further than **BALNEÁRIO CAMBORIÚ**, an effervescent resort town 112km south of São Francisco do Sul with a distinctly hedonistic approach to life often dismissed by Cariocas as the "poor man's Copacabana". Either way it's a popular summer destination with young Brazilians, Paraguayans and Argentines, and the town is packed out during the peak season with sunbathers and fun-seekers.

WHAT TO SEE AND DO

Camboriú has something of a Mediterranean holiday resort feel to it, with its high-rise buildings and pedestrian streets lined with artists peddling souvenirs; walking around town, you could be forgiven for thinking that you were on the Portuguese Algarve. The place is not without its charms – not least its 7km-long **Praia Central**, offering safe swimming and golden sand. **Praia do Pinho**, on the other side of the peninsula west of town, is the site of Brazil's first nudist beach.

Camboriú even has its own 33m-high Rio-style Christ statue, the **Cristo Luz** (April & Sept Wed–Sat 4pm–midnight; Oct, Nov & July Tues–Sat 4pm–midnight; Dec–March Mon–Sat 4pm–midnight; June & Aug Thurs–Sat 4pm–midnight; Sun 10am–midnight year-round; R$12 10am–7pm, R$24 after 7pm; ⓦ cristoluz .com.br), illuminated at night and casting a faint greenish glow over the town. The forested hillside of Morro da Aguada in the south of town is a nature reserve-cum-theme park, the **Parque Unipraias** (daily 9.30am–6pm; closed Mon Nov–April; cable car R$36; ⓦunipraias.com.br). You can reach it via a 3.25km cable car (same hours) that starts at the Estação Barra Sul on the Praia Central before shooting up to the Estação Mata Atlântica on the summit (240m), offering glorious views over the town, beaches and out to sea. From here you can stroll the trails in the Parque Ambiental (same hours; included in price), enjoy the Zip Rider zipline (R$39) or the Youhooo! 60km/hr toboggan ride ($25). The cable car continues down to the beach at Praia Laranjeiras.

ARRIVAL AND INFORMATION

By bus Camboriú sits on the main Curitiba–Florianópolis highway (BR-101), and is just 80km north of Florianópolis. Buses arrive at the *rodoviária* (☏47 3367 2901) on Av Santa Catarina, at the edge of town close to the highway.

Destinations Buenos Aires (1 daily; 28hr); Curitiba (22 daily; 2hr 30min); Florianópolis (38 daily; 1hr 30min); Joinville (26 daily; 1hr 30min); Porto Alegre (9 daily; 8–9hr); São Paulo (13 daily; 8–9hr).

Tourist information There is a tourist information office at Rua 3300, no. 360 (Mon–Sat 8am–8pm; ☏47 3363 7976, ⓦvisitebalneariocamboriu.com.br).

ACCOMMODATION

You'd be wise to book ahead in the peak season when block bookings take up the majority of the more affordable hotels. If you're in a group, ask at the tourist office about renting a house – it's cheaper than you might think.

Hostel & Pousada Rezende Rua 3100, no. 780 ☏47 3361 9815, ⓦhotelpousadarezende.com.br. Standard HI hostel (internet, kitchen, breakfast) a few blocks back from the beach. It's decent value for money, and dorms are small and uncrowded. Dorms R$60, doubles R$80

Hotel Topázio Rua 11, no. 15 ☏47 3367 1022, ⓦhtopazio .com.br. Another small, basic hotel but a reasonable deal and in the centre of town, 50m from the beach. En-suite rooms come with a/c, cable TV and free wi-fi. R$149

EATING

In addition to the proliferation of fast-food joints and *lanchonetes*, there are some excellent restaurants around if you look hard enough, with seafood platters featuring heavily on most menus.

Guacamole Av Beira Rio 1122 ☏47 3366 0311, ⓦguacamolemex.com.br. Charismatic Mexican mini-chain with live music, mariachis and "tequileros" who are only too happy to wet your whistle. Latin dance shows every Tuesday night add to the experience. Spicy mains from R$25. Daily 7.30pm–2am.

O Pharol Av Atlântica 5740 ☏47 3367 3800, ⓦpharol .com.br. Smart seafood restaurant, well worth the extra reais. The seafood *rodizio* (R$55 per person) is something special and includes prawns, lobster, oysters and more; *feijoada* served Wed & Sat. Daily 11.30am–midnight.

NIGHTLIFE

Camboriú has a vibrant, young nightlife scene. Most places are on or around Av Atlântica, especially at the southern end, the Barra Sul, where you'll find a huge array of beach bars and discos. Things don't start to get lively until well after midnight and the action continues until after the sun comes up.

Cachaçaria Uai Av Atlântica 2334 ☏47 3367 4978. Bar-style hangout on the beach, specializing in caipirinhas, the Brazilian cocktail made with *cachaça* and crushed limes, and food from Minas Gerais. Live music Tues–Sun. Daily 6pm–6am.

Woods Av Atlântica 4450, Barra Sul ☏47 7812 3475, ⓦwoodsbar.com.br. This popular country-style pub is a good place to start the evening off, with cold beers served in a beachfront location. Live music. Entry is R$40 (women) and R$80 (men). Wed, Fri & Sat 11pm–5am.

ILHA SANTA CATARINA

Joined to the mainland by suspension bridges, **ILHA SANTA CATARINA** is noted throughout Brazil for its gorgeous scenery and beaches, ideal climate, attractive fishing villages and the city of **Florianópolis**, the small and prosperous capital of Santa Catarina state (half of the city lies on the mainland and the other half on the island).

The island is peppered with resorts – the **north** of the island is the most developed while the extreme **south** remains the quietest and most unspoilt – while central **Lagoa da Conceição** is a great spot for budget accommodation and bar hopping. There are some 42 **beaches** around Ilha Santa Catarina, which means even the most crowded are rarely unbearably so. Anywhere on the island can be reached by bus within an hour or so from Florianópolis, although **renting a car** (see p.358) is a good idea if you have limited time, allowing you to explore the island more thoroughly. Note, however, that parts of Santa Catarina are notorious for bad traffic, especially on the weekends and in the summer. Also, locals often refer to the whole island as Florianópolis, with the city known simply as *centro*.

Florianópolis

Founded in 1675, **FLORIANÓPOLIS** (aka "Floripa") boomed 75 years later thanks to an influx of immigrants from the Azores. With the construction of the bridges linking the island with the mainland, Florianópolis as a port has all but died, and today it thrives as an administrative, commercial and tourist centre. It's a modern city, but the late nineteenth-century pastel-coloured, stuccoed buildings of the centre still have a whiff of old-world appeal, and it's worth taking time to have a look around. Few people visit Ilha Santa Catarina for the express purpose of seeing the city, however, and to see the natural beauty for which the island is renowned, you need to head out to the beaches.

WHAT TO SEE AND DO

On the former waterfront, you'll find two ochre-coloured buildings: the 1889 **Mercado Público** (Mon–Fri 7am–7pm & Sat 7am–3pm), which contains some excellent bars and small restaurants, and the **Casa da Alfândega** (Mon–Fri 2am–6pm & Sat 9am–noon), a former customs house dating from 1875 that has been converted

---

BEER DRINKING IN BLUMENAU

Founded by German immigrants in 1850, the affluent city of Blumenau is best known today for its annual **Oktoberfest** (ⓦoktoberfestblumenau.com.br), the biggest German festival in South America, attracting over 500,000 revellers annually to its vast beer tents, folk dancing, shooting matches and German singing contests. For accommodation options check out ⓦblumenau.sc.gov.br, but you'll need to book in advance; the cheapest option is usually the *Pousada e Hostel Vento Minuano* (Rua Lydia Zwicker 271; ☏47 9191 4422; dorms around R$35), 9km from the bus station (taxis are around R$15). Blumenau is just one hour thirty minutes from Camboriú, three hours by hourly bus from Florianópolis, and four hours from Curitiba.

---

for use as a crafts market. Most sights of interest, however, are centred on the lush square **Praça XV de Novembro**, at the centre of which is the enormous, gnarled "**Centenary Fig**" tree. According to legend, walking three times around the tree will guarantee you fame and fortune.

On one side of the square is the **Palácio Cruz e Souza**, an imposing pink building built between 1770 and 1780 as the seat of provincial government – it houses the **Museu Histórico de Santa Catarina** (Tues–Fri 9am–5pm, Sat & Sun 10am–4pm; R$5, free on Sun; ⓦfcc.sc.gov.br/mhsc), whose nineteenth-century interior is more engaging than its collection of military memorabilia. The **Catedral Metropolitana** (Mon–Fri 6.15am–8pm, Sat 8am–noon & 4–8pm, Sun 7am–noon & 4–9pm), overlooking the square, dates back to the eighteenth century but has been modified many times since; the only church in the city centre virtually unchanged since the colonial era is the **Igreja de Nossa Senhora do Rosário**, built between 1787 and 1830 and approached by a flight of steps at Rua Marechal Guilherme 60, two blocks north of the Praça.

ARRIVAL AND INFORMATION

By plane The airport (☏48 3331 4000) is 12km south of the city, with daily flights from Buenos Aires, São Paulo, Rio and Porto Alegre. You can get into the centre by taxi (around R$38 to the city centre or R$50 to Lagoa), or catch green bus #183 or #186 (every 10–30min and labelled "Corredor do Sudoeste"; R$2.90), which will end up at the Terminal de Integração Centro (TICEN) in the centre (around 45min).

By bus Buses arrive at the Terminal Rodoviária Rita María (☏48 3212 3100) at the foot of the road bridge that links the island to the mainland. Cross Av Paulo Fontes and it's a short walk to the centre; the local bus terminal (TICEN) is one long block east at Paulo Fontes 701.

Destinations Blumenau (hourly; 3hr); Buenos Aires (1 daily; 25hr); Curitiba (hourly; 4–5hr); Foz do Iguaçu (14 daily; 14–16hr); Joinville (hourly; 2hr 30min–3hr); Porto Alegre (12 daily; 6–7hr); Rio (1 daily; 17hr); São Paulo (hourly; 11–12hr).

Tourist information There's a tourist information kiosk at the *rodoviária* (daily 8am–6pm; ☏48 3228 1095, ⓦvisitefloripa.com.br). Santa Catarina's state tourist board is based at Rua Felipe Schmidt 249, on the 9th floor (Mon–Fri 8am–7pm; ☏48 3212 6300, ⓦwww.santur.sc.gov.br).

GETTING AROUND

By bus The island has several local bus terminals, so be prepared to change if travelling by bus a lot (transfers are free). The central local bus terminal is Terminal de Integração Centro (or TICEN) at Paulo Fontes 701, which serves most of the island (fares R$2.90; R$2.70 with a *cartão magnético*, stored-value card). Faster, a/c yellow minibuses – *executivas* (R$6) – also zip between the main beaches.

Routes From Terminal de Integração Centro (TICEN): #311, #330 or #320 to Lagoa Da Conceição (TILAG); #231 or #233 to Canasvieiras (TICAN). From Lagoa Da Conceição (TILAG): #360 to Barra da Lagoa; #363 to Joaquina via Praia Mole; #842 to Canasvieiras (TICAN). From Canasvieiras (TICAN): #276 to Balneário Canasvieiras.

ACCOMMODATION

Most tourists choose to stay at the island's beaches and resorts (see p.360), but staying in Florianópolis itself has the benefit of direct bus services to other parts of the island. It's not cheap, though, and accommodation is snapped up quickly in high season.

Hotel Central Sumaré Rua Felipe Schmidt 423 ☎48 3222 5359, ⓦhotelcentralsumare.com.br. The cheapest of the central hotels, in a secure area of town. The minimal rooms are nothing to write home about, but will do if you'd rather spend your money on enjoying yourself than on your digs. There is an R$25 discount for the rooms with shared bathrooms, and cheaper single rates. R$120

Floripa Hostel Rua Duarte Schuttel 227 ☎48 3225 3781, ⓦfloripahostel.com.br. Everything you would expect from an HI hostel (free wi-fi, linens and lockers), though more expensive than elsewhere on the island. It fills rapidly in summer, so get here early. Cheaper for HI members. Dorms R$60, doubles R$125

Valerim Center Rua Felipe Schmidt 554 ☎48 3225 1100, ⓦhotelvalerim.com.br. The largest of the mid-range hotels, with clean comfortable rooms (some of which sleep up to six people), all with a sleek modern design, a/c, TV and minibar. R$163

EATING AND DRINKING

Getting a snack in Florianópolis is no problem, but finding a decent meal sometimes can be, and many of the better restaurants are some way from the centre along Av Beira Norte (take bus #134 from the local bus terminal) – expect prices similar to upmarket areas of Rio de Janeiro. The best place for cheap eats is the Mercado Público (see p.357).

Botequim Floripa Av Rio Branco 632 ☎48 3333 1234. Old-fashioned bar with a lively happy hour and cold beer on tap. Serves up a Brazilian classic *feijoada* on Saturdays (R$29.90). Mon–Fri 5.30pm–1am & Sat 4.30pm–1am.

Box 32 Mercado Público ☎48 3224 5588, ⓦwww.box32 .com.br. Seafood specialist and meeting place of the local glitterati who come to slurp oysters and munch prawns

(try the *pastel de camarão*). That said, it's not as expensive as you might fear, with most meals setting you back R$25–30. Mon–Fri 10am–8pm & Sat till 3pm.

★**Café das Artes** Rua Esteves Júnior 734. Located in a beautifully restored, early nineteenth-century building, delicious pasta dishes and salads are served, though the cakes and premium-quality coffee are especially recommended. Mon–Fri 11.30am–11pm, Sat 3–10pm.

Cervejaria Original Rua Altamiro Guimarães 126 ☎048 3207 3177, ⓦcervejariaoriginal.com.br. Fun and always heaving pub, with a choice of over 200 beers; food served and live music ranges from blues and soft rock to bossa nova and MPB. Daily 5pm–2am.

DIRECTORY

Banks and exchange Banks are located on Rua Felipe Schmidt and by Praça XV de Novembro.

Boat trips Scuna Sul, Av Osvaldo Rodrigues Cabral s/n (☎48 3225 1806, ⓦscunasul.com.br), offer boat trips around the island for around R$50/person.

Car rental Avis, Av Deputado Diomicio Freitas s/n ☎48 3331 4176; Hertz, Rua Bocaiuva 2125 ☎48 3224 9955; Localiza, Rua Henrique Valgas 112A ☎48 2107 6464; YES, Av Deputado Diomicio Freitas ☎048 3236 0229. All are represented at the airport and can arrange delivery in the city centre. During the peak summer season advance reservations are essential.

Internet Gaming café Adrenaline Lan House at Rua Tenente Silveira 155 has a decent, cheap connection (R$3/hr; Mon–Fri 9am–6am, Sat & Sun 1pm–6am).

Pharmacies Farmacia Bela Vista, Rua Tenente Silveira 110. For homeopathic remedies try Farmacia Homeopática Jaqueline, Rua Felipe Schmidt 413.

Post office The main post office is at Praça XV de Novembro 242 (Mon–Fri 9am–5pm, Sat 8am–noon).

Lagoa da Conceição

A large saltwater lagoon in the centre of the island, **Lagoa da Conceição** is popular for swimming, canoeing and windsurfing, with the bustling downtown area known as **Centrinho da Lagoa** (usually simply referred to as Lagoa) at the southern end. The town is both an attractive and convenient place to stay: there are good bus services from here into the centre of Florianópolis and to the east-coast beaches, and the main road is lined with restaurants and bars. This is arguably the liveliest place for nightlife on the island during the summer and at weekends throughout the year, with restaurants always crowded and people overflowing into the streets from the bars.

ACCOMMODATION

Lagoa da Conceição has plenty of good-value options, although you'll need to book ahead in high season.

Estrela do Mar Rua Antônio da Silveira 282 ☎ 48 3232 1079, ⊛ estreladomar.net. Bright and kitsch *residencial* complete with Disney character gnomes in the garden. The six apartments, which all have kitchens, cable TV and free wi-fi, are named after different species of fish. Apartments R$130

Lagoa Hostel Rua José Henrique Veras 469 ☎ 48 3234 4466, ⊛ lagoahostel.com.br. Friendly hostel where staff make you feel part of the extended family, convenient for the local bus station (TILAG) in Centrinho. There's a sundeck, jacuzzi, pool table, huge widescreen TV and free wi-fi. Dorms (with a/c) R$45, doubles (with a/c) R$110

Pousada e Camping Lagoa da Conceição Av das Rendeiras 1480 ☎ 48 3232 5555, ⊛ pousadaecamping lagoadaconceicao.net. Decent campsite shaded by trees, with hot showers, outdoor barbecues and free wi-fi. Camping/person R$30

★ **Tucano House Backpackers** Rua das Araras 229 ☎ 48 3207 8287, ⊛ tucanohouse.com. Popular place with six dorms and five doubles, some with lagoon views and private bathrooms. The hostel serves meals (R$15) every night in an outside patio area, a great place to meet fellow travellers. There are also half-price drinks at the bar between 5pm and 7pm. Other services include a pool, free internet and free surfboard rental. Dorms R$50, doubles (shared bath) R$160

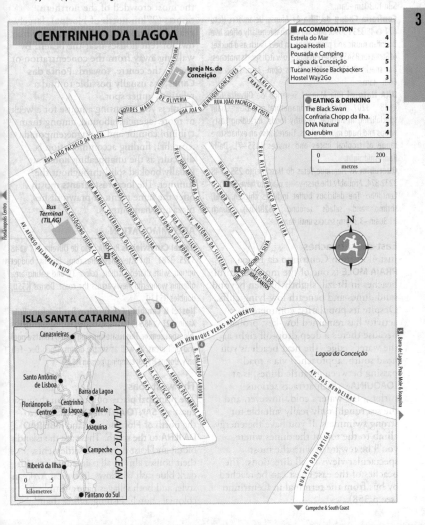

CENTRINHO DA LAGOA

Igreja Ns. da Conceição

Bus Terminal (TILAG)

ISLA SANTA CATARINA

Canasvieiras

Santo Antônio de Lisboa

Florianópolis Centro

Barra da Lagoa

Centrinho da Lagoa — Mole

Joaquina

Campeche

Ribeirã da Ilha

Pântano do Sul

ATLANTIC OCEAN

Lagoa da Conceição

0 — 5 kilometres

0 — 200 metres

N

■ ACCOMMODATION	
Estrela do Mar	4
Lagoa Hostel	2
Pousada e Camping Lagoa da Conceição	5
Tucano House Backpackers	1
Hostel Way2Go	3

● EATING & DRINKING	
The Black Swan	1
Confraria Chopp da Ilha.	2
DNA Natural	3
Querubim	4

Florianópolis Centro

Barra de Lagoa, Praia Mole & Joaquina

Campeche & South Coast

3

Hostel Way2Go Rua Rita Lourenço da Silveira 139 ☎ 48 3364 6004, ⓦ hostelway2go.com. Well-located hostel near the bridge in Centrinho. Washing machines available for guests' use, free wi-fi, TV room and excellent kitchen space. No curfew. Dorms R$50

EATING AND DRINKING

The Black Swan Rua Manoel Severino de Oliveira 592 ☎ 48 3234 5682, ⓦ theblackswan.com.br. Faux-English pub and sports bar run by a British expat, popular with Brazilians and an international crowd. Standard priced local beer on tap, plus a range of expensive imported beer from Europe. Happy hour 5–9.30pm, live music on Saturdays (cover R$20). Mon–Fri 5pm–midnight, Sat & Sun 10.30am–2am.

Confraria Chopp da Ilha Av Afonso Delambert Neto 671 ☎ 48 3334 3696. Buzzing bar that regularly offers live Brazilian music and promotions on beer (such as a bucket of Stella for R$45). A decent place to watch sports matches. Bar snacks R$12–26. Mon–Thurs 6pm–2am, Fri & Sat 6pm–4am.

DNA Natural Rua Manoel Severino de Oliveira 680 ☎ 48 3207 3441, ⓦ dnanatural.com.br. Chain specializing in natural, healthy foods, including tasty wraps and huge mixed salads. There's also an exhaustive range of tropical juices and shakes (R$5–7). Daily 8am–midnight.

Querubim Av Henrique Veras do Nascimento 255 ☎ 48 3232 874. Arguably the best-value place to have lunch in Centrinho. The delicious buffet includes chicken, beef, shrimp and salads (around R$28/kilo). Lunch 11.30am–3.30pm; snacks until 4am.

East-coast beaches

Just 4km from Centrinho da Lagoa, **PRAIA MOLE** is one of the most beautiful beaches in Brazil, slightly hidden beyond sand dunes and beneath low-lying cliffs. Despite its popularity, commercial activity has remained low-key, probably because there's a deep drop-off right at the water's edge. The next beach as you head south, approached via a road passing between gigantic dunes, is at **JOAQUINA**, which attracts serious surfers. The water's cold, however, and the sea rough, only really suitable for strong swimmers. If you have the energy, climb to the top of the dunes where you'll be rewarded with the most spectacular views in all directions. The beaches of the east coast can be reached by bus from the terminal in Centrinho (see p.358).

ACCOMMODATION

Backpackers Sunset Rodovia Jornalista Manoel de Menezes 631 ☎ 48 3232 0141, ⓦ sunsetbackpackers.com. Chilled-out hostel overlooking the bay from a ridge near Praia Mole, with a mix of private rooms and dorms with fans and a/c, free caipirinha (daily 7.30–8.30pm), hearty Brazilian buffet for R$14.90 and the friendly *Sunset Bar* (daily 10am–1am). Dorms R$25, doubles R$75

Canasvieiras

The island's built-up **north coast** offers safe swimming in calm, warm seas and is popular with families. The long, gently curving bay of **CANASVIEIRAS** is the most crowded of the northern resorts (27km north of Floripa), largely geared towards Argentine families who own or rent houses near the beach. By walking away from the concentration of bars at the centre, towards **Ponta das Canas**, it's usually possible to find a relatively quiet spot.

Unless you're renting a house for a week or more (agencies abound, among them ⓦ ibiubi.com.br and ⓦ aluguetemporada .com.br), finding accommodation is difficult, as the unappealing hotels are usually booked solid throughout the summer. The local **restaurants** mostly offer the same menu of prawn dishes, pizza and hamburgers.

ACCOMMODATION

Hostel Canasvieiras Rua Dr João de Oliveira 517 ☎ 48 3225 3781, ⓦ hostelcanasvieiras.com. Decent budget option, with shared kitchen, colour TV and eating area offering wonderful views across the coast. Dorms R$50, doubles R$130

Hostel & Camping Canasvieiras Rua Tertuliano Brito Xavier 521 ☎ 48 9111 9574, ⓦ hostelcampingcanasvieiras .blogspot.com.br. This rustic camping option boasts a pool and grill areas, as well as simple dorms. Open Dec–Feb only. Dorms R$30; camping/person R$25

The west coast

The principal places of interest on the west coast are **SANTO ANTÔNIO DE LISBOA** to the north of Florianópolis and **RIBEIRÃO DA ILHA** to the south. These are the island's oldest and least developed settlements, their houses almost all painted white with dark blue sash windows, in typical Azorean style, and both villages have a simple colonial church. Fishing, rather than

Ostradamus Rodovia Baldicero Filomeno 7640, Ribeirão da Ilha ☎ 48 3337 5711, ⓦostradamus.com.br. Justly popular spot serving up creative dishes such as a dozen oysters with martini and lemon, as well as delicious mains – despite the high prices and long waits for tables, this is easily one of the island's best restaurants. Try the seafood risotto, washed down with local wine (mains R$65–99). Tues–Sat noon–11pm, Sun noon–5pm.

catering to the needs of tourists, remains the principal activity, and the waters offshore from Santo Antônio are used to farm mussels and oysters, considered the best on the island. Because the beaches are small and face the mainland, tourism has remained low-key, accommodation is limited and the few visitors here tend to be on day-trips, staying just long enough to sample oysters at a local bar.

ACCOMMODATION

Pousada Mar de Dentro Rua Caminho dos Açores 1929, Santo Antônio ☎ 48 3235 1521, ⓦpousadamardedentro .com.br. Gorgeous setting overlooking the waterfront, with comfy a/c rooms (with free wi-fi, TV and fridge) and a tiny pool. Rates halve in low season (March–Nov). **R$170**
Pousada do Museu Ribeirão da Ilha ☎ 48 3237 8148, ⓦpousadadomuseu.com.br. In the heart of Ribeirão da Ilha, try this simple option, which has some rooms with glorious sea views and a decent restaurant. **R$170**

PORTO ALEGRE

The booming capital of Rio Grande do Sul, **PORTO ALEGRE** lies on the eastern bank of the Rio Guaíba, some 450km south of Florianópolis. Settlers from the Azores arrived here in 1752, but it wasn't until Porto Alegre became the gateway for the export of beef that it developed into Brazil's leading commercial centre south of São Paulo, with a population today of some 4.5 million. Like most major Brazilian cities it's not especially attractive, with a skyline of primarily tired 1960s high-rises, but the **Fundação Iberê Camargo** is a must-see for art lovers, it's a fun place to eat and drink, and the *centro histórico* is undergoing

something of a renaissance in part thanks to the 2014 football World Cup.

WHAT TO SEE AND DO

Everything in the centre worth seeing is within an easy walk, and a day or so is enough to visit most places of interest. For city tours, the tourist board operates "Linha Turismo", an open-top double-decker bus with two circuits that take in the historic centre and southern zone. Tours leave from outside the main office, Travessa do Carmo 84 (hourly Tues–Sun 9am–4pm; Tues–Fri R$18, Sat & Sun R$20; ⓦportoalegre.travel).

Mercado Público and around

The golden-coloured **Mercado Público** (Mon–Fri 7.30am–7.30pm, Sat 7.30am–6.30pm) stands at the heart of Porto Alegre's commercial district, located alongside Praça Rui Barbosa and Praça XV de Novembro. A replica of Lisbon's Mercado da Figueira, this imposing building contains an absorbing mix of stalls selling household goods, food and regional handicrafts. Upstairs are restaurants offering traditional Brazilian all-you-can-eat lunch buffets which stay open after the market stalls shut. Next to the market is the ochre **Paço Municipal**, the old *prefeitura* (town hall), built in Neoclassical style between 1898 and 1901, its impressive proportions an indication of civic pride and self-confidence during Porto Alegre's golden age.

West of here along Rua Sete de Setembro is the pleasantly verdant **Praça da Alfândega**, home of the grand **Museu de Arte do Rio Grande do Sul** (Tues–Sun 10am–7pm; free; ⓦmargs.rs.gov.br). You can spend an hour or so admiring the local modern art here, combined with a visit to the **Memorial do Rio Grande do Sul** next door (Tues–Fri 10am–7pm, Sat 2–5pm; free), which houses pictorial exhibitions on the history of the state.

Praça da Matriz

A short walk uphill from the Praça da Alfândega via Rua General Câmara leads to the **Praça da Matriz**, home to Porto Alegre's oldest buildings, though they have been so heavily altered over the last

3

few centuries that few retain their original character (the Catedral Metropolitana was only completed in 1986). The **Palácio Piratini**, the state governor's residence (tours every 30min Mon–Fri 9–11.30am & 2–5pm; free), dates from 1909, while the **Teatro São Pedro** (tours by reservation only; Tues–Fri 1–7pm, Sat 4–9pm, Sun 4–6pm; free; ⓦteatrosaopedro.com.br) opposite was inaugurated in 1858.

Casa de Cultura Mário Quintana

The **Casa de Cultura Mário Quintana**, Rua dos Andradas 736 (Mon 2–9pm, Tues–Fri 9am–9pm, Sat & Sun noon–9pm; free; ⓦccmq.com.br), a beautifully restored warren of art galleries, libraries and theatres, was a hotel between 1918 and 1980; the poet Mário Quintana was a long-time resident. Pride of place is given to his room on the second floor (no. 217, **Quarto do Poeta**), which is maintained in the state it was in when he lived here.

Fundação Iberê Camargo

Porto Alegre's under-visited crown jewel, the **Fundação Iberê Camargo** lies 5km south of the *centro histórico* at Av Padre Cacique 2000 (Tues, Wed & Fri–Sun noon–7pm, Thurs noon–9pm; free; ⓦiberecamargo.org.br). The fascinating Modernist building is itself part of the attraction, vaguely reminiscent of the Guggenheim in New York, with a gleaming all-white interior and a spiral layout. The contemporary art exhibits here are usually impressive; displays revolve, but there's always work from Rio Grande do Sul artist **Iberê Camargo** (1914–94), whose unsettling Expressionist images have become some of Brazil's most revered art. The café here is the best place to **watch the sunset** over the Guaíba. Take any bus towards the Zona Sul (from Av Senador Salgado Filho to Juca Batista, Serraria, Padre Réus or Camaquá); to return you'll have to walk back along the highway to the bus stop, and then take any bus headed to town; a taxi from the bus station should be R$22.

ARRIVAL AND DEPARTURE

By plane Aeroporto Internacional Salgado Filho, 6km northeast of downtown Porto Alegre, receives flights from all major national destinations and nearby capitals. Taxis (meter starts at R$4.22) cost around R$20 to Moinhos de Vento and around R$25 into the old centre; you can also take the metrô from the Estação Aeroporto into the city (5am–11.20pm; R$1.70) in just 10min (to the Mercado station).

By bus The *rodoviária* (☎51 3210 0101) is northeast of the centre at Largo Vespasiano Júlio Veppo 11, but within walking distance; after dark it's safer, and easier to ride the metrô to the Mercado Público or take a taxi (around R$7; ☎51 3221 9371).

Destinations Canela (hourly; 2hr); Curitiba (8 daily; 11hr); Buenos Aires (1 daily; 18hr); Florianópolis (14 daily; 7–8hr); Foz do Iguaçu (8 daily; 14–16hr); Gramado (hourly; 2hr); Montevideo (1 daily; 11hr); Rio de Janeiro (1–2 daily; 24–25hr); Santo Ângelo (13 daily; 6–7hr); São Paulo (4 daily; 18hr).

INFORMATION AND TOURS

Tourist information The local Secretaria Municipal de Turismo (ⓦportoalegre.travel) has very helpful branches at the airport, *rodoviária* (7am–10pm), the Centro Cultural Usina do Gasômetro (Tues–Sun 9am–6pm; ☎0800 517 686) and at the Mercado Público (Store 99, Ground Floor; Mon–Sat 9am–6pm; ☎0800 517 686). The main municipal office is in the city centre at Travessa do Carmo 84, Cidade Baixa (Mon 8am–noon & 1.30–6pm, Tues–Sun 8am–6pm; ☎51 3289 0176).

Boat tours Excursions (1hr 30min) on the Rio Guaíba with Barco Cisne Branco leave from the tour-boat berth (Cais do Porto) on Av Mauá 1050, near the metro station (Tues–Fri 10.30am, 3pm & 4.30pm, Sat & Sun also 6pm; R$28; ☎51 3224 5222, ⓦbarcocisnebranco.com.br). There are also similar excursions from the Cais da Usina do Gasômetro, Av Presidente João Goulart 551 (Tues–Fri 3.30pm & 5.30pm; Sat & Sun 7 daily).

ACCOMMODATION

Hostels are scattered all over the city centre, but it's a relatively small area and it's possible to walk to most places – though you should take a taxi after dark.

Casa Azul Rua Lima e Silva 912 ☎51 3084 5050, ⓦcasaazulhostel.com. Popular hostel in a house in Cidade Baixa with bar open to the public (Tues–Sun 6.30pm–1am). There's a spacious outside area, flat-screen TV, free wi-fi, pool table and friendly staff who can organize excursions. Dorms __R$38__

Minuano Express Av Farrapos 31 ☎51 3226 3062. Despite the ugly high-rise building in which they are housed, rooms here are pleasant and surprisingly modern, and the soundproof windows ensure a good night's sleep regardless of the traffic outside (it's a short walk from the bus station). Free wi-fi and filling buffet breakfast. __R$139__

Porto Alegre Eco Hostel Rua Luiz Afonso 276 ☎51 3019 2449, ⓦportoalegreecohostel.com.br. Justly the

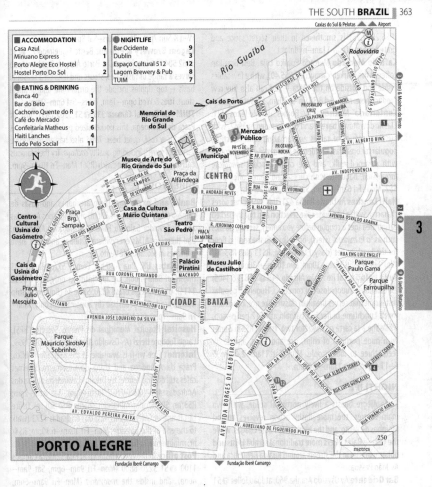

PORTO ALEGRE

Caxias do Sul & Pelotas ▲▲ Airport

■ ACCOMMODATION	
Casa Azul	4
Minuano Express	5
Porto Alegre Eco Hostel	1
Hostel Porto Do Sol	2

● NIGHTLIFE	
Bar Ocidente	9
Dublin	3
Espaço Cultural 512	12
Lagom Brewery & Pub	8
TUIM	7

■ EATING & DRINKING	
Banca 40	1
Bar do Beto	10
Cachorro Quente do R	5
Café do Mercado	2
Confeitaria Matheus	6
Haiti Lanches	4
Tudo Pelo Social	11

0 ___ 250
metres

most popular hostel in the city, with excellent staff and comfy dorms right in Cidade Baixa. Extras include a swimming pool, free wi-fi, games room, garden and bike rental. Breakfast included. Dorms R$35, doubles R$140

Hostel Porto Do Sol Rua Mariante 958 ☎ 51 3330 1324, ⓦ hostelportodosol.com.br. One of the quieter hostels, but a hike from the centre (R$15–20 by taxi; R$2.95 by bus). Mixed and female-only dorms with tiled floors, fans and free wi-fi – a simple breakfast is served on the patio. Pool table, TV room (with DVDs) and kitchen available. Dorms R$33

EATING

As the home of Brazilian *churrasco* (barbecue), Porto Alegre has some excellent places to eat, especially in the Cidade Baixa and Moinhos de Vento neighbourhoods. As always, the best-value places to eat are buffets (especially in the Mercado Público), serving a plentiful range of food and usually offering good lunchtime deals.

★ **Banca 40** Mercado Público Loja 40 ☎ 51 3226 3533. Open since 1927 (it looks modern, however), this local institution is justly lauded for its *bomba royal* (R$9.50) ice-cream dessert; regular scoops of ice cream start at R$3.50, and you can also order sandwiches (R$4–10). Seating in the centre of the market. Mon–Sat 8am–7.30pm.

Bar do Beto Rua Sarmento Leite 811 ☎ 51 3332 9390, ⓦ bardobeto.com.br. Cidade Baixa restaurant that heaves at lunchtime due to its R$19 buffet special, when waiters walk round tables offering different cuts of beef and chicken. Dinner is à la carte only (mains R$25–55). Daily 11am–2am.

★ **Cachorro Quente do R** Praça Dom Sebastião. This legendary cart has been cooking up hot dogs (*cachorro*) in front of Colégio Rosário since 1962 (several imitators have since emerged). Choose your sausage type (*salsicha* is typical hot dog; *linguiça* is a meatier, cured sausage), then what you want on it; mushy peas, parsley, ketchup, mustard, and chilli. The gut-busting finished product

(R$6.25–7.25) is smothered in their secret sauce and grated cheese. Daily 11am–midnight.

Café do Mercado Mercado Público Loja. Best Brazilian coffee in the market (cappuccino R$5.40), with a few tables inside and outside on the plaza – you can also buy raw produce here. Mon–Fri 8.30am–7.30pm, Sat 9am–5pm.

Confeitaria Matheus Av Borges de Medeiros 421. Classic downtown bakery and café founded in 1947, with bustling interior of tables and amazing cake selection; popular for breakfast – order the *dupla café cortado*, coffee with steamed milk, and the calorie-packed *sanduíche farroupilha*, baguette with cheese and ham. Coffee from R$2. Mon–Fri 6am–10pm, Sat 7am–9pm.

Haiti Lanches Av Otavio Rocha 421. This 1955 diner oozes character, with a bar, huge cake selection and tightly packed eating area (get a coupon before you enter), serving classics such as "*a la minuta*" (stew), or walk up to the second floor for the lunch buffet (daily 11am–3pm; R$13 plus R$3.10/kilo). Mon–Sat 6.30am–10pm, Sun 10am–6.30pm.

Tudo Pelo Social Rua João Alfredo 448 ☎ 51 3226 4405, ⓦ restaurantetudopelosocial.com.br. Hugely popular restaurant that serves Brazilian classics like rice, beans and meat. Lunchtime buffet is a bargain at R$12 per person, while the à la carte *picanha* "for two" (steak; R$32) comes with huge portions of chips, rice and salad, and easily feeds three to four people. Mon–Sat 11am–2.45pm & 6–11.45pm, Sun 11am–2.45pm.

NIGHTLIFE

Porto Alegre boasts a lively nocturnal scene, with two main centres: the more flashy action revolves around Moinhos de Vento, and the hub of Rua Padre Chagas, while the Cidade Baixa offers more traditional samba joints and bohemian bars in the streets around Rua da República and Av João Pessoa.

Bar Ocidente Av Osvaldo Aranha 960, at João Telles ☎ 51 3312 1347, ⓦ barocidente.com.br. Legendary former meeting place of dissidents since 1980, now best known for good veggie lunches (R$10–16), its art gallery and lively party nights: Friday is LGBT night, while Saturday is always a themed club night. Mon–Sat 11.45am–2.30pm & 6pm–2am.

Dublin Rua Padre Chagas 342, Moinhos de Vento ☎ 51 3268 8835, ⓦ dublinpub.com.br. Every city must have one: this is your standard faux-Irish bar and the current place where well-to-do "gauchos" look to enjoy themselves. Live bands play daily and an entry fee is charged after 9pm (Sun–Wed R$7; Thurs–Sat R$10 for women, R$20 for men). Mon–Wed & Sun 6pm–3am, Thurs–Sat 6pm–5am.

★ **Espaço Cultural 512** Rua João Alfredo 512 ☎ 51 3212 0229, ⓦ espaco512.com.br. Popular live music bar with a busy weekly programme of performances and a popular house cocktail the *maracangalha* (*cachaça*, pineapple, ginger, passion fruit and red pepper). Cover R$5–15. Tues,

Wed & Sun 7pm–2am, Thurs–Sat 8pm–3am.

Lagom Brewery & Pub Rua Bento Figueiredo 72 ☎ 51 3062 5045, ⓦ lagom.com.br. Porto Alegre's first brew pub serves a range of tasty ales, stouts and IPAs on a seasonal basis – top tipples include the amber ale and oatmeal stout. Tues & Wed 6pm–1am, Thurs–Sat 6pm–2am.

TUIM Rua General Câmara 333 ☎ 51 9962 8851. Just off Praça de Alfândega, this pocket-sized pub in the centre is ideal for a cool, quiet beer. *TUIM* also has an impressive variety of spirits, including quality *cachaça*. Try their famous anchovy and mustard sandwich (R$6). Mon–Fri 10am–9pm.

DIRECTORY

Banks and exchange There are banks and casas de câmbio (Mon–Fri 10am–4.30pm) along Rua dos Andradas and Av Senador Salgado Filho near Praça da Alfândega, and there are ATMs everywhere. Citibank and HSBC have branches in Moinhos de Vento.

Consulates UK, Rua Antenor Lemos 57/conjunto 303 (Mon–Fri 9am–noon, by appointment only; ☎ 51 3232 1414); USA, Av Assis Brasil 4320, Store 84 (Boulevard Strip Mall), Parque Sao Sebastiao (by appointment only; Mon–Fri 9am–1pm; ☎ 51 3226 3344).

Hospital Hospital Municipal de Pronto Socorro (HPS), Largo Teodore Herzl (Av Osvaldo Aranha) ☎ 51 3289 7999.

Internet Free wi-fi is available at the Mercado Público, Praça da Alfândega and Usina do Gasômetro. Internet cafés still dot the centre: try Dreams Lavanderia at Rua dos Andradas 405 (Mon–Fri 7.30am–9pm, Sat 8am–2pm; R$3/hr, $0.05/min; minimum charge R$0.50), or Office Lan House at Galeria Edith, Rua dos Andradas 1273 (walk to the end of the passage; Mon–Fri 10am–6.30pm; R$4/hr; minimum R$1 for 15min).

Post office In the *centro historico* at Rua Siqueira Campos 1100 ☎ 51 3220 8800 (Mon–Fri 9am–6pm, Sat 9am–noon), and inside the *rodoviária* (Mon–Fri 9am–6pm; ☎ 51 3225 1945).

GRAMADO AND CANELA

Some 120km north of Porto Alegre, **GRAMADO** is Brazil's best-known mountain resort – famous for its Natal Luz (Christmas lights) and its annual film festival (ⓦ festivaldegramado.net), held in August. Architecturally, Gramado tries hard to appear Swiss, with "Alpine" chalets and flower-filled window boxes the norm. It's a mere affectation, though, since hardly any of the inhabitants are of Swiss origin – the town was settled by the Portuguese in 1875 and only a small minority is of German extraction; most locals today are of Italian ancestry. The most pleasant time to visit the area is in spring (Oct & Nov) when the parks, gardens and roadsides are full of flowers. At 825m, Gramado is high enough to be refreshingly cool in summer and positively chilly in winter. Marginally cheaper than Gramado, but arranged very much along the same lines, **CANELA** (which means "cinnamon"), 8km further east, is another mountain retreat popular with holidaying Brazilians and better located for visits to the nearby national parks.

★ TREAT YOURSELF

La Caceria Av Borges de Medeiros 3166, Gramado ☎ 54 3295 7575, ⓦ casadamontanha.com.br. An intriguing but expensive restaurant in the classy *Hotel Casa da Montanha*, specializing in game dishes (mains R$70–90) with unusual tropical fruit sauces that complement the often strong-tasting meat. Daily 7pm–midnight.

WHAT TO SEE AND DO

The chief appeal of both towns lies in their clear mountain air and generally relaxed way of life. There really isn't much to do in Gramado other than to admire the houses, enjoy the food and stroll around the large and very pretty flower-filled **Parque Knorr** (daily 10.30am–9.30pm; free; during the festive season the kitsch Santa Claus village is R$18). The surrounding region is magnificent, best appreciated at the **Ecoparque Sperry** (entrance just off Av das Hortênsias on the way to Canela; Tues–Sun 9am–5pm; R$12; ⓦ ecoparquesperry.com .br). Here you can peruse the conservation park's **Centro de Interpretação** or stroll along forest trails and past waterfalls, taking in the local flora. Roads in the mountainous areas around Gramado are unpaved and can be treacherous after rain, so **guided tours** are a safer bet – ask at the tourist office for recommendations.

ARRIVAL AND INFORMATION

By bus Buses (ⓦ citral.tur.br) from Porto Alegre (every 30min–1hr; 2hr 30min) run to Gramado's *rodoviária* (☎ 54 3286 1302) on Av Borges de Medeiros 2100, a couple of minutes' walk south from the town centre. Buses between Porto Alegre and Canela (every 30min–1hr; 3hr; R$27–36) run to Canela's *rodoviária* (☎ 54 3282 1375), just behind the central main street, Av Júlio de Castilhos, a short walk from the main plaza. Buses between Canela and Gramado leave every 10–15min (20min). Citral runs buses to São Francisco de Paula from Canela for the Parque Nacional dos Aparados da Serra (8 daily; 1hr). Buses also depart here for the Parque Caracol.

Tourist information The Gramado tourist office is at Av Borges de Medeiros 1674 (Mon–Thurs 9am–6pm, Fri–Sun 9am–8pm; ☎ 54 3286 1475, ⓦ gramado.rs.gov.br). The Canela tourist office, at Largo da Fama 227 (Mon–Sat 8am–6pm, Sun 8am–1pm; ☎ 54 3282 2200,

ⓦ canelaturismo.com.br) in the town centre, can put you in touch with tour companies arranging trips to the national parks.

ACCOMMODATION

Accommodation is expensive and you should book ahead during peak periods. Outside busy times many hotels offer discounts during the week.

Gramado Hostel Av Das Hortências 3880, Gramado ☎ 54 3295 1020, ⓦ gramadohostel.com.br. About 1.5km outside town on the road to Canela (20min walk or R$1.80 on the Canela bus), this HI hostel is decent value (discounts for members), with dorm rooms and some doubles. Dorms R$65, doubles R$170

Pousada Belluno Rua Nilo Dias 50, Gramado ☎ 54 3286 0820, ⓦ pousadabelluno.com.br. The best of the cheaper hotels in downtown, with elegantly furnished, heated rooms, free wi-fi, LCD TVs and floor-to-ceiling windows. The substantial buffet breakfast will set you up for the day. R$150

Hostel Viajante Rua Ernesto Urbani 132, Canela ☎ 54 3282 2017, ⓦ pousadadoviajante.com.br. Right next to the *rodoviária*, this is the best budget choice, with economical dorms and neat and tidy doubles – perfect for travellers winding down after a hard day's bungee jumping. Dorms R$50, doubles R$120

EATING

Gramado is noted for its handmade chocolate and has some good restaurants (especially fondue places), but expect to pay through the nose for anything resembling a good meal; aim for the buffets or "café colonial" places to fill up for a reasonably good price; Canela is especially known for its apple strudel and other German-inspired sweet treats.

★ **Bela Vista Café Colonial** Av das Hortências 4665, Gramado ☎ 54 3286 1608, ⓦ belavista.tur.br. One of Gramado's classic Alpine-style cafés, offering fabulous "café colonial" spreads of cakes, pastries and meats for a hefty R$58. Mon–Fri 11am–11pm, Sat & Sun 10am–11pm.

ITA Brasil Av São Pedro 1005, Gramado ☎ 54 3286 3833. Off the main drag and very crowded, but well worth seeking out for the cheap lunch buffets (R$16.90) of classic Italian–Brazilian food, fresh juices, strong coffee and home-made *cachaça*. Mon & Wed–Sun 11.15am–2.30pm.

Lá em Casa Rua Jose Luiz Correa Pinto 346, Canela ☏ 54 3278 1049. Rustic, home-made Brazilian food served buffet style, where around R$30 gets you all the food you can eat. Leave room for the delicious *pudim de leite* (milk pudding). *Feijoada* on Saturday. Tues–Fri 11.30am–2pm, Sat & Sun 11.30am–3pm.

Restaurante da Torre (Cervejaria Farol) Rua Severino Inocente Zini 150, Canela ☏ 54 3282 7007, ⓦ cervejariafarol.com.br. Excellent micro-brewery (marked by a 32m "lighthouse"), offering the chance to tour (R$10) the facilities before sampling the beers – the IPA is especially tasty. It also serves a decent menu of German dishes and snacks, and provides free lifts to and from your hotel. Live music (Tues, Fri & Sat). Tues–Fri 5pm–midnight, Sat 11am–12.30am, Sun 11am–5pm.

★**Schnitzelstubb** Rua Baden Powell 246, Canela ☏ 54 3282 9562. This German-inspired restaurant is the place to sample that schnitzel, wurst and apple strudel. Mains R$20–35. Tues 8–10.30pm, Wed–Fri noon–2.30pm & 8–10.30pm, Sat noon–3pm & 8–11pm, Sun 11.45am–3pm.

PARQUE ESTADUAL DO CARACOL

Just 7km outside Canela on RS-466 (aka Estrada do Caracol), the highlight of the **PARQUE ESTADUAL DO CARACOL** (Mon–Fri 8.45am–5.45pm, Sat & Sun 8.45am–6pm; R$18) is the spectacular **Cascata do Caracol**, a stunning waterfall on the Río Caracol that plunges dramatically over a 131m-high cliff of basaltic rock in the middle of dense forest. The hike to the foot of the falls involves over 700 exhausting steps, but you can also take a lift ("elevador panorâmico") up the 27-m high **Observatório Ecológico** (daily 8.30am–6pm; R$9, in addition to park entry; ⓦ observatorioecologico.com.br), which will give you a 360-degree bird's-eye view of the park and falls over the tree-tops. Binoculars are available for close-up sightings of flora and fauna. For even more scintillating views of the waterfall take the 830m **Teleférico de Canela** 500m further along the road from the park entrance, a nerve-jangling chair lift (daily 9am–5pm; 20min; R$36; ☏ 54 3504 1405).

Further along the main road (now the gravel-surfaced Estrada da Ferradura), at Km15 is the entrance to the **Parque Vale da Ferradura** (daily 8.30am–5.30pm;

R$8), where three viewpoints cover the dramatic 420m "horseshoe" canyon of the Río Caí.

Heading back to Canela you'll pass the araucaria wood **Castelinho** (RS-466 Km3; daily 9am–1pm & 2.20–5.40pm; R$10; ⓦ castelinhocaracol.com.br), a fairy-tale German-style mansion dating from 1915 and now a memorial to German immigration to the area (which serves incredible *apfelstrudel* in the tea rooms).

ARRIVAL AND DEPARTURE

By bus Buses run from the *rodoviária* in Canela to the park entrance (Mon–Sat 8.15am, 12.10pm & 5.30pm; returning at 8.35am, 12.15pm & 6pm; Sun 8am, 1.30pm & 5.30pm, returning 8.40am, 1.55pm & 6pm; R$2.20) or you can take a taxi.

PARQUE NACIONAL DOS APARADOS DA SERRA

Around 150 million years ago, lava slowly poured onto the surface of the Brazilian Shield, a vast **highland plateau**, developing into a thick layer of basalt rock. At the edge of the plateau, vast canyons puncture the basalt and the largest of these is protected within the predominantly untouched wilderness of the **Parque Nacional dos Aparados da Serra** (Tues–Sun 8am–5pm; R$13/person, plus R$5/car), some 100km east of Canela.

Approaching the park from any direction, you pass through rugged cattle pasture, occasionally interrupted by the distinctive umbrella-like araucaria pine trees and solitary farm

WHEN TO VISIT

The Parque Nacional dos Aparados da Serra can be visited throughout the year, but is at its best during spring (Oct and Nov) when the blooming flowers create a spectacular effect. In the winter (June to Aug), it can get very cold, though visibility is often excellent. Summers are warm, but heavy rainfall sometimes makes the roads and trails impassable and fog and low-level cloud sometimes completely obscure what should be spectacular views. Avoid April, May and September, the months with the most sustained rainfall.

buildings. As the dirt road enters the park itself, forest patches appear, suddenly and dramatically interrupted by a canyon of breathtaking proportions. Some 5.8km in length, between 600m and 2000m wide and 720m deep, **Itaimbézinho** is a dizzying sight. On the higher levels, with relatively little rainfall, but with fog banks moving in from the nearby Atlantic Ocean, vegetation is typical of a cloudforest, while on the canyon's floor a mass of subtropical plants flourishes.

Three trails are open to visitors, the most difficult of which is the **Trilha do Rio do Boi** (8hr) – an option for experienced hikers that must only be attempted with a guide. It involves a 5m vertical descent of a rock face by rope and a complete descent to the rocky river in the canyon floor. Rather easier is the **Trilha do Vértice** (1.4km), which affords views of Itaimbézinho and two spectacular waterfalls **Véu da Noiva** and **Andorinhas**. If this isn't challenging enough for you, try the **Trilha do Mirante do Cotovelo** (6.3km return), which runs along the rim of the canyon and provides some glorious photo opportunities.

ARRIVAL AND DEPARTURE

By bus Getting to the park via public transport is tough – organized tours are worth considering here. First, take a bus (🌐citral.tur.br) from Gramado or Canela to São Francisco de Paula. From here take another bus 60km northeast to Cambará do Sul (Mon–Sat 9.15am & 5pm, Sun 11am; 1hr 30min) and ask to be let off at the entrance to the park. Citral also has one bus to Cambará from Porto Alegre (Mon–Sat 6am; 5hr). From Cambará it's a further 17km to the park entrance along Estrada do Itaimbézinho (RS-427) towards Praia Grande (taxis charge around R$60 round-trip), and another 2km from there to the edge of the canyon. There is no bus service direct to the park, though Expresso São Marcos has been running local buses from Cambará to the entrance at 8am (Mon–Sat; 35min; R$5.85; 🌐expressosaomarcos.com.br) – check the website for the latest.

By car If you intend to make the trip in your own vehicle it is imperative that you call ☎54 3251 1230 for up-to-date information on local road conditions.

INFORMATION AND TOURS

Tourist information There is a visitors' centre (☎54 3251 1262, 🌐guiaaparadosdaserra.com.br) and a snack bar at the main entrance. Only a thousand visitors are permitted to enter the park each day, so it's advisable to phone the visitors' centre in advance to reserve a place.

Tour operators Trying to visit the park on your own is difficult and barely cheaper than doing it with a tour. Try ecotourism specialists Canyons do Sul (🌐canyonsdosul .com.br).

ACCOMMODATION

Camping is prohibited in the park, so if you decide to visit independently, you'll need accommodation – the most convenient place is Cambará do Sul, aka the "capital of honey" thanks to its numerous bee farms.

Pousada João de Barro Rua Pe. João Francisco Ritter 631 ☎54 3251 1216, 🌐joaodebarropousada.com.br. This cosy little hotel in the centre of Cambará is superb value, with just five en-suite rooms, TVs, free wi-fi and delicious, wholesome breakfasts. The living room and fireplace is popular in winter. **R$150**

ROTA MISSÕES (MISSION ROUTE)

Though less well known than those in Argentina and Paraguay, Rio Grande do Sul is home to no fewer than seven **Jesuit Missions**, with four of the ruins in an excellent state of preservation and grouped together on what is called the **ROTA MISSÕES**. The Jesuits arrived here in 1626 determined to convert the Guarani Indians, with the missions founded between 1682 and 1706 in nominal Spanish territory. In fact the region was virtually independent of both Spain and Portugal, a state of affairs ended by the 1750 Treaty of Madrid when the missions became definitively Portuguese; this led to the Guarani War of 1756, devastating the region (and dramatized in the film *The Mission*).

The best place to base yourself is the town of **SANTO ÂNGELO** in the far southwest of the state, where there is a cluster of accommodation options around Praça Rio Branco. The most accessible and best of the missions is **SÃO MIGUEL ARCANJO** (daily 9am–noon & 2–6pm, Oct–Feb till 8pm; R$5; 🌐missoesturismo .com.br), founded in 1687 in the village of São Miguel da Missões. Guided tours are available, and the small Museu das Missões (same times) and a kitschy nightly light show (Aug–Feb 9pm; March & April 8pm; May–July 7pm; R$9) brings the story of the Jesuits to life.

3

3

CROSSING THE BORDERS TO URUGUAY AND ARGENTINA

Most overland travellers cross the southern Brazilian borders via long-distance bus – in this case formalities are fairly straightforward and you just need to know the entry requirements for Uruguay (see p.833) and Argentina (see p.45). The borders here are generally open, meaning anyone can just walk across – if you are a foreigner, however, you need to find the nearest immigration post to have passports stamped.

TO URUGUAY

Chuí/Chuy (340km northeast of Montevideo). By far the most travelled route, 527km south of Porto Alegre. Buses entering and leaving Brazil stop at an immigration office a short distance north of the town itself (Chuí/Chuy is actually divided by the border) on BR-471. The Uruguayan customs is 3km further south on Rte-9.

Santana do Livramento (497km west of Porto Alegre). There's no duty-free here or passport controls – the town simply merges into the Uruguayan city of Rivera (500km north of Montevideo). Before leaving Livramento you'll need a Brazilian exit (or entry) passport stamp from the Polícia Federal, at Rua Uruguai 1177, near the central park, and a stamp from Uruguay's Dirección Nacional de Inmigración, at Av Presidente Viera s/n. If you have any problems, head for the Uruguayan consulate in Livramento at Av Tamandaré 2101, 4th floor (☎ 55 3242 1416).

TO ARGENTINA

Most people heading to Argentina from Brazil cross the frontier at Foz do Iguaçu (see p.351), but if you find yourself in the south of the country, **Uruguaiana** (694km west of Porto Alegre) is the most convenient crossing – with Paso de los Libres on the other side (around 740km north of Buenos Aires). Customs formalities take place at either end of the 1400m-long road bridge across the Rio Uruguai. Accommodation and restaurant options are both better on the Argentine side of the border. The Argentine consulate is at Rua 13 de Mayo 1674 (☎ 55 3412 1925).

ARRIVAL AND DEPARTURE

By bus The *rodoviária* at Santo Ângelo is 1km west of Praça Pinheiro Machado at Sete Povos das Missões 419. Antonello runs buses to and from São Miguel (Mon–Fri 7.15am, 11am, 3.30pm & 4.45pm; Sat 10am, 1.30pm & 3.30pm; Sun 9.30am & 6.20pm; last bus returning Mon–Fri 6.15pm, Sat 5.30pm, Sun 5pm; 1hr 20min; R$11.10; ⓦ turismoantonello.com.br). For Foz do Iguaçu you'll need to take a bus to Santa Rosa (1hr) and change there.

Destinations Curitiba (1 daily; 13hr); Porto Alegre (10 daily; 6–7hr); Rio (1 daily; 28hr).

ACCOMMODATION

There are also decent options in Santo Ângelo.

Pousada das Missões Rua São Nicolau 601 ☎ 55 3381 1202, ⓦ pousadadasmissoes.com.br. Right next to the ruins, this is a smart choice if you intend to stay for the sound-and-light show, an excellent HI hostel that has clean dorm rooms as well as doubles (with a/c and TV) and a relaxing pool. Dorms R$65, doubles R$160

THE ELQUI VALLEY

Chile

HIGHLIGHTS

❶ **Valparaíso** Stunning setting, bohemian atmosphere and vibrant nightlife. **See p.392**

❷ **The Elqui Valley** Laidback villages, pisco tasting and stargazing. **See p.404**

❸ **San Pedro de Atacama** Gateway to spectacular desert landscapes. **See p.411**

❹ **Iquique** Chile's top paragliding destination. **See p.415**

❺ **Pucón** Volcano climbing, white-water rafting and hot springs. **See p.433**

❻ **Parque Nacional Torres del Paine** World-class hiking amid majestic scenery. See p.472

HIGHLIGHTS ARE MARKED ON THE MAP ON P.371

ROUGH COSTS

Daily budget Basic US$50

Drink Pisco sour US$4

Food *Pastel de choclo* US$9

Camping/hostel/budget hotel US$10/20/45

FACT FILE

Population 17.6 million

Languages Spanish; indigenous languages Aymará, Huilliche, Kawéscar, Mapudungun, Quechua, Rapanui and Yámana

Currency Chilean Peso (CH$)

Capital Santiago (population: 6.3 million)

International phone code ☎56

Time zone GMT -4hr; GMT -3hr from second Sunday in October to second Sunday in March

Introduction

Chileans will tell you that when God created the world, he had a little bit of everything left over, and put pieces of desert, rivers, lakes and glaciers together to make Chile. From the world's driest desert – the Atacama – in the north to the volcanic peaks and verdant landscapes of the Lake District and the icy wilderness of Patagonia In the south, it is perhaps the most geographically diverse and fascinating country in Latin America. Snaking between the snowcapped Andes and the Pacific Ocean, Chile is a fantastic playground for lovers of the outdoors and adrenaline junkies, with world-class skiing, surfing, white-water rafting, climbing and paragliding. The country's plentiful national parks and nature reserves also boast an astounding array of plant and animal life.

Today, despite its troubled past under the brutal Pinochet dictatorship, Chile is among the most politically and economically stable of all Latin American countries. For the most part, it is westernized and affluent, and its excellent bus network makes it an easy country to navigate.

Cosmopolitan **Santiago** is a very manageable starting point, with plenty of excellent hostels, restaurants and bars, as well as easy access to superb ski resorts and the vineyards of **Middle Chile**. Nearby, in the beguiling coastal city of **Valparaíso**, you can ride the *ascensores* (funiculars), soak up the bohemian atmosphere, or relax on the sandy beaches of neighbouring **Viña del Mar**. Head further north to the **Norte Chico** to knock back a pisco sour in the sublime

Elqui Valley, or stargaze in some of the world's clearest skies. Further north still is the **Norte Grande**, where the strong breaks of the Pacific Ocean meet the moonscape scenery of the Atacama Desert. Visit gleaming lagoons and steaming geysers in the backpacker oasis of **San Pedro de Atacama**, and get your fill of sun and surf in the beach towns of **Iquique** and **Arica**.

South of Santiago and Middle Chile, the **Lake District** – a region of lush forests and snowcapped volcanoes – exudes opportunities for rafting, cycling and mountaineering, while the fascinating archipelago of **Chiloé** has beautiful wooden churches and a distinct culture. Towering granite pillars and blue-tinged glaciers draw thousands of visitors to **Chilean Patagonia**, and the excellent trekking routes of **Parque Nacional Torres del Paine**. Last, but definitely not least, for serene beauty, ancient mystery and giant *moai* statues, head to the one of the world's most remote inhabited islands, **Rapa Nui** (Easter Island).

WHEN TO VISIT

If you want to experience the whole of Chile in all its diversity you'll need to come prepared for both extreme cold and extreme heat. The **Lake District**, **Patagonia** and **Tierra del Fuego** are best explored from October through to April, since the Chilean winter effectively shuts down much of the south and transport can be very limited. **Norte Grande**, **Norte Chico**, **Middle Chile** and the **Pacific island** territories, however, can be accessed all year round.

CHRONOLOGY

1520 Ferdinand Magellan is the first European to sail through what is now the Magellan Strait.

1536 Expedition from Peru to Chile by conquistador Diego de Almagro and his four hundred men ends in death for most of the party.

1541 Pedro de Valdivia, a lieutenant of Francisco Pizarro, founds Santiago de Chile; a feudal system in which

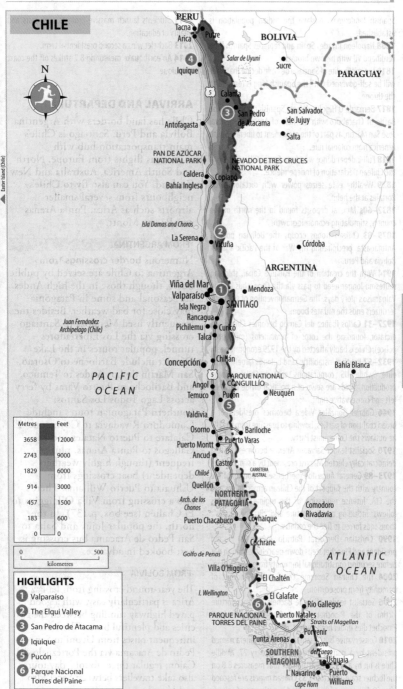

CHILE

N

PERU
Tacna
Arica
Putre
BOLIVIA
Salar de Uyuni
Sucre
Iquique
PARAGUAY
Calama
San Pedro
de Atacama
San Salvador
de Jujuy
Antofagasta
Salta
PAN DE AZÚCAR
NATIONAL PARK
NEVADO DE TRES CRUCES
NATIONAL PARK
Caldera
Copiapó
Bahía Inglesa
Isla Damas and Choros
La Serena
Vicuña
Córdoba
ARGENTINA
Viña del Mar
Mendoza
Valparaíso
Isla Negra
SANTIAGO
Juan Fernández
Archipelago (Chile)
Rancagua
Pichilemu
Curicó
Talca
Chillán
Concepción
Bahía Blanca
PACIFIC
OCEAN
PARQUE NATIONAL
CONGUILLÍO
Angol
Temuco
Pucón
Neuquén
Valdivia
Osorno
Bariloche
Puerto Varas
Puerto Montt
Ancud
Castro
Chiloé
CARRETERA
AUSTRAL
Quellón
NORTHERN
PATAGONIA
Arch. de los
Chonos
Comodoro
Rivadavia
Puerto Chacabuco
Coyhaique
Cochrane
Golfo de Penas
Villa O'Higgins
ATLANTIC
OCEAN
I. Wellington
El Chaltén
El Calafate
Río Gallegos
PARQUE NACIONAL
TORRES DEL PAINE
Puerto Natales
Straits of Magellan
Porvenir
Punta Arenas
Tierra
del Fuego
SOUTHERN
PATAGONIA
I. Navarino
Ushuaia
Puerto
Williams
Cape Horn

Metres	Feet
3658	12000
2743	9000
1829	6000
914	3000
457	1500
183	600
0	0

0   500
kilometres

HIGHLIGHTS
1 Valparaíso
2 The Elqui Valley
3 San Pedro de Atacama
4 Iquique
5 Pucón
6 Parque Nacional
Torres del Paine

Easter Island (Chile)

4

Spanish landowners enslave the Indian population is established.

1808 Napoleon invades Spain and replaces Spanish King Ferdinand VII with his own brother.

1810 The *criollo* elite of Santiago de Chile decide that Chile will be self-governed until the Spanish king is restored to the throne.

1817 Bernardo O'Higgins defeats Spanish royalists in the Battle of Chacabuco with the help of Argentine general José San Martín, as part of the movement to liberate South America from colonial rule.

1818 Full independence won from Spain. O'Higgins signs the Chilean Declaration of Independence.

1829 Wealthy elite seizes power with dictator Diego Portales at the helm.

1832–60s Mineral deposits found in the north of the country, stimulating economic growth.

1879–83 Chilean troops occupy the Bolivian port of Antofagasta, precipitating the War of the Pacific against Bolivia and Peru.

1914 With the creation of the Panama Canal, shipping routes no longer need to pass via the Cape, thus ending Valparaíso's glory days. The German invention of synthetic fertilizers ends the nitrates boom.

1927–31 Carlos Ibáñez del Campo becomes Chile's first dictator, founding the corps of *carabineros* (militarized police); Chile is badly affected by the 1929 economic crash.

1932–52 Political instability: land belongs largely to the elite, while US corporations control Chile's copper production. Seeds are sewn of a political divide between left and conservative right.

1946 Gabriel González Videla becomes president of a broad coalition of parties; bowing to pressure from the US, he outlaws the Communist Party.

1970 Socialist leader Salvador Allende becomes the first democratically elected Marxist president by a slim margin.

1973–89 General Augusto Pinochet seizes control of the country with the support of the Chilean armed forces and the CIA. Intense repression of the regime's opponents follows, including arrests, torture and "disappearances"; thousands forced to flee the country.

1990 Christian Democrat Patricio Aylwin is elected president and Pinochet steps down peacefully, though not before securing constitutional immunity from prosecution.

2004 The Chilean Supreme Court strips Pinochet of immunity from prosecution.

2006 Socialist leader Michelle Bachelet, former torture victim of the Pinochet regime, is elected president. Pinochet dies under house arrest.

2010 Conservative businessman Sebastián Piñera named president by a narrow margin. On February 27, Middle Chile is hit by a massive earthquake that measures 8.8 on the Richter scale. In October, 33 Chilean miners are rescued after 69 days trapped underground in a mine near Copiapó.

2011 Students launch massive protests over costs and quality of education.

2013 Bachelet wins a second presidential term.

2014 An earthquake measuring 8.2 strikes off the coast of Iquique.

ARRIVAL AND DEPARTURE

Chile has land borders with Argentina, Bolivia and Peru. Santiago is Chile's main transportation hub with numerous flights from Europe, North and South America, Australia and New Zealand. You can also fly to Chile's neighbours from several smaller airports such as Arica, Punta Arenas and Puerto Montt.

FROM ARGENTINA

Numerous **border crossings** from Argentina to Chile are served by public buses, though those in the high Andes are seasonal and some in Patagonia may close for bad weather. Besides the frequently used Mendoza to Santiago crossing via the Los Libertadores tunnel, popular routes in the Lake District include Bariloche to Osorno, San Martín de Los Andes to Temuco, and Bariloche to Puerto Varas by ferry across Lago Todos Los Santos. Southern Patagonian routes include Comodoro Rivadavia to Coyhaique, El Calafate to Puerto Natales and Río Gallegos to Punta Arenas, plus frequent (though highly weather-dependent) boat crossings from Ushuaia to Puerto Williams. There's also a crossing from Villa O'Higgins to El Chaltén (see box, p.137). In the north, the popular Jujuy and Salta to San Pedro de Atacama bus crossing is best booked in advance.

FROM BOLIVIA

The year-round crossing from La Paz to Arica is particularly easy, with a good paved highway running between the two cities and plentiful buses. There are infrequent buses from Uyuni to San Pedro de Atacama via the Portezuelo del Cajón; regular three- to four-day tours also take travellers between San Pedro and Uyuni.

FROM PERU

Frequent buses, *colectivos* and taxis serve the year-round crossing from Tacna to Arica.

VISAS

Citizens of the European Union, the United States, Canada, South Africa, Australia and New Zealand do not require **visas**, though citizens of Canada (US$132) and Australia (US$95) are subject to **one-off arrival fees**; at the time of writing there was talk of abolishing these fees. Tourists are routinely granted ninety-day entry permits and must surrender their tourist cards upon departure. In theory, visitors can be asked to produce an onward ticket and proof of sufficient funds, though that rarely happens. Ninety-day **visa extensions** can be granted by the Departamento de Extranjería, San Antonio 580, Piso 2, Santiago Centro (Mon–Fri 8.30am–2pm, calls taken 9am–4pm; ☎600 626 4222, ⓦextranjeria.gob.cl/ingles/), at a cost of US$100, although it may be cheaper and easier simply to cross the border into a neighbouring country and back again. If you lose your tourist card, you can get a replacement from the Policía Internacional, Morande 672, Santiago (☎2 2690 1010, ⓦpolicia.cl).

GETTING AROUND

Most Chileans travel by bus, and it's such a reliable and inexpensive option that you'll probably do the same. However, domestic flights are handy for covering long distances in a hurry.

BY PLANE

Several airlines offer frequent and reasonably priced flights within Chile. You'll often find better fares by booking locally, rather than in advance from home. **LAN** (☎600 526 2000, ⓦlan.com) is the most established airline with efficient online booking, last-minute discounts and a good-value "Visit South America Air Pass". **Sky Airline** (☎600 600 2828, ⓦwww.skyairline.cl) also has daily flights between Chile's major cities, and is

generally cheaper. Punta Arenas-based **Aerovías DAP** (☎61 261 6100, ⓦaeroviasdap.cl) flies to various destinations in Chilean and Argentine Patagonia and Tierra del Fuego; it's best to book tickets directly at the airline offices as their website is inefficient.

BY TRAIN

Chile has a very limited railway network. In Middle Chile a reliable and comfortable service operated by Terrasur (ⓦwww.tmsa.cl) usually runs several times a day between Santiago and Chillán, with stops at intermediate stations including Rancagua and Talca.

BY BUS

Bus travel is popular, affordable and convenient. The level of comfort depends on how much you are prepared to pay, with the *cama* buses generally being the plushest, their seats reclining almost horizontally. The cheapest seats from Santiago to Arica cost around CH$42,000, and from Santiago to Puerto Montt CH$18,000; shop around as there are often promotions.

Bus tickets are valid only for specified buses, and the major bus companies, such as **Tur-Bus** (☎600 660 6600, ⓦturbus.cl) and **Pullman** (☎600 320 3200, ⓦpullman.cl), require you to buy your ticket before you board – though for most routes you'll have no trouble purchasing tickets at the bus station shortly before your departure. That said, south of Puerto Montt, and especially during the peak months, demand outstrips supply, so it is advisable to book in advance if you are on a tight schedule. Bus station kiosks are the easiest option – online booking services are available but usually cannot process foreign credit cards. If crossing **international** borders by bus, remember that it's prohibited to transport animal and plant matter to neighbouring countries, and luggage searches are frequent.

Smaller **local buses** and minibuses (*micros*) connect city centres with outlying neighbourhoods and smaller towns with villages. In some parts of Chile, especially in the north, *colectivos*

4

4

PACHAMAMA BY BUS

The hop-on, hop-off **Pachamama by Bus** service is tailored for independent travellers and designed to cover the most scenic spots in the Lake District and the Atacama Desert. You purchase a pass for the number of days you wish to travel – a seven-day pass costs CH$138,000 – and you can stay at any of the given stops. There are weekly departures on both routes; too book a pass, contact the office inside the *Casa Roja* hostel (see p.388) in Santiago in advance (☏ 2 2688 8018, ⓦ pachamamabybus.com).

(shared taxis with fixed fares) provide a faster and only slightly pricier service between towns than local buses.

BY FERRY

South of Puerto Montt, where Chile breaks up into a plethora of islands and fjords, you will have to take a **ferry**, whether to continue along the Carretera Austral or to work your way down to Southern Patagonia. Travelling south by boat is more expensive than going by bus, but it allows you access to some of the remotest and most beautiful parts of Chile. Popular routes include Puerto Montt to Puerto Natales, Puerto Montt to Chacabuco and Chacabuco to Laguna San Rafael.

BY CAR

Car rental is costly (around CH$30,000–40,000/day) and complicated, with expensive insurance due to the varying condition of the dirt roads. Carrying spare tyres, a jack, extra petrol and plenty of drinking water is essential for driving around more remote parts of Chile, and punctures are frequent. Since public transport is perfectly adequate in most parts of the country, the only places where it may make sense to rent a **4WD vehicle** is on Easter Island, and perhaps to some national parks. To rent a car, you need to be over 21 years old; take your passport as ID, and have a national driver's licence and major credit card on hand.

HITCHING

Hitchhiking remains popular in Chile, especially in rural areas. While it's never an entirely safe method of travel, Chile is probably the safest country in Latin America in which to hitch, although it's always best to do so at least in pairs.

BY BIKE

Cycling can be a good way of getting to the more remote national parks, some of which are inaccessible by public transport. It's a good idea to carry spare parts, although bike repair shops are found in most medium-sized towns. While in the south of Chile **drinking water** can typically be acquired from streams, in the northern half of the country it is highly advisable to carry your own, and essential if cycling anywhere in the arid Atacama region. There are few cycle lanes, and for the most part cyclists share the road with motorists; at least traffic outside cities tends to be light. Stray dogs can also be a nuisance in populated areas.

ACCOMMODATION

Chile has a wide range of **budget accommodation**. Prices are highest during the peak season from December to February, when Chileans go on summer holiday; in shoulder seasons, they generally drop by around twenty percent. Many lodgings in the south of Chile close down during the winter months, so check ahead. Prices are normally listed inclusive of tax (or IVA: 19 percent) but it is best to establish this at the start of your stay; many hotels give foreigners the opportunity to pay in US dollars, which exempts you from paying IVA – they may need to be reminded of this.

RESIDENCIALES, CABAÑAS AND REFUGIOS

Residenciales are the most commonly available budget lodgings, found in both large cities and villages. Typically they consist of furnished rooms in someone's home, often with breakfast included; not surprisingly, the quality varies enormously. A basic double room will cost about CH$20,000; single rooms can cost as much as two-thirds the price of doubles.

Cabañas are usually found in well-visited spots, particularly by the ocean. They tend to come with a fully equipped kitchen, bathroom and bedrooms, and can be a great option for those travelling in groups. Depending on the time of year, a cabaña for two people costs from about CH$30,000. Lower rates can be negotiated for larger groups.

Refugios are inexpensive (except those in Torres del Paine National Park), bare-bones lodgings found in national parks, usually consisting of several bunk beds in a wooden hut. Most have clean bedding, showers and flushable toilets; some require you to bring your own sleeping bag. Costs are around CH$5000–15,000 per person. Many *refugios* stay open year-round, but if you are planning on wilderness trekking, or on travelling in the south of Chile in the winter, try to arrange lodgings by calling the local **Conaf** office (⟟www .conaf.cl), Chile's national forestry service, in advance; individual offices are listed on its website.

HOSTELS AND CAMPING

Hostel options are plentiful across the country, especially in well-visited cities and popular outdoor destinations; dorm beds cost around CH$10,000. Some independent hostel groups compile booklets listing the best hostels, which are worth picking up. **Backpackers Chile**, for example (⟟backpackerschile.com), offer a reliable benchmark for high-quality hostels. The booklet is available from any of the hostels listed on the site, and at major information offices. Also worth picking up is the **Get South** booklet (⟟getsouth.com), which offers discounts and freebies for various hostels across Chile, as well as Argentina and Uruguay.

Most major cities and key tourist centres have a **Hostelling International**-affiliated hostel (⟟hihostels.com), for which member discounts will be available. The quality of HI hostels is not necessarily better than independent hostels, though they do tend to meet basic standards, so can be preferable to some budget hotels.

Note that in some widely visited places, such as Pucón and San Pedro de Atacama, a **hostal** may not necessarily mean a bona fide youth hostel – in many cases they are simply family homes.

Chile has marvellous opportunities for **camping**, with a proliferation of both fully equipped campsites (which can be somewhat pricey) and beautiful wilderness spots. There is ample free camping on empty beaches, although in most national parks you should only camp in designated spots. *Campings y Rutas Chile*, published only in Spanish by Turistel, and updated annually, has an extensive, though not entirely complete, list of campsites around Chile.

FOOD AND DRINK

Chile has an abundance of fresh produce, but outside the bigger cities and tourist destinations **food** can be a little bland, though *pebre* (a spicy salsa served with bread) and *ají chileno*, served with barbecued meat, can liven things up. **Breakfast** (*desayuno*) consists of coffee and the ubiquitous pockmarked bread with butter and jam. **Lunch** (*almuerzo*) is the main meal of the day, typically made up of three courses; at lunchtime most restaurants offer a good-value fixed-price *menú del día*. **Dinner** (*cena*) is usually served late, rarely before 9pm, and in Chilean households is often replaced by a lighter **evening snack** (*once*). Restaurants generally open from around 7pm but don't start to fill up until around 9pm.

Chicken and beef are the commonest **meats**, the latter often served boiled or grilled with a fried egg on top (*lomo a lo pobre*) or as part of a *parillada* (mixed grill). Two dishes found on menus across the country are *cazuela*, a hearty meat casserole, and *pastel de choclo*, a sweet-tasting corn and beef pie. When in Patagonia, do not miss the *asador patagónico*, spit-roasted lamb (*cordero*) and wild boar (*jabalí*) steaks, while llama and alpaca steaks and stew are a staple of *altiplano* cuisine in the north of Chile. Both Chiloé and Easter Island serve up *curanto*, an elaborately prepared dish of meat and seafood.

4

There is a fantastic range of **fish and seafood**. Fish are typically served *frito* (battered and deep-fried), or *a la plancha* (grilled) with different sauces, and trendy sushi bars are springing up everywhere. Alternatively, try the *ceviche* – raw fish marinated in lemon juice with coriander. Excellent seafood dishes include *machas a la parmesana*, baked razor clams covered with parmesan cheese, *chupe de locos*, creamy abalone casserole topped with breadcrumbs, and *paila marina*, seafood soup.

Some excellent vegetarian restaurants have appeared in recent years, but decent vegetarian cuisine may be hard to find outside major cities and tourist destinations. Delicious **fruit and vegetables** are abundant in most parts of Chile, barring Patagonia and Tierra del Fuego. The north of the country grows exotic delights like scaly green *chirimoya* (custard apple), papaya, *tuna* (cactus fruit) and melon-like *pepino dulce*. Easter Island cuisine incorporates Polynesian tubers such as the *camote* (sweet potato).

DRINK

Tap water is generally drinkable all over Chile, with the exception of the Atacama, though Santiago's high mineral content may upset some stomachs. **Mineral water** is inexpensive and comes *sin gas* (still) or *con gas* (carbonated). **Soft drinks** (*gaseosas* or *bebidas*) are plentiful and very popular, and freshly squeezed **fruit juices** (*jugos*) are abundant, especially in the fertile region of Middle Chile; most Chileans like their juice sweetened, so if you don't want a half-juice, half-sugar concoction, ask for it *sin azúcar* (without sugar).

Licuados are fruit smoothies mixed with water or *leche* (milk). *Mote con huesillo*, a drink made from boiled, dried apricots, is popular, especially in Middle Chile.

It can be surprisingly difficult to find real **coffee** (*café de grano*) in smaller towns, with Nescafé unfathomably popular, but coffee shops are appearing thick and fast across Santiago and other cities. In the Lake District and Patagonia, thanks to the influence of Argentine culture, you are likely to encounter *yerba mate*, an antioxidant-rich, energizing herb drunk from a gourd through a metal straw.

Chile has several generic lager **beers** including Escudo, Cristal and Austral; the best beers come from microbreweries, with Kunstmann being the pick of the bunch. Chileans often start meals with a refreshing **pisco sour**, the national drink (see box, p.404).

Chilean **wine**, renowned worldwide, features on many restaurant menus. Wine tourism is also on the rise, with the Rutas del Vino (Wine Routes) in the Maule and Colchagua valleys giving visitors easy access to both the process of wine-making and the sampling of many different varieties.

CULTURE AND ETIQUETTE

Chilean city lifestyle, superficially at least, has more similarities with Europe than with neighbouring Bolivia or Peru. Bargaining is not common and rarely done, even in marketplaces, though Chileans are often excellent at seeking out bargain prices. When eating out, a ten-percent **tip** in restaurants is normal and appreciated.

EATING ON A BUDGET

Prices at some restaurants in places like Santiago and Valparaíso can give the impression that you have to break the bank to enjoy good food in Chile, but there are cheaper options.

In coastal towns, you can pick up superb fish at bargain prices at little **marisquerías**, rustic fish eateries usually found at the busiest point of the seafront. In most large cities, look out for the **market** area where you'll get excellent deals on fruit and vegetables.

Small **kiosks** along city streets and country roads will often sell delicious and filling snacks like *empanadas* (savoury pasties filled with meat or fish) and *humitas* (ground corn wrapped in leaves).

American-style **diners** and home-grown fast-food chains across Chile sell huge *completes*, hot dogs, and *italianos*, hot dogs covered in mayonnaise, ketchup and avocado, as well as a range of sandwiches, like *barros jarpa* (melted cheese and ham), as alternative cheap eats.

Chileans are family- and **child-oriented**, and young people tend to live with their parents until they get married. The predominant religion is **Catholicism**, though the Church is not as influential as it used to be. Machismo is not as prevalent here as in other parts of Latin America; **women** are more respected and a lone woman travelling around the country is not likely to encounter any trouble beyond catcalls. While **homosexuality** is still frowned upon, it is tolerated, and there is a thriving gay scene in larger cities.

Chileans are very **sociable** and will go out of their way to greet you in the street if they know you. If arranging to go out with Chileans, be aware that they may turn up later than the arranged time. When it comes to topics of conversation, Pinochet's brutal rule often provokes a heated discussion.

SPORTS AND OUTDOOR ACTIVITIES

While Chile is not quite in the same league as Argentina or Brazil when it comes to **football**, the game is taken very seriously and attending a live match in Santiago is very worthwhile for the atmosphere alone. Be aware, though, that the passion for football can turn aggressive, and be ready to make an exit. Santiago team Colo Colo has the largest and most enthusiastic following.

Every year, over three hundred **rodeos** are staged during the season (Sept–May) in Middle Chile and Aisén in particular. Evolved from the rural *huaso* (cowboy) culture, the rodeo is a spectacle worth going out of your way for.

La cueca, Chile's national **dance**, is also firmly rooted in *huaso* culture; it re-enacts the courting ritual between a rooster and a hen. Men and women clad in traditional outfits dance largely to guitar-led ballads, though the tempo and the instruments vary from region to region. *La cueca* is most commonly seen during the Chilean independence celebrations in September, when troupes perform on streets and stages across the country, though Chileans often take little

persuading to show off their beloved dance whatever the opportunity.

WATERSPORTS

The mighty rivers of the Lake District and Patagonia offer excellent **white-water rafting** and **kayaking**, with Río Trancura, Río Petrohué and Río Futaleufú offering class V challenges. Futaleufú in particular is hailed as one of the top white-water runs in the world.

Sea kayakers can choose between multi-day paddling in the Patagonian fjords, shorter trips to small islands off the coast of Chiloé and wildlife-viewing on Isla Damas near La Serena.

Surfers head to Chile's top spot, Pichilemu, just south of Santiago, though there are excellent surfing and **windsurfing** opportunities all along the coast north of the capital, around Iquique in particular, and year-round swells on Easter Island.

In the northern half of the country, lack of rain makes for good visibility and abundant marine life for **divers** and **snorkellers**, while Easter Island and the Juan Fernández Archipelago both have world-class dive spots.

HIKING, CLIMBING AND SKIING

Hiking in the Torres del Paine National Park, on Isla Navarino or anywhere in the south is limited to the summer, spring and autumn, but the rest of Chile can be visited at any time of year. There are currently 65 **Rutas Patrimoniales** (ⓦwww .bienesnacionales.cl) covering the whole of Chile as part of a government initiative to preserve and develop land that has natural and historical value. These can all be explored on foot, by bike or on horseback. Another ambitious project, **Sendero de Chile** (ⓦwww.senderodechile .cl), consists of 35 trail sections intended to span the whole of Chile, including its Pacific islands. Once completed, it will become the longest trekking route in the world, but progress on the project is currently slow.

Ice climbers will find excellent **climbing** routes in the Central and Patagonian Andes from November to March, with plenty of accessible glaciers, while the granite towers of Torres del Paine rank among the world's most challenging rock climbs. Middle Chile and the Lake District, however, have the greatest variety of climbing and mountaineering spots.

Along with Argentina, Chile has world-class powder snow, with some of the best **skiing** spots found within easy reach of Santiago (see box, p.391). The Lake District's Villarica-Pucón and Osorno give you the opportunity to whizz down the slopes of volcanoes.

CYCLING

Spectacular **cycling** terrain can be found from Norte Grande to Tierra del Fuego, though you will need a sturdy mountain bike to cope with the potholed trails. While the best time to cycle around much of Chile is between October and March, Norte Chico and Norte Grande can be explored year-round, though altitude is often a consideration, especially if you're planning on exploring Parque Nacional Lauca. Norte Chico offers easy and enjoyable coastal rides, while the Lake District and Chiloé have the greatest variety of cycling routes, and the Carretera Austral is a challenging undertaking that rewards with amazing scenery.

COMMUNICATIONS

Overseas mail sent from any part of Chile via Correos de Chile, Chile's **postal service**, generally takes two or three weeks to reach its destination. Important shipping to Chile is best sent via registered mail.

Chile has a number of different telecoms operators, and in order to make an **international call**, you dial the three-digit carrier code of the telecom, followed by 0, then the country code and finally the phone number itself. Most local numbers consist of seven or eight digits, preceded by the city/area code; if dialling from the same area, drop the city or area code and dial the six or seven digits directly. In 2013, the government completed the roll-out of a new numbering system, adding a 2 to the start of every fixed-line number; many

businesses have still not updated their details. Mobile phone numbers are eight digits and start with a 9, 8, 7, 6 or 5; if you're phoning from a landline, you need to use the prefix "09". Calls abroad from the numerous **centros de llamadas** to most European countries and North America cost around CH$150–250/min, although prices vary from area to area. Many internet cafés in Chile are Skype-equipped. Alternatively, get an inexpensive Chilean **SIM card** for an "unlocked" mobile phone.

Internet/wi-fi is widely available across Chile and provided by virtually all hotels and hostels. Most towns and villages have **internet cafés**, where access costs around CH$300–600/hr, although on Isla Navarino and Easter Island it is considerably pricier.

CRIME AND SAFETY

The risk of **violent crime** in Chile is very low; in larger cities pickpocketing and petty thievery are minor concerns, but assaults are practically unknown, and there is very little corruption among Chilean police.

CHILE ONLINE

Chilean Austral ⓦ chileaustral.com. Dedicated to tourism in Chilean Patagonia, including city guides, national parks, hotels and weather forecasts.

I Love Chile ⓦ ilovechile.cl. Useful site with news, features, music and blogs, plus its own online radio station.

Latin America Bureau ⓦ lab.org.uk. Site of a well-respected UK-based charity has the latest news, analysis and information from across the region, including Chile.

Santiago Times ⓦ santiagotimes.cl. English-language newspaper, based in the capital.

South American Explorers ⓦ saexplorers.org. Useful site of the long-established travel NGO. Offers travel advisories and warnings, trip reports and a bulletin board.

Turismo Chile ⓦ chiletourism.travel. Descriptions of the major attractions in each region, with some historical and cultural background.

HEALTH

There are no compulsory **vaccinations** for Chile, though there have been reported incidents of mosquito-borne **dengue fever** on Easter Island; use insect repellent. **Hantavirus**, caused by inhaling or ingesting rat droppings, is uncommon but deadly: when staying in rural buildings that could potentially have rodents, air them out thoroughly and do not sleep on the floor. Chile has two species of **spider** with a venomous and potentially dangerous bite: the black widow (found in parts of Torres del Paine National Park, among other areas) and the Chilean recluse spider (found throughout Chile). The recluse – or *araña del rincón,* literally "corner spider" – is commonly found in houses. Though bites from either spider are relatively rare, they can prove fatal – if you think you may have been bitten, seek medical help immediately.

INFORMATION AND MAPS

Official **Sernatur** tourist offices (Servicio Nacionalde Turismo; ⊛www.sernatur.cl) are found in all the major cities and towns. They produce a plethora of brochures on local attractions, accommodation and outdoor activities, though some are better stocked than others. Some regions also have a **municipal tourism office** run by the regional authorities. For information on Chile's natural attractions, as well as maps and up-to-date trekking conditions for specific areas, you should head to the local **Conaf** office (Corporación Nacional Forestal, ⊛www.conaf.cl), again found in most towns.

JLM Cartografía maps are usually accurate and helpful, and can be found in most bookshops; they cover both cities and trekking routes in Chile. The Instituto Geográfico Militar (⊛igm.cl) produces detailed topographic maps of the entire country, but they can be pricey.

MONEY AND BANKS

The **peso** is the basic unit of Chilean currency, and it comes in 1000, 5000, 10,000 and rare 20,000 denomination notes, and 10, 20, 50, 100 and 500 peso coins. It is usually represented with the $ sign, not to be confused with US$. Few places will accept US dollars or other foreign currencies, though some hostels and hotels may suggest you pay in dollars to avoid the nineteen percent IVA tax (value added tax) on accommodation, from which foreigners are exempted when paying in dollars. Chile is fairly expensive compared to its Latin American counterparts (besides Brazil), with prices comparable to those in North America and Europe.

At the time of writing, the exchange rate was £1 = CH$954; US$1 = CH$612 and €1 = CH$752.

Large and medium-sized cities have plentiful **banks** and **ATMs**; Banco de Chile and Santander are good bets for withdrawing cash with debit cards. Santiago and most of the more visited destinations have casas de cambio which can change travellers' cheques and foreign currencies at a reasonable rate. Some smaller towns only have Banco Estado ATMs, which generally accept

4

4

PUBLIC HOLIDAYS

January 1 New Year's Day (*Año Nuevo*)
Easter (*Semana Santa*) national holidays on Good Friday, Holy Saturday and Easter Sunday
May 1 Labour Day (*Día del Trabajo*)
May 21 Navy Day (*Día de las Glorias Navales*) marking Chile's naval victory at Iquique during the War of the Pacific
June 29 St Peter and St Paul (*San Pedro y San Pablo*)
July 16 Our Lady of Mount Carmel (*Solemnidad de la Virgen del Carmen, Reina y Patrona de Chile*)
August 15 Assumption of the Virgin Mary (*Asunción de la Virgen*)
September 17 If it falls on a Monday, an extension of Independence celebrations

September 18 National Independence Day (*Fiestas Patrias*) celebrates Chile's proclamation of independence from Spain in 1810
September 19 Armed Forces Day (*Día del Ejército*)
September 20 If it falls on a Friday, an extension of Independence celebrations
October 12 Columbus Day (*Día del Descubrimiento de Dos Mundos*) celebrates the European discovery of the Americas
November 1 All Saints' Day (*Día de Todos los Santos*)
December 8 Immaculate Conception (*Inmaculada Concepción*)
December 25 Christmas Day (*Navidad*)

only Cirrus and MasterCard. If you are heading to small towns off the beaten track, it's wise to carry enough cash to cover a few days as ATMs are not always reliable. **Credit cards** can also be widely used to pay for purchases, especially in larger towns, though budget lodgings and eating places rarely accept them.

OPENING HOURS AND HOLIDAYS

On weekdays, most services and **shops** tend to be open from 9 or 10am to 6 or 7pm; Saturday hours are usually 10 or 11am to 2pm. In smaller towns, **restaurants** are often closed in the afternoon between the lunchtime hours of 1 to 3pm and the dinnertime hours of 8 to 11pm. An increasing number of restaurants, bars and shops open on Sundays, but smaller places, particularly in more rural areas, generally remain closed.

Banks typically operate from 9am to 2pm on weekdays only, while post offices generally open Monday to Friday from 9am to 6pm; in larger towns, they also open Saturdays from 9am to 1pm. Monday is a day off for most **museums**; they are, however, usually open on Sundays, often with free entry. Shops and services are closed during national holidays, local festivals and on local and national election days.

Santiago

Towered over by the snow-streaked Andes, **SANTIAGO** has a distinctly European feel. Its rich pockets of culture and history are often overlooked by travellers frustrated by a lack of iconic sights, and put off by the smog that hangs over the city. Yet those prepared to venture beyond the grid of central shopping streets will be rewarded with quirky, vibrant neighbourhoods filled with a huge variety of lively bars and excellent restaurants. Streetscapes flit between elegant colonial buildings and high-rise office blocks. The city is a microcosm of the country's contrasting ways of life, with ramshackle markets, smart office buildings, rough-and-ready bars and plush shopping malls all just a short metro ride from the main square.

Home to more than a quarter of Chile's population, the capital is crowded but easy to navigate with a clean and efficient metro system. And even if the city itself fails to impress, Santiago is an excellent base from which to explore, with world-class ski resorts, sun-kissed beaches and beautiful vineyards all within easy reach.

WHAT TO SEE AND DO

Downtown Santiago is loosely bordered by the **Río Mapocho** to the north, and the central thoroughfare of Avenida Libertador

Bernado O'Higgins – commonly known as **La Alameda** – to the south. The city's accommodation and most inviting *barrios* are all a short distance from this central section. Bohemian **Barrio Lastarria** is home to a wealth of art museums, cool restaurants and boutique shops with bags of character. North of the river, grungy **Barrio Bellavista** offers buzzing nightlife as well as the city's best viewpoint at **Cerro San Cristóbal**. In the west, down-to-earth **Barrio Brasil** and **Barrio Yungay** are home to many budget hostels and good-value restaurants, while out east, the tree-lined streets of upmarket **Providencia** and plush **Las Condes** are pocketed with luxury hotels and shopping malls.

Plaza de Armas

Pedro de Valdivia, the city's founder, intended the lush tree-studded **Plaza de Armas** to be a centrepiece for Chile, surrounding it with splendid colonial architecture. The oldest building is the **Catedral Metropolitana** (1748), on the west side of the plaza, its Neoclassical facade designed by the Italian architect Joaquín Toesca. To the north is the **Palacio de la Real Audiencia** (1804), housing the Museo Histórico Nacional, and the **Correo Central**. A lively gathering point since the mid-1800s, the plaza's flower gardens and the fountain in the centre honouring Simón Bolívar attract a multitude of chess players, mimes, buskers, vagrants, stray dogs, soap-box preachers, strolling families and giggling children, making the square an ideal place to linger on a bench and people-watch.

Mercado Central and La Vega

By the south bank of Río Mapocho lies the lively **Mercado Central** (daily 6am–4pm), a mass of stalls spilling over with wondrous fish and seafood, dotted with busy little *marisquerías* whose delicious smells draw crowds of customers at lunchtime. All of this is gathered inside an elaborate metal structure prefabricated in Birmingham, England, and erected in Santiago in 1868. Cross the Río Mapocho and you reach **La Vega** (daily: roughly 6am–5pm), an enormous roofed market surrounded by outdoor stalls, selling all kinds of fresh produce, with fruit and vegetables at rock-bottom prices. La Vega is full of local character, giving you a glimpse of "real" Santiago: fragrant, pungent and chaotic. It's also the best place in town to grab a giant fruit smoothie, as well as excellent seafood.

Museo Chileno de Arte Precolombino

The excellent **Museo Chileno de Arte Precolombino** (Tues–Sun 10am–6pm; CH$3500, ⓦmuseoprecolombino.cl), at Bandera 361, is housed in the elegant late-colonial Real Casa de Aduana (Royal Customs House, 1807). The unparalleled collection of pre-Columbian artefacts spans around ten thousand years and covers the whole of Latin America, from Mexico down to the south of Chile. More than 1500 examples of pottery, finely woven textiles and jewellery are on display, including permanent collections from the Andes, Mesoamerica, the Amazon and the Caribbean, and there are outstanding temporary exhibitions.

La Moneda

The restored **Palacio de la Moneda**, (☎2 2690 4000) on the large **Plaza de la Constitución**, is the presidential palace and site of the dramatic siege that brought Pinochet to power on September 11, 1973, and led to the death of President Salvador Allende. A wide, squat Neoclassical construction, originally built to house the Royal Mint, the palace stages an elaborate **changing of the guard** on alternating days at 10am (weekdays) or 11am (weekends), featuring white-jacketed officers, cavalry and an inspired brass band. The palace's inner courtyards can be accessed through the North Gate (Mon–Fri 10am–6pm), and the basement features a huge relief map of Chile that allows visitors to get an accurate impression of the country's size. There are four free tours each day (ⓔvisitas @presidencia.cl). The **Centro Cultural Palacio La Moneda** (daily 9am–9pm; exhibitions CH$5000, half-price Mon–Fri before noon; ⓦccplm.cl), a smart, arty space, is home to exhibitions, craft shops and cafés and is accessed by steps to the left and right of the palace's main frontage.

4

Cerro Santa Lucía

Six blocks east of Palacio de la Moneda along the Alameda, Santiago's main thoroughfare (officially Avenida Libertador Bernardo O'Higgins), the splendidly landscaped **Cerro Santa Lucía** (Dec–Feb 9am–8pm; rest of the year 9am–7pm; free), is the historically significant promontory where Pedro de Valdivia defeated the indigenous forces (to whom it is known as Huelén – "the curse"), and where Santiago was officially founded on February 12, 1541. The barren hill was transformed into a lush

SANTIAGO

■ ACCOMMODATION
Casa Bonita	6
Casa Condell	1
La Casa Roja	2
Hostel Cienfugos	3
EcoHostel	5
Landay Barceló	4

0 500 metres

retreat through the labour of 150 prisoners in the 1870s. The park's peaceful winding footpaths and the ornate Terraza Neptuno fountain draw amorous couples, while visitors take the steep footpaths to the top to be rewarded with **panoramic views** of the city.

Parque Forestal

It's hard to believe that the tranquil green space of the **Parque Forestal**, stretching along the Río Mapocho's south bank, was once a floodplain covered in rubbish dumps. Top attraction here is the grand and airy Neoclassical Palacio de Bellas

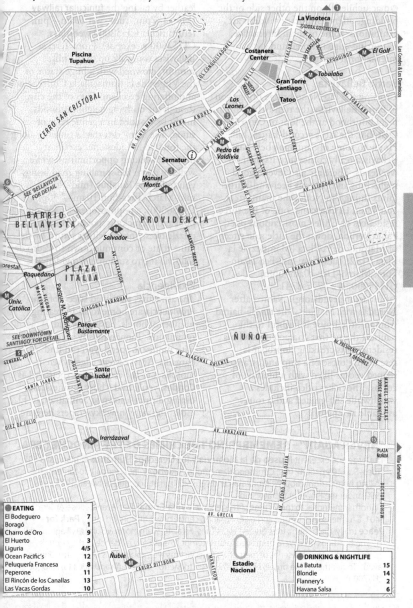

4

● EATING	
El Bodeguero	7
Boragó	1
Charro de Oro	9
El Huerto	3
Liguria	4/5
Ocean Pacific's	12
Peluquería Francesa	8
Peperone	11
El Rincón de los Canallas	13
Las Vacas Gordas	10

● DRINKING & NIGHTLIFE	
La Batuta	15
Blondie	14
Flannery's	2
Havana Salsa	6

Artes, housing the **Museo de Bellas Artes** (Tues–Sun 10am–6.50pm; free; ☎2 2499 1600, ⓦmnba.cl), which features paintings, sculptures, prints and drawings by predominantly Chilean artists. The **Museo de Arte Contemporáneo**, or **MAC** (same hours and price; ☎2 2977 1741, ⓦmac.uchile.cl), on the other side of the building, offers temporary modern art exhibitions, some of them interactive, by cutting-edge national and international artists.

Barrio Bellavista

Crossing the Pío Nono bridge brings you to **Barrio Bellavista**, the trendy bohemian neighbourhood at the foot of **Cerro San Cristóbal**, the city's second-largest hill. Home to some of Santiago's best **bars**, Bellavista really comes into its own on weekends. There are also several good nightclubs and raucous beer-and-burger joints lining Pío Nono, the main street. You'll find **La Chascona**, one of the three residences of Chile's most famous poet, **Pablo Neruda**, down the little side street of Márquez de la Plata (Márquez de la Plata 0192; Tues–Sun: Jan–Feb 10am–7pm; March–Dec 10am–6pm; CH$5000; ☎2 2777 8741, ⓦfundacionneruda.org). Named after Neruda's wife Matilde, "the tangle-haired woman", the house is faithful to the nautical theme that characterizes all his residences, its creaking floorboards resembling those of a ship and strangely shaped rooms filled with a lifetime of curios. The ticket price includes a worthwhile self-guided audio tour, available in English.

Cerro San Cristóbal

A path winds up from Barrio Bellavista's Plaza Caupolicán to Terraza Bellavista, passing Santiago's modest **zoo** (Tues–Sun: April–Sept 10am–6pm; Oct–March 10am–7pm; CH$3000, students CH$1500). Or you can save some shoe leather by taking the **funicular railway** (Mon 1–7pm; Tues–Sun 10am–7pm; return ticket CH$2000 weekdays, CH$2600 weekends). From Terraza Bellavista you walk up to the hill's summit, crowned with a huge statue of the Virgen de la Immaculada Concepción and offering excellent views of the city, though the outlying neighbourhoods might be clouded in a gentle haze of smog. The many dirt tracks running along the forested hillsides offer excellent mountain-biking opportunities, while walking down the spiralling road brings you to **Piscina Tupahue** (mid-Nov to mid-March Tues–Sun 10am–7.30pm; CH$6000), a popular open-air swimming pool and picnicking spot amid monkey puzzle trees. You can either return by the same route or continue down to Pedro de Valdivia metro station in Providencia.

Providencia

The attractive, tree-lined streets of chic **Providencia** are home to an increasing number of hotels, businesses and restaurants. Though mostly aimed at those with money to spend, you can find bargains. At its eastern edge, where it morphs into the even more expensive **Las Condes**, you'll find a busy business and dining district known as Sanhattan, or El Golf. The shiny new skyscrapers here are

---

"NEVER AGAIN" – REMEMBERING THE CRIMES OF THE PINOCHET ERA

The large and excellent **Museo de la Memoria y los Derechos Humanos** at Matucana 501 (Tues–Sun 10am–6pm; free; ⓦmuseodelamemoria.cl; Metro Quinta Normal) documents the chilling human rights abuses, repression and censorship that occurred between 1973 and 1990 under the Pinochet dictatorship.

Another memorial to the victims of the regime is **Villa Grimaldi** at Avenida José Arrieta 8401, a former secret torture and extermination centre now transformed into a **Park for Peace** (daily 10am–6pm; free; guided tours Tues–Fri at 10.30am, noon & 3pm; ⓦvillagrimaldi .cl). The buildings here were destroyed in an attempt to erase any evidence of the centre's existence, but among a series of memorials to its victims are explanations of the site's original layout. To get there, take bus #513, or #D09, or go to Metro Plaza Egaña and get a taxi (about CH$7000).

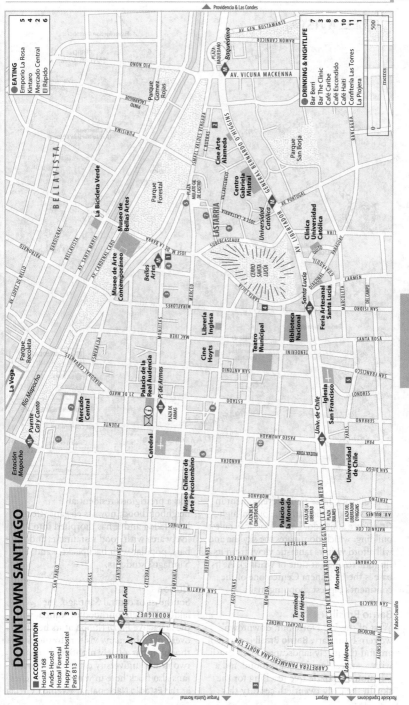

DOWNTOWN SANTIAGO

■ **ACCOMMODATION**
Hostal 168 — 4
Andes Hostel — 1
Hostal Forestal — 2
Happy House Hostel — 3
París 813 — 5

● **EATING**
Emporio La Rosa — 5
Kintaro — 4
Mercado Central — 2
El Rápido — 6

● **DRINKING & NIGHTLIFE**
Bar Berri — 7
Bar The Clinic — 3
Café Caribe — 8
Café Escondido — 9
Café Haití — 10
Confitería Las Torres — 11
La Piojera — 1

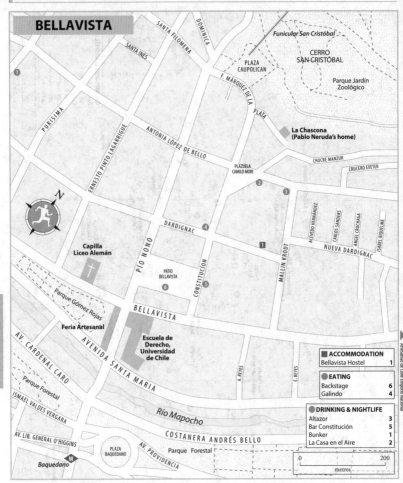

BELLAVISTA

4

ACCOMMODATION
Bellavista Hostel ... 1

EATING
Backstage ... 6
Galindo ... 4

DRINKING & NIGHTLIFE
Altazor ... 3
Bar Constitución ... 5
Bunker ... 1
La Casa en el Aire ... 2

0 ——— 200
metres

symbolic of Chile's rapid development in recent years, particularly the 300m-high **Gran Torre Santiago**, Latin America's tallest building, which dominates the skyline and will afford visitors fantastic views from its tip (due to open at time of writing). At its base is the Costanera Center, one of the continent's biggest shopping malls.

Barrio Brasil

West of the Vía Norte Sur, downtown's western boundary, **Barrio Brasil** is centred around the nicely landscaped Plaza Brasil, with a surreal-looking playground and a tall monkey puzzle tree reaching for the sky. In the early twentieth century this

was a prestigious residential neighbourhood; now its elegant streets have faded and it has morphed into a lively area with good restaurants and bars, popular with backpackers and Santiago's students.

Ñuñoa

Southeast of central Santiago, the laidback neighbourhood of **Ñuñoa**, with the attractive **Plaza Ñuñoa** at its heart, is overlooked by many visitors to the city, though it has a lively **nightlife** thanks to two nearby university campuses. Football fans also flock here to watch the matches at the **Estadio Nacional**, at Avenida Grecia

2001. The stadium has a grim past – it was once used by Pinochet as a torture centre and prison.

ARRIVAL AND DEPARTURE

By plane Aeropuerto Arturo Merino Benítez (☎ 2 2690 1752, ⓦ aeropuertosantiago.cl), 30min from the city centre, has ATMs, currency exchange and a tourist information kiosk. The Centropuerto bus (daily 6am–11.30pm, every 10min; CH$1450 one-way), just outside the terminal doors, is the cheapest way to get to the city centre and stops at Los Héroes metro station. Tur-Bus has transfers to Terminal Alameda (see below) downtown (daily 5am–midnight, every 20min; midnight–5am, hourly; CH$1500; ☎ 2 2822 7448), while TransVip (☎ 2 2677 3000) and Transfer Delfos (☎ 2 2913 8800) charge from CH$7000 to drop you off at your destination.

Destinations LAN and Sky Airline have multiple daily flights to all major Chilean destinations: Arica (hourly; 2hr 45min); Calama (every 30min; 2hr 5min); Iquique (hourly; 2hr 25min); La Serena (hourly; 1hr 5min); Puerto Montt (every 30min; 1hr 40min); Punta Arenas (every 30min; 3hr 25min).

By train Estación Central, Alameda 3322 (ticket sales ☎ 2 2585 5000, ⓦ www.tmsa.cl). Trains leave twice a day for Chillán, stopping at Central Valley towns.

Destinations Chillán (2 daily; 4hr 30min); Curicó (2 daily; 2hr); Rancagua (2 daily; 1hr); Talca (2 daily; 2hr 50min). A slower Metrotrén has hourly departures to Rancagua (6.55am–10pm; 1hr 20min).

By bus The main bus station is the Terminal Buses Estación Central, also known as Terminal Santiago (☎ 2 2376 1755), at Alameda 3850, near the Universidad de Santiago metro station, which handles international routes, and journeys to the west and south. The Terminal Alameda, next door at Alameda 3750 (☎ 2 2822 7400), is served by Pullman and Tur-Bus, who also have some international departures. The two terminals have ATMs,

snack shops and luggage storage, as well as easy access to public transport along Alameda. Buses from northern and central Chile use Terminal San Borja (☎ 2 2776 0645), at San Borja 184, near the Estación Central metro station, while the smaller Terminal Los Héroes, at Tucapel Jiménez 21 (☎ 2 2420 0099), near Los Heroés metro station, serves a range of destinations in both northern and southern Chile.

Destinations Arica (8 daily; 28hr); Chillán (8 daily; 6hr); Copiapó (5 daily; 10hr); Iquique (10 daily; 24hr); La Serena (15 daily; 7hr); Pucón (every 30min; 12hr); Puerto Montt (8 daily; 13hr); Rancagua (every 15min; 1hr); Valparaíso and Viña del Mar (every 10min; 1hr 45min). Terminal Buses Estación Central has international departures to various South American countries including Argentina (Buenos Aires, Mendoza), Brazil (Saõ Paulo, Río de Janeiro) and Peru (Lima, Cusco, Tacna, Arequipa).

INFORMATION AND TOURS

Tourist information An excellent source of tourist information (with bilingual staff) is the municipal tourism office on the north side of the Plaza de Armas (Mon–Fri 9am–6pm, Sat & Sun 10am–4pm; ☎ 2 2713 6745). There's also a small municipal office at the foot of Santa Lucia on Terraza Neptuno. The main Sernatur office is at Av Providencia 1550, near the Manuel Montt metro station, east of the city centre (Mon–Fri 9am–6pm, Sat 9am–2pm; ☎ 2 2731 8300). It provides maps of the city and is well stocked with brochures on the surrounding area. Conaf has an office at Av Bulnes 265 (Mon–Thurs 9am–5.30pm, Fri 9am–4.30pm; ☎ 2 2663 0125, ⓦ www.conaf.cl), which provides information on national parks and reserves, as well as some pamphlets and inexpensive maps.

Listings For entertainment listings, check Friday's *El Mercurio* or *La Tercera*, Santiago's main newspapers.

Tours Free walking tours of the city are provided by the local authorities, and are a good way to take in the city's main sights (enquire at the tourist office). Bike tours are also a good option (see box below).

4

SANTIAGO TOUR OPERATORS

Attractions around Santiago include wineries, thermal baths, the outdoor enthusiast's paradise of the mountainous Cajón del Maipo valley, and more.

La Bicicleta Verde Loreto 6, at Av Santa María, Bellavista ☎ 2 2570 9338, ⓦ labicicletaverde.com. See Santiago at a different pace with a range of bike tours in the city, and around nearby vineyards. Also arranges bike rental. Morning tour of Santiago's sights CH$18,000/person.

Monteagudo Aventura ☎ 2 2346 9069, ⓦ monteagudoaventura.cl. Experienced outfit running full-day horseriding and white-water rafting trips in the

Cajón del Maipo, as well as treks to the San Francisco and Morado glaciers and night excursions to the Colina thermal baths. Full-day horseriding including an *asado* (barbecue) CH$80,000/person.

Rockside Expediciones Constantino 96 ☎ 2 2401 9564. Adrenaline-filled outdoor adventure, including rafting, kayaking, rock climbing and mountain biking in the Cajón del Maipo.

GETTING AROUND

By bus Fleets of "TranSantiago" (ⓦ www.transantiago.cl) buses run around the city. To use them, you need to purchase a "BIP" transit card (CH$1400), sold in most metro ticket booths, which you can then add credit to (at the same booths, and at BIP centres across the city). Bus destinations are posted on window signs and at marked stops; a standard fare is CH$620, which will last up to 2hr, maximum two changes.

By colectivo Slightly pricier than buses, *colectivos* have their destinations displayed on their roofs and carry passengers on fixed itineraries, reaching their destination quicker than regular transport, though you need to know where you are going; useful for destinations outside the city centre.

By metro The metro (Mon–Fri 6am–11pm, Sat 6.30am–11pm, Sun 9am–10.30pm; ⓦ metrosantiago.cl) is the quickest way to get around the city, with just five lines that are easy to navigate, though it gets rather cramped during rush hour and does not serve all neighbourhoods. BIP cards (see above) are the easiest way to use the metro, with each journey costing CH$590–700 depending on the time of day. Single-use tickets are also available at metro stations.

ACCOMMODATION

There are a number of accommodation options in Santiago to suit budget travellers although really cheap places are scarce. Good inexpensive lodgings are mostly to be found in the city centre and Barrio Brasil.

DOWNTOWN

Hostal 168 Santa Lucía 168, Metro Santa Lucía ☏ 2 2664 8478; map p.385. Welcoming hostel just beneath Cerro Santa Lucía with excellent facilities, free internet and breakfast included. Dorms CH$11,000, doubles CH$30,000

EcoHostel General Jofré 349B, Metro Universidad Católica ☏ 2 2222 6833, ⓦ ecohostel.cl; map pp.382–383. With its clean and spacious dorms, chilled-out common areas and fully equipped guest kitchen, this hostel and its

environment-friendly ethic attracts mostly younger travellers. Lockers, wi-fi, good breakfast and knowledgeable bilingual staff are a big plus. Dorms CH$10,000, doubles CH$27,000

París 813 París 813, Metro Universidad de Chile ☏ 2 2664 0921, ⓦ hotelparis813.com; map p.385. Atmospheric, centrally located budget hotel with cheaper rooms to suit backpackers and a newer annexe featuring comfortable rooms and spotless bathrooms. Continental breakfast CH$1500 extra. Doubles CH$26,000

BARRIO LASTARRIA

Andes Hostel Monjitas 506, Metro Bellas Artes ☏ 2 2632 9990, ⓦ andeshostel.com; map p.385. Centrally located hostel with modern decor, bright dorms with individual lockers, and a whole range of facilities – guest kitchen, lounge with pool table and cable TV, free internet, laundry service and a fully stocked bar. Can get noisy. Dorms CH$13,000, doubles CH$48,000

Hostal Forestal Coronel Santiago Bueras 122, Metro Baquedano ☏ 2 2638 1347, ⓦ hostalforestal.cl; map p.385. Perpetually popular, *Hostal Forestal* throws impromptu barbecues and the bilingual staff can advise on sightseeing. Luggage storage, outdoor patio, guest kitchen and lounge with cable TV are some of the perks. Dorms CH$6500, doubles CH$27,000

BELLAVISTA

Bellavista Hostel Dardignac 0184, Metro Baquedano ☏ 2 2899 7145, ⓦ bellavista.hostel.com; map p.386. It's easy to see why this hostel is extremely popular with younger travellers – a stone's throw from some of Santiago's best nightlife, it's cosy, colourful, run by helpful bilingual staff and has all the standard backpacker conveniences. Dorms CH$12,000, doubles CH$33,000

Casa Condell Condell 114, Metro Salvador ☏ 2 2717 8592, ⓦ casacondell.com; map pp.382–383. Brightly coloured and spotlessly clean guesthouse with very good breakfasts (included), and a congenial hostess. Situated on a quiet street just off bustling Av Providencia. Doubles CH$30,000

BARRIO BRASIL

La Casa Roja Agustinas 2113, Metro República ☏ 2 2696 4241, ⓦ lacasaroja.cl; map pp.382–383. Sprawling, Aussie-owned converted mansion firmly established as backpacker party central, with spacious dorms and rooms. There's a jacuzzi, pool with swim-up bar, large common areas, free internet, kitchen and an on-site travel agency. A top budget choice, though not a place to catch up on your sleep; breakfast not included in dorms. Dorms CH$9000, doubles CH$26,000

Hostel Cienfuegos Cienfuegos 151, Metro Los Héroes ☏ 2 2671 8532, ⓦ hostelcienfuegos.cl; map pp.382–383. Large, professionally run, HI-affiliated hostel with clean

TREAT YOURSELF

Casa Bonita Pasaje República 5, Metro República ☏ 2 2672 7302, ⓦ bbcasabonita .com; map pp.382–383. If you're tired of night buses, and in need of good coffee, try a few nights at this beautifully restored, centrally located bed and breakfast with spotless rooms. It's owned by a Dutch-Chilean couple, who are only too happy to help their guests make the most of Santiago. Doubles CH$54,000

TRAITORS' CORNER

For an unusual eating experience, try **El Rincón de los Canallas** ("Traitor's Corner"), at Tarapacá 810 (entry only by prior reservation on ☎ 2 2632 5491, ⓦ canallas.cl; map pp.382–383). It was once a secret meeting place for the opposition during Pinochet's dictatorship, and though this is not the original site, you still need a password to enter. When asked, "*Quién vive, canalla?*", respond "*Chile libre, canalla.*" (Pinochet called his detractors "*canallas*", so the exchange roughly means: "Who's there, traitor?" "Free Chile, traitor.") Against a nostalgic backdrop including wall-to-wall rallying slogans, this intimate bar offers traditional Chilean grub served up under names like *Pernil Canalla* ("Traitor's Ham", a roasted leg of pork). Mains CH$4000–7000.

dorms, plush bunk beds, spacious dining room and bonuses including internet and wi-fi, book exchange, breakfast and laundry service. Dorms CH$8000, doubles CH$27,000

Happy House Hostel Moneda 1829, Metro Los Héroes ☎ 2 2688 4849, ⓦ happyhousehostel.cl; map p.385. Travellers are made to feel really welcome at this beautifully decorated, spacious hostel, with large private rooms, attractive common areas, large kitchen, terrace bar and pool. Breakfast and internet included. Dorms CH$20,000, doubles CH$40,000

Landay Barceló Erasmo Escala 2012, Metro Los Héroes ☎ 2 2671 0300, ⓦ landaybarcelo.cl; map pp.382–383. Attractively renovated house with gleaming bathrooms, wooden floors, colourful rooms with lockers, and a comfy DVD room. Breakfast and internet included. Dorms CH$7000, doubles CH$22,000

EATING

Santiago has a proliferation of good restaurants. Most of the better ones are concentrated in Barrio Lastarria and Providencia, with some cheap options, popular with backpackers and students, in Bellavista, Barrio Brasil and up-and-coming Barrio Yungay.

DOWNTOWN AND BARRIO LASTARRIA

Emporio La Rosa Merced 291; map p.385. Coffee and ice-cream haven with tables out onto the street. The hot chocolate comes highly recommended. One ice-cream scoop CH$2600. Mon–Thurs 8am–9pm, Fri 8am–10pm, Sat 9am–10pm, Sun 9am–9pm.

TREAT YOURSELF

Boragó Nueva Costanera 3467, Vitacura ☎ 2 2953 8893, ⓦ borago.cl; map pp.382–383. Considered one of Latin America's best restaurants, the chefs here use native ingredients to whip up an inventive and delicious multi-course tasting menu (from CH$35,000), pairing the dishes with appropriate local wines. Reservations required. Mon–Sat 8–11pm.

Kintaro Monjitas 460; map p.385. Tasty and authentic sushi, along with teriyaki and udon dishes, all at very reasonable prices. Very popular at lunchtimes. Mains around CH$4500. Mon–Fri 12.30–3pm & 7.30–11pm, Sat 7.30–11.30pm.

Mercado Central Puente and San Pablo; map p.385. The best place for large portions of inexpensive fish and seafood, the fish market's bustling eateries offer such delights as *pastel de jaiva* (creamy crab pie) (CH$4800) and *machas a la Parmesana* (CH$4500); *Donde Augusto* is a popular spot. Daily lunch only.

El Rápido Bandera 371; map p.385. Perfectly prepared *empanadas* and sandwiches, served at a snack counter rather than a restaurant. *Empanadas* from CH$1000. Mon–Fri 9am–9pm, Sat 9am–3.30pm.

BELLAVISTA AND PROVIDENCIA

Backstage Patio Bellavista; map p.386. Half bar, half decent pizzeria, popular *Backstage* has an open-air patio, perfect for enjoying live jazz on Sat nights. Pizza from CH$4000. Daily 10am–late.

El Bodeguero Manuel Montt 382; map pp.382–383. Rough-and-ready bar with cheap lunch and happy hour deals: an excellent place to experience eating and drinking like a Santiago student. Giant *chorrillana* – a pile of fried beef, chips, onions and eggs – and a pitcher of beer for CH$6000. Mon–Sat 10am–late.

Galindo Constitución, at Dardignac; map p.386. Perpetually packed spot serving traditional Chilean food, such as hearty *pastel de choclo, cazuela* and *lomo a la pobre*, along with beers until late, even on weekdays. If sitting outside, you *will* be entertained by street musicians. Mains from CH$4000. Mon–Sat 10am–2am.

El Huerto Orrego Luco 054; map pp.382–383. An excellent choice for a wide variety of lovingly prepared vegetarian dishes, such as hearty burritos. Mains from around CH$6000. Mon–Sat noon–11pm, Sun 12.30–4.30pm.

Liguria Av Providencia 1373; map pp.382–383. Large portions of Chilean and Italian dishes are on offer in this ever-popular and charming bar-bistro, as well as large sandwiches, good salads and superb pisco sours. Clams in parmesan cheese CH$8500. Also has a sister restaurant at Pedro de Valdivia 47. Mon–Sat 11am–2am.

4

4

BARRIO BRASIL AND BARRIO YUNGAY

Charro de Oro Av Ricardo Cumming 342A; map pp.382–383. Spicy and inexpensive Mexican quesadillas (from CH$4000) and burritos served in an intimate, no-frills setting; happy hour until 9pm. Tues–Sat 5.30pm–late, Sun noon–late.

Ocean Pacific's Av Ricardo Cumming 221; map pp.382–383. Popular restaurant serving consistently good fish dishes (though not the cheapest), including an excellent salmon platter for two, with a backdrop of elaborate nautical decoration. Mains CH$7000–10,000. Daily noon–11.30pm.

Peluquería Francesa Compañia de Jesús 2789 ☎2 2682 5243; map pp.382–383. Take a trip back in time at this charming restaurant above a nineteenth-century hair salon, where each table literally bursts with quirky memorabilia. Excellent French cuisine (*coq au vin* CH$7500), and good cocktails. Mon–Fri 10am–8pm, Sat 10am–2pm, Sun 11am–5pm.

Peperone Huérfanos 1954; map pp.382–383. Excellent *empanadería* dishing out baked *empanadas* with myriad fillings, including scallops. Cheese and crab *empanada* CH$1500. Mon–Sat lunch only.

Las Vacas Gordas Cienfuegos 280 ☎2 2697 1066; map pp.382–383. Probably the best restaurant for carnivores in the city, with steaks grilled to perfection at very reasonable prices (from CH$7000). Extremely popular, especially on weekends. Mon–Sat 12.30pm–12.30am, Sun 12.30–5pm.

DRINKING AND NIGHTLIFE

Santiago is not a 24-hour party town, and compared to other Latin capitals can seem rather tame. However, Thursdays, Fridays and Saturdays are lively, with crowds pouring into the streets and bars of the nightlife *zonas*.

DOWNTOWN AND BARRIO LASTARRIA

Bar Berri Rosal 321; map p.385. Great long-running bohemian bar filled with antique furniture. There's a good, reasonably priced drinks menu (skip the food); the upstairs has more character but is slightly more expensive. Mon–Sat 7pm–late.

COFFEE WITH LEGS

In downtown Santiago you may encounter the strange Chilean phenomenon of *café con piernas*, or "coffee with legs" – cafés where businessmen (and often women) are served some of the city's best coffee by skimpily clad waitresses at stand-up counters. *Café Caribe*, at Ahumada 120 (map p.385), and *Café Haiti*, at Ahumada 336 (map p.385), are both examples of the genre.

Bar The Clinic Monjitas 578; map.385. Large café-bar, popular with students and left-wing intellectuals, run by the people behind *The Clinic* newspaper, an alternative humorous take on the events of the day. Some of the jokes on the menu and plastered on the walls about Chilean politicians may go over your head, but you can enjoy the friendly atmosphere, and inexpensive beer and meals (about CH$4000 for a burger). Daily 12.30pm–2am.

Café Escondido Rosal 346; map p.385. If you want cheap beer and bar snacks in a less than raucous environment, this intimate bar is the perfect spot. Mon–Sat 6pm–2.30am.

La Piojera Aillavilú 1030; map p.385. Carve your name into the wooden tables at this rough-and-ready bar with a loyal clientele, and knock back a *terremoto* (earthquake) – a powerful wine and ice-cream mix. Drinks CH$2000. Daily noon–late.

BELLAVISTA AND PROVIDENCIA

Altazor Antonia López de Bello 0189 ☎2 2732 3934; map p.386. Popular bar packed on weekends, often featuring live folk music and blues. Cover CH$2000. Thurs–Sat from 10.30pm.

Bar Constitución Constitución 67, near Patio Bellavista ☎2 2244 4569; map p.386. A friendly international bar-cum-club with a dancefloor that fills up every Friday and Saturday night to an eclectic choice of music. Tues–Sat until around 4am.

Bunker Bombero Núñez 159 ☎2 2737 1716; map p.386. Giant dancefloor with varied alternative music events. A devoted young following makes this one of the most popular places on the gay night scene. Fri & Sat 11pm–late.

La Casa en el Aire Antonia López de Bello 125 ☎2 2735 6680, ⊛lacasaenelaire.cl; map p.386. Inviting candlelit venue offering poetry reading, contemporary theatre performances, film screenings and folk music; check the website for listings. Daily 8pm–2am.

Flannery's Encomenderos 83 ☎2 2233 6675, ⊛flannerys .cl; map pp.382–383. Extremely popular with expats, this pub has authentic Irish charm and a welcoming staff. While the exotic cocktails are not their strong suit, it's a great spot for a beer and surprisingly tasty fajitas. Mon–Fri noon–2.30am, Sat 5.30pm–3am, Sun 5.30pm–12.30am.

Havana Salsa Dominica 142 ☎2 2737 1737, ⊛havanasalsa.cl; map pp.382–383. If you want to shake your hips to some salsa beats, this is the place. Cover and Cuban-style buffet dinner CH$12,000. Fri & Sat until 4am.

BARRIO BRASIL

Blondie Alameda 2879 ⊛blondie.cl; map pp.382–383. Large and popular four-floor dance club featuring techno, goth, indie and other musical styles (depending on the night), as well as occasional live music. Thurs–Sat from midnight.

Confitería Las Torres Alameda 1570 ☎ 2 2668 0751; map p.385. Elegant, nineteenth-century building hosting spellbinding live tango shows on weekends to accompany the expertly cooked traditional Chilean dishes. Dishes CH$5800–10,000. Mon–Sat 10.30am–midnight.

PLAZA ÑUÑOA

La Batuta J. Washington 52 ⓦ batuta.cl; map pp.382–383. A thriving gem of Santiago nightlife, where Chilean and British rock music attract a dedicated following. Drinks around CH$4000. Wed–Sat from 10pm.

ENTERTAINMENT

Cine Arte Alameda Alameda 139, Metro Baquedano ⓦ centroartealameda.cl. An arts cinema showing independent and avant-garde films.

Cine Hoyts Moneda 835, Metro Santa Lucía ⓦ cinehoyts .cl. Multiplex cinema showing the latest releases; English-language films are usually subtitled, although those of interest to young audiences may be dubbed (*doblada*).

Teatro Municipal Agustinas 794, Metro Universidad de Chile ☎ 2 2463 8888, ⓦ municipal.cl. You can find the best of Chile's classical music, opera and ballet inside this magnificent historical building.

SHOPPING

In general, the prices of manufactured goods are expensive in Chile compared to Europe and the US, but cost and choice wise Chile compares well to other South American countries, so its capital is a good place to stock up on any essentials.

Feria Artesanal Santa Lucía, Cerro Santa Lucía. Large crafts market stocking indigenous crafts, tie-dyed clothing and T-shirts featuring the Chilean flag. Mon–Sat 10am–7pm.

Los Dominicos market Apoquindo 9085, Las Condes. Take the metro up to Los Dominicos to visit this large, pretty (if slightly pricey) crafts market next to the *barrio*'s copper-topped church. Daily around 10am–7pm.

Librería Inglesa Huérfanos 669, Downtown. English-language bookshop; prices aren't the cheapest, but you should find a book here you need for that long-distance bus journey. Mon–Fri 10am–7.30pm, Sat 10.30am–1pm.

Mall Sport Av Las Condes 13451. Mall dedicated to sports and outdoor pursuits, with mainly expensive and imported, but good-quality, trekking and climbing gear as well as sleeping bags, backpacks etc.

Patio Bellavista Between Constitución and Pío Nono, Barrio Bellavista ⓦ patiobellavista.cl. Open-air space with a concentration of gift shops selling high-quality crafts and clothing, postcards, jewellery and home-made honey. Daily 11am–10pm.

DIRECTORY

Banks and exchange There are plenty of ATMs downtown, especially along Huérfanos, Agustinas, Bandera, Moneda and Av Alameda, as well as at the large bus terminals. There are exchange houses on Agustinas,

4

SKIING NEAR SANTIAGO

It's easy to arrange day-trips from Santiago to experience some world-class powder snow. The **ski season** lasts from mid-June to early October. All resorts rent ski equipment and clothing, and day passes cost CH$20,000–33,000. High in the Andes Mountains, 36km east of Santiago, three large ski resorts are clustered in the Tres Valles area: **El Colorado**, **La Parva** and **Valle Nevado**; all three can be accessed from **Farellones**, a village (2400m above sea level) at the foot of Cerro Colorado (3333m). The journey from Santiago takes about one hour thirty minutes along a winding road (don't attempt it with a hangover). A fourth resort, **Portillo**, is set on the banks of the stunning Laguna del Inca on the Argentine border, a two-hour drive from Santiago.

OPERATORS

Ski Total Av Apoquindo 4900, local 40-46 ☎ 2 2246 0156, ⓦ skitotal.cl. Operates daily departures to all four resorts, and is a good choice for renting equipment and clothing.

Ski Van ☎ 2 2219 2672, ⓦ skivan.cl. Daily departures to El Colorado, Valle Nevado and La Parva, from General Bustamente 10, just off Plaza Italia.

RESORTS

El Colorado ⓦ elcolorado.cl. The most accessible and busiest resort houses 19 chairlifts and 21 runs, largely aimed at beginners to intermediate level.

La Parva ⓦ laparva.cl. The Cerro Franciscano (3608m) and Cerro La Falsa Parva here offer 30 runs for skiers of all abilities, with some excellent long advanced runs.

Portillo ⓦ skiportillo.com. Chile's most exclusive resort is used for training by international ski teams and boasts 23 runs that cater to intermediates and experts alike, with ample backcountry terrain and heli-skiing opportunities.

Valle Nevado ⓦ vallenevado.com. With the best skiing conditions in Tres Valles and modern lifts, this resort has a good mixture of runs for all abilities, as well as a snow-board park and half-pipe.

between Ahumada and Bandera, which give a reasonable rate on foreign currencies and travellers' cheques (Mon–Fri 9am–2pm & 4–6pm, Sat 9am–2pm).

Embassies and consulates Argentina, Miraflores 285 (☎2 2582 2500, ⊛ehile.mrecic.gov.ar); Australia, Isidora Goyenechea 3621 (☎2 2550 3500, ⊛chile.embassy .gov.au); Bolivia, Av Santa María 2796, Providencia (☎2 2232 8180, ⊛consuladobolivia.cl); Brazil, Padre Alonso de Ovalle 1665 (☎2 2876 3400, ⊛santiago.itamaraty .gov.br); Canada, Nueva Tajamar 481, 12th floor (☎2 2652 3800, ⊛canadainternational.gc.ca/chile-chili); New Zealand, Isidora Goyenechea 3000, 12th floor (☎2 2616 3000, ⊛nzembassy.com/chile); Peru, Antonio Bellet 444 (☎2 2873 1700, ⊛conpersantiago.cl); South Africa, Apoquindo 2827, 4th floor (☎2 2820 0300, ⊛embajada-sudafrica.cl); UK, Av El Bosque Norte 125 (☎2 2370 4100, ⊛ukinchile.fco.gov.uk/en); US, Av Andrés Bello 2800 (☎2 2330 3000, ⊛chile.usembassy.gov).

Hospitals Clínica Las Condes, Lo Fontecilla 441 (☎2 2210 4000); Clínica Universidad Católica, Marcoleta 367, downtown (☎2 2633 4122); Clínica Alemana, Av Vitacura 5951, Vitacura (☎2 2210 1111).

Language schools Bridge Linguatec Language Center, at Los Leones 439, Providencia (☎2 2233 4356 or ☎+1 303 495 5963 in the US, ⊛bridgechile.com), offers intensive immersion Spanish courses, group tutorials and private lessons. Instituto Chileno-Suizo de Idioma, at José Victorino Lastarria 93, 2nd floor (☎2 2638 5414, ⊛www .chilenosuizo.tie.cl), combines Spanish language courses of varying intensity with homestays, city tours and an introduction to Chilean culture.

Laundry Try Lavandería Autoservicio, Monjitas 507, or Lavandería Lolos, Moneda 2296, Barrio Brasil.

Pharmacies There are plenty of Farmacias Ahumada and Cruz Verde pharmacies all over Santiago; Farmacia Ahumada at Av Portugal 125 is open 24hr.

Post offices Correo Central, Plaza de Armas 559 (Mon–Fri 8am–7pm, Sat 9am–2pm). Other branches are at Moneda 1170, near Morandé; Local 503, Exposición 51 Paseo Estación; and Av 11 de Septiembre 2092.

Valparaíso and Viña del Mar

Draped in a crescent shape around the Bahía de Valparaíso, the captivating UNESCO World Heritage-listed city of **Valparaíso** is just 120km from Santiago. "Valpo" – as it's affectionately known – is Chile's principal port and naval base, and also the country's liveliest and most vibrant city. The **nightlife** and excellent cuisine attract much of Santiago to its bars and restaurants at the weekend, as does the nearby beach resort of **Viña del Mar**. Viña's attractions are wide, white beaches surrounded by expensive high-rise apartments, casinos and pricey, touristy restaurants. It has none of the character that distinguishes Valparaíso, but as they're so close together, it's easy enough to stay in Valparaíso and visit Viña's beaches for the day.

VALPARAÍSO

Few travellers fail to be inspired by the ramshackle beauty of **VALPARAÍSO**, whose mishmash patchwork of brightly coloured houses is built across a series of hills; steep stairways and the city's famous **ascensores** (elevators) link the hills to the port area. Still a major port today, the city came into its own during the California Gold Rush, and in the mid-nineteenth century was the main hub for ships crossing between the Atlantic and Pacific oceans. Valparaíso's narrow labyrinth of atmospheric alleyways offers glimpses of the city's decline from the grandeur of its former glories.

WHAT TO SEE AND DO

Valparaíso is effectively split into two halves: the hills (*cerros*), and the flat El Plan. Most restaurants and hostels can be found on the former, especially on **Cerro Concepción** and **Cerro Alegre**. Visitors usually spend their time here meandering along the winding passageways, and enjoying the spectacular views from the rickety *ascensores*. **El Plan**, which includes the busy port area, is home to an extensive nightlife quarter as well as the shopping and administrative districts, all linked by traffic-choked narrow streets.

The hills

Without a doubt, Valparaíso's biggest attraction is its **cerros** (hills). Few pastimes are as enjoyable as meandering up and down the area's winding narrow streets, or riding its antique funiculars.

Visitors can stop to marvel at the impressive views of the city from a multitude of **miradores** (viewpoints), or duck into little shops and cafés to admire the colourful **murals** – a striking example of the city's bohemian culture. It is easy to see how Valparaíso has produced more writers, artists and poets than any other Chilean city.

Cerro Concepción and **Cerro Alegre** are the best known of the hills, with the highest concentration of churches and museums, but they are by no means the only gems. Nearby **Cerro Panteón**, reached by a network of winding paths, is home to three colourful cemeteries, the most interesting of which is the **Cementerio de Disidentes**, resting place of non-Catholic European immigrants. Nearby **Cerro Cárcel** is the site of a former prison, now decorated with colourful graffiti and a hangout for artists and thespians. Its **Parque Cultural de Valparaíso** (☏32 225 8567, ⓦpcdv.cl) hosts (often free) cultural events.

La Sebastiana

La Sebastiana, Ferrari 692, off Alemania (Tues–Sun: Jan & Feb 10.30am–6.50pm; March–Dec 10am–6pm; CH$5000; ☏32 225 6606, ⓦfundacionneruda.org), was the least lived-in of the poet **Pablo Neruda**'s three residences, but it offers incredibly picturesque views of the city and the interior design reflects the poet's quirky tastes. Like his other homes, the five-storey house has a nautical theme and is crammed with knick-knacks that Neruda picked up on his travels; unlike the others, you can explore this one without a guide. The vista from his bedroom window is nothing short of spectacular. To get here, take a short ride on *colectivo* #39 from Plaza Ecuador or bus #612 or "0" from Avenida Argentina or Plaza San Luis at the top of Templeman; if you stay on the latter for the whole route you get a low-cost city tour.

Barrio Puerto

El Plan consists of long east–west streets, crossed by shorter north–south streets leading into the hills, and is divided into two halves, with **Barrio Puerto** located northwest of Cerro Concepción. Its centrepiece, the pedestrianized **Plaza Sotomayor**, is lined with a mixture of modern concrete blocks and grand early twentieth-century buildings, and is home to the **Primera Zona Naval**, the country's naval headquarters. At the port end of the plaza, near the Metrotrén Estación Puerto, is **Muelle Prat**, the passenger pier, from where you can take boat trips out into the harbour (CH$3000/person; 45min). West of the pier, the five-block port-side stretch of Avenida Errázuriz and parallel Blanco make up Valparaíso's principal nightlife

4

LOS ASCENSORES DE VALPARAÍSO

Valparaíso's **ascensores**, or funiculars, were built between 1883 and 1916. As well as being one of the city's enduring attractions, they remain an essential way of getting about, and have recently been renovated. Most run daily from 7am to 11pm and cost CH$100–300 per journey. Below are some of the best.

Ascensor Polanco The only *ascensor* that is an actual elevator, Polanco is reached through a long underground tunnel from Calle Simpson, off Avenida Argentina. It rises vertically through the yellow tower to a *mirador* offering excellent views of the port; there's also some high-class graffiti, though bear in mind that the area is a bit sketchy.

Ascensor Concepción (also known as Ascensor Turri). The city's oldest funicular, built in 1883 and originally steam-powered, is one of the most popular. It climbs up to Paseo Gervasoni on Cerro Concepción, a delightful residential area and the start of many walking tours that cover Cerro Alegre as well. The lower entrance is opposite the Relój Turri clock tower.

Ascensor Artillería Extremely popular with visitors, this funicular should not be missed. It runs from Plaza Aduana up to Cerro Playa Ancha, and offers a beautiful panoramic view of the city and coastline, with Viña del Mar in the distance. The Museo Naval y Marítimo (see p.394) is nearby.

4

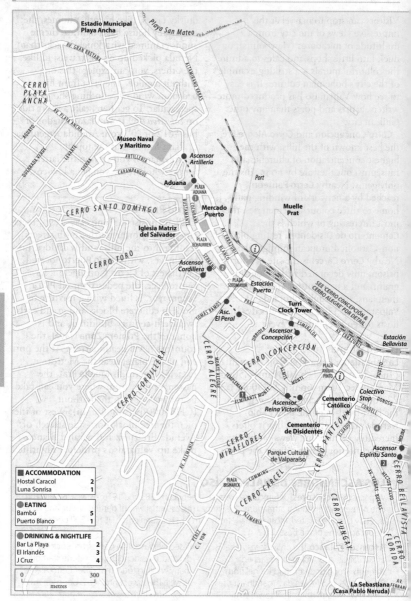

ACCOMMODATION
Hostal Caracol	2
Luna Sonrisa	1

EATING
Bambú	5
Puerto Blanco	1

DRINKING & NIGHTLIFE
Bar La Playa	2
El Irlandés	3
J Cruz	4

district, with **Mercado Puerto** and its plethora of fishy places to eat at the northwest corner. A couple of blocks south of the market is the elegant **Iglesia Matriz del Salvador**, built in 1842, while the **Plaza Aduana** and Ascensor Artillería (see box, p.393) lie two blocks west.

Museo Naval y Marítimo

The **Museo Naval y Marítimo** at Paseo 21 de Mayo 45 (Tues–Sun 10am–5.30pm; CH$1000; ☎32 243 7018, ⓦmuseonaval.cl) houses an extensive collection of artefacts related to Chile's famous military figures, including Arturo

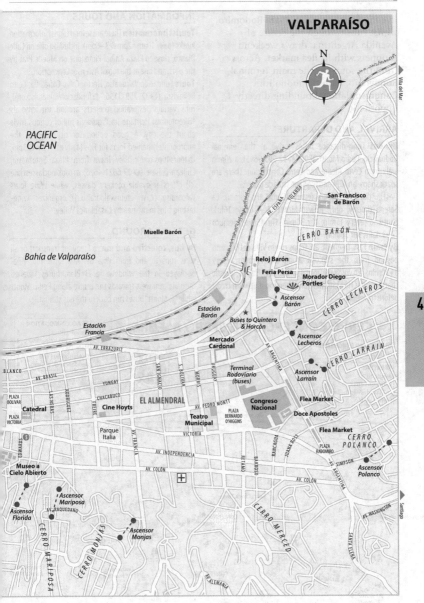

VALPARAÍSO

N

PACIFIC OCEAN

Bahía de Valparaíso

Muelle Barón

San Francisco de Barón

CERRO BARÓN

Reloj Barón

Feria Persa

Morador Diego Portles

AV. ESPAÑA YOLANDA

Ascensor Barón

CERRO LECHEROS

Estación Barón

Buses to Quintero & Horcón

Ascensor Lecheros

CERRO LARRAÍN

Estación Francia

Mercado Cardonal

AV. ERRAZURIZ

Terminal Rodoviario (buses)

Ascensor Larraín

BLANCO

AV. BRASIL

SAN IGNACIO

J. BOLÍVAR

MORRIS

AV. ARGENTINA

YUNGAY

RODRÍGUEZ

LAS HERAS

CHACABUCO

FREIRE

AV. PEDRO MONTT

Congreso Nacional

Flea Market

PLAZA BOLÍVAR

Catedral

Cine Hoyts

EL ALMENDRAL

PLAZA BERNARDO O'HIGGINS

Doce Apostoles

PLAZA VICTORIA

Teatro Municipal

VICTORIA

Flea Market

CERRO POLANCO

Parque Italia

RANCAGUA

JUANA ROSS

PLAZA RADOMIRO

EDWARDS

AV. FRANCIA

AV. INDEPENDENCIA

RETAMO

BARROSO

AV. SIMPSON

Ascensor Polanco

Museo a Cielo Abierto

AV. COLÓN

AV. ARGENTINA

Ascensor Mariposa

AV. BAQUEDANO

CERRO MERCED

AV. COLÓN

Ascensor Florida

Ascensor Monjas

CERRO MARIPOSA

CERRO MONJAS

AV. ALEMANIA

SANTA ELENA

AV. WASHINGTON

Viña del Mar

Santiago

4

Prat and Bernardo O'Higgins, and focuses most attention on the War of the Pacific. The museum is divided into four halls around an immaculate courtyard, each devoted to a different naval conflict and displaying original documents, uniforms and medals.

El Almendral

El Almendral, east of Cerro Concepción, is the bustling commercial district, where lively stalls selling all manner of goods spill out onto the streets. **Plaza O'Higgins** is home to a huge **antiques market** on weekends and doubles as a live music venue, while **Plaza Rodomiro**, which runs through the centre of Avenida Argentina, draws weekend shoppers with its **flea market**. Across from the square is the main **Terminal Rodoviario**, with the monolithic **Congreso National** building directly opposite it.

ARRIVAL AND DEPARTURE

By bus Long-distance buses arrive at the Terminal Rodoviario, Pedro Montt 2800 (📞 32 293 9695), a 20min walk from Cerro Alegre and Cerro Concepción. There are snack shops, an ATM and luggage storage inside.

Destinations Isla Negra (every 15min; 1hr 30min); La Serena (hourly; 6hr); Puerto Montt (3–4 daily; 16hr); Santiago (every 15min; 1hr 30min–1hr 45min); Temuco (2–3 daily; 9hr 30min).

By train Fast, frequent, a/c trains run to Viña del Mar and beyond from the stations along the harbour (every 5–20min; 🌐 www.metro-valparaiso.cl). Buy a plastic charge card (CH\$1350) first, and then top it up with credit before travelling.

INFORMATION AND TOURS

Tourist information There are several tourist information kiosks (daily 10am–2pm & 3–6pm), including one on Calle Blanco, close to Plaza Aníbal Pinto, one on Muelle Prat by the port, and one at the top of Ascensor Concepción.

Tours Fundación Valparaíso, Héctor Calvo Cofre 205, Cerro Bellavista (📞 32 259 3156, 🌐 fundacionvalparaiso.org), runs various restoration projects around the city; its "Bicentennial Heritage Trail" guide is full of curious trivia about the city. A good option for city tours is the appropriately named Tours for Tips (daily at 10am & 3pm; 🌐 tours4tips.com); they leave from Plaza Sotomayor. Chilean Cuisine (📞 09 6621 4626, 🌐 cookingclasseschile .cl) offers enjoyable cookery classes, while Wine Tours Valparaíso (🌐 winetoursvalparaiso.cl) organizes wine-tasting trips in the nearby Casablanca Valley.

GETTING AROUND

By bus, colectivo and micro Frequent transport of all sorts runs to and from Viña del Mar; look for "Viña" displayed in the window. In El Plan, buses labelled "Aduana" run west towards the centre along Pedro Montt while "P. Montt" buses run back to the bus station.

4

CERRO CONCEPCIÓN & CERRO ALEGRE

■ **ACCOMMODATION**
Casa Aventura	5
Hostel Casa Valparaíso	2
Hotel Da Vinci	3
La Maison du Filou	1
Residencia en el Cerro	4

● **DRINKING & NIGHTLIFE**
El Cinzano	2

● **EATING**
Alegretto	3
Café Con Letras	4
Le Filou de Montpellier	5
Pasta e Vino	1

Train Station

ERRÁZURIZ
GÓMEZ CARREÑO
MARTÍNEZ
MELGAREJO
BLANCO

BLANCO
ESMERALDA

PLAZA SOTOMAYOR
SENERO
UMIDLA
COCHRANE
Turri Clock Tower
PRAT

Ascensor Concepción
PASEO GERVASONI
PASEO ATKINSON
PLAZA ANÍBAL PINTO

PAPUDO
CERRO CONCEPCIÓN
Lutheran Church
Lavandería Jerasalem

Ascensor El Peral
PASEO YUGOSLAVO
ABTAO
CONCEPCIÓN
CUMMING

PILCOMAYO
TEMPLEMAN
St Paul's Anglican Church

CERRO ALEGRE
MONTE ALEGRE
PASAJE GÁLVEZ
LEIGHTON
Pasaje Templeman
Ascensor Reina Victoria
ALMIRANTE MONTT

Pasaje Bavestrello
MIRAMAR
URRIOLA
Pasaje Pisa
GALVARINO
ELÍAS
ALMTE MONTT
PASEO DIMALOW

- - - **Walking Tour**

0   100
metres

By tram Antique trams offer limited but cheap service around El Plan; just look for the rails.

ACCOMMODATION

Hostal Caracol Hector Calvo 371, Cerro Bellavista ☎32 239 5817, ⓦhostalcaracol.cl; map pp.394–395. A clean, friendly, popular hostel, located on an up-and-coming *cerro* offering a seven-bed dorm and private rooms. Dorms CH$10,000, doubles CH$30,000

Casa Aventura Pasaje Gálvez 11, Cerro Alegre ☎32 275 5963, ⓦcasaventura.cl; map opposite. Hostel with friendly and knowledgeable staff, spotless dorms, a sunny lounge and kitchen, all of which make it popular with backpackers. Dorms CH$9000, doubles CH$25,000

Hostel Casa Valparaíso Pasaje Gálvez 173, Cerro Alegre ☎32 319 4072, ⓦcasavalparaisohostel.blogspot.com; map opposite. Cheerful, family-run hostel with homey communal spaces, wi-fi and a hearty breakfast included. Dorms CH$7000

Hotel Da Vinci Urriola 426, Cerro Alegre ☎32 317 4494, ⓦhoteldavincivalparaiso.cl; map opposite. A cross between an art gallery and a hotel: the en suites are set around a central atrium, bathed with light from a towering window, while carefully placed photos and paintings provide a mellow ambience. Doubles CH$52,000

★**Luna Sonrisa** Templeman 833, Cerro Alegre ☎32 273 4117, ⓦlunasonrisa.cl; map pp.394–395. Minimalist but comfortable rooms and dorms, pristine facilities, fine breakfast, book exchange and a sociable atmosphere make *Luna Sonrisa* an excellent choice. Staff are very friendly and knowledgeable – the hostel is owned by a travel writer, so you would expect nothing less. Dorms CH$9000, doubles CH$25,000

La Maison du Filou Papudo 579, Cerro Concepción ☎32 212 4681, ⓦlamaisondufilou.over-blog.com; map opposite. Colourful double and twin rooms with high ceilings and wonderful views; kitchen privileges, laundry service and a book exchange are among the perks. French and a smattering of English spoken. Doubles CH$20,000

Residencia en el Cerro Pasaje Pierre Loti 51, Cerro Concepción ☎32 249 5298, ⓦresidenciaenelcerro.cl; map opposite. Large, wonderfully friendly family-run place, with a good breakfast, and a number of cats to keep you company. Dorms CH$9000, doubles CH$24,000

EATING

Alegretto Pilcomayo 529, Cerro Concepción ☎32 296 8839, ⓦallegretto.cl; map opposite. Complete with an entertaining vintage jukebox, this British-Chilean-run spot serves good pizza (from CH$5200), excellent gnocchi and an economical weekday set lunch (CH$5900). Often screens live football. Daily noon–4pm & 7–11pm.

Bambú Independencia 1790 ☎32 223 4216; map pp.394–395. Good-value vegetarian food (CH$2000 upwards) in a

city-centre location. Cookery, yoga, pilates and tai chi classes are also available. Mon 10.30am–6pm, Tues 10.30am–8pm, Wed–Fri 10.30am–6pm, Sat 10.30am–5pm.

Café Con Letras Almirante Montt 316, Cerro Alegre; map opposite. A popular artsy café with quirky decor and a small selection of books; serves a good range of real coffee, too (CH$1200–2900). Mon–Sat 11am–10pm, Sun 4–10pm.

Le Filou de Montpellier Almirante Montt 382, Cerro Concepción ☎32 222 4663; map opposite. A delightful little piece of France in Valpo: the ever-changing set lunch (CH$7200) may include quiche lorraine and boeuf bourguignon. Tues–Thurs 1–4pm, Fri & Sat 1–4pm & 8–11.30pm, Sun 1–4pm.

Puerto Blanco Cochrane 25 ☎32 225 0106, ⓦfacebook.com/puertoblancocafe; map pp.394–395. An unprepossessing location, but a first-class coffee shop: inside you'll find exposed brick walls, MacBooks, hip(ster) clientele and excellent coffee (CH$1100–2800). Tues–Sun 10am–8pm.

DRINKING, NIGHTLIFE AND ENTERTAINMENT

Bar La Playa Serrano 567 ☎32 225 9426; map pp.394–395. This historic bar with a wood-panelled interior is an excellent spot for a quiet beer in the afternoon, and at night transforms into a buzzing dance spot. Thurs 10am–2am, Fri & Sat 10am–5am.

El Cinzano Plaza Aníbal Pinto 1182 ☎32 221 3043, ⓦbarcinzano.cl; map opposite. Hugely popular restaurant-bar (set lunch CH$3900) with a fantastic atmosphere, especially on Thursday, Friday and Saturday nights. Mon–Wed 10am–1am, Thurs 10am–2am, Fri & Sat 10.30am–4.30am.

El Irlandés Blanco 1279 ☎32 254 3592; map pp.394–395. A fairly raucous Irish pub run by an actual Irishman, and offering a large selection of beers (from CH$2000). Daily 5pm–4am.

J Cruz Condell 1466 ☎32 221 1225; map pp.394–395. A legendary bar with glass cabinets filled with all kinds of strange memorabilia. It's an excellent place to enjoy a glass of wine (from CH$1500) and share a greasy pile of *chorrillana* (steak strips with chips, onion and fried egg). Mon–Thurs noon–2am, Fri & Sat noon–4.30am, Sun 1pm–2am.

DIRECTORY

Banks and exchange Prat has a number of banks, ATMs and cambios; Banco de Chile, at Prat 698, also has an ATM and there is a cambio at Plaza Sotomayor 11 which offers a decent exchange rate (Mon–Fri 9am–6pm Sat 10am–1pm).

Hospital Hospital Carlos van Buren, San Ignacio 725, has modern facilities (☎ 32 236 4000, ⓦ hospitalcarlosvanburen.cl).

Language courses Interactive Spanish School, C Elias 571, Cerro Cárcel (☎ 09 9286 4973, ☎ 32 273 5351, ⓦ interactive-spanish.cl). Spanish lessons of varying intensity offered with or without homestay options.

Laundry Lavanderia Jerusalem, Condell 1176, Local 3 (☎ 32 221 9216).

Post office Prat 856 (Mon–Fri 9am–6pm, Sat 10am–1pm).

VIÑA DEL MAR

Though only fifteen minutes from Valparaíso, **VIÑA DEL MAR** could hardly be more different from its grittier neighbour. Purpose-built in the late nineteenth century as a weekend getaway for wealthy Santiago and Valparaíso residents, it draws thousands of holidaymakers during the summer and on weekends. Viña makes for an enjoyable day-trip to the beach, and is worth a visit during the week-long **Festival de la Canción** in the second or third week of February, which draws top Latino and international artists. The city also hosts spectacular Año Nuevo (New Year) celebrations. Other festivals include the two-week-long **Feria del Libro** (Jan), which attracts important literary figures and hosts live readings, and the acclaimed **Festival Cine Viña del Mar** film festival (Oct or Nov; ⓦ cinevina.cl).

WHAT TO SEE AND DO

The city is split in two by the broad, none-too-clean **Marga Marga** estuary, with a largely residential area to the south and most of the beaches in the northern half. **Avenida San Martín**, parallel to the beach, and the side streets off it feature numerous dining and nightlife options. At the heart of Viña lies the large, shady **Plaza Vergara**, a popular spot with the occasional busker or *capoeira* demonstration and horse-drawn carriages

parked around it. Several blocks of **Avenida Valparaíso**, Viña's main thoroughfare, which runs from the square's southwest corner, have been pleasantly pedestrianized, with a number of shops and places to eat.

Museo Francisco Fonck

Museo Francisco Fonck (4 Norte 784; Mon 10am–2pm & 3–6pm, Tues–Sat 10am–6pm, Sun 10am–2pm; CH$2500; ☎ 32 268 6753, ⓦ museofonck.cl) has one of Chile's most important **Easter Island collections**, plus some fascinating pre-Hispanic exhibits. One of the museum's best pieces stands by the entrance in the garden: a giant stone *moai*, one of just six that exist outside Easter Island.

The beaches

Playa Caleta Abarca lies in a sandy cove south of **Castillo Wulff**, an impressive castle-like structure built on a rocky outcrop at the mouth of the estuary by a Valparaíso businessman in 1906. Located next to the large **Reloj de Flores** ("flower clock"), the beach draws a lively picnicking crowd on weekends. Just north of the estuary, Avenida Perú runs parallel to the sea, past the brash **Casino Viña del Mar**. Beyond you will find an almost unbroken line of sandy beaches, backed by high-rise apartment buildings, stretching all the way to the smaller resort of **Reñaca**, which itself has more good beaches and nightlife.

Quinta Vergara

The one spot besides the beaches where you might want to spend some time in Viña del Mar is the lovely **Quinta Vergara** park (daily 7am–7pm), where the manicured grounds are home to a vast array of exotic imported plants. It's a couple of blocks south of Plaza Vergara behind the Estación Viña, with the futuristic-looking **Anfiteatro**, home to the annual music festival, its centrepiece.

ARRIVAL AND INFORMATION

By bus Long-distance buses pull up at Terminal Rodoviario (☎ 32 275 2000) at Av Valparaíso 1055. Buses/*micros* up the coast don't stop at the bus terminal, but at Libertad (just north of Puente Libertad).

VIÑA DEL MAR

ACCOMMODATION

Jaguar Hostel	1
Kalagen Hostel	2
My Father's House	3

EATING

Cevasco	4
Entre Masas	3
La Flor de Chile	1
Jerusalem	7
Panzoni	5

DRINKING & NIGHTLIFE

Café Journal	6
Scratch	2

0 — 250 metres

PACIFIC OCEAN

Reñaca

Playa Los Marineros

Playa El Sol

Muelle Vergara

Playa Acapulco

AV. SAN MARTIN

AVENIDA LIBERTAD

15 NORTE
14 NORTE
13 NORTE
12 NORTE
11 NORTE
10 NORTE
9 NORTE
8 NORTE
7 NORTE
6 NORTE
5 NORTE
4 NORTE
3 NORTE
2 NORTE
1 NORTE

Museo Francisco Fonck

Casino Viña del Mar

Castillo Wulff

Estero

PUENTE CASINO
PUENTE ECUADOR
PUENTE VILLANELO
PUENTE QUINTA
PUENTE LIBERTAD
PUENTE QUILLOTA

Marga Marga

IBERIA
ARLEGUI
VON SCHROEDERS
ECUADOR
TRASLAVIÑA
AV. VALPARAISO
VILLANELO
ETCHEVERS
QUINTA
ÁLVARES
VIANA
BOHN
COUSIÑO

Playa Caleta Abarca

Reloj de Flores

LIBERTAD
BALMACEDA
ÁLAMOS

Teatro

PLAZA VERGARA

Terminal Rodoviario

Estación Miramar

Estación Viña del Mar

Palacio Vergara

El Mercurio

QUINTA VERGARA

Anfiteatro

RECREO

LOS TILOS
GONZÁLEZ
AV. AGUA SANTA

AV. MARINA
AV. ESPAÑA

Cementerio

Santiago

Valparaíso

Jardín Botánico (6km)

Hospital Gustavo Fricke (1km)

Cinemark

4

Destinations Cachagua (hourly; 1hr 30min); Concón (every 15min; 15min); Horcón (hourly; 1hr); La Ligua (hourly; 2hr); Maitencillo (hourly; 1hr 20min); Papudo (2–3 daily; 1hr 45min); Reñaca (every 15min; 25min); Santiago (every 15min; 1hr 30min–1hr 45min); Zapallar (hourly; 1hr 30min).

By train Trains (ⓦ www.metro-valparaiso.cl) depart for Valparaíso (every 5–20min) from the centrally located Miramar and Viña del Mar stations. Buy a plastic charge card (CH$1350) first, and then top it up with credit before travelling.

Tourist information The tourist office is at Arlegui 715 (Mon–Fri 9am–2pm & 3–7pm, Sat & Sun 10am–2pm & 3–6pm; ☎ 32 218 5709, ⓦ visitevinadelmar.cl).

ACCOMMODATION

Jaguar Hostel Pasaje Massot 12, small street off 2 Poniente, between 4 Norte and 5 Norte ☎ 09 9727 9219, ⓦ hosteljaguar.com. Elegant house in a quiet neighbourhood just five blocks from the beach with four-bed dorms and smart private rooms. Dorms CH$15,000, doubles CH$45,000

Kalagen Hostel Av Valparaíso 618 ☎ 32 299 1669, ⓦ kalagenhostel.com. Smart, large and lively hostel on Viña's main shopping drag, with spacious communal areas, and organized tours. Expect parties. Dorms CH$1000, doubles CH$25,000

My Father's House Gregorio Marañón 1210 ☎ 32 261 6136, ⓦ myfathershouse.cl. Spacious, quiet single, double and triple rooms, swimming pool, and gracious owners. It's about 2km from the centre; catch *colectivo* #31, #82 or #131. Doubles CH$40,000

EATING

Cevasco Av Valparaíso 694–700. Bustling *fuente de soda* serving up tasty – if decidedly unhealthy – *completos*, burgers and *barros lucos* (CH$1350–5000). Mon–Sat 10am–10pm.

Entre Masas 5 Norte 235 ☎ 32 297 9919. Excellent little bakery, specializing in *empanadas* (CH$1500–2200): there are dozens of varieties including chorizo and goat's cheese. Daily 10am–10pm.

La Flor de Chile 8 Norte 601 ☎ 32 268 9554, ⓦ laflordechile.cl. Atmospheric restaurant with a Spanish-influenced menu and a good-value set lunch (CH$48,000). Mon–Sat 10am–midnight.

Jerusalem Quinta, at Alvarez ☎ 32 247 4704. Popular with students, this no-frills Middle Eastern place offers inexpensive juices, falafel wraps and kebabs (from CH$2000). Mon–Sat 11.30am–9.30pm.

Panzoni Paseo Cousino 12B ☎ 32 271 4134. This charming Italian joint has a handful of tables, great service and inexpensive pastas and salads (set lunch CH$3800). Mon–Sat noon–4pm & 8pm–midnight.

DRINKING, NIGHTLIFE AND ENTERTAINMENT

Café Journal Agua Santa 2 ☎ 32 266 6654. Thriving university student haunt, complete with pub grub and regular live music. Mon–Thurs 10am–4am, Fri & Sat 10am–5am, Sun 7pm–4am.

Scratch Quillota 830 ☎ 32 238 1381, ⓦ scratch.cl. For more than 20 years this club has been pulling in the crowds, and on weekends it is packed to capacity until sunrise. DJs play a mix of reggaeton, dance, electronica and pop. Thurs, Fri & Sat 10pm–5/6am.

DIRECTORY

Banks and exchange Numerous banks, most with ATMs and cambios, are found along Av Arlegui.

Hospital Hospital Gustavo Fricke is on Álvarez 1532, at Simón Bolívar (☎ 32 267 5067); for emergencies call ☎ 32 265 2328, ⓦ hospitalfricke.cl).

Post office Plaza La Torre 32, just off the main square (Mon–Fri 9am–7pm Sat 10am–1pm).

ISLA NEGRA

The seaside village of **ISLA NEGRA** (not, incidentally, an island), about 80km south of Valparaíso, was the site of Pablo Neruda's favourite home. The **Casa Museo Pablo Neruda**, Calle Poeta Neruda s/n (Tues–Sun: Jan & Feb 10am–8pm; March–Dec 10am–6pm; CH$5000 including tour in English; students CH$1500, reservations essential in summer; ☎ 2 2777 8741, ⓦ fundacionneruda.org), lies down a wooded trail by the sea, a short walk from the main road. Larger than his other two homes, Isla Negra is fascinating for the sheer amount of **exotic objects** that Neruda accumulated here, and the consideration that went into every aspect of the design – from the arrangement of wooden ships' figureheads in the living room, to the positioning of blue glass bottles along the seaward side of the house. The poet's collection includes African wooden carvings, ships in bottles and an amazing array of seashells, housed in a purpose-built room that Neruda designed but never completed. A strong nautical theme runs throughout; there is even a small boat on the terrace so that the poet could be "a sailor on land".

ARRIVAL AND DEPARTURE

By bus Pullman (ⓦ www.pullman.cl) and Tur-Bus (ⓦ turbus.cl) run buses from Santiago's Terminal Alameda to Isla Negra (every 30min; 2hr). There are also services (every 15min; 1hr 30min) from Valparaíso.

Norte Chico

Dominated by dry scrubland and sparse vegetation, the **Norte Chico** region, which stretches roughly from the northern tip of Santiago to the southern reaches of the Atacama, might seem unremarkable from a bus window. Visitors are, however, drawn here for its **stargazing**, long sandy beaches, and trips to its far-flung national parks. The biggest population centre is the relaxed seaside town of **La Serena** with its bustling market and colonial-style architecture, while the fertile **Elqui Valley**, which once inspired Nobel-Prize-winning poet Gabriela Mistral, is now the focal point for the country's favourite tipple, pisco. The islands of **Damas** and **Choros** brim over with seals, penguins and cormorants. Further north, the mining town of **Copiapó**, currently undergoing one of its regular copper-induced booms, is the jumping-off point for the stunning kaleidoscopic landscapes of **Parque Nacional Nevado de Tres Cruces** and **Parque Nacional Pan de Azúcar**. Horseriding, trekking and kayaking are all attractions which are likely to keep tourists in this region longer than they expected.

LA SERENA

LA SERENA, 474km north of Santiago, is one of Chile's prime **beach resorts**, though its charms also include an impressive number of churches and several worthwhile museums. It is also an excellent base for exploring the surrounding countryside. The city was founded in 1544, and during the following century it was the target of multiple raids by the French and British, including the pirate Francis Drake.

Downtown La Serena

With a tranquil vibe, La Serena's central streets are easy to wander around on foot. The town's largest church is the Neoclassical **Iglesia Catedral**, at the corner of Los Carrera and Cordovez, off the Plaza de Armas, which has a beautiful, marble-decorated interior. **Iglesia de San Francisco**, Balmaceda 640, was the first church here to be built out of stone, and **Iglesia Santo Domingo**, Cordovez s/n, dates back to 1673.

The **Casa Gabriel González Videla**, Matta 495, on the west side of the Plaza de Armas (Mon–Fri 10am–6pm, Sat 10am–1pm; CH$600), is well worth a visit. Originally the home of former president González Videla, who was born in the town, it is now a museum housing an impressive collection of fine art and contemporary painting.

At the junction of Cienfuegos with Cordovez, the **Museo Arqueológico** (Tues–Fri 9.30am–5.50pm, Sat 10am–1pm & 4–7pm, Sun 10am–1pm; CH$600, Sun free, ticket also valid for Casa Gabriel Gonzáles Videla) displays elaborate Diaguita ceramics, as well as a 2.5m *moai* statue from Easter Island.

About two blocks west from Paza de Armas, the tranquil and beautifully sculpted Japanese-style **Jardín El Corazón** (Tues–Sun 10am–6pm; CH$1000) is the perfect place to while away a sunny afternoon.

The beaches

While reasonably crowded in the summer, the **beaches** are quiet for the rest of the year. The nearest beach area is a half-hour walk west from the city centre from Jardín El Corazón along Francisco de Aguirre.

Between La Serena and the town of Coquimbo, a **cycle lane** runs beside a dozen or so wide, sandy beaches lined with pricey condominiums, hotels and restaurants – an easy and enjoyable day-trip. Many hostels and travel agencies have bikes to rent. Most of the beaches are suitable for swimming and windsurfing,

4

TOUR OPERATORS

From La Serena, a number of tour companies run excursions in the surrounding area. Popular tours (CH$15,000–50,000) of the **Elqui Valley** include pisco-tasting, stargazing at the **Observatorio Mamalluca** and penguin-watching at **Reserva Nacional Pingüino de Humboldt**.

Daniel Russ ☎09 9454 6000, ⊛jeeptour-laserena .cl. An experienced and extremely knowledgeable man (with a jeep), who runs standard excursions for small groups, as well as trips to Paso del Agua Negra and tailor-made outings.

Kayak Australis ☎2 2334 2015, ⊛kayakaustralis .com. Specializes in multi-day sea-kayak trips around Chile, including one to Isla Damas. Book through their Santiago office at El Bosque Sur 65, Piso 2, Oficina 3,

Las Condes, or online.

Mundo Caballo Km27, along the road between La Serena and Vicuña ☎09 9219 7872, ⊛mundocaballo .cl. Stables 20km outside La Serena offering various horseriding trips, including one at night (CH$12,000– 50,000). Best contacted by phone.

Turismo Delfines Matta 655 ☎51 222 3624, ⊛turismodelfines.cl. Established operator specializing in bilingual guided trips to Isla Damas.

DOWNTOWN LA SERENA

0 200 metres

N

RN Pingüino de Humboldt & Copiapó

Río Elqui

Capilla de Santa Inés

ALMAGRO

COLÓN

Parque Pedro de Valdivia

P. PABLO MUÑOZ

AV. JUAN BOHON (PANAMERICANA)

BRASIL

Supermarket

Mercado La Recova

ZORRILLA

CANTOURNET

Iglesia de la Merced

BALMACEDA

CIENFUEGOS

RENGIFO

MATTA

LOS CARRERA

PRAT

O'HIGGINS

Iglesia San Agustín

GANDARILLAS

Plaza de Armas

Iglesia Catedral

LAN Office

CORDOVEZ

Museo Arqueológico

Jardín El Corazón

Iglesia Santo Domingo

Casa Gabriel González-Videla

Banco de Chile

Supermarket Santa Isabel

LAS CASAS

DE LA BARRA

Iglesia de San Francisco

CIENFUEGOS

VICUÑA

LAUTARO

BENAVENTE

La Florida Airport (5km)

Turismo Delfines

Colectivos for Coquimbo

DOMEYKO

Colectivos to Valle Elqui

COLO COLO

INFANTE

AV. FRANCISCO DE AGUIRRE

2 & Avenida del Mar

A. BELLO

JUAN DE DIOS PEÑI

8 & Coquimbo

Boats to Elqui Valley

ÁNFION MUÑOZ

■ **ACCOMMODATION**
Aji Verde Hostel	1
Hostal Family Home	5
Hostal Maria Casa	4
Hostal El Punto	3
Sole di Mare	2

● **EATING & DRINKING**
Café Centenario	3
La Casa del Guatón	1
La Mia Pizza	4
Rapsodia	2

4, 5 & Bus terminal (500m)

although Playa Cuatro Esquinas is known to have strong rip currents.

ARRIVAL AND INFORMATION

By plane Aeropuerto La Florida is 5km east of town along Ruta 41; catch a taxi (CH$6500), transfer (CH$2500) or *micro* to the centre.

Destinations Antofagasta (2 daily; 1hr 25min); Santiago (6 daily; 1hr).

By bus The main bus terminal is located on corner Amunátegui, at Av El Santo, a 20min walk south of the centre.

Destinations Antofagasta (20 daily; 12hr); Arica (5 daily; 24hr); Calama (11 daily; 15hr); Copiapó (every 30min–1hr; 5hr); Iquique (8 daily; 18hr); Montegrande (every 30min–1hr; 1hr 50min); Ovalle (every 15min; 1hr 20min); Pisco Elqui (every 30min–1hr; 2hr); Santiago (every 30min; 7hr); Valparaíso (6 daily; 5hr); Vicuña (every 30min–1hr; 1hr).

By colectivo Coquimbo (frequent daily departures from Av Francisco de Aguirre, between Los Carrera and Balmaceda; 20min); Elqui Valley (several departures daily from Domeyko in the centre; 1hr).

Tourist information Sernatur, Matta 461, Plaza de Armas (Dec–Feb daily 9am–9pm; March–Nov Mon–Fri 9am–6pm, Sat 10am–4pm; ☎ 51 222 5199).

ACCOMMODATION

Aji Verde Hostel Vicuña 415 ☎ 51 248 9016, ⓦ ajiverdehostel.cl. A fun atmosphere pervades this central, HI-affiliated hostel with young staff, a roof terrace, kitchen and plenty of common areas for connecting with fellow travellers. Dorms CH$8500, doubles CH$22,000

Hostal Family Home Av El Santo 1056 ☎ 51 221 2099, ⓦ www.familyhome.cl. Good-value *hostal* that lives up to its name and is conveniently located close to the bus terminal (albeit on a busy road), with singles, doubles and triples (some en suite), plus use of a kitchen. CH$25,000

Hostal Maria Casa Las Rojas 18 ☎51 222 9282, ⓦhostalmariacasa.cl. Small guesthouse with an effusive hostess, kitchen access, bikes to rent, and a relaxing garden; popular with backpackers. A 3min walk from the main bus station – so good for late arrivals. Dorms CH$10,000, doubles CH$20,000

★**Hostal El Punto** Andres Bello 979 ☎51 222 8474, ⓦhostalelpunto.cl. German-run hostel with friendly and knowledgeable staff, daily excursions, an on-site café, laundry service and spotless rooms; popular with travellers of all ages. Call ahead if arriving later than 10pm. Dorms CH$9000, doubles CH$21,000

Sole di Mare Parcela 66, Peñuelas ☎51 231 2531. Lovely, grassy campsite down at the quieter end of the beach, halfway between La Serena and Coquimbo (buses between the two stop nearby). Per person CH$5000

EATING AND DRINKING

The city's main places to eat are along Calle Prat. Coquimbo, however, is livelier for drinking and nightlife.

Café Centenario Cordovez 391. Lavazza coffee (CH$1500–3000), regional wines and local beer are served in this chic corner spot on the southeast corner of Plaza de Armas. Mon–Fri 8am–8pm.

La Casa del Guatón Brasil 750 ☎51 221 1519. Lively, friendly and intimate, this colonial-style restaurant serves the town's best *parrilladas* (from CH$15,000). There's often live music. Mon–Sat 12.30pm–12.30am, Sun 12.30–6pm.

La Mia Pizza Av del Mar 2100. Seafront pizzeria that offers excellent fish dishes as well as large portions of tasty pizza (from CH$5000). Mon–Sat 12.30pm–midnight, Sun 12.30–4.30pm.

Rapsodia Prat 470 local 19. Dine alfresco on expertly prepared meat and fish dishes in one of La Serena's traditional courtyards (dishes CH$3000–9000). Mon–Wed 9am–9pm, Thurs & Fri 9am–11pm; Jan & Feb also Sat 9am–11pm.

COQUIMBO

A fifteen-minute *colectivo* ride south from La Serena lies its rougher, livelier twin: **Coquimbo**, the region's main port. The beautifully restored historical district of **Barrio Inglés** comprises several plazas with a far more exciting eating and nightlife scene than La Serena. Coquimbo's only real drawback is the lack of budget accommodation, though there is one exception.

The most striking landmark, looming over town, is a huge 93m cross, the **Cruz del Tercer Milenio** (ⓦcruzdeltercermilenio .cl). This slightly bizarre construction, the base of which provides a great viewpoint over town, was funded by the King of Morocco for the benefit of the town's Lebanese Muslim community.

ACCOMMODATION

Hostal Nomade C Regimento Coquimbo 5 ☎51 231 5665 or ☎09 9369 5885. HI-affiliated hostel in the large and rambling former residence of the French ambassador, which has a slightly haunted-house feel. It has informative staff, large rooms with exceptionally high ceilings, internet, kitchen facilities and other backpacker conveniences. Dorms from CH$13,000, doubles CH$26,000

STARGAZING IN CHILE

With an average of 360 cloudless nights per year, northern Chile has some of the clearest skies in the world, so it's little wonder that it's home to some of the world's most powerful telescopes. The larger observatories allow public visits free of charge during the day, allowing you to view the equipment, though not to use it. There are an ever-increasing number of small centres offering nocturnal stargazing facilities expressly for tourists, though the best set up for visits are **Cerro Mamalluca** (see p.405) and **Del Pangue** (see p.405) in the Elqui Valley.

The following places are the best of the big Elqui observatories; there is no public transport other than organized tours and you need to reserve in advance.

OBSERVATORIES

Cerro Paranal ☎55 243 5335, Ⓔvisits@eso.org, ⓦeso.org. 130km south of Antofagasta, the observatory sports four VLTs (Very Large Telescopes), each with an 8m mirror. Tours Sat 10am & 2pm..

Cerro Tololo Office at Casilla 603, La Serena ☎51 220 5200, ⓦwww.ctio.noao.edu. Some 70km east of La Serena, this Inter-American observatory features an impressive 8.1m Gemini telescope. Tours Sat 9.15am–noon & 1.15–4pm.

La Silla Office near the airport at Panorámica 4461 ☎51 227 2601, ⓦeso.org. 147km northeast of La Serena, and home to 14 telescopes. Tours Aug–May Sat 2–4pm.

EATING, DRINKING AND NIGHTLIFE

With many fish restaurants, Coquimbo is a seafood-lover's paradise, and also comes alive at night with lively pubs and clubs – a popular drinking area is along Alduante between Freire and Argandoña.

Dolce Helado Aldunate 862. If the ice-cream stand out front doesn't tempt you in, then live music wafting from the terrace will. Filling and reasonably priced Italian dishes (CH$5000–8000) includes seafood lasagne. Mon–Fri 10am–11pm, Sat 1–11pm, Sun 1–8pm.

Pub Aduana Argandoña 360. Cold beer, pisco-based cocktails and people-watching are the orders of the night at this popular bar with street-side tables and live music. Drinks from CH$2000. Thurs–Sat 10pm–5am.

ELQUI VALLEY

East of La Serena, the 62km journey to **Vicuña** is a scenic trip with breathtaking vistas of the tranquil **Elqui Valley**. Its fertile greenery contrasts with the valley's sandy sides, its slopes a spectrum of red, green and gold due to the mineral-rich soil. The ribbon of the highway, lined with pink peppercorn trees, runs along the valley floor, past vineyards and grapes drying on canvas sheets by the roadside. Tours of the valley typically take in the giant dam and man-made **Lago Puklara**, popular with windsurfers and kitesurfers, the historical village of **Vicuña**, the laidback community of **Pisco Elqui** and a pisco-tasting distillery, before finishing with stargazing at the **Observatorio Mamalluca**.

Vicuña

Sleepy **Vicuña** makes a convenient stopover for exploring the Elqui Valley. Formerly home to Nobel Prize-winner **Gabriela Mistrál**, it has a **museum** at Gabriela Mistrál 759 (Jan & Feb Mon–Sat 10am–7pm, Sun 10am–6pm; March–Dec Mon–Fri 10am–5.45pm, Sat 10.30am–6pm, Sun 10am–1pm; CH$600), dedicated to her. **Planta Capel** (daily 10am–5pm; CH$2500–15,000; ☎ 51 255 4337, ⦿ piscocapel.cl), the valley's largest **pisco distillery**, lies just south of town, and has half-hourly bilingual tours tracking the Muscatel grape's journey from the vine to the pisco bottle, culminating in a small free sample at the end.

ARRIVAL AND INFORMATION

By bus Vicuña's main terminal is one block south of the Plaza de Armas, on O'Higgins, at Prat (☎ 51 241 1348). For Santiago and other major cities, it is easiest to return to La Serena.

Destinations Coquimbo (20 daily; 1hr 30min); Pisco Elqui (every 30min–1hr; 1hr); La Serena (every 30min–1hr; 1hr).

By colectivo *Colectivos* to La Serena and Coquimbo leave from the bus station when full (daily 7am–9pm).

Tourist information Inside the Torre Bauer, San Martín s/n, in the northwest corner of the Plaza de Armas (Mon–Fri 8.30am–6pm, Sat 9am–6pm, Sun 9am–2pm; ☎ 51 220 9125).

ACCOMMODATION

Hostal Donde Rita Condell 443 ☎ 51 241 9611, ⦿ hostaldonderita.com. A comfortable set of rooms surrounded by a leafy garden, complete with pool and terrace area. Overseen by a charming German hostess, who prepares delicious breakfasts. Doubles CH$28,000

Hostal Valle Hermoso Gabriela Mistral 706 ☎ 51 241 1206, ⦿ hostalvallehermoso.com. Motherly Lucia presides over this restored century-old adobe house with a bright central patio. Minimalist but sweet rooms have comfortable beds and private bathrooms complete with piping-hot showers. Doubles CH$25,000

PISCO

The climatic conditions in the Elqui Valley are ideal for growing the sweet Muscatel grapes from which the clear, brandy-like **pisco**, Chile's national drink, is derived. Pisco is a constant source of **dispute** between Chile and Peru. Peru claims that the drink originates from the Peruvian port of the same name, and some historical records demonstrate that pisco has been consumed in that area since the Spaniards introduced vineyards in the early 1600s.

Chileans claim that they have also been producing pisco for centuries, that their pisco is of better quality and that it plays a greater role in Chilean society. In both Chile and Peru, pisco is normally consumed in a **pisco sour** – a mix of pisco, lemon juice, sugar syrup, egg white, crushed ice and a drop of angostura bitters. It goes down deceptively smoothly, but packs a real punch.

EATING

Chaski O'Higgins 159 ☎09 9793 7237. This restaurant's rustic outdoor setting belies its sophisticated cuisine (CH$3000–9000). The owners also offer cycling and horseriding tours. Mon & Wed–Sat 10am–4pm & 6–9.30pm, Sun noon–6pm.

Soledad y Yo Carrera 320. A typical *picada* or family restaurant-bar, popular with locals, serving up substantial servings of Chilean favourites, and decent drinks (from CH$1500). Mon–Thurs 11am–1am, Fri–Sun 11am–3am.

Del Pangue Observatory

In a spectacular mountaintop setting 17km south of Vicuña, **Del Pangue** offers an intimate and personalized stargazing experience specifically designed for amateur astronomers. Two-hour tours (Jan & Feb 9pm & 11pm; June–Aug 6pm; rest of year 8pm; no tours five days around the full moon; tour times often change depending on planet positions; CH$18,000) are conducted by bona fide astronomers, and Del Pangue's state-of-the-art 63cm Obsession telescope is light years ahead of other public observatories. Book tours at the office at San Martin 233, Vicuña (daily 10am–7pm; ☎51 241 2584, ⓦobservatoriodelpangue.blogspot.com).

Observatorio Cerro Mamalluca

The **Observatorio Cerro Mamalluca** is located 9km northeast of Vicuña. Compared to other nearby observatories, its 30cm telescope is tiny, but it still offers magnification of 150 times – sufficient to look closely at the craters on the moon and to view nebulae, star clusters and Saturn. There are two tours offered (Oct–April 8.30pm, 10.30pm & 12.30am; May–Sept 6.30pm & 8.30pm; CH$4500): "Basic Astronomy" and "Andean Cosmovision", looking at the night sky as seen by the pre-Columbian inhabitants of the area. Shuttles to and from the observatory (CH$1500 return) depart from the Cerro Mamalluca office in Vicuña (Gabriela Mistrál 260, office 1; Mon–Fri 8.30am–8.30pm, Sat & Sun 10am–2pm & 4–8pm; ☎51 267 0330 or ☎51 241 1352) half an hour before the tour starts. Reserve tickets in advance, especially in the peak months from December to February.

Pisco Elqui

The green and laidback village of **PISCO ELQUI** boasts a beautiful hillside setting alongside the Río Clara, with unparalleled views of the Elqui Valley. The shaded **Plaza de Armas**, with its brightly painted Gothic church, hosts the **Mercado Artesanal** in the summer. A block away, the Destileria **Pisco Mistral** is Chile's oldest pisco distillery, and offers guided tours (O'Higgins 746; Jan–Feb daily 11.30am–9pm; March–Dec Tues–Sun 10am–6pm; CH$6000; ☎51 245 1358, ⓦdestileriapiscomistral.cl) complete with tastings. **Los Nichos** (tours daily: April–Nov 10am–6pm; Dec–March 11am–7pm; CH$1,000; ☎51 245 1085, ⓦfundolosnichos.cl) is an old-fashioned distillery 3km south of Pisco Elqui, and worth visiting to see pisco processed by hand.

ARRIVAL, INFORMATION AND ACTIVITIES

There are currently no ATMs here; bring plenty of cash.

By bus Buses stop in by the plaza and also go up into the village.

Destinations La Serena/Coquimbo (every 1–2hr; 2hr–2hr 30min); Vicuña (every 30min–1hr; 50min).

Horseriding Alcohuaz Expediciones, in Montegrande, 4km before Pisco (☎09 8788 1978, ⓦcaballo-elqui.cl), is run by a genuine *huaso* (Chilean cowboy) and offers excellent horseriding trips.

Tourist information Hostel owners will be able to help you with information, but an excellent option for local knowledge of the area is the tour agency Turismo Migrantes, O'Higgins s/n (☎51 245 1917, ☎09 9829 5630, ⓦturismomigrantes.cl), where Bárbara and Pablo organize pisco tours, horseriding and bike rides in the surrounding area, and even stargazing tours at their own home.

ACCOMMODATION

Refugio del Angel El Condor s/n, 1km southeast of the plaza ☎51 245 1292, ⓦcampingrefugiodelangel.cl. This pretty riverside campground has shady camping spots, with picnic tables and hot showers. The "teahouse" provides breakfast, drinks and snacks. Per person `CH$7000`

El Tesoro de Elqui Prat s/n ☎51 245 1069, ⓦtesoro-elqui.cl. Cosy adobe dorms and rooms – one with a skylight for stargazing – and excellent food. The owners can help organize motorbike rental and tours. Dorms `CH$11,000`, doubles `CH$35,000`

4

Hostal Triskel Baquedano s/n ☎09 9418 8680, ⓦhostaltriskel.cl. Lovingly decorated rooms and decent breakfasts. They can arrange hiking, biking and horseriding too. Dorms CH$15,000 doubles CH$30,000

RESERVA NACIONAL PINGÜINO DE HUMBOLDT

The **Reserva Nacional Pingüino de Humboldt** (April–Nov Wed–Sun 9am–5.30pm; Dec–March daily 9am–5.30pm; CH$2500) is a remarkable marine wildlife reserve 110km north of La Serena, which comprises three islands jutting from the cold Pacific waters: Isla Chañaral, Isla Choros and Isla Damas. The islands are home to *chundungos* (sea otters), a noisy colony of **sea lions**, the **Humboldt penguin**, four species of cormorants, clamouring **Peruvian boobies** and countless seagulls.

Unless you plan to stay the night at Isla Chañaral (see below), it is much easier to visit as part of a tour from La Serena (see box, p.40). **Boats** sail (CH$8000/person; sailings dependent on conditions) from **Caleta de Choros**, the small fishing community closest to the islands, along the steep jagged coastline of **Isla Choros**. You get close enough to see the wildlife in great detail, and on the way to the island, pods of curious **bottlenose dolphins** often frolic around the boat; it's also possible to spot humpback, blue and killer **whales**. On the way back, visitors are allowed a short ramble on sandy **Isla Damas**, whose pristine beaches are home to a smaller penguin population.

INFORMATION

Tourist information There is a Conaf-run Centro de Información Ambiental (April–Nov Wed–Sun 9am–5.30pm; Dec–March daily 9am–5.30pm; ☎51 261 1555 or ☎09 9544 3052, ⓦwww.conaf.cl) at Caleta de Choros, with informative displays on local flora and fauna, and another smaller one at Caleta Chañaral.

ACCOMMODATION

Several people on Isla Chañaral rent out simple rooms in their homes (around CH$20,000 a double). There is a basic campsite at Caleta Chañaral, but camping is not permitted on Isla Damas.

COPIAPÓ

The prosperous mining town of **COPIAPÓ**, 333km north of La Serena, was founded in 1744 and benefited greatly from the **silver boom** of the 1830s. Today, Copiapó still makes its living from mining, nowadays for **copper**. It will forever be linked in many people's minds with the 2010 rock collapse at the nearby San José mine, which left 33 miners ("Los 33") trapped underground for 69 days before the world cheered their safe rescue.

At the heart of Copiapó is the large **Plaza Prat**, dotted with pepper trees; handicraft stalls line the plaza's east side, facing the mall. The Neoclassical **Iglesia Catedral Nuestra Señora de Rosario** graces the southwest corner, while on the corner of Atacama and Rancagua, a ten-minute walk from the plaza, the **Museo Regional de Atacama** (Tues–Fri 9am–5.45pm, Sat 10am–12.45pm & 3–5.45pm, Sun 10am–12.45pm; CH$600, free on Sun; ☎52 221 2313, ⓦmuseodeatacama.cl) has a display on the trapped miners of the San José mine, which includes their fateful hand-written note: "We are fine in the shelter – the 33". The other well-presented displays cover the exploration of the desert, the War of the Pacific,

---

COPIAPÓ TOUR OPERATORS

The main full-day destinations are located east into the cordillera, taking in **Parque Nacional Nevado de Tres Cruces** and sometimes **Laguna Verde** and **Ojos del Salado**; and north to **Parque Nacional Pan de Azúcar**. Half-day trips go north into the Atacama dunes, west to the beaches around Bahía Inglesa, or east up the Copiapó River Valley.

Atacama Chile ☎56 221 1191, ⓦatacamachile .com. This agency runs a range of trips, including to Parque Nacional Nevado de Tres Cruces, Pan de Azúcar and Llanos de Challe.

Aventurismo ☎09 9599 2184, ⓦaventurismo.cl. Mountaineering outfit specializing in multi-day ascents of the Ojos de Salado volcano between November and March.

pre-Columbian peoples of the region and the Inca road system.

ARRIVAL AND DEPARTURE

By plane Aeropuerto Desierto de Atacama is around 50km northwest of the city; both the Manuel Flores Salinas minibus and Casther bus meet arriving planes and travel into town; taxis cost around CH$25,000.

Destinations Some of these routes require stopovers, which the travel times listed take into account. Calama (1–2 daily; 1hr 10min–4hr); Santiago (5–7 daily; 1hr 20min).

By bus Copiapó's main bus terminal is at Chañarcillo 655, two blocks south of Plaza Prat. Across the road, also on Chañarcillo, is the Tur-Bus terminal; one block south, at Freire and Colipí, is the Pullman Bus terminal. For Caldera and Bahía Inglesa, Casther (☎ 52 221 8889), Expreso Caldera (☎ 09 6155 8048) and Trans Puma (☎ 52 223 5841) run a frequent service from the small bus station on the corner of Esperanza and Chacabuco, opposite the Líder Hypermarket (you can also catch a Casthar transfer to the airport here). Alternately you can catch one of the yellow *colectivos* that wait on the same corner opposite Líder.

Destinations Antofagasta (15 daily; 7hr); Arica (11 daily; 17hr); Calama (15 daily; 10hr); Caldera (every 30min; 1hr); Iquique (12 daily; 13hr); La Serena (every 30min–1hr; 5hr); Santiago (22 daily; 12hr); Valparaíso (6 daily; 12hr).

INFORMATION

Tourist information The well-organized Sernatur office is at Los Carrera 691 on Plaza Prat (Mon–Fri 8.30am–7pm, Sat 10am–2pm, ☎ 52 221 2838). Conaf is at Juan Martínez 56 (Mon–Thurs 8.30am–5.30pm & Fri 8.30am–4pm; ☎ 52 221 3404).

ACCOMMODATION

Hotel Palace Atacama 741 ☎ 52 221 2852, ⌨ palacehotel.cl. Copious wood-panelling gives *Hotel Palace* a vaguely 1970s feel. The carpeted rooms are comfortable enough, though overpriced (try haggling). CH$38,000

Residencial Benbow Rodriguez 541 ☎ 52 221 7634. Clean, no-frills rooms (CH$6000 extra for an en suite) around a narrow courtyard. Breakfast costs extra. Doubles CH$18,000

EATING

Café Columbia Plaza Prat on Colipi, at Carrera. Pricey but excellent, this place serves good coffee (CH$1000–2100), plus cakes, ice-cream sundaes, sandwiches and pizzas. Mon–Sat 9am–9pm.

Flor de la Canela Chacabuco 710 ☎ 52 221 9570. This cheerful Peruvian joint offers a change from the Copiapó norm, with tasty dishes like *ceviche* and *lomo saltado* (mains CH$8300–14,900). Daily 1–3pm & 8–11pm.

AROUND COPIAPÓ

The landscape surrounding Copiapó is astonishingly varied, with the salt flats of the **Parque Nacional Nevado de Tres Cruces**, mesmerizing **Laguna Verde**, active volcano **Ojos de Salado** and, to the west, the fine white sands of **Bahía Inglesa** and **Caldera**.

Parque Nacional Nevado de Tres Cruces

Remote and ruggedly beautiful **Parque Nacional Nevado de Tres Cruces** (daily 8.30am–6pm; CH$4000) is located east of Copiapó via Ruta 31, which winds through the mercilessly desolate desert landscape. The road climbs steeply before reaching the **Salar de Maricunga** – a great field of white crystals on the edge of the park, dotted with emerald-coloured salt pools – and continuing on towards **Paso San Francisco** on the Argentine border.

The park consists of two separate parts. The larger is the 490-square-kilometre **Laguna Santa Rosa** sector, 146km east of Copiapó at an altitude of 3700m, which comprises half of the salt flat and the namesake lake, with roaming herds of **vicuñas** and **guanacos** feeding on the abundant grasslands. The pale blue lagoon, dotted with flamingos and giant coots, is set against a backdrop of snow-streaked volcanoes, including the grand **Nevado Tres Cruces** (6749m). On the west side of the lake is a small and very rustic Conaf-run *refugio*, consisting of bare floorspace, basic cooking facilities and a privy out back.

Cutting across a vast expanse of parched brown land, dotted with hardy yellow *altiplano* plants, you reach the 120-square-kilometre **Laguna del Negro Francisco** sector, around 85km south. In summer it becomes a sea of pink and beige, thanks to the presence of eight thousand or so Andean, Chilean and James **flamingos** that migrate here from neighbouring Argentina, Bolivia and Peru. On the west side of the lake, Conaf's *Refugio Laguna del Negro Francisco* has beds and kitchen facilities; make reservations with Copiapó's Conaf office (CH$10,000/person).

4

Laguna Verde and Volcán Ojos de Salado

The magnificent spectacle of the misnamed **Laguna Verde** lies 65km beyond Laguna Santa Rosa, at a whopping altitude of 4325m. The first flash of its brilliant turquoise waters, around a bend in the road, is breathtaking. On the lake's salty white shore are some rustic and relaxing **hot springs** inside a little wooden shack. It's possible to camp here: you must bring all necessary supplies with you, including water, and remember that night-time temperatures drop well below freezing. Beyond the lake loom three volcanoes, including the second-highest peak in Latin America – **Ojos de Salado**. At an elevation of 6887m, it trails just behind Argentina's 6962m Aconcagua as the tallest mountain in the Americas. It is also the world's highest active volcano, with recent eruptions in 1937 and 1956.

Caldera and Bahía Inglesa

The towns of Caldera and Bahía Inglesa, 7km apart and 75km west of Copiapó, are both popular **beach resorts** famous for their large, delicious **scallops**. **CALDERA** itself is an unremarkable little town, though the Gothic **Iglesia San Vicente** (1862) on Plaza Condell is worth a look. Pedestrianized **Gana**, lined with craft stalls in the summer, makes for a nice stroll between the square and the waterfront **Costanera** (pier) – home to the oldest railway station in Chile, dating back to 1850, and now a museum (Tues–Sun 10am–2pm & 4–7pm; CH$600) and events centre. The pier is the best place to sample inexpensive seafood *empanadas* and other fishy delights.

Caldera's main beach, small seaweed-tinted Copiapina, is not the best in the area. For crystal-clear turquoise waters and long stretches of white sand, head to nearby **Bahía Inglesa**, either by *colectivo* or along the cycle path parallel to the road, which is immensely popular in summer for its laidback atmosphere, the proximity of the ocean and an abundance of cheap seafood *empanadas* vendors

along the seafront. There are several small and sheltered beaches along the main Avenida El Morro, with the wide crescent of **Playa Las Machas** stretching into the distance.

ARRIVAL AND INFORMATION

By bus Buses to Copiapó leave from a small terminal at the corner of Cifuentes and Ossa Varas. Long-distance services to Chañaral and further north are provided by Pullman Bus and Tur-Bus, from Caldera's main terminal at Gallo and Vallejos.

Destinations Chañaral (12 daily; 1hr); Copiapó (every 30min; 1hr).

By micro and colectivo Micros for Bahía Inglesa leave from the Plaza de Armas every 15min in Jan and Feb. The rest of the year, black taxi *colectivos* leave from the plaza.

Tourist information On Plaza Carlos Condell in Caldera (daily 9am–2pm & 4–7pm; ☏ 52 231 6076, ⓦ caldera.cl).

ACCOMMODATION AND EATING

All these options are in Bahía, which has a greater selection of accommodation than Caldera, though it tends to be overpriced during peak season.

Camping Bahía Inglesa Off Playa Las Machas, just south of the town ☏ 52 231 6399 or ☏ 52 231 5424. An excellent place to camp, with hot showers, picnic tables and restaurants. Pitch for up to six people CH$26,000, cabin CH$40,000

Los Jardines de Bahía Inglesa Copiapó 100 ☏ 52 231 5359, ⓦ jardinesbahia.cl. These smart cabañas sleep up to eleven people. There's a good-sized pool, a table-tennis table and a decent Italian restaurant. Cabins for two people CH$41,000

El Plateao El Morro 756 ☏ 09 8826 0007. Restaurant-bar with a terrace overlooking the beach, good service and an innovative menu offering exceptional seafood dishes (around CH$8000–10,000). Daily 1–5pm & 5pm–midnight.

PARQUE NACIONAL PAN DE AZÚCAR

About 180km north of Copiapó, **Parque Nacional Pan de Azúcar** entices visitors with its spectacular coastal desert landscape, which alternates between steep cliffs, studded with a multitude of cactus species, and pristine white beaches. A small gravel road leads into the park from the compact town of Chañaral and continues past Playa Blanca and Playa Los Piqueros to **Caleta Pan de Azúcar**, a small fishing village inside the park. **Isla Pan de Azúcar**, home to Humboldt penguins, sea lions, sea otters and a wealth of marine birds, lies a short distance offshore. Although landing on the island is forbidden, fishing boats (daily: March–Nov 9am–6pm; Dec–Feb 9am–7pm; CH$50,000 for up to ten people, or whatever deal you can strike) get visitors close enough to see (and smell) the wildlife. A 9km trail runs north from the village to the **Mirador Pan de Azúcar**, a lookout point offering staggering panoramic views of the coastline. Also heading north from the village, towards Ruta 5, is a dirt road with a 15km trail branching off to the west that leads you through the arid landscape to **Las Lomitas**, an outlook point often visited by inquisitive **desert foxes** and shrouded in rolling *camanchaca* (sea mist), the main water source for all the coastal vegetation.

ARRIVAL AND INFORMATION

By bus There are no public buses to the park, though northbound buses from Copiapó can drop you off in Chañaral, the nearest town. Ask around at the bus terminal in Chañaral, and you should be able to get someone to take you to the park. Taxis cost CH$15,000 each way – worth it for a group. Alternatively, take a day-trip tour from Copiapó (see box, p.406).

Tourist information Conaf's Centro de Información Ambiental (daily 8.30am–12.30pm & 2–6pm) is opposite Playa Los Piqueros and has maps and information on the park, as well as a display of local cacti. The park fee of CH$4000 is payable here; no fee is charged if entering the park from the east.

ACCOMMODATION AND EATING

Rough camping is not allowed in the park, but there are a number of authorized camping areas. In Caleta Pan de Azúcar, a handful of restaurants on the water's edge serve fried fish, rice and *empanadas*.

Camping Los Pingüinos Just north of the Caleta Pan de Azúcar ☎52 248 1209. If you've got your own camping gear, this campsite has decent facilities. Per person CH$5000

Pan de Azúcar Lodge Playa Piqueros, south of Caleta Pan de Azúcar ☎52 221 9271, ⊛pandeazucarlodge.cl. *Pan de Azúcar Lodge* has the national park's best camping facilities, with barbecues and picnic tables, as well as cabañas sleeping up to eight. Camping per person CH$7000, cabins CH$60,000

Norte Grande

In some parts of the vast Atacama Desert, which covers almost all of the Norte Grande region, there are areas where no rainfall has ever been recorded. With such an inhospitable landscape, it is no wonder that most of the population is squeezed into the more moderate climes along the coast. The sprawling port city of **Antofagasta** is the largest population centre, while other major towns include the beach resort of **Iquique** – popular with surfers and paragliders – and **Arica**, home to the iconic cliff of El Morro. The best base from which to enjoy the spectacular desert scenery is the laidback backpacker haven of **San Pedro de Atacama**, where visitors flock to whizz down dunes on sandboards, admire the steam rising from geysers in the early morning sun, and spot flamingos on Chile's largest salt flat.

ANTOFAGASTA

ANTOFAGASTA is the biggest city in northern Chile; a busy port and major transportation hub, it has few attractions to detain travellers, though it's a good place to stock up on necessities. James Bond fans may recognize flashes of the city from the film *Quantum of Solace*, part of which was filmed here.

WHAT TO SEE AND DO

Antofagasta's compact centre boasts the surprisingly lovely **Plaza Colón**, the apparent British influence accentuated by its centrepiece, the **Torre Reloj**, a small-scale Big Ben replica. To the north, three blocks of Arturo Prat are pedestrianized and feature shops and cafés, while three blocks south along Matta is a large pedestrian square presided over by the impressive pink, grey and cream **Mercado Central**, with its evocative smells of fresh produce and frying fish.

At the port end of Bolívar, you'll find the oldest building in the city, the former **Aduana**, now housing the **Museo Regional** (Tues–Fri 9am–5pm, Sat & Sun

4

11am–2pm; free), with exhibitions on regional natural history, archeology and the War of the Pacific, and an outstanding mummified babies exhibit. *Colectivos* run along Matta to the often-crowded Balneario Municipal, and further south to the Balneario El Huáscar and Caleta Coloso. These are Antofagasta's better **beaches**, lined with places to eat, bars and discos, though not really suitable for swimming.

Ruinas de Huanchaca and the Museo Desierto de Atacama

On a hilltop a short distance inland, 3km south of the city centre near Universidad del Norte, the **Ruinas de Huanchaca** (no fixed opening hours; free; ⓦ ruinasdehuanchaca.cl) are the remains of an old Bolivian silver refinery. It was built to process the silver brought down from the Potosí mine, before being shipped out of Antofagasta. Looking at the square and circular walls of the complex from below, you'd be forgiven for thinking they were ruins of a pre-Columbian fortress. On the same site is the impressive **Museo Desierto de Atacama** (Tues–Sun 10am–1pm & 2.30–7pm; CH$2000).

La Portada

Much featured on postcards, the natural monument of **La Portada**, 15km north of Antofagasta, is a giant rock eroded into a natural arch. To get there, take a Mejillones-bound bus and ask to be dropped off at the junction (10min), from where it is a half-hour walk towards the ocean.

ARRIVAL AND INFORMATION

By plane Aeropuerto Cerro Moreno is 25km north of the city, right on the Tropic of Capricorn. Regular *colectivos* and infrequent *micros* head to the centre or you can take a minibus directly to your accommodation (they await every arrival).

Destinations Iquique (4–6 daily; 55min); La Serena (2 daily; 1hr 25min); Santiago (9–20 daily; 1hr 50min–3hr).

By bus The main Terminal Carlos Oviedo Cavada is on Pedro A. Cerda 5750, about a 15min drive from the centre – a taxi costs about CH$6000. A much cheaper option is to take *colectivo* #111 from right outside the terminal which will drop you off in the centre.

Destinations Arica (every 1–3hr; 10hr); Calama (every 1–2hr; 3hr); Caldera (hourly; 6hr); Copiapó (15 daily; 7hr); La Serena (20 daily; 12hr); Santiago (hourly; 20hr).

Tourist information Prat 384 (Mon–Thurs 8.30am–5.30pm, Fri 8.30am–4.30pm; ☎ 55 245 1820, ⓔ infoantofagasta@sernatur.cl).

ACCOMMODATION

Hotel Colón San Martín 2434 ☎ 55 226 1851, ⓔ colonantofagasta@gmail.com. Decent option with clean, fairly comfortable and light en-suite rooms with TVs. Those facing the road can be rather noisy though. Doubles CH$35,000

Hotel Ibis Av Jose Miguel Carrera 1627 ☎ 55 245 8200, ⓦ ibis.com. This mid-range hotel is a reassuring, good-value choice: staff are professional and the en suites are well equipped. It's around 1.5km southwest of the main plaza. Doubles CH$34,000

Residencial El Cobre Arturo Prat 749 ☎ 55 222 5162. Centrally located option with a grubby-looking exterior and no-frills rooms, with shared bathrooms. Doubles CH$18,000

EATING AND DRINKING

Bavaria Latorre 2618 ☎ 55 228 3821, ⓦ www.bavaria.cl. Two-tiered grill-cafeteria, the latter serving inexpensive fast food, and the former specializing in tasty *parrilladas* (CH$15,500 for two) and German-style dishes. Daily noon–midnight.

Majuyen San Martín 2326 ☎ 55 282 8318. Set back from the road in the Patio Alcántara, this tiny Japanese-Peruvian joint has tasty sushi, sashimi and *ceviche* (CH$1800–6500). Daily 1–4pm & 7–11pm.

CALAMA

The busy city of **CALAMA**, at the heart of the Atacama **copper mining** industry, is a convenient transportation hub and an almost inevitable stop for travellers heading to San Pedro de Atacama.

WHAT TO SEE AND DO

Calama may lack the natural marvels of San Pedro de Atacama, but it does boast the giant Chuquicamata copper mine. State copper company Codelco offers tours, including views of the kilometre-deep open pit and the now abandoned company town. Free, bilingual English and Spanish tours leave from Calama (1.30pm, Jan & Feb also 3.30pm; 2hr; book in advance; call ☎ 55 232 2122 or email ⓔ visitas@codelco.cl).

ARRIVAL AND DEPARTURE

By plane Aeropuerto El Loa is 5km south of the centre; a taxi costs around CH$6000.

Destinations Copiapó (1–2 daily; 1hr 10min–4hr); Santiago (4–12 daily; 2hr).

By bus Arriving by bus, you'll be dropped at your bus company's office, generally near the city centre. Pullman Bus and Tur-Bus both have terminals of their own, the latter inconveniently situated more than 1km north of town. Hail down *colectivo* (shared taxi) #5 or #11 right outside the Tur-Bus terminal to get to the centre, or take a taxi (around CH$3500).

Destinations Antofagasta (every 1–2hr; 3hr); Arica (5–6 daily; 10hr); Chuquicamata (every 30min; 30min); Copiapó (15 daily; 10hr); Iquique (3–4 daily; 6–7hr); La Serena (11 daily; 12hr 30min–15hr); San Pedro de Atacama (every 2–3hr; 1hr 30min); Santiago (hourly; 22hr 30min).

ACCOMMODATION

Hostal Nativo Sotomayor 2215 ☎ 55 231 0377, ⓦ nativo.cl. This centrally located, family-run hotel offers friendly service and plain, immaculately clean rooms with wi-fi and TVs. Doubles CH$30,000

Hostal Toño Vivar 1970 ☎ 55 234 1185, ⓔ david6013@live.com. Secure and spacious rooms with TVs. The walls are thin so it can get noisy. Doubles CH$18,000

EATING

Bavaria Sotomayor 2093 ☎ 55 341 496, ⓦ www.bavaria.cl. Decent if very predictable mid-price mains (CH$4500–11,000) and sandwiches from its downstairs café and upstairs restaurant. Restaurant daily noon–4.30pm & 7.30pm–midnight; café daily 8am–midnight.

Restaurant Paladar Vivar 1797 ☎ 55 292 6554. The swish *Paladar* has an imaginative menu (mains CH$5000–15,000), comprising sharing platters and international cuisine with a French twist. Mon–Sat 12.30–1.30am.

SAN PEDRO DE ATACAMA AND AROUND

SAN PEDRO DE ATACAMA, a little oasis town of single-storey adobe houses and unpaved streets, is situated 75km east of Calama, the nearest city. No other northern destination can compete with the sheer number of natural attractions in the surrounding area: the stunning *altiplano* scenery draws scores of travellers year-round, while volcanoes, sand dunes, geysers and lagoons will keep any nature lover busy.

One of the oldest settlements in Chile, San Pedro was originally a stop on a pre-Columbian trade route between the highland and coastal communities; in 1547, the Spanish established their first mission here and subjugated the locals. The town later became an important rest stop for cattle drives from Salta, Argentina, when the nitrate industry took off in Chile and fresh meat was needed for the workers.

Despite being somewhat crowded during the peak season, San Pedro retains a friendly and relaxed vibe, and has an excellent assortment of budget accommodation and facilities for visitors, as well as the widest range of cuisine north of Santiago.

WHAT TO SEE AND DO

The centre of town is the cheery little **Plaza de Armas**, framed by *algarrobo* and pink peppercorn trees. The whitewashed **Iglesia de San Pedro** (1641) stands on the west side of the square, while most places to eat and other services are found along nearby Caracoles.

Museo Arqueológico Gustavo Le Paige

The intriguing **Museo Arqueológico Gustavo Le Paige** (Mon–Fri 9am–6pm, Sat 10am–6pm; CH$2500), northeast of the square, is well worth a visit, though it no longer displays its famous prehistoric mummy exhibit. Founded by a Belgian Jesuit, after whom it is named, it is home to more than 380,000 clearly labelled pre-Columbian artefacts, perfectly preserved in the dry desert air, including ceramics, gold work and a wide range of tablets and straws for the ritual inhalation of hallucinogenic cacti.

ARRIVAL AND DEPARTURE

By bus Several companies have regular services from Calama to San Pedro; they all arrive at and depart from the bus terminal on Tumiza, a 10min walk southeast from the plaza. You have to change at Calama (often with a delay) for major destinations, including Iquique, Arica and Santiago. Most travellers cross the border to Uyuni in Bolivia on a tour, though it's possible to do so by public transport on a bus from Calama to the border town of Ollagüe; you can also get buses to Salta and Jujuy in Argentina.

Destinations Antofagasta (3 daily; 5hr 30min–6hr); Arica (1–2 daily; 14hr); Calama (every 2–3hr; 1hr 30min); Salta and Jujuy (Argentina; 4–8 weekly; 14–16hr).

SAN PEDRO DE ATACAMA

▲ Pukará de Quitor

Termas de Puritama & El Tatio Geysers ▲

Food Stalls

LICANCÁBUR

Calama

DOMINGO ATIENZA

CALAMA

Museo Arqueológico

GUSTAVO LEPAIGE

Municipalidad

N

Banco Estado (ATM)

Hospital

Iglesia de San Pedro

PLAZA DE ARMAS

Valle de la Luna

Azimut 360

Space Obs

Maxim Experience

Les Copains

CARACOLES

ATM

Cosmo Andino

Vulcano Expediennes

Rancho Cactus

TOCOPILLA

DOMINGO ATIENZA

TOCONAO

PALPANA

0   100
metres

Customs Post, Argentina & Bus Terminal

■ ACCOMMODATION
Camping Los Perales	5
Hostal Elim	6
Mama Tierra	3
Hostal Sonchek	2
Hostal Takha-Takha	4
Vilacoyo Residencial	1

● EATING & DRINKING
Babalu	3/4
Blanco	7
Chela Cabur	2
Pizzeria El Charrúa	1
Salon de Té O2	6
Tierra Todo Natural	5

INFORMATION

Bike rental Many places rent bikes, notably along Caracoles; most charge around CH$4000/half-day or CH$6000/day; try to get an emergency bike-repair kit too.

Money BCI bank on Caracoles and several ATMS dotted around the small centre. Several casas de cambio, on Toconao and Caracoles; tour agencies running trips to Salar de Uyuni can often provide better rates for Bolivianos.

Tourist office Toconao, at Gustavo Le Paige, on the main plaza (Mon, Tues, Thurs & Fri 9.15am–8.15pm, Wed 9.15am–6pm, Sat & Sun 10am–8.15pm; ☎ 55 851 420, ✉ sanpedroatacama@gmail.com). Hands out regional maps and lists of tour companies. Check ⊕ sanpedroatacama.com for more information.

ACCOMMODATION

Camping Los Perales Tocopilla 481 ☎ 55 285 1114. The best campsite in San Pedro, located a short distance south of the plaza, with lots of trees, hot water, a climbing wall and an outdoor kitchen. Per person CH$5000

Hostal Elim Palpana 6 ☎ 55 285 1567, ⊕ hostalelim.cl.

Quiet hostel whose friendly owners offer ten lovingly decorated and furnished doubles, quads and family rooms, with private bathrooms, in a garden setting with fruit trees and hammocks. Laundry service available. Doubles CH$45,000

Mama Tierra Pachamama 615 ☎ 55 285 1418, ⊕ hostalmamatierra.cl. A 10min walk from the centre, this tidy hostel is popular with backpackers and offers dorms, singles and doubles with private or shared bathrooms. Extras include laundry service, and the congenial hostess can help organize volcano climbs in the area. Dorms CH$16,000, doubles CH$42,000

★**Hostal Sonchek** Gustovo Le Paige 198 ☎ 55 285 1112, ⊕ hostalsonchek.cl. With a welcoming and helpful English- and French-speaking hostess, this extremely popular and conveniently located hostel has cosy rooms, kitchen use, a courtyard with hammocks, laundry service and a café next door. Doubles CH$20,000

Hostal Takha-Takha Caracoles 101a ☎ 55 285 1038, ⊕ takhatakha.cl. Small but tidy and quiet rooms giving onto a pleasant garden. There's a lovely (but small) pool and you can also camp here. Also some good-value,

though basic, singles (CH$18,000). Camping per person <u>CH$10,000</u>, double <u>CH$53,000</u>
Vilacoyo Residencial Tocopilla 387 ☎55 285 1006, ✉vilacoyo@sanpedroatacama.com. Very friendly, comfortable hostel with private and shared rooms set around a relaxing hammock-strewn courtyard. Kitchen and shared bathrooms are spotless. Twelve hours of hot water per day. Dorms <u>CH$8000</u>, doubles <u>CH$16,000</u>

EATING AND DRINKING

Prices are notably higher than in other parts of the country. For cheaper, filling set meals, try one of the handful of restaurants at the top end of Licancabur or near the bus station.
Babalu Caracoles 160. Tiny *heladería* offering home-made ice creams (from CH$1500): try the pisco sour or chirimoya flavours. There's another branch at the other end of Caracoles (#419). Daily 10am–8pm.
Blanco Caracoles 195 ☎55 285 1164. Conceived in white minimalist-chic adobe, this stylish joint certainly stands out from the crowd and is arguably the best restaurant in town (mains CH$7900–9400). Daily 6pm–12.30am.
Chela Cabur Caracoles 211 ☎55 285 1576. The name says it all: *Chela Cabur* translates as "mountain of beer" in Kunza-Chilean. Owned by a Finnish beer aficionado (beer CH$2500–3500). Mon–Thurs & Sun noon–1am, Fri & Sat noon–2am.
Pizzeria El Charrúa Tocopilla 442 ☎55 285 1443. The wonderful aroma wafting out of this intimate pizzeria entices hungry punters inside (from CH$4500). Daily 11am–11pm.
Salon de Té O2 Caracoles 295B. This unpretentious café, right in the centre of town, serves up good-value, hearty breakfasts (from CH$2500), tasty quiches and home-made cakes. Daily 8am–8pm.
★**Tierra Todo Natural** Caracoles 46 ☎55 285 1585. Friendly restaurant specializing in wholesome home-made

food (mains CH$5000–11,000; set menu CH$8000), including wholemeal bread, pizzas, *empanadas*, fish, fantastic salads and pancakes. Daily 8.30am–12.30am.

DAY-TRIPS FROM SAN PEDRO

Beyond San Pedro, the scenery is dramatic, dominated by large volcanic peaks, **Valle de la Luna**'s magnificent lunar landscape, the red rock of the **Valle de la Muerte**, the famous **El Tatio geysers**, Chile's largest salt flat **Salar de Atacama** and dazzling **lagoons**. With the exception of the village of **Toconao**, and Valle de la Muerte and Valle de la Luna, both of which can be visited by bike, these places are only accessible on a tour.

Valle de la Muerte

The easiest attraction to cycle to – only 3km from San Pedro – is the **Valle de la Muerte**, with its narrow gorges, peculiar **red rock formations** and 150m-high **sand dunes**. It is also a prime **sandboarding** destination, with scores of enthusiasts whizzing down the slopes in the early mornings and late afternoons. The rest of the time an exquisite silence reigns over the still sand and rocks, and you can often enjoy the views of the snow-peaked volcanoes in the distance entirely undisturbed.

Valle de la Luna

Most people come here for the

4

SAN PEDRO TOUR OPERATORS

Choosing a reputable **tour operator** in San Pedro can be difficult, but at least the competition keeps prices fairly stable. Talk to travellers who have done the tours recently, and look at the comments book in the tourist information office. Expect to pay around CH$10,000 to visit the Valle de la Luna, CH$22,000 for a tour to the Tatio geysers, and around CH$30,000 for a full-day tour of the lakes and oases (excluding entrance fees); three- to four-day tours (around CH$100,000–124,000/US$185–220) that finish in Bolivia and take in the spectacular Salar de Uyuni are popular.

Cosmo Andino Caracoles s/n ☎55 285 1069, ⓦcosmoandino.cl. Well-established and respected company offering interesting variations on the most popular tours, as well as off-the-beaten track expeditions.
Rancho Cactus Tocanao 568 ☎55 285 1506, ⓦrancho-cactus.cl. For an alternative San Pedro experience, try the horse treks (from CH$15,000) run by Rancho Cactus. Treks last from a few hours to three days.

Space Obs Caracoles 166 ☎55 256 6278, ⓦspaceobs .com. Excellent, highly memorable tours (in English, French, Spanish and German; CH$18,000/2hr 30min) of Northern Chile's night sky led by enthusiastic and personable astronomers. Book in advance.
Vulcano Expediciones Caracoles 317 ☎55 285 1023, ⓦvulcanochile.com. The best operator for mountain and volcano ascents, trekking, sandboarding (CH$15,000) and bike tours.

spectacular sunsets with one of a plethora of tour groups, but the lunar landscape of **Valle de la Luna** (summer 8.30am–7.30pm; winter 8.30am–5.30pm; CH$2000), at the heart of the Cordillera del Sal, is as impressive at sunrise, when the first rays of sunlight turn the surrounding jagged red peaks various shades of pink and gold. At dawn there are far fewer spectators, and after making your way up the giant sand dune along a marked trail, you can walk up the crest of the dune for a better vantage point. If cycling the 14km to the valley, go west along Caracoles out of town, turn left at the end and carry straight on; plenty of water, sunscreen and a torch are essential.

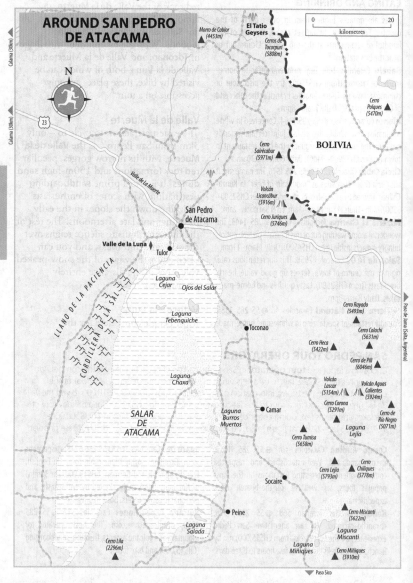

AROUND SAN PEDRO DE ATACAMA

Toconao

Toconao, 38km from San Pedro, is a small village nestled in an idyllic spot surrounded by sandy hills, with houses built entirely of volcanic liparita stone. A cool stream runs through the valley and the surrounding fertile soil supports lush vegetation, including fig, pear and quince trees, as well as a hallucinogenic type of cactus. The site has been inhabited since 11,000 BC, and its present population of around seven hundred villagers make traditional crafts. It is possible to stay in several rustic *hospedajes* here, and there are delicious *humitas* (corn paste wrapped in corn leaves) for sale. Buses Atacama and Buses Frontera each run twice-daily bus services to Toconao from San Pedro.

Salar de Atacama

The edge of Chile's largest salt flat, the **Salar de Atacama** (daily: summer 9am–7pm; winter 8am–6pm; CH$2500), lies 50km south of San Pedro. It may disappoint those expecting a sparkling white field, but still makes an unforgettable spectacle: a jagged white crust, resembling dead coral, created by water flowing down from the mountains, stretches as far as the eye can see. Several shallow lakes dot the Salar, including **Laguna Chaxa**, made bright by the resident Andean, Chilean and James flamingos, which spend up to fourteen hours a day feeding on tiny saltwater shrimp. Many excursions will also take in **Laguna Cejar** – where salt content is so high that you can float on the surface – and gleaming **Laguna Tebenquiche**. Also look out for the **Ojos del Salar** – two small, and almost perfectly round, cold-water pools set amid the arid plain.

El Tatio geysers

The **El Tatio geysers** (CH$5000), 90km north of town, are a morning attraction, with tours setting off at 4am in order to reach them by sunrise, when the fumaroles that spew steam and the jets of scalding water that shoot up from the geysers are at their most impressive. At dawn, there is a surreal quality to the plateau: dark shadowy figures move through the mist and the sunlight glints on patches of white ground frost. When walking around, stick to marked paths, since the ground crust can be very fragile – breaking it might result in a plunge into near-boiling water. The temperature here, at the world's highest geothermal field (4320m), is often below freezing, so warm clothes are essential. A soak in the nearby thermal pool is a must.

Lagunas Miscanti and Miñiques

These two *altiplano* **lagoons** (CH$2500) lie 134km from town, at an elevation of around 4200m. Visitors here are left breathless not just by the altitude, but also by the first sight of the huge shimmering pools of deep blue, ringed with white ribbons of salt. There's abundant bird and animal life as well, and it is possible to see both flamingos and the inquisitive *zorro culpeo*, a type of **fox** that often approaches the area's picnic site to look for scraps.

IQUIQUE

The approach to the busy coastal city of Iquique is unforgettable, especially if coming from the east. The highway along the plateau suddenly gives way to a spectacular 600m drop, looking down onto the giant **Cerro Dragón** sand dune which in turn towers over the city. At sunset, the dune and the surrounding cliffs turn various shades of pink and red, giving the city an almost unearthly feel. Almost 500km north of Antofagasta, Iquique prospered in the nitrate era, between 1890 and 1920. Most of the grand buildings in the city's historical centre date back to that heyday. The town's biggest draws nowadays are its **beaches**, though the huge duty-free Zona Franca in the north of the city also attracts visitors. The city is also one of the top destinations in Latin America for **paragliders**.

Plaza Prat

At the heart of Iquique's centre **Plaza Prat** is lined with banks and restaurants, with the tall white **Torre Reloj**, the city's symbol, built in 1877, as its centrepiece and the Neoclassical **Teatro Municipal** on the south side. The **Casino Español**, a 1904 Moorish-style wooden building with an opulent interior, graces the northeast corner of the square and is worth a visit both for the interior decorations and for the delicious pisco sours.

Calle Baquedano

Heading south from Plaza Prat towards Playa Bellavista, quiet pedestrianized **Calle Baquedano**, with its elevated boardwalks and grand wooden buildings, is strikingly different from the modern parts of Iquique, with a faded colonial feel about it. The **Museo Regional**, at no. 951 (Tues–Sat 9am–5.30pm, Sat 10am–2pm; CH$1500), is home to a number of curious pre-Columbian artefacts, the most impressive of which are the Chinchorro mummies and skulls, deliberately

deformed by having bandages wrapped tightly around them. The natural history section features a sea-lion embryo pickled in formaldehyde and an informative exhibition on nitrate extraction in the area, along with a scale model of the ghost town of Humberstone.

The beaches

Iquique's most popular beach, **Playa Cavancha** is sheltered in a bay alongside the busy main thoroughfare of Avenida Arturo Prat, about 2km from the main plaza. It is particularly popular with sunbathers and boogie-boarders and is safe for swimming. The boardwalk, which winds along the beach amid the palm trees and giant cacti, is always teeming with bikers, rollerbladers and sun worshippers. At the north end of Playa

EATING	
Cafeteria Cioccolata	1
Dona Filomena	5
El Tercer Ojito	4
El Wagon	3

DRINKING & NIGHTLIFE	
Casino Español	2
Los Tres Diablos	6

ACCOMMODATION	
Backpacker's Hostel Iquique	4
Hostel La Casona 1920	3
Hostal Cuneo	2
Flight Park	5
Hotel de la Plaza	1

IQUIQUE

4, 5, 3, 6, Conaf & Beaches

Cavancha lies rocky **Playa Bellavista**, with several good surf breaks, while the large stretch of **Playa Brava**, lined by fun-fairs and themed restaurants, is south of the Peninsula de Cavancha, and is a popular landing spot for paragliders. The less crowded **Playa Huayquique** is located to the very south of the city; it also has good waves for surfers and can be reached by *colectivos* from the centre.

ARRIVAL AND INFORMATION

By plane Aeropuerto Diego Arecena lies 41km south of Iquique; you can get to the centre by transfer (CH$5000; ☎57 231 0800), regular taxi (CH$8000 shared, or CH$16,000 private) or *colectivo*.

Destinations Antofagasta (4–6 daily; 55min); Arica (4 daily; 45min); Santiago (6–11 daily; 2hr 15min–3hr 15min).

By bus The main terminal is inconveniently located at the north end of Patricio Lynch; numerous *colectivos* run to the city centre and some bus companies pick up passengers at their central offices around Mercado Centenario. The Tur-Bus terminal is slightly more central, on Esmeralda, at Ramírez.

Destinations Antofagasta (17 daily; 7hr); Arica (every 30min; 4hr 30min); Calama (3–4 daily; 6–7hr); Caldera (12 daily; 12hr); Copiapó (12 daily; 13hr); La Serena (8 daily; 18hr); Pica (7 daily; 2hr); Santiago (hourly; 25hr).

Tourist information Anibal Pinto 436 (Mon–Fri 9am–5pm, Sat & Sun 10am–2pm; ☎57 241 9241, ✉infoiquique@sernatur.cl). The Conaf office at Juan Antonio 2808 (Mon–Fri 8.30am–1.30pm & 3–5pm; ☎57 243 2085) can provide information on the Volcán Isluga National Park and arrange accommodation there.

ACCOMMODATION

Backpacker's Hostel Iquique Amunátegui 2075, about 2km south of Plaza Prat ☎57 232 0223, ⓦhosteliquique .cl. With English-speaking staff who help organize trips, a

friendly atmosphere and a superb beachside location, this hostel remains a firm backpacker favourite. Kitchen facilities and frequent barbecues. Dorms CH$7500, doubles CH$22,000

★ **Hostel La Casona 1920** Barros Arana 1585 ☎57 241 3000, ⓦcasonahostel.com. Once the family residence of the very personable owner Isabel, *La Casona 1920* is an original nitrate-era building. A home away from home, this hostel has a lovely outdoor patio, an attractive, well-equipped kitchen and, best of all, a very pleasant, friendly atmosphere. Dorms CH$8000, doubles CH$15,000

Hostal Cuneo Baquedano 1175 ☎57 242 8654, ✉hostalcuneo@hotmail.com. With a good location in an old timber building painted a striking turquoise on the historic stretch of Calle Baquedano, this hospitable and good-value *hostal* has small and neat if slightly dark rooms. Doubles CH$25,000

Flight Park Via 6, Manzana Am Sitio 3, Bajo Molle, about a 15min bus ride from town ☎57 238 0110, ☎09 9886 2362, ⓦaltazor.cl. Built almost entirely of ship containers, the rooms at this international paragliding centre are surprisingly inviting, with shared kitchen, and chilled-out communal areas. Check their website for directions. Camping/person CH$5000, doubles CH$14,000, apartments CH$25,000

Hotel de la Plaza Paseo Baquedano 1025 ☎57 241 7172, ✉contacto@kilantur.cl. An airy and light Georgian building on the main stretch with pictures of old Iquique adorning the walls and some racially dubious statues in the lobby. A leafy staircase leads up to pleasant, clean rooms, and there's a restaurant and bar. Doubles CH$30,000

EATING

Cafeteria Cioccolata Av Anibal Pinto 487 ☎57 253 2290. This sweet, old-fashioned tearoom opposite the tourist office serves up good coffee (CH$1400–3100) and obscenely huge slices of cake, waffles and pancakes. *Menu del día* CH$4500. Mon–Fri 8.45am–10pm, Sat 11am–10pm.

PARAGLIDING IN IQUIQUE

Few things compare to the sheer rush of running off the cliff at **Alto Hospicio** on the plateau above Iquique. Once the butterflies settle, you find yourself soaring gently with white-headed eagles as tiny houses with minute turquoise swimming pools, ocean-side high-rises, beaches and the giant sand dune of Cerro Dragón spread out beneath you. You **paraglide** in tandem with an experienced instructor, who guides you through the entire procedure from take-off to landing.

The pros at **Puro Vuelo** (☎57 231 1127, ⓦpurovuelo.cl) come highly recommended. A tandem flight will set you back CH$40,000 and includes a set of photos of you flying, which you can download from their website afterwards. **Altazor** (☎09 9886 2362, ⓦaltazor.cl) also has a good reputation; if you want to enjoy a beer with some of the world's best paragliding talent, consider staying at *Flight Park Altazor* (see above). For the more faint of heart, tour companies will also help you organize a **sandboarding** trip on the dunes.

Dona Filomena Filomena Valenzuela 298 ☎57 231 1235. Reliable *empanada*, beer and pizza joint, popular with a young-ish crowd (dishes from CH$3000). Simple wooden decor and attractive outside seating. Mon–Sat 12.30pm-12.30am.

★ **El Tercer Ojito** Patricio Lynch 1420a ☎57 242 6517, ⓦeltercerojito.cl. This peaceful garden oasis is the mellowest place to spend a shady afternoon or candle-lit evening. A healthy menu (mains CH$4900–11,000) darts from Chilean seafood to Thai curries, via salads, pasta and various veggie options. Tues–Sat 12.30–5pm & 7.30pm–1am, Sun 12.30–5pm.

El Wagon Thomson 85 ☎57 234 1428. Nitrate-era paraphernalia lines the walls of this warm and friendly restaurant with imaginative fish and seafood dishes (CH$6000–12,000): the spicy *pescado a la Huara-Huara* is particularly good. Mon–Sat 1–4pm & 8pm–2am, Sun 1–4pm.

DRINKING AND NIGHTLIFE

Casino Español Plaza Prat 584. The food here is pricey (mains CH$7000–12,000), but it's worth a visit for some of the best pisco sours in Chile. Mon, Sat & Sun noon–3.30pm, Tues–Fri noon–3.30pm & 8–10.30pm.

Los Tres Diablos Filomena Valenzuela 784 ☎57 248 0530. This smart resto-bar is one of Iquique's places to be seen. Come here for a pisco cocktail and snack on fusion food with a Mexican slant. Mon–Wed 1–4pm & 8pm–1am, Thurs–Sat 1–4pm & 8pm–2am.

AROUND IQUIQUE

The nitrate pampas inland from Iquique is dotted with **ghost towns** left over from the area's mining heyday, with the biggest and best-preserved example being **Humberstone** (daily: Jan–March 9am–7pm; April–Dec 9am–6pm; CH$3000, also covers entry to Santa Laura), 45km to the east. Established in the middle of parched desert land in 1862, this once-thriving mining town bears the name of Briton James Humberstone, a nitrate entrepreneur famous for introducing the "Shanks" ore-refining system to the industry. Visitors can wander the eerie streets where squalid and partially wrecked worker barracks contrast sharply with the faded glamour of the theatre and the well-maintained church. Workers here, mostly Chilean but some foreign, earned a pittance putting in long hours in a hot and dangerous environment.

Around 2km down the road is the much smaller **Santa Laura**, where you'll see a couple of remaining houses (one of which has been turned into a small museum), and an amazing processing plant, seeming to loom into the air like a rusty old dinosaur. As you walk around the site, listening to the endless clanging of machinery banging in the wind, the sense of abandonment is nigh-on overwhelming.

The thermal springs at **Pica**, 114km southeast of Iquique, are well worth a visit for a relaxing splash around; the most popular is **Cocha Resbaladero** (daily 8am–9pm; CH$1000). The small, pre-Hispanic town is also famed for producing limes widely believed to make the perfect pisco sour, and the pretty **Iglesia de San Andrés**.

IQUIQUE TOUR OPERATORS

Apart from sandboarding and **paragliding** on Cerro Dragón, and **surfing** all along Iquique's coast, the area around the city has a wealth of attractions on offer, including trips to the **ghost town** of Humberstone, the Gigante de Atacama **geoglyph**, the **hot springs** of Mamiña and the Pica oasis, the **burial site** of an Inca princess at the village of La Tirana, and the sobering **mass graves** from the Pinochet era at the tiny settlement of Pisagua. The cheapest – though perhaps not the most satisfying – tours combine a whistle-stop trip through all these attractions in a day (about CH$25,000). We recommend the following operators:

Avitours Baquedano 997 ☎57 241 3334, ⓦavitours.cl.

Iquitour Patricio Lynch 563, ☎57 242 8772, ⓦiquitour.cl.

Magical Tour Chile Baquedano 1035 ☎57 221 7290, ⓦmagicaltour.cl. Also offers cycling tours.

Surire Tours Baquedano 170 ☎57 244 5440, ⓦsuriretours.cl.

Uma Jaqi Obispo Labbé 1591 ☎09 8771 5768, ⓔumajaqi@gmail.com. Offers surfing lessons.

ARICA

ARICA, Chile's northernmost city, 316km from Iquique, benefits greatly from tourism, with foreign visitors flocking to its pleasant sandy beaches in the summer, and with a smattering of good museums. The city was the principal port exporting silver from Bolivia's Potosí mines until 1776, and only became part of Chile in the 1880s after the War of the Pacific. Aside from its own attractions, Arica makes a good base for the beautiful Parque Nacional Lauca (see p.422).

WHAT TO SEE AND DO

The compact city centre is easy to explore on foot, though a visit to Arica isn't complete without climbing **El Morro**, the dramatic cliff that looms high over the city.

El Morro

A steep path leads to the top of **El Morro** from the southern end of Calle Colón. From the clifftop, home to a number of turkey vultures and a giant Jesus statue that lights up at night, you can enjoy a magnificent panoramic view of the entire city. Also up here, with cannons stationed outside, is the **Museo Histórico y de Armas** (daily 8am–8pm; CH$600), with displays of weaponry, uniforms and other artefacts from the War of the Pacific.

The city centre

Below El Morro is the large, palm-tree-lined **Plaza Vicuña Mackenna**, and alongside that lies Avenida Máximo Lira, the main coastal road. On the east side is the attractive **Plaza Colón**, decorated with pink flowers and ornate fountains. The plaza is home to one of Arica's most celebrated buildings, the Gothic **Iglesia de San Marcos**, designed by Gustave Eiffel (of Eiffel Tower fame), made entirely out of iron and shipped over from France in 1876. Eiffel was also responsible for the grand 1874 **Ex-Aduana** building nearby, alongside the Parque General Baquedano. This now houses the Casa de Cultura, which regularly hosts art and photo exhibitions. The main thoroughfare, **21 de Mayo**, heads east from here before becoming a pedestrian strip, lined with restaurants and banks. Just off it, at Sangra 315, the **Museo del Mar** (Mon–Fri 11am–7pm, Sat 11am–2.30pm; CH$2000; wmuseodelmardearica.cl) houses the impressive, personal collection of Nicols Hrepic Gutunic, who has spent much of his life collecting more than one thousand species of shells from Chile and across the globe. To the west is the bustling **Terminal Pesquero**, where sea lions compete with pelicans for scraps from the dockside fish stalls.

The beaches

North of the centre and west of the bus terminals lies the popular **Playa Chinchorro**, which is ideal for swimming, sunbathing and body-boarding. The city's northernmost beach, **Playa Las Machas**, is not suitable for swimming because of the strong undertow but has some good surf breaks. A twenty-minute walk south of the centre will bring you to the sandy **Playa El Laucho** and **Playa La Lisera**, both popular and good for swimming, followed by the pretty **Playa Brava** and the dark-sand **Playa Arenillas Negra**, which has rougher waves. Finally, there's **Playa Los Corazones**, a beautiful expanse of clean sand flanked by cliffs 8km south of town. The southern beaches can be reached by *colectivo*, though these tend to run only during the summer season.

Museo Arqueológico

The excellent **Museo Arqueológico** (daily: Jan & Feb 10am–7pm; March–Dec 10am–6pm; CH$2000; ☎58220 5551, wwww.uta.cl/masma/) lies 12km from Arica in the green **Azapa Valley**. The museum traces the history of the valley's inhabitants, from the earliest hunter-gatherers, via a remarkably thorough collection of regional pre-Hispanic artefacts. Most impressive of these are the four elaborately prepared **Chinchorro mummies** – a male, a female and two young children, which are believed to be around seven thousand years old, making them by far the oldest mummies in the world. To get there, catch one of the yellow *colectivos* labelled "Azapa" which run along Avenida Diego Portales past the bus terminals.

4

ARICA

ACCOMMODATION

Arica Surfhouse Hostel	4
Doña Inés	3
End of the Trail	1
Hostal Jardín del Sol	5
Sunny Days Hostel	2

EATING & DRINKING

El Arriero	2
Café del Mar	3
Govinda	5
Terminal Pesquero	1
Vereda Bolognesi	4

Playa Chinchorro, Playa Las Machas, Tacna & Airport

Río San José

Terminal Rodoviario

Terminal Internacional

AV SANTA MARÍA

JUAN ANTONIO RÍOS

NICOLÁS HIDALGO

RÓMULO PEÑA

MIGUEL AGUIRRE

SANTA ISABEL

JAVIER FRÁZAR

LUIS VICENTINI

J A RÍOS

Universidad de Tarapacá

INDEPENDENCIA

GENERAL VELÁSQUEZ

GENERAL LAGOS

BLANCO ENCALDA

OLAYO

ÁNGAMOS

PACIFIC OCEAN

Casino Municipal

LASTARRIA

Parque Brasil

ESMERALDA

JUAN NOE

Parque General Ibañez

CHACABUCO

BLANCO ENCALDA

AV VICUÑA MACKENNA

GALLO

Conaf

Arica-Tacna Train Station

O'HIGGINS

MÁXIMO LIRA

FERIA INTERNACIONAL

PEDRO MONTT

ARTURO PRAT

GENERAL VELÁSQUEZ

COLÓN

PATRICIO LYNCH

MAIPU

GENERAL LAGOS

SAN MARTÍN

Terminal Pesquero

Mercado Colón

Vientos del Norte Adventure

THOMPSON

Turismo Lauca

Farmacía Cruz Verde

18 DE SEPTIEMBRE

BOLOGNESI

SANGRA

BAQUEDANO

21 DE MAYO

Banco Santander

Ex-Aduana building

Museo del Mar

Municipalidad

SOTOMAYOR

Parque General Baquedano

PLAZA COLÓN

COLÓN

Teatro Municipal

PLAZA VICUÑA MACKENNA

Iglesia de San Marcos

SAN MARCOS

YUNGAY

AVENIDA SAN MARTÍN

EL MORRO

HÉROES DEL MORRO

EJERCITO

Raíces Andinas

Museo Histórico y de Armas

El Morro

0   200   metres

Playa El Laucho, Playa La Lisera, Playa Brava, Playa Arenillas Negras & Playa Los Corazones

ARRIVAL AND DEPARTURE

By plane Aeropuerto Internacional Chacalluta is 18km north of Arica; a radio taxi downtown costs around CH$6000–7000, or take a cheaper transfer or *colectivo*. Destinations Iquique (4 daily; 45min); Santiago (4–7 daily; 2hr 30min–3hr 35min).

By train The Arica–Tacna train station is located at Máximo Lira 889, on the northwest edge of the city centre: services have been suspended since 2012, but are scheduled to resume.

By bus Terminal Rodovario, at Diego Portales 948 northeast of the centre, is the main stop for local arrivals, plus a few international; inside there are cash machines and snack kiosks. Terminal Internacional is immediately adjacent, with arrivals from La Paz and numerous *micros* and *colectivos* crossing the border from Tacna, Peru. Destinations Antofagasta (every 1–3hr; 10hr); Calama (5–6 daily; 10hr); Chañaral (7 daily; 15hr); Copiapó (11 daily; 17hr); Iquique (every 30min; 4hr 30min); Putre (1 daily; 3hr); San Pedro de Atacama (1–2 daily; 14hr); Santiago (10 daily; 29hr); Vallenar (10 daily; 20hr).

INFORMATION

Tourist information The tourist office is at San Marcos 101 (March–Dec Mon–Thurs 9am–6pm, Fri 9am–5pm; Jan & Feb also Sat & Sun 9am–5pm; ☎58 225 2054, ✉infoarica@sernatur.cl). Helpful staff provide maps of town and a plethora of brochures on local attractions. Conaf has an office at Av Vicuña Mackenna 820 (☎58 220 1200). Staff provide information on, and maps of, local national parks; reserve beds at regional Conaf *refugios* here.

ACCOMMODATION

You can camp for free at the Playa Las Machas.

Arica Surfhouse Hostel O'Higgins 661 ☎58 231 2213, ⓦaricasurfhouse.cl. This centrally located hostel has spacious rooms, and caters well to its surfer clientele, as well as organizing other activities including horseriding and paragliding. Dorms CH$12,000, doubles CH$30,000
Doña Inés Manuel Rojas 2864 ☎58 224 8108, ✉hiarica@ hostelling.cl. The inconvenient location of this hostel is compensated for by the owner's hospitality, knowledge and insatiable enthusiasm. Pluses are bike rental and a cosy common room with TV. To get there, take *colectivo* #4 from the bus station to Chapiquiña (corner of Blest Gana); the hostel is on the left. Dorms CH$9500, doubles CH$25,000
End of the Trail Esteban Alvarado 117 ☎58 231 4316, ☎09 7786 3972, ⓦendofthetrail-arica.cl. A congenial American owner runs this hostel, which has comfortable, quiet rooms around an indoor courtyard, amazing showers and a specially designed roof that keeps the house cool. Breakfast included. To get there from the bus station, walk two blocks west on Diego Portales, then four blocks north on Pedro de Valdivia. Dorms CH$9000, doubles CH$22,000

Hostal Jardín del Sol Sotomayor 848 ☎58 223 2795, ⓦhostaljardindelsol.cl. Central *hostal* run by a very helpful and welcoming couple who organize all manner of outdoor activities for guests. Most rooms are en suite; shares arranged. Kitchen, lounge, TV, bike rental and a laundry service are some of the bonuses. Breakfast included. Doubles CH$33,000
★**Sunny Days Hostel** Tomas Aravena 161 ☎58 224 1038, ⓦsunny-days-arica.cl. Extremely friendly and knowledgeable Kiwi-Chilean hosts preside over travellers of all ages in this custom-built hostel. An excellent breakfast, kitchen and lounge facilities and a relaxed communal atmosphere all add to its appeal. Dorms CH$9000, doubles CH$22,000

EATING AND DRINKING

El Arriero 21 de Mayo 385 ☎58 223 2636, ⓦrestaurantelarriero.cl. Recommended grill house serving tasty fillet steaks and other meat dishes (from CH$7000); often has live folk music at the weekends. Book ahead. Mon–Sat noon–4pm & 7–11pm.
Café del Mar 21 de Mayo 260. Popular restaurant with a bargain *menú del día*, plus large salads and good quiches (from CH$2500). Mon–Sat 9.30am–midnight.
Govinda Blanco Encalada 200. Zen-like place a short walk from the centre, with tasty, vegetarian set menu lunches (from around CH$2500) that include soup, salad and a main dish. Mon–Fri 12.30–3.30pm.
Terminal Pesquero Off Av Máximo Lira, across from entrance to C 21 de Mayo. Several no-frills oceanside eateries here cook up hearty portions of inexpensive fish dishes; *Mata Rangi*, in particular, stands out. Set lunches around CH$5000. Daily noon–3.30pm.
Vereda Bolognesi Bolognesi 340 ⓦveredabolognesi.cl. By night, from about 8pm, this smart little shopping gallery in town turns into a buzzing patio bar zone – several restaurant-bars compete with their happy hours so it's easy to get a good cocktail at a decent price. Mon–Sat 9am–midnight.

TOUR OPERATORS AROUND ARICA

A number of tour companies offer trips into the **national parks** outside Arica. The standard three- to four-day trip takes in Parque Nacional Lauca, Reserva Nacional Las Vicuñas, Salar de Surire and Parque Nacional Volcán Isluga, with overnight stops in the *altiplano* villages of Putre and Colchane. Most tours either return to Arica or drop passengers off in Iquique. Tour operators do offer day-trips taking in Parque Nacional Lauca, and Putre, but this is not recommended as the altitude change is extreme, and is at best likely to make you feel queasy.

Raices Andinas Héroes de Morro 632 ☎58 223 3305, ⓦraicesandinas.com. Tour operator with close links to the local Aymará communities, promoting ecotourism and Aymará culture. Also offers a trip through Parque Nacional Lauca into Bolivia.

Turismo Lauca Thompson 200, at Bolognesi ☎58 222 0067, ⓦturismolauca.cl. Standard trips around the national park circuit, as well as city tours, and archeological interest trips.

ALTITUDE SICKNESS

Known here as *puna* or *soroche*, **altitude sickness** affects roughly a quarter of all travellers who venture above the altitude of about 2500m, regardless of age or fitness, though people with respiratory problems tend to suffer more. It is rarely life-threatening, though is dangerous for people suffering from hypothermia. Symptoms include vertigo, headaches, nausea, shortness of breath, lethargy and insomnia. Keeping properly hydrated and taking aspirin can alleviate some of the symptoms; **mate de coca** (tea brewed from coca leaves) is also widely believed to help. Avoid alcohol consumption, overeating and over-exertion; if symptoms persist, try to move to a lower elevation. The best way to avoid altitude sickness is to acclimatize gradually by breaking up your journey to higher regions into segments.

4 PUTRE

The highland village of **PUTRE** sits at an altitude of 3500m and provides an ideal acclimatization point for venturing into the Parque Nacional Lauca. Populated by the indigenous Aymará people, Putre consists of basic stone houses centred around a square. It is a tranquil place to spend a few days, and is becoming an increasing must-see on the backpacker trail, with a growing number of accommodation options.

ARRIVAL AND INFORMATION

The only bank, on the square's southeast corner, does not accept Visa.

By bus Buses La Paloma, Germán Riesco 2071 (☎58 222 2710), has a daily bus to Putre from Arica (3hr).

Tourist information The tourist office is on the south side of the square (Mon–Fri 10am–2pm & 3–6pm). The Conaf office is at Teniente Del Campo, between La Torre and O'Higgins (☎09 7773 3032).

ACCOMMODATION

La Chakana A 20min walk from the plaza; head downhill past the church ☎09 9745 9519, ⓦla-chakana.com. German-Chilean-run option, with comfy beds, filling breakfasts and a cosy atmosphere. Doubles CH$33,000

Terrace Lodge 5km outside Putre ☎58 258 4275, ⓦterracelodge.com. This charming guesthouse is the best place to stay in and around Putre, boasting a tranquil location

outside town, comfortable en suites, helpful staff and a range of tour options. Book ahead. Doubles CH$34,000

EATING

Kuchu Marka Baquedano s/n ☎09 9011 4007. At this cosy place, you can get alpaca stew and other hearty mountain dishes like *picante de conejo* (a sort of rabbit curry), llama steaks and trout in a butter sauce (mains around CH$8000). Mon–Sat noon–11.30pm.

PARQUE NACIONAL LAUCA

From Putre, Ruta 11 leads up onto the *altiplano* to the **Parque Nacional Lauca**, a region of rich flora and fauna, shimmering lakes and snowcapped volcanoes 4300m above sea level. The most visited village at these dizzying heights is the little whitewashed settlement of **Parinacota**, accessible by public transport, though it's far easier to see the sights of Lauca on an organized tour.

Las Cuevas

The Conaf-run **Las Cuevas** *refugio* is located 9km into the park, and the nature trail near it is the best place to see **viscachas**, the long-tailed, rabbit-like relatives of chinchillas, as they use their powerful hind legs to leap from boulder to boulder. The well-watered *bofedal* (alluvial depression) here provides permanent grazing for herds of **vicuñas**, the wild relatives of llamas and alpacas, which are commonly seen. In addition, you'll find numerous examples of the *llareta* plant, which takes three hundred years to grow to full size; the plant looks like a pile of oddly shaped green cushions but is actually rock-hard. The local Aymará break up the dead plants with picks for use as firewood. Just off the *refugio*'s nature trail are some rustic thermal baths.

Parinacota

The **Conaf** headquarters (daily 9am–12.30pm & 1–5.30pm) are located in the tiny Aymará village of **Parinacota**, 19km east of the Las Cuevas *refugio*. Parinacota is worth a stop for its cheerful, whitewashed little **church**, reconstructed in 1789, and for the stalls opposite, selling colourful local **artesanía**. Besides a fetching bell tower with a tiny doorway, the church (ask around for the guardian of the key) has murals depicting scenes of Jesus being borne to the cross by soldiers resembling Spanish conquistadors, as well as sinners burning in hell. A small wooden table is tethered to the wall to the left of the altar; legend has it that the table wandered around the village, causing the death of a man by stopping in front of his house – the chain prevents the table from escaping again.

Parinacota can be reached by **public bus** from the Terminal Internacional in Arica (departs Tues–Fri at 11am, returning at 9am the following day). It may be possible to rent a very basic **room** from a villager, or stay in the basic hostel opposite the church (ask at Raíces Andinas in Arica).

Lago Chungará

Some 18km east of Parinacota, at a breathtaking altitude of 4600m, lies the stunning **Lago Chungará**. With its brilliant blue waters perfectly reflecting the towering snowcapped cone of **Volcán Parinacota** (6350m), this is undoubtedly one of the highlights of the national park. The roadside **Conaf refugio** here has six basic beds (CH$5500/person), kitchen facilities and three **camping** spaces (free). There is a short lakeside **nature trail**, which provides a good vantage point for viewing the giant coots, flamingos and Andean geese that nest here.

RESERVA NACIONAL LAS VICUÑAS AND SALAR DE SURIRE

A southbound turn-off from Ruta 11 by Lago Chungará heads through the 2091-square-kilometre **Reserva Nacional Las Vicuñas** towards the Salar de Surire salt lake. The *reserva* is made up of seemingly endless marshes and grasslands where herds of vicuñas can be seen grazing in the distance.

At an altitude of 4295m, the enormous, dirty-white **Salar de Surire** is home to up to ten thousand **flamingos** – mostly Chilean, but with a smattering of James and Andean species. Surire means "place of the rhea" in Aymará, and it's also possible to catch

glimpses here of these swift, ostrich-like birds. On the southeast side of the salt flat are the **Termas de Polloquere**, several hot thermal pools amid a small geyser field, which are a good spot to soak and pamper yourself using the mud at the bottom of the pools. It is possible to **camp** at a rustic site near the pools.

There is no public transport to either the *reserva* or *salar*, and a tour is the easiest option.

PARQUE NACIONAL VOLCÁN ISLUGA

South of Las Vicuñas, the dirt track drifts eastwards, passing by large herds of **llamas** and their shorter and hairier **alpaca** cousins, as well as tiny, seemingly deserted Aymará hamlets. All these are overshadowed by the towering **Volcán Isluga** (5218m), from which the park takes its name. The little village of **Enquelga** is home to a small Conaf-run **refugio** with five beds and hot showers (CH$5500/ person), as well as a free **campsite** (1km east of town) with Conaf-maintained shelters alongside a stream and some hot springs. One warm pool here, against the impressive backdrop of the volcano, is large enough for swimming.

Just outside the park, the small farming settlement of **COLCHANE**, surrounded by fields of bright red quinoa and *kiwicha* (a highly nutritious local staple), has several basic **guesthouses** providing simple home-cooked food. It is possible to get on a bus from Iquique to Colchane (daily 1pm & 9pm; 3hr), and get dropped off at the park, but it is best to contact Conaf in advance for advice. For drivers, the road condition is poor and requires a 4WD vehicle.

Middle Chile

As the southernmost reaches of Santiago's sprawling suburbs fade away, a vast expanse of fields, orchards and vineyards serves as a transition area between the bustling metropolitan borough and the natural landscapes of the Lake District.

This is Chile's most fertile region, and home to the country's world-famous **wineries**, which are accessible by day-trip from Santiago but are much less rushed if taken from the quaint town of **Santa Cruz**. West of Santa Cruz is the country's surf capital of **Pichilemu**, where some of the world's biggest breaks crash along vast sandy beaches. Further south, **Concepción**, Chile's second-largest city and an important university town, is picking itself up after it was rocked by a massive **earthquake** in 2010, although the surrounding area is likely to show the scars of the destructive quake for some years to come. **Talca** and **Chillán** are useful stop-offs along the long Panamericana – here, the Ruta 5 – as well as good bases for exploring the wineries, hot baths and natural attractions in the local area.

RANCAGUA

RANCAGUA is a busy agricultural city that lies 87km south of Santiago. The best time for a day-trip here is either in April, to witness the **National Rodeo Championships**, or the last weekend in March, during the **Fiesta Huasa**, a three-day celebration of cowboy culture held in the main square, involving traditional food and wine. Alternatively, if you are coming in November, try to catch the **Encuentro Internacional Criollo**, a demonstration of spectacular horse-breaking and lassoing skills from expert riders from all over Latin America.

ARRIVAL AND INFORMATION

By bus The Terminal O'Higgins (☎72 222 5425) hub for long-distance destinations lies northeast of town, just off Ruta 5. Tur-Bus, at O'Carrol 1175, has a more convenient, central location. Expreso Santa Cruz and Pullman Del Sur run buses on to Santa Cruz.

By train The hourly Metrotrén from Santiago and the faster train to Chillán stop at the Estación Rancagua (☎600 585 5000), on Av Estación, between O'Carrol and Carrera Pinto, at the western edge of downtown.

Tourist information The helpful Sernatur office at Germán Riesco 277, 1st floor (Mon–Thurs 8.30am–5.30pm, Fri 8.30am–4.30pm; ☎72 223 0413, ⓦturismolibertador.cl), can provide plenty of information on the city and its festivals.

SANTA CRUZ

About 90km southwest of Rancagua, the attractive little town of **SANTA CRUZ** lies at the heart of the fertile Colchagua Valley, home to Chile's best-organized *Ruta de Vino*. The hot climate here has proved to be perfect for growing Carmenère, Cabernet, Malbec and Syrah grapes. The ideal time to visit is during the first weekend in March, when the **Fiesta de la Vendimia del Valle de**

RUTA DEL VINO DE COLCHAGUA

The **Colchagua Valley** has some of the best red wines in the world, not to mention the most professionally run **wine route** in Chile. There are fourteen **wineries** in all, including both large, modern producers and small-scale, traditional *bodegas*; many of them can be visited on a drop-by basis or at short notice. The Ruta del Vino agency (☎72 282 3199, ⓦrutadelvino.cl) organizes full-day and half-day tours that take in two or three wineries with tastings and can include lunch, museum visits, and/or transfers from Santiago. Rates depend on the number of people and type of tour; a half-day tour will cost around CH$50,000. The agency can also book (mostly luxury) accommodation in the area.

WINERIES

Viña Casa Silva Hijuela Norte s/n Angostura, Km132, Ruta 5, San Fernando ☎72 291 3117, ⓦcasasilva.cl. Award-winning winery with an excellent restaurant, set in a colonial-style hacienda, using modern technology to produce Carmenère, as well as the less common Viognier, Sauvignon Gris and Shiraz. Tours CH$20,000/person.

Viña Laura Hartwig Camino Barreales s/n ☎72 282 3179, ⓦlaurahartwig.cl. Small, family-owned,

boutique winery producing only reserve-quality wines; the owners directly oversee each stage of production. Book in advance. Tours CH$10,000/person.

Viña Viu Manent Carretera del Vino Km37 ☎72 285 8751, ⓦviumanent.cl. Family-owned winery close to Santa Cruz, famous for its excellent reds, especially Malbec, offering horse-drawn carriage tours as part of its attraction. Tours CH$16,000/person.

Colchagua (grape harvest festival) is held, allowing you to sample the best wines and the region's typical dishes.

WHAT TO SEE AND DO

The heart of Santa Cruz is the gorgeous **Plaza de Armas**, dotted with araucarias, conifers and palm trees, with an ornate fountain at its centre and drinking fountains around its periphery. Within a couple of blocks of the plaza are numerous places to eat and *hospedajes*.

The excellent, privately run **Museo de Colchagua**, at Errázuriz 145 (daily: Sept–Feb 10am–7pm; March–Aug 10am–6pm; CH$7000; ⓦmuseocolchagua.cl), displays the unmatched private collection of Carlos Cardoen, which includes pre-Columbian artefacts from around Latin America, conquistador weaponry, exquisite gold work, Mapuche weavings, a re-creation of the San José mine rescue and much more. Cardoen himself is a highly controversial figure: still wanted by the FBI for allegedly selling weapons to Iraq in the 1980s, the former arms dealer has transformed himself into a successful businessman and philanthropist with extensive interests in wine and tourism.

ARRIVAL AND INFORMATION

By bus Terminal Municipal is on Casanova 478, four blocks southwest of the Plaza de Armas.
Destinations Pichilemu (10 daily; 2hr); Santiago (frequent; 3hr).
Tourist information The tourist office is at Plaza de Armas 242 (Mon–Fri 8.30am–4pm). The Ruta de Vino headquarters on the east side of the Plaza de Armas 298 (Mon–Fri 9am–6pm, Sat & Sun 10am–6pm; ☎72 282 3199, ⓦrutadelvino.cl) is an excellent source of information on the Valle Colchagua (see box opposite).

ACCOMMODATION

Gomero Capellania 327 ☎72 282 1436. Unremarkable hotel with clean but not particularly inviting rooms, and friendly staff. Breakfast included. Rooms CH$36,000

EATING AND DRINKING

Café Sorbo Casanova 158, on the 2nd floor of a cultural centre. Extremely friendly café/restaurant with quality coffee, and great choice for vegetarians. Soya hamburger CH$6800. Daily 11am–8.30pm.
Pizzeria Refranes Diaz Besoain 176. Opposite the fire

★TREAT YOURSELF

Casa de Campo Los Pidenes, Km40 Ruta 50 ☎72 282 3540, ⓦhotelcasadecampo.cl. If you're going to treat yourself anywhere, Santa Cruz is the place to do it, with a wealth of attractive lodgings, many in the vineyards themselves (the Ruta del Vino has a list). *Casa de Campo* is a wonderful family-run place just outside of town that won't blow the budget as much as some, with charming rural-chic rooms. Ask for one with a verandah or balcony overlooking the attractive gardens, vineyards and pool. Doubles CH$89,000

station. Traditional Chilean dishes combine with an excellent range of *empanadas* and divine slabs of pizza in a pleasant ambience. Large pizza CH$5990. Mon–Sat 1–4pm, 8pm–midnight, Sun 1–4pm.
Vino Bello Barreales s/n, 1.5km outside of town. Run by the nearby Laura Hartwig winery (see box opposite), you can dine on decent Italian food including pasta, pizzas and salads on a candlelit terrace, with the impossibly romantic backdrop of the vineyards. Mains from around CH$8000. Mon–Sat 11.30am–11pm, Sun 11.30am–3.30pm.

PICHILEMU

The drive to the surfing magnet of **PICHILEMU**, 90km west of Santa Cruz, is particularly scenic. The Ruta 90 meanders past sun-drenched vineyards before snaking in and out of patches of pine forest. "Pichi", as it's known, was planned as an upmarket vacation spot by the local land baron Agustín Ross Edwards, though in recent years it's become ever more popular with a motley crew of **surfers** and local beach bums.

WHAT TO SEE AND DO

A spread-out town, Pichilemu has numerous guesthouses and places to eat concentrated along the east–west Avenida Ortúzar, and the north–south Aníbal Pinto, a couple of blocks from the sea. The water is always chilly (12–18°C) so you'll need a wetsuit if you want to do more than take a quick dip.

Playa Las Terrazas

Avenida Costanera Cardenal Caro runs alongside the black-sand expanse of

---

SURF'S UP!

Budding surfers wanting to get in on the action can hone their skills with the help of several surfing schools:

Lobos del Pacífico Av Costanera ☎09 506 2127, ⓦ lobosdelpacifico.cl. Experienced surfing instructor charges CH$12,000 per lesson (2hr 30min), which includes board and wetsuit rental. Equipment rental alone costs CH$8000.

Manzana 54 Surf School Av Costanera, next to *Waitara Restaurant* ☎09 574 5984, ⓦ manzana54.cl. Professional surf school and equipment rental offering lessons for CH$18,000 (2hr), all equipment included. Equipment rental alone is CH$7000–8000 for a full day.

Playa Las Terrazas, Pichilemu's principal beach. Good for both sunbathers and surfers, it has a cluster of places to eat and **surf schools** concentrated towards its southern end, at the rocky promontory of La Puntilla. Steps lead up to the meticulously landscaped **Parque Ross**, dotted with palm trees and boasting an excellent view of the coast.

Punta de Lobos

Chile's most famous wave, **Punta de Lobos**, where the National Surfing Championships are held every summer, can be found 6km south of downtown Pichilemu; to get there, take a *colectivo* along Jorge Errázuriz (CH$800), or cycle down Comercio until you reach the turn-off towards the coast and make your way to the end of the jutting, cactus-studded headland. At the tip of the promontory, intrepid surfers descend via a steep dirt path before swimming across the short churning stretch of water to **Las Tetas**, the distinctive sea stacks, and catching the powerful, consistent left break just beyond.

ARRIVAL AND INFORMATION

By bus The main Terminal Municipal is located on Millaco, at Los Alerces, though unless you're staying in Pichi's southeastern quarter it's more convenient to disembark at the bus stop on Angel Gaete. There are hourly departures to Santiago (daily 4.30am–6.40pm; about 3hr 30min; Buses Cruz Mar and Buses Nilahue stop in Santa Cruz and Rancagua). Buy your ticket at the bus offices on Angel Gaete at Aníbal Pinto, and catch them at the bus stop on Santa María, four blocks northeast.

Spanish school Pichilemu Languages Institute (☎72 284 2449, ⓦ studyspanishchile.com) offers short- and longer-term Spanish classes.

Tourist information There is a helpful booth on Angel Gaete, between Montt and Rodríguez (Mon–Fri 8am–1pm

& 2.30–7pm; ⓦ pichilemu.cl), which gives out maps of town and can help with accommodation.

ACCOMMODATION

Hostal Casa Verde Camino Vecinal 295, opposite Dunamar Cabanas, on Playa Hermosa Pasaje San Alfonso s/n; walk up the track opposite Verde Mar supermarket ☎09 9299 8866, ⓦ hostalcasaverde.cl. About 3km from town, this small but popular hostel has good breakfasts, surfing classes, free bike rental, and a chilled-out vibe. Dorms CH$12,000, doubles CH$36,000

Hotel Chile España Av Ortúzar 255 ☎72 284 1270, ⓦ chileespana.cl. Smart, central guesthouse with clean and comfortable rooms; breakfast is included and there's a pleasant patio area. Doubles CH$50,000

EATING, DRINKING AND NIGHTLIFE

El Balaustro Av Ortúzar 289. Conveniently located, two-tiered pub which serves excellent lunchtime specials, both meat and fish, and has nightly drinks deals. Set lunch CH$4900. Daily lunch & dinner.

La Casa de las Empanadas Aníbal Pinto, between Aguirre & Acevedo. Takeaway with amazing range of excellent *empanadas* (CH$1500). Daily noon–midnight.

Disco 127 Av Angel Gaete s/n. Pounding venue that acts as a magnet for Pichilemu's youth and surfing population. Doesn't kick off until after midnight.

Waitara Av Costanera 1039d ☎72 284 3004, ⓦ waitara .cl. The restaurant here is more appealing than the cabañas – its lunchtime menu features tasty and well-cooked fish dishes, and it turns into a party place later in the evening. Mains CH$5000.

TALCA

Some 250km south of Santiago, the agricultural city of **TALCA** has little in the way of its own attractions but makes a good stop-off along the long Ruta 5 between the capital and Patagonia. It also serves as a base for exploring the **Valle del Maule** and its **Ruta de Vino**, as well as for treks into the nearby sierra.

The city's streets are on a numbered grid, making it very easy to navigate. Most of the commercial activity revolves around the **Plaza de Armas**, dominated by the cathedral, between 1 Norte, 1 Sur, 1 Poniente and 1 Oriente. Banks and pharmacies line 1 Sur, and there are numerous inexpensive places to eat and *completo* stands within a couple of blocks of the square. Unfortunately, the Museo O'Higgiano, at 1 Norte 875, where the national hero Bernardo O'Higgins spent his childhood and signed the Declaration of Independence in 1818, remains closed due to severe damage suffered in the 2010 quake.

ARRIVAL AND DEPARTURE

By train The station (☎2 2585 5927) is at 11 Oriente 1000; there is no luggage storage.

Destinations Santiago (2 daily; 3hr); Chillán (2 daily; 1hr 50min).

By bus Most long-distance and local buses arrive at the Terminal Rodoviario at 2 Sur 1920 (☎71 224 3270), ten blocks east of the Plaza de Armas; the Tur-Bus terminal (☎71 241 4807) is at 13 Oriente No 1962 on the corner with 3 Sur. Frequent *colectivos* go back and forth along 1 Sur to and from the train and bus stations.

Destinations Chillán (every 30min; 2hr); Puerto Montt (5 daily; 10hr); Santiago (hourly; 3hr 30min); Temuco (8 daily; 6hr).

INFORMATION

Tourist information The well-stocked and very useful Sernatur office is in the Correos, on the east side of Plaza de Armas, at 1 Oriente 1150 (Mon–Fri 8.30am–5.30pm, Sat 10am–2pm; ☎71 223 3669; ✉infomaule@sernatur.cl). The helpful Conaf office, at 2

Poniente/3 Sur (☎71 222 8029), has information on the Reserva Nacional Altos de Lircay and Radal Siete Tazas.

ACCOMMODATION

Casa Chueca Camino Las Rastras s/n ☎71 197 0096, ☎09 9419 0625, ⒲trekkingchile.com. Located on the banks of the Río Lircay, a short distance out of Talca, this German/Austrian-run guesthouse is a peaceful retreat, with comfortable and charmingly decorated rooms, delicious, home-cooked, mainly vegetarian meals and a swimming pool set amid its lush gardens. Franz Schubert, its knowledgeable owner, also runs excellent guided excursions into the little-visited and under-appreciated protected areas nearby. To get here, take a "Taxutal A" bus from the bus stop at the southeast corner of the main bus terminal to the end of the route; if possible, call beforehand so they can pick you up. Otherwise, follow the dirt road from Taxutal for about 20min. Closed June–Aug. Dorms CH$12,500, doubles CH$49,000

Hostal del Puente 1 Sur 407 ☎71 222 0930. Small but elegant rooms set around a beautiful leafy courtyard, in a traditional adobe house just two blocks from the Plaza de Armas. Doubles CH$28,000

Refugio del Tricahue ✉refugio.tricahue@yahoo.fr, ⒲refugio-tricahue.cl. Run by French-Belgian couple Betty and Dimitri, this nature lover's retreat has simple wooden chalets set against a beautiful backdrop of tree-covered mountains, with opportunities for fishing, trekking and cycling. Take Bus Interbus towards Armerillo (5 buses daily; 1hr 30min). Camping/person CH$4000, dorms CH$7500, doubles CH$22,000

EATING

La Buena Carne 1 Norte 1305. Large restaurant specializing in grilled meat, owned by the butchers on the opposite corner. Excellent cuts at bargain prices. Humitas CH$1000. Mon–Sat 9am–9.30pm.

RUTA DEL VINO DEL MAULE

Valle del Maule is rapidly developing a **Ruta del Vino** involving nine wineries, most of which require reservations to visit. The Ruta del Vino del Maule headquarters at Avenida Circunvalacion Oriente 1055 in the lobby of Talca's casino (Mon–Sat 8.30am–2pm & 5–8pm; ☎09 8157 9951, ⒲valledelmaule.cl) can help to arrange full-day and half-day visits to the nearby wineries. Good options include:

Viña Balduzzi Av Balmaceda 1189, San Javier ☎73 232 2138, ⒲balduzzi.cl. Operating since the seventeenth century, this family winery runs interesting guided tours (CH$5500/person) and tastings in English, and is the easiest to visit by public transport: take the San Javier bus from Talca. No need to reserve. Mon–Sat 9.30am–6.30pm.

Viña Gillmore Camino a Constitución Km20, San Javier ☎73 197 5539, ⒲tabonko.cl. Also known as Tabonko, this boutique winery produces Cabernet Franc, Carignan, Malbec, Syrah, Carmenère and Merlot, with a fine on-site restaurant. Call to arrange a tour (CH$6000/person).

Via Lactea 1 Sur 1339, local 10. Restaurant serving a range of meat and fish dishes and an excellent selection of ice cream. Tables fill up in the evenings. Mains CH$3500–CH$7000.

PARQUE NACIONAL ALTOS DEL LIRCAY

The **Parque Nacional Altos del Lircay** (daily: March–Nov 8.30am–5pm; Dec–Feb 8.30am–7pm; CH$4000), about 70km east of Talca and 2km from the village of **Vilches Alto**, is one of the best trekking destinations in the central part of Chile, with hikes that snake through native forest before emerging above the tree line with spectacular views of snowcapped mountains and volcanoes. The area is also famous as a magnet for UFO sightings and enthusiasts. Multi-day trails around the area or linking Lircay with the nearby **Parque Nacional Radal Siete Tazas** – named for the "cups" (*tazas*) carved by a series of seven waterfalls out of the rock – are also possible; contact a local guide.

ARRIVAL AND INFORMATION

By bus Around 10–14 buses a day (☏71 220 3992, ⓦvilchesalto.com) ply the route – in the process of being paved – between Talca and Vilches Alto.
Tourist information The staff at *Casa Chueca* and *Refugio Don Galo* can advise on treks in the park and help organize excursions.

ACCOMMODATION

Refugio Don Galo Hijuela R, Vilches Alto ☏2 2196 0619, ⓦrefugiodegalo.com. Simple but pleasant pine-walled refuge right by the reserve, with a restaurant and owners who are a good source of local information. CH$35,000

CHILLÁN

CHILLÁN lies 150km south of Talca in the middle of the green **Itata Valley**, a stopover on the Panamericana or launchpad for visiting the nearby skiing and hot-springs area of Nevados de Chillán. A nondescript town rebuilt time and time again after earthquake damage and Mapuche attacks, Chillán is famous as the birthplace of Chile's national hero and founding father, Bernardo O'Higgins. Its market is worth a visit, overflowing with an abundance of fresh produce and handicrafts. The centre of town is the **Plaza Bernardo O'Higgins**, featuring a towering 36m cross commemorating the thirty thousand victims of the 1939 earthquake, which largely destroyed the city. **Escuela Mexico**, a school built with Mexico's donations in the wake of the earthquake, draws visitors with its frescoes, painted by the famous **Mexican muralists** David Alfaro Siqueiros and Xavier Guerrero, and depicting famous figures from Latin American history.

ARRIVAL AND INFORMATION

By bus Most long-distance buses arrive at the Terminal María Teresa at Av O'Higgins 10 (☏42 227 2151), while the regional firm Linea Azul operates its own terminal at Constitución 1 (☏42 220 3800). Buses from local destinations, such as the Valle Las Trancas, arrive at the rural bus terminal at the market.
Destinations Concepción (8 daily; 1hr 30min); Santiago (every 50min; 6hr); Talca (8 daily; 3hr).
By train The station is at Av Brasil s/n (☏600 585 5000). Trains run a couple of times a day between Santiago and Chillán, stopping at several Central Valley towns.
Destinations Santiago (2 daily; 4hr 30min); Talca (2 daily; 2hr 20min).
Tourist information The helpful and well-stocked Sernatur office is located at 18 de Septiembre 455 (March–Nov Mon–Fri 8.30am–5pm; Dec–Feb Mon–Fri 8.30am–8pm, Sat 10am–8pm, Sun 10am–2pm; ☏42 222 3272).

ACCOMMODATION

Sonia Itata 288 ☏42 221 4879, ⓦhospedajesonia.cl. It doesn't get much cheaper than this *hospedaje*, with its friendly owners offering slightly tatty but clean rooms with shared facilities. Doubles CH$10,000

EATING

Arcoiris Roble 525. Excellent vegetarian restaurant specializing in delicious juices, crêpes and salads. Veggie burger CH$3500. Mon–Fri 8.30am–7pm, Sat 9am–5pm.
Mercado Municipal Bordered by Roble, Riquelme, Prat and 5 de Abril. Inexpensive, traditional Chilean dishes, such as *pastel de choclo* and *completos*, are served at the multitude of *cocinerías* here. *Longaniza y pure* (Chilean bangers and mash) CH$2500.

NEVADOS DE CHILLÁN

The biggest attraction in the area is the hot-springs resort of **Nevados de Chillán** (☏42 243 4200, ⓦnevadosdechillan.com), which, with 29 runs, most of intermediate level, becomes a bona fide **ski resort** in the winter. There is also ample off-piste terrain, ideal for **snowboarders**, who are not allowed on some of the resort's runs. During the summer, in the valley overlooked by the looming **Volcán Chillán** (3212m), hiking, horseriding and downhill biking are all popular activities. The four open-air hot baths at the *Parque de Agua* in the resort are open to non-guests (CH$8000/person).

ARRIVAL AND DEPARTURE

By bus Regular Rem Bus (☏ 42 222 9377) services go to nearby Valle Las Trancas between 6.50am and 7.20pm from Chillán's rural bus terminal. For the 8km between Las Trancas and the resort you will need to hitchhike or pay for a private transfer (about CH$20,000).

ACCOMMODATION AND EATING

Staying in the resort itself is very expensive, so the majority of holidaymakers stay at the cheaper lodgings in Valle Las Trancas, which offers a scattering of *hospedajes*, campsites and restaurants, surrounded by immense mountains. Prices are considerably lower outside the ski season.

Chil'In Km72.5, Valle Las Trancas ☏ 42 224 7075, ⊕ chil-in.com. Well-run hostel with its own pizzeria, attractive dorms and Skype-equipped free internet. Dorms CH$18,000, doubles CH$45,000

Riding Chile Km73, Valle Las Trancas ☏ 09 779 1973, ⊕ ridingchile.com. Recently renovated budget accommodation, with a good on-site restaurant in a wood cabin and helpful owners. Doubles CH$29,000

CONCEPCIÓN

CONCEPCIÓN is Chile's second-largest city, a bustling sprawl some 112km southwest of Chillán. It has little in the way of tourist sights, though its huge student population ensures a high concentration of lively bars. Founded in 1550, the city was the administrative and military capital of colonial Chile. It suffered considerable structural damage in the huge 2010 earthquake.

WHAT TO SEE AND DO

The heart of Concepción's walkable city centre, lined with a mixture of elegant old buildings and modern concrete blocks, is the carefully landscaped **Plaza de la Independencia**. Partially pedestrianized Barros Arana, the main thoroughfare, has shops and places to eat, while at the western end lies the lively **Barrio Estación**, whose trendy bars and restaurants are centred on **Plaza España**. A four-block walk south from the Plaza de la Independencia along Aníbal Pinto brings you to the long green stretch of **Parque Ecuador**.

You can also catch a bus from Chacabuco street to Tomé and Dichato, small local coastal resorts with sandy beaches 30km or so north of the city.

Galería de la Historia

Three blocks west of the Parque Ecuador, at the corner of Lamas and Lincoyán, is the **Galería de la Historia** (Mon 3–6.30pm, Tues–Fri 10am–1.30pm & 3–6.30pm, Sat & Sun 10am–2pm & 3–7pm; free), which showcases the region's turbulent history through a series of interactive dioramas, with voice-overs dramatizing the scenes. There's also a large collection of ornate silver *mate* gourds.

Casa del Arte

Three blocks south of the Plaza de la Independencia, you can catch a *colectivo* or walk eastwards to the **Casa del Arte** (Tues–Fri 10am–6pm, Sat 10am–5pm, Sun 11am–2pm; free), just inside the grounds of the Universidad de Concepción. This museum displays a modest collection of Chilean art, but its highlight is the giant **mural**, *La Presencia de América Latina*, by Mexican muralist Jorge Gonzáles Camarena. Latin America – its conquest, its cultural and agricultural wealth – is captured in a series of densely packed images oriented around the main figure of an *indígena* (a native woman). Interwoven throughout are colourful ribbons representing every Latin American flag and numerous national symbols.

ARRIVAL AND INFORMATION

By plane Aeropuerto Internacional Carriel Sur (☏ 41 273 2000) is 5km northwest of downtown; a door-to-door airport transfer service is available (CH$5000; ☏ 41 224 8776).

Destinations Santiago (10 daily, 1hr 5min) with LAN (☎ 600 526 2000) and Sky Airline (☎ 41 221 8941).

By bus Most long-distance buses arrive at the Terminal de Buses Collao, Tegualda 860 (☎ 41 274 9000), from where numerous local buses run downtown.

Destinations Angol (6–8 daily; 2hr); Chillán (every 50min; 1hr 30min); Los Ángeles (hourly; 1hr 30min); Santiago (every 30min; 7hr); Talca (6–8 daily; 4hr).

Tourist information The Sernatur office is at Aníbal Pinto 460 (Mon–Fri 10am–6pm; ☎ 41 262 4000, ⓦ descubrebiobio.cl) and has plenty of information on the region surrounding Concepción. Conaf has an office at Barros Arano 215 (Mon–Fri 8.30am–1pm & 2.15–5.25pm).

ACCOMMODATION

Apart Hotel Don Matías Colo Colo 155 ☎ 41 225 6846, ⓦ aparthoteldonmatias.cl. An attractive B&B with friendly service, large rooms, some with private bathrooms, and a good breakfast. Doubles CH$55,000

San Sebastian Rengo 463 ☎ 41 295 6719, ⓦ hotelsansebastian.cl. Somewhat flowery but perfectly adequate and clean budget hotel, with breakfast. Doubles CH$25,000

EATING

Hiper Lider on Prat/Freire is a massive supermarket with an excellent selection of fresh produce, as well as rare Thai and Chinese cooking ingredients.

Mercado Central Rengo, between Maipú and Freire. The informal cocinerías here are a good spot for inexpensive Chilean standards, such as cazuela (CH$3000).

Il Padrino Barros Arana, at Plaza España. Bustling Italian restaurant and bar, serving generous portions of pasta and pizza. Mains CH$6000–8000. Tues–Sat 6.30pm–late.

DIRECTORY

Banks and exchange There are numerous banks with ATMs on Barros Arana and O'Higgins; Afex, at Barros Arana 565, Local 57, changes foreign currencies.

Hospital Hospital Regional is on San Martín, at Av Roosevelt (☎ 41 272 2500).

Laundry Try Limposco y Lavendería, Colo Colo 148.

Post office Colo Colo 417 (Mon–Fri 9am–7pm, Sat 9.30am–1pm).

The Lake District

Stretching south from the end of the Río Bío Bío to the large port of Puerto Montt, THE LAKE DISTRICT falls within the region of La Araucanía, one of the last parts of Chile to be colonized by Europeans thanks to fierce resistance by the Mapuche that lasted until 1880. While not as challenging as Patagonia, the area's multitude of snowcapped volcanoes, sparkling lakes and dense forest make it a vastly rewarding place to explore.

The Lake District's two biggest adventure sports hubs are **Pucón** and **Puerto Varas**, with numerous hiking, volcano-climbing, rafting, kayaking and horseriding options. From Pucón, you can explore the Mapuche culture of **Villarrica** and **Temuco**, and go trekking in Huerquehue, Conguillío and Villarrica national parks. Further south, the Spanish forts and excellent beer make lively university town **Valdivia** worth a visit, while the sparkling **Lago Llanquihue** by Puerto Varas beckons with its surrounding volcanoes and waterfalls. From the busy port of **Puerto Montt** it's easy to reach **Cochamó Valley** with its ancient trees and superb hiking, horseriding and rock climbing.

TEMUCO

The busy market city of **TEMUCO** was founded in 1881 towards the end of the "pacification" of the Mapuche, the indigenous people who still inhabit the area – Temuco remained a frontier town well into the early twentieth century, when poet Pablo Neruda grew up here.

WHAT TO SEE AND DO

A single compelling reason for visiting Temuco is the superb **Museo Regional de la Araucanía** (Mon–Fri 9.30am–5.30pm, Sat 11am–5pm, Sun 11am–2pm; CH$600), which charts the history and migration of the Araucanían people. Beautifully presented exhibits include displays of asymmetric metawe pottery, funeral urns and sceptre-like sacred stones. Standout exhibits include an enormous seventeenth-century wuampo (hollow log canoe), traditional weavings and ceremonial masks and drums, but the stars are the **Mapuche jewellery**; the Mapuche learned silverwork from the Spanish, and fine examples, including heavy silver collares, passed on from mother to daughter, are on display here.

The museum is a ten-minute walk along Avenida Alemana from the centre; most of the city's best restaurants are also located on Avenida Alemana.

Museum aside, it's worth strolling through the lively and extensive **Feria Libre** (daily: summer 8.30am–6pm; winter 8.30am–5pm), a Mapuche fruit and veg **market** that stretches for several blocks of Aníbal Pinto between Lautaro/Barros Arana and Balmaceda.

ARRIVAL AND DEPARTURE

By plane The new Temuco airport is located 17km away from the city, served by LAN and Sky Airlines flights to Santiago and Concepción, and connected to it by transfer minibuses (CH$5000). In peak season, there are direct transfers to Pucón.

By bus From Pucón or Villarica (you can visit on a day-trip), use Buses JAC as their bus terminal at Balmaceda 1005 is central and convenient. Most other long-distance buses use the Terminal Rodoviario, 5km north of the city centre on Vicente Pérez Rosales – taxis, buses and micros run every few minutes to the city centre. The Terminal Buses Rurales, near the market, at Aníbal Pinto 032, serves smaller destinations in the region.

Destinations Concepción (6 daily; 5hr); Pucón (every 30min; 1hr 45min); Puerto Varas (hourly; 5hr); Santiago (every 30min; 9hr); Valdivia (every 30min; 3hr); Villarrica (every 30min; 1hr 15min).

PARQUE NACIONAL CONGUILLÍO

A vast expanse of old lava fields, extending from the very active Llaima volcano, pristine lakes and araucaria forest, the **PARQUE NACIONAL CONGUILLÍO** (CH$4500; ⓦparquenacionalconguillio.cl) is all the more rewarding because of the relative remoteness and difficulty of access by pitted dirt road. The park offers a good selection of hikes for all abilities. For incredible views of the Sierra Nevada range through araucaria forest, take the 7km (2hr 30min) trail from Playa Linda, at the east end of Lago Conguillío, to the base of the Sierra Nevada. The challenging **Travesía Río Blanco** (5km; 5hr), which crosses a small glacier before continuing into the Sierra Nevada proper, is recommended for very experienced trekkers only. From the western shores of Laguna Verde, the 11km (5hr) **Sendero**

Pastos Blancos runs to the Laguna Captrén, traversing spectacular scenery and rewarding you with panoramic views of Sierra Nevada, Lago Conguillío and the Truful-Truful valley.

ARRIVAL AND DEPARTURE

By car It's possible to traverse the park by regular car, though you'll need a high-clearance vehicle outside the December–March season to cope with the snow.

By bus You can take Nar Bus (☎45 221 1611) from Temuco's Terminal Buses Rurales to Melipeuco (6 daily; 2hr), where, in high season, the tourist office can help arrange transport to the southern entrance of the park via taxi. To reach the northern entrance at Laguna Captrén, take Buses Erbuc (☎09 7632 5232) from Temuco's Terminal Buses Rurales to Curacautín (hourly; 1hr 30min), from where a shuttle runs to the *guardería* (ranger station) at Captrén (Dec–Feb: Mon & Fri at 6am & 5pm; double-check departure times at bus station).

INFORMATION

Tourist information You can pick up maps of the park at the Conaf-run Centro de Información Ambiental (Oct–March daily 9am–1pm & 3–6.30pm; ☎65 297 2336) by Lago Conguillío.

ACCOMMODATION

La Baita ☎045 416 410, ⓦlabaitaconguillio.cl. La Baita ecotourism project has a beautiful lodge (with hot tub), great restaurant and a cluster of cabañas in the southern section of the park; restaurant open during high season. Doubles CH$58,000, cabañas CH$50,000

Camping El Hoyón and **La Caseta** ☎65 229 8100. The tranquil Hoyón campsite is located on the shores of Laguna Conguillío, 2km from the main entrance – each of the ten pitches has its own bathroom. Adjacent La Caseta offers ten similar pitches on the lake, also with private bathrooms. Open Nov–March. Pitch for up to 5 people CH$35,000

Camping Los Ñirres, El Estero and **Los Carpinteros** ☎65 229 8100. These three campsites are located a short walk away from the lake, in the forest, all with shared bathrooms. El Estero also has a basic backpacker dorm. Open Nov–March. Camping/pitch for up to five people CH$20,000, dorms CH$5000

VILLARRICA

Some 87km southeast of Temuco on the western shores of tranquil Lago Villarrica, the colonial town of **VILLARRICA** was destroyed several times by volcanic eruptions and abandoned after being captured by the Mapuche in 1603. What you see today has been built since the 1880s, when Swiss, German and Austrian immigrants resettled the area. Thanks to the railway, completed in 1933, the town was attracting well-heeled Chilean holidaymakers with its gorgeous lakeside views of the Volcán Villarrica long before Pucón (see opposite). The appealing and thoroughly modern lakeside is popular, while in the centre, the **Museo Histórico Municipal** (Mon–Fri 9am–1pm & 2.30–6.30pm; free), at Valdivia 1050, offers a crash course in Mapuche culture. You can acquaint yourself with *ñillawaka* (food storage bags), musical instruments such as the *trutruca*, silver jewellery and traditional weaving: you can tell a Mapuche woman's marital and social status just by looking at her embroidered belt. Next door to the museum on Valdivia, at Zegers, the stalls of the **Centro Cultural Mapuche** (daily 9am–5pm) sell some decent *raulí* woodcarvings, trinkets and delicious *empanadas* (CH$350) around a *ruka* – a traditional Mapuche dwelling with walls and roof tightly woven from reeds.

ARRIVAL AND INFORMATION

By bus Tur-Bus at Muñoz 657 and Pullman (opposite) serve all major central Chile destinations on the way to Santiago. Buses JAC at Bilbao 610 serve all major Lake District destinations, while Igi Llaima at Valdivia 615 crosses the border to San Martín de Los Andes in Argentina.

Destinations Pucón (every 20min; 45min); Puerto Montt (hourly; 5hr); Santiago (4 daily; 10hr); San Martín de Los Andes (4 weekly; 10hr); Temuco (every 30min; 1hr 15min); Valdivia (7 daily; 2hr 15min).

Tourist information The helpful tourist office, at Pedro de Valdivia 1070 (Mon–Fri 8.30am–1pm & 2.30–6pm; Sat & Sun 9am–1pm & 3.30–5.30pm; ☏45 220 6619, ⌨ visitvillarrica.cl), offers free maps of the town.

ACCOMMODATION, EATING AND DRINKING

Several supermarkets are conveniently located in the centre of Villarrica.

Hostal Don Juan Körner 770 ☏45 241 1833, ⌨ hostaldonjuan.cl. Boasting great views of Volcán Villarrica, this cosy hotel has an assortment of rooms and cabañas, plus table tennis and table football for the guests. Doubles (private bath) CH$35,000, shared bath CH$27,000

Fuego Patagón Montt 40 ☏45 241 2207, ⌨ fuegopatagon.cl. From the lovely, glassed-over patio with faux-rustic decor to the expertly seared cuts of meat, this steakhouse means business. Try the signature dish of bacon-wrapped veal with quinoa and wild mushrooms and the tender lamb in a garlicky merkén (smoked chilli) sauce. Daily 12.30–3.30pm & 7.30–11pm.

La Torre Suiza Bilbao 969 ☏45 241 1213, ⌨ torresuiza .com. The wood-shingled interior of this legendary, biker-friendly hostel hides snug twins, doubles and quads with flowery bedspreads, a lounge where lingering is encouraged and a good ratio of guests per shared bathroom. Bikes available for rent. Dorms CH$12,000, doubles (private bath) CH$25,000

The Travellers Letelier 753 ⌨ thetravellers.cl. Boasting a menu that spans the globe – from Mexican burritos to Thai curry (mains from CH$7000) – it's also a top spot for coffee or one of the absolutely superb signature cocktails. Daily 9.30am–midnight.

DIRECTORY

Banks and exchange There are several banks (Bank of Chile, Santander) with ATMs and money exchange places along Valdivia.

Post office Anfión Muñoz 315.

MUSHER FOR A DAY

Based near Villarrica, **Aurora Austral Patagonia Husky** (☏09 8901 4518, ⌨ novena-region .com), is home to a mix of Siberian and Alaskan huskies, and Konrad is the only operator in the whole of South America who leads **multi-day husky sledding expeditions** that allow you to drive your own sled. You can choose either a day-trip in the vicinity of Volcán Villarrica or one of the multi-day expeditions – either to the Termas Geométricas hot springs or across the mountains into Argentina.

The sledding season runs from May to October, September being an excellent time to visit. Summer visitors (Dec–March) can test the half-tricycle, half-chariot contraptions (CH$305,000 per person, two-person minimum). They also rent out three beautiful 2–6-person cottages with skylights (CH$40,000–60,000) on the their peaceful property, complete with wandering pets. Pickup from Villarrica arranged.

PUCÓN

On a clear day, you will spy the mesmerizing snowy cone of the **Volcán Villarrica** long before the bus pulls into **PUCÓN**, 25km east of Villarrica. This small lakeside resort town, awash with the smells of wood smoke and grilled meat, has firmly established itself as a top Chilean and backpacker destination in the last decade. Each November to April season brings scores of adventure sports fanatics looking to climb the volcano, brave the **rapids** on the Río Trancura and Río Liucura or explore the nearby Parque Nacional Huerquehue. A day outdoors is usually followed by eating, drinking and partying in the town's restaurants and bars, or by a soak in the nearby **thermal springs**.

Pucón's wide, tree-lined streets are arranged in a compact grid, and most amenities and bars are located along frenzied **Avenida O'Higgins**, which bisects the town. O'Higgins ends by **La Poza**, a black-sand beach on the lake. Try to avoid February if you can, when central Pucón can make parts of downtown Santiago seem fairly tranquil in comparison.

ARRIVAL AND DEPARTURE

By plane There are twice-weekly flights between Santiago and Pucón airport (5km east of the town), with LAN and Sky Airline (Dec–Feb). The closest airport otherwise is Temuco's (see p.431).

By bus The three main long-distance carriers have separate terminals: Buses JAC (and Condor), Palguín 505 (☎ 45 299 0880), serves Villarrica, Temuco, Valdivia and Puerto Montt; Pullman Bus, Palguín 555 (☎ 45 244 3331), and Tur-Bus, O'Higgins 910 (☎ 45 244 3328), are best for long-distance journeys to Santiago; Igi Llaima (Palguín 595) runs frequent services across the border to Junín de los Andes and San Martín de los Andes; Buses Caburgua (Uruguay 540, at Palguín) serves Parque Nacional Huerquehue (8.30am, 1pm & 4pm) and the Ojos de Caburgua.

Destinations Puerto Montt (4 daily; 5hr 30min); Puerto Varas (4 daily; 5hr); San Martín de los Andes (1–2 daily; 5hr); Santiago (3–4 nightly; 11hr); Temuco (every 30min; 1hr 30min); Valdivia (6 daily; 3hr); Villarrica (every 20min; 45min).

4

OUTDOOR ACTIVITIES

Pucón operators offer a vast range of adventure tours and activities; the nearby **Río Trancura** offers a popular Class III run on the lower part of the river, with the more challenging Class VI upper Trancura run made up almost entirely of drop pools; some operators allow you to combine the two. Since the activities on offer involve an element of risk, it is important to use a reliable operator like those listed below. We don't recommend Trancura, the largest agency, due to its poor safety record.

TOUR OPERATORS

Aguaventura Palguín 336 ☎ 45 244 4246, ⓦ aguaventura.com. Established French outfit specializing in rafting trips, canyoning and watersports (such as hydrospeeding for CH$30,000), as well as winter activities. English spoken.

Antilco Campo Antilco, S-919 (12km northeast of Pucón) ☎ 09 9713 9758, ⓦ antilco.com. This German-Chilean operator is recommended for horse treks in the valleys around Pucón with bilingual guides and horses suitable for beginners. Half-day CH$25,000.

Elementos Pasaje Las Rosas 640 ☎ 45 244 1750, ⓦ elementos-chile.com. This friendly, German-run operator offers tours with an emphasis on small group size and with plenty of options to do with Mapuche culture – from cooking with the Mapuche to homestays and multi-day options. Standard tours also organized.

Paredon Andes Expeditions Variante Internacional, Pasaje Artemio Carrillo s/n ☎ 45 444 663, ⓦ paredonexpeditions.com. A small team of expert trekking and mountaineering guides leads small group ascents up Volcán Villarrica (Sept–April) and other Lake District volcanoes, and also offers tailormade excursions around Chile. English and French spoken. Volcano ascent CH$45,000 (plus CH$7000 chairlift ticket); minimum 3 people.

Summit Chile Tours General Urrutia 585 ☎ 45 244 3259, ⓦ summitchile.org. Headed by bilingual, internationally qualified mountain guide Claudio, who leads small group (six maximum) treks in Villarrica National Park – from the standard ascent of Volcán Villarrica (CH$45,000) to the more technical two-day ascent of Volcán Lanín (CH$180,000) on the border with Argentina. Also offers half-/full-day (CH$24,000/30,000) rock-climbing trips in the area, suitable for beginners and advanced climbers, and ski touring.

INFORMATION AND GETTING AROUND

Tourist office The Oficina de Turismo Municipal is on the corner of O'Higgins, at Palguín (daily: March–Nov 8.30am–5pm; Dec–Feb 8.30am–10pm; ☎ 45 229 3002).

Travelaid Ansorena 425, Local 4 (Mon–Sat 10am–1.30pm & 3.30–7pm; ☎ 45 244 4040, ✆ travelaid .cl). Knowledgeable Swiss-run travel agency that sells guidebooks and detailed maps of different Chilean regions, and can help you book passage on the Navimag tour boat (see p.445).

Bike rental Sierra Nevada on O'Higgins 524a (☎ 45 244 4210) rents mountain bikes. Full day CH$12,000; 5hr CH$7000.

ACCOMMODATION

Camping Parque La Poza Costanera Roberto Geiss 769 ☎ 45 244 4982. Large, shaded campsite near the lake with hot showers, a well-equipped cooking hut/dining area, and a picnic table per camping site. Popular with overland expeditions, cycling tourists and backpackers. Per person CH$5000

Chili Kiwi Hostel O'Higgins 20 ☎ 45 244 9540. Right on the lakefront, this place features Tiki the dog and is great for meeting fellow backpackers without being a party hostel; barbecues and group outings encourage guest camaraderie. Homey dorms come with comfortable bunks and lockers; you can also bed down

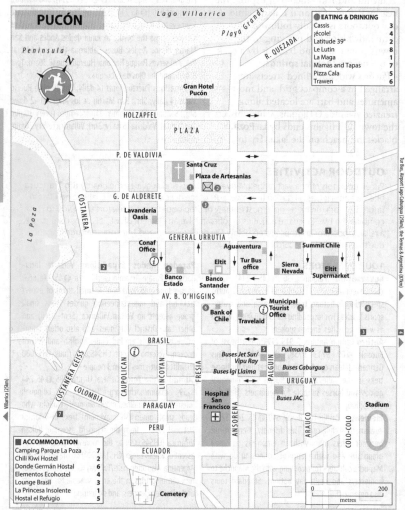

PUCÓN

EATING & DRINKING
Cassis	3
¡école!	4
Latitude 39°	2
Le Lutin	8
La Maga	1
Mamas and Tapas	7
Pizza Cala	5
Trawen	6

ACCOMMODATION
Camping Parque La Poza	7
Chili Kiwi Hostel	2
Donde Germán Hostal	6
Elementos Ecohostel	4
Lounge Brasil	3
La Princesa Insolente	1
Hostal el Refugio	5

in a converted van or in a lofty treehouse double. Dorm CH$10,000, doubles CH$26,000

Donde Germán Hostal Brasil, at Arauco ☏ 45 244 2444, ⓦ dondegerman.cl. *Donde Germán* is a beautiful, wood-shingled building with portholes, spacious rooms with rustic decor, a garden and even a pool with a sun deck. Doubles CH$30,000

Elementos Ecohostel Las Rosas 640 ☏ 45 441 750, ⓦ elementos-chile.com. This rambling house, south of the centre and with a friendly menagerie of dogs, cats and sheep, has just four spacious, spartan rooms named after the elements, as well as a budget bunkhouse (bring own bedding; you can use the guest kitchen and showers). The owner's tour agency has strong links with the Mapuche community and can organize cultural trips as well as outdoor adventures. Bunkhouse/person CH$5000, doubles CH$25,000

Lounge Brasil Colo Colo 485 ☏ 45 244 4035, ⓦ cafeloungebrasil. Not only is there an adorable wood-fire-heated café on the premises, but prices at this intimate, central guesthouse, run by a friendly Brazilian proprietress, are an absolute steal for the six snug singles and doubles (all en suite). CH$25,000

La Princesa Insolente Urrutia 660 ☏ 45 244 1492, ⓦ tpihostels.cl. Part of a five-hostel empire and run by energetic staff, this lively hostel has two cosy, fireplace-warmed common rooms, a restaurant, hot tub in the hammock-festooned garden, guest kitchen and free breakfast, plenty of information on local attractions and occasional barbecues. Most of the snug doubles and dorms have their own bathroom. Dorms CH$7000, doubles CH$25,000

Hostal el Refugio Palguín 540 ☏ 45 244 1596, ⓦ hostalelrefugio.cl. This friendly, efficiently run hostel is super-central and sociable, with one eight-bed dorm and three private rooms, as well as two kitchens. Dorms CH$12,000, doubles CH$28,000

EATING AND DRINKING

There's a large Eltit supermarket on O'Higgins at Colo Colo (daily 8.30am–10.30pm).

Cassis Fresia 223, at Alderete. This trendy café is often full; the clientele comes for the filling multigrain sandwiches and the impressive array of desserts. Try the crêpe cassis – a pancake you'll have to excavate from under a caramel brownie piled high with chocolate and *dulce de leche* ice cream. Desserts from CH$3500. Daily 8.30am–midnight.

★ **¡école!** Urrutia 592 ⓦ ecole.cl. Locally popular vegetarian restaurant serving consistently superb, hearty dishes made from local organic produce, accompanied by home-made bread. Try the sublime vegetable lasagne, or the yellow Thai vegetable curry with quinoa. Mains from CH$4500. Daily 8am–11pm.

Latitude 39° Alderete 324. Run by friendly Californian transplants, this is your home away from home for fish burritos, heaped breakfast burritos, imaginative burgers (the Buddha Burger with Asian slaw is a winner), and other Tex-Mex, accompanied by generous lemonades and regional Chilean beers. Mains from CH$4100. Daily 9.30am–11.30pm.

Le Lutin Colo Colo, at O'Higgins. Located at the strip mall on the corner, this bakery is the place to come in Pucón for proper bread and huge pain au chocolat (CH$1000). Mon–Sat noon–4pm & 7.30pm–midnight.

La Maga Alderete 276, at Fresia ☏ 45 244 4277, ⓦ lamagapucon.cl. Sate all your carnivorous cravings here. While not budget, this Uruguayan steakhouse really delivers when it comes to expertly cooked *bife de chorizo*, and the service is excellent. Steak from CH$10,000. Daily noon–4pm & 7.30pm–midnight.

Mamas and Tapas O'Higgins 587. A well-established watering hole that consistently entices a large clientele nightly with their excellent selection of beers (from CH$1800), and two-for-one cocktail specials; after a few, the "Mexican" food will seem less mediocre. Mon–Thurs & Sun noon–1am, Fri & Sat noon–2am.

Pizza Cala Lincoyán 361. Pucón's best pizzeria serves excellent thin-crust pizza, baked in a brick oven in front of you. The place really fills up when American football or baseball is on TV. Mains from CH$6000. Daily 12.30pm–midnight.

★ **Trawen** O'Higgins 311. One of the friendliest places in town, this offbeat restaurant tantalizes your tastebuds with imaginative, organic and internationally inspired dishes, such as goat's-cheese gnocchi, bacon-wrapped venison with polenta, quinoa salad and ample fresh fruit juices. Great spot for granola breakfasts, too. Mains from CH$7000. Daily 8am–11.30pm.

DIRECTORY

Banks and exchange There are several banks with ATMs and money exchange places along O'Higgins, and an exchange desk inside the Supermercado Eltit (daily 8.30am–10.30pm).

Hospital Hospital San Francisco, Uruguay 325 (☏ 45 244 1177).

EATING THE MAPUCHE WAY

An easy bus ride from Pucón (at least hourly; 45min), the highlight of the Mapuche town of Curarrehue is a meal at **Mapu Lyagl**, Camino internacional s/n (☏ 09 8788 7188), with celebrated Mapuche chef Anita Epulef at the helm. You may taste roasted *piñones* (fruit of the araucaria tree), roasted cornbread, quinoa creations and more. Dec–Feb daily noon–3pm (call ahead to confirm).

Laundry Lavandería Oasis on Lincoyán 272 (Mon–Sat 10.30am–1.30pm & 4–7pm).
Post office Fresia 183.

PARQUE NACIONAL VILLARRICA

The **Volcán Villarrica** (2847m) is the crown jewel of the **PARQUE NACIONAL VILLARRICA** (daily 8.30am–6pm) and undoubtedly the biggest attraction from Pucón; in the winter it becomes a ski and snowboard destination. To do the climb, unless you have mountaineering experience, you should go with a guide (see p.433); they will provide all the necessary equipment and transportation. It's a fairly challenging four- to five-hour ascent (plus 3hr down), starting at the chairlift at the base of the volcano (at the end of the road), with much of the walking done on snow. If the chairlift is running, it cuts an hour off the climb. At the top, by the lip of the (sometimes) smoking crater, you'll be rewarded with unparalleled views across the Lake District, with lakes and distant volcanoes stretching out before you. The sulphuric fumes mean you cannot linger long over the spectacle though. Check the weather forecast before embarking on the climb, as many tour companies take groups out even in cloudy weather, only to turn back halfway.

Volcano ascent aside, the backcountry around the volcano makes for some superb multi-day hiking in January and February when the snow is gone; register with the rangers and get a proper map of the park before setting off.

OJOS DEL CABURGUA

The azure **Ojos del Caburgua** pool, fed by several small but enchanting waterfalls (Oct–March daily 8am–8pm; CH$1000), is relatively easy to access via the Caburgua bus from Pucón. There are two privately managed viewing points (both charge the same), but the second is by far the best (get off the bus at "El Cristo", a statue of Christ on the cross on the main road, 18km from Pucón, and follow the signs for around 2km). The loop also makes an excellent day-trip for bikers. The signposted dirt trail winds along the Río Liucura, passing the falls, before emerging at the Pasarela Quelhue (hanging bridge) 8km later, and just 2km from the paved road back to Pucón.

PARQUE NACIONAL HUERQUEHUE

The compact but dazzling 125-square-kilometre **PARQUE NACIONAL HUERQUEHUE** (daily 8.30am–6pm, till 8pm high season; high season CH$4500, low season CH$2000) comprises densely forested **precordillera** (foothills), highland araucaria groves, several waterfalls and many entrancing **lakes**, making it a perfect destination for day-hikes.

The prettiest of the lakes – Chico, Toro and Verde – are accessed via the popular **Sendero Los Lagos** trail, which climbs steeply to a height of 1300m from the park office at Lago Tinquilco, past two waterfalls (14km return) – expect sensational views back towards the **Volcán Villarrica** on a clear day. You can extend the loop by taking in the tiny Lago de los Patos and Lago Huerquehue (2hr extra) before re-joining the main path, or you can continue along the **Sendero Los Huerquenes** to Termas de San Sebastián and the stunning Renahue viewpoint overlooking the lakes below. It's possible to hike to the Termas in one day (23km; 8–9hr), since much of the Sendero Los Huerquenes is downhill (but only in January and February, when there's little snow on the trail), and stay at the excellent campsite here.

ARRIVAL AND INFORMATION

By bus About 30km northeast of Pucón (and 14km off the Caburgua highway via gravel road), Huerquehue is accessible by Buses Caburgua (3–4 daily, last bus back at 5.10pm; fewer buses out of season). At the Conaf guardería at the Lago Tinquilco entrance, you'll find a trail map; all the trails are clearly signposted.

ACCOMMODATION

Cabañas San Sebastián Termas de San Sebastián ☏ 45 238 1272, ⓦ termassansebastian.cl. Serene campsite and cabañas at the end of the Sendero Los Huerquenes; the rustic wood cabins can accommodate two or five people, all equipped with bathrooms and showers supplied by the hot springs. Day use CH$5000, cabañas from CH$35,000, camping/person CH$8000

LAGO VILLARRICA & AROUND

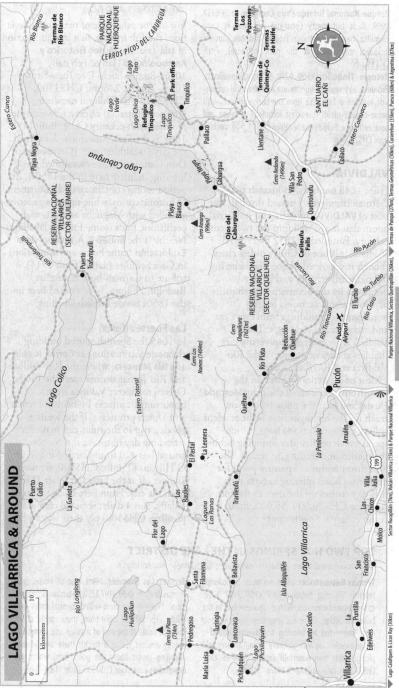

Map labels:

Río de Río Blanco
Termas de Río Blanco
Termas Los Pozones
Termas de Huife
PARQUE NACIONAL HUEREQUEHUE
CERROS PICOS DEL CABURGUA
Lago Toro
Termas de Quimey-Co
Estero Cunco
Park office
Tinquilco
SANTUARIO EL CANI
Lago Chico
Refugio Tinquilco
Lago Verde
Lago Tinquilco
Estero Coñaraco
Playa Negra
Pailaco
Llentante
Coilaco
Piedra Alta
Caburgua
Villa San Pedro
Cerro Redondo (1496m)
Quetroleufú
Lago Caburgua
RESERVA NACIONAL VILLARICA (SECTOR QUILEMBE)
Playa Blanca
Cerro Amargo (996m)
Ojos del Caburgua
Carileufu Falls
Río Pucón
Puerto Trafampulli
Río Tralcupulli
Río Liucura
Río Pucón
El Turbio
Río Turbio
RESERVA NACIONAL VILLARICA (SECTOR QUELHUE)
Cerro Chaquilcura (1621m)
Río Claro
Río Trancura
Pucón Airport
Lago Colico
Cerro Los Nuevos (1404m)
Reducción Quelhue
Río Plata
Pucón
Estero Totoral
Quelhue
La Península
Amulén
Puerto Colico
La Gaviota
El Pastal
La Leonera
Trancaleufú
Trarileufú
Villa Julia
199
Los Chicos
Los Raulíes
Flor del Lago
Laguna Las Ranas
Moto
Río Longlong
Santa Filomena
Bellavista
Isla Aliaquillén
San Francisco
Lago Villarrica
Lago Huilipilun
Loncovaca
Turingia
Punta Sueño
La Puntilla
Cerro La Plaza (734m)
Pedregoso
Pichilafquén
Lago Pichilafquén
Maria Luisa
Edelweiss
Villarrica

Scale: 0 — 10 kilometres

Margin directions:
Termas de Panqui (27km), Termas Geométricas (30km), Curarrehue (35km), Puesco (60km) & Argentina (87km)
Parque Nacional Villarrica, Sectors Quetrupillán (26km)
Parque Nacional Villarrica & Parque Nacional Villarrica
Sector Rucapillán (7km), Volcán Villarrica (15km) & Parque Nacional Villarrica
Lago Caldeleu & Lican Ray (30m)
Valdivia (104km)
Temuco (104km)
Santiago & Temuco (82km)

4

Parque Nacional Huerquehue Camping ☎ 09 6157 4089. Basic but pretty Conaf-run campsite at Lago Tinquilco, near the entrance (toilets and hot showers included; pay Conaf at the park entrance). Pitch CH$15,000

Refugio Tinquilco ☎ 09 9278 9831, ⓦ tinquilco.cl. Excellent, airy wooden guesthouse in a beautiful stream-side location a 2km hike from the park entrance, with home-cooked meals (breakfast included), a sauna and book exchange. Bunks in basic cabins CH$11,500, doubles from CH$27,900

VALDIVIA

From 1848 onwards, thousands of German immigrants passed through the port of **VALDIVIA**, initiating an industrial boom that lasted well into the twentieth century. Founded in 1552 by Pedro de Valdivia, it is one of Chile's oldest cities, though it was razed by the Mapuche in the sixteenth century and largely destroyed by the devastating earthquake of 1960, which accounts for the hotchpotch of buildings from every era and architectural style here. Today Valdivia is an energetic university city that lies at the confluence of the Río Valdivia and Río Calle Calle.

Most of the action centres on the **waterfront**; you'll smell the fishy **Mercado Fluvial** and hear the noise before you reach it. The highlight here is the resident colony of enormous **sea lions**, which spend much of their day lounging behind the market and feeding on scraps. The waterfront is also a departure point for numerous boats offering entertaining half-day cruises up the river to the fort ruins for CH$20,000–35,000, though commentary is Spanish only.

WHAT TO SEE AND DO

Just on the other side of the Río Valdivia from the fish market, in a tranquil section of Isla Teja, the **Museo Histórico y Antropológico** (Jan & Feb daily 10am–8pm; March–Dec Tues–Sun 10am–1pm & 2–6pm; CH$1500, CH$2500 with Philippi museum; ⓦ museoaustral.cl) offers a rare glimpse of nineteenth-century Chile. Built in 1861 as the Casa Anwandter for one of the city's wealthiest men (German-born Don Carl Anwandter established the brewing industry here in the 1850s), its period rooms contain an odd assortment of historic curios, while upstairs galleries are filled with Mapuche artefacts and prehistoric finds (some English labelling). Nearby is the **Museo R. A. Philippi de la Exploración** (same hours and admission) in Casa Schüller (dating from 1914), a tribute to German-born naturalist Rudolph Philippi, who worked here in the 1850s (some English labelling).

Las Fuertes (forts)

In 1645 the Spanish started building elaborate fortifications at **Corral**, **Niebla** and **Isla Mancera**, where the Río Valdivia and Río Tornagaleones meet the Pacific Ocean, to protect Valdivia from opportunistic attacks by British, French and Dutch privateers. If the weather is good, a trip to the ruins can make for a refreshing day out; take the Niebla-bound bus #20 from Carampanque, at O'Higgins (25min; CH$700, frequent), and get off at the little ferry pier 18km from the city. From here boats (Mon–Sat 5 daily, Sun 4 daily; seasonal changes possible; CH$500) ply their way to Isla

---

TOP TWO HOT SPRINGS IN THE LAKE DISTRICT

Most tour companies in Pucón run daily trips to these hot springs.

Termas Geométricas 16km northeast of Coñaripe towards Villarrica National Park ☎ 09 7477 1708, ⓦ termasgeometricas.cl. With a Japanese feel to the beautiful design, there are seventeen thermal pools here, connected by winding boardwalks around a ravine overflowing with greenery, as well as three cold plunge pools, two waterfalls and an excellent café. CH$24,000. Jan–late March 10am–11pm.

Termas Los Pozones 34km east of Pucón, past Termas de Huife ☎ 09 9197 2350, ⓦ termas.cl/pozones .html. Probably the most-visited thermal baths near Pucón, especially on night tours, these consist of hot riverside pools at the end of a steep and sometimes muddy descent (bring a torch); there are wooden changing rooms above the pools from which you descend via a trapdoor. CH$7500. Daily 11am–3am.

Mancera and the ruins of the **Castillo San Pedro de Alcántara** (Jan & Feb daily 10am–8pm; March–Dec Tues–Sun 10am–1pm & 2–6pm; CH$1000).

You can also take a ferry (daily 9am–5.40pm; 30min; CH$650) across the Bahía de Corral to the **Castillo San Sebastián de la Cruz** (Nov–March daily 10am–6pm; April–Oct Tues–Sun 10am–5.30pm; CH$1300), reinforced in the 1760s; it's the most intact of all the forts, and a short walk from the pier in Corral.

To get an overview of the whole system visit **Fuerte Niebla**, 2km beyond the ferry pier (ask the bus driver to drop you off), built between 1647 and 1672 and now the **Museo de Sitio Castillo de Niebla** (April–Oct Tues–Sun 10am–5.30pm; Nov–March Tues–Sun 10am–7pm;

CH$1000; ⓦ museodeniebla.cl). Only the battlements, a battery of rusty cannons and a few grassy foundations remain, but the views of the bay are magnificent and the museum, in the restored commander's house, covers colonial military history in detail (Spanish text only). The fort saw action only once – in 1820, when it was captured by Lord Cochrane's naval flotilla.

ARRIVAL AND INFORMATION

By plane Aeropuerto Pichoy lies 32km northeast of the city; a Transfer Valdivia minibus (ⓣ 63 222 5533) into town will set you back CH$5000. Sky Airline serves Santiago and Concepción, while LAN serves Santiago (2 daily; 1hr 35min).

By bus The main Terminal de Buses (ⓣ 63 222 0498, ⓦ terminalvaldivia.cl) is located at Anfión Muñoz 360, by Río Calle Calle.

Destinations Bariloche (4 weekly at 8.45am; 7hr); Osorno (every 30min; 1hr 45min); Pucón (5–6 daily; 3hr); Puerto

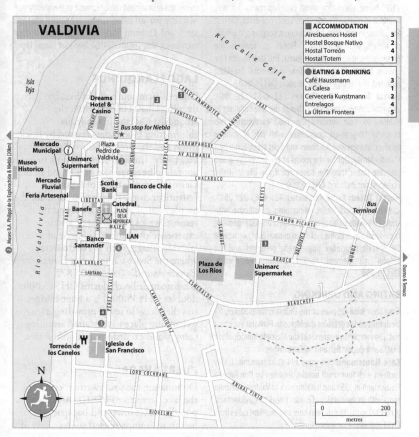

VALDIVIA

Montt (every 30min; 3hr 30min); Santiago (30 daily, mainly departing 7–10am & 7–11pm; 11hr); San Martín de los Andes, Argentina (Wed, Fri & Sun 7.30am; 8hr); Villarrica (4–5 daily; 2hr 15min).

Tourist information There is a helpful Sernatur office at Arturo Prat s/n (on the Costanera, just north of the fish market; Mon–Fri 9am–6pm, Sat & Sun 10am–4pm; ☎63 223 9060, ⓦvaldiviaturismo.cl).

ACCOMMODATION

Airesbuenos Hostel García Reyes 550 ☎63 222 2202, ⓦairesbuenos.cl. Central, eco-aware American-owned hostel with a burgeoning permaculture project on the side. Colourful, secure dorms and spartan private rooms are popular, the communal spaces include a guest kitchen (they'll even let you use herbs from their garden) and breakfast includes proper coffee and good bread. Dorms CH$10,000, doubles CH$28,000

Hostel Bosque Nativo Fresia 290 (off Janequeo) ☎63 243 3782, ⓦhostelnativo.cl. This beautifully restored 1920s house offers cosy wood-panelled rooms, kitchen, lounge and rooftop terrace; there's only one dorm; the rest are private rooms, with solo travellers, couples and groups of friends well catered for. Profits go towards the preservation of native Chilean forest. The staff couldn't be lovelier but don't speak English; continental breakfast included. Dorms CH$10,000, doubles CH$26,000

Hostal Torreón Pérez Rosales 783 ☎63 221 3069, ⓔhostaltorreon@gmail.com. One of the few buildings in Valdivia to have survived the 1960 earthquake, this beautiful 90-year-old guesthouse with lots of antique touches, uneven wooden floors and a pet tabby is run by a friendly family. Opt for the rooms at the top of the grand staircase rather than the basement if you like daylight. Breakfast not included. CH$30,000

Hostal Totem Carlos Anwandter 425 ☎63 229 2849, ⓦturismototem.cl. Quiet, welcoming guesthouse with squeaky wooden floors and spacious, en-suite doubles, triples and quads (some lacking in natural light) with cable TV. Breakfast includes home-made preserves and the helpful management speaks English and French. CH$30,000

EATING AND DRINKING

Grab basic food supplies at the Unimarc supermarket; for fresh fruit and vegetables the Mercado Fluvial is your best bet. The inexpensive eateries at the Mercado Municipal (on Prat) serve decent fish and seafood dishes.

Café Haussmann O'Higgins 394 ⓦhaussmann.cl. Tiny canteen with four small booths, founded by Don Ricardo Haussmann in 1959 and harking back to Valdivia's German roots with its specialities of *crudos* (steak tartare) on toast (CH$1900 each), Kunstmann beer and excellent cakes from CH$1600. Mon–Sat 8am–9pm.

La Calesa O'Higgins 160 ☎63 222 5467. Peruvian restaurant in a quiet neighbourhood putting some spice in your life with its *ají de gallina* (spicy garlic chicken stew), excellent *ceviche* and *suspiro limeño*. Mains CH$7000–9000. Tues–Sat 1–4pm & 7–11.30pm, Sun 1–4pm.

★**Cervecería Kunstmann** 950 Ruta T-350 ⓦlacerveceria.cl. German-style beerhall serving monster portions of smoked meat, sauerkraut and potatoes to accompany its ten celebrated beers (from CH$2300). Tours of this celebrated brewery available daily in peak season. To get here, take bus #20 bound for Niebla (CH$700). Daily noon–midnight.

Entrelagos Pérez Rosales 622. Lauded chocolatier and bakery selling all sorts of delectable cakes, pastries, chocolates and *gelato* (CH$1200 per scoop). Next door is the sit-down "salon de thé" which serves the cakes but also full meals and tea sets. Mon–Fri 9am–9pm, Sat 9am–10pm, Sun 11am–9pm.

La Última Frontera Pérez Rosales 787 Everything about this café screams "bohemian", from the reggae on the stereo and mismatched colour scheme to the grungy staff who serve you real coffee, sandwiches named after Etta James and Chairman Mao, and a selection of local microbrews. Mains from CH$4500. Mon–Sat 10am–11pm.

LAGO LLANQUIHUE

Some 170km south of Valdivia lies dazzling **LAGO LLANQUIHUE**, the second-largest lake in Chile, its shimmering blue waters framed by thick forest and the peaks of snow-tipped volcanoes. The lake draws visitors to its appealing **beaches**, the best found in the German lakeside town of **Frutillar** (ⓦfrutillar.com). People also come for the ample natural attractions around the resort town of **Puerto Varas**, and to experience the laidback lifestyle of lakeside villages such as **Puerto Octay**, where the Swiss-Chilean-run *Hostal Zapato Amarillo* (☎64 210 787, ⓦzapatoamarillo.cl; dorms CH$13,000, doubles CH$35,000) is a huge budget-traveller draw in itself, providing a welcoming place to stay amid stunning scenery and excursions around the area.

PUERTO VARAS

Dominating the southwestern corner of the lake, attractive **PUERTO VARAS** is a popular resort town and backpacker haunt, with unparalleled sunset views of the two nearby volcanoes, Osorno and Calbuco. Rivalling Pucón in terms of nearby **outdoor attractions**, Puerto Varas makes an excellent base for volcano climbing, white-water rafting, kayaking and cycling; it also serves as a popular stopover on the way to Patagonia.

ARRIVAL AND INFORMATION

By plane The nearest airport is at Puerto Montt, but there's a LAN office at Gramados 560 and Sky Airline at San Bernardo 430. Transfers to the airport charge CH$18,000.

By bus Cruz del Sur (serving Chiloé and the Lake District up to Santiago) shares a bus terminal with Bus Norte (with services to Bariloche, Argentina) at San Francisco 1317. Tur-Bus, Intersur, JAC, Tas Choapa, Andersmar and Cóndor Bus are all scattered about the outskirts of town, having been banished from the centre; check locations with the tourist office.

Destinations Ancud (8 daily; 2hr 30min); Castro (8 daily; 4hr 30min); Puerto Montt (every 15min; 35min); Santiago (6 daily; 18hr); Valdivia (2–3 daily; 3hr).

By minibus Those for Ensenada (1hr), Frutillar (40min), Petrohué and the Saltos de Petrohué (45min) leave from San Bernardo 240, just north of Walker Martínez; frequent minibuses to Puerto Montt head up San Francisco.

Tourist information The Casa del Turista is at the foot of a pier (Muelle Piedraplan) on Av Costanera (Mon–Fri 9.30am–6.30pm, Sat & Sun 10am–6.30pm; ☎65 223 7956, ⓦpuertovaras.org).

ACCOMMODATION

Casa Azul Manzanal 66, at Rosario ☎65 223 2904, ⓦcasaazul.net. Firm backpacker favourite a short walk uphill from the centre, run by a German-Chilean couple who offer comfortable rooms, kitchen privileges and an excellent breakfast buffet that includes muesli and home-made bread (CH$3000 extra). Dorms <u>CH$10,000</u>, doubles (shared bath) <u>CH$26,000</u>

Casa Margouya Santa Rosa 318 ☎65 223 7640, ⓦmargouya.com. Lively backpacker hostel with guest kitchen, comfortable lounge area and a big emphasis on outdoor adventures. Bathroom queues are the only drawback. Dorms <u>CH$10,000</u>, doubles <u>CH$24,000</u>

PUERTO VARAS

EATING & DRINKING
Caffé El Barista	1
Dane's Café	4
Donde El Gordito	3
La Gringa/Mercado 605	5
La Marca	2

ACCOMMODATION
Casa Azul	4
Casa Margouya	2
Compass Del Sur	1
Hospedaje Ellenhaus	3
Hostal Margouya II	6
Hostal Melmac	5

Disused Train Station

Puma Verde

Lago Llanquihue

Casa de Turista

Tierra Outdoors & Ko'Kayak

Casino

Buses to Petrohué
Centro Médico
Lavandería Alba

Banco Santander

Banco de Chile

Buses to Frutillar & Llanquihue
Sky Airlines
LAN
Mercado

Banco Santander

Buses to Puerto Octay

Buses to Puerto Montt

Supermarket Santa Isabel

Supermarket Express Lider

Iglesia del Sagrado Corazón de Jesús

Tur Bus/Tas Choapa/ Buses JAC terminal

0   300
metres

Panamericana, Cruz del Sur Bus Terminal, Osorno, Temuco (north) & Puerto Montt (south)

★**Compass Del Sur** Klenner 467 ☎65 223 2044, ⓦcompassdelsur.cl. Lovely three-storey hostel with creaky wooden floors, powerful showers and communal vibe. The helpful staff and friendly Chilean-Swedish owners can help you organize tours. Camping CH$9000, dorms CH$12,000, doubles CH$35,000

Hospedaje Ellenhaus San Pedro 325 ☎65 223 3577, ⓦellenhaus.cl. The place may be quiet on a Saturday night, but the service is friendly and this central labyrinth of compact, spotless rooms is your best bet for a cheap single (facilities shared) or double (some en suite). Breakfast CH$3000 extra. CH$17,000

Hostal Margouya II Purísima 681 ☎65 223 7695, ⓦmargouya2.com. Moonlighting as a language school, the second branch of *Casa Margouya*, housed in a historic 1932 building, offers spacious, quiet rooms, with priority given to those wishing to study Spanish. Dorms CH$10,000, doubles CH$22,000

Hostal Melmac Santa Rosa 608, access off Salvador ☎65 223 0863, ⓦmelmacpatagonia.com. Up a steep staircase, this self-proclaimed "hostel from another world" is in a new location. It has a snug three-bed dorm, two individually decorated doubles and a twin, and plenty of *buena onda* (good vibes). The Argentine-Colombian owner sometimes throws barbecues in the garden (or you can use the grill yourself). Dorms CH$13,000, doubles CH$40,000

EATING AND DRINKING

Self-caterers can try the Santa Isabel on Del Salvador (Mon–Sat 9.30am–10pm).

Caffè El Barista Martínez 211 ⓦelbarista.cl. A great spot for people-watching, this trendy café serves some of the best coffee in town, with large slices of tasty cake, sandwiches and great lunch specials. It's also the hottest nightspot after dark, with everyone piling in for beer and cocktails. Daily 9am–late.

Dane's Café Del Salvador 441. This established favourite reflects the town's hybrid history, with *empanadas de horno* sitting on the menu alongside superb *apfelstrudel*. A great spot for coffee with cake (around CH$2300) or an inexpensive lunch. Daily 9am–10pm.

★**Donde El Gordito** San Bernardo 560. Busy little local institution inside the market, serving large portions of inexpensive fish and seafood to hungry locals. Squid in *pil-pil* sauce, clams baked with parmesan, grilled fish – it's all fresh and fantastic. Mains from CH$6000. Daily 11am–10pm.

★**La Gringa/Mercado 605** Imperial 605 ☎09 7801 0314. *La Gringa's* expat owner from Seattle has successfully created a café that provides the perfect hideaway on rainy days, with sticky, gooey cinnamon rolls, melt-in-your-mouth brownies and chocolate chip cookies to go with your coffee, imaginative lunch specials, great salads and pulled pork sandwiches. After 8pm, the action moves next door where you can indulge yourself by ordering Catalonian-style tapas and sophisticated mains. Café Mon–Sat 9am–8pm; restaurant 8pm–late.

La Marca Santa Rosa 539 ☎65 223 2026, ⓦwww .lamarca.cl. With gaucho music on the stereo and cowboy paraphernalia on the wall, this is one of the best steakhouses in the Lake District. *The bife de chorizo* is mouth-wateringly juicy and there are some rare items on the menu, such as *criadillos* (bull's testicles). Mains from CH$7500. Mon–Sat 7–11pm, Sun 1–4pm.

DIRECTORY

Banks and exchange There are several banks with ATMs downtown, including the reliable Banco de Chile at Del Salvador 201 and Santander at San Francisco and Del Salvador.

Hospital Centro Médico Puerto Varas is at Walker Martínez 576 (☎65 223 2792).

Laundry Lavandería Alba at Walker Martinez 511.

Post office San José 242.

TAKING THE BOAT TO ARGENTINA

Puerto Varas lies on the well-beaten path between Puerto Montt and Bariloche in Argentina (see p.117). If you're Argentina-bound, a **lake crossing** that allows you to experience the beauty of Chile's oldest national park – **Parque Nacional Vicente Pérez Rosales** – is an excellent alternative to a long bus journey. Starting out at 8am, you are first driven along the banks of Lago Llanquihue to **Petrohué**, before boarding the ferry that takes you across **Lago Todos Los Santos**, a spectacular expanse of clear blue-green water. As you sail along the densely forested shores, the volcanoes Osorno (2660m) and Puntiagudo (2190m) loom to the north, with the majestic Tronador (3491m) to the east. The only lunch option in Peulla is an overpriced and mediocre restaurant at *Hotel Peulla*; bring a picnic lunch instead. After going through **Chilean customs** at Peulla, you then cross the Argentine border at Paso Pérez Rosales, and get stamped in at tiny Puerto Frías. At this point you'll board the ferry again for the short crossing of Laguna Frías, then transfer by bus to Puerto Blest and your final nautical leg of the journey, a boat across the stunningly beautiful **Lago Nahuel Huapi** (departing around 6pm), arriving at Puerto Pañuel. From here another bus should get you into Bariloche around 9pm. Book in advance, especially during the peak season, with Turistour (CH$175,000; ☎65 243 7127, ⓦtraveladventure.cl).

PUERTO VARAS TOUR OPERATORS

The area around Puerto Varas offers a variety of outdoor adventures, from challenging climbs up the nearby volcanoes Osorno and Calbuco to rafting on the turbulent turquoise waters of the Río Petrohué and exploring the surrounding Parque Nacional Vicente Pérez Rosales on horseback. The operators listed below are reputable.

Al Sur Aconcagua, at Imperial ☏65 223 2300, ⓦalsurexpeditions.com. Top rafting adventures along the Class III rapids of the Río Petrohué, with half-day and full-day trips available.

Ko'Kayak San Pedro 210 ☏09 9310 5272, ⓦkokayak.cl. Excellent French-run outfit with fun-loving bilingual guides and an emphasis on safety, specializing in half- to four-day rafting trips in the Lake District as well as one- or three-day sea-kayaking trips, and more challenging multi-day

expeditions in the Patagonian fjords. New thrills include smaller rafts and riding a whitewater kayak as a passenger. Half-day rafting on the Río Petrohué CH\$35,000.

Yak Expediciones ☏09 8332 0574, ⓦyakexpediciones.cl. Long-standing operator specializing in outstanding sea-kayaking excursions – from one-day trips to Lago Todos Los Santos (CH\$62,000) to multi-day adventures in the fjords around Parque Pumalín.

SALTOS DE PETROHUÉ

Chile boasts hundreds of waterfalls, but none quite like the **Saltos de Petrohué** (daily: summer 8.30am–7pm; winter 9am–6pm; CH\$1500). Some 50km from Puerto Varas, this series of boiling, churning rapids and falls shoots through eroded lava tubes and bizarrely shaped rocks. With the Osorno volcano as a backdrop, it's hard to imagine a more enchanting location. According to local legend, these rapids are the home of a monster, Cuchivilu, which resembles a giant puma with a claw on the end of its tail. Regular minibuses run here from Puerto Varas (every 30min; 45min) on the way to **Petrohué**. The visitor centre here offers adventure activities in the area.

LAGO TODOS LOS SANTOS

From the **Saltos de Petrohué** the road turns to gravel and continues for another 6km to the tiny village of **Petrohué** itself, embarkation point for boat trips around the mesmerizing waters of **Lago Todos Los Santos** inside the **Parque Nacional Vicente Pérez Rosales** (trips from CH\$8000–20,000). Minibuses connect Puerto Varas with the falls and **Petrohué**.

PUERTO MONTT

Established in the 1850s by German settlers, **PUERTO MONTT** is beautifully situated on the **Seno de Reloncaví** (Strait

of Reloncaví), with snowcapped mountains clearly visible beyond the sound on a good day. Pretty backdrop aside, Puerto Montt is a large, busy city with traffic-choked streets, a place to stock up on provisions and equipment on the way to Patagonia, a major transport hub, and a place to catch the latest blockbuster in English but little else.

The town stretches along the bay, with Avenida Diego Portales running east along the seafront towards the **Plaza de Armas** – the centre, surrounded by banks, cheap bars and restaurants. West of the main bus terminal, Avenida Costanera takes you to the busy passenger port with a **feria artesanal** (craft market) and the Angelmó fishing village.

ARRIVAL AND INFORMATION

By plane Aeropuerto El Tepual (☏65 229 4161, ⓦaeropuertopuertomontt.cl) is located 16km northwest of the city. Buses Andrestur run to and from the airport hourly and meet flights. Daily flights serve Santiago (1hr 50min), Punta Arenas (2hr 10min), Balmaceda (Coyhaique; 1hr 10min) and Temuco (45min) with LAN, at O'Higgins, and Sky Airline, at Benavente 405, Local 4.

By bus Long-distance and local buses arrive at the large Terminal de Buses (ⓦterminalpm.cl), at Av Diego Portales 1001 on the waterfront. The bus station has an information office, ATMs, food stalls and luggage storage. Cruz del Sur (ⓦwww.busescruzdelsur.cl) serves Chiloé; Turibus (☏65 225 4731) runs to Punta Arenas; Tur-Bus (ⓦwww.turbus .cl) and Pullman Bus (ⓦpullman.cl) serve all major destinations en route to Santiago; Tas-Choapa (☏65 225 4828) and Inter Sur (☏65 225 9320) cross the border to

4

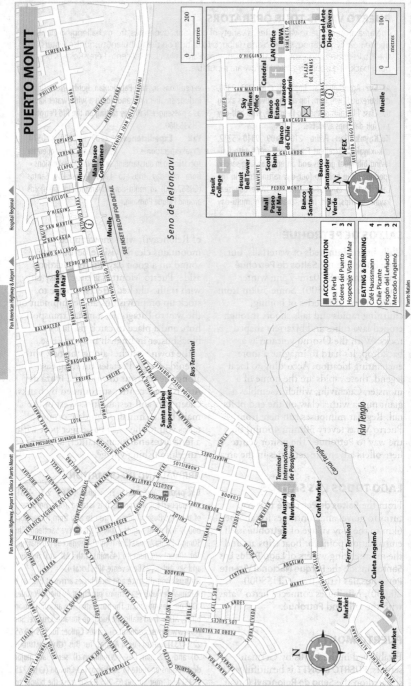

PUERTO MONTT

ACCOMMODATION
Casa Perla	1
Colores del Puerto	3
Hospedaje Vista Al Mar	2

EATING & DRINKING
Café Haussmann	4
Chile Picante	1
Fogón del Leñador	3
Mercado Angelmó	2

Argentina; and Kemelbus runs to Chaitén via Cochamó. Minibuses to Puerto Varas (CH$800) depart from the eastern side of the terminal.

Destinations Ancud (every 30min; 2hr); Bariloche, Argentina (2 daily; 6hr); Castro (every 30min; 3hr 30min); Chaitén (1 daily at 7am; 9hr); Cochamó (1 daily at 7.45am; 2hr); Coyhaíque (4 weekly; 24hr); Futaleufú (2 weekly; 12hr); Osorno (every 30min; 1hr 30min); Pucón (hourly; 5hr 30min); Puerto Varas (every 15–20min; 30min); Santiago (every 30min; 14hr); Valdivia (every 30min; 3hr).

By ferry The Terminal de Transbordadores lies at Angelmó 1735, several blocks west of the main bus terminal; Navimag (☎65 243 2360, ⓦnavimag.com) and Naviera Austral (☎65 227 0430, ⓦwww.navieraustral.cl) ferries have offices here. Navimag has departures to Puerto Chacabuco (Wed & Sat night) and Puerto Natales (1–2 weekly; 3–4 days; US$450 for shared cabin). Naviera Austral has departures for Chaitén (Mon, Thurs & Fri; 9hr; seat/berth CH$16,000/35,000).

Tourist information There is a well-stocked and helpful Turismo Municipal office on the Plaza de Armas, on Varas at San Martín (Dec–March daily 9am–9pm; April–Nov Mon–Fri 9am–1pm & 2.30–6.30pm, Sat 9am–1pm; ☎65 225 4580).

ACCOMMODATION

Unless you're catching a ferry or flight, nearby Puerto Varas is a much more congenial place to stay.

Casa Perla Trigal 312 ☎65 226 2104, ⓦcasaperla.com. Filled with knick-knacks and showing its age, *Casa Perla* is one of the friendliest homes in town, where you're treated like one of the family. English and German spoken and you can use the kitchen, and even camp in the yard. Camping/person CH$7000, dorms CH$10,000, doubles CH$23,000

Colores del Puerto Schwerter 207 ☎65 248 9360, ⓦcoloresdelpuerto.cl. Run by the wonderfully friendly and helpful Tomás, this hostel is only a 5min walk from the port and a 10min walk from the bus station, down a quiet street in Puerto Montt's historic neighbourhood. Three twin rooms share facilities and your host can fix up a simple breakfast; let him know in advance what time you're arriving. CH$30,000

Hospedaje Vista Al Mar Vivar 1337 ☎65 225 5625. Justly popular guesthouse overlooking the city from a high vantage point and offering excellent value, especially for single travellers (CH$15,000), with cosy en-suite rooms. A really good breakfast includes eggs and home-made bread. CH$25,000

EATING AND DRINKING

There's a vast Unimarc supermarket in the basement of Paseo Costanera mall.

Café Haussmann San Martín 185. This branch of the Valdivia original is the place to sample *crudos* (steak tartare on toast with lemon juice, capers and minced onion; CH$1900), tuck into smoked meat with spuds and sauerkraut or indulge in some of the delicious cakes on display. Mains from CH$6000. Mon–Sat 9.30am–8.30pm, Sun 11am–8.30pm.

★**Chile Picante** Rosales 567 ☎09 8454 8923, ⓦchilepicanterestoran.cl. Up a very steep street in Puerto Montt's historic neighbourhood, this superb little place punches way above its weight. The three-course menu changes daily and is a steal at CH$8500; you might be treated to the likes of risotto with lamb and the chef's take on the *caldo de congrio*. Reservations highly recommended. Mon–Sat 12.30–3.30pm & 7.30–10pm.

Fogón del Leñador Rancagua 245. The wrought-iron chandeliers, cow-hide seats and blazing fireplace set the scene for this carnivorous experience. You're warned that your steak will take at least 30min to cook to perfection, and while you wait, you can tuck into home-made *sopaipillas* with an assortment of fresh salsas. Steak from CH$8000. Mon–Sat 12.30–3.30pm & 7.30–11pm.

Mercado Angelmó Av Angelmó, to the west of the ferry terminal; catch any of the Angelmó-bound *colectivos* along Av Diego Portales if you don't want to walk (CH$500). Don't miss this lively fish market and the nearby two-storey cluster of cheap *marisquerías*, an ideal place to sample super-fresh fish and seafood dishes, such as *machas a la parmesana* (razor clams baked with cheese) and *curanto*, all for under CH$5000. Daily noon–8pm.

DIRECTORY

Banks and exchange There is an ATM at the main bus terminal and several banks with ATMs downtown; try BBVA on Urmeneta, at O'Higgins, or Santander on Urmeneta, at Montt.

Hospital Hospital Regional, Seminario s/n (☎65 249 0213), handles medical emergencies.

Laundry Lavaseco y Lavandería Fast Clean, at San Martín 167.

Post office Rancagua 126.

Shopping The Paseo Costanera on the waterfront has an extensive food court, multi-screen cinema screening blockbusters in English, and an "Andesgear" outlet, which stocks high-quality outdoor and camping gear. Unimarc supermarket is in the basement.

COCHAMÓ

Sitting on the gorgeous Estuario de Reloncaví, against the backdrop of snow-tipped mountains 33km south of Lago Llanquihue and reachable by bus from Puerto Montt via Puerto Varas, the appealing fishing village of **COCHAMÓ** is the springboard for the popular hike into the Río Cochamó valley, known as "the Yosemite of the South".

TREKKING IN THE RÍO COCHAMÓ VALLEY

With the temperate rainforest's gnarly trees clothed in lichen, towering *alerces* and granite mountains rising above the forest, it's easy to see how the **Río Cochamó valley** acquired its "Yosemite of the South" moniker. The valley is bisected by the remnants of a nineteenth-century logging road (little more than a muddy footpath in places) that now serves as a popular 12km hiking trail to the valley of **La Junta**, surrounded by mountains that are hugely popular with rock climbers. The **trail**, which takes a full day to hike, is stunning and mostly easy to follow, but can be extremely muddy, as the horses bringing supplies to the two guesthouses churn up the path in rainy weather. If you're not a climber, there is plenty of scope for day hikes in the valley and more adventurous travellers can even continue on foot to Argentina.

The trailhead for the Rió Cochamó valley is at the end of an 8km dirt road that branches off the main road through Cochamó 4km south. Locals offer lifts up to the trailhead for CH$3000 in the summer months.

ACCOMMODATION

Campo Aventura Mountain Lodge La Junta valley ⓦ campoaventura.cl. A converted farmhouse with bunkrooms, simple rooms and camping spots; *asados* can be organized for guests. Camping CH$4000, bunkroom/person CH$12,000, doubles CH$45,000

Refugio Cochamó La Junta valley ⓦ cochamo.com.

Run by effusive Argentine-American hosts, this has long been a haven for climbers; contact them via email in advance to book accommodation/request meals. They also run *Camping La Junta* nearby, with solar-heated showers and composting toilets. Dorms CH$12,000, doubles CH$34,000, camping/person CH$3500

ARRIVAL, INFORMATION AND TOURS

By bus Buses Río Puelo (ⓣ 09 9323 0838) pass through Cochamó at least twice daily en route between Puerto Montt (2hr) and Río Puelo.

Tourist office The municipal office (daily: Jan & Feb 9am–9pm; March–Dec 10am–5pm; ⓣ 65 235 0271) on the main street, close to the entrance of town, has surprisingly good maps of the Río Puelo region.

Tours Southern Trips (ⓣ 09 8407 2559 or ⓣ 09 9919 8947, ⓦ southern-trips.com) offer some fantastic horseriding in the area. Campo Aventura specialize in multi-day horse treks in the region.

ACCOMMODATION AND EATING

Campo Aventura ⓣ 09 9289 4314 or ⓣ 09 9289 4318, ⓦ campoaventura.cl. Around 4km south of Cochamó, near the turn-off for Río Cochamó valley, this beautiful, rustic, American-run lodge sits on a vast riverside property. There is a cluster of compact rooms or you can camp by the river. *Campo Aventura* specialize in horseriding adventures, particularly multi-day explorations. Camping per person CH$5000, doubles CH$38,000

Eco Hostal Las Bandurrias Sector El Bosque s/n ⓣ 09 9672 2590, ⓦ hostalbandurrias.com. High up on a hill above Cochamó (arrange pick-up in advance), this gorgeous little hostel consists of a single four-bed dorm, a twin and a double, all with down duvets and run by a friendly and knowledgeable Swiss-Chilean couple. The excellent breakfast includes home-made bread, and there's luggage storage for those who want to travel light when hiking the Río Cochamó valley. Dorms CH$14,000, doubles (shared bath) CH$32,000

La Ollita Calle Principal s/n. Right on the main street, this local favourite tends to be open and serves simple dishes, such as grilled *congrio* or *lomo a lo pobre*. Mains from CH$5500. Daily 12.30–10pm.

Chiloé

As the ferry ploughs through the grey waters of the Canal de Chacao that separates the **CHILOÉ** archipelago from the mainland, an island appears out of the mist. **Isla Grande de Chiloé** is the second-largest island in South America, a patchwork of forests and fields, with traditional villages nestling in sheltered inlets. Chiloé draws visitors to its two main towns, **Ancud** and **Castro**, lined with distinctive shingle houses and waterside *palafitos*, as well as its remote national parks with plenty of scope for trekking and its precious cache of uniquely constructed wooden **churches**, sixteen of which are UNESCO monuments.

Originally populated by the Huilliche (southern Mapuche) Indians, most of whom died from a smallpox epidemic shortly after European contact, Chiloé was colonized by the Spanish as early as 1567. Scores of refugees fled the fierce

Mapuche on the mainland to the island, and Chiloe's very distinct culture evolved in relative isolation, resulting in a diverse and rich mythology that permeates people's lives to this day.

ANCUD

Tucked away on Chiloé's northern coast, **ANCUD** is the island's second-largest settlement and was the last stronghold of the Spanish, who held out against hostile forces for almost a decade after Chile's

declaration of independence in 1818. Ancud's heart is the little **Plaza de Armas**, where there are crafts and book stalls in the summer.

WHAT TO SEE AND DO

The small but illuminating **Museo Regional de Ancud** on the plaza (Jan & Feb Mon–Fri 10.30am–7.30pm, Sat & Sun 10am–7.30pm; March–Dec Tues–Fri 10am–5pm, Sat & Sun 10am–2pm; CH$600; ⦿museoancud.cl) consists of partly interactive Spanish-language

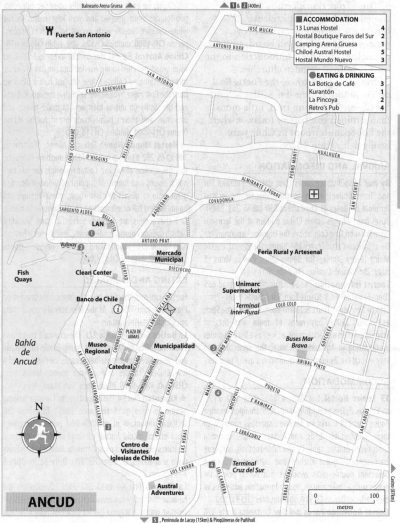

Balneario Arena Gruesa ▲   ▲ **1** & **2** (400m)

ANCUD

ACCOMMODATION
13 Lunas Hostel	4
Hostal Boutique Faros del Sur	2
Camping Arena Gruesa	1
Chiloé Austral Hostel	5
Hostal Mundo Nuevo	3

EATING & DRINKING
La Botica de Café	3
Kurantón	1
La Pincoya	2
Retro's Pub	4

Fuerte San Antonio

JOSÉ MUCKE
ANTONIO BURR
SAN ANTONIO
CARLOS BERENGUER
LORD COCHRANE
O'HIGGINS
BELLAVISTA
HUALHUÉN
PEDRO MONTT
ALMIRANTE LATORRE
SARGENTO ALDEA
BELLAVISTA
BAQUEDANO
COVADONGA
SAN VICENTE
LAN
ARTURO PRAT
Walkway
Mercado Municipal
LIBERTAD
DIECIOCHO
Feria Rural y Artesenal
Fish Quays
Clean Center
Unimarc Supermarket
Banco de Chile
BLANCO ENCALADA
Terminal Inter-Rural
COLO COLO
PLAZA DE ARMAS
CHIRRIBULOS
Bahía de Ancud
Museo Regional
AV. COSTANERA (SALVADOR ALLENDE)
BLANCO ENCALADA
MONSEÑOR AGUILERA
Municipalidad
PEDRO MONTT
Buses Mar Brava
GOYCOLEA
Catedral
CHACAO
ANIBAL PINTO
MAIPU
MOCOPULLI
PUDETO
E RAMIREZ
SAN CARLOS
N
CHACABUCO
LAS HERAS
F ERRÁZURIZ
Centro de Visitantes Iglesias de Chiloe
LOS CAVADA
LOS CARRERA
Terminal Cruz del Sur
YERBAS BUENAS
Austral Adventures

| 0 | | 100 |
metres

▼ **5** , Península de Lacuy (15km) & Pinqüineras de Puñihuil

Castro (87km) ▶

4

exhibits, covering traditional Chilote industries such as fishing, crafts, Chiloé's environment and wildlife, European conquest, archeology and religious art, with striking photographs illustrating the impact of the 1960 earthquake which devastated much of the island. Don't miss the blue whale skeleton or the replica of the *Goleta Ancud* outside, the locally built ship that led the expedition to take control of the Strait of Magellan for Chile in 1843.

Make time also for the **Iglesias de Chiloé Centro de Visitantes** (daily 9.30am–7pm; donations; ⓦiglesiasdechiloe.cl) at Errázuriz 227. Intricate scale models, carved doors, windows and explanation boards (much in English) are a great introduction to the island's beloved wooden churches.

Overlooking the town, the **Fuerte Real de San Antonio** (Mon–Fri 8.30am–9pm, Sat & Sun 9am–8pm; free), little more than a ruined gun battery today, is where the last Spanish troops in Chile were finally defeated in 1826.

ARRIVAL AND INFORMATION

By bus Long-distance buses (Cruz del Sur, Pullman Sur and Trans Chiloé) arrive at the conveniently located Terminal de Buses at Los Carrera 850 (ⓣ65 262 2249). Buses from villages across Chiloé pull up at the Terminal Inter-Rural on Colo Colo, above the Unimarc supermarket. Destinations Castro (every 15–30min; 1hr 15min); Puerto Montt (every 30min; 1hr 30min–2hr); Puerto Varas (5 daily; 2hr 30min); Quellón (16 daily; 4hr).

Tourist information The Sernatur office, Libertad 665 (Dec–Feb Mon–Fri 8.30am–7pm, Sat & Sun 9.30am–7pm; March–Nov Mon–Thurs 8.30am–6pm, Fri 8.30am–5pm; ⓣ65 262 2800), has maps of town and lists of accommodation and attractions, as well as a list of families participating in Agroturismo Chiloé, the opportunity to stay in rural family homes. ⓦchiloe.cl is a useful website.

ACCOMMODATION

13 Lunas Hostel Los Carrera 855 ⓣ65 262 2106, ⓦ13lunas.cl. This beautifully renovated, shingled wooden house gets full marks for facilities: spacious rooms with large, comfortable beds and lockers, ample common spaces with guitars, cable TV and table football, barbecue area, spacious guest kitchen and outdoor terraces. A basement double lacks windows, but bonus points for extras such as bike rentals, tour information and spirit of camaraderie. Dorms CH$10,500, doubles CH$33,000

Hostal Boutique Faros del Sur Costanera Norte 320

ⓣ65 262 5799, ⓦfarosdelsur.cl. Decked out in placid creams and with homey touches such as locally woven bedcovers, the thirteen rooms at this cliff-top guesthouse all have sea views; for the best views, snag the corner suite. The most striking feature, however, is the splendid wood-panelled guest lounge with tall ceilings, chunky stone fireplace and light streaming in from the vast windows. Guest kitchen available. CH$35,000

Camping Arena Gruesa Costanera Norte 290 ⓣ65 262 3428, ⓦhotelarenagruesa.cl. At this great cliff-top location, a few minutes' walk from the Arena Gruesa beach, there are three choices of accommodation: a large campsite with excellent sea views, hot water and individual shelters with lights for each site; several fully equipped cabins for two/four/six/eight people; and well-kept rooms in the white-shingled hostel with access to wi-fi. Camping/person CH$4500, doubles CH$26,000, cabin CH$38,000

Chiloé Austral Hostel Yungay 282 ⓣ65 262 5818. Its snug, wood-panelled rooms overlooking the Bay of Ancud, this blue-shingled Chilote house sits just half a block up from the Costanera. While little English is spoken, Roberto and his family go out of their way to make guests feel welcome, and there's home-made bread for breakfast. Dorms CH$6000, doubles CH$15,000

★ **Hostal Mundo Nuevo** Salvador Allende (Costanera) 748 ⓣ65 262 8383, ⓦnewworld.cl. Longtime favourite, this guesthouse along the Costanera offers bright, top-notch dorms and rooms with polished wooden floors, a great ratio of guests per bathroom, guest kitchen and handy folders full of information on the surrounding area, and the owners are helpful. Serves a good breakfast (which includes home-made bread), and there's a hot tub (CH$12,000/hr) overlooking the waves. Dorms CH$13,000, doubles CH$34,000

EATING AND DRINKING

For self-caterers, there's a huge Unimarc supermarket on Prat (daily 9am–10pm). At the Mercado Municipal there are simple eateries upstairs.

La Botica de Café Pudeto 277. Cheerful café that brews excellent coffee to go with the home-made cheesecake and other sweet offerings. Inexpensive sandwiches and a few Chilean staples also on the menu. Mains from CH$4000. Mon–Sat 9.30am–8pm, Sun 11am–4pm.

★ **Kurantón** Prat 94. The legend reads: "Curanto: helping people to have good sex since 1826". Tuck into this veritable mountain of shellfish and potato dumplings amid photos of old Ancud, carvings of Chilote mythical creatures and nautical paraphernalia. *Kurantón* is reliably open year-round. *Curanto* CH$7700. Daily 12.30–3pm & 7–11.30pm.

La Pincoya Prat 61 ⓣ65 262 2613. Overlooking the harbour, this family-run restaurant with an old-school, bow-tie-clad waiter, is a good bet for excellent fishy offerings,

such as *curanto en olla* and salmon *cancato* (CH$7700). Daily noon–3pm & 7–11pm; erratic hours in the off-season.
Retro's Pub Ramírez 317. Whether you come to this intimate pub to ward off homesickness with their monster burgers, home-made gnocchi, overflowing burritos or immense pizzas, or to court oblivion by knocking back *Retro's* potent Green Demon cocktails at the bar, you're in good company: you're surrounded by images of Bob Marley, Jim Morrison and James Dean. Pizzas CH$9000–12,300. Daily noon–11.30pm.

DIRECTORY

Banks and exchange There is an ATM in Banco de Chile at Chorillos 621 (Plaza de Armas).
Laundry Clean Center, Pudeto 45 (Mon–Sat 9.30am–1pm & 3–7.30pm).
Post office Pudeto, at Blanco Encalada.

PINGÜINERAS DE PUÑIHUIL

Pingüineras de Puñihuil is a large colony of Humboldt and Magellanic penguins spread over three tiny islands off the coast some 28km southwest of Ancud, and reachable via the beach of little fishing village **Puñihuil**. Monitored by Ecoturismo Puñihuil, a local organization dedicated to the protection of the penguins, the colony can be visited between December and March. The adults fish most of the day, so the optimum visiting time is either in the morning or mid- to late afternoon.

Three companies based in the guesthouse and restaurants on the beach pool their customers and run well-explained trips in twenty-person boats to see the penguins and other marine fauna, including the sleek *chungungos* (sea otters). The excursions depart directly from the beach at least once hourly and

last around forty minutes; it's best to reserve in advance (☎09 8317 4302, ⓦpinguineraschiloe.cl) during peak season. Buses Mar Brava (☎65 262 2312) runs three buses daily except Sunday from Ancud (last bus back at 3pm); or share a taxi for CH$16,000–20,000 one-way.

VALLE DE CHEPU

Around 25km south of Ancud, a turn-off leads to the **Valle de Chepu**, a large stretch of wetlands created during the 1960 tsunami, whose sunken forest provides a thriving habitat for hundreds of bird species and superb hiking trails as far as the Parque Nacional Chiloé.

ARRIVAL AND DEPARTURE

By bus Buses Peter (☎09 8383 1172) run from Ancud's Terminal Inter-Rural (Mon, Wed & Fri at 4pm; 1hr).

ACCOMMODATION

★**Chepu Adventures** ☎09 9227 4517, ⓦchepuadventures.com. This wonderful, self-sufficient ecolodge is a destination in its own right, set on a gorgeous bluff overlooking the river, all their energy needs supplied by solar panels and a wind turbine. There's room for nine guests in the snug, en-suite two-/three-person cabins and cheaper *dormis* (mini-cabins with bunk beds; bring your own sleeping bag). Accommodation packages include the self-guided "Kayaking at Dawn" in the sunken forest below, and all meals; book in advance. If you don't have your wheels, pick-up from "Cruce de Chepu", Km25, can be arranged. *Dormi* package CH$25,000, cabin package CH$161,000

CASTRO

The third-oldest continuously inhabited city in Chile, **CASTRO** was founded by the Spanish in 1567 and survived a

---

CURANTO – WHAT'S IN A DISH?

Chiloé's signature dish, **curanto**, has been prepared for several centuries using cooking methods very similar to those used in Polynesia. First, extremely hot rocks are placed at the bottom of an earthen pit; then, a layer of shellfish is added, followed by chunks of meat, *longanisa* (sausage), potatoes, *chapaleles* (potato dumplings) and *milcaos* (fried potato pancakes). The pit is then covered with *nalca* (Chilean wild rhubarb) leaves, and, as the shellfish cooks, the shells spring open, releasing their juices onto the hot rocks, steaming the rest of the ingredients. *Curanto en hoyo* is slow-cooked in the ground for a day or two, but since traditional cooking methods are only used in the countryside, you will probably end up sampling *curanto en olla*, oven-baked in cast-iron pots. The dish comes with hot broth, known to the locals as "liquid Viagra", that you drink during the meal.

number of calamities through the centuries: being pillaged by English and Dutch pirates, numerous fires and the great earthquake of 1960, which largely destroyed it, though these days it's the bustling capital of Chiloé.

WHAT TO SEE AND DO

A large **Plaza de Armas** surrounded by bars and restaurants is Castro's focal point. The UNESCO-listed, yellow-purple neo-Gothic **Iglesia San Francisco** (daily 9.30am–12.30pm & 3–8.30pm) stands on the northeastern corner of the plaza and its all-wood interior is well worth admiring. Down by the water, along Eusebio Lillo, is a number of simple seafood restaurants tucked away behind the large **Feria Yumbel** (daily 9am–6pm) that sells all sorts of woollen goods (not all are from Chiloé).

Palafitos

Chiloé's famous **palafitos** (stilt houses) are still found at several locations around Castro. Perched precariously above the water, these brightly painted, traditional wooden fishermen's dwellings are an unforgettable sight. The idea was that you could moor your boat at your back door and walk out onto the street through the front one. Some impressive examples are found at the north end of town, off Pedro Montt, where they are perfectly reflected in the mini-lake by the roadside. More *palafitos* are found slightly south along the same street, while others at the southern end of town, by the Feria Yumbel, are used as restaurants. A final batch can be seen from the western end of Eusebio Lillo, across the Río Bamboa, and a number have been converted into lodgings and cafés.

ARRIVAL AND INFORMATION

By plane Castro is connected to Santiago and Puerto Montt by regular LAN flights. Transfers to the airport can be organized by your accommodation (CH$4000).

By bus Cruz del Sur (ⓦ www.busescruzdelsur.cl) has its own bus terminal at San Martín 486 which serves numerous long-distance destinations up to and including Puerto Montt, Santiago, Punta Arenas and Ancud. The Terminal de Buses Municipal, at San Martín 667, has services to smaller destinations around Chiloé, including Cucao (Parque Nacional Chiloé), Dalcahue and Achao.

Destinations from Cruz del Sur terminal Ancud (hourly; 1hr 15min); Chonchi (every 30min; 30min); Puerto Montt (12 daily; 3hr); Punta Arenas, via Argentina (3 weekly; 28hr); Quellón (hourly; 1hr 30min); Santiago (4 daily; 18hr).

Destinations from Terminal Municipal Achao (every 30min; fewer on Sun; 1hr 50min); Cucao and the Parque Nacional Chiloé, sector Anay (up to 15 daily; 1hr 15min); Dalcahue (every 30min; 30min).

By ferry Naviera Austral (ⓦ www.navieraustral.cl) runs one weekly boat to Chaitén (time and day subject to change, so check in advance; 5hr 30min) from Castro's passenger terminal. Book tickets via Turismo Pehuén. From Chaitén you can connect with buses south along the Carretera Austral (see p.455).

Tourist office The tourist information centre (daily 10am–8pm, though erratic) on the Plaza de Armas is large and well stocked, though you need to know what to ask for.

TOUR OPERATORS

Altué Expeditions Dalcahue ☎ 09 9419 6809, ⓦ seakayakchile.com. Offers multi-day trips around the Chiloé archipelago complete with lodging at their kayak centre near Dalcahue. Multi-activity combination trips in the Lake District and Patagonia are also on offer.

Chiloé Natural Montt 201B ☎ 65 297 1878, ⓦ chiloenatural.com. An experienced, English-speaking outfit offering day-trips and multi-day treks in Parque Tantauco, as well as trips to Parque Tepuhueico, Parque Nacional Chiloé, *curanto*-eating outings to Chelín by catamaran, and day visits to seven churches on the Ruta de las Iglesias. Tailor-made trips arranged and kayaks, mountain bikes and camping equipment available for rent.

Chiloétnico Riquelme 1228 ☎ 65 263 0951, ⓦ chiloetnico.cl. Juan Pablo is an enthusiastic, English-speaking, experienced guide who arranges anything from trips to Parque Tantauco, Tepuhueico and Parque Nacional Chiloé to multi-day cultural immersion in traditional Chilote culture, half-day horseriding in Nercón and mountain bike rental (CH$12,000/day).

Turismo Pehuén Latorre 238 ☎ 65 263 5254, ⓦ turismopehuen.cl. Established company specializing in day-trips, from boat outings to Isla Mechuque, complete with *curanto*, to gastronomic tours, church tours and outings to the Pinguinera de Punihuil.

ACCOMMODATION

Hostal Cordillera Barros Arana 175 ☎ 09 9512 2667, ⓦ hostalcordillera.cl. The seemingly inexhaustible energy and warmth of the owner is evident, though she speaks little English. The remodelled rooms (some en suite) are centrally heated, solo travellers pay exactly half the price of a double and there's a useful rent-a-car service available. CH$37,000

Hostal Entretenido Almirante Latorre 139 ☎65 253 1677, ⓦhostalentretenido.blogspot.com. Small, centrally located hostel with simple doubles, shared bathrooms, free wi-fi, games room with cable TV and a sunny back terrace. Doubles CH$25,000

★ **Palafito Hostel** Riquelme 1210 ☎65 253 1008,

ⓦpalafitohostel.com. Its curved wooden walls reminiscent of a ship, this revamped *palafito* has just eight beautiful rooms (two with sea view balconies, all private rooms en suite), an appealing common space upstairs, adorned with contemporary art and woollen hangings, and an outdoor deck overlooking the water. Breakfast includes home-made bread and the staff can help organize horseriding in Parque Nacional Chiloé. Dorms CH$15,000, doubles CH$42,000

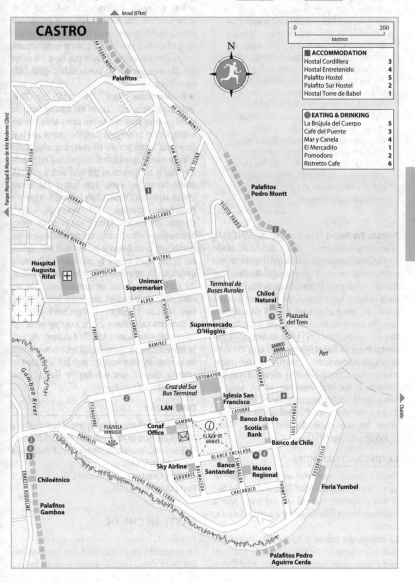

CASTRO

▲ Ancud (87km)

0 — 200 metres

N

■ ACCOMMODATION
Hostal Cordillera	3
Hostal Entretenido	4
Palafito Hostel	5
Palafito Sur Hostel	2
Hostal Torre de Babel	1

● EATING & DRINKING
La Brújula del Cuerpo	5
Café del Puente	3
Mar y Canela	4
El Mercadito	1
Pomodoro	2
Ristretto Cafe	6

4

◀ Parque Municipal & Museo de Arte Moderno (2km)

AV PEDRO MONTT
Palafitos
O'HIGGINS
SAN MARTIN
EL TEJAN
SAMUEL ULLOA
SERRAT
MAGALLANES
PILOTO PARDO
Palafitos Pedro Montt
GALVARINO RIVEROS
G MISTRAL
Hospital Augusta Rifat ✚
CAUPOLICAN
Unimarc Supermarket
ALDEA
O'HIGGINS
Terminal de Buses Rurales
Chiloé Natural
AV PEDRO MONTT
Plazuela del Tren
LOS CARRERA
FREIRE
RAMIREZ
Supermercado O'Higgins
BARROS ARANA
Port
SERRANO
Gamboa River
SOTOMAYOR
EYZAGUIRRE
Cruz del Sur Bus Terminal
Iglesia San Francisco
LAN
GAMBOA
LATORRE
Banco Estado
LUIS ESPINOZA
PLAZUELA HENRIQUE
Conaf Office
ℹ️
PLAZA DE ARMAS
Scotia Bank
Banco de Chile
PORTALES
BLANCO ENCALADA
ESMERALDA
Sky Airline
Banco Santander
Museo Regional
EUSEBIO LILLO
Chiloétnico
PEDRO AGUIRRE CERDA
ALDUNATE
BALMACEDA
CHACABUCO
THOMPSON
Feria Yumbel
ERNESTO RIQUELME
Palafitos Gamboa
Palafitos Pedro Aguirre Cerda

► Chaitén

CHILOTE CHURCHES

It is impossible to visit Chiloé and not be struck by the sight of the archipelago's **wooden churches**, some of which have a vaguely Scandinavian rather than Spanish look. In 2001 UNESCO accepted sixteen of them on to its prestigious World Heritage list. The exterior is almost always bare, and the only thing that expresses anything but functionality is the three-tiered, **hexagonal bell tower** that rises up directly above an open-fronted portico. The facades, doors and windows are often brightly painted, and the walls clad with plain clapboard or wooden tiles. The roofs are built like traditional Chilote boats and then turned upside down. The ceilings are often painted too, with allegorical panels or golden constellations of stars painted on an electric blue background. Of the sixteen churches, fourteen are on mainland Chiloé; the other two are on remote islets. For more information on Chiloé's churches, check out the informative ⓦinterpatagonia .com/iglesiaschiloe.

Palafito Sur Hostel Pedro Montt 465 ☎65 253 6472, ⓦpalafitosur.hostel.com. With its hard-earned "sustainability" credentials and shingle-clad exterior, this *palafito* hostel comes with many thoughtful touches. Snug four-bed dorms come with individual reading lights, the guest kitchen is fully equipped, the waterfront lounge is full of light, and you can kayak right off the waterfront deck. The simple doubles are a little overpriced for what they are, though. Dorms CH$14,000, doubles CH$35,000

Hostal Torre de Babel O'Higgins 965 ☎65 253 4569, ⓦhostaltorredebabel.com. Contrary to the name, travellers from all over the world are able to find a common language in the vast, wood-stove-heated, beanbag-strewn lounge of this welcoming hostel. The owner is happy to give advice, and the wood-panelled rooms are simple but comfortable. Breakfast included. Dorms CH$15,000, doubles CH$30,000

EATING AND DRINKING

There's a Unimarc supermarket on O'Higgins (Mon–Sat 9am–9.30pm, Sun 10am–9pm). The produce market next to Feria Yumbel sells fruit and veg, and several *palafito* restaurants behind Feria Yumbel are a good bet for cheap lunches.

La Brújula del Cuerpo O'Higgins 308. Travellers and locals alike gravitate to "The Body's Compass" – a busy café on the main square specializing in inexpensive Chilean

takes on fajitas, burgers, salads and sandwiches. Burger and fries CH$4200. Daily 11am–midnight.

Café del Puente Riquelme 1180B. This great little café overlooking the water attracts an international clientele with its generous American breakfasts, muesli, good (if not very strong) coffee and 30 types of tea including the odd "Mums Bums". Homesick Brits will appreciate the tea with scones (CH$3100) and proper high tea served from 5pm onwards. Mon & Wed–Sun 8am–9pm.

★**Mar y Canela** Riquelme 1212 ☎65 253 1770, ⓦmarycanela.cl. This homey, bright, cute *palafito* café serves a short-but-sweet menu that tantalizes with such imaginative offerings as smoked pork loin with plums and sheep's cheese or conger eel with crab curry. The coffee and cakes are a great bet too. Mains CH$7000–9000. Daily noon–10pm.

★**El Mercadito** Montt 210 ☎65 253 3866, ⓦelmercaditodechiloe.cl. Crayons and drawing paper are placed on every table to entertain diners while they are waiting for the picture-perfect *ceviche*, chorizo and beef burger, crab "bombs" or any of the other imaginative, playful fusion creations conjured up from local, seasonal ingredients. The decor is as whimsical as the food, with a colourful, shingle-covered bar, wacky light fixtures and knitted jellyfish. Mains from CH$6500. Daily 1–4pm & 8–11pm.

Pomodoro Sotomayor 520 ☎65 263 4141, ⓦpomodorotrattoria.cl. Castro's answer to an Italian trattoria shines when it comes to home-made pasta like gnocchi with pesto Genovese and agnolotti with spinach and ricotta. Don't be shy to ask about off-the-menu specials, which sometimes include king crab cannelloni. The thin-and-crispy pizzas are more authentic than any other pizzas on the island, too. Mains from CH$6500. Mon–Sat 12.30–3.30pm & 7–11.30pm. Sun 1–4pm.

★**Ristretto Caffé** Blanco 264. In a country where real coffee is becoming easier to find, this dark wood café, with 57 different coffees on the menu, still holds its own against the competition. Great foccacias, fresh fruit juices and an extensive range of teas, including the likes of Italian almond. Mon–Sat 8am–9pm.

DIRECTORY

Banks and exchange There are several banks within a block of the Plaza de Armas, all with ATMs. Try Banco de Chile on Blanco Encalada, at Serrano, or Scotiabank half a block north on Serrano.

Laundry Clean Center, at Balmaceda 220.

Post office O'Higgins 388.

EASTERN CHILOÉ

Eastern Chiloé remains a bastion of traditional village life, and the location of many of those famed wooden churches.

Dalcahue is a good spot to base yourself, and **Achao** on Isla Quinchao makes an easy day-trip from Dalcahue or Castro.

Dalcahue

The bustling waterfront town of **DALCAHUE** lies 20km northeast of Castro via the turn-off at Llau-Llao. It is famous for its thriving traditional boat-building industry and the **Feria Artesanal**, open all week but busiest on Sundays, when artisans come from nearby islands to sell woollen crafts, wood-carvings and hand-woven baskets. The attractive Plaza de Armas features the imposing, UNESCO-listed **Iglesia de Nuestra Señora De Los Dolores**, which boasts a unique nine-arched portico (under extensive renovation at research time).

Achao

Twenty-seven kilometres southeast of the ferry terminal on Isla Quinchao the fishing village of **ACHAO** boasts a scattering of houses, famous for their colourful *tejuelas* (shingles), and for its 1764 **Iglesia Santa Maria de Loreto** (Tues–Sun 11am–12.45pm & 2–4pm; free), the oldest Chilote church and a prime example. The other big draw is February's Muestra Gastronómica y Artesanal, which gives you a chance to both sample traditional Chilote cuisine and pick up local handiwork.

ARRIVAL AND DEPARTURE

By bus Buses Dalcahue Expreso run daily (Mon–Sat every 15min; Sun every 30min; 30min) from Castro to Dalcahue.
By ferry and bus for Achao Ferry services (every 30min 7am–11pm; foot passengers free) connect Dalcahue to Isla Quinchao. Achao's Terminal de Buses (Miraflores at Zañartu) has regular departures for Dalcahue (every 20min 7.15am–8.30pm; 40min).

ACCOMMODATION

Hostal Encanto Patagon Montt 146, Dalcahue ☎65 264 1651, ⓦhostalencantopatagon.blogspot.com. Sitting right on the *costanera* (waterfront), this venerable 120-year-old house with sloping wooden floors has a clutch of singles, doubles and triples named after locations on the Carretera Austral. The owners, Carlos and Cecilia, whip up delicious home-cooked meals and can help you if you're planning an adventurous getaway to some of the far-flung islands of the Chiloé Archipelago. Per person CH$12,000

Hostal Lanita O'Higgins 50, Dalcahue ☎65 264 2020, ⓦlanitahostal.blogspot.com. You'll be made to feel part of the family. Besides the snug five-bed dorm there's a double and a twin, and breakfast includes freshly baked bread. The only downside is the occasional queue to the two bathrooms. Dorms CH$10,000, doubles CH$32,000

EATING

★**Café Artesanías Casita de Piedra** Montt 144. Bringing urban sophistication to Dalcahue's *costanera*, at this split-level boutique/café you can purchase woollen goods downstairs (credit cards accepted) and then head up to the cheerful yellow café for a hit of espresso or a ristretto, summoning the waitress with the press of a handy button on each table. Tues–Sat 10.30am–2pm & 3.30–8pm, Sun 10.30am–2pm.

Las Cocinera Dalcahue Next to the Feria Artesanal. This food stalls inside an establishment that resembles an upside-down boat is an excellent place to try inexpensive Chilote specialities. Shop around as local women dish up *curanto*, *empanadas*, *milcaos* (flat potato dumplings studded with smoked pork) and sweet baked twists known as *calzones rotos* (literally "torn underpants"). *Doña Lula*, Puesto 8, does fabulous *empanadas*; *Tenchita*, Puesto 2, is a favourite for *canacato* and other substantial mains, while *La Nenita*, Puesto 4, offers very fresh salmon *ceviche*. Daily 8am–9pm.

PARQUE NACIONAL CHILOÉ

On the island's mountainous western coast, the **PARQUE NACIONAL CHILOÉ** comprises vast areas of native evergreen forest, covering the slopes and valleys of the **Cordillera de Piuchén**, as well as wide deserted beaches and long stretches of **rugged coastline**. The dense vegetation hides the elusive *pudú* (pygmy deer) and the shy Chilote fox. The park is divided into three sectors, though by far the most popular and accessible is Sector Anay.

Sector Anay

To reach Sector Anay, take a bus to the tumbledown village of **Cucao** from Castro's Terminal Municipal (14–16 daily in peak season; 1hr). Pay the park entrance fee at **Chanquín** (daily 9am–7pm; CH$1500), across the river from the village, where Conaf's **Centro de Visitantes** provides visitors with a detailed map of the park. Bring supplies with you if you plan to trek and camp rather than just do a day-trip.

4

Hike-wise, there's the circular, 770m "**El Tepual**" trail that runs through an area of *tepu* forest, a tree which thrives in this humid bogland; there are log walkways across the wetter sections of these enchanted-looking woods, with twisted moss-covered trunks intertwined with other native species. The second hike is the **Sendero La Playa**, which leads you through patches of *nalca* (native rhubarb) and tunnels of dense vegetation before emerging on the regenerating scrubland that takes you via sand dunes to the exposed Pacific coast. A little more taxing is the 3km (one-way) walk along the beach to Lago Huelde, where you pick up the 9km **Sendero Rancho Grande**, along the Río Deñal up to the edge of the tree line, revealing beautiful views below. The park's longest hike is the beautiful 25km (6hr) **Sendero Chanquín**, which alternates between stretches of coastline, pounded by the fierce Pacific surf, and dense, native evergreen forest, before finishing up at the Conaf *refugio* (bring own bedding) and campsite (CH$2000 per person) at Cole Cole.

Punta Pirulil

Reached via a rough, unpaved 45-minute drive south from Cucao, this privately owned headland is the stage for a beautiful, wind-whipped, two-hour walk over the hills and along wave-battered cliffs. Indigenous Huilliche tales have it that this part of the island acts as a bridge between this world and the next, with souls of the dead calling out to the boatman to ferry them across. A symbolic **Muelle de las Almas**, a bridge to nowhere that ends halfway, has been built here facing the bay. It's easiest to visit on a half-day tour with **Palafito Trip** (☏09 8849 5522, ⓦpalafitotrip.cl), based out of *Hostel Palafito Cucao*.

ACCOMMODATION AND EATING

El Arrayán Near the park entrance, this is the only reliable restaurant around, with rough-hewn wooden furniture, friendly service and a menu full of simple but well-executed meat and seafood dishes. Mains from CH$5500. Daily noon–10pm in high season.

Camping Chanquín 200m past the Conaf visitors' centre ☏09 9507 2559. This campsite offers 25 camping spots with fire pits, showers and picnic tables provided. There are also four fully equipped cabins for up to six guests each. Camping/person $\overline{\text{CH\$2500}}$, cabin $\overline{\text{CH\$40,000}}$

Cucao Love ☏09 6751 3222, ⓦcucaolove.com. You'll spot the large geodome before you cross the river to Chanquín. Run by transplants from the Canary Islands, this option consists of camping spots dotted amid the shrubbery and basic bunkrooms, with dinner option (CH$4000). The geodome serves as a cavernous hangout area, complete with internet, bar and kayaks, mountain bikes and paddleboards for rent. Camping/person $\overline{\text{CH\$4500}}$, dorms $\overline{\text{CH\$10,000}}$

★ **Hostel Palafito Cucao** ☏65 297 1164 or ☏09 8403 4728, ⓦhostelpalafitocucao.cl. This shingled guesthouse is ideally situated 200m from the park entrance. It boasts views of Lago Cucao from its centrally heated rooms and dorm. Guests congregate in the cosy lounge, heated by a wood-burning stove, watch the sunset from the deck or simmer in the hot tub. Nab the corner room for the best views. Dorms $\overline{\text{CH\$13,000}}$, doubles $\overline{\text{CH\$48,000}}$

PARQUE TANTAUCO

At the very south of Chiloé, the remote 1200-square-kilometre private reserve of **PARQUE TANTAUCO**, created by the current president of Chile, Sebastián Piñera, is completely uninhabited apart from the fishing hamlet of **Caleta Inío** on the southern coast. The park consists of **Zona Norte**, accessible only by high-clearance vehicle, and **Zona Sur**, accessible by boat from port town Quellón, which is 93km south of Castro, with over 130km of well-signposted, meticulously maintained hiking trails of varying length and difficulty between the two, encompassing both the coastal areas and Chilote rainforest. It's possible to do some **day-hikes** in Zona Norte, 14km north of Quellón along a gravel road, basing yourself at Lago Chaiguata, 20km west of the Lago Yaldad ranger station on the road from Quellón (9am–5pm; CH$6000; get your map of the park here). Alternatively, you can tackle the two long trails in the park which form a T-shape: the east–west Ruta Caleta Zorra from Lago Chaiguata (41km one-way; seven-day return), and the north–south Ruta Transversal (52km; five days one-way) from Lago Chaiguata to Caleta Inío, which turns south halfway along to Caleta Zorra.

ARRIVAL AND INFORMATION

By bus Quellón is connected to Castro by bus (2 hourly; 1hr 30min). In Jan and Feb, there are three buses weekly from Quellón to Zona Norte (Mon, Wed & Sat at 9am, returning at 4pm; CH$15,000/25,000 return to Lago Yaldad and Lago Chaiguata; book via Chiloétnico or Chiloé Natural).

By boat A private boat (CH$60,000/person) can be chartered from Quellón either to drop people off at Caleta Inío or pick people up;. It's sometimes possible to catch a ride from Caleta Inío to Quellón with one of the local fishing boats, but you have to have plenty of time to spare.

Park office Ruta 5 Sur 1826, Castro (Dec–March daily 9am–6pm; April–Nov Mon–Fri 9am–6pm; ☎65 263 3805, ⓦparquetauco.cl). The main park office is just south of Castro, across the street from the casino.

Tours Chiloétnico and Chiloé Natural in Castro (see p.450) offer day- and multi-day tours of Parque Tantauco.

ACCOMMODATION

Refugios (CH$8000, bring own bedding) are deliberately arranged with a day's hike between each site. Drinking water is found at every site apart from Refugio Mirador Inío, the highest of the sites. Accommodation at Lago Chaiguata and Caleta Inió – campsites and geothermal domes, plus a guesthouse at Caleta Inió – must be booked in advance at the park office or via the tour companies.

Northern Patagonia: Aysén

Comprising the northern half of Patagonia, **AYSÉN** is a land of spell-binding glaciers, soaring fjords and snowcapped mountains, still sufficiently remote to attract more adventurous travellers. The **Carretera Austral**, the partially paved, partly dirt-and-gravel "Southern Highway", stretches for 1240km down from Puerto Montt to tiny **Villa O'Higgins** – a popular destination for cyclists – interrupted in places by various

bodies of water and supplemented by short ferry rides. This really is the end of the road – to get further south you'll need to fly, take a boat or travel through Argentina. The only town of any size is **Coyhaique**, roughly in the middle of the "Southern Highway" – a springboard for launching trips north and south.

CHAITÉN

On May 2, 2008, **Volcán Chaitén**, at the foot of which nestles its namesake town, **erupted** for the first time in over nine thousand years, taking everyone by surprise, as the volcano was thought to be dormant. **CHAITÉN** and much of the surrounding area was evacuated and a mudslide caused floods which devastated the town. Vital services have now been reinstated and the town largely rebuilt, though you still see a number of eerie, wrecked houses half-buried in volcanic detritus. Chaitén now makes an excellent base for ventures into Parque Pumalín (see p.456).

ARRIVAL, INFORMATION AND TOURS

By bus Buses Becker (☎67 223 2167) run to Coyhaique (Wed & Sun at noon; 9hr); Buses Cardenas and Buses Cumbres Nevadas serve Futaleufú (2–3 daily; 2hr 30min–4hr); Kemel Bus (☎65 225 3530) runs to Puerto Montt via Hornopirén (daily noon; 7hr).

By ferry Naviera Austral (Av Corcovado 466; ☎65 273 1011, ⓦwww.navieraustral.cl) sails to Castro (Sat noon; 5hr 30min) and Quellón on Chiloé (Mon 10am; 5hr); and also Puerto Montt (Fri & Sun 10am; 8hr); double-check timetables as they're prone to change.

Information and tours Chaitur, O'Higgins 67 (☎65 27 31429 or ☎09 7468 5608, ⓦchaitur.com), run by American Nicolas, doubles as the local bus terminal and he runs day tours to Parque Pumalín (CH$40,000) and Termas el Amarillo. Chaiten Nativo, Libertad 253 (☎65 2731 3333 or ☎09 7764 5891, ⓦchaitennativo.cl), organizes kayaking and mountain biking excursions, as well as tours to Parque Pumalín.

4

"DOING" THE CARRETERA AUSTRAL

Though having your own wheels makes it easier to get around, the majority of the **Carretera Austral**'s attractions are reachable by public transport; all you need is a bit of time and some organizational skills, since not all buses run daily. Bear in mind that Coyhaique is the only place where you can reliably withdraw money, so bring plenty of cash. Be prepared for delays (landslides block the road during heavy rains) and keep in mind that transport can be less frequent outside the November to March high season. Book bus tickets in advance for routes less travelled, as buses tend to fill up.

ACCOMMODATION AND EATING

Hostería Llanos Corcovado 387 ☎09 8826 0448. Seafront residence with wood-panelled en-suite rooms and frilly bedspreads. Per person CH$12,000

Pizzeria Reconquista Portales at O'Higgins. Returning to re-conquer Chaitén after years of volcanic-eruption-induced absence, this locally loved pizzeria has a cute little bar dispensing Espumalín and two other local brews and solidly Chilean pizzas (very little tomato sauce) CH$7000. Daily 12.30–3.30pm & 7–10pm.

El Quijote O'Higgins s/n. This cheery, family-run restaurant serves heaped portions of super-fresh grilled fish or chicken and chips. Owner Javier has several basic but comfortable rooms for rent, too. Daily 12.30–3.30pm & 7–10pm. Rooms/person CH$12,000

PARQUE PUMALÍN

Accessible from Chaitén, **PARQUE PUMALÍN** is the world's largest privately owned conservation area, covering 2900 square kilometres of land, founded by North American billionaire philanthropist Douglas Tompkins to protect one of the world's last strongholds of temperate rainforest. It's a place of overwhelming natural beauty, with pristine lakes reflecting stands of endangered, millennia-old *alerce* trees, ferocious waterfalls gushing through chasms of dark rock, and high, snowy-peaked mountains. Parque Pumalín consists of three sectors, with the southern sector being the most-visited one.

Southern sector

The **southern section** has the most trails and campsites, all branching off the 58km of the Carretera Austral. Highlights include the **Sendero Cascadas** near **Caleta Gonzalo** (where the bus from Chaitén to Puerto Montt boards the ferry north), which climbs steeply through a canopy of overhanging foliage up to a 15m waterfall (3hr round-trip); the challenging **Sendero Laguna Tronador**, 12km south, taking you to a lookout point with fabulous views of Volcán Michinmahuida, ending at the pristine lake with a camping area alongside (3hr round-trip); the twenty-minute **Sendero Los Alerces** loop that runs through a grove of ancient, colossal *alerces*; and the **Sendero Cascadas Escondidas**, an easy hour's walk that takes in three waterfalls.

Closer to Chaitén, the **Sendero Volcán Michimahuida** is a 12km ramble to the base of the namesake volcano, and the **Sendero Volcán Chaitén** is a popular hike up to the rim of the eponymous volcano (2hr 30min round-trip).

Sector El Amarillo

Next to the village of the same name, 24km south of Chaitén, the star of the **El Amarillo sector** is the flat 10km **Sendero El Amarillo Ventisquero**, which runs to the base of the Michimahuida glacier from the Ventisquero campsite, with superb views en route, making it a really good, easy day hike. Another ambitious trail (25–30km) is due to be completed in 2016 with a *refugio* halfway along, connecting the two main sectors of the park via the mountain pass that lies between the Michimahuida and Chaitén volcanoes.

ARRIVAL AND INFORMATION

By bus Buses between Chaitén and Puerto Montt (daily; 9hr) can drop you off in the southern sector anywhere along that stretch of the Carretera Austral, including Caleta Gonzalo. Buses between Chaitén and any destination south can drop you off in El Amarillo; book onward bus tickets in Jan and Feb.

Information There are two Centros de Visitantes: one at Caleta Gonzalo and the other at El Amarillo, (Dec–Feb Mon–Sat 9am–7pm, Sun 10am–4pm; ⓦ www .parquepumalin.cl). There's also Casa Puma in Puerto Varas, Klenner 299 (Mon–Fri 9am–5pm; ☎65 225 0079), where you can get information on the park.

ACCOMMODATION AND EATING

SOUTHERN SECTOR

Café Caleta Gonzalo At Caleta Gonzalo, this appealing restaurant serves Chilean dishes that use organic vegetables, and the delicious bread is home-made. There are also picnic boxes to take away. Summer daily 9am–10pm.

Camping Cascadas Escondidas 14km south of Caleta Gonzalo. Small campsite with showers and sheltered cooking area. Per site CH$7500

Camping Lago Blanco 36km north of Chaitén. This campsite has fantastic views of Lago Blanco from the covered sites, as well as hot showers and fire pits. Per site CH$7500

Camping El Volcán Halfway between Chaitén and Caleta Gonzalo. Large, tree-fringed campsite; each site comes with its own cooking area, barbecue and drinking water access. Per person CH$2500

EL AMARILLO SECTOR

Camping Grande Attractive campsite, 3.3km from the park entrance, with sites scattered around giant patches of native rhubarb and surrounded by trees. Comes with bathrooms and area for cooking. Per person CH$2500

Camping Ventisquero "The most beautiful campsite in Chile", 9km from the park entrance, comes with spectacular views of the hanging glacier, as well as cooking shelters and bathrooms. Per person CH$2500

FUTALEUFÚ

An attractive little town, **FUTALEUFÚ** serves as a popular summer base for rafting, kayaking, hiking and horseriding. Its proximity to the Argentine border also makes it handy for an easy transfer to Esquel (see p.122).

With its big "explosion waves" and massive "rodeo holes", the Río Futaleufú is regarded by many professional rafters and kayakers as one of the most challenging whitewater rivers in the world, with sections of the river known as "Hell" and "The Terminator". A number of Chilean and US operators offer **rafting** trips down the river, a body of water which runs through a basalt gorge known as the "Gates of Hell", and boasts over forty class IV–V rapids; rafting season is between November and March.

ARRIVAL AND INFORMATION

By bus All buses apart from those to Esquel depart from the corner of Prat and Balmaceda.

Destinations Chaitén (daily; 2hr 30min; Buses Cardenas; ☎ 09 9545 4891; and Cumbres Nevadas; ☎ 67 272 1208); Coyhaique (Fri 11.45am; 10hr; Buses Becker; ☎ 67 223 2167); Esquel, Argentina, leaving from Cerda between Prat and Aldea (Mon, Wed & Fri: 9am & 6.45pm; Transporte Internactional); Puerto Montt via Argentina (Sun & Wed 7.30am; 14hr; Buses Transaustral; ☎ 67 272 1360).

Information The tourist office at O'Higgins 536, south side of the Plaza de Armas (summer only; daily 9am–8pm), dishes out maps of town. There's a single ATM at Banco Estado, on the Plaza de Armas, but it doesn't accept some foreign cards so bring plenty of cash.

ACCOMMODATION AND EATING

Camping Puerto Espolón Next to the bridge, just south of town ☎ 65 272 1509. This tree-dotted riverfront campsite is a 10min walk from the plaza, and has its own little beach, as well as accommodation inside two geodomes (up to eight people in each). They also brew their own Futaalhue pale ale and stout. Camping per person CH$5000, domes per person CH$12,000

★**La Gringa Carioca** Aldea 498 ☎ 65 272 1260, ⓦ hostallagringacarioca.cl. An intimate cottage that sits in the middle of a large garden. The four light, bright, spacious doubles are all individually decorated and a delicious American-style breakfast seals the deal. CH$25,000 discount for solo travellers. CH$60,000

Hostal Las Natalias O'Higgins 302 ☎ 09 9631 1330, ⓦ hostallasnatalias.info. A 10min walk west along Cerda, this rambling hostel has a huge open-plan communal area/kitchen and is very sociable with occasional barbecues. Dorms CH$10,000, doubles CH$25,000

Siete Siete Aldea 346 ☎ 09 5980 1039. This newcomer on the scene is poised to win fans with his innovative takes on fish, pasta and meat dishes. Mains from CH$6500. Mon–Fri noon–3pm & 7–10pm, Fri & Sat 11am–10pm.

Sur Andes Cerda 308. Real coffee, freshly squeezed juice and numerous vegetarian options contribute to the popularity of this tiny café, which serves lentil and chorizo stew, home-made pasta and hefty burgers. Mains CH$5000. Daily 9am–11pm.

4

RAFTING OPERATORS

Futaleufú is a challenging river and tour operators take safety seriously. The most common trip for novices is the "Bridge to Bridge" section; it's wet, heart-stopping fun and occasionally people fall out of rafts and rafts flip; you are taught what to do in each situation. The following reputable operators offer half- (from CH$50,000) and full-day (from CH$90,000) rafting trips down the Futaleufú and the less challenging Río Espolón (from CH$25,000).

Patagonia Elements Cerda 549 ☎ 09 7499 0296, ⓦ patagoniaelements.com. Reputable, safety-conscious Chilean operator right on the plaza.

Expediciones Chile Mistral 296 ☎ 65 272 1386, ⓦ exchile.com. This American-Chilean rafting outfit also teaches white-water kayaking, and offers small-group, multi-day trekking, staying overnight at remote ranches.

PUYUHUAPI

Sitting at the head of the narrow Ventisquero fjord, surrounded by steep, wooded hills and frequently shrouded in low-hanging mist, **PUYUHUAPI**, founded in 1935 by four young German immigrants, is a great place to break your journey along the Carretera Austral. The main attraction here are the **Termas Ventisquero** (Dec–Feb daily 7am–9pm; shorter hours rest of year; CH$17,000; ☎09 7666 6862), 6km south of town, which has two simple outdoor pools fed by thermal springs.

ARRIVAL AND INFORMATION

By bus Puyuhuapi is connected to Coyhaique by Buses Terraustral (daily 6am; 4hr 30min; ☎67 225 4335); Buses Becker (☎67 272 1248) passes through en route from Coyhaique to Chaitén (Tues & Sat; 4hr 30min) and Futaleufú (Thurs; 4hr), returning the following day in the afternoon.

Information This small but well-stocked and helpful tourist office is located on Avenida Übel (daily 10.30am–1pm & 3–8pm; ☜puertopuyuhuapi.cl).

ACCOMMODATION AND EATING

★**Casa Ludwig** Otto Uebel 202 ☎67 232 5220, ☜casaludwig.cl. This rambling yellow chalet has comfortable singles and doubles, some en suite, polished wooden floors, a library and great views. **CH$26,000**

Hostal Augusto Grosse Camilo Henríquez 4 ☎67 232 5150, ☜hostalaugustogrosse.cl. This tiny hostel consists of a couple of dorms and doubles, all decked out with beautiful wooden furniture hand-carved by the owner. Guests gather in the tiny wood-stove-heated living area and are welcome to use the kitchen. Breakfast costs an extra CH$1000. Dorms **CH$10,000**, doubles **CH$24,000**

El Muelle Otto Uebel ☎09 7654 3598. The wonderfully fresh catch-of-the-day dishes at this fjordside restaurant do not disappoint. Their grilled hake is a winner and the home-made *kuchen* really hits the spot. Mains from CH$6000. Daily 12.30–3.30pm & 7–10pm.

PARQUE NACIONAL QUEULAT

Consisting of rugged mountains, dense forest, raging glacial rivers and its namesake hanging glacier, the 1540-square-kilometre **PARQUE NACIONAL QUEULAT** is named after the incredible **Ventisquero Colgante**, or "hanging glacier". Wedged between two peaks, forming a V-shaped mass of blue-white ice, the glacier seems to hang suspended over a sheer rock face. From the parking area 2km beyond the **ranger post** (which is 2.5km from the Carretera Austral), cross the suspension bridge over the river, and turn right, taking the 600m **Sendero Laguna Témpanos** (15min one-way) through overgrown woods to the glacial emerald lagoon, fed by two thundering waterfalls plummeting 150m down from the glacier. Left of the bridge, the steep **Sendero Ventisquero Colgante** climbs 3.2km (2hr return) to a higher viewpoint overlooking the glacier.

Buses between Coyhaique and Puyuhuapi or destinations further north can drop you off by the entrance (45min from Puyuhuapi; 4hr from Coyhaique); book onward bus tickets in advance. Pay the park entrance fee (CH$4000) at the ranger post; the attractive camping spots near the trailheads (CH$6000 per site) come equipped with picnic tables, barbecue areas and icy showers.

COYHAIQUE

The town of **COYHAIQUE**, 634km south of Puerto Montt, sits roughly in the middle of the Carretera Austral, at the confluence of the Simpson and Coyhaique rivers. It is a welcome pocket of civilization if you've just passed through numerous little outposts along the Southern Highway, but beyond its services as a major transport hub, a place to withdraw money and eat out at a clutch of good restaurants, its charm is limited.

The heart of the city is the hexagonal **Plaza de Armas**, which resembles a wheel with ten spokes stretching out in various directions, making navigation confusing even for people who have maps.

ARRIVAL AND INFORMATION

By plane Aeropuerto de Balmaceda is 55km south of town; all flights are met by three minibus companies that do door-to-door drop-offs (all CH$5000/person. Daily flights serve Puerto Montt and Santiago with LAN (Moraleda 402) and Sky Airline (Prat 203), and there are several weekly flights to Punta Arenas. Aeródromo Teniente Vidal, 7km out of town, handles Aerocord (General Parra 21 ☎67 224 6300, ☜aerocord.cl) flights to Villa O'Higgins (2 weekly; 1hr 15min; CH$36,000), Cochrane (CH$35,000) and charter flights to Laguna San Rafael.

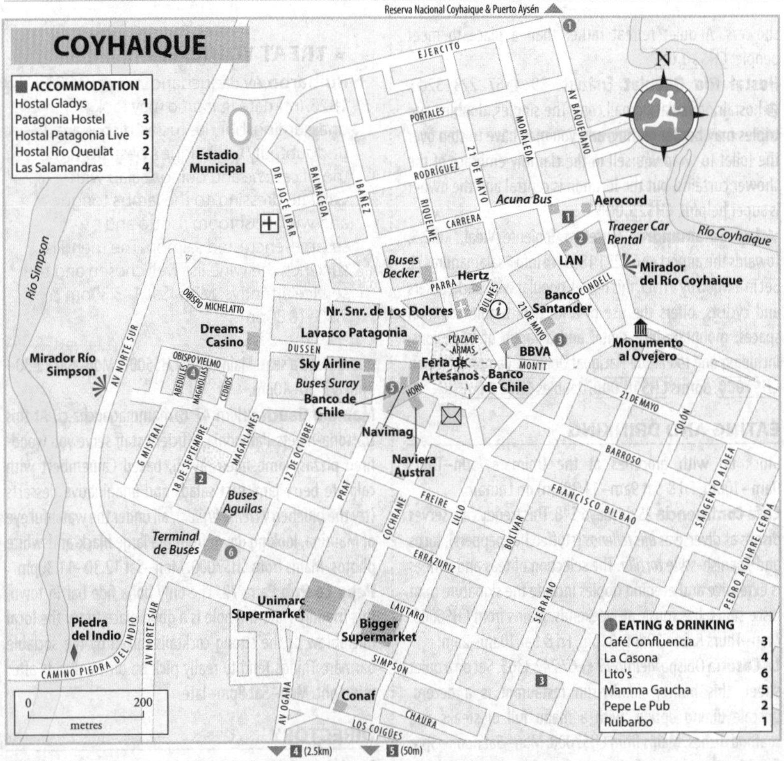
Reserva Nacional Coyhaique & Puerto Aysén
COYHAIQUE
ACCOMMODATION
Hostal Gladys 1
Patagonia Hostel 3
Hostal Patagonia Live 5
Hostal Río Queulat 2
Las Salamandras 4
Estadio Municipal
EJERCITO
PORTALES
RODRÍGUEZ
CARRERA
PARRA
DR. JOSE IBAR
BALMACEDA
IBAÑEZ
RIQUELME
21 DE MAYO
MORALEDA
AV BAQUEDANO
Acuna Bus
Aerocord
Traeger Car Rental
LAN
Río Coyhaique
Mirador del Río Coyhaique
Río Simpson
Buses Becker
Hertz
OBISPO MICHELATTO
Nr. Snr. de Los Dolores
BULNES
CONDELL
Banco Santander
Dreams Casino
Lavasco Patagonia
PLAZA DE ARMAS
Monumento al Ovejero
DUSSEN
BBVA
Mirador Río Simpson
AV NORTE SUR
OBISPO VIELMO
Sky Airline
Feria de Artesanos
MONTT
Banco de Chile
ABEDULES
MAGNOLIAS
CEDROS
Buses Suray
Banco de Chile
HORN
21 DE MAYO
COLÓN
6 MISTRAL
18 DE SEPTIEMBRE
MAGALLANES
12 DE OCTUBRE
Navimag
Naviera Austral
BARROSO
PRAT
FREIRE
FRANCISCO BILBAO
SARGENTO ALDEA
Buses Aguilas
COCHRANE
LILLO
BOLIVAR
PEDRO AGUIRRE CERDA
Terminal de Buses
ERRÁZURIZ
SERRANO
Unimarc Supermarket
LAUTARO
Piedra del Indio
Bigger Supermarket
EATING & DRINKING
Café Confluencia 3
La Casona 4
Lito's 6
Mamma Gaucha 5
Pepe Le Pub 2
Ruibarbo 1
CAMINO PIEDRA DEL INDIO
SIMPSON
AV OGANA
Conaf
CHAURA
LOS COIGÜES
0 200 metres
4 (2.5km)
5 (50m)

By bus Most buses arrive at the main Terminal de Buses on Lautaro 109, at Magallanes, five blocks from the Plaza de Armas.

Destinations Caleta Tortel (Mon 8.30am; 10hr; Buses Patagonia; ☎09 7521 9478); Castro via Ancud, Puerto Montt & Osorno (Mon & Fri 4pm; 28hr; Queilen Bus; ☎67 224 0760); Chaitén (Tues & Sat 8am; 12hr; Buses Becker, General Parra 335; ☎09 8465 2959); Cochrane (1–2 daily, 9am & 9.30am; Buses Acuario 13; ☎67 252 2143; Buses Don Carlos; ☎67 252 2150; Buses Sao Paolo; ☎67 225 5726); Comodoro Rivadavia, Argentina (Mon & Fri, 8–9am; 9hr; Transaustral; ☎67 223 2067); Futaleufú (Sat 8am; 12hr; Buses Becker); Puerto Aysén & Puerto Chacabuco (every 30min, Buses Syray, Prat 265; ☎67 223 8387); Puerto Ibáñez (1–2 daily; 2hr 30min; Miguel Acuña; ☎67 225 1579; Buses Carolina; ☎09 8952 1592); Puyuhuapi (1–2 daily; 4hr 30min; Buses Terraustral; ☎67 225 4335).

By ferry Navimag ferries to Puerto Montt (Tues & Fri; 20hr; Paseo Horn 47-D; ☎67 223 306, Ⓦwww.navimag.cl); and Naviera Austral boats to Quellón on Chiloé (Mon & Fri; 28hr; Paseo Horn 40; ☎67 221 0727, Ⓦnavieraustal.cl), sail from Puerto Chacabuco's Terminal de Transbordadores, 82km from Coyhaique, connected by frequent buses via Puerto Aysén.

Tourist office The well-stocked and super-helpful Sernatur office at Bulnes 35 (Dec–Feb daily 8.30am–8.30pm, Sat & Sun 10.30am–6pm; March–Nov Mon–Fri 8.30am–5.30pm; ☎67 227 0290, Ⓦexploreaysen.com) has a wealth of information on the region.

ACCOMMODATION

Hostal Gladys General Parra 65 ☎67 224 5288, Ⓦhostalgladys.cl. Welcoming, quiet, central guesthouse with twelve spotless rooms (most with bathrooms), complete with cable TV, breakfast and wi-fi, run by a friendly family. CH$30,000

★ **Patagonia Hostel** Lautaro 667 ☎09 6240 6974, Ⓦpatagonia-hostel.com. The only proper backpacker/cyclist hostel in town, so it's frequently booked up. The beds and bunks are large and comfortable, with personal reading lights; the lounge encourages socializing and the young, energetic German owners can assist with kayaking trips and more. Dorms CH$14,000, doubles CH$34,000

Hostal Patagonia Live Lillo 826 ☎67 223 0892, Ⓔhostalpatagonialive@gmail.com. This secure guesthouse consists of a handful of cream-coloured, spacious rooms with modern bathrooms and powerful showers. A quiet retreat rather than a place to meet people. CH$30,000

Hostal Río Queulat Errázuriz 39 ❶67 223 3200, ✉ hostalrioqueulat@gmail.com. The singles, doubles and triples may border on tiny, and you may have to step over the toilet to wrap yourself in the clammy embrace of the shower curtains, but the location is central and the owner is super helpful. CH$25,000

★ Las Salamandras Carretera Teniente Vidal, Km2.5, towards the airport ❶67 221 1865, ✉ info@salamandras.cl. Set in a wood by a river, this hostel, popular with backpackers and cyclists, offers the use of a kitchen, ample common spaces, mountain-bike rental and a range of excursions, including one to Parque Nacional Queulat. Camping/person CH$7000, dorms CH$10,000, doubles CH$25,000

EATING AND DRINKING

Stock up with groceries at the Unimarc (Sun–Thurs 9am–10pm, Fri & Sat 9am–11.30pm) on Lautaro.

Café Confluencia 25 de Mayo 548. This trendy café serves dishes as diverse as *ajís rellenos* (stuffed hot peppers), tacos and Spanish-style *tortilla*. The selection of teas and coffees is extensive and evening tipples include the signature mint pisco sours; live music at weekends. Mains from CH$6000. Mon–Thurs & Sun 10am–11pm, Fri & Sat 10am–2am.

La Casona Obispo Vielmo 77 ❶67 242 3365. Set on a quiet street, this homey, family-run restaurant is a decent, upscale dining option, with a menu full of steaks and seafood dishes. Mains from CH$7000. Mon–Sat noon–3pm & 7.30pm–midnight, Sun noon–3pm & 8pm–midnight.

Lito's Lautaro 147. This local joint looks like a dive from the outside but the focus is delicious fish and seafood, including the less typical steamed barnacles. Very popular with locals, so get here before 1pm for lunch to be

guaranteed a seat. Mains from CH$5000. Mon–Sat 12.30–3pm & 7.30–10pm.

Mamma Gaucha Horn 47 ⊚ mammagaucha.cl. At this trattoria-meets-Patagonia, efficient staff serve you wood-fired pizzas, lamb-filled ravioli, baked Camembert with calafate berry jam, vast salads and imaginative desserts (try the blueberry *crème brûlée*), all under the watchful eye of Mamma, looking down from the large black-and-white photos. Mains from CH$7000. Mon–Sat 12.30–11.30pm.

Pepe Le Pub Parra 72. The only bona fide bar in town, this friendly watering hole is a good place to try the local microbrew or the strong cocktails mixed by the sociable barman. Things tend to really pick up on weekends after midnight. Mon–Sat 8pm–late.

DIRECTORY

Banks and exchange Banco de Chile, BBVA and Santander, all located along Condell, have global ATMs.
Hospital Jorge Ibar 168 (❶67 221 9100), 24hr.
Laundry Lavaseco All Clean, General Parra.
Post office Cochrane 22.

VISITING LAGUNA SAN RAFAEL

If you only see one glacier in Latin America, make it **Laguna San Rafael**, 200km southeast of Coyhaique. It is estimated that in the next twenty years or so it will be completely gone.

As you pass through the tight squeeze of Río Témpanos ("Iceberg River"), and sail past the silent, densely forested shores of the long, narrow inner passage of **Estero Elefantes**, you catch numerous glimpses of marine wildlife. Nearing the impossibly huge glacier, over 4km in width and 60m in height, the boat dodges massive bobbing icebergs, some the size of small houses. Most boat trips allow the passengers to get close to the glacier in inflatable **Zodiacs**, and one of the trip's highlights is drinking whisky on the rocks – using the millennia-old ice, of course. Laguna San Rafael is accessible via the Valle Exporadores road from Puerto Río Tranquilo (see opposite); you need your own wheels to reach Bahía Exploradores, from where **Río Exploradores** (❶09 8259 4017, ⊚ exploradores-sanrafael.cl) whisk you off in Zodiac boats on a three-hour journey to the glacier (CH$140,000). Alternatively, **Catamaranes del Sur** (CH$190,000; ❶2 2231 1902, ⊚ www.catamaranesdelsur.cl) run high-speed catamaran day-trips (5hr each way) from Puerto Chacabuco's *Hotel Loberías del Sur* to the glacier; check website for departure dates. To reach Puerto Chacabuco from Coyhaique take buses by Buses Suray to Puerto Aisén (Prat 265; 2 hourly; 45min; ❶67 223 8387); from here the same company runs frequent buses to Puerto Chacabuco (25min).

TO THE RUTA 40 VIA CHILE CHICO

On the eastern shore of Lago General Carrera, the small agricultural town of **Chile Chico** sits only 11km west of the Argentine border (3 buses daily) and makes a convenient crossing point to Los Antiguos (see p.133), on the famous Ruta 40. Its proximity to the **Reserva Nacional Jeinemeni** also lets you access the northernmost trail of Parque Patagonia (see p.462). In Chile Chico there are several **guesthouses** offering basic rooms for CH$10,000–12,000 per person. To reach Chile Chico you can either take a bus from Puerto Río Tranquilo (see below) or from Cochrane (see p.462), or else take *La Tehuelche* car ferry run by Sotramin (☎67 241 1003, ⊛sotramin.cl) across Lago General Carrera from Puerto Ibañez (daily departures; see website for schedule; 2hr 30min; passengers CH$2100). Puerto Ibañez is easily reachable from Coyhaique with Miguel Acuña (☎67 225 1579) and Buses Carolina (☎09 8952 1592), the minibuses timed to coincide with the arrival and departure of the ferry.

VILLA CERRO CASTILLO

Ninety-six kilometres south of Coyhaique, you pass through **VILLA CERRO CASTILLO**, a rather bleak pioneer settlement whose sole draw is the rugged hiking in the adjoining Reserva Cerro Castillo with its eponymous centrepiece, **Cerro Castillo** (2700m) whose needlepoint spires loom over the valley like the turrets of a Transylvanian castle.

The rewarding 40km **Sendero Cerro Castillo** hike, which takes four days to complete, starts at Villa Cerro Castillo before heading steeply up and passing the stunning **Laguna Cerro Castillo** at the foot of a glacier suspended from the mountainside before following Río La Lima upstream to a 1450m pass on the east side of Cerro Castillo (2300m) through *coigüe* and *ñire* forest. You eventually emerge at Km75, 6km south of the reserve's Conaf ranger station.

ARRIVAL AND INFORMATION

By bus Twice-daily buses pass through on the way between Coyhaique (1hr 30min) and Cochrane (3hr 30min).

ACCOMMODATION AND EATING

Cabañas El Tropero Carretera Austral 305 ☎09 7759 5766, ⊛eltropero.cl. This friendly, family-run place offers two cabins for up to six people each, fully equipped with wood-burning stove for heating, cable TV and small kitchen. Cabin for two CH$30,000

Camping Baqueanos de la Patagonia O'Higgins s/n, sector El Bosque ☎09 7898 8550, ⊛baqueanosdelapatagonia.cl. Besides basic camping spots, this friendly outfit offers recommended horseriding excursions in the area (2–6hr). Camping per person CH$5000

El Puesto Huemul Camino Estero del Bosque ☎09 9218 3250. This homey restaurant really delivers when it comes to imaginative dishes such as lamb ravioli, freshly baked *empanadas* and gnocchi with wild mushrooms. Mains from CH$6500. Daily 8am–10pm.

PUERTO RÍO TRANQUILO

Some 125km south of Cerro Castillo, **Puerto Río Tranquilo**, a picturesque village on the shore of Lago General Carrera, has long been a popular traveller stop thanks to its proximity to the **Capilla de Mármol** ("Marble Chapel"), an impressive limestone cliff streaked with blue-and-white patterns and gashed with caves. It can be visited by boat (CH$5000–8000/person; try any kiosk along the main road) or by kayaking excursion. The opening up of **Valle Exploradores**, a stupendously scenic road that snakes its way past glacial lakes and mountains for 82km to Bahía Exploradores, has made Laguna San Rafael considerably more accessible to visitors from here (see box opposite). Some 55km west along the Valle Exploradores road is the starting point for the guided trek and ice hike run by El Puesto (see p.462) on the vast **Glaciar Exploradores**, the northern tongue of ice that extends from the Campo de Hielo San Valentín.

ARRIVAL AND DEPARTURE

By bus Buses Acuario 13, Don Carlos and Sao Paolo all stop along the main road en route between Coyhaique (5hr 30min) and Cochrane (2hr 30min) with at least two departures daily each way. There's also a bus service to Chile Chico (Mon, Thurs & Sat 4pm; 4hr 30min).

4

ACCOMMODATION AND EATING

Camping Pudú 1km south of Puerto Río Tranquilo ☎ 67 257 3003, ⓦ puduexcursiones.cl. Attractive lakeside campsite with hot showers. Owners are happy to organize excursions to the Capilla de Mármol, into Valle Exploradores and more. Camping per person **CH$5000**

★ **El Puesto** Lagos 258 ☎ 09 6207 3794, ⓦ elpuesto.cl. Specializing in multi-activity itineraries which include hiking on the Glaciar Exploradores (CH$45,000/person) and kayaking to the Capillas de Mármol (CH$30,000/person), this boutique guesthouse consists of nine beautiful en-suite rooms with crisp linens and down duvets. Packed lunch and other meals available on request and there are bikes and kayaks for rent. **CH$65,000**

Restaurant Costanera Carretera Austral 243. The simple menu at this central restaurant includes grilled fish and *lomo a lo pobre*. *Menú del día* CH$8000. Also has rooms. Singles **CH$25,000**, doubles **CH$50,000**

COCHRANE

The last major stop on the Carretera Austral if you're travelling southbound, the ranching settlement of **COCHRANE** lies 50km south of Puerto Bertrand. The town's paved, orderly grid of streets spreads out from the neat Plaza de Armas. There are limited services, which makes it a useful spot to rest up after the wildness of the Carretera Austral, or to pick up provisions if you're planning to hike to Parque Patagonia (see below).

ARRIVAL AND DEPARTURE

By bus Buses depart from the northwest corner of the Plaza.

Destinations Caleta Tortel (Tues, Thurs & Sun 9.30am, Fri 4pm; 3hr; Buses Aldea; ☎ 09 6232 2798; and Patagonia; Wed & Fri 6am; ☎ 09 7521 9478); Chile Chico (Wed & Sun 4pm; 5hr; Buses Baker; ☎ 09 8464 1067; and Mon & Fri 4pm; Buses Malfer; ☎ 09 7756 8234); Coyhaique (1–2 daily 8am; 6–7hr; Acuario 13; ☎ 67 252 2143; Don Carlos; ☎ 67 252 2150; and São Paolo; ☎ 67 252 2143); Villa O'Higgins (Thurs & Sun 8am; 7hr; Katalina; ☎ 09 7961 3358).

ACCOMMODATION AND EATING

Ada's Café Restaurant Teniente Merino 374. This large, family-run restaurant attracts hungry cyclists and locals with their nicely cooked steaks, standard fish dishes, strong signature cocktails and pints of beer. Mains from CH$6000. Daily 7–11pm.

Café Tamango Esmeralda 464. Just off the main square, this light and bright café dishes up hearty burgers, moreish crêpes with sweet fillings and even fresh fruit juice. Mon–Sat 9am–8.30pm.

Latitud 47 Sur Lago Brown 564 ☎ 09 8829 0956. Next to this rambling house, a block of several en-suite rooms boasts excellent power showers, as well as fridges and kitchenettes, while the cheaper rooms (CH$10,000/person) in the house share facilities and have low ceilings. No wi-fi (yet). **CH$25,000**

Residencial Cero a Cero Lago Brown 464 ☎ 67 252 2158. This maze-like family home caters to backpackers and cyclists with their clutch of small, unheated twins and doubles. It's run by a friendly family, breakfast is basic and wi-fi works in the tiny lounge area by the stove. Per person **CH$12,000**

RESERVA TAMANGO

Reserva Nacional Tamango, 6km east of Cochrane, sits on the banks of **Lago Cochrane**. Of the eight trails varying in length and difficulty, the longest trail leads to Laguna Tamanguito, seamlessly connecting Reserva Tamango with Parque Patagonia's Lagunas Altas trail (see below). The reserve is notable for its population of around eighty *huemúl* (native deer); if you're lucky, you may spot one. There's no public transport, but it's possible to walk to the park entrance from Cochrane by taking Pasaje 1 north and then east from San Valentín and Colonia.

PARQUE PATAGONIA

Seventeen kilometres north of Cochrane, the former-*estancia*-cum-nature reserve **Parque Patagonia** is the result of ten years of hard work by Conservacion Patagonia (ⓦ conservacionpatagonica.org). This stunning 690-square-kilometre reserve comprises mountains, highland lagoons, Patagonian steppe and forest-covered hills and acts as a wildlife corridor between Reserva Tamango (see above) and Reserva Nacional Jeinimeni near Chile Chico. There are currently two trails. The 21km **Sendero Lagunas Altas** (6hr) starts by the *Westwinds Campsite* and climbs gently through scrubland and forest to a cluster of ten pristine highland lakes, with superb views of the valley en route and plentiful wildlife including guanacos. This trail is connected by another trail to Reserva Tamango. Parque Patagonia's second trail is **Sendero Los Áviles**, a three-day hike from Casa Piedra along the Áviles river valley to Reserva Nacional Jeinimeni. In 2016 another trail is due to be built, connecting the two trails and allowing for a spectacular week-long hike from Cochrane to Reserva Nacional Jeinimeni.

ARRIVAL AND INFORMATION

On foot There is no public transport to Parque Patagonia, but you can hike in from Cochrane via Reserva Tamango (see opposite): a 7–8hr hike connects RN Tamango to the Lagunas Altas trail from where it's another 2–3hr down to the park headquarters.

Information Check in at the Administration Centre (17km from the entrance to the park; Mon–Fri 8.30am–12.30pm & 2–6pm; Sat 8.30am–1pm; ☎ 65 297 0829) on arrival and pay for camping here.

ACCOMMODATION AND EATING

Casa Piedra New campground at the start of the Los Leones trail. A *refugio* is also in the planning. CH$5000

★ **El Rincón Gaucho** The park restaurant makes full use of greens from the on-site greenhouses, local lamb, and more. You can expect anything from Patagonian-style *asado* buffet in the evenings to goat's cheese and caramelized onion sandwiches for lunch. Lunch CH$12,000, dinner buffet CH$17,000.

Westwinds Campground Tree-shaded campsite has sheltered areas for cooking and bathrooms with solar-power-heated showers. October–late April. Per person CH$5000

CALETA TORTEL

Located at the mouth of the Río Baker between the northern and southern ice fields and a logging spot for a lumber company, **CALETA TORTEL** is perhaps the most unusual village in Chile, with a scattering of houses on forested slopes surrounding a pale emerald bay, linked by a network of walkways and bridges made of fragrant cypress. There are no streets here, and even the police car and the fire engine are boats. Tortel is a great detour from the Carretera Austral, and a jumping-off point for boat trips to two

glaciers: **Ventisquero Steffens**, which originates in the northern ice field (3hr north by boat; speedboat CH$220,000; *lancha* CH$250,000), and **Ventisquero Jorge Montt**, an enormous bluish ice wall that comes from the southern ice field (5hr by *lancha*; CH$280,000; 2hr by motorboat; CH$250,000), best done in a group of eight to ten people, as the trip is charged per vessel.

ARRIVAL AND INFORMATION

By bus Buses stop in the car park in Rincón Alto, the upper section of the village.

Destinations Cochrane (Tues, Thurs, & Sun 3pm, Fri 6pm; 3hr; Buses Aldea; ☎ 09 6232 2798; Wed & Fri 4pm; Buses Patagonia; ☎ 09 7521 9478); Coyhaique (Wed 8.30am, 10hr; Buses Patagonia).

Information The very helpful office with plenty of information on Tortel and glacier excursions is in the car park (daily 10am–8pm in peak season).

ACCOMMODATION AND EATING

Hospedaje Brisas Del Sur Playa Ancha ☎ 09 5688 2723. Sparkling, simple rooms, most with shared bathrooms, colourful bedspreads and sea views, presided over by hospitable Señora Landeros. Meals available on request. CH$24,000, en suite CH$34,000

Hospedaje Hielo Sur Rincón Bajo ☎ 09 5634 6080. Wood-shingled guesthouse run by friendly Señora Ortega; compact rooms (CH$12,000 per person) share facilities, and home-cooked meals are available on request. Don Ortega operates a water taxi and does trips to Isla de los Muertos. CH$24,000

★ **Sabores Locales** Sector Rincón Bajo. The indomitable Maritza cooks up large portions of ultra-fresh fish dishes, hearty shellfish soup and more, and is a great source of local information. Daily 12.30–9pm.

VILLA O'HIGGINS

Continuing south from Cochrane to **VILLA O'HIGGINS**, a simple grid of wooden houses huddled against a sheer mountain face, the Carretera Austral winds its way around hairpin bends with sheer drops and spectacular vistas of glacial rivers cutting through endless forest. Once here, there are two choices: turn back, or cross **Lago O'Higgins** into Argentina.

A footpath off Calle Lago Cisnes runs through Parque Cerro Santiago up to a *mirador* overlooking the village; from

4

there, the path continues on to a higher *mirador* and then towards the ice "tongue" of the **Ventisquero Mosco**, the nearest hanging glacier. It's a rugged 25km trail; you can camp wild halfway. Several glaciers, including the pristine **Ventisquero O'Higgins**, spill into Lago O'Higgins, but these can only be accessed via boat trips in the summer (Nov–April) with Robinson Crusoe (☎67 243 1821, ⊛hielosur.com), Carretera Austral Km1240.

ARRIVAL AND INFORMATION

By plane Transportes Aéreos Don Carlos has charter flights from Coyhaique (Mon & Thurs 9am, return 11am; 1hr 15min) to the airstrip just to the west of town.
By bus Buses Katalina (☎09 7961 3358) leave from Calle Río Mayer (buy your ticket in advance at the little office), running to Cochrane (Mon & Fri 8am; 7hr), and arriving in O'Higgins the day before.
By ferry (see box opposite).
Tourist information On the plaza (summer only; Mon–Fri 10am–2pm & 3–7pm; ⊛villaohiggins.com). The staff provide plenty of information on the town and the surrounding area. Since there are no banks or ATMs, bring plenty of cash. You can change a limited amount of cash on the *Quetru* boat (see opposite); if heading to Argentina, take plenty of US$.

ACCOMMODATION, EATING AND DRINKING

Several guesthouses offer basic rooms for CH$10,000 per person.
Camping Los Ñires Hernan Merino s/n ☎67 243 1811,⊛campinglosnires@gmail.com. This centrally located campsite is spacious and tree-lined with a cooking hut for campers and hot showers. Per person CH$4000
★**El Mosco** Carretera Austral Km1240 ☎67 243 1819, ⊛patagoniaelmosco.blogspot.com.es. With its hammock-festooned porch and guitars in the snug living area, the town's only hostel acts as a hiker and cyclist magnet. Campers can use the hot showers and kitchen, the dorms are spacious and there are doubles upstairs. Breakfast CH$3000 extra. Camping per person CH$5000, dorms CH$10,000, doubles CH$32,000
Restaurante Entre Patagones Carretera Austral 1 ☎67 243 1810. This large wooden lodge dining hall fills up nightly with locals and travellers; food is simple and portions are large. Expect the likes of noodle soup and grilled hake; if you're lucky, you'll be there on *asador patagónico* (spit-roasted lamb) night. Meals around CH$8000. Mon–Sat 7.30–11pm, Sun 1–3.30pm.

Southern Patagonia

Enormous glaciers calving icebergs the size of houses, pristine fjords and dozens of islands make up the otherworldly vistas of Magallanes province, or **SOUTHERN PATAGONIA**. Add in forbidding craggy peaks, impossibly blue glacial lakes, a wealth of wildlife and the sheer size and majesty of the internationally renowned **Torres del Paine** national park, and it's easy to see why Patagonia captures the imagination. Cut off from the rest of Chile by the giant Campo de Hielo Sur (Patagonian Ice Fields) to the northeast, the locals have a strong camaraderie with their counterparts across the Andes; many consider themselves to be Patagonians first, Chileans or Argentines second.

PUNTA ARENAS

On the shores of the turbulent Magellan Strait, Patagonia's largest city, **PUNTA ARENAS**, benefits from its proximity to penguins, glaciers and Tierra del Fuego. Established in 1843, nearby Fuerte Bulnes was Chile's first outpost in the region, but the city itself has its roots in a penal colony founded five years later. The port provided a convenient stopover for ships heading to California during the gold rush of 1849, and then grew in size and importance with the introduction of sheep from the Falkland Islands to the Patagonian plains. Punta Arenas emerged as a wool empire, drawing migrant workers from Croatia, Italy, Spain and especially Britain. Following the decline of the wool economy after World War II, the city benefited from the discovery of petroleum in Tierra del Fuego in the 1940s, and now makes its living from a combination of petroleum production, commercial fishing and tourism.

WHAT TO SEE AND DO

The city centre is compact and easy to navigate, its streets laid out in a grid. Most facilities lie within a few blocks of the main square.

TO ARGENTINA ON FOOT AND BY BOAT

Every year, a few dozen travellers tackle the boat-hike-boat route between **Villa O'Higgins** and Argentina's **El Chaltén**. A minibus (CH$2500) run by Robinson Crusoe connects Villa O'Higgins to the dock at Bahía Bahamóndez, 7km east of town for Argentina. The sixty-passenger *Quetru* leaves here at 8.30am (Jan & Feb Mon, Wed & Sat; Nov, Dec & March Sat only; CH$44,000) and arrives at the hamlet of **Candelario Mancilla** at around 11am. The only accommodation option is a basic **campsite** (CH$4000) and two basic rooms inside the owner's house (CH$8000/person). Get your passport stamped by **Chilean border control** further up the main road.

A gravel road winds uphill for 13km to the international border. Beyond the border, the 7.5km stretch of trail to the **Argentine Gendarmería** on the banks of the **Lago del Desierto** becomes a narrow, muddy footpath snaking its way through hilly forest and scrubland. After getting stamped into Argentina, you can either pitch a tent at *Camping Lago del Desierto* (CH$3500), or stay in the basic **cabaña** run by the gendarmes. The next day, catch the motor launch *Huemul* across the lake (late Dec–late Feb Tues, Thurs & Sun 6.30pm; Dec & March Thurs & Sun; mid-March to early April Sun only; 30–45min; CH$18,000) or hike the remaining 16km (5hr) along a steep, thickly forested path on the left side of the lake, emerging by the pier on the south side.

Minibuses to **El Chaltén** meet the arriving motor launches (1.30pm, 4pm & 8pm; AR$270). To book a guide and packhorses (CH$20,000 per packhorse, two-horse minimum), visit ⓦvillaohiggins.com.

Plaza Muñoz Gamero

The heart of the city is the tranquil, shady square **Plaza Muñoz Gamero**, centred around a fierce-looking statue of **Ferdinand Magellan**, with a **Tehuelche Indian** at his feet. Local lore has it that if you touch the Tehuelche's big toe, you will one day return to Punta Arenas. The plaza is surrounded by several grand Art Nouveau mansions, evidence of the great wealth accumulated here in the 1890s.

Palacio Sara Braun

A visit to opulent Neoclassical French **Palacio Sara Braun** on the plaza (Mon–Fri 10.30am–1pm & 4pm–midnight, Sat 10.30am–1pm & 8–10pm; CH$1000), built for wealthy widow Sara Braun between 1895 and 1905 (a section of which has been the posh Club de la Unión since 1960), provides a fascinating glimpse into the homes of the city's elites during the boom years. Visitors can stroll through elegant, period furniture-lined rooms and marvel at the cornucopia of richly carved ceilings, imported artworks and frescoes.

Mirador Cerro La Cruz

A five-block walk along Calle Fagnano from the southeast corner of the plaza brings you up to the **Mirador Cerro La Cruz**, offering a stupendous view of the brightly coloured, galvanized metal rooftops of Punta Arenas and the deep blue Magellan Strait beyond.

Palacio Braun-Menéndez

Completed in 1906, the **Palacio Museo Braun-Menéndez**, Magallanes 949, is the former family residence of Mauricio Braun, and Josefina Menéndez – a marriage that united the two wealthiest and most powerful families in Punta Arenas. Inside, the **Museo Regional de Magallanes** (Oct–April Mon & Wed–Sun 10.30am–5pm; May–Sept Mon & Wed–Sun 10.30am–2pm; CH1000; ⓦmuseodemagallanes.cl) showcases beautifully preserved private quarters, lavishly decorated with French Art Nouveau furnishings. Several rooms are devoted to a permanent exhibition detailing the colonization of Patagonia and Tierra del Fuego.

Museo Naval y Marítimo

Two blocks east of the plaza, at Pedro Montt 981, the small but illuminating **Museo Naval y Marítimo** (Tues–Sat 9.30am–12.30pm & 2–5pm; CH$1200) focuses on Punta Arenas's naval history and exploration of the southern oceans. The ground floor features scale models of famous ships, including Sir Ernest

4

Cemetery main enterance, Ferry Terminal (5km), Museo Nao Victoria (7km) & Airport (20km)

PUNTA ARENAS

ACCOMMODATION
Hostal Al Fin del Mundo	4
Hostal La Estancia	3
Hospedaje Independencia	5
Hospedaje Magallanes	2
Hostel Keokén	1

DRINKING
Santino	3
Taberna del Club de la Unión	4

EATING
Brocolino	8
Café Tapiz	9
History Coffee	6
Los Inmigrantes	1
La Marmita	2
La Mesita Grande	5
Toques de la Patagonia	7

Shackleton's *Endurance*, as well as a block of Antarctic ice. Upstairs you can play around in the area decked out as a ship, complete with nautical equipment, maps and interactive displays of sailing routes and Chile's southernmost lighthouses.

Museo Salesiano Maggiorino Borgatello

Located seven blocks north of the plaza, at Avenida Bulnes 336, absorbing **Museo Salesiano Maggiorino Borgatello** (Tues–Sun 10am–12.30pm &

3–5.30pm; CH$2500) focuses largely on the indigenous peoples of Southern Patagonia and Tierra del Fuego (Kawéshkar, Selk'nam, Yámana and Tehuelche) and the decimation of their population after the arrival of European missionaries. The unparalleled collection of photographs of the region taken by the Italian mountaineering priest Alberto de Agostini is particularly worth seeing.

Cementerio Municipal

The city's magnificent **Cementerio Municipal** (daily: Dec–March 7.30am–8pm; April–Nov 7.30am–6pm; free) extends over four city blocks to the northwest of the centre. Crisscrossed by a network of footpaths lined with immaculately clipped cypresses, it reflects the turbulent history of Patagonia. The monumental tombs of the city's ruling families – some made from Italian marble and elaborately engraved with the English and Spanish names – mingle with the Croatian and Scandinavian names of immigrant labourers, etched on more modest gravestones and locker-sized funerary urn receptacles.

Museo Nao Victoria

Seven kilometres north of the centre, the interactive **Museo Nao Victoria** (daily 9am–7pm; CH3000; ⓦnaovictoria.cl) gives you the chance to scramble aboard Magellan's *Nao Victoria* carrack, which took him around Cape Horn, the surprisingly compact *Goleta Ancud* that brought the original colonists to Punta Arenas, and to check out Shackleton's lifeboat that carried him and five crew members through the most violent stretch of ocean on earth after the *Endurance* was crushed by ice. Buses run to Río Seco, where the museum is, from the corner of Carrera Pinto and Chiloé.

ARRIVAL AND INFORMATION

By plane Aeropuerto Presidente Ibáñez is 20km north of town. Flights are met by taxis (CH$6000), minibuses (CH$4000) and Buses Fernández (CH$3500). LAN and Sky Airline offer daily flights to Santiago, Puerto Montt and Balmaceda/Coyhaique. Aerovías DAP (ⓦaeroviasdap.cl) has flights to Puerto Williams (summer Mon–Sat at 10am;

winter 3 weekly; 40min–1hr 20min; CH$67,000) and Porvenir (2–3 daily except Sun; 12min; CH$26,000).

By bus Each bus company has its own terminal in the centre of Punta Arenas. If you are taking a bus to Ushuaia (see p.145) it's crucial to book ahead in the summer; this journey involves a 40min ferry crossing of the Magellan Strait and doesn't always include a meal stop, so bring food with you. Take US$ with you as the Argentine peso is a very unstable currency. Buses Tecni Austral, Navarro 975 (ⓣ61 261 3420), Buses Pacheco, Av Colón 900 (ⓣ61 224 2174, ⓦwww.busespacheco.co.cl), Buses Barria, Av España 264 (ⓣ61 224 0646), and Bus Sur, Menéndez 552 (ⓣ61 261 4224, ⓦbussur.com), serve Ushuaia via Río Grande. Bus Sur, Buses Fernández, Sanhueza 745 (ⓣ61 224 2313, ⓦbusesfernandez.com), and Buses Pacheco go to Puerto Natales. Buses Queilen, Navarro 975 (ⓣ61 222 2714, ⓦqueilenbus.cl), Turibus/Cruz del Sur, Sanhueza 745 (ⓣ61 222 7970, ⓦwww.busescruzdelsur.cl), and Pullman, Av Colón 568 (ⓣ61 222 3359, ⓦpullman.cl), run to Osorno, Puerto Montt, Ancud and Castro.

Destinations Ancud and Castro via Puerto Montt & Osorno (5 weekly 8/9am; 27hr); Puerto Natales (16 daily; 3hr); Río Gallegos, Argentina (1–2 daily; 4hr); Ushuaia, Argentina, via Río Grande (daily 8.30–9am; 12hr).

By ferry Ferries from Puerto Williams and Porvenir arrive at the Terminal Tres Puentes 5km north of the plaza; frequent *colectivos* (CH$1000) shuttle between the docks and the centre. Transbordadora Austral Broom, at Juan Williams 6450 (Mon–Fri 8.30am–12.15pm & 2–6.15pm; ⓣ61 272 8100, ⓦtabsa.cl), operates ferries to Puerto Williams (Nov–March weekly on Thurs at 6pm; 30hr; Pullman seat CH$98,000, berth CH$137,000) and Porvenir (1 daily except Mon; 2hr 30min; CH$6200).

Tourist office The well-stocked Sernatur office is at Navarro 999 (April–Sept Mon–Fri 8.30am–6pm; Oct–March Mon–Fri 8.30am–8pm, Sat & Sun 10am–6pm; ⓣ61 224 1330).

ACCOMMODATION

Hostal Al Fin del Mundo O'Higgins 1026 ⓣ61 271 0185, ⓦalfindelmundo.hostel.com. The rooms here are basic, of varying sizes and some windowless, and it's not always easy to tell who's staff and who's a guest. However, perks include pool table, book exchange and a comfy lounge with massive TV, and the location is very central. Dorm CH$14,000, doubles CH$37,000

Hostal La Estancia O'Higgins 765 ⓣ61 224 9130, ⓦestancia.cl. Many travellers end up using this restored 1920s house as a home away from home, attracted by its high-ceilinged dorms and bright rooms with cable TV. The large common area features table football and small book exchange, and the owner is happy to assist with onward travel. Dorm CH$12,500, doubles CH$38,000

4

Hospedaje Independencia Independencia 374 ☎ 61 227 572, ⓦ chileaustral.com/independencia. Friendly young owners allow camping in the yard and can rent out equipment and organize tours of the area. Dorms and rooms are too small to swing a cat but the warmth of the owners and generous breakfast (CH$1000) make up for it. Camping per person CH$2000, dorms CH$6000, doubles CH$12,000

★**Hospedaje Magallanes** Magallanes 570 ☎ 61 222 8616, ⓦ aonikenk.com. Just four simple doubles and a six-bedded dorm on offer at this German–Chilean-run spot. Sebastian is a wilderness expert who's happy to impart his advice, and there's plenty of socializing, fuelled by the occasional impromptu barbecue. Dorm CH$14,000, doubles CH$34,000

Hostel Keokén Magallanes 209 ☎ 61 224 6376, ⓦ hostelkeoken.cl. Comfortable singles, doubles, triples and quads, a book exchange and kitchen privileges are all on offer at this welcoming family-run guesthouse a few blocks from the plaza. English, French and Italian spoken. Doubles (shared bathroom) CH$28,000

EATING

Unimarc supermarket at Bories 647 (Mon–Sat 9am–10pm, Sun 10am–9pm) is useful for self-caterers.

Brocolino O'Higgins 1049 ☎ 61 222 4989. *Brocolino* is a Punta Arenas institution, found inside an unassuming-looking historic wooden building. Tuck into lamb sweetbreads in champagne sauce, perfectly seared steak "in the style of Paris Hilton" or kick-start your libido with "aphrodisiac soup". Mains CH$4600–8500. Daily 1–3pm & 7–11.30pm.

Café Tapiz Roca 912. This wood-shingled café has been drawing in locals and travellers alike with its salads, sandwiches (try the smoked salmon with capers and cream cheese), grilled cheese toasties, real coffee and excellent home-made cake selection. Mon–Sat 10.30am–6pm, Sun 11am–5pm.

History Coffee Navarro 1065. At this aptly named café you're surrounded by history (ye olde photos of Punta Arenas, antique coffee grinders) and coffee (beans embedded in your table). The brew is decent, there's a good selection of sweet and savoury crêpes, *churrascos* and burgers (CH$3200–4000), and the service is sweet and prompt. Mon–Sat 9am–9pm.

Los Inmigrantes Quillota 559 ⓦ inmigrante.cl. Homey café filled with knick-knacks and sporting sepia prints of historic Punta Arenas. It serves chunky sandwiches overflowing with locally smoked salmon, meats and more. Don't leave without sampling the home-made cakes. Mains from CH$5500. Mon–Sat 12.30–10pm.

★**La Marmita** Plaza Sampaio 678 ☎ 61 222 2056. Among the eclectic decor you'll find some of the best flavours in the region. The pisco sours are the finest in town, and you can feast on the likes of *ceviche*, vegetable risotto and hare casserole with beer. The chef's signature chocolate pyramid with calafate berry mousse should be compulsory. Mains CH$6000–9000. Mon–Sat 12.30–3pm & 6.30–11.30pm.

La Mesita Grande O'Higgins, at Montt. This Puerto Natales transplant has taken this city by storm, with its beautiful thin-and-crispy pizzas and the lively, communal ambience. Pizzas from CH$8500. Daily 12.30–3pm & 7–11.30pm.

★**Toques de la Patagonia** España 1175 ☎ 09 8534 8690. The hard-working chef whips up the likes of smoked salmon and scallop skewers with pineapple chutney and hare stew with polenta, and just wait till you see what he can do with chocolate. The lunchtime *menú* (Mon–Sat) is an absolute steal at CH$4000; mains from CH$7000. Reserve ahead. Daily 12.30–3.30pm & 7–10pm.

DRINKING

Santino Colón 657 ⓦ santino.cl. One of the very few proper watering holes in Punta Arenas, this Italian-owned bar offers typical Chilean food, such as *lomo a la pobre*, has

---

PUNTA ARENAS TOUR OPERATORS

Most tour companies offer trips to the Seno Otway penguin colony (CH$19,000) and Fuerte Bulnes (CH$28,000).

Kayak Agua Fresca ☎ 09 9655 5073, ⓦ kayakaguafresca.com. Highly recommended outfit specializing in sea kayaking trips – from a half-day paddle along the Magellan Strait (CH$55,000) to a serious 4-day kayaking expedition to Cabo Froward (CH$550,000).

Solo Expediciones Nogueira 1255 ☎ 61 271 0219, ⓦ soloexpediciones.com. With their fast, covered speedboat, these guys whisk passengers off on half-day-trips to Isla Magdalena, stopping at the sea-lion

colony of Isla Marta. They sail from Laredo pier, rather than Punta Arenas itself, which means far less time on the boat than with Comapa, though their boat is more weather-dependent.

Turismo Comapa Magallanes 990 ☎ 61 220 0200, ⓦ comapa.com. Long-standing operator offers ferry excursions to Isla Magdalena (CH$30,000) that involve four hours on the boat in total. Land excursions to Fuerte Bulnes and Reserva Magallanes also on offer.

a good beer selection and live music on Saturdays. Beers CH$1500. Daily 6pm–3am.

Taberna del Club de la Unión Palacio Sara Braun, Plaza Muñoz Gamero. You can nurse a whisky or cocktail at this atmospheric former gathering spot for the city's most powerful men, decorated with black-and-white maritime photographs. Daily 7pm–2am.

DIRECTORY

Banks and exchange There are several banks with ATMs around Plaza Muñoz Gamero, and cambios along Roca and Lautaro Navarro.

Hospital Hospital Regional at Angamos 180 (❶61 220 5000) deals with 24hr emergencies.

ISLA MAGDALENA

In the middle of the stormy Magellan Strait lies **Isla Magdalena** – the largest Magellanic **penguin colony** in all of Chile, with an estimated 120,000 nesting birds residing on a one-kilometre-square cliff by the old lighthouse. The monogamous birds spend the September-to-March breeding season here, living in burrows in the ground. The female lays two eggs in October, with both parents taking turns looking after the chicks once they've hatched in December, while the other fishes for food. In early February you'll find the grown chicks huddled near the sea, as large as their parents but still growing the adult feathers necessary for swimming. The **best time to visit** the colony is January, when the population is at its largest. Though you have to stick to the designated walking routes, the penguins don't fear humans and will come quite close to you. You can visit here with **Turismo Comapa** or with **Solo Expediciones** (see opposite).

PINGÜINERA SENO OTWAY

If you can't make the boat trip to Isla Magdalena, then don't miss the land-based excursion to the colony of **Seno Otway**, 70km northwest of Punta Arenas. Hosting around ten thousand Magellanic penguins at its peak, the breeding site is fenced off and visitors must stick to the 1.5km wooden boardwalk that runs between the penguin burrows. While not as up-close as Isla Magdalena, you still get excellent views

of the penguins, especially at the viewpoint by the beach, where you can watch them frolic in the waves just a few metres away. Several tour operators in Punta Arenas run tours (mid-Oct to April daily at 3pm, 2hr at the colony, returning 7.30pm; CH$16,000; CH$6000 entry charge and CH$1500 toll road fee not included).

PUERTO NATALES

Some 241km northwest of Punta Arenas, the town of **PUERTO NATALES** is situated in relative isolation on the **Seno Última Esperanza** ("Last Hope Sound"). Officially founded in 1911, it was used primarily as a port for exporting wool and beef from the nearby Puerto Prat cattle *estancia*, built by German explorer **Hermann Eberhard** in 1893. The town's proximity to one of the continent's most gasp-inducing national parks – Torres del Paine – combined with the popular Navimag ferry from Puerto Montt, has firmly established Puerto Natales as one of Patagonia's top destinations for outdoor enthusiasts and backpackers.

Faced with a motley collection of tin and wooden houses, a visitor's first impression of Puerto Natales is invariably coloured by the weather. On a clear day, Seno Última Esperanza is a remarkably vivid, tranquil blue, with magnificent views of the snowcapped **Cordillera Sarmiento** and **Campo de Hielo Sur** visible across the bay.

WHAT TO SEE AND DO

The town is centred on the **Plaza de Armas**, with its main commercial thoroughfares north–south Baquedano and east–west Bulnes. The worthwhile **Museo Histórico**, at Bulnes 285 (Mon–Fri 9am–7pm, Sat 10am–1pm & 3–7pm; CH$1000), has attractive bilingual exhibits on the region's **indigenous tribes**, illustrated with artefacts and black-and-white photos of Aónikenk and Kawéshkar Indians, as well as on European settlement, the story of the Milodon's cave, and the region's first German settler, Hermann Eberhard; look out for his ingenious collapsible boat that turns into a suitcase.

4

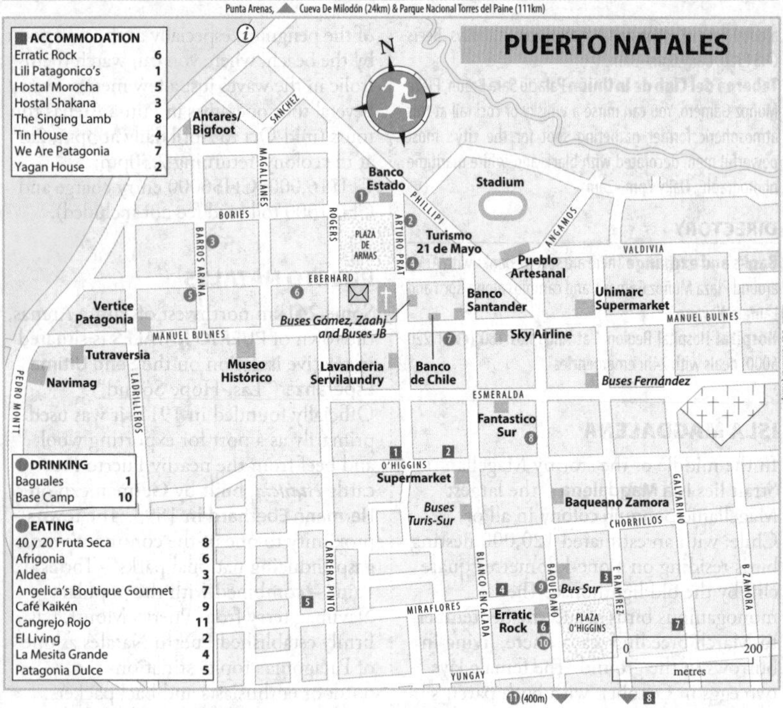

ARRIVAL AND INFORMATION

By bus The new main bus terminal, Rodoviario Puerto Natales is at Av España 1455. It's a 10–15min walk from the centre; taxis cost CH$1000 within town. Services to El Calafate (Argentina) and Torres del Paine only operate Oct–April. Buses Cootra, Baquedano 244 (T 61 241 2785), runs to El Calafate; Buses Fernández, Ramírez 399 (T 61 241 1111, W www.busesfernandez.com), and Buses Magallanes (T 61 241 0101) serve Punta Arenas; Buses Pacheco, Ramírez 224 (T 61 241 4800), runs to Punta Arenas, El Calafate, Ushuaia and Río Gallegos; Bus Sur, Baquedano 668 (T 61 241 0784, W bussur.com), runs to Punta Arenas, Río Gallegos and Ushuaia; Turismo Zaahj, Arturo Prat 236 (T 61 241 1355, W www.turismozaahj.co.cl), Buses JB, Prat 258 (T 61 241 0242), and Buses Gómez, Prat 234 (T 61 241 1971, W busesgomez.com), run to Torres del Paine, while Turismo Zaahj also serves El Calafate. Pullman, Baquedano 668 (T 61 241 3203, W pullman.cl), runs weekly trips to Castro via Puerto Montt and Osorno.

Destinations Castro (1 weekly; 38hr); El Calafate, Argentina (2–3 daily; 5hr); Parque Nacional Torres del Paine; (numerous daily, departures at 7.30am & 2.30pm; 2hr 30min); Punta Arenas (hourly; 3hr); Río Gallegos, Argentina (3 weekly; 5hr); Ushuaia, Argentina (1–2 daily; 12hr).

By ferry From the Navimag ferry terminal (Pedro Montt 308; T 61 241 2554, W navimag.cl) the MV *Edén* sails to Puerto Montt (Tues 6am; from US$450; 4 days). Book a couple of weeks in advance in summer.

Tourist information Sernatur is at Pedro Montt 19 (Mon–Fri 8.30am–8pm, Sat & Sun 9am–1pm & 3–6pm; T 61 241 2125, W sernatur.cl), with very helpful staff. Erratic Rock (W erraticrock.com) at Baquedano 719 holds excellent bilingual daily talks at 3pm at the *Base Camp* pub next door on hiking in Torres del Paine, covering logistics as well as park etiquette and required gear.

ACCOMMODATION

★ **Erratic Rock** Baquedano 719 W erraticrock.com. Run by a hugely experienced trekking guide, this hostel is a Puerto Natales institution. The atmosphere here is laidback – with hostel cats wandering in and out. Dorms and rooms are snug and there's a real sense of camaraderie among the guests. Besides the great breakfast, the daily 3pm talk gives you the lowdown on trekking in the park; onward transport and tours can now also be booked here. Walk-ins only. Dorms CH$10,000, doubles CH$25,000

Lili Patagonico's Arturo Prat 479 T 61 241 4063, W lilipatagonicos.com. This brightly painted backpacker magnet has a cavernous dining and lounge area, an indoor climbing wall, equipment for rent and good breakfasts.

More expensive doubles come with their own bathroom, and they organize half- and full-day tours of the surrounding area. Dorms CH$8000, doubles CH$22,000

Hostal Morocha Barros Luco 688 ☎09 9708 1250, ⊛hostalmorocha.com. With just five individually decorated rooms, a most satisfying breakfast spread, and welcoming, knowledgeable owners (Pablo is a Sherpa in Torres del Paine), this is an excellent choice for those who want some privacy without breaking the budget. The twin and a single share a bathroom. CH$35,000

Hostal Shakana Miraflores 798 ☎61 241 3291, ⊛shakanahostel.com. Small and personal: your host, Torres del Paine guide Chacana, will cook you eggs for breakfast (and real coffee) over a wood stove, offer advice and generally organize your trip. His rooms are compact, warm and cosy. Dorms CH$10,000, doubles CH$25,000

★**The Singing Lamb** Arauco 779 ☎61 241 0958, ⊛thesinginglamb.com. This well-designed hostel is a cut above the rest: nine-, six- and four-bed dorms with comfortable beds rather than bunks, homey common area, good showers and a block of private doubles with windows that open into the corridor. At breakfast, guests can fill up on fresh porridge, home-made bread and jam and scrambled eggs. Dorms CH$15,000, doubles CH$52,000

Tin House Miraflores 616 ☎61 261 4201, ⊛tinhousepatagonia.com. This snug eight-bedder hostel is run by friendly young hosts: David, a trekking guide in

Torres del Paine, and his wife Laura. The two cosy doubles share a bathroom, and while the four-bedded dorm is on the small side, there's plenty of space to hang out in the lounge and there's a kitchen for self-caterers. Dorm CH$11,000, doubles CH$25,000

We Are Patagonia Galvarino 745 ☎09 7389 4802, ⊛wearepatagonia.com. Run by a young, friendly local couple, this gorgeous guesthouse has a clutch of warm, colourful rooms, with excellent beds (some share facilities). CH$35,000

Yagan House O'Higgins 584 ☎61 241 4137, ⊛yaganhouse.cl. Excellent beds with down duvets, warm red-and-cream decor, eco-friendly practices and a guest lounge with a roaring fire distinguish this popular hostel. They throw a great Patagonian barbecue, and other extras include equipment rental, on-site restaurant and bar, and laundry service. Dorms CH$12,000, doubles CH$30,000

EATING

40 y 20 Fruta Seca Baquedano 443. Also known as "the dried fruit guy", this is the place to stock up on a bewildering array of dried fruit and nuts for the forthcoming hike. CH$500/100g. Mon–Sat 10am–8pm.

★**Afrigonia** Eberhard 343 ☎61 241 3609. Natales's most imaginative restaurant serves delectable African–Patagonian fusion dishes. Standout dishes include *ceviche* with mango, melt-off-the-bone Patagonian lamb and spicy seafood curry with *wali* (rice with almonds and

4

PUERTO NATALES TOUR OPERATORS AND TRIPS

Antares/Bigfoot Montt 161 ☎61 241 4611, ⊛antarespatagonia.com. Based out of *Refugio Grey* in Torres del Paine (see p.477), this long-standing operator offers 5hr ice hikes on Glaciar Grey as well as kayaking amid the house-sized chunks of ice. You have to overnight at *Refugio y Campamento Grey* in order to take part.

Baqueano Zamora Baquedano 534 ☎61 261 3531, ⊛baqueanozamora.cl. Horse-trekking in Torres del Paine (CH$25,000/45,000 for half-/full-day-trip) arranged by this long-standing operator.

Erratic Rock Baquedano 719 ⊛erraticrock.com. Experienced operator with an excellent reputation runs multi-day trekking trips to Cabo Froward, the southernmost mainland point on the continent, for a 50km, two-day wild hike on pristine beaches, through forest, scrambling among rocks and following weather-beaten cliffs, and in Torres del Paine, as well as rock-climbing ascents of Torre Norte.

Fantastico Sur Esmeralda 661 ☎61 261 4184, ⊛fantasticosur.com. Makes bookings for the Torre

Norte, Torre Central, Chileno and Los Cuernos *refugios* and campsites, as well as the Campamento Serón and Camping Francés, new as of December 2014.

Turismo 21 de Mayo Eberhard 560 ☎61 261 4420, ⊛turismo21demayo.cl. Runs trips to the Serrano Glacier (with views of the Balmaceda Glacier), on the edge of Parque Nacional Bernardo O'Higgins, via stunning fjords, cormorant and sea-lion colonies and gliding condors. Boats take four hours to reach the glacier dock, where you walk the last 1km to the base. The CH$75,000 includes lunch at a local *estancia*.

Tutravesia Manuel Bulnes 47 ☎61 241 5747, ⊛tutravesia.com. Established kayaking outfit offers multi-day trips for beginner and advanced kayakers – from a gentle paddle along the Río Serrano to the spectacular four-day Ice Route, which ends in a lake filled with icebergs.

Vertice Patagonia Bulnes 100 ☎61 241 2742, ⊛verticepatagonia.com. Makes bookings for Paine Grande, Lago Grey, Los Perros and Dickson *refugios* and campsites in Torres del Paine.

raisins). Mains from CH$8000. Daily 12.30–3pm & 7.30–11.30pm.

★**Aldea** Barros Arana 132 ☎61 241 4027. The menu at this intimate, vegetarian-friendly spot changes daily and consists of just a few beautifully executed dishes. Choose from the likes of hare loin with *platano* purée and vegetable tajine, and finish off with a sublime *arroz con leche*. Mains CH$7000–8000. Daily 12.30–3pm & 7–11pm.

Angelica's Boutique Gourmet Bulnes 501. This bakery-cum-coffee shop serves real coffee, gooey brownies, home-made cheesecake (try chocolate orange) and inexpensive daily specials, such as calzones, Greek salad, and pizza with goat's cheese (from CH$5800). Daily 9am–4pm & 5–10pm.

Café Kaikén Baquedano 699 ☎09 8295 2036. This small café is showered with praise by travellers for its wonderful home-made food – from lamb with gnocchi and heaped portions of *ceviche* to chunky sandwiches. There are only half a dozen tables, so reservations are a good idea in the evenings. Mains from CH$5000. Daily 9am–11pm.

Cangrejo Rojo Santiago Bueras 782. Strategically hung with nautical paraphernalia, this cute little restaurant specializes in fish. However, among the likes of super-fresh *ceviche* and grilled conger eel you'll find more unusual items, such as sheep's testicles. Mains from CH$7000. Tues–Sun 10am–3pm & 5.30–10.30pm.

★**El Living** Arturo Prat 156. An excellent vegetarian restaurant and lounge café, with chill-out music in the background and comfortable sofas to sink into. Treats include pumpkin and walnut ravioli, Caribbean *pepperpot* and bean tacos with guacamole, and their cakes and home-made honeycomb ice cream are equally good. Mains from CH$5500. Closed April–Nov. Mon–Sat 11am–10pm.

La Mesita Grande Eberhard 508. Hordes of hungry hikers stage a daily invasion of the best pizzeria in Patagonia, drawn by the generous portions of superb thin-crust pizzas (from CH$6500) and home-made pasta. Two long wooden tables for communal dining. Daily 12.30–3.30pm & 7–11.30pm.

Patagonia Dulce Barros Arana 233. For home-made chocolate, cookies, excellent cakes and home-made ice cream, head to this gingerbread-house-like café. Mon–Sat 10am–6pm, Sun 11am–3pm.

DRINKING

Baguales Bories 430 ◍www.cervezabaguales.cl. If the one thing that would make your Patagonian hiking experience complete is returning to a cosy microbrewery serving ample platters of fiery buffalo wings, quesadillas, tacos and assorted Tex-Mex food, accompanied by a home-made light or dark brew, then you're in luck. Beers CH$2500; mains from CH$6000. Mon–Sat noon–late.

Base Camp Baquedano 719. This former-brothel-cum-lively-pub (which doubles as an equipment rental centre) is often full to the brim with pre- and post-Torres hikers, contentedly drinking local brews and eating thin-and-crispy pizzas. Saturday is taco night. Expect occasional performances by local bands, themed nights and spontaneous barbecues. Daily 5pm–1am.

DIRECTORY

Banks and exchange Banco Santander, on Blanco Encalada, at Bulnes, and Banco de Chile, at Bulnes 544, both have ATMs.

Hospital Hospital Puerto Natales (☎61 241 1583), at Pinto and O'Higgins, handles basic medical emergencies.

Laundry Lavandería Servilaundy at Prat 332 (daily 9am–10pm.

Post office Eberhard 429, on the plaza.

PARQUE NACIONAL TORRES DEL PAINE

The great massif contained within the **PARQUE NACIONAL TORRES DEL PAINE**, 112km northwest of Puerto Natales, with the sheer granite towers of **Las Torres** to the east, and the multicoloured **Los Cuernos** to the west, is one of Patagonia's most jaw-dropping sights. The park offers incomparable opportunities for backcountry hiking, as well as animal spotting; you are likely to see **guanacos** – wild relatives of llamas – and *ñandú* or rhea (like a small ostrich). Pumas also live in the park, though they're shy, as well as foxes, the elusive *huemúl* deer and condors. There is also a host of other outdoor activities – from ice-trekking on Glacier Grey and kayaking in the icy Lago Grey to horseriding in the outlying hills.

> ### HIKING THE "W"
>
> Though Torres del Paine offers numerous hiking trails, the most popular is undoubtedly the "**W**", a four- to five-day hike that takes in the park's highlights: the massive **Glacier Grey**, steep **Valle Francés** and, finally, the **mirador Las Torres**. It makes sense to hike the "W" from west to east, tackling the steepest ascent last, especially if you're carrying camping gear, as you will have eaten most of your provisions by the time you approach the challenging Las Torres *mirador*.

LAGO GREY AND GLACIER GREY BY BOAT, KAYAK AND CRAMPON

From the *Hostería Lago Grey* it's possible to take a spectacular three-hour **boat ride** up Lago Grey to Glacier Grey (twice daily 8am & 3.30pm; 3hr return; CH$55,000). If staying overnight at *Refugio y Campamento Grey*, you can go kayaking between icebergs on the icy lake or else go ice trekking on the glacier itself with Antares/Bigfoot (see p.471).

Glacier Grey

From the pier at Pudeto where the catamaran drops you off at the *Paine Grande Lodge* (see p.477), a trail runs north through the scrubland, past a small lagoon and into the remnants of a *lenga* forest (damaged by a fire caused by human negligence in 2011). The trail emerges at the **Quebrada de los Vientos** ("Windy Gorge"), an hour or so into the hike, where your first glimpse of **Glacier Grey** – more than 7km wide at its largest point – stops you in your tracks. For the next couple of hours, you walk across exposed terrain, beside the pale water of Lago Grey and its house-sized chunks of blue ice. The glacier peeks from behind the dark rock of **La Isla Nunatak** on the lake's far side.

The trail then descends steeply through the silent *lenga* woods, crossing a wooden bridge over a gushing torrent, before arriving at a shaded lakeside clearing housing the **Refugio y Campamento Grey**, which marks the end of the first leg of the "W".

Valle Francés

You need to double back on yourself for the second leg of the "W". Back at the *Paine Grande Lodge*, a two-and-a-half-hour-long, eastbound trail heads through scrubland and prickly calafate bushes along Lago Pehoé before leading north with glimpses of **Lago Skottsberg** on your right-hand side. A hanging bridge brings you to the *Campamento Italiano*, where you can leave most of your gear before scrambling up the steep, rocky path leading up the **Valle Francés**, the middle part of the "W". The turbulent **Río del Francés** churns on your left-hand side and there are spectacular views of Glacier Francés and Glacier Los Perros.

After two hours hiking through enchanted-looking woods, you reach the very basic *Campamento Británico*, from where it's an hour's hike up to the steep lookout that gives you an excellent close-up view of the multicoloured Los Cuernos, as well as the aptly named 2800m-high **Fortaleza** ("fortress"), northeast of the *mirador*. From *Campamento Italiano*, allow two and a half hours for the hike through the forested backcountry to the *Refugio y Campamento Los Cuernos*; it's a long, steep descent on a scree-strewn trail followed by a brief stretch along the pale blue waters of Lago Nordenskjöld; you'll pass the turn-off for *Camping Francés* shortly after leaving *Campamento Italiano*.

Los Cuernos to Las Torres

From the *Refugio y Campamento Los Cuernos*, the trail runs through hilly scrubland, with Lago Nordenskjöld on your right. Shortly after you depart Los Cuernos, you cross to the **Río del Valle Bader**, a rushing glacial stream; the rest of the trail meanders gently up and down foothills. The hike takes around four and a half hours and you cross a bridge over the Río Asencio just before you reach the *Hostería Las Torres*.

Mirador Las Torres

To see the sunrise at the famous **Mirador Las Torres**, some make their way up the Valle Ascencio from the *Hostería Las Torres* the night before, spending the night at *Campamento Torres*. The hike itself is a steep, three-hour thirty-minute ascent alongside the Río Ascencio. You'll need to rise before daybreak to tackle the steepest part of the journey – an hour-long scramble up boulders – to witness the spectacle of the sun's first rays colouring the magnificent Torres, perfectly reflected in the still waters of **Laguna Torres**. Alternatively, you can break your journey by staying at the

4

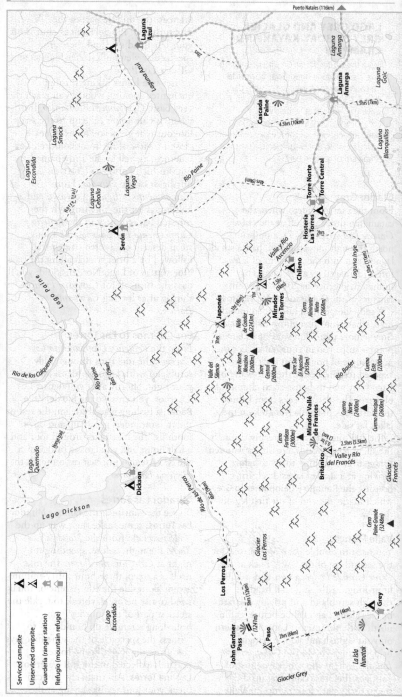

Puerto Natales (116km)

Laguna Azul

Laguna Azul

Laguna Amarga

Laguna Goic

Laguna Smock

Laguna Escondida

Cascada Paine

4.5hrs (10km)

Laguna Amarga

1.5hrs (7km)

Laguna Blanquillos

Río Paine

Horse trail

Laguna Cebolla

Laguna Vega

Serón

Torre Norte

Torre Central

Hostería Las Torres

2hrs

4hrs (9km)

Valle y Río Ascencio

Chileno

Laguna Inge

Lago Paine

1.5hr (5km)

1hr

Torres

Mirador las Torres

Cerro Almirante Nieto (2668m)

Laguna (11km)

1hr (4km)

Japonés

Nido de Cóndor (2243m)

3hrs

Río de los Calqueres

Valle del Silencio

Río Paine

3hrs (9km)

Torre Norte Monzino (2600m)

Torre Central (2600m)

Torre Sur Di Agostini (2650m)

Río Bader

Cuerno Este (2200m)

Lago Quemado

Horse trail

Mirador Valle de Frances

Cerro Fortaleza (3000m)

Cuerno Norte (2400m)

Cuerno Principal (3600m)

Britânico

0.5 hr

2.5hrs (5.5km)

Valle y Río del Francés

Glaciar Francés

Dickson

Río de los Perros

Lago Dickson

Río de los Perros

5hrs (12km)

Los Perros

Glacier Los Perros

Cerro Paine Grande (3248m)

Lago Escondido

John Gardner Pass (1241m)

Paso

2hrs (6km)

Grey

1hr (4km)

La Isla Nunatak

Glacier Grey

Serviced campsite

Unserviced campsite

Guardería (ranger station)

Refugio (mountain refuge)

4

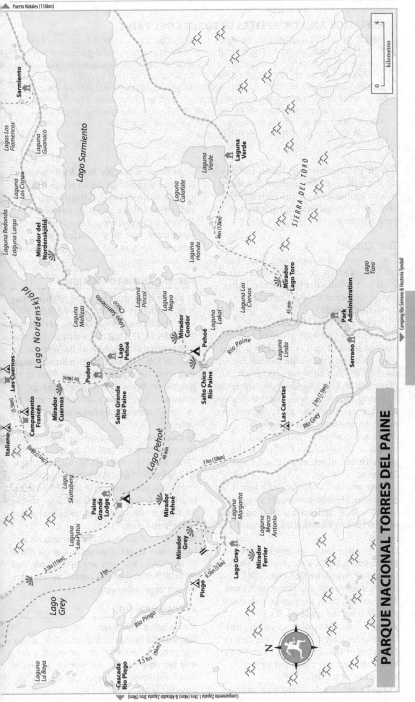

Puerto Natales (116km)

PARQUE NACIONAL TORRES DEL PAINE

Camping Río Serrano & Hostería Tyndall

Compamento Zapata 1.5hrs (4km) & Mirador Zapata 3hrs (9km)

REFUGIOS AND CAMPSITES IN TORRES DEL PAINE

Most of the park's **campsites** and **refugios** (see below) are open only from October to April. Some basic *refugios* are run by Conaf, but the rest belong either to Vertice Patagonia or Fantástico Sur, both in Puerto Natales (see p.471). *Refugios* provide hot meals for around CH\$7000 for lunch and CH\$11,000 for dinner. Book your *refugio* space in advance, especially between December and March. You can rent (limited) camping equipment at most serviced sites, but it's far cheaper to bring your own from Puerto Natales. There are several un-serviced campsites in the park which are free of charge and consist of a clearing with a fire pit; these include *Campamento Paso, Campamento Italiano, Campamento Británico* and *Campamento Torres*. Wild camping inside the park is not permitted.

Refugio y Campamento Chileno, halfway up the trail. The "W" ends with a short trek or minibus ride from *Torre Norte* and *Torre Central refugios* back to the park entrance.

The "Circuit"

The "Circuit" is an extended version of the "W", a seven- to ten-day hike that leads you around the back of the Torres, giving you some respite from the inevitable crowds.

It's best to do the "Circuit" anti-clockwise, so you have views of Glacier Grey in front of you rather than behind you. Start from the *Paine Grande Lodge*, do the "W" and then carry on from *Hostería Las Torres* to *Campamento Serón* – an easy four-hour walk northwards up and down gentle inclines. From here, it's a five- or six-hour hike to *Refugio Dickson*. Finally, the trail descends steeply to *Refugio Lago Dickson* at the southern end of iceberg-flecked Lago Dickson.

Campamento Los Perros lies a four-hour hike from *Dickson* southwest along a largely uphill trail, with a fabulous view of Glaciar Los Perros above a round lagoon.

The weather has to be in your favour before you start on a three-hour climb to the top of **Paso John Gardner** (1241m) from *Campamento Los Perros*, as it's too dangerous to cross the pass in gale-force wind. Above the tree line, it's a straightforward uphill slog. The reward is the sudden, staggering view over the icy pinnacles of **Glaciar Grey** and **Campo del Hielo Sur**, over ten thousand square kilometres of icecap.

On the other side of the pass crude steps descend steeply into *lenga* forest. It takes a couple of hours to reach the small and unserviced *Campamento Paso* and around three hours to descend to *Refugio y Campamento Lago Grey*. In two places, you have to ascend or descend along metal ladders attached to vertical slopes.

ARRIVAL AND INFORMATION

By bus The only entrance to the park for those coming by bus from Natales (daily at 7.30am & 2.30pm; 3hr) is 117km from the town at Laguna Amarga, where you pay the park fee (CH\$18,000) at the Conaf station. From here, minibuses meet bus arrivals for the transfer to *Hostería Las Torres* (CH\$2000). The buses from Natales continue along Lago Nordenskjöld for another 19km to the *guardería* at Pudeto, the departure point for the catamaran to *Paine Grande Lodge* and the start of the "W". The bus continues to the Park Administration 18km further on.

By catamaran From the *guardería* at Pudeto, a Hielos Patagónicos catamaran (mid-Nov to mid-March daily 9.30am, noon & 6pm; early Nov & late March noon & 6pm; Oct & April noon; 30min; CH\$15,000 one-way, CH\$24,000 return; tickets sold on board ☎61 241 1380) runs across Lago Pehoé. Return trips from *Paine Grande Lodge* are 30min after the arrival times and are met by buses heading back to Puerto Natales.

Conaf The Conaf *guardería* at Laguna Amarga has basic information on the park's fauna and flora, as well as basic trekking maps. You must register and pay your CH\$18,000/8000 peak/off-peak entrance fee here before watching the park safety video.

ACCOMMODATION

All prices quoted are per person.

Campamento Francés (Fantástico Sur). New campsite with geodomes overlooking Lago Nordenskjöld, a short, steep hike down from the trail between *Campamento Italiano* and *Refugio Los Cuernos*. Camping CH\$7500, domes CH\$34,000

Campamento Los Perros (Vértice Patagonia). Last campsite before the John Gardner pass, situated in a wooded area, with a small food shop, cold showers and a cooking hut. CH$4300

Campamento Serón (Fantástico Sur). Partially shaded campsite beside the Río Paine with picnic tables, cold showers and a small shop in a pleasant meadow setting. CH$7500

Refugio y Campamento Dickson (Vertice Patagonia). On the shores of Lago Dickson, this is the most remote refuge in the park; there's a well-stocked shop. The campsite has basic facilities only. Camping CH$4300, refugio CH$18,400

Refugio y Campamento Grey (Vertice Patagonia). A popular refugio overlooking Lago and Glacier Grey. Beachside campsite includes hot showers and a small on-site grocery store. Camping CH$4300, refugio CH$18,400

Refugio y Campamento Paine Grande (Vertice Patagonia). This modern structure has a scenic location and a café, restaurant and small store within the lodge. You can camp in the adjoining grassy fields and there are separate toilets and hot showers, as well as a cooking hut for campers. Camping CH$5200, refugio CH$28,400

Refugio y Campamento Torre Norte & Torre Central (Fantástico Sur). Near the entrance to the park and the Hostería Las Torres, this refugio is split between two buildings and has comfortable bunks, a cafeteria, a small shop and gear rental. Campsite has hot showers, picnic tables and fire pits. Camping CH$7500, refugio Torre Norte CH$26,000, refugio Torre Central CH$40,000

Refugio y Campamento Chileno (Fantástico Sur). A popular stop halfway along the Valle Ascencio, this small refugio offers just 32 beds, hot meals, and has a small provisions shop. Camping CH$7500, refugio CH$26,000

Refugio y Campamento Los Cuernos (Fantástico Sur). This refugio sits on the northern shore of Lago Nordenskjöld, with geodomes and private cabins as well as a cafeteria, cooking room for campers, tree-shaded campsite with platforms and hot showers. Camping CH$7500, refugio CH$26,000, domes CH$30,500, cabañas CH$86,500

Tierra del Fuego

The remotest and least visited of Chile's land territories, **TIERRA DEL FUEGO** was named "Land of Fire" by Fernando Magellan, who sailed through the strait that now bears his name in 1520, and saw a multitude of cooking fires lit by the indigenous hunter-gatherers. From then on until the opening of the Panama Canal in 1914, the frigid waters around Cape Horn – the largest ship graveyard in the Americas – formed a link in the perilous yet lucrative trade route from Europe to the west coast of the Americas.

Tierra del Fuego's Isla Grande is split between Chile and Argentina; the Chilean half features the nondescript town of **Porvenir**, settled by a mixture of Chilote and Croatian immigrants in the late nineteenth century. The Argentine half includes the lively town of **Ushuaia** (see p.145), the base for Antarctic voyages. The region's biggest natural draw is southern Tierra del Fuego – a scattering of rocky islands, separated by labyrinthine fjords, home to the craggy Darwin Range and the southernmost permanently inhabited town in the world – Isla Navarino's **Puerto Williams**.

PUERTO WILLIAMS

PUERTO WILLIAMS is home to just over two thousand people, including the last descendants of the **Yámana**. The windblown town has a desolate quality to it, though the community itself is warm and close-knit. Many travellers come to

---

THE DIENTES DE NAVARINO CIRCUIT

Many travellers come to Puerto Williams to complete the **Dientes de Navarino Circuit**, a strenuous four- to seven-day hike in the Isla Navarino wilderness. This is for experienced hikers only – the 53km route includes a particularly steep and treacherous descent at **Arroyo Virginia**.

Fuegia & Co, Partrullero Ortiz 49 (☎ 061 262 1251), offer guided treks and logistical support in the Dientes de Navarino. The best map is the Tierra del Fuego & Isla Navarino satellite map by Zagier & Urruty Publications, available in Ushuaia, in conjunction with GPS. Make sure you have plentiful food and water supplies, sunscreen and warm and waterproof outdoor gear, and inform people in town of your plans.

Puerto Williams to complete the challenging **Los Dientes de Navarino Circuit** – a strenuous four- to seven-day clockwise trek in the Isla Navarino wilderness for experienced hikers only (see box, p.477).

WHAT TO SEE AND DO

The worthwhile **Museo Antropológico Martin Gusinde**, at Aragay 1 (Mon–Fri 9am–1pm & 2.30–7pm; donations), features informative and well-laid-out displays on the native Kawéshkar, Selk'nam and Yámana Indians, complete with a replica of a Selk'nam ritual hut, as well as exhibits on local geology, flora and fauna.

ARRIVAL AND INFORMATION

By plane Aerovías DAP (Centro Comercial Sur 151; ⓦaeroviasdap.cl) flights from Punta Arenas are met by local minivans (CH$2500). One-way flights to Punta Arenas (1 daily except Sun at 11.30am) cost around CH$50,000; book well ahead for the December–February peak season.

By boat From Ushuaia, Ushuaia Boating (see p.149) run highly weather-dependent Zodiac boats to Isla Navarino (Nov–March; 45min; one-way US$125, The boats do not sail when it's windy, so be prepared to spend an extra day or two on either side of the channel. The Transbordadora Austral Broom office at Costanera 435 (☎61 621 015, ⓦwww.tabsa.cl) sells tickets for the Punta Arenas-bound ferry (every Sat at 6pm; 30hr; CH$98,000/137,000 for semi-reclining/reclining seats); it's better to sail *from* Punta Arenas in order to see the glaciers in daytime.

Tourist information Inside the Municipalidad on O'Higgins (Mon–Fri 8.30am–1pm & 2–5pm; ☎61 241 2125). The helpful tourist information desk offers brochures on Puerto Williams and Cape Horn, but not maps of the Dientes de Navarino circuit. Banco de Chile has a global ATM on a narrow passageway towards the waterfront from the Centro Comercial.

ACCOMMODATION

Hospedaje Akainij Austral 22 ☎61 262 1173, ⓦturismoakainij.cl. Cosy en-suite rooms with down duvets, a cheerful living room filled with plants, and friendly owners happy to arrange a plethora of excursions make this an ideal mid-range guesthouse. CH$35,000

Refugio al Padrino Costanera 276 ☎61 262 1136, ⓔceciliamancillao@yahoo.com.ar. A snug backpacker haven, this colourful hostel has a sign on the door

inviting you to let yourself in and decide if you wish to stay. Most do; Cecilia, the owner, may not speak much English, but her genuine warmth transcends language barriers. Dorms CH$12,000

Residencial Pusaki Piloto Pardo 222 ☎61 262 1116, ⓔpattypusaki@yahoo.es. A perpetual traveller favourite with a warm family atmosphere and excellent home-cooked food. Even if you are not staying here, you can arrange to come for dinner, provided you give Patty a couple of hours' warning; *centolla* night is best. Dorms CH$10,000, doubles CH$30,000

EATING AND DRINKING

Micalvi Costanera s/n. Docked at the west end of the Costanera, this ex-Navy supply ship with flags of different countries covering the walls and a well-stocked bar often plays host to an eclectic mix of hikers, Antarctic explorers, international yachtsmen and local navy personnel. Nov–March Mon–Sat 9pm–2am.

El Resto del Sur Ricardo Maragano 146. This is as close as Puerto Williams gets to dining sophistication, with pizzas sitting side by side on the menu with king crab dishes, locally caught trout and more. Mon–Sat noon–10pm.

Easter Island

One of the most remote island territories on earth, over 2000km from the nearest inhabited part of the world, **EASTER ISLAND** entices visitors with the enduring mystery of its **lost culture**. A remarkable civilization arose here, far from outside influence on an island only 163 square kilometres in extent. It apparently declined rapidly and had all but disappeared by the time Europeans first arrived here. Originally known as "Te Pito O Te Henua", or "the navel of the world", due to its isolation, and now called "Rapa Nui" by its inhabitants (*Pascuenses*), the island is home to a culture and people with strong Polynesian roots and a language of their own, which sets it well apart from mainland Chile. Archeological mysteries aside, the island has much to offer: year-round warm weather, excellent diving and surfing conditions and plenty of scope for leisurely exploration of the more out-of-the-way attractions, both on foot and on

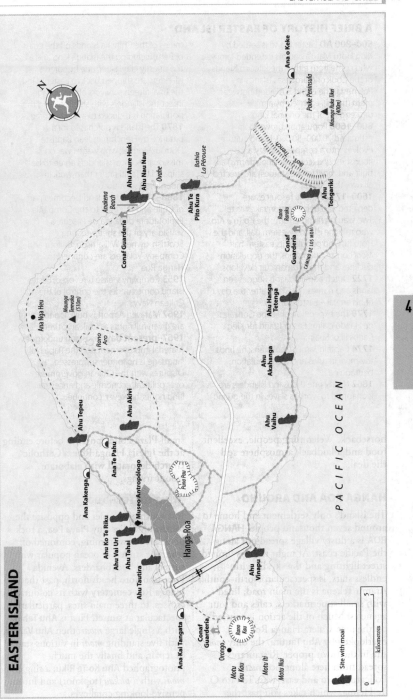

EASTER ISLAND

Ana o Keke

Poike Peninsula

Maunga Puka Tike (400m)

Roiho Trench

Ahu Tongariki

Ahu Ature Huki

Ahu Nau Nau

Ovahe

Bahia La Pérouse

Andkena Beach

Conaf Guarderia

Ahu Te Pito Kura

Rano Raraku

Conaf Guarderia

CAMINO DE LOS MOAI

Ahu Hanga Tetenga

Maunga Terevaka (510m)

Ana Nga Heu

Rano Aro

Ahu Akahanga

Ahu Akivi

Ahu Vaihu

Ahu Tepeu

PACIFIC OCEAN

Ana Kakenga

Ana Te Pahu

Museo Antropólogo

Puna Pau

Ahu Ko Te Riku

Ahu Vai Uri

Ahu Tahai

Ahu Tautira

Hanga-Roa

Ahu Vinapu

Ana Kai Tangata

Conaf Guarderia

Rano Kau

Orongo

Motu Kau Kau

Motu Iti

Motu Nui

Site with moai

0   5
kilometres

4

A BRIEF HISTORY OF EASTER ISLAND

500–800 AD Easter Island is settled by King Hotu Matu'a and his extended family, who come from either the Pitcairn Islands or the Cook or Marquesas Islands in Polynesia. The island is divided between *mata* (tribes), each led by a male descendant of the original king.

800–1600 Population grows to an estimated 20,000–30,000. Island culture evolves into a complex society and flourishes; *ahu* (ceremonial platforms) are built and *moai* (stone statues) are erected all over the island.

1600–1722 Natural resources are depleted and deforestation takes its toll. Two warring factions form: the Ko Tu'u Aro, who rule the island's western half, and the Hotu Iti, who populate its eastern half. *Moai* construction stops, the population declines and the Birdman cult develops.

1722 Dutch admiral Jacob Roggeveen lands and names the island after the day of his arrival – Easter Sunday.

1770 The expedition of Felipe Gonzáles de Haedo claims Easter Island for King Carlos III of Spain.

1774 Captain James Cook visits; he finds the *moai* in ruins and the population bedraggled.

1862 Nearly one thousand islanders are kidnapped to work as slaves in the guano mines of the Chincha Islands off the coast of Peru, including the island's king and all the priestly elite. Later, one hundred islanders are shipped back to Easter Island; the final fifteen survivors of this voyage infect the islanders with smallpox and the population is reduced to a few hundred.

1870 The island is purchased for a pittance by Frenchman Jean Baptiste Dutroux-Bornier, who wages war on missionaries. Most islanders agree to be shipped to Tahiti rather than work in indentured servitude.

1888–1953 Easter Island becomes part of Chile and is leased to the Compañía Explotadora de la Isla de Pascua, a subsidiary of the sheep-rearing Scottish-owned Williamson, Balfour and Company. Villagers are confined to Hanga Roa.

1953 Company's lease is revoked; Easter Island comes under the control of the Chilean Navy.

1967 Mataveri Airport is built. Islanders are given full rights as Chilean citizens.

1967–present day The island undergoes material improvement and the Rapa Nui language is no longer suppressed. Disputes with the Chilean government over political, economic and ancestral land rights, however, continue.

horseback. Welcoming people, excellent food and a laidback atmosphere seal the deal.

HANGA ROA AND AROUND

The island's only settlement and home to around seven thousand people, **HANGA ROA** is a dusty village spread out along the Pacific coast. At night there is limited street lighting and the sky, lit with endless stars, is spectacular. North–south Atamu Tekena is the main road, lined with small supermarkets, cafés and tour agencies. Much of the action is centred on the pier, Caleta Hanga Roa, overlooked by **Ahu Tautira**, the only *moai* site in the town proper. Restaurants spread from here along oceanside Policarpo Toro and east–west Te Pito O Te Henua, which takes you past the small Plaza Policarpo Toro before ending at the Iglesia Hanga Roa, a Catholic **church** decorated with elaborate woodcarvings.

WHAT TO SEE AND DO

Just south of the pier and opposite the tourist office lies tiny **Playa Pea**, a rock pool safe for swimming, cordoned off from the stretch of ocean popular with surfers and bodyboarders. Avenida Policarpo Toro heads north, past the Hanga Roa **cemetery** with its colourful crosses, to three main sites, particularly spectacular at sunset. First is **Ahu Tahai**, with a single large *moai*, then **Ahu Vai Uri**, with five free standing *moai* in various states of repair, and finally the much-photographed **Ahu Ko Te Riku**, a single *moai* with a *pukao* (topknot) and intact, pensive-looking coral eyes.

THE RISE AND FALL OF THE MOAI OF EASTER ISLAND

The giant stone statues, around 887 of which litter the island, are a unique symbol of a lost civilization, whose existence raises many questions. Why were they made? By whom? How were they transported around the island and erected without the benefit of machinery? Why was their construction suddenly abandoned?

Believed to be representations of **ancestors**, the statues range from 2m to 10m in height, with an average weight of 12 tonnes. The majority of the *moai* share a similar appearance: elongated features and limbs, prominent noses, heavy brows and rounded bellies. Most are male, and some wear *pukao*, topknots carved of red stone in a separate quarry. Most *moai* once had coral-and-rock eyes, though now the only intact example is Ahu Ko Te Riku.

Carved from the slopes of the **Rano Raraku quarry**, the *moai* were buried upright in earthen pits so that their sculptors could shape their facial features with basalt *toki* (chisels), and then lowered down the volcano's slopes, presumably using ropes. Most archeologists believe that to transport them to the coastal *ahu* (platforms) the islanders used wooden rollers or sledges – a practice which resulted in complete deforestation – and that once at the foot of the *ahu*, the *moai* were lifted into place using wooden levers. All *moai*, apart from those at Ahu Akivi, were positioned around the coast facing inland, so as to direct their *mana* (life energy) towards their creators and to bless them with plentiful food and other bounties.

It is known that at the height of Easter Island's civilization (800–1500 AD), the tiny island supported a large and complex multi-tiered society, with a ruling class who worshipped **Make-Make**, the creator, and oversaw the construction of these statues. A phenomenal amount of energy must have gone into their creation and transportation, fatally depleting the island's resources and causing acute food shortages. Full-scale warfare erupted when farmers and fishermen couldn't or wouldn't support the *moai*-carving workforce any longer. The carving ceased and the *moai* were toppled from their pedestals. That which gave the civilization purpose was ultimately also its undoing.

Museo Antropológico Padre Sebastían Englert

Amid gentle hills dotted with numerous *hare paenga* (boat-shaped foundations of traditional houses), off the coastal road just north of Ahu Tahai, lies the excellent **anthropological museum** (Tues–Fri 9.30am–5.30pm, Sat & Sun 9.30am–12.30pm; CH\$1000; ☏ 32 255 1020, ☺museorapanui.cl). Not to be missed, it gives a thorough, informative introduction to the island's geography, history, society, Birdman cult (see box, p.482) and the origins and significance of the *moai*. The displays include a rare female *moai*, a wooden carving of a *moai kavakava* – a gaunt figure, believed to represent the spirits of dead ancestors – and replica *rongorongo* tablets (no original examples remain on the island). *Rongorongo* script is one of only four written languages in the world that developed independently of outside influence; the tablets were first mentioned in the nineteenth-century accounts of French missionary Eugene Eyraud, and their purpose remains unclear. It seems that only a small priestly elite was literate and that the knowledge perished with them during the slave raids and smallpox epidemic of the early 1860s. The script remains undeciphered to this day.

Rano Kau crater and Orongo ceremonial village

South of Hanga Roa, a dirt road climbs steeply past a *mirador* offering an excellent panoramic view of the island, to one of Easter Island's most awe-inspiring spots – the giant crater of the extinct **Rano Kau volcano**. The dull waters of the volcano's reed-choked lake contrast sharply with the brilliant blue of the Pacific, visible where a great chunk of the crater wall is missing. A ten-minute walk from here is the **Orongo ceremonial village** (daily: Dec–March 9am–7pm; April–Nov 9am–6pm; your entry permit will be checked at the ranger's office here; the site of the Birdman cult consists of 53 restored houses with tiny doorways, made of horizontally overlapping flat stone slabs, hugging the side of the cliff. A winding labelled footpath leads past them to the edge of Rano Kau, where a cluster of **petroglyphs** depicting the half-bird, half-human Birdman, as well as Make-Make, the creator, overlooks a sheer drop, with the islets Motu Kao Kao, Motu Iti and Motu Nui jutting out of the azure waters below.

THE SOUTHERN COAST

Heading east out of Hanga Roa, Hotu Matu'a leads you towards the **southern coast**. A right turn at the end, followed by an almost immediate left by the fuel storage tanks, takes you to **Vinapu**, an important site consisting of three *ahus* (stone platforms) with a number of broken *moai* scattered around. The *ahus* are made of overlapping stone slabs, seemingly similar in construction to those built by the Inca in Cusco, Peru, leading some archeologists to believe that Easter Island culture has Latin American roots. Continuing east along this coast, you reach **Ahu Vaihu**, with its eight toppled *moai* and their scattered *pukao* (stone topknots). Up the road, the large **Ahu Akahanga** is widely believed to be the burial place of Hotu Matu'a, the first king of the island. The site features a dozen *moai*, lying face down, with petroglyphs carved into one of the platforms. There are also the remains of a village, consisting of *hare paenga* outlines, as well as a number of *pukao*.

Another 3km east, the almost utterly ruined **Ahu Hanga Tetenga** consists of two toppled and shattered *moai*. Beyond, the

PARQUE NACIONAL RAPA NUI ESSENTIALS

There is a CH$30,000 fee to enter **Parque Nacional Rapa Nui**, which covers most of the island's archeological sites. You can buy your entry permit from the Conaf kiosk at the airport just after you land, or at the Conaf office on the outskirts of Hanga Roa (see opposite); most hotels and travel agencies will also purchase them for you. Along with the permit, you'll receive leaflets warning you not to touch or interfere in any way with the *moai* or the other archeological sites.

road forks, the northern branch looping inland toward Rano Raraku, while the east-bound branch continues to **Ahu Tongariki**, one of the island's most enduring and awe-inspiring images. Consisting of fifteen *moai*, one significantly taller than the rest and another sporting a topknot, the island's largest *moai* site was destroyed by a tsunami in 1960, and re-erected by the Japanese company Tadano between 1992 and 1995.

Rano Raraku

Just inland of Ahu Tongariki lies the unforgettable spectacle of **Rano Raraku** (daily: Dec–March 9am–7pm; April–Nov 9am–6pm; your entry permit will be checked at the ranger's office here): the gigantic quarry where all of Easter Island's *moai* were chiselled out of the tuff (compressed volcanic ash) that makes up the sides of the crater. From the Conaf ranger station, a dirt path leads up to the volcano's slopes, littered with dozens of

---

THE CULT OF THE BIRDMAN

The Birdman cult venerating the creator Make-Make flourished in the eighteenth and nineteenth centuries, up until the 1860s. An important element of the religion was a brutal and dangerous **competition** staged each year between July and September to pick the Tangata Manu, or **Birdman**. Only military chiefs were allowed to compete; they would send their representatives, or *hopu*, on a swim through shark-infested waters to the *motu* (islets) off the coast. The *hopu* would often attempt to stab their rivals on the way. Once on the *motu* the competitors would wait for days to retrieve the first Manutara (sooty tern) egg of the season; the winner would then communicate his victory to those waiting in Orongo. The chosen Birdman then spent the year in complete seclusion, either in one of the houses in the Orongo village or in Anakena, attended to only by a priest, while his family enjoyed an elevated social status and special privileges.

completed *moai*, abandoned on the way to their *ahus*. The right branch meanders between the giant statues, buried in the ground up to their necks, their heads mournfully looking out to sea. You pass *moai* in various stages of completion, including the largest one ever carved, **El Gigante**, 21m tall and 4m wide, its back still joined to the stone from which it was carved. The east end of the path culminates in the kneeling, round-headed **Moai Tukuturi**, the only one of its kind, discovered by Thor Heyerdahl's expedition in 1955.

To the west, the trail winds its way up between wild guava trees into the crater itself, with a dirt path running through knee-high shrubbery alongside the large reed-strewn lake. You may take the footpath up to the crater's eastern rim for unparalleled views of the bay and Ahu Tongariki in the distance, but only if accompanied by a ranger or a guide. There has been increased concern regarding visitor behaviour ever since a Finnish tourist was caught in 2008 while trying to break an ear off a *moai* to take home as a souvenir.

Ovahe Beach

This small, sheltered **beach** is located off a dirt road just before Anakena Beach, on the other side of the Maunga Puha hillock. Backed by tall cliffs, its pristine sands are very popular with locals who come here to picnic, swim and snorkel. It's best earlier in the day, before the cliff blocks the afternoon sun.

Anakena Beach

Easter Island's largest and most popular beach is on the northeast side of the island, and can be reached directly by the paved, cross-island road. A white-sand beach dotted with coconut trees, it has picnic tables and fire pits, public toilets and showers, as well as food stands offering drinks and snacks. The beach is also home to the largest *hare paenga* (boat-shaped house) on the island and is believed to have been the landing point for the legendary King Hotu Matu'a. To the east stands the large, squat *moai* on **Ahu Ature Huki**, re-erected by Thor

Heyerdahl's expedition of 1955 with the help of some islanders, while nearby stand the seven *moai* of **Ahu Nau Nau**, four sporting *pukaos* and two badly damaged. The best time for photographers to visit is in the mid-afternoon.

THE NORTHERN COAST AND THE INNER LOOP

Heading up the coast from the north end of Hanga Roa, a rutted dirt-and-gravel road takes you past **Ana Kakenga**, or Caverna Dos Ventanas – a cave set in the cliff with a spectacular view of the coast. Look for two offshore **islets**, Motu Ko Hepko and Motu Tautara; the cave is directly opposite them, with a cairn indicating the location. Bring a torch if you wish to explore. Further along, at the site of **Ahu Tepeu**, the road turns inland while a path carries on up to a copse of trees. The inland road leads you along fenced-off pasture land to **Ana Te Pahu** on your right-hand side – one of many underground **lava caves** on the island, used as a *manavai* (underground garden) to cultivate bananas, sweet potatoes, taro and other tropical plants due to its moisture and fertile soil.

At the southwestern base of **Maunga Terevaka**, the island's highest point (507m), is **Ahu Akivi**, with seven intact *moai*, the only ones on the island to be looking out to sea. As the road heads south to link up with the island's main thoroughfare, a dirt track to the west takes you to **Puna Pau**, the quarry where the *pukao* were carved.

ARRIVAL AND INFORMATION

By plane LAN, currently the only airline serving Easter Island, has seven to eight weekly flights to/from Santiago (4hr 50min–5hr; 40min), and one to two weekly to/from Papeete, Tahiti (5hr 50min). Return flights from Santiago cost around US$800–1500 if booked from outside Chile; cheaper deals are generally available if you buy your ticket at a LAN office in Chile, via a Chilean travel agent, or in conjunction with a long-distance LAN flight. Mataveri airport is on the southern edge of Hanga Roa, about 1km from the centre; most hotels/hostels will pick you up, if you've booked ahead. The LAN office is at Atamu Tekena and Pont (☎ 32 210 0279, ⓦ lan.com).

4

Conaf Mataveri Otai s/n, south of Hanga Roa (Mon–Sat 9am–3.45pm; ☎ 32 210 0236, ⊛ www.conaf.cl), has information on the Rapa Nui National Park. Conaf ranger stations are found at Rano Raraku, Anakena Beach and Orongo.

Tourist office Policarpo Toro at Tu'u Maheke (Mon–Fri 8.30am–1pm; ☎ 32 210 0255, ✉ ipascua@sernatur.cl). Helpful staff provide detailed information on the island's attractions and can help you organize camping, activities such as horseriding, and vehicle rental. There is a tourist information booth at the airport providing brochures on the island.

GETTING AROUND AND ACTIVITIES

Car, scooter and bicycle rental Many travellers rent a car (from around CH$45,000/day), motorbike (around CH$27,000/day) or even a quad bike (around CH$38,000/day) to explore the island. Book a vehicle as soon as you can after arrival (or even before). Outlets include Oceanic Rent a Car, Atamu Tekena s/n (☎ 32 210 0985, ⊛ rentacaroceanic.cl). Note that there is no car insurance on the island. You can visit some sites on a mountain bike or on foot, though walking around the whole island would present quite a challenge. Several stores on Atamu Tekena, and many hotels, have bikes for rent (generally CH$12,000–15,000/day).

Surfing and diving The established Orca Diving Center (☎ 32 255 0877 or ☎ 32 255 0375, ⊛ orcadivingcenter.cl) and Mike Rapu Diving Centre (☎ 32 255 1055, ⊛ mikerapu.cl), both with offices on the *caleta*, offer a range of scuba-diving (CH$30,000–50,000) and snorkelling (CH$15,000) trips. Hare Orca, next door and attached to the Orca Diving Center, rents out surfboards (CH$15,000/4hr), boogie boards (CH$10,000/4hr) and snorkelling gear (CH$10,000/8hr);

the shop can put you in touch with surfing instructors. Mike Rapu Diving Centre rents out kayaks (CH$15,000/3hr).

ACCOMMODATION

Aloha Nui Guest House Av Atamu Tekena s/n ☎ 32 210 0274, ✉ haumakatours@gmail.com. Run by the couple behind the excellent Haumaka Tours, this tastefully decorated guesthouse has comfortable en suites, a tropical garden, and a well-stocked library filled with books, music and pieces of artwork. Doubles CH$80,000

Aukara Lodge Av Pont s/n ☎ 32 210 0539, ⊛ aukara .cl. Follow the signs for the Aukara art gallery, which showcases the owner's pieces, to this small guesthouse, hidden in the midst of the beautiful garden. The six rooms are comfortable, there's a small kitchen for guests and guided tours of the gallery are available. Doubles CH$60,000

Camping Mihinoa Pont s/n ☎ 32 255 1593, ⊛ mihinoa .com. Large campsite with an excellent ocean view, run by a friendly family, with adjoining showers, kitchen facilities, dining room and car rental; a complete lack of shade is the only drawback. The adjoining guesthouse has basic, clean rooms and a five-bed dorm; you can rent camping gear (CH$6500). Camping/person CH$6500, dorms CH$10,000, doubles CH$20,000

Inaki Uhi Av Atamu Tekena s/n ☎ 32 210 0231, ⊛ inakiuhi.com. As central as it gets, this guesthouse consists of self-contained apartments (for two and five people) and pristine rooms and fully equipped kitchens in two low-slung buildings, with an attractive garden/ sitting area in between and a dining area upstairs where breakfast is served. What the rooms lack in character,

---

EASTER ISLAND TOUR OPERATORS

There is a proliferation of tour operators in Hanga Roa, and touring the archeological sites with a knowledgeable guide, especially if you have limited time on Easter Island, can be very worthwhile. If you are not thrilled at the idea of being cooped up in a minivan, horseriding can be an excellent way of seeing the sites instead. A full-day car tour costs around CH$25,000–40,000, while a day's horseriding can set you back around CH$40,000–50,000.

Aku Aku Turismo Av Tu'u Koihu s/n ☎ 32 210 0770, ⊛ akuakuturismo.cl. Established operator offering standard guided day- and half-day tours of the island's sites, both in 4WDs and on horseback.

Cabalgatas Pantu ☎ 32 210 0577, ⊛ pantupikerauri .cl. Reputable operator offering half- and full-day horseback tours of the west and north coasts, including the ascent of Maunga Terevaka, the island's highest point.

Kia Koe Tour Atamu Tekena s/n ☎ 32 210 0852, ⊛ kiakoetour.cl. Bilingual archeological tours of the island.

Haumaka Archaelogical Tours Puku Rangi Uka s/n ☎ 32 210 0274, ✉ haumakatours@gmail.com. Offers excellent, small-group tours of the island's sites in English, French and German, with extremely well-informed and friendly guides.

Taura'a Tours Atamu Tekena s/n ☎ 32 210 0463, ⊛ tauraahotel.cl. Excellent operator offering full-day, small-group tours of the south coast, including Anakena Beach as well as the principal sites, or the west coast, incorporating the inland *moai* site of Ahu Akivi. English and French spoken; tailor-made tours possible.

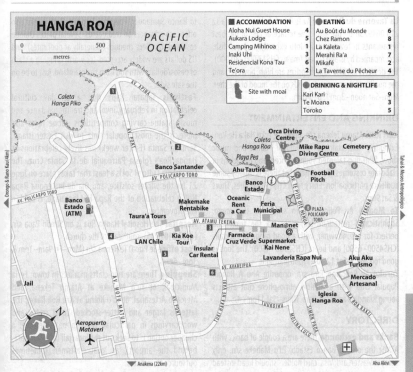

HANGA ROA

PACIFIC
OCEAN

ACCOMMODATION	
Aloha Nui Guest House	4
Aukara Lodge	5
Camping Mihinoa	1
Inaki Uhi	3
Residencial Kona Tau	6
Te'ora	2

EATING	
Au Boût du Monde	6
Chez Ramon	8
La Kaleta	1
Merahi Ra'a	7
Mikafé	2
La Taverne du Pêcheur	4

DRINKING & NIGHTLIFE	
Kari Kari	9
Te Moana	3
Toroko	5

Site with moai

0   500
metres

Caleta Hanga Piko

AV. APINA

Caleta Hanga Roa

Orca Diving Centre

Mike Rapu Diving Centre   Cemetery

Playa Pea

Banco Santander   Ahu Tautira

AV. POLICARPO TORO   Banco Estado   Football Pitch

Banco Estado (ATM)   Makemake Rentabike   Oceanic Rent a Car   Feria Municipal

AV. POLICARPO TORO   PLAZA POLICARPO TORO

Taura'a Tours   Man@net

AV. ATAMU TEKENA

Kia Koe Tour   Farmacia Cruz Verde   Supermarket Kai Nene

LAN Chile   Insular Car Rental   Lavandería Rapa Nui   Aku Aku Turismo

AV. AVAREIPUA   Mercado Artesanal

Jail   Iglesia Hanga Roa

Aeropuerto Mataveri

Anakena (22km)   Ahu Akivi

4

---

the owners more than make up for by being extremely accommodating. Doubles <u>CH$70,000</u>, apartments <u>CH$100,000</u>

Residencial Kona Tau Avareipua s/n ☎ 32 210 0321. HI-affiliated hostel in a large family home with a friendly atmosphere, with thirteen comfortable dorm beds, as well as basic en-suite rooms set in a mango-strewn garden. Large breakfasts are a bonus, but the staff can be hard to find. Dorms <u>CH$15,000</u>, doubles <u>CH$45,000</u>

Te'ora Apina s/n ☎ 32 255 1038, ⌨ rapanuiteora.com. This friendly, good-value Canadian-run place has, amid its gardens, a handful of delightful, spotlessly clean cabins; all come with kitchenettes, private patios and sea views. A laundry service (CH$5000 per load) is also available. <u>CH$40,000</u>

EATING

Chez Ramon Av Te Pito Te Henua s/n. Friendly little restaurant with an overgrown garden, friendly service and a short, straightforward menu. There are five dishes of the day – like fried fish or *cazuela* – for CH$5000 each. Mon–Sat noon–3pm & 7.30–10pm.

La Kaleta Caleta Hanga Roa ☎ 32 255 2244. *La Kaleta*'s wooden deck, right on the water, is a wonderfully romantic place for a meal, particularly around sunset.

The menu is strong on seafood, and dishes (CH$8000–15,000) are beautifully presented. Daily 12.30–3.30pm & 7.30–11pm.

Merahi Ra'a Te Pito O Te Henua s/n. This is the place to come for large servings of the freshest grilled fish, the *mahi mahi* (dorado) being particularly tasty. Fish dishes from CH$10,000. Daily noon–10pm.

Mikafé Caleta Hanga Roa s/n. Tiny café with outdoor seating overlooking the bay featuring the tastiest home-made ice cream (from CH$1800) on the island, as well as exotic fruit juices and banana cake to die for. Mon–Sat 9am–1.30pm & 4.30–9pm.

★ TREAT YOURSELF

Au Boût du Monde Policarpo Toro s/n, north of Caleta Hanga Roa ☎ 32 2552 060. Enjoy excellent sunset views from the extensive upstairs terrace while tucking into inspired dishes (mains CH$10,000–20,000) such as tuna steak in Tahitian vanilla sauce accompanied by island vegetables. The chocolate mousse is also superb. Mon & Wed–Sun 1–2.30pm & 7–10.30pm.

La Taverne du Pêcheur Av Te Pito O Te Henua s/n ☎ 32 210 0619. Sit on the attractive terrace at one of the best restaurants in town and dig into expertly prepared fish, accompanied by island tubers (mains CH$13,000–30,000). The desserts are also superb; prices are high, however, and the quality of the service depends on the mood of the chef. Mon–Sat noon–3pm & 6–11pm.

DRINKING AND ENTERTAINMENT

Kari Kari Atamu Tekena s/n, opposite Tuku Haka He Vari. Extremely entertaining traditional dance-and-music show, featuring talented young dancers and musicians in elaborate costumes. Be warned that there is usually some audience participation. Entry from CH$12,000. Tues, Thurs & Sat 9pm.

Te Moana Av Policarpo Toro s/n, near the *caleta*. Sophisticated restaurant-bar, right on the front and perfect for a sundowner, with a good range of cocktails (CH$4500–6500) and beers (CH$2500–4500). The food is good too. Mon–Sat 12.30–11pm/midnight.

Toroko Av Policarpo Toro s/n, opposite Ahu A Rongo. Popular club with a mellow atmosphere that attracts young islanders and travellers. Thurs–Sat 11pm–4/5am.

DIRECTORY

Banks and exchange There are a couple of banks with ATMS: the one at Banco Estado, Tu'u Maheke s/n, only accepts MasterCard; Visa-card holders should head instead to Banco Santander, Policarpo Toro s/n. Both banks also offer cash advances on credit cards. Several places change cash and travellers' cheques (generally at poor rates), and US dollars are widely accepted. It's worth bringing a stash of pesos/dollars with you from the mainland, just to be on the safe side.

Festivals Tapatai Rapa Nui, a ten-day cultural celebration in February, involving traditional dance and music, statue-carving competitions, canoe races and more, is the most popular time to visit Easter Island. Semana Santa (Easter week) has lively celebrations at Hanga Roa's Iglesia Parroquial de la Santa Cruz. The Ceremonia Culto al Sol is a feast that takes place on June 21 for the winter solstice, and Día de la Lengua Rapa Nui, a celebration of the Rapa Nui language, is held in late November.

Hospital The Hospital Hanga Roa is on Simón Paoa s/n (☎ 32 210 0215), southeast of the church.

Post office Te Pito O Te Henua s/n (Mon–Fri 9am–1pm & 3pm–6pm).

Shopping There are two crafts markets in town: Feria Municipal, at Tu'u Maheke at Atamu Tekena, and Mercado Artesanal, at Tu'u Koihu at Ara Roa Rakei; the latter is larger and better-stocked. Local crafts, and woodcarvings in particular, tend to be expensive; a cheaper option is to seek out the local jail (off Manutara, behind the airport), as local craftsmen sometimes outsource to inmates.

OLD CITY, CARTAGENA

Colombia

HIGHLIGHTS

❶ San Gil The best white-water rafting in Colombia. **See p.512**

❷ Cartagena's old city Spain's most enduring architectural legacy in Latin America. **See p.517**

❸ Parque Nacional Tayrona A paradise of white sandy beaches and falling coconuts. **See p.529**

❹ Providencia Experience the unique Raizal culture on this tiny island. **See p.535**

❺ La Zona Cafetera Stay on an authentic coffee plantation and go hiking in the lovely Valle de Cócora. **See p.546 & p.549**

❻ San Agustín Ponder the mystery behind the Parque Arqueológico's curious statues. **See p.557**

HIGHLIGHTS ARE MARKED ON THE MAP ON P.489

ROUGH COSTS

Daily budget Basic US$50, occasional treat US$90

Drink Fresh fruit juice US$2

Food *Pargo frito con arroz con coco* (fried snapper with coconut rice) US$8

Hostel/budget hotel US$20/40

Travel Bogotá–Cartagena bus (663km; 19hr) US$75

FACT FILE

Population 46.3 million

Languages Spanish (official), plus various indigenous languages

Currency Colombian peso (C$ or COP$)

Capital Bogotá (population: 7.6 million)

International phone code ☏57

Time zone GMT -5hr

5

Introduction

Home to a traumatic but rich history, stunning scenery and some of the continent's most welcoming and sophisticated people, Colombia is a natural draw for travellers to South America. Despite its four-decade-long civil war and reputation for violence, improved security conditions have led to a sharp increase in tourism. Foreigners and Colombians alike are now far more able to explore this thrilling paradise of cloudforested mountains, palm-fringed beaches and gorgeous colonial cities. The only country in South America to border both the Pacific and the Caribbean, Colombia offers a huge range of ecosystems, from the Amazon rainforest near Leticia to the snowcapped mountains of the Sierra Nevada de Santa Marta and the tropical islands of San Andrés and Providencia.

Cosmopolitan **Bogotá** is, like most capitals, a busy commercial centre, with a vibrant cultural scene and festive nightlife. The two other major cities, **Medellín** and **Cali**, are also lively but less overwhelming. Better still are the small towns scattered throughout the country that could turn out to be the highlight of your visit. **Popayán** and **Mompox**, for example, are famed for raucous Semana Santa (Easter week) celebrations, and Mompox has a timeless beauty to it. Colombia's coffee-growing region, the **Zona Cafetera**, offers breathtaking walks in the foothills where the bean is grown, accommodation in authentic *fincas* (coffee farms) and excellent trekking.

Most visitors make time – and rightfully so – to head north to the Caribbean for the sun. Just a stone's throw from the beach, the walled city of **Cartagena** is the biggest Spanish colonial port in South America. A few hours east, the less scenic **Santa Marta** and fishing village of **Taganga** are near **Parque Nacional Tayrona**, whose picturesque sandy beaches are unrivalled. The two are also great bases for a five-day trek to the archeological ruins of **La Ciudad Perdida**, the Lost City.

Almost un-Colombian in their feel, the remote Caribbean islands of **San Andrés** and **Providencia** both offer great diving, crystal-clear waters and – particularly in Providencia's case – a unique Raizal culture.

As you head north from Bogotá through the Andes to **Bucaramanga**, picturesque colonial villages like **Villa de Leyva** give way to more tropical, river-fed bastions of adventure tourism such as **San Gil**.

In the southeast, Colombia's stake of the Amazon, centred on **Leticia**, may not be as well known as Peru's or Brazil's but it offers a slice of jungle adventure and a gateway into the neighbouring countries. The southwest, near Popayán, boasts some wonderful scenery as well as the monumental stone statues and burial chambers of the forgotten cultures of **San Agustín** and **Tierradentro**.

WHEN TO VISIT

Colombia's proximity to the equator keeps regional **temperatures** stable throughout the year, around 24°C (75°F) along the coast and 7–17°C (45–63°F) as you move higher inland. However, **rainfall** does vary with the seasons. In the Andean region there are two dry and two wet seasons per year, the driest months being from December to March and July to August. In low-lying areas, especially southern Colombia, rainfall is more constant but showers never last very long. The Amazon climate is uniformly wet the entire year. Bear in mind that the most intense **tourist seasons**, with the highest prices, are from December to February and Semana Santa (Easter Week), the week before Easter.

CHRONOLOGY

10,000 BC Earliest evidence of human habitation at El Abra in present-day Bogotá.

1200 BC–1525 AD Indigenous cultures – including the Tayrona, Calima, Muisca, Quimbaya, Nariño and others – live scattered across the country.

700 AD The Tayrona build the Ciudad Perdida – their largest city.

1499 Alonso de Ojeda sets foot at Cabo de la Vela.

1525 Rodrigo de Bastidas establishes the first Spanish settlement in Santa Marta, kicking off the hunt for El Dorado.

1533 The Spanish found Cartagena.

1537–38 Spanish conquistador Gonzalo Jiménez de Quesada wrests power (and staggering amounts of gold and emeralds) from the native Chibchas and founds Santa Fe de Bogotá, now known simply as Bogotá.

1717 The Spanish consolidate their colonial holdings, creating the viceroyalty of Nueva Granada from the land now occupied by the independent nations of Colombia, Ecuador, Panama and Venezuela.

1819 Simón de Bolívar overthrows Spanish rule and founds Gran Colombia, comprised of Colombia, Ecuador, Venezuela and Panama. He becomes its first president, thus fulfilling his desire for a united, independent South America.

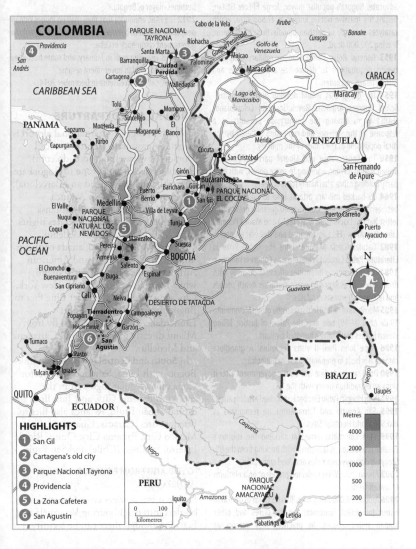

HIGHLIGHTS

1. San Gil
2. Cartagena's old city
3. Parque Nacional Tayrona
4. Providencia
5. La Zona Cafetera
6. San Agustín

5

1830 Ecuador and Venezuela secede from Gran Colombia. Bolívar dies in self-imposed exile in Santa Marta.

1853 Colombia adopts a constitution that includes a prohibition against slavery.

1886 Nueva Granada becomes the Republic of Colombia, after Christopher Columbus.

1899–1902 The War of a Thousand Days, the bloody three-year-long civil war born of escalated antagonism between the Conservative and Liberal political parties.

1903 With the support of the US navy, Panama secedes from Colombia.

1948 The assassination of the working class's greatest advocate, Bogotá's populist mayor, Jorge Eliécer Gaitán, begins the massive rioting known as *El Bogotazo*, which catalyzes a decade of partisan bloodletting, *La Violencia*, leaving 200,000 dead.

1953 General Rojas Pinilla leads a military coup and begins negotiations to demobilize armed groups and restore peace and order.

1954 The group that would develop into Communist-linked Fuerzas Armadas Revolucionarios Colombianos (FARC) forms among the countryside peasants as a response to the violence and repression suffered by the rural population at the hands of the military.

1958 The Conservative and Liberal parties become a united National Front, agreeing to share power, with each party holding office alternately for four years.

1964 US-backed military attacks lead to violent clashes between the government and armed guerrilla groups. The leftist National Liberation Army (ELN) and Maoist People's Liberation Army (EPL) are founded and civil war erupts.

1982 Gabriel García Márquez wins the Nobel Prize in Literature. Pablo Escobar is elected as a Congress member.

1984 The government intensifies efforts to do away with drug cartels, as violence by narco-trafficker death squads and left-wing terrorists escalates.

1985 Members of radical leftist guerrilla group Movimiento 19 de Abril (M-19) take over the Palace of Justice, killing eleven judges and nearly a hundred civilians.

1986 Pope John Paul II visits Colombia. A grandiose cathedral is built in preparation in Chiquinquirá.

1990 Drug cartels declare war on the government after it signs an extradition treaty with the US.

1993 Drug kingpin Pablo Escobar is shot dead evading arrest.

1995 San Agustin and Tierradentro are recognized as UNESCO World Heritage Sites.

1999 Plan Colombia, aimed at tackling the country's cocaine production, is launched, with backing from the US. Spraying destroys coca fields and food crops alike.

2002 Álvaro Uribe Vélez is elected president on a platform of law and order.

2006 Around 20,000 AUC paramilitaries claim to disarm in return for lenient sentences for massacres and other human rights abuses. In practice, they reform as neo-paramilitary groups such as Los Rastrojos, and the drug trafficking, murders and land grabbing continues.

2008 The US and Venezuela assist in a government-orchestrated operation to free high-profile kidnapping victims. French-Colombian presidential candidate Ingrid Betancourt, held hostage for six years, and fifteen other captives are liberated. FARC founder Manuel Marulanda dies.

2010 Following Uribe's failed attempt to run for a third term, former Defence Minister Juan Manuel Santos is elected president.

2011 Former leader of the M-19 guerrillas, Gustavo Petro, becomes mayor of Bogotá.

2012 The FARC announce that they shall no longer kidnap people. Negotiations between the FARC and the Colombian government commence in Cuba.

2013 FARC ceasefire ends in January, and some hostilities against the Colombian government resume.

2014 FARC calls for a ceasefire in December 2014.

ARRIVAL AND DEPARTURE

Colombia's biggest international **airport** is Bogatá's Aeropuerto Internacional El Dorado (Ⓦwww.elnuevodorado.com). Direct services **from Europe** to Bogotá are offered by Iberia (Madrid and Barcelona), Air France/KLM (Paris), Avianca (Barcelona and Paris) and Lufthansa (Frankfurt). Avianca also operates flights from Madrid to Cali and Medellín.

In **North America**, Air Canada connects Toronto to Bogotá, Lan and American Airlines connect Bogotá with Miami, while Delta links Bogotá with New York, Chicago and Atlanta, and Jet Blue flies to Bogotá from Orlando and Fort Lauderdale. It's also possible to fly from Miami directly to Santa Marta, Cartagena and Medellín.

In **South and Central America**, Lan links Bogotá with Lima, Santiago and Quito; Copa offers regular flights from the capital to Panama City, and Tam links the capital to São Paulo. Avianca also flies to Buenos Aires, Caracas, Guayaquil, Lima, Mexico City, Panama City, Quito, Rio de Janeiro, Santiago (Chile) and São Paulo.

OVERLAND FROM ECUADOR AND VENEZUELA

Frequent bus services cross Colombia's borders into neighbouring Venezuela and Ecuador, though there can be security

5

issues with both borders, so check in advance. Ormeño buses cover several international routes to and from Bogotá, including Quito, Caracas and Lima.

There are three main overland **border crossings** with Venezuela (see box, p.516), the most popular being Cúcuta–San Antonio/San Cristóbal. The **Maicao–Maracaibo** crossing at Paraguachón is useful if you are travelling directly to or from Colombia's Caribbean coast. Expreso Brasilia (Ⓦexpresobrasilia .com) operates a coastal bus service between Cartagena, via Barranquilla and Santa Marta, which passes through Maicao in the remote Guajira Peninsula to Maracaibo (1 daily at 7am; 20hr).

The Panamerican Highway runs south into **Ecuador**, with the Ipiales–Tulcán crossing being the most popular and straightforward (see box, p.560).

There is no overland crossing between Colombia and Panama due to the presence of drug traffickers, paramilitaries and smugglers, and the threat of kidnapping in the Darién Gap.

BY BOAT TO/FROM BRAZIL, PERU AND PANAMA

From the Amazon region it's possible to cross to or from Colombia into Manaus, Brazil, and Iquitos, Peru, by taking a **riverboat** (see p.564).

From Cartagena, adventurous travellers can take the new **ferry service** to Colón in Panama with Success Panama Tours (18hr; from COP$108,000 one-way/ person; Ⓦsuccesspanamatours.com).

VISAS

A passport and onward ticket are the sole entry requirements for nationals of most Western European countries, Canada, the US, Australia, New Zealand and South Africa.

Upon arrival, all visitors receive an entry stamp in their passports, usually for **sixty days**. You can request up to ninety days but this is rarely granted. Double-check the stamp straightaway for errors. Make sure you get an entry stamp if coming in overland and that you get a departure stamp upon exiting to avoid trouble.

Thirty-day **extensions** cost COP$78,300 (Ⓦwww.migracion colombia.gov.co). You'll need two passport photos with a white background, copies of your passport and entry stamp as well as the original, and an onward ticket.

GETTING AROUND

Colombia's generally reliable and numerous **buses** are your best bet for intercity travel, though increased competition between domestic airlines means that **air travel** is frequently only slightly more expensive and far faster and more comfortable.

BY BUS, PICK-UP TRUCK AND JEEP

There's a wide range of options in comfort and quality for **buses**; it's a good idea to shop around at different companies' kiosks within larger stations. Generally, the larger, long-distance buses have reclining seats, toilets, loud cheesy music and videos; wear warm clothing as air-conditioning is guaranteed to be arctic. Some recommended companies are: Expreso Bolívariano (Ⓦbolivariano .com.co), Expreso Brasilia (Ⓦexpresobrasilia.com), Expreso Palmira (Ⓦexpresopalmira.com.co), Berlinas (Ⓦwww.berlinasdelfonce.com), Copetran (Ⓦcopetran.com.co) and Flota Magdalena (Ⓦflotamagdalena.com), though different companies cover different parts of the country. Long-distance buses tend to stop at *requisas* (military checkpoints), sometimes at night; the soldiers sometimes search everyone's possessions and make everyone disembark and show their ID. Each city has a *terminal de buses* (bus terminal) where the intercity buses arrive; Bogotá has more than one.

For shorter trips, you're better off sacrificing comfort and price for speed by buying a ticket on a *buseta*, *colectivo* or any similarly sized minibus or minivan that departs when full. If you don't want to be waiting around for ages, don't hand over your luggage or pay unless you can see that a bus is nearly full and ready to depart.

In the coffee-growing areas in particular, the most common mode of transport is

5

the hardy **Willy jeeps**, with two rows of seats in the covered interior and more passengers clinging to the back. These tend to be inexpensive, but the ride can be bumpy and you are squeezed in with mounds of luggage.

BY PLANE

There are more than half a dozen domestic airlines. Avianca (Wavianca .com) serves the greatest number of domestic destinations. Copa (Wcopaair .com), the second-largest airline, covers largely the same destinations and flies to San Andres. Satena (Wsatena.com) offers flights to the Amazon, the Pacific coast and between San Andrés and Providencia.

Budget carrier EasyFly (Weasyfly.com .co) serves Bogotá, Barranquilla, Cartagena, Cúcuta, Medellín and Santa Marta; Lan (Wlan.com) flies to all the major cities as well as smaller regional destinations, while new VivaColombia (Wvivacolombia.co) is the only one to connect Medellín directly to Santa Marta.

A useful website to compare airline fares is Wlostiquetesmasbaratos.com.

Booking in advance doesn't necessarily guarantee a low fare (except during Semana Santa). A one-way fare between Santa Marta and Bogotá purchased a day – or a month – in advance costs about COP$200,000–300,000 (in high season).

ACCOMMODATION

Accommodation ranges considerably, but given the country's relative prosperity you'll be pleasantly surprised at the bargains available. **Backpacker hostels** are prolific, particularly in larger cities such as Bogotá, Medellín, Cali and Santa Marta, and prices start at around COP$19,000 for dorms and COP$45,000 for double rooms. Comfortable beds, shared kitchens, free wi-fi, book exchanges, laundry, cable TV and stacks of DVDs are common, and hostels are often the best places to find out about local attractions; some rent bicycles and even horses. **Guesthouses** rarely cost more than COP$90,000 for a double room with private bathroom.

Camping is an option in some rural areas and national parks, particularly Parque Nacional Tayrona on the Caribbean coast and Parque Nacional Cocuy in the highlands. Be aware that many campsites don't rent tents (or rent substandard ones), so it's best to bring your own if you plan to camp regularly. If you hike to the Ciudad Perdida (see p.531) you'll get to sleep in hammocks with mosquito nets.

In the coffee-growing region, you can stay on one of the stately **fincas**, coffee-growing plantations that have barely changed over the decades. Though these farms range from tiny to sleek, modernized operations, the majority are small estates that offer comfortable accommodation for a moderate price (COP$25,000–45,000 per room). Meals prepared from locally grown food as well as numerous outdoor activities, like farm tours and horseriding, are often included or available.

FOOD AND DRINK

Whether it's a platter full of starch or a suckling pig stuffed with rice, Colombian **food** is anything but light. Breakfast usually consists of *huevos pericos*, scrambled eggs with onion and tomatoes, accompanied by a fried maize pancake (*arepa*) stuffed with chopped pork, rice, potatoes and more. The midday *almuerzo* or *comida corriente* consists of soup, a main course and dessert. Dinners, after 6pm, also tend to involve meat or fish.

In Bogotá and other major cities there is an excellent array of Western and international cuisine.

LOCAL SPECIALITIES

Each region in Colombia has its own local speciality. The national dish is the *bandeja paisa* – an enormous platter of ground beef, chorizo, beans (*frijoles*), rice, fried banana (*plátano*), a fried egg, avocado and fried pork – usually found at inexpensive **market stalls** (*fondas*).

In rural areas, vegetarians will be hard-pressed for options, but in medium and large cities you can find a decent spread of vegetarian dishes.

Other Colombian favourites include *ajiaco* (a thick chicken stew replete with vegetables, maize, three types of potato, cream, capers and sometimes avocado), and *mazamorra* (a similar meat and vegetable soup but with beans and corn flour). Both are often served with *patacón*, a mashed and heavily salted cake of fried plantain.

More unusual regional specialities include *hormigas culonas* – fried giant ants, found in the Santander area. In Cali and southern Colombia, grilled guinea pig, known as *cuy* or *curi*, sometimes crops up on the menu. The coast is renowned for its fish and shellfish, served with aromatic *arroz con coco*, slightly sweet rice with caramelized coconut, while the Amazon is known for its unusual and delicious fish. The islands of San Andrés and Providencia specialize in locally caught crab dishes and lobster.

DRINKING

Though Colombia used to export its best **coffee**, demand from travellers has led to a proliferation of Juan Valdéz café branches; good coffee is now available in other establishments as well, though the majority of Colombians still drink heavily sugared, watered-down black coffee (*tinto*).

If there's one thing you'll pine for when you've returned home it's Colombia's exotic variety of **fresh fruit juices**. Some are completely foreign to Western palates and lack English translations. Worth trying are *guanábana*, *lulo*, mango, *feijoa*, *maracuyá*, *mora* and *guayaba*.

Beer is reasonably good and inexpensive (try light, fizzy lagers like Dorado, Club and Aguila). Far more popular among locals is the anise-flavoured *aguardiente*, pure grain alcohol, and rum (*ron*), both of which are drunk neat. Brave souls won't want to pass up any offer to try *chicha*, a frothy drink, often prepared with maize or yucca, found in rural areas and made with the fermenting enzyme found in saliva: pieces of the peeled root are chewed, spat into a bowl and the juice is left to ferment.

CULTURE AND ETIQUETTE

In Colombia you will notice a great disparity between the wealthiest members of society – who live a lifestyle akin to that of their counterparts in Europe's capitals – and the rest of the population: the poor city residents who live in dangerous neighbourhoods, and below them on the poverty scale the rural poor, particularly those who live in isolated areas where armed conflict still goes on.

When interacting with Colombians, Westerners will note that sincerity in expression, often expressed via good eye contact, is valued more highly than the typical steady stream of pleases and thank yous.

Tipping ten percent at mid-range restaurants is the norm; some establishments will ask you if you'd like for the tip to be included when you ask for the bill, while some add it on

---

TROPICAL FRUIT TREAT

Dotting the country's streets are vendors who will happily blend drinks for you from the juicy bounty in their baskets, either with milk (*con leche*), or the standard ice and sugar (*con agua*).

Corozo A round, maroon-skinned fruit, not unlike a cranberry in tartness.

Guanabaná Pulpy, yellow fruit that tastes like a mild guava, with a touch of grapefruit.

Lulo Resembling a vivid yellow persimmon, this tangy fruit is perfectly balanced sweetness and tartness.

Mora Close cousin of the blackberry.

Níspero This combination of pear and musky, and goes really papaya is rich and musky, and goes really

well with milk.

Tomate de árbol Literally, "tree tomato", this orange-red fruit blurs the line between fruit and vegetable, being sharp and only faintly sweet.

Zapote This luscious orange fruit's uncanny resemblance to sherbet is confirmed by the tendency of some locals to freeze its pulp to eat as dessert.

5

LOCAL SLANG

Colombians take much joy in their particular style of linguistic acrobatics and slang. Colombians freely convert verbs to nouns and vice versa, so take each word as a fluid concept.

Un camello (n), **camellar** (v) Work, or working. A good way to refer to a particularly trying task.

La/una chimba (adj) Used to describe a situation or thing that is wonderful. Roughly synonymous with the youthful American usage of "awesome". Variations include "Qué chimba!" ("Nice!").

Chucha (n) Body odour. A crass but still useable term.

Elegante (adj) "Cool", loosely. Used to describe the subset of cool things – or happenings – that's particularly classy, well executed or elegant. Think football passes or a good outfit. *Chevere* and *bacán* are other words for "cool".

Paila (adj) "That really sucks". Used in response to a comment or situation that's aggressively bad or heavy.

Perico (n) Cocaine. Regional translations include scrambled eggs, coffee with milk or (as here) a parakeet.

Al pelo (adj) Common response to a question like "How was your day?" that means "Good!" or "Perfect!"

---

automatically. For short taxi trips, round up to the nearest thousand pesos.

The **machismo** often ascribed to Latin American culture is present in Colombia, though a significant number (around 30 percent) of politicians and diplomats are female. The country's Catholic roots run quite deep and are apparent in sexual attitudes among both men and women, though there is some flexibility – and contradiction – in views toward gender and sexual orientation.

SPORTS AND OUTDOOR ACTIVITIES

Adrenaline junkies might hyperventilate when they discover Colombia. From almost every vantage point there's a snowcapped peak to climb, an untamed river to ride or some sunken coral reef to explore.

Colombia's waters are a good (and cheap) place to learn to **scuba dive**. All along its 3000km of coastline, but especially around Santa Marta and Taganga, and also on the islands of San Andres and Providencia – home to the world's third-largest barrier reef – operators offer week-long PADI certification courses for around COP$650,000. Be sure to enquire about the reputation of dive operators before signing up, check their PADI or NAUI accreditation, the instructor-to-student ratio and ask for recommendations from other divers. Snorkelling is also particularly good on the islands.

There is a concentration of Class II–IV rapids among the many rivers in the *departamento* of Santander – three intersect near San Gil – that offer some spectacular challenges to **white-water rafting** enthusiasts (see p.512), while the river near San Agustin gives you a somewhat tamer ride.

Hiking in Colombia is second to none: there are demanding week-long adventures in Parque Nacional de Cocuy (see p.515), jungle treks to the spectacular ruins of Ciudad Perdida (see p.531), and shorter but no less attractive rambles around Manizales and Salento in coffee country.

TEJO

Colombia's own native sport is **tejo**, which involves throwing a hefty iron puck at a target embedded in a box of clay. In the middle is the bull's-eye (*balazo*), with four little packets of gunpowder (*mecha*) placed around it. The game works on a system of points – hitting the bull's-eye gets six points, exploding one of the *mechas* scores three, and getting closer to the bull's-eye than any other player nets one point. You'll find *tejo* bars in most towns and cities. Beginners are best off playing together rather than trying to pitch in with local *tejo* experts. Normally it's free to play and you just pay for your drinks.

Football is the national sport and Colombians have a reputation for being some of South America's most skilled players. Cycling is also a common passion – the mountainous land here is made for rugged biking – and Colombians regularly compete in the Tour de France.

COMMUNICATIONS

The three major **mobile phone** networks are Movistar, Claro and Tigo, and it's inexpensive to purchase a local mobile phone: a basic handset will set you back around COP$50,000–60,000; if you have an unlocked phone, a SIM card will set your back around COP$12,000, with around COP$5000 worth of credit, with top-up credits sold in every corner shop. However, it's cheapest to make **domestic long-distance calls** using the mobile phones in corner stores that buy minutes in bulk (look for the word "*minutos*"). Call centres (*telecentros*) allow you to make inexpensive calls both to local numbers and abroad, though Skype is by far the cheapest way to go, given the proliferation of free wi-fi.

Internet cafés can be found even in small towns (from COP$3000/hr), and free wi-fi spots are becoming easier to find.

For **postal services**, packages are best sent via private companies such as Avianca (Ⓦaviancaexpress.com) and Deprisa (Ⓦdeprisa.com).

CRIME AND SAFETY

Colombia today is far safer and more accessible than it has been in decades. That said, pockets of guerrilla activity remain in remote parts of the country, particularly the jungle – a haven for drug-running activities – both by the rebels and particularly by the paramilitary groups who have the tacit support of the government, and who have been criticized for using techniques as dirty as those employed by the rebels. The FARC have renounced **kidnappings** for financial or political ends, but it remains to be seen whether they'll remain true to their word. Although, reassuringly, tourists have not been targeted specifically in the country's

civil war, **certain areas should still be avoided**, including most of the Chocó, parts of Nariño, Putumayo, most of Meta, Arauca and rural parts of Cauca. Most guerrilla/paramilitary activity is confined to rural areas near the border with Panama and Venezuela. However, it's imperative that you stay abreast of current events: for up-to-date travel advice check Ⓦwww.travel.state.gov or Ⓦwww.gov.uk/fco.

Violent crime does exist, particularly in poor neighbourhoods of the big cities, but visitors are far more likely to encounter pickpockets, so keep a sharp eye on your belongings. Beware of **scams** – such as criminals posing as plain-clothes policemen and asking to inspect your passport and money, allegedly in search of counterfeit notes, which they then confiscate. Counterfeit notes do exist, so ask locals how to identify them.

When out and about, take only as much cash as you need for the outing, and leave the rest (as well as your passport) in a safe in your lodgings. Always carry **a photocopy of your passport** with you – the main page and the page with your entry stamp. Local police have a mixed reputation for corruption.

Drugs are a sensitive subject in Colombia, and considering the harm it's done to their country, both in terms of criminal activity and environmental damage, it's no surprise that the majority of Colombians are strongly against cocaine use in particular. Even so, drugs are widely available, cocaine and marijuana especially. Possession of both is illegal and could result in a prison

5

EMERGENCY NUMBERS
Police/ambulance/fire ☎ 123

sentence, and being caught with drugs while trying to cross a border can have very serious consequences. If you do decide to take drugs, be very careful: they are much stronger than in Europe and the US.

Some tourists try the psychedelic jungle brew, *ayahuasca*, which is not illegal but can be potentially hazardous. While some *ayahuasca* ceremonies are indeed conducted by genuine indigenous shamans, there are a lot of cowboys about, and going off with such people can be dangerous. Take this seriously: in 2014 a British tourist died after taking *ayahuasca* in Colombia, as did an American tourist in Peru in 2012.

Do not accept drinks, snacks or cigarettes from strangers as there have been reports of these being spiked with the tasteless and smell-free drug *burundanga*, or "zombie drug", that leaves victims conscious but incapacitated and susceptible to robbery and rape.

HEALTH

Vaccinations against hepatitis A, hepatitis B and typhoid are strongly recommended and rabies should also be considered; consult a travel health clinic weeks in advance. Vaccinations against **yellow fever** are necessary if visiting coastal national parks; some countries, such as Australia and Brazil, will not let you into the country without a yellow fever certificate if you're travelling directly from Colombia. Insect-borne diseases such as **malaria** and **dengue fever** are present, particularly in the Amazonas, Chocó, Antioquia, Córdoba, Bolívar, Putomayo and Atlántico departments. A new mosquito-borne illness **Chikungunya** has mostly affected the Caribbean region of Colombia. The illness is characterized by sudden onset of very high fever, rash, and severe joint pain usually lasting a week. Although non-fatal, the joint pain can be so severe it can be hard to walk. Victims are usually bed-bound. Seek medical help immediately to combat the fever and pain. Bring plenty of mosquito repellent (50 percent DEET, unavailable in Colombia) and cover up with long sleeves and trousers.

Altitude sickness (*soroche*) may affect travellers at altitudes over 2500m, including those flying directly to Bogotá – take time to acclimatize before continuing your journey, drink plenty of water and avoid alcohol.

Colombia offers some of the best healthcare in South America; all major cities have **hospitals**, while in rural areas healthcare is more difficult to come by. In the case of serious health issues, you may be transferred to a larger hospital with more specialized doctors and facilities.

INFORMATION AND MAPS

Despite the significant rise in tourism to Colombia in recent years, the practical information available at tourist offices is often rudimentary. Almost every town has a tourist office, although their staff often don't speak English, and hostels are often much more helpful.

PUBLIC HOLIDAYS

January 1 New Year's Day (*Año Nuevo*)
January 6 Epiphany (*Día de los Reyes Magos*)
March 21 St Joseph's Day (Father's Day)
March or April Easter (*Semana Santa*)
May 1 Labour Day (*Día del Trabajo*)
May Ascension Day (the Monday six weeks and a day after Easter Sunday)
May/June Corpus Christi (the Monday nine weeks and a day after Easter Sunday)
June 29 Saint Peter and Saint Paul (*San Pedro y San Pablo*)
July 20 Independence Day
August 7 Battle of Boyacá
August 15 Assumption of the Virgin Mary (*Asunción de la Virgen*)
October 12 Columbus Day (*Día de la Raza*)
November 1 All Saints' Day (*Día de Todos los Santos*)
November 11 Independence of Cartagena
December 8 Immaculate Conception (*Inmaculada Concepción*)
December 25 Christmas Day (*Navidad*)

5

COLOMBIA'S FESTIVAL PLANNER

Colombia knows how to party and does so year-round. You can join in the following:

January *Carnaval de Blancos y Negros*. Pasto's un-PC celebrations dating back to the days of slavery, with revellers with whitened and blackened faces throwing chalk and flour over each other.

February *Carnaval de Barranquilla*. Second-biggest carnival in South America, complete with parades, dancing, drinking and music, held forty days before Easter.

March *Semana Santa*. Holy Week celebrated with night-time processions by the faithful; particularly impressive in Popayán and Mompox

June/July *Rock al Parque*. Massive free

thee-day pop/rock/funk/metal/reggae concert in Bogotá's Parque Simón Bolívar.

August *Feria de las Flores*. Medellín's big bash, culminating in a parade of peasants bearing flowers down from the mountains.

September *Festival Mundial de Salsa*. Cali's salsa festival, with the hottest moves on show at the Teatro al Aire Libre Los Cristales

November *Reinado Nacional de Belleza*. Cartagena crowns Miss Colombia amid parades, street dancing and music

December *Feria de Cali*. Epic street parties.

March 21 St Joseph's Day (Father's Day).

In Colombia, the annually updated (Spanish only) *Guía de Rutas*, sold at tollbooths and some tourist offices, has excellent maps, as well as potential road-trip routes and extensive local listings.

MONEY AND BANKS

Colombia's national currency is the **peso** (**COP**), divided into 100 centavos. Coins are for 50, 100, 200, 500 and 1000 pesos and notes for 1000, 2000, 5000, 10,000, 20,000 and 50,000 pesos. At the time of writing, rates were: US$1=COP$2400; £1=COP$3600; €1=COP$2800.

Changing large notes can be problematic outside big cities.

ATMs are plentiful, with at least one even in small towns. For **changing money**, casas de cambio offer slightly better rates, have more flexible hours and provide quicker service than most banks. Travellers' cheques can also be exchanged at casas de cambios and banks, but few businesses accept them. Using moneychangers on the street is not recommended.

OPENING HOURS

Shops are open 8am until 6pm, Monday to Friday. Many businesses also often open on Saturdays until mid-afternoon. Outside Bogotá many businesses close at noon for a two- or three-hour siesta. Commercial hours in cities in warmer

areas such as Cali often get started and end earlier. Government offices often follow the same pattern. Banks open around 9am and close at 4pm.

Bogotá and around

Colombia's capital, **BOGOTÁ**, is a city that divides opinion. Its detractors cite poverty, gridlock traffic and crime, as well as depressingly regular rain, and with 7.6 million tightly packed inhabitants and some decidedly drab neighbourhoods, Bogotá rarely elicits love at first sight. Given a day or two, however, most people do fall for this cosmopolitan place with its colonial architecture, numerous restaurants and raucous nightlife. Besides, love it or hate it, odds are you'll have to pass through it at some stage during your travels in Colombia.

Situated on the **Sabana de Bogotá**, Colombia's highest plateau at 2600m, the city was founded on August 6, 1538 by Gonzalo Jiménez de Quesada in what was a former citadel belonging to the Muisca king **Bacatá**, from whom the city's name is derived. For many years, Bogotá's population did not expand in step with its political influence, and even in the 1940s the city had just 300,000 inhabitants. That all changed in the second half of the twentieth century, thanks to industrialization and civil war, which prompted a mass exodus of peasants from rural areas who live in dire conditions in the slums on the southern approach to the city – in marked contrast to the affluent neighbourhoods in the northern part of town. Today, Bogotá is South America's fourth-largest city and home to one of the continent's most vibrant cultural scenes.

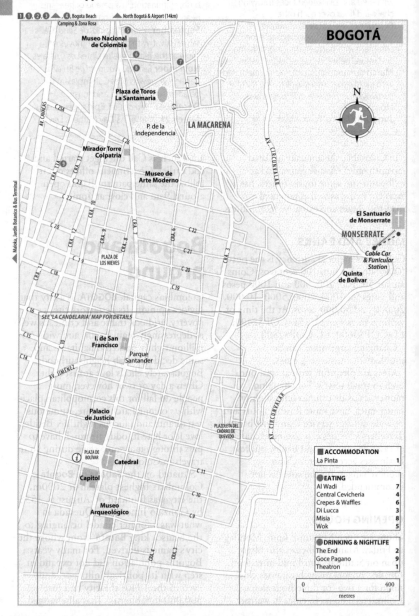

BOGOTÁ

Bogota Beach Camping & Zona Rosa

North Bogotá & Airport (14km)

Museo Nacional de Colombia

Plaza de Toros La Santamaria

LA MACARENA

P. de la Independencia

Mirador Torre Colpatria

Museo de Arte Moderno

El Santuario de Monserrate

MONSERRATE

Cable Car & Funicular Station

Quinta de Bolívar

PLAZA DE LOS NIEVES

Maloka, Jardín Botanico & Bus Terminal

SEE 'LA CANDELARIA' MAP FOR DETAILS

I. de San Francisco

Parque Santander

AV. JIMENEZ

Palacio de Justicia

PLAZOLETA DEL CHORRO DE QUEVEDO

PLAZA DE BOLÍVAR

Catedral

Capitol

Museo Arqueológico

ACCOMMODATION	
La Pinta	1

EATING	
Al Wadi	7
Central Cevicheria	4
Crepes & Waffles	6
Di Lucca	3
Misia	8
Wok	5

DRINKING & NIGHTLIFE	
The End	2
Goce Pagano	9
Theatron	1

0   400
metres

A WORD ON GETTING AROUND

Getting around Bogotá – and all Colombian cities for that matter – is facilitated by a foolproof **numbering system**, derived from the original Spanish grid layout, which makes finding an address virtually arithmetic. The names of the streets indicate their direction: **calles** (abbreviated C) run at right angles to the hills, from east to west, while **carreras** (abbreviated Cra) run from north to south. Addresses are a function of both, with the prefix indicating the cross street. For example, the address Cra 73 no. 12–20 can be found on Carrera 73 at number 20, between calles 12 and 12B. To make matters a little confusing, in La Candelaria, C 13 doesn't follow C 12; there are streets labelled 12 A–12 D in between.

WHAT TO SEE AND DO

The city's historic centre, **La Candelaria**, is full of colourfully painted colonial residences. It begins at Plaza de Bolívar and stretches northward to Avenida Jiménez de Quesada, and is bordered by Cra 10 to the west and the mountains to the east. **Downtown Bogotá** is the commercial centre, with office buildings and several museums, while **North Bogotá**, a catch-all term for the wealthier neighbourhoods to the north of the centre, offers stylish shopping districts and enough dining options to suit most palates and wallets.

Plaza de Bolívar

The heart of La Candelaria is the **Plaza de Bolívar**, awhirl with street vendors, llamas, pigeons and visitors; in the evenings, street-food carts set up shop by the cathedral. A pigeon-defiled statue of El Libertadór stands at its centre, surrounded by monumental buildings in disparate architectural styles spanning more than four centuries, most covered with political graffiti.

On the south side stands the Neoclassical **Capitol**, where the Congress meets, with its imposing, colonnaded stone facade. On the plaza's north side is the modern **Palacio de Justicia**, which was reconstructed in 1999 after the original was damaged during the army's much-criticized storming of the building in 1985, in response to the M-19 guerrilla takeover, with more than a hundred people killed in the raid.

Every Friday from 5pm, Cra 7 is closed to traffic from Plaza de Bolívar all the way to C 26, and the streets fill with performers, food vendors and *Cachacos* (Bogotá natives). The **Septimazo**, as it is called, is people-watching at its best.

Catedral

Looming over the Plaza de Bolívar, Bogotá's Neoclassical **Catedral** (daily 9am–5pm; free; ⓦcatedraldebogota.org) supposedly stands on the site where the first Mass was celebrated in 1538. Rebuilt over the centuries after several collapses, it was completed in 1823, and while its interior is gold-laced, it's still relatively austere compared to the capital's other churches. You'll find the tomb of Jiménez de Quesada, Bogotá's founder, in the largest chapel.

Casa de Nariño

A couple of blocks south of Plaza de Bolívar, between Cra 7 and 8, is the heavily fortified presidential palace and compound, **Casa de Nariño**, done in the style of Versailles. This is where President Santos currently lives and works. To take part in a guided visit (3–6 visits daily; ID required; ⓦwww.presidencia.gov.co), book online – look for "Visitas Casa de Nariño" on the website. It's also possible to watch the ceremonial changing of the guard three times a week (Wed, Fri & Sun at 4pm) – best viewed from the east side of the palace.

Museo Botero

Housed in a fine colonial mansion surrounding a lush courtyard, the **Museo Botero** (C 11 no. 4–41; Mon & Wed–Sat 9am–7pm, Sun 10am–5pm; free; ⓦbanrepcultural.org/museo-botero) contains one of Latin America's largest collections of modern and Impressionist art, donated in 2000 by Colombia's most celebrated artist, Fernando Botero. There are no fewer than 123 paintings and sculptures by Medellín-born Botero himself, which rather upset the residents of his home city. Botero's trademark is the often satirical

5

depiction of plumpness – he claims to find curvy models more attractive than slim ones – and here you will find fatness in all its forms, from a chubby Mother Superior to rotund guerrilla fighters.

Also on display are works by Picasso, Miró, Monet, Renoir and Dalí, as well as a sculpture room featuring works by Henry Moore and Max Ernst.

Casa de Moneda

The stone-built **Casa de Moneda**, or mint (C 11 no. 4–93; Mon & Wed–Sat 9am–7pm, Sun 10am–5pm; free;

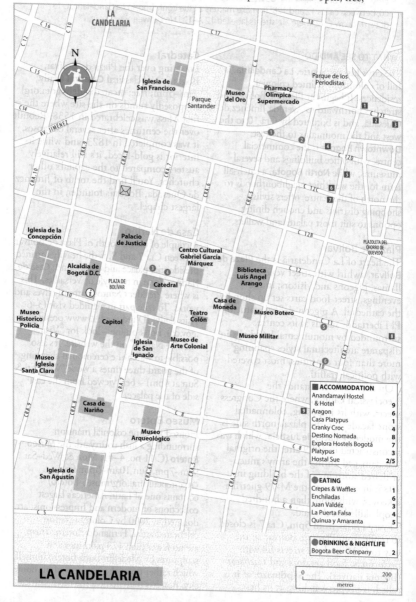

LA CANDELARIA

ACCOMMODATION

Anandamayi Hostel & Hotel	9
Aragon	6
Casa Platypus	1
Cranky Croc	4
Destino Nomada	8
Explora Hostels Bogotá	7
Platypus	3
Hostal Sue	2/5

EATING

Crepes & Waffles	1
Enchiladas	6
Juan Valdéz	3
La Puerta Falsa	4
Quinua y Amaranta	5

DRINKING & NIGHTLIFE

Bogota Beer Company	2

0   200

metres

ⓦbanrepcultural.org/museos-y-colecciones/casa-de-la-moneda), is home to the **Colección Numismática**, its displays chronicling the history of money in Colombia from the barter systems of indigenous communities to the design and production of modern banknotes and coins. Ramps lead to the **Colección de Arte**, featuring a permanent exhibition of works owned by the Banco de la República. The focus here is on contemporary Colombian artists, but the pieces on display range from seventeenth-century religious art through to works by twentieth-century painters. Behind the permanent collection is the **Museo de Arte**, a modern, airy building that houses free, temporary exhibitions of contemporary art, photography and challenging installations.

Museo de Arte Colonial

Set around a beautiful leafy courtyard, the **Museo de Arte Colonial** (Cra 6 no. 9–77; closed for renovation at time of writing) displays fine colonial-era religious and portrait art, as well as sculptures and furniture.

Museo Histórico Policía

Friendly young English-speaking police officers provide free guided tours of the **Museo Histórica Policía** (C 9 no. 9–27; Tues–Sun 8am–5pm; free), which are really worthwhile just to hear about their

experiences. The basement is largely given over to a display on the notorious 499-day police hunt for drug lord Pablo Escobar, and includes his Bernadelli pistol, also known as his "second wife", and there's a great view across the city from the roof.

Museo Militar

Run by the military, the **Museo Militar** (C 10 no. 4–92; Tues–Sun 9am–4.30pm; free; ID required) showcases weaponry through the ages, jaunty military uniforms, model battleships, anti-aircraft guns and other articles relating to the art of war.

Plazoleta del Chorro de Quevedo

Nowhere is La Candelaria's grittier, bohemian side better captured than on the streets surrounding the **Plazoleta del Chorro de Quevedo** (C 12 B and Cra 2). The tiny plaza is said to be the site of the first Spanish settlement, though the tiled-roof colonial chapel on the southwest corner was built much later.

Monserrate

Perched above La Candelaria is the rocky outcrop that is one of Bogotá's most recognizable landmarks: **Cerro de Monserrate**. The hilltop, crowned by **El Santuario de Monserrate** church, offers spectacular views back down on the seemingly endless urban sprawl that is Bogotá. It is easily reached by the frequent *teleférico* cable car (Mon–Sat

---

THE CHURCHES OF LA CANDELARIA

In addition to its cathedral, La Candelaria is teeming with some of the best-preserved colonial-era **churches and convents** found in Latin America:

Museo Iglesia de Santa Clara Cra 8 no. 8–91 (Tues–Fri 9am–5pm, Sat & Sun 10am–4pm; COP$3000; ⓦwww.museoiglesia santaclara.gov.co). Overlooking Casa de Nariño, the austere exterior, built in the early part of the seventeenth century and formerly part of the convent of Clarissa nuns, contrasts sharply with its opulent gold-plated interior and Day of the Dead-looking anaemic Christ.
Iglesia de San Francisco Cra 7, at Av Jiménez (Mon–Fri 6.30am–6.30pm, Sat 6.30am–12.30pm & 4–6.30pm, Sun 7.30am–2pm & 4.30–7.30pm; free; ⓦtemplodesanfrancisco.com). Across from

the Gold Museum, San Francisco is appropriately noted for its particularly splendid golden altar.
Iglesia de la Concepción C 10 no. 9–50 (Mon–Sat 7am–6pm, Sun 7am–1pm; free). The soaring vault here is a fine example of the Moorish-influenced Mudéjar style popular in the sixteenth century.
Iglesia de San Ignacio C 10 no. 6–35 (closed for restoration at the time of writing). The largest and most impressive of the colonial-era churches is the domed San Ignacio, founded in 1610 as the first Jesuit church in Nueva Grenada.

5

noon–midnight, Sun 9am–5pm; return prices: COP$16,400 before 5.30pm, COP$17,700 after, Sun COP$9400; ⓦcerromonserrate.com) or by funicular railway (Mon–Sat 7.45am–11.45am, Sun 6am–6.30pm; prices same as *teleférico*). Alternatively, it's a ninety-minute trek up the 1500-step stone path that begins at the base of the hill and leads to the summit 600m above.

Be aware that there have been a few reports of **robberies** both on the way up the hill and on the walk between the Quinta and its base. The safest (and cheapest) time to go is before 4pm, or Sunday, when you'll be accompanied by thousands of pilgrims hoping for miracles from the church's dark-skinned Christ.

Quinta de Bolívar

At the foot of Monserrate is the **Quinta de Bolívar** (C 20 no. 2–91 Este; Tues–Fri 9am–5pm, Sat & Sun 10am–4pm; English guided tour Wed 11am; COP$3000; ⓦwww.quintadebolivar .gov.co), a spacious colonial mansion with beautiful gardens where Simón Bolívar lived sporadically between 1820 and 1829. The informative museum retells the story of Bolívar's final, desperate days in power before being banished by his political rivals, in a collection that includes a plethora of Bolívar paraphernalia including his military medals, billiard table and bedpan. One object you won't see here is the sword El Libertadór used to free the continent from four centuries of Spanish rule. It was stolen in 1974 from the collection in the now legendary debut of urban guerrilla group **M-19**. When they handed in their arsenal in 1991, the sword was quickly shuttled into the vaults of the Banco Repúblíca.

Museo del Oro

On the northeastern corner of Parque de Santander, at Cra 6 and C 16, is Bogotá's must-see **Museo del Oro**, or Gold Museum (Tues–Sat 9am–6pm, Sun 10am–4pm; COP$3000, Sun free; ⓦbanrepcultural.org/museo-del-oro). The world's largest collection of gold ornaments, some 55,000 pieces strong, is spread out over three floors, with extensive displays on Colombia's indigenous cultures, cosmology and symbolism, techniques used in working with gold, and a region-by-region breakdown of the use of various pieces. Note the recurring symbolism of animals (jaguars, birds, monkeys, human/animal hybrids), the very fine filigree earrings, gold offerings used in rituals and elaborate ornamentation worn by chieftains and those who communed with deities. Free one-hour tours are available (in English Tues–Sat 11am & 4pm; in Spanish Tues–Fri 11am, 3pm & 4pm, Sat 10am, 11am, 3pm & 4pm).

Museo Nacional de Colombia

Inside a fortress-like building, the **Museo Nacional de Colombia** (Cra 7, at C 28; Tues–Sat 10am–6pm, Sun 10am–5pm; free; ⓦmuseonacional.gov.co) provides a detailed chronological look at the country's tumultuous history. The converted jailhouse's most impressive exhibits relate to the conquest and the origins of the beguiling El Dorado myth that so obsessed Europe. The second floor houses an extensive collection of paintings by modern Colombian artists, including Fernando Botero, while on the third floor, don't miss the exhibit on Jorge Gaitán, the populist leader assassinated in 1948. Descriptions are in Spanish only, but you can pick up English-language placards. There's an on-site restaurant and a Juan Valdez café. At the time of writing, some rooms were shut for refurbishment.

Mirador Torre Colpatria

Fantastic 360-degree views can be had from the **Mirador Torre Colpatria** (Cra 7 no. 24–89; Fri & Sat 2–8pm; COP$4500), Colombia's tallest skyscraper (162m). Here you can catch a glimpse of the **Plaza de Toros La Santamaría**, the Moorish-style bullring.

Museo de Arte Moderno

The **Museo de Arte Moderno** (C 24, at Cra 6; Tues–Sat 10am–6pm, Sun noon–4.30pm; COP$4000; ⓦmambogota.com) has the largest

BOGOTÁ FESTIVALS

Colombia's capital has no shortage of festivals. **Semana Santa** (Holy Week; March or April) brings processions, re-enactments and religious pomp. Every other year around Holy Week the city also hosts the **Ibero-American Theater Festival**, one of the continent's biggest festivals of theatre, a fortnight of international performing art and street processions. In April/May, there's the **Feria Internacional del Libro** (international book fair). Perhaps the highlight of the annual calendar is **Rock al Parque** (Rock in the Park; June/July; @rockalparque.gov.co), South America's biggest rock music festival, which lasts three days, before the **Festival de Verano** (summer festival; Aug) to commemorate Bogotá's founding and **Salsa al Parque** (Salsa in the Park; Aug) heats things up. September heralds the **Festival de Jazz** at the *Teatro Libre*, followed by the **Festival de Cine** (film festival; Oct), which includes open-air screenings. Soon after that, the city begins gearing up for a truly South American **Christmas**.

collection of contemporary Colombian art in the country, running the gamut from photography and painting to sculpture and graffiti. Frequently changing exhibits tend to focus on Latin American artists, such as the psychedelic works of Jairo Maldonado. There's also a bookshop and a *cinemateca* that shows art films on weekends (3–5pm).

ARRIVAL AND DEPARTURE

By plane Most international flights land at El Dorado International Airport (@eldorado.aero), 14km northwest of the city centre, currently being rebuilt, though some domestic flights use the Puente Aéreo terminal, 1km from the international one. A taxi downtown costs around COP$25,000. Make sure the taxi meter is turned on. Bus rides into town cost COP$1500, or COP$1800 during rush hour, and can take about an hour (do not attempt if you have a lot of luggage). The airport is served by the following domestic airlines: Avianca, Copa, EasyFly, LAN and Satena.
Destinations There are multiple flights daily to Bucaramanga (1hr); Cali (1hr); Cartagena (1hr 20min); Leticia (1hr 50min); Manizales (50min); Medellín (40min); Pasto (1hr 30min); Pereira (50min); Popayán (1hr 15min); San Andres (2hr); Santa Marta (1hr 30min). International routes include: Buenos Aires (6hr); Caracas (2hr); Frankfurt (10hr); Guayaquil (1hr 50min); Lima (3hr); Santiago (6hr); São Paulo (5hr).
By bus The huge long-distance bus terminal, Terminal de Transporte (Diagonal 23 no. 69–60, off Av de la Constitución; @1 423 3600, @terminaldetransporte .gov.co), is around 5km southwest of the city centre. It's divided into five hubs, three of them colour-coded, roughly serving destinations north (No.3; red), south (No. 1; yellow), east and west of the city and international departures (No. 2; blue). A taxi to the centre costs about COP$17,000. You can also get there from the centre by

hailing any *buseta* from Cra 10 between C 17 and 26, marked "Terminal" (COP$1500, or COP$1800).
Destinations from No. 1 (yellow) Cali (hourly; 8–10hr); Medellín (hourly; 8–9hr); Pasto (8 daily; 18–20hr); Pereira (hourly; 7–9hr); Popayán (7 daily; 12–16hr); San Agustín (11 daily; 9–10hr).
Destinations from No. 2 (blue) Domestic: Cali (hourly; 10hr); Cartagena (14 daily; 12–19hr); Manizales (10 daily; 18hr); Medellín (hourly; 8–9hr); Popayán (7 daily; 12–16hr); Santa Marta (11 daily; 16–18hr). International: Buenos Aires (Tues & Sun; 6 days); Caracas (Thurs; 32hr); Lima (Tues & Sun; 2.5 days); Quito (Tues & Sun; 28hr); Santiago (Tues & Sun; 5 days).
Destinations from No. 3 (red) Cartagena (14 daily; 12–19hr); Cúcuta (several daily; 15–16hr); Manizales (10 daily; 8–9hr); San Gil (3 daily; 6–7hr); Santa Marta (11 daily; 16–18hr); Villa de Leyva (4 daily; 4hr).

INFORMATION

Tourist information Bogotá's tourist bureau produces city maps complete with Transmilenio bus routes. The most useful *Puntos de Información Turística* are at the airport, bus station and the southwest corner of Plaza Bolívar at Cra 8 no. 10–65 (Mon–Sat 8am–6pm, Sun 10am–4pm; @1 283 7115, @pitcentrohistorico @idt.gov), although there are plans to move to a different location.
National park information For up-to-date safety information on Colombia's 51 national parks and protected areas, visit the ecotourism office of Unidad de Parques Nacionales at Cra 10 no. 20–34 (Mon–Fri 8am–5.30pm; @1 353 2400, @parquesnacionales.gov.co).
Publications Pick up a copy of *Plan B* (@planb.com.co) – a monthly what's-on publication and website. On Fridays, Bogotá's leading newspaper, *El Tiempo*, publishes *Qué Hacer*, a weekend entertainment guide. The monthly free English-language *The City Paper* (@thecitypaperbogota .com) is also a useful resource, as is *GO* magazine, featuring a monthly cultural programme in English.

5

GETTING AROUND

Most of Bogotá's attractions are in or near La Candelaria and can be reached on foot (unless you're staying uptown). The area west of Cra 10 and below Av Jimenez is best avoided.

Buses Besides the chaotic minibuses, Bogotá is covered by an extensive, efficient and ever-spreading bus system called TransMilenio (Mon–Sat 5am–11pm, Sun 10am–6pm), with a flat fare of COP$1500 (COP$1800 during rush hour) per journey; buy a *Tu Llave* card (COP$3500) to be loaded up with credit at any of the stations on the website (@ www.tullaveplus.com) and pick up a bus route map from the tourist office. Bus lines are a little confusing, as some express buses miss out a number of stops. The most useful routes include the J buses, which run to Candelaria (otherwise change at Jiménez), and the B lines running north–south along Av Carcas to Portal del Norte via the Zona Rosa. Best avoided during rush hour.

Taxis Taxis in Bogotá are yellow, small and relatively inexpensive. Fares correspond to the number of units on the taxi meter, with a small surcharge (COP$1600) levied between 8pm and 5am, on Sundays and holidays; ask the driver to turn the taxi meter on and check the fare table as some drivers overcharge. It's safer to call a taxi company rather than grab one off the street; you'll need to give the driver the passcode – the last two digits of the phone number you call from. Try Radio Taxi (@ 1 288 8888), Taxi Real (@ 1 333 3333) or Taxi Express (@ 1 411 1111).

ACCOMMODATION

Most budget accommodation is concentrated in La Candelaria. All listed offer free internet and/or wi-fi. Most have private rooms with either shared or private bathrooms; prices below are for doubles with shared bathroom in high season (single rooms are often around two-thirds the price of a double).

Anandamayi Hostel & Hotel C 9 no. 2–81 @ 1 341 7208, @ anandamayihostel.com; map p.500. This hostel is pure Zen, set in a restored colonial house around three flower-filled, hammock-strung courtyards frequented by hummingbirds. Rustic dorms and private rooms come with lockers, and shared bathrooms have spacious stone showers. At night, guests gather around the wood-fire stove in the communal kitchen. Basic breakfast included. Dorms COP$35,500, doubles COP$140,500

Aragon Cra 3 no. 14–13, La Candelaria @ 1 342 5239; map p.500. While this bare-bones hotel has zero atmosphere, the warm rooms with shared bathrooms are clean, most have wi-fi access and cost far less than their youth hostel equivalent. Singles COP$26,500, doubles COP$42,500

Cranky Croc C 12D no. 3–46 @ 1 342 2438, @ crankycroc .com; map p.500. A friendly, Australian-owned place with sparklingly clean dorms, basic rooms around a courtyard, a well-equipped shared kitchen, Friday-night barbecue and daily group outings. Free wi-fi plus computer terminals. Dorms COP$24,500, doubles COP$85,500

Destino Nomada C 11 no. 00–38 @ 1 352 0932, @ destinonomada.com; map p.500. This hostel is guaranteed to leave you breathless (thanks to the uphill walk). It's a compact place with guest kitchen, small bar (offering a daily happy hour), TV lounge, and a small but sweet inner courtyard. Dorms COP$23,500, doubles COP$62,500

Explora Hostels Bogotá C 12C no. 3–19 @ 1 282 9320, @ explorahostels.com; map p.500. An unassuming exterior hides this appealing hostel with an indoor hammock-festooned common space. The kitchen is minuscule but there's a café that cooks up breakfast. Some of the rooms face the covered courtyard and dorms feature nice touches such as large lockers and individual reading lights. Dorms COP$20,500, doubles COP$74,500

La Pinta C 65 no. 5–67 @ 1 211 9526, @ lapinta.com.co; map p.498. If you want to be closer to the nightlife, then this wonderfully friendly hostel (complete with two labradors) on the outskirts of the Zona Rosa is a great bet. Bunks and rooms are comfortable (though don't expect to get much sleep on weekends), a good breakfast is thrown in, and while the hostel is a 15min walk from the nearest

---

BOGOTÁ TOURS

The cheapest way to tour the city is to devise a self-guided **bus** tour. For the price of a single Transmilenio ticket, you can ride the buses for as long as you like, as long as you don't leave the stations.

Bogotá Graffiti Tour @ 321 297 4075, @ bogotagraffiti.com. This excellent three-hour walking tour takes in Bogotá's not inconsiderable collection of street art (daily 10am–12.30pm; free, but suggested donation of COP$20,000–30,000); reserve ahead.

Cycling Every Sunday morning (until 2pm), there is much good-natured fun to be had as many of Bogotá's main roads close to traffic in a civic attempt to get people cycling, known as *Ciclovía*. Bogotá Bike Tours rents bikes (Cra 3 no. 12–72; COP$20,000/35,000 per half/full day; @ 1 281 9924, @ bogotabiketours.com), and runs informative guided tours of the city (COP$35,000, 4hr approx).

Casa Platypus C 12F no. 28, La Candelaria ☎ 1 281 1801, ⊕ casaplatypusbogota.com; map p.500. Located in a beautiful colonial house overlooking Parque de los Periodistas, *Casa Platypus* (same owner as the hostel *Platypus*) combines many of the comforts of a boutique hotel with backpacker-friendly facilities. Rooms are compact but stylish and there's a huge dining room/lounge where a hefty breakfast including fresh fruit and juice, eggs, granola and yoghurt is served up (included in room rate). Add to this a roof terrace, communal kitchen, free coffee, wi-fi and public computers, cold beers on an honour system plus information and friendly advice from super-knowledgeable owner Germán, and you really do have the best of both worlds. Dorms **COP$44,000**, doubles **COP$166,000**

Transmilenio stop, regular minibuses along Cra 7 connect it to La Candelaria. Dorms **COP$26,500**, doubles **COP$96,500**
Platypus C 12F no. 2–43, La Candelaria ☎ 1 341 3104, ⊕ platypushotel.wix.com/hostalplaty; map p.500. An institution, mostly because the English/French/German-speaking owner Germán warmly shares knowledge of Colombia accumulated from extensive travels. Comfortable shared and private rooms with kitchen facilities. Dorms **COP$22,500**, doubles **COP$60,500**
Hostal Sue C 12F no. 2–55 ☎ 1 334 8494, ⊕ suecandelaria .com; map p.500. This well-maintained hostel with a party vibe has neat dorms, three doubles with TVs, on-site bar, bean-bag-stacked TV lounge, kitchen, free coffee, laundry service, ping-pong table and regular pub crawls. There's a second location in La Candelaria at Cra 3 no. 12C–18 (☎ 1 341 2647). Dorms **COP$22,500**, doubles **COP$60,500**

EATING

While the traditional highlander diet consists of meat and starch, middle-class *Cachacos* prefer the same cosmopolitan cuisine as their counterparts in London or New York. Bogotá has four main restaurant zones, from south to north: gritty La Candelaria; yuppie La Macarena (Cra 4 between calles 23 & 28); gay-friendly Chapinero, also called the "G-Zone" (between calles 58 & 72 and carreras 3 & 7); and upmarket Zona Rosa (concentrated in the "T Zone" at C 82 and Cra 12).

Al Wadi C 27 no. 4A–14, La Macarena; map p.498. A compact, cave-like Middle Eastern place serving heaped plates of falafel and moussaka with the trimmings, as well as shawarma and good, tooth-achingly sweet baklava for dessert. Mains from COP$17,500. Mon–Thurs noon–10pm, Fri–Sun noon–11pm.
Central Cevicheria Cra 14 no. 85–14, Zona Rosa; map p.498. Look no further to sate your cravings for fish and seafood – be it laced with spicy sauce or cut into thin *tiradito* slices. Busy and popular, it also serves cooked mains such as prawn curry. Expensive, but worth it. *Ceviche* from COP$19,500. Daily noon–10pm.
Crepes & Waffles Av Jimenez no. 4–55; map p.500; Cra 12 no. 83–40 in the Zona Rosa; map p.498; and more than 30 other city outlets ⊕ crepesywaffles.com. A hugely popular chain restaurant that fulfils every savoury and sweet craving with a monster menu of crêpes and waffles, plus ice-cream sundaes. Savoury crêpes COP$8900–10,200, sweet treats start at COP$4500. Mon–Thurs & Sat 11.45am–8.30pm; Fri 11.45am–9pm, Sun 11.45am–5pm.
Di Lucca Cra 13 no. 85–33, Zona Rosa; map p.498. Munch on wood-fired pizzas, home-made pasta and expertly cooked risotto at this smart Italian restaurant. Given its trendy Zona Rosa location, the prices are extremely good value and dishes such as sepia pasta with seafood sauce stand out. Mains from COP$19,500. Daily noon–10pm.
Enchiladas C 10 no. 2–12, La Candelaria; map p.500. Tuck into enchiladas, burritos and other Mexican staples at this colourful spot festooned with Day of the Dead paraphernalia and black-and-white film photos. The home-made salsas have a real kick to them and the *sopa de tortilla* really hits the spot. Mains from COP$14,500. Mon & Sun noon–9.30pm, Tues–Sat noon–5pm.
Juan Valdéz Cra 7 at C 11, La Candelaria; map p.500. Colombia's answer to Starbucks, with good hot and cold caffeine drinks, muffins, sandwiches and more. Be prepared to pay top dollar for it, though. Also has wi-fi. Coffees COP$5500. Mon–Sat 9am–8pm, Sun until 5pm.
Misia Trv 6 no. 27–50, Local 3; map p.498. Owned by celebrity chef Leonor Espinosa, this trendy spot with wooden crater lights and kitchen utensils on the walls cooks up Colombian street food from their open kitchen. Tapas-style portions cost around COP$4,500, and mains such as the prawn and plantain rice are COP$25,500. There's a long list of exotic juices too. Mon–Sat 7am–10pm, Sun 9am–4pm.
La Puerta Falsa C 11 no. 6–50, La Candelaria; map p.500. This 1816 establishment is where the good citizens of Bogotá come for snacks such as *chocolate completo* (hot chocolate with cheese and bread, COP$6300) and colourful sweets that beckon you through the window. Mon–Sat 7am–10pm, Sun 8am–8pm.
★ **Quinua y Amaranto** C 11 no. 2–95, La Candelaria; map p.500. A tiny place with an open kitchen and delicious, largely organic and vegetarian set lunches (COP$14,500). Sample dishes include black bean soup and mushroom risotto. Also sells wholewheat *empanadas*, bread, eggs and coffee. Mon & Sat 8am–4pm, Tues–Fri 8am–7.30pm.

5

Wok Cra 13 no. 82–74, Zona Rosa, also next to the Museo Nacional ⓦ wok.com.co; map p.498. This chain of trendy restaurants has all-white modern decor and a menu that was clearly constructed by someone who knows about Asian food. Choose from heaped noodle salads, Thai curry, sushi, tempura and much more. The shrimp speared on sugar-cane stalks with Vietnamese dipping sauce are seriously tasty, and the lemonade is among the best in town. Spice fans should ask for extra chilli. Mains start around COP$17,000. Mon–Wed noon–10.30pm, Thurs–Sat noon–11pm, Sun noon–8pm.

DRINKING AND NIGHTLIFE

Rumbear, literally to dance the rumba, is how locals refer to a night's partying, which invariably involves heavy doses of dancing. Bars and discos in La Candelaria attract a somewhat bohemian, often studenty, crowd, while their fluorescent-lit counterparts in the Zona Rosa in North Bogotá (around C 83 and Cra 13) appeal to the city's beautiful people. Virtually everywhere shuts down at 3am. Take taxis to and from your destination.

Bogotá Beer Company C 12D no. 4–02, La Candelaria; map p.500; Cra 12 no. 83–33, Zona Rosa ⓦ bogotabeercompany.com. Artisan brews including stout and wheat beer, served in bottles and on tap, fourteen seasonal microbrews, plus excellent pub grub to soak them up. One of the few places that is busy even on a Mon night. Daily noon–2am.

The End Aparte Suites Tequendema, Cra 10 no. 27–51; map p.498. After all the clubs close and Bogotá's night owls go home, *The End* (aka Piso 30) is where the after-party continues until past sunrise. With great views of the city from its 30th-floor location, this spot attracts a diverse crowd. Fri & Sat 8pm–very, very late.

Goce Pagano Cra 13A no. 23–97, Downtown; map p.498. Less is more in this divey watering hole, which has a simple dancefloor and Bogotá's largest rack of golden-era salsa LPs. Owner Gustavo is a throwback to the era when the revolution was fought listening to salsa. Take a taxi as the area is unsafe at night. Thurs–Sat only.

Theatron C 58 no. 10–42, Chapinero ⓦ theatron.co; map p.498. A neon-lit wonderland, this colossal gay club is spread over three floors and six rooms, some of which are men only. Also hosts live shows, which attract a mixed audience. The COP$25,000 cover charge on Saturday night gets you a cup and access to an open bar (until 2am).

SHOPPING

Artesanías de Colombia Cra 2 no. 18A–58 ⓦ artesaniasdecolombia.com.co. Not cheap, but has beautiful, high-quality handicrafts and jewellery from all over Colombia that's far nicer than the tat you'll find in the tourist traps around the Museo del Oro. Two other branches in north Bogotá.

Flea markets There are some gems to discover amid the more rough-and-ready Sunday flea markets at Parque de los Periodistas and Mercado de San Alejo on Cra 7 (between calles 24 & 26).

Paloquemao C 19 & Cra 24. The largest and most bustling market in the city, where you can stock up on supplies to cook at your hostel. Fantastic veg and tropical fruit, a somewhat gory meat section and plenty of dry goods. Tuesdays and Fridays are when the flower-sellers show up: get there by about 8am to catch the best of their displays. It's safe enough to take a camera if you are sensible with it: be discreet and ask permission before taking photos of people. Mon–Sat 4.30am–4.30pm, Sun 5am–2.30pm.

DIRECTORY

Banks and exchange ATMs are available throughout the city – along Cra 2A in La Candelaria and all over the Zona Rosa. Currency exchanges are found at most hotels, the airport, and on Cra 2A, right near the Museo de Oro.

★ TREAT YOURSELF

Andrés Carne de Res C 3 no. 11A–56, Chía ⓦ andrescarnederes.com. Suburban legend *Andrés Carne de Res* must be seen to be believed. A 1000-capacity restaurant and salsa club that looks like something from a Tim Burton film, it is the biggest all-singing, all-dancing party in the Colombian capital. The four floors (Hell, Earth, Purgatory and Heaven, the last with large roof terrace) are decked out in a kind of gothic burlesque, with live salsa music and staff dressed as circus performers and coquettish chambermaids who parade around dragging non-dancers to their feet. The menu is 62 pages long and features no fewer than nine pages of alcoholic drinks as well as countless eating options, such as the steaks they are famous for. There's live music, and the party runs until 3am Fri & Sat (cover COP$20,000), finishing a bit earlier the rest of the week (COP$10,000 after 10pm Thurs). The location is far out – 23km north of the city, and if you don't want to splurge on a taxi (around COP$190,000 return, including waiting time), many hostels run party buses to *Andrés* on Saturday nights; for COP$50,000, you get the transport there and back and booze along the way. For those who can't make it to the original and best, there's a more sedate version at C 82 no. 12–21, Zona Rosa.

Embassies Australia, C 16 no. 86A–05 (📞1 236 2828); Brazil, C 93 no. 14–20, 8th floor (📞1 218 0800); Canada, Cra 7 no. 115–33, 14th floor (📞1 657 9800); Ecuador, C 72 no. 6–30 (📞1 317 53289); Peru, C 80A no. 6–50 (📞1 257 0505); UK, Cra 9 no. 76–49, 9th floor (📞1 326 8300); US, C 24 no. 48–50 (📞1 275 2000); Venezuela, Cra 11 no. 87–51 (📞1 644 5555).

Hospital Clínica Marly, C 50 no. 9–67 (📞1 343 6600, 🌐marly.com.co), and San Ignacio, Cra 7 no. 40–62 (📞1 594 6161, 🌐www.husi.org.co), are well-equipped medical facilities accustomed to attending foreigners.

Immigration For visa extensions (COP$78,300) visit the Ministerio de Relaciones Exteriores, C 100 no. 11B–27 (Mon–Fri 7.30am–4.30pm; 📞1 595 3525, 🌐migracioncolombia.gov.co).

Pharmacy There is a pharmacy in the Olimpica supermarket at Av Jimenez no. 4 (Mon–Sat 7am–9pm, Sun 9am–4pm).

Police Headquarters of the tourist police is at Cra 13 no. 26–62 (daily 7am–noon & 2–7pm; 📞1 337 4413).

Post office The main post office is in La Candelaria; Cra 8 and C 12A. A popular option is 4-72 (🌐4-72.com.co), which has offices around town including at Cra 7 no. 12–13.

DAY-TRIPS FROM BOGOTÁ

The **Zipaquirá salt cathedral** and the up-and-coming adventure sports town of **Suesca** are both within easy day-trip distance of the capital.

The Zipaquirá salt cathedral

The most popular day-trip from Bogotá is a visit to the salt cathedral of **ZIPAQUIRÁ** (daily 9am–5.30pm; COP$23,000; 🌐catedraldesal.gov.co), some 50km north of the city. Inaugurated in 1995 to great fanfare – having replaced an earlier one that closed because of collapse – the cathedral lies completely underground, topped by a hill that was mined by local Indians before the Spanish arrived in the seventeenth century. As you descend 180m into the earth, you'll pass fourteen minimalist chapels built entirely of salt that glow like marble in the soft light, each a different combination of colours. The main nave is a feat of engineering, complete with the world's largest subterranean cross, and the vast salty cavern is impressive, though the changing lighting is very gimmicky.

Above ground, there's a **museum** (same hours as cathedral) explaining the history of salt extraction; more expensive ticket combinations include museum entry. You must enter the salt cathedral with a **guided tour** that's included in the entrance fee, but once inside, you're free to escape. To get there from Bogotá, take the TransMilenio to the Portal del Norte station at the end of the B line and from here a *buseta* (COP$4200) to Zipa or Zipaquirá. From the centre of Zipaquirá, it's a short taxi ride or fifteen-minute walk to the entrance.

Suesca

Some 65km north of Bogotá, the small town of **SUESCA** is one of Colombia's top rock-climbing destinations. Adventure-sports enthusiasts of all persuasions will feel at home here, but it is the sandstone cliffs on the town's doorstep that steal the show, offering traditional and sport rock-climbing with more than six hundred routes including multi-pitch.

The majority of the rock-climbing and adventure-sports operators are located at the entrance to the rocks, a fifteen-minute walk from the town centre (day climb around COP$130,000).

ARRIVAL AND DEPARTURE

By bus To get to Suesca from Bogotá, take the TransMilenio to the northern terminus at Portal del Norte and then jump on one of the regular buses marked "Alianza" or "Ayacucho" (40min).

ACCOMMODATION

El Vivac Hostal Autopista Norte 📞311 480 5034, 🌐elvivachostal.com. Fifteen minutes on from the rocks, this is a cosy place to stay and recharge, with a communal kitchen, fireplace, good mattresses and camping pitches. Tents COP$15,000, dorms COP$25,000, doubles COP$70,000

North of Bogotá

Away from Bogotá, the smog and busy streets give way to the bucolic countryside of Colombia's central Andean departments Boyacá, Cundimarca and Santander, which mark the geographical heart of the country. First inhabited centuries ago by the gold-worshipping Muisca Indians, these mountainous highlands played a pivotal role in forging

5

Colombia's national identity. **Tunja**, one of Colombia's oldest cities, is famous for its architecture, while an hour further northwest is one of Colombia's best-preserved colonial towns, **Villa de Leyva**, its surrounding countryside studded with archeological treasures.

Tiny **Barichara**, just a steep 22km from the burgeoning adventure centre of **San Gil**, is a compact colonial beauty. Further north again, the modern city of **Bucaramanga** or the colonial town of **Girón** are both decent midway points if you're heading to Venezuela or the coast. Follow a different road from Bogotá, and eight hours later you arrive at the high-altitude splendours of **Parque Nacional El Cocuy**, with its glacial lakes and snowcapped peaks.

TUNJA

Founded in 1539 on the ruins of the ancient Muisca capital of Hunza, **TUNJA** is not the region's most exciting city, though its historic centre is one of the foremost preserves of the country's colonial heritage, and is worth a quick stop on the way to Villa de Leyva.

WHAT TO SEE AND DO

The mansions around the Plaza de Bolívar are particularly splendid. The **Casa del Fundador Suárez Rendón** (Cra 9 no. 19–68; daily 8am–6pm; COP$2000), home of the town's founder, was built in the Moorish Mudéjar style in 1540 and features interesting scenes on its ceiling, while the **Casa de Don Juan de Vargas** (C 20 no. 8–52; Tues–Fri 9am–noon & 2–5pm; COP$3000) also stands out for its eighteenth-century ceiling frescoes. The motifs are a curious mishmash of imagery – from Greek gods to exotic animals and coats of arms, combined in unusual settings.

The town's churches are no less interesting, with **Iglesia de Santo Domingo** (Cra 11 no. 19–55; daily 8.30am–noon & 2.30–6pm) known for its Rosario Chapel, richly decorated with religious paintings and magnificent gilded woodcarving by Gregorio Vásquez de Arce y Ceballos. **Iglesia y Convento de Santa Clara de Real** (Cra 7 no. 19–58;

daily 9am–noon & 2–6pm; COP$3000 entry to the cloister) was the first convent in Nueva Granada, and combines indigenous and Catholic imagery in its elaborate decor; note the sun on the ceiling, the main god of the Muisca.

About 16km south of Tunja on the main road back to Bogotá is a reconstructed colonial-era bridge, **El Puente de Boyacá**, commemorating the Battle of Boyacá of August 7, 1819, which cleared the way for Bolívar and his freedom fighters to march triumphantly into Bogotá. Any Bogotá–Tunja bus will drop you off/pick you up (provided there's room).

ARRIVAL AND DEPARTURE

By bus The bus terminal is on Av Oriental, several blocks uphill from Plaza de Bolívar. Buses north to Bucaramanga (hourly; 6–7hr), the main jumping-off point for the Caribbean coast, travel via San Gil (4hr 30min). Small buses – some direct, some not – to Villa de Leyva leave every 15min (45min), while Bogotá departures are every 15min (3hr).

ACCOMMODATION

Hotel Casa Real C 19 no. 7–65 ☎8 743 1764, ⓦhotelcasarealtunja.com. Atmospheric place with attractive en-suite rooms in an old colonial building between the bus station and Plaza de Bolívar. COP$75,000

VILLA DE LEYVA

Tucked against the foot of spectacular mountains, scenic **VILLA DE LEYVA**, founded in 1572, is a must-see showcase of colonial architecture. The untroubled ambience and mild, dry climate make it a perfect place to relax – sitting in the 400-year-old plaza drinking sangria, you'll be able to appreciate why many describe it as Colombia's most beautiful town. In the mountains around (see p.511), you can go hunting for fossils, bathe in waterfalls or enjoy the countryside on horseback. The narrow streets throng with day-trippers from Bogotá on weekends, but the rest of the time, this lovely town reverts to its former tranquil, timeless self.

WHAT TO SEE AND DO

Villa de Leyva looks and feels immaculately preserved, right down to hand-painted tiles prohibiting horseriding and car traffic along the main plaza. A lively **market**, mostly featuring fruit, veg and clothing, is held in the Plaza de Mercado on Saturday morning. There's a smaller, organic food market on Thursday mornings.

Plaza Mayor

The impressive **Plaza Mayor** is one of the largest in the Americas, paved with large cobblestones, centred on a stone Mudéjar well and surrounded by attractive colonial buildings. Dominating the plaza is the huge stone portal of the seventeenth-century **Catedral**, rebuilt after an 1845 earthquake.

Casa-Museo Luis Alberto Acuña

Facing the Plaza Mayor is the **Casa-Museo Luis Alberto Acuña** (daily 10am–12.30pm & 2–7.30pm; COP$4000), which houses the most comprehensive collection of sculptures and other artwork by influential, avant-garde twentieth-century artist Luis Alberto Acuña, who lived here for the last fifteen years of his life. The large, colourful murals in the courtyard, depicting Muisca mythological figures, are a highlight.

Museo del Carmen

Facing the imposing **Monasterio de las Carmelitas** and its attached church is the **Museo del Carmen** (Plazuela del Carmen; Sat, Sun & hols only 10am–1pm & 2–5pm; COP$3000), justifiably famous for its collection of religious art. Here you'll find large numbers of wooden icons from the Church's early years of proselytizing in the New World, as well as altarpieces and paintings that date back to the sixteenth century.

Casa de Antonio Ricaurte

Once home to a national hero who fought for Bolívar, and operated by the Colombian armed forces since 1970, the house where **Antonio Ricaurte** was born (Wed–Fri 9am–noon & 2–5pm, Sat & Sun 9am–1pm & 2–6pm; free) contains

Santuario de Iguaque, Arcabuco & Museo Paleontológico

VILLA DE LEYVA

0   100
metres

5

some personal objects and documents (in Spanish only), plus modern military paraphernalia, but the best reason for coming here is the beautiful garden.

ARRIVAL AND INFORMATION

By bus The bus station is three blocks southwest of the Plaza Mayor, towards the road to Tunja. Direct buses run to Bogotá (6–8 daily; 4–5hr) between 5am and 5pm, and plentiful minibuses connect Villa de Leyva with Tunja (every 15min; 1hr). To continue north to San Gil or Bucaramanga, it's better to backtrack to Tunja and catch a bus from there as they are more frequent, though it's also possible to go via Arcabuco or Chiquinquirá and transfer there.

Tourist information The helpful tourist information office at Cra 9 no. 13–04 (Mon–Sat 8am–12.30pm & 2–6pm, Sun 9am–1pm & 3–6pm; ☎8 732 0232) has maps and lots of information.

GETTING AROUND AND TOURS

Taxis You can hire a taxi for the day to drive you from site to site around the city (approx. COP$20,000 per site, but negotiate). Alternatively, you can travel by horseback or walk to some sites, though the winding roads can be dangerous for unwary pedestrians.

Tours Colombian Highlands, based at the *Renacer* hostel (☎ colombianhighlands.com), is an excellent stop to pick up information on outdoor excursions. They can organize hiking, abseiling and horseriding, and they offer ten percent discounts to those who stay at their hostel.

ACCOMMODATION

There are several campsites around town, but you need your own tent. Discounts of up to thirty percent are often available during the week; book early for weekends and holidays.

Casa Viena Cra 10 no. 19–114 ☎8 732 0711, ☎ casaviena.com. Friendly little hostel – two doubles, a single and a three-bed dorm – run by Hans and his family.

It's on the same road as *Hostal Renacer* and they'll refund you the taxi fare from the bus station (except in high season) if staying for more than one night (COP$4000). Dorms COP$17,000, doubles COP$42,000

Hospedería La Roca Plaza Mayor ☎8 732 0331. This place has a fantastic location on the main square, plus a pretty courtyard and 23 rooms (including one for up to six people) with private bathrooms and TV. Prices rise twenty percent at the peak of high season. COP$130,00

★**Hostal Renacer** 1.2km northeast of Plaza Mayor ☎8 732 1201, ☎ colombianhighlands.com. Owned by Oscar Gilède, the English-speaking biologist behind Colombian Highlands tour operators, *Hostal Renacer* is a haven surrounded by trees and mountain views. A TV room, hammocks, free wi-fi and hot drinks, a fridge full of beer and heaps of information, plus rooms with huge windows and comfortable beds, make it popular with backpackers who aren't precious about the odd creepy-crawly. You can also camp. The location, about 1km uphill from the centre, is a bit of a pain, but if you call when you arrive in town they'll pay for your taxi. Camping per person with own tent COP$14,000, without tent COP$28,000, dorms COP$22,000, doubles COP$70,000

Zona de Camping C 11, at Cra 10 ☎311 530 7687. No-frills camping, with a wall set up around a large patch of grass and a basic toilet/shower block. Great mountain views. Per person COP$11,000

EATING AND DRINKING

If you can spare the pesos, you will eat very well here, as the food scene is very diverse; the best gourmet food courts are Casona La Guaca (Cra 9 between C 13 & C 14) and Casa Quintero (Cra 9, at C 12). The nightlife is centred on Plaza Mayor. You can find information about the town's culinary options on ☎ villadeleyva.net.

★**La Bonita** Casa Quintero, Cra 9, at C12. If you're craving some spice, then get your fix at this colourful, genuine Mexican restaurant. There is some real heat to the salsas, and while the mains are not cheap (around COP$25,000), you can't go wrong with the sublime *cochinita pibil* (slow-roasted pork) tacos, and the soups are very affordable (from COP$12,000). Mon, Tues & Thurs–Sun noon–10pm.

Carnes y Olivas Cra 10 no. 11–55 ☎8 732 1368. Offers a fantastic-value, three-course *menu del día* (COP$8000), including traditional dishes such as tender braised *sobrebarriga* (flank steak), cooked with considerable skill and flair. Also international dishes such as pizza and hamburgers. Daily 9am–9pm.

Dortkneipe Cra 9, Plaza Mayor, no. 12–88. The nicest bar on the main square draws beer connoisseurs with its selection of unusual (mostly German) beers on tap, as well as the ubiquitous Aguila. Daily from 6pm.

Restaurante Savia Casa Quintero, Cra 9, at C 12. The organic dishes at this fantastic little spot will delight vegetarians and vegans alike. Huge mains (big enough for two) include the likes of vegetable and lentil quinoa and mega salads. Mains from COP$13,000. Thurs–Sun noon–10pm.

La Waffleria La Casona de Arroyo, Cra 9 no. 14–14. Cute little café dishing up all the crêpes and waffles your heart may desire – sweet and savoury. Waffles from COP$7000. Daily 11.30am–6pm.

AROUND VILLA DE LEYVA

Attractions surrounding Villa de Leyva include giant fossils, archeological sites, nature reserves and a town specializing in local crafts. They can be reached on horseback, by bicycle, bus or taxi or via a tour. If making an arrangement with a taxi, make sure the driver knows exactly which sites you want to see, and agree on the price beforehand.

Centro de Investigaciones Paleontológicas

About 5km from Villa de Leyva and just down the road from El Fósil on Km4, this interactive museum and centre of palaeontology research (Tues–Thurs 8am–noon & 2–5pm, Fri–Sun 8am–5pm; COP$8,000) exhibits wonderfully preserved fossils of species that inhabited the area 110 million years ago, among them the marine ichthyosaurs, kronosaurus and pliosaurus. The sabre tooth tiger fossil is a highlight, and a camera link to the lab shows palaeontologists hard at work.

El Fósil

The arid desert highlands surrounding Villa de Leyva attract trekkers, but 120 million years ago the huge flood plain would have been better suited to scuba diving. The ocean waters have since retreated, leaving the country's largest repository of **fossils**. Five kilometres out of town along the road to Santa Sofía, the star of the **El Fósil** museum (daily 8am–6pm; COP$6000; ⍵museoelfosil .com) is the most complete fossil of a 120-million-year-old baby kronosaurus, a prehistoric marine lizard found by a *campesino* here in 1977. The 12.8m-long lizard is one of only two in the world excavated in its entirety, but on display you'll find it without the 5m tail, which was lost.

Estación Astronómica Muisca

Also known as El Infernito, this **Muisca observatory** (Tues–Sun 9am–noon & 2–5pm; COP$6000), dating back to early centuries AD and located around 2km on from El Fósil, is Colombia's answer to Stonehenge. Pathways run between the 115-odd stone monoliths, the larger ones strongly resembling enormous stone phalluses. The Muisca used to decide when to start planting crops by measuring the length of the shadows between the stones.

El Santuario de Iguaque

Around 15km north of town, the large nature reserve of **El Santuario de Iguaque** has excellent hiking. It's named after the park's most sacred lake, Laguna de Iguaque – believed by the native Muiscas to be the birthplace of humanity – which can be visited as a day-trip; there are eight lakes altogether in the park at an altitude between 3550m and 3700m, and it can be cold and wet (the best time to come is Jan, Feb, July & Aug), so come equipped accordingly.

A **visitor centre**, 12km northeast out of Villa de Leyva, offers basic shared accommodation (COP$45,000 per person) and food. The entrance fee for the reserve is COP$38,000 for foreigners. Take one of the buses that leave for Arcabuco (up to 7 daily) and ask to be dropped off at Casa de Piedra (aka Los Naranjos) at Km12; from here it's a 3km walk to the visitor centre.

Ráquira

Tiny **Ráquira**, 25km from Villa de Leyva to the west, is famous countrywide for its pottery. If you're looking for crafts to take home, besides perusing the many pottery workshops, you can raid the craft shops around the main square for hammocks, jewellery, woodcarvings and ponchos. Sunday is **market day** and a particularly good time to visit. Ráquira can be reached by bus from Villa de Leyva (4–5 daily; 45min) or by taxi (around COP$45,000 one-way).

5

SAN GIL

An adventure-sports hotspot, **SAN GIL** is one of the biggest backpacker draws in northern Colombia. The compact town is a premier destination for white-water rafting and paragliding, as well as hiking and other outdoorsy activities that take place in the surrounding countryside, and for day-trips to quiet colonial Barichara. For those craving a spot of culinary adventure, fried *hormigas culonas*, or fat-bottomed ants, a Santander delicacy, can be bought from a few places around town including the market and the street by the river.

San Gil's main attractions lie outside town, but if you want a quiet moment in between adventures, make your way to the large riverside **Parque El Gallineral** (daily 8am–5pm; COP$6000), its trees atmospherically festooned with tendrils of "old man's beard" moss. There's a natural spring-fed swimming pool, and the entrance fee gets you a wristband that means you can go in and out of the park all day. To get here, head to the river and turn left along the Malecón to its end.

ARRIVAL AND DEPARTURE

By bus San Gil has several bus stations, though the main terminal is around 2km southwest of town; a taxi to the centre costs around COP$3500. Buses to Barichara (every 30min; 45min) leave from the terminal at C 15 and Cra 10, while Bucaramanga-bound buses (every 30min; 2hr 30min) leave from the terminal at Cra 11 and C 8, and Bogotá-bound buses depart from the main terminal (several daily; 6–8hr).

ACCOMMODATION

★ **Macondo Guesthouse** C 8 no. 10–35 ☎ 7 724 8001, ⓦ macondohostel.com. Australian-owned *Macondo* has a homey, laidback atmosphere, with guests relaxing in the jacuzzi after an adrenaline-packed day. An excellent place to organize your outdoor adventures. Dorms COP$20,000, doubles COP$50,000

La Mansión de Sam Gil C 12 no. 8–71 ☎ 7 724 6044. There's no stopping Sam of *Sam's VIP*: this colonial mansion on the corner of Parque Central features attractive singles and doubles arranged around a central courtyard. There's a decent gastropub downstairs too. Doubles COP$50,000

Sam's VIP Cra 10 no. 12–33 ☎ 7 724 2746, ⓦ samshostel .com. This lively hostel with particularly attractive decor has a balcony overlooking the main square, poker table and even a small swimming pool. Dorms are on the small side, but there's a superb guest kitchen and the double rooms downstairs are great value. Dorms COP$22,000, doubles COP$45,000

Hostel San Gil C 12 no. 7–63 ☎ 7 724 2535, ⓦ hostelsangil.com. With great views from its terrace, this hostel with a sociable atmosphere appeals to those who want a quiet night after the day's adventures. Great open-air shower, jacuzzi and a DVD player plus film collection (including in English). Breakfast from COP$4500. Dorms COP$17,000, doubles COP$45,000

EATING AND DRINKING

By far the liveliest place to drink on most evenings is the main plaza, which is usually full of families and young people. In the evenings, vendors grill meat skewers and corn on the cob. The central market between calles 13 and 14 is the best bet for self-catering supplies, as well as fresh fruit juice, and is open until 2pm daily. By the riverside park, vendors sell a local speciality – fried giant ants.

ADVENTURE SPORTS

Adrenaline junkies are spoilt for choice by the array of **adventure sports** on offer in San Gil. There are two main **white-water rafting** routes: a hair-raising day-trip down the Class IV/V (depends on the season) Río Suarez costs about COP$130,000, while a more sedate half-day on the Río Fonce is COP$35,000. **Abseiling** down the Juan Curí waterfalls will set you back COP$40,000, or you can take flight with a tandem **paraglide** (COP$65,000–175,000 depending on location). **Spelunkers** have the choice of several caves to explore (around COP$25,000). Other sporty options include kayaking, horseriding and extreme mountain biking.

Most accommodation can arrange any of the above, and you should pay the same as if you book direct. The staff at *Macondo Guesthouse* are particularly helpful if you're trying to decide what to opt for. Alternatively, **recommended operators** are:

Colombian Bike Junkies ☎ 316 327 6101, ⓦ colombianbikejunkies.com.
Colombia Rafting Expediciones Cra 10 no. 7–83 ☎ 311 283 8647, ⓦ colombiarafting.com.

Nativox Cra 11 no. 7–14 ☎ 318 777 9999, ⓦ nativoxsangil.com.
Páramo Santander Extremo Cra 4 no. 4–57 ☎ 7 725 8944, ⓦ paramosantanderextremo.com.

Donde Betty Cra 10, cnr Parque Central. The best place for fruit juices (COP$3000) and superb scrambled eggs, each portion cooked and served in its own miniature frying pan; try the *huevos rancheros* (with fresh tomato, chorizo and coriander) or the *huevos Israeelis* (with onions and spinach). Mains COP$3500. Mon–Sat 7am–11pm, Sun 8am–1pm.

★**Gringo Mike's** C 12 no. 8–35. Sooner or later, everyone makes their way to this candlelit courtyard for the mega breakfast burritos, brie-and-bacon burgers the size of your head, doorstop sandwiches and that old gringo dessert favourite, brownie with ice cream. Mains COP$17,000. Daily 8am–noon & 5–11pm.

El Maná C 10 no. 9–12. Ask a local for advice on restaurants and you'll probably be directed here: *El Maná* is extremely popular for its dependable set meals (COP$11,500), which come with a choice of dishes such as grilled trout and *carne asado* (grilled meat). You won't leave hungry. Mon–Sat 11am–2.30pm & 6–9pm, Sun 11am–3pm.

AROUND SAN GIL

Cascadas de Juan Curí

For a spectacular swim in a natural pool at the base of a 180m-high waterfall, or to abseil down its face (see box opposite), take a trip out of town to the **Juan Curí waterfalls**. Take a bus to Charalá (35min) from Calle 10 on the east side of the bridge, and ask to be let off at the *Las Cascadas* sign. From here it's a 25-minute walk to the waterfalls along either of the two trails; you will be asked to pay COP$7000 by the owners of the land.

Parque Nacional del Chichamocha

About an hour from San Gil on the road to Bucaramanga, Colombia's newest **national park** (Tues–Thurs 9am–6pm, Fri–Sun 10am–7pm; COP$17,000, or COP$30,000 including entrance to the waterpark; ⓦparquenacionaldelchicamocha.com) holds a collection of tacky, forgettable attractions situated next to a beautiful canyon. The *teleférico*, a cable car which runs down into the canyon and over to the other side, is the best way to get sweeping views (Wed & Thurs 9–11am & 1–5.30pm, Fri–Sun 9am–4.30pm; park entrance with *teleférico* COP$42,000). You can also watch the scenery whizz by at much higher speed while hurtling along a zipline (COP$26,000), or get a bird's-eye view by paragliding above the valley (COP$180,000).

BARICHARA

With its undulating stone-slab roads, clay-tiled *tejas* roofs draped in bougainvillea blossoms and single-storey adobe homes, the sedate colonial town of **BARICHARA** looks like it hasn't changed much in its 250 years. So well kept is the town that it was declared a national monument in 1978 and, with its historical buildings restored, it now makes a popular set for Spanish-language films. Barichara is considerably less crowded than similarly picturesque Villa de Leyva, making it a peaceful, if expensive, resting spot for travellers. Indeed, the town's name comes from an Indian word, *Barachala*, meaning "a good place to rest". Alternatively, it makes for a great day-trip from San Gil.

WHAT TO SEE AND DO

Barichara's quiet streets, lined with beautiful architecture, and tranquil vibe are its biggest attraction. Once you've checked out the striking **Catedral de la Inmaculada Concepción**, which stands on fluted sandstone columns on the Parque Principal, the leafy main square, take a look at the elaborate marble tombs at the **Capilla de Jesús Resucitado cemetery**. Surrounding an attractive patio at **Casa de la Cultura** (Mon & Wed–Sat 9am–noon & 2–5pm, Sun 9am–noon; COP$1000) is a collection of regional photos, Guane pottery, fossils and various early twentieth-century paraphernalia.

Very popular with hikers is the 9km **Camino Real**, an ancient stone-paved trail used by the indigenous Guane people, leading down through a cactus-filled valley with great mountain views to the tiny village of **Guane** (2hr one-way). To join the path, head uphill along C 5 from the cathedral before taking a left along Cra 10 to the edge of Barichara. From Guane, there are five buses daily back to Barichara, the last leaving at 6pm; bring plenty of water and wear sturdy footwear.

5

ARRIVAL AND DEPARTURE

By bus Buses run between Barichara's Parque Central and San Gil's local bus terminal (every 30min 5am–6.30pm; 45min).

ACCOMMODATION

There is far more choice for budget accommodation in San Gil than there is in Barichara.

Casa de Hercilia C 3 no. 5–33 ☎315 641 1841, ⊛lacasadehercilia.com. A light and airy guesthouse that oozes tranquillity, with hammocks, beanbags and leafy pot plants liberally scattered throughout. Also has a well-equipped communal kitchen. No dorms, but in low season it's worth asking about renting a single bed in one of their bigger rooms. COP$100,000

Color de Hormiga Hostel C 6 no. 5–35 ☎7 726 71 56, ⊛colordehormiga.com/hostel.html. Set in an old colonial house half a block from the central square, this light and airy hostel in pretty pastels has a courtyard dotted with hammocks. There's a shared kitchen and TV room. No breakfast service, a/c or activities, but if you're looking for a tranquil stay, this place will do nicely. Dorms COP$25,000, doubles COP$70,000

EATING

Some restaurants only open at weekends, and many are shut on Tuesdays.

La Casona C6 no. 5–68. Just off the main square, this popular lunch spot with an inner courtyard serves up traditional Santander cuisine such as *cabrito* (baby goat) to a backdrop of *vallenato* music. The Botero replicas that cover the walls are for sale. Daily 9am–6pm.

Panadería Central C 6, at Cra 6, no. 5–82. This lovely bright bakery on the main square selling bread, cheese, ham and cream-filled puffs and doughnuts is a useful spot for walkers in search of picnic provisions. Daily 7am–9pm.

BUCARAMANGA

Founded in 1622, **BUCARAMANGA** has shed much of its colonial heritage and evolved into one of Colombia's largest, most modern cities. The centre might be low on attractions, but it makes a great jumping-off point for visits to nearby Girón, the mountains surrounding the city are superb for paragliding and it is a convenient stopover for anyone travelling to the coast or Venezuela.

WHAT TO SEE AND DO

Simón Bolívar (El Libertador) spent a grand total of seventy days living in Bucaramanga in 1828, enough for the locals to rename the beautiful house where he stayed, at C 37 no. 12–15, **Casa de Bolívar** (Mon–Fri 8am–noon & 2–6pm, Sat 8am–noon; COP$2000). It contains a small historical museum, the highlight of which is the Guane mummies and artefacts. Across the street another colonial mansion houses the **Casa de la Cultura** (Mon–Fri 8am–noon & 2–6pm, Sat 8am–noon; free), which holds displays of regional art. Also of interest to art lovers is the **Museo de Arte Moderno** (C37 no. 26–16; Mon–Fri 8am–noon & 2–6pm, Sat 8am–noon; free), featuring temporary exhibitions of contemporary painting and sculpture.

Bucaramanga is justifiably taking off as a **paragliding** destination, thanks to Colombia Paragliding (☎312 432 6266, ⊛colombiaparagliding.com), which offers everything from one-off ten-minute tandem flights (COP$50,000) to ten-day courses for those who want their international licence (COP$2,500,000). The owners, who run *Kasa Guane*, also have a hostel at their flight site outside town, which means you can be airborne within about ten minutes of getting out of bed.

ARRIVAL AND DEPARTURE

By plane Palonegro International Airport lies about 30km southwest of the downtown area. The taxi fare to downtown is fixed at COP$30,000. You can also take one of the *colectivos* that run to and from Parque Santander on Cra 20 (COP$10,000). Alternatively, your accommodation can arrange a lift in a shared taxi. There are ten flights daily to Bogotá (1hr).

By bus The Terminal de Transportes is about 5km southwest of the city, and is accessible by city bus marked "Terminal" from Cra 15, or by taxi (COP$6500).

Destinations Bogotá (every 15min; 10hr); Cartagena (8 daily; 12hr); Cúcuta (several daily; 6hr); Santa Marta (2 daily; 9hr).

ACCOMMODATION

Balmoral C 21, at Cra 35 ☎7 630 4663. Lacking in style, but has very cheap double rooms which are clean, secure and have private baths and TVs. Many also have fridges, and there's internet and a restaurant serving cheap breakfasts and lunches on the ground floor. COP$55,000

★**Kasa Guane** C 49 no. 28–21 ☎7 657 6960, ⊛kasaguane .com. *Kasa Guane* has airy dorms, basic doubles, a good communal kitchen, TV area, hammocks, a pool table, free wi-fi and enthusiastic staff happy to share with you the wonders of the surrounding area, including hikes in the nearby mountains. The top-floor bar is great if you want to socialize. Its sister hostel, *Nest*, perched on a hilltop, is more expensive, but there's no better base if paragliding is your passion. Dorms COP$23,000, doubles COP$45,000

EATING AND DRINKING

Keep an eye out for regional specialities such as *cabra* (goat). You'll find a proliferation of bars near Parque Las Palmas.

Govinda Cra 20 no. 34–65. Cheap-as-chips Hare Krishna spot, offering good-value set vegetarian meals, with a daily main and side dishes costing you no more than COP$6500. Mon–Sat 8am–3pm.

Rio Palma Cra 29, at C 48. An extremely popular two-storey bar with live music upstairs at weekends and canned tunes the rest of the week. Full of lively groups swigging beer from early in the evening. Open until 2am.

El Viejo Chiflas Cra 33 no. 34–10. *Comida típica* including *cabra en salsa* (goat in sauce; COP$20,000) and nibbles such as chorizo or *papas criollos* (COP$5500); perfect for night owls. Mon–Wed 7am–midnight, Thurs–Sun 24hr.

GIRÓN

With its whitewashed colonial buildings, leafy main square, stone bridges and elegant churches, pretty **GIRÓN** makes for a great day-trip from nearby Bucaramanga, and is particularly worthwhile for those who don't have time to visit other colonial gems like Villa de Leyva and Barichara. The pace of life here is extremely relaxed, and the narrow cobbled streets are perfect for a wander. Keep an eye out for the main **Catedral del Señor de los Milagros** and the attractive eighteenth-century **capilla de las Nieves** on the tiny namesake square.

ARRIVAL AND DEPARTURE

By bus Buses from Bucaramanga drop you off on the corner of Cra 26 and C 32 and pick you up from C 29 and Cra 26.
By taxi A taxi from Bucaramanga's bus terminal to Girón costs COP$12,000; from the airport it's around COP$24,000.

ACCOMMODATION AND EATING

Girón Chill Out Cra 25 no. 32–06 ☎7 646 1119, ⓦ gironchillout.com. The Italian-run hotel offers cosy rooms. Breakfast included. Single occupancy COP$120,000, doubles COP$174,000

Restaurante La Casona C 28 no. 28–05. Just off the Plazuela de los Nieves, this rustic-style restaurant set in a colonial house specializes in regional Santander dishes,

served by staff in traditional costumes. The goat with yucca (COP$19,900) and the trout dishes come recommended. Daily noon–8pm.

PARQUE NACIONAL EL COCUY

PARQUE NACIONAL EL COCUY (entrance for foreigners COP$50,000) rises to a high point of 5330m above sea level, taking in 32 glacial lakes and 22 snowcapped peaks, and is a hiker's dream. Be prepared for any climatic conditions and be aware that at night it gets bitterly cold, so pack plenty of warm gear and a four-season sleeping bag (you can rent sleeping bags from tour companies, but they may not be as warm as you need). By far the best weather is from December to February.

At the time of writing, the main seven-day circuit trek was closed to hikers as the indigenous U'wa tribe have revoked access to the eastern section of the park. Check ⓦ parquesnacionales .gov.co for updates before visiting.

WHAT TO SEE AND DO

Although the full seven-day circuit trek is currently closed, you can still visit the western section of the circuit: from Lagunillas to Boqueron de Cusiri (4410m), and Kanwara to Boqueron de Cardenillo (4460m). The starting points for any trip to the park are the towns of **El Cocuy** and **Güicán**. You can do day-long forays into the park from the gateway villages, or from a few mountain cabañas inside the park itself that can be used as bases for day walks, or as a place to acclimatize to the altitude before embarking on a longer hike.

The southern sector is the most popular. *Cabañas Sisuma* (☎321 345 7076; COP$40,000/person), near Las Lagunillas at the south end of the park, is a good base for walks to the stunning **Laguna de la Plaza**, a beautifully situated glacial lake, and **El Pulpito del Diablo** (The Devil's Pulpit), a column of rock that sits dramatically in the middle of a glacier. The park's central sector contains its most challenging peaks, notably the two peaks of San Pablín (5200m), but you need to be an experienced climber even to think about taking these on. You can also visit

5

Ritacuba Blanco, the park's highest peak (5330m), in the northern sector. Another possible trek, taking 6hr each way (so plan for an overnight stay), is over the Boquerón del Cardenillo pass to Laguna Grande de los Verdes.

Get in touch with a tour operator to arrange a guide (recommended).

ARRIVAL AND DEPARTURE

By bus From Bogotá, there are around six El Cocuy-bound buses daily, the first leaving around 5am (11hr). Returning from El Cocuy, overnight Libertadores buses to Bogotá depart at 4.30pm and 7pm daily from the main square, while Concorde buses leave at 4.30pm and 7pm and cheaper Fundadores minibuses leave from Cra 5 no. 5–38 (3 daily). From Bogotá, there are morning departures for Güicán with either Libertadores or Fundadores (12hr), the return buses leaving Güicán's main square around 7pm. To get from El Cocuy to Güicán there are three Cootradatil buses daily (30min).

To the park From Güicán it takes 5hr to hike to the park entrance, while hiring private transport to take you up there will set you back around COP$85,000–100,000. It's cheaper to hitch a ride on a *lechero* (milk truck; COP$6000–10,000) to the mountain farms; they depart from the main square in Güicán at 5.30am, then at 6am from El Cocuy plaza. Since there are several milk trucks, ask around to make sure you're going to the right place; they tend to drop you off at the intersection nearest to the cabañas, so you'll have to hike the rest of the way.

Park entrance Pay the entrance fee at the park offices in the town of El Cocuy (Calle 5 no. 4–22) or Güicán (Transversal 4a no. 6–60) the day before you plan to enter the park. Both offices close at 4.45pm. If you don't have personal travel insurance, you will be asked to purchase it at the office for COP$7000/day per person.

GUIDES

Ecoturismo Comunitario Sisuma ☎311 885 4263, ⓦelcocuyboyaca.com. You can hire guides from this guide cooperative within the park boundaries – for around COP$90,000 per day for an accredited guide for up to six people.
Colombia Trek ☎320 339 3839, ⓦcolombiatrek.com. Bilingual climber Rodrigo Aria comes highly recommended; he rents out equipment and arranges personalized packages (3–4 days) for up to four people and a guide (cheaper if it's a Spanish-speaking guide).

ACCOMMODATION

The village of Güicán makes for a closer and easier hike into the park, while El Cocuy has the lion's share of facilities (including an ATM) and accommodation. Most places to eat are inside hotels.

GÜICÁN
Brisas del Nevado Cra 5 no. 4–5 ☎310 629 9001, ⓦbrisasdelnevado.com. Quite possibly the best hotel in town, complete with restaurant serving delicious takes on local specialities (COP$10,000 per meal) and private baths in most rooms. Per person C̲O̲P̲$̲3̲5̲,̲0̲0̲0̲
El Eden Transversal 2 no. 9–58 ☎311 808 8334. Family-run guesthouse popular with travellers, with assorted wildlife in the garden and (mostly) en-suite rooms filled with the smell of pine. It's a 10min walk from the main square; turn right onto the dirt road from Cra 4 past the basketball court, then first right and second left. Campsite C̲O̲P̲$̲1̲0̲,̲0̲0̲0̲, rooms per person C̲O̲P̲$̲2̲5̲,̲0̲0̲0̲

EL COCUY
Hotel Casa Muñoz Cra 5 no. 7–26 ☎8 789 0328, ⓦhotelcasamunoz.com. Modern, not terribly memorable hotel on the main square, with functional, clean rooms around a flower-filled courtyard and reliable hot showers. Rooms per person C̲O̲P̲$̲3̲0̲,̲0̲0̲0̲

CROSSING INTO VENEZUELA: CÚCUTA

The only reason to visit the border town of **Cúcuta** is if you're heading by land to Venezuela. The city is polluted, hot and crime-ridden and not a place to linger, with a dodgy bus station to boot, so exercise utmost caution. Frequent buses and *colectivos* run across the border from Cúcuta's bus terminal and also from the corner of Av Diagonal Santander and Calle 8 to Venezuela's San Antonio de Táchira or San Cristóbal, one hour from Cúcuta (around COP$3000), or else you can take a taxi (COP$18,000). The border is open 6am–6pm, seven days a week. At the time of writing, citizens of the US, Canada, Australia, New Zealand, the UK and much of Western Europe do not require visas to enter Venezuela (see p.860). You must disembark at the DAS post just before the bridge to get your Colombian exit stamp. Once over the border, remember to put your watch forward thirty minutes and pick up a tourist card at the DIEX office on Carrera 9 between Calles 6 and 7.

It's best to take as much cash in US dollars to Venezuela as you can (see p.861).

From San Cristóbal there are around seven overnight departures daily for **Caracas** (14hr), all leaving late afternoon or early evening.

5

La Posada del Molino Cra 3 no. 7–51 ☎ 310 494 5076, 🖰 elcocuycasamuseo.blogspot.com. An allegedly haunted colonial mansion featuring patios, a handful of en-suite rooms with some period furniture and unusual bathrooms. Rooms per person COP$40,000

Cartagena and the Caribbean

Ever since Rodrigo de Bastidas became the first European to set foot on Colombian soil in Santa Marta in 1525, there's been a long history of foreigner fascination with the country's Caribbean coastline, and hundreds of thousands – Colombian holidaymakers chief among them – follow in his footsteps annually. In addition to hot weather and cool breezes, **Cartagena** boasts splendours from the town's past role as the main conduit for the Spanish Crown's imperial plundering. For its extensive fortifications and colonial legacy, the walled city was declared a UNESCO World Heritage Site in 1984.

The 1600km coast holds a wide variety of landscapes from the inaccessible dense jungles of the **Darién Gap** on the border with Panama to the arid salt plains of the **Guajira Peninsula**. If it's a tropical paradise you're after, try the white, jungle-fringed beaches of **Tayrona National Park** and **Palomino** near **Santa Marta**. The translucent waters around the fishing village of **Taganga** number among the most inexpensive places in the world to learn to scuba dive. Inland, travel back to the sixteenth century in sleepy **Mompox** and cross paths with coca-chewing Kogis on a mesmerizing five-day trek to the **Ciudad Perdida**.

While the vast majority of travellers come straight to Cartagena by night bus from Medellín, it's possible to break your journey in the appealing beach town of **Tolú** and do a day-trip to the **Islas de San Bernardo** archipelago.

CARTAGENA DE INDIAS

Without a doubt the Caribbean's most beautiful city, **CARTAGENA DE INDIAS** offers stunning colonial architecture, gourmet dining, all-night partying and beaches. Cartagena literally embodies Colombia's Caribbean coast, with many of the city's colourful, weathered buildings built using coral from the surrounding reefs.

Founded in 1533, Cartagena was one of the first Spanish cities in the New World and served as the main port through which the continent's riches were shipped off to the mother country. Not surprisingly, the city proved an appetizing target for English pirates prowling the Caribbean, and it suffered several sieges in the sixteenth century, the most infamous led by Sir Francis Drake in 1586, during which he held the town hostage for more than a hundred days. After "the Dragon" was paid a hefty ransom to withdraw, the Spaniards began constructing the elaborate fortifications that are now the city's hallmark. Cartagena's monopoly on the Caribbean slave trade in the early seventeenth century is evident in its diverse population, the rhythms of its music, its songs, dances and traditions.

WHAT TO SEE AND DO

Bursting with history, Cartagena's supremely photogenic walled **Old City** is a colourful assault on the senses and where the bulk of the sightseeing is. The greatest pleasure here is wandering the narrow streets, lined with colonial buildings painted in bold colours with their wrought-iron detail, bougainvillea tumbling down from balconies, peddlers trying to sell you all manner of tat, and horse-drawn carriages passing by. You might get a little lost, but the city's many **plazas** can guide you, acting not only as convenient landmarks but also as distinct social hangouts. You can take in the city by strolling the 11km of stone **ramparts** that encircle it, though it's best to avoid this late at night.

San Diego, home to a good number of mid-priced *hostals* and several hostels, offers a more mellow, though still lively, version of the Old City. Grittier **Getsemaní**, where *cumbia* music blasts out in the plazas, lacks some of the architectural grandeur of the walled city but offers a better taste of local life. The most raucous nightlife and nearly all budget accommodation are found here. South of the Old City is **Bocagrande**, Cartagena's modern tourist sector, a thin isthmus dotted with high-rise hotels.

Plaza de los Coches and around

The city's main entranceway is the triple-arched **Puerta del Reloj**, which gives way to the **Plaza de los Coches**, a triangular former slave-trading square. Today, it's where horse-drawn carriages can be hired for tours of the city and the stage for street performances. In the centre stands a statue

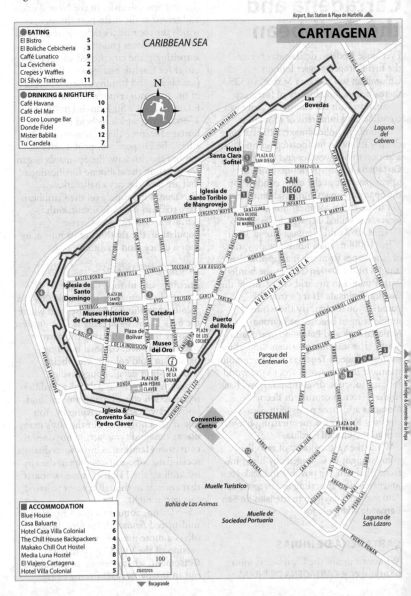

EATING

El Bistro	5
El Boliche Cebicheria	3
Caffé Lunatico	9
La Cevicheria	2
Crepes y Waffles	6
Di Silvio Trattoria	11

DRINKING & NIGHTLIFE

Café Havana	10
Café del Mar	4
El Coro Lounge Bar	1
Donde Fidel	8
Mister Babilla	12
Tu Candela	7

ACCOMMODATION

Blue House	1
Casa Baluarte	7
Hotel Casa Villa Colonial	6
The Chill House Backpackers	4
Makako Chill Out Hostel	3
Media Luna Hostel	8
El Viajero Cartagena	2
Hotel Villa Colonial	5

CARIBBEAN SEA

CARTAGENA

Airport, Bus Station & Playa de Marbella

Castillo de San Felipe & Convento de la Popa

Las Bovedas

Laguna del Cabrero

Hotel Santa Clara Sofitel

PLAZA DE SAN DIEGO

SAN DIEGO

Iglesia de Santo Toribio de Mangrovejo

7 INFANTES

PLAZA DE JOSE FERNANDEZ DE MADRID

AVENIDA VENEZUELA

Iglesia de Santo Domingo

PLAZA DE SANTO DOMINGO

Museu Historico de Cartagena (MUHCA)

Catedral

Plaza de Bolívar

C DE LA INQUISICION

Museo del Oro

Puerto del Reloj

PLAZA DE LOS COCHES

Parque del Centenario

PLAZA DE LA ADUANA

Iglesia & Convento San Pedro Claver

PLAZA DE SAN PEDRO CLAVER

Convention Centre

GETSEMANÍ

PLAZA DE LA TRINIDAD

Muelle Turistico

Bahía de Las Animas

Muelle de Sociedad Portuaria

Laguna de San Lázaro

PUENTE ROMAN

0   100
metres

Bocagrande

of the city's founder, **Pedro de Heredia**, while in the plaza's covered arcade, **Portal de los Dulces**, vendors adeptly pluck sweets of your choice out of a sea of huge glass jars. In the evening, several lively bars open up above the arcade.

Plaza de la Aduana and around

The largest and oldest square, the **Plaza de la Aduana**, once used as a parade ground, features the restored Royal Customs House, now the City Hall, and a statue of Columbus.

Convento and Iglesia de San Pedro Claver

Standing on the quiet plaza of the same name, the imposing **Convento de San Pedro Claver** (Mon–Fri 8.30am–5.30pm, Sat & Sun 8am–4.30pm; COP$9000) was founded by Jesuits in 1603, and is where Spanish-born priest Pedro Claver lived (and died, in 1654). Called the "slave of the slaves" for his lifelong ministering to the city's slaves, aghast at the conditions in which they lived, the ascetic monk was canonized two centuries after his death. His skull and bones are guarded in a glass coffin at the altar of the adjacent **church** (9.30am–noon & 3–5pm; free). The convent itself is a grand three-storey building surrounding a large courtyard bursting with greenery; besides exhibits of religious art and pre-Columbian ceramics, there's a superb display on the top floor featuring colourful, contemporary Haitian art and intricate African wooden masks and carvings.

Plaza de Bolívar

Locals and tourists alike come to find respite from the heat in this leafy, shaded square, with a statue of **Simón de Bolívar** as its centrepiece. Formerly the Plaza de Inquisición, the square is surrounded by some of Cartagena's most opulent buildings.

Museu Historico de Cartagena (MUHCA)

On the west side of Plaza de Bolívar stands MUHCA, formerly known as the **Palacio de la Inquisición** (Mon–Sat 9am–6pm, Sun 10am–4pm; COP$16,000), a splendid block-long example of late colonial architecture. The seat of the dreaded Inquisition for two hundred years from 1611 onwards, it wasn't completed until 1776, and is believed to be the site where at least eight hundred people were sentenced to death. Heretics were denounced at the small window topped with a cross, around the corner from the entrance, and culprits found guilty of witchcraft and blasphemy were sentenced to public autos-da-fé (executions) until independence in 1821. The museum within features a particularly interesting display of torture implements favoured by the Inquisition, as well as scale models of Cartagena, pre-Columbian pottery and displays on the city's history.

Museo de Oro

If you're haven't yet visited Bogotá's larger counterpart, this excellent **gold museum** (Tues–Fri 10am–1pm & 3–7pm, Sat 10am–1pm & 2–5pm, Sun 11am–4pm; free), off the Plaza de Bolívar, will whet your appetite. The displays feature the intricate gold creations of pre-Columbian cultures, particularly the Zenú. Look out for their intricate "woven" earrings and mammal-bird hybrids, as well as the elaborate gold and copper figures of the Tayrona and the schematic representations of shamans from the San Jacinto range.

Catedral

Looming above the northeast corner of the Plaza de Bolívar is the fortress-like **Catedral** (Mass only: Mon–Sat 10am & noon; Sun 8am, 2pm & 7pm), whose construction began in 1575, but which wasn't completed until 1612 due to setbacks such as its partial destruction by cannon fire in 1586 by Sir Francis Drake when Cartagena was slow to come up with the extortionate ransom he demanded. The interior is airy and pleasantly austere.

Iglesia de Santo Toribio de Mangrovejo

The compact church of **Iglesia de Santo Toribio de Mangrovejo** (Mass only: Mon–Fri 6.30am, noon & 6.15pm) on Calle del Sargento Major, built between

5

1666 and 1732, has a particularly attractive interior, with splendid Mudéjar panelling and a striking altar. During the failed attack on the city by Vernon in 1741 a cannonball landed inside the church but didn't cause casualties; you can see it in a glass display case on the left wall.

Iglesia de Santo Domingo

On the lively **Plaza de Santo Domingo** and fronted by Fernando Botero's voluptuous *La Gorda* sculpture, the church of **Santo Domingo** (Mass only: Mon 6am, 11am & 5pm; Tues–Sun 11am & 5pm) constitutes the plaza's main draw. Completed in 1579, the fortress-like structure's austere interior belies its status as Cartagena's oldest church. On the Baroque altar there's a sixteenth-century carved Christ.

Las Bovedas

In the northeast corner of the walled city, these mustard-coloured dungeons, built into the city walls between 1792 and 1796, have been used variously as munitions storage, a jail and – their current incarnation – as craft shops.

Convento de la Popa

For a bird's-eye view of Cartagena, take a taxi (30–45min; around COP$45,000 return; haggle) up the hill 2km northeast of the Castillo de San Felipe to the **Convento de la Popa** (Mon–Fri 8.45am–5.30pm; COP$8000), outside the city's walls. Alternatively, take a city tour (COP$45,000) on one of the brightly coloured buses known as chivas leaving daily from the Torre del Reloj. Don't walk: robberies have been reported along that zigzagging road. The restored whitewashed chapel, built in 1608, is clearly visible from almost anywhere in the city. In addition to offering spectacular panoramic views of the city, photos of Pope John Paul II's 1986 visit to Cartagena are also on display in the small chapel. On February 2, when the city celebrates the day of its patron saint, the **Virgin of Candelaria**, protector against pirates and the plague, a candle-lit procession of pilgrims storms the hill.

Castillo de San Felipe de Barajas

More than a single, uniform wall, Cartagena is surrounded by a series of impressive fortresses, most of which are still standing. The largest and most important was **Castillo de San Felipe de Barajas** (daily 8am–6pm; COP$17,000), a towering stone fort just east of the walled city along Avenida Pedro de Heredia. The sacking of the city by Sir Frances Drake highlighted the need for protection, and so this mighty fort was built between 1656 and 1798 with plans from a Dutch engineer. The fort is an ideal spot from which to watch the sunset, and getting the audioguide is well worth it while you walk around the fort walls and underground passages, learning about its important landmarks, such as the leper hospital. Alternatively, you can talk to one of the guides who hang around at the entrance.

Other forts

The majority of Cartagena's other remaining defences, most of them nearer to the sea than San Felipe, were built much later, during the dawning of the Spanish Empire in the late eighteenth century. Visible on excursions to Islas del Rosario, the **Fuerte de San Fernando** on Tierrabomba Island was built to seal off Bocachica, which, after a sandbar blocked Bocagrande in 1640, was the only access to the city's harbour. As part of the complex engineering, a heavy bronze chain was dangled across the entrance beneath the water to the restored **Batería de San José**. Boats to Tierrabomba Island depart every 30–45 minutes from the Muelle Turística, also known as La Bodegita (15min; COP$13,000; entrance to both forts COP$8000).

Islas del Rosario

At least fifty minutes out to sea from Cartagena, 35km southwest of the city lies an archipelago of small coral islands known as the **Islas del Rosario**, in transparent turquoise waters. In total there are 27 islands, many of them private islets barely large enough for a bungalow. Not technically part of the chain, **Playa Blanca**, on Barú island, is one of the more popular beach spots.

For **day-trips by boat**, all of which depart in the morning around 8–9.30am and return around 4–5pm, you can either book through your accommodation or head straight to the **Muelle Turística**, the wharf across from the Convention Center. For COP$60,000 you can get a round-trip ride on a boat to Playa Blanca with about twenty others, including a lunch of fried fish, *patacones* (smashed, fried plantains), rice and salad. Larger boats, such as the *Alcatraz*, are cheaper (COP$40,000) but tend to be slower, and you do spend a lot of time on the boat.

The boats sail through Bocachica Strait, passing between Fuerte de San Fernando and Batería de San José, and stopping for lunch on Playa Blanca on Isla de Barú where you're let loose for a couple of hours. If you're short of time, ask if there's a boat heading straight to Playa Blanca and missing out the "panoramic tour" on the way.

There are a few basic **accommodation** options on the island, with hammocks available for around COP$15,000 and rustic huts for around COP$25,000. Snorkelling costs COP$30,000 – COP$5000 if you bring your own gear – and entrance to the open-water aquarium that's a stop on some trips (ask ahead) is COP$25,000. A COP$13,500 park fee applies to all those leaving from the port.

Volcán de Lodo El Totumo

The small, mud-blowing **Volcán de Lodo El Totumo**, 50km northeast of Cartagena, makes for another popular day-trip. You can clamber down into the crater for a refreshing wallow in the mud (COP$5000) that allegedly has therapeutic properties, while helpful locals gather nearby, offering to photograph you in your *Creature From the Black Lagoon* guise, and to give you an energetic but not terribly professional massage. Most hostels arrange this trip (around COP$55,000, including lunch at La Boquillo beach).

ARRIVAL AND DEPARTURE

By plane Cartagena's Rafael Nuñez International Airport is 10min by taxi (COP$12,000) or a slightly longer bus ride (COP$1700) from the city centre.

Destinations Multiple flights daily to Bogotá (1hr 20min), Cali (1hr 25min) and Medellín (1hr 20min). Twice-daily flights to San Andrés (2hr).

By bus The city's large bus terminal is 1hr by bus northwest from the city centre; a taxi is quicker (30min) and will set you back COP$15,000; otherwise catch one of the frequent green Metrocar buses from Av Santander (40min; COP$2200).

Destinations Barranquilla (every 30min 5am–10pm; 2hr); Bogotá (every 2hr 6am–7pm; 22hr); Caracas (1 daily at 7am; 20hr); Medellín (6 daily 5am–9pm; 13hr); Mompox (1 daily at 7.30am; 8hr); Riohacha (every 2hr 5am–8pm; 7hr); Santa Marta (every 1–2hr 4.30am–8pm; 4hr).

By boat There's a ferry service to Colón in Panama (18hr; from COP$108,000 one-way/person; ⓦ successspanamatours .com), which departs from the Muelle de Sociedad Portuaría.

INFORMATION AND GETTING AROUND

Most visitors will get around by foot, though the streams of available taxis make a trip to the other end of town after a long night out easy.

Tourist information Turismo Cartagena de Indias (daily 9am–noon & 2–6pm; ☎ 5 660 1583, ⓦ cartagenadeindias .travel) is located in Plaza de la Aduana and stocks maps of the city.

ACCOMMODATION

Budget lodgings are spread out equally over the attractive San Diego neighbourhood in the heart of the historical centre, as well as grittier Getsemaní, a short walk from the Old City. Prices during the high season (Dec–Feb) usually surge ten to twenty percent.

Blue House Plaza Fernández Madrid, no. 38–08, San Diego ☎ 5 668 6501. For wonderfully friendly, personalized service from owner Alexandra, an unbeatable central location and three supremely comfortable rooms with balconies, this pint-sized hotel is attached to a jewellery shop and rum bar. Colombian breakfast is served in the tiny downstairs café, and you certainly can't miss the bright blue exterior. If you need a break from hostel dorms, this is an excellent bet. Doubles COP$200,000

Casa Baluarte C Media Luna no. 10–81, Getsemaní ☎ 5 664 2208, ⓦ hostalcasabaluarte.com. One of the more airy and upmarket guesthouses in the area, housed in an attractive colonial building. The 24 a/c rooms with terracotta floors are well kept and it's attached to the excellent *Caffé Lunatico*. COP$80,000

Hotel Casa Villa Colonial C de la Media Luna no. 10–89, Getsemaní ☎ 5 664 5421, ⓦ www.casavilla colonial.com. Quiet colonial house with spacious en-suite rooms (all have a/c), friendly staff and attractive communal areas to lounge around in. The small kitchen dispenses free coffee all day long. *Hotel Villa Colonial*, their sister hotel round the corner on the quieter C de las

5

Maravillas (no. 30–60) has simpler a/c rooms for COP$100,000. Doubles COP$170,000

The Chill House Backpackers C de la Tablada no. 7–12, San Diego ☎ 5 660 2386, ⓦ chillhousebackpackers.hostel .com. In a wonderfully central location, overlooking a small leafy square, this compact hostel's chilled vibe is reflected in its decor – retro posters, hammock in the indoor chillout area – and good bars and restaurants are just footsteps away. Dorms COP$22,000, doubles COP$80,000

Makako Chill Out Hostel C Quero no. 9–54, San Diego ☎ 5 660 6231. Located along one of the loveliest streets in the historical centre, the common area of this spacious colonial house is a great place to kick back and relax. Wonderfully tranquil yet also close to the action. Dorms COP$22,000, doubles COP$80,000

★**Media Luna Hostel** C Media Luna no. 10–46, Getsemaní ☎ 5 664 3423, ⓦ www.medialunahostel.com. Popular with young travellers, this smart super-hostel (with 160 beds) has rooms and dorms all overlooking the central courtyard with pool. There are plenty of tours on offer, and bicycles for rent (COP$3000/hr). Frequent parties on the enormous roof terrace – with a bar open until 3.30am – go on until the early hours. Dorms COP$50,000, doubles COP$100,000

El Viajero Cartagena C 7 Infantes no. 9–45, San Diego ☎ 5 660 2598. At this sociable hostel, the a/c rooms and dorms, decked out with comfortable beds and safe boxes, are clustered around a couple of inner courtyards with colourful murals where everyone meets to socialize and, on some nights, learn salsa. There's a small bar on-site as well as a tour agency. Don't count on getting much sleep on weekends. Dorms COP$30,000, doubles COP$136,000

EATING

Among Cartagena's greatest charms is its array of fine restaurants catering to all palates, though most are expensive.

El Bistro C de Ayos no. 4–46, El Centro ⓦ el-bistro-cartagena.com. German-owned bistro, bar and bakery popular with travellers, serving a Caribbean-Mediterranean fusion menu, including excellent curries. Mains are COP$13,000–20,000 and happy hour is 4–7pm daily. Mon–Sat 9am–11pm.

El Boliche Cebicheria Cra 8 no. 38–17, San Diego. Although not cheap, this thimble-sized *cevicheria* with an open kitchen dishes out delicious crabmeat *empanadas* (COP$37,000). The Costeño *ceviche* made with octopus, shrimp, squid and white fish (COP$39,000) served with sour cream and a crispy cassava roll are highly recommended. Daily 12.30–3pm & 7–11pm.

★**Caffé Lunatico** C de la Media Luna no. 10–81, Getsemaní. This Spanish-Colombian husband-and-wife team bring the best of their respective country's cuisine in tapas form to this compact café-restaurant-bar. Colourful decor – mismatched hanging lights, wall poetry and

vintage posters – adds to the bohemian atmosphere. Weekday lunch menu is COP$15,000, and there are excellent burgers and salads on the à la carte, plus a tapas tasting menu for two (COP$39,000). Mon–Sat 8am–11pm.

La Ceviceria C Stuart no. 7–14, San Diego. Small, smart *cevicheria* with lively outdoor seating, with music from passing street musicians filling the air. Innovative takes on *ceviche* – including shrimp, octopus and squid combos in coconut-lime and mango sauces. The Vietnamese-style grilled seafood on brown rice is nothing short of inspired. Mains around COP$40,000. Mon & Wed–Sun noon–11pm.

Crepes y Waffles C Baloco, at C Sta Teresa. A variety of crêpes, sweet and savoury, plus ice-cream sundaes and sweet waffles with a choice of toppings. Avoid on weekends when the harried staff find it difficult to keep up with orders. Waffles from COP$6000. Mon–Sat 10am–10pm, Sun 11am–6pm.

Di Silvio Trattoria C de la Sierpe no. 9A–08, Getsemaní. Spread across two buildings (one has a garden), this popular Italian trattoria off the vibrant Plaza de la Trinidad is a wonderful place to watch the world go by. The authentic pasta and pizzas are well priced at around COP$20,000–23,000, plus there's live music on Friday and Saturday nights. Tues–Sun 6.30–11pm.

DRINKING AND NIGHTLIFE

A concentration of tourist bars and dance clubs above the Portal de los Dulces overlooks the Plaza de los Coches; most charge a small cover. Locals gather at the cheaper clubs in Getsemaní along Calle del Arsenal. Another option for a night out is a *chiva* ride – essentially a party bus in an old-fashioned, luridly decorated trolley that takes you on a late-night city tour fuelled by rum, fried finger foods, and *vallenato* music. *Chivas* depart at 8–8.30pm from Bocagrande locations such as *Hotel Capilla del Mar*, at Cra 1 no. 8–12, or from Torre del Reloj at 7.30pm (☎ 5 650 1500; rides around COP$30,000, return at midnight).

Café Havana C de la Media Luna, at C del Guerrero, Getsemaní. You'll be transported to Old Havana at this packed Getsemaní spot, where black-and-white photos of Cuban music legends line the walls and thumping live Cuban beats get the crowd's hips swinging. Excellent mojitos (COP$14,000). Thurs–Sun 7pm–4am.

Café del Mar Baluarte de Santo Domingo, Old Town. Perched on the city's stone fortress walls, with spectacular 360-degree views of the Caribbean and the Old City's elegant colonial buildings, this is the perfect spot to lounge on an open-air couch with a sunset martini (COP$14,000) surrounded by cool locals. Food is served until 1am and DJs take over from 10pm. Dress nicely. Mon–Wed & Sun 5pm–3am, Fri & Sat until 5am.

Donde Fidel Portal de los Dulces no. 32–09, Old Town. These outdoor tables, between the city wall and the Plaza de los Coches, are the place to people-watch over a beer. Inside, every centimetre of the walls is covered with

★TREAT YOURSELF

El Coro Lounge Bar *Santa Clara Sofitel, C del Torno no. 39–29, San Diego* ☎ 5 650 4700, ⊛ www.sofitel.com. Lounge on a luxurious white leather sofa with an exclusive cocktail at this hotel bar. Housed in a former monastery dating from 1621, *El Coro* (the Choir), named after its original use, is a chic bar where you can immerse yourself in the architectural splendour of the city. The room itself evokes the sense of a grand library, with a majestic vaulted ceiling and giant wooden doors, and is the perfect place to curl up with a book during the day. At night, trendy locals arrive for the quality live music from Thursday to Saturday and regular house DJs. Expect to pay around COP$23,000 per cocktail.

pictures of owner Fidel and friends. Pounding Cuban music from an extensive salsa collection is the soundtrack to which couples get romantic. Open until 2am.

Mister Babilla *Av del Arsenal no. 8B–137, Getsemaní.* The tacky jungle-themed decor aside, this massive multi-floor club will get you dancing to at least one of its music genres, be it salsa, rock or house. The party usually extends until the wee hours of the morning. Entry COP$12,000. Tues–Sat 7pm–4am.

Tu Candela *Above the Portal de los Dulces no. 32–25, Old City.* One of Cartagena's wildest and most popular clubs, frequented by tourists and Colombian jet-setters, who dance the night away predominantly to salsa, though reggaeton, *merengue* and other genres creep on to the playlist. Entry COP$13,000. Daily 8pm–4am.

DIRECTORY

Banks and exchange Several banks with 24hr ATMs and casas de cambio are on the Plaza de la Aduana and adjoining streets, as well as along Av San Martín in Bocagrande.

Immigration For visa extensions, DAS has an office in the airport and at C Gastelbondo near the ramparts. Otherwise dial ☎ 153 for any immigration-related emergencies.

Medical Hospital Bocagrande on C 5 and Cra 6 (☎ 5 665 5270).

TOLÚ

Popular with holidaying Colombians but practically undiscovered by overseas travellers, the seaside town of **TOLÚ** is a pleasant, laidback spot to break your journey from Medellín to Cartagena. Bicycles rather than than cars fill the streets, though the brightly decorated *bicitaxis*, each one blaring its own choice of upbeat music, make up in volume for the lack of motorized traffic. While Tolú's beaches are nondescript in comparison to the ones in Parque Nacional Tayrona (see p.529), you can reach those 20km south, near Coveñas, by *colectivos* from the corner of Cra 2 and C 17 in Tolú. The town's malecón, lined with restaurants, craft stalls and bars, makes for a nice stroll, but Tolú's main attraction – the Islas de San Bernardo – lies off the coast.

LAS ISLAS DE SAN BERNARDO

An archipelago of ten islands, the **Islas de San Bernardo** are wonderfully tranquil (when not overrun by Colombian holidaymakers), and their teal waters and blinding-white beaches make for a great day-trip. Boats leave Tolú's Muelle Turístico at around 8.30/9am, returning around 4pm. Tours (COP$60,000) take in **Santa Cruz del Islote** – an island populated by fishermen – **Isla Tintípan**, the largest of the islands, and mangrove-fringed **Isla Múcura**, where you get to linger the longest – around three hours – to have lunch, sip a cold beer or go snorkelling. Tours finish on **Isla Palma**, which is the best of the lot when it comes to snorkelling, with greater visibility and an abundance of fish.

ACCOMMODATION

Casa en El Agua ⊛ casaenelagua.com. True to its name, *Casa en El Agua* ("house in the water") is a rustic hostel on stilts just off Isla Tintipan. Surrounded by coral reef, the wooden structure is the best budget accommodation in the paradisiacal archipelago. Spend your days snorkelling, sunbathing, and dodging scuttling crabs. The hostel offers trips out to nearby beaches, and night swims with the plankton. Delicious lobster dinners can be whipped up on demand, although it's best to bring at least some food supplies, along with water and cash. To get here, a public boat from Tolú leaves every morning for the islands, or splash out on a speedboat (COP$150,000) from Rincon del Mar (2hr from Cartagena). Wayyu hammocks COP$40,000, dorms COP$50,000, doubles per person COP$75,000

5

ARRIVAL AND DEPARTURE

By bus The bus station is on the southwest side of Plaza Pedro de Heredia.
Destinations Bogotá (2 daily; 19hr); Cartagena (several daily; 3hr); Medellín (5 daily; 10hr); Santa Marta (2 daily).

ACCOMMODATION AND EATING

There are plenty of informal places to eat along the malecón, most serving fried fish and *ceviche*, while around the main plaza there are several bakeries and *arepa* stalls.

Villa Babilla C 20 no. 3–40 ☎312 677 1325, ⓦvillababillahostel.com. A few minutes' walk from the waterfront, this German-owned guesthouse features airy, spotless rooms named after locations around the world. The ones on the first floor are somewhat pricier, but they do come with a nice terrace. There's free coffee all day and they'll wash your dirty togs, too. COP$80,000

MOMPOX

Marooned on a freshwater island in the vast low-lying wetlands of the Rio Magdalena's eastern branch, **MOMPOX** (also spelt Mompós) was founded in 1537 by Don Alonso de Heredia (brother of Cartagena's founder). It served as the lynchpin for the mighty river's trade network between coastal Cartagena and the country's interior, and remained one of Colombia's most prosperous commercial centres until the silt-heavy river changed its course in the late nineteenth century and Mompox was left to languish as a forgotten backwater. Simón Bolívar raised an army here and Mompox was the first town in Colombia to declare complete independence from Spain in 1810.

Its beauty has remained practically untouched ever since, and **UNESCO** declared it a World Heritage Site in 1995 in recognition of its outstanding colonial architecture. It was also the setting for **Gabriel García Márquez**'s classic novella *Chronicle of a Death Foretold*. Time seems to stand still here: locals unhurriedly putter around the unpaved streets and fishing boats ply the network of rivers and lakes. The town's remoteness has kept it out of mainstream travel but its appeal as the "anti-Cartagena" – architecture to rival the coastal city but none of the hustle – has seen a recent influx of visitors.

WHAT TO SEE AND DO

Mompox's grid of streets stretches out alongside the river and is easy to explore on foot. Its sprawl of grand Catholic churches and elaborate colonial mansions is a constant reminder of the town's faded glory and wealth. The town is also famous for its **wooden rocking chairs**, which residents drag on to the streets in the evenings to watch the world go by, as well as **filigree silver and gold** work sold around Calle Real del Medio, and **Vinimompox** – fruit wines made from banana, guava, orange and tamarind.

The best way to explore is to wander the streets, peeking at the whitewashed colonial houses with wrought-iron grilles, intricately carved doorways, clay-tile roofs and fragrant flower-draped balconies.

The churches

Of its six churches, the finest is **Iglesia de Santa Bárbara**, at the end of Calle 14 on the riverfront plaza of the same name. With its Baroque octagonal bell tower and Moorish balcony adorned with ornate mouldings of flowers and lions, it resembles a fancy cake. **Iglesia de San Agustín**, on Calle Real del Medio, houses several richly gilded religious objects, most notably the Santo Sepulcro, used in the traditional Semana Santa processions.

Cementerio Municipal

Hiding behind Mompox's most attractive leafy square, the atmospheric **cemetery** (C 18; daily 8am–noon & 2–5pm), where elaborate white marble tombs stand alongside more modest graves in the unkempt grass, will appeal to those with a taste for the macabre.

Museo Cultural

The **Museo Cultural**, at Cra 2 no. 14–15 (Mon–Fri 8am–noon & 2–5pm, Sat & Sun 8am–5pm; COP$3500), where Simón Bolívar once stayed, has a small collection of religious art. Bolívar's statue graces the small namesake square, while the inscription on the plinth of another Bolívar-related statue in a tiny nearby square reads (in Spanish): "To Caracas I owe my life but to Mompós I owe my glory."

Boat tours

Particularly worthwhile if you're interested in local birds and wildlife, **boat trips** are a great way to spend an afternoon and are best booked through *La Casa Amarilla*. Tours leave around 3pm, generally take four hours and cost COP$25,000–30,000, depending on the number of people. Your guide will point out numerous animals and birds that live alongside the river, such as giant iguanas, howler monkeys, herons, fishing eagles and kingfishers, and there's usually an opportunity for a swim in one of the lakes, such as the **Ciénaga de Pijino**, reachable by narrow channels from the main waterway. Returning by boat to Mompox after a quick sunset dip, you'll be greeted by a sixteenth-century vision of how the town would have appeared to new arrivals (if you discount the anachronistic mounds of twenty-first-century trash on the riverbank), with all six of its imposing churches facing the river to welcome you.

ARRIVAL AND INFORMATION

By bus Buses arrive and depart from the Expreso Brasilia/ Unitransco terminal, three blocks from the riverfront on C Atras and Santa Barbara. From Bogotá take a bus to El Banco, Magdalena (1–3 daily; 14hr), followed by a 4WD to Mompox (1hr). From Bucaramanga take a night bus to El Banco (3 daily; 9hr), then a 4WD. From Cartagena a direct bus leaves at 6.30am (8hr); for a faster route (5–6hr), take a direct bus to Managué, then a *chalupa* water taxi to Bodegá-Mompox (30min).

By van A door-to-door van (*"puerta a puerta"*) can be arranged from Cartagena with Toto Express (⊕ 310 707 0838; COP$75,000), and with a different company from Santa Marta (6–10hr; COP$80,000) and Taganga (6–10hr; COP$90,000), with 3am or 11am pick-up. Call *La Casa Amarilla* to book, or ask for more information at your hostel.

Tourist information There is no tourist office but Richard McColl at *La Casa Amarilla* is very knowledgeable. The three ATMs on Plaza Bolívar often run out of money, so arrive with plenty.

ACCOMMODATION

★**La Casa Amarilla** Cra 1 no. 13–59 ⊕ 5 685 6326, ⊚lacasaamarillamompos.com. Hands down the best place to stay in Mompox, this scenic guesthouse in a beautifully restored, riverfront colonial building has ten clean and stylish rooms, all en suite with a/c, cable TV and colourful murals. The bright, plant-filled courtyard is great for an afternoon hammock snooze, and the open-air shared kitchen, rooftop terrace, bike rental, book exchange, cable TV and stacks of DVDs make backpackers feel welcome. The owner – British journalist Richard McColl – is an excellent source of information and can arrange transport and tours. Single COP$50,000, doubles COP$60,000

Casa Hotel La Casona Cra 2 (C Real del Medio) no. 18–58 ⊕ 5 685 5307. The place to go if *La Casa Amarilla* is full, this atmospheric colonial building has a maze of communal areas, including pretty courtyards, lots of scattered rocking chairs and basic rooms. COP$60,000

EATING AND DRINKING

In the evenings, Plaza de Concepción is the best place to people-watch while sitting in one of the rocking chairs next to the huddle of open-air restaurants and sipping an ice-cold beer, while Plaza Santo Domingo bustles with popular food stands, selling juice, beer, pizzas, grilled meats and more.

★**Comedor Costeño** Cra 1 (Calle de la Albarrada). Informal outdoor eatery on the breezy riverfront serving excellent-value set meals. Try the mouthwatering *bagre* (catfish) with coconut rice, fried plantain and yucca, which comes with a fish soup starter and drink (COP$12,000). Daily noon–4pm.

Luna de Mompox Cra 1, Albarrada de Los Angeles. This lively bar on the riverfront can get cramped but has tables outside and is fun for a late-night drink. Daily until 1am, later on weekends.

BARRANQUILLA

Despite being Colombia's fourth-largest city and main port, **BARRANQUILLA**, on the mouth of the Río Magdalena, would be all but overlooked if it were not for its annual **Carnaval** (⊚carnavaldebarranquilla .org) – Colombia's biggest street party. For four days, this swelteringly hot, industrial city drapes itself in a riot of vibrant colours, playful costumes and pulsating music: salsa, *cumbia*, *vallenato* and African drumming. Preparations begin much earlier, in mid-January, and once the festivities begin, the town converts into one huge street party, kicked off by traditional parades like the "Battle of the Flowers" and "Dance of the Caiman". Parallel to the festivities, the city-sponsored gay Carnaval, though less publicized, is equally bacchanalian. Although barely known outside Latin America, Barranquilla's festivities are second only to Rio's Carnaval in size. Outside festival time, you'll only want to pass through on the way to either Cartagena or Santa Marta without stopping.

ARRIVAL AND DEPARTURE

By bus The bus terminal is 7km out of the city centre (COP$16,000 by taxi; 30min).

Destinations Bogotá (several daily; 18hr); Cartagena (every 30min; 2hr); Santa Marta (every 30min; 2hr).

ACCOMMODATION AND EATING

Arrange accommodation well in advance if you visit during Carnaval. The centre can be unsafe at night but this is where you'll find the cheapest options.

Hotel Colonial Inn C 42 no. 43–131 ☎ 5 379 0241. A reasonable bet in the centre, with clean and simple rooms, some with a/c; Carnaval parades pass nearby. Doubles COP$55,000

Sancochos y Asados de la 74 C 74 no. 49–10. Serves generous portions of Colombian favourites (mains COP$14,000–17,000).

SANTA MARTA AND AROUND

Although Colombia's oldest city, founded in 1525, **SANTA MARTA**'s colonial heritage was all but swept away at the hands of English and Dutch pirates. The result is a busy beach city geared to middle-class Colombians on holiday and international backpackers in search of jungle adventure. Though its narrow streets are clogged with traffic, restoration in the city centre over the past few years has created attractive public spaces, such as the Parque de los Novios, a pedestrian area surrounded with bustling restaurants, and an international marina full of yachts.

Not far away are some of the country's best beaches, particularly in and near **Parque Nacional Tayrona**, Colombia's most popular national park. Also close by is the fishing/party village of **Taganga**, ultra-popular with backpackers, hippies and holidaying Colombians. Santa Marta

also acts as the hub for organizing hikes (see p.531) to the **Ciudad Perdida**.

WHAT TO SEE AND DO

Although better known as the jumping-off point for the region's attractions, Santa Marta does have several sights of its own.

Casa de la Aduana and Museo del Oro Tairona

A striking building with wooden garrets underneath a pitched tile roof, the well-maintained **Casa de la Aduana** (Customs House; C 14 & Cra 2; Tues–Sat 9am–5pm, Sun 10am–3pm; free) is the city's oldest building, dating from 1531. Simón Bolívar stayed here briefly, and his body lay in state in an upstairs gallery after his death. On its ground floor, the recently renovated **Museo del Oro Tairona** has extensive displays on ancient Tayrona culture and its modern-day descendants – the Kogis, Arhuacos and Arsarios. A large-scale model of the Ciudad Perdida provides a valuable introduction for anyone planning to visit the ruins.

Quinta de San Pedro Alejandrino

Whether or not you have a particular interest in Colombia's liberation hero, the hacienda and sugar plantation 5km south of town where Simón Bolívar spent his last agonizing days makes for a great visit (daily 9am–5pm; COP$12,000; guided tours in Spanish included in the price). The lush grounds, with an enchanting forest of twisted trees and creeping vines, are a pleasure to wander, and you are likely to spot numerous giant iguanas perched on the trees. Peek into the

---

MAGICAL MACONDO

Before you came to Colombia, you may have read about the town of **Macondo** in *One Hundred Years of Solitude* by Gabriel García Márquez. Now you can visit it. Yes, officially it's called **Aracataca**, but the birthplace of the author seems to blur the lines between reality and magical realism. Aan't Goor (a.k.a. Tim Buendía) is a Dutchman who claims to be the last surviving member of the Buendía family from the novel and whose enthusiasm for the book knows no limits. For a fee (US$50 plus COP$30,000 for walking tour; ☎ timbuendia@gmail.com), he organizes guided walking tours around Aracataca which take in a plethora of García Márquez-themed attractions including the re-creation of the author's family home, followed by trips to nearby towns of Macondo and Sevilla. Homestays (COP$60,000 for two) can also be arranged.

Regular **buses** run to Aracataca from Santa Marta's market (1hr 30min).

mustard-coloured buildings for a glimpse of the Libertadór's personal effects – an Italian marble bathtub, miniature portraits of the Bolívar family and military badges. Just to the right of the imposing Altar de la Patria memorial, the **Museo Bolívariano** features contemporary works by artists from countries liberated by Bolívar – Colombia, Peru, Bolivia, Ecuador, Panama and Venezuela. Buses leaving the waterfront main drag (Cra 1) for the Mamatoco suburb will drop you off at the Quinta if you ask the driver (COP$1400), or take a taxi for COP$4500.

Catedral

The large whitewashed **catedral** (Cra 4, at C 17) is the oldest church in Colombia, though the current structure, with its bulky bell tower and stone portico, dates mostly from the seventeenth century. Just to the left of the entrance are the ashes of Rodrigo de Bastidas, the town's founder. Simón Bolívar's remains were kept here until 1842, when they were repatriated to his native Caracas.

ARRIVAL AND INFORMATION

By plane Santa Marta's Simón Bolívar airport is 16km south of the city centre. Taking a taxi to the airport costs COP$25,000.

Destinations Bogotá (12 daily; 1hr 30min); Medellín (3 daily; 1hr 30min).

By bus The Terminal de Transportes (main bus station) lies 5km to the southeast of the city centre and taxis cost around COP$8000.

Destinations Barranquilla (hourly; 2hr); Bogotá (hourly 2–8pm; 17hr); Bucaramanga (3 daily; 10hr); Cartagena (hourly 5am–8pm; 4hr); Medellín (11 daily; 15hr). Buses run between Taganga and Cra 5 in Santa Marta (every 10min 5am–10pm; COP$1400); and also to Palomino.

Taxis A taxi to Taganga costs COP$9000.

Tourist information There is a tourist office at C 16 no. 4–15 (Mon–Fri 8am–noon & 2–6pm; ☎5 438 2587), on the Plaza de la Catedral, where you can pick up free maps. Several tour operators (see box, p.531) in Santa Marta arrange trips to Ciudad Perdida and the Guajira Peninsula.

ACCOMMODATION

Hostels are numerous, but book in advance in December and January. Prices can double in peak season.

★**Aluna** C 21 no. 5–72 ☎5 432 4916, ⓦalunahotel.com. Feel well looked after and rested at this peaceful hostel, beautifully designed by Dublin-born architect and owner

Patrick Flemming. Paintings by local artists line the walls, rooms are spotless and fresh, thanks to wooden slats that allow air to circulate, and a bamboo roof offers welcome shade from the blazing midday sun. Excellent book exchange and a great little café on the premises. Pricier rooms have a/c. Dorms COP$25,000, doubles COP$70,000

★**La Brisa Loca** C 14 no. 3–58 ☎5 431 6121, ⓦlabrisaloca.com. This sprawling converted mansion, named after Santa Marta's wild coastal wind, is owned by two party-loving Californian dudes and has firmly established itself as a backpacker haven, with spacious dorms, a roof terrace, lively late-night bar, billiards and a well-used pool. The helpful bilingual staff are a plus. Dorms COP$20,000, doubles COP$90,000

★**The Dreamer** C 51 no. 26D–161, Magdalena ☎5 433 3264, ⓦthedreamerhostel.com. Some 5km out of town but closer to Tayrona and more than worth it for the atmosphere, this backpacker favourite has a pool in a hammock-bedecked courtyard, Italian and Mexican food on the menu and a plethora of day-trips (including Bahía Concha and diving outings) organized by friendly staff. Take a Mamatoco-bound bus (COP$1400) or a taxi (COP$5000). Social activities include poker nights. Dorms COP$20,000, doubles COP$70,000

Hostal Parque Real C 21 no. 2A–05 ☎5 431 0016, ⓦhostalparquereal.com. You won't find lively common areas here, but you will find three floors of spotless, tiled, en-suite a/c rooms with cable TV and excellent wi-fi on every floor – more a hotel than hostel. Ideal for a quiet stay and for getting away from the backpacker scene. COP$150,000

EATING, DRINKING AND NIGHTLIFE

★**Agave Azul** C 14 no. 3–58. New York-trained chef Michael McMurdo uses locally sourced ingredients to prepare a quality spin on Mexican food at reasonable prices. You can't go wrong with the ceviches (COP$18,000), fish tacos with mango salsa (COP$23,000) or the cocktails with a twist (try the lulo daiquiri). Tues–Sat noon–10pm.

Crab's Bar C 18 no. 3–69. If you like old-school music videos, this is the bar for you. Owner Oscar takes rock and

5

blues very seriously – and likes a bit of kitsch too. Signed vintage albums and plastic crabs hang on the walls, and there's a bathtub in the middle of the bar. Live blues band on Wednesday evenings. Wed–Sat 8pm–3am.

Lulo Cra 3 no. 16–34 ⓦ lulocafebar.com. Friendly owners Melissa and David whip up fantastic breakfasts at this excellent café. Try the delicious "Lula la Ranchera" *arepa* made from natural corn, served with egg, beans, cheese and chorizo (COP$12,000). Great smoothies from COP$5500, happy-hour cocktails Mon–Fri 7–9pm, and free wi-fi. Mon–Fri 8am–11pm, Sat & Sun 9am–10pm.

Ouzo Cra 3 no. 19–29, Parque de los Novios ☎ 423 0658, ⓦ ouzosantamarta.com. By far the classiest option on the square, this Greek/Mediterranean restaurant is reasonably priced considering what you get. Pizzas from COP$20,000, or try the aubergine croquettes with feta and tzaziki (COP$12,000) followed by crispy pork belly (COP$14,000) or Greek paella (COP$30,000). Pizzas from COP$20,000 and happy hour offers. Mon–Sat 5.30–11pm.

La Placita C 20 no. 3–16. Gourmet burgers attract locals and visitors alike to this small, friendly joint. Choose from the likes of lamb burger and beef burger stuffed with caramelized onion and melted cheese, with spicy potato wedges or fries on the side. Mains COP$17,000. Daily 5–11pm.

La Puerta C 17 no. 2–29. Local students and foreign backpackers in their 20s and 30s frequent this jam-packed, sexy club. Salsa, electronica and international club hits will have you sweating on the narrow dancefloor that snakes into one of the club's many nooks and crannies. Cool off on the outdoor patio if the crowd gets too much. Tues & Wed 6pm–1am, Thurs–Sat 6pm–3am.

TAGANGA

Once upon a time a pristine fishing village, lively **TAGANGA**, 4km north of Santa Marta (between it and Parque Nacional Tayrona), is where backpackers come to party. Built on the side of a mountain, the town has unpaved dirt streets, a busy beach, and arid hills surrounding the horseshoe-shaped bay. For budget travellers, it's an alternative to Santa Marta before or after tackling the Ciudad Perdida

hike (see p.531) and other surrounding attractions. There have, however, been reports of muggings in recent years and it's not the safe haven it used to be.

WHAT TO SEE AND DO

Everything here is pretty much water-related, whether diving or hitting the beach. Fishermen ply an easy alternative access route to Tayrona National Park's southern beaches, the most popular being the crystalline waters of **Bahia Concha**, about an hour away by boat. Costing at least COP$120,000, this is a good excursion for small groups. Accessible by boat (5min; COP$5000) and foot (20min) is the much closer **Playa Grande**, which is modestly sized, heavily touristed and a bit pebbly, but still has the makings for a day of sun and sea. Taganga's main beach is awash with small boats, many available for hire, though you'll find people swimming at the southern end.

Conveniently, Ciudad Perdida treks and a whole manner of adventure travel options are on offer too at bigger shops on the main drag, along the beach.

ARRIVAL AND INFORMATION

By plane A taxi from Santa Marta's Simón Bolívar Airport (14km) will cost around COP$35,000.

By boat A daily speedboat runs to Cabo de San Juan in Parque Nacional Tayrona from the waterfront by the tourist information kiosk at 10.30am (1hr; COP$40,000); book in advance at your hostel as spaces are limited.

By bus Frequent buses (every 10min 6am–9pm; 15min; COP$1400, COP$1500 on Sun) run along Cra 2 to Santa Marta's Cra 1C. Daily minibus transfers to Parque Nacional Tayrona (COP$17,000 one-way) are arranged through your accommodation.

By taxi A taxi between the centre of Santa Marta and Taganga costs COP$10,000. If you're coming from the bus terminal, it will be around COP$13,000.

DIVING IN TAGANGA

One of the cheapest spots in the world for **scuba** certification, both PADI and NAUI, Taganga has so many dive shops that the prices and services offered by each are pretty competitive. A three-day certification course costs about COP$650,000 and often includes English- or Spanish-speaking dive masters, and six open water dives. Try Ocean Scuba (ⓦ oceanoscuba .com.co) or Poseidon (ⓦ poseidondivecenter.com). Always check the dive school's PADI or NAUI accreditation, your instructor's credentials, the instructor-to-student ratio, and ensure that equipment is well maintained.

Tourist information There's a tourist information kiosk on the waterfront (9am–7pm) where you can pick up maps of Taganga. The only ATM, on Cra 2 next to the police station, often runs out of money, so it's best to load up in Santa Marta.

ACCOMMODATION

Casa de Felipe Cra 5A no. 19–13 ☎5 421 9101, ⓦlacasadefelipe.com. Three blocks uphill from the beach, with beautiful views of the bay and a lush, greenery-filled garden, the rustic rooms at this long-time backpacker favourite fill up quickly so book in advance. Plenty of information on exploring the area available. Dorms COP$19,000, rooms COP$75,000, private apartments for two COP$110,000

Hostel Divanga B&B C 12 no. 4–07 ☎5 421 9092, ⓦdivanga.com. This French-run hostel has a small pool surrounded with hammocks, an upstairs bar, a sociable vibe and wonderfully friendly staff. Rooms are compact but spotless and the restaurant is one of the best in town. There's another branch a block away. Dorms COP$25,000, doubles COP104,000

Hostal Techos Azules Sector Dunkarinca, cabaña no. 1–100 ☎5 421 9141, ⓦtechosazules.com. Sitting high above Taganga, just off the main road to Santa Marta, this rambling blue-roofed guesthouse offers a plethora of rooms for individuals and groups and great views of the town. Some rooms have kitchenettes, some share bathrooms, and all have access to the airy, hammock-festooned patio. The road leads steeply down to the beach. More expensive with a/c. Dorms COP$30,000, doubles COP$50,000

EATING, DRINKING AND NIGHTLIFE

The waterfront is lined with fruit juice and fried snack sellers, as well as *palapas* specializing in fish-heavy lunches. The menus (*ceviche*, fried fish, *arroz de coco*) are comparable.

Baba Ganoush Cra 1 no. 18–22. Huge diner overlooking the sea serving culinary creations from Thai green curries to Mediterranean-inspired dishes. Daily 6–11pm.

Los Baguettes de María C 18 no. 3–47. Stuff yourself with giant 30cm-long chicken, tuna or beef baguettes (COP$12,000) and thirst-quenching giant fruit juices before stumbling into one of the hammocks here. Mon–Fri & Sun 9am–10pm, Sat 2–10pm.

★**Café Bonsai** C 13 no. 1–7 ⓦcafebonsai.com. This cool Swedish-run café serves delicious home-made treats (around COP$2500), including brownies in chocolate sauce, fresh sandwiches on crusty home-baked bread, healthy muesli breakfasts with yogurt and blackberry jam, organic local coffee and an array of over twenty teas. Happy-hour cocktails (5–8pm) and mains are around COP$17,000. Mon–Sat 8am–10.30pm.

El Miradór Cra 1 no. 18–117. The frisson sparked by the mix of locals and backpackers that fill this club favourite makes this place taxi-worthy even if you're staying in Santa Marta. A disco with a great view, this spot throbs with mainstream pop. Mon–Wed & Sun 8.30pm–1am, Thurs–Sat 8.30pm–3am.

★**Pachamama** C 16 no. 1C–18. Off a quiet backstreet, this Tiki bar-cum-tapas bar serves some of the most imaginative offerings in town. The dishes (COP$8000–10,000) are small, so you can have quite a few. Choose from the likes of *kefta* (spiced lamb meatballs), prawns wrapped in bacon, fish in passion-fruit sauce, scallop tartare and grilled camembert. Mon–Sat 6–11pm.

PARQUE NACIONAL TAYRONA

Colombia's most unspoilt tropical area, **PARQUE NACIONAL TAYRONA**, a 45-minute drive east of Santa Marta, is a wilderness of beaches, with lush jungle running right down to the sand. The laidback attitude of the place makes it feel like a paradisiacal summer camp, though it does get overcrowded during the holidays so it's best to avoid coming in peak season if you can.

The park gets its name from the Tayrona Indians, one of South America's greatest pre-Columbian civilizations. This area was a major trading centre for the Tayrona, whose population once exceeded a million. With the arrival of the Spanish, their peaceful existence came to an end. The Spanish governor ordered their annihilation in 1599 on the trumped-up charge that the Tayrona men practised sodomy; the brutal massacre that followed forced the remaining Tayronas to seek refuge high in the Sierra Nevada de Santa Marta, whose foothills flank the park to the south. Rising from sea level, these snowcapped sierras reach their apex just 42km from the coast, at the 5775m-high **Cristóbal Colón**, Colombia's tallest peak. Tayrona stretches over 120 square kilometres on land, with an additional 30 square kilometres of marine reserve, but since much of the park isn't easily accessible, visitors find themselves sticking largely to the string of beaches that stretch for around 8km from the entrance of the park, bounded by **Cañaveral** to the east and with **Cabo San Juan** to the west.

5

Beaches

Tayrona's beaches and the jungle that edges them are the irrefutable stars of the park. If arriving by boat, you'll get dropped off at **Cabo San Juan**, an attractive palm-fringed beach where many budget visitors stay; further west into the park from here are two more beaches, the second being a **nudist beach** (30min). Twenty minutes' walk east of Cabo San Juan brings you to **La Piscina**, a beach good for swimming and snorkelling, with calm, deep water. From there, it's another twenty-minute stroll east to **La Aranilla**, a narrow strip of sand framed by huge boulders, fine for swimming, followed almost immediately by the long, beautiful, wave-lashed stretch of **Arrecifes** where signs warn you that over two hundred tourists have drowned here; rip tides and strong currents make swimming extremely dangerous. Another forty minutes or so east along a wooded, muddy trail takes you to **Cañaveral** and the entrance to the park, where the beach is good for sunbathing but the rip tides make it unsuitable for swimming.

Pueblito

A clear and physically demanding uphill path from Cabo San Juan brings you to the archeological site of **Pueblito**, a former Tayrona village with a large number of terrace dwellings, sometimes called a mini Ciudad Perdida. Although it's possible to complete an Arrecifes–Cabo San Juan–Pueblito circuit in one long, strenuous day, the trip is better made as part of a multi-day stay on the beaches in the park. From Pueblito, you can also hike two hours through the jungle down to the road and catch a bus back to Santa Marta from that park exit point, instead of returning along your original route to Cabo San Juan. That said, you may be better off hiring a guide for this hike, which has no signs and is quite taxing.

ARRIVAL AND INFORMATION

By boat Regular speedboats run from Taganga to Cabo San Juan, arriving at around 11am and departing at around 4pm (see p.528). Rangers collect the park entrance fee (COP$38,000) when you disembark. From Cabo San Juan it's around a 4hr walk east to the park entrance via various beaches.

By bus Buses run from Santa Marta (every 30min; 1hr) from the market at the corner of Cra 11 and C 11 to El Zaino, 35km away, which is the main entrance to Tayrona, where your passport will be checked, and entrance fee (COP$38,000) collected. From here, take one of the jeeps that regularly traverse the 4km to the entrance proper at Cañaveral for COP$2000. From Cañaveral to Cabo San Juan the walk takes around 4hr, but make sure you start off in the morning to avoid the midday heat. From Taganga, hostels arrange daily minibus transfers to Tayrona for around COP$17,000.

Park information Opening times are 8am–5pm. Bring plenty of cash – only the Aviatur-run restaurant and accommodation accept credit cards – and lots of insect repellent. Bring as little as possible to the park to avoid trekking in the heat with a heavy load. Most hostels in Santa Marta/Taganga will let you leave your backpack for a few days.

ACCOMMODATION AND EATING

The two main beaches offering budget accommodation are Arrecifes and Cabo San Juan; both offer the option of renting tents and hammocks, and cabañas are a good alternative for medium to large groups at Arrecifes. Lockers are available too. There are basic restaurants at Cabo San Juan, food shacks at La Aranilla, serving *empanadas* and *ceviche*, and another restaurant at Arrecifes.

CABO SAN JUAN

Cabo San Juan del Guía The downside to the hammocks here – both on the beach and in a gazebo on a small hillock – is that they offer no mosquito netting, so bring your own, and it can get quite chilly at night. Seek out the information hut next door to the restaurant (mains from COP$12,000), the only real building in sight. Camping COP$15,000, hammock on the beach COP$15,000, hammock in gazebo COP$25,000

ARRECIFES

Finca El Paraiso Rents hammocks and tents close to the beach, and has a basic restaurant and shop. Hammocks COP$15,000, tent for two COP$26,000, with own tent COP$13,000

Yuluka Has options of hammocks, camping and five-person cabañas with luxury bathrooms. Also has a well-priced restaurant – the only one in the park that accepts credit cards; mains are around COP$15,000. Hammocks COP$20,000, camping per person COP$12,000, cabaña for five COP$355,000

PALOMINO

Located 70km from Santa Marta past the Parque Tayrona entrance towards Riohacha, the small town of **PALOMINO** has in recent years become popular with travellers craving Caribbean beach time. Once associated with paramilitary action, Palomino is now safe, with a number of beachfront hostels and cabins, while retaining the atmosphere of a perfect peaceful haven, much like Taganga once was. The town itself is not much more than a few dusty roads just off the highway, lined with basic restaurants and homes, but it's the stunning palm-fringed beach and jungle backdrop just behind the town that's responsible for Palomino's speedy rise to fame. It affords fantastic views of the Sierra Nevada de Santa Marta mountain range: on a clear day you can see Colombia's highest peaks, the snowcapped Pico Cristóbal Colón and Pico Simón Bolívar, both over 5700m high. Things to do include **tubing** on the Palomino River and excursions to **Quebrada de Valencia**, a waterfall, and several natural swimming holes in the middle of the jungle, thirty minutes away by bus. If you want to visit a traditional Kogi or Arhuaco village, hostels such as *The Dreamer* can arrange trips to the Sierra Nevada de Santa Marta national park (horseriding optional). Note that the sea current can be strong, particularly where the Palomino River meets the Caribbean, so be cautious – on certain days, it's best to avoid swimming in the sea altogether – or stick to a dip in one of the two rivers.

ARRIVAL AND DEPARTURE

By bus To get here, take a bus with the sign "Tayrona/Palomino" from Santa Marta (Cra 11, at C 11). It's a 20min walk down to the beach, or take a *mototaxi* for COP$2500.

ACCOMMODATION AND EATING

There's no ATM in Palomino, although many accommodation options accept credit cards. There are basic restaurants dotted around town serving typical Colombian fare (cash only), or eat at one of the hostels or cabins along the beach.

★**The Dreamer on the Beach** Playa Donaire s/n ☎ 300 609 7229, ⓦ thedreamerhostel.com/onthebeach. Following the success of their Santa Marta branch (see p.527), *The Dreamer on the Beach* was one of the first hostels to set up in Palomino. It's more of a boutique hostel, with a pool area surrounded by palm trees and hammocks, and a bar with a lounge area that gets busy when happy hour starts at 6pm. There's also a garden, a volleyball court and a restaurant. Tastefully decorated doubles are enormous and all have en-suite bathrooms and private terraces. Dorms COP$25,000, doubles COP$110,000

CIUDAD PERDIDA

The "Lost City" of the Tayronas, **CIUDAD PERDIDA** ranks among South America's most magical spots. More than a lost city, it's a lost world. Although its ruins are more understated than Machu Picchu in Peru, thanks to its geographic isolation the once-teeming city perched high in the Sierra Nevada de Santa Marta manages to preserve the natural allure that the overrun Inca capital has lost. While climbing the sierra's luxuriant foothills,

---

CIUDAD PERDIDA: TOUR GUIDES AND TIPS

As of 2008, the area has been safe from paramilitaries, but you can only do the hike as part of an **organized group**. There are four tour companies authorized to lead tours, all with offices in Santa Marta, the most reputable being **Magic Tour** (C 16 no. 4–41, Santa Marta; ☎ 5 421 5820, ⓦ magictourcolombia.com) and **Expotur** (C 3 no. 17–27, Santa Marta; ☎ 5 420 7739, ⓦ expotur-eco.com), though you may find that guides from different companies swap clients to accommodate those who wish to do the tour in more or fewer days, and during low season the four companies pool clients. The official **price** of the tour is set at COP$600,000 and includes all meals, accommodation along the trail, the entrance fee to the ruins and transport to and from the trailhead. Guides generally don't speak English. Groups consist of four to twelve hikers.

The hike can be done all year; the driest period is between late December and March, while during the wet months from May to November the trail can get exceedingly muddy. It's a reasonably challenging trek and a reasonable level of **physical fitness** is required.

Expect to get wet at any time of the year and pack everything you'll need, especially: **sturdy footwear** suitable for river crossings (either waterproof trekking sandals or hiking boots and flip-flops); 50 percent DEET **insect repellent** (not available in Colombia); **water-purifying tablets**; **anti-malarial prophylactics** (there's low risk of malaria but if you want to err on the side of caution); **waterproof bag** and **poncho**, and **sunscreen**.

5

THE KOGI INDIANS

Although now uninhabited, Ciudad Perdida is in many respects a living monument. It's surrounded by villages of **Kogi Indians**, who call the revered site Teyuna. You may be able to interact with the Kogis as they drift on and off the main trail you'll traverse as part of the trek, though as it comprises only a fraction of the wilderness they call home, and they are increasingly less present. The men are recognizable by their long, black hair, white (or off-white) smocks and trousers, a woven purse worn across one shoulder and trusty *póporo*, the saliva-coated gourd holding the lime that activates the coca leaves they constantly chew. Women also dress in white, and both women and girls wear necklaces; only the men own *póporo*. About nine thousand Kogis are believed to inhabit the Sierra Nevada.

In the 1970s, the Sierra Nevada became a major marijuana factory, and an estimated seventy percent of its native forests were burned to clear the way for untold amounts of the lucrative Santa Marta Gold strand. As the forest's prime inhabitants, the Kogis suffered dearly from the arrival of so many fast-buck farmers, one of the reasons why they're sceptical of the outside world; while Kogi children may well approach you, asking for sweets, don't take pictures of adults without their permission.

you'll get a chance to bathe in idyllic rivers, visit inhabited indigenous villages and marvel at the swarms of monarch butterflies and beautiful jungle scenery.

Built sometime after 500 AD, the Tayrona capital is less than 50km southeast of Santa Marta and is believed to have been home to around four thousand people before the Spanish wiped the Tayrona out. The ruins weren't "discovered" until the early 1970s, when a few of the more than ten thousand *guaqueros* (tomb raiders) from Santa Marta chanced upon the city while scavenging for antiquities. Perched atop a steep slope 1300m high in the vast jungle, the site consists of more than a thousand circular stone **terraces** – with more still being uncovered – that once served as foundations for Tayrona homes. Running throughout the city and down to the Buritaca river valley is a complex network of paved footpaths and steep stone steps – more than 1350 – purportedly added later to obstruct the advance of Spanish horsemen.

The hike

The trek covers 40km, with most hikers opting for the five-day version. You get picked up in Santa Marta for the three-hour drive to **Machete**, the village where the hike begins after lunch. From here it's four to five hours to **Camp 1** – mostly a steep uphill slog with a long, steep descent towards the camp. There's a

swimming hole close to the start of the trail and another at Camp 1, where there are hammocks with mosquito nets. **Day two**'s four- to five-hour hike to Camp 2 is an hour's ascent, a steep hour's descent, and an attractive flat stretch that takes you past a Kogi village. At the camp there's good swimming in the river and relatively comfortable bunks with mosquito nets. **Day three** consists of a four-hour hike that includes a narrow path overlooking a sheer drop and ups and downs along a narrow jungle trail, and a bridge across the main river. Camp 3, Paraíso, tends to be the most crowded, and has hammocks, bunks and musty tents with mattresses. Weather permitting, some groups press on to the Ciudad Perdida in the afternoon (four-hour round trip), an hour's ascent from Camp 3, most of it up a very steep bunch of uneven and slippery stone steps – particularly challenging on the way down. And then it's there – your prize – stone terrace upon stone terrace, tranquil and overgrown with jungle, with splendid views of the main terrace from the military outpost. The alternative is to hike to Ciudad Perdida on the morning of day four. On your return, you either stay overnight in Camp 2 at the end of **day four** or, if you made it to Ciudad Perdida on day three, you make the eight- to nine-hour hike from Camp 3 back to Camp 1. **Day five** is then either a very early start and a gruelling seven-hour hike from Camp 2 back to Machete before lunch, or

– if you're already at Camp 1 – a somewhat less gruelling four-hour slog, with the steepest part at the very beginning. Hearty victory lunch at Machete follows, and a transfer back to Santa Marta.

THE GUAJIRA PENINSULA

Colombia's northernmost point, **Guajira Peninsula** has a hostile desert climate that has kept it largely isolated since colonial times. As a result it's one of those places where independent travellers can still feel as if they're leaving fresh tracks. Some 240km long and no more than 50km wide, the barren peninsula is empty except for the semi-nomadic Wayuu, and is a beguiling mix of desert and sea, a smugglers' haven that English pirates once tried to conquer. More challenging to explore than the rest of the Caribbean coast, the Guajira Peninsula rewards those who make the effort with the end-of-the-world feel of **Cabo de la Vela** and **Punta Gallinas**. Cabo de la Vela is a remote Wayuu fishing village, 180km northwest of **Riohacha**, the capital of the Guajira Peninsula, which is 175km northeast of Santa Marta. On the journey to Cabo you pass through a landscape of sand, baked mud huts and goats grazing under the sparse shade of the acacia trees.

Cabo de la Vela

A dusty one-street settlement strung out along an aquamarine bay, **CABO DE LA VELA**'s main draw is the spectacular landscape: a long sliver of beach, rocky cliffs and cactus-studded arid plains. In December and January the village is inundated with holidaying Colombians, but the rest of the year it's a tranquil spot for sunset viewing, particularly from the westernmost hill at the far end of the bay, El Faro, kitesurfing and lazing on the sand.

ARRIVAL AND INFORMATION

It's easiest to go with a tour company such as Expotur or Magictour from Santa Marta (see p.531).

By bus Catch an early morning bus from Santa Marta's Terminal de Transportes to Riohacha (3hr); from Riohacha, Cootrauri (C 15 no. 5–39; ☎5 728 0000) runs shared cars to Uribia (1hr; COP$15,000) where the driver will drop you off at the pick-up truck departure point.

The last trucks head for Cabo at 1pm at the latest (2hr; COP$15,000). Coming back, trucks leave Cabo between 4 and 4.30am.

ACCOMMODATION AND EATING

There's plentiful accommodation consisting of hammocks (CH$15,000), traditional Wayuu *chinchorros* (warmer hammocks; COP$20,000), Wayuu huts made of *yotojoro* (the inner core of the cactus) and basic concrete rooms (around COP$40,000/ person). Showers tend to be bucket-style affairs. Most guesthouses have generators that only work between 6 and 10pm, and many double as restaurants serving goat and locally caught fish and lobster.

Punta Gallinas

If Cabo is insufficiently remote, then perhaps **Punta Gallinas** will suffice – intrepid travellers who make it to this otherworldly spot are unlikely to regret their efforts. What awaits is a turquoise bay fringed by what is arguably Colombia's most beautiful beach, home to a large colony of pink flamingos and around sixty Wayuu. Colombia's northernmost tip is only reachable by organized tour. Contact **Kaí Ecotravel** in Riohacha (☎311 436 2830, ⌨www .kaiecotravel.com), a reputable operator that also runs trips to Cabo, or Expotur in Santa Marta (see p.531).

San Andrés and Providencia

A world apart from the rest of Colombia, both geographically and culturally, the San Andrés and Providencia islands sit in the Caribbean sea near Nicaragua, with Providencia atop the third-largest barrier reef in the world. Visitors come all this way for the fantastic beaches, the best diving in Colombia, and the unique Raizal culture; 300-year-old ties to England mean that the residents of **Providencia** in particular speak an English-based Creole with a Caribbean lilt. On larger, busier **San Andrés** the Raizal culture is much more diluted, and for many Colombians, one of the island's draws is its duty-free status, making it a much cheaper place to shop than the mainland.

5

SAN ANDRÉS

Seahorse-shaped **SAN ANDRÉS** is a full-on Colombian resort island with gorgeous (if often crowded) white-sand beaches, surrounding azure waters and fantastic diving (see box opposite). Budget accommodation is concentrated in **San Andrés Town**, the capital – a busy whirl of unattractive concrete buildings, duty-free shops and careering scooters.

WHAT TO SEE AND DO

Though San Andrés Town has a main beach of its own, the best beach is on **Johnny Cay**, the palm-shaded, iguana-inhabited island visible directly across the water. Numerous boats depart from San Andrés beach for Johnny Cay in the mornings around 9am; a return trip costs around COP$12,000, with the last boats returning around 3.30pm (make sure you remember on which boat you came). Visits to Johnny Cay can be combined with a stop at **Acuario** – a sliver of sand off the east coast of the island next to Haynes Cay, where the water is swimming-pool clear – though on busy days you'll find yourself fighting for space – and its three shacks poking out of the water (one for snacks and drinks, one for lockers and one for toilets; trips to both places cost around COP$25,000.

If you rent a bicycle or scooter, you can do an easy loop around the island, following the coastal road. Along the west coast, south of El Cove, you'll pass **West View** (daily 9am–6pm), a beachside restaurant and snorkelling combo: for COP$4000 entry, you can swim with the many fishes who'll eat out of your hand (further south is the similar **Piscinita**). At the southern tip of the island is **Hoyo Soplador** (free) – a natural blowhole surrounded by makeshift bars, gift shops and restaurants; when the tide and wind conditions are right, a jet of water shoots up to 20m up out of the hole in the rock. On the east side of the island, you're often likely to have the white-sand, windswept beaches of **San Luis** all to yourself.

ARRIVAL AND DEPARTURE

By plane San Andrés airport, a short walk from San Andrés Town, is served by numerous daily Avianca and Copa flights from the mainland and is connected to neighbouring Providencia by SATENA flights. You have to buy a tourist card (COP$48,000; cash only) on the mainland when you check-in for your San Andrés flight. Taxis from the airport to the heart of San Andrés Town cost COP$12,000, or else you can walk in 15min.

Destinations Bogotá (4–5 daily; 2hr); Cartagena (1 daily; 1hr 25min); Cali (1 daily; 2hr); Medellín (1 daily; 1hr 45min); Panama City (2 daily; 1hr 20min); Providencia (2–4 daily; 15–20min).

By boat Weather permitting, a catamaran service to Providencia runs several times a week (Sun, Mon, Wed & Fri at 7.30am; 3hr 30min; $130,000 one-way; ☎ 310 222 5403 or ⊚ catamaransanandresyprovidencia.com). Boats return at 3pm from Providencia.

GETTING AROUND AND INFORMATION

Buses Local buses leave every 20–30min (7.30am–8.30pm) from near the *Hotel Hernando Henry* in San Andrés Town and cost COP$1700 per ride; there are basically two routes: the "San Luis" bus and the "Loma/Cove" bus that runs all the way along the coast road to the Hoyo Soplador.

Bicycle/scooter/golf carts Several outlets in San Andrés Town rent bicycles (COP$20,000/day) and scooters (COP$60,000/day). Souped-up golf carts are COP$80,000/day. Cycling is a good way to explore the rest of the island, as the roads are paved and there's not much traffic. Most scooter rental places won't ask you for your licence and they won't provide you with a helmet, either; be prepared for some erratic local driving.

Tourist information On Av Newball, almost directly opposite *Restaurante La Regatta* (Mon–Fri 8am–noon & 2–6pm; ☎ 8 513 0801).

ACCOMMODATION

★**Blue Almond Hostel** Los Almendros, Manzana 4, Casa 3 ☎ 8 512 3746, ⊚ bluealmondhostel.com. Small, charming hostel run by the amicable Juan Velasquez (who speaks English) and Jennifer Muñoz, around a 15min walk from the town centre, with functional kitchen, four simple but clean rooms and dorms (no a/c, fans only) with shared bathroom, communal computer and TV room. Free lockers and surfboards; bike rentals for COP$25,000/day. Dorms COP$35,000, doubles COP$65,000

The Rock House C 8 no. 18A–59, Cabañas Altamar ☎ 316 579 1342, ⊚ therockhouse1.webs.com. In a quiet residential area behind the airport, a 25min walk to town, Doña Luz and her family greet you with open arms for a bit of homey comfort. The en-suite rooms are spotless and the atmosphere just wonderful. Doubles COP$90,000

El Viajero San Andrés Av 20 de Julio no. 3A–12 ☎ 8 512 7497, ⊚ sanandreshostel.com. Thoughtfully designed, this upscale hostel occupies an entire multi-storey building. Expect a/c dorms and doubles, and all the perks you can think of – daily tours organized, a movie room, chill-out bar area, large guest kitchen, balconies to hang out on – all within a slick, dark interior. Dorms COP$45,000, doubles COP$90,000

EATING AND DRINKING

The town's fruit-and-veg market on the corner of C 2 and Cra 11, where self-caterers can stock up, is open daily but liveliest Saturday to Monday.

Fisherman Place Av Colombia, just behind the airport. Aka "El Pescadero", this is a large, casual, open-air restaurant, founded by local fishermen in 1975, and still serving the best of the local catch every lunchtime. The grilled fish in garlic sauce with all the trimmings comes in a heaped platter, and the *rondón* (local seafood stew with coconut milk) is flavourful and filling. Mains from COP$15,000. Daily noon–4pm.

★**Kella Reggae Bar** Carretera Circunvalar, Sector San Luis. This long-running favourite (run by Kella Williams since 1980) is an old-style beach shack and reggae bar offering a real taste of the Caribbean with authentic reggae, dance-hall music and a Rastafari vibe right on the shoreline. Things don't really get going till after midnight. Daily 6pm–4am.

Miss Celia O'Neill Taste Av Colombia, at C 2. The decor gives the game away at this friendly little place: the fishing nets hanging from the ceiling, nautical memorabilia and plastic fish aplenty suggest that the specialities here come from the sea. You can't go wrong with the curry crab (or any other curried seafood, for that matter), and the service is relaxed and friendly. Mains from COP$25,000. Daily noon–11pm.

PROVIDENCIA

Tiny **PROVIDENCIA** is the antithesis of its sister island: a sleepier, friendlier place with a population of around five thousand, where everyone knows everyone else, and where most speak an English-based Creole; with a mountainous interior covered with lush vegetation, and the world's third-largest barrier reef beckoning divers from all over the world.

WHAT TO SEE AND DO

Providencia is circled by a 16km loop of a coastal road, so it's easy to see all the sights along it. At the north tip of the island is **Santa Isabel**, the main "town", with ATMs and other services. A pedestrian bridge takes you across to the minute **Santa Catalina Island** – after dark, it's possible to see manta rays swimming under the bridge. On Santa Catalina Island, a footpath leads past the mangroves and a ramshackle village to Morgan's Cannon on the right, while a slightly longer walk to the left leads you up to the ruins of Fort Warwick and down to **Fort Beach** where it's possible to snorkel. A narrower path leads on from here (15min or so) to **Morgan's Head**, a jagged outcrop that is said to resemble the infamous pirate's head.

THE BEST OF ISLAND DIVING

The islands' biggest attractions are to be found under the sea, and both Providencia and San Andrés have several reputable diving outfits that can introduce you to a whole new world, even if you're a first-time diver.

GREAT DIVE SITES

Cantil de Villa Erica Turtles, manta rays and eagle rays to be found around this reef southwest of San Andrés; 12–45m depths.

Manta's Place Southern stingrays (rather than mantas) congregate at this Providencia spot.

Palacio de la Cherna Exciting wall dive that drops from 12m to over 300m, with reef and nurse sharks, lobster and king crab among its denizens; southeast of San Andrés.

Piramide Large numbers of morays, octopus and shoals of fish make this shallow reef dive in San Andrés one of the most exciting.

Tete's Place An abundance of schoolmasters, goat fish, parrotfish and more makes you feel as if you're swimming in a giant aquarium southwest of Providencia.

DIVE OPERATORS ON SAN ANDRÉS

Banda Dive Shop Av Colombia, San Andrés Town ☎ 8 513 1080, ⓦ bandadiveshop.com. A friendly, central choice.

San Andrés Divers Av Circunvalar Km9 ☎ 312 448 7230, ⓦ sanandresdivers.com. Particularly recommended for their professional approach.

DIVE OPERATORS ON PROVIDENCIA

Felipe Diving Shop in Freshwater Bay ☎ 8 514 8775, ⓦ felipediving.com.

Sirius Dive Shop Southwest Bay, next to *Sirius Hotel* ☎ 8 514 8213.

5

Back on Providencia and heading clockwise, a road loops off from the main coastal road through Maracaibo, where the pricey but good seafront restaurant *Deep Blue* is a fantastic spot for an oceanside drink. Directly across the water is **Crab Cay**, a tiny island with some superb snorkelling and a great view of Providencia from the top (boat trips to Crab Cay are easily arranged through your accommodation for COP$35,000; admission is another COP$14,500).

In the south of the island, a hiking trail leads from **Casabaja** village up **El Pico** (360m), the island's only mountain, with superb 360-degree views from the top. The hike takes around ninety minutes one-way; be sure to ask for directions and bring plenty of water.

From Casabaja, another road leads south to **Manchineel Bay** (Bahía Manzanillo), a rustic, unspoiled stretch of palm-backed sand, home to *Roland's* bar (see below). Further west long the coastal road, you pass the turn-off to **Southwest Bay** (Bahía Suroeste), the island's best beach, with a couple of hotels and places to eat. On the west side of the island, **Freshwater Bay** (Aguadulce) is the main hotel strip (though still low-key), with just a small beach at the southern end.

ARRIVAL AND DEPARTURE

By plane Several Satena (w satena.com) flights daily (15–20min) connect Providencia with San Andrés only; there are no flights from the mainland. Luggage allowance is 10kg. Pick-up trucks meet flights and will drop you off anywhere on the island for a non-negotiable COP$23,000; if there are several people going to the same place, costs are shared.
By boat See p.534.

GETTING AROUND AND INFORMATION

By bus Small buses do make circuits around the island (COP$2500), but are not very reliable (they are supposed to run hourly); you can also flag down passing vehicles who might give you a lift (confirm the price first).
By bike/scooter You can rent bicycles or a scooter (around COP$60,000) from operators in Freshwater Bay and Santa Isabel.
Tourist information There's a helpful tourist booth in Santa Isabel by the bridge to Santa Catalina island (daily 8am–noon & 2–5pm).

ACCOMMODATION

Blue Almond Hostel (inside Cabañas Agua Dulce), Freshwater Bay ☏ 317 654 7117, w bluealmondhostel .com. Solid budget option, with one mixed dorm (one double bed and single beds, for a maximum of six people) with two full bathrooms in one of the Cabañas Agua Dulce cabins; no lockers, no wi-fi as yet, and no kitchen. Breakfast is COP$15,000. __COP$75,000__
Hostal Flaming Tree Santa Isabel ☏ 8 514 8049. Well-run family-owned guesthouse in the middle of town (handy for the boat), with nine spacious rooms, all with a/c. Doubles __COP$100,000__
Mr Mac Freshwater Bay ☏ 8 514 8366, e posadamistermack@hotmail.com. Large, simple rooms right by the water. Ideal for self-caterers, as rooms come with kitchenettes; discounts for solo travellers. Doubles __COP$80,000__

EATING AND DRINKING

The liveliest part of the island is Freshwater Bay, though the best beach restaurants and bars can be found down the road at Southwest Bay.
★ **Café Studio** Maroon Hill (200m along the main road from Southwest Bay to Freshwater Bay) ☏ 8 514 9076. The best restaurant on the island, run by a Canadian-Raizal couple; try anything in Creole sauce and don't leave without sampling either the cappuccino pie or the lemon pie. Mon–Sat 11am–10pm.
Old Providence Taste Signposted off the road from Freshwater Bay to Santa Isabel in the Pueblo Viejo area. Run by the fishing co-op, serving a fantastic value *menú* for COP$14,000, which includes soup and a heaped plate of fish or curry crab with all the trimmings. Daily noon–4pm.
Roland Roots Bar Manchineel Bay ☏ 8 514 8417. This Rasta-themed bar rocks to a thumping reggae soundtrack and there are even swings from which to fling yourself into the sea. Nominally 24hr, or whenever Roland is around.

Tierra Paisa

Nominally a slang term to describe anyone from the mountainous region of Antioquia, **paisas** are alternately the butt of jokes and the object of envy for many Colombians. What makes them stand out is their rugged individualism and reputation for industriousness. Their fame dates back to the early nineteenth century, when they cleared Colombia's hinterland for farming in exchange for the government's carrot of free land.

5

Perhaps the biggest *paisa* contribution to Colombia is its role in the spread of coffee.

The heart of *paisa* country is the metropolis of **Medellín**, which has made a remarkable turnaround since its days as Colombia's murder capital in the early 1990s, and a is now thriving and attractive cosmopolitan city. The picturesque coffee-growing *fincas* near the modern cities of **Manizales** and **Pereira** were almost all established by *paisa* homesteaders and some growers have opened their estates to tourists, who during harvest time can partake in the picking process. Easily accessible from Pereira, the incredibly photogenic village of **Salento** is the gateway to some great hiking in the misty **Valle de Cócoro**. The so-called **Zona Cafetera**, or "Coffee Zone", is the base for exploring one of Colombia's most postcard-perfect national parks, **Parque Nacional Natural Los Nevados**.

MEDELLÍN

It's hard to think of a city that was more in need of a public relations makeover than **MEDELLÍN**. When turf wars between rival drug gangs became public in the 1980s and 1990s, Colombia's second-largest city was rampaged by teenage hitmen, called *sicarios*, who, for as little as US$30, could be hired to settle old scores.

But when cocaine kingpin **Pablo Escobar** was snuffed out in 1993, Medellín began to bury its sordid past, though the notorious Mr Escobar remains an infamous attraction (see p.540). These days, the increasing number of travellers who come here find an inviting, modern city with one of the country's best climates – year-round temperatures average 24°C.

WHAT TO SEE AND DO

Pleasant green spaces, interesting museums, a bustling centre and thriving commercial areas make Medellín an exciting place to explore, while top-notch restaurants, vibrant bars and a pumping club scene provide non-stop fun until the early hours. The reliable metro makes it easy to get around. **El Poblado**, an upmarket area in the southeastern part of Medellín, has the highest concentration of lodgings, restaurants and nightlife.

Museo de Antioquia

Medellín is the birthplace of sculptor and painter **Fernando Botero**, known for his satirical representation of all things fat – oranges, priests, even a chubby Mona Lisa. Although Medellín residents felt miffed by Botero's donation of his extensive European art collection to the Museo Botero in Bogotá (see p.499), the highlight of the **Museo de Antioquia** (Cra 52 no. 52–43; Mon–Sat 10am–5.30pm, Sun 10am–4.30pm; COP$10,000;

COFFEE AND COCAINE

It's hard to say which of Colombia's two cash crops garners more international attention, the white or the black one. One thing is for certain: both are synonymous with quality. The country's first bumper crop was **coffee**. Colombia is the second-largest producer of Arabica coffee after Brazil and the third-largest overall coffee producer in the world (behind Vietnam and Brazil). High temperatures, heavy rainfall and cool evening breezes make Colombia the bean's ideal habitat.

Cocaine was perceived as an innocuous stimulant until the twentieth century. Two US presidents, several European monarchs and even a pope were early addicts (and vocal advocates) of Vin Tonique Mariani, a nineteenth-century liqueur made from coca extract. The "real thing" that Coca-Cola initially pushed on its customers was cocaine. For Sigmund Freud, a spoonful of coke each day was the cure for depression. Plan Colombia, the US-backed programme to combat cocaine production, has seen some decline in coca cultivation, though coca growers have merely moved on to producing hardier coca crops that give four times as much yield and grow far faster than old crops. However, the cocaine-related cartel violence that used to plague the cities of Medellín and Cali has been "exported" to Mexico, where drug trade-related murders have risen dramatically.

5

MEDELLÍN: CENTRE

Jardin Botanico de Medellin Joaquín, Antonio Uribe & Parque Arvi

VILLA NUEVA

Catedral Metropolitana

LOS ANGELES

AVENIDA DE GREIFF

Museo de Antioquia

Plazuela de Nutibara

Plaza Bolívar

AVENIDA BOLÍVAR

Parque Berrio

Parque Berrio

AVENIDA JUNIN

CALLE 52

AVENIDA ORIENTAL

Basílica Nuestra Señora de la Candelaria

AVENIDA LA PLAYA

San Antonio

AVENIDA CARABOBO

Parque San Antonio

AVENIDA ORIENTAL

LA CANDELARIA

BOMBONA I

AVENIDA BOLÍVAR

AVENIDA SAN JUAN

Alpujarra

COLON

0 — 250 metres

Museo de Arte Moderno de Medellin

T1. 2 & Parque de Los Pies Descalzos

2 & Pueblito Paisa

El Poblado (3.5km)

■ ACCOMMODATION			● EATING				● DRINKING & NIGHTLIFE	
Black Sheep Hostel	5	Tiger Paw Hostel	3	The Flip Flop		Royal Thai	8	3 Cordilleras	2
Casa Blanca	4	Urban Buddha	2	Sandwich Shop	6	Señor Itto	4	El Blue	5
Casa Kiwi	7	Wandering Paisa	1	Il Forno	10	Verdeo	7	El Eslabón Prendido	1
Pit Stop Hostel	6			Hummus	9			Luxury	3

Centre (3.5km), Jardines de Montesauro cemetery & 3

MEDELLÍN: EL POBLADO

EXITO

CALLE 10

CALLE 10A

Parque El Poblado

CARRERA 43C

CARRERA 43B

CARRERA 43D

CARRERA 45

ASTORGA

CALLE 9

CALLE 8

AVENIDA EL POBLADO

CALLE 9

Parque Lleras

CARRERA 41

CARRERA 40

CARRERA 38

CARRERA 37

EL POBLADO

CARRERA 39

Divina Eucaristia

CALLE 5E

CALLE 7

0 — 250 metres

5

ⓦmuseodeantioquia.co) is the largest collection of his works, including paintings, sculptures and sketches. Another twenty Botero sculptures are on display outside the museum in the busy **Plaza Botero**, including a rotund Roman legionary.

Basílica Nuestra Señora de la Candelaria

A few churches from the late colonial era survive. The most important is the **Basílica Nuestra Señora de la Candelaria** (Cra 50, at C51 Boyacá), whose Baroque interior dates from 1776. Its most impressive feature is a German pipe organ that made its way here on the backs of long-suffering horses.

Catedral Metropolitana

The fortress-like **cathedral** at **Plaza Bolívar** (between Cra 48 & 49), four blocks from Basílica de la Candelaria along a pedestrian walkway, was constructed between 1875 and 1931 and claims to be the largest church in the world built entirely of bricks – 1.2 million of them. A large **handicraft fair** is held on the first Saturday of every month in the plaza.

Parque San Antonio

If your appetite for Botero isn't sated, check out his *Pájaro de Paz* (Bird of Peace) sculpture at **Parque San Antonio**, on Carrera 46 between calles 44 and 46. When a guerrilla bomb destroyed the bronze sculpture in 1996, Botero ordered the skeleton to be left in its shattered state and a replica of the original was placed alongside it as an eloquent protest against violence.

Museo de Arte Moderno de Medellín

Housed in an attractively restored industrial warehouse in the Ciudad del Río neighbourhood, the **Museo de Arte Moderno de Medellín** (Cra 44 no. 19A–100; Tues–Fri 9am–5.30pm, Sat 10am–5.30pm, Sun 10am–5pm; COP$8000; ⓦelmamm.org; metro Poblado) features an impressive selection of contemporary art by international and national artists, including prolific Medellín painter Débora Arango.

Pueblito Paisa

The geographical limitations of so many people living in a narrow valley mean that many residents live in overcrowded conditions, with homes running up 45-degree slopes. Within the city centre itself there's a huge shortage of open recreational spaces. An exception is **Pueblito Paisa** at C 30A no. 55–64 (daily 5am–midnight, restaurants open from 10am; free), a replica of a typical Antioquian village that's situated atop Cerro Nutibara, a hilly outcrop downtown that offers fabulous panoramic views of the city. At the bottom of the hill is the **Parque de las Esculturas**, a sculpture park where the imagination of South American artists takes on abstract form. The closest metro station is Industriales, from where it's a ten-minute walk up Cerro Nutibara.

Jardín Botánico de Medellín Joaquín Antonio Uribe

This lush **botanical garden** (C 73 no. 51D–14; daily 9am–5pm; free; ⓦbotanicomedellin.org; metro Universidad) is one of Colombia's oldest, dating from 1913 and home to over six hundred plant species as well as a butterfly enclosure. Don't miss a visit to the stunning Orchideorama – a weaving structure of steel trunks and towering wooden petals – where plants are showcased and the garden's annual orchid exhibition is held in August during the Feria de las Flores flower festival.

Parque Arví

On the eastern slopes of the Aburrá Valley, **Parque Arví** (Tues–Sun 9am–6pm; free; ⓦparquearvi.org) is an ecological nature reserve and archeological site. It forms part of the network of pre-Hispanic trails of Parque Ecológico Piedras Blancas (see p.542), which can be reached from the park in an hour on foot. Other attractions include canopy ziplines and a butterfly enclosure, and you can easily spend the day exploring this welcome bit of wilderness. The park is connected to downtown Medellín via the Cable Arví Metrocable (Linea L; closed for maintenance on Mon) from the

5

ESCOBAR'S LEGACY

Few individuals have had as great (and negative) an impact on Medellín in recent history as **Pablo Escobar Gaviria**, the most successful of the cocaine barons. After years of inflicting violence on the city's civilians because of the Medellín cartel's rivalry with the Cali cartels – his brutality included a willingness to blow up a plane just to get at a single passenger – Escobar was unceremoniously shot down on the roof of a house on December 2, 1993, while on the run from the police.

ESCOBAR TOURS

Though many Medellín citizens find the idea of this godfather of crime posthumously becoming a major tourist attraction distasteful, a number of **tours** have sprung up that take you around the city to various Escobar-associated sights. You get to see the building he lived in, apartment blocks he built, the rooftop on which he was shot, and, finally, his gravestone at the Jardines de Montesacro cemetery. Tours cost around COP$55,000 per person and the best of the operators is **Paisa Road** (☏ 317 489 2629, ⓦ paisaroad.com), known for their sensitive and balanced tours.

ESCOBAR'S HIPPOS

Escobar is also the reason why there are feral hippos in the mountains around Medellín. To find out why, you can visit one of the more bizarre sites in Colombia – **Hacienda Nápoles** (Tues–Sun 9am–5pm; COP$32,000; ☏ 1800 510 344, ⓦ haciendanapoles.com), the huge farm that was once Escobar's private kingdom, complete with mansions, menagerie of exotic animals, bullring and more. Once Escobar was on the run, the abandoned hippos broke out of their enclosure, fled into the wild and bred, thus giving rise to dangerous non-native mammals in Colombia. This strange attraction sits halfway between Medellín and Bogotá, off the highway 1km from Dorodal. Today you can wander through the abandoned mansion, check out the displays on Escobar's reign of terror, and there are even some rides for children.

Metro Santo Domingo interchange; the fifteen-minute ride up glides over the mountain ridge and into the park, affording spectacular views of the city.

ARRIVAL AND INFORMATION

By plane Medellín's futuristic José María Córdova Airport (☏ 4 562 2818) lies a hilly 28km from the city along a scenic highway; it services all international and most domestic flights. Taxis to the city cost COP$60,000. Conbuses, at Cra 50a no. 53–13, run between the *Nutibara Hotel*, across the street from Plaza Botero, and the airport (every 20min roughly 5am–9pm; 1hr; COP$8600; ☏ 4 311 5781). The city's smaller second airport is Olaya Herrera (☏ 4 365 6100), located beside the southern bus terminal and serving domestic destinations; taxis to El Poblado cost around COP$10,000.

Domestic destinations Barranquilla (12 daily; 1hr 45min); Bogotá (hourly; 50min); Bucaramanga (6 daily; 50min); Cali (2 daily; 50min); Cartagena (3 daily; 1hr 20min); Manizales (2 daily; 30min); Pereira (7 daily; 35min); San Andrés (1 daily; 1hr 50min).

International destinations Caracas (daily; 2hr); Lima (daily; 4hr 30min); Quito (1–2 daily; 1hr 30min).

By bus Depending on which part of the country you're coming from, long-distance buses arrive either at the Terminal del Norte (Metro Caribe) or the Terminal del Sur.

Terminal del Norte handles traffic from the north, east and southeast, while Terminal del Sur has departures for destinations south and west. A taxi from the northern terminal to El Poblado, where most of the hostels are, costs about COP$18,000, but it is cheap and easy to get the metro (station: metro Polado). A taxi from the southern terminal to El Poblado is COP$6000.

Terminal del Norte destinations Bogotá (every 30min; 9–10hr); Cartagena (15 daily; 13hr); Ipiales (5 daily; 20–22hr); Magangué for Mompox (2 daily; 12hr); Santa Marta (12 daily; 16hr).

Terminal del Sur destinations Cali (50 daily; 9hr); Manizales (hourly; 5hr); Pasto (5 daily; 18hr); Pereira (twice hourly; 5hr); Popayán (3–4 daily; 10hr).

Tourist information There are information stands at both airports as well as a small tourist office inside the Palacio de Exposiciones at C 41 no. 55–35 (daily 9am–5pm; ☏ 4 261 7277). The main office is at Alpujarras, piso 10 (daily 9am–5pm; ☏ 4 385 6966).

GETTING AROUND

Metro The city's excellent metro system (Mon–Sat 4.30am–11pm, Sun 5am–10pm; COP$1900; ⓦ www .metrodemedellin.gov.co) is clean and efficient; included in the price of a metro ride are cable cars that leave from Acevedo, Santo Domingo and San Javier metro stations, carrying passengers high above the city for remarkable

5

views of the city and close-up views of the hilltop shanty towns. Ticket booth queues can be long, so if you're in the city for a few days, it's worth asking for a "Tarjeta Civica" from any of the metro stations, a card that you load up with however much money you want (minimum COP$3000) and which saves you 200 pesos per journey.

Buses The safety and efficiency of the metro means that you're far less likely to use buses, but at COP$1700 a ride they're a cheap – though not recommended – option after the metro closes. Bus #133 runs between Parque Berrío and C 10 in El Poblado, and to get from the Zona Rosa to Metro Poblado, just hop on any bus running along C 10A.

Taxi Taxis are cheap and plentiful and there is no surcharge for journeys to the bus terminal, airports or at night.

ACCOMMODATION

Most of the good budget accommodation is close to the night-time action in El Poblado and Patio Bonito.

HOSTELS

★Black Sheep Hostel Transversal 5A no. 45–133, Patio Bonito ☎4 311 1589, ⓦblacksheepmedellin.com. This sociable backpackers' pad has all bases covered, including Spanish classes, high-pressure showers and weekly barbecues. The Kiwi owner has travelled extensively in Colombia and is happy to share his knowledge. Single rooms available. Dorms `COP$24,000`, doubles `COP$50,000`

Casa Blanca Transversal 5A no. 45–256 ☎4 586 5149, ⓦcasablancamedellin.com. In a quiet, attractive neighbourhood, only 15min walk to the Zona Rosa, you can take advantage of the little extras that this homey hostel offers – from free Spanish classes to the sociable barbecues on Sundays. Dorms `COP$20,000`, doubles `COP$55,000`

Casa Kiwi Cra 36 no. 7–10 ☎4 268 2668, ⓦcasakiwi.net. Owned by a motorcycle-loving American, this excellent party hostel has clean dorms, DVD room, pool table, kitchen, massage room, bar and restaurant, laundry

service, and an adjoining luxury wing with fancy doubles, some en suite. They also run their own bike tour. Dorms `COP$20,000`, doubles `COP$60,000`

Pit Stop Hostel Cra 43E no. 5–110 ☎4 352 1176, ⓦpitstophostel.com. Right near the Zona Rosa, this lively place is aimed at travellers who play hard – with pool and basketball court complemented by the chillout areas – one with steam room, another with hammocks. Dorms `COP$21,000`, doubles `COP$60,000`

Tiger Paw Hostel Cra 36 no. 10–49 ☎4 311 6079, ⓦtigerpawhostel.com. Right in the middle of the Zona Rosa, this lively hostel has its own bar, lounge and pool table. The rooms are colourful but a bit basic – not that it matters, since you won't be spending much time sleeping. Dorms `COP$20,000`, doubles `COP$70,000`

Urban Buddha Circular 73A no. 38–55, Laureales ☎4 413 9322, ⓦbuddhahostel.com. This colourful hostel with quirky sculptures and murals is located in the up-and-coming Laureales district. There's a Zen garden, complete with pond and hammocks, and a retro communal area with artisan beer on tap. Breakfast is included. Dorms `COP$24,000`, doubles `COP$85,000`

Wandering Paisa C 44A no. 68A–76 ☎4 436 6759, ⓦwanderingpaisahostel.com. A little out of the way, this hostel goes the extra mile when it comes to arranging social events for its guests. There's an on-site bar to assist with the social lubrication. Dorms `COP$21,000`, doubles `COP$60,000`

EATING

Paisa cuisine, among Colombia's most distinctive, is heavy on the *frijoles* (black beans), grilled meat, plantains and rice. Perhaps no dish is more characteristic of the region than the *bandeja paisa*, a large bowl filled with ground beef, chorizo sausage, *frijoles*, rice, fried green bananas, a fried egg, avocado and fried pork. The city's trendiest restaurants are around leafy Parque Lleras in El Poblado, also known as the Zona Rosa.

★The Flip Flop Sandwich Shop Cra 36 no. 8A–92. Homesick travellers (or anyone in search of real bacon) gravitate towards this excellent breakfast/sandwich joint. Chris, the owner, is a treasure-trove of local information, his sandwiches (try the "Buffalo chicken") hit the spot and the vibe is wonderfully relaxed. Sandwiches COP$9000. Mon–Sat 8am–6pm.

Il Forno Cra 37A no. 8–9. A modern, open-air Italian place and El Poblado institution with plenty of mood lighting and satisfying pizza, home-made pasta and salads. Mains COP$14,000–23,000. Mon &Thurs–Sun noon–10pm, Fri & Sat noon–11pm.

★Hummus C 6 no. 43C–16. Not only are there plenty of vegetarian options at this classy Lebanese restaurant, their *limonada de coco* is also easily the best in town, and if you're extra hungry, go for the *mixto platter* – complete with *kofta*, *tabouleh*, *swarma*, *kibbeh* and rice.

5

Mains from COP$20,000. Mon–Sat noon–10.30pm, Sun noon–4.30pm.

Royal Thai C 8A no. 37A–05. Though there are Japanese elements to the decor upstairs, the food here is authentic Thai. The curries, though not cheap, are beautifully flavoured and hit that spice spot, and the dessert menu features the classic sticky rice with mango. Mains COP$25,000. Mon–Sat 11am–3pm & 6–10pm, Sun 5–9.30pm.

Señor Itto C 9 no. 43B–115. For a taste of beautifully prepared raw fish, try what is considered to be the best sushi joint in town. The "Dinamita Especial" deserves applause and there are plenty of noodle and teriyaki dishes. Lunch *menú* COP$12,000, mains COP$25,000–30,000. Mon–Sat noon–3pm & 7–10pm, Fri & Sat till 11.30pm.

★**Verdeo** Cra 35 no. 8a–3; ☎444 0934, ⬤ricoverdeo .com. This plant-filled vegetarian spot with colourful murals and quirky decor serves up imaginative juices (COP$4000) to wash down the delicious veggie burgers (COP$14,500), soups and salads. They also do a mean banana cake with Nutella. Mon–Thurs noon–10pm, Fri & Sat noon–11pm, Sun noon–9pm.

DRINKING AND NIGHTLIFE

A cluster of thumping bars and clubs – most of them catering to a young clientele – is in El Poblado. If you fancy something a bit more authentic, start with a beer on C 70 (Metro El Estadio) and listen to local musicians playing *vallenato* before heading on to C 33 (Metro Floresta) for a dance. Bars usually close around 2am Mon–Wed and 4am Thurs–Sat.

3 Cordilleras C 30 no. 44–176 ☎4 444 2337. If you take beer seriously and want to learn a thing or two about how it's made, this brewery offers weekly tours (COP$20,000), including five free beers, to help you appreciate Medellín's finest. Thurs only 5.30–9pm.

Blue C 10 no. 40–20. Giant speakers pump hard electro beats to a student and backpacker-centric crowd who wave along to flashing green laser lights. Entry COP$10,000. Thurs–Sat until late.

★**El Eslabón Prendido** C 53 no. 42–55. Renowned for its live music on Tuesday nights, when the tightly packed crowd goes wild to Colombia salsa. Entry COP$8000. Tues–Sat 8pm–2am.

Luxury Cra 43G no. 24–15. This is where a young, tipsy crowd gets down and dirty to reggaeton, hip-hop and more. Luxury it ain't, but it sure is lively. Entry COP$10,000. Thurs–Sun 10pm–4am.

DAY-TRIPS FROM MEDELLÍN

A few nearby parks make good if not absolutely essential stops within range of Medellín.

Parque Ecológico Piedras Blancas

The **Parque Ecológico Piedras Blancas** (daily 9am–5pm; free), 26km east of the city, serves as the lungs of Medellín. Set at the cool height of 2500m, much of this nature reserve has been reforested with native species, attracting butterflies and birds such as the brilliant blue soledad and the toucanet. Well-preserved pre-Columbian stone trails constructed between 100 BC and 700 AD weave through the park, while there is a butterfly gallery and a slick **insect museum** close to the official entrance.

To **get to the park**, board a bus from the corner of Ayacucho and Córdoba in the city centre (leaves every 30min) to the village of Santa Elena (30min), where another bus runs (every 30min) to the park. The metro cable car that runs from Santo Domingo to Parque Arví (see p.539) also connects the city to the park.

Piedra del Peñol and Guatapé

Bearing a freakish resemblance to Rio de Janeiro's Sugar Loaf Mountain, **Piedra del Peñol**, or simply "the rock", rises spectacularly from the edge of Embalse del Peñol, an artificial lake some 70km east of Medellín, studded with islands. Locals may tell you that the 200m granite and quartz monolith is a meteorite. Whatever geological or intergalactic anomaly brought it here, it's well worth climbing the 649 stone steps to the rock's peak for phenomenal 360-degree views of emerald-green peninsulas jutting into the azure Embalse del Peñol – a hydroelectric dam that submerged the original town of El Peñol in the 1970s.

There are a handful of restaurants and tourist stalls at the base of the rock, but it's better to walk or take a jeep (COP$3500 per person) to the delightful lakeside village of **Guatapé**, 3km away, which is full of restaurants serving trout fresh from the lake. The palm-lined main square, Plaza Simón Bolívar, is well preserved, with its crowning glory the Iglesia La Inmaculada Concepción; throughout you'll find colourful colonial houses adorned with intricate artistic motifs.

The best places to eat are along the lakefront Avenida Malecón (also known as Calle 32), all serving more or less the same menu. You'll get filling trout mains with a salad, plantain and fries for COP$12,000, or opt for the three-course lunch menus for around COP$8000–10,000. **Buses** leave for Guatapé roughly every half-hour from Medellín's northern bus terminal (2hr; COP$12,000, although you can haggle). Ask the driver to let you off at "La Piedra".

ACCOMMODATION

El Encuentro Vereda Quebrada Arriba, Guatapé ☏ 4 861 1374, ⊕ hostelelencuentro.com. This sweet little hostel overlooking the lake is about 10min from town and offers kayaking, mountain bike rentals, boat tours and hiking tours to the nearby waterfalls. Some rooms have lake views. Dorms COP$22,000, doubles COP$60,000, camping COP$18,000

MANIZALES AND AROUND

Founded in 1849 by migrating *paisas*, **MANIZALES** developed in the late nineteenth century with the growth of the coffee industry. One legacy is the numerous Neoclassical buildings in the city centre, which has been declared a national monument. This high-mountain city (altitude 2150m) sits at the base of the snowcapped Nevado del Ruiz volcano, which on a clear day you can sometimes see burping vapour, from the bridge in front of the Teatro Los Fundadores. Manizales owes its hilly topography to the geologically volatile earth beneath it, and small earthquakes occur with some frequency.

WHAT TO SEE AND DO

Much of the town's charm lies in its large student population, who helps create a festive atmosphere, with night-time entertainment centred mostly on the Zona Rosa district, also known as El Cable. The party comes to a head in the first weeks of January during the **Fería de Manizales**, when there are colourful parades, a beauty pageant in search of a new Coffee Queen and bloody bullfights staged in the Plaza de Toros (C 10 and Cra 27). Manizales also makes an excellent base for exploring the surrounding **coffee farms** (see p.546) and

the **Parque Nacional Natural Los Nevados** (see p.545).

Plaza de Bolívar

In the centre of the city, the main square is dominated by the vast **Catedral de Manizales** (tower: daily 8am–8pm; COP$10,000), made of reinforced concrete and featuring a vertigo-inducing, 106m-tall tower that you can ascend with a guide; tours start on the hour, and there's also a coffee shop inside the cathedral. In the centre of the plaza stands an obligatory **statue of Simón Bolívar**, but with a twist – *Bolívar-Cóndor*, the creation of Rodrigo Arenas Betancur, is half-man, half-condor.

Torre Mirador

In the northwest suburb of Chipre, on a high bluff at the end of Avenida 12 de Octubre, the 45m-tall **Torre Mirador** (daily 10am–10pm; COP$3000) is the town's best lookout. On a clear day you can see seven *departamentos* and three mountain ranges. Buses run to Chipre from the Cable Plaza along Avenida Santander every minute or so.

Reserva Ecológica Río Blanco

Around 3km northeast of Manizales, the **Reserva Ecológica Río Blanco** is home to 380 bird species, 180 butterfly species and around 60 mammals. Tranquil orchid-lined uphill hikes through impressive cloudforest reveal dense jungle flora entwined in a battle for a place in the sun; if you are lucky, you may catch a glimpse of the reserve's endangered spectacled bear. There is also a hummingbird farm. You'll need to request permission to enter the reserve from the Fundación Ecológica Gabriel Arango Restrepo (☏ 6 887 9770, ext 72185, ⊕ cerestrepo@aguasdemanizales .com.co, ⊕ aguasdemanizales.com.co). They will book the compulsory guides (COP$20,000 for up to fifteen people). A taxi to the entrance costs around COP$35,000 (20min); arrange a return trip.

Recinto del Pensamiento

Butterflies and birds are the main attraction at this nature park (Tues–Sun

5

9am–4pm; COP$13,500, COP$17,500 including cable-car ride; ☎6 889 7070, ext 2990, ⓦ recintodelpensamiento.com), 14km from Manizales. As well as visiting the colourful butterfly enclosure, you can also wander through a medicinal herb garden, have lunch at the restaurant, enjoy a stroll through the orchid forest and marvel at the gigantic *guadua* bamboo gazebo, used for conventions and wedding ceremonies. Guides are compulsory and included in the admission price. Buses (marked Sera Maltería; every 5min; 40min; COP$1600) leave from along Avenida Santander, or you can catch a taxi (20min; COP$12,500).

ARRIVAL AND DEPARTURE

By plane La Nubia Airport is about 9km southeast of the city centre. A taxi costs around COP$15,000 or you can jump on one of the frequent buses for COP$1600 from three blocks from the airport to the centre.
Destinations Bogotá (10 daily; 50min); Cartagena (daily; 1hr 20min); Medellín (2 daily; 30min).
By bus The bus terminal (☎6 878 5641) is at Cra 43 no. 65–100. Ride the cable car to the centre of town from where regular buses (COP$1500) run to Cable Plaza, or jump in a taxi (COP$10,000).
Destinations Bogotá (hourly; 8–9hr); Cali (hourly; 5hr); Medellín (hourly; 4hr 30min); Pereira (every 5min; 1hr 20min).

GETTING AROUND AND INFORMATION

Cable car The city's cable-car line runs from the bus station (Cambulos stop) to Cra 23 in the centre of town (Fundadores stop) in less than 10min and costs COP$1500. You can also ride the cable car to Villa Maria.
Tourist information Parque Benjamin López on the corner of Cra 22 and C 31 (daily 7am–7pm; ☎6 873 3901) dishes out maps.

ACCOMMODATION

Kaleidoscopio C 20 no. 21–15 ☎8 901 702, ⓦ hostal kaleidoscopio.com. Just two blocks from the cathedral, the location of this simple and central *hostal* is its main selling point. It might not offer any social activities or tours, but the rooms are clean (two have balconies), there's a laundry for guest use (COP$10,000), and breakfast is included. Dorms COP$25,000, doubles COP$56,000
★**Mirador Andino** Cra 23 no. 32–20 ☎6 882 1699, ⓦ miradorandino-hostel.com. Just steps from the cable car's Fundadores stop, this spacious hostel is a great city-centre option, immaculately clean and with a stylish retro design. The roof terrace has stunning views across the city

and is perfect for a sunset beer. The owners are outdoor enthusiasts and can organize multiple-day hikes to Los Nevados. Dorms COP$28,000, doubles COP$80,000
★**Mountain Hostel** C 66 no. 23B–91 ☎6 887 4736, ⓦ mountainhostels.com.co. On a quiet suburban street just two blocks from the buzzing Zona Rosa, this lively backpackers' hostel has comfortable dorms, a cosy TV room stocked with DVDs, free breakfast and all-day coffee, kitchen, a large backyard with a barbecue area, hammocks, and – best of all – all kinds of outdoor ventures organized by helpful staff. Dorms COP$24,000, doubles COP$68,000

EATING, DRINKING AND NIGHTLIFE

The city centre clears out at night and most eating and drinking is done in the suburbs. The liveliest area, popular with students, is around Cable Plaza, between calles 60 and 75 along Cra 23 (the Zona Rosa), where you'll find the best restaurants, bars and clubs.
★**La Clave del Mar** C 69A no. 27–100, Barrio Palermo ☎6 887 5528. Excellent fresh seafood delivered from Tumaco or Buenaventura on the Pacific coast. Try the delicious *cazuela de mariscos* seafood casserole (COP$26,500) or the *sancocho del bagre* (COP$21,500), a potato, cassava and catfish soup. Mon & Sun 11am–4pm, Tues–Sat 11am–9.15pm.
★**Juan Sebastian-Bar** Cra 23 no. 63–66. Charismatic owner Elmer Vargas has a passion for jazz and an awesome CD collection. Popular with artists, writers and university lecturers, this intimate spot has great views of the city and fine cocktails. Mon–Thurs & Sun 6pm–midnight, Fri & Sat 6pm–2am.
Limonaria C 58 no. 24–15, Barrio Estrella. The owner of this gourmet café uses mostly home-grown, organic produce to cook up healthy meals and snacks such as stuffed Portobello mushrooms (COP$16,500), salads (COP$14,000) and juices (COP$3500). The cheesecake is to die for. A pretty outdoor terrace is lit up with fairy lights in the evenings. Mon–Thurs 3–10pm, Fri & Sat 3–11pm.
Restaurante y Asadero Típico El Zaguán Paisa Cra 23 no. 31–27. Enter through the never-ending bamboo corridor for a hearty *menú del día* (COP$6500); it's conveniently located for the cable car to the bus station. Daily 11am–8.30pm.
Santelmo Cra 23B no. 64–80. Heaving with students who down cocktails (COP$13,000) and jugs of sangria (COP$33,000), then dance the night away between the tables. Wed–Sat from 6pm until late.
Spago C 59 no. 24A–10 ☎6 885 3328. A stylish Italian restaurant that offers great home-made pasta, wood-fired pizza and expertly cooked meats. Mains COP$17,000. Mon–Thurs noon–3pm & 6–10pm, Fri & Sat noon–3pm & 6–11pm, Sun noon–3pm.
La Suiza Cra 23 no. 26–57 & Cra 23B no. 64–06. Two branches of a superb bakery where you can grab breakfast

or a light lunch – crêpes, sandwiches – or treat yourself to home-made chocolates and sweet pastries. Mon–Sat 9am–8.30pm, Sun 10am–7pm.

PARQUE NACIONAL NATURAL LOS NEVADOS

The **PARQUE NACIONAL NATURAL LOS NEVADOS** (entry COP$34,500, including guide), 40km southeast of Manizales, protects some of the last surviving snowcapped peaks in the tropics. Three of the five volcanoes are now dormant, but **Nevado del Ruiz** – the tallest at 5321m – remains an active threat, having killed 22,000 people and buried the now extinct town of Armero when it erupted in 1985. Sadly, though, for a park whose name, Nevado, implies perpetual snow, climate change has lifted the snow line to almost 5000m on most peaks. Note that the most spectacular part of the park, the Nevado del Ruiz, has been closed since 2012 because of volcanic activity. Weekly bulletins on its status are posted (in Spanish) on the Colombian National Parks website (ⓦparquesnacionales.gov.co).

The best months to visit are January and February – clear days make for spectacular views of the volcanic peaks. March, July, August and December can also be ideal, while the rest of the year sees a fair amount of rain.

WHAT TO SEE AND DO

Since 2012, the Nevado del Ruiz volcano has been off-limits due to a resurgence of volcanic activity. Tours go as high as Valle de las Tumbas at 4350m, but hikers will be disappointed as much of it is by 4WD. Instead, alternative tours to **Volcano Santa Isabel** have become far more popular, stopping off at waterfalls, and to admire condors and other birds and mammals, before finally reaching the glaciers at the 4800m summit. Day visits start at 4.30am, and include breakfast and lunch, ending at 7pm (approx COP$170,000). You can also do two- and three-day treks, staying overnight with a local family in a mountain cabin, or camping. As there is no public transport to the park, many visitors come as part of a day-trip, and then arrange to be picked up by a tour

company a day or so later. In low season, tours don't run every day so check beforehand.

The dramatic **southern end**, where a dense wax-palm forest slowly metamorphoses into *páramo* near the cobalt-blue **Laguna del Otún** (3950m), can only be accessed on foot – many people can make a single trip, taking in both this and Volcano Santa Isabel. You can reach the trout-stuffed Laguna del Otún from Villamaria (10min from Manizales), taking in Laguna Verde and Volcano Santa Isabel on the way. You can also approach from Salento (see p.547).

At 5220m, the park's second-highest peak is **Nevado de Tolima**, rated its most beautiful, in the southeast corner, which can be accessed from Salento or Ibagué. Climbing it is no mean feat and would involve a four-day expedition with the right equipment and permits.

No longer a *nevado* (snowcapped peak), the **Paramillo del Quindio** has been demoted thanks to global warming, but is a relatvely easy climb at 4750m, and affords views of the park's three white-topped volcanoes: Nevado del Ruiz, Nevado de Santa Isabel and Nevado de Tolima. It can be reached on a three-day excursion from Salento. Contact a tour operator as all visits must be accompanied by guides.

TOUR OPERATORS

Ecosistemas Cra 21 no. 20–45, Manizales ☎6 880 8300. Runs a daily trip from Manizales, leaving at 6.30am, for COP$130,000, including transport, breakfast, lunch, park entrance, partial ascent of Ruiz in a 4WD, and a visit to the thermal baths at the park's entrance. Also runs 1–3-day hiking treks up Volcano Santa Isabel, where you'll see birds, mammals, waterfalls and glaciers.

Kumanday C 66 no. 23B–40, Manizales ☎6 887 2682, ⓦkumanday.com. Runs a host of regional tours including the Laguna del Otun and Santa Isabel in the Parque Nevado, plus a range of mountain bike tours. They also have a modern hostel near Zona Rosa.

Páramo Trek C 5 no. 1–37, Salento ☎311 745 3761, ⓦparamotrek.com. Well-informed operator offering easy two-day visits to the southern part of the park along with the Valle de Cócora for COP$390,000 per person (less for groups of more than two). They also offer more challenging three-day visits including the peak of the Paramillo del Quindio.

5

PEREIRA

Just 56km south of Manizales, **PEREIRA** makes an equally suitable base for exploring the Zona Cafetera. The region's largest city, it shares Manizales' history as a centre for the coffee industry, and though its historic centre has been repeatedly destroyed by earthquakes, the most recent striking in 1999, it's closer to many of the region's coffee *fincas* and thermal springs.

Pereira's **Plaza de Bolívar** is unique among the uniformly named central plazas of Colombia for Rodrigo Arenas Betancourt's modern sculpture of *Bolívar Desnudo* – El Libertadór nude on horseback, a controversial pose when it was unveiled in 1963 but now a beloved city symbol. Also on the plaza is the town's magnificent **Catedral**, built in 1875. Nondescript from the outside, the Catedral's single-nave interior is supported by an elaborate latticework of twelve thousand wooden beams forming a canopy like a spider's web.

ARRIVAL AND INFORMATION

By plane Pereira's international Aeropuerto Matecaña (☎6 314 8151) is 5km west of the city centre. A taxi downtown costs around COP$12,000, or jump on one of the frequent buses for COP$1700.

Destinations Bogotá (8 daily; 50min); Cali (4 daily; 30min); Medellín (5 daily; 35min).

By bus The bus terminal (☎6 315 2323) lies 1.5km south of the city centre at C 17 no. 23–157. A taxi to the centre is COP$4000; a bus will set you back COP$500.

Destinations Armenia (every 10min; 1hr); Bogotá (hourly; 9hr); Cali (hourly; 3hr 30min); Manizales (every 15min; 1hr 15min); Medellín (hourly; 6hr); Salento (3 daily, hourly on weekends; 50min); Santa Rosa de Cabal (every 10min; 45min).

Tourist information The very helpful tourist office (Mon–Fri 7.30am–noon & 2–6.30pm; ☎6 324 8753, ⓦpereira.travel) is on the corner of C 17 and Cra 10 on the first floor of the Centro Cultural Lucy Tejada. There's another branch at the airport (daily 10am–5pm).

ACCOMMODATION

Pereira has few accommodation options for budget travellers, so it's worth staying at one of the converted *fincas*, many of them former coffee plantations, between 5km and 35km from the city (see below).

STAYING ON A COFFEE FARM

Coffee is the planet's most-traded commodity after oil and Colombia is one of its largest producers, with 500,000-plus growers and the unique benefit of two annual harvests. Recognized for producing world-class coffee, **coffee fincas** in the Zona Cafetera are now following in the footsteps of the wine industry and opening their doors to curious tourists.

Fincas range from traditional estates still attended by their owner to deceptively modern rural hotels where the only coffee you'll find comes served with breakfast. Scenically, the farms look out on lush slopes, overgrown with the shiny-leaved coffee shrubs and interspersed with banana plants and bamboo-like *guadua* forests. Many will also arrange horseriding and walks, and they make an ideal base to explore the region's many attractions.

To locate the best *fincas* for your needs, ask other travellers; you can also enquire at the local tourist offices or hostels in Manizales (see p.544) or Pereira (see above).

FINCAS

Hacienda Guayabal Cra 3 no. 15–72 Chinchiná ☎314 772 4856, ⓦwww.haciendaguayabal.com. Runs tours, in English, of their postcard-perfect coffee farm (COP$25,000). Guests can stay in the main house, and the price includes a tour, three meals and use of the swimming pool. To get there, take a bus from Manizales or Pereira to Chinchiná (30min) and then travel the last 3km by taxi or catch a bus from in front of the church to the farm. Per person COP$55,000

★**Hacienda Venecia** C 59 no. 24A–18 ☎6 885 0771, ⓦhaciendavenecia.com. This fourth-generation, family-owned working coffee farm is an essential stop for anyone who wants to learn more about coffee

production, roasting techniques, trade and aromas. Proud owner Juan Pablo exports coffee as well as roasting for the domestic market. Tours (COP$45,000 including pick-up from Manizales, COP$35,000 if staying overnight) of his sprawling plantation allow visitors to observe the production process from start to finish. Spend a night at the guesthouse or *hostal*, swinging in a hammock on the veranda, firefly-spotting and listening to the croaks of happy frogs in the swimming pool. Breakfast included. To get there from Medellín, ask the bus to drop you off at Puente San Pellegrino. Someone from the farm can pick you up from the restaurant by the bridge (they can make the call for you). Dorms COP$35,000, doubles COP$90,000, main guesthouse COP$280,000

5

Hotel Cumanday Cra 5 no. 22–54 ☏ 6 324 0416. Solid downtown option, with reliable hot showers, cable TV and a place to wash your dirty togs. If you ask nicely, the staff will let you cook in their kitchen. **COP$50,000**

Kolibrí Hostel C 4 no. 16–35 ☏ 6 331 3955, ⓦ kolibrihostel .com. Hostel run by a wonderfully friendly Dutch–Colombian couple. The rooms are bright, the atmosphere sociable and the location is great for going out in the Sector Circunvalar. Dorms **COP$22,000**, doubles **COP$50,000**

Hotel Mi Casita C 25 no. 6–20 ☏ 6 333 9995. Close to Parque El Lago Uribe and used to dealing with travellers, this no-frills option is one of the better budget spots in town, with cable TV and a garish colour scheme. Free wi-fi; breakfast is included. **COP$85,000**

EATING AND DRINKING

The majority of good eating and drinking options are located in the Sector Circunvalar, on or near the Av Circunvalar.

Crepes & Waffles Cra 8 no. 19–17. Branch of the ubiquitous chain where the myriad sweet and savoury offerings are always a crowd-pleaser. Waffles from COP$6000. Daily 11am–8pm.

★ **Leños y Parilla** Cra 12 no. 2–78. This Argentine-style steakhouse specializes in what is possibly the best grilled meat in Colombia. You are presented with a beautifully cooked cut of your choice with all the trimmings by smartly attired waiters, and it's all amazing value for the quality and quantity. Sirloin steak COP$22,500. Mon–Fri noon–3.15pm & 6.30–10.30pm, Sat noon–7pm, Sun noon–5.30pm.

★ **El Parnaso** Cra 6 no. 23–35. Enjoy a cocktail (COP$15,000) in this cool outdoor garden bar, with fairy lights strung between guava trees, to a rock-indie soundtrack over which you can still make yourself heard. Mon–Thurs 3pm–1am, Fri & Sat 3pm–midnight.

DAY-TRIPS FROM PEREIRA

Pereira makes a good base for striking out on numerous ventures to the nearby hot springs, hiking trails and coffee *fincas*.

Termales Santa Rosa

Sitting at the foot of a 25m-high waterfall and surrounded by lush greenery, these attractive **hot springs** (daily 9am–midnight; COP$32,000) consist of four thermal pools and a visitor centre with cafeteria and massages on offer, and you can also take a dip in the natural pool directly beneath the waterfall. Just a little further down the dirt road are the **thermal springs** (daily 9am–midnight; COP$42,000; ⓦ termales.com.co) attached to the *Hotel Termales*, which resembles an alpine chalet, with one large pool and two thimble-sized hot tubs available to non-guests, set against a spectacular backdrop of three tall waterfalls. There's also a lavish spa on site.

The springs are easily reachable from Santa Rosa de Cabal, 9km west. Frequent buses run from Pereira to Santa Rosa de Cabal (COP$2500, 40min). From the corner of Santa Rosa's *la galería* (marketplace), opposite the police station, *chivas* and buses (try to catch a *chiva* if possible) leave for the hot springs (every 2hr 7am–6pm; 45min; double-check timetables before departure), coming back pretty much straight after. If you miss the bus, one of the Willy Jeeps parked by the market will take you there for around COP$20,000.

Termales San Vicente

These lavishly landscaped **hot springs** (daily 8am–midnight; COP$30,000; ☏ 6 333 6157, ⓦ sanvicente.com.co), 35km northeast of Pereira via the town of Santa Rosa de Cabal, feature a selection of steaming medicinal thermal pools scattered across some five square kilometres of cloudforest, river, waterfalls and luxuriant countryside. At 2330m, it gets pretty chilly up here, so it helps that the average pool temperature is 38°C. A variety of spa treatments is offered, including massage (COP$45,000) and mud therapy (COP$20,000). If you want to **spend the night** at the springs, the most cost-effective option is camping (COP$85,000 including entrance fee and breakfast). Further up the accommodation ladder are cabañas (COP$238,000 per person) or single rooms (COP$220,000).

There's no public transport to the spa but you can make your own way by catching a bus to Santa Rosa from the bus terminal in Pereira and grabbing a seat on a Willy Jeep (ex-US military 4WD) from *la galería* (market) for Termales San Vicente (COP$160,000 return for four people).

SALENTO

In the heart of coffee country, the adorable village of **SALENTO** is one of

5

the region's earliest settlements, and its slow development means the original lifestyle and buildings of the *paisa* journeymen who settled here in 1842 have barely been altered since. Rural workers clad in cowboy hats and *ruanas* (Colombian ponchos) are a common sight. The colourful, wonderfully photogenic one-storey homes of thick adobe and clay-tile roofs that surround the plaza are as authentic as it gets.

WHAT TO SEE AND DO

Salento is a popular destination for weary backpackers who linger here to soak up the town's unpretentious charms and hike in the spectacular Valle de Cócora or to use the town as a base to explore the rest of the Zona Cafetera. The town is also the second most popular weekend destination in the country for Colombians, and on Saturdays and Sundays the main plaza hosts a **food and handicrafts fair**. Salento's annual fiesta falls in the first week of January, when the town kicks up its heels for a week of horse processions, mock bullfighting and folk dancing.

From the top of Calle Real, steps lead to **Alto de la Cruz**, a hilltop *mirador* offering unbeatable vistas of the Valle de Cócora and, on a clear day, the peaks of snow-clad volcanoes in Parque Nacional Natural Los Nevados (see p.545).

ARRIVAL AND INFORMATION

By bus Buses arrive at Salento's main plaza and depart from Cra 2, at C 4. Willy Jeeps (daily at 6.10am, 7.30am, 9.30am, 11.30am; 20min) run to Cócora. They return when full at around 3 or 4pm.

Destinations Armenia (every 20min from 6am–9pm; 1hr); Pereira (3 daily at 7.50am, 2.50pm & 5.50pm, more frequent on weekends; 50min). Going to/from Pereira, you can also take an Armenia-bound bus to the Las Flores junction and then catch one of the frequent buses from Armenia to Salento or Pereira.

Information The English-speaking staff at *Tralala* and *Plantation House* are particularly knowledgeable about the area. The ATM on the main square often runs out of money, so it's best to arrive with cash.

ACCOMMODATION

Book ahead if you plan to visit during the annual fiesta at the start of January.

Hostal Ciudad de Segorbe C 5 no. 4–06 ☎6 759 3794, ⓦhostalciudaddesegorbe.com. Stylish rooms offer stunning views of the Valle de Cócora and balconies overlook the spacious flower-filled central courtyard, which is a great place to unwind with a book. The Spanish/Colombian owners are just wonderful. Breakfast is included. Doubles COP$100,000

Plantation House C 7 no. 1–04 ☎316 285 2603, ⓦtheplantationhousesalento.com. An old colonial house set on a picturesque coffee plantation near town, the best thing about this British/Colombian-run hostel is the owners' fountain of regional knowledge. An adjacent building accommodates guests when the main house is full and the owners can let you stay on their coffee farm. Dorms are plain and some rooms are en suite. Dorms COP$19,000, doubles COP$45,000

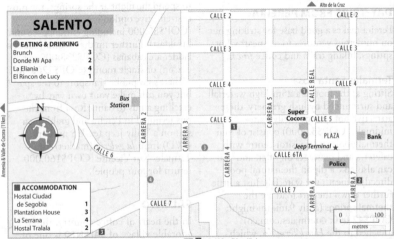

SALENTO

● **EATING & DRINKING**
Brunch	3
Donde Mi Apa	2
La Eliania	4
El Rincon de Lucy	1

■ **ACCOMMODATION**
Hostal Ciudad de Segobia	1
Plantation House	3
La Serrana	4
Hostal Tralala	2

5

★**La Serrana** Via Palestina Km1.5 🕿316 296 1890, ⓦlaserrana.com.co. Eco-friendly working farm and hostel with faux-rustic rooms, 1.5km from Salento, with spectacular views of the surrounding Cócora mountains and valleys. Horseriding and mountain biking are offered and there's a campfire every night. End your day on a comfy sofa enjoying the great music selection. Willy Jeeps from town cost COP$6000. Dorms COP$23,000, doubles COP$80,000, camping (if you bring your own tent) COP$15,000

★**Hostal Tralala** C 7 no. 6–45 🕿314 850 5543, ⓦhostaltralalasalento.com. Friendly Dutch owner, Hemmo Misker, has worked hard to convert this traditional *paisa*-style house into a beautiful, modern hostel. The spotless rooms with ultra-comfortable beds and smart bathrooms retain original features, like the wooden floors with furnishings made by local artisans. Bonus features include a fully equipped guest kitchen, DVD lounge, library and sun terrace. Dorms COP$20,000, doubles COP$50,000

EATING AND DRINKING

Fresh trout is on the menu in all the town's restaurants and is usually served with big crunchy *patacones* (fried plantains). The main square has several lively bars with outside tables. Or meet locals to play *tejo* (see p.494) at Cra 4, C 3–32.

★**Brunch** C 6 no. 3–25 ⓦbrunchsalento.com. This American-run spot has been winning rave reviews from an international crowd for its burgers, fajitas and delectable peanut butter brownies, among other things. They'll whip up packed lunches for Cócora-bound hikers and there's even a little cinema room for nightly screenings. Daily 6.30am–10pm.

★**Donde Mi Apá** Cra 6 no. 5–24, main square. Perfect for people-watching on the square and hanging out with locals having a drink. The interior is packed with stacked vinyls, old photos and a glaring stuffed bull's head. Mon–Thurs & Sun 4pm–midnight, Fri & Sat 4pm–2am.

La Eliania Cra 2 no. 6–65. If you're craving proper Indian curry, gourmet pizza or doorstop sandwiches with inventive fillings, look no further. Given the high cooking standards, the prices are a bargain. Mains from COP$12,000; lunch menu COP$8000. Daily noon–9pm.

El Rincón de Lucy Cra 6 no. 4–02. A whizz in the kitchen, Lucy serves the best set lunches in town. For COP$6000 you get juice, soup and a heaped plate of beans, vegetables and fish or meat. Daily 6am–3.30pm & 6–8.30pm; shut Sun eve.

DAY-TRIP FROM SALENTO: VALLE DE CÓCORA

Salento sits atop the **VALLE DE CÓCORA**, which contains a thick forest of the skyscraper wax palm, Colombia's national plant, which grows up to 60m high. The valley, which offers picturesque hikes, is easily explored in a day-trip from Salento. The hamlet of **Cócora**, with a handful of restaurants, small shops and hotels, lies 11km east of Salento. From Cócora a well-trodden path leads into misty, pristine cloudforest, scattered with the remains of pre-Columbian tombs and dwellings. Orchids, bromeliads and heliconias are just some of the plant species that thrive here, and the fauna includes spectacled bear, native deer and puma, along with hundreds of bird species such as toucans, eagles and motmots.

A five- to six-hour **loop walk** starts from the blue gate in Cócora; the muddy track passes a trout farm and runs through farmland for around 45 minutes before reaching the park entrance, after which you're following an uneven, slippery trail through cloudforest. The trail eventually branches, with one track leading up to the extremely worthwhile **Reserva Acaime** (entrance COP$5000), home to eighteen species of hummingbirds that flock to its bird feeders. The price includes a large mug of revitalizing hot chocolate and a chunk of locally produced cheese. You then retrace your steps to the main trail that crosses nine rickety wooden Indiana Jones-style bridges over the Río Quindío before the Finca La Montaña branch culminates at a mountain-top viewing platform with exhilarating valley views. The way down along a wide gravel road takes you past a cluster of wax palms.

To **get to Cócora**, take one of the four Willy Jeeps (ex-US military 4WDs) that leave daily from Salento's main plaza (daily at 6.10am, 7.30am, 9.30am, 11.30am; 20min; COP$3000 one-way). They return when full at around 3 or 4pm. Jeeps can also be hired for COP$30,000 one-way.

The southwest

Leaving the snowy white caps of the "Coffee Zone" behind, the Cauca River Valley descends south and widens until you reach **Cali**, gateway to Colombia's southwest and the self-proclaimed world

5

capital of salsa music. A knuckle-whitening detour from Cali takes you to the tiny town of **San Cipriano**. Further south, the Panamerican Highway stretches past steamy fields of sugar cane to the serene, colonial town of **Popayán**, known for its blindingly white Rococo colonial architecture. The verdant rolling countryside around **San Agustín** is some of Colombia's finest, and would be worth a visit even without the enigmatic stone statues – remnants of a mysterious civilization – that pepper the hillsides. **Tierradentro**'s ancient tombs are less well known but no less fascinating. Heading further south from the overlooked town of **Pasto**, you ascend a ridge dominated by volcanoes all the way to Ecuador.

CALI

Colombia's third-largest city, with a population of 2.3 million, **CALI** was founded in 1536 but only shed its provincial backwater status in the early 1900s, when the profits brought in by its sugar plantations prompted industrialization. Today it's one of Colombia's most prosperous cities, in part because of its central role in the drug trade since the dismantling of the rival Medellín cartel in the early 1990s; however, Cali is now more famous for salsa dancers than white powder.

The low-lying and extremely hot city (with temperatures routinely surpassing 40°C) straddles the **Río Cali**, a tributary of the Río Cauca, surrounded by the sugar plantations of the marshy Cauca Valley. The large numbers of African slaves brought to work the sugar mills left a notable impact on Cali's culture, nowhere more so than in its music.

Parts of central Cali are **unsafe** to walk around; be sure to get up-to-date advice on where not to go.

WHAT TO SEE AND DO

The city stakes a powerful claim to being Colombia's party capital, and you'll hear Cuban-style **salsa** music blaring from the numerous *salsatecas* throughout the day and night. If you're here in September, don't miss the Festival Mundial de Salsa.

Plaza de Caycedo and around

The city's centre is **Plaza de Caycedo**, which has a statue of independence hero Joaquín de Caycedo y Cuero in the middle. On the plaza's south end is the nineteenth-century **Catedral San Pedro**, with its elaborate stained-glass windows.

Iglesia de la Merced

The oldest church in the city is the **Iglesia de la Merced**, on the corner of Cra 4 and C 7, built from adobe and stone shortly after the city's founding. In the adjoining former convent – Cali's oldest building – is the **Museo Arqueológico la Merced** (Mon–Sat 9am–1pm & 2–6pm; COP$4000), which has displays of pre-Columbian pottery including funerary urns and religious objects unearthed throughout central and southern Colombia.

Museo del Oro

This small museum at C 7 no. 4–69 (Tues–Sat 10am–5pm; free) has a well-presented collection of gold and ceramics from the Calima culture from the region northwest of Cali.

Museo de Arte Moderno La Tertulia

Cali's **Museo de Arte Moderno La Tertulia** (Av Colombia no. 5–105 Oeste; Tues–Sun 10am–6pm; COP$4000; ⓦmuseolatertulia.com) shows changing exhibitions of contemporary photography, sculpture and painting, sometimes featuring high-profile international names, as well as arthouse film screenings in the adjoining *cinemateca*. Walk along Río Cali for fifteen minutes from the city centre to get here.

ARRIVAL AND INFORMATION

By plane The best way to and from Cali's Aeropuerto Alfonso Bonilla Aragon (ⓣ 2 666 3200), 16km northeast of the city, is to catch one of the regular minibuses that run to and from the bus terminal (40min; COP$4300). A taxi is COP$55,000.

Destinations Bogotá (daily; 50min); Cartagena (daily; 1hr 25min); Medellín (4 daily; 40min); Pereira (4 daily; 30min); Pasto (2 daily; 1hr); San Andrés (daily; 2hr). Also international departures for Lima, Panama City, Madrid and Miami.

By bus The city's gigantic bus terminal at C 30N no. 2AN–29, 2km north of the centre, is connected to downtown by

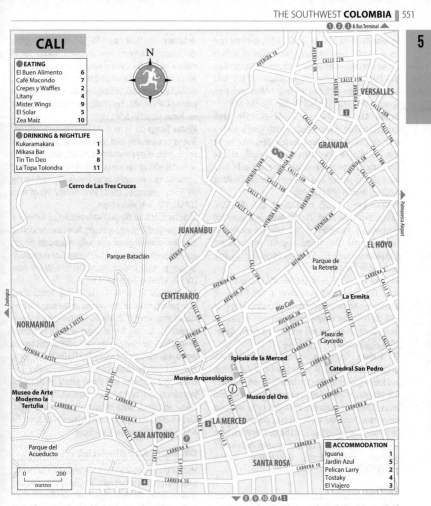

CALI

N

● EATING

El Buen Alimento	6
Café Macondo	7
Crepes y Waffles	2
Litany	4
Mister Wings	9
El Solar	5
Zea Maiz	10

● DRINKING & NIGHTLIFE

Kukaramakara	1
Mikasa Bar	3
Tin Tin Deo	8
La Topa Tolondra	11

Cerro de Las Tres Cruces

VERSALLES

GRANADA

JUANAMBU

Parque Bataclán

EL HOYO

Parque de la Retreta

CENTENARIO

NORMANDIA

Rio Cali

La Ermita

Plaza de Caycedo

Iglesia de la Merced

Catedral San Pedro

Museo Arqueológico

Museo del Oro

Museo de Arte Moderno la Tertulia

SAN ANTONIO

LA MERCED

■ ACCOMMODATION

Iguana	1
Jardin Azul	5
Pelican Larry	2
Tostaky	4
El Viajero	3

Parque del Acueducto

SANTA ROSA

0	200
metres	

Zoológico

Palmaseca Airport

❽ ❾ ❿ ⓫ & ❺

Mio, the efficient integrated bus system (see below). A taxi into downtown costs COP$6000. There's a left luggage office at the terminal (24hr; COP$2700/12hr).

Destinations Armenia (hourly; 4hr); Bogotá (hourly; 12hr); Manizales (hourly; 5hr); Medellín (8 daily; 9hr); Pasto (hourly; 9hr); Pereira (several daily; 4hr); Popayán (every 30min; 3hr).

Tourist information The Secretaria de Cultura y Turismo is on Cra 4, at C 6 (Mon–Fri 8am–noon & 2–5pm, Sat 10am–2pm; ☎ 2 885 6173).

GETTING AROUND

Much local sightseeing can be done on foot, provided you're staying in the Granada or San Antonio neighbourhoods and are prepared to walk a lot.

By bus The main route of the efficient Mio network of

electric buses (ⓦ www.metrocali.gov.co), akin to Bogotá's TransMilenio, runs along the river, and also passes through the centre and along the Av Quinta (Av 5). It costs COP$1700 per ride (COP$1600 weekdays); you need to buy a swipecard.

By taxi Some outlying attractions are best reached by inexpensive taxi. Always take a taxi at night. Try Taxi Libre (☎ 2 444 4444) or Taxi Libre Aeropuerto (☎ 2 555 5555).

ACCOMMODATION

Cali's backpacker hostels are concentrated in two clusters, one around the Granada neighbourhood with good access to nightlife on Avenida 6N and the restaurants around Avenida 8N, and the other in the characterful (but slightly less secure at night) colonial neighbourhood of San Antonio.

5

Iguana Av 9N no. 22N–46 ☎ 2 660 8937, ⊛ iguana.com .co. A friendly, Swiss-run youth hostel with all facilities spread over two houses: garden barbecues on Wednesdays, plus loads of information on the region and free salsa lessons for those with two left feet. A short walk from Granada. Dorms COP$20,000, doubles COP$65,000

Jardin Azul Cra 24A no. 2A–59 ☎ 2 556 8380, ⊛ jardinazul.com. A wonderfully friendly guesthouse in a quiet neighbourhood a short ride from the centre on the Mio. The bilingual proprietress is super-helpful, and the large, bright rooms and small swimming pool make this a great place to unwind after the heat of the city. Breakfast included. Doubles COP$150,000

Pelican Larry C 20N no. 6AN–44 ☎ 2 382 7226, ⊛ hostelpelicanlarry.com. The big beds, DVD room and twice-weekly barbecues at this fabulous location in Granada make this hostel popular with younger backpackers who are in Cali to party. Dorms COP$20,000, doubles COP$50,000

Tostaky Cra 10 no. 1–76 ☎ 2 893 0651, ⊛ tostakycali .com. There's a refined atmosphere at this French-run hostel in San Antonio, which probably has something to do with the coffee bar complete with chess sets in the front room. Guest kitchen for self-caterers is a bonus. Dorms COP$20,000, doubles COP$50,000

El Viajero Cra 5 no. 4–56 ☎ 2 893 8342, ⊛ elviajerohostels.com. If you're looking to dance, chill and have a good time, then this hostel's for you: they offer free salsa classes (Mon–Sat), yoga three times a week, and circus shows every Saturday night. The circus and salsa theme runs throughout the hostel, with posters of singers and clowns. The pool is lovely, and happy hour at the bar is 7–9pm. Hot water can at times be sporadic as it's heated by solar panels. Dorms COP$24,000, doubles COP$94,000

EATING

El Buen Alimento C 2 no. 4–53. Popular vegetarian restaurant serving fresh juices and tasty fusion food, such as stir-fries, paella and lasagne, plus a take on Colombian classics including a chicken-free *ajiaco*. Mains from COP$10,000. Delivery service available. Tues–Sat 11.30am–10pm, Sun 11.30am–5pm.

Café Macondo Cra 6 no. 3–03 ☎ 2 893 1570. This cosy café with a jazz and blues soundtrack offers sandwiches, salads and burgers (from COP$16,000) plus delicious carrot muffins with an oozy *mora* centre (COP$3000) and a decent list of coffees and stronger tipples. Free film screenings daily. Mon–Fri noon–midnight, Sat & Sun 4pm–midnight.

Crepes y Waffles Av 6AN no. 24A–70. Everyone's favourite crêpe and waffle joint, serving a predictably good array of sweet and savoury offerings and ice creams. Waffles from COP$45,000. Mon–Sat 11.30am–8pm, Sun 11.30am–5pm.

★**Litany** C 15AN no. 9N–35 ☎ 2 661 3736, ⊛ restaurantelitany.com. Flavour-starved foodies should make a beeline for this acclaimed Lebanese restaurant, which serves up mouthwatering platters featuring *tabouli*, falafel, vine leaves (COP$25,000) and top-notch *shawarma* (around COP$20,000). Better still, you can BYO alcohol for no charge. Closed Fri & Sun night.

Mister Wings Cra 34 no. 4–12 Esq ⊛ misterwings.com. True to its name, this joint serves several styles of wings (we dare you to try the *endiabladas*), ribs, heaped platters of nachos with all the works, slabs of steak and jalapeño cheese sticks – enough to make anyone homesick for the US. You're guaranteed not to leave hungry. Wings from COP$11,800. Daily noon–11pm.

El Solar C 15N no. 9N–62B ⊛ faroelsolar.co. Imagine a large courtyard filled with greenery. Now imagine some of the best seafood pasta and wild mushroom risotto appearing before you, with a tall, frothy glass of *limonada de coco* to wash it down with. This is it. Mains from COP$18,000. Mon–Sat noon–11pm.

Zea Maiz Cra 12 no. 1–21, San Antonio. Singer Manu Chao put this colourful little *arepera* on the map when he started frequenting it during his Cali tours. It's a simple proposition: lots and lots of *arepas* with varied fillings, ranging from the classic to the more adventurous and all served with a selection of sauces. The Fin Del Mundo *arepa* with sour cream, caramelized onions, mushroom and chicken is a bestseller, and there's plenty of choice for vegetarians, such as the Turca – hummus, basil, tomato, cheese and olives. Finish off with a Nutella-filled *arepa*. Grab a seat outside if you can. Wed & Thurs 6–10.30pm, Fri & Sat 6.30–11.30pm, Sun 5.30–10pm.

DRINKING AND NIGHTLIFE

Much of the late-night action is just beyond the city limits. Cover charges, where they exist, are usually converted into drinks vouchers. The clubs around Avenida 6N are liveliest at the weekends. Single male travellers should find themselves a mixed group to go out with or risk being refused entry.

Kukaramakara C 28N no. 2bis–97 ⊛ kukaramakara .com. There's rock, pop and electronica at this large, rowdy disco, but the live bands, who usually blast out salsa, are the biggest draw. Cover COP$12,000. Thurs–Sat.

Mikasa Bar C 26N no. 5AN–51. Friday is the night to go to this alternative bar/club, playing a mix of dancehall, cumbia, indie music and electronic music. Emerging artists are invited to play, and when the dancefloor gets too much, take a break under the mango tree on the terrace, check out the local artwork for sale, or chill on one of the beds (yes, beds) downstairs, cocktail in hand. Tues–Sat 8pm–late, Sun noon–9pm.

★**Tin Tin Deo** C 5 no. 38–71 ⊛ tintindeo.com. Unpretentious salsa temple where the odd reggae tune also sneaks onto the playlist and dancers sing along to the music. Particularly popular with foreigners on Thursdays. Entrance is COP$5000 for women, COP$10,000 for men. Thurs 7pm–2am, Fri & Sat 7pm–3am.

La Topa Tolondra C 5 no. 13–27, ⓦ latopatolondra.com. Frequented by tourists and locals young and old, this lively little salsa spot draws in the dancing crowds every night of the week with predominantly old-school salsa by the likes of Willie Colón and Rubén Blades. Tuesdays are bolero nights, while Thursday is a mix of Boogaloo, mambos and Cuban salsa.

SAN CIPRIANO

Cali is a good springboard from which to launch yourself to the unusual riverside village of San Cipriano, en route to the Pacific coast (see p.561). Set in the sweltering tropical jungle 128km northwest of Cali, the straggly jungle community of **SAN CIPRIANO** offers an entertaining change of pace for those who need time out from city life. The crystalline river here provides plentiful secluded cooling-off opportunities, but it is the unique journey to the 300-strong community of African slave descendants that has put San Cipriano on the traveller's map. There's no road and only a forest-flanked railway line linking San Cipriano with the town of Córdoba, 6km away, and since it sees very little train action, to bring visitors from Córdoba, inventive locals have attached motorcycle-powered wooden carts to the tracks. The journey down is nothing short of hair-raising and exhilarating; since it's a single-track railway, and there might be traffic coming the other way, be prepared to leap off in case of emergency.

San Cipriano lies at the confluence of the Escalarete and San Cipriano rivers and there are nine sites for safe **river swimming**, as well as opportunities for **tubing** (COP$6500). Follow the only road out of the settlement (the river will be on your right); well-signed tracks positioned every few hundred metres lead down to the river.

ARRIVAL AND DEPARTURE

To reach San Cipriano, catch any Buenaventura bus from Cali's bus terminal and ask to be let out at the junction to Córdoba (3hr). Walk down the hill (10min) to the train tracks from where carts leave roughly every hour. The carts leave when they are full; agree the price of your cart trip before setting off (around COP$10,000 return). San Cipriano is just inland from the port city of Buenaventura, making it a convenient stopover for adventurous souls heading to the Pacific coast.

ACCOMMODATION AND EATING

A number of restaurants serve meals and many also offer basic accommodation. If you do plan to spend the night here, bring a mosquito net.

Hotel David ☎ 312 815 4051. The rooms here come with fans, and shared or private bathrooms with cold water only; the food is hearty and tasty. Per person COP$14,000

POPAYÁN

Although less illustrious than Cartagena, Colombia's other open-air colonial museum, **POPAYÁN**, has little reason to envy its more celebrated rival. Founded in 1537 by Sebastián de Belálcazar on his march northward from Quito, the "White City" was a powerful counterweight to Bogotá's dominance during the colonial era and a bastion of Spanish loyalty during the wars of independence. Unlike Cartagena, which saw its influence wane after independence, Popayán's aristocrats remained very active in politics, and no fewer than eleven presidents have emerged from their ranks.

When a disastrous earthquake destroyed most of the historic centre in 1983, collapsing the cathedral's roof onto the worshippers just before the Maundy Thursday celebrations, residents banded together to rebuild. The result is one of the most attractive cities in Colombia, its streets flanked by single-storey houses and whitewashed mansions and its churches lit up beautifully at night. During Easter week the city is cordoned off to make way for thousands of parading worshippers brandishing candles and colourful flowers. Popayán's Semana Santa celebrations are the second largest in the world, after Seville in Spain.

WHAT TO SEE AND DO

Besides its attractive architecture and leafy main square, most of Popayán's

5

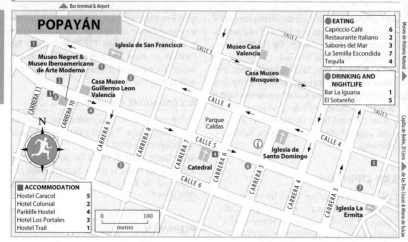

▲ Bus terminal & Airport

POPAYÁN

N

Museo de Historia Natural

Capilla de Belén, El Cerro de las Tres Cruces & Morro de Tulcán

Iglesia de San Francisco

Museo Negret & Museo Iberoamericano de Arte Moderno

Casa Museo Guillermo Leon Valencia

Museo Casa Valencia

Casa Museo Mosquera

Parque Caldas

Catedral

Iglesia de Santo Domingo

Iglesia La Ermita

CARRERA 11
CARRERA 10
CARRERA 9
CARRERA 8
CARRERA 7
CARRERA 6
CARRERA 5
CARRERA 4
CARRERA 3

CALLE 2
CALLE 3
CALLE 4
CALLE 5
CALLE 6

EATING	
Capriccio Café	6
Restaurante Italiano	2
Sabores del Mar	3
La Semilla Escondida	7
Tequila	4

DRINKING AND NIGHTLIFE	
Bar La Iguana	1
El Sotareño	5

ACCOMMODATION	
Hostel Caracol	5
Hotel Colonial	2
Parklife Hostel	4
Hotel Los Portales	3
Hostel Trail	1

0   100
metres

attractions lie outside the city. The museums are of limited interest to visitors, though you can kill a couple of hours on a rainy day there.

The churches
The town's leafy main square, Parque Caldas, is overlooked by the whitewashed **Catedral**. Although the biggest and most frequently used of the churches, architecturally it's the least important, built around 1900 on the site where two earlier structures stood. Four blocks east, on C 5 and Cra 2, is the city's oldest standing church, **La Ermita**, which features an austere single-naved chapel comprised of wooden ribbing and a golden altar dating from 1564.

On C 4 and Cra 5, the **Iglesia de Santo Domingo**'s Baroque stone portal is an excellent example of Spanish New World architecture. Equally ornate is the staircased pulpit of **Iglesia de San Francisco**, situated on a quiet plaza on C 4 and Cra 9, where several of Popayán's patrician families are buried. La Ermita and Iglesia de Santo Domingo are beautifully lit up at night.

Museo de Historia Natural
A few blocks east of the historic centre, the **Museo de Historia Natural** (Cra 2 no. 1A–25; 9am–noon & 2–5pm; COP$3000; ⊛museo.unicauca.edu.co) is worth visiting to see its rich collection of taxidermied animal and bird species, many of which are endemic to Colombia – just to see what they look like, as it's difficult to spot many of them in the wild.

Morro de Tulcán, El Cerro de las Tres Cruces and Capilla de Belén
For a tremendous view of the town, follow Cra 2 north to the **Morro de Tulcán**, once the site of a pre-Columbian pyramid and now a hill capped by an equestrian statue of Sebastián de Belalcázar, who founded Popayán in 1537. Near El Morro is **Pueblito Patojo**, a slightly bizarre set of buildings that are smaller copies of Popayán's most famous landmarks. From the top of El Morro, a path continues to the three crosses of **El Cerro de las Tres Cruces** and on to the hilltop chapel of **Capilla de Belén**, accessible via a steep cobbled path from the eastern end of C4; the entire walk takes a couple of hours. There are usually people on El Morro, whereas the Capilla de Belén is more isolated; leave valuables behind if visiting either.

Casa Museo Mosquera
If you're interested in a glimpse of the salon society of the colonial and early independence era, the **Casa Museo Mosquera**, C 3 no. 5–14 (Tues–Sun 8am–noon & 2–5pm; COP$2000), the childhood residence of Tomás Cipriano de Mosquera, four times Colombia's

president, offers just that. On a macabre note, Mosquera's heart is kept in an urn in the wall.

Museo Negret and Museo Iberoamericano de Arte Moderno

The home of modernist sculptor Edgar Negret, **Museo Negret** (C 5 no. 10–23; Mon, Wed & Fri–Sun 8am–noon & 2–5.30pm; COP$2000) is now a museum exhibiting his work. Next door the **Museo Iberoamericano de Arte Moderno** (same opening hours; included in entry to Museo Negret) exhibits Negret's private collection of works by Picasso and other important artists from Spain and Latin America.

ARRIVAL AND INFORMATION

By plane Popayán's airport is just a 20min walk north of the centre of town, opposite the bus terminal.

By bus The bus station is a 15min walk north of the centre along Autopista Norte and opposite the airport.

Destinations Bogotá (5 daily; 12hr); Cali (every 15min; 2–3hr); Pasto (hourly; 6hr; travel during daylight hours); San Agustín (6 daily; 5–6hr); Silvia (every 30min; 1hr 30min); Tierradentro (4 daily; 5–6hr).

Taxi COP$1700 is the minimum charge on the taxi meter.

Tourist information The tourist office is at Cra 5 no. 4–68 (daily 9am–12.30pm & 2–6pm; ☎2 824 2251). Staff hand out a good free city guide/map, bus and flight timetables, and can help arrange guided tours in the region.

Tour agency Run by the couple who own *Hostel Trail* and *Hostel Caracol*, Popayan Tours (ⓦpopayantours.com) organizes bike tours, night trips to the thermal baths and hikes up Volcano Puracé.

ACCOMMODATION

Popayán boasts a good selection of budget options, including several excellent hostels. Accommodation is particularly expensive during Semana Santa; book well ahead.

Hostel Caracol C 4 no. 2–21 ☎2 820 7335, ⓦhostelcaracol.com. *Hostel Trail*'s offshoot, popular with travellers who like a quiet place to retreat to at the end of the day, offers cosy rooms clustered around a covered courtyard and all the information you need on the area, courtesy of the helpful staff. Dorms COP$20,000, doubles COP$48,000

Hotel Colonial C 5 no. 10–94 ☎2 831 7848. A comfortable central hotel with clean and bright en-suite double rooms with cable TV. Upstairs rooms are naturally brighter. COP$75,000

Parklife Hostel C 5 no. 6–19 ☎300 249 6240, ⓦparklifehostel.com. Besides its super-central location right on the main square, *Parklife* is appreciated for its attractive glassed-over communal space, movie night and large kitchen as well as its colour-coded private rooms and large (though dark) dorms. Dorms COP$20,000, doubles COP$44,000

Hotel Los Portales C 5 no. 10–125 ☎2 821 0139. A great-value hotel in an attractive colonial building. The 29 rooms all come with cable TV and private bathrooms, and are nicely set around three pretty patios. Cheaper to pay cash. COP$75,000

★**Hostel Trail** Cra 11 no. 4–16 ☎314 696 0805, ⓦhosteltrail.com/hostels/hosteltrail. Friendly Scottish owners Tony and Kim run an excellent hostel with clean, bright rooms, free coffee, DVD room and a sociable atmosphere. There's heaps of information on the walls about Popayán and the region, and cycling trips are organized, as well as visits to a local coffee farm. They run their own tour agency, Popayan Tours (see above). Dorms COP$20,000, doubles COP$48,000

EATING

For self-caterers, there's an enormous *Exito* supermarket next door to the bus station.

Capriccio Café C 5 no. 5–63. Fabulous *granisados* (iced coffee drinks) and more at this little café that roasts its own coffee beans. Mon–Sat 8am–noon & 2–8.30pm.

Restaurante Italiano C 4 no. 8–83 ☎2 824 0607. A two-floor, Swiss-owned restaurant serving good Italian standards as well as fondues – expect a leisurely meal. Good-value set lunch COP$9000, mains from COP$15,000. Mon–Sat noon–3pm & 5.30–10pm, Sun noon–11pm.

Sabores del Mar C 5 no. 10–97. Decked out with all sorts of nautical paraphernalia, this little place lures you in with delicious smells. Unusually for a *menú del día* you can enjoy decent fish or seafood. Lunch COP$6000. Daily 7am–7pm.

★**La Semilla Escondida** C 5 no. 2–28. A self-styled slice of France in a small Colombian town, *La Semilla* serves sweet and savoury crêpes, chunky sandwiches and Colombian lunch specials, with the likes of *crème brûlée* sneaking onto the dessert menu. Free wi-fi. Crêpes COP$7000. Set lunch COP$7700. Mon noon–3pm, Tues–Sat noon–3pm & 6–10pm.

Tequila C 5 no. 9–25. A jaunty Tex-Mex café that is not going to win any fine-dining awards, but does get a prize for its burritos (COP$1100), quesadillas (COP$10,300), cheap beer, good cocktails, lively music and very friendly service. Set lunch COP$6500. Mon–Fri noon–10pm, Sat 4–10pm.

DRINKING AND NIGHTLIFE

Bar La Iguana C 4 no. 9–67. This dimly lit bar has a good cocktail list (around COP$10,000), funky salsa soundtrack, projector screen for showing videos, and trendy clientele. Live music on Wednesdays. Daily 8pm til late.

5

★ **El Sotareño** C 6 no. 8–05. Head through *El Sotareño's* swing doors and the first thing you'll see is the owner quietly sitting behind his compact bar, surrounded by a vinyl collection of vintage salsa, tango and other Latin music. Order a cold beer, bag one of the booths, then sit back and listen as the tunes are spun. Mon–Sat until 1am.

AROUND POPAYÁN

The colourful market village of **Silvia**, an outstanding **natural park** and some invigorating **thermal springs** are all within 60km of Popayán.

Silvia

Well worth a detour is the rural village of **SILVIA**, 60km northeast of Popayán, which fills up with Guambiano Indians, with the men in blue skirts with fuchsia trim and bowler hats (don't take photos as they can become aggressive), every Tuesday morning for market day. The market focuses on fruit, veg and basic household goods rather than handicrafts, but the Guambiano, who arrive from their homes in the mountain villages above Silvia, make it a great opportunity for people-watching. **Buses** (every 30min; 1hr 15min) leave for Silvia from Popayán's bus terminal. If coming from Cali, take a Popayán-bound bus to Piendamó (2hr), then grab a bus to Silvia (30min). Once here, it's possible to hire horses (COP$6000/hr) by the small lake and ride up to the village of Guambia (1hr) where the Guambiano cook up fried trout, plucked fresh from nearby trout farms.

Parque Natural Puracé

Once a national park, but now run by the indigenous community, the high-altitude **Parque Natural Puracé** (COP$10,000), 58km east of Popayán, encompasses 860 square kilometres of volcanoes, snowcapped mountains, sulphurous springs, waterfalls, canyons, trout-stuffed lagoons and grasslands. The park's literal high point is **Volcán Puracé** (4700m), which last blew its top in 1956. It's a lung-straining four-hour climb to the steaming crater where, on a clear day, there are sensational views of Cadena Volcánica de Los Coconucos – a chain of forty volcanoes. There are also less strenuous trails, including an orchid walk, and thermal baths. Enquire at the visitor centre near the park entrance if you want to hire a guide. The weather is best for climbing the volcano in December and January; it is worst from June to August.

Four **buses** daily leave Popayán for the park entrance at El Cruce de San Juan (2hr), though if you're planning a day-trip you should catch the bus at 4.30am or 6.30am; double-check timetables before departure. Sometimes one of the early buses is cancelled at the last minute, which makes a day-trip challenging. The last bus back to Popayán passes El Cruce at 5pm. For a more relaxed ascent of the volcano, it's best to stay **overnight** in the park in basic cabañas (☎313 680 0051) or camp.

Thermal springs at Coconuco

The village of **Coconuco**, 26km from Popayán, is near two rudimentary outdoor thermal baths. The better maintained and more pleasant of the two is **Termales Agua Tibia** (daily 8am–6pm; COP$12,000; ☎315 578 6111), 5km southwest of Coconuco on the road to San Agustín. Set at the base of a steep-sided valley with great views, the complex has five lukewarm pools, a bottom-jarring concrete waterslide and a mud spring rich in rejuvenating minerals. There is no place to lock up valuables.

The indigenous-run **Agua Hirviendo** (Tues–Sun 24hr; COP$8000), 3km east of Coconuco, is less picturesque than Agua Tibia but it's open around the clock, its sulphur-reeking pools are far toastier, and the on-site waterfall is a refreshing shock to the system. Basic cabins are available for rent and a restaurant serves meals until late.

To **get to either baths**, take the bus from Popayán to Coconuco (hourly, more frequently on weekends; 45min; COP$6000), from where it's a short walk to Agua Hirviendo and about thirty minutes to the Termales Agua Tibia; a *mototaxi* will take you for COP$2000, or hire a jeep for COP$7000. The owners of *Hostel Trail* in Popayán organize cycling trips that involve driving you and a rented bicycle to the thermal baths from COP$45,000. Having enjoyed the waters, you can then pedal your way back to town, mostly downhill.

SAN AGUSTÍN AND PARQUE ARQUEOLÓGICO

The thoroughly laidback little town of **SAN AGUSTÍN**, 140km southeast of Popayán, has everything a budget traveller could want: awesome landscape, cryptic remains of a forgotten civilization, bargain-basement prices and a plethora of outdoor activities. Some 3300 years ago the jagged landscape around the town was inhabited by masons, whose singular legacy is the hundreds of monumental fanged stone statues, many of them in the **archeological park**, comparable in detail to the more famous Moai statues found on Chile's Easter Island.

Much mystery still surrounds the civilization that built the monoliths, though the surreal imagery of sex-crazed monkeys, serpent-headed humans and other disturbing zoomorphic glyphs suggests that the hallucinogenic San Isidro mushroom may have been working its magic when the statues were first created. What is known is that the priestly culture disappeared before the Spanish arrived, probably at the hands of the Inca, whose empire stretched into southern Colombia. The statues weren't discovered until the middle of the eighteenth century.

To see San Agustín and its surroundings properly, you ideally need three days: one for the archeological park, one for a day-long jeep tour of the outlying sights, such as the Alto de los Idolos, and one for a horseback tour of El Tablón, La Chaquira, El Purutal and La Pelota.

Parque Arqueológico

Unmissable for its wealth of statues, the **Parque Arqueológico**, which was declared a UNESCO World Heritage Site in 1995 (daily 8am–6pm; COP$20,000), sits 2.5km west of San Agustín. The park contains over a hundred stone creations, the largest concentration of statues in the area. Many of them are left as they were found, linked by trails A, B and C, while

others, like the ones in the wooded sector known as the **Bosque de las Estatuas**, are rearranged and linked by an interpretative trail. The statues are beguiling – their fanged faces, the animal-human hybrids, the stylized animal carvings – and they are all very much intact, though their purpose remains a mystery. Don't miss the **Fuente de Lavapatas**, a maze of terraced pools, covered with clearly visible images of reptiles and human figures, thought to have been used for ritual ablutions. Further along, and up, is the furthest point of the park, **Alto de Lavapatas**, the oldest of the sites, with statues sitting forlornly on a hilltop, their brooding gaze sweeping over the countryside.

There's also a **Museo Arqueológico** (8am–5pm) featuring pottery, jewellery, smaller statues and background information on the San Agustín culture; visit it before hitting the statue sites if possible.

El Tablón, La Chaquira, La Pelota and El Purutal

Hundreds more statues are littered across the colourful hillside on either side of the Río Magdalena. Some of the most popular destinations are **El Tablón**, **La Chaquira**, **La Pelota** and **El Purutal**, which most visitors see as part of a four-hour horseriding tour. While the four sites are also doable as part of a day-long hike from town, riding through spectacular scenery is one of the highlights of San Agustín, and knowledgeable guides can shed some light on what you are seeing. Of the four sites, La Chaquira is the most impressive, with deities carved into the sheer rock above the beautiful Río Magdalena gorge. Horses and guides can be booked through your accommodation, or try Pacho Muñoz (☏ 311 827 7972), Abay Menezes (☏ 311 453 3959), or Chaska Tours (☏ 311 271 4802); around COP$30,000/person plus COP$50,000 per guide.

Alto de los Ídolos, Alto de las Piedras and around

Alto de los Ídolos (daily 8am–4.30pm; COP$10,000 or combination ticket with Parque Arqueológico COP$20,000) is the area's second most

5

important site after the Parque Arqueológico, and its two hills lined with tombs are home to the region's tallest statue, 7m high. Four kilometres southwest of the village of San José de Isnos (26km northeast of San Agustín), it can be reached by joining a day-long **jeep tour** (around COP$45,000/person), which is easily arranged through your accommodation. Jeep tours also take in the **Alto de las Piedras**, another important archeological site, its highlight being *Doble Yo*, a statue that is half-man, half-beast. If you look closely, you'll see that there are four figures carved on that rock. Other stops include Colombia's tallest waterfall and a smaller waterfall viewpoint.

White-water rafting

Though they play second fiddle to the archeological attractions, **white-water rafting** and **kayaking** are also popular in San Agustín, thanks to ready access to the Class II–IV Río Magdalena. Magdalena Rafting offers excursions (COP$53,000/ half-day; ☎311 271 5333, ⓦmagdalenarafting.com); trips can also be arranged via your guesthouse.

ARRIVAL AND INFORMATION

By bus Buses depart in the centre of town near the corner of C 3 and Cra 11, where there is a cluster of bus company offices. On arrival, most companies drop you off at junction (Km7) and from there you get a jeep into town (included in your bus ticket and simpler than it sounds).

Destinations Bogotá (5 daily; 10–12hr; afternoon and

DESIERTO DE TATACOA

The bizarre **Tatacoa Desert** makes for a worthwhile detour en route from Bogotá to San Agustín or Tierradentro. Measuring just 300 square kilometres, tiny Tatacoa's arid topography – cracked earth, giant cacti, orange-and-grey soil and towering red rock sculptures – is all the more astonishing because it lies only 37km northeast of Neiva, a city encircled by fertile coffee plantations. Scorpions, spiders, snakes, lizards, weasels and eagles have all found a home here, while fossils indicate that the area was an ancient stomping ground for monkeys, turtles, armadillos and giant sloths.

Some of the fossils are on display at the paleontology museum (daily 8.30am–noon & 2–5pm; COP$2000), on the main plaza in the village of **Villavieja**, 4km from the desert. Villavieja has a few basic hotels and restaurants, but since one of Tatacoa's chief attractions is the amazing night sky, it pays to stump up for one of the basic four-walls-and-a-corrugated-iron-roof deals in the desert itself; accommodation is scattered along the road just past the **observatory**, the desert's focal point. In the evenings, don't miss local astronomer Javier Fernando Rua Restrepo's star show, where you get to observe the night sky from his three powerful telescopes (weekends 7–9.30pm; by appointment on weekdays; COP$10,000; ☎310 465 6765). Across the road from the observatory, there's a lookout point over the Laberintos de Cusco – the maze of otherworldly red rock formations. A 45-minute trail runs down from the red-roofed bar through this labyrinth to the main road; a number of locals also offer guided **desert tours** by car, *mototaxi* or horseback. The best time to explore the desert is early morning before the heat becomes intolerable (temperatures frequently reach 43°C).

Villavieja is an hour **by bus** from Neiva, which in turn is 6hr by bus from Bogotá and 5hr from San Agustín on the main Bogotá–San Agustín road. Buses and vans from Neiva (COP$6000, 1hr) run frequently early in the morning and late in the afternoon; a taxi from Neiva to Villavieja costs COP$60,000 and COP$70,000 to the desert itself; since a *mototaxi* from Villavieja to the desert costs a stiff COP$15,000–20,000 for up to three people, it pays to take a taxi all the way to the desert if you've taken it from Neiva to Villavieja.

ACCOMMODATION

Accommodation tends to be basic and overpriced for what it is, though with some negotiation you can bring the prices down.

Estadero Doña Lilia ☎313 311 8828. 400m past the observatory; camping also possible and meals available on request. Shared room COP$15,000,

doubles COP$50,000

Noches de Saturno ☎313 305 5898. A little further up the road from the observatory, with very basic rooms and camping; there's a small swimming pool for COP$3000 per use. Rooms for around COP$30,000, camping COP$15,000

evening only); Neiva (5 daily; 4–5hr); Pitalito (several daily; 45min); Popayán (at least 7 daily; 4hr 30min). The road to Popayán is still pretty ghastly. Getting to Tierradentro from San Agustín involves two bus transfers, which can extend the journey time to around 7hr. The first transfer is at Pitalito, then at La Plata (after 3hr). From La Plata it's 1hr 30min to El Cruce de San Andrés (or directly to the museum). There are many more buses to destinations (including Bogotá) from Pitalito.

Tourist information The helpful tourist office (C 3 at Cra 12; Mon–Fri 8am–noon & 2–5pm; ☎ 8 837 3062) is inside the town hall.

ACCOMMODATION AND EATING

There is an abundance of budget accommodation in San Agustín, including some fantastic-value *fincas* in stunning locations just outside town.

La Casa de Francois 250m along Via El Tablón ☎8 837 3847, ⊛ lacasadefrancois.com. Situated on a bluff over-looking the city, this ecologically friendly and sociable place offers airy dorms (one with fantastic views), an excellent communal kitchen and a couple of private doubles. The enthusiastic owner offers home-made bread, jam and other goodies, plus hearty breakfasts (COP$7000). There's also a camping area. Camping COP$10,000, dorms COP$20,000, doubles COP$55,000

Casa de Nelly Via La Estrella 1.5km along Av 2 ☎310 215 9057, ⊛ hotelcasadenelly.co. Tricky to find, as the route along a poorly lit dirt track from town is not brilliantly signposted, but lovely once you've made it. Romantic cabins surrounded by trees make this a great spot for those who want to hide away and relax for a couple of days. Has a restaurant serving breakfasts and "whatever's available" for dinner. Dorms COP$18,000, doubles per person COP$22,000

★**Finca El Maco** 750m along the road to the Parque Arqueológico and then 500m up a rough road ☎8 837 3437, ⊛elmaco.ch. This working organic farm with a gaggle of friendly dogs offers a range of sleeping options from camping and simple dorms to luxurious *casitas* (literally "small houses"). The restaurant serves up good-value Thai curries, great crêpes and massive breakfasts. Alternatively, you can buy home-made cheese, pasta sauces and yoghurt and make your own meals in the basic communal kitchen, then retire to a hammock and admire the surrounding hills. Camping COP$10,000, dorms COP$20,000, doubles COP$34,000

EATING

The town's fruit-and-veg market on the corner of C 2 and Cra 11, where self-caterers can stock up, is open daily but liveliest Sat, Sun & Mon when the *campesinos* come to sell their wares.

★**Donde Richard** 750m along the road to the Parque Arqueológico at C 5 no. 23–45. The best spot to chow down

in town serves high-quality, carnivore-friendly food such as barbecued pork, chicken, beef and fish, all cooked on a big grill at the front of the restaurant (mains COP$24,000). Don't miss the Sunday special of *asado huilense* (slow-cooked pork marinated overnight). Daily noon–8pm.

El Fogón C 5 no. 14–30. Extremely popular restaurant that serves up a better-than-average *menú del día* (COP$7000) to scores of hungry locals every day of the week. Daily 6am–11pm.

Restaurante Italiano Vereda el Tablón. A short taxi ride out of town (COP$4500), this authentic Italian spot with the most imaginative name ever delivers consistently good dishes, including home-made pasta, that have earned the praise of Italian and non-Italian travellers alike. Mains from COP$18,000. Tues–Sun 11–10.30pm.

TIERRADENTRO

After San Agustín, **Tierradentro** is Colombia's most treasured archeological complex, though far less visited. Its circular tombs, some as deep as 9m and reachable by steep, smooth original steps through trapdoors, are decorated with elaborate geometric iconography. Monumental statues have also been found here, indicating a cultural influence from San Agustín, though again little is known about the tomb-building civilization other than that it flourished around 700–900 AD, with the statue phase occurring around 500 years later.

No large population centres have been discovered, lending credence to the belief that the original inhabitants belonged to a dispersed group of loosely related farmers. The modern **Paez Indian** population, 25,000 of whom live in the surrounding hillside, is not thought to be related to the creators of the tombs.

Tierradentro means "Inner Land", an appropriate nickname to describe the rugged countryside of narrow valley and jagged summits. The area receives far fewer visitors than San Agustín, thanks to the poor quality of the road from Popayán, though that's likely to change, given the ongoing road improvements and with the area currently safe from guerrillas.

WHAT TO SEE AND DO

The main village is tiny **San Andrés de Pisimbalá**, 4km from El Cruce de San Andrés, the junction on the main

5

Popayán–La Plata road. San Andrés has a picturesque thatched-roof chapel that dates from the seventeenth-century mission. Two kilometres along the road to San Andrés, where you'll find a smattering of guesthouses, starts the **Parque Arqueológico Tierradentro** (daily 8am–4pm; COP$10,000), which comprises the five burial sites. The trail begins behind the **Museo Etnográfico** (daily 8am–4pm), where you pay the park entry fee and receive a wristband, valid for two days. The well-presented displays in the museum focus on the history and customs of the indigenous Paez, while the **Museo Arqueológico** across the road has an archeological display including funeral urns, some statuary and information about the park's tombs; both are worth visiting before you visit the sites.

It's possible to visit all five sites, spread out over a sublime landscape, on a full-day, 14km walk that runs in a loop from the Museo Etnográfico and the Museo Arqueológico, with San Andrés making a convenient lunch stop. Be sure to bring your own torch to explore the tombs, as some are unlit, as well as plenty of water, and wear sturdy footwear. The guards at each site who open the tombs for you can answer most questions (in Spanish). It's best to do the loop anticlockwise, since a

clockwise route would mean tackling a long, tough uphill climb first thing.

Start with **Segovia** (20min walk uphill), the most important of the tomb sights. There are 29 of them; you descend into the trapdoors and down large, steep stone steps to peer into the gloom; note the black, red and white patterns that have survived the centuries. From here, it's fifteen minutes up to **El Duende**, a smaller site with four tombs and very little colour on the walls of the tombs. It's then a 25-minute walk to **El Tablón** – where you'll fine nine weather-worn stone statues which look similar to the ones found in San Agustín. To get here, go up to the main road and head left; El Tablón will be well signposted on your left. From here you can either take the main road into the village or else descend down the muddy trail that joins the other road that runs up into San Andrés from the two museums.

The best place for lunch is *La Portada*, after which you can pick up the trail again along the side of the restaurant. A ten-minute walk gets you to **Alto de San Andrés**, its six tombs boasting well-preserved wall paintings. From here, it's a good hour and a half to the last and most remote site, **El Aguacate**, with spectacular views of the valley and a style of tomb painting not found in the others. Allow plenty of daylight time for the

---

CROSSING INTO ECUADOR: PASTO

Pasto is the commercial hub of southern Colombia – a bustling town devoid of major sights and likely to be visited only in passing on the way to Ecuador, 88km further south along the Panamerican Highway, unless you happen to be travelling through during the Carnaval de Blancos y Negros (see p.497).

The Colombian town of **Ipiales**, a 2hr bus ride from Pasto, is 2km from the **Rumichaca Bridge**, which has Colombian and Ecuadorian border control offices on either side. . From Ipiales, you can catch a minibus (which leaves when full from half a block north of the marker on C 14) or a *colectivo* (COP$1500; departs from the bus terminal near the corner or C 14 and Cra 10) to the border, which is open 24hr.

You will need to cross into Ecuador on foot and take a new *colectivo* from there; the town of **Tulcán** is 2km from the bridge (see box, p.590), and from there you can connect to Quito, Otavalo and elsewhere. Check the **safety** situation on the Ecuadorian side before travelling. There are moneychangers on both sides of the border on and close to the bridge

ACCOMMODATION IN PASTO

Koala Inn C 18 no. 22–37 ☎ 3 722 1101. If you have to stay overnight in Pasto, this long-established backpackers' hostel two blocks from the main square is a convenient spot. Dorms <u>COP$20,000</u>, doubles <u>COP$35,000</u>

hour-and-a-half walk down to the museums as in the past there have been several robberies along this isolated trail.

ARRIVAL AND DEPARTURE

By bus Tierradentro is 113km from Popayán along a rough mountain road that's currently undergoing improvement. There is one direct bus at 10.30am daily (5hr 30min) from Popayán (COP$20,000) and three daily (5am, 8am & 1pm) that pass El Cruce de San Andrés – a road junction. From here it's a 2km walk to the museums and 4km uphill to San Andrés de Pisimbalá. There's a direct bus to Popayán daily from San Andrés at 6am, and from El Cruce de San Andrés at 9am, 11am & 1pm. Buses and pick-ups run from San Andrés to La Plata (6.30am, 8.30am, 1pm; 2hr) where you can pick up connections to San Agustín and Bogotá via Neiva (and Tatacoa).

ACCOMMODATION AND EATING

There are several basic guesthouses of comparable standards right near the two museums; meals available on request in most places.

★ **La Portada** ☎ 311 601 7884. Located along the main road in the village, *La Portada* has attractive, clean rooms with reliably hot showers. The excellent, home-cooked food on offer in the pretty restaurant (breakfast COP$4500, lunch and dinner COP$6000) is the best in town and the gregarious owner is a treasure trove of local knowledge. Doubles COP$35,000

Hotel El Refugio ☎ 312 811 2395. A 2min walk from the museums, this hotel with a pool and small musty rooms is the swishest option besides *La Portada*. Doubles COP$40,000

Residencias Ricabet ☎ 312 795 4636. A short walk up from the museums, with small, basic rooms with shared or private bath, set around a pretty cobbled courtyard. Doubles COP$25,000

The Pacific coast

One of the least-visited parts of the country, and a ruggedly beautiful one at that, the Pacific coast is where the jungle and ocean meet alongside grey-sand beaches, where you can go whale- and dolphin-spotting, or stay in small villages, the majority of whose residents are of African descent. You will need plenty of time and patience to explore this region, as the majority of the settlements, such as laidback **El Valle**, are reachable only by boat from the main port of **Buenaventura**.

BUENAVENTURA

A busy, gritty and charmless port city, **BUENAVENTURA** is the only gateway to the region, so you will end up overnighting here. The boats to various coastal destinations run from the *muelle turístico* (tourist wharf); the area around it is reasonably safe (which is more than can be said for much of the rest of town), and you'll find a number of guesthouses and eateries nearby.

Buenaventura doesn't lend itself to sightseeing, though if you're a surfer it's well worth visiting **Ladrilleros**, an hour's boat ride north, where enormous 2–3m waves lash the shore during the August–November rainy season and where you can stay in a number of basic digs. To reach Ladrilleros, take a boat to Juanchaco, from where you can either walk the 2.5km or get a ride on the back of someone's motorbike.

ARRIVAL AND DEPARTURE

By bus Numerous buses run between Buenaventura and Cali (3–4hr) and you can stop in San Cipriano (see p.553) on the way.

By boat Speedboats for various coastal destinations leave from the *muelle turístico*.

ACCOMMODATION AND EATING

In Buenaventura, as the cheapest digs are downright unsavoury, it's worth paying a little more for comfort. Cheap eats are to be had at *la galería* (market) in Pueblo Nuevo; the stalls on the second floor serve the likes of fish stewed in coconut milk and other coastal specialities. A taxi here costs around COP$3800.

Hotel Titanic C 1A no. 2A-55 ☎ 2 241 2046. Conveniently located just a block from the *muelle turístico*. Comfortable rooms come with a/c, cable TV and internet, though many lack windows, and the rooftop restaurant is good for people-watching. Doubles COP$86,000, room for one COP$76,000

EL VALLE AND AROUND

Way north up the coast, and near **Bahía Solano**, a town famous for sports-fishing and whale-watching, compact **EL VALLE** is a good spot for surfing, as well as visiting **Parque Nacional Natural Ensenada de Utría**, where it's possible to see whales close to the shore during calving season. Entry to the park costs COP$37,000 and you can stay overnight in one of the

5

cabins in the park (COP$120,000/person); group trips can be arranged from El Valle, with boats costing around COP$200,000 (minimum three people per boat).

In En Valle, there's some good **surfing**, and between September and December it's possible to see **turtles** nesting at Estación Septiembre, a sanctuary (COP$10,000) 5km south along the coast. You can also do a day hike through the jungle to the **Cascada del Tigre**, a splendid waterfall with a refreshing waterhole (guide necessary).

ARRIVAL AND DEPARTURE

By plane To reach El Valle, you can fly from Medellín with Satena into Bahía Solano's tiny airport, with flights very much weather-dependent, and then take a Jeep from opposite the school (around COP$10,000; 1hr).

By boat Cargo boats leave Buenaventura every Saturday (24hr; around COP$150,000 including three meals and a bed) to Bahía Solano and then take a Jeep. Return journey from Bahia Solano also leave on Saturday.

ACCOMMODATION

Humpback Turtle on Playa Almejal, El Valle ☎ 312 756 3439, ⊚ humpbackturtle.com. Complete with beach bar, hammock room, rustic camping, a plethora of tours, surfboard rental, on-site restaurant and even an organic farm. Owner Tyler is a fount of knowledge on the area. To get there, take a Jeep from Bahia Solano and tell them to take you to "Donde Tyler". Dorms COP$30,000, doubles/person COP$45,000, hammock/camping COP$15,000

Amazonas

Accounting for around a third of Colombia in size and largely inaccessible to visitors, the **Amazon basin** feels unlike any other part of the country, with its pristine rainforest, fantastic wildlife and indigenous groups living deep in the jungle, their cultures still preserved intact. The capital of the Amazonas province, the bustling jungle town of **Leticia**, is only accessible by air and river, and thus retains a somewhat isolated feel. Travellers come to Leticia for a taste of jungle adventure and also to cross over into Brazil or Peru, as this is where the three countries meet.

LETICIA

This compact riverside town, its partially unpaved streets abuzz with a fleet of scooters and motorcycles – the local transport of choice – has worn many hats during its lifetime. Founded in 1867, **LETICIA** was part of Peru until it was awarded to Colombia in 1933 in a ceasefire agreement following a war between the two countries in 1932. A den of iniquity and sin (well, drug trafficking) in the 1970s, Leticia had to clean up its act when the Colombian army moved in, though visitors are still warned not to wander out into the outskirts of Leticia after dark. Today it's a hot, humid, yet relatively tranquil place, with a lively waterfront and houses hidden amid the greenery. It makes a good base for short trips up the Amazon and for crossing over into Brazil or Peru.

WHAT TO SEE AND DO

The main attractions lie outside the town, but in Leticia proper you can stop by the **Museo Etnográfico Amazónico** (Cra 11 no. 9–43; Mon–Fri 8.30–11.30am & 1.30–5pm, Sat 9–11am; free) to check out the collection of indigenous weaponry, splendid (and scary) ceremonial masks, pottery and more. For high-quality crafts made by local indigenous tribes, the best selection is at the **Galería Arte Uirapuru** (C 8 no. 10–35; Mon–Sat 8.30am–noon & 3–7pm, Sun 8.30am–12.30pm).

ARRIVAL AND INFORMATION

By plane Leticia is served by several flights daily from Bogotá (2hr) with LAN and Avianca. All visitors must pay COP$20,000 tourist tax upon landing at the tiny Aeropuerto Nacional Alfredo Vásquez Cobo. From the airport, you can walk (20min), catch a taxi (COP$8000) or a *mototaxi* (motorbike taxi; COP$2000) into town. Tabatinga International Airport, 4km south of Tabatinga (take *colectivos* marked "Comara" from Leticia), has daily flights to Manaus with Azul.

By boat (see box, p.564).

Tourist information The helpful tourist office (C 8 no. 9–75; Mon–Fri 8am–noon & 2–5pm; ☎ 8 592 7569) can provide onward transport info and maps.

Visas Both locals and foreigners are allowed to move between Leticia, adjoining Tabatinga, and Peru's Isla Santa Rosa without visas or passport control (though you should

5

keep your passport on you). If heading further into Brazil or Peru, you'll need to get a Colombian exit stamp from the immigration office at Leticia Airport (daily 8am–6pm), and then an entry stamp from the Brazilian Policía Federal in Tabatinga (Av de Amizade 26; 8am–noon & 2–6pm; ☎97 3 412 2180 in Brazil) or the Peruvian immigration office on Isla Santa Rosa (daily 8am–1pm & 2–6pm). Some nationalities need a visa to enter Brazil; try to get it before coming to Leticia; otherwise, visit the Brazilian consulate (C9 no. 9–73; 8am–noon & 1–3pm; ☎8 592 7755). All travellers require a yellow fever certificate to enter Brazil.

ACCOMMODATION

★**Amazon B&B** C 12 no. 9–30 ☎8 592 4981, ⓦamazonbb.com. If you have just got off the boat from Brazil or Peru, this lovely hotel will seem like paradise. Think minimalist chic, ceiling fans, crisp white sheets and plenty of space in both rooms and bungalows to throw your gear about. Doubles COP$169,000

La Jangada Cra 9 no. 8–106 ☎311 498 5447, ⓔlajangadaleticia@gmail.com. This Swiss-Colombian run hostel wins extra points for friendliness and helpfulness; the fan-cooled rooms and dorms are clean and airy, you can book your jungle adventures here and the kitchen whips up a simple breakfast. Dorms COP$25,000, doubles COP$50,000

Mahatu Jungle Hostel C 7 no. 1–40 ☎8 592 7384, ⓦmahatu.org. On the outskirts of town, this hostel boasts its own lake and lush grounds filled with fruit trees and the odd animal. Gustavo the owner is a no-nonsense character with a wealth of local knowledge, the rooms are somewhat musty and pricey for what they are, but there's a large guest kitchen and it's a great spot to meet fellow travellers. Dorms COP$20,000, doubles COP$60,000

EATING

In Leticia you'll find culinary delicacies you won't encounter elsewhere in Colombia – an abundance of river fish and a vast variety of fruit juices. The most delicious fish include *gamitana* and *pirarucú*, though you should avoid eating the latter during its breeding season (mid-Nov to mid-March), when fishing it is banned to conserve stocks. Places to eat are concentrated along C 8 and Cra 10, off C 8.

★**Tierras Amazónicas** C 8 no. 7–50. Cool, open-fronted restaurant serving huge slabs of perfectly cooked *pescado a la pupeca* (fish steamed in a banana leaf) for COP$18,000. Wash it down with *borojó* or *copoazú* juice (COP$3000). Tues–Sun 11.30am–10.30pm.

AROUND LETICIA

Amazonas' biggest attractions are found outside Leticia. These include the

---

> ### EXPLORING THE UNKNOWN
> While parts of Peruvian and Brazilian jungle are quite well trodden by now, Colombian jungle remains pristine, and Leticia can be your launching point for multi-day jungle adventures: just you, your indigenous guide, and indigenous communities as yet virtually untouched by the outside world. **Travel the Unknown** (☎+44 20 7183 6371, ⓦtraveltheunknown.com) can help you arrange your jungle trip, including local guide.

abundant wildlife of Parque Nacional Natural Amacayacu, jungle hikes and stays in Puerto Nariño, upstream of Leticia – a great base for dolphin-spotting trips.

Jungle trips

There are numerous tour agencies in Leticia that can organize **jungle and river trips** of virtually any length, taking in flora, fauna and the area's indigenous communities. However, that also means that there are a number of unscrupulous operators, so make sure you've agreed on exactly what's included and avoid pushy "guides" who approach you in the street. Since the Amazon is such a vast area, odds are, you won't see any big mammals, but you're very likely to see monkeys and numerous bird species, and a three-day stint in the jungle is great exposure to a unique environment. Recommended operators include Amazon Jungle Trips (Av Internacional no. 6–25; ☎8 592 7377, ⓦwww.amazonjungletrips.com.co), going strong after more than 25 years, and Tanimboca (Cra 10 no. 11–69; ☎8 592 7679, ⓦtanimboca.org), both with English-speaking guides.

Parque Nacional Natural Amacayacu

Around ninety minutes upstream from Leticia, the 3000-square-kilometre **Parque Nacional Natural Amacayacu** is a spectacular slice of wilderness, home to five hundred bird species, plenty of crocodiles, anacondas and other reptiles and 150 mammal species, including big cats. The park is officially closed at

5

INTO BRAZIL AND PERU BY BOAT

Many travellers come to Leticia en route to Brazil or Peru. To get to the former, you need only head to the port of **Tabatinga**, just across the border, which has virtually fused with the Colombian town; there are no checkpoints between the two and all you have to do is walk south along Av Internacional.

Boats leave for **Manaus** from Tabatinga's port on Wednesdays and Saturdays at around noon (double-check times in advance and remember that the time in Brazil's Amazonas state is 1hr ahead of Colombia time), taking three days and four nights and costing around R$200 if you have your own hammock, or around R$1000 for a double cabin. The reverse journey (upstream) takes around six days and is more expensive.

High-speed passenger boats connect Leticia and **Iquitos** in Peru, leaving from Isla Santa Rosa; since the boats depart early in the morning, it's easiest to stay in Santa Rosa the night before, and note that in dry season boats may not be able to cross over to Santa Rosa from Leticia, so you may have to take one from Tabatinga. Boats depart around 5am (double-check departure times), with Transtur (Wed, Fri & Sun; ☎97 3412 2945, ⊛transtursa.com), and Transportes Golfinho (Tues, Thurs & Sat; ☎97 3412 3186, ⊛transportegolfinho.com). Price includes breakfast and lunch. Don't forget to get an exit stamp and relevant visa (see p.228 & p.718) before departing Leticia.

present due to flooding, but it is still possible to enter with guides from the neighbouring villages of San Martín and Mocagua; come prepared for squadrons of mosquitoes. A particularly worthwhile visit is to the Fundación Maikuchiga, a project for rehabilitating monkeys – visits can be arranged through *La Jangada* hostel (see p.563) for COP$85,000 per person for transport, food and guide, plus COP$120,000 for up to six people for entrance to the monkey sanctuary.

Puerto Nariño

Eco-friendly **PUERTO NARIÑO** sits around 75km upstream of Leticia and makes a great base for spotting the Amazon's pink dolphins; half-day excursions to Lago Tarapoto cost around COP$60,000 for up to six people. You can learn more about the endangered creatures at the riverfront Fundación Natütama

(⊛natutama.org), located near the dock. The town itself, peopled mostly by the indigenous Yagua, Tikuna and Cocoma, is a shining example of recycling, organic waste management and rainwater collection; other Colombian towns could learn a great deal here, and this may well be the only Colombian settlement with zero motorized traffic.

ARRIVAL AND DEPARTURE

By boat Three high-speed boats run daily from Leticia at 8am, 10am and 1.30pm (COP$29,000; 2hr), returning at 7.30am, 11am and 3.30pm. Bring plenty of cash, as there are no banks here.

ACCOMMODATION AND EATING

Las Margaritas C 6 no. 6–80. This thatch-roofed place does a great home-cooked buffet.
Moloka Napü C 4 no. 5–72 ☎ 310 488 0998. A friendly place to stay, with sparse yet cosy rooms, those upstairs at the back being the best. Dorms **COP$20,000**

CROWD AT ZUMBAGUA ANIMAL MARKET

Ecuador

HIGHLIGHTS

❶ **Quito** Explore the capital's Baroque squares, churches and palaces. **See p.573**

❷ **Avenue of the Volcanoes** Experience the bustle of indigenous markets under soaring ice-covered summits. **See p.586 & p.591**

❸ **Páramo del Angel** Hike off the beaten track amid a bizarre landscape that looks straight out of Star Wars. **See p.590**

❹ **Cuenca** Quito's southern rival is one of Latin America's best-preserved colonial cities. **See p.603**

❺ **Amazon lodges** No longer a tropical "green hell" but a place to explore for its exotic wildlife and ancient rainforest cultures. **See p.617**

❻ **Galápagos Islands** Witness the miracle of evolution. **See p.633**

HIGHLIGHTS ARE MARKED ON THE MAP ON P.567

ROUGH COSTS

Daily budget Basic US$25, occasional treat US$40

Drink Cerveza Pilsener US$1

Food Set menu two-course lunch US$2.50

Hostel/budget hotel US$6–12

Travel Quito–Baños: 3hr 30min, US$4

FACT FILE

Population 16.1 million

Languages Spanish, Kichwa, Shuar

Currency US dollar

Capital Quito (population: 2,240,000)

International phone code ☎593

Time zone GMT -5hr

Introduction

In Ecuador it's possible to wake up on the Pacific coast, drive through the snowcapped Andes and reach the edge of the Amazon jungle by sundown. Although Ecuador is only slightly larger than the UK, its vastly different terrains have enough to keep visitors occupied for months. It's one of the world's most biodiverse countries, with some 25,000 species of plants, more than the species found in all North America, and 1600 species of birds. It's entirely fitting, therefore, that the Galápagos Islands, where Charles Darwin developed his theory of evolution, belong to Ecuador.

Mainland Ecuador is divided into three geographically distinct regions: Pacific coast, Andean highlands and Amazon jungle. The highlands are the most popular, with **Quito** a convenient starting point. The capital's historic sights, range of day-trips and excellent facilities can keep you busy for over a week.

Northwest of Quito are the cloudforest reserves around **Mindo** and to the north the indigenous market town of **Otavalo**, whose woven crafts are a shopper's dream.

Ecuador's most dramatic mountain scenery rises up to the south of Quito, including **Volcán Cotopaxi**, the highest active volcano in the world, and the extinct volcanic lake **Laguna Quilotoa**. Further south is the popular spa town of **Baños**, and **Riobamba**, the best base to explore Ecuador's highest mountain, **Chimborazo** (6310m), and the **Nariz del Diablo** train ride. In the southern highlands are Ecuador's best-preserved Inca ruins, **Ingapirca**, its beautiful third city, **Cuenca**, and the relaxing "Valley of Longevity", **Vilcabamba**.

Excursions can take you deep into wildernesses of primary jungle, including **Cuyabeno Natural Reserve** and **Yasuní National Park**, along the majestic Napo River, while shorter trips and stays with Amazon indigenous communities are best via **Puyo** and **Tena**, Ecuador's white-water-rafting capital and the most appealing jungle town.

On the coast, visit Ecuador's largest city, **Guayaquil**, to see its regenerated waterfront, then head for the beach: eco-city **Bahía de Caráquez**, surfer hangouts **Montañita** and **Canoa**, or the unspoilt beaches of **Parque Nacional Machalilla** and **Mompiche**.

Some 1000km west of mainland Ecuador lie the country's tourism crown jewels, **the Galápagos Islands**, which remain among the world's top destinations for watching wildlife and are easy to explore independently.

WHEN TO VISIT

Because of Ecuador's diverse landscapes, the best time to visit varies by region. On the **coast**, temperatures are typically 25–35°C. The rainy season is dramatic, with downpours between January and April. This is the hottest time of the year, at times uncomfortably humid, but also the best months for the beach. It's cooler and cloudier between June and December. In the **highlands**, the temperature is on average 15°C, but due to the altitude it gets hot at midday and cold at night, particularly above 2500m. The driest, warmest season is June to September. In the **Oriente** the temperature is generally 20–30°C with high levels of rainfall and humidity. The driest season is December to March. In the **Galápagos**, the temperature peaks at over 30°C in March and cools to the low 20s in August. It's best to avoid the rough seas and cold between June and September.

CHRONOLOGY

8000 BC The oldest archeological evidence of human settlement found in today's Ecuador dates from around 8000 BC.

4000 BC The Valdivia culture develops one of the earliest ceramic techniques in the Americas.

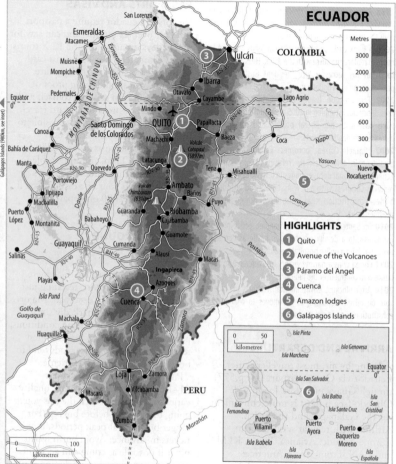

ECUADOR

HIGHLIGHTS

1 Quito
2 Avenue of the Volcanoes
3 Páramo del Angel
4 Cuenca
5 Amazon lodges
6 Galápagos Islands

1460 AD Tupac Yupanqui leads the first Inca invasion of Ecuador.

1495 Huayna Capac conquers territory up to Pasto, now in Colombia, despite violent resistance. He dies in Quito.

1532 Atahualpa defeats his half-brother Huascar in an Inca civil war, but is captured and executed by Spanish conqueror Francisco Pizarro.

1541 Francisco de Orellana journeys down the Amazon and reaches the Atlantic.

1809 On August 10, Quito declares independence from Napoleonic Spain.

1822 On May 24, Quito wins independence at the Battle of Pichincha. Bolívar's dream of a united continent dies and Ecuador secedes from Colombia in 1830.

1861 Ultramontane Gabriel García Moreno gains power, quashes rebellions and makes Catholicism a prerequisite for all citizens. He is assassinated in Quito in 1875.

1895 Liberal Eloy Alfaro becomes president and introduces sweeping reforms, ending the connection between Church and state. He is assassinated in 1912.

1941 Peru invades Ecuador and forces it to recognize as Peruvian 200,000 square kilometres of jungle, almost half its claimed territory.

1967 Oil is discovered in the Ecuadorian Oriente, ushering in an oil boom.

1979 Left-winger Jaime Roldós is elected president, ending military rule. He emphasizes human rights and dies in a mysterious plane crash two years later.

1996 Self-styled *loco* (crazy) Abdalá Bucharam wins the presidency but quickly becomes engulfed in corruption scandals. Protests lead to his ouster by Congress, ushering in a decade of instability.

6

1998 After a brief war, President Jamil Mahuad and Peruvian President Fujimori sign a peace treaty, which ends the long-running border dispute.

2000 A bank crisis and hyperinflation leads Mahuad to move to replace the sucre with the dollar. He is ousted in a coup but his successor Vice President Gustavo Noboa presses ahead with dollarization.

2002 Former coup leader Lucio Gutiérrez wins the presidency but is toppled in 2005 after infuriating his left-wing base with neo-liberal policies and attempts to increase presidential powers.

2007 Rafael Correa becomes Ecuador's seventh president in ten years. He refuses to pay part of Ecuador's national debt, engages in left-wing populism, replaces Congress with a new Assembly and introduces a new constitution that centralizes power in the president's hands.

2010 On September 30, a badly handled police protest escalates into a deadly evening gun battle as Correa is extracted from a police hospital by soldiers.

2011 Correa wins a narrow victory in a referendum that hands him control over the judiciary.

2014 After blocking environmentalist efforts to force a vote on oil development, Correa moves to change the constitution to end term limits.

ARRIVAL AND DEPARTURE

Arriving by **air**, most travellers enter Ecuador via Quito's airport (see p.577), though Guayaquil's José Joaquín de Olmedo (see p.626) is more convenient for the Galápagos and the beach. Airlines with regular services from Europe include: Avianca, Iberia, KLM, and LAN. From North America: American Airlines, Continental Airlines, Delta, COPA and LAN.

OVERLAND FROM PERU

You can reach Ecuador by **bus** from Peru via Tumbes and Huaquillas on the coast, with frequent bus connections. It's also possible to cross via Macará or Zumba in the highlands, which are more scenic.

OVERLAND FROM COLOMBIA

Travelling to and from Colombia overland is only possible via Tulcán in the northern highlands. The border region has a troubled history, so many travellers fly to Colombia from Quito.

PASSPORTS AND VISAS

Visitors to Ecuador require a passport valid for over six months and can stay for **ninety days** on an automatic 12-X tourist visa. Visitors receive a T3 tourist card, which must be kept until departure. Officially, you should bring proof of sufficient funds to support yourself and a return ticket or proof of onward travel, but it's rarely demanded. It's possible to extend your visa to 180 days but complicated and costs at least $230 for a 12-IX visa in Quito, and impossible to re-enter more than once for 90 days within a year. If your visa expires, you'll be fined $200–2000 on departure.

GETTING AROUND

BY BUS

Ecuador's cheap **buses** are the easiest form of public transport, reaching just about everywhere there's a road. Major roads have improved markedly since 2000. However, poor driving conditions, particularly in the rainy season, often result in **delays**; the worst roads tend to be in Esmeraldas and the Oriente.

Public buses are typically about $1–1.50 per hour of travel, but quality varies so if possible check the bus you're going to travel on before buying. For longer bus rides at peak periods, buy tickets in advance. Avoid bus travel at night if possible as **crime** and accidents are more common. Pickpocketing is rife on public buses, especially popular tourist routes out of Quito; never stow valuables in your bag above your head or under your seat – always keep them on you.

Another option is **van services** ordered by phone that are more expensive, but quicker and safer and cut down on travel to bus stations in major cities, likely saving you one or two taxi fares.

BY CAR AND TAXI

Renting a car is possible but not recommended because of the expense. Rental charges are $300–500 per week, with an alarming excess of $1000 in case of damage. A better option is a **taxi**. In bigger cities this is the best way to get around, though always check credentials, avoid unmarked cabs and use the meter, which in theory is obligatory but often turned off at night (if there isn't one, negotiate in advance). The safest option is to book a cab from a reputable company. Hotels and restaurants can help. Smartphone application Easy Taxi is recommended. Short trips in small towns cost $1–2, around double in cities. Taxi drivers in tourist towns will often offer longer trips, but rates are obviously higher than for buses.

BY AIR

Since Quito opened a new airport, domestic flights have lost some of their appeal given the $25 taxi fare and inconvenience of $2.50–8 buses. But flights are necessary to reach the Galápagos, and often convenient to the Amazon. Prices of internal flights are $50–100 one-way, with some cheaper deals possible by booking well ahead. TAME (𝕋02 2397 7100, 𝕎www.tame.com.ec) offers flights from Quito to Coca, Cuenca, Esmeraldas, Galápagos, Guayaquil, Lago Agrio, Loja, Manta, Salinas, Santa Rosa and Tulcán. There are flights from Guayaquil to Coca, Cuenca, Esmeraldas, Galápagos and Loja. Avianca Ecuador (𝕋1 800 003434, 𝕎www.avianca.com) and LAN Ecuador (𝕋1 800 842526, 𝕎lan.com) both serve Quito, Guayaquil, Cuenca and the Galápagos. Small planes serve jungle hamlets from Mera.

ACCOMMODATION

Ecuador has a wide variety of **accommodation**, from dirt-cheap rickety shacks to comfortable mid-range hotels and luxury high-rise options. A basic dorm in a cheap *pensión*, *residencial* or *hostal* can cost just $5. The mid-range is where Ecuador offers best value. In most destinations $20–40 gets you a good-sized double room with comfortable beds, private bathroom, hot water and cable TV. The $40–100 range gets you a swankier international city hotel, a colonial hacienda or a secluded jungle lodge.

Cities such as Quito, Guayaquil and Cuenca are slightly more expensive but competition keeps the prices down. On the coast, air-conditioning costs extra, and budget places sometimes have no hot water, although the climate renders it unnecessary. Consider bringing your own mosquito net if you plan to spend time in the jungle or on the coast during the rainy season. Deep in the jungle, budget options are harder to find so expect to pay more as part of a tour. **Camping** is not widely available but possible in some areas for $5 per person, but you must usually bring your own gear unless you book a tour.

FOOD AND DRINK

There's a lot more to Ecuadorian cuisine than roasted guinea pig. Rice and potatoes are staples, and rice is often served with everything. Budget travellers can enjoy cheap set menu *almuerzos* (lunches) and *meriendas* (dinners), which serve a soup, main course and drink for $2–3. *Sopa* (soup), *caldo* (broth) and *seco* (stew) are cheap ways to stay full. *Locro de papa* is a hearty potato soup with cheese and avocado; *chupe de pescado* is a thick fish-and-vegetable soup. *Seco de pollo* (chicken stew with coriander) or *lomo salteado* (salted beef steak) are common main courses, whereas *caldo de pata* (cow's foot soup) is for the more adventurous. In the highlands and Oriente the fish of choice are tilapia and river trout. The famous *cuy* (guinea pig) and *hornado* (roast pork) are Andean delicacies and are often roasted whole on a spit.

On the coast, the **seafood** is among the best in the world. *Ceviche*, a cold seafood soup marinated with lemon and onion, is excellent, but only served until mid-afternoon. *Encebollado*, a fish and onion soup, is often eaten to stave off a hangover. Another interesting option is *cazuela*, a seafood and vegetable broth made with plantains and peanut. In Manabí try *biche*, a sweeter fish soup with corn and *maduros* (sautéed plantains). The best white fish is *corvina* (sea bass), which can be *frito* (fried), *apanado* (breaded), *a la plancha* (grilled) or *al vapor* (steamed). Note that

6

shellfish is a common cause of illness, so take care.

If you're on a tight budget, **snacks** come in handy, but avoid meat cooked on the street and avoid hot snacks sold on public transport. Popular treats from bakeries include *empanadas* (meat- or cheese-filled pastries), *tortillas de verde* (fried mashed green bananas) or *yuca* (cassava, a starchy tropical root) and delicious *humitas* (mashed corn with cheese wrapped in a corn husk and steamed). *Pan de yuca* (cassava bread), eaten with cheese, is a common snack.

Always buy **bottled water** and never drink from the tap. Avoid ice in cheaper places. Abundant tropical fruits make fresh *jugos* (juices) and *batidos* (milkshakes) great breakfast options. Alongside pineapple, melon, papaya and banana are more unusual fruits such as *naranjilla* (a sour orange) and *tomate de árbol* (a bittersweet tomato). Sodas are everywhere, while coffee is of variable quality. The most common beers are the standard local Pilsener and slightly more expensive Club Verde, but a craft beer scene is emerging. Domestic rum and the local firewater *Agua Ardiente* are cheap and strong enough to give you a stonking hangover. *Chicha*, made from fermented corn or potato, is drunk by indigenous people in the Andes. The Amazon version is made from chewed cassava, and it's impolite to refuse it. Note that when going out at night, in Ecuador the expression "nightclub" means brothel, so don't get caught out – use the word *discoteca*.

CULTURE AND ETIQUETTE

A highlight of Ecuador is the hospitable, fun-loving people. Ecuador's population of more than sixteen million is divided equally between the coast and highlands, with 5 percent in the Oriente. Some 65 percent are *mestizo* (mixed race), 25 percent indigenous, 3 percent Afro-Ecuadorian and 7 percent white. While many Indians hold on to traditional customs and dress, the mainstream population use Western dress. The 1998–2000 crisis led many to emigrate,

while some 500,000 Colombians live in Ecuador.

More than eighty percent of Ecuadorians are Roman Catholic, although evangelical Christianity is increasing. Rivalry between the mountains and coast is strong. Many *Costeños* consider *Serranos* (mountain people) to be conservative, uptight and two-faced. *Serranos* sometimes call *Costeños* "monos" (monkeys) and consider them rude, uncultured, immoral gossips. The rivalry ranges from banter to deep resentment.

Ecuadorians' lax attitude to time is notorious. At social gatherings, add at least an hour to the agreed meeting time. However, scheduled departures such as buses and tours are usually punctual, so don't be caught out.

Greetings are essential for Ecuadorians – a kiss on each cheek for women and a handshake between men. If you don't know any Spanish, it's worth learning basic greetings and pleasantries.

Tipping is not essential in most situations but advisable in higher-end hotels for bellboys (50 cents to $1). If your guide is good, show your appreciation. Supermarket bag carriers and parking attendants require a tip (up to $1).

SPORTS AND OUTDOOR ACTIVITIES

TEAM SPORTS

Football is the number one sport in Ecuador and watching a major local match at a stadium in Quito or Guayaquil is unforgettable. Quito has three major teams: Liga, Nacional and Deportivo Quito, while Guayaquil has two: Emelec and Barcelona. Football, volleyball and basketball can be played in many parks, while other sports include rugby and hockey (on ice only in Quito).

HIKING AND CLIMBING

The highlands' open spaces offer a vast range of **hiking** – the Quilotoa Loop, Parque Nacional Cotopaxi, the hills around Baños, Parque Nacional Cajas and Vilcabamba are but a few. On the coast, Parque Nacional Machalilla near Montañita offers good hiking. The best **climbing** is on Cotopaxi and Chimborazo, although ensure you are fit, acclimatized and with a qualified guide.

WATERSPORTS

For watersports, including **rafting** and **kayaking**, Tena and Baños are best for trips on fast-flowing rapids and gentler tributaries. The best **surfing** is at the resorts of Montañita, which holds a famous surfing competition around Carnaval, and Canoa and Mompiche. **Scuba-diving** and **snorkelling** opportunities are limited on the mainland. Parque Nacional Machalilla has a few operators but the best place by far is the Galápagos Islands, whose amazing marine life makes it one of the world's top underwater destinations.

WILDLIFE

Birdwatching enthusiasts should head to the cloudforests of Mindo, which have more than 400 bird species and 250 species of butterfly. The tiny hummingbirds are a highlight, commonly seen in the cloudforests and the jungle. The Andean condor is a rare but unforgettable sight, occasionally seen in Parque Nacional Cotopaxi. For other **wildlife-watching**, the Oriente offers opportunities to observe sloths, otters, caymans, tapirs and many species of monkey. The Galápagos is of course unbeatable for wildlife.

COMMUNICATIONS

The **postal** system in Ecuador is adequate in major towns, but unreliable in rural areas. If you need to send or receive something important, use an international courier service such as DHL or Fedex, but minimum charges are about $50.

There are countless **phone** offices in towns, which are the best places for conventional calls. There are also cellular public phones, which use prepaid phone cards available at shops or kiosks. Calling North America costs as little as $0.10–0.20/minute and Europe $0.30–0.40/minute, but there is usually a connection charge. Most travellers staying longer than a few weeks invest in a mobile phone from Claro or Movistar. Phones start at $35 including SIM cards.

You're never far from **internet cafés** in tourist towns, and even remote places have a connection. Expect to be charged $1–1.50/hour, although many hotels, hostels and cafés have free **wi-fi**. Skype calls are obviously far cheaper than telephone but connections can be poor.

CRIME AND SAFETY

Sneak theft is common for travellers across Ecuador. Expert pickpockets target tourists, particularly in Quito. Be vigilant in crowded areas and on public transport, keep your money out of sight and be wary of strangers engaging you in conversation, a common diversionary tactic. Don't carry large amounts of cash. **Armed robbery** is less common but increasing. Sadly, the tourist district of Mariscal Sucre in Quito is now the most common place for tourists to be mugged. There have also been some reports of violent attacks on tourists. Gangs look for easy targets, so don't wander around alone and always take a licensed taxi back to your hotel at night, no matter how close it is. Other crime hot spots in Quito include parts of the Old Town, the walk up to El Panecillo (take a taxi) and Parque Carolina.

In Guayaquil, be extra vigilant at night, particularly downtown. Esmeraldas and Atacames also have problems with theft and robbery; avoid the northern coastal town of San Lorenzo completely. Drug smuggling, Colombian guerrilla activity and risk of kidnappings in the northern border areas have made areas of Sucumbíos (capital Lago Agrio), Carchi (capital Tulcán) and Esmeraldas (capital Esmeraldas) provinces unsafe. On the southern border, the Cordillera del Cóndor, southeast of Zamora, contains landmines from the conflicts with Peru.

EMERGENCY NUMBERS

Call ☎ **911** for police, fire and ambulance services.

By law you must carry **identification** – this means your passport. If you can't produce it, you may be detained by the police. Carry **drugs** in Ecuador and you may end up in jail for up to fifteen years, so avoid contact with drug dealers. Foreigners are sometimes vulnerable to drug set-ups and a bail-out is an easy way for corrupt police officials to make money.

HEALTH

Vaccinations that are recommended include typhoid, hepatitis A and yellow fever. Others to consider are hepatitis B and rabies. **Malaria** is present (but rare) in the Oriente and on the northern coast. Wear long sleeves, light-coloured clothes and use repellent to avoid mosquito bites. Malarone is the best anti-malarial medication, and must be taken daily. **Dengue fever** is spread by day-biting mosquitoes, mainly during the rainy season, and is an increasing problem in urban areas on the coast. There is no vaccine, so seek medical help immediately if you show symptoms (high fever, aching limbs, vomiting and diarrhoea).

The most common problem is **travellers' diarrhoea**. Minimize risks of bacterial and parasitic infections by avoiding bus vendor/street food; also try to eat in clean restaurants. Tap water, ice, salad, ice cream, unpeeled fruit and seafood are common culprits. Eat plenty of carbohydrates, drink water and pack oral rehydration and Imodium.

Another common problem is **altitude sickness**, which can be dangerous. When arriving at altitudes over 2000m (most of the highlands), don't over-exert yourself, avoid alcohol and don't attempt to climb mountains without sufficient time to adjust to the altitude.

Sunburn and **sunstroke** are also very common because the equatorial sun is fiercely strong. Apply sunblock regularly and don't be fooled by cool temperatures in the mountains – because of the altitude, the sun is stronger.

Ecuador's public health system is poor and **emergency care** particularly bad.

Travelling with valid insurance is essential. If you have an emergency, try to head for a private hospital. In Quito, Hospital Metropolitano is good, and in Guayaquil, Clínica Kennedy has several branches. Pharmacies dish out some medicines without prescription, so you are responsible for knowing what you're taking – opt for brand names rather than generic drugs and bring essential medicine from home.

INFORMATION AND MAPS

Ministry of Tourism iTur offices (🅦ecuador.travel), in provincial capitals and the main tourist centres, supply maps, lists of hotels, restaurants and sights, and the website is a good source of information. Quito's tourist office is the best in Ecuador, with a very good website (🅦quito.com).

The Instituto Geográfico Militar in Quito, Seniergues E4-676 y Gral. Telmo Paz y Miño, sells topographical maps for $3 and a giant map of Quito for $10 (bring your passport as ID to enter the institute). For tablets and smartphones, apps using OpenStreetMap (🅦openstreetmap.org) tend to be slightly superior to Google Maps. Waze is excellent for finding your way.

MONEY AND BANKS

Ecuador replaced the plummeting sucre with the **US dollar** as its currency amid an economic crisis in 2000. There are 1, 5, 10, 25, 50 cent and 1 dollar coins, the smaller denominations often minted in Ecuador. Notes come in 1, 5, 10 and 20 dollars. Avoid 50 and 100 dollar bills, and even 20 dollar bills cause problems in small towns. Dollarization has made Ecuador more expensive but it's still cheap.

Carry enough cash for a few days; a credit card is recommended as backup. Visa, MasterCard, Cirrus and Maestro are commonly accepted at ATMs. In larger agencies, you can pay for tours with a credit card but you may be charged five to ten percent more. Note rates of exchange for currencies outside South

PUBLIC HOLIDAYS

Most of the following are national holidays, although some are celebrated in certain areas of the country. The government habitually changes the dates of national holidays to tag them onto the weekend.

January 1 New Year's Day (*Año Nuevo*).
January 6 Epiphany (*Reyes Magos*). Celebrated mainly in the highlands.
February/March Carnival (*Carnaval*). The week before Lent is Ecuador's biggest party. Monday and Tuesday are holidays. The beaches are packed and in the highlands Ambato and Guaranda are famous for celebrations. Don't be surprised to get wet, as throwing water is part of the fun.
March/April Holy Week (*Semana Santa*). The big processions in Quito are on Good Friday, a public holiday.
May 1 Labour Day (*Día del Trabajo*).
May 24 Battle of Pichincha (*La Batalla del Pichincha*). Celebrating the decisive battle for independence in 1822 (highlands only).
July 24 Birthday of Simón Bolívar, the man who dreamed of a united South America and helped liberate Ecuador.

August 10 Quito Independence Day (*Día de la independencia*).
October 9 Independence of Guayaquil (Guayaquil only).
October 12 Columbus Day (*Día de la Raza*).
November 2 All Souls' Day or Day of the Dead (*Día de los Muertos*).
November 3 Independence of Cuenca (Cuenca only).
December 6 Foundation of Quito. Bullfights are the order of the day (Quito only).
December 25 Christmas Day (*Navidad*). Most Ecuadorians celebrate Christmas on Christmas Eve night and relax on Christmas Day.
December 31 New Year's Eve (*Nochevieja* or *Años viejos*). New Year rivals Carnaval as the country's biggest party. Locals burn effigies of well-known characters. Note that safe use of fireworks is absent.

America (eg British pounds) are often poor, so bring cash in US dollars wherever possible. Travellers' cheques are often expensive and a hassle to use.

OPENING HOURS AND HOLIDAYS

Most shops and public offices are open Monday to Saturday 9am to 5pm or 6pm, but family-owned businesses open at the owner's discretion. Most banks are open 8 or 9am to 4pm Monday to Friday and until noon weekends in shopping malls. Call centres open 8am to 10pm. Restaurant and bar opening hours vary and museums are usually open weekends and closed Mondays. On weekends and public holidays government offices and some shops are closed.

The majority of national holidays mark famous historical events as well as Catholic festivals. Ecuadorians love to party with lots of food, drink and late nights, so it's a great experience. Tourist resorts, especially beach towns, are extremely busy on national holidays, with sky-high prices.

Quito

At a dizzying elevation of 2850m, **QUITO** is the second-highest seat of government in the world after Bolivia's La Paz. It has a dramatic location, with active Volcán Pichincha, which covered the city in ash in 1999, looming to the west and two valleys descending east separated by the snowcapped Antisana from the Amazon basin. If the altitude doesn't leave you breathless then the architecture will. Founded by the Spanish in 1534, Quito rapidly became a major colonial centre, and its churches, monasteries, cobbled streets and wide plazas have been beautifully preserved. The warmest, driest time is June to September, but the rest of the year can be chilly, especially at night, with frequent rain in the afternoons.

WHAT TO SEE AND DO

Although most visitors stay in the centre-north, the **Old Town**, mostly known as "El Centro Histórico", is what

6

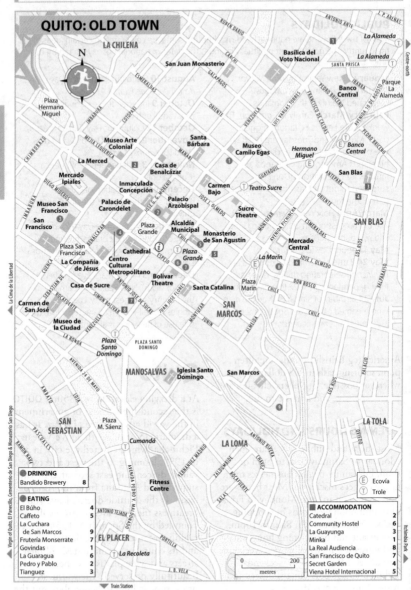

QUITO: OLD TOWN

N

▲ La Cima de la Libertad

Virgin of Quito, El Panecillo, Cementerio de San Diego & Monasterio San Diego

Itchimbía Park

Train Station

● DRINKING	
Bandido Brewery	8

● EATING	
El Búho	4
Caffeto	5
La Cuchara de San Marcos	9
Frutería Monserrate	7
Govindas	1
La Guaragua	6
Pedro y Pablo	2
Tianguez	3

■ ACCOMMODATION	
Catedral	2
Community Hostel	6
La Guayunga	3
Minka	1
La Real Audiencia	8
San Francisco de Quito	7
Secret Garden	4
Viena Hotel Internacional	5

E	Ecovía
T	Trole

0 ——— 200
metres

makes Quito special. Highlights include the two main squares **Plaza Grande** and **Plaza San Francisco**, the **Palacio de Carondelet**, the **Catedral**, the gaudy gold church **La Compañia** and the **Church of San Francisco**. For great views, take a taxi up to the top of **El Panecillo** or climb the stairs of the neo-Gothic **Basílica del Voto Nacional**, the earlier, the better.

The **centre-north** has a generous range of accommodation, restaurants and bars. Cheaper options abound in the area dubbed "La Mariscal", but it has noise and safety issues, especially after dark. La Floresta and other parts of the centre-north are thus gaining in popularity.

Modern Quito has plenty of attractions, but they are spread out, which makes sightseeing more complicated than in the Old Town. Highlights include Ecuador's biggest art museum, **El Museo Nacional**, Oswaldo Guayasamín's extraordinary work of art **La Capilla del Hombre** and a trip up to 4100m on the **Teleférico**.

Plaza Grande and around

This picture-perfect sixteenth-century plaza forms the political and religious focal point of Quito, linking the cathedral, Presidential Palace, Archbishop's Palace and city hall. You can visit the **Palacio de Carondelet** (Presidential Palace; tours Tues–Sun 8.30am–6pm, except when the cabinet is in session; free) on a guided tour to see the staterooms, a stunning mosaic and various indigenous artefacts. On the south side of the square is the **Catedral**, entered through the museum (entrance on Venezuela; Mon–Sat 9.30am–5pm; $1.50, Sun services free). Its interior features seventeenth- and eighteenth-century religious art, the tombs of liberator Mariscal José Antonio Sucre and ultramontane president Gabriel García Moreno, who was hacked to death under here (an inscription marks the spot).

On the corner of García Moreno and Espejo is the **Centro Cultural Metropolitano**, with regular exhibitions and performances in its courtyard. The centre also houses the **Museo Alberto Mena Caamaño** (Tues–Sat 9am–5.30pm, Sun 10am–4.30pm; $1.50), which has waxwork depictions of Quito life from 1700 to 1830, including the battles for independence.

Walk half a block south from Plaza Grande along Calle García Moreno to reach Quito's most extravagant church, **La Compañía de Jesús** (Mon–Fri 9.30am–5.30pm, Sat 9.30am–4.30pm, Sun 1.30–4.30pm; $4), built by Jesuits in the seventeenth and eighteenth centuries. It took 163 years to construct, with seven tonnes of gold to cover the interior from top to bottom. It's a wonder to behold, despite bordering on opulence gone mad.

Continue south down García Moreno to reach the **Museo de la Ciudad** (Tues–Sun 9.30am–5.30pm; $3; free last Sat of every month). Aside from a confusing layout, it's rewarding, depicting life in Quito through the centuries.

Plaza San Francisco

From La Compañía head northwest to Plaza San Francisco, one of Ecuador's most beautiful squares. The sixteenth-century **Iglesia de San Francisco** is Quito's oldest church and its twin bell tower is one of the city's most famous sights. Recent painstaking restoration has left the interior nearly as resplendent as that of La Compañía, although some work remains to be done. Behind the impressive facade is the largest religious complex in South America. The **Museo Fray Pedro Gocial/San Francisco** (Mon–Sat 9am–5.30pm, Sun 9am–1pm; $2) is housed in the cloisters and has an impressive collection of religious sculptures, paintings and furniture. Through the museum, you can enter the choral room of the church with a statue of the "dancing virgin" and depictions of planets on the ceiling.

Plaza Santo Domingo and La Ronda

Follow Simón Bolívar east of Plaza San Francisco to reach Quito's third impressive square, Plaza Santo Domingo, dominated by the sixteenth-century **Iglesia Santo Domingo**. From this square take Guayaquil south to reach the winding alley of **La Ronda**, one of Quito's oldest streets. This formerly seedy area has been renovated; the result is a pleasant walkway of tiny art galleries,

---

SIX SCENIC VIEWS OF QUITO

Quito's stunning location in a valley surrounded by volcanoes means you are spoilt for choice for the finest views of the city. Here are six of the best. All are most easily accessed by taxi (La Basílica can be reached on foot from Plaza Grande).

1. El Panecillo, Old Town
2. La Basílica, Old Town
3. Parque Itchimbía, Old Town
4. Guápulo, centre-north
5. Parque Metropolitano, Northeast
6. El Teleférico, Volcán Pichincha

6

bakeries and traditional cafés. La Ronda has become a popular spot at night to listen to live music or have a *canelazo* (a hot mix of *naranjilla*, cinnamon water and *aguardiente*).

El Panecillo

Old Quito's skyline is dominated by the 40m-high statue of the **Virgin de Quito**, on the hill known as El Panecillo ("little bread loaf") to the southwest. It's not safe to walk, so take a taxi (about $3 single from the Old Town or $8 return including waiting time). From the top, the view over the city is spectacular and the close-up of the statue with a chained dragon at her feet is equally impressive. You can climb up the statue for $2 (daily 9am–5pm).

Basílica del Voto Nacional

Take Calle Venezuela uphill from Plaza Grande to admire the neo-Gothic grandeur of the **Basílica del Voto Nacional** (daily 9am–5pm; $2). Construction took place over the past century, beginning in 1892. Instead of gargoyles, the church has iguanas and Galápagos tortoises protruding from its sides. Climbing the steep stairs and ladders up the 115m towers is unnerving, so take the lift if you're afraid of heights. The views across the city are fantastic.

Itchimbía Park and Cultural Centre

Perched high on a hill east of the Old Town, the glass-and-steel cultural centre inside the park hosts occasional exhibitions, but the main draw is the view and a chance to escape the city on footpaths winding through the extensive natural landscape. A taxi from the Old Town costs $2–3.

La Casa de la Cultura

To the northeast of Parque El Ejido, the modern oval building of **La Casa de la Cultura** (Patria between 6 de Diciembre and 12 de Octubre; ☎02 222 0967, ⓦcasadelacultura.gob.ec) contains cinemas, theatres, auditoriums and, of most interest to tourists, the **Museo Nacional** (Mon–Fri 9am–5pm, Sat & Sun 10am–4pm; $1). This is Ecuador's

premier museum, with an astonishing collection of pre-Columbian ceramics and artefacts as well as colonial, early republican and modern art. The museum is divided into four sections: archeology, colonial art, contemporary art and the Gold Room, which displays a majestic Tolita culture sun-mask.

Museo Fundación Guayasamín and the Capilla del Hombre

Oswaldo Guayasamín is Ecuador's most famous modern artist, and Quito's Bellavista district, where he used to live, houses two collections of his art. The **Museo Fundación Guayasamín** (José Bosmediano 543; Mon–Fri 10am–5pm; $3; ⓦguayasamin.org) exhibits many paintings as well as his enormous collection of pre-Columbian ceramics and colonial religious art. A further ten-minute walk up the hill is the far more impressive **Capilla del Hombre** or "Chapel of Man" (Lorenzo Chávez EA18-143, Tues–Sun 10am–5.30pm; $6), one of South America's most important works of art. This was Guayasamín's final great project, initiated in his last years and not fully completed until after his death in 1999. From the museum you can walk up to the garden of Guayasamín and see where his ashes are buried under the "Tree of Life". Just up from the Capilla del Hombre is the **Parque Metropolitano**, Quito's largest park, with forested trails, picnic areas and sweeping views. There are occasional buses up to Bellavista but it's best to take a taxi ($2).

Parque Carolina

Quito's modern mid-town central park is **Parque Carolina**. This is where locals come to walk and play sports. The park contains a beautiful set of **Botanical Gardens** (Tues–Sun 8am–4.45pm; $3), which showcases Ecuador's array of flowers and trees, including more than five hundred orchid species in greenhouses. Next door, the **Vivarium** (Tues–Sun 9.30am–5.30pm; $3) features more than forty species of reptiles including caimans, turtles and snakes. The highlights are the 6m-long python and the boa constrictor, which you can be photographed holding ($3). Across the park, the **Museo de Ciencias Naturales** (Mon–Fri 8.30am–4.30pm; $2) has a huge collection of dead insects and arachnids.

Guápulo

On an eastern slope of the centre-north, this pretty neighbourhood is a world away from downtown. With steep cobbled streets, historic houses and pleasant cafés, it's a relaxing place with squares and a major park. The focal point is the beautiful seventeenth-century Iglésia de Guápulo, a jewel box of Baroque colonial sculpture.

The Teleférico

Quito's most dizzying tourist attraction is the **Teleférico** (daily 9am–8pm; $4), a cable-car ride high above the city. The main attraction is the fifteen-minute ride up to 4100m, from where the views are spectacular on a clear day. At the top, take in the views, relax in the café or tackle the hike to Rucu Pichincha, 3km away (do not attempt this walk alone as robberies have been reported). Bring warm clothes and take care not to over-exert yourself at this altitude if you've just arrived in Quito. Teleférico shuttles run from Rio Coca, at 6 Diciembre (Ecovía) and Estación Norte (Trole); or take a taxi ($3.50).

ARRIVAL AND DEPARTURE

By plane Aeropuerto Internacional Mariscal Sucre (☏ 02 294 4900, ⓦ quiport.com) is in the suburb of Tababela. The airport has regular flights to Europe, North America, Central America and other destinations in South America. The journey from Quito (45–120min) costs $25 by taxi. Shuttle buses ($8) connect it to the centre-north, but the city arrival area is unsafe after dark. Cheap but slower local buses are also available for $0.25.

By train Trains from Quito leave from Chimbacalle station, south of the old town, which can be reached on the trolleybus or via a taxi from La Mariscal District ($4–5). These trains aren't really travel options; advanced booking is advised, as services are popular. The Latacunga service (Thurs–Sun 8am; 4hr) passes through Machachi and Boliche, but there are separate services to each of these towns on weekends (see ⓦ trenecuador.com). The train (see box, p.594) has a four-day luxury service to Guayaquil.

By bus Quito has three bus terminals. All destinations from the south, including the coast and jungle, use the main terminal, Quitumbe, in the far south of Quito. It's complicated, involves changes and takes over an hour to reach central Quito by trolleybus, so consider a taxi ($8–10). From Otavalo and the northern highlands, you arrive at Carcelén terminal, at the northern end of the Metrobus line. From Mindo, you arrive at Ofelia in the far north on the Metrobus line. It takes an hour to get to the centre-north from these stations by Metrobus or taxi ($5–7).

Destinations from Quitumbe Ambato (hourly; 2hr 30min); Atacames (daily; 7hr); Baños (hourly; 3hr); Coca (daily; 9hr); Cuenca (hourly; 9hr); Guaranda (daily; 5hr); Guayaquil (hourly; 8hr); Lago Agrio (daily; 9hr); Latacunga (hourly; 1hr 30min); Santo Domingo (hourly; 3hr); Tena (hourly; 5hr).

Destinations from Carcelén Note, heavy traffic amid ongoing road widening means that travelling north can face delays, but these will decline once work is completed. Atacames (daily; 7hr); Ibarra (hourly; 2hr 30min–3hr 30min); Los Bancos (indirect to Mindo, daily; 2hr); Otavalo (hourly; 2–3hr); Tulcán (hourly; 5–6hr).

Destinations from Ofelia Cayambe (hourly; 1hr 30min–2hr 30min); Mindo (direct, daily; 2hr); Mitad del Mundo (via Metrobus line, hourly; 1hr).

By van Door-to-door van services include Taxi Lagos (Otavalo and Ibarra, $15; ☏ 02 256 5992; Guaytambos (Ambato, $12; Riobamba, $15; ☏ 098 710 0679); Grey (Guayaquil, $30; ☏ 098 402 8211).

INFORMATION

Tourist information The Quito Visitors Bureau (ⓦ quito .com.ec) has several offices in the city with brochures, maps and information on Ecuador. In the Old Town the office is on Venezuela, at Espejo, on Plaza Grande (Mon–Fri 9am–6pm, Sat 10.30am–9.30pm, Sun 9am–5pm; ☏ 02 257 2445). There's an office in the Casa de La Cultura Ecuatoriana (6 de Diciembre, at Patria; Mon–Fri 9am–5pm, Sat & Sun 10am–4pm; ☏ 02 222 1116) and in La Mariscal (Reina Victoria, at Luis Cordero; ☏ 02 255 1566). Also check out the travellers' club South American Explorers on Av Mariana de Jesus OE3-32 (Mon–Fri 9.30am–5pm & Sat 9am–noon, Thurs until 8pm; ☏ 02 222 5228, ⓦ saexplorers.org), which has a huge amount of information on Quito and Ecuador in the form of trip reports, and free information sheets for non-members. Membership costs from $60 per year.

GETTING AROUND

By bus These cost only $0.25 per trip and while hit and miss are useful for travelling short distances up main avenues such as 12 de Octubre, 6 de Diciembre, 10 de Agosto, and Colón.

By electric bus There are three main electric bus routes running north to south, with designated stations and car-free lanes, making them the most efficient way to get around. All charge $0.25 flat fare (bought at kiosks or machines in advance). The three services rarely link up, so changing routes

6

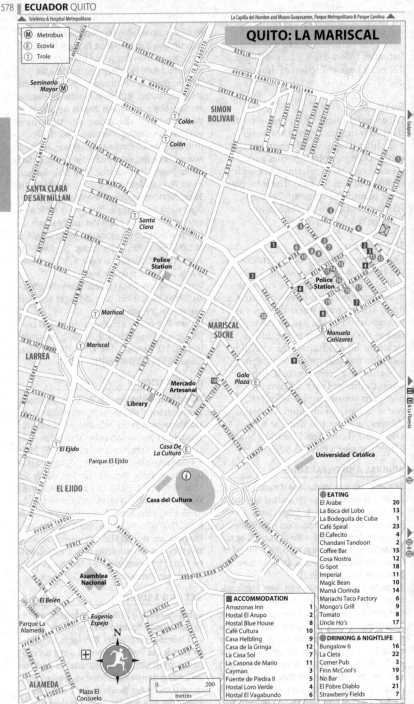

QUITO: LA MARISCAL

■ Teleférico & Hospital Metropolitano

La Capilla del Hombre and Museo Guayasamín, Parque Metropolitano & Parque Carolina ▲

M Metrobus
E Ecovía
T Trole

■ ACCOMMODATION

Amazonas Inn	1
Hostal El Arupo	2
Hostal Blue House	8
Café Cultura	10
Casa Helbling	9
Casa de la Gringa	12
La Casa Sol	7
La Casona de Mario	11
Cayman	3
Fuente de Piedra II	5
Hostal Loro Verde	4
Hostal El Vagabundo	6

● EATING

El Arabe	20
La Boca del Lobo	13
La Bodeguita de Cuba	1
Café Spiral	23
El Cafecito	4
Chandani Tandoori	2
Coffee Bar	15
Cosa Nostra	12
G-Spot	18
Imperial	11
Magic Bean	10
Mamá Clorinda	14
Mariachi Taco Factory	6
Mongo's Grill	9
Tomato	8
Uncle Ho's	17

● DRINKING & NIGHTLIFE

Bungalow 6	16
La Cleta	22
Corner Pub	3
Finn McCool's	19
No Bar	5
El Pobre Diablo	21
Strawberry Fields	7

0 — 200 metres

often involves walking several blocks. They generally run every 10min Mon–Fri 6am–midnight, Sat & Sun 6am–10pm. El Trole is the trolleybus system that runs down 10 de Agosto to the Old Town; stops are easy to spot because of their distinctive green raised platforms. In the Old Town buses travel south along Guayaquil and return north on Flores and Montúfar. Ecovía are buses that run mainly along 6 de Diciembre from Río Coca in the north to Plaza la Marín in the Old Town. Metrobus runs from Carcelén bus terminal down Avenida América to Universidad Central. Pickpocketing is a chronic problem on Quito's trolleybuses so be vigilant and don't carry valuables.

By car Many reputable international rental companies have offices outside the international terminal of the airport, including Avis (☎ 02 244 0270) and Hertz (☎ 02 225 4258).

By taxi It's often easier to take a taxi and is recommended at night. Check that the meter is reset when you get in. It's very cheap – from the Old Town to La Mariscal should be only $2–3. Fares increase at night, when most drivers don't use the meter (in which case, agree the price beforehand). Most hoteliers and bars have numbers of trusted companies. Reliable 24hr services include Central Radio Taxis (☎ 02 250 0600) and Teletaxi (☎ 02 222 2222). Easy Taxi is a very good smartphone app that charges a $0.50 surcharge and mostly works better than calling a cab.

ACCOMMODATION

Many visitors stay in La Mariscal in the centre-north, which is geared up for tourists with a wide selection of hotels, restaurants, bars and tour operators. The area gets very noisy at the weekends and can be dangerous, especially at night. There are quieter alternatives in La Floresta, among others. Staying in the Centro Histórico is a better option than it used to be and convenient for sightseeing – though there are fewer tourist amenities.

CENTRE-NORTH

Amazonas Inn Joaquín Pinto 471, at Av Amazonas ☎ 02 222 5723; map opposite. Friendly hotel with comfortable if compact rooms with private bath and cable TV. **$26**

Hostal El Arupo Juan Rodríguez E7-22, at Reina Victoria ☎ 02 255 7543, ⒲ hostalelarupo.com; map opposite. An attractive renovated house with TV room, free internet and colourful rooms. Breakfast included. **$45**

Hostal Blue House Pinto, at Diego de Almagro ☎ 02 222 3480, ⒲ bluehousequito.com; map opposite. Very popular backpacker hostel with a kitchen, bar, free internet and breakfast included. Dorms **$9**, doubles **$30**

★**Casa Helbling** Veintimilla E8-152 ☎ 02 222 6013, ⒲ casahelbling.de; map opposite. Relaxed bed and breakfast with excellent service and better quality than more expensive places, including double glazing to keep the street noise out. There's a garden to the back, kitchen facilities and a roofed sitting area around a huge palm.

Breakfast $3.80–6.90. Dorms **$12**, doubles **$21**

Casa de la Gringa Guipuzcoa E16-55 ☎ 02 223 7298, ⒲ hostel.lacasadelagringa.com; map opposite. If La Mariscal is not for you, stay in the quieter neighbourhood of La Floresta. A small and welcoming budget place in a traditional house with a courtyard, but still near cafés and restaurants. Dorms **$9**, doubles **$26**

La Casa Sol Calama 127 ☎ 02 223 0798, ⒲ lacasasol.com; map opposite. Cosy, quiet, brightly coloured guesthouse with comfortable rooms set around an attractive courtyard. Breakfast included. **$68**

La Casona de Mario Andalucia 213, at Galicia ☎ 02 254 4036, ⒲ casonademario.com; map opposite. This welcoming home away from home in La Floresta, run by an Argentine, has a communal kitchen and comfortable lounge area. **$20**

Cayman Juan Rodríguez 270, at Reina Victoria ☎ 02 256 7616, ⒲ hotelcaymanquito.com; map opposite. Attractive renovated old house with a huge fireplace, large garden and good restaurant. Free wi-fi and breakfast. **$53**

★**Fuente de Piedra II** Juan León Mera, at Baquedano ☎ 02 290 0323, ⒲ ecuahotel.com; map opposite. Take a step up from Mariscal's budget options and treat yourself at this colonial-style mid-range hotel. It's elegantly furnished and has attentive service, wi-fi and a gourmet restaurant (breakfast is included). A sister hotel is on Tamayo, at Wilson. **$56**

Hostal Loro Verde Juan Rodríguez, at Diego de Almagro ☎ 02 222 6173; map opposite. A hotel as colourful as its name (green parrot), with indigenous artefacts and comfortable rooms. **$30**

Hostal El Vagabundo Wilson E7-45 ☎ 02 222 6376; map opposite. A dependable budget option with a friendly atmosphere, small café and table tennis. **$25**

OLD TOWN

Catedral Mejía 638, at Benalcázar ☎ 02 295 5438, ⒲ hotelcatedral.ec; map p.574. Comfortable hotel in the heart of the Old Town; facilities include cable TV, sauna and steam room. **$55**

★**Community Hostel** Pedro Fermín Cevallos N6-78, accross from the Mercado Central ☎ 09 5904 9658, ⒲ communityhostel.com; map p.574. Excellent, friendly central option for the Old Town, with the Bandido Brewery almost across the street. Well-appointed rooms, easily among

---

> ★**TREAT YOURSELF**
>
> **Café Cultura** Robles 513, at Reina Victoria ☎ 02 222 4271, ⒲ cafecultura.com; map opposite. An elegant place to stay in the Mariscal, this restored old mansion mixes grandeur with intimacy. The roaring fires in the lounge, the large bathtubs and a gourmet café are the perfect repose after a hard day's sightseeing. **$122**

the best hostels in Quito. Dorms $\overline{$10}$, doubles $\overline{$30}$

La Guayunga Antepara E4-27 ☎02 228 8544, ⓦlaguayungaquito.com; map p.574. Cheery family-run hostel in the central La Tola neighbourhood, with gorgeous views of the centre from the glass-topped rooftop terrace. Dorms $\overline{$10.50}$, doubles $\overline{$35}$

Minka Matovelle 219 ☎02 255 3953, ⓦminkahostel .com; map p.574. Excellent, relaxed hostel near the basilica, with beanbags to lounge in and a pool table and table football while you wait for the afternoon rain to end. Breakfast included. Dorms $\overline{$10.50}$, doubles $\overline{$30}$

La Real Audiencia Bolívar 220, at Guayaquil ☎02 295 0590, ⓦrealaudiencia.com; map p.574. Try this upmarket option with stylish rooms, black-and-white photography and a fabulous view of Plaza Santo Domingo from the restaurant (open to non-guests). Breakfast included. $\overline{$55}$

★**San Francisco de Quito** Sucre 217, at Guayaquil ☎02 228 7758, ⓦsanfranciscodequito.com.ec; map p.574. The pick of the Old Town mid-range options with pleasant rooms set around a cosy courtyard, a fountain, rooftop patio and great views. Breakfast included. $\overline{$47}$

Secret Garden Antepara E4-60, at Los Rios ☎099 602 3709, ⓦsecretgardenquito.com; map p.574. Hidden away south-east of the historic centre in a listed building, this is a great Aussie-run budget hostel set on five floors with basic rooms and a rooftop terrace serving big breakfasts. There's also a Spanish school and tour operator. Dorms $\overline{$9}$, doubles $\overline{$24}$

Viena Hotel Internacional Flores 600, at Chile ☎02 295 4860; map p.574. A good-quality three-star hotel with well-appointed rooms set around an enclosed courtyard. $\overline{$30}$

EATING

Quito boasts the best selection of international restaurants in Ecuador – from Asian to Middle Eastern and Mediterranean. Most are in the centre-north, with Old Town eating options restricted. For those on a budget, fill yourself up at lunch, as most restaurants offer specials for $2–4. Many places are closed Sunday evenings.

CENTRE-NORTH

El Arabe Reina Victoria 627 between Veintimilla and Carrión ☎02 254 9414; map p.578. Authentic Syrian kebabs, falafel and pita. Daily noon–10pm.

La Bodeguita de Cuba Reina Victoria N26-105; map p.578. Tasty Cuban specialities ($4–5) with live Cuban music on Thursday nights, when drinking and dancing continues into the early hours. Mon & Tues noon–11pm, Wed & Thurs noon–1am, Fri & Sat noon–2am.

Café Spiral Mallorca N24-266 in La Floresta; map p.578. Varied vegetarian, Ecuadorian and American food with lunch menus for $5–9 in this charming traditional house, with an outdoor fountain and a small upstairs lounge. Mon–Thurs noon–10pm, Fri noon–11pm; sporadically open Sat.

El Cafecito Luis Cordero 1124; map p.578. Cosy café with

great coffee, home-made cakes, crêpes and vegetarian meals for around $3–5. Daily 8am–11pm.

Chandani Tandoori Juan León Mera, at Luis Cordero; map p.578. Head here for authentic Indian food at low prices. Masala, korma, dupiaza, balti and hot vindaloo – all the classics are done well for only $3–5. Mon–Thurs 12.30pm–midnight, Fri & Sat 12.30pm–1am, Sun 12.30pm–4pm.

Coffee Bar Foch, at Reina Victoria; map p.578. A long-standing café on Plaza Foch, great for people-watching over a coffee or cocktail. Daily 24hr.

Cosa Nostra Moreno, at Diego de Almagro; map p.578. Italian-owned restaurant with some of the best pizzas in town ($6–18); another location at República de El Salvador N34-234. Tues–Sun 12.30–3pm & 6.30–10.30pm.

G-Spot Diego de Almagro, at Calama; map p.578. Its name may leave you nonplussed but this fast-food joint has cheap burgers with trimmings galore ($2–3). Mon–Sat 9.30am–6.30pm, Sun 9.30am–3pm.

Imperial Juan Rodríguez, at Reina Victoria; map p.578. Eat alfresco in this restaurant's garden terrace. Choose from an imaginative menu of mainly chicken and meat dishes ($5–6) and a great-value set lunch ($3). Mon–Thurs 12.30pm–midnight, Fri & Sat 12.30pm–1am.

Magic Bean Foch, at Juan León Mera; map p.578. Hugely popular café with great breakfasts, pancakes and fresh juices from $3–6 and mains $9–14. Café branch also at Portugal E9-106. Daily 7am–11pm.

Mamá Clorinda Reina Victoria 1144; map p.578. Well-prepared but pricey Ecuadorian specialities. Try half a guinea pig (*cuy*) for $13. Mon–Sat 11am–10pm.

Mariachi Taco Factory Foch, at Juan León Mera; map p.578. A good Mexican place – burritos, chimichangas, fajitas, etc, for $5–8, all washed down with cocktails and sangria. Mon–Wed 12.30–10pm, Thurs 12.30–11pm, Fri & Sat 12.30pm–1am, Sun 12.30–7pm.

Mongo's Grill Calama; map p.578. This hugely popular Mongolian barbecue offers sizzling meat and vegetable dishes such as chicken teriyaki and lamb in spicy yogurt, all cooked in front of you. Excellent-value buffets from $6. Uptown branch at Shyris N34-300. Mon–Thurs 11am–11pm, Fri & Sat noon–2am.

Tomato Juan León Mera, at Calama; map p.578. A great place for pizza ($5–7) and pasta. The *calzone* is particularly good. Daily noon–11pm.

★**TREAT YOURSELF**

La Boca del Lobo Calama 284, at Reina Victoria; map p.578. With a brightly coloured glass-encased patio, flamboyant decor and Mediterranean menu, this is the place to indulge. You'll be amazed at how many ways they cook mushrooms. Mains $8–12. Mon–Sat 5pm til late.

★**Uncle Ho's** Calama E8-40; map p.578. Vietnamese restaurant run by a friendly Irish guy who serves up a range of great cocktails, followed by a feast of Asian food – from coconut curry to Imperial rolls and beef noodle soup. Mains $5–7. Mon–Sat noon–10.30pm.

OLD TOWN

El Búho José Moreno, at Espejo; map p.574. Inside the Centro Cultural Metropolitano, this is a pleasant stop for soups, salads, sandwiches and pasta. $3–6. Mon–Sat 8am–8pm.

Caffeto Chile, at Guayaquil; map p.574. Little gem of a café at the entrance to San Agustín Monastery specializing in coffee and hot chocolate served with *humitas*, *tamales*, *empanadas* and cakes for $3–5. Mon–Sat 8am–10pm, Sun 9.30am–3pm.

★**La Cuchara de San Marcos** Junín E3-121, map p.574. Occupying the upstairs and courtyard of a large old-town house, this restaurant has a real old-world vibe and features gourmet organic meals around $7 and craft beers. Tues–Sat noon–10pm, Sun 11am–5pm.

Frutería Montserrate Espejo Oe2-12; map p.574. The perfect place to take a break from sightseeing with an extravagant helping of fruit salad and ice cream ($2–5). Cheap *almuerzos* and sandwiches also available. Mon–Sat 9am–7.30pm, Sun 9am–5pm.

Govindas Esmeraldas 853; map p.574. Very good vegetarian option in the Old Town. Healthy breakfasts and specialities such as vegetarian risotto for lunch. Mains $2–4. Mon–Sat 9am–3pm.

La Guaragua Espejo Oe2-40; map p.574. Appealing little restaurant just down from Plaza Grande. Ecuadorian specialities such as *seco de pollo* (chicken stew) and *chuleta* (fried pork chops); the great-value set lunches will set you back $3–6. Mon–Sat 11.30am–7pm.

Pedro y Pablo Chile, at Plaza Grande; map p.574. Just one of the many cafés in a delightful food court hidden in a historic building on Plaza Grande, serving mainly seafood. Mains $4. Daily 8.30am–4.30pm.

Tianguez Plaza de San Francisco; map p.574. Right on the square, this is a perfectly situated café in which to take a break from sightseeing. Well-prepared local specialities and indulgent desserts are slightly pricey ($3–8) but worth it for the great setting. It also houses one of Quito's best stores for Ecuadorian crafts. Mon–Wed & Sun 9.30am–6pm, Thurs 9.30am–6pm, Fri & Sat 9.30am–8.30pm.

DRINKING AND NIGHTLIFE

MODERN QUITO

La Mariscal has a vibrant nightlife and gets packed Thursday to Saturday nights. The most happening area is along Calama and Foch between avenidas Amazonas, Juan León Mera and Reina Victoria. Bars are busy from 8pm onwards with the clubs filling up towards midnight and winding down around 3am. Take a taxi at night. La Mariscal is quiet and feels dangerous on Sundays, except for Plaza Foch.

Bungalow 6 Calama, at Diego Almagro; map p.578. A mixture of locals and tourists flock to enjoy the great atmosphere and dance to Latin and pop classics in this hugely popular bar/disco (entrance $5 including one drink). Wed–Sat 8pm–2am.

★**La Cleta** Lugo N24-250, at Guipuzcoa; map p.578. Bicycle-themed bar with outdoor terrace in La Floresta. Excellent stone-baked pizzas, $16 for a large with three large beers. Mon–Sat 3–11pm.

Corner Pub Amazonas, at Calama; map p.578. A small bar on the corner of La Mariscal's main drag, popular with expats and locals alike. Mon–Thurs 12.30pm–midnight, Fri & Sat 12.30pm–1am.

Finn McCool's Almagro, at Pinto; map p.578. The most popular expat pub, with draught beer, pool, quiz nights, movie nights and plenty of rock music. Thurs–Sat 8.30am–2am.

No Bar Calama 380; map p.578. Raucous Mariscal disco with a large dancefloor. It gets very loud and crowded at weekends (entrance $5 including one drink). Thurs–Sat 8.30pm–2am.

El Pobre Diablo Isabel La Católica, at Galavis; map p.578. A Quito institution in La Floresta with a bohemian atmosphere, cocktails, a good restaurant and live music. Mon & Tues 12.30–3.30pm & 6–10pm, Wed–Sat 12.30–3.30pm, 6pm–2am.

Strawberry Fields Calama E5-23; map p.578. A world away from *No Bar* next door, this tiny rock bar, brimming with Beatles memorabilia, is great to escape the disco craziness. Much larger, upscale branch at González Suárez N27-171. Wed–Sat 6pm–2am.

OLD TOWN

★**Bandido Brewery** Olmedo E1-136; map p.574. One of the best spots in Ecuador's upstart craft brewing scene, with seven beers on tap, right across from the Mercado Central. Good atmosphere and pizzas in an old building. Co-owner Ryan promises Rough Guide readers a discount. Mon–Sat 4–11pm.

DIRECTORY

Banks and exchange There are plenty of banks and ATMs in the centre-north, fewer in the Old Town. They are normally open Mon–Fri 8.30am–4pm and Sat am. Try Banco de Guayaquil, Reina Victoria, at Colón, or Banco del Pacífico, 12 de Octubre, at Cordero.

Books The English Bookshop (Calama, at Diego de Almagro) is the best place in Mariscal to pick up fiction and travel books, to buy, sell or borrow. Libri Mundi (J Mera, at Wilson; ☎02 223 4791, ⓦlibrimundi.com) is the best place for new books, and Confederate Books (Calama, at Mera; ☎02 252 7890) is also good for secondhand books.

Embassies and consulates Argentina, Amazonas

6

21–147, at Roca (☎02 250 1106); Bolivia, Eloy Alfaro 2432, at Fernando Ayarza (☎02 244 6652); Brazil, Amazonas N39-123, Edificio Amazonas Plaza (☎02 227 7300); Canada, Amazonas 4153, Edificio Eurocenter (☎02 245 5499); Chile, Juan Pablo Sanz 3617, at Amazonas (☎02 225 6947); Colombia, 12 de Octubre N24-528 World Trade Centre Torre B (☎02 222 2486); Peru, República de El Salvador 495, at Irlanda (☎02 246 8411); UK, Naciones Unidas, at República de El Salvador, Edificio Citiplaza, 14th floor (☎02 297 0801, ⓦukinecuador.fco.gov.uk); US, Avigiras E12-170 (☎02 398 5000, ⓦecuador.usembassy .gov); Venezuela, Amazonas N30-240 Edificio Comonsa (☎02 255 7209).

Hospital Hospital Metropolitano, Av Mariana de Jesús, at Av Occidental ☎02 226 1520, emergency and ambulance ☎02 226 5020.

Internet Wi-fi is almost ubiquitous. Sambo.net (JL Mera, at J Pinto; $0.70–$1/hr; ☎02 290 1315).

Police La Policía de Turismo (Reina Victoria, at Roca; ☎02 254 3983).

Post offices The most convenient office for La Mariscal is on the corner of Reina Victoria, at Colón (Mon–Fri 8am–7pm, Sat & Sun 8am–noon; ☎02 250 8890).

Shopping Mercado Artesanal (Juan León Mera, at Jorge Washington, La Mariscal), weekend market at Parque El Ejido, and Mercado Ipiales (Chile, at Imbabura, Old Town).

Telephones Fixed-line CNT (ⓦwww.cnt.com.ec), an office on Eloy Alfaro near 9 de Octubre.

QUITO EXCURSIONS

Visitors can reach many attractive sites within a few hours from central Quito: Papallacta, Mindo and Cotopaxi are all less than three hours from the city.

Pululahua and Mitad del Mundo

Best visited early mornings for spectacular views, the extinct volcanic crater of **Pululahua** forms a 32-square-kilometre nature reserve, with small farms at the bottom, making this one of the very few inhabited craters on the planet. Excellent for hiking, biking or horseriding, it takes about three hours for the steep climb down and back from the most easily accessible scenic overlook on its east side. Near the rim, the **Museo Templo del Sol** (daily 9am–6pm; $3), a museum of contemporary indigenous art, is housed in a massive stone building reminiscent of Inca and medieval fortresses. Much of the area has been marred by haphazard development, particularly quarries. There are no direct buses from Quito; local buses along the highway connect Pululahua with the touristy

---

ACTIVITIES IN QUITO

After a few days of sightseeing and acclimatization, you will be ready to take advantage of the huge range of activities in the mountains near the city. The most popular one-day tours are cycling and horseriding. For **cycling**, Cotopaxi National Park and Ilinizas are firm favourites (average cost $65/day). There are numerous locations south of Quito offering **horseriding** (average cost $45/day). For **rafting and kayaking**, day tours in valleys north and west of Quito cost $70–80. The most popular **trekking** route is around Lake Quilotoa (see p.593). One- and two-day tours can be booked from Quito. If you fancy **climbing**, the easier peaks include Pasochoa (4199m), El Corazón (4788m) and the more challenging Iliniza Norte (5126m). All cost $65 for a one-day tour. Cotopaxi (5897m), Cayambe (5790m), Antisana (5755m) and Chimborazo (6310m) are tough and can all be climbed by well-prepared, fit people on two-day tours ($175–215).

TOUR OPERATORS

Alta Montaña Jorge Washington 8–20 ☎02 255 8380, ⓦclimbing-ecuador.com. Climbing and trekking.

Biking Dutchman Foch 714, at Juan León Mera ☎02 254 2806, ⓦbiking-dutchman.com. Mountain-biking tours.

Ecuadorian Alpine Institute Ramírez Dávalos 136, at Amazonas ☎02 256 5465, ⓦvolcanoclimbing.com. Top-class climbing tours.

Enchanted Expeditions De las Alondras N45–102, at Los Lirios ☎02 334 0525, ⓦenchantedexpeditions .com. Wide range of tours. Specialists in Galápagos

yachts and haciendas in the highlands.

Gulliver JL Mera, at Calama ☎02 252 9297, ⓦgulliver .com.ec. Popular Mariscal operator with climbing, hiking, biking and jungle tours as well as Galápagos visits.

Surtrek Reina Victoria N24–151 ☎02 255 3658, ⓦsurtrek.com. Offers a comprehensive selection of tours throughout Ecuador, including loads of adventure hiking, biking, and birdwatching.

Yacu Amu Foch 746, at Juan León Mera ☎02 290 4055, ⓦyacuamu.com. White-water rafting and kayaking specialist.

Mitad del Mundo ("The Middle of the World"; Mon–Fri 9am–6pm, Sat & Sun 9am–8pm; $3; ⓦwww.mitaddelmundo .com). Its 30m-high equator **monument** ($3 to go inside), topped by a brass globe, can be climbed and also includes an **Ethnographic Museum**. There are various other small exhibitions dotted around the complex, the highlight being the France building with a good exhibition on the measurement of the equator by Charles Marie de La Condamine. Although everybody wants to get a photo straddling the equator in front of the monument, this is not actually the real equator, which lies approximately 300m along the main road to the east at the **Museo Solar Inti Ñan** (daily 9.30am–5pm; $3; ⓦmuseointinan.com.ec). It's particularly fun to see the experiments to prove you are standing on the equator (though Ecuador's best equatorial site is Quitsato near Cayambe). It's worth taking a short taxi ride to the nearby fifteenth-century ruins of the small Inca fortress of **Rumicucho**, overlooking the Guayllabamba River as it heads north.

To get to Mitad del Mundo, take the Metrobus on Avenida America north to the Ofelia terminal and then a green Mitad del Mundo **bus** ($0.50). The trip from north-central Quito takes about an hour.

Volcán Pichincha
Two summits crown the active **Volcán Pichincha** overlooking Quito. **Rucu**, meaning Elder in Kichwa, and **Guagua** (baby) make good hikes, but each has its problems (both are over 4700m). Rucu, which is easily accessed from the top of the *Teleférico*, has suffered from muggings, but there is usually police presence on the trail at weekends. Guagua is badly behaved and a violent eruption showered Quito in ash in 1999. It's still officially active and harder to climb. Ask at a tour operator in Quito for the latest situation.

Papallacta
About 65km (two hours) from Quito, the road to Lago Agrio and Tena passes through the town of **Papallacta**, home to the best thermal baths in Ecuador. The entrance to **Las Termas de Papallacta** (daily 6am–9pm; $7; ☎02 232 0040) is a thirty-minute walk up a dirt road, so consider a $2 taxi. The complex is impressive, with 25 baths of different temperatures. On clear days there are great views of snowcapped Volcán Artisana. At 3300m it gets cold outside the baths, so bring warm clothes.

ACCOMMODATION
Hostal Coturpa ☎ 06 289 5000. The best budget option, with a charming interior, so don't let the ugly cement exterior put you off. Singles $\overline{23}$, doubles $\overline{32}$, with jacuzzi $\overline{56}$

The Northern Highlands and Western Andean slopes

North of Quito lie two dramatically different regions. To the northwest are verdant **cloudforests**, filled with birdlife. The small town of **Mindo** is the best base to explore the forest's biodiversity and indulge in adrenaline-pumping adventure sports. To the north, magnificent Andean scenery populated by proud indigenous cultures extends to the Colombian border. The most popular destination is **Otavalo**, north of the snowcapped **Volcán Cayambe**, whose colourful Saturday market is one of the largest in South America and heaven for lovers of indigenous crafts and clothing. Some 30km north stands the stately Ciudad Blanca, **Ibarra**, the largest city in the region. Between Ibarra and **Tulcán** on the border with Colombia are Afro-Ecuadorian villages and **Páramo del Ángel**, an extraordinary, otherworldly landscape.

6

MINDO

Snuggled in a cloudforest at a pleasant elevation of 1200m, **MINDO** is a truly idyllic destination. Whether you want to watch for some of the 400 species of birds and 250 species of butterfly, swing above the forest canopy on zip-lines, plunge down the rivers on rubber tubes or simply gaze at the waterfalls, there's something for everyone. The cool climate means that this is a far more comfortable region to explore pristine forest than the Oriente. Tourism has developed relatively slowly in Mindo so you can usually avoid the crowds, although weekends get busy with day-trippers. Many attractions are a one- or two-hour walk from town. To save time, share a taxi for $5–10.

Mariposas de Mindo

The town is surrounded by the Bosque Protector Mindo-Nambillo cloudforest but most accessible areas are due south. The dirt road leading out of town forks after about 1km. To the left is the butterfly farm **Mariposas de Mindo** (daily 9am–6.30pm; $5; ⓦ mariposasdemindo .com), which breeds 25 species, including the Brown Owl Eye and the Peleides Blue Morpho, the latter with a wingspan of 20cm. Come in the early morning and you may be lucky and see them hatch.

Mindo Canopy Adventure

Take a right when the dirt road out of town forks, and you reach **Mindo Canopy Adventure** ($10; ☎ 098 542 8758, ⓦ mindocanopy.com). Adrenaline lovers can get their fix by zinging along cables from 20m to 400m in length, high above the forest, either solo or accompanied by a guide. The thirteen-line circuit takes about one hour thirty minutes ($10), or do three lines for $5.

About 1km up the hill is a more relaxed way to traverse the treetops. **La Tarabita** cable car ($5/person) cruises 150m above a river basin. On the other side are trails to seven waterfalls. The paths are confusing in places but you can't really get lost as there is only one exit – wear boots as it's muddy. The entire circuit takes two hours and goes deep inside the cloudforest; hiring a birdwatching guide is a great way

to learn more. Most charge $50/half-day and $100/full-day (cheaper in a group).

Tubing and canyoning

For adventure-sports lovers, there's plenty in Mindo. An unusual alternative to rafting is tumbling down river rapids in an inflatable **tube** ($8 for a couple of hours including transport). **Canyoning** is also available ($10/half-day).

ARRIVAL AND DEPARTURE

By bus Cooperativa Flor del Valle (☎ 02 252 7495, ⓦ flordelvalle.com.ec) runs buses from Quito's Ofelia bus station (daily 8am, 9am, 3pm & 4pm, returning 6.30am, 1.45pm & 3pm; Sat & Sun more frequent; 2hr). If you miss the morning bus from Quito, go to Carcelén terminal and take any bus heading to Los Bancos and ask the driver to let you off at the turn-off to Mindo, where you can usually hire a taxi to town ($1–2).

INFORMATION AND TOURS

Information The Centro de Información is on Quito near the main plaza (Wed–Sun 8.30am–12.30pm & 1.30–5pm). It has lists of recommended guides.

Tours The owner of *Birdwatcher's House* is an experienced guide. Other recommended tour operators include *La Isla Mindo* (☎ 02 217 0481, ⓦ laislamindo.com) and *Mindo Bird* (☎ 099 735 1297, ⓦ www.mindobirds.com.ec), both on Avenida Quito.

ACCOMMODATION

Mindo has a wide selection of accommodation but it's more enjoyable to stay in one of the lodges on the edge of town, surrounded by cloudforest.

Arco Iris Quito, at 9 de Octubre ☎ 02 390 0405. A basic option in town, with comfortable rooms and a central location on the main square. $̲1̲8̲

Cabañas Armonía Lluvia de Oro, south of the football stadium ☎ 02 217 0131. Already on the outskirts of town, these comfortable cabins have all come with hammocks and feature a shady orchid garden full of hummingbirds. Doubles $̲3̲0̲

Cabañas la Estancia ☎ 099 878 3272, ⓦ mindohosterialaestancia.com. Cross the rickety bridge to these spacious cabins, set in landscaped gardens with outdoor restaurant, a swimming pool and even a waterslide. $̲1̲7̲, camping from $̲3̲

Casa de Cecilia End of 9 de Octubre ☎ 02 217 0243. On the eastern edge of town, these great-value rustic cabins stand on the banks of a roaring river. $̲1̲5̲

Dragonfly Inn Quito, at Sucre ☎ 02 217 0426, ⓦ dragonflyinn-mindo.com. This wooden cabin-style hotel is one of the best options in town, with balconies

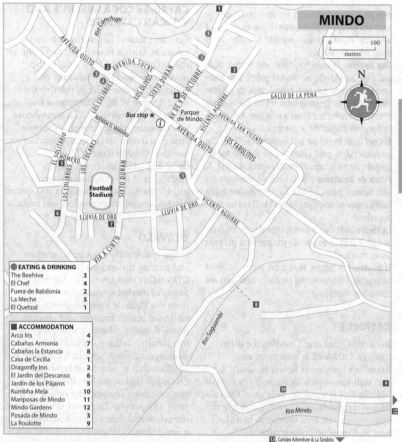

MINDO

0   100
metres

N

Bus stop ★
Parque de Mindo

Football Stadium

12, Canopy Adventure & La Tarabita ▼

● **EATING & DRINKING**
The Beehive	3
El Chef	4
Fuera de Babilonia	2
La Meche	4
El Quetzal	1

■ **ACCOMMODATION**
Arco Iris	4
Cabañas Armonía	7
Cabañas la Estancia	8
Casa de Cecilia	1
Dragonfly Inn	2
El Jardín del Descanso	6
Jardín de los Pájaros	5
Kumbha Mela	10
Mariposas de Mindo	11
Mindo Gardens	12
Posada de Mindo	3
La Roulotte	9

overlooking a garden patio along the river and a very good restaurant. $28.50

El Jardín del Descanso Los Colibríes ☎ 099 482 9587. Near the southern edge of town, birdwatcher Rodny Garrido enthusiastically shows guests the plethora of birds that visit his garden (a very worthwhile $3 without staying overnight). Book ahead for the four lodge-type rooms. $20

Jardín de los Pájaros Los Colibríes ☎ 099 175 6688. Well-presented hotel with carpeted rooms, and a balcony lounge with hammocks and outdoor swimming pool. $15

Kumbha Mela ☎ 099 405 1675. Deep in the forest with a selection of cabins and rooms nestled in extensive gardens. There's a good restaurant, swimming pool and even a private lagoon. Dorms $18, doubles per person $35

Mariposas de Mindo ☎ 02 224 2712, ⓦ mariposasdemindo.com. Pleasant cabins 2km from town near the butterfly farm (entrance included in price, as well as breakfast). $34.50

Mindo Gardens ☎ 099 722 3260, ⓦ mindogardens.com. One of Mindo's most popular mid-range hotels, 1km past the butterfly farm and set in a private reserve of forest and waterfalls. Brightly coloured cabins sit beside the river and there's a comfortable lounge and games area. Breakfast included. $50.50

Posada de Mindo End of Vicente Aguirre ☎ 02 217 0199. One of the most comfortable options in town, these new spotless cabins have a good restaurant attached. $40

La Roulotte ☎ 098 976 4484. On lush grounds, charming, novel all-wood, spotless gypsy wagons with double bunk beds set this place apart from all the cabins elsewhere. Bread is baked on-site and the restaurant is excellent, particularly the slow-cooked pork *bondiola*. It also has a roofed pétanque court, so you can play in the rain. $63

EATING AND DRINKING

There are plenty of restaurants on the main street offering Ecuadorian standards for $5. Many lodges also have good

6

restaurants. Most restaurants are open noon–2pm for lunch and 6–10pm for dinner, often staying open all day at weekends. Mindo has little nightlife, but after-dinner drinks are readily available.

The Beehive Av Quito. Vegetarian and German might sound like an odd mix, but this lounge/café with a nice terrace view gives you both options. Ingo, its talkative owner (also of the *Dragonfly Inn* across the street), serves Mindo's best coffee and brews a tasty beer. He can also help you pick tours off the beaten track. Mains $4–8.

El Chef Quito. One of the best restaurants in Mindo. The set lunch ($4) is good value. To treat yourself, try the speciality *lomo a la piedra* (barbecued steak). Mains $4–8.

Fuera de Babilonia 9 de Octubre. An alternative bar with assorted Indian artefacts on the walls, misshapen tables, a wide-ranging menu (dishes $4–7) and live music at weekends.

La Meche Quito. On the eastern edge of town, this is the best place to fill up on carefully prepared pizza and pasta dishes, from $6–10.

El Quetzal 9 de Octubre. Head to this organic restaurant for vegetarian specialities, big breakfasts, fresh juices and tasty snacks. Mains $6–8.

CAYAMBE

Between Quito and Otavalo, the little town of **CAYAMBE** is the centre of Ecuador's important flower industry. It's also well known for its *bizcochos*, a type of biscuit, and is a quieter base than Otavalo to explore surrounding peaks, notably the eponymous volcano. **Quitsato**, Ecuador's best and most precise equatorial monument, is a $4 round-trip taxi ride away. Cayambe celebrates the festival of Inti Raymi fervently in late June.

ARRIVAL AND DEPARTURE

By bus There are direct buses to Cayambe from Quito's Ofelia terminal (hourly; 1hr 20min) and regular buses from Otavalo (hourly; 30min).

ACCOMMODATION

Hacienda Guachalá Panamericana Norte Km70 ☎02 361 0908, ⓦguachala.com. By far Cayambe's best lodgings are haciendas, and this, one of Ecuador's oldest, is among the most accessible, with cheaper rooms in the former stables, all with fireplaces. Doubles $57, quad $84

Hotel La Gran Colombia Av Natalia Jarrín S3-74 ☎02 236 1238. Mid-range comfort just south of the centre with TV, private bathrooms and a playground at the back (get in touch with your inner child). Back rooms are quieter. $22.50

CAYAMBE COCA RESERVE AND VOLCÁN CAYAMBE

Ecuador's second-largest Andean reserve ranges in altitude from 600m to 5790m at the top of Cayambe itself – the highest point in the world that straddles the equator. It's a tough climb, possibly the most difficult in the country, so is for advanced climbers only. It's a seven-hour trek from the refuge through constantly changing terrain and frequent snowstorms. Contact Alta Montaña in Quito (☎02 252 4422) to arrange a trek. Highlights of the surrounding reserve include more than 80 lakes and 900 species of birds, among them condors and toucans.

OTAVALO

If you love wandering around markets and picking up *artesano* bargains, then **OTAVALO** is your town. The famous **Saturday market** spreading across town from the Plaza de Ponchos (from 7am) is easily the best in Ecuador and possibly South America. There's a wide range of handicrafts, clothing, hammocks, weavings, carvings, jewellery, ceramics and oddities such as fake shrunken heads. The *Otavaleño* traders are friendly and greet you as "amigo"; behind the smiles, they're savvy salespeople. Take your time gauging the prices and then knock them down by a few dollars, but bear in mind that while this is part of the fun, the extra dollar means more to the locals than to you.

During the week the town is quieter but the market is open. Outside the market, the **Museo de Tejidos el Obraje** (Mon–Sat 9am–1pm & 3–5pm; $2) is worth a visit for its demonstrations of textile production. Otavalo's surroundings are also impressive – the town is nestled between the extinct volcanic peaks of Imbabura and Cotacachi on opposite ends of town. Some 4km out of town is the **Parque Cóndor** (Tues–Sun 9.30am–5pm; $2.50; ☎02 292 4429, ⓦparquecondor.org), which rehabilitates owls, eagles, falcons and condors. It makes a pleasant walk with views over Otavalo, though robberies have been reported and the route can be hard to find so consider a taxi ($4). If walking, start from the south end of town along Piedrahita and follow the signs past a eucalyptus grove and up a hill. Along the way is **El Lechero**, a tree revered by locals for its healing powers, named because of the milky liquid found in its leaves.

ARRIVAL AND INFORMATION

By bus Buses to Otavalo leave from Quito's Carcelén terminal several times each hour (2hr). There are also services from Ibarra (hourly; 40min). The bus station is on Atahualpa, at Neptali Ordoñez, a couple of blocks northeast of the central Plaza de Ponchos market – a short walk but take a taxi for $1 if you're laden with luggage or if you arrive at night.

Tourist office For information and maps, try the Cámara de Turismo office (Quiroga, at Modesto Jaramillo; Mon–Fri 8.30am–1pm & 2.30–5.30pm, Sat 9am–2pm, Sun 9am–noon; ☎ 06 292 7230).

GETTING AROUND

Otavalo is small enough to walk around, but a taxi across town costs just $1 and is recommended at night. Taxis to surrounding attractions like Peguche, Parque El Cóndor and Laguna San Pablo cost $3–4. A taxi to attractions further away, including Lagunas de Mojanda, costs $10/hr.

ACCOMMODATION

Otavalo has a lot of hotels for such a small town, most of which have low weekday occupation rates but fill up at weekends (book ahead for Fri & Sat). The area near the market can be noisy and the best hotels are in the south of the centre.

Hostal Los Andes Quiroga and Sucre ☎ 06 292 1057. One of the cheapest options in town, overlooking the market. Great view but the simple rooms can be noisy. $15

Chasqui Piedrahita 141 ☎ 06 292 1826. A ten-minute walk south of the Plaza del Poncho, this three-storey hostel has clean, rustically decorated rooms. Upstairs rooms have great views, but their water pressure can be a little low. Double $24

Hostal Doña Esther Montalvo 4-44 ☎ 06 292 0739, ⓦ otavalohotel.com. Owned by a Dutch family, this small colonial-style hotel has friendly service, a verdant courtyard and a great restaurant with Mediterranean specialities. $34.20

★**Flying Donkey** Abdón Calderón 510 ☎ 06 292 8122, ⓦ flyingdonkeyotavalo.com. Spacious, light dorm rooms and, the highlight of this hostel, a rooftop terrace with great views of the town and surrounding mountains. Wi-fi and

---

SPORTS AND ACTIVITIES AROUND OTAVALO

While most travellers come to Otavalo for a day or two, you could easily fill a week exploring the stunning mountains and valleys that surround it, and trying out adventure sports. A $50 new rail excursion to Salinas north of Ibarra is scheduled to begin working in 2015. The nearest attraction is the **Laguna de San Pablo**, fifteen minutes from town by bus from the terminal (take any bus heading to Araque). Hike around the lake, visit small indigenous communities or arrange watersports. It's very popular with locals at weekends.

Of the many indigenous communities near Otavalo, the best known is **Peguche**, a five-minute journey by bus (Coop Imbaburapac at the terminal does this route). The town is famed for its weavers and musicians, and for a 20m-high waterfall. Peguche, the waterfall and surrounding weaving communities can be visited on a tour ($30/person) with Runa Tupari (see below). Further afield are the three **Lagunas de Mojanda**, considered sacred by many locals. There are trails around the lakes and up to the peak of **Fuya Fuya** (4275m), which is good practice for climbing higher peaks. Another popular trip is the stunning **Laguna Cuicocha**, a 3km-wide extinct volcanic crater lake with steep forested islands in the middle. It sits at the foot of Cotacachi Volcano and can be reached by taxi from the leatherworking town of Cotacachi (a 30min bus ride from the Otavalo terminal). Tours to Mojanda and Cuicocha can be organized with tour operators in Otavalo for $25. Hiking or cycling tours cost $30–40.

The valleys and rivers around Otavalo offer great adventure-sports opportunities. **Canyoning** is possible in Peguche and in Taxopamba ($30–35). There is class III–IV **white-water rafting** in Río Chota, Río Mira and Río Intag ($30). The best **mountain-biking** tour descends into the Intag Valley to the west ($50). For those well acclimatized and fit, the mountains around Otavalo offer unforgettable climbing. **Imbabura** (4690m; $60) is the easiest climb, **Cotacachi** (4944m; $80) has technical climbing at the summit, and **Cayambe** (5789m; $190) is Ecuador's third-highest peak and takes a minimum of two days.

TOUR OPERATORS

Runa Tupari Plaza de Ponchos ☎ 06 292 2320, ⓦ runatupari.com.

Ecomontes Sucre, at Morales ☎ 06 292 6244, ⓦ ecomontestour.com.

6

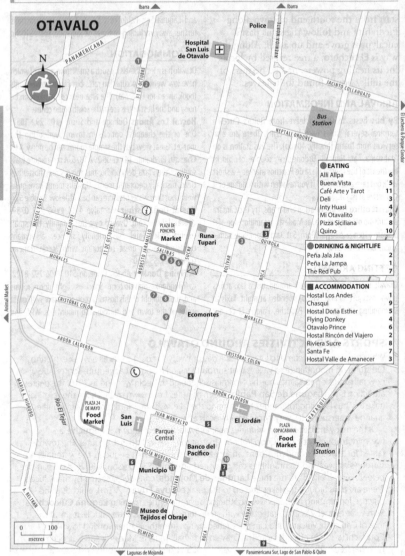

OTAVALO

EATING

Alli Allpa	6
Buena Vista	5
Café Arte y Tarot	11
Deli	3
Inty Huasi	4
Mi Otavalito	9
Pizza Siciliana	8
Quino	10

DRINKING & NIGHTLIFE

Peña Jala Jala	2
Peña La Jampa	1
The Red Pub	7

ACCOMMODATION

Hostal Los Andes	1
Chasqui	9
Hostal Doña Esther	5
Flying Donkey	4
Otavalo Prince	6
Hostal Rincón del Viajero	2
Riviera Sucre	8
Santa Fe	7
Hostal Valle de Amanecer	3

kitchen available. Offers 20 percent off on week nights if you reserve three weeks in advance. Dorms $8.50, doubles $24

Otavalo Prince Sucre, at Garcia Moreno ☎ 06 292 3200. Extravagant exterior but cosy interior with low ceilings. The low prices mean this place fills up fast. $23

Hostal Rincón del Viajero Roca 11–07 ☎ 06 292 1741. This is a hospitable option for budget travellers, with artwork on the walls, a TV lounge with fireplace, rooftop terrace with hammocks, games room and restaurant. Includes breakfast. $24

Riviera Sucre Roca, at Garcia Moreno ☎ 06 292 0241, ⓦ www.rivierasucre.com. Relaxing lounge area, beautiful garden and colourful, comfortable rooms. $26

Santa Fé Roca, at Garcia Moreno ☎ 06 292 3640, ⓦ hotelsantafeotavalo.com. The quiet location, excellent-quality rooms furnished in pine and eucalyptus, good restaurant and reasonable prices make this one of the best deals in town. Includes breakfast. $16

★ **Hostal Valle del Amanecer** Roca, at Quiroga ☎ 06 292 0990, ⓦ valledelamanecer.com. The most pleasant budget accommodation in town with rooms set around a cobbled, leafy courtyard. Outdoor fireplace and hammocks. $20

EATING

Alli Allpa Plaza de Ponchos, at Salinas. Endearing little café with great-value Ecuadorian meals and fresh lemonade. Three-course set lunch $4.

Buena Vista Plaza de Ponchos, at Salinas. From the balcony you can observe the market from afar and choose from a wide-ranging menu. The brownies are a speciality. $4–6.

Café Arte y Tarot Garcia Moreno, at Bolívar. A quirky, creative atmosphere and a range of tasty crêpes ($3–5). The most popular spot is the toilet seat at the upstairs table.

★ **Deli** Quiroga, at Bolívar. Little gem of a café a block from the market specializing in Tex-Mex and Italian (main dishes $4–8). Also crêpes, desserts and delicious hot chocolate with marshmallows. Mon–Thurs & Sun 9.30am–9pm, Fri & Sat 9.30am–11pm.

Inty Huasi Plaza de Ponchos, at Salinas. Locals head to this well laid-out, large restaurant to fill up on meat and seafood dishes priced around $5–7.

Mi Otavalito Sucre, at Morales. The best place in town to enjoy well-presented Ecuadorian dishes ($7.50–9) in an elegant but cosy setting. Live Andean music at weekends.

Pizza Siciliana Morales, at Sucre. Out of all the pizza places in town, this has the best reputation with a rustic atmosphere and roaring fire. Pizzas $7–12.

Quino Roca, at García Moreno. If you're craving seafood, try the *ceviche* and fresh mountain trout here. Juices, cocktails and mulled wines are also good. Mains $7–10.

DRINKING AND NIGHTLIFE

Peña Jala Jala 31 de Octubre, at Quito. Head north of the centre to catch live music and dance the night away to a mix of local and international tunes. Fri & Sat 7pm–2am.

Peña La Jampa 31 de Octubre near Panamericana. Three blocks north of the market, this is another great place to catch energetic live performances from traditional Andean bands. Fri & Sat 9pm–2am.

The Red Pub Morales 507, at Jaramillo. English-style pub with plenty of beer, burgers, rock music and live bands at weekends. Daily 4pm–late.

IBARRA

Forty minutes by bus northeast of Otavalo lies **IBARRA**, the largest town in the northern highlands, known as La Ciudad Blanca (white city). While Otavalo is famous for its unique culture, Ibarra deserves a visit for its much more attractive architecture, including beautiful squares, as well as for ice cream famous throughout Ecuador.

WHAT TO SEE AND DO

Parque La Merced is impressive, fronted by the nineteenth-century Basílica La Merced, but eclipsed in terms of beauty by **Parque Pedro Moncayo**, dominated by the Baroque-influenced **cathedral** adorned with a golden altar. The **Museo de la Sierra Norte** on Sucre and Oviedo (Mon–Sat 8.30am–5pm; $0.50) has an exhibition of archeology from prehistory to colonial times. Three kilometres south, in the Caranqui neighbourhood, the **Museo Arqueológicoa Atahualpa** (Wed–Sun 9am–noon & 3–5pm; $1) showcases Caranqui and Inca artefacts, near a site called Inka Huasi, where excavations revealed some fine imperial Inca stonework.

A popular excursion is to **Laguna Yahuarcocha**, which means Lake of Blood, a reference to its violent history (tens of thousands of dead Cara soldiers were dumped into the lake after an Incan victory in 1495). You can rent boats or just walk around and enjoy the beautiful setting. Buses run regularly at weekends from the obelisk on Sánchez and Cifuentes. A **train service** that used to run all the way to San Lorenzo now does a 15km excursion from Ibarra's train station to Salinas (Wed–Sun10.30am–4.30pm; $20; ☎06 295 0390, ⊛trenecuador.com).

ARRIVAL AND INFORMATION

By bus Aerotaxi and Expreso Turismo have regular services to and from Quito's Carcelén terminal (hourly; 2hr 30min) and Atacames (daily; 9hr); Trans Otavalo goes to and from Otavalo (hourly; 35min); Expreso Turismo and Flota Imbabura head to and from Tulcán for the Colombian border (hourly; 2hr 30min). Services depart from the terminal 1km out of town, so to/from the centre take a bus ($0.25) or a taxi ($1).

Tourist information García Moreno on Parque La Merced (Mon–Fri 8.30am–1pm & 2–5pm; ☎06 295 5711).

Internet Zonanet, Moncayo 5–74 ($1/hr).

ACCOMMODATION

While Ibarra beats Otavalo for beauty, Otavalo has better hotel options, so many travellers prefer a day-trip. Many of the more attractive places are haciendas well outside the centre.

Hostería Cananvalle Línea Ferrea Km167 ☎098 260 9132, ⊛hosteria-cananvalle.com. The easily accessible

6

hacienda on organic farmland is a 10min taxi ride just west of downtown. It has traditionally styled rooms, an outdoor whirlpool, and is a perfect base to explore Ibarra's environs, including hot springs and the Páramo del Ángel. Doubles $60, extra beds $15

Casa Aida La Esperanza ☎ 06 266 0221, ⓦ casaaida.com. Fabled, rustic hippie hangout just south of Ibarra (taxi $5), an excellent base to explore the much less touristy east of mount Imbabura. Breakfasts from 5am. Camping per person $10

Hotel Madrid Pedro Moncayo 7-41, at Olmedo ☎ 06 295 6177. Quiet, basic and inexpensive downtown hotel with decent rooms. $16

★ **Hotel Montecarlo** Rivadeneira 5-55, at Oviedo ☎ 06 295 8266, ⓦ hotelmontecarloibarra.ec. One of the few upmarket hotels in the centre of Ibarra. Well-appointed rooms with cable TV, a small pool and spa. $44

Hotel Nueva Estancia Garcia Moreno 7-58, at Parque La Merced ☎ 06 295 1444. Quiet, ideally located midtown hotel across from Basílica La Merced. It has spacious, carpeted rooms, cable TV, laundry service and a good restaurant. Breakfast included. Single $23, double $40

EATING AND DRINKING

There are plenty of cheap restaurants serving filling *almuerzos* and *meriendas* for $2.

Antojitos de mi Tierra Plaza de la Ibarreñidad. Traditional Ecuadorian dishes and tasty snacks such as *humitas* and *quimbolitos* ($1–3).

Café Arte Salinas 5-43, at Oviedo. A wide variety of international food – from burgers to tacos to filet mignon – in a vibrant setting, with live music at weekends. Mains $3–6. Mon–Sat 5pm till late.

La Hacienda Sucre, at Oviedo. Lively in the evening, this hacienda-themed restaurant has pizzas, sandwiches and large salads. Mains $6–12.

Donde El Argentino Plaza de la Ibarreñidad. Facing the square, this Argentine-owned place specializes in barbecued steaks, ideal for eating alfresco on sunny days. Mains $5–9.

★ **Heladería Rosalía Suárez** Oviedo, at Olmedo. The best place to try Ibarra's famous sorbet. Ice creams $0.50–3.

Suaya Café Parque San Augustín. Charming café in a nineteenth-century mansion, which does good breakfasts and sandwiches – try their *suaya* (chicken in basil sauce), or enjoy a carafe of mulled wine on the square in the evening.

PÁRAMO DEL ÁNGEL

Near the border with Colombia, giant furry flower-like plants (actually sub-shrubs) called *Frailejónes* create an alien landscape, the **Páramo del Ángel** (Angel Steppe), amid soaring peaks above 4000m and lagoons in the mist. When the sun breaks through the clouds, hikers can see all the way to Imbabura and Cayambe. Polylepis trees, with twisted branches and soft brown bark that peels away like paper, create fairy-tale forests in ravines sheltered from the wind.

These unique areas are protected by the 15,700-hectare **Reserva Ecológica El Ángel**, a cold, high-altitude area just south of the Colombian border.

ARRIVAL AND INFORMATION

By bus Access via El Angel 14 km away costs $15 for a camioneta. Day-trips are possible from Otavalo or Ibarra, with several buses daily from each city (2hr 30min) but most easily done on a tour.

ACCOMMODATION

Polylepis Lodge ☎ 06 263 1819, ⓦ polylepislodgeec .com. The only place to stay overnight is this magnificent, but pricey, lodge, a group of thatched-roof, rustic stone cabins, including spa usage. Dinners are $24. $168

CROSSING INTO COLOMBIA

Seven kilometres east of the town of **Tulcán**, which is 2–3hr by bus from Otavalo and Ibarra, the **Rumichaca Bridge** forms the entry into **Colombia**, open daily 24hr. To cross, obtain an **exit stamp** from Ecuadorian customs, in the *Migración* building, and an **entry stamp** from the Colombians on the other side of the bridge. The entry stamp for Colombia is valid for 90 days (arriving from Colombia, the Ecuadorians will also give you up to 90 days and a tourist card, which you retain until you leave the country). **Buses to the border** leave from Parque Isidro Ayora (15min; $0.80), while a taxi costs about $4. From the border, **Ipiales** is the nearest town with decent hotels. It is 3km away and you can take a taxi shuttle ($1), bus ($0.50) or taxi (around $2). Official **moneychangers** abound on the border, but check the calculations before handing money over. You should get a slightly better rate in Tulcán than at the border, so try the official moneychangers on Plaza de la Independencia, where there are also ATMs.

The Central Highlands

South of Quito lies Ecuador's most dramatic Andean scenery, where the Panamericana winds between two parallel mountain chains. Ecuador's highest peaks are here so it's unsurprising that nineteenth-century German explorer Alexander von Humboldt named the region "the Avenue of the Volcanoes". On the eastern side, the most popular peak to visit (and climb if you're fit enough) is **Cotopaxi** (5897m), which dominates the surrounding valley. To the southwest lies the turquoise luminescence of **Lake Quilotoa**, one of Ecuador's most stunning natural sights. The region's principal towns are **Latacunga**, **Ambato** and **Riobamba**, all of which are at altitudes similar to Quito and provide convenient bases. The spa town of **Baños**, with its ideal climate, beautiful setting, thermal baths and adventure sports, is a highlight. Nearby **Volcán Tungurahua** has been erupting regularly for the past decade and is an attraction in itself. South of Riobamba, the relaunched **Nariz del Diablo train ride** remains popular.

PARQUE NACIONAL COTOPAXI

About 60km south of Quito, **Volcán**

Cotopaxi (5897m) is everybody's idea of a picture-perfect volcano, its symmetrical cone-shaped peak dominating the landscape. But Cotopaxi's beauty belies its destructive heritage – it has erupted on ten occasions since 1742, destroying Latacunga several times. Luckily for local inhabitants, it has been quiet since 1904, although it's still officially active, with plumes of smoke visible to climbers reaching the crater. Thanks to its proximity to Quito, **Parque Nacional Cotopaxi** (daily 8am–5pm) is also Ecuador's most-visited park. The volcano offers a spectacular climb (see box below), but for a more relaxed experience, the surrounding *páramo* (Andean grasslands) offers great opportunities for trekking and cycling. Inhabitants of the park include deer, rabbits, foxes, pumas and ninety species of birds, among them the endangered Andean condor. Several ancient haciendas dot the countryside and San Agustín de Callo, a former monastery, has small but well-preserved Inca remains, and a chapel open to visitors ($4).

INFORMATION AND TOURS

Most people take a guided tour from Quito, although they are possible from other locations. A one-day hiking and cycling tour costs $50, taking in the museum, Limpiopungo Lake and going up to the edge of the ice. A two-day climbing tour costs from $170 and the better three-day tour about $200–250. In Quito, try Gulliver (see p.582). All the accommodation

---

CLIMBING COTOPAXI

Climbing Cotopaxi can be done with little technical mountaineering experience. However, it's not a challenge to be taken lightly. You must be in good physical shape, acclimatized and travel with a qualified guide, preferably certified by ASEGUIM (Asociación Ecuatoriana de Guías de Montaña) and arranged through a tour operator (see p.582).

The importance of **acclimatization** cannot be stressed enough. If you're pushed for time and feeling bold, it's tempting to get up in the morning and think: "let's climb a volcano today". Unscrupulous guides won't hesitate in taking your money and going to the high-altitude refuge. But above 3000m you need to ascend slowly over a few days. A couple of days in Quito (2800m) is not enough to tackle Cotopaxi (5897m). Lake Quilotoa (3800m) is good preparation and a three-day, rather than two-day, climbing tour of Cotopaxi is recommended.

The best preparation is to climb lower peaks first. The most popular option is Rumiñahui (4712m), mainly a steep hike. You can also try Corazón (4788m) or the more challenging Illiniza Norte (5126m).

When **climbing Cotopaxi** itself, beginning from the José Rivas refuge at 4800m, it's six to eight strenuous hours to the top, negotiating snow, ice and several crevices. The views of Ecuador's other major peaks are breathtaking, as is the view down into the steaming crater. The descent takes three to four hours. December to April is usually the best time to climb Cotopaxi, when the snow is hardest, but it can be climbed year-round.

6

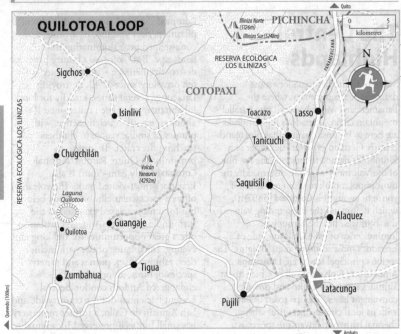

options listed below can arrange tours. A good tour operator in Latacunga is Volcan Route (see opposite).

ACCOMMODATION

Cuello de Luna El Chasqui, Panamerican Highway South Km44 ☎099 970 0300, ⓦcuellodeluna.com. Lovely hacienda setting, just 6km from the park entrance, this place offers simple dorms or private rooms with fireplaces. Dorms $20, doubles $56

Hacienda La Ciénega ☎03 271 9052, ⓦhaciendalacienega.com. A 400-year-old hacienda, 2km from Lasso, with period furnishings and a good restaurant. Breakfast included. $100

Secret Garden Cotopaxi ☎099 357 2714, ⓦsecretgardencotopaxi.com. An ecolodge set in the foothills of Pasochoa, near the village of Pedregal, overlooking the national park. The price includes three meals, snacks, drinks and use of mountain bikes. Many rooms have their own fireplace to keep warm. Dorms $40, doubles $97

SAQUISILÍ

SAQUISILÍ holds a popular Thursday market, a less known but more authentic indigenous market than Otavalo. On market day, eight plazas in the centre flood with tradespeople selling foodstuffs, herbal remedies, household goods and live animals. It's also a social gathering for the locals, many of whom arrive in their best traditional dress and felt hats. For tourists, the main attraction is the shopping. There are also plenty of tasty *tortillas de maíz* to snack on.

Saquisilí is a few kilometres off the Panamericana, two hours south of Quito. Ask the bus driver to drop you at the junction and take another bus – or catch a regular bus from Latacunga (30min).

LATACUNGA

Some 30km south of Cotopaxi National Park, **LATACUNGA** doesn't look inviting from the highway, but venture towards the centre of town with quaint cobbled streets and friendly people. There's not a huge amount to do, but the town serves as the best base to explore **Quilotoa** and **Cotopaxi**, with good local tour operators (see opposite) and decent accommodation.

WHAT TO SEE AND DO

The town has been rebuilt in colonial style after being destroyed several times by Cotopaxi's eruptions. The main square

– **Parque Vicente León** – forms the town's focal point, flanked by the cathedral and town hall. A few blocks to the west, next to the river Cutuchi, is **Museo de la Casa de la Cultura** (Vela, at Salcedo; Tues–Fri 8am–6pm; $0.50), which has a small ethnography and art museum. In late September and again in early November (usually the Saturday before November 11) Latacunga parties hard for **La Fiesta de la Mama Negra**, which features a parade of colourful costumed characters and culminates in the arrival of the Mama Negra, a man dressed up as a black woman in honour of the liberation of African slaves in the nineteenth century. The November celebration is secular and more raucous.

ARRIVAL AND INFORMATION

By bus Latacunga's bus station is on the Panamericana, five blocks west of town. If Latacunga is not the final destination of your bus, you'll be dropped off 400m further west (take a taxi to the centre for $1, or walk over the bridge). There are hourly services from the bus station to Quito's Quitumbe terminal (1hr 30min) and Ambato (1hr). For the surrounding indigenous villages there are buses to Saquisilí (hourly; 20min). To get to Quilotoa, there is only one direct bus per day (around noon). If you miss it, take a bus to Zumbahua and take a taxi from there.
Tourist information Captur (Orellana, at Guayaquil; ☎ 03 281 4968).

ACCOMMODATION

Hotel Central Orellana, at Salcedo ☎ 03 280 2912. Along with *Hotel Cotopaxi* next door, this is the best-located budget option in Latacunga. Rooms have private bathroom and cable TV, and some have a great view of the main square. $20
Rosim Quito 16-49 ☎ 03 280 2172, ⓦ hotelrosim.com. A quieter option than the *hostals* on the main square, with well-equipped rooms and high ceilings. Good value. $26
Hostal Tiana Vivero, at Ordoñez ☎ 03 281 0147, ⓦ hostaltiana.com. This friendly backpacker favourite has a range of colourful rooms and its own tour operator. Breakfast included. Dorms $9.50, doubles $22
Cabañas los Volcanes Ciudadela Estrella Pamba in Lasso, 20km north of Latacunga ☎ 03 271 9524. This family-run budget option is a great setting for a quiet base camp to explore Cotopaxi and the Illinizas, plus it has wi-fi. $28

EATING

Chifa Miraflores Salcedo, at 2 de Mayo. The best Chinese restaurant in town, with a wide range of soup, rice, noodles and sweet and sour for $3–5.

El Gringo y La Gorda Padre Salcedo, at Quito. Charming colonial setting in the middle of Latacunga, with Ecuadorian and Lousiana cuisine. $6–7.
La Mama Negra Ordoñez, at Rumiñahui. The best place to try the local speciality *chugchucara* (fried pork with fried potatoes, plantains and corn). $6–7.
Pizzería Buon Giorno Orellana, at Maldonado. A friendly place to escape the pork and rice highland staples, with great lasagne and large pizzas ($7) to share.

LAKE QUILOTOA AND THE QUILOTOA LOOP

The luminous turquoise water of volcanic crater lake **Laguna Quilotoa** is one of Ecuador's most awe-inspiring sights. The lake was formed 800 years ago by a massive eruption and subsequent collapse of the volcano. The caldera is 3.2km wide and the lake 250m deep. You can visit from Latacunga on a day-trip but it's better to at least stay overnight or spend a couple of days hiking parts of the **Quilotoa Loop**.

WHAT TO SEE AND DO

The first town after leaving Latacunga is **Tigua** (3500m), famous for indigenous arts and handicrafts. Another 30km further is **Zumbahua**, a small village that gets boisterous at the weekend with its busy Saturday market and accompanying merriment. A further 14km north is the sleepy village of **Quilotoa** (3800m), perched above the lake. A great base for exploring, it costs $2 to enter the village,

TOURS TO QUILOTOA

If you're travelling alone or want to see Quilotoa without the inconvenience of relying on public transport, take a **guided tour** from Latacunga. A one-day tour to the lake costs $40, or three days to do the entire loop costs $130. These operators also offer hiking and climbing tours to Cotopaxi.

TOUR OPERATORS

Tierra Zero Padre Salcedo, at Quito ☎ 099 953 7846, ⓦ tierrazerotours.com.
Tovar Expeditions Guayaquil 5-38, at Quito ☎ 03 281 1333, ⓦ tovarexpeditions.com.
Volcan Route Quevedo, at Guayaquil ☎ 03 281 2452, ⓦ volcanroute.com.

6

BACK ON TRACK

Ecuador's **rail network** took nearly forty years of toil before completion in 1908, when President Eloy Alfaro rode triumphantly from Guayaquil to Quito. But as the twentieth century rolled on, Ecuador's train service rolled backwards; by the 1990s one of the few lines still running was the short section along the famous Nariz del Diablo (Devil's Nose) south of Riobamba (see p.601).

Current President Rafael Correa, who idolizes Alfaro, announced ambitious plans to revitalize the entire rail network. The $240 million effort has resulted in a luxury service linking Durán (across from Guayaquil) to Latacunga and bus entry into Quito in the form of a $1000, four-day "rail cruise".

Much cheaper, popular **tourist trips** are nonetheless available along short stretches of restored railway. Note that these are round-trip tours rather than point-to-point transport options. For information visit ⊛trenecuador.com. Nearest to Cotopaxi is the **Quito–El Boliche–Quito (via Machachi)** trip (Thurs–Sun; 4hr; $39).

---

including unlimited access to the lake (8am–8pm). You can hike down into the crater to the waterside in forty minutes (it's an hour to come back up). The water's high sulphurous content makes it unsuitable for swimming, and it's quite cold, but there are canoes for rent. For a longer walk to appreciate the lake from all angles, allow four hours to walk around the perimeter. The most popular hike on the Quilotoa Loop is the dramatic route from Quilotoa to Chugchilán. It takes about five hours, but don't attempt it alone and do not set off after 1pm.

GETTING AROUND

The biggest problem in this region is getting around because public transportation is infrequent and often full. During the rainy season, bus routes are sometimes cancelled and roads impassable. It is strongly advised that you don't attempt lonely parts of the loop alone because of its remoteness.

By bus The Latacunga–Zumbuhua–Quilotoa–Chugchilán bus leaves Latacunga daily at noon. It is 2hr to Quilotoa and a further 1hr 30min to Chugchilán. If you miss the bus from Latacunga, get the first bus to Zumbahua, and hire a taxi to Quilotoa (about $5/person). Coming back, the Chugchilán–Quilotoa–Zumbuhua–Latacunga bus leaves Chugchilán at 4am. There are buses later in the morning on Sundays only, otherwise take a taxi to Zumbuhua ($35 from Chugchilán, $10 from Quilotoa), where there are more frequent buses back to Latacunga (hourly; 2hr).

ACCOMMODATION

The Quilotoa Loop has a few accommodation options, including in Quilotoa proper.

Hostal Cabañas Quilotoa ☎099 212 5962. The best budget option in Quilotoa is owned by local artist Humberto Latacunga. It has comfortable rooms, hot showers and woodburners (it gets very cold at night). $16

Hostal Cloud Forest ☎03 281 4808. A backpacker favourite in Chugchilán, with simple rooms and a common room with fireplace to warm up. $24

★ **Llullu Llama** ☎099 258 0562, ⊛llullullama.com. In the village of Isinliví, and a tongue-twister to say even for Ecuadorians, Llullu Llama boasts a smart, ultra-cosy converted farmhouse. Includes breakfast and dinner. Dorms $18, doubles $46

Mama Hilda ☎03 281 4814, ⊛mamahilda.com. A good-value option in Chugchilán, with cosy rooms. $34

Princesa Toa A simple, budget option in the village of Quilotoa, with warm, comfortable rooms just across from the best lake-viewing area. $16

AMBATO

Some 47km south of Latacunga, most tourists bypass **AMBATO** en route to Baños or Riobamba. A massive earthquake destroyed much of the city in 1949, but parts of the "city of fruit and flowers", particularly around the main square, are attractive enough for a brief visit.

WHAT TO SEE AND DO

Of most interest in the **Parque Juan Montalvo** is the **Casa de Montalvo** (Mon–Fri 9am–6pm, Sat 9am–2pm; $1), the former residence of Juan Montalvo, Ambato's most famous literary son. A liberal, he was forced into exile by conservative president Gabriel García Moreno in 1869. The house has a collection of photos, manuscripts, clothing and a life-size portrait. Unnervingly, Montalvo's body is on display in the mausoleum. Across the square is the city's modern **cathedral**, rebuilt after the devastating 1949 earthquake, one Ecuador's leading Art Deco constructions. The interior has huge bronze statues and fabulous acoustics during Mass. Escape the downtown bustle by visiting the riverside gardens of **La Quinta de Juan León Mera** (Av Los Capulíes; Wed–Sun 9.30am–5.30pm; $1), just 2km from the centre (30min walk or $1 taxi ride), the former farm of another important Ambato author.

ARRIVAL AND INFORMATION

By bus Ambato's bus station is 2km north of the centre and an important hub. There are regular services to and from Quito, Guayaquil, Latacunga, Riobamba, Puyo, Cuenca and Loja. A taxi to the centre costs $1.50 or you can catch a local bus. Buses to Baños don't leave from the bus station: take a taxi ($1.50) to Mercado Mayorista where buses to Baños pass several times per hour (45min).
Tourist information The tourist office on Guayaquil, at Rocafuerte (Mon–Fri 8am–5pm; ☎03 282 1800), has maps and brochures.

ACCOMMODATION

Accommodation in Ambato tends to cater for the business community, so mid-range hotels are more expensive, while cheaper options tend to be seedy. You're better off heading to Baños or Riobamba.
Hotel Ambato Guayaquil, at Rocafuerte ☎03 242 1791, ⓦhotelambato.com. The best in town, with spectacular views of the river and a gourmet restaurant. Breakfast included. $68
La Florida Av Miraflores in front of Inmaculada school ☎03 242 2007. Accessibly priced for well-appointed, carpeted rooms with cable TV. $34

EATING AND DRINKING

Café la Catedral Bolívar. This friendly little café, in a small mall opposite the cathedral entrance, is ideal for good-value lunches ($2.50–4).
La Fornace Av Cevallos 17–28. Delicious pizza baked in a massive brick oven as well as great pasta dishes ($3–6).
Marcelos Kfetería Castillo, at Rocafuerte ☎03 282 8208. Renowned locally as one of the best places to eat in town. Choose from a wide range of meats, snacks and delicious ice cream. $6–10.
Parrilladas El Gaucho Bolívar, at Quito. The best spot to pig out on huge portions of steak and barbecued meats ($7–10).

SALASACA

On the road between Ambato and Baños, it's worth stopping briefly at **SALASACA**, famous for its tapestries. The indigenous people who live here look noticeably different, dressed in black ponchos and white hats. They originate from Bolivia, forced here by the Incas in the fifteenth century. There is a craft market every Sunday; on other days, it's best to browse the tapestry stores. About 6km from Salasaca is **Pelileo**, with surely more cut-price jeans per square metre than anywhere else in South America. To visit Pelileo and Salasaca, hop off the bus from Ambato to Baños. There are several buses per hour.

BAÑOS, TUNGURAHUA

In the shadow of lava- and ash-spewing **Volcán Tungurahua** (see p.599), **BAÑOS DE AGUA SANTA** has grown from a sleepy spa town into Ecuador's hub of adventure tourism. With an ideally warm climate, a stunning location in a verdant valley surrounded by steep hills, an excellent choice of hotels and restaurants, great walking and adventure sports, plus, of course, the thermal baths that give the town its name, Baños is ideally located between the Avenue of the Volcanoes and Amazonia. Tungurahua has been erupting regularly since 2000. Luckily, the crater is on the opposite side to the town, and Baños has added volcano-watching to its list of activities.

WHAT TO SEE AND DO

In town, don't miss the **Basílica de Nuestra Señora de Agua Santa** on the main Ambato street. This massive church is dedicated to the Virgin Mary, credited with several miracles including saving the town from Tungurahua's eruption in 1773. The facade is attractive when lit up at night, dominating the town's skyline. Inside are ten huge, amusing naive paintings depicting the Virgin saving the town and its citizens from various calamities, while upstairs a small **museum** (daily 8am–4pm; $0.50) houses a collection of the Virgin's processional clothes, religious art and a bizarre collection of stuffed animals.

Piscinas de la Virgen

The most popular baths are the **Piscinas de la Virgen** (daily 5am–4pm & 6–10pm; $2

6

BAÑOS

Puyo

Rio Pastaza

AVENIDA AMAZONAS

Bus Terminal

CALLE EUGENIO ESPEJO

CARRERA ORIENTE

CALLE AMBATO

CALLE VICENTE ROCAFUERTE

Parque Central

Market

Basilica

Parque de la Basilica

CALLE LUIS A. MARTÍNEZ

CALLE JUAN MONTALVO

CALLE VELASCO IBARRA

Bellavista

Piscinas de la Virgen

CARRERA ELOY ALFARO

AVENIDA ORIENTE

CALLE 16 DE DICIEMBRE

PABLO ARTURO SUAREZ

Ambato & San Martin Zoo

Piscinas El Salado

PLAZA 5 DE JUNIO

0   100
metres

■ **ACCOMMODATION**
Hostal Casa Real	7
Hostal Edén	5
Hospedaje Santa Cruz	3
Hostería Isla de Baños	9
Hotel Mariane	6
Plantas y Blanco	2
Posada del Arte	8
Hostal Rosita	4
Transilvania	1

● **EATING**
La Abuela Café	5
Café Good	10
Casa Hood	6
El Chozón de la Molienda	12
El Jardín	7
Pancho Villa	9
Quilombo Steak House	11
Swiss Bistro	8

● **DRINKING**
Jack Rock	4
Leprechaun Bar	3
Peña Ananitay	1
Volcan Peña	2

daytime, $3 at night) at the foot of a small waterfall to the eastern end of Avenida Martínez. The cloudy yellow waters are high in minerals. There are three pools – freezing cold, warm and hot (45°C: just a little too hot to linger for more than a few minutes). The baths get very busy so it's best to go either early morning or early evening to avoid the crowds.

Piscinas El Salado
About 2km out of town, **Piscinas El Salado** (daily 5am–5pm; $3) are the more attractive, modern public baths, with five pools ranging from 16 to 42°C and the water visibly bubbling up from underground. They're a twenty-minute walk from town, or take a taxi for $1.50.

Around Baños
The best way to take in the town's stunning setting is to walk to **Bellavista**,

high above the town. It's a steep forty-minute climb up a rocky, muddy path, rewarded with spectacular panoramic views over Baños and the Pastaza valley leading down to the Oriente. There are a couple of cafés at the top selling light lunches and drinks. You can continue on the path uphill for a further hour to the hamlet of **Runtún** at 2600m, then loop around to the other side of Baños, passing the statue of La Virgen del Agua Santa and back to town. The entire walk takes about four hours, or you can **hire horses** ($12/2hr, $22/ 4hr, including guide). Uphill at Runtún, small meets stunning in the form of the Casa del Árbol (daily 9am–5pm; $2), or tree house, where an enterprising local has built a small tree house at a spectacular scenic overlook. You can watch eruptions from there while enjoying (if you're unafraid of heights) a spectacular swing over a steep slope. On the western edge of town is the **San Martín Zoo** (daily 8am–5pm; $2.50), originally founded by Dominican monks. Its denizens include condors in a nice ravine aviary, spectacled bears and a jaguar. There is a small aquarium opposite.

When Tungurahua blows its lid, it becomes a star attraction. **Las Antenas** up the mountain just north of Baños has spectacular night viewing during eruptive activity. Tour operators offer $5 viewing tours in open chiva buses.

ARRIVAL AND INFORMATION

By bus Baños's bus terminal is a few blocks north of the main square surrounded by stalls selling *jugo de caña* (sugar-cane juice). Central Baños is so compact that you can walk everywhere, and a taxi across town costs just $1.
Destinations There are services to Puyo (hourly; 2hr), Riobamba (hourly; 2hr 30min) and Ambato (hourly; 1hr). For most other destinations, including Quito (several daily; 4hr) and Guayaquil (several daily; 6–7hr), there are hourly services by changing at Ambato. The direct road to Riobamba is often closed due to Tungurahua's eruptions.
Tourist information Purchase guidebooks and pick up free maps at the municipal tourist office on Halflants near Rocafuerte (Mon–Fri 8am–5pm; ☎03 274 1660, ⊚banos-ecuador.com) on the east side of Parque Central.

ACCOMMODATION

Hostal Casa Real Montalvo, at Pasaje Ibarra ☎03 274 0215, ⊚banios.com/casareal. This is a good-value mid-range option close to the waterfall. Rooms are simple but brightened up by murals of wildlife. Breakfast included. **$16**
Hostal Edén 12 de Noviembre ☎03 274 1046. Among the cheapest options, this hostel has basic rooms with cable TV set on a small garden courtyard. There's a cheap restaurant next door. **$14**
Hospedaje Santa Cruz 16 de Diciembre ☎03 274 3527. A funky little place with simple but colourfully decorated rooms. **$19**
Hostería Isla de Baños Halflants, at Montalvo ☎03 274 0609, ⊚isladebanios.com. An excellent-value mid-range option with comfortable rooms, balconies, a leafy garden and spa ($10/person). **$52**
Hotel Mariane Montalvo, at Halflants ☎03 274 1947, ⊚hotelmariane.com. Large colourful rooms with balconies in a quiet, leafy courtyard setting offer one of the best-value mid-range deals in town. **$25**
★**Hostal Plantas y Blanco** Martínez, at 12 de Diciembre ☎03 274 0044. This backpacker favourite is the ideal place to swap stories with kindred spirits. Relax on the rooftop terrace, make your own meals in the kitchen, and soak in the Turkish baths. There's also free internet. Rooms are small but adequate. Dorms **$7**, doubles **$24**
Posada del Arte Pasaje Ibarra ☎03 274 0083, ⊚posadadelarte.com. As its name suggests, this comfortable place offers a feast of South American art. The invitingly colourful rooms all have fireplaces with chimneys. The good restaurant has craft beers and is worth a visit even if you don't stay. **$64**

THE ROAD FROM BAÑOS TO PUYO

One of Ecuador's most beautiful routes, the road from Baños to Puyo, drops nearly 1000m following the Río Pastaza down from lush Andean foothills, through cloudforest to the edges of the tropical jungle. It's best admired from the saddle of a bike, which can be rented from any agency in Baños for $8/day, including helmet, map and repair kit. A guided tour costs $40. Leaving Baños, you cross the Agoyan hydroelectric project and it's about forty minutes until the impressive **Manto de La Novia** (Bride's Veil) waterfall. You can take the cable car ($2) 500m across the river gorge for a closer look. The second waterfall in the same location was caused by a landslide here in 2010. A 25-minute ride then brings you to the village of Río Verde, where you can lock your bike and hike 15 minutes downhill to see the even more spectacular **Pailón del Diablo** (Devil's Cauldron) waterfall. View it from a rickety suspension bridge or pay $1.50 to get a closer look from the panoramic balcony. There is also a path cut into the rock so you can go inside the cave behind the waterfall. Cycling half an hour uphill from Río Verde, you reach **Machay**. From here, hike a 2.5km trail into the cloudforest past eight waterfalls, the most beautiful of which is Manantial del Dorado. From Machay, it's downhill to **Río Negro** where the surroundings begin to feel tropical with bromeliads, giant tree ferns and colourful orchids. The final highlight is the spectacular view of the Pastaza as it broadens out into Amazonia. Start early if you want to cover the entire 61km but bear in mind the route is far more scenic than the end destination of **Puyo**. Most people hop on a bus back to Baños from Río Verde or Río Negro or Mera if you ride down into the Oriente proper. Note that in February 2010 two locals were killed by a landslide in Río Verde, so exercise caution visiting during the rainy season.

6

ACTIVITIES AND TOURS

Adventure sports are popular in the Pastaza valley between Baños and Puyo. **Rafting** is particularly good. A half-day on the class III part of the Río Pastaza costs $30 including transport, equipment, licensed guide and lunch. A half-day on the faster class IV part of the river costs $45. Other adrenaline-filled activities include **bridge jumping** (rather like bungee except you swing like a pendulum) off the 100m Puente San Francisco for $20, as well as zipping across the valley on **canopy lines** ($10–15). You can also rent noisy *Cuadrones* (quad bikes; $8 /hr; $20/3hr). Canyoning trips cost $30, taking in four waterfalls. You can book tours to many jungle destinations including Coca and Lago Agrio, but these generally go through Quito so it's better booking there (see p.582). For a more accessible jungle experience, there are good trips via Puyo.

TOUR OPERATORS

Córdova Tours Maldonado, at Espejo ☎ 03 274 0923, ⊕ cordovatours.banios.com.

Expediciones Pailontravel 12 de Diciembre, at Montalvo ☎ 03 274 0899.

Geotours Ambato, at Thomas Halflants ☎ 03 274 1344, ⊕ geotoursbanios.com. In the business for nearly 20 years and highly recommended.

Rainforestur Ambato, at Maldonado ☎ 098 446 9884, ⊕ rainforestur.com. Jungle and rafting tour specialist.

Wonderful Ecuador Maldonado, at Oriente ☎ 03 274 1580. Plenty of adventure tour options including canyoning.

MASSAGE

Baños has many skilled professionals and you can get all types of massage treatments here. Most charge around $20 for an hour's massage plus $15 for a facial.

Chakra Alfaro, at Luis Martínez ☎ 03 274 2027.

Stay in Touch Montalvo ☎ 03 274 0973.

Hostal Rosita 16 de Diciembre, at Martínez ☎ 03 274 0396. One of the best-value budget options in town, with free internet. There are two larger apartments for longer stays. $15

Transilvania 16 de Diciembre, at Oriente ☎ 03 274 2281, ⊕ hostal-transilvania.com. If you can get past the rather bizarre name, you'll find this Israeli-owned *hostal* a great deal, with bright, simple rooms and a café where big breakfasts are served on petrified wooden tables. There's also a pool table and a Middle Eastern menu. It's popular and fills up fast. Breakfast included. $17

EATING

Baños offers some of the best international cuisine outside Quito. Most of the finest restaurants are away from the main street. The town is also famous for dozens of stalls selling *membrillo* (a gelatinous red block made with guayaba) and *milcocha*, chewy sugar-cane bars that you can watch being made, swung over petrified wooden pegs. Outside the market, there's also the memorable sight of *cuy* (guinea pig) being roasted on a spit.

La Abuela Café Ambato, at 16 de Diciembre ☎ 099 965 4365. Many of the restaurants on the main street are uninspiring but this is one of the best options, with a wide-ranging menu and a balcony to watch the world go by. Mains $6.

Café Good 16 de Diciembre ☎ 03 274 0592. Specializes in vegetarian and Asian food. The Indian curry is good. Mains $3–7.

★**Casa Hood** Martínez, at Alfaro ☎ 03 274 2668. This is a great place for a meal or a drink, with a vibrant atmosphere and a wide-ranging menu of international food including Mexican, Middle Eastern and Asian dishes, plus smoothies and hot drinks. Mains $4–5. Closed Tues.

El Chozón de la Molienda Montalvo, at Pasaje Ibarra ☎ 03 274 1816. Enjoy excellent barbecued dishes such as *lomo volcánico* (steak in ginger sauce) served in a thatched hut set in a large garden. Mains $5–8. Evenings only.

El Jardín 16 de Diciembre, at Ambato ☎ 03 274 1686. A popular place to eat breakfast or afternoon snacks alfresco in the leafy garden, with a wide selection of dishes and an economical set menu. Mains $6–9.

Pancho Villa Martínez, at 16 de Diciembre ☎ 03 274 2138. Run by a friendly local couple, this is the best Mexican in town with great *enchiladas*, *fajitas*, *tacos* and *burritos*. Mains $5–8.

Quilombo Steak House Montalvo, at 12 de Noviembre ☎ 098 553 2144. A quirky, humorous place set in a wooden cabin decked out with eclectic decor, from hammocks to horseshoes. The menu comes on cubes in little bags and the barbecued steaks and chicken dishes ($6–8) are cooked to perfection. Wed–Sun.

★**Swiss Bistro** Martínez, at Alfaro ☎ 03 274 2262. One of the best places in Ecuador for a sumptuous fondue. The cow skins on the walls and even cow-patterned lampshades place you in the heart of the Swiss Alps. The cheese and meat fondues ($6–8) are fabulous, rounded off by stewed pears in red wine for dessert.

NIGHTLIFE

Nightlife in Baños is rather sleepy during the week, but it can get very busy at weekends, particularly on Saturday night. Most of the liveliest places are situated on the stretch of Alfaro north of Ambato.

Jack Rock Alfaro. Start the evening off with some rock classics at this bar, which is decked out with music memorabilia.

Leprechaun Bar Alfaro. A popular spot with backpackers, it has a dancefloor that gets busy at weekends and a roaring bonfire out back.

Peña Ananitay 16 de Diciembre, at Espejo. The best place in town to catch some traditional folk music.

Volcan Peña Alfaro. Stands out on Ambato for offering more of an authentic flavour with mainly Latin music. It's popular with locals.

VOLCÁN TUNGURAHUA

Tungurahua, which means "throat of fire", has a troubled relationship with Baños. The volcano supplies the **hot springs** that make the town famous, but eruptions have caused regular alerts in recent years. The volcano awoke from years of dormancy in October 1999 with a spectacular eruption that covered Baños in ash. However, because the crater is on the opposite side, the town escaped further damage. There have been subsequent eruptions in August 2006 and at regular intervals in 2008, 2009 and in May 2010, when a 10km-high ash cloud reached as far as Guayaquil, over 200km away. The volcano remains highly active at the time of writing.

Bañenos have been living in Tungurahua's shadow for centuries, and now it's constantly monitored. Check the national press, Instituto Geofísico's Spanish website (⊚igepn.edu.ec) or the Smithsonian Institution's English site (⊚volcano.si.edu). Only in extreme cases will authorities – and then with good reason – warn against visiting Baños.

RIOBAMBA

Near the centre of Ecuador, **RIOBAMBA**, almost in the shadow of giant **Volcán Chimborazo**, Ecuador's highest mountain, is the best base from which to climb it. Riobamba is also one of Ecuador's coldest cities, and night temperatures can drop near freezing in cold snaps. Though restoration has spruced up much of the city's nineteenth-century architecture, it offers fewer facilities geared towards foreign travellers and has a strong indigenous flavour, making it feel more authentic than Baños.

WHAT TO SEE AND DO

The best sightseeing is centred around **Parque Maldonado**. The facade of the **Catedral** is all that remains of the original building after a 1797 earthquake and was painstakingly moved and reconstructed when the town was rebuilt at a new location (the old spot is nearby Cajabamba). Inside the Monasterio de las Conceptas, the **Museo de Arte Religioso** has a large collection of religious art (entrance on Argentinos; Tues–Sat 9am–12.30pm & 3–6.30pm; $3). On Saturdays, Riobamba has one of the

largest **markets** in the region, spreading out northeast of Parque de la Concepción.

Twenty kilometres southwest on the Panamericana, **Colta** on the eponymous lagoon features the charming Balbanera church, Ecuador's oldest, dating back to 1534. On clear days, the walk along the south shore of the lagoon offers beautiful views of Chimborazo. There's a government-run **train tour** to Colta (daily noon–4pm; 4hr; $15), and a half-day "Ice Train" excursion to Urbina, the highest spot on the railway (daily 8am–11.40am; $12 half-day, $15 full day from Ambato).

ARRIVAL AND DEPARTURE

By bus Riobamba's main bus terminal is 2km northwest of the centre. From the Oriente you arrive at the Terminal Oriental (Espejo, at Luz Elisa Borja); take a regular bus ($0.25) to the centrally located train station. A taxi into town from the terminal costs $1.

Destinations Ambato (hourly; 1hr); Baños (hourly via Ambato; 2hr); Cuenca (hourly; 5hr); Guayaquil (hourly; 4hr 30min); Quito (hourly; 4hr).

ACCOMMODATION

Most accommodation is situated close to the train station. The area can be noisy so it's best to stay off the main road or ask for a back room.

Inti Sisa Vargas Torres, at García Moreno, Guamote, between Riobamba and Alausí ☏ 03 291 6529, ⊚ www .intisisa.org. Very friendly, rustic guesthouse with private bathrooms and a fireplace, part of a community tourism initiative deeply involved with the local Kichwa. Tours available. Dorms $19, doubles $53

★ **El Libertador** Av Daniel León Borja 29–22 ☏ 03 294 7393, ⊚ hotelellibertador.com. The best mid-range deal. For more comfort, this colonial-style hotel has spacious, tastefully furnished rooms with cable TV. $30

Montecarlo 10 de Agosto 25–41 ☏ 03 296 1557, ⊚ hotelmontecarlo-riobamba.com. To treat yourself, try this restored historic house around a pleasant flower-filled courtyard. Breakfast included. $33

Oasis Veloz, at Almagro ☏ 03 296 1210, ⊚ oasishostelriobamba.com. South of the Basílica in a quiet area of town, this is an excellent mid-range choice.

★ **TREAT YOURSELF**

El Troje Km4.5 Via Riobamba a Chambo ☏ 03 262 2201, ⊚ eltroje.com. If you have spare cash, go south of town to enjoy the sauna and spacious grounds of this upmarket *hostería*. Breakfast included. $55

Tastefully decorated rooms, with a garden, courtyard and kitchen. Book in advance as there are only eight rooms. $24

Rincón Alemán Remigio Romero Mz H, Casa 9 at Alfredo Pareja ☏ 03 260 3540, ⊚ hostalrinconaleman.com. The excellent value and tranquillity of this European-style guesthouse makes up for being out of the way near Av Leonidas Proaño. Rooftop terrace views of Chimborazo. Kitchen use available. Singles $31, doubles $51

Los Shyris 10 de Agosto, at Rocafuerte ☏ 03 296 0323, ⊚ hotellosshyris.com. Good budget deal with private baths, cable TV and hot water. $18

Tren Dorado Carabobo 22–35, at 10 de Agosto ☏ 03 296 4890, ⊚ hoteltrendorado.com. Popular budget option right across from the station, with compact but perfectly adequate rooms and a friendly atmosphere. A cheap, filling buffet breakfast ($3) is available. $22

EATING AND DRINKING

★ **El Delirio** Primera Constituyente 28–16 ☏ 03 296 6441. Visited by Bolívar himself, this traditional colonial house is the perfect place for a romantic meal accompanied by live music, set inside a sleepy courtyard with a log fire to ward off the chills. Mains, including filet mignon, $9–12.

Pizzeria d'Baggio Av León Borja 33–24 ☏ 03 296 1832. Unbeatable for sumptuous pizzas and *calzone* hand-made in front of you. Pizzas $4–8.

El Rey de Burrito Borja 38–36 ☏ 03 295 3230. The best bet for burritos and enchiladas with plenty of vegetarian options. $3–5.

San Valentín Av León Borja, at Torres ☏ 03 296 3137. For something cheap and cheerful, try the Tex-Mex and varied fast food served in an informal atmosphere. Mains $5–10.

Sierra Nevada Primera Constituyente 27–38 ☏ 03 295 1542. A good-value eatery offering imaginative seafood and meat dishes. Mains $5–7.

El Tentadero Av León Borja. Nightlife is limited in Riobamba but this club on the main drag, just up from *San Valentín*, pumps out reggaeton, *merengue* and salsa until late ($3). Thurs–Sat.

VOLCÁN CHIMBORAZO

Just 30km northwest of Riobamba, the extinct **Volcán Chimborazo** looms large. At 6310m, it's Ecuador's highest peak and the furthest point from the centre of the Earth due to the equatorial bulge. The nature reserve has good roads so it can be easily visited from Riobamba. On a day-trip you can walk from the lower refuge (4800m) to the second refuge (5000m), but bear in mind that the climb in altitude from Riobamba could leave you suffering, and only experienced mountaineers should

6

THE DEVIL'S NOSE TRAIN RIDE

Not quite as adventurous as it used to be after a complete modernization, the **Devil's Nose Train Ride** still offers fabulous mountain views. The ride now takes you down from Alausí to Sibambe in the valley. The main event is a hair-raising 800m descent through a series of tight switchbacks carved out of the steep mountainside, viewable through panoramic windows from inside the modern rail cars. Tourists used to ride on the roof to get the full dramatic effect but this ended after the deaths of two Japanese people in 2007.

Tickets ($25) can be purchased at Alausí's train station in a somewhat comical procedure of providing your name, passport details and having the ticket stamped and then reviewed when boarding, so you should get there thirty minutes before departure (daily 8am, 11am & 3pm; 2hr 30min; $25). The tour includes a stop at the restored Sibambe station on the Guasuntos River, featuring folkloric dances and friendly llamas, before returning up the Devil's Nose to Alausí. Tickets are also bookable online at ⊛trenecuador.com/en/

tackle the summit. For this, there are several tour operators in Riobamba charging $220 for a two-day tour. Recommended operators include: Alta Montaña, on Avenida Daniel León Borja at Diego Ibarra (☎03 294 2215); and Andes Trek, on Colón 22–25, at 10 de Agosto (☎03 294 0964, ⊛andes-trek.com), which also offers ski mountaineering.

For non-climbers, enjoy the unworldly moonscapes and sweeping *páramo* that are home to thousands of vicuñas, brought back from the brink of extinction, and other wildlife. This enormous reserve stretches over 580 square kilometres in three provinces. It also contains Carihuairazo (5020m), a summit often tackled as a preparation climb. One-day hiking tours to Chimborazo National Park cost from $50 per person with tour operators in Riobamba. Alternatively, take a bus to Guaranda and ask to be let off near the refuge (8km from the main road) or take a taxi from Riobamba ($35).

ALAUSÍ

The regeneration of the train line has brought some sparkle back to the small Andean town of **ALAUSÍ**. Situated in a verdant valley with steep hills rising up on all sides, Alausí is a very pleasant town to base yourself for the most exhilarating train ride in Ecuador: the **Devil's Nose train ride** (see box above). Many of the old houses lining the rail line as well as the old metal bridge and main squares have been restored. The walk up to the huge statue of Saint Peter ten minutes from the centre offers excellent views over the town and

valley. For even better views, head to *Hostería Pircapamba* and hire horses to ride around the hills.

ARRIVAL AND DEPARTURE

By bus There are regular bus services to Alausí from Riobamba (hourly; 2hr); Cuenca (daily; 4hr); Quito (daily; 5hr); and Guayaquil (daily; 5hr).

By truck or taxi To begin the Inca Trail to the south, occasional trucks head to Achupallas from 5 de Junio, or you can take a taxi.

ACCOMMODATION

Hotel Europa 5 de Junio ☎03 293 0200. Dependable budget option on the main street but fills up fast. Choose from shared or private bath. **$12**

Hostal San Pedro 5 de Junio ☎03 293 0089. Hotel in the centre with comfortable rooms with private bath and cable TV, which are great value. **$30**

EATING

Alausí has plenty of budget eateries but few stand out. If money is tight, choose from various set menus on Av 5 de Junio.

Chifa Pekín 5 de Junio. A break from the usual Andean fare. Choose from noodles, fried rice and a range of Chinese soups. Mains $3–6.

★TREAT YOURSELF

Hostería Pircapamba Colombia, at Calle 25 ☎03 293 0180, ⊛pircapamba.com. Friendly ranch high above Alausí with breathtaking views of the valley (taxi $1 from the centre). Horseriding and hiking will keep you busy during the day, and for the evening there's a games room. Piping-hot showers, and breakfast is included. Doubles **$50**

El Mesón del Tren Ricaurte, at Eloy Alfaro ☎ 03 293 0243. The best restaurant in town offers a wide range of meat and fish specialities. Try the tilapia, pork chops or roast lamb at weekends. Mains $5–7.

The Southern Highlands

South of Riobamba, the snowcapped summits of the Andes fade from you, replaced by undulating green mountains. The hub of the region is **Cuenca**, Ecuador's third-largest city and one of Latin America's best-preserved colonial cities. Cuenca is also the most convenient base to explore the Inca archeological site **Ingapirca**, and the rugged moors and lakes of **Parque Nacional El Cajas**.

South of Cuenca, distances between towns lengthen and the climate warms up. The historic plazas and award-winning parks of the provincial capital of **Loja** are worth visiting before heading to the relaxing backpacker favourite of **Vilcabamba**, nicknamed the "Valley of Longevity". Recharge your batteries and take advantage of great hiking and horseriding trails in the surrounding hills.

INGAPIRCA

Between Riobamba and Cuenca lies the site of **Ingapirca** (daily 8am–6pm; $6 including guide), Ecuador's only major Inca ruins. Those who've already visited Peru may be disappointed by this more modest site; however, the complex boasts the Inca Empire's sole remaining sun temple. The site's strategic position is impressive, at a height of over 3200m with panoramic views over the surrounding countryside.

Ingapirca was built at the end of the fifteenth century by Huayna Capac on top of the ruins of a Cañari site. The stone of the Cañari moon temple, which the Inca preserved from its earlier construction, is still visible. Sadly, much of the site is now little more than stone foundations and it takes imagination and a guided tour to bring it to life.

WHAT TO SEE AND DO

Points of interest include the **calendar stone** and sacrificial site, but the highlight is the well-preserved **Temple of the Sun**, constructed with more than three thousand intricately carved blocks. It's entertaining to stand in the sentry posts of the temple and hear your whispers reverberate through the walls. Just outside

THE INCA TRAIL TO INGAPIRCA

Though by no means as famous or impressive as the trail in Peru, keen hikers can tackle the three-day trail from near Alausí to Ingapirca. The start of the trail is at **Achupallas**. To get there, take a bus from Riobamba towards Cuenca and get off at La Moya, 10km south of Alausí. From there, it's a steep climb – or you can hitch a ride to Achupallas. Alternatively, a taxi from Alausí direct to Achupallas costs $7. On the first day, head south down the Río Cadrul valley and through a narrow gap between two hills, Cerro Mapahuiña and Cerro Callana Pucará. Continue towards Laguna Tres Cruces and camp nearby. This hike is about six hours in total through parts of Sangay National Park.

On day two, continue southwest and up along Cuchilla Tres Cruces, which commands great views of the Quebrada Espíndola valley. Descend into the valley to the left of the final peak, Quillo Loma. There are remains of an Inca road, protected as a UNESCO site since 2014, and the foundations of an Inca bridge. You'll also find a trail to Laguna Culebrillas and more ruins at **Paredones**.

On day three, head southwest from Paredones on the 7m-wide Inca road. After the village of **San José** turn right to **El Rodeo**, then follow the road to **Ingapirca**. It takes nearly five hours in total. Take plenty of food, water and camping equipment and ensure you are prepared as the entire trail is not well marked. Alternatively, take a guided tour. Several tour operators based In Riobamba and Cuenca (see p.605) operate tours.

the complex is a **museum** (included in the
entrance fee), which houses a small
collection of objects found at the site.

ARRIVAL

By bus To get to Ingapirca, take a Transportes Cañar bus
from Cuenca's bus terminal (9am & 1pm; 2hr). The return
service is at 1pm & 4pm (weekends 1pm only). Guided
tours from Cuenca cost $45/person. If you're travelling
south from Alausí, get off the bus at El Tambo.

ACCOMMODATION

Options to stay overnight are limited and a day-trip is most
common.

Hostal Inti Huasi ☎07 229 2940. Very basic rooms in
Ingapirca village, 5min from the site. Bring warm clothes,
as it gets cold at night. **$15**

CUENCA

CUENCA is Ecuador's third-largest city,
with a population of 330,000, but it
doesn't feel that way, retaining the
atmosphere of a traditional Andean
town. The Incas established **Tomebamba**
in the late fifteenth century, one of the
most important cities in the Inca
Empire. It was destroyed shortly
afterwards in the civil war between
brothers Atahualpa and Huascar, and the
Spanish later founded Cuenca in 1557.
Little remains of the city's Inca past,
although ruins have been excavated
behind the **Museo Pumapungo**. Most
museums and restaurants are closed on
Sundays, which is the best day to take a
trip outside the city to **Cajas** or **Ingapirca**.

WHAT TO SEE AND DO

The cobbled streets, charming squares,
traditional architecture and magnificent
cathedral make the historic centre a
delight to explore; Cuenca was declared a
UNESCO World Heritage Site in 1996.

The historic city centre

The focal point of Cuenca's centre is
Parque Calderón, an elegant square filled
with flower beds and palm trees,
dominated by the towering nineteenth-
century **Catedral Nueva**. The interior is
relatively bare except for the stunning
gold-leaf altar and the massive sky-blue
domes, best viewed from the side or rear.
To the left of the cathedral entrance, along
Calle Sucre on the Plazoleta del Carmen, is
a flower market. Turn left along Padre
Aguirre to the ramshackle market
(scheduled for renovation) on **Plaza San
Francisco** and the peach-and-white **Iglesia
San Francisco**. Five blocks west on a quiet
square is the seventeenth-century **Iglesia
San Sebastián**. Opposite is the **Museo de
Arte Moderno** (Mon–Fri 9am–5.30pm, Sat
9am–1pm; free), which houses temporary
exhibitions of Latin American modern art.

Along the Río Tomebamba

Busy Calle Larga forms the southern
fringe of the historic centre. At the west
end is **Museo del Sombrero** (Mon–Fri
9am–6pm, Sat 9.30am–5pm, Sun
9.30am–1.30pm; free) where you can
learn about the process of making
Panama hats, which are actually from
Ecuador. The **Museo Remigio Crespo Toral**
(Mon–Fri 9am–5pm, Sat 9am–4.30pm,
Sun 10am–1pm; free) exhibits
pre-Columbian ceramics as well as
colonial and modern art in a restored
nineteenth-century house. A couple of
blocks further east, the excellent **Museo
de las Culturas Aborígenes** (Mon–Fri
8.30am–6pm, Sat 9am–1pm; $4) has an
enormous collection of pre-Hispanic
artefacts – second only to the Casa del
Alabado in Quito – from Stone Age tools
to Inca ceramics. Calle Larga has three
staircases, the largest of which is **La
Escalinata**, down to the riverbank,
pleasant for walking or biking between El
Vado (the ford) in the west and
Pumapungo and beyond in the east.

Museo Pumapungo

Museo Pumapungo (C Larga, at Huayna
Capac; Mon–Fri 9am–6pm, Sat
9am–1pm; $3; ☎07 283 1255) is Cuenca's
biggest museum and worth the

6

6

twenty-minute walk east of the centre (taxi $1.50). The three floors include a large collection of colonial art, an archeology room and an exhibition of indigenous costumes and masks. The highlight is the **ethnographic** exhibition of Ecuador's indigenous cultures with animated dioramas, re-created dwellings and a stunning display of five *tsantsas* (shrunken heads) from the Shuar culture. Entrance includes access to the **Pumapungo archeological site** behind the museum, where the most important buildings of the Inca city of Tomebamba were located, although mainly only foundations remain. Below the ruins are landscaped gardens and a bird rescue centre.

Mirador de Turi

For great views over Cuenca, take a taxi ($3) or a bus from 12 de Abril, at Solano ($0.25), to the **Mirador de Turi**, a lookout point on a hill 4km south of the centre. Views are particularly good in the evening when the churches are lit up.

ARRIVAL AND DEPARTURE

By plane Cuenca's airport (Mariscal Lamar; ☎ 07 286 7120) is 2km northeast of the centre. There are daily flights to and from Quito by Tame (Av Florencia Astudillo; ☎ 07 288 9581, ⓦ tame .com.ec), LAN (Bolívar 9–18, at Benigno Malo; ☎ 07 282 2783, ⓦ lan.com) and Avianca (Av España 1114; ☎ 07 286 1041, ⓦ www.aerogal.com.ec). TAME also flies to Guayaquil. From the airport buses run on Av España to the northern edge of central Cuenca or it's a 10min walk to the main bus terminal.
By bus The bus terminal is near the airport, northeast of the centre. A new tram running through the centre and stopping at the bus and airport terminals is scheduled to begin running in 2016.

Destinations Quito (hourly; 10hr); Guayaquil (hourly; 4hr 30min); Ambato (hourly; 7hr); Riobamba (hourly; 6hr); and Loja (hourly; 4hr).

CUENCA

● EATING
La Brasserie — 1
Cacao y Canela — 9
Café Austria — 5
El Cafécito — 11
Los Capulíes — 6
Moliendo Café — 13
El Pedregal Azteca — 4
Raymipamba — 3
Taj Mahal — 10
Tiestos — 8

● NIGHTLIFE
Café Eucalyptus — 2
Far Out — 7
Monday Blue — 12
Wunderbar — 14

■ ACCOMMODATION
El Cafécito — 10
La Casa Cuencana — 13
Hostal Casa del Barranco — 11
Hostal Casa Naranja — 2
Hostal Chordeleg — 4
Hostal La Cigale — 9
Hostal Colonial — 6
Hotel Forum — 3
Macondo — 1
Hostal Monarca — 8
Monasterio de Colección — 12
Orquidea — 7
Hostal Posada del Ángel — 5

Taxi Taxis cost about $2 from the airport to Cuenca. Minimum charges around town are $1.40.

INFORMATION

Tourist information The iTur office on the main square (Mariscal Sucre; Mon–Fri 8am–8pm, Sat 8.30am–1.30pm; ☎07 282 135, ⓦ www.cuenca.com.ec) has friendly staff providing maps and regional information. It also has an office at the airport, which opens for flight arrivals. Cuenca offers good-value $8 double-decker city bus tours from Parque Calderón (hourly: Mon–Sat 9am–noon & 2–7pm, Sun 9am-3pm, covering the centre and Turi.

TOUR OPERATORS

The following offer tours to Ingapirca, Cajas and elsewhere. Trips to Cajas and Ingapirca cost $40–50/person.

Expediciones Apullacta Gran Colombia 11-02, at General Torres ☎07 283 7815, ⓦ apullacta.com.

Metropolitan Touring Mariscal Sucre 6-62, at Hermano Miguel ☎07 283 1463, ⓦ metropolitan-touring.com.

Monodedo Av 12 de Abril, at Guayas ☎07 288 5909, ⓦ monodedoecuador.com. Rock-climbing and canyoning pioneers.

Terra Diversa Travel and Adventure Hermano Miguel 5-42, at Honorato Vásquez ☎07 282 3782, ⓦ terradiversa.com.

ACCOMMODATION

Cuenca has a wide range of hotels in charming colonial buildings. The best area to stay is in the centre between Calle Larga and Sangurima. Book ahead at weekends and on national holidays.

El Cafécito Honorato Vasquez 7–36, at Cordero ☎07 283 2337, ⓦ cafecito.net. A friendly café with basic rooms at the back. Dorms $8, doubles $25

La Casa Cuencana Hermano Miguel 4–45 ☎07 282 6009. With terracotta walls adorned with artwork, and a friendly family atmosphere, these simple rooms with private bathrooms are excellent value for the price. $17

Hostal Casa del Barranco C Larga 8–41, at Cordero ☎07 283 9763, ⓦ casadelbarranco.com. Many of the hotels on Calle Larga come at a premium, but this historic house displaying paintings by local artists is a great-value mid-range option. Breakfast included. $30

★ TREAT YOURSELF

Hotel Forum Borrero 10-91, at Lamar ☎07 28 28 801. Splash out on one of Cuenca's finest new hotels, in a beautifully restored, centrally located mansion full of understated elegance. Very competitively priced doubles including buffet breakfast. $79

Hostal Casa Naranja Lamar 10-38, at Padre Aguirre ☎07 282 5415. Inside a traditional house, modern decor and spacious bathrooms put this centrally located place somewhere between hostel and cheap boutique hotel. $39

Hostal Chordeleg Gran Colombia, at General Torres ☎07 282 2536. An attractive converted colonial home on a corner in the city centre with decent mid-range rooms set around a pleasant courtyard and garden. Breakfast included. $40

Hostal La Cigale Vásquez, 7-80 at Cordero ☎07 283 5308. Simple rooms and a popular courtyard café with frequent weekend live events attached. Dorms $10, doubles $22

Hostal Colonial Gran Colombia 10-13, at Padre Aguirre ☎07 2841 644. Compact mid-range rooms in an eighteenth-century house set around a small courtyard. Breakfast included. $34

★ Macondo Tarqui 11-64, at Mariscal Lamar ☎07 284 0697. Another colonial-style favourite with artwork on the walls, a spacious lawn in the back garden and a choice of private or shared bathrooms. Breakfast included. $31

Hostal Monarca Borrero 5-47, at Honorato Vásquez ☎07 283 6462. Loud, bright decor but a quiet family atmosphere, with great-value budget rooms and shared bathroom. $15

Monasterio de Colección Hermano Miguel 4-79, at Honorato Vásquez ☎07 282 7827. Hostel with giant beds in a restored colonial house just a block away from happening Calle Larga (entrance through Marea pizzeria). Doubles $50

Orquidea Borrero 931, at Bolívar ☎07 282 4511. A converted colonial home in the centre of the city, and one of the cheapest mid-range options. $24

Hostal Posada del Ángel Bolívar 14-11, at Estévez y Toral ☎07 284 0695, ⓦ hostalposadadelangel.com. It's difficult to paint a hotel orange and blue and still maintain a charming elegance, but this endearing place pulls it off. Free internet and breakfast served in the spacious, enclosed courtyard. $66

EATING

You're never far from a stall or bakery selling cakes and confectionery, including the ubiquitous *membrillo* (a gelatinous red block made with guayaba). Cuenca has a varied offering of international and local cuisine.

La Brasserie Borrero 10-91, at Lamar. *Hotel Forum*'s surprisingly accessibly priced restaurant, a mix of modern decor with classic touches. French cuisine with the odd, hearty German dish. Perfect for a romantic meal. Mains $12. Daily noon–10pm.

★ Cacao y Canela Jaramillo, at Borrero. Snug little café serving a huge selection of hot chocolate drinks ($2–3) – rum, cinnamon, almonds and mozzarella are just a few of the flavours available. Great cakes and snacks too. Mon–Sat 4pm–late.

Café Austria Hermano Miguel, at Simón Bolívar. Tasty Central European specialities such as roulade and goulash, plus tasty cakes and ice creams for dessert. Mains $6–8. Daily

6

(including Sun). Mon–Sat 9am–midnight, Sun 9am–11pm.

El Cafécito Honorato Vásquez 7-36, at Luis Cordero. A backpacker hangout, this is a good place to meet like-minded travellers over a coffee and a game of chess. Burgers, pasta and Tex-Mex are great value at around $3. Daily 8am–11pm.

Los Capuliés Córdova, at Borrero. Well-priced Ecuadorian specialities ($4–6) served in a pleasant enclosed courtyard. Daily 9am–10pm.

Moliendo Café Honorato Vásquez 6–24. Huge selection of cheap Colombian *arepas* (corn tortillas) and filling *almuerzos* ($2–4). Mon–Sat 9am–9pm.

El Pedregal Azteca Estévez de Toral 860 ☎ 07 282 3652. The best place in town for high-quality Mexican cuisine. Especially good is the *pollo mole poblano* (chicken with chocolate sauce). $5–10. Tues–Sat noon–3pm & 6.30–10.30pm, Sun noon–3pm.

Raymipamba Benigno Malo, at Bolívar, Parque Calderón. Bustling café under the colonnaded arches of the Catedral Nueva, offering large portions of filling Ecuadorian staples and sweet and savoury crêpes for $4–6. Mon–Fri 8.30am–11pm, Sat & Sun 9.30am–10pm.

★ **Taj Mahal** C Larga, at Benigno Malo. *Jalfrezi*, *biryani* and a range of Indian dishes are done extremely well in this friendly Pakistani-run place. They also do good kebabs. Don't miss the traditional yogurt or the Bollywood on the big screen. $3–5. Mon–Thurs noon–10pm, Fri & Sat noon–midnight, Sun noon–8pm.

NIGHTLIFE

It's not as raucous as Guayaquil or Quito but there are enough options, mostly south of downtown and along Calle Larga.

★ **Café Eucalyptus** Gran Colombia, at Benigno Malo. Lively, fun café-bar with a diverse tapas menu (dishes $5–6), draught beer, couches to lounge on and live music Wed–Sat. Mon–Wed noon–10pm, Thurs noon–11pm, Fri & Sat noon–2am, Sun 5–10pm.

Far Out Jaramillo 7-36, at Borrero. Ecuador's baddest stereo speakers per square metre in a tiny rock music café. Huge high-sampling music collection and German-made craft beers on tap. Wed–Sat 7pm–late.

Monday Blue C Larga, at Cordero. Funky little bar with walls covered in art and eclectic memorabilia, serving

cheap Mexican and Italian food. Thurs–Sat 8pm–late.

Wunderbar Escalinata, off C Larga. Popular place in a large red-brick building with a small garden nestled above the river. The bar serves Ecuador's best pisco sours by a mile and is lively in the evenings, with occasional live music and billiards. Mon–Wed noon–midnight, Thurs–Sat noon–2am.

DIRECTORY

Banks and exchange Banco de Guayaquil on Mariscal Sucre, at Hermano Miguel; Banco de Austro on M. Sucre, at Borrero; Banco de Pacífico on Benigno Malo 9-75.

Hospitals Hospital Santa Ines on Av Daniel Cordova Toral 2-113, at Augustian Cueva (☎ 07 281 7888); Hospital Monte Sinai at Miguel Cordero 6-111, at Av Solano (☎ 07 288 5595).

Internet Cuenc@net at C Larga, at Hermano Miguel; ExploreNet on Padre Aguirre 10-96, at Lamar.

Police Benigno Malo & Antonio Muñoz (☎ 07 281 0068).

Post offices Post office on Presidente Borrero, at Gran Colombia; Fedex on Miguel Cordero 350, at Alfonso Cordero.

Phone Etapa on Benigno Malo, at Sucre, on the west side of the city hall building.

BAÑOS (CUENCA)

The ideal way to relax after sightseeing is to visit **BAÑOS** (not to be confused with its namesake between Ambato and Puyo), once a hamlet and now a suburb of Cuenca, a fifteen-minute uphill drive from the centre. A number of baths and spas have been established here, two of which are head and shoulders above the rest.

Hostería Durán (Av Ricardo Durán; prices start at $3; ☎07 289 2301, ⊛hosteriaduran.com), founded in the 1920s, sprawls over ten acres, with a hotel and large pool in the middle of an Andalucian-style colonnade, and a modern spa, Novaqua. This is rivalled by *Piedra de Agua* (Paseo de la Guadalupana; pool $10, spa service $30, massages $20/30min, $40/hr; ☎07 289 2496), a more modern, intimate setting of several mid-sized pools amid warm, red stone.

ARRIVAL

By bus The bus ($0.25) departs from Vega Muñoz, at Padre Aguirre, or Av 12 de Abril, at Av Fray Vicente Solano, south of the river.

By taxi A taxi from Cuenca to Baños costs $5.

PARQUE NACIONAL EL CAJAS

Just 30km northwest of Cuenca, the

enormous **PARQUE NACIONAL EL CAJAS** (daily 6am–5pm) spans nearly 300 square kilometres of spectacular moor-like *páramo*. With two hundred lakes shining beneath rugged hillsides, this is one of Ecuador's most compelling wildernesses, offering great hiking and trout-fishing opportunities. Highlights include wild llamas, which were introduced to the park in the late 1990s. There are eight hiking trails, ranging from three hours to two full days. The short hike around Laguna Toreadora is the most popular, while the trail to Laguna Totoras takes six hours. However, the wind, rain and fog can often make visits uncomfortable so come prepared with rainproof gear, snacks, warm clothing and walking boots. Most of the park lies above 4000m so ensure you are properly acclimatized before tackling long hikes.

It's easy to visit independently by taking a Cooperativa Alianza bus from the terminal (1hr) and walking 100m to the Laguna Toreadora refuge station, which has maps and information on popular hiking trails. The station also has a few beds, or you can camp in the recreation area for about $5 per person, but it gets very cold. Cuenca-based tour operators (see p.605) offer guided tours costing about $40 per person.

VILLAGES AROUND CUENCA

There are several interesting indigenous villages close to Cuenca, famous for handicrafts. **Gualaceo** (45min east of Cuenca; bus from the terminal) has the largest indigenous market in the area on Sundays with a range of woven textiles – from shawls to tapestries. **Chordeleg** is 5km further and renowned for jewellery. A further fifteen minutes by bus is **Sigsig**, well known for the Panama hat factory on the edge of town, where you can make considerable savings on hats compared with Cuenca. On a separate route, southeast of Cuenca, the village of **San Bartolomé** (30min by bus) is famous for handmade guitars.

LOJA

South of Cuenca, the road winds through varied Andean dry-and-warm or cold-and-wet microclimates until **LOJA**, some 200km away. Loja was founded in 1548 and today boasts a well-preserved historic centre, thriving music scene and spectacular parks.

WHAT TO SEE AND DO

Begin at the **Parque Central**, dominated by the towering yellow and white **Catedral**. On the south side, the **Museo de Loja** (Mon–Fri 9am–5pm; free) has a small collection of pre-Columbian ceramics and religious art. Walk south on Bolívar, and you reach the beautiful **Iglesia Santo Domingo**, which houses more than one hundred oil paintings. A couple of blocks further, the highlight of central Loja, the **Plaza de la Independencia** (also known as Plaza San Sebastián), is lined by brightly coloured colonial buildings. On the southwest corner is the **Iglesia San Sebastián**, while the square's focal point is an impressive clock tower with stone depictions of the battles for Ecuador's independence. Don't miss charming Calle Lourdes, which runs past San Sebastián.

Loja's delightful parks are easily reached by a short taxi ride ($2). The best is the **Parque Universitario de Educación Ambiental y Recreación** (PUEAR; daily 9am–6pm; $1), which has trails up through the forest and impressive views over Loja and the valley. Across the road is the **Jardín Botánico Reynaldo Espinosa** (daily 8am–6pm; $1), which has more than two hundred species of orchids.

ARRIVAL AND INFORMATION

By plane Daily flights from Quito and Guayaquil arrive at the Aeropuerto Ciudad de Catamayo, 33km west in the town of Catamayo. A shared taxi (about $5/person) is the only way to get directly to Loja from the airport, or take a taxi to the town of Catamayo ($2) and a bus from there to Loja.

By bus Loja's bus terminal is 2km north of the centre on Av Cuxibamba, with plenty of taxis ($1) and buses ($0.30) to the centre. There is an hourly bus to Vilcabamba from the bus terminal (75min, $1.25). Or go to Iberoamérica, at Chile, and take a shared taxi with Taxi Ruta (45min; $1.50).

Tourist information iTur office on Bolívar, at Eguiguren (Mon–Fri 8am–6pm; ☎ 07 257 0407).

ACCOMMODATION

Hostal El Inca Av Universitaria at 10 de Agosto, at Bolívar ☎ 07 256 1103. Decoration-wise, stuck

6

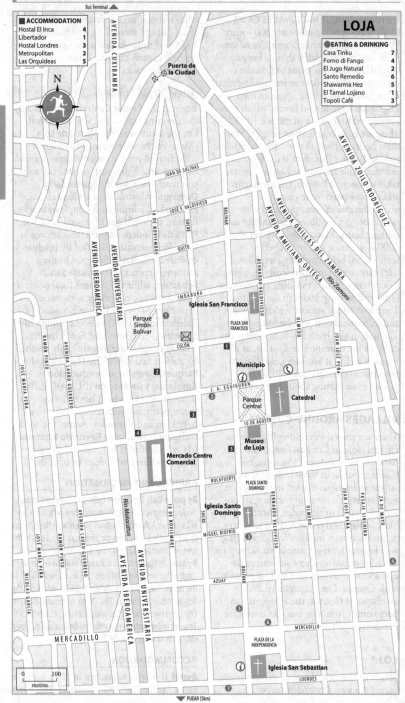

Bus Terminal

LOJA

N

Puerta de
la Ciudad

AVENIDA CUXIBAMBA

JUAN DE SALINAS

JOSÉ F. VALDIVIESO

18 DE NOVIEMBRE

SUCRE

BOLÍVAR

QUITO

AVENIDA IBEROAMÉRICA

AVENIDA UNIVERSITARIA

AVENIDA ORILLAS DEL ZAMORA

AVENIDA AMILIANO ORTEGA

AVENIDA ZOILO RODRÍGUEZ

Río Zamora

BERNARDO VALDIVIESO

IMBABURA

Iglesia San Francisco

Parque
Simón
Bolívar

PLAZA SAN
FRANCISCO

OLMEDO

COLÓN

Municipio

JUAN JOSÉ PEÑA

RAMÓN PINTO

JOSÉ MARÍA PEÑA

AVENIDA LAURO GUERRERO

J. A. EGUIGUREN

Parque
Central

Catedral

10 DE AGOSTO

**Museo
de Loja**

ROCAFUERTE

PLAZA SANTO
DOMINGO

Mercado Centro
Comercial

Río Malacatos

18 DE NOVIEMBRE

SUCRE

**Iglesia Santo
Domingo**

MIGUEL RIOFRÍO

BERNARDO VALDIVIESO

OLMEDO

JUAN JOSÉ PEÑA

PASAJE SINCHINA

24 DE MAYO

AZUAY

BOLÍVAR

JOSÉ MARÍA PEÑA

RAMÓN PINTO

AVENIDA LAURO GUERRERO

NICOLÁS GARCÍA

AVENIDA IBEROAMÉRICA

AVENIDA UNIVERSITARIA

MERCADILLO

MERCADILLO

PLAZA DE LA
INDEPENDENCIA

Iglesia San Sebastián

LOURDES

0   100
metres

PUEAR (5km)

somewhere in the 1970s, but adequate for the price and central location. Ask for a room away from the main street on a higher floor. **$20**

Libertador Colón 14-30 ☎07 256 0779, ⓦ hotellibertador.com.ec. The best option to treat yourself, with plush decoration, swimming pool, sauna and steam bath. Breakfast included. **$65**

Hostal Londres Sucre 07-51 ☎07 256 1936. Very basic rooms with shared bath for those on a tight budget. **$10**

Metropolitano 18 de Noviembre 06-31 ☎07 257 0007, ⓦ hotelmetropolitanoloja.com. A solid mid-range choice, with wooden floors and good-sized rooms with cable TV and private bath. **$25**

★**Las Orquideas** Bolívar, at 10 de Agosto ☎07 258 7008. The best of the budget options, with clean, neat rooms with TV and private bathroom. **$18**

EATING AND DRINKING

Casa Tinku Lourdes, at Bolívar. In a colonial-style setting, a good place to catch live music at weekends.

Forno di Fango 24 de Mayo, at Azuay. A local favourite for great pizza and pasta dishes at $4–8. Daily.

El Jugo Natural Eguiguren, at Bolívar. A huge range of fresh fruit and vegetable juices, plus fresh bread, veggie specialities and ice cream. $1–3. Daily.

Santo Remedio Plaza de la Independencia. Nightlife is limited in Loja, but this popular bar with the city's most elegant, modern lounge-type decor is a good option for a drink and dance.

★**Shawarma Hez** Bolívar near Plaza de la Independencia. Enjoy something different in this beautifully decorated restaurant with tasty Arabic food (mains $2–4) and seating on traditional floor cushions. Closed Sun.

El Tamal Lojano 18 de Noviembre. The best place to sample local specialities like *humitas*, *tamales* and *empanadas* for $1–2. Another branch on 24 de Mayo.

Topoli Café Bolívar, at Riofrío. Sandwiches, burgers, crêpes, cakes and ice cream, all for less than $5.

VILCABAMBA

VILCABAMBA has been attracting travellers for years in search of relaxation and the apparent secret to a long, healthy life. Backpackers, hikers and hippies flock to the "Valley of Longevity" to enjoy the region's perfect climate and spectacular scenery. The town itself is not brimming with tourist attractions; the main draw is in the surroundings, which offer great **hiking** and **horseriding** opportunities.

Vilcabamba has also long been associated with the hallucinogenic San Pedro cactus, which grows in this region. Be warned that consuming San Pedro is illegal and local police may deal severely with anyone found taking it.

WHAT TO SEE AND DO

The most impressive hiking trail is up to the jagged hill **Cerro Mandango**. Walk south of town along Avenida Eterna Juventud to find the trail entrance ($1.50). It's a steep 45-minute climb to the first peak and then an unnerving trek across the very narrow ridgeline to the second peak. You can loop around descending slowly towards town, which means the entire walk is about four hours. To shorten it, retrace your steps back down from the first peak.

Easier trails are found at Rumi Wilco Nature Reserve (ⓦ rumiwilco.com), just ten minutes east of town. There are half a dozen trails through the protected forest beside the river Chamba.

Many hotels have excellent **massage** facilities attached; the best option in town is Karina at Massage Beauty Care (Diego Vaca de Vega, at Bolívar; $15/hr; ☎07 264 0359).

6

CROSSING INTO PERU

If you're in the southern sierra, it's better to cross to Peru via **Macará**, 190km southeast of **Loja**, than go down to the coast and cross via frenetic Huaquillas. A bus service operated by Cooperativa Loja (☎07 257 9014) travels from Loja to Piura in Peru via Macará (7am, 1pm & 11pm; 6hr). Buy tickets in advance if possible. The company has offices in Loja bus terminal and next to Vilcabamba's bus terminal. From Vilcabamba take a bus to Loja and change. In Macará the bus stops at the 24hr Migración office for your exit stamp. Walk across the bridge, which forms the border, to get the entry stamp on the other side, and then get back on the bus. An alternative route is gaining popularity at **Zumba** because it is more convenient if visiting the Chachapoyas ruins in Peru. There are three night buses from Loja to Zumba via Vilcabamba (6hr), and one bus passing Vilcabamba at 6am.

6

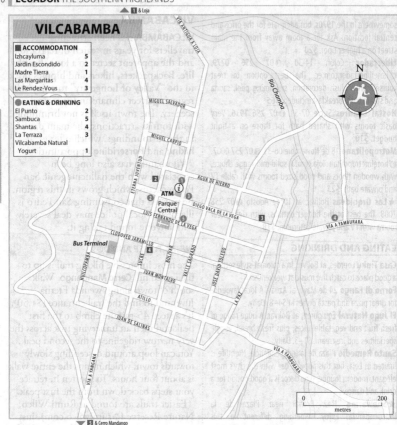

ARRIVAL AND DEPARTURE

By bus Buses run to and from Loja (every 30min; 75min) from the corner of Av de la Eterna Juventud and C Jaramillo. To go to Peru, buses to the crossing at Zumba pass through Vilcabamba. To cross via Macará, take a bus from Loja.

By taxi Pick-up trucks act as taxis and charge $1–1.50 to most of the accommodation in and around Vilcabamba.

INFORMATION AND TOURS

Money There is a Banco de Guayaquil cash machine on the main square in Vilcabamba but no bank; the nearest is in Loja. The machine frequently runs out of money at weekends.

Tourist information The tourist office, on the northeast corner of Parque Central (daily 8am–1pm & 3–6pm; ☎07 264 0090), provides maps and information on hikes and excursions around Vilcabamba.

Tour operators Caballos Gavilán (Sucre, at Diego Vaca; ☎07 264 0281) organize half-day/full-day ($20/30) horseriding tours with a guide, and two- and three-day tours to a cloudforest cabin in Podocarpus; Monta Tour

(☎098 914 4812) next door and Apache Tour on Sucre (☎07 264 0415) also offer tours to Podocarpus.

ACCOMMODATION

Expect to pay a little more for accommodation in Vilcabamba than in other parts of Ecuador unless you stay at one of the town's grubbiest dives.

★ **Izhcayluma** ☎07 264 0095, ⓦizhcayluma.com. About 2km south of town, this friendly German-owned *hostería*, whose name means "between two hills" in Inca, has rustic cabins, a small spa and a great view. The owners have mapped out trails around Vilcabamba for hikers. Don't miss the Bavarian stroganoff or the German Weissbier in the restaurant. Breakfast included. Dorms $10, doubles $26

Jardín Escondido Sucre, at Diego Vaca ☎07 264 0281. Simple but spacious rooms around a garden with lemon trees, a small pool and jacuzzi. The hotel's Mexican restaurant is excellent and the service friendly. $25

Las Margaritas Sucre, at C Jaramillo ☎07 264 0051. This large white house feels like a family residence, with a cosy

★**TREAT YOURSELF**

Madre Tierra ☎ 07 264 0269,
Ⓦ madretierra.com.ec. For more comfort, stay at this award-winning spa hotel 1km north of town. Enjoy the view from the balcony of your comfortable cabin and take advantage of the jacuzzi, pool and huge range of spa treatments on offer. Breakfast and soft drinks included. Room prices vary considerably. Single **$19**, junior suite **$89**

atmosphere and well-maintained rooms. Excellent value for the price, and breakfast is included. **$20**
Le Rendez-Vous Diego Vaca de la Vega ☎ 099 219 1180, Ⓦ rendezvousecuador.com. East of the town centre, this French-owned guesthouse has good-value, comfy rooms with hammocks on the terrace overlooking the garden. Breakfast included. **$20**

EATING AND DRINKING

Many hotels have good restaurants attached, particularly Mexican food at *Jardín Escondido* and German food at *Izhcayluma*. Nightlife is almost non-existent in Vilcabamba. Many restaurants outside the hotels are closed Sundays.
El Punto Sucre, at Diego Vaca. Popular café with expats, ideal to watch the world go slowly by over pizza, local fare, a coffee, juice or dessert ($3–5).
Sambuca Bolívar. Good choice for organic vegetarian specialities, soups, salads, Mexican and a wide range of juices. $4–7.
Shantas Diego Vaca de la Vega. On the road east out of town, this informal place offers a wide selection of dishes, including trout and frog's legs ($4–6). The more adventurous can try snake juice ($2), made from pickled coral snake, sugar cane and *aguardiente*.
La Terraza Parque Central. This restaurant serves good *almuerzos* as well as tasty Mexican, Italian and Chinese dishes ($5–7). The set lunch ($2.50) is great value.
Vilcabamba Natural Yogurt Bolívar. One of the cheapest places in town, great for crêpes, burgers, breakfasts, home-made yogurt and juice for $2–3.

PODOCARPUS AND YACURI

Ecuador's southernmost national parks contain remarkable diversity from high *páramo* to tropical jungle. The parks are comparatively remote, but visitors are rewarded with pristine lakes, hillsides covered in cloudforest, waterfalls, and thousands of species of plants. There are six hundred species of birds, including 61 species of hummingbirds, as well as

spectacled bear, tapirs and deer, although you will be very lucky to see them.

ARRIVAL AND TOURS

Cajanuma ranger station between Loja and Vilcabamba is the most popular and accessible entrance to Podocarpus.
By bus Buses from Vilcabamba drop you on the main road 9km from the entrance (tell the driver you are going to Podocarpus).
By taxi A taxi from Vilcabamba is approximately $15.
Tours There are hikes ranging from one hour to several days. If you are planning to stay longer, you are better off arranging a tour in Vilcabamba.

The Oriente

East of Quito, the Andes drop dramatically and snowcapped mountains give way to verdant swathes of tropical rainforest stretching 250km to the Colombian and Peruvian borders. Ecuador's chunk of the Amazon basin, known as the Oriente ("The East"), constitutes almost half of the country's territory, although only five percent of the population lives here, in oil towns and remote indigenous communities. However, with oil exploration increasing and roads improving, the population is expanding fast. Sadly, areas of pristine jungle remain as under threat here as elsewhere in South America, with one of the region's highest rates of deforestation.

The **Eastern Oriente** offers the most spectacular opportunities for visitors to encounter an array of flora and fauna in primary rainforest. The highlights are huge protected areas – **Parque Nacional Yasuní** and the **Reserva Faunística Cuyabeno** and lodges in indigenous communities to the south. Reaching these unforgettable wildernesses usually involves travelling through the forgettable hubs of **Lago Agrio** or **Coca**. For those with limited time seeking an accessible experience, much more pleasant towns of **Tena** and **Macas** and perhaps Puyo are surrounded by secondary rainforest with chances to stay with **indigenous communities**. The higher elevation of these towns makes **white-water rafting** and **kayaking** popular activities in rapids

6

JUNGLE TOURS

If you dream of striking out on your own and hacking through dense jungle like a modern-day explorer, dream on. Unguided travel is strongly discouraged by the government and not advisable, considering how inhospitable and inaccessible parts of the Oriente remain. **Guided tours** are the best option and are relatively cheap, costing $30–50 per person per day. Prices rise if you stay in a luxurious lodge or air-conditioned river cruiser, but bear in mind that some discomfort is part of the jungle experience. Always check that your guide has a **permit** from the Ministry of Tourism. Generally the larger the number of people in your group, the lower the price. Solo travellers usually have to share a cabin or pay a higher rate for a separate room. Tours range from two to eight days and can often be booked at the last minute. For tours around Puyo and Tena, a couple of days will give you an insight into life in the Oriente, but if you are travelling deep into the jungle, more than four days is recommended, because nearly two days will be spent travelling.

You must prepare thoroughly and pack **essentials** before heading into the jungle. Take plenty of insect repellent, long-sleeved tops, trousers, waterproofs, a torch and boots. A first-aid kit is also advisable, although the guide will carry one. Anti-malarials and yellow fever vaccinations are recommended (see p.32). You must carry your original **passport**, as copies are not sufficient at military checkpoints.

TOUR OPERATORS

It's easiest to book your tour in Quito, particularly for those going via Coca and Lago Agrio. For shorter tours to secondary jungle, operators in Tena (see p.616) and Baños (see p.598) are also useful. Booking locally in Coca and Lago Agrio is more difficult so it's better to make arrangements beforehand. The following Quito operators are recommended:

Dracaena J Pinto E4-453, at Amazonas ☎02 254 6590, ⓦamazondracaena.com. Offers tours of Cuyabeno, staying at *Nicky Amazon Lodge and Dracaena Camp Site* (5 days; $240).

Gulliver Travels Juan León Mera N24-156 ☎02 252 9297, ⓦgulliver.com.ec. Tours in Cuyabeno from $220 for four days.

Latitud0 Mallorca N24-500 at Francisco Salazar ☎02 290 6039, ⓦlatitud0.com. Offers strenuous eight-day deep Yasuní camping trips including visits to Huaorani communities. Prices vary depending on the season; through the Cononaco, two-person tours run $1590 per person. Other tailor-made Amazon trips possible.

Magic River Tours 18 de Diciembre, at C Primera, Pacayacu ☎02 262 9303, ⓦmagicrivertours.com. German-owned company specializing in canoe trips in the Cuyabeno reserve. Five days from $330.

Neotropic Turis J Pinto E4-340 near Amazonas and Wilson ☎02 252 121, ⓦneotropicturis.com. Four-day tours to Cuyabeno Reserve, staying in *Cuyabeno Lodge*, from $350.

Rainforestur Amazonas 410, at Robles ☎02 223 9822, ⓦrainforestur.com. Wide range of jungle tours throughout the Oriente via Lago Agrio, Coca, Puyo and Tena. Four days in Jamu Lodge from $220.

Safari Tours Reina Victoria N25-33, at Av Colón ☎02 255 2502, ⓦsafari.com.ec. Wide range of jungle tours through Puyo, Tena, Coca and Lago Agrio.

Tropic Ecological Adventures Av República 307, at Almagro, Edif Taurus ☎02 222 5907, ⓦtropiceco.com. Tours and ecotourism projects throughout the Oriente. Four days on the edge of Yasuní from $670 in *Sani Lodge*; from $860 in *Huaorani Eco Lodge* (not including flights from Puyo). Indigenous community stays available.

---

tumbling down to the Amazon basin. From **Mera** near Puyo, small aircraft provide short flights to remote indigenous villages.

LAGO AGRIO

LAGO AGRIO, also known as Nueva Loja, was used by Texaco in the 1960s as a base for oil exploration in the Oriente and takes its name (meaning "sour lake") from the company's original

headquarters in Texas. The town epitomizes the power struggle between oil companies keen to get their hands on the "black gold" underneath the jungle and tour operators keen to preserve the once pristine forests of the **Cuyabeno Reserve**. More worryingly, the infiltration of Colombian FARC guerrillas along the border just 21km to the north makes this a **dangerous area**. A FARC leader and sixteen rebels were killed in a bombing raid northeast of

THE ROAD TO LAGO AGRIO

The bus ride from Quito to Lago Agrio (7hr) is long and arduous and you might consider flying. If you take the bus, it makes sense to break the journey up with visits to **Papallacta** (see p.583) and **San Rafael Falls**, Ecuador's largest waterfalls. The latter are located three hours after Baeza, 2.5km along a trail from the main road (ask the bus driver). You should allow yourself about one hour thirty minutes to walk down to the falls and back.

Lago Agrio in March 2008 and two tourists were kidnapped (and released) in 2012. It's best not to hang around waiting for a tour; book from Quito and consider flying in or out to avoid spending time in the area. Don't wander from the centre (most hotels, restaurants and tourist agencies are located along Av Quito), and take care at night. At the time of writing, the British Foreign Office advises travellers to avoid Lago Agrio and all areas in Sucumbíos province bordering Colombia.

ARRIVAL AND DEPARTURE

By plane The airport is 4km east of Lago Agrio. TAME (9 de Octubre, at Orellana; ☎ 06 283 0113) has a morning flight Mon–Sat from Quito. Take a taxi to the town centre ($3) unless your tour operator has arranged a transfer.

By bus The bus station is 2km northeast of the town centre. Destinations Quito (hourly; 8hr); Tena and Puyo (overnight).

ACCOMMODATION

Gran Colombia Av Quito 265 ☎ 06 283 1032. Well-equipped but rather characterless rooms with fans (a/c extra) and cable TV. $28

Gran Hotel de Lago Av Quito km 11/2 ☎ 06 283 2415. Best hotel in town, with a bar, cable TV, swimming pool, a/c and free internet, but book ahead because it can be fully booked by oil companies. Breakfast included. $50

RESERVA FAUNÍSTICA CUYABENO

This beautiful reserve (admission $20) of unique **flooded rainforest** spreads out over 6000 square kilometres east of Lago Agrio, extending to the Peruvian border. It contains an astonishing biodiversity of plants, trees, mammals and aquatic wildlife. Meandering down the Río Aguarico through huge areas of inundated forest and passing countless lagoons is unforgettable. Pink freshwater **dolphins**, white and black **caiman**, **anacondas**, **giant otters** and many species of **monkeys** are commonly seen, while the jaguar will likely prove elusive.

The borders of the reserve were expanded in the early 1990s, partly in response to damaging oil exploration. Sadly, areas of Cuyabeno have been badly polluted, but vocal indigenous protest has improved the situation and there remain areas of unspoilt jungle. You need a guided tour (see opposite) to explore this remote region.

COCA

The capital of Orellana province has grown rapidly since the 1970s into a sprawling oil town. It's much more pleasant than Lago Agrio, with a riverfront malecón, but there's little to tempt you to stay long. **COCA** is the last major town on the Río Napo, the gateway to the enormous **Parque Nacional Yasuní**, and is also emerging as a route over the border to Peru via **Nuevo Rocafuerte**. Local operators are thin on the ground so it's best to organize a tour from Quito.

ARRIVAL AND DEPARTURE

By plane Tame (☎ 06 288 1078) and Avianca (☎ 06 288 0997) both operate daily flights from Quito to Coca, which is tempting to avoid the gruelling bus ride. The terminal is 2km from the central riverfront on the Napo (taxi $1).

By boat Coop de Transportes Fluviales Orellana (☎ 06 288 0087) has an office on the riverside and operates boat services to Nuevo Rocafuerte on the Peruvian border (Sun, Tues, Thurs & Fri at 7am; 10hr). Advance booking advised. The office doubles as a tourist information point.

By bus Coca's modern bus terminal is 500m north of town but most bus companies have offices in the centre of town. Trans Baños (Napo & Bolívar) offers several services daily to Quito (9hr), Tena (5hr) and Baños (7hr). Transportes Loja and Transportes Esmeraldas also go to Quito.

By taxi Taxis will take you from the terminal and around town from $1.

ACCOMMODATION

El Auca Rocafuerte, at García Moreno ☎ 06 288 0127. Choose from rustic cabins or upscale hotel rooms with a garden courtyard and good restaurant. $46

6

6

CROSSING INTO PERU: NUEVO ROCAFUERTE

For adventurers wanting to emulate Francisco de Orellana and float deeper down the Río Napo into the Amazon Basin, improved relations between Ecuador and Peru in the past decade have made it easier to cross the border via Nuevo Rocafuerte. There are even plans afoot to make the trip possible all the way to Brazil's Atlantic coast, although this remains to be seen. This is not a trip for those who like comfort, as it's some eight hours downstream from Coca. Boats leave Coca at 7am (Sun, Tues, Thurs & Fri; $15 one-way), usually stopping off at Pañacocha. (On the return journey from Nuevo Rocafuerte to Coca there are usually departures Wed & Sun.) Come prepared with adequate supplies of food, water purification tablets and insect repellent. In Nuevo Rocafuerte there are a few basic, cheap places to stay but nowhere good enough to linger long. From Nuevo Rocafuerte you receive an **exit stamp** and boats cross the border to Pantoja, where you get an **entry stamp**. Pantoja also has a small amount of basic accommodation. Boats leave to Iquitos (Peru) from Coca via Nuevo Rocafuerte only once a month, a trip that takes six days.

La Misión Camilo de Torrano ☎ 06 288 0260. Next to the river, this is one of Coca's more upscale hotels, with well-tended rooms, swimming pool, steam baths, good restaurant and squirrel monkeys roaming the grounds. $38

Oasis Camilo de Torrano ☎ 06 288 0206. The pick of the cheap options. Rooms are basic and don't face the river, but the terrace does. $12

EATING AND DRINKING

Ear-piercing music blares away at the Napo Malecón, but otherwise there are several pleasant cheap places to eat near the modern waterfront.

El Auca Napo, at Rocafuerte. The best upscale place in town, with a varied menu – from shrimps in garlic to pork chops with pineapple. $8–11.

La Casa de Maito Espejo. Good place for cheap, delicious fish ($4–6).

Emerald Forest Blues Bar Espejo, at Napo. A place to drink with fellow jungle-seekers at this backpacker hangout.

PARQUE NACIONAL YASUNÍ

YASUNÍ is one of Ecuador's last great wildernesses and the country's largest mainland national park. The terrain of nearly 10,000 square kilometres ranges from upland tropical forest to seasonally flooded forest, marshes, swamps, lakes and rivers. This region remained jungle through the last Ice Age and therefore has staggering biodiversity – more than five hundred species of **birds** and sixty percent of Ecuador's **mammals**, including jaguar, puma and tapir. A highlight is the spectacle at the clay licks where dozens of parrots and parakeets congregate daily to feed.

UNESCO declared it an International Biosphere Reserve in 1979 but this didn't prevent oil exploration. The construction of a road, Vía Maxus, through parts of the park and pollution from irresponsible oil companies has damaged some areas. However, large sections remain unscathed and Yasuní still offers the best opportunity in Ecuador to experience pristine rainforest. Most tours coming through Coca include a visit to the park.

TENA

TENA is the most pleasant town in the Oriente to be based for a few days. Rather than being merely a gateway to the jungle, it's a destination in itself, with a slightly cooler climate, good hotels and restaurants, and an impressive setting on the river surrounded by lush forest. Nearby **Misahuallí** also offers a convenient place to dip into the jungle experience.

Aside from wandering around the centre and relaxing in a riverside restaurant, the main attraction in town is **Parque Amazónico La Isla** (daily 8.30am–6pm; $1), just south of the main pedestrian bridge. This park has several self-guided forested trails, diverse plants and wildlife.

ARRIVAL AND INFORMATION

By bus The terminal is 1km south of the centre. A taxi from here or anywhere in town costs $1.

Destinations Quito via Baeza (hourly; 4hr 30min); Puyo (hourly; 2hr 30min); Baños (daily; 4hr); Coca (daily; 4hr 30min).

Tourist information Agusto Rueda (Mon–Fri 8am–5pm; ☎ 06 288 8046).

ACCOMMODATION

Brisas del Río Av Francisco de Orellana 248 ☎ 06 288 6208. One of the best-located budget hotels on the river, and with a friendly owner. Pricier rooms have a/c, cable TV and private bath. **$16**

La Casa del Abuelo Sucre 432 ☎ 06 288 6318. This mid-range choice is as cosy and friendly as the name ("grandfather's house"), with well-furnished rooms, high ceilings and a pleasant rooftop terrace. Rooms upstairs are better. **$25**

Limoncocha Av del Chofer ☎ 06 288 7583 ⓦ hostallimoncocha.com. A popular backpacker option is this German-run *hostal* on the southeast edge of town (20min walk from the centre), with a travel agency, guest kitchen and free internet. Dorms $7.

Travellers Lodging Av 15 de Noviembre 438, at 9 de Octubre ☎ 06 288 6372. Budget travellers will feel right at home here. The rooms in three different price ranges are good value, with hot water, private bathroom and cable

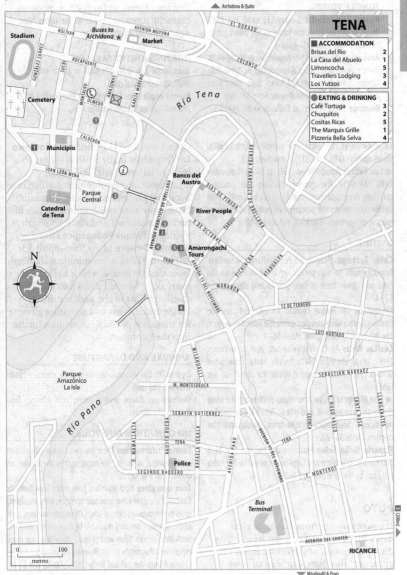

6

6

TOUR OPERATORS

Tena-based operators offer jungle tours, most of which are all-inclusive of transport, accommodation, food and guides. Tena is also the best place in Ecuador for **white-water rafting** and **kayaking** on the countless tributaries surrounded by spectacular jungle scenery. There are plenty of tour operators in town, but ensure you book with an experienced, well-equipped organization, ideally accredited by AGAR. The most famous stretches of river are the Jondachi and Jatunyacu or Upper Napo (both class III) and the wilder Misahuallí and Hollín (class IV). Day-trips are generally $55–70, and longer trips with overnight accommodation are from $130.

JUNGLE TOURS

Agency Limoncocha Sangay 533 ☎06 288 7583. Based in the *hostal* of the same name; offers jungle tours of 1–4 days at $35–45/day.

Amarongachi Tours 15 de Noviembre ☎06 288 6372. Tours staying in *Cabañas Amarongachi* or, preferably, *Cabañas Shangri-La*, perched 100m above Napo River and commanding wonderful views. From $40/day.

Ricancie Av El Chofer, at Pullurcu ☎06 284 6262,

ⓦ ricancie.nativeweb.org. Coordinates ten indigenous community ecotourism projects in the upper Napo region. Tours cost around $30/day.

RAFTING AND KAYAKING

Ríos Tarqui 230 ☎06 288 6727 or Quito ☎02 260 5828, ⓦ riosecuador.com.

River People 15 de Noviembre, at 9 de Octubre ☎06 288 7887, ⓦ riverpeopleecuador.com.

TV. River views cost extra. The reputable Amarongachi travel agency (☎06 288 6372) is attached. **$15**

★**Los Yutzos** Agusto Rueda 190, at 15 de Noviembre ☎06 288 6717. The riverside location and spacious, tastefully decorated rooms make this the best mid-range option. Lounge on the balcony overlooking the river or relax in the gardens. Breakfast included. **$40**

EATING

Café Tortuga Francisco de Orellana. Travellers' favourite with friendly service, an ideal location on the river and great fresh coffee, snacks and desserts for $2–4.

Chuquitos Off Parque Central. An excellent riverside position, with a wide-ranging menu and attentive service. The fish is particularly good. Mains $6–7.

Cositas Ricas Av 15 de Noviembre, at 9 de Octubre. This cheap, cheerful place serves tasty Ecuadorian staples ($3–7) and is a good option for the cheap set lunch.

★**The Marquis Grille** Amazonas, at Olmedo. The ideal choice to treat yourself, and one of Tena's few upmarket restaurants. Specialities include trout, paella and filet mignon. Mains $8–20.

Pizzeria Bella Selva Francisco de Orellana. The best place in town for pizza and large plates of pasta. They also sell pizza by the slice (mains $3–14).

PUYO

If you're arriving from Baños or even Tena, **PUYO** will at first sight be a disappointment, as the centre is less than attractive. But 3km southeast of town

(take a taxi for $1) is the **Jardín Botánico Las Orquídeas** (daily 8.30am–4pm; $5 book in advance; ☎03 253 0305, ⓦjardinbotanicolasorquideas.com). These botanical gardens, set among lush hills, boast more than two hundred species of native Amazonian orchids. Also worth visiting is **Parque Pedagógico Etno-Botánico Omaere** (daily 9am–5pm; $3; ☎03 288 3174), a ten-minute walk north from the city centre, which has guided tours along forested paths past indigenous dwellings. Part of the park is primary jungle and it offers an interesting glimpse for those not planning to venture further into the rainforest.

ARRIVAL AND DEPARTURE

By bus The bus station is 1km west of the centre, a 15min walk or $1 by taxi.

Destinations Baños (every 30min; 1hr 30min); Tena (hourly; 2hr 30min).

INFORMATION AND TOURS

Tourist information There are two tourist offices, one on Atahualpa, at Marin, the other next to the market on Orellana, at 9 de Octubre.

Tour operators Most travellers book tours from Quito or Baños but there are a few good tour operators in Puyo offering tours to communities close to town. Other communities, such as the Huaorani, are only reachable by light aircraft from the Shell-Mera airport 10km west of town; these tours are more expensive. Information about Huaorani communities can be obtained from the political body ONHAE (☎03 288 6148).

TEN OF THE BEST JUNGLE LODGES

Prices include all accommodation, food, guides and tours. Transfers are extra. Contact details given are for the Quito offices of each operator. Most lodges do last-minute deals when you can save up to thirty percent, but you risk coming up empty-handed.

Cotococha Lodge Amazonas, at Wilson ☎02 223 4336, ⓦcotococha.com. Located on the Napo River between Tena and Puyo, with 21 comfortable bungalows and a lounge area. Five days from $435.

Cuyabeno Lodge Pinto, at Amazonas ☎02 252 121, ⓦneotropicturis.com. The first lodge in Cuyabeno Reserve, these simple eco-cabins are still one of the cheapest ways to experience primary jungle. Four days from $250.

Huaorani Ecolodge Pasaje Sánches Melo OE1-37, at Av Galo Plaza ☎02 281 4658, ⓦhuaorani.com. Environmentally and sustainability conscious lodge on the upper part of the Shiripuno River. Huaorani guides help point out Amazon wildlife. Five days including transport from Quito $1260.

Itamandi Eco Lodge Tamayo N24-96, at Foch ☎02 222 0827, ⓦitamandi.com. Elegant lodge near Tena with swimming pool, but reachable by river only. The best quick jungle experience, starting from two days/one night from $114 (10 percent discount for cash).

Jamu Lodge Calama, at Reina Victoria ☎02 222 0614, ⓦcabanasjamu.com. One of the best-value budget lodges in the jungle, with nine thatched cabins in the Cuyabeno Reserve. Five days from $260.

Kapawi Lodge Foch, at Reina Victoria ☎02 600 9333, ⓦkapawi.com. High-end ecolodge owned by the Achuar people and situated on the Pastaza River near the Peruvian border. Five days from $999.

Napo Wildlife Center Av de la Prensa, at Av de America ☎02 600 5893, ⓦnapowildlifecenter.com. Ten deluxe cabins and a 15m viewing tower two hours from Coca by boat. Part-owned by the Kichwa Añangu community. Four days from $839.

Sani Lodge Roca, at Amazonas ☎02 255 8881, ⓦsanilodge.com. Cabins owned by the Quechua community, set on a secluded lagoon on the Napo River, three hours from Coca. Four days from $670 (camping from $440).

La Selva Jungle Lodge San Salvador E7-85, at Carrión ☎02 255 0995, ⓦlaselvajunglelodge.com. One of the cheaper options deep in primary jungle next to Yasuní National Park. Its location on a lake is spectacular and the food is particularly good. Four days from $720.

Yachana Lodge Vicente Solano, at Oriental ☎02 256 6035, ⓦyachana.com. Award-winning higher-end lodge with comfortable accommodation on the Napo River near Coca. Four nights from $660.

Amazonía (Atahualpa, at 9 de Octubre; ☎03 288 3219) offers a range of tours to indigenous communities close to Puyo from $35/day. Papangu (27 de Febrero, at Sucre; ☎03 288 7684, ⓦpapangutours.com) is an indigenous-run agency offering tours to nearby Quechua communities and further afield to Sarayacu and Río Curaray (travel by light aircraft). Tours $65/day not including flights. Selva Vida (Ceslao Marín, at Villamil; ☎03 288 9729, ⓦselvavidatravel.com) offers two- and three-day jungle trips from $35/day, plus five-day trips deeper into the rainforest.

ACCOMMODATION

You don't come to Puyo to stay in the bland, central hotels, so it's better to stay on the outskirts of town or head straight to a jungle lodge.

Hostal Araucano Ceslao Marín, at 27 de Febrero ☎03 288 5686. Worn, weathered rooms but very friendly service in this cosy, basic budget option in town. Breakfast included. $16

★ **El Jardín** Barrio Obrero ☎03 288 7770, ⓦeljardinrelax .com.ec. North of the centre towards Parque Omaere, this rustic wooden building, set in a large garden with chirpy parrots, is a real find. The restaurant is one of the best in the region. Breakfast included. $66

Las Palmas 20 de Julio, at 4 de Enero ☎03 288 4832. This pleasant yellow building on the edge of town has economical rooms; breakfast included. $24

EATING

El Fogón Atahualpa. Barbecued meat dishes and jungle specialities, including *guanta* (a type of large spotted Amazonian rodent). Mains $4–6.

★ **El Jardín** Barrio Obrero. In the lodge of the same name, this is the best restaurant locally, with specialities including *pollo Ishpingo* (chicken with cinnamon). Mains $5–10.

MACAS

MACAS, capital of the strongly Shuar province of Morona-Santiago, lies five hours south of Puyo and seven hours northeast of Cuenca. Most travellers enter the jungle via the northern towns, but quieter Macas has a certain charm. In the midst of Shuar territory, a people once renowned for headhunting, indigenous pride burns strongly and there have been confrontations with the

6

OIL AND THE ENVIRONMENT

Oil has provided lifeblood for Ecuador's economy since 1972, when the military dictatorship paraded around the first barrel of oil to herald the country's future prosperity. This dream failed. Today, the Oriente, which produces almost all of Ecuador's oil, has some of the poorest areas of Ecuador, though those depending on oil – from governments to contractors, all the way down to drivers working for oil companies – can't imagine doing without it. The sad legacy of the industry's first two decades can be seen on the road between Lago Agrio and Coca in the form of open pits and numerous spills that continue to happen with depressing regularity. Between courtroom battles and street protests, the struggle over responsibility has drawn on for many years. In 2007, Rafael Correa floated an idea to keep the oil in the northeastern part of Yasuní National Park underground as an anti climate-change initiative. Named after the Ishpingo, Tambococha and Tiputini (ITT) oilfields, Correa sought $3.6 billion in donations in exchange for leaving the oil *in situ*. But design flaws and doubts about Ecuador's reliability kept the money to a trickle. Blaming stingy foreigners, Correa U-turned in 2013. But while he is pressing ahead with oil development, hundreds of thousands of angry Ecuadorians no longer believe in the promise of black gold and want what remains of Yasuní protected.

government. Tourists can only visit the traditional villages that surround Macas with approved guides. Local tour agencies also arrange jungle treks.

WHAT TO SEE AND DO

In the centre of Macas, the main attraction is the large modern **Catedral** on Parque Central, which commands good views of the town. A block southwest of the park is the small **archeological museum** (Museo Arqueológico; 10 de Agosto, at Soasti; Mon–Fri 8am–5pm; free), which has Shuar exhibits including headdresses, blowpipes and a replica of a shrunken head. To the north is the **Parque Recreacional Campo Alegre**, which has even better views than the cathedral.

ARRIVAL AND INFORMATION

By plane Tame (☎02 397 7100) flies Mon–Fri to Macas.
By bus The bus terminal is on Amazonas, at 10 de Agosto, in the centre.
Destinations There are several daily buses to Cuenca (7hr), Puyo (3hr) and Quito (8hr).
By taxi Taxis around town cost $1.
Tourist information There is a tourist office on Comin (Mon–Fri 8am–8pm; ☎07 270 0143).

ACCOMMODATION

Casa Blanca Soasti, at Sucre ☎07 270 0195. Has decent rooms with private bath, cable TV and breakfast included. $25

La Orquídea 9 de Octubre, at Sucre ☎07 270 0970. A basic boarding house with firm beds, run by a friendly family. $22

EATING AND DRINKING

La Maravilla Soasti, at Sucre. Adorned with indigenous artefacts, and serving a variety of meat dishes and snacks (mains $3–6).
La Napolitana Amazonas, at Tarqui. Serves pizza, pasta and barbecue as well as great fish dishes, including tilapia and trout. Mains $3–8.

The northern coast and lowlands

Travelling up the Ecuadorian coast, the scenery gets greener and the vibe more Caribbean. The Afro-Ecuadorians who make up a large part of the population of **Esmeraldas** province give the region a different cultural feel to the rest of the country. The locals are exuberant, extrovert and talkative, a refreshing change from the mountains.

The main route from the Sierra descends dramatically via **Santo Domingo de los Colorados**, an unattractive transport hub. Avoid the dangers of grim **Esmeraldas** town and head south to a string of beach resorts. **Atacames** is the most popular party town. Further south, the beautiful beach at **Mompiche** is emerging as a popular spot for budget travellers. In the province of **Manabí**, head to **Canoa**, a haven for surfers and sunseekers. Nearby, the elegant resort **Bahía de Caráquez** juts out dramatically on a slim peninsula, close to mangroves and tropical forest. Further south is Ecuador's second-largest port, **Manta**, a bustling city that is unfortunately plagued by security problems.

SANTO DOMINGO DE LOS COLORADOS

This transport hub is the most convenient route from the Sierra to the coast. From here you can head north to Esmeraldas and Pedernales or south to Bahía de Caráquez, Manta and Guayaquil. Parts of town are dangerous, so take care at night. Santo Domingo has little to offer other than Tsátchila communities, but most places on the coast have direct buses, making an overnight stay unnecessary.

ARRIVAL

By bus The bus terminal is 1.5km north of the town centre (take a taxi for $1 or a public bus).

ACCOMMODATION

Hotel Diana Real Corner 29 de Mayo, at Loja ☎02 275 1380. The best mid-range option in the centre, with spacious rooms and a restaurant attached. **$24**

EATING

Gran Hotel Santo Domingo Río Toachi, at Galápagos ☎02 276 7950. This hotel has a good restaurant *La Tonga* inside. Choose from veggie, local and international food for around $7.

Timoneiro Av Quito, at Tsátchila. Just one of the good restaurants east of the centre serving chicken, soups and filling set meals. $3–5.

ATACAMES

ATACAMES is the busiest, brashest beach resort on the north coast and, along with Salinas, the most popular in Ecuador. Most hotels, restaurants and bars are situated on the thin peninsula, which forms the **Malecón**. The long sandy beach is lined with bamboo bars serving up fruit shakes by day and cocktails by night. During the week it's relatively quiet and a bit depressing, with staff desperately trying to lure you into their empty bars, but at the weekends and on national holidays Atacames turns into a heaving party town. Boom boxes pump out ear-splittingly loud salsa and reggaeton, while bars are packed with revellers until dawn. Note that tourists, particularly women, get hassled more here than in the southern resorts. **Muggings** have also been reported, so avoid taking valuables onto the beach, take taxis at night and stay in well-lit areas.

WHAT TO SEE AND DO

There are a few interesting excursions, including boat trips to nearby **Isla Encantada** ($3), which has abundant birdlife. From June to September, you can watch humpback whales off the coast; tours can be organized through *Le Castell Hotel*, on the Malecón (☎06 273 1476). The town of Atacames is inland over the bridge but it's a dusty unpleasant place, which only necessitates a visit if you need a bank.

ARRIVAL AND INFORMATION

By bus There are buses to and from Quito (several daily; 7hr) and Guayaquil (several daily; 8hr). If you can't get a direct bus, change at Esmeraldas (the bus station is a few kilometres outside the city, which it's preferable to avoid). Use Trans Esmeraldas, Aerotaxi or Trans Occidentales (offices across the footbridge). At weekends and during national holidays you must book in advance as demand is high. Atacames has no central bus terminal so you usually need to stand on the dusty main street inland to hail one. Trans La Costeñita and Trans Pacífico buses run several times an hour to Súa, Same and Muisne (1hr 30min). For Mompiche (2hr 30min), there are three or four direct buses a day, or you can catch a bus heading to Pedernales and be dropped off nearby.

By tricycle taxi The town is compact enough to walk around, but if you're laden with luggage, and particularly at night, take one of the motorized tricycle taxis ($0.50).

Tourist information There is a small iTur office stocked with brochures on the corner of the main road inland from Malecón.

ACCOMMODATION

Atacames has a vast amount of accommodation ranging from dirt-cheap cabins to luxurious tourist complexes. It can be surprisingly hard to find anything decent during peak periods, so book ahead. Prices can rise by around fifty percent in high season.

6

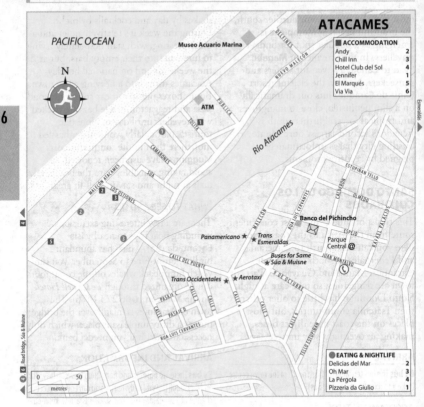

Andy Malecón, at Los Ostiones ☎06 276 0221. This beach-front hotel is cleaner than other budget options and has good, well-kept rooms (for the price) with fans and TV, although it gets noisy. **$20**

Chill Inn Los Ostiones, at Malecón ☎06 276 0477, ⓦchillinnecuador.com. Comfortable rooms, communal TV, kitchen for guest use and a small bar make for a homey atmosphere at this Swiss-run hostel. It's the best-placed hostel in Atacames, but there are only four rooms so book in advance. **$20**

Hotel Club del Sol 21 de Noviembre s/n, Barrio Nueva

★ TREAT YOURSELF

El Marqués Malecón ☎06 276 0182. Set back from the beach, the towering glass facade of this hotel stands out above anything else in Atacames. It's hardly full of character but it's the most upscale place in town, with spacious, impeccable rooms, a small gym and pool, plus breakfast is included. **$75**

Granada ☎06 276 0660, ⓦhotelclubdelsol.com. A square three-storey compound perfectly located on the beach, and with a large and pleasant pool. Rooms are good-sized, with more expensive suites on the top floor. **$65**

Jennifer Malecón, at C La Tolita ☎06 273 1055, ⓦhostaljennifer.com. A dependable budget choice just off the Malecón, with peach-coloured, clean rooms equipped with fans. **$15**

Via Via Tonsupa ☎06 246 5014, ⓦelflamenco.ec. Smaller and much more pleasant than Atacames, you may prefer the resort of Tonsupa. *Via Via* is the best hostel in town but fills up quickly. **$14**

EATING AND NIGHTLIFE

You're spoilt for choice for seafood restaurants. The beach stalls at the south end of the Malecón sell cheap *ceviche* (a popular hangover cure for breakfast) and most of the restaurants offer good fish and shellfish dishes. After dinner there are scores of beach bars in which to enjoy cocktails and dancing. One of those most popular is Caída del Sol (sunset). All restaurants are on the Malecón unless otherwise indicated.

Delicias del Mar Malecón. Out of the many seafood

restaurants along the seafront, this is the most popular budget choice, always jam-packed with locals and tourists wolfing down fish soup and breaded shrimps. Set menu just $3.

Oh Mar Principal. For a feast of seafood in a more refined setting head a block inland. *Ceviche*, *encocado*, shrimps, as well as steaks and pork chops all cooked well. $6–9.

La Pérgola Tonsupa. Among the best in the resort of Tonsupa, in a rustic garden setting. Besides the fresh seafood, *La Pérgola* specializes in Italian, from stone-baked pizzas and home-made pasta to pork in red wine. End with a tasty tiramisu. Mains $6–10.

Pizzeria da Giulio Malecón. For a break from seafood, head to this Italian-Ecuadorian place, which offers sumptuous fresh pizza and pasta dishes (mains $4–12).

MOMPICHE

The tiny little village of **MOMPICHE** is home to one of the most beautiful beaches in Ecuador. This, combined with great surfing conditions, has made it increasingly popular with both backpackers and higher-end tourists, in part thanks to the luxury hotel, *Royal Decameron*, on the hill above town, increasing tourist traffic and helping to improve the town's facilities.

ARRIVAL AND DEPARTURE

By bus Getting to Mompiche is not that easy. There are a few buses daily from Esmeraldas via Atacames (3hr). If you just miss one, either take a bus to Muisne and change at El Salto, or take a bus to Pedernales and ask the driver to drop you off at the entrance to Mompiche. From there, you can hitch a ride or sweat it on a 30min walk. From the south, travel via Pedernales and then Chamanga.

ACCOMMODATION

Unless you have hundreds to spend per night, the town has limited accommodation options and is booked up during busy periods.

La Facha ☎ 06 244 8024, ⓦ lafachahostel.com. This Argentine-owned place is a good choice, with

great-value rooms and pizza and barbecues in the small restaurant. **$15**

Gabeal ☎ 06 244 8060. The best budget option in town, located up the beach to the right. This ecolodge has rooms in bamboo cabins, each with a private bathroom. The building next to the beach is more basic, while the newer building has more spacious mid-range rooms. **$35**

San Marena ☎ 06 244 8032. A 5min walk inland, this budget hotel has large rooms with TV. **$20**

EATING

La Langosta A block inland to the south of the main road, this is renowned as the best place in town for lobster, *ceviche* and fried fish. $4–7.

El Punto Encuentro You can get your seafood fill at any of the restaurants on the beachfront. This is a dependable option. $4–6.

CANOA

CANOA is rather like the original Montañita – a quiet fishing village that has developed into a laidback resort by virtue of its beautiful beach and great surfing conditions. It has a dramatic setting, with waves crashing upon long stretches of sand flanked by steep cliffs. At present, it's probably Ecuador's best beach resort for budget travellers without the overblown craziness of Atacames or Montañita, but it's changing fast and can get pretty crowded on high season weekends.

An interesting excursion from Canoa is **Río Muchacho Organic Farm** (ⓦ riomuchacho.com), where you can see sustainable farming in practice and learn about the culture of the *Montubios* (lowland farmers). Guided hikes, horseriding and birdwatching are available.

ARRIVAL AND DEPARTURE

By bus From Quito there are direct buses with Transvencedores and Reina del Camino from Quitumbe bus station (daily; 7hr). There are more regular buses from Quito to Bahía de Caráquez; from there take a bus to Canoa (twice hourly; 20min). From Pedernales, there are buses to Canoa every 30min.

INFORMATION AND TOURS

Tourist information There is no tourist office, though the Rio Muchacho Office a block inland on Av 3 de Noviembre, at Javier Santos, has plenty of information and friendly staff. The guys at *Surf Shak* are also full of advice on local tours.

★ **TREAT YOURSELF**

Royal Decameron Mompiche ☎ 06 299 7300, ⓦ decameron.ec. Blow your budget completely on the swankiest hotel on the Ecuadorian coast. Perched on a headland above town, it boasts six swimming pools, four restaurants, and boats to a private beach on island Portete. Discounts for longer stays. **$150**

Tour operators Guacamayo Bahiatours offers all-inclusive tours (1 day $30, 3 days $115). Its offices are in Bahía de Caráquez (Bolívar 902; ☎ 05 269 1107) and Canoa (☎ 099 147 9849).

ACCOMMODATION

Accommodation prices are seasonal. The prices given are for high season (Dec–April & national holidays). They are about 50 percent cheaper out of season.

Bambú ☎ 05 258 8017, ⓦ hotelbambuecuador.com. At the north end of the beach is Canoa's most happening hotel. Rooms are small but the vibrant atmosphere and beautiful beachfront gardens make up for it. The restaurant is worth visiting even if you don't stay. Surfboards are available for rent. Camping $3.50, doubles $22

Canoa's Wonderland Malecón, at C San Andrés ☎ 05 2581 8163, ⓦ hotelcanoaswonderland.com.ec. This hotel stands out as one of the few plush options in Canoa, with a pleasant bar, restaurant, rooftop terrace, swimming pool and a/c rooms. $90

Coco Loco Malecón ☎ 099 243 6508, ⓦ hostalcocoloco .weebly.com. Two blocks left of the junction with the beach are these basic rooms in a large thatched bamboo house with fans, hammocks on the balconies, kitchen, bar with cocktails and a friendly atmosphere. Dorms $8, doubles $25

★ **País Libre** Filomeno Hernández at San Andrés ☎ 05 258 8187. This very popular hotel is run by friendly local surfer Favio Coello. Rooms are well kept, the hotel is decorated with artwork, there's a disco/bar next door and a small pool set in leafy gardens. Dorms $7, doubles $20

Posada Olmito Javier Santos ☎ 099 553 3341, ⓦ olmito .org. An endearing Dutch-owned place with basic rooms in an intricately constructed wooden building. $20

Sundown Beach Hostel Km2 Via San Vicente ☎ 099 364 5470, ⓦ ecuadorbeach.com. A 20min walk from town, this quiet beachfront hostel is a good spot to get away from it all, with private patio, garden and communal atmosphere. Dorms $8, doubles $24

La Vista Hotel ☎ 098 647 0222. Next to *Coco Loco*, this mid-range beachfront hotel offers comfortable, airy rooms, all with sea view and private bathroom. $24

EATING AND NIGHTLIFE

Canoa has plenty of restaurants – mainly informal beachfront places offering fresh seafood. Nightlife is restricted but quite busy in the bars on the main street at weekends and on national holidays.

Adicto Surf Café A rare vegetarian option, even with home-made vegan ice cream, plus sushi, on the north side of the beach close to Bambú. The perfect beach-bum spot to chill, hammocks included. $3–10.

Amalur C San Andrés. A few blocks from the beach, this is one of Canoa's few upmarket options and specializes in Spanish food such as tortillas, meatballs and octopus

(dishes $5–8). They have a small but great-value hostel at the back ($20).

Cevichería Saboréame Malecón. The best seafood in town according to locals – and they should know. Seafood soups and *encocado*, all delicious. Mains $3–5.

Coco Bar Javier Santos. On the main street leading to the beach, this is the hub of Canoa's nightlife – dead during the week but hot at weekends and in high season, with a packed dancefloor and free-flowing cocktails.

★ **Surf Shak** Malecón. This American-owned place is the centre of the expat community in Canoa. Choose from big breakfasts, big burgers, pizzas and fresh coffee. Wi-fi is available as well as plenty of advice on tours from Pete the owner. Mains $5–13.

BAHÍA DE CARÁQUEZ AND AROUND

The most dramatic location of Ecuador's coastal resorts, **BAHÍA DE CARÁQUEZ** sits on a slim sand peninsula jutting out from the mouth of the River Chone into the Pacific. The city, known simply as Bahía to locals, endured two disasters in 1998, when the El Niño rains washed away roads and triggered massive landslides before an earthquake in August destroyed two hundred buildings and left twenty people dead. The city recovered, however, and introduced a wide-ranging environmental programme, converting itself into an "eco-city" with recycling, sustainable development and reforestation. The result is that, unlike many of Ecuador's resorts, Bahía is a clean and pleasant place to stroll around.

WHAT TO SEE AND DO

The **Museo Bahía de Caraquez** (Tues–Fri 10am–5pm, Sat & Sun 10am–4pm; free) has a very good collection of pre-Columbian artefacts including tools, gold pectorals and ceramics. The **Mirador La Cruz**, a large cross above the south end of town, offers wonderful views over the city and surrounding bay. Some 15km south of town is the **Chirije archeological site**, which has countless ancient artefacts such as ceramics and burial sites dating from 500 BC. Inland from Bahía, the River Chone has some excellent unspoilt mangroves inhabited by abundant birdlife, including a colony of frigate birds to rival those found in the Galápagos.

ARRIVAL AND DEPARTURE

By boat It's a short walk to the passenger ferry dock, which has regular boats speeding across the bay to San Vicente, from where you can continue north up the coast.

By bus Buses to the terminal run up and down Malecón. There are regular services to and from Portoviejo, Manta and Guayaquil, and four a day from Quito (or travel via Pedernales). Reina del Camino is the biggest bus company with the best services.

By taxi There are plenty of tricycle taxis to get around town (most fares $0.50–$1).

INFORMATION AND TOURS

Tourist information The tourist information office is on Bolívar, at Malecón (☎ 05 269 1044). The next best thing is to visit Guacamayo Tours.

Tour operators The Chirije archeological site can be visited through Bahía Dolphin Tours (Bolívar 1004; ☎ 05 269 0257, ⓦ bahiadolphintours.com), which owns the site. A half-day nature tour with Guacamayo Tours (Bolívar 902, at Arenas; ☎ 05 269 1412) costs $25/person.

ACCOMMODATION

Most budget travellers prefer to stay in Canoa, but Bahía is a pleasant alternative. Accommodation ranges from cheap and basic to rather overpriced at the higher end. Hotels fill up quickly during high season (Dec–April) and on national holidays.

Bahía Bed and Breakfast Inn Ascazubi 316, at Morales ☎ 05 269 0146. The best rock-bottom budget option in town, with basic rooms with fans and cable TV in the lounge. Not to be confused with the more upscale *Bahía B&B*. $10

★ **Hostal Coco Bongo** Intriagi, at Arenas ☎ 05 269 1084, ⓦ cocobongohostel.com. Run by a friendly Aussie lady, this converted house overlooking the park has rooms with hot water, private bath, wi-fi and cable TV. It´s a good place to hang out and the breakfasts are top-notch. Dorms $6, doubles $25

Hotel Italia Bolívar, at Checa ☎ 05 269 1137. A cut above the budget options, this mid-range place has clean, simple rooms with private baths and a café downstairs. $40

★ **TREAT YOURSELF**

La Herradura Bolívar, at Daniel Hidalgo ☎ 05 269 0266, ⓦ laherradurahotel.com. At the northwest end of town, this charming old Spanish house is a delight. Nooks and crannies are filled with colonial artefacts from wagon wheels and saddles to statues and artwork. Rooms are comfortable with a/c and cable TV, and the restaurant is renowned as one of the best in town. Book in advance, 50 percent discount in low season. Doubles $60

EATING AND DRINKING

Arena Bar Pizzeria Marañon, at Bolívar. Good pizza and lasagne ($5–7) plus eclectic celebrity decor.

Colombius Bolívar. A cheap place for set lunches of chicken and fish ($2–3).

Muelle Uno Malecón. One of a string of restaurants on the pier near the docks, serving man-sized barbecue platters and seafood dishes for $4–8.

Puerto Amistad Malecón. This place is owned by an American sailor and offers *quesadillas* and crêpes as well as meat and fish dishes ($5–10).

Tropihelados Bolívar. Indulgent ice-cream sundaes and filling fast food ($2–3).

MANTA

Ecuador's second port used to be a pleasant expat haven, but a deteroriating security situation means that the city is best avoided. There are far better beaches elsewhere too. However, you may need to pass through Manta on your way up or down the coast and change at its unsightly bus terminal in front of the fishing boat harbour on Calle 7 and Avenida 8. If stuck for a few hours, head for the seafood promenade at Playa Murciélagos.

ARRIVAL AND DEPARTURE

By bus There are regular services to Bahía de Caráquez (hourly; 3hr), Puerto López (hourly; 2hr) and Montañita (daily; 3hr 30min), as well as departures to Guayaquil (hourly; 4hr) and Quito (hourly; 8hr). There are also daily buses up the coast to Esmeraldas.

Guayaquil

GUAYAQUIL is Ecuador's largest city and handles most of the country's imports and exports. The heat, dirt and danger used to be reasons enough to stay away, but the city has undergone quite a facelift in the past two decades and the waterfront and city centre have enough to keep visitors occupied for a day or two.

Arriving from the mountains, the contrast is striking between Quito's cool colonial charms and Guayaquil's hot, humid vivacity. *Guayaquileños* (or *Guayacos*) are fiercely proud of their city and they have a centre that is worth

6

6

showing off. Guayaquil's 3km-long **Malecón** and renovated artistic district of **Las Peñas** are great achievements, as are the new airport, bus terminal and museums.

Be aware that the heat and traffic pollution can make sightseeing an uncomfortable experience, so get up early. The weekend, when the city is quieter, is the best time to explore. Outside the centre and Urdesa, Guayaquil is not picturesque and remains dangerous, particularly at night.

El Malecón

The **Malecón** (daily 7am–midnight) running alongside the river is a public space that is easily the highlight of the city – enclosed, pedestrianized and patrolled by security guards. The best point to enter is **La Plaza Cívica** at the end of 9 de Octubre. Start at **La Rotonda**, a statue of South America's liberators, José de San Martín and Simón Bolívar, shaking hands in front of a semicircle of marble columns. Past the plush Guayaquil Yacht Club is the 23m-high Moorish Clock Tower, and further south **The Henry Morgan**, a replica of a seventeenth-century pirate ship, is docked. A one-hour trip on the river costs $5 (hourly departures afternoons and evenings).

Further south is **Plaza Olmedo**, with its contemplative monument of José Joaquín de Olmedo (1780–1847), the first mayor of Guayaquil. The southern end of Malecón reaches La Plaza de la Integración and an artisans' market, selling traditional indigenous clothing and crafts.

Botanical gardens

North from La Rotonda is a large children's play area packed with families at weekends. Further on is a stunning set of **botanical gardens** with more than three hundred species of coastal vegetation. The gardens are divided into four zones: ornamental trees, humid forest, palms and conifers. There are two plazas within the gardens: the

Pre-Columbian Plaza, with Manteña balsa wood and palm trees, and the Neoclassic Plaza, with a bronze fountain surrounded by lanterns. Above the gardens is a set of 32 transparent panels with the names of some 48,000 citizens who contributed to the construction of the Malecón.

IMAX and Museo Guayaquil en La Historia

At the north end of Malecón is an **IMAX cinema** (☎04 256 3078, ⊛cinemamalecon.com) with a 180-degree screen. Below the cinema is **Museo Guayaquil en La Historia** (Tues–Sun 9am–1.30pm, 4.30–8pm; free), which condenses a compact history of the city in English and Spanish, from prehistory to the present day, into fourteen dioramas.

Centro Cultural Simón Bolívar

The north end of Malecón culminates in the spacious **Centro Cultural Simón Bolívar** (Tues–Fri 9am–5pm, Sat & Sun 10am–5pm; free), which has regular exhibitions and a huge collection of pre-Columbian ceramics and first-rate modern art.

Mercado Artesanal (Artisans' market)

A couple of blocks inland along Calle Loja from the IMAX is the huge, enclosed **Mercado Artesanal** (Mon–Sat 9am–7pm, Sun 10am–5pm), which has a wide selection of traditional handicrafts and clothing. Prices are slightly higher than in the Sierra and haggling is obligatory.

Malecón del Salado

At the opposite end of 9 de Octubre (a 20min walk or short taxi ride) is the **Malecón del Salado**, next to the Estero Salado, a tributary of the River Guayas. It's a picturesque place to stroll, and for great views of the river you can cross the bridges (which tower over 9 de Octubre). Otherwise, take a boat trip or relax in one of the seafood restaurants.

Las Peñas

Rising above the north end of Malecón is the colourful artistic district of **Las Peñas**, a formerly run-down area that's been revamped. Like the Malecón, it's patrolled by security guards. Round the corner to the right of the steps is the historic, cobbled street of Numa Pompilio Llona, named after the *Guayaco* lawyer and poet. The street leads from old to new, reaching **Puerto Santa Ana**, the city's latest grand project with waterfront shops, restaurants, luxury apartments and an extensive marina. There are a couple of interesting museums, the best of which is **Museo de la Música Popular Julio Jaramillo** (Wed–Sat, 10am–5pm; free), dedicated

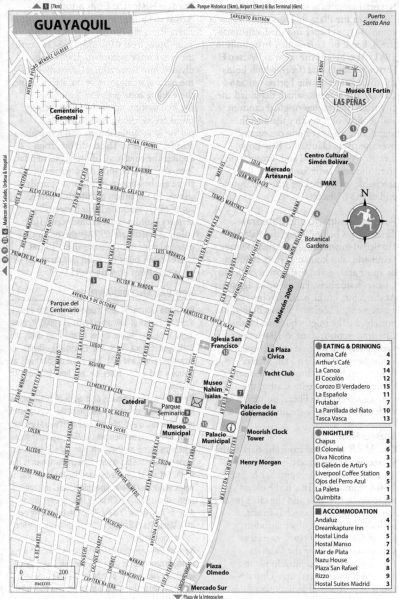

GUAYAQUIL

Parque Historica (5km), Airport (5km) & Bus Terminal (6km)

Puerto Santa Ana

Cementerio General

Museo El Fortín

LAS PEÑAS

Mercado Artesanal

Centro Cultural Simón Bolívar

IMAX

Botanical Gardens

Parque del Centenario

Iglesia San Francisco

La Plaza Cívica

Yacht Club

Museo Nahim Isaias

Catedral

Parque Seminario

Palacio de la Gobernación

Museo Municipal

Palacio Municipal

Moorish Clock Tower

Henry Morgan

Plaza Olmedo

Mercado Sur

Plaza de la Integración

Malecón del Salado, Urdesa & Hospital

Malecón 2000

● EATING & DRINKING	
Aroma Café	4
Arthur's Café	2
La Canoa	14
El Cocolón	12
Corozo El Verdadero	15
La Española	11
Frutabar	7
La Parrillada del Ñato	10
Tasca Vasca	13

● NIGHTLIFE	
Chapus	8
El Colonial	6
Diva Nicotina	3
El Galeón de Artur's	3
Liverpool Coffee Station	9
Ojos del Perro Azul	5
La Paleta	1
Quimbita	3

■ ACCOMMODATION	
Andaluz	4
Dreamkapture Inn	1
Hostal Linda	5
Hostal Manso	7
Mar de Plata	2
Nazu House	6
Plaza San Rafael	8
Rizzo	9
Hostal Suites Madrid	3

0   200
metres

6

to the city's most famous singer. Next door is **Museo Pilsener** for everything on Ecuador's most popular beer.

For spectacular views of Guayaquil, climb the 444 steps up Las Peñas to the peak of **Cerro Santa Ana** (en route, there's a wide selection of craft shops, restaurants, cafés and bars). At the top of the hill in the Plaza de Honores is a new colonial-style chapel and the **Lighthouse** (free), based on Guayaquil's first, built in 1841. Also here is the open-air **Museo El Fortín del Santa Ana** (free), which holds the foundations of the Fortress of San Carlos. The fortress, which defended the city from pirates, has original cannons and replicas of Spanish galleons. The highlight is the sweeping panoramic view over the rivers Daule and Babahoyo, downtown Guayaquil and, across the river, the reserve of Santay Island, reachable via footbridge from the south end of the Malecón.

Parque Seminario and Catedral
Three blocks behind the grand **Palacio Municipal** (town hall) is the small **Parque Seminario**, also known as Parque Bolívar or, more aptly given that dozens of urban iguanas reside here, Parque de las Iguanas. At the centre of the park is an imposing monument of liberator Simón Bolívar on horseback. The huge white neo-Gothic **Catedral**, reconstructed in 1948 after a fire, towers over the west side of the square.

Northeast, Plaza San Francisco is dominated by the church of the same name, a statue of Pedro Carbo, the nineteenth-century liberal politician and writer, and a large fountain.

Museo Municipal
One block southeast from the park is the **Museo Municipal** (Sucre, at Chile; Tues–Fri 8.30am–4.30pm; Sat & Sun 10am–2pm; free). This is the oldest museum in Ecuador and the city's best. The pre-Hispanic room has fossils, including the tooth of a mastodon, dating back 10,000 years, as well as sculptures created by the Valdivia – Ecuador's oldest civilization – and a huge Manteña funeral urn. Upstairs is a room of portraits of Ecuadorian

presidents, nicknamed "the room of thieves", plus a small exhibition of modern art. There are five shrunken heads on display in a closed room, which is only viewed on guided tours. Free tours in English are recommended.

Parque Histórico Guayaquil
Across the bridge in the wealthy district of Entre Rios, the **Parque Histórico** (daily 9am–5pm; free; ☎04 283 2958) is worth the trip from downtown. The park is divided into three zones. Created out of the natural mangroves of the River Daule, the **wildlife zone** provides a snapshot of the Ecuadorian jungle with deer, tapirs, monkeys, sloths, ocelots, tortoises, parrots, toucans, caimans and fermenting termite mounds. The **traditions zone** depicts the rural way of life via haciendas, "peasant" houses and crops. At weekends, there are boisterous music and comedy shows. In the **urban architecture zone**, some of Guayaquil's late nineteenth-century buildings are reproduced. The colonial-style *Café 1900* is the perfect place to gaze out over the river. To **get there**, catch bus #81 from the terminal or get a taxi from downtown ($4–5).

ARRIVAL AND DEPARTURE

By plane Guayaquil's José Joaquín de Olmedo airport, about 5km north of downtown (☎04 216 9000, ⓦwww .tagsa.aero), has regular flights to and from Quito, the Galápagos, Cuenca, Loja and Esmeraldas. There's an exchange bureau and ATM. Take a taxi to your hotel, as Metrovía and public buses are not best tackled with luggage.

By bus The bus terminal is 6km north of downtown, a brief albeit uncomfortable walk from the airport, with many food courts and shops. The cheapest way to get into town from here is the Metrovía ($0.25), a rapid transit bus system modelled on Quito's. It runs from Terminal Río Daule opposite the bus station through downtown to the south. Get off at La Catedral stop for the main tourist sights. Watch your belongings as pickpockets are common.

Destinations Bahía de Caráquez (hourly; 7hr); Baños (3 daily; 6–7hr); Canoa (2 daily; 7hr); Puerto López (8 daily; 4hr); Montañita (3 daily; 3hr 30min); Quito (hourly; 9hr); Salinas (hourly; 2hr).

By taxi There are plenty of taxis but few of them use a meter, so negotiate the price first. Taxi drivers in Guayaquil will nearly always try to overcharge foreigners. You should pay $3–4 from the bus terminal to the centre and $4–5 from the airport. Do not take unmarked or informal cabs. Short taxi rides around the city centre should cost about $2–3.

INFORMATION AND TOURS

Tourist information The Dirección Municipal de Turismo office at 10 de Agosto and the Malecón (Mon–Fri 9am–5pm; ☎04 259 9100, ⊛turismo.guayaquil.gob.ec) has friendly staff and up-to-date maps and brochures. The tourist site also produces seven downloadable guidebooks. Another useful website is ⊛inguayaquil.com.

Tour operators Canodros (Urb. Santa Leonor Mz 5 Solar 10 ☎04 228 0880); Chasquitur (Acacias 605, at Las Monjas ☎04 288 8988); Ecoventura (Miraflores Av Central 300A ☎04 283 9390, ⊛ecoventura.com); Metropolitan Touring (Francisco de Orellana, World Trade Centre Millennium Gallery, ground floor; ☎04 263 0000, ⊛metropolitan-touring.com).

ACCOMMODATION

Guayaquil has plenty of hotels but is still not well geared up for the backpacker market. Many of the budget hotels are of a very poor standard in unappealing areas, while the top-end hotels charge high rates. It's best to stay near to Parque Bolívar or Parque Centenario. The centre can get very noisy so ask for a back room or a higher floor. It doesn't make much sense to stay in the suburbs because there are few tourist sights, although there is one good backpacker hostel, *Dreamkapture Inn*.

★**Andaluz** Baquerizo Moreno, at Junín ☎04 230 5796. Located just a few blocks from Malecón and 9 de Octubre, this bright, breezy hotel has comfortable rooms with a/c and hot water, a splash of artwork on the walls, a relaxing rooftop terrace and a lounge area with leather sofas and TV. $40

Dreamkapture Inn Alborada Doceava Etapa ☎04 224 2909, ⊛dreamkapture.com. A few kilometres from the centre, this is one of the city's few backpacker haunts. Secure, well maintained and friendly, the comfortable rooms have a/c and there's a small pool. The hostel also owns its own travel agency. Dorms $10, doubles $25

Hostal Linda Lorenzo de Garaicoa 809 ☎04 256 2495. Hotel overlooking Parque Centenario with marble floors and plush, well-furnished rooms. $40

Hostal Manso Malecón 1406, at Aguirre ☎04 252 6644, ⊛manso.ec. A slice of Arabian boutique chic in Guayaquil with individually designed rooms, seated cushions and regular performances in the lounge area. $42

Mar de Plata Junín 718, at Boyacá ☎04 230 7610. Many of Guayaquil's budget hotels border on intolerable but this is a good deal. Rooms are basic but clean and come equipped with fans, cable TV and private bathrooms (a/c $5 extra). $30

Nazu House Av C J Arosemena km 3.5, Cuidadela La Cogra ☎04 220 1143, ⊛nazuhouse.com. The hilltop location of this hostel offers a different experience of Guayaquil, with friendly service, a fine lounge and small

pool, charming tiled rooms and a great view. Doubles $85

Plaza San Rafael Chile 414 ☎04 232 7140. Smallish but comfortable rooms with a/c, cable TV and hot water. Breakfast included. $55

Rizzo Clemente Ballén 319, at Chile ☎04 601 7500. Adequate rooms, some with small balconies, ideally situated next to Parque Bolívar. $44

Hostal Suites Madrid Quisquis 305, at Rumicacha ☎04 230 7804, ⊛hostalsuitesmadrid.com. Not the best location but certainly one of the best-value options in the city, with colourful decor, patterned bedspreads, spacious rooms, background music, a feast of artwork covering the walls and very friendly service. $30

EATING AND DRINKING

Guayaquil has a wide range of restaurants spread around the city. Downtown, there are plenty of cheap, basic places, while restaurants attached to hotels are overpriced. Las Peñas is the most pleasant area to eat, with a cluster of traditional cafés. An alternative is to take a taxi ($2–3) to the fashionable neighbourhood of Urdesa, where there's a wide range of restaurants, particularly along main street Victor Emilio Estrada.

★**Aroma Café** Jardines del Malecón 2000. The best place to eat on the Malecón, with a wide selection of Ecuadorian specialities ($5–8) served in the cool, shaded atmosphere of the botanical gardens. Daily noon–midnight.

Arthur's Café Numa Pompillo, Las Peñas. Dramatically located restaurant perched over the river. The open windows make for a fresh, breezy experience and the menu offers local staples such as grilled fish, *ceviche* and fried pork chops for $6–9. Daily 6.30pm–late.

La Canoa At *Hotel Continental*, 10 de Agosto at Chile. Probably Ecuador's most popular restaurant, serving coastal and Andean staples to around a thousand people a day, along with sandwiches and *humitas*. Mains $12. Daily 24hr.

El Cocolón Pedro Carbo, at 9 de Octubre; also Plaza Orellana in Urdesa Norte. Named for crusty rice, this is the best place to indulge in huge portions of imaginative Pacific Lowlands specialities, with plenty of *bolón*, *maduro*, secos and verde dishes. Mains $6–12. Mon–Fri & Sun 11am–6pm, Sat 11.30am–10pm.

Corozo El Verdadero Av Pedro Carbo 103, at Roca. Fabled downtown Afro-Ecuadorian seafood restaurant, with a 40-year track record. Mains $4–9. Mon–Sat 7.30am–4pm.

La Española Junín, at Boyacá. Excellent bakery with a wide selection of delicious cakes, pastries, sandwiches and big breakfasts for $1–3. Mon–Fri 8am–7pm, Sat 8am–3pm.

Frutabar Malecón, at Martínez. Misshapen tables, surfboards, tropical murals, a huge selection of *batidos* (fruit shakes) and imaginative burgers and sandwiches make this the perfect repose after a hard morning's sightseeing.

6

6

$4–6. Daily 8am–midnight.

La Parillada del Ñato Estrada, at Laureles, Urdesa. Treat yourself to a huge plate of barbecued meats in this enormously popular Urdesa institution. There's a branch in the centre at Luque, at Pichincha. Mains $5–12. Mon–Sat 11am–1am, Sun noon–11pm.

Tasca Vasca Ballén 422, Parque Seminario. Beautifully laid-out Spanish restaurant with a cosy cellar-like ambience and waiters in traditional dress. Large menu of tapas and Spanish specialities with mains at $6–10.

NIGHTLIFE

Guayaquileños love to party, and the city has a nightlife to rival Quito's. Las Peñas has a wide selection of café-bars and Urdesa is also a good place for a few drinks after dinner. To hit the dancefloor, go to the Zona Rosa, between downtown and Las Peñas, around Rocafuerte and Panamá. Most bars open at 8pm and clubs at 10pm. Bars stop serving alcohol at midnight Mon–Thurs and at 2am Fri–Sat and most discos only open Thurs–Sat. There's usually a minimum consumption charge of $10 for discos, which includes entrance.

Chappus Estrada, Urdesa. A Guayaquil institution. Have a few drinks on the wooden balcony or hit the dancefloor – one of the few in Urdesa. Thurs–Sat 10pm–4am.

El Colonial Rocafuerte, at Imbabura, Zona Rosa. A traditional Peñas bar with Ecuadorian specialities and live music at weekends. Mon–Thurs 4pm–midnight, Fri & Sat 4pm–2am.

Diva Nicotina La Escalinata, Las Peñas. At the bottom of the steps of Las Peñas, you can catch some great live music here – from Cuban Habanera to jazz – accompanied by whisky and cigars. Mon–Thurs 7pm–midnight, Fri & Sat 7pm–2am.

El Galeón de Artur's La Escalinata, Las Peñas. With its maritime decor and live music at weekends, this is a good place for a drink and a light meal. Daily 7pm–2am.

Liverpool Coffee Station Av Las Monjas 402, Urdesa. Bright, vibrant café-bar packed with Beatles memorabilia. Live music Tues–Sat. Mon 5–11pm, Tues 5pm–midnight, Wed–Fri 5pm–1am, Sat 7pm–2am.

Ojos del Perro Azul Panamá, at Padre Aguirre. Named for a short story by Colombian writer Gabriel García Márquez, it's a good place to catch live rock and Latin music at weekends. Wed & Thurs 8pm–midnight, Fri & Sat 8pm–2am.

★ **La Paleta** Numa Pompillo Llona, Las Peñas. One of the city's most aesthetically pleasing watering holes with a bohemian atmosphere, cosy corners and bars on two floors. Tues–Sat 8pm–2am.

Quimbita Galeria La Escalinata, Las Peñas. At the bottom of the steps, this art gallery doubles as a café-bar with live folk music at weekends. Wed & Sun 5pm–1am, Thurs–Sat 5pm–3am.

DIRECTORY

Banks and exchange The most convenient banks are Banco del Pacífico, Banco de Guayaquil and Banco Pichincha, all on Icaza and Pichincha.

Consulates Australia, Rocafuerte 20, at Tomás Martínez (☎ 04 601 7529); Canada, Blue Towers 6th floor office 604, Av Francisco de Orellana 234 (☎ 04 263 1109 ext 101); UK, General Córdova 623, at Padre Solano (☎ 04 256 0400); US, Santa Ana, at Rodríguez Bonín (☎ 04 232 3570).

Hospital Clínica Kennedy, Av del Periodista, Kennedy (☎ 04 224 7900).

Internet Internet 50C, Rumichaca, at Rendón.

Post office The main office is at Aguirre 301 and Pedro Carbo, just off the Parque Bolívar. Branches are also at the bus and airport terminals.

The south coast beaches

At weekends, *Guayacos* flee the city's heat in droves and head west to the cooler Pacific beaches of the **Ruta del Sol**. It gets very crowded in peak season between Christmas and Easter, when the weather is hottest. Among the beach resorts, **Playas** is the closest to Guayaquil, **Salinas** is the playground of wealthy *Guayacos*, and surfer hangout **Montañita** draws in backpackers. Further north is the beautiful province of Manabí, which contains Ecuador's only protected coastal area, the **Parque Nacional Machalilla**. The port of **Puerto López** is the most convenient base to explore the park and Isla de la Plata, billed as the "poor man's Galápagos" because of its birdlife. **Whale-watching** is a highlight between June and September.

PLAYAS AND PUERTO EL MORRO

PLAYAS, one hour thirty minutes from Guayaquil by bus, attracts lower-middle-class *Guayacos*. Like all south-coast resorts, it's jammed in high season and quiet the rest of the year. The beach is very long but not sheltered and currents are strong, so take care in the water.

A few kilometres east of Playas is the small port of **Puerto El Morro**, which makes a great day-trip. To get here from Guayaquil, change at Playas. The main attractions are mangroves, birdlife and dolphins in the estuary, as well as Islas de los Pájaros, which has a large population of magnificent frigatebirds and pelicans.

TOUR OPERATOR

Ecoclub Los Delfines ☎ 04 252 9496, ⓦ puertoelmorro .blogspot.com. Arranges tours of Puerto El Morro (1hr 30min, $5; 3hr, $8). A short tour takes in the mangroves, lets you see dolphins and even do a spot of fishing, and a longer tour includes an extended boat trip and a walk on the Isla de los Pájaros.

ACCOMMODATION

Hostal Cattan Malecón ☎ 04 276 0179. ⓦ hostalcattanplayas.com. This cheapie budget hotel is past *Dorado*. **$20**
Hotel Dorado Malecón ☎ 04 276 0402. A good mid-range choice with a/c, private bath and cable TV. **$35**

EATING

Cabins line the beach selling great fresh seafood.
Los Ajos Jaime Roldós, at C 8. One of the best in town, with a more upscale atmosphere and range of fish, chicken and meat dishes. $8–12.
La Cabaña Típica Malecón. A cosier alternative to the beach, serving seafood specialities at $4–6.

SALINAS

To new arrivals **SALINAS** looks like a wannabe Miami Beach with high-rise apartment blocks and expensive yachts. But it's worth stopping here, at least for a day-trip, to walk along the attractive waterfront and swim in the calm waters. The resort has plenty of great restaurants and nightlife. West of the Malecón is a second beach, **Chipipe**, which is quieter and has a plaza, church and park.

ARRIVAL AND INFORMATION

By bus Comfortable CLP buses run to and from Guayaquil (hourly; 2hr 30min); most come equipped with a/c, TV and seat belts. Change at Santa Elena for Montañita.
Tourist information The tourist information office (Enriquez Gallo, at C 30) is open sporadically in high season.

ACCOMMODATION

Book hotels well ahead in high season, particularly at weekends and on national holidays. Hotels on the waterfront come at a premium, while inland from the waterfront, Salinas is rather ugly.
Chescos Malecón, near the western end of the main

beach, next to Banco Guayaquil ☎ 04 277 1334. The best backpacker option, with the most international flair. The first-floor balcony has hammocks to watch goings-on at the beach. The blue-and-white rooms have a/c and dorms with interesting "wavy" wooden bunks. **$30**
Cocos Malecón, at Fidón Tomalá ☎ 04 277 0361, ⓦ hostal-cocos.com. The most economical of the options on the waterfront, with a restaurant, bar, disco and games room. **$40**
Francisco II Enríquez, at Rumiñahui ☎ 04 277 4133, ⓦ cadenahotelesfrancisco.com. Tacky but dependable mid-range option, with a/c and a small pool. Its sister hotels, *Francisco I* and *Francisco III*, are nearby. **$50**
Yulee Eloy Alfaro, at Mercedes Molina ☎ 04 277 4325. In the more pleasant area of Chipipe, this brightly painted colonial-style hotel is a break from the high-rise concrete. It has three levels of rooms and you won't find a cheaper option. **$16**

EATING

You're spoilt for choice on where to eat, particularly seafood. Avoid the seafood stalls, nicknamed "Cevichelandia", as sanitation is a problem. Salinas' nightlife heats up in high season.
Amazon Malecón ☎ 04 277 3671. International cuisine in a rustic ambience with mains for around $6–10.
La Bella Italia Malecón ☎ 04 277 1361. For a break from Ecuadorian fare, watch mouth-watering pasta and pizza prepared in front of you in this comfortable restaurant – and then devour. Mains $4–7.
La Ostra Nostra Eloy Alfaro, at Las Almendras ☎ 04 277 4028. Choose from a wide range of seafood, soups and meat (mains $5–10) at this extremely popular restaurant out towards Chipipe. Oysters ($12 per dozen) are a particular speciality.

MONTAÑITA

Perhaps there should be a sign at the entrance to **MONTAÑITA** that reads: "You are now leaving Ecuador". Such is the international vibe that you could be anywhere. At first sight, the town feels like countless backpacker havens, but whether you love it or hate it, you can't deny the place's infectious energy. The surfing contingent has been joined in recent years by hippies and partygoers, making it the coast's most buzzing resort for budget travellers. Many people stay for months, while others get out after a couple of excessive nights – if you're seeking a relaxing beach break, go elsewhere. Surfers can enjoy rideable breaks most of the year, frequently

6

6

2–3m on good days. It's not the best place to learn but there are plenty of experienced teachers. There's a renowned international surf competition around Carnaval (Feb/March).

ARRIVAL

By plane Tame operates flights to and from Quito (Thurs, Fri & Sun). Deep discounts available if booking ahead.

By bus The bus stop is a couple of blocks inland from the beach on the corner of Rocafuerte. Comfortable CLP buses leave Guayaquil at 5am, 1pm and 5pm (3hr 30min). If you can't catch one of these, take a bus from Guayaquil to Salinas (hourly; daytime only) and ask the driver to drop you at Santa Elena (1hr) to catch a connection. Buses north to Puerto López pass hourly (1hr). For Quito, go to Manta or Puerto López and change.

TOUR OPERATORS

Montañitours Guido Chiriboga, at Rocafuerte ☎04 206 0043. Offers a wide range of tours – everything from fishing, diving and snorkelling, to organized tours of Isla de la Plata and Galápagos.

Sweet Surf C Quatro ☎099 738 9089. Run by a friendly Swedish-Ecuadorian couple, *Sweet Surf* offers surfboard rentals for $15/day ($4/hr) and 2hr lessons for $15, as well as tours ranging from day-trips to a week-long surf tour of the coast.

ACCOMMODATION

Montañita has a huge amount of accommodation and where you stay depends mainly on how much sleep you want to get. You can find a basic room for $5–7/person, but bear in mind the centre is often very noisy and at weekends partying continues until after dawn. The north end is quieter with the best-quality mid-range accommodation. Prices double on high season weekends and it's hard to find a room in the centre. You can negotiate prices in low season.

Abad Lounge Av Costanera, at Malecón ☎04 230 7707. Right on the beach, this new family-run hotel has tidy rooms, many with sea views and balconies. $20

★**Casa del Sol** ☎099 248 8581, ⓦcasadelsolmontanita .com. Walk north all the way to the point to this very popular hangout run by a Californian surfer. The rooms are bright and breezy, and there's a great restaurant and bar area. Sea view costs extra. $40

El Centro de Mundo Malecón, at Rocafuerte ☎099 728 2831. Look no further for cheap, basic rooms than this three-storey, wooden beachfront building, just to the right of the junction of Rocafuerte with the beach. Dorms $3.50, doubles $14

Charos Malecón between 15 de Mayo & Rocafuerte ☎04 206 0044, ⓦcharoshostal.com. Just inland to the left of the beachfront. One of the most comfortable places to stay in the

centre, with a/c rooms, a bar, restaurant and small pool. $45

Kamala Hostería ☎099 942 3754, ⓦkamala-hosteria .minihostels.com. Escape the noise of Montañita completely at this hippy haven just north of Manglaralto. The individual cabins are set around a small swimming pool in front of the beach and there's also a bar, restaurant and dive school. $30

Hostal Pakaloro Av Costanera at the north end of Chiriboga ☎04 206 0092. A great budget deal, featuring newly refurbished rooms with private bath and cable TV. $18

Paradise South ☎04 290 1185. For something quieter and more upmarket, go north of town (past the second bridge) to enjoy the comfortable thatched cottages and large lawns of this tranquil, welcoming place. $25

EATING

There are scores of good restaurants in the centre of town. Montañita throws quite a party at weekends, particularly in high season (Dec–April). Most bars on the main street, Guido Chiriboga, offer two-for-one happy hours on cocktails ($3), but take it slow until things get going towards midnight.

Cañagrill Av Costanera. Round the corner from the main street Guido Chiriboga, this is the town's busiest disco, with two dancefloors playing a mix of electronic and Latin music. It gets packed in the early hours and the partying continues until after dawn. From 10pm at weekends; entrance $5.

★**Hola Ola** 10 de Agosto. Two blocks inland, *Hola Ola* is the centre of the town's social scene. Big breakfasts in the morning, a wide range of cocktails in the evening, parties at weekends and great international food in between. Mains $5–10.

Karukera Guido Chiriboga. A great choice for breakfast, this place specializes in crêpes and also serves up Caribbean cuisine such as fish in orange sauce. Mains $4–8.

Papillon Guido Chiriboga, at Rocafuerte, on the corner of the main street. Indulge in a range of sweet and savoury pancakes or relax with an ice-cream sundae. Mains $4–8.

Tiki Limbo Guido Chiriboga. This backpackers' favourite takes pride in its food ($6–9) and you´re bound to find something tantalizing on its imaginative, eclectic menu. Asian and vegetarian dishes are particular specialities. The brightly coloured rooms in the hostel upstairs are very popular ($25).

DOS MANGAS

DOS MANGAS is the best base to explore the tropical dry forest of the Cordillera Chongón. This community of 950 people makes a living from crafts and agriculture. It has a small information centre, and two paths through the forest to waterfalls and natural pools. Trucks from the main coast road head to Dos Mangas every hour and you can hire guides and horses (around $10/person). The park entrance fee is $1. Alternatively, book a tour in Montañita.

OLÓN

This tranquil village on the other side of the point is developing as a quiet alternative to Montañita; it has a long beach and a few good hotels and restaurants. The sea isn't suitable for surfing but you could just about swim in it.

ACCOMMODATION

Hostería N&J ☎ 04 239 0643, ⓦ hosterianj.com. This friendly place is on the beachfront. Breakfast included. **$25**

Quimbita ☎ 04 278 8019, ⓦ quimbita.com. The most interesting accommodation option is this charming, colourful hotel with a permanent art exhibition two blocks from the beach. **$25**

MONTAÑITA TO PUERTO LÓPEZ

Head north from Montañita and cross into the province of **Manabí**. This is probably the most beautiful stretch of Ecuador's coastline – so if you prefer peace to partying and watching wildlife rather than people this is the place to come. On the road to Parque Nacional Machalilla, you pass a succession of fishing villages – **Ayampe**, **Las Tunas**, **Puerto Rico** and **Salango**. Tourist facilities are still underdeveloped, but the area does contain some good-quality accommodation and the beaches are often deserted.

ACCOMMODATION

Between Montañita and Puerto López there are several highly recommended *hosterías*.

★ **La Barquita** ☎ 04 278 0051, ⓦ hosterialabarquita.com. Near the tiny village of Puerto Rico. The main attraction is the wooden, boat-shaped restaurant, worth a visit even if you don't stay. The rooms are set in idyllic gardens with a small adventure playground and swimming pool. **$20**

Cabañas La Tortuga ☎ 04 278 0613, ⓦ latortuga .com.ec. These comfortable cabins are the only beachfront accommodation in Ayampe. For those on a budget there are bunk beds with shared bath and camping. Camping/person **$10**, dorms **$10**, doubles **$30**

Mantaraya Lodge ☎ 02 336 0887. Inside Machalilla National Park, this is a brightly coloured neo-colonial style

resort, rather than the typical thatched-roof lodge. Fantastic ocean views, excellent food available in package deals, shuttles to Salango beach, and excursions along the coast and into the park's dry forest. **$90**

PUERTO LÓPEZ

PUERTO LÓPEZ is the tourism hub for the Machalilla area and the best base to explore **Parque Nacional Machalilla** and **Isla de la Plata**. The town isn't pretty but boasts one of the most attractive locations on the coast, set in a wide bay surrounded by the green hills of Ecuador's largest protected coastal forest. The dusty Malecón has a certain beaten-down charm, with fishermen heading out from the bay every morning. The town gets very busy on weekends during the whale-watching season (June–Sept), when you should book accommodation in advance.

ARRIVAL AND INFORMATION

By bus Buses drop passengers by the terminal on the main road, General Córdova, from where it's a short walk to the waterfront. Alternatively, you can take a tricycle taxi ($0.50).

Destinations There are regular buses to Jipijapa (hourly; 1hr 30min), where you change for Guayaquil, La Libertad (daily; 3hr) or Salinas; Manta (hourly; 2hr). Reina del Camino (☎ 05 230 0207) offers relatively comfortable services to Quito (8am & 8pm; 10hr).

Tourist information The local iTur office on Av Machalilla, at Atahualpa (daily; ☎ 099 199 5390, ⓦ puertolopez.gob.ec), is two blocks inland and has plenty of leaflets and attentive service.

ACCOMMODATION

Hostal Itapoa Malecón ☎ 05 230 0071, ⓦ itapoareserve .com. North of town, these Brazilian-run cabins set in a small garden are an endearing budget hideaway; they offer their own locally produced organic chocolate. **$20**

★ **Hostería Mandala** Malecón ☎ 05 230 0181, ⓦ hosteriamandala.info. North of town along the Malecón is this very popular travellers' option with beachfront cabins set in beautiful gardens, plus a games room, small library and a good restaurant. **$58**

Maremonti Bed & Breakfast C San Francisco, Colina Central ☎ 099 173 1325, ⓦ maremonti.com.ec. A 15min uphill walk from the centre, meaning they have the best views and most spectacular sunsets in Puerto López from the rustic wooden balcony. Almost all the rustic rooms share the view, with hammocks slung on their individual balconies. **$35**

6

6

Hostería Nantu Malecón ☎05 230 0040, ⓦ hosteriananntu.com. This hotel is excellent value, offering mid-range rooms at a low price. Firm beds, hot water, as well as a small pool and games room to keep you busy. $30

Piedra del Mar General Córdova accross from the fire station ☎05 230 0250 ⓦ piedradelmarhotel.com. To call it boutique style is a bit exaggerated but the colonial-style courtyard, pebble-dashed walls and small pool make this a good-value option in the centre of town. $50

Sol Inn Juan Montalvo, at Eloy Alfaro ☎05 230 0248. The basic wooden cabins and laidback vibe are ideal for those on a tight budget. Camping/person $3, dorms $6, doubles $14

EATING AND DRINKING

Espuma del Mar Malecón. The decor is a bit tacky but this spacious restaurant does most dishes well, from breakfasts to snacks and evening meals. Mains $4–5.

Patacón Pisa'o General Córdoba. For something different, try Colombian specialities such as *arepas* at this friendly little place where mains are $3–5.

Restaurante Carmita Stands out from the cluster of restaurants along the Malecón with a great selection of seafood (mains $6) in a polished setting.

★ **The Whale Café** At the south end of Malecón. This is a great place to eat and chat, where the friendly American owners whip up everything from Thai noodles to pancakes and veggie specialities for around $6–9. Home-made bread for breakfast too.

PARQUE NACIONAL MACHALILLA

Ecuador's only coastal national park was set up in 1979 to preserve the rapidly disappearing tropical dry forest that once stretched north all the way to Costa Rica. It's a dramatic setting with thickly forested hills crowned by candelabra cacti, dropping down to pristine, peaceful beaches. The park headquarters (daily 8am–5pm; ☎05 230 0102) is based in Puerto López, opposite the market, just off the town's main road, where you pay your entrance fee (valid for five days; mainland only $12; Isla de la Plata only $15; combined ticket $20).

WHAT TO SEE AND DO

The best place to explore the park's dry forest is **Agua Blanca**, a village inhabited by some 280 indigenous people and an important archeological site of the Manteño culture that lived here from 800 to 1500 AD. Getting to Agua Blanca involves either taking a bus north from Puerto López and then walking the unpleasant 5km trail up a dirt track, or hiring a *mototaxi* ($5 one-way, $10 return). The museum houses an interesting

---

CROSSING THE PERUVIAN BORDER

The only significant coastal town between Guayaquil and the Peruvian border is the banana hub, **Machala**. Some 75km south of here is the grubby border town of **Huaquillas**, the busiest crossing point from Ecuador to Peru. Spend as little time as possible here; Cuenca and Guayaquil are both at an easy distance by bus so there should be no need to stay overnight.

ACCOMMODATION AND EATING IN HUAQUILLAS

Grand Hotel Hernancor 1 de Mayo 323, at Hualtaco ☎07 299 5467, ⓦ hotelhernancord.blogspot.com.

This hotel has decent guest rooms with private bath and a/c. $24

La Habana T. Córdovez, at Santa Rosa. A good choice for Ecuadorian meat and fish dishes and a filling set meal ($3).

INTO PERU

What was once one of the worst border crossings in South America is now hugely improved, thanks to a new "CEBAF Huaquillas-Aguas Verdes" joint Ecuadorian-Peruvian migration control centre just inside Peru, open 24hr. The main road bypasses the grubby border towns entirely. Cross-border buses stop and handle their paperwork separately while travellers exit through the building, first getting Ecuadorian exit stamps and then Peruvian entry stamps, or of course vice versa. Lines are long, however, and it can take 2hr 30min or more to clear on a normal day.

INTO ECUADOR

For those arriving in Ecuador, **buses** from Huaquillas leave from depots a few blocks from the international bridge. Co-op CIFA (☎07 293 0260, ⓦ cifainternacional.com) goes to Machala (frequent; 1hr), the closest city. CIFA also goes to Guayaquil (4hr 30min), as does Ecuatoriano Pullman (☎07 293 0197) and Rutas Orenses (☎07 293 7661). Panamericana (☎07 293 0141) has comfortable buses to Quito (6 daily; 12hr). For Cuenca (8 daily; 5hr) use Trans Azuay (☎07 293 0539). If you intend to go to Loja, it's better to cross from Peru at Macará.

collection of sculptures, funeral urns and pickled snakes. A guided tour ($5) includes museum entry followed by a two-hour forest walk. Highlights include the towering ceibos, barbasco and fragrant Palo Santo trees whose wood is burnt as incense and to repel mosquitoes. Take in the spectacular views up to San Sebastián before a refreshing soak in a pungent but relaxing sulphur pool, considered sacred by local indigenous people.

San Sebastián

The landscape rises to 800m inland, where the dry forest turns into the cloudforest of **San Sebastián**, with lush vegetation including orchids, bamboo and wildlife such as howler monkeys, anteaters and 350 species of birds. This virgin forest can be explored on a 20km hike with a mandatory guide hired in Agua Blanca ($20). You can camp overnight or stay with local villagers.

Playa Los Frailes

A few kilometres further north is the entrance to **Playa Los Frailes**, a stunning virgin beach, often deserted in early mornings. Present your park ticket or pay the entrance fee at the kiosk, then either head straight for Los Frailes on a thirty-minute hike or take the 4km circular trail via the black-sand cove of La Payita and Playa La Tortiguita. To get straight to the beach, take a taxi from Puerto López ($5 one-way).

ISLA DE LA PLATA

The tounge-in-cheek tag of "poor man's Galápagos" refers to the fantastic amount of wildlife visitors can find on the small island of **ISLA DE LA PLATA**. Just 37km from Puerto López, it's by all means worth a day-trip to see its birdlife, which is easy to combine with whale-watching in the summer months. The island is home to numerous blue-footed boobies, masked boobies and frigate birds. Red-footed boobies and waved albatrosses are also seen from April to October. The island has a small colony of sea lions, though it's rare to see them. You can only visit the island with a tour operator.

WHAT TO SEE AND DO

From the landing point in Bahía Drake, there are two circular **footpaths** around the island, the 3.5km Sendero Machete and the 5km Sendero Punta Escaleras. The hikes are about three hours long and there's no shade, so bring sunscreen, water and a hat. The close encounters with the friendly boobies, which peer at you with mild curiosity, are the main highlight, but also watch out for colourful caterpillars crossing your path. Cool off after the hike with some snorkelling among an array of marine life including parrotfish and clownfish. Peak season is June to September (particularly July & Aug) when humpback whales arrive for the mating season, which is an awesome spectacle.

TOUR OPERATORS

The day-trip to Isla de la Plata can be arranged at several local tour operators and hotels on the Malecón in Puerto López. It generally costs $35–40/person including guide and light lunch. Recommended companies include:

Bosque Marino ☎ 05 230 0004, ⓦ bosquemarino.com. Offers a wide range of tours including Isla de la Plata and Isla Salango and onshore activities like horseriding.

Exploramar Diving ☎ 05 230 0123, ⓦ exploradiving .com. Specializes in diving trips along the coast.

Naturis ☎ 05 230 0218, ⓦ machalillatours.com. Specializes in community tourism and offers a wide range of multi-activity trips including kayaking, fishing and snorkelling ($25/person) as well as tours to San Sebastián.

The Galápagos Islands

Charles Darwin developed his monumental theory of evolution after travelling to the **GALÁPAGOS** in the 1830s, and it's no exaggeration to say that the creatures of these unworldly volcanic islands, 1000km west of the Ecuadorian coast, were fundamental in changing the way we view ourselves.

The array of **wildlife** in the Galápagos is spellbinding. From giant tortoises to marine iguanas, sea lions to sharks and blue-footed boobies to magnificent frigate birds, it's hard to know which way to turn. Nowhere else on earth can you

6

WHERE TO SEE WILDLIFE IN THE GALÁPAGOS

Blue-footed boobies Most easily viewed on North Seymour, Punta Pitt (San Cristóbal), Española or Genovesa.

Frigate birds Try Seymour Norte, Punta Pitt or Española.

Galápagos penguins Colonies on Floreana, Bartolomé, Fernandina and Isabela.

Giant tortoises See them in the wild in the Santa Cruz highlands or at the breeding centres in Puerto Ayora and on Isabela and San Cristóbal.

Green sea turtles The best-known nesting sites are Bartolomé, Tortuga Bay (Santa Cruz) and Gardner Bay (Española).

Iguanas The marine variety is found on all major islands; see their land cousins on Seymour Norte, South Plaza or Santa Fé.

Sea lions To see them underwater, the best snorkelling spots are Champion Island (Floreana) and La Isla de los Lobos (San Cristóbal). Or walk among a colony at South Plaza or La Lobería (San Cristóbal). Males are territorial, so keep your distance.

Sharks Docile white-tipped and black-tipped reef sharks are best viewed off Floreana, North Seymour, Bartolomé and León Dormido (San Cristóbal), while hammerhead sharks are mainly seen by divers (also at León Dormido).

Waved albatross Exclusively found on Española from April to November.

view wild mammals, reptiles and birds that are utterly unconcerned by human presence – a legacy of there being few natural predators on the islands.

Visiting the Galápagos independently is now relatively easy and last-minute deals are better than ever. However, a week in the Galápagos will cost much more than one on the Ecuadorian mainland. The **low season** is May/June and September/October, while December to mid-April and July/August is **high season**, though cheap deals can still be found.

The Galápagos is a year-round destination, but conditions are most balmy between December and April, with calmer seas and sunny weather with occasional rain on larger islands. From June to October the weather is cooler and the sea rougher, but colder waters mean more wildlife. Whenever you choose to visit, you can only see a tiny percentage of the islands because 97 percent of the area is protected by the national park and the 70 registered visitor sites comprise only 0.01 percent of the landmass, a comforting fact for environmentalists.

ARRIVAL AND DEPARTURE

By plane Return flights to San Cristóbal or Baltra start at about $350 plus around $150 taxes and fees with TAME (Quito ☎ 02 396 6300, ☎ 1700 500 800, ⊛ tame.com.ec), Avianca (Quito ☎ 02 294 2800, ☎ 1800 237 6425, ⊛ avianca.com) or LAN (☎ 1800 842 526, ⊛ lan.com). If booking online, you must indicate your nationality; if you

mistakenly book as an Ecuadorian resident, you will have to pay surcharges.

In San Cristóbal it's a $1.50 taxi ride to town, i.e. Puerto Baquerizo Moreno. If arriving on Baltra, it's more complicated. To get to the main port Puerto Ayora involves a free 10min bus ride south, a $1, 10min ferry crossing and then a $2.50 bus (45min) or $18 taxi (40min). Note that to return to the airport from Puerto Ayora, the last bus usually leaves about 8am, after which a taxi or private transfer is the only option.

INFORMATION

Tourist information The Ministry of Tourism (☎ 05 252 6174, ⊛ www.turismo.gob.ec) has iTur offices in Puerto Ayora, Puerto Baquerizo Moreno and Puerto Villamil. Alternatively, contact the Galápagos National Park (☎ 05 252 6511, ⊛ galapagospark.org). The Galápagos National Park entrance fee is $100 for foreign adults, payable in cash on arrival. There is also a $20 transit card, which must be purchased before check-in at Quito or Guayaquil airport counters, regulating the length of stay in the archipelago (90 days maximum).

TOUR OPERATORS

The price of tours, accommodation and cruises varies hugely. When booking from abroad, tours cost $2000–5000 for a week. Booking last-minute in Quito and Guayaquil brings the prices down to $500–1500 (not including flights). However, the most common way for backpackers to visit is to buy flights, stay in budget accommodation ($20–40/night), eat at cheap restaurants and pick up day-trips locally ($50–150/day). Doing it this way, it's possible to spend a week on the islands for less than $1400 total, including flights.

In Quito Galápagos Tours (Amazonas N23-71, at Wilson; ☎ 02 254 6028, ⊛ galapagostours.net); Metropolitan Touring (Av Amazonas N20-39, at 18 de Septiembre;

02 250 6650, www.metropolitantouring.com); Ninfa Tour (Av Amazonas N24-62, at Pinto; 02 222 3124, galapagosninfatour.com); Nuevo Mundo Expeditions (18 de Septiembre E4-161 at JL Mera; 02 256 5261, nuevomundoexpeditions.com).

In Guayaquil Centro Viajero (Baquerizo Moreno 1119, at 9 de Octubre; 04 230 1283); Ecoventura (04 283 9390, ecoventura.com); Metropolitan Touring (Francisco de Orellana, World Trade Centre Millennium Gallery, ground floor; 04 263 0000, metropolitan-touring.com); Via Natura (Junín 114, at Malecón, Ed. Torres del Rio, Floor 7; 04 256 9052, vianatura.com).

In Puerto Ayora Galapatour (Av Rodríguez Lara; 05 252 6088); Galapagos Voyager (Av Charles Darwin, at Colono; 05 252 6833, galapagos-voyager.com); Moonrise Travel (Av Charles Darwin; 05 252 6348, galapagosmoonrise .com); Scuba Iguana (Av Charles Darwin; 05 252 6497); Galapagos Sub-Aqua (Av Charles Darwin; 099 919 8798, galapagos-sub-aqua.com); Metropolitan Touring (*Finch Bay Eco Hotel;* 05 252 6297, metropolitan-touring.com); We are the Champions Tours (Av Charles Darwin; 05 252 6951, wearethechampionstours.com).

GETTING AROUND

By plane Airlines EMETEBE (Galápagos 05 252 1183, Guayaquil 04 230 9209, emetebe.com.ec) and Air ZAB (05 301 0267, airzab.net) fly small eight-seater planes between San Cristóbal, Baltra and Isabela (several times per week; $160 one-way or $260 return, plus $15 taxes). The weight limit is 10kg, but penalties for more are only $0.85/kg.

By ferry Daily services on small launches connecting Santa Cruz with San Cristóbal and Isabela (all routes $30 one-way; 2hr–2hr 30min). The ferries leave Isabela at 6am and 3pm; San Cristóbal at 7am and 3pm; and depart Santa Cruz for both islands at 7am and 2pm. There are usually at least two boats, but you should book one day in advance at an agent in the main ports. Note that it's a bumpy ride, particularly at 2pm. Pharmacies sell inexpensive anti sea-sickness pills.

ISLA SANTA CRUZ

This is the most developed island in the Galápagos and its capital **PUERTO AYORA** is the central tourism hub where most island-hoppers arrive. It's by no means the highlight of the archipelago, but the central location and wide range of hotels, restaurants and tour operators make it the most convenient base to explore surrounding islands.

Puerto Ayora

In Puerto Ayora you can arrange tours and pick up last-minute deals. A visit to the Charles Darwin Research Station to see the tortoises is worth it, and there are some interesting short hikes out of town.

WHAT TO SEE AND DO

There are various attractions close to Puerto Ayora, but for some you need to take the **Bay Tour** ($35 from most local operators). The tour takes in La Lobería, where you can snorkel with sea lions, Playa de los Perros, where marine iguanas and various birds are seen, Las Tintoreras, channels where sharks are often found, and Las Grietas.

A fifteen-minute walk east of town is the **Charles Darwin Research Station** (daily 7am–6pm; free; 05 252 6146, darwinfoundation.org), which contains an information centre and a museum. The highlight is the giant tortoise enclosure where you can view the Galápagos giants close-up. Of the original fourteen subspecies, eleven have survived. "Lonesome George" was the most famous resident until his death in 2012 meant the extinction of his Pinta island subspecies. The station gets quite busy with tour groups so come early if possible, and you can also see tortoises at the breeding centres in San Cristóbal and Isabela.

If you're in Puerto Ayora and want to kill a few hours, then the best option is **Tortuga Bay.** Follow the trail from the western edge of town along a paved path through cactus forest (a 45min walk with little shade). The first bay is not actually Tortuga Bay, but one of the longest beaches in the archipelago, popular with surfers but dangerous to swim. Walk to the end of this beach and cross over to a lagoon to find the bay where marine turtles come to lay their eggs. The beach closes at 6pm.

Las Grietas

Another side trip from the port with a relaxing dip at the end is the walk to **Las Grietas,** a crevice in the rocks that supplies the port with much of its fresh water. Take a water taxi ($0.60) across the bay towards Playa de Los Alemanes, then venture along rocky trails for a further twenty minutes to reach Las Grietas. Fissures in the lava rocks have created two layers of brackish water – saline and fresh.

6

ACCOMMODATION

Casa Natura	1
Cormorant Lodging House	6
España	3
Estrella del Mar	7
Galápagos Best Homestay	2
Lirio del Mar	5
Las Palmeras	4

● EATING & DRINKING

Café Hernán	9
Chifa Asia	3
Chocolate	1
El Descanso del Guía	8
Galápagos Deli	6
La Garrapata	7
Il Giardino	2
Isla Grill	5
La Panga	7
The Rock	10
Servisabrosón	4

It's a beautiful, sheltered place for a swim. Be aware that the rocky trails are a bit tricky; walking shoes will come in handy.

The highlands

The highlands offer a very different experience to the beaches on Santa Cruz and it's worth venturing inland to see the diversity of the island. At El Chato, you can observe giant tortoises in their natural habitat in the reserve (entrance $3 including guide). Nearby are the lava tunnels, which are naturally formed and have lighting so you can walk through them. Note that you need to crawl under a low wall to get out unless you walk back to the entrance. Either side of the main road which cuts through Santa Cruz are the Gemelos (twins), collapsed 30m-deep craters. The sheer drop into the craters, covered in vegetation, makes them an impressive sight; tour groups often stop on the way to or from the airport. All of the attractions above can be seen on a guided tour with any of the tour operators in Puerto Ayora ($80 for groups up to 14), or, to save money, hire a taxi in the port to take you to all of

them ($30), which can be done in two or three hours.

Las Bachas

On the north coast, **Las Bachas**, once a base for the US military, is a long white-sand beach often covered in Sally Lightfoot crabs; flamingos also abound in the lagoons inland. Tour operators often combine a visit here with other excursions such as North Seymour (see p.638).

ACCOMMODATION

Santa Cruz has the largest selection of accommodation on the islands and it's even possible to find budget rooms in peak periods. If you have your eye on a specific hotel, book in advance as places fill up fast. Prices start from $15–25/person for budget rooms up to $100–200/night in the higher-range hotels, mainly filled by tour groups.

Casa Natura Petrel, at Isla Floreana ☎02 246 9846, ⌨ vianatura.com. To enjoy a little comfort in charming surroundings, stay at this friendly hotel 10min out of town and enjoy the buffet breakfast and small pool at the back. **$160**

Cormorant Lodging House Av Darwin, at 12 de Febrero ☎05 252 4343. Centrally located and with great views of the bay from the top-floor terrace, a/c and towels folded into swan shapes. The brighter superior doubles are worth the $10 extra. Doubles **$25**

España Thomas de Berlanga, at 12 de Febrero ☎ 05 252 6108, ⓦhotelespanagalapagos.com. One of the most popular budget hotels, with neat rooms around a colourful courtyard with hammocks. Doubles $\overline{\$65}$

Estrella del Mar 12 de Febrero, next to police station ☎ 05 252 6427. The cheapest hotel on the waterfront has great views and simple rooms with a/c and cable TV. Book early to get a view of Academy Bay. Double $\overline{\$50}$

Galápagos Best Homestay Piqueros, Barrio Escalesia ☎ 05 3015345, ⓦgalapagosbesthomestay.com. Hands down the best Puerto Ayora hostel experience. Well equipped with microwaves, small fridges, a/c. Easy walking distance from Av Darwin. Owner Kevin will give you a free walking tour. Dorms $\overline{\$20}$

Lirio del Mar Islas Plaza, at Thomas de Berlanga ☎ 05 252 6212. Another dependable budget option with a small terrace but basic, no-frills rooms. A/c extra. Dorms $\overline{\$17}$, doubles $\overline{\$45}$

Las Palmeras Thomas de Berlanga, at Islas Plaza ☎ 05 252 6139, ⓦhotelpalmeras.com.ec. This is one of the best mid-range options in town. Rooms are plushly decorated and there's a large pool on the terrace. Doubles $\overline{\$100}$

EATING AND DRINKING

Puerto Ayora is a very pleasant resort with a wide range of restaurants, mostly in the slightly higher range ($15–25 for dinner). There are also quite a few cheap places, particularly the *kioskos* along Charles Binford (pedestrianized in evenings), where you can get a good meal for $5 and $20 lobster in season (June–Dec). Some restaurants also do set lunches and dinners for just $3.50.

Café Hernán Av Baltra, at Av Darwin. This waterfront favourite does the best pizza in town (mains $6–12) and indulgent desserts such as black forest gateau.

Chifa Asia Binford. Backpackers flock to the *kioskos* restaurants on this street to grab a delicious budget meal. For something a little spicier try this popular Chinese. Mains $4–6.

Chocolate Darwin. Very good-value set lunch ($5) and more expensive specialities such as *ceviche* and beef in chocolate sauce.

El Descanso del Guía Av Darwin (next to the church). A popular option for locals to fill up on Ecuadorian staples such as *bolón* (fried plantain ball) for breakfast and chicken stew or a variety of white fish for lunch. The juices are excellent and the two-course set meals are well above average and cost just $3–4.

Galápagos Deli Tomás de Berlanga, between Baltra and Islas Plaza. Very pleasant modern café featuring excellent home-made ice cream and sandwiches and Puerto Ayora's best thin-crust pizza. For those nostalgic for the UK, fish and chips are $8.75.

La Garrapata Av Darwin, near Berlanga. Laidback local favourite with a varied menu including excellent seafood, as well as set lunches. Mains $5–15.

★**Il Giardino** Darwin, at Binford. The town's most popular gourmet restaurant does not disappoint, with a menu featuring home-made panini and crêpes, plus delicious ice creams and sorbets. But wear insect repellent outdoors. Mains $9–16.

Isla Grill Av Charles Darwin, opposite *Solymar Hotel*. Excellent grilled seafood and meats including steaks and barbecued ribs. Mains $8–15, lobster $24.50.

La Panga Darwin, at Thomas de Berlanga. The town's main disco, which pumps out Latin and international music until 2am. *Bongo*, the archipelago's most elegant late-night bar, is upstairs.

The Rock Darwin, at Islas Plaza. Named after the first Galápagos bar set up on Baltra in the 1940s, this endearing

6

THE GALÁPAGOS IN DANGER

From the 1980s onwards, Galápagos tourism has experienced explosive growth. But the influx of humans, both transient and permanent, has done huge damage to parts of the fragile ecosystem and the islands were placed on the **UNESCO Danger List** in April 2007. The key problems included: uncontrolled immigration; high traffic levels; an inadequate sewage system; invasive species such as livestock, pets and fruits; and overfishing.

The Ecuadorian government took action by deporting hundreds of illegal Ecuadorian immigrants back to the mainland and using satellite technology to stop illegal fishing. Recycling and renewable energy are being rolled out. Isabela, Floreana and Santiago have seen goat extermination programmes, with more than 250,000 killed since 2006. Other harmful invasive species are fruit flies, fire ants and rats, the last of which have proved the most difficult to exterminate.

Emergency measures were deemed successful, and, to the dismay of scientists and environmentalists, the Galápagos Islands were removed from the UNESCO Danger List in July 2010. The islands' problems are far from over and tourists can help by following the strict rules on waste disposal and recycling. Sadly, in 2014, the government lifted restrictions on hotel construction again, without comment on environmental impact.

place serves up a feast, from Mexican *quesadillas* to teriyaki fish fillets ($6–10). The wide variety of juices, shakes and cocktails washes it all down.

Servisabrosón Binford. One of the many cheap and informal places on the *kioskos* offering filling plates of chicken, pork and seafood (mains $4–7). The fish in coconut is particularly popular.

AROUND ISLA SANTA CRUZ

Isla North Seymour

Off the north coast of Santa Cruz is the tiny island of **NORTH SEYMOUR**, which offers some of the best opportunities in the archipelago to watch frigate birds and get close to blue-footed boobies. Follow the 2.5km circular trail around the island to see frigates nesting and the amusing courtship of the boobies. Sea lions and iguanas are also common. A day tour is comparatively pricey ($125/person with Puerto Ayora tour operators) due to restricted access.

Islas Plazas

Off the east coast of Santa Cruz are the two tiny islands of **Plazas**, home to a large sea-lion colony and a great place to observe these animals up close on land. You can only visit the south island, where a 1km trail around the cliffs offers good views of birdlife including pelicans and frigate birds. There's also a sea-lion bachelor colony, where defeated males congregate. Like North Seymour, day tours cost $125/person, combined with Punta Carrión.

Isla Santa Fé

Southeast of Puerto Ayora, the small island of **SANTA FÉ** has great snorkelling as well as opportunities to see white-tipped reef sharks, marine iguanas, sea lions and stingrays. Santa Fé land iguanas laze around the trails that wind through a forest of 10m-high *Opuntia* cacti. Access to the island's land sites is restricted to

---

CRUISES

Although many budget travellers now choose to travel independently and stay in hotels, in many ways the best way to see the Galápagos is on a **cruise**. If you can deal with the seasickness, which is likely on all but the most luxurious boats, then you'll be rewarded with more quality time at sites and be spared the daily return journey to a port. There are also many sites only accessible to cruise boats.

Vessels that tour the Galápagos range from small boats to luxury cruise yachts carrying ninety passengers. Five-day tours allow visitors to explore the islands close to Santa Cruz, while eight-day tours include islands further afield. Single-cabin supplements are usually very high. If you have some flexibility, you can make substantial **savings** on cruises by booking last-minute in Quito or Guayaquil. Prices are even lower booking last-minute in Puerto Ayora and you could be lucky enough to get the higher-level cruises on the cheap. Always check the official grading of the boat before booking. Prices below are full prices for eight days based on two sharing (last-minute discounts can be as little as 50 percent of these prices). Boats listed are not necessarily recommended. The rock-bottom economy-class boats have all but disappeared as budget travellers increasingly opt for land-based tours.

Tourist class boats cost from $2000 for eight days and offer a basic level of comfort. They have Class II guides with a good level of knowledge and English-language skills. Boats include *Floreana*, *Darwin*, *Encantada* and *Golondrina*.

Tourist-superior boats start at $2900 for eight days and have more comfortable cabins, better food and Class II guides. Boats include *Archipel I* and *II*, *Aida Maria*, *Eden*, *Daphne* and *Yolita II*.

First-class yachts cost $3600–4800 for eight days, can travel faster and have a

decent level of comfort, high-quality food and Class III guides, the highest level of accreditation. Boats include *Anahí*, *Eric*, *Letty*, *Flamingo I*, *Ecogalaxy*, *Majestic*, *Tip Top II*, *III* and *IV* and *Seaman Journey*.

Deluxe vessels start around $5000 for eight days. These are the largest yachts and ships with the most stability and have extra facilities such as jacuzzis and more spacious social areas. Boats include *Galápagos Legend*, *Silver Galápagos* and *Santa Cruz II*.

cruise boats, but there are day-trips from Puerto Ayora (around $60), which are of limited appeal because you can only visit selected offshore sites.

ISLA SAN CRISTÓBAL

The most easterly island of the archipelago, this is the administrative centre of the islands. It's quieter than Santa Cruz, which may appeal, and the large population of sea lions in the main port is a particular highlight.

WHAT TO SEE AND DO

The most popular boat trip ($80) combines Isla de Los Lobos, where you can snorkel with playful sea lions, and León Dormido, one of the best snorkelling and diving sites in the archipelago, with great opportunities to see reef sharks, turtles, stingrays and even hammerhead sharks. Inland, highlights include El Junco Lagoon, one of the few freshwater lakes in the islands, with abundant birdlife. Nearby is the Galapaguera, a giant-tortoise reserve set in dry forest. To visit these two attractions as well as nearby beach Puerto Chino, either take a guided tour ($50) or hire a taxi. On the far east of the island is Punta Pitt, an excellent dive site, also reachable on day-trips.

Puerto Baquerizo Moreno

The islands' capital is smaller and calmer than Puerto Ayora. It has its share of tourism infrastructure, however, with hotels, restaurants, tour operators, a

EATING & DRINKING
Casa Blanca Café	3
Iguana Rock	1
Mi Grande	6
La Playa	7
Rosita	4
Rosley	2
Tongo Reef Bar	5

ACCOMMODATION
Casa Blanca	2
Gosen Guest House	1
Hostal León Dormido	4
Hotel Mar Azul	5
Hostal San Francisco	3

PACIFIC OCEAN

Playa de los Marinos

Centros de Interpretación and Playa Cabo de Horno

La Lobería & Airport

PUERTO BAQUERIZO MORENO

6

smart waterfront and a beach usually covered in sea lions.

A fifteen-minute walk north of town past the small, popular Mann Beach is the **Centro de Interpretación** (daily 6am–6pm; free), which provides a more in-depth overview than the exhibition at Charles Darwin Station in Puerto Ayora, covering the islands' history, development and current environmental problems, split into three galleries. Continue walking past the centre and you will find a forked path that leads to Cerro Tijeretas (Frigatebird Hill) to observe the birds and enjoy sweeping views over the bay below. Then take the other path down to Playa Cabo de Horno, which has good snorkelling. On the opposite end of town, it's a hot, thirty-minute walk to La Lobería, a large sea-lion colony, which is not technically on national parkland. There's also good surfing nearby (taxi from port $2).

TOUR OPERATORS

Tours to León Dormido and the highlands can be arranged with most tour operators in town, including Sharksky (Española, at Darwin; ☎ 099 954 0596, ⊛ sharksky.com), Chalo Tours (Española, at Hernández; ☎ 05 252 0953) and Galakiwi (Darwin at Malecón; ☎ 05 252 1562, ⊛ galakiwi.com). The best diving option is Dive and Surf Club (Melville; ☎ 098 087 7122, ⊛ divesurfclub.com).

ACCOMMODATION

Casa Blanca Malecón, at Melville ☎ 05 252 0392, ⊛ casablancagalapagos.com. This Moorish Moroccan throwback is the most elegant mid-range place in town with rustic a/c rooms, wide balconies and an art gallery downstairs. $50

Gosen Guest House Carlos Mora, at Northia ☎ 05 252 0328. Attractive murals of Galápagos wildlife distinguish this small, friendly place on a side street. Large kitchen, good wi-fi, fans. Double $40

Hostal León Dormido José de Villamil, at Malecón ☎ 05 252 0169. The best-value budget option – clean rooms with private bath, fans and TV. $40

Hotel Mar Azul Alsacio Northia, at Esmeraldas ☎ 05 252 0139. The inland location on the main road is a short walk from the Malecón. Cheap clean rooms with a/c and cable TV and a breezy covered seating area. $35

Hostal San Francisco Malecón ☎ 05 252 0304. A cheap option with no-frills, basic rooms, ideal for those on a tight budget. $20

EATING AND DRINKING

Compared to Puerto Ayora, cheap meals are less easy to find, but there are some inexpensive places spread out along the central Av Alsacio Northia.

★ **Casa Blanca Café** Malecón, at Melville. Good place to start the day or while away the evening. They serve traditional *tamales* or *humitas* (mashed corn), burgers and a range of cocktails. $3–5.

Iguana Rock J José Flores, at Av Quito. After dinner, head here, three blocks inland, to shoot pool, have a few beers and dance until the early hours at the town's most popular bar.

Mi Grande Villamil. A good place for fresh juices and shakes as well as burgers and breakfasts for $2.50–6.

La Playa Av de la Armada. If you don't mind the wait, this open-fronted space on the western edge of the Malecón is worth it for its delicious seafood (mains $7–12).

Rosita Ignacio Hernández, at Wolf. A former surfers' haunt now going upscale and popular with tour groups. Decorated in football jerseys and nautical symbols, it has both à la carte seafood and meats and both lunch and dinner menus ($5). Mains $9–16.

Rosley Española, at Ignacio Hernández. This local favourite is one of the few places in town that offers a $2.50 two-course set lunch and dinner of standard Ecuadorian fare – chicken stew, fried beef and grilled fish.

Tongo Reef Bar Malecón. One of a few cheap, simple snack bars along the waterfront, it serves breakfasts, burgers, sandwiches and fruit juices for $3–7.

ISLA ISABELA

This is by far the largest island in the Galápagos and the most westerly of the populated islands. It also has the most dramatic landscapes because of its recent volcanic activity. **Puerto Villamil** is the only town with accommodation on the island.

Puerto Villamil

Much smaller than Puerto Ayora, with a sleepy atmosphere and charming sandy streets, this town is an ideal place to relax for a longer stay ($5 municipal dock fee on arrival). There are also plenty of attractions close to town to keep you busy.

Five minutes' walk west of town is a set of pozas (lagoons), where flamingos are often seen. Continue walking along the trail for twenty minutes to reach the **Centro de Crianza de Tortugas** (Tortoise Breeding Centre; daily 9am–5pm; free), which has 850 tortoises separated into eight separate enclosures. An information centre has details of the giant tortoise's life cycle and the programme to boost the populations of the five subspecies endemic to Isabela. To avoid the round trip, take a taxi ($2) to the centre and walk back past the lagoons.

Continuing along the coast to the west, it's a pleasant but longer walk to reach the Wall of Tears, built by a penal colony in the 1940s. It may be just a wall but the story of the convicts who were forced to build it in the 1940s is interesting (a taxi here costs $5 or a guided tour $20). Southeast of town is a set of islets called **Las Tintoreras**, named after the reef sharks that frequent them. This is a very good snorkelling spot, with opportunities to watch sea lions, turtles, penguins and white-tipped sharks, which sometimes rest in the canals. There's also a short trail around the islets.

Volcán Sierra Negra

A trek around the volcano is the highlight of a trip to Isabela. You can trek there yourself, but it's far better and safer to take a guided tour. There are two routes – the shorter, known as **Volcán Chico**, takes about four hours, usually on foot and horseback. You can see small lava cones and impressive views over the north of the island and Fernandina. The visibility tends to be better on this side. The longer trek to **Las Minas de Azufre** (Sulphur Mines) takes around seven hours and is tougher, especially in the rainy season. However, the extra effort is rewarded with a more spectacular experience. The walk around the crater, which is the second largest in the world after Ngorongoro in Tanzania, is followed by a descent into the yellow hills of the sulphur mines, which spew out pungent sulphuric gas. Note that the longer trek is less popular so you may need to book ahead.

TOUR OPERATORS

Tours of Villamil cost around $25. A good tour operator is Nautilus (Antonio Gil, at Las Fragatas; ☎ 05 252 9076). Tours of Volcán Sierra Negra are around $40, the sealife marvel Los Tuneles snorkelling site $80.

ACCOMMODATION

There is quite a large accommodation offering for such a small town and it may be possible to negotiate because hotels don't fill up that often. Accommodation on the beach tends to be a bit more expensive than inland.

Caleta Iguana Antonio Gil, at the western end of town ☎ 05 252 9405, ⊛ iguanacove.com. A surfers' place a good cut above the norm, with seven pleasant white or colourful rooms right on a beach frequented by marine iguanas. Doubles $60

★ **La Casa de Marita** El Gaviotín at the eastern entrance of town ☎ 05 252 9301, ⊛ galapagosisabela.com. Seven large oceanfront and twelve garden-view rooms, each individually styled in Mediterranean-inspired fashion. Relax on the palm-shaded deck. Fine restaurant featuring locally produced ingredients. $120

Dolphin House Antonio Gil ☎ 05 252 9138. Great for dramatic views of the ocean. Rooms are adequate – you're paying extra for the location. Breakfast included. $65

Posada del Caminante Near Cormorant ☎ 05 252 9407, ⊛ posadadelcaminante.com. For those on a tighter budget in search of an informal atmosphere, try this place, a 15min walk inland with one low-rise compound and a three-storey building nearby. Most clean, bright rooms have a kitchen and there's a communal fridge and free laundry. $20

EATING AND DRINKING

Bar Beto Antonio Gil. At the far end of the main road, one of the few open-air bars in town; a place where you can sip pricey cocktails on wooden tables overlooking the beach.

★ **La Choza** Malecón. Puts on a barbecued feast (mains $8–15) in a colourful, rustic setting.

El Encanto de la Pepa Antonio Gil. A good option for seafood at $5–7. *Ceviche* to breaded shrimps and grilled fish.

Tres Hermanos Antonio Gil. Among the cheaper places to eat across from the main square with simple but good meals, ranging from breakfasts, burgers and sandwiches to fish with *patacones*, rice and salad ($3–6).

NORTHERN ISLANDS

Isla Santiago

Northwest of Santa Cruz are the blackened lava fields of **ISLA SANTIAGO**, also known as San Salvador, only accessible to cruises. Highlights of the island include the lava trails of **Sullivan Bay**. On the western side is **Puerto Egas**, the best landing point to hike along the lava flow and watch countless crabs and marine iguanas. On the southeastern tip of Santiago, the waters around the

6

volcanic cone of **Sombrero Chino** are also excellent for snorkelling.

Bartolomé, just off the east coast, is available on day-trips. It contains the Galápagos's most famous landmark, **Pinnacle Rock**, a partially eroded lava formation. Climb up 108m to a viewpoint commanding spectacular views over the 40m-high rock with two horseshoe-shaped beaches in the foreground and the blackened lava of Santiago's Sullivan Bay beyond. There's very good snorkelling below and opportunities to see the Galápagos penguins and marine turtles. Bartolomé can be visited on a day-trip from Puerto Ayora ($125/person with Puerto Ayora tour operators).

Genovesa

This is one of the remotest northern islands, only included on cruises. However, it is worth the eight-hour overnight trip to see the largest red-footed booby population in the archipelago. The two visitor sites are Darwin Bay Beach, with a trail to see boobies and frigates, and a boat trip along the cliffs at Prince Philip steps, named after a royal visit in the 1960s.

SOUTHERN ISLANDS

Isla Floreana

The southern island of **FLOREANA** has a hamlet at Puerto Velasco Ibarra. It was actually the first island to be populated thanks to its freshwater supply, and a descendant of the German Wittmer family runs *Hotel Wittmer* (☏05 252 0150; $50), but the infrequent transportation and strict regulations mean that the most practical way to visit is on a cruise or a day tour. Post Office Bay is the most common landing point for cruises, with its quirky post office barrel – leave a postcard, hoping a fellow tourist will post it, and take letters to post in your country. In the highlands, there is a small tortoise-breeding centre and caves that were

inhabited by pirates in the sixteenth century. Punta Cormorant is a good place to observe flamingos and various wading birds. The islands of Enderby and Champion are excellent spots for snorkelling, while nearby Devil's Crown, a half-submerged volcanic cone, is one of the top snorkelling and diving sites in the archipelago, with reef sharks, turtles and rays. A day-trip from Puerto Ayora costs about $75, but only includes the highlands, Enderby and Champion. The tour misses out many of the most famous sites, which are restricted to cruises.

Isla Española

ESPAÑOLA is the southernmost island and can only be visited via a cruise. The island is the sole place in the Galápagos with a colony of waved albatrosses, which flock here between April and November. Seeing them land at one of the "albatross airports" is quite a sight. As well as sea lions, iguanas and boobies, there are opportunities to see the rare hood mockingbird and the finches made famous by Charles Darwin's studies. Punta Suárez is the most popular landing point, and there is excellent snorkelling at Turtle Island.

ISLA FERNANDINA AND OUTLYING ISLANDS

West of Isabela is the volcanic **FERNANDINA**, which can only be visited on a cruise. The highlight is the huge population of marine iguanas sunning themselves on the rocks of **Punta Espinoza**, the only visitor site; there are also trails through the recently formed lava fields. Fernandina's volcano La Cumbre was the most recent eruption in the Galápagos, in April 2009. Further north are the tiny, remote islands of **Darwin** and **Wolf**. These are restricted to specialist diving trips to see large populations of hammerhead and whale sharks.

The Guianas

HIGHLIGHTS

❶ **Kaieteur Falls** One of the world's highest
single-drop waterfalls. **See p.655**

❷ **Rupununi Savannah** Friendly Amerindian
villages and fantastic wildlife viewing. **See p.656**

❸ **Awarradam** Unique Saramaccan culture and
jungle walks. **See p.670**

❹ **Galibi Nature Reserve** Watch baby turtles
hatch on the beach. **See p.671**

❺ **Centre Spatial Guyanais** View a space
rocket being launched into orbit. **See p.680**

❻ **Îles du Salut** Spot fearless wildlife and learn
about the history of these former French prison
islands. **See p.681**

**HIGHLIGHTS ARE MARKED ON THE MAP ON
PP.646–647**

ROUGH COSTS

Daily budget Basic G: US$40; S: US$45; FG: US$100
Drink Beer G: US$2; S: US$1.50; FG: US$5
Food G: *Pepperpot* (stew) US$4; S: Saoto soep US$3;
FG: Blaff (soup) US$12
Guesthouse/budget hotel G: US$15–45;
S: US$18–35; FG: US$70–90
Travel Georgetown–Lethem, bus: 18hr, US$60

FACT FILE

Population G: 795,000; S: 567,000; FG: 250,000
Official languages G: English; S: Dutch; FG: French
Currencies G: Guyanese dollar (G$); S: Suriname
dollar (SRD); FG: euro (€)
Capitals G: Georgetown; S: Paramaribo; FG: Cayenne
International phone codes G: ☎592; S: ☎597;
FG: ☎594
Time zones GMT -3hr (-4hr in Guyana)

Introduction

The Guianas, which comprise the independent nations of Guyana and Suriname and the French overseas département of French Guiana, feel more Caribbean than South American. As a result of colonial legacies the official languages are English (Guyana), Dutch (Suriname) and French (French Guiana), and each has an ethnically diverse population, a mix of indigenous peoples, descendants of European colonizers and their slaves, East Indians, Indonesians, Brazilians, Southeast Asian refugees and Haitians.

7

Tucked between Brazil's Amazonian region and the continent's northeast coast, the verdant Guianas are criss-crossed by rivers; indeed, the Amerindian word *guiana* means "land of many waters". Between eighty and ninety percent of the area is covered by dense tropical forests. Jaguars, pumas, caimans, iguanas, ocelots, tapirs and other diverse wildlife thrive in this environment, making the Guianas an ecotourism haven. That said, wildlife can remain stubbornly elusive, and though you're bound to see birds, monkeys and small rodents, you'll be very lucky to spot a big cat. It's worth the expense to stay in a **jungle lodge**, to take a **river trip** down some of its majestic waterways, or to witness **sea turtles** laying their eggs.

The towns take a back seat to nature in the Guianas, but the capital cities of **Georgetown** (Guyana), **Paramaribo** (Suriname) and **Cayenne** (French Guiana) have a certain charm and are worth exploring for a day or two. Paramaribo is the best preserved, Georgetown is the most lively and

dynamic, and edgy Cayenne offers an authentic taste of colonial-era life. These three capitals comprise the main international gateways from the Caribbean, North America and Europe. Within South America, you can fly directly to all three from Belém and Boa Vista in Brazil.

Borders between the Guianas are marked by rivers, and crossing involves taking scheduled ferries and go-when-full motorized boats. From Guyana to Suriname, you'll need to cross the Corentyne River from Molson Creek to South Drain near Nieuw Nickerie (see box, p.662); and from Suriname to French Guiana, the Maroni River from Albina to Saint-Laurent du Maroni (see box, p.685).

SURFING, SWINGING AND SLEEPING

The Guianas are not a traditional budget destination so traveller hospitality websites such as Ⓦcouchsurfing.org (see p.32) are a good option for those on tight budgets. It's also well worth investing in a hammock (easily available in any of the three capital cities) and accompanying mosquito net if you can spare the room.

WHEN TO VISIT

Temperatures in the Guianas vary little from one month to the next: generally 20°C to 33°C, with a mean temperature of around 27°C (slightly hotter in the interior owing to the absence of the cooling coastal trade winds). Planning a trip should be based around the region's two annual **wet seasons**, which pummel the region from December to January and from May to July. While the tropical forest is lush and green during the wet season, navigating the many unsealed roads that govern land access to the interior can be extremely difficult (if not impossible). As such, late summer/early autumn and late winter/early spring are the optimum times for a visit – the latter particularly, as this is when many carnival celebrations take place.

Guyana

GUYANA, the largest and most populous nation of the three Guianas, is a rum-drinking and cricket-loving country, and the only English-speaking nation in South America. **Georgetown**, the capital, typifies this with its cosmopolitan mix of black, white, East Indian, Asian and Amerindian ethnicities and a laidback Caribbean attitude.

Guyana's principal attractions are its rainforests (part of the Guyana Shield and some of the oldest and most pristine on earth), its wildlife and its indigenous culture. Guyana's greatest natural wonder is the majestic Kaieteur Falls – among the tallest and most powerful in the world – made all the more dramatic by their isolated location at the end of an immense jungle gorge.

Going down the middle of the country from north to south is the **Iwokrama Rainforest**. Gold and diamond mining are very common throughout the interior and independent travel within the region is easiest along "pork-knocker" (Guyanese term for freelance gold miner) routes. Further southwest, the jungle gives way to the wide-open spaces of the **Rupununi Savannah**, dotted with Amerindian villages. Here you can immerse yourself in indigenous culture and go in search of caimans, giant anteaters and giant river otters.

CHRONOLOGY

10,000 BC Amerindians arrive, having crossed a land bridge from Asia.

1492 Christopher Columbus sets foot in the region. Unsuccessful Spanish exploration in search of the Lost City of Gold.

1595 Sir Walter Raleigh visits Guyana and publishes *The Discoverie of the Large, Rich and Bewtiful Empyre of Guiana*, igniting European interest in the region.

1613–21 The Dutch found Fort Kyk Over Al, build trading posts, and establish sugar-cane plantations.

1650s African slaves replace Amerindian ones; Amerindians assist the Dutch in capturing runaway slaves.

1763 A slave revolt is led by Guyana's national hero, Cuffy, though quelled in 1764; 125 slaves executed.

1796 Dutch lose control of colony to the British.

1802 Dutch regain control of Guyana.

1814 Treaty of Paris grants the British control of the area.

1823 Demerara slave revolt brutally suppressed.

1834 Slavery abolished. Thousands of indentured labourers from India, China, England, Ireland, Portugal and Africa are brought to Guyana to work the sugar-cane plantations.

1870s Charles Barrington Brown is the first European to find Kaieteur Falls. Gold found in Guyana's interior.

1950 The People's Progressive Party (PPP) is established.

1953 PPP wins first elections allowed by British. Jagan becomes leader. Britain suspends constitution and sends in troops, fearing plans to establish Guyana as a communist state.

1955 PPP splits and Burnham forms the People's National Congress (PNC).

1957 Elections permitted and PPP wins. Jagan becomes first premier in 1961.

1966 Guyana achieves independence.

1978 More than 900 members of Rev. Jim Jones' People's Temple religious sect commit mass suicide in Jonestown (see box, p.651).

1980 Guyana gets a controversial new constitution and Burnham becomes president.

1985 Burnham dies; Prime Minister Hugh Desmond Hoyte becomes president.

1992 Cheddi Jagan's PPP wins election.

1997 Jagan dies. His American widow, Janet Jagan, is elected president.

1999 Janet Jagan resigns and is succeeded by Bharrat Jagdeo.

2001 Violent demonstrations follow the elections.

2009 Norway agrees to invest US$250m to preserve Guyana's rainforests.

2012 Protests in Linden leave three people dead. Police questioned over killings.

2014 The remains of nine people who perished in the Jonestown massacre are discovered in a house in Delaware.

ARRIVAL AND DEPARTURE

Guyana's **Cheddi Jagan International Airport**, 41km from Georgetown, receives direct **flights** from Suriname, Brazil, Barbados, Trinidad, Panama, New York, Miami, Fort Lauderdale and Toronto. Some flights from Suriname and domestic flights arrive at the smaller **Ogle International Airport**, ten minutes east of Georgetown's centre.

Guyanese authorities levy a G$4000 (or US$21) exit tax for those departing the country by air.

OVERLAND FROM BRAZIL

Travellers arriving overland from Brazil enter Guyana at the town of **Lethem**,

7

about 130km northeast of the Brazilian town of Boa Vista. It is a cramped and bone-jarring eighteen-hour **minibus** ride (see p.659) from Lethem to Georgetown along a dirt logging road that slices the country in half. Two small airlines also run daily flights from Lethem to Georgetown, and tickets can be bought in their offices beside the town's airstrip with Brazilian, Guyanese or US currency.

(see p.659)

OVERLAND FROM SURINAME

Travellers from Suriname must board a **ferry** at South Drain, near Nieuw Nickerie, and make the thirty-minute

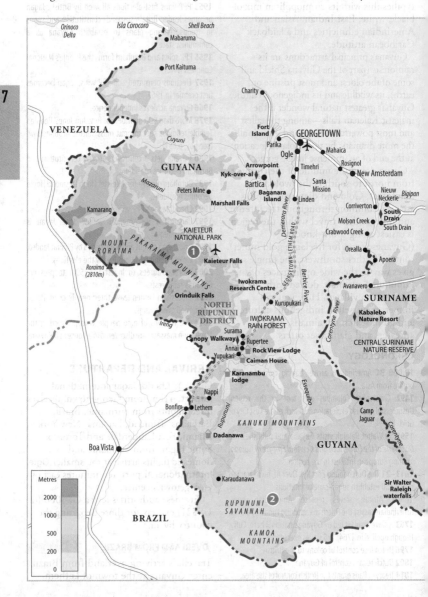

journey across the Corentyne River to **Molson Creek** on the Guyana border before taking a local minibus to Georgetown (see box, p.662). It's possible to arrange direct transport from Paramaribo to Georgetown (total travel time 10hr).

VISAS

You must have a passport with six months' validity and a return ticket if arriving by air. Guyanese immigration grants visitors stays of up to ninety days. To extend your stay, contact the Ministry of Home Affairs (6 Brickdam St; ☎226 2445, ⓦmoha.gov.gy) or the Central

THE GUIANAS

HIGHLIGHTS

1. Kaieteur Falls
2. Rupununi Savannah
3. Awarradam
4. Galibi Nature Reserve
5. Centre Spatial Guyanais
6. Îles du Salut

7

ATLANTIC OCEAN

Matapica Beach
WIA WIA NATURE RESERVE
GALIBI NATURE RESERVE
Leonsburg Nieuw Amsterdam Plage les Hattes
Zorg en Hoop Alliance Awala-Yalimapo
Totness PARAMARIBO Meerzorg Christiaankondre Mana
Zanderij Langamankondre Javouhey
COMMEWIJNE Moengo Iracoubo
Colakreek Albina Sinnamary RN 1 Îles de Salut
Jodensavanne St Laurent Space Centre Kourou CAYENNE
Witagron Brownsweg Blakawatra du Maroni
Brokopondo Apatou Voltaire Ilet la Mère
BROWNSBERG Falls Montsinéry Remire-Montjoly
NATURE Blonnestein Tonnegrande Matoury
RESERVE Meer Cacao RN 2 Roura Kaw
Pokigron Cabo Orange
Voltzberg RALEIGHVALLEN Regina Approuague River Ouanary
NATURE Grand Santi FRENCH Cisame
RESERVE GUIANA Saint-Georges-
TAFELBERG Botopasi de-l'Oyapok Oiapoque
NATURE Tafelberg
RESERVE (1026m) Kajana
Juliana Top Awarradam
(1280m) Maripasoula Saül
Palumeu SURINAME
Camopi
EILERTS DE Kasikasima
HAAN NATURE St Maroni BRAZIL
RESERVE (635m)

Coppename
Suriname
Gran Rio
Saramacca
Maroni
Lawa
Tapanahony
Oyapock

N

0 — 100
kilometres

Office of Immigration (Camp St; ☎226 4700), both in Georgetown.

Visas are required for all visitors except those from the USA, Commonwealth, most European and CARICOM (Caribbean community) countries. Contact your nearest Guyanese embassy/ consulate for more details.

GETTING AROUND

Privately owned **minibuses** operate to nearly all destinations accessible by road, including Lethem close to the Brazilian border (US$60). Roads are paved from Georgetown to towns along the coast and inland as far as Linden; beyond, it's dirt roads only, which sometimes become impassable during rainy season.

Hitchhiking is common outside of the capital. Independent travel in the interior requires cash (no ATMs) to pay for boats, minibuses and 4WD vehicles with a driver. Motorcycle rides are often given freely (see box, p.657). Daily **flights** in small aircraft connect Georgetown to settlements in the Rupununi and elsewhere; these are reliable and relatively cheap (US$125 to Lethem).

Travel along Guyana's main rivers involves **river taxis** (speedboats), whereas locals tend to use dugout canoes and motorboats when travelling along the smaller rivers.

ACCOMMODATION

There are plenty of good, reasonably priced **guesthouses** and **hotels** in Georgetown, where G$6000 will get you a spacious, clean room with a mosquito net, TV, running water and air-conditioning. Prices are cheaper outside the capital, but accommodation more limited. In the Rupununi Savannah there are several excellent ecolodges and ranches that offer an introduction to traditional savannah life as well as outdoor pursuits such as wildlife-watching and fishing. Most villages will have a *benab* (wooden shelter with thatched roof) where you can hang your hammock (bring your own and make sure you invest in a mosquito net, cost/night US$10); in

the absence of a *benab*, you may well be able to hang it on someone's porch.

In Guyana a "single room" will usually have a double or queen-sized bed and a "double room" may come with two beds of varying sizes. Not all establishments accept foreign credit cards, so check when making a booking. Call rather than email.

FOOD AND DRINK

Curries, roti, cassava, rice and coconut milk reign over **Guyanese cuisine**. Chicken, pork and beef are fried Creole-style, and then curried with East Indian spices. **Rice** is ubiquitous, boiled with coconut milk, black-eyed peas, lentils, *channa* (chickpeas), okra or *callaloo* (spinach), such medleys are referred to as *Cookup*. Other staples include roti and *dhal puri* (akin to a tortilla wrap).

Bakes, a fried and puffed-up bread of Trinidadian origin are also cut open and stuffed with all manner of Creole fillings.

Saltfish, fish fillets salted for preservation, is common in the interior. Make sure you ask for your fish to be washed free of the salt before it is cooked.

The Amerindian contribution to Guyanese cuisine is *pepperpot* – made with stewed meat (or fish), coloured, preserved and flavoured with *cassareep* (a thick dark sauce made from cassava juice), cinnamon and hot peppers.

Locals consider **wild meat** a delicacy and adventurous eaters will have the opportunity to try deer, capybara, iguana, wild pig, *manicou* (opossum) and *labba* or agouti (jungle rat).

Snacks such as patties, buns, potato balls, *pholouri* (seasoned flour and lentil balls), pineapple tarts, *salara* (red coconut rolls) and *cassava pone* (like bread pudding but made with coconut and cassava) are sold in bakeries (G$200–300 each).

In Georgetown you'll also find Brazilian and Chinese restaurants as well as Western-style international cafés. A hot meal costs G$400–500 from a market *cook shop*; in local cafés it costs twice that, and in upmarket restaurants you'll spend over G$1300.

DRINK

Alcoholic drinks worth trying include local award-winning **Banks Beer** (G$400) and Demerara Distillers' El Dorado fifteen-year-old, reputedly the best rum in the world.

Fizzy soft drinks (many from Brazil) are sold everywhere, along with regional brands such as Busta and I-Cee. Chilled drinks like Mauby (a tree bark-based beverage), Cherry and Sorrel (each flavoured with their eponymous ingredient) are very refreshing, as are coconut water and ginger juice. Drinking tap water is inadvisable.

CULTURE AND ETIQUETTE

English is the national **language** but locals tend to converse in *Creolese* (as the locals refer to their dialect), an English-based Creole influenced by the Amerindian, African, Dutch and Indian languages.

The nine Amerindian communities speak several dialects including Arawak, Macushi and Warao, while the prominent Brazilian population speaks Portuguese. The three dominant **religions** are Christianity, Hinduism and Islam.

Women can expect to get plenty of loud comments and persistent kissing noises. It's best not to wear excessively revealing clothing. Guyanese dress stylishly for work, church, visiting government offices and dining out. **Tipping** is not compulsory though it is appreciated.

SPORTS AND OUTDOOR ACTIVITIES

The country's national sport is cricket, though visitors are more likely to come for the outdoor activities such as canoeing, birdwatching, wildlife-spotting and mountain climbing in the interior. **Horseriding** in the Rupununi Savannah is easily accessible and a visit to the annual **Rupununi Rodeo** in Lethem (see p.659) is recommended.

COMMUNICATIONS

Sending **letters and postcards** from Guyana is cheap (G$80–180) but slow.

> ### GUYANA ON THE NET
> ⓦ **exploreguyana.org** Directory of accommodation, restaurants, airlines and travel agencies run by the Tourism and Hospitality Association of Guyana.
> ⓦ **guyanalive.com** Social site providing forums and info on festivals and events.

Guyana's country code is 592. To use your unlocked **mobile phone**, buy a local SIM card (G$2000) from either GT&T or Digicel outlets. Mobile internet plans are available, although you don't get much for your money.

In Georgetown, there are several internet cafés. Internet and/or **wi-fi** is available in most hotels and guesthouses (mostly for free) and some cafés, but is less readily available outside the capital.

CRIME AND SAFETY

Most visits to Guyana are trouble-free. Still, opportunistic **petty crime** (particularly theft) is rife, particularly in Georgetown, so avoid displaying valuable items. Pickpockets are particularly active around Stabroek Market. At night robberies at gun or knife point are not uncommon, often targeting tourists. Take taxis if going more than a few blocks after dark and avoid walking alone down deserted, sparsely lit streets.

HEALTH

There is one public and several private **hospitals** in Georgetown. Rural and outlying areas are served by municipal hospitals and health centres; Medivac services (emergency air ambulance) are also available in emergencies. Medical facilities at Georgetown public hospital (see p.655) are rather limited; serious injury or illness may require an airlift to Port of Spain, Trinidad.

Avoid drinking tap water, and pack sunscreen and a broad-rimmed hat, as well as rehydration mix for severe cases of travellers' diarrhoea.

Consult your doctor regarding vaccinations; advice currently includes hepatitis A and B, typhoid,

7

tetanus-diphtheria and rabies. Malaria is found in all parts of the interior, for which prevention is the best cure; mosquito nets, repellent and long-sleeved clothing are essentials, and get anti-malaria tablets (see p.33) before you set off.

In the interior, travellers must be wary of several types of venomous snakes as well as black caimans.

INFORMATION AND MAPS

There is no tourist information office in Guyana, but the **Tourism and Hospitality Association of Guyana** (THAG; 157 Waterloo St; Mon–Fri 9am–5pm; ☏225 0807, ⓦexploreguyana.org) produces the ubiquitous annual **magazine**, *Explore Guyana*, full of **general information** about the country as well a new tourism options. G.E.M.S. Inc also publishes a pocket-sized listings guide called *Guyana: where & what*. Both are available at hotels and tourism agents around the city. **Permits** are required to visit Amerindian villages, arranged by tour operators for organized trips. Independent travellers should contact the Ministry of Amerindian Affairs, at 251–252 Quamina, at Thomas (☏227 5067, ⓦamerindian.gov.gy).

MONEY AND BANKS

The unit of **currency** is the Guyanese dollar (G$), available in 20, 100, 500 and 1000 notes. Stabroek market has the best exchange rates. Most businesses and hotels accept US$, while fewer may accept euros. While major **credit cards** such as MasterCard, Visa and American Express are accepted in some restaurants and hotels, take plenty of Guyanese dollars if travelling in the interior. Scotiabank ATMs accept foreign cards. At the time of writing, US$1=G$208, €1=G$276, £1=G$345.

OPENING HOURS

Banks: Monday to Thursday 8am–2pm, Friday 8am–2.30pm. Government offices: Monday to Thursday 8am–noon and 1–4.30pm, Friday 8am–noon and 1–3.30pm. Shops and businesses: Monday to Friday 8.30am–4pm and Saturday 8am–noon.

GEORGETOWN

GEORGETOWN is the colourful, gritty, commercial and administrative heart of Guyana. Set on the east bank of the Demerara estuary, the capital is a grid city designed largely by the Dutch in the eighteenth century, originally nicknamed "The Garden City" because of its parks, tree-lined streets and an abundance of flowers. Today, there is still a definite charm despite its rubbish-strewn streets,

Georgetown is the gateway to Guyana's true attractions and likely to be your base for several days.

The capital is worth exploring for its diverse cultural, religious and historical landmarks.

Main Street and around
One of downtown's most distinctive buildings, the towering **St George's Cathedral** on Church Street is one of the world's tallest freestanding wooden structures at 44m, with an attractive, airy interior (daily 9am–2pm, except public hols). A couple of blocks south along the Avenue of the Republic is the turreted City Hall, built in the Victorian Gothic style.

The **Walter Roth Museum of Anthropology** (61 Main St; Mon–Thurs 8am–4.30pm, Fri 8am–3.30pm, Sat 9am–2pm; entry by donation) is a good introduction to the culture of Guyana's nine Amerindian tribes, showcasing everything from cassava-processing, traditional fishing and hammock-making to the medicinal use of plants and ceremonial wear, which includes some splendid macaw-feather headgear.

The **Guyana National Museum** (North Rd; Mon–Fri 9am–4pm, Sat 9am–2pm; entry by donation) showcases the history of slavery in Guyana, the gold-mining industry, including a demonic-looking

(and pretty accurate) statue of a "pork-knocker", and an enormous replica of the extinct giant sloth which once roamed the Guyanese bush. There is a tourist market in front of the museum selling purple heart hardwood walking sticks, handmade leather sandals and other souvenirs.

Stabroek Market and around
The busy-as-bedlam focal point for *higglers* (fruit and vegetable sellers), moneychangers, beggars and jewellers, **Stabroek Market** on Water Street is dominated by its four-faced clock tower. Originally the site of the slave market where the exhausted survivors of the Middle Passage first faced a hostile New World, Stabroek now supports slavery of the sweatshop variety, spilling over with knock-off designer gear, jewellery and watches. It's also a great place for a cheap lunch at a *snackette*. East of Stabroek, off North Street, is the small but lively **Bourda Market**, a colourful shantytown filled with 24-hour fruit and vegetable vendors.

The National Art Gallery and around
Located in Castellani House on Vlissengen Road – once the official residence of the prime minister of Guyana – is the **National Art Gallery** (Mon–Fri 10am–5pm, Sat 2–6pm; free). The collection features African-inspired masks, carvings and paintings,

7

JONESTOWN MASSACRE
The chilling events of November 18, 1978, when more than 900 members of a sect died in an apparent mass suicide in northwestern Guyana, about 80km southwest of the town of Mabaruma, have been the subject of many books. In 1974, American **Reverend Jim Jones**, the leader of a sect called **The People's Temple**, chose Guyana to establish a self-sufficient community of about 1100 based on utopian socialist ideals, which he humbly named Jonestown. Referring to an unnamed enemy that would come to destroy Jonestown, he told his flock that "revolutionary suicide" was the only way to combat this threat. When US Congressman Leo Ryan and a party of journalists and concerned family members visited Jonestown in November 1978 to investigate alleged human rights abuses, the enemy had apparently arrived. Ryan and others were shot and killed at Port Kaituma airstrip as they tried to leave, while back at Jonestown the men, women and children were instructed to drink poison. A total of 913 people died, although a coroner's report suggested that many were forcibly killed, including at least 200 children. A few managed to escape and later wrote about their experiences. Today the Jonestown site is overrun by bush and there is no monument or other reminders of its existence.

7

including the psychedelic works of celebrated local artist Philip Moore. Don't miss the collection of *balata* (hardened, shaped tree sap) Amerindian figurines in the attic, taking part in traditional pastimes such as hunting and cassava processing. Just south of the gallery is the **1763 Monument**, a 5m-high bronze memorial to Cuffy, an African slave who led an unsuccessful slave rebellion in 1763. Behind the art gallery are the botanical gardens, home to some tame manatees in its central pond (daily 9.30am–5.30pm).

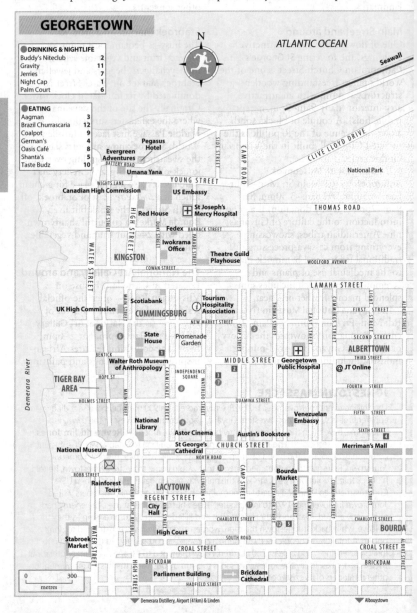

GEORGETOWN

DRINKING & NIGHTLIFE
Buddy's Niteclub	2
Gravity	11
Jerries	7
Night Cap	1
Palm Court	6

EATING
Aagman	3
Brazil Churrascaria	12
Coalpot	9
German's	4
Oasis Café	8
Shanta's	5
Taste Budz	10

ATLANTIC OCEAN

Seawall

N

CLIVE LLOYD DRIVE

National Park

Pegasus Hotel
Evergreen Adventures
BATTERY ROAD
Umana Yana
WIGHTS LANE
Canadian High Commission
YOUNG STREET
US Embassy
THOMAS ROAD
SIDE STREET
CAMP ROAD

FORT STREET
HIGH STREET
Red House
St Joseph's Mercy Hospital
Fedex
DUKE STREET
PARADE STREET
BARRACK STREET
Iwokrama Office
KINGSTON
Theatre Guild Playhouse
COWAN STREET
WOOLFORD AVENUE
WATER STREET

LAMAHA STREET

MAIN STREET
Scotiabank
Tourism Hospitality Association
CUMMINGSBURG
UK High Commission
NEW MARKET STREET
THOMAS STREET
EAST STREET
CUMMINGS STREET
FIRST STREET
ALBERT STREET
LIGHT STREET

State House
Promenade Garden
CAMP STREET
SECOND STREET
ALBERTTOWN
BENTICK
Walter Roth Museum of Anthropology
CARMICHAEL STREET
MIDDLE STREET
Georgetown Public Hospital
THIRD STREET
@ JT Online
TIGER BAY AREA
HOPE ST
MAIN STREET
INDEPENDENCE SQUARE
WATERLOO STREET
FOURTH STREET
HOLMES STREET
QUAMINA STREET
National Library
Venezuelan Embassy
FIFTH STREET
Astor Cinema
Austin's Bookstore
SIXTH STREET
National Museum
St George's Cathedral
CHURCH STREET
Merriman's Mall
NORTH ROAD
ROBB STREET
Rainforest Tours
Bourda Market
CAMP STREET
ALEXANDER STREET
BOURDA STREET
ORANGE WALK
CUMMINGS STREET
LIGHT STREET
LACYTOWN
WELLINGTON ST
REGENT STREET
City Hall
AVENUE OF THE REPUBLIC
KING STREET
High Court
CHARLOTTE STREET
CHARLOTTE STREET
BOURDA
SOUTH ROAD
Stabroek Market
WATER STREET
CROAL STREET
CROAL STREET
ALBERT STREET
BRICKDAM
HIGH STREET
Parliament Building
Brickdam Cathedral
BRICKDAM
HADFIELD STREET

Demerara River

0   300
metres

Demerara Distillery, Airport (41km) & Linden

Albouystown

The seawall

Despite being on the coast, Georgetown is a few metres below sea level. The Dutch-built seawall which keeps the Atlantic at bay produces a bizarre sight at high tide, when you can stand on the wall and look at the water at a higher level than the town on the other side. On Sunday nights the whole town turns out to drink, flirt and strut their stuff along the promenade. Not a sight to be missed if you're in town. On any other day the safest times to go are around 4.30–6pm.

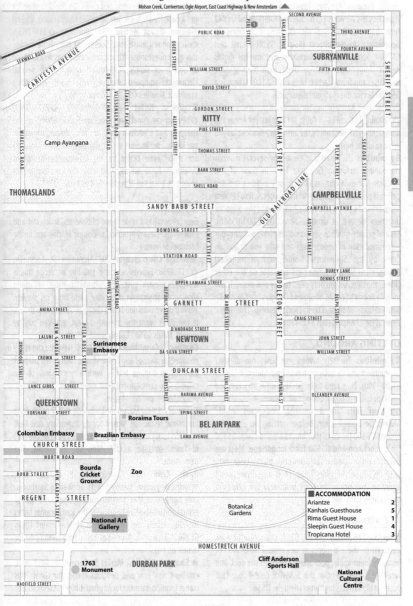

Molson Creek, Corriverton, Ogle Airport, East Coast Highway & New Amsterdam

■ ACCOMMODATION	
Ariantze	2
Kanhais Guesthouse	5
Rima Guest House	1
Sleepin Guest House	4
Tropicana Hotel	3

ARRIVAL AND DEPARTURE

By plane Cheddi Jagan International Airport (⊚cjairport-gy.com) is located at Timehri, 41km south of the centre. International carriers currently serving CJIA include Delta Airlines, Caribbean Airlines, LIAT, Meta Airlines and Suriname Airways. Domestic airlines include Air Guyana (⊚airguyana.biz), Air Services Ltd (⊚aslgy.com), Roraima Airways (⊚roraimaairways.com) and Trans Guyana Airways (⊚transguyana.net). Minibus #42 runs from in front of the Parliament building in Georgetown to the airport (45min; G$280); taxis cost G$5000. Some flights to Suriname and internal flights depart from Ogle airstrip, 8km from Georgetown; minibuses run from Market; taxis cost G$1000. There is a G$4000 tax for international departures.

Destinations Annai (daily; 1hr 30min); Karanambu (daily; 1hr 20min); Lethem (3–4 daily; 1hr 30min). For Annai and Karanambu you must notify the airline in advance that you want to alight here.

By minibus The interior is served by several minibus companies, including Guy-Braz from in front of the Brazilian bar on Light, at Church; buy a ticket the day before if possible. Minibuses from Georgetown to Lethem leave around 6pm, while those travelling in the opposite direction depart at around 5pm (G$12,000/US$60). Several private minibus services offer pick-ups from your accommodation in Georgetown and take you to Molson Creek by the Surinamese border with a reciprocal arrangement with a Surinamese operator on the other side of the river, so you only need to buy one ticket. These include Bobby's (☎226 8668) and Douglas (☎226 2843).

Destinations Molson Creek (3hr); Lethem (16–18hr); Timehri for CJ Airport (bus #42; 45min).

GETTING AROUND

By minibus Privately owned minibuses run all over Georgetown and its outlying towns from Stabroek Market (G$80–100). They tend to be packed, drive very fast and are impossible to board during rush hour.

By taxi Taxis are unmetered, and fares should always be agreed upon before getting in. Fares are around G$300 for up to four blocks around town, G$400 for a short hop and G$500 for a longer one. Most are painted yellow and display number plates beginning with "H". Taxis are ubiquitous, so if one driver won't agree to your price, there are invariably five others in the vicinity who will.

ACCOMMODATION

Ariantze 176 Middle St T227 0152, ⊚ariantzesidewalk.com. While the a/c rooms at this central hotel are not instantly memorable, pool access sweetens the deal, and weekly entertainment at the *Sidewalk Café & Jazz Club* occasionally attracts highbrow clientele. US$67

Kanhais Guesthouse 210 Charlotte St, Lacytown ☎231 6058, ⊚kanhais.com. Secure guesthouse above a hardware store, with helpful staff and clean but characterless a/c en-suite doubles. Wi-fi available. Basic breakfast included. US$60

Rima Guest House 92 Middle St ☎225 7401, ✉rima@networksgy.com. This is the main backpacker lodging in town and it's comfortable and clean. On the downside it's not a good idea to leave any valuables lying around. US$30

Sleepin Guest House 151 Church St ☎231 7667, ⊚sleepinguesthouse.com. Somewhat out of the centre, this quiet guesthouse attracts self-caterers as well as those in search of simple, fan-cooled rooms, with several kitchenette-equipped studios. Free wi-fi and basic breakfast. Doubles US$35, studios US$65

Tropicana Hotel 177 Waterloo St ☎227 5701, ⊚newtropicanahotel.com. *Tropicana*, aka *Jerries*, is the cheapest and friendliest hotel in town, although noisy on weekends. Free internet access, mosquito nets, fans (no a/c) are made even better by the 24-hour bar/restaurant downstairs. Make sure you meet Jerry, who loves to entertain his guests. Local taxi drivers know it as *Jerries*. US$18

EATING

Georgetown has a wide range of bakeries, *snackettes* and *cook shops* – many attached to Bourda Market and inside Stabroek Market.

★**Brazil Churrascaria** 208 Alexander St, Lacytown ☎231 1268. Expensive, but if you like barbecue this is worth the extra cost. The pitmaster slices unlimited sizzling meat straight onto your plate from his skewer. Wash it down with good (and cheap at G$500) caipirinhas. If you don't want the all-you-can-eat, you can pay by weight. Meals G$5000. Daily noon–10pm.

Coalpot 98 Carmichael St ☎225 8556. Here you can enjoy *metagee*, *pepperpot* and Creole dishes such as red snapper steamed in banana leaf – with a great view of the cathedral to complement your meal. Mains from G$800. Daily 11am–3pm & 6–11pm.

German's 8 New Market, at Mundy St ☎227 0079. Busy lunchtime restaurant famed for its legendary cow-heel soup (G$1500) and Creole dishes. Located in a sketchy part of town, so take a taxi. Mon–Sat 8am–6pm, Sun 8am–4pm.

Oasis Café 125 Carmichael St ☎226 9916, ⊚oasiscafegy.com. Georgetown's answer to Starbucks, only much nicer, this is an air-conditioned "oasis" where expats and locals alike linger over the iced caramel lattes (G$650), salads and inventive lunchtime mains (from G$2000). Free wi-fi. Mon–Sat 9am–5pm (also open for dinner on Fri).

★**Shanta's** 225 New Market St. Serving up fresh rotis, excellent *dhal puri* and delicious curries for cheap, this corner location is a must for any first-timer to Creole Indian food. Ask what's good at the counter if you can't make sense of the scrawled menu. Meals around G$800. Mon–Sat 7.30am–6pm.

Taste Budz 54 Robb St ☎ 231 0885. Friendly owner Brian runs this proper Creole joint doing big breakfasts, cold beers and the best *coocup* (national dish of rice and beans in coconut milk) you'll find around town. Free wi-fi. Daily 7am–10pm.

DRINKING AND NIGHTLIFE

The bars and clubs are mostly concentrated along Sheriff and Main streets. The real action in the clubs starts around midnight on weekends. On Sunday nights the seawall is the place to be, with stands selling drinks and food all along the road.

Buddy's Niteclub 137 Sheriff St ☎ 231 7260. A multi-storey club attracting a young crowd with "Shooter Fridays": a melange of hip-hop, r'n'b, chutney (the music style, not the condiment) and reggae. Bring your confidence. Free entry before 10.30pm. Thurs–Sat.

Gravity Lounge Top Floor of Foot Steps Mega Store, corner of Regent St and Camp St. The GT spot on Saturday nights, this cool rooftop bar in the centre commands great views over the town as well as a higher class of clientele than you are likely to come across on Sheriff St. Dress to impress. Mon–Sat noon–late, Sun 5pm–late.

Jerries 177 Waterloo St ☎ 227 5701. This Georgetown institution is a 24-hour bar/restaurant with unabashed Creolese soul. Sit at the bar or the mercifully fanned terrace to consume a changing range of tasty Creole or curry. Karaoke and oldies on Friday and Saturday. Open 24hr.

★ **Night Cap** 8 Pere St, Kitty ☎ 231 8644. An enchanting garden bedecked with Christmas lights, nestling inside the walls of the Russian embassy. Swing in a hammock, lounge on the patio, or sit in the wi-fi-enabled a/c cool of the café. Sip a classic rum punch, or try out the odder

---

★ TREAT YOURSELF

Aagman 28A Sheriff St ☎ 225 0601. Probably the best curry available in South America. The first-generation Indian management operate a real tandoor oven, make desserts the traditional way and take obvious pride in their business. The Guyanese president is a regular diner, so don't be surprised if you end up having a drink with him (mains from G$1800 but big enough for two).

---

peanut butter frappes and espresso martinis. Sandwiches are also pretty good. Daily 5–11pm.

Palm Court 35 Main St ☎ 231 8144. Popular local nightspot with electric palms lining its breezy courtyard. Makes a good rum punch and stays open as long as the clients are having fun. Mon–Sat 5pm–late.

DIRECTORY

Banks and exchange Scotiabank at 104 Carmichael St, Pegasus Hotel and various along Robb St. Ask about the cambio nearest to your lodgings.

Embassies and Consulates Brazil, 308 Church St (☎ 225 7970); Canada, High, at Young St (☎ 227 2081); Suriname, 171 Peter Rose St, at Crown St (☎ 226 7844); UK, 44 Main St (☎ 226 5881); US, Young St, at Duke St (☎ 226 3938); Venezuela, 296 Thomas St (☎ 226 1543).

Hospital St Joseph's Mercy Hospital, 130–132 Parade St (☎ 227 2072). Private hospital with 24hr emergency room.

Internet Hotels tend to have wi-fi. Otherwise try JT Online Internet Café at 38 Cummings St.

Pharmacies Medicare Pharmacy at 18 Hinck St or The Medicine Chest at 315 Middle St.

KAIETEUR FALLS

One of the world's most beautiful waterfalls, 226m **Kaieteur Falls** are in a cavernous gorge surrounded by the dense rainforest of the **Kaieteur National Park**. The region's most popular attraction, their isolation, power and pristine surroundings make them a heart-stopping sight.

Operators (see p.656) offer flights to Kaieteur Falls in twelve-seater planes from Georgetown's Ogle airport (from US$195). A day-trip usually involves a brief guided tour of the three viewpoints from which you can admire the sight of 30,000 gallons of water per second crashing down into the valley below (with the more intrepid visitors crawling to the cliff edge to watch the rainbows play on the water spray). Your guide will point out interesting animal life, such as the tiny golden frogs, the toxins from which are used in Haitian voodoo ceremonies.

Alternatively, you can take a five-day/four-night overland journey involving a 4WD drive, boat trip and a fairly strenuous hike, with rustic accommodation thrown in along the way (from US$700). If you want to visit independently, the only overnight accommodation is a rustic lodge near the falls (G$4000/person), booked through Air Services Ltd (🌐 aslgy.com). You will be rewarded with views of the falls at dusk and dawn without the crowds. Air Services Ltd, together with Roraima Airways (🌐 roraimaairways.com), are responsible for flights to the falls. Flights run year-round on weekends, with one to three flights during the week depending on the season.

DAY-TRIPS FROM GEORGETOWN

Georgetown makes a good base for ventures into the interior to visit **Kaieteur Falls** (see box, p.655) as well as trips up Essequibo River for an appreciation of the country's colonial past and mining present, and to Santa Mission, for a taste of Amerindian life.

Essequibo and Mazaruni rivers

This popular day-trip involves a boat journey on the **Essequibo**, one of Guyana's main waterways. First stop is the market town of Parika, then a visit to **Kyk Over Al**, a seventeenth-century Dutch fort, and a stopover in **Bartica**, a gritty gold-mining town and a wonderful place to get an insight into one of Guyana's main trades. This is followed by a boat trip up the smaller Mazaruni River to the Bara Cara Falls or else Marshall Falls – both great spots for a dip – and a short hike through the jungle for a chance to see some of the country's fabled wildlife.

THE INTERIOR: IWOKRAMA RAINFOREST AND THE RUPUNUNI SAVANNAH

Visitors come to Guyana for two things: pristine nature and Amerindian culture. Both are found in the interior, reachable either by Guyana's north–south highway that runs all the way to the Brazilian border, or by frequent flights made by small aircraft. Much of the road passes through some of the oldest and most pristine jungle on earth, home to jaguar, tapir, ocelot, puma, peccary and anaconda. In the heart of the country lies Guyana's only official nature reserve: the vast **IWOKRAMA RAINFOREST**, known for the incredible biodiversity of its plant, bird and animal species. Beyond Iwokrama, dense jungle dramatically gives way to the **RUPUNUNI SAVANNAH**, Guyana's cowboy country – scrubland and grassland that stretches as far as the eye can see, punctuated with giant anthills, the odd cattle ranch and a smattering of thatched roofs, which announce the presence of an

---

TOURS OF THE INTERIOR

While travels in the interior are cheapest if you have the time and flexibility to arrange it all independently (see box opposite), there are several reputable tour operators in Georgetown who specialize in nature and adventure tours throughout Guyana's hinterland and who can also arrange day-trips to Kaieteur Falls and other destinations within easy reach of the capital. Prices are roughly as follows: tour of the city (US$30–40); day-trip to Bartica (US$120); day-trip to Santa Mission (US$120); flight to Kaieteur Falls (US$195–240).

TOUR OPERATORS

A common ruse among Georgetown travel agents is to name a price and then try to have the client pay the extra 5–7 percent fee for paying with a credit or debit card. This is prohibited under their banking terms and shouldn't be agreed to.

Bushmasters ⓦ bushmasters.co.uk. Extreme jungle survival course, which includes paintball and rainforest hunting, led by an ex-SAS commando. The tour ends with two days of solo survival, armed with nothing but a knife and the clothes on your back. Not for wimps.

Evergreen Adventures *Pegasus Hotel*, Seawall Rd ⓣ 225 4484, ⓦ evergreenadventuresgy.com. City tours, four types of Kaieteur Falls trips, day-trips up Essequibo River and to Berbice.

Rainforest Tours 5 Av of the Republic, 1st floor ⓣ 231 5661, ⓦ rftours.com. Proprietor of the original and excellent Kaieteur overland tour, Frank Singh's office above a fried chicken shop can customize tours to suit you. Ask for discounts as prices are a bit steep.

Roraima Tours 8 Eping Av, Bell Air Park ⓣ 225 9648, ⓦ roraimaairways.com. Offers the cheapest flights (US$195) to Kaieteur Falls because it's an arm of Roraima Airways. Also does day-trips around the region.

Wilderness Explorers ⓣ 227 7698, ⓦ wilderness -explorers.com. Now operating solely online, this company can arrange more complex tours of the interior suited to your interests. Specializes in adventure and bushman skills.

INDEPENDENT TRAVEL IN THE INTERIOR

Independent travel in Guyana's interior requires forward planning, time and flexibility, but it's possible to visit all main attractions without having to go with a tour operator. Overland travel away from the Lethem–Georgetown highway is along Guyana's many rivers, and boatmen need to be negotiated with over prices. If you can't give them a specific date to be collected from where they drop you, it's advisable to take a radio for communication. To visit most Amerindian villages (barring Annai and Rupertee), you first have to get permission from either the Amerindian Affairs office (see p000) in Georgetown or its equivalent in Lethem. Book accommodation well in advance instead of just rocking up. If travelling overland, it is essential that you have your **passport** (or at least a photocopy) with you, as there are several police checkpoints in the interior.

GETTING AROUND

By plane See p.654

By minibus Georgetown–Lethem minibuses can stop en route at Annai or drop you at the turn-offs to Surama or the Iwokrama Research Centre and Canopy Walkway (make arrangements to be picked up from the turn-off or walk in). Since minibuses tend to overflow with passengers and luggage, to board a bus from a location in between Lethem and Georgetown, reserve a seat in advance by calling the minibus company directly or through your lodgings.

By 4WD and boat There is no public transport from the main "highway" to remote lodges and villages, so you have to hire a 4WD (around US$200/day; less for short distances) or motorbike. In the rainy season, you will find yourself travelling more by motorboat. 4WDs are easy to arrange in Lethem, but all lodges can help you with onward travel arrangements.

By motorbike The least expensive way of getting around the Rupununi is on the back of someone's motorbike. Most people own one, and wherever you may be staying, it's always possible to arrange onward transport by motorbike just by asking around. It's considerably cheaper than going by 4WD, especially if you're a solo traveller: several hours' ride or hiring someone to take you around for a day will set you back no more than US$40. You have to travel light, though.

By bicycle Most Amerindians in the Rupununi cycle long distances on their sturdy, fixed-gear Brazilian bikes. While cycling from Georgetown to Lethem has been done by several intrepid travellers, there is a long stretch of uninhabited jungle between Linden and Kurupukari, and you have to carry all the water you need. Cycling around the Rupununi Savannah is a possibility in the dry season, though.

Amerindian village. Here you can sling your hammock in the hospitable villages of Annai, Yupukari, Shulinab and Nappi, linger in the friendly frontier town of Lethem or go wildlife-spotting from one of the local ecolodges. The savannah's grasslands abound with giant anteaters, while the many rivers are home to the black caiman, giant river otter and aparaima.

Iwokrama Research Centre and Canopy Walkway

The pristine, 400-square-kilometre **Iwokrama Rainforest** is home to a staggering 474 bird species, 130 different mammals, 420 types of fish and 132 species of reptile. It's possible to stay at the eight attractive solar-powered riverside cabins at the **Research Centre**

itself (rooms US$120; meals US$45/day; ☎225 1504, ⊛iwokrama.org), an internationally funded project to research forest management and sustainable development, with participation from local Amerindian communities. Visitors share lodgings and meals with visiting biologists, botanists and journalists, and can take part in visits to nearby Amerindian villages, night-time caiman spotting, and multi-day excursions into the jungle and up Turtle Mountain.

A ninety-minute drive from the Research Centre is the **Canopy Walkway** (⊛iwokramacanopywalkway.com), a 140m network of aluminium suspension bridges set amid the treetops, 30m from the forest floor. Its three observation platforms provide excellent vantage points to spot birds, howler monkeys and other fauna within the forest canopy – but only if you're there at dusk or dawn, when animal life is at its most active. An overnight stay at the luxurious **Atta Rainforest Camp**, at the foot of the canopy walk trail, costs US$260 for a room, including all meals, the canopy user fee and a trained guide. Day visitors pay G$5000. Booking in advance is vital.

Surama Village and Ecolodge

An ecotourism success story, the Surama Village (☎548 9262, ⓦsuramaecolodge .com) is a spread-out Makushi settlement of some 300 people and thatch-roofed huts connected by dusty paths, 45 minutes' drive west of the Canopy Walkway. You can stay in one of the two ecolodges in the village, each consisting of several traditional huts (rooms US$150), learn about medicinal plants from local guides, or hike up Surama Mountain (230m) and go wildlife-watching along the Burro Burro River. Alternatively, camp in one of the two basic camps along the river (US$15) and go jungle trekking.

Annai and Rupertee

The first Makushi village you reach after emerging from the jungle is **Rupertee**, famous for its craft shop (if it's closed, ask around for Gloria Duarto) where you can pick up carvings made of a local red hardwood, as well as intricate woven goods and bows and arrows (still used for hunting in these parts). Jeep tracks and footpaths connect it to **Annai**, around 2km off the main road – a compact, attractive village of around 300 people. Across the road from *Oasis* is the Uncle Dennis Trail (45min), which snakes up the forest-covered hill; from the top there's a splendid view of the savannah.

ACCOMMODATION

Oasis The budget-friendly sister to *Rock View Lodge* is a 10min walk away. Just off the main road, it's a popular stop for minibuses. Comprises spacious, airy en-suite rooms with mosquito nets, a hammock *benab* and an eatery with simple, inexpensive meals. Doubles <u>US$70</u>, hammocks <u>US$10</u>

Karanambu Lodge ⓦwww .karanambutrustandlodge.org. Sitting in a clearing near the Rupununi River, this one-of-a-kind lodge consists of six luxurious cabins. A bell summons guests to the table, presided over by the formidable 82-year-old Diane McTurk – a local legend, best known for her work with orphaned giant river otters. Wild animals abound in the savannah, wetlands and rainforest around the lodge, and there's a good chance of seeing jaguars, giant anteaters, tapirs and caimans during guided walks and river trips. The meals are excellent, the rate is inclusive of everything and the staff are wonderful. You can either fly into Karanambu or take a boat from Guinep landing (1hr 30min); Karanambu is 30min by boat from Caiman House. Cabañas <u>US$200</u>

Rock View Lodge ⓦrockviewlodge.com. This British-run option has clean and comfortable en-suite rooms and is set in large grounds with a swimming pool. Owned by local character Colin Edwards; even if you don't stay here, he will arrange activities, including visits to the nearby village of Wowetta. Wi-fi when the generator is running. Triples make this option a little more affordable for groups. Doubles <u>US$300</u>, triples <u>US$360</u>

Yupukari and Caiman House

Yupukari (ⓦrupununilearners.org) is a mostly Makushi village of around 500 inhabitants, a couple of hours' drive along a rutted dirt track from Annai; it's also possible to reach it by boat along the Rupununi River from Guinep Landing, 21km west of Annai (2hr). The main attraction here is the **Caiman House Field Station**, whose main purpose is to study the black caiman. If you're lucky, you will join the local caiman research crew in the evening when they go out to capture, weigh, measure and tag the fearsome creatures.

ACCOMMODATION

Caiman House This guesthouse has en-suite rooms with mosquito nets, a hammock *benab* and some of the best home-cooked food in the savannah (meals are included). The place is a constant hub of activity, with knowledgeable Fernando to talk to and a lively learning centre for the local children next door (book donations very welcome). Doubles <u>US$85</u>, hammocks <u>US$30</u>

LETHEM AND AROUND

With its wide dirt streets, unhurried pace of life and an everybody-knows-everybody feel, **LETHEM** is a great little place to linger en route to Brazil or Venezuela and a good base from which to launch your exploration of the southern **Rupununi Savannah**. Moco Moco and Kumu Falls (30min drive each) are both great for swimming, and it's possible to arrange horseriding near the Kumu Mountains at the village of **Shulinab** (1hr 30min drive). There's easy access to the village of **Nappi**, 30km away – a great place for wildlife-watching – and you can live out your cowboy fantasy at the remote Dadanawa Ranch.

Lethem really comes alive during Easter weekend, when cowboys from all around (including the Brazilian *vaqueros*) gather in town for bull-riding, calf-roping and stallion-taming competitions (book accommodation weeks in advance).

ARRIVAL AND INFORMATION

By plane Four airlines fly between Lethem and Georgetown (4 departures daily, more during rainy seasons; 1hr 30min), and all four offices are located next to the airstrip. TGA and Roraima airlines will stop at Annai and Karanambu on request. Ticket prices (one-way) cost around US$125. Check-in two hours before the flight. Flying is sometimes the only mode of travel between Georgetown and Lethem during the rainy season, when sections of the route become impassable for days.

By minibus Various minibus companies from Georgetown arrive and depart from different places around town (departing Georgetown 5–7pm, arriving noon–2pm; 18hr). Guy Braz is probably the most convenient one, as its office is the most central (10min walk from the airstrip). The journey is slow because,

aside from the paved stretch between Georgetown and Linden, the rest of the "highway" is unpaved and rutted, and the car ferry at Kurupukari runs only between 6am and 6pm; the minibuses break their journey near the ferry dock. Most passengers end up sleeping in the cramped bus.

Tourist information Your one essential contact in Lethem is Shirley Melville, usually found either in the craft shop next to the airstrip or in the grocery store next door. She produces maps of Lethem and has started her own tour company, so she'll either be able to personally assist you in your onward travels, or will point you in the right direction.

ACCOMMODATION AND EATING

At time of research there was talk of *Mann's Cafe* beside the airstrip opening a twelve-bed backpacker hostel (G$2000/night) with laundry facilities.

Betty's Creole Corner The lovely Betty cooks up a roti storm at her little *cook shop* on the corner. Portions are generous (try her excellent *pepperpot*) and there are fruit juices and snacks if you're not looking for a full meal (meals G$600–800). Daily 6am–8pm.

Dadanawa Ranch 📞 0044 7961 521 951 (UK number), 🌐 rupununitrails.com. Situated against the dramatic backdrop of the Kanuku Mountains, this is the largest and most isolated ranch in Guyana, a 3hr drive southeast of Lethem. You're treated like family by Sandy, Duane and their team of workers and guides, and the ranch is a good base to help cowboys work the cattle, as well as for trekking, horseriding, nature walks, birdwatching, swimming and fishing. Meals included. **US$120**

Maipaima Eco-Lodge 🌐 wildrupununi.com. Surrounded by pristine rainforest and located at the foot of the Kanuku Mountains, 10km south of Nappi village, this lovely spot consists of traditional wood-and-thatch buildings on stilts and a central *benab* for dining. There's limited electricity and the rustic setting is perfect for wildlife-watching: jaguar, monkeys and tapir have been sighted in the vicinity. Stays include a village tour and introduction to balata craft – making figurines and scenes out of hardened tree sap. **US$125**

CROSSING INTO BRAZIL

To get from Lethem to the Brazilian town of Bonfim, cross the Takutu River Bridge about 1.5km north of Lethem either on foot or by taxi. Pick-ups from the airstrip to the crossing cost around G$1200. **Guyanese immigration formalities** should be completed either at the airstrip when there are flights, or at the Lethem immigration office. Get your passport stamped on the Brazilian side of the border before you make your way to **Bonfim**, from where there are buses to **Boa Vista**, some 150km away, with connections to Manaus (Brazil) and Caracas (Venezuela). There is a GBTI **bank** in Lethem (Lot 121; Mon–Fri 8am–1pm), which offers foreign exchange. **Moneychangers** on the Lethem side of the river will also change Guyanese dollars for Brazilian reais and vice versa. Make sure that you have enough reais to get you to Bonfim, if not Boa Vista.

Ori Hotel ☎ 772 2124. The loveliest hotel in town, with wonderfully friendly service and en-suite rooms (with wi-fi) hidden within a tranquil blooming garden. The restaurant serves delicious Creole dishes. G$5000.

Takutu Hotel ☎ 772 2034. ✉ takutuhotel@gmail.com. Friendly hotel 5min from the airstrip, with spic-and-span, tiled en-suite rooms with a/c and wi-fi and a bar/restaurant in a flowering garden. You can meet some interesting characters on karaoke nights. G$6000.

Suriname

SURINAME, formerly Dutch Guiana, is South America's smallest independent nation and has a lot in common with its neighbours – a brutal history of slavery, for one. Though it predominantly attracts tourists and volunteers from Holland, English-speaking travellers are also made to feel welcome. The capital, **Paramaribo**, is the most attractive city in the Guianas, with much of its eighteenth- and nineteenth-century wooden architecture still intact; it also makes a good base for visiting the former plantations nearby and river dolphin-watching on the Commewijne River.

While ecotourism is still in its fledgling state, and facing constant challenges (thirteen percent of Suriname's land surface area is under official environmental protection but that hasn't stopped illegal gold mining), there are two excellent ecolodges in the interior – *Awarradam* and *Palumeu* – that act as springboards for exploration of the unique Amerindian and Saramaccan (Maroon) communities. There are great opportunities for hiking and wildlife watching at the Central Suriname Nature Reserve, while on the coast **Galibi Nature Reserve** offers the chance to observe giant sea turtles laying their eggs. If you're short of time, **Brownsberg Nature Park**, easily accessible from Paramaribo, gives you a taste of Suriname's wilderness.

CHRONOLOGY

10,000 BC Suriname's earliest inhabitants are thought to be the Surinen Indians after whom the country is named.

1498 Columbus sights Surinamese coast.

1602 Dutch begin to settle the land.

1651 England's Lord Willoughby establishes first permanent settlement – Willoughbyland, with 1000 white settlers and 2000 slaves.

1654 Jews from Holland expelled from Brazil arrive.

1667 Suriname becomes Dutch Guiana with the Treaty of Breda, after conquest of Willoughbyfort (now Fort Zeelandia) by Dutch Admiral Crynssen.

1700s–1800s Slavery under the Dutch particularly harsh, with rape, maiming and killing of slaves common. Many run away into the interior and form Maroon communities, conducting occasional murderous raids on the plantations and their owners.

1799 Suriname reconquered by the British.

1814 Suriname given back to Holland as part of the Treaty of Paris.

1853 Chinese plantation labourers arrive.

1863 Formal abolition of slavery (though slaves not released for another 10 years as part of transition period).

1873 Labourers from India, and later Indonesia, arrive.

1941 US troops occupy Suriname to protect bauxite mines.

1949 First elections based on universal suffrage held.

1975 Suriname wins independence.

1980 Military coup led by Sergeant Major Dési Bouterse topples government. Socialist republic declared.

1982 Fifteen prominent leaders of re-democratization movement executed.

1986 Civil war begins between military government and Maroons, led by Bouterse's former bodyguard, Ronnie Brunswijk. At least 39 unarmed inhabitants of the N'Dyuka Maroon village, Moiwana, mostly women and children, are murdered by military.

1987 Civilian government installed with new constitution for Republic of Suriname, but Bourterse remains in charge of army.

1990 Bouterse dismisses civilian government with phone call in "telephone coup".

1991 Bouterse holds elections under international pressure. The New Front coalition wins; Ronald Venetiaan is elected president.

1996 National Democratic Party (founded by Bouterse in 1987) wins election.

1999 Bouterse convicted of drug smuggling in Holland in absentia.

2000 Venetiaan and the New Front coalition regains presidency (and again in 2006).

2004 Surinamese dollar introduced as currency.

2007 UN maritime border tribunal awards both Guyana and Suriname a share of the potentially oil-rich offshore basin under dispute.

2008 Trial begins of Bouterse and others accused of

involvement in executions of opponents of military regime in 1982.

2010 Bouterse elected president.

2012 Fire in Paramaribo destroys a number of historical wooden buildings.

ARRIVAL AND DEPARTURE

Johan Adolf Pengel International Airport (also known as Zanderij), an hour south of Paramaribo, receives direct **flights** from Aruba, Amsterdam, Belém and Boa Vista (Brazil), Cayenne (French Guiana), Curaçao, Georgetown, Miami and Port of Spain (Trinidad). **Zorg en Hoop**, a smaller airport about fifteen minutes from the capital, receives small domestic aircraft, as well as daily flights to and from Guyana.

OVERLAND FROM GUYANA

From Georgetown it's a three-hour **bus** ride to the **ferry** port at Molson Creek, with three crossings per day (9.30am, noon & 4.30pm), then a three-hour **bus** ride from South Drain to Paramaribo (see box, p.662).

OVERLAND FROM FRENCH GUIANA

Travellers from French Guiana must cross the Maroni River from St Laurent du Maroni to Albina by **ferry** or motorized canoe, before continuing the three-hour drive by **minibus** or **taxi** to Paramaribo (see box, p.685).

VISAS

Visas are required for all visitors except nationals from CARICOM countries, and a few Asian and South American countries. Visitors may apply for a Tourist Card, valid for thirty days, single entry only (US$25). Tourist Cards may be obtained at Paramaribo airport (Johan Adolf Pengel International Airport) on arrival, whereas overland travellers need to secure theirs in advance at the consulates in Guyana (see p.655) and French Guiana (see p.678); processing takes around twenty minutes. For stays of longer than thirty days or multiple entry, visas must be obtained (from US$45 upwards), which may not be processed on the same day for certain nationalities. For updated information on visa requirements, check ⓦsurinameembassy.org.

GETTING AROUND

While commuting around the capital and outlying areas is reasonably easy, there are no major highways in Suriname except for the Oost–Westverbinding (East–West Highway) that runs between Albina and Nieuw Nickerie. Scheduled state-run buses and private minibuses run to most destinations, though for many remote interior destinations you'll need to travel by 4WD, small plane or motorized dugout canoe (or a combination of all three); it's cheaper and easier to go as part of a tour.

BY PLANE

There are some **scheduled internal flights**, but tour operators tend to charter planes to visit parks and reserves, and this limits their frequency to the number of tourists wishing to make a trip. Suriname Airways (ⓦwww.slm.firm.sr) offers organized tours to Kasikasima, Palumeu and Awarradam through its tour division METS (see p.667).

BY BUS

Brightly decorated, crowded **private minibuses** are numbered and run along assigned routes both between the capital and smaller cities near the coast, and to Paramaribo's neighbourhoods. These don't leave until they are completely full, but are more frequent than the scheduled state-run services and stop wherever you want along the road. Journeys are of the sardine-tin variety, so if you don't want to ride with your backpack on your lap shared taxis are a more comfortable option. The plainer **state-run buses** (*staatsbus*; ⓦwww.nvbnvsuriname.com) have a dedicated bus station, follow a schedule and use bus stops.

BY SHARED TAXI

Shared taxis (essentially private vehicles) run to Albina and are far more comfortable than minibuses (your guesthouse can recommend a reliable operator).

7

CROSSING BETWEEN SURINAME AND GUYANA

Getting to Guyana involves crossing the Corantijn (Corentyne) River on the ferry, with daily departures at 11am and 3pm (SRD48 single) from **South Drain**, an hour west of Nickerie. If you arrive after the last boat has left you must stay in Nickerie and leave early for the 11am boat. Ticket sales on the Surinamese side open at 8am. Taxis will collect from your Nickerie hotel and take you to the ferry (SRD100). Numerous minibuses make the early morning journey from Paramaribo to catch the 11am boat (3hr; SRD70); some minibus companies work in partnership with Guyanese tour companies (see p.656). You will need time to clear customs and a valid passport. Once you arrive at **Molson Creek, Guyana**, you must clear customs again and get your passport stamped before taking one of the waiting minibuses for the three-hour journey to Georgetown (G$2400). There is no currency exchange or ATM at South Drain or Molson Creek, but euros or US$ (preferably the latter) can be easily exchanged at either location with unofficial (and costly) moneychangers for Surinam/Guyanese dollars, respectively. If going from Guyana to Suriname, most minibus companies pick up passengers at around 4–4.30am in order to make the 9.30am ferry to Suriname.

BY BOAT

Navigating the Suriname and Commewijne rivers around Paramaribo is done by public ferry. Normally used to cross the water at specific points, fees for journeys to other towns along the rivers' banks can be negotiated at the docks, where boatmen wait for customers.

ACCOMMODATION

Accommodation in Paramaribo consists of **guesthouses** and mid-range hotels. Almost all rooms will come equipped with running water, fans and mosquito nets. Outside the capital accommodation is rather basic. A comprehensive list of guesthouses can be found at ⓦsuriname-tourism.org.

If you travel into the interior, you're likely to stay in **lodges** in Suriname's nature parks and reserves, which vary from rustic (a place to hang your hammock and shared facilities) to the more luxurious (en-suite rooms with mosquito nets). This is usually on an all-inclusive basis and bookings are best made through tour operators.

FOOD AND DRINK

The food in Suriname is fairly inexpensive, tasty and influenced by its ethnically diverse population. Informal Javanese (Indonesian) eateries known as **warungs** (in the Blauwgrond area) and

Hindustani **roti shops** sit alongside Chinese, sushi, European-style and Creole restaurants. Meals cost around SRD15–25.

Kip (chicken) is very popular and typical Surinamese dishes include *moksie alesie* (rice, beans, chicken and vegetables) and *pom* (chicken baked with a root vegetable). Indonesian specialities include *saoto* (chicken soup, beansprouts, potatoes and a boiled egg), *bami* (fried noodles) and *nasi goreng* (fried rice). Two tasty peanut soups are *pindasoep*, made with tom-tom (plantain noodles), and *petjil*, made with vegetables. *Bakabanna* (plantain slices, dipped in a pancake batter and fried) is an established crowd-pleaser. Traditional Dutch favourites like *bitterballen* (breaded and fried minced meat balls) and *poffertjes* (sugared pancakes) are plentiful. If travelling in the interior, you may well get to try various game dishes.

DRINK

Suriname produces some of the Caribbean's best rum, and both Borgoe and Black Cat brands are worth a try; the lethal 90 percent proof stuff is usually used to mix cocktails. Imported and local beer (Parbo is the very drinkable local tipple of choice), soft drinks and bottled water are widely available, as is **dawet**, a very sweet, pink concoction of coconut milk and lemongrass. In Paramaribo you can also find decent **coffee**.

CULTURE AND ETIQUETTE

Suriname's diverse population is 37 percent Hindustani (the local term for East Indian); 31 percent Creole (people of mixed European and African origin); 15 percent Javanese (Indonesian); 10 percent Maroon (Bush Negro). The main **religions** are Hinduism, Christianity and Islam.

The official **language** in Suriname is Dutch but the common language is Sranan Tongo (Surinamese Creole), also known as Taki-Taki. Several Maroon languages, including Saramaccan and Aukan, are spoken, as are Amerindian languages such as Carib. A reasonable number of people speak some English, particularly in Paramaribo. Always ask permission before taking pictures of people, buildings and sacrificial areas when visiting Maroon villages. For **tipping**, ten percent is the norm if a service charge hasn't been included.

COMMUNICATIONS

The country code is 597. To use your **mobile phone**, get it unlocked, then purchase a Telesur or Digicel SIM card and some prepaid charge cards costing SRD5, 10, 20 or 50. **Internet cafés** are dying out due to proliferation of (mostly) free internet/wi-fi in many hotels/ guesthouses.

Postal services are provided by the Central Post Office, Surpost, near RBTT in Kerkplein 1.

CRIME AND SAFETY

Locals are proud of saying that tourists can walk safely from one end of Paramaribo to the other at night. Take this with a pinch of salt; as in most cities, burglary, armed robbery and other **petty crime** do take place. Avoid flaunting valuables and don't walk down inadequately lit streets after dark.

Travel to the interior is usually without incident, although there have been some reports of independent tourists being robbed. Be careful on the **roads**, as drivers can be reckless, and mopeds, scooters and motorcycles always have the right of way.

SURINAME ON THE NET

ⓦ **suriname-tourism.org** The Suriname Tourism Foundation has information on what to do, where to stay and how to get around in Suriname.
ⓦ **ci-suriname.org** Information on Suriname's protected areas by Conservation International.
ⓦ **whc.unesco.org/en/list/940** Information on Paramaribo's historic city centre.

HEALTH

Medical care is limited, as is the small ambulance fleet. **Academisch Ziekenhuis** (Fluestraat; ☎113, ⓦazp.sr) has the only 24-hour emergency room service in Paramaribo as well as general practitioners who speak English. Drink bottled water where possible. Insect repellent is essential as there are reported cases of mosquito-borne dengue fever. Consult your doctor regarding malaria tablets (malaria is present in some parts of the interior) and the various **vaccinations** required, which include hepatitis A, hepatitis B, yellow fever, typhoid, tetanus-diphtheria and rabies.

INFORMATION AND MAPS

For information and to pick up a copy of *Suriname's Destination Guide*, visit the Toeristen Informatie Centrum in Paramaribo (see p.667).

MONEY AND BANKS

The unit of **currency** is the Suriname dollar (SRD), which comes in 1, 2.50, 5, 10, 20, 50 and (rare) 100 notes and 1, 5, 10, 25, 100 and 250 cent coins. Prices are often given in euros, which are readily accepted (as are US$), and cambios (money exchanges) offer better exchange rates than banks. Major **credit cards** are

EMERGENCY NUMBERS

Fire services ☎**110**
Ambulance ☎**113**
Police ☎**115**

7

PUBLIC HOLIDAYS

January 1 New Year's Day
March Holi Phagwa (Hindu festival; date varies)
March/April (varies) Good Friday
March/April (varies) Easter Monday
May 1 Labour Day
July 1 Keti Koti (Emancipation Day)
August 8 Emancipation of the Javanese
August 9 Day of the Indigenous People
September Eid Ul Fitr (Muslim festival; date varies)
November 25 Srefidensi. Independence Day
December 25 Christmas Day
December 26 Second Christmas Day

FESTIVALS AND CELEBRATIONS

In addition to national holidays, many important events are celebrated among the resident ethnic communities. These include Chinese New Year (Feb); Jewish New Year (Sept); Loweman Dei, celebrating all things Maroon (Oct); and Diwali (Nov). Other festivities include the Brazilian carnival (Feb); French Music Festival (June); Back to School Festival (Sept); Salsuri Music and Suriname Jazz Festivals (Oct); and Surifesta, the end of year festival (Dec). On New Year's Eve (Owru Jari) there is a spectacular fireworks display in the capital.

accepted by most tour operators and in some restaurants and hotels in Paramaribo. Some **ATMs** in Paramaribo accept foreign bankcards; elsewhere ATMs are sparse, so carry extra **cash**. At the time of writing, €1=SRD4.33, US$1=SRD3.27 and £1=SRD5.42.

OPENING HOURS AND HOLIDAYS

Government institutions: Monday to Friday 7am–2.30pm. Shops and other businesses: Monday to Friday 9am–4.30pm and Saturday 9am–1pm; Chinese corner shops tend to be open daily. Banks: Monday to Friday 9am–2pm.

PARAMARIBO

PARAMARIBO ("Parbo" to the locals) is by far the most pleasant of the three Guyanese capitals. The administrative, much fought-over capital of the Guianas

during the colonial era, Parbo's historic inner city became a UNESCO World Heritage Site in 2002. Its streets are lined with attractive eighteenth- and nineteenth-century colonial Dutch, British, Spanish and French wooden buildings, you can take refuge from the heat in the beautiful palm tree grove that is Palmentuin (Palm Garden), and the riverfront near the historical **Fort Zeelandia** is a romantic spot at sunset.

You can eat well in Parbo, its vast mix of cultures reflected in the capital's diverse cuisine.

The Waterkant (waterfront), the bus station and the markets seem just as colourful and chaotic as their equivalents in the two neighbouring countries, but Paramaribo is generally **safe**. Steer clear of the unlit Palmentuin after dark, as well as the residential area east of Van Sommelsdijkstrant Straat and its intersection with Kleine Dwarsstraat. Taxis are the best way to get around town in the evening.

WHAT TO SEE AND DO

Paramaribo's principal charm lies in the unhurried exploration of its Old Town. It's easy to organize cycling tours of nearby plantations, as well as river dolphin-spotting on the Commewijne River.

Onafhankelijkheidsplein and around

The centrepiece of the historic inner city is **Onafhankelijkheidsplein** (**Independence Square**), an expanse of green lawn near the Waterkant overlooked by several state buildings, a statue of a rather round Johan Adolf Pengel (former prime minister) and the **Presidential Palace**.

Early on Sunday mornings (around 7–8am) Independence Square plays host to competitive **bird-singing contests**. Here, *picolets* and *twa twas* are persuaded to sing in turns, the winning bird earning a payout for its owner.

Fort Zeelandia

The tree-shaded colonial buildings of Fort Zeelandia (originally Fort Willoughby) overlook the Suriname River. One of the darkest spots in the fort's recent history was the 1982 "December murders", when

7

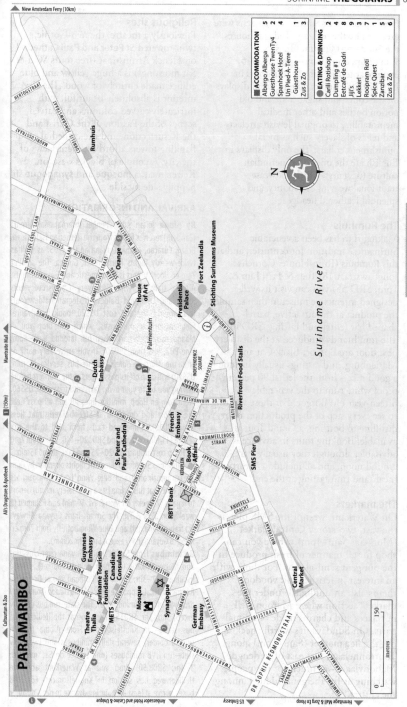

PARAMARIBO

▲ Niew Amsterdam Ferry (10km)

■ ACCOMMODATION
Albergo Alberga	5
Guesthouse TwenTy4	2
Spanhoek Hotel	4
Un Pied-A-Terre	1
Guesthouse	3
Zus & Zo	

● EATING & DRINKING
Carili Rotishop	2
Dumpling #1	4
Eetcafé de Gadri	8
Jjil's	9
Lekker!	3
Roopram Roti	7
Spice Quest	1
Zanzibar	5
Zus & Zo	6

Suriname River

Rumhuis

Fort Zeelandia
Stichting Surinaams Museum

House of Art

Presidential Palace

Palmentuin

Orange

Dutch Embassy

Fietsen

Independence Square

Riverfront Food Stalls

French Embassy

St. Peter and Paul's Cathedral

Book Affairs

SMS Pier

RBTT Bank

Central Market

Guyanese Embassy
Suriname Tourism Foundation
Canadian Consulate

METS

Theatre Thalia

Mosque

Synagogue

German Embassy

▲ Maretraite Mall
▲ (150m)
◄ Ali's Drugstore & Apotheek
◄ Culturtuin & Zoo

◄ Ambassador Hotel and Casino & Unique
◄ Hermitage Mall & Zorg En Hoop
◄ US Embassy

0 ———— 150
metres

fifteen prominent Surinamese citizens were executed by the military. Today it houses the **Suriname Museum** (Tues–Sat 9am–2pm, Sun 10am–2pm; SRD15; enquire at tourist office about tours in English), its exhibits ranging from displays on the coffee and sugar trade and old potion bottles and other medical memorabilia, to original Jewish artefacts and relics of slavery such as metal punishment collars. The only displays in English are the ones on Amerindian culture (upstairs), which showcase traditional weaving, weaponry, and splendid feathered headgear.

The Rumhuis

Making rum has been a venerable Surinamese tradition for centuries, and at this **Rumhuis** (Rum House; Cornelis Jongbawstraat 18; Tues & Fri 11am & 1pm; SRD 55) you can visit its well-designed interactive museum then sample the product at the attractive, barrel-shaped bar (entry and tastings SRD50). The rum brands produced at the distillery next door are Borgoe, Black Cat and Mariënburg, and tastings usually include a good mix – from the lethal 90 percent proof white rum to the venerable fifteen-year-old Borgoe. For those wanting to see every step of the production from distilling to bottling, a Grand Tour is available. Booking tours in advance is advisable, although they usually start around noon, and all include a "hearty meal" and rum tasting at the end.

The markets

On Waterkant, west of the SMS pier, is the vast, two-storey **Central Market** (Mon–Sat 5am–4pm), where you can shop for all manner of fresh produce in the pungent semi-gloom. For those with an interest in fetishes and voodoo, there's also an unofficial "under the market" section where Maroons sell necklaces and charms made of animal parts. On Sundays, it's worth checking out the **flea market** (8am–1pm) along Tourtonnelaan, just east of Verlengde Mahonylaan – as much for the people-watching as for the gems hidden among the clutter.

Religious sites

Previously a theatre, the neo-Gothic, twin-towered **St Peter and Paul Cathedral** on Henck Arronstraat (free tours Wed & Sat mornings) is a huge yellow and blue edifice made entirely of wood. The airy interior is absolutely beautiful, with intricately carved columns and carved scenes of the Passion of the Christ and the Resurrection, and the cathedral's four flanking towers afford excellent views of the city. A couple of blocks west, on Keizerstraat, a **mosque** and **synagogue** sit happily side by side.

ARRIVAL AND INFORMATION

By plane Johan Adolf Pengel International Airport (Zanderij) receives flights from the Netherlands, Trinidad, Brazil, Curaçao, Aruba, Guyana and the US, as well as twice-weekly flights from French Guiana. The smaller Zorg en Hoop Airport is for domestic and Guyana flights. Airport transfers with Buscovery (W buscoverytours .com) and Le Grand Baldew (W legrandbaldew.com) take around 1hr and cost US$20; book in advance. Frequent private minibuses, which will drop you in Maagdenstraat, depart when full (around 8am–8pm; Line POZ, less than SRD10). If you arrive very early or late, the *Marriott Hotel*'s shuttle-bus service (45min; US$20) will drop off its passengers at the *Marriott* before driving you on to your own. Taxis into town cost US$60. From Zorg en Hoop, minibus lines #8 and #9 pass near the airport and drop you at Steenbakkerijstraat (less than SRD10). Unmetered taxis from JAPI to the city centre (45min) cost around SRD120–140. Taxis from Zorg en Hoop cost around SRD20–25 and take about 15min.

Destinations Scheduled domestic flights operated by Gum Air (W gumair.com) and Blue Wing (W bluewingairlines .com; note that this airline has a poor safety record) depart to Kajana (2 weekly on Mon & Fri; 50min) and Palumeu (2 weekly on Mon & Fri; 1hr 5min). Trans Guyana Airways (W transguyana.net) and Blue Wing both fly from Zorg en Hoop to Guyana (daily except Sun; 1hr 20min).

By minibus From South Drain (Guyana river crossing) and Nieuw Nickerie (car park next to market), private minibuses (2–3hr; SRD60) will offload you at Dr Sophie Redmondstraat, opposite *Hotel Ambassador* (some may drop you off at your lodgings). The state-run bus (2 daily except Sun; 3hr; SRD15) drops you at the Heiligenweg bus station in Knuffelsgracht. From Albina (French Guiana border) several daily minibuses and two daily state-run NVB minibuses (one service on Sat and Sun; 3–4hr; SRD8.50) drop you at Waterkant and the Heiligenweg bus station in Knuffelsgracht. For NVB buses, arrive at least an hour in advance to get a number from the ticket office; you then present the number to the minibus driver and pay for your seat when you board. Private minibuses such as Lada & Son have a reciprocal arrangement with minibus companies in Guyana, so you can buy a ticket all the way to Georgetown if you use their services to get to South Drain.

Destinations Albina (NVB state bus from Heiligenweg, minibus #PA from Central Market; 3–4hr); Nieuw Nickerie and South Drain (NVB state bus from Heiligenweg or minibus #PN from Dr. Sophie Redmondstraat; several daily; 2hr–3hr 30min).

By taxi To and from South Drain unmetered taxis cost SRD70–200 depending on passenger numbers (2–3hr). Taxis to Albina (for the French Guiana border crossing) cost SRD70–200 depending on passenger numbers (3hr); ask your guesthouse to book a reputable one.

Tourist information The Toeristen Informatie Centrum is at Fort Zeelandia Complex, Waterkant 1 (Mon–Fri 8am–3.30pm; ☎479 200). Staff are very helpful and speak English. They provide free maps and information in Dutch and English on transport, restaurants, nightlife, day-trips and tours.

GETTING AROUND

By bicycle You can rent bikes from SRD15/day from Fietsen, at Grote Combeweg 13a (ⓦfietseninsuriname .com), as well as from Cardy Adventures at Cornelis Jongbawstraat 31 (ⓦcardyadventures.com).

By bus The larger, cheaper but less frequent scheduled state buses (*staatsbus*) leave from the bus station at Heiligenweg in Knuffelsgracht. Fares in and around Paramaribo cost about SRD1.50.

By taxi Taxis wait for passengers in front of Central Market (Waterkant). Registered, unmetered taxis use fixed rates, measuring distance by their vehicles' mileage clocks and referring to their price list to charge upon arrival. Taxi drivers often try to cheat tourists, so if your

phone has GPS capabilities, monitor their route from the back seat. If they cheat you (look with suspicion on them driving you into heavy traffic), you don't have to pay. Trips within the city should cost SRD7.50–15. Recommended taxi firms include Djo's Taxi (☎471 048) and Sheriff Taxi (☎410 241).

ACCOMMODATION

All accommodation options below have wi-fi.

Albergo Alberga Mr F.H.R. Lim A Postraat 13 ☎520 050, ⓦguesthousealbergoalberga.com. Lovely nineteenth-century wooden house in the city centre with a button-sized swimming pool. Rooms (some with a/c) are bright but could be cleaner. €17

Guesthouse TwenTy4 Jessurunstraat 24 ☎420 751, ⓦtwenty4suriname.com. Under the same management as *Zus & Zo*, this comfortable guesthouse on a peaceful street is a little bit plusher than its sister business (most rooms are en suite). Friendly staff can help arrange tours and there's a small bar open until 11pm. €15

Spanhoek Hotel Domineestraat 2–4 ☎477 888, ⓦwww.spanhoekhotel.com. Smack-bang in the middle of town, this hotel's stylish rooms, blasting a/c and professional service make the high price more palatable if you need a break from ramshackle guesthouses. Buffet breakfast included. €110

★**Un Pied-À-Terre Guesthouse** Costerstraat 59 ☎470 488, ⓦguesthouse-un-pied-a-terre.com. A quaint guesthouse which attracts young clientele. Breezy verandas, four-poster beds, beers on the honour system and breakfast from €4. Alternatively, hang a hammock (don't forget your mosquito net) in the garden (€2 discount if you hang your own). Rooms €22, hammocks €12

Zus & Zo Grote Combéweg 13a ☎520 905, ⓦzusenzosuriname.com. The traveller hub of Parbo, comprising several compact, brightly painted rooms with

---

7

SURINAME TOURS

In the off-season, the tour operators work together and share customers in order to make up minimum group numbers. Price-wise, there isn't much difference between operators. Unless you have a lot of time to spare, you'll need a tour operator for excursions into the interior.

TOUR OPERATORS

METS Dr J F Nassylaan 2, Parbo ☎477 088, ⓦsurinamevacations.com. One of the longest-running, reputable operators; specializes in visits to the interior and manages jungle lodges in Awarradam, Kasikasima and Palumeu, but also does day-trips around Parbo.

Orange Van Sommelsdijkstraat 1 ☎421 984, ⓦorangesuriname.com. Professional, English-speaking staff, and a plethora of tours – from day-trips

to Brownsberg and the Commewijne River to multi-day adventures in Galibi, Central Suriname Nature Reserve and much more.

Irvin Ristie ☎823 4879, ✉irvinristie@gmail.com. An independent guide who organizes excellent and inexpensive multi-day expeditions into relatively unknown bush. White-water kayaking, abseiling and other adrenaline-pumping activities can be worked in. Get in touch in advance since he needs at least two weeks' notice to put a trip together.

7

shared bath, helpful staff, tour agency, bike rental agency next door and one of the best chillout spots in town. Clientele varies between international travellers and screeching Dutch teenagers. Book in advance as it fills up quickly. **€25**

EATING AND DRINKING

Take a taxi to the Blauwgrond neighbourhood to eat at one of the many *warungs* (Javanese restaurants) here. Check ⓦ eteninsuriname.com for a restaurant list and online menus.

Carili Rotishop Julianastraat ☎ 470 055. Family-run roti place with fresh bread, tasty fillings and low prices. It opens really early so it's a good breakfast option if you have an early tour departure. Meals from SRD6. Mon–Fri 6.15am–2.30pm & Sat 6.45am–1.30pm.

Dumpling #1 Dr J Nassylaan 168 ☎ 477 904. Breezy Chinese restaurant in a courtyard set back from the tree-lined street, serving dumplings, grilled seafood and more. Meals from SRD35. Daily 11am–3pm & 6–11pm.

Eetcafé de Gadri Zeelandiaweg 1 ☎ 420 688. Generous portions of Creole and Indonesian food (SRD15–30), served at tables overlooking the Suriname River. Mon–Fri 8am–10pm & Sat 11am–10pm.

Jiji's SMS Pier Waterkant 2nd floor. At this breezy location overlooking the river, this is the best of the places to eat, serving generous portions of Surinamese and international dishes. Meals around SRD30. Daily 5–11pm.

Lekker! Van Sommelsdijckstraat 22 ☎ 472 722. Aptly named, trendy café and bistro ("lekker" is Dutch for "delicious"), with the best coffee in town, create-your-own-salad option, toasties and treats such as bagels with grilled goat's cheese and honey and real lemonade. You can linger with your laptop, too. Mon–Sat 8am–4pm & Sun 10am–5pm.

★ Roopram Roti Several sites across town including Zwartenhovenbrugstraat 23. Visit for generous portions of roti (Indian pancake) stuffed with various curried meats (or vegetables) with all the trimmings for around SRD15.

Daily 9am–10pm (varies by location).

Zanzibar Van Sommelsdijkstraat 1. This lively outpost with a DJ (Fri & Sat) has outdoor seating and an open-air bar serving food and strong cocktails from SRD8. Daily 6pm until late.

★ Zus & Zo Grote Combéweg 13a ☎ 520 905. This garden café decorated with Christmas lights serves great international tapas (grilled plantain, tasty *sate*, *patatas bravas*) as well as more substantial mains – noodles, grilled meats and more, accompanied by tangy ginger juice and Parbo beer. Wednesday night is movie night and the little stage hosts live music on the weekends. Daily 9am–11pm.

SHOPPING

Book Affairs Kerkplein 8. Run by the wonderful Debby, this small secondhand bookshop may have what you need.

Zus & Zo Grote Combéweg 13a. Quality Saramaccan and Amerindian handicrafts – from carved, decorated calabashes to intricate jewellery and woodcarvings.

DIRECTORY

Banks and exchange Several RBTT ATMs in the centre accept foreign cards. A convenient cambio is on Kleine Waterstraat, at Van Sommelsdijckstraat: outside working hours, you can exchange your cash directly at the ATM-like exchange machine next to it.

Embassies and Consulates Brazil, Maratakastraat 2 (☎ 400 200); Canada, Wagenwagstraat 50 (☎ 424 527); France, Henck Arronstraat 5–7 (☎ 475 222); Guyana, Gravenstraat 82 (☎ 477 895); Netherlands, Van Roosevelt-kade 5 (☎ 477 211); UK, c/o VSH United Bldgs, Van't Hogerhuysstraat 9–11 (☎ 402 558); US, Dr. Sophie Redmondstraat 129 (☎ 472 900).

Pharmacies Ali's Drugstore & Apotheek, at Tourtonnelaan 127; Apotheek Sibilo, at Koningstraat 90.

DAY-TRIPS FROM PARAMARIBO

From Paramaribo you can do numerous interesting day-trips; some destinations are reachable by public transport or by bike, whereas others are more easily accomplished by organized tours (see p.667).

Brownsberg Nature Park

About 130km south of Paramaribo on the Mazaroni Plateau, **BROWNSBERG NATURE PARK** is the only protected area in Suriname that can be visited from Paramaribo as a day-trip (10hr). On a lucky day, you might see howler and spider monkeys, deer, agouti, and birds such as woodpeckers, macaws and parrots. There are also fine views from the plateau of the rainforest and the vast **Van Blommestein Lake**, created to provide electricity for the Alcoa aluminium industry (which resulted in the displacement of several Maroon villages and inadequate government compensation for its residents). Several tour companies, including Orange (see p.667), offer day-trips to the reserve (US$60), with transport, lunch and a hike to one of the three waterfalls included (bring your bathing suit). It's technically possible to stay overnight, as STINASU operates a lodge on the plateau (rooms from SRD400), as well as hammock and camping facilities (SRD35–45); however, travellers have complained about the run-down rooms and inadequate cleanliness of the facilities.

Suriname and Commewijne rivers

Paramaribo stands on the banks of the Suriname River, which joins Commewijne River a short distance east. The area is littered with the remnants of plantations (alongside a few working ones) and wonderful colonial architecture. The dilapidated **Pepperpot Plantation** is an old coffee and cocoa plantation that's great for birdwatching, and Frederiksdorp Plantation has stone and wooden buildings that have been fully renovated and converted into a delightful hotel and restaurant. The star-shaped **Fort Nieuw Amsterdam** (Mon–Fri 9am–6pm, Sat & Sun 10am–6pm; SRD10; ⓦfortnieuwamsterdam.com) is located at the meeting point of the Commerwijne and Suriname rivers. It houses an entertaining open-air museum with highlights including the Coach House, the temporary art/ photography exhibitions held in the former jail cells and the impressive American World War II cannons.

North of Fort Nieuw Amsterdam, near the mouth of Suriname River, is **Matapica Beach**, a reserve established in 1966 to protect the nesting places of the sea turtles. Nowadays, much of the beach has eroded, though some turtles still visit the shores to lay their eggs between April and August, and it is also the habitat of many species of waterfowl. Since the only accommodation on the beach has been swept away, staying overnight to watch the turtles is problematic, even if you can arrange boat transport out there. Still, it's worth enquiring about.

To explore the rivers and plantations you can either go by organized **boat tour** (see p.667), which typically includes Fort Nieuw Amsterdam, lunch at Frederiksdorp and a spot of dolphin-watching (the rivers are home to pink river dolphins), by **bike** (see box below), either as a group tour or solo, or by **public transport** (see ⓦwww .nvbnvsuriname.com for bus schedules within Commewijne).

CYCLING NEAR PARIMARIBO

The region around Parbo, once packed with highly profitable sugar-cane plantations and rum distilleries, is easily navigable by bicycle and makes for a great day-trip. Grab a map from your bicycle rental place (see p.667) – both Fietsen and Cardy Adventures can help with maps and independent trip planning – and cycle north (10km) along the river road to the **Nieuw Amsterdam ferry crossing**. Picnic on the riverfront (plenty of shops around for supplies) or cycle on to **Marienburg** (5km) where a guide will show you around a plantation that produced sugar and rum until as recently as 1998 – the abandoned, rusted machinery (made in Liverpool) looks far older. Delicious smoked catfish is readily and cheaply available along the route. On the northern side of the Commewijne River (which involves taking another ferry north of Marienburg, there are functioning plantations, from where you can cycle back to the Paramaribo ferry, and take in the bizarre sight of a Nazi German ship which the captain blew up and sank at the outbreak of World War II in an attempt to block the river, curbing bauxite exports from Suriname and thus hindering the Allies' war effort. The complete route is around 30km of cycling.

7

Colakreek

Just 5km from the international airport lies **COLAKREEK** (SRD15), a recreation park centred on a river the colour of Coca-Cola. The well-managed site is great for swimming and there are also water bikes for rent, a good cafeteria and overnight facilities including five-person cabins (SRD295) and camping sites (SRD20/person). To **get here**, take one of the state buses (or a taxi) to the airport, from where you can either walk or take another taxi.

NIEUW NICKERIE AND BIGIPAN

Though easily bypassed if you're taking a direct minibus between the border and Paramaribo, the orderly grid of **Nieuw Nickerie**'s streets with its palm tree-lined boulevard is worth an overnight stay, if only to visit **Bigipan**, a coastal area overgrown with mangroves, known for its abundance of birds, particularly the scarlet ibis. If you have your own wheels, you can try asking the local fishermen in the area to take you birdwatching. METS (see p.667) offer two-day tours of the Bigipan area and the coast west of Paramaribo (US$260).

ARRIVAL AND DEPARTURE

Nickerie is reachable by NVB state buses and private minibuses from Paramaribo (2hr–3hr 30min) and by minibus from South Drain (1hr). Taxis to South Drain cost SRD100 and will pick you up early form your hotel to catch the morning ferry to Guyana.

ACCOMMODATION

Residence Inn R. B. Bharostraat 84 ☎ 210 950, ⓦ www .resinn.com. This centrally located hotel is a good place to stay. There is a decent fusion restaurant and the helpful staff can arrange a day-trip to Bigipan. US$60

AWARRADAM AND PALUMEU

One of Suriname's highlights is a visit to the Saramaccan and Amerindian villages in the country's interior.
AWARRADAM is a community made up of eight villages populated by Saramaccan Maroons, descendants who fled deep into the jungle; it lies in the Gran Rio River near a rapid of the same name. There is a wonderful ecolodge located on an island in the river, consisting of a number of self-contained huts with mosquito nets owned by METS (see p.667) and run by members of a local Saramaccan village. From here a knowledgeable guide can take you wildlife-spotting along the river, swimming in the nearby rapids and to the four Saramaccan villages nearby – a slice of Africa in the depths of the Surinamese jungle. The women still carry large loads on their heads, and the Saramaccan tongue spoken is based on the dialects spoken in Ghana over 300 years ago; most of the villages still follow traditional religions and practise traditional dance, which you may be able to see – and participate in. While modernity is creeping in (many men now work in Paramaribo or in the gold mines, and many villages now have mobile phone reception), it's still a unique culture and tours of the villages are very sensitively conducted.

PALUMEU is a village located at the beginning of the Tapanahony River, deep within the Amazon rainforest, populated by Trio and Wajana Amerindians. Visitors stay in the METS-owned traditional lodge by the airstrip and activities offered include a boat trip along the Tapanahony River to Poti Hill, hikes in the rainforest and a two-day trip by dugout canoe to Mount Kasikasima.

ARRIVAL AND TOURS

By plane There are flights to both Awarradam and Palumeu on Mon and Fri from Zorg en Hoop airport.
Tour operators Trips to either community are usually booked through METS (see p.667), which offers four-/five-day stays at either location (combined visits to both can be arranged), though if you're looking to hike up Mt Kasikasima, it's an eight-day trip.

THE CENTRAL SURINAME NATURE RESERVE

Occupying nine percent of Suriname, the **Central Suriname Nature Reserve** is a diverse and popular destination for single - to multi-day trips into the interior.

Though illegal gold-mining is rife and poorly controlled, it is nevertheless a staggeringly beautiful part of the country, home to diverse fauna such as spider monkeys, ocelot and the world's largest-known species of the cock-of-the-rock bird. Highlights include Ralleighvallen (Raleigh Falls) and Voltzberg mountain.

Visitors stay at the basic lodge on Foengoe Island next to Ralleighvallen, reachable either by short flight (50min) or five hours overland. Tours can be organized through Orange (see p.667), among others.

GALIBI NATURE RESERVE

Situated in the northeastern corner of Suriname at the mouth of the Maroni River, the **GALIBI NATURE RESERVE** is a major nesting ground for leatherback and green turtles between March and August. Several tour operators (see p.667) run two- to three-day trips to Galibi (€180–210), which involve a bus ride to Albina, followed by a night in the Amerindian village of Christiankondre. The visit to the Galibi site itself is at night, when the newly hatched baby turtles make a break for the water.

French Guiana

FRENCH GUIANA is a strange beast. It's a tropical corner of France that is staunchly proud of its connection to the old country, despite few French mainlanders paying it much attention. The country speaks, eats and thinks French, though the majority of its population hail from African-Caribbean stock.

One of the most expensive countries in South America, it's nevertheless worth visiting for **Cayenne** – a colonial outpost masquerading as a French seaside town.

The country also has significant Laotian, Chinese, Haitian and Brazilian populations, which is evident in the capital's varied cuisine.

A notorious penal colony for much of its existence, French Guiana's muggy, oppressive climate, malaria-ridden forests and inhospitable terrain were considered an ideal way to punish French criminals (as well as World War II prisoners of war). French Guiana next came to international attention in the 1960s, when the European Space Agency cleared a patch of jungle and built a **space centre** to launch satellites into orbit from the town of **Kourou**. A rocket launch is one of the country's biggest attractions, along with the **Îles du Salut**, rocky islets that were once home to French criminal deportees.

French Guiana is perfect for adventurous travellers; it helps to have your own transport and to speak a little French. You'll find the three towns of Cayenne, Kourou and St Laurent fairly straightforward to visit. The attractions of the Hmong village of Cacao and the turtle-watching beach, Plage Les Hattes, lie in the interior or somewhat off the beaten path. Finally, there are expeditions down the country's rivers deep into the jungle and visits to remote Amerindian communities – which means flights by tiny plane, nights in hammocks and long boat journeys into the unknown.

CHRONOLOGY

10,000 BC Originally settled by various Amerindian groups, such as the Arawak and the Caribs.

1498 AD Columbus briefly sets foot in Guiana and dubs it "the land of pariahs".

1604 First attempts at French settlement made difficult by tropical diseases and native resistance.

1643 Cayenne founded but French soon forced out by hostile Amerindians.

1664 Cayenne finally established as a permanent settlement.

1665 Dutch occupy Cayenne.

1667 Colony awarded to France under the Treaty of Breda. All inhabitants now French citizens.

1676 Brief Dutch occupation and expulsion.

1763–65 France sends around 12,000 immigrants as part of the Kourou Expedition to develop the region, but 10,000 die of yellow fever and typhoid.

1809 Combined Anglo-Portuguese naval force captures the colony for Portugal.

7

7

1814 Guiana restored to France as part of the Treaty of Paris but Portuguese remain until 1917.

1848 Slavery is abolished. The colony's fragile plantation economy collapses. Ex-slaves establish Maroon communities in the jungle.

1852 Region designated a penal colony by Napoleon; more than 70,000 French convicts transported to the area.

1853 Gold discovered in the interior.

1946 French Guiana becomes an overseas *département* of France.

1947 Penal colony abolished but the last convicts only leave in 1952.

1964–68 ESA (European Space Agency) establishes space station in Kourou to launch communications satellites.

1974 French Guiana gains own *Conseil Régional* with some autonomy in social and economic matters.

1997 Independence leader Jean-Victor Castor arrested by police, leading to civil violence in Cayenne.

2000 Riots occur in Cayenne following an organized march calling for greater autonomy.

2008 President Sarkozy dedicates 1000 troops to combat growing immigration problems.

2009 The largest space telescope yet created is launched from Kourou.

2010 The option of increased autonomy rejected in referendum.

2011 Russian rocket "Soyuz" launched from Kourou.

2013 The False-Form Beetle, a new species which coexists with fire ants, is discovered in interior.

ARRIVAL AND DEPARTURE

French Guiana's main international airport, **Aéroport de Félix Eboué**, is some 17km south of Cayenne, near the town of Matoury. It receives direct flights from France, Martinique, Guadeloupe, Haiti, Brazil, Suriname and the Dominican Republic.

OVERLAND FROM BRAZIL

Travellers arriving from Brazil enter French Guiana via a boat across the Oyapok River to the town of **Saint-Georges** (see p.680) and then continue their journey via road by bus or car.

OVERLAND FROM SURINAME

Travellers from Suriname must take a **ferry** or **dugout canoe** across the Maroni River to **St Laurent du Maroni** (see box, p.685) then continue via road by bus or car.

VISAS

As French Guiana is an overseas *département* of France, **visas** are only required for those travellers who would also need a visa for France. Non-EU nationals unsure of their visa requirements should check ⓦdiplomatie .gouv.fr/en.

GETTING AROUND

Shared taxis or minibuses are the best and most economic way to move around the country. **Minibuses** will pick up and drop off passengers at their hotels around town. Reservation numbers change periodically, although hotels and guesthouses are kept up to date.

While the government-run TIG buses exist in theory (ⓦcg973.fr/Lignes-de-transport-prevues), the services are so unreliable that they can be disregarded as a viable means of transport.

Hitchhiking is widely practised by locals outside Cayenne; common-sense precautions apply.

Renting a car is relatively inexpensive – cheaper than the bus if there are two of you sharing the costs – and pretty much essential if you wish to travel beyond the coastal towns or even around Cayenne and Kourou. Prices start from around €30 per day and you can rent cars in Cayenne, Saint Laurent and at Félix Eboué Airport. The main roads are paved and well signed. Keep your passport with you, as there are occasional *gendarme* checkpoints.

Travel into and within the interior involves taking tiny planes and motorized *pirogues* (dugout canoes). Your *pirogue* travel will usually be part of an organized tour.

ACCOMMODATION

Accommodation in French Guiana is limited and very expensive, with the budget end geared towards independent travellers with their own transport. In large towns, you're likely to be confined to unremarkable business-oriented hotels (from €60/double). On the outskirts of towns and in rural areas you'll find *gîtes* (family-run lodgings), which range from simple to fairly luxurious (from €30/double). Adventurous and budget-conscious travellers may choose to opt for **carbets** – wooden shelters for hammocks. Check the excellent ⓦescapade-carbet .com for a definitive guide to the country's swinging accommodation, free or charged. Many are unmanned and free of charge, located by the sides of roads or on beaches, and have no facilities attached; for these you'll need your own hammock and two lengths of rope to hang it (easily purchased in Cayenne). Others are found in villages and even in some towns; some come with an attached shower/toilet block and provide hammocks at extra cost (€10–15/night).

FOOD AND DRINK

Those on a tight budget will look to street vendors, markets, well-stocked supermarkets (in Cayenne) and small takeaway joints. The preferred fast foods are Chinese and pizza, as well as proper coffee, baguettes with Caribbean Creole fillings, crêpes and croissants in the capital's cafés and bakeries. Cayenne offers the best variety of cuisines, with French, Laotian, Chinese, North African, Indonesian, Japanese, Vietnamese, Brazilian and Creole options (although you may find yourself paying Parisian prices), some of which you'll also find in St Laurent and Kourou. The best Laotian food is found in the Hmong village of Cacao (see p.679).

Fish dishes are plentiful, one of the more typical being *blaff*: a stock heavily seasoned with onion, garlic, celery, basil and spices. Another typical stock, used mostly at Easter and the Pentecost, is *bouillon d'awara*, made from the *awara* palm tree fruit and cooked with chicken, shrimp, crab and vegetables. *Fricassée* and *colombo* are typical Creole stews, the latter a meat- and vegetable-based curry stew. Wild meat like capybara, peccary and paca can also be found on the menu. Adventurous eaters will be presented with the chance to sample iguana, beetles and various species of rodent, although most of these generally come in curries.

DRINK

The authentic drink here is the sweet French aperitif **Ti' punch**: lime, sugar-cane syrup and rum, without ice, downed in one. Fresh fruit juices are popular and found at the Cayenne market, in Cacao and in some restaurants, or mixed with rum to create the ubiquitous fruit punch. You can find an excellent selection of French wines, and French beer is a popular import, expats appreciating the presence of Kronenbourg 1664.

CULTURE AND ETIQUETTE

Amerindian tribes and Maroons largely maintain their own cultural traditions, as does the immigrant population of Hmong from Laos in villages such as Cacao and Javouhey. The majority of the population is **Creole**, and mixed-Creole culture is dominant in the metropolitan areas; there is also an increasing number of immigrants from Brazil, Colombia and other South American countries, whose presence is evident in Cayenne and St Laurent. All teachers, police, *gendarmes* and other civil functionaries are recruited in mainland France. Note that the French generally don't tip.

COMMUNICATIONS

The efficient postal system is integrated with that of metropolitan France, so deliveries to Europe are quick and cheap. Digicel or Orange SIM cards can be purchased for unblocked mobile phones in any of the three major towns. When

> ### LANGUAGE
>
> French is the most widely spoken language, though a significant proportion of the population also speaks a French-based patois or Creole, with Chinese, *Neg Maron* (Bush Negro or Maroon), Portuguese and Amerindian languages spoken in certain areas. In St Laurent, due to the number of Surinamese and Guyanese immigrants, some English is also spoken, and the one language common to all three Guianas – Taki-Taki – is spoken along the rivers.

7

calling French Guiana from abroad, you must dial 594 (country code) followed by a nine-digit number also beginning 594 (or 694 for mobiles). For international calls it's better to buy phone cards that work with PINs (*libre service*), available from convenience stores, or else opt for Skype. Most hotels offer wi-fi and there are internet cafés in both Cayenne and St Laurent.

CRIME AND SAFETY

There are certain areas of Cayenne that are best avoided, such as the area immediately south of the canal, Laussat. At night it's best to stick to Place des Palmistes and the better-lit main streets of the centre. Drug addicts and beggars can be a nuisance both in Cayenne and in St Laurent. If spending the night in a *carbet* on a deserted beach, keep your valuables in the hammock with you.

HEALTH

Malaria prophylactics are recommended for all areas, though the risk is thought to be low along the coast. A number of vaccinations, including hepatitis A, hepatitis B, typhoid, yellow fever, tetanus-diphtheria and rabies, are also strongly recommended. Vaccination against yellow fever is compulsory if you're arriving from certain South American countries. There have also been recent outbreaks of dengue fever and Q fever, so mosquito repellent is essential.

While the locals claim that the coastal **tap water** is drinkable, you're best off sticking to bottled water.

European-standard **medical care** is available in Cayenne, Kourou and St Laurent du Maroni. The European Health Insurance Card (ⓦwww.ehic.org.uk) that allows travellers to

EMERGENCY NUMBERS

Ambulance ❶15
Police ❶17
Fire service ❶18

FRENCH GUIANA ON THE NET

ⓦ**tourisme-guyane.com** Official site providing information on accommodation, transport, tour agencies and life in French Guiana.

ⓦ**cg973.fr** Culture, sport and a general overview of French Guianese life.

ⓦ**www.terresdeguyane.fr/guyane** News, politics, history, nature and some helpful links.

receive free medical treatment in participating member states works in French Guiana.

INFORMATION AND MAPS

Printed information (mostly in French) is readily available in tourist offices in Cayenne and St Laurent, where you will also find good city maps. Ask for a copy of *Le Guide*, a handy annual guide, which lists hotels, restaurants, bars and clubs throughout French Guiana in French and English. If you can read French, it's well worth buying the *Guide Guyane* by Philippe Boré – a labour of love and a detailed and entertaining guidebook to French Guiana.

MONEY AND BANKS

The currency of French Guiana is the **euro** (€), and credit/debit cards are widely accepted in the urban centres. **ATMs** generally accept Visa, MasterCard or Eurocard, and hotels usually take American Express. Few banks have foreign exchange facilities; Cayenne has more than one bureau de change but St Laurent has none. At the time of writing, US$1.31=€1, £0.79=€1.

OPENING HOURS AND HOLIDAYS

Many businesses and shops shut for two to three hours over lunch. Most **shops** are open Monday to Saturday 8/9am to 1pm and 3/4 to 6.30/7pm. Supermarkets remain open until around 9pm and open on

PUBLIC HOLIDAYS

January 1 New Year's Day
February (varies) Ash Wednesday
March/April (varies) Good Friday
March/April (varies) Easter Monday
May 1 Labour Day
May 8 WWII Victory (VE) Day
May/June (varies) Ascension Day
May/June (varies) Whit Monday

June 10 Abolition of Slavery Day
July 14 Bastille Day
August 15 Assumption Day
November 1 All Saints' Day
October (varies) Cayenne festival
November 11 Armistice (Remembrance Day)
December 25 Christmas Day

FESTIVALS AND NATIONAL CELEBRATIONS

The major festival in French Guiana is **Carnival**, which begins after Epiphany in the first week of January and goes on for about two months until Ash Wednesday. On Friday and Saturday nights during Carnival you can witness the tradition of **Touloulou balls**, when women (*Touloulou*), heavily disguised and wearing masks, are given the sole, non-reciprocal right to ask the men to dance; guys are not allowed to refuse. Women disguise their faces, bodies and voices so the men are incapable of recognizing even their own wives. Mardi Gras (Carnival Monday and Tuesday) takes place during the last five days of Carnival, which ends on Ash Wednesday. It features colourful street parades with music, dancing, exotic costumes and merriment.

7

Sunday 9am to around lunchtime. **Banks** open Monday to Friday 7.30am to noon & 2.30 to 5.30pm.

CAYENNE

In your travels around French Guiana **CAYENNE** is likely to be your base for exploration of the surrounding sights. This sprawling city, slowly rotting in the tropical heat, has a compact centre with an attractive main square which becomes the focal point of community activity in the evenings. Its eighteenth-century colonial buildings, French mainlanders on overseas postings and a lively market make it the most European experience on the South American continent and well worth a visit.

WHAT TO SEE AND DO

The view overlooking Cayenne and the ocean from the hill at the end of Rue de Rémire, west of the Place des Palmistes, is the best place to get your bearings before exploring.

Place des Palmistes and around

Place des Palmistes, on Avenue du Général de Gaulle, is a refreshing green space sparsely covered with palms, where you can catch an impromptu football game or live music performance some weekends. It includes a statue of Felix Éboué (1884–1944), a black French Guianese who governed various French territories in Africa and the Caribbean. Just off the square, the **Musée Départemental**, 1 Avenue du Général de Gaulle (Mon 10am–1.30pm & 3–6pm, Wed–Fri 8am–2pm & 3–6pm, Sat 9am–1.15pm; €3, under 18s free; ☎594 295 913), in one of the original wooden colonial mansions, contains taxidermied examples of local fauna and, in the upstairs gallery, terrifying paintings of the brutalities of penal colony life.

Fort Céperou

For a sweeping view of Cayenne, climb up the hill at the end of Rue de Rémire to the crumbling remains of **Fort Céperou**, the first building to appear in Cayenne after the Compagnie de Rouen purchased the hill from a Galibi Amerindian chief named Céperou in 1643.

Musée des Cultures Guyanaises and around

For a good introduction to Amerindian, Maroon and Creole languages and culture through artefacts, crafts, costume and art, check out the **Musée des Cultures Guyanaises**, 78 Rue Madame-Payé (Mon–Fri 8am–1pm & 3.30–5.30pm, Sat 8–11am; €2, 18–25-year-olds €1).

Centre Hospitalier Andre-Rosemon de Cayenne, Motel Beauregard & Break Club

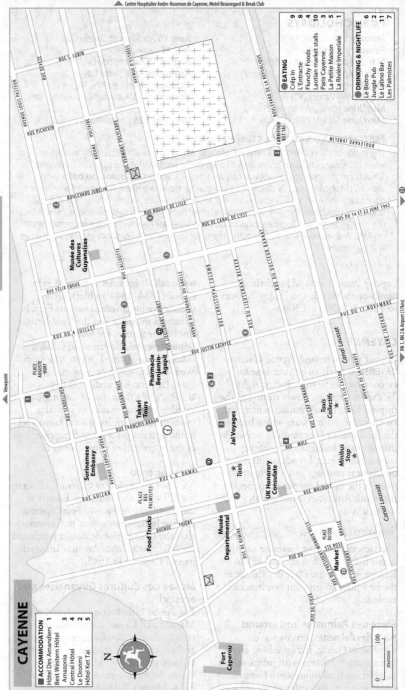

CAYENNE

ACCOMMODATION
Hôtel Des Amandiers	1
Best Western Hôtel	
Amazonia	3
Central Hôtel	4
Le Dronmi	2
Hôtel Ket Tai	5

EATING
Crép In	9
L'Entracte	8
Flunchy Foods	4
Laotian market stalls	10
Paris Cayenne	3
La Petite Maison	5
La Rivière Imperiale	1

DRINKING & NIGHTLIFE
Le Bistro	6
Jungle Pub	2
Le Latino Bar	11
Les Palmistes	7

FN 1, FN 2 & Airport (17km)

FRENCH GUIANA TOURS

If you wish to explore Guiana's jungle and rivers, virtually the only way to do so is to join an **organized excursion**, although it's cheaper to hire local guides by asking around. High season is from July to November, outside of which time you can generally show up at the travel agent's on spec.

TOUR OPERATORS

JAL Voyages 26 Av du Général de Gaulle, Cayenne ☎ 594 316 820, ✉ jal@jal-voyages.com, ⓦ jal-voyages .com. Specializes in birdwatching river trips to Kaw and the Maroni aboard floating *carbets* (houseboats with both hammock spaces and cabins) but also arranges trips to Kourou's space centre, Cacao and Îles du Salut.

Takari Tour 17 Rue Lallouette, Cayenne ☎ 594 311 960, ⓦ www.takaritour.com. The oldest of the tour operators, offering everything from a 3hr history tour of Cayenne (from €20), trips to Îles du Salut and Cacao (from €42) to multi-day adventures on the Oyapock and Maroni rivers (from €598).

ARRIVAL AND INFORMATION

By plane Félix Eboué International Airport (ⓦ www .guyane.cci.fr/fr/aeroport) is in Matoury, 17km south of Cayenne. Taxis to Cayenne cost €30–35.

Destinations Air France (ⓦ airfrance.com) has regular flights to Paris, Guadeloupe and Martinique; Air Caraïbes (ⓦ aircaraibes.com) flies to Brazil and France and connects French Guiana with Haiti, Martinique, Guadeloupe and the Dominican Republic; Surinam Airways (ⓦ slm.nl) connects Belem in Brazil to Paramaribo twice a week and can stop over in Cayenne. Air Guyane (ⓦ airguyane.com) provides domestic services to Maripasoula, Saül and St Laurent du Maroni.

By minibus Minibuses will drop passengers at their hotels or the Place des Palmistes. Departing minibuses leave when full (Mon–Sat 7am–6pm) from the bus stop on the north side of the Canal Laussat.

Destinations Kaw (1hr 50min); Kourou (1hr 15min); Matoury (45min); Roura (40–50min); Saint-Georges de l'Oyapock via Régina (2hr 30min); Saint Laurent du Maroni via Iracoubo (4hr).

Tourist information Comité du Tourisme de la Guyane, 12 Rue Lallouette (Mon, Tues & Thurs 7.30am–1pm & 2.30–5.30pm; Wed & Fri 7.30am–1pm; ☎ 594 296 500, ⓦ tourisme-guyane.com), has helpful staff and a plethora of maps and brochures.

GETTING AROUND

By bus SMTC, 2682 Route de la Madeleine (☎ 594 254 928), runs a small network of local buses around Cayenne (Mon–Sat); call for details. Most of the buses leave from Place du Coq near the market.

By taxi Taxis in Cayenne are metered; there's a taxi stand just off the Place de Palmistres. Rates are around €1.75 to hire, plus €0.65/km (double on Sun and 7pm–6am).

ACCOMMODATION

Budget accommodation is limited. Solo travellers usually pay as much for single occupancy as for a double,

although, if your French is good enough to haggle, prices can drop. All accommodation below has a/c and en-suite bathrooms.

Hôtel Des Amandiers Place Auguste-Hort ☎ 594 289 728. Rambling colonial house on a pleasant seafront park complete with confused staff, worn but serviceable rooms and wi-fi on the terrace. Plenty of parking space – a rarity in Cayenne. **€60**

Best Western Hôtel Amazonia 28 Av du Général de Gaulle ☎ 594 310 000, ⓦ bestwestern.fr. Good option for groups of three or more as triple rooms are good value. Right in the centre of town, but otherwise unremarkable. Wi-fi. Doubles **€120**, triples **€130**

Central Hôtel Rue Molé, at Becker ☎ 594 256 565, ⓦ centralhotel-cayenne.fr. The central location, friendly service and clean, tiled rooms make this place an under-stated winner; kitchenettes in some rooms are a bonus for self-caterers. Levies a tourist tax of €0.80/person/ night. **€75**

Le Dronmi 42 Av du Général de Gaulle ☎ 594 317 770, ⓦ ledronmi.com. A brothel in a previous incarnation, this trendy and central hotel is just a few staggers from the liveliest bar in town. It has flat-screen TVs, kitchenettes and wi-fi. Great value for groups; breakfast included. Doubles **€95**, suites **€150**

Hôtel Ket Tai 72 Blvd Jubelin ☎ 594 289 777, ✉ g.chang @wanadoo.fr. Brazilian *telenovelas* in the lobby, friendly service and compact, featureless, tiled rooms with struggling a/c. If every other hotel in town is full, there's a good chance you can still find a bed at this cheapie. Wi-fi extra. **€55**

EATING

Self-caterers will find fresh produce at the market on Avenue du Président Monnerville (Mon, Wed & Sat), fresh bread in the *boulangerie* next to the market, and pretty much everything else at the enormous *Carrefour* and *Géant* supermarkets on the southern approach to town. In the centre, there are small shops with limited choice. Most restaurants are closed on Sundays. Food trucks producing everything from ham baguettes to Chinese fast food set up nightly from 6pm along the Place des Palmistes.

Crêp In 5 Rue Lieutenant Becker. It just wouldn't be France without crêpes made by Chinese immigrants, and this little place serves up a fine choice, along with a good selection of fresh fruit juice, *croque monsieurs* and salads. Meals €8. Mon–Sat 8am–8pm.

L'Entracte 65 Rue Justin Catayée ☎ 594 300 137. At this pseudo-Italian joint you can consume (actually pretty decent) pizza, pasta and salads under the watchful eyes of Marlon Brando and Brigitte Bardot. A number of veggie options on the menu. Mains from €8. Daily noon–2.30pm & 6–10.30pm.

Flunchy Foods 24 Rue Rouget de Lisle ☎ 594 281 038. Hole-in-the-wall takeaway serving up heaped portions of curry and rice, *porc caramel*, spring rolls and more; delivery available. Mains €8. Daily 10am–3pm & 6.30–10.30pm.

★ Laotian market stalls Av du Président Monnerville. Feast on *nems* (spring rolls), *phô* soup and other Laotian dishes at the market. Portions are generous and the dishes are full of flavour, with plenty of fresh herbs. Meals from €5. Wed, Fri & Sat, lunchtime only.

La Petite Maison 23 Rue Félix Eboué ☎ 594 385 839. Its popularity justifying that fact that it's hardly ever open, this restaurant serves up imaginative cuisine in a beautifully restored colonial mansion. Meals around €25. Mon, Tues, Thurs & Fri noon–2pm & 8–10pm. Wed & Sat 8–10pm, closed Sun.

La Rivière Imperiale 10 Rue J. Catayée. Crispy *nems* (spring rolls), noodles, *fricassée* and conch stew are all on the menu at this small, friendly restaurant specializing in Vietnamese, Creole and Haitian dishes. Mon, Tues &Thurs–Sat noon–2.30pm & 7–11pm, Sun noon–2.30pm.

DRINKING AND NIGHTLIFE

Le Bistro 42 Av du Général de Gaulle. Perch on the terrace of Cayenne's most popular bar for an afternoon beer, a pre-dinner short drink, or even a liquid breakfast (coffee, that is). There is a small dancefloor with an adjoining chill-out lounge. Daily 7am–1am.

Jungle Pub 10 Blvd Jubelin. Not the place for a quiet drink, this lively expat joint specializes in reggae and rock with salsa classes on Thursday nights. Daily 7pm–1am.

Le Latino Bar 493 Route de la Madeleine. True to its name, this is the place to show off your salsa and *merengue* moves (or else watch someone else's moves over a cocktail). Karaoke some nights. Tues–Sun 6pm–1am.

Les Palmistes 10 Rue de Remire. Sit on the attractive terrace of this colonial mansion overlooking the Place des Palmistes and sip a delicious (and highly decorative) *Punch des Palmistes*. A popular spot for French expats to meet. Daily 6.30am–1am.

★ TREAT YOURSELF

Paris Cayenne 59 Rue Lalouette ☎ 594 317 617. All dark-wood-meets-anaconda-skin chic and giant prints on the walls; this eclectic bar/restaurant is *the* place to be on a Friday night. The staff operate on Zen time, but it's worth stopping by for the ambience and the signature Paris-Cayenne cocktail alone. Meals around €40, cocktails €10. Mon–Sat noon–3pm & 8–10.30pm; closed Mon & Sat lunch.

DIRECTORY

Banks and exchange ATMs along Av du Général de Gaulle and on the corner with Rue Mole. Change Caraïbes offers good exchange rates at 64 Av du Général de Gaulle (Mon–Fri 7.30am–12.30pm & 3.30–6.30pm, Sat 8am–12.30pm).

Car rental C.L.A.S (the cheapest by far). 58 Rue de Christoph Colomb (☎ 594 315 750, ☎ fg1109@aol.com); Avis, 58 Blvd Jubelin (☎ 594 302 522); Budget, 55 Artisanal Zone Galmot (☎ 594 351 020).

Embassies and consulates Brazil, 444 Chemin Saint-Antoine (☎ 594 296 010); Suriname, 3 Av Leopold Héder (☎ 594 282 160); UK, Honorary British Consul, 16 Av du Président Monnerville (☎ 594 311 034).

Hospital Centre Hospitalier de Cayenne Andrée Rosemon, 3 Av des Flamboyants (☎ 594 395 050, ☎ ch-cayenne.com).

Internet PC Yuan Yuan, southeast corner of Place des Palmistes.

Laundry Rue Catayée, at Rue Lalouette; Laverie, 28 Rue Cayee, 8am–8pm, self-service.

Pharmacies Pharmacie Benjamin-Agapit, 23 Av du Général de Gaulle.

Post office Opposite Place Léopold Heder near Place des Palmistes, also at east end of Av du Général de Gaulle (Mon–Fri 7.30am–1pm; Sat at 11.30am).

DAY-TRIPS FROM CAYENNE

There are a number of varied attractions outside Cayenne that make for easy day-trips – from a sloth sanctuary, monkey island and morass rich with birdlife to a Hmong Laotian village – though you need to have your own wheels to reach most of them.

Sloth sanctuary

If you've ever seen a sloth cross a road, you'll understand the need for this sanctuary (Wed & Thurs 1.45–4pm; €5; ☎ 694 906 923, ☎ www.chouai.free.fr) that takes in injured and orphaned sloths and nurses them back to health before releasing them. Here you get to cuddle several of its three-toed members (the *ai*), and learn about the less cuddly, larger and omnivorous two-toed sloths (the *unau*). To **get here** from Cayenne, take the bridge across the Cayenne River towards Kourou and take the first left immediately, then turn right.

Îlet la Mère

This small island, 13km from the coast and reachable from Cayenne's Marina de Degrad-des-Cannes (to the east of the city centre) is home to an abundance of squirrel monkeys, iguanas, caimans and red ibis. You can either walk around the island's perimeter (3.5km; 1hr 30min), with its various viewpoints and picnic spots, or else hike up to the 88m peak (2.5km; 1hr 15min) to admire the environs. Or both. Count on making this a day-trip, since the boat (€35; ☎694 222 253) departs the marina at around 8–8.30am and returns at around 4pm.

Cacao

A slice of Asia in Guyana's interior, and only really open to visitors on Sundays, about 75km southwest of Cayenne, **CACAO** was settled in 1977 by refugees from Laos. Since then, this small Hmong community has become the fruit and vegetable basket of the *département* because of the extensive cultivation of Cacao's steep hillsides. Chow down on large bowls of *phô*, *porc caramel*, spring rolls and other outstanding Laotian dishes. Don't miss the wonderful **Le Planeur Bleu** museum (Sun 9am–1pm & 2–4pm; other days by appointment; €3.50; ☎594 270 034), opposite the market, where you'll gape in wonder at the wealth of insects and butterflies, hold live tarantulas and get a brief introduction to gold mining, Hmong handicrafts and other aspects of French Guiana's culture.

ARRIVAL AND DEPARTURE

By car Take the RN2 towards Saint-Georges before turning off along the beautiful, winding, signposted road to Cacao.
By minibus Minibuses (8am–11pm) depart from the stands on the north side of the canal.

ACCOMMODATION

Quimbe Kio ☎594 270 122, ✉infos@quimbekio.com. Overnight stays on a wooded hill near the centre, either in a *carbet* (€5 discount if you bring your own hammock) or in one of the en-suite rooms (breakfast included). Kayaking, boat and quad tours available. Doubles €45, carbets €10

ROURA AND KAW

Some 75km east of Cacao, across the heavily forested Kaw Hills, the Everglades-style swamp Marais De Kaw covers around one thousand square kilometres and makes an excellent place to spot water birds, including flamingos. Tour operators in Cayenne such as JAL Voyages (see p.677) offer wildlife-spotting boat trips along the river, after-dark *pirogue* trips to spot black caiman and overnight stays in a floating *carbet*. When driving to Kaw, you pass through the pleasant village of **Roura**, where it's possible to arrange boat trips to various destinations, including the Îlet la Mère (see opposite).

ARRIVAL AND DEPARTURE

Visitors to Kaw arrive as part of an organized tour, by rented car or via the few minibuses which make the trip from Cayenne daily.
By minibus Shared transport will drop passengers off at requested locations within the town, while departure must be reserved ahead of time to organize where you'll be collected for the outward journey.

ACCOMMODATION AND EATING

If staying overnight, arrangements must be made in advance; Kaw is not a place to turn up on spec.
Auberge de Camp Caïman PK 36, Route de Kaw ☎594 307 277. In between Roura and Kaw, this eco-friendly large wooden hostel with a library offers basic doubles and a large *carbet*. Butterfly-catching, marsh walks and caiman-spotting trips on demand. Meals available on request. Closed Wed. Doubles €35, carbets (including hammock rental) €17
★**Malou** Route de Kaw ☎694 210 712. A short distance east of Roura, this new roadside eatery has a breezy terrace overlooking the large garden where they grow their own fruit for the fresh juices. The crêpes are perfection and there's a nice little sandwich selection too. Wed–Sun 10am–5pm.

7

CROSSING INTO BRAZIL

From Cayenne, take bus #17 to Régina and then switch to bus #18 to **Saint-Georges** (check timetable in advance). *Do not* drive between Cayenne and Saint-Georges at night or pick up hitchhikers along the Régina/Saint-Georges road; French authorities periodically clamp down on those seen to assist illegal immigrants. Saint-Georges is a small border town with a lively Brazilian feel, used as the jumping-off point for Brazil and tours (see p.677) of local Amerindian villages along the Oyapok River.

To cross over **to Brazil**, non-EU passport holders must get their passport stamped at the **Douane** by the river (8am–6pm; closed for lunch). Then take one of the **motorized canoes** across the river to **Oiapoque** in Brazil (15–20min; €4–6; negotiate price beforehand). Once in Brazil, get your passport stamped by the **Policia Federal**; follow the main street until you see a road to your left with a church in its middle. The office is on the right side of the road, past the church. **Moneychangers** operate on the Brazilian side of the river, but not in Saint-Georges.

If travelling further into Brazil, there is a morning bus and an evening bus daily from Oiapoque to Macapá (10hr); pack a sweater as they tend to crank up their a/c.

ACCOMMODATIN IN SAINT-GEORGES

Chez Modestine ☎ 594 370 013. Clean a/c en-suite rooms in a traditional house on the main square; book in advance. **€45**

Ilha do Sol ☎ 694 407 311. Take a boat (5min) to the tiny Ilha do Sol to swing a hammock at their *carbet* or stay in a basic double. Doubles **€25**, *carbets* **€12**

KOUROU

There's not much to **KOUROU**, a seaside town built mainly to service the **Centre Spatial Guyanais** – the space station that employs the majority of its residents. The town is not designed for pedestrians, and is difficult to navigate. If your timing is right, you can witness one of the most impressive spectacles you're ever likely to see: the fiery launching of a rocket into space.

The town is also the departure point for French Guiana's next biggest tourist attraction – the **Îles du Salut**.

Centre Spatial Guyanais

The sight of the launch towers surrounded by tropical forest at the **CENTRE SPATIAL GUYANAIS** (3hr guided tours Mon–Thurs 8.15am & 1.15pm, Fri 8.15am; free but advance reservation by phone is *essential* due to the tours' popularity; visitors must be over 8 years old and provide ID; ☎594 326 123, ⓦwww.cnes-csg.fr) is like something out of a Bond film. The CSG occupies an area of 850 square kilometres and has sent more than five hundred rockets (most carrying satellites) into orbit since Véronique blasted off on April 9, 1968. **Tours** include a film charting the site's history and a visit to the Jupiter Control Centre, though no tours take

place on launch days. There are three types of tours: one takes in all three rocket sites, Ariane 5, Vega and Soyuz; another focuses on just the Soyuz site (Mon & Wed pm); while a third takes you to the Ariane 5 and Vega sites (Tues & Thurs pm).

The partially interactive, state-of-the-art **Musée de l'Espace** (Mon–Fri 8am–6pm, Sat 2–6pm; €7 or €4 if on a guided tour of the CSG), next to the CSG welcome centre, introduces visitors to space exploration, with exhibitions on human space flight, the history of the base, the universe and more, through multimedia animations, space-related artefacts and temporary exhibits. The museum is sometimes closed on launch days.

Unless visiting the CSG via a tour operator, make your own way by car, or else take a bus (see below) from Cayenne to Kourou and then a taxi to the site.

ARRIVAL AND INFORMATION

Kourou is difficult to navigate on foot, with no public transport to speak of.

By minibus Minibuses from Saint Laurent and Cayenne will drop passengers off at their hotels. Getting away from Kourou is a matter of reserving a place on a minibus (Saint Laurent 4am & 4.30pm; Cayenne 6 daily) which will collect you from your location. Bear in mind that collection times will be vague and it's advisable to be ready for an hour on either side of the agreed time. If the minibus passes and you aren't there, you'll miss your ride.

Tourist information Place de l'Europe, C2 Rue Palika (Mon, Tues & Thurs 8am–1.30pm, Wed & Fri 8am–2pm; ☎594 329 833, ✉tourisme@kourou.info). Impressive collection of information in French and English on the space centre, Îles du Salut and Kourou.

ACCOMMODATION

Budget travellers into swinging (in hammocks) can stay at the *carbets* on the attractive beach off Av des Roches. Accommodation is more limited than in Cayenne and tends to be booked up weeks in advance if there's a rocket launch due.

Hôtel Le Ballahou 1–3 Rue Amet-Martial ☎594 220 022, ⊛www.ballahou.com. On the beach's western end, so don't stay here if you plan on the penal colony tour given the distance from the jetty and the tour's early start time. Clean en-suite rooms presided over by the reception-dodging Marie. Make sure you request the gate code. Open noon–2pm & 6–8pm. Studios €68, doubles €53

Chez Taliko ☎694 212 328. On the beach-side road parallel to Hotel Le Ballahou, Mr Taliko's charming family, good location and chilled-out attitude make this the best option for those toting their own hammocks. €7

Résidence le Gros Bec 56 Rue D. Floch ☎594 329 191, ✉hotel.legrosbec@wanadoo.fr. Only three blocks from the catamaran departure point for the Îles du Salut, this is a brightly painted, family-friendly place offering studios equipped with kitchenettes. Studios €69.90

EATING

You'll find a number of places to eat, drink and be reasonably merry on the seafront Av de l'Anse and along Av du Général de Gaulle.

Le Baraka 37 Av du Général de Gaulle ☎594 323 323. This inviting spot lit with Christmas lights serves Moroccan tagines and the like from €15. Daily 12.30–11pm.

L'orchidée Off Av F. Kennedy, opposite the post office. Heaped portions of delicious Vietnamese food – it's difficult to go wrong with the *phô* or any of the noodle dishes. Mains from €10. Daily noon–10.30pm.

Violeta 12 Av de l'Anse ☎594 228 580. A seafront snackery, with a two-course set meal for €11 until 6pm; later it turns into a bar, much like numerous others along this strip. Daily 11am–late.

ÎLES DU SALUT

The **ÎLES DU SALUT**, 15km off the coast, comprise three beautiful islands shaded with coconut trees and surrounded by azure waters: Île Royale, Île Saint-Joseph and Île du Diable. Their English name – Salvation Islands – is an ironic misnomer, given their use as a penal colony responsible for the deaths of over 50,000 of its 70,000 prisoners between 1852 and 1953. Thanks to Henri Charrière's book, *Papillon*, which recounts the horrors of life in the colony

BLAST OFF! VISITING A ROCKET LAUNCH

Few spectacles compare to the sight of a rocket leaving the atmosphere for outer space. There's a launch pretty much every month, usually scheduled on a weekday night (visit ⊛www.cnes-csg.fr for details), and the one you're most likely to see is Ariane 5 – the French rocket that frequently launches satellites into orbit. The Centre Spatial Guyanais has seven official observation sites from which you can watch the rocket launch: Agami, Carapa, Venus, Ibis, Jupiter, Colibri and Toucan; access is limited and by invitation only. To obtain an **invitation** (you must be over 16), email either ✉liza.greene@cnes.fr (in English or French) or ✉helene.hernandez-garcia@cnes.fr (in French) at least a month in advance of your setting foot in the country. Give your full name, date/place of birth, passport number and contact details, including address, email and telephone number. Once you've obtained an invitation, either ask for it to be emailed to you (you'll need to print it out) or pick it up from the assigned point (usually the Musée de l'Espace) the day before the launch. Delays of up to two weeks are possible, so it helps if your schedule is flexible. On the day of the launch, visitors assemble at the Médiathèque du Kourou, from where they are taken to the assigned observation sites by a convoy of coaches. Few visitors make it to the Jupiter Control Room (the spaces tend to be snapped up by family and friends of the space station employees), so you'll most likely end up at Agami, Toucan or Colibri (5.5–7.5km from the launch site), where you'll watch the countdown on the giant screen and have an unobstructed view of the rocket itself for a spectacle lasting between seven and thirty minutes. Finally, even if you can't obtain an invitation, it's possible to drive up the Montagne des Singes, just to the southwest of Kourou, where anyone can view the launch from one of two observation spots, connected by a twenty-minute hiking trail.

7

ÎLES DU SALUT TOURS

Return **ferry trips** to Île Royale (no matter how long your stay) cost €42. Jaunts across to Île Saint-Joseph leave from the same arrival jetty on Île Royale at no extra cost. If you wish to stay overnight, make arrangements with the Royal Ti' Punch/Îles du Salut operator, directly connected to the island's lodgings. Catamarans leave from Kourou's *appontement des pêcheurs* (fishermen's jetty) at the end of Avenue du Général de Gaulle (daily at 8.30am & 11am, returning 4pm & 6pm).

TOUR OPERATORS

Havas Voyages 10 Av de France ☎ 594 223 101, ✉ scubas@havas-voyages.fr, ⊛ www.havas-voyages .fr.

La Hulotte ☎ 594 323 381, ⊛ www.lahulotte-guyane.fr.

and his various attempts at escape, the islands are the country's most popular attraction.

WHAT TO SEE AND DO

Catamaran tours take you directly to the jetty on Île Royale from where visitors wanting to get to Île Saint-Joseph can board the free crossings. The **Île du Diable** is off-limits to visitors, although the swimming area on the northeast side of the Île Royale offers views of its wrecked prison buildings.

Île Royale, the main and most-visited island, was used for administration and housing common-law criminals. You can peer at the ruins of old buildings and go swimming either off the small pier (on the opposite side of the island from the boat landing) or in the small bay sheltered from the sea by rocks. The fearless wildlife is another attraction and you're certain to spot monkeys and agouti. Île Royale is home to the islands' only hotel and excellent restaurant, as well as the small Musée du Bagne (10.30am–12.30pm & 2.30–4pm; free), in the old colony administrator's mansion beside the jetty.

"Incorrigible" convicts and those who tried to escape were sent to **Île**

Saint-Joseph. Today it's home to a small naval base, and visitors can take the tranquil, coconut-tree-lined path around the perimeter of the island, passing the ruins of the penal colony overgrown with vegetation.

ACCOMMODATION

Auberge des Îles Île Royale ☎ 594 321 100, ✉ sothis2 @wanadoo.fr. At the only lodgings on the islands, you have a choice between delightfully clean, bright and breezy rooms, cheaper digs in the guards' barracks, or a space to sling a hammock (as long as you have your own) with access to bathroom facilities. During high season (July–Nov) reserve ahead of arrival, outside these months you can show up on spec. Suite €̶1̶7̶0̶, guards' quarter €̶6̶0̶, hammocks €̶1̶0̶

SAINT LAURENT DU MARONI

Outside **SAINT LAURENT DU MARONI**'s tourist office is a statue of a convict with his head in his hands – an apt monument to despair, given that this town was a transportation camp for prisoners until the middle of the twentieth century. Saint Laurent is less homogeneous than the capital, thanks to the porous border between French Guiana and Suriname; the large number of illegal Surinamese, Brazilian and Guyanese residents accounts for the melange of languages spoken and the laidback feel of this riverside frontier town. The town is the best base for excursions up the **Maroni River**, visits to the **Amerindian** and **Maroon communities** or the beautiful **Voltaire Falls**.

SAINT LAURENT FESTIVALS

Saint Laurent has a festival or three happening pretty much every month, all celebrated in the sandy Place de la Republique. Festivities not to miss include January's **Carnaval**, October's **Les Journées de la Culture Bushinengué** (a celebration of traditional Maroon culture) and November's biennial **Le Festival des Transamazoniennes**, an international extravaganza that spans the music of South America and the Caribbean.

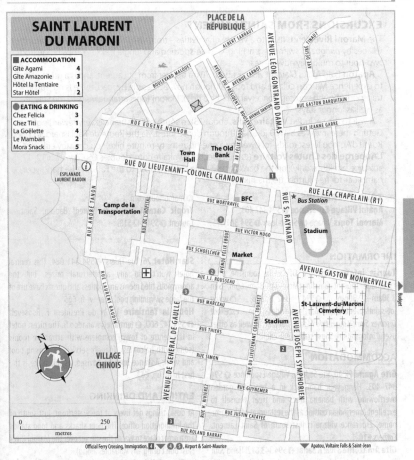

SAINT LAURENT DU MARONI

ACCOMMODATION
Gîte Agami	4
Gîte Amazonie	3
Hôtel la Tentiaire	1
Star Hôtel	2

EATING & DRINKING
Chez Felicia	3
Chez Titi	1
La Goëlette	4
Le Mambari	2
Mora Snack	5

Official Ferry Crossing, Immigration, 4, 4, 5, Airport & Saint-Maurice · Apatou, Voltaire Falls & Saint-Jean

WHAT TO SEE AND DO

Saint Laurent has some fine colonial architecture in the triangular "Petit Paris" area north of Rue du Lieutenant-Colonel Chandon, such as the old bank and town hall.

Camp de la Transportation

The **Camp de la Transportation**, where prisoners were processed before their final destinations, is an imposing complex. You can walk around the grounds and check out the permanent free exhibition of photos in the camp's former kitchen and chapel, but access to the cells is by guided tour only and not to be missed (Mon 3pm & 4.30pm, Tues–Sat 9.30am, 11am, 3pm &

4.30pm, Sun 9.30am & 11am; 1hr 15min; €6; tours in English available on weekdays; tickets sold at the tourist office). An informed peek into the horrors of French transportation puts everything into chilling context. Cell no. 47 allegedly once held Papillon.

ARRIVAL AND DEPARTURE

By plane There are four flights weekly to/from Cayenne with Air Guyane (w airguyane.com).
By boat See box, p.684.
By minibus Minibuses depart from the bus station (*gare routière*) on Rue Léa Chapelain, or will collect you at your hotel if you reserve ahead (ask your hotel for current phone numbers). They depart when full from 7am until 4.30pm.
Destinations Awala-Yalimapo (1hr 10min); Cayenne (4hr); Kourou (2hr 30min).

EXCURSIONS FROM SAINT LAURENT

The **Maroni River** lends itself to a variety of activities – from visits to Amerindian and Maroon villages by *pirogue* to swimming, fishing, wildlife-spotting and jungle trekking. Trips range from two-hour to multi-day adventures.

Apatou is an Aluku Maroon village, about 70km upriver from St Laurent, and is a great place to experience Maroon culture and food. Although now accessible by road, there is no public transport (though you can conceivably hitch a ride). Maroni Tours arrange visits to the village as well as longer stays.

A visit to the secluded **Voltaire Falls**, about 73km south of St Laurent, is very rewarding. Getting there involves a 4WD journey through dense forest via the Route de Paul Isnard and Route d'Apatou forest roads, followed by a one-hour-thirty-minute hike. You can stay either at **L'Auberge des Chutes Voltaire** (@ aubergechutesvoltaire.com; doubles €60, *carbets* €12–17; advance bookings only), on the banks of the Voltaire River, close to the Falls, or else hang your hammock for free further up the hiking trail.

TOUR OPERATORS

Agami Village Espérance @ 594 347 403.

Maroni Tours Village de Saint-Jean @ 594 341 175,

@ maronitours.com.

Tropic Cata 1 Esplanade Laurent Baudin, Saint Laurent @ 594 342 518.

INFORMATION

Tourist information The Office du Tourisme at 1 Esplanade Laurent Baudin (Mon–Sat 8am–6pm, Sun 8.30am–12.30pm; @ 594 342 398, @ www .ot-saintlaurentdumaroni.fr) provides the excellent *Discover Saint-Laurent du Maroni* booklet, as well as other useful information. Some staff speak English.

ACCOMMODATION

Gîte Agami Pk 10, Rte St Jean, Village Espérance @ 594 347 403. Hang your hammock in a beautiful garden overflowing with banana trees and treat yourself to excellent Amerindian cuisine at the restaurant of the same name. Espérance village is just south of Saint Laurent. *Carbets* **€10**

Gîte Amazonie 3 Rue R Barrat @ 594 343 612. Hang your hammock along with other backpackers (mainly French). Adequate bathroom facilities, and the talkative owner's wife will cook delicious Creole food at any time of day as long as she isn't busy in her hair salon on the same site. Laundry service available. €5 discount if you have your own hammock. *Carbets* **€15**

Star Hôtel 26 Rue Thiers @ 594 341 084. This central hotel won't win any architectural prizes, but the anonymous tiled rooms are spotless and guests have use of the large swimming pool. Free wi-fi. **€65**

Hôtel la Tentiaire 12 Av du President F. Roosevelt @ 594 342 600, @ tentiarie@wanadoo.fr. The nicest hotel in the centre of town, complete with attractive rooms (some with balconies), friendly service, swimming pool and wi-fi. Advance booking advised, as this place is the first to fill up. **€63**

EATING AND DRINKING

At dusk, things get lively at the waterfront, just south of the immigration office. The beer shacks and food stands are a great place to watch the sun set over the Maroni River (just don't bring any valuables along).

★**Chez Felicia** 23 Av du Général de Gaulle. A local institution, still going strong after 25 years. The basic menu focuses on generous portions of Creole dishes, such as *fricassée*, and wild game. Mains €9–12. Generally Mon–Sat noon–10pm, Sun noon–4pm.

Chez Titi 11 Rue de Victor Hugo. Open-air pizzeria with outdoor tables, pizza that's decent without wowing, and an assortment of French, Creole and grilled dishes (mains €10–20). A bakery attached to the restaurant will give you love handles. Tues–Sat 4–10.30pm.

★**La Goëlette** Balaté Plage @ 594 342 897. This boat-cum-restaurant, complete with frolicking cats and dogs, is the most atmospheric place for a meal for miles around. The quality of the Creole and French dishes matches the ambience and there are music sessions on Sunday nights. Mains €13–17. Tues & Sun 6–11pm, Wed–Sat 11am–3pm, 6–11pm.

CONVICT ART

If you happen to be driving between St Laurent and Cayenne, you'll invariably pass through Iracoubo. The **Eglise Saint Joseph d'Iracoubo** by the roadside is a church famed for its amazing interior covered with brightly coloured frescoes, painted by French convict and painter Pierre Huguet between 1892 and 1898. Well worth getting out of the car for.

Le Mambari 7 Rue JJ Rousseau. Perch at one of the picnic-style tables outside or prop up the bar at this French/Creole joint; mains €8–18. DJs on Thursdays, while on Fridays and Saturdays it's time for "soirée NO STRESS". Tues–Sat 11am–2pm & 4.30–11pm.

Mora Snack Rue Louise Orsini. Pull up a plastic chair at this informal little spot, decked out in fairy lights, and chow down on the excellent *saté*, burgers and sausages (but avoid the insipid French fries). Mains €3–4. Daily 5–11pm.

DIRECTORY

Banks and post office The post office at the north end of Av du Général du Gaulle (Mon–Fri 8am–1pm 3–5pm, Sat 8am–noon, closed Sun) also has the town's only reliable ATM. There is no currency exchange.

Car rental Budget (☏594 340 294, ⌨budget-guyane .com) has an office by the Texaco service station (closed noon–2.30pm).

Internet Upgrade Computer, at 25 Rue Félix Eboué.

Pharmacy Pharmacie Centrale, 22 Av du Général de Gaulle.

PLAGE LES HATTES

From roughly March to July, the wide, clean stretch of sand that is **Plage Les Hattes**, at the mouth of the Maroni River a few kilometres from the Suriname border, is French Guiana's best place to view endangered **leatherback turtles** laying their eggs.

Leatherbacks are massive – they can grow up to 2m in length and weigh almost 900kg. During peak egg-laying season, an estimated 200 turtles crawl up onto the beach each night to lay their eggs. In August and September thousands of baby turtles can be seen hatching at night and dashing towards the water to escape predators.

The small Amerindian village of **Awala-Yalimapo** is 4km from the beach. Unless you are part of an organized tour, it's best to rent a car and base yourself here, or in the pleasant town of Mana 20km away. You can also stay on the beach itself (in which case bring food, water, a hammock and mosquito protection).

ARRIVAL AND DEPARTURE

By minibus Minibuses marked for Awala-Yalimapo depart the bus station in St Laurent (7am–4pm; returning 9am–6pm).

By car Plage Les Hattes is some 60km from St Laurent, accessible via a turn-off along the D9 from the RN1 via Mana and then a 20km single-track access road to Awala-Yalimapo.

ACCOMMODATION AND EATING

Several local spots in Awala-Yalimapo, such as *Chez Judith et Denis* and *Yalimalé*, offer *carbets* with basic facilities.

CROSSING BETWEEN FRENCH GUIANA AND SURINAME

The **ferry** runs between Saint Laurent and **Albina** in Suriname (3–7 daily; 7am–5.30pm; €4 one-way for foot passengers; motorbike/car €15/€33; euros only). Unless you have a vehicle (and rental vehicles may not cross borders), the quickest way to cross the Maroni River is to take one of the many **motorized dugout canoes** (10–15min; €5 or SRD15). When crossing the river in either direction, ask to be dropped off either at the **Surinamese Immigration office** (daily 7am–6pm) or the **French Immigration office** (daily 6am–7pm) – both located at the ferry piers – to get your visa checked and passport stamped. For Suriname, most passport holders require either a visa or a Tourist Card (see p000). You'll find that non-tourists travelling across the river tend to ignore border formalities, but if you're looking to travel further into either country, your paperwork must be in order.

There is a **cambio** at the Albina ferry terminal, which gives good rates when exchanging Suriname and US dollars for euros: change your money here, as in Saint Laurent there are no money-changing services. The French Immigration office is around 2km south of the centre of Saint Laurent; taxis are hard to find, so you may have to walk for twenty minutes. Unlike Saint Laurent, Albina is not a town to linger in; minibuses (SRD50–70) and taxis (SRD70–250) meet the ferries and take passengers to Paramaribo (3–4hr). State buses (see p.666) between Albina and Paramaribo run from the centre of Albina; take a taxi (SRD5) to and from the pier.

★**Le Buffalo** Rue A. M. Javouhey, Mana ☎ 594 344 280. An unexpectedly sophisticated restaurant in small-town Guiana that would give Cayenne's best a run for its money: great service, steak and other French delights cooked to perfection, complemented by a good range of French wines and cocktails. Dessert? Profiteroles to die for. Mains €12–15. Tues–Sun noon–10pm.

Hôtel Le Samana Mana ☎ 694 382 294, ✉ lesamanahotel@hotmail.fr. This cheery yellow hotel near the bridge is a real find: the spotless en-suite rooms and studios all have facilities for self-caterers,

there are pleasant common areas for lounging around with a laptop, and some rooms offer river views. Studios €70, doubles €60

Simili Youth Hostel Rte de Yalimapo, Awala-Yalimapo ☎ 594 341 625. Beachside accommodation to suit all tastes, from basic bungalows sleeping 2–6 people to a large *carbet* with hammocks (mosquito net extra €8 each); meals provided on request. Reservations must be made in advance as the place is deserted outside turtle season. Bungalow/person €18, *carbets* €7

7

SUNSET AT YPACARAI LAKE IN SAN BERNARDINO

Paraguay

HIGHLIGHTS

❶ **Laguna Blanca** A crystal-clear lake, perfect for birdwatching. **See p.693**

❷ **Asunción** Learn about Paraguay's history by day and bar-hop by night. **See p.695**

❸ **San Bernardino** Watch the sunset over the great lake in this tranquil holiday town. See p.701

❹ **The Ruta Jesuítica** Stargaze at remote Jesuit missions and explore under-threat Atlantic Forest. **See p.704**

❺ **The Chaco Mennonites** The Mennonites share this immense wilderness with indigenous tribes and jaguars. **See p.711**

HIGHLIGHTS ARE MARKED ON THE MAP ON P.689

ROUGH COSTS

Daily budget basic US$30, occasional treat US$50

Drink 1 litre Pilsen beer US$4

Food *Sopa paraguaya* US$0.75, *asado* US$10

Hostel/budget hotel US$10–15/US$25–40

Travel Asunción–Encarnación (365km): bus US$12

FACT FILE

Population 6.8 million

Language Guaraní and Castellano (Spanish). The blending of the two languages is known as *Jopará*.

Currency Guaraní (Gs)

Capital Asunción (population: 2.3 million)

International phone code ☎595

Time zone GMT -4hr

Introduction

Paraguay is billed as the "Heart of South America", but perhaps "South America's forgotten corner" is more appropriate. Despite being one of the most traditional countries on the continent and the only one with an indigenous tongue as its official language (Guaraní), Paraguay is far too often passed over by travellers. Those who do stop here may find themselves pleasantly surprised by the rich culture, host of under-promoted natural attractions, fascinating and bloodthirsty history and real feeling of being "off the beaten track".

Paraguay combines the scorching, arid wilderness of the **Chaco** – one of the best places in South America to see large mammals – with the wet and humid **Atlantic Forest** of eastern Paraguay; the rampant commercialism of **Ciudad del Este** with the muted, backwater feel of colonial towns like **Concepción**. Paraguay is difficult to pin down, in part due to its mixed immigrant intake over the past century; you're as likely to stumble across a colony of Japanese migrants, Mennonites or Australian socialists as you are to meet an indigenous tribe. The small country is not lacking in attractions – it is part-owner of the second-largest hydroelectric dam in the world and home to superbly preserved **Jesuit-Guaraní missions** – but tourism is undeveloped. Don't let this deter you, though; if you've a sense of adventure and crave a real, uncommercialized South American experience, get off the beaten path in Paraguay.

CHRONOLOGY

1537 The Spanish found the city of Nuestra Señora de Asunción.

1609 Jesuit missionaries arrive with the aim of converting indigenous tribes.

1767 The Jesuits are expelled from Paraguay by King Charles III of Spain.

1811 Paraguay declares its independence from Spain in a bloodless revolution.

1814 Dr José Gáspar Rodríguez de Francia is chosen as the first president and takes Paraguay into a period of isolation and industrialization.

1816 Rodríguez de Francia declares himself "El Supremo" – dictator for life, becoming progressively more arbitrary through his reign, suppressing the Church, isolating the country and taking to torturing opposition.

1844 Rodríguez de Francia is succeeded by Carlos Antonio López and Paraguay enters its period of greatest prosperity.

1862 Francisco Solano "Mariscal" López takes over as president from his ailing father, who leaves him with the deathbed advice that the pen is mightier than the sword.

1865–70 López launches Paraguay into the disastrous War of the Triple Alliance against Brazil, Argentina and Uruguay, which sees the country lose much of its territory and suffer many losses.

1927 The first Mennonites arrive in Paraguay, part of a campaign to colonize the Chaco.

1932–37 The Chaco War breaks out after rumours of undiscovered oil reserves provoke a violent reaction from the Paraguayan government at Bolivian army presence in the Paraguayan Chaco.

1954 After 22 presidents in 31 years, General Alfredo Stroessner seizes power and goes on to become the longest-lasting dictator in South American history, holding power for 34 years.

1989 Stroessner is driven into exile and Paraguay declares itself a Republic.

WHEN TO VISIT

Paraguay is an extremely hot country for most of the year. Eastern Paraguay can be very humid, while the Chaco (northwest) is dry. The hottest time is from November to February, when daytime temperatures can peak at around 45°C (or hotter in the Chaco) and high atmospheric pressure makes just walking along the street a tough task. Winter (June–Aug) is often pleasantly warm during the day (around 20–25°C), generally sunny and dry, though can get as cold as 5°C. Between September and November spectacular electric storms become more frequent and travelling off-road can be difficult.

1993 The first democratic elections are held, and are won by the quasi-liberal Colorados, effectively returning Stroessner's political party to power.

1999 Eight protesters are shot dead by snipers during pro-democracy protests during a month of unrest now referred to as the Marzo Paraguayo.

2008 Fernando Lugo, an ex-Catholic priest with a socialist agenda, defeats the Colorado Party candidate, ending 61 years of Colorado party rule.

2012 Lugo is impeached in a 24hr period in what many consider to have been a "parliamentary" coup d'état. His vice president, Federico Franco, continues the presidency until the 2013 general elections.

2013 The leader of the Colorado Party, Horacio Cartes, wins the general election and becomes president.

ARRIVAL AND DEPARTURE

A **passport** valid for six months after entry is required by all visitors, except residents of Argentina or Brazil who can use their national identity documents. Australian, Canadian and US citizens need to get an **entry visa** before travelling; Western European, UK and Japanese citizens do not (see ⓦworldtravelguide .net/paraguay/passport-visa for a list of countries not requiring visas).

If you're **arriving by land**, be aware that buses frequently cross the border without stopping at the customs post. It is your responsibility to get exit stamps from Bolivia, Brazil and Argentina and the required entry stamp for Paraguay or you risk a substantial fine – inform your driver that you need stamps and take your bags with you as buses won't always wait. The entry stamp entitles you to a ninety-day stay in Paraguay and this can be renewed once without cost at an immigrations post. A **yellow fever certificate** may also be demanded at border control.

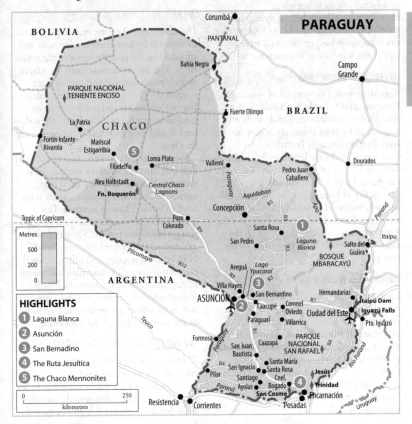

PARAGUAY

8

HIGHLIGHTS

1 Laguna Blanca
2 Asunción
3 San Bernadino
4 The Ruta Jesuítica
5 The Chaco Mennonites

BY PLANE

Those arriving on international flights will land at Aeropuerto Internacional Silvio Pettirossi (☎021 688 2000, ⓦwww .dinac.gov.py), 15km northeast of Asunción in the suburb of Luque. The main **airlines** operating in and out of Paraguay are: TAM (flies internally to Ciudad del Este and externally to Brazil, Bolivia, Argentina and Chile; ⓦtam .com.br); Aerolineas Argentinas (to Buenos Aires; ⓦaerolineas.com.ar); Copa (to Panama where there are connecting flights within Central America; ⓦcopa .com); Taca (ⓦtaca.com) and Avianca Peru (ⓦavianca.com) to Lima; GOL (to Buenos Aires and various Brazilian cities; ⓦvoegol.com.br); Buquebus flies to Uruguay (ⓦflybqb.com) and Avianca Peru to Lima (ⓦwww.avianca.com). It's a good idea to confirm your flight 24 hours in advance, as there are often cancellations. Check before flying that your ticket includes the US$41 **departure tax** (*tasa de embarque*) or you'll have to pay at the window at the airport.

OVERLAND FROM ARGENTINA

Argentina wraps around all of southern Paraguay and is easily accessible. From Asunción many international buses make a quick exit out of Paraguay across the river headed towards Formosa, Resistencia and Corrientes in Argentina. The border city of Encarnación sits across the River Paraná from **Posadas**; international buses connect the terminals on each side of the border. Similar buses run from Ciudad del Este in Paraguay to **Puerto Iguazú**, making day-trips to the falls – or onwards into Argentina – easy (see p.709).

OVERLAND FROM BOLIVIA

Land crossings from Bolivia are fairly straightforward in good weather, less so during heavy rains. A paved road branches off from the Trans-Chaco to cross the border at **Fortín Infante Rivarola**; international buses stop here en route from Santa Cruz to Asunción, but there is no passport control, so border formalities need to be done in another town (see p.712).

OVERLAND FROM BRAZIL

The busiest border crossing with Brazil is the **Puente de la Amistad** ("friendship bridge") linking Ciudad del Este with Foz do Iguaçu. Regular buses make the short crossing, and it is also possible to cross by taxi, motorcycle-taxi (much cheaper) or even on foot (see p.709). Many other border crossings with Brazil, such as that at Pedro Juan Caballero, are popular smuggling routes and considered unsafe.

GETTING AROUND

Buses in Paraguay are cheap and easy, although they may stop short of national parks, *estancias* or other isolated attractions. Renting a car is extremely expensive and many provisions need to be taken if driving alone. It is not recommended for non-Spanish speakers.

BY BUS

The easiest and cheapest way to get around Paraguay is by **bus**; there are frequent and affordable services daily between the major cities. Visiting areas away from the major cities is more difficult and bus services – when they exist – are uncomfortable. Journey durations and departure times tend to be erratic, as buses leave when they are full and may pick further passengers up en route.

Asunción is the country's major transport hub and there are so many companies at the main "Terminal" (see p.698) that, outside of the holiday seasons, there is no need to book tickets in advance. The quality of service varies greatly: in general, you get what you pay for. Pluma (ⓦwww .pluma.com.br) offers services to Brazil, NSA (ⓦwww.nsa.com.py) offers national bus services as well as international routes to Argentina, while Crucero del Norte (ⓦcrucerodelnorte.com.ar) is an Argentine company whose bus services link up most of the southern half of the continent.

BY CAR

Renting a **car** is possible only in Asunción, Ciudad del Este or Encarnación, and a 4WD is necessary for the dirt roads that crisscross the country away from the national highway system.

Rental is expensive (around Gs1,000,000 per day or more for a 4WD with unlimited mileage), making it difficult to see more remote areas of the country cheaply, though petrol costs are low (around Gs6700 a litre for unleaded). An **international driving licence** is required.

Heading off the Ruta Trans-Chaco on your own is strongly discouraged. If you plan on going deeper into the Chaco than the Mennonite colonies, you should take a guided tour (see p.712) – many tourists come to grief by embarking on poorly planned journeys in an effort to save a little money. Once past the Mennonite colonies there is nowhere to stay or buy food, and very few places to refuel.

There are rental agencies at the airport in Asunción, including international chains, but the only company that currently serves all three of the main cities is Localiza (0800 979 2000, www.localiza.com); 24hr breakdown cover is provided by the Touring y Automovil Club Paraguayo (TACPy; 021 210 550, tacpy.com.py).

BY TAXI

Taxis are well organized in Paraguay and there is not as much need to barter. *Taxistas* are assigned a rank to wait at, and these are clearly marked in towns by a yellow shelter saying "Taxi". Ask for the meter (*contadora*) to be switched on (*prendida*), or at least agree on a price before embarking. Journeys in small towns or around central Asunción will cost around Gs10,000–25,000, while trips out of towns or to airports may be up to Gs100,000.

BY BOAT

Most of the **boats for tourists** in Paraguay are very expensive, but ferries do run to Brazil, Argentina and Bolivia. For the budget traveller there is just one boat trip from Asunción up the Río Paraguay to Concepción (or the reverse). From Concepción it is possible to take another cheap boat further upstream into the Paraguayan Pantanal.

ACCOMMODATION

On the whole **accommodation** in Paraguay is good value for money, and you'll usually get air-conditioning, TV, en-suite bathroom and breakfast included. You don't usually need to book in advance, except in Caacupé during the weeks surrounding the Immaculate Conception (Dec 8), during the Carnaval in Encarnación (Feb) and in the Mennonite colonies during the Trans-Chaco Rally (last weekend in Sept), when prices are higher.

In Asunción there are twenty or so **youth/backpacker hostels** that have opened in recent years. Don't bank on **camping** in Paraguay as campsites are few and far between and in rural areas most land is in private hands and you risk being accused of trespassing if you do not have the permission of the landowner. Times are changing, however, and SENATUR is trying to develop a camping culture to attract tourists, so it's always worth asking them for updates if you're determined.

FOOD AND DRINK

At first glance, **Paraguayan cuisine** may appear to be based entirely on junk-food joints selling hamburgers, *milanesas* (schnitzels) and pizza. However, a little exploring will uncover a number of excellent restaurants, at least in the major cities. The mainstay of the Paraguayan diet is **asado** – essentially barbecue – almost always accompanied by *mandioca* (manioc, also known as cassava or yucca). The best cuts are *tapa de cuadril*, *corte Americano* and *colita de cuadril*. Those with a weak stomach should avoid *mondongo* (tripe), *lengua* (tongue), *chinchulín* (small intestine) and *tripa gorda* (large intestine). *Morcilla* is black pudding and *chorizo* is sausage – but no relation to Spanish chorizo. *Pollo asado* (grilled chicken) is often sold on roadside grills, and don't forget to try *corazoncitos* (chicken hearts).

Fish is generally expensive and at least twice the price of beef, *surubí* being the most frequently available. For a cheap, tasty snack, *empanadas* (pasties) are widely available and there is almost always somebody selling **chipa** (cheese bread made with manioc flour) – it is best when hot (*caliente*). Oddly, *chipa* in Asunción is frequently disappointing, so don't let it put you off trying it elsewhere.

Sopa Paraguaya is not soup, but a savoury cheese cornmeal cake, delicious when warm. *Chipa Guazu* is similar, but made with fresh corn and egg. Both come as accompaniments to meals.

Ask around for unmarked eating houses, which local people always know about, where you may be able to find home-cooked Paraguayan food such as *bori-bori* (soup with corn balls), *guiso de arroz* (a sort of Paraguayan paella) and *so'o apu'á* (meatball soup).

Paraguayan **desserts** include *ensalada de frutas* (fruit salad), which you can buy from street sellers after lunch, the sandwich spreads *dulce de leche* and *dulce de guayaba*, as well as *dulce de batata con queso paraguayo* (a candied sweet potato accompanied with cheese).

DRINK

Wondering what those wildly decorated thermos flasks contain? It's **tereré**, or ice-cold *yerba mate*, a refreshing and addictive herbal tea, undoubtedly the most widely consumed drink in Paraguay. It is sometimes drunk mixed with fruit juice (*tereré Ruso*) or with milk and desiccated coconut (*tereré dulce*). Look out for street vendors with baskets of **yu-yos**: native plants with medicinal properties. Whether you have a hangover or want to lose weight, let the vendor know and he'll add the appropriate plant mix to your *tereré*. Ask a "*yuyero/a*" if they sell the *tereré por el vaso* (by the cup) if you want to try some.

The preferred **local beer** is Pilsen. *Chopp* is a generic term for draught beer, although beer is more widely available in returnable litre bottles.

CULTURE AND ETIQUETTE

Paraguay is generally a safe, informal and laidback country. Men greet each other with a shake of the hand and women are greeted with a kiss on each cheek. The main **religion** is Roman Catholicism. As in many Latin American countries, there is a typically macho attitude to **women**, who may be seen as "fair game" when travelling alone; try to avoid any behaviour or clothing that may be misconstrued as "flirty", especially away from the major cities. Equally, it's not considered appropriate for women to be drunk in public. If you wish to take a photo of somebody, ask permission and don't offer payment if it's not asked for.

Tipping is not expected but is always appreciated. A tip of Gs2000–3000 is appropriate for a meal; as most museums are free, a tip to the guide is always welcome.

SPORTS AND OUTDOOR ACTIVITIES

As in most South American countries, **soccer**, or *fútbol*, is the main sporting obsession and Paraguay's special claim is that it now houses the **Museo del Fútbol Sudamericano**, near Asunción's airport (Av Sudamericana 595, Autopista Aeropuerto Internacional Km12, Luque; Mon–Sat, call in advance; free; ☎02 164 5781; bus #30 from Oliva/Cerro Corá). For football fans this museum has become a pilgrimage to see the trophy room containing all the most important cups South American teams play for. Regular matches are played on Sundays and the two biggest clubs are Olimpia and Cerro Porteño. Tickets are bought at the stadium upon entry. **Motor racing** fans will want to look into the **Trans-Chaco Rally**, one of the most demanding motor races on earth (see p.711).

COMMUNICATIONS

Postal services, run by Correo Paraguayo (ⓦwww.correoparaguayo.gov.py), are unreliable, so important mail should always be sent registered (*certificado*) or by international courier. There are no post boxes – you have to go into the post office. For **public telephones** you need to look out for *cabinas telefónicas*, telephone booths inside a shop. Copaco (ⓦwww.copaco.com.py) are the national phone company and they have an office in most towns with *cabinas* that tend to open roughly between 8am and 8pm. If you are going to be in the country a while, think about getting a pay-as-you-go **mobile phone** (from around Gs200,000)

PARAGUAY'S DIFFICULT NATURAL WONDERS

The immense range of **flora and fauna** in Paraguay should be drawing tourists from all over the world; the Chaco is one of the best places in South America to see large mammals, while the Atlantic Forests of eastern Paraguay are the most threatened natural habitat on the planet. Paraguay also has a sizeable slice of the mighty Pantanal, a wildlife wonderland normally associated with Brazil. Paraguay suffers from aggressive deforestation and encroaching agrarian interests, but luckily, people are starting to catch on that the country needs protecting. All of the options below are worth investigating, but many – in the Chaco in particular – are notoriously difficult to access. **Fauna Paraguay** (ⓦfaunaparaguay.com) provide an impressive number of ecologically sensitive tours with extremely knowledgeable English-speaking guides (including all of the below). Many of the Asunción-based tour companies (see p.698) will also arrange tours.

Central Chaco Lagoons Correctly the Cuenca del Riacho Yacaré Sur, a series of temporal saline lakes east of the Mennonite colonies, whose presence depends on rainfall in previous months. In winter they can be occupied by ducks and Chilean flamingos; from September to December, huge flocks of sandpipers and plovers are attracted to the water. To visit without a tour agency, get in touch with the Mennonites (see p.711) who may be able to provide transport, accommodation and food (upwards of US$200/day).

Laguna Blanca One of the most beautiful and peaceful places in Paraguay, with crystal-clear water offering much-needed "beaches". Activities such as birdwatching (with a chance of seeing the world's rarest bird, the white-winged nightjar), kayaking, snorkelling, fishing and horseriding are available. Accommodation is either in cabins, or camping. Only possible with prior arrangement (ⓣ021 424 760, ⓦlagunablanca.com.py). The area remains fairly inaccessible and remote, with dirt tracks for over 70km the only possible route. Those particularly interested in animals should get in touch with conservation group Para la Tierra (ⓦparalatierra.org), who welcome people for longer periods as volunteers.

Bosque Mbaracayú This forest reserve, consisting of over 640 square kilometres of Atlantic Forest and *cerrado* habitat, is accessible to tourists (though not cheap) thanks to the Fundación Moises Bertoni (Prócer Carlos Argüello 208, Asunción;

ⓣ021 608 740, ⓦwww.mbertoni.org.py). It's home to over 400 bird species, and 89 different mammals, including pumas and jaguars. FMB run a lodge for tourists, and you can hike, canoe, abseil or mountain bike with guides. Buses from Asunción go to Villa Ygatimi, 25km from the forest, where FMB can pick you up (Gs10,000 entry; Gs275,000/night B&B for two, or Gs45,000 to camp; pickup from Villa Ygatimi costs Gs300,000).

The Pantanal Paraguay's part of this enormous marshland spanning Brazil and Bolivia is difficult to reach (a more accessible route is from Corumba, Brazil), and not tourist-friendly. However, thanks to its remoteness, people who do make it here will be rewarded with many of nature's giants, including giant otters, giant armadillos, giant tegus and giant anteaters. Again, you're best off going with Fauna Paraguay between April and September – the roads are impassable at other times.

Parque Nacional San Rafael Set in 730 square kilometres of Atlantic Forest, this national park contains some 300 species of bird, big mammals such as pumas, ocelots and tapirs, nestling in a unique ecosystem where you'll also find rare orchids. Pro Cosara (ⓣ076 829 5046, ⓦprocosara.org) are the main NGO working here and they can provide food and accommodation (US$30/day full board in cabins plus US$10 transportation into the park from nearest town; minimum two-day stay) as well as guided tours of the park. If you need an English-speaking guide; organize it through Fauna Paraguay.

8

which may include some credit.

Internet access is ubiquitous in the major cities and very cheap (around Gs4000/hr), with generally good connections; most hotels and hostels offer wi-fi. The most popular **newspapers** (*diarios*) are the tabloids *Crónica* and *Popular*, both written in Jopará, a mixture of Spanish and Guaraní. For a more serious read try *ABC* or *Última Hora*.

EMERGENCY NUMBERS

In an emergency requiring police, firefighters or ambulance, dial ☎911.

CRIME AND SAFETY

Paraguay is generally a safe country to visit; with so few tourists around they are rarely targeted by thieves. The usual precautions regarding personal safety and protecting your belongings should be taken, and it's unwise to wander alone after dark in unpopulated areas of the capital. If you report a crime, don't expect the **police** to offer more assistance than the taking of your statement for insurance purposes.

The border area in **Ciudad del Este** is occasionally unsafe and you should take a taxi if you have all your belongings with you. Further afield, the vast, largely unpopulated wilderness of the **Chaco** is an extremely desolate and hostile environment, and you should not go off the beaten track without a local guide and substantial preparation and supplies.

HEALTH

Travellers coming to Paraguay should be **vaccinated** against diphtheria, yellow fever and hepatitis A. Your doctor may also recommend malaria, rabies, hepatitis B and typhoid vaccines, depending on your travel plans. Take the usual precautions against mosquitoes; while malaria is uncommon, dengue fever is on the rise here. The tourist board says all running **tap water** is safe; however, bottled or sterilized water is preferable and essential in more rural areas, where you may also want to avoid eating prepared salads.

Bed bugs are an increasing problem internationally, so scour mattresses for signs of them; they hide in the seams and you might notice blood spots from bites.

INFORMATION AND MAPS

The tourist board is run by **SENATUR** (Secretaría Nacional de Turismo; ⓦwww .paraguay.travel). They produce some good leaflets and maps; be sure to drop into their Asunción office (see p.698).

Asatur's website (ⓦasatur.org.py) lists all tour agents in Paraguay. Fauna Paraguay (see box, p.693) provides accurate lists and image galleries of the majority of the species present in the country.

For detailed **maps**, try the Touring y Automovil Club Paraguayo (TACPy; 25 de Mayo 1086, at Brasil, Asunción; ☎021 210 550, ⓦwww.tacpy.com.py). Most Paraguayans locate places by landmarks, so addresses are often vague. Paraguayans know places by being "almost at" a crossroad (usually indicated by the word *casi*, shortened to c/), or, if they are at a street corner, the address will say *esquina* (or esq.).

MONEY AND BANKS

The **guaraní** has been relatively stable in recent years. Notes are issued in denominations of 1000, 5000, 10,000, 20,000, 50,000 and 100,000. Coins come in denominations of 50, 100, 500 and 1000. Note that the Gs2000 note is plastic currency, while other notes are paper. It is almost impossible to change the guaraní outside Paraguay. **Credit cards** are not widely accepted outside the capital and incur a charge of five to ten percent – plan on paying in cash wherever you go. There are 24hr **ATMs** which will accept international cards in all sizeable towns and cities, though an administration charge of Gs20,000–30,000 is usually applied.

You'll get the best exchange rates if you **exchange money** midweek at a casa de cambio; prices tend to rise at weekends. Do not use street moneychangers – when you are dealing with hundreds of thousands of guaraníes you can be easily tricked. The chain MaxiCambios (ⓦmaxicambios.com .py) has branches in Asunción and Ciudad del Este and is reliable for both exchanging money and cashing travellers' cheques.

OPENING HOURS

Opening hours for shops are generally Monday to Friday 8am until 6pm, plus Saturday until early afternoon. Restaurants are open around 11.30am to 2.30pm and 6.30pm to midnight. Banks are typically open Monday to Friday 8am

PUBLIC HOLIDAYS

In addition to the national holidays listed below, some local anniversaries or saints' days are also public holidays, when everything in a given town may close down.

January 1 New Year's Day (Año Nuevo)
February 3 Day of San Blas, patron saint of Paraguay (Día de San Blas)
March 1 Heroes' Day (Día de los Héroes)
March/April Easter and Holy Week (Pascua y Semana Santa)
May 1 Labour Day (Día del Trabajador)
May 15 Independence Day (Día de la Independencia Patria)
June 12 Commemoration of the end of the Chaco War (Paz del Chaco)
August 15 Founding of Asunción (Fundación de Asunción)
December 8 The Immaculate Conception and the Virgin of Caacupé (Concepción Immaculada y la Virgen de Caacupé)
December 25 Christmas Day (Navidad)

to 1pm and closed at weekends, though ATMs can be used at any time. Many **museums** are only open in the mornings, or not at all unless you find the guide or guardian, but persevere.

Asunción

Less intimidating than many South American capital cities, **ASUNCIÓN** sits astride a broad bay on the Río Paraguay. Once the historic centre of government for the Spanish colonies of Río de la Plata, the city declined in importance with the founding of Buenos Aires, while the impenetrable Chaco prevented it from becoming the envisioned gateway to the riches of Peru. The quirky city brims with the history of its despots and dictators, but the real stars are its friendly and accommodating citizens, whom you'll meet if you take advantage of the city's fun nightlife.

WHAT TO SEE AND DO

While Asunción offers the usual Latin American urban dichotomy of a crumbling

historical centre and modern, wealthy suburbs, its personality shines through once you start getting your head around the country's crazy history. The **historic centre**, or *casco histórico*, is spookily deserted in the evenings and at weekends, but it provides enough cultural attractions for at least a couple of days of wandering. The action is centred on **Plaza Uruguaya**, **Plaza de los Héroes** and the **waterfront**. Many of the city's high-end restaurants are in the area around the mammoth **Shopping del Sol** complex in the suburb of **Villa Mora**, but the old centre is still the best place to look for cheap accommodation, as well as cutting-edge nightlife. A visit to the multi-coloured *barrio* of **Loma San Jerónimo**, with its cobbled streets and lively markets, is also not to be passed up on.

Those seeking more tranquil surroundings will find solace in the arty towns around the peaceful **Lago** (**Lake**) **Ypacaraí**, easily reached as a day-trip from the city.

Note that in the centre, the street names running east–west change after Independencia Nacional, which cuts them north–south, so Cerro Corá and Oliva, for example, are the same street.

Plaza de los Héroes

The *casco histórico* is easy to explore on foot and a good starting place is the main square, **Plaza de los Héroes**. A lively place, filled with *lapacho* trees that bloom a dramatic pink in July and August, it's a frequent concert venue and attracts tourists, protesters and pedlars alike. Made up of four squares, each with its own name, it's generally referred to as a whole as the Heroes' Square thanks to the redoubtable **Panteón de los Héroes** (daily 8am–6pm; free) in its northwestern corner. In a country lacking in postcard-perfect moments, it's Paraguay's most instantly recognizable monument and it contains the remains of former presidents: Carlos Antonio López, his son Francisco Solano López and the dictator Dr Rodríguez de Francia. The Panteón faces onto the busy commercial and shopping street **Palma**, where you'll find plenty of *artesanía* stalls.

8

CENTRAL ASUNCIÓN

ACCOMMODATION
Arandú Hostal	3
Black Cat Hostel	1
Circo Hostel	2
El Jardin Hostal	5
Urbanian Hostel	4

DRINKING & NIGHTLIFE
Britannia Pub	13
La Cachamba	6
La Casa del Mojito	1
Hippie Chic	9
Kilkenny	7
El Poniente	2

EATING
Bar San Roque	12
Be Okay	8
Bolsi	5
Café Literario	11
Lido Bar	3
La Piccola Trattoria	10
Sukiyaki	14
Taberna Española	4

The Costanera

Northwest of Plaza de los Héroes the **Costanera** (waterfront) runs along the banks of the Río Paraguay. As you walk here from the centre, you'll pass the squat yet overblown **Palacio de Gobierno** (presidencia.gov.py), which will come as something of a shock. Often referred to as the Palacio de los López, the seat of government was started in the 1850s by the elder of the López dictators who wanted to bring a touch of Europe to Paraguay. He hired an English contractor to whip up a palace with a touch of Versailles, the White House and Westminster, but for all its grand pretensions, the resulting building is almost friendly and, thanks to the lack of fencing, you can walk almost right up to it.

A few blocks west of the Palace, down El Paraguauo Independiente, brings you to the **puerto** (port; at the corner with

Colón), where you can catch boats across the Paraguay (daily 6.30am–7pm; 30min; Gs3500 one-way; ☎0983 127 965) to the small town of Chaco'i from where you'll get lovely views of Asunción, as well as respite from its smog. Once a week boats also leave for Concepción in the north (see p.709).

Immediately opposite the palace is a terrace of old buildings with Italianate facades which are known collectively as the **Centro Cultural Manzana de la Rivera** (Ayolas 129; daily 8am–6pm; free; ☎021 442 448, ⊕centroculturalmanzanarivera .blogspot.com), a series of restored houses dating from 1750, housing the **Museo Memoria de la Ciudad**, with artefacts from the city, a gallery space with temporary exhibitions, a library and a bar which fills with people having after-work drinks overlooking the beautifully lit palace.

Plaza de Armas

A two-block walk east along El Paraguayo Independiente from Palacio de Gobierno will bring you to the unofficially named **Plaza de Armas** (also known as Plaza Mayor, Plaza de la Independencia, Parque de la República or Plaza del Marzo Paraguayo). The square, home to some of the most important buildings in the city, feels sleepy and almost forgotten. It's dominated by the **Cabildo**, which housed the national congress until 2004 when a modern building was completed just off the northwestern corner of the square along Avenida República. Built in the 1840s, the Cabildo now houses the **Centro Cultural de la República** (Mon–Fri 9am–8pm, Sat & Sun 9.30am–5.30pm; free; ☎021 443 094, ⑩www.cabildoccr .gov.py), which exhibits important historical pieces, such as the López presidential throne alongside displays about famous national musicians and actors, while there are often free concerts and talks in the evenings. On the plaza's southeastern corner stands the uninteresting Neoclassical **Catedral** (officially Mon–Fri 9.30am–noon & 1–5pm, Sat & Sun 10am–noon, though unreliable; ☎021 449 512), built in the same decade as the Cabildo. It's not safe for tourists to walk in the slums that lead from this plaza down to the bay.

A few blocks away, the **Casa de la Independencia** (14 de Mayo esq. Presidente Franco; Mon–Fri 8am–6pm, Sat 8am–1pm; free; ☎021 493 918, ⑩casadelaindependencia.org.py), dating back to 1811, is one of the oldest and most important buildings in the country. It was here that the architects of Paraguayan independence secretly met to discuss their plans. Today it houses a museum with artefacts from the time of the declaration of independence, and there is a lovingly preserved colonial alleyway alongside.

Plaza Uruguaya

With several bookshops in the middle, leafy **Plaza Uruguaya** has an appealingly gentle pace, encapsulated by the nostalgic and elegant **Estación de Ferrocarril** (México 145, entrance on Eligio Ayala; Mon–Fri 7am–5pm;

Gs10,000; ☎021 447 848, ⑩www .fepasa.com.py), the city's old railway station, which dates back to 1861. It now serves as a museum to Paraguay's historic railway, with grand old carriages in the station hall to wander around. Things get slightly seedier in the Plaza at night, but the surrounding streets become the centre of the city's nightlife.

Other museums in the centre

Five blocks east along Eligio Ayala from the Plaza Uruguaya is the modest **Museo Nacional de Bellas Artes** (Eligio Ayala 1345, at Curupayty; Tues–Fri 7am–6pm, Sat & Sun 8am–2pm; free; ☎021 211 578), which primarily displays artworks collected by Paraguayan intellectual Juan Silviano Godoy (1850–1926). It includes some European art, but the real draw is the strong selection of national art evoking a bygone Paraguay.

A little further out of the centre, in an unassuming terraced house, sits the former torture centre of the Stroessner dictatorship, now home to the moving **Museo de las Memorias** (Chile 1066 between Manduvirá and Jejuí; Mon–Fri 9am–4pm; free; ☎021 493 873). The museum's displays are based on the "terror archives" discovered in 1992 detailing the human rights abuses carried out under the 35-year dictatorship. You'll see the cells where up to a hundred people at a time were kept, as well as a bathtub used for water torture and other gruesome implements used by the regime.

Loma San Jerónimo

A lookout point for ships during the nineteenth-century Spanish occupation, the colourful little neighbourhood of **Loma San Jerónimo** lies to the west of the centre and towards the port at Remigio Cabral, Diaz de Pefaur and Avenida Stella Maris, and is reminiscent of La Boca in Buenos Aires. Once a particularly poor and run-down *barrio*, a government incentive saw houses painted bright colours, streets strung with bunting and many homespun businesses popping up (often in locals' front rooms), attracting tourism and turning the area into one of Asunción's gems. Wander through the winding

8

cobbled alleyways and ask a local for directions to the church, which you can climb to the top of for the best views of the city (the neighbouring mirador is more expensive, but the church only asks for a donation). On Sunday, the area buzzes with artisanal stalls, street performers and food stands.

Villa Mora and the Museo del Barro

Like many Latin American countries, Paraguay's elite have left the crumbling splendour of the historic centre for flashy modernity at arm's length from their past. Most buses going away from the centre up España will go through the neighbourhood of **Villa Mora** and its beating heart, the mall **Shopping del Sol** (see p.700), as well as Paseo Carmelitas, which has restaurants and bars and is popular in the evening.

If you're not a shopaholic, the best reason to make the trip here is to visit arguably Paraguay's best museum, the **Museo del Barro** (Grabadores del Cabichui 2716; free; Tues 3.30–8pm, Wed–Sat 9am–noon & 3.30–8pm; ☏021 607 996, ⓦmuseodelbarro.org; bus #28, #30 or #56 from any corner of Oliva, which becomes Cerro Corá). Dedicated to Paraguay's indigenous, folk and urban/contemporary visual arts, it is housed in an interesting modern building with a good shop selling folk art. Don't miss the eighteenth-century *ñandutí* (spiderweb lace specific to Paraguay). The museum is a couple of blocks east after Shopping del Sol; when Avenida España splits in two, take the left fork – Aviadores del Chaco – two blocks further, and turn right down Cañada.

ARRIVAL AND DEPARTURE

By plane Aeropuerto Internacional Silvio Pettirossi (☏021 646 094) is 15km northeast of the city along Av España and its continuation Aviadores del Chaco. Taxis from the airport are extremely expensive (Gs100,000 to central Asunción); if you arrive by day, walk to the avenue outside the airport and take a taxi there (approx. Gs60,000 to city centre), or even better, get the bus (#30; 30min–1hr depending on traffic; Gs2400), which takes you directly into the centre.

By bus The two-tiered intercity bus terminal (☏021 551 740/1, ⓦwww.mca.gov.py/webtermi.html), at the junction of Fernando de la Mora and República de Argentina, is in the southeast of the city. A taxi from the terminal to the centre will cost around Gs40,000.

International destinations Buenos Aires (several daily; 21hr); Córdoba (2–5 weekly; 20hr); Rio de Janeiro (weekly; 26hr); Salta (weekly; 20hr); Santa Cruz, (daily; 20hr); Santiago (2 weekly; 30hr); São Paulo (daily; 22hr).

Domestic destinations Ciudad del Este (hourly; 4–5hr); Concepción (hourly; 7hr); Encarnación (hourly; 6hr); Filadelfia (2 daily; 7hr); San Bernardino (every 1–2hr; 2hr); San Cosme y San Damian (daily; 6hr); San Ignacio (5 daily; 4hr).

By boat There are expensive cruise boats (such as Crucero Paraguay; ☏021 446 974, ⓔcomercial@cruceroparaguay .info) that have all the mod cons, leave infrequently and often require large group bookings. The *Cacique II* (☏021 524 961), however, is for locals and goes from Asunción to Concepción every Tues at 7am (22hr; Gs80,000) from Playa Montevideo in the harbour, in theory: it's best to go down to the port in advance and enquire in person.

INFORMATION AND TOURS

Tourist information The Turista Róga (Palma 468, at 14 de Mayo; daily 7am–7pm; ☏021 494 110, ⓦparaguay .travel), run by SENATUR, is packed with maps, information and high-quality handicrafts. Staff are extremely helpful and there are computers with internet access to use free of charge. SENATUR also run a booth at the airport (daily 10am–6pm; ☏021 645 600).

Tour operators DTP, Gral. Brúguez 353, at 25 de Mayo (☏021 221 816, ⓦwww.dtp.com.py); and Mavani, Palma, at 14 de Mayo Galeria Palma, Local 39 (☏021 493 580, ☏021 446 654, ⓦmavani.com.py). Both offer some of the best tours all over the country as well as Asunción and Lago Ypacaraí tours, and both also have offices in Ciudad del Este; DTP is also in Encarnación.

APPRECIATING MERCADO 4

Asunción's **Mercado Cuatro** (4) is one of those sprawling Latin American markets where you can buy anything and everything (not to mention delicious and dirt-cheap street food). There are seemingly endless passageways in and out of this part-covered, part-street market and it's easy to get lost in the bustle. In 2012, a film based entirely in the market, *7 Cajas* (Maneglia & Schémboli), or "7 Boxes" as it's known in English, brought the world's attention to Paraguay's great market. As with any market, keep your wits about you and belongings close (or leave them in the hostel). The market is a twenty-minute uphill trudge from the centre via Pettirossi, or hop on any bus going southwest with "Mercado" in the window.

GETTING AROUND

The city centre is compact and easily walkable, as is Mercado 4. You'll want to take a bus to the Villa Mora area.

Buses You can flag down buses at all street corners. Destinations are advertised on the front (better to go by this than the number) and there is a flat fare of Gs2400. From the centre, buses to most parts of town run along Oliva, which becomes Cerro Corá. Buses #31 and #8 go to the bus terminal; #30A goes to the airport via Villa Mora; #28, #30, #37B and #56 all go to Villa Mora from the centre; #13, #14, #33 and #38 go from Herrera/Haedo in the centre to Mercado 4.

Taxis A journey within the centre shouldn't come to more than about Gs25,000; there are ranks every few streets in the centre and in Plaza de los Héroes. The radio taxi number is ☎ 021 311 080.

ACCOMMODATION

For people on a budget, there is far more choice and quality in the historic centre than Villa Mora. Breakfast, internet and/or wi-fi, a/c and hot water is included unless otherwise stated.

Arandú Hostal 15 de Agosto 783, at Humaitá ☎ 021 449 712, ⊛ aranduhostal.com. A boutique hostel in the owner's refurbished family home, with lovely facilities including robust, generous bunks each with locker, a roof terrace with great views west over the city and cosy communal areas. Dorms Gs70,000, rooms Gs160,000

Black Cat Hostal Eligio Ayala 129, between Yegros and Indepencia Nacional ☎ 021 449 827, ⊛ hostelblackcat .com. While the *Black Cat* – Paraguay's first backpacker hostel – is shabbier than some of the newcomers, it boasts all the features backpackers love, including a roof terrace with barbecue and a/c in every room; there's even a small pool. The mother–daughter team running the place speak good English, provide great customer service and can organize tours. Dorms Gs50,000, doubles Gs190,000

Circo Hostel Manuel Gondra, at Mcal. Lopez ☎ 021 441 000. Housed in an old radio station studio, this circus-themed hostel is basic but lively thanks to its excellent downtown location near the sights and nightlife. Large kitchen; breakfast included. Dorms Gs50,000

★ **El Jardín Hostal** Azara 941, between EEUU and Tacuary ☎ 098 236 9487, ⊛ eljardinhostal.com. Rooms here are adorned with interesting fabrics and Paraguayan *artesanía*, while bathrooms have some of the best showers around, and the garden is convivial. Run by a Paraguayan–Swedish couple, whose friendly policies, like no checkout time, and singles not having to pay double for a private room (write rather than use a booking website), set this place apart. Dorms Gs50,000, doubles Gs180,000

★ **Urbanian Hostel** Montevideo 1029, between Jejui and Manduvira ☎ 021 441 209, ⊛ urbanianhostel.com. Modern, Scandinavian-style decor and custom-built beds so you can sit up on the bottom bunk, and with a small pool surrounded by swinging chairs. No kitchen but there is a good restaurant-bar. Dorms Gs75,000

EATING

At lunchtime it is easy to find cheap filling food – simply look out for the barbecues outside restaurants all over the centre, chalk boards displaying the *menú del día*, or head over to Mercado 4.

Bar San Roque Eligio Ayala 792, at Tacuary ☎ 021 446 015. Classic Paraguayan food in a classic Paraguayan restaurant – it claims to be the oldest in the country. Service by the bow-tied waiters is slow, but sometimes the best things are worth waiting for. Mains from Gs35,000. Mon–Fri 8am–3pm & 6pm–midnight, Sat 9am–3pm & 7pm–12.30am, Sun 10am–3.30pm.

Be Okay Hassler and Cruz del Chaco ☎ 021 327 5667. One of the first health-food restaurants in the city, this vegetarian-vegan joint provides welcome respite from stodgy Paraguayan food. The imaginative wraps, veggie burgers and juices make it popular with young Asunceños. Mon–Wed & Sun 11am–11pm, Thurs–Sat 11am–midnight.

★ **Bolsi** Estrella 339, at Alberdi ☎ 021 491 841, ⊛ www .bolsi.com.py. Heralded as Asunción's best restaurant, this lively bistro serves traditional Paraguayan dishes alongside a large selection of fresh salads and other international dishes. Don't miss the sensational *Parisienne*-style pastry counter. Mains Gs40.000. Daily 24hr.

Café Literario Mcal. Estigarribia 456 ☎ 021 491 640. Nestled on a downtown side street, this cosy coffee house is equipped with reading lamps, comfy armchairs and shelves of books waiting to be read while sipping on the city's best cappuccino.

★ **Lido Bar** Av Mariscal José Felix Estigarribia, at Chile. Make this your first stop in Asunción to get a taste for Paraguayan food and the locals. It's as central as you can get – right in front of the Panteón de los Héroes – and packed day and night. It has a diner-style interior with everyone sitting around the bar barking their orders at gingham-capped waitresses who are a vision in peach. *Empanada* Gs8000, mains Gs30,000. Daily 7.30am–1am.

La Piccola Trattoria Yegros 335, at 25 de Mayo ☎ 021 446 051. The only clue to this tiny pasta restaurant is the brightly painted mural on the wall outside. Serving fresh pasta only, with simple but exquisitely flavoured sauces alongside a shot of *Limoncello*. Menu changes daily; around Gs30,000. Mon–Sat lunch.

Sukiyaki Constitución 763, at Pettirossi. Walkable from the centre, towards Mercado Cuatro, this is a genuine sushi restaurant that offers some of the best food in Asunción for decent prices. Bento box Gs70,000. Closed Sun.

Taberna Española Ayolas 631, at Gral. Díaz ☎ 021 441 743. Excellent tapas, hearty portions of paella and flowing sangría at this cosy and eccentrically decorated Spanish restaurant. Plate of mixed tapas Gs50,000. Open daily.

8

DRINKING AND NIGHTLIFE

Asunción has a thriving nightlife, especially at weekends, though things only really get going after midnight. The centre offers the coolest and most exciting places while Villa Mora is more upmarket. The biggest live music events are held at the Jockey Club, also known as the Hipódromo, at Eusebia Ayala Km4.5 (☎021 553 326, ✆jcp.com.py).

★**Britannia Pub** Cerro Corá 851, between EEUU and Tacuary. There are two other good bars on this block of Cerro Corá, but *Britannia* is the best; despite being over twenty years old, this British-themed pub still heaves with Asunceños. Unlike most Asunción bars it's busy on week nights and the action starts earlier than elsewhere, with bingo to win your bar tab Tues–Thurs from 6.30pm, Fri–Sun from 8pm.

La Cachamba Manuel Gondra, at Mcal. Lopez ☎021 441 000. Set in a train graveyard adorned with fairy lights and mismatched furniture, the "wagon bar" serves imaginative cocktails and has fast become a favourite among Asunción's cool cats. Head down at the weekend to party on the sunken open-air dancefloor. Wed–Sun 6pm–3am.

La Casa del Mojito Loma San Jerónimo ☎098 594 5711. Watch the sunset from the roof terrace while sipping on exquisite herb-infused cocktails made by Carlos and taking in breathtaking views of the city.

Hippie Chic Av España, at Dr Bestard ✆reservashippiechic @hotmail.com. Lanterns, disco balls and sparkly peace signs give this tented bar a festival feel. Reasonably priced drinks and delicious *lomitas* make it the perfect place to stop en route to Villa Mora. Wed, Thurs & Sun 8.30pm–3am, Fri & Sat 8.30pm–5am.

Kilkenny Malutín, at Av España alongside Paseo Carmelitas ✆kilkenny.com.py. Every city must have one, and this is a typical faux-Irish bar with drunken revelry guaranteed. Although themed and expensive, good for the live music, rowdy atmosphere and huge beer menu. Beer from Gs9000. Daily 6pm–5am.

El Poniente Palma, at Montevideo ☎097 178 0643. This downtown dive wouldn't look out of place in Berlin. Set in a colonial townhouse, the exposed brickwork, scrubbed wood and industrial lighting are softened by the palatial beauty of the house's former glory. Local DJs play modern house music at the weekend, making it *the* place to be seen. Thurs & Sun 6pm–2am, Fri & Sat 6pm–4am.

SHOPPING

Artesanía The website ✆www.artesania.gov.py has a rundown of arts and crafts by department. Good and high-quality selection sold at the Turista Róga (see p.698); cheapest in Asunción is in Mercado 4 (see box, p.698), clustered inside the market close to Pettirossi at Gral. Aquino.

Bookshops Many in and around the Plaza Uruguaya, but not much in English. Books (✆libreriabooks.com), with

one shop in the centre on Mcal. López 3791, at D. Morra, and in Shopping del Sol, Local 154, has a good variety of English-language titles.

Shopping centres Asunción has many "shoppings" (malls): Shopping del Sol (Av Aviadores del Chaco), ✆www.delsol.com.py), the most famous, will fulfil your every consumer dream.

DIRECTORY

Banks and exchange Branches of all major banks in Shopping del Sol. In the centre there's 24hr ATMs at BBVA, Yegros 435, at 25 de Mayo; HSBC, J.E.O' Leary 302, at Palma; Sudameris Bank, Independencia Nacional 513. The casas de cambio are clustered around Palma and Aberdi. There are MaxiCambios (which change travellers' cheques) in Shopping Asunción Super Centro at Oliva, at 14 de Mayo, and in Shopping del Sol.

Embassies and consulates Canada, Prof. Ramirez, at J. de Salazar (☎021 227 207); New Zealand, O'Leary 795, Humaitá (☎021 496 951); South Africa, Fulgencio R. Moreno 509 – Piso 8 (☎021 441 971); UK, J. Eulogio Estigarribia 4846, at Mons. Bogarín (☎021 210 405); USA, Mariscal López 1776 (☎021 490 686).

Hospital Centro Medico Bautista, Av República de Argentina, at Andrés Campos Cervera (☎021 688 9000, ✆cmb.org.py).

Internet Easy Internet on Plaza Uruguaya, 25 de Mayo, at Antequera, has internet and telephone *cabinas* (Gs15,000/hr; closed Sat pm & all day Sun). There is free wi-fi in any plaza where you see the wi-fi/Tigo sign.

Language school Idipar, Manduvirá 979/963, at Colón (☎021 447 896, ✆idipar.net), provide lessons in Spanish and Guaraní.

Laundry Lavandería Shalom, 15 de Agosto 230.

Pharmacy Punto Farma is a slick chain with 24hr delivery service (☎021 607 500, ✆puntofarma.com.py), and many stores open 24hr. Central branch: Estrella 480, at 14 de Mayo (daily 7am–midnight).

Phone Copaco, 14 de Mayo, at Oliva.

Police Tourist police, Chile, at Presidente Franco ☎021 446 608.

Post office 25 de Mayo, at Yegros (Mon–Fri 7am–7pm, Sat 7am–noon).

DAY-TRIPS FROM ASUNCIÓN

Respite from Asunción's oppressive heat is easier than you might imagine, and just a short distance from the city limits the buildings clear, the pace of life slows to a more typically Paraguayan tempo, while the lushness of the area is immediately striking. Two of the most interesting nearby towns are situated on the cool (but contaminated) waters of **Lago Ypacaraí**, a huge lake with attached national park. Although it's easy (and cheap) to hop on local buses between the towns (you can see them both in a day), tours are available (see p.698).

Areguá

A pleasant town full of big old houses located among the lush hills above the lake, arty **AREGUÁ** is noted for its ceramics, but has drawn all kinds of artists and literary types over the years. It has a small "**beach**" by the lake (a 5min walk down Mcal. Estigarribia) with a picturesque pier, which becomes crowded from December to February with Asunceños escaping the city. The town is also known for its huge strawberry (*frutilla*) crops, and every September it holds the Festival de las Frutillas. Don't miss the outstanding **craft shops** El Cántaro (Mcal. Estigarribia; ⓦel-cantaro.com) and the Centro Cultural del Lago (Yegros 855, at Mcal. López; ⓦccdl.com.py). There is **tourist information** at La Candelaria 515 (☎0291 433 500). To get there, catch bus #11 from Mercado 4 (Gs2400; 1hr 30min).

San Bernardino

From Areguá you can get two buses (changing at the main crossroads in Ypacaraí town; takes less than 1hr), or in summer, a boat, to the shady town of SAN

BERNARDINO (or "SanBer"), on the eastern shore of the lake. Founded in the 1880s by five German families, the town has retained an orderly feel. In the winter it is a ghost town full of exotic birdsong, bromeliads, and sprinklers maintaining the perfect lawns of Asunción's elite's second homes, but in summer it springs to life, although prices soar. Outside town there's fantastic walking in the mix of valleys and wooded slopes, while in town there are rowing boats and pedalos for rent, as well as craft stalls at Playa la Rotonda near the main square.

Tourist information is at Casa Hassler on 14 de Mayo, at Luís F. Vaché one block from the plaza (Mon–Fri 8am–3pm, Sat & Sun 8am–1pm; ☎051 223 2974, ⓦsanbernardino.gov.py), and Aventura Xtrema (Ntra. Señora de la Asunción, at Hassler; ☎098 168 2243, ⓦaventuraxtrema.com.py) can sort out all your extreme sporting needs, including waterskiing, even when their shop shuts in winter. Buses depart every one to two hours from Asunción's main terminal (see p.698).

ACCOMMODATION AND EATING

Brisas del Mediterraneo ☎051 223 2459, ⓦparaguay -hostel.com. A space to camp 2km north of town, still on the shores of the lake. Dorms (at weekend in high season) Gs80,000, camping Gs60,000

El Café Francés Av Luis Vaché 1005, ☎051 223 2295, ⓦcafefrances.com. Lovely little French restaurant serving everything from crêpes to fondue, or meat to cook on your own hotplate. Possibly the best crème brûlée outside of France. Mains Gs50.000. Tues–Sun 10am–10pm.

East of the Paraguay

The Río Paraguay slices the country into two distinct landscapes. The wild west of the Chaco couldn't be more different to the populous, diverse east. Some 97 percent of the population live on this side of the river, and it holds the majority of Paraguay's tourist draws. Whether you experience the human influence of the **Jesuit missions**, the **Itaipú hydroelectric dam**, Encarnación's fabulous **Carnaval**, or the under-promoted and under-explored

8

wildlife of the Atlantic Forest, in either the **Parque Nacional San Rafael** or **Bosque Mbaracayú** (see box, p.693), you'll leave wondering why more people don't come to Paraguay. The exquisite **Laguna Blanca** (see box, p.693), and the tranquil town labelled the "pearl of the north", **Concepción**, will only confirm the feeling that you've stumbled across some of the world's last secret spots.

ENCARNACIÓN

Known as the "Perla del Sur" (Pearl of the South), **ENCARNACIÓN** is Paraguay's third-largest, but second-wealthiest, city outside of the capital, and you'll notice some extraordinary houses as you walk around its streets. However, unlike its commerce-hungry fellow border town of Ciudad del Este, Encarnación has a laidback modernity that makes it much more likeable.

WHAT TO SEE AND DO

Although it's a pleasant, cosmopolitan town, there's not much to do here outside of **Carnaval** but enjoy the benefits of the town's immigrant populations – which include Germans, Eastern Europeans and Japanese – in the city's **restaurants**, and become a river-beach bum lazing on the sandy **beach** looking over to Posadas in Argentina. If you're visiting in winter, you're probably better off enjoying the countryside and staying nearer the reductions (see p.704), but it's worth stopping by to get some good food and to visit the tourist information, which specializes in the Jesuit missions.

ARRIVAL AND DEPARTURE

By bus Most visitors arrive at the bus terminal on General Cabañas at Mariscal Estigarribia, six blocks downhill from the Plaza de Armas. If you're coming from Argentina you'll arrive at the San Roque González International Bridge in the south of the city.

Destinations Asunción (hourly; 5–6hr); Ciudad del Este (6 daily; 4–5hr); Posadas (every 15min; 1hr); San Cosme (3 daily; 2hr).

INFORMATION AND TOURS

Tourist information Good English is spoken at the Ruta Jesuítica tourist office run by SENATUR, Mcal. Estigarribia 1015, at Curupayty (daily 7.30am–6pm; ☎071 205 021, ✉lamisiongroup@gmail.com). They can help with booking Carnaval tickets, reserving posadas and luggage storage. There's another office at customs at Puente San Roque González de Santa Cruz (daily 7.30am–5.30pm; ☎098 579 4595). Good road maps can be bought at Touring and Automovil Club Paraguayo (Gral. Artigas, at Villarrica).

Tour operators Most of the tour operators in Asunción will do one- or two-day tours to the Jesuit ruins, but they tend to be prohibitively expensive unless you are in a large group. The tourist office can provide an English-speaking guide to take you to them on public transport, for a fee.

Taxi Central Encarnación is easily walkable, but there are taxi ranks every few streets; no journey within the city should cost more than Gs25,000. Taxista Diosnel Cabral has a nice taxi fully equipped with seat belts. He'll do a return trip to Jesús and Trinidad for Gs300,000 (one-way Gs150,000).

ACCOMMODATION

Book well ahead for Carnaval, when prices rise considerably. Avoid the hotels around the bus terminal (except *Germano*) and those along Tómas Romero Pereira in the centre. The former attract an undesirable clientele, the latter have serious noise issues at weekends.

CARNAVAL

For most Paraguayans, Encarnación is synonymous with **Carnaval** (◍carnavalencarnaceno.com), a spectacular celebration transforming the city into a whirlpool of frivolity during four weekends from January to February. Some claim the Carnaval here is better than Rio's thanks to the crowd and community participation. Things begin to hot up during the week with bands of children roaming the streets armed with spray-snow and water balloons, looking to make a fool out of the unwary, but the main events are the weekend *corsos* (parades) in the Sambodromo on Av Rodriguez de Francia. The action begins around 9pm each night in the Sambódromo on the Costanera, and lasts through to the early hours. Tickets (Gs30,000–200,000, some with after-party entrance) sell out rapidly, so book ahead via the tourist office, or in person at the TIGO store at Mcal. Estigarribia, at Av Caballero, or at their store in Asunción, Av Mcal. López, at República de Argentina.

8

● **EATING & DRINKING**

Benndo	3
Camelot	1
Hiroshima	2
La Piccola Italia	1

■ **ACCOMMODATION**

Casa de la Y	4
Colonial Hostel and Camping	3
Germano	2
Hostel Kerana	1

4 (8 blocks), La Placita (5 blocks) & Post Office (3km) ▼

Casa de la Y Carmen de Lara Castro, at Yegros ☎ 098 577 8198, ⓦ casadelay.wix.com/casa-de-la-y. Doña Yolanda will make you feel like part of the family in this cosy homestay with dorms. Space is tight, and booking ahead is essential, but a good choice for a bed with breakfast in the city. Dorms Gs70,000, doubles Gs180,000

Colonial Hostel and Camping General Artigas 762, at Cabañas ☎071 201 500, ⓔ colonialhostelencarnacion@gmail.com. With beautiful views of the Río Parana and excellent transport links to the sights, this bright and airy hostel is a favourite among budget travellers. Gs60,000

Germano General Cabañas, at C.A. López ☎071 203 346. Conveniently located right in front of the bus station, this is the city's best-value budget option. It is basic (fans only, no a/c, breakfast not included), but it's a good place to get your head down for the night. Shared bath Gs70,000, en-suite Gs100,000

Hostel Kerana Juan Leon Mallorquin 590 ☎071 201 073, ⓦ keranahostel.com. Walking distance to the bus terminal, river-beach and attractions, this friendly hostel has a nice outside area, well-equipped kitchen and an excellent breakfast included. Dorms Gs65,000, doubles Gs180,000

EATING AND DRINKING

There are surprisingly good eating options in Encarnación, thanks to its multicultural population. For cheap food fast, the *comedor* (dining hall) behind the bus station has lots of little restaurants, as does La Placita indoor market. Encarnación's nightlife revolves around one or two bars for most of the year, but during the summer everything moves to the beach and there are always new pop-up bars there.

CROSSING TO ARGENTINA

Buses between **Encarnación** and **Posadas** in Argentina start from Ruta 1 at the junction with Caballero (opposite *Camelot Pub*) and go down Mallorquín through the centre where you can catch the bus on most corners every 10min (5am–11pm; 1hr; Gs5000). Make sure to get off the bus at both ends of the bridge for **customs** formalities. The bus won't wait for you to get your stamps, but your ticket remains valid for the next service.

Benndo 25 de Mayo, at Tte. Horario Gonzalez ☎ 098 581 8916. With a huge array of sandwiches, *empanadas*, Mexican food and pizza, *Benndo* is a cheesy-meaty-carb-lover's dream. Pizzas from Gs25,000. Daily 11am–3pm, 6pm–1am.

Camelot Ruta 1, at Caballero ☎ 098 655 6688. Next to *Piccola Italia*, and run by the same people, this is the most consistent bar/disco in town and is always popular. Fri & Sat 10pm–7am.

★**Hiroshima** 25 de Mayo, at Lomas Valentinas ☎ 071 206 288. What this place lacks in character, it makes up for with good service, fresh ingredients and excellent quality. Superb selection of bento boxes. Mains Gs30,000–50,000. Also runs a pop-up restaurant by the beach in summer. Daily 11.45am–2pm & 7–11pm.

Piccola Italia Ruta 1, at Caballero ☎ 071 202 344. Faux Mediterranean surroundings and a cheery Paraguayan/ Italian host at this popular trattoria. Pig out on huge portions of pizza and pasta – one plate is easily enough for two. Mains Gs40,000. Mon, Tues, Thurs & Fri 6.30–11pm, Sat & Sun 9.30am–1.30pm & 6.30–11pm.

DIRECTORY

Banks and exchange Sudameris Bank and Banco Familiar on the Plaza de Armas both have ATMs.

Hospital Clínica Tajy, Gral. Artigas 1772, at Constitución ⓦ clinicatajy.com.

Laundry Salon de Belleza Meri, Gral. Cabañas, at C.A. López.

Post office Nuevo Circuito on the Ruta Internacional, at San José.

Tourist police Wear light blue shirts with chequered hat; the main police station is at Tte. H. Gonzalez, cnr 25 de Mayo.

THE RUTA JESUÍTICA

No trip to Paraguay is complete without visiting at least a few of the seven towns that make up the **RUTA JESUÍTICA** (Jesuit route; ☎ 021 210 0550; see ⓦ rutajesuitica. com.py for details of museums, ruins and accommodation; see also ⓦ misiones.gov. py), so dubbed by SENATUR to promote the route between Asunción and Encarnación. There are four towns with Jesuit connections in the department of **Misiones** (see box, p.706), while in neighbouring Itapúa, there are the remains of three **Jesuit-Guaraní missions**. While **Trinidad** is the most well known, neglecting its neighbour **Jesús**, or the further-afield **San Cosme**, the other side of Encarnación, would be a great loss. It's worth timing trips to Trinidad and San Cosme for an evening, as both have special events. There is a **joint ticket**

(Gs25,000) for all three as long as you go within 72 hours. The best places to stay are in posadas (see box opposite), or one of the fancy or unusual hotels (see box opposite) along the way. There are no ATMs in any of the villages, so carry cash.

Trinidad

The mission of **Trinidad**, or **La Santísima Trinidad del Paraná** to give it its full unwieldy name (English-speaking guides available; daily 7am–7pm, Luz y Sonido show Thurs–Sun 7/8pm; Gs25,000 joint ticket; ☎ 098 577 2803, ⓔ trinidad @senatur.gov.py), is the most complete and important of all the *Treinta Pueblos*, and retains its magic (despite being just 700m from Ruta 6) thanks to its hilltop location. It best provides a sense of how full life would have been for the inhabitants of the missions. The most impressive structure is the **Iglesia Mayor**, filled with fantastically ornate stone carvings, the most famous being the **frieze of angels** stretching around the altar (look up). Try and time your visit to see the *Luz y Sonido* which, at nightfall, provides – you've guessed it – lights and sounds re-creating daily life in the mission.

Trinidad is easily reached on **public**

THE ENTRANCE AND EXIT OF THE JESUITS

The **Jesuits**, a religious order of Catholic missionaries, came to Paraguay in 1607 and based seven of their *Treinta Pueblos* (the thirty towns they built in South America between Brazil, Argentina, Bolivia and Paraguay) within the modern borders of the country. In the missions (also known as reductions), isolated from the colonial world, the arts flourished and the Jesuit-Guaraní partnership produced music, a printing press (the first in South America), sculpture and architecture. The missions survived and grew for 160 years, but the Jesuits were finally expelled in 1768, having plagued the colonial rulers for too long for their insular governance and protection of the indigenous community from exploitation. The Oscar-winning film *The Mission* (Roland Joffe; 1986), starring Robert De Niro, explores many of the reasons for their expulsion.

transport travelling in either direction on Ruta 6 (ask to be dropped at Trinidad at Km31, clearly signposted next to an incongruous power plant). Buses and *colectivos* to Trinidad leave the Terminal in Encarnación regularly (hourly; 30min–1hr). It's 250km from here to Ciudad del Este and you can flag down any of the larger buses, which will probably be heading there.

Jesús

Some 13km from the ruins at Trinidad lie those of **Jesús** (Jesús del Tavarangüe; daily 8am–5.30/7pm; ☎071 270 038, ☎098 573 4340, ✉jesus@senatur.gov.py), in rolling agricultural lands punctuated by palm trees and the simple wooden houses, painted in shades of blue and green. The mission is, again, set on a hill above the modern village and has enough original buildings to give visitors a feel for how the inhabitants lived. Although there would have been a great workforce living here, it was not completed before the expulsion of the Jesuits, and the church is unfinished, but it was on track to be one of the greatest.

To get between the sites, men with *mototaxis* hover (20–30min; Gs40,000 round trip), or there are *colectivos* that leave from the petrol station on Ruta 1, at the turning to Jesús, every hour or two (Mon–Sat 8am–7pm; Gs5000).

San Cosme

From Santiago in Misiones department, it's possible to get to **SAN COSME Y SAN DAMIÁN** (to give it its full name) along a new road from Ayolas, making a full circuit of Jesuit missions possible. The **mission** here (buy tickets from the astronomical observatory; there is usually a peace corps volunteer in town who can help translate into English if you let the staff know in advance; on the main plaza; daily 7am–5pm; ☎098 573 2956) is well worth the detour as it has two unique draws. Firstly, it is the only working mission from that period: the main building, dating to 1760, is still used as the town's main church. A restored doorway (don't miss the cheeky bat guarding the top) and the original structure of most of the mission still stands. You'll see original painted

> ### STAYING IN A POSADA
> To help local communities and tourists alike, the **posadas** scheme was established as a way of integrating the two. To open as a posada, the homeowner must have an en-suite guestroom, sometimes away from the rest of the house. Rooms cost Gs40,000–70,000, and SENATUR provides details (☎021 494 110, ⓦwww.paraguay .travel). There are posadas in Jesús, Trinidad and San Cosme. It's always best to call ahead to book; if you can't speak Spanish, call or email the Encarnación tourist office (see p.702), who can help.

wooden ceilings, as well as the only ironwork left in any of the missions on one of the windows.

The second attraction here is the **Centro Astronómico Buenaventura Suárez** (daily 7am–8pm or later in summer; included in joint ticket; ☎073 275 315), which promotes the work of the eponymous Jesuit astronomer who worked from this mission and developed the incredibly accurate sundial in the mission's plaza, among other celestial discoveries; he was the first person to document the Paraguayan sky. You'll be shown a documentary on the Guaraní understanding of the stratosphere and then taken to a little **planetarium**. Spending time in San Cosme's plaza or down by the river, experiencing the

8

> ### ★ TREAT YOURSELF
> There are two really good hotels on the road between Encarnación and Ciudad del Este, after Jesús and Trinidad. All buses heading between the two cities pass both hotels.
> **Papillon** Ruta 6, Km45 ☎076 724 0235, ⓦpapillon.com.py. With modern facilities, a lovely pool and pretty grounds, locals prefer this spotless choice. **Gs363,000**
> **Hotel Tirol** Ruta 6, Km20 ☎071 211 054, ⓦhoteltirol.com.py. Set within Atlantic Forest, its grounds are home to capuchin monkeys and some 190 bird species. Even if you don't stay here, you can use the (four) pools and walk around the forest for a minimal fee (Gs10,000). **Gs300,000**

8

THE MUSEUMS OF MISIONES

It's all well and good roaming the ruins of Itapúa department, but if these have piqued your interest there is a lot more to see in the neighbouring Misiones department with its four **museums** containing some of the finest remaining Jesuit-Guaraní art of all the *Treinta Pueblos*. There are five designated buses daily to San Ignacio, or any bus heading south along Ruta 1 will drop you there (3–4hr from Asunción). From here it's easy to hop on local *colectivos* to the other towns; taxis between the towns will cost upwards of Gs75,000.

Museo Diocesano del Arte Jesuítico Guaraní Two blocks from Ruta 1 South at Iturbe 870, San Ignacio ☎097 563 1352, ☎078 223 2223, ✉museoartejesuitico@ hotmail.com. San Ignacio was the first Jesuit-Guaraní mission established in Paraguay. The museum here contains art and history from this mission (it's the best place to see carved woodwork from the Jesuit period) and is housed in a seventeenth-century adobe building, which was the Jesuit college then and, amazingly, now. Daily 8–11.30am & 2–5.30pm. Gs15,000.

Museo de Santa María de Fe To the right of the church in the fenced building in Santa María ☎078 128 3332, ☎098 578 8011. The unrivalled collection of carved wooden statues displays the Guaraní Baroque style at its best, and you can see the differences between the carvings done by the Italian–Jesuit masters and those done

by their indigenous pupils. Tues–Sun 8.30–11.30am & 1.30–5pm (you may need to ask for a guide from their home across the plaza to get in). Gs15,000.

Loreto Chapel On Santa Rosa's main square ☎0858 285 221. The village of Santa Rosa has the only remaining Jesuit Loreto Chapel, with beautiful, muralled walls and some more fine carved pieces, as well as a full terrace of *casas de indios* from the original mission and a surviving high bell tower. Mon–Sat 7.30–11.30am; ask at the parochial office next door for it to be opened. Free.

Museo Tesoros Jesuíticos In Santiago, 18km south of Ruta 1 on the road to Ayolas next to the church on the main plaza ☎097 510 1120, ☎097 576 2008. Museum where the only remaining wooden altarpiece of any of the Jesuit ruins is displayed, along with other Jesuit treasures. Mon–Sat 8–11am & 2–5pm, Sun 9–11am. Gs15,000 for the guide.

ACCOMMODATION

★**Santa María Hotel** Opposite the museum across the plaza in Santa María ☎0781 283 311, ⓦsantamariahotel.org. The best place to stay in Misiones department, started by a Brit (Margaret, a travel writer with extensive knowledge of Paraguay) with the aim of generating employment for locals, this pint-size hotel has great food, excellent English is spoken, and country-wide tours are offered. Includes American breakfast. Rooms (per person) Gs140,000

enormity of the sky here, is an unforgettable Paraguayan experience.

There are direct **buses** from Encarnación (2–3 daily; Gs50,000; 2hr), or catch a *colectivo* (every 1hr 30min–2hr, 6am–6pm; Gs20,000) to San Cosme from Coronel Bogado's bus terminal (any bus passing along Ruta 1 between Asunción and Encarnación will stop in Coronel Bogado).

Coronel Bogado is a sizeable town with ATM and money-changing facilities. San Cosme's only **accommodation** option (and a good one) is its posada (see box, p.705).

CIUDAD DEL ESTE

Commercial, tacky, frequently intimidating and occasionally sordid, **CIUDAD DEL ESTE** ("city of the east") is a

shock to the system for many entering Paraguay for the first time; you'd be forgiven if your first instinct is to escape across the Puente de la Amistad into Brazil. Paraguay's second city, with a population of some 220,000, is hard to love, but do stick around and explore the sights: it does get better. Founded in 1957 as a garden city named Puerto Presidente Stroessner, it grew rapidly as people flocked to the jobs and homes created by the **Itaipú Dam**. Capitalizing on its position on the triple frontier, the town provides cheap duty-free – and frequently contraband – goods to Brazilians and Argentines hungry for bargains; almost everything is priced in US dollars.

WHAT TO SEE AND DO

The city's relative modernity means that it has little in the way of sights, but don't miss the **Museo de la Tierra Guaraní** (Hernandarias; Mon 2.30–5pm, Tues–Sat 8–11.30am & 2.30–5pm, Sun 8–11.30am; ☎061 599 8638), an excellent new museum charting 200 years of indigenous Guaraní culture through interactive multimedia displays.

CDE's **malls** (or *shoppings*) provide the real entertainment, with shops, bars, clubs, arcades and cinemas. **Shopping Zuni** and **Shopping Corazón**, both on Avenida San Blas alongside the Ruta Internacional, are two of the best for entertainment (Corazón has better eating and drinking, Zuni has one of Paraguay's few cinemas out of the capital). The real attractions, however, lie in the surrounding area, including the dam and numerous nature reserves.

ARRIVAL AND INFORMATION

By plane Aeropuerto Internacional Guaraní, 30km west of town on Ruta 7, has regular flights to Asunción, as well as destinations in Brazil and Argentina (ⓦtam.com.br), but suffers from frequent unexplained cancellations. A taxi to most points in the city costs Gs150,000.

By bus The bus terminal (☎061 510 421) is some way south of the centre on Chaco Boreal y Capitán del Puerto, adjacent to the Estadio P. Sarubi on Gral. Bernardino Caballero. There are *colectivos*, but if you arrive with luggage it's safer to take a taxi (Gs25,000 to Centro).

Destinations Asunción (hourly; 5hr); Encarnación (hourly; 4–5hr); Foz do Iguaçu (every 15min, 45min if no traffic); Puerto Iguazú (every 30min–1hr, 1hr if no traffic).

Tourist information SENATUR's office (daily 7am–7pm; ☎061 508 810, ⓔsenaturcde@senatur.gov.py) is at Av Adrian Jara y Mcal. Estigarribia, just off Ruta Internacional down Av del Lago next to the bus stands opposite Shopping Corazón. They have good free maps of the city. Good road maps can be bought at Touring and Automovil Club Paraguayo (Av San Blas Km1.5 in petrol station).

Tours Mariza Martinez (☎098 365 4619, ⓔmariza@cosmos.com.py) organizes tours for two agencies and can arrange English-speaking guides to most of the surrounding places if you write in advance. You could also try Mavani, who work in CDE with Exchange Tours (offices next to each other in Edificio Saba, Av Nanawa 90, at Jara, ☎061 500 766, ⓦmavani.com.py).

ACCOMMODATION

Mid-range accommodation in Ciudad del Este is widely available, but cheap options are thin on the ground and seedy. Avoid the area around the bus station and head for the cluster of decent hotels that line E. R. Fernández, two blocks north of the Ruta Internacional near the bridge. All prices include breakfast, wi-fi, TV and a/c unless stated.

★**Austria** E. R. Fernández 165 ☎061 504 213, ⓦhotelaustriarestaurante.com. Excellent rooms with TV, minibar and a spacious terrace with majestic views out over the river. The restaurant is also recommended, even if you do not plan to stay, for its pleasant faux-alpine ambience and good range of food. Gs220,000

Casa Alta Hostel Tacuru Pucu 20 at Avenida del Lago ☎097 350 8022, ⓦcasaaltahostel.com. Its location outside the city centre (25min walk) means this hostel has plenty of space for a swimming pool, barbecue area, several chill rooms and a sunset terrace with hammocks: a welcome oasis of calm after a hectic day in the city. Dorms Gs70,000, doubles Gs150,000

Hummingbird Hostel Los Sauces 220 ☎097 364 0397. Away from the bustle but close to the city centre, this basic hostel has all the necessary amenities. Welcoming hostess speaks excellent English, and you can spot hummingbirds in the tranquil garden. Dorms Gs70,000

8

CIUDAD DEL ESTE ORIENTATION

The **Ruta Internacional**, running east–west through the centre of town, leads to the rest of Paraguay one-way, and Brazil via the bridge over the Río Paraná the other. It is flanked by **Av San Blas** going east and **Av Monseñor Rodríguez** going west. Nearly all the malls, markets and shops are along this mammoth avenue. At the roundabout, just before the Ruta leads down to the bridge, **Pioneros del Este** runs south and splits around one of the parks into Alejo Garcia and Gral. Bernadino Caballero (which goes to the bus station). Most hotels and restaurants are based in the **Centro**, which comprises the blocks south of the Ruta Internacional and east of Pioneros del Este running to the river – Gral. A. Jara is the main street in the Centro – or **San Blas** neighbourhood, which is immediately north of the Centro across the Ruta Internacional.

E.R. Fernández is packed with hotels with stunning views over the Río Acaray at its juncture with the Paraná. The Centro becomes deserted in the evenings as trading stops, and nightlife is based in the **Boquerón** neighbourhood, southwest of the centre off Gral. Bernadino Caballero.

EATING AND DRINKING

Food tends to be pricier here than elsewhere in Paraguay. For cheap food, try the *comedor* for workers between the southbound Ruta Internacional and Av Monseñor Rodriguez. Restaurants in the Centro tend to close around 9pm.

★**Época** Av Rogelio Benítez 439, approx 700m up Av Bernardino Caballero from the Centro ☎061 514 984. Not cheap, but this 1950s Americana-themed bar/restaurant is a stand-out bar in distinctly un-cool Paraguay. There's a dancefloor with mirror-ball, stage and live music (with small entrance fee), and the food has names like the "Steak 'n' Shake", while cocktails are named after movies. Worth booking a table if you want to go for the music. Tues–Thurs 6pm–midnight, Fri & Sat 6pm–5.30am.

Fast Way Av Rogelio Benitez ☎061 500 763, ⓦfastway .com.py. It won't win any prizes for imagination, but this restaurant has a buzzy atmosphere (sometimes with live music) and a nice terrace; a solid bet for international fast food. Daily 11am–2am.

Gouranga Av Eugenio Pampliega, at Eusebio Ayala, behind the Municipalidad complex ☎061 510 362. An Indian vegetarian restaurant with bargain set lunches (Gs30,000) including veggie takes on Paraguayan classics and inventive fresh juices. Daily 7am–3pm.

Ña Morocha Choferes del Chaco and Campo Vía ☎061 500 005. Best place in the city for *empanadas* and other traditional snacks. Mon–Sat 7.30am–9pm, Sun 8am–3pm.

Tia Lili Carlos Antonio López, at Oscar Rivas ☎061 509 444, ⓦtialili.lgdsa.com.py. A great place to sample exactly the kind of typical – and cheap – Paraguayan food that can be hard to find elsewhere, like *Caldo de Surubí* (fish stew) and *Chipa Guazú* (an eggy corn bread). This also serves as a relaxed bar in the evening, when tables spring up on the street. Mains Gs20,000. Daily 24hr.

SHOPPING

CDE is known as the "Supermarket of South America", and just about everything you can think of can be purchased here at prices well below market rates. Electronics, alcohol and perfumes provide the best deals, but beware of substandard goods and don't be afraid to haggle. Compare prices beforehand and ask for products to be tested; not all dealers are honest. Most bargains are found in the maze of shops and stalls on either side of Ruta Internacional, though the area attracts thieves – do not carry valuables with you.

DIRECTORY

Banks and exchange Many on Av Jara.
Car rental Various options at the airport, or Localiza (☎061 572 456) on Av San Blas (Ruta Internacional) Km4.
Hospital Fundación Tesai on Av Caballero behind the bus terminal.
Internet *Shopping Mirage* Gs5000/hr.
Laundry At least three laundries along E.R. Fernandez two blocks north of the Ruta Internacional.
Post office Alejo Garcia, at Centro Democrático (Mon–Fri 7am–6pm, Sat 7am–noon).

AROUND CIUDAD DEL ESTE

The main reasons for staying in CDE are to visit **Iguazú Falls** – both the Brazilian (see p.353) and Argentine (see p.86) sides are an easy day-trip from here – and the **Itaipú Dam**, the second-largest dam in the world (and the largest producer of hydroelectric power), and an extraordinary engineering feat. The Itaipú Dam company oversees eight small nature reserves, but if you have time, head straight for the **Reserva Bosque Mbaracayú** (see box, p.693).

Itaipú Dam

Sited 20km north of Ciudad del Este, **ITAIPÚ** (in Hernandarias 10km from CDE; ☎061 599 8069, ⓦwww.itaipu.gov.py) was once referred to as one of the seven wonders of the modern world. With a maximum height of 195m and generating up to 75,000GWh of energy per year (and fulfilling 87 percent of Paraguay's energy needs), it's still something to behold. Visits are by **guided tour only** (on the hour: summer daily 8am–5pm, winter 8am–4pm; free, passport required; 1hr 30min), with a short documentary shown first. There are tours from the Brazilian side where you can pay to see the inner workings of the colossal 1km-long machine room, which is fantastic, but as tours from the Paraguay side are free, those on a budget will be more than satisfied with the enormous vistas outside. There are also spectacular light shows on Friday and Saturday nights at 7.30pm (free, but reserve in advance with passport details).

The project's backers had to invest heavily in ecological damage-limitation projects, establishing the **Centro Ambiental** (Tues–Sun 8am–6pm; free), a few kilometres south of the dam's entrance (back towards CDE) and easily reached by taxi. It contains a good museum about the Guaraní peoples, as well as an excellent zoo by South American standards, set up to house animals rescued from the flooding. The Dam also runs several **nature reserves**

CROSSING TO BRAZIL AND ARGENTINA

The Puente de la Amistad (Ponte da Amizade in Portuguese, or Friendship Bridge), across the Río Paraná, marks the border with the Brazilian town of **Foz do Iguaçu**. Immigration formalities take place at either end of the bridge. This is Paraguay's busiest border crossing, and there are frequently huge queues in either direction (if crossing by bus, try to go before midday and return after 2pm). A local bus runs from the bus terminal along Av Gral. Bernardino Caballero, Pioneros del Este, then to the Ruta Internacional to the terminal in "Foz", as it's known locally (every 15min; duration depends on bridge traffic; Gs8000). Often crossing on foot is quicker, but be sure to obtain all necessary entrance and exit stamps; you need them even if you are just visiting the waterfalls. Traffic police do not help matters by putting pressure on buses to speed up, occasionally directing them away from the customs checkpoint. A taxi will cost around Gs90,000, while a cheaper (and certainly more hair-raising) option is a motorcycle-taxi (Gs45,000).

The company Río Uruguay runs buses daily between CDE and **Puerto Iguazú** in Argentina (every 30min–1hr, 7am–6pm, duration depends on bridge traffic; Gs10,000 or AR$10). It starts from the Terminal, but you can catch it anywhere along Av Gral. Bernardino Caballero, or on the Ruta Internacional. You'll have to get stamps before the bridge to leave Paraguay, and again at the Argentine border, some 20min later. You do not need to get stamps to go in and out of Brazil if you do not plan to get off the bus before Argentina. Even if the buses tell you they will not wait, be sure that your paperwork is in order; another bus will come along.

in this area, but these are really only worth looking into if you won't have time to make it to Mbaracayú or San Rafael (see box, p.693).

The Dam is easily accessed by **public transport**; simply jump on any bus marked "Hernandarias" from the bus stands next to the SENATUR office (Gs3000; 20min) and get off at Km17 where you'll see the entrance on your right. There is also a taxi stand here for the return journey.

CONCEPCIÓN

From CDE it's possible to catch a connecting bus from transport hub Coronel Oviedo up to **CONCEPCIÓN**, although it's a comfier journey from Asunción. A cultured, peaceful and historic port town on the bank of the Río Paraguay, Concepción is the main trading centre in the northeast of the country. It has a wealth of **museums** for a town of its size and has become popular with tourists as a centre for rustic but picturesque **river trips** along the Río Paraguay to the Paraguayan **Pantanal** (see box, p.693).

WHAT TO SEE AND DO

Concepción is best known by Paraguayans for its graceful Italianate and Art Deco turn-of-the-twentieth-century **mansions**, with Villa Heyn (set back from C.A. López

between Brasil and Otaño), housing the regional government, arguably the finest example. The bulk of the tourist sights are in the centre, concentrated on the main street Avenida Pinedo, which runs north–south, with east–west streets running from Pinedo to the river. Presidente Franco goes from Pinedo to the port and is mainly commercial, Mariscal Estigarribia and Mariscal López run parallel to the south of Franco, and have three plazas between them, containing the bulk of the museums with beautiful nineteenth-century mansions on the streets between. While here, don't miss hanging out at the port at sunset with a *termo* of *tereré*, watching locals swimming in the river and the sun setting over the Chaco.

The museums

The town's small but high-quality museums are mostly only open in the morning. The ones not to miss include the **Museo del Cuartel de Villa Real** (Mcal. Estigarribia, at C.A. López; Mon–Sat 8am–noon; free; ☎097 180 3951), with a motley collection of historical artefacts housed in a refurbished part of the army barracks dating back to the Triple Alliance war. Nearby is the stately yellow and white **Palacio Municipal** dating from 1898 (pop in to see two enormous murals in the main hall), while the **Museo Cívico Municipal** (☎097 180 3951) houses a fascinating haul of paintings, fossils, musical instruments, items of clothing and furniture. One block south of the palace, on Mcal. López between Cerro Corá and Gral. Garay, is the **Teatro Municipal**, which currently plays host to the tourist information office.

ARRIVAL AND INFORMATION

By boat The Aquidabán (☎ 033 124 2435) goes upriver to Bahía Negra in the Paraguayan Pantanal once a week. In theory it leaves Concepción every Tues around 11am, arriving at dawn on Fri. It costs Gs100,000, or Gs180,000 with a bed (you'll need to take a hammock if not). Boats are uncomfortable, and while they should have basic food for sale, it's best to take your own food and water. The *Cacique II* leaves on Sun nights for Asunción (see p.698).

By bus Buses arrive at the terminal on Asunción, between Gral. Garay and Andrés Miancoff, eight blocks north of the town centre. NSA (☎ 021 289 1000, ⓦ nsa.com.py) and La Santaniana (☎ 021 558 961, ⓦ lasantaniana.com.py) are the best companies, offering national and international routes.

Destinations Asunción (7 daily; 7hr); Buenos Aires (daily; 24hr); Campo Grande, Brazil (4 daily; 7–10hr); Coronel Oviedo (daily; 6–7hr); Filadelfia (daily; 8hr); Pedro Juan Caballero (11 daily; 4–5hr); Vallemí (2 daily; 5hr); São Paulo, Brazil (daily; 24hr).

Tourist information Tourism is run by Elva Ruíz on behalf of the municipality, at the Teatro Municipal (Mon–Fri 8am–1pm). She speaks good English and Italian, and can offer the best service if you email or call her in advance (☎ 097 124 7648, ☎ 098 399 4372, ✉ eruizmendez @yahoo.com). She is able to help with booking accommodation, and provides information on the Pantanal.

ACCOMMODATION

There is a good range of accommodation in town, and a great *estancia* in the countryside. Hotels listed below include breakfast, TV, wi-fi and a/c unless specified.

IN TOWN

Francés Franco, at C.A. López ☎ 0331 242 383, ⓦ hotelfrancesconcepcion.com. The best bet in town, in a charming old building with a swimming pool and a good restaurant. Rooms with fan Gs120,000, a/c Gs150,000

Victoria Franco and Pedro Caballero ☎ 0331 242 256, ✉ hotelvictoria@hotmail.es. While sparklingly refurbished on the outside, the rooms may have seen better days, but it's great value, with a patio with orchids and ferns and two decent restaurants. Rooms with fan Gs90,000, with a/c Gs140,000

ESTANCIAS NEAR CONCEPCIÓN

Granja El Roble Km16 towards Belén ☎ 098 589 8446, ⓦ paraguay.ch. This farm offers treehouses, camping

space or cabins, and is very well set up for tourism. The owner offers all kinds of excursions – including the Chaco – as well as rafting and fishing. The website is in English and gives excellent details on how to get there. Camping Gs15,000, cabins Gs120,000

EATING AND DRINKING

There are numerous *copetíns* (snack bars) in town which serve juices, *empanadas* and sandwiches for next to nothing, and a market two blocks east of Pinedo on Don Bosco (extension of Franco), plus a supermarket at the corner of Pinedo and Estigarribia.

Palo Santo restaurant and chopería Franco, at Pedro Caballero, next to the *Hotel Victoria* ☎ 033 124 1454. Brazilian-run place in central Concepción, serving the best caipirihnas in town alongside traditional dishes. Tues–Sun 6.30pm–midnight.

★ **Toninho y Jandira** Mcal Estigarribia between Iturbe and Cerro Corá, in front of the Municipalidad ☎ 033 124 1415. An excellent Brazilian restaurant where a set price of Gs55,000 gives you a simple choice of beef or fish accompanied with a personal feast of rice, beans and five types of salads and vegetables. One portion is more than enough for two people. Closed Sun.

Hotel Victoria & La Quincha de Victoria Franco, at Pedro Caballero. The lunchtime restaurant is in the hotel itself and is a pleasant place for a Gs15,000 set lunch. The evening restaurant is right across the street, and is a popular outdoor spot to have a grill, steak, burger or beer, and listen to Paraguayan music. Mains Gs20,000–45,000.

DIRECTORY

Banks and exchange Avenidas Franco and Pinedo are lined with casas de cambio and banks, most of which have 24hr ATMs that accept international cards.

Hospital State-run hospital at Guillermo Cabral, at Doctor Macial Roig.

Internet Cyberplanet on Gral. Garay between Brasil and Mayor Julio Otaño. Gs5000/hr.

Laundry On Gral. Garay between Mayor Julio Otaño and Tte. 1 Eugenio Aguero.

Phone Copaco office on Franco between Pinedo and Yegros. Daily 7am–8.45pm.

Post office Correo Paraguayo, 485 Mcal. J.F. Estigarribia, at Gral. Garay.

West of the Paraguay

West of the Río Paraguay lies the area of the country that accounts for over sixty percent of the land, but with just two to three percent of the population, **THE CHACO**. The main route north from the capital is Ruta 9 – the "Trans-Chaco" – which takes you straight up through this "inferno verde", or "green inferno", as it is popularly known, and beyond to Bolivia. It is split into three departments, Presidente Hayes, Alto Paraguay and Boquerón, but it is more helpful to think of it as two climate zones – the **lower Chaco** being humid, and the **upper Chaco** being dry. Where they meet in the central Chaco there is a cluster of fascinating **Mennonite colonies** which provide the only real urban tourism in the whole place.

Vast swathes of the Chaco are uninhabited, and this, along with the extreme heat, makes it very dangerous to travel around, even for those who live here; locals always travel in groups. **Guided tours** are the easiest (and safest) way to see the highlights, which include stunning birdlife at the **Central Chaco Lagoons** (see box, p.693); however, these can be cripplingly expensive and difficult to organize. Exploring independently is not recommended.

THE MENNONITE COLONIES

While indigenous tribes still make up just over fifty percent of the Chaco's denizens (some 28,000 people), the German Mennonites, who first came to Paraguay in 1927 as a group of just 1700 or so to escape persecution or enforced participation in national service (Mennonites are pacifists), are now the largest minority group here. Despite their early struggles, today the Mennonites are some of the most prosperous people in Paraguay. They are the major dairy producers in the country and their three colonies operate with an efficiency that belies their isolated location, with beautifully kept gardens, ruler-straight streets and solidly made brick houses, interspersed with parks and pavements. The Mennonites here are relatively liberal, modern and open, and have embraced tourism and relish the opportunity to show off their achievements to the few visitors who pass through.

WHAT TO SEE AND DO

The **three Mennonite colonies** who settled here each established one of the central Chaco towns, and the only thing to do in the towns, other than seeing how the Mennonites, indigenous peoples and *mestizo* Paraguayans rub along together, is to visit the interesting **Mennonite museums**, monuments and cooperative supermarkets in each.

Unless you are a motor-racing fanatic, the area is best avoided in the last week of September when it becomes gripped by **Trans-Chaco Rally** fever (ⓦrally.com.py). Billed as one of the toughest motorized events on earth, it is accompanied by a considerable hike in hotel prices and you will have to book well in advance.

Filadelfia

Thanks to its proximity to the Ruta Trans-Chaco, **FILADELFIA**, home to the Fernheim Colony, has grown to be the capital of the Boquerón department and receives all the long-distance buses, as well as being the hub for "local" buses, for the Chaco. Of all the colonies, it also has the most to do in town, with several museums, most on or around the main Avenida Hindenburg. In a prim park at the corner of Calle Unruh sit the **Museo Jakob Unger**, which houses taxidermy of Chaco wildlife, and the **Museo de la Colonia** (both Mon–Sat 7–11.30am; free; ☎0491 417 380), housed in the only surviving building from the original pioneers. In the same park is a **tourist information** office run by very helpful Gati Harder, who speaks perfect English (daily 7–11am; ☎0491 417 380, ☎098 582 0746, ☎turismo @fernheim.com.py) and will happily give talks on Mennonite history, and her other speciality, the trees of the Chaco. A half-day guided tour, arranged through the Cooperative Fernheim (☎049 141 7000, ⓦwww.fernheim.com.py), costs Gs150,000.

Loma Plata and Neu Halbstadt

The largest of the Mennonite towns is **LOMA PLATA**, home to the Menno Colony, whose Chortitzer Cooperative makes Paraguay's largest dairy brand, Trébol, but other than the small **Museo**

8

8

de Historia Mennonita (next to the cooperative on the main street; daily 7–11.30am; ☎098 356 9922), it's the least interesting of the colonies, but Patrick Friesen is an excellent guide (✉patrick@chortitzer.com.py).

The Neuland Colony's main town, **NEU HALBSTADT** (locally known as Neuland; ⊛neuland.com.py), has more to offer tourists thanks to its dynamic tourist officer Heinz Wiebe (information office next to the coop; ☎097 170 1634, ✉hwiebe@neuland.com.py). Although he only speaks Spanish, if you get in touch with him before you go he can arrange a translator for his tours of all three colonies.

ARRIVAL AND INFORMATION

Although all three Mennonite cities are populous (and growing rapidly), all maintain a very suburban feel with wide streets and huge blocks. They are tiring to walk around and can feel inaccessible at times, but people tend to be very helpful. There are ATMs which accept foreign cards on the principal avenue in each town, and each has a post office and a supermarket.

By bus There is a bus terminal in Filadelfia, of sorts, on Chaco Boreal, one block west of Hindenburg. Most services from Filadelfia pass through Loma Plata en route to the capital.
Destinations Asunción (5 daily; 7hr); Concepcion (daily; 4–5hr); Mariscal Estigarribia (2 daily); Neuland and Loma Plata (2 daily to each; 30min).

Taxi There is a taxi rank on Hindenburg in Filadelfia of 4WDs who charge some Gs140,000 to Loma Plata, Gs200,000 to Neuland, or Gs30,000 within town.

Tours Other than the guides mentioned, it's worth looking at Paraguay Salvaje, ⊛paraguay-salvaje.com.py, and ⊛chaco-wildlife.org, while Stel Turismo have an office in Filadelfia (☎049 143 2670).

ACCOMMODATION

The Mennonites run mid-range, spotless, efficient hotels in all three colonies. All are en-suite, have wi-fi, TV, a/c, and offer very good buffet breakfasts, as well as having dining options.
Boquerón Opposite the Coop on main street Av 1 de Febrero, Neu Halbstadt ☎049 324 306, ✉hotel@neuland .com.py. Recently refurbished, this lovely Mennonite hotel has lawns and flower beds flanking spacious rooms with pine beds. Double Gs180,000
Estancia Iparoma ☎098 194 0050, ⊛estanciaiparoma .com. Worth investigating if you want to stay out in the Chaco

CROSSING TO BOLIVIA

At the small town of **La Patria**, a fully paved road (formerly Picada 108) branches off the Trans-Chaco to the border crossing of **Fortín Infante Rivarola**. There is a small guard post here that does not have exit stamps; you have to stop in Mariscal Estigarriba en route to do immigration formalities, using the NSA bus service to get there. This bus will only stop to pick up passengers in Filadelfia if there are enough people waiting. The border point here is extremely isolated and a popular smuggling route, so you are not advised to attempt to cross the border here by yourself. The best-known bus from Filadelfia to Santa Cruz in Bolivia is Stel Turismo (Av Hindenburg), but you still have to go via Mariscal Estigarribia. Alternatively, buses from Asunción (1–2 daily; 30hr) are run by the companies Yacyretá, Pycasu and Río Paraguay. Bus tickets from Filadelfia and Asunción are the same price.

without straying so far you could put yourself in danger, this Mennonite-run working farm, 19km from Filadelfia, provides accommodation, food, horseriding and other activities. Best organized through Gati at the Filadelfia tourist office (see above). B&B Gs200,000, camping Gs20,000
Golondrina Av Hindenburg 365-Sur, at Palo Santo, Filadelfia ☎049 143 3111, ⊛hotelgolondrina.com. Run by Paraguayans, laid out in a motel style, with clean but soulless rooms; it's one of the cheaper B&Bs with wi-fi in Filadelfia. Doubles Gs180,000

EATING AND DRINKING

Boquerón Boquerón, at Miller, Filadelfia. Big and bright restaurant with a good choice of food including everything from Mexican to pizza, and from buffet (Gs60,000/kg) to burgers (Gs18,000). Daily from 7pm.
Hotel Florida Av Hindenburg 165–S, Filadelfia ☎049 143 2151. International buffet of meats and salads (Gs58.000/kg) alongside traditional dishes. Nice outdoor patio and excellent service from trilingual staff. Daily lunch & dinner.
Girasol Unruh 122, at Av Hindenburg, Filadelfia ☎049 143 2078. Regarded as the best restaurant in the colonies, this place does a great range of grills, as well as a buffet (Gs62,000/kg). Lovely garden for drinks, too. Mon–Sat lunch & dinner, Sun lunch.

MACHU PICCHU

Peru

HIGHLIGHTS

❶ **Machu Picchu** Walk the Inca Trail to these legendary ruins. **See p.759**

❷ **Nazca Lines** Dazzling geometric designs etched into the desert. **See p.774**

❸ **Colca Canyon** At its deepest point the canyon reaches 4km. **See p.782**

❹ **Huaraz** Trek the stunning snowcapped peaks of the Andes. **See p.789**

❺ **Cajamarca** Outstanding architecture, great food and the Northern Highlands. **See p.809**

❻ **Madre de Dios** Lush rainforest home to the world's largest macaw clay lick. **See p.824**

HIGHLIGHTS ARE MARKED ON THE MAP ON PP.716–717

ROUGH COSTS

Daily budget Basic US$25, occasional treat US$35

Drink Cristal beer US$1–2

Food Lunchtime menu US$3–5

Hostel/budget hotel US$7–12

Travel Tumbes–Lima: 18hr, US$20–40, Lima–Cusco: 22hr, US$25–55

FACT FILE

Population 30.3 million

Language Spanish, Quechua, Aymara

Currency Nuevo Sol (S)

Capital Lima (population: 8.5 million)

International phone code ☎51

Time zone GMT -5hr

9

Introduction

Peru is the most varied and exciting of all the South American nations, with a combination of Inca relics, immense desert coastline and vast tracts of tropical rainforest, divided by the Andes, its chain of breathtaking peaks, over 7km high and 400km wide in places, rippling the length of the nation. So distinct are these regions that it is very difficult to generalize about the country, but one thing for sure is that Peru offers a unique opportunity to experience an incredibly wide range of spectacular scenery, a wealth of heritage and a vibrant living culture.

Hedonists will head for the beaches of **Máncora**, the nightclubs of **Lima** and the bars of **Cusco** – the latter a city where a cosmopolitan lifestyle coexists alongside pre-Columbian buildings and ancient festivals. Just as easily, you can retreat from civilization, travelling deep into the remote parts of the **Peruvian Amazon** or walking in the footsteps of the Incas, taking on the challenge of the **Inca Trail** to reach the ancient citadel of **Machu Picchu**. You can take flight over the **Nazca Lines** to ponder the meaning of the giant figures etched into the desert and hike the canyons and snow-tipped peaks around **Arequipa** and **Trujillo**.

In the more rural parts of Peru, local life has changed little in the last four centuries, though roads and tracks now connect almost every corner of the country, making travel quite straightforward. Nevertheless, you should be prepared to accept the occasional episode of social unrest or travel delays caused by natural disasters with the good humour of the locals.

CHRONOLOGY

c.40,000–15,000 BC The first Peruvians, descendants of nomadic tribes, cross into the Americas from Asia during the last ice age.

2600 BC The complex civilization at the site of Caral develops, lasting for an estimated 500 years.

200–600 AD Emergence and growth of the Moche and Nazca cultures.

1200 The Inca Empire begins to emerge.

1438–70 Pachacutec becomes ruler of the Inca Empire. Machu Picchu and the Inca capital of Cusco are constructed.

1500–30 The Inca Empire stretches over 5500km, from southern Colombia right down to northern Chile.

1532 Francisco Pizarro leads his band of 170 conquistadors from Tumbes to Cajamarca, capturing the Inca ruler Atahualpa and massacring thousands of Inca warriors.

1533 Atahualpa is executed and the Spaniards install a puppet Inca ruler, Manco Inca.

1535 Lima is founded by Pizarro as the "City of Kings".

WHEN TO VISIT

The best time to visit Peru will depend upon which areas of the country you intend to visit, and what activities you plan on doing. **The coast** tends to be mostly dry year-round, but sits under a blanket of fog from April to November each year (especially in Lima); the driest, sunniest months here (Dec–March) tend to coincide with the rainiest weather elsewhere.

In the **Andes** the seasons are more clearly marked, with heavy rains from December to April and a relatively dry period from June to September, which, although it can be cold at night, is certainly the best time for trekking and most outdoor activities. In much of the **jungle**, rainfall is heavier and more frequent, and it's hot and humid all year. In the lowland rainforest areas around Iquitos water levels are higher between December and January, which offers distinct advantages for spotting wildlife and accessing remote creeks by canoe.

Those wishing to avoid the crowds will prefer to visit during the shoulder seasons of May and September to November, as from May to August many popular tourist attractions are packed with tour groups.

1538–41 Conquistadors fight for control of the colony. Diego de Almagro is executed by Pizarro, who in turn is assassinated by Almagro's son.

1542 The Viceroyalty of Peru is established by Spain's King Charles I, with Lima as its capital.

1571 Unsuccessful rebellion by the last Inca, Túpac Amaru, results in his execution.

1821 Argentine general José de San Martín declares Peruvian Independence on July 28.

1824 The last of the Spanish forces are defeated at the battles of Junín and Ayacucho. Peru becomes an independent state.

1879–83 The War of the Pacific with Chile. Chile is victorious, annexing a large chunk of southern Peru, including the nitrate-rich northern Atacama desert.

1911 Hiram Bingham discovers Machu Picchu.

1948–56 The economy spirals into ruin and a military junta takes control.

1969–75 Massive economic crisis occurs after General Juan Velasco nationalizes foreign-owned businesses, bans foreign investors and gives all the hacienda land to workers' cooperatives.

1980–92 The Maoist Sendero Luminoso ("Shining Path"), led by Abimael Guzman, carries out terrorist attacks against the government. The conflict causes 69,000 deaths and "disappearances", at least 75 percent of them Quechua-speaking highlanders.

1985 Socialist Alan García comes to power. Financial reforms cause massive hyperinflation and trigger the worst economic crisis Peru has ever experienced.

1990 Surprise presidential victory by Alberto Fujimori over renowned author Mario Vargas Llosa. Privatization of state-owned companies improves economic conditions.

1994 Amnesty offered to Shining Path members; more than 6000 surrender.

2000 Fujimori re-elected amid allegations of electoral fraud, but flees to Japan shortly after due to revelations of corruption, extortion, arms trafficking and human rights abuses.

2001–06 Alejandro Toledo becomes Peru's first full-blooded indigenous president. Protests against the US-backed eradication of coca plantations and nationwide strikes ensue, but the economy remains stable.

2007 Massive earthquake devastates the coastal province of Ica, killing 520 people.

2007–09 Fujimori extradited to Peru. After a lengthy public trial he is convicted to 25 years in prison for authorizing death squad killings in 1991–92.

2010 Mario Vargas Llosa wins the Nobel Prize for Literature.

2011 Ollanta Humala wins the presidential election in a run-off vote.

2012 Shining Path faction leader Artemio is captured and charged with terrorism and drug trafficking.

ARRIVAL AND DEPARTURE

Peru has land borders with Chile, Ecuador, Bolivia, Brazil and Colombia. While the borders with Chile, Ecuador and Bolivia are easily negotiated, the borders with Brazil and Colombia are deep in the jungle and less easily reached. Lima is a major transport hub with international flights from the US and Europe; there are also good connections from Lima to other South American countries. International flights within South America tend to be expensive, while national flights within Peru average around US$90 to any destination. Save money by crossing borders by land and only flying within Peru.

Major operators include LAN Peru and Avianca; also American Airlines from the US, Iberia from Europe via Madrid, and KLM from Europe via Amsterdam. Local airlines include Star Peru and Peruvian Airlines. US citizens are required to show a return ticket if flying in.

If crossing land borders from Chile, Bolivia or Ecuador, aim to take a long-distance bus that goes directly to your destination across the border – it may be a little pricier, but that way you avoid hanging around dodgy border crossing areas and the drivers can assist you with border formalities.

FROM BOLIVIA

The southern cities of Puno, Cusco and Arequipa are easily reached overland from Bolivia. There are two crossings: **Yungayo** from Copacabana on Lake Titicaca, and **Desaguadero** from La Paz; Yungayo is marginally less chaotic. Regular buses run direct to Puno (and some to Cusco) from both destinations. It's difficult, though not impossible, to take a boat to Puerto Maldonado from Bolivia's Puerto Heath via Puerto Pardo.

FROM BRAZIL

It's a simple bus journey along the Interoceanic Highway and across the bridge from the Brazilian border post of **Assis Brasil** to the Peruvian village of Iñapari, which is three hours by bus from Puerto Maldonado (see p.826). You can also reach Iquitos via the Amazon from

9

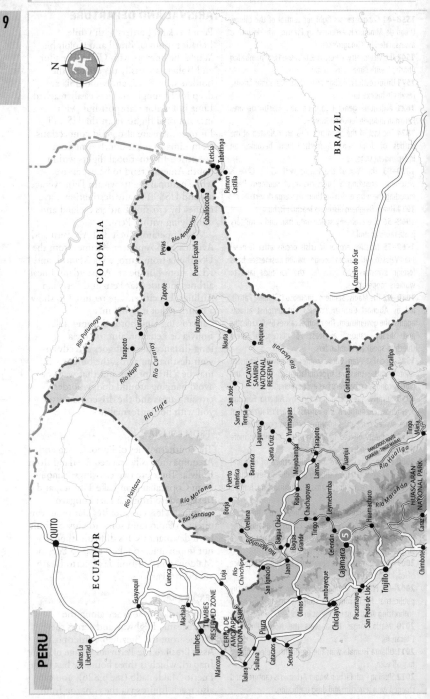

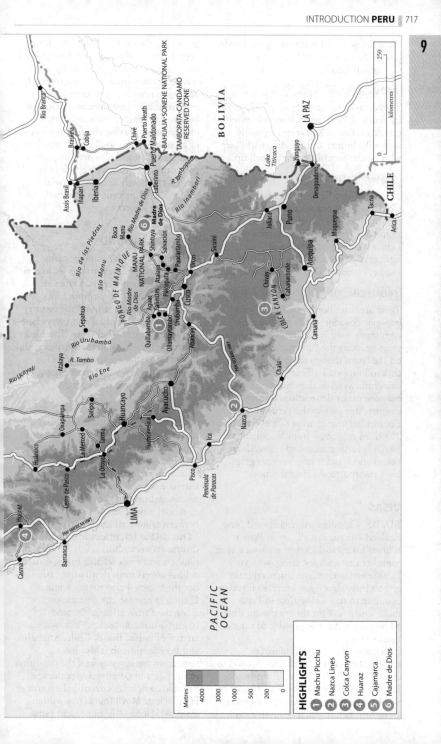

BOLIVIA

LA PAZ

CHILE

Rio Branco
Cobija
Assis Brasil
Iberia
Iñapari
Brasiléia
Puerto Heath
Chivé
Puerto Maldonado
Laberinto
TAMBOPATA-CANDAMO
RESERVED ZONE
BAHUAJA-SONENE NATIONAL PARK
R. Tambopata
Rio Inambari
Lake Titicaca
Yunguyo
Desaguadero
Puno
Juliaca
Arequipa
Moquegua
Tacna
Arica
Camaná
Chala
Nazca
Ica
Pisco
LIMA
Barranca
Casma
Huaraz
Cerro de Pasco
Huánuco
La Oroya
Tarma
La Merced
San Ramón
Satipo
Oxapampa
Huancayo
Huancavelica
Ayacucho
Abancay
Cusco
Urubamba
Ollantaytambo
Pisac
Aguas Calientes
Quillabamba
Paucartambo
Pilcopata
Atalaya
Shintuya
Salvación
Boca Manu
Colca Canyon
Chivay
Cabanaconde
Sicuani
Vitos
Madre de Dios
MANU NATIONAL PARK
PONGO DE MAINIQUE
Rio Madre de Dios
Rio de las Piedras
Rio Manu
Sepahua
Rio Urubamba
R. Tambo
Rio Ucayali
Rio Ene
Atalaya
Peninsula de Paracas
PACIFIC OCEAN
PAN-AMERICAN HWY
PAN OCEAN HWY

HIGHLIGHTS
1 Machu Picchu
2 Nazca Lines
3 Colca Canyon
4 Huaraz
5 Cajamarca
6 Madre de Dios

Metres
4000
3000
1000
500
200
0

0   250
kilometres

9

the small port of **Tabatinga** via the border post of Santa Rosa, just like from Colombia's Leticia.

FROM CHILE

The **Arica–Tacna** border (see p.782) in the far south of Peru causes few problems for travellers. Taxi *colectivos* run regularly across the border and the driver will help with border formalities for a small tip.

FROM COLOMBIA

The easiest way to reach Peru from Colombia is by bus via Ecuador, but if in the Amazon, you can also take a boat from the Colombian border town of Leticia to Iquitos via the small immigration post of Santa Rosa; river journeys take two and a half to three days.

FROM ECUADOR

There are three border crossings open between Ecuador and Peru. The most commonly used is the **Tumbes–Machala** crossing along the Panamerican Highway on the coast, though the crossing from **Loja** to Piura via La Tina is also straightforward, as there are direct buses between major destinations in each country, stopping at the Peruvian and Ecuadorian immigration offices en route. The third crossing – from Vilcabamba to Jaén – is further inland where roads are not so good, and it involves changing basic transportation several times.

VISAS

EU, US, Canadian, Australian and New Zealand citizens can all stay in Peru as tourists for up to 183 days without a visa; for other nationalities, check with your local Peruvian embassy. You're typically given ninety days upon entry, so if you're planning to stay a long time in Peru, make sure to ask for the maximum time allowance, as it is not possible to extend tourist visas.

All nationalities need a **tourist or embarkation card** (*tarjeta de embarque*) to enter Peru, which is issued at the border or on the plane before landing. In theory you have to show an outbound ticket (by air or bus) before you'll be given a card,

but this is almost never checked. Keep a copy of the tourist card and your passport on you at all times – particularly when travelling away from the main towns. It is very important that you keep your original tourist card safe, since you will be asked to return it to immigration officials when leaving the country. Fines of around S15 are applicable if you lose your card. You will also need to present your card every time you check in at hostels and hotels in order to avoid paying the 18 percent tax that national citizens are subject to.

GETTING AROUND

Given the size of the country, many Peruvians and holiday-makers fly to their destinations, as all Peruvian cities are within a two-hour flight from Lima. Most budget travellers get around the country by bus, as these go just about everywhere and are extremely good value. There is a limited rail service along some routes, and though often picturesque they are considerably slower and more expensive than the equivalent bus journey.

BY BUS

Peru's privately operated buses offer remarkably low fares. Buses range from the efficient and relatively luxurious *cama* or *semicama* buses with air conditioning, snacks/meals included and on-board entertainment, to the more basic *económico* buses, to the scruffy old ex-school buses used on local runs between remote villages.

Cruz del Sur (⟲cruzdelsur.com.pe) and **Oltursa** (⟲www.oltursa.com.pe) offer the plushest and most reliable buses; Cruz del Sur covers most destinations (though not the Cusco–Puno route), while Oltursa is best for any destination along the Panamericana. **Ormeño** (⟲grupo-ormeno.com.pe) has routes as far as Colombia, Brazil, Chile, Argentina and Bolivia, though it also has a reputation for lateness, and the condition of the buses has declined over the years. Reliable companies covering the north of Peru include **Movil Tours** (⟲moviltours .com.pe), **Línea** (⟲linea.pe) and **Tepsa**

(🌐www.tepsa.com.pe), while the south is covered by the cheaper **Flores** (🌐floreshnos.net), **TransMar** (🌐transmar .com.pe) and **Soyuz** (🌐www.soyuz .com.pe). For intercity rides, it's best to buy tickets in advance direct from the bus company offices; for local trips, you can buy tickets on the bus itself.

If storing main luggage in the hold, you should get a receipt, which you'll need to hand in at the end of your journey to claim your luggage. Keep your hand luggage with you at all times, particularly if travelling on cheaper buses like Soyuz.

BY TAXI, MOTOTAXI AND COLECTIVO

Taxis are easily found at any time in almost every town. Any car can become a taxi simply by sticking a taxi sign up in the front window; a lot of people take advantage of this to supplement their income. However, this has led to an increase in crime, so if possible call a radio taxi from a recommended company. Always fix the price in advance, since few taxis have meters. Relatively short journeys in Lima generally cost around S7, but it's cheaper elsewhere. Taxi drivers in Peru do not expect tips.

In many towns, you'll find small cars and *mototaxis* (**motorcycle rickshaws**). The latter are always cheaper than taxis, if slightly more dangerous and not that comfortable. Outside Lima, you will almost never pay more than S5 for a ride within a town.

Colectivos (shared taxis) are a very useful way of getting around. They look like private cars or taxis but run a fixed route; each has a small sign in the window with the destination and can squeeze in up to six passengers. They connect all the coastal towns, and many of the larger centres in the mountains, and tend to be faster than the bus, though they often charge twice as much. *Colectivos* can be found in the centre of a town or at major stopping places along the main roads. The price is generally double that of *combis*, depending on distance travelled. *Colectivo* minibuses, also known as **combis**, can squeeze in twice as many people, or often more. They cost on average S5 per person, per hour travelled. Do keep in mind that in the cities, particularly in Lima, *colectivos* (especially *combis*) have a poor reputation for safety. They frequently crash, turn over and knock down pedestrians.

BY TRAIN

Peru's spectacular train journeys are in themselves a major attraction. **Peru Rail** (🌐perurail.com) runs passenger services from Puno to Cusco, from where another line heads down the magnificent Urubamba Valley as far as Machu Picchu (see box, p.764). **Inca Rail** (🌐incarail .com) also operates the Cusco-Machu Picchu route. The world's second-highest railway route, from Lima to Huancayo, is considered to be among the most scenic in the world, but it only runs once a month or so; check departure dates and times at 🌐www.ferrocarrilcentral.com.pe.

Trains tend to be slower than buses and considerably more expensive, but they do allow ample time to enjoy the scenery, and are quite comfortable. If you're planning on visiting Machu Picchu but don't intend to hike the Inca Trail, you have no option but to take a tourist train priced in US dollars.

At the time of writing, the Cusco–Puno service costs S490, while a bus costs S50; the cheapest train fare from Ollantaytambo in the Sacred Valley to Machu Picchu costs US$52, while from Cusco's Poroy station it is US$73. If possible, tickets should be bought at least a day in advance, and a week in advance on the Cusco–Machu Picchu route.

BY AIR

Peru is so vast that the odd flight can save a lot of time, and flights between major towns are frequent and relatively inexpensive. The most popular routes usually need to be booked at least a few days in advance (more at the time of major fiestas). For the best fares to popular destinations, either book your flights in advance with Chilean-owned LAN (🌐lan.com), the main airline, or with the smaller Peruvian subsidiaries of Star Peru (🌐starperu.com), Peruvian Airlines (🌐peruvianairlines.pe) or LC Perú (🌐lcperu.pe).

9

Some places in the jungle, such as Iquitos, are more easily accessible by plane, as land and river routes take much longer and can cost as much as a plane ticket.

Flights are sometimes cancelled, delayed or leave earlier than scheduled, so it is important to reconfirm your flight 48 hours before departure. If a passenger hasn't shown up twenty minutes before the flight, the company can give the seat to someone on the waiting list.

BY BOAT

There are no coastal boat services in Peru. In the jungle, river travel is of enormous importance, and cargo boats are an excellent way of travelling along the Amazon – though you have to have plenty of time at your disposal. The facilities are basic (bring your own hammock to hang on deck or rent a cabin), as is the food. The most popular routes are either from Pucallpa or Yurimaguas to Iquitos, from where you can then go on to Colombia or Brazil. On smaller rivers, motorized dugout canoes are the preferred local mode of transport and come in two basic forms: those with a large outboard motor, and slow and noisy *peke-peke* (the name describes the sound of the engine).

ACCOMMODATION

Peru has the typical range of Latin American accommodation, from top-class international hotels to tiny rooms at the back of someone's house for around ten soles a night. Virtually all upmarket accommodation will call itself a hotel or, in the countryside regions, a posada. Lodges in the jungle can be anything from quite luxurious to an open-sided, palm-thatched hut with space for slinging a hammock. *Pensiones* or *residenciales* tend to specialize in longer-term accommodation and may offer discounts for stays of a week or more.

GUESTHOUSES AND HOTELS

Budget **guesthouses** (usually called *hospedajes* or *hostales* and not to be confused with youth hostels) are generally old – sometimes beautifully so, converted from colonial mansions with rooms grouped around a courtyard – and tend to be quite central. At the low end of the scale, which can be basic with shared rooms and a communal bathroom, you can usually find a bed for S20–30, the price often including breakfast. Rooms with private bath tend to cost about S20 more. *Hostales* can be great value if you're travelling with one other person or more; you can often get a good, clean en-suite room for less than two or three bunk beds in a youth hostel. A little haggling is often worth a try, particularly in the low season.

HOSTELS AND CAMPING

A list of the HI-affiliated **youth hostels** in Peru is at ⓦhihostels.com/dba/country-Peru-PE.en.htm. These are relatively cheap and reliable; expect to pay around S15–25, more in Lima. All hostels are theoretically open 24hr. There are also many non-HI-affiliated hostels throughout the country (try ⓦhostels .com, ⓦhostelbookers.com or ⓦhostelworld.com). **Camping** is possible all over Peru. In towns and cities you may be charged the same amount to put up a tent in the grounds of a hostel as for a dorm bed. Organized campsites are gradually being established on the outskirts of popular tourist destinations, though these are still few and far between. Outside urban areas, apart from some restricted natural reserves, it's possible to camp amid some stunning scenery along Peru's vast coast, in the

---

TAX HOAX

If any restaurant tries to add an extra "tax" to your bill, be aware that in Peru, the 18 percent VAT is automatically added to the cost of the dishes and that you shouldn't have to pay anything extra. Also, for a bill to be legal, it has to be either a *boleto de venta* or a *factura*, with the name and address of the restaurant on it. Should any establishment insist that you pay an illegal bill or tax, you have the right to report them to SUNAT, the local regulating board (ⓦwww.sunat.gob.pe).

mountains and in the jungle. It's best not to camp alone, and if you are setting up camp anywhere near a village or settlement, ask permission or advice from the nearest farm or house first.

FOOD AND DRINK

Peruvian cuisine is wonderfully diverse, and essentially a *mestizo* creation, merging indigenous Indian cooking with Spanish, African, Chinese, Italian and Japanese influences. Along the coast, *ceviche* is the classic Peruvian seafood dish, consisting of raw fish, assorted seafood or a mixture of the two, marinated in lime juice and chilli and with corn, sweet potato and onions. You'll also find *arroz con mariscos* (rice with seafood), *tiradito* (like sashimi, served with a spicy sauce), *conchitas a la parmesana* (scallops baked with cheese) and fish prepared a dozen different ways. In coastal areas you'll also find numerous *chifas* (Chinese eateries) serving ample portions of inexpensive Chinese dishes, including vegetarian options.

Food in the Andes includes delicious, hearty soups, such as *sopa de quinoa* (quinoa soup), *chupe de camarones* (shrimp chowder) and *sopa criolla* (beef noodle soup with vegetables). Peru is home to hundreds of potato varieties, the standout dishes from which include *ocopa* (potato with spicy peanut sauce), *papa a la Huancaína* (potato in a spicy cheese sauce) and *causa* (layers of mashed potato with countless fillings). Other popular dishes include *lomo saltado* (stir-fried beef), *ají de gallina* (chicken in a mild chilli sauce), *arroz con pato* (rice with duck, simmered in dark beer with coriander) and the ubiquitous *cuy* (seared guinea pig).

In the jungle, the succulent local fish, such as *dorado* and *paiche*, comes grilled, as *patarashka* (spiced, wrapped in banana leaves and baked on coals) or as *paca* (steamed in a banana tube). Fried and mashed plantain figures highly, along with *yuca* (a manioc rather like a yam) and *juanes* (banana leaves stuffed with chicken, rice and spices). There is often game on the menu, but beware of eating turtle or other endangered species. It is best not to eat fish along the River Tambopata due to the high levels of mercury used extensively in river mining activities.

In big cities, there are often a handful of vegetarian restaurants, though vegetarian food may be quite difficult to find elsewhere. If you ask for your dish *sin carne* (without meat), that may only exclude red meat, but not chicken or fish.

Dessert-wise, Peru offers a wide array of tropical fruit, such as *lúcuma*, *chirimoya* (custard apple) and *grenadilla* (passion fruit), as well as *mazamorra morada* (purple corn pudding with cloves and pineapple) and *suspiro limeño* (caramelized condensed milk topped with meringue).

In Peru, lunch is the main meal of the day, and the time to grab the best food bargains. In coastal areas, some of the best food is found in *cevicherías*, simple seafood restaurants open at lunchtime only. Ask for the *menú marino* – a lunchtime seafood menu that typically consists of two courses, such as *ceviche* and *arroz con mariscos*, and costs around S15–20. Elsewhere, most restaurants will offer a *menú* – a three-course set lunch from S10 upwards.

DRINK

In Peru you can find all the popular soft drink brands, though Peruvians prefer the neon-yellow Inca Kola, which tastes like liquid bubblegum. Fresh fruit juices (*jugos*) are abundant, with *jugerías* (juice stalls) in markets and elsewhere offering a variety of flavours, such as papaya,

---

PERU'S CULINARY SUPERSTAR

No foodie should come to Peru without sampling the gastronomic delights of **Gastón Acurio**, the chef who put Peruvian cuisine on the world map. His restaurants include *ChiCha* in both Cusco and Arequipa, *La Trattoria del Monasterio* in Arequipa, *La Mar* in Lima and his flagship restaurant, *Astríd y Gastón*, also in the capital. The food ranges from superb takes on regional cuisine to original and innovative fusion creations. Not to be missed.

9

maracuyá (passion fruit), *plátano* (banana), *piña* (pineapple) and *naranja* (orange); specify whether you want yours *con azúcar* (with sugar) or *sin azúcar* (without sugar). Another excellent non-alcoholic drink is *chicha morada*, made from purple corn – not to be confused with *chicha*, home-made corn beer popular in the Andes (look out for a red flag outside homes).

Surprisingly for a coffee-growing country, Peruvians tend to drink either *café pasado* (previously percolated coffee mixed with hot water to serve) or simple powdered Nescafé, though it is possible to find good coffee in big cities. A wide variety of herbal teas is also available, such as *muña* (Andean mint), *manzanilla* (camomile) and the extremely popular *mate de coca* – tea brewed from coca leaves that helps one acclimatize to high altitude.

Peru brews some excellent beer, the most popular brands being *Cristal, Pilsen* and *Cusqueña* – all light lagers, though you can also get Pilsen *cerveza negra* (dark beer). Good regional brews include *Arequipeña* and *Trujillana* (named after the cities they're brewed in). Most Peruvian wine tends to be sweet and almost like sherry. Among brands more attuned to the Western palate are *Tabanero, Tacama* and *Vista Alegre*. The national beverage and a source of great pride is pisco, a potent grape brandy with a unique and powerful flavour. Pisco sour – a mix of pisco, lime juice, ice and sugar – is a very palatable and extremely popular cocktail found on menus everywhere.

Bars and pubs tend to be open from 11am until midnight or later on weekends. Clubs typically open at 8pm or 9pm, though things don't kick off until after midnight, and the revelry continues until 4am or 5am.

CULTURE AND ETIQUETTE

Due to the huge variety of geographical conditions found within Peruvian territory, culture and traditions tend to vary between regions. On the whole, coastal people tend to be more outgoing

and vivacious, while the mountain people of Quechua descent are more reserved and modest. The jungle is still home to many indigenous groups who keep their ancestral traditions and way of life. All Peruvians are family-oriented and tend to be close to large extended families. *Machismo* is alive and well in Peru, though women travelling alone are not likely to encounter much trouble. Note that whistling in the north of Peru can be a greeting rather than an attempt at harassment.

One of the most common things travellers do that offends local people is to take their picture without asking – so always ask first, and respect a negative answer. At tourist sites all over Peru, you'll encounter women and children in stunning traditional dress who expect a tip for having their photo taken (1–2 soles is a reasonable amount). In the highlands in particular there is a strong culture of exchange, meaning that if you receive something, you are expected to give in return. This can be as simple as giving someone coca leaves in exchange for directions on a trail.

Tipping is the norm in more upmarket restaurants, where a ten percent gratuity is expected and sometimes automatically added to the bill; in cheap local eateries, tips are received with surprise and gratitude. It's worth bearing in mind that some unscrupulous travel agencies pay their guides very low wages, meaning that they rely on tips, as do freelance guides in museums (agree on a fee before a tour). You should always tip your guide and porters on the Inca Trail (see box, p.758).

GAY AND LESBIAN TRAVEL IN PERU

Being gay in Peru is still very much frowned upon due to a culture infused with *machismo* and fervent Catholicism, though tolerance is slowly improving. **Epicentro** (Jr Jaén 250A, Barranco, Lima; ☎01 247 2755, ⓦepicentro.org.pe) is a not-for-profit community centre that organizes a range of events including dance, theatre, cinema outings and more.

SPORTS AND OUTDOOR ACTIVITIES

When it comes to exploring the wilderness, few of the world's countries can offer anything as varied, rugged and colourful as Peru.

TREKKING AND HIKING

Peru offers a spectacular variety of trekking routes; the main hiking centres are Cusco and Arequipa in the south and Huaraz in the north. The most popular trekking route is, of course, the famous Inca Trail, but other trails in and around the Sacred Valley are rapidly gaining popularity, partly because you get to experience fantastic Andean scenery without being overrun by hordes of tourists. From Arequipa, you can descend into two of the world's deepest canyons – Cañón de Colca and the more remote Cañón de Cotahuasi – which are accessible all year, unlike the Sacred Valley. The Cordillera Blanca near Huaraz lures hikers and climbers alike with its challenging peaks, many of them over 5000m high.

Guides are required for some trekking routes, such as the Inca Trail, and for some challenging routes you'll need to hire mules and *arrieros* (muleteers). You can rent trekking gear or join guided treks at all the major hiking centres; good topographic maps are available from the Instituto Geográfico Nacional (IGN) or the South American Explorers' Club (see p.725). Always make sure you're properly equipped, as the weather is renowned for its dramatic changeability, and properly acclimatized.

MOUNTAIN BIKING

Bike shops and bicycle repair workshops are easy to find throughout Peru, though you should bring your own bike if you're planning on some major cycle touring, as mountain-bike rental is pretty basic. Various tour companies (see p.748) offer guided cycling tours, which can be an excellent way to see the best of Peru. Huaraz and Cusco are both popular and challenging destinations for experienced bikers, while the Colca Canyon is a better bet for novices although it also has its fair share of advanced biking activities too.

WATERSPORTS

Cusco is one of the top white-water rafting and kayaking centres in South America, with easy access to a whole range of river grades, from Class II to V on the Río Urubamba (shifting up grades in the rainy season) to the most dangerous white water on the Río Apurímac, only safe for rafting during the dry season. Río Chili near Arequipa offers good rafting for beginners, with half-day trips passing through Class II and III rapids. A superb multi-day rafting expedition from Cusco goes right down into the Amazon Basin on the Tambopata River.

Bear in mind that rafting is still not a regulated sport in Peru, so it's very important to go with a responsible and eco-friendly operator (see p.748). Also see ⓦ peruwhitewater.com.

SURFING

Surfing is a popular sport in Peru, with annual national and international championships held in Punta Rocas, south of Lima. You can find good breaks even in Lima itself, particularly in the Miraflores area, though Punta Hermosa, further south, is less crowded. Peru's north coast offers some world-class breaks, with Puerto Chicano boasting the world's longest left-hand wave, whereas Santa Rosa and Pacasmayo outside Chiclayo also have excellent waves. Equipment rental is abundant and it's possible to take surfing lessons. Check out ⓦ vivamancora .com for more information.

SANDBOARDING AND DUNE BUGGYING

The best places to ride the sand are in Nazca (see p.775), home of the world's largest dune, Cerro Blanco, and Huacachina, near Ica (see p.771). You can either rent a board from the numerous agencies or go out on the dunes with one of them; snowboarding experience is helpful but not necessary. Also in Huacachina, you can experience the stomach-churning adrenaline rush of dune-buggy rides. While in Nazca they are used as the most efficient means of reaching distant desert sites, in Huacachina they are used for the thrill alone.

9

COMMUNICATIONS

Postal services are slow and very expensive but quite acceptable for normal letters and postcards.

All public phones are operated by coins or phone cards (*tarjetas telefónicas*), which are available in 3, 5, 10, 15, 20, 40 and 50 sol denominations. You can buy cards at little *tiendas* (corner shops) or at *farmacias* (pharmacies) or on the street from cigarette stalls in the centres of most towns and cities. Both 147 and Hola Peru cards are good for local, national and international landline calls. A number of shops, restaurants and corner shops in Peru have a phone available for public use, which you can use for calls within Peru only. If you need to contact the international operator, dial ☎ 103. Collect calls are known either simply as *collect* or *al cobro revertido*.

If you have an unlocked mobile phone, it's cheap and easy to get a Peruvian SIM card (S15); alternatively, you can buy a cheap mobile for the duration of your stay (S80). The networks with the most extensive coverage of the country are Movistar and Claro; the latter allows you to send free text messages via their website.

Peru has good internet connections, with internet cafés abundant in big cities and found even in the most unlikely of small towns (though the connection may be slow). The general rate is S1/hr, though in touristy places you may end up paying as much as S5. Virtually all hotels, hostels and cafés have free wi-fi.

CRIME AND SAFETY

Perhaps the most common irritants are the persistent **touts** found at bus stations and other tourist spots, offering anything from discount accommodation to tours; be very wary of accepting their services, and don't give them money up front. Also don't take **unlicensed taxis** if possible.

You're most likely to come into contact with **police** at the border posts. While they have a reputation for being corrupt, they will mostly leave tourists alone, though some travellers may experience petty harassment aimed at procuring a bribe. If they search your luggage, be scrupulously polite and be aware that possession of any drugs is considered an extremely serious offence in Peru – usually leading to at least a ten-year jail sentence.

Violent crime, such as muggings, is relatively rare. Robberies occasionally occur on overnight buses and there have been isolated attacks on hikers in the area around Huaraz, so it's best not to hike alone. It's not advisable to travel at night between Abancay and Ayacucho, around the Apurímac Valley near Ayacucho or in the Río Huallaga area in the north, between Tingo María and Juanjui, as those areas are notorious for drug trafficking. If you're unlucky enough to have anything stolen, your first port of call should be the **tourist police** (*policía de turismo*), from whom you should get a written report. Bear in mind that the police in popular tourist spots, such as Cusco, have become much stricter about investigating reported thefts, after a spate of false claims by dishonest tourists. This means that genuine victims may be grilled more severely than expected, and the police may even come and search your hotel room for the "stolen" items.

HEALTH

In most cities there are **private clinics** (*clínicas*) with better medical facilities than general hospitals, and if given the choice in a medical emergency, opt for a *clínica*. The EsSalud national hospitals

---

PERU ON THE NET

🌐 **andeantravelweb.com/peru** Links to a whole range of travel-related features and listings.
🌐 **perulinks.com** English-language pages on art, entertainment and travel.
🌐 **virtualperu.net** Peruvian geography, history and people, plus satellite photos, maps and other information.

EMERGENCY NUMBERS

All services ☎ **105**

SOUTH AMERICAN EXPLORERS' CLUB

The non-profit-making **South American Explorers' Club** (ⓦsaexplorers.org) is a good bet for getting information both before you leave home and when you arrive in Lima or Cusco (membership starts at US$60 a year). In its clubhouses in Lima (see p.736) and Cusco (see p.747), members can make use of free internet, a library, book exchange, a variety of **maps** and extensive booklets and folders full of member reviews and information on different parts of the country. Bear in mind, however, that some of the information may be out of date. Membership also gives you discounts on a plethora of accommodation, restaurants and tours.

have undergone drastic improvements in the last few years, and although they are supposed to be for Peruvians who pay into an insurance scheme with them, they can take independent patients (who pay a higher price). Even in relatively small villages there is a *posta médica* where you can get basic medical attention and assistance in getting to a larger medical facility. The South American Explorers' Clubs in Lima and Cusco as well as iPerú offices can provide you with a list of recommended doctors and clinics.

INFORMATION AND MAPS

The government iPerú offices present in every large city are useful for basic information and advice, as well as free local maps and leaflets (24hr hotline: ⓣ01 574 8000, ⓦperu.info); they are also the place to go if you need to make a formal complaint about dishonest guides, tour companies not meeting their obligations, and so on.

Good bookshops stock the Lima 2000 series, which produces the best maps of the major cities as well as the best road map of Peru. For excellent topographic maps of remote places, try Lima's Instituto Geográfico Nacional (ⓦign.es).

MONEY AND BANKS

The current Peruvian currency, the **nuevo sol**, whose symbol is S/ (or S), is simply called a "sol" on the streets and has so far remained relatively steady against the US dollar. The bills come in denominations of 10, 20, 50, 100 and 200 soles; there are coins of 1, 2 and 5 soles, and the sol is divided into céntimos, in values of 5, 10, 20 and 50. Beware of counterfeit bills, which feel smooth and glossy to the

touch, rather than crisp and coarse; genuine bills should have watermarks and thin ribbons when held up against a light source, and when tilted from side to side, the reflective ink on the number denomination should change colour.

Changing foreign currencies is easy in all major cities; you will find casas de cambio around the Plaza de Armas or along the main commercial streets. They readily change euros and British pounds, though the preferred currency is US dollars. You'll find that some tour companies and hotels still quote prices in US dollars, and happily accept them as long as the notes are new; few places will accept US$100 bills.

Banks and ATMs are numerous in cities; if travelling to remote villages, take plenty of cash in small denomination bills and coins with you. BCP (Banco de Crédito) accepts all major credit cards and is the best bank for cash withdrawals, as it doesn't charge a fee for the transaction, whereas the Global Net network can charge up to US$2.50 per withdrawal.

OPENING HOURS AND HOLIDAYS

Most shops are open from around 9am to 9pm, and many are open on Sunday as well, if for more limited hours. Peru's more important ancient sites and ruins usually have opening hours that coincide with daylight – from around 7am until 5pm or 6pm daily.

FESTIVALS AND CELEBRATIONS

Peru is a country rich with culture and traditions, and on any given day there is a town or village celebrating their anniversary or similar occasion. Festivals

PUBLIC HOLIDAYS

January 1 New Year's Day.
March/April Easter; Semana Santa (Holy Week). Maundy Thursday and Good Friday are national holidays, Easter Monday is not.
May 1 Labour Day.
July 28–29 National Independence Day. Public holiday with military and school processions.
October 8 Anniversary of Battle of Angamos.
November 1–2 Day of the Dead, and All Souls' Day.
December 8 Immaculate Conception.
December 25 Christmas Day.

can be spectacular events with processions, usually with live music and dancing, and a proud usage of traditional dress. Carnival time (generally late February) is especially lively almost everywhere in the country. During fiesta times small towns become completely booked up, hotel prices go up significantly, transport services stop running or prices double, and often most people will stop work and celebrate for a few days either side of the festival. Below are some of the major events:

February Carnaval. Wildly celebrated immediately prior to Lent, throughout the whole country.
February 2 Virgen de la Candelaria. Celebrated in the most spectacular way in Puno (known as the folklore capital of the country) with a week of colourful processions and dancing.
March/April Semana Santa (Holy Week). Superb processions all over Peru (the best are in Cusco and Ayacucho), the biggest being on Good Friday and Easter Saturday night.
Late May/early June Q'oyllor Riti. One of the most breathtaking festivals in Peru; thousands of people make the overnight pilgrimage up to Apu Ausangate, a shrine located on a glacier just outside of Cusco.
Early June Corpus Christi. Takes place nine weeks after Maundy Thursday and involves colourful processions with saints carried around on floats and much feasting. Particularly lively in Cusco.
June 24 Inti Raymi is Cusco's main Inca festival.
June 29 St Peter's Day. Fiestas in all the fishing villages along the coast.
July 15–18 Virgen del Carmen. Celebrated in style in the town of Paucartambo, on the road between Cusco and

Manu Biosphere Reserve. Dancers come from surrounding villages in traditional dress for the celebration, which lasts several days. There's a smaller celebration in the Sacred Valley town of Pisac.
August 13–19 Arequipa Week. Processions, firework displays, plenty of folklore dancing and craft markets in Arequipa.
August 30 Santa Rosa de Lima. The city of Lima stops for the day to worship their patron saint, Santa Rosa.
Late September Spring Festival. Trujillo festival involving dancing, especially the local Marinera dance and popular Peruvian waltzes.
October 18–28 Lord of Miracles. Festival featuring large and solemn processions (the main ones take place on October 18, 19 & 28); many women wear purple.
November 1–7 Puno Festival. Celebrates the founding of Puno by the Spanish and of the Inca Empire by Manco Capac. Particularly colourful dancing on the fifth day.
November 1–30 International Bullfighting Competitions. Spectacular in the Plaza da Ancho in Lima.

Lima

LIMA, "City of Kings", was founded in 1535 by **Francisco Pizarro** and rapidly became the capital of a Spanish viceroyalty that included Ecuador, Bolivia and Chile. By 1610 its population had reached 26,000 and it had become an international trading port, the city's centre was crowded with stalls selling produce from all over the world and it was one of the most beautiful and wealthy cities in Spanish America. It then grew steadily until the twentieth century, when the population exploded. Today, many of its eight and a half million inhabitants are *campesinos* (rural folk) who fled their homes in the countryside to escape the civil war that destroyed many Andean communities in the 1980s and 1990s.

Some say that Lima is Peru. And given its wealth of museums, nightlife, architecture and world-class food, plus its position as the nation's transport hub, the city makes the perfect base from which to explore the rest of the country. Ignore Lima's grey and polluted facade, ride the *combis* and get stuck in – no visit to Peru is complete without time well spent in Lima.

WHAT TO SEE AND DO

Lima is very much a city of neighbourhoods, and it's worth visiting several before making up your mind about this huge capital. You can't beat **Central Lima** for sights or architecture, while up-and-coming neighbourhood **Pueblo Libre** to the southwest has some excellent museums loaded with pre-Hispanic artefacts. Coast-hugging **Miraflores** and neighbouring **San Isidro** are certainly the most modern and commercial areas of the city and you'll find many designer stores, gourmet restaurants and sophisticated lounge bars here, as well as some of the best tourist attractions and nightlife. Arty and colourful **Barranco** feels like a sleepy seaside town by day, and is fantastic for escaping the chaos of central Lima, but at night comes alive and is packed with bars and clubs.

Plaza Mayor

Lima's main square, known as the **Plaza Mayor** or the Plaza de Armas, boasts UNESCO World Heritage status due to its former colonial importance – Lima was capital of the Spanish Empire in South America – and its colours and famous wooden balconies are kept in beautiful condition accordingly. It is one of the largest squares in South America and has some of the most important government and religious buildings in Peru.

On the eastern corner of the plaza stands the austere Renaissance-style **Catedral** (open for Mass Sat 9am & Sun 11am). The interior retains some of its appealing Churrigueresque (highly elaborate Baroque) decor and it houses the **Museo de Arte Religioso** (Mon–Fri 9am–5pm & Sat 10am–1pm; S10; ☎01 427 9647), which contains paintings from the seventeenth century as well as the remains of Francisco Pizarro.

The original **Palacio del Gobierno** was built on the site of Pizarro's adobe house, where he spent the last few years of his life until his assassination in 1541. The present building was only built in 1938 (the older palace was destroyed by an earthquake). It's possible to arrange a free tour, on Saturdays only, although this can take a few days to sort out (contact the Jefatura de Turismo, English spoken, on ☎01 311 3900, extension 523, ✉scuadros@ presidencia.gob.pe). The **changing of the guard** takes place outside (daily 11.45am & 5.45pm), which always draws a crowd to watch the marching soldiers and listen to the military brass band.

Museo de la Iglesia y Convento San Francisco

East of the Palacio del Gobierno along Jr Ancash is the majestic **Museo de la Iglesia y Convento San Francisco** (daily 9.30am–5.30pm; S7 for 40min guided tour; ☎01 426 7377, ⊕museocatacumbas.com). The large seventeenth-century church has an attached **monastery**, which contains a superb library, a room of paintings by (or finished by) Rubens, Jordaens and Van Dyck, some pretty cloisters and, the main highlight, the vast crypts with gruesome **catacombs**, which contain the skeletons of some seventy thousand people – well worth a visit.

Museo de la Inquisición

A couple of blocks southeast of San Francisco, the **Museo de la Inquisición y del Congreso**, Jr Junín 548 (daily 9am–5pm; free, by regular guided tours only, available in English; ☎01 311 7777, ⊕www .congreso.gob.pe/museo.htm), was the headquarters of the Inquisition for the whole of Spanish America from 1570 until 1820. The museum includes the original tribunal room, with its beautifully carved mahogany ceiling, and beneath the building you can look round the dungeons and torture chambers, which contain a few gory, life-sized human models.

Mercado Central and Chinatown

Walk south on Avenida Abancay from the Museo de la Inquisición, take a left on Ucayali and after a couple of blocks you'll see the fascinating **Mercado Central** on your left, where you can buy almost anything (keeping one eye open for pickpockets). A little further east, an ornate Chinese gateway ushers visitors into Lima's **Barrio Chino**. This pedestrianized section of the street is,

9

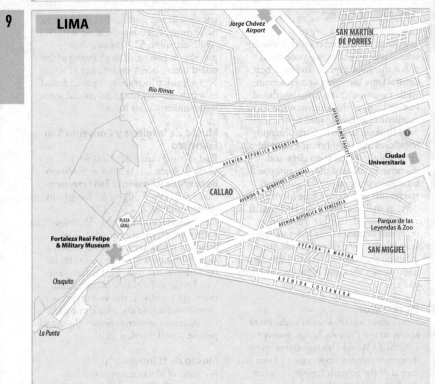

LIMA

Jorge Chávez Airport

SAN MARTÍN DE PORRES

Río Rimac

AVENIDA ELMER FAUCETT

AVENIDA REPÚBLICA ARGENTINA

Ciudad Universitaria

CALLAO

AVENIDA O. R. BENAVIDES (COLONIAL)

AVENIDA REPÚBLICA DE VENEZUELA

PLAZA GRAU

Parque de las Leyendas & Zoo

Fortaleza Real Felipe & Military Museum

AVENIDA LA MARINA

SAN MIGUEL

AVENIDA COSTANERA

Chuquito

La Punta

PACIFIC

N

■ ACCOMMODATION	
Hostal Barranco	2
Domeyer	3
The Point	1

● NIGHTLIFE	
La Candelaria	9
La Noche	5
De Rompe y Raja	4
Wahio's Bar	6

● EATING	
Anticuchos Tío Jhony	3
El Grifo	1
Expreso Virgen de Guadalupe	7
Mi Carcochita	8
Punto Azul	2

0 _____ 2
kilometres

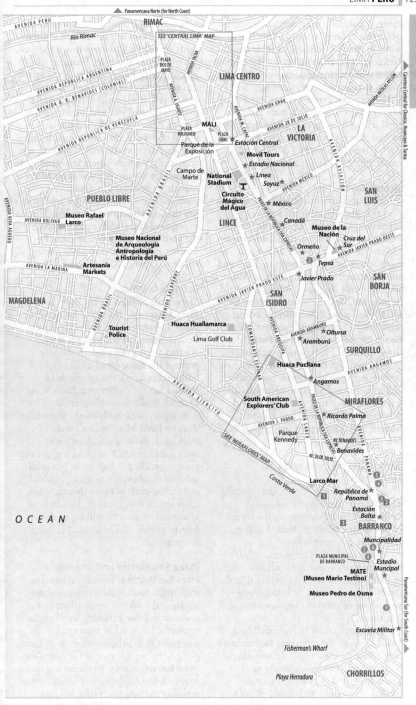

Panamericana Norte (for North Coast)

RÍO RIMAC

AVENIDA PERÚ

RIMAC

SEE 'CENTRAL LIMA' MAP

PLAZA BOS DE MAYO

AVENIDA TACNA

LIMA CENTRO

AVENIDA REPÚBLICA ARGENTINA

AVENIDA O. R. BENAVIDES (COLONIAL)

AVENIDA A. UGARTE

AVENIDA GRAU

AVENIDA 28 DE JULIO

AVENIDA REPÚBLICA DE VENEZUELA

PLAZA BOLOGNESI

MALI

PLAZA GRAU

LA VICTORIA

Parque de la Exposición

Estación Central

AVENIDA M. CÁPAC

AVENIDA MÉXICO

AVENIDA AVIACIÓN

Campo de Marte

Movil Tours ★

Estación Nacional ★

Línea Soyuz ★

SAN LUIS

AVENIDA BRASIL

National Stadium

PUEBLO LIBRE

Circuito Mágico del Agua

México ★

AVENIDA RIVA AGÜERO

Museo Rafael Larco

AVENIDA BOLÍVAR

LINCE

Canadá ★

Museo de la Nación

Cruz del Sur ★

AVENIDA JAVIER PRADO OESTE

Museo Nacional de Arqueología Antropología e Historia del Perú

PASEO DE LA REPÚBLICA (VÍA EXPRESA)

Ormeño ★

②

Tepsa ★

AVENIDA LA MARINA

Artesanía Markets

AVENIDA SALAVERRY

Javier Prado ★

SAN BORJA

MAGDELENA

AVENIDA JAVIER PRADO ESTE

SAN ISIDRO

AVENIDA BRASIL

Tourist Police

Huaca Huallamarca ★

Lima Golf Club

COMANDANTE ESPINAR

AVENIDA ARAMBURÚ

AVENIDA AREQUIPA

Oltursa ★

Aramburú ★

SURQUILLO

Huaca Pucllana ★

AVENIDA ANGAMOS

AVENIDA EJÉRCITO

Angamos ★

South American Explorers' Club

PASEO DE LA REPÚBLICA (VÍA EXPRESA)

AVENIDA LARCO

MIRAFLORES

Ricardo Palma ★

AVENIDA J. PARDO

Parque Kennedy

AV. BENAVIDES

AVENIDA PANAMÁ

SEE 'MIRAFLORES' MAP

Benavides ★

③ ④

AV. 26 DE JULIO

Larco Mar

República de Panamá ★

⑤ ②

OCEAN

①

Estación Balta

③

BARRANCO

Muncipalidad

⑦ ⑧

PLAZA MUNICIPAL DE BARRANCO

Estadio Municipal

MATE (Museo Mario Testino)

Museo Pedro de Osma

Panamericana Sur (for South Coast)

⑨

Escuela Militar ★

Fisherman's Wharf

Playa Herradura

CHORRILLOS

9

rather graphically, commonly referred to as Calle Capón (Castration Street) after some of the practices the Chinese used to fatten up their animals. As you'd expect, this is where many of Lima's best (from cheap to super-swanky) Chinese restaurants are, crammed into a few bustling streets. There's also an indoor mall selling Asian goods, and don't forget to look down at the modest walk of fame paying tribute to many *Limeños* who could afford to pay for a tile.

Jirón Ucayali

Walking back towards Plaza Mayor, you'll find that Jirón Ucayali has a few interesting buildings. The **Iglesia San Pedro**, on the corner with Jirón Azángaro (Mon–Sat 9.30–11.30am & 5–6pm; free), was built by the Jesuits in 1636 and the plain exterior is completely at odds with its richly decorated interior, a world of gold leaf, ornate tiles and impressive altars. A short walk west on the corner with Jirón Lampa is the excellent **Museo Banco Central de Reserva del Perú** (Mon, Tues, Thurs & Fri 10am–5pm, Wed 10am–7pm, Sat & Sun 10am–1pm; free; ⓦwww.bcrp.gob.pe), whose permanent collection includes textiles, ceramics and a security-heavy room full of gold and precious artefacts, as well as a short history of Peruvian painting, with good information in English.

Santa Rosa de Lima and Las Nazarenas

Heading west down Jirón Lima from the Plaza Mayor you'll pass the **Iglesia y Convento Santo Domingo** on the corner with Camaná (daily 9.30am–5.30pm; monastery S7, church free; ⓦconventosantodomingolima.org). It's here that you can see the skull and other remains of the first saint canonized in the Americas, Santa Rosa de Lima, along with those of another Peruvian saint, Martín de Porres.

If you continue on to Avenida Tacna, you'll come to the terracotta **Santuario de Santa Rosa de Lima** (daily 7am–noon & 5–8pm; free), birthplace of the saint. Directly behind the church, a small garden (9am–1pm & 3–6pm) offers a pleasant escape from the chaos of Lima, and many Peruvians come here to drop cards with their wishes on down the well.

A few blocks south on Tacna, at the junction with Huancavelica, is the **Iglesia de Las Nazarenas** (daily 6am–noon & 4–8.30pm; free), small and outwardly undistinguished but with an interesting history. After the 1655 earthquake, a mural of the crucifixion, painted by an Angolan slave on the wall of his hut, was apparently the only object left standing in the district. Its survival was deemed a miracle – the cause of popular processions ever since – and it was on this site that the church was founded. The widespread and popular processions for the **Lord of Miracles**, to save Lima from another earthquake, take place every autumn (Oct 6, 7, 18, 19, 28 & Nov 1).

Jirón de la Unión

The stretch of Jirón de la Unión between Plaza Mayor and Plaza San Martín is the main shopping street, with everything from designer brands to thrift stores. Nestled among the modern shops is perhaps the most noted of all religious buildings in Lima, the **Iglesia de La Merced**, on the corner with Jirón Miro Quesada (daily 8am–12.30pm & 4–8.30pm; free). Built on the site where the first Latin Mass in Lima was celebrated, the original church was demolished in 1628 to make way for the present building. Much of its beautiful colonial facade is not original, but look out for the **cross of Padre Urraca**, whose silver staff is smothered by hundreds of kisses every hour and witness to the fervent prayers of a constantly shifting congregation.

Plaza San Martín and around

Plaza San Martín is virtually always busy, with traffic tooting its way around the square and buskers, mime artists and soapbox *políticos* attracting small circles of interested faces. It has been (and continues to be) the site of most of Lima's political rallies. Of note is the huge **Gran Hotel Bolívar**, not for its rooms but for its streetside bar *El Bolivarcito*, which serves arguably the best pisco sour in Lima.

One block east of the Plaza, Avenida Nicolás de Piérola runs towards the **Parque Universitario**, with the grand old buildings of the first university in the Americas, San Marcos. The buildings now house the **Centro Cultural de San Marcos** (Mon–Sat 9am–1pm & 2–5pm; free or S5 with guided visit of historic building; ⓦccsm-unmsm.edu.pe), the cultural centre of the modern university, now sited in Pueblo Libre. It hosts many interesting talks and events and also contains a gallery, focusing on Peruvian folk and contemporary art, and an archeological and anthropology museum with rotating exhibits on Peruvian history, as well as a permanent collection of textiles and ceramics.

Plaza Grau and around

The Jirón de la Unión becomes Jirón Belén and leads down to the **Plaza Grau** and the **Paseo de la República** (also known as the Vía Expresa), an enormous dual carriageway that cleaves through the city. Underneath the plaza is the Estación Central of the Metropolitano bus service (see p.735).

Just south of the plaza at Paseo Colón 125 is the **Museo de Arte Lima** (MALI; Tues–Sun 10am–8pm, Sat until 5pm; S12; English-speaking guides available

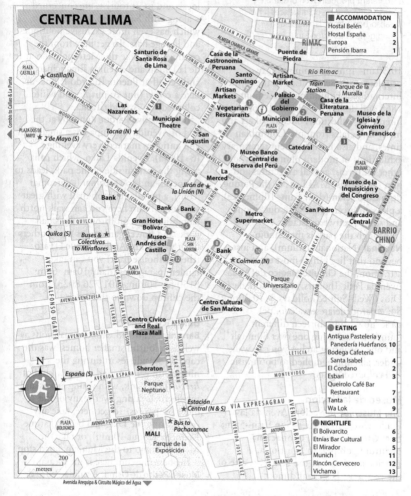

9

10.30am–4pm; S3; minimum two people; Ⓦmali.pe), housed in the former International Exhibition Palace built in 1868 and designed by Eiffel. It contains interesting collections of colonial art and many fine crafts from pre-Columbian times, and also hosts frequent temporary exhibitions of modern photography and other art forms, as well as lectures and film screenings. MALI sits in the **Parque de la Exposición** (daily 8am–10pm; free), a pleasant green space with duck ponds and some pretty bandstands.

Through the park is the **Estadio Nacional** (National Stadium), and just beyond that lies Lima's most eccentric attraction, the **Circuito Mágico del Agua**, Avenida Petit Thouars, at Jr Madre de Dios (Wed–Sun & holidays 3–10.30pm; S4; Ⓦparquedelareserva.com.pe). It's a park showcasing thirteen different fountains, including one over 80m tall and one sprouting arches you can walk under, all choreographed to pop music and coloured lights.

Museo de la Nación

The **Museo de la Nación**, Avenida Javier Prado Este 2465 (Tues–Sun 9am–5pm; free; ☎01 476 9933, ✉mnacion@mcultura.gob.pe), in San Borja, a district southeast of the centre, is one of the country's largest and most important museums and has an outstanding and very moving exhibition about the devastation caused by the Sendero Luminoso group, which terrorized the country in the 1980s and 1990s (see p.715).

To **get here**, take the Metropolitano bus from the centre or from Miraflores to the huge intersecting Avenida Javier Prado. Then take any bus east marked "todo Javier Prado" and ask for the museum.

Miraflores

Miraflores, its streets lined with cafés and flashy shops, is the major focus of Lima's gastronomy and nightlife as far as affluent locals and most tourists are concerned – along with San Isidro, further north, which has even more exclusive boutiques and lounge bars. To get here from the centre, either take the Metropolitano at Jr de la Unión and Avenida Emancipación and get off at Puente Ricardo Palma, or take a *combi* (line A; purple and white coloured) on Avenida Tacna.

The attractive **Parque Kennedy** at the end of Avenida Arequipa has a small craft and antiques market every evening (6–10pm). Avenida Larco, which runs along the eastern side of the park, leads to the ocean and to **Larcomar** (Ⓦlarcomar.com), a popular clifftop mall with great sea views. From here you can walk north along the Malecón through the small parks and flower gardens, as many others do at weekends. At the **Parque El Faro** (the lighthouse park) you can take tandem paraglides (daily 10am–6pm; S150 for 10min; ☎01 726 8023) from the clifftop down to the beach.

Barranco

Barranco, scattered with old mansions as well as colourful smaller homes, was the capital's seaside resort during the nineteenth century and is now a kind of *limeño* Left Bank, with young artists and intellectuals taking over many of the older properties. To get here, take any *combi* along the Diagonal beside Parque Kennedy (about 10min), or take the Metropolitano to the Municipalidad stop.

The best museum here is the pleasant **Museo Pedro de Osma**, Avenida Pedro de

EATING
La Lucha	2
La Luchita	3
Manolo	6
Patagonia: Soul Food	7
El Príncipe	1
Punto Azul	9
Thani Wasi	5

NIGHTLIFE
Downtown Vale Todo	4
Jazz Zone	8

MIRAFLORES

ACCOMMODATION
Casa del Mochilero	2
Explorer's House	3
Flying Dog Hostels	7/8/9
The House Project	5
HQ Villa	4
Kokopeli Backpackers	6
The Lighthouse	1

Osma 421 (Tues–Sun 10am–5.30pm; S20; ☎01 467 0141, ⓦmuseopedrode osma.org), which houses a good collection of religious art, silver and antique furniture in a stunning French-style mansion with stained-glass windows designed by the eponymous collector. Another highlight is the **Museo Mario Testino**, or MATE, Avenida Pedro de Osma 409 (Tues–Sun 11am–8pm; S20; ⓦmate.pe), housed in another beautifully restored colonial town house and the first permanent exhibition to the UK-based fashion photographer in his home town.

A walk across the **Puente de Suspiros** (The Bridge of Sighs) to the cliffside bars and cafés is a favourite pastime for locals – as well as checking out some of the colourful houses, often daubed with graffiti, on streets such as Calle Cajamarca – but otherwise there's little else to see specifically; the main highlight of Barranco is its bars, clubs and cafés clustered around the attractive **Plaza Municipal**.

Pueblo Libre

This upcoming neighbourhood, southwest of the centre, hosts two world-class museums. The **Museo Nacional de Arqueología, Antropología e Historia del Perú** (Plaza Bolívar s/n; Tues–Sat

9

9am–4pm, Sun 9am–3pm; S10; @mnaahp@mcultura.gob.pe) has an extensive collection of pre-Hispanic and colonial artefacts, helpfully laid out in chronological order. It also houses the two most important relics from the Chavín de Huántar site near Huaraz: the Raimondi Stela, a 2m-tall piece of granite with intricate carvings, and the Tello Obelisk, which once lurked underground, worshipped by priests of the Chavín cult. Part of the museum is in a mansion once inhabited by the liberators Simón Bolívar and José de San Martín.

Follow the (sometimes worn) blue line outside the museum for a pleasant 25-minute walk to the expensive but excellent **Museo Rafael Larco** at Avenida Bolívar 1515 (daily 9am–10pm; S30; guided tour in English S25, reserve in advance; ☎01 461 1835, Ⓦmuseolarco .org). Situated in a viceroy's mansion, which in turn was built on a pre-Columbian pyramid, it displays the enormous private collection of Peruvian archeologist Rafael Larco, which includes textiles, jewellery, gold, silver and ceramics. Best of all, you can explore the vast storage rooms, packed to the rafters with more than 45,000 pre-Columbian objects. It's also famous for an extensive erotic ceramics section.

These museums are close to both the **artisan stalls** on blocks 6–8 of Avenida La Marina known as the Mercado Inca (9am–8.30pm) and the **Parque de las Leyendas**, Avenida Las Leyendas 580 (daily 9am–6pm; S10; Ⓦleyendas.gob.pe), a family-orientated zoo landscaped to represent the three zones in Peru – coast, mountains and jungle. The site also contains more than thirty pre-Columbian *huacas* (see box below), all in differing stages of excavation, as well as a botanical garden and boating lake.

ARRIVAL AND DEPARTURE

BY PLANE

All flights leave and depart from Jorge Chávez Airport (Ⓦwww.lap.com.pe) in Callao, 10km northwest of the city centre – departure and arrival taxes are included in the price of tickets. The two main carriers serving the rest of the country are LAN (Ⓦlan.com) and the cheaper StarPerú (Ⓦstarperu.com).

FROM THE AIRPORT INTO TOWN

By taxi The quickest and safest way to get into central Lima (45min) is to take an official taxi from one of the companies with desks at the airport on street level – pay there and you'll be assigned a driver. Green Taxis is the cheapest (S45–55 to downtown). The family-run RGM Secure Taxi service is also recommended; the father and sons are very knowledgeable about the city (S40–55; English spoken; ☎997 380 389).

HUACAS

There are reminders of Lima's pre-Columbian past all over the capital in the form of adobe **huacas** – sacred places – also referred to as pyramids. They are mostly associated with the Lima culture, which dominated in the area from 200 to 700 AD. Two of the most impressive sit wonderfully at odds with the modern monstrosities around them. The **Huaca Pucllana**, at General Borgoño block 8, Miraflores (Wed–Mon 9am–4pm; S12; ☎01 617 7138, @huacapucllana@hotmail.com), the larger of the two, was thought to have been a major administrative centre. It's a short walk from Av Arequipa at block 44 (off to the right if you're coming from central Lima). **Huaca Huallamarca**, Nicolás de Ribera 201, San Isidro (Tues–Sun 9am–5pm; S5), is three blocks from Camino Real along Choquehuanca. It's thought to be a little older than Pucllana and pertains to the Hualla tribe. The spaceship-like ramp can be scaled to get great views of the neighbourhood. Both tickets include entrance to small site museums.

The most wonderful of all Lima's *huacas*, **Pachacamac**, lies just outside the city at Km31.5 off the Antigua Panamericana Sur, Lurín (Tues–Sun 9am–5pm; S8; ☎01 430 2115, @museopachacamac@mcultura.gob.pe). It's easily reached by public transport – you can do it in half a day. Get there from Lima centro by catching the brown *combi* marked San Bartolo from outside MALI and double-check that it's going to Lurín. Alternatively, you can get this same *combi* nearer Miraflores by taking any bus marked "todo Benavides" from Miraflores to the Panamericana; go down the steps to the busy motorway and wait at the stop under the bridge. From here it's about 30min away and you can be dropped off right outside the Museo de Sitio (site museum).

DESTINATIONS

Arequipa (10 daily; 1hr 20min); Cajamarca (5 daily; 1hr 20min); Cusco (15 daily; 1hr 15min); Iquitos (8 daily; 1hr 45min); Tumbes (daily; 1hr 50min).

BY BUS

Unfortunately Peru doesn't have central terminals – each bus company has its own private terminal. Buses to Lima usually arrive and depart in the district of La Victoria, near central Lima, or at the other end of La Victoria on Av Javier Prado. Whichever terminal, it's best to hail the first decent-looking taxi you see and fix a price – about S12–15 from or to anywhere in the centre, or S15–18 from or to anywhere else in Lima. Many buses can't be booked online, so you'll have to visit the office in person – it's worth booking in advance if you want the best seats (ie *cama*, with fully reclining seats). A good option is to find a decent travel agent – the in-house agency in the *Hotel España* (see p.736) is recommended and they can advise about different companies, hours and prices.

BUS COMPANIES

The following bus companies have the best fleets and services.

Cruz del Sur Av Javier Prado 1109 (☎01 311 5050, ⓦ www.cruzdelsur.com.pe)

Línea Av Paseo de la República 941–959 (☎01 424 0836, ⓦ linea.pe)

Movil Tours Paseo de la República 749 (☎01 716 8000, ⓦ moviltours.com.pe)

Oltursa Av Aramburu 1160, San Isidro (☎01 708 5000, ⓦ oltursa.pe)

Ormeño Av Javier Prado Oeste 1057 (☎01 472 1710)

Soyuz Perú Av México 280 (☎01 205 2370, ⓦ www.soyuz.com.pe)

Tepsa Av Javier Prado Este 1091 (☎01 617 9000, ⓦ www.tepsa.com.pe)

DESTINATIONS

Ayacucho (9hr 30min): Cruz del Sur (3 daily)

Arequipa (15hr): Cruz del Sur (7 daily), Oltursa (6 daily), Ormeño (1 daily), Tepsa (2 daily)

Cajamarca (14hr): Cruz del Sur (1 daily), Línea (2 daily), Tepsa (1 daily)

Chachapoyas (20hr): Movil Tours (1 daily)

Chiclayo (12hr): Cruz del Sur (4 daily), Línea (2 daily), Movil Tours (2 daily), Oltursa (4 daily), Tepsa (3 daily)

Cusco (22hr): Cruz del Sur (2 daily), Oltursa (1 daily), Movil Tours (1 daily), Tepsa (2 daily)

Puno (20hr): Ormeño (1 daily)

Huaraz (7hr 30min): Cruz del Sur (4 daily), Oltursa (4 daily), Movil Tours (5 daily)

Nazca (7hr 30min): Cruz del Sur (5 daily), Oltursa (3 daily), Ormeño (2 daily), Soyuz Perú (hourly), Tepsa (3 daily)

Tacna (19hr): Cruz del Sur (2 daily), Oltursa (2 daily), Tepsa (1 daily)

Trujillo (9hr): Cruz del Sur (4 daily), Oltursa (3 daily), Línea (9 daily), Movil Tours (1 daily), Tepsa (2 daily)

Tumbes via Máncora (18–20hr): Cruz del Sur, Línea, Oltursa, Ormeño, Tepsa (all 1 daily).

BY TRAIN

Apart from a small local service, the only train from Lima goes to Huancayo twice a month (see p.719). It departs from Desamparados station (Jr Ancash 207).

GETTING AROUND

By bus *Combis* race from one street corner to another along all the major arterial city roads. Wave one down and pay the flat fare (S1–1.50 within Lima, depending on distance) to the driver or *cobrador* (conductor). A fantastic unofficial map of Lima's most useful and safe *combis* (many are more than a little ropey) can be purchased for US$2.50 at ⓦ rutasrecomendables.com.

By colectivo A useful form of transport for getting to outer districts of the capital such as Chosica and Comas, mostly leaving from Plaza Bolognesi (S4–8).

By taxi Taxis should not cost more than S30 within the city (except to/from the airport). Most are unofficial, although the yellow ones with a licence plate number on the side are, in theory, regulated. It is, perhaps, better to look at the condition of the car and always agree on a price beforehand as they don't have meters. As a guide, taxis within a district (such as anywhere within central Lima) should be S4–7, while Miraflores to the centre should be S12–15. Private companies are few and far between, change numbers regularly and charge a lot more.

METROPOLITANO

Lima may be one of the largest cities in the world without an underground metro, but it now has the very modern **Metropolitano** bus service (daily 6am–9.50pm, express service during rush hours 7–9.30am & 5–8.30pm; ⓦ metropolitano.com.pe). This bus runs through the city north to south and connects the main tourist areas of Barranco, Miraflores and San Isidro along the Paseo de la República with central Lima. It uses a rechargeable card which subtracts S1.50 per ride, and it's the quickest, easiest and certainly the safest way to get around Lima as the buses use special lanes and the fleet is new. Check the website (under "rutas") for any changes before you use the service.

9

INFORMATION

Tourist information The municipal tourist office is just off the Plaza Mayor behind the Palacio Municipal (Pasaje Los Escribanos 145; Mon–Fri 8.30am–6pm, Sat & Sun 9am–5pm; ☎ 01 314 1542). iPerú is the national tourist info provider, and can also help if you need to make a complaint, visit the police or simply book accommodation. iPerú has desks in Lima airport (open 24hr; ☎ 01 574 8000) and Miraflores (Larcomar, stand 10; daily 11am–2pm & 3–8pm; ☎ 01 445 9400), as well as San Isidro (Jorge Basadre 610; daily 9am–1pm & 2–6pm; ☎ 01 421 1627). Callao has a basic tourist information booth on the road between Plaza Grau and Chuquito (daily 10am–5pm), which has information about the museums in the area. The South American Explorers' Club, C Piura 135, Miraflores (Mon–Fri 9.30am–5pm, Sat 9.30am–1pm; ☎ 01 444 2150), has good information including maps, listings and travel reports available to non-members for a higher fee.

TOUR OPERATORS

Bike Tours of Lima C Bolívar 150, Miraflores ☎ 01 445 3172, ⓦ biketoursoflima.com. Does what it says on the tin, as well as bike rentals.

Ecocruceros Av Arequipa 4960, Miraflores, and a stand by the port in Callao ☎ 01 226 8530, ⓦ islaspalomino.com. Runs trips to the Islas Palominos.

Fertur Peru Jr Junín 211, Central Lima ☎ 01 427 2626, ⓦ fertur-travel.com. Offers nationwide package tours and some local tours.

Kolibri Expeditions ☎ 01 273 7246, ⓦ kolibriexpeditions .com. Recommended for birdwatching tours locally and across Peru.

Lima Vision Jr Chiclayo 444, Miraflores ☎ 01 447 7710, ⓦ limavision.com. The best choice for Lima tours, including Pachacamac and the museums.

Mirabús Stalls in both Parque Kennedy and Plaza Mayor ☎ 01 242 6699, ⓦ mirabusperu.com. Runs open-top bus tours of Lima by day/night, as well as Callao (Sun only 10.15am). Also does boat trips to the Islas Palominos (bi-monthly) and a land and sea excursion (Thurs, Fri & Sat 2pm).

ACCOMMODATION

There are good budget options throughout the city, although Central Lima works out slightly cheaper and offers hostels within walking distance of some of the most important tourist sights. Barranco has a relaxed bohemian atmosphere and is close to the sea, but the most popular district for tourists is still Miraflores; with bright lights and fast-food joints on every corner, it has a cosmopolitan feel, plus plenty of chain backpacker hostels providing mainly dorm-style accommodation. There are no campsites, official or otherwise.

CENTRAL LIMA

Hostal Belén Nicolás de Piérola 953, Plaza San Martín ☎ 01 427 7391, ⓔ ryexport2000@yahoo.es; map p.731. One of the best-value budget options in Central Lima – a well-maintained colonial gem with a restaurant (Mon–Sat) serving bargain set lunches. Try to get a room with views of the plaza. ~~S60~~

★ **Hostal España** Jr Azángaro 105 ☎ 01 428 5546, ⓦ hotelespanaperu.com; map p.731. The main courtyard, filled with antique oil paintings, marble statues and trailing pot plants, is quite stunning. There's also a verdant rooftop patio where breakfast is served (S6–6.50) – look out for peacocks strutting about. *España* is perhaps a little old-school, but it's secure and has wi-fi, a book exchange and a tour operator service for onward travel anywhere in the country. Dorms ~~S25~~, doubles ~~S65~~

Europa Jr Ancash 376 ☎ 01 427 3351; map p.731. A very basic and slightly run-down building opposite the San Francisco church, with a pretty internal courtyard. The rooms are worthy of a monastery in their simplicity (most have shared bathroom), but it's good value (although can be cold in winter). ~~S40~~

Pensión Ibarra Av Tacna 359 apt.1402 ☎ 01 427 8603, ⓔ pensionibarra@gmail.com; map p.731. For a different type of experience, try staying with the very welcoming Ibarra couple in two apartments on the fourteenth and fifteenth floor. The rooms are simple but the views are spectacular and the place is kept tidy. Breakfast (S8–10) and laundry can be arranged, use of the kitchen is permitted and there's no curfew. Very cheap rates can be arranged for long stays. ~~S40~~

MIRAFLORES

Casa del Mochilero Jr Cesareo Chacaltana 130a, upstairs ☎ 01 444 9089, ⓔ pilaryv@hotmail.com; map p.733. This safe place is remarkably good for the price, with hot water, cable TV and a stainless-steel kitchen. It's not right at the centre of Miraflores's action, but it's close enough. Don't confuse it with the similarly named and decorated hostel next door; ask for Pilar or Juan to be sure you're in the right place (it's the green building). Dorms ~~S15~~, doubles ~~S50~~

Explorer's House Av Alfredo Leon 158 ☎ 01 241 5002, ⓔ evaaragon_9@hotmail.com; map p.733. Out of the centre of Miraflores but close to the sea, *Explorer's House* is a good old-fashioned hostel. Breakfast is included, and internet, wi-fi, hot water and a rooftop terrace add to the charm; there's also a small kitchen for guests to use. Book ahead as it is small and popular. Dorms ~~S21~~, doubles ~~S60~~

Flying Dog Hostels ⓦ flyingdogperu.com; map p.733. The *Flying Dog* is the most established backpacker joint in the city, with several outlets: *Backpackers*, Diez Canseco 117 (includes breakfast); *Bed and Breakfast*, C Lima 457; *Hostel*, Olaya 280. All locations offer cheap accommodation, kitchen use, TV room, storage service and internet access, as well as being hugely popular and therefore a great place to meet people. Dorms $33, doubles $99

The House Project Bellavista 215 ☎01 446 2941, ⓦthehouseproject.pe; map p.733. A backpacker option near the Miraflores strip with a focus on adventure sports. Nice touches include a barbecue, fresh sushi and smoothies, pizza oven and an outdoor bar. Dorms $40, doubles $130

★ **HQ Villa** C Independencia 1288 ☎01 651 2320, ⓦhq-villa-hostel.minihostels.com; map p.733. While this is a bit out of the way in a quiet residential neighbourhood – in between Miraflores and San Isidro, parallel to Cuadra 40 of Arequipa and about a 20min walk to the centre of either neighbourhood – it's worth it. A British/Peruvian-owned boutique hostel with loads of character, including a huge garden and open-plan kitchen/living area with moodily lit bathrooms, chandeliers, photography and a packed social calendar, on top of all the usual extras. Dorms $19

Kokopeli Backpackers C Berlin 259 ☎01 242 5665, ⓦhostelkokopeli.com; map p.733. Another top spot for meeting people, with the social life revolving around a rooftop bar that is always buzzing. Dorms $32, doubles $95

★ **The Lighthouse** Jr Cesareo Chacaltana 162 ☎01 446 8397, ⓦthelighthouseperu.com; map p.733. Spacious comfortable rooms in this B&B (one with a balcony) with cable TV – good for those looking for a more tranquil stay. A patio with barbecue plus a communal area with DVDs, books and internet offer the budget traveller some real creature comforts. Kitchen use and a generous breakfast all add to the experience. Book in advance as there are only six rooms. $102

BARRANCO

Hostal Barranco Jr Ignacio Mariategui 105 ☎01 247 5412, ⓦhostalbarranco.com; map pp.728–729. You won't be hanging out with other travellers here, but there are plenty of bars nearby. The clean rooms and en-suite bathrooms make up for the thin walls and slight street noise. Off Av Bolognesi, northeast of the Plaza de Armas. $60

Domeyer C Domeyer 296 ☎01 247 1413, ⓦdomeyerhostel.net; map pp.728–729. This hostel has a bohemian feel (there's normally one or two long-stayers here), shared kitchen and living room plus laundry service (and a decent breakfast included with room price). Rooms include cable and wi-fi, and there is a cheaper dorm room. Gay friendly. Dorms $50, doubles $150

The Point Malecón Junín 300 ☎01 247 7997, ⓦthepointhostels.com; map pp.728–729. Boasts lots of facilities including internet, TV room and kitchen, as well as the on-site *Pointless Bar*, a great place to meet other travellers and have a good time. Relaxed garden with hammocks is a boon. Dorms $27, doubles $70

EATING

Lima has seen its gastronomy boom in the past few years, partly thanks to Peruvian celebrity chef and international restaurateur Gastón Acurio (see box, p.721); the swell in national pride surrounding Peruvian cuisine is palpable, nowhere more so than in Lima. Many of the more upmarket restaurants fill up very quickly, so it's advisable to reserve in advance.

CENTRAL LIMA

There is a Metro supermarket on Jr Cusco 245 (between Lampa and Augusto Wiese) and two enormous supermarkets opposite each other on Alfonso Ugarte, where it is crossed by Uruguay. Most *chifas* (Chinese restaurants) in Chinatown are good and very cheap. There is also a whole street full of vegetarian restaurants one block from the Plaza de Armas on Camaná.

★ **Antigua Pastelería y Panadería Huérfanos** Azángaro ☎01 428 6273; map p.731. This cake shop has been here for over one hundred years – and is easily the best place in central Lima for bread. It also makes its own fresh pasta and you can buy pastries and biscuits by weight. Also has a small restaurant. Plate of lasagne with wine and bread $18. Daily 6.40am–8.50pm.

★ **Bodega Cafetería Santa Isabel** Jr Carabaya 520 ☎01 426 0058; map p.731. Recharge after sightseeing in this tiny *huarique* that serves some of the best coffee in Lima. Excellent chocolates and drinks are available, and they also specialize in regional cheeses and hams – their sandwiches and *empanadas* ($3) are excellent. Mon–Sat 8am–8.30pm.

El Cordano Jr Ancash 202 ☎01 427 0181, ⓔrestcordano@hotmail.com; map p.731. Beside the Palacio del Gobierno, this is one of the city's last surviving traditional bar-restaurants, open since 1905. The food is overpriced, but go for a drink, soak up the atmosphere and feel yourself slip back in time. Does a roaring trade in local ham sandwiches ($10). Daily 8am–8pm.

Esbari Jr de la Unión 574; map p.731. Primarily an ice-cream parlour with fabulous flavours and sundaes ($13.50), good coffee and cheap food – look for the "*ofertas*" section in the back of the menu where everything is less than $10. Daily 8am–11.30pm.

Queirolo Café Bar Restaurant Quilca 201; map p.731. Arguably there is no place that better represents old bohemian Lima; this bar has seen every artist and writer in the city come through its doors for lunch or drinks since 1880. They serve a good set lunch ($9), as well as sandwiches and the usual *criolla* favourites. Mon–Fri 9am–11pm.

Tanta Pasaje Nicolás de Rivera 142–148 ☎01 428 3115; map p.731. If you can't afford a whole Gastón Acurio meal, his café chain *Tanta* can give you a taste of what he has to offer. This one, opposite the tourist information office, is a

9

very pleasant place to refuel while sightseeing. Serves breakfasts, sandwiches, soups, salads and mains. Try the *ají de gallina* (S29) or the fruit juice mixes (S12–14). Mon–Sat 9am–10pm, Sun 9am–6pm.

Wa Lok Jr Paruro 864, Chinatown ☎01 427 2656; map p.731. An excellent and traditional Chinese restaurant, consistently recommended by many Peruvians. It offers a range of authentic *chifa* dishes, and although it's not the cheapest, there are good vegetarian and dim sum options under S20. Come for an early dinner as it closes at 9pm.

MIRAFLORES

Eating options tend to be a little more expensive out of the centre, but there are a lot of good set menus for S8–12 on Los Pinos (even at dinner) and in the small passage connecting Manuel Bonilla to Esperanza (go for the ones that are full of locals). Both streets are off Parque Kennedy. There is also a huge food market between the Ovalo Parque Kennedy and Paseo de la Republica at Jr Eledoro Romero, and supermarkets everywhere.

La Lucha & La Luchíta Av Diagonal at the corner with C Olaya & Pasaje Champagnant 139; map p.733. These two sandwich joints just around the corner from each other may be diminutive, but their oversized sandwiches with a variety of meaty fillings and sauces certainly aren't – the *chicharrón* (deep-fried pork) is particularly delicious at S9.10 for a large portion. Mon–Thurs 8am–1am, Fri & Sat 8am–3am, Sun 8am–1am.

Manolo Av Larco 608 ☎01 44 2244, ⓦmanolochurros .com; map p.733. This Miraflores institution is all about the Spanish-style *churros con chocolate* – a thin doughnut that comes with hot chocolate for dipping; heaven for just S12.80. Also does breakfasts, mains, burgers and the like. Daily 7am–1am.

Patagonia: Soul Food C Bolívar 164 ☎01 446 8705, ⓦpatagoniarestaurante.net; map p.733. Colourful mixture of Peruvian and Argentine influences (the owner is from Buenos Aires so expect everything from juicy steaks to *chifa*) – there are bright Andean throws, walls crammed with photos and a rooftop terrace. Does an excellent lunch-time menu for S25. Mon–Sat noon–2am.

El Príncipe Berlín 250 ☎01 241 4332; map p.733. A standout weekday lunchtime menu (S9) with Peruvian fish and meat dishes that are tastier and more generous than similar deals on the same street. Many wash it all down with a stein of beer and return at night for a pisco sour. Mon–Thurs noon–1am, Fri & Sat noon–3am, Sun 3pm–1am.

★**Punto Azul** Benavides 2711 and San Martín 595, Miraflores ☎01 445 8078, ⓦpuntoazulrestaurante.com; map pp.728–729 & p.733. This *cevichería* is a real gem. As well as *ceviche* (S23) it serves other Peruvian classics involving fish or seafood, such as *causas* (tuna with mashed potato and lime) and *chupes* (chowder). The

original site, a *huarique* on the busy Javier Prado in San Isidro, has you sitting on stools outside, while those in Miraflores are more restaurant-like. Tues–Sun 11am–4pm.

Thani Wasi C Manuel Bonilla 176; map p.733. Locals pack out the small wooden tables here at lunchtime for the tasty and healthy food on good-value menus (S8–12), featuring everything from *bistec a la pobre* (steak, egg and chips) to *trucha* (trout). Daily noon–5pm.

BARRANCO AND OTHER SUBURBS

Anticuchos Tio Jhony Catalina Miranda 101, at Av Paseo de la República; map pp.728–729. This authentic *huarique* serves some of the best *anticuchos* (beef heart kebabs) in the capital. Don't be put off by the unusual meat – *anticuchos* are the most flavourful beef you'll ever try, especially here (S15–30). "Uncle" Jhony's special chilli sauce is spectacular. Daily 5pm–1am.

Expreso Virgen de Guadalupe Av Prolongación San Martín 15-A, next to the Municipalidad ☎01 252 8907; map pp.728–729. A unique vegetarian restaurant in an old tram car right on the main square. Lunchtime buffet S16 (S18 at weekends) for a great selection of meat-free and some vegan dishes. Mon–Thurs & Sun 9am–2am, Fri & Sat 9am–3am (live music most nights from 10pm).

Mi Carcochita Av Pedro de Osma, at Malecón Castilla ☎01 248 7826; map pp.728–729. Friendly corner bar and café that does a good range of snacks, sandwiches and juices – but the main draw is the fact that it's open 24hr. Lunch menu S14 (S15 at weekends).

NIGHTLIFE

The daily newspaper *El Comercio* provides good entertainment listings and its Friday edition carries a comprehensive supplement on Lima's nightlife. The Plaza San Martín is a frenetic nightlife spot, with enough bars and clubs there to take you through until dawn. Barranco is also trendy and the liveliest place to hang out at weekends, while Miraflores has the highest concentration of cheap bars around the Parque Kennedy. There are good places for live music in all three areas. As you would expect, Friday and Saturday nights are the most popular, and many bars and clubs only open on those days. Most bars have Facebook pages to check what's on.

BARS AND CLUBS

The distinction between a bar and a club in Lima is often blurred, as bars become dancefloors and stay open all night. A good guide as to which is which is the opening times – many of the clubs only open at weekends. Lima has a fun and rapidly growing gay and lesbian scene; see ⓦ lima .gaycities.com for current information about what's on.

El Bolivarcito Jr de la Unión 926, Central Lima ⓦ granhotelbolivar.com.pe; map p.731. Come to the "catedral" of pisco sour, part of the *Gran Hotel Bolívar*, for probably the best in Lima (the classic house pisco will set you back S20). Also does an excellent set lunch (S14; except Sun). Mon–Sat noon–midnight, Sun noon–11pm.

Downtown Vale Todo Pasaje Los Pinos 168, Miraflores ⓦ peruesgay.com; map p.733. The name means "everything's allowed downtown" and it certainly is here at Lima's most established gay/lesbian club. Often has live drag or strip shows. Usually free Mon–Thurs, entrance fee at weekends. Daily from 9pm.

Etnias Bar Cultural Jr Carabaya 815, Central Lima; map p.731. A highly atmospheric multipurpose space with muralled walls, folk art and a chequered dancefloor. *Etnias* is a café/nightclub which often has live world music/reggae or film showings. Thurs–Sat 9.30pm until dawn.

★ **El Mirador** Jr de la Unión 892, 7th floor, Central Lima ⓦ barelmirador.com; map p.731. Without doubt the bar with the best view in Lima. Walk confidently up to the bouncer and take the lift up to the seventh floor, where you'll find a cool crowd listening to a mix of rock and Latin music surrounded by incense and Hindu imagery. Get there before 10pm to grab a table with views of the plaza. Entry S10. Thurs–Sat 8pm until dawn.

Munich Jr de la Unión 1044, Central Lima; map p.731. German-themed underground piano bar with a barrel for a doorway and bar food, a live pianist and nostalgic European landscapes on the walls. Mon–Sat 7pm–3am.

Rincón Cervecero Jr de la Unión 1045, Central Lima ☎ 01 428 1422, ⓦ rinconcervecero.com.pe; map p.731. Another German-themed bar opposite *Munich*, where you can order beer in containers of all forms, including a 5-litre barrel (S77), from Peruvian waiters in lederhosen. Mon–Thurs 3pm–midnight, Fri & Sat noon–3am (closed Sun).

Vichama Jr Carabaya 945, Central Lima; map p.731. A seriously cool rock bar/club in a huge colonial space, with many small art-filled rooms containing a mix of shabby-chic furniture. Free entry. Thurs–Sat 10pm until very late.

Wahio's Bar Pasaje Espinoza 111 on the Plaza de Bomberos ☎ 01 247 2592; map pp.728–729. Cosy bar club with several rooms playing different sounds, though you'll mostly hear reggae and electronic pop. Walls are packed with photos and artwork, there's comfy seating and bar food is served. Free entry. Thurs–Sat from around 9.30pm until the last people leave.

LIVE MUSIC

The great variety of traditional and hybrid sounds is one of the most enduring reasons for visiting the capital. The best place to go for an evening's entertainment is a *peña* – a live music spectacular featuring many styles of national song and dance with an MC, live band, some audience participation and much dancing. *Peñas* are great fun for all ages – they start late and the dancing can last all night. The Lima versions are very expensive compared to the rest of the country (you can pay up to S60 just to enter) – so if you can't go here, be sure to seek one out elsewhere.

La Candelaria Av Bolognesi 292, Barranco ☎ 01 247 1314, ⓦ lacandelariaperu.com; map pp.728–729. Impressive costumes, choreography and plenty of audience participation mark this place out as one of Barranco's most popular *peñas*. The amazingly decorated room adds to the atmosphere. Entrance fee (depending on the show) S35–45, including a pisco sour. Shows Thurs and Sat starting at 9.30pm.

Jazz Zone Av La Paz 646, Pasaje El Suche, Miraflores ☎ 01 241 8139, ⓦ jazzzoneperu.com; map p.733. Live music (most often rock, jazz and *música criolla*) from local and international groups in this atmospheric joint upstairs. Entrance fee varies depending on the show. Tues–Sat from 8pm.

★ **La Noche** Av Bolognesi 307, at El Boulevard, Barranco ⓦ lanoche.com.pe; map pp.728–729. At the top end of the Boulevard, this bar is really packed at weekends and is the top nightspot in the neighbourhood. There's a section with a stage for live music, with free jazz sessions on Mon eve. Free entry to bar, cover charge for live music. Mon–Sat from 7pm.

De Rompe y Raja C Manuel Segura 127, Barranco ☎ 01 247 3271, ⓦ derompeyraja.pe; map pp.728–729. This moodily lit *peña* is especially famous for Afro-Peruvian rhythms, but you'll hear salsa and *música folklórica* too. Entry is S30, but always check the website as flyers can be printed off for discounts. Lunchtime shows with food included are cheaper. Thurs–Sun from around 10pm.

SHOPPING

Artesanía All types of Peruvian *artesanía* are available in Lima, including woollen goods, crafts and gemstones.

9

Some of the best in Peru are on Av Petit Thouars, which is home to a handful of markets between Av Ricardo Palma and Av Angamos, all within easy walking distance of Miraflores centre. Often considerably cheaper are the artisan markets on blocks 9 and 10 of Av La Marina in Pueblo Libre, as well as the good craft and antique market in the Miraflores Park between Diagonal and Av Larco, which takes place every evening (6–9pm). In central Lima the Artesanía Santo Domingo, opposite the church of the same name, houses a range of suppliers to suit all budgets, just a stone's throw from the Plaza Mayor; it is especially good for loose beads.

Clothing Polvos Azules (Av Paseo de le República, 2 blocks from Plaza Grau) and Gamarra (Prolongación Gamarra 712, La Victoria) are huge shopping centres/ markets where you can pick up very cheap branded clothing and footwear. Both areas can be dangerous and are rife with pickpockets, so take only the money you want to spend and try to visit early in the morning.

DIRECTORY

Banks and exchange Central Lima, Miraflores, Barranco and San Isidro all have several casas de cambio, and Interbank will change money and travellers' cheques. Moneychangers on the streets will often give a slightly better rate but will try all sorts of tricks, from doctored calculators to fake money. Official money changers on the streets around Parque Kennedy offer good rates. Ensure that they are wearing the official blue vests and laminated badges. Often the best way to change money in Lima is by buying things in supermarkets with large US$ notes and asking them for the change in soles – they usually give the best rates.

Embassies and consulates Australia, Av La Paz 1049, 10th floor, Miraflores (☎01 630 0500); Canada, Bolognesi 228, Miraflores (☎01 319 3200); Ireland (consulate), Av Paseo de la Republica 5757b, Miraflores (☎01 242 9516); South Africa, Av Víctor Andrés Belaunde, Edificio Real 3, Office 801, San Isidro (☎01 440 9996); UK, Torre Parque Mar, Av Larco 1301, 22nd floor, Miraflores (☎01 617 3000); USA, Av La Encalada, block 17, Surco (☎01 618 2000).

Internet Internet cafés are available throughout the capital, most equipped for chat, with several 24hr places in Miraflores. A large percentage of bars, restaurants and accommodation also have wi-fi.

Police Tourist Police, Jr Moore 268, Magdalena del Mar (☎01 460 1060 or ☎980 121 462, ✉divtur@pnp.gob.pe). English spoken.

Postal services Not overly reliable, the principal postal company is SERPOST whose main office is on Pasaje Piura s/n off Jr de la Unión, one block from the Plaza de Armas (8am–8.30pm; ☎01 511 5110). SERPOST also has an office in Miraflores at Petit Thouars 5201.

CALLAO

Still the country's main commercial harbour, and one of the most modern ports in South America, **Callao** lies about 14km west of central Lima. Its main attraction is the pentagonal **Fortaleza del Real Felipe**, on Plaza Independencia, which houses the **Museo del Ejército** (Military Museum; Tues–Sun 9.30am–4pm; S15 by 1hr 30min guided tour in Spanish or English; ☎01 429 0532). The collection of eighteenth-century arms and rooms dedicated to Peruvian heroes are interesting, but the real star is the fort itself, a superb example of the military architecture of its age. A short walk from the fort, at the dock on Plaza Grau, you can take **boat tours** (see p.736) out around local islands. Book ahead for trips further out to the **Islas Palomino** (4hr; around S115), where you'll see sea birds, dolphins and sometimes whales.

A twenty-minute walk southwest of the fort are the crumbling but charming neighbourhoods of **Chuquito** and **La Punta**, where you can dream away an afternoon on the pebble beach, eat mouth-wateringly fresh *ceviche* or go for a rowing-boat ride out to sea.

ARRIVAL

By bus or colectivo To get to Callao from central Lima, take a *colectivo* from Plaza Dos de Mayo running down Avenida Oscar R. Benavides, or a bus from Avenida Tacna (line Roma 1). Note that Callao can be dangerous in the evening.

Ayacucho

Beautiful **AYACUCHO** (2761m) played a vital role for the fifteenth-century Spanish conquistadors, thanks to its strategic location between Lima and Cusco and between Potosí (Bolivia) and Antofagasta (Chile-Argentina), home to gold, silver and mercury mines. Ayacucho attracted rich miners and landowners who financed the construction of the beautiful churches and colonial buildings that are still standing today. More recently, the region was one of the worst hit in the 1980s when the Maoist revolutionary movement Sendero Luminoso, or Shining Path, launched mass internal conflict leading to the death of thousands. The city's isolation and its recent turbulent history mean that the area has mostly remained off the backpacker trail. Nonetheless, since the late 1990s, the region has become as safe as the rest of Peru and travellers have begun to explore the city's treasures and enjoy the surrounding Andean landscape.

WHAT TO SEE AND DO

The heart of the city is the Plaza Mayor, with its sixteenth- and seventeenth-century buildings characterized by stone arches, pillars with balustrades and red-brick clay roofs. The plaza is home to the seventeenth-century **Catedral**, which combines Renaissance and Baroque elements. Despite its somewhat sombre facade, its rich interior is home to ten beautiful gold-leaf altarpieces.

Visitors should not miss the **Museo de la Memoria** (Prolongación Libertad 1229; Mon–Fri 9am–1pm & 3–6pm, Sun call in advance; S2; ☎066 317 170), which focuses on the socio-political violence inflicted by the Shining Path revolutionary movement in the 1980s and 90s. The little museum is home to a number of displays including photographs of the dead and missing, as well as artworks on the conflict and a replica of a torture cell. A wall chart details the history of ANFASEP, the non-profit organization that runs the museum. Mothers and wives of the deceased and missing meet here regularly to share their experiences and lend support to one another. You can purchase the women's handmade clothes and crafts in the little shop upstairs.

ARRIVAL AND DEPARTURE

By plane The Alfredo Mendívil Duarte airport is 4km east of town, a 10–15min taxi ride (S8). Regular *combis* (every 15min; 10min) connect the airport to Puente Nuevo on Jr Vivanco. LAN, LC Perú and Star Perú serve Lima (5 daily; 1hr). Star Perú are due to launch a direct service to Cusco at the end of 2015.

By bus Most buses use the Terminal Municipal Los Libertadores de America on Av Pérez de Cuellar s/n (☎066

312 666), with the exception of the well-established Cruz del Sur which serves Lima (3 daily) from its own terminal at Jr Mariscal Cáceres 1264 (☎066 312 813).

Destinations Cusco (daily; 12–16hr); Huancayo (3 daily; 10hr); Ica (3 daily; 6hr); Lima (several daily; 8–9hr).

INFORMATION

Tourist information The friendly and helpful iPerú office is at Portal Municipal 45 on the eastern side of the main plaza (Mon–Sat 9am–6pm, Sun 9am–1pm; ☎066 318 305, ✉iperuayacucho@promperu.gob.pe).

ACCOMMODATION

La Colmena Cusco 140 ☎066 311 318, ⊚hotel-colmena.com. Formerly the home of a Spanish General, La Colmena has clean tiled rooms spread out over three levels, most giving onto a leafy interior courtyard. All have private bath and rates include breakfast and wi-fi. There's also a pleasant outdoor restaurant serving Creole dishes. S70

Tres Máscaras Jr Tres Máscaras 194 ☎066 312 921, ⊚hoteltresmascaras.galeon.com. Colourful birds tweet in cages as three little dogs supervise the premises of this welcoming hostel with a pleasant lush courtyard area with prickly pears, cacti and orange trees. Rooms are spacious and all have TV and private bath. Free wi-fi. S71

EATING

Niñachay Centro Turístico Cultural, San Cristóbal de Huamaga, Jr 28 de Julio 178. Located within the San Cristóbal cultural centre that also houses a number of other restaurants, this pleasant laidback option offers courtyard seating and the menu encompasses a range of tasty local dishes. Mains S16. Daily 8am–10pm.

Via Via Café Portal Constitución 4. This welcoming Belgian-owned restaurant/café with great views over the square serves excellent grub, including quinoa risotto (S15) and alpaca-based mains (S12). They also rustle up healthy freshly made fruit-and-veg juices (S7), too. Free wi-fi. Daily 7am–midnight.

DIRECTORY

Banks and exchange BCP and Banco Continental are both on the northern side of the square; both have ATMs. There are casas de cambio and money exchangers just by La Miel café.

Internet Conquistadores, Dos de Mayo 172 (daily 8am–9pm; S1/hr; ☎066 527 683).

Laundry LHL, Garcilazo de la Vega 265 (Mon–Sat 8am–9pm).

Police The tourist police are at Dos de Mayo 113, at Jr Arequipa (daily 8am–10pm; ☎066 315 845).

Post office Asamblea 293 (Mon–Fri 8am–7pm, Sat 8am–6pm).

9

Cusco and around

The former capital of the Inca empire, modern **CUSCO** is an exciting and colourful city, enclosed between high hills and dominated by the imposing ceremonial centre and temple of **Sacsaywamán**. It's one of South America's biggest tourist destinations, thanks to its narrow whitewashed streets, thriving culture, lively nightlife, substantial Inca ruins and architectural treasures from the colonial era.

Once you've acclimatized to the 3400m altitude, there are dozens of enticing destinations within easy reach. For most people the **Sacred Valley** is the obvious first choice, with the citadel of **Machu Picchu** as the ultimate goal. The mountainous region around Cusco boasts some of the country's finest trekking, and beyond the **Inca Trail** to Machu Picchu are hundreds of lesser-known paths into the mountains, including the **Salcantay** and **Ausungate** treks, which are even more stunning and challenging. Cusco is also a convenient jumping-off point for the exploration of the lowland **Amazon rainforest** in Madre de Dios, such as the Tambopata-Candamo Reserved Zone, or the Manu Biosphere Reserve, among the most biodiverse wildernesses on Earth.

SOME HISTORY

Legend has it that Cusco was founded by **Manco Capac** and his sister **Mama Occlo** in around 1100 AD. Over the next two centuries, the **Cusco Valley** was home to the Inca tribe, but it wasn't until

WHEN TO VISIT

The best time to visit the area around Cusco is during the dry season (May–Sept), when it's warm with clear skies during the day but relatively cold at night. During the wet season (Oct–April) it rarely rains every day or all week, but the heavy downpours trigger landslides, making it difficult and dangerous to travel in the nearby mountains.

Pachacutec assumed power in 1438 that Cusco became the centre of an expanding empire. The new ruler designed the city in the shape of a puma, with its head incorporating some of its most important sites. Of all the Inca rulers, only **Atahualpa**, the last, never actually resided in Cusco, and even he was en route there when the conquistadors captured him at Cajamarca. **Francisco Pizarro** reached the native capital on November 15, 1533, after holding Atahualpa to ransom, then killing him anyway. The city's beauty surpassed anything the Spaniards had seen before in the New World, the stonework was better than any in Spain and precious metals were used in a sacred context throughout the city. As usual, they lost no time in looting it.

Like its renowned art, the Cusco of today is dark yet vibrantly coloured, reflecting its turbulent legacy. It's a politically active, left-of-centre city where the streets are often alive with fiestas and demonstrations.

WHAT TO SEE AND DO

The city divides into several distinct zones, with the **Plaza de Armas** at the heart of it all.

The **Boleto Turístico** Tourist Ticket (see box opposite) will give you an idea of some of the most popular city and Sacred Valley sites, but it does not include entry to the one unmissable Cusco site, the Inca sun temple at **Q'orikancha**. Around the city there are opportunities for tours, hikes and extreme sports, as well as the fascinating Inca sites of **Sacsaywamán** and **Tambomachay**.

Plaza de Armas

Cusco's ancient and modern centre, **Plaza de Armas** corresponds roughly to the ceremonial *Huacaypata*, the Incas' ancient central plaza, and is a constant hub of activity, its northern and western sides filled with shops and restaurants. Here you'll be approached by touts, waiters and shoe-shine boys, and here is where you'll come to watch the parades during Cusco's festivities. You'll see two flags flying here – the Peruvian one and the rainbow flag of Tuhuantinsuyo, which

THE CUSCO TOURIST TICKET AND BOLETO INTEGRAL

The **Boleto Turístico** (S130 for ten days, students with ISIC card S70) is a vital purchase for most visitors, as you can't visit most important sites without it. It covers the Sacsaywamán, Q'enqo, Pukapukara and Tambomachay ruins near the city, as well as those in Ollantaytambo, Chinchero, Písac, Moray, Tipón and Pikillacta, plus the optional extras of Museo Histórico Regional, Museo de Arte Contemporáneo, Museo de Arte Popular, Centro Qosqo de Arte Nativo, the Pachacutec monument and the Q'orikancha site museum (though not the Q'orikancha itself). It's available from all of the sites on the ticket, or from the issuing COSITUC offices at Av Sol 103, office 102 (daily 8am–6pm; ☎084 261 465, ⓦ www.cosituc.gob.pe). You can also buy three partial *boletos*, valid for one or two days (S70), one covering the ruins immediately outside Cusco, another the above museums, and the third, the Sacred Valley ruins. The **Boleto Religioso** (S50, or S25 for students; valid for ten days; ⓦ cra.org.pe), which must be purchased at one of the following sites, covers the star attraction of the Catedral, as well as the Iglesia de San Blas, the Templo de San Cristóbal and the Museo de Arte Religioso.

represents the four corners of the Inca empire (not to be confused with the gay pride flag). On the northeastern side stands the imposing cathedral, flanked by the Jesús María and El Triunfo churches, with the Compañía de Jesús church on the eastern side.

La Catedral

The plaza's exposed northeastern edge is dominated by the fortress-like Baroque-style **Catedral** (daily 10am–6pm; S25). Inside you'll find some of the best examples of art from the *Escuela Cusqueña* (Cusco School): look out for *The Last Supper*, with Christ sitting down to a feast of *cuy* (guinea pig), and the portrayals of the Virgin Mary as Pachamama (Mother Earth). Also check out the cathedral's finely carved granite altar and oldest surviving painting in Cusco, depicting the terrible 1650 earthquake, as well as a Neoclassical high altar made entirely of finely beaten embossed silver. Ten smaller chapels surround the nave, including the Chapel of El Señor de los Temblores (The Lord of Earthquakes), which houses a 26kg crucifix made of solid gold and encrusted with precious stones.

Iglesia de la Compañía de Jesús

As you look downhill from the centre of the plaza, the **Iglesia de la Compañía de Jesús** (Mon–Sat 9am–5.30pm, Sun 9–11.30am & 1–5.30pm; S15, S10 with ISIC card) dominates the skyline, and is often confused with the cathedral on first

glance due to the splendour of its highly ornate facade. First built in the late 1570s, it was resurrected after the earthquake of 1650 in a Latin cross shape, over the foundations of Amara Cancha – originally Huayna Capac's Palace of the Serpents. Cool and dark inside, with a grand gold-leaf altarpiece and a fine wooden pulpit displaying a relief of Christ, its transept ends in a stylish Baroque cupola.

Museo Inka

North of the cathedral, slightly uphill, you'll find one of the city's most beautiful colonial mansions, **El Palacio del Almirante** (The Admiral's Palace), which now houses the **Museo Inka** (Mon–Fri 8am–7pm, Sat 9am–4pm; S10). The museum itself is the best place in Cusco to see exhibits of Inca pottery, textiles, trepanned skulls, finely crafted metalwork (including miniature metal llamas given as offerings to the gods) and the largest range of wooden *quero* vases in the world.

Q'orikancha

If you visit one site in Cusco it should be **Q'orikancha**. The Convento de Santo Domingo at the intersection of Avenida El Sol and Calle Santa Domingo rises imposingly but rudely from the impressive walls of the Q'orikancha complex (Mon–Sat 8.30am–5.30pm, Sun 2–5pm; S10; S5 with ISIC card), which the conquistadors laid low to make way for their uninspiring Baroque seventeenth-century church. Before the

9

Spanish set their gold-hungry eyes on it, the temple must have been even more breathtaking, consisting of four small sanctuaries and a larger temple set around the existing courtyard, which was encircled by a cornice of gold made of seven hundred solid gold sheets (Q'orikancha means "golden enclosure"). Below the temple was an artificial garden in which everything was made of gold or silver and encrusted with precious jewels, from llamas and shepherds to the tiniest details of clumps of earth and weeds, including snails and butterflies. The Incas used the Q'orikancha as a solar observatory to study celestial activities, and archeologists believe that the mummies of the previous Incas were brought here and ritually burned.

Visitors need to use their imagination when they enter the courtyard inside the site, although surviving sections of the original Inca wall, made of tightly interlocking blocks of polished andesite, stand as firmly rooted as ever, completely

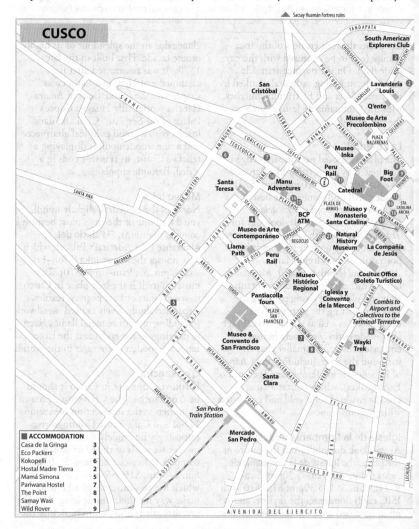

▲ Sacsay Huamán Fortress ruins

CUSCO

ACCOMMODATION	
Casa de la Gringa	3
Eco Packers	4
Kokopelli	6
Hostal Madre Tierra	2
Mamá Simona	5
Pariwana Hostel	7
The Point	8
Samay Wasi	1
Wild Rover	9

unshaken by the powerful earthquakes that have devastated colonial buildings.

Museo de Sitio del Q'orikancha

The underground **Museo de Sitio del Q'orikancha**, Santo Domingo s/n (daily 9am–6pm; entry with Boleto Turístico), consists of five rooms, containing various relics such as pottery shards, Inca weaponry, mummies and a section on the practice of trepanning, complete with medical instruments and several examples of trepanned skulls from the

Paracas area. Guides are available for a small fee.

Museo Machu Picchu

A number of artefacts including beautiful Inca ceramics that Hiram Bingham unearthed during the 1911 expedition to Machu Picchu are now on display at the fascinating **Museo Machu Picchu** (Mon–Sat 9am–5pm; S20) at C Santa Catalina Ancha 320. There are a number of informative videos too – it's worth visiting before travelling to the ruins to

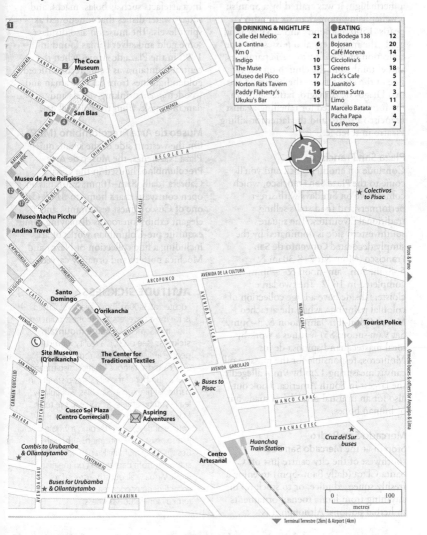

● DRINKING & NIGHTLIFE		● EATING	
Calle del Medio	21	La Bodega 138	12
La Cantina	6	Bojosan	20
Km 0	1	Café Morena	14
Indigo	10	Cicciolina's	9
The Muse	13	Greens	18
Museo del Pisco	17	Jack's Cafe	5
Norton Rats Tavern	19	Juanito's	2
Paddy Flaherty's	16	Korma Sutra	3
Ukuku's Bar	15	Limo	11
		Marcelo Batata	8
		Pacha Papa	4
		Los Perros	7

Terminal Terrestre (2km) & Airport (4km)

9

get a clearer idea of what lies behind the Incan marvel that is Machu Picchu.

Iglesia y Convento de La Merced

Just southwest from the Plaza de Armas along Calle Mantas is the **Iglesia y Convento de La Merced** (Mon–Sat 8am–12.30pm & 2–5.30pm; S6). Founded in 1536, it was rebuilt after the 1650 earthquake in a rich combination of Baroque and Renaissance styles. While its facade is exceptional, the highlight is a breathtaking 1720s **monstrance** standing a metre high; it was crafted by a Spanish jeweller using more than six hundred pearls, 1500 diamonds and 22kg of solid gold. The monastery also possesses a fine collection of *Escuela Cusqueña* paintings, and entombed in the church on the far side of the cloisters are the bodies of the two Diegos de Almagro, father and son, the former executed for rebelling against Francisco Pizarro and the latter for killing Pizarro in revenge.

Plaza San Francisco

Continue on another block and you'll come to the **Plaza San Francisco**, which comes alive on Sundays with street performers and food stalls selling traditional favourites. The square's southwestern side is dominated by the simply decorated **Convento de San Francisco** (Mon–Sat 7–8.30am & 5–8pm, Sun 7am–noon & 5–8pm; free), completed in 1652. The two large cloisters inside have a large collection of colonial paintings, while the attached **Museo** (Mon–Fri 9am–noon & 3–5pm, Sat 9am–noon; S5) features a work by local master Juan Espinosa de los Monteros, responsible for the massive oil canvas measuring 12m by 9m – allegedly the largest in South America. Look out also for an unusual candelabra made out of human bones.

Mercado San Pedro

Stop in at the **Mercado San Pedro** southwest of the city centre just off C Santa Clara (daily 8am–5pm) to enjoy a freshly squeezed juice, or to stock up on anything from llama toenail ornaments to herbal potions. Although it is principally a food market, there are several stalls selling traditional costumes. Leave your valuables behind, as pickpockets are rife here.

Museo Histórico Regional y Casa Garcilaso

At the southern corner of Plaza Regocijo, the **Museo Histórico Regional y Casa Garcilaso** (daily 8am–5pm; entry with Boleto Turístico) is home to fascinating pre-Inca ceramics, plus a Nazca mummy with 1.5m-long hair, and a number of Inca artefacts such as bolas, maces, and square water dishes that functioned as spirit levels. The museum also displays some gold and silver llamas found in 1996 in the Plaza de Armas when the central fountain was being reconstructed, golden figurines from Sacsaywamán and wooden *quero* drinking vessels and dancing masks from the colonial era.

Museo de Arte Precolombino (MAP)

On the western side of the small, quiet Plaza Nazarenas, the **Museo de Arte Precolumbino**, housed in the Casa Cabrera (daily 8am–10pm; S20), has an open courtyard that's home to *MAP Café*, one of Cusco's finest restaurants, and elegant exhibition rooms displaying some exquisite pre-Columbian works of art, including a fine collection of Nazca and Mochica pottery and ornately carved

---

ALTITUDE SICKNESS

Located at 3400m above sea level, Cusco is, for most travellers, the highest point on their trip. *Soroche*, or **acute mountain sickness** (see p.33), is a reality for most people arriving by plane from sea level. Cusco's mountainous location also means that a number of the city's steep streets, in particular high up in San Blas, will quickly leave you breathless as you explore town. Make sure to take it easy for the first couple of days, even sleeping a whole day just to assist acclimatization. Although Cusco's lively nightlife is an obvious draw, stay away from bars at least on the first night. Virtually all guesthouses offer complimentary coca tea, a traditional remedy for altitude sickness.

Mochica ceremonial staffs, all labelled in English, French and Spanish.

San Blas

Just around the corner from Plaza Nazarenas you come to the narrow alley of **Hathun Rumiyoq**, the most famous Inca passageway of all. Within its impressive walls lies the celebrated **Inca stone**; the twelve-cornered block fits perfectly into the original lower wall of what used to be the Inca Roca's old imperial palace.

From here, walk north up the Cuesta de San Blas, and you come to the Plazoleta de San Blas, which hosts a Saturday handicrafts market (9am–4pm). Also on the tiny square is the small **Chapel of San Blas** (daily 8am–6pm; S10 or free with Boleto Religioso). The highlight here is an incredibly intricate pulpit, carved from a block of cedar wood in a complicated Churrigueresque style by an indigenous man who allegedly devoted his life to the task and whose skull rests in the topmost part of the carving.

Museo de la Coca

Just up Calle Suytuqatu from Plazoleta San Blas lies the fascinating little **Museo de la Coca** (daily 9am–7pm; S10), devoted to the history of the coca leaf through the ages. The exhibits explore the significance of the plant in Peru from its first known ceremonial use by the Andean people to the present day through a series of displays, from ancient ceramic figures with cheeks bulging from chewing coca leaves to nineteenth-century texts on research into the medical use of cocaine. The curator is happy to answer any questions you may have.

ARRIVAL AND DEPARTURE

By plane Cusco Airport (Alejandro Velasco Astete International Airport; ☎084 222 611) is 4km south of the city centre. You can either take a taxi from outside the arrivals hall (S20–30 to the city centre), or hop on a Correcaminos *colectivo* (S0.70) from outside the airport car park, which goes along Av Sol to C Ayacucho, two blocks from the Plaza de Armas.

Destinations LAN, Peruvian Airlines, Star Peru, Andes and Avianca have regular flights to major national destinations, including Lima (every 30min; 1hr 20min); Puerto

Maldonado (3 daily; 55min), Arequipa (2 daily; 2hr 15min) and Juliaca (for Puno; 1 daily; 1hr). Amaszonas flies to La Paz (daily except Sat; 1hr 55min) in Bolivia.

By bus Most international and inter-regional buses use the Terminal Terrestre (☎084 224 471) at Vía de Evitamiento 429, 2km southeast of the centre. *Colectivos* (S0.70) marked "Correcaminos" run from one block north of the station dropping passengers off at C Almadro between Sol and Bernardo. To get to the bus station catch the same *colectivo* from Ayacucho between Sol and Andrés; a taxi will set you back S5–8. Recommended bus companies include: Cruz del Sur, which has its own bus depot at Av Industrial 121 (☎084 243 261) and at the Terminal Terrestre (☎084 248 255); Ormeño (☎084 227 501); Inka Express (☎084 247 887); Tour Peru (☎084 236 463); Litoral (☎084 281 920); Movil Tours (☎084 262 526); Cial (☎084 256 216); San Martín (☎097 970 9615).

Destinations Arequipa (hourly between 6–9am and 7pm–midnight; 10hr); Ayacucho (2 daily; 17hr); Copacabana, Bolivia (1 daily; 10hr); La Paz, Bolivia (daily at 10pm; 12hr); Lima (at least hourly; 20hr); Puerto Maldonado (10pm and 5–6 daily between 6.30–9pm; 7hr); Puno (4 early departures between 7 and 8am, one departure at 10pm; 8hr); Rio Branco, Brazil (2 weekly; 20hr). Cruz del Sur to: Arequipa (daily at 8pm & 8.30pm; 9hr); Lima via Nazca (daily at 2pm & 6pm; 18hr).

By train If you're coming from Puno, you'll arrive at the Wanchaq station in the southeast of the city. From here you can hail a taxi on the street outside (around S5 to the centre), catch the airport *colectivo*, or walk the eight or nine blocks up a gentle hill to the Plaza de Armas. If you're coming by train from Machu Picchu, you'll disembark at Estación Poroy, east of the centre; arrivals are met by a bus (S8) that can drop you off at the Plaza Regocijo, or else take a taxi (S15–20). Peru Rail has offices in town at Plaza Regocijo 202 and Plaza de Armas (both daily 7am–10pm), though it's also easy to buy tickets directly through ⊛ perurail.com. For Machu Picchu, it's best to buy at least a week in advance in peak season.

Destinations Wanchaq station to: Puno (April–Oct Mon, Wed, Fri & Sat at 8am; Nov–March Mon, Wed & Sat; 10hr). Poroy station to: Machu Picchu (Vistadome daily at 6.40am & 8.25am; Expedition daily at 7.42am; Hiram Bingham daily at 9.05am; 3hr 30min–4hr).

INFORMATION

Tourist information iPerú is at Portal de Harinas 177 on the Plaza de Armas (Mon–Fri 9am–7pm, Sat & Sun 9am–1pm; ☎084 252 974, ⊜iperucusco@promperu .gob.pe); they also have a couple of kiosks in the main hall of the airport as well as at arrivals (daily 6am–5pm; ☎084 237 364).

South American Explorers' Club (Atoqsaycuchi 670; Mon–Fri 9.30am–5pm, Sat 9.30am–1pm; ☎084 245 484,

9

TOURS IN AND AROUND CUSCO

Tours in and around Cusco range from a half-day city tour to a full-on adventure down to the Amazon. Service and facilities vary considerably, so check exactly what's provided. **Standard tours** around the city, Sacred Valley and to Machu Picchu range from a basic bus service with fixed stops and little in the way of a guide, to luxury packages including guide, food and hotel transfers. The two- to four-day **Inca Trail** is the most popular of the **mountain treks**; many agencies offer trips with guides, equipment and fixed itineraries; do a lot of research deciding when and how to do the Inca Trail (see p.756).

Other popular **alternative Inca trails** (see p.765) are around the snowcapped mountains of Salcantay (6264m) to the north and Ausangate (6372m) to the south, a more remote trek, which needs at least a week plus guides and mules. You can also rent out **mountain bikes** for trips to the Sacred Valley and around, and some operators arrange guided tours. Many **jungle trip** operators are also based in Cusco (see p.828 & p.830).

TOUR OPERATORS

The Cusco area is an adrenaline junkie's paradise, with a huge range of adventure sports on offer. As well as trekking expeditions in the Sacred Valley, there's world-class river rafting on the Apurimac River, climbing and canyoning in the nearby mountains, and mountain biking.

Amazonas Explorer Av Collasuyo 910, Miravalle ☎ 084 252 846, ⓦ amazonas-explorer.com. Internationally renowned operator offering multi-activity trips, combining hiking and rafting on the Apurimac, as well as mountain biking and horseriding excursions.

Aspiring Adventures Apartado 611 ☎ +64 3 489 7474, ⓦ aspiringadventures.com. Aspiring offers gastronomic and "off-beat Cusco" tours to discover more about the city's hidden attractions, as well as unique 3–4-day trips to mysterious religious festivities such as Qoyllur Riti where entranced costume dancing goes on for days.

Andina Travel Plazoleta Santa Catalina 219 ☎ 084 251 892, ⓦ andinatravel.com. Andina are the pioneers in real alternative treks and are constantly working at opening and developing new alternatives to remote

areas, including Quillatambo. Part of the profits goes towards community projects including building new schools, reforestation projects and the reintroduction of native Andean alpacas and llamas.

Big Foot Triunfo 392, 2nd floor ☎ 084 233 836, ⓦ bigfootcusco.com. Specialists in multi-day expeditions, such as trekking in Ausangate and to Vilcabamba (see p.766).

Llama Path San Juan de Dios 250 ☎ 084 223 448, ⓦ llamapath.com. One of the newer Inca Trail trekking operators in town, Llama Path has quickly established itself as a more affordable, high-quality, responsible outfit.

Q'ente Choquechaca 229 ☎ 084 222 535, ⓦ qente.com. Responsible adventure travel company specializing in alternative treks as well as the traditional Inca Trail.

Wayki Trek Quera 239 ☎ 084 224 092, ⓦ waykitrek .net. Professional company supporting many community projects in the area and offering some off-the-beaten-trail treks. Also offers a "wayki option" on the Inca Trail whereby groups spend the night in a porter community prior to starting the trail.

ⓦ saexplorers.org) is an excellent source of information about Cusco and around, with trip reports compiled by fellow travellers, as well as good trekking maps and a good book exchange.

Andean Travel Web (ⓦ andeantravelweb.com) has up-to-date information about events and festivities in the Cusco area.

GETTING AROUND

By bus and colectivo The city bus and *colectivo* networks are incredibly complicated, though cheap and fast once you learn your way around, and charge S0.70 per person. If you don't have much luggage, you can take a Correcaminos *colectivo* from the eastern side of C Ayacucho, half a block south of Av El Sol, to the airport and the Terminal Terrestre.

By taxi Rides within Cusco cost around S3 or S6–10 for trips to the suburbs or up to Sacsaywamán and Q'enqo (some *taxistas* may charge S20 and wait for you, in which case give them half in advance and half later).

ACCOMMODATION

There are numerous budget options around the Plaza de Armas and in the quieter artists' quarter of San Blas uphill from the square.

Casa de la Gringa Tandapata, at Pasnapacana 148 ☎ 084 241 168, ⓦ casadelagringa.com. Cactus pots and a colourful mural decorate the hall of this pleasant guesthouse. Try and stay in the main building as the annexe has darkish rooms. There's a kitchen for guests' use and a communal area with TV and wi-fi. Rates include breakfast. **S90**

★**Eco Packers** Santa Teresa 375 ☎084 231 800, ⓦecopackersperu.com. This fun and colourful hostel has clean dorms set around a leafy interior courtyard. There is table football and billiards to unwind, as well as a laid-back bar with live rock music on Saturday evenings. Wi-fi in the rooms and breakfast included. Dorms $33, doubles $120

Kokopelli San Andres 260 ☎084 224 473, ⓦhostelkokopelli.com. Set in a beautiful colonial house, this new addition to town has female only and mixed dorms, as well as doubles with private bath. There's table tennis, mini-football, a TV lounge, billiards and a cosy wooden bar. Wi-fi and breakfast included. Dorms $25, doubles $140

★**Hostal Madre Tierra** Atoqsaycuchi 647 ☎084 248 452, ⓦhostalmadretierra.com. A wonderful little guesthouse offering brightly coloured doubles, all with private bath, set on two floors. The interiors are decked out in local wood and the fireplace adds to the home-like atmosphere. Breakfast is served at the convivial communal table, and there's free wi-fi and all-day coca tea. $183

Mamá Simona Ceniza 364 ☎084 260 408, ⓦmamasimona.com. A laidback place with an internal patio featuring armchairs, fun murals and colourful beanbags and masks. Doubles and dorms have lovely parquet floors and light wooden beds, and are kept spick-and-span. There's a bright red kitchen for guests' use, too. Dorms $30, doubles $80

Pariwana Hostel Mesón de la Estrella 136 ☎084 233 751, ⓦpariwana-hostel.com. A long-standing favourite among backpackers, *Pariwana* has dorms and doubles set around a lovely interior courtyard dotted with colourful beanbags. Table tennis, mini-football, TV lounge, book exchange and drinking games are sure to keep you busy. Wi-fi, free breakfast and 24hr security. Dorms $27, doubles $130

The Point Mesón de la Estrella 172 ☎084 252 266, ⓦthepointhostels.com. Cusco's party hostel hits it hard every night at the lively bar upstairs. Luckily there's a verdant garden at the back to get some air and come back to your senses in the morning. Dorms are mostly dark as they all give onto the interior courtyard and the premises could do with a bit more of a clean. Dorms $22

Samay Wasi C Atoqsaycuchi 416, San Blas ☎084 253 108, ⓦsamaywasiperu.com. This wonderful little place high up in San Blas has clean and tidy rooms set on two floors. All have private bath, there's a kitchen for guests' use, all-day coca tea, wi-fi, free continental breakfast and free airport pick-up. Ask for a room on the second floor, from where there are spectacular views over Cusco. Dorms $33, doubles $82

Wild Rover C Matará 261 ☎084 221 515, ⓦwildroverhostels.com. Cusco's other lively party hostel has a fiesta every night. Rooms at the back are slightly quieter although lack sunlight; on the plus side, this

means they are the perfect spot to kick that hangover. Free wi-fi and breakfast included. Dorms $21, doubles $80

EATING

There are dozens of stalls at the Mercado San Pedro where you can get hearty dishes for a bargain S4. Self-caterers can stock up on fresh produce here too, as well as at Orion Supermarket, just opposite the San Pedro market.

★**La Bodega 138** Herrajes 138. This welcoming restaurant attracts a young, laidback crowd who enjoy the pizzas (S29) and pastas (S25) in a couple of dining areas. The salads (S23) are made with organic ingredients from the Sacred Valley, and the delicious Nutella cheesecake (S15) is large enough to share. Daily noon–10.30pm.

Bojosan C San Agustín 275 ☎084 246 502. This little udon bar with an open kitchen that aims to re-create Japanese ambience and cuisine is the perfect spot for a warming bowl of noodles on a cold Cusco evening. There are several types of udon (S20) to choose from, namely beef, duck, curry, chicken, seaweed and pork, accompanied by Japanese green tea, beer or sake. Mon, Tues & Thurs–Sun 12.30–3.30pm & 6.30–10.30pm.

Café Morena C Plateros 348B ☎084 437 832. This café lit by dozens of dangling light bulbs specializes in tasty sandwiches with a great choice of fillings including pork, chicken and a veggie option served on focaccia bread. Other light dishes include soups (S19), salads (S20) and empanadas (S10). Mon–Sat 9.30am–10pm.

Greens Santa Catalina Angosta 235, 2nd floor. This bustling café and restaurant has bright wooden interiors and potted plants dotted about; a farm in the Sacred Valley supplies the organic food, and there are plenty of veggie dishes to choose from. Mains S30–45. Daily 11.30am–10.30pm.

★**Jack's Cafe** Choquechaca 509. A real gringo hangout – don't be surprised to see customers standing in line. The ingredients here come from local suppliers and the coffee is family grown. Plenty on offer, from big tasty sandwiches (S19) to hearty home-made soups (S16). Daily 7am–11.30pm.

Juanito's Qanchipata 596. This tiny sandwich joint serves the best sandwiches (S10–22) in town – just point at what ingredients take your fancy and it'll all come nicely served in a large bun. It's the perfect spot to grab a sandwich before a long bus journey. Mon–Thurs 11am–11pm, Fri & Sat 11am–midnight.

Korma Sutra Tandapata 909, San Blas. Cusco's Indian restaurant attracts crowds of Brits itching for generous portions of onion bhajis (S12) and chicken tikka masala (S27), all to be washed down with a refreshing mango lassi (S8). More adventurous types can go for the crispy tandoori guinea pig (S24). Mon–Sat 1–10pm.

Marcelo Batata Palacio 121. The real draw at *Marcelo's* is the wonderful roof terrace with breathtaking views of the

9

town, where you can enjoy a postprandial beer (S8) or a pisco sour (S18). The international menu includes grilled lamb ribs served with mash (S44) and spicy pork adobo (S43). Daily 12.30–11pm.

Pacha Papa Plazoleta San Blas 120. Set in a pleasant courtyard, *Pacha Papa* is one of Cusco's few restaurants with outdoor seating. The cuisine is Peruvian, with a variety of meats, including lamb, alpaca and *cuy* grilled in the outdoor clay oven. Mains S40. Daily 11.30am–10pm.

Los Perros Tecsecocha 436. This relaxed restaurant/bar with dark red undertones, hanging lamps and comfortable sofas is the perfect spot to grab a beer (S9). You can nibble on some tasty oriental snacks here too, including chilli rolls (S19) and spicy wonton (S19). Daily 11am–midnight.

DRINKING AND NIGHTLIFE

Apart from Lima, no Peruvian town has as varied a nightlife as Cusco. Clubs open early, around 9pm, but don't start getting lively before 11pm, and close in the wee hours. Pubs and clubs alike often offer 2-for-1 drink deals during happy hour. Beware of your drink being spiked in crowded nightspots.

PUBS AND BARS

★**Calle del Medio** Calle del Medio 113. The welcoming bar and lounge of this appealing restaurant is decked out in recycled furniture with a touch of retro, and features over thirty colourful pisco jars lining the bar. The drinks menu exclusively features pisco-based drinks (S22). There's a small balcony area overlooking the plaza, which is the perfect spot for a sundowner. Daily 11am–3am.

La Cantina Saphi 554. This Italian-run wine bar is a great

spot to sit back and enjoy a glass of Italian red (S15) on a cold Cusco evening. There are great cheese and salami platters (S60) too. Daily 6–11pm.

Indigo Tecsecocha 415. It's always happy hour at this laidback bar with swinging chairs and comfortable couches. The Thai food (S20–27), hookahs, board games, background classics and friendly staff will ensure you stay for a good while. Free wi-fi, too. Daily 4pm–2am.

Norton Rats Tavern Santa Catalina Angosta 116, 2nd floor, Plaza de Armas. This spacious, low-key pub/bar with flags draped on the ceiling attracts crowds of young blokes keen for a game of darts or billiards. The beer is home-brewed (S12), the burgers (S12) are some of the best in town, and the chilli con carne burrito (S14) sells like hot cakes. Daily 7.30am–2am.

★**Paddy Flaherty's** Triunfo 124. At 3347m, Paddy's proudly boasts that it is the highest 100-percent Irish owned pub on the planet. The pub attracts a melting pot of Peruvians and tourists alike and the menu offers all sorts of home favourites, such as shepherd's pie (S17.50) and cheese burgers (S17). Daily 10am–2am.

CLUBS AND LIVE MUSIC

Km 0 Tandapata 100, San Blas. This chilled-out bar with a relaxed lounge area upstairs hosts live bands (daily 10.30pm–midnight) playing an eclectic mix from reggae to funk. Hookahs (S15), darts, tapas (from S6) and more substantial mains including Thai curry (S24). Daily 6pm–2am.

The Muse Triunfo 338, 2nd floor. Belt your favourite songs out in the karaoke room, catch up on some footie or hit the dancefloor at this alternative joint. A Cuban salsa band kicks off at 11.30pm on Wed, Fri and Sat, and it livens up substantially on weekends. Daily 9am–late.

★**Museo del Pisco** Santa Catalina Ancha 398 ☎084 262 709, ⊛museodelpisco.org. Not exactly a museum, but nearly – with three types of Pisco from over forty *bodegas*, this is Cusco's Pisco bar *par excellence*, offering pisco tastings and live music – criolla, jazz, rock and blues – daily (9.30–11pm). There are tapas (S16) to accompany the drinks, as well as more substantial mains, too (S24). Daily noon–12.30pm, Thurs–Sat noon–1am.

Ukuku's Bar Plateros 316. This is one of the oldest and largest bars in town, with a world collection of liqueur bottles dating back over one hundred years. It really gets going at 10.30pm, with live music and dance shows. Profits go towards preserving the Andes by planting native trees, as well as helping children in local communities. Happy hour 7.30–10.30pm. Drinks start at S9. Daily 7.30pm–4am.

SHOPPING

The best shopping area is around Plazoleta San Blas – Tandapata, Cuesta San Blas and Carmen Alto.

Books The best bookshops with extensive English-language sections are Jerusalén at Heladeros 143, with a large book exchange (if you give two books you can take one) and guidebooks, and the smaller SBS Bookshop on Av El Sol 781A.

Clothing Buy quality T-shirts with unique designs at Andean Expressions on Choquechaca 213.

Crafts Mercado Modelo de Huanchac stocks a good range of crafts and you can find quirky gifts at Mercado San Pedro. Try Aymi Wasi on Nueva Alta for handmade fairtrade gifts – anything from jewellery to ceramics to art.

Food Self-caterers can stock up on fruit and veg at the Mercado de Wanchaq on Av Garcilazo, at Huascar (daily 6am–6pm). The best supermarket is Orion, just opposite the Mercado San Pedro.

Textiles Centro de Textiles Tradicionales del Cusco, on Av El Sol 603A (daily 7.30am–8.30pm), promotes traditional weaving techniques, so not only can you purchase textiles of excellent quality, but you may also watch weavers demonstrate their skill. The Centro Artesanal on Av Tullumayo (daily 8am–9pm) is home to dozens of stalls selling similar products, including blankets, jumpers and colourful woolly hats.

DIRECTORY

Banks and exchange BCP has a global ATM (Plateros, at Espaderos on the Plaza de Armas), and there are ATMs in the BCP and BBVA bank branches along Av El Sol. Up in San Blas, there is a BCP on Plazoleta San Blas. The best place to exchange foreign currency is along Av El Sol, where there are dozens of money exchangers. *Cambistas* (moneychangers along the pavement) may offer slightly better rates than foreign-exchange bureaus, but rip-offs are common.

Camping equipment Most tour agencies rent out tents, sleeping bags, sleeping mats and cooking equipment. There are also several shops on Procuradores and Plateros. Try Camping Equipment Rosly, C Procuradores 394 (☏ 084 248 042). Make sure to always thoroughly check the equipment before renting.

Consulates Most embassies are in Lima, though there are several honorary consul representatives in Cusco: UK (☏ 084 239 974); US (☏ 084 231 474); Finland (☏ 084 252 721); Germany (☏ 084 235 459); Holland (☏ 084 224 322).

Hospital and pharmacies Clínica Peruana Suiza (☏ 084 242 114, ⊛ cps.com.pe) on Av Perú K-3, Urbanizacion Quispicanchis, is well equipped to deal with 24hr emergencies. There are pharmacies along Av El Sol.

Laundry The cheapest laundry places are along C Choquechaca. Try Lavandería Louis at Choquechaca 264 (Mon–Sat 8am–8pm; S3/kg).

Post office The main office is at Av Sol 800 (Mon–Sat 7.30am–8pm, Sun 9am–2pm).

Taxis Reliable companies include AloCusco (☏ 084 222 222).

Tourist police Plaza Túpac Amaru s/n (24hr; ☏ 084 235 123).

INCA SITES OUTSIDE CUSCO

There are four major Inca sites, all an energetic day's **walk** from Cusco: the megalithic fortress of **Sacsaywamán**, which looms high above the city, the great *huaca* of **Q'enqo**, the fortified hunting lodge of **Pukapukara** and the nearby imperial baths of **Tambomachay**. To start from the top and work your way downhill, take one of the regular **buses** to Pisac leaving from Avenida Tullumayo or Calle Puputi every twenty minutes throughout the day and ask to be dropped off at the highest of the sites, Tambomachay, from where it's an easy two-hour walk back into the centre of Cusco, visiting the above sites in reverse order. The **opening times** for all the sites are daily 7am–6pm and entry is by Boleto Turístico only (see box, p.743).

Sacsaywamán

From central Cusco, it's quite a steep 2km climb up to the ruins of Sacsaywamán from the Plaza de Armas. Take Calle Suecia, then the first right along Huaynapata until it meets the even narrower Pumacurco going steeply up (left) to a small café-bar. From there, follow the signposted steps all the way up to the ruins.

Because **SACSAYWAMÁN** was protected by such a steep approach from the town, it only needed defensive walls on one side, and three massive parallel walls zigzag together for some 600m. Little of the inner structures remains, yet these enormous ramparts stand 20m high, unperturbed by past battles, earthquakes and the passage of time. The strength of the mortar-less stonework – one block weighs more than 300 tonnes – is matched by the brilliance of its design: the zigzags expose the flanks of any attackers trying to clamber up. The Inca Pachacutec began work on Sacsaywamán in the 1440s, although it took the labour of some twenty thousand men and nearly a century of work to finish it.

A flat expanse of grassy ground divides the temple from a large outcrop of volcanic rock, called the **Rodadero** ("precipice"), which is used today during the colourful spectacle of the **Inti Raymi**

9

festival held annually during the summer solstice in June.

Q'enqo

From the warden's hut on the northeastern edge of Sacsaywamán, take the track towards the Cusco–Pisac road; **Q'ENQO** is just over the other side of the main road.

This great stone or *huaca* revered by the Inca is carved with a complex pattern of steps, seats, geometric reliefs and puma designs, and illustrates the critical role of the Rock Cult in the realm of Inca cosmological beliefs; the name of the temple means "zigzag" and refers to the patterns carved into the upper western edge of the stone. At an annual festival priests would pour *chicha* or sacrificial llama blood into a bowl at the serpent-like top of the main channel; if it flowed out through the left-hand bifurcation, this was a bad omen for the fertility of the year to come. If, on the other hand, it continued the full length of the zigzag and poured onto the rocks below, this was a good omen.

Pukapukara

A relatively small ruin named **PUKAPUKARA** ("Red Fort", due to the pinkish hue of the rock) is situated right beside the main Cusco–Pisac road, a two-hour cross-country walk uphill from Q'enqo. Although in many ways reminiscent of a small European castle, Pukapukara is more likely to have been a hunting lodge, or out-of-town lodgings for the emperor, than simply a defensive position. Thought to have been built by the Emperor Pachacutec, it commands views towards glaciers to the south of the Cusco Valley.

Tambomachay

TAMBOMACHAY, otherwise known as "El Baño del Inca" ("The Bath of the Inca"), less than fifteen minutes' walk away along a signposted track from Pukapukara, is an impressive temple, evidently a place for ritual as well as physical cleansing and purification.

The ruins consist of three tiered platforms. The top one holds four trapezoidal niches that may have been used as seats; on the next level, underground water emerges directly from a hole at the base of the stonework, and from here cascades down to the bottom platform, creating a cold shower just about high enough for an Inca to stand under. On this platform the spring water splits into two channels, both pouring the last metre down to ground level. The superb quality of the stonework suggests that its use was restricted to the higher nobility, who perhaps used the baths only on ceremonial occasions.

Tipón

Around 25km east out of Cusco, the town of **TIPÓN** is famous for its Sunday lunches, featuring oven-roasted *cuy* (guinea pig), and its ruins – a large structure made up of several terraces and one of the few working examples of Inca irrigation systems, with fountains and water channels covering the area. From the town, it's a steep one-hour-thirty-minute climb (or 20min taxi ride; S20 each way) to the ruins. To get here take an Urcos-bound *colectivo* from Avenida de la Cultura, one block west of the Hospital Regional, and ask to be let out at the Tipón turn-off (45min; S5). To get back, squeeze onto a passing bus on the main road.

Pikillaqta and Rumicolca

One of the few well-preserved pre-Inca sites in the area, **Pikillaqta** was built by the Wari culture and comprises a sprawling residential compound surrounded by a defensive wall in the midst of rolling grasslands. It is the earliest example in the region of two-storey buildings. Further on, on the opposite side of the road, is **Rumicolca**, the huge Inca gateway to Cusco, built on top of what used to be a massive Wari aqueduct. The contrast between the fine Inca stonework and the cruder earlier constructions of the Wari is quite striking. You can easily visit this site together with Tipón in a day-trip from Cusco; otherwise, stay on an Urcos-bound bus for an extra 5km; the site is 1km from the main road.

The Sacred Valley and Machu Picchu

The Río Urubamba valley, also known as El Valle Sagrado or the **Sacred Valley**, traces its winding, astonishingly beautiful course to the northwest of Cusco. Standing guard over the two extremes of the Sacred Valley road, the ancient **Inca citadels** of Pisac and Ollantaytambo are among the most evocative ruins in Peru, while the small Andean towns of Pisac and Chinchero really come into their own on Tuesdays, Thursdays and Sundays – market days – when villagers in colourful regional dress gather to sell their crafts and produce.

Beyond Ollantaytambo the route becomes too tortuous for any road to follow, the valley closes in around the rail tracks, and the Río Urubamba begins to race and twist below **Machu Picchu** itself, the most famous ruin in South America and a place that – no matter how jaded you are or how commercial it seems – stops you in your tracks.

Unless you're walking the Inca Trail, you will inevitably spend at least one night in Machu Picchu town, commonly referred to as **Machu Picchu Pueblo**. Given the town's brutalist architecture and overpriced accommodation and eating establishments, it's best not to linger here for too long.

A plethora of tour companies runs day-trips to Machu Picchu (which have to be booked in advance), as well as whirlwind day tours of the Sacred Valley (from S30 upwards, plus entry to the sites). While guiding standards vary, it's a good way of seeing sights that are far apart, especially if you don't have much time, though it's more rewarding to linger and explore the valley at your leisure.

PISAC

A vital Inca road once snaked its way up the canyon that enters the Sacred Valley at **PISAC**, and the ruined citadel that sits at the entrance to the gorge controlled a route connecting the Inca Empire with Paucartambo, on the borders of the eastern jungle. Nowadays, the village is best known for its Tuesday, Thursday and Sunday craft **market**, held on the town's main square, the Plaza Constitución, though most stalls are open all week, with fewer crowds on non-market days. The main local **fiesta** – Virgen del Carmen (July 15–18) – is a good alternative to the simultaneous but more remote and raucous Paucartambo festival of the same name, with processions, music, dance groups, the usual firecracking celebrations, and food stalls around the plaza.

WHAT TO SEE AND DO

It takes roughly two hours to climb directly to the **citadel** (daily 8am–4pm; entry by Boleto Turístico), heading up through the agricultural terraces still in use at the back of Plaza Constitución. A better option is to take a taxi to the top of the ruins (20min; from S20 one-way, or negotiate a return fare with waiting time) and then walk back down, visiting all four archeological complexes on the way.

Set high above a valley floor patchworked by patterned fields and rimmed by centuries of terracing amid giant landslides, the stonework and panoramas at the citadel are magnificent. On a large natural balcony, a semicircle of buildings is gracefully positioned under row upon row of fine stone terraces thought to represent a partridge's wing (*pisac* means "partridge"). In the upper sector of the ruins, the main **Temple of the Sun** is the equal of anything at Machu Picchu. Above the temple lie still more ruins, largely unexcavated, and the honeycombed cliff wall opposite the fortress is the handiwork of agile grave robbers who desecrated the cliff tombs.

ARRIVAL AND DEPARTURE

By colectivo From Cusco, catch a *colectivo* throughout the day from Calle Puputi (every 15min; 45min); they drop you off and you can pick a returning one up on Pisac's main street.

9

ACCOMMODATION AND EATING

Hospedaje Chaska Wasi Av Amazonas s/n ☎985 903 868, ⊕pisachotel.com. A great backpacker pad just a short walk from the main square with warm and welcoming rooms set around a large courtyard. There's a kitchen for guests' use, an outdoor lounge hut with cushioned seating and a meditation room decked out in mellow colours. Dorms <u>S30</u>, doubles <u>S110</u>

Intihuatana Lounge Calle Pardo 601 ☎993 075 352. A laidback veggie place with colourful dining areas that give onto an interior garden dotted with beanbags. The menu includes healthy juices (S6), as well as vegetarian tacos with guacamole, black beans, cheese and tortilla (S14). They also rent tastefully furnished – albeit pricey – rooms that are kept in spick-and-span condition (S190). Mon–Fri & Sun 9.30am–7.30pm.

Hotel Royal Inka 2km out of the village ☎084 203 064, ⊕royalinkahotel.pe. An excellent place to camp, just out of town. Not only do you get access to the club's facilities, such as the restaurant and Olympic-sized pool, but the camping area comes with barbecue, electricity sockets and lights. Camping/person <u>S25</u>

Ulrike's Café C Pardo 613. Set over two floors and a roof-top terrace, this German-run restaurant with wi-fi is a pleasant place to hang out. Thin-crust pizzas are baked in the wood-burning oven (Tues, Thurs, Sat & Sun), and the menu also includes curries (S15), salads (S15) and a home-made carrot cake (S7) that remains their bestselling dessert. Set menu S22. Daily 8am–9pm.

URUBAMBA AND AROUND

Spread-out **URUBAMBA** lies about 80km from Cusco via Pisac or around 60km via Chinchero. Although it has little in the way of obvious historic interest, the town has numerous connections to other parts of the Sacred Valley and is situated in the shadow of the beautiful Chicon and Pumahuanca glaciers.

The attractive Plaza de Armas, dominated by the red sandstone **Iglesia San Pedro**, is laidback and attractive, with palm trees, a couple of pines and surrounded by interesting topiary, while at its heart is a small fountain topped by a maize corn. At weekends there's a large **market** on Jirón Palacio, which serves the local villages.

WHAT TO SEE AND DO

Urubamba makes an ideal base from which to explore the mountains and lower hills around the Sacred Valley, which are filled with sites. The eastern side of the valley is formed by the **Cordillera Urubamba**, a range of snowcapped peaks dominated by the summits of Chicon and Veronica. Many of the ravines can be hiked, and on the trek up from the town you'll have stupendous views of Chicon. **Moray**, a stunning Inca site, lies about 6km north of Maras village on the Chinchero side of the river, within a two- to three-hour walk from Urubamba. Make a circuit to include the spectacular Maras salt flats.

ARRIVAL AND DEPARTURE

By bus *Colectivos* leave from Calle Pavitos in Cusco (every 20min from about 5–6am; 2hr). Buses also connect Urubamba with Pisac (every 20min; 1hr 30min); Ollantaytambo (20min; 30min); for Calca (40min) and Chincero (1hr) catch a Cusco-bound bus. They use the Urubamba Terminal Terrestre on the main highway, 1km west of town. A *mototaxi* into town will set you back S2.

ACCOMMODATION

Hostal Los Jardines Av Convención 459 ☎084 201 331, ⓦlosjardines.weebly.com. A very pleasant budget choice a few blocks east of the main square with rooms giving onto a verdant garden area dotted with chairs and parasols. Rooms are simply furnished but welcoming, and all feature private facilities and hot-water showers. __S90__

Hostal Los Perales Pasaje Arenales 102 ☎084 201 151, ⓦecolodgeurubamba.com. This pleasant guesthouse features six neat rooms set around a large overgrown garden. There's table tennis and a billiards table, too. The congenial owner, who speaks some English, also offers apartments sleeping six, all fully equipped with kitchen. __S70__

EATING

Los Geranios Av Cabo Conchatupa s/n ☎084 201 093. Secluded booths at this restaurant are set around an interior garden humming with caged canaries, parakeets and parrots. The food is local and good value, with dishes such as *pollo a la plancha* (grilled chicken; S18) and *trucha frita* (fried trout; S20). Tues–Sun noon–5pm.

★ Tres Keros Av Sr de Torrechayoc ☎084 201 701. This superb restaurant is one of the very best in the Sacred Valley and is not to be missed. The warm atmospheric interior features candle-lit tables and a fireplace, while beautiful ceramic plates adorn the walls. The food is all home-made – the *lomo saltado* (S42) is exceptional, and the pisco sours are great, too. Mon & Wed–Sun 12.30–3.30pm & 6.30–9.30pm.

OLLANTAYTAMBO

On the approach to **OLLANTAYTAMBO** from Urubamba, the river runs smoothly between a series of fine Inca terraces that gradually diminish in size as the slopes get steeper and rockier. Built as an Inca administrative centre rather than a town, it's hard not to be impressed by the two huge Inca ruins that loom above the village, or by the foundations that abound in the cobbled backstreets radiating up from the plaza, especially in Calle Medio. Laid out in the form of a maize corncob – and one of the few surviving examples of an Inca grid system – the plan can be seen from vantage points high above it, especially from the hill opposite the fortress. Ollanta is an attractive, laidback village, and a wonderful place in which to linger.

WHAT TO SEE AND DO

The hubs of activity in town are the main **plaza** – the heart of civic life and the scene of traditional folk dancing during festive occasions – and the Inca fortress.

Downhill from the plaza, just across the Río Patacancha, is the old Inca Plaza Mañya Raquy, dominated by the town's star attraction – the astonishing Inca ruins atop some steep terraces. Climbing up through the **fortress** (daily 7am–5pm; entrance with Boleto Turístico), the solid stone terraces, jammed against the natural contours of the cliff, remain frighteningly impressive and the view of the valley from the top is stupendous. Not only was this the site of a major battle in 1536 between the Spaniards and the rebellious Manco Inca, who fought them off before being forced to retreat to the jungle stronghold in Vilcabamba, but this was also a ceremonial centre; note the particularly fine stonework towards the top of the ruins.

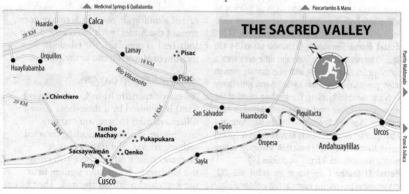

9

Directly across, above the town, are rows of **ruined buildings** originally thought to have been prisons but now believed to have been granaries. To the front of these it's quite easy to make out a gigantic, rather grumpy-looking profile of a face carved out of the rock, possibly an **Inca sculpture** of Wiracochan – commonly referred to as Tunupa – the mythical messenger from Wiracocha, the major creator god of the Incas. It's a stiff forty-minute climb to the viewpoint; follow the signpost from Waqta, off the Plaza de Armas.

ARRIVAL AND DEPARTURE

By bus and colectivo From Cusco, several buses daily go via Urubamba from Av Grau 525, as well as numerous *colectivos* and *combis* from Pavitos in Cusco (6am–5pm; 1hr 30min–2hr) and Urubamba (30min). From Ollanta, Cusco-bound tourist buses (2hr) leave from the small yard just outside the train station. For Urubamba catch a *combi* or *colectivo* from the Mercado Central, off the southeastern corner of the plaza (every 15min; 30min).

On foot Public buses leave from the plaza at 10am and 3pm to Santa María; from here you can catch a *combi* to the HydroElectric Station, from where it is a 3hr hike along the railway tracks to Machu Picchu Pueblo.

By train The train station is 1km from town, or a 10min walk along Av Ferrocarril from the main part of the village. A *mototaxi* into town is S1 per person. There are at least ten trains daily each way between Cusco and Machu Picchu via Ollanta (check ⓦperurail.com for schedule); book tickets in advance, particularly the return, since trains going back to Cusco fill up with hikers coming off the Inca Trail.

ACCOMMODATION

Hostal Iskay Patacalle s/n ☎084 204 004, ⓦiskaygroup .com. Tucked away on a quiet alleyway, this welcoming place offers a series of rustic rooms on an old Inca site, all with private bathrooms and some with bare stone walls. Some of the single rooms can be a bit of a squeeze. **S120**
Hostal Mamá Simona Av Ocobamba s/n ☎084 436 383, ⓦmamasimona.com. This calm little oasis with a pretty garden area complete with river running through offers comfortable four- and six-bed dorms with sturdy beds and colourful blankets. The soothing sound of the water is heard from most rooms, some of which have balconies. There's a fully equipped kitchen, hammocks and a barbecue set for guests, along with all-day coca tea and lockers for those wanting to leave their belongings as they head to Machu Picchu. Dorms **S36**, doubles **S90**
Hostal El Tambo C del Horno s/n ☎084 385 770, ⓦhostaleltambo.com. The rooms at this wonderful place

are set on two floors and look over a pleasant interior garden with hammocks. Local fabrics and paintings decorate the interiors, all with beautiful hardwood floors. Rates include breakfast and wi-fi. Discounts for large groups. **S60**

EATING

Hearts Café Av Ventiderio s/n. This wonderful little café serves chunky home-made soups (S10), huge salads (S16), and a range of international dishes (mains from S16), including plenty of veggie options. The bread is freshly baked and the cookies and pies (S8) are all home-made. Profits go out to the local community. Free wi-fi. Daily 7am–8.45pm.
Il Piccolo Forno C del Medio 120. This Italian-Peruvian owned place is a great spot for a pizza (S15), lasagne (S23) or one of the many home-made desserts that can be consumed at little wooden tables. The shelves are lined with home-made pasta sauces and local coffee – available for purchase – and there are plenty of gluten-free options, too. Tues–Sun 1–9pm.
Tutti Amore Av Estación s/n. This little ice-cream joint produces over eighty flavours a year, solely using local produce including all manner of seasonal fruits. S5/scoop or two for S8. Daily 8am–5pm.

THE INCA TRAIL

The world-famous **Inca Trail** is set in the **Santuario Histórico de Machu Picchu**, an area set apart by the Peruvian state for the protection of its flora, fauna and natural beauty. Acting as a bio-corridor between the Cusco Andes, the Sacred Valley and the lowland Amazon forest, the National Sanctuary of Machu Picchu has a huge biodiversity, with species including the cock-of-the-rock (known as *tunkis* in Peru), spectacled bear (*tremarctos ornatus*) and condor (*vultur gryphus*). Although just one of a multitude of paths across remote areas of the Andes, what makes the 33km Inca Trail so popular is the fabulous treasure of **Machu Picchu** at the end.

SETTING OFF AND DAY ONE

An early departure from Cusco (around 5am) is followed by a three-hour drive to Ollantaytambo (where you can buy last-minute supplies, including recycled walking sticks). The trail begins at **Piscacucho**, at Km82, where you cross the Urubamba River after signing in at the first checkpoint on the trail. The first

THE INCA TRAIL: WHEN AND HOW TO DO IT

Consider the **season** when booking your Inca Trail. The dry season runs approximately from May to October – expect blistering sun during the daytime and sub-zero temperatures at night. During the rainy season of November to April the temperature is more constant but, naturally, the path is muddier and can be slippery, and afternoon thunderstorms are the norm. The trail is closed for restoration during the entire month of February.

In recent years, due to the growing popularity of the Inca Trail, the sanctuary authority, the Unidad de Gestión del Santuario Histórico de Machu Picchu, has imposed a **limit of 500 people a day** on the Inca Trail, and they must be accompanied by a registered tour operator. By law, permits must be purchased thirty days before departure on the trail with the name and passport number of each trekker. In practice, however, it is usually necessary to book four to six months in advance to make sure you get a space on the trail. Currently permits cost around US$100 per person, including entrance to Machu Picchu – this permit should always be included in the price of your trek. Check the government website ⓦwww.machupicchu .gob.pe for permit availability. Always carefully research the **tour company** (see p.748) that you choose, and make sure you know exactly what you are paying for, as well as what conditions your porters will be working under (see box, p.758). Make sure you enquire about the toilets used on the trek, as more reliable companies use portable toilets, thereby avoiding the facilities at the campsites that are used by hundreds of people every day.

Prices vary considerably between US$300 and US$750, and although a higher price doesn't always reflect genuine added value, usually the better and more responsible companies will have higher expenses to cover (for better food, equipment, fair wages, and so on). Check what's included in the price: train tickets, quality of tent, roll mat, sleeping bag, porter to carry rucksack and sleeping bag (or if not, how much a personal porter will cost), bus down from ruins, exactly which meals, drinking water for the first two days, and what transport to the start of the trail.

As far as **preparations** go, the most important thing is to acclimatize, preferably allowing at least three days in Cusco if you've flown straight from sea level, because altitude sickness will seriously ruin your travel plans.

If you don't want to hike for four days, the **two-day Inca Trail** is a good option. It starts at Km104 of the Panamerican Highway, 8km from Machu Picchu; the footbridge here leads to a steep climb (3–4hr) past Chachabamba to reach Wiñay Wayna (see p.758), where you join the remainder of the Inca Trail.

day consists of a 12km stretch, beginning at an elevation of 2600m and gaining 400m during the course of the day. The gentle incline of the trail first follows the river and passes a viewpoint with the terraced Inca ruins of the **Llaqtapata** fortress below, before it descends past rock formations to the first night's campsite at **Huayllabamba**. Along the way you pass the villages of Miskay and Hatunchaca, where you can buy (overpriced) snacks and water, as well as *chicha* (traditional fermented corn beer).

The campsite at Huayllabamba is very basic, and there are no showers, though you may consider bathing in the icy stream. If you haven't acclimatized and don't feel well, then Huayllabamba is the last place from which it's fairly easy to return to Cusco; beyond, it's nearly impossible.

DAY TWO

The second day is the toughest part of the hike – an ascent of 1100m to the Abra Huarmihuañusca, or **Dead Woman's Pass** (4200m), the highest point on the trail, followed by a steep descent to the second night's campsite at Paq'aymayo. There is little shade or shelter, so prepare for diverse weather conditions, as cold mist sometimes descends quickly, obscuring visibility.

After an hour or so, you reach the campsite of Ayapata (where some groups camp on the first night), where there are bathrooms and a snack stall. Another one hour thirty minutes to two hours along a combination of dirt path and steep stone steps through mossy forest takes you up to the second campsite of Lluluchapampa, your last chance to purchase water or snacks.

9

PORTER WELFARE

Even though the Peruvian government has introduced regulations, stipulating that the Inca Trail porters must be paid a set minimum wage and only carry a set amount, abuses of staff by unscrupulous tour agencies still occur, especially on the alternative trails, where you may find your porters eating leftovers, carrying huge weights and sleeping without adequate cold-weather gear. Avoid doing the Inca Trail for the cheapest price possible, and be prepared to pay more by going with a reputable company that treats its staff well (see box, p.748). When trekking, keep an eye on the working conditions of the porters, offer to share your snacks and water, ask the porters about how they are treated, and don't forget to **tip** them at the end of the trek (around US$20 per porter is fair; a bit more if you had a personal porter). If you find evidence of abuse, don't hesitate to report it at your nearest iPerú office.

The views from the pass itself are stupendous, but it gets cold rapidly. From here the trail drops down into the Paq'aymayo Valley. The descent takes up to two hours, but you're rewarded by sight of the attractive **campsite** by the river (3600m), complete with showers (cold water only).

DAY THREE

This is the longest day but also the most enjoyable, with some of the loveliest scenery. It takes forty minutes up the steep, exposed trail to reach the ruins of the Inca fortress of Runkurakay, then another twenty minutes of stone steps and steep dirt track before you pass the false summit with a small lake before arriving at the **second pass** – Abra de Runkuracay (3950m), from which you can see the snow-covered mountains of the Cordillera Vilcabamba.

About an hour's descent along some steep stone steps leads to the Inca ruins of **Sayaqmarka**, a compact fortress perched on a mountain spur, overlooking the valley below. From Sayaqmarka you make your way down into increasingly dense cloudforest where delicate orchids begin to appear among the trees, and then up to the Chaquicocha campsite, where some groups break for lunch. The one-hour hike between Chaquicocha and the **third pass** – Abra de Phuyupatamarka (3650m) – is the loveliest bit of the hike; the trail runs through stretches of cloudforest, with hummingbirds flitting from flower to flower and stupendous views of the valley. The trail winds down to the impressive ruin of **Phuyupatamarca** – "Town Above the Clouds" – where there are five small ceremonial baths and, in the wet season, fresh running water. Some groups camp here on the third night and wake to a starry milky way at 4am, followed by breathtaking views of the surrounding range of glaciers at sunset.

It's a rough two- to three-hour descent to the final campsite. The first section comprises steep stone steps for forty minutes, followed by gentler stretches of dirt track. When you come to the fork in the trail, the right branch goes down to the next ruin, a citadel almost as impressive as Machu Picchu, **Wiñay Wayna** ("Forever Young"), where most groups will spend their third night. There is basic **accommodation** here and a large restaurant/bar area where you can treat your group and porters to a round of drinks. Most groups will **camp** outside the structure, but still enjoy the hot showers.

DAY FOUR

To reach **Intipunku** ("The Sun Gate") for sunrise the next day, most groups form a bottleneck at the Wiñay Wayna guard post long before it opens at 5.30am; groups aren't allowed to leave the campsite any earlier. A well-marked track from Wiñay Wayna skirts the mountain, leading you along some gentle ups and downs for about an hour before you reach a spectacularly steep set of stone steps – the last ascent of the hike – which leads to a pathway paved by the Inca. This in turn culminates in a large stone archway, Intipunku, where you catch your first sight of Machu Picchu – a stupendous moment, however exhausted you might be. From Intipunku, to reach the main ruins, it's an easy thirty- to forty-minute descent.

MACHU PICCHU

The most dramatic and enchanting of the Inca citadels lies suspended on an extravagantly terraced saddle between two prominent peaks. **MACHU PICCHU** (daily 6am–5pm; S126; students with ISIC card S63) is one of the greatest of all South American tourist attractions, set against a vast, scenic backdrop of forested mountains that spike up from the deep valleys of the Urubamba and its tributaries.

With many legends and theories surrounding the position of Machu Picchu (meaning "ancient mountain"), most archeologists agree that the sacred geography of the site helped the Inca Pachacutec decide where to build it. Its intactness owes much to the fact that it was never discovered by the Spaniards, and the atmosphere, as you wander around, drinking it all in, is second to none.

SOME HISTORY

Unknown to the outside world, for many centuries the site of Machu Picchu lay forgotten, except by local Quechua people. In the 1860s it was first looted by a pair of German adventurers and then rediscovered by the US explorer **Hiram Bingham**, who came upon it on July 24, 1911.

It was a fantastic find, not least because it was still relatively intact, without the usual ravages of either conquistadors or tomb robbers. Bingham was led to the site by an 11-year-old local boy, and it didn't take long for him to see that he had come across some important ancient Inca terraces. After a little more exploration Bingham found the fine white stonework, which led him to believe (incorrectly, as it transpired) that Machu Picchu was the lost city of Vilcabamba, the site of the Incas' last refuge from the Spanish conquistadors. Bingham returned in 1912 and 1915 to clear the thick forest from the site and in the process made off with thousands of artefacts; the Peruvian government is currently trying to reclaim the remainder from Yale University, where some are still kept.

While archeologists are still not clear as to what Machu Picchu's purpose was, there is a general consensus that it was an important religious and ceremonial centre, given the layout and quantity of temples, as well as the quality of the

---

ARRIVING AT MACHU PICCHU

If coming from the Inca Trail, you'll need to descend to the main entrance and register your entrance ticket before doubling back to the ruins. Or, if you're arriving from Machu Picchu Pueblo, you can either hike up to the ruins (1–3hr, depending on how fit you are) along a clearly marked footpath that's much shorter than following the winding paved road, or take one of the **buses** that run throughout the day (every 10min, 5.30am–5.30pm).

If you're travelling independently, it's best to buy your **entrance ticket** to Machu Picchu at the INC (Instituto Nacional de Cultura) office in the main square before going up to the ruins; that way you'll avoid the long queues at the ticket office at the site itself.

There is no **accommodation** near Machu Picchu itself apart from the hideously overpriced *Machu Picchu Sanctuary Lodge*, located right at the entrance to the ruins. The lodge serves up a good lunchtime buffet that will set you back US$40; otherwise, there are expensive sandwiches (S20–25) to be had at the hotel's sister café by the gate. It's best to bring your own packed lunch from Machu Picchu Pueblo, although bear in mind you must consume your food outside the ruins. Water bottles are allowed in.

There are two **left-luggage** offices: one next to the entrance to the ruins (S5) and one just as you go inside (S3); you must check in any large rucksacks and camping equipment. There are toilets just outside the entrance (S1) and this is where you can also hire a guide (approximately S100 for a 2hr tour, per group), though they tend to be of varying quality.

When walking around the ruins, stick to the designated trails, or the zealous wardens will blow their whistles at you.

9

stonework. The citadel may have been built as an administrative, political and agricultural centre, while the existence of numerous access routes to Machu Picchu has led others to believe that it was a trading post between the Andes and the Amazon. Conflicting theories aside, there is no denying Machu Picchu's great importance to the Inca culture.

WHAT TO SEE AND DO

Though more than 1000m lower than Cusco, Machu Picchu seems much higher, constructed as it is on dizzying slopes overlooking a U-curve in the Río Urubamba. More than a hundred flights of stone steps interconnect its palaces, temples, storehouses and terraces, and the outstanding views command not only the valley below in both directions but also extend to the snowy peaks around Salcantay. Wherever you stand in the ruins, spectacular terraces (some of which are once again being cultivated) can be seen slicing across ridiculously steep cliffs, transforming mountains into suspended gardens.

Unless you're coming off the Inca Trail, you'll be following the footpath from the main entrance to the ruins proper. For a superb view of the ruins, take the staircase up to the thatched guardian's hut and the **funerary rock** behind it; this is thought to have been a place where mummified nobility were laid due to its association with a nearby graveyard where Bingham found evidence of many burials, some of which were obviously royal.

Temple of the Sun and the Royal Tomb

Entering the main ruins through the ancient doorway, you soon come across the **Temple of the Sun** on your right, also known as the *Torreón* – a wonderful, semicircular, tower-like temple displaying some of Machu Picchu's finest stonework and built for astronomical purposes. Its carved steps and smoothly joined stone blocks fit neatly into the existing relief of a natural boulder, which served as some kind of altar. During the June and December solstices, the first rays of the sun shine directly into the eastern and

western windows respectively, illuminating the tower perfectly. The temple is cordoned off, but you can appreciate it from above.

Below the Temple of the Sun is a cave with a stepped altar and tall niches, known as the **Royal Tomb**, despite the fact that neither graves nor mummies have ever been found here. Along the staircase leading up to the Temple of the Sun, you'll find sixteen small **fountains**, the most beautiful at the top.

The Sacred Plaza

Another staircase ascends to the old quarry, past the **Royal Area**, so-called due to the imperial-style Inca stonework. Turn right and cross the quarry to reach the **Sacred Plaza**, flanked by an important temple complex. Dominating the southeastern edge of the plaza, the attractive **Three-Windowed Temple** has unusually large windows, perfectly framing the mountains beyond the Urubamba river valley. Next to it is the **Principal Temple**, so-called because of the fine stonework of its three high main walls; the damage to the rear right corner was caused by the ground sinking. Directly opposite the Principal Temple, you'll find the **House of the High Priest**.

Intihuatana

An elaborately carved stone stairway behind the **Sacristy** brings you to one of the jewels of the site, the **Intihuatana**, loosely translated from Quechua as the "hitching post of the sun". This fascinating carved rock, sometimes mistakenly referred to as a sundial, is one of the very few not to have been discovered and destroyed by the conquistadors in their attempt to eradicate sun worship. Its shape resembles Huayna Picchu and it appears to be aligned with the nearby mountains. Inca astronomers are thought to have used it as an astro-agricultural clock for viewing the complex interrelationships between the movements of the stars and constellations.

Sacred Rock

Following the steps down from the Intihuatana and passing through the

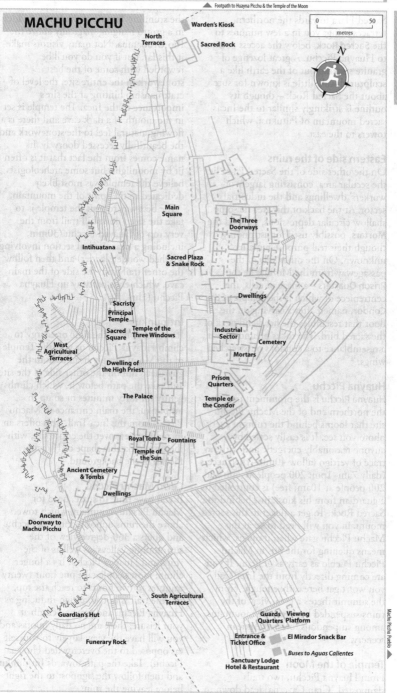

MACHU PICCHU

Footpath to Huayna Picchu & the Temple of the Moon

Warden's Kiosk

North Terraces

Sacred Rock

N

0   50
metres

Main Square

The Three Doorways

Intihuatana

Sacred Plaza & Snake Rock

Sacristy

Principal Temple

Sacred Square

Temple of the Three Windows

Dwellings

Industrial Sector

Cemetery

West Agricultural Terraces

Dwelling of the High Priest

Mortars

Prison Quarters

The Palace

Temple of the Condor

Royal Tomb

Fountains

Temple of the Sun

Ancient Cemetery & Tombs

Dwellings

Ancient Doorway to Machu Picchu

South Agricultural Terraces

Guardian's Hut

Guards Quarters

Viewing Platform

Entrance & Ticket Office

El Mirador Snack Bar

Funerary Rock

Buses to Aguas Calientes

Sanctuary Lodge Hotel & Restaurant

Footpath to Inca Drawbridge

Machu Picchu Pueblo

Machu Picchu Mountain, Inti Punku gateway, Inca Trail & Wiñay Wayna

9

Sacred Plaza towards the northern terraces brings you in a few minutes to the **Sacred Rock**, below the access point to Huayna Picchu. A great lozenge of granite sticking out of the earth like a sculptured wall, little is known for sure about the Sacred Rock – though its outline is strikingly similar to the Inca's sacred mountain of Putukusi, which towers to the east.

Eastern side of the ruins

On the other side of the Sacred Plaza lies the secular area, consisting largely of workers' dwellings and the industrial sector. At the back of this area lie some shallow circular depressions, dubbed the **Mortars**, possibly used for astronomy, though their real purpose remains unknown. On the other side of the passageway from the Mortars lie the **Prison Quarters** – a maze of cells, the centrepiece of which is the **Temple of the Condor**, named after a carving on the floor that resembles the head and neck of the sacred bird. The rocks behind it bear a resemblance to a condor's outstretched wings.

Huayna Picchu

Huayna Picchu is the prominent peak at the northern end of the Machu Picchu site that looms behind the ruins in every photo you see. It is easily scaled by anyone reasonably energetic and with no trace of vertigo (allow 40min–1hr); access (daily 7am–1pm; 200 people at 7am and 200 people at 10am; free) is controlled by a guardian from his kiosk just behind the Sacred Rock. To get a ticket to this sacred mountain you will need to be at the Machu Picchu gate when it opens, which means queuing for the bus in Machu Picchu Pueblo as early as 4.30am. If you are coming directly from the Inca Trail, you won't get here early enough. From the summit there's a great view of the ruins suspended between the mountains among stupendous forested Andean scenery.

Temple of the Moon

From Huayna Picchu, two trails signposted "Gran Caverna" lead down to the stunning **Temple of the Moon**, hidden in a grotto hanging magically above the Río Urubamba. Not many visitors make it this far, but if you do you'll be rewarded with some of the best stonework in the entire site, the level of craftmanship hinting at the site's importance to the Inca. The temple is set in the mouth of a dark cave and there is a flowing, natural feel to the stonework and the beautifully recessed doorway. Its name comes from the fact that it is often lit by moonlight, but some archeologists believe the temple was most likely dedicated to the spirit of the mountain.

The best way to visit the temple is to take the steep downhill trail from the very top of Huayna Picchu (30min, including a near-vertical section involving a lashed wooden ladder) and then follow the other trail from the side of the main cave, which ends partway up Huayna Picchu (1hr).

Intipunku

If you don't have the time or energy to climb Huayna Picchu or visit the Temple of the Moon, simply head back to the guardian's hut on the other side of the site and take the path below it, which climbs gently for forty minutes or so up to **Intipunku**, the main entrance to Machu Picchu from the Inca Trail. This offers an incredible view over the entire site, with the unmistakeable shape of Huayna Picchu in the background.

Cerro Machu Picchu

If you have time to spare, head for Machu Picchu mountain, which towers above the ruins opposite Huayna Picchu and offers a 360-degree view of the surrounding valleys, as well as of the ruins and Huayna Picchu. It's a longer climb; most people take one hour twenty minutes to two hours to reach the top, but the trail is not as vertigo-inducing as Huayna Picchu and you can climb at your leisure; there are no daily quotas and you will have the view largely to yourself (as opposed to the overcrowded Huayna Picchu). Take the path towards Intipunku and then follow the signpost to the right before leaving the ruins.

Inca drawbridge

If you don't suffer from vertigo, there's an excellent scenic and level twenty-minute walk that you can take from the Hut of the Caretaker of the Funerary Rock through the cemetery to the Inca drawbridge. Follow the narrow path along the tops of the southern terraces, along the side of the cliff, and over a man-made ledge until you reach the barrier several hundred metres above the bridge, which spans the gap in the Inca road that was built on a sheer cliff face. You're not allowed to get close to it, as someone fell to their death from it a few years ago, but it's certainly an impressive sight.

MACHU PICCHU PUEBLO

Anyone wishing to come to Machu Picchu will invariably pass through the settlement of **MACHU PICCHU PUEBLO** (often referred to as Aguas Calientes), which is connected to the ruins by bus, though the town itself is only accessible by train from Cusco via the Sacred Valley.

Its warm, humid climate and surrounding landscape of towering mountains covered in cloudforest make it a welcome change to Cusco, though it has even more of a touristy feel to it: every other building in this little town seems to be either a hotel, restaurant or a souvenir shop and you constantly run the gauntlet of touts. If you wish to see Machu Picchu at sunrise and enjoy the surrounding scenery when it is not overrun by day-trippers, you'll need to stay here for at least one night.

WHAT TO SEE AND DO

The town's main attraction (besides Machu Picchu) is the natural **thermal bath** east of town (daily 5am–8pm; S10), which is particularly welcome after a few days on the Inca Trail. Several shops rent towels and bathing suits near the entrance.

There is also a **hiking trail** (around 90min each way; closed on rainy days) up the sacred mountain of Putukusi, starting just outside of town, a couple of

MACHU PICCHU PUEBLO

■ ACCOMMODATION

Camping Municipal	5
Eco Packers	4
Hostal El Místico	1
Pirwa	3
Rupa Wasi Lodge	2
Super Tramp Hostel	6

● EATING & DRINKING

Bistro Indio Feliz	2
La Boulangerie de Paris	4
Incontri del Pueblo Viejo	3
Palate	6
Toto's	5
Tree House	1

0   50
metres

Sacred Valley (Cusco)

9

TRAIN JOURNEY TO MACHU PICCHU PUEBLO

Two companies serve the Ollantaytambo–Machu Picchu Pueblo route: Peru Rail and Inca Rail, with Peru Rail also offering services from Cusco. Rumbling out of **Cusco** daily (see p.747), the train zigzags its way through the backstreets, where little houses cling to the steep valley slopes. It takes a while to rise out of the teacup-like valley, but once it reaches the high plateau above, the train rolls through fields and past highland villages before eventually dropping rapidly down into the Urubamba Valley using several major track switchbacks, which means you get to see some of the same scenery twice. It reaches the Sacred Valley floor just before getting into **Ollantaytambo**, where you can already see scores of terraced fields and, in the distance, more Inca temple and storehouse constructions. The train continues down the valley, stopping briefly at Km88, where the Inca Trail sometimes starts, then following the Río Urubamba as the valley gets tighter and the mountain more forested and precipitous. The end of the line is at Machu Picchu Pueblo.

---

hundred metres down on the left if you follow the railway track towards the ruins. The walk offers stupendous views of the town and across to Machu Picchu, but watch out for the small, venomous snakes. It is also not for the faint-hearted as the trail is very steep in parts (some sections have been replaced by ladders) and very narrow.

ARRIVAL AND INFORMATION

By train You are most likely to arrive in Machu Picchu Pueblo by train (see box above). To get to the heart of the town, walk through the market and cross one of the bridges. Peru Rail and Inca Rail trains connect Ollantaytambo to Machu Picchu Pueblo. Peru Rail also has services from Cusco's Poroy station. The cheapest option from Ollantaytambo with Peru Rail is the Expedition train (S209), which can be booked online (w perurail.com).

Tourist information iPerú is at Av Pachacutec s/n just by the main square (Mon–Sat 9am–1pm & 2–6pm, Sun 9am–1pm; ☎084 211 104, e iperumachupicchu@ promperu.gov.pe).

Machu Picchu Tickets The INC (Instituto Nacional de Cultura) office, just off the main square at Av Pachacutec 123 (daily 5.20am–8.40pm; ☎084 211 067), sells tickets for Machu Picchu S63; combined entry with Wayna Picchu S150, students S75). If you stay overnight in Machu Picchu Pueblo before visiting the site, buy your ticket as soon as you arrive in town as this will save you time in the morning.

ACCOMMODATION

Although there is an overwhelming choice of accommodation options, most hostels in Machu Picchu Pueblo lack charm; there can be a lot of competition for lodgings during the high season (June–Sept) and the better places need booking a week or two in advance. The check-out time at most hostels is 9–9.30am.

Camping Municipal The municipal campsite is just before the bridge over the Río Urubamba, a 20min walk from Machu Picchu Pueblo. The campsite has toilets, showers with intermittent hot water, and cooking facilities. Camping S15

Eco Packers Av Imperio de los Incas 136 ☎084 211 121, w ecopackersperu.com. A popular place with dorms and doubles giving onto narrow corridors that wind their way up to the rooftop terrace with billiards table and cable TV. Dorms have wooden beds tightly packed together, while the more comfortable doubles feature en-suite bathrooms – if you're after some quiet, ask for a room facing the back of the building. Dorms S43, doubles S150

Hostal El Místico Av Pachacutec 814 ☎084 011 107, w elmisticomachupicchu.com. This pleasant guesthouse decorated with psychedelic paintings features ten rooms spread across three floors with a little lounge area on each. The friendly owner, who runs a jewellery shop right next door, organizes complimentary mystical tours around town. S90

Pirwa Tupuc Yupanqui 103 ☎084 244 315, w pirwahostelscusco.com. No-frills hostel with dorms and doubles, some with private baths. There's a kitchen for guests' use, free breakfast and wi-fi. Call ahead and a staff member will pick you up from the train station. Dorms S35, doubles S105

Super Tramp Hostel C Chaska Tika, Plaza de la Cultura ☎084 435 830, w supertramphostel.com. This friendly, brightly painted hostel offers a range of dorm rooms sleeping eight to twelve. Doubles, all with shared bathrooms, are small but comfortable. There's a communal kitchen, a lounge area with cable TV, book exchange, wi-fi, all-day coffee and tea and an attached burger joint. Dorms S30, doubles S85

EATING AND DRINKING

Since there is enormous competition for customers, you'll perpetually find yourself running the gauntlet of over-eager

Rupa Wasi Lodge C Huanacaure 180 ☎ 084 211 101, ⊛ rupawasi.net. The young conservationist owners here have tried to preserve the original design of the house and maintain the surrounding natural environment; the result is a beautiful eco-friendly lodge with avocado, walnut and native trees. Rooms are small and cosy with wooden interiors and en-suite facilities; some have private balconies with lovely views over the surrounding cloudforest. The rustic **Tree House** restaurant is one of the best in town, featuring *novoandina* cuisine, which combines local ingredients with international influences to great effect. They also offer cooking lessons (S210). **S240**

waiters, all trying to entice you into their particular restaurant, which looks and offers exactly the same dishes as most places within sight. These are the exceptions.

★ **Bistro Indio Feliz** Lloque Yupanqui 103 ☎ 084 211 090. The best restaurant in town has been going for over two decades, serving top-notch French and Peruvian dishes in a unique nautical setting. The set menu (S64.50) is exceptional value and the pisco sours the largest you'll ever come across. Book ahead. Daily noon–10pm.

La Boulangerie de Paris Jr Sinchi Roca. This French-run bakery serves superb freshly baked sweet and savoury pastries, including quiche (S10.50) and croissants (S2.50); there's hot chocolate (S11.50) too that can be enjoyed at one of the little tables. The best spot in town to pick up a packed lunch for Machu Picchu or for the train journey back to Machu Picchu. Daily 5am–9pm.

Incontri del Pueblo Viejo Av Pachacutec s/n ☎ 084 211 072. This Italian- and Peruvian-owned place is a great spot to grab a delicious thin-crust pizza (S25) or a plate of home-made tagliatelle (S33) or *gnocchi al ragù* (gnocchi in bolognaise sauce; S30). The handmade pastas are kneaded right in front of you, and there are great organic beers from Peru and beyond, too. Daily noon–10pm.

Palate Chaska Tika, Plaza de la Cultura. This cosy burger joint adjacent to *Super Tramp* hostel serves excellent burgers (S20) served with fries; there are veggie burgers too, as well as pizzas (S20). They also prepare Machu Picchu lunch boxes for S30. Tues–Sun noon–10pm.

Toto's Imperio de los Incas s/n. This warm, rustic restaurant with a crackling open fire to grill meats and views over Urubamba River offers a huge buffet lunch (noon–4pm; S60). There's a popular evening show upstairs (Mon–Fri at 8pm; 45min), featuring a contemporary circus performance. Daily noon–10pm.

DIRECTORY

Banks BCP, Av Los Incas 600, next to *Toto's*, Banco de la Nación, Av Los Incas 540 by the police station, and Caja Municipal by the Mercado Artesanal all have ATMs, but sometimes run out of money, especially at weekends.

Hospital Ministerio de la Salud by the Mercado Artesanal has a 24hr emergency room (☎ 084 211 161).

Internet Cyber World, on the plaza, has reliable internet (daily 8am–10pm; S3/hr). Most restaurants offer wi-fi.

Laundry Mariana on the eastern end of Av Pachacutec (Mon–Sat 7am–9pm; S8/hr).

Police Av Imperio de Los Incas 401 (☎ 084 211 178).

Post office On the western end of the plaza, with erratic (infrequent) opening hours.

ALTERNATIVE INCA TRAILS

As permits to walk the famous Inca Trail become more expensive and the Trail more crowded, many tour operators and individuals have started exploring **alternative Inca Trails**. Many of these offer stunning scenery to rival that of the Inca Trail, as well as ecological biodiversity and, in the case of **Choquequirao**, an archeological site larger than Machu Picchu itself. Of the several established alternative trails, only one (**Salcantay**) takes you close to the site of Machu Picchu.

Salcantay

The most popular of the alternatives, this five- to seven-day hike takes you either as far as the hydroelectric plant (from where it's a short bus and train ride to Machu Picchu Pueblo), or to the village of Huayllabamba, where you can join the regular Inca Trail. Beginning in Mollepata, the **first day** is a gentle climb through winding cloudforest trails to Soraypampa. On the **second day** there's a steep climb up to the only high pass on the trail (4750m), at the foot of the Salcantay glacier; the landscape here is sparse and dry. From the pass you descend into cloudforest with views of the verdant canyon below, camping that evening at Colcapampa. On the **third day** a five-hour walk takes you to the jungle town of La Playa, and then it's either an hour's bus ride to the town of Santa Teresa, or a six- to seven-hour walk. From Santa Teresa, you walk along the valley to the hydroelectric plant, from where there

9

are trains to Machu Picchu Pueblo (check for the latest schedules).

Alternatively, on the second day you'll descend along the right-hand side of the pass into the valley towards the village of Huayllabamba, and join the Inca Trail there. Buses run from Cusco's Avenida Arcopata to Mollepata every morning (hourly from 5.30am; 3hr).

Choquequirao

A trek to the archeological site of **Choquequirao** and back will take four or five days. Believed to be much larger than Machu Picchu, Choquequirao is only forty percent uncovered, and is a much more authentic experience as it still receives few visitors and you can find yourself wandering alone among huge ruined walls covered with cacti and exotic flowers. There are four trekking options, all starting at **Cachora**, which involves crossing the Apurimac Canyon. Day one is a steep descent of around 2000m, and day two a steep climb up the other side. It is recommended to spend one whole day (day three) at the ruins, and then either return on the same route, or via Huanipaca. It is also possible to link this trail to the last day of the Salcantay via Yanama, or to Hancacalle, returning to Cusco via Quillabamba (allow at least eight days for these options).

Hiring *arrieros* and mules is highly recommended for the above treks, as the area is very remote. To **get to Cachora**, take an Abancay-bound bus from Cusco and ask to be dropped off at the Cachora turn-off (4hr), from where you can catch a taxi to the village, where there is basic accommodation, *arrieros* and mules for hire.

Ausangate

This incredible high-altitude trek takes five to six days, plus two more days for travel, and provides the chance to see herds of vicuña wander among glacial lakes with the imposing snowcapped **Ausangate mountain** towering above you. The entire trek is above 4000m and includes several high passes over 5000m. Beginning at the town of **Tinqui**, you make a loop around the Ausangate

mountain, in either direction, passing through small Andean villages with great views of nearby glaciers. There are morning buses to Tinqui from Cusco's Calle Tomaso Tito Condemayta at around 10am (5hr).

Lares

There are several options for trekking in the **Lares valley**, lasting two to five days, and all offer splendid views of snow-capped peaks and green valleys. The hikes allow you to properly experience village life in the Andes. You'll pass through communities where you can stay with local families and purchase traditional crafts. The hot springs in Lares make for a relaxing end to any trek in the area. Some tour operators sell a three-day Lares trek with a day-trip to Machu Picchu on the fourth day, but do not be misled; in most cases you will still need to travel for two to five hours by bus and/or train before arriving at Machu Picchu Pueblo from the end point of your trail.

Espíritu Pampa/Vilcabamba

To visit the least frequented but most rewarding of the alternative Inca Trails, Espíritu Pampa or **Vilcabamba**, believed to be the last stronghold of the Inca, deep in the jungle and as remote as it gets, you need ten to sixteen days. Only accessible in the dry season, the trail begins at Huancacalle, 60km east of Machu Picchu, from where you can visit the sites of **Vitcos** (a huge fortress) and **Yurac Rumi** (the White Rock – a huge rock with steps and seats carved into it, thought to have been used for ceremonial purposes). It usually takes around three days to trek to the site of Vilcabamba, which is mostly covered by jungle vegetation. It is a further day's walk to the village of **Kiteni**, from where there is regular transport to Quillabamba (6hr); regular buses from Quillabamba go to Cusco (7–9hr). It is highly recommended that you hire a local guide and *arrieros* in Huancacalle.

THE INKA JUNGLE TRAIL

The Inka Jungle Trail lasts three to four days, going south to Machu Picchu via

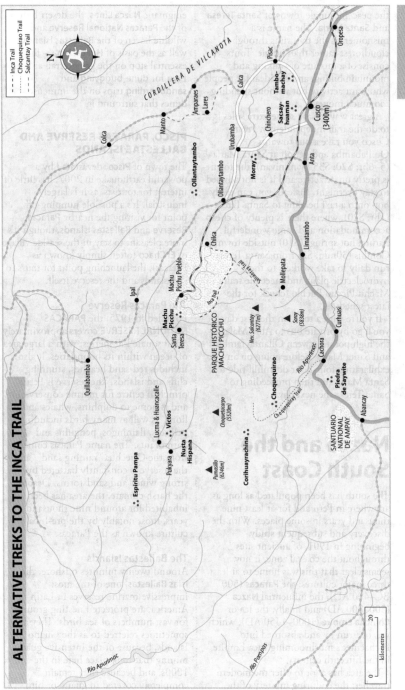

ALTERNATIVE TREKS TO THE INCA TRAIL

- – – – Inca Trail
- ········ Choquequirao Trail
- – ·· – Salcantay Trail

N

CORDILLERA DE VILCANOTA

Oropesa
Pisac
Calca
Tambo-machay
Amparaes
Lares
Chinchero
Sacsay-huaman
Cusco (3400m)
Manto
Urubamba
Anta
Colca
Ollantaytambo
Moray
Ollantaytambo
Limatambo
Chita
Ipal
Mollepata
Machu Picchu Pueblo
Salcantay Trail
Curhuasi
Nev. Salcantay (6371m)
Songo (5838m)
Machu Picchu
Inca Trail
Cachora
Río Apurímac
Santa Teresa
PARQUE HISTÓRICO MACHU PICCHU
Quillabamba
Choquequirao
Piedra de Sayhuite
Abancay
Lucma & Huancacalle
Victos
Choquetacarpo (5520m)
Choquequirao Trail
Pulkyra
Nústa Hispana
SANTUARIO NATIONAL DE AMPAY
Corihuayrachina
Espiritu Pampa
Pumasillo (6246m)

Río Apurímac

Río Pampas

0   20
kilometres

9

the peaceful jungle towns of **Santa Teresa** and **Santa María**. The name is a misnomer, as the trail runs through cloudforest rather than jungle. Tours consist of a mixture of walking and mountain biking, and are ideal for people who want activity but without spending too much money.

A great way to save some extra soles is to do the trail independently. From Cusco you take a bus towards Quillabamba and get off at Santa María (5–6hr; S20; S35 by minivan); the town is pretty unattractive and it is not advised to stay overnight. Instead, you can easily hop onto a taxi heading to Santa Teresa (1hr; S20), where there is plenty of cheap accommodation and some wonderful natural hot springs (S10) outside town. Combis (30min; S2) from Santa Teresa run daily to take workers to the hydroelectric plant and meet the trains to Machu Picchu Pueblo (check for the latest schedule).

If you're with a tour, on the first day you'll go by private bus to Abra Málaga, the high point between Ollantaytambo and Santa María, before going on an exhilarating four-hour downhill ride to Santa María and then proceeding to Santa Teresa the next day.

Nazca and the South Coast

The south has been populated as long as anywhere in Peru and for at least nine thousand years in some places. With the discovery and subsequent study, beginning in 1901, of ancient sites throughout the coastal zone, it now seems clear that this was home to at least three major cultures: the **Paracas** (500 BC–400 AD), the influential **Nazca** (500–800 AD) and finally, the **Ica** or **Chincha Empire** (1000–1450 AD), which was overrun by and absorbed into Pachacutec's mushrooming Inca Empire in the fifteenth century.

The area has a lot to offer the modern traveller: the enduring mystery of the enigmatic **Nazca Lines**, the desert beauty of the **Paracas National Reserve** and wildlife haven of the **Ballestas Islands**, as well as the oasis of **Huacachina** – the essential stop on the gringo trail around Peru for **dune-buggying** and **sandboarding** trips on the immense dunes that surround it.

PISCO, PARACAS RESERVE AND BALLESTAS ISLANDS

The town of **Pisco**, devastated by a powerful earthquake in 2007, has little of interest for tourists, as it is largely industrial. It's a possible jumping-off point for visiting the nearby **Paracas Reserve** and **Ballestas Islands**, though it's more pleasant to stay in the seaside village of **El Chaco** (often simply known as Paracas), the launching point for tours to the islands and the reserve itself.

The Paracas Reserve

Founded in 1975, the **PARACAS NATIONAL RESERVE** covers approximately 3350 square kilometres; with a large area of ocean within its boundaries, it also includes red-sand beaches, stunning cliffs and islands. The reserve is Peru's principal centre for marine conservation and is home to dolphins, whales and sea lions, as well as many birds including pelicans, flamingos, penguins and cormorants. The name Paracas comes from the Quechua "raining sand", and the reserve is constantly battered by strong winds and sandstorms. Despite the harsh climate, the area has been inhabited for around nine thousand years, most notably by the pre-Inca culture known as the Paracas.

The Ballestas Islands

Around twenty minutes offshore, the **Islas Ballestas**, one of the most impressive marine reserves in Latin America, are protected nesting grounds for vast numbers of sea birds. They are sometimes referred to as the Guano Islands, because of the intensive guano mining that took place here in the 1800s, and because they remain completely covered in guano or bird

TOURS OF THE PARACAS RESERVE AND BALLESTAS ISLANDS

There are several local **tour operators** running standard speedboat tours to the Ballestas Islands, leaving early in the morning and returning a couple of hours later. Many people choose to do an afternoon tour of the Paracas National Reserve with the same operator, making a whole-day trip. The boat trips to the **Ballestas Islands** cost S35, not including the S15 entrance fee, to be paid on the pier. They last two hours and take in the giant Candelabra geoglyph on the northern part of the Paracas Peninsula, 124m tall and 78m wide, before bobbing very close to the islands to give you the full measure of the impressive stench, the rocks alive with wildlife and the sky dark with birds. You can sometimes see sea lions, penguins and bottlenose dolphins.

Excursions into the **Paracas Reserve** typically cost S35, not including the S10 entry fee or lunch. Tours begin at around 11am to coincide with the return of the boats from the Ballestas Islands and take in a stretch of desert with 40-million-year-old fossils, two attractive beaches, the popular "La Catedral" rock formation just off the shore, which collapsed after the 2007 earthquake, and a couple of fantastic viewpoints overlooking the desert scenery. Tours end with lunch at the tiny fishing village of Lagunillas (*menú marino* S25).

It's best to buy **tickets** the day before, as boats leave at around 8am and you can arrange to be picked up at your hotel if you already have tickets. There is a discount for doing a combined tour to the islands and the reserve.

TOUR OPERATORS

Most companies also organize cycling and camping trips into the reserve, tours to other nearby attractions, such as Tambo Colorado – adobe ruins built by the Chinca culture – and dune-buggy excursions into the desert.

Paracas Overland San Francisco 111, Pisco (T 056 533 855, W paracasoverland.com.pe), or El Chaco, just as you enter the village (T 056 545 141).

Paracas Explorer Av Paracas MzD L5, El Chaco (T 056 531 487, W paracasexplorer.com).

droppings. Today the islands are alive with a mass of sea lions soaking up the sun, and birds, including pelicans, Humboldt penguins, Inca terns, Peruvian boobies and cormorants.

ARRIVAL AND DEPARTURE

Under 4hr south of Lima, the Paracas Reserve is easily reached via the Panamerican Highway.

By bus Only two bus companies, Oltursa and Cruz del Sur, run directly to El Chaco. The rest drop you off at El Cruce de Pisco, in the middle of the Panamericana, from where you can take a *colectivo* to Pisco (S3) or to El Chaco (S5); taxis to El Chaco will cost (S15). If travelling from Ayacucho, buses drop you off at San Clemente, from where you will need to catch a *colectivo* to El Cruce. Oltursa has an office in town at Av Paracas 6 (T 994 616 492), while Cruz del Sur stops at the northern entrance to the village (T 056 536 636).

Destinations Oltursa to: Nazca (daily at 11am; 3hr); Arequipa (daily at 11am; 12hr); Lima (at 9.50am, Sun at 8pm; 3hr); Ica (daily at 7am, 3pm & 4pm; 1hr 30min). Cruz del Sur to: Lima (7 daily; 3hr); Nazca (6 daily; 3hr 45min); via Ica (7 daily; 1hr); Arequipa (daily at 11am; 12hr).

By colectivo *Colectivos* to Paracas leave from outside Pisco's central market when full, throughout the day (15min; S3). To head back into Pisco, grab a *colectivo* at the entrance of El Chaco.

ACCOMMODATION

As Pisco is a rather unattractive dusty town, it is best to base yourself in the laidback fishing village of El Chaco. All guesthouses here can arrange trips to the Ballestas Islands and the Paracas Reserve.

Hospedaje Backpacker Soler Av Los Libertadores s/n T 056 798 200, E hospedajesolerparacas@hotmail.com. This airy hostel with wind chimes gently singing in the sea breeze offers accommodation in rustic wooden and bamboo huts. All have shared bathrooms and wi-fi. Ask for a dorm *descuento* in low season. Dorms S20, doubles S40

Icthus Paracas Asociacion San Martin Mz J1 Lt 29 T 989 178 278. All you need for your stay – cheap, clean dorms and rooms, wi-fi and a well-equipped shared kitchen. The owners are nearly always present and can help arrange tours. Dorms S18, doubles S50

Paracas Backpackers House Av Los Libertadores MzJ–1 T 056 773 131, W paracasbackpackershouse.com.pe. Cheaper accommodation here is in little wooden huts with clean, shared bathrooms, while the tiled en suites with marine-themed blankets are at the back in a concrete block. There's a sandy chill-out area with deckchairs, a communal kitchen and wi-fi. Dorms S17, doubles S45

Residencial Los Frayles José de San Martín, Mz J–1 Lote 4 T 056 531 487, W hotelresidenciallosfrayles.com. Welcoming and well located in the centre of town, this is one of the best options for those not splashing out on one of the expensive resorts. The rooms are standard, the wi-fi

9

STAY IN THE PARACAS RESERVE

You can **camp** for free on the beaches inside the reserve and it is a wonderful way to experience the peace and the wildlife around you. Be warned that the sun and wind can be quite harsh, and come prepared with food and water.

Inti Mar Playa Atenas ☎ 991 350 656, ⊕ inti-mar .com. A simple but special place to stay right on Atenas beach. Great food, especially the scallops farmed by the owners. Pricey but worth it for the location. **S240**

decent and the pool area with bar and sun loungers good after a day of tours. **S170**

EATING AND DRINKING

Aquamarine On the street behind the seafront. This is the only place in El Chaco offering desserts, including ice cream (three scoops S8), crêpes (S12) and fruit salads (S6–8), as well as breakfasts (S8–10) and sandwiches (S5–8). Daily 7am–noon & 6–10pm.

Brisa Marina Right on the seafront. The most Peruvian of all the touristy restaurants along the seafront, this place serves a variety of *pescados a la plancha* (grilled fish; S22–27), chicken dishes (S19) and a limited selection of

vegetarian options, which mostly comprise salads (S5–17). A *menú marino* will set you back S25. Daily 11am–3pm.

Cevicherías Off the southern end of the Malecón El Chaco (boardwalk). This row of no-frills fish and seafood eateries offers the cheapest set menus in town and they usually include *ceviche* followed by a fish or seafood main (*menú marino*; S20–25).

ICA

The city of **ICA** lies 50km inland, in a fertile valley surrounded by impressive sand dunes. It suffered considerable damage in the 2007 earthquake and several buildings were completely destroyed, including almost one entire side of the Plaza de Armas. In the city itself, the **Museo Regional** is excellent, and the surrounding area offers **vineyard tours** to wineries and pisco *bodegas*. It's better to stay in nearby Huacachina.

WHAT TO SEE AND DO

Ica's busy streets do not lend themselves to leisurely strolls; however, it is easy to get around using the numerous *tico* taxis that will take you anywhere in the city for around S5.

PARACAS, ICA & NAZCA

Museo Regional de Ica

Located in an Ica suburb, the superb **Museo Regional** (Jr Ayabaca, block 8; Mon–Fri 8am–7pm, Sat & Sun 9am–6pm; S12) is one of the best in Peru, housing important Nazca, Ica and Paracas cultural artefacts. The exhibits range from mummies (including those of children and parrots), trophy heads and trepanned skulls to examples of Nazca pottery and Paracas weavings; a scale model of the Nazca lines is out back. To get there, take a *mototaxi* from the centre of Ica (S3).

Bodega and vineyard tours

Ica's main tourist attraction and principal industry is the many *bodegas* and vineyards nearby, which can be visited on tours, both from the city and from Huacachina, and which usually involve a look around the vineyard followed by wine tasting and the chance to buy. The most commonly visited are: Bodega Ocucaje (🖰 ocucaje .com), Bodega Vista Alegre (🖰 vistaalegre .com.pe), Bodega Tacama (🖰 tacama.com), Bodega Lazo (🖰 bodega.lazotur.com) and Bodega El Catador (☎ 056 403 427), where the visitors are allowed to join in the stomping of the grapes in February and March. Great to visit on your own are Distilería La Caravedo (reservations essential; ☎ 056 313 963), for a full hacienda tour and tasting, and Tres Generaciones (☎ 056 403 565), for great pisco, a good explanation of how pisco is made and their excellent restaurant.

ARRIVAL AND DEPARTURE

By bus Most bus companies have their own terminals in the unsavoury area along Manzanilla and Lambayeque;

there are numerous departures in both directions along the Panamericana during the day. Recommended companies include Ormeño, Lambayeque 180 (☎ 056 215 600); Cruz del Sur, Fray Roman Rojas (☎ 056 223 333); and Oltursa, Av Ayabaca 974 (☎ 056 211 960). If travelling with Soyuz (Av Manzanilla 130; ☎ 056 224 138), go with the quicker, direct busses.

Destinations Arequipa (several daily; 10–12hr); Lima (several daily; 4hr); Nazca (several daily; 2hr 30min); Paracas (several daily; 2hr).

By mototaxi A *mototaxi* to Huacachina will set you back S4.

HUACACHINA

Since Ica itself is not terribly attractive, it's preferable to base yourself at the nearby village of **HUACACHINA**, as it's just as easy to do *bodega* tours from here. This once peaceful oasis, nestled among huge sand dunes and boasting a lake with curative properties, has been overrun with travellers, eager for adrenaline-packed adventures (in particular **sandboarding** and **dune-buggying**) and all-night parties around dimly lit pools.

ARRIVAL AND DEPARTURE

By taxi A taxi from town should be around S10.

By colectivo *Colectivos* leave when full, from near the kiosks at the entrance of the lagoon in Huacachina to the Plaza de Armas in Ica (S2).

By mototaxi A *mototaxi* between Ica and Huacachina should cost no more than S5.

ACCOMMODATION

Most hostels either run their own sandboarding, dune-buggy and *bodega* tours, or they can organize them for you. Much of the nightlife in Huacachina revolves around the hostels, which usually have their own

---

ICA AND HUACACHINA TOURS

Most hostels in Huacachina rent out **sandboards** and run late-afternoon **dune-buggy tours**. Those looking to cut costs may want to rent a board and go it alone, but bear in mind that it soon gets very tiring dragging a board up a sand dune in the scorching sun.

TOUR OPERATORS

Irresponsible dune-buggy drivers are known to drive quite recklessly, so it's best to book your trip with a reputable agency such as:

Curasi Balneario de Huacachina 197 ☎ 056 216 989, 🖰 huacachinacurasi.com. A reliable outfit running sandboarding and dune-buggy tours (S35 plus S3.80

entry tax payable as you enter the dunes).

Desert Adventures Hostal Desert Nights ☎ 056 228 458, 🖰 desertadventure.net. An established Huacachina-based tour company, offering the standard half-day dune-buggy tours of the dunes (S50), with sandboarding included. Also runs vineyard tours (S35) and a dune-buggy trip with an overnight stay in the desert (S180).

9

restaurants and bars, and throw raucous pool parties in the evenings.

Casa de Arena Perotti s/n ☏ 056 215 274, ⌨ casadearena .net. Huacachina's party hostel has raucous nightly pool parties and an affiliated club (with free entry for guests) playing electronica and Peruvian tracks. The party goes on all night – join in or bring earplugs. The simple yet colourful rooms (with wi-fi) are mostly set around the pool and there's a large eighteen-bunk dorm too. Dorms $\overline{S25}$, doubles $\overline{S60}$

★ **La Casa de Bamboo** Av Perotti behind the *Hostería Suiza* ☏ 056 776 649. Small family place for those looking to escape the party, but not pay a fortune. Rooms are small and simple, but light and cool, and some even have a balcony. The owners are great and the garden restaurant/café is a treat. Excellent wi-fi. $\overline{S80}$

Curasi Balneario de Huacachina 197 ☏ 056 216 989, ⌨ huacachinacurasi.com. Slightly less backpacker-focused than the other options in that it is a quiet three-star hotel including more of a Peruvian clientele, the secure *Curasi* has neat and tidy rooms giving onto a pleasant pool area with deckchairs. $\overline{S100}$

Hostal Desert Nights By the lagoon ☏ 056 228 458, ⌨ desertadventure.net. This popular backpacker choice has four eight-bunk dorms (no doubles) and a perpetually packed restaurant serving international grub such as burgers (S15–20; veggie burger S15) and sandwiches (S6–15). Thirsty gullets can opt for a jug of pisco sour (S35). Dorms $\overline{S20}$

EATING

La Casa de Bamboo Av Perotti s/n, behind the *Hostería Suiza*. This laidback family-run veggie restaurant with tables dotted around the garden offers healthy breakfasts (S9), delicious chocolate fudge brownies (S8) and green tea (S5). Veggie and vegan dishes include Thai curry (S18) and pasta dishes (S12–16), as well as exquisite home-made hummus (S8). Mon–Wed 8.30am–3pm, Thurs–Sat 8.30am–3pm & 6–10pm.

Desert Nights Balneario de Huacachina ☏ 056 228 458. A simple place that serves a bit of everything at a good price (S15–30) – you can't really go wrong. Daily 8am–10pm.

NAZCA AND AROUND

The small, sun-baked town of **NAZCA** spreads along the margin of a small coastal valley. Although the river is invariably dry, Nazca's valley remains green and fertile through the continued use of ancient subterranean aqueducts. The town is one of Peru's major attractions, and though most travellers come here solely to take a flight over the enigma that is the Nazca Lines (see p.774), other local attractions include the excellent **Museo Didáctico Antonini**, the adobe Inca ruins of **Paredones** on the outskirts, and the popular (if somewhat macabre) outlying archeological sites, such as the nearby **Chauchilla Cemetery** and the **Cahuachi pyramids**, an hour's drive into the desert.

WHAT TO SEE AND DO

Plaza de Armas is the heart of Nazca, with main street Jr Bolognesi connecting it to Plaza Bolognesi three blocks to the west. Numerous restaurants, bars and hostels are all within a couple of blocks of the two plazas.

Museo Didáctico Antonini

Heading east five blocks from the Plaza de Armas along Bolognesi you will find the fascinating **Museo Didáctico Antonini** (daily 9am–7pm; S15). The museum stretches over six blocks and presents interpretative exhibits covering the evolution of Nazca culture, with superb examples of pottery, household tools and trophy skulls with pierced foreheads. There's a good audiovisual show and scale-model reconstructions of local ruins such as the Templo del Escalonado at Cahuachi. The museum complex includes an archeological park that contains the Bisambra aqueduct (once fed by the Bisambra reservoir higher up the valley) and some burial reconstructions. The exhibit labels are in Spanish but you can pick up translation booklets at the front desk.

María Reiche Planetarium

For those with a particular interest in the Nazca Lines, a trip to the **María Reiche Planetarium** in the *Nazca Lines Hotel* (Bolognesi 147; showings in English daily at 7pm and in Spanish at 8.15pm; S20) is a good idea. The shows last about 45 minutes and focus primarily on María Reiche's theories about the Lines, and their correspondence to various constellations, followed by a quick look through a powerful telescope.

Didáctico Museo Antonini & CantayocAqueducts ▲

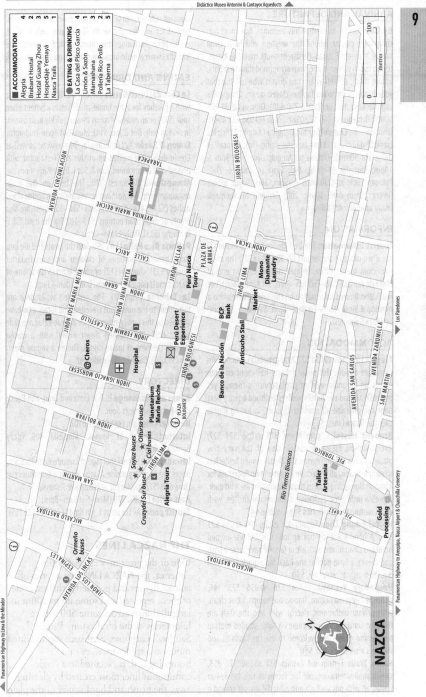

ACCOMMODATION
Alegria	4
Brabant Hostal	2
Hostal Guang Zhou	5
Hospedaje Yemayá	3
Nasca Trails	1

EATING & DRINKING
La Casa del Pisco García	4
Limón & Sazón	1
Mamashana	3
Pollería Rico Pollo	2
La Taberna	5

NAZCA

100 metres

▲ Panamerican Highway to Lima & the Mirador

▲ Panamerican Highway to Arequipa, Nasca Airport & Chauchilla Cemetery

Los Paredones ▶

9

ARRIVAL AND DEPARTURE

By bus There's no central bus terminal, but most bus companies cluster around the western end of Jr Lima where it meets Bolívar. Persistent touts meet all buses, trying to sell you anything from accommodation to flights; ignore them, as well as any taxi drivers who tell you that your hostel is dirty/too far/has closed down. Companies include: Cruz del Sur (☎ 056 720 440); Oltursa (☎ 01 708 5000); Ormeño (☎ 056 522 058); Soyuz (☎ 056 521 464).
Destinations Cruz del Sur to: Arequipa (4 daily, 10hr); Ica (several daily; 2hr); Lima (several daily; 7hr); Paracas (4 daily; 3hr 30min). Oltursa to: Arequipa (daily at 3pm & 10pm; 9hr); Ica (3 daily; 2hr); Lima (4 daily; 6–7hr); Paracas (daily at 6.30am & 4.45pm; 2hr). Soyuz to: Ica (every 30min 6am–10pm; 2hr); Ormeño to: Arequipa (daily at midnight; 10hr).

INFORMATION

Tourist information The best choice for information is the iPerú office at the airport (☎ 979 980 622). The main municipal tourist office, located on the eastern end of Plaza de Armas (Mon–Fri 8am–8pm, Sat 8am–noon), has maps and limited information on the town. There's also a municipal kiosk (Mon–Fri 8am–8pm, Sat 8am–3.30pm) on Plaza Bolognesi.

ACCOMMODATION

Alegría Lima 166 ☎ 056 522 702, ⊕ hotelalegria.net. An upmarket option, this popular hotel has clean en-suite rooms set around a verdant pool; service is friendly yet professional and the hotel's well-established agency next door can organize all manner of tours, including flights over the Nazca Lines. **S̄135**
Brabant Hostal C Juan Matta 878 ☎ 056 524 127, ⊕ brabanthostalnasca.webklik.nl. One of the very few places in town offering dorms, this Dutch-owned hostel has six simple rooms, all with cable TV, set on two floors; ask for a pad on the second floor as those downstairs are a bit dark. There's a little book exchange, a communal kitchen, wi-fi and a rooftop terrace. Dorms **S̄16**, doubles **S̄45**
Hostal Guang Zhou Fermín de Castillo 494 ☎ 056 521 391. A good-value central option, this Chinese-owned hotel has clean rooms with a/c or fan. All have private bath and there's a little pool at the back for a quick afternoon dip. Wi-fi only at reception. **S̄40**
Hospedaje Yemayá Callao 578 ☎ 056 523 146, ⊕ hospedajeyemaya.com. Rooms are compact but clean, with private bathrooms, decent wi-fi and the staff are friendly. Centrally located, there's a large shaded rooftop terrace and guests are welcome to use the facilities and showers after check-out. **S̄50**
Nasca Trails Fermín del Castillo 637 ☎ 056 522 858, ⊕ nascatrails@terra.com.pe. The rooms at this family-run hostel, all with private bath and cable TV, are set around a

pleasant outdoor area with sofas, armchairs and hammocks, perfect for an afternoon siesta. There's also table football, wi-fi, book exchange and home-cooked dinners. The friendly owner is multilingual and runs good local tours. **S̄70**

EATING AND DRINKING

La Casa del Pisco García Bolognesi 298. Head to this bar with a jukebox for some home-made pisco, a potent pisco sour (S12) or an excellent *tunas* frozen (prickly pear frozen; in season only, Dec & Jan; S14). Mon–Sat 6pm–midnight.
Limón & Sazón Av Los Incas s/n. Great *ceviche* as well as Creole dishes are rustled up at this airy restaurant with *peña* shows at lunchtime (Sat & Sun). Daily 9am–6pm.
Mamashana Bolognesi 270. The best on the main restaurant strip, *Mamashana* serves great fish and seafood dishes (S24–34) and meat mains (S20–35); there are also plenty of vegetarian options (S10–18). Try the mild *fish a lo macho* (S33). Daily 11am–late.
Pollería Rico Pollo Lima 190. Join the locals and dig into some generous portions of chicken and fries (quarter chicken S13), chorizo (S12) or *salchipapas* (S10) at one of Nazca's most popular *pollerías*. Daily 10am–1am.
La Taberna Lima 321. The scribbled walls here are testament to the numerous travellers and locals who have stopped by this family-run place for a great-value *menú de casa* (S8.50–10), washed down nicely with a *chicha morada* (fermented maize drink). There's a veggie menu too (S13.50). Daily 11am–midnight.

DIRECTORY

Banks and exchange BCP at Lima and Grau, and Banco de la Nación just next door.
Hospital Callao s/n (☎ 056 522 010).
Internet Cheros at Ignacio Morseski 408 (daily 8am–11pm; S1/hr).
Laundry There's a real shortage of *lavanderías* in Nazca so prices are high; try inside *Mono Diamante Guesthouse* at Lima 660 (S7/kg; 24hr) or at *Hospedaje Yemayá*.
Post office Castillo 379 (Mon–Sat 8am–8pm).
Tourist police Av Los Incas 1, s/n Km447 (☎ 056 522 105).

THE NAZCA LINES

One of the great mysteries of South America, the **NAZCA LINES** are a series of animal figures and geometric shapes, none of them repeated and some up to 200m in length, drawn across some 500 square kilometres of the bleak, stony Pampa de San José. Each one, even such sophisticated motifs as a spider monkey or a hummingbird, is executed in a single continuous line, most created by clearing away the brush and hard stones of the plain

TOURS AROUND NAZCA

Some well-established companies arrange **tours** to the major sites around Nazca, all offering similar trips to Los Paredones, Cantalloc, Cahuachi, Chauchilla and the Lines. Tours around Chauchilla Cemetery last 2hr 30min for about S35–45, while a trip to the viewing tower and the Casa Museo María Reiche also takes 2hr 30min and costs around S40. Tours out to the ruined temple complex in the desert at Cahuachi (see below) are 4hr and cost around S150–225 for four people; these need to be arranged in advance.

TOUR OPERATORS

Alegría Tours Lima 166 ☏ 056 522 497, ⓦ alegriatoursperu.com. Well-established company.

Perú Nasca Tours Bolognesi 449 ☏ 056 523 300, ⓦ perunascatours.com.

Perú Desert Experience Bolognesi 299 ☏ 56 771 900, ⓦ perudesert.com. For sandboarding tours and buggy rides.

to reveal the fine dust beneath. Theories abound as to what their purpose was – from landing strips for alien spaceships to some kind of agricultural calendar, aligned with the constellations above, to help regulate the planting and harvesting of crops. Perhaps at the same time some of the straight lines served as ancient sacred paths connecting *huacas*, or power spots. Regardless of why they were made, the Lines are among the strangest and most unforgettable sights in the country.

At Km420 of the Panamerican Highway, 20km north of Nazca, a tall metal **viewing tower** (or *mirador*, S2) has been built above the plain, from which you get a partial view of a giant tree, a pair of hands and a lizard, though the experience does not compare to a **flight** over the Lines (see box, p.776).

Around 5km south along the Panamericana from the *mirador*, you'll find the **Museo María Reiche** (Mon–Sat 9am–15pm; S15), the former home of the German mathematician who made research into the Lines her life's work. Here you can see her possessions and sketches and visit her tomb.

AROUND NAZCA

Chauchilla and **Cahuachi**, after the Lines the most important Nazca sites, are both difficult to reach by public transport, so you may want to consider a tour.

Cerro Blanco

You can easily see **Cerro Blanco**, the world's largest sand dune, from anywhere in the city. Formerly used as a religious

centre, it's now the site for extreme dune-buggy rides and sandboarding. Several tour agencies (see box above) run morning trips here, typically leaving at 5am and returning at lunchtime.

Chauchilla Cemetery

Roughly 30km south of Nazca, **Chauchilla Cemetery** is an atmospheric sight. Scattered about the dusty ground are thousands of graves, dating back to the Nazca culture (400 BC–800 AD), which have been cleaned up in recent years and organized for visitors, though bits of human bone and broken pottery shards still litter the ground, left there by grave robbers from decades ago.

There are clear walkways from which you must not stray, and open graves have roofs built over them to save the mummies, skeletons, shroud fabric and lengths of braided hair from the desert sun. The mummies with the longest hair are the chiefs, and the Nazca mummified animals as well; look for a child's pet parrot. It is an impressive experience, intensified by the curator's decision to arrange the mummies into positions intended to represent their daily lives. Tours of the cemetery last around three hours and take in a pottery workshop and a gold-processing centre on the way back to town.

Cahuachi

Currently being excavated by an Italian archeological team, **Cahuachi** is an enormous ceremonial centre of great importance to the Nazca culture, consisting of 44 pyramids, only one of which has been renovated; the rest are

9

still hidden under the sand. There is also a llama cemetery and a site called Estaquería – a possible place of mummification. It lies in the middle of the desert, 25km west of Nazca along a dirt track; on the way, you pass ransacked ancient graveyards with scattered human remains. Tours normally take place in the morning, as sandstorms can pick up in the afternoon.

Paredones and Aquaductos de Cantalloc

These two sites are normally seen as part of one tour as they are close together. The **Paredones ruins**, 2km southeast of town, are the crumbling remains of an Inca fortress and administrative centre (and now home to desert owls). The **Cantalloc Aqueducts** lie 5km further on; constructed by the Nazca, they consist of stone spirals going deep into the ground, thought to be air vents for a vast underground system of aqueducts bringing water from higher in the valley, or, some theorize, from a large underground well in Cerro Blanco. They are still used to irrigate the nearby fields. It is possible to circle down to the openings at the bottom and dip your fingers in this cool, well-travelled water.

Arequipa and around

The country's second-biggest and arguably, after Cusco, most attractive city, **AREQUIPA** sits some 2400m above sea level with **El Misti**, the dormant volcano poised above, giving the place a rather legendary appearance. An elegant yet modern city, with a relatively wealthy population of more than 750,000, it has a relaxed feel and maintains a rather aloof attitude towards the rest of Peru.

The spectacular countryside around Arequipa rewards a few days' exploration, with some exciting trekking and rafting possibilities (best in the dry season, May–Sept). Around 200km to the north of the city is the **Colca Canyon**: called the "valley of marvels" by the Peruvian novelist Mario Vargas Llosa, it is nearly twice the size of Arizona's Grand Canyon and one of the country's most extraordinary natural sights. Further north, the remote **Cotahuasi Canyon** offers even more remote and challenging treks for those with plenty of time. Around 120km west of Arequipa, you can see the amazing petroglyphs of **Toro Muerto**, perhaps continuing on to hike amid the craters and cones of the **Valley of the Volcanoes**.

WHAT TO SEE AND DO

The city centre is compact and walkable, spreading out in a grid shape from the Plaza de Armas. Arequipa's architectural beauty comes mainly from the colonial period, characterized here by white *sillar* stone, which gives the city the name "Ciudad Blanca" ("White City"). Of the huge number of religious buildings spread about the old colonial centre, the **Monastery of Santa Catalina** is the most outstanding. Within a few blocks of the Plaza de Armas are half a dozen churches that merit a brief visit, and a couple of superb old mansions. You can walk to the attractive suburb of **Yanahuara**, renowned for its dramatic views of the valley with the volcanoes.

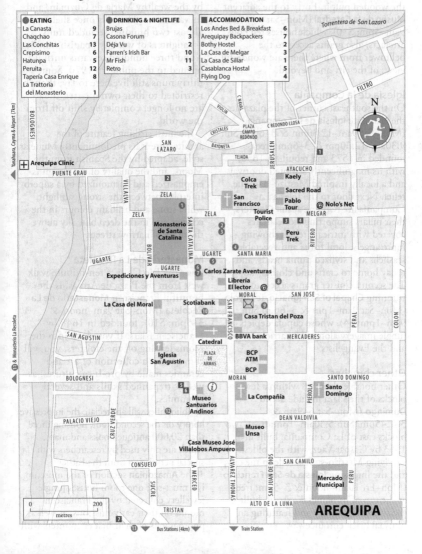

EATING
La Canasta	9
Chaqchao	7
Las Conchitas	13
Crepísimo	6
Hatunpa	5
Peruita	12
Tapería Casa Enrique	8
La Trattoria del Monasterio	1

DRINKING & NIGHTLIFE
Brujas	4
Casona Forum	3
Déja Vu	2
Farren's Irish Bar	10
Mr Fish	11
Retro	3

ACCOMMODATION
Los Andes Bed & Breakfast	6
Arequipay Backpackers	7
Bothy Hostel	2
La Casa de Melgar	3
La Casa de Sillar	1
Casablanca Hostal	5
Flying Dog	4

AREQUIPA

9

The Plaza de Armas and Catedral
The **Plaza de Armas**, one of South America's grandest, comprises a particularly striking array of colonial architecture, dotted with palms, flowers and gardens. It is dominated by the arcades and elegant white facade of the seventeenth-century **Catedral** (Mon–Sat 7–10am & 5–7pm, Sun 9am–1pm; free), which has one of the largest organs in South America, imported from Belgium. Note the serpent-tailed devil supporting the wooden pulpit. Entry to the adjacent **Museo de la Catedral** (Mon–Sat 9am–5pm; S10), which houses religious artefacts, also grants access to the belltower from where there are wonderful views of the city and beyond.

Iglesia de la Compañía
On the southeast corner of the plaza lies the elaborate **Iglesia de la Compañía** (Mon–Sat 9am–12.30pm & 3–6pm, Sun 9.30am–12.30pm & 3–6pm; free), founded in 1573 and rebuilt in 1650, with its magnificently sculpted doorway, and a locally inspired Mestizo-Baroque relief. Next door to the Iglesia La Compañía are two fine **Jesuit Cloisters**, their pillars supporting stone arches covered with intricate reliefs showing more angels, local fruits and vegetables, seashells and stylized puma heads, and today home to crafts and clothes shops. The second cloister grants access to the stunning **Chapel of San Ignacio de Loyola** (Mon–Sat 9am–1pm & 3–6pm, Sun 9am–1pm; S4), whose cupola depicts jungle imagery alongside warriors, angels and the Evangelists.

Other churches
Other notable churches within a few blocks of the Plaza include **Santo Domingo** (Mon–Sat 6–9am & 3–7.45pm, Sun 5.30am–1pm; free), two blocks east of La Compañía, built in 1553 by Gaspar Vaez, with the oldest surviving Mestizo-style facade in the city; and the imposing **Iglesia de San Francisco** (Mon–Fri 10am–noon & 3–5pm; free), at the top of its namesake street, built in the sixteenth century and featuring an unusual brick entranceway.

Monasterio de Santa Catalina
Just two blocks north of the Plaza de Armas, the **Monasterio de Santa Catalina** (daily 8am–5pm, Tues & Thurs until 8pm; S40, multilingual guides available for about S20) is the most important and prestigious religious building in Peru – a citadel within a city – and its enormous complex of rooms, cloisters, streets and tiny plazas is perfect to explore at a leisurely pace.

The monastery was founded in 1580 by the wealthy María de Guzmán, and its vast protective walls once sheltered almost two hundred secluded nuns – daughters of wealthy Spanish families – and three hundred servants until it opened to the public in 1970. Some thirty nuns still live here today; though restricted to their own quarter, they are no longer completely shut off from the world.

The most striking feature of the architecture is its predominantly Mudéjar style, adapted by the Spanish from the Moors, and the quality of the design is emphasized and harmonized by a superb interplay between the strong sunlight, white stone and brilliant colours in the ceilings and in the deep blue sky above the maze of narrow streets.

Monasterio de La Recoleta
Over the Río Chili, a ten-minute walk west from the Plaza de Armas, is the beautiful Franciscan **Monasterio de La Recoleta** (Mon–Sat 9am–noon & 3–5pm; S10), founded in 1648 by Franciscan friars. If you duck into the rooms leading off the cloisters, you will come across a collection of art and ceramics made by pre-Inca cultures, as well as trepanned skulls and several mummies.

Bibliophiles will appreciate the impressive **library** on the second floor, housing more than 20,000 antique books and maps, which are only used by researchers with special permission from the Father.

The **Amazonian section** of the museum is a must-see; one room houses jungle jewellery collected by the Franciscan monks on their early missions, as well as photographs of their first encounters with the "natives". The second room displays a large variety of stuffed birds and animals from the Amazon, as well as traditional weapons, some still used today, and maps of early exploration of the Manu and Madre de Dios areas. Make sure to head up to the belfry, from where there are wonderful views of Arequipa and beyond.

Museo Santuarios Andinos

Often referred to as the "Juanita" or "Ice Princess" museum after its most famous exhibit – the immaculately preserved mummy of a 12- to 14-year-old girl sacrificed to a mountain deity around five hundred years ago – the superb little **Museo Santuarios Andinos** lies just off the plaza at Calle La Merced 110 (Mon–Sat 9am–6pm, Sun 9am–3pm; S20). After a dramatic twenty-minute National Geographic video about the discovery of Juanita, a multilingual guide talks you through the exhibits related to the sacrificial and burial practices of the Incas before finally unveiling the museum's star attraction. The intricate tiny offerings to the gods, made of gold and precious stones, are particularly fine, and ice-covered Juanita is very well preserved,

although note that her body is on display for only six months of the year. Bring warm clothes, as it's rather cold inside, and don't forget to tip the guide (S10).

Museo Arqueológico UNSA

A block and a half south of the plaza along Álvarez Thomas, you'll find the small yet fascinating **archeological museum** (Mon–Fri 9am–4pm; S2), which gives a glimpse into the local pre-Inca culture. The displays, labelled in Spanish only, feature Nazca, Chiribaya and Wari pottery; Nazca mummies and ritually deformed skulls; fine cloaks adorned with parrot feathers; and Inca and Spanish weaponry.

Museo José Villalobos Ampuero

Built in the early twentieth century, the former home of José Villalobos, the wealthy former mayor of Arequipa, is now open to the public as the **Museo José Villalobos Ampuero**, Alvarez Thomas 206 (Mon–Sat 9.30am–5pm; S20, includes 45min guided tour). The building's Art Nouveau facade with curving wavy columns was built using materials exclusively from Europe, including Italian

---

TOURS, TREKKING AND CLIMBING AROUND AREQUIPA

Most companies offer trips of one to three days out to the **Colca Canyon** for S90–250 (sometimes with *very* early morning starts) or to the petroglyphs at **Toro Muerto** for S60–120. Trips to the **Valley of the Volcanoes**, as well as specialist adventure activities (such as rafting in the Colca Canyon, mountaineering or multi-day trekking), can cost anything from S200 up to S1200 for a three- to six-day outing.

TOUR OPERATORS

Carlos Zarate Aventuras Santa Catalina 204 ☎ 054 202 461, ⓦ zarateadventures.com. Knowledgeable guide Carlos offers climbs of nearby peaks, canyoning, and cycling excursions, as well as archeological tours.
Colca Trek Jerusalén 401b ☎ 054 206 217, ⓦ colcatrek .com.pe. An excellent trekking, climbing, mountain-biking and canoeing operator that specializes in customized tours permitting a mix of these, as well as three-day tours of the Colca Canyon. Also sells maps and has equipment rental for independent trekkers.
Expediciones y Aventuras Santa Catalina 219 ☎ 054 221 653, ⓦ expedicionesyaventuras.com. Specialists in rafting and kayaking trips along the Chili River, the Majes River, the Canyon del Colca and Cotahuasi. They also arrange downhill and cross-country

mountain-biking trips, including to Chachani Volcano (6057m), where experienced bikers can descend all the way to Arequipa from an altitude of 4000m.
Pablo Tour Jerusalén 400 ☎ 054 203 737, ⓦ pablotour.com. Run by friendly multilingual Edwin, this company runs all manner of tours, from 4WD trips to the salt lake Laguna de Salinas, to trekking and cultural trips into the Colca Canyon using new alternative routes, thereby avoiding the crowds. Slightly pricier than the rest, but worth the extra expense.
Sacred Road Jerusalén 400 ☎ 054 330 408, ⓦ sacredroad.com. This company offers a wide range of tours to satisfy all tastes: mountain biking, canyoning, rock climbing, trekking and mountaineering, as well as the standard Colca Canyon tours.

9

granite and marble, while the sumptuous interiors contain antique wooden furniture, porcelain ornaments, a Titian and a one-tonne chandelier embellished with statuettes of the Greek goddess Minerva. Note the seventeenth-century cross in the bedroom, which is decorated with diamond nails. The house continues to be used by family members on special occasions.

Mercado Municipal

For a taste of local life, check out the covered **market** (daily 6am–5pm), which takes up an entire block between San Camillo and Alto de la Luna. Lose yourself amid the stalls piled high with local produce, the smells of cooking, *juguerías*, the vendors of jungle potions and wandering musicians. Just leave your valuables behind.

The views: Yanahuara and Mirador de Carmen Alto

A jaunt across the Río Chili via Puente Grau followed by a fifteen-minute uphill stroll brings you to the attractive plaza of the Yanahuara neighbourhood. It features a **viewing point** (*mirador*), with a postcard panorama of Misti framed behind by the white stone arches. The elaborately carved facade of the small eighteenth-century **Iglesia San Juan Bautista** nearby is a superb example of Mestizo art.

From here, a five-minute taxi ride (S5–8) takes you to the **Mirador del Carmen Alto**, which features a stupendous view of the city and all the volcanoes surrounding it.

ARRIVAL AND DEPARTURE

By plane Flights land at Arequipa airport (☎054 443 464), 8km northwest of the town. A taxi to downtown Arequipa will set you back S25 (30min).

By bus There are two main bus terminals in Arequipa: the Terminal Terrestre (☎054 427 798), Av Cáceres, at Arturo Ivañez, which mainly receives buses from Puno, Cusco and the Colca Canyon; and the Terrapuerto (☎054 348 810), just next door at Av Arturo Ivañez, with buses travelling mainly west to destinations such as Lima and Nazca. Leaving from the Terrapuerto for destinations including Lima, Nazca and Cusco are Cruz del Sur (☎054 427 375) and Cial (☎054 429 090). Flores (☎054 431 717) has its own terminal just opposite the Terminal Terrestre and has

numerous services to Puno and to Lima via Nazca and Ica. If you're going to the Colca Canyon, use Andalucía (☎054 445 089), Milagros (☎054 298 090) or Reyna (☎054 430 612). Both terminals are around 4km from the centre of town; there are regular buses from outside the station to Av La Marina west of the city centre (30–40min); a taxi to the Plaza de Armas is about S15.

Destinations Cusco (8 daily, mostly with night-time departures; 9–11hr); Desaguadero (4 daily; 8–9hr); La Paz, Bolivia (daily; 12–14hr); Lima (hourly; 16hr) via Nazca (9hr 30min) and Ica (12hr); Puno (7 daily; 6–7hr); Tacna (hourly; 6–7hr).

INFORMATION AND GETTING AROUND

Tourist information iPerú are on the Plaza de Armas (Mon–Sat 9am–8pm, Sun 9am–1pm; ☎054 223 265, ✉iperuarequipa@promperu.gov.pe). They also have a branch at the airport that meets incoming flights. For topographic maps of the Colca Canyon, try Pablo Tour or Colca Trek (see box, p.779), while Librería El Lector on San Francisco 213 (Mon–Sat 9am–8pm) has an extensive English-language book section, as well as detailed city maps.

Taxis If you want a taxi make sure you order a cab over the phone; taxis on the city streets are not necessarily safe – many are illegal and robberies have taken place in the past. To call a taxi, there's Aló Cayma (☎054 458 282), Aló 45 (☎054 454 545) or Taxi Plus (☎054 438 070).

ACCOMMODATION

Los Andes Bed & Breakfast La Merced 123 ☎054 330 015, ✇losandesarequipa.com. This welcoming place has spacious rooms with parquet flooring and a rooftop terrace with views over town. Self-caterers will delight at the huge open-plan kitchen with a large outdoor seating area, complete with TV lounge. Wi-fi; rates include breakfast. Dorms S̲2̲5̲, doubles S̲8̲5̲

Arequipay Backpackers Pasaje O'Higgins 224 ☎054 234 560, ✇arequipaybackpackers.com. A fun hostel with brightly painted walls featuring two movie rooms with flatscreen TVs and PlayStation, a pool room and a pleasant patio with hammocks and barbecue set. Dorms are comfortable if a bit cramped, with sturdy beds, lockers and shared bathrooms. Dorms S̲2̲0̲, doubles S̲7̲0̲

Bothy Hostel Puente Grau 306 ☎054 282 438, ✉bothyhostel@gmail.com. This colourful laidback hostel in a seventeenth-century building just a few steps from Arequipa's nightlife centre features quirky murals and beanbags where travellers sit back and socialize at all times of the day. Dorms, mixed and female-only, have lockers and colourful linen. Dorms S̲2̲7̲, doubles S̲7̲0̲

La Casa de Sillar Rivero 504 ☎054 284 249, ✇lacasadesillar.com. This pleasant guesthouse in a beautiful colonial building with a leafy patio is an excellent

choice for those wanting to stay somewhere quiet.
Doubles with private bath are more welcoming than those
with shared bath, with decorative wall paintings, lamps
made using natural materials and clay floors. The
quadruple mezzanine room (S140) with a vaulted ceiling is
a great choice for groups, there's a small rooftop terrace
with hammock and a kitchen for guests' use, too. **S70**

★ **Casablanca Hostal** Puente Bolognesi 104 ☎054 221
327, ⓦcasablancahostal.com. This very agreeable place
constructed with volcanic blocks of stone right by the main
plaza features eight spacious rooms with private
bathrooms and lovely parquet floors. Some rooms have
private balconies overlooking the street, and there's an
open-plan kitchen that guests are welcome to use. **S120**

★ **Flying Dog** Melgar 116 ☎054 231 163,
ⓦflyingdogperu.com. Misti the dog and Chacani the cat
patrol the premises of this pleasant hostel located in a
colonial building just a couple of blocks east of the
Monastery of Santa Catalina. Rooms are warm and clean,
there's a kitchen for guests' use and a lounge area with a
pool table, as well as a bar for evening drinks. Dorms **S30**,
doubles **S75**

EATING

La Canasta Jerusalén 115 ☎054 211 820. This popular
bakery tucked away off Calle Jerusalén offers *empanadas*
(S3.80), sandwiches (S8), savoury pastries (S5) and quinoa
and cheese croissants (S1.50), which can be enjoyed at
little tables in the peaceful courtyard. Mon–Sat
8.30am–8pm.

★ **Chaqchao** Santa Catalina 204 ☎054 234 572,
ⓦchaqchao.com. A chocolate lover's paradise specializing
in chocolate and only chocolate – there's even
(complimentary) chocolate tea, made from cocoa husks,
and chocolate lip balm and soap available for purchase.
You can feast on home-made brownies (S6), double
chocolate cake (S8) and exquisite hot chocolate (S8) as you
watch life go by from the little balcony overlooking Calle
Santa Catalina. There are daily chocolate-making classes
(S60), too. Daily 11am–9pm.

★ **Las Conchitas** Av San Martín 200 ☎054 223 672. This
small and friendly local hangout serves excellent fresh fish

and seafood dishes at very reasonable prices. The crab
empanadas (S5) are delicious, as are the *ceviche* (S21) and
steamed fish with yucca or rice (S35). Tues–Sun
10am–4pm.

Crepísimo Santa Catalina 208. This Swiss-run café serves
one hundred varieties of sweet and savoury crêpes to be
enjoyed with a refreshing home-made Andean ice tea
(S4). The *crepísimo* with ham, cheese and egg (S16)
remains their bestseller, and they have a great lunch deal
for S26, which includes salad, crêpe, dessert and drink.
Mon–Sat 8am–midnight, Sun 8am–10pm.

Hatunpa Ugarte 208 ☎054 212 918. This cheap and
cheerful restaurant attracts a young foreign crowd for its
potato-based dishes (S12.50). Everything on the menu
features potatoes with a topping of choice, including meat
or vegetarian. The food is rustled up in front of customers'
eyes at the little open-plan kitchen. Mon–Sat
12.30–9.30pm.

Peruita Palacio Viejo 321A. One of southern Peru's very
few Italian-run pizzerias, here you will see the Italian
pizzaiolo spinning all sorts of exotically flavoured thin-
crusted (or more thickly so, depending on customers'
preference) pizzas (S26), while at lunch time there's an
excellent-value set lunch for only S15. Mon–Sat 1–3pm &
5.30–10.30pm.

Tapería Casa Enrique Jerusalén 212 ☎054 213 060.
This laidback place offers Spanish favourites including
tortilla, chorizo and manchego (cheese or meat platters
S60). There are Spanish and South American wines and an
excellent-value set lunch for S12 (Mon–Sat), which
includes a starter, main (normally *paella*) and dessert.
Daily noon–10pm.

DRINKING AND NIGHTLIFE

Brujas San Francisco 300. On Arequipa's busy nightlife
strip, this laidback bar with wooden interiors and low
lighting is a great spot for those wanting to enjoy a beer
(S10; 3 for S25) and a chat without their voices being
drowned by pumping music. Daily 6pm–3am.

Casona Forum San Francisco 317. This three-storey
complex houses some of Arequipa's best nightspots, such as

9

Zero Pub & Pool, with pool tables, and the *Terrasse* lounge restaurant, offering fine dining and stunning views of the city through 360-degree windows. The jewel in the crown – the basement *Forum* disco – is the place to see and be seen among young *Arequipeños*, with a lively tropical decor including palm trees, pools and a large artificial waterfall.

★**Déja Vu** San Francisco 319B ☎054 221 904, ⊛dejavuaqp.com. This popular place gets particularly busy in the evenings thanks to its appealing terrace with sofas and views over town, which is a particularly pleasant spot for a sundowner. It morphs into a club at night, mainly playing an eclectic mix of salsa and dance music on the ground floor and electronica on the first floor. There's a S10 entry charge on weekends after 11.30pm. Daily 11am–3am, Thurs, Fri & Sat until 5am.

Farren's Irish Bar Pasaje Catedral 107. Just behind the plaza, this little Irish bar/pub with outdoor seating is the perfect spot to grab a refreshing beer as you explore town. There's a screen for sporting events, and if you're around on St Patrick's Day you can enjoy a few pints of Guinness. Local beers (S6), as well as Belgian and English brews (Old Speckled Hen S18). Happy hour 6–10pm. Mon–Sat 10am–midnight.

Mr Fish Av Variante Uchumayo s/n. This large club located on the outskirts of Arequipa is the city's hottest nightlife spot. Young *Arequipeños* dance away on Thursday from as early as late afternoon, on Friday it's Creole music while on Saturday revellers go wild to club beats. Entry S60. Thurs 3pm–5am, Fri & Sat 9pm–5am.

Retro San Francisco 317. Located in the Casona Forum, this is Arequipa's only bar hosting bands early on in the week. Rock groups hit the stage Tuesday through to Saturday at 10pm, occasionally backed up by some salsa, reggaeton, and 1970s, 80s and 90s tunes. Mon–Sat 7pm–2am.

DIRECTORY

Banks and exchange BCP at San Juan de Dios 125 and Scotia Bank on Moral, at San Francisco, have ATMs and can change/dispense US dollars. There are *cambios* on the Plaza de Armas, on Jerusalén and on San Juan de Dios.

Hospital Clínica Arequipa, Av Bolognesi con Puente Grau (☎054 599 000, ⊛www.clinicarequipa.com.pe).

Internet There are a handful of internet cafés north of town on Melgar, Rivero and Jerusalén. Try Nolo's.net, Rivero 400, at Melgar (daily 7.30am–9pm; S1/hr).

Laundry There are plenty of laundry places on Jerusalén to the north of the plaza. Try Kaely, Jerusalén 412 (Mon–Sat 8am–8pm, Sun 8am–5pm; S3/kg; ☎054 691 777).

Police The 24hr tourist police is at Jerusalén 315 (☎054 201 258).

Post office Moral 118 (Mon–Sat 8am–8pm, Sun 9am–1pm).

THE COLCA CANYON

The sharp terraces of the **COLCA CANYON**, the world's deepest at more than 4km from cliff edge to river bottom, are still home to more-or-less traditional Indian villages, despite the canyon's growth into one of Peru's most popular tourist attractions. The **Mirador Cruz del Condor** is the most popular viewing point – the canyon is around 1600m deep at this point – from where you can almost guarantee seeing condors circling up from the depths against breathtaking scenery (best spotted 7–9am; in May, June and July sightings are 9–11am).

The entry point for the Colca Canyon is the market town of **Chivay**, 150km north of Arequipa (3–4hr by bus). The pleasant little town of **Cabanaconde** (3300m) serves as an excellent base to descend into the canyon, and is about 10km further down the road.

You'll need a couple of days to begin exploring the area and three or four to do it any justice, but several tour companies offer punishing one-day tours as well as extended trips with overnight stops. When you enter the canyon, you need to purchase the Boleto Turístico (Tourist Ticket; S70) from the control point just before the entrance to Chivay. Only buy tickets from Autocolca authorities, as counterfeit tickets do exist.

Chivay

This is the largest village in the Colca Valley, although note it is not in the canyon itself. Its attractions include the

---

CROSSING INTO CHILE

The **border with Chile** (Mon–Fri 8am–midnight, Sat & Sun 24hr) is about 40km south of Tacna (a 6–7hr bus ride from Arequipa). Regular buses and *colectivos* to **Arica** (see p.419) leave from the modern bus terminal on Hipolito Unanue in Tacna; the *colectivos* (S25) are a particularly quick and easy way to cross the border. For a small tip, the drivers will assist you with border formalities. **Coming back into Peru** from Arica is as simple as getting there; *colectivos* run throughout the day from the Terminal Internacional de Buses on Diego Portales 1002.

COLCA CANYON

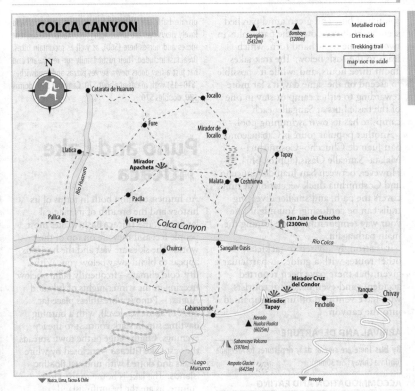

Legend:
- Metalled road
- Dirt track
- Trekking trail

map not to scale

N

Sepregina (5432m)
Bomboya (5200m)
Catarata de Huaruro
Tocallo
Fure
Mirador de Tocallo
Llatica
Mirador Apacheta
Tapay
Malata
Coshñirwa
Río Huaruro
Padla
Pallca
Geyser
Colca Canyon
San Juan de Chuccho (2300m)
Chuirca
Sangalle Oasis
Río Colca
Mirador Cruz del Condor
Yanque
Chivay
Mirador Tapay
Pinchollo
Cabanaconde
Nevado Huaca Huaca (6025m)
Sabancaya Volcano (5976m)
Lago Mucurca
Ampato Glacier (6425m)

Nazca, Lima, Tacna & Chile ▼

Arequipa ▼

hot springs, 3km northeast of town (daily 4am–7pm; S15), with a zip-line (@colcaziplining.com) next to it. *Colectivos* run from the Plaza de Armas (daily every 20min; 5min). There are also several hiking trails here, although as **CHIVAY** is not so attractive, most visitors continue on to the laidback village of Cabanaconde.

ARRIVAL AND DEPARTURE

By bus Regular buses connect Chivay with Arequipa (every 2hr or so; 3hr) and Cabanaconde (6 daily; 2hr 30min). The bus companies 4MM and Sillustani have daily departures to Puno (6hr), leaving around lunchtime.

ACCOMMODATION

Hostal La Casa de Lucila Grau 131 @ 054 284 211. This small but homey place offers comfortable rooms set on two floors that look onto a leafy garden area with stone walkway and potted plants. It's by far the best budget place in town. **S150**

Hostal La Pascana Siglo XX 106 @ 054 531 001, @ hostal-lapascana.com. A pleasant respite from the endless concrete blocks, *La Pascana* has rooms giving onto a central flowering courtyard, although these could do with a splash of paint and a revamp. Rates include breakfast. Free wi-fi. **S120**

EATING

Q'anka Salaverry 105, 3rd floor @ 958 296 914. This atmospheric little place specializes in hot stone steaks, with a particularly tasty *lomito de alpaca* (S30), and pizzas (S15), also served sizzling on hot stones. The walls are decorated with masks and mud vases adorn the tables. Daily 11am–10pm.

Urinsaya Francisco Bolognesi 1026. Serving one of the best all-you-can-eat lunchtime buffets (S30), the grub here includes a variety of hearty soups, as well as fish and meat dishes. Daily 11am–3pm.

Cabanaconde

An attractive village in the heart of the canyon, surrounded by Inca terracing, **CABANACONDE** makes an excellent base for hiking down into the canyon. Follow fellow hikers through the fields to a steep trail leading down to **Sangalle Oasis** – a

9

splotch of blue and green amid parched scenery. Halfway down, the path splits in two; take the right-hand turn, which leads to the oasis below. The trek takes about three hours, and, while it's possible to ascend on the same day, it's far more rewarding to either camp or stay in one of the basic huts at Sangalle; each campsite has its own swimming pool.

Another popular route is Cabanaconde–San Juan de Chuccho–Coshñirhua–Malata–Sangalle Oasis (approx 6hr). However, between San Juan de Chuccho and Coshñirhua thick vegetation at times covers the path, and smaller diverging trails can be confusing. You might lose your way temporarily before joining the main path again.

It is strongly advised to tackle all other routes with a guide, in particular given that there have been reported accidents and even deaths of tourists who have ventured off unaccompanied into the canyon.

ARRIVAL AND DEPARTURE

By bus There are several daily departures to Arequipa (6hr) via Chivay (2hr 30min).

ACCOMMODATION AND EATING

La Casa de Santiago ☎ 054 203 737, ⓦ lacasadesantiago .com. This calm little oasis with clean and tidy rooms has a verdant garden with hammocks and wonderful views over the surrounding mountains. **S100**

★**Oasis Paraíso Camping Lodge** Sangalle Oasis ☎ 054 630611 or ☎ 054 797 485. Deep in the canyon in the lush Sangalle Oasis, this rustic place has a lush garden area with a very inviting pool that will make sure you linger here for longer than planned. Meals are served in the open-fronted restaurant, it's happy hour 4–6pm, and there are cooking classes (S30) that kick off with guests picking their ingredients from the vegetable garden. Camping **S10**, dorms **S15**, doubles **S60**

Pachamama ☎ 054 767 277, ⓦ pachamamahome.com. The main area of this hostel is warm and welcoming with a wood-fire pizza oven that keeps the room toasty and plenty of board games and a book exchange to keep travellers happy. Rooms here are rather plain but pleasant enough; those with a private bath will set you back a bit more. Dorms **S25**, doubles **S60**

★**Valle del Fuego** ☎ 054 668 910, ⓦ valledelfuego .com. Laidback and friendly owner Yamil will welcome you with a potent pisco sour ("the authentic pisco sour, not the one for tourists…"). The brick and stone rooms, all with

private bath, are warm and welcoming and command lovely views over the surrounding mountains. You can rent mules and horses here (S60), as well as mountain bikes. Breakfast included. Their rustic family-run restaurant and bar just a few doors down serves pizzas and sandwiches (S10–15) with mains at about S20. Camping **S10**, dorms **S20**, doubles **S70**

Puno and Lake Titicaca

An immense region both in terms of its history and the breadth of its magical landscape, the **Titicaca Basin** makes most people feel as if they are on top of the world. The skies are vast and the horizons appear to blend away below you. With a dry, cold climate – frequently falling below freezing in the winter nights of July and August – **Puno** is a breathless place (at 3870m above sea level), with a burning daytime sun in stark contrast to the icy evenings. On the edge of the town spreads the vast **Lake Titicaca** – enclosed by white peaks and dotted with unusual **floating islands**. The lake is home to the Uros culture, as are the beautiful island communities of **Amantani** and **Taquile**, which can all be visited by boat from Puno.

PUNO

The first Spanish settlement at **PUNO** sprang up around a silver mine discovered by the infamous Salcedo brothers in 1657, a camp that forged such a wild and violent reputation that the Lima viceroy moved in with soldiers to crush the Salcedos before things got too out of hand. In 1668 he created Puno as the capital of the region and from then on it developed into Lake Titicaca's main port and an important town on the silver trail from Potosí. Rich in traditions, Puno is also famed as the folklore capital of Peru. During the first two weeks of February, fiestas are held in honour of the **Virgen de la Candelaria** – a great spectacle, with incredible dancers wearing devil masks, which climaxes on the second Sunday of February.

WHAT TO SEE AND DO

Puno is a congested, chaotic but friendly town, compact enough to walk around. Most travellers use it as a stopover on their way to see the islands, but there are a couple of sites of interest in the town itself. There are four main points of reference in Puno: the spacious **Plaza de Armas**, the cosmopolitan strip of **Jirón Lima** on which most restaurants and bars can be found, tiny **Parque Pino** and the bustling **port** area.

The Plaza de Armas and around

The seventeenth-century **Catedral** on the Plaza de Armas (Mon–Fri 8am–noon & 3–6pm, Sat 8am–noon & 3–7pm, Sun 7.30am–noon & 3–5pm; free) is surprisingly large, with an exquisite

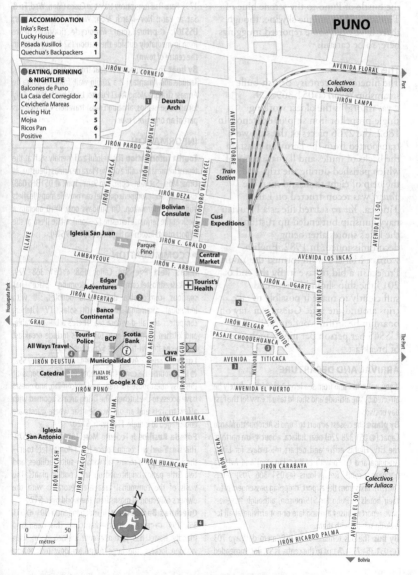

PUNO

ACCOMMODATION
Inka's Rest	2
Lucky House	3
Posada Kusillos	4
Quechua's Backpackers	1

EATING, DRINKING & NIGHTLIFE
Balcones de Puno	2
La Casa del Corregidor	4
Cevichería Mareas	7
Loving Hut	5
Mojsa	5
Ricos Pan	6
Positive	1

JIRÓN M. H. CORNEJO
AVENIDA FLORAL
Colectivos to Juliaca
JIRÓN LAMPA
Port
Deustua Arch
AVENIDA LA TORRE
JIRÓN PARDO
JIRÓN INDEPENDENCIA
JIRÓN TARAPACÁ
Train Station
JIRÓN DEZA
JIRÓN TEODORO VALCARCEL
Bolivian Consulate
Cusi Expeditions
AVENIDA EL SOL
Iglesia San Juan
Parque Pino
JIRÓN C. GRALDO
LAMBAYEQUE
JIRÓN F. ARBULU
Central Market
AVENIDA LOS INCAS
ILLAVE
Edgar Adventures
JIRÓN LIBERTAD
Banco Continental
Tourist's Health
JIRÓN A. UGARTE
JIRÓN PINEDA ARCE
JIRÓN CAHUIDE
JIRÓN MELGAR
PASAJE CHOQUEHUANCA
Huajsapata Park
GRAU
Tourist Police
BCP
Scotia Bank
All Ways Travel
JIRÓN DEUSTUA
Municipalidad
Lava Clin
JIRÓN AREQUIPA
JIRÓN MOQUEGUA
AVENIDA TITICACA
WENDOREE
The Port
Catedral
PLAZA DE ARMES
Google X
JIRÓN PUNO
AVENIDA EL PUERTO
Iglesia San Antonio
JIRÓN LIMA
JIRÓN CAJAMARCA
JIRÓN TACNA
JIRÓN ANCASH
JIRÓN AYACUCHO
JIRÓN HUANCANE
JIRÓN CARABAYA
Colectivos for Juliaca
N
0   50
metres
JIRÓN RICARDO PALMA
AVENIDA EL SOL
Bolivia

9

Baroque facade and, unusually for Peru, a very simple interior, in line with the local Aymara Indians' austere attitude to religion. High up, overlooking the town and Plaza de Armas, **Huajsapata Park** sits on a prominent hill, a steep ten-minute climb up Jirón Deustua, right into Jirón Llave, left up Jirón Bolognesi, then left again up the Pasaje Contique steps. Huajsapata offers stupendous views across the bustle of Puno to the serene blue of Titicaca and its unique skyline, though there have been some reported muggings here, so be careful.

The Yavari

The nineteenth-century British-built steamship **Yavari** (☎051 369 329, ⊛yavari.org) is the oldest working single-propellor iron ship in existence. In 1862, the 2766 pieces of the ship were transported from the Peruvian coast on the backs of mules and llamas, many of which perished during the trip, and with the help of eight thousand men the *Yavari* was reconstructed on Lake Titicaca. *Yavari* started life as a Peruvian navy gunship but ended up rusting on the lake's shores after being decommissioned. In 1982, English-woman Meriel Larkin formed the Yavari Project in a bid to save it. By the end of 2015 the ship should be repaired sufficiently to make it possible to take trips around the lake. Guests can stay on board in beautiful wooden cabins for US$45 per person per night, inclusive of breakfast.

ARRIVAL AND DEPARTURE

If you arrive in Puno from sea level, you'll immediately be affected by the altitude and should take it easy for the first day or two.

By plane The closest airport to Puno is Aeropuerto Manco Capac (☎051 328 226) near Juliaca, about 49km north of the city. Flights arrive and depart most days for Lima, Arequipa and Cusco with LAN (⊛lan.com) and Avianca (⊛avianca.com). Rossy Tours (☎051 366 709) offers *colectivo* taxis from the airport, dropping passengers off at their hotels in Puno for S15/person, although travellers have reported buses arriving late or not arriving at all for pick-up service with them.

By bus The bus terminal is at Jr Primero de Mayo 703 (☎051 364 733). A taxi to the centre is S5. Recommended

companies include: Cruz del Sur (☎051 205 824), Ormeño (☎051 352 780) and Transzela (☎051 353 822).
Destinations Arequipa (hourly; 6hr); Cusco (hourly; 6hr); La Paz (daily at 7.30am & 2.30pm; 6–7hr) via Copacabana (3hr); Lima (4 daily; 18–21hr); Puerto Maldonado (3 daily; change at Juliaca; 15hr). 4M Express (⊛4m-peru.com) and Turismo Sillustani (⊛turismosillustani.com) both run a tourist bus (daily at 6am; 5hr) to Chivay, picking passengers up from their respective hotels.

By train The train station is at Av La Torre 224 (☎051 369 179). Peru Rail runs pricey trains to Cusco (Mon, Wed, Fri & Sat at 8am; Nov–March Mon, Wed & Sat only; 10hr; US$161; ⊛perurail.com). Motorcycle rickshaws leave from immediately outside the station (S2 to anywhere in the centre of town).

By boat The main port for boat trips to the Uros Islands, Taquile and Amantani is a 20min walk from the Plaza de Armas, straight along Av El Puerto. Local boats leave daily for all three islands, although most travellers visit these as part of an organized tour.

INFORMATION

Tourist information The helpful and friendly staff at the tourist information office on the Plaza de Armas (Deustua, at Lima; Mon–Sat 9am–6pm, Sun 9am–1pm; ☎051 365 088, ✉iperupuno@promperu.gob.pe) can provide maps, leaflets and other information. On Sundays only iPerú operate a kiosk at the Terminal Terrestre (2–4pm), while iPerú at the airport meets incoming flights (☎051 639 549).

ACCOMMODATION

Inka's Rest Psje San Carlos 158 ☎051 368 720, ⊛inkasresthostel.com. This welcoming place has spacious, comfortable dorms and doubles, all with individual communal areas with sofas, TV, kitchen, computers and all-day coca tea. There's a billiards table, and kitchen for guests' use, too. Rates include breakfast and there's free wi-fi. Dorms S̲2̲6̲, doubles S̲6̲0̲
Lucky House Av Titicaca 144 ☎051 353 552, ⊛luckyyourhouse.com. The simply furnished rooms at this cosy guesthouse are clean and welcoming, and guests have access to the kitchen. The living area is adorned with a few trinkets and an old wooden bar where guests are encouraged to mingle. Free wi-fi. S̲1̲2̲0̲
Posada Kusillos Jr Federico More 162 ☎051 364 579. This small and welcoming place has a homey feel to it – there are only ten rooms, all with en-suite facilities, and two little patios brightened up with potted plants. The walls of the communal area are decorated with the owner's collection of masks from the world over. S̲1̲2̲0̲
Quechua's Backpackers Jr Independencia 301 ☎051 352 194, ⊛quechuasbackpackers.com. This clean and friendly hostel has just one cosy six-bed dorm with wooden lockers; the large round window overlooking

TOURS AROUND PUNO

There are four main tours on offer in Puno, all of which will reward you with abundant bird and animal life, immense landscapes and indigenous traditions. The trip to the ancient burial towers or *chullpas* at **Sillustani** normally involves a three- to four-hour tour by minibus and costs S55 including the entrance fee and guide. Most other tours involve a combination of visits to the nearby **Uros Floating Islands** (half-day tour; S45) and **Taquile and the Uros Islands** (full day from S85, or from S288 overnight). The best way to see the lake and experience life on Titicaca is to take a two-day tour, which stops at the Uros Islands then goes to Amantaní, where you spend the night, and then continues to Taquile on the second day; a day-trip is very rushed, as it takes three hours to reach Amantaní from Puno.

TOUR OPERATORS

Many agencies run formulaic tours and some companies have a reputation for ripping off the islanders. The following show a more sensitive approach:

All Ways Travel Deustua 576, 2nd floor ☎051 353 979, ⓦtiticacaperu.com.
Cusi Expeditions Teodoro Valcarcel 155 ☎051 369 072.
Edgar Adventures Lima 328 ☎051 353 444, ⓦedgaradventures.com.

town means it has plenty of light, and there's a small balcony with lake views. There's free all-day tea, book exchange, laundry service (S7/kg) and a fully equipped open-plan kitchen that guests are encouraged to use. Dorms S̲3̲5̲, doubles S̲8̲7̲

EATING, DRINKING AND NIGHTLIFE

Balcones de Puno Jr Libertad 354 ☎051 365 300, ⓦbalconesdepuno.com. The real draw at this restaurant is the daily folkloric dance shows (7.30–9pm) featuring beautiful traditional costumes. The food is excellent too – try the alpaca medallions (S40) and don't forget to order the quinoa ice cream (S15) and the coca mousse (S11). Daily 10am–10pm.
La Casa del Corregidor Jr Deustua 576 ☎051 351 921, ⓦcafebar.casadelcorregidor.pe. A welcoming café and bar with a quirky room with upturned funnels as lampshades and walls plastered with vinyl discs. The food is nothing to write home about, but the sunny courtyard is a pleasant spot to kick back with a freshly squeezed juice (S7) or a beer (S10). Mon–Sat 9am–9pm.
Cevichería Mareas Jr Cajamarca 448 ☎051 777 000. A popular open-fronted *cevichería* that gets packed at lunchtime for its tasty *ceviche* (S11) and other fish-based dishes including rice with seafood (S16). Daily 9am–4pm.
Loving Hut Psje Choquehuanca 188 ☎051 353 523, ⓦlovinghut.com/pe. Offering tasty vegan cuisine at extremely reasonable prices, this place understandably gets very busy at lunchtime. The lunch menu will set you back S15, or you can choose individual dishes for about S7. Mon–Sat 8am–6.30pm.
★**Mojsa** Jr Lima 635, 2nd floor ☎051 363 182. It translates as "delicious" in Aymara and so it is – local and international dishes here are prepared using highland produce, and the pizzas (S12–38) are cooked in the wood-fire oven that keeps the place snug on cold winter evenings. Try the *palta mojsa* (avocado and marinated

chicken in tomato served with Creole sauce; S16). Book ahead. Daily 10am–10pm.
Ricos Pan Jr Moquegua 334. A local favourite, this café/bakery serves all manner of tasty pies (S6), cakes (S6) and teas (S2.50), as well as breakfasts (S8) and freshly baked *empanadas* (S2.50). Mon–Sat 6am–9.30pm, Sun 3–9.30pm.
Positive Lima 378. This well-established bar has nightly DJs playing all sorts from electronica to reggae. After a few drinks, the neon lighting at the back will wreak havoc with your retinas. Happy hour 4–7pm. Beer S15. Daily 7am–2am.

DIRECTORY

Banks and exchange Banco Continental, Lima at Libertad, and BCP, Lima at Grau, both have ATMs. There are plenty of casas de cambio along Lima.
Consulate Bolivia, Arequipa 136, 2nd Floor (Mon–Fri 8.30am–2pm; ☎051 351 251).
Hospital Tourist's Health, Moquegua 191 (☎051 365 909, ⓦth.pe).
Internet Try Google X, Jr Arequipa 666, at Jr Puno (daily 7am–10pm; S1/hr).
Laundry Lava Clin, Deustua 323 (Mon–Sat 8am–noon & 2.30–7pm; S6/kg).
Post office Moquegua 269 (Mon–Fri 8am–7pm, Sat 8am–noon).
Taxis Millennium (☎051 353 134); Taxi Tour Puno (☎051 369 000).
Tourist police Deustua 538, open 24hr (☎051 352 303).

LAKE TITICACA

An undeniably impressive sight, **Lake Titicaca**'s skies are vast, almost infinite, and deep, deep hues of blue; below this

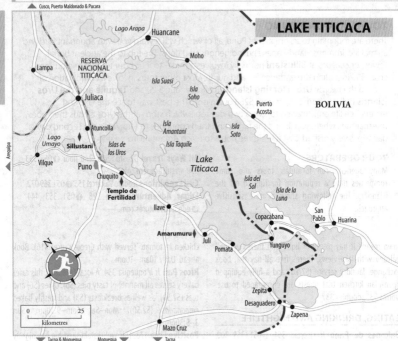

Cusco, Puerto Maldonado & Pucara

LAKE TITICACA

Lago Arapa
Huancane
Moho
RESERVA
NACIONAL
TITICACA
Lampa
Isla Suasi
Isla Soho
Juliaca
Puerto Acosta
BOLIVIA
Atuncolla
Isla Amantaní
Isla Soto
Lago Umayo
Sillustani
Islas de los Uros
Isla Taquile
Vilque
Lake Titicaca
Puno
Chuquito
Isla del Sol
Isla de la Luna
Templo de Fertilidad
Ilave
San Pablo
Huarina
Copacabana
Amarumuru
Juli
Yunguyo
Pomata
Zepita
Desaguadero
Zapena
Zapata
Mazo Cruz

Arequipa

La Paz (Bolivia)

0   25
kilometres

Tacna & Moquegua   Moquegua   Tacna

sits a usually placid mirror-like lake, reflecting the big sky back on itself. A national reserve since 1978, the lake has more than sixty varieties of birds, fourteen species of native fish and eighteen types of amphibians. It's also the world's largest high-altitude body of water, at 284m deep and more than 8500 square kilometres in area.

The unique, man-made **Uros Floating Islands**, which have been inhabited since their construction centuries ago by Uros Indians, are an impressive sight. Tour groups only visit a couple of the islands where the people are used to tourism; they will greet you, offer you handicrafts for sale and possibly suggest a tour on one of their boats, made from the same totora reeds as their island homes, for a small fee. For a more authentic experience, visit the communities who live on the fixed islands of **Taquile** and **Amantaní**, who still wear traditional clothes and follow ancient local customs. There are, in fact, more than seventy islands in the lake, the largest and most sacred being the **Isla del Sol** (see p.180), an ancient Inca temple site on the Bolivian side of the border that divides the lake's southern shore. Titicaca is an Aymara word meaning "Puma's Rock", which refers to an unusual boulder on the Island of the Sun. The Bolivian islands can only be visited from Copacabana.

CROSSING INTO BOLIVIA

The most popular routes to Bolivia involve overland road travel, crossing the frontier either at **Yunguyo/Kasani** (best for Copacabana) or at the principal border of **Desaguadero** (best for La Paz). En route to either you'll pass by some of Titicaca's more interesting colonial settlements, each with its own individual styles of architecture. By far the easiest way is to take a direct bus from Puno to either Copacabana or La Paz, which will stop for the formalities at the border. Otherwise, from Puno you can take a *combi* to Yunguyo, then another to Kasani, then walk across the border and take a Bolivian *combi* for the ten-minute ride to Copacabana. From Copacabana it is approximately five hours to La Paz.

Huaraz and the Cordillera Blanca

Sliced north to south by the parallel **Cordillera Blanca** and **Cordillera Negra** (the white and black mountain ranges), the department of Ancash offers some of the best hiking and mountaineering in the Americas. Its capital **Huaraz** – eight hours by bus from Lima – is tourist-friendly, has a lively atmosphere and makes an ideal base for exploring some nearby lagoons, ruins, glaciers and remote trails. Through the valley known as the Callejón de Huaylas is the pretty town of **Caraz**, which offers a taste of traditional Andean life.

HUARAZ

With glaciated peaks and excellent trekking nearby, **HUARAZ** is a place to stock up, hire guides and equipment, and relax with great food and drink after a breathtaking expedition. While there are only a couple of tourist attractions to visit in the city itself, the spectacular scenery and great cafés make it a pleasant stop for even non-adventurous spirits. Make sure to acclimatize before trying any hikes; Huaraz is 3090m above sea level.

WHAT TO SEE AND DO

Huaraz was levelled by an earthquake in 1970 and today most of the houses are single-storey modern structures topped with gleaming tin roofs. The one surviving pre-earthquake street, **Jiron José Olaya**, serves as a sad reminder of Huaraz's colonial past and is worth a stroll down to see what this city was once like. The **Museo Arqueologico de Ancash**, at Avenida Luzuriaga 762 on Plaza de Armas (Tues–Sat 8.30am–5.15pm & Sun 9am–2pm; S5; ☏ 043 721 551), is worth a look for its attractive landscaped gardens and superb collection of ceramics, as well as some trepanned skulls. On the other side of the Plaza de Armas is the **Catedral**; the vast blue-tiled roof makes a good landmark and, if you look closely, appears to mirror the

glaciated Nevado Huanstán to the east.

There's an easy day trek (7km; 3hr) from Huaraz to the remains of a Wari mausoleum, **Wilcawain** (Mon–Sat 9am–5pm & Sun 9am–2pm; S5). From here there's a non-covered road that leads to the nearby thermal springs at **Monterrey**, a relaxing afternoon. Be sure to check details with the tourist office before you go, as attacks on tourists have been reported on this route.

ARRIVAL AND DEPARTURE

By plane LC Perú operates daily flights from Lima. The small airstrip is close to the village of Anta, some 23km north of Huaraz; a 30min ride into the city from the side of the road by *combi* (S2.50) or taxi (S35).

By bus Most bus companies have terminals a street or two from the main drag of Av Luzuriaga on Jr Comercio which becomes Jr Lucar y Torre.

Destinations Lima (18 daily; 8hr); Chimbote (3 daily; 7hr); Trujillo (4 daily; 9hr).

GETTING AROUND

Av Luzuriaga is the north–south axis of the town centre, where most of the restaurants, nightlife and tour operators are based. Much of Huaraz town can be negotiated on foot once you've acclimatized to the altitude; however, some of the more remote sectors around the urban area should not be walked alone at night.

By taxi For short journeys within the city, the best option is to use one of the regular *taxi colectivos* that run on fixed routes along Av Luzuriaga and Av Centenario (S0.80). A taxi ride anywhere in the city should not cost more than S3–4.50. Companies include Phono Taxi (☏ 043 428 800) and Taxi Plus (☏ 043 792 111).

INFORMATION

Tourist information iPerú, at Pasaje Atusparia just off the Plaza de Armas (Mon–Sat 9am–6pm, Sun 9am–1pm; ☏ 043 428 812). Make sure to pick up the free mini-booklet *Map Guide Huaraz-Peru*, produced by ⊛ andeanexplorer.com, with excellent information on local treks and lots of maps; it's also available in many of the tourist restaurants in Huaraz.

Huascarán National Park office Jr Federico Sal y Rosas 555 (Mon–Fri 8.30am–1pm & 2.30–6pm, Sat 9am–noon; ☏ 043 422 086).

Tourist police Av Luzuriaga 724, at the Plaza de Armas (daily 8am–8pm; ☏ 043 421 351). Some English spoken.

ACCOMMODATION

Even in high season, around August, it's rarely difficult to find accommodation at a reasonable price, and except during high season it's definitely worth bargaining.

Airport (23km) ▲

▲ Monterrey, Anta, Yungay, Caraz & Wikahuain

HUARAZ

0   200
metres

CARHUAZ
GUZMAN BARRON
JIRON DANIEL VILLAIZAN
LIBERTADORES
JIRON VICTOR VELEZ

AVENIDA CONFRATERNIDAD OESTE
SEBASTIAN DE ALISTE
AVENIDA MANCO CAPAC

Río Quillcay
AVENIDA GRAN CHAVIN
AVENIDA MANCO CAPAC

AVENIDA CONFRATERNIDAD INTERNACIONAL ESTE

13 DICIEMBRE
AVENIDA PRIMAVERA
PERLAS
ASUNCION

HUASCARAN
HUALCAN
SAN SUSTENAL
CARAZ
COMERCIO
AVENIDA FITZCARRALD
13 DICIEMBRE
CALAMARCA
CARAZ
CARAZ

AVENIDA RAIMONDI
AVENIDA LAS AMERICAS

Movil Tours ❶ ❷ Linea

Stadium
AVENIDA BOLOGNESI
CACCRES
Mercado Central ❷
JIRON JOSE DE LA MAR ❸ Cruz del Sur
Parque del Periodista ❹
JIRON MORALES ❺ Civa
ALAMEDA GRAU

AVENIDA 27 DE NOVIEMBRE
AVENIDA TARAPACA
Tourist Police Station ✉
Casa de Guias ❻
Parque Ginebra ❼

Río Santa
Museo Arqueológico de Ancash ℹ
PLAZA DE ARMAS
Bank ■
JIRON JOSE DE SUCRE
AVENIDA A FIGUERAO ❹
❺

Catedral ■

■ **ACCOMMODATION**
B&B My House — 6
Benkawasi Albergue — 7
Churup Guest House — 5
El Jacal Guest House — 4
Jo's Place — 1
Hostal Raimondi — 2
The Way Inn — 3

28 DE JULIO
AVENIDA CONFRATERNIDAD OESTE
JIRON DE LA CRUZ
URIBE
28 DE JULIO
VILLANUEVA
AVENIDA GAMARRA
ALVA CURADO

❽
JIRON LUZURIAGA
JIRON SIMON BOLIVAR
DAMASCO
SAL Y ROSAS
VALENZUELA
JIRON RAMON CASTILLA

● **EATING**
La Brasa Roja — 9
Café Andino — 5
California Café — 8
Chilli Heaven — 7
El Horno — 1
Portal de Los Andes — 2

FEDERICO
Huascarán Nacional Park Office

✚ Hospital Regional
AVENIDA ATUSPARIA

Andino Club Hotel

● **DRINKING & NIGHTLIFE**
El Tambo — 4
Xtreme Bar — 6
Zion Bar — 3

AVENIDA VILLON
JIRON BELEN
LAS MAGNOLIAS

Mirador de Rataquena ▼

B & B My House Av 27 de Noviembre 773 ☎ 043 423 375, ⊕ micasahuaraz.jimdo.com. A pleasant family-run B&B with a flower-filled courtyard and bright dining room. $\overline{S80}$

★ **Benkawasi Albergue** Parque Santa Rosa 928 ☎ 043 423 150, ⊕ huarazbenkawasi.com. This hostel is run by a friendly Huaraz family who have done a lot for the area – the owners built Huaraz's first hotel after the 1970 earthquake (now *Andino Club Hotel*). The communal areas are pleasant, with table tennis and games, and there's a shared kitchen. If you're into adventure sports, owner Benquelo Morales is the man to see. Dorms $\overline{S20}$, doubles $\overline{S80}$

Churup Guest House Jr Amadeo Figueroa 1257 ☎ 043 424 200, ⊕ churup.com. A good base for trekkers, with luggage storage as well as reference maps and a book exchange. Although it's an uphill walk from the centre, they'll pick you up from the bus station for free and the views from the terrace are great. Breakfast included. Dorms $\overline{S28}$, doubles $\overline{S120}$

★ **El Jacal Guest House** Jr José de Sucre 1044 ☎ 043 424 612, ⊕ jacalhuaras.com. This place is amazing value,

with friendly owners and lots of extras like laundry, wi-fi, kitchen use and cable TV. But above everything (literally) there's a terrace with unbelievable 360-degree views. Breakfast included. $\overline{S70}$

Jo's Place Jr Daniel Villaizan 276 ☎ 043 425 505, ⊕ huaraz.com/josplace. Although ramshackle and somewhat chaotically managed, *Jo's Place* is a die-hard backpacker joint, with functional rooms and dorms, some with wonderful views. It's always popular and there's internet, wi-fi, a common room with TV and a terrace with hammocks. Full English breakfast (S10), thanks to the British owner. Camping/person $\overline{S10}$, dorms $\overline{S15}$, doubles $\overline{S35}$

Hostal Raimondi Av Raimondi 820 ☎ 043 421 082. An old-fashioned place with real character. Large rooms that stay cool in summer. Those on a tight budget can take the cheaper rooms without hot water. $\overline{S50}$

★ **The Way Inn** Carretera Huaraz–Pitec Km22 ☎ 043 466 219, ⊕ thewayinn.com. Built and owned by a Brit, this mountain lodge about 40min from the city offers a true

TOURS AND ACTIVITIES IN AND AROUND HUARAZ

Most of the tour operators in Huaraz can be found along Avenida Luzuriaga, or the two small squares that join it to the Plaza de Armas, and are open from 7am until late, closing between 1pm and 4pm. Most specialize in hiking and mountaineering. Popular excursions include the 8hr **Llanganuco Lakes** (see p.793), the 9–11hr **Chavín de Huantar** (see p.792) and the edge of the **Pastoruri Glacier** at 5240m (8hr). Most operators can also arrange trips to the Monterrey **thermal baths** (2hr) and some offer **adventure activities** in the area. Costs usually exclude entrance fees and food; make sure your guide can speak English if you need them to. If you're hiring your own guide, always check for certification and that they're registered at the Casa de Guías (see below). iPerú can help with any complaints.

TREKKING

If you're organizing your own trek in Huascarán National Park, register beforehand with the Park Office (see p.789), where you should buy your permit (S65; valid for six days) to enter the park; if you're trekking with an agency then they should sort all of this for you. In theory you're not meant to enter the park without one of these agencies – unless you're a professional. Also visit the Casa de Guías (Parque Ginebra 28-G; ☎043 421 811) for the best information about local trails, current climatic conditions and advice on hiring guides, equipment and mules – they also organize rock- and ice-climbing courses. They have a useful noticeboard, worth checking to see if there are any groups about to leave on treks that you might want to join, and they sell detailed trekking maps.

TOUR OPERATORS

★**Andean Kingdom** Parque Ginebre 120 ☎043 425 555, ⓦandeankingdom.com. Argentine-run tour operator specializing in climbing and trekking. Has its own centre out in the Cordillera Negra, where they offer lodging and rock-climbing courses.

Galaxia Expeditions Parque del Periodista, Lote 36 ☎043 425 355, ⓦgalaxia-expeditions.com. The biggest and most popular tour office in town offers a variety of treks, mountaineering trips and day tours as well as horseriding, mountain biking and canyoning. Also owns a guesthouse (*Aldo*; see Galaxia website). Four-day Santa Cruz trail US$120 all-inclusive; a day trek to Laguna 69 costs US$35–50. Daily 6am–10pm.

Mountain Bike Adventures Jr Lucar y Torre 530, 2nd floor (one block east of Av Luzuriaga) ☎043 424 259, ⓦchakinaniperu.com. Customizable guided bike tours and hikes, with English-speaking guides. Also rents bikes and sells local *artesanía* in the office. Good reputation for safety.

alternative from normal hostels, with orthopaedic beds, down duvets, a climbing wall and a sauna. Camping/person $15, dorms $35, doubles $230

EATING

There's no shortage of restaurants in Huaraz, with a huge number of budget options, but the places aimed at tourists tend to be better (albeit pricier). Mercado Central is good for cheap fresh food and there are a few mini-marts on Luzuriaga.

La Brasa Roja Av Luzuriaga 915 ☎043 427 738. Very popular and always busy, serving cheap and generous plates of chicken, pizza, grills and hamburgers. Pasta dishes from $15; chicken and chips with salad $19.50. Daily noon–midnight.

★**Café Andino** Jr Lucar y Torre 530 ⓦcafeandino.com. This top-floor café with amazing views is a true gem. It serves a range of international dishes and great breakfasts with pizza-sized pancakes. There's wi-fi and not only a book exchange, but a substantial library of guides on the area, as well as maps. Try the *shara shara* herbal tea for altitude sickness; mains $8–25. Daily 7am–10pm.

★**California Café** Jr 28 de Julio 562 ⓦhuaylas.com. One of several very pleasant cafés in town, this one predictably has West Coast vibes, which makes it a relaxing spot to refuel at any time. The food, including American breakfasts, soups, salads and sandwiches (mains $12–18; American-style pancakes $13), is great, and they also have a good book exchange as well as games, wi-fi and maps. Daily except Wed 7.30am–6.30pm, Sun 7.30am–2pm.

Chilli Heaven Parque Ginebra ☎043 396 085. Fun, popular place that draws an international crowd, run by a Peruvian/British couple. Spicy dishes from around the world are on the menu, including Indian and Thai curries (mains $25–40). Owner Simon is also a motorbike fanatic and organizes tours. Mon–Sat 11am–10pm.

El Horno Parque del Periodista (off the 6th block of Luzuriaga) ☎043 424 617. The best wood-fired pizzas in town, as well as charcoal grills and a mean pasta carbonara. Pizzas $18–25. Mon–Sat noon–11pm.

Portal de Los Andes Jr José de la Mar 437 ☎043 426 983. This place is a gem for a good set lunch at either $5, $7 or $12. You won't find any gringos here – this is as real as it

9

gets. Enjoy the enormous portions of tasty traditional Peruvian food and Andean music playing in the background. Daily 7am–9.30pm.

DRINKING AND NIGHTLIFE

El Tambo Jr José de la Mar 776 ☎ 043 423 417. One of Huaraz's best nightspots, spinning Western music with Latino beats and occasional live music. Food also served. Daily 11am–2am.

★**Xtreme Bar** Av Luzuriaga 646, 2nd floor. This is a true Huaraz institution, run by the owners of *Benkawasi*. There's often live music, food and a quirky rock'n'roll shrine to icons such as Bob Marley and Amy Winehouse. Daily 5pm–late.

Zion Bar Jr José de la Mar 773. A French/Peruvian-run bar that aims to be the most chilled-out space in town. Friendly atmosphere, cheap drinks and plenty of reggae make this place a good bet. Drinks two for S15 before 10pm. Daily from 7pm.

CHAVÍN DE HUANTAR

One of the most popular day-trips from Huaraz is to **Chavín de Huantar** (Tues–Sun 8.30am–1pm & 2.30–5pm; S10; ☎ 043 454 042), a mysterious stone temple complex that was at the centre of a puma-worshipping religious movement some 2500 years ago. The pretty village of **Chavín**, with its whitewashed walls and traditional tiled roofs, is a gruelling but stunning drive from Huaraz; from here the complex is a few hundred metres away. The same distance in the other direction is the accompanying **museum** (same hours; free), which displays some of the most important finds from the site, including most of the famous tenon heads that originally adorned the walls of the temple.

Most people arrive on a **full-day tour** (S45 excluding lunch and entrance), although the distance can make visits feel rushed and many agencies only provide Spanish-speaking guides. To visit independently, take one of the buses that leave Huaraz for Chavín daily around 8am (3–4hr; S10) from small terminals on Jr Andres Avelino Cáceres. Buses return from Chavín more or less on the hour from 3–6pm. It's a small village, but there are a couple of hostels, and you can camp by the Baños Quercos thermal springs, a twenty-minute stroll from the village.

THE CORDILLERA BLANCA

The highest range in the tropical world, the **Cordillera Blanca** consists of around 35 peaks poking their snowy heads over the 6000m mark, and until early in the

---

HIKING IN THE HUARAZ REGION

Given the scope of the mountain ranges and the passion of mountaineers, it's not surprising that there is an enormous range of **hikes** and guides in the area. Anyone interested in really getting stuck in should arm themselves with good maps and detailed guidebooks, and talk to everyone in town, from hostel owners to expats. Wherever you end up, be sure to pay heed to the rules of **responsible trekking**: carry away your waste, particularly above the snow line, where even organic waste does not decompose. And always carry a camping stove – campfires are strictly prohibited in Huascarán National Park. It's also vital to be fit, particularly if you are going it alone.

It's essential to spend at least a couple of days **acclimatizing** to the altitude before attempting a hike; if you intend high mountain climbing, this should be extended to at least five days. Although Huaraz itself is 3060m above sea level, most of the Cordilleras' more impressive peaks are over 6000m.

HIRING A GUIDE

Going hiking alone without an agency is possible, but not recommended to anyone but the most experienced hikers and climbers, and you'll likely end up paying a lot more as you'll be shouldering the costs alone. Be very careful when hiring an independent guide and always check them out with the Casa de Guías (see p.791), which has a list of all qualified guides in the area. On top of the national park fee (S65) and guide's fee (around US$60 per day for someone certified), you'll be expected to foot the bill for return transport, accommodation and food for everyone hired to help. Auxiliary porters, mule drivers (*arrieros*) and cooks will each cost you around US$10 a day, plus an additional US$10 per day per pack-carrying mule or llama.

twentieth century, when the glaciers began to recede, this white crest could be seen from the Pacific. Above Yungay, and against the sensational backdrop of Peru's highest peak, **Huascarán** (6768m), are the magnificent **Llanganuco Lakes**, whose waters change colour according to the time of year and the movement of the sun.

Fortunately, most of the Cordillera Blanca falls under the auspices of the **Huascarán National Park**, and the habitat has been left relatively unspoiled. Among the more exotic **wildlife** are viscacha (Andean rabbit-like creatures), vicuña, grey deer, pumas, foxes, the rare spectacled bear and several species of hummingbirds.

To get here without an organized trek, take a *combi* along the valley to Yungay or Caraz and ask around for recommended guides (check them out first with the Casa de Guías in Huaraz).

CARAZ

Further along the valley north from Huaraz are the distinct settlements of **Yungay** and the much prettier and friendly **CARAZ**. The town sits at an altitude of 2285m, making it much warmer than Huaraz, and palm trees and flowers adorn a classic colonial **Plaza de Armas**. While most people come for the hiking or cycling trails around the town, there's enough here to divert you for a day or so, most notably the pre-Chavín era remains of **Tumshukayko** (daily 8am–5pm; free), an archeological structure about 1km uphill from the Plaza de Armas (turn right once you hit Av 28 de Julio). This impressive series of stone walls, stairways and terraces (the layers have been dated to between 2500 BC and 300 AD) needs a huge amount more excavation to make greater sense of it, but is nevertheless fascinating to wander around. Finally, no stay in Caraz would be complete without careful consideration of the dessert menu: Caraz is famous for its **manjar blanco** – a caramel-like substance similar to *dulce de leche*; all bakeries in town sell it.

ARRIVAL AND DEPARTURE

By plane Anta Airport is 45km from Caraz and has a daily flight to and from Lima (50min). There's a regular bus service to town (S5) or Pony Exhbitions can organize a minibus (for groups).

By bus Most of the bus terminals are along Daniel Villar and Córdova, within a block or two of the Plaza de Armas. From anywhere in the Callejón de Huaylas, it's best to go back through Huaraz and down the main road to the coast. The only other alternative is to take the road north from Caraz via the Cañon del Pato down to Chimbote on the coast, where you'll have to change buses.

Destinations The main routes are Chimbote via Cañon del Pato (2 daily; 7–10hr); Lima (7 daily; 8hr); Trujillo (5 daily; 8–10hr).

GETTING AROUND

By mototaxi Everywhere in Caraz is walkable; don't let the *mototaxis* charge you more than S1 for anywhere in town (S2 to bus terminals outside the centre).

By combi *Combis* pull in at Av Sucre, three blocks south of the Plaza de Armas.

INFORMATION AND TOURS

Tourist office In the municipality building on the Plaza de Armas. Keeps sporadic hours, but try it for maps and brochures covering the attractions and hikes in the area.

Pony Expeditions Jr Sucre 1266, at Plaza de Armas. ☎043 391 642, ⍟ponyexpeditions.com. A professional and knowledgeable organization good for local information. Offers tours of the area (including the stunning Cañón del Pato) as well as guides for trekking. Prices get cheaper the larger the groups are.

ACCOMMODATION

Hostal La Casona Jr Raimondi 319 ☎043 391 334. Shabby but full of character, this place is set around a nice courtyard and the prices cannot be argued with – although if you do you'll find they become even cheaper. **S20**

★ **Los Pinos Lodge** Parque San Martín 103 ☎043 391 130, ⍟lospinoslodge.com. This hostel on a little plaza five minutes' walk from the centre has colourful and tastefully decorated common areas with a retro feel. The bedrooms are not as impressive, but offer basic accommodation at reasonable rates. Also offers camping space and wi-fi. Breakfast included. Camping/person **S20**, doubles **S120**

San Marco Jr San Martín 1133 ☎043 391 558. Just off the plaza, this hostel in a pretty colonial building has quiet, light-filled rooms at the back around gorgeous courtyards. Even cheaper dark, front rooms lack private bathrooms and TVs. Breakfast not included. **S40**

EATING

Eating in Caraz is basic. The small daily market, three blocks north of the plaza, is good for fresh food and traditional Andean goods.

9

Café de Rat Above Pony Expeditions on Jr Sucre 1266 ☏ 043 391 642. It may sound unsanitary, but Cafferata is the owner's surname and the place has the joint appeal of cheap, good food (including vegetarian) and a cosy feeling like that of being in someone's kitchen. The little balcony overlooks the main square. Best for pizza (S15–29) and breakfasts (S5–12). Has wi-fi too. Mon–Sat 8am–11am & 6–10pm.

Café La Terraza Jr Sucre 1107 ☏ 043 301 226, ⓦ hostalcarazdulzura.com. Probably the best place in town to grab a cappuccino or espresso. Also does excellent artisan ice cream (S2) using regional fruits. Daily 7am–11pm.

Restaurant Jeny Plaza de Armas ☏ 043 391 101. Offers tasty good-value set menus (S8) as well as some traditional and Chinese dishes plus sandwiches and breakfasts. Daily 8am–9pm.

Trujillo and the North

Pizarro, on his second voyage to Peru in 1528, sailed by the ancient Moche site of **Chan Chan**, then still a major city and an important regional centre of Inca rule. He returned to establish a Spanish colony in the same valley, naming it **Trujillo** after his birthplace in Extremadura. Despite two Inca rebellions, the Spanish hold was lasting and Trujillo grew to become the main port of call for the Spanish treasure fleets. It still boasts one of the most impressive colonial centres in Peru, as well as some of the grandest pre-Inca remains, but this city of more than one million feels modern and there's plenty to keep visitors occupied.

North of Trujillo the vast desert stretches all the way to the Ecuadorian frontier just past **Tumbes**, passing the modern and ever hectic city of **Chiclayo** as well as Peru's liveliest beach town, **Máncora** – and some genuinely unspoilt stretches for the adventurous. This area has an incredible wealth of pre-Inca pyramids, tombs and temple sites to explore, as well as world-class museums, many of which can be easily visited in day-trips from the main cities. From here you can travel on to the Northern Highlands (see p.809), which will give you a totally different angle to travellers only doing the traditional gringo trail.

TRUJILLO

Traditionally a trading point for coastal and jungle goods, **TRUJILLO** retains a cosmopolitan atmosphere and a welcoming attitude towards visitors. The climate is usually pleasant all year, although in winter it can be grey and sometimes fresh.

WHAT TO SEE AND DO

From the graceful colonial mansions and Baroque churches at its heart, Trujillo's commercial buildings, light industry and shantytown suburbs give way to rich sugar-cane fields that stretch far into the neighbouring Chicama Valley. Everything within the circular **Avenida España** is considered the centre and this is where most of the colonial buildings and museums lie. **Gamarra** is the main commercial street, dominated by modern buildings, shops, hotels and restaurants. The other main street, older and more attractive, is **Jirón Pizarro**, which has been pedestrianized from the eighth block to the pleasant **Plazuela El Recreo**. But it is the large and graceful **Plaza Mayor** that is the deserved star and heart of the city.

The city also boasts the largest mural in Latin America; it runs along the walls of the Universidad de la Nación (worth seeing at night when lit up).

Around Plaza Mayor

Trujillo's **Plaza Mayor** (Plaza de Armas) is often packed with street vendors and entertainers. The city's **Catedral** (daily 7–11.45am & 4–7pm; free), built in the mid-seventeenth century and then rebuilt the following century after earthquake damage, sits in one corner of the plaza. Beside the cathedral is its **museum** (Mon–Fri 9am–1pm & 4–7pm, Sat 9am–1pm; S4), which exhibits a sombre range of mainly eighteenth- and nineteenth-century religious paintings and sculptures.

Also on the square at Jr Pizarro 313 sits the **Casa Urquiaga** (Mon–Fri 9am–3pm & Sat 9.30am–1pm; free; take your passport), a colonial mansion owned by the Peruvian Central Reserve, which is worth a visit – despite the rather rigid thirty-minute tour you have to take – for its well-kept interiors and historical importance. Simón Bolívar stayed here while he organized his final push for liberation.

East of Plaza Mayor

East of the plaza, on the corner of Jr Pizarro and Gamarra, stands another of Trujillo's impressive mansions, **La Casa de la Emancipación**, Jr Pizarro 610 (Mon–Fri 9am–1pm & 4–8pm; free). The building is now head office of the Banco Continental but hosts contemporary art displays in its colonial rooms, where the enormous windows make for great people-watching.

Further down the same road, two blocks east of the Plaza Mayor, is the **Palacio Iturregui**, at Jr Pizarro 668 (Mon–Fri 8.30–10am; S5), a striking mid-nineteenth-century mansion whose

highlight is a pseudo-Classical courtyard, with tall columns and an open roof.

At the eastern end of Jr Pizarro, five blocks from the Plaza Mayor, there's a small but attractive square known as the **Plazuela El Recreo** where, under the shade of some vast 130-year-old fig trees, a number of bars and food stalls provide a place to meet in the evenings. The waterworks for colonial Trujillo can be seen in the plaza, where the Spaniards extended Moche and Chimu irrigation channels to provide running water to the city.

Museo de Arqueología, Antropología e Historia

The **Museo de Arqueología, Antropología e Historia**, at Jr Junín 682 (Mon–Fri 9am–5pm, Sat & public holidays 9am–2pm; S5; ☏044 474 850), is housed

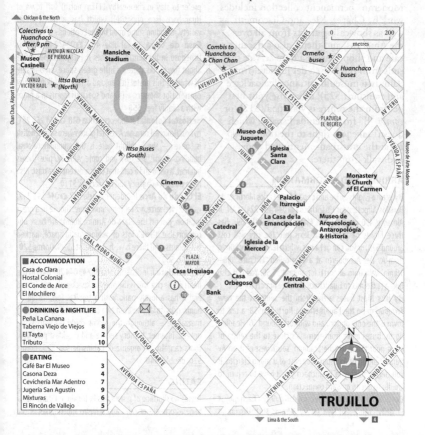

ACCOMMODATION

Casa de Clara	4
Hostal Colonial	2
El Conde de Arce	3
El Mochilero	1

DRINKING & NIGHTLIFE

Peña La Canana	1
Taberna Viejo de Viejos	8
El Tayta	2
Tributo	10

EATING

Café Bar El Museo	3
Casona Deza	4
Cevichería Mar Adentro	7
Jugería San Agustín	9
Mixturas	6
El Rincón de Vallejo	5

TRUJILLO

9

in a colonial mansion; among the highlights are some beautiful anthropomorphic ceramics. The entry fee includes a guide (some speak English).

Museo de Arte Moderno

The substantial and beautiful **Museo de Arte Moderno**, at Avenida Villarreal just after the crossroads with the carretera Industrial (Mon–Sat 9am–5pm; S10), was opened in 2006 by one of Peru's most successful artists, Gerardo Chávez, who lives next door, and is also the man behind the quirky toy museum **Museo del Juguete**, Jr Junín 713 (Mon–Thurs & Sat 10am–6pm, Fri 10am–10pm, Sun 10am–1pm; S5; ☎044 208 181), crammed with antique toys from all over the world. A world-class gallery with colonial and postmodern architecture set in lush grounds, the Museo de Arte Moderno's permanent collection includes work by Chávez, Klee and Giacometti, as well as showcasing artists from all over the Americas, and there's also a decent café and shop. There's a tram service that runs from the Museo del Juguete (from 9am; two museum entrance fee package and transport S25), otherwise your best bet from the centre is via a taxi (S12), or *combi* "B" from Avenida España, which doesn't take you right to the door – hop off at the crossroads mentioned above and walk from there.

ARRIVAL AND INFORMATION

By plane Flights arrive and depart from Carlos Martínez de Penillos Airport, near Huanchaco (☎044 464 224). LAN, Jr Almagro 490 on the Plaza Mayor (☎044 221 469), has three flights daily to Lima. Taxis into the city will cost around S20, or you can get a bus, which leaves every 20min from Av Del Aeropuerto at a stop called "El Cruce" (10–15min walk from airport), for around S1.50. You can also take a taxi direct to Huanchaco from the airport for S10.

By bus Most buses arrive from the south at the new *Terrapuerto* on the Panamericana Norte Km558; a taxi to town is the only option, and will cost around S6. Heading north, buses leave from terminals close to the centre of town near the Mansiche Stadium, southwest of it on Av Daniel Carrión or Av España, or east of it along Ejército. If you decide to stay in Huanchaco you'll have to return to Trujillo to get an onward connection.

Destinations Cajamarca (several daily; 6hr); Chachapoyas (1 daily; 14hr); Chiclayo (every 30min; 3hr); Huaraz (4

daily; 9hr); Lima (hourly; 9hr); Máncora (several daily; 6hr); Tumbes (7 daily; 10hr). Ormeño runs buses from Trujillo to Guayaquil, Ecuador, via Piura, Máncora and Tumbes (midnight Mon, Wed, Fri & Sun; 18hr; US$55).

By combi and taxi *Combis* cannot enter within Av España, but if you walk to this boundary you can find one to most places. If you're arriving by day it's fine to walk to the city centre, though at night it's best to take a taxi (around S4 for a ride within Trujillo, S20 to Huanchaco, S25 to the airport). Navy blue and white coloured *combis*, and a special orange and yellow bus, go to Huanchaco (S1.50). Of the taxi companies, Sonrisa (☎044 233 000) and Tele Taxi (☎044 694 747) are recommended by iPerú.

Tourist information iPerú, Jr Diego de Almagro 420 on Plaza Mayor (Mon–Sat 9am–6pm, Sun 10am–2pm; ☎044 294 561).

ACCOMMODATION

The majority of Trujillo's hotels are within a few blocks of the central Plaza Mayor; however, there are surprisingly few good-value hotels for a city this size. Many people prefer to stay in the nearby (11km north) surf town of Huanchaco (see opposite), which has a much wider variety, including some good budget options.

Casa de Clara Jr Cahuide 495 ☎044 243 347. Jr Orbegoso in the centre becomes Jr Huayna Capac; after about five blocks there's a little green space, on one side of which is this hostel (it's around a 10min walk from the centre). Hot showers, wi-fi and spacious rooms in a place with a family feel. S50

★ **Hostal Colonial** Jr Independencia 618 ☎044 268 261, ⒲ hostalcolonial.com.pe. A central place where some English is spoken – the highlight here is the stunning colonial building. Rooms are cosy and come with TV, plus there's internet, a patio and a café that does a decent breakfast. Also has a cheap tour agency and taxi service. S110

El Conde de Arce Jr Independencia 577 ☎044 295 117, ⒲ elcondedearce.hostel.com. Small guesthouse in a great location, just off the Plaza de Armas. Rooms are basic but comfortable, there's lots of outdoor patio space, packed with plants, and there is wi-fi. Breakfast S5–9. Dorms S20, doubles S60

El Mochilero Jr Independencia 887 ☎044 297 842. In the heart of the city, this is the only backpacker place in Trujillo and it has a lovely patio with a tropical feel, including hammocks, sofas and even two cabin rooms on a bamboo mezzanine – although the rooms could do with some upkeep. Internet, laundry service and breakfast provided. Tours can also be organized. Cabins/person S25, dorms S20, doubles S40

EATING

There's no shortage of restaurants in Trujillo. Jr Pizarro has a huge assortment of cafés and a Metro supermarket at no.

700. A speciality of the area is seafood, which is probably best appreciated on the beach at the nearby resort of Huanchaco.

★**Café Bar El Museo** Jr Independencia, at Jr Junín ☏ 044 346 741. In the same building as the Museo del Juguete, this plush café-bar with an old-world vibe is cluttered with posters and features a saloon bar. The menu is limited to sandwiches (S10–14), coffee, juices and alcohol but it's worth it for the atmosphere alone (expect an ever-so-cool jazz soundtrack, and live jazz on Thursdays). Mon–Thurs 9am–11pm, Fri & Sat 9am–1am.

Casona Deza Jr Independencia 630 ☏ 044 474 756. A first-rate Italian restaurant set in a building dating back to 1635. Two gorgeous open-air patios to dine in, and the walls are decorated with impressive artwork. Daily noon–midnight.

Cevichería Mar Adentro Jr Diego de Almagro 311. Look for the sample plates of food on a pavement table and then follow the passageway to a bright, large room with cheap *ceviche*, as well as other classic Peruvian dishes. *Ceviche* S6, set lunch S4. Daily 10am–4.30pm.

Jugería San Agustín Jr Bolívar 522 ☏ 044 259 591. Trujillo's most famous juice bar, a few blocks from the plaza, it's best known for its unmissable *sandwich de pavo* (turkey sandwich). Daily 8am–1pm & 4.15–8.30pm.

Mixturas Jr de Orbegoso 319 ☏ 044 205 946. This café-bar serves good Peruvian snacks – try the fried yucca (S4) – and is decorated with colourful local artworks. There's a relaxing garden to escape from Trujillo's busy centre. Set lunch S12. Mon–Sat 7am–11pm.

El Rincón de Vallejo Jr Orbegoso 303 ☏ 044 292 972. Cesar Vallejo, Peru's most famous poet, was brought up in the house that now hosts this café. Really good, well-priced *criollo* food, so predictably this place gets packed and rushed at lunch. Set menu S6.90–8.90 and a great selection of breakfasts (S12). Mon–Sat 7am–3pm & 5–11pm, Sun 7am–3pm.

DRINKING AND NIGHTLIFE

★**Peña La Canana** Jr San Martín 791 ☏ 044 232 503. A highly popular restaurant-*peña* serving excellent meals, with a great atmosphere and shows with bands, dancing and audience participation, usually culminating in a disco. The music and dances are fantastic and you'll be amazed at Peruvian stamina. Meals from S16, cocktails S20. Wed–Sat from 6pm for food, from 10.30pm for show until the last people leave; best on weekends.

Taberna Viejo de Viejos Jr San Martín 323. This rustically decorated place is a truly Peruvian experience; a specialist pisco bar serving cocktails as well as local wines. Try the "Viejo" deals: from S50 you get a whole bottle of pisco and everything you need to make various cocktails, and you'll be shown how to make them at your table. Great for groups. Tues–Thurs 7pm–2am, Fri & Sat 6pm–3am.

El Tayta Jr Pizarro 926, Plazuela El Recreo. Bar-restaurant with soft rock vibes and art on the walls. Drinks are good value, and while main dishes are a little pricier, there are plenty of sandwiches under S10. Daily 6pm–midnight.

Tributo Jr Pizarro 389 ☏ 989 969 050. Featuring live music nightly with regular drinks specials, this is one of the most happening places in Trujillo. Thurs 10pm–4am, Fri & Sat 10pm–5am.

DIRECTORY

Banks and exchange Banco Continental, Jr Pizarro 620; BCP, Jr Gamarra 562; Scotiabank, Jr Pizarro 314; Interbank, Jr Gamarra 463; Banco de la Nación, Av Almagro s/n; BBVA, Real Plaza mall and Av Pizarro 620. There are also several casas de cambio on the Pizarro side of the Plaza Mayor, and on block 6 of Pizarro.

Embassies and consulates UK (consulate), Jr Alfonso Ugarte 310 (☏ 044 245 935).

Hospital Hospital Belén de Trujillo, at Jr Bolívar 350 (☏ 044 245 748). Open 24hr.

Laundry Lavandarias Unidas, Jr Pizarro 683.

Post office SERPOST, Jr Independencia 286.

Tourist police Jr Independencia 630 (☏ 044 291 705).

HUANCHACO

A traditional fishing village turned popular surfing resort, **HUANCHACO** is the perfect base for exploring nearby ruins while relaxing by the beach and enjoying excellent seafood. Just fifteen minutes from the centre of Trujillo, Huanchaco has exploded in terms of popularity and growth in the last thirty years. While prices do rise in summer, it's nowhere near as overpriced as some other beach towns.

There is a multitude of **surf and language schools** in town; Espaanglisch (⊛espaanglisch.com) does both and is recommended (English spoken). Another option is with the excellent Otra Cosa network, which offers well-priced classes as preparation for volunteer work with them (⊛otracosa.org). If you're not a surfer, another way to catch some waves is with a local fisherman in their traditional *caballitos de mar* – hand-made reed fishing boats first used by the Moche culture; you'll see them lined up along the front. There is a long beachfront promenade and a rickety pier, as well as an unusual church-less Plaza de Armas away from the

9

seafront. Reggae parties on the beach are commonplace, and Latino music blasts from the many beachfront restaurants.

ARRIVAL AND DEPARTURE

By taxi or combi Taxis to and from Trujillo should cost no more than S15, or it's easy enough to take any one of the frequent *combis* (yellow & orange) from Av España on the corner with Jr Junín, or at Av Juan Pablo II and Jesus Nazereth near the university (S1.50). *Combis* come in along Av La Rivera, by the sea.

ACCOMMODATION

Every other house in Huanchaco seems to offer lodging of some sort. For those on a really tight budget, there are many no-frills places that charge S10 per person for small and often dark rooms with shared bath. Los Pinos, the street that all the buses turn down away from the sea, has a few hostels and many signs saying *alquilo habitaciones* ("I rent rooms"). Prices drop outside high season. Many places do not have hot water – fine in the summer but miserable in winter.

★**Casa Fresh** Av La Rivera 322 ☎945 917 150, ⓦcasafresh.pe. A small hostel with the friendliest vibe in town and a great terrace overlooking a quieter part of the beach near the beginning of Rivera – less traffic noise and more sound of the sea. They have boards for rent and offer Spanish classes. Dorms S̲20̲, doubles S̲60̲

La Casa Suiza C Los Pinos 308 ☎044 461 285, ⓦcasasuiza.com. Popular budget accommodation with many of the extra services loved by backpackers – internet, cable TV, laundry, book exchange and a balcony. A few blocks from the seafront. Also has hot water and a friendly atmosphere. Dorms S̲25̲, doubles S̲85̲

Oceanus Los Cerezos 105 ☎044 461 653, ⓦhospedajeoceano1.com. Family run and deservedly popular, the easily recognized blue-fronted *Oceanus* is a block away from the beachfront, which can be a blessing on busier days. There is a shared kitchen and the rooms are spacious, well lit, all have private baths and are spotless thanks to daily cleaning. Don't miss the *cremoladas* (S3, a rough fruity sorbet) downstairs; the *lúcuma* and *coco* are spectacular. Dorms S̲15̲, doubles S̲50̲

★**Surf Hostel Meri** Av La Rivera 720 ☎044 538 675, ⓦsurfhostelmeri.com. A perfect hangout with loungers on the deck, hammocks sprinkled judiciously all over the place and a central, beachside location. The restaurant is one of the best in town with menus scribbled on blackboards offering backpacker favourites like Thai curries, tacos and banana pancakes for breakfast. Busy and sociable, a place to meet fellow travellers and talk surf. Dorms S̲30̲, doubles S̲60̲

EATING

There are restaurants all along the front in Huanchaco, many of them with balconies overlooking the beach. Not surprisingly, seafood is the local speciality, including excellent crab; *ceviche* is traditionally only served at lunch.

★**Chocolate Café** Av La Rivera 752 ☎044 462 420. Really good Peruvian hot chocolate for the low season when Huanchaco gets pretty cold. Breakfasts, soups, wraps and inventive sandwiches are served up in a cheerful incense-scented café. Full English breakfast S15. Organizes a tea party on Thursdays where Peruvians and foreigners can practise each others' language. Owner Choco also organizes archeological tours. Mon & Wed–Sun 8.30am–8.30pm.

Estrella Marina Av Larco 740. Very good, fresh *ceviche* (S15) served in a seafront restaurant, which often plays loud salsa music and is popular with locals. Daily 10am–11pm.

Menu Land C Los Pinos 250. Run by a friendly German-Peruvian couple, the name refers to the set lunch *menú* you'll find all over Peru. Food is basic, but you won't find bigger or cheaper portions anywhere else; great for refuelling on a very tight budget. Daily 8am–10pm.

Surf Hostel Meri Av La Rivera 720. Even if you're not staying there, go for breakfast. There's a sunny outdoor seating area and they offer everything from bacon and eggs, to granola and banana pancakes (S9–15).

DRINKING AND NIGHTLIFE

Huanchaco has a buzzing nightlife, with many bars and clubs. Always ask around to see if there's a pop-up party on the beach going on, or to find the coolest bar (these can open and close quickly). Outside of peak season nightlife will certainly be calmer.

My Friend C Los Pinos 533 ☎044 461 080. A good restaurant as well as a cheap hostel, but it is definitely the most well-known meeting spot in town and serves cheap drinks; happy hour 7–10.30pm (Thurs evening, all cocktails are S3). Daily 8am–10.30pm.

Sabes? Av Larco 804 ⓦsabesbar.com. This place is either great fun or fairly quiet, as it's right down at the end of the main drag past *Big Ben* restaurant. When it's the former it's a fantastic place to meet people, relax on the outdoor terrace with a happy-hour cocktail and munch on a pizza (S25–30). Mon–Sat 7pm–1am.

ANCIENT SITES AROUND TRUJILLO

One of the main reasons for coming to Trujillo is to visit the numerous **archeological sites** dotted around the nearby Moche and Chicama valleys. For anyone even remotely interested in Peruvian history these should not be missed.

Huacas del Moche

Five kilometres south of Trujillo, beside

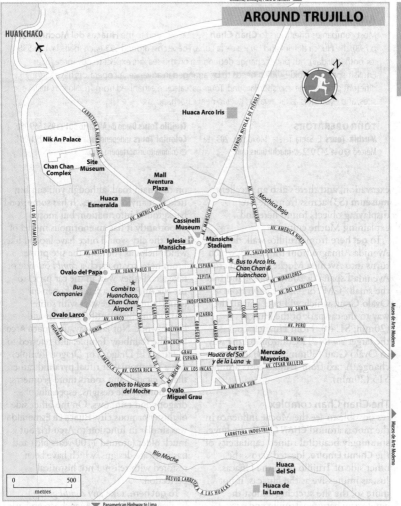

AROUND TRUJILLO

9

Chicama, Chiclayo, Piura & Tumbes

HUANCHACO

Huaca Arco Iris

Nik An Palace

Chan Chan Complex

Site Museum

Mall Aventura Plaza

Huaca Esmeralda

Cassinelli Museum

Iglesia Mansiche

Mansiche Stadium

Ovalo del Papa

Bus Companies

Combi to Huanchaco, Chan Chan Airport

Ovalo Larco

Mercado Mayorista

Bus to Arco Iris, Chan Chan & Huanchaco

Bus to Huaca del Sol y de la Luna

Combis to Hucas del Moche

Ovalo Miguel Grau

Carretera Industrial

Río Moche

Huaca del Sol

Huaca de la Luna

DESVÍO CARRETERA A LAS HUACAS

Panamerican Highway to Lima

0   500   metres

Museo de Arte Moderno

Museo de Arte Moderno

the Río Moche in a barren desert landscape, are two temples that really bring ancient Peru to life. The stunning complex known as the **HUACAS DEL MOCHE** (daily 9am–4pm; S10 including guided tour in English or Spanish, tip expected; ☎ 044 297 430, ⊛ huacasdemoche.pe) is believed to have been the capital, or most important ceremonial and urban centre, for the **Moche** (Mochica) culture at its peak between 400 and 600 AD. It contains two temples: the **Huaca del Sol** (Temple of the Sun) is perhaps the most impressive of the many pyramids on the Peruvian coast, set over 12,000 square metres. Its twin, **Huaca de la Luna** (Temple of the Moon), is smaller, but more complex and brilliantly frescoed; it's thought to have been a sacrificial centre. For now, the Huaca del Sol remains closed to visitors, still being studied by archeologists, but it's an amazing sight from the Huaca de la Luna, 500m away. In between the two you can see the remains of a town in the midst of

ANCIENT SITES

Most companies offer tours to **Chan Chan** (see below) and to the **Huacas del Moche** (see p.798), the Huaca del Sol and Huaca de la Luna. These cost around S25 each (half-day), or S35 for both (full day), but prices change depending on the season; expect to pay more for an English-speaking guide, which needs to be arranged in advance. All operators have slightly different programmes, so shop around. Tours can also be organized from Trujillo for Chiclayo sites, and even sites as far away as Kuelap near Chachapoyas.

TOUR OPERATORS
Muchik Tours C Santa Teresa 146 depto. 203, La Merced ☎ 044 243 022, ⓦ muchiktours.com.

Trujillo Tours Diego de Almagro 301 ☎ 953 559 980.
Colonial Tours Independencia 616 ☎ 044 291 034, ⓦ colonialtoursnorteperu.com.

excavation, and there's also an excellent **museum** (S3) across from the site, displaying objects found here and explaining Moche culture.

To **get here** from Trujillo, walk down Avenida Almagro from the centre, which turns into Avenida Moche once you cross Avenida España (a 20min walk), and take the small "CM" or "SD" *combis* from Ovalo Grau, which will take you all the way to the car park of the Huacas (20min; S1.40). From Huanchaco, take the larger *combi* "H Corazón" all the way to Ovalo Grau (30min; S1.50) and change. A taxi from Trujillo costs around S15 (20min).

The Chan Chan complex

It's possible to see the Moche influence in the motifs around **CHAN CHAN**, the huge, stunningly beautiful ruined capital city of the **Chimú Empire**, located across the other side of Trujillo from the Huacas. Just as impressive as the Huacas, if not more so, the site stretches almost the whole way between Trujillo and Huanchaco and represents the largest pre-Columbian ruins in the whole of South America. While most of the area is little more than melted mud walls, there are a few remarkably well-preserved areas, giving a great insight as to what the city may have looked like. The main areas to see are spread out and comprise the Nik An temple complex, a site museum, the Huaca El Dragon and the Huaca La Esmeralda (all daily 9am–4pm; S10 for 2-day pass to all sites; ☎ 044 206 304).

It's best to start at the **museum**, which you'll find about halfway to Huanchaco

on the main road, although you can buy tickets at any of the sites. It has some good background information, but most importantly it has an enormous model of what the city would once have looked like, which helps as you tour the site proper. From here, try to catch a *combi* outside or take a taxi (they wait in the car park) to the **Nik An Palace**, a series of open-air temples and passageways with some extraordinarily beautiful patterns and lattice-work. Not far away, the **Huaca Arco Iris** (The Rainbow Temple; also referred to as Huaca El Dragón, or Dragon Temple) was a ceremonial or ritual pyramid rather than a citadel, and sports more geometric and zoomorphic designs, especially of dragons and rainbows. On the other side of this enormous city, **Huaca La Esmeralda** was similar in function to Arco Iris but is much older (around 1100 years old) and has intricate designs, which have been restored with relish if not historical perfection.

To **get here**, take any *combi* going between Trujillo and Huanchaco and ask the driver to drop you at the Museo de Chan Chan. There is no public transport between the different sites, so hire a taxi from Trujillo (see p.796) to take you round and wait (depending on sites visited and distance covered, expect to pay S30/hr), or take a hat and lots of water if you plan to walk; the sun is unforgiving.

Huaca Cao Viejo

Equally impressive but less visited (perhaps because it's 60km northwest of Trujillo) lies another fascinating Moche ruin, the **HUACA CAO VIEJO**, part of an archeological site known as "El Brujo" (The Wizard). Only discovered in 2006, the huaca contained a mausoleum in which an extremely well-preserved woman was found, buried with enough pomp to suggest that she was an important Moche leader (the first female discovery of this type in Peru). The site is run by the Fundación Wiese, and the heavily tattooed *señora* is due to go on display in the adjoining modernist museum, along with other discoveries from the area (daily 9am–5pm; S10; ⓦ fundacionwiese.com).

To **get here** from Trujillo either visit with an organized tour or take a bus or *colectivo* from the Santa Cruz stop to Chocope (45min; S3). From Chocope take another bus to Magdalena de Cao (20min; S1.50).

CHICLAYO

Apart from building a few convents, the Spanish never really bothered with **CHICLAYO**, and tourists, too, would be forgiven for missing out Peru's fourth-largest city if it were only for the city itself. Though not an unpleasant place to spend a day or so, it's full of casinos, banks and bus stations and pressing, noisy traffic. The attractions here are the remarkable **archeological finds** in the nearby countryside, which are of huge importance to Peruvian culture and identity. It's well worth spending at least a few days in the area getting to grips with the different groups that formed part of the pre-Inca landscape here, and seeing their intriguing tombs, temples and pyramids, many still in the process of being uncovered.

WHAT TO SEE AND DO

The Plaza de Armas, or **Parque Principal**, is still very much the centre of Chiclayan life, with the huge commercial Avenue Balta running north to the fascinating witches' market and south to the main bus stations.

The only real point of interest in town is the **Mercado Modelo** – a good general market – but if you turn left on Arica, walk another block and enter where you

see the plants outside, you'll reach the **witches' market**. Here the stalls sell shaman's tools, elixirs, swords, taxidermied snakes and voodoo aids. Avoid the northern end of the market as it's seedy, and watch out for pickpockets.

A good place to stay overnight in Chiclayo is nearby **La Pimentel**, a soothing seaside village with a long boardwalk and pier. The few accommodation options aren't cheap, but out of season you can get a bargain. Regular *combis* leave from Avenida Pedro Ruiz and Simon Bolivar (15min; S2), while a taxi costs S15.

ARRIVAL AND INFORMATION

By plane The airport is 2km east of town and is served by LAN which flies to Lima (daily; 1hr 30min). From here, a taxi to town should cost S10. Chiclayo Taxi is recommended by the tourist board (☎ 074 265 410).

By bus Most bus companies have terminals along Av Bolognesi, the main road at the end of Av Balta Sur. From here it's a 10min walk to the Plaza de Armas.

Destinations Cajamarca (10 daily; 6hr); Chachapoyas (2 daily; 9hr); Lima (10 daily; 10hr); Piura (every 30min; 4hr); Trujillo (every 30min; 3.5–4hr); Tumbes (8 daily; 7hr).

Tourist information iPerú, on C 7 de Enero 579 (Mon–Sat 9am–6pm, Sun 9am–1pm; ☎ 074 205 703). English spoken.

Tour operators Moche Tours, at C 7 de Enero 638 (☎ 074 232 184, ⓦ www.mochetourschiclayo.com.pe), offers reliable tours around the area with good English-speaking guides and their own transport.

GETTING AROUND

By combi *Combis* skirt around the centre; simply walk down Balta to Bolognesi, or east from the Plaza to Av Sáenz Peña, to pick one up (S1 within town).

By taxi or mototaxi Taxis should cost no more than S3.50 anywhere within the city. Always go for one with the municipal shield stencilled on the doors. *Mototaxis* are not allowed in the centre, so walk out to the post office or the Av Bolognesi at the end of Balta Sur to find one. Within the city limits they should cost no more than S1.50–2.50.

ACCOMMODATION

CHICLAYO

★**Casa Cima** Chiclayo C Los Mangos 161, apt 501, Urb Santa Victoria ☎ 074 602 244, ⓔ infocima.ingles.cix@ gmail.com. A few rooms in the owner's penthouse with a terrace that has great views over the city. Hosts Liam and Teófila are great company and eager to help you get the

AVENIDA AUGUSTO B. LEGUÍA

AVENIDA NICOLÁS DE PIÉROLA

COIS

■ ACCOMMODATION
Casa Cima	3
Muchik Hostel	1
Hostal Victoria	2

ANDRES RASURI

● EATING, DRINKING & NIGHTLIFE
900's Café	6
Fiesta Chiclayo Gourmet	1
La Naturaleza	7
Restaurant Mi Tía	5
Rico Mar	2/3/4
Romana	8

M. PARDO

M. PARDO

ANGAMOS

UNIVERSO

AMAZONAS

Mercado Modelo

0   50
metres

PEDRO RUIZ

ALFONSO UGARTE

AVENIDA LUIS GONZALES

Witches' Market

ARICA

LETICIA

AVENIDA SAÉNZ PEÑA

★ Colectivos to Lambayeque

R. CIVILES

T. PINGLO

★ Combis to Pimentel

SAN MARTIN

FERRE

BDE OCTUBRE

7 DE ENERO

★ Combis to Ferreñafe

LEONCIOPRADO

LEONCIO PRADO

LORA Y CORDERO

JIRON JUAN CUGLIEJAN

Mercado Central

Terminal Terrestre Oeste

VICENTE DE LA VEGA

★ Combis to Lambayeque & Pimentel

SAN JOSE

Bank

Palacio Municipal

M. CAPAC

Airport (2km)

PLAZA ELÍAS AGUIRRE

Metro Supermarket

ELIAS AGUIRRE

Parque Principal

Catedral

Bank ✉

Centro Civico

Hospital Las Mercedes

UGARTE

Bank

AVENIDA LEONARDO ORTIZ

N

MARIA IZAGA

ℹ

7 DE ENERO

AVENIDA SAÉNZ PEÑA

TORRES PAZ

AVENIDA JOSE BALTA SUR

FCO. CABRERA

R. LA POINT

COLON

TACNA

CHICLAYO

Artisan Market

AVENIDA BOLOGNESI

★ Línea buses

Cruz del Sur buses

Tepsa buses ★

Emtrafesa buses & **3** ▼

Trujillo & The South ▼

---

best out of your time in the region. The three rooms (one with en-suite bathroom) are comfortable and there is a kitchen you can use. Great wi-fi, cheap laundry and a solid breakfast. **S96**

Muchik Hostel Jr Vincente de la Vega 1127 ☎ 074 272 119, ⓦ muchik-hostel.minihostels.com. This place is trying to set itself up as the backpackers' choice in Chiclayo with a dorm and other traveller conveniences like lockers, free internet and a laundry service. Other rooms are bright, clean and the whole building's very safe. Private rooms are all en suite and come with cable TV. Dorms **S25**, doubles **S60**

Hostal Victoria Av Izaga 933 ☎ 074 225 642, ⓔ victoriastar2008@hotmail.com. Pleasant, friendly hostel with cable TV, laundry service, wi-fi, a luggage depot and communal kitchen. All rooms are en suite and there are homey touches everywhere. Book ahead, as it can be popular. **S35**

LA PIMENTEL
Casona del Muelle C Nueva Estación 116 ☎ 074 458 168, ⓦ casonadelmuelle.com. Pricier, but more pleasant than staying in the city, this 1920s seaside home is right near the

main beach and pier. Comfortable rooms with wooden floors and a jumble of antique furniture with a slight tendency towards kitsch. Good breakfast and wi-fi. **S100**

EATING, DRINKING AND NIGHTLIFE

Go to Centro Comercial (CC) Real Plaza on the edge of town for all the Western chain restaurants, as well as shopping. Good local specialities include *tortilla de raya* (ray omelette), *arroz con pato* (duck with rice) and *King Kong*, a pastry thick with *manjar blanco* (caramel), peanuts and pineapple flavouring.

★ **900's Café** Av Izaga 900 ☎ 074 209 268, ⊚ cafe900 .com. A really pleasant place any time of day, this café-bar does good breakfasts, snacks, salads, pastas, *criollo* mains (S17.50–28; try the *spaguetti a la huancaina con lomo al pisco*) and cocktails. But better than anything, this place has truly great coffee – there are around 25 different concoctions on the menu. Mon–Sat 8am–3.30pm & 5.30–11pm (open until 1am Fri & Sat).

La Naturaleza Jr Juan Cuglievan 619 ☎ 074 233 060. A good little vegetarian place – one of few places in town – that serves breakfast, lunch and dinner, and, in theory, a wide range of veggie takes on classic Peruvian dishes. Does a good set menu that includes salad, soup and a drink (S7). Mon–Fri 8am–9pm, Sat 8am–3pm.

Restaurant Mi Tía C Elías Aguirre 662 ☎ 074 205 712. Easy to find by the queue outside in the evenings, but they are there for the burgers; skip that, take a seat inside and order with relish any of the traditional local dishes like the tender beer-marinated goat stew, *seco de cabrito* (S25). Mon–Sat 8am–11pm.

Rico Mar Saenz Peña 841, San José 476, at Elias Aguirre 241. A chain of *cevicherías* with a good range of little dishes, ideal for trying different classic Peruvian starters like *papa rellena* (stuffed potato), *tamales* and of course *ceviche*. Lunch from S3.50. Daily 9am–4pm.

Romana Av Balta 512. This place specializes in northern Peruvian cuisine and is a solid choice for good food and a buzzing atmosphere. Classic dishes include *arroz con pato* (duck with rice) and *ceviche*, plus there's a cheaper set lunch and good-value sandwiches. Mains S15–25. Daily 7am–1am.

DIRECTORY

Banks and exchange You'll find all the banks and moneychangers by walking south on Balta from the Plaza de Armas. It's always better to exchange in a bank – count money carefully if on the street.

Hospital Hospital Nacional Almanzo Aguinaga Asento, at C Hipólito Unanue 180 (☎ 074 237 776). Open 24hr; you'll need to present insurance documents for treatment.

Laundry Lavandería Diamante, at C 7 de Enero 639.

Post office Jr Elías Aguirre 140.

Tourist police Av Saenz Peña 830 (☎ 074 235 181). Open 24hr.

AROUND CHICLAYO

There are several sites around Chiclayo that are definitely worth seeing, all offered on organized tours, though it can get confusing as some sites have several names, while different places have similar names. The most easily confused are **Sipán**, where remains from the **Moche** culture were discovered, and the **Sicán** (or Lambayeque) culture. Add to the mix the fact that several Sipán sites are located in the town of Lambayeque and it all becomes too much. The sights below are essential viewing, but there are many, many more. You can visit the sights independently, but it is easier, quicker and cheaper to go with a tour company.

Huaca Rajada

The Moche culture (100–800 AD) was based all along the coast in northern Peru. The tombs found at the **Huaca Rajada** in Sipán (site museum daily 9am–5pm; S8) are vital to Moche history, as, unlike the *huacas* near Trujillo, they were never plundered by treasure hunters. Excavation began in 1987 and continues to this day. Walk around the site to see the archeologists at work and the real tombs, where the extraordinary treasures now mostly displayed at the Museo Tumbas Reales in Lambayeque were discovered. There's a small museum documenting the digs, but it is best combined with a visit to the larger museum. It's fascinating to think that there's still so much more to be found.

9

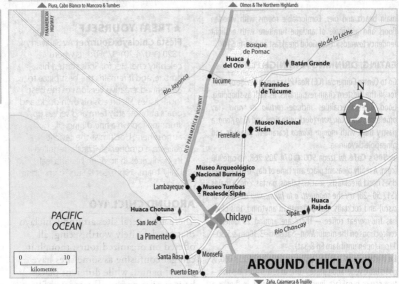

PANAMERICAN HIGHWAY

▲ Piura, Cabo Blanco to Mancora & Tumbes

▲ Olmos & The Northern Highlands

Bosque
de Pomac

Río de la Leche

Huaca
del Oro

◆ Batán Grande

Túcume

Río Joyanca

OLD PANAMERICAN HIGHWAY

◆ Piramides
de Túcume

Ferreñafe

Museo Nacional
Sicán

N

► Bambamarca

Museo Arqueológico
Nacional Burning

Lambayeque ●

Museo Tumbas
Realesde Sipán

Huaca Chotuna ◆

San José ●

Chiclayo

Sipán ●

Huaca
Rajada

**PACIFIC
OCEAN**

Río Chancay

La Pimentel ●

Santa Rosa ●

Monsefú

0   10
kilometres

AROUND CHICLAYO

Puerto Eten ●

▼ Zaña, Cajamarca & Trujillo

To **get to Sipán**, take a *combi* from the Terminal EPSEL on Avenida Nicolás de Piérola in Chiclayo (25min; S2.50).

Lambayeque museums

The treasures from the Huaca Rajada's multiple tombs are displayed at the world-class **Museo Tumbas Reales de Sipán** in Lambayeque (Av Juan Pablo Vizcardo y Guzmán; Tues–Sun 9am–5pm; S10; ⓦmuseotumbasrealessipan.pe). Although the museum is quite an eyesore from the outside, it is impossible to do justice to the wonders within. The hauls from the various digs are laid out as they were discovered, and there are an overwhelming number of sacred objects all intricately made from precious metals, shells and stones.

The **Bruning National Archeology Museum**, also in Lambayeque (Parque Infantil; daily 9am–5pm; S8; ☏074 282 110), contains displays on all Peru's ancient cultures and spans five millennia. Housed in a modernist building, the collection is displayed over four floors and even has a "Sala de Oro" (room of gold), full of Sipán and Sicán treasures.

To **get to Lambayeque**, take a *combi* from the corner of Calle San José (leading off the northwest corner of the Plaza de Armas) with Avenida Leonardo Ortíz

(15min). The museums are within walking distance of each other and everyone in town knows where they are.

Museo Nacional Sicán

Little is known about the Sicán, or Lambayeque, culture, even though it existed as recently as the fourteenth century AD. Some suggest Sicán culture was simply an extension of Moche culture, which makes it fascinating to compare the haul at the **Museo Nacional Sicán** in Ferreñafe (Tues–Sun 9am–5pm; S8; ☏074 286 182) with its counterpart in Lambayeque, as it's clear there are similarities between the two in terms of their belief and adornment. Although this museum is the less well presented of the two and the treasures fewer, the metalwork here is finer and the use of semi-precious stones just as remarkable. There's also a reconstruction of the surreal tomb of the Señor de Sicán; his body was discovered decapitated, upside down and with huge gauntlets laid out beside him.

To **get to the museum**, take a *combi* from the corner of Avenida Sáenz Peña and Calle Leoncio Prado in Chiclayo (approx 25min; S2.50) to the town of Ferreñafe and then a *mototaxi* to the museum (approx 5min; S1.50).

Bosque de Pómac

The major treasures from the Sicán culture on display in Ferreñafe were discovered in the Huaca del Oro (Temple of Gold) in the **Bosque de Pómac** (Pomac Forest) in Batán Grande. This is considered to be the seat of the Sicán empire, with a host of other *huacas* rising majestically out of the verdant forest – it's worth scaling the **Huaca las Ventanas** (Temple of the Windows) to get a wonderful view of them.

The forest is a great place for a picnic, birdwatching or horseriding – Rancho Santana (☏979 712 145, ⓦcabalgatasperu.com) offers different riding tours of the area from S45 for four hours. Don't miss the **Árbol Milenario**, an ancient, enormous carob tree which locals believe has magic and religious powers; it's situated along the main road through the forest.

Tours will take you here from Chiclayo, usually combined with a visit to one or two of the museums, but if you want to go alone, get a *combi* from the Terminal EPSEL in Chiclayo (45min; S4) and head for the Centro de Interpretación, at the entrance to the forest on the main road from Chiclayo, for information.

Valle de los Pirámides

The Sicán culture was also responsible for the extraordinary **Valle de los Pirámides** (Valley of the Pyramids) at Túcume (museum daily 9am–4.30pm; two sites S8, or S10 for a full tour; ☏074 830 250, ⓦmuseodesitiotucume.com). This site consists of a cluster of a few of the 26 trapezoidal structures that fan out around the countryside here – you can see many of them for miles around if you scale the tallest in the complex. There's a small museum and a great craft shop selling individual pieces made by locals.

Combis to Túcume cost S2.50 and leave from the Terminal Leguía at the Ovalo del Pescador in Chiclayo (take a taxi there, as it's a 30min walk from the centre and in a rough neighbourhood). Ask for "los pirámides" and the *combi* will drop you on the main road about 1km from the site. A *mototaxi* from there will cost S1.50 per person.

MÁNCORA AND AROUND

Just a small fishing village until about twenty years ago, **MÁNCORA** has become Peru's most popular beach resort – justifiably so, as the sea is warm most of the year, the beaches are white and the waves near perfect. It's definitely worth a stop to relax on the beach, eat to your heart's content at the great restaurants and try the outdoor sports. Máncora's **nightlife** is also famous, but can definitely make you feel that sleep is for the weak. Between the loud music and the busy main road, *la bulla* (the ruckus) puts many off, but there are more peaceful resorts along this stretch of coast between here and Tumbes – such as Pocitas, Vichayito, Cabo Blanco, Canoas de Punta Sal and Zorritos – where it's possible to find quieter, unspoilt stretches of coastline.

WHAT TO SEE AND DO

Máncora itself is a small settlement based along Avenida Piura (the stretch of the Panamericana that passes through) and the few side roads and passageways (many without an official name) that lead to the beach. There are no real **sights** other than some small mud baths about forty minutes away by *mototaxi*; hit the waves, wander around the multitude of *artesanía* stalls along the main avenue, have a cocktail and watch the spectacular sunsets.

Outdoor activities

Long famed for its **surf**, the area is now also a world-class destination for **kite-surfing**, and regularly hosts national and international competitions. The long beach and warm water make for a great place to learn and there's no shortage of teachers. You can rent gear and take lessons from several places along the beach from around S50/hr for surfing or US$45/hr for kite-surfing (cheaper if you buy package deals).

Horseriding is also popular, and you'll see touts along the beach offering ragged-looking ponies for S15–30/hr; it's preferable to go through your hostel or use a tour agency listed with the tourist office, as the animals may be better treated. It's

9

THE TURTLES AT EL ÑURO

A great day-trip when the surf is flat is the fishing village of **El Ñuro** 7km past Los Organos. Here, around the pier you can usually see numerous turtles lazing around in the clear aquamarine water, waiting for scraps from the fishermen. You can jump in off the pier and swim with them – just don't get too close; these are wild animals, and you may get a deserved nip. There is a S5 entrance fee to the beach. Go early for best visibility and to avoid crowds. Get there with an EPPO bus south to Los Organos (15min; S1.50) and then a *mototaxi* to the beach (S5).

also possible to arrange tours to see marine wildlife, including **humpback whale spotting** from August to October.

ARRIVAL AND DEPARTURE

By plane Piura Airport is 3hr 30min by bus, or 2hr 30min in a minivan, which is more expensive (S35) and leaves directly from the airport or from a terminal on Sanchez Cerro. (While Tumbes is closer, flights are considerably cheaper to Piura.)

By bus The bus companies have terminals all over town, but rarely more than a S4 taxi ride from the centre.

Destinations Most buses to Lima (9 daily; 18–20hr) leave Tumbes in the afternoon and may stop at Máncora (2hr), Piura (6hr), Chiclayo (8hr), Trujillo (10hr), or go straight there. International buses go to Machala, Ecuador (8 daily; 1hr 30min once through immigration), or Guayaquil (5 daily; 8hr). EPPO buses leave very 30min to Piura, stopping along the way at Los Organos, El Cruce (for Cabo Blanca) and Talara (for Lobitos). Only some are air-conditioned.

By colectivo and combi *Colectivos* depart every 30min 4am–7pm from EPPO, at Av Grau 470, to nearby beach Los Organos (20min; S1.50) and most resorts south to Piura (4hr). *Combis* drive up and down Av Piura throughout the day, picking up passengers until they are full for the trip to Tumbes (2hr; S7). *Colectivos* to Punta Sal leave from outside the Cruz del Sur station on Av Piura 208 (40min; S5). There are also companies along Av Piura offering a comfortable trip to Piura or Tumbes in modern people carriers; much faster than coaches, but they cost a lot more (S35 to Piura).

INFORMATION AND TOURS

Check ⓦ vivamancora.com for up-to-date information about the area, including upcoming surfing events.

Tourist information There's a small office on Av Piura 352 (daily 8am–1pm & 2–4pm). The main iPerú office in Piura can supply information (☎073 320 249, ⓔ iprompiura@promperu.gob.pe).

Tour operators Iguana's Trips (Av Piura 233; ☎073 632 762, ⓦ iguanastrips.com) offers horseriding, hikes to national parks and trips to mud baths; Eco Fundo La Caprichosa (Av Grau s/n; ☎073 258 574, ⓦ ecofundolacaprichosa.com) is a great one-stop shop – they have an ecolodge and also specialize in adventure tourism, including motorbike rental (S250/hr with kit and instructors).

GETTING AROUND

By mototaxi *Mototaxis* are a standard S1–2 in town (look for those with the official jacket), although many will try to charge you more – fix a price before riding. Don't take one of the taxis without an official-looking sticker on the front, especially if you are going out of town, as there have been incidences of tourists getting robbed.

ACCOMMODATION

Those looking for peace and quiet will do better staying on the edges of town, although take care when returning late at night, as attacks on tourists are not unheard of. Note that prices are given for high season (Nov–March); out of season you can get a great deal. Avoid peak public holidays.

Laguna Surf Camp Acceso Veraniego s/n ☎994 015 628, ⓦ lagunasurfcamp.insta-hostel.com. Half a block from the beach and a short stroll into town (but far enough to escape the noise), this is unbeatable value and location for the price. Bamboo-roofed bungalows surround a small pool and lounging area and the in-house restaurant run by Dutch cook Pepe serves amazing food. Energetic and friendly owner Pilar offers quality surf lessons. Dorms S30, doubles S90

Misfit Hostel Playa del Amor ☎073 496 938, ⓦ misfithostel.com. Four friends from different parts of the world built four wood and bamboo A-frame bungalows on the isolated Playa del Amor. Each is distinct, with rather trippy murals inside, and they sit right on the sand. A great, social atmosphere and hugely popular; book well in advance. Dorms S32, doubles S102

★**Waltako Beach Town** Av Panamericana Norte Km1199, Canoas de Punta Sal ☎998 141 976, ⓦ waltakoperu.com. For those looking for an unspoilt stretch of beach away from the craziness of Máncora, this is a sure bet. Here it's all about eating fresh *ceviche*, chilling in hammocks and enjoying the bungalows, complete with kitchen, cable TV and fans. Take a bus from Máncora towards Tumbes and ask to be dropped in Canoas de Punta Sal (30min); from here it's a short *moto* ride (S5). Camping/person S20, bungalows S120

EATING

Many of the restaurants aimed at gringos are along the Panamericana and serve excellent international cuisine, but none is cheap. Better-priced grub can be found towards the market at the north end of town, where Av

Piura becomes Av Prolongación Grau. Here you can find S5
menus, *pollo a la brasa* (spit-roast chicken) joints, *ceviche*
for S12, and fresh fruit and veg.

El Ají Pasaje 8 de Noviembre s/n (between Papa Mo's & Del
Wawa) ☎998 488 325. Down a little passageway that
leads to the sea – from the beach looking back towards the
main drag it's to the right of *Birdhouse*. A tiny little Mexican
restaurant that serves great burritos, tacos and quesadillas
for around S23, not forgetting some mean cocktails.
Daily 12.30pm–11pm.

La Bajadita Av Piura 424 ☎073 258 385. For a decent
espresso and a huge selection of home-made cakes and
desserts, this place can't be beaten. Also serves reasonably
priced sandwiches, cocktails and combos. Main courses
S25–28. Tues–Sun 10.30am–10pm.

Birdhouse complex On a balcony overlooking the sea
next to *Hostal Sol y Mar* is this colourful three-in-one
restaurant with wi-fi access. *Green Eggs and Ham*
(7am–5pm) does the best breakfasts in town, including
waffles and fantastic American pancakes (S12); *Papa Mo's*
(open all day) does milkshakes and nothing but milkshakes;
and *Surf & Turf* is open for lunch and dinner and does, as the
name suggests, fish and steak plates (S25–35).

La Espada Av Piura 501 & 655 ☎073 258 334. This
restaurant with two locales is the best for very large
portions of seafood such as *ceviche* and *parihuela espada*
(stew). Mains average S20–30, daily lunch menu for S15.
Daily 8am–11pm.

★**Tao** Av Piura 228 ☎073 258 056. This place gets packed
every night, as word is spreading about its great Thai and
Chinese food. The tuna steak pad thai (S35) is exquisite and
the service excellent. Mains S20–40. Daily 11am–11pm.

DRINKING AND NIGHTLIFE

Eating might be expensive in Máncora, but drinking
certainly is not. Every bar in town has a very flexible
"happy hour", which usually runs all night; you can get two
cocktails or beers for S10 in many bars. After-hours
nightlife tends to take place in the hostels, especially *Sol y
Mar*, *Loki* and *The Point*, whose full-moon party every
month has become a town fixture.

Iguana's Bar Av Piura 223 ☎073 632 762. The oldest bar
in town and a friendly place to have a drink, where every
hour is happy hour. Daily 6pm–3am.

Surfers Bar Block 3 of Av Piura. One of the few bars in
Máncora that isn't just a roadside shack, this place has Elvis
posters and kitsch on the walls, and rock and pop on the
stereo. Happy hour is two drinks for S15. Daily from 6pm.

DIRECTORY

Banks and exchange Banco de la Nación, Av Piura
525–527; Globalnet ATM outside Minimarket Marlon, Av
Piura 520.

Health Clínica Emergencias, Av Piura 641 (☎073 258
713). Open 24hr.

Laundry Mil@net, Av Piura 408, will do your laundry
cheaply, but it takes a couple of days; make sure it's your
own clothes you get back.

Tourist police Av Piura 330 (☎073 496 926).

TUMBES

Unlike most border settlements, tropical
TUMBES, about 30km from the
Ecuadorian border, is a surprisingly
friendly place, but away from the plaza
the city is shabby and chaotic. Tumbes is
close to some of Peru's finest **beaches** and
three national parks of astounding
ecological variety: the arid **Cerros de
Amotape**, the mangrove swamps of the
Santuario Nacional Manglares de Tumbes
and the tropical rainforest of the **Zona
Reservada de Tumbes**. Unfortunately, as
so few tourists explore this part of Peru,
tours are less frequent and expensive.

WHAT TO SEE AND DO

Tumbes is good for a stroll to see its
bright, almost gaudy, modern
architecture around the centre. The large
Plaza de Armas feels very tropical, with
sausage trees, a huge rainbow archway
and a stripy cathedral. Next to the plaza
runs the pedestrianized **Paseo de la
Concordia** (also known as Av San
Martín), which has huge sculptures and
more colourful architecture. **Calle Grau**,
which leads east off the plaza, has
unusual rickety wooden buildings, while
the southern end leads to the malecón
(boardwalk) along the river. Getting to
the parks is almost impossible without a
tour company or car, but you can ask at
the tourist information office.

9

ARRIVAL AND INFORMATION

By plane There's a daily flight from Lima with LAN to and from Tumbes (1hr 45min). Note that Tumbes Airport is often very quiet, particularly at night, when there's no access to food or drink. A taxi into town should cost S20; it's about a 15min journey.

By bus or colectivo Most buses and colectivos coming to Tumbes arrive at offices along Av Tumbes Norte. From here it's a couple of blocks to the Plaza de Armas. You can reach Tumbes from Lima (18hr) and many of the major coastal cities. From Máncora, you can get a bus, but it is a quicker and more pleasant journey in a colectivo or minivan. Busses from Guayaquil, Ecuador are also an option.

Tourist information iPerú (Malecón III Milenio, 3rd floor; Mon–Sat 8am–1pm & 2–6pm, ☎ 072 506 721).

Tour operators Preference Tours (C Grau 427 ☎ 072 525 518, ✉ turismomundial@hotmail.com) and Tumbes Tours (Av Tumbes Norte 355; ☎ 072 524 837, ⓦ tumbestours .com) all offer trips to the mangroves and the national parks, but none is cheap.

ACCOMMODATION

While there are many budget hotels in Tumbes, few of them are recommendable. If you don't have mosquito repellent, go for places with windows that close and fans.

Hospedaje Amazonas Av Tumbes Norte 317 on the corner of the Plaza de Armas ☎ 072 525 266 or ☎ 972 683 780. One of the more pleasant of the budget places, with cable TV, fans and light en-suite rooms. S10 extra for hot water. **S40**

Hospedaje Franco Paseo la Concordia 105 ☎ 072 525 295. On the pedestrian avenue off the Plaza de Armas, it is considerably quieter here. Big rooms with ceiling fans; cold water only. **S80**

EATING AND DRINKING

Tumbes is the best place in Peru to try conchas negras – the black clams found only in these coastal waters, where they grow on the roots of mangroves.

Bahia Lounge Av Grau 307 ☎ 072 526 038, ⓦ bahialoungetumbes.com. Styles itself as a trendy fusion bar and restaurant, but the reality is an average interior but with tables on a cool terrace right on the plaza. Serves international and local cuisine, and a passable breakfast. Mon–Sat 8am–1am & Sun 8am–4pm.

★ **Bohemia/Eduardo (El Brujo)** Jr Malecón Benavides 850 ⓦ eduardoelbrujo.com. One of the best restaurants in this part of the world, this place serves exquisite seafood in a light, open restaurant spanning two floors, including a rooftop terrace with river views. Try the fantastic sudado de conchas negras, a thick seafood stew served with rice, with supposedly aphrodisiac properties. A little pricey (mains S30–40), but portions are big enough to share. Mon–Sat 9am–midnight.

Misky Bolognesi 221. Good-value snack bar offering breakfasts, snacks, burgers, sandwiches, milkshakes, juices, cakes, sundaes and smoothies. Everything less than S15. Daily 7am–11pm.

DIRECTORY

Banks and exchange All banks are along C Bolívar (on the side of the plaza). Moneychangers can also be found on this street at the crossroads with Av Piura.

Post office San Martín 208.

CROSSING INTO ECUADOR

Crossing the border from Tumbes can be complicated and has caught many tourists, especially non-Spanish-speaking ones, adrift in a no-man's land with a lot of canny locals trying to make as much as they can fleece you for. Make sure you get some US dollars for Ecuador in Tumbes, as exchange rates in **Aguas Verdes** (the closest town to the border) can be extortionate. There is an iPerú office at the border (☎ 072 632 537).

By far the easiest, and in the end, the cheapest way to cross the border is to take an **international bus service** from Tumbes, such as Ormeño, Cruz del Sur or the Ecuadorian company Cifa, which take you straight through to Machala (S6–20) or Guayaquil (S105), waiting at the new CEBAF border control while you get your exit and entry stamps (in the same building, located on the Ecuadorian side). If you can't do this, you'll have to go it alone. Combis (S2.50) and colectivo cars (S4) for the border leave Tumbes from block four of Av Mariscal Castillo, just past the market, and drop you in Aguas Verdes. Once here, it is a short stroll across the Puente Internacional (international bridge) and on the other side you take one of the yellow taxis to the CEBAF control point (10min; US$3–5). Get your stamps and return to Huaquillas (the Ecuadorian equivalent of Aguas Verdes) and choose a bus for any Ecuadorian destination. If you're coming into Peru from Ecuador, it's simply a reversal of the above procedure – note that Tumbes is a much nicer place to stay than Aguas Verdes – and in both directions the authorities occasionally require that you show an onward ticket out of their respective countries. **Do not take photographs** anywhere near the border or immigration offices.

The Northern Highlands

The **Northern Highlands** offers some of the least-explored areas in Peru. The two main cities, **Cajamarca** and **Chachapoyas**, are welcoming and peaceful. Each makes a fantastic springboard for exploring the wealth of archeological sights in the countryside around them.

CAJAMARCA

Nestling in a fertile rolling valley of eucalyptus and pine, 2720m above sea level, **CAJAMARCA** is a charming colonial town shrouded in legend, most famously – or infamously – known as the place of Inca ruler **Atahualpa's last stand** against Pizarro in 1532, signalling the end of the Inca Empire. While its Spanish colonial ambience, along with its one remaining Inca building and Andean location, have earned it the title "the Cusco of the north", Cajamarca has a character all of its own. Relatively small until Peru's largest gold mine (within driving distance) was discovered, the city's population has grown rapidly in the last decade to around 220,000. Despite this, Cajamarca is still surprisingly low-key; the liveliest time to visit is during the week-long Carnaval, complete with parades, music and water fights.

WHAT TO SEE AND DO

Cajamarca's sights lie in the centre around the **Plaza de Armas**, in the swish suburb of **Baños del Inca** and **outside the city**, where the attractions are all accessible on half-day tours.

Around the Plaza de Armas

The **Plaza de Armas** lies at the centre, and most of the sights in the city are nearby in the easy-to-navigate surrounding streets. On the plaza sit the **Catedral** (open during Mass times Mon–Sat 6pm, Sun 7.30am, 11am & 6pm) and **Iglesia San Francisco** (daily 10am–noon & 4–6pm). The adjoining **Convento San Francisco** (Mon–Sat 9am–noon & 4–6pm; S5), whose entrance is on Amalia Puga, houses an interesting selection of religious art in a rambling run of rooms, crypts and cloisters in a working monastery.

Cerro Santa Apolonia

South from the Plaza de Armas, a steep walk up Jr 2 de Mayo takes you past sellers flogging crafts, children playing, gussied-up llamas and Quechua ladies in their ten-gallon hats up to the pretty white church on the hill of **Cerro Santa Apolonia**. Next to the church, pay S1 (daily 7am–7pm) to go right to the top through pretty gardens, and see the rock formation known as the **Silla del Inca** (Inca chair), reputed to be a place where the Inca ruler would sit and gaze out over his empire.

El Cuarto del Rescate (Atahualpa's Ransom Room)

One **joint ticket** (S5, available from all sites) gives you entrance to several sights. The most famous is the only surviving Inca structure in Cajamarca – a modest stone room known as **El Cuarto del Rescate** (the ransom room), at Jr Amalia Puga 722 (Tues–Sat 9am–1pm & 3–8pm, Sun 9am–noon). It was the room, legend has it, that Atahualpa was forced by the conquistadors to fill with gold in order to save his life, although in reality it is probably just the room in which he was held prisoner.

Compejo Belén

The gorgeous Baroque **Complejo Belén** (Mon–Fri 8.30am–noon & 4–6pm, Sat & Sun 8.30am–noon; same ticket as Cuarto del Rescate) includes two former hospitals on either side of the **Iglesia Belén**, on the corner of Calle Belén and Jr Junín. One is now an archeology and ethnography museum, displaying ceramics and weavings from pre-Inca civilizations (don't miss the two four-breasted women flanking the gate, allegedly symbols of fertility). The other is a vaulted space with small alcoves that would have held patients, with a room dedicated to the colourful Andean scenes painted by Cajamarcan artist Andrés Zevallos. The church is worth seeing for its ornate carved interiors and particularly graphic portrayal of the Crucifixion.

9

Airport, Ventanillas de Otuzco & El Quinde Mall

CAJAMARCA

● EATING
Cascanuez	4
Chifa Hong Kong	2
Don Paco	7
Heladería Holanda	3
El Marengo/	
Marenguito Pizzeria	10/11
Om Gri	5
Pez Loco	8
Q'illpu Café Lounge	12
Salas	6
Sanguchon.com	9

● DRINKING & NIGHTLIFE
Peña Tisné	13
Peña Usha Usha	1

■ ACCOMMODATION
Albergue Baños del Inca	5
Hospedaje Los Jazmines	4
Hostal Jusovi	2
Miriam Alcalde	
Figueroa's place	6
Hostal Plaza	3
Los Pinos Inn	1

Baños del Inca

The hugely popular and thoroughly relaxing **Baños del Inca** (Tues–Thurs, Sat & Sun 5am–6.30pm, until 5pm Thurs; public pool S5, private bath S6–25, massage S20/30min; ⓦctbinca.com.pe) are 6km east of the centre. As you walk around the area you'll see steam rising from the streams – the water reaches up to 72°C. At the tourist complex this water is channelled into private and communal baths, a pool, jacuzzis and even an aromatic sauna filled with orange peel and eucalyptus.

Combis to the baths depart from Jr Sabogal, one block north of the Plaza de Armas (20min; S1.50).

ARRIVAL AND DEPARTURE

By plane The airport, 5km out of town, is served by LC Perú and LAN. There are five flights a day to Lima (1hr 20min) with LAN (ⓦlan.com) and LC Perú (ⓦlcperu.pe).
By bus Most bus terminals are located around the third block of Avenida Atahualpa. Cruz del Sur, Av Atahualpa 844

(☎076 362 024), Civa, Ayacucho 753 (☎067 361 460), Tepsa, Sucre 422 (☎067 363 306), and Línea, Atahualpa 306 (☎076 366 100), all run overnight buses (with reclining seats) to Lima via Trujillo, with Línea being the most comfortable; Línea also runs services to Chiclayo; Transportes Chiclayo, Atahualpa 283 (☎067 364 628), runs a night service to Chiclayo with good onward connections to Tumbes via Máncora; Virgen del Carmen, Atahualpa 333A (☎067 413 243), runs direct services to Cajamarca via Leymebamba.
Destinations Chachapoyas (2 daily at 4am & 3pm; 10–11hr); Chiclayo (8 daily; 6hr); Lima (at least 10 daily; 16hr); Trujillo (at least 10 daily; 6hr).

INFORMATION AND TOURS

Tourist information The helpful tourist office, inside the Belén Complex (Mon–Sat 7.30am–1pm & 3–5pm; ☎076 362 903), has basic maps of the region. Staff are happy to explain how to reach outlying attractions independently. Some English spoken.
Tour operators All the companies offer pretty much the same array of tours. Bike Cajamarca (☎076 506 354, ⓦbikecajamarca.blogspot.com) offers mountain-bike trips in the surrounding mountains; Catequil Tours

(☎076 363 958, ⊕catequiltours.com) organizes everything from guided city tours to community tourism in the nearby countryside; Cumbe Mayo Tours (Jr Amalia Puga 635 ☎076 362 938) offers the normal range of excursions.

GETTING AROUND

By combi *Combis* cost S1–2 within the city.

By taxi or mototaxi Taxis should cost no more than S4 in the city centre and as far as the bus stations. Baños del Inca or the airport will cost S8–15. *Mototaxis* are a standard S3 per journey within the city.

ACCOMMODATION

A few families in Cajamarca offer cheap homestays (*turismo vivencial*), which the tourist board has information about. They are mostly outside the city with local communities – most notably in Huayanay (1hr from town) and Namora (40min from town).

Albergue Baños del Inca Located behind the Baños del Inca ☎076 348 385, ⊕ctbinca.com.pe. This place has doubles and family rooms, as well as two-person bungalows, all very comfortable and with their own built-in thermal bathrooms, and TV. Free access to the main thermal pool at the baths complex. **S60**, bungalows **S150**

★**Hospedaje Los Jazmines** Jr Amazonas 775 ☎076 361 812, ⊕hospedajelosjazmines.com.pe. A comfortable hostel in a converted colonial house surrounds a leafy courtyard, and the excellent Espresso Bar on the premises serves some of the best coffee in town. Rooms are simple en suites. This place is associated with a charity that supports patients who can't afford cancer treatment. **S80**

Hostal Jusovi Jr Amazonas 637 ☎076 362 920. This place looks like a concrete monstrosity from the outside, but inside the singles, doubles and triples are pleasant and spotless and come with cable TV and wi-fi. **S70**

Miriam Alcalde Figueroa's place Ayacucho 319 ☎076 362 932. This homestay is very central, with six dorm-like rooms – and there's hot water and space to do laundry. Dorms **S20**

Hostal Plaza Amalia Puga 669 ☎076 362 058. At this House of Chintz, rooms are basic but generous and come with plastic flowers and teddy bears. Some of the rooms look out over the plaza from the little balconies and there's hot water in the shared baths only in mornings and evenings. **S45**

Los Pinos Inn Jr La Mar 521 ☎076 365 992, ⊕lospinosinn .com. This mansion combines Old World elegance in the form of gilded mirrors and antique furniture, a touch of kitsch (the suits of armour) and modern amenities (cable TV, wi-fi). Bed down in the cheaper old wing or the more elaborate new wing; suites are great value for groups of three to four. Doubles **S120**, suites **S270**

EATING

Cajamarca is famous for its dairy products – including some of the best cheese in Peru. It's often served as *choclo con queso*, a slab of cheese with a big cob of corn. Other dishes include *caldo verde* (green broth made from potato, egg, herbs and *quesillo* cheese) and *picante de papas con cuy* (potatoes with peanut and chilli sauce with fried guinea pig). There is a mall housing a supermarket, El Quinde, at Av Hoyos Rubios blocks 6 and 7, a 20min walk from the Plaza de Armas.

Cascanuez Amalia Puga 554 ☎076 946 089. Some of the best coffee and cake in town, in a refined café. Also good for lunchtime sandwiches, *humitas* and three types of breakfast (S14–16). Daily 7.30am–7pm.

Chifa Hong Kong Jr Batán 133 ☎076 340 932. Its decor may be "generic Chinese" but the menu consists mostly of genuine Cantonese dishes as well as *chifa* (Peruvian-Chinese) creations. If you've been living on a diet of yucca and potatoes, you may be thrilled to see glass noodles, fresh broccoli and a dozen flavours of bubble tea. Mains from S12. Daily noon–11pm.

★**Don Paco** Amalia Puga 726 ☎076 362 655. The menu at this popular hangout is among the most imaginative in town. Choose from the likes of Philly cheese steak and a quarter *cuy* with spicy potatoes, or opt for the signature *Novocaxamarquino* (New Cajamarcan) dishes such as seared duck breast with elderberry sauce and fish fillet with Andean mash and oyster-and-passionfruit sauce. Mains S13–30. Daily 9am–10pm.

Heladería Holanda Amalia Puga 657, on the plaza. There's a real artisan at work here preparing some excellent ice cream using local milk and fresh tropical fruit. It's hard to go wrong with *maracuyá* or *lucuma*. Cones from S3. Daily 10am–8pm.

El Marengo/Marenguito Pizzeria Jr Junín 1201 ☎076 368 045, & Junín 1184 ☎076 344 251. This tiny pizzeria is so popular it has two locales around the corner from each other; both get packed with locals after the best pizza in town (around S16), washed down with sangria. Daily 5–11pm.

Om Gri Jr Amazonas 858. Modesty is not one of chef/owner Tito's virtues – he claims to cook "the best pasta in the world". That might be stretching it, but it certainly is some of the best pasta in town, served while he chats to you. Mains from S15. Daily noon–11pm.

Pez Loco Jr San Martín 333 ☎076 361 806. This smart little restaurant is a lunchtime favourite, serving ample portions of a dozen or so different *ceviches*, as well as vast plates of rice dishes (try the *arroz con conchas negras*) and *chicharrón de pescado* (fried, battered fish bits). In the evenings, the menu turns meaty with mixed grill offerings and *anticuchos* (skewers). Mains from S15. Mon–Sat noon–4pm & 7–11pm.

Q'illpu Café Lounge Jr Santisteban 105 ☎076 313 327. With its crimson-coloured easy chairs, an extensive selection of coffees, frappés, hot chocolates and a smattering of international nibbles (lasagne, ciabatta

9

chicken sandwiches, waffles, cupcakes), this is a good spot to linger, though continents may drift before you get served. Coffees S10. Mon–Sat 9am–8pm.

Salas Cruz de Piedra 639 ☎076 362 867. *Salas* has been around since 1947 and is a local institution; their repertoire of regional dishes is hard to fault. There's *cuy* with potato and rice stew (S28), dish-of-the-day specials are a steal at S7, and sandwiches and light bites as well. Daily 7am–10.30pm.

Sanguchon.com Jr Junín 1137 ☎076 343 066. This lively hole-in-the-wall-cum-bar specializes in huge sandwiches. Choose from overflowing burgers, grilled chicken sandwiches (the "Californichicken" stands out) or really push the boat out with "Vito Corleone" – an epic creation comprising steak, double cheese, eggs and more. Sandwiches S9–15. Mon–Sat 7–11.30pm.

DRINKING AND NIGHTLIFE

Peña Tisné Jr San Martín 265. This is neither a real *peña* nor a real bar, but a one-of-a-kind Peruvian experience that should not be missed. Knock on the unmarked door and Don Victor will lead you through his house to his bohemian back garden, full of cosy tables and memorabilia soaked in Cajamarcan history. Try the home-made *macerado* – a delicious liquor made from fermenting tomatillo (an exotic fruit) and sugar (pitcher S14). Daily 9am–midnight.

★ **Peña Usha Usha** Amalia Puga 142. This is the best venue in town for live Peruvian music, especially *criolla* music, as well as Cuban troubador-style performances. A small space particularly busy at weekends but also entertaining during the week when owner Jaime Valera entertains locals and tourists alike with his incredibly talented and versatile guitar playing and singing. Often lit only by candle, this bar has a cosy and inviting atmosphere. Entry S5. Wed–Sat 8pm–2am.

SHOPPING

Cajamarca is known for its high-quality pottery, and the general standard in some of the small shops here is excellent – there is some unique craftwork you'll not find elsewhere.

Cajamarca Colors & Creations Jr Belén 628 ☎076 343 875, ⓦ cajamarcacyc.com. Wonderfully imaginative jewellery, ceramics, shawls and gifts for children.

Mercado Artesanal Jr 2 de Mayo 255. This collection of stalls is a good bet for quality ponchos, sweaters and other woollen goods. Daily 10am–7pm.

Quinde Ex Jr 2 de Mayo 264 ☎942 025 555. Colourful textiles, cushion covers and handbags made of Andean woven belts.

DIRECTORY

Banks and exchange BCP at Jr Apurimac 717; Interbank, Jr 2 de Mayo 546 (good for changing money); Banco de La Nación, Jr Pisagua 552; Banco Continental, Jr Tarapaca 747.

Hospital Clínica Limatambo, Jr Puno 263 (☎076 362 241). Private, high-standard 24hr care.

Post office SERPOST, Jr Apurimac 626.

Tourist police Jr El Comercio 1013 (☎076 507 826).

DAY-TRIPS FROM CAJAMARCA

There are several sites of interest easily accessible from Cajamarca. One is the aqueduct of **Cumbe Mayo**, thought to be perhaps the oldest man-made structure in South America. From the parking area, a 2km trail loops past the Bosque de Piedras (Forest of Stones), where huge clumps of eroded limestone taper into some fanciful shapes. A little further on, you'll see the well-preserved and skilfully constructed **canal**, built almost 1200 years before the Incas arrived here. Dotted along the canal there are some interesting **petroglyphs** attributed to the early Cajamarca culture. The easiest way to visit is with a half-day tour (around S25).

Another interesting half-day excursion is to the **Ventanillas de Otuzco** (daily 9am–5pm; S5), a hillside necropolis 8km away whose graves resemble little alcoves or windows (*ventanillas*). Combis go here from Plaza de la Recoleta in Cajamarca (20min; S1.50); you can take an organized tour or do a two-hour walk from the Baños del Inca. Twelve kilometres further east from the Ventanillas de Otuzco are the **Ventanillas de Combayo**, an even bigger necropolis; *combis* pass nearby but you have to ask the driver to drop you off in the right place.

CHACHAPOYAS

The thriving market town of **CHACHAPOYAS**, high up in the Andes at 2334m, is first and foremost a springboard for a wealth of nearby pre-Columbian remains that litter the Utcubamba valley. The city itself is a colonial delight and its citizens are known for their friendliness. But what "Chachas" really offers is the chance to see some extraordinary sights, not least the marvellous remains of the **Kuelap** fortress, that easily rival their southern counterparts.

WHAT TO SEE AND DO

The town is centred on the tranquil **Plaza de Armas**, surrounded by the cathedral and municipal buildings and with a colonial bronze fountain, a monument to Toribio Rodríguez de Mendoza, as its centrepiece. Born here in 1750, he is considered the main ideological inspiration for Peru's independence from Spain. The town's main church of interest, **Iglesia de Santa Ana**, Jr Santa Ana 1056, was built in 1569. There is also a *mirador* (viewpoint) that you can reach if you walk west along Jr Santa Ana to the end of the road and take the steps.

ARRIVAL AND DEPARTURE

By bus The best of the bus companies, the comfortable Movil Tours buses at Libertad 464 (☎041 478 545), serve Lima (11am), Chiclayo (8pm) and Trujillo (7.30pm), while Civa at Salamanca 956 (☎041 478 048) also run to Lima (1pm) and Chiclayo (6.30pm). To get to Tarapoto, take a direct *colectivo* or switch to a bus in Pedro Ruíz.
Destinations Chiclayo (4 daily; 9hr); Trujillo (2–3 daily; 12hr); Lima (2 daily; 22hr).
By combi/colectivo Minibuses and shared cars to regional destinations depart from the Terminal Terrestre, around ten blocks from Plaza de Armas. Vírgen del Carmen (☎041 413 243) serves Cajamarca via Leymebamba; Turismo Selva (☎961 659 443) serves Tarapoto, where you can catch a bus to Yurimaguas for boats to Iquitos (see p.818).
Destinations Cajamarca (2 daily at 5.30am & 7pm; 10–12hr); Lamud (several daily; 2hr); Tarapoto (5 daily; 8hr).

INFORMATION AND TOURS

Tourist information Jr Ortiz Arrieta 5 (Mon–Sat 9am–6pm, Sun 9am–1pm; ☎041 477 292). Run by iPerú; some English spoken.
Tour operators There are numerous tour operators dotted around the Plaza de Armas, all of which offer standard day-trips to Kuélap (S35); Karajía, combined with either Pueblo de Los Muertos or the Quiocta Cave (S70); and Gocta waterfall (S70). Turismo Explorer, at Jr Grau 509 on the plaza (☎041 478 162, ⓦturismoexplorerperu .com), is highly recommended and the guides speak excellent English. Amazon Expeditions, at Jr Ortiz Arietta 508 (☎041 798 718, ⓦamazonexpedition.com.pe), is a very professional outfit that also runs four-day treks to Gran Vilaya (S800), four-day treks to Laguna de Los Cóndores combined with Kuélap (S900), and the more adventurous day trek to the Gocta waterfall.

ACCOMMODATION

★**Chachapoyas Backpackers** Jr Dos de Mayo 639 ☎041 478 879, ⓦchachapoyasbackpackers.com. Run by an effusive, English-speaking host, this central hostel is a great budget choice. The simple rooms (some with own bathrooms) come with cool lamps in the shape of Karajía sarcophagi, guests congregate in the kitchen and small lounge, and laundry service is a welcome perk. Dorms S18, doubles S40
Hostal Ñunurco Jr Ortíz Arrieta 186 ☎041 477 845, ⓦnunurcotravellers.com. This rambling guesthouse is run by several friendly, helpful guys (no English spoken) who organize tours to all major nearby sites. Breakfast is simple and the rooms are spacious, tiled and spic-and-spank. Wi-fi works in the dining room only. S100
Hostal Revash Jr Grau 517, Plaza de Armas ☎041 477 391. Centred around a greenery-filled courtyard featuring a replica Karajía sarcophagus, this guesthouse is renowned for the having the best hot showers in town, and the spacious rooms (the cheapest singles are S40) come with properly comfortable beds. There's a buffet breakfast and a rather persistent in-house tour agency. S120
Hostal Rumi Huasi Ortiz Arrieta 365 ☎041 791 100. In keeping with its name (literally "stone house"), this place is a bit bare, but it's clean, light, has hot water, a laundry service, wi-fi and TV in all rooms. S50

TWO ROADS BETWEEN CHACHAPOYAS AND CAJAMARCA

There are two routes between Chachapoyas and Cajamarca. The far longer and less exciting route is the road that passes through Chiclayo (changing buses at Pedro Ruíz); this route has fewer and lower passes but is more prone to landslides during the rainy season.

A fascinating **alternative route to Chachapoyas** is the direct scenic route taken by the Virgen del Carmen bus company – a paved yet precarious one-lane highway from Cajamarca that passes through the village of **Leymebamba**, winding its way up and down several massive valleys and passes. There's a reason why the driver's assistant hands out travel sickness bags: the curves can be nausea-inducing and it's best if you have a head for heights, given the sheer drop to one side (which is stunning or terrifying, depending on your outlook). This scenic route is also run overnight (wear warm clothes and bring a blanket). It's well worth stopping in Leymebamba to visit the fantastic Museo de Leymebamba (5km from town), home to 219 remarkably well-preserved Chachapoyas mummies, found in 1996 at the Laguna de Los Condores – itself reachable via a very scenic three- or four-day guided trek either from Leymebamba proper or from Chachapoyas (in which case it incorporates a visit to Kuélap (see p.815).

9

CHACHAPOYAS

●EATING & DRINKING		■ ACCOMMODATION	
El Batán del Tayta	5	Chachapoyas Backpackers	4
Café Fusiones	1	Hostal Ñunurco	1
Silvias Pub	3	Hostal Revash	3
El Tejado	2	Hostal Rumi Huasi	2
Terra Mia	4		

EATING AND DRINKING

The Mercado Central, one block north of Plaza de Armas between Grau and Ortiz Arrieta, sells fresh produce.

El Batán del Tayta Jr La Merced 604 ☎ 959 865 539. A corridor inscribed with messages from happy customers greets you as you enter, and the menu is as eclectic as the decor, including steak flambéed in pisco, rice with duck and wonderful, imaginative salads. Wash it down with pineapple sangria or one of their signature sours. Mains from S15. Daily noon–11pm.

★**Café Fusiones** Chincha Alta 445 ☎ 041 479 170. This bohemian hangout specializes in largely organic "slow food". Come here for spicy lentil burgers, fresh guacamole and hummus, fresh juices, chunky sandwiches, ample breakfasts and great teas and coffees. Wi-fi and book exchange make it even more worth spending some time here. Mains from S10. Mon–Sat 7am–noon & 3–9pm.

Silvias Pub Jr Ayacucho 822. A time warp of a bar, with posters of John Lennon, Kurt Cobain and Bon Jovi on the walls, and English-language pop on the sound system. Go for their good selection of locally made *macerado* (fermented fruit rum). Daily 9pm–1am.

El Tejado Santo Domingo 424 ☎ 041 477 592. Really good traditional Peruvian and local cuisine served in a warm and friendly place set around a patio. The speciality here is several takes on *tacu tacu* (S10), a rice-and-beans dish. Mon–Sat noon–4pm & 7–9pm.

★**Terra Mia** Jr Chincha Alta 557 ☎ 041 477 217. A cultured hangout with an artistic air – walls are painted a deep red hue and there are colourful Andean cushions. But what marks this place out are the breakfasts (from S14) – a welcome change from bread, juice and coffee. Try the spinach and cheese omelette or waffles. Daily 7am–10.30pm.

DIRECTORY

Banks and exchange BCP is on Triunfo, seven blocks from the Plaza de Armas and next to the hospital. Banco de la Nación is at Ayacucho and 2 de Mayo. Both have global ATMs.
Hospital The public hospital (open 24hr) is on the corner of the plaza (☎ 041 477 017).
Post office Grau 561 (Mon–Sat 8am–7pm).

DAY-TRIPS FROM CHACHAPOYAS

There are many remote ruins dotted around the stunning countryside, all easily reachable by day tour. West of Chachapoyas lie the **Pueblo de los Muertos** and **Karajía**, two impressive cliff-face burial centres for the elite of the Chachapoyas peoples; southeast are the marvellous remains of the **Kuélap** citadel, second only to Machu Picchu in terms of location and magnificence, while northeast is **Gocta**, Peru's tallest waterfall.

Kuélap

If you only see one sight in the northern highlands, make it **KUÉLAP** (daily 8am–5pm; S15). This impressive pre-Inca fortress, 3100m up in the clouds, 700m long and with 20m-tall walls, was built around 500 AD and would have housed around four thousand people in circular thatched huts. The remains of these houses are decorated with characteristic Chachapoyas diamond and zigzag patterns. Elsewhere, you may spot small, carved animal heads, condor designs and intricate serpent figures. The site is atmospherically overgrown with trees, bromeliads and mosses. The upper part of the citadel was restricted to the most privileged ranks in Chachapoyas society and one of the most interesting buildings is the temple, containing *El Tintero* ("the ink well"), a large, bottle-shaped cavity, possibly a place of sacrifice, since archeologists have found human bones there, accessed via a hole in the roof.

You can get to Kuélap by day tour or as part of a four-day trek that passes by the collection of ruins known as **Gran Vilaya** – some tour companies in Chachapoyas run excursions (around S200 per person per day and includes food, accommodation and transport).

Cateratas de Gocta

About a two-hour road trip from Chachapoyas, the waterfalls at **GOCTA** (771m) are believed to be the fifth tallest in the world. Getting to a good viewpoint – from where you can make out the main two tiers of the falls (231m above and another 540m below) – requires a two-hour hike through the cloudforest either from the village of San Pablo or from Cocachimba. It's easiest with a tour as it's mandatory to go with a guide; the more adventurous tour companies do the walk from San Pablo to Cocachimba via the falls.

Karajía and the Pueblo de los Muertos

Two cliffside mausoleums, Karajía and the Pueblo de los Muertos ("town of the dead"), are both easiest reached by day tour, as public transport to the nearest villages is scarce. From the plaza in the village of Cruz Pata, it's a 1km (20min) descent via dirt road to **KARAJÍA**. Thirty metres above the walkway is a row of six sarcophagi, up to 2m in height, elaborately painted clay coffins moulded around a cone made of wooden poles, with heads reminiscent of Easter Island's moai. Up to 2m in height, they house the mummies of the most important individuals, such as chieftains, warriors and shamans, as well as their most prized belongings. The two skulls above them are thought to be trophy skulls. From the far end of the walkway you can see another five sarcophagi to the left of the main group – these are far less elaborate and have been thoroughly desecrated. To the left of those there's a solitary sarcophagus, hidden in the shrubbery.

The **PUEBLO DE LOS MUERTOS** is similarly interesting, with more sarcophagi and also burial houses, again perched precariously on a ledge with a huge drop into the valley below. It's a 45-minute walk downhill from Lamud, and one hour thirty minutes back up.

During the rainy season, the walk to the Pueblo de Los Muertos becomes a mud bath and tour companies visit **CAVERNA DE QUIOCTA** (10km northwest of Lamud; 2hr walk each way) instead. It's an impressive (and extremely muddy) cave with jaw-dropping stalagmites and stalactites, also the site of some Chachapoyas human remains; tour companies supply rubber boots.

The Northern Jungle

Over half of Peru is covered by rainforest, with its eastern regions offering easy access to the world's largest and most famous jungle, the **Amazon**. Of the Amazon's original area, around six million square kilometres (about eighty percent) remains intact, fifteen percent of which lies in Peru. It's the most biodiverse region on earth, and much that lies beyond the main waterways remains relatively untouched and unexplored.

9

Although far easier to access by air from Lima, you can get to the northern jungle from the northern Peruvian coast via an adventurous three-day boat journey up the Río Marañon from Yurimaguas to **Iquitos**. This will take you close to an animal-rich national reserve the size of many European countries, **Pacaya Samiria**.

IQUITOS

The largest city in the world not accessible by road, **IQUITOS** began life in 1739 when the Jesuits established settlements on the Río Mazán. By the end of the nineteenth century, it was, along with Manaus in Brazil, one of the great rubber towns – as depicted in Werner Herzog's 1982 film *Fitzcarraldo* – but during the last century has oscillated between prosperity and depression. Yet its role as Peru's busiest river port and the nearby three-way frontier with Colombia and Brazil (see box, p.826) has ensured both its economic and strategic importance.

Iquitos is a busy, cosmopolitan town of about 500,000 and growing (people from smaller jungle villages flock here looking for a better life), with elegant architectural reminders of the rubber boom years, eccentric expats and the atmospheric *barrio* of **Puerto Belén**.

WHAT TO SEE AND DO

Iquitos is easily overlooked in favour of the surrounding jungle, but don't be too quick to dismiss this steamy metropolis. It has a few sights, more than its fair share of quirks, surprisingly good food and a lively nightlife.

Plaza de Armas

The only real sight on **Plaza de Armas** is the unusual **Casa de Fierro** (Iron House). Originally created by Eiffel for the 1889 Paris exhibition, it was shipped out to Iquitos in pieces by one of the rubber barons and erected here in the 1890s.

Along the river

The two best sections of the **old riverfront** run parallel to the Plaza de Armas. Malecón Maldonado, locally known as

El Boulevard, is the busier of the two, especially at night, as it's full of bars and restaurants and there's a small dugout amphitheatre hosting street performers. The other section, **Malecón Tarapaca**, has fine old mansions with Portuguese *azulejos* (tiles), brilliantly extravagant in their Moorish inspiration. The impressive **Museo de las Culturas Indígenas Amazónicas** (Malecón Tarapacá 332; daily 8am–7.30pm; S15) showcases the culture and rituals of forty different indigenous peoples of the Amazon Basin, including pre-Columbian funerary urns, splendid ceremonial feathered headgear of the Wayana-Apari and the Kaiapo and a totem-pole-like mask of the Tikuna. You can also check out a trophy shrunken head of the Jivaro and learn about the Matses poison frog ceremony.

The nearby municipal **Museo Amazónico** (Malecón Tarapacá 386; Mon–Fri 9am–12.30pm & 2–5pm; S3) is less impressive, but look out for the collection of fibreglass statues modelled on more than eighty people from different indigenous groups residing in the surrounding jungle.

Museo Barco Histórico "Ayapua"

Docked by the waterfront across the little Plaza Ramón Castilla from Casa Morey is this triple-decked 1906 **steamer**, the *Ayapua* (daily 9am–5pm; S15), dating back to the height of the rubber boom. Inside the cabins are displays that cover the European exploration of the Amazon, missionaries, the rubber boom and the

---

WHEN TO VISIT

The city of Iquitos is good to visit year-round. There is no rainy season as such; instead, the year is divided into "high water" (Dec–May) and "low water" (June–Nov) seasons. The weather is always hot and humid, with temperatures averaging 23–30°C and an annual rainfall of about 2600mm. Most visitors come between June and August, but the high-water months can be the best time for **wildlife**, because the animals are crowded into smaller areas of dry land and more rivers can be navigated.

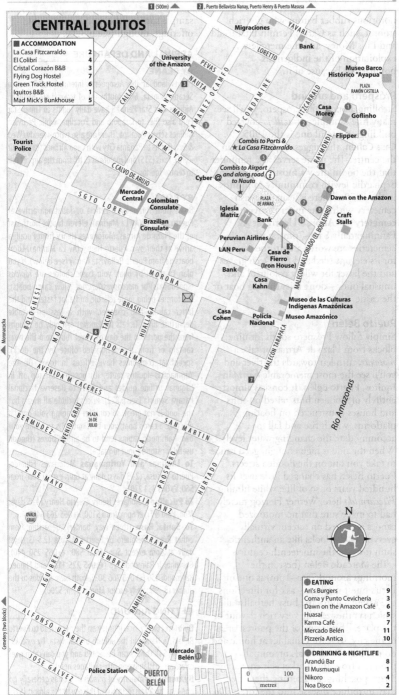

CENTRAL IQUITOS

■ ACCOMMODATION

La Casa Fitzcarraldo	2
El Colibrí	4
Cristal Corazón B&B	3
Flying Dog Hostel	7
Green Track Hostel	6
Iquitos B&B	1
Mad Mick's Bunkhouse	5

1 (500m)
2, Puerto Bellavista Nanay, Puerto Henry & Puerto Masusa

Migraciones

YAVARI

LORETO

Bank

University of the Amazon

Museo Barco Histórico "Ayapua"

PLAZA RAMÓN CASTILLA

Casa Morey

Goflinho

Flipper

Tourist Police

Combis to Ports & ★ La Casa Fitzcarraldo

Combis to Airport and along road to Nauta

Cyber @

Mercado Central

Colombian Consulate

Brazilian Consulate

Iglesia Matriz

PLAZA DE ARMAS

Bank

Dawn on the Amazon

Craft Stalls

Peruvian Airlines

LAN Peru

Casa de Fierro (Iron House)

Bank

Casa Kahn

Museo de las Culturas Indígenas Amazónicas

Casa Cohen

Policía Nacional

Museo Amazónico

MORONA

BRASIL

HUALLAGA

TACNA

RICARDO PALMA

AVENIDA M CACERES

BERMUDEZ

PLAZA 26 DE JULIO

SAN MARTIN

2 DE MAYO

GARCIA SANZ

OVALO GRAU

J C ARANA

9 DE DICIEMBRE

ABTAO

ALFONSO UGARTE

JOSE GALVEZ

Police Station

Mercado Belén

PUERTO BELÉN

Río Amazonas

N

0   100
metres

Maroncocha

Cemetery (two blocks)

▼ Airport, Nauta, Mercado Artesanal (4km) & Centro Rescate Manati (8km)

● EATING

Ari's Burgers	9
Coma y Punto Cevichería	3
Dawn on the Amazon Café	6
Huasaí	5
Karma Café	7
Mercado Belén	11
Pizzería Antica	10

● DRINKING & NIGHTLIFE

Arandú Bar	8
El Musmuqui	1
Nikoro	4
Noa Disco	2

9

notorious rubber barons who got rich from it, such as Carlos Fermín Fitzcarrald and Luis Morey, and the merciless exploitation of the indigenous populations because of it.

Próspero and around

Strolling along Calle Próspero, you'll see many fine examples of *azulejo*-covered buildings; a useful one is the 1905 **Casa Cohen**, the biggest supermarket in the centre. The name serves as a reminder that the boom drew a mostly Moroccan, Sephardic Jewish community to Iquitos in the 1870s. There is a small Jewish cemetery within the main Peruvian **cemetery** (Av Alfonso Ugarte, at Av Fanning; daily 8am–7pm); both cemeteries are worth a visit, the former for its elegant tiled and Art Deco graves and the latter for wildly colourful and unusual ones – don't miss the tug boat or the castle.

Puerto Belén

Simply follow Próspero south for nine blocks from Plaza de Armas or take a *motokar*, turn left towards the river and you'll see the most memorable *barrio* in Iquitos, **Puerto Belén**. It consists almost entirely of wooden huts raised on stilts and houses constructed on floating platforms, which rise and fall to accommodate the changing water levels. When the tide is high enough, get a canoe to take you out on the flooded streets. Puerto Belén has changed little over its hundred years or so of life; while filming *Fitzcarraldo* here, Werner Herzog merely had to make sure that no motorized canoes appeared on screen; virtually everything else looks like an authentic slum town of the nineteenth century.

The **Mercado Belén** (best in the mornings around 7am–1pm) is one of Peru's finest markets – ask for directions to Pasaje Paquito, the busy herbalist alley, which synthesizes the very rich flavour of the place. This is one of the poorest areas of the city, so leave valuables at home and do not buy any animals or animal products from the market – it encourages illegal poaching, and setting them free may introduce disease into the forest. Do

sample some of the more exotic edible offerings, though (see p.820).

ARRIVAL AND DEPARTURE

BY PLANE

Flights land at the Aeropuerto Internacional Francisco Secada Vigneta, 6km southwest of town. LAN, Peruvian Airlines and Star Perú all have daily flights to Lima; Star Perú also flies to Tarapoto and Pucallpa, while Peruvian Airlines serves Pucallpa. There are also twice-weekly (Wed & Sat) flights to Panama City with Copa Airlines (w copaair .com). Taxis ($15) and *mototaxis* ($10) from the airport run to central Iquitos.

BY BOAT

Boats from Yurimaguas, Leticia or Tabatinga arrive at Puerto Masusa (Av La Marina), eleven blocks northeast of the Plaza de Armas. Motonaves Henry from Pucallpa arrive at their own Puerto Henry (Av La Marina). Local boats go from Puerto Bellavista Nanay (see below). If you plan to travel by boat, your basic choices are *rápidos* (speedboats) or *motonaves/lanchas* (slow cargo boats), the former being more reliable and a lot faster, and the latter calmer and cheaper, with a less predictable departure time. Tickets for *lanchas* can only be bought from the ports on the day of travel (buy from the boat captain or from the designated office by the dock); speedboat companies have offices in town. On the Yurimaguas–Iquitos route, it's possible to stop off in Lagunas to find guides and tours to Reserva Nacional Pacaya Samiria (see p.822). Prices include all meals but the food is not great, so consider bringing your own. If you take a cargo boat, your best option is to swing your own hammock; cabins tend to be airless boxes (though useful for storing your luggage).

To Lagunas and Yurimaguas Motonaves Eduardo, Puerto Masusa, (2–3 days; daily at 6pm except Sun; from S60; ☎ 065 351 270).

To Pucallpa Motonaves Henry, Puerto Henry (4–5 days; Mon, Wed & Fri at 6pm; from S100; ☎ 065 263 948).

To Santa Rosa (three-way border): departing from either Puerto Pesquero or Puerto Masusa (2.5–3 days; daily at 6pm except Sun; from S80; ☎ 065 250 440); Golfinho, Jr Raimondi 378 (☎ 065 225 118), and Flipper, Raymondi 350 (☎ 065 766 303), both have *rápidos* to the border (8–9hr; daily except Mon at 5am; S200).

GETTING AROUND

By boat For any local journey on the river, head to Puerto Bellavista Nanay, in the suburb of Bellavista, by *motokar* (10min; S4). Canoes can be rented and you can catch river *colectivos* to islands and other villages nearby.

By combi The majority of *combis* in Iquitos generally go one-way back and forth out of the city to the airport (S1).

By mototaxi *Mototaxis* are ubiquitous and can be taken everywhere. Short hops are S2; in the city the most expensive ride would be to Bellavista Nanay (S4).

INFORMATION

Dawn on the Amazon Café (see p.820) acts as an unofficial clearing house of information; owner Bill is happy to recommend ecologically friendly attractions and steer people away from less-than-reputable *ayahuasca* retreats.

Tourist information There's a helpful tourist information kiosk at the airport (daily 8am–9pm; ☎ 065 260 251), and the main iPerú tourist office is at C Napo 161 (Mon–Sat 9am–6pm, Sun 9am–1pm; ☎ 065 236 144). The staff provide free advocacy should you run into any problems with tour companies. The monthly English-language newspaper *The Iquitos Times* (ⓦ iquitostimes.com) is also a good source of information, and is available at most hotels and restaurants. There's also the monthly English-language *The Amazon River* (ⓦ theamazonrivermonthly.com), with an entertaining collection of articles on all things Amazonian and a breakdown of restaurant listings.

Tourist permits If you are planning a trip into the jungle with just a guide (as opposed to a group) or to Pacaya Samiria National Reserve, then talk to SERNANP (☎ 065 223 555), located at C Chávez 930–942 (behind the military base).

ACCOMMODATION

El Colibrí Jr Nauta 172 ☎ 065 241 737. A modern, clean and pleasant guesthouse right in the centre. Rooms have cable TV and private bath with hot water, as well as a/c or fans. There's also a decent breakfast (S7). S̲6̲5̲

Cristal Corazón B&B C Nanay 130 ☎ 065 222 070, ⓦ cristalcorazon.com. A cosy B&B with orthopaedic beds, healthy breakfasts, a large communal kitchen and a patio. Mosquito nets and repellent can be provided. Host Miguel Pizango can organize expeditions, lodge stays and *ayahuasca* ceremonies. Dorms S̲2̲5̲, doubles S̲6̲0̲

Flying Dog Hostel Malecón Tarapacá 592 ☎ 065 223 755, ⓦ flyingdogperu.com. Bona fide offshoot of the Lima/Cusco/Arequipa hostel chain, complete with colourful rooms (some with bathroom), spacious guest lounge with graffitied testimony from happy guests, guest kitchen and plenty of *buena onda* (good vibes). Dorms S̲2̲5̲, doubles S̲9̲0̲

★**Green Track Hostel** Jr Palma 516 ☎ 065 600 805, ⓦ greentrack-jungle.com. Popular backpacker haunt a short distance from the plaza with all facilities that backpackers expect, as well as an appealing courtyard filled with greenery. Green Track also have their own jungle lodge (see p.823) in the Tapiche Reserve and the owner is renowned for his efforts to protect the local wildlife. Dorms S̲2̲5̲, doubles S̲1̲0̲5̲

Iquitos B&B Jr Prado 231 ⓦ iquitosbnb.com. Run by a friendly Dutch jungle guide and ayahuasca enthusiast, this is one of the best backpacker digs in town. Rooms are modest en suites, quiet and clean, and your host is a treasure trove of local information. S̲3̲5̲

Mad Mick's Bunkhouse Putumayo 163 (upstairs 202) ☎ 992 193 726. British expat Mad Mick will welcome you with a smile to his one room with eight beds, behind the office for his jungle supplies store. Not for those who need personal space, but you can't fault it at the price. Dorms S̲1̲5̲

EATING

Ari's Burgers Prospero 127 ☎ 065 241 124. An American-style diner serving more than just burgers, including a mind-boggling variety of jungle superjuices (from S9) as well as traditional dishes; it's particularly well known for its ice cream. The most popular meeting spot in Iquitos and good for late-night munchies. Ice-cream scoop S2. Daily 7am–2am.

Coma y Punto Cevichería Jr Napo 488 ☎ 065 225 268. A popular lunchtime place that serves some of Iquitos' best *ceviche*, made from different types of river fish. Other dishes include generous portions of *arroz con mariscos* (seafood rice) and *chicharrón de pescado* (chunks of fried,

---

★**TREAT YOURSELF**

La Casa Fitzcarraldo Av La Marina 2153, Punchana ☎ 065 601 138, ⓦ casafitzcarraldo.com. For your own slice of Amazonian and movie history, stay in this luxurious B&B where the cast and crew of *Fitzcarraldo* lodged during the filming (Mick Jagger stayed in the Blue Room before he quit to tour with the Stones). The owner, Walter, was the producer on the film and speaks five languages. It's slightly out of the centre (5min by *motokar*; S4), so you'll feel you've stumbled out of the city and into an orchid-rich jungle oasis. If you can't afford the stay, S10 will get you in to use their pool (9am–6pm) and treehouse or to eat in their excellent restaurant. Book ahead as there are only four rooms; airport pick-up included. S̲3̲0̲0̲

9

ANIMAL RESCUE CENTRES

There are three reputable, genuine animal rescue centres around Iquitos: the **Pilpintuwasi Butterfly Farm and Animal Orphanage** (see opposite), the **Centro Rescate de Manatí** (see opposite) and the **Isla de los Monos** (see p.822). However, numerous tour companies offer less salubrious animal encounters in the form of visits to self-proclaimed "animal rescue centres" where you're offered the opportunity to wrap an anaconda or python around yourself or hold a sloth or monkey for that exotic holiday snap. These are nothing more than decrepit zoos and are best avoided, since visiting them perpetuates the illegal animal trade in endangered species and dooms the unhappy monkeys, sloths, macaws and snakes to a short life in a cage.

battered fish). Mains from S15. Daily noon–5pm.

★ **Dawn on the Amazon Café** Malecón Maldonado 185 ⓣ 065 234 921, ⓦ dawnontheamazoncafe.com. This wonderfully relaxed spot on the waterfront is hugely popular, not just for its varied menu, which makes great use of fresh local produce and runs the gamut from American-style breakfasts and ample salads to spicy Mexican fajitas, falafel burgers and grilled fish – but also for the genuine warmth of owner Bill, who's a fantastic source of local information. Mains around S15. Mon–Sat 7.30am–11pm.

Huasaí Jr Fizcarrald 131 ⓣ 065 242 222. Family-run traditional Peruvian restaurant, always heaving with locals. Serves an excellent and huge S12 lunch *menú* including starter, main and jug of juice. Simply delicious. Daily 7am–4.30pm (sometimes later).

★ **Karma Café** Napo 138 ⓣ 065 223 663. All psychedelic wall hangings, incense and bright colours, the only thing missing from this "Eastern" ambience are the delicate strains of the sitar. There's plenty to please vegetarians (falafel burgers, veggie curry) and spice lovers (Thai curries), huge fruit juices and salads, and in the evening the place gets so packed with offbeat travellers that you'll be lucky to find a spare beanbag to sprawl on. Mains from S15. Daily 12.30pm–midnight.

Mercado Belén Puerto Belén. The chaotic Mercado Belén is a great spot for cheap eats, particularly generous helpings of fresh fruit juices (try the *jugo especial* – jungle juice), and real jungle staples of juicy Amazon grubs on a stick, *sikisapa*, fried leafcutter ants, rice-studded *morcilla* (black pudding) and more. From S2. Daily 7am–5pm.

Pizzeria Antica Jr Napo, between the plaza and the Malecón ⓣ 065 241 988. A large space with ceiling fans and driftwood decor, this Italian joint has an extensive menu of wood-fired pizzas, pasta and immense calzones, including good vegetarian options and some dishes incorporating jungle ingredients. Mains from S19. Daily 11am–1am.

DRINKING AND NIGHTLIFE

Arandú Bar Malecón Maldonado 113. With a prime location on the Boulevard, this bar is often packed in the evenings, with seating spilling outside. Serves a range of drinks (pisco sour S14, large beer S7) and a few snacks. Daily 4pm–midnight.

★ **El Musmuqui** Raymondi 382. A specialist in exotic cocktails, this tiny but lively bar is packed with locals every night of the week. Come here to try traditional jungle liquors, many of which are said to have strong aphrodisiac properties (S4–7) – try the house speciality *charapita ardiente*. Also serves snack food. Mon–Thurs & Sun 5pm–midnight, Fri & Sat 5pm–3am.

★ **Nikoro** Down the steps at the end of Pevas. This is one special bar: a huge wooden hut on the river (though in low water, you're 15m up on stilts) serving jungle drinks and cocktails (S10). Sit on the balcony for unrivalled views of the river and the stars. Iquitos' most bohemian and diverse crowd can be found here, from hippies to botanists. Daily 7pm–1am.

Noa Disco Fitzcarrald 298 ⓣ 065 222 555, ⓦ noadisco.com. Easily identified after midnight by the huge number of flashy motorbikes lined up outside, this is the most popular and lively of the clubs in Iquitos. It has five bars and plays lots of Latino music. S15 entrance includes one beer. Thurs–Sat 10pm–7am.

SHOPPING

Craft stalls Malecón Maldonado s/n. The craft stalls on the waterfront sell a really good selection of psychedelic Shipibo embroidery, the designs allegedly inspired by *ayahuasca* visions.

Mercado Artesanal San Juan Near the airport. Some 2km east of the airport along the main road is this popular souvenir market where you can pick up some Shipibo embroidery. Other items not to miss are the vases carved out of beautiful tropical hardwoods, some of them true works of art.

DIRECTORY

Banks and exchange Banco de Crédito, Jr Putumayo 201; Banco de la Nación, Jr Condamine, cuadra 4; Banco Continental, Jr Próspero, cuadra 4; and Interbank, Jr Próspero, cuadra 1, all have global ATMs (the moneychangers on Próspero can't always be trusted).

Consulates Brazil, Jr Lores 363 (ⓣ 065 235 151); Colombia, C Calvo de Araujo 431 (ⓣ 065 231 461).

Health Clinica Ana Stahl, Av La Marina 285 (ⓣ 065 252 535) is a good 24hr private clinic. TrámazonDoctor, Jr Bolívar 222 (ⓣ 959 464 131, ⓦ tramazondoctor.com), provides a 24hr emergency callout service.

Immigration You can extend or renew your Peruvian tourist card or visa at Migraciónes, Cáceres, cuadra 18 (☏ 065 235 371).

Internet Cyber, Putumayo at Condamine.

Jungle supplies Mad Mick's Trading Post, Putumayo 184b. Provides everything you need for a jungle trip, for purchase or rent, including rubber boots, rainproof ponchos, sunhats and fishing tackle.

Laundry Lavandería Imperial, Jr Nauta, cuadra 1 (Mon–Sat 8am–8pm).

Police Tourist Police, C Lores 834 (☏ 065 242 081).

Post office SERPOST, C Arica 402 (Mon–Fri 8am–6pm, Sat to 4.30pm).

DAY-TRIPS FROM IQUITOS

For those who want to experience a bit of the jungle without straying too far from the city, there are several easy day-trips from Iquitos. It's simple to hop over to a nearby island for some monkeying around or visit rescued jungle species at the Amazon Animal Orphanage, while the Centro de Rescate de Manatí is easily reached by *mototaxi*.

Pilpintuwasi Butterfly Farm & Amazon Animal Orphanage

One of the most popular day-trips from Iquitos is to the **Pilpintuwasi Butterfly Farm & Amazon Animal Orphanage** in Padre Cocha (Tues–Sun 9am–4pm; S20, S10 for students; ☏ 965 932 999, ⓦ amazonanimalorphanage.org). The life's work of Austrian expat Gudrun (she speaks excellent English), this is a butterfly farm and also a sanctuary for orphaned jungle animals bought illegally and subsequently confiscated, such as Pedro Bello the jaguar, giant anteater, sloths, coatí, howler monkeys and red aukari monkeys. **To get here**, take a river *colectivo* from the Bellavista Nanay port in Iquitos to Padre Cocha (S5; 20min); once there, it's a fifteen-minute walk (straight, then left towards the water tower, then straight) or a S1 *motokar* journey. Tour companies also run day-trips combined with pink river dolphin spotting at the confluence of Río Nanay and Río Amazonas.

Centro de Rescate de Manatí

This hard-working animal rescue centre (Mon noon–3pm, Tues–Sun 9am–3pm; S20) specializes principally in the rehabilitation of orphaned baby manatees whose mothers are killed by poachers. They are nursed back to health and released into the wild when they are ready to fend for themselves. Entry is by Spanish-speaking tour and there are a few other rescued animals – a tailless macaw and some monkeys. You can also purchase a pot full of aquatic plants that the manatees particularly like, and feed them by hand. It's 2km past the airport; a *mototaxi* from the centre costs S10.

SHAMANS AND AYAHUASCA SESSIONS

Ayahuasca retreats have long been a booming business in Iquitos, and account for a third of its tourism industry. A jungle vine (*Banisteriopsis caapi*) that grows in the Western Amazon region, *ayahuasca* has been used for thousands of years as a "teacher plant", gaining a worldwide reputation for divination, inspiration and healing of physical, emotional and spiritual ailments. The vine is generally mixed with other jungle plants to transform it into a bitter-tasting hallucinogenic brew, usually taken in a public session with a shaman.

While each indigenous community in the area has a shaman, not all practitioners who offer *ayahuasca* sessions in and around Iquitos are qualified to do so. If mixed with a particular plant, or if you have an allergic reaction, *ayahuasca* can lead to dangerously high blood pressure and even death, though this is rare. Since the plant is a powerful hallucinogen, participants may undergo hours of intense visions, along with intense purging (vomiting). The business is currently not regulated at all; ⓦ ayaadvisor.org is a good starting point if you want to read about the experiences of others and decide what's right for you.

There are dozens of *ayahuasca* retreats around Iquitos, some of them very upmarket, with plush accommodation and a cleansing superfood diet, and while it's difficult to give specific recommendations, the **Temple of the Way of Light** (ⓦ templeofthewayoflight.org) has female Shipibo shamans and a good reputation for combining *ayahuasca* ceremonies with charitable and environmental work.

9

La Isla de los Monos (Monkey Island)

The wonderful family-run initiative of **La Isla de los Monos** (office in town at Sargento Lores 752; ☎065 235 529, ⓦmonkeyislandperu.com) is located on an island a couple of hours upriver from Iquitos, where they have planted all the fruit trees that eight species of monkey feed from. The organization takes in animals rescued from poachers and releases them into the wild if feasible when they are well. Otherwise, the howlers, tamarins, spider monkeys, woolly monkeys and others are free to roam the island and many of them interact with humans. It's a fantastic day out; they don't charge entry but they greatly appreciate donations and take in volunteers. Beware of fake Monkey Island: some boat operators in Iquitos balk at the long journey (2hr–2hr 30min upriver, 1hr 30min back) and instead take you to a place close to Iquitos that's a disreputable "animal rescue centre". To get to the genuine one, take a speedboat from the Puerto de Productores to Varadero and call ☎965 779 610 when setting off so that they can pick you up at Varadero, or else take a tour with Dawn on the Amazon (see opposite) or another reputable tour company ($79/person).

PACAYA SAMIRIA NATIONAL RESERVE

Around 130km southwest of Iquitos, **RESERVA NACIONAL PACAYA SAMIRIA** comprises over 20,000 square kilometres (about 1.5 percent of the landmass of Peru) of virgin rainforest and is home to the Cocama peoples. The reserve is a swampland during the rainy season

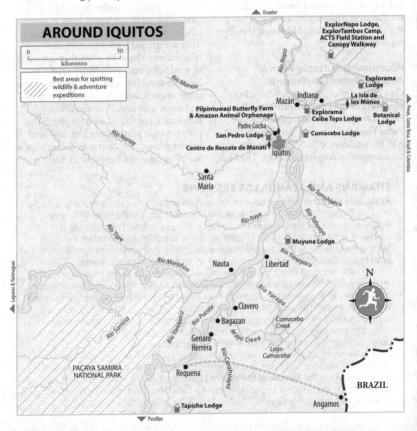

AROUND IQUITOS

Ecuador

0 — 50 kilometres

Best areas for spotting wildlife & adventure expeditions

ExplorNapo Lodge, ExplorTambos Camp, ACTS Field Station and Canopy Walkway

Río Napo

Río Momón

Explorama Lodge

Mazán   Indiana   La Isla de los Monos

Pilpintuwasi Butterfly Farm & Amazon Animal Orphanage

Explorama Ceiba Tops Lodge

Botanical Lodge

Río Nanay

Padre Cocha

San Pedro Lodge

Cumaceba Lodge

Centro de Rescate de Manatí

Iquitos

Santa María

Río Tamshiyacu

Río Itaya

Río Tahuayo

Río Tigre

Muyuna Lodge

Río Yanayacu

Río Marañón   Nauta   Libertad

Río Yarapa

Clavero

Río Pucate   Bagazan   Cumaceba Creek

Río Samiria

Río Yanayacu

Genaro Herrera

Mayo Creek

Río Curahuayra

Lago Cumaceba

PACAYA SAMIRIA NATIONAL PARK

Requena

N

BRAZIL

Tapiche Lodge   Angamos

Pucallpa

Pevas, Santa Rosa, Brazil & Colombia

Lagunas & Yurimaguas

IQUITOS TOURS AND JUNGLE LODGES

The massive river system around Iquitos offers some of the best access to indigenous villages, lodges and primary rainforest in the entire Amazon. It's usually best to travel with one of the many lodges or tour companies. Some tours include a visit to the nearby Bora and Yaguar communities where the locals put on traditional costume and a song and dance for visitors; the experience is contrived, but it's also become a way to preserve what's left of their culture, and they still speak their original languages.

If you've come to Iquitos to see jungle wildlife in the wild, staying at a jungle lodge is by far the best option. When choosing a lodge, consider its distance from Iquitos, the company's commitment to conservation, the level of comfort you want and what's included in the price. Most lodge itineraries will include dolphin-watching, fishing, visiting an indigenous village, jungle walks and caiman-spotting on the river by night. The best companies should be booked in advance, have fixed prices and never tout for business in the street. Prices below are based on a three-day/two-night stay for two people, per person, and the addresses included are for the Iquitos-based booking offices.

TOUR OPERATORS AND LODGES

Cumaceba Lodge Putumayo 184 ☎065 232 229, ⓦcumaceba.com. A highly recommended budget option on the Río Yanayacu, 35km downriver from Iquitos (45min by speedboat), with accommodation in private rustic bungalows with individual bathrooms. Cumaceba has another lodge, Botanical Lodge, 90km downstream, with a large swimming pool and own botanical garden. US$370.

Dawn on the Amazon Malecón Maldonado 185 ☎065 223 730, ⓦdawnontheamazon.com. Passionate about the local ecology, Bill Grimes and his team are happy to organize custom-made tours depending on your interests – be it day-trips in the surrounding area, or multi-day cruises into the Pacaya Samiria Reserve (from US$159/person per day), swinging a hammock on the *Dawn on the Amazon*.

★**Explorama** Av la Marina 340 ☎065 252 530, ⓦexplorama.com. Explorama is the top operator in the region and has a good reputation for responsible tourism; not cheap but worth it. It has four sites in the jungle offering everything from remote camping to the most luxurious lodge in the Amazon. It's possible to go between sites and tailor your stay to include an excursion to the company's canopy walkway. Ceiba Tops (the most luxurious option, with a/c & pool) US$475.

★**Muyuna** Putumayo 163 ☎065 242 858, ⓦmuyuna.com. Located close to the Pacaya Samiria Reserve, 120km from Iquitos, *Muyuna* offers attractive, en-suite, mosquito-proof cabins and activities such as jungle walking and dolphin-spotting river safaris. The lodge works hard to distinguish itself as a protector of wild animals and most of their guides come from nearby indigenous communities. US$890.

★**Tapiche Lodge** Ricardo Palma 516 ☎065 600 805, ⓦtapichejungle.com. Located 404km upriver from Iquitos inside the Tapiche Reserve, this fantastic lodge is second to none when it comes to proximity to rare and endangered wildlife. Accommodation is not ultra-luxurious (oversized Brazilian hammocks or private, mesh-protected cabins), but the owners, Deborah and Katoo, are really passionate about conservation and keeping wild animals in the wild. Trekking and canoeing in the reserve are on offer and the emphasis is on animal- and bird-spotting. Five days/four nights US$600.

(Dec–March), when the streams and rivers all rise; as such you'll see different wildlife in the high-water and low-water seasons (both good in different ways). The reserve is famous for its abundance of fauna, particularly pink and grey dolphins, river turtles, manatees, caimans, numerous species of monkeys and an astounding 450-plus bird species. Away from human settlement, there's a good chance of spotting jaguars and other big mammals.

To do the reserve justice you ideally need a week, or at least five days. There are three ways of visiting: by staying in remote jungle lodges near the reserve (see above), aboard boats from Iquitos (see p.818) or (far cheaper) independently via dugout canoe with a guide from the town of **Lagunas**, two days downstream from Iquitos towards Yurimaguas (see p.818), which requires more time and effort and costs around S150–170/day for guide, boat and simple lodgings (food is extra) but is very worthwhile. Come well prepared with mosquito nets, hammocks, insect repellent, and all the necessary food and medicines. SERNAMP charges S30/day for visiting the reserve; this is normally included in organized tours.

9

The Southern Jungle

Part of the Peruvian Amazon basin – a large, forested region with a searingly hot and humid climate, punctuated with sudden cold spells (*friajes*) between June and August – the **southern selva** regions of Peru have only been systematically explored since the 1950s and were largely unknown until the twentieth century, when rubber began to leave Peru through Bolivia and Brazil, eastwards along the rivers. Cusco (see p.742) is the best base for trips into the jungles of the southern selva, with road access to the frontier town of **Puerto Maldonado**, itself a good base for budget travellers. The nearby forests of Madre de Dios are rich in flora and fauna, especially in the **Manu Biosphere Reserve**.

MADRE DE DIOS

Named after the broad river that flows through the heart of the southern jungle, the still relatively wild *departamento* of **MADRE DE DIOS** is changing rapidly, with agribusinesses moving in to clear mahogany trees and set up brazil-nut plantations, and prospectors panning for gold dust along the riverbanks. Nearly half of Madre de Dios *departamento*'s 78,000 square kilometres are accounted for by national parks and protected areas such as **Manu Biosphere Reserve**, **Tambopata-Candamo Reserved Zone** and **Bahuaja-Sonene National Park**, between them containing some of the richest flora and fauna in the world.

Madre de Dios still feels very much like a frontier zone, centred on the rapidly growing river town of **Puerto Maldonado**, supposedly founded by legendary explorer and rubber baron Fitzcarraldo.

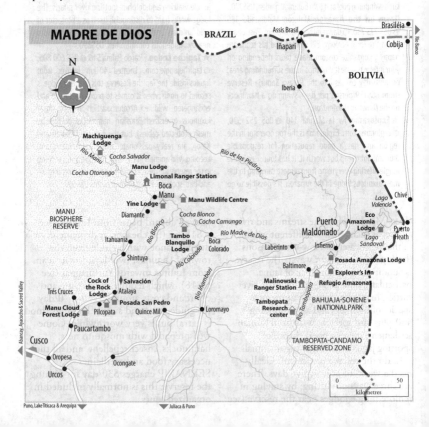

Puerto Maldonado

Despite its position firmly on the Interoceanic Highway, connecting the Peruvian and Brazilian coasts, the jungle town of **PUERTO MALDONADO** still has a raw feel to it, its *mototaxi*-clogged streets often culminating in pitted dirt tracks. With an economy based on gold panning, logging, cattle ranching and brazil-nut gathering, it has grown enormously over the last twenty years, becoming the thriving capital of a region that feels very much on the threshold of major upheavals.

The town is centred on a pleasant **Plaza de Armas**. Ten blocks from the plaza is the large, bustling **market**, which covers an entire block, and if you follow Fitzcarraldo beyond it, you'll reach the **Obelisco** (daily 9am–5pm; S2), a phallic tower offering an expansive panorama of the entire city and the jungle beyond.

ARRIVAL AND DEPARTURE

By plane Puerto Maldonado International Airport is 4km from the centre of town. *Mototaxis* cost around S7 for the ride. LAN and Star Perú have daily flights to Cusco (50min) and Lima (1hr 40min).

By bus All buses arrive at the Terminal Terrestre, located 2km away from the airport, along Carretera Tambopata. A dozen bus companies run overnight services to Cusco (Movil Tours is the most comfortable); there are also direct departures to Juliaca, with connections to Puno and Arequipa. Transportes M. D'Acre makes daily trips in shared cars from their office at Av Fitzcarrald 704 to Iñapari, by the Brazilian border, less then 3hr drive away, and Assis across the border, with onward connections to Brasiléia and Rio Branco.

Destinations Cusco (numerous daily, departing either at around 8.30pm or 9pm; 10hr); Juliaca (5–6 daily 6pm & 6.30pm; 10hr).

By boat Puerto Maldonado has two main river ports: one on the Río Tambopata, at the southern end of León de Velarde, the other on the Río Madre de Dios, at the northern end of León de Velarde. From the latter you can hire a boatman and canoe for a river trip (around S120/boat for up to five people). From the Tambopata dock there are twice-weekly passenger boats that go as far as the indigenous community of Baltimore. Jungle lodges use both docks, and transfers are included in the price of your stay. From the Madre de Dios dock you can hire private boats to take you to the Bolivian border, although this is an expensive option (around S550; 6hr).

GETTING AROUND

By mototaxi and motorbike The quickest way of getting around town is to hail a *mototaxi* (S2–6, depending on where you're going; ask first) or passenger-carrying motorbikes (S1–2). You can rent mopeds along Prada between Puno and Velarde (from S5/hr; passports and driving licences required) if you can handle the erratic local driving.

INFORMATION AND TOURS

Tourist information There's a small tourist information kiosk at the airport which meets oncoming flights. The SERNANP office at Av 28 de Julio, 8th block (☎082 573 278), has handouts on the nearby national park and reserve; it collects entrance fees (S30) for a permit, for those planning on going independently.

Tour operators *Tambopata Hostel* (☎082 574 201), run by a former Rainforest Expedition guide, offers authentic backpacker jungle tours between one and five days and popular trips to Lago Sandoval and Lago Valencia, as well as *ayahuasca* ceremonies at the indigenous community of Infierno. *Anaconda Lodge* organizes kayak tours and trips to Sandoval Lake, Tambopata and Madre de Dios, as does *Tarantula Hostel*.

ACCOMMODATION

★**Anaconda Lodge** 600m away from the airport, along Av Aeropuerto s/n ☎082 792 726, ⓦanacondajunglelodge .com. Occupying an area of just under four acres, this Swiss-Thai lodge is home to rustic bungalows surrounded by a verdant tropical garden. Monkeys, sloths, porcupines, agoutis and armadillos – to name a few – roam the premises and there's a little pool at the back to cool off. The restaurant offers superb Thai food. **S160**

Kapievi Eco Village Carretera Tambopata Km1.5 ☎082 795 650, ⓦecoaldeakapievi.blogspot.com. Part-yoga and part-*ayahuasca* retreat, this chilled-out place sits in its own patch of jungle off the dirt road leading to Infierno (10min by *mototaxi*). Expect rustic cabins with mosquito nets, solar heated showers, wind chimes dangling from trees and home-cooked meals on request. Per person **S100**

Hostal Paititi Jr Velarde 290, at Jr Prada ☎082 574 667. Colourful central guesthouse on a busy street, with spacious rooms and large windows, guest internet and even a small gym. The on-site café is decent and a basic breakfast is included. You can opt for cheaper fan-cooled rooms. **S140**

★**Tambopata Hostel** 26 de Diciembre 234 ☎082 574 201, ⓦtambopatahostel.com. A great-value pad for budget travellers in a very central cedarwood house with dorms, private rooms (some with own bathrooms) with mosquito nets and hammocks in the garden. There's free wi-fi, a communal kitchen, and an outside terrace. Breakfasts are included in the price, you can bone up on your Peruvian slang by reading the wall, and take a wildlife tour. Dorms **S30**, doubles **S80**

9

CROSSING INTO COLOMBIA OR BRAZIL: THE THREE-WAY FRONTIER

Leaving or entering Peru via the Amazon means experiencing the **three-way frontier** between Santa Rosa (Peru), Tabatinga (Brazil) and Leticia (Colombia). **Leticia** (see p.562) is a lively jungle town with a good selection of guesthouses and restaurants, while **Tabatinga** (see box, p.316) is an unpretty urban sprawl a few blocks away (the two towns blend into one another), from where you can take a boat to Manaus if continuing on in Brazil.

The route by river from Iquitos to **Santa Rosa** takes some eight or nine hours by *rápida* (speedboat; S200 one-way) or 2.5–3 days in a standard cargo boat (from S90 hammock one-way; cabin from S150). Bring own hammock.

Boats drop you off at immigration in Santa Rosa where you must obtain an **exit stamp** from Peru if you're leaving (show your tourist card to do this), or get an **entry stamp and tourist card** if arriving. Larger boats may take you all the way to Tabatinga (Brazil) or Leticia (Colombia), in which case an immigration official may board the vessel and do the paperwork there and then. If not, Brazilian entry and exit formalities are processed at the Policia Federal office, Av da Amizade (daily 7am–noon & 2–6pm; ☎ 097 3412 2180) in Tabatinga. US citizens need a visa to enter Brazil, which must be obtained in Lima or the United States in advance. To officially enter Colombia, take a short *mototaxi* ride to Leticia's airport and get a Colombian tourist card from the immigration office there (daily 8am–6pm). Motorized canoes connect Santa Rosa with Tabatinga and Leticia (15–20min).

Tarantula Hostel Av Aeropuerto s/n ☎ 082 632 334, ⓦ tarantulaecohostel.com. Located at just 500m from the airport, *Tarantula* is set on a verdant plot of land, home to plenty of wildlife including monkeys and macaws. Guests have access to the barbecue, kitchen and large pool, and owners organize *ayahuasca* ceremonies as well as wildlife-watching trips. Free wi-fi and airport pick-up. Breakfast included. Dorms $\overline{S35}$, doubles $\overline{S105}$

EATING, DRINKING AND NIGHTLIFE

★ **Burgos** Av 26 de Diciembre, Cuadra 1 ☎ 082 502 373. This open-fronted restaurant with woven prickly-pear lamps and dangling clay pots serves a range of regional dishes heavily influenced by jungle ingredients (*juanes* with wild pig and *criollo* salad, grilled fish with star-fruit sauce) and an evening buffet (pick a main and then help yourself to fried yucca and sweet potato, salads and more). The exotic cocktails (star-fruit sour, for example) pack a punch. Mains S20–28. Daily noon–3pm & 6–10pm.

La Casa de la Cerveza Jr Velarde, at Jr Carrión. Popular two-storey watering hole right on the Plaza, with a good range of beers and some stronger options if you feel like courting oblivion. Daily 6pm–late.

La Casa Nostra Jr Velarde 515 ☎ 082 573 833. A popular little café that serves a range of tasty cakes, tropical fruit juices, including mango, passionfruit, pineapple and local favourite *carambola*, for around S3 a glass, as well as *tamales* and *papas rellenas* (stuffed potatoes). It also serves pretty good coffee and Peruvian breakfasts. Daily 7am–1pm & 4–11pm.

Cevichería El Califa Jr Piura 266 ☎ 082 571 119. This Puerto Maldonado favourite has been going strong for over three decades and specializes in river fish *ceviche* (though you can also find bush meat on the menu (not all

of it legal). The fresh juices are made with fruits from the back garden. Mains S17–20. Mon–Sat 11am–5pm.

Heladería Gustitos del Cura Jr Loreto 286. Run by a Swiss priest, the profits at this pleasant café help fund a local orphanage. Friendly staff serve a selection of home-made ice creams (S2/scoop) in seventeen exotic fruit flavours, as well as delicious cakes (S5) and light bites. Free wi-fi. Daily 8am–8pm.

El Hornito Pizzeria Jr Carrión 271 1 ☎ 082 572 082. This is arguably Puerto Maldonado's best pizzeria, with ample portions of wood-fired pizza, calzones and an array of pasta dishes. Only open in the evening. Pizzas from S20. Daily 6–10pm.

Witite Jr Velarde 151. This popular club packs with 20-somethings for some pop, rock and salsa tunes on Friday and Saturday nights and keeps going until the early hours of the morning. Entry is sometimes S10. Fri & Sat 11pm–6am.

DIRECTORY

Banks and exchange There are three banks on the plaza: Scotiabank, Interbank and BCP, all with ATMs. Casa de Cambio on C Prada, at C Puno, changes foreign currency at good rates (Mon–Sat 8am–8pm).

Hospital Hospital Santa Rosa at Cajamarca 171 (☎ 082 571 019).

Internet Mundo Net on León Velarde 613 (Mon–Sat 7am–midnight, Sun 10am–midnight).

Laundry Lavandería Jhonatan, C Cusco s/n (Mon–Sat 7.30am–9pm, Sun 8.30am–9pm).

Post office Velarde 675 (Mon–Sat 8am–8pm).

Visas Oficina de migraciones, Av 28 de Julio 467 (Mon–Fri 8am–1pm; ☎ 082 571 069). Get your passport stamped here if leaving for Bolivia by river.

Wildlife reserves around Puerto Maldonado

Madre de Dios boasts spectacular virgin lowland rainforest and exceptional wildlife. Brazil-nut-tree trails, a range of lodges, some excellent local guides and ecologists plus indigenous and colonist cultures are all within a few hours of Puerto Maldonado. There are two main ways to explore: either by arranging your own boat and boatman, or by taking an excursion up to one of the lodges, which is more expensive but also more convenient.

Less than one hour downriver from Puerto Maldonado (1hr 30min return) is **Lago Sandoval**, a large oxbow lake, home to caimans, giant otters and a host of birds. It's best to stay here overnight and do a boat ride on the lake in the early morning – the best time for

wildlife-spotting, though it's also possible to do the lake as a day-trip. Take one of the recommended tours (see p.828) or hire a boat (around S120 for up to five people) to drop you off at the start of the trail (1hr walk to the lake) and to pick you up later. Bring your own food and water.

Further along the river, 60km from Puerto Maldonado, lies the huge **Lago Valencia**. It's easiest to visit it from one of the lodges along Río Madre de Dios; its remoteness increases your chances of seeing wildlife and the lake is also good for fishing.

South of Puerto Maldonado, Río Tambopata flows into the heart of the **Reserva Nacional Tambopata**, where you'll find several excellent lodges, as well as the indigenous communities of Infierno and Batimore. The remote **Parque Nacional**

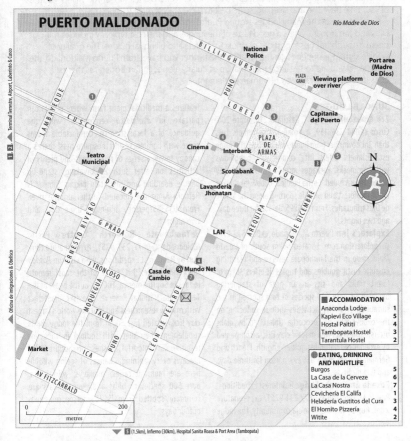

PUERTO MALDONADO

Río Madre de Dios

National Police

Port area (Madre de Dios)

PLAZA GRAU — Viewing platform over river

Capitania del Puerto

Cinema — Interbank

PLAZA DE ARMAS

Teatro Municipal

Scotiabank

BCP

Lavandería Jhonatan

LAN

Casa de Cambio

@ Mundo Net

Market

BILLINGHURST

PUNO

LORETO

LAMBAYEQUE

CUSCO

CARRION

PIURA

2 DE MAYO

ERNESTO RIVERO

G PRADA

J TRONCOSO

MOQUEGUA

TACNA

ICA

PUNO

LEÓN DE VELARDE

AREQUIPA

26 DE DICIEMBRE

AV FITZCARRALD

Terminal Terrestre, Airport, Laberinto & Cusco

Oficina de imigraciones & Obelisco

N

0   200
metres

■ **ACCOMMODATION**
Anaconda Lodge   1
Kapievi Eco Village   5
Hostal Paititi   4
Tambopata Hostel   3
Tarantula Hostel   2

● **EATING, DRINKING AND NIGHTLIFE**
Burgos   5
La Casa de la Cerveze   6
La Casa Nostra   7
Cevichería El Califa   1
Heladería Gustitos del Cura 3
El Hornito Pizzería   4
Witite   2

5 (1.5km), Infierno (30km), Hospital Sanita Roasa & Port Area (Tambopata)

9

Bahuaja-Sonene is even further upstream (6hr minimum) and features some of the best wildlife in the Peruvian Amazon as well as the Tambopata Research Centre, located next to the Colpa de Guacamayos – one of the largest macaw clay licks in the Amazon. To visit the reserve and the national park, book a guided tour at one of the lodges.

MANU BIOSPHERE RESERVE

Encompassing almost 20,000 square kilometres (about half the size of Switzerland) on the foothills of the eastern Andes, **MANU**, declared a Biosphere Reserve by UNESCO in 1977, features a uniquely varied environment of pristine rainforest, from crystalline cloudforest streams and waterfalls down to slow-moving rivers in the dense lowland jungle. Manu is one of the most biologically diverse places in South America; rich in macaw clay licks and otter lagoons, it's also home to thirteen species of monkey and seven species of macaw.

PUERTO MALDONADO JUNGLE LODGES

Compared with independent travel, a stay at a jungle lodge saves time and adds varying degrees of comfort. It also ensures that you're exploring the jungle with someone who knows the area, who speaks English and can introduce you to the flora, fauna, culture and regions. It's best to book a trip in Cusco directly through the lodge offices or online before travelling to Puerto Maldonado. The cheapest option with jungle lodges is a two-day and one-night tour, but you will spend most of your time travelling and sleeping, so it's best to allow at least three to four days.

A stay at one of the many lodges around Puerto Maldonado, mainly on the ríos Madre de Dios and Tambopata, offers a good taste of the jungle, and the cost typically includes full board (though not tips for guides or drinks), transfers and bilingual guides. The quality of wildlife sightings depends on the location; the further you travel from Puerto Maldonado, the more likely you are to see large mammals, particularly along Río Tambopata, as there's considerably less in the way of human settlement.

JUNGLE LODGES

Eco Amazonia Lodge C Garcilaso 210, office 206, Cusco ☏ 084 236 159, ⓦ ecoamazonia.com.pe. Less than 2hr downriver from Puerto Maldonado, this large establishment offers fifty comfortable bungalows with hammocks. Packages include visits to Monkey Island, the secluded "Cocha Perdida" oxbow lake, hikes in the rainforest and wildlife spotting along the Madre de Dios tributaries. From US$295/person for three days and two nights.

Explorer's Inn Puerto Maldonado ☏ 082 572 078, ⓦ explorersinn.com. Located 58km south of Puerto Maldonado in the Tambopata reserve and featuring en-suite rustic doubles and triples. It offers 38km of forest trails and sits in an area of staggering biodiversity, with 620 species of bird spotted in the surrounding jungle. Activities include canoeing on the oxbow lake of Cococcocha (inhabited by giant otters), and visits to a macaw clay lick, accompanied by experienced naturalist guides. English, French and German spoken. From US$299/person for three days and two nights.

Posada Amazonas Lodge Rainforest Expeditions, Puerto Maldonado ☏ 0877 231 9251, ⓦ perunature .com. Run by the local Ese'eja community, the lodge features a medicinal plant farm where guests can partake in *ayahuasca* ceremonies with the guidance of a local shaman. Comfortable rooms come with hammocks and mosquito nets, there's a canopy tower, a series of forest trails and plenty of activities on offer such as kayaking, stand-up paddle boarding and mountain biking. Similar is Refugio Amazonas, located further up the river. From US$385/person, minimum three days and two nights.

★ Tambopata Research Centre Puerto Maldonado ☏ 0877 231 9251, ⓦ perunature.com. Run by Rainforest Expeditions, who also run *Posada Amazonas Lodge*, this is one of the most remote lodges in South America, TRC lies at the heart of the Tambopata National Reserve. Guests can interact with macaw researchers and visit the world's largest clay lick, located just 500m from the lodge. Birds supplement their diet with sodium in the clay, resulting in colourful flashes of hundreds of macaws every morning. Chances of seeing wildlife here are high: peccaries, monkeys, wild boars, over 500 species of birds and even jaguars are commonly spotted. From US$785/person, minimum of four days.

Manu is reachable via a six-hour bus journey from Cusco along a partially paved road, followed by several hours along Río Madre de Dios, making it a destination for serious jungle enthusiasts with at least a week to spare. The reserve is divided into three parts: the **Cultural Zone**, encompassing the bus route and several villages within the cloudforest; the **Reserved Zone**, with the jungle lodges and oxbow lakes, located along Río Madre de Dios and Río Manu, accessible only as part of a guided tour (see box, p.830); and the **Restricted Zone**,

WHEN TO VISIT

The Manu region experiences a **rainy season** from December to March, when the road into the park is particularly susceptible to landslides, so is best visited between May and August when it's much drier, although at that time the temperatures often exceed 30°C. Bring a jacket just in case, as roughly once a month the jungle experiences several days of *friaje* – a cold spell that can bring the temperature down as low as 12°C.

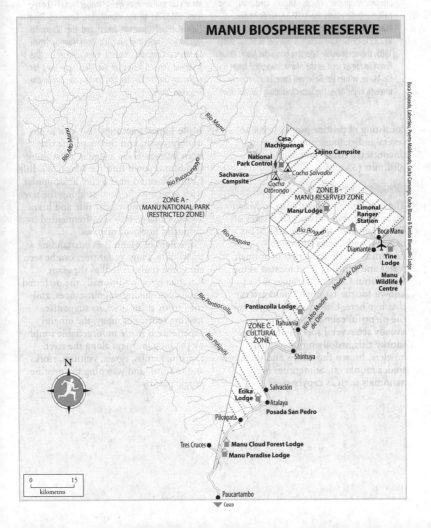

MANU BIOSPHERE RESERVE

MANU TOURS

The companies below have a responsible attitude towards the Manu reserve and are keen to keep the impact of tourism to a minimum. Transport here is by land from Cusco.

TOUR OPERATORS

Manu Adventures Plateros 356, Cusco ☎084 261 640, ⓦmanuadventures.com. Popular, reputable operator offering four-day trips into the Cultural Zone and eight-day adventures to the Reserved Zone. Optional extras include rafting, zipping down a canopy line and a visit to the clay lick near their own *Erika Lodge* in the Cultural Zone, as well as stays at their *Sajino Campsite* in the Reserved Zone, on the banks of Cocha Salvador. Five-day "esoteric" trips are also available and involve shamanic rituals using medicinal and hallucinogenic plants. From US$820 for eight days.

Manu Nature Tours Av Pardo 1046, Cusco ☎084 252 721, ⓦmanuperu.com. A pioneer in Manu since 1985, this responsible operator owns the *Manu Cloud Forest Lodge* as well as the *Manu Lodge*, the latter on Río Manu, within the Reserved Zone. Tours range from three to eight days, the latter including birdwatching

along the 20km worth of trails around *Manu Lodge* spotting giant otters on the oxbow lakes in Zone B. They can also incorporate white-water rafting and mountain biking into their tours for an extra fee. Seven-night tours from US$934/person.

Pantiacolla Tours Garcilaso 265, 2nd floor, Cusco ☎084 238 323, ⓦpantiacolla.com. A company with a reputation for serious eco-adventure tours. This company offers three- to five-day trips (from US$450) to the cloudforest and Pantiacolla mountain range of Manu's Cultural Zone, as well as longer trips (7–9 days; from US$1570) to the cloudforest, Reserved Zone (Salvador and Otorongo lakes) and the Blanquillo macaw lick. Their *Yine Lodge* near Boca Manu and their *Sachavaca Campsite*, located even deeper in the Reserved Zone, 6 hours up Río Manu, are used for exploring Cocha Salvador and Cocha Otorongo in the Reserved Zone.

consisting of pristine jungle, home to several indigenous communities and uncontacted tribes, and completely off-limits to visitors.

WHAT TO SEE AND DO

The highlights of most visits to Manu include the trail network and lakes of **Cocha Salvador** (the largest of Manu's oxbows) and **Cocha Otorongo** – bountiful jungle areas rich in animal, water and birdlife, both located along Río Manu. Cocha Otorongo is best known for the family of **giant otters** that live here. Other wildlife includes the plentiful **caimans** and you can usually see several species of **monkey** (dusky titis, woolly monkeys, red howlers, brown capuchins and the larger spider monkeys). Sometimes big mammals such as **capybara** or

white-lipped peccaries also lurk in the undergrowth, and the fortunate have been known to see a jaguar. Also along Río Manu you'll find the Manu Wildlife Centre, located near a clay lick popular with tapirs, while further along the river to the east, a short boat ride and hike away, is a large clay lick, frequented by colourful flocks of macaws.

The **flora** of Manu is as outstanding as its wildlife. Huge cedar trees can be seen along the trails, as well as the giant Catahua trees, traditionally the preferred choice for making dugout canoes, and the "erotic palm" with its suggestive-looking roots. For many, the jungle experience is made unforgettable simply by the long journeys along the river, spotting herons, egrets, vultures, storks and toucans, and watching the pristine jungle pass by.

STREET IN COLONIA DEL SACRAMENTO

Uruguay

HIGHLIGHTS

❶ **Montevideo** Eclectic architecture, sweeping beaches and hip nightlife. **See p.837**

❷ **Colonia del Sacramento** Picturesque and historical town with excellent food. **See p.845**

❸ **Carmelo** Sleepy town, home to vineyards and riverside beaches. **See p.848**

❹ **Minas** Ride with gauchos through Uruguay's vast interior. **See p.849**

❺ **Punta del Este** Flashy beach resort with surf and celebrities. **See p.851**

HIGHLIGHTS ARE MARKED ON THE MAP ON P.833

ROUGH COSTS

Daily budget Basic US$40, occasional treat US$60

Drink Pilsen beer (1 litre) US$3

Food *Asado de tira* steak US$10

Hostel/budget hotel US$15–40

Travel Montevideo–Colonia del Sacramento (150km) by bus: 2hr 45min, US$11

FACT FILE

Population 3.4 million

Language Spanish

Currency Peso Uruguayo (UR$)

Capital Montevideo (population: 1.3 million)

International phone code ☎598

Time zone GMT -3hr

Introduction

If, as the saying goes, countries get the government they deserve, then Uruguay's most popular former president José Mujica was a great fit for Uruguay – modest, but sure of himself, progressive, but totally laidback; it's no wonder that this country is often referred to as the Switzerland of South America.

10

Through misfortune and good times, Uruguayans maintain their traditionally relaxed and cheerful attitude, and it's not hard to see why. From the secluded **surfing beaches** of the Atlantic coast, to the rolling pastoral land of the interior tended by **gauchos**, or the picturesque streets of **Colonia del Sacramento** and the buzzing nightlife of **Montevideo**, theirs is a gem of a nation set between the South American giants of Brazil and Argentina. "*Tranquilo*" (peaceful) could be Uruguay's national motto, and, after witnessing the beauty of the land and the relaxed kindness of its people, you are unlikely to be in any hurry to leave.

CHRONOLOGY

Pre-1600 Uruguay is home to the Charrúa Indians, a hunter-gatherer people hostile to the European invaders.

Early 1600s Spanish settlers introduce cattle to Uruguay and the gaucho lifestyle of cattle-ranching develops.

1680 The Portuguese establish Colonia del Sacramento as the first major colony in Uruguay.

1726 The Spanish retaliate by founding Montevideo in an attempt to cement their power in the region. Their wars with the Portuguese continue for the next century.

1811 José Artigas begins an independence campaign against the Spanish, who finally leave Uruguay in 1815, only for Brazil and Argentina to fight over control of the territory.

1820 Artigas, defeated by the Portuguese, is exiled to Paraguay, where he stays until his death.

1825 Juan Lavalleja leads the legendary Treinta y Tres Orientales (a group of 33 revolutionaries) to victory over the Brazilians. Uruguay gains its independence a year later.

1831 Uruguay's 500 remaining Charrúa are massacred by the government.

1834–51 Uruguay plunged into civil war pitting the Colorados against the Blancos, names that have survived as political parties to this day.

1903–15 President José Batlle y Ordoñez of the Colorado Party makes sweeping social reforms, effectively making Uruguay South America's first welfare state.

1950–60s Inflation and political corruption leads to the stagnation of Uruguay's industries, and social unrest ensues.

1973 The Congress is dissolved and the army takes control of the government. Twelve years of military dictatorship ensue.

1984 The military allows free elections to take place. Colorado wins, Dr Julio Sanguinetti becomes president and holds office until 1989, only to return to power from 1995 until 2000.

2000 Personal possession and use of marijuana is legalized.

2001 The economic crisis in Argentina leads to a collapse in the value of the Uruguayan peso; inflation and widespread unemployment ensues.

2009 José Mujica, a former militant leftist taken prisoner and tortured during the military regime, easily wins the presidency.

2012 Uruguay becomes the second Latin American country, after Cuba, to legalize abortion.

2013 A year later, it becomes the first country in the world to legalize marijuana sales.

2014 Mujica's successor Tabaré Vázquez wins the November election.

ARRIVAL AND DEPARTURE

The majority of visitors to Uruguay arrive via **ferry** from Buenos Aires to Colonia del Sacramento as an easy day-trip. Those **flying** into Uruguay usually arrive at Montevideo's **Aeropuerto de Carrasco** (see p.841); check online for the full list of airlines flying here (ⓦ aeropuertodecarrasco.com.uy). Those coming by bus will be dropped at Tres Cruces bus terminal (ⓦ trescruces.com.uy) in downtown Montevideo.

WHEN TO VISIT

One of Uruguay's main draws is its beaches, so it's best to visit from **November to February** when it's warm, although bear in mind that prices in beach towns soar. Winters in Uruguay can be downright frigid, with cold wet air blowing in from the ocean, but you should still get some sunny days.

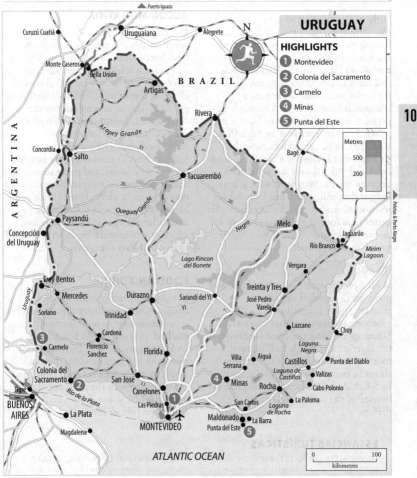

URUGUAY

HIGHLIGHTS

1 Montevideo
2 Colonia del Sacramento
3 Carmelo
4 Minas
5 Punta del Este

VISAS

Citizens of the EU, US, Australia, New Zealand, South Africa and Canada, among others, do not need a visa to visit Uruguay. Check the *Preguntas Frecuentes* (FAQ) section of ⓦwww.mrree.gub.uy for a full list of countries.

GETTING AROUND

BY BUS

The most convenient and cheapest means of transport in Uruguay are **intercity buses**, which operate from the bus terminal (*terminal de ómnibus*) in

most towns. Montevideo's main terminal Tres Cruces has an excellent website (ⓦtrescruces.com.uy) with details of all the companies and timetables operating there.

BY CAR

Uruguay is an easy country to drive around; all the major routes are asphalted, well signposted, and, outside of summer along the coast, there are very few drivers on the roads. Non-paved roads off the numbered routes tend to be in pretty good shape, except after rain when they may become too muddy without a 4WD. Even Montevideo is

10

fairly straightforward to get in and out of, thanks to the coastal road (the *ramblas*) linking the airport with the centre and old town. In low season you can find **rental cars** for as little as UR$1900/day, and from UR$6000 in high season (all the major international car rental companies have offices in Uruguay), but petrol costs are equivalent to European prices. Fines for speeding are high (from US$250), so be sure to adhere to the national speed limits of 45km/hr in inner cities and 90km/hr on the main roads between towns. **Taxis** tend to be safe as long as they're licensed, but look out for *remises* (minicabs), which sometimes offer better rates for fixed distances as they are booked in advance – ask at your hostel for reliable companies.

BY BIKE

With a predominantly flat landscape and good-quality roads, Uruguay is a tempting place for cyclists.

Accommodation is never more than 50km apart along the coast (although in the interior and north facilities are much more sparse) and there are repair shops in many cities. As with elsewhere in South America, however, you must beware of the recklessness of local drivers.

ACCOMMODATION

Uruguay's coastal towns house plenty of **youth hostels** and other towns will offer basic hotels for those on a budget. Off the main tourist routes, however, places to stay can be few and far between; it's also worth checking if your trip coincides with a public holiday as accommodation can book up fast. Tourist information offices are usually happy to help find accommodation. During the summer holidays from December to February you need to book ahead, and prices soar, so that a dorm bed can be as expensive as sharing a double room in a basic hotel. Hotels and hostels often have a set dollar exchange rate, rather than going by the daily rate, which can mean you'll be slightly better off paying in dollars than pesos.

FOOD AND DRINK

Uruguay may not provide the most cosmopolitan of culinary experiences, but if you enjoy **beef** or most kinds of **seafood**, you will not go hungry. Uruguayan steakhouses (*parrillas*) serve steaks that are larger and (as the locals insist) more tender than their Argentine counterparts, with the most popular cuts being the ribs (*asado de tira*) and tenderloin (*bife de chorizo*).

ESTANCIAS TURÍSTICAS

No visit to the interior of the country would be complete without a stay or at least a daytime visit to an *estancia* – a working ranch – but although staying overnight can be magical, the experience does not come cheap and there is a huge variation in authenticity; note that *estancias turísticas* are essentially rural hotels (you can download a list from ⓦturismo.gub.uy).

If you can't afford to stay overnight, most will arrange (much cheaper) day stays which include horseriding, farm activities and a meal or two. The following are a couple of suggestions and demonstrate the huge variety you can choose from:

El Galope 50km from Colonia near Colonia Suiza, ⓦelgalope.com.uy. One of the few *estancias* run with backpackers in mind, owners Miguel and Mónica (who speak English) aim to provide "a holiday from your holiday", offering R'n'R, Uruguayan style. With horse-riding, a sauna and great food all priced separately, you can choose how much or how little you do (meals UR$200–300, horseriding UR$850). Dorms UR$600, doubles UR$1700

Guardia del Monte Ruta 9, Km261.5, ⓦguardiadelmonte.com. If you can shell out for a

night at a traditional *estancia*, none offers a better location (overlooking Laguna de Castillos) or more rugged elegance than this one. The cosy farmhouse, with fantastic birdwatching and horseriding opportunities, is a taxi ride from Castillos (around UR$350), 10km down a dirt track. English is spoken, and while it is relatively expensive, you'll get an incomparable taste of rural Uruguay. Closed May–Sept. Full board with all activities per person (less if B&B only, or without activities) UR$3900

The best dining option for **vegetarians** tends to be the ubiquitous pizza and pasta restaurants. **Desserts** (*postres*) also bear an Italian influence and Uruguay's *confiterías* (patisseries) and *heladerías* (ice-cream parlours) are bursting with delicious treats. *Dulce de leche* is an irresistible type of caramel that you'll find in almost any form on dessert menus (and as part of your hostel breakfast to spread on toast). The national snack is the **chivito**, essentially a whopping burger stacked with fried egg, ham, cheese and bacon, but with a whole steak instead of ground beef.

Uruguayans don't really do breakfast – most cafés open around 10am, but almost all hotels and hostels provide a basic breakfast for tourists. Lunch is eaten early, between noon and 1pm, making time for the *merienda* or *te*: a sumptuous afternoon tea – usually advertised for two – full of sweet and savoury snacks along with tea or coffee, which is taken around 5pm. Thanks to this tradition, dinner is always late; you'll normally be eating on your own if you arrive at a restaurant before 9pm.

Restaurant **prices** are fairly high for South America: the average price for a lunch set menu is around UR$250–350 in Montevideo, and *à la carte* prices can be much higher.

DRINK

Mate (pronounced mah-tey) is the national drink and involves a whole set of paraphernalia to partake in drinking it. Coffee is the other non-alcoholic drink of choice here, and teas and bottled water are always available, along with fresh juices and smoothies (*licuados*).

When not clutching their thermos, Uruguayans enjoy the local beers – especially the ubiquitous **Pilsen** – which come in one-litre bottles (UR$70) fit for sharing. Uruguayan wine is becoming more prominent, especially the Tannat grape which makes a fine red (*tinto*). You may also see wine offered as *medio y medio* which is a blend of sparkling and slightly sweet white wine. **Tap water** is fine to drink.

THE ART OF DRINKING MATE

You are unlikely to walk down a single street in Uruguay without seeing someone carrying the thermos, pots and metal straw (*bombilla*) required for *mate*. In a tradition that goes back to the earliest gauchos, Uruguayans are said to drink even more of the grassy tea than Argentines, and a whole set of social rituals surrounds it. At the close of a meal, the *mate* is meticulously prepared before being passed round in a circle; the drinker makes a small sucking noise when the pot needs to be refilled, but if this is your position, beware making three such noises: this is considered rude.

CULTURE AND ETIQUETTE

Uruguayans of all ages tend to be warm, relaxed people, fond of lively conversation over a beer or barbecue (*asado*). As a nation in which the overwhelming majority of people are descended from Italian and Spanish immigrants, Uruguay also maintains some conservative **Catholic** religious and social practices, especially in the countryside, although the coastal towns are very liberal by South American standards. Uruguayans display a rugged sense of independence that recalls the romantic figure of the **gaucho**, the cowboys who still roam the grassy plains of the interior. Women and men alike greet each other with one kiss on the cheek. It's usual to leave a ten percent **tip** anywhere with table service.

SPORTS AND OUTDOOR ACTIVITIES

Ever since the first football World Cup, in 1930, was held in Uruguay and won by the national team, **football** has been the sport to raise the passions of the normally laidback Uruguayans. In the countryside, **horseriding** (*cabalgata*) is more a part of working life than a sport, but there are many opportunities for tourists to go riding – many hostels and most *estancias* (see box opposite) offer horseriding. **Cycling** is a popular way of seeing the cities (many hostels provide free or cheap bikes), while **fishing** is another favoured afternoon pursuit.

10

Surfing is increasing in popularity, thanks to fantastic Atlantic waves, and many beach hostels will rent out boards or advertise lessons.

A widely accepted translation of the Guaraní word *uruguay* is "river of painted birds", so it's no surprise that the country offers fantastic **birdwatching** opportunities, including flamingos, vultures, hawks, rheas and Magellanic penguins. Tourist information offices have excellent leaflets about twitching in Uruguay.

COMMUNICATIONS

The **national post office**, *Correo Uruguayo* (Ⓦ correo.com.uy), provides an expensive and sometimes unreliable service for international mail; for urgent deliveries, you are much better using a private mailing company like FedEx, at Juncal 1321 in Montevideo's old town. There are no postboxes on the street; you either need to go to a post office branch, or in Montevideo most museums have *buzones* (boxes) in their foyers. Antel run the **public phone** service and you'll find street phones and *cabinas telefónicas* (booths inside shops) wherever you go. You can buy phone cards (*tarjeta telefónica*), available wherever you see the Antel signs, or use change.

Internet cafés charge UR$20–30/hr and are present in all towns.

CRIME AND SAFETY

Uruguayans pride themselves on how safe their country is, although statistically crime is on the rise. **Thefts** from dorms, as well as pickpocketing, do occur, especially in Montevideo and the beach resorts during the summer months. Store your valuables in lockers whenever possible, but you shouldn't feel worried carrying valuables around with you during the day. The Uruguayan police are

EMERGENCY NUMBERS

❶ **911** is the general emergency number for the police, ambulance and fire services. You may need to dial ❶ **42911** from mobiles.

MARIJUANA

When Uruguay's much-heralded former president José Mujica passed a law in December 2013 allowing the purchase of **marijuana** grown by certified producers, 3.4 million Uruguayans heaved a sigh of relief and sparked up a joint. Or so the rest of the world thought.

In fact, around 60 percent opposed the law prior to its approval and consensus still hasn't been reached on the fine print about how to implement sales. Throw into the mix a change of leadership – even before he won the presidential election in November 2014, Mujica's successor Tabaré Vázquez had suggested he would tinker with the law – and it still isn't yet possible to buy weed legally.

The upshot for visitors? Even if the purchase of marijuana is implemented, it will be **illegal for tourists** to buy or consume the local produce.

courteous, but unlikely to speak English. As well as the emergency phone number (see box below), there is a national number for **tourist police** ❶ 08008226.

HEALTH

Uruguay's public healthcare system is in pretty good shape; there are adequate public **hospitals** in the major cities. Contact your embassy, or ask locals, for advice on the best facilities, and check that they will accept your insurance.

INFORMATION AND MAPS

The national **tourist board**, run by the Ministerio de Turismo y Deporte (Minitur; ❶ 02 1885100, Ⓦ turismo.gub .uy), is branded as **Uruguay Natural**, and they run offices in all of Uruguay's major towns, alongside local tourist offices run by the municipality. Uruguay Natural in Montevideo (see p.841) can give you free maps of every department, or you can buy high-quality road maps in petrol stations and bookshops. Uruguayans often write addresses using the abbreviations "esq.", meaning "at the corner with", and "c/", meaning "almost at", or "nearby".

MONEY AND BANKS

The unit of currency is the **peso uruguayo** (UR$). Coins come as 50 centimos and 1, 2, 5 and 10 pesos; notes as 10, 20, 50, 100, 200, 500 and 1000 pesos. At the time of writing, the **exchange rate** was £1 = UR$37, €1 = UR$29 and US$1 = UR$24.

Money changing is stress-free as everyone has to buy at the same rate, which varies slightly day to day (you can always find it displayed on the front of the daily newspapers). Breaking large banknotes is less of a problem than in most South American countries, though you are still advised to carry smaller notes in the countryside.

While major **credit cards** are widely accepted, and **ATMs** are common in cities (look out for the Banred and RedBrou ATMs which accept international cards), you should always carry a relatively large supply of **cash** for places where this is not the case. This applies especially to the beach villages of Eastern Uruguay, such as Punta del Diablo, which don't have ATMs. ATMs charge around UR$85 per withdrawal.

OPENING HOURS AND HOLIDAYS

Most **shops and post offices** open on weekdays from 8am until noon, before closing for lunch, reopening around 4pm until 7 or 8pm. Most businesses work at least a half-day on Saturday, but most close on Sundays. Banks are usually open Monday to Friday 1 to 5pm and closed at weekends. The exception to this is many shops in Montevideo, the main coastal tourist centres, and **supermarkets** in general; the latter are often open as late as 11pm during the week.

Most **museums and historic monuments** are open daily, though times vary, and tend to close once a week for maintenance. **Public holidays** are: January 1, January 6, Maundy Thursday, Good Friday, Easter Monday, April 19, May 1, May 18, June 19, July 18, August 25, October 12, November 2, December 25.

Montevideo

With a population of around 1.4 million, over fifteen times larger than the second city of Paysandú, **Montevideo** is Uruguay's political, economic and transport hub. Founded in 1726 as a fortress against Portuguese encroachment on the northern shore of the **Río de la Plata**, it had an excellent trading position and, following a turbulent and often violent early history, its growth was rapid. The nineteenth century saw mass immigration from Europe – mostly Italy and Spain – that has resulted in a vibrant mix of architectural styles and a cosmopolitan atmosphere.

Far more relaxed, but less affluent than its Argentine neighbour across the river, the Uruguayan capital has nevertheless seen an economic improvement in recent years, and wisely invested in its culture, infrastructure and beaches. Montevideo may appear humble at first, but this is a seriously cool, confident city.

10

WHAT TO SEE AND DO

Montevideo can sometimes be overshadowed by its snazzier neighbour Buenos Aires, but this, Uruguayans will tell you, is the true home of the **tango**, with plenty of free classes and *milongas* – bars playing traditional music – not to mention the best place to experience South America's longest **Carnaval** season (see box, p.838). There are tons of quirky **museums**, especially in the charming **Ciudad Vieja** and east to the **Centro**, based around Avenida 18 de Julio. Close to here, **Calle Tristan Narvaja** is filled with independent bookshops and cultural spaces, and holds a huge weekly flea market (see p.840). You may well stay in **Barrio Sur** – a traditionally Afro-Uruguayan neighbourhood where **candombe** drumming was cultivated – or chic and affluent areas **Punta Carretas** or **Pocitos**, where you'll find some of the best food and nightlife.

Ciudad Vieja

If you've ever seen a fictionalized version of Havana on TV or film, it's quite possible it was actually shot in

10

CARNAVAL

You will not truly understand the lure of Montevideo unless you experience **Carnaval**. It's a three-month celebration of Uruguayan culture with parades, neighbourhood stages known as *tablados* which host *murgas* (street bands where singing groups are accompanied by wild drumming – *candombe* – originating in the African rhythms brought over by slaves), plays, parodists and comedians, all wildly dressed and there to entertain. The spectacular opening and closing parades take place on Avenida 18 de Julio and the biggest events are held at the **Teatro de Verano** (see p.844). If you plan to be in Montevideo during Carnaval, email the tourist office to find out key dates.

Montevideo's **Ciudad Vieja**, so reminiscent are its streets of those in the Cuban capital. Dotted among the crumbling houses and cobbled streets are endearingly bizarre (and mostly free) **museums** and galleries, while the highlight is the glorious **Mercado del Puerto**.

Plaza Independencia and around

A good place to start a walking tour of the Ciudad Vieja is the **Puerta de la Ciudadela**, dating to 1746, marking the original site of the Citadel of Montevideo on the **Plaza Independencia**. This square commemorates the emergence of Uruguay as a sovereign nation, and a 17m-high statue and mausoleum (under the statue; Mon noon–6pm, Tues–Sun 10am–6pm) of **José Artigas**, the man credited with kick-starting Uruguay's independence campaign against Spain and Portugal, stands aptly in the centre.

The area around the plaza contains eclectic architectural styles, from the rather ugly **Torre Ejecutiva** where the president performs his duties, to the bulbous tower of the **Palacio Salvo**, built on the reported site of the first ever performance of tango.

Tucked behind the plaza's southwestern corner is the celebrated **Teatro Solís** (see p.844), the most prestigious theatre in the country, completed in 1856 and remodelled a few times thereafter. The guided tours (Tues & Thurs 4pm, Wed & Fri–Sun 11am, noon & 4pm; UR$20 in Spanish, UR$50 in English; tours in all available languages are free on Wed) are a fun way to see behind the scenes, but to experience its full splendour, you really have to watch a performance.

On the south side of the plaza, the old Presidential palace, a Neoclassical building from 1873, now houses the intriguing **Museo Casa de Gobierno** (Mon–Fri 10am–5pm; free; ☎02 1515902), which charts the history of the country via its often eccentric presidents.

Plaza de la Constitución and around

Lively pedestrian boulevard **Sarandí** cuts through the centre of the old city – starting at the Puerta de la Ciudadela – with its street-sellers, artisans, buskers and frequent parades, to the **Plaza de la Constitución**. Also referred to as the Plaza Matríz, this is Uruguay's oldest square, dating back to 1726. It's dominated by the **Catedral Metropolitana** (also known as Iglesia Matríz), which, despite dating back to 1790, is underwhelming by Latin American standards.

Museo Torres García and Museo Gurvich

Two of Uruguay's finest art galleries are near Plaza de la Constitución. **Museo Torres García**, at Sarandí 683 (Mon–Sat 10am–6pm; UR$100; ☎29162663, ⓦwww.torresgarcia.org.uy), is devoted to the work of Uruguay's visionary artist Joaquín Torres García, who championed the creation of a Latin American art form and created the upside-down image of South America that is so prevalent in *artesanía* in Uruguay. Torres García's most famous pupil is honoured on the Plaza Matríz around the corner at the excellent **Museo Gurvich** (Ituzaingó 1377; Mon–Fri 10am–6pm, Sat 11am–3pm; UR$65, free on Tues; ☎29157826, ⓦmuseogurvich.org). Lithuanian Jewish immigrant José Gurvich gained fame in his own right with elaborate murals and sculptures, reminiscent of Chagall and Miró.

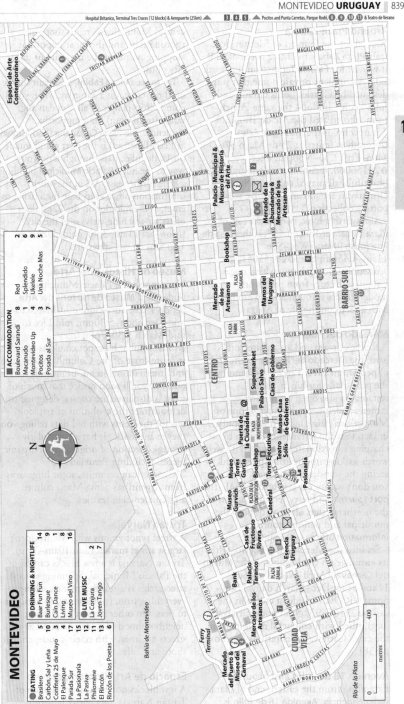

Hospital Britanico, Terminal Tres Cruces (12 blocks) & Aeropuerto (25km) ▲ 3, 4, 5 ▲ Pocitos and Punta Carretas, Parque Rodó, 8, 9, 10, 11 & Teatro de Verano

MONTEVIDEO

● EATING	
Brasilero	5
Carbón, Sal y Leña	10
Confitería 25 de Mayo	3
El Palenque	4
Parada Sur	17
La Pasionaria	15
La Pasiva	12
Philomène	11
El Rincón	13
Rincón de los Poetas	6

● DRINKING & NIGHTLIFE	
Baar Fun Fun	14
Burlesque	9
Caín Dance	3
Living	8
Museo del Vino	16

● LIVE MUSIC	
La Conjura	2
Joven Tango	7

■ ACCOMMODATION		
Boulevard Sarandí	8	Red	2
Macanudo	1	Splendido	6
Montevideo Up	4	Ukelele	9
Pocitos	3	Una Noche Mas	5
Posada al Sur	7	

N

Espacio de Arte
Contemporáneo

CENTRO

CIUDAD
VIEJA

BARRIO SUR

Bahía de Montevideo

Río de la Plata

0   400
metres

Ferry
Terminal

Mercado
del Puerto &
Museo del
Carnaval

Mercado de los
Artesanos

Bank

Palacio
Taranco

Casa de
Fructuoso
Rivera

Esencia
Uruguay

Museo
Gurvich

Museo
Torres
García

Catedral

La
Pasionaria

Puerta de
la Ciudadela

Bookshop

Torre
Ejecutiva

Teatro
Solís

Museo Casa
de Gobierno

Palacio Salvo

Supermarket

Casa de Gobierno

Palacio Municipal &
Museo de Historia
del Arte

Mercado de la
Abundancia &
Mercado de los
Artesanos

Bookshop

Mercado
de los
Artesanos

Manos del
Uruguay

10

Around Plaza Zabala

Named for the founder of Montevideo, leafy **Plaza Zabala** might be overlooked if it weren't for **Palacio Taranco** on the north side. An opulent private home that was designed by Charles Louis Girault and Jules Leon Chifflot – the same French team who created the Arc de Triomphe – it now holds the **Museo de Artes Decorativas** (entry at 25 de Mayo 376; Mon–Fri 12.30–5.30pm; free; ☎29156060, ⊛cultura.mec.gub.uy). The beautifully displayed collection includes Uruguayan art and an expansive world pottery collection.

Also worth a look, two blocks east of Plaza Zabala at Rincón 437, is the **Casa de Fructouso Rivera** (Wed–Sun 11am–4.45pm; free; ☎29151051, ⊛www .museohistorico.gub.uy), which traces Uruguay's history from prehistoric to modern times through art and artefacts, with a focus on the life of Artigas.

Mercado del Puerto

A foodie's dream and an architectural gem, the **Mercado del Puerto**, at the end of pedestrian street Pérez Castellano by the port (daily for lunch, some restaurants also open for dinner; ⊛mercadodelpuerto.com.uy), is one of Montevideo's highlights. It's so popular, in fact, that the restaurants cash in by charging extortionately; however, it's well worth soaking up the atmosphere and seeing the wandering minstrels, even if you don't stay to eat (see box, p.843). The port (*puerto*) and ferry terminal are on the northern edge, along with both the municipal and national **tourist information offices** (see opposite).

Set into the Mercado del Puerto, with its entrance on the Rambla, is the **Museo del Carnaval** (April–Nov Wed–Sun 11am–5pm; Dec–March daily 11am– 5pm; UR$90, includes a coffee in the café; ☎29165493, ⊛museodelcarnaval .org), filled with colourful exhibits from the city's Carnaval celebrations (see box, p.838).

Avenida 18 de Julio and around

Extending from the eastern end of Plaza Independencia, **Avenida 18 de Julio** is central Montevideo's main shopping thoroughfare and the most important stopping point for the majority of the city's buses.

Try to pass **Plaza Fabini**, a verdant square on the avenue, on a Saturday, when you'll come across people of all ages dancing tango (from 4pm) for a supportive audience. The **Plaza Cagancha** (also known as Plaza Libertad) is the next grand square on 18 de Julio; pass through it on your way to the huge **Palacio Municipal** building a little further east. Ask at the tourist information office at its base for a ticket to enter, as the **mirador** on the 22nd floor offers far-reaching views over the city (Mon–Sat 11am–3pm; guided tours at 11.15am on weekdays; free).

Museo de Historia del Arte

Underneath the Palacio Municipal the underrated **Museo de Historia del Arte** (Ejido 1326; Tues–Sun: mid-March to mid-Dec noon–5.30pm; mid-Dec to mid-March 1.30–7pm; free; ⊛museomuhar.blogspot.co.uk) is a treasure-trove of pre-Columbian, colonial and international items, beautifully laid out, but you'll soon notice that much of what is displayed are copies, designed to demonstrate the evolution of art; look out for the items with red dots telling you they're authentic. It has a particularly strong collection of original pre-Hispanic pieces, including Peruvian and Mesoamerican ceramics, some huge urns from Argentina's Santa María culture, and Guatemalan textiles.

Tristan Narvaja

A street synonymous with Montevideo's largest **street market** (Sun 10am–3pm), Tristan Narvaja is a few blocks east from the Palacio Municipal. Spanning several streets, this is a real flea market selling everything from fruit and veg to antiques to pets. On other days, it's a pleasant neighbourhood to wander around as the streets are lined with eclectic independent shops and cafés.

Espacio de Arte Contemporáneo

A few blocks northeast from the top of Tristan Narvaja, in a partly refurbished prison dating to 1888, you'll find the **Espacio de Arte Contemporáneo** (Arenal Grande 1930; Wed–Sat 2–8pm, Sun 11am–5pm; free; ⓦeac.gub.uy), exhibiting beautifully curated, world-class contemporary art. You can see resident artists at work in the old cells.

ARRIVAL AND DEPARTURE

By plane The Aeropuerto de Carrasco (ⓦaeropuertodecarrasco.com.uy) is 25km east of the city centre. Eschew the extortionately priced taxis (30min; UR$1200) and take a bus (every 15min; 24hr, reduced service overnight and at weekends; 25min; UR$120) run by COT (ⓦcot.com.uy) or COPSA (ⓦcopsa.com.uy) to Tres Cruces bus station. There is a US$41 tax on international flights (US$19 to Buenos Aires), and US$2 on internal flights, usually included in your ticket price, but if not, payable at the airport.

Destinations There are several daily flights with Aerolineas Argentinas (ⓦaerolineas.com.ar) and SOL (ⓦsol.com.ar) to Buenos Aires' Aeroparque and Ezeiza airports (the former is better for central BA). Buquebus (ⓦflybqb.com.uy) run the only domestic flights. International flights to: Asunción (daily; 3hr); Lima (daily; 5hr); Miami (daily; 9hr); Madrid (3 weekly); Panama City (daily; 7hr 30min); Rio de Janeiro (daily; 2hr 40min); Santiago, Chile (4 daily; 2hr 40min); São Paulo (4 daily; 2hr 30min).

By bus All intercity buses operate out of Tres Cruces bus station (ⓦtrescruces.com.uy), 2km northeast of the centre. From here bus CA1 (every 15min; 15min; UR$16) goes to the centre, down Av 18 de Julio to the Plaza Independencia, loops around the Ciudad Vieja, then returns via the same route.

Destinations International: Asunción, Paraguay (2 weekly; 22hr); Buenos Aires, Argentina (3 daily; 8–10hr); Córdoba, Argentina (daily; 15hr); Porto Alegre, Brazil (daily; 12hr); Rosario, Argentina (daily; 8–10hr); Santiago, Chile (weekly; 28hr). National: Cabo Polonio (daily; 5hr); Carmelo (hourly; 3hr 30min); Colonia del Sacramento (hourly; 2hr 45min); Minas (hourly; 1hr 40min–2hr 30min); Punta del Diablo (every 2hr; 5hr);

Punta del Este (every 30min–every 2hr, 24hr a day; 2hr); Valizas (3 daily; 4–5hr).

Backpacker bus Summer Bus (ⓣ42775781, ⓦsummerbus.com) is a beach-hopping backpacker bus which conveniently picks you up from your hostel during summer months (Nov–April; hop-on-hop-off ticket to 12 beaches US$95).

By ferry (see box below).

INFORMATION

Information and listings The website ⓦdescubrimontevideo.uy has comprehensive tourist information, including an excellent downloadable guide in English (under Montevideo – *Guía Práctica* – *Guía en Inglés*). Look out for the *Friendly Map Magazine* (ⓦfriendlymap.com.uy) at tourist information offices for LGBT listings. The government site ⓦcultura.montevideo .gub.uy (only in Spanish) is great for cultural listings.

Tourist information The Minitur office on La Rambla 25 de Agosto de 1825 at the end of Yacaré (daily 8am–10pm; ⓣ021885100, ⓦturismo.gub.uy) has the best range of maps, leaflets and information in English in Uruguay. There are also information kiosks at the airport (ⓣ26040386), and at Tres Cruces bus station (ⓣ24097399). There are municipal tourist offices (daily: April–Nov 9am–5.30pm; Dec–March 11am–5pm; ⓣ29168434) on the port side of the Mercado del Puerto, as well as outside the Palacio Municipal (ⓣ19508363).

City tours LB Tour (18 de Julio 1044, office 702, ⓣ29007159, ⓦlbtour.com.uy) run some of the most popular city tours in Montevideo, also available in Colonia; MVD Walking Tour (ⓣ096535284, ⓦmvdtour.com) does what it says on the tin as well as street art tours for around US$35. Soccer fans won't do better than Fanaticos Fútbol Tours (ⓣ099862325, ⓦfutboltours.com.uy), who live and breathe the beautiful game. *Hostel Posada al Sur* (see p.842) have responsible tourism in mind with tours that benefit locals.

GETTING AROUND

Most of the points of interest in the city are within walking distance of Plaza Independencia, while Pocitos and Punta

10

CROSSING THE RÍO DE LA PLATA

Every day, two Buquebus **ferries** leave from Montevideo (in the morning and late afternoon) to Buenos Aires (2hr 12min; UR$600–1200 one-way). For a more frequent service, both Buquebus and Seacat do a combined bus and ferry ticket to Colonia del Sacramento (see p.846), where there are ferries every couple of hours which take just one hour (around the same price) to the Argentine capital. Although less convenient and less used, the most picturesque ferry crossing is operated by Cacciola between Tigre, a northern suburb of Buenos Aires, and Carmelo, a one-hour bus ride to the west of Colonia (daily; 2hr 30min; UR$850 one-way; ⓦcacciolaviajes .com). They also run connecting buses to Montevideo. Note that there is a one-hour time difference between the countries, so check which time is being quoted on the websites.

10

TOUR URUGUAY

Uruguay's large countryside makes it difficult to tackle without a car, but there are some excellent tour operators who can get you out in the sticks.

TOUR OPERATORS

Biking Uruguay ☏ 27090636, ⊛ bikinguruguay .com; & **Bike Tours Uruguay** (☏ 099592709, ⊛ biketoursuruguay.com. Both companies run cycling tours in Montevideo and Punta del Este.

Caballos de Luz ☏ 099400446, ⊛ caballosdeluz.com. Recommended, good-value horseriding tours in Rocha department.

Lares W. Ferreira Aldunate 1322, office 14, Montevideo ☏ 29019120, ⊛ larestours.com. A popular nationwide tour operator, specializing in outdoor activities and nature.

The Wine Experience ☏ 097348445, ⊛ thewine -experience.com. South African Ryan runs raved-about gourmet food and vineyard tours from both Montevideo and Colonia; prices depend on number of people in tour.

Carretas are easily reached by bus. Note that the roads crossing Av 18 de Julio north–south change names either side of the main road.

By bus There are no route maps available, but there is a bus journey planner at ⊛ montevideo.gub.uy/aplicacion/ como-ir and a list of inner-city route numbers with destinations at ⊛ cutcsa.com.uy. You can catch buses to most parts of the city from outside the Teatro Solís. Buses heading for the centre are marked "Aduana" or "Ciudad Vieja". Ask for a "centrico" ticket (UR$16) if you're only going within the *centro*, or a "común" (UR$23) otherwise. Buses run regularly from 6am until midnight, when the service starts to thin out dramatically.

By bike Renting a bike is a popular way to see the city, and the lovely Ramblas hugging the estuary beaches makes it easy. Most hostels rent bikes cheaply. If you're staying for a while, it might be worth signing up to the free (after a one-off UR$110 fee) bike scheme. ⊛ Movete .montevideo.gub.uy (Spanish only).

By taxi Journeys within the city rarely amount to more than UR$200 in hailed street taxis or *remises* (minicabs). The meter does not give the fare but rather the distance, which corresponds to a pre-fixed rate (taxis should always have the rates displayed).

ACCOMMODATION

Although the Ciudad Vieja is dotted with cheap hotels and hostels, away from the pedestrianized Sarandí it can be unsafe at night. The Barrio Sur is a good bet for character and excellently placed for the old town and nightlife, while Punta Carretas and Pocitos are best for safety, shopping, beaches and partying. Hostels will usually offer bikes for rent and tango classes, and you can also assume that breakfast, internet and wi-fi, a/c and heat are provided unless otherwise mentioned. Prices are given for the cheapest bed or double room in high season, which starts in mid-Nov.

BARRIO VIEJO AND CENTRO

Boulevard Sarandí Sarandí 405, at Zabala ☏ 029153765, ⊛ boulevardsarandihostel.com. This

friendly family-run hostel on Ciudad Vieja's pedestrian drag has a cosy layout and is outfitted with gaucho-themed items. The living room has a bar and holds events such as jam sessions. Dorms UR$360

Macanudo Paysandu 889 ☏ 290085810. ⊛ macanudohostel.com. A 1890s house turned sleek hostel a stone's throw from the old town; rooms are spacious and beds comfy. Throw in a great roof terrace, large breakfast and friendly staff, and it's no wonder this is considered one of Montevideo's best hostels. Dorms UR$500

★**Posada al Sur** Pérez Castellano 1424 ☏ 29165287, ⊛ posadaalsur.com.uy. The most ethically conscious choice in Montevideo, with organic breakfasts and community-oriented tours. Light common areas enhance the *buena onda* ("good vibes"). Its location close to the port is great during the day, but you might want to take a taxi back at night. Dorms UR$380, doubles UR$1500, en-suite apartment UR$2000

Red San José 1406 ☏ 29088514, ⊛ redhostel.com. Up a grand staircase in a building with nice architectural flourishes, this hostel is a 20min walk to the old city, but still very central, just off Av 18 de Julio. With various communal areas, including a roof terrace and living room with fireplace, it is a nice place to relax. Dorms UR$400, doubles UR$1450

★**Splendido** Bartolomé Mitre 1314 ☏ 29156171, ⊛ splendidohotel.com.uy. This budget hotel with retro styling is truly splendid. All twenty rooms overlook Teatro Solís, and each has a different shabby-chic personality. There's a kitchen you can use and the breakfast is good; the only downside is that it's above the most popular bars in the Ciudad Vieja, so bring earplugs. Rooms sleep 1–5 people. Singles UR$850, doubles UR$1200

Ukelele Maldonado 1183 between Michelini and Ruíz ☏ 29027844, ⊛ ukelelehostel.com. You can really relax in what was the family home of owner Patricia. This enormous house with soaring ceilings eschews the institutional feel and, unusually for Montevideo, has a large pool and pretty patio garden. Breakfast is simple, and, with no central heating, the place becomes a little fridge-like in winter. Dorms UR$420, doubles UR$1500

POCITOS AND PUNTA CARRETAS

Montevideo Up Riachuelo 175 ☎27123463, ⓦmontevideoup.com.uy. A somewhat chaotic place run by a likeable family who make you feel welcome, with no set times for breakfast and free use of the washing machine. In a pleasant neighbourhood just one block from the water. Dorms UR$420, doubles UR$900

Pocitos Sarmiento 2641 ☎27118780, ⓦpocitoshostel .com. Let the good times roll in one of the city's most likeable – if cramped – backpacker joints, with a lovely garden and good rates on private rooms. The young owners also have a hostel in Colonia. Dorms UR$420, doubles UR$1500

Una Noche Mas Patria 712, Punta Carretas ☎96227406, ⓦunanochemas.com.uy. Delightful B&B in upmarket Punta Carretas in Carla and Eduardo's home. Cosy rooms, a lovely roof terrace and an abundant breakfast. Doubles UR$1440

EATING

Café culture is big in Montevideo, with several galleries and design stores doubling as cafés and small restaurants, and there are some truly great eating experiences.

BARRIO VIEJO AND CENTRO

★**Brasilero** Ituzaingó 1447 ⓦcafebrasilero.com.uy. Established in 1877, this is the most classic café in Montevideo, with cosy dark wooden walls and furniture. With its good, fresh food and huge selection of tea and coffee, it's no wonder it has been favoured by Uruguayan literary giants such Mario Benedetti and Eduardo Galeano. Coffee and cake UR$75. Daily 9am–10pm.

Confitería 25 de Mayo 25 de Mayo 655, at Bartolomé Mitre. A patisserie/bakery with an unbeatable selection of snacks and takeaway lunches, but what it's really known for are the mouth-watering pastries, sold by weight, adorning the windows. Mon–Sat 7am–9pm.

Parada Sur Paraguay, at Gardel. A neighbourhood *parrilla* with friendly service, and whose walls and food are infused with Uruguayan gaucho tradition. For the less carnivorous there is fish, pasta and salads too. Steak from UR$200. Mon & Sat 8pm–1am, Tues–Sun noon–4pm & 8pm–1am.

★**La Pasionaria** Reconquista 587. This gourmet café, beloved among the city's arty crowd, serves fresh, seasonal and inventive dishes and is tucked away in La Pasionaria art complex. Mains UR$250. Mon–Fri 10am–6pm, Sat 11am–5pm.

La Pasiva Sarandí 600, Plaza de la Constitución. A national institution for one thing and one thing only; *panchos* (hot dogs) and beer at the bar. This one is the original, but it is now a nationwide chain offering other reliable fast food. Mon–Thurs 8am–1am, Fri 8am–2am, Sat 8am–3am.

El Rincón Rincón, at Zabala, Ciudad Vieja & Buxareo 1321, Pocitos. Those really on a budget cannot do better than this *empanada* joint where everything is made to order and

arrives piping hot. There are twenty fillings to choose from, both savoury and sweet. The molten *dulce de leche* filling is divine. *Empanadas* UR$25–45. Lunch only, Mon–Fri 11.30am–2.30pm.

Rincón de los Poetas San José 1312, at Yaguarón. For big, cheap plates of comfort food, try this popular lunch and dinner spot above the artisan market in the beautiful old Mercado de la Abundancia. *Menú del día* UR$220–240. Mon–Sat 11.30am–11.30pm.

POCITOS AND PUNTA CARRETAS

Carbón, Sal y Leña España 2688, at Fco. Aguilar, Pocitos. A highly recommended *parrilla* run by a friendly husband and wife who cook arguably the best steak in the city on their wood-fired grill. Imaginative sides, stir-fries and home-made pasta too. Mains UR$200–400. Mon–Sat from 8pm. Closed Jan.

Philomène Solano García 2455, at Miñones. An elegant, but cosy, French-style café serving some great light bites – including gourmet soups, sandwiches and salads (UR$200) – as well as the finest real tea in the city. Mon–Fri 9am–8.30pm, Sat 11am–8.30pm.

DRINKING AND NIGHTLIFE

There are a number of good bars in the Ciudad Vieja, mainly along Bartolomé Mitre and Ciudadela. The area known as the "World Trade Centre" in Pocitos (Av Dr Luís A. de Herrera leading up from the Rambla República del Perú) has a huge number of bars and clubs, but they tend to be more expensive than in the centre. Bars open in the early evening and close in the early hours, when, at weekends, clubs will open.

BARS AND CLUBS

Baar Fun Fun Soriano 922 ⓦbaarfunfun.com.uy. Open since 1895, *Fun Fun* recently moved premises from its original spot, which was steeped in the history of tango,

---

★TREAT YOURSELF

El Palenque ☎29170190, ⓦelpalenque .com.uy. The fantastically atmospheric Mercado del Puerto (see p.840) has become a victim of its own success with most restaurants offering overpriced and distinctly average food. While *El Palenque* may be a little overpriced (the UR$100 cover charge could almost buy you a whole meal elsewhere), it bucks the trend by serving truly excellent food. You'll end up spending at least UR$500 for the fresh seafood and meat, cooked on the grill in front of you, but it's worth it. Usually Mon–Sat lunch & dinner, Sun lunch only; closed Sun or Mon (depending on time of year).

10

and had been visited by the likes of the Chilean president to Bryan Adams. You can watch some top tango singers and dancers while you try the house speciality drink, *uvita* (similar to grappa), for just UR$100.

Burlesque Av Dr Luís A de Herrera 1136. One of the most popular bars in Pocitos, this Americana-themed place has a massive range of whiskies (over 40), good Tex-Mex food and is a great place to start – or finish – on this buzzing nightlife boulevard. Daily from 6.30pm.

Caín Dance Cerro Largo 1833 ⊛ caindance.com. Uruguay is one of the most gay-friendly countries in South America and *Caín* is the most friendly gay club in town, getting its groove on every Friday and Saturday night. Opens at midnight, though no one goes before 3am.

Living Paulier 1050. A chilled-out grungy bar, between the centre and Pocitos, that will make you feel at home in Montevideo. The staff will join you for a shot of the house Grappamiel (UR$60), and DJs might take over the downstairs room. Wed–Sun 9pm–3/6am.

★**Museo del Vino** Maldonado 1150 ☎ 29083430, ⊛ museodelvino.com.uy. Despite its name, this is no museum but a wine (only national wines are sold) and tango bar. Live music can command covers of up to UR$250, but the ambience is well worth it. There are free *milongas* (community tango dances) every week. Tues–Sat from 9pm; tango classes Wed 8pm.

LIVE MUSIC AND CULTURE

★**La Conjura** Tristán Narvaja 1634, at Uruguay ☎ 24021245. A secondhand bookstore that also sells locally made clothes and has a cheap café (daily noon–8pm; *menú del día* UR$1300), plus live *Candombe*, tango and Afro-Uruguayan beats (Thurs–Sat from 10.30pm & Sun lunchtime).

Joven Tango Mercado de la Abundancia, San José 1312 ☎ 09015561, ⊛ joventango.org. If you are a tango enthusiast, head to the food court of this market, which is converted into a dance-floor for classes followed by dancing most nights of the week.

Teatro Solís Reconquista s/n, corner of Mitre ☎ 19503323, ⊛ teatrosolis.org.uy. Uruguayans are justly proud of their historic theatre. Shows the best of Uruguayan opera, music and theatre at subsidized prices. Tickets start at around UR$150.

Teatro de Verano Rambla Wilson, at Cachón ☎ 27124972, ⊛ www.teatrodeverano.org.uy. For some of the biggest moments during Carnaval and to see international music stars, try this big outdoor amphitheatre in Parque Rodó.

CINEMAS

Most films are shown in their original language with Spanish subtitles. The best choice of films is at Life Cinemas (ex Casablanca, 21 de Septiembre 2838, at Ellauri; ☎ 27123795, ⊛ lifecinemas.com.uy) in Punta Carretas, and the enormous

Movicenter in Montevideo Shopping (Luis Alberto de Herrera 1290; ☎ 29003900, ⊛ movie.com.uy) in Pocitos.

SHOPPING

Av 18 de Julio is Montevideo's main commercial street, while there are some large malls located in the upmarket neighbourhoods of Pocitos and Punta Carretas.

Bookshop Central shops at Sarandí 640 and at 18 de Julio 1296 with Yaguarón (shops 4–5). See ⊛ bookshop.com.uy for locations ("surcursales"). Stocks a good range of English-language novels.

Esencia Uruguay Sarandí 359. If you can't get out to the *bodegas* in the countryside, sampling Uruguay's fine wine selection at this pleasant shop may well be the next best thing.

Manos del Uruguay San José 1111. The discount store of the international brand with a range of high-quality woollen clothes, all of which are handmade in Uruguay. Open Mon–Sat.

Mercado de los Artesanos Mercado de la Abundancia, San José 1312; Mercado de la Plaza, Plaza Cagancha; Espacio Cultural Barradas, Pérez Castellano 1542, ⊛ mercadodelosartesanos.com.uy. Three excellent indoor artisan markets where you can find original, high-quality souvenirs.

La Pasionaria Reconquista 587 ⊛ lapasionaria.com.uy. A sophisticated multipurpose art complex housing a design store, boutique clothing shop, small gallery, and the excellent café *Doméstico*.

DIRECTORY

Banks and exchange You'll find ATMs in Tres Cruces Terminal, and branches of all the major banks along Av 18 de Julio in the centre, or at the World Trade Centre in Pocitos.

Embassies and consulates Argentina, Wilson Ferreira Alduante 1281 (☎ 29028623); Australia, Cerro Largo 1000 (☎ 29010743); Brazil, Convención 1343–6 (☎ 279012024); Canada, Plaza Independencia 749, office number 102 (☎ 29022030); South Africa, Dr. Gabriel Otero 6337 (☎ 26017591); UK, Marco Bruto 1073 (☎ 26223630); US, Lauro Muller 1776 (☎ 17702000).

Hospital Hospital Británico, near the Tres Cruces Bus Station on Italia 2400 (☎ 24871020), offers good private healthcare.

Internet and phone Phone Box, Av 18 de Julio, at Andes, is open 24hr.

Laundry Most of the hostels have cheap laundry services. There are no self-service laundrettes but Lavadero Mis Niños, at Andes 1333, charges UR$210 to wash and dry a backpack full of clothes.

Left luggage There is 24hr left-luggage at Tres Cruces bus terminal (UR$120/24hr). Most hostels will let you store things for free.

Post office Misiones 1328 (Ciudad Vieja), at Ejido; between San José and Soriano (central).

Tourist police Uruguay 1667, at Minas (☎ 08008226).

Western Uruguay

Although Western Uruguay in general has often been neglected by visitors heading for the eastern beaches, **Colonia del Sacramento**, just one hour away from Buenos Aires, is the most common point of entry for tourists – especially Argentine day-trippers – as well as being one of the most beautiful and intriguing towns on the whole continent. The even sleepier **Carmelo** is small Uruguayan town personified, where you can get out into the vineyards or relax at the quiet riverside beaches.

COLONIA DEL SACRAMENTO

Originally a seventeenth-century Portuguese smuggling port designed to disrupt the Spanish base of Buenos Aires across the Río de la Plata, **COLONIA DEL SACRAMENTO** (often referred to simply as "Colonia") is a picturesque town with charming little museums, plenty of outdoor activities and some of the best foodie culture in Uruguay. Despite an increasing number of tourists visiting, the town retains a sleepy indifference to the outside world and merits more than just a day-trip to get to know it.

WHAT TO SEE AND DO

Start your trip at **BIT**, the "Uruguay experience", the country's flagship tourist information centre (Odriozola 434; daily 10am–7pm; ☎45221072, ⓦbitcolonia .com; free wi-fi), two blocks from both the bus terminal and ferry port. It's architecturally interesting – built in a modernist glass box at the old railway station, beautifully integrated with the disused tracks – and is also a fantastic source of information for both Colonia and the whole country. From there it's an easy stroll around the atmospheric **Barrio Histórico** (old quarter), or there's an easy half-day excursion on foot or by bus to the eerie abandoned resort of **Real de San Carlos**.

Plaza Mayor and around

At the southwestern corner of the plaza is the 1857-constructed **lighthouse** (daily noon–6pm; UR$15), which affords great views from the cupola, while at the southeastern corner lie the remains of the old (if heavily restored) city gateway, the **Portón de Campo**. Once charged with protecting the important trade centre from invading forces, now they permanently separate old Colonia from the "new" city.

A few blocks north of the plaza, along Vasconcellos, the **Iglesia Matríz** claims to be the oldest church in Uruguay, with some columns from the original Portuguese building constructed in 1730.

The central museums

Dotted around the Barrio Histórico, a UNESCO World Heritage Site, is a series of nine modest **museums** (all 11.15am–4.45pm, each closed one day a week on different days; joint ticket UR$50; ⓦmuseoscolonia.blogspot.com). The **Museo Municipal** (closed Thurs), on the west side of Plaza Mayor, is the only place you can buy the joint ticket. It houses town treasures and a small natural history museum and is worth a peek around. A few of the other museums deserve a look if you have time, especially the restored **Casa Nacarello** (closed Tues), next to the Museo Municipal, whose tiny rooms, with period furnishings, give you a taste of colonial life. The **Museo del Período Histórico Portugés** (between De Solís and De los Suspiros on the Plaza; closed Fri) is also worth a visit; you'll find some fine *azulejos* here, and the internal walls are constructed in rectangular and diagonal brick patterns, dating back to around 1720.

The similarly named **Museo del Período Histórico Español** (De España, at De San José; closed Wed), at the north end of the Barrio Histórico, also exhibits colonial items, but, most interestingly, has seven evocative oil paintings by Uruguay's most famous contemporary painter, Carlos Páez Vilaró, creator of Casapueblo (see p.852), depicting important moments in Colonia's history.

Bastión del Carmen

If you wander along the piers on the northern edge of the Barrio Histórico, you'll notice the striking red-brick **Bastión del Carmen** (Rivadavia 223; Tues–Sun 1–8pm; free; ☎45227201), with walls dating from the time of

10

10

COLONIA DEL SACRAMENTO

Real de San Carlos (5km) ▲ 🔟

Río de la Plata

DAYMAN

CORONEL ARROYO

Feria de los Artesanos

DOCTOR DANIEL FOSALBA

PLAZA DE DEPORTES

Colonia Shopping (1km)

ACCOMMODATION	
El Capullo	4
El Nido	1
Rivera	5
Sur	2
El Viajero B&B Posada	6
El Viajero Hostel & Suites	3

EATING	
La Bodeguita	4
Buen Suspiro	7
Lentas Maravillas	3
Mi Carrito	2
Viejo Barrio	5

DRINKING & NIGHTLIFE	
Barbot	6
Tr3s Cu4tro	1

Bastión del Carmen

RIVADAVIA

Museo del Período Español

Motorent **Mini-Market**

El Abrazo **Iglesia Matriz** **Police** **Hostel Colonial**

18 DE JULIO **Motorent**

Museo Municipal Casa Nacarelo

Lighthouse

Portón de Campo

Museo del Período Portugués

Bus Terminal

Ferry Terminal

Port

B.I.T

N

0   100
metres

Governor Vasconcellos (1722–49). Once a fortress, it was converted into a factory producing soap and gelatine products in the 1880s, and a chimney from that period still stands. Today it operates as a cultural centre, with a theatre, gallery and a small museum dedicated to its history.

Real de San Carlos

Outside of Colonia's centre, the only other attraction is the **Real de San Carlos.** The brainchild of millionaire Nicolas Mihanovic, who conceived it as an exclusive tourist complex for rich Argentines, it now lies largely deserted. Between 1903 and 1912, he constructed a magnificent bullring, which was used only eight times in two years, a *frontón* (Basque pelota) court which now lies decaying, and a racecourse, which is the only part of the resort still operational.

Regular **horse races** take place, and the horses can frequently be seen exercising along the nearby beach. If you fancy a ride yourself, the *Hostel Colonial* organizes **horseriding** trips for up to two hours (UR$850) to forests and

wineries outside town. To get there either walk the 5km north along the *rambla*, or catch a bus (10min) from the bottom end of Avenida General Flores.

ARRIVAL AND DEPARTURE

By bus and ferry The terminal and port are located next to each other three blocks to the south of Av General Flores (the main street). The town centre is a 10min walk to the west along Manuel Lobo. Ferries run by Buquebus, Colonia Express and Seacat run to Buenos Aires every couple of hours (1–3hr; UR$550–1300 one-way).

Destinations by bus Carmelo (every 2hr Mon–Sat, 5 daily Sun; 45min–1hr 30min); Montevideo (every 1–2hr; 2hr 45min).

> ### ★ TREAT YOURSELF
>
> If you are tired of tackling Colonia's cobbles on foot, several companies offer **motor-scooters** (UR$190/hr), two-person **buggies** or even four-person **golf carts** (both UR$360/hr) to rampage around the streets. Motorent (Manuel Lobo 505 & Virrey Cevallos 223; ☎45229665, ⦿ motorent.com.uy) have the best prices. Relevant driving licence needed.

INFORMATION

Tourist information Colonia has no shortage of tourist information centres. BIT is the main one (see p.845); there's another branch on Manuel Lobo by the Portón de Campo, run by the Intendencia (daily 9am–6pm; ☎ 45226886, ⓦ coloniaturismo.com), and smaller offices in the bus and ferry terminals.

Tour operators Local operator Feeling Uruguay (☎ 093724893, ⓦ feelinguruguay.com.uy) can take you on city tours, as well as to vineyards on the outskirts for around US$25/person. City walks with professional guides start at the tourist information office on Lobo daily at 11am and 3pm (UR$100 in Spanish or UR$150 in English with prior reservation; ☎ 099379167). Bus Turístico Colonia (ⓦ busturistico.com.uy) runs a bus tour (US$25) and walking tour (US$20).

ACCOMMODATION

The standard of budget accommodation in Colonia is dire and prices are higher than elsewhere, though most are very central. It's worth investigating the out-of-town *estancia El Galope* (see box, p.834). Breakfast is included unless otherwise stated. For a comprehensive list of hotels and hostels by star rating, try ⓦ hotelesencolonia.com.

HOSTELS

★**Sur** Rivadavia 448, at Mendez ☎ 45220553, ⓦ surhostel.com. The lovely lads who run this and *Pocitos Hostel* in Montevideo have made it their mission to spread *buena onda* ("good vibes") among their guests, and the staff are always on hand to socialize and give a local perspective. Dorms UR$380, doubles UR$1300

El Viajero Hostel & Suites/B&B Posada W. Barbot 164 ☎ 45222683; Florida 269 ☎ 45228645, ⓦ elviajerohostels .com. Success has made this Uruguayan chain of HI hostels feel a little formulaic and institutional, but it is always a reliable choice. In Colonia, there is a hostel with some "suites" (private rooms), and around the corner is a "B&B Posada" offering very nice private rooms with TV and DVDs, some with river views. Dorms UR$410, suites UR$840, B&B Posada doubles UR$2000

HOTELS AND B&BS

These hotels provide rooms with TV, private bathrooms and a free breakfast.

★**El Capullo** 18 de Julio 219 ☎ 45230135, ⓦ elcapullo .com. Run by a British–American couple, this boutique hotel is stylish yet cosy, with a gorgeous garden and a great breakfast buffet. Not cheap, but head and shoulders above other places which charge only a couple of hundred pesos less. Doubles UR$3200

El Nido Tula Suárez de Cutinella s/n, Paraje El Caño ☎ 45203223. An adorable if remote country cottage overlooking vineyards for the ultimate laidback experience 8km from downtown Colonia. Own transport essential. There

are also two unique treehouses for rent. Doubles UR$1800

Rivera Rivera 131 ☎ 45220807, ⓦ hotelrivera.com.uy. A comfy hotel with an Alpine feel, conveniently located a block from the bus terminal and port. Doubles UR$1700

EATING

Although the restaurants in the Barrio Histórico are pricey, the quality on the whole is excellent and the ambience is hard to beat.

La Bodeguita Del Comercio 167. Buzzing, stylish place whose three terraces overlooking the river get crowded with people who've heard rumours of the best pizzas in town (UR$150). Tues–Sun from 8pm, Sun also 12.30–3.30pm.

Buen Suspiro C de los Suspiros 90 ☎ 45226160. On the most photographed street in Uruguay, only recognizable by a discreet sign, this intimate foodie heaven specializes in fine wines, cheeses, charcuterie and preserves attractively served on platters for sharing (as a main for two UR$360–580). Reservations recommended. Daily 11am–midnight.

★**Lentas Maravillas** Santa Rita 61. If you've got an afternoon to relax you won't find a cosier way to do it than perusing owner Maggie's English-language books in front of the fire or on the riverside deck. Inventive baked goods with a superb carrot cake, gourmet sandwiches (UR$290) and hot drinks. Daily noon–8pm, weekends only April–Nov.

★**Mi Carrito** Rivadavia 302. There is nowhere locals rave about for budget food more than this food truck selling the best bad food you'll ever eat. Try the epic *milanesa* for two with every topping imaginable (UR$180), or the *pancho* wrapped in bacon with mozzarella (UR$90). Daily 11.30am–4pm & 8.30pm–1am.

Viejo Barrio Vasconcellos 169. This otherwise decent Italian restaurant serves the best veal *milanesas* (like a schnitzel) this side of Vienna, including one stuffed with ham and cheese (UR$240). Mon & Thurs–Sun 11am–midnight, Tues & Wed 11am–4pm.

DRINKING AND NIGHTLIFE

Barbot Washington Barbot 160. Notable for being the first craft brewer in town, *Barbot* is buzzy, friendly and pulls a mean pint of IPA. Its central location in a revamped colonial house means there are plenty of corners to kick back in. Also serves up decent pizza and Tex-Mex (UR$150–400). Wed–Sun from 6pm.

Tr3s Cu4tro Alberto Mendez 295, ⓦ trescuarto.com. Their website says it all: "One building, two courtyards, three dancefloors, four bars, steaming hot". A great Uruguayan *"boliche"* (bar/nightclub), good for just a few drinks, or for staying up all night. There is an entry fee (UR$50–100), but once you get in, food and drinks are reasonably priced. There's often live music too. Thurs "After office" from 9pm, Fri & Sat from 11pm.

10

SHOPPING

The Barrio Histórico is littered with fashionable, pricey boutiques selling locally made as well as more generic leather goods, but the best deals for handicrafts are to be found at either the *feria* or the artisans' market (Dr Daniel Fosalba; daily 10am–6pm).

El Abrazo Flores 272. A commendable little shop selling Uruguay-specific books, including English translations of national authors Bennedetti and Galeano, music, and locally made gifts and clothes.

Colonia Shopping Roosevelt 458 ⓦ coloniashopping.com .uy. Mall with all the expected facilities, including a cinema.

DIRECTORY

Banks Av General Flores is the main commercial street and has many banks, casas de cambio and ATMs.
Hospital 18 de Julio between Rivera and Mendez.
Internet Free wi-fi in the Plaza 25 de Mayo, computers either at the main Antel office, or there's an internet café at Flores 172, open until 9pm every night.
Laundry Arco Iris on Suárez between Flores and 28 de Julio.
Left luggage Facilities at the bus terminal, and at BIT.
Post office and telephone Correo Uruguayo and Antel have main offices next to each other on Lavalleja on Plaza 25 de Agosto, and share an office in the ferry terminal.
Taxi A 24hr service is run from the corner of Flores with Mendez (ⓣ 45222920).
Tourist Police At the main *comisaría* on Flores opposite Plaza 25 de Mayo (ⓣ 45222962).

CARMELO

Despite being the only town founded by Uruguayan hero General Artigas in 1816, CARMELO isn't as historically rich as nearby Colonia del Sacramento. However, it does offer a good supply of natural resources, from quiet and pristine riverside beaches to rolling hills and boutique wineries. Carmelo is slowly picking up speed as a popular, if pricey, destination for those in the know. The town is also a good base from which to visit legendary meat-extraction town Fray Bentos, 136km up river.

WHAT TO SEE AND DO

Local **wineries** (see box opposite) welcome visitors to wine and olive-oil tastings; once the hard work is out the way, kick back on one of the sandy beaches. **Playa Sere**, at Av Grito de Asencio and Avenida Del Exodo, a fifteen-minute walk from downtown, is a shady and peaceful part of the coastline, with uninterrupted expanses of white sand.

Fray Bentos

When the Anglo meat-packing factory opened in Fray Bentos in 1858, it proved the industrial revolution had arrived on the shores of the River Plate. The plant-turned-museum **Museo de la Revolución Industrial**, Rambla Andrés Montaño, Fray Bentos (daily 9.30am–5.30pm; UR$50; ⓣ 45622918, ⓔ museo.anglo@rionegro .gub.uy), showcases the beginnings of Uruguay's beef industry – as well as offering a trip down foodie memory lane for Brits of a certain age. Agencia Central buses leave Carmelo twice a day for Fray Bentos (18 de Julio 811; ⓣ 45422987).

ARRIVAL AND INFORMATION

By plane Carmelo has a small international airport, Zagarzazú, with small charter flights and private planes arriving from San Fernando in Argentina.
By bus Although plans are afoot for a central bus station, buses arrive and depart at their own office. Berrutti is located at Uruguay 337 (ⓣ 45422504), while Chadre is at 18 de Julio 411 (ⓣ 454222987).
Destinations Colonia (hourly; 1hr 30min); Montevideo (every 2hr; 3hr).
By boat The *Cacciola* arrives twice daily to Carmelo from Tigre in Argentina.
Tourist information 19 de Abril 246, Casa de la Cultura (daily 9am–6pm).

ACCOMMODATION

If it's time to splash out, the delightful *Narbona Wine Lodge* (see box opposite) is a real treat.
Camping Náutico Carmelo Rambla de Carmelo, south of the stream ⓣ 45422058, ⓔ dnhcarmelo@adinet .com.uy. Well-sized campsite close to Playa Sere beach catering for up to 300 people. Clean bathrooms are a bonus, while *asadores* in the making can make use of the grills. Two-man tent __UR$150__
CampoTinto Camino de los Peragrinos, Colonia Estrella ⓣ 45427744, ⓦ posadacampotinto.com. A few kilometres out of town, treat yourself to one of the four rooms at this posada set among Tannat vineyards – one is a glamping safari tent. Breakfast is abundant, service professional, and there's an on-site restaurant, swimming pool and bikes for borrowing. Doubles __UR$4000__
Posada del Navegante Rodó 383 ⓣ 45423973, ⓦ posadadelnavegante.com. A stone's throw from the beach, this simple eight-room hotel comes with most mod cons such as wi-fi and a/c. Doubles __UR$1000__

WINERIES NEAR CARMELO

Bodega Familia Irurtia Ing. Quim. Dante Irurtia & Paraje Curupí ☎99692545, ⓦirurtia.com.uy. Founded in 1913 by Don Lorenzo Irurtia, this winery remains in the family's capable hands. Book ahead for a guided tour of the vineyards and *bodega* before tasting some of their wares, such as Tannat, Pinot Noir and Malbec, in a cellar steeped in history. **Narbona Wine Lodge** Av Ruta 21, Km268 ☎45404778, ⓦnarbona.com.uy. If staying at this stunning complex is way out of your budget at UR$5500 for a double room, at the very least a wine tasting is within reach. Comprising the old cellar dating back to 1909 and a more contemporary one, sample a variety of Narbona's wines at a tasting.

EATING

El Horno 19 de Abril 251, at Ignacio Barros. Locals rave about the wood-oven pizzas and *chivito* at this place. Great service helps tip the balance at this joint. UR$150–UR$3500. Daily for lunch and dinner.

Piccolino 19 de Abril, at Roosevelt. More of the same fodder at this decent diner opposite the main square serving up well-priced Uruguayan staples (UR$250–UR$300). Daily for lunch and dinner.

The Interior

Some of South America's most undiscovered natural beauty awaits you in Uruguay's interior. This is real **gaucho country** and it's easily accessible, if little known about. While most of the interior is unknown to tourists, largely because it's mostly covered in vast ranches, some of Uruguay's finest and least explored pastoral landscapes are within reach of **Minas**, a small town with a big history.

MINAS AND AROUND

Just 120km from Montevideo, but far from the usual backpacker trail, **MINAS**, the capital of the Lavalleja department, is an excellent base for exploring the rolling hills and romantic traditions of Uruguay's interior – you won't have to go far before you see a genuine mounted gaucho wearing a poncho and clutching his *mate*. Delving into this region's history can give you a deeper understanding of the Uruguayan mentality and the nation's history.

WHAT TO SEE AND DO

In Minas, there are some interesting **museums** worth visiting, as well as pleasant parks, but around Minas is where the real fun lies. **Parque del Salto Penitente**, in craggy moor-like countryside, offers outdoor adventures aplenty, while **Villa Serrana** is a copse of isolated houses offering complete rest and relaxation in pretty surroundings.

Central Minas

Most of the region's draw lies in the rolling hills surrounding the town, but there are some cultural surprises here that warrant a pause before heading out into the countryside. The city is easily navigated; the main shopping street, 18 de Julio, is parallel with Avenida Treinta y Tres which runs along the north side of the main square, **Plaza Libertad**, and onwards to the bus terminal. Full of palm trees and with a horseback statue of the national hero Juan Lavalleja, who lends his name to the department, Plaza Libertad is a pleasant place to sit and enjoy a pastry from one of the country's most renowned patisseries.

Casa de Cultura

One block south of the main plaza is the excellent series of museums housed in the **Casa de Cultura** (Lavalleja 572, at Rodó; daily 9am–7pm; free), including rooms displaying gaucho artefacts from the nineteenth century and a room dedicated to Uruguayan composer Eduardo Fabini. Independence leader Lavalleja's childhood house sits in the central courtyard; one of the forty original houses from the town's foundation, it has been restored, but its original ceiling beams made from palm trees are intact.

Teatro Lavalleja

The city's most surprising building is the grand old **Teatro Lavalleja** (Batlle y Ordoñez between Florencio Sánchez and Sarandí), a magnificent brick construction finished in 1909, with regular productions and also housing the odd **Museo del Humor y la Historieta** (Mon–Fri 8am–6pm, Sat & Sun 1–6pm; free), dedicated to caricatures.

10

10

Cerro Artigas

The city is surrounded by some very pleasant parks. **Cerro Artigas** is worth visiting for its great views of the city and surrounding hills, as well as its imposing 10m-high concrete statue of the liberator Artigas on his horse, said to be one of the largest equine statues in the world. Avenida Varela goes all the way to Cerro Artigas from central Minas – around a 45-minute walk – or a taxi costs UR$120.

Parque del Salto Penitente

At the heart of this private natural reserve is a delicate waterfall, the eponymous **Salto del Penitente**, which falls some 60m before following its course. Here there is a restaurant (open daily for lunch), precariously cantilevered off the hillside over the falls, as well as a hostel and terrace affording graceful views across the park, all under the same management (☎44403096, ⓦsaltodelpenitente.com). Sleeping is in shared wood cabins (UR$350/450 without/with linen), or you can camp, and there's a rustic common room with an open fire. Activities include horseriding, rock-climbing, zip-wiring and abseiling (all UR$150–200), as well as hiking and birdwatching. It's tricky to get to without a car, but the management can collect you from Minas or a taxi is around UR$800.

Villa Serrana

With zero amenities, other than a couple of places to stay, it's hard to even award **Villa Serrana** village status; it's more a cluster of houses 25km from Minas. However, its location is Elysian, perching on top of a horseshoe string of hills around a lake, with splendid walking, fishing and horseriding opportunities – not to mention magical sunsets. Its other major attraction is a remarkable historic hotel, the **Ventorrillo de la Buena Vista** (☎44402109, ⓦventorrillodelabuenavista.com.uy), designed by Uruguayan architect Julio Vilamajó, which attracts architecture fans from across the world. Built in 1946, its brilliance lies in its synthesis with its surroundings, and it has been tastefully restored to run as a splendid inn (see below). There are just four **buses** a week from Minas to Villa Serrana (Tues & Thurs

9am & 5.30pm, returning shortly after that; 30min), but if you're staying there you'll probably be able to arrange a lift with your hosts. Taxis cost UR$1000.

ARRIVAL AND INFORMATION

By bus Intercity and local buses arrive and depart from the Terminal de Omnibuses (☎44423178), three blocks west of Plaza Libertad on Treinta y Tres between Claudio Williman and Sarandí.

Destinations Montevideo (hourly; 1hr 40min–2hr 30min); Punta del Este (10 daily; 2hr); Villa Serrana (4 weekly; 30min).

Taxi 24hr service from the Plaza Libertad (☎095749380). Set prices to surrounding areas.

Tourist information At the bus station (daily 8am–7pm; ☎44429796, ⓦwww.destinominas.com.uy, ⓦlavalleja .gub.uy).

ACCOMMODATION

It's worth booking ahead; accommodation is limited and fills up fast, especially during Minas' large festivals over nine days in October and on April 9.

Camping Arequita 10km north of town on Ruta 12 ☎44402503, ⓦwww.lavalleja.gub.uy/web/lavalleja/ campingarequita. Set in pleasant grounds at the foot of Cerro Verdún (a grand rocky peak with caves to explore), each plot has electricity and a barbecue. Horseriding can be arranged, but there's no internet. 12km from town; buses from Minas run Dec–Feb. Self-catering cabins UR$1200, mini-cabins (beds only) UR$500, camping/person UR$100

Posada Verdún Dr Washington Beltrán 715, at Beltrán ☎44424563, ⓦhotelposadaverdun.com. The same family has run this posada, the best-value place in town, for more than two decades. The rooms are clean with private bathrooms and TV; there's also a recommended restaurant. Doubles (includes breakfast) UR$1250

★**Villa Serrana B&B** The green thatched house in Villa Serrana ☎098280811, ⓦvillaserrananp.com. Owned by the exuberant Zen López, who speaks fluent English, the house has three spacious rooms and is decorated with flea-market finds and bright colours. There is also an adjacent self-catering bungalow for groups. Horseriding and other day-trips in the country can be arranged. Breakfast included and other meals can be provided. Doubles UR$1400, bungalow (up to 8 people, breakfast not included) UR$2600

EATING

★**Confitería Irisarri** Treinta y Tres 618, Plaza Libertad. A family business originating in 1898, this confectionery shop and tearoom is one of the great treats in the region. Try their speciality – yemas – bonbons designed to look like egg yolks. Selection of pastries with coffee UR$70. Daily 9am–9pm.

Ki-Joia Domingo Pérez 489, Plaza Libertad. A surprisingly modern, decent-value parrilla with quick and friendly service and alfresco tables overlooking the plaza. The meat is good and the home-made pasta is excellent. Mains UR$170–500. Daily from 6pm; *parrilla* open from 8pm.

★**Ventorrillo de la Buena Vista** Villa Serrana. The name means "Good View Inn", and if you can't afford the UR$2200 for a double designer room (each has a living room with working fireplace as well as bed and bath), at least eat at the restaurant and enjoy one of the best views and meals in Uruguay (mains UR$200–300). Try the *Borego Confitado* – lamb, date and walnuts with beetroot pasta. Mon–Fri 10am–9pm, or 11.30pm at weekends for dinner.

DIRECTORY

Banks Av 18 de Julio is the main commercial street and has many banks, casas de cambio and ATMs.

Hospital On Av Pedro Varela between Maldonado and Dighiero ☎ 44422058.

Internet Cyber Peatonal on 25 de Mayo charges UR$20/hr.

Left luggage Facilities at the bus terminal.

Police Off Plaza Libertad down Vidal y Fuentes.

Post office Correo Uruguayo, Wáshington Beltrán, at 25 de Mayo.

The eastern beaches

Uruguay's biggest draw is its vast, and largely unspoilt, coastline. Humans have made their mark with *balnearios* (coastal resorts or villages), each with a very different feel to them. Between Maldonado and Rocha departments you can choose between the hedonistic party life in **Punta del Este**, the isolated and rugged **Cabo Polonio**, the blissful beaches and dunes of **Valizas** or wild surfing and nightlife in **Punta del Diablo**, all with shimmering lagoons full of birdlife in between.

The towns are easy to hop between, especially in the summer, but they change drastically off-season; in winter everything shuts down and they can feel completely deserted. Other than in luxurious Punta del Este, be sure to come with enough **cash** to fuel your stay; there are no banks or ATMs in the smaller villages.

PUNTA DEL ESTE

Situated on a narrow peninsula 140km east of Montevideo, **PUNTA DEL ESTE** – often written as PdE or simply called Punta – is a jungle of high-rise hotels, expensive restaurants, casinos and designer stores bordered by some of the finest beaches on the coast. Exclusive, luxurious and often prohibitively expensive, between this and the nearby towns of **La Barra** and **José Ignacio**, this is *the* place to be seen for many South American celebrities in summer.

WHAT TO SEE AND DO

The best thing to do in PdE is what everyone else does: go to the beach during the day and go drinking at night. Within striking distance and well worth the trip is the whitewashed **Casapueblo**, a remarkable villa and art gallery.

The beaches

These are what attract most visitors to Punta del Este, and two of the best are on either side of the neck of the peninsula. **Playa Mansa** on the bay side is a huge, arcing stretch of sand, with plenty of space for sunbathing and gentle waves, while **Playa Brava** on the eastern side is where you go if you're serious about **surfing**, or simply to compare your height to the fingers of the uncanny **Hand in the Sand** sculpture, one of Uruguay's most famous sights. Both sides are commonly referred to by these names, although there are actually many beaches with their own names.

Off the coast

From Playa Mansa, there are excellent views out to the wooded **Isla de Gorriti**, once visited by Sir Francis Drake (boats daily in high season if sufficient demand; UR$300/person). Slightly further off the coast lies the **Isla de Lobos**, home to one of the largest **sea-lion colonies** in the world. Calypso (opposite *La Galerna* at the entrance to the harbour; ☎ 42446152) offer expensive tours, though if you just want to see sea lions, it's worth heading down to the port itself in the early morning: they are often out sunbathing as the fishermen set sail.

On the peninsula

Life on the peninsula offers a glimpse of what the town must have been like when it was a modest holiday village a few decades back – the **port** area up to **Plaza**

10

10

el Faro is charmingly old-world and the houses represent a host of architectural styles not present in the identikit luxury developments that have sprung up all along the adjacent coastal roads.

Casapueblo

The area's best sight is the vision of Uruguayan artist Carlos Páez Vilaró – **Casapueblo** (daily 10am–sunset; UR$150 for entry to museum; upwards of UR$6000 for a room out of high season; ☎42578041, ⒲carlospaezvilaro.com.uy & ⒲clubhotelcasapueblo.com). He started the construction himself in the late 1950s, and today it's an unwieldy yet strangely beautiful villa, restaurant, hotel and art gallery clinging to the side of a craggy peninsula 15km west of Punta. Bright white and lacking any right angles, it's well worth a visit to see Vilaró's artwork and have a cocktail in the bar at sunset. To get there, take any bus from the terminal towards Montevideo and ask to be dropped at the entrance to Punta Ballena, from where you'll have a thirty-minute walk up along the peninsula. A taxi will cost UR$600–700.

La Barra

Sandwiched between forested hills on one side and golden beaches on the other, **La Barra** took over as the fashionable place to stay for those tired of the crowds of PdE, and its characterful houses are set along tree-lined dirt tracks which preserve its rustic feel. With gentrification, hippy cafés have been replaced with designer clothing stores, but it's still the place for summer nightlife, with new "it" clubs, bars and restaurants springing up each year. One kilometre from the famous **undulating bridge** connecting PdE with La Barra, you'll find the frankly bizarre **Museo del Mar & Insectario** (well signposted; daily 10.30am–5.30pm/8.30pm; UR$160; ☎42771817, ⒲museodelmar.com.uy), whose intriguing collection of marine artefacts includes a mind-boggling array of seashells, insects, and a 19m whale skeleton.

ARRIVAL AND DEPARTURE

Addresses are often given by their *parada* -- or bus stop number – which you'll see on poles in the middle of the large dual carriageway – the Costanera – which hugs the coast

either side of PdE. The streets in the peninsula have names and numbers, but addresses usually give their numbers.

By bus Punta del Este's bus station lies at the top end of Av Gorlero, just past the roundabout, at the neck of the peninsula. It's a 10min walk to the port along Av Gorlero, or a 5min walk to Playas Mansa or Brava. To reach the beaches further east, you need to get back to the main Ruta 9 by catching the #1 or #2 bus from Punta del Este to San Carlos (every 15min–1hr; 50min) from C 20 (winter), or C 26 (summer). From there most buses with Chuy as the destination will stop in Punta del Diablo (2hr 30min), or get off at Castillos for connecting buses to Cabo Polonio or Valizas. Alternatively, there are two buses direct to Castillos each day (11am & 5pm) from PdE's terminal.

Destinations Minas (4–7 daily; 2hr); Montevideo (every 30min; 2hr).

GETTING AROUND

Local buses #9, #12, #17, #19 and #24 go from C 20 (winter), or C 26 (summer) to Maldonado via Punta Shopping (every 30min; daily 6am–11pm; 20min). Codesa buses go from the terminal to La Barra, Manantiales and José Ignacio (Mon–Sat hourly 5.20am–midnight; Sun 6am–9pm; more buses in summer). See ⒲maldonado.gub.uy and ⒲codesa.com.uy for timetables (*horarios*).

Taxis Taxi stands by the beaches, on Gorlero and at the bus terminal. Minicabs are sometimes cheaper than metered cabs – PdE can get snarled up with traffic. Try Punta Remises at Artigas, at Chiverta (☎42498585), or driver José Techera (☎098447000).

INFORMATION AND ACTIVITIES

Surfing Sunvalley Surf (☎42448622, ⒲sunvalleysurf.com) have two stores in PdE, one at Playa El Emir (C 28, at Rambla Artigas) on the peninsula and the other at Playa Brava, between *paradas* 3 and 4 (daily 11am–7pm all year), and another opposite the Nike shop in La Barra (daily 11am–11pm all year).

Tourist information National tourist office at Gorlero 942, at C 30 (high season: daily 10am–1.30pm & 2.30–6pm; low season: Mon–Sat 10am–5pm, Sun noon–4pm). Local tourist office in Plaza Artigas (daily 8am–5pm or later in high season; ☎42446510), and in the bus terminal. The website ⒲vivapunta.com has good information in English.

Tour operators Most tour companies offer city tours (usually including Casapueblo), boat trips, vineyard and ranch tours, as well as organizing motorized transport such as Segways and quad bikes, or renting cars or bikes. Hostels generally provide the most backpacker-friendly tours, but try A.G.T. (☎42490570, ⒲alvarogimenoturismo.com) in the bus terminal, or DW Service (Artigas, at Chiverta; ☎42491749, ⒲dwservice.com.uy). Nationwide tour operators covering PdE are also worth checking out (see box, p.842).

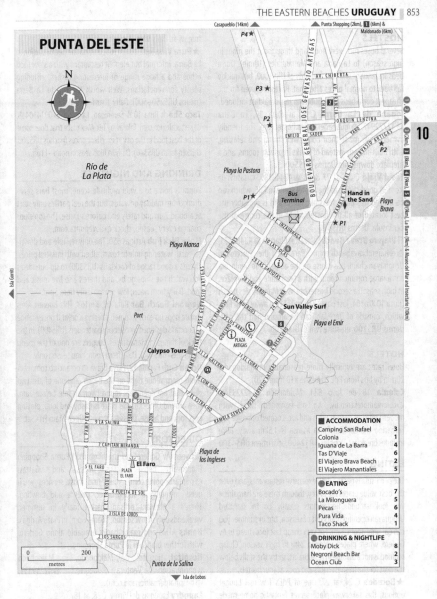

PUNTA DEL ESTE

Casapueblo (14km) ▲   ▲ Punta Shopping (2km), **1** (6km) & Maldonado (6km)

Río de La Plata

Isla Gorriti

Playa la Pastora

Bus Terminal

Hand in the Sand

Playa Mansa

Playa Brava

Sun Valley Surf

Playa el Emir

Port

Calypso Tours

PLAZA ARTIGAS

El Faro

PLAZA EL FARO

Playa de los Ingleses

0   200
metres

Punta de la Salina

▼ Isla de Lobos

■ ACCOMMODATION

Camping San Rafael	3
Colonia	1
Iguana de La Barra	4
Tas D'Viaje	6
El Viajero Brava Beach	2
El Viajero Manantiales	5

● EATING

Bocado's	7
La Milonguera	5
Pecas	6
Pura Vida	4
Taco Shack	1

● DRINKING & NIGHTLIFE

Moby Dick	8
Negroni Beach Bar	2
Ocean Club	3

ACCOMMODATION

In the summer months (Dec–Feb) accommodation is wildly overpriced (you may pay upwards of US$40 for a dorm bed), yet this does not put people off; book at least a month in advance. In winter you won't need to book and prices will be affordable again, but most hostels close down completely. Options listed here are open year-round (except the campsite). If you're stuck, try the tourist information offices, who can help with accommodation.

CAMPING

San Rafael Aparicio Saravia (no number), 800m from Parada 30 ☎ 42486715, ⊛ campingsanrafael.com.uy. Set in pleasant woods, this campsite has a minimart and wi-fi, and lies just 1km from La Barra. It's 15 percent cheaper off season and there are other discounts for longer stays; closed April–Oct. Camping/person <u>UR$250</u>, self-catering cabin (sleeps 4) <u>UR$2000</u>

10

HOSTELS

Several buses run every hour (and throughout the night in high season) to La Barra and Manantiales (10min). Dorm beds in January will cost upwards of UR$1000, but quickly fall back to normal prices after that. Prices are given for the cheapest dorm beds and doubles in Jan, breakfast included.

Iguana de La Barra C 8, at Ruta 10, La Barra ☎ 42772947, ⊛ iguanadelabarra.hostel.com. The friendly owners have made their home welcoming and relaxing, with built-in beds instead of bunks in private rooms, and a fireplace downstairs. Dorms UR$500

Tas d'Viaje C 25, at 27 & 28 ☎ 42448789, ⊛ tasdviaje .com. A good choice in the hostel scene in PdE, which can be grotty. This place feels like home and is probably the best located of all the hostels, right in the centre of the peninsula. Dorms UR$660

El Viajero Brava Beach Salazar, at Charrua ☎ 42480331, ⊛ elviajerobravabeach.com. Part of the successful Uruguayan chain, this house on the edge of the peninsula has a large common room with a pool table and fireplace. In high season a second hostel opens at Manantiales beach (Ruta 10 Km164, just past La Barra), 11km away from PdE, which, outside of Dec–Jan, can be around half the cost. Dorms UR$700, en-suite twins UR$1100

HOTELS

Hotel rates are typically more reasonable in Maldonado, 20min by bus from PdE (take the #10 from C 20).

Colonia 18 de Julio 884, Maldonado ☎ 42223346, ⊛ coloniahotel.com.uy. An old-fashioned hotel with modern touches such as wi-fi and a/c. Located opposite San Fernando church, and Playa Mansa is 1.5km away. Price includes breakfast. Doubles UR$2400, apartment UR$4300

EATING

The peninsula is packed with expensive restaurants, and even the best-value places are pricey, though there are bargains if you look around. Restaurants usually go by standard Uruguayan opening hours out of season, but in summer you can eat until about 2am. For very cheap fast food, head to Av Gorlero, where places are open 24hr in high season. Cheap seafood is not available in restaurants, so try the stalls below the port for the freshest hauls and cook at your hostel.

★**Bocado's** C 24, at 27. One of PdE's few real budget options, this takeaway place serves fantastic home-made quiches, *empanadas*, pastas, pizza and sandwiches, as well as a *menú del día*. Everything UR$200 or less. Daily from midday.

La Milonguera Joaquín Lenzina, at Blvd Artigas. The big wagon wheel outside characterizes this rustic *parrilla*, popular with locals, which serves tasty grilled meat such as *vacío* and pastas at fair prices. Mains UR$250–450. Daily noon–1am.

Pecas Golero, at Las Focas. Better than its rivals across the street, and slightly cheaper (ice cream: two flavours and two toppings UR$85), *Pecas* also serves breakfasts and has

free wi-fi. Daily 9am–late.

★**Pura Vida** Ruta 10 Km160, behind the petrol station in La Barra. Informal but elegant restaurant with a slow food ethos and a huge range of interesting dishes, including plenty for vegetarians. Well worth the trip to La Barra (mains UR$250–500). Daily 10am–midnight.

Taco Shack Ruta 10 & Serenidad, La Barra ☎ 091410448, ⊛ restocalexico.com. Takeaway Tex-Mex place that does some of the best food in the city at excellent prices (nachos UR$200, chicken fajita UR$340). Daily in high season noon–11pm.

DRINKING AND NIGHTLIFE

Punta is home to a wild nightlife scene; most bars serve drinks from midday onwards, but the real parties only start at around 2am and rarely end before sunrise. The top clubs change every season; check ⊛ ilovepunta.com.

Moby Dick Pub Artigas 650. The only reliable and down-to-earth watering hole in town, albeit with inflated prices. There's a good range of cocktails (UR$300) to sip outside as you watch the ships go by, and there's also live music and food. Daily from noon; low season daily from 5pm.

Negroni Beach Bar Ruta 10, Km163. This Buenos Aires fixture pops up each summer, offering a great if pricey range of cocktails designed by celebrity bartenders (UR$400). In the thick of things in Manantiales, burgers are one of the menu highlights (UR$400). Daily from noon; high season only.

Ocean Club Parada 12, Playa Brava ⊛ oceanclub.com.uy. A multi-room venue right on the beach, and one of just two clubs that are open year-round (women free before 2am, men around UR$300), this place is flashy and loud, playing pop, rock and house. Dress to impress. Opens 1am Fri–Sat.

DIRECTORY

Between Av Gorlero and the huge mall Punta Shopping (Roosevelt between Los Alpes and Gattas; ⊛ puntashopping.com), you'll find most services you'll need, including a supermarket, cinema and bowling. There's a pleasant artisan market (daily in summer, weekends only in low season, 10am–6pm) in Plaza Artigas.

Banks ATMs and major banks available along Gorlero, with further branches in Punta Shopping.

Hospital Hospital de Maldonado, in Maldonado (Continuación Ventura Alegre; ☎ 42559137, ⊛ hospitaldemaldonado.com).

Laundry Espumas del Virrey, C 28, at 18.

Police Colonia 1021 (☎ 08008226).

Post office Correo Uruguayo, Golero 1037.

CABO POLONIO

Moving east from brash Punta del Este can be quite a shock to the system – the *balnearios* thin out and become increasingly rustic – but even the most hardy rural-dweller would find the lack of infrastructure in **CABO POLONIO** surprising. Originally no more than a few fishermen's huts, the settlement consists of some eighty permanent residents who still live in extremely rustic dwellings; the cape with its dunes and forests is protected as a national park and camping is not allowed.

There's nothing to see or do other than soak up the beauty of the cape, spot **sea lions** near the 120-year-old **lighthouse**, or hike (you can walk unobstructed both ways along the coast to Valizas 10km to the east, or as far as La Pedrera 43km to the west). Ask around to arrange horseriding, or trips to the **Laguna de Castillos** with its strange *ombú* trees. Although in high season it can be inundated with tourists during the day, it still exudes a dreamy, other-worldly isolation, thanks to its lack of roads and electricity, best experienced by staying overnight.

ARRIVAL AND DEPARTURE

To get to the cape from Valizas it's possible to hike, ride or pay someone with a rowing boat, but most guests arrive via the visitor centre (☏ 095643217, ⌨ turismorocha.gub.uy) at the entrance to the national park at Km264.5 of Ruta 10. This is where any bus from Montevideo (daily) or Castillos (at least 3 daily; more during summer) to Cabo Polonio will drop you (the car park here costs UR$185/24hr). From here walk the final 7km (over sand), or pay one of the 4WD drivers to take you (30min drive; hourly 7am–10pm Dec–Feb, less frequent March–Nov; UR$170 round trip).

ACCOMMODATION AND EATING

Cabo Polonio Hostel ☏ 099445943, ⌨ cabopoloniohostel.com. A rustic place with solar-powered electricity and a pedal-powered washing machine. Meals can be arranged here, at other lodging/ restaurants in the village, or bring your own supplies. Dorms UR$800, doubles UR$2400

Lo de Dani Plaza Principal. Sweet wooden and tin roof eatery on the main square serving up *chivitos*, pizza, fresh fish and *milanesas*. Dishes from UR$180. Open all year round.

BARRA DE VALIZAS

In the summer, Cabo Polonio's slightly more grown-up next-door neighbour, **VALIZAS** (as it's more commonly known), feels like you're at one big festival. You'll either love or hate the hazy, dreadlocked, guitar-strumming vibes, with people practically living on the enormous and

ancient sand dunes from Christmas until Carnaval in February, but it's worth staying both for its beauty and because in January, when prices along the coast soar, you'll find better value here. Out of season you'll have the sweeping sun-bleached beaches completely to yourself.

ARRIVAL AND DEPARTURE

By bus There are local buses from Castillos (every 2–3hr; 30min) and Montevideo (4 daily; 4–5hr).

ACCOMMODATION AND EATING

Lucky Valizas No address; simply stroll across the football pitch one block to the right of where the bus will drop you ☏ 44754070, ⌨ luckyvalizas.com. Stay with Lucky in her home-turned-eco-hostel; she knows everyone in town and can arrange horseriding or boats to Cabo Polonio. Prices include breakfast and are halved, or more, off-season. Dorms UR$580, cabins for two UR$1470, camping/pitch UR$350

El Rabuk By the lake. The only restaurant open year-round, this husband-and-wife team serve excellent fresh fish at bargain prices. Grilled fish with salad UR$190.

PUNTA DEL DIABLO

For a similar mix of remoteness and natural beauty to Cabo Polonio but within reach of a supermarket, electricity and heady nightlife, **PUNTA DEL DIABLO** is the place to go. Stay in a hostel or beach cabin; relax in a hammock or go out and hit the waves.

WHAT TO SEE AND DO

During the summer months the population swells from some 1500 inhabitants to over 20,000 and you'll find pop-up businesses, hostels and internet facilities appear – they even wheel in an ATM. The rest of the year you're pretty much stuck with a handful of restaurants by the **Playa Pescadores**, the main beach strewn with fishing boats (a tourist information office springs up here during summer months).

The **surfing** is excellent all year, and the hostels are the best place to rent gear out of season. There are other beaches either side of Pescadores: northeast the **Playa Grande** is vast and will lead you to the **Parque Santa Teresa** 10km away (around a 3hr walk), a small national park with some easy forest treks and an impressive fort. Along the southwest edge of town, the **Playa de la Viuda** tends to get the biggest

10

waves, although all are good for surfing and the abundance of wide beaches means it never gets unbearably crowded.

Don't miss the twenty-minute walk up Avenida Central (starts at the northern end of the Playa Pescadores) until the houses start to thin out. Keep looking to your right, and soon you'll come across **La Casa Mágica** – the Magic House. Built by a local woodworker, it's in the shape of a head, the steps leading up to the door form the tongue, and it's made entirely from carved wood and found objects. When someone's in, you'll be welcomed inside to admire the workmanship and artwork.

ARRIVAL AND DEPARTURE

By bus In high season, buses stop at the new terminal on Bulevar Santa Teresa, about 3km from the centre. In low season, they all go into town to Av los Pescadores, the street that leads to the main beach, from where you'll be able to spot the hostels off to the right when you look back. Offices for the three bus companies which serve the town are located at the terminal; however, you can pay on board, though you might lose your seat to a pre-paid traveller.

Destinations Chuy (5 daily; 2hr); Montevideo (10-plus daily; 5hr); Rocha (12-plus daily; 2hr); San Carlos (for Punta del Este; 6 daily; 3hr 30min).

ACCOMMODATION

Hostels have sprung up in the last few years; check online before you go for hostels which open seasonally. Locals throughout the town also rent out their cabañas for tourists – look out for the signs saying *se alquila*, but these are generally only cheaper if you're in a group. Expect the prices to be more than halved outside of Dec–April.

Botella al Mar @ marosierras@gmail.com, @ marosierras .blogspot.com. Two sweet white cabins just 150m from the Playa Pescadores right in the centre of town; one sleeps 2 and the other 4. They come fully equipped (apart from sheets and towels), and have sea views. Cabin for two per day, min stay 7 days **UR$1900**

★**La Casa de las Boyas** C 5 s/n, also access from Av Central ☎ 44772624, @ lacasadelasboyas.com. This well-equipped hostel – the oldest in town – sprawls over several buildings all connected with wooden walkways. Kitchenettes in the dorms furthest away from the house, lots of bathrooms and a swimming pool elevate this from the rest. Dorms **UR$375**, lofts (sleeps up to 10) with kitchenette **UR$1800**

★**El Diablo Tranquilo Hostel & Suites** Hostel on Av Central, Suites opposite on beach ☎ 44772647, @ eldiablotranquilo.com. Bright red hostel with open-plan common areas and a fun terrace kitchen with sea views, which compensate for the rather cramped dorms.

CROSSING THE BRAZILIAN BORDER

Crossing the border is straightforward if you catch an international **bus** from Montevideo or any major town (the last of which is San Carlos) on the Ruta 9 heading north: the bus driver will take your passport details at the start of the journey and get all the required stamps for you en route. If you want to stop in Chuy itself (a haven for duty-free and electrical shops and not much else), or are planning to cross the border from any of the beach towns on the northern coast, it becomes more complicated. It is essential that you have all the correct visas in place, and receive all necessary **entrance and exit stamps** from both the Uruguayan and Brazilian border controls before entering Brazil.

All local buses heading north stop at the Brazilian border, 2km to the north of Chuy, but Uruguayan bus drivers do not routinely stop at the Uruguayan border control, so you'll have to ask to get off. The **tourist office at customs** (daily 9am–5pm; ☎ 44743627, @ turismorocha.gub.uy) can assist with information regarding crossings.

There are boutique en-suite rooms and dorms in both locations; the newer building is on the beach with a funky bar for guests. Dorms **UR$1300**, doubles **UR$2400**

EATING AND DRINKING

The best place to start for food or drink is the Av los Pescadores, leading down to Playa Pescadores. In high season bars and clubs open down by Playa de la Viuda and at the top of Av Central (there are huge parties held near the old bus station). Everywhere runs on less than reliable opening hours out of season. In summer everything opens late and closes late.

Cero Stress Close to the police station, Av los Pescadores. Suitably nautical and also nice, this space is one of the better dining options in Punta del Diablo, plus it boasts a deck with a sea view. Tuck into the catch of the day dressed up in a hearty stew (UR$410), or one of the many beef cuts (UR$250). Friendly staff is a bonus. Open all year round.

Lo de Olga Av los Pescadores. Olga has over 30 years' experience serving up the freshest fish in town with an excellent range of seafood, fish, pastas and Uruguayan staples like *chivitos*, all under UR$350. Service can be haphazard. Ask for the *menú turístico*, which will be much cheaper than *à la carte*.

Mirjo Av los Pescadores. A classy joint serving fine food and Italian coffee right by the beach. Grilled fish with side dish UR$300.

ORINOCO DELTA

Venezuela

HIGHLIGHTS

❶ **Mérida** A high-altitude adventure sports paradise. **See p.891**

❷ **Los Llanos** Endless horizons, stunning wildlife, and cowboys. **See p.896**

❸ **The Amazon** Tropical rainforest and otherworldly geography. **See p.899**

❹ **Angel Falls** The world's tallest waterfall. **See p.905**

❺ **Orinoco Delta** A vast region of waterways and indigenous tribes. **See p.909**

❻ **Parque Nacional Mochima** Deserted beaches, luminescent plankton and fantastic seafood. **See p.912**

HIGHLIGHTS ARE MARKED ON THE MAP ON P.859

ROUGH COSTS

Daily budget Basic US$20, occasional treat US$30 (see box, p.861)

Drink Polar beer (300ml) US$0.20

Food *Arepa* US$0.80

Budget hotel US$5

Travel Caracas–Mérida (680km) by bus, US$25

FACT FILE

Population 30 million

Language Spanish

Currency Bolívar Fuerte (BsF). See box, p.861

Capital Caracas (population: 2.1 million)

International phone code ☏ 58

Time zone GMT -4hr 30min

Introduction

One of the most underrated destinations in South America, today Venezuela is not only a fantastically cheap destination, but also one of the most rewarding for those who like to get off the beaten track. An outdoor-lover's paradise, the country boasts nearly every natural environment: towering mountains, mini-deserts, endless plains, Caribbean beaches, lush green jungle and wildlife-rich wetlands. You'll also find a passionate and welcoming people, proud of their nation and keen to showcase it to foreign visitors. While the Colombian borderlands and Caracas are not particularly welcoming, those who venture to destinations better equipped for foreign visitors will discover a culture like no other. Venezuela, still mourning the loss of President Hugo Chavez, is an eye-opening experience of one of the last surviving socialist regimes.

With 43 **national parks** preserving the country's natural beauty, Venezuela's prime attractions lie outside its major urban areas. Its capital, **Caracas**, a lively city of petrol-financed concrete, is towered over by the jungled **Ávila**, a stunning mountain range separating the city from the Caribbean coast – a geographical feature which affords the capital one of the planet's most agreeable year-round climates. Most visitors explore at least part of Venezuela's stunning 2600km-long Caribbean **coast**. Several hours east of the capital, **Parque Nacional Mochima** boasts red-sand beaches, fishing villages, fantastic seafood and playful dolphins, while **Parque Nacional Henri Pittier**, about three hours west, offers wildlife-spotting opportunities, crystal-clear lagoons and a lively social life. Further west is **Parque Nacional Morrocoy**, which features picturesque white-sand cays. More exclusive, the **Los Roques Archipelago** in the Caribbean contains the country's most pristine beaches with fewer crowds, given the off-mainland transport issues.

An overnight bus ride from the coast will take you to **Mérida**, in the northern extent of the continent-spanning Andes range. Mérida is also the best place to arrange trips to **Los Llanos**, the extensive plains that provide some of the best wildlife and birdwatching opportunities on the continent. The enormous region of **Guayana** encompasses most of the south and east portions of the country and boasts a number of adventure-based attractions. Here you'll find the **Orinoco Delta**, a labyrinth of jungle waterways formed as the enormous river reaches the Atlantic Ocean. Further up the Orinoco, the historic town of **Ciudad Bolívar** is the most

WHEN TO VISIT

Venezuela can be visited year-round, but you are most likely to get the best out of visiting during the November-to-May **dry season**. On **the coast**, there is less rain and fewer mosquitoes, although humidity is an issue year-round. Wildlife spotting in **Los Llanos** is much better in the dry season, when animals congregate at the few watering holes, while the abundance of mosquitoes during the wet season makes walking very unpleasant. Travel in the **Guayana** region is more comfortable during the dry season, though Angel Falls tends to be fuller and therefore more spectacular during the wet season.

If you are after beach time, it is best to come outside the national holiday periods of Easter, Carnaval (which begins at the end of Feb or beginning of March), Christmas (Dec 15–Jan 15) and the summer holidays (July 15–Sept 15). Venezuelans generally spend their holidays at the beach and the hordes drive prices up and the tranquillity down.

VENEZUELA

CARIBBEAN SEA

Aruba
Paraguaná Peninsula
Bonaire
Curaçao
Punto Fijo
Golfo de Venezuela
Malcao
Coro
Los Roques Archipelago
Chichiriviche
PARQUE NACIONAL MORROCOY
Maracaibo
Lago de Maracaibo
Barquisimeto
Choroní
Maracay
PARQUE NACIONAL HENRI PITTIER
CARACAS
Puerto La Cruz
Santa Fe
Chacopata
Isla de Margarita
Porlamar
Guiria
Tobago
Trinidad
El Vigía
Trujillo
Mérida
Barcelona
Canipe
Maturin
PARQUE NACIONAL MOCHIMA
Cúcuta
Bañas
San Cristóbal
Tucupita
Orinoco Delta
Bucaramanga
San Fernando de Apure
Los Llanos
Apure
Orinoco
Puerto Ordáz
San Félix
Ciudad Bolívar
La Paragua
PARQUE NACIONAL CANAIMA
Tunja
Puerto Páez
Puerto Carreño
Puerto Ayacucho
COLOMBIA
Angel Falls
Canaima
GUYANA
Mt Roraima (2810m)
Santa Elena de Uairén
Boa Vista
BRAZIL
San Carlos de Río Negro
San Simón de Cocuy

HIGHLIGHTS

1 Mérida
2 Los Llanos
3 The Amazon
4 Angel Falls
5 Orinoco Delta
6 Parque Nacional Mochima

Metres
4000
2000
1000
500
200
0

N

0   100 kilometres

11

economical base from which to explore **Parque Nacional Canaima**, where **Angel Falls**, the world's highest waterfall, plunges a vertical kilometre into the jungle below.

CHRONOLOGY

C.13,000 BC–1498 AD Roughly 500,000 indigenous people live in the area today covered by Venezuela, belonging to three principal ethno-linguistic groups: Carib, Arawak and Chibcha.

1498 Christopher Columbus arrives August 4 at the eastern tip of the Paria Peninsula and continues south to the Orinoco Delta.

1502 Italian Amerigo Vespucci sees the Arawak houses on wooden stilts in Lake Maracaibo and calls the place Venezuela, or "little Venice". Enslavement of the indigenous population for pearl harvesting begins.

1521 The first European settlement is established at Cumaná, on the northeast coast, serving as a base for Catholic missionaries and further exploration.

Late 1500s The Creoles, Spanish descendants born in the New World, accumulate slaves, agricultural wealth and a large degree of autonomy.

1819–21 Simón Bolívar, a wealthy Creole landowner from Caracas, wins several naval battles against the Spanish and liberates the territory of Colombia. Bolívar proclaims the new Republic of Gran Colombia, an independent nation made up of modern-day Venezuela, Colombia and Ecuador.

1829 Gran Colombia disbands in the face of irreconcilable internal disputes, and Bolívar, bitterly disappointed by the dissolution of his dream, succumbs to tuberculosis.

1859–63 A power struggle between Liberals and Conservatives, known as the Federal War, results in Liberal control of Venezuela for forty years.

1908–35 General Juan Vicente Gómez rules the country and becomes one of Venezuela's most brutal dictators. Press and public freedoms are curtailed and political dissidents murdered.

1918 Oil is discovered in Venezuela along the Caribbean coastline, and ten years later the country is the largest producer in the world. Gómez pays off foreign debts and invests in infrastructure.

1973 Carlos Andrés Pérez is elected and governs Venezuela through one of its most prosperous periods, during which the petroleum industry is nationalized.

Late 1970s–80s Increased oil production in other countries sends prices spiralling downwards. Inflation and unemployment increase and Venezuela sells much of its precious oil reserves to pay its debts.

1992 A mid-level military officer named Hugo Chávez launches an unsuccessful coup attempt against Pérez and is imprisoned; soon after, Pérez is found guilty of corruption charges.

1994 Chávez is pardoned for his coup attempt and continues gathering support around the country.

1998 In a landslide victory over former Miss Universe Irene Sáez, Chávez is elected president and, through a referendum, establishes a new constitution that dismantles the Senate, increases state control over the oil industry and grants the military greater autonomy.

2000 Chávez wins a new election.

2002 Government officials and the middle class, angered by Chávez's reform laws and a weakening economy, incite massive, violent protests on April 11; the next day, Chávez is taken into military custody. Two days later the interim government collapses and Chávez regains control.

2007 Chávez attempts to pass, by national referendum, a constitutional reform that would facilitate federal expropriation of private property and, most controversially, allow him to be re-elected indefinitely. He is narrowly defeated. Shortly after, Chávez turns the clocks back a half-hour, claiming it will increase the country's productivity.

2010 The opposition overturns Chávez's two-thirds majority in Parliament, reducing the president's sway on the National Assembly.

2012 Hugo Chávez wins his third presidential election, defeating his closest challenger yet, Henrique Capriles. The victory extends Chávez's term as president until 2018, although he misses his January inauguration due to ill health.

2013 Hugo Chávez's death to cancer is announced by the Venezuelan government. Following a closely fought emergency presidential election, former foreign minister and Chavez's anointed heir, Nicolas Maduro, wins the presidency by less than one percent. Over 25,000 murders are committed in Venezuela during the year.

2014–15 Inflation in Venezuela hits sixty percent and keeps rising – the highest in the world. Black market rates reach fifteen times the official and shortages throughout the country cause 5hr queues to get hold of staples such as flour and oil. Global oil prices hit a fifty-year low.

ARRIVAL AND DEPARTURE

Venezuela can be reached by land from neighbouring Colombia and Brazil, but not from Guyana to the east, and by sea, usually from Isla de Margarita (see p.915) from surrounding Caribbean islands.

BY AIR

Nearly all international flights land at Simón Bolívar International Airport in Maiquetía (often known simply as **Maiquetía Airport**), between 45 minutes and an hour from central Caracas. Services and public transport are available at the airport (see p.872).

BY BUS

Long-distance international buses arrive from neighbouring **Colombia** and **Brazil** and head for Caracas, nine to fifteen hours from the Colombian border crossings, depending on where you cross (see box, p.888), and up to 24 hours from the main Brazilian crossing. Border formalities for international bus passengers are generally straightforward, though you are responsible for arranging any necessary visas, vaccinations and exit/entry stamps.

PASSPORTS AND VISAS

Citizens of the US, Canada, Australia, New Zealand, South Africa, Ireland, the UK and other EU countries do not need a **visa** to enter Venezuela. Upon arrival from Brazil you may be asked for a certificate of yellow fever vaccination. You will need to present a passport valid for at least six more months and they will often ask to see an onward ticket.

Always keep multiple photocopies of your passport to hand as Venezuelan officials can be fastidious. Make sure you have your passport number memorized, as you will be asked to supply it for nearly every transaction you make in the country.

To extend your stay for an additional ninety days, go to SAIME, the country's immigration agency, in Caracas (see p.878). Bring your passport, two photos and your return or onward ticket. The process takes a maximum of 72 hours (although it is usually issued the same day) and costs roughly US$50.

GETTING AROUND

Travellers are best off using the convenient and inexpensive public transport system of buses and *por puestos*. Internal flights

MUCH ADO ABOUT MONEY

Visitors to Venezuela should not use ATMs, pay with bank cards or use any form of electronic payment which will incur charges at the official exchange rate, a rate which will have you paying $30 for a simple arepa. Instead, travellers should sell international currency (either in the form of cash or international bank transfers) at **black market rates**. This is due to the country's current economic situation:

Venezuela's government sets a value for its currency (BsF6.3 to US$1 at time of writing) rather than floating it on the international market. At the same time the state controls which citizens are allowed to exchange their Bolívars for other currencies. This means that ordinary Venezuelans without political connections cannot get hold of international currency, and are desperate to exchange a currency whose inflation rate tops 60 percent.

While exchanging money in this manner – known as the *mercado negro*, *oscuro* or *paralelo* – is technically illegal for Venezuelans, it should be no cause of concern for international travellers, who will not incur punishments for doing so.

Dollars are easily exchanged with Venezuelans (every hotel listed in this guide will exchange at paralelo rates), and the only issue you will encounter will be at what price to sell.

The website **dolartoday** gives the daily value of the Bolívar against the dollar (the number represents how many BsF you can expect per single dollar exchanged). The website is constantly being shut down by the government, although an internet search will direct you to its latest location. Don't accept anything less than five points off the dolartoday price for bank transfers, or ten points less for cash. If your hotel is offering you less, any independent business may offer more favourable rates.

Do not change money in the airport or border towns. If unavoidable, change only enough to reach a hotel where more favourable rates will be available. Unfortunately, carrying large amounts of cash is often unavoidable, as it is often better to change large amounts while a favourable rate is available. Ensure that your stash is divided between different locations in your luggage.

As a result of **massive inflation** in Venezuela it is unlikely that, although accurate at the time of research, hotel and restaurant prices listed in this guide will be accurate.

You do not have to declare carrying cash up to the value of US$10,000 when entering the country.

are an unreliable alternative if you wish to avoid the longer overland routes.

BY AIR

Flying within Venezuela is a stressful experience, made more difficult for international travellers subject to the whims of uncompromising airline staff. Booking domestic flights online yourself is best avoided as you need a Venezuelan *cédula* (national identity card). You can reserve flights in person through airline offices in major cities and at airports, or – the least stressful option – have a Venezuelan travel agency do it for you. Flights are often booked up many weeks in advance during the high season.

Always call to confirm flight times, and arrive at airports up to two hours in advance, as queues can be formidable. Bring your passport and two photocopies. Domestic flights are usually subject to a *tasa* (tax) of around BsF60.

BY BUS

Buses are the primary mode of transport throughout Venezuela and invariably the cheapest. Tickets go on sale on the day of departure and are bought from the various private company ticket booths in the bus terminals. In smaller towns your hotel can reserve your ticket ahead of time. Venezuelans book all bus travel with their national identification numbers (*cédula*), for which you should use your passport number. You'll usually have to pay a *tasa*, or tax, on top of the bus fare; costing around BsF4, the *tasa* is a ticket bought from the dedicated terminal booth and presented when you board the bus or depart the terminal. Most regional bus services end at around 6pm or 7pm; overnight services to more distant destinations sometimes depart as late as midnight or 1am.

Local buses, or *busetas*, are minibuses, recognizable by the myriad destination cards stuck to the inside of the windscreens, which can be hailed from roadsides along their routes. Payment is either collected when the bus is in motion or when you alight. If you want to get off at a specific point, shout "*parada!*" (meaning "stop") at the driver, who will let you off at the nearest possible place. Economical buses, or *servicio normal* (roughly BsF60/hr), are common for shorter distances. These are often cramped, with no toilet or air conditioning; when choosing your seat, try to select one away from the sound system as music is blasted at deafening volumes. More comfortable executive buses, or *servicio ejecutivo* (about BsF100/hr), run longer distances and have toilets. Air conditioning, however, is so intense that you'll need a blanket or sleeping bag. If you're travelling overnight, be sure to take a *bus-cama*, with almost fully reclining seats (about BsF150/hr).

BY POR PUESTO

Another economical option is the ubiquitous **por puesto** or **carrito**. Essentially shared taxis, *por puestos* are gas-guzzling American sedans in which you pay for one of four or five places and depart when the car is full. They are generally twice the price of a bus ride, but take half the time and are sometimes the only available option. "*¿Cuantos faltan?*" is a useful expression to ask how many places are still to be filled before the car can depart.

BY TAXI

Taxis never have meters, so you should agree on a price before your journey. In towns where public buses are rare, taxis are the established way of getting around. In these cases, fares within the town are set; ask a local beforehand. Don't get into the car until you've agreed upon the price.

VENEZUELA TOURS

Hugo Chávez famously said, "we don't need tourism, we have oil!". Ten years on, despite the country's tanking economy caused by dropping oil prices, Venezuela has yet to develop any passable infrastructure for budget holidaymakers. This means that independent travellers often turn to **agencies** for assistance in arranging trips and activities to the country's top attractions. Booking tours is always cheapest in the closest town to the attraction itself, but if your time is limited, or if you're looking for a multi-destination tour, the following Caracas- and Mérida-based companies can arrange trips anywhere. Companies will require payment either in cash or to an international bank account (see p.861), allowing you to pay at *mercado paralelo* rates. Don't pay with credit cards within Venezuela.

TOUR OPERATORS

Akanán C Bolívar, Ed Grano de Oro, Ground Floor, Chacao ☎0212 715 5433, ⓦakanan.com. Akanán's office has plenty of material for researching trips, and Rough Guide readers can use the internet for free. Clients who opt not to hire a guide are lent a mobile phone for use on their travels.

Andes Tropicales ☎0274 263 8633, ⓦandestropicales .org. A Mérida-based company devoted to helping local communities protect the natural environment while promoting tourism in remote areas.

Angel Eco-Tours Av Casanova, at 2da Av de Bello Monte, Ed La Paz, Oficina 51, Sabana Grande ☎0212 762 5975, ⓦangel-ecotours.com. British expat Paul Stanley runs this excellent agency specializing in slightly more luxurious travel than affiliate Osprey. The company also does a huge amount of community work

wherever its tours go, and is particularly active with the indigenous Pemón community of Parque Nacional Canaima (see p.905). Payments in US dollars.

Club Aventurismo Av Andres Bello and 2nd Transversal, Los Palos Grandes ☎0212 285 8541, ⓔclubaventusimo@gmail.com. A tour company covering the entire country, Club Aventurismo offers complete packages ranging from Los Roques beach breaks to exploring the heart of Venezuela's Amazon. Pricing in Bolívars make this a very economical option.

Osprey Expeditions Same office as Angel Eco-Tours ☎0212 762 5975 or ☎0414 310 4491, ⓦospreyexpeditions.com. The most economical option for backpacker-friendly, nationwide trips, with exceptionally friendly staff. They can also organize pick-ups from Caracas airport.

ACCOMMODATION

Naturally enough, you'll find Venezuela's best low-end **accommodation** in the towns that attract the most backpackers. Consequently Mérida (see p.891), Choroní (see p.881) and Ciudad Bolívar (see p.901) have excellent budget options. Cheap accommodation is generally poor in larger cities such as Caracas and Puerto La Cruz. It's not uncommon for budget hotels in larger towns to rent out rooms by the hour, and although this is no cause for safety concern, it may offer a clue as to how backpacker-friendly your hotel is. Nevertheless, you can always expect clean sheets and towels. Hot water is rare outside Mérida and other Andean towns.

Dormitories are not common, while youth hostels are virtually non-existent; solo travellers are often stuck paying for a *matrimonial* (double), cheaper than a twin but more expensive than a single. Quality is much higher beyond the big cities and usually appears in the form of **posadas**, affordable family-owned guesthouses, often with lots of individual character. Many posadas and backpacker spots are run by French and German expats.

Camping hasn't caught on among Venezuelans, and in general is not recommended because of the risk of robberies, even on isolated beaches and cays. The safest time to camp is on weekends and during national holidays. For more information, contact Inparques (☎0212 273 2701, ⊚inparques.gob.ve).

FOOD AND DRINK

Venezuelan cuisine centres around **meat**, with the most common accompaniments being rice, black beans and *tajadas* (fried plantain strips). Corn flour is the carbohydrate staple of all Venezuelan cooking, the base (and often sole) ingredient in **arepas** (fried cornbread disks), **empanadas** (fried savoury turnovers), **bollos** (boiled corn dough) and the **cachapa** (a sweet-meal pancake folded over a slab of cheese). The **arepa**, the quintessential Venezuelan food, is ubiquitous and given variety by the endless number of fillings which are

available. Among the most common are *carne mechada* (shredded beef), *quest amarillo* (yellow cheese) and *reina pepeada* (shredded chicken, mayonnaise and avocado). *Arepa* can be very thick, and those with smaller appetites should tell the restaurant to "*saca la masa*" (scoop out the uncooked interior) before inserting the filling. *Areperas*, restaurants serving up the staple, are generally open 24 hours.

Though rather difficult to find, **vegetarian food** (*comida vegetariana*) and health food (*comida dietética*) are usually available in larger cities, often in restaurants dedicated to these cuisines.

Breakfasts are generally small, usually little more than an *empanada* or *arepa*, and always accompanied by a thimble-sized cup of scalding-hot coffee. Lunch is generally lighter – a good economic choice is the *menú ejecutivo* (soup, main dish and a drink) which many restaurants offer. Common dinner options include fried fish, rotisserie chicken and southern-fried chicken. Italian, Portuguese, Spanish and Arabic food are popular international dishes, thanks to large immigrant communities.

The Venezuelan national dish is **pabellón criollo**, which consists of shredded beef, plantain, cheese, rice and beans; a breakfast version of this is the *desayuno criollo*. Pabellón-stuffed *empanadas* are particularly good and should be sampled if stumbled upon.

The ocean, abundant rivers and mountain lakes afford plenty of fresh **fish**, the most common varieties being *mero* (grouper), *dorado* (dolphin fish), *pargo* (red snapper), *trucha* (trout), *corvina* (sea bass) and *corocoro* (grunt).

Common **desserts** are strawberries and cream, *dulce de leche* (caramel) and sweets made from guava or plantains. Venezuelan *cacao* (cocoa) is considered among the best in the world, but, as nearly all of it is exported to Europe, Venezuelan chocolate is difficult to find. Two particularly good products are the *CriCri* bars and the *Pirulin* chocolate-filled wafer rolls.

Restaurants tend to open around 6am for breakfast and stay open for dinner, which ends around 8pm. Although

11

restaurants close early, burger and condiment-heavy hotdog stands keep serving until around midnight on main streets. Ask a local for the best in the area as quality varies tremendously.

In most restaurants, it's customary to leave a tip of around ten percent. Restaurants may also add the 13.5 percent tax to the bill.

DRINK

Fruit juices, or *jugos* (also known as *batidos*), are delicious, inexpensive and safe to drink; combined with milk and whipped, they become *merengadas*. The most common flavours are *lechosa* (papaya), *parchita* (passion fruit), mango, *piña* (pineapple), *guayaba* (guava), *guanábana* (soursop) and *tamarindo* (tamarind). Another sweet, refreshing drink is *papelón con limón* (lemonade made with unrefined brown sugar). Bottled water is inexpensive and available everywhere.

Coffee in Venezuela is served very strong, black, sweetened and in small amounts. The tiny red straws that come with the drink are for stirring rather than drinking through. If you want it with milk, ask for *marrón* (brown).

Although you can always depend on being served an ice-cold one, Venezuelan **beer** is bad compared to what you'll drink elsewhere. The major brand is Polar, with several varieties, distinguished informally by colour: the watery Solera comes in *verde* (green) and the weaker azul (blue) varieties, negra (black) refers to the pilsener, and blanca (white) denotes either the light or "ice" varieties. Beer, a price-controlled product, costs around BsF20 in liquor stores and BsF25 in a bar.

Dark rum is generally the liquor of choice – try the Santa Teresa 1796 – mixed with cola, lime and plenty of ice to produce the "Cuba Libre", the nation's most popular cocktail. Whisky is popular among the more affluent set (particularly Buchanan's 12 Year and Old Parr).

SELF-CATERING

Given Venezuela's immense **shortages** of every staple from milk to shampoo, those who prefer to self-cater may find serious challenges.

Many supermarkets in the country now resort to rationing in order to provide for everyone who braves the six-hour queues, and foreign tourists may not be allowed to buy certain basic items if they are particularly in demand. A good option for those who are determined not to eat out are the road-side bus stops, which sell groceries at an inflated rate compared with the government-controlled supermarket prices, but where prices are nevertheless far cheaper than anywhere else on the continent.

CULTURE AND ETIQUETTE

Thanks to its location at the crown of South America, Venezuela combines distinctive elements of Caribbean and Latin American **culture**. Visitors familiar with these regions won't be surprised to find the country a fairly relaxed place, whose warm, cheerful nationals place a high value on socializing, recreation, food and (loud) music. By the same token, **machismo** is an inescapable aspect of Venezuelan society, and women will experience cat-calling throughout the day. However, Venezuelan law places a high price on female integrity, and should harassment persist past casual flirtation the individual should be reported to the authorities.

Venezuelans are a passionate people, and while a conversation between family members may seem to verge on violence, conversation on any topic invariably leads to raised voices and aggressive gestures. Do not be offended if a Venezuelan interrupts you in the middle of a sentence; simply continue speaking at a higher volume.

Understandably, given their government's notoriety, Venezuelans are **politically aware** and eager to discuss their thoughts about their country. Even in death, President Hugo Chávez excites both zealous fervour and fearful hatred. Venezuelans will listen with good grace to anything you may have to say on the subject of politics, but it's best to be asked before sharing. Don't share any negative opinions about the current government unless you are sure of your company. Anyone dressed in a red T-shirt should be regarded with caution.

11

LANGUAGE

Not many Venezuelans speak English – a general knowledge of Spanish will serve you well. **Venezuelan Spanish** is notable for its dropped "S" and the constant use of the "-*ito/a*" diminutive. European-Spanish speakers should note that the personal pronoun "*vosotros*" is not generally used, "*ustedes*" being the standard for third person plural.

Slang is a major feature of Venezuelan Spanish; some of the most common words are "*chévere*" (pronounced che-ver-ey, meaning great or excellent), "*chamo/a*" (meaning kid) and "*chimbo*" (meaning bad).

SPORTS AND OUTDOOR ACTIVITIES

Close to Caribbean nations such as Cuba and the Dominican Republic, Venezuela's primary sporting obsession is **baseball**. You'll see fans across the country wearing gear from both Venezuelan and American Major League Baseball teams. There is a long history of players heading to the major leagues in the US; the Detroit Tigers are particularly favoured due to Venezuela's large representation on the team. The LVBP (Liga Venezolana de Beisbol Profesional) consists of eight teams, the most prominent being the Caracas Leones and Valencia's Navegantes del Magallanes. The regular season runs from October until December, and attending a game (see p.877) is an excellent experience.

Despite baseball's dominance, **football** has a large following, particularly when the national side, nicknamed the *Vinotinto* (red wine) because of the colour of their strip, plays.

The country is also an **outdoor** enthusiast's paradise, with a variety of landscapes and climates offering the ideal conditions for hiking, paragliding, kite-surfing, snorkelling, scuba diving, white-water rafting and more. Most outdoor activities are concentrated in the few backpacker-friendly destinations, namely Mérida (see p.891), Caripe (see p.914), Ciudad Bolívar (see p.901) and Santa Elena de Uairén (see p.906).

COMMUNICATIONS

Venezuela is relatively technologically savvy, and call centres and internet cafés are found in all major towns; except in the most remote outposts, you should have no trouble finding a reasonable **internet** connection. Rates are BsF20/hr on average.

Movistar and CANTV are the most visible **telecommunications** providers, while Movilnet is government-owned and therefore the cheapest. All three have call centres and outlets in most towns and cities. Pre-paid SIM cards cost around BsF150. These can be topped up online, by street vendors or in your provider's store. Calls are inexpensive: around BsF1.40/min within the country, BsF2.50/min for international. Data plans are available on every network, generally costing BsF800 per GB and include texts, local and international calls. To place an international call, first dial 00 and then the code of the country you are calling.

Ipostel, the Venezuelan national **postal service**, is fairly unreliable. If you have an important letter or package to send, do so through an international carrier like MRW or DHL, which have offices in most major cities. Ipostel charges BsF1.70 for a postcard to the US, BsF2 to Europe and BsF2.20 to the rest of the world. Ipostel branches are typically open weekdays from 8am to 4pm.

CRIME AND SAFETY

Despite its reputation, Venezuela is a relatively **safe** place to travel. Certain regions such as the Colombian borderlands – which the FCO currently recommend avoiding – and areas of Caracas are tense and uninviting, mainly due to a corrupt police force which sees backpackers as easy targets for extortion.

Opportunistic crime is common in Venezuela, and travellers should always keep an eye on their belongings while using public transport. Do not walk

11

USEFUL NUMBERS

All-purpose, nationwide emergency
hotline ☎171
All-purpose, nationwide information
hotline ☎131

down poorly lit streets after dark and
leave your valuables in the hotel.

If you are unlucky enough to be
robbed, calmly accede to the criminal's
demands before reporting the crime
immediately.

Police corruption is a fact of life in
Venezuela: police officers earn less than
US$50 a month and see bribery as a
legitimate subsidy to their wages. Bribes
should never be openly offered to police
officers, and never suggested at all to
anyone in plain clothes. If stuck with a
police officer who refuses to let you go,
the suggestion of a "*propinita*" (a tip) for
a few hundred Bolívars may be what he is
waiting for. Bribery is not condoned, but
can make for an easier travel experience
in the country.

Illegal drugs are common in
Venezuela, most notably *creepy* (a potent
strain of cannabis), cocaine and *base*
(crack cocaine). Although it's unlikely
that you will be offered any, illicit
substances should be avoided due to
unpredictable police searches and
serious penalties for possession.

HEALTH

The main illnesses in Venezuela are
dengue fever, yellow fever, hepatitis A,
hepatitis B and malaria. Make sure you
consult a doctor before travelling; they
will be able to recommend which
vaccinations to get pre-trip. If entering
the country from Brazil you may be asked
for a certificate of **yellow-fever**
vaccination. The vaccination should be
procured four weeks in advance to ensure
effectiveness. **Malaria** is a risk in rural
parts of the country, particularly
Amazonas and the Orinoco Delta.
Prevention is the best cure with malaria,
so take plenty of repellent and long-
sleeved clothing. If you plan on a longer
stay, consider a course of anti-malarials.

Good **medical care** is available in
Venezuela, although this tends to be of
a higher standard in Caracas than in the
rest of the country. It may be very hard
to find a hospital with good facilities,
let alone good doctors, in remote
areas. Foreigners tend to rely on
private clinics, which offer high-quality
service.

INFORMATION AND MAPS

What Venezuela's tourism officials – all
overseen by the national body Mintur
(Ⓦmintur.gob.ve) – lack in useful
knowledge for budget travellers, they
make up for with charm and enthusiasm.
Unfortunately, many offices don't abide
by any logical schedule. Additionally,
most states have their own tourism entity
located in its capital city. Though
information provided by private tour
agencies is rarely unbiased, independent
travellers will find them useful, as they
are more in touch with current public
transport schedules and black market
exchange rates.

A variety of country and regional **maps**
is available in Venezuela, the best being
Miro Popic's *Guia Vial de Venezuela/Atlas
de Carreteras* and individual city maps.

VENEZUELA ON THE NET

Ⓦ**www.mintur.gob.ve** Official site of the
government's tourism arm, with current,
tourism-related news and links to similar
federal agencies.
Ⓦ**inparques.gob.ve** Official site of the
national parks agency, with contact info
and descriptions of parks and reserves.
Ⓦ**miropopic.com** Website for the
publisher of Venezuelan maps and
reference books, with an online
"gastronomic guide".
Ⓦ**venezuelatuya.com** Decent
overview of travel and accommodation
in Venezuela, with a smattering of
country facts.
Ⓦ**valentinaquintero.com.ve** An
extensive and detailed guide covering all
parts of the country, particularly useful for
out-of-the-way towns away from the
tourist trail.

Elizabeth Klein's guidebooks to Venezuela are also an excellent source of information, and these, along with maps, are available in most bookshops.

MONEY AND BANKS

Money – and how to get the most value from it – is likely to be your biggest concern while in Venezuela (see box, p.861). The country's economy – entirely dependent on oil exports – has the world's highest inflation and a black market with runaway prices. Consequently, Venezuelans and foreigners alike resort to foreign currency transactions through the **black market**, or *mercado paralelo*. This is both a blessing and a curse for international travellers: it makes Venezuela the cheapest country on the continent to travel in with black market rates upwards of twenty times the official, but also means having to keep all one's money in the form of cash.

Travellers should never use ATMs, pay with credit cards or use any form of electronic payment, as this will incur charges at the official exchange rate. Bank hours vary hugely, but are generally open Monday to Friday, 8am to 4pm. Two reliable banks are BBVA Provincial and Banco Mercantíl (ⓦbancomercantil.com), both found in most sizeable towns.

OPENING HOURS AND HOLIDAYS

Most **shops** are open from 8am until 7pm on weekdays, often closing for lunch from around 12.30pm until 2 or 3pm. **Shopping centres**, however, generally stay open until 9 or 10pm. In addition to their regular business hours, **pharmacies** operate on a "*turno*" system, with a rotating duty to stay open all night; the designated pharmacy will advertise *turno* in neon. All **banks** take a bank holiday on one Monday each month, although these off-days have no fixed timings since they are often scheduled to coincide with other public holidays. Businesses are generally closed on Sunday, while hours are unpredictable if they do open – don't expect to get much done.

Festivals, most with a religious basis, seem to occur constantly. Some are national, while others are local, as each town celebrates its patron saint.

11

PUBLIC HOLIDAYS

In addition to the events listed here, Caracas celebrates the anniversary of its foundation every year from July 21 to July 29 with a series of cultural events that include theatre presentations, painting and sculpture exhibits, concerts and sports.

Reyes Magos January 6. Twelfth Night or Epiphany. Choroní, Mucuchíes and Caracas.

Carnaval February. The most famous celebrations are in Carupano and El Callao.

Nuestra Señora de La Candelaria February 2. Virgin of the Candlemas, with offerings and folk singing. Mérida and Caracas.

Semana Santa Easter. Large processions involve re-enactments of Jesus' last days and resurrection; most Venezuelans, however, celebrate by heading to the beach. Several small towns in the state of Mérida, as well as El Hatillo (see p.872).

San Isidro Labrador May 15. Honours agriculture and animal husbandry; produce is carted through the streets and animals are blessed.

Corpus Christi Late May or early June. The most famous celebration on this day is Diablos Danzantes (Dancing Devils) in San Francisco de Yare (see p.878).

Día de San Juan Bautista June 24. Choroní, El Higuerote and Ocumare del Tuy. Venezuelans celebrate the arrival of the summer solstice and rejoice the birth of San Juan, with drumming and dancing on the streets.

Día de Todos los Santos and Día de los Muertos November 1–2. All Saints' Day. Venezuelans pay tribute to the deceased by adorning their tombs with flowers and offerings.

La Navidad December. Christmas – the entire country essentially shuts down for a week.

Caracas

The Venezuelan capital gets something of a bad rap, and while expensive living costs, poor budget accommodation and higher crime rates than the rest of the country have tended to deter visitors, this cosmopolitan capital nevertheless has some diverting attractions. *Caraqueños* are proud of their vibrant city with its excellent artistic, culinary and social scenes; you'll be surprised at how readily and enthusiastically they are willing to help a foreign traveller.

Caracas's most famous native, **Simón Bolívar**, was born to an influential Creole (Spanish descendant) family in 1783. After several years abroad he returned in 1813 and captured the city from the Spanish. He had to abandon it a year later, but Bolívar had already earned the epithet "El Libertador". When Venezuela became fully independent in 1830, Caracas was made the capital of the new nation. Since then, various political eras have left their mark on the city's architecture, though the predominant aesthetic is the mid-twentieth-century concrete high-rise.

WHAT TO SEE AND DO

The bustling and attractive district of **El Centro** has some excellent museums and budget restaurants, perfect for getting an authentic taste of Venezuela if Caracas is your first port of call in the country. Street vendors and heavy traffic along the wider arteries can be an irritation, but the area is interesting enough for a day's wandering. Sightseeing around this area is best kept to daylight hours as it has a reputation for street crime after dark. Away from El Centro, visitors can take in the gritty street life of **Sabana Grande**, enjoy the business end of town in **Altamira**, immerse themselves in the restaurant scene around residential **Los Palos Grandes**, or party with the beautiful people until the morning in **Las Mercedes**. Slow the pace slightly with a trip to the arty suburb of **El Hatillo**, or treat your lungs to some fresh air with an excursion to **Parque Nacional El Ávila**.

Plaza Bolívar

As with all Venezuelan towns, the **Plaza Bolívar** is the main square, and Caracas's version, a leafy hub northeast of the Capitolio/El Silencio metro station, is a good starting spot for a walking tour. The south side of the square features the **Consejo Municipal** (City Hall), which doubles as the **Museo Caracas** (Tues–Sat 9am–4pm; free), containing artefacts from the city's history as well as seasonal art exhibitions.

Built in 1575, the colonial-style **Catedral de Caracas** on the east side of the plaza houses Bolívar's parents and wife, who are buried in a chapel on the right-hand side. Next door at the **Museo**

CARACAS METROPOLITAN AREA

Airport (26km)

LA PASTORA

Teleférico

Parque Nacional El Ávila

N

SAN BERNARDINO

AVENIDA BOYACA

LOS PALOS GRANDES

LA FLORIDA

AVENIDA ANDRES BELLO

LA CASTELLANA

CENTRO

SEE 'SABANA GRANDE' MAP

ALTAMIRA

AVENIDA LIBERTADOR

AV. RÓMULO GALLEGOS

SEE 'EL CENTRO/PARQUE CENTRAL' MAP

SABANA GRANDE

AV. FRANCISCO DE MIRANDA

Jardín Botanico

Parque del Este

EL ROSAL

AV. NUEVA GRANADA

AVENIDA LOS ILUSTRES

LA CARLOTA

BELLO MONTE

SEE 'EASTERN CARACAS' MAP

Terminal La Bandera

SANTA MÓNICA

CHUAO

0   2
kilometres

VALLE ARRIBA

EL CAFETAL

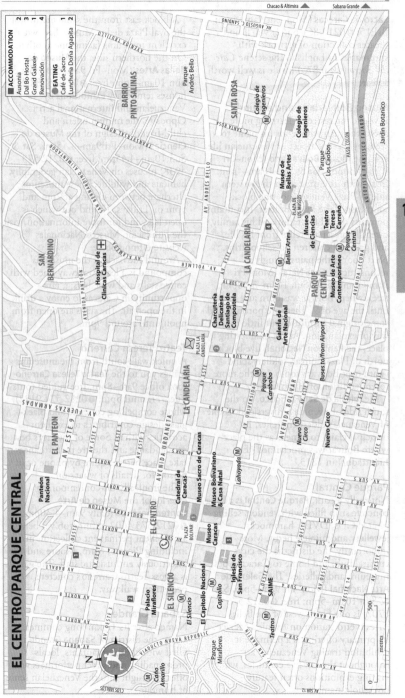

EL CENTRO/PARQUE CENTRAL

ACCOMMODATION	
Ausonia	2
Dal Bo Hostal	3
Grand Galaxie	1
Renovación	4

EATING	
Café de Sacro	1
Lunchería Doña Agapita	2

Chacao & Altimira

Sabana Grande

11

Sacro de Caracas (Mon–Sat 9am–4pm; BsF15; ☎0212 861 6562) you'll find a greater collection of artwork with summaries in English. The serene *Café del Sacro* (see p.875) inside is well worth a visit.

Museo Bolivariano and around

If you're interested in learning more about the man who lends his name to seemingly every aspect of Venezuelan life, visit the **Museo Bolivariano** (Mon–Fri 9am–4.30pm, Sat & Sun 10am–4pm; free), with its entrance on the western side of Plaza Venezolano, one block southeast of the Plaza Bolívar. It contains portraits of El Libertador and his family, carefully preserved relics from his life, and gangs of children on school trips. Next door is the painstakingly reconstructed **Casa Natal** (Mon–Fri 9am–4pm, Sat & Sun 10am–3.30pm; free), where Bolívar was born and lived until the age of 9. There are portraits and some original furniture, but little in the way of explanation. At his final resting place, the **Panteón Nacional**, five blocks north of Plaza Bolívar, soldiers stand guard over Bolívar's tomb and the more recent addition of Hugo Chávez.

The **Iglesia de San Francisco**, on the south side of Avenida Universidad, is one of Venezuela's oldest churches. Its principal claim to fame is as the place where Bolívar was proclaimed "El Libertador" in 1813.

Parque Central

Not really a park, **Parque Central** is a long concrete strip filled with vendors selling pirated CDs, DVDs, hammocks, jewellery and miracle herbs. More importantly, the district is the city's cultural hub, and home to Caracas's best museums and galleries. The **Galería de Arte Nacional** (Mon–Fri 9am–5pm, Sat & Sun 10am–5pm; free; ☎0212 576 8707) is one block west of the Bellas Artes metro station on Avenida México. Its primary offering is a permanent exhibition tracing Venezuelan art throughout the last five centuries, while visiting exhibitions often feature household names.

A block east from the same metro stop, the oval Plaza de los Museos has two excellent museums facing one another. On the northern side, the **Museo de Bellas Artes** (Mon–Fri 9am–5pm, Sat & Sun 10am–5pm; free; ☎0212 578 0275) houses temporary exhibitions by Venezuelan and international artists. Opposite, the more modern and child-friendly design of the **Museo de Ciencias** (Mon–Fri 9am–4.45pm, Sat & Sun 10am–4.45pm; free; ☎0212 573 4938) focuses on Venezuelan geography, habitats and wildlife. These museums alternate between closing at 2pm and 9pm on Fridays. To find out which is open late, and for more information, visit the Fundación Museos Nacionales website ⊛fmn.gob.ve.

Around the back of the museums' compound is a leafy walkway lined with coffee stalls and wine bars: a rare opportunity in Caracas to enjoy a drink in the open air. The stalls are open from noon until around 9pm.

Teatro Teresa Carreño

A quick walk south from the museums brings you to the **Teatro Teresa Carreño** (box office 9am–8pm, free guided tours Tues–Fri until 5pm; ☎0212 574 9122), whose compelling concrete and black-glass design contributes to excellent acoustics within. Some of the city's best music, dance and theatre performances take place here; enquire by phone or in person for details of what's on.

The ironically un-contemporary exterior of the **Museo de Arte Contemporáneo** (daily 9am–4.30pm; ☎0212 573 4602, ⊛fmn.gob.ve) belies an excellent permanent collection inside, including Picasso, Miró, Moore and infectiously enthusiastic staff. The gallery is across Teatro Carreño's concrete pedestrian walkway.

Sabana Grande

Named after its 1.5km-long commercial artery, the district of **Sabana Grande** is filled with cheap restaurants, locals promenading and street performers who offer an insight into the Venezuelan sense of humour.

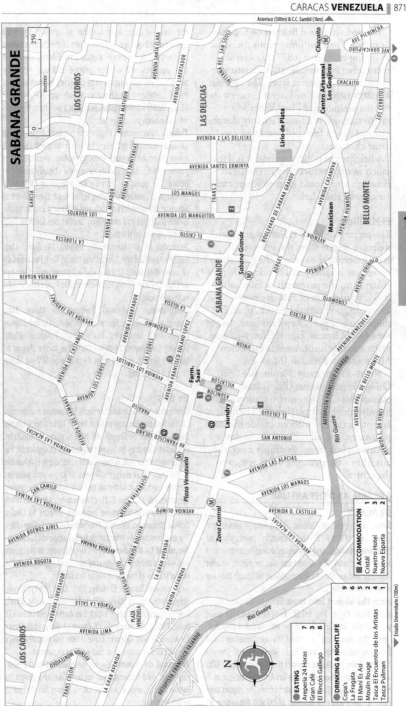

Asterisco (500m) & C.C. Sambil (1km)

SABANA GRANDE

0 250

metres

LOS CEDROS

AVENIDA SANTA CLARA

INTERDAL RES. SAN SOUCI

AVE PICHINCHA

AVE GUAICAIPURO

Chacaito (M)

CHACAITO

LOS CERRITOS

Centro Artesanal
Los Goajiros

AVENIDA LIBERTADOR

AVENIDA SANTA CLARA

LAS DELICIAS

LAS DELICIAS

AVENIDA MATURIN

AVENIDA LAS TRINITARIAS

AVENIDA 2 LAS DELICIAS

Lirio de Plata

AVENIDA SANTOS ERMINYA

AVENIDA EL MIRADOR

LOS MANGOS

TRANS 2

AVENIDA LOS MANGUITOS

GARCIA

LOS HUERTOS

LA FLORESTA

EL CRISTO

BOULEVARD DE SABANA GRANDE

AVENIDA CASANOVA

AVENIDA HUMBOLT

Maxiclean

BELLO MONTE

AVENIDA 2

Sabana Grande

SABANA GRANDE (M)

BORGES

AVENIDA 1

AVENIDA ORINOCO

AVENIDA NEGRIN

AVENIDA LOS JARDINES

AVENIDA LOS CASTAÑOS

AVENIDA LIBERTADOR

S. GERONIMO

LA IGLESIA

EL RECREO

COROMOTO

AVENIDA VENEZUELA

AUTOPISTA FRANCISCO FAJARDO

Río Guaire

AVENIDA LOS CEDROS

AVENIDA LOS JABILLOS

LAS FLORES

AVENIDA FRANCISCO SOLANO LOPEZ

UNION

AVENIDA PRAL. DE BELLO MONTE

AVENIDA LAS ACACIAS

AVENIDA LOS SAMANES

PARAISO

VILLAFLOR

ASUNCION

Farm.
Saas

Laundry

EL COLEGIO

SAN ANTONIO

AVENIDA L. DA VINCI

AVENIDA FRANCISCO SOLANO

AV FRANCISCO SOLANO

Plaza Venezuela (M)

AVENIDA VENEZUELA

AVENIDA LAS ACACIAS

SAN CAMILO

AVENIDA LAS PALMAS

AVENIDA VALPRAISO

AVENIDA LOS MANGOS

AVENIDA BUENOS AIRES

AVENIDA OLIMPO

AVENIDA O. CASTILLO

AVENIDA LAS ACACIAS

AVENIDA BOGOTA

AVENIDA PANAMA

AVENIDA BOLIVIA

LA GRAN AVENIDA

Zona Central (M)

AVENIDA CASANOVA

AUTOPISTA FRANCISCO FAJARDO

LOS CAOBOS

AVENIDA LIBERTADOR

AVENIDA LA SALLE

AVENIDA QUITO

PLAZA
VENEZUELA

Plaza
Venezuela (M)

AVENIDA LIMA

Río Guaire

TRANS COLON

LA GRAN AVENIDA

AVENIDA MONTEVIDEO

N

Estadio Universitario (100m)

11

The pedestrianized **Bulevar de Sabana Grande** is lined with numerous specialist shopping malls (see p.877), as well as every other conceivable trade, legitimate or otherwise, on street level. The callejón, a graffiti-rich bar-lined street between the Sabana Grande and Plaza Venezuela metro stations, is a fun, if slightly sketchy, place to have a few cold beers and meet some characters.

A heightened police presence has done much to improve security in the area, although you should keep to where there are crowds after dark.

11 El Hatillo

The pretty suburb of **El Hatillo** provides a welcome respite from the intense atmosphere of the centre. The only street noise here is gallery and boutique owners chatting on the pavement or faint salsa music wafting out of café doorways. There are good eating (see p.876) and shopping (see p.877) options here. To **get here** from Caracas, take the forty-minute metrobus ride from Avenida Sur below Altamira metro station (Mon–Fri 5.30am–11pm; every 30min; BsF1.50). On weekends, *busetas* (BsF4) leave from outside the Chacaíto metro station – look for windshields displaying "El Hatillo". Get off at the roundabout beside the large pharmacy. The suburb is at the end of a circuitous bus route, so simply catch the bus from where you got off to return to the centre.

ARRIVAL AND DEPARTURE

BY PLANE

26km northwest of Caracas, Maiquetía International Airport (☎ 0212 303 1329) is the country's primary hub for international flights, and also serves domestic destinations across the country. The airport has two terminals, one for domestic and another for international, although they are in the same building.

From the airport into town Buses to Parque Central (daily 5am–10pm; 1hr; BsF25; ☎ 0212 352 4140) leave every 20min from in front of the international terminal. From the bus stop, it's best to continue to your accommodation by taxi. Red Sitssa buses (hourly 7.30am–9pm; BsF8) also connect the airport to *Hotel Alba* in Parque Central, from where Bellas Artes metro station is two blocks away. Official taxis to and from the airport take about an hour and cost upwards of BsF800 depending on

the time of day. Taxis waiting at arrivals are 4WD *camionetas*; buy a prepaid ride at one of the clearly marked counters inside the terminal upon arrival. Many hotels and tour agencies will arrange private pick-ups from the airport, or you can arrange to be collected by trusted driver Pedro Castellano by phone or WhatsApp (☎ 0414 247 5555). Under no circumstances accept a ride from the touts who approach you in the terminal.

Tickets International flights are impossible to buy in advance using Venezuelan currency; any international travel must be booked through airline websites. It is possible to fly domestically extremely cheaply paying in Bolívars by going on standby for a flight at Maiquetía, although it requires showing up at least three hours in advance, bringing lots of cash and making it known to the airline staff that you are willing to offer tips for their help in putting you on the flight.

Destinations (international) Bogotá (4 daily; 1hr); Buenos Aires (2 daily; 10hr); Lima (daily; 4hr); Panama City (2 daily; 4hr); Quito (2 daily; 4hr w/connection); Santiago de Chile (2 daily; 9hr w/connection); São Paulo (daily; 10hr w/connection).

Destinations (domestic) Barquisimeto (daily; 1hr); Canaima (4 weekly; 5hr w/connection); Ciudad Bolívar (daily; 1hr); Maracaibo (daily; 1hr); Porlamar (daily; 50min); Los Roques (4 daily; 1hr). Due to the closure of Mérida's airport, visitors must fly to nearby El Vigía (daily; 1hr) and take a bus.

BY BUS

Caracas has two major bus terminals, La Bandera and Oriente. La Bandera has luggage storage for BsF10/hr after an initial BsF20, Terminal de Oriente will hold luggage for BsF20/hr. Bus tickets can only be bought on the day of departure. For less-served destinations (particularly Mérida) it is advisable to buy your ticket early. You'll need to know your passport number (or have it to hand) to book tickets. Aeroexpresos Ejecutivos (☎ 0212 266 2321, ⊛ aeroexpresos.com.ve) offers very comfortable but more expensive services to Ciudad Bolívar, Maracaibo, Valencia, Puerto La Cruz and other cities. The terminal is on Av Principal de Bello Campo in Chacao.

Terminal La Bandera Serves destinations to the south and west of the capital. Situated two blocks uphill from the metro station of the same name (on line 3).

Destinations Barinas (3 daily; 7hr); Coro (every 30min; 9hr); Maracaibo (4 daily; 12hr); Mérida (3 daily; 15hr); Puerto Ayacucho (1 daily; 14hr); San Antonio del Táchira (2 daily; 20hr); San Fernando de Apure (3 daily; 8hr). Buses for Maracay and Valencia leave when full (usually every 15min); simply take a seat and wait for departure.

Terminal de Oriente Serves destinations to the east, southeast and international routes. Take the metro to Petare station, where you can take a 15min *buseta* (BsF5) to the terminal.

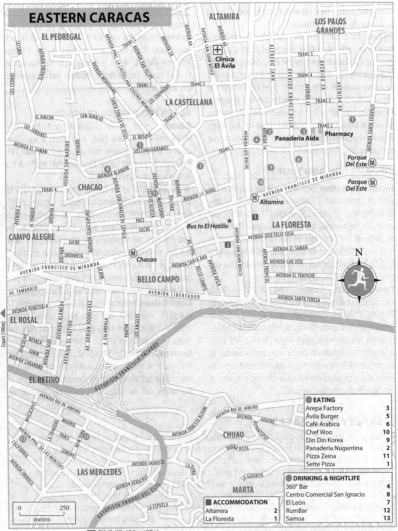

EASTERN CARACAS

EATING

Arepa Factory	3
Ávila Burger	5
Café Arabica	6
Chef Woo	10
Din Din Korea	9
Panadería Nugantina	2
Pizza Zeina	11
Sette Pizza	1

DRINKING & NIGHTLIFE

360° Bar	4
Centro Comercial San Ignacio	8
El León	7
RumBar	12
Samoa	13

ACCOMMODATION

Altamira	2
La Floresta	1

▼ El Hatillo (12km) & Hannsi (12km)

Destinations Barcelona (several daily; 5hr); Carúpano (several daily; 10hr); Ciudad Bolívar (5 daily; 9hr); Cumaná (6 daily; 8hr); Puerto La Cruz (several daily; 5hr); Puerto Ordáz (5 daily; 10hr); Santa Elena de Uairén (1 daily at 3.45pm; 22hr); which continues on to Manaus in Brazil.

GETTING AROUND

By bus Olive-green metrobuses, running 5.30am–11pm, connect metro stations with outlying destinations. There's a set fare of BsF1.50. There is also a virtually infinite number of unofficial *busetas* running their own routes, with stops listed on their windshields. Fares depend on distance travelled, but usually don't exceed BsF10.

By metro Operates from 5.30am to 11pm daily and is cheap, efficient and safe – by far the best way to get around the city, although it can be extremely crowded during peak times. Line 1, the most useful, runs east to west. Lines 2 and 3 run south from the line 1 transfer stations of Capitolio/El Silencio and Plaza Venezuela respectively. The best ticket options are the single-ride *boleto* (BsF1.50) or the ten-ride *abono integrado* (BsF13.50). Beware at peak hours as pickpockets intentionally cause jams between boarding and alighting passengers to create a distraction.

By taxi Official taxis are white with yellow licence plates; take these rather than their unmarked *pirata* ("pirate") counterparts. Taxis do not have meters and fares should be agreed before you get in. Ask a local what the price should be before bartering with a *taxista*. Most rides within the city should cost under BsF50, more for journeys at night. A cheaper and quicker option is the two-wheeled *mototaxi*, on which helmets come provided. Look for the riders wearing hi-vis orange jackets (who are hailed like a regular taxi) advertising the service.

INFORMATION AND TOURS

Tourist information There are two Venetur desks in the airport's international terminal (both daily 7am–midnight; ☎0212 355 1326 or ☎0212 355 1765) and another in the domestic terminal (7am–8pm). There's also an office on the first floor of the Torre Venetur, on Av Francisco de Miranda in Altamira (Mon–Fri 8.30am–4pm; ☎0212 208 4652), though this is more administrative and they'll be surprised to see you.

Travel agents Candes (☎0212 953 1632, ⓦcandesturismo.com) in Edificio Roraima Av Francisco de Miranda; Club del Trotamundo (☎0212 283 7253) in Centro Comercial Centro Plaza, Los Palos Grandes. English-speaking taxi driver Eustoquio Ferrer (☎0412 720 3805, ⓔferrermiranda@hotmail.com) comes recommended by the owners of *Nuestro Hotel* (see opposite) and can take you on day-trips out of town. Caracas also has a number of reputable tour operators (see p.862).

ACCOMMODATION

Budget accommodation in Caracas is overpriced and underwhelming. For your safety and comfort after dark you should look for accommodation in the Chacao/Altamira district. If you're particularly nervous about Caracas, stay at *Dal Bo Hostal*, although you can expect to pay in dollars.

EL CENTRO/PARQUE CENTRAL

Ausonia Corner of Av Urdaneta (next to Palacio Miraflores) ☎0212 864 3931; map p.869. A spanking-clean lobby belies grimier rooms upstairs (all with TV), although the position beside Miraflores Palace affords it a certain level of security. __BsF600__

★ **Dal Bo Hostal** Av Sur 2, at Av Universidad ☎0424 215 0799, ⓦwww.dalbohostal.hostel.com; map p.869. Gustavo Dal Bo's dedicated homestay is an excellent option for those who are nervous about Caracas. Right in the centre of town, the entrance is trickily positioned next door to a shoe shop. There's capacity for six, while the apartment is equipped with every imaginable gadget. Gustavo has a couple of pleasant surprises including lending out pre-paid mobile phones. Breakfast included. Dorm __US$35__

Grand Galaxie Av Baralt Truco, at Caja de Agua ☎0212 864 9011; map p.869. This basic hostel has a bustling lobby, wi-fi throughout and a good bakery next door; the rooms themselves have a/c and hot water. __BsF800__

Renovación Av Este 2, 154 ☎0212 571 0133; map p.869. The upside is the proximity of the city museums, the downside is putting up with the sour-faced staff. Some of the rooms (all en suite) have comically ostentatious

---

SAFETY IN CARACAS

While Caracas is not as dangerous as its dreadful international reputation would have you believe, **crime rates** in the capital are the country's highest and **robberies** are not uncommon. Simple common sense is the policy: don't carry around excessive cash or anything you can't afford to lose. Don't venture up deserted side streets and stick to where there are crowds after dark, especially in and around El Centro and Sabana Grande. Dress down; wearing overtly touristy clothes will earn you odd looks even from those who don't pose a threat, though grimy backpacker-chic is best saved for towns more accustomed to budget travellers. Change money calmly, in a secure place, and only once you've had a chance to gauge current *paralelo* rates (see p.861). Don't change money in the street; you'll be an easy target for passing opportunists and could also get landed with fake notes.

While not as overtly aggressive as in previous years, the Caracas **police** are a constant presence. Street-level officers are usually very helpful, while the bored staff manning the red or blue police gazebos in pedestrianized areas (particularly common in Sabana Grande) are best avoided; giving them a wide berth is usually enough to avoid unwanted interaction. Spot searches are rare, but if you are unlucky enough to be pulled into a gazebo for an inspection, insist that you unpack your things yourself, one item at a time – things are less likely to go missing if you don't allow yourself to be rushed. Never offer bribes. If you are asked to pay a fine, always ask for the official paperwork.

All that said, there is no reason for paranoia and Caracas is one of South America's friendlier capital cities; exercise your common sense, don't take unnecessary risks, stay alert to your surroundings at all times and you're likely to have an incident-free stay.

bathtubs and there's a great place to eat on the nearby corner. BsF1000

SABANA GRANDE

Cristál Pasaje Asunción, at Bulevar Sabana Grande ☎0212 761 9131; map p.871. A good option for sampling the Caracas nightlife as the location on the graffiti-strewn *callejón* is a popular and friendly spot with numerous bars, although you should avoid it if getting an early night is a higher priority. Avoid the drug dealers who loiter about the entrance. Expect adequate service and clean rooms, all with a/c, en suite and TV. BsF600

Nuestro Hotel C El Colegio, at Av Casanova ☎0212 761 5431; map p.871. The cheapest accommodation in town, the starkly basic rooms in this security-conscious place are pretty grimy, although you can guarantee clean sheets and towels. The reception doubles up as a sort of shop – although anyone other than guests must make their purchases from the other side of the barred entrance. Some of the staff speak English and are good sources of information, and there is wi-fi. Do not venture downhill on foot. BsF500

Nueva Esparta Av Los Manguitos, between Libertador and Solano ☎0212 761 5732; map p.871. The ostentatious entrance sets this pristine lodging back from a bustling side street. Rooms are all en suite, with a/c and TV, but otherwise basic. The hotel also has a decent pizzeria opposite the tiny reception booth. BsF800

ALTAMIRA

Caracas's business district, Altamira is far safer to walk around after dark than other areas of the city.

★**Altamira** Av José Félix Sosa, at Av Altamira Sur ☎0212 267 4255; map p.871. Secure, stylish and relaxed, this friendly place on a quiet side street has homely rooms with hot showers, a/c, TV and wi-fi throughout. A short walk from Altamira metro station, the rates are a bargain given the high-end nature of accommodation in the area. BsF800

La Floresta Av Ávila Sur below Plaza Altamira ☎0212 263 1955; map p.871. Perfectly decent rooms all have a/c, en suite and wi-fi, while some have balconies. Don't expect quality service; the shifty and disinterested staff can be comically rude. Breakfast in the hotel restaurant included. BsF1871

EATING

In addition to established cafés and restaurants, there is no shortage of street vendors hawking burgers and hot dogs for around BsF50. Street food, including fresh fruit juice, is generally safe when prepared in front of you.

EL CENTRO/PARQUE CENTRAL

Café de Sacro Inside Museo Sacro; map p.869. A haven of serenity on the raucous Plaza Bolívar. Grab a coffee and

cake and sit back to admire the pretty surroundings. You'll have to pay the BsF50 entry fee whether you're interested in the art gallery or not, although the peace and quiet are well worth it. Mains are more gourmet, and start from BsF350. Mon–Fri noon–3.30pm.

Luncheria Doña Agapita Av Sur 13 south of Plaza la Candelaria; map p.869. If you've not eaten a *cachapa* (sweetmeal pancake folded over a thick slab of cheese), this is the place to have your first. Grab a seat, enjoy the banter between the staff and their patrons, and watch your meal cooked on the hot plate at the entrance. BsF140 for a *cachapa con queso de mano*. Mon–Sat 7am–8pm.

SABANA GRANDE

★**Arepería 24 Horas** Av Casanova, at Av Las Acacias ☎0212 793 7961; map p.871. Open 24hr for when you need your *arepa* fix, this open-fronted diner brims with colourful characters. Look behind the glass counters to select your fillings, which include octopus, tuna and roast pork (BsF65–100). For more leisurely dining, the table service area has slick waiters and sports channels rolling on the numerous TVs, although the other patrons are far more interesting. Also does excellent *batidos* from BsF40. 24hr.

Gran Café Boulevard de Sabana Grande, at C Pascual Navarro ☎0212 763 6792; map p.871. Grand it ain't, but this popular lunch destination serves potent coffee, sandwiches (around BsF120 with fries), ice cream, pastries and more. Mon–Sat 7am–6pm, Sun 7am–3pm.

El Rincón Gallego Av Francisco Solano López, at C Los Manguitos ☎0212 762 8307; map p.871. The unstoppably chatty owner Lola emigrated from Spain over fifty years ago and is still dishing out traditional favourites from her homeland as well as friendly security advice. A cosy place that stays open until the early hours if the punters are having fun. Paella BsF400 per person. Mon–Sat noon–late.

ALTAMIRA/LOS PALOS GRANDES

Arepa Factory 2da Transversal, at 2da Av, Los Palos Grandes ☎0212 285 1125; map p.873. They've fixed what isn't broken with artesanal, slim or wholemeal *arepa* options, although the staff admit nothing beats the original. The fillings menu is extensive (BsF26–45), while a yummy local favourite is the *capresa con queso planchado* (BsF42), a caprese salad with grilled cheese. Bag a seat first and order at the counter. Mon–Thurs 8am–9pm, Fri–Sun 8am–1pm.

Ávila Burger C Chaguaramo, behind CC San Ignacio, Chacao ☎0212 264 3434; map p.873. Massive and juicy burgers served with enormous sides of fried *yucca*, bacon-cheese fries and washed down with ice-cold beer. Who said Creole-Americana wasn't a wonderful fusion? The service is also excellent by Venezuelan standards. Burgers from BsF360. Daily noon–10pm, Fri & Sat closes 11pm.

Café Arabica Av Andres Bello, at 1ra Transversal, Los Palos Grandes ☎0212 286 3636; map p.873. A famous opposition

11

hangout in Caracas, so expect to get kicked to the kerb for expounding the merits of petro-socialism. Good food (get the jam-packed *empanadas*), excellent coffee and beers later on, although don't expect much from the service. DOC restaurant next door does a great steak. Mon–Fri 6.30am–11pm, Sat & Sun 6.30am–midnight.

Chef Woo 1ra Av, above Av Francisco de Miranda, Los Palos Grandes; map p.873. Students and businessmen alike flock to this Chinese restaurant (and neighbouring *Lai Cen*) for cheap beers, lively conversation and sometimes even Chinese food, though this is usually lower down the list of priorities. Closes 11pm.

★Din Din Korea 1ra Av, at 1ra Transversal, Los Palos Grandes ☎0212 285 4853; map p.873. Sick of the flavourless Venezuelan food? Head to this basement restaurant run by Venezuela's only expat Korean family. All the kimchi-munching delights of Korean cuisine, authentically prepared. Ask the English-speaking staff for that day's off-menu items. Daily 11.30am–10pm.

Panadería Nugantina 1ra Av, at 3ra Transversal, Los Palos Grandes ☎ 0212 284 8034; map p.873. One of Caracas's best pastry bakeries, this is the place to take your time over breakfast with a ham and cream cheese-filled croissant or attempt one of their enormous cuban sandwiches for lunch. Does great coffee and squeezes fresh orange juice to go. Weekdays 6.30am–8pm, weekends 7am–8pm.

Pizza Zeina Av Mohedano beside Plaza Chacao ☎0212 267 8320; map p.873. Not a pizzeria as the name suggests, rather an informal lunch spot serving up authentic Lebanese food, prepared fresh daily. The *Plato Mixto* (BsF260) gives a rounded taste of the kitchen's delights, washed down with refreshing yoghurt drinks. Gets very busy at lunchtime. Daily 9am–8pm, Mon until 5pm.

Sette Pizza 4a Av between 2da and 3ra Transversals, Los Palos Grandes ☎0212 283 6608; map p.873. Down a side street, this over-staffed pizza joint stone-bakes tasty artisan pizzas to compensate for underwhelming service. The pasta menu operates on a "choose your shape, choose your sauce" basis. Individual pizza from BsF79, family-size from BsF196, pasta dishes from BsF85. There's live music Thurs–Sat with a BsF40 cover charge. Daily 2pm–midnight.

EL HATILLO

Dulces Criollos C La Paz on Plaza Bolívar ☎0212 961 3198. Come in for a gawp at the sweets and pastries that run three rows deep at this rustically contemporary (or contemporarily rustic) cake shop. A slice of cake is BsF100 and the coffee is excellent. Scoff it down at a bar stool or enjoy it outside in the leafy Plaza Bolívar. Daily 8am–11pm.

DRINKING AND NIGHTLIFE

Caracas has bars and clubs for virtually anyone, and at any time – many establishments stay open until the last patron leaves. Being a large and cosmopolitan city, it also

has a decent selection of gay and lesbian nightclubs. Check ⊕rumbacaracas.com for a variety of club and event listings. As most streets empty out after dark, especially in the western districts, it's wise to take taxis to and from your destination.

SABANA GRANDE

★El Maní Es Así C El Cristo; map p.871. This self-proclaimed "temple of salsa" is a Caracas legend where they relish gringos getting involved. Thursday to Saturday sees live bands fill the wide dancefloor from 9pm, while the enormous sound system thumps out salsa the rest of the time. Tues–Sat 7pm–3am; arrive early for occasional salsa lessons.

Moulin Rouge Av Francisco Solano; map p.871. With a giant, two-dimensional windmill for a facade, you can't miss this ever-popular dive bar, where the city's rockers, ravers and gutter-punks convene for live alternative music. Mon–Thurs 10pm–2am, Fri–Sun until 5am; see the website for who's performing soon.

Tasca El Encuentro de los Artistas Pasaje la Asunción, Sabana Grande; map p.871. This is the best of the bars along a street lined with many. Take a seat at the long bar, or head upstairs for the DJ sets from 8pm. Many punters get their drinks to go, preferring the reveller-filled street. Ice-cold beers (BsF12) are fished out of the cooler by staff who are always keen to talk politics. Daily 4pm–1am, Fri & Sat until 3am.

ALTAMIRA/LOS PALOS GRANDES

★360° Bar Hotel Altamira Suites, 1ra Av at 1a Transversal; map p.873. The coolest bar in Caracas, right above the Plaza Altamira, this rooftop bar affords stunning views of the city in all directions as well as of the beautiful clientele within. Throw yourself into a hammock, order a mojito (BsF200) and feel yourself a world apart from the intensity of Caracas life below. Daily 5pm–late.

Centro Commercial San Ignacio Av Blandín ⊕centrosanignacio.com; map p.873. An upmarket shopping centre with a wide selection of bars and clubs where wealthy *Caraqueños* come to show off their latest moves and fashionable purchases. Try *Suka*, which gets particularly busy on Wednesday nights, and hosts regular DJs, or neighbouring *Pi'Sko*, the building's *merengue* dancing spot. There are plenty of eating options here too. Opening hours vary, although generally daily from 7pm until late.

El León 2da Transversal de la Castellana ☎0212 263 6014; map p.873. A popular bar (and pizzeria) where the waiters keep the drinks coming. Grab a seat at the wide outdoor patio, relax and watch the Venezuelan motorists crossing the poorly designed roundabout nearby. Keep note of how many beers you've had, as the waiters have been known to add a couple to the bill. Daily until 3am.

TAKE ME OUT TO THE BALL GAME

It won't take you long to notice Venezuela's **baseball** obsession, with what seems like every fifth person sporting club gear. If you're in town during the October-to-December season, attending an **LVBP** (Liga Venezolana de Beisbol Profesional) game in the capital is a good way to see what all the fuss is about. The two local teams, the Leones and Tiburones (Lions and Sharks), share the **Estadio Universitario** in Sabana Grande, and there are games on most days of the week. The biggest fixture of the year pits the Caracas Leones against their fiercest rivals, Valencia's Navegantes del Magallanes.

Tickets can be bought in advance at one of the numerous Leones merchandise shops around town; there's one in the Centro Comercial Sambil in Chacao (see below). You can also buy them online at ⍟leones.com, although you'll need a local friend to reserve them, as the site doesn't accept international credit cards.

Alternatively, you can buy tickets from the stadium box office from 9am on game days. Arrive early as service at the four ticket windows is slow. Tickets for the *tribuna* (main stand) start at BsF50; unreserved-seating tickets for the *grada* (terrace) around the outfield are cheaper and you can jump the queue to buy them.

The stadium is a ten-minute walk south of Plaza Venezuela metro station. Walk to Arepería 24 Horas and you'll see the floodlights. Check ⍟lvbp.com for upcoming fixtures.

If you fail to get tickets in advance, show up to the *grada* gate beside the ticket office and slip the attendant BsF200 to let you through.

LAS MERCEDES

RumBar C Nueva York, at C Madrid; map p.873. Sweaty, crowded and excellent fun; party to salsa, reggaeton and *merengue*. An outdoor patio offers a breather from the constantly rammed dancefloor. It's at its best from Thursday onwards. Tues–Sat 9pm–late.

Samoa Av Principal de Las Mercedes, at C Mucuchíes ☎0212 261 6949; map p.873. An increasingly popular chain of bars, *Samoa* stands out for its bizarre South Pacific theme, where the locals go crazy for the plastic palm trees, looped surf videos and swings instead of seats at the bar. Daily 5pm until late.

GAY AND LESBIAN

Copa's C Guaicaipuro, close to Chacaíto metro station ☎0212 951 3947; map p.871. Caracas's best (possibly only) lesbian spot, the overzealous security is worth putting up with for the friendly crowd, which has become more mixed in recent years. BsF50 cover charge. Wed–Sat 10.30pm–6.30am.

La Fragata C Villa Flor, Sabana Grande; map p.871. This popular club brings in a friendly, mostly male clientele, although the good location and party-hard reputation are beginning to attract a fun-loving straight crowd as well. Excuse the cheesy, neon-heavy decor and focus instead on the cheap drinks and crowded dancefloor. Daily 6pm–3am.

Tasca Pullman Av Francisco Solano, Sabana Grande; map p.871. One of Caracas's oldest gay bars, and still sporting a distinctly Eighties vibe, this dimly lit place draws a friendly, working-class crowd and the occasional drag queen. Mostly male, though women are welcome. Daily until late.

SHOPPING

Shopping culture in Caracas is dominated by mega-malls, where your chances of finding unique, inexpensive crafts are virtually nonexistent. Street shopping is a bit more promising, at least in terms of prices, and the Hannsi crafts outlet in El Hatillo (see p.872) is your best source for souvenirs.

Centro Artesanal Los Goajiros Next to Chacaíto metro station. This alleyway of stalls is the closest Caracas gets to backpacker-chic and the place to come if you have a pressing need for Hugo Chávez baseball caps. Mon–Sat 7am–7pm, Sun 9am–4pm, although individual vendors keep their own hours.

Centro Comercial Lido Av Francisco de Miranda. A good place to get things done; services include Continental, Copa and Santa Barbara airline offices, major phone network outlets and various ATMs. *South Beach* is a good spot to stock up on women's beachwear before a trip to the coast. Mon–Sat 10am–7pm.

Centro Comercial Sambil Chacao. The most famous of the city's malls, this mind-bogglingly enormous complex hosts every conceivable amenity, including top international brands. Mon–Sat 10am–9pm, Sun & holidays noon–8pm.

Hannsi C Bolívar No 12, El Hatillo ⍟hannsi.com.ve. This enormous craft shop sprawls through several buildings, filled throughout with astonishing amounts of chintzy junk, although the occasional gem is buried beneath it all. You can choose your own coffee beans to grind at the café, which also has wi-fi, pastries and savoury snacks. Daily 10am–1pm, 2.30–7pm.

Libreria Tecni-Ciencias In Centro Comercial Sambil and around the city ⍟tecniciencia.com. The prices are a bit high, but this chain is one of the best options for books in Caracas, with more than a dozen outlets (including one in Centro Lido in El Rosal).

SBS Sports Business In Centro Comercial Sambil or Centro Comercial El Recreo. Come here for official Caracas Leones baseball gear, including jerseys, T-shirts, caps, pins, stickers and game tickets (see box, p.877).

DIRECTORY

Banks and exchange There are plenty of banks, not that you should ever consider using their ATMs (see p.861). The international airport terminal has a Banco de Venezuela (and others), as well as an Italcambio for exchanging travellers' cheques; visit ⓦ www.italcambio.com for other locations around town.

Embassies and consulates Brazil, Av Mohedano, at C Los Chaguaramos in La Castellana (Mon–Fri 9am–1pm; ☎0212 981 6000, ✉brasembcaracas@embajadabrasil .org.ve); Canada, Av Francisco de Miranda at Av Sur, Altamira (Mon–Thurs 7.30am–4.30pm, Fri 7.30am–1pm; ☎0212 600 3000, ⓦcaracas.gc.ca); Colombia, 2e Av de Campo Alegre at Av Francisco de Miranda, Torre Credival (Mon–Fri 8am–1pm; ☎0212 515 9596, ✉ecaracas@ cancillera.gov.co); Guyana, Av El Paseo, Quinta Roraima in Prados del Este (Mon–Thurs 8.30am–3.30pm, Fri 8.30am–3pm; ☎0212 977 1158, ✉embaguy@cantv .net); Ireland, Av Venezuela, Torre Clement, 2nd Floor, Office 2-A in El Rosal (Mon–Fri 8am–12.30pm; ☎0212 951 3645, ✉irlconven@cantv.net); UK, Av Principal de La Castellana, Torre La Castellana 11th Floor (Mon–Fri 8am–4.30pm; ☎0212 263 8411, ⓦukinvenezuela.fco .gov.uk); USA, Colinas de Valle Arriba, C F at C Suapure (Mon–Fri 8am–5pm; ☎0212 975 6411, ⓦcaracas .usembassy.gov).

Hospitals Two recommended clinics are Hospital de Clínicas Caracas, on Av Panteón, five blocks north of Metro Bellas Artes (☎0212 508 6111, ⓦwww.clinicaracas.com), and Clinica El Ávila, on Av San Juan Bosco, at 6ta Transversal in Altamira (☎0212 276 1111, ⓦclinicaelavila.com).

Immigration office SAIME (El Servicio Administrativo de Identificación, Migración y Extranjería) at Av Baralt in front of Plaza Miranda opposite Teatros metro station (Mon–Fri 8.30am–3.30pm; ☎0212 483 2070, ⓦsaime .gob.ve).

Internet There are numerous internet cafés in Caracas, especially in pedestrian-heavy Sabana Grande. Most charge BsF10/hr. Two reliable options are MSX Cybershop, at C San Antonio above Bulevar de Sabana Grande, and Ciberplace, at C Villa Flor below Bulevar de Sabana Grande. Both daily 8.30am–8.30pm.

Laundry Many hotels will do your laundry (generally for around BsF100/load). Otherwise, try Maxiclean, which has branches around the city including on Av Casanova in Sabana Grande.

Left luggage Both La Bandera and Oriente bus terminals offer luggage storage. Most accommodation will hold luggage for you as well.

Pharmacy Pharmacies are just as ubiquitous as banks and internet cafés. On Bulevar de Sabana Grande, Farmacia Saas is at C Villa Flor. In Altamira, Farmacia San Andrés is on the corner of 3a Av at 2da Transversal, or there's a large Farmatodo on Av Andres Bello and 3ra Transversal in Los Palos Grandes.

Phones CANTV, Digicel and Movistar have shops throughout the city for buying SIM cards and credit; all three have outlets around Plaza Bolívar and Centro Plaza in Altamira, and the latter also has phone booths and photocopiers (daily 8am–4pm). There's a CANTV office (daily 8am–5pm) on C San Antonio above Av Francisco Solano, which also offers internet.

Post office Ipostel beside the cathedral in Plaza la Candelaria (Mon–Fri, 8am–noon & 1–4pm). There's another post office at the international airport, and others in *Puntos de Gestión* (administration offices) around the city. Better, private alternatives, such as MRW (ⓦmrw .com.ve) and DHL (ⓦdhl.com.ve), both have numerous offices around the city.

FESTIVAL DE LOS DIABLOS DANZANTES

The otherwise nondescript town of **San Francisco de Yare**, 60km southeast of Caracas, is the site of one of Venezuela's most famous spectacles, the **Festival de los Diablos Danzantes** ("dancing devils"). In observance of the Catholic holy day Corpus Christi (in late May or early June; check with Caracas tourism offices for exact dates), townspeople don elaborate devil costumes and engage in highly ritualized performances. While similar festivals occur in other parts of Venezuela, including Ocumare de la Costa, Chuao, Naiguatá and Cuyagua, Yare's is considered the definitive.

To get here from Caracas, take the **metro** to the Nuevo Circo station and walk one block to the bus terminal of the same name. From here, **buses** (every 15min until 9pm; 1hr 30min) leave for Ocumare del Tuy from the designated stand. From the Ocumare terminal, frequent *busetas* to Santa Teresa drop passengers at Yare's Plaza Bolívar (20min). To return to Caracas, Ocumare-bound *busetas* pass one block northeast of the Plaza Bolívar. Buses from Ocumare to Caracas leave every 15min until 9pm.

DAY-TRIPS FROM CARACAS

For a quick escape from the hustle and bustle of Caracas, ride the cable car that ascends the slopes of **Parque Nacional El Ávila**, with its spectacular views and hiking trails. If you've got more time, consider visiting **Colonia Tovar**, a Black Forest-style village built by nineteenth-century German immigrants. On the other side of the coastal range, Caracas boasts some fabulous beaches, particularly popular with surfers from the capital.

Parque Nacional El Ávila

The lush mountain ridge that separates Caracas from the coast, **PARQUE NACIONAL EL ÁVILA** is a popular escape from the urban mayhem for *Caraqueños*. On clear days there are stunning views of the city to the south and the Caribbean to the north.

There are several ways to explore the park. For those who want to explore on foot there are four well-marked hiking trails accessible via Avenida Boyacá – best accessed via taxi/*mototaxi*, although infrequent *busetas* do go from points along the Avenida Liberator – the most popular of which is **Sabas Nieves**, a fairly strenuous hour-long trail, packed with posing fitness buffs, with refreshing home-made ice cream at the end. From here the trail continues up the mountain to the **Silla de Caracas** (4hr) and the spectacular summit at the **Pico Oriental** (6hr). All routes are well signposted and the trails well trodden. For similarly stunning views with less exertion, the **Cotamil** is a 5km path that traverses the Ávila at a height of 1000m above sea level, from Altamira to Plaza Venezuela. Access points at both ends are guarded by Inparques checkpoints.

However, the most popular option is the **teleférico** (box office Tues noon–6pm, Wed–Sun 9.30am–6pm, closed Mon; BsF45; last return 10pm), a high-speed cable car. To get to the base station, go to Colegio de Ingenieros metro station and take a BsF80 taxi from outside the entrance. There's an ice-rink at the top as well as some more predictable attractions, while a steep trail leads down to the pretty village of **Galipán**. Jeeps wait at either end to ferry passengers up and down the trail for BsF20 each way. Numerous roadside stands sell strawberries and cream and local honey, while restaurants in the village have superb views.

To explore the park further, contact Akanán Tours (see p.862). Alternatively, take a taxi to San Bernadín at the foot of the hill at weekends, where jeeps leave for Galipán when full (BsF15/person one-way).

The northern coast

The coast of Vargas state, separated from Caracas by Parque Nacional El Ávila, provides a good sample of Venezuela's **beaches** if you don't have time to venture further afield. The surfing here is particularly good, with some of the best breaks at Anare, Los Caracas and Playa Pantaleta. To **get here** under your own steam, catch the bus from Parque Central to the airport and continue 35km by taxi to La Guaira or Macuto (around BsF600). Here you can flag down one of the numerous *busetas* that ply the seaside highway in both directions; hop off and on wherever you choose.

Colonia Tovar

Founded by German immigrants in 1843, the small mountain village of **COLONIA TOVAR**, 60km west of Caracas, is still inhabited by their descendants. Most of the houses have been built in traditional Black Forest style, and restaurants selling German-style bratwurst line the main roads of the village. "Colonia" is a popular weekend destination, when it becomes packed with bemused *Caraqueños*, who turn the whole place into a Deutsch Disneyland. The **Museo de Historia y Artesanía** (Sat, Sun & festivals 9am–6pm; BsF50) features a small collection of documents, clothes, tools, guns and other relics of the village's early days.

ARRIVAL AND DEPARTURE

By metro and buseta To get here from Caracas, take the metro to La Yaguara station. Join the queue around the corner for a *buseta* to El Junquito (every 15min; 1hr),

★TREAT YOURSELF: LOS ROQUES

An underwater extension of the Andes range, the **Los Roques** archipelago is Venezuela's closest thing to desert-island paradise. Populated mostly by posada owners and boatmen, the high cost of flying to Los Roques has helped keep them both exclusive and unspoilt. Most Caracas travel agencies (p.874) and tour operators (see p.862) offer package trips, but you'll save a lot of money organizing things yourself.

Trips are cheaper during the week, when the major carrier for the archipelago, Aereotuy (ⓦtuy.com), offers return flights and a night's accommodation for BsF5000/person. Chapi Air (ⓞ0212 355 1965, ⓦchapiair.com) serves Los Roques with two flights daily each way.

Two good **posadas** are *El Botuto* (ⓞ0416 621 0381, ⓦposadaelbotuto.com; generally part of a package with plane or US$85/person with breakfast), which has great service and lovely outside showers, and *Doña Carmen* (ⓞ0414 318 4926, ⓦturismodonacarmen.com; BsF800/ person with dinner).

Camping is a safer option than on the mainland, although you'll need a permit from the Inparques office (at the far end of town from the landing strip). Camping is restricted to a designated area on Gran Roque and a few of the smaller, uninhabited islands, for a maximum of eight days. Contact Libya Parada (ⓞ0414 291 9240, ⓔlibyapara@hotmail.com) for tent rentals.

A boatmen's cooperative for transport around the islands operates out of Oscar Shop next to the landing strip, which also rents snorkelling gear (BsF200/day). Arrecife Divers, near Inparques, runs **scuba-diving** trips and courses. Tourist numbers and prices rise substantially in the June-to-September high season.

---

and then change at the same spot for an onward bus to Colonia Tovar (every 15min; 1hr). To return to Caracas, *busetas* leaving Colonia Tovar depart 300m outside the village on the road to El Junquito; many of them go directly to Caracas for BsF80. The last *buseta* leaves Colonia at 6pm. If you want to move on to the western coast, take a *buseta* to La Victoria from the other end of town. From La Victoria buses leave regularly for Maracay, the access point for Parque Nacional Henri Pittier (see opposite).

TOUR OPERATORS

Douglas Pridham ⓞ0416 743 8939, ⓦvivatrek.com. An expert paraglider who can get you airborne from the steep hillsides around Colonia Tovar (BsF1500). His outfit also offers guided excursions into Parque Nacional Henri Pittier.

Rustic Tours ⓞ0244 355 1908, ⓔrustictours@cantv.net. One of several companies with stalls around the village, which run jeep outings through the mountainous countryside (2hr; BsF400).

EATING

Lunchería Schmuk 100m uphill from the church. Specializes in German-style meats, which come in a variety of forms ranging from simple hot-dogs (BsF75) to the *Plato Especial Schmuk* sausage-fest (BsF240). Daily 6am–9pm.

Zu Hause Next to the car park. Offers good-value breakfasts, again involving sausages, and lunch combos such as *sandwich de pernil* (BsF220), all of which include a drink. Fri–Sun 8am–5pm.

The northwest coast

Some of Venezuela, and indeed the Caribbean's, finest beaches stretch along the country's **northwest coast**, where pretty colonial towns, two fine national parks and spectacular landscapes inland also bid for visitors' attention.

Parque Nacional Henri Pittier, roughly 150km from Caracas, has palm-lined sands, striking mountain ranges and four vegetation zones, which are home to a tremendous array of birds and plant life. If taking a speedboat to the beach appeals, then make for popular **Parque Nacional Morrocoy**, a few hours to the west, for its offshore cays surrounded by crystalline water. Three hours closer to Colombia from Morrocoy, the well-preserved colonial town of **Coro** serves as a good breather between the coast and the Andes, while a short hop across a land bridge to the **Paraguaná Peninsula** will reward visitors with some of the country's finest aquatic sports. For those heading directly to Colombia, Coro is the most backpacker-friendly spot en route to the border (see p.888) 360km away.

PARQUE NACIONAL HENRI PITTIER

Venezuela's first national park, created in 1937, **PARQUE NACIONAL HENRI PITTIER** was named after the Swiss geographer and botanist who classified more than thirty thousand plants in the region. Despite the park's great biodiversity, the vast majority of visitors come for its **beaches**, which can be overrun on weekends but are generally quiet the rest of the time.

Pittier's wide array of **flora and fauna** is a result of the relatively short space in which it climbs from sea level to 2430m, producing distinct vegetation zones. The park's wildlife is best experienced from the Universidad Central de Venezuela's **Estación Biológica**. The area is renowned among birdwatchers, having one of the highest densities of birds in the world, with at least 582 species including the stunning red ibis. The park also has large reptile and mammal populations; noteworthy residents include sea turtles, jaguars, pumas, spider monkeys and rattlesnakes.

Entry to the park is free, and most people access the beach communities of **Choroní** and **Ocumare de la Costa** by bus from the terminal in uninspiring **Maracay**. Choroní, on the eastern side of the park, is the nicer of the two, with lots of places to stay and a lively atmosphere. Ocumare, named after the indigenous Cumarí people, is only worth visiting in order to reach the stunning La Ciénaga lagoon around the coast. Guided tours of the park are organized from Choroní or Ocumare, rather than Maracay.

Estación Biológica Rancho Grande

The park can be explored along hiking trails from Choroní or the extensive mangroves around La Ciénaga, but the best base for serious wildlife-spotting is the atmospheric **Estación Biológica Rancho Grande**, a complex which has sadly fallen out of regular use by the Universidad Central de Venezuela. Visits must be arranged in advance – contact Oskar Padilla (see below) – and visitors are likely to see an incredible variety of fauna, including sloths, anteaters and howler monkeys. The station has a dormitory, although guests must bring their own sheets or a sleeping bag and food.

ARRIVAL AND DEPARTURE

By bus Maracay is the access point for Henri Pittier and has a busy terminal serving country-wide locations. The Estación Biológica's entrance is a nondescript gate beside a bus stop on the road between Maracay and Ocumare de la Costa; to get there, board the hourly bus heading in either direction and ask the bus driver to let you off at Rancho Grande. To get away, hail a passing bus from beside the entrance. Buses for Choroní and Ocumare de la Costa depart from the terminal when full (usually every 30min) until 9pm.

Destinations from Maracay Caracas (every 20min; 1hr 30min); Coro (several daily; 7hr); Maracaibo (2 daily; 9hr); Mérida (3 daily; 12hr); San Cristóbal (3 daily; 12hr); Puerto la Cruz (2 daily; 10hr); Puerto Ordaz (2 daily; 14hr); San Fernando de Apure (3 daily; 6hr); Valencia (every 15min; 45min).

INFORMATION AND TOURS

Tourist information Don't show up at the Estación Biológica unannounced, as it's likely that you'll find the gates locked and the building unoccupied. You should advise Inparques in Maracay (☎0243 889 3242) if you plan to walk the trails, although you're better off getting in touch with Oskar Padilla.

Tour operators Oskar Padilla, a helpful, experienced and English-speaking guide (☎0412 892 5308, ✉oskarpadilla@hotmail.com), offers hiking and birdwatching around Rancho Grande, and will happily do your permit administration for you. *Casa Luna Espinoza* in Choroní (see below) can also arrange stays and activities at the research centre.

Choroní

Choroní actually consists of two parts: the colonial town of **CHORONÍ** and **PUERTO COLOMBIA**, a beach town 2km away where the action is concentrated. Puerto Colombia's beating heart is its lively **malecón** (seafront) where the fishing boats dock, revellers congregate and on weekends it's common to see *tambores*, a coastal tradition of African drum-playing, singing and energetic dancing.

WHAT TO SEE AND DO

The **Mirador de Cristo** on the eastern headland (named *Papelón*, or Sugar Loaf) offers a view over the tiny town and stunning relief surrounding it. A path

11

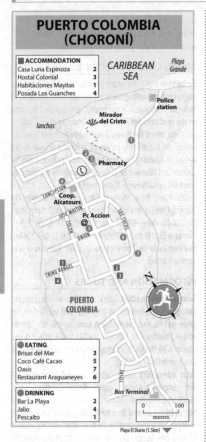

PUERTO COLOMBIA (CHORONÍ)

ACCOMMODATION
Casa Luna Espinoza	2
Hostal Colonial	3
Habitaciones Mayitas	1
Posada Los Guanches	4

CARIBBEAN SEA

Playa Grande

Police station

Mirador del Cristo

lanchas

Pharmacy

Coop. Alcatours

Pc Acción

PUERTO COLOMBIA

EATING
Brisas del Mar	3
Coco Café Cacao	5
Oasis	7
Restaurant Araguaneyes	6

DRINKING
Bar La Playa	2
Jalio	4
Pescaíto	1

Bus Terminal

0   100
metres

Playa El Diario (1.5km)

weaves towards it from the Playa Grande side of the bridge.

The one beach easily reached on foot is **Playa Grande**, a sheltered bay of jungled hills and a curving sandbar, which consequently attracts the most visitors.

About the same distance to the west, but harder to reach, **Playa El Diario** is a 45-minute walk from the village. To get here from the midpoint of the main Choroní–Puerto Colombia road, follow Calle Cementerio past the cemetery, bear left at the split and follow it around the headland to the sea.

To access the other nearby beaches you will need to take a *lancha*, which can be arranged at the malecón. To the east, the closest beach is **Playa Valle Seco** (BsF200/person return), which has some coral reefs and decent snorkelling.

Farther east, **Playa Chuao** (BsF250/person return) offers postcard good looks and a path that runs inland to Chuao town. Some of the world's best cacao is grown here. If you don't visit, you can still stock up on their fantastic chocolate from Sabor A Cacao (see opposite) in Puerto Colombia. Still farther east is equally nice **Playa Cepe** (BsF300/person return), which is generally the least crowded.

To combine these beaches in a single trip, negotiate a price (aim for around BsF1200 for the day) with the *lanchero*. Pack a lunch.

ARRIVAL AND DEPARTURE

By bus The only road to Choroní is from Maracay. Buses (every 2hr; 2hr) leave when full until 8pm and cost BsF60. Puerto Colombia is a safe 15min stroll from the bus terminal. Take a left out of the entrance and follow the other passengers.

By boat If you're coming from or going to Ocumare de la Costa, a rapid and scenic alternative is to negotiate a ride with a *lanchero* from either end. The price should be around BsF800 and the trip takes an hour. It's also possible to get to and from Caracas (via Catia el Mar or La Guaira) by sea, a 2hr speedboat trip (around BsF4000) which takes in the stunning northern coast of the continent. Ask the boatmen hawking beach trips at either end of the journey before noon, and haggle hard on price.

By taxi Taxis from Maracay cost around BsF800 and take half the time. Alternatively, take a seat in a *por puesto* (shared taxi) for BsF220. Both depart regularly from the Maracay terminal.

INFORMATION AND TOURS

Claudia, the owner of *Casa Luna Espinoza*, can organize tours of the park, the chocolate plantations in Chuao and speedboat trips to various beaches along the coast.

ACCOMMODATION

Camping isn't especially worthwhile as there is a good selection of budget accommodation in Puerto Colombia – the location of all those listed below. Reservations are recommended in the high season.

Casa Luna Espinoza C Morillo ☎0243 951 5318, ⓦjungletrip.de. Knowledgeable German *dueña* Claudia speaks English (though staff may not). This hostel is a good choice with a communal kitchen, dining table, wi-fi and hammocked courtyard, although the dormitory is next to the noisy main road. Also runs two other posadas in town and can sort out an exploration of Henri Pittier. Don't be surprised if the needy cat gets into bed with you in the morning. Dorms <u>BsF300</u>, doubles <u>BsF600</u>

★**Hostal Colonial** C Morillo ☎0243 431 8757, ✉colonialchoroni@gmail.com. Rooms are stylish, good value and numerous at this friendly guesthouse with fountains, wi-fi and a good restaurant. The affable staff speak English, Italian and German while the spacious rooms (some with en suite and a/c) are fan-cooled and thankfully set back from the noisy main road. <u>BsF500</u>

Habitaciones Mayitas C Rangel 12 ☎0243 991 1141. Look for the dolphins stencilled on the wall rather than a sign in this cluttered family-run homestay. The friendly atmosphere and over-equipped kitchen makes up for the five rather cramped rooms, some with a/c, ranging in size from a double to a sextuple. <u>BsF600</u>

Posada Los Guanches C Colón. The only noise you'll be disturbed by in this mercifully cool building is your own echo. Run by the welcoming family that lives on the opposite side of the flowery backstreet, rooms are fan-cooled, en suite and basic. Have a browse of the bamboo jewellery on sale. <u>BsF800</u>

EATING

The following options are all in Puerto Colombia, and here you'll also find a small courtyard opposite the malecón where kitchens open in the evenings and serve up excellent hamburgers and hotdogs. There are numerous shacks lining the path to Playa Grande that sell plates of fish, rice and salad for around BsF160 until the foot traffic coming back from the beach slows down.

Brisas del Mar Av Los Cocos ☎0243 991 1268. Not the most peaceful place in town to eat, being next to *Bar La Playa*, but *Brisas* offers calamarí five ways (all BsF200) as well as non-seafood options such as *pabellón* and pasta. Locals also recommend the soups at *Restaurant Puerto Colombia* next door. Daily 8.30am–11pm.

★**Coco Café Cacao** C Union at Plaza Bolívar ☎0426 833 7920. The pastries, cakes and coffee are good here, but people queue up for the signature ice creams (BsF40). You can choose from a variety of flavours, but given that they use the locally grown cacao to make the chocolate popsicle, it's a good test of free will. It puts a percentage of its profits into local community projects. Daily 8am–10pm, Sat until midnight.

Oasis Av Los Cocos ☎0243 711 1666. Anglophile owner Raúl, who studied art in London in the 1980s, whips up delicious seafood dishes from his bamboo-walled kitchen. Excellent Creole breakfasts (BsF80), fresh juices (BsF30) and healthy touches such as bran *arepas*. His artwork adorns the walls of the attractive covered courtyard. Daily 8am–10pm.

Restaurant Araguaneyes Av Los Cocos ☎0243 991 1166. Enjoy huge portions of fresh fish and seafood (BsF250) on the large upstairs terrace while listening to music that for once isn't salsa. Also open for breakfast. Daily 8am–11pm.

DRINKING

Nightlife, if you can call it that, is very casual – most people just buy a few beers and drink them on the malecón.

Bar La Playa At the beach end of Av Los Cocos. By day, holidaymakers laze about in the plastic chairs on the covered patio, sipping beers and watching the fishermen come and go. At night, the focus is on rum, high-volume salsa and getting flirty. Daily until late.

Jalio C Concepción. The most upscale option in town, promising tapas by day and cocktails by night. Thurs–Sat, if the owners feel like it.

Pescaíto Along the path to Playa Grande. The closest that Puerto Colombia gets to a club, atop a low hill across the bridge. Open until dawn when the fishermen head out to catch its namesake.

SHOPPING

For food to cook in your posada's kitchen, you can buy fish directly from the fishermen on the malecón or go to Pescadería Choroní down the side of *Bar La Playa*. There are numerous fruit and veg stands at the sea-end of Av Los Cocos.

Cooperativa Alcatours C Morillo, at Independencia ☎0414 237 0797, ✉alcatours14@hotmail.com. Interesting "cacao-arte" and *artesanía* made by the husband-wife owners. Daily 8am–6pm.

Sabor A Cacao C José Maitín ☎0243 673 1449. Excellent chocolate products, including cocoa butter lip-salve from nearby Chuao. Daily 9am–1pm, 3–7pm.

DIRECTORY

Bank There is a BNC ATM at the bus terminal. You can change dollars at some hotels.

Internet *Hostal Colonial* has a computer you can use for BsF4/hr until 10pm, or wi-fi which you can jump onto for free if you're nice to the owner.

Pharmacy There's a small pharmacy next door to *Brisas del Mar* (Mon–Sat 8.30am–9pm).

Phones Movistar, C Concepción, for mobile phone credit. Otherwise, ask at your accommodation or head for the malecón, where there will usually be someone with a phone on a plastic table to rent by the minute.

Post office Half a block south of the Plaza Bolívar in Choroní. Theoretically open Mon–Fri 10am–4pm.

Ocumare de la Costa

The main reason to visit **OCUMARE DE LA COSTA** is for the stunning lagoon around the coast, where sea turtles, red ibis and barracuda abound. Only accessible by *lancha*, **La Ciénaga** used to be a safe haven for pirates while today it's a peaceful spot where day-trippers come to sunbathe, snorkel, kayak and swim.

11

Around 5km east of the town is **Playa Cata**, which is one of the country's finest beaches hidden between bulky headlands, accessible via an hour-long hike or short boat ride (BsF100/person). Farther east, surfing beach **Playa Cuyagua** can get fairly large waves, so swimmers should exercise caution.

ARRIVAL AND DEPARTURE

By bus Buses (BsF80) run to and from Maracay (hourly; 90min). The ride is a rough one, so if there's enough of you, share a taxi.

By taxi Taxis (BsF900) from Maracay depart from the gas station outside the terminal entrance (*por puestos* don't operate this route).

GETTING AROUND

By bus All buses stop at Ocumare de la Costa's main plaza. Buses depart regularly to Playa Cata (every 20min; 30min) and Playa Cuyagua (every 20min; 40min).

By boat *Lanchas* to the various destinations around the Ocumare hub depart from La Boca at the eastern end of Ocumare's malecón and should cost around BsF800 for the day (negotiate depending on where you want to go). The staff at *Eco-Lodge* can arrange trips for you.

ACCOMMODATION

Eco-Lodge ☎0243 993 1986, ⊛ecovenezuela.com. The best accommodation in El Playón is the luxurious *Eco-lodge* at the western end of the malecón. This posada also runs *Coral Lagoon Lodge* (see box below). Breakfast included. **BsF1400**

★TREAT YOURSELF

Coral Lagoon Lodge La Ciénaga ⊛corallagoonlodge.com. Located right on the shores of La Ciénaga lagoon, *Coral Lagoon Lodge* might just be the most relaxing place on Venezuela's northwest coast. An all-inclusive overnight package here includes boat transfers, kayaks and snorkelling equipment, and fantastic meals involving plenty of fresh fish and drinks. For two days, life won't get any more taxing than deciding between a swim, early morning turtle-spotting or that hammock under a tree. During the week, particularly outside the July–September school holiday season, you'll probably have the whole magical lagoon almost to yourself. If your budget won't stretch to an overnight stay, note that the owners at Ocumare's *Eco-Lodge* organize day-trips to La Ciénaga. All-inclusive package/person **US$160**

Habitaciones Caribe C Vargas ☎0243 993 1496. Resembling the set of a slasher film, this bare-minimum establishment offers the cheapest rooms in town, although it's still vastly overpriced. A good option if you don't intend spending much time in your hotel, the rooms all have private showers, fans and clean, if moth-bitten, sheets. **BsF500**

Hotel Monte Mar C Vargas ☎0243 993 1173. A motel-style complex set around a wide courtyard, this colourful and relatively quiet hotel is a short stroll from the beach. All rooms are en suite and have wi-fi, while rooms on the upper floors have a/c. Ocumare's best mid-range option. **BsF900**

PARQUE NACIONAL MORROCOY

Gorgeous white-sand cays surrounded by azure water are the highlights of **PARQUE NACIONAL MORROCOY**, one of the most popular national parks in Venezuela. The 300-square-kilometre reserve, spread primarily over water, was created in 1974, but today it doesn't feel much like a national park. Hordes of eco-unfriendly Venezuelans are a weekend presence year-round, although some of the more remote cays still have that remote desert island feel. The park is home to nearly four-fifths of Venezuela's aquatic **bird species**, as well as several types of mammal.

Chichiriviche and **Tucacas** both serve as bases for forays into the park. Neither is particularly attractive, although the profusion of decent budget accommodation options and restaurants in Chichiriviche makes it a better base for further exploration.

WHAT TO SEE AND DO

There is a total of 22 **cays**, or cayos, in the park, most differing only in size and facilities. Day-trips can be arranged by most posadas for no extra charge, while *lancheros* hawk return trips from the malecón end of Calle Zamora in the mornings. If you want snorkelling gear it should come included in the journey price for no extra charge. Prices listed are for the boat, not per person, and include return; all are negotiable and a jokey attitude will be a great help when bargaining.

Dotted with shade-giving palms, **Cayo Sombrero** (BsF1700), halfway between

Chichiriviche and Tucacas, is the most popular of the cays, although with beaches on all sides you can still find uncrowded parts. There are numerous food stands as well as *lancha*-restaurants, boats with rudimentary kitchens that bring the meal directly to your sun lounger. Food is expensive, however, so it's a good idea to pack a lunch. There are some good snorkelling spots, although it's generally better around **Cayo Sal** (BsF900). *Lanchas* also make trips to cayos Muerto (BsF800), Pelón (BsF1000), Peraza (BsF1000) and Varadero (BsF1200). You can combine multiple spots on either a short (BsF3000) or long (BsF5000) day tour, which includes visiting the two-hundred-year-old shipwrecked *Barco Hundido*, the questionably romantic "tunnel of love" through thick mangroves and Piscina Los Juanes, sapphire-blue shallows where you can hunt for clams.

Chichiriviche

Chichiriviche's spread-out format, numerous *liquorerías* and gritty street style render it an unexceptional town. It nevertheless attracts plenty of tourists who come for its useful proximity to the cays. Calle Zamora, the town's main artery, dead-ends at the malecón, where most activity is centred. By day it's bustling with *lancha* passengers headed to the cays; by night hippie street vendors descend to sell handmade jewellery, strum guitars and watch the fishing boats rocking beside the sea wall.

ARRIVAL AND INFORMATION

By bus Only three destinations are served from Chichiriviche, of which Valencia has the most onward connections, serving Caracas, Mérida, Coro and other major cities. Buses arrive and depart 500m inland on C Zamora from 5.30am. Sanare is a junction where a road breaks off from the Coro–Maracay highway and heads to Chichiriviche. For routes between Coro and Chichiriviche, ask your driver to let you off here. Move to the corresponding bus stop, where you shouldn't have to wait more than half an hour to hail a passing bus for either destination. Hitchhiking is also common from this spot.
Destinations Barquisimeto (every 30min; 45min); Puerto Carreño (every 30min; 45min); Valencia (every 30min; 1hr). All pass through Sanare junction.

Tourist information There's a red-roofed Corfaltur kiosk outside the petrol station 50m inland from where the bus stops on C Zamora, though it has no reliable schedule of opening hours.

ACCOMMODATION

Most accommodation is within a couple of blocks of the malecón, a generally safe part of town with lots of foot traffic. *Panadería El Centro* and *Rancho Andino* also have rooms. Camping in the national park is banned.

Capri C Zamora ☎0259 818 6026, ✉hotelcaprica@ yahoo.com. With eight water tanks on the roof, water rationing won't affect you in this Italian-run Art Deco hotel. Some rooms have psychedelic beach-scene murals, while all come with en suite and a/c. Wi-fi on site. BsF500

Morena's Place Sector Playa Norte ☎0259 815 0936, ✉posadamorenas@hotmail.com. Just one street in from the beach, *Morena's* has the only dorms in town, making this a good-value spot for solo travellers. A friendly English-speaking family runs the place, and can prepare meals on request. There's a laundry service, communal kitchen, barbecue and relaxed atmosphere. Dorms BsF150, doubles BsF600

Posada La Negra C Mariño ☎0259 815 0476. The place to come if you need a bed or a haircut, *La Negra* is the only posada-hairdressers you're likely to encounter on your trip. Friendly, brightly coloured rooms around a communal kitchen come with a/c, en suite and TVs. There's a five-person apartment for BsF300. BsF600

★Posada Villa Gregoria C Mariño ☎0259 818 6359. A secure Mediterranean-style building with coconut trees in the wide courtyard, a profusion of hammocks and aloe vera plants, useful if you've skimped on the sunscreen. English-speaking staff provide spotless rooms (a/c, TV, en suite) and showers, which, although cold, amount to more than pipes sticking out of the wall. Also has apartments for five (BsF1400) and seven (BsF1800). BsF600

EATING AND DRINKING

Chichiriviche's nightlife amounts to hanging around the liquor stores while they're open and drinking on the malecón when they're closed. Your best bet for a drink in more relaxed settings is *Txalupa* and its neighbouring seafront restaurants.

Panadería El Centro C Zamora opposite *Hotel Capri* ☎0259 818 6906. Now on the corner next to the old shop, impressively moustachioed José serves up good coffee and inexpensive bread. The mini cinnamon rolls, enormous bags of crisps and bottled juices will be all you need for a trip to the cays. Rooms available upstairs for BsF500, with capacity for eighty people. Daily 7am–9pm.

★Rancho Andino C Mariño ☎0259 815 0897. The town's most chilled-out restaurant is positioned away from the *lancha* touts and serves up excellent *batidos*

11

(BsF50). Manuel, the Colombian owner, stakes a claim to the town's best *pasta marinera* (BsF180) and makes a passable stab at a full English breakfast (BsF140). Rooms in town are available for BsF800. Daily 8am–9pm, closed Thurs in low season.

Restaurant La Esquina de Arturo C Plantél. "Art's Corner" is a good place to sit and watch the world go by, positioned as it is on the town's busiest intersection. Good *comida criolla* comes cheap and the set breakfasts (around BsF100) include juice. The *desayuno marinero* is particularly good, while there's a great-value *menu del día* (BsF140) for every day of the week, served from noon. Daily 7.30am–6pm.

Txalupa Av Principal, at C Zamora ☎0259 818 6425. The portions are big but pricey at this first-floor balcony restaurant overlooking the malecón. Dinner will be around BsF400, but beers are only BsF20 and the staff are happy to keep them coming. Daily noon–10pm.

DIRECTORY

Banks and exchange Bancoro, C Plantél, at C Calvario; Banco Industrial (and others) on C Zamora.

Internet Byte Quest, on the south side of Paseo Bolívar (daily 8am–8pm; BsF8/hr).

Pharmacy Several options on C Zamora, one next to Oasis Sport (daily 8am–9pm).

Phones Comunicación los Cayos, on the west side of C Zamora (daily 8am–8pm), offers calls, internet access, and sells mobile phone credit for all the major networks. There's also a Movistar call centre about 100m further inland (Mon–Sat 8am–noon & 3–7pm).

CORO

CORO, Venezuela's prettiest colonial town, was named a national monument in 1950 and a World Heritage Site in 1993. A pleasant stopover between the coast and the mountains, Coro contains some of the country's best backpacker accommodation. The town is at its prettiest in the **casco histórico**, where a number of colonial mansions have opened their doors to the public as museums. The nearby **Parque Nacional Médanos de Coro** lies on the edge of town, a mini-desert of golden sand dunes and wild goats.

WHAT TO SEE AND DO

You only need wander the sleepy streets of central Coro to get a flavour of the town's Spanish imperial heritage. If you're in town on a Tuesday, head over to the Museo de Arte de Coro at 6pm, when **Cine en la Calle** hosts a weekly showing of classic movies in a makeshift street cinema.

Churches

The centre of the *casco histórico* is the Plaza Bolívar, on the east end of which stands Venezuela's oldest **Cathedral**, begun in 1583 and finished in 1634. Two blocks north on Plaza San Clemente, the **Iglesia San Clemente** was originally built in 1538 by the town's founder, Juan de Ampíes. Totally rebuilt in the eighteenth century, San Clemente is one of three churches in the country built in the shape of a cross. Beside it, a small monument contains the **Cruz de San Clemente**, the wooden cross used in the first Mass after the town was founded.

Colonial mansions

El Balcón de los Arcaya (Mon–Sat 9am–noon & 2.30–5.30pm, Sun 9am–noon; free), at the western edge of the Plaza San Clemente on Calle Zamora, is a mansion once owned by the affluent Arcaya family; it houses impressive mastodon excavations and some less-than-scientific diagrams. Further down the road, the **Casa de las Ventanas de Hierro** (Tues–Sun 9am–5pm; free) is a colonial museum where the staff are kitted out in period dress. The work of local artists is displayed at the **Casa del Tesoro** (Tues–Sun 9am–5pm; free), another stately mansion next door. A block and a half to the northeast of Plaza Bolívar on Avenida Talavera, the **Museo de Arte de Coro** (Mon–Sat 9am–6pm, Sun 9am–1pm; free) has temporary exhibits featuring international names in a beautifully restored eighteenth-century townhouse.

Parque Nacional Médanos de Coro

A short taxi ride (BsF60) will take you to the entrance of the eighty-square-kilometre **Parque Nacional Médanos de Coro**, a mini-desert where you can stroll the sand dunes, spy on wild goats or go sandboarding with the staff of *Posada El Gallo* (see p.888). To get back to town try hitching a ride with any of the numerous visitors at the entrance, otherwise it's a 500m stroll to the main road where you can hail a taxi. Robberies have occurred here, so don't linger long after dark and be discreet with any valuables.

ARRIVAL AND DEPARTURE

It is possible to cross into Colombia from this region (see box, p.888).

By bus The bus terminal is 2km east of town on Av Los Médanos. Taxis to and from the *casco histórico* should cost BsF60. There's an exit tax of BsF3.50 to pay, with three booths dotted around the terminal. There's an ATM but no luggage storage. *Por puestos* run regularly from the terminal until around 5pm for closer destinations like Punto Fijo and Maracaibo.

Destinations Caracas (several daily; 9hr); Mérida (daily at 6pm; 10hr); Maracay (several daily; 7hr); Maracaibo (several daily; 3hr); Puerto La Cruz (daily at 6.30pm; 12hr); San Cristóbal (2 daily; 12hr).

INFORMATION AND TOURS

Tourist information The Corfaltur kiosk beside the old cross (Paseo Alameda; ☎0268 251 8033) has maps,

English-speaking staff and very unreliable opening hours. There's an identical kiosk at the entrance to Parque Médanos de Coro, although opening hours are similarly lax.

Tour operators Araguato Expeditions (☎0426 866 9328, ⓦ araguato.org), in *La Casa del Mono*, does day-trips to the Paraguaná Peninsula, San Luís mountains (including the "Spanish trail", a jungle path once used by European explorers), Maracaibo's flea market and the eerie Catatumbo lightning (see p.893). *Posada El Gallo* can take you sandboarding on the Parque Médanos de Coro dunes.

ACCOMMODATION

La Casa del Mono C Federación 16 ☎0268 251 1590, ⓔ info@araguato.org. A well-equipped and attractive posada run by Araguato Expeditions (see above). Stylishly decorated rooms (with shared or private bathrooms) come with mosquito nets, and there is a courtyard with hammocks, kitchen, public computer and wi-fi. <u>BsF700</u>

Casa Tun Tun C Zamora ☎0268 404 4260, ⓔ casatuntun @hotmail.com. A relaxed atmosphere generated by Parisian owner Damien and his wife Norka, *Tun Tun* has everything you could want from a posada: hammocks, wi-fi, kitchen, barbecue, clean rooms with a/c (some en

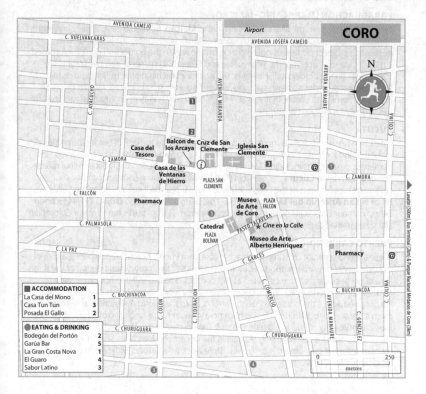

CORO

ACCOMMODATION
La Casa del Mono	1
Casa Tun Tun	3
Posada El Gallo	2

EATING & DRINKING
Bodegón del Portón	2
Garúa Bar	5
La Gran Costa Nova	1
El Guaro	4
Sabor Latino	3

suite) and a good selection of board games. The only room without a/c is a triple, costing Bs1200, a particularly good deal for groups. BsF800

★**Posada El Gallo** C Federación 26 ☎0268 252 9481, ✉posadaelgallo@gmail.com. This beautiful French-run colonial townhouse is a popular spot for backpackers (including non-guests) to hang out in. Beer is on the honour system and there is an abundance of hammocks to swing in. Two dorm rooms are useful for solo travellers, while the intimate doubles are fan cooled, some with en suite. The friendly owners organize sandboarding (BsF140) and other trips throughout the area. Dorms BsF200, doubles BsF700

EATING AND DRINKING

There are a number of inexpensive restaurants in Coro, many doubling as bars in the evening, although opening hours are generally lax. Be sure to try *chivo* (goat), the regional speciality.

Bodegón del Portón C Falcón, at Toledo ☎0426 268 7593. A big saloon serving up great seafood and meat, as well as Creole classics. There's an ample and friendly bar where Coro natives of all generations will happily join you for a few drinks. Mon–Wed 11am–7pm, Thurs–Sat 11am–5am.

Garúa Bar C Manzo y Colón. Claiming the title of Coro's oldest bar, this working man's saloon is a safe place to sit and talk rubbish with barman and owner Luis. Beers are at

---

CROSSING INTO COLOMBIA

There are three main **border crossings** between Venezuela and Colombia. The northernmost, at Paraguachón, offers the best connections to coastal cities like Cartagena; Cúcuta has onward services to Bogotá. Before leaving Venezuela you must pay the BsF140 **exit tax** (in bolívares) and get your passport stamped by the nearest SAIME emigration office. Once you cross the border, immediately visit the nearest Colombian immigration office for an entry stamp and set your watch back a half-hour.

Relations between Venezuela and Colombia are volatile, and can deteriorate at short notice. It is wise to seek up-to-date advice on the current political situation, and on **security**, before using any of the three crossings.

PARAGUACHÓN (MARACAIBO–MAICAO)

Take a *por puesto* from the **Maracaibo** terminal to **Maicao**, Colombia (several daily until 4pm; 3hr). From here you can switch to a bus for Santa Marta (4hr), Cartagena (8hr) and other destinations. Expect numerous police checks on the way to the border and don't be surprised if they decide to search you. The Venezuelan and Colombian passport stamping points are 200m apart on the border itself. However, the point for purchasing the BsF140 *tasa de salida* is 2km before the border, so make sure you ask your driver to stop briefly so you can buy it. Set off in the morning to ensure that you arrive in Maicao with plenty of time to catch an onward bus. The border is open 6am–9pm.

CÚCUTA

Open 24 hours, this border is more popular with shoppers, so the lack of border formalities can make it trying for those leaving Venezuela. Take a bus to **San Cristóbal**, which is served by numerous destinations including Mérida and Caracas. From the San Cristóbal terminal take a bus or *por puesto* to **Cúcuta** in Colombia (1hr). On Mon–Sat 8am–6pm you can pay your exit tax and get your stamps at the border; outside these times you'll need to go to the SAIME office in **San Antonio del Táchira** (Carrera 9 between calles 6 and 7; ☎0276 771 4453; open 24hr), buy your exit tax at the print shop opposite. From Cúcuta buses run to major Colombian cities; Bucaramanga (3hr); Bogotá (12hr); Medellín (12hr) and Cali (18hr).

PUERTO CARREÑO/CASUARITO

These are two separate crossings, both accessible from Puerto Ayacucho (see p.898), although the difficulty of onward transport in Colombia makes this the most difficult option of the three. No exit tax or border fees are collected at this border. Go to the SAIME office on Avenida Aguerrevere in Puerto Ayacucho to get your Venezuelan exit stamp; Colombia entry stamps are obtained across the border in Puerto Carreño. From the Puerto Ayacucho bus terminal, catch a *por puesto* for El Burro (45min); from here you can take a *lancha* across the Orinoco to the Colombian city of Puerto Carreño (10min). The onward journey by road from Puerto Carreño to Bogotá is long and only feasible in the December–March dry season. Outside of these months the only option is to fly, with three weekly departures with Satena (Tues, Wed & Fri; ☎satena.com) for Bogotá.

socialist prices and the patrons will be happy to act as taxi drivers for your return to the hotel when you're finished. Mon–Fri 6pm–late.

La Gran Costa Nova Av Manaure opposite *Hotel Intercaribe*. This *panadería* makes good coffee and bakes great bread, *pastelitos* and cakes. It's also a good spot to stock up on provisions for your posada's kitchen. If you're eating in, pay at the till first and give your receipt to the staff behind the counter. Daily 6am–9pm.

Los Guaros C Ampíes, at Maparari ☏ 0268 989 0333. The name means a native of Barquisimeto, and the food perfectly represents the taste of that ranching hub: big plates of tasty Creole food for cheap. Come on a Thursday to sample the *chivo*, while the chicken is particularly good the rest of the week. Daily 6am–3pm, although the menu is more limited on Sun.

★**Sabor Latino** Paseo Alameda ☏ 0268 252 4139. Miniature houses and marginally amusing jokes scrawled across the walls (test your Spanish to see how many you understand) at this popular joint, which takes its "Latin Flavour" name from more than the food. Staff are friendly and the grub is cheap. The *chivo* (BsF300) comes a few different ways, while the juices (BsF20) are bigger and better than you'll get in the street. Mon–Thurs 6am–4pm, Fri 6am–8pm.

SHOPPING

Artesanía There are a few places selling *artesanía* in Coro, though none of it is very compelling. Local potters sell their wares in Plaza Falcón, and the Centro Artesanal next to Plaza San Clemente has a momentarily diverting array of paintings, dioramas and *dulce de leche* made from goat's milk. Officially, it's open daily 9am–6pm, though the vendors tend to operate on their own schedules.

Market There's a small food market on C Garcés at C Colón (daily until about 7pm), where you can pick up supplies for self-catering.

DIRECTORY

Banks and exchange Banco Venezuela on Av Talavera, Banco Mercantil on C Falcón.

Internet *Hotel Intercaribe* opposite La Gran Costa Nova on Av Manaure has a popular internet café next door, BsF5/hr. Daily 8am–8pm.

Laundry All the listed accommodation choices have laundry services. Otherwise, Lavatín on C Falcón (Mon–Fri 8am–6pm, Sat 8am–2pm; ☏ 0268 251 671) has an English-speaking owner and will wash clothes for BsF30/load.

Pharmacy Farmacia Santa Catalina, C Federación, on Falcón (Mon–Fri 8am–3pm). There's another two blocks south of *La Gran Costa Nova* on Av Manaure.

Phones Movistar call centre at C Falcón between Plaza Falcón and Av Manaure, Mon–Sat 8am–6pm. Also Digitel, at Paseo Talavera.

Post office Ipostel, Casa de las 100 Ventanas, C Ampíes. Mon–Fri 8am–4pm.

PARAGUANÁ PENINSULA

A Caribbean island connected to mainland South America by a thin land bridge, the **PARAGUANÁ PENINSULA** is a tax-free watersports haven. It's also the site of Venezuela's last functioning oil refinery, though this is nowhere near its tourist centres.

The island's only city is on its western shores, **Punto Fijo**, a shopping haven where government-enforced "fair prices" allow international visitors to buy designer goods for astonishingly low prices. On the breezier eastern edge, the sleepy town of **Adícora** offers surf enthusiasts the country's best kite- and windsurfing, while backpackers can catch an island-feel breather from the intensity of the mainland on their way to or from Colombia.

WHAT TO SEE AND DO

Crossing the land bridge from Coro to Paraguaná is like a scene out of Mario Kart. Belting the motor along at breakneck speeds, your battered bus or shared taxi will dodge around wandering goats and encroaching sand dunes in order to get to **Adícora**, the best town to base yourself as a budget traveller. The sleepy town is a peninsula on a peninsula, jutting out east into the Caribbean, with beaches five blocks apart on both north and south sides. It's on the wide and windswept **Playa Sur** that the wind- and kitesurfing takes place, while **Playa Norte** is the social hub, with a posada- and restaurant-lined seafront and more shelter from the elements.

Across the peninsula is **Punto Fijo**, an ugly city and the island's administrative hub, where you will have to go if you want either to take advantage of the island's tax-free shopping, or journey directly to anywhere further afield than Coro.

ARRIVAL AND DEPARTURE

By shared taxi The only way to get directly to Adícora from the mainland is via shared taxi (BsF140) from Coro. Cars arrive and depart from the Coro bus terminal and the

Adícora bus shelter on the main road. If coming from further afield, you should go to Punto Fijo before catching an onward bus to Adícora from the same terminal.

By bus The Punto Fijo bus terminal is an airport-like structure serving nationwide destinations as well as towns along Colombia's northern coast.

Destinations Adícora (every 15 min; 1hr); Caracas (several daily; 12hr); Maracaibo (every 30min; 3hr); Maracay (several daily; 10hr); Mérida (3 daily; 7hr); Puerto La Cruz (2 daily; 16hr).

INFORMATION AND ACTIVITIES

Tourist information There's a tourist information desk inside the Punto Fijo bus terminal, although you'll be lucky to find it manned. Hotel operators in Adícora are more on the ball, and can organize tours.

Watersports Chicho's School (☎ 0424 439 6240), Playa Sur, or at *Chicho's Posada*, one of the watersports institutions along the beach, is one of the few to offer both wind- and kitesurfing in the same place. Rents equipment (Kitesurf rental BsF1500/hr, windsurf BsF400/hr) and offers 8hr courses (kitesurfing BsF13,000, windsurfing BsF4000). North Shore Windsurf (☎ 0424 627 0359), located next to the police station on Playa Norte; friendly windsurf champion Carlos and his crew offer 8hr courses spread over two days (BsF3000) and rentals (BsF500/hr).

ACCOMMODATION

La Casa Rosada Boulevard de Adícora ☎ 0269 988 8004, ⓦ posadalacasarosada.com. A lovely colonial building in a great position on the pedestrian seafront. All rooms have a/c and there's a good restaurant specializing in seafood. Free wi-fi. BsF850

Chicho's Posada C La Pastora ☎ 0269 988 8886, ✉ chichosposada@gmail.com. Italian Francesco, known as Chicho, runs this chilled-out spot in the centre of town alongside his surf school. It boasts pool tables, a lively bar and local kids hanging out. The place to stay if you're in town for the watersports. Does a good deal (BsF1800) for parties of four. BsF1500

Posada Los Reyes C Geraldo Silva ☎ 0414 610 6025. A no-frills, although pleasant, family home beside the south beach; prices aren't as high as along the malecón and the friendly owners can help organize surf lessons. BsF400

EATING AND DRINKING

A lot of restaurants don't open on weekdays, so you may have to resort to the various burger stands on the north beach malecón, which operate nightly until late.

Rancho Cacique Boulevard de Adícora ☎ 0269 988 8093. One of various restaurants along the north beach, this open-kitchen serves up the freshest seafood. Indeed, if the dish you want is out of stock, it may be a matter of waiting for the fishermen to walk through the

door with their day's catch. Meals from BsF400. Daily noon–9pm.

SHOPPING

Tax-free If you want to take double advantage of Paraguaná's tax-free status and Venezuela's tanking socialist economy, head to the CC Sambil in Punto Fijo, where international designer brands are forced to sell their high-end wares for "fair prices" dictated by the government. Take plenty of cash.

DIRECTORY

Banks and exchange Adícora has no banks, although the CC Sambil in Punto Fijo has a Mercantil and Banco Venezuela.

Pharmacy Farmacia Santa Catalina, C Federación, on Falcón (Mon–Fri 8am–3pm). There's another one two blocks south of *La Gran Costa Nova* on Av Manaure.

Phones Movistar and CANTV outlets in the CC Sambil in Punto Fijo.

Post office Ipostel, C Bolívar in Punto Fijo.

Mérida and the Andes

Occupying the northernmost limit of the Andes range, the mountainous state of **Mérida** is a region of lofty peaks and raw natural beauty. The region has long been Venezuela's most popular backpacker destination, and facilities for budget travellers are among the best in the country. The state capital, also called Mérida, has a sizeable student population, resulting in some of the country's most entertaining nightlife, an excellent place to blow off steam after the various adventure sports the region is known for. To the city's south and east, the **Parque Nacional Sierra Nevada**, dominated by the famed Pico Bolívar (5007m) and Pico Humboldt (4920m), offers some of the finest hiking opportunities in the region. To the north, the Carretera Transandina, or the Trans-Andean Highway, passes several charming mountain towns on its weaving way to Barinas, including **Apartaderos**, which has one of the world's highest observatories, the **Observatorio Astronómico Nacional**.

MÉRIDA

From the bottom of a deep valley, the city of **MÉRIDA** enjoys stunning views of the surrounding mountains. Based in Mérida, **La Universidad de los Andes** is one of the country's most prestigious universities and runs numerous international exchange programmes, adding undergraduates of all backgrounds to its already sizeable student population. Despite its cosmopolitan sensibilities, Mérida offers reasonable prices, safe streets and a block numbering system that makes the town easily navigable.

Owing to its natural endowment as well as the efforts of several excellent tour operators, Mérida's chief attraction is **adventure sports** (see box, p.892). However, if you've got some down time, or if you're allergic to adrenaline, the city offers a couple of sights, as well as some diverting **day-trips**.

WHAT TO SEE AND DO

The old town around Plaza Bolívar makes for a pleasant half-day's wandering. The town has a small old-fashioned zoo at its northern limit with some impressive species on show.

The Old Town

Walking the streets of the **old town** to admire its colonial houses, pretty parks and inordinate number of shoe shops will only take a few hours. Right on the Plaza Bolívar, the impressive **Catedral** was only completed in 1958, after over 150 years of stalled construction. Of the several decent museums in the area, the most interesting is the **Museo Arqueológico** (Tues–Sun 8–11.30am & 2–5.30pm;

11

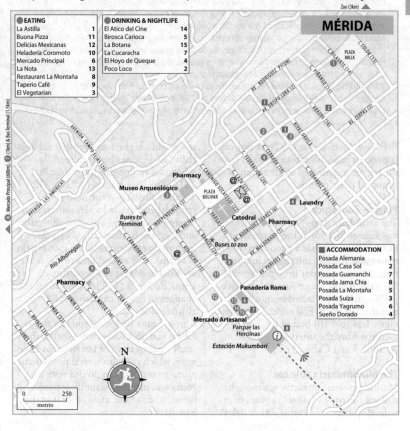

EATING
La Astilla	1
Buona Pizza	11
Delicias Mexicanas	12
Heladería Coromoto	10
Mercado Principal	6
La Nota	13
Restaurant La Montaña	8
Taperio Café	9
El Vegetarian	3

DRINKING & NIGHTLIFE
El Atico del Cine	14
Birosca Carioca	5
La Botana	15
La Cucaracha	7
El Hoyo de Queque	4
Poco Loco	2

MÉRIDA

ACCOMMODATION
Posada Alemania	1
Posada Casa Sol	2
Posada Guamanchi	7
Posada Jama Chia	8
Posada La Montaña	5
Posada Suiza	3
Posada Yagrumo	6
Sueño Dorado	4

ADVENTURE SPORTS AND TOURS

Mérida's surroundings provide the perfect conditions for an astounding range of **adventure sports**. There's an equally amazing array of tour companies in town, so it's a good idea not to jump at the first tour offered (usually by your accommodation). Companies compete particularly hard for your business outside of the July–September high season, and the more you shop around, the more likely you are to find an itinerary, group or price that suits you.

Tour prices generally decrease as more customers register, so ask your company about joining an existing group. Many trips require a minimum number of customers, so it's a good move to check availability before you arrive in town, easily done through the companies' websites. Paying in cash is the most cost-efficient option, but bank transfers can be arranged for better rates than you would pay on a credit card. Except on one-day trips, all meals and accommodation are included in tour prices.

Due to Venezuela's volatile economy and fierce competition among companies, **prices** listed here are approximate. For the latest rates, contact the tour operators directly. Most operators offer all of the following activities, though some claim individual specialities.

ACTIVITIES

Canyoning A combination of abseiling, scrambling and climbing around and under waterfalls. Full-day rates are BsF2000 per person, typically with a two-person minimum.

Climbing and trekking There are numerous less challenging treks than the popular Pico Humboldt (see p.897) and Pico Bolívar (see p.897) routes. These include Pico Pan de Azúcar (BsF8000/day) or Los Nevados (BsF7500/day); both routes take three to four days to complete.

It is possible for experienced hikers to trek independently, although they should notify Inparques at the base station of the *teleférico* beforehand.

Mountain biking Many companies rent out good bikes for BsF700/day, and will happily indicate where to head for the best routes. If you want to use a guide, day tours cost from BsF2000–2500/person depending on whether you want a jeep to access the more remote trails. Some companies also offer horseriding for similar rates.

Paragliding The slopes above Mérida are the jumping-off point for a thrilling thirty-minute descent by paraglider. Tandem rates are around BsF2500/person. Be sure to bring a jacket and don't eat before going if you're prone to motion sickness. Some agencies also offer paragliding courses.

BsF1) on Avenida 3 at the Plaza Bolívar. It presents pre-Columbian artefacts from the region, augmented by thorough historical descriptions.

Parque Zoologico

The zoo (daily 8am–5pm, closed Mon in low season; BsF50) at the northeastern limit of the town has a good selection of native and foreign animals including a tiger, a lion, a condor brought down from the refuge above Apartaderos (see p.896), and a spectacled bear, which is pictured on the BsF50 note. To get here take a bus (BsF10) bound for Los Chorros from the intersection of Avenida 5 and Calle 23.

The Mukumbarí cable car

Mérida's greatest attraction, although still yet to reopen following years of redevelopment and construction delays, the world's highest and longest cable car rising to 4893m above sea level, is scheduled to open to the public in 2016. The base station (☏0274 252 5080) is situated at the newly refurbished Parque Las Heroínas, from where the car climbs 3000m vertically and 12.5km horizontally across three intermediate stations to the **Pico Espejo** (4865m). It is a good idea to pause for acclimatization at the penultimate, Loma Redonda (4045m), as the rapid changes in height can cause mild altitude sickness.

From Loma Redonda, you can also follow various hiking trails (4hr) to the small Andean town of **Los Nevados** 13km away, which contains several posadas and places to eat. You can do this walk on your own, but should notify Inparques beforehand, whose main office is at the base station.

Rafting Rivers in Mérida and Barinas states have Class III to V rapids. Rafting season is from June to November; it's possible in December but companies don't generally take advance bookings due to unpredictable water levels. Two-day trips cost around BsF6000/person for five people; four-day trips cost double. Some agencies have private camps in Barinas where you'll spend the night.

Los Llanos and Catatumbo Mérida is the main staging point for guided trips to Los Llanos (see p.896), the wildlife-filled wetlands east of the Andes. Prices for a four-day trip, which often include some rafting, are around BsF12,000. The natural phenomenon of the Catatumbo lightning occurs on average three out of every four nights of the year. Most companies only go for one night and prices are around BsF5000. If you want to double your chances of seeing it, Alan Highton (see below) goes for two nights.

TOUR OPERATORS

Colibrí In Posada Suiza ☎0274 252 4961, ⊛www .colibri-tours.com. This expert outfit is one of Mérida's oldest and can sort out every activity including tailor-made trips. Ask about the owner's signature Jají day-trip and he'll draw you a map.

Fanny Tours C 24 between Av 8 and Parque Las Heroínas ☎0274 252 2952, ⊛fanny-tours.com. Specializes in mountaineering; also offers trips to Los Llanos. Multiple languages spoken, including English.

Gravity Tours C 24 between Av 7 and 8 ☎0274 251 1279, ⊛gravity-tours.com. Offers a popular two-day combo of mountain biking and rafting for BsF8000, as well as trips throughout the country. Very helpful, English-speaking staff.

Guamanchí Expeditions C 24 between Av 8 and Parque Las Heroínas ☎0274 252 2080, ⊛guamanchi.com. With more than 20 years of experience in the Andes and Los Llanos, this company supplies quality equipment for its specialities of climbing and trekking. Also offers day-trips to Laguna Negra (see p.897) and birdwatching tours.

Alan Highton ☎0414 756 2575. Local community worker who runs the best available tour to the Catatumbo lightning, a three-day/two-night expedition for US$120/person for groups of six or more. Alan's also a butterfly expert and will share his passion with you: he's even had a species named after him.

Tony Martin ☎0416 973 1682. A Los Llanos native and jack-of-all-trades, Tony is an experienced, enthusiastic and knowledgeable English-speaking guide who runs four-day trips to his home region.

ARRIVAL AND INFORMATION

By plane The closest functioning airport to Mérida is El Vigía two hours away, where dedicated shared taxis (private BsF3000, shared BsF600) or buses (BsF80) wait to ferry visitors up to the mountain town. Buses arrive into the terminal, while shared and private cars will drop you off at your destination. Conviasa (⊛conviasa.aero) and Laser (⊛laser.com.ve) are the main operators to El Vigía.
Destinations Bogotá (3 weekly); Caracas (4 weekly); Porlamar (3 weekly); and others.

By bus The bus terminal is 2km outside the city centre. Take a bus (BsF10) into town from the stop on the opposite side of the main road to the terminal. Buses back to the terminal pass via Av 2 beside the bridge.
Destinations Caracas (several daily; 13hr); Coro (1 night bus; 10hr); Maracaibo (several nightly; to go by day take a *por puesto*; 6hr); Maracay (several daily; 8hr); Puerto La Cruz (daily at 10am; 18hr) with Expresos Mérida (☎0414 737 1075); San Cristóbal (every 30min; 5hr). For Ciudad Bolívar you have to change at Puerto La Cruz or Barinas, although onward connections are far more reliable from the former.

Tourist information Cormetur (☎0274 263 4701) has offices in several locations around town, including the bus terminal, the airport and the Mercado Principal on Av Las Américas. The most reliable booth is in the bus terminal (daily 7am–7pm). The town's main central tourist office is at the base station of the cable car, as well as the Inparques office.

ACCOMMODATION

Mérida has a good selection of budget hostels and posadas. Most of the cheapest options are conveniently found near Parque Las Heroínas, a sort of backpacker ghetto where nearly all the tour agencies have their offices. Mid-range options can be up to forty percent cheaper during the Nov–June low season, although the posadas tend to remain the same price year-round. Unlike the rest of the country, hot water is taken as given in Mérida. To camp in the surrounding national parks, contact the Inparques office at the *teleférico*.

Posada Alemania Av 2 between calles 17 and 18 ☎0274 252 4067. A hangout at the back with communal kitchen, hammocks and chunky furniture gives this

★TREAT YOURSELF

Posada Casa Sol Av 4 between calles 15 and 16 ☎0274 252 4164, ⓦposadacasasol .com. Mérida's best attempt at the boutique hotel, this haven of serenity has an excellent restaurant, balconies suited to Shakespearean soliloquy and an interesting water feature full of carp. Rooms are elegant, the wi-fi reaches throughout, beds are super-soft and showers are excellent – the perfect spot to reward yourself after an arduous trek or bus journey. Breakfast included. BsF2050

otherwise basic posada a friendly feel. Spacious dorm beds go for BsF400, there's wi-fi, a computer, and the friendly owners cook up big breakfasts from BsF38. BsF600

★Posada Guamanchi C 24 between Av 8 and Parque las Heroínas ☎0274 252 2080, ⓦguamanchi.com. This three-floor building has a nice location beside Parque las Heroínas. The wi-fi reaches to the top-floor terrace, which contains some of the hammocks that are slung throughout. Probably the only place in the country you can snag a double bed in a dormitory. Also has a posada in Los Nevados (see p.892). Dorms BsF300, doubles BsF900

Posada Jama Chia C 24 across from the *teleférico* base ☎0274 252 5767. Look for the gold-painted metalwork on this unmarked posada overlooking the *teleférico* and run by affable owner Benedicta. Communal bathrooms, a light-filled seating area and cheaper rates for those who stay longer. Posadas *Paty* and *Mara* in the same block are similarly decent and cheap fall-back options. Dorms BsF150, doubles BsF800

Posada La Montaña C 24 no. 6–47 ☎0274 252 5977, ⓦposadalamontana.com. *La Montaña* looks rather like a posada that set up shop in a botanical garden; bursting with greenery, its upper-balcony rooms have stunning views of the even lusher scenery outside. Rates drop significantly in the low season and there's a very nice restaurant on the ground floor. BsF1000

Posada Suiza Av 3 between calles 17 and 18 ☎0274 252 4961, ⓦcolibri-tours.com. Professional and friendly staff run the Colibrí tours company from the large reception, while a courtyard at the back is ringed by dorms and pleasant rooms, all with colourful tartan blankets and en suite. There's wi-fi and it's a short walk back from the bars. Dorms BsF150, doubles BsF700

Posada Yagrumo C 24, at Av 8, next door to *Posada Guamanchi*. ☎0274 252 9539, ⓦposadayagrumo.com. The cheapest dorm in town is found in sterile settings where you'll also find en-suite doubles without natural light. Cable TVs, communal kitchen, wi-fi, laundry service

and a few internet booths for BsF5/hr which stay open until 11pm. Dorms BsF100, doubles BsF600

Sueño Dorado Av 6 between calles 19 and 20 ☎0274 251 1192, ⓦhotelsuenodorado.com.ve. A smart hotel with steel banisters and plate glass cleverly designed into more rustic architecture. Rooms upstairs have great views of the mountains as well as safes and cable TV. The restaurant downstairs is a good place for a coffee break while wandering the hilly backstreets. Breakfast included. BsF1500

EATING

The cuisine from Mérida and the Andes is famous throughout the country. Some specialities include *arepas de trigo* (made from wheat flour), *queso ahumado* (smoked cheese) and *trucha* (trout). *Vino de mora* is wine made from blackberries.

★La Astilla C 14 between Av 2 and 3 ☎0274 251 0832. They eventually decided on every colour when they chose the paint scheme for this place. Positioned on the leafy Plaza Milla, much of the vegetation has made its way inside. Friendly staff, tiled tabletops, local specialities like trout (BsF350), plus pizza (BsF180) and the best *batidos* you'll find in town. Across the way, *El Andino* is another good option in a less colourful setting. Daily 8am–10pm.

Buona Pizza Av 7 between calles 24 and 25 ☎0274 251 2420. Chunks of gooey mozzarella on crunchy-crusted pizzas follow Nonna's original recipe. This long-standing restaurant dresses itself up for the holidays and offers some quirky toppings; who knew guava was good on a pizza? There's an "Express" version across the street for takeaway. Daily noon–11pm.

Delicias Mexicanas Ground floor of *Hotel Altamira*, C 25 between Av 7 and 8 ☎0274 252 8677 (for hotel reception). Pricey, but if you need your taco fix this stylish eatery is the place to come. Does the Tex-Mex classics alongside a few interesting attempts at Andean-fusion, mainly involving trout. Daily noon–10pm.

★Heladería Coromoto Av 3 between calles 28 and 29. This Mérida institution holds the Guinness World Record for the most ice-cream flavours (over 900!), although with a menu including sardines-in-brandy, *pabellón criollo* and beer, the importance of the record clearly got a bit out of hand. A quintessential Mérida experience, only around 60 flavours are available daily. BsF80 for 2 scoops. Tues–Sun 2.15–9pm.

Mercado Principal Av Las Américas, at Viaducto Miranda. Shop for blackberry wine and magic herbs then head up to the fun food court on the second floor, which has competitive outlets serving up good set menus for around BsF120. The area becomes rammed at lunchtime. Mon–Sat 7am–5pm, Sun until 1.30pm.

La Nota Av 8 by Parque las Heroínas, beside the bus terminal and several other locations about town. Popular local chain which *Mérideños* promote as "how McDonald's should be" (although the excellent street-level burger stands do just as good a job). Meal combos for BsF160 alongside subs, teriyaki and steaks. Daily until 11pm.

★ **Restaurant La Montaña** In *Posada La Montaña*, C 24 no. 6–47. Roses on the tables, an open-fronted kitchen and an excellent *menú del día* for BsF45 at lunch make this modest trattoria-style place a fine-dining choice for relative peanuts. The menu changes daily, scrawled on the blackboard out front. Daily 8am–9.30pm.

Taperio Café Av 3, at C 29. An atmospheric street-corner joint with iron-grille walls and a café-culture crowd. A very chilled spot for a beer in the evening; there's live music on the weekends and tasty food, while the *merengadas* are big and bad in a good way. Mon–Sat 11am–10pm.

El Vegetariano Av 4, at C 18. This small, split-level place features a far more interesting menu than usual for an all-veggie venue. You can also buy artisan honey and other high-quality consumables from behind the counter. Menu options include aubergine carpaccio with pumpkin and pesto (BsF200) and an appealing list of salads. Mon–Sat 7.30am–8.45pm.

DRINKING AND NIGHTLIFE

In large part because of the immense student population, Mérida enjoys an active nightlife, particularly between Wednesday and Saturday. Expect to pay cover charges of around BsF100 in the evenings, although this often includes a drink.

El Atico del Cine C 25 next to *La Nota*. Beer comes in coffee mugs and the cocktails are named after classic movies (see if you can translate them all) in this trendy little café-bar. Plays a wide range of music and is a popular starting point for students on a night out. Does a good late-lunch menu for BsF180. Mon–Sat 4–11pm.

Birosca Carioca Av 2, at C 24. Pounding samba and students define this friendly, ever-popular club, as do the red buckets of "La Bomba", a rum-and-beer concoction for sharing. Open until the crowd goes home – it's situated on a shady street so be careful outside when leaving. Daily from 5pm.

La Botana Parque las Heroínas, beside the *Mercado Artesanal*. A rasta-themed bar popular for its pizza, which they keep producing even when it's rammed. A good bar to spend the evening at if you can secure one of the few tables. Tues–Sun 6.30pm–12.30am.

La Cucaracha In Centro Comercial Las Tapias on Av Urdaneta. One of Mérida's oldest nightspots, this large but always crowded disco has two floors, one with techno and the other with salsa and *merengue*. The chain caters to various budgets and clienteles around town. Daily until late.

★ **El Hoyo de Queque** Av 4, at C 19. You can't miss Mérida's most popular student bar a few blocks up from the Plaza Bolívar; for starters it's painted bright purple. DJs

pack the place from 8pm, while the draught beer and a *menú ejecutivo* for BsF250 make it a good spot for an easy afternoon. After hours numerous burger stands accumulate outside. Mon–Sat noon–1am.

Poco Loco Av 3 between calles 18 and 19. Although it's a little odd for a bar in Andean Venezuela to be staunchly FC Barcelona, this is Mérida's best alternative venue, with cheap draught beer and a friendly crowd. Dare you to show up in a Real Madrid shirt. Mon–Sat 1pm–1am, DJs from 8pm.

SHOPPING

Mérida is a decent place to buy souvenirs or stock up on travel essentials.

Antiques You can find a number of antique shops along the road to Apartaderos, which specialize particularly in wooden furniture, preserves and fruit liquors.

Food and drink For food to cook at your posada, there's a nameless *frutería* on the corner of Av 7 and C 24, while Panadería Roma (Mon–Sat 7am–8pm, Sun until noon) next to *Posada Yagrumo* is a useful spot for supplies as well as breakfast.

Markets The most renowned destination among bargain-hunters is the green-and-yellow-striped Mercado Principal. This three-storey, tourist-oriented market (Mon–Sat 7am–6pm, Sun until 1.30pm) on the other side of the river sells quality Andean produce and there's a good food court on the second floor for lunch. More *artesanía* can be found at the much smaller Mercado Artesanal in front of Parque Las Heroínas, where a permanent installation of stalls sells ceramics, jewellery, blackberry wine, leather goods and woodcarvings.

DIRECTORY

Banks and exchange Banco de Venezuela, Av 4 between calles 23 and 24; various ATMs dotted around town and in the bus terminal. Various agencies and hotels around town offer international bank transfers for vastly superior rates.

Camping equipment Cumbre Azul, Av 8 between calles 23 and 24, is a good place to rent or buy camping and hiking equipment.

Internet and phones Several useful *centros de conexiones* offer internet, phone services and photocopying. There's a CANTV centre (Mon–Sat 7am–5pm) beside *Posada Guamanchi*. There's another *centro* in the bus terminal, and a handful more internet cafés around the *teleférico* base. Internet costs around BsF5/hr.

Laundry An unnamed laundry on Av 6, between C 19 and Hotel Sueño Dorado, does a same-day service for BsF100/load (Mon–Sat 8am–noon & 2–6pm). Most accommodation will wash guests' clothes for around BsF100.

Medical care A reputable clinic with some English-speaking doctors is Clínica Mérida (☎ 0274 263 0652) on Av Urdaneta next to the airport.

Pharmacy Farmacía Central (daily) on Av 3, at Plaza Bolívar; Farmacía 6ta Avenida (Mon–Sat) on Av 6, at C 22. Both 8am–7pm.

Police The main station is on Av Urdaneta, adjacent to Parque Gloria Patrias (☎ 0274 263 6722).

Post office Ipostel, C 21 between Av 4 and 5, and in the bus terminal. Mon–Fri 8am–4.30pm.

APARTADEROS AND AROUND

Most of the quaint Andean towns northeast of Mérida are set alongside the Carretera Transandina (Trans-Andean Highway), with beautiful views of the Sierra Nevada range to the south and the Sierra Culata range to the north. Two hours up the valley, the mountain town of **APARTADEROS** makes a diverting day-trip from Mérida, although you should head out early as it tends to rain in the afternoons. The strip of houses here looks a lot like a town in the Scottish Highlands; there are fabulous views of the valley below when it's clear, although, like bonny Scotland, it's utterly dismal when the rain comes down.

The nearby **Refugio del Cóndor**, best accessed by hailing a passing cab from the main road (daily 7am–5pm; no phone, contact Inparques in Mérida for more details), is home to the Andean condor conservation and research project. Only one condor remains in the dome-cage at the top of the mountain road. It's one of only fifteen remaining in Venezuela, all of which live in captivity around the country. If you want to see a condor without making the trip, visit Mérida Zoo (see p.892), which is home to a condor from this project. Visitors are shown an instructional five-minute video in English or Spanish.

Two kilometres away, the **Observatorio Astronómico Nacional** (Aug & Sept daily 5–11pm; ☎ 0274 245 0106, ✆ cida.gob .ve) opens its doors to the public during August and September to showcase its work in one of the world's highest observatories.

The Carretera Transandina highway eventually crosses the highest driveable summit in Venezuela, at Pico El Águila, and begins the spectacular descent to Barinas and Los Llanos (see below).

ARRIVAL AND DEPARTURE

By bus From the Mérida terminal buses for Apartaderos (every 15min; 2hr) leave from the designated platform until 6pm. You don't need to pay a *tasa de salida* to ride this route. To return to Mérida, flag down one of the buses which pass along the route every 20min or so until 6.30pm.

By taxi From Apartaderos taxis will take tourists to the condor refuge or the observatory for BsF200. Getting back is as simple as walking the kilometre (or paying anyone with a car to drive you) back to the bus route.

PARQUE NACIONAL SIERRA NEVADA

Looming above Mérida to the south and east, the Sierra Nevada runs northeast

---

LOS LLANOS

Taking up nearly a third of the country, the immense plains and wetlands of **Los Llanos** are one of the continent's premier wildlife-viewing areas. Some of the most abundant species are alligators, anacondas and capybaras, the world's largest rodent. Other common species are river dolphins, jaguars, pumas, howler and capuchin monkeys and anteaters. However, the livelihood of the region's human inhabitants, the Llaneros, is most closely linked with domesticated animals. Los Llaneros are extremely skilled horsemen and work in secluded groups on **hatos**, enormous ranches with cattle often numbering in the tens of thousands. Many comparisons have been drawn between the **llaneros** and the cowboys of the American West. Known for being tough and independent, both are portrayed as embodying the spirit of their countries.

Los Llanos has two very pronounced **seasons**. During the wet season, from May to November, much of the land becomes flooded and extremely verdant. In the dry season the land becomes parched and dusty, and vegetation changes colour to match the dry surroundings. The best wildlife viewing comes when water is scarce, when animals congregate at the few watering holes.

Unless you have a wad of cash to spend on a stay at one of the *hatos*, you'll most likely visit Los Llanos as part of a **multi-day tour** from Mérida (see p.893).

along the Carretera Transandina and through the 2760-square-kilometre **PARQUE NACIONAL SIERRA NEVADA**. There is great diversity in flora and fauna here, but the park's most famous inhabitant, the threatened spectacled bear, is a shy creature that you'll be lucky to see, although Mérida's zoo (see p.892) has one. The park features the country's highest mountains, which reach over 5000m, as well as its best **adventure activities**. You can easily explore the lower reaches on your own, but guides (see box, p.893) are recommended for the two higher peaks unless you are an experienced mountaineer.

Just inside the northern entrance to the park, a few kilometres along the highway from Apartaderos, is **Laguna Mucubají**. Camping is allowed here; you will need permission from the Inparques office near the entrance. A good hiking trail connects Laguna Mucubají with **Laguna Negra**, a trout-filled lake with dark water. The beautiful hike takes two hours, and you can continue another one hour thirty minutes to the pretty **Laguna Los Patos**. In the wet season, it's best to leave early to avoid rain and fog that could limit visibility considerably. Just outside the park entrance is *Refugio Mucubají*, a restaurant that sells good picnic supplies as well as excellent *arepas*, soups and coffees.

Pico Bolívar

At 5007m, **Pico Bolívar** is the country's highest and most hiked peak. There are multiple routes up, varying in difficulty and length of ascent. When the *teleférico* is operational, many walkers get off at the last station, Pico Espejo, and make the five-hour ascent along the Ruta Weiss. This is not very technical in the dry season (Dec–May). The Ruta Sur Este and North Flank are two more challenging routes, which involve ice-climbing and require ice axes and crampons. Views from the top are spectacular – on a clear day, you can see the city of Mérida, the Colombian Andes and the vast expanse of Los Llanos.

Pico Humboldt

Another renowned peak, **Pico Humboldt** can be combined with a climb of Pico

Bolívar or tackled on its own. Starting at the entrance of Parque Nacional La Mucuy, about 10km to the northeast of Mérida, the first day's ascent is 1000m; after the six-hour, 9km walk, most people camp around the picturesque Laguna Coromoto. The ascent on the second day is shorter but steeper as you get into the rocky terrain above the tree line. The final day's ascent to the peak and return to the campsite usually takes at least eight hours, depending upon your ice-climbing ability. The fourth day is for the descent back to La Mucuy.

ARRIVAL AND DEPARTURE

By bus The park entrance is on the Apartaderos route from Mérida; simply stay on the bus for a few kilometres after Apartaderos. To get back to Mérida or onwards to Barinas, flag down a passing bus in either direction, which pass every 20min or so until 6.30pm.

INFORMATION AND TOURS

Tourist information As well as the Inparques offices in Mérida at the base station of the *teleférico* (see p.892), there is one near the park entrance that can issue camping permits and dispense advice (Spanish only).

Tour operators Companies (see box, p.893) organize groups on a one-guide-to two-clients ratio; cost is BsF600 per day and all equipment is included. Routes (Weiss, Sur Este, North Flank) can be selected depending on experience and generally take six days, a time which can be cut to four with higher levels of expertise.

Guayana

Covering the southern and southeastern half of Venezuela, **Guayana** (not to be confused with the country Guyana) is comprised of three of Venezuela's largest states – Amazonas, Bolívar and Delta Amacuro. The region contains the vast majority of Venezuela's natural resources such as gold, iron ore, bauxite and diamonds. It also supplies hydroelectricity for large swathes of the country. Despite the immensity of Guayana, there are only two real cities, **Puerto Ordáz** and **Ciudad Bolívar**, which are vastly outnumbered by indigenous communities belonging to the Yanomami, Pemón, Warao and Piaroa,

11

all of whom have retained many of their customs.

The region is estimated to have been above sea level for three billion years; the resulting landscape is the area's biggest tourist draw, although its size means the individual sights are spread far apart. Attractions include the **tropical rainforests** of the Amazon, the mighty **Orinoco Delta**, the breathtaking **Angel Falls** and the magnificent *tepuis*, or flat-topped mountains. *Tepuis* means "Houses of the Gods" in the indigenous Pemón language, and the two most popular are the beautiful and isolated **Autana**, deep in the heart of thick jungle, and the immense **Mount Roraima** – the inspiration for Sir Arthur Conan Doyle's *The Lost World*.

PUERTO AYACUCHO

A sleepy town that's home to half the inhabitants of Amazonas, **PUERTO AYACUCHO** is the state's only major

municipality, founded in 1924 as a port for shipping timber downriver. Across the Orinoco from Colombia, it is the access point for the most southerly of the three Colombian border crossings (see box, p.888), although the difficulty of onward transport makes it the least convenient. Puerto Ayacucho is also the principal entry point for the Amazon region.

WHAT TO SEE AND DO

Like many other Venezuelan municipalities, Puerto Ayacucho itself has almost no intrinsic appeal, but there are several nearby attractions, the most popular of which is the immense **Autana**, a sole *tepui* which towers above the jungle around it.

In town, the **Museo Etnológico de Amazonas** (Tues–Fri 8.30am–noon & 2.30–5.45pm, Sat 8.30am–noon; BsF10), on Avenida Río Negro, showcases the culture and history of the region's indigenous tribes. In front of the

▲ Border at Casuarito (1km)

PUERTO AYACUCHO

ACCOMMODATION
Gran Hotel Amazonas	2
Posada Manapiare	4
Residencia Internacional	3
Residencias Michelangelli de Pozo	1

Mercado Municipal

AVENIDA ORINOCO
AVENIDA AGUERREVERE
ATATAPO
EVELIA ROA

Pharmacy

Laundry

BOLÍVAR
PIAR

AVENIDA RÍO NEGRO
CALLE AMAZONAS
LA GUARDIA

Centro Cultural Amazonas

Río Orinoco

Museo Etnológico de Amazonas

PLAZA DE LOS INDIOS

SAIME Office
Coyote Expediciones
AVENIDA AGUERREVERE
Banesco

Bank

Pharmacy

Cerro Perico ▲

AVENIDA 23 DE ENERO
UNIÓN

Bank

AVENIDA ORINOCO

El Mercadito

N

Banco de Venezuela

LUISA CÁCERES
CARABAÑO

EATING & DRINKING
Café Rey David	5
El Guariqueño	3
El Mercadito	4
Panadería Amazonas	2
Royal Pool	1

0   200
metres

(1km), Hospital (2km), Bus Terminal (4km) & Eco-Destinos

Mercatradona (300m), El Mirador (700m), Airport (6km) & Tourist Info ▼

museum is **Plaza de los Indios**, a market selling local handicrafts including *catara*, a delicious hot sauce made from leafcutter ants; like peanut butter, it comes either crunchy or smooth.

One block east of the plaza on Avenida Amazonas is the **Centro Cultural Amazonas** (Mon–Sat 8am–6pm; free), where the art gallery has an indigenous-themed permanent exhibit. Styles range from classical to quasi-pornographic absurdism. Ask the friendly staff for what's on at the amphitheatre next door.

The town's most popular attraction lies 30km away at the **Parque Tobogán de la Selva**, where a natural waterslide has been dammed at the bottom to create a rustic infinity pool. A return trip in a taxi to the park costs about BsF600 – make sure you arrange for pick-up.

ARRIVAL AND INFORMATION

You can cross into Colombia (see box, p.888) or Brazil (see box, p.908) from this region.

By plane Puerto Ayacucho Airport is 6km southeast of town. Conviasa (ⓦ conviasa.aero) operates flights to and from Caracas (3 weekly; 1hr 30min). Buses from the airport into town are rare; it's much easier to take a taxi (roughly BsF100).

By bus The bus terminal is 4km east of the centre and has nowhere to leave luggage. Taxis into town are hailed from the road outside the main entrance and cost BsF60.

Destinations Caracas (daily at 6pm; 15hr); Ciudad Bolívar (hourly with several night buses; 12hr); San Fernando de Apure (several daily until 5pm; 6hr); Valencia (daily at 6.30pm; 13hr).

Tourist information The Secretaría de Turismo is at the airport (Mon–Fri 8am–5pm; ☏ 0248 521 0033).

GETTING AROUND

By taxi Although Puerto Ayacucho does have city buses, you rarely see them and schedules are unpredictable. Most locals take taxis (in and around town BsF50); look for the "taxi" window-stickers rather than the rooftop signs. *Mototaxis* are a good option for when traffic clogs the city streets at peak hours.

ACCOMMODATION

Gran Hotel Amazonas Av Emilio Roa, at C Amazonas ☏ 0248 521 5633. The best hotel in town isn't that expensive. An attractive Amazon-themed reception is decorated with wooden parrots, tribal masks and tropical flowers, with spacious rooms set around the perimeter. There's a big swimming pool at the back, which you can pay BsF50 to use if you aren't staying there. BsF1200

★ **Posada Manapiare** Urb Alto Parima, Entrada no. 2 ☏ 0248 686 0062, ⓔ posadamanapiare@gmail.com. You'll have to remember your animal rather than room

---

AMAZON TOURS

Squeezing all of the Amazon's wonders into a three-day tour is impossible, but a few companies in Ayacucho do their best. The classic tour is a three-day/two-night trip up the Sipapo and Autana rivers to **Cerro Autana**, a 1200m-high *tepui* seen from an adjacent vantage point. You'll spend the nights in hammocks with an indigenous community, explore waterways in small boats and fish for exotic species which you can eat for dinner if successful. More in-depth and expensive options include the ten- to twelve-day **Ruta Humboldt**, following in the footsteps of the famous explorer, and even longer journeys to meet the Yanomami and other isolated tribes.

All-inclusive prices, for groups of four or more people, are US$60–80 per day per person for three or four days, usually more for longer trips. Companies provide any necessary jungle access permits and can often help you plan a journey into Brazil.

Finally, a **disclaimer**: many people expect to see amazing wildlife in the Amazon, but in reality the density of the jungle and the reclusiveness of the animals make this quite difficult. If you're set on wildlife-watching, save your money for a trip to Los Llanos (see p.896).

TOUR OPERATORS

Coyote Expediciones Av Aguerrevere 75 ☏ 0414 486 2500, ⓔ coyoteexpedition@cantv.net. Rarely in the office, Luis Coyote is better contacted by phone. He arranges tours throughout the region as well as trips along the narrow Río Casiquiare, on which the indigenous Báquiro live, a good alternative to Autana

if the weather isn't cooperating.

Eco-Destinos Ent. Urbanización Bolivariana, Quinta Los Abuelos ☏ 0416 448 6394 or ☏ 0248 521 3964, ⓦ amazonasvenezuela.com. Lets customers fully customize trips, for instance by suggesting they bring and prepare their own food to mitigate expenses.

number at this stylish posada between the bus terminal and town. Nice rooms are set around a terracotta-roofed courtyard and the restaurant is popular even with non-guests. Book ahead, preferably via email. Breakfast included. BsF800

Residencia Internacional Av Aguerrevere 18 ☎0248 521 0242. A colourful and cheap option in a quiet part of town. Some rooms have a/c and private bathrooms for BsF30 extra, and there's a matriarchal atmosphere from the indulgent grandmother who runs the place. A good *panadería* two doors down is a prime breakfast option. BsF500

Residencias Michelangelli de Pozo C Evelio Roa 35 ☎0248 521 3189. You may find yourself showering out of a bucket, since the plumbing occasionally gives out at this otherwise peaceful posada. Rooms (some with a/c) are very basic and set around a courtyard that's more concrete than greenery. BsF500

EATING AND DRINKING

In addition to the range of inexpensive restaurants about town, there is a string of food stalls along Av Aguerrevere, west of Av Orinoco, hawking *empanadas*, burgers, fried chicken and fish each evening.

Café Rey David Av Orinoco, south of the *mercadito* ☎0248 521 0074. Self-titled "King David" is something of a silver fox, and regally presides over his popular open-fronted place positioned right in the thick of it. Tasty *pollo asado* (BsF120), sandwiches (BsF80), *empanadas* (BsF60) and *arepas* (BsF80). Mon–Sat 7am–11pm.

El Guariqueño Av 23 de Enero ☎0248 521 4940. A popular place with *Ayacuchans* thanks to its big portions of *pollo al ajillo* or *pollo a la plancha* (both BsF250). Numerous ceiling fans make this an excellent spot to duck out of the heat and grab a refresher from the long list of juices (BsF60). Mon–Sat 10am–6pm.

El Mercadito Between Av Orinoco and Av Amazonas, south of Av 23 de Enero. The destination of choice for workers on a lunch break. Various indoor restaurants at the east end of the market serve inexpensive *comida criolla*, but for the real deal slurp down a steaming bowl of *sopa de gallina* (around BsF80) surrounded by knock-off DVD salesmen in the market itself.

Panadería Amazonas Av Rómulo Gallegos south of C Constitución. Regarded as the best *panadería* in town, the bread and pastries are nothing to write home about. However, the coffee is excellent and the gossipy staff provide ample entertainment. Daily 6.30am–8.30pm.

Royal Pool C Evelia Roa next to *Residencias Michelangelli*. The friendly and excitable patrons at this pool hall knock back cheap beers while casual games of pool, dominoes or cards proceed until late. There's a little-used jenga set behind the bar that will inspire fierce competition and jubilant celebration. Mon–Sat 6pm–1am.

DIRECTORY

Banks and exchange Banesco, Av Orinoco south of Av Aguerrevere; Banco de Venezuela on Av Orinoco south of Av 23 de Enero.

Hospital Clínica Amazonas, Av Rómulo Gallegos (☎0248 521 2454); Clínica Zerpa, Av 23 de Enero (☎0248 521 2815).

Immigration SAIME, Av Aguerrevere 60 (Mon–Fri 8am–4.30pm). For a Colombian visa (see p.491), the consulate is at C Yapacana, Quinta Beatriz (Mon–Fri 8am–1pm & 3–6pm; ☎0248 521 0789).

Internet Don't expect to be streaming YouTube in Ayacucho as connections are extremely slow if they work at all. Inversiones Friends (no sign), above CANTV, Av Orinoco, at Av Aguerrevere (Mon–Fri 8am–6pm; BsF4/hr); Servinet, C Atabapo, at Evelio Roa (daily 8am–8pm).

Laundry Lavandería Automática Acuario, Av Aguerrevere next to *Residencias Internacional* (Mon–Fri 8am–noon & 2–6pm, Sat 9am–noon & 2–5pm).

Pharmacy Farmacia Autana, Av Río Negro, at C Evelio Roa (Mon–Sat 8am–8pm); FarmaLlanos, Av Orinoco south of Av Aguerrevere (Mon–Sat 8am–6pm). On Sunday one of the two pharmacies is open.

Phones CANTV, Av Orinoco, at Av Aguerrevere; Movistar, Av Orinoco south of C Carabobo; Movilnet, C Evelio Roa, at C Atabapo.

Post office Ipostel, Av Amazonas, at C Roa (Mon–Fri 8am–noon & 2–5pm).

Shopping Mercatradona on Av Orinoco, at C Constitución (daily 8am–8pm, Sun until 1pm), is a Wal-Mart-sized monster for everything you might need. For local artisan jewellery head to Plaza de los Indios (Mon–Sat 8am–6pm, Sun until noon).

PUERTO ORDÁZ

Most of the visitors who pass through **PUERTO ORDÁZ** are on their way to Ciudad Bolívar, a much better jumping-off point for the main attractions in the state. The town is the base for Venezuela's aluminium, steel and iron industries, as well as a large producer of hydroelectric power from various dams in the area. It is consequently of little interest to the backpacker and is more of a transport hub. Nearby **San Félix**, an indecorous and seedy town, is best avoided entirely.

WHAT TO SEE AND DO

Built on an industrial scale, Puerto Ordáz's few sights are spread kilometres apart. Taxis are the easiest and safest way

GUAYANA TOURS

Most of the Ciudad Bolívar agencies also sell tours of the Orinoco Delta (see p.909) and Gran Sabana (see p.909), although for the latter you'll find better tour prices in Santa Elena. All agencies offer pretty much the same packages, so make sure you shop around for the best deal.

While it's possible to cobble together a trip to **Angel Falls** (see p.905) on your own, the small amount of money you save hardly warrants the effort of arranging all the various components (flights, boats, accommodation, food). Local tourism operates on the basis of package tours arranged elsewhere (usually Ciudad Bolívar), and the needs of maverick travellers are generally an afterthought. The standard three-day/two-night budget tour, with flights in and out of Canaima, should cost around BsF10,000. Prices are all-inclusive except for the BsF150 national park fee payable when you land in Canaima, and the Ciudad Bolívar airport tax (BsF30).

TOUR OPERATORS

Amor Patrio In *Posada Amor Patrio*, C Amor Patrio ☎0414 854 4925, ⓦposadaamorpatrioaventura.com. Specializes in Río Caura trips, rugged camping and visits to indigenous villages.

Eco-Adventures In the bus terminal ☎0285 651 9546, ⓦadventurevenezuela.com. Often mistaken for a pirate outfit due to its location, it's actually a great option for travellers who are keen to get things sorted once they've hopped off the bus.

Energy Tours At the airport ☎0285 617 4530, ⓦenergytour.com. Italian-owned company that offers Angel Falls trips combined with other destinations, usually the Gran Sabana, Orinoco Delta, Isla Margarita and Los Roques. Office hours are not strictly kept and they are best contacted through the website.

Excursiones Don Carlos In *Posada Don Carlos*, C Boyacá ☎0285 632 6017, ⓦposada-doncarlos.com.

Organizes tours throughout the country with reputable operators, as well as offering bank transfers at *mercado paralelo* rates if you're running short on cash.

Excursiones Salto Ángel C Libertad 31 ☎0412 190 5084, ⓦsaltoangel.com.ve. English-speaking Rodman covers the whole state with a range of activities, although, as the name suggests, he specializes in the waterfalls. Tailor-made packages range from luxury to basic.

Sapito Tours At the airport ☎0285 632 7989, ⓦsapitotours.com. The tour agency arm of *Campamento Bernal* in Canaima, specializing in tourism around the village.

Turi Express Dorado At the airport ☎0285 634 1243. Long-established company that has been operating for over two decades, offering the usual packages as well as tours of Ciudad Bolívar itself.

---

popular spot for picnicking locals, while deeper into the gardens, which should be toured with a guide (free, although a BsF10 tip is appropriate), is an impressive array of plants from around the world. The park's main entrance is on Avenida Bolívar at the intersection with Calle Caracas.

ARRIVAL AND INFORMATION

By plane The airport (Tomás de Heres Airport; ☎0285 632 6635) is at the southeastern edge of town, on Av Táchira, at Av Aeropuerto. Taxis to and from the *casco histórico* cost around BsF160. Buses displaying Ruta 1 or Ruta 2 in the windscreen go via the airport and cost BsF4; hail one from the shopping side of the Paseo Orinoco.

Destinations Caracas (daily; 1hr); Maturín (daily; 1hr). For Canaima, numerous companies fly daily for BsF6000 return; tickets can be bought in advance at the airport or organized by your hotel.

By bus The terminal lies southwest of the centre on Av República, at Av Sucre. Taxis to or from the centre cost BsF120, while buses heading to the terminal can be hailed

from the river side of Paseo Orinoco. Tickets can only be bought on the day of departure; for less-served destinations (particularly Santa Elena and Barinas) you should buy your night bus ticket in the morning.

Destinations Barinas (2 daily; 15hr); Caracas (several daily; 9hr); Puerto Ayacucho (several daily; 14hr); Puerto La Cruz (4 daily; 5hr); Puerto Ordáz (every 30min; 1hr); Santa Elena de Uairén (6 daily, mostly night buses; 12hr); Valencia (several daily; 10hr).

Tourist information The Secretaría de Turismo and its extremely enthusiastic staff are in the main entrance of the Jardín Botánico (daily 8am–5pm; ☎0800 674 6626, ⓔsecretariadeturismoyambiente@gmail.com); there's also a Venetur desk at the airport (daily 8am–5pm; ☎0800 462 8871).

ACCOMMODATION

Ciudad Bolívar is rivalled only by Mérida in its selection of great, cheap accommodation.

Posada Amor Patrio C Amor Patrio, at Plaza Bolívar ☎0414 854 4925, ⓦposadaamorpatrioaventura.com. In a building that's nearly 300 years old, this German-owned

11

★ **TREAT YOURSELF**

La Casa Grande C Venezolana, at C Boyacá ☎ 0424 851 2295, ✉ angostura@cacaotravel.com. Utterly peerless in Ciudad Bolívar, if not in Venezuela, this luxurious boutique hotel seamlessly blends graceful modern flair with charming imperial decadence in the former headquarters of the Red Cross. A skylit atrium contains plants and a fountain, and a rooftop pool has expansive views of the Orinoco. En-suite rooms have a/c, flat-screen TVs, exposed original stonework and safes. The staff provide free transport to and from the bus terminal and airport. A stately breakfast is included. **BsF4500**

posada rocks a chilled vibe throughout. Rooms are named after exotic locations across the globe and the atmospheric *salón del ritmo* brims with Caribbean personality. There's a kitchen, laundry service and internet (but no wi-fi). Also has a tour agency. **BsF600**

★ **Posada Don Carlos** C Boyacá, at C Amor Patrio ☎ 0285 632 6017, ⊛ posada-doncarlos.com. You can just picture Venezuelan gentry sipping on some dark rum at the bar of this characterful posada. Rooms are off the large colonial courtyard, dotted with all sorts of nineteenth-century knick-knacks. There's a dormitory/balcony area with bunk beds and hammocks for BsF400. Also runs a reputable tour agency. **BsF600**

Posada Doña Carol C Libertad 28 ☎ 0285 634 0989. Wacky grandma Doña Carol welcomes you into her oddly decorated house with a friendly smile. There's a bright colour scheme, wi-fi, five spotless rooms (some with a/c) and a balcony upstairs that overlooks the surrounding roofs. **BsF500**

Posada Turística Sousa C Libertad, at C Venezuela ☎ 0426 799 7663. The cheapest rooms in town, although you may find yourself with neighbours who are paying by the hour. Nevertheless, tight security makes it a safe option. **BsF450**

EATING

Ciudad Bolívar is not particularly noted for its food, but a few decent options exist. Local fish such as *dorado*, *palometa* and *sapoara* are fresh and tasty.

El Caribeño C Igualdad between Paseo Orinoco & C Venezuela ☎ 0285 444 8166. A very simple, very cheap cafeteria serving breakfasts (*pastelitos*, *empanadas*, *jugos*) and full meals (*pollo a la brasa*, *bisteck*, *pescado*) with sides of rice, salad, yucca and more – nothing over BsF180. Daily 6am–7pm.

★ **Comidas Margarita** C Bolívar, at C Libertad ☎ 0285 617 8424. The juice (BsF40) comes in jam jars and the

coffee comes free at this bright blue lunch option. Grab a spare seat at one of the few tables and browse the day's menu on the whiteboard out front. Chat with the friendly lunchers or watch the world go by while you tackle the big portions (all BsF220). Mon–Sat 6.30am–3pm.

Mini-lunch Arabian Food C Amor Patrio, at C Igualdad ☎ 0285 632 7208. A little corner café that provides a fix of Middle Eastern fare for when you can't handle beans and rice any more. Beef, chicken or mixed *shawarma* goes for BsF120, while the large platter of falafel, *kibbe*, tabbouleh, meat and hummus is BsF380. Mon–Sat 7am–7pm, occasionally Sun.

Restaurant Vegetariano C Amor Patrio, at C Dalla Costa ☎ 0285 632 6381. A four-course vegetarian meal for BsF160 is not to be sniffed at, while the friendly owner runs four daily yoga classes for which contributions are encouraged but not enforced. An oasis of patrician calm; grab a few guavas from the tree in the courtyard on your way in or out. Mon–Fri noon–3pm.

Restaurante Caribe C Libertad 33 ☎ 0416 697 4707. Two large rooms full of tables occupy the front of this family home, where you can bang on the door after hours as they're usually willing to feed you. Basic food at basic prices: soups BsF100, mains BsF320. Mon–Sat 11am–8pm.

Tostadas Juancito's Av Cumaná, at C Bolívar. Fun and friendly outdoor terrace with stone tables, offering cheap and tasty street food, including *arepas* (BsF80), *pabellón criollo* (BsF170, and *pollo a la brasa* (quarter BsF140). Pay at the cash register first and hand your ticket to the counter staff. Mon–Sat 7am–6pm.

DIRECTORY

Banks and exchange Banco de Venezuela, Paseo Orinoco, at C Constitución; Banesco, C Dalla Costa, at C Venezuela.

Hospital Hospital Ruiz y Páez, Av Germania (☎ 0285 632 0041).

Internet Val Web, C Venezuela, at C Libertad (Mon–Fri 8am–5.30pm; BsF6/hr).

Pharmacy Numerous around town, *por turno* (only one open at a time) on Sun. Farmacia Unión, C Venezuela, at C Libertad (Mon–Sat 8am–6pm); Hospifárma, Paseo Orinoco at C Carabobo (Mon–Sat 8am–5.30pm).

Phones Movistar, Paseo Orinoco between calles Dalla Costa and Libertad. There's another *centro de llamadas* on C Dalla Costa between calles Venezuela and Bolívar.

Police In the Jardín Botánico by the tourist office (daily 8am–8pm, no phone).

Post office Ipostel, Av Táchira, 1km south of the *casco histórico*.

Shopping For groceries there's a fruit/veg market along C Venezuela until 4pm daily; numerous stands and shops along the Paseo Orinoco sell *artesanía*, cheap clothing and electronics.

PARQUE NACIONAL CANAIMA

One of the world's largest national parks, **PARQUE NACIONAL CANAIMA** is Venezuela's number one tourist attraction, due entirely to the world's tallest waterfall, the astonishing Salto Ángel, or **Angel Falls**. The park is inhabited by roughly twenty thousand Pemón Indians, made up of three major tribes: Kamakoto, Arekuna and Taurepan. Most live in small villages of between 100 and 200 people. At the centre of it all is **Canaima Village**, originally a small Pemón settlement that is now the hub of a tourism industry vastly superior to those you are likely to witness elsewhere in Venezuela. The falls are a world-class attraction without the accompanying crowds – perhaps due in part to a reliance on local guides and agencies that have garnered reputations for unprofessionalism.

Canaima Village

The most visited village in the park, **Canaima** is the principal base for trips to Angel Falls. On the other side of **Laguna de Canaima** from the lodges are four postcard-worthy waterfalls – **Salto Ucaima**, **Salto Golondrina**, **Salto Guadima** and **Salto Hacha** – the latter being the largest, discharging enough water to fill an Olympic-sized swimming pool in a single second. The lagoon has a sandy beach and palm trees jutting out of the water, at the end of which is the hydroelectric power station that supplies the village and surrounding area with electricity. It can be visited at all hours, but is usually seen on the way to the jetty above the falls from where the boats depart upriver.

Tour packages (see box, p.903) include a short excursion to another nearby waterfall, **Salto El Sapo**, which you can actually walk right behind (make sure you protect your camera properly, as you will get soaked).

Angel Falls

At nearly a vertical kilometre (980m), **ANGEL FALLS** (Salto Ángel in Spanish) is the world's tallest waterfall – around sixteen times the height of Niagara Falls and twelve times the height of Iguazú Falls. It is created by the Churún River,

which makes a dramatic plunge from the edge of the enormous Auyantepui and into the verdant jungle below.

Seeing the falls is one of the highlights of a trip to Venezuela, and you can arrange a visit through tour agencies in Ciudad Bolívar (see p.903) and even Caracas (see p.862). The first leg of the trip is a three-hour, 70km and very wet boat ride up the Caroní and Carrao rivers from Canaima Village; the second leg is an hour's hike through the jungle, ending at the falls' principal vantage point. The falls themselves are generally fuller, and therefore more spectacular, during the rainy season; the trade-off is less visibility, as the top of the falls can be covered in clouds during those months.

In the **dry season** (Jan–May), low water levels in the access rivers can complicate the journey, sometimes requiring passengers to unload and push the boat. Tour agencies are usually diligent about warning customers of such conditions, but it's a good idea to ask anyway.

ARRIVAL AND TOURS

By plane Canaima is primarily accessed by small planes, and in most cases moving on is simply a matter of boarding your pre-arranged return flight to Ciudad Bolívar. The airstrip is on the village's main road. The main airline is Transmandu (⊛transmandu.com); if you're arranging your own transport expect to pay BsF6000 return from Ciudad Bolívar. Tickets can be purchased at the airport's various airplane desks. In theory you can charter a plane to Santa Elena, although the high prices and five-passenger minimum make the twelve-hour overnight bus ride (see p.906) from Ciudad Bolívar a more viable option. There are no direct flights to Caracas.

Destinations Ciudad Bolívar (4 daily; 1hr 30min) and Puerto Ordáz (2 daily; 2hr).

Tour operators If you've come to Canaima on a tour, a guide will have been arranged for you; if you're on your own, seek out English-speaking Materson Nathaniel (☎0426 997 2879, ✉kaikuse_68@yahoo.es) or Yosmary López (☎0416 852 1558, ✉amanon983@gmail.com), who both run tours to Angel Falls and Salto el Sapo, as well as to other lesser-known sights around the region.

ACCOMMODATION

Like transport, accommodation in Canaima is included in pre-arranged tour packages. All lodgings, save the exclusive luxury ones, are *campamentos* of varying simplicity (the cheapest are listed here; they charge per person rather than per room). On the excursion to Angel Falls you'll spend the night in one of the various camps built close to the falls, usually around an hour's walk to the viewing point. Note that tour prices from Canaima exclude flights.

Tiuna 🕿 0414 864 0033, 🖂 tiunatours@hotmail.com. By far the most receptive option (as well as the cheapest) for independent travellers, *Tiuna* has a serene location at the edge of Canaima Lagoon. The 3-day/2-night Angel Falls tour is BsF1000. Hammocks BsF400, dorms BsF1200

Wey Tupuy 🕿 0414 191 8708, 🖂 weytupui@hotmail .com. Expanding to triple in size at the time of research, this high-capacity place beside the lagoon has perfectly decent rooms and a good restaurant. An extra BsF1000 if you want three square meals. BsF1400

EATING AND DRINKING

Food is included in tour prices; vegetarians should notify the agency when purchasing a tour. *Posada Kusari* (which is a poor accommodation option for BsF1400) close to *Tiuna* runs a general store, though prices are outrageous since all stock is flown in. As a tourist hub, Canaima has a fairly decent social life, with locals, tourists and guides always up for a party.

Bar Morichal At *Campamento Morichal*. A beach bar popular with the locals, guides and tourists alike. The dancefloor has disco lights, an impressive sound system and DJs. If your salsa isn't up to scratch, grab a few unsurprisingly expensive beers from the bar, take a seat in one of the parked boats and watch the waterfalls across the lagoon. Daily noon until the last patron leaves.

Salon Ikupai At *Venetur Campamento Canaima*. Occupying the best spot on the lagoon, the state-owned resort's restaurant and bar has unreal views of Canaima's waterfalls across the water. Come to watch the sunset from the specially designed viewing terrace, order a cocktail and soak it all in. Beers BsF80, cocktails BsF200. Daily 6am–midnight.

SANTA ELENA DE UAIRÉN

SANTA ELENA DE UAIRÉN grew significantly when the paved road connecting it with the rest of the country was completed, but, with a population of only eighteen thousand, it's still a quiet town. Many of its inhabitants are originally from Brazil, whose border is just 15km away. The town serves as a good base for exploring the awe-inspiring *tepuis*, as well as being a **good access point for Brazil** (see box, p.908), where Manaus is the closest major city. Although there's little to do, Santa Elena is a very backpacker-friendly town, with reasonably priced accommodation and restaurants. Two blocks southeast of the Plaza Bolívar a **baseball field** hosts local matches in the evenings, where the party atmosphere is fun, beers are cheap and gringos are warmly welcomed whether or not they can follow what's going on. The town is the best place to book tours to the **Gran Sabana** and up **Mount Roraima** (see p.709).

ARRIVAL AND INFORMATION

By plane Flights arrive from Ciudad Bolívar and Puerto Ordáz, though schedules are unpredictable and planes tend to be relatively old and very small.

By bus The bus terminal is 3km from the town centre, a short BsF100 taxi ride; there are no city buses. From Ciudad

---

EXCHANGING BRAZILIAN REAIS FOR BOLÍVARES

The Brazilian town of Pacaraima's designation as "**puerto libre**" – permitting visitors across the border without immigration formalities if they return the same day – allows you to replenish funds without resorting to Venezuela's unfavourable official exchange rate at an ATM or bank. The border is open 7am–10pm.

Grab your passport and bankcard and head to the intersection of calles Icabaru and Roscio, where *por puestos* leave regularly for the border (20min; BsF60). In the unlikely event that you're stopped when crossing, explain to officials that you're returning to Venezuela the same day; make sure they **do not stamp** your passport (if they do, you'll have to wait a day to return to Venezuela). Once you're over, visit one of several available ATMs and withdraw Brazilian reais (current exchange rate US$1 = R$2.5).

Back in Santa Elena, head to the intersection of calles Urdaneta and Bolívar, where unofficial moneychangers congregate. You can change cash on the street, although they often have better rates at the open-fronted offices where you can sit and take your time over the transaction. You should be able to exchange R$1 for at least BsF80, maximizing the value of your money within Venezuela.

Bolívar there are two checkpoints on the way to Santa Elena as well as a full baggage search when you arrive at the terminal, so keep your passport handy.

Destinations Caracas (daily; 22hr); Ciudad Bolívar (4 daily; 12hr), stopping in Puerto Ordáz; Manaus (daily at 1pm; 12hr); Puerto la Cruz (2 daily; 16hr).

Tourist information Vía La Línea, on the way to the Brazilian border (☎0414 998 7167).

ACCOMMODATION

The best places, along with most other backpacker services, are on C Urdaneta between C Icarabú and Av Perimetral.

Lucrecia Av Perimetral ☎0289 995 1105. Spacious plot, popular with Brazilians and Venezuelans. The rooms are pleasant, and there's a good-sized swimming pool out back. BsF800

★Posada Backpackers C Urdaneta ☎0289 995 1430, ⓦbackpacker-tours.com. Easily the best spot in town for backpackers, this colourful German-owned posada is covered with murals, has spotless rooms and dormitories on the upper floor, and shares the building with an excellent bar. There's a reputable tour agency (see p.709) and wi-fi. Dorms BsF200, doubles BsF700

Posada Hotel Michelle C Urdaneta ☎0289 416 1257. A good choice on the backpacker strip with clean, although somewhat gloomy, rooms. Laundry service (BsF50/kg), kitchen and book exchange. BsF600

Posada Moronkatok C Urdaneta ☎0289 995 1518. The staff here aren't exactly sure what the place is called, there being no sign; just look for a gated entrance with red pillars across from Lavandería Pereira. There's a communal kitchen surrounded by decent rooms, all with cable TV and some with hot water. BsF600

Posada Los Pinos ☎0289 995 1430 or ☎0414 886 7227, ⓦposadapinos.com. Under the same management as *Posada Backpackers*, this pricier option a 10min walk from town has nineteen rooms, each inspired by Indian tribes and Venezuelan plants. There's also a fun Flintstones-esque pool with a slide. BsF800 extra for dinner and breakfast. BsF1800

EATING

Santa Elena has some good eating options, particularly if you want to sample authentic Brazilian fare. After dark, numerous burger stands set up along C Icabarú between calles Urdaneta and Zea and serve up tasty grub until around midnight.

11

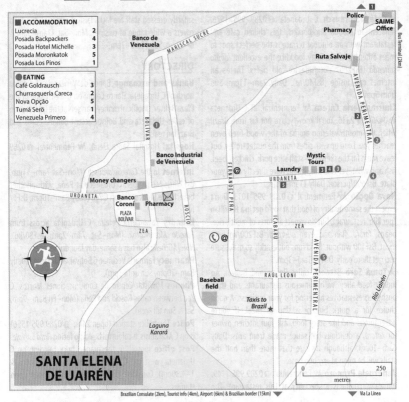

ACCOMMODATION
Lucrecia	2
Posada Backpackers	4
Posada Hotel Michelle	3
Posada Moronkatok	5
Posada Los Pinos	1

EATING
Café Goldrausch	3
Churrasquería Careca	1
Nova Opção	5
Tumá Serö	2
Venezuela Primero	4

SANTA ELENA DE UAIRÉN

Police

SAIME Office

Pharmacy

Ruta Salvaje

Banco de Venezuela

MARISCAL SUCRE

AVENIDA PERIMETRAL

Bus Terminal (2km)

BOLÍVAR

Banco Industrial de Venezuela

Mystic Tours

Laundry

URDANETA

FERNANDEZ PENA

Money changers

URDANETA

Banco Coroní

Pharmacy

PLAZA BOLÍVAR

ROSCIO

ZEA

ZEA

ICABARÚ

AVENIDA PERIMETRAL

N

Baseball field

RAÚL LEONI

Taxis to Brazil

Laguna Karará

Río Uairén

0 250 metres

Brazilian Consulate (2km), Tourist info (4km), Airport (6km) & Brazilian border (15km) ▼   ▼ Vía La Línea

11

CROSSING INTO BRAZIL

There are two main border crossings between Venezuela and Brazil. The primary crossing is at **Santa Elena de Uairén** (see p.906), a simple affair with good onward connections to Manaus. The other, at **San Simón de Cocuy**, involves a twelve-day boat journey only possible from November–May at around US$150/day. For more information on this trip see ⓦ selvadentro.com.

Citizens of the US, Canada and Australia need a visa to enter Brazil; European, South African and New Zealand nationals do not, although citizens of Spain must register at the nearest police station upon entry. For a list of all countries' visa requirements, visit ⓦ dpf.gov.br. All visitors must have a valid yellow-fever vaccination certificate. Advance your watch half an hour when entering Brazil (or 1hr 30min depending on daylight saving time).

SANTA ELENA DE UAIRÉN

The Brazilian Consulate in Santa Elena, on C Los Castaños (Mon–Fri 8am–2pm; ☏ 0289 995 1256), supplies visas within 72hr, although they usually process them the same day. You must provide a passport photo and give the address for your first port of call in Brazil. Visa fees vary by country of citizenship. If you have a problem, there's a SAIME office behind the police station in Santa Elena.

The border at Santa Elena is open 7am–10pm. There is one daily bus at 1pm from Santa Elena to Manaus in Brazil (16hr; BsF1600).

From within Brazil regular buses run to Manaus from Boa Vista, the terminal of which you can get to from the border in a taxi for R$40. TAM (ⓦ tam.com.br) also flies from Boa Vista to Manaus (daily; 1hr).

You can also cross the border simply to change money (see box, p.906).

★**Café Goldrausch** C Urdaneta ☏ 0289 995 1576. Adjacent to *Posada Backpackers*, this chilled café and restaurant with an outdoor terrace is the perfect spot to meet other travellers. Tasty food like the excellent *lomito salteado* (BsF280) alongside ice-cold beers. There's an internet café inside (BsF40/hr). Daily 7am–11pm, Sun from 5pm.

Churrasquería Careca Av Perimentral, at C Urdaneta ☏ 0426 294 2336. You'll know you're not far from Brazil when the mouthwatering aroma of the wood-fired oven reaches you. Load up with sides from the buffet trolley, but leave room for the skewers – staff slice pork, chicken, beef, fish and whatever else they might have directly onto your plate. BsF600/person. Daily 11am–5pm.

Nova Opção Av Perimentral ☏ 0289 995 1013. Don't expect the same quality of food that you'd get in a Brazilian "per kilo" restaurant, but do expect all sorts of meats, rice, beans, *farofa*, flan and even *guaraná*. BsF200/kg with meat, BsF100 without. Food runs out quickly so make sure you get there early. Daily 11am–3pm.

★**Tumá Serö** Between calles Roscio and Bolívar. An indoor food-alley, with numerous restaurants and their pushy representatives hollering for your business. A good choice for a quick bite or a slap-up meal. If you're adventurous and like spicy food, ask your kitchen owner for *catara*, a delicious hot sauce made from ants. Daily 6am–10pm, although it's rare that more than half the stalls will be open at any one time.

Venezuela Primero Av Perimentral ☏ 0289 995 1149. Ironically, paella is a speciality at this restaurant. The smartly dressed staff are lackadaisical although the food covers a wide range of cuisines. Mon–Sat 11am–3pm & 6–10pm, Sun 11am–2pm.

DIRECTORY

Banks and exchange Banco de Venezuela, C Bolívar north of C Urdaneta; Banco Coroní on the east side of the Plaza Bolívar. Unofficial moneychangers at the intersection of calles Urdaneta and Bolívar accept dollars, euros and Brazilian reais.

Hospital Hospital Santa Elena, Av Perimentral ☏ 0289 995 1155.

Internet In the *Café Goldrausch* (Mon–Sat 7am–11pm, BsF7/hr); Megacyber, C Urdaneta at Peña, with another branch one block south on C Zea (daily 8am–10pm, BsF6/hr).

Laundry Lavandería Pereira, C Urdaneta across from *Posada Moronkatok* (Mon–Sat 7am–7pm; BsF80/kg). *Hotel Michelle* also has a same-day laundry service.

Pharmacy Farmacía Vecimar, C Bolívar, at Urdaneta (daily 8am–10pm, Sun until 3pm).

Phones Movistar/Centro de Comunicaciones Marcos, C Zea between calles Roscio and Peña (Mon–Fri 8am–9pm, Sat & Sun till 8pm).

Police The police station (open 24hr; ☏ 0289 995 1556) is on C Akarabisis, a colourful building facing *Ruta Salvaje*.

Post office Ipostel, in the orange brick building on C Urdaneta west of C Roscio (Mon–Fri 8am–noon & 1–4.30pm). Consider yourself lucky if you happen upon stamps.

LA GRAN SABANA AND RORAIMA

While few Venezuelans have ever visited the vast region of lush grassland, deep primary rainforest and mighty *tepuis* that is the **GRAN SABANA**, it is nevertheless one of the grandest natural spectacles their country has to offer. At the triple frontier of Venezuela, Brazil and Guyana lies the area's principal attraction: the beautiful and climbable **MOUNT RORAIMA**, a flat-topped mountain with 400m-high cliffs protecting its summit, which is renowned for its otherworldly landscape and was the inspiration for Sir Arthur Conan Doyle's *The Lost World*. The entire region is filled with other magnificent *tepuis* and waterfalls, separated by vast expanses of grasslands.

One of the most famous waterfalls is **Quebrada de Jaspe**, noted for its bright red jasper rock. Other well-known waterfalls in the region include the 105m-high **Salto Aponguao**, where you can swim in the nearby **Pozo Escondido**, and **Quebrada Pacheco**, two pretty falls with natural waterslides.

THE ORINOCO DELTA

A unique phenomenon, the enormous **Orinoco Delta** is formed as Venezuela's mightiest river reaches the Atlantic below Trinidad, finishing its 2736km course through the country. It is here that it divides and seeps through a 44,000-square-kilometre area of jungle, forming a network of navigable waterways (known as *caños*) on which the Warao Indians have lived for millennia. Trips to the Orinoco Delta go to tourist *campamentos* built on the riverbanks, although all are very basically equipped.

11

GRAN SABANA AND RORAIMA TOURS

The classic six-day trek to the top of **Mount Roraima**, considered by many to be one of the best hikes in South America, is now also one of the cheapest (around BsF12,000) if you book using Bolívars, thanks to the state of Venezuela's economy. Since the price is based on distance rather than time, agencies are usually willing to add or subtract a day to fit your schedule. Multi-day **Gran Sabana** tours typically take a minimum of five people and include all meals. One- or two-day trips to **El Pauji**, **El Abismo**, **Salto Aponguao** and other specific sites cost around BsF2500/day/person, meals included, although prices drop as group size increases. If you want to visit multiple sites on the same day, rates increase considerably. The following are operators in Santa Elena:

TOUR OPERATORS

Backpacker Tours C Urdaneta ☎ 0289 995 1430, ⓦ backpacker-tours.com. The most expensive of the bunch, but has a permanent guide staff, sells air tickets and supplies its own equipment, including high-quality tents, bicycles and trucks. Offers shorter alternatives (Mantopai and Chiricayén) to the six-day Roraima trek that costs BsF12,000.

Mystic Tours C Urdaneta ☎ 0289 416 1081 or ☎ 0289 416 0686, ⓦ mystictours.com.ve. Said to be along one of the world's major energy meridians, which also passes through Machu Picchu and Stonehenge, Gran Sabana has caused many visitors to experience extremely lucid dreams, spiritual rejuvenations and even to see UFOs. Mystic Tours has built a solid reputation on its unique mystical approach to the Gran Sabana and in particular to Roraima – the owner is a scholar of the paranormal and has written guidebooks on the area.

Ruta Salvaje Av Mariscal Sucre, at C Akarabisis ☎ 0289 995 1134 or ☎ 0414 889 4164, ⓦ rutasalvaje .com. From a hut beside the police station, Ruta Salvaje sells art painted by the owner's family and organizes adrenaline-boosting activities around the Gran Sabana including paragliding (BsF1600), rafting (BsF1400) on class I to IV rapids and paramotoring (BsF4000) on all-inclusive day tours. Prices listed are per person for a group of two; rates go down the larger the group gets.

Turísticos Álvarez In the bus terminal ☎ 0414 385 2846, ⓦ saltoangelrsta.com. Francisco Álvarez has wallpapered his bus terminal office with information flyers, and can be found inside organizing trips for budget-conscious travellers. Sorting out bare-bones packages, he also rents tents and offers trips to Gran Sabana from just BsF800/day.

ORINOCO DELTA TOURS

There are various lodges within the delta, which you can contact directly, as well as agencies throughout the country that organize trips in the region. The region is generally accessed from the cities of Ciudad Bolívar and Puerto Ordaz, from which boats are taken down the mighty Orinoco before it reaches the delta.

Activities generally include visiting indigenous Warao villages, canoeing through the small *caños*, fishing for piranha and observing local flora and fauna on jungle walks. Packages cost US$100–140 per person per day (far less if you book in Bolívars within the country) and are all-inclusive.

TOUR OPERATORS

Orinoco Queen ✆ 0414 871 9339, 🌐 lobo-tours.de. Built and run by the owner of *Casa del Lobo* in Puerto Ordáz, the *Orinoco Queen* is the smallest and most personal of the numerous camps in the area. A three-night stay, one of them spent in the hammocks at a nearby Warao village, costs US$300 and includes all food and activities; piranha fishing, jungle walks and expeditions in dugout canoes. Can also organize customized tours throughout the country.

Tucupita Expeditions Boulevard Playa El Agua, Isla Margarita ✆ 0295 249 1823 or ✆ 0414 794 0172, 🌐 orinocodelta.com. Margarita Island-based company operating trips to the Orinoco with stays in three different lodges, some more rustic than others. English-speaking guides available. Free pick-up from Maturín, Puerto Ordáz or Tucupita.

Waro Waro Lodge ✆ 0424 162 1960, 🌐 orinocodeltatours.com. Named after the Warao word for the electric-blue butterflies that flutter around the region, this intimate rustic French-Argentine owned lodge is located on the Jaropuna channel northwest of the delta. The lodge arranges transport either from Maturín on the northeast coast or from Ciudad Bolívar (BsF400 extra, book in advance).

The northeast coast and islands

The **northeast coast** is home to some of the country's most ruggedly beautiful coastline, where sleepy fishing villages lie unperturbed by the proximity of some of the country's most energetic cities. **Puerto La Cruz**, a high-rise fast-food paradise, is the coastline's main hub, and makes for a diverting afternoon's people-watching on the seafront. A short ferry ride away is **Isla Margarita**, Venezuela's largest island, whose mega-resorts and island vibe are a huge magnet for Venezuelans taking a break from the mainland.

Between Puerto La Cruz and Cumaná (the continent's first European settlement, although there's little to see) is **Parque Nacional Mochima**, loved for its uninhabited cays and under-the-radar charm. Still further east, **Caripe** is a pretty mountain town nestled away at chillier altitudes, where mountain sports, volunteer work and the astonishing Cueva del Guácharo are excellent diversions.

PUERTO LA CRUZ

The bustling collection of high-rises that calls itself **PUERTO LA CRUZ** isn't that long removed from being a fishing village. Not that you'll notice much to give away its rural past; it acts primarily as a hub for tourists heading to Parque Nacional Mochima (see p.912) or taking the ferry to Isla Margarita (see p.915). There's little reason to spend long here, although the wide seafront promenade makes for an enjoyable afternoon of strolling and people-watching, especially when there's a cool breeze rolling in off the Caribbean.

WHAT TO SEE AND DO

There's really nothing much to see in Puerto La Cruz itself – most **activities** take place outside the urban limits. For beaches and boat rides in Parque Nacional Mochima, you're better off organizing excursions from Santa Fe or Mochima within the park.

Los Altos de Sucre

A do-it-yourself diversion is to head to the bus terminal for the frequent shared jeeps (40min; BsF80) to **Los Altos de Sucre**, a small community hidden in the hills above Puerto La Cruz, near the

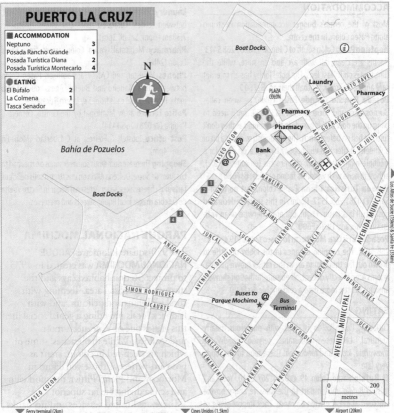

PUERTO LA CRUZ

■ ACCOMMODATION	
Neptuno	3
Posada Rancho Grande	1
Posada Turística Diana	2
Posada Turística Montecarlo	4

■ EATING	
El Bufalo	2
La Colmena	1
Tasca Senador	3

N

Bahía de Pozuelos

Boat Docks

Boat Docks

Boat Docks

Laundry

PLAZA COLON

Pharmacy

Pharmacy

Pharmacy

Bank

Buses to Parque Mochima

Bus Terminal

PASEO COLON

CARABOBO
ALBERTO RAVEL
FLORES
GUARAGUAO
ARISMENDI
MIRANDA
FREITES
AVENIDA 5 DE JULIO
MANEIRO
BOLIVAR
LIBERTAD
BUENOS AIRES
JUNCAL
SUCRE
GIRARDOT
ANZOATEGUI
AVENIDA 5 DE JULIO
SIMON RODRIGUEZ
RICAURTE
VENEZUELA
CEMENTERIO
DEMOCRACIA
ESPERANZA
CONCORDIA
LA PROVIDENCIA
AVENIDA MUNICIPAL
DEMOCRACIA
ESPERANZA
BUENOS AIRES
SUCRE
MANEIRO
AVENIDA MUNICIPAL

Los Altos de Sucre (15km) & Santa Fe (35km)

11

0   200
metres

Ferry terminal (2km)   Cines Unidos (1.5km)   Airport (20km)

border of Anzoátegui State. The lush, rural roads couldn't be further in spirit from the city's mayhem, and are known for their numerous pastry and *artesanía* shops and spectacular views of the bay below. Shout "*¡parada!*" at the bus driver wherever you want to get off along the Via Principal de los Altos.

ARRIVAL AND INFORMATION

By plane The nearest airport is in Barcelona, roughly 20km southwest of Puerto La Cruz and served by frequent buses. From the Barcelona terminal, numerous local bus routes cover the airport. A taxi from Puerto La Cruz costs around BsF600.

Destinations Caracas (6 daily; 45min); Maracaibo (2 daily except Sat; 3hr); Mérida (daily except Sun; 2hr 30min with 1 connection); Porlamar (2 daily; 30min); Puerto Ordáz (2 daily; 40min); Valencia (3 daily Sun–Fri, 1 daily Sat; 40min). Avior flies to Miami at 9.30am on Wed–Fri and Mon.

By bus The bus terminal is on C Democracia at C Concordia, an easy walk from most accommodation. Playa Colorada, Santa Fe and Mochima are all served along the same route. *Busetas* depart (6am–8pm) when full from C Democracia beside the liquor shop outside the terminal.

Destinations Barinas (3 daily; 12hr); Barquisimeto (4 daily; 5hr); Caracas (hourly; 6hr); Ciudad Bolívar (8 daily; 5hr) also serving Puerto Ordáz; Coro (daily at 3pm; 11hr); Cumaná (half-hourly; 2hr); Maracaibo (4 daily; 15hr); Mérida (daily at 10am; 17hr); Santa Elena de Uairén (daily at 3pm; 18hr); Valencia (several daily; 7hr).

By ferry The port terminal is about 3km west of the town centre. Ferries arrive and depart daily from Isla Margarita with Conferry (☎0281 267 7847, ⊛conferry.com), Naviarca/Gran Cacique (☎0281 267 7286, ⊛grancacique.com.ve) and Navibus (☎0295 500 6284, ⊛www.navibus.com.ve).

Tourist information In the lobby of *Hotel Venetur* (Paseo La Cruz y El Mar; Mon–Fri 9am–noon & 1–5.30pm; ☎0281 500 3675, ⊛venetur.gob.ve).

ACCOMMODATION

Most of the centre's budget accommodation is strung along Paseo Colón, in the centre.

Neptuno Paseo Colón south of C Juncal ☎ 0281 268 5413. Rooms are clean, all with a/c and en suite, while the furniture is on its last legs. The hotel lobby has an internet café and is, bizarrely, football themed. <u>BsF800</u>

Posada Rancho Grande Paseo Colón, between calles Buenos Aires and Sucre ☎ 0414 093 4020. You'll need to bang on the door of this posada in the morning as they don't turn the bell on before lunch. The outlandish owner is a bit of a wheeler-dealer and will happily bargain a discount for a multiple-night stay. Small, clean rooms (en suite, TV, a/c), although none with windows facing outside. <u>BsF680</u>

Posada Turística Diana Paseo Colón, just north of C Sucre ☎ 0281 265 3517. Rooms in this sparsely decorated posada all lack natural light, but are otherwise clean with en suite, a/c and TV. <u>BsF600</u>

Posada Turística Montecarlo Paseo Colón 119 ☎ 0281 268 5677. The chirping canaries in the lobby do little to drown out the thundering a/c in this rather brown posada. Rooms are perfectly decent, all en suite, although showers amount to little more than a cold dribble. <u>BsF600</u>

EATING

Curiously, Paseo Colón is lined with numerous, nearly identical, Lebanese restaurants serving good-value *shawarma*, *kibbe* and *tabbouleh*. These tend to stay open very late.

El Bufalo Paseo Colón 49 ☎ 0281 267 2210. You can't miss *El Bufalo*, due in part to the massive angry bovine stuccoed above the wide entrance. They import some of their more gourmet cuts from Argentina, while the outside terrace is a popular night spot for cheap beers, sea views and live music on the weekends. Daily 11am–midnight.

La Colmena Paseo Colón, west of C Miranda ☎ 0281 265 2751. A little health-food shop serving up vegetarian food in the back at lunchtime only. Mon–Fri 11.30am–2.30pm.

Tasca Senador C Miranda north of C Alberto Ravel ☎ 0414 825 8044. This restaurant has a rather sultry atmosphere, which nonetheless attracts plenty of office workers on their lunch break for a good-value *menú ejecutivo* (BsF180). There's a DJ on weekends, when things get rowdy. Mon–Thurs noon–midnight, Fri noon–3am, Sat 8pm–3am.

DIRECTORY

Banks and exchange Banco de Venezuela, C Libertad, at C Miranda; Banco Banesco, C Freites, at C Bolívar.

Hospital Policlínica Puerto La Cruz, Av 5 de Julio at C Arismendi, open 24hr (☎ 0281 266 6833).

Internet In *Hotel Neptuno* (daily 8am–9pm). Sky Intern@tional, C Maneiro, at Paseo Colón (daily 9am–9pm, Sun from 1pm). Both cost BsF40/hr.

Laundry There is a nameless *lavandería* on Av Ravél, between calles Carabobo and Las Flores (Mon–Fri 7.30am–6pm, Sat till 3pm).

Pharmacy Meditotal, Paseo Colón across from Plaza Colón (24hr).

Phones Movistar and CANTV are both on Paseo Colón between calles Maneiro and Buenos Aires. You can also make international calls from Sky Intern@tional.

Police Located at Av Municipal by the Centro, Comercial Regina (☎ 0281 266 1414).

Post office Ipostel, C Freites, at C Libertad (Mon–Fri 8am–4pm).

Shopping There are numerous souvenir shops on the road to Los Altos de Sucre. Dulcería Alicia on this stretch sells delicious tarts and cheesecakes. Taller Artesanal Bogar in Sector Vuelta de Culebra makes local liquor, sweets and preserves.

PARQUE NACIONAL MOCHIMA

The 950-square-kilometre **PARQUE NACIONAL MOCHIMA** was created in 1973 to protect 36 uninhabited cays and the surrounding coastal area. Teeming with coral, dolphins and pelicans, and with laidback locals providing a genial social life, this area is one of Venezuela's most undervalued. While the beaches, some of which are deep-red in colour, aren't as postcard-perfect as those you'll find in Morrocoy and Henri Pittier, the snorkelling and scuba diving are far superior.

There are limited services and no banks or ATMs in Playa Colorado, Santa Fe or Mochima – stock up on cash in Puerto La Cruz (see p.910) or Cumaná.

Playa Colorada

In a protected cove lined with swaying palm trees, **PLAYA COLORADA** is rather winding down from the glory days of Venezuelan tourism, but nevertheless offers a welcome retreat from the more intense coastal towns. Deriving its name from the stretch of terracotta sand, few day-trippers ever venture to the other side of the highway where the town's numerous posadas and single restaurant are to be found. The sandbar's visitors triple at the weekends, but during the week you'll be left pretty much alone.

ARRIVAL AND DEPARTURE

By bus Buses operating the coastal highway between Puerto La Cruz, Santa Fe and Cumaná all pass through

Playa Colorada. Shout "*¡parada!*" at the driver to alight when you see the red sand. Buses from Puerto La Cruz depart from beside the liquor store on C Demoncracia outside the terminal. To get out of town, simply hail a passing bus (every 30min) in the direction you need.

ACCOMMODATION

Most of Playa Colorada's accommodation consists of purpose-built posadas that rent budget rooms and apartments for longer stays.

★**Jakera Lodge** On the main highway across from the beach ☎0293 808 7057, ⓦjakera.com. Resembling the secret retreat from *The Beach*, Scottish-owned *Jakera Lodge* looks and feels every centimetre the backpacker accommodation. There are hammocks (BsF400 with a private locker), dorms and doubles are clean, and mosquito nets are provided. Prices are per person and include breakfast and dinner. Spanish courses are also on offer. Dorms BsF600, doubles BsF1200

Villa Nirvana C Marchán ☎0293 808 7844, ⓔrita .pascal@hotmail.com. Straight-talking owner Rita built this beautiful posada after moving from Zürich. She offers the cheapest rooms in town, with apartments, roomy doubles and two little units without a/c for those on a tight budget. Apartments BsF2000, doubles BsF800

EATING

Other than the stalls lining the beach, there's only one place in the village at which to eat.

Las Carmitas 3a Transversal ☎0416 322 8887. There are only five tables, so you often need to wait for a seat at weekends, not that grabbing a beer and chatting with the other waiting people is much of an inconvenience. Serves pretty good burgers (BsF120), sandwiches (BsF140), pizzas (BsF250) and the like. Daily noon–8.30pm.

Santa Fe

One of the best spots along Venezuela's coastline, **SANTA FE**'s thin strip of sand is lined with good-value accommodation, crystal-clear water and hordes of pelicans whose signature fishing style is very entertaining to watch. The atmosphere is a little sketchier away from the well-populated seafront, and you should stick to the beach and road behind it (Calle Cochaima) after dark. At the far end of the beach, Santa Fe's bright-blue **market** makes for entertaining wandering, as well as a good spot to shop for fresh produce for your posada's kitchen.

The area's best activity is a day's island-hopping in which you'll cruise alongside dolphins, snorkel in coral reefs, visit island fishing outposts and barbecue your lunch on a secluded beach. You can also hop across to popular individual destinations such as **Isla Arapo** and **La Piscina** from the *lancheros* (return trip around BsF300/ person) outside the market.

ARRIVAL AND TOURS

By bus The terminal is a 500m walk from the beach on C La Plata. *Busetas* come and go regularly (5am–7pm).

Destinations Cumaná (every 30min; 1hr) passing via Mochima 30min away; Puerto La Cruz (every 30min; 40min) passing Playa Colorada 10min away.

Tour operators You can arrange island-hopping through your posada; one excellent guide is Jhonny (☎0293 808 0793) at *Posada Bahía del Mar*, who does full-day trips for BsF500/person. Local guide Sergio (☎0293 231 0058, ⓔsergioj38@hotmail.com) offers tours of the land behind Santa Fe for around BsF800/person. He takes tourists to coffee, mango and cacao plantations as well as visiting local Indians and swimming at a beautiful waterfall.

ACCOMMODATION

Camping on the beach is discouraged for safety reasons. All listings below are on the C Cochaima beach road. *Café del Mar* also runs a posada.

Hotel Cochaima ☎0293 642 0728. Matriarch Margot runs the town's first posada, which has cheap rooms and a family atmosphere. Numerous white-tiled rooms (a/c, en suite) are faded but spotless, while the upper floor has excellent sea views. Discounts negotiable for multiple nights and guests. BsF600

★**Posada Bahía del Mar** ☎0293 231 0073, ⓦposadabahiadelmar.com. Charming French couple Mado and Jean (and their friendly pets) run this delightful posada with its entrance right on the beach. Rooms are nicely decorated, clean and spacious; ask for no. 7 or no. 8, open-fronted doubles with fantastic views. Fast wi-fi, delicious smells from the outdoor kitchen, and the laundry service comes included in the room fee. BsF800

Posada Sierra Inn ☎0293 231 0042, ⓔposadasdeamigos@gmail.com. The family atmosphere is infectious in this colourful beach posada where chunky rocking chairs are favoured. There's a communal kitchen below an outpost-like beach lookout, decent rooms with a/c and TV, and hot water when the electricity permits. BsF600

EATING AND DRINKING

Seafood-lovers are in for a treat in Santa Fe, where the produce is freshly caught daily.

Café del Mar Far end of the beach ☎0293 231 0009. With tables on top of the sand, this palm-roofed restaurant serves up delicious platters made with fresh ingredients from the market nearby. Does soups from BsF100, but the

11

real triumph is the *parrilla Café del Mar* (BsF350), a seafood platter that you'll be thinking about until dinnertime the next day, when you'll probably be back. Also runs a posada upstairs with doubles for BsF600. Tues–Sun 11am–9pm.

El Mercado On the beach past *Café del Mar*. An excellent breakfast option, as well as a place to stock up on supplies (you can buy fish directly from the fishermen outside in the mornings). Numerous stands where *empanadas* and *arepas* are made to order while you sit back and watch the pelicans sneaking up on the fishermen. Daily breakfast & lunch.

DIRECTORY

Internet *Posada Bahía del Mar* has a computer you can use for BsF40/hr until 8pm, or for free if you're staying there.
Pharmacy Medicinas Santa Elena, C Las Mercedes, east of Av Principal (daily 7am–7pm, although they take a siesta around noon–2.30pm).
Police Station at beach end of Av Principal.

Mochima

The village after which the national park is named occupies a pretty inlet 3km from the main coastal road. Originally a fishing village, **MOCHIMA** has a lively malecón, though no beach, and is tricky to get to.

The main activity in Mochima is, once again, **boat trips** to the cays of the national park, all of which depart from the Terminal de Lanchas in the town centre. Prices for each destination are written on a board above the booth where you buy your tickets. If there's a group of you, you may want to rent a *lancha* (speedboat) for the day (BsF10,000 on the weekends, less during the week). Alternatively, consider the friendly Los Buzos dive centre (☎0293 416 0856, ✉mochimadivecenter@hotmail.com), which offers kayaking, trekking, climbing, rafting and dolphin-spotting in addition to one-day scuba trips (BsF3000) and a four-day scuba SSI certification course (BsF25,000, accommodation included).

ARRIVAL AND DEPARTURE

By bus and jeep The road to Mochima breaks off from the main coastal highway (heading towards Puerto La Cruz or Cumaná) beside various food stands; shout "¡parada!" at the bus driver to let you off, or hail a bus from the roadside to get on. Walking the road to Mochima is not recommended as robberies have occurred. Intermittent jeeps and *busetas* (BsF80) shuttle back and forth along the road daily until 8pm. Otherwise, drivers who know the road's reputation are usually happy to give you a lift if you flag them down.

ACCOMMODATION

Casa Cruz ☎0293 416 0810, ✉posadacasacruzmochima@hotmail.com. Plenty of fish motifs to remind you of the beach location at this welcoming little posada with five rooms. Also has a separate house for groups of six for BsF600. Book ahead. **BsF1000**
Posada El Mochimero ☎0293 643 5797. An oversized ceramic toad, elevated views from the big rooftop terrace and a trippy painting of marine life brighten up this otherwise dull posada. Rooms are clean, all with a/c; ask for room no. 10 or no. 17 as they have natural light. All rooms are triple. **BsF680**

EATING

Restaurant El Mochimero ☎0293 644 3200. They boast a Basque chef (which means delicious food) at this pleasant waterside restaurant, who serves up excellent seafood and grumbles over anything land-based, although the menu is extensive. Daily 11am–9pm.
Restaurant Puerto Viejo ☎0293 416 0810. Right next to the jetty, you'll get splashed at your table if a boat roars away quickly enough. The three-in-one platter serves up fresh octopus, squid and shrimp for BsF600. Also mixes up an excellent *piña colada* if your vitamin C count is running low. Daily 11am–8pm, Thurs–Sun in low season.

CARIPE

Tucked away in the mountainous state of Monagas, the rounded limestone hills and lush forest around **CARIPE** offer respite from the heat of the coast. The town is famous for the **Cueva del Guácharo**, a 10km-long cave home to screeching nocturnal birds that add an unearthly atmosphere to an astonishing natural phenomenon.

WHAT TO SEE AND DO

The pretty town centre is easily walkable and safe at all times of day. The region is renowned across the country for its fruit; make sure you sample the strawberries and cream on offer from vendors around town.

Venezuela's first national monument, the **Cueva del Guácharo** is a cave set deep in the limestone mountainside inhabited by oilbirds. You can take a tour (daily 8am–4pm; BsF100; ☎0291 641 7543) through the first 1200m of the cave, during which gas-lamp-toting guides point out distinctively shaped rock formations. At the entrance there's a museum dedicated to Alexander Von Humboldt, who first made oilbirds known to science. Taxis will take you to the entrance of Parque Nacional El Guácharo from the centre for BsF100.

Hiking opportunities abound in Monagas and a popular walk is the **Cerro Turumiquire**, the region's highest point at 2600m. Contact Viajes y Turismo WM (Av Enrique Chaumer; ☎0292 415 0428) in the *centro comercial* for more information on activities.

ARRIVAL AND DEPARTURE

By bus The bus terminal is a BsF25 taxi ride from the centre. Buses run to state capital Maturín (every 2hr; 6.30am–4pm), which has connections throughout the country. To head directly to Puerto Ordáz or Cumaná, *por puestos* depart intermittently from the terminal. To get here from the coast, take a bus from Cumaná in the morning (3 daily until 1pm; 3hr), or, if you miss the direct morning buses, *por puestos* leave irregularly from Cumaná bus terminal, or you can take a bus to Maturín from where buses run regularly to Caripe.

ACCOMMODATION

Campamento Kenya Sector El Guácharo ☎0416 396 8376, ✉kenya002@hotmail.com. Friendly tour guide and local legend Carlos Kenya runs his "Lost Boys"-style homestay close to the Guácharo cave. There's a dormitory and four cosy doubles which are en suite. Carlos also runs tours and volunteering projects throughout the region. Dorms BsF100, doubles BsF450

Hotel El Nuevo San Fransisco Av Enrique Chaumer, at Plaza Bolívar ☎0414 996 9047. Clean rooms have hot showers, cable TV and fans. The hotel is opposite the Plaza Bolívar, giving a very central location, useful for the weekend when locals converge on the area to drink and socialize. You won't see the hotel's name displayed anywhere on this brown-tiled building, only the word "hotel" written a number of different ways. BsF700

EATING AND DRINKING

On weekends, welcoming revellers tend to hang out with bottles of rum in the pedestrianized middle of C Bolívar until the early hours.

Ké Pollo C Ribero ☎0412 498 9244. Two colourful – if not artistically adept – murals are signature features at the town's most popular chicken joint. Whole (BsF400), half (BsF220) or quarter (BsF140) bird servings come accompanied with mini *arepas* and fries; also does excellent juices. Daily 11am–8pm.

Neno's Pizza C Bolívar ☎0292 808 8478. A pizzeria that's very popular with the locals. Excellent deep-dish-style pizzas come with all the usual toppings and boxes for takeaway. Personal size from BsF160, family size from BsF300. Daily noon–10.30pm.

DIRECTORY

Bank Banco Coroní on C Bolívar has a 24hr ATM.
Internet Centro de Conexiones, C Bolívar (daily 8am–8pm; BsF30/hr).
Pharmacy Farmacia El Cristo, Av Enrique Chaumer (daily 8am–4pm).
Police Av Guzman Blanco (daily 8am–8pm).
Shopping You can buy artisan jewellery in the pedestrian park in the middle of C Bolívar beside the Plaza Bolívar most evenings.

ISLA DE MARGARITA

The 940-square-kilometre island of **ISLA DE MARGARITA** mainly attracts well-to-do Venezuelan holidaymakers. While the island's rampant commercialism means that prices are inflated, Margarita can still provide an entertaining taste of mainstream Venezuelan-style tourism.

WHAT TO SEE AND DO

Isla de Margarita has many beach communities and just a few developed urban centres, **PORLAMAR** being the largest and containing the lion's share of inexpensive services. It's therefore best to base yourself here and take day-trips to the island's other attractions.

Ten kilometres north of Porlamar lies the more peaceful town of **Pampatar**. Founded in 1530, it was one of the first settlements in Venezuela, and even today it retains some of its former charm, with the remains of a Spanish fortress, Castillo de San Carlos Borromeo, completed in 1684 (daily 8am–5pm; free).

Margarita's most famous beach, **Playa El Agua** (1hr from Porlamar by bus), is 3km of white sand, palm trees and plenty of tourists. Less rammed beaches around the island include playas Manzanillo, El Yaque, Caribe, Guayacán, Puerto Abajo and Cardón.

ARRIVAL AND INFORMATION

By plane Santiago Mariño Airport is about 27km southwest of Porlamar; a taxi ride into town costs BsF600. Destinations Barcelona (3 daily; 30min); Caracas (several daily; 45min); Maracaibo (4 daily; 2–3hr with connection); Puerto Ordáz (2 daily; 1hr); and San Antonio del Táchira (1 daily; 3hr with connection).
By ferry The cheapest way to get to and from Isla de Margarita is by ferry (see box, p.917). Buses to the ferry

11

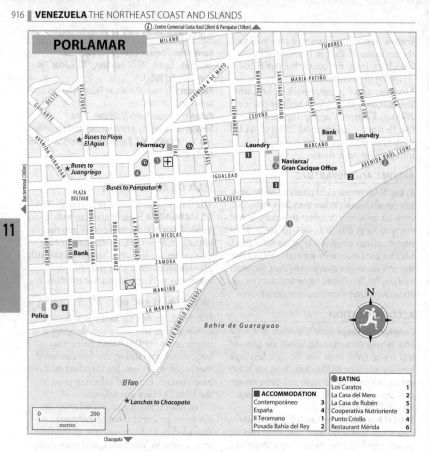

PORLAMAR

ⓘ Centro Comercial Costa Azul (2km) & Pampatar (10km)

Bus terminal (300m)

★ Buses to Playa El Agua
★ Buses to Juangriego
Pharmacy
★ Buses to Pampatar
PLAZA BOLÍVAR
Bank
Police
El Faro
★ Lanchas to Chacopata
Chacopata ▼

Laundry
Bank
Laundry
Naviarca/ Gran Cacique Office

Bahia de Guaraguao

N

0   200
metres

■ ACCOMMODATION
Contemporáneo   3
España   4
Il Teramano   1
Posada Bahía del Rey   2

■ EATING
Los Caratos   1
La Casa del Mero   2
La Casa de Rubén   5
Cooperativa Nutrioriente 3
Punto Criollo   4
Restaurant Mérida   6

dock at Punta de Piedras (which stop at the top of the jetties) come and go from the bus terminal in Porlamar five blocks west of the Plaza Bolívar between calles Velasquez and Igualdad until 7pm. A taxi either way costs BsF600 after hours. Keep in mind that ferry companies leave from different jetties at Punta de Piedras, so ensure you tell your bus driver which company you are travelling with.

Tourist information Corpotur, Centro Artesanal Gilberto Menchini in Los Robles (☎ 0295 262 2322 or ☎ 262 3638, ⓦ corpoturmargarita.gov.ve), roughly 3km from the centre. There's also an information point at the airport (daily 5am–11pm; ☎ 0295 400 5057).

GETTING AROUND

By bus Buses (daily 6am–9pm) are the cheapest way to explore the island. The primary bus terminal is five blocks west of the Plaza Bolívar, serving Punta de Piedras and various locations in the north of the island. Otherwise, bus stops throughout Porlamar's centre correspond to the island's more popular locales.

By taxi Taxis within Porlamar cost around BsF100 during the day, BsF140 at night. Otherwise the city's centre is easily walkable.

ACCOMMODATION

PORLAMAR

Porlamar is the undisputed commercial centre of the island and rocks a distinctly more Caribbean vibe than the mainland. It's also the best spot for reasonably priced accommodation and dining options. Make sure to ask for low-season discounts outside the island's peak periods of Dec–Jan and Easter.

Contemporáneo Av Santiago Mariño between calles Igualdad and Velásquez ☎ 0295 988 4978. A decent option in a safe setting, although you'll have to shout upstairs to be let in. The rooms (en suite, a/c, TV) are made darker by windows that don't open, and making a reservation over the phone can prove troublesome. Nevertheless, its location beyond the centre is a plus. BsF600

España C Mariño, at Av La Marina ☎ 0295 261 2479. An alarm clock is unnecessary in this friendly establishment as the frisky canaries (and one mad parrot) don't shut up after their covers come off. The rooms are decent enough, with fan, TV and en suite, and there's also free wi-fi. BsF600

Il Teramano C Marcano between calles Narváez and Hernández ☎0424 811 6485. Larger-than-life owner Walter has travelled extensively and knows what backpacking's all about. His spanking-clean establishment shows it. With three floors of dorms, private rooms and a communal kitchen, this is a good, secure option a short walk from the centre. Dorms BsF250, doubles BsF1000

★**Posada Bahía del Rey** C Fermín, at Av Raúl Leoni ☎0295 264 8947, ✉posadabahiadelrey@gmail.com. Bright yellow posada away from the chaos of the city, and only five steps from the seashore. Catch some rays on their lounge chairs on the beach before heading back to the warm and welcoming rooms (en suite, TV). There are plans to build a four-person apartment and swimming pool. BsF1200

EATING

PORLAMAR

Los Caratos C Marcano, at C Fajardo. A tiny juice joint selling delicious, freshly made *merengadas* and *batidos* (BsF60). Also does a good *cachapa* (sweetmeal pancake) (BsF100). Mon–Sat 7am–7pm.

La Casa del Mero Av Raul Leoni ☎0295 263 0105. Right on the beach, this tiki-themed restaurant serves up huge plates of the freshest fish and seafood from its open-front kitchen. The service is also efficient and friendly, making the place something of a diamond in the rough. Mon–Sat 11am–10pm.

La Casa de Rubén C Santiago Mariño ☎0295 264 5969. Rubén, whose smiling countenance grins at you from all over his establishment, is the author of several traditional Venezuelan cookbooks. The eatery serves meat, but the emphasis is on the locally sourced seafood (around BsF520). Mon–Sat 11am–6pm.

Cooperativa Nutrioriente C Santiago Mariño, at C Igualidad. A very clean, very cheap self-service restaurant, with plates of beef, vegetarian, chicken, fish and sides for BsF60. As the name suggests, some options are healthy and low-fat. Mon–Sat 7.30am–5pm.

★**Punto Criollo** C Igualdad, at C Fraternidad ☎0295 263 6745. Towering plates of mixed seafood and *comida criolla* at every table of this constantly packed local joint. Meat dishes feature heavily (*bistec* BsF280, *medallones* BsF340, beef stroganoff BsF280), the seafood is excellent (from BsF87) and the choice of sides is endless. Daily 10.30am–10pm.

Restaurant Mérida C Arismendi, south of C Maneiro. Though naming a tropical island restaurant after Venezuela's most renowned mountain town is an odd decision, this is a

11

BOAT TRANSPORT TO AND FROM ISLA DE MARGARITA

The three ferry companies which operate to the island depart from either Puerto La Cruz or Cumana on the mainland, the towns at either end of Parque Mochima. All ferries dock on the island at **Punta de Piedras**, an hour's bus ride from Porlamar. Speedboats, which are half the price and twice as bumpy, are also an option and depart from the mainland's closest point at Chacopata (easily reached by bus from Cariaco), arriving at El Faro dock in Porlamar. All companies run 2hr "express" services, while Conferry and Naviarca run the cheaper 5hr "conventional" trips, although they're scheduled at inconvenient times. You're asked to arrive 1hr 30min prior to departure to "confirm" your ticket at a company booth. Like bus tickets, you'll need your passport number to book a ticket. Rates are the same both to and from the island; prices quoted are one-way.

FROM PUERTO LA CRUZ

Puerto La Cruz's port is roughly 3km west of the centre, to which a taxi from the town should cost BsF100. Services are: Naviarca/Gran Cacique (4 daily express, BsF800; ☎0281 267 7286, ✇grancacique.com.ve); Conferry (3 daily express, BsF640; 2 daily conventional, BsF480; ☎0281 267 784); Navibus (2 daily express, BsF780; ☎0295 500 9284, ✇navibus.com.ve).

FROM CUMANÁ

Cumaná's terminal is 1km from the town's centre. Naviarca/Gran Cacique and Navibus run express boats (both 2 daily; BsF640); Naviarca also has conventional boats (3 daily; BsF420). An additional departure is added to each type of service in the high season.

FROM ISLA DE MARGARITA

If you didn't buy a return ticket on the mainland, make sure you visit a ferry office in Porlamar a day before you wish to leave. From Isla de Margarita, the following services run: Conferry (3 daily express for Puerto La Cruz; 4 daily conventional); Naviarca/Gran Cacique (3 daily express to Puerto La Cruz in high season; 2 daily in low season). You can also take cheaper *lanchas* (speedboats) from the El Faro dock in Porlamar, which act like *por puestos*, departing when full between Porlamar and Chacopata on the mainland (daily 6am–2pm; 1hr; around BsF500; ask your fellow passengers how much they are paying as drivers have been known to hike prices for foreigners). *Por puestos* serve Chacopata from Maturín and Cumaná bus terminals.

friendly budget option with communal atmosphere. Tuck into the day's menu (BsF150) scribbled on a board, as you share a table with other diners in the pleasant courtyard of the owners' home. Mon–Sat 10am–3pm.

DRINKING AND NIGHTLIFE

Night owls are in for a treat on the island. Most action takes place in Pampatar or in the Centro Comercial Costa Azul, a 2km taxi ride east of Porlamar (BsF200). Most clubs have no cover charge.

CENTRO COMERCIAL COSTA AZUL

Aldea Beach Complejo Margarita Village, behind the Centro Comercial Costa Azul. The main musical flavour is electronica at this open-air club by the seashore with three dance areas. Thurs–Sat 9am–3pm.

British Bulldog ☎ 0295 267 1527. You've got to give the place credit for trying so hard with the pub theme – with memorabilia, advertisements for drinks they don't serve and an enormous Union Jack. At weekends, local bands play amazingly accurate renditions of European and American hard-rock classics. Mon–Wed 9pm–midnight, Thurs–Sat 9pm–4am.

Opah ☎ 0295 262 8186. Your best bet for traditional salsa dancing with a local crowd, though the giant video screen and fog machines remind you that you're in the twenty-first century – or maybe the 1980s. Thurs–Sat 9pm–3am.

PAMPATAR

Beach Bar C El Cristo, La Caranta ☎ 0295 267 2392, ⓦ beachbar.com.ve. Have a few refreshing cocktails *après-plage* at this laidback bar with bamboo gazebos facing the beach. Tues–Sun 7pm–3am.

Latitud Diez °59 C El Cristo, Sector La Caranta ☎ 0295 267 1850. Snazzy club with an outdoor terrace where you can have a boogie or a cocktail as you check out the view. Thurs–Sat until late.

DIRECTORY

Banks and exchange Banco Universal, C Marcano between C Santiago Mariño and C Malave; Banco Mercantil, C San Nicolás, at C Mariño.

Hospital Clínica Margarita, C Marcano, at C Díaz (☎ 0295 264 9158).

Internet Grafica Multicolor (Mon–Sat 8.30am–5.30pm; BsF20/hr), C Fajardo between calles Marcano and Igualdad.

Laundry Lavanderia HR, C Marcano, at C Santiago Mariño (Mon–Fri 8am–5.30pm, Sat 8am–noon; BsF80/kg; ☎ 0295 264 9158); Edi's Lavandería, C Marcano between calles Campo Sur and Fermín (self service; Mon–Sat 7.45am–7.30pm, Sun 7.45am–1pm), also has an internet café while you wait (BsF2089/hr).

Pharmacy FarmaSigo, C Marcano, at C Díaz (daily 8.30am–6.30pm).

Police Station on C Arismendi, just south of C Maneiro (☎ 0295 264 1494).

Post office Ipostel, C Maneiro between C Fraternidad and Bulevar Gómez.

Shopping Margarita is famed for its duty-free shopping. Two pedestrianized streets, Bulevar Gómez and Bulevar Guevara, are lined with vendors selling mostly knockoff items and pirated CDs – though the occasional used-book vendor may be holding some treasures.

Language

Spanish

Although there are dozens of indigenous tongues scattered throughout South America – some thirty in the Peruvian Amazon alone – this is, in general, a Spanish-speaking continent. The Spanish you will hear in South America does not always conform to what you learned in the classroom, and even competent speakers of peninsular Spanish will find it takes a bit of getting used to. In addition to the odd differences in pronunciation – discussed in detail below – words from native languages as well as various European tongues have infiltrated the different dialects of South American Spanish, giving them each their own unique character.

For the most part, the language itself is the same throughout the continent, while the pronunciation varies slightly. In parts of Argentina, for example, the *ll* and *y* sound like a *zh* (the English equivalent is the *s* in "treasure"), while the final *s* of a word is often not pronounced.

Spanish itself is not a difficult language to pick up and there are numerous learning products on the market. You'll be further helped by the fact that most South Americans, with the notable exception of fast-talking Chileans, speak relatively slowly (at least compared with Spaniards) and that there's no need to get your tongue round the lisping pronunciation. *Spanish: The Rough Guide Phrasebook* is a concise and handy **phrasebook**.

Pronunciation

The rules of Spanish **pronunciation** are pretty straightforward. All syllables are pronounced. Unless there's an accent, words ending in d, l, r and z are **stressed** on the last syllable, all others on the second last. All **vowels** are pure and short.

A somewhere between the "A" sound of back and that of father.

E as in get.

I as in police.

O as in hot.

U as in rule.

C is soft before E and I, hard otherwise: cerca is pronounced "serka".

G works the same way: a guttural H sound (like the ch in loch) before E or I, a hard G elsewhere – gigante becomes "higante".

H is always silent.

J is the same sound as a guttural G: jamón is pronounced "hamón".

LL sounds like an English Y: tortilla is pronounced "torteeya".

N is as in English unless it has a tilde (accent) over it, when it becomes NY: mañana sounds like "manyana".

QU is pronounced like an English **K**.

R is rolled, RR doubly so.

V sounds more like **B**, vino becoming "beano".

X is slightly softer than in English – sometimes almost SH – except between vowels in place names where it has an "H" sound – for example México (Meh-Hee-Ko) or Oaxaca.

Z is the same as a soft **C**, so cerveza becomes "servesa".

WORDS AND PHRASES

The following will help you with your most basic day-to-day language needs.

BASIC EXPRESSIONS

Yes, No	Sí, No
Please, Thank you	Por favor, Gracias
Where, When?	¿Dónde, Cuándo?
What, How much?	¿Qué, Cuánto?
Here, There	Aquí, Allí
This, That	Este, Eso
Now, Later	Ahora, Más tarde/Luego
Open, Closed	Abierto/a, Cerrado/a
Pull, Push	Tire, Empuje
Entrance, Exit	Entrada, Salida
With, Without	Con, Sin
For	Para/Por
Good, Bad	Buen(o)/a, Mal(o)/a
Big, Small	Gran(de), Pequeño/a
A little, A lot	Poco/a, Mucho/a
More, Less	Más, Menos
Another	Otro/a
Today, Tomorrow	Hoy, Mañana
Yesterday	Ayer
But	Pero
And	Y
Nothing, Never	Nada, Nunca

GREETINGS AND RESPONSES

Hello, Goodbye	Hola, Adios
Good morning	Buenos días
Good afternoon/night	Buenas tardes/noches
See you later	Hasta luego
Sorry	Lo siento/Discúlpeme
Excuse me	Con permiso/Perdón
How are you?	¿Como está (usted)?
What's up?	¿Qué pasa?
I (don't) understand	(No) Entiendo
Not at all/You're welcome	De nada
Do you speak English?	¿Habla (usted) inglés?
I (don't) speak Spanish	(No) Hablo español
My name is …	Me llamo …
What's your name?	¿Como se llama usted?
I am English/American	Soy inglés(a)/ americano(a)
Cheers	Salud

ASKING DIRECTIONS, GETTING AROUND

Where is…?	¿Dónde está…?
…the bus station	…la estación de autobuses
…the train station	…la estación de ferrocarriles
…the nearest bank	…el banco más cercano
…the post office	…el correo
…the toilet	…el baño/sanitario
Is there a hotel nearby?	¿Hay un hotel aquí cerca?
Left, right, straight on	Izquierda, derecha, derecho
Where does the bus to … leave from?	¿De dónde sale el autobús para…?
How do I get to…?	¿Por dónde se va a…?
I'd like a (return) ticket to…	Quiero un boleto (de ida y vuelta) para…
What time does it leave?	¿A qué hora sale?

ACCOMMODATION

Private bathroom	Baño privado
Shared bathroom	Baño compartido
Hot water (all day)	Agua caliente (todo el día)
Cold water	Agua fría
Fan	Ventilador
Air-conditioned	Aire-acondicionado
Mosquito net	Mosquitero
Key	Llave
Check-out time	Hora de salida
Do you have…?	¿Tiene …?
… a room …	…una habitación
… with two beds/ double bed …	…con dos camas/ cama matrimonial…
It's for one person (two people)	Es para una persona (dos personas)
…for one night …	…para una noche…
…one week	…una semana
It's fine, how much is it?	¿Está bien, cuánto es?
It's too expensive	Es demasiado caro
Don't you have anything cheaper?	¿No tiene algo más barato?

NUMBERS AND DAYS

1	un/uno/una
2	dos
3	tres
4	cuatro
5	cinco
6	seis
7	siete
8	ocho
9	nueve
10	diez
11	once
12	doce
13	trece
14	catorce
15	quince
16	dieciséis
20	veinte

21	veintiuno	**Cerro**	Hill, mountain peak
30	treinta	**Colectivo**	Shared taxi/bus
40	cuarenta	**Combi**	Small minibus that runs
50	cincuenta		urban routes
60	sesenta	**Cordillera**	Mountain range
70	setenta	**Criollo**	"Creole": a person of
80	ochenta		Spanish blood born in
90	noventa		the American colonies
100	cien(to)	**Entrada**	Ticket (for theatre, football
200	doscientos		match, etc)
500	quinientos	**Estancia**	Ranch, or large estate
1000	mil	**Farmacia**	Chemist
		Gaucho	The typical Argentine
Monday	lunes		"cowboy", or rural
Tuesday	martes		*estancia* worker
Wednesday	miércoles	**Gringo**	Foreigner, Westerner
Thursday	jueves		(not necessarily a
Friday	viernes		derogatory term)
Saturday	sábado	**Hacienda**	Large estate
Sunday	domingo	**Mestizo**	Person of mixed Spanish
			and indigenous blood
USEFUL WORDS		**Micro**	City bus
Barrio	Suburb, or sometimes	**Mirador**	Viewpoint
	shantytown	**Peña**	Venue with live music
Carretera	Route or highway	**Soroche**	Altitude sickness

A SPANISH MENU READER

While menus vary by country and region, these words and terms will help negotiate most of them.

BASIC DINING VOCABULARY

Almuerzo	Lunch	**Maracuyá**	Passion fruit
Asada	Barbecue	**Melocotón/durazno**	Peach
Carta (la)/Lista (la)	Menu	**Mora**	Blackberry
Cena	Dinner	**Naranja**	Orange
Comida típica	Typical cuisine	**Pera**	Pear
Cuchara	Spoon	**Piña**	Pineapple
Cuchillo	Knife	**Plátano**	Plantain
Desayuno	Breakfast	**Pomelo/toronja**	Grapefruit
La cuenta, por favor	The bill, please	**Sandía**	Watermelon
Merienda	Set menu		
Plato fuerte	Main course	**VEGETABLES (*LEGUMBRES/VERDURAS*)**	
Plato vegetariano	Vegetarian dish	**Aguacate**	Avocado
Tenedor	Fork	**Alcachofa**	Artichoke
		Cebolla	Onion
		Champiñón	Mushroom
FRUIT (*FRUTAS*)		**Choclo**	Maize/sweetcorn
Cereza	Cherry	**Coliflor**	Cauliflower
Chirimoya	Custard apple	**Espinaca**	Spinach
Ciruela	Plum	**Frijoles**	Beans
Fresa/frutilla	Strawberry	**Guisantes/arvejas**	Peas
Guayaba	Guava	**Hongo**	Mushroom
Guineo	Banana	**Lechuga**	Lettuce
Higo	Fig	**Lentejas**	Lentil
Limón	Lemon or lime	**Menestra**	Bean/lentil stew
Manzana	Apple	**Palmito**	Palm heart

Patata	Potato
Papas fritas	French fries
Pepinillo	Gherkin
Pepino	Cucumber
Tomate	Tomato
Zanahoria	Carrot

MEAT (*CARNE*) AND POULTRY (*AVES*)

Carne de chancho	Pork
Cerdo	Pork
Chicharrones	Pork scratchings, crackling
Chuleta	Pork chop
Churrasco	Grilled meat with sides
Conejo	Rabbit
Cordero	Lamb
Cuero	Pork crackling
Cuy	Guinea pig
Jamón	Ham
Lechón	Suckling pig
Lomo	Steak
Pato	Duck
Pavo	Turkey
Pollo	Chicken
Res	Beef
Ternera	Veal
Tocino	Bacon
Venado	Venison

OFFAL (*MENUDOS*)

Chunchules	Intestines
Guatita	Tripe
Hígado	Liver
Lengua	Tongue
Mondongo	Tripe
Patas	Trotters

SHELLFISH (*MARISCOS*) AND FISH (*PESCADO*)

Anchoa	Anchovy
Atún	Tuna
Calamares	Squid
Camarón	Prawn
Cangrejo	Crab
Ceviche	Seafood marinated in lime juice with onions
Corvina	Sea bass
Erizo	Sea urchin
Langosta	Lobster
Langostina	King prawn
Lenguado	Sole
Mejillón	Mussel
Ostra	Oyster
Trucha	Trout

COOKING TERMS

A la parrilla	Barbecued
A la plancha	Lightly fried
Ahumado	Smoked
Al ajillo	In garlic sauce
Al horno	Oven-baked
Al vapor	Steamed
Apanado	Breaded
Asado	Roast
Asado al palo	Spit roast
Crudo	Raw
Duro	Hard boiled
Encebollado	Cooked with onions
Encocado	In coconut sauce
Frito	Fried
Picant	Spicy hot
Puré	Mashed
Revuelto	Scrambled
Saltado	Sautéed
Secado	Dried

DRINKS (*BEBIDAS*)

Agua (mineral)	Mineral water
Con gas	Sparkling
Sin gas	Still
Sin hielo	Without ice
Aguardiente	Sugar-cane spirit
Aromática	Herbal tea
Manzanilla	Camomile
Menta	Mint
Batido	Milkshake
Café (con leche)	Coffee (with milk)
Caipirinha	Cocktail of rum, lime, sugar and ice
Cerveza	Beer
Chicha	Fermented corn drink
Gaseosa	Fizzy drink
Jugo	Juice
Leche	Milk
Limonada	Fresh lemonade
Mate de coca	Coca leaf tea
Ron	Rum
Té	Tea
Vino blanco	White wine
Vino tinto	Red wine
Yerba (hierba) mate	Herbal infusion with *mate*

FOOD GLOSSARY

Aceite	Oil
Ají	Chilli
Ajo	Garlic
Arroz	Rice
Azúcar	Sugar
Galletas	Biscuits

Hielo	Ice	Chifles	Banana chips/crisps
Huevos	Eggs	Empanada	Cheese/meat pasty
Mantequilla	Butter	Hamburguesa	Hamburger
Mermeleda	Jam	Humitas	Ground corn and cheese
Miel	Honey	Omelet	Omelette
Mixto	Mixed seafood/meats	Palomitas	Popcorn
Mostaza	Mustard	Patacones	Thick-cut dried banana/
Pan (integral)	Bread (wholemeal)		plantain
Pimienta	Pepper	Salchipapas	Sausage, fries and
Queso	Cheese		sauces
Sal	Salt	Sanwiche	Sandwich
Salsa de tomate	Tomato sauce	Tamale	Ground maize with meat/
			cheese wrapped in leaf

SOUPS

		Tortilla de huevos	Firm omelette
Caldosa	Broth	Tostada	Toast
Caldo de gallina	Chicken broth	Tostado	Toasted maize
Caldo de patas	Cattle-hoof broth		
Crema de espárragos	Cream of asparagus	**DESSERT (POSTRES)**	
Locro	Cheese and potato soup	Cocados	Coconut candy
Sopa de bolas de verde	Plantain dumpling soup	Ensalada de frutas	Fruit salad
Sopa del día	Soup of the day	Flan	Crème caramel
Yaguarlocro	Blood sausage (black	Helado	Ice cream
	pudding) soup	Manjar de leche	Very sweet caramel made
			from condensed milk

SNACKS (BOCADILLOS)

		Pastas	Pastries
Bolón de verde	Baked cheese and	Pastel	Cake
	potato dumpling	Torta	Tart

Portuguese

The great exception to the Spanish-speaking rule in South America is, of course, Portuguese-speaking Brazil (that is, putting the Guianas to the side). Unfortunately, far too many people – especially Spanish-speakers – are put off going to Brazil solely because of the language, while this should actually be one of your main reasons for going. Brazilian Portuguese is a colourful, sensual language full of wonderfully rude and exotic vowel sounds, swooping intonation and hilarious idiomatic expressions.

The best **dictionary** currently available is *Collins Portuguese Dictionary*, which has a pocket edition. For a **phrasebook**, look no further than *Portuguese: The Rough Guide Phrasebook*, with useful two-way glossaries and a brief and simple grammar section.

Pronunciation

Although its complex pronunciation is far too difficult to be described in detail here, for the most part, Brazilian Portuguese is spoken more slowly and clearly than its European counterpart. The neutral vowels so characteristic of European Portuguese tend to be sounded out in full; in much of Brazil outside Rio the slushy "sh" sound doesn't exist; and the "de" and "te" endings of words like *cidade* and *diferente* are palatalized so they end up sounding like "sidadgee" and "djiferentchee".

WORDS AND PHRASES

You'll also find that Brazilians will greatly appreciate even your most rudimentary efforts, and every small improvement in your Portuguese will make your stay in Brazil much more enjoyable.

BASIC EXPRESSIONS

Yes, No	Sim, Não
Please	Por favor
Thank you	Obrigado (men)/ Obrigada (women)
Where, When?	Onde, Quando?
What, How much?	Que, Quanto?
This, That	Este, Esse, Aquele
Now, Later	Agora, Mais tarde
Open, Closed	Aberto/a, Fechado/a
Pull, Push	Puxe, Empurre
Entrance, Exit	Entrada, Saída
With, Without	Com, Sem
For	Para/Por
Good, Bad	Bom, Ruim
Big, Small	Grande, Pequeno
A little, A lot	Um pouco, Muito
More, Less	Mais, Menos
Another	Outro/a
Today, Tomorrow	Hoje, Amanhã
Yesterday	Ontem
But	Mas (pronounced like "mice")
And	E (pronounced like "ee" in "seek")
Something, Nothing	Alguma coisa, Nada
Sometimes	Às vezes

GREETINGS AND RESPONSES

Hello, Goodbye	Oi, Tchau (like the Italian "ciao")
Good morning	Bom dia
Good afternoon/night	Boa tarde/Boa noite
Sorry	Desculpa
Excuse me	Com licença
How are you?	Como vai?
Fine	Bem
I don't understand	Não entendo
Do you speak English?	Você fala inglês?
I don't speak Portuguese	Não falo português
My name is …	Meu nome é …
What's your name?	Como se chama?
I am English/American	Sou inglês/americano
Cheers	Saúde

ASKING DIRECTIONS, GETTING AROUND

Where is...?	Onde fica...?
...the bus station	...a rodoviária
...the bus stop	...a parada de ônibus
...the nearest hotel	...o hotel mais próximo
...the toilet	...o banheiro/sanitário
Left, right, straight on	Esquerda, direita, direto
Where does the bus to ... leave from?	De onde sai o ônibus para...?
Is this the bus to Rio?	É esse o ônibus para Rio?
Do you go to...?	Você vai para...?
I'd like a (return) ticket to...	Quero uma passagem (ida e volta) para...
What time does it leave?	Que horas sai?

ACCOMMODATION

Do you have a room?	Você tem um quarto?
...with two beds	...com duas
...with double bed	...camas/cama de casal
It's for one person/ two people	É para uma pessoa/ duas pessoas
It's fine, how much is it?	Está bom, quanto é?
It's too expensive	É caro demais
Do you have anything cheaper?	Tem algo mais barato?
Is there a hotel/ campsite nearby?	Tem um hotel/ camping por aqui?

NUMBERS AND DAYS

1	um, uma
2	dois, duas
3	três
4	quatro
5	cinco
6	seis
7	sete
8	oito
9	nove
10	dez
11	onze
12	doze
13	treze
14	quatorze
15	quinze
16	dezesseis
17	diecisiete
18	dieciocho
19	diecinueve
20	vinte
21	vinte e um
30	trinta
40	quarenta
50	cinquenta
60	sesenta
70	setenta
80	oitenta
90	noventa
100	cem
200	duzentos
300	trezentos
500	quinhentos
1000	mil
Monday	segunda-feira (or segunda)
Tuesday	terça-feira (or terça)
Wednesday	quarta-feira (or quarta)
Thursday	quinta-feira (or quinta)
Friday	sexta-feira (or sexta)
Saturday	sábado
Sunday	domingo

USEFUL WORDS

Azulejo	Decorative glazed tiling
Boîte	Club or bar with dancing
Candomblé	African-Brazilian religion
Capoeira	African-Brazilian martial art/dance form
Carimbó	Music and dance style from the north
Carioca	Someone or something from Rio de Janeiro
Dancetaria	Night spot where the emphasis is on dancing
Favela	Shantytown, slum
Fazenda	Country estate, ranch house
Feira	Country market
Ferroviária	Train station
Forró	Dance and type of music from the Northeast
Frevo	Frenetic musical style and dance from Recife
Gaúcho	Person or thing from Rio Grande do Sul; also southern cowboy
Gringo/a	Foreigner, Westerner (not necessarily derogatory)
Latifúndios	Large agricultural estates
Leito	Luxury express bus
Louro/a	Fair-haired/blonde – Westerners in general
Maconha	Marijuana
Mirante	Viewing point
Paulista	Person or thing from São Paulo state
Rodovia	Highway
Rodoviária	Bus station
Visto/visa	Visa

A BRAZILIAN MENU READER

BASIC DINING VOCABULARY

Almoço/lonche	Lunch
Café de manhã	Breakfast
Cardápio	Menu
Colher	Spoon
Conta/nota	Bill
Copo	Glass
Entrada	Hors d'oeuvre
Faca	Knife
Garçon	Waiter
Garfo	Fork
Jantar	Dinner, to have dinner
Prato	Plate
Sobremesa	Dessert
Sopa/Caldo	Soup
Taxa de serviço	Service charge

FRUIT (*FRUTAS*)

Abacate	Avocado
Abacaxi	Pineapple
Ameixa	Plum, prune
Caju	Cashew fruit
Carambola	Star fruit
Cerejas	Cherries
Côco	Coconut
Fruta do conde	Custard apple (also *ata*)
Goiaba	Guava
Laranja	Orange
Limão	Lime
Maçã	Apple
Mamão	Papaya
Maracujá	Passion fruit
Melancia	Watermelon
Melão	Melon
Morango	Strawberry
Pera	Pear
Pêssego	Peach
Uvas	Grapes

VEGETABLES (*LEGUMES*)

Alface	Lettuce
Arroz e feijão	Rice and beans
Azeitonas	Olives
Batatas	Potatoes
Cebola	Onion
Cenoura	Carrot
Dendê	Palm oil
Ervilhas	Peas
Espinafre	Spinach
Macaxeira	Roasted manioc
Mandioca	Manioc/cassava/yucca
Milho	Corn
Palmito	Palm heart

Pepinho	Cucumber
Repolho	Cabbage
Tomate	Tomato

MEAT (*CARNE*) AND POULTRY (*AVES*)

Bife	Steak
Bife a cavalo	Steak with egg and *farinha*
Cabrito	Kid (goat)
Carne de porco	Pork
Carneiro	Lamb
Costela	Ribs
Costeleta	Chop
Feijoada	Black bean, pork and sausage stew
Fígado	Liver
Frango	Chicken
Leitão	Suckling pig
Lingüiça	Sausage
Pato	Duck
Peito	Breast
Perna	Leg
Peru	Turkey
Picadinha	Stew
Salsicha	Hot dog
Veado	Venison
Vitela	Veal

SEAFOOD (*FRUTOS DO MAR*)

Acarajé	Fried bean cake stuffed with *vatapá*
Agulha	Needle fish
Atum	Tuna
Camarão	Prawn, shrimp
Caranguejo	Large crab
Filhote	Amazon river fish
Lagosta	Lobster
Lula	Squid
Mariscos	Mussels
Moqueca	Seafood stewed in palm oil and coconut sauce
Ostra	Oyster
Pescada	Seafood stew, or hake
Pirarucu	Amazon river fish
Pitu	Crayfish
Polvo	Octopus
Siri	Small crab
Sururu	A type of mussel
Vatapá	Bahian shrimp dish, cooked with palm oil, skinned tomato and coconut milk, served with fresh coriander and hot peppers

COOKING TERMS

Assado	Roasted
Bem gelado	Well chilled
Churrasco	Barbecue
Cozido	Boiled, steamed
Cozinhar	To cook
Grelhado	Grilled
Mal passado/Bem passado	Rare/well done (meat)
Médio	Medium-grilled
Milanesa	Breaded
Na chapa/Na brasa	Charcoal-grilled

SPICES (*TEMPEROS*)

Alho	Garlic
Canela	Cinnamon
Cheiro verde	Fresh coriander
Coentro	Parsley
Cravo	Clove
Malagueta	Very hot pepper, looks like red or yellow cherry

DRINKS (*BEBIDAS*)

Água mineral	Mineral water
Batida	Fresh fruit juice (sometimes with *cachaça*)
Cachaça	Sugar-cane rum
Café com leite	Coffee with hot milk
Cafézinho	Small black coffee
Caipirinha	Rum and lime cocktail
Cerveja	Bottled beer
Chopp	Draught beer
Com gás/sem gás	Sparkling/still
Suco	Fruit juice
Vinho	Wine
Vitamina	Fruit juice made with milk

FOOD GLOSSARY

Açúcar	Sugar
Alho e óleo	Garlic and olive oil sauce
Arroz	Rice
Azeite	Olive oil
Farinha	Dried manioc flour beans
Manteiga	Butter
Molho	Sauce
Ovos	Eggs
Pão	Bread
Pimenta	Pepper
Queijo	Cheese
Sal	Salt
Sorvete	Ice cream

Small print and index

A ROUGH GUIDE TO ROUGH GUIDES

Published in 1982, the first Rough Guide – to Greece – was a student scheme that became a publishing phenomenon. Mark Ellingham, a recent graduate in English from Bristol University, had been travelling in Greece the previous summer and couldn't find the right guidebook. With a small group of friends he wrote his own guide, combining a highly contemporary, journalistic style with a thoroughly practical approach to travellers' needs.

The immediate success of the book spawned a series that rapidly covered dozens of destinations. And, in addition to impecunious backpackers, Rough Guides soon acquired a much broader readership that relished the guides' wit and inquisitiveness as much as their enthusiastic, critical approach and value-for-money ethos.

These days, Rough Guides include recommendations from budget to luxury and cover more than 120 destinations around the globe, as well as producing an ever-growing range of ebooks.

Visit **roughguides.com** to find all our latest books, read articles, get inspired and share travel tips with the Rough Guides community.

HELP US UPDATE

We've gone to a lot of effort to ensure that the fourth edition of **The Rough Guide to South America on a Budget** is accurate and up-to-date. However, things change – places get "discovered", opening hours are notoriously fickle, restaurants and rooms raise prices or lower standards. If you feel we've got it wrong or left something out, we'd like to know, and if you can remember the address, the price, the hours, the phone number, so much the better.

Please send your comments with the subject line "**Rough Guide South America on a Budget Update**" to mail@uk.roughguides.com. We'll credit all contributions and send a copy of the next edition (or any other Rough Guide if you prefer) for the very best emails.

Find more travel information, connect with fellow travellers and plan your trip on ⓦroughguides.com.

READERS' UPDATES

Thanks to all the readers who have taken the time to write in with comments and suggestions (and apologies if we've inadvertently omitted or misspelt anyone's name):
Natalia Bainotti; Ben and Izzy; Marcel Bokhorst; Eleonora Bozzoni; Paul Brown; Jan Brunotte; Hanna Büchler; Amy Coates; Jamila Douhaibi; Pablo Felipe Espinoza Alliende; Scott Fitzgerald; Melissa Graham; Neil Iosson; Emma Jamison; Juan Leon; Hannah Lupien; Ryan Mes; Leena Pandit; Barry Ress; Caroline Robertson; Renata Snow; Mark Stringer Melanie Whitlock

Rough Guide credits

Editor: Alice Park
Layout: Ankur Guha
Cartography: Deshpal Dabas
Picture editor: Aude Vauconsant
Proofreader: Jan McCann
Managing editor: Andy Turner
Assistant editor: Payal Sharotri

Production: Janis Griffith
Cover design: Nicole Newman, Dan May, Ankur Guha
Editorial assistant: Freya Godfrey
Senior pre-press designer: Dan May
Programme manager: Gareth Lowe
Publishing director: Georgina Dee

Publishing information

This fourth edition published August 2015 by
Rough Guides Ltd,
80 Strand, London WC2R 0RL
11, Community Centre, Panchsheel Park,
New Delhi 110017, India
Distributed by Penguin Random House
Penguin Books Ltd,
80 Strand, London WC2R 0RL
Penguin Group (USA)
345 Hudson Street, NY 10014, USA
Penguin Group (Australia)
250 Camberwell Road, Camberwell,
Victoria 3124, Australia
Penguin Group (NZ)
67 Apollo Drive, Mairangi Bay, Auckland 1310,
New Zealand
Penguin Group (South Africa)
Block D, Rosebank Office Park, 181 Jan Smuts Avenue,
Parktown North, Gauteng, South Africa 2193
Rough Guides is represented in Canada by Tourmaline
Editions Inc. 662 King Street West, Suite 304, Toronto,
Ontario M5V 1M7
Printed in Singapore

Acknowledgements

Alasdair Baverstock Thanks to Jerry Bacchus in
Georgetown for being a top bloke, and Oriana Gonzalez de
Caracas quien me abrió su ciudad.
Kiki Deere wishes to thank Ric and Bernard at Peru
for Less; Richard for his company and all the long days'
driving up in the Andes; Mountain Lodges of Peru for
hosting me on such a wonderful trek to Machu Picchu;
Whilder Alarico for being such an excellent guide and for
his jovial company on our trek; Boneth for her patience
and company as she guided me around the Sacred
Valley's beautiful Inca sights; Edwin from Pablo Tours
in Arequipa for helping out with my itinerary and for
his excellent organizational skills; his brother Yamil for
the great pizzas, and Pablo for the fun company on the
trek down to (and back up – just about!) Sangalle Oasis;
Gustavo for kindly taking me around the Colca Canyon;
Mayra for her company in Cotahuasi; all the friendly
helpful staff at the iPerú offices throughout the country;
the Rough Guides team in London for commissioning me
to travel to such a beautiful part of the world; and last but
not least Budgie for his support over the years and for
putting up with a fiancée who nipped off to Peru for over a
month just two days after he proposed.
Daniel Jacobs Thanks to Teri Oliveira (São Paulo), Bob and
Malu Nadkarni (The Maze, Rio), Hervé Neukomm, Alejandra
Currea Dereser and Salome Aramburo Calle (La Jangada,
Leticia), and Lorenzo Tottone (Leticia and Introdacqua).
Clemmy Manzo I'd like to thank Juan Pablo at Hacienda
Venecia for his hospitality and a memorable alfresco movie
night surrounded by his adorable dogs; Ronaldo at El Viajero

for showing me the best of Cali, for trying to teach me
salsa and not laughing at my failures; Alexandra at the Blue
House in Cartagena for her kindness; Shaun at Macondo
hostel for introducing us to the weird and wonderful game
of tejo; Aluna hostel, La Brisa Loca and Tierra Negra in Santa
Marta; Esther at The Dreamer on the Beach; Expotur for an
unforgettable trip to La Guajira; Kim and Tony at HostelTrail
in Popayán for their help and knowledge; RG's Daniel Jacobs
for sharing a few drinks, laughs and notes; and Alice Park for
her superb editing skills. But most of all, thanks goes to Jack
Coleman, the best and most supportive travel companion
anyone could wish for.
Shafik Meghji Thanks to all the locals and travellers that
helped me out along the way. A special muchas gracias must
go to: Mani Ramaswamy, Andy Turner and Olivia Rawes at
RG HQ; Alice Park for her sterling editing work; MaryAnne
Nelson and Laura Rendell-Dunn at Journey Latin America for
all their help with travel bookings; Nicolas Fernandez of Chile
Running Tours; Jaime for showing me Humberstone and
Santa Laura; Janak Jani in Valpo; Jean, Nizar and Nina Meghji;
and Sioned Jones, for all her love and support.
Phillip Tang Muchísimas gracias a Ernesto A. Alanis
Cataño. Tu ayuda fue increíble. Vivan las sánguiches! Thank
you to Alice Park for all her meticulous help and guidance.
Madelaine Triebe I would like to thank Rachel Mills for
the initial commission, Alice for having eyes like a hawk,
and Andy for being Pep Guardiola. Would also like to say
massive thanks to all the beautiful Argentines who hosted
and entertained me on the trip. Also special thanks to
Angélica and my family.

Photo credits

All photos © Rough Guides except the following:
(Key: t-top; c-centre; b-bottom; l-left; r-right)

Index

Maps are marked in **grey**

Map symbols

The symbols below are used on maps throughout the book

Main road	@	Internet café/access	Ski area		Mountain range
Minor road		Post office	Museum		Bridge
Motorway	(i)	Tourist office	Vineyard		Church (regional map)
Pedestrianized road	(C)	Telephone office	Petrol station		Church (town map)
Steps		Hospital	Harbour/port		Building
Unpaved road		Place of interest	Arch		Market
Railway		Cave	Lighthouse		Stadium
Path		Ruin	Mountain refuge/lodge		Park/national park
Wall		Fortress	Park ranger		Beach
Funicular		Tower	Spring		Christian cemetery
Cable car		Viewpoint	Waterfall		Jewish cemetery
Gate		Mosque	Swimming pool		Marsh/swamp
Airport		Campsite	Volcano		Glacier
Bus/taxi		Statue	Mountain peak		Salt flats
(M) Metro/subway stop		Synagogue	Gorge		

Listings key

- Accommodation
- Eating/drinking/nightlife